ISSN 0360-2710

BIBLIOGRAPHIC GUIDE TO
BLACK STUDIES
1989

G.K. HALL & CO.
70 Lincoln Street, Boston, Massachusetts

PREFACE

G. K. Hall *Bibliographic Guides* are comprehensive annual subject bibliographies. They bring together publications cataloged by The Research Libraries of The New York Public Library and the Library of Congress for thorough subject coverage. Included are works in all languages and all forms—non-book materials as well as books and serials.

Bibliographic Guides provide complete LC cataloging information for each title, as well as ISBN and identification of NYPL holdings. Access is by main entry (personal author, corporate body, names of conference, etc.), added entries (co-authors, editors, compilers, etc.), titles, series titles, and subject headings. All entries are integrated into one alphabetical sequence. Full bibliographic information, including tracings, is given in the main entry, with abbreviated or condensed citations for secondary entries. Subject headings appear in capital letters in bold-face type. Cataloging follows the *Anglo-American Cataloging Rules*. Following is a sample entry with full bibliographic information:

(a) **Rapoport, Anatol, 1911–** (b) N-person game theory; (c) concepts and applications. (d) Ann Arbor, (e) University of Michigan Press (f) (1970) (g) 331 p. (h) illus. 22cm. (i) (Ann Arbor science library) (j) Bibliography: p. 317-320. (k) ISBN 0-472-00117-5 (l) LC Card 79-83451 (m) DDC 512/.8 (n) 1. Games of strategy (Mathematics).
(o) I. Title
(p) PA27O.R34 1970   (q) **NYPL (r) [JSD 72-370]**

(a) Author's name.	(i) Series.
(b) Short, or main, title.	(j) Note(s).
(c) Sub-title and/or other title page information.	(k) ISBN.
	(l) LC Card number.
(d) Place of publication.	(m) DDC number.
(e) Publisher.	(n) Subject heading.
(f) Date of Publication.	(o) Added entry.
(g) Pagination.	(p) LC Call number.
(h) Illustration statement.	(q) NYPL indicator.
	(r) NYPL Classmark.

G. K. Hall *Bibliographic Guides* offer easy, multiple access to a wealth of material in each subject area. They serve as authoritative reference sources for librarians and scholars, valuable technical aids for library acquisition and cataloging, and useful research tools for professionals.

Bibliographic Guides for 1989 are available in twenty-one fields:

Anthropology and Archaeology	Latin American Studies
Art and Architecture	Law
Black Studies	Maps and Atlases
Business and Economics	Microform Publications
Computer Science	Music
Conference Publications	North American History
Dance	Psychology
East Asian Studies	Soviet and East European Studies
Education	Technology
Government Publications—Foreign	Theatre Arts
Government Publications—U.S.	

They include material cataloged between September 1, 1988 and August 31, 1989.

INTRODUCTION

The *Bibliographic Guide to Black Studies* lists publications cataloged during the past year by The New York Public Library. The *Guide* also serves as an annual supplement to the *Dictionary Catalog of the Schomburg Collection of Negro Literature and History*, The New York Public Library (G. K. Hall, 1962; *First Supplement*, 1967; *Second Supplement*, 1972). The Guide represents only New York Public Library holdings.

The New York Public Library's Schomburg Center for Research in Black Culture is one of the most important centers in the world for the study of black life and history. Its literature is international in scope and comprehensive in its coverage of black activity wherever peoples of African descent have lived. The Schomburg Collection includes books by authors of African descent, regardless of subject matter or language. The Collection also strives to obtain all significant materials about peoples of African descent. Subject strengths include art, biography, folklore, geography, history (Africa and the Americas), literature and languages, music, religion, and sports.

Unlike other volumes in the *Bibliographic Guide* series, materials in the *Bibliographic Guide to Black Studies* are classified by the Dewey Decimal System. Library of Congress subject headings are supplemented by special headings developed for the Collection.

A. A. I. see **African-American Institute.**

A C R L. see **Association of College and Research Libraries.**

A la source du Nil . Paternostre de La Mairieu, Baudouin. Paris [1985] 108 p., [12] p. of plates : ISBN 2-85244-730-4 : DDC 967/.571 19
DT450.2 .P38 1985 **NYPL [Sc C 88-308]**

A. M. A. see **American Missionary Association.**

A Madagascar /. Planche, Bernard. [Paris] , c1987. 158 p. : **NYPL [Sc D 88-254]**

A. Philip Randolph /. Hanley, Sally. New York [1988], c1989. 110 p. : ISBN 1-555-46607-9 DDC 323.4/092/4 92 19
E185.97.R27 H36 1989 **NYPL [Sc E 88-617]**

A R L. see **Association of Research Libraries.**

Aaab-Richards, Dirg. Tongues untied . London , Boston, MA, USA , 1987. 95 p. ; ISBN 0-85449-053-1 (pbk) : DDC 821/.914/080920664 19
PR1178.H6 **NYPL [JFD 88-7561]**

AAI and Africa. African-American Institute. New York [1986?] 1 v. (various pagings) ;
NYPL [Sc F 88-298]

Aardema, Verna.
Princess Gorilla and a new kind of water : a Mpongwe tale / retold by Verna Aardema ; pictures by Victoria Chess. New York : Dial Books for Young Readers, 1988. [32] p. : col. ill. ; 27 cm. King Gorilla decrees that no one may marry his daughter until a suitor strong enough to consume a barrel of strange, intoxicating water is found. SCHOMBURG CHILDREN'S COLLECTION. ISBN 0-8037-0412-7 : DDC 398.2/0966 E 19
1. Mpongwe (African people) - Folklore. 2. Folklore - Africa, West. I. Chess, Victoria, ill. II. Schomburg Children's Collection. III. Title.
PZ8.1.A213 Pr 1987 **NYPL [Sc F 88-133]**

The sky-god stories / by Verna Aardema ; illustrated by Elton Fax. New York : Coward-McCann, c1960. [50] p. : ill. ; 23 cm. "Based upon an Ashanti story in Akan-Ashanti folk-tales published 1930 by Clarendon Press." SCHOMBURG CHILDREN'S COLLECTION.
1. Anansi (Legendary character) - Juvenile fiction. 2. Ashantis (African people) - Folklore. 3. Tales - Ghana. I. Schomburg Children's Collection. II. Title.
NYPL [Sc D 89-83]

Aarhaug, Aksel, 1921- Mitt Afrika / Aksel Aarhaug. Oslo : Luther Forlag, 1985. 104 p., [17] p. of plates : ill. (some col.) ; 25 cm. ISBN 82-531-4177-7
1. Missions - Cameroon. 2. Cameroon - Description and travel. 3. Cameroon - Social life and customs. I. Title.
NYPL [Sc E 88-149]

Ab Ibadan , 1986. vii. 108 p. : ISBN 978-245-824-4 **NYPL [Sc C 88-358]**

ABACUÁ LANGUAGE.
Cabrera, Lydia. La lengua sagrada de los Náñigos /. Miami, Fla. , c1988. 530 p. ;
NYPL [Sc D 89-585]

The Abagana ambush . Enonchong, Charles. Calabar, Nigeria [197?] 47 p. :
NYPL [Sc C 89-33]

ABANDONED CHILDREN - UNITED STATES - BIOGRAPHY.
Fitts, Hervey. Abraham Vest, or, The cast-off restored. Boston, 1847. 142 p.
T275.V55 F5 1847 **NYPL [Sc Rare C 88-12]**

Abasiattai, Monday B. Akwa Ibom and Cross River States . Calabar [Nigeria] , 1987. 284 p. : ISBN 978-228-320-7 **NYPL [Sc D 88-740]**

Abba island in America [microform] Brooklyn : Ansaru Allah Community, [197-?] 11 p. : ill. ; 38 cm. Cover title. Paging in reverse. Microfilm. New York: New York Public Library, 1982. 1 microfilm reel; 35 mm. (MN *ZZ-23673)
1. Ansaru Allah Community. 2. Muslims, Black - New york (N.Y.) - Brooklyn - Social life and customs.
NYPL [Sc Micro R-4114 no. 19]

Abban, J. B. Prerequisites of manpower and educational planning in Ghana / J.B. Abban. Accra : Baafour Educational Enterprises, 1986. xii, 144 p. ; 21 cm. Includes index. Bibliography: p.132-138. ISBN 996-560-307-6
1. Manpower planning - Ghana. 2. Educational planning - Ghana. I. Title. II. Title: Manpower and educational planning in Ghana. III. Title: Educational planning in Ghana. **NYPL [Sc D 89-496]**

Abbeokoeta. Tucker, Charlotte Maria, 1821-1893. Amsterdam, 1860. viii, 330 p. ;
NYPL [Sc Rare C 88-25]

Abbott, Dorothy, 1944- Mississippi writers . Jackson , c1985- v. ; ISBN 0-87805-232-1 (pbk.) DDC 813/.008/09762 19
PS558.M7 M55 1985 **NYPL [Sc E 88-316]**

Abbott, Elizabeth. Haiti : the Duvaliers and their legacy / Elizabeth Abbott. New York, N.Y. : McGraw-Hill, c1988. xii, 381 p., [8] p. of plates : ill., ports. ; 24 cm. Bibliography: p. 367-381. ISBN 0-07-046029-9 : DDC 972.94/06 19
1. Duvalier, François, 1907-1971. 2. Duvalier, Jean Claude, 1951-. 3. Haiti - Politics and government - 1934-1971. 4. Haiti - Politics and government - 1971-1986. I. Title.
F1928 .A583 1988 **NYPL [Sc E 88-605]**

Abdallah, Mohammed Ben. The trial of Mallam Ilya and other plays / Mohammed ben Abdallah. Accra : Woeli Pub. Services, 1987. 165 p. ; 20 cm. CONTENTS. - The alien king.--Verdict of the cobra.--The trial of Mallam Ilya. ISBN 996-497-076-5
I. Title. **NYPL [Sc D 88-1491]**

Abdin, Hasan. Early Sudanese nationalism, 1919-1925 / Hasan Abdin. [Khartoum?] : Institute of African & Asian Studies, University of Khartoum, [1985?] iv, 167 p. : map ; 24 cm. (Sudanese library series . 14) Based on the author's thesis (Ph.D.)--University of Wisconsin. Bibliography: p. 142-145. DDC 962.4/03 19
1. Nationalism - Sudan - History - 20th century. 2. Sudan - History - 1899-1956. I. Series: Sudanese library series , no. 14. II. Title.
DT156.7 .A23 1985 **NYPL [Sc E 88-335]**

Abdullahi Smith Centre for Historical Research. Smith, Abdullahi, 1920-1984. A little new light . Zaria , 1987- v. :
NYPL [Sc D 88-708]

Abé, K. (Katsuji) Jazz giants. New York , 1988,c1986. 280 p. : ISBN 0-8230-7536-2 : DDC 779/.978542 19
ML3506 .J43 1988 **NYPL [Sc G 89-14]**

Abebe Brehanu. Tadi Liben. Planning and conducting training in communication /. Nairobi, Kenya , 1986. viii, 55 p. : DDC 307.1/4/0706 19
HN780.Z9 C679 1986 **NYPL [Sc F 89-171]**

Abegunrin, Olayiwola. African development . Lawrenceville, Va., U. S. A. , c1985. 241 p. : ISBN 0-931494-57-5 (pbk) DDC 337.1/6 19
HC800 .A565 1985 **NYPL [Sc F 87-376]**

Abejo, Bisi. Love at first flight / Bisi Abejo. Ibadan, Nigeria : Spectrum, 1986. 241 p. ; 18 cm.
1. Nigeria - Fiction. I. Title.
MLCS 87/7911 (P) **NYPL [Sc C 88-367]**

Abel, Christopher. José Martí, revolutionary democrat /. London , 1986. xviii, 238 p. ; ISBN 0-485-15018-2 **NYPL [JFD 86-9243]**

Abénon, Lucien René, 1937- La Guadeloupe de 1671 à 1759 : étude politique, économique et sociale / Lucien René Abenon. Paris : L'Harmattan, c1987. 2 v. : Ill., maps, facsims. ; 24 cm. Includes index. "Sources et bibliographie: v. 2, p. 245-253. ISBN 2-85802-752-8 (v. 1)
1. Guadeloupe - History. I. Title.
NYPL [Sc E 88-248]

ABEOKUTA (NIGERIA) - DESCRIPTION.
Tucker, Charlotte Maria, 1821-1893. Abbeokoeta. Amsterdam, 1860. viii, 330 p. ;
NYPL [Sc Rare C 88-25]

Aberdeen Anti-Slavery Society. West India slavery . Aberdeen , 1825. 24 p. ;
NYPL [Sc Rare G 86-34]

Abeyi, administration and public services [microform] /. Salih, Mohamed Abdel Rahim M. Khartoum , 1978. 27 leaves ;
NYPL [Sc Micro F-11039]

ABIDJAN, IVORY COAST - DESCRIPTION.
Bonnassieux, Alain. L'autre Abidjan . Abidjan , Paris , c1987. 220 p. : ISBN 0-86537-191-3
NYPL [Sc C 88-212]

Abina, Tchalla. L'Afrique face à ses priorités /. Paris , c1987. 144 p. ; ISBN 2-7178-1296-2
NYPL [Sc E 88-291]

La abolición de la esclavitud negra en la legislación española, 1870-1886 /. Navarro Azcue, Concepción, 1952- Madrid , c1987. 296

p. ; ISBN 84-7232-420-6
KG546 .N38 1987 **NYPL [Sc D 89-574]**

ABOLITION OF SLAVERY. see **SLAVERY.**

Abolitionist down South. Texan. The Yankee slave-dealer, or, An abolitionist down South . Nashville, Tenn. , 1860. 368 p. ;
NYPL [Sc Rare C 88-21]

ABOLITIONISTS - BRAZIL - BIOGRAPHY.
Nabuco, Joaquim, 1849-1910. Minha formação /. Rio de Janeiro , 1957. 258 p. :
F2536 .N1425 1957 **NYPL [Sc D 87-1353]**

ABOLITIONISTS - LEGAL STATUS, LAWS, ETC. - SOUTHERN STATES - CASES.
Slave rebels, abolitionists, and southern courts . New York , 1988. 2 v. : ISBN 0-8240-6721-5 (set : alk. paper) : DDC 342.75/0872 347.502872 19
KF4545.S5 A5 1987b **NYPL [Sc D 88-1263]**

ABOLITIONISTS - MASSACHUSETTS.
Massachusetts Anti-Slavery Society. Board of Managers. An address to the abolitionists of Massachusetts, on the subject of political action /. [Boston , 1838] 20 p. ;
NYPL [Sc Rare G 86-10]

ABOLITIONISTS - UNITED STATES.
A Refutation of the charge of abolitionism. Boston, 1845. 32 p.
F69 .M455 **NYPL [Sc Rare C 89-21]**

ABOLITIONISTS - UNITED STATES - BIOGRAPHY - JUVENILE LITERATURE.
Ferris, Jeri. Walking the road to freedom . Minneapolis , 1987. 64 p. : ISBN 0-87614-318-4 (lib. bdg.) : DDC 305.5/67/0924 B 92 19
E185.97.T8 F47 1987 **NYPL [Sc D 88-1046]**

Jakoubek, Robert E. Harriet Beecher Stowe /. New York , c1989. 111 p. : ISBN 1-555-46680-X DDC 813/.3 B 92 19
PS2956 .J35 1989 **NYPL [Sc E 89-144]**

Krass, Peter. Sojourner Truth /. New York , c1988. 110 p. : ISBN 1-555-46611-7 DDC 305.5/67/0924 B 92 19
E185.97.T8 K73 1988 **NYPL [Sc E 88-470]**

Nolan, Jeanette Covert, 1896- John Brown /. New York , 1968, c1950. 181 p. :
NYPL [Sc D 88-665]

Russell, Sharman Apt. Frederick Douglass /. New York , c1988. 110 p. : ISBN 1-555-46580-3 DDC 973.8/092/4 B 92 19
E449.D75 R87 1988 **NYPL [Sc E 88-174]**

ABOLITIONISTS - UNITED STATES - HISTORY - 19TH CENTURY.
Which path to freedom? . Pomona, Calif. , c1986. iv, 60 p. ; DDC 973.7/114 19
E449 .W565 1986 **NYPL [Sc D 88-1154]**

ABORIGINES. see **ETHNOLOGY.**

ABORIGINES, AUSTRALIAN. see **AUSTRALIAN ABORIGINES.**

Aborisade, Oladimeji. Readings in Nigerian local government /. Ile-Ife [1986?] 274 p. ;
NYPL [Sc D 89-501]

ABORTION - RELIGIOUS ASPECTS - CATHOLIC CHURCH.
Njai, D. M. (Daniel Michael) Abortion, the way it is /. Nairobi [198-] 31 p. :
NYPL [Sc D 89-321]

Abortion, the way it is /. Njai, D. M. (Daniel Michael) Nairobi [198-] 31 p. ;
NYPL [Sc D 89-321]

Abosi, Okechukwu C.
Development of special education in Nigeria /. Ibadan , 1988. ix, 132 p. ; ISBN 978-267-703-5
NYPL [Sc E 89-70]

Educating the blind : a descriptive approach / Okechukwu C. Abosi, Emeka D. Ozoji. Ibadan : Spectrum Books, c1985. xiv, 106 p. : ill. ; 22 cm. Bibliography: p.100-105. ISBN 978-226-553-5 (pbk) DDC 371.91/1/09669 19
1. Children, Blind - Education - Nigeria. I. Ozoji, Emeka D. II. Title.
HV2165.5 .A65 1985 **NYPL [Sc D 89-209]**

Aboud, Frances E. Children and prejudice / Frances Aboud. Oxford [Oxfordshire] ; New York, NY : B. Blackwell, 1988. x, 149 p. : ill. ; 24 cm. (Social psychology and society) Includes indexes. Bibliography: p. [134]-142. ISBN 0-631-14939-2 : DDC 305.2/3 19
1. Prejudices in children. 2. Ethnicity in children. 3.

Race awareness in children. I. Title. II. Series.
BF723.P75 A24 1988   *NYPL [Sc E 89-57]*

About the poor . Herzog, Elizabeth.
[Washington] , 1967 [i.e. 1968] 85 p.   DDC
362.5/0973
HC110.P6 H47   *NYPL [Sc E 88-67]*

Aboyade, B. Olabimpe. The provision of
information for rural development / by B.
Olabimpe Aboyade. Ibadan : Fountain
Publications, 1987. xv, 104 p. ; 22 cm.
Bibliography: p. 101-104.   ISBN 978-267-900-3
*1. Communication in rural development - Nigeria. 2.
Rural development - Nigeria - Information services. I.
Title.*   *NYPL [Sc D 88-739]*

Abraham, the patriarch in Islam. see **Abraham,
the patriarch - Islamic interpretations.**

**Abraham, the patriarch - Interpretations,
Islamic.** see **Abraham, the patriarch - Islamic
interpretations.**

**ABRAHAM, THE PATRIARCH - ISLAMIC
INTERPRETATIONS.**
'Isá 'Abd Allāh Muḥammad al-Mahdī, 1945-
The true story of the Prophet Abraham (Pbuh)
[microform] /. Brooklyn, N.Y. [1980?] 96 p. :
NYPL [Sc Micro R-4114 no. 7]

Abraham, the patriarch - Muslim interpretations.
see **Abraham, the patriarch - Islamic
interpretations.**

Abraham Vest, or, The cast-off restored. Fitts,
Hervey. Boston, 1847. 142 p.
T275.V55 F5 1847   *NYPL [Sc Rare C 88-12]*

Abranches, Henrique. Cantico barroco / Henrique
Abranches. Lisboa, Portugal : Edições 70,
c1987. 53 p. : ill. ; 20 cm. (Autores angolanos. 45)
I. Series: Colecção Autores angolanos, 45. II. Title.
NYPL [Sc C 88-322]

Abreu, Antero. Poesia intermitente / Antero
Abreu. Lisboa, Portugal : Edições 70, c1987. 48
p. ; 20 cm. (Autores angolanos. 44)
I. Series: Colecção Autores angolanos, 44. II. Title.
NYPL [Sc C 88-321]

ABRON (AFRICAN PEOPLE) - HISTORY.
Princes & serviteurs du royaume . Paris , 1987.
225 p. :   ISBN 2-901161-29-4
NYPL [Sc E 88-409]

**Abstracts of theses accepted by University of Ife,
1985** /. Hezekiah Oluwasanmi Library. Ile-Ife ,
1986. ii, ii, 95 p. ;   *NYPL [Sc D 89-580]*

Abu, Katharine. Oppong, Christine. Seven roles of
women . Geneva , 1987. xi, 127 p. :
NYPL [Sc E 89-143]

Abu Sabah, Mohammed Azim. Tribal structure of
the Ngok Dinka of southern Kordofan Province
[microform] / by Mohammed Azin Abu Sabah.
Khartoum : Development Studies and Research
Centre, Faculty of Economic & Social Studies,
University of Khartoum, 1978. 20 leaves ; 28
cm. (Working report/Abyei Project. no.1) Microfiche.
New York: New York Public Library, 198 . 1
microfiche: negative; 11 x 15 cm. (FSN Sc 019,061)
*1. Tribes and tribal systems - Sudan - Kordofan. 2.
Dinka (Nilotic tribe). I. Title.*
NYPL [Sc Micro F-11037]

Abucar, Mohamed. Struggle for development : the
Black communities of North & East Preston
and Cherry Brook, Nova Scotia. 1784-1987 /
Mohamed Abucar.1st ed. [S.l. : s.n.], 1988
(Halifax, Nova Scotia: McCurdy Print. &
Typesetting) xiv, 103 p. : ill., map ; 23 cm.
Bibliography: p. 99-103.   ISBN 0-921201-04-4
1. Blacks - Nova Scotia - Social conditions. I. Title.
NYPL [Sc D 89-138]

**ABYEI (SUDAN) - ECONOMIC
CONDITIONS.**
Elkhider, Mohmed Osman. Some aspects of
economic structures [microform] /. Khartoum ,
1978. 27 leaves ;   *NYPL [Sc Micro F-11038]*

Abyssinia. see **Ethiopia.**

**ACADEMIC ACHIEVEMENT - CASE
STUDIES.**
Bullivant, Brian Milton. The ethnic encounter
in the secondary school . London , New York ,
1987. x, 214 p. ;   ISBN 1-85000-255-X :   DDC
371.97/0994 19
LC3739 .B84 1987   *NYPL [JLE 88-2088]*

ACADEMIC ACHIEVEMENT - SENEGAL.
Morin, Melle. Les retards scolaires et les échecs
au niveau de l'ecole primaire du Sénégal /.

[Dakar] [1966?] 143 leaves ;
NYPL [Sc F 87-439]

**ACADEMIC ACHIEVEMENT - SOCIAL
ASPECTS - TRINIDAD AND TOBAGO.**
Osuji, Rose C. The effect of socio-economic
status on the eductional achievement of Form
V students in Trinidad /. St. Augustine,
Trinidad , 1987. xiv, 229 p. ;   ISBN
976-618-002-4   *NYPL [Sc E 88-352]*

ACADEMIC DISSERTATIONS. see
DISSERTATIONS, ACADEMIC.

Accords perdus . Dorsinville, Roger. Montréal,
Québec, Canada , c1987. 190 p. ;   ISBN
2-920862-07-3   *NYPL [Sc C 88-128]*

**An account of the slave trade on the coast of
Africa** /. Falconbridge, Alexander, d. 1792.
London , 1788. 55 p. ;
NYPL [Sc Rare F 88-63]

ACCUMULATION, CAPITAL. see **SAVING
AND INVESTMENT.**

Ace.
Sotheby, Madeline. The Bob Marley story /.
London , 1985. 64 p. ;   ISBN 0-09-160031-6
(pbk) :   DDC 428.6/2 19
PE1121   *NYPL [Sc C 88-141]*

Achebe, Chinelo. The last laugh and other stories
/ Chinelo Achebe. Ibadan : Heinemann
Educational Books (Nig.), 1988. 79 p. ; 18 cm.
ISBN 978-12-9853-7
1. Nigeria - Fiction. I. Title.
NYPL [Sc C 89-152]

Achebe, Chinua.
Hopes and impediments : selected essays,
1965-1987 / Chinua Achebe. London :
Heinemann, 1988. x, 130 p. ; 22 cm. Includes
index. Bibliography: p. 122-126.   ISBN 0-435-91000-0
(cased) :   DDC 823/.914/09 19
*1. West African literature (English) - History and
criticism. 2. Africans in literature. I. Title.*
PR881   *NYPL [Sc D 88-1265]*

Things fall apart. Wren, Robert M. Chinua
Achebe, Things fall apart / Robert M. Wren.
London , 1980. vi, 56 p. ;   ISBN 0-582-60109-6
NYPL [Sc C 88-88]

[Things fall apart. German]
Okonkwo, oder, Das Alte stürzt : roman /
Chinua Achebe. Stuttgart : H. Goverts,
c1958. 230 p. ; 20 cm. Translation of: Things fall
apart.
*1. Igbo (African people) - Fiction. 2. Nigeria - Fiction.
I. Title. II. Title: Alte stürzt.*
NYPL [Sc C 88-357]

[Things fall apart. Spanish]
Todo se derrumba / Chinua Achebe ;
traducción de Fernando Santos. 1st ed.
Madrid : Ediciones Alfaguara, 1986. 198 p. ;
22 cm. Translation of: Things fall apart.   ISBN
84-204-2323-8
*1. Igbo (African people) - Fiction. 2. Nigeria - Fiction.
I. Title.*   *NYPL [Sc D 88-1415]*

The university and the leadership factor in
Nigerian politics / Chinua Achebe. Enugu,
Nigeria : ABIC Books & Equipment, c1988. 22
p. ; 19 cm. (Strategies for Nigerian development)
ISBN 978-226-907-7
*1. Political leadership - Nigeria. 2. Higher education
and state - Nigeria. I. Title. II. Series.*
NYPL [Sc D 89-28]

Achebe, Chinwe. The world of the Ogbanje / by
Chinwe Achebe. Enugu, Nigeria : Fourth
Dimension Publishers, 1986. iv, 68 p. : ill. ; 22
cm. Bibliography: p. 67-68.   ISBN 978-15-6239-0
DDC 616.89/1 19
*1. Cultural psychiatry - Nigeria. 2. Igbo (African
people) - Psychology. I. Title.*
RC455.4.E8 A34 1986
NYPL [Sc D 88-1246]

ACHIEVEMENT, ACADEMIC. see
ACADEMIC ACHIEVEMENT.

Achime, Nwafueze H. Oyaide, William John,
1936- Presidentialism . Benin City, Nigeria ,
c1987. xi, 133 p. ;   ISBN 978-300-550-2
NYPL [Sc D 88-917]

Achode, Codjo. The Negro renaissance from
America back to Africa : a study of the Harlem
Renaissance as a Black and African movement
/ by Codjo Achode. Ann Arbor, Mich. :
University Microfilms International, 1986. viii,
306 p. ; 22 cm. Thesis (Ph.D.)-University of

Pennsylvania,1986. Includes index. Bibliography: p.
272-284.
1. Harlem Renaissance. I. Title.
NYPL [Sc D 89-291]

Acholonu, Catherine Obianuju. Into the heart of
Biafra / [Catherine Obianuju Acholonu.]
Owerri, Nigeria : Totan Publishers, c1985. 86
p. ; 18 cm. ISBN 978-244-914-8
*1. Nigeria - History - Civil War, 1967-1970 - Drama. I.
Title.*   *NYPL [Sc C 88-337]*

Aclarações . Costa, Antonio Maria Judice da.
Lisboa , 1898. 28 p. ;
NYPL [Sc Micro F-10,894]

Acquah, Kobena Eyi. The man who died : poems
1974-1979 / Kobena Eyi Acquah. Accra :
Asempa Publishers, 1984. 94 p. : ill. ; 20 cm.
ISBN 996-478-065-6 (pbk.)   DDC 821 19
I. Title.
PR9379.9.A27 M3 1984
NYPL [Sc D 88-247]

Acquier, Jean-Louis, 1946- Le Burundi /
Jean-Louis Acquier ; dessins de Christian
Seignobos. Marseille, France : Editions
Parenthèses, c1986. 129 p. : ill. ; 21 x 25 cm.
(Collection Architectures traditionnelles, 0291-4921 . 3e
v.) Includes glossary. Bibliography: p. 125-126.   ISBN
2-86364-030-5 :   DDC 728/.67/0967572 19
*1. Dwellings - Burundi. 2. Vernacular architecture -
Burundi. I. Series: Collection Architectures
traditionnelles , 3e v. II. Title.*
GT377.B94 A27 1986   *NYPL [Sc E 88-568]*

Across the great craterland to the Congo . Barns,
Thomas Alexander, 1880- London , 1923. 271,
[1] p., [64] leaves of plates, 2 folded leaves :
NYPL [Sc E 88-252]

The act /. Mwiwawi, Andrew M., 1952- Nairobi,
Kenya , 1976. 76 p. ;   DDC 823
PZ4.M9933 Ac PR9381.9.M93
NYPL [Sc B 89-22]

ACTING - COSTUME. see **COSTUME.**

Action (Parti communiste martiniquais) Nicolas,
Armand. Le combat d'André Aliker /.
Fort-de-France , 1974. 108 p. :
NYPL [Sc D 88-1189]

Activism in American librarianship, 1962-1973 /
edited by Mary Lee Bundy and Frederick J.
Stielow. New York : Greenwood Press, 1987. x,
207 p. : ill. ; 25 cm. (Contributions in librarianship
and information science, 0084-9243 . no. 58) Includes
index. Bibliography: p. [197]-198.   ISBN
0-313-24602-5 (lib. bdg. : alk. paper)   DDC 021
19
*1. Libraries and society - United States - History - 20th
century. 2. Library science - Political aspects - United
States - History - 20th century. 3. Library science -
Social aspects - United States - History - 20th century.
4. Librarians - Professional ethics - United States -
History - 20th century. I. Bundy, Mary Lee, 1927-. II.
Stielow, Frederick J., 1946-.*
Z716.4 .A27 1987   *NYPL [JFE 87-6266]*

**Activities of the Knights of the Ku Klux Klan in
Southern California, 1921-1925** /. Salley,
Robert Lee. 1963. v, 199 leaves ;
NYPL [Sc F 88-119]

ACTORS - HAITI - BIOGRAPHY.
Fouchard, Jean. Artistes et répertoire des
scènes de Saint-Domingue /. Port-au-Prince,
Haiti , 1988. 195 p. ;   *NYPL [Sc D 89-410]*

**ACTORS - UNITED STATES - BIOGRAPHY -
JUVENILE LITERATURE.**
Bergman, Carol. Sidney Poitier /. New York ,
c1988. 110 p. :   ISBN 1-555-46605-2   DDC
791.43/028/0924 B 92 19
PN2287.P57 B47 1988   *NYPL [Sc E 88-171]*

Acts . Smith, Obediah Michael. [Nassau? , c1983]
56 p. ;
MLCS 85/735 (P)   *NYPL [Sc D 88-494]*

Adam and the roof /. Simon, Leonard J. [New
Jersey? , 198-?] 36 p. :   *NYPL [Sc B 89-28]*

Adam Clayton Powell, Jr. /. Jakoubek, Robert E.
New York , c1988. xiv, 252 p. ;   ISBN
1-555-46606-0   DDC 973/.0496073024 B 92 19
E748.P86 J35 1988   *NYPL [Sc E 88-372]*

Adam, Hassan. Kiswahili : elementary course with
key / by Hassan Adam. Hamburg : Helmut
Buske, 1987. 208 p. : map ; 24 cm. English and
Swahili. Bibliography: p. 207-208.   ISBN
3-87118-843-3

1. Swahili language - Text-books for foreign speakers - English. 2. Swahili language - Self-instruction. I. Title.
NYPL [Sc E 88-433]

Adama. Ilboudo, Pierre Claver, 1948- Adama, ou, La force des choses . Paris , 1987. 154 p. ;
ISBN 2-7087-0484-2
PQ3989.2.I43 A65x 1987
NYPL [Sc C 88-316]

Adama, ou, La force des choses . Ilboudo, Pierre Claver, 1948- Paris , 1987. 154 p. ; ISBN 2-7087-0484-2
PQ3989.2.I43 A65x 1987
NYPL [Sc C 88-316]

ADAMAWA DIALECT. see FULAH LANGUAGE.

Adamou, Aboubacar. Atlas du Niger /. Paris , c1980. 64 p. : ISBN 2-85258-151-5 : DDC 912/.6626 19
G2660 .A8 1980   *NYPL [Sc F 84-232]*

Adamou, Ndam Njoya. see Ndam Njoya, Adamou, 1942-

Adams, Robert Hugo. The little black book of business inspirations / by Robert Hugo Adams Hempstead, NY : Minority Business Review, 1987. vi, 74 p. : ill. ; 22 cm.
1. Minority business enterprises - United States. I. Title.
NYPL [Sc D 88-440]

ADAMS, TOM, 1931-1985.
Hoyos, F. A. Tom Adams . Basingstoke , 1988. x, 198 p., [32] p. of plates : ISBN 0-333-46332-3 (pbk) : DDC 972.98/1/00994 19
NYPL [Sc D 88-1275]

Adams, W. M. (William Mark), 1955-
Environmental issues in African development planning /. Cambridge , c1988. v, 84 p. : ISBN 0-902993-21-6 (pbk) : DDC 330.96/0328 19
HC502   *NYPL [Sc D 88-1233]*

Adapting to drought . Mortimore, M. J., 1937- Cambridge , New York , 1989. xxii, 299 p. : ISBN 0-521-32312-6 DDC 333.73 19
HC1055.Z7 N6755 1988
NYPL [Sc E 89-191]

Adassa and her hen. McCall, Virginia, 1909- [New York, 1971] 79 p. DDC [Fic]
PZ7.M12295 Ad   *NYPL [Sc D 89-100]*

Adasu, Moses Orshio. Understanding African traditional religion / Moses Orshio Adasu. Sherborne, Dorset, England : Dorset Pub. Co., 1985- v. ; 21 cm. Bibliography: part 1, p. 47-48.
ISBN 0-902129-68-6
1. Christianity - Africa. 2. Africa - Religion. I. Title.
NYPL [Sc D 88-856]

Adawaisi, Linus C. The inmates : a play / Linus C. Adawaisi. [Maiduguri? : s.n.]. 1987 (Maiduguri : Uncle Oguns Press) 72 p. ; 19 cm. Cover title.
I. Title.   *NYPL [Sc C 89-104]*

Addai, G. K. Langley, Ph. Managing the Botswana brigades . Douala, U.R.C. [1983] 93 p. : DDC 658.3/12404/096811 19
HD5715.5.B55 L36 1983
NYPL [Sc E 88-483]

Addison, Joan. A historical survey of facilities for handicapped people in Zimbabwe / by Joan Addison. Harare, Zimbabwe : NASCOH [National Association of Societies for the Care of the Handicapped], [1986] 36 p. : ill., map ; 30 cm. Includes index. Bibliography: p. 29.
1. Handicapped - Services for - Zimbabwe. I. Title.
NYPL [Sc F 88-266]

Addleson, Mark. Regional restructuring under apartheid . Johannesburg , 1987. xxii, 317 p. ; ISBN 0-86975-327-4   *NYPL [Sc D 89-16]*

Addo, N. O. West African Seminar on Population Studies, University of Ghana, 1972. Interdisciplinary approaches to population studies . Legon , 1975. ix, 333 p. :
HB21 .W38 1972   *NYPL [JLD 78-861]*

The Address and reply on the presentation of a testimonial to S.P. Chase by the colored people of Cincinnati. Cincinnati : H. W. Derby, 1845. 35 p. ; 23 cm. Cover title. Includes an account of the case of Samuel Watson, an escaped slave, for whom Chase acted as counsel.
1. Watson, Samuel, fugitive slave. 2. Slavery - Ohio. I. Chase, Salmon Portland, 1808-1873. II. Title.
NYPL [Sc Rare G 86-15]

Address by His Excellency the Life President, Ngwazi Dr. H. Kamuzu Banda, to open the 1978 convention of the Malaŵi Congress Party, Zomba Catholic Secondary School, September 24, 1978 [microform] Banda, Hastings Kamuzu, 1905- Blantyre [1978] 16 p. ;   *NYPL [Sc Micro F-11123]*

Address by Prime Minister Maurice Bishop at the opening of the Socialist International meeting held in Grenada, July 23-24 [microform]. Bishop, Maurice. [St. George's, Grenada] [1981?] 12 leaves ;
NYPL [Sc Micro R-4108 no.29]

Address of the Board of Managers of the American Colonization Society, to the auxiliary societies and the people of the United States. American Colonization Society. Board of Managers. Washington , 1820. 32 p. ;
NYPL [Sc Rare G 86-23]

Address of the Conference on Development Problems of Small Island States, July 13, 1981 /. Bishop, Maurice. [St. George's, Grenada , 1981] 9 p. ;   *NYPL [Sc Micro R-4108 no.26]*

An address on slavery, and against immediate emancipation . Citizen of New-York. New-York , 1834. 16 p. ;
NYPL [Sc Rare G 86-19]

An Address to Her Royal Highness the Dutchess of York, against the use of sugar. [London? : s.n.], 1792. 20 p. ; 21 cm.
1. Slavery - West Indies, British. 2. Sugar trade - West Indies, British. I. Frederica Charlotte Ulrica Catherina, Duchess of York, 1767-1820.
NYPL [Sc Rare G 86-31]

An address to the abolitionists of Massachusetts, on the subject of political action /. Massachusetts Anti-Slavery Society. Board of Managers. [Boston , 1838] 20 p. ;
NYPL [Sc Rare G 86-10]

An Address to the citizens of the United States, on the subject of slavery / reported to the Association of Friends, for advocating the cause of the slave, and improving the condition of the free people of color, by a committee appointed to collect and disseminate information on that subject. [Philadelphia] : Published by direction of the Association, 1838 ([Philadelphia] : Neall & Shann, printers) 24 p. ; 18 cm.
1. Slavery - United States - Emancipation. I. Association of Friends for Advocating the Cause of the Slave, and Improving the Condition of the Free People of Color. II. Title.   *NYPL [Sc Rare G 86-12]*

Ade, Femi Ojo- see Ojo-Ade, Femi.

Adebagbo, S. A. Family and social change . Lagos, Nigeria , 1986. vi, 96 p. ;
NYPL [Sc D 88-794]

Adebo, Simeon O., 1913- Our international years / Simeon Ola Adebó. Ibadan : Spectrum Books, 1988. xi, 281 p., [10] p. of plates : ill., ports. ; 22 cm. Includes index. ISBN 987-246-025-7
1. Statesmen - Nigeria - Biography. 2. Ambassadors - Nigeria - Biography. I. Title.   *NYPL [Sc D 89-75]*

Adebowale, Bayo. Out of his mind/ Bayo Adcbowale. Ibadan : Spectrum Books Limited, 1987. 149 p. ; 18 cm. ISBN 978-246-160-1
1. Nigeria - Fiction. I. Title.
NYPL [Sc C 88-168]

Adedeji, Adebayo. The political class, the higher civil service and the challenge of nation-building [microform] / by Adebayo Adedeji. Addis Ababa, Ethiopia : United Nations Information Service, Economic Commission for Africa, [1981?] 24 p. ; 22 cm. "Text of a paper delivered at the workshop on the Relationship between Policy-makers and the Higher Civil Service under the Nigerian Executive Presidential System of Government held at the Administrative Staff College, Badagry from 4-7 March 1981." Microfiche. New York: New York Public Library, 198 . 1 microfiche: negative; 11 x 15 cm. (FSN Sc 019,105)
1. Civil service - Nigeria. I. Title.
NYPL [Sc Micro F-11062]

Adefuye, Ade. History of the peoples of Lagos State /. Ikeja, Lagos , 1987. xii, 378 p. ; ISBN 978-228-148-4   *NYPL [Sc D 88-731]*

Adekanye, Femi. The elements of banking / Femi A. Adekanye. 2d ed. Leighton Buzzard : G. Burn, [1984] xxvi, 461 p. : ill. ; 21 cm. Bibliography: p. 527-528. ISBN 0-907721-19-2 (pbk)

1. Banks and banking - Nigeria. I. Title.
NYPL [Sc D 88-1139]

Adélaïde-Merlande, Jacques. Histoire des communes . [S.l.] , c1986. 6 v. : ISBN 2-88218-800-4 (set) DDC 972.97/6 19
F2151 .H575 1986   *NYPL [Sc F 88-98]*

Adele, Lynne. Black history, black vision : the visionary image in Texas / Lynne Adele ; exhibition organized by the Archer M. Huntington Art Gallery ... January 27-March 19, 1989 : The University of Texas, Institute of Texan Cultures at San Antonio ... April 11-June 11, 1989 : Amarillo Art Center ... July 1-August 6, 1989. / by Lynne Adele ; exhibition organized by the Archer M. Huntington Art Gallery, The University of Texas at Austin. [Austin] : Archer M. Huntington Art Gallery, College of Fine Arts, University of Texas at Austin, 1989. 93 p. : ill. (some col.) ; 28 cm. ISBN 0-935213-15-5
1. Afro-American art - Texas - Exhibitions. 2. Art, Modern - 20th century - Texas - Exhibitions. 3. Afro-American artists - Texas - Biography. I. Archer M. Huntington Art Gallery. II. Institute of Texas Cultures at San Antonio. University of Texas. III. Amarillo Art Center. IV. Title.
NYPL [Sc F 89-155]

Adeniran, Tunde.
[Poems. Selections]
Fate unearthed! : selected poems / by Tunde Adeniran. Ibadan : Aderet Publishers Ltd., 1982. 71 p. ; 21 cm.
I. Title.   *NYPL [Sc C 88-56]*

Adenubi, A. Solarin, Tai. Timeless Tai /. Lagos, Nigeria , 1985. x, 232 p. ;
NYPL [Sc D 89-371]

Adenuga, Adebisi Fola. Odunuga, S. A. F. (Samuel Adedoyin Folafunmi), 1902- [Sermons. Selections.] The life of Venerable Archdeacon S.A.F. Odunuga /. [Nigeria] , 1982. xiii, 175 p., [2] p. of plates : DDC 252/.03 19
BX5700.7.Z6 O28 1982
NYPL [Sc E 89-142]

Adepegba, Cornelius Oyeleke, 1941- Decorative arts of the Fulani nomads / C. O. Adepegba. Ibadan, Nigeria : Ibadan University Press, 1986. 48 p. : ill. (some col.) ; 22 cm. Bibliography: p. [45]-48. ISBN 978-12-1195-4
1. Decorative arts, Fulah. 2. Fulahs. I. Title.
NYPL [Sc D 88-735]

Adepoju, Aderanti. Seminar on Internal Migration in Nigeria (1975 : University of Ife) Internal migration in Nigeria . [Ife] , 1976. iii, 300 p. :
NYPL [Sc E 88-489]

Aderibigbe, A. B. A History of the University of Lagos, 1962-1987 /. Lagos, Nigeria , 1987. xiii, 600 p. :   *NYPL [Sc F 89-82]*

Aderinlewo, 'Dele. Youths in revolt : a drama commentary on education / 'Dele Aderinlewo. Ibadan, Oyo State, Nigeria : Stevelola Educational Publishers, 1985. 63 p. : ill. ; 19 cm. (Lola frontline drama series) ISBN 978-18-0006-2
I. Title. II. Series.   *NYPL [Sc C 88-293]*

Aderinto, Adeyemo. Manpower development and utilization in Nigeria . Lagos, Nigeria , 1986. xiii, 240 p. ; ISBN 978-226-441-5
NYPL [Sc D 88-1077]

Aderounmu, Olusola. Managing the Nigerian education enterprise / Olusola Aderounmu and Olusola Aina. Ikeja, Lagos, Nigeria : John West Publications, 1986. 230 p. : ill. ; 27 cm. Includes bibliographical references.
1. School management and organization - Nigeria. 2. Universities and Colleges - Nigeria - Administration. 3. Education - Nigeria. I. Aina, Olusola. II. Title.
NYPL [Sc F 88-171]

Aderounmu, Olusola W. An introduction to the administration of schools in Nigeria / Olusola W. Aderounmu, Egbe T. Ehiametalor. Ibadan, Nigeria : Evans Brothers (Nigeria Publishers), 1985. xiii, 271 p. : ill. ; 22 cm. Includes bibliographical references. ISBN 978-16-7241-2
1. School management and organization - Nigeria. I. Ehiametalor, Egbe T. II. Title.
NYPL [Sc D 88-730]

Adesina, Segun. Hanson, John Wagner. Secondary level teachers: supply and demand in Nigeria. [East Lansing, c1973] 1 v. (various pagings) DDC 331.1/26
LB2833.4.N6 H36   *NYPL [Sc F 88-151]*

Adesua, Adeleye. Administrative problems in Nigerian schools / Adeleye Adesua. Agege-Lagos [Nigeria] : Ibijoke Publications, c1987. vii, 136 p. ; 22 cm. Bibliography: p. 134-135. ISBN 978-302-711-5
1. School management and organization - Nigeria - Problems, exercises, etc. I. Title.
NYPL [Sc D 88-789]

Adewole, Ayo. A philosophy of education for Nigeria : Including a treatise of the social, economic and political perspectives / Ayo Adewole. Onitsha : Leadway Books, 1988, c1987. 131 p. ; 21 cm. Includes bibliographical references and index. ISBN 978-254-972-X
1. Education - Nigeria. I. Title.
NYPL [Sc D 89-85]

Adéwọlé, Lásún. Àlàyé Akéwi / Lásún Adéwọlé. Ibàdàn : Onibonoje Press & Book Industries, 1987. v. 90 p. ; 19 cm. ISBN 978-14-5062-2
1. Yoruba language - Texts. I. Title.
NYPL [Sc C 88-217]

Adewọle, Lawrence Olufemi. The Yoruba language : published works and doctoral dissertations 1843-1986 / Lawrence Olufemi Adewọle. Hamburg : Helmut Buske Verlag, c1987. 182 p. ; 21 cm. (African linguistic bibliographies . v. 3) Includes indexes. ISBN 3-87118-842-5
1. Yoruba language - Bibliography. I. Title. II. Series.
NYPL [Sc D 88-821]

Adewunmi, Wole. Twenty five years of merchant banking in Nigeria / by Wole Adewunmi. Akoka : Lagos University Press, 1985. xvi, 136 p. ; 23 cm. "Published to commemorate the 25th anniversary of NAL Merchant Bank Limited." Spine title: 25 years of merchant banking in Nigeria. Bibliography: p. 130-136. ISBN 978-226-475-X : DDC 332.66/09669 19
1. NAL Merchant Bank - History. 2. Merchant banks - Nigeria - History. I. NAL Merchant Bank. II. Title. III. Title: 25 years of merchant banking in Nigeria.
HG1971.N6 A34 1985
NYPL [Sc D 88-1020]

Adger, John Bailey, 1810-1899.
The religious instruction of the colored population : a sermon / preached by the Rev. John B. Adger, in the Second Presbyterian Church, Charleston, S.C., May 9th, 1847 ; published by request. Charleston : T.W. Haynes, 1847. 19 p. ; 19 cm.
1. Afro-Americans - South Carolina - Charleston - Religion. 2. Slavery - South Carolina - Charleston - Condition of slaves. I. Title.
NYPL [Sc Rare G 86-6]

A REVIEW OF REPORTS TO THE LEGISLATURE OF S.C., ON THE REVIVAL OF THE SLAVE TRADE. B. Notice of the Rev. John B. Adger's article on the slave trade Charleston, S.C. , 1858 (Charleston, S.C. : Steam Power Press of Walker, Evans) 28 p. ;
NYPL [Sc Rare G 86-8]

Adire, a living craft /. Okuboyejo, Betti. [Nigeria] , c1987. 55 p. :
NYPL [Sc C 89-16]

Adjanoumelezo . Franketienne. [Port-au-Prince?] 1987. 522 p. ;   *NYPL [Sc D 88-466]*

Adler, Alfred. Princes & serviteurs du royaume . Paris , 1987. 225 p. : ISBN 2-901161-29-4
NYPL [Sc E 88-409]

Adler, B. Tougher than leather : the authorized biography of Run-DMC / B. Adler. New York : New American Library, c1987. viii, 191 p., [14] p. of plates : ill. ; 18 cm. ISBN 0-451-15121-6 (pbk.) :
1. Rapping (Music). 2. Rock musicians - Biography. 3. Afro-American singers - Biography. I. Title.
NYPL [Sc C 88-271]

Adler, David A. Jackie Robinson : he was the first / by David A. Adler ; illustrated by Robert Casilla.1st ed. New York : Holiday House, c1989. 48 p. : ill. ; 26 cm. Includes index. Traces the life of the talented and determined athlete who broke the color barrier in major league baseball in 1947 by joining the Brooklyn Dodgers. ISBN 0-8234-0734-9 DDC 796.357/092/4 B 19
1. Robinson, Jackie, 1919-1972 - Juvenile literature. 2. Baseball players - United States - Biography - Juvenile literature. 3. Afro-American baseball players - Biography - Juvenile literature. I. Casilla, Robert, ill. II.

Title.
GV865 .A37 1989   NYPL [Sc F 89-137]

Adloff, Richard. Thompson, Virginia McLean, 1903- Historical dictionary of the People's Republic of the Congo /. Metuchen, N.J. , 1984. xxi, 239 p. : ISBN 0-8108-1716-0 DDC 967/.24 19
DT546.215 .T47 1984   NYPL [Sc D 85-104]

Administering management development institutions in Africa /. Rwegasira, Kami S. P. Aldershot, England , Brookfield, Vt. , 1988. vi, 112 p. ; ISBN 0-566-05501-5 DDC 658.4/07124/096 19
HF5549.5.A78 R94 1988
NYPL [Sc D 88-458]

ADMINISTRATION. see CIVIL SERVICE; MANAGEMENT; POLITICAL SCIENCE; STATE, THE.

ADMINISTRATION OF CRIMINAL JUSTICE. see CRIMINAL JUSTICE, ADMINISTRATION OF.

ADMINISTRATION OF JUSTICE. see JUSTICE, ADMINISTRATION OF.

ADMINISTRATION, PUBLIC. see PUBLIC ADMINISTRATION.

ADMINISTRATIVE AGENCIES - UNITED STATES. Walton, Hanes, 1941- When the marching stopped . Albany , c1988. xxiv, 263 p. : ISBN 0-88706-687-9 DDC 353.0081/1 19
E185.615 .W325 1988   NYPL [Sc E 89-10]

Administrative decentralisation in the Zambian bureaucracy . Lungu, Gatian F. Gweru, Zimbabwe , c1985. 85 p. :
NYPL [Sc D 89-318]

Administrative problems in Nigerian schools /. Adesua, Adeleye. Agege-Lagos [Nigeria] , c1987. vii, 136 p. ; ISBN 978-302-711-5
NYPL [Sc D 88-789]

Administrators of special education . Ihenacho, Izuka John. [Nigeria] , c1986. 208 p. ; ISBN 978-239-609-5 (pbk) DDC 371.9/09669 19
LC3988.N6 I44 1986   NYPL [Sc C 89-145]

ADOLESCENT PARENTS - UNITED STATES. Hendricks, Leo E. A comparative analysis of three select populations of Black unmarried adolescent fathers /. Washington, D.C. , 1982. ix, 129 p. :   *NYPL [Sc F 88-222]*

Adolf Hitler et les accords de Locarno. Durant, Franck Alphonse. Rétrospectives [microform] . Port-au-Prince, Haiti , 1977. 16 p. ;
NYPL [Sc Micro F 10,933]

Adolf Loos . Groenendijk, Paul. Rotterdam , 1985. 39 p., [6] leaves of plates : ISBN 90-6450-027-4 DDC 728.3/72/0228 19
NA1011.5.L6 G76 1985 NYPL [Sc F 89-67]

Adolf Loos : house for Josephine Baker. Groenendijk, Paul. Adolf Loos . Rotterdam , 1985. 39 p., [6] leaves of plates : ISBN 90-6450-027-4 DDC 728.3/72/0228 19
NA1011.5.L6 G76 1985 NYPL [Sc F 89-67]

ADOPTION - JUVENILE FICTION. Myers, Walter Dean, 1937- Me, Mop, and the Moondance Kid /. New York , 1988. 154 p. : ISBN 0-440-50065-6 DDC [Fic] 19
PZ7.M992 Me 1988   NYPL [Sc D 88-1457]

Adotevi, Bénédicta. Christianisme en Afrique noire . Dakar , 1979. 162 p. ;
NYPL [Sc F 89-17]

Adouknou, B. Mort dans la vie africaine. Spanish. La Muerte en la vida africana. Barcelona , París , 1984. 314 p. : ISBN 84-85800-81-8
NYPL [Sc D 88-601]

ADULT EDUCATION - ANTIGUA AND BARBUDA - DIRECTORIES. Wolfe, David. Adult education in Antigua and Barbuda . St. John's, Antigua , 1985. 61 p. ; DDC 379/.97297/4 19
L912.A63 W65 1983   NYPL [Sc E 88-119]

Adult education in Antigua and Barbuda . Wolfe, David. St. John's, Antigua , 1985. 61 p. ; DDC 379/.97297/4 19
L912.A63 W65 1983   NYPL [Sc E 88-119]

ADULT EDUCATION - NIGERIA. Odokara, E. O. Outreach . Nsukka [between 1976 and 1981] 67 p. : *NYPL [Sc E 88-275]*

ADULT EDUCATION - UGANDA. Kakooza, Teresa. The problems of the university's role in adult education in Uganda /. [Kampala?] , 1987. 20 p. ;
NYPL [Sc F 89-92]

An adult functional literacy manual /. Asiedu, Kobina. Ibadan , 1985. ix, 148 p. ; ISBN 978-15-4737-5 (Nigeria)
NYPL [Sc D 88-799]

Adulthood rites . Butler, Octavia E. New York, NY, c1988. 277 p. ; ISBN 0-446-51422-5 : DDC 813/.54 19
PS3552.U827 A65 1988
NYPL [JFE 88-6322]

ADULTS, EDUCATION OF. see ADULT EDUCATION.

ADVENTURE AND ADVENTURERS - GREAT BRITAIN - BIOGRAPHY. Thesiger, Wilfred, 1910- The life of my choice /. London , 1987. 459 p., [32] p. of plates : ISBN 0-00-216194-X :
G525 .T415x 1987   NYPL [Sc E 88-222]

Adventure in black and white /. Gatti, Attilio. New York , 1943. 172 p. :
NYPL [Sc D 88-1169]

ADVENTURERS. see ADVENTURE AND ADVENTURERS.

Adventures of a bank inspector /. Umobuarie, D. O. Nigeria , 1988. 168 p. ; ISBN 978-300-323-2
NYPL [Sc C 88-339]

The adventures of Dan Aiki /. Powe, Edward L. (Edward Llewellyn), 1941- Paterson, N.J. , c1987. 32 p. :   *NYPL [Sc D 88-489]*

ADVERTISING, CONSUMER. see ADVERTISING.

ADVERTISING - EXHIBITIONS. Negripub . [Paris] [1987] 157 p. : ISBN 2-7012-0580-8   *NYPL [Sc E 88-234]*

Advertising in Nigerian perspective /. Doghudje, Chris. Lagos , c1985. 85 p. ; ISBN 978-249-700-2   *NYPL [Sc D 88-785]*

ADVERTISING - MEDIUMS - RADIO. see RADIO ADVERTISING.

ADVERTISING - NIGERIA. Doghudje, Chris. Advertising in Nigerian perspective /. Lagos , c1985. 85 p. ; ISBN 978-249-700-2   *NYPL [Sc D 88-785]*

ADVERTISING, RADIO. see RADIO ADVERTISING.

ADVERTISING, RETAIL. see ADVERTISING.

ADVERTISING - RETAIL TRADE. see ADVERTISING.

Adzei, Morgan. A burning desire / Morgan Adzei ; foreword by Dr. John Henrik Clarke. New York N.Y. : M. Adzei, 1984. 145 p. ; 22 cm. Cover title. With autograph of author. ISBN 0-910437-01-7
1. Ghana - Fiction. I. Title.
NYPL [Sc D 89-192]

AERONAUTICS - TRINIDAD AND TOBAGO - HISTORY. Airports Authority of Trinidad and Tobago. The history of aviation in Trinidad & Tobago 1913-1962 /. Port-of-Spain, Trinidad , 1987. xxv, 59 p., [77] p. of plates : ISBN 976-8054-24-2   *NYPL [Sc D 87-1398]*

AEROSTATION. see AERONAUTICS.

Äthiopien -- Unterentwicklung und radikale Militärherrschaft . Brüne, Stefan. Hamburg , 1986. viii, 372 p. ; ISBN 3-923519-63-X
NYPL [L-11 2640 Bd. 26]

Äthiopistische Forschungen.
(Bd. 20) Sumner, Claude. The source of African philosophy . Stuttgart , 1986. 153 p. : ISBN 3-515-04438-8 DDC 199/.63 19
B5409.M27 S86 1986   NYPL [Sc E 89-260]

Affirmation de l'identité culturelle et la formation de la conscience nationale dans l'Afrique contemporaine. Spanish. La Afirmación de la identidad cultural y la formación de la coniencia nacional en el África contemporánea / H. Aguessy ... [et al.] 1a ed. Barcelona : Serbal ; Paris : Unesco, 1983. 220 p. ; 20 cm. (Colección de temas africanos . 13) Papers presented at a conference which was organized jointly by Unesco and the Congolese government, and held in Brazzaville, 13-17 February 1978. Translation of: L'Affirmation de l'identité culturelle et la formation de la conscience nationale dans l'Afrique contemporaine. 1981. Includes bibliographies. ISBN 84-85800-57-5

1. Nationalism - Africa - Congresses. 2. Africa - Politics and government - 1960- - Congresses. I. Aguessy, Honorat, 1934-. II. Unesco. III. Title. IV. Series.
NYPL [Sc D 88-597]

Affirmative action and minorities . Dworaczek, Marian. Monticello. Ill., USA [1988] 63 p. ;
ISBN 1-555-90638-9 (pbk.) : DDC 016.33113/3 19
Z7164.A26 D87 1988 HF5549.5.A34
NYPL [Sc f 89-39]

AFFIRMATIVE ACTION PROGRAMS - BIBLIOGRAPHY.
Dworaczek, Marian. Affirmative action and minorities . Monticello. Ill., USA [1988] 63 p. ; ISBN 1-555-90638-9 (pbk.) : DDC 016.33113/3 19
Z7164.A26 D87 1988 HF5549.5.A34
NYPL [Sc f 89-39]

AFFIRMATIVE ACTION PROGRAMS - LAW AND LEGISLATION - UNITED STATES.
Schwartz, Bernard, 1923- Behind Bakke . New York , c1988. x, 266 p. ; ISBN 0-8147-7878-X : DDC 347.73/0798 347.304798 19
KF228.B34 S39 1988　NYPL [JLE 88-4158]

Afonja, Simi.
Social change in Nigeria /. Harlow, Essex, England , 1984. 261 p. ; ISBN 0-582-64434-8 (pbk.) : DDC 306/.09669 19
HN831.A8 S63 1984　NYPL [Sc D 88-880]

Social change in Nigeria /. London , 1986. 261 p. ; ISBN 0-582-64434-8 (pbk.) : DDC 306/.09669 19
HN831.A8 S63 1986　NYPL [JLE 87-3643]

Afonso, o africano [microform] /. Oliveira, Mário António Fernandes de, 1934- Braga , 1980. 30 p. ; *NYPL [Sc Micro F-10927]*

Africa. Allen, William Dangaix, 1904- Grand Rapids [c1972] 172, 20 p. DDC 916
DT5 .A53 1972　NYPL [Sc F 88-377]

Africa . Coquery-Vidrovitch, Catherine. Berkeley , c1988. x, 403 p. ; ISBN 0-520-05679-5 (alk. paper) DDC 967 19
HC800 .C67513 1988　NYPL [Sc E 89-221]

Africa . Fenton, Thomas P. Maryknoll, N.Y. , c1987. xiv, 144 p. ; ISBN 0-88344-542-8
NYPL [Sc D 88-398]

Africa . Haeger, Barbara. Ibadan, Nigeria , 1982. xiii, 105 p. : *NYPL [Sc D 87-759]*

AFRICA.
Potekhin, I. I. (Ivan Izosimovich), 1903-1964. African problems: analysis of eminent Soviet scientist. Moscow, 1968. 141 p. DDC 320.9/6
DT30 .P59　NYPL [Sc C 88-86]

AFRICA - ADDRESSES, ESSAYS, LECTURES.
African studies. Berlin, 1973. xi, 400 p.
NYPL [JLK 73-249 Bd. 15]

Africa, America, and central Asia : formal and informal empire in the nineteenth century / edited by Peter Morris. [Exeter, Devon] : University of Exeter ; [Atlantic Highlands, N.J. : Distributed in the U. S. A. by Humanities Press], 1984. 107 p. : maps ; 21 cm. (Exeter studies in history, 0260-8626 . no. 9) Distributor from label on t.p. Includes bibliographical references. ISBN 0-85989-295-6 (pbk.) : DDC 330.9/034 19
1. Colonies - Economic conditions. 2. Africa - Economic conditions - To 1918. 3. Latin America - Economic conditions. 4. Asia, Central - Economic conditions. I. Morris, Peter. II. Series.
HC53 .A35 1984　NYPL [Sc D 88-1315]

Africa and its refugees : Africa Refugee Day, June 20, 1975. [Addis Ababa] : Organization of African Unity, Bureau for the Placement and Education of African Refugees, [1975] 76 p. : ill. ; 22 cm. Cover title. Errata slip laid in. DDC 362.8/7/096 19
1. Refugees - Africa. I. Organisation of African Unity. Bureau for Placement and Education of African Refugees.
HV640.4.A35 A35 1975
NYPL [Sc D 88-198]

Africa and the islands / by R. J. Harrison Church ... [et al.]. 3d. impression with rev. maps. London : Longmans, 1966. xiv, 494 p. : ill. ; 22 cm. (Geographies: an intermediate series)

Includes bibliographies and index.
1. Africa - Description and travel - 1951-1976. 2. Africa - History. I. Church, Ronald James Harrison. II. Title.
NYPL [Sc D 88-352]

Africa and the modern world /. Wallerstein, Immanuel Maurice, 1930- Trenton, N.J. , c1986. 209 p. ; ISBN 0-86543-024-1 (pbk.) : DDC 337.6 19
HF1611 .W35 1986　NYPL [Sc D 89-378]

Africa and the Renaissance . Bassani, Ezio. New York City , c1988. 255 p. : ISBN 0-945802-00-5 : DDC 736/.62/096607401471 19
NK5989 .B37 1988　NYPL [Sc F 89-30]

Africa and the world today /. Rosberg, Carl G. [Chicago?] , 1960. 66 p. : *NYPL [Sc B 88-5]*

AFRICA - AUDIO-VISUAL AIDS - CATALOGS.
Fenton, Thomas P. Africa . Maryknoll, N.Y. , c1987. xiv, 144 p. ; ISBN 0-88344-542-8
NYPL [Sc D 88-398]

AFRICA - BIBLIOGRAPHY.
Fenton, Thomas P. Africa . Maryknoll, N.Y. , c1987. xiv, 144 p. ; ISBN 0-88344-542-8
NYPL [Sc D 88-398]

Africa, Black. see Africa, Sub-Saharan.

AFRICA - BOUNDARIES.
Bono, Salvatore. Le frontiere in Africa. [Milano], 1972. xix, 284 p.
NYPL [JFD 75-1056]

AFRICA, CENTRAL - COLONIZATION - CONGRESSES.
Les Réactions africaines à la colonisation en Afrique Centrale . Ruhengeri , 1986. 478 p. ;
NYPL [Sc G 87-9]

AFRICA, CENTRAL - FICTION.
Dongala, Emmanuel B. Le feu des origines . Paris , 1987. 255 p. ; *NYPL [Sc D 87-1396]*

AFRICA, CENTRAL - HISTORY - CONGRESSES.
Les Réactions africaines à la colonisation en Afrique Centrale . Ruhengeri , 1986. 478 p. ;
NYPL [Sc G 87-9]

AFRICA, CENTRAL - LANGUAGES - DETERMINERS.
La maison du chef et la tête du cabri . Paris , c1987. 125 p. : ISBN 2-7053-0339-1
NYPL [Sc E 88-292]

Africa che cambia . Valsecchi, Silvestro. Bologna , 1979. 204 p. : DDC 337.6 19
HC800 .V34 1979　NYPL [Sc D 87-1375]

AFRICA - CHURCH HISTORY.
Hickey, Raymond. Two thousand years of African Christianity /. Ibadan, Nigeria , 1987. viii, 54 p. : *NYPL [Sc C 88-207]*

Luneau, René. Laisse aller mon peuple! . Paris , c1987. 193 p. ; ISBN 2-86537-173-5 DDC 282/.6 19
BX1675 .L86 1987　NYPL [Sc D 88-315]

AFRICA - CIVILIZATION.
Afrika /. Frankfurt am Main , New York , c1986. 413 p. : ISBN 3-88655-212-8 DDC 960 19
DT14 .A3747 1986　NYPL [Sc D 89-311]

Black women in antiquity /. New Brunswick, [N.J.] , London , 1988. 192 p. : ISBN 0-87855-982-5　*NYPL [Sc D 89-351]*

Concept de pouvoir en Afrique. Spanish. El concepto del poder en Africa /. Barcelona , París , 1983. 178 p. ; ISBN 92-3-301887-3 (Unesco)　*NYPL [Sc D 88-604]*

Introduction à la culture africaine. Spanish. Introducción a la cultura africana . Paris , 1982. 176 p. ; ISBN 92-3-301478-9 (Unesco)　*NYPL [Sc D 88-600]*

AFRICA - CIVILIZATION - STUDY AND TEACHING.
University of Illinois at Urbana-Champaign. African Studies Program. Curriculum-related handouts for teachers . Urbana, Illinois [1981] ca. 500 p. ; *NYPL [Sc F 88-215]*

AFRICA - COLONIAL INFLUENCE - BOOK REVIEWS.
Heinecke, P. Twenty-two reviews /. Kaduna, [Nigeria] [1986?] 69 p. ;
NYPL [Sc E 88-284]

AFRICA - COLONIZATION.
MacKenzie, John M. The partition of Africa,

1880-1900 and European imperialism in the nineteenth century /. London , New York , 1983. x, 48 p. : ISBN 0-416-35050-X DDC 960/.23 19
DT29 .M33 1983　NYPL [Sc D 88-268]

Rummelt, Peter. Sport im Kolonialismus, Kolonialismus im Sport . Köln , 1986. 341 p. : ISBN 3-7609-5213-5 DDC 796/.096 19
GV665 .R85 1986　NYPL [Sc D 88-973]

AFRICA - COLONIZATION - COMIC BOOKS, STRIPS, ETC.
Comics für Afrika . Dormagen [West Germany] [1986] 96 p. : *NYPL [Sc G 88-27]*

AFRICA - COLONIZATION - CONGRESSES.
Centenaire de la Conférence de Berlin (1884-1885) (1985 : Brazzaville, Congo) Centenaire de la Conférence de Berlin (1884-1885) . Paris , 1987. 469 p. ; ISBN 2-7087-0481-8　*NYPL [Sc E 88-101]*

AFRICA - COLONIZATION - HISTORY.
Brooke-Smith, Robin. The scramble for Africa /. Basingstoke, Hampshire , 1987. viii, 134 p. ; ISBN 0-333-42491-3　*NYPL [Sc D 88-98]*

AFRICA - DESCRIPTION AND TRAVEL - 1951-1977.
Wästberg, Per. [Afrika, ett uppdrag. English.] Assignments in Africa . London , 1986. viii, 231 p. ; ISBN 0-946889-11-2 (pbk.)
NYPL [JFD 87-7408]

AFRICA - DESCRIPTION AND TRAVEL - 1951-1976.
Africa and the islands /. London , 1966. xiv, 494 p. : *NYPL [Sc D 88-352]*

AFRICA - DESCRIPTION AND TRAVEL - 1977-
Baeriswyl-Nicollin, Dominique. Afrika . Lausanne , c1983. 148 p. : DDC 916/.0448 19
DT12.25 .B32 1983　NYPL [Sc F 88-67]

Hampton, Charles. A family outing in Africa /. London , 1988. 267 p., [16] p. of plates : ISBN 0-333-44190-7 : DDC 916/.04328 19
DT12.25　NYPL [Sc D 88-1274]

Jahn, Wolfgang. Afrika anders erlebt /. Hannover , 1986. 207 p. : ISBN 3-7842-0336-1
NYPL [Sc D 88-806]

Montgomery, Denis. The reflected face of Africa /. Bolton, England , 1988. 288 p. : ISBN 1-85421-008-4　*NYPL [Sc E 88-535]*

Taylor, Jane. Fielding's literary Africa /. New York, N.Y. , 1988. xv, 506 p. : ISBN 0-688-05071-9 DDC 960 19
DT12.25 .T39 1988　NYPL [Sc D 88-1361]

AFRICA - DICTIONARIES AND ENCYCLOPEDIAS.
Afrika . Berlin , 1985. 520 p. :
NYPL [Sc C 88-144]

AFRICA, EAST.
Knappert, Jan. East Africa . New Delhi , c1987. 383 p. ; ISBN 0-7069-2822-9 : DDC 967.6 19
DT423 .K56 1987　NYPL [Sc D 88-852]

AFRICA, EAST - DESCRIPTION AND TRAVEL.
Le Roy, Alexandre, abp., 1854-1938. Sur terre et sur l'eau . Tours , 1894. 350 p. :
NYPL [Sc F 88-13]

Pruen, Septimus Tristram (Septimus Tristam) The Arab and the African . London , 1896. vii, 338 p. [8] p. of plates : *NYPL [Sc D 88-387]*

AFRICA, EAST - DESCRIPTION AND TRAVEL - 1951-
Waters, Grahame H. C. (Grahame Hugh Clement), 1923- Geography of Kenya and the East African region /. London , 1986. 252 p. : ISBN 0-333-41564-7 (pbk) : DDC 916.76 19
DT427　NYPL [Sc E 88-370]

AFRICA, EAST - DESCRIPTION AND TRAVEL - 1981- - VIEWS.
Beddow, Tim. East Africa . New York, N.Y. , 1988. 21 p., [80] p. of plates : ISBN 0-500-24131-7　*NYPL [Sc F 88-291]*

AFRICA, EAST - DESCRIPTION AND TRAVEL - GUIDE-BOOKS.
Crowther, Geoff. East Africa . South Yarra , 1987. 373 p., [16] p. of plates : ISBN 0-86442-005-6　*NYPL [Sc C 88-332]*

AFRICA, EAST - DISCOVERY AND EXPLORATION - JUVENILE

LITERATURE.
African adventures and adventurers /. Boston , 1880. 393 p. : *NYPL [Sc C 88-60]*

AFRICA, EAST - ECONOMIC CONDITIONS.
Nabudere, D. Wadada. Imperialism in East Africa /. London , Westport, Conn. , 1981- v. ; *NYPL [Sc Ser.-L .N238]*

Africa, East - Government. see Africa, East - Politics and government.

AFRICA, EAST - HISTORY.
Nabudere, D. Wadada. Imperialism in East Africa /. London , Westport, Conn. , 1981- v. ; *NYPL [Sc Ser.-L .N238]*

AFRICA, EAST - LANGUAGES.
Whiteley, Wilfred Howell. To plan is to choose /. Bloomington , 1973. vii, 50 p. ; *NYPL [Sc D 88-213]*

AFRICA, EAST - POLITICS AND GOVERNMENT.
Nabudere, D. Wadada. Imperialism in East Africa /. London , Westport, Conn. , 1981- v. ; *NYPL [Sc Ser.-L .N238]*

Rothchild, Donald S. From federalism to neo-federalism in East Africa [microform] /. Nairobi , 1966. 19 leaves ; *NYPL [Sc Micro R-4108 no.30]*

AFRICA, EAST - SOCIAL LIFE AND CUSTOMS.
Pruen, Septimus Tristram (Septimus Tristam) The Arab and the African . London , 1896. vii, 338 p. [8] of plates : *NYPL [Sc D 88-387]*

AFRICA, EAST - SOCIAL LIFE AND CUSTOMS - JUVENILE LITERATURE.
Young people of East and South Africa . New York , c1962. vii, 211 p. ; *NYPL [Sc D 88-660]*

AFRICA, EASTERN - HISTORY - CONGRESSES.
Relations historiques à travers l'océan Indien. Spanish. Relaciones históricas a través del océano Índico . Barcelona , Paris , 1983. 224 p. ; ISBN 84-85800-51-6 *NYPL [Sc D 88-593]*

AFRICA, EASTERN - LANGUAGES.
Etudes sur le bantu oriental . Paris , 1982 [i.e. 1983] 158 p. ; ISBN 2-85297-144-5 : DDC 496/.39 19
PL8025 .E84 1983 *NYPL [Sc E 88-357]*

AFRICA - ECONOMIC CONDITIONS.
Diakité, Tidiane. L'Afrique malade d'elle-même /. Paris , c1986. 162 p. ; ISBN 2-86537-158-1 DDC 960/.32 19
DT31 .D5 1986 *NYPL [Sc D 88-1351]*

La economía /. Madrid , c1986. 109, [4] p. ; *NYPL [Sc C 88-186]*

Fonkoué, Jean. Différence & identité . Paris , c1985. 202 p. : ISBN 2-903871-46-9 : DDC 301/.096 19
HM22.A4 F66 1985 *NYPL [Sc D 88-1151]*

Hazoumé, Alain T. Afrique, un avenir en sursis /. Paris , c1988. 214 p. ; ISBN 2-7384-0068-X *NYPL [Sc D 89-290]*

Hope born out of despair . Nairobi , 1988. xv, 123 p. ; ISBN 996-646-456-5 *NYPL [Sc D 89-477]*

Nafziger, E. Wayne. Inequality in Africa . Cambridge [Cambridgeshire] , New York , c1988. xii, 204 p. : ISBN 0-521-26881-8 DDC 339.2/096 19
HC800.Z9 I5136 1988 *NYPL [Sc E 88-521]*

Rosenblum, Mort. Squandering Eden . San Diego , c1987. x, 326 p., [32] of plates : ISBN 0-15-184860-2 : DDC 960/.3 19
GF701 .R67 1987 *NYPL [Sc E 88-24]*

AFRICA - ECONOMIC CONDITIONS - TO 1918.
Africa, America, and central Asia . [Exeter, Devon] [Atlantic Highlands, N.J.] 1984. 107 p. : ISBN 0-85989-295-6 (pbk.) : DDC 330.9/034 19
HC53 .A35 1984 *NYPL [Sc D 88-1315]*

AFRICA - ECONOMIC CONDITIONS - 1945-
Harrison, Paul, 1945- The greening of Africa . London , 1987. 380 p. : ISBN 0-586-08642-0 (pbk) : DDC 330.96/0328 19
HC502 *NYPL [Sc C 88-327]*

AFRICA - ECONOMIC CONDITIONS - 1945- - ADDRESSES, ESSAYS, LECTURES.

Indian Council for Africa. India and Africa. [New Delhi, 1967] 57 p.
HF1590.15.A3 I5 *NYPL [JLE 72-1609]*

AFRICA - ECONOMIC CONDITIONS - 1960-
L'Afrique face à ses priorités /. Paris , c1987. 144 p. ; ISBN 2-7178-1296-2 *NYPL [Sc E 88-291]*

The Challenge of employment and basic needs in Africa . Nairobi , New York , 1986. xii, 379 p. ; ISBN 0-19-572559-X *NYPL [Sc E 88-419]*

Kennedy, Paul M., 1945- African capitalism . Cambridge, Cambridgeshire , New York , 1988. x, 233 p. ; ISBN 0-521-26599-1 DDC 332/.041/096 19
HC800 .K46 1988 *NYPL [Sc E 88-520]*

Morel, Yves. Homme, sociétés et développement /. Douala , 1980- v. : DDC 338.9 19
HD83 .M59 *NYPL [Sc F 87-415]*

Obasanjo, Olusegun. Africa embattled . Agodi, Ibadan , 1988. xi, 118 p. ; ISBN 978-267-924-0
DT30.5 .O23x 1988 *NYPL [Sc E 88-574]*

Onimode, Bade. A political economy of the African crisis /. London , Atlantic Highlands, N.J. , 1988. 333 p. ; ISBN 0-86232-373-8 DDC 330.96/0328 19
HC800 .O55 1988 *NYPL [JLD 88-4614]*

Organization of African Unity 25 years on . London , 1988. vii, 175 p. : ISBN 0-948583-05-3 (Hardback) *NYPL [Sc D 89-556]*

Pisani, Edgard. Pour l'Afrique /. Paris , 1988. 251 p. ; ISBN 2-7381-0026-0 *NYPL [Sc E 88-249]*

Prospects for Africa . London , 1988. 97 p. : ISBN 0-340-42909-7 (pbk) : DDC 330.96/0328 19
HC800 *NYPL [Sc E 89-34]*

Rural transformation in tropical Africa /. London , 1988. 177 p. : ISBN 1-85293-012-8 : DDC 330.96/0328 19
HC800 *NYPL [JLE 88-4346]*

Die UNO-Sondersitzung über Afrika 1986 in der afrikanischen Presse /. Hamburg , 1986. ii, 104 p. : ISBN 3-923519-66-4 *NYPL [Sc F 88-229]*

Valsecchi, Silvestro. Africa che cambia . Bologna , 1979. 204 p. ; DDC 337.6 19
HC800 .V34 1979 *NYPL [Sc D 87-1375]*

Vingt questions sur l'Afrique . Paris , 1988. 238 p. ; ISBN 2-7384-0048-5 *NYPL [Sc D 88-1390]*

AFRICA - ECONOMIC CONDITIONS - 1960- - ADDRESSES, ESSAYS, LECTURES.
African crisis areas and U. S. foreign policy /. Berkeley , c1985. xiv, 374 p. : ISBN 0-520-05548-9 (alk. paper) DDC 327.7306 19
DT38.7 .A39 1986 *NYPL [JLE 85-4182]*

The USSR and Africa. Moscow , 1983. 205 p. ; DDC 303.4/8247/06 19
DT38.9.S65 U86 1983 *NYPL [Sc D 88-980]*

AFRICA - ECONOMIC DEVELOPMENT.
Prospects for Africa . London , 1988. 97 p. : ISBN 0-340-42909-7 (pbk) : DDC 330.96/0328 19
HC800 *NYPL [Sc E 89-34]*

AFRICA - ECONOMIC INTEGRATION - BIBLIOGRAPHY.
Kersebaum, Andrea. Integrationsbestrebungen in Afrika . Hamburg , 1986-1987. 2 v. ; ISBN 3-922852-13-0 *NYPL [Sc F 88-33]*

AFRICA - ECONOMIC INTEGRATION - CONGRESSES.
African development . Lawrenceville, Va., U. S.A. , c1985. 241 p. : ISBN 0-931494-57-5 (pbk.) DDC 337.1/6 19
HC800 .A565 1985 *NYPL [Sc F 87-376]*

AFRICA - ECONOMIC POLICY.
Katapu, Agbeko. Workable strategies to end Africa's poverty . Syracuse, N.Y. , c1986. xxiv, 288 p. ; ISBN 0-944338-00-3 DDC 338.96 19
HC800 .K37 1988 *NYPL [Sc D 89-610]*

Sawadogo, Abdoulaye. Un plan Marshall pour l'Afrique? /. Paris , c1987. 119 p. ; ISBN 2-85802-816-8 *NYPL [Sc D 88-911]*

AFRICA - ECONOMIC POLICY - CONGRESSES.
African development . Lawrenceville, Va., U.

S.A. , c1985. 241 p. : ISBN 0-931494-57-5 (pbk.) DDC 337.1/6 19
HC800 .A565 1985 *NYPL [Sc F 87-376]*

Africa embattled . Obasanjo, Olusegun. Agodi, Ibadan , 1988. xi, 118 p. ; ISBN 978-267-924-0
DT30.5 .O23x 1988 *NYPL [Sc E 88-574]*

Africa en armas /. Cabrera, M. A. Madrid [1986] 163 p. ; ISBN 84-85436-37-7
NYPL [Sc D 88-757]

AFRICA - FICTION.
Agokla, K. M., 1955- L'aube nouvelle . Lomé , 1982. 94 p. ; ISBN 2-7236-0850-6
NYPL [Sc D 88-1018]

Baldé de Labé, Sirah. D'un Fouta-Djalloo à l'autre /. Paris , c1985- v. ; ISBN 2-214-06108-8 (v. 1) : DDC 843 19
PQ3989.2.B26 D86 1985 *NYPL [Sc C 88 103]*

Condé, Maryse. [Une Saison à Rihata. English.] A season in Rihata /. London , 1988. 192 p. ; ISBN 0-435-98832-8 (pbk) :
PQ3949.2.C65 *NYPL [Sc C 89-90]*

Doumbi-Fakoly. La retraite anticipée du Guide suprême /. Paris , c1984. 209 p. ; ISBN 2-85802-382-1 DDC 843 19
PQ3989.2.D639 R48 1984 *NYPL [Sc C 88-78]*

Fall, Aminata Sow. Ex-père de la nation . Paris , 1987. 189 p. ; ISBN 2-85802-875-3
NYPL [Sc D 88-1360]

Hopkins, David, 1936- African comedy /. London , 1988. 224 p. ; ISBN 0-00-223235-9 : DDC 823/.914 19 *NYPL [Sc D 89-162]*

Kimbidima, Julien Omer, 1961- Les filles du président . Paris , c1986. 138 p. ; ISBN 2-85802-769-2
MLCS 87/2312 (P) *NYPL [Sc D 88-1083]*

Laleye, Barnabé. Une femme dans la lumiére de l'aube . Paris , c1988. 228 p. ;
NYPL [Sc D 88-1407]

Ly, Ibrahima. Les noctuelles vivent de larmes /. Paris , c1988- v. ; ISBN 2-7384-0066-3
NYPL [Sc D 88-1338]

Nyika, Oliver P. Old Mapicha, and other stories /. Gweru, Zimbabwe , 1983. 102 p. ; ISBN 0-86922-263-5 (pbk.) : DDC 823 19
PR9390.9.N93 O4 1983
NYPL [JFC 86-1443]

Rawiri, Ntyugwetondo. G'amèrakano . Paris , c1988. 197 p. ; ISBN 2-87693-021-8
NYPL [Sc D 89-202]

Sessi, Kpanlingan. Les eunuques /. Paris , c1984. 71 p. ; ISBN 2-903871-56-6
NYPL [Sc D 88-1231]

Tchichellé Tchivéla, 1940- L'exil, ou, La tombe . Paris , c1986. 239 p. ; ISBN 2-7087-0473-7 *NYPL [Sc C 88-289]*

Waweru, Mwaura. The siege /. Nairobi , 1985. 273 p. ; *NYPL [Sc C 88-287]*

AFRICA - FILM CATALOGS.
University of Illinois Film Center. Film and video resources about Africa available from the University of Illinois Film Center /. Champaign, Ill. [c1985] 34 p. : DDC 016.96 19
Z3501 .U64 1985 DT3 *NYPL [Sc F 88-335]*

AFRICA - FORECASTING.
Africa in the 1990s and beyond . Algonac, Mich. , 1988. 309 p. : ISBN 0-917256-44-1 (pbk.) : DDC 303.4/8273/06 19
DT38 .A44 1988 *NYPL [Sc E 89-98]*

Reclaiming the future . Oxford , Riverton, N.J. , c1986. xvi, 197 p. : ISBN 1-85148-010-2 (pbk.) : DDC 303.4/96 19
DT4 .R43 1986 *NYPL [Sc D 88-584]*

AFRICA - FOREIGN ECONOMIC RELATIONS.
Valsecchi, Silvestro. Africa che cambia . Bologna , 1979. 204 p. ; DDC 337.6 19
HC800 .V34 1979 *NYPL [Sc D 87-1375]*

Wallerstein, Immanuel Maurice, 1930- Africa and the modern world /. Trenton, N.J. , c1986. 209 p. ; ISBN 0-86543-024-1 (pbk.) : DDC 337.6 19
HF1611 .W35 1986 *NYPL [Sc D 89-378]*

AFRICA - FOREIGN ECONOMIC RELATIONS - INDIA - ADDRESSES, ESSAYS, LECTURES.

Indian Council for Africa. India and Africa. [New Delhi, 1967] 57 p.
HF1590.15.A3 I5 **NYPL [JLE 72-1609]**

AFRICA - FOREIGN OPINION.
Die UNO-Sondersitzung über Afrika 1986 in der afrikanischen Presse /. Hamburg , 1986. ii, 104 p. : ISBN 3-923519-66-4
NYPL [Sc F 88-229]

AFRICA - FOREIGN PUBLIC OPINION, AMERICAN.
Magubane, Bernard. The ties that bind . Trenton, N.J. [1987] xi, 251 p. ; ISBN 0-86543-037-3 (pbk.) DDC 305.8/96073 19
E185.625 .M83 1987 **NYPL [Sc D 88-1348]**

AFRICA - FOREIGN RELATIONS.
Chan, Stephen. Issues in international relations . London , 1987. viii, 206 p. ; ISBN 0-333-44102-8 (pbk.) **NYPL [Sc D 88-371]**

Wallerstein, Immanuel Maurice, 1930- Africa and the modern world /. Trenton, N.J. , c1986. 209 p. ; ISBN 0-86543-024-1 (pbk.) : DDC 337.6 19
HF1611 .W35 1986 **NYPL [Sc D 89-378]**

AFRICA - FOREIGN RELATIONS - 1960-
Africa in world politics . Houndmills, Basingstoke, Hampshire , 1987. xvi, 214 p. : ISBN 0-333-39630-8 **NYPL [Sc D 88-220]**

Agbi, Sunday O. The Organization of African Unity and African diplomacy, 1963-1979 /. Agodi, Ibadan , 1986. x, 166 p. ; ISBN 978-238-601-4 (pbk.) DDC 960/.326 19
DT30.5 .A374 1986 **NYPL [Sc D 89-124]**

Chan, Stephen. Issues in international relations . London , 1987. viii, 206 p. ; ISBN 0-333-44102-8 (pbk.) **NYPL [Sc D 88-371]**

Valsecchi, Silvestro. Africa che cambia . Bologna , 1979. 204 p. ; DDC 337.6 19
HC800 .V34 1979 **NYPL [Sc D 87-1375]**

AFRICA - FOREIGN RELATIONS - 1960- - ADDRESSES, ESSAYS, LECTURES.
African crisis areas and U. S. foreign policy /. Berkeley , c1985. xiv, 374 p. : ISBN 0-520-05548-9 (alk. paper) DDC 327.7306 19
DT38.7 .A39 1986 **NYPL [JLE 85-4182]**

AFRICA - FOREIGN RELATIONS - UNITED STATES.
Transafrica Forum (Organization) A retrospective . [Washington, D.C.] , c1987. 32 p. : **NYPL [Sc E 88-163]**

AFRICA - FOREIGN RELATIONS - UNITED STATES - ADDRESSES, ESSAYS, LECTURES.
African crisis areas and U. S. foreign policy /. Berkeley , c1985. xiv, 374 p. : ISBN 0-520-05548-9 (alk. paper) DDC 327.7306 19
DT38.7 .A39 1986 **NYPL [JLE 85-4182]**

AFRICA, FRENCH-SPEAKING EQUATORIAL - DICTIONARIES AND ENCYCLOPEDIAS.
L'Afrique noire de A à Z. Paris, 1971. 317 p.
NYPL [Sc F 88-75]

AFRICA, FRENCH-SPEAKING EQUATORIAL - GOVERNMENT PUBLICATIONS - BIBLIOGRAPHY - UNION LISTS.
Witherell, Julian W. French-speaking central Africa. Washington, 1973. xiv, 314 p. ISBN 0-8444-0033-5
Z3692 .W5 **NYPL [JLF 74-197]**

AFRICA, FRENCH-SPEAKING WEST - DICTIONARIES AND ENCYCLOPEDIAS.
L'Afrique noire de A à Z. Paris, 1971. 317 p.
NYPL [Sc F 88-75]

Africa, French-speaking West - Government. see Africa, French-speaking West - Politics and government.

AFRICA, FRENCH-SPEAKING WEST - POLITICS AND GOVERNMENT - 1884-1960.
Harrison, Christopher, 1958- France and Islam in West Africa, 1860-1960 /. Cambridge [Cambridgeshire] , New York , 1988. xi, 242 p. : ISBN 0-521-35230-4 DDC 966/.0097451 19
DT530.5.M88 H37 1988
NYPL [Sc E 88-484]

Africa from the seventh to the eleventh century / UNESCO International Scientific Committee for the Drafting of a General History of

Africa ; editor, M. El Fasi ; assistant editor, I. Hrbek. London : Heinemann Educational Books ; Berkeley : University of California Press ; xxv, 869 p. : ill. ; 24 cm. (General history of Africa . 3) Includes index. Bibliography: p. [799]-847. ISBN 0-435-94809-1
1. Africa - History - 1498. I. Fāsī, Muḥammad. II. Hrbek, Ivan. III. Unesco. International Scientific Committee for the Drafting of a General History of Africa. IV. Series. **NYPL [Sc E 88-384]**

AFRICA Fund.
Africa Fund : action for resisting invasion, colonialism and apartheid. [Zimbabwe?] : Visual Communication, [1986?] [24] p. : ill. ; 30 x 21 cm. Title on cover: Africa Fund summit.
1. Apartheid - South Africa. I. Title: Africa Fund summit. **NYPL [Sc D 88-1201]**

Southern Africa film guide [microform] New York [1982] 12 p. ;
NYPL [Sc Micro F-11052]

Africa Fund summit. AFRICA Fund. Africa Fund . [Zimbabwe?] [1986?] [24] p. :
NYPL [Sc D 88-1201]

AFRICA - GAZETTEERS.
Kirchherr, Eugene C. Place names of Africa, 1935-1986 . Metuchen, N.J. , c1987. viii, 136 p. : ISBN 0-8108-2061-7 DDC 911/.6 19
DT31 .K53 1987 **NYPL [Sc D 88-813]**

Africa, German Southwest. see **Namibia.**

Africa (Group 3) missions. Church Missionary Society. Africa (Group 3) Committee. Catalogue of the papers of the missions of the Africa (Group 3) Committee /. London , 1981. 8 v. ; DDC 266/.3 19
CD1069.L715 C47 1981 **NYPL [Sc F 88-78]**

AFRICA - HISTORICAL GEOGRAPHY - MAPS.
McEvedy, Colin. Atlas of African history /. New York , c1980. 142 p. : ISBN 0-87196-480-5 : DDC 911/.6
G2446.S1 M3 1980 **NYPL [Sc D 89-395]**

AFRICA - HISTORY.
Africa and the islands /. London , 1966. xiv, 494 p. : **NYPL [Sc D 88-352]**

Sweeting, Earl. African history . London , 1988. 31 p. : **NYPL [Sc D 89-505]**

AFRICA - HISTORY - 1498.
Africa from the seventh to the eleventh century /. London : Berkeley : xxv, 869 p. : ISBN 0-435-94809-1
NYPL [Sc E 88-384]

AFRICA - HISTORY - 19TH CENTURY.
Njiro, Esther I. A history of Africa in the 19th century /. Nairobi , 1985. viii, 291 p. : DDC 960/.23 19
DT28 .N55 1985 **NYPL [Sc D 88-322]**

AFRICA - HISTORY - 1884-1918.
MacKenzie, John M. The partition of Africa, 1880-1900 and European imperialism in the nineteenth century /. London , New York , 1983. x, 48 p. : ISBN 0-416-35050-X DDC 960/.23 19
DT29 .M33 1983 **NYPL [Sc D 88-268]**

AFRICA - HISTORY - 20TH CENTURY.
Ganiage, Jean. L'Afrique au XXe siècle /. Paris , 1966. 908 p. : **NYPL [Sc D 88-236]**

Hargreaves, John D. Decolonization in Africa /. London , New York , 1988. xvi, 263 p. : ISBN 0-582-49150-9 DDC 960/.32 19
DT29 .H37 1988 **NYPL [Sc D 89-315]**

AFRICA - HISTORY - 1960-
Reed, John Neville. Mercenary activity in Africa since 1960 /. 1982. vi, 342 leaves ;
NYPL [Sc F 88-121]

Africa - History - Atlases. see **Africa - Historical geography - Maps.**

AFRICA - HISTORY - AUTONOMY AND INDEPENDENCE MOVEMENTS.
Aquarone, Marie-Christine. Les frontières du refus . Paris , 1987. 133 p. : ISBN 2-222-03962-2
NYPL [Sc F 89-112]

AFRICA - HISTORY - AUTONOMY AND INDEPENDENCE MOVEMENTS - DRAMA.
Faces of African independence . Charlottesville , 1988. xxxvi, 127 p. ; ISBN 0-8139-1186-9 DDC 842 19
PQ3987.5.E5 F33 1988 **NYPL [Sc D 89-32]**

AFRICA - HISTORY - COLLECTED WORKS.
Geschichte Afrikas. Afrika . Köln , 1979- v. : ISBN 3-7609-0433-5 (v. 1) : DDC 960 19
DT20 .G47 1979 **NYPL [JFK 82-28]**

Africa - History - Maps. see **Africa - Historical geography - Maps.**

AFRICA - HISTORY, MILITARY.
Cabrera, M. A. Africa en armas /. Madrid [1986] 163 p. ; ISBN 84-85436-37-7
NYPL [Sc D 88-757]

Reed, John Neville. Mercenary activity in Africa since 1960 /. 1982. vi, 342 leaves ;
NYPL [Sc F 88-121]

AFRICA - HISTORY, MILITARY - 20TH CENTURY.
Donders, Joseph G. War and rumours of war . Eldoret, Kenya , 1986. 51 p. :
NYPL [Sc D 88-1467]

AFRICA IN MOVING-PICTURES - BIBLIOGRAPHY.
Southern Africa film guide [microform] New York [1982] 12 p. ;
NYPL [Sc Micro F-11052]

Africa in the 1990s and beyond : U. S. policy opportunities and choices / edited by Robert I. Rotberg. Algonac, Mich. : Reference Publications, 1988. 309 p. : ill. ; 23 cm. (A World Peace Foundation Study) Papers from a conference held on Lake Winnipesaukee, N.H., in Oct. 1987 under auspices of World Peace Foundation. Includes bibliographies and index. ISBN 0-917256-44-1 (pbk.) : DDC 303.4/8273/06 19
1. Africa - Relations - United States. 2. United States - Relations - Africa. 3. Africa - Forecasting. I. Rotberg, Robert I. II. World Peace Foundation. III. Series.
DT38 .A44 1988 **NYPL [Sc E 89-98]**

Africa in U. S. schools, K-12 [microform] . Hall, Susan J. New York , c1978. 39 p. ;
NYPL [Sc Micro R-4202 no. 2]

Africa in world politics : changing perspectives / edited by Stephen Wright and Janice N. Brownfoot. Houndmills, Basingstoke, Hampshire : Macmillan, 1987. xvi, 214 p. : maps ; 23 cm. Includes index. Bibliography: p. 207-209. ISBN 0-333-39630-8
1. Africa - Politics and government - 1960-. 2. Africa - Foreign relations - 1960-. I. Wright, Stephen, 1954-. II. Brownfoot, Janice. **NYPL [Sc D 88-220]**

AFRICA - INTELLECTUAL LIFE.
Benson, Peter. Black Orpheus, Transition, and modern cultural awakening in Africa /. Berkeley , c1986. xiii, 320 p. : ISBN 0-520-05418-0 DDC 820/.8 19
PL8000.B63 B4 1986 **NYPL [Sc E 88-354]**

N'Da, Paul, 1945- Pouvoir, lutte de classes, idéologie et milieu intellectuel africain. /. Paris , c1987. 107 p. ; ISBN 2-7087-0485-0
NYPL [Sc D 88-918]

Africa internacional .
(2) Surafrica. Madrid , 1986. 160 p. : ISBN 84-245-0469-0; 84-85436-39-3
NYPL [Sc D 88-296]

(3) La economía /. Madrid , c1986. 109, [4] p. ; **NYPL [Sc C 88-186]**

AFRICA - JUVENILE FICTION.
Coatsworth, Elizabeth Jane, 1893- Ronnie and the Chief's son. New York, 1962. 38 p.
PZ7.C6294 Ro **NYPL [Sc E 89-23]**

Elkin, Benjamin. Why the sun was late /. New York , 1966. [40] p. :
PZ7.#426 Wh **NYPL [Sc F 88-105]**

Fleming, Elizabeth P. The Takula tree. Philadelphia, 1964. 175 p.
PZ7.F5995 Tak **NYPL [Sc D 88-508]**

The Jeep. Leicester [Eng.] , Montreal Canada [195-?] [8] p. ; **NYPL [Sc C 88-325]**

Mwenye Hadithi. Tricky Tortoise /. Boston , c1988. [32] p. : ISBN 0-316-33724-2 : DDC [E] 19
PZ7.M975 Tr 1988 **NYPL [Sc F 88-389]**

Osahon, Naiwu. The hawk and the eagle /. Apapa, Lagos, Nigeria , 1981. [22] p. : ISBN 978-18-6007-3 **NYPL [Sc D 89-225]**

Osahon, Naiwu, 1937- The land of the spirits /. Apapa, Lagos, Nigeria , 1981. [30] p. : ISBN 978-18-6008-1 **NYPL [Sc D 89-226]**

Osahon, Naiwu, 1937- Laruba and the two

wicked men /. Apapa, Lagos, Nigeria , 1981.
[22] p. : ISBN 978-18-6004-9
NYPL [Sc D 89-224]

Osahon, Naiwu, 1937- The missing gold ring /.
Apapa, Lagos, Nigeria , c1981. [24] p. : ISBN
978-18-6000-6
MLCS 85/698 (P) *NYPL [Sc D 89-222]*

Osahon, Naiwu, 1937- Odu and Onah /.
Apapa, Lagos, Nigeria , 1981. [22] p. :
NYPL [Sc D 89-227]

AFRICA - JUVENILE LITERATURE.
Allen, William Dangaix, 1904- Africa. Grand
Rapids [c1972] 172, 20 p. DDC 916
DT5 .A53 1972 *NYPL [Sc F 88-377]*

**AFRICA - MILITARY RELATIONS -
FOREIGN COUNTRIES.**
Cabrera, M. A. Africa en armas /. Madrid
[1986] 163 p. ; ISBN 84-85436-37-7
NYPL [Sc D 88-757]

AFRICA - MORAL CONDITIONS.
Diakité, Tidiane. L'Afrique malade d'elle-même
/. Paris , c1986. 162 p. ; ISBN 2-86537-158-1
DDC 960/.32 19
DT31 .D5 1986 *NYPL [Sc D 88-1351]*

Africa must be free /. Jibrin, Sani A. Kano State,
Nigeria , 1987. x, 48 p. :
NYPL [Sc C 88-302]

AFRICA - NATIONAL SECURITY.
Cabrera, M. A. Africa en armas /. Madrid
[1986] 163 p. ; ISBN 84-85436-37-7
NYPL [Sc D 88-757]

The Africa News cookbook : African cooking for
Western kitchens / Africa News Service, Inc. ;
edited by Tami Hultman ; designed and
illustrated by Patricia Ford. New York, NY :
Penguin, 1987, c1985. xxix, 175 p. : ill. ; 26
cm. Includes index. ISBN 0-14-046751-3 (pbk.)
DDC 641.596 19
*1. Cookery, African. I. Hultman, Tami. II. Africa News
Service.*
TX725.A4 A35 1986b *NYPL [Sc E 88-371]*

Africa News Service. The Africa News
cookbook . New York, NY , 1987, c1985. xxix,
175 p. : ISBN 0-14-046751-3 (pbk.) DDC 641.596
19
TX725.A4 A35 1986b *NYPL [Sc E 88-371]*

AFRICA, NORTH - CONGRESSES.
Contemporary North Africa . London , c1985.
271 p. ; ISBN 0-7099-3435-1 : DDC 961 19
DT181.5 .C66 1985b *NYPL [Sc D 88-1017]*

**AFRICA, NORTH - DESCRIPTION AND
TRAVEL.**
Ogrizek, Doré, 1899- (ed) North Africa. New
York [1955] 447 p. DDC 916.1
DT165 .O372 *NYPL [Sc C 88-362]*

**AFRICA, NORTH - DICTIONARIES AND
ENCYCLOPEDIAS.**
The Cambridge encyclopedia of the Middle
East and North Africa /. Cambridge
[England] , New York , 1988. 504 p. : ISBN
0-521-32190-5 DDC 956 19
DS44 .C37 1988 *NYPL [*R-BCF 89-551]*

**AFRICA, NORTHEAST - FOREIGN
RELATIONS - SOVIET UNION.**
Sauldie, Madan M. Super powers in the Horn
of Africa /. New York , c1987. ix, 252 p. ;
ISBN 0-86590-092-2 DDC 320.960 19
DT367.8 .S28 1987 *NYPL [Sc D 89-488]*

**AFRICA, NORTHEAST - FOREIGN
RELATIONS - UNITED STATES.**
Sauldie, Madan M. Super powers in the Horn
of Africa /. New York , c1987. ix, 252 p. ;
ISBN 0-86590-092-2 DDC 320.960 19
DT367.8 .S28 1987 *NYPL [Sc D 89-488]*

**AFRICA, NORTHEAST - POLITICS AND
GOVERNMENT.**
Markakis, John. National and class conflict in
the Horn of Africa /. Cambridge , New York ,
1987. xvii, 314 p. : ISBN 0-521-33362-8 DDC
960/.3 19
DT367.75 .M37 1987 *NYPL [JFE 88-364]*

**AFRICA, NORTHEAST - POLITICS AND
GOVERNMENT - 1974-**
Sauldie, Madan M. Super powers in the Horn
of Africa /. New York , c1987. ix, 252 p. ;
ISBN 0-86590-092-2 DDC 320.960 19
DT367.8 .S28 1987 *NYPL [Sc D 89-488]*

**AFRICA - PERIODICALS - BIBLIOGRAPHY -
CATALOGS.**

Institut für Afrika-Kunde (Hamburg, Germany).
Bibliothek. Verzeichnis der
Zeitschriftenbestände . Hamburg , 1986. 100
p. ; *NYPL [Sc F 88-209]*

Universität Kiel. Institut für Weltwirtschaft.
Bibliothek. Verzeichnis, Afrika bezogener
Zeitschriften in Auswahl /. Kiel , 1984. 161 p.,
[117] columns ;
Z3503 .U54 1984 DT1 *NYPL [Sc F 88-213]*

AFRICA - POETRY.
El Mahmud-Okereke, N. O. E. (Noel Olufemi
Enuma), 1948- Nancy Reagan's red dress ;
Previewing UK's King Charles ; Israel's
indigenous black minority : & other poems of
Pan-Afrikan expression /. London , 1988,
c1987. xxi, 179 p. ; ISBN 978-242-304-1 (pbk) :
DDC 821 19 *NYPL [Sc C 88-182]*

AFRICA - POLITICS AND GOVERNMENT.
Biarnès, Pierre. Les Français en Afrique noire,
de Richélieu à Mitterand . Paris , 1987. 447
p. :bill., maps, ports. ; *NYPL [Sc D 88-562]*

Bono, Salvatore. Le frontiere in Africa.
[Milano], 1972. xix, 284 p.
NYPL [JFD 75-1056]

Concept de pouvoir en Afrique. Spanish. El
concepto del poder en Africa /. Barcelona ,
París , 1983. 178 p. ; ISBN 92-3-301887-3
(Unesco) *NYPL [Sc D 88-604]*

Democracy in developing countries /. Boulder,
Colo. , 1988- v. : ISBN 1-555-87039-2 (v. 2) :
DDC 320.9173/4 19
D883 .D45 1988 *NYPL [Sc E 88-201]*

The Democratic theory and practice in Africa
/. Nairobi , 1987. vi, 208 p. ;
NYPL [Sc D 89-569]

Hazoumé, Alain T. Afrique, un avenir en sursis
/. Paris , c1988. 214 p. ; ISBN 2-7384-0068-X
NYPL [Sc D 89-290]

Hope born out of despair . Nairobi , 1988. xv,
123 p. ; ISBN 996-646-456-5
NYPL [Sc D 89-477]

Oshisanya, Samuel Adekoya. The ultimate end
of Pan-Africanism /. [Lagos], Nigeria , 1983]
105 p. : *NYPL [Sc E 86-472]*

Socio-political aspects of the palaver in some
African countries. Spanish. Aspectos
sociopolíticos del parlamento tradicional en
algunos países africanos /. Barcelona , Paris ,
1979. 95 p. ; ISBN 84-85800-24-9
NYPL [Sc D 88-599]

**AFRICA - POLITICS AND GOVERNMENT -
20TH CENTURY.**
Donders, Joseph G. War and rumours of war .
Eldoret, Kenya , 1986. 51 p. :
NYPL [Sc D 88-1467]

**AFRICA - POLITICS AND GOVERNMENT -
1945-1960.**
Decolonization and African independence .
New Haven , 1988. xxix, 651 p. ; ISBN
0-300-04070-9 DDC 960/.32 19
DT30.5 .D42 1988 *NYPL [Sc E 88-517]*

Kirchherr, Eugene C. Place names of Africa,
1935-1986 . Metuchen, N.J. , c1987. viii, 136
p. : ISBN 0-8108-2061-7 DDC 911/.6 19
DT31 .K53 1987 *NYPL [Sc D 88-813]*

Sevillano Castillo, Rosa. Los Orígenes de la
descolonización africana a través de la prensa
española (1956-1962) /. Madrid , 1986. 158 p. ;
NYPL [Sc E 88-94]

**AFRICA - POLITICS AND GOVERNMENT -
1960-**
Africa in world politics . Houndmills,
Basingstoke, Hampshire , 1987. xvi, 214 p. :
ISBN 0-333-39630-8 *NYPL [Sc D 88-220]*

Agbi, Sunday O. The Organization of African
Unity and African diplomacy, 1963-1979 /.
Agodi, Ibadan , 1986. x, 166 p. ; ISBN
978-238-601-4 (pbk) DDC 960/.326 19
DT30.5 .A374 1986 *NYPL [Sc D 89-124]*

Aurillac, Michel. L'Afrique à coeur . Paris ,
1987. 264 p., [8] p. of plates : ISBN
2-7013-0739-2 *NYPL [Sc E 88-203]*

Decolonization and African independence .
New Haven , 1988. xxix, 651 p. ; ISBN
0-300-04070-9 DDC 960/.32 19
DT30.5 .D42 1988 *NYPL [Sc E 88-517]*

Diakité, Tidiane. L'Afrique malade d'elle-même
/. Paris , c1986. 162 p. ; ISBN 2-86537-158-1
DDC 960/.32 19
DT31 .D5 1986 *NYPL [Sc D 88-1351]*

El Mahmud-Okereke, N. O. E. (Noel Olufemi
Enuma), 1948- Nancy Reagan's red dress ;
Previewing UK's King Charles ; Israel's
indigenous black minority : & other poems of
Pan-Afrikan expression /. London , 1988,
c1987. xxi, 179 p. ; ISBN 978-242-304-1 (pbk) :
DDC 821 19 *NYPL [Sc C 88-182]*

Garba, Joeseph Nanven, 1943- Diplomatic
soldiering . Ibadan , 1987. xviii, 238 p., [9] p.
of plates : ISBN 978-246-176-8 (limp)
NYPL [Sc D 88-726]

Kirchherr, Eugene C. Place names of Africa,
1935-1986 . Metuchen, N.J. , c1987. viii, 136
p. : ISBN 0-8108-2061-7 DDC 911/.6 19
DT31 .K53 1987 *NYPL [Sc D 88-813]*

Mahmud-Okereke, N. Enuma, 1948-
OAU--time to admit South Africa /. Lagos,
Nigeria , 1986. xxvi, 57, 190 p. : ISBN
978-242-302-5 *NYPL [Sc C 88-204]*

Obasanjo, Olusegun. Africa embattled . Agodi,
Ibadan , 1988. xi, 118 p. ; ISBN 978-267-924-0
DT30.5 .O23x 1988 *NYPL [Sc E 88-574]*

Organization of African Unity 25 years on .
London , 1988. vii, 175 p. : ISBN 0-948583-05-3
(Hardback) *NYPL [Sc D 89-556]*

Pisani, Edgard. Pour l'Afrique /. Paris , 1988.
251 p. ; ISBN 2-7381-0026-0
NYPL [Sc E 88-249]

Revolution and counter-revolution in Africa .
London , 1987. x, 130 p. ; ISBN 0-86232-750-4
(cased) : DDC 320.96 19
JQ1872 *NYPL [Sc D 88-637]*

Sevillano Castillo, Rosa. Los Orígenes de la
descolonización africana a través de la prensa
española (1956-1962) /. Madrid , 1986. 158 p. ;
NYPL [Sc E 88-94]

Touré, Ahmed Sékou, 1922- [Conférences,
discours, et rapports] Conakry [1958?]- v.
NYPL [Sc F966.52-T]

Vingt questions sur l'Afrique . Paris , 1988. 238
p. ; ISBN 2-7384-0048-5
NYPL [Sc D 88-1390]

**AFRICA - POLITICS AND GOVERNMENT -
1960- - ADDRESSES, ESSAYS,
LECTURES.**
African crisis areas and U. S. foreign policy /.
Berkeley , c1985. xiv, 374 p. : ISBN
0-520-05548-9 (alk. paper) DDC 327.7306 19
DT38.7 .A39 1986 *NYPL [JLE 85-4182]*

The USSR and Africa. Moscow , 1983. 205 p. ;
DDC 303.4/8247/06 19
DT38.9.S65 U86 1983 *NYPL [Sc D 88-980]*

**AFRICA - POLITICS AND GOVERNMENT -
1960- - CONGRESSES.**
Affirmation de l'identité culturelle et la
formation de la conscience nationale dans
l'Afrique contemporaine. Spanish. La
Afimación de la identidad cultural y la
formación de la coniencia nacional en el África
contemporánea /. Barcelona , Paris , 1983. 220
p. ; ISBN 84-85800-57-5 *NYPL [Sc D 88-597]*

Regional Seminar for Africa (Mogadishu :
1975) On African women's equality, role in
national liberation, development and peace .
[Mogadishu] , 1975. 123 p. ;
NYPL [Sc E 88-138]

**AFRICA - POLITICS AND GOVERNMENT -
CONGRESSES.**
Décolonisation de l'Afrique. Spanish. La
Descolonización de Africa : Africa austral y el
Cuerno de Africa . Barcelona , Paris , 1983.
197 p. ; ISBN 92-3-301834-2 (Unesco)
NYPL [Sc D 88-590]

**AFRICA - POLITICS AND GOVERNMENT -
JUVENILE LITERATURE.**
Hollings, Jill. African nationalism. New York
[1972, c1971] 128 p. DDC 320.5/4/096
DT31 .H577 1972 *NYPL [Sc D 88-1496]*

**AFRICA - POLITICS AND GOVERNMENT -
PHILOSOPHY.**
Obi, Chike. Our struggle . Enugu, Nigeria ,
1986. 76 p. ; ISBN 978-15-6187-4
NYPL [Sc D 88-753]

Africa Regional Project on Technological Change, Basic Needs and the Condition of Rural Women. Improved village technology for women's activities . Geneva , 1984. vi, 292 p. : ISBN 92-2-103818-1   *NYPL [JLF 85-625]*

AFRICA - RELATIONS - FRANCE.
Aurillac, Michel. L'Afrique à coeur . Paris , 1987. 264 p., [8] p. of plates :   ISBN 2-7013-0739-2   *NYPL [Sc E 88-203]*

Vingt questions sur l'Afrique . Paris , 1988. 238 p. ;   ISBN 2-7384-0048-5
NYPL [Sc D 88-1390]

AFRICA - RELATIONS - FRANCE - CONGRESSES.
Francophonie & géopolitique africaine . Paris , c1987. 156 p. ;   ISBN 2-906861-01-4
NYPL [Sc D 88-1448]

AFRICA - RELATIONS - SOVIET UNION - ADDRESSES, ESSAYS, LECTURES.
The USSR and Africa. Moscow , 1983. 205 p. ; DDC 303.4/8247/06 19
DT38.9.S65 U86 1983   NYPL [Sc D 88-980]

AFRICA - RELATIONS - SWEDEN.
Jinadu, Adele. Idealism and pragmatism as aspects of Sweden's development policy in Africa /. Lagos [1982?]. 107 p. ;   ISBN 978-227-698-7   *NYPL [Sc D 88-355]*

AFRICA - RELATIONS - UNITED STATES.
Africa in the 1990s and beyond . Algonac, Mich. , 1988. 309 p. :   ISBN 0-917256-44-1 (pbk.) :   DDC 303.4/8273/06 19
DT38 .A44 1988   NYPL [Sc E 89-98]

Watson, Denton L. Reclaiming a heritage . New York, N.Y. , c1977. 63 p. :
NYPL [Sc F 89-78]

AFRICA - RELIGION.
Adasu, Moses Orshio. Understanding African traditional religion /. Sherborne, Dorset, England , 1985- v. ;   ISBN 0-902129-68-6
NYPL [Sc D 88-856]

Mbiti, John S. Bible and theology in African Christianity /. Nairobi , 1986. xiv, 248 p., [16] p. of plates :   ISBN 0-19-572593-X
NYPL [Sc D 89-296]

Metuh, Emefie Ikenga. Comparative studies of traditional African religions /. Onitsha, Nigeria , 1987. xi, 288 p.   ISBN 978-244-208-9
NYPL [Sc D 88-800]

Mort dans la vie africaine. Spanish. La Muerte en la vida africana. Barcelona , París , 1984. 314 p. :   ISBN 84-85800-81-8
NYPL [Sc D 88-601]

Spiritualité et libération en Afrique /. Paris , c1987. 123 p. ;   *NYPL [Sc D 88-1416]*

AFRICA - RELIGION - INFLUENCE.
Castellanos, Isabel, 1939- Elegua quiere tambó . Cali, Colombia , 1983. 84 p. ;
NYPL [Sc D 88-534]

AFRICA - RURAL CONDITIONS.
Rural transformation in tropical Africa /. London , 1988. 177 p. :   ISBN 1-85293-012-8 : DDC 330.96/0328 19
HC800   NYPL [JLE 88-4346]

AFRICA - SOCIAL CONDITIONS.
Fonkoué, Jean. Différence & identité . Paris , c1985. 202 p. :   ISBN 2-903871-46-9 :   DDC 301/.096 19
HM22.A4 F66 1985   NYPL [Sc D 88-1151]

Rosenblum, Mort. Squandering Eden . San Diego , c1987. x, 326 p., [32] p. of plates :   ISBN 0-15-184860-2 :   DDC 960/.3 19
GF701 .R67 1987   NYPL [Sc E 88-24]

AFRICA - SOCIAL CONDITIONS - 1960-
Onimode, Bade. A political economy of the African crisis /. London , Atlantic Highlands, N.J. , 1988. 333 p. ;   ISBN 0-86232-373-8   DDC 330.96/0328 19
HC800 .O55 1988   NYPL [JLD 88-4614]

Socio-political aspects of the palaver in some African countries. Spanish. Aspectos sociopolíticos del parlamento tradicional en algunos países africanos /. Barcelona , Paris , 1979. 95 p. ;   ISBN 84-85800-24-9
NYPL [Sc D 88-599]

AFRICA - SOCIAL CONDITIONS - CONGRESSES.
Social development and rural fieldwork .

Zimbabwe [1986]. 96 p. ;
NYPL [Sc D 88-1153]

AFRICA - SOCIAL LIFE AND CUSTOMS.
Loth, Heinrich. [Frau im Alten Afrika. English.] Woman in ancient Africa /. Westport, Conn. , c1987. 189 p. :   ISBN 0-88208-218-3   DDC 305.4/096 19
HQ1137.A35 L6813 1987
NYPL [Sc F 88-132]

Loth, Heinrich. [Frau im Alten Afrika. English.] Woman of ancient Africa. Westport, Conn. , c1987. 189 p. :   ISBN 0-88208-218-3   DDC 305.4/096 19
HQ1137.A35 L6813 1987
NYPL [Sc F 88-114]

Sandoval, Alonso dc, 1576-1652. Naturaleza, policia sagrada i profana, costumbres i ritos, disciplina i catechismo evangelico de todos etiopes /. En Sevilla , 1627. [23], 334 p., 81 leaves /.   *NYPL [Sc Rare F 82-70]*

AFRICA - SOCIETIES, ETC. - DIRECTORIES.
Fenton, Thomas P. Africa . Maryknoll, N.Y. , c1987. xiv, 144 p. ;   ISBN 0-88344-542-8
NYPL [Sc D 88-398]

AFRICA, SOUTHERN - CHURCH HISTORY.
Chirenje, J. Mutero, 1935- Ethiopianism and Afro-Americans in southern Africa, 1883-1916 /. Baton Rouge , c1987. xii, 231 p. :   ISBN 0-8071-1319-0   DDC 276.8/08 19
BR1450 .C45 1987   NYPL [Sc E 88-336]

AFRICA, SOUTHERN - DESCRIPTION AND TRAVEL.
Baines, Thomas, 1820-1875. Baines on the Zambezi 1858 to 1859 /. Johannesburg , c1982. 251 p. :   ISBN 0-909079-17-X (Standard ed.)
NYPL [Sc F 83-34]

Procter, Lovell James. The Central African journal of Lovell J. Procter, 1860-1864. [Boston] 1971. xvii, 501 p.   DDC 916.8
DT731 .P75   NYPL [Sc D 88-977]

AFRICA, SOUTHERN - ECONOMIC CONDITIONS.
SADCC . Tokyo, Japan : London ; xi, 256 p. ;   ISBN 0-86232-748-2 :   DDC 337.1/68 19
HC900 .S23 1987   NYPL [Sc D 89-50]

AFRICA, SOUTHERN - ECONOMIC CONDITIONS - 1975-
South Africa in southern Africa . Pretoria , 1988. viii, 266 p. :   ISBN 0-7983-0102-3
NYPL [Sc F 89-50]

AFRICA, SOUTHERN - ECONOMIC INTEGRATION.
SADCC . Tokyo, Japan : London ; xi, 256 p. ;   ISBN 0-86232-748-2 :   DDC 337.1/68 19
HC900 .S23 1987   NYPL [Sc D 89-50]

AFRICA, SOUTHERN - ECONOMIC POLICY.
Poverty, policy, and food security in southern Africa /. Boulder , 1988. xii, 291 p. :   ISBN 1-555-87092-9 (lib. bdg.) :   DDC 363.8/56/0968 19
HD9017.A26 P68 1988   NYPL [Sc E 88-355]

AFRICA, SOUTHERN - FOREIGN RELATIONS - 1975-
Hanks, Robert, 1923- Southern Africa and Western security /. Cambridge, Mass. , c1983. vii, 74 p. :   ISBN 0-89549-055-2 :   DDC 355/.033268 19
UA855.6 .H36 1983   NYPL [Sc D 85-489]

Legum, Colin. The battlefronts of Southern Africa /. New York , c1988. xxix, 451 p. :   ISBN 0-8419-1135-5 (alk. paper)   DDC 327.68 19
DT746 .L425 1987   NYPL [Sc E 88-468]

Vanneman, Peter. Soviet foreign policy in Southern Africa . Pretoria, Republic of South Africa , 1982. 57 p. ;   ISBN 0-7983-0078-7 (pbk.) DDC 327.68047 19
DT747.S65 V36 1982   NYPL [Sc D 88-1155]

AFRICA, SOUTHERN - FOREIGN RELATIONS - BOTSWANA.
Black, David R. (David Ross), 1960- Foreign policy in small states . Halifax, N.S. , 1988. viii, 83 p. :   ISBN 0-7703-0736-1 :   DDC 327.681068 19
NYPL [Sc D 89-564]

AFRICA, SOUTHERN - FOREIGN RELATIONS - LESOTHO.
Black, David R. (David Ross), 1960- Foreign

policy in small states . Halifax, N.S. , 1988. viii, 83 p. :   ISBN 0-7703-0736-1 :   DDC 327.681068 19
NYPL [Sc D 89-564]

AFRICA, SOUTHERN - FOREIGN RELATIONS - SOUTH AFRICA.
Poverty, policy, and food security in southern Africa /. Boulder , 1988. xii, 291 p. :   ISBN 1-555-87092-9 (lib. bdg.) :   DDC 363.8/56/0968 19
HD9017.A26 P68 1988   NYPL [Sc E 88-355]

AFRICA, SOUTHERN - FOREIGN RELATIONS - SOVIET UNION.
Vanneman, Peter. Soviet foreign policy in Southern Africa . Pretoria, Republic of South Africa , 1982. 57 p. ;   ISBN 0-7983-0078-7 (pbk.) DDC 327.68047 19
DT747.S65 V36 1982   NYPL [Sc D 88-1155]

AFRICA, SOUTHERN - FOREIGN RELATIONS - SWAZILAND.
Black, David R. (David Ross), 1960- Foreign policy in small states . Halifax, N.S. , 1988. viii, 83 p. :   ISBN 0-7703-0736-1 :   DDC 327.681068 19
NYPL [Sc D 89-564]

AFRICA, SOUTHERN - FOREIGN RELATIONS - UNITED STATES.
Schümer, Martin. Die amerikanische Politik gegenüber dem südlichen Afrika /. Bonn [1986]. v, 183 p. :   ISBN 3-7713-0275-7
NYPL [Sc D 88-983]

Africa, Southern - Government. see Africa, Southern - Politics and government.

AFRICA, SOUTHERN - HISTORIOGRAPHY - CONGRESSES.
Historiographie de l'Afrique australe. Spanish. La historiografía del Africa austral . Barcelona , Paris , 1983. 128 p. ;   ISBN 92-3-301775-3 (Unesco)   *NYPL [Sc D 88-598]*

AFRICA, SOUTHERN - INDUSTRIES.
SADCC . Tokyo, Japan : London ; xi, 256 p. ;   ISBN 0-86232-748-2 :   DDC 337.1/68 19
HC900 .S23 1987   NYPL [Sc D 89-50]

AFRICA, SOUTHERN - MILITARY RELATIONS - SOUTH AFRICA.
Frontline Southern Africa . New York , 1988. xxxv, 530 p., [16] p. of leaves :   ISBN 0-941423-08-5 :   DDC 322/.5/0968 19
DT747.S6 F76 1988   NYPL [JLE 89-595]

AFRICA, SOUTHERN - POLITICS AND GOVERNMENT - 1975-
Die Bischofskonferenzen Angolas und Südafrikas zu Frieden und Gerechtigkeit in ihren Länder. Bonn , 1986. 54 p. ;
NYPL [Sc D 88-929]

Hanks, Robert, 1923- Southern Africa and Western security /. Cambridge, Mass. , c1983. vii, 74 p. :   ISBN 0-89549-055-2 :   DDC 355/.033268 19
UA855.6 .H36 1983   NYPL [Sc D 85-489]

Legum, Colin. The battlefronts of Southern Africa /. New York , c1988. xxix, 451 p. :   ISBN 0-8419-1135-5 (alk. paper)   DDC 327.68 19
DT746 .L425 1987   NYPL [Sc E 88-468]

Mangope, Lucas. Mandatory sanctions . Lagos, Nigeria , 1988. v. 110, a-t p. of plates :   ISBN 978-242-313-0   *NYPL [Sc C 88-181]*

AFRICA, SOUTHERN - POLITICS AND GOVERNMENT - DICTIONARIES.
Williams, Gwyneth, 1953- The dictionary of contemporary politics of southern Africa /. London , New York , 1988. xi, 339 p. :   ISBN 0-415-00245-1   DDC 320.968/03 19
JQ2720.A127 W55 1988   NYPL [Sc D 89-2]

AFRICA, SOUTHERN - RACE RELATIONS.
Brown, Alex. Southern Africa. Ottawa [1973] 43 p.
DT746 .B76   NYPL [JLD 75-1128]

AFRICA, SOUTHERN - RELATIONS (GENERAL) WITH CANADA.
Brown, Alex. Southern Africa. Ottawa [1973] 43 p.
DT746 .B76   NYPL [JLD 75-1128]

AFRICA, SOUTHERN - RELATIONS - UNITED STATES.
Diggs, Charles C. Report of Special Study Mission to Southern Africa, August 10-30, 1969/. Washington , 1969. vi, 179 p. :   DDC 301.29'68'073
DT733.D5   NYPL [Sc E 89-39]

AFRICA, SOUTHERN - SOCIAL CONDITIONS - CONGRESSES.
Class formation and class struggle . [Roma? Lesotho] [1982] 211 p. ;
NYPL [Sc D 89-25]

AFRICA, SOUTHERN - SOCIAL LIFE AND CUSTOMS - JUVENILE LITERATURE.
Young people of East and South Africa . New York , c1962. vii, 211 p. ;
NYPL [Sc D 88-660]

AFRICA, SOUTHERN - STRATEGIC ASPECTS.
Hanks, Robert, 1923- Southern Africa and Western security /. Cambridge, Mass. , c1983. vii, 74 p. : ISBN 0-89549-055-2 : DDC 355/.033268 19
UA855.6 .H36 1983   *NYPL [Sc D 85-489]*

Vanneman, Peter. Soviet foreign policy in Southern Africa . Pretoria, Republic of South Africa , 1982. 57 p. ; ISBN 0-7983-0078-7 (pbk.) DDC 327.68047 19
DT747.S65 V36 1982   *NYPL [Sc D 88-1155]*

Africa, Southwest. see Namibia.

AFRICA - STUDY AND TEACHING - DIRECTORIES.
Baker, Philip. International guide to African studies research =. London , New York , 1987. 264 p. ; ISBN 0-905450-25-6
NYPL [Sc E 88-218]

AFRICA - STUDY AND TEACHING - UNITED STATES.
Hall, Susan J. Africa in U. S. schools, K-12 [microform] . New York , c1978. 39 p. ;
NYPL [Sc Micro R-4202 no. 2]

AFRICA, SUB-SAHARAN - ARMED FORCES - APPROPRIATIONS AND EXPENDITURES.
Disarmament and development . Lagos, Nigeria , 1986. ix, 117 p., 1 folded leaf : ISBN 978-13-2828-2   *NYPL [Sc D 88-783]*

AFRICA, SUB-SAHARAN - CIVILIZATION.
Makinde, M. Akin. African philosophy, culture, and traditional medicine /. Athens, Ohio , 1988. xvii, 154 p., [2] leaves of plates : ISBN 0-89680-152-7 DDC 199/.6 19
B5375 .M35 1988   *NYPL [Sc D 88-1273]*

AFRICA, SUB-SAHARAN - COLONIAL INFLUENCE - HISTORY.
Coquery-Vidrovitch, Catherine. Africa . Berkeley , c1988. x, 403 p. : ISBN 0-520-05679-5 (alk. paper) DDC 967 19
HC800 .C67513 1988 *NYPL [Sc E 89-221]*

AFRICA, SUB-SAHARAN - DESCRIPTION AND TRAVEL - 1981-
Shoumatoff, Alex. African madness /. New York , 1988. xviii, 202 p. ; ISBN 0-394-56914-8 : DDC 967/.0328 19
DT352.2 .S48 1988   *NYPL [Sc D 89-160]*

AFRICA, SUB-SAHARAN - DESCRIPTION AND TRAVEL - JUVENILE LITERATURE.
Caldwell, John C. (John Cope), 1913- Let's visit middle Africa. New York [1961] 96 p. DDC 916.7
DT352 .C3   *NYPL [Sc D 88-507]*

AFRICA, SUB-SAHARAN - ECONOMIC CONDITIONS.
Coquery-Vidrovitch, Catherine. Africa . Berkeley , c1988. x, 403 p. : ISBN 0-520-05679-5 (alk. paper) DDC 967 19
HC800 .C67513 1988 *NYPL [Sc E 89-221]*

AFRICA, SUB-SAHARAN - ECONOMIC CONDITIONS - 1918-1960.
Mutations économiques et sociales à la campagne et à la ville . Paris , 1980. 258 p. ;
NYPL [Sc F 87-437]

AFRICA, SUB-SAHARAN - ECONOMIC CONDITIONS - 1960-
Wanjui, J. B. From where I sit . Nairobi, Kenya , 1986. xi, 88 p. ; *NYPL [Sc C 88-90]*

AFRICA, SUB-SAHARAN - FICTION.
Pliya, Jean, 1931- Les tresseurs de corde . Paris , 1987. 239 p. ; ISBN 2-218-07841-X
NYPL [Sc C 88-9]

AFRICA, SUB-SAHARAN - FOREIGN RELATIONS - ISRAEL.
Mahmud-Okereke, N. Enuma el, 1948- Israel and Black Africa . Lagos, Nigeria , 1986. xxxiv,

211 p. : ISBN 978-242-301-7
NYPL [Sc C 88-205]

Africa, Sub-Saharan - Government. see Africa, Sub-Saharan - Politics and government.

AFRICA, SUB-SAHARAN - HISTORY.
Pouvoirs et sociétés dans l'Afrique des grands lacs /. Bujumbura , 1986. 146 p. ;
NYPL [Sc F 89-62]

Rosberg, Carl G. Africa and the world today /. [Chicago?] , 1960. 66 p. : *NYPL [Sc B 88-5]*

Suret-Canale, Jean. [Essais d'histoire africaine. English.] Essays on African history . London , 1988. 242 p. : ISBN 0-905838-43-2 : DDC 960/.3 19
DT29   *NYPL [Sc D 88-1314]*

AFRICA, SUB-SAHARAN - HISTORY - 1960-
Blanc, Paul. Le prince et le griot . Paris , c1987. 250 p., [4] p. of plates : ISBN 2-7013-0719-8   *NYPL [Sc E 88-345]*

AFRICA, SUB-SAHARAN - LANGUAGES.
Les Langues de l'Afrique subsaharienne /. Paris , 1981. 2 v : ISBN 2-222-01720-3 :
NYPL [JFN 81-11 v.1]

AFRICA, SUB-SAHARAN - POLITICS AND GOVERNMENT - 1960-
Blanc, Paul. Le prince et le griot . Paris , c1987. 250 p., [4] p. of plates : ISBN 2-7013-0719-8   *NYPL [Sc E 88-345]*

AFRICA, SUB-SAHARAN - POLITICS AND GOVERNMENT - DRAMA.
Mboya, Alakie-Akinyi. Ontongolia /. Nairobi , 1986. xiv, 92 p., [4] p. of plates ; ISBN 0-19-572615-4   *NYPL [Sc C 88-138]*

AFRICA, SUB-SAHARAN - POLITICS AND GOVERNMENT - FICTION.
Olinto, Antônio. Trono de vidro . Rio de Janeiro , 1987. 382 p. ; ISBN 85-7007-110-8
NYPL [Sc D 88-76]

AFRICA, SUB-SAHARAN - POPULATION - HISTORY.
Coquery-Vidrovitch, Catherine. Africa . Berkeley , c1988. x, 403 p. : ISBN 0-520-05679-5 (alk. paper) DDC 967 19
HC800 .C67513 1988 *NYPL [Sc E 89-221]*

AFRICA, SUB-SAHARAN - RELATIONS - ARAB COUNTRIES - CONGRESSES.
Arabs & Africa. French. Les arabes et l'Afrique . Paris , 1986. 2 v. ; ISBN 2-85802-589-1   *NYPL [Sc E 88-390]*

AFRICA, SUB-SAHARAN - RELIGION.
Brezault, Alain. Missions en Afrique . Paris , c1987. 193 p. : ISBN 2-86260-209-4 : DDC 266/.267 19
BV3520 .B74 1987   *NYPL [Sc E 89-163]*

Christianisme en Afrique noire . Dakar , 1979. 162 p. ;   *NYPL [Sc F 89-17]*

Gallardo, Jorge Emilio. Presencia africana en la cultura de América Latina . Buenos Aires, Argentina , c1986. 123 p. ; ISBN 950-643-006-3 DDC 299/.69 19
BL2490 .G33 1986   *NYPL [Sc D 89-358]*

AFRICA, SUB-SAHARAN - RELIGIOUS LIFE AND CUSTOMS.
Glantz, Stephan Hamilton. Spirit heads . New York , 1987. 133 p. : *NYPL [Sc F 88-103]*

Heusch, Luc de. Le sacrifice dans les religions africaines /. Paris , 1986. 354 p. :
NYPL [Sc D 88-941]

AFRICA, SUB-SAHARAN - RURAL CONDITIONS.
Coquery-Vidrovitch, Catherine. Africa . Berkeley , c1988. x, 403 p. : ISBN 0-520-05679-5 (alk. paper) DDC 967 19
HC800 .C67513 1988 *NYPL [Sc E 89-221]*

AFRICA, SUB-SAHARAN - SOCIAL CONDITIONS.
Mutations économiques et sociales à la campagne et à la ville . Paris , 1980. 258 p. ;
NYPL [Sc F 87-437]

AFRICA, SUB-SAHARAN - SOCIAL CONDITIONS - 1960-
Blanc, Paul. Le prince et le griot . Paris , c1987. 250 p., [4] p. of plates : ISBN 2-7013-0719-8   *NYPL [Sc E 88-345]*

AFRICA, SUB-SAHARAN - STUDY AND TEACHING.

Rosberg, Carl G. Africa and the world today /. [Chicago?] , 1960. 66 p. : *NYPL [Sc B 88-5]*

Africa, the gospel belongs to us . Salvoldi, Valentino. [Africa, il vangelo ci appartiene. English.] Ndola [Zambia] , 1986. 187 p ;
NYPL [Sc D 89-568]

AFRICA - VIDEO TAPE CATALOGS.
University of Illinois Film Center. Film and video resources about Africa available from the University of Illinois Film Center /. Champaign, Ill. [c1985] 34 p. : DDC 016.96 19
Z3501 .U64 1985 DT3 NYPL [Sc F 88-335]

AFRICA, WEST - BIBLIOGRAPHY.
Jones, Adam. Brandenburg sources for West African history, 1680-1700 /. Stuttgart , 1985. xiv, 348 p., [14] p. of plates : ISBN 3-515-04315-2   *NYPL [Sc E 88-84]*

AFRICA, WEST - BIOGRAPHY.
Okonkwo, Rina. Heroes of West African nationalism /. Enugu, Nigeria , 1985. x, 128 p. ; ISBN 978-233-596-7   *NYPL [Sc C 88-95]*

AFRICA, WEST - COLONIAL INFLUENCE.
La Colonisation, rupture ou parenthèse /. Paris , c1987. 326 p. :   *NYPL [Sc D 88-727]*

AFRICA, WEST - COLONIZATION.
Allison, Philip. Life in the white man's grave . London , 1988. 192 p. : ISBN 0-670-81020-7 : DDC 966 19
DT476.2   *NYPL [Sc F 88-174]*

La Colonisation, rupture ou parenthèse /. Paris , c1987. 326 p. :   *NYPL [Sc D 88-727]*

AFRICA, WEST - DESCRIPTION AND TRAVEL.
Niven, Cecil Rex, 1898- The lands and peoples of West Africa /. London [1961] vii, 84 p. :
NYPL [Sc D 88-669]

AFRICA, WEST - DESCRIPTION AND TRAVEL - 1851-1950.
Bicknell, Leona Mildred. How a little girl went to Africa . Boston , 1904. 172 p. :
NYPL [Sc C 88-368]

AFRICA, WEST - DESCRIPTION AND TRAVEL - 1981-
Dodwell, Christina, 1951- Travels with Pegasus . London , 1989. 208 p., [16] p. of plates : ISBN 0-340-42502-4 : DDC 916.6/04 19
NYPL [JFE 89-902]

AFRICA, WEST - DESCRIPTION AND TRAVEL - JUVENILE LITERATURE.
Davis, Russell G. Land in the sun. Boston [1963] 92 p.   *NYPL [Sc F 88-365]*

AFRICA, WEST - ECONOMIC POLICY.
African-American Institute. A system approach to the implications of national school-leaver problems in Dahomey, Ivory Coast, Niger, Togo and Upper Volta . Washington , 1970. 1 v. (various pagings), [7] folded leaves :
NYPL [Sc F 88-84]

AFRICA, WEST - FICTION.
Kanté, Cheik Oumar. Douze pour une coupe . Paris , c1987. 159 p. ; ISBN 2-7087-0490-7
NYPL [Sc D 88920]

AFRICA, WEST - FOREIGN ECONOMIC RELATIONS - GERMANY.
Jones, Adam. Brandenburg sources for West African history, 1680-1700 /. Stuttgart , 1985. xiv, 348 p., [14] p. of plates : ISBN 3-515-04315-2   *NYPL [Sc E 88-84]*

AFRICA, WEST - HISTORY.
Allison, Philip. Life in the white man's grave . London , 1988. 192 p. : ISBN 0-670-81020-7 : DDC 966 19
DT476.2   *NYPL [Sc F 88-174]*

AFRICA, WEST - HISTORY - 1884-1960.
La Colonisation, rupture ou parenthèse /. Paris , c1987. 326 p. : *NYPL [Sc D 88-727]*

Person, Yves. Samori: une révolution dyula. Dakar, 1968- v. (2377 p.) DDC 966/.2601/0924 B
DT475.5.S3 P47 1968   NYPL [Sc F 87-398]

AFRICA, WEST - HISTORY - CONGRESSES.
Peuples du golfe du Bénin . Paris , c1984. 328 p. : ISBN 2-86537-092-5 DDC 966/.8004963 19
DT510.43.E94 P48 1984
NYPL [Sc E 88-449]

AFRICA, WEST - HISTORY, MILITARY.
Ukpabi, Sam C. The origins of the Nigerian

army . Zaria, Nigeria , 1987. 194 p. : ISBN
978-19-4128-6   *NYPL [Sc D 88-1489]*

**AFRICA, WEST - KINGS AND RULERS -
BIOGRAPHY.**
Person, Yves. Samori: une révolution dyula.
Dakar, 1968- v. (2377 p.) DDC 966/.2601/0924
B
DT475.5.S3 P47 1968   NYPL [Sc F 87-398]

**AFRICA, WEST - POPULATION -
CONGRESSES.**
West African Seminar on Population Studies,
University of Ghana, 1972. Interdisciplinary
approaches to population studies . Legon ,
1975. ix, 333 p. ;
HB21 .W38 1972   NYPL [JLD 78-861]

**AFRICA, WEST - POPULATION POLICY -
CASE STUDIES.**
Sex roles, population and development in West
Africa . London , Portsmouth, N.H. , 1987. xiii,
242 p. ; ISBN 0-435-08022-9 DDC 304.6/0966 19
HB3665.5.A3 S49 1988
NYPL [Sc E 88-318]

AFRICA, WEST - RELIGION - TEXT-BOOKS.
Quarcoopome, T. N. O. West African
traditional religion /. Ibadan , 1987. viii, 200
p. : ISBN 978-14-8223-8   *NYPL [Sc D 88-819]*

**AFRICA, WEST - SOCIAL LIFE AND
CUSTOMS.**
Niven, Cecil Rex, 1898- The lands and peoples
of West Africa /. London [1961] vii, 84 p. :
NYPL [Sc D 88-669]

**AFRICA, WEST - SOCIAL LIFE AND
CUSTOMS - CONGRESSES.**
Peuples du golfe du Bénin . Paris , c1984. 328
p. ; ISBN 2-86537-092-5 DDC 966/.8004963 19
DT510.43.E94 P48 1984
NYPL [Sc E 88-449]

L'africain et le missionnaire . Laverdière, Lucien,
1940- Montr´eal , 1987. 608 p. ; ISBN
2-89007-640-7   *NYPL [Sc D 88-343]*

African adventures and adventurers / edited by
G.T. Day. Boston : Lothrop, 1880. 393 p. : ill. ;
19 cm.
*1. Livingstone, David, 1813-1873 - Journeys - Africa,
East - Juvenile literature. 2. Explorers - Africa, East -
Juvenile literature. 3. Nile River - Discovery and
exploration - Juvenile literature. 4. Africa, East -
Discovery and exploration - Juvenile literature. I. Day,
George Tiffany, 1822-1875.   NYPL [Sc C 88-60]*

African all-stars . Stapleton, Cris. London , 1987.
373 p., [16] p. of plates : ISBN 0-7043-2504-7
NYPL [Sc E 88-137]

African-American Institute.
AAI and Africa. New York : Afro-American
Institute, [1986?] 1 v. (various pagings) ; 29 cm.
1. African-American Institute. I. Title.
NYPL [Sc F 88-298]

African universities . Lagos, Nigeria , 1968. iii,
80 p. ;   *NYPL [Sc F 88-81]*

Mother and child in African Sculpture . New
York , 1987. [16] p. :   *NYPL [Sc F 88-3]*

A system approach to the implications of
national school-leaver problems in Dahomey,
Ivory Coast, Niger, Togo and Upper Volta :
research, development, evaluation /
African-American Institute. Washington : The
Institute, 1970. 1 v. (various pagings), [7]
folded leaves : ill. ; 29 cm. Cover title. "May,
1970." Includes bibliographical references.
*1. Educational planning - Africa, West. 2. Africa,
West - Economic policy. I. Title.*
NYPL [Sc F 88-84]

AFRICAN-AMERICAN INSTITUTE.
African-American Institute. AAI and Africa.
New York [1986?] 1 v. (various pagings) ;
NYPL [Sc F 88-298]

African American life.
Denby, Charles. Indignant heart . Detroit ,
1989, c1978. xvi, 303 p. : ISBN 0-8143-2219-0
(alk. paper) DDC 331.6/396073 B 19
HD8039.A82 U633 1989
NYPL [Sc D 89-563]

African American life series.
Denby, Charles. Indignant heart . Detroit ,
1989, c1978. xvi, 303 p. : ISBN 0-8143-2219-0
(alk. paper) DDC 331.6/396073 B 19
HD8039.A82 U633 1989
NYPL [Sc D 89-563]
Rich, Wilbur C. Coleman Young and Detroit

politics . Detroit, Mich. , 1989. 298 p. : ISBN
0-8143-2093-7 DDC 977.4/34043/0924 B 19
F474.D453 Y677 1989   NYPL [Sc E 89-208]

**AFRICAN-AMERICANS. see AFRO-
AMERICANS.**

**African and Asian Inter-regional Workshop on
Strategies for Improving the Employment
Conditions of Rural Women (1984 : Arusha,
Tanzania)** Resources, power and women :
proceedings of the African and Asian
Inter-regional Workshop on Strategies for
Improving the Employment Conditions of Rural
Women, Arusha, United Republic of Tanzania,
20-25 August 1984. Geneva : International
Labour Office, 1985. ix, 82 p. ; 30 cm. (A WEP
study) ISBN 92-2-105009-2 (pbk.) : DDC
331.4/83/095 19
*1. Rural women - Employment - Africa - Congresses. 2.
Rural women - Employment - Asia - Congresses. 3.
Women in rural development - Africa - Congresses. 4.
Women in rural development - Asia - Congresses. I.
Title. II. Series.*
HD6207 .A78 1984   NYPL [JLF 87-1038]

African and western legal systems in contact
Bayreuth, W. Germany : Bayreuth University,
c1989. 89 p. ; 21 cm. (Bayreuth African studies
series, 0178-0034 . 11) Bibliography: p. 85-89. ISBN
3-927510-01-7 :
*1. Law - Africa - History and criticism. 2. Law -
Nigeria. I. Series.   NYPL [Sc D 89-465]*

AFRICAN ART. see ART, AFRICAN.

**African art from the Rita and John Grunwald
collection** /. Pelrine, Diane. Bloomington ,
c1988. 159 p. : ISBN 0-253-21061-5 (I.U. Press :
pbk.) : DDC 730/.0966/0740172255 19
N7398 .P44 1988   NYPL [Sc F 89-158]

**AFRICAN-ASIAN POLITICS. see AFRO-
ASIAN POLITICS.**

**African Association for Training and
Development. Conference (6th : 1986 :
Badagry, Nigeria)** Human resources
development and utilization in Africa /. Maseru
[Lesotho] , 1988. vi, 160 p. ; ISBN
0-620-12102-5   *NYPL [Sc D 89-558]*

African Biosciences Network. The State of
medicinal plants research in Nigeria .
[Ibadan?] , c1986. vi, 404 p. : ISBN
978-302-850-2   *NYPL [Sc E 88-305]*

African capitalism . Kennedy, Paul M., 1945-
Cambridge, Cambridgeshire , New York , 1988.
x, 233 p. ; ISBN 0-521-26599-1 DDC
332/.041/096 19
HC800 .K46 1988   NYPL [Sc E 88-520]

An African Chris[t]mas? / edited by Brian
Hearne ; contributors, Pol Vonck ... [et al.].
Eldoret, Kenya : Gaba Publications, AMECEA
Pastoral Institute, 1983. 53 p. ; 21 cm.
(Spearhead. no. 77) Bibliography: p. 51-53. DDC
263/.91/096 19
*1. Bible. N.T. Matthew II, 1-12 - Criticism,
interpretation, etc. 2. Bible. N.T. Luke II, 1-20 -
Criticism, interpretation, etc. 3. Christmas - Africa. I.
Hearne, Brian, 1939-. II. Vonck, Pol. III. Title: African
Christmas?. IV. Series: Spearhead (Eldoret, Kenya) , no.
77.*
BS2575.2 .A37 1983   NYPL [Sc D 88-195]

African Christmas? An African Chris[t]mas? /.
Eldoret, Kenya , 1983. 53 p. ; DDC 263/.91/096
19
BS2575.2 .A37 1983   NYPL [Sc D 88-195]

African comedy /. Hopkins, David, 1936-
London , 1988. 224 p. ; ISBN 0-00-223235-9 :
DDC 823/.914 19   *NYPL [Sc D 89-162]*

**AFRICAN COOPERATION -
BIBLIOGRAPHY.**
Kersebaum, Andrea. Integrationsbestrebungen in
Afrika . Hamburg , 1986-1987. 2 v. ; ISBN
3-922852-13-0   *NYPL [Sc F 88-33]*

African creations : an anthology of Oxike short
stories / selected and introduced by E.N.
Obiechina. Enugu, Nigeria : Fourth Dimension
Publishers, 1985, c1982. 180 p. ; 21 cm. ISBN
978-15-6181-5
*1. Short stories, African (English). I. Obiechina,
Emmanuel N., 1933-. II. Okike.*
NYPL [Sc D 88-436]

African crisis areas and U. S. foreign policy /
edited by Gerald J. Bender, James S. Coleman,
Richard L. Sklar. Berkeley : University of
California Press, c1985. xiv, 374 p. : maps ; 24

cm. Includes index. Bibliography: p. 343-347. ISBN
0-520-05548-9 (alk. paper) DDC 327.7306 19
*1. Africa - Foreign relations - United States -
Addresses, essays, lectures. 2. United States - Foreign
relations - Africa - Addresses, essays, lectures. 3.
Africa - Foreign relations - 1960- - Addresses, essays,
lectures. 4. Africa - Politics and government - 1960- -
Addresses, essays, lectures. 5. Africa - Economic
conditions - 1960- - Addresses, essays, lectures. I.
Bender, Gerald J. II. Coleman, James Smoot. III. Sklar,
Richard L.*
DT38.7 .A39 1986   NYPL [JLE 85-4182]

African debt and financing / edited by Carol
Lancaster and John Williamson. Washington,
D.C. : Institute for International Economics,
1986. 223 p. : ill. ; 23 cm. (Special report . 5)
Conference held by the Institute for International
Economics in Washington, D.C., Feb. 20-22, 1986.
Includes bibliographies. ISBN 0-88132-044-7 : DDC
336.3/435/096 19
*1. Debts, External - Africa - Congresses. 2. Loans,
Foreign - Africa - Congresses. I. Lancaster, Carol. II.
Williamson, John, 1937-. III. Institute for International
Economics (U. S.). IV. Series: Special reports (Institute
for International Economics (U. S.)) , 5.*
HJ8826 .A36 1986   NYPL [JLE 87-3261]

African development : the OAU/ECA Lagos Plan
of Action and beyond / by Ralph I. Onwuka,
'Layi Abegunrin, and Dhanjoo N. Ghista,
editors.1st original ed. Lawrenceville, Va., U.
S.A. : Brunswick Pub. Co., c1985. 241 p. : ill. ;
26 cm. Bibliography: p. 220-241. ISBN
0-931494-57-5 (pbk.) DDC 337.1/6 19
*1. Lagos Plan of Action - Congresses. 2. Africa -
Economic policy - Congresses. 3. Africa - Economic
integration - Congresses. I. Onwuka, Ralph I. II.
Abegunrin, Olayiwola. III. Ghista, Dhanjoo N.*
HC800 .A565 1985   NYPL [Sc F 87-376]

The African diaspora . Ifill, Max B. Port-of-Spain,
Trinidad , 1986. vii, 118 p. : ISBN
976-8008-00-8 (pbk.) DDC 382/.44/09729 19
HT1072 .I35 1986   NYPL [Sc D 88-934]

**AFRICAN DRAMA (FRENCH) - 20TH
CENTURY - TRANSLATIONS INTO
ENGLISH.**
Faces of African independence .
Charlottesville , 1988. xxxvi, 127 p. ; ISBN
0-8139-1186-9 DDC 842 19
PQ3987.5.E5 F33 1988   NYPL [Sc D 89-32]

African environments and resources /. Lewis,
Lawrence. Boston , 1988. xii, 404 p. : ISBN
0-04-916010-9 (alk. paper) DDC 333.7/096 19
HC800 .L48 1987   NYPL [Sc E 89-50]

The African exchange : toward a biological
history of Black people / Kenneth F. Kiple,
editor. Durham N.C. : Duke University Press,
1987, c1988. vi, 280 p. : ill ; 23 cm. Includes
bibliographies and index. ISBN 0-8223-0731-6 DDC
614.4/273/08996073 19
*1. Blacks - Diseases - America - History. 2. Slavery -
America - Condition of slaves - History. 3. Health and
race - America - History. I. Kiple, Kenneth F., 1939-.*
RA442 .A37 1988   NYPL [Sc D 88-541]

**AFRICAN FICTION (ENGISH) - HISTORY
AND CRITICISM.**
Studies in the African novel /. [Ibadan]
[1985?] viii, 258 p. ;   *NYPL [Sc D 88-1316]*

**AFRICAN FICTION (ENGLISH) -
CRITICISM AND INTERPRETATION.**
Pifferi, Annisa. La donna nel romanzo africano
in lingua inglese . Calliano (Trento) , c1985.
143 p. ; ISBN 88-7024-258-7
NYPL [Sc D 89-102]

**AFRICAN FICTION (ENGLISH) - SOCIAL
ASPECTS.**
Agovi, Kofi Ermeleh, 1944- Novels of social
change /. Tema, Ghana , 1988. xxviii, 290 p. ;
ISBN 996-410-332-8
NYPL [Sc D 88-1410]

**AFRICAN FICTION - HISTORY AND
CRITICISM.**
Ricard, Alain. Naissance du roman africain .
Paris , Dakar , c1987. 228 p., [4] p. of plates :
ISBN 2-7087-0494-X   *NYPL [Sc D 89-46]*

An African "Florence Nightingale" . Akinsanya,
Justus A. Ibadan, Nigeria , 1987. xii, 224 p. :
ISBN 978-245-826-0 (hard back ed.)
NYPL [Sc D 88-895]

**AFRICAN FOLK LITERATURE. see FOLK
LITERATURE, AFRICAN.**

African heritage : a public auction : featuring contemporary fine art on pots by artists for the Cape / to be conducted by Stephen Welz of Sotheby's in aid of "Operation Hunger." Cape Town : Sotheby's, 1987. 24 p. : col. ill. ; 30 cm. "A public exhibition at the New Forum Gallery, lower mall, Cavendish Square, Claremont, Cape Town, 17 July - 1 Aug. 1987."
1. Art, African - Exhibitions. 2. Pottery - Africa - Exhibitions. I. Welz, Stephan. II. Sotheby's.
NYPL [Sc F 89-117]

African historical dictionaries.
(no. 2 2) Thompson, Virginia McLean, 1903- Historical dictionary of the People's Republic of the Congo /. Metuchen, N.J. , 1984. xxi, 239 p. : ISBN 0-8108-1716-0 DDC 967/.24 19
DT546.215 .T47 1984 NYPL [Sc D 85-104]

(no. 36 36) Wucher King, Joan. Historical dictionary of Egypt /. Metuchen, N.J. , 1984. xiii, 719 p. : ISBN 0-8108-1670-9 DDC 962/.003/21 19
DT45 .W83 1984 NYPL [Sc D 85-101]

(no. 11) Imperato, Pascal James. Historical dictionary of Mali /. Metuchen, N.J. , 1986. xvii, 359 p. ; ISBN 0-8108-1885-X DDC 966/.23 19
DT551.5 .I46 1986 NYPL [Sc D 87-5]

(no. 21) Liniger-Goumaz, Max. Historical dictionary of Equatorial Guinea /. Metuchen, N.J. , 1988. xxx, 238 p. : ISBN 0-8108-2120-6 DDC 967/.18/00321 19
DT620.15 .L57 1988 NYPL [Sc D 89-528]

(no. 22) Lobban, Richard. Historical dictionary of the Republic of Guinea-Bissau /. Metuchen, N.J. , 1988. xx, 210 p. : ISBN 0-8108-2086-2 DDC 966/.57 19
*DT613.5 .L62 1988 NYPL [*R-BMP 88-5080]*

(no. 37) Saunders, Christopher C. Historical dictionary of South Africa /. Metuchen, N.J. , 1983. xxviii, 241 p. ; ISBN 0-8108-1629-6 DDC 968/.003/21 19
*DT766 .S23 1983 NYPL [*R-BN 89-3347]*

(no. 38) Dunn, D. Elwood. Historical dictionary of Liberia /. Metuchen, N.J. , 1985. xx, 274, [7] p. of plates : ISBN 0-8108-1767-5 DDC 966.6/2/00321 19
DT631 .D95 1985 NYPL [Sc D 86-127]

(no. 39) McFarland, Daniel Miles. Historical dictionary of Ghana /. Metuchen, N.J. , 1985. lxxx, 296 p. : ISBN 0-8108-1761-6 DDC 966.7/003/21 19
*DT510.5 .M38 1985 NYPL [*R-BMK 89-3348]*

(no. 40) Oyewole, A. Historical dictionary of Nigeria /. Metuchen, N.J. , c1987. xvii, 391 p. : ISBN 0-8108-1787-X DDC 966.9/003/21 19
*DT515.15 .O94 1987 NYPL [*R-BMM 89-3341]*

(no. 42) Lobban, Richard. Historical dictionary of the Republic of Cape Verde /. Metuchen, N.J. , 1988. xix, 171 p. : ISBN 0-8108-2087-0 DDC 966/.57/00321 19
DT613.5 .L62 1988b NYPL [Sc D 88-1311]

(no. 7) Decalo, Samuel. Historical dictionary of Benin /. Metuchen, N.J. , 1987. xxvii, 349 p. : ISBN 0-8108-1924-4 DDC 966/.83 19
DT541.5 .D4 1987 NYPL [Sc D 88-982]

[African historical documents series.
(2]) Procter, Lovell James. The Central African journal of Lovell J. Procter, 1860-1864. [Boston] 1971. xvii, 501 p. DDC 916.8
DT731 .P75 NYPL [Sc D 88-977]

African history . Sweeting, Earl. London , 1988. 31 p. : *NYPL [Sc D 89-505]*

African Institution, London.
Reasons for establishing a registry of slaves in the British colonies : being a report of a committee of the African Institution. London : The Institution, 1815 (London : Printed by Ellerton and Henderson) 118 p. ; 22 cm. Written by James Stephen.--Dict. of natl. biog.
1. Slavery - West Indies, British - Condition of slaves. 2. Slave-trade - Great Britain. I. Stephen, James, 1758-1832. II. Title. *NYPL [Sc Rare G 86-4]*

A review of the colonial slave registration acts : in a report of a committee of the Board of Directors of the African Institution, made on the 22d of February, 1820, and published by order of that Board. London : Printed by

Ellerton and Henderson and sold by Hatchard, 1820. 139, 11 p. ; 21 cm. Includes bibliographical references.
1. Slavery - West Indies, British. I. Title.
NYPL [Sc Rare G 86-24]

Special report of the directors of the African Institution, made at the annual general meeting, on the 12th of April, 1815 : respecting the allegations contained in a pamphlet entitled "A letter to William Wilberforce, Esq. &c. by R. Thorpe, Esq. &c." London : J. Hatchard, 1815 (London : Printed by Ellerton and Henderson) 157 p. ; 22 cm.
1. Thorpe, Robert. A letter to William Wilberforce ... containing remarks on the reports of the Sierra Leone Company and African Institution. 2. Sierra Leone Company. I. Title. *NYPL [Sc Rare G 86-5]*

AFRICAN INSTITUTION, LONDON.
Antidote to West-Indian sketches, drawn from authentic sources. London , 1816-1817. 7 nos. ;
NYPL [Sc Rare G 86-16]

African junior library .
(13) Chukwuka, J. I. N. Zandi and the wonderful pillow /. Lagos, Nigeria , 1977. 48 p. : ISBN 0-410-80099-6 *NYPL [Sc C 88-76]*

(14) Iroaganachi, John. A fight for honey /. Lagos, Nigeria , 1977. 30 p. : ISBN 0-410-80181-X *NYPL [Sc C 88-77]*

(6) Appiah, Peggy. Why there are so many roads /. Lagos , 1972. 62 p. :
NYPL [Sc C 88-12]

AFRICAN LANGUAGES.
Diop, Cheikh Anta. Nouvelles recherches sur l'égyptien ancien et les langues négro-africaines modernes /. Paris , c1988. 221 p. ; ISBN 2-7087-0507-5 *NYPL [Sc D 89-550]*

Les Langues de l'Afrique subsaharienne /. Paris , 1981. 2 v : ISBN 2-222-01720-3 :
NYPL [JFN 81-11 v.1]

Mann, Michael. A thesaurus of African languages . New York , 1987. 325 p. ; ISBN 0-905450-24-8 *NYPL [Sc F 88-142]*

AFRICAN LANGUAGES - CLASSIFICATION.
La méthode dialectometrique appliquée aux langues africaines /. Berlin , 1986. 431 p. : ISBN 3-496-00856-3 *NYPL [Sc E 88-46]*

AFRICAN LANGUAGES - DIALECTOLOGY.
La méthode dialectometrique appliquée aux langues africaines /. Berlin , 1986. 431 p. : ISBN 3-496-00856-3 *NYPL [Sc E 88-46]*

AFRICAN LANGUAGES - INFLUENCE ON SPANISH.
Alvarez, Alexandra, 1946- Malabí Maticulambí . Montevideo, Uruguay? , c1987. 191 p. ; *NYPL [Sc D 88-1012]*

African librarianship . Prichard, R. J. Aberystwyth, Dyfed, Great Britain , 1987. 35 p. ; ISBN 0-904020-21-5 (pbk.) DDC 016.02706 19
Z857.A1 P75 1987 NYPL [Sc D 88-1518]

African linguistic bibliographies .
(v. 3) Adewole, Lawrence Olufemi. The Yoruba language . Hamburg , c1987. 182 p. ; ISBN 3-87118-842-5 *NYPL [Sc D 88-821]*

AFRICAN LITERATURE.
February, V. A. (Vernie A.) And bid him sing . London , 1988. xvi, 212 p. : ISBN 0-7103-0278-9 : DDC 306 325/.32 19
NYPL [Sc D 88-1363]

African literature, African critics . Bishop, Rand. New York , 1988. xii, 213 p. ; ISBN 0-313-25918-6 (lib. bdg. : alk. paper) DDC 820/.9/96 19
PR9340 .B5 1988 NYPL [Sc E 89-129]

AFRICAN LITERATURE - BIBLIOGRAPHY.
Michael, Colette Verger, 1937- Negritude . West Cornwall, CT , 1988. xvii, 315 p. ; ISBN 0-933951-15-9 (lib. bdg. : alk. paper) : DDC 016.909/04924 19
Z6520.N44 M53 1988 PN56.N36 NYPL [Sc D 88-1470]

AFRICAN LITERATURE - CONGRESSES.
Forces littéraires d'Afrique. Bruxelles , c1987. 238 p. ; ISBN 2-8041-0965-8
NYPL [Sc E 88-442]

La Tradition orale, source de la littérature contemporaine en Afrique. Dakar , c1984. 201 p. : ISBN 2-7236-0899-9 *NYPL [Sc E 89-55]*

AFRICAN LITERATURE (ENGLISH)
Mambo book of Zimbabwean Verse in English /. Gweru, Zimbabwe , c986. xxix, 417 p. ; ISBN 0-86922-367-4 (pbk.)
NYPL [JFD 88-10986]

AFRICAN LITERATURE (ENGLISH) - COLLECTED WORKS.
Literature and society . Oguta, Nigeria , 1986. iv, 303 p. ; *NYPL [Sc D 88-639]*

AFRICAN LITERATURE (ENGLISH) - HISTORY AND CRITICISM - THEORY, ETC.
Bishop, Rand. African literature, African critics . New York , 1988. xii, 213 p. ; ISBN 0-313-25918-6 (lib. bdg. : alk. paper) DDC 820/.9/96 19
PR9340 .B5 1988 NYPL [Sc E 89-129]

AFRICAN LITERATURE (FRENCH)
Anthologie africaine d'expression française /. Paris , c1981- v. ; ISBN 2-218-05648-8 (v. 1) :
NYPL [Sc C 89-80]

AFRICAN LITERATURE (FRENCH) - 20TH CENTURY - HISTORY AND CRITICISM.
Interviews avec des écrivains africains francophones /. [Bayreuth, W. Germany , c1986. 95 p. ; *NYPL [Sc D 88-906]*

Locha Mateso. Littérature africaine et sa critique . Paris , c1986. 399 p. ; ISBN 2-86537-153-0 DDC 840/.9/896 19
PQ3981 .L6 1986 NYPL [Sc D 88-1392]

AFRICAN LITERATURE (FRENCH) - BLACK AUTHORS.
Littérature négro-africaine francophone . [Pau] , 1986. 137 p. ; DDC 840/.9/896 19
PQ3980.5 .L56 1986 NYPL [Sc D 89-316]

AFRICAN LITERATURE (FRENCH) - BLACK AUTHORS - HISTORY AND CRITICISM.
Littérature négro-africaine francophone . [Pau] , 1986. 137 p. ; DDC 840/.9/896 19
PQ3980.5 .L56 1986 NYPL [Sc D 89-316]

AFRICAN LITERATURE (FRENCH) - HISTORY AND CRITICISM.
Laverdière, Lucien, 1940- L'africain et le missionnaire . Montr´eal , 1987. 608 p. : ISBN 2-89007-640-7 *NYPL [Sc D 88-343]*

Literature and African identity. Bayreuth , c1986. 125 p. ; *NYPL [Sc D 89-369]*

Locha Mateso. Littérature africaine et sa critique . Paris , c1986. 399 p. ; ISBN 2-86537-153-0 DDC 840/.9/896 19
PQ3981 .L6 1986 NYPL [Sc D 88-1392]

Réception critique de la littérature africaine et antillaise d'expression française. Paris , 1979. 272 p. ; *NYPL [Sc E 87-557]*

AFRICAN LITERATURE (FRENCH) - HISTORY AND CRITICISM - THEORY, ETC.
Bishop, Rand. African literature, African critics . New York , 1988. xii, 213 p. ; ISBN 0-313-25918-6 (lib. bdg. : alk. paper) DDC 820/.9/96 19
PR9340 .B5 1988 NYPL [Sc E 89-129]

AFRICAN LITERATURE - HISTORY AND CRITICISM.
African writers on the air. Köln , c1984. 119 p. : *NYPL [Sc D 88-674]*

John, Elerius Edet. Topics in African literature /. Lagos , 1986. 3 v. ; ISBN 978-244-610-6 (v. 1)
NYPL [Sc D 89-370]

Literature and African identity. Bayreuth , c1986. 125 p. ; *NYPL [Sc D 89-369]*

Morán, Fernando, 1926- Nación y alienación en la literatura negroafricana. [Madrid, 1964] 90 p.
PL8010 .M65 NYPL [Sc C 88-347]

AFRICAN LITERATURE - PERIODICALS - HISTORY.
Benson, Peter. Black Orpheus, Transition, and modern cultural awakening in Africa /. Berkeley , c1986. xiii, 320 p. : ISBN 0-520-05418-0 DDC 820/.8 19
PL8000.B63 B4 1986 NYPL [Sc E 88-354]

AFRICAN LITERATURE - SOCIAL ASPECTS.
Ogidan, Anna. Thememschwerpunkte im Werk Ayi Kwei Armahs /. Wien , 1988. ii, 202 p. ; ISBN 3-85043-046-4
NYPL [Sc D 88-1035]

AFRICAN LITERATURE - TRANSLATIONS INTO ENGLISH.

Voices from twentieth-century Africa .
London , Boston , 1988. xl, 424 p. ; ISBN
0-571-14929-4 (cased) : DDC 808.8/9896 19
NYPL [Sc D 89-174]

**AFRICAN LITERATURE - WOMEN
AUTHORS - HISTORY AND CRITICISM.**
Women in African literature today . London ,
Trenton, N.J. , 1987. vi, 162 p. ; ISBN
0-85255-500-8 (pbk) : DDC 809/.89287 19
PL8010   *NYPL [Sc D 88-984]*

African lives . Boyles, Denis. New York , c1988.
xi, 225 p., [8] p. of plates : ISBN 1-555-84034-5
DDC 960/.04034 19
DT16.W45 B69 1988   *NYPL [Sc E 88-503]*

African madness /. Shoumatoff, Alex. New York ,
1988. xviii, 202 p. ; ISBN 0-394-56914-8 : DDC
967/.0328 19
DT352.2 .S48 1988   *NYPL [Sc D 89-160]*

African medicine in the modern world :
proceedings of a seminar held in the Centre of
African Studies, University of Edinburgh, 10
and 11 December, 1986 / [edited by Una
Maclean and Christopher Fyfe] Edinburgh :
Centre of African Studies, University of
Edinburgh, [1987] 222 p. : ill. ; 21 cm. (Seminar
proceedings . no. 27) Errata slip inserted. Includes
bibliographies. DDC 615.8/82/096 19
I. Maclean, Una. II. Fyfe, Christopher. III. University
of Edinburgh. Centre of African Studies. IV. Series:
Seminar proceedings (University of Edinburgh. Centre
of African Studies) , no. 27.
GR350   *NYPL [Sc D 87-1283]*

**African Methodist Episcopal Church. General
Conference.** Combined minutes of the general
conferences 1948-1952-1956 / African
Methodist Episcopal Church ; compiled by
Russell S. Brown. [Nashville, Tenn. : The
Conference, 1956?] 503 p. ; 23 cm. Official
minutes of the 33rd, 34th, and 35th conferences.
I. Brown, Russell S.   *NYPL [Sc D 87-1381]*

**AFRICAN METHODIST EPISCOPAL
CHURCH - MISSIONS - AFRICA,
SOUTHERN.**
Chirenje, J. Mutero, 1935- Ethiopianism and
Afro-Americans in southern Africa, 1883-1916
/. Baton Rouge , c1987. xii, 231 p. : ISBN
0-8071-1319-0 DDC 276.8/08 19
BR1450 .C45 1987   *NYPL [Sc E 88-336]*

African music; meeting in Yaoundé (Cameroon)
23-27 February 1970. Organized by UNESCO.
Paris, La Revue musicale [c1972] 154 p. music
27 cm. Issued also in French under title: La musique
africain; no. 288-289 of La Revue musicale. Includes
bibliographical references.
I. Music, African - Congresses.
     NYPL [JMF 74-320]

**African myth and black reality in Bahian
Carnaval /.** Crowley, Daniel J., 1921- [Los
Angeles, Calif.] [1984] 47 p. :
     NYPL [Sc F 86-281]

**AFRICAN MYTHOLOGY. see MYTHOLOGY,
AFRICAN.**

**AFRICAN NATIONAL CONGRESS -
HISTORY.**
Meli, Francis, 1942- South Africa belongs to
us . Harare , 1988. xx, 258, [8] p. of plates :
     NYPL [Sc D 89-308]

African nationalism. Hollings, Jill. New York
[1972, c1971] 128 p. DDC 320.5/4/096
DT31 .H577 1972   *NYPL [Sc D 88-1496]*

African Negro art . Museum of Modern Art
(New York, N.Y.) New York [c1935] 58 p. :
     NYPL [Sc F 88-125]

African outreach series .
(no. 5) University of Illinois Film Center. Film
and video resources about Africa available from
the University of Illinois Film Center /.
Champaign, Ill. [c1985] 34 p. : DDC 016.96 19
Z3501 .U64 1985 DT3   *NYPL [Sc F 88-335]*

**African philosophy, culture, and traditional
medicine /.** Makinde, M. Akin. Athens, Ohio ,
1988. xvii, 154 p., [2] leaves of plates : ISBN
0-89680-152-7 DDC 199/.6 19
B5375 .M35 1988   *NYPL [Sc D 88-1273]*

African poetry and the English language /.
Haynes, John. Basingstoke , 1987. 165 p. :
ISBN 0-333-44928-2 (pbk) : DDC 821 19
PR9342   *NYPL [Sc D 88-717]*

**AFRICAN POETRY (ENGLISH) - HISTORY
AND CRITICISM.**
Haynes, John. African poetry and the English
language /. Basingstoke , 1987. 165 p. : ISBN
0-333-44928-2 (pbk) : DDC 821 19
PR9342   *NYPL [Sc D 88-717]*

AFRICAN POETRY (FRENCH)
Senghor, Léopold Sédar, 1906- Anthologie de la
nouvelle poésie nègre et malgache de langue
française /. Paris , 1985, c1948. xliv, 227 p. ;
ISBN 2-13-038715-2   *NYPL [Sc C 88-134]*

**African problems: analysis of eminent Soviet
scientist.** Potekhin, I. I. (Ivan Izosimovich),
1903-1964. Moscow, 1968. 141 p. DDC 320.9/6
DT30 .P59   *NYPL [Sc C 88-86]*

**AFRICAN PROSE LITERATURE (ENGLISH) -
HISTORY AND CRITICISM.**
Sandiford, Keith Albert, 1947- Measuring the
moment . Selinsgrove , c1988. 181 p. ; ISBN
0-941664-79-1 (alk. paper) DDC 828 19
PR9340 .S26 1988   *NYPL [Sc E 88-467]*

**AFRICAN PROVERBS. see PROVERBS,
AFRICAN.**

African psychology . Nobles, Wade W. Oakland,
California , 1986. 133 p. ; ISBN 0-939205-02-5
     NYPL [Sc D 88-696]

**African reactions to colonization in Central
Africa.** Les Réactions africaines à la
colonisation en Afrique Centrale . Ruhengeri ,
1986. 478 p. ;   *NYPL [Sc G 87-9]*

African resistance in Liberia . Akpan, Monday B.
Bremen , 1988. 68 p. : ISBN 3-926771-01-1
     NYPL [Sc D 89-347]

African Rural Economy Program.
**Working paper - African Rural Economy
Program .**
(no. 9) Michigan State University. Dept. of
Agricultural Economics. An analysis of the
Eastern ORD rural development project in
Upper Volta. East Lansing , 1976. v, 103
p. : DDC 338.1/866/25
HD2135 .U63 1976   *NYPL [Sc F 89-170]*

**AFRICAN SCULPTURE. see SCULPTURE,
AFRICAN.**

**AFRICAN SEMINAR ON THE CHANGING
AND CONTEMPORARY ROLE OF
WOMEN IN SOCIETY, ADDIS ABABA,
1975.**
Pala, Achola O. A preliminary survey of
avenues for and constraints on women's
involvement in the development process in
Kenya [microform] /. [Nairobi? , 1975] 26 p. :
     NYPL [Sc Micro R-4108 no.14]

**AFRICAN SHORT STORIES (ENGLISH) see
SHORT STORIES, AFRICAN (ENGLISH)**

The African slave trade : The secret purpose of
the insurgents to revive it. No treaty
stipulations against the slave trade to be
extended into with the European powers :
Judah P. Benjamin's intercepted instructions to
L.Q. Lamar, styled commissioner, etc.
Philadelphia : C. Sherman, Son & Co., printers,
1863. 24 p. ; 24 cm. "A reproduction of some recent
editorials of the National intelligencer."
I. Confederate States of America - Politics and
government. 2. Slave-trade. I. Benjamin, J. P. (Judah
Philip), 1811-1884. II. Lamar, Lucius Q. C. (Lucius
Quintus Cincinnatus), 1825-1893. III. National
intelligencer.   *NYPL [Sc Rare F 89-5]*

African society today.
Freund, Bill. The African worker /. Cambridge
[Cambridgeshire] , New York , 1988. viii, 200
p. ; ISBN 0-521-30758-9 DDC 305.5/62/096 19
HD8776.5 .F74 1988   *NYPL [Sc C 88-334]*

Kennedy, Paul M., 1945- African capitalism .
Cambridge, Cambridgeshire , New York , 1988.
x, 233 p. ; ISBN 0-521-26599-1 DDC
332/.041/096 19
HC800 .K46 1988   *NYPL [Sc E 88-520]*

Nafziger, E. Wayne. Inequality in Africa .
Cambridge [Cambridgeshire] , New York ,
c1988. xii, 204 p. : ISBN 0-521-26881-8 DDC
339.2/096 19
HC800.Z9 I5136 1988   *NYPL [Sc E 88-521]*

African special bibliographic series, 0749-2308 .
(no. 9) Bullwinkle, Davis. African women, a
general bibliography, 1976-1985 /. New York ,
1989. xx, 334 p. ; ISBN 0-313-26607-7 (lib. bdg.

alk. paper) DDC 016.3054/096 19
Z7964.A3 B84 1989 HQ1787
     NYPL [Sc E 89-173]

AFRICAN STUDENTS - INDIA - FICTION.
Agburum, Ezenwa. Broken graduate /. Orlu,
Imo State, Nigeria , 1986. 96 p. ;
     NYPL [Sc C 88-193]

African studies. Afrika-Studien. Dedicated to the
IIIrd International Congress of Africanists in
Addis Abeba / edited by Thea Büttner and
Gerhard Brehme. [Translated from the German
by Ria and Christopher Salt] Berlin,
Akademie-Verlag, 1973. xi, 400 p. 22 cm.
(Studien über Asien, Afrika und Lateinamerika. Bd. 15)
"Published by the Sektion Afrika- und
Nahostwissenschaften of The Karl-Marx-University
Leipzig on behalf of The Central Council of Asian,
African and Latin American Sciences in the GDR."
Includes bibliographical references.
1. Africa - Addresses, essays, lectures. I. Büttner, Thea.
II. Brehme, Gerhard. III. International Congress of
Africanists, 3d, Addis Abeba, 1973. IV. Title:
Afrika-Studien. V. Series.
     NYPL [JLK 73-249 Bd. 15]

African studies. University of Illinois at
Urbana-Champaign. African Studies Program.
Curriculum-related handouts for teachers .
Urbana, Illinois [1981] ca. 500 p. ;
     NYPL [Sc F 88-215]

African studies by Soviet scholars .
(no. 3) The USSR and Africa. Moscow , 1983.
205 p. ; DDC 303.4/8247/06 19
DT38.9.S65 U86 1983   *NYPL [Sc D 88-980]*

**African studies in curriculum development &
evaluation .**
(no. 133) Mombod, Josephine Ntinou.
Developing models/techniques in the teaching
of English as a second foreign language in
senior secondary schools in the Congo /.
Nairobi , 1983. ii, 67 leaves ; DDC
428/.007/126724 19
PE1068.C74 M67 1983   *NYPL [Sc F 88-200]*

African studies (Lewiston, N.Y.) .
(v. 2) Oral histories of three secondary school
students in Tanzania /. Lewiston/Queenston ,
1987. 248 p. ; ISBN 0-88946-179-1 (alk. paper) :
DDC 306/.0967/8 19
LA1842 .O73 1987   *NYPL [Sc E 88-267]*

(v. 5) New religious movements in Nigeria /.
Lewiston, N.Y. , c1987. xvi, 245 p. ; ISBN
0-88946-180-5 (alk. paper) DDC 291.9/09669 19
BL2470.N5 N49 1987   *NYPL [Sc E 88-266]*

(v. 6) Texts on Zulu religion . Lewiston, NY ,
Queenston, Ont. , 1987. 488 p. ; ISBN
0-88946-181-3 : DDC 299/.683 19
BL2480.Z8 T48 1987   *NYPL [Sc E 88-463]*

African studies series.
(no. 5) Peil, Margaret. The Ghanaian factory
worker. [Cambridge, Eng.] 1972. ix, 254 p.
     NYPL [Sc 331.7-P]

(55) Markakis, John. National and class conflict
in the Horn of Africa /. Cambridge , New
York , 1987. xvii, 314 p. : ISBN 0-521-33362-8
DDC 960/.3 19
DT367.75 .M37 1987   *NYPL [JFE 88-364]*

(56) Joseph, Richard A. Democracy and
prebendal politics in Nigeria . Cambridge
[Cambridgeshire] , New York , 1987. x, 237
p. : ISBN 0-521-34136-1 DDC 966.9/05 19
DT515.84 .J67 1987   *NYPL [JFE 88-4953]*

(59) Martin, Susan M. Palm oil and protest .
Cambridge [Cambridgeshire] , New York ,
1988. xi, 209 p. : ISBN 0-521-34376-3 DDC
338.4/76643 19
HD9490.5.P343 N66 1988
     NYPL [JLE 88-3417]

(60) Harrison, Christopher, 1958- France and
Islam in West Africa, 1860-1960 /. Cambridge
[Cambridgeshire] , New York , 1988. x, 242
p. : ISBN 0-521-35230-4 DDC 966/.0097451 19
DT530.5.M88 H37 1988
     NYPL [Sc E 88-484]

(61) Clapham, Christopher S. Transformation
and continuity in revolutionary Ethiopia .
Cambridge [Cambridgeshire] , New York ,
1988. xviii, 284 p. : ISBN 0-521-33441-1 DDC
963.07 19
JQ3752 .C55 1988   *NYPL [Sc E 88-446]*

**African Unity, Organization of. see Organization
of African Unity.**

African universities : a summary of collected information / prepared by The African-American Institute. Lagos, Nigeria : The Institute, 1968. iii, 80 p. ; 26 cm. Cover title.
1. Universities and colleges - Africa - Directories. I. African-American Institute.   ***NYPL [Sc F 88-81]***

The African Wesleyan Methodist Episcopal Church : known as Bridge Street AWME Church, org. 1766- inc. 1818. Brooklyn, N.Y. : The Church, c1980. 288 p. : ill., map, ports. ; 29 cm. Bibliography: p. 83.
1. African Wesleyan Methodist Episcopal Church (Brooklyn, New York, N.Y.) - History. I. African Wesleyan Methodist Episcopal Church (Brooklyn, New York, N.Y.).   ***NYPL [Sc F 88-385]***

African Wesleyan Methodist Episcopal Church (Brooklyn, New York, N.Y.)
The African Wesleyan Methodist Episcopal Church . Brooklyn, N.Y. , c1980. 288 p. :
NYPL [Sc F 88-385]

AFRICAN WESLEYAN METHODIST EPISCOPAL CHURCH (BROOKLYN, NEW YORK, N.Y.) - HISTORY.
The African Wesleyan Methodist Episcopal Church . Brooklyn, N.Y. , c1980. 288 p. :
NYPL [Sc F 88-385]

African witers series.
Karodia, Farida. Coming home and other stories /. London , 1988. v, 185 p. ; ISBN 0-435-90738-7 (pbk) :
PR9369.3.K3   ***NYPL [Sc C 89-88]***

African women, a general bibliography, 1976-1985 /. Bullwinkle, Davis. New York , 1989. xx, 334 p. ; ISBN 0-313-26607-7 (lib. bdg. : alk. paper) DDC 016.3054/096 19
Z7964.A3 B84 1989 HQ1787
NYPL [Sc E 89-173]

The African worker /. Freund, Bill. Cambridge [Cambridgeshire] , New York , 1988. viii, 200 p. ; ISBN 0-521-30758-9 DDC 305.5/62/096 19
HD8776.5 .F74 1988   ***NYPL [Sc C 88-334]***

African writers on the air. Köln : Deutsche Welle, c1984. 119 p. : ports. ; 21 cm. (DW-Dokumente . 3) Twelve radio broadcasts based on readings and interviews held as part of the "Horizons '79" cultural festival in Berlin.
1. African literature - History and criticism. I. Series.
NYPL [Sc D 88-674]

Africana, an exhibit of West African art : Jackson College, Jackson, Mississippi, February 17-18-19, 1950. [Jackson, Miss. : Jackson College, 1950] 23 p. : ill. ; 30 cm. Cover title.
1. Art - Africa, West - Exhibitions. I. Jackson College for Negro Teachers.   ***NYPL [Sc F 85-236]***

Africana Saraviensia linguistica, 0724-0937 .
(nr. 14) Eklou, Akpaka A. Satzstruktur des Deutschen und des Ewe . Saarbrücken , 1987. 262 p. ;   ***NYPL [Sc D 89-203]***

The AfriCanadian church . Shreve, Dorothy Shadd. Jordan Station, Ontario, Canada , c1983. 138 p. : ill. ISBN 0-88815-072-5 (pbk.) DDC 277.1/008996 19
BR570 .S53 1983   ***NYPL [Sc D 86-305]***

Africanity and the Black family . Nobles, Wade Winfred, 1945- Oakland, Calif. , 1985. 116 p. ; ISBN 0-939205-01-7 ***NYPL [Sc D 88-760]***

AFRICANIZATION - NIGERIA - CONGRESSES.
Development of management education in Nigeria /. Ikeja, Nigeria , 1985. 555 p. : ISBN 978-14-0017-X   ***NYPL [Sc E 89-161]***

AFRICANS - FRANCE - PARIS - FICTION.
Simon, Njami. [Cercueil & Cie. English.] Coffin & Co. /. Berkeley, CA , c1987. 195 p. ; ISBN 0-88739-049-8 (pbk).
NYPL [Sc C 89-144]

AFRICANS - GREAT BRITAIN - HISTORY - 18TH CENTURY.
Sandiford, Keith Albert, 1947- Measuring the moment . Selinsgrove , c1988. 181 p. ; ISBN 0-941664-79-1 (alk. paper) DDC 828 19
PR9340 .S26 1988   ***NYPL [Sc E 88-467]***

AFRICANS IN FRANCE.
Makanda Duc d'Ikoga, André. Non, Monsieur Giscard [microform] /. Paris [1980] 23 p. ;
NYPL [Sc Micro F-11014]

AFRICANS IN LITERATURE.
Achebe, Chinua. Hopes and impediments .

London , 1988. x, 130 p. ; ISBN 0-435-91000-0 (cased) : DDC 823/.914/09 19
PR881   ***NYPL [Sc D 88-1265]***

Barthelemy, Anthony Gerard, 1949- Black face, maligned race . Baton Rouge , c1987. xi, 215 p. ; ISBN 0-8071-1331-X DDC 822/.3/093520396 19
PR678.A4 B37 1987
NYPL [MWET 87-5064]

Africans in the New World, 1493-1834 . Brown, Larissa V. Providence, Rhode Island , 1988. 61 p. : ISBN 0-916617-31-9 ***NYPL [Sc D 88-624]***

Africa's struggle for freedom, the USA and the USSR : a selection of political analyses / assembled and with an introd. by Henry Winston. New York : New Outlook Publishers, 1972. 96 p. : ill. ; 19 cm. Includes a selection of speeches delivered by African delegates at the 24th Congress of the Communist Party of the Soviet Union, March 30-April 9, 1971. PARTIAL CONTENTS. - To my brothers and sisters / a letter from Henry Winston.--International Trade Union Committee of Negro Workers / by Lily Golden.--Speech by Comrade Sharaf Rashidov ... at the 24th Congress of the Communist Party of the Soviet Union.--Speeches and greetings of African liberation leaders and organizations to the 24th Congress of the Communist Party of the Soviet Union.--Dear Eartha Kitt : an open letter to Jeremy Thorpe and Eartha Kitt.--U. S. imperialism in Africa / by Gus Hall.--Dr. W.E.B. Du Bois' letter of application to join the Communist Party, U. S.A. and Gus Hall's reply. ISBN 0-87898-096-2
1. Communism - Africa. I. Winston, Henry.
NYPL [Sc C 88-139]

Africasouth paperbacks.
Plomer, William, 1903-1973. Cecil Rhodes /. Cape Town , 1984. xvii, 179 p. ; ISBN 0-86486-018-8   ***NYPL [Sc C 88-64]***
Plomer, William, 1903-1973. Cecil Rhodes /. Cape Town , 1984. xvii, 179 p. ; ISBN 0-86486-018-8   ***NYPL [Sc C 88-64]***

Afrika / kleines Nachschlagewerk / herausgegeber Gerhard Brehme, Hans Kramer. Berlin : Dietz, 1985. 520 p. : maps ; 20 cm. Map on lining papers.
1. Africa - Dictionaries and encyclopedias. I. Brehme, Gerhard. II. Kramer, Hans.   ***NYPL [Sc C 88-144]***

Afrika / herausgegeben von Hans-Jürgen Heinrichs. Frankfurt am Main ; New York : Edition Qumran im Campus Verlag, c1986. 413 p. : ill. ; 21 cm. Bibliography: p. 404-407. ISBN 3-88655-212-8 DDC 960 19
1. Africa - Civilization. I. Heinrichs, Hans-Jürgen, 1945-.
DT14 .A3747 1986   ***NYPL [Sc D 89-311]***

Afrika . Baeriswyl-Nicollin, Dominique. Lausanne , c1983. 148 p. : DDC 916/.0448 19
DT12.25 .B32 1983   ***NYPL [Sc F 88-67]***

Afrika /. Deutsches Ledermuseum. Offenbach am Main , 1988. 227 p. : ISBN 3-87280-042-6
NYPL [Sc D 89-506]

Afrika . Geschichte Afrikas. Köln , 1979- v. : ISBN 3-7609-0433-5 (v. 1) : DDC 960 19
DT20 .G47 1979   ***NYPL [JFK 82-28]***

Afrika anders erlebt /. Jahn, Wolfgang. Hannover , 1986. 207 p. : ISBN 3-7842-0336-1
NYPL [Sc D 88-806]

Afrika für dich : afrikanische Weisheit aus allen Zeiten des Kontinents von der Sahara bis zur Kalahariwüste, von Angola bis Abessinien : afrikanische Bilder und Ornamente / Auswahl und Gestaltung: Charlotte Widmer. St. Gallen : Amboss Verlag, [1986]. [43] p. : ill. ; 21 x 11 cm.
1. Proverbs, African. I. Widmer, Charlotte. II. Title.
NYPL [Sc D 88-675]

Afrika-Studien. African studies. Berlin, 1973. xi, 400 p.   ***NYPL [JLK 73-249 Bd. 15]***

Afrika-Studien.
(nr. 104 104) Kiwanuka, M. S. M. Semakula. Amin and the tragedy of Uganda /. München , 1979. ix, 201 p. : ISBN 3-8039-0177-4
DT433.283 .K58   ***NYPL [L-10 9005 nr. 104]***
(nr. 37) Amann, Hans. Energy supply and economic development in East Africa. München, (1969). 254 p. with maps, 7 inserts (in pocket) DDC 333
HD9557.A32 A6   ***NYPL [Sc E 88-226]***

Afrika-Studien. Sonderreihe Information und Dokumentation.
(no. 5 5) Marquardt, Wilhelm. Seychellen, Komoren und Maskarenen . München , c1976. 346 p. : ISBN 3-8039-0117-0
DT469.S4 M37   ***NYPL [JFC 77-3948]***

Afrika sucht sein Menschenbild : afrikanischer Humanismus und Sozialismus. Freiburg : Schweizerischer Katholischer Missionsrat ; Basel : Schweizerischer Evangelischer Missionsrat, 1974. 112 p. : ill. ; 23 cm. (Missionsjahrbuch der Schweiz . 1974, Jahrg. 41)
1. Schweizerischer Katholischer Missionsrat. II. Schweizerischer Evangelischer Missionsrat. III. Series.
DT351 .A38   ***NYPL [Sc D 87-1433]***

AFRIKAANS LANGUAGE - TEXTS.
De Villiers, Helene. (comp) Die Sprokiesboom en ander verhale uit Midde-Afrika. Kaapstad, 1970. 84 p.;
P214 .D43   ***NYPL [Sc D 89-373]***

Afrikan lullaby . Chisiya, 1960- London , 1986. 60 p. : ISBN 0-946918-45-7 (pbk) : DDC 398.2/1/096891 19
PZ8.1   ***NYPL [Sc D 88-436]***

Afrikan matriarchal foundations . Amadiume, Ifi. London , 1987. [120] p. : ISBN 0-907015-27-1 (pbk) : DDC 966.9/004963 19
DT515.45.I33   ***NYPL [Sc D 89-112]***

AFRIKANERS - ECONOMIC CONDITIONS.
Keegan, Timothy J. Rural transformations in industrializing South Africa . Basingstoke ; London , 1987. xviii, 302 p. : ISBN 0-333-41746-1   ***NYPL [Sc D 88-1228]***

Afrikanische Fabeln und Mythen / [Herausgeber], Friedrich Becker. Frankfurt am Main ; New York : P. Lang, c1987. vi, 233 p. ; 21 cm. (Artes populares, 0170-8198 . Bd. 13) ISBN 3-8204-8641-0 DDC 398.2/0966 19
1. Folk literature, African - Africa, West. 2. Tales - Africa, West. I. Becker, Friedrich, 1942-.
GR350.3 .A35 1987   ***NYPL [JFD 88-8333]***

Afrikanische Frisuren . Frehn, Beatrice, 1948- Köln , c1986. 147 p. : ISBN 3-7701-1619-4 DDC 391.5/0966 19
GT2295.A358 F74 1986
NYPL [Sc C 88-153]

Afrikanische Nationalunion von Simbabwa. see Zimbabwe African National Union.

"Afrikanische Theologie" . Rücker, Heribert. Innsbruck , 1985. 271 p. ; ISBN 3-7022-1548-4
BT30.A438 R83 1985   ***NYPL [Sc D 88-868]***

La Afirmación de la identidad cultural y la formación de la coniencia nacional en el África contemporánea /. Affirmation de l'identité culturelle et la formation de la conscience nationale dans l'Afrique contemporaine. Spanish. Barcelona , Paris , 1983. 220 p. ; ISBN 84-85800-57-5   ***NYPL [Sc D 88-597]***

L'Afrique à coeur . Aurillac, Michel. Paris , 1987. 264 p., [8] p. of plates : ISBN 2-7013-0739-2
NYPL [Sc E 88-203]

L'Afrique au XXe siècle /. Ganiage, Jean. Paris , 1966. 908 p. :   ***NYPL [Sc D 88-236]***

Afrique du Sud . Cukierman, Maurice. Paris , c1987. 279 p. : ISBN 2-209-05983-6
NYPL [Sc D 88-756]

Une Afrique entre le village et la ville . Franqueville, André. Paris . 646 p. : ISBN 2-7099-0805-0   ***NYPL [Sc E 88-325]***

L'Afrique face à ses priorités / Bertrand Schneider. Paris : Economica, c1987. 144 p. ; 24 cm. At head of title: Club de Rome, "Ce livre a été realisé grace aux travaux préparatoires du séminaire de Lusaka (Zambie) et à ceux de la conférence du Club de Rome à Yaoundé décembre 1986, avec la contribution des personnalités suivantes : Tchalla Abina ... [et al.]" ISBN 2-7178-1296-2
1. Africa - Economic conditions - 1960-. I. Schneider, Bertrand. II. Abina, Tchalla.
NYPL [Sc E 88-291]

L'Afrique malade d'elle-même /. Diakité, Tidiane. Paris , c1986. 162 p. ; ISBN 2-86537-158-1 DDC 960/.32 19
DT31 .D5 1986   ***NYPL [Sc D 88-1351]***

L'Afrique noire de A à Z: Cameroun. RCA, Congo, Côte d'Ivoire, Dahomey, Gabon, Haute-Volta, Mali, Mauritanie, Niger, Sénégal, Tchad, Togo. Paris, Édiafric, 1971. 317 p. 27 cm. Cover title. "Numéro spécial du Bulletin de

l'Afrique noire."
1. Africa, French-speaking West - Dictionaries and encyclopedias. 2. Africa, French-speaking Equatorial - Dictionaries and encyclopedias. I. Bulletin de l'Afrique noire. ***NYPL [Sc F 88-75]***

Afrique plurielle, Afrique actuelle : hommage à Georges Balandier / [contributors, Pierre Bonnafé ... et al.]. Paris : Éditions Karthala, c1986. 272 p. ; 24 cm. (Hommes et sociétés) Includes bibliographies. ISBN 2-86537-151-4
1. Balandier, Georges. 2. Ethnology - Africa, Sub-Saharan. I. Bonnafé, Pierre. II. Series.
NYPL [Sc E 88-349]

Afrique, un avenir en sursis /. Hazoumé, Alain T. Paris , c1988. 214 p. ; ISBN 2-7384-0068-X
NYPL [Sc D 89-290]

AFRO-AMERICAN ACTORS - BIOGRAPHY - JUVENILE LITERATURE.
Bergman, Carol. Sidney Poitier /. New York , c1988. 110 p. : ISBN 1-555-46605-2 DDC 791.43/028/0924 B 92 19
PN2287.P57 B47 1988 ***NYPL [Sc E 88-171]***

AFRO-AMERICAN AGED - DISEASES - CONGRESSES.
The Black American elderly . New York , c1988. xvi, 383 p. ; ISBN 0-8261-5810-2 DDC 362.1/9897/00973 19
RA448.5.N4 B56 1988 ***NYPL [JLE 88-5391]***

AFRO-AMERICAN AGED - HEALTH AND HYGIENE - CONGRESSES.
The Black American elderly . New York , c1988. xvi, 383 p. ; ISBN 0-8261-5810-2 DDC 362.1/9897/00973 19
RA448.5.N4 B56 1988 ***NYPL [JLE 88-5391]***

AFRO-AMERICAN AGED - PSYCHOLOGY - CONGRESSES.
The Black American elderly . New York , c1988. xvi, 383 p. ; ISBN 0-8261-5810-2 DDC 362.1/9897/00973 19
RA448.5.N4 B56 1988 ***NYPL [JLE 88-5391]***

AFRO-AMERICAN AIR PILOTS - HISTORY.
Francis, Charles E. The Tuskegee airmen . Boston, MA , c1988. 300, [33] p. : ISBN 0-8283-1386-5 : DDC 940.54/4973 19
D790 .F637 1988 ***NYPL [Sc E 89-164]***

AFRO-AMERICAN ART - EXHIBITIONS.
American visions Afro-American art, 1986 /. Washington, D.C. , 1987. 57 p. :
NYPL [Sc F 87-438]

AFRO-AMERICAN ART - HISTORY AND CRITICISM.
American visions Afro-American art, 1986 /. Washington, D.C. , 1987. 57 p. :
NYPL [Sc F 87-438]

AFRO-AMERICAN ART - MASSACHUSETTS - EXHIBITIONS.
Gaither, Edmund B. Massachusetts masters . Boston [1988] 48 p. : ***NYPL [Sc F 89-159]***

AFRO-AMERICAN ART - TEXAS - EXHIBITIONS.
Adele, Lynne. Black history, black vision . [Austin] , 1989. 93 p. : ISBN 0-935213-15-5
NYPL [Sc F 89-155]

AFRO-AMERICAN ART - WASHINGTON (D. C.) - EXHIBITIONS.
Morrison, Keith. Art in Washington and its Afro-American presence 1940-1970 /. Washington, D.C. , 1985. 109 p. :
NYPL [Sc F 88-34]

AFRO-AMERICAN ARTISTS - EXHIBITIONS.
Augusta Savage and the art Schools of Harlem. New York, N.Y. , 1988. 27 p. :
NYPL [Sc F 89-45]

AFRO-AMERICAN ARTISTS - MASSACHUSETTS - BIOGRAPHY.
Gaither, Edmund B. Massachusetts masters . Boston [1988] 48 p. : ***NYPL [Sc F 89-159]***

AFRO-AMERICAN ARTISTS - TEXAS - BIOGRAPHY.
Adele, Lynne. Black history, black vision . [Austin] , 1989. 93 p. : ISBN 0-935213-15-5
NYPL [Sc F 89-155]

AFRO-AMERICAN ARTS.
Dodson, Jualynne E. Black stylization and implications for child welfare . Atlanta, Georgia , 1975. 1 v. (various pagings) ;
NYPL [Sc F 88-223]

AFRO-AMERICAN ARTS - NEW YORK (N.Y.)
Wintz, Cary D., 1943- Black culture and the Harlem Renaissance /. Houston, Tex. , 1988. 277 p. ; ISBN 0-89263-267-4 : DDC 810/.9/896073 19
PS153.N5 W57 1988 ***NYPL [Sc E 89-106]***

AFRO-AMERICAN ARTS - NEW YORK (N.Y.) - CONGRESSES.
The Harlem renaissance . New York , 1989. xv, 342 p. ; ISBN 0-8240-5739-2 (alk. paper) DDC 810/.9/896073 19
PS153.N5 H264 1989 ***NYPL [Sc D 89-591]***

AFRO-AMERICAN ATHLETES.
Ashe, Arthur. A hard road to glory . New York, NY , 1988. 3 v. : ISBN 0-446-71006-7 DDC 796/.08996073 19
GV583 .A75 1988 ***NYPL [IEC 89-1295]***

AFRO-AMERICAN ATHLETES - BIOGRAPHY.
Ritchie, Andrew. Major Taylor . San Francisco , New York , 1988. 304 p., [32] p. of plates : ISBN 0-933201-14-1 (hardcover)
NYPL [Sc E 88-570]

AFRO-AMERICAN ATHLETES - BIOGRAPHY - JUVENILE LITERATURE.
Biracree, Tom, 1947- Wilma Rudolph /. New York , 1988. 111 p. : ISBN 1-555-46675-3 DDC 796.4/2/0924 B 92 19
GV697.R8 B57 1988 ***NYPL [Sc E 88-172]***

AFRO-AMERICAN AUTHORS - 20TH CENTURY - BIOGRAPHY.
Black writers . Detroit, Mi. , c1989. xxiv, 619 p. ; ISBN 0-8103-2772-4 ***NYPL [Sc F 89-57]***

AFRO-AMERICAN AUTHORS - BIOGRAPHY.
Delany, Samuel R. The motion of light in water . New York , c1988. xviii, 302 p. : ISBN 0-8795-947-1 : DDC 813/.54 19
PS3554.E437 Z475 1988
NYPL [JFD 88-7818]

Johnson, James Weldon, 1871-1938. Along this way . New York , 1933. 418 p., [16] leaves of plates : ***NYPL [Sc Rare F 89-9]***

AFRO-AMERICAN AUTHORS - BIOGRAPHY - JUVENILE LITERATURE.
Tolbert-Rouchaleau, Jane. James Weldon Johnson /. New York , c1988. 110 p. : ISBN 1-555-46596-X DDC 818/.5209 B 92 19
PS3519.O2625 Z894 1988
NYPL [Sc E 88-164]

AFRO-AMERICAN AUTHORS - SOUTHERN STATES - BIOGRAPHY - DICTIONARIES.
Foster, Mamie Marie Booth. Southern Black creative writers, 1829-1953 . New York , 1988. xvii, 113 p. ; ISBN 0-313-26207-1 (lib. bdg. : alk. paper) DDC 016.81/09/896073 19
Z1229.N39 F67 1988 PS153.N5
NYPL [Sc E 88-495]

AFRO-AMERICAN AUTOMOBILE INDUSTRY WORKERS - BIOGRAPHY.
Denby, Charles. Indignant heart . Boston , c1978. 295 p. : ISBN 0-89608-092-7 DDC 331.6/3/960730774340924 B 19
HD8039.A82 U633 1978
NYPL [Sc D 88-853]

Denby, Charles. Indignant heart . Detroit , 1989, c1978. xvi, 303 p. : ISBN 0-8143-2219-0 (alk. paper) DDC 331.6/396073 B 19
HD8039.A82 U633 1989
NYPL [Sc D 89-563]

AFRO-AMERICAN BAPTISTS.
Smith, Sid. 10 super Sunday schools in the Black community /. Nashville, Tenn. , c1986. 178 p. : ISBN 0-8054-6252-X : DDC 268/.861/08996073 19
BV1523.A37 S65 1986 ***NYPL [Sc C 88-229]***

AFRO-AMERICAN BAPTISTS - DOCTRINES - HISTORY - 20TH CENTURY.
Fluker, Walter E., 1951- They looked for a city . Lanham, MD , c1989. xiv, 281 p. ; ISBN 0-8191-7262-6 (alk. paper) DDC 307/.092/2 19
BX6447 .F57 1988 ***NYPL [Sc D 89-492]***

AFRO-AMERICAN BAPTISTS - HISTORY.
Brooks, Evelyn, 1945- The women's movement in the Black Baptist church, 1880-1920 /. [Rochester, N.Y.] c1984. viii, 342 leaves ;
NYPL [Sc D 88-938]

AFRO-AMERICAN BASEBALL PLAYERS.
Robinson, Frank, 1935- Extra innings /. New York , c1988. x, 270, [8] p. of plates. : ISBN 0-07-053183-8 DDC 796.357/08996073 19
GV863.A1 R582 1988 ***NYPL [Sc E 88-382]***

AFRO-AMERICAN BASEBALL PLAYERS - BIOGRAPHY.
Holway, John. Blackball stars . Westport, CT , c1988. xvi, 400 p. : ISBN 0-88736-094-7 (alk. paper) : DDC 796.357/08996073/0922 B 19
GV865.A1 H614 1988 ***NYPL [JFE 88-6437]***

Honig, Donald. Mays, Mantle, Snider . New York, N.Y. , London , c1987. vii, 151 p. : ISBN 0-02-551200-5 DDC 796.357/092/2 B 19
GV865.A1 H6192 1987
NYPL [JFF 87-1461]

Peterson, Robert, 1925- Only the ball was white. Englewood Cliffs, N.J. [1970] vii, 406 p. ISBN 0-13-637215-5 DDC 796.357/09
GV863 .P4 ***NYPL [Sc 796.357-P]***

Riley, James A. Dandy, Day and the Devil /. Cocoa, FL , 1987. xiii, 153 p. : ISBN 0-9614023-2-6 ***NYPL [Sc D 88-104]***

Robinson, Jackie, 1919-1972. Jackie Robinson . New York , 1948. 170 p. :
NYPL [Sc C 88-61]

Winfield, Dave, 1951- Winfield . New York , c1988. xvi, 274 p., [22] p. of plates : ISBN 0-393-02467-9 : DDC 796.357/092/4 B 19
GV865.W57 A3 1988
NYPL [JFD 88-11493]

AFRO-AMERICAN BASEBALL PLAYERS - BIOGRAPHY - JUVENILE LITERATURE.
Adler, David A. Jackie Robinson . New York , c1989. 48 p. : ISBN 0-8234-0734-9 DDC 796.357/092/4 B 19
GV865 .A37 1989 ***NYPL [Sc F 89-137]***

Devaney, John. Bo Jackson . New York , 1988. 110 p. : ISBN 0-8027-6818-0 DDC 796.332/092/4 B 92 19
GV865.J28 D48 1988 ***NYPL [Sc E 89-12]***

Humphrey, Kathryn Long. Satchel Paige /. New York , 1988. 110 p. : ISBN 0-531-10513-X DDC 796.357/092/4 B 92 19
GV865.P3 H86 1988 ***NYPL [Sc E 88-481]***

Scott, Richard, 1956- Jackie Robinson /. New York , 1987. 110 p. : ISBN 1-555-46208-1 : DDC 796.357/092/4 B 92 19
GV865.R6 S36 1987 ***NYPL [Sc E 88-168]***

AFRO-AMERICAN BASEBALL PLAYERS - CASE STUDIES.
Moore, Joseph Thomas. Pride against prejudice . New York , c1988. 195 p., [8] p. of plates : ISBN 0-313-25995-X (lib. bdg. : alk. paper) DDC 796.357/092/4 B 19
GV865.D58 M66 1988 ***NYPL [Sc E 88-272]***

AFRO-AMERICAN BASKETBALL PLAYERS - BIOGRAPHY.
Webb, Spud. Flying high /. New York , c1988. xv, 208 p., [16] p. of plates : ISBN 0-06-015820-4 : DDC 796.32/3/0924 B 19
GV884.W35 A3 1988 ***NYPL [Sc D 89-375]***

AFRO-AMERICAN BOXERS.
Reading the fights . New York , c1988. viii, 305 p. : ISBN 0-8050-0510-2 : DDC 796.8/3 19
GV1121 .R4 1988 ***NYPL [Sc D 88-899]***

AFRO-AMERICAN BOXERS - BIOGRAPHY.
Barrow, Joe Louis. Joe Louis . New York , c1988. xvii, 270 p., [8] leaves of plates : ISBN 0-07-003955-0 : DDC 796.8/3/0924 B 19
GV1132.L6 B37 1988 ***NYPL [Sc E 88-566]***

AFRO-AMERICAN BOXERS - BIOGRAPHY - JUVENILE LITERATURE.
Rummel, Jack. Muhammad Ali /. New York , c1988. 128 p. : ISBN 1-555-46569-2 DDC 796.8/3/0924 B 19
GV1132.A44 R86 1988
NYPL [Sc E 88-175]

AFRO-AMERICAN CATHOLICS - BIOGRAPHY.
Johnson, MayLee. Coming up on the rough side . South Orange, N.J. , c1988. vii, 88 p. ; ISBN 0-944734-01-4 ***NYPL [Sc D 89-190]***

AFRO-AMERICAN CATHOLICS - HISTORY - 20TH CENTURY.
Nickels, Marilyn Wenzke. Black Catholic protest and the Federated Colored Catholics, 1917-1933 . New York , 1988. ix, 325 p. ; ISBN 0-8240-4098-8 (alk. paper) : DDC

282/.73/08996073 19
BX1407.N4 N5 1988   *NYPL [Sc E 89-85]*

AFRO-AMERICAN CHILDREN - BIBLIOGRAPHY.
Washington, Valora. Black children and American institutions . New York , 1988. xv, 432 p. ; ISBN 0-8240-8517-5 : DDC 305.2/3/08996073 19
Z1361.N39 W34 1988 E185.86
NYPL [Sc D 89-385]

AFRO-AMERICAN CHILDREN - EDUCATION.
Visible now . New York , 1988. xvi, 344 p. ; ISBN 0-313-25926-7 (lib. bdg.: alk. paper) DDC 371./02/0973 19
LC2761 .V57 1988   *NYPL [Sc E 98-257]*

AFRO-AMERICAN CHILDREN - FICTION.
Myers, Walter Dean, 1937- Me, Mop, and the Moondance Kid /. New York , 1988. 154 p. : ISBN 0-440-50065-6 DDC [Fic] 19
PZ7.M992 Me 1988   *NYPL [Sc D 88-1457]*

AFRO-AMERICAN CHILDREN - GEORGIA - ATLANTA - CASE STUDIES.
Dettlinger, Chet. The list /. Atlanta , c1983. 516 p., [4] p. of plates : ISBN 0-942894-04-9 : DDC 364.1/523/09758231 19
HV6534.A7 D47 1983   *NYPL [Sc E 86-40]*

AFRO-AMERICAN CHILDREN - JUVENILE FICTION.
Alcock, Gudrun. Turn the next corner. New York [1969] 160 p. DDC [Fic]
PZ7.A332 Tu   *NYPL [Sc D 88-1471]*

Babcock, Bernie Smade, 1868-1962. Hallerloogy's ride with Santa Claus. Perry, Ark., c1943. 48 p.
PZ7.B12 Hal   *NYPL [Sc D 88-1285]*

Bradman, Tony. Wait and see /. New York, NY , 1988. [28] p. : ISBN 0-19-520644-4 DDC [E] 19
PZ7.B7275 Wai 1988   *NYPL [Sc D 89-255]*

Brothers, Aileen. Just one me /. Chicago , c1967. 32 p. :   *NYPL [Sc D 88-376]*

Burchardt, Nellie. Project cat /. New York, N.Y. , c1966. 66 p. :   *NYPL [Sc D 89-435]*

Caines, Jeannette Franklin. I need a lunch box /. New York , c1988. [32] p. : ISBN 0-06-020984-4 : DDC [E] 19
PZ7.C12 Iaan 1988   *NYPL [Sc D 88-1504]*

Cameron, Ann, 1943- Julian, secret agent /. New York , 1988. 62 p. : ISBN 0-394-91949-1 (lib. bdg.) : DDC [Fic] 19
PZ7.C1427 Jt 1988   *NYPL [Sc C 89-123]*

Cameron, Ann, 1943- Julian's glorious summer /. New York , c1985. 62 p. : ISBN 0-394-89117-1 (pbk.) : DDC [Fic] 19
PZ7.C1427 Ju 1987   *NYPL [Sc C 89-99]*

Cameron, Ann, 1943- The stories Julian tells /. New York : c1987, c1981. 71 p. : ISBN 0-394-82892-5   *NYPL [Sc C 89-93]*

Chandler, Ruth Forbes. Ladder to the sky /. London , New York , c1959. 189 p. :
NYPL [Sc D 88-1107]

Clymer, Eleanor (Lowenton) 1906- The house on the mountain. New York [1971] 39 p. ISBN 0-525-32365-1 DDC [Fic]
PZ7.C6272 Ho   *NYPL [Sc D 88-445]*

Dragonwagon, Crescent. Strawberry dress escape /. New York [1975] [32] p. : ISBN 0-684-13912-X :   *NYPL [Sc F 88-126]*

Durham, John, fl. 1960- Me and Arch and the Pest. New York [1970] 96 p. DDC [Fic]
PZ7.D9335 Me   *NYPL [Sc E 88-416]*

Elting, Mary, 1909- Patch /. Garden City, N.Y. , 1948. 156 p. :
PZ7.E53Pat   *NYPL [Sc C 89-14]*

Fields, Julia. The green lion of Zion Street /. New York , c1988. [32] p. : ISBN 0-689-50414-4 DDC [E] 19
PZ8.3.F458 Gr 1988   *NYPL [Sc F 88-186]*

Gerber, Will. Gooseberry Jones /. New York , c1947. 96 p. :   *NYPL [Sc D 89-442]*

Gles, Margaret. Come play hide and seek /. Champaign, Ill. [1975] 32 p. : ISBN 0-8116-6053-2
PZ7.G4883 Co   *NYPL [Sc D 89-119]*

Gray, Genevieve. A kite for Bennie. New York,

1972. [40] p. ISBN 0-07-024197-X DDC [Fic]
PZ7.G7774 Ki   *NYPL [Sc E 88-422]*

Greenfield, Eloise. First pink light /. New York , c1976. [39] p. ISBN 0-690-01087-7 DDC [E]
PZ7.G845 Fi   *NYPL [Sc D 89-60]*

Greenfield, Eloise. Grandpa's face /. New York , 1988. [32] p. : ISBN 0-399-21525-5 DDC [E] 19
PZ7.G845 Gs 1988   *NYPL [Sc F 88-387]*

Greenfield, Eloise. Talk about a family /. New York , c1978. 60 p. : ISBN 0-590-42247-2
NYPL [Sc C 89-79]

Hodges, Elizabeth Jamison. Free as a frog. [Reading, Mass., c1969] [32] p. DDC [Fic]
PZ7.H6634 Fr   *NYPL [Sc D 88-1126]*

Horvath, Betty F. Hooray for Jasper. New York [1966] 1 v. (unpaged)
PZ7.H7922 Ho   *NYPL [Sc F 88-252]*

Horvath, Betty F. Jasper makes music. New York [1967] [38] p. DDC [E]
PZ7.H7922 Jas   *NYPL [Sc F 88-343]*

Howard, Elizabeth Fitzgerald. The train to Lulu's /. New York , c1988. [32] p. : ISBN 0-02-744620-4 : DDC [E] 19
PZ7.H8327 Tr 1988   *NYPL [Sc F 88-219]*

Isadora, Rachel. Willaby /. New York , c1977. [32] p. : ISBN 0-02-747746-0 DDC [E]
PZ7.I763 Wi   *NYPL [Sc F 88-374]*

Jensen, Virginia Allen. Sara and the door /. Reading, Mass. , c1977. [32] p. : ISBN 0-201-03446-8 DDC [E]
PZ8.3.J425 Sar   *NYPL [Sc B 89-17]*

Johnson, Eric W. The stolen ruler. Philadelphia [1970] 64 p. DDC [Fic]
PZ7.J631765 St   *NYPL [Sc D 88-1114]*

Justus, May, 1898- New boy in school. New York [1963] 56 p. DDC [Fic]
PZ7.J986 Ng   *NYPL [Sc E 89-25]*

Keats, Ezra Jack. Da Snøen Kom /. [Norway] , 1967. [20] p. :   *NYPL [Sc D 88-467]*

Lang, Don. Strawberry roan /. New York , 1946. 218 p. :   *NYPL [Sc D 88-646]*

Lawrence, James Duncan, 1918- Binky brothers, detectives. New York [1968] 60 p. DDC [Fic]
PZ7.L4359 Bi   *NYPL [Sc D 89-118]*

Lewis, Richard W. A summer adventure /. New York , c1962. 105 p. :
NYPL [Sc D 89-405]

Lexau, Joan M. Don't be my valentine /. New York, N.Y. , c1985. 64 p. : ISBN 0-06-023872-0 : DDC [E] 19
PZ7.L5895 Dp 1985   *NYPL [Sc D 89-58]*

Lipkind, William, 1904- Four-leaf clover /. New York , 1959. [32] p. :
NYPL [Sc F 89-22]

Lovelace, Maud Hart, 1892- The valentine box /. New York , 1966. [48] p. :
PZ7.L9561 Val   *NYPL [Sc D 89-115]*

McKissack, Pat, 1944- Nettie Jo's friends /. New York , 1989. [33] p. : ISBN 0-394-89158-9 DDC [E] 19
PZ7.M478693 Ne 1989   *NYPL [Sc F 89-143]*

Martin, Patricia Miles. The little brown hen. New York [1960] 23 p.
PZ7 .M36418 Li   *NYPL [Sc D 88-1495]*

Molarsky, Osmond. Where the good luck was. New York [1970] 63 p. ISBN 0-8098-1158-8 DDC [Fic]
PZ7.M7317 Wh   *NYPL [Sc E 88-552]*

Morse, Evangeline. Brown Rabbit: her story. Chicago [1967] 191 p.
PZ7.M84586 Br   *NYPL [Sc D 89-89]*

Napjus, Alice James. Freddie found a frog. New York [1969] [29] p. DDC [Fic]
PZ7.N148 Fr   *NYPL [Sc C 89-27]*

Rinkoff, Barbara. Rutherford T. finds 21 B. New York [1970] [47] p. DDC [Fic]
PZ7.R477 Ru   *NYPL [Sc D 88-1404]*

Rose, Karen. A single trail. Chicago [1969] 158 p. ISBN 0-695-44082-9 DDC [Fic]
PZ7.R717 Si   *NYPL [Sc D 89-91]*

Scott, Ann Herbert. Let's catch a monster. New

York [1967] 1 v. (unpaged)
PZ7.S415 Le   *NYPL [Sc F 88-342]*

Springer, Nancy. They're all named Wildfire /. New York , 1989. 103 p. ; ISBN 0-689-31450-7 DDC [Fic] 19
PZ7.S76846 Th 1989   *NYPL [Sc D 89-498]*

Steptoe, John, 1950- Baby says /. New York , 1988. [24] p. : ISBN 0-688-07423-5 DDC [E] 19
PZ7.S8367 Bab 1988   *NYPL [Sc D 88-1257]*

Stolz, Mary, 1920- Storm in the night /. New York , 1988. [32] p. : ISBN 0-06-025912-4 : DDC [E] 19
PZ7.S875854 St 1988   *NYPL [Sc F 88-181]*

Taylor, Mildred D. The friendship /. New York , 1987. 53 p. : ISBN 0-8037-0418-6 (lib. bdg.) : DDC [Fic] 19
PZ7.T21723 Fr 1987   *NYPL [Sc D 88-126]*

Walter, Mildred Pitts. Mariah loves rock /. New York , c1988. 117 p. : ISBN 0-02-792511-0 DDC [Fic] 19
PZ7.W17125 Mar 1988   *NYPL [Sc C 89-29]*

Weir, LaVada. Howdy! Austin, Tex. [1972] 32 p. ISBN 0-8114-7735-5 DDC [E]
PZ7.W4415 Ho   *NYPL [Sc E 88-613]*

Woody, Regina Llewellyn (Jones) Almena's dogs /. New York , c1954. 240 p. :
NYPL [Sc D 88-648]

Yarbrough, Camille. The shimmershine queens /. New York , c1988. 142 p. ; ISBN 0-399-21465-8 DDC [Fic] 19
PZ7.Y1955 Sh 1988   *NYPL [Sc D 89-283]*

AFRO-AMERICAN CHILDREN - JUVENILE LITERATURE.
Shackelford, Jane Dabney. My happy days /. Washington, D.C. , c1944. 121 p. :
NYPL [Sc F 88-337]

AFRO-AMERICAN CHILDREN - JUVENILE POETRY.
Carma, Jemel. Happy birthday everybody . New York, N. Y. [1988] [24] p. :
NYPL [Sc H 89-1]

AFRO-AMERICAN CHILDREN - MENTAL HEALTH SERVICES.
Gary, Lawrence E. The delivery of mental health services to Black children . Washington, D.C. , 1982. vi, 111, 19 p. :
NYPL [Sc F 88-66]

AFRO-AMERICAN CHILDREN - NEW YORK (N.Y.) - JUVENILE FICTION.
Huston, Anne. Ollie's go-kart. New York [1971] 143 p. DDC [Fic]
PZ7.H959 Ol   *NYPL [Sc D 88-1472]*

Weiss, Edna S. Truly Elizabeth /. Boston , 1957. 178 p.   *NYPL [Sc D 88-663]*

AFRO-AMERICAN CHILDREN - NORTH CAROLINA - FICTION.
Burgwyn, Mebane (Holoman) Lucky mischief /. New York , 1949. 246 p. :
NYPL [Sc D 88-1513]

AFRO-AMERICAN CHILDREN - POETRY.
Little, Lessie Jones. Children of long ago . New York , 1988. [32] p. : ISBN 0-399-21473-9 DDC 811/.54 19
PS3562.I78288 C5 1988
NYPL [Sc F 88-276]

AFRO-AMERICAN CHILDREN - SERVICES FOR.
Dodson, Jualynne E. Black stylization and implications for child welfare . Atlanta, Georgia , 1975. 1 v. (various pagings) :
NYPL [Sc F 88-223]

AFRO-AMERICAN CHILDREN - SOUTH CAROLINA - JUVENILE FICTION.
Lattimore, Eleanor Frances, 1904- Indigo Hill. New York, 1950. 128 p. DDC [Fic]
PZ7.L37 In   *NYPL [Sc D 88-1428]*

AFRO-AMERICAN CHILDREN - SOUTHERN STATES - JUVENILE FICTION.
Hays, Wilma Pitchford. The goose that was a watchdog. Boston [1967] 41 p. DDC [Fic]
PZ7.H31493 Go   *NYPL [Sc D 88-1426]*

AFRO-AMERICAN CHURCHES.
Bechler, Le Roy, 1925- The Black Mennonite Church in North America, 1886-1986 /. Scottdale, Pa. , 1986. 196 p. : ISBN

0-8361-1287-3 :   DDC 289.7/08996073 19
BX8116.3.A37 B43 1986
                    NYPL [Sc E 89-134]

Bosch Navarro, Juan. La Iglesia negra .
Valencia , 1986 (Valencia : Imprenta Nácher).
57 p. ;   *NYPL [Sc D 87-1154]*

Harris, James H., 1952- Black ministers and
laity in the urban church . Lanham, MD ,
c1987. xi, 133 p. :   ISBN 0-8191-5823-2 (alk.
paper) :   DDC 253/.2/08996073 19
BR563.N4 B575 1987   NYPL [Sc D 89-127]

**AFRO-AMERICAN CHURCHES - ATLANTIC
STATES - HISTORY.**
Smith, Edward D. Climbing Jacob's ladder .
City of Washington , 1988. 143 p. :   ISBN
0-87474-829-1   *NYPL [Sc E 88-505]*

**AFRO-AMERICAN CHURCHES -
MASSACHUSETTS - BOSTON -
HISTORY.**
Hayden, Robert C. Faith, culture, and
leadership . [Boston, MA , c1983] iv, 56 p. :
DDC 280/.08996073074461 19
BR560.B73 H39 1983   NYPL [Sc F 88-269]

AFRO-AMERICAN CLERGY.
Harris, James H., 1952- Black ministers and
laity in the urban church . Lanham, MD ,
c1987. xi, 133 p. :   ISBN 0-8191-5823-2 (alk.
paper) :   DDC 253/.2/08996073 19
BR563.N4 B575 1987   NYPL [Sc D 89-127]

AFRO-AMERICAN COLLEGE STUDENTS.
Recruitment and retention of Black students in
higher education /. Lanham, MD , c1989. viii,
135 p. :   ISBN 0-8191-7292-8 (alk. paper)   DDC
378/.1982 19
LC2781 .R43 1989   NYPL [Sc D 89-590]

Wesley, Charles H., 1891- The history of Alpha
Phi Alpha . Chicago , 1981, c1929. xiv, 567 p. :
                    NYPL [Sc D 89-135]

**AFRO-AMERICAN COLLEGE STUDENTS -
CONGRESSES.**
Black student retention in higher education /.
Springfield, Ill., U. S. A. , c1988. xvi, 111 p. :
ISBN 0-398-05477-0   DDC 378/.198/2 19
LC2781 .B465 1988   NYPL [Sc F 89-139]

**AFRO-AMERICAN COLLEGE STUDENTS -
HISTORY.**
Toward Black undergraduate student equality in
American higher education /. New York ,
1988. xvii, 217 p. :   ISBN 0-313-25616-0 (lib. bdg. :
alk. paper)   DDC 378/.1982 19
LC2781 .T69 1988   NYPL [Sc E 88-507]

**AFRO-AMERICAN COLLEGE STUDENTS -
MASSACHUSETTS - CAMBRIDGE.**
Varieties of black experience at Harvard .
Cambridge [Mass.] , 1986. v, 180 p. ;
LD2160 .V37x 1986   NYPL [Sc D 88-672]

**AFRO-AMERICAN COLLEGE STUDENTS -
PSYCHOLOGY.**
Hillman, Chrisanthia. The relationship between
self-esteem and academic achievement among
Black students in remedial reading instruction
at a community college [microform] /. 1981. 60
leaves.   *NYPL [Sc Micro R-4686]*

**AFRO-AMERICAN COLLEGES. see AFRO-
AMERICAN UNIVERSITIES AND
COLLEGES.**

**AFRO-AMERICAN COMMUNISTS -
BIOGRAPHY.**
Denby, Charles. Indignant heart . Boston ,
c1978. 295 p. :   ISBN 0-89608-092-7   DDC
331.6/3/960730774340924 B 19
HD8039.A82 U633 1978
                    NYPL [Sc D 88-853]

Denby, Charles. Indignant heart . Detroit ,
1989, c1978. xvi, 303 p. :   ISBN 0-8143-2219-0
(alk. paper)   DDC 331.6/396073 B 19
HD8039.A82 U633 1989
                    NYPL [Sc D 89-563]

**AFRO-AMERICAN COMPOSERS -
BIOGRAPHY.**
Arvey, Verna, 1910- William Grant Still. New
York, 1939. 48 p.
ML410.S855 A8   NYPL [Sc D 89-3]

Green, Jeffrey P. Edmund Thornton Jenkins .
Westport, Conn. , 1982. xii, 213 p. :   ISBN
0-313-23253-9 (lib. bdg.)   DDC 780/.92/4 B 19
ML410.J44 G7 1982   NYPL [Sc D 86-413]

**AFRO-AMERICAN COMPOSERS -
BIOGRAPHY - JUVENILE LITERATURE.**

Preston, Katherine. Scott Joplin /. New York ,
c1988. 110 p. :   ISBN 1-555-46598-6   DDC
780/.92/4 B 92 19
ML3930.J66 P7 1988   NYPL [Sc E 88-170]

AFRO-AMERICAN CRIMINALS.
Marowitz, Roberta Lee. Psychosocial dynamics
of Black rapists [microform] . 1982. x, 216
leaves ;   *NYPL [Sc Micro R-4806]*

**AFRO-AMERICAN CRIMINALS - CIVIL
RIGHTS.**
Gross, Samuel R. Death & discrimination .
Boston , c1989. xvi, 268 p. ;   ISBN
1-555-53040-0 (alk. paper) :   DDC 364.6/6/0973
19
HV8699.U5 G76 1989   NYPL [Sc D 89-493]

**AFRO-AMERICAN CRIMINALS - GEORGIA -
BIBLIOGRAPHY.**
Haith, Dorothy May. State of Georgia v.
Vincent Derek Mallory M.D. . Washington ,
1988. 12 leaves ;   *NYPL [Sc D 88-131]*

Afro-American culture and society, 0882-5297 .
(v. 6) Marotti, Giorgio. [Negro nel romanzo
brasiliano. English.] Black characters in the
Brazilian novel /. Los Angeles , c1987. ix, 448
p., [18] p. of plates ;   ISBN 0-934934-24-X :
DDC 869.3/093520396 19
PQ9607.B53 M3713 1987
                    NYPL [Sc E 87-334]

**AFRO-AMERICAN DANCING. see AFRO-
AMERICANS - DANCING.**

**AFRO-AMERICAN DIALECT. see BLACK
ENGLISH.**

**AFRO-AMERICAN DRAMA (ENGLISH) see
AMERICAN DRAMA - AFRO-
AMERICAN AUTHORS.**

**AFRO-AMERICAN DRAMATISTS - 20TH
CENTURY - BIOGRAPHY -
DICTIONARIES.**
Peterson, Bernard L. Contemporary Black
American playwrights and their plays . New
York , 1988. xxvi, 625 p. ;   ISBN 0-313-25190-8
(lib. bdg. : alk. paper)   DDC 812/.54/09896 19
PS153.N5 P43 1988   NYPL [Sc E 88-378]

AFRO-AMERICAN DROPOUTS.
Lewis, Geraldine Fambrough. An analysis of
interviews with urban Black males who dropped
out of high school [microform] /. 1983. iii, 123
leaves :   *NYPL [Sc Micro R-4791]*

**AFRO-AMERICAN EDUCATION. see AFRO-
AMERICANS - EDUCATION.**

**AFRO-AMERICAN ENGINEERS -
MISSOURI - ST. LOUIS - BIOGRAPHY.**
Young, F. Weldon (Frank Weldon), 1902- The
30's, donnybrook decade in St. Louis public
school power plants . St. Louis, Mo. , c1984. 96
p. :   ISBN 0-87527-331-9 (pbk.) :   DDC
621.31/2132/0924 B 19
TA140.Y68 A33 1984   NYPL [Sc D 89-256]

**AFRO-AMERICAN ENGLISH. see BLACK
ENGLISH.**

**AFRO-AMERICAN ENTERTAINERS -
BIOGRAPHY.**
Grupenhoff, Richard, 1941- The black
Valentino . Metuchen, N.J. , 1988. xi, 188 p. :
ISBN 0-8108-2078-1   DDC 790.2/092/4 B 19
PN2287.T78 G78 1988
                    NYPL [Sc D 88-1029]

**AFRO-AMERICAN ENTERTAINERS -
BIOGRAPHY - JUVENILE LITERATURE.**
Haskins, James, 1941- Bill Cosby . New York ,
1988. 138 p. :   ISBN 0-8027-6785-0   DDC
792.7/028/0924 B 92 19
PN2287.C632 H37 1988
                    NYPL [Sc D 88-1162]

**AFRO-AMERICAN ENTERTAINERS - NEW
YORK (N.Y.) - BIOGRAPHY.**
Buckley, Gail Lumet, 1937- The Hornes . New
York , 1986. 262 p. :   ISBN 0-394-51306-1 :
DDC 974.7/2300496073/00922 B 19
F129.B7 B83 1986   NYPL [Sc E 86-286]

**AFRO-AMERICAN EPISCOPALIANS - NEW
YORK (N.Y.)**
Memories and records of St. Jude's Chapel
[microform] . [New York , 1982] [18] p. ;
                    NYPL [Sc Micro F-11024]

**AFRO-AMERICAN EVANGELISTS -
BIOGRAPHY.**
Smith, Amanda, 1837-1915. An autobiography .
New York , 1988. xlii, 506 p. [23] p. of plates :

ISBN 0-19-505261-7 (alk. paper)   DDC
269/.2/0924 B 19
BV3785.S56 A3 1988   NYPL [JFC 88-2154]

**AFRO-AMERICAN EXECUTIVES -
ILLINOIS - CHICAGO.**
Salmon, Jaslin U. Black executives in
white-owned businesses and industries in the
Chicago metropolitan area [microform] /. 1977.
197 leaves.   *NYPL [Sc Micro R-4703]*

**AFRO-AMERICAN EXECUTIVES - UNITED
STATES.**
Logan, Harold G. A study of the inclusion of
Black administrators in American medical
schools, 1968-78, and their perception of their
roles [microform] /. 1982. v, 90 leaves :
                    NYPL [Sc Micro R-4793]

**AFRO-AMERICAN FAMILIES - JUVENILE
FICTION.**
Clifton, Lucille, 1936- Everett Anderson's nine
month long /. New York , c1978. [31] p. :
ISBN 0-03-043536-6   DDC [E]
PZ8.3.C573 Evk   NYPL [Sc D 89-30]

Greenfield, Eloise. Talk about a family /. New
York , c1978. 60 p. :   ISBN 0-590-42247-2
                    NYPL [Sc C 89-79]

**AFRO-AMERICAN FAMILIES - JUVENILE
LITERATURE.**
Shackelford, Jane Dabney. My happy days /.
Washington, D.C. , c1944. 121 p. :
                    NYPL [Sc F 88-337]

**AFRO-AMERICAN FAMILIES -
MASSACHUSETTS - BOSTON.**
Overbea, Luix V. (Luix Virgil) Black Bostonia
/. Boston, Mass. , c1976. 39 p. :
                    NYPL [Sc C 89-44]

**AFRO-AMERICAN FOLK ART - SOUTHERN
STATES EXHIBITIONS.**
Baking in the sun . Lafayette , c1987. 146 p. :
ISBN 0-295-96606-8   *NYPL [Sc F 88-197]*

**AFRO-AMERICAN FOOTBALL PLAYERS -
BIOGRAPHY.**
Pennington, Richard, 1952- Breaking the ice .
Jefferson, N.C. , c1987. ix, 182 p. :   ISBN
0-89950-295-4 :   DDC 796.332/72/0973 19
GV939.A1 P46 1987   NYPL [Sc E 88-35]

**AFRO-AMERICAN FOOTBALL PLAYERS -
BIOGRAPHY - JUVENILE LITERATURE.**
Devaney, John. Bo Jackson . New York , 1988.
110 p. :   ISBN 0-8027-6818-0   DDC 796.332/092/4
B 92 19
GV865.J28 D48 1988   NYPL [Sc E 89-12]

**AFRO-AMERICAN FOOTBALL PLAYERS -
JUVENILE BIOGRAPHY.**
Terzian, James P. The Jimmy Brown story /.
New York , c1964. 190 p. :
                    NYPL [Sc D 89-432]

**AFRO-AMERICAN GAYS - CALIFORNIA -
FICTION.**
Hansen, Joseph, 1923- Pretty boy dead . San
Francisco , 1984. 203 p. ;   ISBN 0-917342-48-8 :
DDC 813/.54 19
PS3558.A513 P7 1984   NYPL [JFD 87-9537]

**AFRO-AMERICAN GAYS - NEW YORK (N.Y.)
- FICTION.**
Baxt, George. A queer kind of death /. New
York , 1986, c1966. 249 p. ;   ISBN
0-930330-46-3 (pbk.) :   *NYPL [Sc C 88-132]*

**AFRO-AMERICAN GENERALS -
BIOGRAPHY.**
Fletcher, Marvin. America's first Black general .
Lawrence, Kan. , c1989. xix, 226 p. :   ISBN
0-7006-0381-6 (alk. paper) :   DDC
355/.008996073 19
U53.D38 F57 1989   NYPL [Sc D 89-276]

McGovern, James R. Black Eagle, General
Daniel "Chappie" James, Jr. /. University, AL ,
c1985. 204 p. :   ISBN 0-8173-0179-8   DDC
355/.0092/4 B 19
UG626.2.J36 M34 1985
                    NYPL [JFD 85-7082]

Afro-American history : primary sources / edited
by Thomas R. Frazier.2nd ed. Chicago, Ill. :
Dorsey Press, c1988. xv, 464 p. ; 24 cm.
Includes bibliographies.   ISBN 0-256-06306-0 (pbk.)
DDC 973/.0496073 19
1. Afro-Americans - History - Sources. I. Frazier,
Thomas R.
E184.6 .A35 1988   NYPL [Sc E 89-44]

AFRO-AMERICAN HOMOSEXUALS - FICTION.
Preston, John. Stolen moments /. Boston , 1985. 125 p. ; ISBN 0-932870-71-6
NYPL [Sc D 88-3]

AFRO-AMERICAN - ILLINOIS - CHICAGO - FICTION.
Brown, Frank London. The myth maker. Chicago [1969] 179 p. DDC 813/.5/4
PZ4.B8774 My PS3552.R6855
NYPL [Sc D 88-1118]

AFRO-AMERICAN - ILLINOIS - FICTION.
Gilbert, Herman Cromwell. The uncertain sound. Chicago [1969] 349 p. DDC 813/.5/4
PZ4.G4647 Un PS3557.I342
NYPL [Sc D 88-1117]

AFRO-AMERICAN-INDIAN RELATIONS. see AFRO-AMERICANS - RELATIONS WITH INDIANS.

AFRO-AMERICAN INTELLIGENCE. see INTELLIGENCE LEVELS - AFRO-AMERICANS.

AFRO-AMERICAN INVENTORS - BIOGRAPHY - JUVENILE LITERATURE.
Sweet, Dovie Davis. Red light, green light . Smithtown, N.Y. , 1978 (1980 printing) 39 p. : ISBN 0-682-49088-1 *NYPL [Sc D 89-70]*

AFRO-AMERICAN-JEWISH RELATIONS. see AFRO-AMERICANS - RELATIONS WITH JEWS.

AFRO-AMERICAN JOURNALISTS - BIOGRAPHY.
Waters, Enoch P., 1909- American diary . Chicago , c1987. xxiii, 520 p. ; ISBN 0-910671-01-X : DDC 070.4/1/0924 B 19
PN4874.W293 A33 1987
NYPL [Sc E 88-270]

AFRO-AMERICAN JOURNALISTS - UNITED STATES - BIOGRAPHY.
Suggs, Henry Lewis. P.B. Young, newspaperman . Charlottesville , 1988. xxii, 254 p. ; ISBN 0-8139-1178-8 DDC 070.4/1/0924 B 19
PN4874.Y59 S84 1988 *NYPL [JFE 89-97]*

AFRO-AMERICAN JUDGES - BIOGRAPHY.
McGuire, Phillip, 1944- He, too, spoke for democracy . New York , c1988. xvii, 154 p. ; ISBN 0-313-26115-6 (lib. bdg. : alk. paper) DDC 355/.008996073 B 19
KF373.H38 M35 1988 NYPL [Sc E 88-347]

AFRO-AMERICAN JUDGES - NEW YORK (N. Y.) - BIOGRAPHY.
Wright, Bruce, 1918- Black robes, white justice /. Secaucus, N.J. , c1987. 214 p. ; ISBN 0-8184-0422-1 : DDC 345.73/05/08996073 347.305508996073 19
KF373.W67 A33 1987 NYPL [JLE 87-2842]

AFRO-AMERICAN LEGISLATORS - BIOGRAPHY - JUVENILE LITERATURE.
Jakoubek, Robert E. Adam Clayton Powell, Jr. /. New York , c1988. xiv, 252 p. ; ISBN 1-555-46606-0 DDC 973/.0496073024 B 92 19
E748.P86 J35 1988 NYPL [Sc E 88-372]

AFRO-AMERICAN LITERATURE (ENGLISH) see AMERICAN LITERATURE - AFRO-AMERICAN AUTHORS.

AFRO-AMERICAN LUTHERANS - CONGRESSES.
Theology and the Black experience . Minneapolis , c1988. 272 p. ; ISBN 0-8066-2353-5 DDC 284.1/08996 19
BX8065.2 .T48 1988 NYPL [Sc D 89-353]

AFRO-AMERICAN MAYORS - MICHIGAN - DETROIT - BIOGRAPHY.
Rich, Wilbur C. Coleman Young and Detroit politics . Detroit, Mich. , 1989. 298 p. : ISBN 0-8143-2093-7 DDC 977.4/34043/0924 B 19
F474.D453 Y677 1989 NYPL [Sc E 89-208]

AFRO-AMERICAN MEN.
Crisis in Black sexual politics /. [San Francisco, Calif.] c1989. iv, 184 p. ; ISBN 0-9613086-2-1
NYPL [Sc D 89-152]

AFRO-AMERICAN MEN - FICTION.
Wright, Richard, 1908-1960. Eight men. Cleveland [1961] 250 p.
PZ3.W9352 Ei NYPL [Sc Rare F 88-59]

Wright, Richard, 1908-1960. Eight men . New York , c1987. xxv, 250 p. ; ISBN 0-938410-39-3 : DDC 813/.52 19
PS3545.R815 E4 1987 NYPL [Sc D 89-376]

AFRO-AMERICAN MEN - NEW YORK (N.Y.) - PHOTOGRAPHS.
Vincent, Alan W. The bangy book . Berlin , 1988. [80] p. : ISBN 3-924040-62-1
NYPL [Sc F 89-115]

AFRO-AMERICAN MEN - PICTORIAL WORKS.
Mapplethorpe, Robert. Black book /. New York , c1986. 91 p. : *NYPL [Sc F 87-42]*

AFRO-AMERICAN MEN - PSYCHOLOGY.
Herbert, James I. Black male entrepreneurs and adult development /. New York , 1989. xviii, 235 p. ; ISBN 0-275-93023-8 (alk. paper) : DDC 155.8/496073 19
E185.625 .H44 1989 NYPL [Sc E 89-256]

AFRO-AMERICAN MEN - SEXUAL BEHAVIOR.
Brown, Leroy. Black sexual power /. Cleveland, Ohio , c1970. 220 p. ; *NYPL [Sc C 88-274]*

AFRO-AMERICAN MENNONITES.
Bechler, Le Roy, 1925- The Black Mennonite Church in North America, 1886-1986 /. Scottdale, Pa. , 1986. 196 p. : ISBN 0-8361-1287-3 : DDC 289.7/08996073 19
BX8116.3.A37 B43 1986
NYPL [Sc E 89-134]

AFRO-AMERICAN MERCHANT SEAMEN - LEGAL STATUS, LAWS, ETC. - SOUTH CAROLINA.
United States. President, 1841-1845 (Tyler) Colored mariners in ports of South Carolina. [Washington, D. C.] 18. 18 p.;
NYPL [Sc Rare F 88-23]

Afro-American military personnel. see United States - Armed Forces - Afro-Americans.

AFRO-AMERICAN MISSIONARIES - BIOGRAPHY.
[Broughton, Virginia W] Twenty year's [!] experience of a missionary [microform]. Chicago, 1907. 140 p.
NYPL [Sc Micro R-1445]

AFRO-AMERICAN MORTALITY. see AFRO-AMERICANS - MORTALITY.

AFRO-AMERICAN MOTION PICTURE PRODUCERS AND DIRECTORS - EXHIBITIONS.
Black visions '87 . New York , 1987. 32 p. :
NYPL [Sc F 88-258]

AFRO-AMERICAN MOTION PICTURE PRODUCERS AND DIRECTORS - INTERVIEWS.
Black visions '87 . New York , 1987. 32 p. :
NYPL [Sc F 88-258]

AFRO-AMERICAN MUSIC - EXHIBITIONS.
Muse presents Jazz in the first person . [Brooklyn, N.Y. , c1972] 31 p. :
NYPL [JNF 85-14]

AFRO-AMERICAN MUSICIAN - BIOGRAPHY.
Armstrong, Louis, 1900-1971. Satchmo . New York, N.Y. , 1986, c1954. xib, p. 7-240 : ISBN 0-306-80276-7 (pbk.) : DDC 785.42/092/4 B 19
ML419.A75 A3 1986 NYPL [Sc D 88-339]

AFRO-AMERICAN MUSICIANS - BIOGRAPHY.
Backus, Rob, 1946- Fire music . Chicago, Ill. , 1976. vii, 104 p. : ISBN 0-917702-00-X
NYPL [Sc D 88-337]

Brown, Marion, 1935- Faces and places . 1976. 2 v. (289 leaves) : *NYPL [Sc F 88-101]*

Brown, Scott E., 1960- James P. Johnson . Metuchen, N.J. , 1986. viii, 500 p., [12] p. of plates : ISBN 0-8108-1887-6 DDC 786.1/092/4 B 19
ML417.J62 B76 1986 NYPL [Sc D 88-1435]

Chilton, John, 1931 or 2- Sidney Bechet, the wizard of jazz /. Basingstoke , 1987. xiii, 331 p., [32] p. of plates : ISBN 0-333-44386-1
NYPL [Sc E 88-33]

Collier, James Lincoln, 1928- Duke Ellington /. New York , 1987. viii, 340 p., [16] p. of plates : ISBN 0-19-503770-7 (alk. paper) DDC 785.42/092/4 B 19
ML410.E44 C6 1987 NYPL [JNE 87-49]

Gammond, Peter. Duke Ellington /. London , 1987. 127 p. : ISBN 0-948820-00-4 (pbk.) :
NYPL [JNC 87-8]

Horricks, Raymond, 1933- Quincy Jones /.

Tunbridge Wells, Kent , New York , 1985. 127 p., [8] p. of plates : ISBN 0-87052-215-9 (Hippocrene Books) : DDC 785.42/092/4 B 19
ML419.J7 H67 1985 NYPL [Sc E 87-36]

Ingram, Adrian. Wes Montgomery /. Gateshead, Tyne and Wear, England , 1985. 127 p. : ISBN 0-9506224-9-4
NYPL [Sc F 88-61]

Koch, Lawrence O. Yardbird suite . Bowling Green, Ohio , c1988. 336 p. : ISBN 0-87972-259-2 (clothbound)
NYPL [Sc E 89-48]

Lees, Gene. Meet me at Jim & Andy's . New York, N.Y. , c1988. xviii, 265 p. ; ISBN 0-19-504611-0 (alk. paper) DDC 785.42/092/2 B 19
ML394 .L4 1988 NYPL [JND 89-5]

Lyons, Leonard. Jazz portraits . New York , c1989. 610 p. : ISBN 0-688-04946-X DDC 785.42/092/2 B 19
ML394 .L97 1989 NYPL [Sc E 89-91]

Palmer, Richard (Richard Hilary), 1947- Oscar Peterson /. Tunbridge Wells , New York , 1984. c. 93 p. : ISBN 0-87052-011-3 (Hippocrene Books) : DDC 785.42/092/4 B 19
ML417.P46 P3 1984 NYPL [Sc C 88-142]

Pinfold, Mike. Louis Armstrong, his life and times /. New York , c1987. 143 p. : ISBN 0-87663-667-9 DDC 785.42/092/4 B 19
ML419.A75 P55 1987 NYPL [Sc F 88-65]

Southall, Geneva H. Blind Tom . Minneapolis , 1979- v. : DDC 786.1/092/4 B
ML417.B78 S7 1979
NYPL [Sc Ser.-L .S674]

Swenson, John. Stevie Wonder /. London , c1986. 160 p. : ISBN 0-85965-076-6 (pbk.) : DDC 784.5/4/00924 B 19
ML410.W836 S9 1986b
NYPL [Sc F 88-363]

AFRO-AMERICAN MUSICIANS - BIOGRAPHY - JUVENILE LITERATURE.
Collier, James Lincoln, 1928- Louis Armstrong . New York , c1985. 165 p. : ISBN 0-02-722830-4 DDC 785.42/092/4 B 92 19
ML3930.A75 C67 1985
NYPL [Sc D 86-229]

Tanenhaus, Sam. Louis Armstrong /. New York , c1989. 127 p. : ISBN 1-555-46571-4 DDC 785.42/092/4 B 92 19
ML3930.A75 T3 1989 NYPL [Sc E 89-170]

AFRO-AMERICAN MUSICIANS - BIOGRAPHY - PICTORIAL WORKS.
Giddens, Gary. Satchmo /. New York , 1988. 239 p. : ISBN 0-385-24428-2 : DDC 785.42/092/4 B 19
ML410.A75 G5 1988 NYPL [Sc F 89-73]

AFRO-AMERICAN MUSICIANS - JUVENILE BIOGRAPHY.
Frankl, Ron. Duke Ellington /. New York , c1988. 110 p. : ISBN 1-555-46584-6 DDC 785.42/092/4 B 92 19
ML3930.E44 F7 1988 NYPL [Sc E 88-381]

AFRO-AMERICAN MUSICIANS - JUVENILE FICTION.
Thomas, Ianthe, 1951- Willie blows a mean horn /. New York , c1981. 22 p. : ISBN 0-06-026106-4 : DDC [E]
PZ7.T36693 Wi NYPL [Sc E 89-22]

AFRO-AMERICAN MUSICIANS - PORTRAITS.
Alexander, Jim. Duke and other legends . Atlanta, GA. , c1988. 63 p. : ISBN 0-945708-03-3 *NYPL [Sc E 89-63]*

Jazz giants. New York , 1988, c1986. 280 p. : ISBN 0-8230-7536-2 : DDC 779/.978542 19
ML3506 .J43 1988 NYPL [Sc G 89-14]

Wilmer, Valerie. The face of Black music ; photographs /. New York , 1976. [118] p. : ISBN 0-306-70756-X. DDC 780/.92/2 B
ML87 .W655 NYPL [Sc F 88-207]

Afro-American nationalism . Herod, Agustina. New York , 1986. xvi, 272 p. ; ISBN 0-8240-9813-7 (alk. paper) DDC 016.3058/96073 19
Z1361.N39 H47 1986 E185.625
NYPL [Sc D 87-1338]

AFRO-AMERICAN NEWSPAPERS - HISTORY.

Waters, Enoch P., 1909- American diary .
Chicago , c1987. xxiii, 520 p. ;　ISBN
0-910671-01-X :　DDC 070.4/1/0924 B 19
PN4874.W293 A33 1987
　　　　　　　　　　NYPL [Sc E 88-270]

AFRO-AMERICAN NEWSPAPERS -
MISSISSIPPI - BIBLIOGRAPHY -
UNION LISTS.
Thompson, Julius Eric. The Black press in
Mississippi, 1865-1985 . West Cornwall, CT ,
1988. xxiv, 144 p. :　ISBN 0-933951-16-7 (alk.
paper) :　DDC 015.762035 19
Z1361.N39 T52 1988 PN4882.5
　　　　　　　　　　NYPL [Sc D 89-34]

AFRO-AMERICAN NEWSPAPERS -
MISSISSIPPI - DIRECTORIES.
Thompson, Julius Eric. The Black press in
Mississippi, 1865-1985 . West Cornwall, CT ,
1988. xxiv, 144 p. :　ISBN 0-933951-16-7 (alk.
paper) :　DDC 015.762035 19
Z1361.N39 T52 1988 PN4882.5
　　　　　　　　　　NYPL [Sc D 89-34]

AFRO-AMERICAN NOVELISTS -
BIOGRAPHY.
Walker, Margaret, 1915- Richard Wright,
daemonic genius . New York , c1988. xix, 428
p., [8] leaves of plates :　ISBN 0-446-71001-6
DDC 813/.52 B 19
PS3545.R815 Z892 1988
　　　　　　　　　　NYPL [Sc E 88-604]

AFRO-AMERICAN NOVELISTS -
BIOGRAPHY - JUVENILE LITERATURE.
Bishop, Jack, 1910- Ralph Ellison /. New
York , c1988. 110 p. :　ISBN 1-555-46585-4
DDC 818/.5409 B 19
PS3555.L625 Z59 1988　NYPL [Sc E 88-165]
Wilson, M. L. (Matthew Lawrence), 1960-
Chester Himes /. New York , c1988. 111 p. :
　ISBN 1-555-46591-9　DDC 813/.54 B 92 19
PS3515.I713 Z93 1988　NYPL [Sc E 88-373]

AFRO-AMERICAN PAINTING -
LOUISIANA - NATCHITOCHES.
Wilson, James L. (James Lynwood) Clementine
Hunter, American folk artist /. Gretna , 1988.
160 p. :　ISBN 0-88289-658-X　DDC 759.13 B 19
ND237.H915 A4 1988　　NYPL [Sc F 89-94]

AFRO-AMERICAN PENTECOSTALS -
HISTORY.
MacRobert, Iain, 1949- The Black roots and
white racism of early Pentecostalism in the
USA /. Basingstoke , 1988. xv, 142 p. ;　ISBN
0-333-43997-X :　DDC 277.3/082 19
BR1644.5.U6　　　NYPL [Sc D 89-131]

AFRO-AMERICAN PERIODICALS -
MISSISSIPPI - BIBLIOGRAPHY -
UNION LISTS.
Thompson, Julius Eric. The Black press in
Mississippi, 1865-1985 . West Cornwall, CT ,
1988. xxiv, 144 p. :　ISBN 0-933951-16-7 (alk.
paper) :　DDC 015.762035 19
Z1361.N39 T52 1988 PN4882.5
　　　　　　　　　　NYPL [Sc D 89-34]

AFRO-AMERICAN PERIODICALS - UNITED
STATES.
Knox, Ellis Oneal. A study of Negro periodicals
in the United States /. 1928. 77 leaves ;
　　　　　　　　　　NYPL [Sc F 88-264]

AFRO-AMERICAN PHILOSOPHY.
Hatchett, John F. Notes from the mind of a
Black philosopher /. [New York?] , c1979. iv,
112 p. :　　　　　　*NYPL [Sc F 89-21]*

AFRO-AMERICAN PHOTOGRAPHERS.
Willis-Thomas, Deborah, 1948- An illustrated
bio-bibliography of Black photographers,
1940-1988 /. New York , 1989. xiv, 483 p. :
　ISBN 0-8240-8389-X (alk. paper)　DDC
770/.92/2 19
TR139 .W55 1988　　　NYPL [Sc F 89-156]

AFRO-AMERICAN PHYSICIANS -
BIOGRAPHY.
Wynes, Charles E. Charles Richard Drew .
Urbana , c1988. xvi, 132 p., [14] p. of plates :
　ISBN 0-252-01551-7　DDC 610/.92/4 B 19
R154.D75 W96 1988　　NYPL [Sc E 89-65]

AFRO-AMERICAN PILOTS - BIOGRAPHY.
Johnson, Hayden C. The Fighting 99th Air
Squadron, 1941-45 /. New York , c1987. 49
p. :　ISBN 0-533-06879-7 :　DDC 940.54/4973 19
D790 .J57 1987　　　NYPL [Sc D 88-1192]

Afro-American poetics . Baker, Houston A.

Madison, Wis. , c1988. x, 201 p. ;　ISBN
0-299-11500-3 :　DDC 810/.9/896073 19
PS153.N5 B22 1988　NYPL [Sc D 88-1356]

AFRO-AMERICAN POETRY (ENGLISH) see
AMERICAN POETRY - AFRO-
AMERICAN AUTHORS.

AFRO-AMERICAN POETS - BIOGRAPHY.
Meltzer, Milton, 1915- Langston Hughes . New
York [1968] xiii, 281 p.　DDC 811/.5/2 B
PS3515.U274 Z68　　NYPL [Sc D 89-329]
Rampersad, Arnold. The life of Langston
Hughes /. New York , 1986-1988. 2 v. :　ISBN
0-19-504011-2 (v. 1)　DDC 818/.5209 B 19
PS3515.U274 Z698 1986
　　　　　　　　　　NYPL [Sc E 87-44]

AFRO-AMERICAN POETS - BIOGRAPHY -
JUVENILE LITERATURE.
Gentry, Tony. Paul Laurence Dunbar /. New
York , c1989. 110 p. :　ISBN 1-555-46583-8
DDC 811/.4 B 92 19
PS1557 .G46 1989　　NYPL [Sc E 88-514]
Richmond, M. A. (Merle A.) Phillis Wheatley
/. New York , 1988. 111 p :　ISBN
1-555-46683-4　DDC 811/.1 B 92 19
PS866.W5 Z683 1987　NYPL [Sc E 88-173]
Rummel, Jack. Langston Hughes /. New York ,
c1988. 111 p. :　ISBN 1-555-46595-1　DDC
818/.5209 B 92 19
PS3515.U274 Z775 1988
　　　　　　　　　　NYPL [Sc E 88-166]

AFRO-AMERICAN POETS - FICTION.
Shange, Ntozake. Melissa & Smith /. St. Paul,
Mn. , 1976. [13] p. ;　ISBN 0-09-377807-6
　　　　　　　　　　NYPL [Sc Rare C 86-6]

AFRO-AMERICAN PRESS - HISTORY -
19TH CENTURY.
Kinshasa, Kwando Mbiassi. Emigration vs.
assimilation . Jefferson, N.C. , 1988. xiv, 234
p. ;　ISBN 0-89950-338-1 (lib. bdg.)　DDC
973/.0496073 19
E185 .K49 1988　　　NYPL [IEC 88-2401]

AFRO-AMERICAN QUILTMAKERS -
ALABAMA - HISTORY.
Callahan, Nancy. The Freedom Quilting Bee /.
Tuscaloosa, Ala. , c1987. xi, 255 p., [8] p. of
plates :　ISBN 0-8173-0310-3　DDC
976.0/3800496073 19
NK9112 .C34 1987　NYPL [3-MOT 88-1171]

AFRO-AMERICAN QUILTS.
Leon, Eli. Who'd a thought it . San Francisco,
CA , c1987. 87 p. :　　　*NYPL [Sc F 88-235]*

AFRO-AMERICAN RADIO STATIONS.
Newman, Mark. Entrepreneurs of profit and
pride . New York , 1988. xvi, 186 p., [4] p. of
plates :　ISBN 0-275-92888-8　DDC 305.8/96073 19
PN1991.8.A35 N49 1988
　　　　　　　　　　NYPL [Sc E 89-88]

AFRO-AMERICAN - RELIGION.
MacRobert, Iain, 1949- The Black roots and
white racism of early Pentecostalism in the
USA /. Basingstoke , 1988. xv, 142 p. ;　ISBN
0-333-43997-X :　DDC 277.3/082 19
BR1644.5.U6　　　NYPL [Sc D 89-131]

AFRO-AMERICAN SERMONS (ENGLISH)
see SERMONS, AMERICAN - AFRO-
AMERICAN AUTHORS.

AFRO-AMERICAN SINGERS - BIOGRAPHY.
Adler, B. Tougher than leather . New York ,
c1987. viii, 191 p., [14] p. of plates :　ISBN
0-451-15121-6 (pbk.) :　*NYPL [Sc C 88-271]*
Kliment, Bud. Ella Fitzgerald /. New York ,
c1988. 112 p. :　ISBN 1-555-46586-2　DDC 784.5
B 19
ML420.F52 K6 1988　　NYPL [Sc E 88-611]
LaBrew, Arthur R. The Black Swan . Detroit ,
1969. 86 p. :　　　*NYPL [JND 82-30]*
Patterson, Charles. Marian Anderson /. New
York , 1988. 154 p. :　ISBN 0-531-10568-7　DDC
782.1/092/4 B 92 19
ML420.A6 P4 1988　　　NYPL [Sc E 89-4]

AFRO-AMERICAN SINGERS - BIOGRAPHY -
JUVENILE LITERATURE.
Ehrlich, Scott. Paul Robeson /. New York ,
c1988. 111 p. :　ISBN 1-555-46608-7　DDC
782.1/092/4 B 92 19
E185.97.R63 E35 1988　NYPL [Sc E 88-167]
Greenberg, Keith Elliot. Whitney Houston /.
Minneapolis , c1988. 32 p. :　ISBN 0-8225-1619-5

(lib. bdg.) :　DDC 784.5/0092/4 B 92 19
ML3930.H7 G7 1988　NYPL [Sc D 88-1459]
Mabery, D. L. Janet Jackson /. Minneapolis ,
c1988. 32 p. :　ISBN 0-8225-1618-7 (lib bdg.) :
　DDC 784.5/4/00924 B 920 19
ML3930.J15 M3 1988
　　　　　　　　　　NYPL [Sc D 88-1460]
Stevenson, Janet. Marian Anderson /. Chicago
[1963] 189 p. :　　　*NYPL [Sc D 88-377]*

AFRO-AMERICAN SLAVEHOLDERS -
SOUTH CAROLINA - HISTORY.
Koger, Larry, 1958- Black slaveowners .
Jefferson, N.C. , 1985. xiii, 286 p. ;　ISBN
0-89950-160-5 :　DDC 975.7/00496073 19
E445.S7 K64 1985　　　NYPL [Sc E 88-473]

AFRO-AMERICAN SOLDIERS - CIVIL
RIGHTS.
McGuire, Phillip, 1944- He, too, spoke for
democracy . New York , c1988. xvii, 154 p. ;
　ISBN 0-313-26115-6 (lib. bdg. : alk. paper)　DDC
355/.008996073 B 19
KF373.H38 M35 1988　NYPL [Sc E 88-347]

AFRO-AMERICAN SOLDIERS - FICTION.
Covin, David, 1940- Brown sky . Chicago ,
c1987. 274 p. ;　ISBN 0-910671-11-7 :　DDC
813/.54 19
PS3553.O875 B7 1987　NYPL [JFD 88-427]

AFRO-AMERICAN SOLDIERS - GREAT
BRITAIN.
Smith, Graham. When Jim Crow met John
Bull . London , c1987. 265 p. ;　ISBN
1-85043-039-X　　　NYPL [Sc D 88-55]*

AFRO-AMERICAN SPIRITUALS. see
SPIRITUALS (SONGS)

AFRO-AMERICAN STUDIES.
Newsum, H. E., 1951- The politics of
"scholarship" in Black intellectual discourse
[microform] . 1977 116 leaves.
　　　　　　　　　　NYPL [Sc Micro R-4689]

AFRO-AMERICAN STUDIES -
BIBLIOGRAPHY.
Sloan, Irving J. The Negro in modern American
history textbooks . Chicago, Ill. , 1966. 47 p. ;
　　　　　　　　　　NYPL [Sc D 89-262]

AFRO-AMERICAN SUFFRAGE. see AFRO-
AMERICANS - POLITICS AND
SUFFRAGE.

AFRO-AMERICAN SUNDAY SCHOOLS.
Smith, Sid. 10 super Sunday schools in the
Black community /. Nashville, Tenn. , c1986.
178 p. :　ISBN 0-8054-6252-X :　DDC
268/.861/08996073 19
BV1523.A37 S65 1986　NYPL [Sc C 88-229]

AFRO-AMERICAN SURGEONS - UNITED
STATES - BIOGRAPHY.
A Century of Black surgeons . Norman, Okla. ,
c1987. 2 v. (xx, 973 p.) :　ISBN 0-9617380-0-6
(set)　DDC 617/.092/2 B 19
RD27.34 .C46 1987　　NYPL [Sc E 88-216]

AFRO-AMERICAN SURGEONS - UNITED
STATES - DIRECTORIES.
A Century of Black surgeons . Norman, Okla. ,
c1987. 2 v. (xx, 973 p.) :　ISBN 0-9617380-0-6
(set)　DDC 617/.092/2 B 19
RD27.34 .C46 1987　　NYPL [Sc E 88-216]

AFRO-AMERICAN TEACHERS - DIARIES.
Forten, Charlotte L. [Journals.] The journals of
Charlotte Forten Grimké /. New York , 1988.
xlix, 609 p. ;　ISBN 0-19-505238-2 (alk. paper)
DDC 371.1/0092/4 B 19
LA2317.F67 A3 1988　NYPL [JFC 88-2152]

AFRO-AMERICAN TEENAGE MOTHERS -
WASHINGTON (D.C.) - CASE STUDIES.
Dash, Leon. When children want children .
New York , c1989. 270 p. :　ISBN 0-688-06957-6
DDC 306.7/088055 19
HQ759.4 .D37 1989　　NYPL [Sc E 89-151]

AFRO-AMERICAN TEENAGERS -
WASHINGTON (D.C.) - SEXUAL
BEHAVIOR - CASE STUDIES.
Dash, Leon. When children want children .
New York , c1989. 270 p. :　ISBN 0-688-06957-6
DDC 306.7/088055 19
HQ759.4 .D37 1989　　NYPL [Sc E 89-151]

AFRO-AMERICAN THEATER.
Grupenhoff, Richard, 1941- The black
Valentino . Metuchen, N.J. , 1988. xi, 188 p. :

ISBN 0-8108-2078-1   DDC 790.2/092/4 B 19
PN2287.T78 G78 1988
                    NYPL [Sc D 88-1029]
Marshall, Alex C. (Alexander Charles)
Representative directors, Black theatre
productions, and practices at historically Black
colleges and universities, 1968-1978
[microform] /. 1980. ix, 141 leaves.
                    NYPL [Sc Micro R-4807]

**AFRO-AMERICAN THEATER -
   CHRONOLOGY.**
Sampson, Henry T., 1934- The ghost walks .
Metuchen, N.J. , 1988. ix, 570 p. : ISBN
   0-8108-2070-6   DDC 792/.08996073 19
PN2270.A35 S25 1988
                    NYPL [Sc D 88-1145]

**AFRO-AMERICAN THEATER -
   DIRECTORIES.**
Peterson, Bernard L. Contemporary Black
American playwrights and their plays . New
York , 1988. xxvi, 625 p. ; ISBN 0-313-25190-8
   (lib. bdg. : alk. paper)   DDC 812/.54/09896 19
PS153.N5 P43 1988   *NYPL [Sc E 88-378]*

AFRO-AMERICAN THEATER - HISTORY.
Sanders, Leslie Catherine, 1944- The
development of black theater in America .
Baton Rouge , c1988. 252 p. : ISBN
   0-8071-1328-X   DDC 812/.009/896073 19
PS338.N4 S26 1987
                    NYPL [MWED 88-1125]

AFRO-AMERICAN THEATER - REVIEWS.
Sampson, Henry T., 1934- The ghost walks .
Metuchen, N.J. , 1988. ix, 570 p. : ISBN
   0-8108-2070-6   DDC 792/.08996073 19
PN2270.A35 S25 1988
                    NYPL [Sc D 88-1145]

**AFRO-AMERICAN UNIVERSITES AND
   COLLEGES - CONGRESSES.**
Inside black colleges and universities /.
Chicago , c1986. 153 p. ; ISBN 0-695-60051-6
                    NYPL [Sc D 88-951]

**AFRO-AMERICAN UNIVERSITIES AND
   COLLEGES.**
The Black/white colleges . Washington, D.C. ,
1981. v, 46 p. :   *NYPL [Sc F 89-48]*

**AFRO-AMERICAN UNIVERSITIES AND
   COLLEGES - ADMINISTRATION.**
Hoskins, Robert L. Background characteristics
and selected perceptions of Black administrators
working at Black and white land-grant
institutions of higher education [microform] /.
1977. 213 leaves.   *NYPL [Sc Micro R-4226]*

Lundy, Harold Wayne. A study of the
transition from white to Black presidents at
three selected schools founded by the American
Missionary Association [microform] /. 1978.
676 leaves.   *NYPL [Sc Micro R-4216]*

**AFRO-AMERICAN UNIVERSITIES AND
   COLLEGES - CONGRESSES.**
Black colleges and public policy /. Chicago ,
c1986. 99 p. ; ISBN 0-695-60050-8
                    NYPL [Sc D 88-947]

**AFRO-AMERICAN UNIVERSITIES AND
   COLLEGES - FINANCE - CONGRESSES.**
Black colleges and public policy /. Chicago ,
c1986. 99 p. ; ISBN 0-695-60050-8
                    NYPL [Sc D 88-947]

**AFRO-AMERICAN UNIVERSITIES AND
   COLLEGES - TENNESSEE - HISTORY.**
A School for freedom . [Knoxville] , 1986. xiii,
60 p. :   *NYPL [Sc D 88-417]*

**AFRO-AMERICAN UNIVERSITY
   STUDENTS. see AFRO-AMERICAN
   COLLEGE STUDENTS.**

**AFRO-AMERICAN VOTING RIGHTS. see
   AFRO-AMERICANS - POLITICS AND
   SUFFRAGE.**

AFRO-AMERICAN WIT AND HUMOR.
Cosby, William H. The wit and wisdom of Fat
Albert. New York [1973] [64] p. ISBN
   0-525-61004-9   DDC 818/.5/407
PZ8.7.C6 Wi   *NYPL [Sc C 89-26]*

**AFRO-AMERICAN WOMEN ATHLETES -
   HISTORY - 20TH CENTURY.**
Blue, Adrianne. Faster, higher, further .
London , 1988. ix, 182 p. : ISBN 0-86068-648-5
   (pbk.) :
GV721.5 .B58x 1988   *NYPL [Sc E 89-82]*

AFRO-AMERICAN WOMEN AUTHORS.
Juncker, Clara. Black roses . København ,
c1985. 158 p. : ISBN 87-7565-316-8 (styksalg)
                    NYPL [Sc E 88-441]
Lewis, Vashti Crutcher. The mulatto woman as
major female character in novels by Black
women, 1892-1937 [microform] /. [Iowa City,
Ia.] 1981. iv, 182 leaves ;
                    NYPL [Sc Micro R-4792]

**AFRO-AMERICAN WOMEN AUTHORS -
   BIOGRAPHY.**
Afro-American women writers, 1746-1933 .
Boston , 1988. xxviii, 465 p. ; ISBN
   0-8161-8823-8   *NYPL [Sc E 88-428]*

**AFRO-AMERICAN WOMEN -
   BIBLIOGRAPHY.**
Redfern, Bernice, 1947- Women of color in the
United States . New York , 1989. vii, 156 p. ;
   ISBN 0-8240-5849-6 (alk. paper)   DDC
   016.3054/8/0973 19
Z7964.U49 R4 1989 HQ1410
                    NYPL [Sc D 89-562]

AFRO-AMERICAN WOMEN - BIOGRAPHY.
Hill, Pauline Anderson Simmons. Too young to
be old . Seattle, Washington , c1981. xiv, 58
p. : ISBN 0-89716-098-3
                    NYPL [Sc D 88-1214]

Homespun heroines and other women of
distinction /. New York , 1988. xxxv, viii, 248
p., [25] leaves of plates : ISBN 0-19-505237-4
   (alk. paper)   DDC 920.72/08996073 19
E185.96 .H65 1988   *NYPL [JFC 88-2157]*

Johnson, MayLee. Coming up on the rough
side . South Orange, N.J. , c1988. vii, 88 p. ;
   ISBN 0-944734-01-4   *NYPL [Sc D 89-190]*

Shakur, Assata. Assata, an autobiography /.
Westport, CT , 1987. xiv, 274 p. ; ISBN
   0-88208-221-3 : DDC 973/.0496073024 19
E185.97.S53 A3 1987   *NYPL [Sc E 88-21]*

Spiritual narratives /. New York , 1988. 489 p.
in various pagings : ISBN 0-19-505266-8 (alk.
   paper)   DDC 209/.22 B 19
BR1713 .S65 1988   *NYPL [JFC 88-2189]*

Tyson, Jennifer. Claudia Jones, 1915-1964 .
London , c1988. 16 p. :
                    NYPL [Sc D 89-553]

**AFRO-AMERICAN WOMEN - BIOGRAPHY -
   JUVENILE LITERATURE.**
Krass, Peter. Sojourner Truth /. New York ,
c1988. 110 p. : ISBN 1-555-46611-7 DDC
   305.5/67/0924 B 92 19
E185.97.T8 K73 1988   *NYPL [Sc E 88-470]*

AFRO-AMERICAN WOMEN - CALIFORNIA.
Gray, Mattie Evans. Images . Sacramento,
Calif. , c1988. 185 p. : ISBN 0-8011-0782-2
                    NYPL [Sc F 89-134]

AFRO-AMERICAN WOMEN - CONGRESSES.
Black working women . Berkeley, Calif.
[1981?] vii, 222 p. :   *NYPL [Sc F 89-33]*

**AFRO-AMERICAN WOMEN -
   EMPLOYMENT - HISTORY.**
Black workers . Philadelphia , 1989. xv, 733 p. ;
   ISBN 0-87722-592-3   *NYPL [Sc E 89-206]*

AFRO-AMERICAN WOMEN EXECUTIVES.
Malone, Beverly Louise. Relationship of Black
female administrators' mentoring experience and
career satisfaction [Microform] /. 1982. 165
leaves.   *NYPL [Sc Micro R-4804]*

AFRO-AMERICAN WOMEN - FICTION.
Dickens, Nathaniel A. The gospel Singer /.
New York , c1987. 187 p. ; ISBN 0-533-07387-1
                    NYPL [Sc D 88-1450]

Douglas, Ellen, 1921- Can't quit you, baby /.
New York , 1988. 256 p. ; ISBN 0-689-11793-0
   DDC 813/.54 19
PS3554.O825 C3 1988
                    NYPL [JFD 88-11335]

Edwards-Yearwood, Grace. In the shadow of
the Peacock /. New York , c1988. 279 p. ;
   ISBN 0-07-019037-2   DDC 813/.54 19
PS3555.D99 I5 1988   *NYPL [JFE 88-4421]*

Komo, Dolores. Clio Browne . Freedom, Calif. ,
c1988. 193 p. ; ISBN 0-89594-320-4 (pbk.) :
   DDC 813/.54 19
PS3561.O4545 C55 1988
                    NYPL [Sc C 89-50]

Morrison, Toni. Sula /. New York [1987],
c1973. 174 p. ; ISBN 0-452-26010-8 DDC

813/.54 19
PS3563.O8749 S8 1987
                    NYPL [Sc D 88-633]

Walker, Alice, 1944- The color purple . New
York , c1982. 245 p. ; ISBN 0-15-119153-0 :
   DDC 813/.54 19
PS3573.A425 C6 1982
                    NYPL [Sc Rare F 88-3]

Walker, Alice, 1944- The color purple /.
London , 1983 (1986 [printing]) 245 p. : ISBN
   0-7043-3905-6 (pbk)   DDC 813/.54 19
                    NYPL [Sc C 88-143]

Walker, Alice, 1944- You can't keep a good
woman down . New York , c1982, c1981. 167
p. ; ISBN 0-15-699778-9 *NYPL [Sc D 87-684]*

Walker, Alice, 1844- [Color purple. Portuguese.]
A Cor púrpura /. Lisboa , 1986. 244 p. ;
                    NYPL [Sc D 88-388]

West, Dorothy, 1909- The living is easy /.
London , 1987, c1982. 362 p. ; ISBN
   0-86068-753-8   *NYPL [Sc C 88-165]*

AFRO-AMERICAN WOMEN - HISTORY.
Brooks, Evelyn, 1945- The women's movement
in the Black Baptist church, 1880-1920 /.
[Rochester, N.Y.] c1984. viii, 342 leaves ;
                    NYPL [Sc D 88-938]

**AFRO-AMERICAN WOMEN IN
   LITERATURE.**
Angelou, Maya. Conversations with Maya
Angelou /. Jackson , c1989. xvi, 246 p. ; ISBN
   0-87805-361-1 (alk. paper)   DDC 818/.5409 19
PS3551.N464 Z4635 1989
                    NYPL [Sc E 89-225]

Awkward, Michael. Inspiriting influences . New
York , 1989. x, 178 p. ; ISBN 0-231-06806-9
   DDC 813/.5/099287 19
PS153.N5 A94 1989   *NYPL [Sc E 89-188]*

**AFRO-AMERICAN WOMEN -
   INTELLECTUAL LIFE.**
Awkward, Michael. Inspiriting influences . New
York , 1989. x, 178 p. ; ISBN 0-231-06806-9
   DDC 813/.5/099287 19
PS153.N5 A94 1989   *NYPL [Sc E 89-188]*

**AFRO-AMERICAN WOMEN - LITERARY
   COLLECTIONS.**
Afro-American women writers, 1746-1933 .
Boston , 1988. xxviii, 465 p. ; ISBN
   0-8161-8823-8   *NYPL [Sc E 88-428]*

Scott, Kesho. Tight Spaces /. San Francisco ,
1987. 182 p. ; ISBN 0-933216-27-0
                    NYPL [Sc D 88-12]

**AFRO-AMERICAN WOMEN - MIDDLE
   WEST.**
The Black women in the Middle West Project .
Indianapolis, Ind. (140 N. Senate Ave., Room
408, Indianapolis 46204) , 1986. xi, 238 p. :
   DDC 977/.00496073 19
E185.915 .B52 1986   *NYPL [Sc F 88-141]*

**AFRO-AMERICAN WOMEN - MIDDLE
   WEST - ARCHIVAL RESOURCES -
   MIDDLE WEST.**
The Black women in the Middle West Project .
Indianapolis, Ind. (140 N. Senate Ave., Room
408, Indianapolis 46204) , 1986. xi, 238 p. :
   DDC 977/.00496073 19
E185.915 .B52 1986   *NYPL [Sc F 88-141]*

**AFRO-AMERICAN WOMEN - MIDDLE
   WEST - BIOGRAPHY.**
The Black women in the Middle West Project .
Indianapolis, Ind. (140 N. Senate Ave., Room
408, Indianapolis 46204) , 1986. xi, 238 p. :
   DDC 977/.00496073 19
E185.915 .B52 1986   *NYPL [Sc F 88-141]*

**AFRO-AMERICAN WOMEN - MIDDLE
   WEST - RESEARCH - MIDDLE WEST -
   HANDBOOKS, MANUALS, ETC.**
The Black women in the Middle West Project .
Indianapolis, Ind. (140 N. Senate Ave., Room
408, Indianapolis 46204) , 1986. xi, 238 p. :
   DDC 977/.00496073 19
E185.915 .B52 1986   *NYPL [Sc F 88-141]*

**AFRO-AMERICAN WOMEN MUSICIANS -
   BIOGRAPHY.**
Harrison, Daphne Duval, 1932- Black pearls .
New Brunswick [N.J.] , c1988. xv, 295 p. :
   ISBN 0-8135-1279-4 : DDC 784.5/3/0922 19
ML3521 .H38 1988   *NYPL [JNE 88-21]*

AFRO-AMERICAN WOMEN MUSICIANS - EXHIBITIONS.
Black visions '88 . New York [1988] 44 p. :
NYPL [Sc D 88-1200]

AFRO-AMERICAN WOMEN - NEW YORK (N.Y.) - SOCIETIES AND CLUBS.
National Association of Negro Business and Professional Women's Club. New York Club. Annual founder's day . [New York , 1961] [68] p. : *NYPL [Sc F 87-379]*

Afro-American women of the South and the advancement of the race, 1895-1925 /.
Neverdon-Morton, Cynthia, 1944- Knoxville , c1989. 272 p. : ISBN 0-87049-583-6 (alk. paper) : DDC 305.4/8896073/075 19
E185.86 .N48 1989   NYPL [Sc E 89-218]

AFRO-AMERICAN WOMEN - POETRY.
Collected Black women's poetry /. New York , 1988. 4 v. : ISBN 0-19-505253-6 (v. 1) DDC 811/.008/09287 19
PS591.N4 C57 1988   NYPL [JFC 88-2144]

Mossell, N. F., Mrs., 1855- The work of the Afro-American woman /. New York , 1988. xlii, 178 p. : ISBN 0-19-505265-X (alk. paper) DDC 305.8/96073 19
E185.86 .M65 1988   NYPL [JFC 88-2155]

AFRO-AMERICAN WOMEN POETS - NEW YORK (N.Y.) - BIOGRAPHY.
Hull, Gloria T. Color, sex, and poetry . Bloomington , c1987. xi, 240 p. : ISBN 0-253-34974-5 DDC 811/.52/099287 19
PS153.N5 H84 1987   NYPL [Sc E 88-72]

AFRO-AMERICAN WOMEN - RELIGION.
Spiritual narratives /. New York , 1988. 489 p. in various pagings : ISBN 0-19-505266-8 (alk. paper) DDC 209/.22 B 19
BR1713 .S65 1988   NYPL [JFC 88-2189]

AFRO-AMERICAN WOMEN - SOCIAL CONDITIONS.
Slipping through the cracks . New Brunswick, N.J. , 1986. 302 p. ; ISBN 0-88738-662-8
NYPL [Sc D 88-767]

AFRO-AMERICAN WOMEN - SOUTHERN STATES - FICTION.
Youngblood, Shay. The big mama stories /. Ithaca, N.Y. , c1989. 106 p. ; ISBN 0-932379-58-3 (alk. paper) : DDC 813/.54 19
PS3575.O8535 B5 1989
NYPL [Sc D 89-530]

AFRO-AMERICAN WOMEN - SOUTHERN STATES - HISTORY.
Fox-Genovese, Elizabeth, 1941- Within the plantation household . Chapel Hill , c1988. xvii, 544 p. : ISBN 0-8078-1808-9 (alk. paper) DDC 305.4/0975 19
HQ1438.A13 F69 1988   NYPL [JLE 89-21]

Neverdon-Morton, Cynthia, 1944- Afro-American women of the South and the advancement of the race, 1895-1925 /. Knoxville , c1989. 272 p. : ISBN 0-87049-583-6 (alk. paper) : DDC 305.4/8896073/075 19
E185.86 .N48 1989   NYPL [Sc E 89-218]

AFRO-AMERICAN WOMEN - SOUTHERN STATES - HISTORY - 19TH CENTURY.
Cooper, Anna J. (Anna Julia), 1858-1964. A voice from the South /. New York , 1988. liv, 304 p. ; ISBN 0-19-505246-3 (alk. paper) DDC 975/.00496073 19
E185.86 .C587 1988   NYPL [IEC 88-1201]

AFRO-AMERICAN WOMEN - SOUTHERN STATES - INTERVIEWS.
Telling memories among southern women . Baton Rouge , c1988. xi, 279 p. : ISBN 0-8071-1440-5 (alk. paper) : DDC 305.4/3 19
HD6072.2.U52 A137 1988
NYPL [Sc E 89-124]

Afro-American women writers, 1746-1933 : an anthology and critical guide / [edited by] Ann Allen Shockley. Boston : G.K. Hall, 1988. xxviii, 465 p. ; 25 cm. Bibliography: p.456-465. ISBN 0-8161-8823-8
1. American literature - Women authors. 2. Afro-American women authors - Literary collections. 3. Afro-American women authors - Biography. I. Shockley, Ann Allen.   NYPL [Sc E 88-428]

AFRO-AMERICAN YOUTH - CALIFORNIA.
Thomas, Joyce Carol. Water girl /. New York, N.Y. , c1986. 119 p. ; ISBN 0-380-89532-3 :
NYPL [Sc C 88-115]

AFRO-AMERICAN YOUTH - FICTION.
Graham, Lorenz B. [North Town. German.] Stadt im Norden /. Stuttgart , 1973, c1965. 157 p. ; ISBN 3-8002-5087-X
NYPL [Sc D 88-1171]

Hamilton, Virginia. A white romance /. New York , 1987. 191 p. ; ISBN 0-399-21213-2 : DDC [Fic] 19
PZ7.H1828 Wh 1987   NYPL [Sc D 88-221]

AFRO-AMERICAN YOUTH - FLORIDA - JUVENILE FICTION.
Ball, Dorothy Whitney. Hurricane . Indianapolis [c1964] 147 p. ; *NYPL [Sc D 88-486]*

AFRO-AMERICAN YOUTH - HARLEM (NEW YORK, N.Y.) - JUVENILE FICTION.
Moore, Emily. Whose side are you on? /. New York , 1988. 133 p. ; ISBN 0-374-38409-6
NYPL [Sc D 88-1330]

AFRO-AMERICAN YOUTH - JUVENILE FICTION.
Christopher, Matt. The basket counts. Boston [1968] 125 p. DDC [Fic] 19
PZ7.C458 Bash   NYPL [Sc C 89-15]

Cooper, Page. Thunder /. Cleveland , 1954. 218 p.   *NYPL [Sc D 88-661]*

Farley, Carol J. The most important thing in the world /. New York , 1974. vi, 133 p., ISBN 0-531-02663-9 *NYPL [Sc D 88-431]*

Madden, Betsy. The All-America Coeds /. New York [1971] 143 p. ; ISBN 0-200-71785-5
NYPL [Sc D 88-432]

Myers, Walter Dean, 1937- Scorpions /. New York , c1988. 216 p. ; ISBN 0-06-024364-3 : DDC [Fic] 19
PZ7.M992 Sc 1988   NYPL [Sc D 88-1146]

Naylor, Phyllis Reynolds. Making it happen. Chicago [1970] 128 p. ISBN 0-695-80144-9 DDC [Fic]
PZ7.N24 Mak   NYPL [Sc D 88-446]

Williams-Garcia, Rita. Blue tights /. New York , c1987. 138 p. ; ISBN 0-525-67234-6 DDC [Fic] 19
PZ7.W6713 Bl 1987   NYPL [Sc D 88-939]

Willis, Priscilla D. The race between the flags /. New York , 1955. 177 p. :
NYPL [Sc D 88-1508]

Wilson, Johnniece Marshall. Oh, brother /. New York , c1988. 121 p. ; ISBN 0-590-41363-5 : DDC [Fic] 19
PZ7.W696514 Oh 1988
NYPL [Sc D 88-699]

AFRO-AMERICANS - AESTHETICS.
Baker, Houston A. Afro-American poetics . Madison, Wis. , c1988. x, 201 p. ; ISBN 0-299-11500-3 : DDC 810/.9/896073 19
PS153.N5 B22 1988   NYPL [Sc D 88-1356]

AFRO-AMERICANS - ANECDOTES, FACETIAE, SATIRE, ETC.
Short, Sam B. 'Tis so . Baton Rouge, La. , c1972. 114 p. :   *NYPL [Sc D 89-63]*

AFRO-AMERICANS - ARKANSAS - PHILLIPS COUNTY - HISTORY.
Cortner, Richard C. A mob intent on death . Middletown, Conn. , c1988. xii, 241 p., [24] p. of plates : ISBN 0-8195-5161-9 (alk. paper) : DDC 976.7/88052 19
F417.P45 C67 1988   NYPL [Sc E 88-362]

AFRO-AMERICANS - ATTITUDES.
Magubane, Bernard. The ties that bind . Trenton, N.J. [1987] xi, 251 p. ; ISBN 0-86543-037-3 (pbk). DDC 305.8/96073 19
E185.625 .M83 1987   NYPL [Sc D 88-1348]

AFRO-AMERICANS - BIBLIOGRAPHY.
Rollins, Charlemae Hill. We build together. [Champaign, Ill. , 1967] xxviii, 71 p. ; DDC 016.818
Z1361.N39 R77 1967   NYPL [Sc D 89-387]

AFRO-AMERICANS - BIOGRAPHY.
Black leaders of the nineteenth century /. Urbana , c1988. xii, 344 p. ; ISBN 0-252-01506-1 (alk. paper) DDC 920/.009296073 19
E185.96 .B535 1988   NYPL [Sc E 89-365]

Branchcomb, Sylvia Woingust. Son, never give up /. [Yonkers, N.Y.?] , 1979. 36 p. :
NYPL [Sc D 88-568]

Cheek, William F., 1933- John Mercer Langston and the fight for Black freedom, 1829-65 /. Urbana , c1989. 478 p. ; ISBN 0-252-01550-9 (alk. paper) DDC 973/.0496073/0924 B 19
E185.97.L27 C48 1989   NYPL [Sc E 89-255]

Colaiaco, James A., 1945- Martin Luther King, Jr. . New York , 1988. x, 238 p. ; ISBN 0-312-02365-0 : DDC 323.4/092/4 B 19
E185.97.K5 C65 1988   NYPL [Sc D 89-231]

Comer, James P. Maggie's American dream . New York, N.Y. , c1988. xxiv, 228 p., [4] leaves of plates : ISBN 0-453-00588-8 DDC 973/.0496073022 B 19
E185.97.C68 C66 1988   NYPL [Sc D 89-335]

Duberman, Martin B. Paul Robeson /. New York , 1988, c1989. xiii, 804 p., [48] p. of plates : ISBN 0-394-52780-1 : DDC 790.2/092/4 B 19
E185.97.R63 D83 1988   NYPL [Sc E 89-108]

Harlan, Louis R. Booker T. Washington . New York , 1983. xiv, 548 p. : ISBN 0-19-503202-0 : DDC 378/.111 B 19
E185.97.W4 H373 1983
NYPL [Sc E 83-233]

Harlan, Louis R. Booker T. Washington in perspective . Jackson , c1988. xii, 210 p., [8] p. of plates : ISBN 0-87805-374-3 (alk. paper) DDC 378/.111 B 19
E185.97.W4 H36 1988   NYPL [Sc E 89-217]

Jackson, Clyde Owen. In this evening light /. Hicksville, N. Y. , c1980. xiii, 113 p. ; ISBN 0-682-49479-8 *NYPL [Sc D 88-1213]*

Kletzing, Henry F., 1850- Progress of a race. Atlanta, Ga., 1897. xxiv, 23-663 p.
NYPL [Sc 973-K]

Larison, Cornelius Wilson, 1837-1910. Silvia Dubois . New York , 1988. xxvii, 124 p. : ISBN 0-19-505239-0 DDC 305.5/67/0924 B 19
E444.D83 L37 1988   NYPL [JFC 88-2191]

Lee, George L. Interesting people . Jefferson, N.C. , London , c1989. xiii, 210 p. : ISBN 0-89950-403-5 : DDC 973/.0496073022 19
E185.96   NYPL [Sc E 89-240]

Lipsitz, George. A life in the struggle . Philadelphia , 1988. viii, 292 p. : ISBN 0-87722-550-8 (alk. paper) DDC 973/.0496073024 B 19
E185.97.P49 L57 1988   NYPL [Sc E 89-43]

Mickey, Rosie Cheatham. Russell Adrian Lane, biography of an urban negro school administrator [microform] /. 1983. xiii, 275 leaves : *NYPL [Sc Micro R-4813]*

Narratives of colored Americans. New York , 1877. 276 p. ; *NYPL [Sc Rare C 88-4]*

Narratives of colored Americans. New York , 1882. 276 p. ; *NYPL [Sc Rare C 88-26]*

Stewart, Rowena. A heritage discovered . Providence, R.I. [1975] 39 p. :
NYPL [Sc E 89-110]

Urban, Joan, 1950- Richard Wright /. New York, N.Y. [1989] 111 p. ; ISBN 1-555-46618-4 DDC 813/.52 19
PS3545.R815 Z85 1989
NYPL [Sc E 89-196]

AFRO-AMERICANS - BIOGRAPHY - HISTORY AND CRITICISM.
Starling, Marion Wilson, 1907. The slave narrative . Washington, D.C. , 1988. xxx, 375 p. ; ISBN 0-88258-165-1 : DDC 973/.0496073 19
E444 .S8 1988   NYPL [Sc E 89-185]

AFRO-AMERICANS - BIOGRAPHY - JUVENILE LITERATURE.
Altman, Susan R. Extraordinary Black Americans from colonial to contemporary times /. Chicago , 1988. 240 p. : ISBN 0-516-00581-2 DDC 973/.0496073022 B 920 19
E185.96 .A56 1988   NYPL [Sc E 89-177]

Ehrlich, Scott. Paul Robeson /. New York , c1988. 111 p. : ISBN 1-555-46608-7 DDC 782.1/092/4 B 19
E185.97.R63 E35 1988   NYPL [Sc E 88-167]

Ferris, Jeri. Go free or die . Minneapolis , 1987. 63 p. : ISBN 0-87614-317-6 (lib. bdg.) : DDC 305.5/67/0924 B 92 19
E444.T82 F47 1987   NYPL [Sc D 88-620]

Ferris, Jeri. Walking the road to freedom . Minneapolis , 1987. 64 p. : ISBN 0-87614-318-4

(lib. bdg.) : DDC 305.5/67/0924 B 92 19
E185.97.T8 F47 1987   NYPL [Sc D 88-1046]

Halasa, Malu. Mary McLeod Bethune /. New
York , c1989. 111 p. : ISBN 1-555-46574-9
DDC 370/.92/4 B 92 19
E185.97.B34 H35 1989   NYPL [Sc E 88-616]

Hanley, Sally. A. Philip Randolph /. New York
[1988], c1989. 110 p. : ISBN 1-555-46607-9
DDC 323.4/092/4 92 19
E185.97.R27 H36 1989   NYPL [Sc E 88-617]

Jakoubek, Robert E. Adam Clayton Powell, Jr.
/. New York , c1988. xiv, 252 p. : ISBN
1-555-46606-0 DDC 973/.0496073024 B 92 19
E748.P86 J35 1988   NYPL [Sc E 88-372]

Krass, Peter. Sojourner Truth /. New York ,
c1988. 110 p. : ISBN 1-555-46611-7 DDC
305.5/67/0924 B 92 19
E185.97.T8 K73 1988   NYPL [Sc E 88-470]

Lawler, Mary. Marcus Garvey /. New York ,
c1988. 110 p. : ISBN 1-555-46587-0 DDC
305.8/96073/024 B 92 19
E185.97.G3 L39 1988   NYPL [Sc E 88-156]

Russell, Sharman Apt. Frederick Douglass /.
New York , c1988. 110 p. : ISBN 1-555-46580-3
DDC 973.8/092/4 B 92 19
E449.D75 R87 1988   NYPL [Sc E 88-174]

**AFRO-AMERICANS - CALIFORNIA - LOS
ANGELES - FICTION.**
Himes, Chester B., 1909- Lonely crusade . New
York , c1986. x, 398 p. ; ISBN 0-938410-37-7
(pbk.) : DDC 813/.54 19
PS3515.I713 L6 1986   NYPL [Sc D 88-1362]

**AFRO-AMERICANS - CALIFORNIA - SAN
FRANCISCO - DISEASES.**
A baseline survey of AIDS risk behaviors and
attitudes in San Francisco's Black communities
/. San Francisco, Calif. [1987] vii, 74, [59]
leaves :   *NYPL [Sc F 88-232]*

**AFRO-AMERICANS - CARICATURES AND
CARTOONS.**
Alley, J. P. The meditations of "Hambone".
Memphis, Tenn. [1918] 104 p.
NYPL [Sc Rare C 89-28]

**AFRO-AMERICANS - CHILDREN. see AFRO-
AMERICAN CHILDREN.**

AFRO-AMERICANS - CIVIL RIGHTS.
Ashmore, Harry S. Hearts and minds . Cabin
John, Md. , c1988. xviii, 513 p. ; ISBN
0-932020-58-5 (pbk. : alk. paper) DDC
305.8/96073 19
E185.615 .A83 1988   NYPL [Sc D 89-382]

Assensoh, A. B. Rev Dr Martin Luther King,
Jr. and America's quest for racial integration .
Ilfracombe, Devon , 1987. 104 p. : ISBN
0-7223-2084-1   *NYPL [Sc D 88-100]*

Bernheim, Nicole. Voyage en Amérique noire /.
Paris , c1986. 254 p. ; ISBN 2-234-01886-2 :
DDC 305.8/96073/073 19
E185.86 .B47 1986   NYPL [Sc E 88-607]

Black, brown and red . Detroit, Mich. , 1975.
77 p. :   *NYPL [Sc D 84-219]*

Black mass revolt [microform]. Detroit , 1967.
23 p. ;   *NYPL [Sc Micro R-4202 no.14]*

Blauner, Bob. Black lives, white lives .
Berkeley , c1989. xii, 347 p. ; ISBN
0-520-06261-2 (alk. paper) DDC 305.8/00973 19
E185.615 .B556 1989   NYPL [Sc E 89-219]

Branch, Taylor. Parting the waters . New
York , c1988- v. : ISBN 0-671-46097-8 (v. 1)
DDC 973/.0496073 19
E185.61 .B7914 1988   NYPL [IEC 88-122]

The Civil rights movement in America .
Jackson , c1986. xii, 188 p. ; ISBN
0-87805-297-6 (alk. paper) DDC 323.1/196073
19
E185.615 .C585 1986   NYPL [IEC 87-273]

Colaiaco, James A., 1945- Martin Luther King,
Jr. . New York , 1988. x, 238 p. ; ISBN
0-312-02365-0 : DDC 323.4/092/4 B 19
E185.97.K5 C65 1988   NYPL [Sc D 89-231]

Haines, Herbert H. Black radicals and the civil
rights mainstream, 1954-1970 /. Knoxville ,
c19. xii, 231 p. : ISBN 0-87049-563-1 (alk. paper) :
DDC 305.8/96073 19
E185.615 .H25 1988   NYPL [Sc E 88-511]

Harlan, Louis R. Booker T. Washington in
perspective . Jackson , c1988. xii, 210 p., [8] p.

of plates : ISBN 0-87805-374-3 (alk. paper) DDC
378/.111 B 19
E185.97.W4 H36 1988   NYPL [Sc E 89-217]

Horne, Gerald. Communist front? . Rutherford
[N.J.] , London , c1988. 454 p. ; ISBN
0-8386-3285-8 (alk. paper) DDC
323.1/196073/073 19
E185.61 .H8 1988   NYPL [Sc E 88-147]

Lipsitz, George. A life in the struggle .
Philadelphia , 1988. viii, 292 p. : ISBN
0-87722-550-8 (alk. paper) DDC
973/.0496073024 B 19
E185.97.P49 L57 1988   NYPL [Sc E 89-43]

Saunders, Doris E. The Kennedy years and the
Negro . Chicago , 1964. xiii, 143 p. :
NYPL [Sc F 89-75]

Smith, J. Owens. Blacks and American
government . Dubuque, Iowa , c1987. xii, 148
p. : ISBN 0-8403-4407-4 (pbk.) DDC 323.1/196073
19
E185.615 .S576 1987   NYPL [Sc E 89-193]

Walton, Hanes, 1941- When the marching
stopped . Albany , c1988. xxiv, 263 p. : ISBN
0-88706-687-9 DDC 353.0081/1 19
E185.615 .W325 1988   NYPL [Sc E 89-10]

**AFRO-AMERICANS - CIVIL RIGHTS -
ADDRESSES, ESSAYS, LECTURES.**
White House Conference "To Fulfill These
Rights", Washington, D. C., 1966. Major
addresses at the White House Conference to
Fulfill These Rights, June 1-2, 1966.
[Washington, 1966] 66 p. DDC 323.4/09174/96
E185.615 .W45 1966c   NYPL [Sc E 88-386]

**AFRO-AMERICANS - CIVIL RIGHTS -
HISTORY.**
Simba, Malik. The Black laborer, the Black
legal experience and the United States Supreme
Court with emphasis on the neo-concept of
equal employment [microform] /. 1977. 357
leaves.   *NYPL [Sc Micro R-4706]*

Swinney, Everette, 1923- Suppressing the Ku
Klux Klan . New York , 1987. ix, 360 p. ;
ISBN 0-8240-8297-4 (alk. paper) : DDC
342.73/0873 347.302873 19
KF4757 .S93 1987   NYPL [Sc D 88-653]

**AFRO-AMERICANS - CIVIL RIGHTS -
HISTORY - 20TH CENTURY -
JUVENILE LITERATURE.**
Rosset, Lisa. James Baldwin /. New York,
N.Y. , 1989. 111 p. : ISBN 1-555-46572-2 DDC
818/.5409 B 92 19
PS3552.A45 Z87 1989   NYPL [Sc E 89-224]

**AFRO-AMERICANS - CIVIL RIGHTS -
JUVENILE LITERATURE.**
Hanley, Sally. A. Philip Randolph /. New York
[1988], c1989. 110 p. : ISBN 1-555-46607-9 DDC
323.4/092/4 92 19
E185.97.R27 H36 1989   NYPL [Sc E 88-617]

**AFRO-AMERICANS - CIVIL RIGHTS -
KENTUCKY.**
Johnson, Lyman T., 1906- The rest of the
dream . Lexington, Ky. , c1988. xiv, 230 p., [8]
p. of plates : ISBN 0-8131-1674-0 (alk. paper) :
DDC 976.9/00496073024 B 19
E185.97.J693 A3 1988   NYPL [Sc E 89-211]

**AFRO-AMERICANS - CIVIL RIGHTS -
MISSISSIPPI.**
McAdam, Doug. Freedom Summer /. New
York , c1988. [xiii], 333 p., [14] p. of plates :
ISBN 0-19-504367-7 (alk. paper) DDC
976.2/00496073 19
E185.93.M6 M28 1988   NYPL [Sc E 88-563]

**AFRO-AMERICANS - CIVIL RIGHTS -
MISSISSIPPI - JACKSON.**
Spofford, Tim. Lynch Street . Kent, Ohio ,
c1988. 219 p., [1] leaf of plates : ISBN
0-87338-355-9 (alk. paper) DDC 976.2/51 19
F349.J13 S66 1988   NYPL [Sc E 89-27]

**AFRO-AMERICANS - CIVIL RIGHTS -
MISSOURI - SAINT LOUIS.**
Lipsitz, George. A life in the struggle .
Philadelphia , 1988. viii, 292 p. : ISBN
0-87722-550-8 (alk. paper) DDC
973/.0496073024 B 19
E185.97.P49 L57 1988   NYPL [Sc E 89-43]

**AFRO-AMERICANS - CIVIL RIGHTS -
SOUTHERN STATES.**
Ashmore, Harry S. Hearts and minds . Cabin
John, Md. , c1988. xviii, 513 p. ; ISBN
0-932020-58-5 (pbk. : alk. paper) DDC

305.8/96073 19
E185.615 .A83 1988   NYPL [Sc D 89-382]

Peake, Thomas R., 1939- Keeping the dream
alive . New York , 1987. xiv, 492 p. : ISBN
0-8204-0397-0 : DDC 323.42/3/06073 19
E185.61 .P4 1987   NYPL [Sc D 88-444]

AFRO-AMERICANS - COLLECTIBLES.
Reno, Dawn E. Collecting Black Americana /.
New York , c1986. vii, 150 p. : ISBN
0-517-56095-X DDC 700/.8996073/075 19
NK839.3.A35 R46 1986   NYPL [Sc F 87-6]

**AFRO-AMERICANS - COLONIZATION -
AFRICA.**
American Colonization Society. Board of
Managers. Address of the Board of Managers of
the American Colonization Society, to the
auxiliary societies and the people of the United
States. Washington, 1820. 32 p. ;
NYPL [Sc Rare G 86-23]

Colonization Society of the County of Oneida.
To the inhabitants of Oneida County. [Utica,
N.Y. , 1838?] 8 p. ;
NYPL [Sc Rare G 86-40]

**AFRO-AMERICANS - COLONIZATION -
AFRICA - HISTORY - 19TH CENTURY.**
Kinshasa, Kwando Mbiassi. Emigration vs.
assimilation . Jefferson, N.C. , 1988. xiv, 234
p. ; ISBN 0-89950-338-1 (lib. bdg.) DDC
973/.0496073 19
E185 .K49 1988   NYPL [IEC 88-2401]

**AFRO-AMERICANS - COLONIZATION -
LIBERIA.**
Birney, James Gillespie, 1792-1857.
Examination of the decision of the Supreme
Court of the United States, in the case of
Strader, Gorman and Armstrong vs.
Christopher Graham . Cincinnati , 1852. iv, [1],
6-46, [1] p. ;
E450 .B57   NYPL [Sc Rare F 88-37]

Johnson, Charles Spurgeon, 1893-1956. Bitter
Canaan . New Brunswick, N.J. , c1987. lxxiii,
256 p. ; ISBN 0-88738-053-0 : DDC 966.6/2 19
DT631 .J59 1987   NYPL [Sc E 88-351]

Rutherfoord, John Coles 1825-1866. Speech of
John C. Rutherfoord, of Goochland, in the
House of Delegates of Virginia, on the removal
from the Commonwealth of the free colored
population . Richmond , 1853. 20 p. ;
NYPL [Sc Rare C 89-10]

Williams, Alfred Brockenbrough, 1856-1930.
The Liberian exodus. Charleston, S.C., 1878. 62
p.
E448 .W53   NYPL [Sc Rare F 88-58]

Worcester County Colonization Society. Report
made at an adjourned meeting of the friends of
the American Colonization Society, in
Worcester County, held in Worcester, Dec. 8,
1830 /. Worcester , 1831. 20 p. ;
NYPL [Sc Rare G 86-29]

AFRO-AMERICANS - CONDUCT OF LIFE.
Coleman, Mel. The Black gestalt . Minneapolis,
Minnesota , 1987. 118 p. :
NYPL [Sc D 88-292]

AFRO-AMERICANS - CONGRESSES.
White House Conference "To Fulfill These
Rights", Washington, D. C., 1966. Major
addresses at the White House Conference to
Fulfill These Rights, June 1-2, 1966.
[Washington, 1966] 66 p. DDC 323.4/09174/96
E185.615 .W45 1966c   NYPL [Sc E 88-386]

AFRO-AMERICANS - CORRESPONDENCE.
Washington, Booker T. 1856-1915. The Booker
T. Washington papers. Urbana [1972- v.
NYPL [Sc B-Washington, B.]

**AFRO-AMERICANS - CULTURAL
ASSIMILATION - HISTORY - 19TH
CENTURY.**
Kinshasa, Kwando Mbiassi. Emigration vs.
assimilation . Jefferson, N.C. , 1988. xiv, 234
p. ; ISBN 0-89950-338-1 (lib. bdg.) DDC
973/.0496073 19
E185 .K49 1988   NYPL [IEC 88-2401]

AFRO-AMERICANS - DANCING.
Haskins, James, 1941- Mr. Bojangles . New
York , 1988. 336 p. : ISBN 0-688-07203-8 :
DDC 793.3/2/0924 B 19
GV1785.R54 H37 1988

NYPL [Sc D 88-851]

AFRO-AMERICANS - DISEASES.
EVAXX. Black Americans' attitudes toward cancer and cancer tests /. [New York], 1981. 1 v. (various pagings) ;   *NYPL [Sc F 88-293]*

AFRO-AMERICANS - DOMESTIC RELATIONS.
Hare, Nathan. The endangered Black family . San Francisco, CA , c1984. 192 p. ;   ISBN 0-9613086-0-5   *NYPL [Sc C 88-307]*

AFRO-AMERICANS - DRAMA.
Totem voices . New York , 1989. lxiii, 523 p. ;   ISBN 0-8021-1053-3 :   DDC 812/.54/080896 19
PS628.N4 T68 1988   *NYPL [Sc D 89-381]*

Wallace, G. L. Them next door [microform] . New York , 1974. 36 p. :
NYPL [Sc Micro F-11011]

AFRO-AMERICANS - ECONOMIC CONDITIONS.
Black economic progress . Washington, D.C. , Lanham, Md. , 1988. xi, 52 p. :   ISBN 0-941410-69-2 (alk. paper)   DDC 330.973/008996073 19
E185.8 .B496 1988   *NYPL [Sc E 89-154]*

Black workers . Philadelphia , 1989. xv, 733 p. ;   ISBN 0-87722-592-3   *NYPL [Sc E 89-206]*

Harris, Abram Lincoln, 1899-1963. Race, radicalism, and reform . New Brunswick, U.S.A. , c1989. viii, 521 p. ;   ISBN 0-88738-210-X   DDC 305.8/96073 19
E185.8 .H27 1989   *NYPL [Sc E 89-166]*

Quiet riots . New York , 1988. xiii, 223 p. ;   ISBN 0-394-57473-7 :   DDC 305.5/69/0973 19
HV4045 .Q54 1988   *NYPL [JLD 89-239]*

Staples, Robert. The urban plantation . Oakland, CA , c1987. 248 p. ;   ISBN 0-933296-13-4 (pbk.)
NYPL [Sc D 88-1021]

Symposium on race and class. Philadelphia , 1984. 62 p. ;   *NYPL [Sc D 88-2]*

AFRO-AMERICANS - ECONOMIC CONDITIONS - HISTORY.
Crew, Spencer R. Field to factory . Washington, D.C. , 1987. 79 p., [4] p. of plates :   *NYPL [Sc F 88-369]*

AFRO-AMERICANS - EDUCATION - ARKANSAS - HISTORY - SOURCES.
United States. Bureau of Refugees, Freedmen and Abandoned Lands. Records of the Superintendent of Education for the State of Arkansas, Bureau of Refugees, Freedmen, and Abandoned Lands, 1865-1871 [microform] 1865-1871. 10 v.   *NYPL [Sc Micro R-4643]*

AFRO-AMERICANS - EDUCATION - DISTRICT OF COLUMBIA - HISTORY - SOURCES.
United States. Bureau of Refugees, Freedmen and Abandoned Lands. Records of the Superintendent of Education for the District of Columbia, Bureau of Refugees, Freedmen, and Abandoned Lands, 1865-1872 [microform] 1865-1872. 11 bound v., 15 ft. of unbound doc.   *NYPL [Sc Micro R-4645]*

AFRO-AMERICANS - EDUCATION (HIGHER)
Recruitment and retention of Black students in higher education /. Lanham, MD , c1989. viii, 135 p. ;   ISBN 0-8191-7292-8 (alk. paper)   DDC 378/.1982 19
LC2781 .R43 1989   *NYPL [Sc D 89-590]*

The Status of Blacks in higher education /. Lanham, MD [Washington, D.C.] , c1989. ix, 110 p. ;   ISBN 0-8191-7286-3 (alk. paper)   DDC 378/.008996073 19
LC2781 .S72 1988   *NYPL [Sc D 89-589]*

AFRO-AMERICANS - EDUCATION (HIGHER) - CONGRESSES.
Economic issues and black colleges /. Chicago , c1986. 59 p. ;   ISBN 0-695-60053-2
NYPL [Sc D 88-950]

AFRO-AMERICANS - EDUCATION (HIGHER) - MASSACHUSETTS - CAMBRIDGE.
Varieties of black experience at Harvard . Cambridge [Mass.] , 1986. v, 180 p. ;
LD2160 .V37x 1986   *NYPL [Sc D 88-672]*

AFRO-AMERICANS - EDUCATION (HIGHER) - UNITED STATES.
The Black/white colleges . Washington, D.C. , 1981. v, 46 p. :   *NYPL [Sc F 89-48]*

AFRO-AMERICANS - EDUCATION - NEW YORK (N.Y.)
Rury, John L. Education and Black community development in ante-bellum New York City /. 1975. 100 leaves ;   *NYPL [Sc F 89-114]*

AFRO-AMERICANS - EDUCATION - NORTH CAROLINA - HISTORY - SOURCES.
United States. Bureau of Refugees, Freedmen and Abandoned Lands. Records of the Superintendent of Education for the State of North Carolina, Bureau of Refugees, Freedmen, and Abandoned Lands, 1865-1870 [microform] 1865-1870. 7 ft. (24 v.)
NYPL [Sc Micro R-4647]

AFRO-AMERICANS - EDUCATION - OKLAHOMA - HISTORY.
Cayton, Leonard Bernard. A history of Black public education in Oklahoma [microform] /. 1976. 170 leaves.   *NYPL [Sc Micro R-4692]*

AFRO-AMERICANS - EDUCATION - READING.
Hillman, Chrisanthia. The relationship between self-esteem and academic achievement among Black students in remedial reading instruction at a community college [microform] /. 1981. 60 leaves.   *NYPL [Sc Micro R-4686]*

AFRO-AMERICANS - EDUCATION - SOUTHERN STATES - HISTORY - 19TH CENTURY.
Anderson, James D., 1944- The education of Blacks in the South, 1860-1935 /. Chapel Hill , c1988. xiv, 366 p. :   ISBN 0-8078-1793-7 (alk. paper)   DDC 370/.0889073075 19
LC2802.S9 A53 1988   *NYPL [Sc E 88-457]*

AFRO-AMERICANS - EDUCATION - SOUTHERN STATES - HISTORY - 20TH CENTURY.
Anderson, James D., 1944- The education of Blacks in the South, 1860-1935 /. Chapel Hill , c1988. xiv, 366 p. :   ISBN 0-8078-1793-7 (alk. paper)   DDC 370/.0889073075 19
LC2802.S9 A53 1988   *NYPL [Sc E 88-457]*

AFRO-AMERICANS - EDUCATION - SOUTHERN STATES - HISTORY - SOURCES.
United States. Bureau of Refugees, Freedmen and Abandoned Lands. Education Division. Records of the Education Division of the Bureau of Refugees, Freedmen, and Abandoned Lands, 1865-1871 [microform] 1865-1871. 23 v.
NYPL [Sc Micro R-4641]

AFRO-AMERICANS - EDUCATION - VIRGINIA - HISTORY - 19TH CENTURY.
Horst, Samuel L., 1919- Education for manhood . Lanham, MD , c1987. viii, 292 p. ;   ISBN 0-8191-6662-6 (alk. paper) :   DDC 370/.89090730755 19
LC2802.V8 H67 1987   *NYPL [Sc D 88-550]*

AFRO-AMERICANS - EMPLOYMENT - CONGRESSES.
Black working women . Berkeley, Calif. [1981?] vii, 222 p. :   *NYPL [Sc F 89-33]*

AFRO-AMERICANS - EMPLOYMENT - HISTORY.
Black workers . Philadelphia , 1989. xv, 733 p. ;   ISBN 0-87722-592-3   *NYPL [Sc E 89-206]*

AFRO-AMERICANS - EMPLOYMENT - ILLINOIS - CHICAGO.
Salmon, Jaslin U. Black executives in white-owned businesses and industries in the Chicago metropolitan area [microform] /. 1977. 197 leaves.   *NYPL [Sc Micro R-4703]*

AFRO-AMERICANS - EMPLOYMENT - LAW AND LEGISLATION - HISTORY.
Simba, Malik. The Black laborer, the Black legal experience and the United States Supreme Court with emphasis on the neo-concept of equal employment [microform] /. 1977. 357 leaves.   *NYPL [Sc Micro R-4706]*

AFRO-AMERICANS - EMPLOYMENT - SOUTH CAROLINA - HISTORY - 19TH CENTURY.
Koger, Larry, 1958- Black slaveowners . Jefferson, N.C. , 1985. xiii, 286 p. ;   ISBN 0-89950-160-5 :   DDC 975.7/00496073 19
E445.S7 K64 1985   *NYPL [Sc E 88-473]*

AFRO-AMERICANS - FAMILIES.
Toward reflective analysis of Black families .

[Atlanta] , 1976. ii, 74 l. :
NYPL [Sc F 88-224]

AFRO-AMERICANS FAMILIES - MENTAL HEALTH.
Boyd-Franklin, Nancy. Black families in therapy . New York, N.Y. , c1989. xiv, 274 p. :   ISBN 0-89862-735-4   DDC 616.89/156/08996073 19
RC451.5.N4 B69 1988   *NYPL [Sc E 89-242]*

AFRO-AMERICANS - FAMILIES - PROBLEMS, EXERCISES, ETC.
Nobles, Wade W. The KM ebit husia . Oakland, California , 1985. 201 p. ;   ISBN 0-939205-03-3   *NYPL [Sc F 88-159]*

AFRO-AMERICANS - FAMILIES - RESEARCH.
Nobles, Wade W. Understanding the Black family . Oakland, California , 1984. 137 p. ;   ISBN 0-939205-00-9   *NYPL [Sc D 88-697]*

AFRO-AMERICANS - FICTION.
Banner, Warren M. Have you got it? . New York , c1987. x, 371 p. ;   ISBN 0-533-07057-0   *NYPL [Sc E 89-68]*

Carn, John, 1947- Stressed out . Indianapolis, Ind. , c1988. vii, 148 p. ;   ISBN 0-916967-03-4 :   *NYPL [Sc D 89-423]*

Cartiér, Xam Wilson. Be-bop, re-bop /. New York , c1987. 147 p. ;   ISBN 0-345-34833-8 (pbk.) :   *NYPL [Sc D 88-716]*

Colter, Cyrus. A chocolate soldier . New York , c1988. 278 p. ;   ISBN 0-938410-42-3 :   DDC 813/.54 19
PS3553.O477 C5 1988
NYPL [Sc D 88-1396]

Cooper, J. California. Some soul to keep /. New York , c1987. xi, 211 p. ;   ISBN 0-312-00684-5 :   DDC 813/.54 19
PS3553.O5874 S6 1987
NYPL [JFD 88-7431]

Fauset, Jessie Redmon. There is confusion. London , 1924. 297 p.
PZ3 .F276.Th   *NYPL [Sc Rare C 88-20]*

Flowers, A. R. De mojo blues . New York , 1986, c1985. 216 p. ;   ISBN 0-525-24376-3 :   DDC 813/.54 19
PS3556.L598 D4 1986   *NYPL [JFD 86-3984]*

Fuller, Louisia. The risks of Ro . Teaneck, N.J. , c1988. 105 p. ;   ISBN 0-945779-00-3
NYPL [Sc D 88-1172]

Harper, Frances Ellen Watkins, 1825-1911. Iola Leroy, or, Shadows uplifted /. New York , 1988. xxxix, 281 p. :   ISBN 0-19-505240-4 (alk. paper)   DDC 813/.3 19
PS1799.H7 I6 1988   *NYPL [JFC 88-2190]*

Hopkins, Pauline E. (Pauline Elizabeth) Contending forces . New York , 1988. xlviii, 402 p., [8] p. of plates :   ISBN 0-19-505258-7 (alk. paper)   DDC 813/.4 19
PS1999.H4226 C66 1988
NYPL [JFC 88-2153]

Hopkins, Pauline E. (Pauline Elizabeth) [Novels. Selections.] The magazine novels of Pauline Hopkins /. New York , Oxford , 1988. l, 621 p. ;   ISBN 0-19-505248-X (alk. paper)   DDC 813/.4 19
PS1999.H4226 A6 1988
NYPL [JFC 88-2195]

McElroy, Colleen J. Jesus and Fat Tuesday . Berkeley, Calif. , c1987. 202 p. ;   ISBN 0-88739-023-4 (pbk.)   *NYPL [Sc D 88-586]*

Millar, Margaret. Spider webs /. New York , c1986. 323 p. ;   ISBN 0-930330-76-5
NYPL [Sc C 88-350]

Morrison, Toni. Tar baby /. New York , 1981. 305 p. ;   ISBN 0-452-26012-4
NYPL [Sc D 88-1105]

Sampson, Emma Speed, 1868-1947. Miss Minerva's baby /. Chicago , c1920. 320 p. :
PZ7.S16 Mis   *NYPL [Sc C 88-71]*

Thomas, Joyce Carol. Journey /. New York , c1988. 153 p. ;   ISBN 0-590-40627-2 :   DDC [Fic] 19
PZ7.T36696 Jo 1988   *NYPL [Sc D 89-235]*

Thomas, Veona. Never too late to love /. Saddle Brook, N. J. , 1987. 69 p. :
NYPL [Sc D 87-1427]

Walker, Alice, 1944- The color purple . New

York , c1982. 245 p. ; ISBN 0-15-119153-0 :
DDC 813/.54 19
PS3573.A425 C6 1982
NYPL [Sc Rare F 88-3]

Walker, Alice, 1944- The color purple /.
London , 1983 (1986 [printing]) 245 p. : ISBN
0-7043-3905-6 (pbk) : DDC 813/.54 19
NYPL [Sc C 88-143]

Wideman, John Edgar. The lynchers /. New
York , 1986. 264 p. ; ISBN 0-8050-0118-2 (pbk.) :
DDC 813/.54 19
PS3573.I26 L9 1986   **NYPL [Sc D 88-306]**

Wideman, John Edgar. Reuben . New York ,
c1987. 215 p. ; ISBN 0-8050-0375-4 DDC
813/.54 19
PS3573.I26 R4 1987   **NYPL [JFE 88-3493]**

AFRO-AMERICANS - FICTIONS.
Walker, Alice, 1844- [Color purple. Portuguese.]
A Cor púrpura /. Lisboa , 1986. 244 p. ;
NYPL [Sc D 88-388]

**AFRO-AMERICANS - FLORIDA - FORT
LAUDERDALE.**
A walk through the neighborhood. Ft.
Lauderdale, Fla. , c1985. 88 p. :
NYPL [Sc D 88-1414]

AFRO-AMERICANS - FOLKLORE.
Branner, John Casper, 1850-1922. How and
why stories /. New York , 1921. xi, 104 p. :
NYPL [Sc D 89-104]

Gates, Henry Louis. The signifying monkey .
New York , 1988. xxviii, 290 p. : ISBN
0-19-503463-5 (alk. paper) DDC 810/.9/896073
19
PS153.N5 G28 1988   **NYPL [Sc E 89-181]**

Lester, Julius. More tales of Uncle Remus .
New York , c1988. xvi, 143 p. : ISBN
0-8037-0419-4 DDC 398.2/08996073 19
PZ8.1.L434 Mo 1988   **NYPL [Sc E 88-458]**

Tracy, Steven C. (Steven Carl), 1954- Langston
Hughes & the blues /. Urbana , c1988. xiii, 305
p. ; ISBN 0-252-01457-X (alk. paper) DDC
818/.5209 19
PS3515.U274 Z8 1988   **NYPL [Sc E 88-506]**

**AFRO-AMERICANS - FRANCE - PARIS -
FICTION.**
Simon, Njami. [Cercueil & Cie. English.]
Coffin & Co. /. Berkeley, CA , c1987. 195 p. ;
ISBN 0-88739-049-8 (pbk.)
NYPL [Sc C 89-144]

AFRO-AMERICANS - GENEALOGY.
Redford, Dorothy Spruill. Somerset
homecoming . New York , c1988. xviii, 266 p. :
ISBN 0-385-24245-X : DDC
929/.3/089960730756 19
E185.96 .R42 1988   **NYPL [Sc E 88-498]**

Woodson, Minnie Shumate. The Sable curtain
/. Washington, D.C. , 1987, c1985. 380, 12 p. :
ISBN 0-943153-00-X   **NYPL [Sc D 88-68]**

**AFRO-AMERICANS - GENEALOGY -
BIBLIOGRAPHY.**
Lawson, Sandra M. Generations past .
Washington , 1988. 101 p. : ISBN 0-8444-0604-X
DDC 016.929/1/08996073 19
Z1361.N39 L34 1988 E185.96
NYPL [Sc D 89-360]

**AFRO-AMERICANS - GENEALOGY -
HANDBOOKS, MANUALS, ETC.**
Boykin, Yogi Rudolph. [Discovering my "AA"
family roots] Winthorp, Wash. , c1978. 106
p. :   **NYPL [Sc F 89-91]**

AFRO-AMERICANS - GEORGIA - FICTION.
Major, Clarence. Such was the season . San
Francisco , c1987. 213 p. ; ISBN 0-916515-20-6 :
DDC 813/.54 19
PS3563.A39 S8 1987   **NYPL [Sc D 88-744]**

**AFRO-AMERICANS - GEORGIA - JUVENILE
FICTION.**
Herlihy, Dirlie. Ludie's song /. New York ,
c1988. 212 p. ; ISBN 0-8037-0533-6 : DDC [Fic]
19
PZ7.H43126 Lu 1988   **NYPL [Sc D 89-132]**

**AFRO-AMERICANS - HARLEM (NEW YORK,
N.Y.) - FICTION.**
McKay, Claude, 1890-1948. Home to Harlem /.
Boston , 1987, c1928. xxvi, 340 p. ; ISBN
1-555-53023-0 (alk. paper) : DDC 813/.52 19
PS3525.A24785 H6 1987
NYPL [Sc D 88-544]

**AFRO-AMERICANS - HEALTH AND
HYGIENE.**
Currents of health policy . New York , 1987. 2
v. :   **NYPL [Sc D 88-1205]**

Williams, Richard, Ed. D. They stole it, but
you must return it /. Rochester, New York ,
c1986. vii, 130 p. ; ISBN 0-938805-00-2 (pbk.)
DDC 306.8/5/08996073 19
E185.86 .W49 1986   **NYPL [Sc D 88-1308]**

**AFRO-AMERICANS - HEALTH AND
HYGIENE - SOUTHERN STATES -
HISTORY - 20TH CENTURY.**
Beardsley, Edward H. A history of neglect .
Knoxville , c1987. xvi, 383 p. : ISBN
0-87049-523-2 (alk. paper) : DDC 362.1/0425
19
RA448.5.N4 B33 1987   **NYPL [Sc E 87-625]**

**AFRO-AMERICANS - HEALTH AND
HYGIENE - UNITED STATES.**
United States. Dept. of Health and Human
Services. Task Force on Black and Minority
Health. Report of the Secretary's Task Force on
Black & Minority Health. Washington, D.C. ,
1985-1986. 8 v. in 9 : DDC 362.1/08996073 19
RA448.5.N4 U55 1985   **NYPL [JLM 86-589]**

**AFRO-AMERICANS - HEALTH AND
HYGIENE - UNITED STATES -
STATISTICS.**
United States. Dept. of Health and Human
Services. Task Force on Black and Minority
Health. Report of the Secretary's Task Force on
Black & Minority Health. Washington, D.C. ,
1985-1986. 8 v. in 9 : DDC 362.1/08996073 19
RA448.5.N4 U55 1985   **NYPL [JLM 86-589]**

AFRO-AMERICANS - HISTORIOGRAPHY.
Quarles, Benjamin. Black mosaic . Amherst,
Mass. , 1988. 213 p. ; ISBN 0-87023-604-0 (alk.
paper) DDC 973/.0496073 19
E185 .Q19 1988   **NYPL [Sc E 88-330]**

AFRO-AMERICANS - HISTORY.
Drimmer, Melvin. Issues in Black history .
Dubuque, Iowa , c1987. xviii, 308 p. ; ISBN
0-8403-4174-1 (pbk.) DDC 973/.0496073 19
E185 .D715 1987   **NYPL [Sc E 88-107]**

Johnson, Edward A. (Edward Augustus),
1860-1944. A school history of the Negro race
in America from 1619 to 1890 . Chicago ,
1894. 200 p. :   **NYPL [Sc Rare F 88-9]**

Kletzing, Henry F., 1850- Progress of a race.
Atlanta, Ga., 1897. xxiv, 23-663 p. :
NYPL [Sc 973-K]

Moore, Richard B. (Richard Benjamin) Richard
B. Moore, Caribbean militant in Harlem .
Bloomington , London , 1988. ix, 324 p. :
ISBN 0-253-31299-0 DDC 970.004/96 19
F2183 .M66 1988   **NYPL [Sc E 89-148]**

Quarles, Benjamin. Black mosaic . Amherst,
Mass. , 1988. 213 p. : ISBN 0-87023-604-0 (alk.
paper) DDC 973/.0496073 19
E185 .Q19 1988   **NYPL [Sc E 88-330]**

Quarles, Benjamin. The Negro in the making of
America /. New York , c1987. 362
p. ; ISBN 0-02-036140-8 DDC 973/.0496073 19
E185 .Q2 1987   **NYPL [Sc C 88-364]**

AFRO-AMERICANS - HISTORY - TO 1863.
Bowen, David Warren, 1944- Andrew Johnson
and the Negro /. Knoxville , c1989. xvi, 206
p. ; ISBN 0-87049-584-4 (alk. paper) DDC
973/.0496073 19
E667 .B65 1989   **NYPL [Sc D 89-508]**

Bullwhip days . New York , c1988. xviii, 460
p. : ISBN 1-555-84210-0 DDC 973/.0496073022 B
19
E444 .B95 1988   **NYPL [IEC 89-3083]**

Cheek, William F., 1933- John Mercer
Langston and the fight for Black freedom,
1829-65 /. Urbana , c1989. 478 p. ; ISBN
0-252-01550-9 (alk. paper) DDC
973/.0496073/0924 B 19
E185.97.L27 C48 1989   **NYPL [Sc E 89-255]**

Kinshasa, Kwando Mbiassi. Emigration vs.
assimilation . Jefferson, N.C. , 1988. xiv, 234
p. ; ISBN 0-89950-338-1 (lib. bdg.) DDC
973/.0496073 19
E185 .K49 1988   **NYPL [IEC 88-2401]**

Werner, John M., 1941- Reaping the bloody
harvest . New York , 1986. 333 p. ; ISBN
0-8240-8301-6 (alk. paper) : DDC 973.5/6 19
E185 .W44 1986   **NYPL [Sc E 88-242]**

Which path to freedom? . Pomona, Calif. ,
c1986. iv, 60 p. ; DDC 973.7/114 19
E449 .W565 1986   **NYPL [Sc D 88-1154]**

**AFRO-AMERICANS - HISTORY - 19TH
CENTURY.**
Black leaders of the nineteenth century /.
Urbana , c1988. xii, 344 p. : ISBN 0-252-01506-1
(alk. paper) DDC 920/.009296073 19
E185.96 .B535 1988   **NYPL [Sc E 88-365]**

AFRO-AMERICANS - HISTORY - 1863-1877.
Bowen, David Warren, 1944- Andrew Johnson
and the Negro /. Knoxville , c1989. xvi, 206
p. ; ISBN 0-87049-584-4 (alk. paper) DDC
973/.0496073 19
E667 .B65 1989   **NYPL [Sc D 89-508]**

Foner, Eric. Reconstruction, America's
unfinished revolution, 1863-1877 /. New York ,
c1988. xxvii, 690 p., [8] p. of plates : ISBN
0-06-015851-4 : DDC 973.8 19
E668 .F66 1988   **NYPL [*R-IKR 88-5216]**

**AFRO-AMERICANS - HISTORY - 1863-1877 -
JUVENILE FICTION.**
Hansen, Joyce. Out from this place /. New
York , 1988. vi, 135 p. ; ISBN 0-8027-6816-4
DDC [Fic] 19
PZ7.H19825 Ou 1988   **NYPL [Sc D 88-1321]**

**AFRO-AMERICANS - HISTORY - 1863-1877 -
PICTORIAL WORKS - EXHIBITIONS.**
Wood, Peter H., 1943- Winslow Homer's
images of Blacks . Austin , c1988. 144 p. :
ISBN 0-292-79047-3 (University of Texas Press)
DDC 759.13 19
ND237.H7 A4 1988a   **NYPL [Sc F 89-133]**

AFRO-AMERICANS - HISTORY - 1877-1964.
Meier, August, 1923- Negro thought in
America, 1880-1915 . Ann Arbor , 1988,
c1963. xii, 336 p. ; ISBN 0-472-64230-8 DDC
973/.0496073 19
E185.6 .M5 1988   **NYPL [Sc D 89-509]**

Pomerance, Alan. Repeal of the blues /.
Secaucus, N.J. , c1988. x, 264 p., [16] p. of
plates : ISBN 0-8065-1105-2 : DDC
792/.08996073 19
PN1590.B53 P6 1988   **NYPL [Sc E 89-90]**

Saunders, Doris E. The Kennedy years and the
Negro . Chicago , 1964. xiii, 143 p. :
NYPL [Sc F 89-75]

**AFRO-AMERICANS - HISTORY - 1877-1964 -
JUVENILE LITERATURE.**
Drisko, Carol F. The unfinished march. Garden
City, N.Y. , 1967. 118 p. : DDC 973.8 (j)
E185.6 .D7   **NYPL [Sc D 88-1429]**

**AFRO-AMERICANS - HISTORY -
ADDRESSES, ESSAYS, LECTURES.**
Washington, Booker T. 1856-1915. A new
Negro for a new century. Miami, Fla., 1969.
428 p. DDC 301.45/22
E185 .W315 1969b   **NYPL [Sc D 89-43]**

**AFRO-AMERICANS - HISTORY -
BIBLIOGRAPHY.**
Moss, S. G. Slavery and emancipation . St.
Michael, Barbados , 1986. 61 l. ;
NYPL [Sc F 88-83]

AFRO-AMERICANS - HISTORY - DRAMA.
The Blacker the berry . [Providence, R.I.]
[1980?] 20 p. :   **NYPL [Sc F 89-80]**

**AFRO-AMERICANS - HISTORY - JUVENILE
LITERATURE.**
Sealy, Adrienne V. The color your way into
Black history book /. Brooklyn, N.Y. , c1980.
51 p. : ISBN 0-9602670-6-9
NYPL [Sc F 89-36]

AFRO-AMERICANS - HISTORY - SOURCES.
Afro-American history . Chicago, Ill. , c1988.
xv, 464 p. ; ISBN 0-256-06306-0 (pbk.) DDC
973/.0496073 19
E184.6 .A35 1988   **NYPL [Sc E 89-44]**

Washington, Booker T. 1856-1915. The Booker
T. Washington papers. Urbana [1972- v.
NYPL [Sc B-Washington, B.]

**AFRO-AMERICANS - HISTORY - STUDY
AND TEACHING.**
Thinking and rethinking U. S. history /. New
York, N.Y. , c1988. 389 p. ;
NYPL [Sc F 89-130]

**AFRO-AMERICANS - HOUSING -
MICHIGAN - DETROIT.**
Detroit, race and uneven development /.
Philadelphia , 1987. xii, 317 p. : ISBN

0-87722-485-4 (alk. paper) DDC
305.8/009774/34 19
HC108.D6 D47 1987   **NYPL [Sc E 88-205]**

**AFRO-AMERICANS - ILLINOIS - CHICAGO -
BIOGRAPHY.**
Monroe, Sylvester. Brothers . New York, N.Y. ,
c1988. 284 p. : ISBN 0-688-07622-X DDC
977.3/1100496073 B 19
F548.9.N4 M66 1988   **NYPL [Sc E 88-356]**

Wilson, Mary, 1938- To Benji, with love /.
Chicago , c1987. p. cm. ISBN 0-910671-07-9 :
DDC 977.3/11043/0924 B 19
F548.9.N4 W559 1987
    NYPL [Sc D 88-1219]

**AFRO-AMERICANS - ILLINOIS - CHICAGO -
DIRECTORY.**
Rhea's new citizen's directory of Chicago, Ill.
and suburban towns . Chicago, Ill. , 1908. 173
p. :   **NYPL [Sc Rare F 89-3]**

**AFRO-AMERICANS - ILLINOIS -
GENEALOGY.**
Tregillis, Helen Cox. River roads to freedom .
Bowie, Md. , 1988. 122 p. : ISBN 1-556-13120-8
DDC 929/.3/08996073 19
F540 .T7 1988   **NYPL [Sc D 88-1442]**

AFRO-AMERICANS IN ART.
Images of Blacks in American culture . New
York , 1988. xvii, 390 p. : ISBN 0-313-24844-3
(lib. bdg. : alk. paper) DDC 700 19
NX652.A37 I43 1988   **NYPL [Sc E 88-466]**

**AFRO-AMERICANS IN ART -
EXHIBITIONS.**
Wood, Peter H., 1943- Winslow Homer's
images of Blacks. Austin , c1988. 144 p. :
ISBN 0-292-79047-3 (University of Texas Press)
DDC 759.13 19
ND237.H7 A4 1988a   **NYPL [Sc F 89-133]**

**AFRO-AMERICANS IN DRAMA. see AFRO-
AMERICANS IN LITERATURE.**

**AFRO-AMERICANS IN FICTION. see AFRO-
AMERICANS IN LITERATURE.**

AFRO-AMERICANS IN LITERATURE.
Baker, Houston A. Afro-American poetics .
Madison, Wis. , c1988. x, 201 p. : ISBN
0-299-11500-3 : DDC 810/.9/896073 19
PS153.N5 B22 1988   **NYPL [Sc D 88-1356]**

Brenowitz, Ruth. A study of the portrayal of
Black Americans in the dramatic literature of
the United States [microform] /. 1969. 92
leaves.   **NYPL [Sc Micro R-4691]**

Brown, Sterling Allen, 1901- Negro poetry and
drama /. Washington, D.C. , c1937. 142 p. ;
    NYPL [Sc D 89-105]

Callahan, John F. In the African-American
grain . Urbana , c1988. 280 p. ; ISBN
0-252-01459-6 (alk. paper) DDC
813/.009/896073 19
PS153.N5 C34 1988   **NYPL [Sc E 88-144]**

Evans, James H., 1950- Spiritual empowerment
in Afro-American literature . Lewiston, NY ,
1987. 174 p. ; ISBN 0-88946-560-6 DDC
810/.9/896073 19
PS153.N5 E92 1987   **NYPL [Sc E 88-265]**

Gates, Henry Louis. The signifying monkey .
New York , 1988. xxviii, 290 p. : ISBN
0-19-503463-5 (alk. paper) DDC 810/.9/896073
19
PS153.N5 G28 1988   **NYPL [Sc E 89-181]**

Harris, Norman, 1951- Connecting times .
Jackson , c1988. 197 p. ; ISBN 0-87805-335-2
(alk. paper) DDC 813/.54/093520396073 19
PS153.N5 H27 1988   **NYPL [Sc E 88-288]**

Harris, Norman, 1951- Understanding the
sixties [microform] . 1980. 202 leaves.
    NYPL [Sc Micro R-4680]

Hull, Gloria T. Color, sex, and poetry .
Bloomington , c1987. xi, 240 p. : ISBN
0-253-34974-5 DDC 811/.52/099287 19
PS153.N5 H84 1987   **NYPL [Sc E 88-72]**

Lewis, Vashti Crutcher. The mulatto woman as
major female character in novels by Black
women, 1892-1937 [microform] /. [Iowa City,
Ia.] 1981. iv, 182 leaves ;
    NYPL [Sc Micro R-4792]

Nielsen, Aldon Lynn. Reading race . Athens,
Ga. , c1988. xii, 178 p. ; ISBN 0-8203-1061-1
(alk. paper) DDC 811/.5/09355 19
PS310.R34 N54 1988   **NYPL [JFE 88-3098]**

Sanders, Leslie Catherine, 1944- The
development of black theater in America .
Baton Rouge , c1988. 252 p. ; ISBN
0-8071-1328-X DDC 812/.009/896073 19
PS338.N4 S26 1987
    NYPL [MWED 88-1125]

Sherman, Joan R. Invisible poets . Urbana ,
c1989. xxxii, 288 p. : ISBN 0-252-01620-3 (alk.
paper) DDC 811/.009/896073 19
PS153.N5 S48 1989   **NYPL [Sc E 89-216]**

Tracy, Steven C. (Steven Carl), 1954- Langston
Hughes & the blues /. Urbana , c1988. xiii, 305
p. ; ISBN 0-252-01457-X (alk. paper) DDC
818/.5209 19
PS3515.U274 Z8 1988   **NYPL [Sc E 88-506]**

Wintz, Cary D., 1943- Black culture and the
Harlem Renaissance /. Houston, Tex. , 1988.
277 p. ; ISBN 0-89263-267-4 : DDC
810/.9/896073 19
PS153.N5 W57 1988   **NYPL [Sc E 89-106]**

**AFRO-AMERICANS IN LITERATURE -
BIBLIOGRAPHY.**
Rollins, Charlemae Hill. We build together.
[Champaign, Ill. , 1967] xxviii, 71 p. ; DDC
016.818
Z1361.N39 R77 1967   **NYPL [Sc D 89-387]**

**AFRO-AMERICANS IN LITERATURE -
BIBLIOGRAPHY - CATALOGS.**
France. Bibliothèque nationale. Département
des livres imprimés. Les auteurs afro-américains,
1965-1982 . Paris , 1985. 28 p., [4] leaves of
plates : ISBN 2-7177-1709-9 :
Z1229.N39 F7 1985 PS153.N5
    NYPL [Sc F 89-5]

**Afro-Americans in military service. see United
States - Armed Forces - Afro-Americans.**

Afro-Americans in New Jersey . Wright, Giles R.
Trenton , c1988. 100 p. : ISBN 0-89743-075-1
DDC 974.9/00496073 19
E185.93.N54 W75 1988
    NYPL [Sc D 89-529]

**AFRO-AMERICANS IN POETRY. see AFRO-
AMERICANS IN LITERATURE.**

**AFRO-AMERICANS IN RADIO
BROADCASTING.**
Newman, Mark. Entrepreneurs of profit and
pride . New York , 1988. xvi, 186 p., [4] p. of
plates : ISBN 0-275-92888-8 DDC 305.8/96073 19
PN1991.8.A35 N49 1988
    NYPL [Sc E 89-88]

**Afro-Americans in the Armed Forces. see United
States - Armed Forces - Afro-Americans.**

**AFRO-AMERICANS IN THE PERFORMING
ARTS.**
Pomerance, Alan. Repeal of the blues /.
Secaucus, N.J. , c1988. x, 264 p., [16] p. of
plates : ISBN 0-8065-1105-2 : DDC
792/.08996073 19
PN1590.B53 P6 1988   **NYPL [Sc E 89-90]**

AFRO-AMERICANS - INDEXES.
Stevenson, Rosemary M. Index to
Afro-American reference resources /. New
York , 1988. xxvi, 315 p. ; ISBN 0-313-24580-0
(lib. bdg. : alk. paper) DDC 973/.0496073 19
Z1361.N39 S77 1988 E185
    NYPL [Sc E 88-220]

AFRO-AMERICANS - INTELLECTUAL LIFE.
Bruce, Dickson D., 1946- Black American
writing from the nadir . Baton Rouge , c1989.
xiii, 272 p. : ISBN 0-8071-1450-2 (alk. paper)
DDC 810/.9/896073 19
PS153.N5 B77 1989   **NYPL [Sc E 89-197]**

Childs, John Brown. Leadership, conflict, and
cooperation in Afro-American social thought /.
Philadelphia , 1989. xii, 172 p. ; ISBN
0-87722-581-8 (alk. paper) : DDC
303.3/4/08996073 19
E185.6 .C534 1989   **NYPL [Sc D 89-497]**

Gates, Henry Louis. The signifying monkey .
New York , 1988. xxviii, 290 p. : ISBN
0-19-503463-5 (alk. paper) DDC 810/.9/896073
19
PS153.N5 G28 1988   **NYPL [Sc E 89-181]**

Meier, August, 1923- Negro thought in
America, 1880-1915 . Ann Arbor , 1988,
c1963. xii, 336 p. ; ISBN 0-472-64230-8 DDC
973/.0496073 19
E185.6 .M5 1988   **NYPL [Sc D 89-509]**

Redding, J. Saunders (Jay Saunders), 1906- To

make a poet Black /. Ithaca , 1988. xxxii, 142
p. ; ISBN 0-8014-1982-4 (alk. paper) DDC
811/.009/896073 19
PS153.N5 R4 1988   **NYPL [Sc D 89-388]**

Sherman, Joan R. Invisible poets . Urbana ,
c1989. xxxii, 288 p. : ISBN 0-252-01620-3 (alk.
paper) DDC 811/.009/896073 19
PS153.N5 S48 1989   **NYPL [Sc E 89-216]**

Wintz, Cary D., 1943- Black culture and the
Harlem Renaissance /. Houston, Tex. , 1988.
277 p. ; ISBN 0-89263-267-4 : DDC
810/.9/896073 19
PS153.N5 W57 1988   **NYPL [Sc E 89-106]**

**AFRO-AMERICANS - INTELLECTUAL LIFE -
JUVENILE LITERATURE.**
Urban, Joan, 1950- Richard Wright /. New
York, N.Y. [1989] 111 p. : ISBN 1-555-46618-4
DDC 813/.52 19
PS3545.R815 Z85 1989
    NYPL [Sc E 89-196]

**AFRO-AMERICANS - INTELLIGENCE. see
INTELLIGENCE LEVELS - AFRO-
AMERICANS.**

**AFRO-AMERICANS - INTELLIGENCE
LEVELS.**
Essays on the nature of intelligence and the
analysis of racial differences in the performance
of IQ tests /. Washington D.C. , c1988. 72 p. :
ISBN 0-941694-32-1   **NYPL [Sc D 89-546]**

AFRO-AMERICANS - JUVENILE FICTION.
Childress, Alice. Those other people /. New
York , c1989. 186 p. : ISBN 0-399-21510-7
DDC [Fic] 19
PZ7.C4412 Th 1988   **NYPL [Sc D 89-327]**

Knott, Bill, 1927- Crazylegs Merrill. Austin
[1969] iv, 155 p. ;   **NYPL [Sc D 88-632]**

McKissack, Pat, 1944- Mirandy and Brother
Wind /. New York , 1988. [32] p. : ISBN
0-394-88765-4 DDC [E] 19
PZ7.M478693 Mi 1988   **NYPL [Sc F 89-58]**

Walker, Alice, 1944- To hell with dying /. San
Diego , 1987. [32] p. : ISBN 0-15-289075-0
DDC [Fic] 19
PZ7.W15213 To 1987   **NYPL [Sc F 88-182]**

**AFRO-AMERICANS - KENTUCKY -
BIOGRAPHY.**
Johnson, Lyman T., 1906- The rest of the
dream . Lexington, Ky. , c1988. xiv, 230 p., [8]
p. of plates : ISBN 0-8131-1674-0 (alk. paper) :
DDC 976.9/00496073024 B 19
E185.97.J693 A3 1988   **NYPL [Sc E 89-211]**

AFRO-AMERICANS - LANGUAGE.
Twum-Akwaboah, Edward. From pidginization
to creolization of Africanisms in Black
American English /. [Los Angeles , 1973] 46
leaves ;   **NYPL [Sc F 88-210]**

**AFRO-AMERICANS - LEGAL STATUS, LAWS,
ETC. - OHIO.**
State Convention of Colored Men (1856 :
Columbus, Ohio) Proceedings of the State
Convention of Colored Men, held in the city of
Columbus, Ohio, Jan. 16th, 17th & 18th, 1856.
[Columbus? , 1856?] 8 p. ;
E185.93.O2 S84 1856
    NYPL [Sc Rare F 89-23]

**AFRO-AMERICANS - LEGAL STATUS, LAWS,
ETC. - SOUTHERN STATES - CASES.**
Slave rebels, abolitionists, and southern courts .
New York , 1988. 2 v. : ISBN 0-8240-6721-5
(set : alk. paper) : DDC 342.75/0872
347.502872 19
KF4545.S5 A5 1987b   **NYPL [Sc D 88-1263]**

AFRO-AMERICANS - LIFE SKILL GUIDES.
McClenney, Earl H. How to survive when
you're the only Black in the office . Richmond,
Va. , c1987. 212 p. ; ISBN 0-9618835-0-2 (pbk.) :
DDC 650.1/3/0240396073 19
HF5386 .M473 1987   **NYPL [Sc D 89-242]**

**AFRO-AMERICANS - LITERARY
COLLECTIONS.**
Bonner, Marita, 1899-1971. Frye Street &
environs . Boston , c1987. xxix, 286 p. ; ISBN
0-8070-6300-2 DDC 810/.8/0896073 19
PS3503 .O439 1987   **NYPL [Sc D 88-683]**

Dunbar-Nelson, Alice Moore, 1875-1935.
[Works. 1988.] The works of Alice
Dunbar-Nelson /. New York , 1988. 3 v. :
ISBN 0-19-505250-1 (v. 1 : alk. paper) DDC

818/.5209 19
PS3507 .U6228 1988   NYPL [JFC 88-2143]

Plato, Ann. Essays. New York , 1988. liii, 122
p. ; ISBN 0-19-505247-1 (alk. paper)   DDC 814/.3
19
PS2593 .P347 1988   NYPL [JFC 88-2156]

AFRO-AMERICANS - MARRIAGE.
Hare, Nathan. The endangered Black family .
San Francisco, CA , c1984. 192 p. ; ISBN
0-9613086-0-5   *NYPL [Sc C 88-307]*

**AFRO-AMERICANS - MARYLAND - ANNE
ARUNDEL COUNTY.**
Clayton, Ralph. Free Blacks of Anne Arundel
County, Maryland 1850 /. Bowie, MD. , 1987.
xiv, 51 p. ; ISBN 1-556-13069-4
NYPL [Sc D 88-64]

**AFRO-AMERICANS - MARYLAND -
BALTIMORE - GENEALOGY.**
Clayton, Ralph. Black Baltimore, 1820-1870 /.
Bowie, MD , 1987. vii, 199 p. ; ISBN
1-556-13080-5 (pbk.) : DDC
929/.3/0899607307526 19
F189.B19 N42 1987
NYPL [APR (Baltimore) 88-868]

**AFRO-AMERICANS - MASSACHUSETTS -
BOSTON.**
Overbea, Luix V. (Luix Virgil) Black Bostonia
/. Boston, Mass. , c1976. 39 p. -
NYPL [Sc C 89-44]

**AFRO-AMERICANS - MASSACHUSETTS -
BOSTON - FICTION.**
West, Dorothy, 1909- The living is easy /.
London , 1987, c1982. 362 p. ; ISBN
0-86068-753-8   *NYPL [Sc C 88-165]*

AFRO-AMERICANS - MEDICAL CARE.
Maida, Carl Albert. Black networks of care
[microform] . 1981. xiii, 276 leaves ;
NYPL [Sc Micro R-4803]

**AFRO-AMERICANS - MEDICAL CARE -
ALABAMA - HISTORY.**
Hasson, Gail Snowden. The medical activities
of the Freedmen's Bureau in Reconstruction
Alabama, 1865-1868 [microform] /. 1982. 252
leaves.   *NYPL [Sc Micro R-4681]*

**AFRO-AMERICANS - MEDICAL CARE -
SOUTHERN STATES - HISTORY - 20TH
CENTURY.**
Beardsley, Edward H. A history of neglect .
Knoxville , c1987. xvi, 383 p. : ISBN
0-87049-523-2 (alk. paper) : DDC 362.1/0425
19
RA448.5.N4 B33 1987   NYPL [Sc E 87-625]

AFRO-AMERICANS - MENTAL HEALTH.
Coleman, Mel. The Black gestalt . Minneapolis,
Minnesota , 1987. 118 p. :
NYPL [Sc D 88-292]

Milburn, Norweeta G. Social support .
Washington, D.C. , 1986. iii, 67 p. ;
NYPL [Sc F 87-428]

**AFRO-AMERICANS - MENTAL ILLNESS. see
AFRO-AMERICANS - MENTAL
HEALTH.**

**AFRO-AMERICANS - MICHIGAN -
DETROIT.**
Blacks in Detroit . Detroit , 1980. 111 p. :
NYPL [Sc G 88-15]

Brown, Earl Louis, 1900- Why race riots
[microform]? [New York] 1944. cover-title, 31,
[1] p.
F574.D4 B58   NYPL [Sc Micro R-3541]

**AFRO-AMERICANS - MICHIGAN -
DETROIT - ATTITUDES.**
Hatchett, Shirley. Black racial attitude change
in Detroit, 1968-1976 [microform] /. 1982. 171
leaves.   *NYPL [Sc Micro R-4682]*

**AFRO-AMERICANS - MICHIGAN -
DETROIT - ECONOMIC CONDITIONS.**
Detroit, race and uneven development /.
Philadelphia , 1987. xii, 317 p. : ISBN
0-87722-485-4 (alk. paper)   DDC
305.8/009774/34 19
HC108.D6 D47 1987   NYPL [Sc E 88-205]

**AFRO-AMERICANS - MICHIGAN -
DETROIT - GENEALOGY.**
Echols, James, 1932- The Echols of Detroit .
[S. l.] 1985 [Port Jefferson Sta., N.Y. :
McPrint Graphics Center] v. :
NYPL [Sc F 88-97]

AFRO-AMERICANS - MISSISSIPPI.
Whitfield, Stephen J., 1942- A death in the
Delta . New York , London , c1988. xiv, 193
p., [8] p. of plates : ISBN 0-02-935121-9 : DDC
345.73/02523 347.3052523 19
E185.61 .W63 1989   NYPL [Sc E 89-140]

**AFRO-AMERICANS - MISSISSIPPI -
HISTORY.**
McMillen, Neil R., 1939- Dark journey .
Urbana, Ill. , c1989. xvii, 430 p., [10] p. of
plates, ISBN 0-252-01568-1 (alk. paper)   DDC
976.2/00496073 19
E185.93.M6 M33 1989   NYPL [Sc E 89-213]

**AFRO-AMERICANS - MISSISSIPPI -
SEGREGATION - HISTORY.**
McMillen, Neil R., 1939- Dark journey .
Urbana, Ill. , c1989. xvii, 430 p., [10] p. of
plates, ISBN 0-252-01568-1 (alk. paper)   DDC
976.2/00496073 19
E185.93.M6 M33 1989   NYPL [Sc E 89-213]

AFRO-AMERICANS - MORTALITY.
Currents of health policy . New York , 1987. 2
v. :   *NYPL [Sc D 88-1205]*

AFRO-AMERICANS - MUSIC.
Ogren, Kathy J. The jazz revolution . New
York , 1989. vii, 221 p., [8] p. of plates : ISBN
0-19-505153-X (alk. paper)   DDC 781/.57/0973
19
ML3508 .O37 1987   NYPL [Sc D 89-451]

**AFRO-AMERICANS - MUSIC - ADDRESSES,
ESSAYS, LECTURES.**
Readings in Black American music /. New
York , c1983. xii, 338 p. : ISBN 0-393-95280-0
(pbk.)   DDC 781.7/296073 19
ML3556 .R34 1983   NYPL [Sc D 85-30]

**AFRO-AMERICANS - MUSIC - HISTORY
AND CRITICISM.**
Finn, Julio. The bluesman . London , New
York , 1986. 256 p., [8] p. of plates : ISBN
0-7043-2523-3   *NYPL [Sc E 88-181]*

George, Nelson. The death of rhythm & blues
/. New York , c1988. xvi, 222 p., [16] p. of
plates : ISBN 0-394-55238-5 : DDC 781.7/296073
19
ML3556 .G46 1988   NYPL [Sc E 88-504]

Lovell, John, 1907- Black song . New York ,
1986, c1972. xviii, 686 p. : ISBN 0-913729-53-1
(pbk.)   DDC 783.6/7/09 19
ML3556 .L69 1986   NYPL [Sc D 88-421]

Pearson, Boyce Neal. A cantomeric analysis of
three Afro-American songs recorded in the
Commerce, Texas, area [microform] /. 1978. 47
leaves.   *NYPL [Sc Micro R-4701]*

Woll, Allen. Black musical theatre . Baton
Rouge , c1989. xiv, 301 p. : ISBN 0-8071-1469-3
DDC 782.81/08996073 19
ML1711 .W64 1989   NYPL [Sc E 89-198]

**AFRO-AMERICANS - NEW ENGLAND -
HISTORY - 18TH CENTURY.**
Piersen, William Dillon, 1942- Black Yankees .
Amherst , 1988. Xii,237 p. ; ISBN 0-87023-586-9
(alk. paper)   DDC 974/.00496073 19
E185.917 .P54 1988   NYPL [Sc E 88-213]

**AFRO-AMERICANS - NEW JERSEY -
HISTORY.**
Wright, Giles R. Afro-Americans in New
Jersey . Trenton , c1988. 100 p. : ISBN
0-89743-075-1 DDC 974.9/00496073 19
E185.93.N54 W75 1988
NYPL [Sc D 89-529]

AFRO-AMERICANS - NEW YORK (CITY)
First National City Bank. Economics Dept.
Profile of a city. New York [1972] x, 273 p.
ISBN 0-07-021066-7
HC108.N7 F57   NYPL [Sc 309.174-F]

New York (City). Housing Authority. Harlem,
1934. [New York, 1934] 20 p.
HD268.N5 N27   NYPL [Sc G 88-30]

**AFRO-AMERICANS - NEW YORK (CITY) -
HARLEM - FICTION.**
Hughes, Langston, 1902-1967. Simple speaks
his mind /. New York , c1950. 231 p. ;
NYPL [Sc Rare C 82-2]

AFRO-AMERICANS - NEW YORK (N.Y.)
Committee of Merchants for the Relief of
Colored People, Suffering from the Late Riots
in the City of New York. Report of the
Committee of Merchants for the Relief of
Colored People, Suffering from the Late Riots

in the City of New York. New York , 1863. 48
p. ;   *NYPL [Sc Rare F 89-2]*

New York (N.Y.) Mayor's Commission on
Black New Yorkers. The report of the Mayor's
Commission on Black New Yorkers. New
York , 1988. xxi, 315 p. ;
NYPL [Sc F 89-96]

Whistelo, Alexander. (defendant) The
Commissioners of the Alms-house, vs.
Alexander Whistelo, a black man . New York ,
1808. 56 p. ;   *NYPL [Sc Rare F 88-21]*

**AFRO-AMERICANS - NEW YORK (N.Y) -
BIOGRAPHY.**
Buckley, Gail Lumet, 1937- The Hornes . New
York , 1986. 262 p. : ISBN 0-394-51306-1 :
DDC 974.7/2300496073/00922 B 19
F129.B7 B83 1986   NYPL [Sc E 86-286]

Walter, John C. (John Christopher), 1933- The
Harlem Fox . Albany, N.Y. , c1989. xv, 287
p. : ISBN 0-88706-756-5 DDC 974.7/1043/0924 B
19
F128.5.J72 W35 1988   NYPL [Sc E 89-107]

**AFRO-AMERICANS - NEW YORK (N.Y.) -
ECONOMIC CONDITIONS.**
New York (N.Y.) Mayor's Commission on
Black New Yorkers. The report of the Mayor's
Commission on Black New Yorkers. New
York , 1988. xxi, 315 p. ;
NYPL [Sc F 89-96]

**AFRO-AMERICANS - NEW YORK (N.Y.) -
FICTION.**
Himes, Chester B., 1909- The real cool killers/.
London , New York , 1985, c1958. 159 p. ;
ISBN 0-85031-615-4   *NYPL [Sc D 88-280]*

Williams, John Alfred, 1925- !Click song . New
York , c1987. 430 p. ; ISBN 0-938410-43-1 :
DDC 813/.54 19
PS3573.I4495 C5 1987
NYPL [Sc D 88-1344]

Wolfe, Tom. The bonfire of the vanities /. New
York , 1987. 659 p. ; ISBN 0-374-11534-6 :
DDC 813/.54 19
PS3573.O526 B6 1987   NYPL [Sc E 88-389]

**AFRO-AMERICANS - NEW YORK (N.Y.) -
POLITICS AND GOVERNMENT.**
Green, Charles (Charles St. Clair) The struggle
for black empowerment in New York City .
New York , 1989. xvi, 183 p. : ISBN
0-275-92614-1 (alk. paper) : DDC
974.7/100496073 19
F128.9.N3 G74 1989   NYPL [Sc E 89-203]

Walter, John C. (John Christopher), 1933- The
Harlem Fox . Albany, N.Y. , c1989. xv, 287
p. : ISBN 0-88706-756-5 DDC 974.7/1043/0924 B
19
F128.5.J72 W35 1988   NYPL [Sc E 89-107]

**AFRO-AMERICANS - NEW YORK (STATE) -
WESTCHESTER COUNTY - HISTORY.**
Caro, Edythe Quinn. "The Hills" in the
mid-nineteenth century . Valhalla, New York ,
c1988. iii, 184 p. :   *NYPL [Sc F 89-71]*

**AFRO-AMERICANS - NORTH CAROLINA -
BIOGRAPHY.**
My folks don't want me to talk about slavery .
Winston-Salem, N.C. , c1984. xiv, 103 p. ;
ISBN 0-89587-038-X DDC
975.6/00496073/0922 B 19
E445.N8 M9 1984   NYPL [JFD 85-1549]

**AFRO-AMERICANS - NORTH CAROLINA -
HALIFAX - GENEALOGY.**
Stephenson, Anne N. Informal history of the
Black people I have known in Halifax /.
[Halifax] c1978. 99 p. ;
NYPL [Sc D 88-1209]

**AFRO-AMERICANS - NORTH CAROLINA -
HISTORY.**
Davis, Lenwood G. The Black heritage of
Western North Carolina /. [Asheville, North
Carolina , 1986?] 78 leaves ;
NYPL [Sc F 88-265]

Redford, Dorothy Spruill. Somerset
homecoming . New York , c1988. xviii, 266 p. :
ISBN 0-385-24245-X : DDC
929/.3/089960730756 19
E185.96 .R42 1988   NYPL [Sc E 88-498]

**AFRO-AMERICANS - NORTH CAROLINA -
JUVENILE FICTION.**
Burgwyn, Mebane (Holoman) River treasure.

New York, 1947. 159 p.
PZ7.B9177 Ri   *NYPL [Sc D 89-512]*

AFRO-AMERICANS - OCCUPATIONS. see AFRO-AMERICANS - EMPLOYMENT.

AFRO-AMERICANS - OHIO.
Joiner, William A., 1868- A half century of freedom of the Negro in Ohio. Xenia, Ohio [1915] 134 p.   *NYPL [Sc Rare F 89-7]*

AFRO-AMERICANS - OHIO - CINCINNATI - FICTION.
Morrison, Toni. Beloved . New York , 1987. 275 p. ; ISBN 0-394-53597-9 : DDC 813/.54 19
PS3563.O8749 B4 1987
                    NYPL [Sc E 88-188]

Morrison, Toni. Beloved /. Thorndike, Me. , 1988. 472 p.; 22 cm. ISBN 0-89621-123-1 (alk. paper) DDC 813/.54 19
PS3563.O8749 B4 1988
                    NYPL [Sc D 88-1503]

AFRO-AMERICANS - OHIO - CLEVELAND REGION - SOCIAL LIFE AND CUSTOMS.
Watson, Wilbur H. The village . Atlanta, Ga. , c1989. xxii, 204 p. : ISBN 0-9621460-0-5 DDC 977.1/3200496073 20
F499.C69 N38 1989   *NYPL [Sc D 89-609]*

AFRO-AMERICANS - OHIO - CONGRESSES.
State Convention of Colored Men (1856 : Columbus, Ohio) Proceedings of the State Convention of Colored Men, held in the city of Columbus, Ohio, Jan. 16th, 17th & 18th, 1856. [Columbus? , 1856?] 8 p. ;
E185.93.O2 S84 1856
                    NYPL [Sc Rare F 89-23]

AFRO-AMERICANS - OHIO - FICTION.
Morrison, Toni. Sula /. New York [1987], c1973. 174 p. ; ISBN 0-452-26010-8 DDC 813/.54 19
PS3563.O8749 S8 1987
                    NYPL [Sc D 88-633]

AFRO-AMERICANS - OHIO - GENEALOGY.
Nitchman, Paul E. Blacks in Ohio, 1880 in the counties of ... /. [Decorah? Iowa] , c1985- v. ; DDC 929/.3/089960730771 19
E185.93.O2 N57 1985
                    NYPL [APR (Ohio) 86-2025]

AFRO-AMERICANS - OHIO - PICKAWAY COUNTY - GENEALOGY.
Buchanan, James. The Blacks of Pickaway County, Ohio in the nineteenth century /. Bowie, Maryland , 1988. iv, 142 p. ; ISBN 1-556-13129-1
                    NYPL [Sc D 89-154]

AFRO-AMERICANS - PENNSYLVANIA - PHILADELPHIA.
Anderson, John, 1954 Mar. 27- Burning down the house . New York , c1987. xv, 409 p. : ISBN 0-393-02460-1 : DDC 974.8/1104 19
F158.9.N4 A53 1987   *NYPL [Sc E 88-332]*

AFRO-AMERICANS - PENNSYLVANIA - PHILADELPHIA - HISTORY.
Nash, Gary B. Forging freedom . Cambridge, Mass. , c1988. xii, 354 p. : ISBN 0-674-30934-0 (alk. paper) DDC 974.8/1100496073 19
F158.9.N4 N37 1988   *NYPL [Sc E 88-594]*

Winch, Julie, 1953- Philadelphia's Black elite . Philadelphia , 1988. x, 240 p. ; ISBN 0-87722-515-X (alk. paper) : DDC 974.8/1100496073 19
F158.9.N4 W56 1988   *NYPL [Sc E 88-198]*

AFRO-AMERICANS - PENNSYLVANIA - PHILADELPHIA - SOCIAL CONDITIONS.
Rose, Dan. Black American street life . Philadelphia, Pa. , c1987. x, 278 p. : ISBN 0-8122-8071-7 DDC 974.8/1100496073 19
F158.9.N4 R67 1987   *NYPL [Sc E 88-76]*

AFRO-AMERICANS - PENNSYLVANIA - PHILADELPHIA - SOCIAL LIFE AND CUSTOMS.
Rose, Dan. Black American street life . Philadelphia, Pa. , c1987. x, 278 p. : ISBN 0-8122-8071-7 DDC 974.8/1100496073 19
F158.9.N4 R67 1987   *NYPL [Sc E 88-76]*

AFRO-AMERICANS - PENNSYLVANIA - PITTSBURGH - FICTION.
Attaway, William. Blood on the forge /. New York , c1987. 315 p. ; ISBN 0-85345-722-0 (pbk.) : DDC 813/.52 19
PS3501.T59 B55 1987
                    NYPL [Sc D 88-1438]

AFRO-AMERICANS - PENNSYLVANIA - WYOMING VALLEY.
Patterson, Christine. The Black experience in Wyoming Valley /. [Pennsylvania] [1987?] 9 p. :   *NYPL [Sc D 89-148]*

AFRO-AMERICANS - POETRY.
Gurus and griots . Brooklyn, N.Y. [1987], c1985. 108 p. : ISBN 0-9618755-0-X (pbk.) DDC 811/.008/0896 19
PS591.N4 G87 1987   *NYPL [Sc E 89-230]*

Patrick, Herbert R. Just being Black . Petersburg, Va. (3406 Union Branch Rd., Petersburg 23805) , c1984. 50 p. : DDC 811/.54 19
PS3566.A778 J87 1984   *NYPL [Sc D 88-668]*

AFRO-AMERICANS - POLITICAL ACTIVITY.
Maish, Kemba Asili. Black political orientation, political activism, and positive mental health [microform] /. 1977. 220 leaves.
                    NYPL [Sc Micro R-4228]

Transafrica Forum (Organization) A retrospective . [Washington, D.C.] , c1987. 32 p. :   *NYPL [Sc E 88-163]*

AFRO-AMERICANS - POLITICS AND GOVERNMENT.
Blacks and the 1984 Republican National Convention . Washington, D.C. (1301 Pennsylvania Ave., N.W., Suite 400, Washington 20004) , 1984. v, 25 p. ; ISBN 0-941410-51-X (pbk.) DDC 324.2734 19
JK2353 1984   *NYPL [Sc F 87-172 rept. 4]*

Carmines, Edward G. Issue evolution . Princeton, N.J. , c1989. xvii, 217 p. : ISBN 0-691-07802-5 : DDC 323.1/196073 19
E185.615 .C35 1989   *NYPL [Sc E 89-214]*

Cavanagh, Thomas E. The impact of the Black electorate [microform] /. Washington, D.C. (1301 Pennsylvania Ave., N.W., Suite 400, Washington 20004) , 1984. v, 28 p. ; DDC 324.973/008896073 19
E185.615 .C364 1984   *NYPL [*Z-4913 no.8]*

Haines, Herbert H. Black radicals and the civil rights mainstream, 1954-1970 /. Knoxville , c19. xii, 231 p. : ISBN 0-87049-563-1 (alk. paper) : DDC 305.8/96073 19
E185.615 .H25 1988   *NYPL [Sc E 88-511]*

Smith, J. Owens. Blacks and American government . Dubuque, Iowa , c1987. xii, 148 p. : ISBN 0-8403-4407-4 (pbk.) DDC 323.1/196073 19
E185.615 .S576 1987   *NYPL [Sc E 89-193]*

AFRO-AMERICANS - POLITICS AND SUFFRAGE.
Epton, William. Electoral politics [microform] . New York , 1980. 33 p. :
                    NYPL [Sc Micro F-10975]

AFRO-AMERICANS - PSYCHOLOGY.
Crisis in Black sexual politics /. [San Francisco, Calif.] c1989. iv, 184 p. ; ISBN 0-9613086-2-1
                    NYPL [Sc D 89-152]

Jenkins, Adelbert H. The psychology of the Afro-American . New York , 1982. xix, 213 p. ; ISBN 0-08-027206-1 DDC 155.8/496073 19
E185.625 .J47 1982   *NYPL [Sc D 88-718]*

Maish, Kemba Asili. Black political orientation, political activism, and positive mental health [microform] /. 1977. 220 leaves.
                    NYPL [Sc Micro R-4228]

Milburn, Norweeta G. Social support . Washington, D.C. , 1986. iii, 67 p. ;
                    NYPL [Sc F 87-428]

AFRO-AMERICANS - RACE IDENTITY - BIBLIOGRAPHY.
Herod, Agustina. Afro-American nationalism . New York , 1986. xvi, 272 p. ; ISBN 0-8240-9813-7 (alk. paper) DDC 016.3058/96073 19
Z1361.N39 H47 1986 E185.625
                    NYPL [Sc D 87-1338]

AFRO-AMERICANS - RELATIONS WITH AFRICANS.
Clarke, John Henrik, 1915- The image of Africa in the mind of the Afro-American . New York , 1973. 32 leaves ; *NYPL [Sc Micro F-9664]*

Magubane, Bernard. The ties that bind . Trenton, N.J. [1987] xi, 251 p. ; ISBN 0-86543-037-3 (pbk.) DDC 305.8/96073 19
E185.625 .M83 1987   *NYPL [Sc D 88-1348]*

AFRO-AMERICANS - RELATIONS WITH INDIANS.
Forbes, Jack D. Black Africans and native Americans . Oxford, UK , New York, NY, USA , 1988. 345 p. ; ISBN 0-631-15665-8 : DDC 973/.0496073 19
E59.M66 F67 1988   *NYPL [HBC 88-2172]*

Katz, William Loren. Black Indians . New York , c1986. 198 p. ; ISBN 0-689-31196-6
                    NYPL [IEC 87-411]

AFRO-AMERICANS - RELATIONS WITH INDIANS - ADDRESSES, ESSAYS, LECTURES.
McLoughlin, William Gerald. The Cherokee ghost dance . [Macon, Ga.] , c1984. xxiv, 512 p. : ISBN 0-86554-128-0 : DDC 975/.00497 19
E78.S65 M37 1984   *NYPL [HBC 85-263]*

AFRO-AMERICANS - RELATIONS WITH JEWS - CONGRESSES.
National Conference on African American/Jewish American Relations (1983 : Savannah State College) Blacks and Jews . [Savannah, Ga.] [1983] iii, 58 p. ;
                    NYPL [Sc D 88-335]

AFRO-AMERICANS - RELATIONS WITH WEST INDIANS.
Rahming, Melvin B., 1943- The evolution of the West Indian's image in the Afro-American novel /. Millwood, N.Y. , c1986. xix, 160 p. ; ISBN 0-8046-9339-0 DDC 813/.009/35203969729 19
PS153.N5 R3 1985   *NYPL [JFD 86-6569]*

AFRO-AMERICANS - RELIGION.
Eckardt, A. Roy (Arthur Roy), 1918- Black-woman-Jew . Bloomington , c1989. 229 p. ; ISBN 0-253-31221-3 DDC 305.4/8896073 19
E185.86 .E28 1989   *NYPL [Sc E 89-209]*

Evans, James H., 1950- Spiritual empowerment in Afro-American literature . Lewiston, NY , 1987. 174 p. ; ISBN 0-88946-560-6 DDC 810/.9/896073 19
PS153.N5 E92 1987   *NYPL [Sc E 88-265]*

West, Cornel. Prophetic fragments /. Grand Rapids, Mich. , Trenton, N.J. , c1988. xi, 294 p. ; ISBN 0-8028-0308-3 : DDC 291/.0973 19
BL2525 .W42 1988   *NYPL [Sc E 88-401]*

AFRO-AMERICANS - RHODE ISLAND - HISTORY.
Stewart, Rowena. A heritage discovered . Providence, R.I. [1975] 39 p. :
                    NYPL [Sc E 89-110]

AFRO-AMERICANS - SOCIAL CONDITIONS.
Ashmore, Harry S. Hearts and minds . Cabin John, Md. , c1988. xviii, 513 p. ; ISBN 0-932020-58-5 (pbk. : alk. paper) DDC 305.8/96073 19
E185.615 .A83 1988   *NYPL [Sc D 89-382]*

Boston, Thomas D. Race, class, and conservatism /. Boston , 1988. xix, 172 p. : ISBN 0-04-330368-4 (alk. paper) DDC 305.5/0973 19
HN90.S6 B67 1988   *NYPL [Sc D 89-107]*

Boyd-Franklin, Nancy. Black families in therapy . New York, N.Y. , c1989. xiv, 274 p. : ISBN 0-89862-735-4 DDC 616.89/156/08996073 19
RC451.5.N4 B69 1988 *NYPL [Sc E 89-242]*

Crisis in Black sexual politics /. [San Francisco, Calif.] c1989. iv, 184 p. ; ISBN 0-9613086-2-1
                    NYPL [Sc D 89-152]

Staples, Robert. The urban plantation . Oakland, CA , c1987. 248 p. ; ISBN 0-933296-13-4 (pbk.)
                    NYPL [Sc D 88-1021]

Symposium on race and class. Philadelphia , 1984. 62 p. ;   *NYPL [Sc D 88-2]*

AFRO-AMERICANS - SOCIAL CONDITIONS - TO 1964.
12 million Black voices /. New York , 1988, c1941. xx, 152 p. : ISBN 0-938410-48-2 : DDC 973/.0496073 19
E185.86 .A13 1988   *NYPL [Sc F 88-315]*

AFRO-AMERICANS - SOCIAL CONDITIONS - TO 1964 - PICTORIAL WORKS.
12 million Black voices /. New York , 1988, c1941. xx, 152 p. : ISBN 0-938410-48-2 : DDC

973/.0496073 19
E185.86 .A13 1988   *NYPL [Sc F 88-315]*

AFRO-AMERICANS - SOCIAL CONDITIONS - 1964-1975.
Dilemmas of the new Black middle class /.
[Pa.?] c1980. v, 100 p. ;
E185.86 .D54x 1980   *NYPL [Sc D 89-24]*

AFRO-AMERICANS - SOCIAL CONDITIONS - 1975-
Bernheim, Nicole. Voyage en Amérique noire /.
Paris , c1986. 254 p. ; ISBN 2-234-01886-2 :
DDC 305.8/96073/073 19
E185.86 .B47 1986   *NYPL [Sc E 88-607]*

Black families in crisis . New York , c1988. xiv,
305 p. ; ISBN 0-87630-524-9 DDC 305.8/96073
19
E185.86 .B5254 1988   *NYPL [Sc E 89-155]*

Davis, Angela Yvonne, 1944- Women,
culture, & politics /. New York, NY , 1989. xv,
238 p. ; ISBN 0-394-76976-8 : DDC
305.4/8896073 19
E185.86 .D382 1989   *NYPL [Sc D 89-275]*

Dilemmas of the new Black middle class /.
[Pa.?] c1980. v, 100 p. ;
E185.86 .D54x 1980   *NYPL [Sc D 89-24]*

Eckardt, A. Roy (Arthur Roy), 1918-
Black-woman-Jew . Bloomington , c1989. 229
p. ; ISBN 0-253-31221-3 DDC 305.4/8896073 19
E185.86 .E28 1989   *NYPL [Sc E 89-209]*

Landry, Bart. The new Black middle class /.
Berkeley , 1987. xi, 250 p. ; ISBN 0-520-05942-5
(alk. paper) DDC 305.8/96073 19
E185.86 .L35 1987   *NYPL [Sc D 87-1006]*

AFRO-AMERICANS - SOCIAL CONDITIONS - HISTORY.
Crew, Spencer R. Field to factory .
Washington, D.C. , 1987. 79 p., [4] p. of
plates :   *NYPL [Sc F 88-369]*

AFRO-AMERICANS - SOCIAL CONDITIONS - JUVENILE FICTION.
Walter, Mildred Pitts. Lillie of Watts takes a
giant step. Garden City, N.Y. [1971] 187 p.
DDC [Fic]
PZ7.W17125 Lk   *NYPL [Sc D 88-1119]*

AFRO-AMERICANS - SOCIAL LIFE AND CUSTOMS.
Dodson, Jualynne E. Black stylization and
implications for child welfare . Atlanta,
Georgia , 1975. 1 v. (various pagings) ;
    NYPL [Sc F 88-223]

Hare, Nathan. The endangered Black family .
San Francisco, CA , c1984. 192 p. ; ISBN
0-9613086-0-5   *NYPL [Sc C 88-307]*

Milburn, Norweeta G. Social support .
Washington, D.C. , 1986. iii, 67 p. ;
    NYPL [Sc F 87-428]

Newman, Mark. Entrepreneurs of profit and
pride . New York , 1988. xvi, 186 p., [4] p. of
plates : ISBN 0-275-92888-8 DDC 305.8/96073 19
PN1991.8.A35 N49 1988
    NYPL [Sc E 89-88]

AFRO-AMERICANS - SOCIAL WORK WITH.
Dodson, Jualynne E. Training of personnel for
services to Black families . [Atlanta] [1976] 1
v. (various foliations) ; *NYPL [Sc F 88-130]*

AFRO-AMERICANS - SOUTH CAROLINA - BIOGRAPHY.
Taylor, Susie King, b. 1848. [Reminiscences of
my life in camp.] A Black woman's Civil War
memoirs . New York , 1988. 154 p. : ISBN
0-910129-85-1 (pbk.) : DDC 973.7/415 B 19
E492.94 33rd .T3 1988
    NYPL [Sc D 88-1473]

AFRO-AMERICANS - SOUTH CAROLINA - CHARLESTON - RELIGION.
Adger, John Bailey, 1810-1899. The religious
instruction of the colored population .
Charleston , 1847. 19 p. ;
    NYPL [Sc Rare G 86-6]

AFRO-AMERICANS - SOUTH CAROLINA - JUVENILE FICTION.
Allen, Merritt Parmelee. Battle lanterns /. New
York , 1949. 278 p. ; *NYPL [Sc D 88-1106]*

AFRO-AMERICANS - SOUTH CAROLINA - SAINT HELENA ISLAND - SOCIAL LIFE AND CUSTOMS.
Daise, Ronald. Reminiscences of Sea Island

heritage /. Orangeburg, S.C. , c1987. xvi, 103,
[13] p. :   *NYPL [Sc F 88-168]*

AFRO-AMERICANS - SOUTHERN STATES.
Davis, Allison, 1902- Deep South. Los Angeles,
CA , 1988. xxiii, 567 p. : ISBN 0-934934-26-6
    NYPL [Sc E 89-45]

AFRO-AMERICANS - SOUTHERN STATES - BIOGRAPHY.
Rouse, Jacqueline Anne. Lugenia Burns Hope,
Black southern reformer . Athens , c1989. xi,
182 p., [8] p. of plates : ISBN 0-8203-1082-4 (alk.
paper) DDC 973/.0496073024 B 19
E185.97.H717 R68 1989
    NYPL [Sc D 89-469]

AFRO-AMERICANS - SOUTHERN STATES - FICTION.
Lincoln, C. Eric (Charles Eric), 1924- The
Avenue, Clayton City /. New York , c1988.
288 p. ; ISBN 0-688-07702-1 DDC 813/.54 19
PS3562.I472 A94 1988
    NYPL [JFE 88-5108]

AFRO-AMERICANS - SOUTHERN STATES - JUVENILE FICTION.
Glasser, Barbara. Bongo Bradley. New York
[1973] 153 p. DDC [Fic]
PZ7.G48143 Bo   *NYPL [Sc D 89-99]*

AFRO-AMERICANS - SOUTHERN STATES - POLITICS AND GOVERNMENT - CONGRESSES.
Blacks in southern politics /. New York , 1987.
vii, 305 p. : ISBN 0-275-92655-9 (alk. paper) :
DDC 323.1/196073/075 19
E185.92 .B58 1987   *NYPL [Sc E 88-196]*

AFRO-AMERICANS - SOUTHERN STATES - SOCIAL CONDITIONS.
Ashmore, Harry S. Hearts and minds . Cabin
John, Md. , c1988. xviii, 513 p. ; ISBN
0-932020-58-5 (pbk. : alk. paper) DDC
305.8/96073 19
E185.615 .A83 1988   *NYPL [Sc D 89-382]*

AFRO-AMERICANS - SOVIET UNION - BIOGRAPHY.
Robinson, Robert, ca. 1902- Black on Red .
Washington, D.C. , 1988. 436 p. : ISBN
0-87491-885-5 DDC 947.084 19
DK34.B53 R63 1988   *NYPL [Sc E 88-377]*

AFRO-AMERICANS - SPORTS - HISTORY.
Ashe, Arthur. A hard road to glory . New
York, NY , 1988. 3 v. : ISBN 0-446-71006-7
DDC 796/.08996073 19
GV583 .A75 1988   *NYPL [IEC 89-1295]*

AFRO-AMERICANS - STUDY AND TEACHING - MARYLAND - BALTIMORE.
Fisher, Walter. Ideas for Black studies.
Baltimore, 1971. vii, 51 p.
E184.7 .F53   *NYPL [Sc 917.306-F]*

AFRO-AMERICANS - STUDY AND TEACHING - NEW YORK (CITY)
New York (N.Y.). Bureau of Curriculum
Development. Black studies. New York [c1970]
vii, 227 p. DDC 375/.0097471 s
LB1563 .N57 1970-71, no. 3
    NYPL [Sc G 87-32]

AFRO-AMERICANS - SUFFRAGE.
Blacks and the 1984 Republican National
Convention . Washington, D.C. (1301
Pennsylvania Ave., N.W., Suite 400,
Washington 20004) , 1984. v, 25 p. ; ISBN
0-941410-51-X (pbk.) DDC 324.2734 19
JK2353 1984   *NYPL [Sc F 87-172 rept. 4]*

Cavanagh, Thomas E. The impact of the Black
electorate [microform] /. Washington, D.C.
(1301 Pennsylvania Ave., N.W., Suite 400,
Washington 20004) , 1984. v, 28 p. ; DDC
324.973/08996073 19
E185.615 .C364 1984   *NYPL [*Z-4913 no.8]*

Cavanagh, Thomas E. Jesse Jackson's
campaign . Washington, D.C. , 1984. 27 p.,
[1] ; ISBN 0-941410-45-5 (pbk.) DDC 324.973 19
JK526 1984c   *NYPL [Sc F 87-172 rept. 2]*

AFRO-AMERICANS - SUFFRAGE - HISTORY.
Walters, Ronald W. Black presidential politics
in America . Albany , c1988. xvii, 255 p. ISBN
0-88706-546-5 DDC 324.6/2/08996073 19
JK1924 .W34 1987   *NYPL [Sc E 88-283]*

AFRO-AMERICANS - SUFFRAGE - MISSISSIPPI.
McAdam, Doug. Freedom Summer /. New

York , c1988. [xiii], 333 p., [14] p. of plates :
ISBN 0-19-504367-7 (alk. paper) DDC
976.2/00496073 19
E185.93.M6 M28 1988   *NYPL [Sc E 88-563]*

AFRO-AMERICANS - TENNESSEE - FRANKLIN COUNTY - HISTORY.
Hill, Arthur Cyrus. The history of the Black
people of Franklin County, Tennessee
[microform] /. 1981. 408 leaves.
    NYPL [Sc Micro R-4685]

AFRO-AMERICANS - UNITED STATES. see AFRO-AMERICANS.

AFRO-AMERICANS - UNITED STATES - BIOGRAPHY - JUVENILE LITERATURE.
Ferris, Jeri. What are you figuring now? .
Minneapolis , c1988. 64 p. : ISBN 0-87614-331-1
(lib. bdg.) : DDC 520.92/4 B 92 19
QB36.B22 F47 1988   *NYPL [Sc D 89-120]*

AFRO-AMERICANS - UNITED STATES - INTERVIEWS.
Govenar, Alan B., 1952- Meeting the blues /.
Dallas, Tex. , c1988. 239 p. : ISBN
0-87833-623-0 : DDC 784.5/3/00922 19
ML3521 .G68 1988   *NYPL [Sc G 89-4]*

AFRO-AMERICANS - VIRGINIA - NORFOLK - SOCIAL CONDITIONS.
Suggs, Henry Lewis. P.B. Young,
newspaperman . Charlottesville , 1988. xxii, 254
p. : ISBN 0-8139-1178-8 DDC 070.4/1/0924 B 19
PN4874.Y59 S84 1988   *NYPL [JFE 89-97]*

AFRO-AMERICANS - VIRGINIA - RICHMOND - HISTORY - TO 1863 - EXHIBITIONS.
McGraw, Marie Tyler. In bondage and
freedom . Richmond, VA. [Chapel Hill, N.C.] ,
1988. 71 p. :   *NYPL [Sc F 89-107]*

AFRO-AMERICANS - VIRGINIA - RICHMOND - SOCIAL CONDITIONS.
Davis, Scott C., 1948- The world of Patience
Gromes . [Lexington, Ky.] , 1988. 222 p. ;
ISBN 0-8131-1644-9 DDC 975.5/45100496073
19
F234.R59 N43 1988   *NYPL [Sc D 88-1302]*

AFRO-AMERICANS - VIRGINIA - RICHMOND - SOCIAL CONDITIONS - TO 1964 - EXHIBITIONS.
McGraw, Marie Tyler. In bondage and
freedom . Richmond, VA. [Chapel Hill, N.C.] ,
1988. 71 p. :   *NYPL [Sc F 89-107]*

AFRO-AMERICANS - VIRGINIA - RICHMOND - SOCIAL LIFE AND CUSTOMS.
Davis, Scott C., 1948- The world of Patience
Gromes . [Lexington, Ky.] , 1988. 222 p. ;
ISBN 0-8131-1644-9 DDC 975.5/45100496073
19
F234.R59 N43 1988   *NYPL [Sc D 88-1302]*

AFRO-AMERICANS - WEST (U. S.) - BIOGRAPHY.
Katz, William Loren. The Black West /. Seattle,
WA , c1987. xiii, 348 p. : ISBN 0-940880-17-2
DDC 978/.00496073 19
E185.925 .K37 1987   *NYPL [Sc E 89-86]*

AFRO-AMERICANS - WEST (U. S.) - FICTION.
Davis, Levaster. Torture /. New York , c1987.
167 p. ; ISBN 0-533-07293-X
    NYPL [Sc D 88-517]

AFRO-AMERICANS - WEST (U. S.) - HISTORY.
Katz, William Loren. The Black West /. Seattle,
WA , c1987. xiii, 348 p. : ISBN 0-940880-17-2
DDC 978/.00496073 19
E185.925 .K37 1987   *NYPL [Sc E 89-86]*

Afro-Asian nations: history and culture.
Knappert, Jan. East Africa . New Delhi ,
c1987. 383 p. : ISBN 0-7069-2822-9 : DDC 967.6
19
DT423 .K56 1987   *NYPL [Sc D 88-852]*

AFRO-ASIAN POLITICS.
Essack, Karrim. The Mathaba International /.
Dar es Salaam [1987?] iv, 81 p. : DDC 325/.32
19
JC359 .E825 1987   *NYPL [Sc C 89-30]*

The Afro-Nicaraguans . Congress, Rick. [Atlanta,
Georgia] , c1987. 88 p. :
    NYPL [Sc D 88-1280]

Afroamerican poetics. Baker, Houston A.
Afro-American poetics . Madison, Wis. , c1988.

x, 201 p. ; ISBN 0-299-11500-3 : DDC
810/.9/896073 19
PS153.N5 B22 1988   *NYPL [Sc D 88-1356]*

Afroamerikanischen Religionen .
(2) Fichte, Hubert. Xango /. Frankfurt am
Main , 1981. 353 p. ; ISBN 3-10-020701-7
NYPL [Sc D 88-1481]

Afrocommunism /. Ottaway, Marina. New York ,
1986. ix, 270 p. : ISBN 0-8419-1034-0 DDC
335.43/096 19
HX438.5 .O87 1985   *NYPL [JLD 86-4056]*

Afrocomunistas. Romero, Vicente, 1947-
Guinea-Bissau y Cabo Verde . Madrid , 1981.
109 p. ; ISBN 84-85761-09-X DDC 966/.5702 19
DT613.78 .R66 1981   *NYPL [Sc C 89-1]*

Afshar, Haleh, 1944- Women, state, and
ideology . Basingstoke, Hampshire , c1987. xii,
245 p. : ISBN 0-333-41389-X
NYPL [JLD 87-2346]

After 4.30 /. Maillu, David G., 1939- Nairobi,
Kenya , 1987. 249 p. ;   *NYPL [Sc C 89-143]*

Against all odds . Hubbard, Stephen, 1961-
Toronto , 1987. 140 p. : ISBN 1-550-02013-7
(bound)   *NYPL [Sc D 88-985]*

Against all odds . Woodling, Chuck. Lawrence,
KS , c1988. 138 p., [16] p. of plates : ISBN
0-7006-0387-5 (pbk.) : DDC
796.32/363/0978165 19
GV885.43.U52 W66 1988
NYPL [JFF 89-236]

Agbà tí ń y Owolabi, Olu. Ibàdàn, Nigeria , 1985.
iii, 117 p. ; ISBN 978-16-7246-3
NYPL [Sc C 88-219]

Agbetiafa, Komla. Les ancêtres et nous : analyse
de la pensée religieuse des Bê de la Commune
de Lomé / Komla Agbetiafa. Dakar : Les
Nouvelles Editions africaines, 1985. 95 p. : ill. ;
21 cm. Bibliography: p. 93. ISBN 2-7236-0929-4
*1. Ewe (African people) - Religious life and customs. 2.
Ancestor worship - Togo. 3. Funeral rites and
ceremonies, Ewe (African people). I. Title.*
NYPL [Sc D 88-7]

Agbi, Sunday O. The Organization of African
Unity and African diplomacy, 1963-1979 / S.O.
Agbi. 1st ed. Agodi, Ibadan : Impact Publishers
Nig., 1986. x, 166 p. ; 22 cm. Includes index.
Bibliography: p. 156-158. ISBN 978-238-601-4 (pbk.)
DDC 960/.326 19
*1. Organization of African Unity - History. 2. Africa -
Politics and government - 1960-. 3. Africa - Foreign
relations - 1960-. I. Title.*
DT30.5 .A374 1986   *NYPL [Sc D 89-124]*

Agbodjan, Combévi. Institutions politiques et
organisation administrative du Togo / Combévi
Agbodjan. [S.l. : s.n., between 1981 and 1984]
134 leaves, [1] folded leaf of plates : ill. ; 21
cm. DDC 320.966/81 19
*1. Local government - Togo. 2. Togo - Politics and
government - 1960-. I. Title.*
JQ3532 .A37 1981   *NYPL [Sc D 88-224]*

Agboola, David. The Seventh Day Adventists in
Yorubaland, 1914--1964 : a history of
Christianity in Nigeria / by David Agboola.
Ibadan : Daystar Press, 1987. ix, 92 p. : ill.,
ports. ; 22 cm. Includes bibliographical references.
ISBN 978-12-2197-6
1. Seventh-Day Adventists - Nigeria - History. I. Title.
NYPL [Sc D 88-1043]

Agburum, Ezenwa. Broken graduate / by Ezenwa
Agburum. Orlu, Imo State, Nigeria : Culson &
Bombay, 1986. 96 p. ; 18 cm.
*1. Students - Nigeria - Fiction. 2. African students -
India - Fiction. I. Title.*   *NYPL [Sc C 88-193]*

AGE GROUPS - KENYA.
Spencer, Paul, 1932- The Maasai of Matapato .
Bloomington , c1988. xii, 296 p. : ISBN
0-253-33625-2 DDC 306/.08996 19
DT433.545.M33 S64 1988
NYPL [JFE 88-7115]

AGE - PHYSIOLOGICAL EFFECT. see
AGING.

AGED - AFRICA (WEST)
Aging in cross-cultural perspective . New
York , c1988. vii, 138 p. ; ISBN 0-940605-51-1
NYPL [Sc D 89-431]

AGED, AFRO-AMERICAN. see **AFRO-
AMERICAN AGED.**

AGED - BRAZIL.
Aging in cross-cultural perspective . New
York , c1988. vii, 138 p. ; ISBN 0-940605-51-1
NYPL [Sc D 89-431]

AGED - CANADA - SOCIAL CONDITIONS.
Driedger, Leo, 1928- Aging and ethnicity .
Toronto , 1987. xv, 131 p. : ISBN 0-409-81187-4
NYPL [Sc E 88-127]

AGED - CROSS-CULTURAL STUDIES.
Aging in cross-cultural perspective . New
York , c1988. vii, 138 p. ; ISBN 0-940605-51-1
NYPL [Sc D 89-431]

AGED - UNITED STATES.
Aging in cross-cultural perspective . New
York , c1988. vii, 138 p. ; ISBN 0-940605-51-1
NYPL [Sc D 89-431]

An agenda for Zimbabwe /. Ushewokunze, H. S.
M. (Herbert Sylvester Masiyiwa), 1938-
[Harare, Zimbabwe] c1984. vi, 198 p. ; ISBN
0-906041-67-8 DDC 361.6/1/096891 19
HX451.A6 U84 1984   *NYPL [Sc D 88-942]*

Agent K-13. Teague, Bob. Garden City, N.Y.,
c1974. 47 p., ISBN 0-385-08704-7 DDC [E]
PZ7.T21937 Ag   *NYPL [Sc E 88-587]*

Agheyisi, Rebecca N. An Ẹdo-English dictionary
/ by Rebecca N. Agheyisi. Benin City,
Nigeria : Ethiope Pub. Corp., 1986. xxiv, 169
p. : ill. ; 21 cm. ISBN 978-12-3293-5 DDC
496/.33 19
1. Bini language - Dictionaries - English. I. Title.
PL8077.4 .A44 1986   *NYPL [Sc D 88-847]*

Aging and ethnicity . Driedger, Leo, 1928-
Toronto , 1987. xv, 131 p. : ISBN 0-409-81187-4
NYPL [Sc E 88-127]

Aging in cross-cultural perspective : Africa and
the Americas / edited by Enid Gort. New
York : Phelps-Stokes Fund, c1988. vii, 138 p. ;
23 cm. "A Phelps Stokes Institute publication."
Includes bibliographies. ISBN 0-940605-51-1
*1. Aged - Africa (West). 2. Aged - Brazil. 3. Aged -
United States. 4. Aged - Cross-cultural studies. I. Gort,
Enid.*   *NYPL [Sc D 89-431]*

AGING PERSONS. see **AGED.**

AGING - SOCIAL ASPECTS - CONGRESSES.
The Black American elderly . New York ,
c1988. xvi, 383 p. ; ISBN 0-8261-5810-2 DDC
362.1/9897/00973 19
RA448.5.N4 B56 1988   *NYPL [JLE 88-5391]*

Agiri, Babatunde Aremu. History of the peoples
of Lagos State /. Ikeja, Lagos , 1987. xii, 378
p. ; ISBN 978-228-148-4   *NYPL [Sc D 88-731]*

Agnes Etherington Art Centre.
Fry, Jacqueline, 1923- Visual variations .
Kingston, Canada , c1987. vii, 63 p. : DDC
730/.0966/074011372 19
NB1098 .F79 1987   *NYPL [Sc F 88-189]*

**AGNES ETHERINGTON ART CENTRE -
EXHIBITIONS.**
Fry, Jacqueline, 1923- Visual variations .
Kingston, Canada , c1987. vii, 63 p. : DDC
730/.0966/074011372 19
NB1098 .F79 1987   *NYPL [Sc F 88-189]*

Agokla, K. M., 1955- L'aube nouvelle : roman /
K.M. Agokla. Lomé : Les Nouvelles Editions
africaines, 1982. 94 p. ; 21 cm. ISBN
2-7236-0850-6
1. Africa - Fiction. I. Title.
NYPL [Sc D 88-1018]

Agony of St. Lucia. DaBreo, D. Sinclair. --of men
and politics . Castries, St. Lucia , c1981. 208
p. : DDC 972.98/43 19
F2100 .D32 1981   *NYPL [Sc D 88-815]*

The agony of Uganda from Idi Amin to Obote .
Bwengye, Francis Aloysius Wazarwahi.
London , 1985. xxii, 379 p. ; ISBN
0-7212-0717-0 ;   *NYPL [Sc D 88-873]*

Agossou, Jacob-Mèdéwalé Jacob. Christianisme
africain : une fraternité au-delà de l'ethnie /
Mèdéwalé Jacob-Agossou. Paris : Editions
Karthala, 1987. 217 p. ; 22 cm. Includes
bibliographical footnotes. ISBN 2-86537-184-0
*1. Christianity - Africa, Sub-Saharan. 2. Theology,
Doctrinal - Africa, Sub-Saharan. I. Title.*
NYPL [Sc D 88-552]

Agostinho Neto /. Khazanov, A. M. (Anatoliĭ
Mikhaĭlovich), 1932- [Agostinó Neto. English.]
Moscow , 1986. 301 p. ; DDC 967/.304/0924 B

19
DT611.76.A38 K4213 1986
NYPL [Sc B 88-47]

Agostinho Neto, António, 1922- Sagrada
esperança / Agostinho Neto. São Paulo :
Editora Atica, 1985. 126 p. ; 21 cm. (Autores
africanos . 24) Introductory matter translated from the
English language ed. with title: Sacred hope.
Bibliography: pp. 124-126. ISBN 85-08-01056-7
I. Title. II. Series.   *NYPL [Sc D 89-64]*

AGOSTINHO NETO, ANTÓNIO, 1922-
Khazanov, A. M. (Anatoliĭ Mikhaĭlovich),
1932- [Agostinó Neto. English.] Agostinho
Neto /. Moscow , 1986. 301 p. ; DDC
967/.304/0924 B 19
DT611.76.A38 K4213 1986
NYPL [Sc B 88-47]

Agosto de Muñoz, Nélida. El fenómeno de la
posesión en la religión Vudú : un estudio sobre
la posesión por los espíritus y su relación con el
ritual en el Vudú / Nélida Agosto de Muñoz.
Río Piedras, P.R. : Instituto de Estudios del
Caribe, Universidad de Puerto Rico, 1975,
c1974. 119 p. ; 24 cm. (Caribbean monograph
series. no. 14) Originally presented as the author's
thesis (bachelor of letters --Oxford, 1969) under title:
The phenomenon of possession in Voodoo religion.
Bibliography: p. 113-119. DDC 299/.64 19
1. Voodooism. 2. Spirit possession. I. Title. II. Series.
BL2490 .A33 1975   *NYPL [TB (Caribbean
monograph series no. 14)]*

Agovi, Kofi Ermeleh, 1944- Novels of social
change / K. E. Agovi. Tema, Ghana : Ghana
Pub. Corp., 1988. xxviii, 290 p. ; 21 cm.
Bibliography: p. 288-290. ISBN 996-410-332-8
*1. English fiction - Social aspects. 2. African fiction
(English) - Social aspects. I. Title.*
NYPL [Sc D 88-1410]

AGRARIAN QUESTION. see **AGRICULTURE
AND STATE; AGRICULTURE -
ECONOMIC ASPECTS; LAND TENURE.**

AGRARIAN REFORM. see **LAND REFORM.**

Agrarstrukturen und Landflucht im Senegal .
Leber, Gisela. Saarbrücken , Fort Lauderdale ,
1979. vii, 142 p. : ISBN 3-88156-125-0
HD2144.5 .L42   *NYPL [JLD 80-2814]*

AGRIBUSINESS. see **AGRICULTURE -
ECONOMIC ASPECTS.**

Agribusiness in Africa /. Dinham, Barbara.
London , 1983. 224 p. : ISBN 0-946281-00-9 :
NYPL [Sc D 84-44]

Agricultural and natural resources [microform] .
Eltayab, Shorhabil Ali. Khartoum , 1978. 29
leaves ;   *NYPL [Sc Micro F-11041]*

AGRICULTURAL BANKS. see **BANKS AND
BANKING.**

**Agricultural commercialization and government
policy in Africa** /. Hinderink, J. (Jan) London ,
New York , 1987. xii, 328 p. : ISBN
0-7103-0205-3   *NYPL [Sc D 88-580]*

AGRICULTURAL CREDIT - SIERRA LEONE.
Johnny, Michael. Informal credit for integrated
rural development in Sierra Leone /. Hamburg ,
1985. xviii, 212 p. : ISBN 3-87895-274-X (pbk.)
HG2146.5.S5 J63x 1985
NYPL [Sc D 88-766]

Agricultural crisis in Africa . Iyegha, David A.,
1949- Lanham, MD , c1988. xx, 246 p. : ISBN
0-8191-7080-1 (alk. paper) DDC 338.1/09669 19
HD2145.5.Z8 I94 1988
NYPL [JLE 88-5390]

**AGRICULTURAL DEVELOPMENT
PROJECTS - NIGERIA -
ANNIVERSARIES,ETC.**
Events that marked the first decade of ADPs in
Nigeria. [Ibadan , 1986] 34 p. ;
NYPL [Sc F 89-74]

**AGRICULTURAL DEVELOPMENT
PROJECTS - SOUTH AFRICA -
HOMELANDS - CASE STUDIES.**
De Wet, C. J. Rural communities in transition .
Grahamstown [1983] iii, 113 p., [6] leaves of
plates : ISBN 0-86810-101-X (pbk.) DDC
307.7/2/0968 19
HD2130.5.Z9 H653 1983
NYPL [Sc F 88-328]

AGRICULTURAL ECONOMICS. see
AGRICULTURE - ECONOMIC ASPECTS.

AGRICULTURAL LABORERS - SOUTHERN STATES - HISTORY - 19TH CENTURY.
Van Deburg, William L. The slave drivers .
New York , 1988. xvii, 202 p. : ISBN
0-19-505698-1 DDC 305.5/67/0975 19
E443 .V36 1988   *NYPL [Sc D 89-424]*

**AGRICULTURAL POLICY. see
AGRICULTURE AND STATE.**

AGRICULTURAL RESOURCES - MALAWI.
Buchanan, John, 1855-1896. The Shirè
highlands. Blantyre [Malawi] , 1982. xii, 260 p.,
[8] p. of plates :   *NYPL [Sc C 87-434]*

**AGRICULTURAL RESOURCES - SUDAN -
ABYEI.**
Eltayab, Shorhabil Ali. Agricultural and natural
resources [microform] . Khartoum , 1978. 29
leaves ;   *NYPL [Sc Micro F-11041]*

AGRICULTURE AND STATE - AFRICA.
Curtis, Donald, 1939- Preventing famine .
London , New York , 1988. xi, 250 p. ; ISBN
0-415-00711-9 DDC 363.8/7/096 19
HC800.Z9 F326 1988 *NYPL [JLD 88-3825]*

**AGRICULTURE AND STATE - AFRICA -
CASE STUDIES.**
Coping with Africa's food crisis /. Boulder ,
c1988. xi, 250 p. : ISBN 0-931477-84-0 (lib. bdg.) :
DDC 338.1/9/6 19
HD9017.A2 C65 1988 *NYPL [Sc E 88-287]*

**AGRICULTURE AND STATE - AFRICA, SUB-
SAHARAN.**
Hinderink, J. (Jan) Agricultural
commercialization and government policy in
Africa /. London , New York , 1987. xii, 328
p. : ISBN 0-7103-0205-3 *NYPL [Sc D 88-580]*

**AGRICULTURE AND STATE - BURKINA
FASO.**
Michigan State University. Dept. of Agricultural
Economics. An analysis of the Eastern ORD
rural development project in Upper Volta . East
Lansing , 1976. v, 103 p. : DDC 338.1/866/25
HD2135 .U63 1976   *NYPL [Sc F 89-170]*

**AGRICULTURE AND STATE - CARIBBEAN
AREA.**
Enjeux fonciers dan la Caraibe, en Amérique
centrale et à la Réunion. . Paris , c1987. 232
p. : ISBN 2-7380-0003-7 *NYPL [Sc E 88-246]*

AGRICULTURE AND STATE - GUINEA.
Guinea. Comité militaire de redressement
national. Premières mesures de mise en
application du programme du CMRN.
[Conakry, R.G. , 1984] 84 p. ;
HD2143.Z8 G85 1984 *NYPL [Sc E 88-306]*

AGRICULTURE AND STATE - KENYA.
Lofchie, Michael F. The policy factor . Boulder,
Colo. , Nairobi , c1989. xii, 235 p. : ISBN
1-555-87136-4 (alk. paper) : DDC 338.1/86762
19
HD2126.5.Z8 L64 1989
                          NYPL [Sc E 89-123]

AGRICULTURE AND STATE - NIGERIA.
Iyegha, David A., 1949- Agricultural crisis in
Africa . Lanham, MD , c1988. xx, 246 p. :
ISBN 0-8191-7080-1 (alk. paper) DDC
338.1/09669 19
HD2145.5.Z8 I94 1988
                          NYPL [JLE 88-5390]

**AGRICULTURE AND STATE - SOUTH
AFRICA.**
Keegan, Timothy J. Rural transformations in
industrializing South Africa . Basingstoke ;
London , 1987. xviii, 302 p. : ISBN
0-333-41746-1   *NYPL [Sc D 88-1228]*

AGRICULTURE AND STATE - TANZANIA.
Lofchie, Michael F. The policy factor . Boulder,
Colo. , Nairobi , c1989. xii, 235 p. : ISBN
1-555-87136-4 (alk. paper) : DDC 338.1/86762
19
HD2126.5.Z8 L64 1989
                          NYPL [Sc E 89-123]

**AGRICULTURE AND STATE - UGANDA -
BUGISU (DISTRICT)**
Bunker, Stephen G., 1944- Double dependency
and constraints on class formation in Bugisu,
Uganda /. Urbana, Ill. , 1983. v, 88 p. : DDC
303.3/09676/1 19
HD1538.U43 B86 1983
                          NYPL [Sc D 88-1054]

AGRICULTURE - CARIBBEAN AREA.
Rural development in the Caribbean /.
London , 1985. xxi, 246 p. : ISBN 0-312-69599-3
                          NYPL [Sc D 88-1309]

**AGRICULTURE - ECONOMIC ASPECTS -
AFRICA.**
Pisani, Edgard. Pour l'Afrique /. Paris , 1988.
251 p. ; ISBN 2-7381-0026-0
                          NYPL [Sc E 88-249]

**AGRICULTURE - ECONOMIC ASPECTS -
AFRICA, SUB-SAHARAN.**
Dinham, Barbara. Agribusiness in Africa /.
London , 1983. 224 p. : ISBN 0-946281-00-9 :
                          NYPL [Sc D 84-44]

Hinderink, J. (Jan) Agricultural
commercialization and government policy in
Africa /. London , New York , 1987. xii, 328
p. : ISBN 0-7103-0205-3 *NYPL [Sc D 88-580]*

**AGRICULTURE - ECONOMIC ASPECTS -
BOTSWANA - CASES STUDIES.**
Hesselberg, J. (Jan) The Third World in
transition . Uppsala , Stockholm, Sweden ,
1985. 256 p. : ISBN 91-7106-243-2 (pbk.) DDC
305.5/63 19
HD1538.B55 H47 1985
                          NYPL [Sc E 88-290]

**AGRICULTURE - ECONOMIC ASPECTS -
BURKINA FASO.**
Michigan State University. Dept. of Agricultural
Economics. An analysis of the Eastern ORD
rural development project in Upper Volta . East
Lansing , 1976. v, 103 p. : DDC 338.1/866/25
HD2135 .U63 1976   *NYPL [Sc F 89-170]*

**AGRICULTURE - ECONOMIC ASPECTS -
BURUNDI.**
Bonvin, Jean. Changements sociaux et
productivité agricole en Afrique Centrale /.
Paris : Centre de développement de
l'orgnisation de coopértion et de développement
économiques, c1986. 140 p. : ISBN
92-64-22803-9   *NYPL [Sc D 88-803]*

**AGRICULTURE - ECONOMIC ASPECTS -
IRAN.**
Jazayeri, Ahmad, 1957- Economic adjustment
in oil-based economies /. Aldershot, Hants,
England , Brookfield, Vt., USA , c1988. xvi,
260 p. : ISBN 0-566-05682-8 : DDC 330.955/054
19
HD9576.I62 J39 1988   *NYPL [JLD 89-202]*

**AGRICULTURE - ECONOMIC ASPECTS -
MALAWI.**
Martin, Michael. Malawi, ein
entwicklungspolitisches Musterland? . Bonn ,
1984. 95 p. : ISBN 3-921614-17-1
                          NYPL [Sc D 88-681]

**AGRICULTURE - ECONOMIC ASPECTS -
NIGERIA.**
Iyegha, David A., 1949- Agricultural crisis in
Africa . Lanham, MD , c1988. xx, 246 p. :
ISBN 0-8191-7080-1 (alk. paper) DDC
338.1/09669 19
HD2145.5.Z8 I94 1988
                          NYPL [JLE 88-5390]

Jazayeri, Ahmad, 1957- Economic adjustment
in oil-based economies /. Aldershot, Hants,
England , Brookfield, Vt., USA , c1988. xvi,
260 p. : ISBN 0-566-05682-8 : DDC 330.955/054
19
HD9576.I62 J39 1988   *NYPL [JLD 89-202]*

**AGRICULTURE - ECONOMIC ASPECTS -
NIGERIA, NORTHERN.**
Mortimore, M. J., 1937- Adapting to drought .
Cambridge , New York , 1989. xxii, 299 p. :
ISBN 0-521-32312-6 DDC 333.73 19
HC1055.Z7 N6755 1988
                          NYPL [Sc E 89-191]

**AGRICULTURE - ECONOMIC ASPECTS -
SENEGAL.**
Leber, Gisela. Agrarstrukturen und Landflucht
im Senegal . Saarbrücken , Fort Lauderdale ,
1979. vii, 142 p. : ISBN 3-88156-125-0
HD2144.5 .L42   *NYPL [JLD 80-2814]*

**AGRICULTURE - ECONOMIC ASPECTS -
SIERRA LEONE.**
Promoting smallholder cropping systems in
Sierra Leone . Berlin , 1985. xiv, 227 p. :
                          NYPL [Sc D 88-817]

**AGRICULTURE - ECONOMIC ASPECTS -
SOUTH AFRICA.**
Bundy, Colin. The rise and fall of the South

African peasantry /. Cape Town , 1988. [21],
276 p. ; ISBN 0-520-03754-5
                          NYPL [Sc D 89-533]

**AGRICULTURE - ECONOMIC ASPECTS -
SOUTH AFRICA - HISTORY.**
Keegan, Timothy J. Rural transformations in
industrializing South Africa . Basingstoke ;
London , 1987. xviii, 302 p. : ISBN
0-333-41746-1   *NYPL [Sc D 88-1228]*

**AGRICULTURE - ECONOMIC ASPECTS -
SOUTH AFRICA - HOMELANDS - CASE
STUDIES.**
De Wet, C. J. Rural communities in transition .
Grahamstown [1983] iii, 113 p., [6] leaves of
plates : ISBN 0-86810-101-X (pbk.) DDC
307.7/2/0968 19
HD2130.5.Z9 H653 1983
                          NYPL [Sc F 88-328]

**AGRICULTURE - ECONOMIC ASPECTS -
TANZANIA.**
Tanzania . Uppsala [Stockholm, Sweden]
1986. 325 p. : ISBN 91-7106-257-2 (pbk.) DDC
330.9678/04 19
HD2128.5 .T36 1986   *NYPL [Sc E 88-450]*

**AGRICULTURE - ECONOMICS. see
AGRICULTURE - ECONOMIC ASPECTS.**

AGRICULTURE - ETHIOPIA.
Minker, Gunter. Burji, Konso-Gidole, Dullay .
Bremen , 1986. vi, 275 p. : ISBN 3-88299-051-1
                          NYPL [Sc E 88-236]

AGRICULTURE - NIGERIA.
Iyegha, David A., 1949- Agricultural crisis in
Africa . Lanham, MD , c1988. xx, 246 p. :
ISBN 0-8191-7080-1 (alk. paper) DDC
338.1/09669 19
HD2145.5.Z8 I94 1988
                          NYPL [JLE 88-5390]

AGRICULTURE - SOMALIA.
Massey, Garth. Subsistence and change .
Boulder , 1987. xvii, 238 p. : ISBN
0-8133-7294-1 (alk. paper) : DDC
338.1/0967/73 19
DT402.4.R35 M37 1987
                          NYPL [Sc D 88-298]

**AGRICULTURE - SOUTHERN STATES -
HISTORY - 19TH CENTURY.**
Mathew, William M. Edmund Ruffin and the
crisis of slavery in the Old South . Athens ,
c1988. xiv, 286 p. : ISBN 0-8203-1011-5 (alk.
paper) DDC 306/.362/0924 19
F230.R932 M38 1988   *NYPL [JFE 88-3149]*

**AGRICULTURE - UGANDA - BUGISU
(DISTRICT) - SOCIETIES, ETC. -
POLITICAL ACTIVITY.**
Bunker, Stephen G., 1944- Double dependency
and constraints on class formation in Bugisu,
Uganda /. Urbana, Ill. , 1983. v, 88 p. : DDC
303.3/09676/1 19
HD1538.U43 B86 1983
                          NYPL [Sc D 88-1054]

AGRONOMY. see AGRICULTURE.

Água-marinha . Teodoro, Lourdes, 1946- Brasília ,
1978. 63 p. ;
PQ9698.3.E6985 A79   *NYPL [Sc D 88-889]*

Aguero, Kathleen. A Gift of tongues . Athens ,
c1987. xii, 342 p. ; ISBN 0-8203-0952-4 (alk.
paper) DDC 811/.5/09920693 19
PS153.M56 G54 1987   *NYPL [Sc E 88-364]*

Aguessy, Honorat, 1934- Affirmation de l'identité
culturelle et la formation de la conscience
nationale dans l'Afrique contemporaine.
Spanish. La Afirmación de la identidad cultural
y la formación de la coniencia nacional en el
África contemporánea /. Barcelona , Paris ,
1983. 220 p. ; ISBN 84-85800-57-5
                          NYPL [Sc D 88-597]

Aguilar, Mila D. A comrade is as precious as a
rice seedling : poems / by Mila D. Aguilar ;
introduction by Audre Lorde.1st ed. New
York : Kitchen Table, Women of Color Press,
c1984. xix, 37 p. : ill. ; 22 cm. ISBN
0-913175-04-8
I. Title.   *NYPL [Sc D 88-1158]*

Agyeman, Dominic Kofi. Ideological education
and nationalism in Ghana under Nkrumah and
Busia / D. Kofi Agyeman. Accra : Ghana
Universities Press, 1988. 81 p. ; 21 cm.
Originally published in 1974 under title: Erziehung und
Nationwerdung in Ghana. Bibliography: p. 76-79.
ISBN 996-430-120-0

1. Nationalism - Ghana. 2. Education - Ghana. 3. Education and state - Ghana. I. Title.
NYPL [Sc D 89-582]

Ah, man, you found me again. Gross, Mary Anne. (comp) Boston [1972] x, 84 p. ISBN 0-8070-1532-6 DDC 810/.8/09282
HQ792.U53 N53 1972 **NYPL [Sc F 88-336]**

Ahmad, Idzia. A Shout across the wall / by Idzia Ahmad. Lagos, Nigeria : Update Communications, 1988. 115 p. ; 18 cm. "A special publication for the Association of Nigerian Authors sponsored by Concord Press of Nigeria." ISBN 978-302-092-7
I. Association of Nigerian Authors. II. Title.
NYPL [Sc C 89-135]

AHMADU BELLO UNIVERSITY.
The pedagogy of a decade of OAU mock-summits at ABU. Zaria [1988] (Zaria : Ahmadu Bello University Press) 64 p. : ISBN 978-301-130-12   **NYPL [Sc G 88-38]**

AHMADU BELLO UNIVERSITY. FACULTY OF ARTS AND SOCIAL SCIENCES.
FASS, a quarter of a century . Zaria , 1988. vi, 82 p. ; ISBN 978-272-500-5
NYPL [Sc E 88-609]

AHMADU BELLO UNIVERSITY - HISTORY.
Silver jubilee . Zaria [1987] 76 p. :
NYPL [Sc D 89-6]

Ahmed, Shama. Social work with Black children and their families /. London , 1986. 207 p. ; ISBN 0-7134-4888-1 (cased)
NYPL [Sc D 89-281]

Ai, 1947-
[Cruelty]
Cruelty ; Killing floor : poems / by Ai ; foreword by Carolyn Forché. New York : Thunder's Mouth Press : Distributed by Persea Books, c1987. xi, 99 p. ; 22 cm. (Classic reprint series) Reprint (1st work). Originally published : Boston : Houghton Mifflin, 1973. Reprint (2nd work). Originally published : Boston : Houghton Mifflin, 1979. ISBN 0-938410-38-5 (pbk.) : DDC 811/.54 19
I. Ai, 1947- Killing floor. 1987. II. Title. III. Title: Killing floor. IV. Series.
PS3551.I2 A6 1987   **NYPL [JFD 88-417]**

Killing floor. 1987. Ai, 1947- [Cruelty.] Cruelty ; Killing floor : poems / by Ai ; foreword by Carolyn Forché. New York , c1987. xi, 99 p. ; ISBN 0-938410-38-5 (pbk.) : DDC 811/.54 19
PS3551.I2 A6 1987   **NYPL [JFD 88-417]**

Aid & development in southern Africa :
evaluating a participatory learning process / edited by Denny Kalyalya ... [et al.]. Trenton, N.J. : Africa World Press, [1988] xi, 148 p. : ill. ; 22 cm. Includes bibliographies and index. ISBN 0-86543-047-0 (pbk.) : DDC 338.968 19
1. Economic assistance - Africa, Southern - Evaluation. 2. Technical assistance - Africa, Southern - Evaluation. 3. Economic development projects - Africa, Southern - Evaluation. I. Kalyalya, Denny. II. Title: Aid and development in southern Africa.
HC900 .A53 1988   **NYPL [Sc D 88-1455]**

Aid and development in southern Africa. Aid & development in southern Africa . Trenton, N.J. [1988] xi, 148 p. : ISBN 0-86543-047-0 (pbk.) : DDC 338.968 19
HC900 .A53 1988   **NYPL [Sc D 88-1455]**

AID TO UNDERDEVELOPED AREAS. see ECONOMIC ASSISTANCE; TECHNICAL ASSISTANCE.

Aide à la migration . DeWind, Josh. [Aiding migration. French.] Montréal, Québec, Canada , 1988. 216 p. :   **NYPL [Sc D 89-441]**

AIDS : sexual behavior and intravenous drug use / Charles F. Turner, Heather G. Miller, and Lincoln E. Moses, editors. Washington, DC : National Academy Press, 1989. xiii, 589 p. : ill. ; 23 cm. "Committee on AIDS Research and the Behavioral, Social, and Statistical Sciences, Commission on Behavioral and Social Sociences and Education, National Research Council"--T.p. Includes bibliographical references and index. ISBN 0-309-03976-2; 0-309-03976-2 (pbk.).
1. AIDS (Disease) - United States - Prevention. 2. AIDS (Disease) - Research. 3. AIDS (Desease) - Epidemiology. I. Turner, Charles F., 1918-. II. Miller, Heather G. III. Moses, Lincoln E. IV. National

Research Council. Committee on AIDS Research and the Behavioral, Social, and Statistical Sciences.
NYPL [Sc D 89-342]

Aids, Africa and racism . Chirimuuta, Richard C. Bretby [England] , 1987. 160 p. ; ISBN 0-9512804-0-6 hardback
NYPL [Sc D 88-1185]

AIDS and the Third World / published [by the Panos Institute] in association with the Norwegian Red Cross. Trade ed. London : The Institute ; Philadelphia : New Society Publishers, 1989. v, 198 p. : ill. ; 23 cm. (Panos dossier . 1) Includes index. Bibliography: p. [180]-194. ISBN 0-86571-143-7 (hardcover)
1. AIDS (Disease). 2. AIDS (Disease) - Developing countries. I. Panos Institute. II. Norges Røde kors. III. Series. **NYPL [Sc D 89-51]**

AIDS (DESEASE) - EPIDEMIOLOGY.
AIDS . Washington, DC , 1989. xiii, 589 p. : ISBN 0-309-03976-2; 0-309-03976-2 (pbk.)
NYPL [Sc D 89-342]

AIDS (DISEASE)
AIDS and the Third World /. London , Philadelphia , 1989. v, 198 p. : ISBN 0-86571-143-7 (hardcover)
NYPL [Sc D 89-51]

Chirimuuta, Richard C. Aids, Africa and racism /. Bretby [England] , 1987. 160 p. ; ISBN 0-9512804-0-6 hardback
NYPL [Sc D 88-1185]

What science knows about AIDS. [New York] 1988. 152 p. :   **NYPL [Sc F 89-163]**

You CAN do something about AIDS /. Boston , 1988. 126 p. : ISBN 0-945972-00-8
NYPL [Sc C 88-290]

AIDS (DISEASE) - AFRICA.
Chirimuuta, Richard C. Aids, Africa and racism /. Bretby [England] , 1987. 160 p. ; ISBN 0-9512804-0-6 hardback
NYPL [Sc D 88-1185]

AIDS (DISEASE) - AFRICA, SUB-SAHARAN.
Shoumatoff, Alex. African madness /. New York , 1988. xviii, 202 p. ; ISBN 0-394-56914-8 : DDC 967/.0328 19
DT352.2 .S48 1988   **NYPL [Sc D 89-160]**

AIDS (DISEASE) - CALIFORNIA - SAN FRANCISCO.
A baseline survey of AIDS risk behaviors and attitudes in San Francisco's Black communities /. San Francisco, Calif. [1987] vii, 74, [59] leaves :   **NYPL [Sc F 88-232]**

AIDS (DISEASE) - CASE STUDIES.
Greenly, Mike, 1944- Chronicle . New York , c1986. 422 p. ; ISBN 0-8290-1800-X : DDC 616.97/92/00922 19
RC607.A26 G73 1986
NYPL [Sc D 88-1087]

Whitmore, George, 1945- Someone was here . New York, N.Y. , c1988. 211 p. ; ISBN 0-453-00601-9 : DDC 362.1/969792/00924 19
RC607.A26 W495 1988
NYPL [JLD 88-4435]

AIDS (DISEASE) - DEVELOPING COUNTRIES.
AIDS and the Third World /. London , Philadelphia , 1989. v, 198 p. : ISBN 0-86571-143-7 (hardcover)
NYPL [Sc D 89-51]

AIDS (DISEASE) - FICTION.
Duplechan, Larry. Tangled up in blue /. New York , 1989. 264 p. ; ISBN 0-312-02650-1 : DDC 813/.54 19
PS3554.U55 T36 1989 **NYPL [Sc D 89-250]**

AIDS (DISEASE) - PATIENTS - FAMILY RELATIONSHIPS.
Ruskin, Cindy. The quilt . New York , 1988. 160 p. : ISBN 0-671-66597-9 :
NYPL [Sc F 88-237]

Whitmore, George, 1945- Someone was here . New York, N.Y. , c1988. 211 p. ; ISBN 0-453-00601-9 : DDC 362.1/969792/00924 19
RC607.A26 W495 1988
NYPL [JLD 88-4435]

AIDS (DISEASE) - POLITICAL ASPECTS - UNITED STATES.
Krieger, Nancy. The politics of AIDS /. Oakland, CA , 19. 60 p. : ISBN 0-913781-06-1
NYPL [Sc D 88-1299]

AIDS (DISEASE) - POPULAR WORKS.
Greenly, Mike, 1944- Chronicle . New York , c1986. 422 p. ; ISBN 0-8290-1800-X : DDC 616.97/92/00922 19
RC607.A26 G73 1986
NYPL [Sc D 88-1087]

Jennings, Chris, 1954- Understanding and preventing AIDS . Cambridge, MA (P.O. Box 2060, Cambridge 02238-2060) , c1988. 230 p. : ISBN 0-936571-01-2 **NYPL [Sc F 88-239]**

Richardson, Diane. Women and AIDS /. New York , 1988. 183 p. ; ISBN 0-416-01741-X : DDC 616.9/792 19
RC607.A26 R53 1988 **NYPL [Sc D 88-987]**

AIDS (DISEASE) - PSYCHOLOGICAL ASPECTS.
Whitmore, George, 1945- Someone was here . New York, N.Y. , c1988. 211 p. ; ISBN 0-453-00601-9 : DDC 362.1/969792/00924 19
RC607.A26 W495 1988
NYPL [JLD 88-4435]

AIDS (DISEASE) - RESEARCH.
AIDS . Washington, DC , 1989. xiii, 589 p. : ISBN 0-309-03976-2; 0-309-03976-2 (pbk.)
NYPL [Sc D 89-342]

AIDS (DISEASE) - SOCIAL ASPECTS.
Blaming others . London , Philadelphia, PA , 1988. [120] p. ; ISBN 0-86571-146-1 (pbk.) DDC 362.1/042 19
RC607.A26 **NYPL [Sc D 88-1215]**

Whitmore, George, 1945- Someone was here . New York, N.Y. , c1988. 211 p. ; ISBN 0-453-00601-9 : DDC 362.1/969792/00924 19
RC607.A26 W495 1988
NYPL [JLD 88-4435]

AIDS (DISEASE) - SOCIAL ASPECTS - UNITED STATES.
Ruskin, Cindy. The quilt . New York , 1988. 160 p. : ISBN 0-671-66597-9 :
NYPL [Sc F 88-237]

AIDS (DISEASE) - UNITED STATES.
Krieger, Nancy. The politics of AIDS /. Oakland, CA , 19. 60 p. : ISBN 0-913781-06-1
NYPL [Sc D 88-1299]

AIDS (DISEASE) - UNITED STATES - PREVENTION.
AIDS . Washington, DC , 1989. xiii, 589 p. : ISBN 0-309-03976-2; 0-309-03976-2 (pbk.)
NYPL [Sc D 89-342]

AIDS-RELATED COMPLEX - CALIFORNIA - SAN FRANCISCO.
A baseline survey of AIDS risk behaviors and attitudes in San Francisco's Black communities /. San Francisco, Calif. [1987] vii, 74, [59] leaves :   **NYPL [Sc F 88-232]**

Aigbe, E. I. Emwẹn Ẹdo na zedu ẹre y'Ebo = Edo English dictionary / E.I. Aigbe. Lagos : Academy Press, [1986?] viii, 62 p. : port. ; 19 cm. Prefatory matter in Bini and English.
I. Bini language - Dictionaries - English. I. Title.
NYPL [Sc C 88-174]

Ailloud, Jean. Le Boulch, Pierre. Today's English . [Dakar] , 1968- v. ;
NYPL [Sc F 87-274]

Aina, Olusola. Aderounmu, Olusola. Managing the Nigerian education enterprise /. Ikeja, Lagos, Nigeria , 1986. 230 p. :
NYPL [Sc F 88-171]

Ainsi parlaient les anciens . Moundjegou-Mangangue, Pierre Edgar. Paris , 1987. 87 p. ; ISBN 2-903871-78-7
NYPL [Sc D 88-393]

Ain't you got no shame? /. Barrett, William M., 1900- Washington, D.C. , 1965. iii, 98 p. :
NYPL [Sc D 88-483]

AIR NAVIGATION. see AERONAUTICS.

Airports Authority of Trinidad and Tobago. The history of aviation in Trinidad & Tobago 1913-1962 / by the Airports Authority of Trinidad & Tobago. Port-of-Spain, Trinidad : Paria, 1987. xxv, 159 p., [77] p. of plates : ill., ports. ; 22 cm. Includes index. Written by Gaylord Kelshall. Bibliography: p. 136-142. ISBN 976-8054-24-2
1. Aeronautics - Trinidad and Tobago - History. I. Kelshall, Gaylord. II. Title.
NYPL [Sc D 87-1398]

Aishatu, and other plays /. Hagher, Iyorwuese H.

Benin City [Nigeria] , c1987. 136 p. ; ISBN
978-235-603-4 *NYPL [Sc D 88-797]*

Aisien, Ekhaguosa. IWU : the body markings of
the Edo people / by Edhaguosa Aisien ;
illustrations by Osemwegie Amadasun. Benin
City, Nigeria : Aisien Publishers, c1986. 64 p. :
ill. ; 22 cm.
*1. Body-marking - Nigeria. 2. Bini (African people) -
Social life and customs. I. Title.*
NYPL [Sc D 88-728]

Aita twake /. Mzemba, C. (Charles), 1955-
Zimbabwe , 1987. 135 p. ; ISBN 0-86922-418-2
NYPL [Sc C 89-119]

AJA (AFRICAN PEOPLE) - CONGRESSES.
Peuples du golfe du Bénin . Paris , c1984. 328
p. : ISBN 2-86537-092-5 DDC 966/.8004963 19
DT510.43.E94 P48 1984
NYPL [Sc E 88-449]

AJA (AFRICAN PEOPLE) - RELIGION.
Mort dans la vie africaine. Spanish. La Muerte
en la vida africana. Barcelona , París , 1984.
314 p. ; ISBN 84-85800-81-8
NYPL [Sc D 88-601]

Ajayi, John Olufemi.
Ebira names in Nigeria : the origin, meaning,
and pronounciation / John Olufemi Ajayi.
Okpella : S. Asekome, 1985. 51 p. : maps ; 23
cm. Bibliography: p. 51. ISBN 978-252-800-5 (pbk.)
DDC 929.4/089963 19
*1. Names, Personal - Igbira. 2. Names, Personal -
Nigeria. I. Title.*
CS2375.N6 A34 1985 NYPL [Sc D 88-1256]

Library education in Nigeria, 1948-1986 / John
Olufemi Ajayi, Moses Adekunle Omoniwa.
Zaria : Sponsored by the University Board of
Research, Ahmadu Bello University, 1987. ii,
81 p. ; 22 cm. Includes index.
*1. Library education - Bibliography. 2. Library
education - Nigeria - Bibliography. I. Omoniwa, Moses
Adekunle. II. Title.* *NYPL [Sc D 88-1376]*

Ajiboye, Josy. Romance of life / by Josy Ajiboye.
1st ed. Lagos, Nigeria : Daily Times of Nigeria,
1985. 108 p. : ill. ; 18 cm. Cover title.
1. Caricatures and cartoons - Nigeria. I. Title.
MLCS 87/7906 (P) NYPL [Sc C 89-85]

Ajose, Audrie. Emo and the Babalawo / Audrie
Ajose. Ibadan : University Press Limited, 1985.
51 p. : ill. (some col.) ; 18 x 22 cm. (Rainbow
series supplementary readers) SHOMBURG
CHILDREN'S COLLECTION. ISBN 978-15-5652-2
(Nigeria)
*1. Nigeria - Juvenile literature. I. Schomburg Children's
Collection. II. Title.*
NYPL [Sc C 88-152]

Akada wokure /. Runyowa, Genius T., 1945-
Gwelo, Zimbabwe , 1981. 123 p. ;
NYPL [Sc C 88-140]

Akakpo-Ahianyo, Anani K. Au hasard de la vie /
Anani K. Akakpo-Ahianyo. [Lomé?] : D'un
monde à l'autre, c1983. 111 p. ; 18 cm. Poems.
I. Title.
MLCS 84/818 (P) NYPL [Sc C 88-54]

Akangbou, Stephen D. The economics of
educational planning in Nigeria / Stephen D.
Akangbou. New Delhi : Vikas Pub. House,
c1985. 150 p. ; 21 cm. Includes bibliographies and
index. ISBN 0-7069-2338-3
*1. Educational planning - Nigeria. 2. Education -
Economic aspects - Nigeria. I. Title.*
NYPL [Sc D 88-289]

Akeh, Afam. Stolen moments / by Afam Akeh.
Lagos, Nigeria : Update Communications, 1988.
66 p. ; 18 cm. "A special publication for the
Association of Nigerian Authors sponsored by Concord
Press of Nigeria." ISBN 978-302-097-8
I. Association of Nigerian Authors. II. Title.
NYPL [Sc C 89-133]

**AKELEY, CARL ETHAN, 1864-1926 -
JUVENILE LITERATURE.**
Sutton, Felix. Big game hunter . New York ,
1960. 192 p. : *NYPL [Sc D 88-659]*

Akeredolu, J. L. The Church and its
denominations in Nigeria / by J.L. Akeredolu.
Ibadan : Dastar [i.e. Daystar] Press, 1986. viii,
68 p. ; 18 cm. ISBN 978-12-2193-3 (pbk.) DDC
280/.09669 19
*1. Christian sects - Nigeria. 2. Nigeria - Church history.
I. Title.*
BR1463.N5 A39 1986 NYPL [Sc C 89-71]

Akéwì ló n'ìtàn . Awóyẹle, Oyètúndé. Ibàdàn ,
1987. iv, 97 p. ; ISBN 978-14-5044-4
NYPL [Sc C 88-216]

Akhenaten, King of Egypt /. Aldred, Cyril.
London, N.Y. , 1988. 320 p. : ISBN
0-500-05048-1 DDC 932/.014/0924 B 19
*DT87.4 .A24 1988 NYPL [*OBX 88-4161]*

AKHENATON, KING OF EGYPT.
Aldred, Cyril. Akhenaten, King of Egypt /.
London, N.Y. , 1988. 320 p. : ISBN
0-500-05048-1 DDC 932/.014/0924 B 19
*DT87.4 .A24 1988 NYPL [*OBX 88-4161]*

Akin, Louis. Chants d'aurore pour Manou :
poèmes / Louis Akin. [Abidjan] : CEDA,
c1983. 68 p. ; 18 cm. (CEDA Poésie) Cover title:
Chant pour Manou. ISBN 2-86394-013-9
I. Title. II. Title: Chant pour Manou.
NYPL [Sc C 88-121]

Akinfeleye, Ralph A. Contemporary issues in
mass media for development and national
security /. Lagos , 1988. xiv, 235 p. ; ISBN
978-228-317-7 *NYPL [Sc D 89-573]*

Akinjogbin, I. A. Concept de pouvoir en Afrique.
Spanish. El concepto del poder en África /.
Barcelona , París , 1983. 178 p. ; ISBN
92-3-301887-3 (Unesco)
NYPL [Sc D 88-604]

Akinlabí, Bánjọ. Nňkan Àṣírí / láti ọw Ibadan,
Oyo State, Nigeria : Abiprint Pub. Co., 1985.
62 p. ; 22 cm. ISBN 978-14-1052-3
1. Yoruba language - Texts. I. Title.
NYPL [Sc D 88-1381]

Akinsanya, Justus A. An African "Florence
Nightingale" : a biography of Chief (Dr) Mrs
Kofoworola Abeni Pratt / by Justus A.
Akinsanya. Ibadan, Nigeria : Vantage
Publishers, 1987. xii, 224 p. : ill., ports. ; 22
cm. Includes index. ISBN 978-245-826-0 (hard back
ed.)
*1. Pratt, Kofoworula Abeni. 2. Nurses - Nigeria -
Biography. I. Title.* *NYPL [Sc D 88-895]*

Akinsemoyin, Kunle.
Building Lagos/ by Kunle Akinsemoyin & Alan
Vaughan-Richards. 2d ed. Jersey: Pengrail,
1977, c1906. 76 p.: ill., maps; 22x32 cm. Cover
title.
*1. Architecture - Nigeria - Lagos (City). 2. Lagos
(City) - History. I. Vaughan-Richards, Alan, joint
author. II. Title.* *NYPL [3-MQWW 79-2215]*

Who are Lagosians? [microform] / by 'Kunle
Akinsemoyin. [Lagos : s.n.],c1979 (Lagos :
Nigerian Security Print. & Minting Co.) 23 p. ;
22 cm. Microfiche. New York: New York Public
Library, 198 . 1 microfiche: negative; 11 x 15 cm. (FSN
Sc 019,132)
1. Lagos (City) - History. I. Title.
NYPL [Sc Micro F-11129]

Akinyemi, A. B. Disarmament and development .
Lagos, Nigeria , 1986. ix, 117 p., 1 folded leaf :
ISBN 978-13-2828-2 *NYPL [Sc D 88-783]*

Akiri, Chris W.A. Essays in African and
European history. Ikeja, Lagos State Nigeria :
Lantern Books, 1984. 143 p.
I. Title. *NYPL [Sc D 88-1132]*

Akójop T.A.A. Ladele ... [et al.] ; olóòtú
gbogbo-gbòò. Lagos : Macmillan Nigeria, 1986.
xi, 324 p., map, ports. ; 22 cm. ISBN
978-13-2563-1
*1. Yorubas. 2. Yoruba language - Texts. I. Ladele, T. A.
A. II. Qlabimtan, Afolabi.* *NYPL [Sc D 88-955]*

Àkójop Àlàbá, 'Gbóyèga. Nigeria , 1985. 118 p. ;
ISBN 978-227-101-2
NYPL [Sc D 88-1373]

Akosa, Chike. Heroes & heroines of Onitsha / by
Chike Akosa. 1st ed. Onitsha, Nigeria : C.
Akosa, 1987 (Etukokwu Press) viii, 344 p. :
ports. ; 21 cm. ISBN 978-303-730-7
*1. Onitsha (Nigeria) - Biography. 2. Onitsha, Nigeria -
History. I. Title. II. Title: Heroes and heroines of
Onitsha.* *NYPL [Sc D 88-1109]*

Akpa, G. O. Udoh, Sunday. Theory and practice
of educational administration in Nigeria /. Jos,
Nigeria , 1987. x, 347 p. :
NYPL [Sc E 88-295]

Akpan, A. O. (Aneidi Okon) ca. 1916-
Zementskulpturen aus Nigeria . Stuttgart ,
c1988. 70 p. : *NYPL [Sc F 89-44]*

**AKPAN, A. O. (ANEIDI OKON), CA. 1916- -
EXHIBITIONS.**

Zementskulpturen aus Nigeria . Stuttgart ,
c1988. 70 p. : *NYPL [Sc F 89-44]*

Akpan, Ekwere Otu. The women's war of 1929 :
preliminary study / by Ekwere Otu Akpan &
Violetta I. Ekpo. Calabar, Nigeria : Govt.
Printer, 1988. vii, 68 p. : ill., maps ; 24 cm.
Bibliography: p. 66-68.
*1. Women - Nigeria. 2. Nigeria - Politics and
government - To 1960. I. Ekpo, Violetta I. II. Title.*
NYPL [Sc E 89-20]

Akpan, Emmanuel D. (Emanuel David), 1938-
Communication and media arts : a new
approach to the basics / Emmanuel Akpan.
Uyo [Nigeria] : Modern Business Press, c1987.
178 p. : ill. ; 23 cm. Includes bibliographical
references. ISBN 978-267-600-4
*1. Communication - Nigeria. 2. Mass media - Nigeria.
I. Title.* *NYPL [Sc D 88-752]*

Akpan, Monday B. African resistance in Liberia :
the Vai and the Gola-Bandi / Monday B.
Akpan. Bremen : Liberia Working Group, 1988.
68 p. : maps ; 21 cm. (Liberia Working Group
papers, 0932-1896 . no. 2) Includes bibliographical
references. ISBN 3-926771-01-1
*1. Gbandi (Liberian people). 2. Vai (African people). 3.
Liberia - History - To 1847. 4. Liberia - History -
1847-1944. I. Title. II. Series.*
NYPL [Sc D 89-347]

Akpan, S. J. (Sunday Jack), ca. 1940-
Zementskulpturen aus Nigeria . Stuttgart ,
c1988. 70 p. : *NYPL [Sc F 89-44]*

**AKPAN, S. J. (SUNDAY JACK), CA. 1940- -
EXHIBITIONS.**
Zementskulpturen aus Nigeria . Stuttgart ,
c1988. 70 p. : *NYPL [Sc F 89-44]*

Aktueller Informationsdienst Afrika. Beiheft .
(9) Die UNO-Sondersitzung über Afrika 1986
in der afrikanischen Presse /. Hamburg , 1986.
ii, 104 p. : ISBN 3-923519-66-4
NYPL [Sc F 88-229]

Aktueller Informationsdienst Afrika, 0720-0471.
Sondernummer .
(5) Senegal . Hamburg , 1983. xxxix, 392 p. :
ISBN 3-922887-28-7 (pbk.) DDC 324.266/3 19
JQ3396.A91 S38 1983 NYPL [JLF 85-1341]

Akwa Ibom and Cross River States : the land,
the people and their culture / edited by
Monday B. Abasiattai. Calabar [Nigeria] :
Wusen Press, 1987. 284 p. : ill., maps ; 21 cm.
Includes index. Bibliographical references. ISBN
978-228-320-7
*1. Akwa Ibom State (Nigeria). 2. Cross River State
(Nigeria). I. Abasiattai, Monday B.*
NYPL [Sc D 88-740]

AKWA IBOM STATE (NIGERIA)
Akwa Ibom and Cross River States . Calabar
[Nigeria] , 1987. 284 p. : ISBN 978-228-320-7
NYPL [Sc D 88-740]

Al África, españoles! . Castillo, Rafael del.
Barcelona-Gracia [1895?]- v.
NYPL [Sc D 88-1097]

**Al Hajj al Imam Isa Abd' Allah Muhammed al
Mahdi.** see 'Isá 'Abd Allāh Muḥammad al-
Mahdi, 1945-

**al Mahdi, Al Hajj al Imam Isa Abd' Allah
Muhammad.** see 'Isá 'Abd Allāh Muḥammad
al-Mahdi, 1945-

al-Numayrī, Ja'far Muḥammad. Text of address
delivered by His Excellency President Gaafar
Mohamed Nimeiry, at the opening sitting of the
first session of the second People's Assembly,
Khartoum, 24th May, 1974 [microform]
[Khartoum] : Democratic Republic of the
Sudan, [1974] 24 p., [1] p. of plates : port. ; 17
cm. Cover title. Microfiche. New York: New York
Public Library, 198 . 1 microfiche: negative; 11 x 15 cm.
(FSN Sc 019,080)
*1. Sudan - Politics and government - Addresses, essays,
lectures. I. Sudan Majlis al-Sha'b. II. Title.*
NYPL [Sc Micro F-11007]

Al Am Ibàdan, Nigeria , 1987, c1978. vi, 136 p. ;
ISBN 978-16-7488-1 *NYPL [Sc D 88-952]*

Àlàbá, 'Gbóyèga. Àkójop 'Gbóyèga Àlàbà.
Nigeria : Ayọ Ṣodimu Publishers, 1985. 118 p. ;
22 cm. ISBN 978-227-101-2
1. Yoruba language - Texts. I. Title.
NYPL [Sc D 88-1373]

**ALADURA CHURCHES. see ZIONIST
CHURCHES (AFRICA)**

Alagoa, Ebiegberi Joe. Noin nẹngıa, bẹre nẹngia . Port Harcourt, Nigeria , 1986. 137 p. ; ISBN 978-232-110-9 *NYPL [Sc E 89-130]*

Alao, Kayode. Makinde, Olu. Profile of career education /. Ibadan, Oyo State, Nigeria , 1987. xv, 308 p. ; ISBN 978-254-605-4 *NYPL [Sc D 89-177]*

ALASKA - DESCRIPTION AND TRAVEL - 1867-1896.
Healy, M. A. (Michael A.) Report of the cruise of the revenue marine steamer Corwin in the Arctic Ocean in the year 1884 /. Washington , 1889. 128 p., [39] leaves of plates : *NYPL [Sc Rare F 88-62]*

Àlayé Akéwi /. Adéwọlé, Lásún. Ibàdàn , 1987. v. 90 p. ; ISBN 978-14-5062-2 *NYPL [Sc C 88-217]*

Albert Buron, ou, Profil d'une "élite" /. Victor, Gary, 1958- [Port-au-Prince , 1988] 230 p. ; *NYPL [Sc D 88-1005]*

Albuquerque, L. M. do Couto de.
Albuquerque, L. M. do Couto de. O escravo branco . Lisboa , 1854. 4 v. : *NYPL [Sc F 82-65]*

O escravo branco : companheiro do tio Thomaz, ou A vida de um fugitivo na Virginia : romance de Hildreth / tradução livre de L.M. do Couto de Albuquerque. Lisboa : Typ. de L.C. da Cunha, 1854. 4 v. : ill. ; 21 cm. Translation of: The slave; or, Memoirs of Archy Moore.
1. Slavery in the United States - Fiction. I. Albuquerque, L. M. do Couto de. II. Hildreth, Richard, 1807-1865. The white slave. III. Title.
NYPL [Sc F 82-65]

Alcock, Gudrun. Turn the next corner. New York, Lothrop, Lee & Shepard [1969] 160 p. 22 cm. When his father is imprisoned, Richie and his mother must move to Chicago's crowded near-north side. Here Richie makes friends with a crippled Negro boy whose toughness and perseverance help Richie deal with the new problems in his life. SCHOMBURG CHILDREN'S COLLECTION. DDC [Fic]
1. Afro-American children - Juvenile fiction. I. Schomburg Children's Collection. II. Title.
PZ7.A332 Tu *NYPL [Sc D 88-1471]*

Aldred, Cyril. Akhenaten, King of Egypt / Cyril Aldred. London, N.Y. : Thames and Hudson, 1988. 320 p. : ill. ; 26 cm. Includes index. Bibliography: p. 308-312. ISBN 0-500-05048-1 DDC 932/.014/0924 B 19
1. Akhenaton, King of Egypt. 2. Egypt - History - Eighteenth dynasty, ca. 1570-1320 B.C. I. Title.
DT87.4 .A24 1988 *NYPL [*OBX 88-4161]*

ALE-HOUSES. see HOTELS, TAVERNS, ETC.

Alexander, Jim. Duke and other legends : jazz photographs / by Jim Alexander. Atlanta, GA. : Blackwood Press, c1988. 63 p. : chiefly ports ; 24 cm. ISBN 0-945708-03-3
1. Jazz musicians - United States - Portraits. 2. Afro-American musicians - Portraits. I. Title. II. Title: Jazz photographs. *NYPL [Sc E 89-63]*

Alexander, Neville. Sow the wind : contemporary speeches/ Neville Alexander. Johannesburg : Skotaville Publishers, c1985 (1987 printing) xi, 180 p. ; 21 cm. ISBN 0-947009-07-8
1. Blacks - South Africa. I. Title.
NYPL [Sc D 88-196]

Alexis, Marcus. Black economic progress . Washington, D.C. , Lanham, Md. , 1988. xi, 52 p. : ISBN 0-941410-69-2 (alk. paper) DDC 330.973/008996073 19
E185.8 .B496 1988 *NYPL [Sc E 89-154]*

ALFRED (SHIP)
Documentos relativos ao apresamento, julgamento e entrega da barca franceza Charles et Georges . Lisboa , 1858. 249, 16 p. ; *NYPL [Sc Rare G 86-1]*

Algeria - Government. see Algeria - Politics and government.

ALGERIA - POLITICS AND GOVERNMENT - 1945-1962.
Journée nationale du premier novembre 1961 [microform] Conakry [1961?] 38 p. ; *NYPL [Sc Micro F-11002]*

ALGERIA - RELIGIOUS LIFE AND CUSTOMS.
Sanson, Henri. Christianisme au miroir de l'Islam . Paris , 1984. 195 p. ; ISBN 2-204-02278-0 : *NYPL [*OGC 85-2762]*

ALGERIA - SOCIAL CONDITIONS.
Bouzar, Wadi, 1938- La culture en question /. Alger , Paris , c1982. 187 p. ; ISBN 2-903871-11-6 (pbk.) : DDC 306/.0965 19
HN980 .B68 1982 *NYPL [JLC 84-337]*

Algranti, Leila Mezan. D. Joao VI e os bastidores da independência / Leila Mezan Algranti. São Paulo : Editora Atica, 1987. 78 p. ; 18 cm. (Série Princípios . 115) Bibliography: p. 72-78. ISBN 85-08-01870-3
1. Brazil - History - 1763-1821. I. Title. II. Series.
NYPL [Sc C 88-15]

Ali, Arif. Third world impact /. London , 1986. 272 p. : ISBN 0-9506664-8-3 *NYPL [Sc F 88-19]*

Ali/Frazier III / [Harold Hayes, ed.] [S.l.] : Don King, 1975. [32] p. : ill. (some col.) ; 29 cm. "Souvenir program courtesy of Cutty Sark, Sept. 30th, 1975.
1. Ali Muhammad, 1942-. 2. Clay, Cassius, 1944-. I. King, Don. *NYPL [Sc F 89-46]*

Ali, Hauwa. Destiny : a novel / by Hauwa Ali. Enugu : Delta Publications (Nigeria), 1988. 101 p. ; 18 cm. ISBN 978-233-583-5
1. Nigeria - Fiction. I. Title.
NYPL [Sc C 89-151]

ALI MUHAMMAD, 1942-
Ali/Frazier III /. [S.l.] , 1975. [32] p. : *NYPL [Sc F 89-46]*

ALI, MUHAMMAD, 1942- - JUVENILE LITERATURE.
Rummel, Jack. Muhammad Ali /. New York , c1988. 128 p. : ISBN 1-555-46569-2 DDC 796.8/3/0924 B 92 19
GV1132.A44 R86 1988
NYPL [Sc E 88-175]

ALI, NOBLE DREW, 1886-
Is a Abd Ali ah Muḥammad al-Hahd i, 1945- Who was Noble Drew Ali? /. [Brooklyn, N.Y.] 1988, c1980. 122 p. : *NYPL [Sc D 89-74]*

'Isá 'Abd Allāh Muḥammad al-Mahdī, 1945- Who was Noble Drew Ali? [microform] /. Brooklyn, N.Y. [1980] 56 p. : *NYPL [Sc Micro R-4114 no. 10]*

Ali, Sidi H. The WAI as an ideology of moral rectitude / by Sidi H. Ali. [Nigeria : S. Ali], 1985 (Lagos : Academy Press) 88 p. : ill. ; 22 cm.
1. Ethics - Nigeria. 2. Nigeria - Moral conditions. 3. Nigeria - Social conditions. I. Title. II. Title: War Against Indiscipline as an ideology of moral rectitude.
NYPL [Sc D 88-869]

Alianza Mundial de Asociaciones Cristianas de Jóvenes. see World Alliance of YMCAs.

ALIEN LABOR - AMERICA.
When borders don't divide . Staten Island, N.Y. , c1988. viii, 220 p. : ISBN 0-934733-26-0 : DDC 325.8 19
JV7398 .W47 1988 *NYPL [Sc E 89-169]*

ALIEN LABOR - EUROPE.
Power, Jonathan, 1941- Western Europe's migrant workers /. London , 1984. 35 p. : ISBN 0-08-030831-7 *NYPL [Sc F 88-231]*

ALIEN LABOR, HAITIAN - DOMINICAN REPUBLIC.
Báez Evertsz, Franc, 1948- Braceros haitianos en la República Dominicana /. [Santo Domingo] , c1986. 354 p. : DDC 331.6/2/729407293 19
HD8218.5 .B34 1986 *NYPL [JLE 88-5011]*

Plant, Roger. Sugar and modern slavery . London , Atlantic Highlands, N.J. , c1987. xiv, 177 p. : ISBN 0-86232-572-2 : DDC 331.7/6361/097293 19
HD8039.S852 D657 1987
NYPL [Sc D 87-1240]

ALIEN LABOR - NIGERIA.
Ukpong, Ignatius I. The contributions of expatriate and indigenous manpower to the manufacturing industry in Nigeria . [Calabar, Cross River State, Nigeria] [c1986] ix, 61 p. ; ISBN 978-227-526-3 DDC 331.12/57/09669 19
HD5848.A6 U37 1986 *NYPL [Sc C 89-128]*

ALIEN LABOR - QUÉBEC - MONTRÉAL.
Histoires d'immigrées . Montréal , 1987. 275 p. : ISBN 2-89052-170-2 *NYPL [Sc D 88-346]*

ALIEN WORKERS. see ALIEN LABOR.

ALIENATION (SOCIAL PSYCHOLOGY) IN LITERATURE.
Lewis, Marvin A. Treading the ebony path . Columbia , 1987. 142 p. ; ISBN 0-8262-0638-7 (alk. paper) DDC 863 19
PQ8172 .L49 1987 *NYPL [Sc D 88-443]*

ALIKER, ANDRÉ, 1894-1934.
Nicolas, Armand. Le combat d'André Aliker /. Fort-de-France , 1974. 108 p. : *NYPL [Sc D 88-1189]*

Aliki. (illus) Sherlock, Philip Manderson, Sir. Ears and tails and common sense: more stories from the Caribbean. London , 1982. xvii, 121 p. *NYPL [Sc D 88-1220]*

Aliu, Y. O. Silver jubilee . Zaria [1987] 76 p. : *NYPL [Sc D 89-6]*

All Africa Conference of Churches. Special Agency for EPEAA. Ecumenical Programme for Emergency Action in Africa : programme list. Nairobi : All Africa Conference of Churches, Special Agency for EPEAA : World Council of Churches, Division of Inter-Church Aid, Refugee and World Service, 1967. [193] p. ; 26 cm.
1. Church work with refugees - Africa. 2. Economic development projects - Africa. 3. Refugees - Charities - Africa. I. World Council of Churches. Division of Inter-church Aid, Refugee and World Service. II. Title.
NYPL [Sc F 88-74]

All-Africa Games (4th : 1987 : Nairobi, Kenya)
4th All Africa Games : 4th July-1st August 1987, Nairobi, Kenya : Torch relay programme. Lausanne : Berg & Associates for Africa, 1987. 64 p. : ill. (some col.), maps, ports. ; 30 cm. Cover title. "Incorporating All Africa Music Festival."
1. Relay races - Kenya. I. Title.
NYPL [Sc F 88-82]

The All-America Coeds /. Madden, Betsy. New York [1971] 143 p. ; ISBN 0-200-71785-5 *NYPL [Sc D 88-432]*

Alladin, M. P. The monstrous angel [microform] : 40 poems / by M. P. Alladin. Maraval, Trinidad : Alladin, [1969] viii, 41 p. ; 22 cm. Microfiche (neg.) 1 sheet. 11 x 15 cm. (NYPL FSN 27,732)
I. Title.
PR9272.9.A4 M6 *NYPL [*XM-10236]*

Allard, Jean-François-Marie, 1806-1889. Records from Natal, Lesotho, the Orange Free State, and Mozambique concerning the history of the Catholic Church in southern Africa . Roma, Lesotho [1974] 2 v. : DDC 282/.68 19
BV3625S67 R43 1974 *NYPL [Sc E 89-47]*

Allegations of corrupt use of powers of detention during 1976 state of emergency [microform]. [Kingston : s.n., 1979?] 70.2 p. ; 33 cm. Microfilm. New York: New York Public Library, 1982. 1 microfilm reel; 35 mm. (MN *ZZ-23051)
1. Jamaica. Emergency powers regulations 1976. 2. Detention of persons - Jamaica.
NYPL [Sc Micro R-4108 no.13]

Allen, Merritt Parmelee. Battle lanterns / by Merritt Parmele Allen ; decorations by Ralph Ray, Jr. New York : Longmans, Green, 1949. 278 p. ; 22 cm.
1. Afro-Americans - South Carolina - Juvenile fiction. 2. South Carolina - History - Revolution, 1775-1783 - Juvenile fiction. I. Title. *NYPL [Sc D 88-1106]*

Allen, Robert Raymond. Singing in the spirit : an ethnography of gospel performance in New York City's African-American church community / Robert Raymond Allen. Ann Arbor, Mich : University Microfilms International, c1987. xii, 424 p. ; 22 cm. Includes index. Thesis (PH. D.)--University of Pennsylvania,1987. Bibliography: p. [409]-420.
1. Gospel music - New York (N.Y.). I. Title.
NYPL [Sc D 88-1212]

Allen, S. W. Sartre, Jean Paul, 1905-1980. [Orphée noir. English.] Black Orpheus. [Paris, 1963?] 65 p. ; *NYPL [Sc C 88-110]*

Allen, William Dangaix, 1904- Africa [by] William D. Allen [and] Jerry E. Jennings. Benjamin E. Thomas, editor. Grand Rapids, Fideler Co. [c1972] 172, 20 p. illus. (part col.) 28 cm. A social studies text for the upper elementary grades, describing the geography, history, people, education, and industries of the countries of the African continent. SCHOMBURG CHILDREN'S COLLECTION. DDC 916

1. Africa - Juvenile literature. I. Jennings, Jerry E., joint author. II. Schomburg Children's Collection. III. Title.
DT5 *.A53 1972* **NYPL [Sc F 88-377]**

Alley, J. P. The meditations of "Hambone", with an introduction by Sara Beaumont Kennedy. Memphis, Tenn., Jahl [1918] 104 p. illus., port. 16 x 19 cm. On cover: Hambone's meditations.
1. Afro-Americans - Caricatures and cartoons. I. Title. II. Title: Hambone's meditations.
NYPL [Sc Rare C 89-28]

Alley, Roderic Martin.
Nuclear-weapon-free zones. Epstein, William, 1912- A nuclear-weapon-free zone in Africa? / William Epstein. Nuclear-weapon-free zones : the South Pacific proposal / Roderic Alley. Muscatine, Iowa , 1977. 52 p. ;
JX1974.7 *.E553* **NYPL [JLK 75-198 [no.]14]**

Alleyne, Mervyn. Roots of Jamaican culture / Mervyn C. Alleyne. London : Pluto, 1988. xii, 186 p. ; 22 cm. Includes index. Bibliography: p. 173-182. ISBN 0-7453-0245-9 DDC 972.92 19
1. Jamaica - Civilization. I. Title.
F1874 **NYPL [Sc D 88-1190]**

Alleyne, Mervyn C. Studies in Saramaccan language structure /. [Amsterdam] , 1987. viii, 112 p. ; ISBN 976-410-004-X
NYPL [Sc D 88-554]

Alleyne, Warren, 1924- Caribbean pirates / Warren Alleyne. London : Macmillan, 1986. v, 113 p. : ill., maps, facsims. ; 23 cm. Bibliography: p. 112-113. ISBN 0-333-40570-6 (cased) : DDC 910.4/53 19
1. Pirates - Caribbean Area - History. I. Title.
F2161 **NYPL [Sc D 88-448]**

Alliance universelle des Unions chrétiennes de jeunes gens. see **World Alliance of YMCAs.**

Allinson, William J. Memoir of Quamino Buccau : a pious Methodist / by William J. Allinson. Philadelphia : H. Longstreth ; London ; C. Gilpin, 1851. 30 p. ; 18 cm.
1. Slaves - United States - Biography. I. Buccau, Quamino. II. Title. **NYPL [Sc Rare G 86-28]**

Allison, Diane Worfolk. (ill) Cameron, Ann, 1943- Julian, secret agent /. New York , 1988. 62 p. : ISBN 0-394-91949-1 (lib. bdg.) : DDC [Fic] 19
PZ7.C1427 Jt 1988 **NYPL [Sc C 89-123]**

Allison, Philip. Life in the white man's grave : a pictorial record of the British in West Africa / Philip Allison. London : Viking, 1988. 192 p. : ill. ; 25 cm. Includes index. Bibliography: p. 187-188. ISBN 0-670-81020-7 : DDC 966 19
1. Africa, West - Colonization. 2. Africa, West - History. 3. Great Britain - History - 19th century. 4. Great Britain - History - 20th century. I. Title.
DT476.2 **NYPL [Sc F 88-174]**

Allo, Lorenzo. Domestic slavery in its relations with wealth : an oration pronounced in the Cuban Democratic Athenaeum of New York, on the evening of the 1st of January, 1854 / by Lorenzo Allo. New York : W.H. Timson, 1855. 16 p. ; 23 cm. Translated by Domingo de Goicouria.
1. Slavery - Cuba - Emancipation. 2. Slavery - Economic aspects. I. Title.
NYPL [Sc Rare G 86-32]

Almena's dogs /. Woody, Regina Llewellyn (Jones) New York , c1954. 240 p. :
NYPL [Sc D 88-648]

ALMSHOUSES - NEW YORK (N.Y.)
Whistelo, Alexander. (defendant) The Commissioners of the Alms-house, vs. Alexander Whistelo, a black man . New York , 1808. 56 p. ; **NYPL [Sc Rare F 88-21]**

Along this way /. Johnson, James Weldon, 1871-1938. New York , 1933. 418 p., [16] leaves of plates : **NYPL [Sc Rare F 89-9]**

ALPHA KAPPA ALPHA.
Parker, Marjorie H. An Alpha Kappa Alpha family album /. [Chicago] , 1984. 210 p. :
NYPL [Sc F 88-17]

An Alpha Kappa Alpha family album /. Parker, Marjorie H. [Chicago] , 1984. 210 p. :
NYPL [Sc F 88-17]

ALPHA KAPPA ALPHA - HISTORY.
Parker, Marjorie H. Alpha Kappa Alpha sorority . [Washington, D.C. , 1958] iii, 108 leaves ; **NYPL [Sc F 89-66]**

Alpha Kappa Alpha sorority . Parker, Marjorie H. [Washington, D.C. , 1958] iii, 108 leaves ;
NYPL [Sc F 89-66]

ALPHA PHI ALPHA.
Wesley, Charles H., 1891- The history of Alpha Phi Alpha . Chicago , 1981, c1929. xiv, 567 p. :
NYPL [Sc D 89-135]

Alphabets and careers /. Osahon, Naiwu. Apapa, Lagos, Nigeria , 1981. [32] p. : ISBN 978-18-6006-5 **NYPL [Sc F 88-295]**

Alschuler, Lawrence R., 1941- Multinationals and maldevelopment : alternative development strategies in Argentina, the Ivory Coast, and Korea / Lawrence R. Alschuler. Basingstoke, Hampshire : Macmillan Press, c1988. xii, 218 p. : ill. ; 23 cm. Includes index. Bibliography: p. 201-208. ISBN 0-333-41561-2
1. Economic development - Case studies. 2. International business enterprises - Case studies. 3. Argentina - Economic policy. 4. Ivory Coast - Economic policy. 5. Korea (South) - Economic policy - 1960-. I. Title. **NYPL [Sc D 88-701]**

Alte stürzt. Achebe, Chinua. [Things fall apart. German.] Okonkwo, oder, Das Alte stürzt . Stuttgart , c1958. 230 p. ;
NYPL [Sc C 88-357]

Alternaties vir apartheid. Eglin, Colin. Die beginsels en belied van die Suid-Afrikaanse Progressiewe Reformisteparty [microform] /. [Cape Town , 1975] 12, 12 p. ;
NYPL [Sc Micro R-4094 no. 4]

Alternative political futures for Nigeria / edited by Stephen O. Olugbemi. Nigeria : Nigerian Political Science Association, 1987. xviii, 565 p. ; 21 cm. "Papers presented at the 13th Annual Conference of the Nigerian Political Science Association, 1986." - p. iii. Bibliography: p. 565. ISBN 978-303-170-8
1. Political planning - Nigeria - Congresses. 2. Nigeria - Politics and government - Congresses. 3. Nigeria - Economic conditions - Congresses. I. Olugbemi, Stephen Oluwole, 1940-. II. Nigerian Political Science Association. **NYPL [Sc D 88-1374]**

Alternative to apartheid. Eglin, Colin. Die beginsels en belied van die Suid-Afrikaanse Progressiewe Reformisteparty [microform] /. [Cape Town , 1975] 12, 12 p. ;
NYPL [Sc Micro R-4094 no. 4]

Altman, Susan R. Extraordinary Black Americans from colonial to contemporary times / by Susan R. Altman. Chicago : Childrens Press, 1988. 240 p. : ill., ports. ; 25 cm. Includes index. Presents short biographies of ninety-five Black Americans from colonial to contemporary times, highlighting their personal achievements and their resulting contributions to the growth of American society. ISBN 0-516-00581-2 DDC 973/.0496073022 B 920 19
1. Afro-Americans - Biography - Juvenile literature. I. Title.
E185.96 *.A56 1988* **NYPL [Sc E 89-177]**

Alvares Maciel no degrêdo de Angola. Lopes, Francisco Antonio, 1882- [Rio de Janeiro] , 1958. 104 p. ;
HD9527.A22 L6 **NYPL [Sc D 88-419]**

Alvarez, Alexandra, 1946- Malabí Maticulambí : estudios afrocaribeños / Alexandra Alvarez. Montevideo, Uruguay? : Monte Sexto, c1987. 191 p. ; 21 cm. (Colección Temas (Monte Sexto (Firm)) . 008) Includes bibliographies. CONTENTS. - El negro como personaje : estudio de tres novelas venezolanos del siglo XX.--Léxico afroamericano en el castellano de Venezuela.
1. Venezuelan fiction - 20th century - History and criticism. 2. Spanish language - Venezuela - Foreign words and phrases - African. 3. African languages - Influence on Spanish. I. Title.
NYPL [Sc D 88-1012]

Alvarez, Tito, 1916- Cuba, a view from inside . New York [1985?] 2 v. :
TR646.U6 N4853x 1985
NYPL [Sc D 88-1511]

Alves, Miriam. Estrelas no dedo / Miriam Alves. São Paulo : M. Alves, 1985. 58 p. : ill. ; 16 cm. Poems.
I. Title. **NYPL [Sc B 88-8]**

Alyson, Sasha. You CAN do something about AIDS /. Boston , 1988. 126 p. : ISBN 0-945972-00-8 **NYPL [Sc C 88-290]**

Am Al Adébísí Am Ibàdan, Nigeria : Evans, 1987, c1978. vi, 136 p. ; 22 cm. (Ojúlówó Yorùbá) ISBN 978-16-7488-1

1. Yoruba language - Texts. I. Title.
NYPL [Sc D 88-952]

Ama goes to the library /. Ntrakwah, Abena. Accra , 1987. 16 p. : **NYPL [Sc F 88-352]**

Amachree, Igolima T. D. Ferns, George W. Secondary level teachers: supply and demand in Liberia. [East Lansing, c1970] xii, 116 p.
LB2833.4.L7 F4 **NYPL [JFM 72-62 no. 6]**

Amadi, John Osinachi. The ethics of the Nigerian broadcaster / John Osinachi Amadi. Rome : [s.n.], 1986. 155 p. [6] p. of plates : ill. ; 24 cm. Bibliography: p. 141-148.
1. Mass media - Nigeria - Moral and religious aspects. 2. Broadcasters - Nigeria. I. Title.
NYPL [Sc E 89-138]

Amadi, L. E. Igbo heritage : curriculum materials for social and literary studies / [L.E. Amadi]. Owerri : I. Onyeukwu Press, 1987. iii, 128 p. ; 21 cm. Bibliography: p. 123-127. ISBN 978-259-801-1
1. Igbo (African people). I. Title.
NYPL [Sc D 89-252]

Amadiume, Ifi. Afrikan matriarchal foundations : the Igbo case / Ifi Amadiume. London : Karnak House, 1987. [120] p. : ill. ; 22 cm. Includes bibliography. ISBN 0-907015-27-1 (pbk) : DDC 966.9/004963 19
1. Igbo (African people) - Nigeria. 2. Matriarchy - Nigeria. I. Title.
DT515.45.I33 **NYPL [Sc D 89-112]**

Amado, Jorge, 1912-
[Capitães da areia. English]
Captains of the sands / Jorge Amado ; translated from Portuguese by Gregory Rabassa. New York, N.Y. : Avon, c1988. 248 p. ; 21 cm. Translation of: Capitães da areia. ISBN 0-380-89718-0 (pbk.) : DDC 869.3 19
1. Salvador (Brazil) - Fiction. I. Title.
PQ9697.A647 C373 1988
NYPL [Sc D 89-198]

[Jubiabá. English]
Jubiabá / Jorge Amado ; translated by Margaret A. Neves. New York : Avon Books, c1984. 294 p. ; 18 cm. "A Bard book." Translation of: Jubiabá. ISBN 0-380-88567-0 (pbk.) : DDC 869.3 19
1. Salvador (Brazil) - Fiction. I. Title.
PQ9697.A647 J813 1984
NYPL [JFC 85-368]

Amagdala und Akawuruk . Brüggemann, Anne. Hohenschäftlarn bei München , 1986. 264 p. : ISBN 3-87673-106-2 **NYPL [Sc D 88-652]**

Amakuru ki? : über leben in Rwanda = vivre au Rwanda / ISOKO (Hg.) Frankfurt : Verlag für Interkulturelle Kommunikation, [1987] 447 p., 1 folded leaf. [8] p. of plates : ill. (some col.), map ; 21 cm. Includes bibliographical references.
I. Internationale Solidarität und Kommunikation.
NYPL [Sc D 88-898]

Amamoo, Joseph G. The Ghanaian revolution / Joseph G. Amamoo. London : Jafint, 1988. 234 p. ; 23 cm. ISBN 1-85421-016-5 : DDC 966.7/05 19
I. Title.
DT512.32 **NYPL [Sc D 89-392]**

Amann, Hans. Energy supply and economic development in East Africa. (With 41 tables, 39 graphs and 2 maps.) München, Weltforum-Verlag (1969). 254 p. with maps, 7 inserts (in pocket) 24 cm. (Afrika-Studien. nr. 37) At head of title: IFO-Institut für Wirtschaftsforschung München. Afrika-Studienstelle. Bibliography: p. 244-247. DDC 333
1. Power resources - Africa, East. I. IFO-Institut für Wirtschaftsforschung, Munich. Afrika-Studienstelle. II. Title. III. Series.
HD9557.A32 A6 **NYPL [Sc E 88-226]**

AMAPÁ BRAZIL TER. - SOCIAL LIFE AND CUSTOMS.
Andrade, Julieta de. Cultura creoula e lanc-patuá no norte do Brasil =. São Paulo , 1984. 310 p. :
F2543 *.A53 1984* **NYPL [HFS 86-2895]**

Amaral, Angelo Thomaz do. Lei de 13 de maio / [Angelo do Amaral] [Fortaleza, Brazil] : Instituto do Ceará, [1907] p. [331]-336 ; 21 cm. Detached from Revista trimestral do Instituto do Ceará, t. 21, 3.e e 4.e trimestres (1907)
1. Slavery - Brazil - Emancipation. I. Title. II. Title: Lei de treze de maio. **NYPL [Sc Rare G 86-30]**

Amaral, Ilidio do. Ensaio de um estudo geográfico da rede urbana de Angola. Lisboa, 1962. 99 p. illus., maps (part fold.) diagrs. 25 cm. (Junta de investigações do Ultramar. Estudos, ensaios e documentos. v. 97) Summary in French and English. Bibliography: p. 91-99. With autograph of author.
1. Cities and towns - Angola. I. Series. II. Series: Estudos, ensaios e documentos , v. 97. III. Title.
HT148.A5 A7　　　　*NYPL [Sc E 98-118]*

Amarillo Art Center. Adele, Lynne. Black history, black vision . [Austin] , 1989. 93 p. : ISBN 0-935213-15-5　　*NYPL [Sc F 89-155]*

AMATOLA WATERSHED (SOUTH AFRICA) - ECONOMIC CONDITIONS.
Bekker, S. B. Socio-economic survey of the Amatola Basin . Grahamstown [South Africa] Institute of Social and Economic Rrsearch, 1981. 58, xxxxiv p. : ISBN 0-86810-073-0
NYPL [Sc F 87-430]

AMATOLA WATERSHED (SOUTH AFRICA) - SOCIAL CONDITIONS.
Bekker, S. B. Socio-economic survey of the Amatola Basin . Grahamstown [South Africa] Institute of Social and Economic Rrsearch, 1981. 58, xxxxiv p. : ISBN 0-86810-073-0
NYPL [Sc F 87-430]

AMBASSADORS - NIGERIA - BIOGRAPHY.
Adebo, Simeon O., 1913- Our international years /. Ibadan , 1988. xi, 281 p., [10] p. of plates : ISBN 987-246-025-7
NYPL [Sc D 89-75]

Ambrus, Victor G. (illus) May, Charles Paul. Stranger in the storm. London, New York [1972] 92 p. ISBN 0-200-71821-5 DDC [Fic]
PZ7.M4505 St　　*NYPL [Sc D 88-1430]*

Amecea Liturgical Colloquium (1985 : Catholic Higher Institute of Eastern Africa) Liturgy : towards inculturation / by AMECEA Liturgical Colloquium. Eldoret, Kenya : Gaba Publications ; AMECEA Pastoral Institute, 1986. viii, 78 p. ; 21 cm. (Spearhead. no. 92) Includes bibliographies.
1. Liturgics - Africa, Eastern - Congresses. 2. Liturgical adaptation - Catholic Church - Congresses. I. Series: Spearhead (Eldoret, Kenya) , no. 92. II. Title.
NYPL [Sc D 88-901]

AMERICA - EMIGRATION AND IMMIGRATION.
When borders don't divide . Staten Island, N.Y. , c1988. viii, 220 p. : ISBN 0-934733-26-0 : DDC 325.8 19
JV7398 .W47 1988　　*NYPL [Sc E 89-169]*

AMERICA - HISTORY - TO 1810 - CONGRESSES.
Colonial identity in the Atlantic world, 1500-1800 /. Princeton, N.J. , c1987. xi, 290 p. ; ISBN 0-691-05372-3 (alk. paper) : DDC 909/.09812 19
E18.82 .C64 1987　　*NYPL [HAB 87-3215]*

AMERICA - LITERATURES - BLACK AUTHORS - HISTORY AND CRITICISM.
La Letteratura della negritudine /. Roma , 1986. 243 p. :　　*NYPL [Sc D 87-1377]*

America needs an ideology /. Campbell, Paul. London , 1957. 184 p. ; DDC 179 170
BJ10.Mb C29　　*NYPL [Sc C 87-467]*

AMERICAN ABORIGINES. see INDIANS OF NORTH AMERICA; INDIANS OF SOUTH AMERICA.

American Anti-slavery Society. Proceedings of the American Anti-slavery Society, at its third decade : held in the city of Philadelphia, Dec. 3d and 4th, 1864 [i.e. 1863] ; phonographic report by Henry M. Parkhurst. New York : The Society, 1864. 175 p. ; 23 cm. "Catalogue of anti-slavery publications in America [from 1750 to 1863]": p. [157]-175.
1. Slavery - United States - Societies, etc. 2. Slavery - United States - Bibliography. I. Title.
NYPL [Sc Rare G 86-43]

American Board of Commissioners for Foreign Missions. Committee on Anti-slavery Memorials. Report of the Committee on Anti-slavery Memorials, September 1845. W ith a historical statement of previous proceedings. Boston, T. R. Marvin, 1845. 32 p. 24 cm.
NYPL [Sc Rare F 88-15]

American Cancer Society. EVAXX. Black Americans' attitudes toward cancer and cancer

tests /. [New York], 1981. 1 v. (various pagings) ;　　*NYPL [Sc F 88-293]*

AMERICAN CIVIL WAR. see UNITED STATES - HISTORY - CIVIL WAR, 1861-1865.

American Colonization Society. Board of Managers. Address of the Board of Managers of the American Colonization Society, to the auxiliary societies and the people of the United States. Washington : Printed by Davis and Force, 1820. 32 p. ; 29 cm.
1. Afro-Americans - Colonization - Africa. I. Title.
NYPL [Sc Rare G 86-23]

American Council on Education. Overseas Liaison Committee.
Ferns, George W. Secondary level teachers: supply and demand in the Gambia. [East Lansing, 1969] xi, 78 p.
LB2833.4.G3 F4　*NYPL [JFM 72-62 no. 2]*

Hanson, John Wagner. Secondary level teachers: supply and demand in Botswana. [East Lansing, 1969, c1968] x, 97, [2] p.
LB2833.4.B55 H3　*NYPL [JFM 72-62 no. 1]*

Hanson, John Wagner. Secondary level teachers: supply and demand in Ghana. [East Lansing, 1971] xv, 130 p.
NYPL [JFM 72-62 no. 12]

Haupt, W. Norman. Secondary level teachers: supply and demand in West Cameroon. [East Lansing, 1971] xii, 45, [20] p.
NYPL [JFM 72-62 no. 13]

American diary . Waters, Enoch P., 1909- Chicago , c1987. xxiii, 520 p. ; ISBN 0-910671-01-X : DDC 070.4/1/0924 B 19
PN4874.W293 A33 1987
NYPL [Sc E 88-270]

AMERICAN DRAMA - 20TH CENTURY - BIO-BIBLIOGRAPHY - DICTIONARIES.
Peterson, Bernard L. Contemporary Black American playwrights and their plays . New York , 1988. xxvi, 625 p. ; ISBN 0-313-25190-8 (lib. bdg. : alk. paper) DDC 812/.54/09896 19
PS153.N5 P43 1988　*NYPL [Sc E 88-378]*

AMERICAN DRAMA - 20TH CENTURY - HISTORY AND CRITICISM.
Brenowitz, Ruth. A study of the portrayal of Black Americans in the dramatic literature of the United States [microform] /. 1969. 92 leaves.　　*NYPL [Sc Micro R-4691]*

Making a spectacle . Ann Arbor , c1989. 347 p. : ISBN 0-472-09389-4 (alk. paper) : DDC 812/.54/099287 19
PS338.W6 M3 1989　　*NYPL [JFE 89-144]*

AMERICAN DRAMA - AFRO-AMERICAN AUTHORS - BIO-BIBLIOGRAPHY - DICTIONARIES.
Peterson, Bernard L. Contemporary Black American playwrights and their plays . New York , 1988. xxvi, 625 p. ; ISBN 0-313-25190-8 (lib. bdg. : alk. paper) DDC 812/.54/09896 19
PS153.N5 P43 1988　　*NYPL [Sc E 88-378]*

AMERICAN DRAMA - AFRO-AMERICAN AUTHORS - HISTORY AND CRITICISM.
Brown, Sterling Allen, 1901- Negro poetry and drama /. Washington, D.C. , c1937. 142 p. ;
NYPL [Sc D 89-105]

Sanders, Leslie Catherine, 1944- The development of black theater in America . Baton Rouge , c1988. 252 p. ; ISBN 0-8071-1328-X DDC 812/.009/896073 19
PS338.N4 S26 1987
NYPL [MWED 88-1125]

AMERICAN DRAMA - JEWISH AUTHORS - HISTORY AND CRITICISM.
Harap, Louis. Dramatic encounters . New York , c1987. xiv, 177 p. ; ISBN 0-313-25388-9 (lib. bdg. : alk. paper) DDC 810/.9/35203924 19
PS173.J4 H294 1987　*NYPL [*PZB 87-5243]*

AMERICAN DRAMA - WOMEN AUTHORS - HISTORY AND CRITICISM.
Making a spectacle . Ann Arbor , c1989. 347 p. : ISBN 0-472-09389-4 (alk. paper) : DDC 812/.54/099287 19
PS338.W6 M3 1989　　*NYPL [JFE 89-144]*

American earlier Black English . Schneider, Edgar W. (Edgar Werner), 1954- [Morphologische und syntaktische Variablen im amerikanischen early black English. English.] Tuscaloosa , 1989. xiv, 314 p. : ISBN

0-8173-0436-3 DDC 427/.973/08996 19
PE3102.N43 S3613 1989
NYPL [Sc E 89-210]

American expansionism vs. European colonialism [microform] . Roark, J. L. [Nairobi] , 1976. 16 leaves ;　　*NYPL [Sc Micro R-4108 no. 34]*

AMERICAN FANTASTIC FICTION. see FANTASTIC FICTION, AMERICAN.

AMERICAN FICTION - 20TH CENTURY.
Kindred spirits . Boston , 1984. 262 p. ; ISBN 0-932870-42-2 (pbk.) :
NYPL [Sc D 89-269]

Worlds apart . Boston, Mass. , 1986. 293 p. ; ISBN 0-932870-87-2 (pbk.) : DDC 813/.0876/08353 19
PS648.H57 W67 1986　*NYPL [JFD 87-7753]*

AMERICAN FICTION - 20TH CENTURY - HISTORY AND CRITICISM.
Awkward, Michael. Inspiriting influences . New York , 1989. x, 178 p. ; ISBN 0-231-06806-9 DDC 813/.5/099287 19
PS153.N5 A94 1989　　*NYPL [Sc E 89-188]*

Callahan, John F. In the African-American grain . Urbana , c1988. 280 p. ; ISBN 0-252-01459-6 (alk. paper) DDC 813/.009/896073 19
PS153.N5 C34 1988　　*NYPL [Sc E 88-144]*

Harris, Norman, 1951- Connecting times . Jackson , c1988. 197 p. ; ISBN 0-87805-335-2 (alk. paper) DDC 813/.54/093520396073 19
PS153.N5 H27 1988　*NYPL [Sc E 88-288]*

Harris, Norman, 1951- Understanding the sixties [microform] . 1980. 202 leaves.
NYPL [Sc Micro R-4680]

AMERICAN FICTION - AFRO-AMERICAN AUTHORS - HISTORY AND CRITICISM.
Awkward, Michael. Inspiriting influences . New York , 1989. x, 178 p. ; ISBN 0-231-06806-9 DDC 813/.5/099287 19
PS153.N5 A94 1989　　*NYPL [Sc E 89-188]*

Callahan, John F. In the African-American grain . Urbana , c1988. 280 p. ; ISBN 0-252-01459-6 (alk. paper) DDC 813/.009/896073 19
PS153.N5 C34 1988　　*NYPL [Sc E 88-144]*

Harap, Louis. Dramatic encounters . New York , c1987. xiv, 177 p. ; ISBN 0-313-25388-9 (lib. bdg. : alk. paper) DDC 810/.9/35203924 19
PS173.J4 H294 1987　*NYPL [*PZB 87-5243]*

Harris, Norman, 1951- Connecting times . Jackson , c1988. 197 p. ; ISBN 0-87805-335-2 (alk. paper) DDC 813/.54/093520396073 19
PS153.N5 H27 1988　*NYPL [Sc E 88-288]*

Harris, Norman, 1951- Understanding the sixties [microform] . 1980. 202 leaves.
NYPL [Sc Micro R-4680]

Lewis, Vashti Crutcher. The mulatto woman as major female character in novels by Black women, 1892-1937 [microform] /. [Iowa City, Ia.] 1981. iv, 182 leaves ;
NYPL [Sc Micro R-4792]

Rahming, Melvin B., 1943- The evolution of the West Indian's image in the Afro-American novel /. Millwood, N.Y. , c1986. xix, 160 p. ; ISBN 0-8046-9339-0 DDC 813/.009/35203969729 19
PS153.N5 R3 1985　　*NYPL [JFD 86-6569]*

Reilly, John Terrence, 1945. The first shall be last [microform] . 1977. 198 leaves.
NYPL [Sc Micro R-4702]

AMERICAN FICTION - WOMEN AUTHORS - HISTORY AND CRITICISM.
Awkward, Michael. Inspiriting influences . New York , 1989. x, 178 p. ; ISBN 0-231-06806-9 DDC 813/.5/099287 19
PS153.N5 A94 1989　　*NYPL [Sc E 89-188]*

AMERICAN INDIANS. see INDIANS OF NORTH AMERICA; INDIANS OF SOUTH AMERICA.

American Jewish Archives. Harap, Louis. Dramatic encounters . New York , c1987. xiv, 177 p. ; ISBN 0-313-25388-9 (lib. bdg. : alk. paper) DDC 810/.9/35203924 19
PS173.J4 H294 1987　*NYPL [*PZB 87-5243]*

American legal and constitutional history.
Swinney, Everette, 1923- Suppressing the Ku Klux Klan . New York , 1987. ix, 360 p. ;

ISBN 0-8240-8297-4 (alk. paper) : DDC
342.73/0873 347.302873 19
KF4757 .S93 1987   **NYPL** *[Sc D 88-653]*

Werner, John M., 1941- Reaping the bloody
harvest . New York , 1986. 333 p. ; ISBN
0-8240-8301-6 (alk. paper) : DDC 973.5/6 19
E185 .W44 1986   **NYPL** *[Sc E 88-242]*

American Library Association. Association of
College and Reference Libraries. see
Association of College and Research
Libraries.

American Library Association. Association of
College and Research Libraries. see
Association of College and Research
Libraries.

American Library Association. College and
Reference Section. see Association of College
and Research Libraries.

AMERICAN LITERATURE - 19TH
CENTURY - HISTORY AND CRITICISM.
Bruce, Dickson D., 1946- Black American
writing from the nadir . Baton Rouge , c1989.
xiii, 272 p. : ISBN 0-8071-1450-2 (alk. paper)
DDC 810/.9/896073 19
PS153.N5 B77 1989   **NYPL** *[Sc E 89-197]*

AMERICAN LITERATURE - 20TH
CENTURY.
Deep down . Boston , c1988. xii, 330 p. ;
ISBN 0-571-12957-9 : DDC 810/.8/03538 19
PS509.E7 D44 1988   **NYPL** *[Sc D 88-1080]*

Ebony and topaz . New York , 1927. 164 p. :
   NYPL *[Sc Rare F 82-72]*

Mississippi writers . Jackson , c1985- v. ; ISBN
0-87805-232-1 (pbk.) DDC 813/.008/09762 19
PS558.M7 M55 1985   **NYPL** *[Sc E 88-316]*

AMERICAN LITERATURE - 20TH
CENTURY - BIBLIOGRAPHY -
CATALOGS.
France. Bibliothèque nationale. Département
des livres imprimés. Les auteurs afro-américains,
1965-1982 . Paris , 1985. 28 p., [4] leaves of
plates : ISBN 2-7177-1709-9 :
Z1229.N39 F7 1985 PS153.N5
   NYPL *[Sc F 89-5]*

AMERICAN LITERATURE - 20TH
CENTURY - HISTORY AND CRITICISM.
Baker, Houston A. Afro-American poetics .
Madison, Wis. , c1988. x, 201 p. ; ISBN
0-299-11500-3 : DDC 810/.9/896073 19
PS153.N5 B22 1988   **NYPL** *[Sc D 88-1356]*

Bruce, Dickson D., 1946- Black American
writing from the nadir . Baton Rouge , c1989.
xiii, 272 p. : ISBN 0-8071-1450-2 (alk. paper)
DDC 810/.9/896073 19
PS153.N5 B77 1989   **NYPL** *[Sc E 89-197]*

Harap, Louis. Dramatic encounters . New
York , c1987. xiv, 177 p. ; ISBN 0-313-25388-9
(lib. bdg. : alk. paper) DDC 810/.9/35203924 19
PS173.J4 H294 1987   **NYPL** *[*PZB 87-5243]*

Wintz, Cary D., 1943- Black culture and the
Harlem Renaissance /. Houston, Tex. , 1988.
277 p. ; ISBN 0-89263-267-4 : DDC
810/.9/896073 19
PS153.N5 W57 1988   **NYPL** *[Sc E 89-106]*

AMERICAN LITERATURE - 20TH
CENTURY - HISTORY AND CRITICISM -
CONGRESSES.
The Harlem renaissance . New York , 1989. xv,
342 p. ; ISBN 0-8240-5739-2 (alk. paper) DDC
810/.9/896073 19
PS153.N5 H264 1989   **NYPL** *[Sc D 89-591]*

The Southern review and modern literature,
1935-1985 /. Baton Rouge , c1988. xvi, 238 p.:
ISBN 0-8071-1424-3 : DDC 810/.9/975 19
PS267.B3 S68 1987   **NYPL** *[Sc E 88-280]*

AMERICAN LITERATURE - AFRICAN
INFLUENCES.
Gates, Henry Louis. The signifying monkey .
New York , 1988. xxviii, 290 p. : ISBN
0-19-503463-5 (alk. paper) DDC 810/.9/896073
19
PS153.N5 G28 1988   **NYPL** *[Sc E 89-181]*

AMERICAN LITERATURE - AFRO-
AMERICAN AUTHORS -
BIBLIOGRAPHY - CATALOGS.
France. Bibliothèque nationale. Département
des livres imprimés. Les auteurs afro-américains,
1965-1982 . Paris , 1985. 28 p., [4] leaves of

plates : ISBN 2-7177-1709-9 :
Z1229.N39 F7 1985 PS153.N5
   NYPL *[Sc F 89-5]*

AMERICAN LITERATURE - AFRO-
AMERICAN AUTHORS - BIO-
BIBLIOGRAPHY.
Foster, Mamie Marie Booth. Southern Black
creative writers, 1829-1953 . New York , 1988.
xvii, 113 p. ; ISBN 0-313-26207-1 (lib. bdg. : alk.
paper) DDC 016.81/09/896073 19
Z1229.N39 F67 1988 PS153.N5
   NYPL *[Sc E 88-495]*

AMERICAN LITERATURE - AFRO-
AMERICAN AUTHORS - CONGRESSES.
Black working women . Berkeley, Calif.
[1981?] vii, 222 p. :   **NYPL** *[Sc F 89-33]*

AMERICAN LITERATURE - AFRO-
AMERICAN AUTHORS - HISTORY AND
CRITICISM.
Baker, Houston A. Afro-American poetics .
Madison, Wis. , c1988. x, 201 p. ; ISBN
0-299-11500-3 : DDC 810/.9/896073 19
PS153.N5 B22 1988   **NYPL** *[Sc D 88-1356]*

Black feminist criticism and critical theory /.
Greenwood, Fla. , c1988. iii, 202 p. ; ISBN
0-913283-25-8   **NYPL** *[Sc D 88-1394]*

Bruce, Dickson D., 1946- Black American
writing from the nadir . Baton Rouge , c1989.
xiii, 272 p. : ISBN 0-8071-1450-2 (alk. paper)
DDC 810/.9/896073 19
PS153.N5 B77 1989   **NYPL** *[Sc E 89-197]*

Evans, James H., 1950- Spiritual empowerment
in Afro-American literature . Lewiston, NY ,
1987. 174 p. ; ISBN 0-88946-560-6 DDC
810/.9/896073 19
PS153.N5 E92 1987   **NYPL** *[Sc E 88-265]*

Redding, J. Saunders (Jay Saunders), 1906- To
make a poet Black /. Ithaca , 1988. xxxii, 142
p. ; ISBN 0-8014-1982-4 (alk. paper) DDC
811/.009/896073 19
PS153.N5 R4 1988   **NYPL** *[Sc D 89-388]*

Williams, Sherley Anne, 1944- Give birth to
brightness. New York, 1972. 252 p.
PS153.N5 W54   **NYPL** *[JFD 72-6307]*

Wintz, Cary D., 1943- Black culture and the
Harlem Renaissance /. Houston, Tex. , 1988.
277 p. ; ISBN 0-89263-267-4 : DDC
810/.9/896073 19
PS153.N5 W57 1988   **NYPL** *[Sc E 89-106]*

AMERICAN LITERATURE - AFRO-
AMERICAN AUTHORS - HISTORY AND
CRITICISM - CONGRESSES.
The Harlem renaissance . New York , 1989. xv,
342 p. ; ISBN 0-8240-5739-2 (alk. paper) DDC
810/.9/896073 19
PS153.N5 H264 1989   **NYPL** *[Sc D 89-591]*

AMERICAN LITERATURE - AFRO-
AMERICAN AUTHORS - HISTORY AND
CRITICISM - THEORY, ETC.
Gates, Henry Louis. The signifying monkey .
New York , 1988. xxviii, 290 p. : ISBN
0-19-503463-5 (alk. paper) DDC 810/.9/896073
19
PS153.N5 G28 1988   **NYPL** *[Sc E 89-181]*

AMERICAN LITERATURE - HISTORY AND
CRITICISM.
Dash, J. Michael. Haiti and the United States .
Basingstoke, Hampshire , 1988. xv, 152 p. ;
ISBN 0-333-45491-X
   NYPL *[Sc D 88-1358]*

AMERICAN LITERATURE - LOUISIANA -
BATON ROUGE - HISTORY AND
CRITICISM - CONGRESSES.
The Southern review and modern literature,
1935-1985 /. Baton Rouge , c1988. xvi, 238 p.:
ISBN 0-8071-1424-3 : DDC 810/.9/975 19
PS267.B3 S68 1987   **NYPL** *[Sc E 88-280]*

AMERICAN LITERATURE - MINORITY
AUTHORS - HISTORY AND CRITICISM.
The Invention of ethnicity /. New York , 1989.
xx, 294 p. ; ISBN 0-19-504589-0 DDC
810/.9/920692 19
PS153.M56 I58 1988   **NYPL** *[Sc D 89-374]*

AMERICAN LITERATURE - MISSISSIPPI.
Mississippi writers . Jackson , c1985- v. ; ISBN
0-87805-232-1 (pbk.) DDC 813/.008/09762 19
PS558.M7 M55 1985   **NYPL** *[Sc E 88-316]*

AMERICAN LITERATURE - NEW YORK (N.
Y.) - HISTORY AND CRITICISM.

Wintz, Cary D., 1943- Black culture and the
Harlem Renaissance /. Houston, Tex. , 1988.
277 p. ; ISBN 0-89263-267-4 : DDC
810/.9/896073 19
PS153.N5 W57 1988   **NYPL** *[Sc E 89-106]*

AMERICAN LITERATURE - NEW YORK (N.
Y.) - HISTORY AND CRITICISM -
CONGRESSES.
The Harlem renaissance . New York , 1989. xv,
342 p. ; ISBN 0-8240-5739-2 (alk. paper) DDC
810/.9/896073 19
PS153.N5 H264 1989   **NYPL** *[Sc D 89-591]*

AMERICAN LITERATURE - SOUTHERN
STATES - BIO-BIBLIOGRAPHY.
Foster, Mamie Marie Booth. Southern Black
creative writers, 1829-1953 . New York , 1988.
xvii, 113 p. ; ISBN 0-313-26207-1 (lib. bdg. : alk.
paper) DDC 016.81/09/896073 19
Z1229.N39 F67 1988 PS153.N5
   NYPL *[Sc E 88-495]*

AMERICAN LITERATURE - SOUTHERN
STATES - HISTORY AND CRITICISM -
CONGRESSES.
The Southern review and modern literature,
1935-1985 /. Baton Rouge , c1988. xvi, 238 p.:
ISBN 0-8071-1424-3 : DDC 810/.9/975 19
PS267.B3 S68 1987   **NYPL** *[Sc E 88-280]*

AMERICAN LITERATURE - WOMEN
AUTHORS.
Afro-American women writers, 1746-1933 .
Boston , 1988. xxviii, 465 p. ; ISBN
0-8161-8823-8   **NYPL** *[Sc E 88-428]*

AMERICAN MISSIONARY ASSOCIATION.
Lundy, Harold Wayne. A study of the
transition from white to Black presidents at
three selected schools founded by the American
Missionary Association [microform] /. 1978.
676 leaves.   **NYPL** *[Sc Micro R-4216]*

AMERICAN PAINTING. see PAINTING,
AMERICAN.

AMERICAN POETRY - 19TH CENTURY.
Collected Black women's poetry /. New York ,
1988. 4 v. : ISBN 0-19-505253-6 (v. 1) DDC
811/.008/09287 19
PS591.N4 C57 1988   **NYPL** *[JFC 88-2144]*

AMERICAN POETRY - 19TH CENTURY -
HISTORY AND CRITICISM.
Sherman, Joan R. Invisible poets . Urbana ,
c1989. xxxii, 288 p. : ISBN 0-252-01620-3 (alk.
paper) DDC 811/.009/896073 19
PS153.N5 S48 1989   **NYPL** *[Sc E 89-216]*

AMERICAN POETRY - 20TH CENTURY.
Gay & lesbian poetry in our time . New York ,
c1988. xxviii, 401 p. : ISBN 0-312-02213-1 :
DDC 811/.54/080353 19
PS595.H65 G39 1988   **NYPL** *[JFE 89-277]*

Gurus and griots . Brooklyn, N.Y. [1987],
c1985. 108 p. : ISBN 0-9618755-0-X (pbk.) DDC
811/.008/0896 19
PS591.N4 G87 1987   **NYPL** *[Sc E 89-230]*

AMERICAN POETRY - 20TH CENTURY -
HISTORY AND CRITICISM.
Drake, William. The first wave . New York ,
London , c1987. xxi, 314 p., [8] p. of plates :
ISBN 0-02-533490-5 : DDC 811/.52/099287 19
PS151 .D7 1987   **NYPL** *[JFD 87-7537]*

A Gift of tongues . Athens , c1987. xii, 342 p. ;
ISBN 0-8203-0952-4 (alk. paper) DDC
811/.5/09920693 19
PS153.M56 G54 1987   **NYPL** *[Sc E 88-364]*

Hull, Gloria T. Color, sex, and poetry .
Bloomington , c1987. xi, 240 p. : ISBN
0-253-34974-5 DDC 811/.52/099287 19
PS153.N5 H84 1987   **NYPL** *[Sc E 88-72]*

Kerlin, Robert Thomas, 1866-1950.
Contemporary poetry of the Negro /. Hampton,
Virginia , 1921. 23 p. ;
   NYPL *[Sc Rare C 89-22]*

Nielsen, Aldon Lynn. Reading race . Athens,
Ga. , c1988. xii, 178 p. : ISBN 0-8203-1061-1
(alk. paper) DDC 811/.5/09355 19
PS310.R34 N54 1988   **NYPL** *[JFE 88-3098]*

Reid, Margaret Ann, 1940- A rhetorical
analysis of selected Black protest poetry of the
Harlem Renaissance and of the sixties /. , 1981.
284 p. [i.e. 216] p.   **NYPL** *[Sc D 88-264]*

AMERICAN POETRY - 20TH CENTURY -
HISTORY AND CRITICISM -
ADDRESSES, ESSAYS, LECTURES.

American poetry observed . Urbana , c1984. xi, 313 p. ; ISBN 0-252-01042-6 DDC 811/.54/09 19
PS129 .A54 1984　　　*NYPL [JFE 84-3478]*

AMERICAN POETRY - AFRO-AMERICAN AUTHORS - HISTORY AND CRITICISM.
Brown, Sterling Allen, 1901- Negro poetry and drama /. Washington, D.C. , c1937. 142 p. ;
NYPL [Sc D 89-105]

Hull, Gloria T. Color, sex, and poetry . Bloomington , c1987. xi, 240 p. : ISBN 0-253-34974-5 DDC 811/.52/099287 19
PS153.N5 H84 1987　　　*NYPL [Sc E 88-72]*

Kerlin, Robert Thomas, 1866-1950. Contemporary poetry of the Negro /. Hampton, Virginia , 1921. 23 p. ;
NYPL [Sc Rare C 89-22]

Redding, J. Saunders (Jay Saunders), 1906- To make a poet Black /. Ithaca , 1988. xxxii, 142 p. ; ISBN 0-8014-1982-4 (alk. paper) DDC 811/.009/896073 19
PS153.N5 R4 1988　　　*NYPL [Sc D 89-388]*

Reid, Margaret Ann, 1940- A rhetorical analysis of selected Black protest poetry of the Harlem Renaissance and of the sixties /. , 1981. 284 p. [i.e. 216] p.　　*NYPL [Sc D 88-264]*

Sherman, Joan R. Invisible poets . Urbana , c1989. xxxii, 288 p. : ISBN 0-252-01620-3 (alk. paper) DDC 811/.009/896073 19
PS153.N5 S48 1989　　　*NYPL [Sc E 89-216]*

AMERICAN POETRY - BLACK AUTHORS. see AMERICAN POETRY - AFRO-AMERICAN AUTHORS.

AMERICAN POETRY - HISTORY AND CRITICISM.
Voices & visions . New York , c1987. xxx, 528 p. : ISBN 0-394-53520-0
NYPL [JFE 87-5435]

AMERICAN POETRY - MINORITY AUTHORS - HISTORY AND CRITICISM.
A Gift of tongues . Athens , c1987. xii, 342 p. ; ISBN 0-8203-0952-4 (alk. paper) DDC 811/.5/09920693 19
PS153.M56 G54 1987　　*NYPL [Sc E 88-364]*

American poetry observed : poets on their work / edited by Joe David Bellamy. Urbana : University of Illinois Press, c1984. xi, 313 p. : ports. ; 24 cm. ISBN 0-252-01042-6 DDC 811/.54/09 19
1. Poets, American - 20th century - Interviews. 2. American poetry - 20th century - History and criticism - Addresses, essays, lectures. I. Bellamy, Joe David.
PS129 .A54 1984　　　*NYPL [JFE 84-3478]*

AMERICAN POETRY - WASHINGTON METROPOLITAN AREA.
Gurus and griots . Brooklyn, N.Y. [1987], c1985. 108 p. : ISBN 0-9618755-0-X (pbk.) DDC 811/.008/0896 19
PS591.N4 G87 1987　　*NYPL [Sc E 89-230]*

AMERICAN POETRY - WHITE AUTHORS - HISTORY AND CRITICISM.
Nielsen, Aldon Lynn. Reading race . Athens, Ga. , c1988. xii, 178 p. ; ISBN 0-8203-1061-1 (alk. paper) DDC 811/.5/09355 19
PS310.R34 N54 1988　　*NYPL [JFE 88-3098]*

AMERICAN POETRY - WOMEN AUTHORS.
Collected Black women's poetry /. New York , 1988. 4 v. : ISBN 0-19-505253-6 (v. 1) DDC 811/.008/09287 19
PS591.N4 C57 1988　　*NYPL [JFC 88-2144]*

AMERICAN POETRY - WOMEN AUTHORS - HISTORY AND CRITICISM.
Drake, William. The first wave . New York , London , c1987. xxi, 314 p., [8] p. of plates : ISBN 0-02-533490-5 : DDC 811/.52/099287 19
PS151 .D7 1987　　　*NYPL [JFD 87-7537]*

Hull, Gloria T. Color, sex, and poetry . Bloomington , c1987. xi, 240 p. : ISBN 0-253-34974-5 DDC 811/.52/099287 19
PS153.N5 H84 1987　　　*NYPL [Sc E 88-72]*

American poets continuum series .
(v. 14) Clifton, Lucille, 1936- Good woman . Brockport, NY , St. Paul, Minnesota , 1987. 276 p. : ISBN 0-918526-59-0 (pbk.)
NYPL [Sc E 88-232]

American singers . Balliett, Whitney. New York , 1988. x, 244 p. ; ISBN 0-19-504610-2 (alk. paper) DDC 784.5 B 19
ML400 .B25 1988　　　*NYPL [JNE 88-46]*

AMERICAN SUNDAY-SCHOOL UNION.
Tappan, Lewis, 1788-1873. Letters respecting a book "dropped from the catalogue" of the American Sunday School Union in compliance with the dictation of the slave power. New York , 1848. 36 p. ;
NYPL [Sc Rare C 89-11]

American University, Washington, D. C. Foreign Area Studies. Nelson, Harold D. Area handbook for Southern Rhodesia /. Washington , 1975. xiv, 394 p.
DT962 .N36　　　*NYPL [JFE 75-2684]*

American visions Afro-American art, 1986 / edited by Carroll Greene, Jr. Washington, D.C. : Visions Foundation, 1987. 57 p. : ill. (chiefly col.) ; 28 cm.
1. Afro-American art - Exhibitions. 2. Afro-American art - History and criticism. I. Green, Carroll. II. Vissions Foundation. (Washington, D.C.). III. Title.
NYPL [Sc F 87-438]

American women of achievement.
Biracree, Tom, 1947- Wilma Rudolph /. New York , 1988. 111 p. : ISBN 1-555-46675-3 DDC 796.4/2/0924 B 92 19
GV697.R8 B57 1988　　*NYPL [Sc E 88-172]*

Jakoubek, Robert E. Harriet Beecher Stowe /. New York , c1989. 111 p. : ISBN 1-555-46680-X DDC 813/.3 B 92 19
PS2956 .J35 1989　　*NYPL [Sc E 89-144]*

Richmond, M. A. (Merle A.) Phillis Wheatley /. New York , 1988. 111 p. : ISBN 1-555-46683-4 DDC 811/.1 B 92 19
PS866.W5 Z683 1987　　*NYPL [Sc E 88-173]*

Americanische Sonntags Schulen Union. see American Sunday-School Union.

America's first Black general . Fletcher, Marvin. Lawrence, Kan. , c1989. xix, 226 p. : ISBN 0-7006-0381-6 (alk. paper) : DDC 355/.008996073 B 19
U53.D38 F57 1989　　*NYPL [Sc D 89-276]*

The Americo-Liberian ruling class and other myths . Burrowes, Carl Patrick. Philadelphia , 1989. 77 leaves ;　*NYPL [Sc F 89-128]*

Amerikai Egyesült Allamok. see United States.

Die amerikanische Politik gegenüber dem südlichen Afrika /. Schümer, Martin. Bonn [1986]. v, 183 p. ; ISBN 3-7713-0275-7
NYPL [Sc D 88-983]

L'Amérique noire. Smith, William Gardner, 1926-1974. [Return to Black America. Frech.] [Tournai, 1972] 149 p.　*NYPL [IEC 79-113]*

Ames, Julius Rubens, 1801-1850. Branagan, Thomas, b. 1774. The guardian genius of the Federal Union, or, Patriotic admonitions on the signs of the times . New York , 1839. 104 p. :
NYPL [Sc Rare G 86-18]

Ami, Gad, 1958- Etrange héritage : roman / Gad Ami. Lomé : Nouvelles Editions africaines, 1986, c1985. 155 p. ; 24 cm. ISBN 2-7236-0931-6
1. togo - Fiction. I. Title.　*NYPL [Sc E 88-427]*

Amin and the tragedy of Uganda /. Kiwanuka, M. S. M. Semakula. München , 1979. ix, 201 p. : ISBN 3-8039-0177-4
DT433.283 .K58　*NYPL [L-10 9005 nr. 104]*

AMIN, IDI, 1925-
Kiwanuka, M. S. M. Semakula. Amin and the tragedy of Uganda /. München , 1979. ix, 201 p. : ISBN 3-8039-0177-4
DT433.283 .K58　*NYPL [L-10 9005 nr. 104]*

Amin, Mohamed, 1943-
Kenya : the magic land / by Mohamed Amin, Duncan Willetts and Brian Tetley. London : Bodley Head, 1988. 191 p. : col. ill. ; 32 cm. ISBN 0-370-31225-2 : DDC 967.6/204/0222 19
1. Kenya - Description and travel - Views. 2. Kenya - Description and travel - 1981-. I. Willetts, Duncan, 1945-. II. Tetley, Brian. III. Title.
DT433.52　　　*NYPL [Sc G 88-33]*

The last of the Maasai / Mohamed Amin, Duncan Willetts, John Eames ; foreword by Elspeth Huxley. London : Bodley Head, 1987. 185 p. : col. ill. ; 33 cm. ISBN 0-370-31097-7
1. Masai. I. Willetts, Duncan. II. Eames, John. III. Huxley, Elspeth Joscelin Grant. IV. Title.
NYPL [Sc G 88-21]

Aminu, Jibril M.,1939- Observations / by Jibril Aminu. [Enugu, Anambra State, Nigeria] :

Delta of Nigeria, [1988] 148 p. ; 23 cm. Includes bibliographical references. ISBN 978-233-531-2
1. Education - Nigeria. I. Title.
NYPL [Sc D 89-483]

Les Amo . Ndam Njoya, Adamou, 1942- Yaoundé , c1982. 29 p. ;
MLCS 84/860 (P)　　*NYPL [Sc D 89-185]*

Amoko and Efua bear /. Appiah, Sonia. New York, NY , 1989, c1988. [30] p. : ISBN 0-02-705591-4 DDC E 19
PZ7.A647 Am 1989　　*NYPL [Sc F 89-138]*

AMOKWE (NIGERIA) - HISTORY.
Onyia, Nathaniel Maduabuchi. Pre-colonial history of Amokwe /. Enugu, Nigeria , 1987. 95 p. : ISBN 978-239-618-4
NYPL [Sc D 89-53]

Amolo, Milcah. Trade unionism and colonial authority [microform] : the example of Sierra Leone up to 1946 / by Milcah Amolo. [Nairobi] : University of Nairobi, Dept. of History, [1978] 16 p. ; 33 cm. (Staff seminar paper / University of Nairobi, Department of History. no. 7, 1978/79) Cover title. Includes bibliographical references. Microfilm. New York: New York Public Library, 1982. 1 microfilm reel; 35 mm. (MN *ZZ-23051)
1. Trade-unions - Sierra Leone - History. I. Series: Nairobi. University. Dept. of History. Staff seminar paper, no. 7. II. Title.
NYPL [Sc Micro R-4108 no. 37]

Amondji, Marcel, 1934-
Côte-d'Ivoire : le P.D.C.I. et la vie politique de 1944 à 1985 / Marcel Amondji. Paris : L'Harmattan, c1986. 207 p. ; 22 cm. (Collection "Points de vue") Bibliography: p. 201-205. ISBN 2-85802-631-6 DDC 324.2666/809 19
1. Parti démocratique de Côte d'Ivoire. 2. Ivory Coast - Politics and government. I. Title. II. Series.
DT545.75 .A46 1986　　*NYPL [Sc D 88-297]*

Côte-d'Ivoire : la dépendance et l'epreuve des faits / Marcel Amondji. Paris : L'Harmattan, c1988. 188 p. ; 22 cm. Includes index. Bibliography: p. 179-181. ISBN 2-7384-0072-8
1. Ivory Coast - Politics and government - 1960-. I. Title.
NYPL [Sc D 89-503]

Amoo, Dawood Ayodele. Sanni, Ishaq Kunle. Why you should never be a Christian /. Ibadan, Nigeria , 1987. ix, 125 p. :
NYPL [Sc C 88-157]

Amos, Gregory. Amos, Wally. The power in you . New York , c1988. xiii, 217 p. ; ISBN 1-556-11093-6 :　　*NYPL [Sc D 89-266]*

Amos, Wally. The power in you : 10 secret ingredients for inner strength / by Wally Amos and Gregory Amos. New York : D. I. Fine, c1988. xiii, 217 p. ; 22 cm. At head of title: Famous Amos. ISBN 1-556-11093-6 :
I. Amos, Gregory. II. Title. III. Title: Ten secret ingredients for inner strength.
NYPL [Sc D 89-266]

Ampene, Esther C. Focus on the early learner : some West African situations / by Esther C. Ampene. Accra-North : Sam Modern Stationary Supplies, 1987. viii, 65 p. : ill. ; 21 cm. ISBN 996-490-189-5
1. Education (Preschool) - Africa, West. I. Title.
NYPL [Sc D 88-1383]

Amsterdam. Instituut voor de Tropen. see Koninklijk Instituut voor de Tropen.

Amucheazi, E. C. (Elochukwu C.) Church and politics in Eastern Nigeria, 1945-66 : a study in pressure group politics / Elochukwu C. Amucheazi. Yaba Lagos : Macmillan Nigeria, 1986. xvii, 256 p. : ill. ; 22 cm. Revision of the author's thesis (M.S.). Includes index. Bibliography: p. 233-244. ISBN 978-13-2786-3 (pbk.) DDC 322/.1/096694 19
1. Church and state - Nigeria, Eastern. 2. Nigeria, Eastern - Politics and government. I. Title.
DT515.9.E3 A66 1986　*NYPL [Sc D 88-992]*

Anacaona . Métellus, Jean, 1937- Paris , 1986. 159 p. : ISBN 2-218-07538-5
NYPL [Sc C 88-6]

Anacostia Museum. Smith, Edward D. Climbing Jacob's ladder. City of Washington , 1988. 143
NYPL [Sc E 88-505]

Anaele, Justin Uchechukwu. The role of the laity in ecumenism with reference to the church in Nigeria / Justin Uchechukwu Anaele. Rome : [s.n.], 1985 (Rome : R. Ambrosini) 146 p.

maps ; 24 cm. Bibliography: p. 139-146.
*1. Ecumenical movement. 2. Laity - Catholic Church. 3.
Christian union - Nigeria. 4. Laity - Nigeria. I. Title.*
NYPL [Sc E 88-608]

Analogía de umbanda . Ronton, Josef. São Paulo ,
c1985. 389 p. : **NYPL [JFD 87-5626]**

**An analysis of continued semi-nomadism of the
Kaputiei Maasai group ranches [microform] .**
Halderman, John M. [Nairobi] [between 1972
and 1974]. 35 p. ; DDC 307.7/2/0967627
DT433.542 .H34
NYPL [Sc Micro R-4108 no.25]

**An analysis of interviews with urban Black males
who dropped out of high school [microform] /.**
Lewis, Geraldine Fambrough. 1983. iii, 123
leaves : **NYPL [Sc Micro R-4791]**

**An analysis of the Eastern ORD rural
development project in Upper Volta .** Michigan
State University. Dept. of Agricultural
Economics. East Lansing , 1976. v, 103 p. :
DDC 338.1/866/25
HD2135 .U63 1976 **NYPL [Sc F 89-170]**

**Analysis of the evidence given before the select
committees upon the slave trade /.** Barrister.
London , 1850. 121 p. ;
NYPL [Sc Rare G 86-11]

ANANSI (LEGENDARY CHARACTER)
Appiah, Peggy. Tales of an Ashanti father /.
Boston , 1989, c1967. 156 p. : ISBN
0-8070-8312-7 DDC 398.2/1/09667 19
PZ8.1.A647 Tal 1989 **NYPL [Sc E 89-87]**

Arkhurst, Joyce Cooper. More adventures of
Spider . New York , c1972. 48 p. :
NYPL [Sc D 88-1449]

Iremonger, Lucille. West Indian folk-tales.
London [1956] 64 p.
GR120 .I7 **NYPL [Sc C 89-157]**

**ANANSI (LEGENDARY CHARACTER) -
JUVENILE FICTION.**
Aardema, Verna. The sky-god stories /. New
York , c1960. [50] p. : **NYPL [Sc D 89-83]**

**ANATOMY FOR ARTISTS. see FIGURE
DRAWING.**

Anatsui, El.
Pieces of wood : an exhibition of mural
sculpture / El Anatsui. [Nigeria] : E. Anatsui,
1987 ; (Enugu : SNAAP Press) 39 p. : ill. ; 17
x 22 cm. Includes bibliographies.
1. Anatsui, El - Exhibitions. I. Title.
NYPL [Sc B 88--59]

ANATSUI, EL - EXHIBITIONS.
Anatsui, El. Pieces of wood . [Nigeria] , 1987 ;
(Enugu : SNAAP Press) 39 p. :
NYPL [Sc B 88--59]

Anaughe, S. W. Better life for Nigerians /.
Lagos , 1987. 56 p. : **NYPL [Sc D 88-796]**

ANCESTOR WORSHIP - AFRICA.
Nyamiti, Charles. Christ as our ancestor .
Gweru [Zimbabwe] , 1984. 151 p. ; DDC 232
19
BT205 .N82 1984 **NYPL [Sc D 88-986]**

ANCESTOR WORSHIP - NIGERIA.
Babayemi, S. O. Egúngún among the Oyǫ
Yoruba /. Ibadan , c1980. ix, 123 p. :
BL2480.Y6 B33 1980 **NYPL [Sc D 88-1149]**

ANCESTOR WORSHIP - TOGO.
Agbetiafa, Komla. Les ancêtres et nous .
Dakar , 1985. 95 p. : ISBN 2-7236-0929-4
NYPL [Sc D 88-7]

**Lo ancestral africano en la narrativa de Lydia
Cabrera /.** Valdés-Cruz, Rosa. Barcelona ,
1974. 113 p. ; ISBN 84-346-0082-X ;
PQ7389.C22 Z94 **NYPL [Sc D 89-36]**

Les ancêtres et nous . Agbetiafa, Komla. Dakar ,
1985. 95 p. : ISBN 2-7236-0929-4
NYPL [Sc D 88-7]

ANCIENT ART. see ART, ANCIENT.

Ancient Ashanti chieftaincy /. Obeng, Ernest E.
Tema, Ghana , 1988. 74 p. : ISBN
996-410-329-8 **NYPL [Sc C 88-343]**

Ancient Egyptian cut and use stencils /. Menten,
Theodore. New York , 1978. [32] leaves :
ISBN 0-486-23626-9 : **NYPL [Sc F 88-366]**

Ancona, George. (ill) Anderson, Joan. A
Williamsburg household /. New York , c1988.
[48] p. : ISBN 0-89919-516-4 : DDC [Fic] 19
PZ7.A5367 Wi 1988 **NYPL [Sc F 88-242]**

And bid him sing . February, V. A. (Vernie A.)
London , 1988. xvi, 212 p. : ISBN
0-7103-0278-9 : DDC 306 325/.32 19
NYPL [Sc D 88-1363]

And the jackal played the masinko. Hopkins,
Marjorie. New York [1969] [41] p. ISBN
0-8193-0271-6
PZ7.H7756 An **NYPL [JFF 72-292]**

And when you come to our house . Berry,
Kelly-Marie. [New York?] , c1987. [35] p. ;
NYPL [Sc D 89-186]

And why not every man? . Phelan, Helene C.
Interlaken, New York , 1987. 247 p. : ISBN
0-9605836-4-5 **NYPL [Sc D 87-1420]**

Anderson, David M. The Ecology of survival .
London, England , Boulder, Colo. , 1988. xii,
339 p. : ISBN 0-8133-0727-9 (Westview) DDC
304.2/096 19
GF720 .E26 1988 **NYPL [Sc D 89-280]**

Anderson, David, 1957- Conservation in Africa .
Cambridge [Cambridgeshire] , New York ,
1987. ix, 355 p. : ISBN 0-521-34199-X DDC
333.7/2/096 19
QH77.A4 C66 1987 **NYPL [Sc E 88-199]**

Anderson, Hope. Slips from grace / Hope
Anderson. Toronto : Coach House Press, 1987.
82 p. : port. ; 22 cm. ISBN 0-88910-352-6
I. Title. **NYPL [Sc D 88-73]**

Anderson, James D., 1944- The education of
Blacks in the South, 1860-1935 / James D.
Anderson. Chapel Hill : University of North
Carolina Press, c1988. xiv, 366 p. : ill. ; 24 cm.
Includes index. Bibliography: p. [313]-351. ISBN
0-8078-1793-7 (alk. paper) DDC
370/.0889073075 19
*1. Afro-Americans - Education - Southern States -
History - 19th century. 2. Afro-Americans -
Education - Southern States - History - 20th century. I.
Title.*
LC2802.S9 A53 1988 **NYPL [Sc E 88-457]**

Anderson, Joan. A Williamsburg household / by
Joan Anderson ; photographed by George
Ancona. New York : Clarion Books, c1988.
[48] p. : col. ill. ; 26 cm. Focuses on events in the
household of a white family and its black slaves in
Colonial Williamsburg in the eighteenth century.
SCHOMBURG CHILDREN'S COLLECTION. ISBN
0-89919-516-4 : DDC [Fic] 19
*1. Slavery - Juvenile fiction. 2. Williamsburg (Va.) -
Social life and customs - Juvenile fiction. I. Ancona,
George, ill. II. Schomburg Children's Collection. III.
Title.*
PZ7.A5367 Wi 1988 **NYPL [Sc F 88-242]**

**ANDERSON, JOHN, B. 1831? - TRIALS,
LITIGATION, ETC.**
Teatero, William, 1953- John Anderson .
[Kingston, Ont.] , c1986. 183 p. : ISBN
0-9692685-0-5 : DDC 345.71/056/0924 19
NYPL [Sc E 89-113]

Anderson, John, 1954 Mar. 27- Burning down the
house : MOVE and the tragedy of Philadelphia
/ John Anderson and Hilary Hevenor.1st ed.
New York : Norton, c1987. xv, 409 p. : ill. ; 24
cm. Includes index. ISBN 0-393-02460-1 : DDC
974.8/1104 19
*1. MOVE (Organization). 2. Black nationalism -
Pennsylvania - Philadelphia. 3. Afro-Americans -
Pennsylvania - Philadelphia. 4. Public relations -
Pennsylvania - Philadelphia - Police. 5. Philadelphia
(Pa.) - Race relations. I. Hevenor, Hilary, 1957-. II.
Title.*
F158.9.N4 A53 1987 **NYPL [Sc E 88-332]**

**ANDERSON, MARIAN, 1902- - JUVENILE
LITERATURE.**
Stevenson, Janet. Marian Anderson /. Chicago
[1963] 189 p. : **NYPL [Sc D 88-377]**

Anderson, Patricia, Dr. Mini bus ride : a journey
through the informal sector of Kingston's mass
transportation system / Patricia Anderson with
Hilary Bailey ... [et al.]. Mona, Kingston,
Jamaica : Institute of Social and Economic
Research, University of the West Indies,
Jamaica, 1987. vii, 179 p. : ill., forms, map ; 23
cm. Bibliography: p. 179. ISBN 976-400-006-1
*1. Bus lines - Jamaica - Kingston Metropolitan Area. 2.
Informal sector (Economics) - Jamaica - Kingston
Metropolitan Area. 3. Bus drivers - Jamaica - Kingston
Metropolitan Area. 4. Kingston Metropolitan Area
(Jamaica) - Economic conditions. I. Bailey, Hilary. II.*

Title.
HE5647.K56 A53x 1987
NYPL [Sc D 89-312]

**ANDEVORANTO (MADAGASCAR) -
DESCRIPTION.**
Delval, Raymond, 1917- Andovoranto, son
passé prestigieux /. Antananarivo , 1985. 106
p. ; DDC 969.7 19
DT469.M38 A543 1985
NYPL [Sc F 88-321]

**ANDEVORANTO (MADAGASCAR) -
HISTORY.**
Delval, Raymond, 1917- Andovoranto, son
passé prestigieux /. Antananarivo , 1985. 106
p. ; DDC 969.7 19
DT469.M38 A543 1985
NYPL [Sc F 88-321]

Andevoranto, son passé prestigieux. Delval,
Raymond, 1917- Andovoranto, son passé
prestigieux /. Antananarivo , 1985. 106 p. ;
DDC 969.7 19
DT469.M38 A543 1985
NYPL [Sc F 88-321]

Andevoranto, son passé prestigieux /. Delval,
Raymond, 1917- Antananarivo , 1985. 106 p. ;
DDC 969.7 19
DT469.M38 A543 1985
NYPL [Sc F 88-321]

Andrada e Silva, José Bonifácio de, 1763-1838.
see **Silva, José Bonifácio de Andrada e, 1763-
1838.**

Andrade, Julieta de. Cultura creoula e lanc-patuá
no norte do Brasil = Culture créole et langue
patúa au nord du Brésil / Julieta de Andrade ;
tradução, Marcel Jules Thiéblot. São Paulo :
Escola de Folclore, 1984. 310 p. : ill., ports. ;
21 cm. (Coleção Pesquisa. vol. 7) Text in French and
Portuguese; summary in English, French, German,
Italian, Lanc-patuá, Portuguese, and Spanish. Cover
title: Cultura crioula e lanc-patuá no norte do Brasil.
Includes index. Errata slip tipped in. Bibliography: p.
[301]-303.
*1. Creoles - Brazil - Amapá (Territory) - Social life and
customs. 2. Karipuna Creole dialect - Brazil - Amapá
(Territory). 3. Amapá Brazil Ter. - Social life and
customs. I. Title. II. Title: Culture créole et langue
patúa au nord du Brésil. III. Title: Cultura crioula e
lanc-patuá no norte do Brasil.*
F2543 .A53 1984 **NYPL [HFS 86-2895]**

André, Jacques. L'inceste focal dans la famille
noire antillaise : crimes, conflits, structure /
Jacques André ; sous la direction de Jean
Laplanche. Paris : Presses universitaires de
France, 1987. 396 p. ; 22 cm. (Voix nouvelles en
psychanalyse) Includes index. Bibliography: p. 385-388.
ISBN 2-13-040101-5
*1. Family violence - West Indies. 2. Blacks - West
Indies - Family relationships. 3. Murder - West Indies.
I. Title. II. Series.* **NYPL [Sc D 88-129]**

Andrew Johnson and the Negro /. Bowen, David
Warren, 1944- Knoxville , c1989. xvi, 206 p. ;
ISBN 0-87049-584-4 (alk. paper) DDC
973/.0496073 19
E667 .B65 1989 **NYPL [Sc D 89-508]**

Andrews, Charles Freer, 1871-1940.
Sadhu Sundar Singh. Wawili, Rafiki. Sadhu
Sundar Singh : mwaminifu mkuu /
Kimetungwa na Rafiki Wawili. London ,
1949. 48 p. ; **NYPL [Sc C 89-111]**

**ANEMIA, DREPANOCYTIC. see SICKLE
CELL ANEMIA.**

Angelou, Maya.
Conversations with Maya Angelou / edited by
Jeffrey M. Elliot. Jackson : University Press of
Mississippi, c1989. xvi, 246 p. ; 24 cm. (Literary
conversations series) Includes index. ISBN
0-87805-361-1 (alk. paper) DDC 818/.5409 19
*1. Angelou, Maya - Interviews. 2. Afro-American
women in literature. 3. Authors, American - 20th
century - Interviews. 4. Entertainers - United States -
Interviews. 5. Women and literature - United States -
History - 20th century. I. Elliot, Jeffrey M. II. Title.
III. Series.*
PS3551.N464 Z4635 1989
NYPL [Sc E 89-225]

Mrs. Flowers : a moment of friendship / Maya
Angelou ; illustrated by Etienne Delessert.
Minneapolis, Minn. : Redpath Press, c1986. 32
p. : ill. (some col.) ; 19 cm. Excerpt from the
author's I know why the caged bird sings. ISBN
1-556-28009-2 (pbk.) : DDC [Fic] 19

I. Delessert, Étienne, ill. II. Title.
PZ7.A5833 Mr 1986
                    NYPL [Sc Rare C 88-28]

ANGELOU, MAYA - INTERVIEWS.
Angelou, Maya. Conversations with Maya
Angelou /. Jackson , c1989. xvi, 246 p. ; ISBN
0-87805-361-1 (alk. paper)   DDC 818/.5409 19
PS3551.N464 Z4635 1989
                    NYPL [Sc E 89-225]

ANGLICAN COMMUNION - SERMONS.
Odunuga, S. A. F. (Samuel Adedoyin
Folafunmi), 1902- [Sermons. Selections.] The
life of Venerable Archdeacon S.A.F. Odunuga
/. [Nigeria] , 1982. xiii, 175 p., [2] p. of plates :
DDC 252/.03 19
BX5700.7.Z6 O28 1982
                    NYPL [Sc E 89-142]

ANGLICAN COMMUNION - ZIMBABWE -
    CLERGY - BIOGRAPHY.
Walker, David A. C. Paterson of Cyrene .
Gweru, Zimbabwe , 1985. xi, 85 p. : ISBN
0-86922-340-2   DDC 283/.3 B 19
BX5700.4.Z8 P378 1985
                    NYPL [Sc D 88-229]

Anglican pioneers in Lesotho . Dove, R.
(Reginald) [s.l. , 1975?] (s.l. - Mazenod
Institute) 216 p., [1] fold. leaf of plates :   DDC
283/.68/6
BX5700.6.A44 L473   *NYPL [JXD 84-17]*

Anglin, Robert Alton, 1910- Jordan, Lawrence V.
Publications of the faculty and staff of West
Virginia State College [microform] /. Institute ,
1960. 23 p. ;   *NYPL [Sc Micro F-11,160]*

ANGLING. see FISHING.

ANGOLA - ECONOMIC CONDITIONS.
Hodges, Tony. Angola to the 1990s . London ,
1987. 145 p. :   *NYPL [Sc F 88-138]*

ANGOLA - FICTION.
Pessoa, Henrique Novais. Comboio comakovi .
[Portugal] , 1987. 147 p. :
                    NYPL [Sc D 88-1010]
Santos, Arnaldo, 1935- O cesto de Katandu e
outros contos /. Lisboa , c1986. 101 p. ;
                    NYPL [Sc C 88-267]
Van-Dúnem, Domingos. Dibundu /. Lisbon
[1988?] 84 p. ;   *NYPL [Sc C 89-134]*
Van-Dúnem, Domingos, 1925- Kuluka /. Lisboa
[1988?] 87 p. :   *NYPL [Sc C 89-129]*
Vieira, José Luandino, 1935- Vidas novas /.
[Porto?] [1975]. 109 p. :
                    NYPL [Sc E 89-14]

ANGOLA - FOREIGN ECONOMIC
    RELATIONS.
Hodges, Tony. Angola to the 1990s . London ,
1987. 145 p. :   *NYPL [Sc F 88-138]*

ANGOLA - HISTORY - CIVIL WAR, 1975-
Dixon, Glen. Hostage /. London , 1986. 189 p.,
[8] p. of plates : ISBN 0-86287-271-5
                    NYPL [Sc E 88-406]
Savimbi, Jonas Malheiro. Por um futuro melhor
/. Lisboa , 1986. 192 p. : DDC 967/.304 19
DT611.8 .S28 1986   *NYPL [Sc D 88-771]*

ANGOLA - HISTORY - SOUTH AFRICAN
    INCURSIONS, 1978-
Bernstein, Keith. Frontline Southern Africa /.
London , c1988. x, 117 p. : ISBN 0-7470-3012-X
(pbk)   DDC 968.06/3 19
HN800.A8   *NYPL [Sc E 89-122]*

ANGOLA - INDUSTRIES.
Hodges, Tony. Angola to the 1990s . London ,
1987. 145 p. :   *NYPL [Sc F 88-138]*

ANGOLA - JUVENILE FICTION.
Wellman, Alice. Time of fearful night. New
York [1970] 158 p.   DDC [Fic]
PZ7.W4578 Ti   *NYPL [Sc D 88-1431]*

Angola. Ministério da Informação. Proclamação
da independência da República Popular de
Angola, 11 de novembro de 1975 . Luanda ,
1975. 166 p., [6] leaves of plates :
                    NYPL [Sc. D 88-245]

Angola, onze de novembro de 1975. Proclamação
da independência da República Popular de
Angola, 11 de novembro de 1975 . Luanda ,
1975. 166 p., [6] leaves of plates :
                    NYPL [Sc D 88-245]

ANGOLA - POLITICS AND GOVERNMENT -
    1961-1975.

Road to liberation . Richmond, B. C. , pref.
1976. viii, 53 p. :   *NYPL [JFD 80-10236]*

ANGOLA - POLITICS AND GOVERNMENT -
    1975-
Savimbi, Jonas Malheiro. Por um futuro melhor
/. Lisboa , 1986. 192 p. : DDC 967/.304 19
DT611.8 .S28 1986   *NYPL [Sc D 88-771]*

ANGOLA - POLITICS AND GOVERNMENT -
    1975- - SOURCES.
Proclamação da independência da República
Popular de Angola, 11 de novembro de 1975 .
Luanda , 1975. 166 p., [6] leaves of plates :
                    NYPL [Sc D 88-245]

Angola to the 1990s . Hodges, Tony. London ,
1987. 145 p. :   *NYPL [Sc F 88-138]*

Angola, 11 de novembro de 1975. Proclamação da
independência da República Popular de Angola,
11 de novembro de 1975 . Luanda , 1975. 166
p., [6] leaves of plates :
                    NYPL [Sc D 88-245]

ANGONI - FOLKLORE.
Elliot, Geraldine. Where the leopard passes .
New York, 1987. x, 125 p. :
                    NYPL [Sc C 88-840]

Anigbedu, Laide. Hero's welcome / [Laide
Anigbedu. Yaba-Lagos, Nigeria : Writers'
Fraternity, 1986. 141 p. ; 20 cm. (Trumpeters)
ISBN 978-256-400-1
1. Nigeria - Fiction. I. Title. II. Series.
                    NYPL [Sc C 88-283]

ANIMAL BEHAVIOR - AFRICA.
YllA, 1910-1955. Animals in Africa /. New
York , 1953. 146 p. : *NYPL [Sc F 88-127]*

Animal jackets. Fisher, Aileen Lucia, 1906-
[Glendale, Calif., 1973] 43 p. ISBN
0-8372-0861-0   DDC [E]
PZ8.3.F634 Ap   *NYPL [Sc F 88-87]*

ANIMAL REMAINS (ARCHAEOLOGY) -
    TANZANIA - OLDUVAI GORGE.
Potts, Richard, 1953- Early hominid activities
at Olduvai /. New York , c1988. xi, 396 p. :
ISBN 0-202-01176-3 (lib. bdg.)   DDC 967.8 19
GN772.42.T34 P67 1988
                    NYPL [Sc E 89-92]

ANIMALS, FOSSIL. see PALEONTOLOGY.

Animals in Africa /. YllA, 1910-1955. New
York , 1953. 146 p. : *NYPL [Sc F 88-127]*

ANIMALS IN ART.
Santa Barbara Museum of Art. Antelopes and
elephants, hornbills and hyenas. [Santa Barbara,
1973] [48] p.   DDC 732/.2/0967
NB1098 .S27 1973   *NYPL [Sc F 88-165]*

ANIMALS - JUVENILE FICTION.
Umeh, Rich Enujioke. Why the cock became a
sacrificial animal /. Enugu, Nigeria , 1985. 38
p. : ISBN 978-239-648-6   *NYPL [Sc C 89-18]*

ANIMALS - JUVENILE POETRY.
Fisher, Aileen Lucia, 1906- Animal jackets.
[Glendale, Calif., 1973] 43 p. ISBN
0-8372-0861-0   DDC [E]
PZ8.3.F634 Ap   *NYPL [Sc F 88-87]*

The animals talk to Gussie /. Sullivan, Sarah A.
[S.l. , c1951 (wilmington, N.C. : Garey-Mintz
Print.) 28 p. :   *NYPL [Sc F 89-2]*

Animalu, Alexander O. E., 1938- Umezinwa,
Willy A. From African symbols to physics .
[Nigeria] c1988. 71 p. : *NYPL [Sc E 89-36]*

ANINI, LAWRENCE.
Enonchong, Charles. The rise and fall of Anini
/. Calabar, Nigeria [1988] 73 p. :
                    NYPL [Sc C 89-8]

ANN ARUNDEL COUNTY (MARYLAND) -
    CENSUS, 7TH, 1850 - INDEXES.
Clayton, Ralph. Free Blacks of Anne Arundel
County, Maryland 1850 /. Bowie, MD. , 1987.
xiv, 51 p. : ISBN 1-556-13069-4
                    NYPL [Sc D 88-64]

Annales martiniquaises. Série sciences humaines .
(no.3) Oralitures et littératures africaines et
caribéennes. [Fort-de-France] [1985] 56 p. :
                    NYPL [Sc F 89-93]

Annie John /. Kincaid, Jamaica. New York ,
1985. 148 p. ; ISBN 0-374-10521-9 : DDC
813/.54 19
PS3561.I425 A55 1985
                    NYPL [JFD 85-2648]

**Annotated list of theses submitted to Makerere
University and held by Makerere University
Library [microform]** /. Makerere University.
Library. [Kampala?] , 1981. 89 leaves ;
                    NYPL [Sc Micro R-4840 no.13]

Annual founder's day . National Association of
Negro Business and Professional Women's Club.
New York Club. [New York , 1961] [68] p. :
                    NYPL [Sc F 87-379]

Another year in Africa /. Zwi, Rose.
Johannesburg , c1980. 172 p. ; ISBN
0-86975-316-9   *NYPL [Sc D 88-1328]*

Ans, André Marcel d'. Haiti, Paysage et Société /
André-Marcel d'Ans. Paris : Karthala, 1987.
337 p. : ill., maps ; 24 cm. (Hommes et sociétés)
Bibliography: p. [331]-337. ISBN 2-86537-190-5
1. Haiti - History. 2. Haiti - Civilization. I. Title. II.
Series.   *NYPL [Sc E 88-251]*

**Ansaru Allāh Community.
Edition.**
    (no. 109) 'Isā 'Abd Allāh Muḥammad
    al-Mahdī, 1945- Who was Noble Drew Ali?
    [microform] /. Brooklyn, N.Y. [1980] 56 p. :
                    NYPL [Sc Micro R-4114 no. 10]
    (no. 109) Īs a Ābd All ah Muḥammad
    al-Hahd i, 1945- Who was Noble Drew Ali?
    /. [Brooklyn, N.Y.] 1988, c1980. 122 p. :
                    NYPL [Sc D 89-74]
    (no. 11) 'Isā 'Abd Allāh Muḥammad
    al-Mahdī, 1945- Who was the prophet
    Muhammad? [microform] /. Brooklyn, N.Y.
    [1980] 96 p. :
                    NYPL [Sc Micro R-4114 no. 11]
    (no. 177) 'Isā 'Abd Allāh Muḥammad
    al-Mahdī, 1945- Who was Marcus Garvey? .
    [Brooklyn, N.Y.] c1988. 101 p. :
                    NYPL [Sc D 89-139]
    (no. 3) 'Isā 'Abd Allāh Muḥammad al-Mahdī,
    1945- Was Christ really crucified?
    [microform] /. Brooklyn, N.Y. [1980] 72 p. :
                    NYPL [Sc Micro R-4114 no. 6]
    (no. 30) 'Isā 'Abd Allāh Muḥammad
    al-Mahdī, 1945- Eternal life after death
    [microform] /. Brooklyn, N.Y. [197-?] 36
    p. ;   *NYPL [Sc Micro R-4114 no.3]*
    (no. 91) 'Isā 'Abd Allāh Muḥammad
    al-Mahdī, 1945- The true story of the
    Prophet Abraham (Pbuh) [microform] /.
    Brooklyn, N.Y. [1980?] 96 p. :
                    NYPL [Sc Micro R-4114 no. 7]
    (no. 92) 'Isā 'Abd Allāh Muḥammad
    al-Mahdī, 1945- Holy war [microform] /.
    Brooklyn, N.Y. , c1979. 68 p. :
                    NYPL [Sc Micro R-4114 no. 8]
    (16) 'Isā 'Abd Allāh Muḥammad al-Mahdī,
    1945- ?Vino el puerco para la humanidad?
    [microform] . [Brooklyn , 197-?] 40 p. :
                    NYPL [Sc Micro R-4114 no. 12]
    (18) 'Isā 'Abd Allāh Muḥammad al-Mahdī,
    1945- The tribe Israel is no more [microform]
    /. Brooklyn [197-?] 62 p. :
                    NYPL [Sc Micro R-4114 no. 13]
    (48) 'Isā 'Abd Allāh Muḥammad al-Mahdī,
    1945- Arabic made easy [microform] /.
    [Brooklyn, N.Y. , 197-?] 2 v. :
                    NYPL [Sc Micro R-4114 no.2]
    (49) 'Isā 'Abd Allāh Muḥammad al-Mahdī,
    1945- Islamic marriage ceremony and
    polygamy [microform] /. Brooklyn , c1977.
    30 p. ;   *NYPL [Sc Micro R-4114 no.1]*
    (52) 'Isā 'Abd Allāh Muḥammad al-Mahdī,
    1945- Islamic cookery [microform] /.
    Brooklyn , c1976. 31 p. :
                    NYPL [Sc Micro R-4114 no. 14]
    (77) 'Isā 'Abd Allāh Muḥammad al-Mahdī,
    1945- Khutbat's of Al Hajj Al Imam Isa
    Abd'Allah Muhammad Al Mahdi
    [microform]. Brooklyn [1978?] 2 v. :
                    NYPL [Sc Micro R-4114 no. 17]
    (83) 'Isā 'Abd Allāh Muḥammad al-Mahdī,
    1945- The true story of Noah (Pbuh)
    [microform] /. Brooklyn, N.Y. [1978] 62 p. :
                    NYPL [Sc Micro R-4114 no. 9]

Mating in Islam! [microform] . Brooklyn
[197-?] 11 p. :
                    NYPL [Sc Micro R-4114 no. 21]

People call him the Son of God [microform]

Brooklyn [197-?] 11 p. :
NYPL [Sc Micro R-4114 no. 20]

ANSARU ALLAH COMMUNITY.
Abba island in America [microform] Brooklyn
[197-?] 11 p. :
NYPL [Sc Micro R-4114 no. 19]

**Antecedentes económicos de la guerra de los diez
años/.** Besada, Benito. La Habana , 1978. 17
p. ; *NYPL [Sc C 88-211]*

**ANTEDILUVIAN ANIMALS. see
PALEONTOLOGY.**

Antelopes and elephants, hornbills and hyenas.
Santa Barbara Museum of Art. [Santa Barbara,
1973] [48] p. DDC 732/.2/0967
NB1098 .S27 1973 NYPL [Sc F 88-165]

Anthologie africaine d'expression française /
[compilée par] Jacques Chevrier. Paris : Hatier,
c1981- v. ; 18 cm. (Collection Monde noir poche.
9-) Includes index. CONTENTS. - v. 1. Le roman et la
nouvelle -- v. 2. La poésie. ISBN 2-218-05648-8 (v.
1) :
*1. African literature (French). I. Chevrier, Jacques, fl.
1974-. II. Series. III. Series: Collection Monde noir
poche, 9, etc.* *NYPL [Sc C 89-80]*

**Anthologie de la nouvelle poésie nègre et
malgache de langue française /.** Senghor,
Léopold Sédar, 1906- Paris , 1985, c1948. xliv,
227 p. ; ISBN 2-13-038715-2
NYPL [Sc C 88-134]

**Anthologie des sculptuers et peintres zaïrois
contemporains /.** Bamba Ndombasi Kifimba,
1937- Paris , 1987. 109 p. : ISBN 2-09-168350-7
NYPL [Sc G 88-11]

Anthony Burns . Hamilton, Virginia. New York ,
c1988. xiii, 193 p. ; ISBN 0-394-88185-0 DDC
973.6/6/0924 B 92 19
E450.B93 H36 1988 NYPL [Sc D 88-1157]

Anthony, Michael. Towns and villages of Trinidad
and Tobago / by Michael Anthony. St. James,
Port of Spain : Circle Press, 1988. v., 342 p. :
ill., maps ; 22 cm. Includes index. Bibliography: p.
333-338.
*1. Cities and towns - Trinidad and Tobago. 2. Villages -
Trinidad and Tobago. I. Title.*
NYPL [Sc D 89-404]

Anthropologie de l'esclavage . Meillassoux,
Claude. Paris , c1986. 375 p. ; ISBN
2-13-039480-9 *NYPL [Sc D 88-768]*

ANTHROPOLOGY.
Anthropology for the nineties . New York ,
London , c1988. xxvii, 561 p. : ISBN
0-02-906441-4 (pbk.) DDC 306 19
GN316 .A574 1988 NYPL [Sc E 88-488]

ANTHROPOLOGY - COLLECTIONS.
Art/artifact . New York , Munich , c1988. 195
p. : ISBN 0-9614587-7-1 DDC 730/.0967/074 19
GN36.A35 A78 1988 NYPL [Sc G 88-25]

Anthropology for the eighties. Anthropology for
the nineties . New York , London , c1988.
xxvii, 561 p. : ISBN 0-02-906441-4 (pbk.) DDC
306 19
GN316 .A574 1988 NYPL [Sc E 88-488]

Anthropology for the nineties : introductory
readings / edited with introductions by
Johnnetta B. Cole. New York : Free Press ;
London : Collier Macmillan, c1988. xxvii, 561
p. : ill. ; 24 cm. "Revised edition of Anthropology for
the eighties." Includes bibliographies and index. ISBN
0-02-906441-4 (pbk.) DDC 306 19
*1. Anthropology. I. Cole, Johnnetta B. II. Anthropology
for the eighties.*
GN316 .A574 1988 NYPL [Sc E 88-488]

**ANTHROPOLOGY - MOZAMBIQUE -
CONGRESSES.**
Seminario Interdisciplinar de Antropologia
(1st : 1982 : Maputo, Mozambique) Primeiro
seminário interdisciplinar de antropologia /.
Maputo , 1987. 153 p. ;
NYPL [Sc F 88-172]

Anthropology of contemporary issues.
Williams, Brett. Upscaling downtown . Ithaca
[N.Y.] , 1988. xi, 157 p. : ISBN 0-8014-2106-3
(alk. paper) DDC 307.3/42/09753 19
HT177.W3 W55 1988 NYPL [Sc E 88-387]

The Anthropology of form and meaning.
Schloss, Marc R. The hatchet's blood . Tucson ,
c1988. xv, 178 p. : ISBN 0-8165-1042-3 (alk.

paper) DDC 966/.3 19
DT549.45.B39 S35 1988
NYPL [Sc E 88-443]

ANTI NAZI LEAGUE (GREAT BRITAIN)
Widgery, David. Beating time /. London ,
1986. 126 p. : ISBN 0-7011-2985-9
NYPL [JMD 88-112]

Anti-Apartheid Movement.
Nelson Mandela . [London , 1988] 61 p. :
NYPL [Sc G 89-3]

**ANTI-APARTHEID MOVEMENT - SOUTH
AFRICA.**
Oliver Tambo and the struggle against apartheid
/. New Delhi , c1987. xii, 172 p., [1] leaf of
plates : ISBN 81-207-0779-6 : DDC
323.1/196/068 19
DT763 .O57 1987 NYPL [Sc D 88-1443]
Südafrika - Widerstand und Befreiungskampf .
Köln , 1987, c1986. 286 p. : ISBN 3-7609-1023-8
NYPL [Sc C 88-190]

**ANTI-APARTHEID MOVEMENT - SOUTH
AFRICA - GRAHAMSTOWN.**
Roux, Andre, 1954- Voices from Rini .
Grahamstown, South Africa , 1986. 107 p. ;
ISBN 0-86810-131-1 *NYPL [Sc F 88-216]*

ANTI-APARTHEID MOVEMENTS.
Phelan, John M. Apartheid media . Westport,
Conn. , c1987. xi, 220 p. ; ISBN 0-88208-244-2 :
DDC 323.44/5 19
PN4748.S58 P4 1987 NYPL [JLD 87-4698]

**ANTI-APARTHEID MOVEMENTS -
BIOGRAPHY.**
Levine, Janet, 1945- Inside apartheid .
Chicago , c1988. xvi, 287 p., [16] p. of plates :
ISBN 0-8092-4544-2 : DDC 968.06/3/0924 B
19
DT779.955.L48 A3 1989
NYPL [JLE 89-122]

**ANTI-APARTHEID MOVEMENTS - SOUTH
AFRICA.**
Cukierman, Maurice. Afrique du Sud . Paris ,
c1987. 279 p. : ISBN 2-209-05983-6
NYPL [Sc D 88-756]
Nelson Mandela . [London , 1988] 61 p. :
NYPL [Sc G 89-3]
Ramusi, Molapatene Collins. Soweto, my love
/. New York , c1988. viii, 262 p. ; ISBN
0-8050-0263-4 DDC 968.06/092/4 B 19
DT779.955.R36 A3 1988
NYPL [Sc E 89-95]

**ANTI-APARTHEID MOVEMENTS - SOUTH
AFRICA - JUVENILE LITERATURE.**
Haskins, James, 1941- Winnie Mandela . New
York , c1988. 179 p., [12] p. of plates : ISBN
0-399-21515-8 DDC 968.06/092/4 B 92 19
DT779.955.M36 H38 1988
NYPL [Sc D 88-1138]

ANTI-COLONIALISM. see COLONIES.

**ANTI-COMMUNIST MOVEMENTS -
UNITED STATES - HISTORY - 20TH
CENTURY.**
Horne, Gerald. Communist front? . Rutherford
[N.J.] , London , c1988. 454 p. ; ISBN
0-8386-3285-8 (alk. paper) DDC
323.1/196073/073 19
E185.61 .H8 1988 NYPL [Sc E 88-147]

**ANTI-COMMUNIST RESISTANCE. see ANTI-
COMMUNIST MOVEMENTS.**

Antidesarrollo, Suráfrica y sus bantustanes /.
Moerdijk, Donald. [Anti-development, South
Africa and its Bantustans. Spanish.] Barcelona ,
Paris , 1982. 222 p. : ISBN 92-3-301888-1
(Unesco) *NYPL [Sc D 88-595]*

**ANTI-DISCRIMINATION LAWS. see RACE
DISCRIMINATION.**

**Antidote to West-Indian sketches, drawn from
authentic sources.** London : Printed for
Whitmore and Fenn, 1816-1817. 7 nos. ; 21
cm. CONTENTS. - No. 1. Condition of the slaves in
the British colonies.--no. 2. A short account of the
African Institution.--no. 3. The actual condition of the
Negroes in the British West India colonies.--no. 4 The
columnies of the African Institution.--no. 5. An
illustration of the principles of the African
Institution.--no. 6. Observations on the ameliorated
condition of the Negroes in the British West India
colonies.--no. 7. Observations on the necessity of a total
change in the system of management of the African
Institution.

*1. African Institution, London. 2. West-Indian sketches,
drawn from authentic sources.* *NYPL [Sc Rare G 86-16]*
British.

Antieau, Chester James. Federal civil rights acts :
civil practice / Chester J. Antieau.2d ed.
Rochester, N.Y. : Lawyers Co-operative Pub.
Co. ; San Francisco, Calif. : Bancroft-Whitney
Co., 1980. 2 v. ; 26 cm. Kept up to date by
cumulative supplements. Includes index. DDC
342.73/085 19
1. Civil rights - United States. I. Title.
KF4749 .A745 1980 NYPL [Sc F 83-46]

ANTIGUA - FICTION.
Kincaid, Jamaica. Annie John /. New York ,
1985. 148 p. ; ISBN 0-374-10521-9 : DDC
813/.54 19
PS3561.I425 A55 1985
NYPL [JFD 85-2648]
Kincaid, Jamaica. A small place /. New York ,
1988. 81 p. : ISBN 0-374-26638-7 : DDC 813 19
PR9275.A583 K5637 1988
NYPL [Sc D 88-1061]

ANTI-IMPERIALIST MOVEMENTS.
Essack, Karrim. The Mathaba International /.
Dar es Salaam [1987?] iv, 81 p. : DDC 325/.32
19
JC359 .E825 1987 NYPL [Sc C 89-30]

Les Antilles /. Benoist, Jean, 1929- [Paris ,
1976?] p. [1372]-1448 :
NYPL [Sc D 87-1164]

Antilles. see West Indies.

Antilles Caraïbes / préface de Jean Raspail ;
texte de Jacques Patuelli ; légendes de Daniel
Van de Valde ; photographies de Claude Rives
et Gérard Sioen. Paris : Éditions Sun, c1982.
157 p. : col. ill., map ; 32 cm. (Collection "Vivre
dans le monde") ISBN 2-7191-0177-0
*1. West Indies - Description and travel. 2. West
Indies - Social conditions. I. Raspail, Jean. II. Patuelli,
Jacques. III. Velde, Daniel Van de. IV. Rives, Claude.
V. Sioen, Gérard. VI. Series.*
NYPL [Sc F 88-347]

Les Antillles . Berney, Henri-Maurice. Paris ,
1977, c1972. 128 p. : ISBN 3-405-11035-1
NYPL [Sc F 89-34]

The antipeople . Sony Lab'Ou Tansi.
[Anté-peuple. English.] London ; New York :
170 p. ; ISBN 0-7145-2845-5 : DDC 843 19
PQ3989.2.S64 A813 1987
NYPL [Sc D 88-835]

**ANTIQUITIES, PREHISTORIC. see MAN,
PREHISTORIC.**

ANTISLAVERY. see SLAVERY.

Anti-Slavery Meeting (1855 : Boston) The
Boston mob of "gentlemen of property and
standing." : Proceedings of the Anti-Slavery
Meeting held in Stacy Hall, Boston, on the
twentieth anniversary of the mob of October
21, 1835 / Phonographic report by J.M.W.
Yerrinton. Boston : Published by R.F. Wallcut,
1855 (Boston : J.B. Yerrinton and Son, printers)
76 p. ; 24 cm.
*1. Garrison, William Lloyd, 1805-1879. 2. Riots -
Massachusetts - Boston. 3. Boston (Mass.) - Garrison
mob, 1835. 4. Boston (Mass.) - History - Anti-slavery
movement, 1830-1863. I. Yerrinton, James M. W. II.
Title. III. Title: Proceedings of the Anti-Slavery
Meeting held in Stacy Hall, Boston.*
E450.B74 NYPL [Sc Rare F 88-44]

The anti-slavery movement in Indiana
[microform] /. Miller, Marion Clinton. 1938.
290 leaves. *NYPL [Sc Micro R-4836]*

Anti-slavery reporter.
(v.1, no.4) Whittier, John Greenleaf, 1807-1892.
Justice and expediency. New-York , 1833.
[49]-63 p. :
E449 .A624 NYPL [Sc Rare F 98-1]

Antonio Maceo, la protesta de Baraguá /.
Caballero, Armando O. La Habana , 1977. 30,
[1] p. : *NYPL [Sc F 88-281]*

**António, Mário. see Oliveira, Mário António
Fernandes de, 1934-**

**ANTONIUS, MARCUS, 83?-30 B.C. -
POETRY.**
Chase-Riboud, Barbara. Portrait of a nude
woman as Cleopatra /. New York , c1987. 110
p. : ISBN 0-688-06403-5 : DDC 811/.54 19
PS3553.H336 P6 1987 NYPL [Sc D 88-329]

Antony, Mark. see **Antonius, Marcus, 83?-30 B. C.**

Antropologia (São Paulo, Brazil) .
(13) Ferrara, Miriam Nicolau. A imprensa negra paulista (1915-1963) /. São Paulo , 1986. 279 p. :   *NYPL [Sc B 88-6]*

(7) Kabengele Munanga. Os Basanga de Shaba . Sao Palulo , 1986. 334 p. :   *NYPL [Sc B 88-7]*

Anukwu, Martin. Eziokwu bụ ndụ / Anukwu, Martin V. Enugu, Nigeria : Cecta, 1986. 110 p. : ill. ; 19 cm. ISBN 978-239-649-4
1. Igbo language - Texts. I. Title.
     NYPL [Sc C 89-12]

Anusionwu, Emmanuel Chukwuma, 1946-
Ukpong, Ignatius I. The contributions of expatriate and indigenous manpower to the manufacturing industry in Nigeria . [Calabar, Cross River State, Nigeria] [c1986] ix, 61 p. ;
ISBN 978-227-526-3   DDC 331.12/57/09669 19
HD5848.A6 U37 1986   *NYPL [Sc C 89-128]*

Anwar, Muhammad. Ethnic minority broadcasting : a research report / Muhammad Anwar.1st ed. London : Commission for Racial Equality, 1983. 80 p. ; 21 cm. Bibliography: p. 72. ISBN 0-907920-39-X
1. Ethnic radio broadcasting - Great Britain. 2. Radio audiences - Great Britain. I. Title.
     NYPL [Sc D 88-573]

Anya, A. O., 1937- Science, development and the future : the Nigerian case : reflections and essays on the Nigerian socio-cultural experience / by A.O. Anya. [Nsukka] : University of Nigeria Press, [1982] v, 90 p. ; 24 cm. Includes bibliographical references and index. ISBN 978-229-902-2
1. Science and state - Nigeria - Addresses, essays, lectures. I. Title.   *NYPL [Sc E 88-136]*

APARTHEID.
Buthelezi, Gatsha. South Africa . Lagos, Nigeria , c1986. xxxvii, 143 p. : ISBN 978-242-308-4   *NYPL [Sc C 88-269]*

Mwaga, D. Z. The crime of apartheid /. Dar es Salaam , c1985. xix, 141 p. ; ISBN 997-660-049-6   DDC 342.68//0873 346.802873 19
LAW   *NYPL [Sc C 89-117]*

Apartheid, imperialism, and African freedom /.
Pomeroy, William J., 1916- New York , 1986. ix, 259 p. ; ISBN 0-7178-0640-5 : DDC 305.8/00968 19
E183.8.S6 P65 1986   *NYPL [Sc D 88-1147]*

Apartheid in India. Rajshekar Shetty, V. T., 1932- Dalit, the black Untouchables of India /. Atlanta, Ga. , c1987. 89 p. ; ISBN 0-932863-05-1 (pbk.) :   *NYPL [Sc D 89-356]*

Apartheid in South Africa. Special report of the Director-General on the application of the declaration concerning the policy of apartheid in South Africa. Geneva , 1986. 186 p. : ISBN 92-2-105167-6 (pbk.)   *NYPL [Sc E 88-179]*

Apartheid in transition /. Lemon, Anthony. Aldershot, Hants , Brookfield, Vt. , c1987. xi, 414 p. ; ISBN 0-566-00635-9
     NYPL [Sc D 88-644]

Apartheid media . Phelan, John M. Westport, Conn. , c1987. xi, 220 p. ; ISBN 0-88208-244-2 : DDC 323.44/5 19
PN4748.S58 P4 1987   *NYPL [JLD 87-4698]*

APARTHEID - MORAL AND ETHICAL ASPECTS.
Motlhabi, Mokgethi B. G. (Mokgethi Buti George), 1944- Challenge to apartheid . Grand Rapids, Mich. , c1988. xii, 243 p. ; ISBN 0-8028-0347-4 : DDC 305.8/00968 19
DT763 .M69 1988   *NYPL [JFD 88-11473]*

APARTHEID - NAMIBIA.
Moorehead, Caroline. Namibia . Oxford [1988] 50 p. : ISBN 0-85598-111-3 :
     NYPL [Sc F 89-120]

Pomeroy, William J., 1916- Apartheid, imperialism, and African freedom /. New York , 1986. ix, 259 p. ; ISBN 0-7178-0640-5 : DDC 305.8/00968 19
E183.8.S6 P65 1986   *NYPL [Sc D 88-1147]*

APARTHEID - SOCIAL ASPECTS - SOUTH AFRICA.
Wolpe, Harold. Race, class & the apartheid state /. London , 1988. viii, 118 p. ; ISBN

0-85255-319-6 (pbk.)   DDC 305.8/968 19
DT763   *NYPL [JLD 88-3222]*

APARTHEID - SOUTH AFRICA.
AFRICA Fund. Africa Fund . [Zimbabwe?] [1986?] [24] p. :   *NYPL [Sc D 88-1201]*

Apartheid, South Africa and international law . New York, NY , 1985. iv, 136 p. ;
     NYPL [Sc F 88-289]

Boon, Rudolf. Over vijf jaar in Johannesburg-- . Amsterdam , 's-Gravenhage [Netherlands] , 1986. 223 p. ; ISBN 90-70509-53-9
     NYPL [Sc D 89-167]

Bot, Monica. Training on separate tracks . Braamfontein, Johannesburg , 1988. iv, 71 p. ; ISBN 0-86982-346-9   *NYPL [Sc D 89-81]*

Cohen, Robin. Endgame in South Africa? . London : Paris : x, 108 p. ; ISBN 0-85255-308-0 (pbk.) : DDC 323.1/68 19
DT763 .C64 1986   *NYPL [Sc D 88-770]*

Commonwealth Group of Eminent Persons. Mission to South Africa . Harmondsworth, Middlesex, Eng. , New York , 1986. 176 p. : ISBN 0-14-052384-7 :   *NYPL [Sc C 88-116]*

Cukierman, Maurice. Afrique du Sud . Paris , c1987. 279 p. : ISBN 2-209-05983-6
     NYPL [Sc D 88-756]

Davies, Robert H. The struggle for South Africa . London , Atlantic Highlands, N.J. , 1988. 2 v. : ISBN 0-86232-760-1 (v. 1) DDC 322/.0968 19
JQ1931 .D38 1988   *NYPL [Sc D 88-1369]*

Frontline Southern Africa . New York , 1988. xxxv, 530 p., [16] p. of leaves : ISBN 0-941423-08-5 : DDC 322/.5/0968 19
DT747.S6 F76 1988   *NYPL [JLE 89-595]*

González, Carmen, 1940- Sobre los hombros ajenos /. La Habana , 1985. 119 p. ; DDC 968 19
DT766 .G66 1985   *NYPL [Sc D 88-416]*

Legum, Colin. The battlefronts of Southern Africa /. New York , c1988. xxix, 451 p. : ISBN 0-8419-1135-5 (alk. paper) DDC 327.68 19
DT746 .L425 1987   *NYPL [Sc E 88-468]*

Lemon, Anthony. Apartheid in transition /. Aldershot, Hants , Brookfield, Vt. , c1987. xi, 414 p. : ISBN 0-566-00635-9
     NYPL [Sc D 88-644]

Levine, Janet, 1945- Inside apartheid . Chicago , c1988. xvi, 287 p., [16] p. of plates : ISBN 0-8092-4544-2 : DDC 968.06/3/0924 B 19
DT779.955.L48 A3 1989
     NYPL [JLE 89-122]

Makhoere, Caesarina Khana. No child's play . London , 1988. 121 p. ; ISBN 0-7043-4111-5 :
     NYPL [Sc C 88-333]

Moerdijk, Donald. [Anti-development, South Africa and its Bantustans. Spanish.] Antidesarrollo, Suráfrica y sus bantustanes /. Barcelona , Paris , 1982. 222 p. : ISBN 92-3-301888-1 (Unesco)
     NYPL [Sc D 88-595]

Motlhabi, Mokgethi B. G. (Mokgethi Buti George), 1944- Challenge to apartheid . Grand Rapids, Mich. , c1988. xii, 243 p. ; ISBN 0-8028-0347-4 : DDC 305.8/00968 19
DT763 .M69 1988   *NYPL [JFD 88-11473]*

Mwaga, D. Z. The crime of apartheid /. Dar es Salaam , c1985. xix, 141 p. ; ISBN 997-660-049-6 DDC 342.68//0873 346.802873 19
LAW   *NYPL [Sc C 89-117]*

The National question in South Africa /. London , Atlantic Highlands, N.J. , 1988. 154 p. ; ISBN 0-86232-794-6 DDC 320.5/4/0968 19
DT763 .N35 1988   *NYPL [JLD 88-4552]*

Oliver Tambo and the struggle against apartheid /. New Delhi , c1987. xii, 172 p., [1] leaf of plates : ISBN 81-207-0779-6 : DDC 323.1/196/068 19
DT763 .O57 1987   *NYPL [Sc D 88-1443]*

Phelan, John M. Apartheid media . Westport, Conn. , c1987. xi, 220 p. ; ISBN 0-88208-244-2 : DDC 323.44/5 19
PN4748.S58 P4 1987   *NYPL [JLD 87-4698]*

Pomeroy, William J., 1916- Apartheid, imperialism, and African freedom /. New

York , 1986. ix, 259 p. : ISBN 0-7178-0640-5 : DDC 305.8/00968 19
E183.8.S6 P65 1986   *NYPL [Sc D 88-1147]*

Poverty, policy, and food security in southern Africa /. Boulder , 1988. xii, 291 p. : ISBN 1-555-87092-9 (lib. bdg.) : DDC 363.8/56//0968 19
HD9017.A26 P68 1988 *NYPL [Sc E 88-355]*

Salazar, Philippe Joseph. L'Intrigue raciale . Paris , 1989. 230 p. : ISBN 2-86563-211-3
     NYPL [Sc D 89-504]

South Africa . Basingstoke, Hampshire , 1988. xxiii, 390 p. : ISBN 0-333-47095-8 (hardcover)
     NYPL [Sc D 89-257]

South Africa in question /. Cambridge, Cambridgeshire , Portsmouth, NH , c1988. x, 244 p. : ISBN 0-85255-325-0 DDC 305.8/00968 19
DT763 .S6428 1988   *NYPL [Sc D 88-841]*

Südafrikas schwieriger Weg . Krefeld , c1988. 167 p., [8] p. of plates : ISBN 3-88289-803-8
     NYPL [Sc D 89-548]

Surafrica. Madrid , 1986. 160 p. : ISBN 84-245-0469-0; 84-85436-39-3
     NYPL [Sc D 88-296]

Tomaselli, Keyan G., 1948- The cinema of apartheid . New York , c1988. 300 p. ; ISBN 0-918266-19-X (pbk.) : DDC 384/.8/0968 19
PN1993.5.S6 T58 1988
     NYPL [Sc D 88-1242]

Torkington, Percy Anthony Thomas, 1931- Love with no regrets . Liverpool , 1988. 232 p. ;   *NYPL [Sc D 89-368]*

Tutu, Desmond. Crying in the wilderness . London , 1986. xix, 124 p., [8] p. of plates : ISBN 0-264-67119-8 (pbk) : DDC 261.7 19
DT737   *NYPL [Sc C 89-10]*

United States. Dept. of State. Advisory Committee on South Africa. A U. S. policy toward South Africa . [Washington, D.C.] [1987] vi, 49 p. :   *NYPL [Sc F 88-300]*

What is apartheid? Geneva , Switzerland [1986]. 72 p. :   *NYPL [Sc D 88-326]*

Apartheid, South Africa and international law : selected documents and papers / edited by Enuga S. Reddy. New York, NY : United Nations, Centre Against Apartheid, 1985. iv, 136 p. ; 28 cm. (Notes and documents) Cover title. "86-02029." "December 1985." Includes bibliographical references.
1. Apartheid - South Africa. I. Reddy, Enuga S. II. United Nations. Centre against Apartheid. III. Series: Notes and documents (United Nations Center against Apartheid).   *NYPL [Sc F 88-289]*

APARTHEID - SOUTH AFRICA - CONGRESSES.
Children of resistance . London , 1988. vii, 146 p. ;   *NYPL [Sc D 88-1286]*

APARTHEID - SOUTH AFRICA - HISTORY.
Meli, Francis, 1942- South Africa belongs to us . Harare , 1988. xx, 258, [8] p. of plates :   *NYPL [Sc D 89-308]*

APARTHEID - SOUTH AFRICA - HISTORY - CARICATURES AND CARTOONS.
Fighting apartheid . London , 1988. 76 p. : ISBN 0-904759-84-9 (pbk) : DDC 323.1/68 19
DT763   *NYPL [Sc D 88-1092]*

APARTHEID - SOUTH AFRICA - NATAL - HISTORY - 19TH CENTURY.
Kline, Benjamin. Genesis of apartheid . Lanham, MD , c1988. xxii, 283 p. ; ISBN 0-8191-6494-1 (alk. paper) : DDC 968.4/04 19
DT872 .K56 1988   *NYPL [JLD 88-4097]*

APARTHEID - SOUTH AFRICA - SOWETO.
Finnegan, William. Dateline Soweto . New York , c1988. x. 244 p. : ISBN 0-06-015932-4 : DDC 070/.92/4 B 19
PN4874.F45 A3 1989 *NYPL [JFE 88-2005]*

Appeal for world peace [microform] : text of an address delivered by Osagyefo D`Kwame Nkrumah, President of the Republic of Ghana, to the Conference of Heads of State or Government of Non-aligned Countries in Belgrade on September 2nd, 1961, together with an appeal for peace and a joint declaration issued by the Conference on September 6th, 1961. Accra : Ministry of Information and Broadcasting, [1961?] 19 p. : ill. ; 26 cm.

Microfiche. New York: New York Public Library, 198 .
1 microfiche: negative; 11 x 15 cm. (FSN Sc 019,093)
1. World politics - 1955-1965 - Congresses. 2. Peace -
Congresses. I. Nkrumah, Kwanie, Pres. Ghana
1909-1972. II. Conference of Heads of State or
Government of Non-aligned Countries. 1st, Belgrade,
1961.   **NYPL** *[Sc Micro F-10978]*

Appiah-Kubi, Kofi. In America in search of gold /
K. Appiah Kubi. 1st ed. Bloomfield, Conn. : K.
A. Kubi, 1985. 103 p. : ill., ports. ; 22 cm.
Cover title.   ISBN 0-9614573-0-9
1. Appiah-Kubi, Kofi. 2. Authors - Ghana - Biography.
I. Title.   **NYPL** *[Sc D 89-583]*

APPIAH-KUBI, KOFI.
Appiah-Kubi, Kofi. In America in search of
gold /. Bloomfield, Conn. , 1985. 103 p. :
ISBN 0-9614573-0-9   **NYPL** *[Sc D 89-583]*

Appiah, Peggy.
Tales of an Ashanti father / Peggy Appiah ;
illustrated by Mora Dickson. Boston : Beacon
Press, 1989, c1967. 156 p. : ill. ; 24 cm. (Beacon
Press night lights) A collection of folktales from Ghana,
centering around the figure of Kwaku Ananse, the
spider man.   ISBN 0-8070-8312-7   DDC
398.2/1/09667 19
1. Anansi (Legendary character). 2. Tales - Ghana. 3.
Folklore - Ghana. I. Dickson, Mora, 1918- ill. II. Title.
III. Series.
PZ8.1.A647 Tal 1989   **NYPL** *[Sc E 89-87]*

Why there are so many roads / by Peggy
Appiah. Lagos : African Universities Press,
1972. 62 p. : ill. ; 19 cm. (African junior library .
6) SCHOMBURG CHILDREN'S COLLECTION.
1. Tales - Ghana. I. Schomburg Children's Collection.
II. Title. III. Series.   **NYPL** *[Sc C 88-12]*

Appiah, Sonia. Amoko and Efua bear / Sonia
Appiah ; illustrated by Carol Easmon. 1st
American ed. New York, NY : Macmillan,
1989, c1988. [30] p. : col. ill. ; 21 x 26 cm.
Amoko, a little girl living in Ghana, takes her favorite
teddy bear everywhere that she goes and is heartbroken
when she thinks he's lost. SCHOMBURG
CHILDREN'S COLLECTION.   ISBN 0-02-705591-4
DDC E 19
1. Ghana - Juvenile fiction. I. Easmon, Carol, ill. II.
Schomburg Children's Collection. III. Title.
PZ7.A647 Am 1989   **NYPL** *[Sc F 89-138]*

Appleman, Rose. Krieger, Nancy. The politics of
AIDS /. Oakland, CA , 19. 60 p. :   ISBN
0-913781-06-1   **NYPL** *[Sc D 88-1299]*

Appleyard, David L. Letters from Ethiopian rulers
(early and mid-nineteenth century) . Oxford ,
New York , c1985. xvii, 197 p. :   ISBN
0-19-726046-2   **NYPL** *[Sc E 88-262]*

APPLIED FOLKLORE - SUDAN.
Folklore and National Development Symposium
(1981 : Khartoum, Sudan) Folklore and
development in the Sudan . Khartoum , 1985.
272 p. :
GR355.8 .F65 1981   **NYPL** *[Sc E 88-333]*

APPRAISAL OF BOOKS. see CRITICISM.

**L'approvisionnement alimentaire de la ville de
Bandundu (Rép. du Zaïre) /.** Mbo-Ikamba,
Iyeti. Bandundu, République du Zaïre , 1987.
58 p. :   **NYPL** *[Sc F 89-63]*

Aqatoor a seereer /. Faye, Suleymane. Kampala,
Ouganda , 1986. 67 p. :
    NYPL *[Sc F 88-263]*

Aquarone, Marie-Christine. Les frontières du
refus : six séparatismes africains / par
Marie-Christine Aquarone. Paris : Éditions
nationales de la recherche scientifique, 1987.
133 p. : ill., maps ; 27 cm. (Mémoires et
documents de géographie) Bibliography: p. 129-132.
ISBN 2-222-03962-2
1. Africa - History - Autonomy and independence
movements. I. Title. II. Series.
    NYPL *[Sc F 89-112]*

The Arab and the African . Pruen, Septimus
Tristram (Septimus Tristam) London , 1896. vii,
338 p. [8] p. of plates :   **NYPL** *[Sc D 88-387]*

**ARAB COUNTRIES - RELATIONS - AFRICA,
SUB-SAHARAN - CONGRESSES.**
Arabs & Africa. French. Les arabes et
l'Afrique . Paris , 1986. 2 v. ;   ISBN
2-85802-589-1   **NYPL** *[Sc E 88-390]*

Arab Republic of Egypt. see Egypt.

Les arabes et l'Afrique . Arabs & Africa. French.
Paris , 1986. 2 v. ;   ISBN 2-85802-589-1
    NYPL *[Sc E 88-390]*

**ARABIC LANGUAGE - TEXT-BOOKS FOR
FOREIGNERS - ENGLISH.**
'Isá 'Abd Allāh Muhammad al-Mahdī, 1945-
Arabic made easy [microform] /. [Brooklyn,
N.Y. , 197-?] 2 v. :
    NYPL *[Sc Micro R-4114 no.2]*

Arabic made easy [microform] /. 'Isá 'Abd Allāh
Muhammad al-Mahdī, 1945- [Brooklyn, N.Y. ,
197-?] 2 v. :   **NYPL** *[Sc Micro R-4114 no.2]*

**ARABIC MANUSCRIPTS. see
MANUSCRIPTS, ARABIC.**

Arabic speaking states. see Arab countries.

Arabs and Africa. Arabs & Africa. French. Les
arabes et l'Afrique . Paris , 1986. 2 v. ;   ISBN
2-85802-589-1   **NYPL** *[Sc E 88-390]*

Arabs & Africa. French. Les arabes et l'Afrique :
compte rendu du séminaire tenu à Amman
(Jordanie) du 24 au 29 avril 1983 / Centre
d'études pour l'unité arabe. Paris : L'Harmattan,
1986. 2 v. ; 24 cm. Translation of: Arabs & Africa.
Includes bibliographical references.   ISBN
2-85802-589-1
1. Arab countries - Relations - Africa, Sub-Saharan -
Congresses. 2. Africa, Sub-Saharan - Relations - Arab
countries - Congresses. I. Markaz Dirāsāt al-Wahdah
al-'Arabiyah (Beirut, Lebanon). II. Title. III. Title:
Arabs and Africa.   **NYPL** *[Sc E 88-390]*

**Araújo Pereira, Arthur Ramos de. see Ramos,
Arthur, 1903-1949.**

ARAWAK INDIANS - DRAMA.
Métellus, Jean, 1937- Anacaona . Paris , 1986.
159 p. :   ISBN 2-218-07538-5
    NYPL *[Sc C 88-6]*

Arbeiten aus dem Institut für Afrika-Kunde .
(50) Liberia . Hamburg , 1986. vi, 292 p., [1]
folded leaf of plates :   ISBN 3-923519-65-6 (pbk.)
DDC 322/.5/096662 19
JQ3923.5.C58 L53 1986
    NYPL *[Sc D 88-1320]*

(55) Rocksloh-Papendieck, Barbara.
Frauenarbeit am Strassenrand Kenkeyküchen in
Ghana /. Hamburg , 1988. iii, 193 p. :   ISBN
3-923519-75-3   **NYPL** *[Sc D 89-575]*

Arbeitspapiere zur internationalen politik.
(39) Schümer, Martin. Die amerikanische
Politik gegenüber dem südlichen Afrika /. Bonn
[1986]. v, 183 p. ;   ISBN 3-7713-0275-7
    NYPL *[Sc D 88-983]*

Arcangeli, Alberto. O mito da terra : uma análise
da colonização da Pré-Amazônia maranhense /
Alberto Arcangeli. São Luís : Universidade
Federal do Maranhão, 1987. 302 p. : maps ; 22
cn, (Coleção Ciências sociais. Série Questão agrária .
3) Bibliography: p. 275-278.
1. Land settlement - Brazil - Maranhão. I. Title. II.
Series.   **NYPL** *[Sc D 89-579]*

ARCHAEOLOGICAL EXPEDITIONS.
Norman, Bruce. Footsteps . London , 1987. 279
p. :   ISBN 0-563-20552-0   **NYPL** *[Sc F 88-18]*

Archbishop Heerey . Idigo, Peter Meze. Enugu,
Nigeria , 1987. 261 p. :   ISBN 978-239-602-8
    NYPL *[Sc C 89-77]*

Archer, Leonie. Slavery and other forms of unfree
labour /. London , New York , 1988. xi, 307
p. ;   ISBN 0-415-00203-6   DDC 306/.362 19
HT855 .S57 1988   **NYPL** *[Sc D 89-334]*

Archer M. Huntington Art Gallery. Adele,
Lynne. Black history, black vision . [Austin] ,
1989. 93 p. :   ISBN 0-935213-15-5
    NYPL *[Sc F 89-155]*

Archibald, Douglas, 1919- Tobago : "melancholy
isle." / by Douglas Archibald. Port-of-Spain :
Westindiana Ltd., 1987- v. : maps ; 22 cm.
Includes index. Bibliography: v. 1, p. [125]-127.
CONTENTS. - Vol. 1. 1498-1771.   ISBN
976-8059-00-1
1. Tobago - History. I. Title.
    NYPL *[Sc D 88-106]*

Archief voor anthropologie, .
(nr. 16) Vansina, Jan. La légende du passé .
Tervuren, Belgique , 1972. ix, 257 p. :
    NYPL *[Sc F 88-193]*

ARCHITECTURAL MODELS - AUSTRIA.
Groenendijk, Paul. Adolf Loos . Rotterdam ,
1985. 39 p., [6] leaves of plates :   ISBN

90-6450-027-4   DDC 728.3/72/0228 19
NA1011.5.L6 G76 1985   **NYPL** *[Sc F 89-67]*

ARCHITECTURE - BENIN.
Cunha, Marianno Carneiro da, 1926-1980. Da
senzala ao sobrado . São Paulo, SP , c1985. 185
p. :   ISBN 85-21-30173-1 :
NA1599.N5 C86 1985   **NYPL** *[Sc E 88-565]*

ARCHITECTURE, BRAZILIAN - BENIN.
Cunha, Marianno Carneiro da, 1926-1980. Da
senzala ao sobrado . São Paulo, SP , c1985. 185
p. :   ISBN 85-21-30173-1 :
NA1599.N5 C86 1985   **NYPL** *[Sc E 88-565]*

ARCHITECTURE, BRAZILIAN - NIGERIA.
Cunha, Marianno Carneiro da, 1926-1980. Da
senzala ao sobrado . São Paulo, SP , c1985. 185
p. :   ISBN 85-21-30173-1 :
NA1599.N5 C86 1985   **NYPL** *[Sc E 88-565]*

**ARCHITECTURE, COLONIAL - ZIMBABWE -
HARARE - CATALOGS.**
Jackson, Peter, 1949- Historic buildings of
Harare, 1890-1940 . Harare, Zimbabwe , 1986.
x, 134 p. :   ISBN 0-908306-03-2 (pbk.)   DDC
720/.96891 19
NA1596.6.R52 H375 1986
    NYPL *[Sc D 89-467]*

**ARCHITECTURE, DOMESTIC - 20TH
CENTURY - DESIGNS AND PLANS.**
Groenendijk, Paul. Adolf Loos . Rotterdam ,
1985. 39 p., [6] leaves of plates :   ISBN
90-6450-027-4   DDC 728.3/72/0228 19
NA1011.5.L6 G76 1985   **NYPL** *[Sc F 89-67]*

**ARCHITECTURE - LIBERIA -
EXHIBITIONS.**
Belcher, Max. A land and life remembered .
Athens , Brockton, Mass. , c1988. [xii], 176 p. :
ISBN 0-8203-1085-9 (alk. paper)   DDC
720/.9666/2074014482 19
NA1599.L4 B4 1988   **NYPL** *[Sc F 89-90]*

**ARCHITECTURE, MODERN - 19TH
CENTURY - ONTARIO - KINGSTON -
EXHIBITIONS.**
Mattie, Joan. 100 years of architecture in
Kingston . [Ottawa] , c1986. 30 p. :   ISBN
0-662-54396-3 (pbk.)   DDC
720/.9713/72074011384 19
NA747.K56 M38 1986   **NYPL** *[Sc F 88-195]*

**ARCHITECTURE, MODERN - 19TH
CENTURY - ZIMBABWE - HARARE -
CATALOGS.**
Jackson, Peter, 1949- Historic buildings of
Harare, 1890-1940 /. Harare, Zimbabwe , 1986.
x, 134 p. :   ISBN 0-908306-03-2 (pbk.)   DDC
720/.96891 19
NA1596.6.R52 H375 1986
    NYPL *[Sc D 89-467]*

**ARCHITECTURE, MODERN - 20TH
CENTURY - ONTARIO - KINGSTON -
EXHIBITIONS.**
Mattie, Joan. 100 years of architecture in
Kingston . [Ottawa] , c1986. 30 p. :   ISBN
0-662-54396-3 (pbk.)   DDC
720/.9713/72074011384 19
NA747.K56 M38 1986   **NYPL** *[Sc F 88-195]*

**ARCHITECTURE, MODERN - 20TH
CENTURY - ZIMBABWE - HARARE -
CATALOGS.**
Jackson, Peter, 1949- Historic buildings of
Harare, 1890-1940 /. Harare, Zimbabwe , 1986.
x, 134 p. :   ISBN 0-908306-03-2 (pbk.)   DDC
720/.96891 19
NA1596.6.R52 H375 1986
    NYPL *[Sc D 89-467]*

ARCHITECTURE - NIGERIA.
Cunha, Marianno Carneiro da, 1926-1980. Da
senzala ao sobrado . São Paulo, SP , c1985. 185
p. :   ISBN 85-21-30173-1 :
NA1599.N5 C86 1985   **NYPL** *[Sc E 88-565]*

**ARCHITECTURE - NIGERIA - LAGOS
(CITY)**
Akinsemoyin, Kunle. Building Lagos/. Jersey,
1977, c1906. 76 p.:
    NYPL *[3-MQWW 79-2215]*

**ARCHITECTURE - ONTARIO - KINGSTON -
EXHIBITIONS.**
Mattie, Joan. 100 years of architecture in
Kingston . [Ottawa] , c1986. 30 p. :   ISBN
0-662-54396-3 (pbk.)   DDC
720/.9713/72074011384 19
NA747.K56 M38 1986   **NYPL** *[Sc F 88-195]*

ARCHITECTURE, RURAL. see
ARCHITECTURE, DOMESTIC.

**ARCHITECTURE - SOUTHERN STATES -
INFLUENCE - EXHIBITIONS.**
Belcher, Max. A land and life remembered .
Athens , Brockton, Mass. , c1988. [xii], 176 p. :
ISBN 0-8203-1085-9 (alk. paper) DDC
720/.9666/2074014482 19
NA1599.L4 B4 1988   NYPL [Sc F 89-90]

**ARCHITECTURE, TROPICAL - ZIMBABWE -
HARARE - CATALOGS.**
Jackson, Peter, 1949- Historic buildings of
Harare, 1890-1940 /. Harare, Zimbabwe , 1986.
x, 134 p. : ISBN 0-908306-03-2 (pbk.) DDC
720/.96891 19
NA1596.6.R52 H375 1986
NYPL [Sc D 89-467]

**ARCHITECTURE - ZIMBABWE - HARARE -
CATALOGS.**
Jackson, Peter, 1949- Historic buildings of
Harare, 1890-1940 /. Harare, Zimbabwe , 1986.
x, 134 p. : ISBN 0-908306-03-2 (pbk.) DDC
720/.96891 19
NA1596.6.R52 H375 1986
NYPL [Sc D 89-467]

Architectuurmodellen .
(7) Groenendijk, Paul. Adolf Loos .
Rotterdam , 1985. 39 p., [6] leaves of plates :
ISBN 90-6450-027-4 DDC 728.3/72/0228 19
NA1011.5.L6 G76 1985   NYPL [Sc F 89-67]

**ARCHIVAL MATERIALS - CONSERVATION
AND RESTORATION.**
Conservation of library and archive materials
and the graphic arts /. London , Boston , 1985.
328 p. : ISBN 0-408-01466-0 : DDC 025.7 19
Z701 .C5863 1985   NYPL [MFW+ 88-574]

**ARCHIVAL RESOURCES - CONSERVATION
AND RESTORATION - AUDIO-VISUAL
AIDS - HANDBOOKS, MANUALS, ETC.**
Harrison, Alice W., 1929- The conservation of
archival and library materials . Metuchen, N.J. ,
1982. xi, 190 p. ; ISBN 0-8108-1523-0 DDC
025.8/4 19
Z701 .H28   NYPL [Cons. Div. 84-252]

Archives de la Martinique.
Bibliographie relative aux Antilles : ouvrages
appartenant aux cotes C et D, selon l'ancien
cadre de classement des Archives
départementales. Fort-de-France : Archives
départementales de la Martinique, 1978- v. ; 30
cm. At head of title: Collections. Fasc. 1 by Charles
Fantaisie. DDC 016.97298/2 19
*1. Archives de la Martinique - Catalogs. 2. West Indies,
French - Bibliography - Catalogs. 3. Martinique -
Bibliography - Catalogs. I. Fantaisie, Charles. II. Title.*
Z1502.F5 A72 1978 F2151
NYPL [Sc F 88-286]

**ARCHIVES DE LA MARTINIQUE -
CATALOGS.**
Archives de la Martinique. Bibliographie
relative aux Antilles . Fort-de-France , 1978-
v. ; DDC 016.97298/2 19
Z1502.F5 A72 1978 F2151
NYPL [Sc F 88-286]

ARCTIC EXPEDITIONS. see ARCTIC
REGIONS.

ARCTIC EXPLORATION. see ARCTIC
REGIONS.

**ARCTIC REGIONS - DESCRIPTION AND
TRAVEL.**
Healy, M. A. (Michael A.) Report of the cruise
of the revenue marine steamer Corwin in the
Arctic Ocean in the year 1884 /. Washington ,
1889. 128 p., [39] leaves of plates :
NYPL [Sc Rare F 88-62]

Area handbook for Southern Rhodesia /. Nelson,
Harold D. Washington , 1975. xiv, 394 p.
DT962 .N36   NYPL [JFE 75-2684]

ARGENTINA - ECONOMIC POLICY.
Alschuler, Lawrence R., 1941- Multinationals
and maldevelopment . Basingstoke, Hampshire ,
c1988. xii, 218 p. : ISBN 0-333-41561-2
NYPL [Sc D 88-701]

ARID REGIONS - CONGRESSES.
Desertification in extremely arid environments
/. [Stuttgart] , 1980. 203 p., [1] folded leaf of
plates : ISBN 3-88028-095-9 (pbk.) DDC 551.4 19
GB611 .D44   NYPL [JFL 74-410 Bd. 95]

**ARID REGIONS FARMING - NIGERIA,
NORTHERN.**

Mortimore, M. J., 1937- Adapting to drought .
Cambridge , New York , 1989. xxii, 299 p. :
ISBN 0-521-32312-6 DDC 333.73 19
HC1055.Z7 N6755 1988
NYPL [Sc E 89-191]

ARID ZONES. see ARID REGIONS.

**ARINDRANO (MADAGASCAR : REGION) -
HISTORY.**
Raherisoanjato, Daniel. Origines et évolution du
Royaume de l'Arindrano jusqu'au XIXe siècle .
Antananarivo , 1984. 334 leaves : DDC 969/.1
19
DT469.M37 A747 1984
NYPL [Sc F 88-390]

**ARIVONIMAMO (MADAGASCAR :
DISTRICT) - HISTORY - SOURCES.**
La Vie quotidienne dans un district,
1913-1935 . Antananarivo , 1984. 53 p., [6]
leaves of plates : DDC 969/.1 19
DT469.M37 A758 1984
NYPL [Sc F 88-241]

Arkhurst, Joyce Cooper. More adventures of
Spider : West African folk-tales / retold by
Joyce Cooper Arkhurst ; illustrated by Jerry
Pinkney. New York : Scholastic Book Services,
c1972. 48 p. : ill. ; 21 cm. SCHOMBURG
CHILDREN'S COLLECTION.
*1. Tales - Africa, West. 2. Anansi (Legendary
character). I. Pinkney, Jerry. II. Schomburg Children's
Collection. III. Title.   NYPL [Sc D 88-1449]*

**ARMAH, AYI KWEI, 1939- - CRITICISM
AND INTERPRETATION.**
Ogidan, Anna. Thememschwerpunkte im Werk
Ayi Kwei Armahs /. Wien , 1988. ii, 202 p. :
ISBN 3-85043-046-4
NYPL [Sc D 88-1035]

**ARMAH, AYI KWEI, 1939- - POLITICAL
AND SOCIAL VIEWS.**
Ogidan, Anna. Thememschwerpunkte im Werk
Ayi Kwei Armahs /. Wien , 1988. ii, 202 p. :
ISBN 3-85043-046-4
NYPL [Sc D 88-1035]

Armah, E. O. A custom broken / E.O. Armah.
Tema : Ghana Pub. Corp., 1978. 87 p. ; 19 cm.
1. Ghana - Fiction. I. Title.   NYPL [Sc C 88-223]

Armand, Alain. Dictionnaire kréol réunioné
français / Alain Armand. Saint-André : Ocean
Editions, [1987?] lxiv, 399, xxxvii p. ; 20 cm.
Includes bibliographical references. ISBN
2-907064-01-0
*1. Creole dialects, French - Réunion - Dictionaries -
French. I. Title.   NYPL [Sc C 88-345]*

Armed robbery in Nigeria /. Idowu, Sina, 1947-
Lagos, Nigeria , c1980. 121 p. : ISBN
978-231-900-7 (pbk.) DDC 364.1/552/09669 19
HV6665.N6 136 1980   NYPL [Sc D 89-264]

Armstrong, Alice. Women and law in southern
Africa /. Harare, Zimbabwe , 1987. xiv, 281
p. : ISBN 0-949225-48-7 NYPL [Sc D 89-297]

Armstrong, John. Birney, James Gillespie,
1792-1857. Examination of the decision of the
Supreme Court of the United States, in the case
of Strader, Gorman and Armstrong, vs.
Christopher Graham . Cincinnati , 1852. iv, [1],
6-46, [1] p. ;
E450 .B57   NYPL [Sc Rare F 88-37]

Armstrong, Louis, 1900-1971.
Satchmo : my life in New Orleans / by Louis
Armstrong ; new introduction by Dan
Morgenstern. New York, N.Y. : Da Capo Press,
1986, c1954. xiii, p. 7-240 : ill. ; 21 cm. (A Da
Capo paperback) Reprint. Originally published: New
York : Prentice-Hall, 1954. With new introd. ISBN
0-306-80276-7 (pbk.) : DDC 785.42/092/4 B 19
*1. Armstrong, Louis, 1900-1971 - Childhood and youth.
2. Jazz musicians - United States - Biography. 3. Jazz
music - Louisiana - New Orleans. 4. Afro-American
musician - Biography. I. Title.*
ML419.A75 A3 1986   NYPL [Sc D 88-339]

ARMSTRONG, LOUIS, 1900-1971.
Pinfold, Mike. Louis Armstrong, his life and
times /. New York , c1987. 143 p. : ISBN
0-87663-667-9 DDC 785.42/092/4 B 19
ML419.A75 P55 1987   NYPL [Sc F 88-65]

**ARMSTRONG, LOUIS, 1900-1971 -
JUVENILE LITERATURE.**
Collier, James Lincoln, 1928- Louis
Armstrong . New York , c1985. 165 p. : ISBN

0-02-722830-4   DDC 785.42/092/4 B 92 19
ML3930.A75 C67 1985
NYPL [Sc D 86-229]

Tanenhaus, Sam. Louis Armstrong /. New
York , c1989. 127 p. : ISBN 1-555-46571-4
DDC 785.42/092/4 B 92 19
ML3930.A75 T3 1989   NYPL [Sc E 89-170]

**ARMSTRONG, LOUIS, 1900-1971 -
CHILDHOOD AND YOUTH.**
Armstrong, Louis, 1900-1971. Satchmo . New
York, N.Y. , 1986, c1954. xiii, p. 7-240 : ISBN
0-306-80276-7 (pbk.) : DDC 785.42/092/4 B 19
ML419.A75 A3 1986   NYPL [Sc D 88-339]

**ARMSTRONG, LOUIS, 1900-1971 -
PICTORIAL WORKS.**
Giddens, Gary. Satchmo /. New York , 1988.
239 p. : ISBN 0-385-24428-2 : DDC 785.42/092/4
B 19
ML410.A75 G5 1988   NYPL [Sc F 89-73]

Armstrong, Robert G., 1917- Socio-political
aspects of the palaver in some African
countries. Spanish. Aspectos sociopolíticos del
parlamento tradicional en algunos países
africanos /. Barcelona , Paris , 1979. 95 p. ;
ISBN 84-85800-24-9 NYPL [Sc D 88-599]

Armstrong, Thomas, 1899- King cotton / Thomas
Armstrong. London : Collins, 1947. 928 p. ; 22
cm.
*1. Cotton trade - Great Britain - Fiction. 2. Slavery -
United States - Economic aspects - Fiction. I. Title.*
NYPL [Sc D 88-97]

Arnold, Marion I. Zimbabwean stone sculpture /
by Marion I. Arnold. Bulawayo : L. Bolze,
1986. xxvi, 234 p. : ill. ; 22 cm. "Reprint of the
1981 edition incorporating place-name changes and a
new postscript." Bibliography: p. 169-181. ISBN
0-7974-0747-2 DDC 730/.96891 19
*1. Sculpture, Shona. 2. Sculpture, Black - Zimbabwe. 3.
Stone carving - Zimbabwe. I. Title.*
NB1209.Z55 A76 1986
NYPL [Sc D 89-326]

Arnold, Millard W. Biko, Steve, 1946-1977. The
testimony of Steve Biko /. London , 1987,
c1978. xxxv, 298 p. ;   *NYPL [Sc C 89-126]*

**ARNOLD, RICHARD JAMES, 1796-1873 -
DIARIES.**
Hoffmann, Charles. North by South . Athens ,
c1988. xxii, 318 p., [8] p. of plates : ISBN
0-8203-0976-1 (alk. paper) DDC
975.8/73203/0924 19
F292.B85 A753 1988   NYPL [Sc E 89-35]

Aròf Ọpadọtun, 'Tunji. Ibàdàn , 1987. v, 82 p. ;
ISBN 978-14-5069-X NYPL [Sc C 88-218]

Arokò . Ọpadọtun, 'Tunji. Ibadan , 1986. viii, 120
p. : ISBN 978-245-840-6 NYPL [Sc D 88-948]

Aron, Janine. Asbestos and asbestos-related
disease in South Africa : an update / Janine
Aron and Jonny Myers. Cape Town : Southern
Africa Labour and Development Research Unit,
1987. 71 p. : ill. ; 21 cm. (Saldru working paper
no. 71) Bibliography: p. 41-48. ISBN 0-7992-1126-5
*1. Asbestos industry - Hygienic aspects - South Africa.
2. Asbestosis - South Africa. I. Myers, Jonathan. II.
Title. III. Series.   NYPL [Sc D 88-1258]*

Around the city / prepared by the Bank Street
College of Education. New York : Macmillan,
c1965. 127 p. : col. ill. ; 24 cm. (The Bank Street
readers) SCHOMBURG CHILDREN'S
COLLECTION.
*1. Readers (Primary). 2. City children - United States -
Juvenile fiction. I. Schomburg Children's Collection.*
NYPL [Sc E 89-17]

ARREST - GREAT BRITAIN.
Demuth, Clare. 'Sus', a report on the Vagrancy
Act 1824 /. London , 1978. 62 p. :
NYPL [Sc D 88-1174]

The arrivants . Race Today Collective. London,
England , 1987. 112 p. : ISBN 0-947716-10-6
(pbk.)   *NYPL [Sc D 88-1206]*

The arrogance of race . Fredrickson, George M.,
1934- Middletown, Conn. , c1988. viii, 310 p. :
ISBN 0-8195-5177-5 DDC 973/.0496 19
E441 .F77 1988   NYPL [Sc E 88-487]

ART - AFRICA.
Essomba, Joseph-Marie. L'art africain et son
message /. Yaoundé, Cameroun , 1985. 73 p. :
ISBN 2-7235-0049-7 *NYPL [Sc D 88-278]*

Glantz, Stephan Hamilton. Spirit heads . New
York , 1987. 133 p. : *NYPL [Sc F 88-103]*

ART - AFRICA - EXHIBITIONS.
Museum of Modern Art (New York, N.Y.)
African Negro art . New York [c1935] 58 p. :
NYPL [Sc F 88-125]

ART - AFRICA, WEST - EXHIBITIONS.
Africana, an exhibit of West African art .
[Jackson, Miss. , 1950] 23 p. :
NYPL [Sc F 85-236]

L'art africain et son message /. Essomba,
Joseph-Marie. Yaoundé, Cameroun , 1985. 73
p. : ISBN 2-7235-0049-7 *NYPL [Sc D 88-278]*

ART, AFRICAN - EXHIBITIONS.
African heritage . Cape Town , 1987. 24 p. :
NYPL [Sc F 89-117]

Museum of Modern Art (New York, N.Y.)
African Negro art . New York [c1935] 58 p. :
NYPL [Sc F 88-125]

Neue Kunst aus Afrika . [Hamburg] , c1984.
111 p. :   *NYPL [Sc G 88-17]*

**ART, AFRICAN - EXHIBITIONS -
CATALOGS.**
Volkstümliche Künste . Reinbek , c1986/87.
135 p. :   *NYPL [Sc D 89-238]*

**ART, AFRICAN - WASHINGTON, D.C. -
EXHIBITIONS.**
Morrison, Keith. Art in Washington and its
Afro-American presence 1940-1970 /.
Washington, D.C. , 1985. 109 p. :
NYPL [Sc F 88-34]

**ART - ANALYSIS, INTERPRETATION,
APPRECIATION. see PAINTING.**

ART, ANCIENT - CYPRUS - CATALOGS.
Karageorghis, Vassos. Blacks in ancient Cypriot
art /. Houston, Tex. , 1988. 62 p. : ISBN
0-939594-13-7 (pbk.) : DDC
704.9/42/093937074 19
N8232 .K37 1988   NYPL [3-MAE 89-1038]

ART, ANCIENT - EGYPT - EXHIBITIONS.
Bourriau, Janine. Pharaohs and mortals .
Cambridge [Cambridgeshire] ; New York : vi,
167 p. : ISBN 0-521-35319-X DDC
709/.32/07402659 19
N5336.G7 C3634 1988
NYPL [3-MAE 88-2748]

ART AND SOCIETY - AFRICA.
Essomba, Joseph-Marie. L'art africain et son
message /. Yaoundé, Cameroun , 1985. 73 p. :
ISBN 2-7235-0049-7 *NYPL [Sc D 88-278]*

**ART AND SOCIOLOGY. see ART AND
SOCIETY.**

Art/artifact : African art in anthropology
collections / with essays by Arthur Danto ... [et
al.] ; introduction by Susan Vogel ; photographs
by Jerry L. Thompson. New York : Center for
African Art ; Munich : Prestel Verlag, c1988.
195 p. : ill. (some col.), map ; 31 cm. Includes
index. ISBN 0-9614587-7-1 DDC 730/.0967/074 19
*1. Anthropology - Collections. 2. Art, Primitive -
Africa - Collections. I. Danto, Arthur Coleman, 1924-.
II. Center for African Art (New York, N.Y.).*
GN36.A35 A78 1988   NYPL [Sc G 88-25]

ART, BLACK - AFRICA. see ART, AFRICAN.

**ART, BLACK - AFRICA, CENTRAL -
EXHIBITIONS.**
Pelrine, Diane. African art from the Rita and
John Grunwald collection /. Bloomington ,
c1988. 159 p. : ISBN 0-253-21061-5 (I.U. Press :
pbk.) : DDC 730/.0966/0740172255 19
N7398 .P44 1988   NYPL [Sc F 89-158]

**ART, BLACK - AFRICA, SUB-SAHARAN -
CATALOGS.**
Celenko, Theodore. A treasury of African art
from the Harrison Eiteljorg Collection /.
Bloomington , c1983. 239 p. : ISBN
0-253-11057-2 DDC 730/.0967/074013 19
NB1091.65 .C46 1983
NYPL [3-MADF+ 88-2098]

**ART, BLACK - AFRICA, SUB-SAHARAN -
EXHIBITIONS.**
The Art of collecting African art /. New York ,
c1988. 64 p. : DDC 730/.0967/07401471 19
N7391.65 .A78 1988   NYPL [Sc G 88-36]

**ART, BLACK - AFRICA, WEST -
EXHIBITIONS.**
Pelrine, Diane. African art from the Rita and
John Grunwald collection /. Bloomington ,
c1988. 159 p. : ISBN 0-253-21061-5 (I.U. Press :

pbk.) : DDC 730/.0966/0740172255 19
N7398 .P44 1988   NYPL [Sc F 89-158]

**ART, BLACK - AFRICA, WEST - THEMES,
MOTIVES.**
The Art of West African kingdoms /.
Washington, D.C. , 1987. 48 p., [4] folded
leaves : ISBN 0-87474-611-6 DDC 709/.01/10966
19
N7398 .A75 1987   NYPL [Sc F 89-26]

**ART, BLACK - SOUTH AFRICA -
HOMELANDS.**
Younge, Gavin. Art of the South African
townships /. New York , 1988. 96 p. : ISBN
0-8478-0973-0 (pbk.) : DDC 704/.03968 19
N7394.H66 Y68 1988   NYPL [Sc F 88-364]

ART - CARIBBEAN AREA.
Juan, Adalaida de. En la Galería
Latinoamericana /. La Habana , 1979. 203 p. :
NYPL [3-MAM 88-2546]

**ART, CARIBBEAN - MUSEUMS -
DIRECTORIES.**
Visual arts collections relating to Caribbean
cultures. New York [198-?] 16 p. :
NYPL [Sc D 88-1177]

**ART, CHRISTIAN. see CHRISTIAN ART
AND SYMBOLISM.**

**ART - COLLECTIONS, PRIVATE. see ART -
PRIVATE COLLECTIONS.**

**ART - CONSERVATION AND
RESTORATION.**
Conservation of library and archive materials
and the graphic arts /. London , Boston , 1985.
328 p. : ISBN 0-408-01466-0 : DDC 025.7 19
Z701 .C5863 1985   NYPL [MFW+ 88-574]

Horie, C. V. (Charles Velson) Materials for
conservation . London , Boston , 1987. xi, 281
p. : ISBN 0-408-01531-4 : DDC 667/.9 19
TP156.C57 H67 1987   NYPL [Sc D 88-558]

ART, CYPRIOTE - CATALOGS.
Karageorghis, Vassos. Blacks in ancient Cypriot
art /. Houston, Tex. , 1988. 62 p. : ISBN
0-939594-13-7 (pbk.) : DDC
704.9/42/093937074 19
N8232 .K37 1988   NYPL [3-MAE 89-1038]

ART, DOGON - EXHIBITIONS.
Ezra, Kate. Art of the Dogon . New York ,
1988. 116 p. : ISBN 0-87099-507-3 : DDC
730/.089963 19
N7399.M3 E97 1988   NYPL [Sc F 88-160]

**ART, ECCLESIASTICAL. see CHRISTIAN
ART AND SYMBOLISM.**

**ART - ECONOMIC AND SOCIAL ASPECTS.
see ART AND SOCIETY.**

ART, EGYPTIAN - EXHIBITIONS.
Bourriau, Janine. Pharaohs and mortals .
Cambridge [Cambridgeshire] ; New York : vi,
167 p. : ISBN 0-521-35319-X DDC
709/.32/07402659 19
N5336.G7 C3634 1988
NYPL [3-MAE 88-2748]

Art et mythologie : figures humaines / [conception
et direction : Christiane Falgayrettes] Paris :
Fondation Dapper, 1988. 117 p. : ill. (some
col.), maps ; 24 cm. "Publié à l'occasion de
l'exposition 'Art et mythologie, figures shokwé ...
présentée du 13 octobre 1988 au 25 février 1989, au
musée Dapper." --T. p. verso. Bibliography: p. 109-111.
ISBN 2-906067-06-7
1. Sculpture, Chokwe (African people) - Exhibitions. I.
Falgayrettes, Christiane.   NYPL [Sc E 89-96]

ART, EUROPEAN - CATALOGS.
Suckale-Redlefsen, Gude. Mauritius, der heilige
Mohr /. Houston , München , c1987. 295 p. :
ISBN 0-939594-03-X DDC 704.9/4863/094 19
N8080.M38 S9 1987   NYPL [Sc D 88-1357]

**ART FESTIVALS - BRITISH VIRGIN
ISLANDS.**
Reminiscences . Road Town, Tortola, British
Virgin Islands , c1981. xii, 94 p. : DDC
700/.97297/25 19
NX430.G72 B757 1981   NYPL [Sc F 88-331]

ART, FOLK. see FOLK ART.

Art for city children. Krinsky, Norman. New
York [1970] 96 p. DDC 372.5/2
N350 .K7   NYPL [Sc F 88-378]

**ART - GERMANY (WEST) - REINBEK -
CATALOGS.**

Volkstümliche Künste . Reinbek , c1986/87.
135 p. :   *NYPL [Sc D 89-238]*

ART, GRAPHIC. see GRAPHIC ARTS.

ART, HAITIAN.
Rodman, Selden, 1909- Where art is joy . New
York , c1988. 236 p. : ISBN 0-938291-01-7 :
DDC 759.97294 19
N6606.5.P74 R64 1988
NYPL [3-MAM+ 89-6425]

**Art in Washington and its Afro-American
presence 1940-1970 /.** Morrison, Keith.
Washington, D.C. , 1985. 109 p. :
NYPL [Sc 88-34]

ART, KENYAN.
Sheikh-Dilthey, Helmtraut, 1944- Kenya .
Köln , 1987. 279 p. :   *NYPL [Sc D 88-935]*

ART - LATIN AMERICA.
Juan, Adalaida de. En la Galería
Latinoamericana /. La Habana , 1979. 203 p. :
NYPL [3-MAM 88-2546]

ART, LIBERIAN - CATALOGS.
Cuttington University College. Africana
Museum. Rock of the ancestors . Suakoko,
Liberia , c1977. 102 p. : DDC
730/.09666/2074096662 19
N7399.L4 C87 1977   NYPL [Sc F 89-27]

**ART, MODERN - 20TH CENTURY - AFRICA -
EXHIBITIONS.**
Neue Kunst aus Afrika . [Hamburg] , c1984.
111 p. :   *NYPL [Sc G 88-17]*

**ART, MODERN - 20TH CENTURY -
AFRICAN INFLUENCES -
EXHIBITIONS.**
Morrison, Keith. Art in Washington and its
Afro-American presence 1940-1970 /.
Washington, D.C. , 1985. 109 p. :
NYPL [Sc F 88-34]

**ART, MODERN - 20TH CENTURY -
CARIBBEAN AREA.**
Juan, Adalaida de. En la Galería
Latinoamericana /. La Habana , 1979. 203 p. :
NYPL [3-MAM 88-2546]

**ART, MODERN - 20TH CENTURY - LATIN
AMERICA.**
Juan, Adalaida de. En la Galería
Latinoamericana /. La Habana , 1979. 203 p. :
NYPL [3-MAM 88-2546]

**ART, MODERN - 20TH CENTURY -
MASSACHUSETTS - EXHIBITIONS.**
Gaither, Edmund B. Massachusetts masters .
Boston [1988] 48 p. :   *NYPL [Sc F 89-159]*

**ART, MODERN - 20TH CENTURY -
NIGERIA.**
Onobrakpeya, Bruce. Bruce
Onobrakpeya--Symbols of ancestral groves .
[Mushin [Nigeria] , 1985. 252 p. : ISBN
978-250-900-0   *NYPL [Sc F 88-169]*

**ART, MODERN - 20TH CENTURY - TEXAS -
EXHIBITIONS.**
Adele, Lynne. Black history, black vision .
[Austin] , 1989. 93 p. : ISBN 0-935213-15-5
NYPL [Sc F 89-155]

**ART, MODERN - 20TH CENTURY -
WASHINGTON (D.C.) - EXHIBITIONS.**
Morrison, Keith. Art in Washington and its
Afro-American presence 1940-1970 /.
Washington, D.C. , 1985. 109 p. :
NYPL [Sc F 88-34]

ART, MODERN - 20TH CENTURY - ZAIRE.
Bamba Ndombasi Kifimba, 1937- Anthologie
des sculpteurs et peintres zaïrois contemporains
/. Paris , 1987. 109 p. : ISBN 2-09-168350-7
NYPL [Sc G 88-11]

ART, MODERN - NIGERIA - EXHIBITIONS.
Eze, Okpu. Timeless search . [Lagos] [1985?]
51 p. :   *NYPL [Sc C 88-170]*

Art Museum Association of America. Sims,
Lowery Stokes. Robert Colescott, a
retrospective, 1975-1986 /. San Jose, Calif. ,
c1987. 34 p. : ISBN 0-938175-01-7 (pbk.) DDC
759.13 19
ND237.C66 A4 1987   NYPL [Sc F 88-317]

ART, OCCIDENTAL. see ART.

The Art of collecting African art / essays by
Robert and Nancy Nooter ; introduction by
Susan Vogel ; with photographs by Jerry L.
Thompson. New York : Center for African Art,
c1988. 64 p. : ill. ; 30 cm. "Ernst Anspach, Arman,

John and Nicole Dintenfass, Jean and Noble Endicott, George and Gail Feher, Gaston T. deHavenon and family, Brian and Diane Leyden, Daniel and Marian Malcolm, Franklin and Shirley Williams." "Published in conjunction with an exhibition of the same title organized by the Center for African Art."--Verso t.p. Includes index. DDC 730/.0967/07401471 19
1. Art, Black - Africa, Sub-Saharan - Exhibitions. 2. Art, Primitive - Africa, Sub-Saharan - Exhibitions. 3. Art - Private collections - United States - Exhibitions. I. Vogel, Susan. II. Center for African Art (New York, N.Y.).
N7391.65 .A78 1988   **NYPL** *[Sc G 88-36]*

Art of the Dogon . Ezra, Kate. New York , 1988. 116 p. : ISBN 0-87099-507-3 : DDC 730/.089963 19
N7399.M3 E97 1988   **NYPL** *[Sc F 88-160]*

Art of the South African townships /. Younge, Gavin. New York , 1988. 96 p. : ISBN 0-8478-0973-0 (pbk.) : DDC 704/.03968 19
N7394.H66 Y68 1988   **NYPL** *[Sc F 88-364]*

The Art of West African kingdoms / project director, Edward Lifschitz. Washington, D.C. : National Museum of African Art, Smithsonian Institution, 1987. 48 p., [4] folded leaves : ill., maps ; 28 cm. Folded leaves in pockets of inside covers. Bibliography: p. 47. ISBN 0-87474-611-6 DDC 709/.01/10966 19
1. Art, Black - Africa, West - Themes, motives. 2. Art, Primitive - Africa, West - Themes, motives. I. Lifschitz, Edward, 1945-. II. National Museum of African Art (U. S.).
N7398 .A75 1987   **NYPL** *[Sc F 89-26]*

ART PATRONAGE - PORTUGAL - EXHIBITIONS.
Bassani, Ezio. Africa and the Renaissance . New York City , c1988. 255 p. : ISBN 0-945802-00-5 : DDC 736/.62/096607401471 19
NK5989 .B37 1988   **NYPL** *[Sc F 89-30]*

ART, POPULAR. see FOLK ART.

ART, PREHISTORIC - ZIMBABWE.
Garlake, Peter S. The painted caves . Harare, Zimbabwe , c1987. iv, 100 p., [8] p. of plates : ISBN 0-908309-00-7 **NYPL** *[Sc D 89-411]*

ART, PRIMITIVE - AFRICA, CENTRAL - EXHIBITIONS.
Pelrine, Diane. African art from the Rita and John Grunwald collection /. Bloomington , c1988. 159 p. : ISBN 0-253-21061-5 (I.U. Press : pbk.) : DDC 730/.0966/0740172255 19
N7398 .P44 1988   **NYPL** *[Sc F 89-158]*

ART, PRIMITIVE - AFRICA - COLLECTIONS.
Art/artifact . New York , Munich , c1988. 195 p. : ISBN 0-9614587-7-1 DDC 730/.0967/074 19
GN36.A35 A78 1988   **NYPL** *[Sc G 88-25]*

ART, PRIMITIVE - AFRICA, SUB-SAHARAN - CATALOGS.
Celenko, Theodore. A treasury of African art from the Harrison Eiteljorg Collection /. Bloomington , c1983. 239 p. : ISBN 0-253-11057-2 DDC 730/.0967/074013 19
NB1091.65 .C46 1983
   NYPL *[3-MADF+ 88-2098]*

ART, PRIMITIVE - AFRICA, SUB-SAHARAN - EXHIBITIONS.
The Art of collecting African art /. New York , c1988. 64 p. : DDC 730/.0967/07401471 19
N7391.65 .A78 1988   **NYPL** *[Sc G 88-36]*

ART, PRIMITIVE - AFRICA, WEST - EXHIBITIONS.
Pelrine, Diane. African art from the Rita and John Grunwald collection /. Bloomington , c1988. 159 p. : ISBN 0-253-21061-5 (I.U. Press : pbk.) : DDC 730/.0966/0740172255 19
N7398 .P44 1988   **NYPL** *[Sc F 89-158]*

ART, PRIMITIVE - AFRICA, WEST - THEMES, MOTIVES.
The Art of West African kingdoms /. Washington, D.C. , 1987. 48 p., [4] folded leaves : ISBN 0-87474-611-6 DDC 709/.01/10966 19
N7398 .A75 1987   **NYPL** *[Sc F 89-26]*

ART, PRIMITIVE - EXHIBITIONS.
Museum voor Volkenkunde (Rotterdam, Netherlands) Expressions of belief . New York , 1988. 248 p. : ISBN 0-8478-0959-5 : DDC 730 19
N5310.75.H68 M876 1988
   NYPL *[Sc G 88-37]*

ART, PRIMITIVE - KENYA.
Sheikh-Dilthey, Helmtraut, 1944- Kenya . Köln , 1987. 279 p. :   **NYPL** *[Sc D 88-935]*

ART, PRIMITIVE - MALI - EXHIBITIONS.
Ezra, Kate. Art of the Dogon . New York , 1988. 116 p. : ISBN 0-87099-507-3 : DDC 730/.089963 19
N7399.M3 E97 1988   **NYPL** *[Sc F 88-160]*

ART - PRIVATE COLLECTIONS - INDIANA - BLOOMINGTON - EXHIBITIONS.
Pelrine, Diane. African art from the Rita and John Grunwald collection /. Bloomington , c1988. 159 p. : ISBN 0-253-21061-5 (I.U. Press : pbk.) : DDC 730/.0966/0740172255 19
N7398 .P44 1988   **NYPL** *[Sc F 89-158]*

ART - PRIVATE COLLECTIONS - UNITED STATES - EXHIBITIONS.
The Art of collecting African art /. New York , c1988. 64 p. : DDC 730/.0967/07401471 19
N7391.65 .A78 1988   **NYPL** *[Sc G 88-36]*

The Art Rust Jr. baseball quiz book /. Rust, Art, 1927- New York, N.Y. , c1985. 184 p., [16] p. of plates : ISBN 0-8160-1147-4 (pbk.) DDC 796.357/0973 19
GV867.3 .R87 1985   **NYPL** *[JFE 85-2627]*

Art Rust Junior baseball quiz book. Rust, Art, 1927- The Art Rust Jr. baseball quiz book . New York, N.Y. , c1985. 184 p., [16] p. of plates : ISBN 0-8160-1147-4 (pbk.) DDC 796.357/0973 19
GV867.3 .R87 1985   **NYPL** *[JFE 85-2627]*

ART, SAN (AFRICAN PEOPLE)
Sampson, C. Garth (Clavil Garth), 1941- Stylistic boundaries among mobile hunter-foragers /. Washington , c1988. 186 p. : ISBN 0-87474-838-0 DDC 968/.004961 19
DT764.B8 S24 1988   **NYPL** *[Sc F 89-97]*

ART SCHOOLS - NEW YORK (N.Y.) - HARLEM.
Augusta Savage and the art Schools of Harlem. New York, N.Y. , 1988. 27 p. :
   NYPL *[Sc F 89-45]*

ART - SOCIAL INFLUENCE. see ART AND SOCIETY.

ART - STUDY AND TEACHING (ELEMENTARY)
Krinsky, Norman. Art for city children. New York [1970] 96 p. DDC 372.5/2
N350 .K7   **NYPL** *[Sc F 88-378]*

ART, ZARIAN.
Bamba Ndombasi Kifimba, 1937- Anthologie des sculpteurs et peintres zaïrois contemporains /. Paris , 1987. 109 p. : ISBN 2-09-168350-7
   NYPL *[Sc G 88-11]*

Arte y Sociedad. [Santo Domingo]. see Santo Domingo. Universidad Autónoma. Publicaciones.

The artful egg /. McClure, James, 1939- London , New York , 1984. 283 p. ; ISBN 0-333-37103-8 : DDC 823 19
PR9369.3.M394 A87 1984
   NYPL *[JFD 88-7714]*

ARTISANS - MALI - MOPTI REGION.
Gardi, Bernhard. Ein Markt wie Mopti . Basel , 1985. 387 p. : ISBN 3-85977-175-2 DDC 745/.0966/23 19
TT119.M34 G37 1985   **NYPL** *[Sc E 87-494]*

Artistes et répertoire des scènes de Saint-Domingue /. Fouchard, Jean. Port-au-Prince, Haiti , 1988. 195 p. ;
   NYPL *[Sc D 89-410]*

ARTISTIC INFLUENCE. see INFLUENCE (LITERARY, ARTISTIC, ETC.)

ARTISTIC PHOTOGRAPHY. see PHOTOGRAPHY, ARTISTIC.

ARTISTS, AFRO-AMERICAN. see AFRO-AMERICAN ARTISTS.

Artists Against apartheid. Nelson Mandela . [London , 1988] 61 p. :   **NYPL** *[Sc G 89-3]*

ARTISTS, BLACK - COLOMBIA - BIOGRAPHY.
Paz Gómez, Enelia. Black in Colombia /. Mexico , c1985. 173 p. :
   NYPL *[Sc D 89-66]*

ARTISTS - ZAIRE.
Bamba Ndombasi Kifimba, 1937- Anthologie

des sculpteurs et peintres zaïrois contemporains /. Paris , 1987. 109 p. : ISBN 2-09-168350-7
   NYPL *[Sc G 88-11]*

ARTS, AFRO-AMERICAN. see AFRO-AMERICAN ARTS.

ARTS AND CHILDREN - UNITED STATES.
Dodson, Jualynne E. Black stylization and implications for child welfare . Atlanta, Georgia , 1975. 1 v. (various pagings) :
   NYPL *[Sc F 88-223]*

ARTS, BLACK - BRITISH VIRGIN ISLANDS.
Reminiscences . Road Town, Tortola, British Virgin Islands , c1981. xii, 94 p. : DDC 700/.97297/25 19
NX430.G72 B757 1981 **NYPL** *[Sc F 88-331]*

ARTS, BLACK - GREAT BRITAIN.
Storms of the heart . London , 1988. 308 p. : ISBN 0-948491-30-2 (pbk) : DDC 700/.8996 19
   NYPL *[Sc D 88-1364]*

ARTS, DECORATIVE. see DECORATION AND ORNAMENT.

ARTS, FINE. see ART; ARTS.

ARTS, GRAPHIC. see GRAPHIC ARTS.

ARTS - NIGERIA.
Tapping Nigeria's limitless cultural treasures /. Ikeja [1987?] 119 p., [2] leaves of plates :
   NYPL *[Sc F 89-1]*

ARTS - NIGERIA - CONGRESSES.
Cultural development and nation building . Ibadan , 1986. xiv, 157 p. : ISBN 978-246-048-6 (pbk.) DDC 338.4/77/0096694 19
NX750.N6 C85 1986   **NYPL** *[Sc D 88-812]*

ARTS - NIGERIA - CROSS RIVER STATE - CONGRESSES.
Cultural development and nation building . Ibadan , 1986. xiv, 157 p. : ISBN 978-246-048-6 (pbk.) DDC 338.4/77/0096694 19
NX750.N6 C85 1986   **NYPL** *[Sc D 88-812]*

Artur, Armando, 1962- Espelho dos dias / Armando Artur. [Maputo?] Associação dos Escritores Moçambicanos, [1986?] 52 p. ; 21 cm. (Colecção Início . 5) Poems
I. Title. II. Series.   **NYPL** *[Sc D 88-536]*

Arundel, Jocelyn, 1930- Mighty Mo : the story of an African elephant / by Jocelyn Arundel ; illustrated by Wesley Dennis.1st ed. New York : Whittlesey House, 1961. 124 p. : col. ill. ; 24 cm. SCHOMBURG CHILDREN'S COLLECTION.
I. Dennis, Wesley. II. Schomburg Children's Collection. III. Title.   **NYPL** *[Sc E 88-228]*

Arvey, Verna, 1910- William Grant Still, by Verna Arvey, with introduction by John Tasker Howard. New York, J. Fischer & bro., 1939. 48 p. illus. (port., music) 23 cm. (Studies of contemporary American composers) "Publications": p. 47.
1. Still, William Grant, 1895-. 2. Afro-American composers - Biography. I. Howard, John Tasker, 1890-1964.
ML410.S855 A8   **NYPL** *[Sc D 89-3]*

Asante brass casting . Fox, Christine. Cambridge , 1988. xii, 112 p. : ISBN 0-902993-24-0 (pbk) : DDC 739.2/27667 19
   NYPL *[Sc D 88-1434]*

Asbestos and asbestos-related disease in South Africa . Aron, Janine. Cape Town , 1987. 71 p. : ISBN 0-7992-1126-5
   NYPL *[Sc D 88-1258]*

ASBESTOS INDUSTRY - HYGIENIC ASPECTS - SOUTH AFRICA.
Aron, Janine. Asbestos and asbestos-related disease in South Africa . Cape Town , 1987. 71 p. : ISBN 0-7992-1126-5
   NYPL *[Sc D 88-1258]*

ASBESTOSIS - SOUTH AFRICA.
Aron, Janine. Asbestos and asbestos-related disease in South Africa . Cape Town , 1987. 71 p. : ISBN 0-7992-1126-5
   NYPL *[Sc D 88-1258]*

Aschwanden, Herbert, 1933- Symbols of death : an analysis of the consciousness of the Karanga / by Herbert Aschwanden ; English translation, Ursula Cooper. Gweru, Zimbabwe : Mambo Press, 1987. 389 p. ; 22 cm. (Shona heritage series. 4) Includes bibliographical references and index. ISBN 0-86922-390-9

1. Karanga (African people). I. Title.
NYPL [Sc D 88-979]

Ase omo osayin-- ewe aye /. Ramos, Miguel.
[S.l.] , 1985, c1982. 113 p. ;
NYPL [Sc D 89-487]

Asein, S. O. Studies in the African novel /.
[Ibadan] [1985?] viii, 258 p. ;
NYPL [Sc D 88-1316]

Ashabranner, Brent K., 1921-
(joint author) Davis, Russell G. Land in the sun.
Boston [1963] 92 p.   *NYPL [Sc F 88-365]*
(joint author) Davis, Russell G. Strangers in
Africa. New York [1963] 149 p.
PZ7.D2993 St   NYPL [Sc D 88-505]

ASHANTI GOLDWEIGHTS. see
GOLDWEIGHTS, ASHANTI.

ASHANTI - KINGS AND RULERS.
Obeng, Ernest E. Ancient Ashanti chieftaincy
/. Tema, Ghana , 1988. 74 p. :   ISBN
996-410-329-8   *NYPL [Sc C 88-343]*

ASHANTIS (AFRICAN PEOPLE) -
FOLKLORE.
Aardema, Verna. The sky-god stories /. New
York , c1960. [50] p. :   *NYPL [Sc D 89-83]*

Ashaolu, Albert Olu. Studies in the African novel
/. [Ibadan] [1985?] viii, 258 p. ;
NYPL [Sc D 88-1316]

Ashby, Timothy. The bear in the back yard :
Moscow's Caribbean strategy / Timothy Ashby.
Lexington, Mass. : Lexington Books, c1987. xii,
240 p. : ill. ; 24 cm. Includes index. Bibliography: p.
[191]-221. ISBN 0-669-14768-0 (alk. paper) DDC
327.470729 19
1. Geopolitics - Caribbean Area. 2. Caribbean Area -
Foreign relations - Soviet Union. 3. Soviet Union -
Foreign relations - Caribbean Area. 4. Caribbean Area -
Foreign relations - 1945-. I. Title.
F2178.S65 A84 1987   NYPL [HNB 87-1399]

Ashe, Arthur. A hard road to glory : a history of
the African-American athlete / Arthur R. Ashe,
Jr ; with the assistance of Kip Branch, Ocania
Chalk, and Francis Harris. New York, NY :
Warner Books, 1988. 3 v. : ill., ports. ; 25 cm.
Includes bibliographies and indexes. CONTENTS. - [v.
1.] 1619-1918 -- [v. 2.] 1919-1945 -- [v. 3.] Since 1946.
ISBN 0-446-71006-7 DDC 796/.08996073 19
1. Afro-Americans - Sports - History. 2. Afro-American
athletes. I. Title.
GV583 .A75 1988   NYPL [IEC 89-1295]

Ashkenazi, Michael. Ethiopian Jews and Israel /.
New Brunswick, NJ, U. S.A. , c1987. 159 p. ;
ISBN 0-88738-133-2 DDC 305.8/924/05694 19
DS113.8.F34 E84 1987   NYPL [Sc E 88-73]

Ashmore, Harry S. Hearts and minds : a personal
chronicle of race in America / Harry S.
Ashmore ; foreword by Harold C. Fleming.Rev.
ed. Cabin John, Md. : Seven Locks Press,
c1988. xviii, 513 p. ; 23 cm. Includes index. "A
Calvin Kytle book." ISBN 0-932020-58-5 (pbk. : alk.
paper) DDC 305.8/96073 19
1. Ashmore, Harry S. 2. Afro-Americans - Civil rights.
3. Afro-Americans - Civil rights - Southern States. 4.
Afro-Americans - Social conditions. 5.
Afro-Americans - Southern states - Social conditions. 6.
United States - Race relations. 7. Racism - United
States - History - 20th century. I. Title.
E185.615 .A83 1988   NYPL [Sc D 89-382]

ASHMORE, HARRY S.
Ashmore, Harry S. Hearts and minds . Cabin
John, Md. , c1988. xviii, 513 p. ;   ISBN
0-932020-58-5 (pbk. : alk. paper) DDC
305.8/96073 19
E185.615 .A83 1988   NYPL [Sc D 89-382]

Ashu, Comfort Eneke. A Junior secondary poetry
anthology /. [Limbe , c1984- v. : DDC 428.6/4
19
PE1126.A44 J86 1984   NYPL [Sc D 88-384]

ASIA, CENTRAL - ECONOMIC
CONDITIONS.
Africa, America, and central Asia . [Exeter,
Devon] [Atlantic Highlands, N.J.] 1984. 107
p. : ISBN 0-85989-295-6 (pbk.) : DDC 330.9/034
19
HC53 .A35 1984   NYPL [Sc D 88-1315]

ASIAN-AFRICAN POLITICS. see AFRO-
ASIAN POLITICS.

Asiedu, Kobina. An adult functional literacy
manual / [Kobina Asiedu, Lekan Oyedeji]
Ibadan : University Press Limited, 1985. ix, 148

p. ; 21 cm. Includes index. Bibliography: p. 143-144.
ISBN 978-15-4737-5 (Nigeria)
1. Reading (Adult education) - Nigeria. I. Oyedeji,
Lekan. II. Title.   *NYPL [Sc D 88-799]*

Ask the humorist : Nigerian jokes / [compiled]
by Rems Nna Umeasiegbu. Enugu : Koruna
Books, 1986. 104 p. : ill. ; 19 cm. Bibliography: p.
104. ISBN 978-225-808-3
1. Nigeria - Anecdotes, facetiae, satire, etc. I.
Umeasiegbu, Rems Nna, 1943-.
NYPL [Sc C 88-240]

Asociación de Graduadas de la Universidad de
Puerto Rico. Feria del Libro (9th: 1967: San
Juan, Puerto Rico) Programa [microform] . [San
Juan , 1967] 37 p. :
NYPL [Sc Micro F-11056]

Asociación de Maestros de Puerto Rico. Feria del
Libro (9th: 1967: San Juan, Puerto Rico)
Programa [microform] . [San Juan , 1967] 37
p. :   *NYPL [Sc Micro F-11056]*

Aspectos sociopolíticos del parlamento tradicional
en algunos países africanos /. Socio-political
aspects of the palaver in some African
countries. Spanish. Barcelona , Paris , 1979. 95
p. ; ISBN 84-85800-24-9 *NYPL [Sc D 88-599]*

Aspects of Dominican history / issued by
Government of Dominica to commemorate fifth
anniversary of associated statehood with Britain,
November 3, 1972. Dominica, W.I. :
Government Printing Division, 1972. 172 p. ;
25 cm. Includes bibliographical references.
CONTENTS. - Columbus saw them first. The
interpretation of some documentary evidence on Carib
culture. Kinship and social structure of the Island Carib.
Tales and legends of the Dominican Carib. A note on
marriage and kinship amng the Island Carib. The Island
Caribs of Dominica, B.W.I. / Douglas Taylor -- Spain
and Dominica 1493-1647. The French and Dominica
1699-1763. Dominica during French occupation
1778-1784. How Crown Colony Government came to
Dominica by 1898 / Joseph Boromé -- Dominica : the
French connexion /Cecil A. Goodridge -- Notes on the
slaves of the French / R. Proesmans.
1. Dominica - History - Addresses, essays, lectures. I.
Taylor, Douglas. II. Dominica.
NYPL [HRG 83-1714]

Aspects of legislative drafting / M/J.C. van den
Bergh. KwaDlangezwa, South Africa :
University of Zululand, 1987. ix, 204 p. ; 20
cm. (Publication series of the University of Zululand.
Series C . no 15) Consists almost entirely of papers
delivered at a workshop organized by the Institute of
Foreign and Comparative Law (Unisa) and the Southern
African Society for Legislative Drafting, and held on
4-5 July, 1985, at the University of South Africa.
ISBN 0-907995-73-X
1. Bill drafting - South Africa - Congresses. 2. Bill
drafting - Africa, Southern - Congresses. I. Van den
Bergh, N. J. C. II. University of South Africa. Institute
of Foreign and Comparative Law. III. Southern African
Society for Legislative Drafting. IV. Series: Publications
series of the University of Zululand. Series C , no.15.
NYPL [Sc C 88-66]

Aspects of slavery, part II . Bahamas. Dept. of
Archives. Nassau, Bahamas [1984] 52 p. :
DDC 306/.362/097296 19
HT1119.B34 B35 1984   NYPL [Sc F 88-346]

Aspects of slavery, part 2. Bahamas. Dept. of
Archives. Aspects of slavery, part II . Nassau,
Bahamas [1984] 52 p. : DDC 306/.362/097296
19
HT1119.B34 B35 1984   NYPL [Sc F 88-346]

Aspects of the biogeography of southern African
butterflies . Cottrell, C. B. Salisbury
[Zimbabwe] , c1978. viii, 100 p. ;
QL557.S65 C68 1978   NYPL [Sc E 88-555]

Assata, an autobiography /. Shakur, Assata.
Westport, CT , 1987. xiv, 274 p. ;   ISBN
0-88208-221-3 : DDC 973/.0496073024 19
E185.97.S53 A3 1987   NYPL [Sc E 88-21]

ASSAULT, CRIMINAL. see RAPE.

Assensoh, A. B. Rev Dr Martin Luther King, Jr.
and America's quest for racial integration :
(with historical testimonies from King's former
class-mate, close friends and colleagues) / A.b.
Assensoh. Ilfracombe, Devon : Arthur H.
Stockwell, 1987. 104 p. : ill. ; 22 cm. Includes
index. Bibliography: p. 83-86. ISBN 0-7223-2084-1
1. King, Martin Luther, Jr., 1929-1968. 2.
Afro-Americans - Civil rights. I. Title.
NYPL [Sc D 88-100]

ASSESSMENT CENTERS (PERSONNEL
MANAGEMENT PROCEDURE)
Rwegasira, Kami S. P. Administering
management development institutions in Africa
/. Aldershot, England , Brookfield, Vt. , 1988.
vi, 112 p. ; ISBN 0-566-05501-5 DDC
658.4/07124/096 19
HF5549.5.A78 R94 1988
NYPL [Sc D 88-458]

Assignments in Africa . Wästberg, Per. [Afrika,
ett uppdrag. English.] London , 1986. viii, 231
p. ; ISBN 0-946889-11-2 (pbk.)
NYPL [JFD 87-7408]

Association des professeurs d'histoire & de
géographie du Togo. Textes et documents sur
l'histoire des populations du nord Togo /. Lomé
[1978] iii, 70 p. :   *NYPL [Sc F 88-332]*

Association générale des étudiants guadeloupéens.
Guadeloupe, 1635-1971 . Tours [1982] 109 p. :
DDC 306/.362/0972976 19
HT1108.G83 G8 1982   NYPL [Sc F 89-141]

Association of College and Research Libraries.
Greater New York Metropolitan Area
Chapter. Women's Resources Group. Library
and information sources on women . New
York , c1988. ix, 254 p. ; ISBN 0-935312-88-9
(pbk.) : DDC 305.4/025/7471 19
HQ1181.U5 L52 1987
*NYPL [*R-Econ. 88-4682]*

Association of Friends for Advocating the Cause
of the Slave, and Improving the Condition of
the Free People of Color. An Address to the
citizens of the United States, on the subject of
slavery /. [Philadelphia] , 1838 ([Philadelphia] :
Neall & Shann, printers) 24 p. ;
NYPL [Sc Rare G 86-12]

Association of Media Women in Kenya. Directory
of media women in Kenya /. [Nairobi] [1985]
48 p. : DDC 001.51/02552 19
P94.5.W652 K43 1985   NYPL [Sc F 88-370]

Association of Nigerian Authors.
Ahmad, Idzia. A Shout across the wall /.
Lagos, Nigeria , 1988. 115 p. ; ISBN
978-302-092-7   *NYPL [Sc C 89-135]*
Akeh, Afam. Stolen moments /. Lagos,
Nigeria , 1988. 66 p. ; ISBN 978-302-097-8
NYPL [Sc C 89-133]
Shehu, Emman Usman. Questions for big
brother /. Nigeria , 1988. 85 p. ; ISBN
978-302-093-5   *NYPL [Sc C 89-121]*

Association of Research Libraries. Office of
University Library Management Studies.
Systems and Procedures Exchange Center.
see Association of Research Libraries.
Systems and Procedures Exchange Center.

Association of Research Libraries. Systems and
Procedures Exchange Center. Preservation
guidelines in ARL libraries /. Washington, D.C.
[1987] 110 p. :   *NYPL [Sc F 88-326]*

Association of Research Libraries. Systems and
Procedures Exchange Program. Organizing
for preservation in ARL libraries /. Washington,
D.C. , 1985. 131 p. :   *NYPL [Sc F 88-327]*

ASSOCIATIONS, INSTITUTIONS, ETC. -
SOUTH AFRICA.
Davies, Robert H. The struggle for South
Africa . London , Atlantic Highlands, N.J. ,
1988. 2 v. : ISBN 0-86232-760-1 (v. 1) DDC
322/.0968 19
JQ1931 .D38 1988   NYPL [Sc D 88-1369]

ASSOCIATIONS, INTERNATIONAL. see
INTERNATIONAL AGENCIES.

Astres si longtemps . Obenga, Théophile. Paris ,
c1988. 123 p. : ISBN 2-7087-0500-8
NYPL [Sc C 89-69]

ASTRONAUTICS - VOYAGES TO THE
MOON. see SPACE FLIGHT TO THE
MOON.

ASTRONOMERS - UNITED STATES -
BIOGRAPHY - JUVENILE LITERATURE.
Ferris, Jeri. What are you figuring now? .
Minneapolis , c1988. 64 p. : ISBN 0-87614-331-1
(lib. bdg.) . DDC 520.92/4 B 92 19
QB36.B22 F47 1988   NYPL [Sc D 89-120]

Asuzu, Boniface Ntomchukwu.
Communications media in the Nigerian Church
today / y Boniface Ntomchukwu Asuzu. 2d ed.
Rome : Tip. Ugo Detti, 1987. 160 p. : ill.,

maps ; 24 cm. Bibliography: p. 155-157.
1. Communication - Religious aspects - Catholic Church. 2. Mass media - Religious aspects - Catholic Church. 3. Mass media in religion - Nigeria. 4. Evangelistic work - Nigeria. I. Title.
NYPL [Sc E 88-297]

Communications strategy in the new era of evangelization : (case for the Catholic Church of Nigeria) / Boniface Ntomchukwu Asuzu.1st ed. Roma : B.N. Asuzu, 1987. xxi, 343 p. : ill., maps ; 25 cm. Bibliography: p. [325]-338.
1. Communication - Religious aspects - Catholic Church. 2. Catholic Church - Nigeria. 3. Evangelistic work - Nigeria. I. Title. **NYPL [Sc E 88-276]**

Atabaques /. Limeira, José Carlos. [Rio de Janeiro? , 1983] 171 p. ;
NYPL [Sc D 88-1096]

Atakora . Maurice, Albert-Marie. Paris , 1986. xxiii, 481 p., clv p. of plates : ISBN 2-900098-11-4 **NYPL [Sc E 88-106]**

ATHLETES, AFRO-AMERICAN. see AFRO-AMERICAN ATHLETES.

ATHLETES - UNITED STATES - BIOGRAPHY - JUVENILE LITERATURE.
Biracree, Tom, 1947- Wilma Rudolph /. New York , 1988. 111 p. : ISBN 1-555-46675-3 DDC 796.4/2/0924 B 92 19
GV697.R8 B57 1988 **NYPL [Sc E 88-172]**

Atieno Odhiambo, E. S., 1946- Cohen, David William. Siaya, a historical anthropology of an African landscape /. London , Athens , 1989. viii, 152 p., [8] p. of plates : ISBN 0-8214-0901-8 DDC 967.6/2 19
DT433.545.L85 C64 1988
NYPL [Sc D 89-354]

Atipa . Parépou, Alfred. Paris , 1987. viii, 231 p. : ISBN 2-85802-965-2 **NYPL [Sc E 88-18]**

Atkinson, Dermot. The meeting / by Dermot Atkinson. [Jamaica?] : D. Atkinson, c1985. 68 p. ; 18 cm.
1. Garvey, Marcus, 1887-1940 - Drama. 2. Jamaica - History - Drama. I. Title. **NYPL [Sc C 88-108]**

Atkinson, Doreen. The search for power and legitimacy in Black urban areas : the role of the Urban Councils Association of South Africa / Doreen Atkinson. Grahamstown [South Africa] : Institute of Social and Economic Research, Rhodes University, [1984] 38, xix, v, [1] p. ; 30 cm. (Development studies . working papers no. 20) "January 1984." Bibliography: p. [1] (4th group). ISBN 0-86810-114-1 (pbk.) : DDC 320.8/0968 19
1. Urban Councils Association of South Africa. 2. Neighborhood government - South Africa. 3. Blacks - South Africa - Politics and government. I. Series. II. Series: Development studies , working paper no. 20. III. Title.
JS7533.A8 A85 1984 **NYPL [Sc F 88-355]**

ATLANTA (GA.) - POLITICS AND GOVERNMENT.
Ball, Thomas E. Julian Bond vs John Lewis . Atlanta, Ga. , 1988. ix, 144 p. : ISBN 0-9621362-0-4 **NYPL [Sc E 88-582]**

ATLANTA UNIVERSITY. SCHOOL OF LIBRARY SERVICE - DISSERTATIONS.
Haith, Dorothy May. Theses accepted by the Atlanta University Graduate School of Library Service, 1950-1975 /. Huntsville, Al , 1977. v, 45 p. ;
Z666 .H25 **NYPL [Sc D 88-69]**

Atlanta University. School of Social Work.
Dodson, Jualynne E. Black stylization and implications for child welfare . Atlanta, Georgia , 1975. 1 v. (various pagings)
NYPL [Sc F 88-223]

Dodson, Jualynne E. Training of personnel for services to Black families . [Atlanta] [1976] 1 v. (various foliations) ; **NYPL [Sc F 88-130]**

Toward reflective analysis of Black families . [Atlanta] , 1976. ii, 74 l. :
NYPL [Sc F 88-224]

ATLANTIC STATES - CHURCH HISTORY.
Smith, Edward D. Climbing Jacob's ladder . City of Washington , 1988. 143 p. : ISBN 0-87474-829-1 **NYPL [Sc E 88-505]**

Atlantic University. School of Library Service.
Haith, Dorothy May. Theses accepted by the Atlanta University Graduate School of Library Service, 1950-1975 /. Huntsville, Al , 1977. v,

45 p. ;
Z666 .H25 **NYPL [Sc D 88-69]**

Atlantis a utopian nightmare / by Moosa Ebrahim ... [et al.] Cape Town : Southern Africa Labour and Development Research Unit, 1986. 114 p. : ill. ; 22 cm. (Saldru working paper . no. 66) Includes bibliographical references. ISBN 0-7992-1070-6
1. Colored people (South Africa) - Atlantis. I. Series. **NYPL [Sc D 89-17]**

Atlas du Niger / sous la direction de Edmond Bernus, Sidikou A. Hamidou, avec la collaboration de Aboubacar Adamou ... [et al.] ; préf. de Idé Oumarou. Paris : Éditions J.A., c1980. 64 p. : col. maps ; 29 cm. (Les atlas Jeune Afrique) Includes index. Bibliography: p. 64. ISBN 2-85258-151-5 : DDC 912/.6626 19
1. Niger - Maps. I. Bernus, Edmond. II. Hamidou, Sidikou A. III. Adamou, Aboubacar.
G2660 .A8 1980 **NYPL [Sc F 84-232]**

Atlas linguistique du Cameroun. Situation linguistique en Afrique centrale . Paris , Yaoundé , 1983. 475 p. :
NYPL [Sc F 88-153]

Atlas of African history /. McEvedy, Colin. New York , c1980. 142 p. : ISBN 0-87196-480-5 : DDC 911/.6
G2446.S1 M3 1980 **NYPL [Sc D 89-395]**

ATOMIC BOMB AND DISARMAMENT. see ATOMIC WEAPONS AND DISARMAMENT.

ATOMIC WEAPONS AND DISARMAMENT.
Epstein, William, 1912- A nuclear-weapon-free zone in Africa? /. Muscatine, Iowa , 1977. 52 p. ;
JX1974.7 .E553 **NYPL [JLK 75-198 [no.]14]**

ATROCITIES - MOZAMBIQUE.
Magaia, Lina. [Dumba nengue. English.] Dumba nengue, run for your life . Trenton, N.J. , 1988. 113 p. : ISBN 0-86543-073-X
NYPL [Sc D 88-1509]

Attas, Ali. Kamusi ya kwanza : kwa wanafunzi / Ali Attas. Nairobi : Macmillan Kenya, 1986. 169 p. : ill. ; 25 cm. ISBN 0-333-42702-5
1. Swahili language - Glossaries, vocabularies, etc. I. Title. **NYPL [Sc E 89-125]**

Attaway, William. Blood on the forge / William Attaway ; foreword by John Oliver Killens ; afterword by Richard Yarborough. New York : Monthly Review Press, c1987. 315 p. ; 21 cm. (Voices of resistance) Bibliography: p. 313-315. ISBN 0-85345-722-0 (pbk.) : DDC 813/.52 19
1. Afro-Americans - Pennsylvania - Pittsburgh - Fiction. I. Title. II. Series.
PS3501.T59 B55 1987
NYPL [Sc D 88-1438]

An attempt to strip Negro emancipation of its difficulties as well as its terrors . Merchant. London , 1824. 48 p. ;
NYPL [Sc Rare G 86-13]

Attenborough, Richard. Richard Attenborough's cry freedom . New York , 1987. [128] p. : ISBN 0-394-75838-2 DDC 791.43/72 19
PN1997.C885 A88 1987 **NYPL [Sc G 89-17]**

ATTITUDE CHANGE.
Hatchett, Shirley. Black racial attitude change in Detroit, 1968-1976 [microform] /. 1982. 171 leaves. **NYPL [Sc Micro R-4682]**

Atuchi, Ugochukwu. Tell it as it is /. Enugu [Nigeria] [1985?]- v. ; ISBN 978-247-202-6
NYPL [Sc C 88-183]

Au hasard de la vie /. Akakpo-Ahianyo, Anani K. [Lomé?] , c1983. 111 p. ;
MLCS 84/818 (P) **NYPL [Sc C 88-54]**

Au temps des isles à sucre . Cauna, Jacques, 1948- Paris , c1987. 285 p., [16] p. of plates : ISBN 2-86537-186-5 **NYPL [Sc E 88-492]**

Au verso du silence /. Pépin, Ernest. Paris , c1984. 108 p. ; ISBN 2-85802-279-8 DDC 841 19
PQ3949.2.P37 A9 1984
NYPL [Sc C 88-273]

Une aube incertaine . Konaté, Moussa, 1951- Paris , c1985. 217 p. ; ISBN 2-7087-0459-1
MLCS 86/6414 (P) **NYPL [Sc E 89-105]**

L'aube nouvelle . Agokla, K. M., 1955- Lomé , 1982. 94 p. ; ISBN 2-7236-0850-6
NYPL [Sc D 88-1018]

AUDIENCES.
Past meets present . Washington, D.C. , 1987. x, 169 p. : ISBN 0-87474-272-2 DDC 069/.9973 19
D16.163 .P37 1987 **NYPL [Sc E 88-577]**

Auf Pad in Südwest . Sauerbier, Udo. [Mainz] c1982. 224 p. : **NYPL [Sc D 88-619]**

Augusta Savage and the art Schools of Harlem. New York, N.Y. : Schomburg Center for Research in Black Culture, The New York Public Library, 1988. 27 p. : ill. ; 28 cm. Catalog of an exhibition, Oct. 9, 1988 - Jan. 28, 1989. Curator: Deirdre L. Bibby. Bibliography: p. 11.
1. Savage, Augusta - Exhibitions. 2. Art schools - New York (N.Y.) - Harlem. 3. Afro-American artists - Exhibitions. I. Bibby, Deirdre L.
NYPL [Sc F 89-45]

Auguste, Michel Hector. Haiti, la lucha por la democracia (clase obrera, partidos y sindicatos) / Michel Hector Auguste, Sabine Manigat. Jean L. Dominique ; coordinación de Michel Hector Auguste. Puebla : Universidad Autónoma de Puebla, [1986]. 244 p. ; 22 cm. (Colección historia /Universidad Autónoma de Puebla) Includes bibliographical references.
1. Labor and laboring classes - Haiti - History. 2. Labor and laboring classes - Haiti - Political activity. I. Manigat, Sabine. II. Dominique, Jean L. III. Title.
NYPL [Sc D 88-761]

Aurillac, Michel. L'Afrique à coeur : la coopération, un message d'avenir / Michel Aurillac. Paris : Berger Levrault, 1987. 264 p., [8] p. of plates : ill. ; 24 cm. (Mondes en devenir . Série Bâtisseurs d'avenir) Includes bibliographical references. ISBN 2-7013-0739-2
1. Africa - Politics and government - 1960-. 2. Africa - Relations - France. 3. France - Relations - Africa. I. Title. II. Series. **NYPL [Sc E 88-203]**

AUSTEN, JANE, 1775-1817 - CRITICISM AND INTERPRETATION.
James, Selma. The ladies and the mammies . Bristol, England , 1983. 96 p. ; ISBN 0-905046-24-2 : **NYPL [JFD 84-4049]**

Austerity and the Nigerian society / edited by G.E.K. Ofomata and N.I. Ikpeze. Nsukka : Faculty of the Social Sciences, University of Nigeria, 1987. vi, 240 p. : ill., maps ; 21 cm. Includes bibliographies. "A conference on 'Austerity and the Nigerian Society' was held at the University of Nigeria, Nsukka under the auspices of the Faculty of the Social Sciences, from 5 to 7 March, 1985." ISBN 978-264-356-4
1. Nigeria - Social conditions - Congresses. 2. Nigeria - Economic conditions - Congresses. I. Ofomata, G. E. K. II. Ikpeze, N. I. III. University of Nigeria, Nsukka. Faculty of the Social Sciences.
NYPL [Sc D 89-205]

Austin, James Trecothick, 1784-1870. REMARKS ON DR. CHANNING'S SLAVERY.
[Simmons, George Frederick] 1814-1855. Review of the Remarks on Dr. Channing's Slavery [microform] . Boston, 1836. 48 p.
E449 .C4562 **NYPL [Sc Micro R-4839]**

Austin, William W. "Susanna," "Jeanie," and "The old folks at home" : the songs of Stephen Foster from his time to ours / William W. Austin.2nd ed. Urbana [Ill.] : University of Illinois Press, 1987. xxiv, 422 p. ; 24 cm. (Music in American life) Includes index. Bibliography: p. 403-404. ISBN 0-252-01476-6 DDC 784.5/0092/4 19
1. Foster, Stephen Collins, 1826-1864 Songs. I. Title.
ML410.F78 A9 1987 **NYPL [Sc E 88-465]**

AUSTRALIAN ABORIGINAL POETRY.
Inside Black Australia . Ringwood, Victoria , 1988. xxiv, 213 p. ; ISBN 0-14-011126-3
NYPL [Sc D 89-547]

AUSTRALIAN ABORIGINES - AUSTRIALIA - NEW SOUTH WALES.
Blomfield, Geoffrey. Baal Belbora, the end of the dancing . Chippendale, N.S.W. [New South Wales] , 1981. 148 p. : ISBN 0-909188-57-2
NYPL [Sc D 82-242]

AUSTRALIAN ABORIGINES - ECONOMIC CONDITIONS.
Stevens, Frank S. Black Australia /. Sydney , 1981. xviii, 248 p. : ISBN 0-909188-43-2
NYPL [Sc D 88-1165]

AUSTRALIAN ABORIGINES - SOCIAL CONDITIONS.

Being Black . Canberra , 1988. xiv, 273 p. :
ISBN 0-85575-185-1 *NYPL [Sc E 88-515]*

Stevens, Frank S. Black Australia /. Sydney ,
1981. xviii, 248 p. : ISBN 0-909188-43-2
NYPL [Sc D 88-1165]

**AUSTRALIAN ABORIGINES - URBAN
RESIDENCE.**
Being Black . Canberra , 1988. xiv, 273 p. :
ISBN 0-85575-185-1 *NYPL [Sc E 88-515]*

**AUSTRALIAN TRIBES. see AUSTRALIAN
ABORIGINES.**

**AUSTRALIANS (NATIVE PEOPLE) see
AUSTRALIAN ABORIGINES.**

Les auteurs afro-américains, 1965-1982 . France.
Bibliothèque nationale. Département des livres
imprimés. Paris , 1985. 28 p., [4] leaves of
plates : ISBN 2-7177-1709-9 :
Z1229.N39 F7 1985 PS153.N5
NYPL [Sc F 89-5]

AUTHORS, AFRICAN - INTERVIEWS.
Interviews avec des écrivains africains
francophones /. [Bayreuth, W. Germany ,
c1986. 95 p. ; *NYPL [Sc D 88-906]*

**AUTHORS, AFRO-AMERICAN. see AFRO-
AMERICAN AUTHORS.**

**AUTHORS, AMERICAN - 19TH CENTURY -
BIOGRAPHY - JUVENILE LITERATURE.**
Jakoubek, Robert E. Harriet Beecher Stowe /.
New York , c1989. 111 p. : ISBN 1-555-46680-X
DDC 813/.3 B 92 19
PS2956 .J35 1989 *NYPL [Sc E 89-144]*

**AUTHORS, AMERICAN - 20TH CENTURY -
BIOGRAPHY.**
Delany, Samuel R. The motion of light in
water . New York , c1988. xviii, 302 p. : ISBN
0-87795-947-1 : DDC 813/.54 19
PS3554.E437 Z475 1988
NYPL [JFD 88-7818]

Johnson, James Weldon, 1871-1938. Along this
way . New York , 1933. 418 p., [16] leaves of
plates : *NYPL [Sc Rare F 89-9]*

Lester, Julius. Lovesong . New York, N.Y. ,
c1988. 248 p., [4] leaves of plates : ISBN
0-8050-0588-9 DDC 296.8/346/0924 B 19
BM755.L425 A3 1988 *NYPL [Sc E 88-317]*

**AUTHORS, AMERICAN - 20TH CENTURY -
BIOGRAPHY - JUVENILE LITERATURE.**
Rosset, Lisa. James Baldwin /. New York,
N.Y. , 1989. 111 p. : ISBN 1-555-46572-2 DDC
818/.5409 B 92 19
PS3552.A45 Z87 1989 *NYPL [Sc E 89-224]*

Tolbert-Rouchaleau, Jane. James Weldon
Johnson /. New York , c1988. 110 p. : ISBN
1-555-46596-X DDC 818/.5209 B 92 19
PS3519.O2625 Z894 1988
NYPL [Sc E 88-164]

Urban, Joan, 1950- Richard Wright /. New
York, N.Y. [1989] 111 p. : ISBN 1-555-46618-4
DDC 813/.52 19
PS3545.R815 Z85 1989
NYPL [Sc E 89-196]

**AUTHORS, AMERICAN - 20TH CENTURY -
CORRESPONDENCE.**
Teague, Bob. The flip side of soul . New York ,
c1989. 201 p. : ISBN 0-688-08260-2 DDC
305.8/96073 19
PS3570.E2 Z495 1989 *NYPL [Sc D 89-303]*

**AUTHORS, AMERICAN - 20TH CENTURY -
INTERVIEWS.**
Angelou, Maya. Conversations with Maya
Angelou /. Jackson , c1989. xvi, 246 p. ; ISBN
0-87805-361-1 (alk. paper) DDC 818/.5409 19
PS3551.N464 Z4635 1989
NYPL [Sc E 89-225]

**AUTHORS AND PRINTERS. see
AUTHORSHIP - HANDBOOKS,
MANUALS, ETC.**

**AUTHORS, BLACK - 20TH CENTURY -
BIOGRAPHY.**
Black writers . Detroit, Mi. , c1989. xxiv, 619
p. ; ISBN 0-8103-2772-4 *NYPL [Sc F 89-57]*

AUTHORS, BLACK - GREAT BRITAIN.
Let it be told . London , 1987. 145, [1] p. ;
ISBN 0-7453-0254-8 *NYPL [Sc E 88-125]*

**AUTHORS, BLACK - SOUTH AFRICA -
CORRESPONDENCE.**
Mphahlele, Ezekiel. Bury me at the

marketplace . Johannesburg , c1984. 202 p. ;
ISBN 0-620-06779-9 *NYPL [Sc D 89-117]*

**AUTHORS, FRENCH - 20TH CENTURY -
BIOGRAPHY.**
Dennis, John Alfred. The René Maran story .
Ann Arbor, Mich. , c1987. viii, 275 p. :
NYPL [Sc D 89-292]

AUTHORS - GHANA - BIOGRAPHY.
Appiah-Kubi, Kofi. In America in search of
gold /. Bloomfield, Conn. , 1985. 103 p. :
ISBN 0-9614573-0-9 *NYPL [Sc D 89-583]*

**AUTHORS - HOMES AND HAUNTS. see
LITERARY LANDMARKS.**

AUTHORS' MARKETS. see AUTHORSHIP.

**AUTHORS, SOUTH AFRICAN - 20TH
CENTURY - CORRESPONDENCE.**
Mphahlele, Ezekiel. Bury me at the
marketplace . Johannesburg , c1984. 202 p. ;
ISBN 0-620-06779-9 *NYPL [Sc D 89-117]*

**AUTHORS, TRINIDADIAN - 20TH
CENTURY - BIOGRAPHY.**
Buhle, Paul, 1944- C.L.R. James . London ,
New York , 1988. 197 p. ; ISBN 0-86091-221-3 :
DDC 818 B 19
PR9272.9.J35 Z59 1988
NYPL [Sc E 89-171]

**AUTHORSHIP - HANDBOOKS, MANUALS,
ETC.**
Nwosu, I. E. A guide to Christian writing in
Africa /. Enugu, Nigeria , 1987. 116 p. ; ISBN
978-262-606-6 *NYPL [Sc C 88-156]*

An autobiography . Smith, Amanda, 1837-1915.
New York , 1988. xlii, 506 p. [23] of plates :
ISBN 0-19-505261-7 (alk. paper) DDC
269/.2/0924 B 19
BV3785.S56 A3 1988 *NYPL [JFC 88-2154]*

**AUTOMATIC DATA STORAGE. see
INFORMATION STORAGE AND
RETRIEVAL SYSTEMS.**

**AUTOMATIC INFORMATION RETRIEVAL.
see INFORMATION STORAGE AND
RETRIEVAL SYSTEMS.**

**AUTOMATION IN DOCUMENTATION. see
INFORMATION STORAGE AND
RETRIEVAL SYSTEMS.**

Autores africanos .
(24) Agostinho Neto, António, 1922- Sagrada
esperança /. São Paulo , 1985. 126 p. ; ISBN
85-08-01056-7 *NYPL [Sc D 89-64]*

Autores de Cabo Verde.
Lopes, Manuel. Os flagelados do vento leste /.
Lisboa , c1985. 216 p. ;
NYPL [Sc D 88-1387]

Autour du feu . Djungu-Simba Kamatenda, 1953-
Kinshasa , 1984. 70 p. : DDC 398.2/09675/1 19
GR357.82.W35 D48 1984
NYPL [Sc C 88-272]

L'autre Abidjan . Bonnassieux, Alain. Abidjan ,
Paris , c1987. 220 p. : ISBN 0-86537-191-3
NYPL [Sc E 88-212]

**Avaliação nutricional da população infantil banto
(0-5 anos) de uma zona suburbana da cidade
Lourenço Marques .** Santos, Norberto Teixeira.
[Lourenço Marques, Moçambique] 1974. 400
p., [40] p. of plates : *NYPL [Sc E 88-143]*

L'avènement de la littérature haïtienne /.
Laroche, Maximilien. Sainte-Foy, Québec ,
1987. 219 p. ; *NYPL [Sc D 88-1462]*

Aventure coloniale de la France.
Biondi, Jean Pierre. Saint-Louis du Sénégal .
Paris , c1987. 234 p., [16] p. of plates : ISBN
2-207-23350-2 *NYPL [Sc D 88-1501]*

Aventures de Yévi au pays des monstres. Zinsou,
Sénouvo Agbota, 1946- La tortue qui chante .
Paris , 1987. 127 p. ; ISBN 2-218-07842-3
NYPL [Sc C 88-8]

The Avenue, Clayton City /. Lincoln, C. Eric
(Charles Eric), 1924- New York , c1988. 288
p. ; ISBN 0-688-07702-1 DDC 813/.54 19
PS3562.I472 A94 1988
NYPL [JFE 88-5108]

Avery-Coger, Greta Margaret Kay McCormick.
Index of subjects, proverbs, and themes in the
writings of Wole Soyinka / compiled by Greta
M.K. Coger. New York : Greenwood Press,
c1988. xxii, 311 p. ; 25 cm. (Bibliographies and
indexes in Afro-American and African studies,

0742-6925 . no. 21) Includes indexes. Bibliography: p.
[291]-311. ISBN 0-313-25712-4 (lib. bdg. : alk. paper)
DDC 822 19
1. Soyinka, Wole - Dictionaries, indexes, etc. I.
Soyinka, Wole. II. Title. III. Series.
PR9387.9.S6 Z54 1988 *NYPL [Sc E 88-496]*

AVIATION. see AERONAUTICS.

Avraham, Shmuel, 1945- Treacherous journey :
my escape from Ethiopia / Shmuel Avraham
with Arlene Kushner.1st ed. New York, NY :
Shapolsky Pub., 1986. xii, 178 p. : ill. ; 24 cm.
ISBN 0-933503-46-6 (jacket); 0-933503-46-5 :
DDC 963/.004924 19
1. Avraham, Shmuel, 1945-. 2. Falashas - Biography. 3.
Jews - Ethiopia - Persecutions. 4. Ethiopia - Emigration
and immigration - Biography. 5. Israel - Emigration and
immigration - Biography. 6. Ethiopia - Ethnic relations.
I. Kushner, Arlene. II. Title.
DS135.E75 A93 1986 *NYPL [Sc E 87-275]*

AVRAHAM, SHMUEL, 1945-
Avraham, Shmuel, 1945- Treacherous journey .
New York, NY , 1986. xii, 178 p. : ISBN
0-933503-46-6 (jacket); 0-933503-46-5 : DDC
963/.004924 19
DS135.E75 A93 1986 *NYPL [Sc E 87-275]*

Avrin, Nancy. A Directory of international
migration study centers, research programs, and
library resources /. Staten Island, N.Y. , 1987.
ix, 299 p. ; ISBN 0-934733-18-X (pbk.) : DDC
325/.07 19
JV6033 .C45 1987 *NYPL [JLF 88-1452]*

Àw on oríkì oríl`e /. Babalọlá, Adébóyè. Glasgow
U.K. , 1967. 160 p. ; *NYPL [Sc C 89-112]*

Away went the balloons. Haywood, Carolyn,
1898- New York, 1973. 189 p. ISBN
0-688-20057-5 DDC [Fic]
PZ7.H31496 Aw *NYPL [Sc D 89-113]*

Awkward, Michael. Inspiriting influences :
tradition, revision, and Afro-American women's
novels / Michael Awkward. New York :
Columbia University Press, 1989. x, 178 p. ; 24
cm. (Gender and culture) Includes bibliographical
notes and index. ISBN 0-231-06806-9 DDC
813/.5/099287 19
1. American fiction - Afro-American authors - History
and criticism. 2. American fiction - Women authors -
History and criticism. 3. American fiction - 20th
century - History and criticism. 4. Women and
literature - United States - History - 20th century. 5.
Afro-American women - Intellectual life. 6.
Afro-American women in literature. 7. Influence
(Literary, artistic, etc.). 8. Intertextuality. I. Title. II.
Series.
PS153.N5 A94 1989 *NYPL [Sc E 89-188]*

Awo & Nigeria . Babatope, Ebenezer. Ikeja
[Nigeria] , 1984. 97 p. : ISBN 3-7830-0100-0
NYPL [Sc D 88-1397]

Awo and Nigeria. Babatope, Ebenezer. Awo &
Nigeria . Ikeja [Nigeria] , 1984. 97 p. : ISBN
3-7830-0100-0 *NYPL [Sc D 88-1397]*

AWOLOWO, OBAFEMI, 1909-
Babatope, Ebenezer. Awo & Nigeria . Ikeja
[Nigeria] , 1984. 97 p. : ISBN 3-7830-0100-0
NYPL [Sc D 88-1397]

Awon olori Yoruba ati isedale won /. Kenyo,
Elisha Alademomi. Lagos, Nigeria , 1952. 96
p. : *NYPL [Sc D 88-818]*

Awonge, Flora. A year for my nation / Flora
Awonge. Calabar : Insideout Publications Ltd.,
c1986. 99 p. ; 18 cm.
1. Nigeria - Fiction. I. Title.
MLCS 87/7812 (P) *NYPL [Sc C 88-155]*

Awoonor, Kofi, 1935- Until the morning after :
selected poems 1963-85 / by Kofi Awoonor.
Greenfield Center, NY : Greenfield Review
Press, 1987. 216 p. ; 22 cm. ISBN 0-912678-69-0
I. Title. *NYPL [Sc D 88-103]*

**Awoonor-Williams, George. see Awoonor, Kofi,
1935-**

Awóyele, Oyètúndé. Aké wì ló n'ìtàn : (apá
kejì :b'óa wì fọmọ ẹni / Oyètúndé Awóyelé.
Ìbàdàn : Oníbonoje Press & Book Industries,
1987. iv, 97 p. ; 18 cm. ISBN 978-14-5044-4
1. Yoruba language - Texts. I. Title. II. Title: B'áa wí f
NYPL [Sc C 88-216]

Axelson, Eric. Baines, Thomas, 1820-1875. Baines
on the Zambezi 1858 to 1859 /. Johannesburg ,
c1982. 251 p. : ISBN 0-909079-17-X (Standard ed.)
NYPL [Sc F 83-34]

The ayah /. Maillu, David G., 1939- Nairobi , 1986. 178 p. ;
MLCS 89/131165 (P) **NYPL** *[Sc C 89-158]*

Aye, Efiong U. Presbyterianism in Nigeria / by E.U. Aye. Calabar, Cross River State : Wusen Press, 1987. 175 p. : ill., maps ; 20 cm.
Bibliography: p. 175. ISBN 978-228-288-X
1. Presbyterian Church - Nigeria - Missions - History.
2. Presbyterians - Nigeria - History. I. Title.
NYPL *[Sc C 88-234]*

Ayeni, Victor. The impact of military rule on Nigeria's administration /. Ile-Ife, Nigeria , c1987. vi, 344 p. ; ISBN 978-266-601-7
NYPL *[Sc D 88-733]*

Ayida, A. A. Reflections on Nigerian development / Allison A. Ayida. Lagos : Malthouse Press ; Ibadan : Heinemann Educational Books (Nigeria), 1987. xxiii, 278 p. ; 22 cm. Includes bibliographical references and index. ISBN 978-260-101-2
1. Nigeria - Economic conditions - 1960-. 2. Nigeria - Economic policy. I. Title. **NYPL** *[Sc D 88-1078]*

Ayomike, J. O. S. A history of Warri / J.O.S. Ayomike. Benin City : Ilupeju Press, 1988. xiii, 198 p. : ill., maps ; 22 cm.
1. Jekri (African people) - History. 2. Warri (Nigeria) - History. I. Title. **NYPL** *[Sc D 88-1370]*

Azevedo, Celia Maria Marinho de. Onda negra, medo branco : o negro no imaginário das elites - século XIX / Celia Maria Marinho de Azevedo ; prefácio de Peter Eisenberg. Rio de Janeiro : Paz e Terra, c1987. 267 p. ; 21 cm. (Coleção Oficinas da história. v.6) Bibliography: p. 259-261.
1. Blacks - Brazil - History - 19th century. 2. Brazil - Race relations. I. Title. II. Series.
NYPL *[Sc D 88-469]*

Azevêdo, Eliane. Raça : conceito e preconceito / Eliane Azevêdo. São Paulo : Editora Atica, 1987. 62 p. ; 18 cm. (Série Princípios . 107) Bibliography: p. 59-62. ISBN 85-08-01878-9
1. Race. 2. Brazil - Race relations. I. Title. II. Series.
NYPL *[Sc C 88-14]*

B. Notice of the Rev. John B. Adger's article on the slave trade Charleston, S.C. : Published for the author, 1858 (Charleston, S.C. : Steam Power Press of Walker, Evans) 28 p. ; 22 cm. Signed: B.
1. Adger, John Bailey, 1810-1899. A review of reports to the legislature of S.C., on the revival of the slave trade. 2. Slavery - United States - Controversial literature - 1858. I. Title.
NYPL *[Sc Rare G 86-8]*

Ba, Amadou Hampaté. Njeddo Dewal : mère de la calamité : conte initiatique peul / Amadou Hampaté Bâ. Abidjan [Ivory Coast] : Nouvelles éditions africaines, c1985. 156 p. ; 24 cm. (Collection orale) A French prose version of a Fulah poetic work of oral tradition. ISBN 2-7236-0732-1
I. Title. II. Series. **NYPL** *[Sc E 88-417]*

Bâ, Ardo Ousmane, 1948- Silamaka fara dikko . Berlin , 1988. xi, 271 p., 1 folded page : ISBN 3-496-00961-6 **NYPL** *[Sc E 88-230]*

Bâ, Mariama.
SI LONGUE LETTRE.
Grésillon, Marie. Une si longue lettre de Mariama Bâ . Issy les Moulineux [France] , c1986. 94 p. : ISBN 2-85049-344-9
NYPL *[Sc D 88-824]*

Baa, Enid M. Theses on Caribbean topics, 1778-1968. Compiled by Enid M. Baa. San Juan, Institute of Caribbean Studies [University of Puerto Rico] 1970. v, 146 p. 24 cm. (Caribbean bibliographic series. no. 1 1)
1. Caribbean area - Bibliography. I. Title. II. Series.
Z1501 .C33 no. 1 **NYPL** *[JFL 74-576 no. 1]*

B'áa wí f Awóyẹlé, Oyètúndé. Akèwì ló n'ìtàn . Ibàdàn , 1987. iv, 97 p. ; ISBN 978-14-5044-4
NYPL *[Sc C 88-216]*

Baal Belbora, the end of the dancing . Blomfield, Geoffrey. Chippendale, N.S.W. [New South Wales] , 1981. 148 p. : ISBN 0-909188-57-2
NYPL *[Sc D 82-242]*

Baar, Liliane, 1928- Baar, Marius. Tschad--Land ohne Hoffnung? . Bad Liebenzell , c1985. 190 p., [6] p. of plates : ISBN 3-88002-270-4
NYPL *[Sc D 88-892]*

Baar, Marius. Tschad--Land ohne Hoffnung? : Erlebnisbericht einer 25jährigen Aufbautätigkeit im Dangaleat-Stamm / Marius und Liliane

Baar. Bad Liebenzell : Verlag der Liebenzeller Mission, c1985. 190 p., [6] p. of plates : ill. ; 21 cm. (Edition C . C 188) ISBN 3-88002-270-4
1. Missions - Chad. 2. Chad - Description and travel. I. Baar, Liliane, 1928-. II. Title. III. Series.
NYPL *[Sc D 88-892]*

BAAYO FAMILY.
A History of the migration and the settlement of the Baayo family from Timbuktu to Bijini in Guine Bissau /. [Banjul? , 1987.] 71 p. :
NYPL *[Sc F 89-146]*

Babalọlá, Adébóyè.
Aw on oríkì oríl`e / láti ow o Adéb oyè Babal olá. 1st ed. Glasgow U.K. : Wm. Collins, 1967. 160 p. ; 20 cm. (Yoruba classics)
1. Yoruba language - Texts.
NYPL *[Sc C 89-112]*

Iwe ede yoruba : fun awọn akẹkọ ni ile-iwe giga :apa kini / Adeboye Babalọla. [Ikeja] : Longmans of Nigeria, [1968] 139 p. : ill. ; 19 cm. Originally published in 1963.
1. Yoruba language - Text-books. I. Title.
NYPL *[Sc C 88-127]*

Babalola, J. A. Past questions and answers for secondary modern schools, 1964-1969 /. Ado-Ekiti [197-?] 301 p. ;
NYPL *[Sc C 86-206]*

Babangida, Ibrahim Badamasi.
Collected speeches of the president / Ibrahim Babangida. Lagos : Federal Ministry of Information and Culture, [1986?] 280 p. : ports. (some col.) ; 25 cm.
1. Nigeria - Politics and government - 1984-. I. Nigeria. President (1985- : Babangida). II. Title.
NYPL *[Sc E 88-303]*

Quotes of a general : selected quotes of Major General Ibrahim Babangida. Surulere [Nigeria] : Terry Publishers, 1987. 90 p. : col. ill. ; 22 cm. Cover title.
1. Nigeria. Army. 2. Nigeria - Military policy - Quotations, maxims, etc. I. Title.
NYPL *[Sc D 88-711]*

Babatope, Ebenezer. Awo & Nigeria : setting the records straight / by Ebenezer Babatope. Ikeja [Nigeria] : Ebino Topsy Publishers, 1984. 97 p. : facsim. ; 22 cm. ISBN 3-7830-0100-0
1. Awolowo, Obafemi, 1909-. 2. Unity Party of Nigeria. 3. Statesmen - Nigeria - Biography. 4. Nigeria - Politics and government - 1960-. I. Title. II. Title: Awo and Nigeria. **NYPL** *[Sc D 88-1397]*

Babayemi, S. O.
Content analysis of oríkì oríl by S.O. Babayemi. [Ibadan : Institute of African Studies, University of Ibadan, 198-?] xi, 352 p. ; 25 cm. In English and Yoruba. Includes bibliographies.
1. Laudatory poetry, Yoruba. 2. Yoruba language - Texts. I. Title. **NYPL** *[Sc E 89-229]*

Egúngún among the Ọyọ Yoruba / by S.O. Babayemi. Ibadan : Ọyọ State Council for Arts and Culture, c1980. ix, 123 p. : ill. ; 21 cm. English and Yoruba. Includes bibliographical references.
1. Egúngún (Cult). 2. Yorubas - Religion. 3. Ancestor worship - Nigeria. I. Ọyọ State Council for Arts and Culture. II. Title.
BL2480.Y6 B33 1980 **NYPL** *[Sc D 88-1149]*

Babcock, Bernie Smade, 1868-1962. Hallerloogy's ride with Santa Claus, by Bernie Babcock. Hand-set special ed. Perry, Ark., printed by Rice Print Shop, c1943. 48 p. plates. ; 23 cm. Title on cover: Hallerloogy; the story of a little Arkansas Negro boy who took a ride with Santa Claus. Inscribed by the author. SCHOMBURG CHILDREN'S COLLECTION.
1. Afro-American children - Juvenile fiction. 2. Christmas stories. I. Schomburg Children's Collection. II. Title.
PZ7.B12 Hal **NYPL** *[Sc D 88-1285]*

Babing, Alfred. Wo die Sonne wohnt / Alfred Babing, Hans-Dieter Bräuer. 1. Aufl. Berlin : Verlag der Nation, 1985. 368 p. : ill., maps ; 21 cm. Bibliography: p. 361-365.
1. Zimbabwe - History. 2. Zimbabwe - Politics and government. I. Bräuer, Hans-Dieter. II. Title.
NYPL *[Sc D 89-72]*

Baby says /. Steptoe, John, 1950- New York , 1988. [24] p. : ISBN 0-688-07423-5 DDC [E] 19
PZ7.S8367 Bab 1988 **NYPL** *[Sc D 88-1257]*

The baby-sitter /. Duczman, Linda. Milwaukee , Chicago , c1977. 30 p. : ISBN 0-8172-0065-7 (lib.

bdg.) : DDC 649/.1
HQ772.5 .D8 **NYPL** *[Sc E 88-588]*

BABY SITTERS - JUVENILE LITERATURE.
Duczman, Linda. The baby-sitter /. Milwaukee , Chicago , c1977. 30 p. : ISBN 0-8172-0065-7 (lib. bdg.) : DDC 649/.1
HQ772.5 .D8 **NYPL** *[Sc E 88-588]*

Baccard, André. Les martyrs de Bokassa / André Baccard. Paris : Editions du Seuil, c1987. 349 p., [16] p. of plates : ill., ports. ; 21 cm. (Collection L'Histoire immédiate) ISBN 2-02-009669-2 : DDC 967/.4105/0924 B 19
1. Bokassa I, Emperor of the Central African Empire, 1921-. 2. Heads of state - Central African Republic - Biography. 3. Central African Republic - Politics and government - 1966-1979. I. Series: Histoire immédiate.
DT546.382.B64 B33 1987
NYPL *[Sc D 88-636]*

Bachelet, Michel. Systèmes fonciers à la ville et au village . Paris , c1986. 296 p. ; ISBN 2-85802-719-6 DDC 346.6704/32 346.706432 19
LAW **NYPL** *[Sc D 89-367]*

BACK TO AFRICA MOVEMENT.
Barron, Charles. Look for me in the whirlwind . [Brooklyn, NY] , c1987. v, 60 p. : DDC 305.8/96073 19
E185.97.G3 B37 1987
NYPL *[Sc D 88-1501]*

Yard, Lionel M. Biography of Amy Ashwood Garvey, 1897-1969 . [S.l.] [198-?] vii, 233 p. :
NYPL *[Sc E 88-541]*

Background characteristics and selected perceptions of Black administrators working at Black and white land-grant institutions of higher education [microform] /. Hoskins, Robert L. 1977. 213 leaves.
NYPL *[Sc Micro R-4226]*

Backus, Rob, 1946- Fire music : a political history of Jazz / by Rob Backus. Chicago, Ill. : Vanguard Books, 1976. vii, 104 p. : ill. music, ports. ; 22 cm. Includes bibliographical references. ISBN 0-917702-00-X
1. Jazz music - History and criticism. 2. Jazz musicians - United States - Biography. 3. Afro-American musicians - Biography. I. Title.
NYPL *[Sc D 88-337]*

Bacmeister, Rhoda Warner, 1893- Voices in the night / by Rhoda W. Bacmeister ; pictures by Ann Grifalconi. 1st ed. Indianapolis : Bobbs-Merrill, 1965. 117 p. : ill. ; 23 cm. SCHOMBURG CHILDREN'S COLLECTION.
1. Underground Railroad - Juvenile fiction. I. Grifalconi, Ann. II. Schomburg Children's Collection. III. Title. **NYPL** *[Sc D 88-382]*

Badian, Seydou, 1928-
Mort de Chaka. English. 1988. Faces of African independence : three plays / translated by Clive Wake ; introduction by Richard Bjornson. Charlottesville , 1988. xxxvi, 127 p. ; ISBN 0-8139-1186-9 DDC 842 19
PQ3987.5.E5 F33 1988 **NYPL** *[Sc D 89-32]*

Baeriswyl-Nicollin, Dominique. Afrika : 45000 KM Abenteuer / Text und Foto, Dominique und Gérald Baeriswyl-Nicollin. Lausanne : Mondo-Verlag, c1983. 148 p. : chiefly ill. (all col.) ; 28 cm. DDC 916/.0448 19
1. Baeriswyl-Nicollin, Dominique. 2. Baeriswyl-Nicollin, Gérald. 3. Africa - Description and travel - 1977-. I. Baeriswyl-Nicollin, Gérald. II. Title.
DT12.25 .B32 1983 **NYPL** *[Sc F 88-67]*

BAERISWYL-NICOLLIN, DOMINIQUE.
Baeriswyl-Nicollin, Dominique. Afrika . Lausanne , c1983. 148 p. : DDC 916/.0448 19
DT12.25 .B32 1983 **NYPL** *[Sc F 88-67]*

Baeriswyl-Nicollin, Gérald. Baeriswyl-Nicollin, Dominique. Afrika . Lausanne , c1983. 148 p. : DDC 916/.0448 19
DT12.25 .B32 1983 **NYPL** *[Sc F 88-67]*

BAERISWYL-NICOLLIN, GÉRALD.
Baeriswyl-Nicollin, Dominique. Afrika . Lausanne , c1983. 148 p. : DDC 916/.0448 19
DT12.25 .B32 1983 **NYPL** *[Sc F 88-67]*

Báez Evertsz, Franc, 1948- Braceros haitianos en la República Dominicana / Franc Báez Evertsz. 2a ed. [Santo Domingo] : Instituto Dominicano de Investigaciones Sociales, c1986. 354 p. : ill., maps ; 23 cm. Bibliography: p. 327-342. DDC 331.6/2/729407293 19

1. Alien labor, Haitian - Dominican Republic. 2. Haitians - Dominican Republic. I. Title.
HD8218.5 .B34 1986   NYPL [JLE 88-5011]

Baez, Joan, 1913- One bowl of porridge : memoirs of Somalia / Joan Baez, Sr. Santa Barbara, Calif. : John Daniel, 1986, c1985. 94 p. : ill. ; 22 cm. ISBN 0-936784-12-1 (pbk.) : DDC 363.8/83/096773 19
1. Food relief - Somalia. 2. Volunteers - Somalia. I. Title.
HV696.F6 B34 1986   NYPL [Sc D 89-333]

Bagaza, Jean-Baptiste. Discours de son Excellence le colonel Jean-Baptiste Bagaza, président de la République du Burundi. Bujumbura : Rébublique du Burundi, Ministère de l'information, Direction générale des publications de presse burundaise, Dépt. de la documentation, 1980. 167 p. : ill. ; 25 cm.
1. Bagaza, Jean-Baptiste. I. Burundi. President (1976- : Bagaza). II. Title.
DT450.853.B34 A5 1980
NYPL [Sc E 88-122]

BAGAZA, JEAN-BAPTISTE.
Bagaza, Jean-Baptiste. Discours de son Excellence le colonel Jean-Baptiste Bagaza, président de la République du Burundi. Bujumbura , 1980. 167 p. :
DT450.853.B34 A5 1980
NYPL [Sc E 88-122]

BAGÉMDER (ETHIOPIA) - ECONOMIC CONDITIONS - CASE STUDIES.
Baker, Jonathan. The rural-urban dichotomy in the developing world . Oslo . 372 p. : ISBN 82-00-07412-9
HC845.Z7 B343 1986   NYPL [JFD 87-3176]

BAGÉMDER (ETHIOPIA) - ECONOMIC CONDITIONS - REGIONAL DISPARITIES - CASE STUDIES.
Baker, Jonathan. The rural-urban dichotomy in the developing world . Oslo . 372 p. : ISBN 82-00-07412-9
HC845.Z7 B343 1986   NYPL [JFD 87-3176]

BAGÉMDER (ETHIOPIA) - SOCIAL CONDITIONS - CASE STUDIES.
Baker, Jonathan. The rural-urban dichotomy in the developing world . Oslo . 372 p. : ISBN 82-00-07412-9
HC845.Z7 B343 1986   NYPL [JFD 87-3176]

BAGIRMI (AFRICAN PEOPLE) see BAGUIRMI (AFRICAN PEOPLE)

BAGUIRMI (AFRICAN PEOPLE)
Princes & serviteurs du royaume . Paris , 1987. 225 p. : ISBN 2-901161-29-4
NYPL [Sc E 88-409]

Bahamas / directed and designed by Hans Johannes Hoefer ; edited by Sara Whittier. 1st ed. Singapore : APA Productions, 1987. 305 p. : ill. (some col.), maps, ports. (some col.) ; 23 cm. (Insight guides) Includes index. ISBN 0-13-056276-9 (pbk.)
1. Bahamas - Description and travel - Guide-books. I. Hoefer, Hans. II. Series.   *NYPL [Sc D 88-477]*

BAHAMAS.
Bothwell, Jean. By sail and wind . London , New York , c1964. 152 p. :
NYPL [Sc D 89-103]
Knights, Ian E. The Bahamas [microform] . London , 1979. 18 p. :
NYPL [Sc Micro R-4108 no.16]

Bahamas. Dept. of Archives. Aspects of slavery, part II : a booklet of the Archives exhibition held in the foyer of the Post Office Building, East Hill Street, 6-25 February, 1984. Nassau, Bahamas : Dept. of Archives, Ministry of Education, [1984] 52 p. : ill. ; 28 cm. "A booklet to commemorate the 150th anniversary of the abolition of slavery"--Cover. "February, 1984." First exhibition booklet, entitled Aspects of slavery, was published in 1974. DDC 306/.362/097296 19
1. Slavery - Bahamas - Exhibitions. 2. Slavery - Bahamas - Emancipation - Exhibition. I. Title. II. Title: Aspects of slavery, part 2.
HT1119.B34 B35 1984   NYPL [Sc F 88-346]

BAHAMAS - DESCRIPTION & TRAVEL.
Defries, Amelia Dorothy, 1882- The Fortunate Islands. London [1929] xxiii, 160 p. DDC 917.296
F1651 .D31   NYPL [Sc D 88-936]

BAHAMAS - DESCRIPTION AND TRAVEL - 1981- - GUIDE-BOOKS.

Moore, James E. Pelican guide to the Bahamas /. Gretna, LA , c1988. 322 p. : ISBN 0-88289-663-6 :   *NYPL [Sc D 89-272]*

BAHAMAS - DESCRIPTION AND TRAVEL - GUIDE-BOOKS.
Bahamas /. Singapore , 1987. 305 p. : ISBN 0-13-056276-9 (pbk.)   *NYPL [Sc D 88-477]*

BAHAMAS - HISTORY.
Bothwell, Jean. By sail and wind . London , New York , c1964. 152 p. :
NYPL [Sc D 89-103]

BAHAMAS - JUVENILE FICTION.
Holdridge, Betty. Island boy /. New York , c1942. 110 p. :   *NYPL [Sc D 88-1181]*

Bahian Carnaval. Crowley, Daniel J., 1921- African myth and black reality in Bahian Carnaval /. [Los Angeles, Calif.] [1984] 47 p. :
NYPL [Sc F 86-281]

Bai-Sharka, Abon. Temne names and proverbs /. Freetown , 1986. 137 p. ;
NYPL [Sc D 89-489]

Baianada .
(3) Gilberto Gil Expresso 2222 /. [Salvador, Brasil?] , 1982. 287 p. ;
NYPL [JMD 83-309]

Baikie, Adamu. The Urban poor in Nigeria /. Ibadan, Nigeria , 1987. xvi, 413 p. : ISBN 978-16-7489-4   *NYPL [Sc D 88-779]*

Los bailes y el teatro de los negros en el folklore de Cuba /. Ortiz Fernández, Fernando, 1881-1969. Habana, Cuba , 1981. 602 p. :
NYPL [JME 82-163]

Bailey, A. Peter. Harlem today : a cultural and visitors guide / A. Peter Bailey ; contributing text, Carol M. Hill, Bob Gumbs. New York : Gumbs & Thomas, c1986. viii, 55 p. : ill. ; 22 cm. Bibliography: p. 52. Presentation copy to the Schomburg Center, with autographs of author and others.   ISBN 0-936073-01-2 (pbk.) :   DDC 917.47/1 19
1. Harlem (New York, N.Y.) - Description - Guide-books. 2. New York (N.Y.) - Description - 1981- - Guide-books. I. Hill, Carol M. II. Gumbs, Bob. III. Title.
F128.68.H3 B3 1986   NYPL [Sc D 88-1402]

Bailey, Frederick Augustus Washington. see Douglass, Frederick, 1817-1895.

Bailey, Hilary. Anderson, Patricia, Dr. Mini bus ride . Mona, Kingston, Jamaica , 1987. vii, 179 p. :   ISBN 976-400-006-1
HE5647.K56 A53x 1987
NYPL [Sc D 89-312]

Le bain des reliques . Rakotoson, Michèle. Paris , c1988. 146 p. ;   ISBN 2-86537-218-9
NYPL [Sc D 89-245]

Baines on the Zambezi eighteen fifty-eight to eighteen fifty-nine. Baines, Thomas, 1820-1875. Baines on the Zambezi 1858 to 1859 /. Johannesburg , c1982. 251 p. :   ISBN 0-909079-17-X (Standard ed.)
NYPL [Sc F 83-34]

Baines on the Zambezi 1858 to 1859 /. Baines, Thomas, 1820-1875. Johannesburg , c1982. 251 p. :   ISBN 0-909079-17-X (Standard ed.)
NYPL [Sc F 83-34]

Baines, Thomas, 1820-1875. Baines on the Zambezi 1858 to 1859 / Edward C. Tabler, Eric Axelson and Elaine N. Katz. Johannesburg : Brenthurst Press, c1982. 251 p. : ill. (some col.) ; 28 cm. (Brenthurst series. 8) Includes index. Bibliography: p. 241-242.   ISBN 0-909079-17-X (Standard ed.)
1. Baines, Thomas, 1820-1875. 2. Zambezi River - Description and travel. 3. Africa, Southern - Description and travel. I. Tabler, Edward C. II. Axelson, Eric. III. Katz, Elaine N. IV. Title. V. Title: Baines on the Zambezi eighteen fifty-eight to eighteen fifty-nine.   *NYPL [Sc F 83-34]*

BAINES, THOMAS, 1820-1875.
Baines, Thomas, 1820-1875. Baines on the Zambezi 1858 to 1859 /. Johannesburg , c1982. 251 p. :   ISBN 0-909079-17-X (Standard ed.)
NYPL [Sc F 83-34]

Bakari, Ishaq Imruh. Sounds & echoes / by Ishaq Imruh Bakari. 1st ed. London : Karnak House 1980. 45 p. ; 21 cm. On cover : Ishaq Imruh Bakari (Imruh Caesar).   ISBN 0-907015-01-8
1. Title. II. Title: Sounds and echoes.
NYPL [Sc D 88-492]

Bakel, Elimane. Bonjour monsieur le ministre : théâtre pour rire / Elimane Bakel.Ed. originale. Paris : Silex, c1983. 75 p. ; 22 cm.   ISBN 2-903871-21-3
1. Title.
MLCS 86/6370 (P)   NYPL [Sc D 88-1036]

Baker, Augusta.
(comp) The golden lynx and other tales, [1st ed.] Philadelphia, Lippincott [1960] 160 p. illus. 23 cm. SCHOMBURG CHILDREN'S COLLECTION.
1. Fairy tales. I. Schomburg Children's Collection. II. Title.
PZ8.1.B172 Go   NYPL [Sc D 88-1492]
Rollins, Charlemae Hill. We build together. [Champaign, Ill. , 1967] xxviii, 71 p. ; DDC 016.818
Z1361.N39 R77 1967   NYPL [Sc D 89-387]
Storytelling : art and technique / by Augusta Baker and Ellin Greene.2nd ed. New York : Bowker, 1987. xvii, 182 p. : ill. ; 24 cm. Includes index. Bibliography: p. 133-168. ISBN 0-8352-2336-1 DDC 808.06/8543 19
1. Storytelling - United States. I. Greene, Ellin, 1927-. II. Title. III. Title: Story telling.
LB1042 .B34 1987   NYPL [Sc E 89-46]

Baker, Houston A.
Afro-American poetics : revisions of Harlem and the Black aesthetic / Houston A. Baker, Jr. Madison, Wis. : University of Wisconsin Press, c1988. x, 201 p. ; ports. : Includes index. Bibliography: p. 181-191. ISBN 0-299-11500-3 : DDC 810/.9/896073 19
1. American literature - Afro-American authors - History and criticism. 2. American literature - 20th century - History and criticism. 3. Afro-Americans in literature. 4. Afro-Americans - Aesthetics. 5. Harlem Renaissance. I. Title. II. Title: Afroamerican poetics.
PS153.N5 B22 1988   NYPL [Sc D 88-1356]
Black feminist criticism and critical theory /. Greenwood, Fla. , c1988. iii, 202 p. ; ISBN 0-913283-25-8   *NYPL [Sc D 88-1394]*

Baker, Jonathan. The rural-urban dichotomy in the developing world : a case study from northern Ethiopia / Jonathan Baker. Oslo : Norwegian University Press : Oxford ; 372 p. : ill. ; 23 cm. Bibliography: p. [365]-372.   ISBN 82-00-07412-9
1. Cities and towns - Ethiopia - Bagémder - Case studies. 2. Urbanization - Ethiopia - Bagémder - Case studies. 3. Rural-urban migration - Ethiopia - Bagémder - Case studies. 4. Bagémder (Ethiopia) - Economic conditions - Case studies. 5. Bagémder (Ethiopia) - Social conditions - Case studies. 6. Bagémder (Ethiopia) - Economic conditions - Regional disparities - Case studies. I. Title.
HC845.Z7 B343 1986   NYPL [JFD 87-3176]

Baker, Josephine, 1906-1975.
Josephine / by Josephine Baker and Jo Bouillon ; translated from the French by Mariana Fitzpatrick. 1st paperback ed. New York : Paragon House, 1988, c1977. xiii, 302 p., [16] p. of plates : ill. ; 24 cm. Reprint. Originally published: New York : Harper & Row, c1977. Includes index. ISBN 1-557-78108-7 (pbk.) DDC 793.3/2/0924 B 19
1. Baker, Josephine, 1906-1975. 2. Dancers - France - Biography. I. Bouillon, Jo, 1908-. II. Title.
GV1785.B3 A3 1988   NYPL [Sc D 88-1476]

BAKER, JOSEPHINE, 1906-1975.
Baker, Josephine, 1906-1975. Josephine /. New York , 1988, c1977. xiii, 302 p., [16] p. of plates : ISBN 1-557-78108-7 (pbk.) DDC 793.3/2/0924 B 19
GV1785.B3 A3 1988   NYPL [Sc D 88-1476]

BAKER, JOSEPHINE, 1906-1975 - HOMES AND HAUNTS.
Groenendijk, Paul. Adolf Loos . Rotterdam , 1985. 39 p., [6] leaves of plates :   ISBN 90-6450-027-4   DDC 728.3/72/0228 19
NA1011.5.L6 G76 1985   NYPL [Sc F 89-67]

Baker, Philip.
International guide to African studies research = Etudes africaines : guide international de recherches / edited by the International African Institute ; compiled by Philip Baker.2nd fully rev. and expanded ed. London ; New York : Published for the International African Institute [by] H. Zell, 1987. 264 p. ; 24 cm. Key to symbols located on pull-out flap inside the back cover. Introductory matter in English and French. Previous ed. (1975) published as: International guide to African studies research = Etudes africaines : guide

international de recherches / International African Research Institute, Research Information Liaison Unit. Includes indexes. ISBN 0-905450-25-6
1. Africa - Study and teaching - Directories. I. Title. II. Title: Etudes africaines. **NYPL [Sc E 88-218]**

Mann, Michael. A thesaurus of African languages . New York , 1987. 325 p. ; ISBN 0-905450-24-8 **NYPL [Sc F 88-142]**

Morisyen - English - français : diksyoner kreol morisyen = dictionary of Mauritian Creole = dictionnaire du créole mauricien / Philip Baker, Vinesh Y. Hookoomsing. Paris : Éditions L'Harmattan, 1987. 365 p. ; 24 cm. Bibliography: p. 355-361. ISBN 2-85802-973-3
1. Creole dialects, French - Mauritius - Dictionaries - English. 2. Creole dialects, French - Mauritius - Dictionaries - French. I. Hookoomsing, Vinesh Y. II. Title. III. Title: Diksyoner kreol morisyen.
NYPL [Sc E 88-407]

Baker, Richard St. Barbe, 1889- Sahara conquest. London, Lutterworth P., 1966. 186 p. 16 plates (incl. ports., map) 18 cm. DDC 333.7/3/096
1. Reclamation of land - Sahara. 2. Natural resources - Africa. 3. Sahara - Description and travel. I. Title.
S616.S16 B3 **NYPL [Sc C 88-117]**

Baker, Tod A. Blacks in southern politics /. New York , 1987. vii, 305 p. ; ISBN 0-275-92655-9 (alk. paper) : DDC 323.1/196073/075 19
E185.92 .B58 1987 **NYPL [Sc E 88-196]**

Baker's dozen : abstracts of 13 doctoral dissertations completed under Manpower Administration research grants. Washington : U. S. Dept. of Labor, Manpower Administration : For sale by The Supt. of Docs., U. S. G. P. O., [1973] 112 p. ; 26 cm. (Manpower research monograph . no. 27) "Editors ... are Allen Abrahamson ... Susan Ghozeil ... and Barry Bainton."
1. Dissertations, Academic - United States - Abstracts. 2. Labor supply - United States. 3. Minorities - Employment - United States. I. Series.
NYPL [Sc F 88-244]

Baking in the sun : visionary images from the South : selections from the collection of Sylvia and warren Lowe. 1st ed. Lafayette : University Art Museum, University of Southwestern Louisiana, c1987. 146 p. : Ill. (some col.), ports. ; 28 cm. Published in connection with an exhibition held at the University Art Museum, Lafayette, La., June 13-July 31, 1987, and scheduled for other locations through Nov. 27, 1988. Exhibition organized by Herman Mhire, director, University Art Museum. Bibliography: p. 144. PARTIAL CONTENTS. - Foreword / Herman Mhire - Aspects of visionary art / Andy Nasisse - Africanisms in Afro-American visionary arts / Maude Southwell Wahlman. ISBN 0-295-96606-8
1. Lowe, Sylvia - Art collections. 2. Lowe, Warren - Art collections. 3. Folk art - Southern States - Exhibitions. 4. Afro-American folk art - Southern States Exhibitions. 5. Eccentrics and eccentricities in art - Exhibitions. I. Mhire, Herman. II. Nasisse, Andy. III. Wahlman, Maude Southwell. IV. University of Southwestern Louisiana. University Art Museum. V. Title. **NYPL [Sc F 88-197]**

BAKKE, ALLAN PAUL - TRIALS, LITIGATION, ETC.
Schwartz, Bernard, 1923- Behind Bakke . New York , c1988. x, 266 p. ; ISBN 0-8147-7878-X : DDC 347.73/0798 347.304798 19
KF228.B34 S39 1988 **NYPL [JLE 88-4158]**

Baku, Shango.
One bad casa. Baku, Shango. 3 plays of our time / by Shango Baku. 1st ed. Belmont, Trinidad , 1984. 116 p. ;
NYPL [Sc D 88-971]

Revo! Baku, Shango. 3 plays of our time / by Shango Baku. 1st ed. Belmont, Trinidad , 1984. 116 p. ; **NYPL [Sc D 88-971]**

Ruby my dear. Baku, Shango. 3 plays of our time / by Shango Baku. 1st ed. Belmont, Trinidad , 1984. 116 p. ;
NYPL [Sc D 88-971]

3 plays of our time / by Shango Baku. 1st ed. Belmont, Trinidad : Baku Publications, 1984. 116 p. ; 21 cm. CONTENTS. - Revo! - Ruby my dear - One bad casa.
1. West Indies - Drama. I. Baku, Shango. Revo!. II. Baku, Shango. Ruby my dear. III. Baku, Shango. One bad casa. IV. Title. V. Title: Three plays of our time. VI. Title: Revo!. VII. Title: Ruby my dear. VIII. Title: One bad casa. **NYPL [Sc D 88-971]**

Bakwena, Stella. Women in development . Gaborone , 1984. 49, 4 p. :
NYPL [Sc F 88-116]

BALANCE OF NATURE. see ECOLOGY.

BALANDIER, GEORGES.
Afrique plurielle, Afrique actuelle . Paris , c1986. 272 p. ; ISBN 2-86537-151-4
NYPL [Sc E 88-349]

Baldé de Labé, Sirah. D'un Fouta-Djalloo à l'autre / Sirah Baldé de Labé. Paris : Pensée universelle, c1985- v. ; 18 cm. ISBN 2-214-06108-8 (v. 1) : DDC 843 19
1. Africa - Fiction. I. Title.
PQ3989.2.B26 D86 1985
NYPL [Sc C 88 103]

Baldwin, James, 1924-
BALDWIN, JAMES, 1924- - CRITICISM AND INTERPRETATION.
Critical essays on James Baldwin /. Boston, Mass. , 1988. ix, 312 p. ; ISBN 0-8161-8879-3 DDC 818/.5409 19
PS3552.A45 Z88 1988 **NYPL [JFE 88-2203]**

Porter, Horace A., 1950- Stealing the fire . Middletown, Conn. , Scranton, Pa. , c1989. xviii, 220 p. ; ISBN 0-8195-5197-X : DDC 818/.5409 19
PS3552.A45 Z85 1989 **NYPL [Sc D 89-468]**

Of the sorrow songs. New Edinburgh review anthology / edited by James Campbell. Edinburgh , 1982. 203 p. ; ISBN 0-904919-56-0 : DDC 082 19
AC5 .N37 1982 **NYPL [Sc D 88-1056]**

BALDWIN, JAMES, 1924- - BIOGRAPHY - JUVENILE LITERATURE.
Rosset, Lisa. James Baldwin /. New York, N.Y. , 1989. 111 p. : ISBN 1-555-46572-2 DDC 818/.5409 B 92 19
PS3552.A45 Z87 1989 **NYPL [Sc E 89-224]**

Baldwin, Lindley. J. The march of faith : the challenge of Samuel Morris to undying life and leadership. / by Lindley J. Baldwin.Victory Center ed. Bronx, N.Y. : Distributed by Soldiers for Christ, 1944. 94 p. : ill., port. ; 20 cm. distributed from stamp on t.p.
1. Morris, Samuel, 1873-1893. I. Title.
NYPL [Sc C 88-13]

Baleine, Philippe de. Goulphin, Fred. Les Veillées de chase d'Henri Guizard /. [Paris] , 1987. 235 p. ; ISBN 2-08-065054-8 **NYPL [Sc D 88-28]**

Balet, Jan B., 1913- (illus) Brothers, Aileen. Just one me . Chicago , c1967. 32 p. :
NYPL [Sc D 88-376]

Ball, Dorothy Whitney. Hurricane : the story of a friendship / by Dorothy Whitney Ball. Indianapolis : Bobbs-Merrill, [c1964] 147 p. ; 22 cm.
1. Afro-American youth - Florida - Juvenile fiction. 2. Florida - Juvenile fiction. I. Title.
NYPL [Sc D 88-486]

Ball, Thomas E. Julian Bond vs John Lewis : on the campaign trail with John Lewis & Julian Bond / by Thomas E. Ball.[Limited copy ed.] Atlanta, Ga. : W.H. Wolfe, 1988. ix, 144 p. : ill., ports. ; 24 cm. Includes index. ISBN 0-9621362-0-4
1. Bond, Julian, 1940-. 2. Lewis, John. 3. United States. Congress. House - Contested elections. 4. Atlanta (Ga.) - Politics and government. I. Title.
NYPL [Sc E 88-582]

Balliett, Whitney. American singers : twenty-seven portraits in song / Whitney Balliett. New York : Oxford University Press, 1988. x, 244 p. ; 25 cm. ISBN 0-19-504610-2 (alk. paper) DDC 784.5 B 19
1. Singers - United States - Biography. 2. Jazz musicians - United States - Biography. I. Title.
ML400 .B25 1988 **NYPL [JNE 88-46]**

Balling, Adalbert Ludwig. Wo Menschen lachen und sich frauen : Begegnungen in der Dritten Welt / Adalbert Ludwig Balling.Originalausgabe. Freiburg im Breisgau : Herder, c1986. 126 p. ; 19 cm. (Herderbücherei. Bd. 1297) ISBN 3-451-08297-7
1. Christianity - Africa, Sub-Saharan. 2. Christianity - Brazil. I. Title. **NYPL [Sc C 89-125]**

A balloon for grandad /. Gray, Nigel. London , New York , 1988. [30] p. : ISBN 0-531-05755-0 : DDC [E] 19
PZ7.G7813 Bal 1988 **NYPL [Sc F 88-345]**

BALLOONS - JUVENILE FICTION.
Gray, Nigel. A balloon for grandad /. London , New York , 1988. [30] p. : ISBN 0-531-05755-0 : DDC [E] 19
PZ7.G7813 Bal 1988 **NYPL [Sc F 88-345]**

Haywood, Carolyn, 1898- Away went the balloons. New York, 1973. 189 p. ISBN 0-688-20057-5 DDC [Fic]
PZ7.H31496 Aw **NYPL [Sc D 89-113]**

Balmes, Jaime Luciano, 1810-1848.
[Protestantismo comparado con el catolicismo en sus relaciones con la civilización europea. Selections. Portuguese]
A Igreja católica em face da escravidão / Jaime Balmes ; tradução de José G. M. Orsini. São Paulo : Centro Brasileiro de Fomento Cultural, 1988. 141 p. ; 21 cm. "Adendo : A Igreja e a escravidão no Brasil / José Geraldo Vidigal de Carvalho." Translation of: El protestantismo comparado con el catolicismo en sus relaciones con la civilização européia, ch. 14-19. Bibliography: p. 133-135.
1. Slavery and the church - Catholic church - History. 2. Slavery - Brazil. 3. Catholic Church - Brazil. I. Carvalho, José Geraldo Vidigal de. Igreja e a escravidão no Brasil. II. Orsini, José G. M. III. Title.
NYPL [Sc D 89-554]

Balsvik, Randi Rønning. Haile Sellassie's students : the intellectual and social background to revolution, 1952-1977 / by Randi Rønning Balsvik. East Lansing, Mich. : African Studies Center, Michigan State University in cooperation with the Norwegian Council of Science and the Humanities, c1985. xix, 363 p. : map ; 23 cm. (Monograph / Committee on Northeast African Studies . no. 16) Includes index. Bibliography: p. 321-354. DDC 378/.198/0963 19
1. Haile Sellassie I University - Students - History. 2. Student movements - Ethiopia - History. 3. College students - Ethiopia - Political activity - History. 4. Education, Higher - Ethiopia - History. 5. Ethiopia - History - 1889-1974. I. Series: Monograph (Michigan State University. Committee on Northeast African Studies) , no. 16. II. Title.
LA1518.7 .B35 1985 **NYPL [Sc D 88-1403]**

BALTIMORE (MD.) - GENEALOGY.
Clayton, Ralph. Black Baltimore, 1820-1870 /. Bowie, MD , 1987. vii, 199 p. : ISBN 1-556-13080-5 (pbk.) : DDC 929/.3/0899607307526 19
F189.B19 N42 1987
NYPL [APR (Baltimore) 88-868]

BALTIMORE (MD.) - POPULATION.
Clayton, Ralph. Black Baltimore, 1820-1870 /. Bowie, MD , 1987. vii, 199 p. : ISBN 1-556-13080-5 (pbk.) : DDC 929/.3/0899607307526 19
F189.B19 N42 1987
NYPL [APR (Baltimore) 88-868]

Bamba Ndombasi Kifimba, 1937- Anthologie des sculpteurs et peintres zaïrois contemporains / Bamba Ndombasi Kufimba, Musangi Ntemo. Paris : Nathan : Agence de Coopération Culturelle et Technique, 1987. 109 p. : ill. (some col.), ports. ; 31 cm. Bibliography: p. 109. ISBN 2-09-168350-7
1. Art, Zarian. 2. Art, Modern - 20th century - Zaire. 3. Artists - Zaire. I. Musangi Ntemo, 1946-. II. Title.
NYPL [Sc G 88-11]

BAMBARA (AFRICAN PEOPLE)
Brüggemann, Anne. Amagdala und Akawuruk . Hohenschäftlarn bei München , 1986. 264 p. : ISBN 3-87673-106-2 **NYPL [Sc D 88-652]**

BAMBARA LANGUAGE - TEXTS.
Silamaka fara dikko . Berlin , 1988. xi, 271 p., 1 folded page : ISBN 3-496-00961-6
NYPL [Sc E 88-230]

Bamboté, Makombo, 1932- Coup d'état nègre : récit / Makombo Bamboté. [Montréal] : Humanitas Nouvelle optique, 1987. 117 p. ; 21 cm. ISBN 2-9800950-7-9 : DDC 843 19
1. Central African Republic - History - 1960-. I. Title.
NYPL [Sc D 89-114]

Bamgbose, Ayo. Yoruba : a language in transition / Ayo Bamgbose ; edited with an introduction by Olatunde O Olatunji. Lagos, Nigeria : J.F. Odunjo Memorial Lectures Organising Committee, 1986. xvii, 83 p. ; 22 cm. (J.F. Odunjo memorial lectures series . no. 1) Includes bibliographical references.
1. Yoruba language - History. I. Olatúnjí, Olatúndé O. II. Title. III. Series. **NYPL [Sc D 88-1091]**

BAMOUN (CAMEROON) - COURT AND COURTIERS - PICTORIAL WORKS.
Geary, Christraud M. Images from Bamum .
Washington, D.C. , 1988. 151 p. : ISBN
0-87474-455-5 (pbk. : alk. paper) DDC
967/.1102/0880621 19
DT574 .G43 1988   *NYPL [Sc F 89-55]*

BAMUM (AFRICAN PEOPLE)
Geary, Christraud M. Mandou Yénou .
München , c1985. 223 p. : ISBN 3-923804-08-3
                    NYPL [Sc E 88-178]

BAMUM (AFRICAN PEOPLE) - PICTORIAL WORKS.
Geary, Christraud M. Mandou Yénou .
München , c1985. 223 p. : ISBN 3-923804-08-3
                    NYPL [Sc E 88-178]

BAMUM (AFRICAN TRIBE)
Princes & serviteurs du royaume . Paris , 1987.
225 p. : ISBN 2-901161-29-4
                    NYPL [Sc E 88-409]

BAMUN (AFRICAN PEOPLE) - HISTORY.
Ndam Njoya, Adamou, 1942- Njoya . Paris (9,
rue du Château-d'Eau, 75010) : Dakar ; [116]
p. : ISBN 2-85809-101-3 : DDC 967/.113 B 19
DT570 .N22   *NYPL [Sc C 88-162]*

BAMUN (AFRICAN PEOPLE) - KINGS AND RULERS - BIOGRAPHY.
Ndam Njoya, Adamou, 1942- Njoya . Paris (9,
rue du Château-d'Eau, 75010) : Dakar ; [116]
p. : ISBN 2-85809-101-3 : DDC 967/.113 B 19
DT570 .N22   *NYPL [Sc C 88-162]*

Bamunoba, Y. K. Mort dans la vie africaine.
Spanish. La Muerte en la vida africana.
Barcelona , París , 1984. 314 p. : ISBN
84-85800-81-8   *NYPL [Sc D 88-601]*

Ban empty barn . Onwueme, Tess Akaeke.
Owerri, Nigeria , 1986. 145 p. ; ISBN
978-244-909-4   *NYPL [Sc C 88-202]*

BANANA TRADE - WINDWARD ISLANDS.
Thomson, Robert. Green gold . London , 1987.
vii, 93 p. : ISBN 0-906156-26-2
                    NYPL [Sc D 88-66]

Banda desenhada .
(3) Motta, Helena. Moçambique por Eduardo
Mondlane /. [Maputo?] [1984] 86 p. : DDC
967/.903/0222 19
DT463 .M64 1984   *NYPL [Sc F 89-172]*

Banda, Hastings Kamuzu, 1905- Address by His
Excellency the Life President, Ngwazi Dr. H.
Kamuzu Banda, to open the 1978 convention of
the Malaŵi Congress Party, Zomba Catholic
Secondary School, September 24, 1978
[microform] Blantyre : Dept. of Information,
[1978] 16 p. ; 25 cm. On cover: His Excellency the
Life President's speeches. Microfiche. New York: New
York Public Library, 198 . 1 microfiche: negative; 11 x
15 cm. (FSN Sc 019,149)
*1. Malawi - Politics and government - 1964-. I. Malawi
Congress Party. II. Title.*
          NYPL [Sc Micro F-11123]

BANDI (LIBERIAN PEOPLE) see GBANDI (LIBERIAN PEOPLE)

Bangou, Henri. Les voies de la souveraineté :
peuplement et institutions à la Guadeloupe (des
origines a nos jours) / Henri Bangou. Paris :
Editions Caribéennes, c1988. 144 p. ; 23 cm.
(Collection Parti-pris) Includes bibliographical footnotes.
ISBN 2-87679-021-1
*1. Guadeloupe - History. 2. Guadeloupe - Race
relations. 3. Guadeloupe - Politics and government. 4.
Guadeloupe - Economic conditions. I. Title.*
          NYPL [Sc D 88-1001]

Bangura, Ibrahim. Temne stories and songs /.
Freetown, Sierra Leone , 1986. 96 p. :
                    NYPL [Sc D 89-427]

The bangy book . Vincent, Alan W. Berlin , 1988.
[80] p. : ISBN 3-924040-62-1
                    NYPL [Sc F 89-115]

Banjo, A. O. Social science libraries in West
Africa : a directory / A. O. Bango. Lagos,
Nigeria : Nigerian Institute of International
Affairs, 1987. iii, 63 p. : map ; 21 cm. (NIIA
monograph series. no. 13) Includes index.
*1. Social science libraries - Africa, West - Directories. I.
Title. II. Series.*   *NYPL [Sc D 88-1204]*

Banjo, A. Olugboyega. Nigerian Institute of
International Affairs, 1961-1986 : the story so
far / by A.O. Banjo. Lagos : Nigerian Institute
of International Affairs, 1986. iv, 34 p. : ill.,

ports. ; 25 cm. (NIIA monograph series. no.12)
Bibliography: p. 29.
*I. Title. II. Title: Nigerian Institute of International
Affairs, 1961-1986. III. Series.*
                    NYPL [Sc E 89-254]

BANK EMPLOYEES - NIGERIA.
Omobuarie, D. O. The cashier and his rubber
stamp /. Benin City, Nigeria , 1987. 79 p. ;
  ISBN 978-300-321-6 *NYPL [Sc D 88-738]*

BANK ROBBERIES - KENYA.
Kimani, John Kiggia. Life and times of a bank
robber /. Nairobi , 1988. 133 p. ; ISBN
996-646-376-3   *NYPL [Sc C 89-97]*

BANK TELLERS.
Omobuarie, D. O. The cashier and his rubber
stamp /. Benin City, Nigeria , 1987. 79 p. ;
  ISBN 978-300-321-6 *NYPL [Sc D 88-738]*

BANKING. see BANKS AND BANKING.

BANKS. see BANKS AND BANKING.

BANKS AND BANKING - NIGERIA.
Adekanye, Femi. The elements of banking /.
Leighton Buzzard [1984] xxvi, 461 p. : ISBN
0-907721-19-2 (pbk) *NYPL [Sc D 88-1139]*

BANKS AND BANKING - NIGERIA - FICTION.
Umobuarie, D. O. Adventures of a bank
inspector /. Nigeria , 1988. 168 p. ; ISBN
978-300-323-2   *NYPL [Sc C 88-339]*

BANKS AND BANKING - TRINIDAD AND TOBAGO - HISTORY.
Republic Bank (Trinidad and Tobago) From
Colonial to Republic . Port-of-Spain, Trinidad,
W.I. [1987] xxii, 206 p. : ISBN 976-8054-05-0
                    NYPL [Sc F 89-119]

BANNED PERSONS (SOUTH AFRICA) - BIOGRAPHY - JUVENILE LITERATURE.
Haskins, James, 1941- Winnie Mandela . New
York , c1988. 179 p., [12] p. of plates : ISBN
0-399-21515-8 DDC 968.06/092/4 B 92 19
DT779.955.M36 H38 1988
                    NYPL [Sc D 88-1138]

BANNEKER, BENJAMIN, 1731-1806 - JUVENILE LITERATURE.
Ferris, Jeri. What are you figuring now? .
Minneapolis , c1988. 64 p. : ISBN 0-87614-331-1
(lib. bdg.) : DDC 520.92/4 B 92 19
QB36.B22 F47 1988   *NYPL [Sc D 89-120]*

Banner, Warren M. Have you got it? :
avez-vous? : ebony and ivory / by Warren M.
Banner.1st ed. New York : Vantage Press,
c1987. x, 371 p. ; 24 cm. ISBN 0-533-07057-0
1. Afro-Americans - Fiction. I. Title.
                    NYPL [Sc E 89-68]

BANNERS. see FLAGS.

Bantoetuislande, South Africa. see Homelands, South Africa.

Banton, Michael P. Racial consciousness /
Michael Banton. London ; New York :
Longman, 1988. ix, 153 p. : ill. ; 23 cm. Includes
index. Bibliography: p. 147-150. ISBN 0-582-02385-8
DDC 305.8 19
1. Race. 2. Race awareness. I. Title.
GN269 .B36 1988   *NYPL [Sc D 89-123]*

Bantu Homelands, South Africa. see Homelands, South Africa.

BANTU LANGUAGES - ADDRESSES, ESSAYS, LECTURES.
Etudes sur le bantu oriental . Paris , 1982 [i.e.
1983] 158 p. : ISBN 2-85297-144-5 : DDC
496/.39 19
PL8025 .E84 1983   *NYPL [Sc E 88-357]*

BANTU LANGUAGES - POSSESSIVES.
Stappers, Leo. Substitutiv und Possessiv im
Bantu /. Berlin [1986] xix, 223 p. : ISBN
3-496-00877-6 DDC 496/.3 19
PL8025.1 .S73 1986   *NYPL [Sc E 88-360]*

BANTU LANGUAGES - PRONOUN.
Stappers, Leo. Substitutiv und Possessiv im
Bantu /. Berlin [1986] xix, 223 p. : ISBN
3-496-00877-6 DDC 496/.3 19
PL8025.1 .S73 1986   *NYPL [Sc E 88-360]*

Bantustans, South Africa. see Homelands, South Africa.

Bañuelos, Juan.
[Poems. Selections]
Poesía / Juan Bañuelos ; selección de Raúl
Hernández Novás. La Habana : Casa de las

Américas, c1987. 58 p. ; 19 cm. (Cuadernos de
la honda)
I. Title.   *NYPL [Sc C 89-41]*

Banza-Lute : 25 ans de présence chrétienne /
[Belengi Nzileyel ... et al.]. Bandundu,
République du Zaïre : [CEEBA], 1983. 251 p. :
ill. ; 27 cm. (Ceeba publications. Série II . vol. 90)
DDC 282/.67513 19
*1. Catholic Church - Zaire - Banza-Lute - History. 2.
Banza-Lute (Zaire) - Church history. 3. Banza-Lute -
Religious life and customs. I. Belengi Nzileyel, 1934-.
II. Series: Publications (Ceeba). Série II , v. 90.*
BX1682.C6 B36 1983   *NYPL [Sc F 89-38]*

BANZA-LUTE - RELIGIOUS LIFE AND CUSTOMS.
Banza-Lute . Bandundu, République du Zaïre ,
1983. 251 p. : DDC 282/.67513 19
BX1682.C6 B36 1983   *NYPL [Sc F 89-38]*

BANZA-LUTE (ZAIRE) - CHURCH HISTORY.
Banza-Lute . Bandundu, République du Zaïre ,
1983. 251 p. : DDC 282/.67513 19
BX1682.C6 B36 1983   *NYPL [Sc F 89-38]*

BAOULÉ (AFRICAN PEOPLE)
Debouvry, Pierre. Contribution à la définition
d'une méthodologie de transfert de populations
paysannes . [Montpellier] [1985] 294 p. :
  ISBN 0-85352-039-0 *NYPL [Sc F 88-302]*

BAPTISTS, AFRO-AMERICAN. see AFRO-AMERICAN BAPTISTS.

BAPTISTS - HYMNS.
Gospel pearls . Nashville, Tenn. , c1921. [152]
p. :   *NYPL [Sc C 86-222]*

BAPTISTS - UNITED STATES - CLERGY - BIOGRAPHY.
Colaiaco, James A., 1945- Martin Luther King,
Jr. . New York , 1988. x, 238 p. ; ISBN
0-312-02365-0 DDC 323.4/092/4 B 19
E185.97.K5 C65 1988   *NYPL [Sc D 89-231]*

Barakat, Halim Isber. Contemporary North
Africa . London , c1985. 271 p. ; ISBN
0-7099-3435-1 : DDC 961 19
DT181.5 .C66 1985b *NYPL [Sc D 88-1017]*

BARBADIAN POETRY.
Worrell, Vernon, 1952- Under the flambo .
Bridgetown, Barbados , 1986. ix, 84 p. : DDC
811 19
PR9230.9.W67 U5 1986
                    NYPL [Sc D 88-945]

Barbados /. Potter, Robert B. Oxford, England ,
Santa Barbara, Calif. , c1987. xxxix, 356 p., [1]
leaf of plates : ISBN 1-85109-022-3
                    NYPL [HRG 87-2371]

BARBADOS - BIBLIOGRAPHY.
Potter, Robert B. Barbados /. Oxford, England ,
Santa Barbara, Calif. , c1987. xxxix, 356 p., [1]
leaf of plates : ISBN 1-85109-022-3
                    NYPL [HRG 87-2371]

BARBADOS - BIOGRAPHY.
Stoute, Edward. Glimpses of old Barbados /.
[Barbados] , 1986. 156 p. ;
                    NYPL [Sc D 88-394]

Barbados comes of age . Hoyos, Alexander, Sir.
London , 1987. ix, 70 p. : ISBN 0-333-43819-1
(pbk) DDC 972.98/1 19
F2041   *NYPL [Sc E 88-326]*

BARBADOS - DESCRIPTION AND TRAVEL.
Stoute, Edward. Glimpses of old Barbados /.
[Barbados] , 1986. 156 p. ;
                    NYPL [Sc D 88-394]

BARBADOS - FICTION.
Callender, Timothy. The watchman /. [St.
Michael, Barbados? , 1978?] [28] p. :
                    NYPL [Sc F 89-52]

BARBADOS - HISTORY.
Hoyos, Alexander, Sir. Barbados comes of age .
London , 1987. ix, 70 p. : ISBN 0-333-43819-1
(pbk) DDC 972.98/1 19
F2041   *NYPL [Sc E 88-326]*

O'Callaghan, Evelyn. The earliest patriots .
London , 1986. 61 p. ; ISBN 0-946918-53-8pb
                    NYPL [Sc C 88-104]

Stoute, Edward. Glimpses of old Barbados /.
[Barbados] , 1986. 156 p. ;
                    NYPL [Sc D 88-394]

BARBADOS - POETRY.
Hawkins, Kathleen. Barbados 1900-1950 .

[S.1.] 1986 (Barbados : Letchworth Press) 23 p. :   **NYPL [Sc D 88-1184]**

Worrell, Vernon, 1952- Under the flambo . Bridgetown, Barbados , 1986. ix, 84 p. : DDC 811 19
PR9230.9.W67 U5 1986
                    NYPL [Sc D 88-945]

Barbados 1900-1950 . Hawkins, Kathleen. [S.1.] 1986 (Barbados : Letchworth Press) 23 p. :
                    NYPL [Sc D 88-1184]

Barbareschi Fino, Maria Antonietta. Il samba : folklore negro M.A. Barbareschi Fino. Milano : G. Miano, 1979. 63 p. ; 21 cm. (Narratori del nostro tempo) CONTENTS. - Josepha.--A companheira.--Il mercato di Caruarù.--La grande illusione.--Magia negra.--I pescecani.
1. Brazil - Fiction. I. Title. **NYPL [Sc D 89-187]**

Barbarie-l'espoir /. Valtis, Laureine. Paris , c1986. 135 p. ; ISBN 2-903871-76-0
MLCS 87/1686 (P)   **NYPL [Sc D 88-232]**

Barbary States. see Africa, North.

The barber's nine children /. Dangana, Yahaya S. Yaba, Lagos , 1987. 17 p. ; ISBN 978-13-2850-9
                    NYPL [Sc C 89-24]

Barbosa, Rogério Andrade. La-le-li-lo-luta : um professor brasileiro na Guiné-Bissau / Rogério Andrade Barbosa. Rio de Janeiro : Achiamé, 1984. 124 p. ; 21 cm. Bibliography: p. 121-124. DDC 371.1/0092/4 B 19
1. Barbosa, Rogério Andrade. 2. Teachers - Brazil - Biography. 3. Education - Guinea-Bissau. 4. Guinea-Bissau - Social conditions. I. Title.
LA2365.B72 B37 1984 **NYPL [Sc D 88-284]**

BARBOSA, ROGÉRIO ANDRADE.
Barbosa, Rogério Andrade. La-le-li-lo-luta . Rio de Janeiro , 1984. 124 p. ; DDC 371.1/0092/4 B 19
LA2365.B72 B37 1984 **NYPL [Sc D 88-284]**

Bardelli, Raimondo. Centro Africa : una giovane Chiesa alla ricerca della sua identità / Raimondo Bardelli. Bologna : Editrice missionaria italiana, 1979. 258 p. : ill. ; 20 cm. Bibliography: p. 255-258.
1. Christianity - Africa, Central. I. Title.
                    NYPL [Sc C 87-359]

Bardill, John E. Class formation and class struggle . [Roma? Lesotho] [1982] 211 p. ;
                    NYPL [Sc D 89-25]

BARI, DJIBRIL ABDOULAYE.
Bari, Nadine. Noces d'absence /. Paris , c1986. 119 p., [8] p. of plates : ISBN 2-227-12607-8
                    NYPL [Sc D 89-61]

Bari, Nadine. Noces d'absence / Nadine Bari. Paris : Centurion, c1986. 119 p., [8] p. of plates : ill., ports. ; 22 cm. Includes bibliographical references. ISBN 2-227-12607-8
1. Bari, Djibril Abdoulaye. 2. Political prisoners - Guinea. 3. Political persecution - Guinea. 4. Guinea - Politics and government - 1958-1984. I. Title.
                    NYPL [Sc D 89-61]

BARINGO DISTRICT (KENYA)
Socio-cultural profiles, Baringo District . [Nairobi?] , 1986. xviii, 268 p. : DDC 967.6/27 19
DT434.B36 S63 1986   **NYPL [Sc F 88-230]**

BARINGO DISTRICT (KENYA) - SOCIAL LIFE AND CUSTOMS.
Socio-cultural profiles, Baringo District . [Nairobi?] , 1986. xviii, 268 p. : DDC 967.6/27 19
DT434.B36 S63 1986   **NYPL [Sc F 88-230]**

Barker, Carol. Village in Nigeria / text and photographs by Carol Barker. London : Black, c1984 25 p. : col. ill. ; 22 cm. (Beans. Geography) Twelve-year-old Thaddeus, son of a doctor with six wives, describes life in his Nigerian village. SCHOMBURG CHILDREN'S COLLECTION. ISBN 0-7136-2391-8 : DDC 966.9/05 19
1. Nigeria - Social life and customs - Juvenile literature. I. Schomburg Children's Collection. II. Title. III. Series.
DT515.8 .B29 1984   **NYPL [Sc D 88-605]**

Barnett, Moneta.
(illus) Elting, Mary, 1909- A Mongo homecoming. New York [1969] 54 p. DDC 309.1/675
DT644 .E4   **NYPL [Sc E 88-578]**

Greenfield, Eloise. First pink light /. New York , c1976. [39] p. : ISBN 0-690-01087-7

DDC [E]
PZ7.G845 Fi   **NYPL [Sc D 89-60]**

Barns, Thomas Alexander, 1880- Across the great craterland to the Congo : sequel to The Wonderland of the Eastern Congo / by T. Alexander Barns ; with an introduction by J.W. Gregory. London : E. Benn, 1923. 271, [1] p., [64] leaves of plates, 2 folded leaves : ill., maps ; 24 cm. Includes index. Bibliography: p. [272].
1. Natural history - Tanzania. 2. Natural history - Zaire. 3. Tanzania - Description and travel. 4. Zaire - Description and travel. I. Title.
                    NYPL [Sc E 88-252]

Barrett, Anthony. English-Turkana dictionary / compiled by A.Barrett. Nairobi : Macmillan Kenya, 1988. xxx, 225 p. ; 22 cm. English and Turkana. Bibliography: p. xxviii. ISBN 0-333-44577-5
1. English language - Dictionary - Turkana. 2. Turkana language - Dictionary - English. I. Title.
                    NYPL [Sc D 89-437]

Barrett, William M., 1900- Ain't you got no shame? / William M. Barrett ; original illustrations by Leonard Guardino. Washington, D.C. : New Merrymount Press, 1965. iii, 98 p. : ill. ; 23 cm. Poems. With autograph of author.
I. Guardino, Leonard J. II. Title.
                    NYPL [Sc D 88-483]

Barricades mystérieuses & pièges à pensée . Boyer, Pascal. Paris , 1988. 190 p. : ISBN 2-901161-31-6 **NYPL [Sc E 88-500]**

Barricades mystérieuses et pièges à pensée. Boyer, Pascal. Barricades mystérieuses & pièges à pensée . Paris , 1988. 190 p. : ISBN 2-901161-31-6   **NYPL [Sc E 88-500]**

Barrister. Analysis of the evidence given before the select committees upon the slave trade / by a barrister. London : Partridge and Oakey, 1850. 121 p. ; 21 cm.
1. Great Britain. Parliament. House of Commons. Select Committee on the Slave Trade. Report. 2. Slave-trade - Africa. I. Title.   **NYPL [Sc Rare G 86-11]**

Barriteau, Eudine. Emmanuel, Patrick. Political change and public opinion in Grenada 1979-1984 /. Cave Hill, Barbados , c1986. xii, 173 p. :   **NYPL [JLM 79-1223 no.19]**

Barron, Charles. Look for me in the whirlwind : a biographical sketch of the Honorable Marcus Mosiah Garvey ... / by Charles Barron.1st ed. [Brooklyn, NY] : African Peoples' Christian Organization, c1987. v, 60 p. : ill. ; 23 cm. "Corrections" note inserted. Transcribed from the African Peoples' Christian Organization radio broadcasts. Bibliography: p. 44-45. Author's autographed presentation copy to the Schomburg Center. DDC 305.8/96073 19
1. Garvey, Marcus, 1887-1940. 2. Universal Negro Improvement Association - History. 3. Back to Africa movement. I. Title.
E185.97.G3 B37 1987
                    NYPL [Sc D 88-1501]

Barrow, Joe Louis. Joe Louis : 50 years an American hero / by Joe Louis Barrow and Barbara Munder. New York : McGraw-Hill, c1988. xvii, 270 p., [8] leaves of plates : ill. ; 23 cm. Bibliography: p. 269-270. ISBN 0-07-003955-0 : DDC 796.8/3/0924 B 19
1. Louis, Joe, 1914-1981. 2. Boxers (Sports) - United States - Biography. 3. Afro-American boxers - Biography. I. Munder, Barbara. II. Title.
GV1132.L6 B37 1988   **NYPL [Sc E 88-566]**

Barrows, William, 1815-1891. The war and slavery; and their relations to each other : a discourse, delivered in the Old South Church, Reading, Mass., December 28, 1862 / by William Barrows. Boston : John M. Whittemore , 1863. 18 p. ; 24 cm. "Published by request."
1. Slavery - United States - Political aspects. I. Title. II. Title: Discourse, delivered in the Old South Church,Reading, Mass.
                    NYPL [Sc Rare F 88-51]

Barry, Boubacar. La Sénégambie du XVe au XIXe siècle : traite négrière, Islam et conquête coloniale / Boubacar Barry. Paris : L'Harmattan, c1988. 431 p., [8] of plates : ill., maps, ports. ; 22 cm. (Racines du présent) Bibliography: p. 409-427.
1. Senegambia - History. I. Title.
                    NYPL [Sc D 89-600]

BARS (DRINKING ESTABLISHMENTS) see HOTELS, TAVERNS, ETC.

Barsanti, Anne. Johnson, MayLee. Coming up on the rough side . South Orange, N.J. , c1988. vii, 88 p. ; ISBN 0-944734-01-4
                    NYPL [Sc D 89-190]

Bart, Simone Schwarz- see Schwarz-Bart, Simone.

Barth, Ernest Kurt. (illus) Clark, Margaret Goff. Freedom crossing. New York [1969] 128 p. DDC [Fic]
PZ7.C5487 Fr   **NYPL [Sc D 88-1121]**

Barthelemy, Anthony Gerard, 1949- Black face, maligned race : the representation of blacks in English drama from Shakespeare to Southerne / Anthony Gerard Barthelemy. Baton Rouge : Louisiana State University Press, c1987. xi, 215 p. ; 24 cm. Includes index. Bibliography: p. 203-209. ISBN 0-8071-1331-X DDC 822/.3/093520396 19
1. English drama - 17th century - History and criticism. 2. Africans in literature. 3. English drama - Early modern and Elizabethan, 1500-1600 - History and criticism. 4. English drama - Restoration, 1660-1700 - History and criticism. 5. Racism in literature. I. Title.
PR678.A4 B37 1987
                    NYPL [MWET 87-5064]

Bartlett, Richard C. (illus) Bateman, Walter L. The Kung of the Kalahari. Boston [1970] 128 p. ISBN 0-8070-1898-8 DDC 301.2
DT764.B8 B3   **NYPL [Sc E 88-550]**

Bartocci, Clara. La Letteratura della negritudine /. Roma , 1986. 243 p. ;
                    NYPL [Sc D 87-1377]

BASA (CAMEROON PEOPLE)
Ndebi Biya, Robert, 1946- Etre, pouvoir et génération . Paris , c1987. 134 p. ;
                    NYPL [Sc D 88-909]

BASA LANGUAGE - TERMS AND PHRASES.
Ndebi Biya, Robert, 1946- Etre, pouvoir et génération . Paris , c1987. 134 p. ;
                    NYPL [Sc D 88-909]

BASAA (CAMEROON PEOPLE) see BASA (CAMEROON PEOPLE)

Os Basanga de Shaba . Kabengele Munanga. Sao Palulo , 1986. 334 p. ; **NYPL [Sc B 88-7]**

BASE-BALL. see BASEBALL.

BASEBALL CARDS - UNITED STATES - COLLECTORS AND COLLECTING.
Slocum, Frank. Classic baseball cards . New York, N.Y. , c1987. ca 600 p. : ISBN 0-446-51392-X DDC 769/.49796357/0973 19
GV875.3 .S57 1987 **NYPL [8-*ISGB 89-500]**

BASEBALL - HISTORY.
Peterson, Robert, 1925- Only the ball was white. Englewood Cliffs, N.J. [1970] vii, 406 p. ISBN 0-13-637215-5 DDC 796.357/09
GV863 .P4   **NYPL [Sc 796.357-P]**

Baseball in the fifties. Honig, Donald. Baseball in the '50s. New York , 1987. 238 p. : ISBN 0-517-56578-1 DDC 796.357/0973 19
GV863.A1 H67 1987   **NYPL [JFF 88-794]**

Baseball in the '50s . Honig, Donald. New York , 1987. 238 p. ; ISBN 0-517-56578-1 DDC 796.357/0973 19
GV863.A1 H67 1987   **NYPL [JFF 88-794]**

BASEBALL - JUVENILE FICTION.
Myers, Walter Dean, 1937- Me, Mop, and the Moondance Kid /. New York , 1988. 154 p. : ISBN 0-440-50065-6 DDC [Fic] 19
PZ7.M992 Me 1988   **NYPL [Sc D 88-1457]**

BASEBALL - JUVENILE LITERATURE.
Robinson, John Roosevelt, 1919-1972. Jackie Robinson's Little League baseball book. Englewood Cliffs, N.J. [1972] 135 p. ISBN 0-13-509232-9
GV867.5 .R6   **NYPL [JFD 72-7423]**

BASEBALL PLAYERS - PUERTO RICO - BIOGRAPHY - JUVENILE LITERATURE.
Walker, Paul Robert. Pride of Puerto Rico . San Diego , c1988. 135 p. ; ISBN 0-15-200562-5 DDC 796.357/092/4 B 92 19
GV865.C45 W35 1988 **NYPL [Sc E 88-452]**

BASEBALL PLAYERS - UNITED STATES - BIOGRAPHY.
Honig, Donald. Mays, Mantle, Snider . New York, N.Y. , London , c1987. vii, 151 p. : ISBN 0-02-551200-5 DDC 796.357/092/2 B 19
GV865.A1 H6192 1987
                    NYPL [JFF 87-1461]

Moore, Joseph Thomas. Pride against prejudice . New York , c1988. 195 p., [8] p. of plates : ISBN 0-313-25995-X (lib. bdg. : alk. paper) DDC 796.357/092/4 B 19
GV865.D58 M66 1988 **NYPL** *[Sc E 88-272]*

Riley, James A. Dandy, Day and the Devil /. Cocoa, FL , 1987. xiii, 153 p. : ISBN 0-9614023-2-6 **NYPL** *[Sc D 88-104]*

Robinson, Jackie, 1919-1972. Jackie Robinson . New York , 1948. 170 p. :
NYPL *[Sc C 88-61]*

Winfield, Dave, 1951- Winfield . New York , c1988. 314 p., [22] p. of plates : ISBN 0-393-02467-9 : DDC 796.357/092/4 B 19
GV865.W57 A3 1988
NYPL *[JFD 88-11493]*

BASEBALL PLAYERS - UNITED STATES - BIOGRAPHY - JUVENILE LITERATURE.
Adler, David A. Jackie Robinson . New York , c1989. 48 p. : ISBN 0-8234-0734-9 DDC 796.357/092/4 B 19
GV865 .A37 1989 **NYPL** *[Sc F 89-137]*

Devaney, John. Bo Jackson . New York , 1988. 110 p. : ISBN 0-8027-6818-0 DDC 796.332/092/4 B 92 19
GV865.J28 D48 1988 **NYPL** *[Sc E 89-12]*

Humphrey, Kathryn Long. Satchel Paige /. New York , 1988. 110 p. : ISBN 0-531-10513-X DDC 796.357/092/4 B 92 19
GV865.P3 H86 1988 **NYPL** *[Sc E 88-481]*

Scott, Richard, 1956- Jackie Robinson /. New York , 1987. 110 p. : ISBN 1-555-46208-1 : DDC 796.357/092/4 B 92 19
GV865.R6 S36 1987 **NYPL** *[Sc E 88-168]*

BASEBALL - UNITED STATES - HISTORY.
Honig, Donald. Baseball in the '50s . New York , 1987. 238 p. : ISBN 0-517-56578-1 DDC 796.357/0973 19
GV863.A1 H67 1987 **NYPL** *[JFF 88-794]*

Robinson, Frank, 1935- Extra innings /. New York , c1988. x, 270, [8] p. of plates. : ISBN 0-07-053183-8 DDC 796.357/08996073 19
GV863.A1 R582 1988 **NYPL** *[Sc E 88-382]*

BASEBALL - UNITED STATES - MISCELLANEA.
Rust, Art, 1927- The Art Rust Jr. baseball quiz book /. New York, N.Y. , c1985. 184 p., [16] p. of plates : ISBN 0-8160-1147-4 (pbk.) DDC 796.357/0973 19
GV867.3 .R87 1985 **NYPL** *[JFE 85-2627]*

BASEBALL - UNITED STATES - RECORDS.
Holway, John. Blackball stars . Westport, CT , c1988. xvi, 400 p. : ISBN 0-88736-094-7 (alk. paper) : DDC 796.357/08996073/0922 B 19
GV865.A1 H614 1988 **NYPL** *[JFE 88-6437]*

BASEKA (BANTU PEOPLE) see EKONDA (BANTU PEOPLE)

A baseline survey of AIDS risk behaviors and attitudes in San Francisco's Black communities / conducted for the AIDS Surveillance Office, San Francisco Department of Public Health by Polaris Research and Development and Research & Decisions Corporation. San Francisco, Calif. : Polaris Research and Development, [1987] vii, 74, [59] leaves : ill. ; 28 cm. "Noel A. Day, project director, James Deslonde, Ph.D., co-principal investigator, Amanda Houston-Hamilton, DMH, co-principal investigator and ... Gary L. Stieger, director of research." Includes bibliographical references.
1. AIDS (Disease) - California - San Francisco. 2. AIDS-related complex - California - San Francisco. 3. Afro-Americans - California - San Francisco - Diseases. 4. Sexual behavior surveys - California - San Francisco. I. Polaris Research and Development (Firm). II. Research & Decisions Corporation (San Francisco, Calif.). III. San Francisco (Calif.). Dept. of Public Health. AIDS Surveillance Office.
NYPL *[Sc F 88-232]*

Basi and company . Tsaro-Wiwa, Ken. Port Harcourt, Nigeria , Epsom,Surrey , 1987. 216 p. ; ISBN 1-87071-600-0 (pbk) : DDC 823 19
PR9387.9.S3 **NYPL** *[Sc C 88-224]*

Basic facts about the southern provinces of The Sudan. Sudan. Maktab al-Isti'lamat al-Markazi. Khartoum , 1964. 114 p., [1] folded leaf :
NYPL *[Sc D 88-449]*

BASIC NEEDS - AFRICA.
The Challenge of employment and basic needs

in Africa . Nairobi , New York , 1986. xii, 379 p. ; ISBN 0-19-572559-X **NYPL** *[Sc E 88-419]*

BASKET-BALL. see BASKETBALL.

The basket counts. Christopher, Matt. Boston [1968] 125 p. DDC [Fic] 19
PZ7.C458 Bash **NYPL** *[Sc C 89-15]*

BASKET MAKING - DOMINICA - SALYBIA.
Découverte de la vannerie caraïbe du Morne des Esses à Salybia /. Martinique , 1984. 60 p. : **NYPL** *[Sc C 88-323]*

BASKET MAKING - MARTINIQUE - SAINTE-MARIE.
Découverte de la vannerie caraïbe du Morne des Esses à Salybia /. Martinique , 1984. 60 p. : **NYPL** *[Sc C 88-323]*

Basketball Association. see National Basketball Association.

BASKETBALL - JUVENILE FICTION.
Lunemann, Evelyn. Tip off. Westchester, Ill. [1969] 70 p. DDC [Fic]
PZ7.L979115 Ti **NYPL** *[Sc E 88-533]*

Madden, Betsy. The All-America Coeds /. New York [1971] 143 p. ; ISBN 0-200-71785-5
NYPL *[Sc D 88-432]*

Neigoff, Mike. Free throw. Chicago [1968] 128 p. DDC [Fic]
PZ7.N427 Fr **NYPL** *[Sc D 88-1427]*

BASKETBALL PLAYERS, AFRO-AMERICAN. see AFRO-AMERICAN BASKETBALL PLAYERS.

BASKETBALL PLAYERS - UNITED STATES - BIOGRAPHY.
Webb, Spud. Flying high /. New York , c1988. xv, 208 p., [16] p. of plates : ISBN 0-06-015820-4 : DDC 796.32/3/0924 B 19
GV884.W35 A3 1988 **NYPL** *[Sc D 89-375]*

BASKETBALL PLAYERS - UNITED STATES - BIOGRAPHY - JUVENILE LITERATURE.
Martin, Gene L. Michael Jordan, gentleman superstar /. Greensboro, N.C. , c1987. 69 p. : ISBN 0-936389-02-8 : DDC 796.32/3/0924 B 19
GV884.J67 M37 1987 **NYPL** *[Sc E 88-320]*

BASKETBALL - STORIES.
Christopher, Matt. The basket counts. Boston [1968] 125 p. DDC [Fic] 19
PZ7.C458 Bash **NYPL** *[Sc C 89-15]*

Olson, Gene. The tall one . New York , 1957, c1956. 211 p. ; **NYPL** *[Sc D 89-428]*

BASKETBALL - UNITED STATES.
Ryan, Bob. Forty-eight minutes . New York , London , c1987. x, 356 p. ; ISBN 0-02-597770-9 DDC 796.32/364/0973 19
GV885.515.N37 R9 1988
NYPL *[JFD 87-10809]*

Basler Beiträge zur Ethnologie.
(Bd. 25) Gardi, Bernhard. Ein Markt wie Mopti . Basel , 1985. 387 p. : ISBN 3-85977-175-2 DDC 745/.0966/23 19
TT119.M34 G37 1985 **NYPL** *[Sc E 87-494]*

BASSA (CAMEROON PEOPLE) see BASA (CAMEROON PEOPLE)

Bassani, Ezio. Africa and the Renaissance : art in ivory / Ezio Bassani and William B. Fagg ; edited by Susan Vogel, assisted by Carol Thompson ; with an essay by Peter Mark. New York City : Center for African Art : Distributed in the U. S. A. and Canada by Neues Pub. Co., c1988. 255 p. : ill. (some col.) ; 31 cm. Catalog of a loan exhibition held at the Center for African Art, New York and the Museum of Fine Arts, Houston. Bibliography: p. 251-254. ISBN 0-945802-00-5 : DDC 736/.62/0966074014711 19
1. Ivories - Africa, West - History - 16th century - Exhibitions. 2. Art patronage - Portugal - Exhibitions. I. Fagg, William Butler. II. Vogel, Susan Mullin. III. Thompson, Carol, 1954-. IV. Center for African Art (New York, N.Y.). V. Museum of Fine Arts, Houston. VI. Title.
NK5989 .B37 1988 **NYPL** *[Sc F 89-30]*

BASSETERRE (SAINT KITTS) - HISTORY.
Inniss, Probyn, Sir. Historic Basseterre . Basseterre, St. Kitts , c1985. 84 p. :
NYPL *[Sc D 88-266]*

Bassolet, Bernard Nébila. Guide pédagogique pour la mise en œuvre des soins de santé primaires au niveau villageois /.

Bobo-Dioulasso, Burkina Faso , 1986. 79 p. :
RA771 .G85 1986 **NYPL** *[Sc D 89-265]*

Bassomb, Nouk. Le crabe noir / Nouk Bassomb. Antony : B et F Editions, c1987. 91 p. ; 21 cm. ISBN 2-906661-00-7
I. Title. **NYPL** *[Sc D 89-446]*

Bastide, Roger, 1898-1974.
[Religions africaines au Brésil. Portuguese]
As religiões africanas no Brasil : contribuição a uma sociologia das interpenetrações de civilizações / Roger Bastide ; tradução de Maria Eloisa Capellato e Olívia Krähenbühl. São Paulo : Pioneira, 1985. 567 p. ; 22 cm. (Biblioteca Pioneira de ciências sociais. Sociologia) Includes bibliographical footnotes.
1. Blacks - Brazil. 2. Blacks - Religion. 3. Brazil - Religion. I. Title. **NYPL** *[Sc D 88-542]*

Bastien, Christine. Folies, mythes et magies d'Afrique noire : propos de guérisseurs du Mali / Christine Bastien ; préface de Jean Bazin. Paris : Edition l'Harmattan, 1988. 230 p. ; 22 cm. (Connaissance des hommes) Bibliography: p. 223-225. ISBN 2-7384-0038-8
1. Healers - Mali. 2. Medicine, magic, mystic, and spagiric - Mali. I. Title. II. Series.
NYPL *[Sc D 89-191]*

Bateman, Walter L. The Kung of the Kalahari, by Walter L. Bateman. Illustrated by Richard C. Bartlett. Boston, Beacon Press [1970] 128 p. illus. (part col.) 24 cm. Describes the environment, daily life, family, and customs of the Kung Bushmen of the Kalahari. Includes bibliographical references. SCHOMBURG CHILDREN'S COLLECTION. ISBN 0-8070-1898-8 DDC 301.2
1. !Kung (African people). I. Bartlett, Richard C., illus. II. Schomburg Children's Collection. III. Title.
DT764.B8 B3 **NYPL** *[Sc E 88-550]*

Bathily, Abdoulaye. Lexique soninke (sarakole)-français / par Abdoulaye Bathily, et Claude Meillassoux. [Dakar] : Centre de linguistique appliquée de Dakar, 1975. xx, 191 p. ; 30 cm. (Les Langues africaines au Sénégal) "No. 64." Soninke and French. Introductory matter in French. Bibliography: p. xi-xii.
1. Soninke language - Dictionaries - French. I. Meillassoux, Claude. II. Centre de linguistique appliquée de Dakar. III. Title. IV. Series.
NYPL *[Sc F 86-166]*

Battle lanterns /. Allen, Merritt Parmelee. New York , 1949. 278 p. ; **NYPL** *[Sc D 88-1106]*

The battlefronts of Southern Africa /. Legum, Colin. New York , c1988. xxix, 451 p. : ISBN 0-8419-1135-5 (alk. paper) DDC 327.68 19
DT746 .L425 1987 **NYPL** *[Sc E 88-468]*

BAULE (AFRICAN PEOPLE) see BAOULÉ (AFRICAN PEOPLE)

Baxt, George. A queer kind of death / George Baxt. New York : International Polygonics, 1986, c1966. 249 p. ; 18 cm. ISBN 0-930330-46-3 (pbk.)
1. Gay men - New York (N.Y.) - Fiction. 2. Afro-American gays - New York (N.Y.) - Fiction. I. Title. **NYPL** *[Sc C 88-132]*

Bayān mā waqa'a. Ḥajj 'Umar ibn Sa'īd al-Fūti, 1794?-1864. [Bayān mā waqa'a. French & Arabic.] Voilà ce qui est arrivé . Paris , 1983. 261 p., [57] p. of plates ISBN 2-222-03216-4
NYPL *[Sc F 88-211]*

Baynham, Simon, 1950- The military and politics in Nkrumah's Ghana / Simon Baynham. Boulder : Westview Press, 1988. xvi, 294 p. ; 23 cm. (Westview special studies in Africa) Includes index. Bibliography: p. 270-285. ISBN 0-8133-7063-9 : DDC 966.7/05 19
1. Nkrumah, Kwame, 1909-1972. 2. Ghana - Politics and government - 1957-1979. 3. Ghana - Armed Forces - Political activity. 4. Ghana - History - Coup d'état, 1966. I. Title.
DT512 .B39 1986 **NYPL** *[JFD 88-10630]*

BAYOT (AFRICAN PEOPLE)
Schloss, Marc R. The hatchet's blood . Tucson , c1988. xv, 178 p. : ISBN 0-8165-1042-3 (alk. paper) DDC 966/.3 19
DT549.45.B39 S35 1988
NYPL *[Sc E 88-443]*

Bayreuth African studies series.
(10) Paulin, Adjai. La Revolte des esclaves mercenaires . Bayreuth, W. Germany , 1987. 96 p. : **NYPL** *[Sc D 88-1326]*

(12) Beier, Ulli. Three Yoruba artists .
Bayreuth, W. Germany , c19. 93 p. ;
NYPL [Sc D 88-1325]

(6) Literature and African identity. Bayreuth ,
c1986. 125 p. ;   ***NYPL [Sc D 89-369]***

Bayreuth African studies series, 0178-0034 .
(11) African and western legal systems in
contact Bayreuth , c1989. 89 p. ;
ISBN 3-927510-01-7 :
NYPL [Sc D 89-465]

(6) Literature and African identity. Bayreuth ,
c1986. 125 p. ;   ***NYPL [Sc D 89-369]***

(8) Interviews avec des écrivains africains
francophones /. [Bayreuth, W. Germany ,
c1986. 95 p. ;   ***NYPL [Sc D 88-906]***

(9) Perspectives on African music /. Bayreuth,
W. Germany , c1989. 139 p., [8] leaves of
plates : ISBN 3-927510-00-9
NYPL [Sc D 89-448]

BAZELAIS, BOYER.
Gilbert, Marcel, 1938- La patrie haïtienne .
Brazzaville , 1984. 60 p. ;
NYPL [Sc D 89-629]

BE BOP MUSIC. see JAZZ MUSIC.

Be-bop, re-bop /. Cartiér, Xam Wilson. New
York , c1987. 147 p. ; ISBN 0-345-34833-8
(pbk.) :   ***NYPL [Sc D 88-716]***

Beacon Hill's Colonel Robert Gould Shaw /.
Smith, Marion Whitney. New York , 1986. 512
p. : ISBN 0-8062-2732-X
NYPL [Sc D 88-414]

Beacon Press night lights.
Appiah, Peggy. Tales of an Ashanti father /.
Boston , 1989, c1967. 156 p. : ISBN
0-8070-8312-7 DDC 398.2/1/09667 19
PZ8.1.A647 Tal 1989   ***NYPL [Sc E 89-87]***

Beans. Geography.
Barker, Carol. Village in Nigeria /. London ,
c19. 25 p. : ISBN 0-7136-2391-8 : DDC 966.9/05
19
DT515.8 .B29 1984   ***NYPL [Sc D 88-605]***

The bear in the back yard . Ashby, Timothy.
Lexington, Mass. , c1987. xii, 240 p. : ISBN
0-669-14768-0 (alk. paper) DDC 327.470729 19
F2178.S65 A84 1987   ***NYPL [HNB 87-1399]***

Beardsley, Edward H. A history of neglect :
health care for Blacks and mill workers in the
twentieth-century South / Edward H.
Beardsley. Knoxville : University of Tennessee
Press, c1987. xvi, 383 p. : ill. ; 25 cm. Includes
index. Bibliography: p. 315-364. ISBN 0-87049-523-2
(alk. paper) : DDC 362.1/0425 19
*1. Afro-Americans - Health and hygiene - Southern
States - History - 20th century. 2. Afro-Americans -
Medical care - Southern States - History - 20th century.
3. Cotton textile industry - Employees - Diseases and
hygiene - Southern States - History - 20th century. 4.
Cotton textile industry - Employees - Medical care -
Southern States - History - 20th century. 5. Textile
workers - Diseases and hygiene - Southern States -
History - 20th century. 6. Textile workers - Medical
care - Southern States - History - 20th century. 7.
Southern States - Social conditions. 8. Southern States -
Economic conditions. I. Title. II. Title: Health care for
blacks and mill workers in the twentieth-century South.*
RA448.5.N4 B33 1987   ***NYPL [Sc E 87-625]***

Bearings /. Hippolyte, Kendel. [St. Lucia?]
c1986. ii, 52 p. : ISBN 976-8036-00-1
NYPL [Sc D 88-802]

BEARS - JUVENILE FICTION.
Warren, Cathy. Springtime bears /. New York ,
c1986. [32] p. : ISBN 0-688-05905-8 DDC [E] 19
PZ7.W2514 Sp 1986   ***NYPL [Sc D 87-622]***

The beast of fame /. Motsi, Daniel, 1964- Harare,
Zimbabwe , 1987. 59 p. : ISBN 0-949225-61-4 :
NYPL [Sc C 89-100]

The beast of the Haitian hills /. Thoby-Marcelin,
Philippe, 1904-1975. [Bête du Musseau.
English.] San Francisco , 1986. 179 p. : ISBN
0-87286-189-9 (pbk.) DDC 843 19
PQ3949.T45 B413 1986
NYPL [Sc D 88-199]

Beating time /. Widgery, David. London , 1986.
126 p. : ISBN 0-7011-2985-9
NYPL [JMD 88-112]

BEATNIKS. see BOHEMIANISM.

BEATS. see BOHEMIANISM.

Beatty, Lula A. Gary, Lawrence E. The delivery
of mental health services to Black children .
Washington, D.C. , 1982. vi, 111, 19 p. ;
NYPL [Sc F 88-66]

Beaujean, Henri. Demain la Guadeloupe unie, la
régionalisation réussie : Mouvement réformateur
Guadeloupéen / Henri Beaujean. Paris :
Marianne Média, c1988. 374 p. ; 23 cm.
Bibliography: p. 367.
*1. Guadeloupe - Economic conditions. 2. Guadeloupe -
Politics and government. I. Title.*
NYPL [Sc D 88-972]

Beauties of philanthropy. Branagan, Thomas, b.
1774. The guardian genius of the Federal
Union, or, Patriotic admonitions on the signs of
the times . New York , 1839. 104 p. :
NYPL [Sc Rare G 86-18]

Beautiful crescent . Garvey, Joan B. New
Orleans, LA , c1988. 249 p. : ISBN
0-9612960-0-3   ***NYPL [Sc E 89-189]***

Beauty care for today's woman /. Bolton, Shelly.
Harare , 1983. 48 p. : ***NYPL [Sc D 88-1444]***

BEBOP MUSIC. see JAZZ MUSIC.

BECHET, SIDNEY, 1897-1959.
Chilton, John, 1931 or 2- Sidney Bechet, the
wizard of jazz /. Basingstoke , 1987. xiii, 331
p., [32] p. of plates : ISBN 0-333-44386-1
NYPL [Sc E 88-33]

Bechler, Le Roy, 1925- The Black Mennonite
Church in North America, 1886-1986 / Le Roy
Bechler ; foreword by Joy Lovett. Scottdale,
Pa. : Herald Press, 1986. 196 p. : ill. ; 24 cm.
Includes index. Bibliography: p. 183. ISBN
0-8361-1287-3 : DDC 289.7/08996073 19
*1. Afro-American Mennonites. 2. Afro-American
churches. I. Title.*
BX8116.3.A37 B43 1986
NYPL [Sc E 89-134]

Becker, Barbara. Wildpflanzen in der Ernährung
der Bevölkerung afrikanischer Trockengebiete :
drei Fallstudien aus Kenia und Senegal /
Barbara Becker. Göttingen : Institut für
Pflanzenbau und Tierhygiene in den Tropen
und Subtropen, 1984. iv, 341 p. : ill., maps ; 21
cm. (Göttinger Beiträge Zur Land- und Forstwirtschaft
in den Tropen und Subtropen . Heft 6)
Thesis-Georg-August-Universität Göttingen. Abstract in
English. Bibliography: p. 278-299.
*1. Wild plants, Edible - Kenya. 2. Wild plants, Edible -
Senegal. 3. Diet - Kenya. 4. Diet - Senegal. I. Title. II.
Series.*   ***NYPL [Sc D 88-682]***

Becker, Friedrich, 1942- Afrikanische Fabeln und
Mythen /. Frankfurt am Main , New York ,
c1987. vi, 233 p. ; ISBN 3-8204-8641-0 DDC
398.2/0966 19
GR350.3 .A35 1987   ***NYPL [JFD 88-8333]***

Beckford, George L. Pathways to progress .
Morant Bay, Jamaica, W.I. , 1985. vii, 128 p. ;
DDC 338.97292 19
HC154 .P38 1985   ***NYPL [Sc D 88-1239]***

Becknell, Charles Edward, 1941-
Black culture in America : an educator's
perspective / Charles E. Becknell. Albuquerque,
New Mexico : Horizon Communications,
c1987. iii, 85, A-J p. ; 28 cm. Body of text is
identical with that of the author's Blacks in the
workforce: a black manager's perspective. ISBN
0-913945-50-1
I. Title.   ***NYPL [Sc F 88-156]***

Blacks in the workforce : a black manager's
perspective / Charles E. Becknell. Albuquerque,
New Mexico : Horizon Communications,
c1987. iii, 85 p., A-D leaves ; 28 cm. Body of
text is identical with that of the author's Black culture
in America: an educator's perspective. ISBN
0-913945-52-8
I. Title.   ***NYPL [Sc F 88-157]***

**BED AND BREAKFAST
ACCOMMODATIONS - CARIBBEAN
AREA - GUIDE-BOOKS.**
Strong, Kathy, 1950- Bed and breakfast in the
Caribbean /. Chester, Conn. , c1987. ix, 278
p. : ISBN 0-87106-764-1 (pbk.) DDC 647/.94729
19
TX910.C25 S77 1987   ***NYPL [Sc D 88-1148]***

Bed and breakfast in the Caribbean /. Strong,
Kathy, 1950- Chester, Conn. , c1987. ix, 278
p. : ISBN 0-87106-764-1 (pbk.) DDC 647/.94729
19
TX910.C25 S77 1987   ***NYPL [Sc D 88-1148]***

Beddow, Tim. East Africa : an evolving landscape
/ Tim Beddow ; introduction by Dominic Sasse.
New York, N.Y. : Thames and Hudson, 1988.
21 p., [80] p. of plates : chiefly col. ill., map ;
25 x 28 cm. ISBN 0-500-24131-7
*1. Africa, East - Description and travel - 1981- - Views.
I. Title.*   ***NYPL [Sc F 88-291]***

Bedell, Madelon. Thinking and rethinking U. S.
history /. New York, N.Y. , c1988. 389 p. ;
NYPL [Sc F 89-130]

BEER - ZAMBIA - GWEMBE DISTRICT.
Colson, Elizabeth, 1917- For prayer and profit .
Stanford, Calif. , 1988. vi, 147 p. : ISBN
0-8047-1444-4 (alk. paper) : DDC 968.94 19
DT963.42 .C65 1988   ***NYPL [Sc D 88-1254]***

Beese, Barbara. Dohndy, Farrukh. The Black
explosion in British schools /. London , 1985.
64 p. ; ISBN 0-9503498-6-0
NYPL [Sc D 88-1030]

Before Stonewall . Weiss, Andrea. Tallahassee,
FL , 1988. 86 p. ; ISBN 0-941483-20-7 : DDC
306.7/66/0973 19
HQ76.8.U5 W43 1988
NYPL [Sc D 88-1125]

Before the birth of the moon /. Mudimbe, V. Y.,
1941?- [Bel immonde. English.] New York ,
c1989. 203 p. ; ISBN 0-671-66840-4 : DDC 843
19
PQ3989.2.M77 B413 1989
NYPL [Sc D 89-236]

Beginning of no end. Fuller, Louisia. The risks of
Ro . Teaneck, N.J. , c1988. 105 p. ; ISBN
0-945779-00-3   ***NYPL [Sc D 88-1172]***

**Die beginsels en belied van die Suid-Afrikaanse
Progressiewe Reformisteparty [microform] /.**
Eglin, Colin. [Cape Town , 1975] 12, 12 p. ;
NYPL [Sc Micro R-4094 no. 4]

Begorrat--Brunton. De Verteuil, Anthony. A
history of Diego Martin 1784-1884 /. Port of
Spain, Trinidad , c1987. viii, 174 p., [96] p. of
plates : ISBN 976-8054-10-7
NYPL [Sc F 88-192]

BEGORRAT, ST. HILAIRE, 1759?-1851.
De Verteuil, Anthony. A history of Diego
Martin 1784-1884 /. Port of Spain, Trinidad ,
c1987. viii, 174 p., [96] p. of plates : ISBN
976-8054-10-7   ***NYPL [Sc F 88-192]***

Behind Bakke . Schwartz, Bernard, 1923- New
York , c1988. x, 266 p. ; ISBN 0-8147-7878-X :
DDC 347.73/0798 347.304798 19
KF228.B34 S39 1988   ***NYPL [JLE 88-4158]***

Behind the frontlines . Dennis, Ferdinand, 1956-
London , 1988. xv, 216 p. ; ISBN 0-575-04098-X
NYPL [JLD 89-210]

Behind the masquerade . Owusu, Kwesi.
Edgware , 1988. 90 p. : ISBN 0-9512770-0-6
(pbk) : DDC 394.2/5/0942134 19
NYPL [Sc E 88-497]

Behind the scenes. Keckley, Elizabeth,
1824-1907. Behind the scenes, or, Thirty years
a slave, and four years in the White House .
New York , 1988. xxxvi, xvi, 371 p. : ISBN
0-19-505259-5 DDC 973.7/092/2 19
E457.15 .K26 1988   ***NYPL [JFC 88-2194]***

**Behind the scenes, or, Thirty years a slave, and
four years in the White House /.** Keckley,
Elizabeth, 1824-1907. New York , 1988. xxxvi,
xvi, 371 p. : ISBN 0-19-505259-5 DDC
973.7/092/2 19
E457.15 .K26 1988   ***NYPL [JFC 88-2194]***

Beier, Ulli. Three Yoruba artists : Twins
Seven-Seven, Ademola Onibonokuta, Muraina
Oyelami / Ulli Beier. Bayreuth, W. Germany :
Bayreuth University, c1988 93 p. ; 21 cm.
(Bayreuth African studies series . 12) Bibliography: p.
91-93.
*1. Onibonokuta, Ademola. 2. Twins Seven-Seven. 3.
Oyelami, Muraina. I. Title. II. Series.*
NYPL [Sc D 88-1325]

Being Black : aboriginal cultures in "settled"
Australia / edited by Ian Keen. Canberra :
Aboriginal Studies Press, 1988. xiv, 273 p. : ill.,
maps ; 24 cm. Includes bibliographies and index.
ISBN 0-85575-185-1
*1. Australian aborigines - Urban residence. 2. Australian
aborigines - Social conditions. I. Keen, Ian.*
NYPL [Sc E 88-515]

Beken, Alain van der, 1935- L'Evangile en
Afrique, vécu et commenté par des Bayaka /

Alain van der Beken. Nettetal [Germany] :
Steyler Verlag, 1986. 328 p. ; 24 cm. (Studia
Instituti Missiologici Societatis Verbi Divini,
0562-2816 . Nr. 38) French and Puna. Bibliography: p.
14. ISBN 3-87787-204-2 :
*1. Missions to Bayaka (African people). I. Title. II.
Series.*

BV3630.B69 B45 1986   *NYPL [Sc E 88-339]*

Bekker, S. B.
Perspectives on rural development in Ciskei,
1983 / [S.B. Bekker and C.E.B. Hughes].
Grahamstown : Institute of Social and
Economic Research, Rhodes University, [1984]
52 p. : ill. ; 30 cm. (Development studies working
paper . no. 17) "March 1984." Bibliography: p. 45.
ISBN 0-86810-103-6 (pbk.) : DDC
307.1/4/0968792 19
*1. Rural development - South Africa - Ciskei. I.
Hughes, C. E. B. (Christopher E. B.). II. Title. III.
Series.*

HN801.C57 B45 1984   *NYPL [Sc F 88-325]*

Socio-economic survey of the Amatola Basin :
interim report / S.B. Bekker, C. de Wet and
C.W. Manona. Grahamstown [South Africa]
Institute of Social and Economic Rrsearch:
Rhodes University, 1981. 58, xxxxiv p. : charts,
maps ; 30 cm. (Development studies working paper .
no. 2) "September 1981." ISBN 0-86810-073-0
*1. Amatola Watershed (South Africa) - Economic
conditions. 2. Amatola Watershed (South Africa) -
Social conditions. 3. Ciskei (South Africa) - Economic
conditions. 4. Ciskei (South Africa) - Social conditions.
I. Wet, C. de. II. Manona, C. W. III. Title. IV. Series.*

NYPL [Sc F 87-430]

Belcher, Max. A land and life remembered :
Americo-Liberian folk architecture /
photographs by Max Belcher ; text by Svend E.
Holsoe and Bernard L. Herman ; afterword by
Rodger P. Kingston. Athens : University of
Georgia Press ; Brockton, Mass. : Brockton Art
Museum/Fuller Memorial, c1988. [xii], 176 p. :
ill. (some col.) ; 23 x 29 cm. Catalog of a loan
exhibition held at the Brockton Art Museum.
Bibliography: p. 171-174. ISBN 0-8203-1085-9 (alk.
paper) DDC 720/.9666/2074014482 19
*1. Architecture - Liberia - Exhibitions. 2. Vernacular
architecture - Liberia - Exhibitions. 3. Architecture -
Southern States - Influence - Exhibitions. 4. Liberia -
Civilization - History - 19th century - Exhibitions. I.
Holsoe, Svend E. II. Herman, Bernard L., 1951-. III.
Brockton Art Museum. IV. Title.*

NA1599.L4 B4 1988   *NYPL [Sc F 89-90]*

Belcher, Wendy Laura.
Honey from the lion : an African journey /
Wendy Laura Belcher.1st ed. New York :
Dutton, c1988. xiv, 188 p. : map ; 22 cm.
ISBN 0-525-24596-0 : DDC 966.7/05 19
*1. Belcher, Wendy Laura - Journeys - Ghana. 2.
Ghana - Social life and customs. 3. Ghana - Religious
life and customs. I. Title.*

DT510.4 .B38 1988   *NYPL [Sc D 88-842]*

**BELCHER, WENDY LAURA - JOURNEYS -
GHANA.**
Belcher, Wendy Laura. Honey from the lion .
New York , c1988. xiv, 188 p. : ISBN
0-525-24596-0 : DDC 966.7/05 19

DT510.4 .B38 1988   *NYPL [Sc D 88-842]*

Belengi Nzileyel, 1934- Banza-Lute . Bandundu,
République du Zaïre , 1983. 251 p. : DDC
282/.67513 19

BX1682.C6 B36 1983   *NYPL [Sc F 89-38]*

BELIZE - HISTORY.
Dobson, Narda. A history of Belize. [Port of
Spain, Trinidad and Tobago, 1973] xiv, 362 p.
ISBN 0-582-76601-X DDC 972.82

F1446 .D56 1973   *NYPL [Sc D 88-649]*

Bellamy, Joe David. American poetry observed .
Urbana , c1984. xi, 313 p. : ISBN 0-252-01042-6
DDC 811/.54/09 19

PS129 .A54 1984   *NYPL [JFE 84-3478]*

Bellegarde, Dantès, 1877-1966. La nación
haitiana / Dantès Bellegarde. Santo Domingo :
Sociedad Dominicana de Bibliófilos, 1984. 429
p. : port. ; 24 cm. (Colección de cultura dominicana.
54) Translation (by Lissette Vega de Purcell) of: La
nation haïtienne. Bibliography: p. [411]-[421]
1. Haiti. 2. Haiti - History. I. Title.

NYPL [Sc E 88-103]

BELLES-LETTRES. see LITERATURE.

Beloved . Morrison, Toni. New York , 1987. 275

p. ; ISBN 0-394-53597-9 : DDC 813/.54 19
PS3563.O8749 B4 1987

NYPL [Sc E 88-188]

Beloved /. Morrison, Toni. Thorndike, Me. ,
1988. 472 p.; 22 cm. ISBN 0-89621-123-1 (alk.
paper) DDC 813/.54 19
PS3563.O8749 B4 1988

NYPL [Sc D 88-1503]

BELSHAZZAR - DRAMA.
Green, Ernest Davis. The King, Belshazzar /.
New York , 1962. 178 p. ;

NYPL [Sc D 88-839]

Bélsiva. Lamentos só lamentos / Bélsiva, poeta
primitivo. [São Paulo? : s.n.], 1973 (São Paulo :
Empresa Gráfica da Revista dos Tribunais). vii,
48 p. ; 21 cm.
I. Title.

NYPL [Sc D 88-1104]

Ben Said, Christine. Le Boulch, Pierre. Today's
English . [Dakar] , 1968- v. ;

NYPL [Sc F 87-274]

Benagh, Jim, 1937- Terzian, James P. The Jimmy
Brown story /. New York , c1964. 190 p. :

NYPL [Sc D 89-432]

Bender, Gerald J. African crisis areas and U. S.
foreign policy /. Berkeley , c1985. xiv, 374 p. :
ISBN 0-520-05548-9 (alk. paper) DDC 327.7306
19

DT38.7 .A39 1986   *NYPL [JLE 85-4182]*

Bender, Louis W. Richardson, Richard C.
Fostering minority access and achievement in
higher education . San Francisco, Calif. , c1987.
xviii, 244 p. ; ISBN 1-555-42053-2 (alk. paper)
DDC 378/.052 19

LC3727 .R53 1987   *NYPL [Sc E 88-472]*

Bender, M. Lionel (Marvin Lionel), 1934- The
Non-semitic languages of Ethiopia /. East
Lansing , c1976. xv, 738 p. ; DDC 492
PL8021.E8 N6   *NYPL [Sc D 88-854]*

Bender, Wolfgang. Perspectives on African music
/. Bayreuth, W. Germany , c1989. 139 p., [8]
leaves of plates : ISBN 3-927510-00-9

NYPL [Sc D 89-448]

Bene gulmanceba = Les gulmancéba du Bénin :
approche sociolinguistique. Cotonou, R.P. du
Bénin : Ministère de l'enseignement supérieur et
de la recherche scientifique, Direction de la
recherche scientifique et technique, Commission
nationale de linguistique, 1983. 101 p., [1] leaf
of plates : ill. ; 22 cm. French and Gurma. DDC
305.8/963 19
*1. Gurma (African people) - Social life and customs. 2.
Gurma (African people) - Folklore. 3. Tales - Benin. 4.
Gurma language - Texts. I. Benin. Commission
nationale de linguistique. II. Title: Gulmancéba du
Bénin.*

DT541.45.G87 B46 1983

NYPL [Sc D 88-202]

Benedict, Michael Les. The fruits of victory :
alternatives in restoring the Union, 1865-1877 /
Michael Les Benedict.Rev. ed. Lanham, MD :
University Press of America, c1986. xiii, 159
p. ; 21 cm. Includes bibliographies. ISBN
0-8191-5557-8 (pbk : alk. paper) : DDC 973.8
19
*1. Reconstruction - Sources. 2. United States -
Politics and government - 1865-1877. 3. United States -
Politics and government - 1865-1877 - Sources. I. Title.*

E668 .B462 1986   *NYPL [IKR 87-1888]*

Benedict, Niyi. The tortoise & the dog : a Yoruba
story / adapted by Niyi Benedict & Titi
Benedict. Ilupeju, Lagos : Friends Foundation
Publishers, 1988. 21 p. : ill. (some col.) ; 25
cm. SCHOMBURG CHILDREN'S COLLECTION.
*1. Tales, Yoruba. I. Benedict, Titi. II. Schomburg
Children's Collection. III. Title.*

NYPL [Sc E 88-599]

Benedict, Titi. Benedict, Niyi. The tortoise & the
dog . Ilupeju, Lagos , 1988. 21 p. :

NYPL [Sc E 88-599]

Benin. Commission nationale de linguistique.
Bene gulmanceba =. Cotonou, R.P. du Bénin ,
1983. 101 p., [1] leaf of plates : DDC 305.8/963
19
DT541.45.G87 B46 1983

NYPL [Sc D 88-202]

BENIN - DIRECTORIES.
Dossier Benin /. Paris , 1987. 225 p. :

NYPL [Sc F 88-176]

BENIN - ECONOMIC CONDITIONS.
Dossier Benin /. Paris , 1987. 225 p. :

NYPL [Sc F 88-176]

BENIN - FICTION.
Bhêly-Quénum, Olympe. [Piège sans fin.
English.] Snares without end /. Charlottesville ,
1988. xxvi, 204 p. ; ISBN 0-8139-1189-3 (pbk.)
DDC 843 19
PQ3989.2.B5 P513 1988

NYPL [Sc D 89-434]

BENIN - HISTORY - TO 1894.
Garcia, Luc, 1937- Le royaume du Dahomé
face à la pénétration coloniale . Paris , c1988.
284 p., [8] p. of plates :

NYPL [Sc E 89-145]

Norris, Robert, d. 1791. Memoirs of the reign
of Bossa Ahádee. London, 1789. xvi, 184 p. ;
DT541 .N85   *NYPL [Sc Rare F 88-64]*

BENIN - HISTORY - DICTIONARIES.
Decalo, Samuel. Historical dictionary of Benin
/. Metuchen, N.J. , 1987. xxvii, 349 p. : ISBN
0-8108-1924-4 DDC 966/.83 19
DT541.5 .D4 1987   *NYPL [Sc D 88-982]*

BENIN POETRY (FRENCH)
Nouvelle poésie du Bénin . Avignon , 1986. 78
p. :   *NYPL [Sc C 88-70]*

BENIN - SOCIAL LIFE AND CUSTOMS.
Maurice, Albert-Marie. Atakora . Paris , 1986.
xxiii, 481 p., clv p. of plates : ISBN
2-900098-11-4   *NYPL [Sc E 88-106]*

Benjamin, J. P. (Judah Philip), 1811-1884. The
African slave trade . Philadelphia , 1863. 24 p. ;

NYPL [Sc Rare F 89-5]

Benji. Scribe sistren : poems / by Benji. London :
Centerprise Trust, 1987. 72 p. ; 21 cm. ISBN
0-903738-72-4
1. Women, Black - Great Britain - Poetry. I. Title.

NYPL [Sc D 88-686]

Benjie Ream /. Hodges, Carl G. Indianapolis ,
c1964. 153 p. ;   *NYPL [Sc D 89-433]*

Benny Moré . Naser, Amín E. (Amín Egeraige),
1936- Ciudad de La Habana , c1985. 231 p. ,
[61] p. of plates : DDC 784.5/0092/4 B 19
ML420.M596 N3 1985 NYPL [Sc C 87-302]

Benoist, Jean, 1929-
Les Antilles / [Jean Benoist] [Paris : Gallimard,
1976?] p. [1372]-1448 : ill., maps ; 22 cm.
(Encyclopédie de la Pléiade) "Ethnologie régionale II -
tirage à part." Bibliography: p. 1441-1448.
*1. Ethnology - West Indies. I. Title. II. Title:
Ethnologie régionale. III. Series.*

NYPL [Sc D 87-1164]

Grandy, Moses, b. 1786? Le récit de Moses
Grandy, esclave en Caroline du Nord
[microform] /. [Montréal] [1977] 45 p. ;
E444 .G7514   *NYPL [*XM-12976]*

Benoit, Marie. Let's visit Haiti. Macmillan, 1988.
96 p. : ill. ; 21 cm. (Let's visit) ISBN
0-333-45692-0 : DDC 972.94/07 19
1. Haiti - Social life and customs. I. Title.

F1916   *NYPL [Sc D 89-73]*

Benson, Brian Joseph. The short fiction of
Richard Wright [microform] / by Brian Joseph
Benson. 1972. 266 leaves. Thesis (Ph.
D.)--University of South Carolina, 1972. Bibliography:
leaves 261-266. Microfilm of typescript. Ann Arbor,
Mich.: University Microfilms International, 1972. 1
microfilm reel; 35 mm.
*1. Wright, Richard, 1908-1960 - Criticism and
interpretation. I. Title.*

NYPL [Sc Micro R-4217]

Benson, Mary. A far cry / Mary Benson.
London,England : Viking, 1989. 254 p., [4]
leaves of plates : ill., ports. ; 24 cm. Includes
bibliographical references and index. ISBN
0-670-82138-1
*1. Benson, Mary. 2. South Africa - Politics and
government - 20th century.*   *NYPL [Sc E 89-228]*

BENSON, MARY.
Benson, Mary. A far cry /. London,England ,
1989. 254 p., [4] leaves of plates : ISBN
0-670-82138-1

NYPL [Sc E 89-228]

Benson, Peter. Black Orpheus, Transition, and
modern cultural awakening in Africa / Peter
Benson. Berkeley : University of California
Press, c1986. xiii, 320 p. : ill., port. ; 24 cm.
Includes index. Bibliography: p. 293-307. ISBN
0-520-05418-0 DDC 820/.8 19
1. Black Orpheus. 2. Transition (Kampala, Uganda). 3.

African literature - Periodicals - History. 4. Africa - Intellectual life. I. Title.
PL8000.B63 B4 1986   **NYPL [Sc E 88-354]**

Bergman, Billy. Hot sauces : Latin and Caribbean pop / by Billy Bergman, with Andy Schwartz ... [et al.].1st Quill ed. New York : Quill, c1985. 144 p. : ill. ; 26 cm. Includes discographies and index. ISBN 0-688-02193-X (pbk.) : DDC 780/.42/09729 19
1. Popular music - West Indies - History and criticism. 2. Popular music - United States - History and criticism. 3. Popular music - Latin America - History and criticism. I. Schwartz, Andy. II. Title.
ML3475 .B47 1985   **NYPL [Sc F 87-19]**

Bergman, Carol. Sidney Poitier / Carol Bergman. New York : Chelsea House Publishers, c1988. 110 p. : ill. ; 25 cm. (Black Americans of achievement) Includes index. Traces the life of the movie actor who won an Academy Award in 1963 and became a symbol of the breakthrough of black performers in motion pictures. Bibliography: p. 108. ISBN 1-555-46605-2 DDC 791.43/028/0924 B 92 19
1. Poitier, Sidney - Juvenile literature. 2. Actors - United States - Biography - Juvenile literature. 3. Afro-American actors - Biography - Juvenile literature. I. Title. II. Series.
PN2287.P57 B47 1988   **NYPL [Sc E 88-171]**

Berg/Unesco studies in development theory and policy. Women and economic development . Oxford [England] ; New York : ix, 231 p. ; ISBN 0-85496-091-0 : DDC 305.4/2 19
HQ1240 .W665 1988   **NYPL [JLD 89-559]**

Berhane Tesfay. Index to livestock literature microfiched in Zimbabwe /. Addis Ababa [1986?] viii, 235 p. ; ISBN 92-9053-064-2
   NYPL [Sc E 89-204]

Berjonneau, Gerald. Chefs-d'ouevre inédits de l'Afrique noire /. Paris , 1987. 320 p. : ISBN 2-04-012941-3   **NYPL [Sc G 88-10]**

Berlin, Edward A. Reflections and research on ragtime / Edward A. Berlin. Brooklyn, N.Y. : Institute for Studies in American Music, Conservatory of Music, Brooklyn College of the City University of New York, c1987. xii, 99 p. : ill. ; 22 cm. (I.S.A.M. monographs . no. 24) Bibliography: p. 93-98. "A list of recordings cited": p. 99. ISBN 0-914678-27-2 (pbk.) DDC 781/.572 19
1. Ragtime music - History and criticism. I. Series. II. Series: Brooklyn College. Institute for Studies in American Music. I. S. A. M. monographs, 24. III. Title.
ML3530 .B5 1987   **NYPL [Sc D 88-410]**

BERLIN WEST AFRICA CONFERENCE (1884-1885) - CONGRESSES.
Centenaire de la Conférénce de Berlin (1884-1885) (1985 : Brazzaville, Congo) Centenaire de la Conférence de Berlin (1884-1885) . Paris , 1987. 469 p. ; ISBN 2-7087-0481-8   **NYPL [Sc E 88-101]**

Berliner Studien zur Politik in Afrika, 0930-7303 .
(Bd. 7) Teubert-Seiwert, Bärbel, 1951- Parteipolitik in Kenya 1960-1969 /. Frankfurt am Main , New York , c1987. 428 p. ; ISBN 3-8204-0151-2 DDC 324.2676/2 19
JQ2947.A979 .T48 1987
   NYPL [Sc D 88-1141]

Berlitz Reiseführer.
McLeod, Catherine. Jamaika /. Lausanne, Switzerland [1985], c1981. 128 p. :
   NYPL [Sc B 88-57]

Berman, Sanford, 1933- Worth noting : editorials, letters, essays, an interview, and bibliography / by Sanford Berman ; with a foreword by Bill Katz. Jefferson, N.C. : McFarland, c1988. viii, 175 p. ; 24 cm. Includes index. Bibliography: p. 137-152. ISBN 0-89950-304-7 (lib. bdg.) : DDC 081 19
1. Creationism. I. Title.
Z674 .B44 1988   **NYPL [JFE 88-5518]**

Bermuda. [Hamilton?, Bermuda : s. n., 198-?] (Bermuda : Island Press) [16] p. : col. ill., map ; 30 cm. Cover title. Map folded as back cover.
   NYPL [Sc F 88-272]

BERMUDA ISLANDS - SOCIAL LIFE AND CUSTOMS.
McCallan, E. A. (Ernest Albert), 1874- Life on old St. David's, Bermuda /. Hamilton, Bermuda , 1986. 258 p., [26] p. of plates :
F1639.S26 M35x 1986 **NYPL [Sc E 88-539]**

Bermudez, José Ignacio Rasco y. see Rasco y Bermudez, José Ignacio.

Bernabé, Jean. Grammaire Créole (Fondas Kréyol-la) : eléments de base des créoles de la zone américano-caraïbe / Jean Bernabé. Paris : L'Harmattan, 1987. 205 p. ; 22 cm. Includes index. Bibliography: p. 198. ISBN 2-85805-734-X
1. Creole dialects, French - Caribbean area - Grammar. I. Title. II. Title: Fondas Kréyol-la.
   NYPL [Sc F 88-99]

Bernadine and the water bucket /. Olsen, Aileen. London , New York , 1966. [41] p :
   NYPL [Sc F 88-99]

Bernard, Alain. Contes et légendes de l'Afrique des grands lacs / Alain Bernard ; préface de Jean-Pierre Allaux ; illustrés par Nicole Pommaux. Arudy, France : Editions d'Utovie, [1984] 79 p. : ill. ; 20 cm. (Collection 180 millions) ISBN 2-86819-011-1
1. Tales - Africa, Central. 2. Tales, Burundi. I. Title.
   NYPL [Sc D 88-309]

Bernard, Patrick, 1956- Les oubliés du temps / Patrick Bernard. Paris : R. Moser, [1984] 160 p. : ill. (some col.) ; 30 cm. ISBN 2-902906-09-9 DDC 306 19
1. Title. II. Title: Oubliés.
GN378 .B45 1984   **NYPL [Sc F 88-69]**

Bernardi, Bernardo. The social structure of the kraal among the Zezuru in Musami (Southern Rhodesia) [Cape Town] 1950. [2], 60, [1] . illus., map. 33 cm. (Communications from the School of African Studies, University of Cape Town. New ser., no. 23) Bibliographical footnotes. DDC 572.9689
1. Ethnology - Rhodesia, Southern. 2. Tribes and tribal system. I. Series: Cape Town. University of Cape Town. School of African Studies. Communications, new ser, no. 23. II. Title.
GN490 .B4   **NYPL [Sc F 88-349]**

Bernardin, Antoine. Pour mon plaisir et pour ma peine / Antoine Bernardin. Port-au-Prince, Haiti : Imprimerie des Antilles, [19]88. 163 p. ; 21 cm. Poems. "Avril 88."
I. Title.   **NYPL [Sc D 88-10003]**

Bernd, Zilá, 1944- Introdução à literatura negra / Zila Bernd. Sao Paulo : Editora Brasiliense, 1988. 101 p. ; 21 cm. Bibliography: p. [100]-101.
1. West Indian literature - Black authors - History and criticism. 2. Brazilian literature - Black authors - History and criticism. I. Title.
   NYPL [Sc D 89-188]

Berney, Henri-Maurice. Les Antillles : archipel tropical de la mer des Caraïbes / Henri-Maurice Berney, Helmut Blume.2e ed. Paris : Elsevier Séquoia, 1977, c1972. 128 p. : col. ill., maps ; 28 cm. Maps on lining papers. ISBN 3-405-11035-1
1. West Indies - Description and travel. I. Blume, Helmut. II. Title.   **NYPL [Sc F 89-34]**

Bernheim, Nicole. Voyage en Amérique noire / Nicole Bernheim. Paris : Stock, c1986. 254 p. ; 24 cm. Bibliography: p. [251]-252. ISBN 2-234-01886-2 : DDC 305.8/96073/073 19
1. Afro-Americans - Social conditions - 1975-. 2. Afro-Americans - Civil rights. 3. United States - Race relations. I. Title.
E185.86 .B47 1986   **NYPL [Sc E 88-607]**

Bernlef, J. Klaasse, Piet. Jam session . Newton Abbot [Devon] , 1985. 192 p. : ISBN 0-7153-8710-3 DDC 785.42/092/2 19
ML3506 .K58 1985   **NYPL [Sc G 88-13]**

Bernstein, Hilda (Watts) No. 46 Steve Biko / by Hilda Bernstein. London : International Defence and Aid Fund, 1978. 150 p., [4] p. of plates : ill., ports ; 21 cm. Includes bibliographical references. ISBN 0-904759-21-0 :
1. Biko, B. S. 2. Blacks - South Africa - Politics and government. 3. Police corruption - South Africa. 4. Political prisoners - South Africa - Biography. I. Title.
DT779.8.B48 B47   **NYPL [JFD 79-52]**

Bernstein, Keith. Frontline Southern Africa / Keith Bernstein and Toni Strasburg ; foreword by Kenneth Kaunda. London : Christopher Helm, c1988. x, 117 p. : chiefly ill., 1 map ; 25 cm. ISBN 0-7470-3012-X (pbk) DDC 968.06/3 19
1. Mozambique - History - 1975-. 2. Angola - History - South African Incursions, 1978-. 3. South Africa - History - 1961-. I. Strasburg, Toni. II. Title.
HN800.A8   **NYPL [Sc E 89-122]**

Bernus, Edmond. Atlas du Niger /. Paris , c1980. 64 p. : ISBN 85258-151-5 : DDC 912/.6626 19
G2660 .A8 1980   **NYPL [Sc F 84-232]**

Berre, Henri, 1911-1984. Sultans dadjo du Sila, Tchad / par Henri Berre. Paris : Editions du Centre national de la recherche scientifique, 1985. xiv, 119 p. : ill. ; 21 cm. (Contributions à la connaissance des élites africaines. fasc. 4e) Includes bibliographical references and indexes. ISBN 2-222-03641-0 : DDC 967/.4302/0922 B 19
1. Sultans - Chad - Biography. 2. Chad - History. I. Title.
DT546.472 .B47 1985 **NYPL [Sc D 87-1421]**

Berry, James.
Chain of days / James Berry. Oxford [Oxfordshire] ; New York : Oxford University Press, 1985. viii, 94 p. ; 22 cm. ISBN 0-19-211964-8 (pbk.) : DDC 821/.914 19
I. Title.
PR9265.9.B47 C5 1985   **NYPL [Sc D 89-45]**

A thief in the village / by James Berry. New York : Orchard Books, 1988, c1987. 148 p. ; 22 cm. A collection of nine short stories about life in contemporary Jamaica, covering such subjects as a young boy's desire to buy shoes for the cricket team and a girl's adventures on a coconut plantation. ISBN 0-531-05745-3 DDC [Fic] 19
1. Children's stories, Jamaican. 2. Jamaica - Juvenile fiction. I. Title.
PZ7.B46173 Th 1988 **NYPL [Sc D 88-1252]**

Berry, Kelly-Marie. And when you come to our house : a Buddy Books production of poems / by Kelly-Marie Berry. [New York?] : K. M. Berry, c1987. [35] p. ; 23 cm. Cover title.
I. Title.   **NYPL [Sc D 89-186]**

Berry, Leonard, 1930- Lewis, Lawrence. African environments and resources /. Boston , 1988. xii, 404 p. : ISBN 0-04-916010-9 (alk. paper) DDC 333.7/096 19
HC800 .L48 1987   **NYPL [Sc E 89-50]**

Berthold Saieh, Laïla. Tourne la peau, elle sera noire : (credo et témoignages) / Laïla Berthold Saieh ; Préface de Roland Dorcély. Port-au-Prince, Haiti : H. Deschamps, 1986. 67 p. : ill. ; 21 cm. Poems.
I. Title.   **NYPL [Sc D 88-183]**

Bertley, Leo W. Montreal's oldest black congregation : Union Church, 3007 Delisle Street / by Leo W. Bertley. Pierrefonds, Quebec : Bilongo Publishers, c1976. 30 p. : ill. ; 28 cm. Cover title. Author's autographed presentation copy to the Schomburg Collection.
1. Union Church (Montréal, Québec) - History. 2. Montréal (Québec) - Church history. I. Title.
BX9882.8.M668 B47 1976
   NYPL [Sc F 89-49]

Besada, Benito. Antecedentes económicos de la guerra de los diez años/ Benito Besada. La Habana : Editorial de Ciencas Sociales, 1978. 17 p. : 18 cm. (Teoría económica) Bibliography: p. 17.
1. Cuba - Economic conditions. I. Title.
   NYPL [Sc C 88-211]

The best of George B. Wallace . Wallace, George B., poet. [Kingston, Jamaica] 1982. 152 p. :
MLCS 84/1847 (P)   **NYPL [JFD 85-8238]**

Bestor, Arthur. State sovereignty and slavery : a reinterpretation of proslavery constitutional doctrine, 1846-1860 / Arthur Bestor. Springfield, IL : A. Bestor, 1961. 64 p. ; 24 cm. Published subsequently in: Journal of the Illinois State Historical Society, Summer 1961. "Complete texts of a paper to be presented vefore the Mississippi Valley Historical Association at its meeting in detroit on April 21, 1961."
1. Slavery - United States - Legal status, laws, etc. 2. State rights. 3. United States - Constitutional history. I. Title.   **NYPL [Sc E 87-669]**

BETHUNE, MARY MCLEOD, 1875-1955 - JUVENILE LITERATURE.
Halasa, Malu. Mary McLeod Bethune /. New York , c1989. 111 p. : ISBN 1-555-46574-9 DDC 370/.92/4 B 92 19
E185.97.B34 H35 1989 **NYPL [Sc E 88-616]**

BETI, MONGO, 1932-
John, Elerius Edet. Topics in African literature /. Lagos , 1986. 3 v. ; ISBN 978-244-610-6 (v. 1)
   NYPL [Sc D 89-370]

BETSILEOS - HISTORY.
Raherisoanjato, Daniel. Origines et évolution du

Royaume de l'Arindrano jusqu'au XIXe siècle . Antananarivo , 1984. 334 leaves : DDC 969/.1 19
DT469.M37 A747 1984
     NYPL [Sc F 88-390]

Bettelheim, Judith, 1944- Nunley, John W. (John Wallace), 1945- Caribbean festival arts . [Saint Louis] , 1988. 218 p. : ISBN 0-295-96702-1 : DDC 394.2/5/07409729 19
GT4823 .N85 1988   **NYPL [Sc F 89-89]**

Better life for Nigerians / editor, S.W. Anaughe. Lagos : Fed. Min. of Information and Culture, 1987. 56 p. : ill., ports. ; 22 cm. Published for the National Day Celebration of 1987.
1. Nigeria - Economic policy. 2. Nigeria - Social policy. I. Anaughe, S. W. II. Nigeria. Federal Ministry of Information and Culture. **NYPL [Sc D 88-796]**

Between now and then . Lee, Leslie. New York , c1984. 108 p., [1] p. of plates : ISBN 0-573-61911-5 (pbk.) DDC 812/.54 19
PS3562.E35435 B4 1984 **NYPL [Sc C 88-55]**

Beyond a Kennedy-backed J. Jackson 1988 ticket. Mahmud-Okereke, N. Enuma, 1948- OAU--time to admit South Africa /. Lagos, Nigeria , 1986. xxvi, 57, 190 p. : ISBN 978-242-302-5   **NYPL [Sc C 88-204]**

Beyond community development . Bratton, Michael. London , 1978. 62 p. :
HN802.Z9 C62   **NYPL [JLD 81-437]**

Beyond the bend in the river . Northrup, David. Athens, Ohio , 1988. xvii, 264 p. : ISBN 0-89680-151-9 DDC 331.11/73/0967517 19
HD8811.Z8 K586 1988
     NYPL [Sc D 88-960]

Beyond the Botha/Buthelezi political debate . El Mahmud-Okereke, N. O. E. (Noel Olufemi Enuma), 1948- London , c1987. v, 177 p. : ISBN 978-242-309-2 (pbk.) DDC 346.802/3 19
     NYPL [Sc C 88-180]

Beyond the mother country . Pilkington, Edward. London , 1988. 182 p. ; ISBN 1-85043-113-2 DDC 305.8/96/041 19
     NYPL [Sc D 89-122]

Beyond the woodfuel crisis . Leach, Gerald. London , 1988. [x], 309 p. : ISBN 1-85383-031-3 (pbk) : DDC 333.75 19
     NYPL [Sc D 89-397]

Bhajan, Selwyn. Whispers of dawn / [Selwyn Bhajan]. [Barbados? : s.n., c1978] (Barbados : Caribbean Graphics) iv, 52 p. : ill. ; 22 cm. Poems.
I. Title.
MLCS 85/658 (P)   **NYPL [Sc D 88-792]**

The bhang syndicate /. Saisi, Frank. Nairobi , 1984. 180 p. ;
MLCS 84/916 (P)   **NYPL [Sc C 88-282]**

Bhat, Ashok. Britain's Black population . Aldershot, Hants, England , Brookfield, Vt., USA , c1988. xv, 298 p. ; ISBN 0-566-05179-6 : DDC 305.8/96/041 19
DA125.N4 B75 1988   **NYPL [Sc E 89-100]**

Bhêly-Quénum, Olympe.
[Piège sans fin. English]
Snares without end / by Olympe Bhêly-Quénum ; translated by Dorothy S. Blair ; introduction by Abioseh Michael Porter. Charlottesville : University Press of Virginia, 1988. xxvi, 204 p. ; 22 cm. (CARAF books) Translation of: Un piège sans fin. ISBN 0-8139-1189-3 (pbk). DDC 843 19
1. Benin - Fiction. I. Title. II. Series.
PQ3989.2.B5 P513 1988
     NYPL [Sc D 89-434]

BIAFRAN CONFLICT, 1967-1970. see NIGERIA - HISTORY - CIVIL WAR, 1967-1970.

The Biafran nightmare . Okpoko, John. Enugu, Nigeria , 1986. x, 76, [4] p. of plates : ISBN 978-233-504-5   **NYPL [Sc C 88-184]**

Biarnès, Pierre. Les Français en Afrique noire, de Richélieu à Mitterand : 350 ans de présence française au sud du Sahara / Pierre Biarnès . Paris : A. Colin, 1987. 447 p. :bill., maps, ports. ; 21 cm. Bibliography: p. 442-445. ISBN 2-200-37115-2
1. French - Africa. 2. France - Colonies - Africa. 3. France - Foreign relations - Africa. 4. France - Foreign relations - France. 5. Africa - Politics and government. I. Title.   **NYPL [Sc D 88-562]**

Bibby, Deirdre L. Augusta Savage and the art Schools of Harlem. New York, N.Y. , 1988. 27 p. :   **NYPL [Sc F 89-45]**

Bibele hi swifaniso . Schnorr von Carolsfeld, Julius, 1794-1872. [Bibel in Bildern. Selections.] Kensington, Tvl. , 1970. 64 p. :
     NYPL [Sc E 89-180]

Bibeli mimo . Bible. Yoruba. 1969. Lagos , 1969. 923 p. : ISBN 0-564-00643-2
     NYPL [Sc C 88-154]

Bibiliokerafi ya puo ya Setswana. Peters, Marguerite Andree. Bibliography of the Tswana language . Pretoria , 1982. 1 [i.e. L], 175 p., [3] leaves of plates : ISBN 0-7989-0116-0 DDC 015.68 19
Z3601 .P47 1982   **NYPL [Sc E 87-667]**

BIBLE - AFRICA.
Mbiti, John S. Bible and theology in African Christianity /. Nairobi , 1986. xiv, 248 p., [16] p. of plates : ISBN 0-19-572593-X
     NYPL [Sc D 89-296]

Bible and theology in African Christianity /. Mbiti, John S. Nairobi , 1986. xiv, 248 p., [16] p. of plates : ISBN 0-19-572593-X
     NYPL [Sc D 89-296]

BIBLE. N. T. JOHN - CRITICISM, INTERPRETATION, ETC.
Kuzenzama, K. P. M. La structure bipartite de Jn 6, 26-71 . Kinshasa , 1987. 124 p. ;
     NYPL [Sc E 88-374]

BIBLE. N.T. LUKE II, 1-20 - CRITICISM, INTERPRETATION, ETC.
An African Chris[t]mas? /. Eldoret, Kenya , 1983. 53 p. ; DDC 263/.91/096 19
BS2575.2 .A37 1983   **NYPL [Sc D 88-195]**

BIBLE. N.T. MATTHEW II, 1-12 - CRITICISM, INTERPRETATION, ETC.
An African Chris[t]mas? /. Eldoret, Kenya , 1983. 53 p. ; DDC 263/.91/096 19
BS2575.2 .A37 1983   **NYPL [Sc D 88-195]**

BIBLE. O. T. GENESIS I-XI - CRITICISM, INTERPRETATION, ETC.
Oduyoye, Modupẹ. The sons of the gods and the daughters of men . Maryknoll, N.Y. , c1984. xi, 132 p. : ISBN 0-88344-467-4 (pbk.) DDC 222/.1106 19
BS1235.2 .O38 1984   **NYPL [Sc D 88-1236]**

BIBLE. O.T. PSALMS - FOLKLORE.
Ofori-Amankwah, E. H. Mystical and sacred uses of the holy book of Psalms /. [S.L. , 1985] Zaria : printed by Gaskiya Corp.) 48 p. ;
     NYPL [Sc B 88-61]

BIBLE - PRAYERS.
Heart of prayer . London , 1985. 175 p. : ISBN 0-00-599841-7 **NYPL [Sc C 88-29]**

Bible. Yoruba. 1969. Bibeli mimo : tabi majemu lailai ati titun. Corr. ed. Lagos : The Bible Societu of Nigeria, 1969. 923 p. : maps ; 19cm. ISBN 0-564-00643-2
I. Title.   **NYPL [Sc C 88-154]**

Bibliograf'ia cubana : 1921-1936 / compilada por Marta Dulzaides Serrate ... [et al. en el Departamento Colección Cubana.] La Habana : Editorial Orbe, 1977-78. [v. 1, 1978] 2 v. ; 30 cm. At head of title of vol. 2: Consejo Nacional de Cultura. CONTENTS: [t. 1] 1921-1924.- t. 2. 1925-1928.
1. Cuba - History - 1909-1933 - Bibliography. 2. Cuba - History - 1933-1959 - Bibliography. 3. Cuba - Bibliography. I. Dulzaides Serrate, Marta. II. Cuba. Consejo Nacional de Cultura. III. Havana. Biblioteca Nacional "José Martí". Departamento Colección Cubana.   **NYPL [HO 80-1472]**

Bibliografia de temas afrocubanos /[revisión técnica, Tomás Fernández Robaina ; edición, Marta Trigo Marabotto y Maria Luisa Acosta]. La Habana : Biblioteca Nacional José Martí, Dpto. de Investigaciones Bibliográficas, 1985. 581 p. ; 23 cm. At head of title: Ministerio de Cultura. Includes indexes. Errata slip inserted.
1. Blacks - Cuba - Bibliography. I. Robaina, Tomás Fernández, 1941-. II. Biblioteca Nacional José Martí. Departamento de Investigaciones Bibliográficas. III. Title.   **NYPL [Sc D 89-510]**

Bibliographie relative aux Antilles . Archives de la Martinique. Fort-de-France , 1978- v. ; DDC 016.97298/2 19
Z1502.F5 A72 1978 F2151
     NYPL [Sc F 88-286]

Bibliographies & documentation series. A Directory of international migration study centers, research programs, and library resources /. Staten Island, N.Y. , 1987. ix, 299 p. ; ISBN 0-934733-18-X (pbk.) : DDC 325/.07 19
JV6033 .C45 1987   **NYPL [JLF 88-1452]**

Bibliographies and indexes in Afro-American and African studies .
(no. 22) Foster, Mamie Marie Booth. Southern Black creative writers, 1829-1953 . New York , 1988. xvii, 113 p. ; ISBN 0-313-26207-1 (lib. bdg. : alk. paper) DDC 016.81/09/896073 19
Z1229.N39 F67 1988 PS153.N5
     NYPL [Sc E 88-495]

Bibliographies and indexes in Afro-American and African studies, 0742-6925 .
(no. 20) Stevenson, Rosemary M. Index to Afro-American reference resources /. New York , 1988. xxvi, 315 p. ; ISBN 0-313-24580-0 (lib. bdg. : alk. paper) DDC 973/.0496073 19
Z1361.N39 S77 1988 E185
     NYPL [Sc E 88-220]

(no. 21) Avery-Coger, Greta Margaret Kay McCormick. Index of subjects, proverbs, and themes in the writings of Wole Soyinka /. New York , c1988. xxii, 311 p. ; ISBN 0-313-25712-4 (lib. bdg. : alk. paper) DDC 822 19
PR9387.9.S6 Z54 1988 **NYPL [Sc E 88-496]**

Bibliographies and indexes in religious studies, 0742-6836 .
(no. 10) Evans, James H., 1950- Black theology . New York , c1987. xii, 205 p. ; ISBN 0-313-24822-2 (lib. bdg. : alk. paper) DDC 016.23/008996073 19
Z7774 .E9 1987 BT82.7
     NYPL [Sc E 87-426]

Bibliographies (South Africa. State Library) .
(no. 25) Peters, Marguerite Andree. Bibliography of the Tswana language . Pretoria , 1982. 1 [i.e. L], 175 p., [3] leaves of plates : ISBN 0-7989-0116-0 DDC 015.68 19
Z3601 .P47 1982   **NYPL [Sc E 87-667]**

BIBLIOGRAPHY - BIBLIOGRAPHY - DEVELOPING COUNTRIES.
Gorman, G. E. Guide to current national bibliographies in the Third World /. London , New York , c1987. xx, 372 p. ; ISBN 0-905450-34-5   **NYPL [Sc E 88-474]**

BIBLIOGRAPHY - BIBLIOGRAPHY - UNITED STATES.
Prucha, Francis Paul. Handbook for research in American history . Lincoln , c19. xiii, 289 p. ; ISBN 0-8032-3682-4 (alk. paper) DDC 016.973 19
Z1236 .P78 1987 E178 **NYPL [Sc D 88-545]**

BIBLIOGRAPHY, CRITICAL. see CRITICISM.

BIBLIOGRAPHY, NATIONAL - BIBLIOGRAPHY.
Gorman, G. E. Guide to current national bibliographies in the Third World /. London , New York , c1987. xx, 372 p. ; ISBN 0-905450-34-5   **NYPL [Sc E 88-474]**

A Bibliography of health and disease in East Africa / editors, A.S. Muller ... [et al.]. Amsterdam ; New York : Elsevier ; 282 p. ; 31 cm. "Royal Tropical Institute, Amsterdam, the Netherlands, Kenya Medical Research Institute, Nairobi, Kenya." Sponsored by the East African Medical Research Council of the East African Community and the Medical Research Centre, Nairobi. Includes index. ISBN 0-444-80931-7 (U. S.) DDC 016.3621/0967 19
1. Public health - Africa, East - Bibliography. 2. Diseases - Africa, East - Bibliography. I. Muller, A. S. (Alexander Samuel), 1930-. II. Koninklijk Instituut voor de Tropen. III. Kenya Medical Research Institute. IV. East African Medical Research Council. V. Medical Research Centre, Nairobi.
Z6673.6.A353 B53 1988 RA552.A353
     NYPL [Sc G 89-6]

Bibliography of official publications of the Black South African homelands /. Kotzé, D. A. Pretoria , 1979. xix, 80 p. : ISBN 0-86981-137-1 DDC 015.68
Z3607.H65 K67 J705.T3;
     NYPL [Sc D 88-1197]

Bibliography of the Tswana language . Peters, Marguerite Andree. Pretoria , 1982. 1 [i.e. L], 175 p., [3] leaves of plates : ISBN 0-7989-0116-0

DDC 015.68 19
Z3601 .P47 1982   *NYPL [Sc E 87-667]*

BIBLIOGRAPHY - REFERENCE BOOKS. see REFERENCE BOOKS.

Biblioteca Conmemorativa de Colón. see Columbus Memorial Library.

Biblioteca Nacional José Martí. Departamento de Investigaciones Bibliográficas. Bibliografia de temas afrocubanos /. La Habana , 1985. 581 p. ;   *NYPL [Sc D 89-510]*

Bibliothèque de l'Ecole des hautes études. Section des sciences religieuses. (v. 88) Sous le masque de l'animal . Paris , c1987. 380 p. :   ISBN 2-13-039831-6   *NYPL [Sc E 88-314]*

Bibliothèque d'histoire antillaise. (10) Pérotin-Dumon, Anne. Etre patriote sous les tropiques . Basse-Terre , 1985. 339 p. :   ISBN 2-900339-21-9   *NYPL [Sc E 88-256]*

Bibliothèque Forney. Negripub . [Paris] [1987] 157 p. :   ISBN 2-7012-0580-8   *NYPL [Sc E 88-234]*

Bibliothèque inguimbertine de Carpentras. Un Flibustier français dans la mer des Antilles en 1618-1620 /. Clamart [France] , c1987. 263 p. :   ISBN 2-9502053-0-5   *NYPL [Sc E 88-247]*

Bibliothèque Peiresc . (4) Tubiana, Marie José. Des troupeaux et des femmes . Paris , 1985. 390 p., [16] p. of plates :   ISBN 2-85802-554-9   *NYPL [Sc E 88-217]*

Bickell, Richard. The West Indies as they are, or, A real picture of slavery : but more particularly as it exists in the island of Jamaica. / by R. Bickell. London : J. Hatchard, 1825. xvi, 256 p. ; 23 cm. "In three parts with notes."
1. Slavery - West Indies. 2. Slavery - Jamaica. I. Title. II. Title: Real picture of slavery.
NYPL [Sc Rare F 88-57]

Bicknell, Leona Mildred. How a little girl went to Africa : told by herself / by Leona Mildred Bicknell. Boston : Lee and Shepard, 1904. 172 p. : ill. ; 20 cm.
1. Africa, West - Description and travel - 1851-1950. I. Title.   *NYPL [Sc C 88-368]*

Bidelman, Patrick Kay. The Black women in the Middle West Project . Indianapolis, Ind. (140 N. Senate Ave., Room 408, Indianapolis 46204) , 1986. xi, 238 p. :   DDC 977/.00496073 19
E185.915 .B52 1986   *NYPL [Sc F 88-141]*

Biehl, João Guilherme. De igual pra igual : um diálogo crítico entre a teologia da libertação e as teologias negra, feminista e pacifista / João Guilherme Biehl. Petrópolis : Vozes ; São Leopoldo, RS, Brasil : Editora Sinodal, 1987. 155 p. ; 21 cm. Bibliography: p. 140-155.
1. Black theology. 2. Feminism - Religious aspects - Christianity. 3. Pacifism - Religious aspects - Christianity. I. Title.
BT83.57 .B54 1987   *NYPL [Sc D 88-1016]*

Bielemeier, Günter. Interviews avec des écrivains africains francophones /. [Bayreuth, W. Germany , c1986. 95 p. ;
NYPL [Sc D 88-906]

Biesele, Megan. The Past and future of !Kung ethnography . Hamburg , 1986. 423 p. :   ISBN 3-87118-780-1   *NYPL [Sc D 88-234]*

The big band years /. Crowther, Bruce, 1933- Newton Abbot , c1988. 208 p. :   ISBN 0-7153-9137-2 :   DDC 785/.06/660973 19
ML3518   *NYPL [JNF 88-254]*

BIG BANDS - UNITED STATES - HISTORY. Crowther, Bruce, 1933- The big band years /. Newton Abbot , c1988. 208 p. :   ISBN 0-7153-9137-2 :   DDC 785/.06/660973 19
ML3518   *NYPL [JNF 88-254]*

Big game hunter . Sutton, Felix. New York , 1960. 192 p. ;   *NYPL [Sc D 88-659]*

The big mama stories /. Youngblood, Shay. Ithaca, N.Y. , c1989. 106 p. ;   ISBN 0-932379-58-3 (alk. paper) :   DDC 813/.54 19
PS3575.O8535 B5 1989
NYPL [Sc D 89-530]

Bigaignon, Romuald. Livre d'or de la République Malgache. [Tananarive? , 1960] 176 p. ;   *NYPL [Sc G 88-18]*

Bigangara, Jean-Baptiste. Eléments de linguistique burundaise / Jean-Baptiste Bigangara. Bujumbura : Expression et valeurs africaines burundaises, 1982. 138 p. ; 24 cm. (Collection Expression et valeurs africaines burundaises . 1) French and Rundi. Bibliography: p. 135. DDC 496/.39 19
1. Rundi language - Grammar. 2. Names, Personal - Rundi. I. Title. II. Series.
PL8611.1 .B54 1982   *NYPL [Sc E 88-403]*

Le fondement de l'imanisme, ou, Religion traditionnelle au Burundi : approche linguistique et philosophique / Jean-Baptiste Bigangara. Bujumbura, Burundi : Expression et valeurs africaines burundaises, 1984. 140 p. ; 24 cm. (Collection Expression et valeurs africaines burundaises . 2) In French and Rundi. Bibliography: p. 130-137.
1. Imana (Rundi deity). 2. Burundi - Religion. I. Title. II. Title: Fondement de l'imanisme. III. Series.
BL2470.B94 B54 1984   *NYPL [Sc E 88-459]*

Bigirumwami, Aloys. Imigani "tima-ngiro" y'u Rwanda =. Butare , 1987. 267, [1] p. ;   *NYPL [Sc D 88-865]*

BIKO, B. S. Bernstein, Hilda (Watts) No. 46 Steve Biko /. London , 1978. 150 p., [4] p. of plates :   ISBN 0-904759-21-0 :
DT779.8.B48 B47   *NYPL [JFD 79-52]*

Biko, Stephen Bantu. see Biko, B. S.

BIKO, STEPHEN, 1946-1977 - DRAMA. Richard Attenborough's cry freedom . New York , 1987. [128] p. :   ISBN 0-394-75838-2   DDC 791.43/72 19
PN1997.C885 A88 1987   *NYPL [Sc G 89-17]*

Biko, Steve, 1946-1977. The testimony of Steve Biko / edited, with an introduction and commentary, by Millard Arnold, and with an appendix on the inquest into the death of Stephen Bantu Biko. London : Grafton Books, 1987, c1978. xxxv, 298 p. ; 18 cm. Includes bibliographical references.
1. Biko, Steve, 1946-1977. 2. Trials (Terrorism) - South Africa - Pretoria. I. Arnold, Millard W. II. Title.
NYPL [Sc C 89-126]

BIKO, STEVE, 1946-1977. Biko, Steve, 1946-1977. The testimony of Steve Biko /. London , 1987, c1978. xxxv, 298 p. ;   *NYPL [Sc C 89-126]*

BILINGUAL EDUCATION. see EDUCATION, BILINGUAL.

Bill and report of John A. Bingham . Bingham, John Armor, 1815-1900. [Washington, D.C. , 1860] 7, [1] p. ;   *NYPL [Sc Rare C 89-2]*

Bill Cosby . Haskins, James, 1941- New York , 1988. 138 p. :   ISBN 0-8027-6785-0   DDC 792.7/028/0924 B 92 19
PN2287.C632 H37 1988
NYPL [Sc D 88-1162]

BILL DRAFTING - AFRICA, SOUTHERN - CONGRESSES. Aspects of legislative drafting /. KwaDlangezwa, South Africa , 1987. ix, 204 p. ;   ISBN 0-907995-73-X   *NYPL [Sc C 88-66]*

BILL DRAFTING - SOUTH AFRICA - CONGRESSES. Aspects of legislative drafting /. KwaDlangezwa, South Africa , 1987. ix, 204 p. ;   ISBN 0-907995-73-X   *NYPL [Sc C 88-66]*

Billi Gordon's You've had worse things in your mouth cookbook /. Gordon, Billi. San Francisco, Calif. , c1985. 96 p. :   *NYPL [Sc F 88-214]*

Billie Holiday, her life & times /. White, John, 1939- Tunbridge Wells, Kent , New York , 1987. 144 p. :   ISBN 0-87663-668-7 (USA)   DDC 784.5/3/00924 B 19
ML420.H58 W5 1987   *NYPL [JNF 88-88]*

Billie Holiday, her life and times. White, John, 1939- Billie Holiday, her life & times /. Tunbridge Wells, Kent , New York , 1987. 144 p. :   ISBN 0-87663-668-7 (USA)   DDC 784.5/3/00924 B 19
ML420.H58 W5 1987   *NYPL [JNF 88-88]*

Billingsley, Andrew. Black colleges and public policy /. Chicago , c1986. 99 p. :   ISBN 0-695-60050-8   *NYPL [Sc D 88-947]*

Blacks on white campuses, whites on black

---

campuses /. Chicago , c1986. 177 p. ;   ISBN 0-695-60052-4   *NYPL [Sc D 88-949]*

Inside black colleges and universities /. Chicago , c1986. 153 p. ;   ISBN 0-695-60051-6   *NYPL [Sc D 88-951]*

Les Bin Kanyok . Wymeersch, Patrick. Bandundu, République du Zaïre , 1983. ix, 368 p. ;   *NYPL [Sc F 89-41]*

BIN KANYOK (AFRICAN PEOPLE) Wymeersch, Patrick. Les Bin Kanyok . Bandundu, République du Zaïre , 1983. ix, 368 p. :   *NYPL [Sc F 89-41]*

Bindman, Geoffrey. South Africa . London , New York , 1988. 159 p. :   ISBN 0-86187-979-1 :   DDC 323.4/0968 19   *NYPL [JLE 88-4543]*

Bingel, Anthony Dung. Jos, origins and growth of the town, 1900 to 1972 / by Anthony Dung Bingel. Jos, Nigeria : Dept. of Geography, University of Jos, 1978. v, 22 p. : ill. ; 30 cm. (Publication / University of Jos, Dept. of Geography . no. 1) Bibliography: p. 21. ISBN 978-16-6000-7
1. Jos (Nigeria) - History. I. Series: Publication / University of Jos, Dept. of Geography , no. 1. II. Title.
MLCM 83/4794 (D)   *NYPL [Sc F 88-249]*

Bingham, John Armor, 1815-1900. Bill and report of John A. Bingham : and vote on its passage, repealing the territorial New Mexican laws establishing slavery and authorizing employers to whip "white persons" and others in their employment, and denying them redress in the courts. [Washington, D.C. : s.n., 1860] 7, [1] p. ; 24 cm. Caption title. Contains the text of the bill and an extract from the report, dated May 10, 1860. "Presidential campaign of 1860. Republican Executive Congressional Committee ... The committee are prepared to furnish the following speeches and documents ..."--p. [8].
1. Slavery - New Mexico. 2. Slavery - United States - Speeches in Congress - 1860. 3. Campaign literature, 1860 - Republican. I. Title.
NYPL [Sc Rare C 89-2]

BINI (AFRICAN PEOPLE) - SOCIAL LIFE AND CUSTOMS. Aisien, Ekhaguosa. IWU . Benin City, Nigeria , c1986. 64 p. :   *NYPL [Sc D 88-728]*

BINI LANGUAGE - DICTIONARIES - ENGLISH. Agheyisi, Rebecca N. An Ẹdo-English dictionary /. Benin City, Nigeria , 1986. xxiv, 169 p. :   ISBN 978-12-3293-5   DDC 496/.33 19
PL8077.4 .A44 1986   *NYPL [Sc D 88-847]*

Aigbe, E. I. Ẹmwẹn Ẹdo na zedu ẹre y'Ebo . Lagos [1986?] viii, 62 p. :
NYPL [Sc C 88-174]

Binky brothers, detectives. Lawrence, James Duncan, 1918- New York [1968] 60 p. DDC [Fic]
PZ7.L4359 Bi   *NYPL [Sc D 89-118]*

Biographical dictionary of American sports. Football / edited by David L. Porter. New York : Greenwood Press, 1987. xvii, 763 p. ; 24 cm. Includes bibliographies and index.   ISBN 0-313-25771-X (lib. bdg. : alk. paper)   DDC 796.332/092/2 B 19
1. Football - United States - Biography - Dictionaries. 2. Football - United States - History. I. Porter, David L., 1941-.
GV939.A1 B56 1987
*NYPL [*R-MVFF 88-6690]*

BIOGRAPHY (AS A LITERARY FORM) Starling, Marion Wilson, 1907. The slave narrative . Washington, D.C. , 1988. xxx, 375 p. :   ISBN 0-88258-165-1 :   DDC 973/.0496073 19
E444 .S8 1988   *NYPL [Sc E 89-185]*

Biography of Amy Ashwood Garvey, 1897-1969 . Yard, Lionel M. [S.l.] [198-?] vii, 233 p. :   *NYPL [Sc E 88-541]*

BIOGRAPHY, WRITING OF. see BIOGRAPHY (AS A LITERARY FORM)

Biologie . Kipasman, Mikalukalu. Kinshasa [1984?] 70 p. :   *NYPL [Sc G 87-46]*

BIOLOGY - ECOLOGY. see ECOLOGY.

BIOLOGY - EXAMINATIONS, QUESTIONS, ETC. Kipasman, Mikalukalu. Biologie . Kinshasa [1984?] 70 p. :   *NYPL [Sc G 87-46]*

BIOLOGY - OUTLINES, SYLLABI, ETC.
Kipasman, Mikalukalu. Biologie . Kinshasa
[1984?] 70 p. : *NYPL [Sc G 87-46]*

Biondi, Jean Pierre. Saint-Louis du Sénégal :
mémoires d'un métissage / Jean-Pierre Biondi.
Paris : Éditions Denoël, c1987. 234 p., [16] p.
of plates : ill., maps ; 24 cm. (Aventure coloniale
de la France) Destins croisés Includes index.
Bibliography: p. [217]-221. ISBN 2-207-23350-2
1. Saint Louis (Senegal) - History. I. Title. II. Series.
NYPL [Sc D 88-1501]

BIONOMICS. see ECOLOGY.

Biracree, Tom, 1947- Wilma Rudolph / Tom
Biracree. New York : Chelsea House, 1988. 111
p. : ill. ; 25 cm. (American women of achievement)
A biography of the woman who overcame crippling
polio as a child to become the first woman to win three
gold medals in track in a single Olympics. Includes
index. Bibliography: p. 108. ISBN 1-555-46675-3
DDC 796.4/2/0924 B 92 19
*1. Rudolph, Wilma, 1940- - Juvenile literature. 2.
Athletes - United States - Biography - Juvenile
literature. 3. Afro-American athletes - Biography -
Juvenile literature. I. Title. II. Series.*
GV697.R8 B57 1988 *NYPL [Sc E 88-172]*

Birbalsingh, Frank. Passion and exile : essays in
Caribbean literature / Frank Birbalsingh.
London : Hansib, 1988. 186 p. ; 21 cm. Includes
bibliographical references. ISBN 1-87051-816-0 (pbk)
: DDC 810.9/91821 19
*1. Caribbean literature (English) - History and criticism.
I. Title.* *NYPL [JFD 89-183]*

Bird, Charles S. Explorations in African systems
of thought /. Washington, D.C. , c1987. xvi,
337 p. : ISBN 0-87474-591-8 (pbk.)
NYPL [Sc D 88-566]

Bird, Van S. Symposium on race and class.
Philadelphia , 1984. 62 p. ;
NYPL [Sc D 88-2]

Birmingfind. The Media and the movement
[microform] . [Birmingham, Ala. , 1981?] [12]
p. : *NYPL [Sc Micro F-10982]*

Birmingham Museum of Art. Spanel, Donald,
1952- Through ancient eyes . Birmingham, AL ,
1988. xiii, 159 p. : DDC 732/.8 19
NB1296.2 .S63 1988
NYPL [3-MAE 88-3366]

Birney, James Gillespie, 1792-1857. Examination
of the decision of the Supreme Court of the
United States, in the case of Strader, Gorman
and Armstrong vs. Christopher Graham :
delivered at its December term, 1850 ;
concluding with an address to the free colored
people, advising them to remove to Liberia / by
James G. Birney. Cincinnati : Truman &
Spofford, publishers, 1852. iv, [1], 6-46, [1] p. ;
23 cm. "Mr. Chief Justice Taney delivered the opinion
of the court."-p. [12]
*1. Slavery - United States - Legal status of slaves in
free states. 2. Ordinance of 1787. 3. Afro-Americans -
Colonization - Liberia. I. Graham, Christopher. II.
Strader, Jacob. III. Gorman, James. IV. Armstrong,
John. V. Taney, Roger Brooke, 1777-1864. VI. Title.*
E450 .B57 *NYPL [Sc Rare F 88-37]*

**BIRTH CONTROL - AFRICA -
BIBLIOGRAPHY.**
Régulation des naissances en Afrique . Abidjan,
Côte d'Ivoire [1987] 74 p. ;
NYPL [Sc F 88-392]

**BIRTH CONTROL - AFRICA, WEST - CASE
STUDIES.**
Sex roles, population and development in West
Africa . London , Portsmouth, N.H. , 1987. xiii,
242 p. ; ISBN 0-435-08022-9 DDC 304.6/0966 19
HB3665.5.A3 S49 1988
NYPL [Sc E 88-318]

**BIRTH CONTROL CLINICS - AFRICA -
ADMINISTRATION.**
Brown, Richard Coleman, 1936- The family
planning clinic in Africa . London , 1987. ix,
102 p. : ISBN 0-333-43658-X
NYPL [Sc D 88-630]

BIRTH CONTROL - KENYA - CONGRESSES.
Women and population . [Nairobi?] [1985] 73
p. ; DDC 363.9/6/096762 19
HQ766.5.K4 W65 1985 *NYPL [Sc F 88-191]*

BIRTH CONTROL - NIGERIA.
Olusanya, P. Olufemi. Nursemaids and the pill .
Legon , 1981. xiii, 157 p. :
NYPL [Sc E 89-249]

The birth of Christian Zionism in South Africa /.
Oosthuizen, G. C. (Gerhardus Cornelis)
KwaDlangezwa, South Africa , 1987. ii, 56 p. ;
ISBN 0-09-079580-2 DDC 289.9 19
BR1450 .O55 1987 *NYPL [Sc D 88-693]*

BIRTH-RATE. see POPULATION.

**Die Bischofskonferenzen Angolas und Südafrikas
zu Frieden und Gerechtigkeit in ihren Länder.**
Bonn : Sekretariat der Deutschen
Bischofskonferenz, 1986. 54 p. ; 21 cm.
(Stimmen der Weltkirche . Nr. 21) Cover title: Die
Bischofskonferenzen von Angola, Kongo und Südafrika
zu Frieden und Gerechtigkeit in ihren Ländern.
*1. Catholic Church - Africa, Sub-Saharan - Pastoral
letters and charges. 2. Church and social problems -
Africa, Southern. 3. Africa, Southern - Politics and
government - 1975-. I. Catholic Church. Deutsche
Bischofskonferenz. Sekretariat. II. Title. III. Title:
Bischofskonferenzen von Angola, Kongo und Südafrika
zu Frieden und Gerechtigkeit in ihren Ländern. IV.
Series.* *NYPL [Sc D 88-929]*

**Bischofskonferenzen von Angola, Kongo und
Südafrika zu Frieden und Gerechtigkeit in
ihren Ländern.** Die Bischofskonferenzen
Angolas und Südafrikas zu Frieden und
Gerechtigkeit in ihren Länder. Bonn , 1986. 54
p. ; *NYPL [Sc D 88-929]*

Bishop, Jack, 1910- Ralph Ellison / Jack Bishop.
New York : Chelsea House, c1988. 110 p. :
ill. ; 24 cm. (Black Americans of achievement)
"Introductory essay by Coretta Scott King"--Cover.
Includes index. A biography of the black author famous
for his 1952 novel "Invisible Man" revealing the realities
of the black experience in America. Bibliography: p.
108. ISBN 1-555-46585-4 DDC 818/.5409 B 19
*1. Ellison, Ralph - Biography - Juvenile literature. 2.
Novelists, American - 20th century - Biography -
Juvenile literature. 3. Afro-American novelists -
Biography - Juvenile literature. I. Title. II. Series.*
PS3555.L625 Z59 1988 *NYPL [Sc E 88-165]*

Bishop, Maurice.
Address by Prime Minister Maurice Bishop at
the opening of the Socialist International
meeting held in Grenada, July 23-24
[microform]. [St. George's, Grenada] :
Government Information Service, [1981?] 12
leaves ; 33 cm. Cover title. Microfilm. New York:
New York Public Library, 1982. 1 microfilm reel; 35
mm. (MN *ZZ-23051)
*1. Socialism in Latin America - Congresses. 2.
Socialism in the Caribbean area - Congresses. I. Title.*
NYPL [Sc Micro R-4108 no.29]

Address of the Conference on Development
Problems of Small Island States, July 13, 1981
/ by Maurice Bishop [microform]. [St. George's,
Grenada : s.n., 1981] 9 p. ; 33 cm. Caption title.
Microfilm. New York: New York Public Library, 1982.
1 microfilm reel; 35 mm. (MN *ZZ-23051)
*1. Underdeveloped areas - Congresses. I. Conference on
the Development Problems of Small Island States
(1981: Grenada, West Indies). II. Title.*
NYPL [Sc Micro R-4108 no.26]

"Forward to 1982--the year of Economic
construction" [microform] : New Year's address
to the nation / by Prime Minister Maurice
Bishop of the People's Revolutionary
Government of Grenada, on 1st January, 1982.
[st. George's], Grenada : Government
Information Service, 1982. 22 leaves ; 33 cm.
Cover title. Microfilm. New York: New York Public
Library, 1982. 1 microfilm reel; 35 mm. (MN
*ZZ-23051)
*1. Grenada, West Indies - Economic policy. 2.
Grenada, West Indies - Economic conditions. I. Title.*
NYPL [Sc Micro R-4108 no. 28]

Imperialism is the real problem [microform] :
address to the Conference on the Development
Problems of Small Island States, 13th July,
1981 / Maurice Bishop. [st. George's],
Grenada : Government Information Service,
1981. 13 leaves ; 33 cm. Cover title. Microfilm.
New York: New York Public Library, 1982. 1
microfilm reel; 35 mm. (MN *ZZ-23051)
*1. Imperialism - Congresses. 2. Underdeveloped areas -
Congresses. I. Conference on the Development
Problems of Small Island States (1981: Grenada, West
Indies). II. Title.*
NYPL [Sc Micro R-4108 no.27]

Bishop, Rand. African literature, African critics :
the forming of critical standards, 1947-1966 /
Rand Bishop. New York : Greenwood Press,
1988. xii, 213 p. ; 25 cm. (Contributions in

Afro-American and African studies, 0069-9624 . no.
115) Includes index. Bibliography: p. [181]-204. ISBN
0-313-25918-6 (lib. bdg. : alk. paper) DDC
820/.9/96 19
*1. African literature (English) - History and criticism -
Theory, etc. 2. African literature (French) - History and
criticism - Theory, etc. 3. Criticism - Africa - History -
20th century. 4. Literature and society - Africa -
History - 20th century. 5. Canon (Literature). I. Title.
II. Series.*
PR9340 .B5 1988 *NYPL [Sc E 89-129]*

BISHOPS - NIGERIA - BIOGRAPHY.
Idigo, Peter Meze. Archbishop Heerey . Enugu,
Nigeria , 1987. 261 p. : ISBN 978-239-602-8
NYPL [Sc C 89-77]

**BISHOPS - NIGERIA - BIOGRAPHY -
JUVENILE LITERATURE.**
Milsome, John, 1924- From slave boy to
bishop . Cambridge , 1987. [96] p. ; ISBN
0-7188-2678-7 (pbk) DDC 283/.092/4 19
BV3625.N6C7 *NYPL [Sc C 88-106]*

BISHOPS - SOUTH AFRICA - BIOGRAPHY.
Du Boulay, Shirley. Tutu . London , 1988. 286
p., [8] p. of plates : ISBN 0-340-41614-9 : DDC
283/.68/0924 19
BX5700.6.Z8T87 *NYPL [*R-ZPZ 88-3127]*

Biso banso lisanga totonga eklezya ya biso .
Matondo kwa Nzambi. Kinshasa [1988] 72 p. :
NYPL [Sc D 89-221]

Bisson, Terry. Nat Turner / Terry Bisson. New
York : Chelsea House Publishers, c1988. 111
p. : ill. ; 25 cm. (Black Americans of achievement)
Includes index. A biography of the slave and preacher
who, believing that God wanted him to free the slaves,
led a major revolt in 1831. ISBN 1-555-46613-3
DDC 975.5/5503/0924 B 92 19
*1. Turner, Nat, 1800?-1831 - Juvenile literature. 2.
Slaves - Virginia - Biography - Juvenile literature. 3.
Southampton Insurrection, 1831 - Juvenile literature. I.
Title. II. Series.*
F232.S7 T873 1988 *NYPL [Sc E 88-454]*

Bissundyal, Churaumanie. Cleavage : (a poem on
East Indian immigration to British Guyana) /
by Churaumanie Bissundyal. East Coast
Demerara, Guyana : C. Bissundyal, c1986. 64
p. ; 22 cm.
I. Title.
MLCS 87/7682 (P) *NYPL [Sc D 88-714]*

Bisuga, Mike. Nigeria on the forward march /
Mike Bisuga. Ikeja, Nigeria : John West, 1984.
v, 119 p. ; 21 cm. "This booklet is a collection of the
monthly articles of Major Mike Bisuga in the SOJA, a
Nigerian army monthly news bulletin..."-P. i. ISBN
978-16-3030-2
I. Title. *NYPL [Sc D 89-65]*

Bitako-A /. Confiant, Raphaël. [Martinique] ,
1985. 77 p. ; *NYPL [Sc D 88-1269]*

Bitter Canaan . Johnson, Charles Spurgeon,
1893-1956. New Brunswick, N.J. , c1987. lxxiii,
256 p. ; ISBN 0-88738-053-0 : DDC 966.6/2 19
DT631 .J59 1987 *NYPL [Sc E 88-351]*

BIYA, PAUL, 1933-
Gwellem, Jerome F. (Jerome Fultang) Paul
Biya, hero of the New Deal /. Limbe,
Cameroon [1984]. 68 p. :
NYPL [Sc D 88-1255]

Paul Biya . Bamenda , 1985. 103 leaves :
NYPL [Sc D 89-278]

Biyidi, D'Alexandre. see Beti, Mongo, 1932-

BIZANGO (CULT)
Davis, Wade. Passage of darkness . Chapel
Hill , c1988. xx, 344 p. : ISBN 0-8078-1776-7
(alk. paper) DDC 299/.65 19
BL2530.H3 D37 1988 *NYPL [Sc E 88-429]*

Bizimana, Nsekuye.
Müssen die Afrikaner den Weissen alles
nachmachen? / Nsekuye Bizimana. Berlin :
Quorum, c1985. 271 p. : ill. ; 21 cm.
Bibliography: p. 270-271. ISBN 3-88726-014-7 DDC
940 19
*1. Bizimana, Nsekuye - Homes and haunts - Germany
(West). 2. Europe - Civilization - 1945-. I. Title.*
D1055 .B57 1985 *NYPL [Sc D 88-995]*

**BIZIMANA, NSEKUYE - HOMES AND
HAUNTS - GERMANY (WEST)**
Bizimana, Nsekuye. Müssen die Afrikaner den
Weissen alles nachmachen? . Berlin , c1985.
271 p. : ISBN 3-88726-014-7 DDC 940 19
D1055 .B57 1985 *NYPL [Sc D 88-995]*

Black Africa. see **Africa, Sub-Saharan.**

Black Africans and native Americans . Forbes, Jack D. Oxford, UK , New York, NY, USA , 1988. 345 p. ; ISBN 0-631-15665-8 : DDC 973/.0496073 19
E59.M66 F67 1988 **NYPL [HBC 88-2172]**

The Black American elderly : research on physical and psychosocial health / James S. Jackson, editor ; Patricia Newton ... [et al.], associate editors. New York : Springer Pub. Co., c1988. xvi, 383 p. ; 24 cm. Collection of papers presented during a workshop held at the National Institutes of Health on Sept. 25-26, 1986. Workshop was co-sponsored by the National Institute on Aging, the American Association of Retired Persons, and the Dept. of Health and Human Services' Minority Health Office. Includes bibliographical references and index. ISBN 0-8261-5810-2 DDC 362.1/9897/00973 19
1. Afro-American aged - Health and hygiene - Congresses. 2. Afro-American aged - Diseases - Congresses. 3. Afro-American aged - Psychology - Congresses. 4. Aging - Social aspects - Congresses. I. Jackson, James S. (James Sidney), 1944-. II. National Institute on Aging. III. United States. Office of Minority Health.
RA448.5.N4 B56 1988 **NYPL [JLE 88-5391]**

Black American pioneers . Johnson, Glenderlyn. New York, N.Y. , c1987. ii, 22 p. :
NYPL [Sc D 88-1284]

Black American street life . Rose, Dan. Philadelphia, Pa. , c1987. x, 278 p. : ISBN 0-8122-8071-7 DDC 974.8/1100496073 19
F158.9.N4 R67 1987 **NYPL [Sc E 88-76]**

Black American writing from the nadir . Bruce, Dickson D., 1946- Baton Rouge , c1989. xiii, 272 p. : ISBN 0-8071-1450-2 (alk. paper) DDC 810/.9/896073 19
PS153.N5 B77 1989 **NYPL [Sc E 89-197]**

Black Americana . Reno, Dawn E. Collecting Black Americana /. New York , c1986. vii, 150 p. : ISBN 0-517-56095-X DDC 700/.8996073/075 19
NK839.3.A35 R46 1986 **NYPL [Sc F 87-6]**

BLACK AMERICANS. see **AFRO-AMERICANS.**

Black Americans' attitudes toward cancer and cancer tests /. EVAXX. [New York], 1981. 1 v. (various pagings) ; **NYPL [Sc F 88-293]**

Black Americans of achievement.
Bergman, Carol. Sidney Poitier /. New York , c1988. 110 p. : ISBN 1-555-46605-2 DDC 791.43/028/0924 B 92 19
PN2287.P57 B47 1988 **NYPL [Sc E 88-171]**

Bishop, Jack, 1910- Ralph Ellison /. New York , c1988. 110 p. : ISBN 1-555-46585-4 DDC 818/.5409 B 19
PS3555.L625 Z59 1988 **NYPL [Sc E 88-165]**

Bisson, Terry. Nat Turner /. New York , c1988. 111 p. : ISBN 1-555-46613-3 DDC 975.5/5503/0924 B 92 19
F232.S7 T873 1988 **NYPL [Sc E 88-454]**

Ehrlich, Scott. Paul Robeson /. New York , c1988. 111 p. : ISBN 1-555-46608-7 DDC 782.1/092/4 B 92 19
E185.97.R63 E35 1988 **NYPL [Sc E 88-167]**

Frankl, Ron. Duke Ellington /. New York , c1988. 110 p. : ISBN 1-555-46584-6 DDC 785.42/092/4 B 92 19
ML3930.E44 F7 1988 **NYPL [Sc E 88-381]**

Gentry, Tony. Paul Laurence Dunbar /. New York , c1989. 110 p. : ISBN 1-555-46583-8 DDC 811/.4 B 92 19
PS1557 .G46 1989 **NYPL [Sc E 88-514]**

Gilman, Michael. Matthew Henson /. New York , c1988. 110 p. : ISBN 1-555-46590-0 : DDC 919.8/04 B 92 19
G635.H4 G55 1988 **NYPL [Sc E 88-169]**

Halasa, Malu. Mary McLeod Bethune /. New York , c1989. 111 p. : ISBN 1-555-46574-9 DDC 370/.92/4 B 92 19
E185.97.B34 H35 1989 **NYPL [Sc E 88-616]**

Hanley, Sally. A. Philip Randolph /. New York [1988], c1989. 110 p. : ISBN 1-555-46607-9 DDC 323/.092/4 92 19
E185.97.R27 H36 1989 **NYPL [Sc E 88-617]**

Jakoubek, Robert E. Adam Clayton Powell, Jr. /. New York , c1988. xiv, 252 p. ; ISBN

1-555-46606-0 DDC 973/.0496073024 B 92 19
E748.P86 J35 1988 **NYPL [Sc E 88-372]**

Kliment, Bud. Ella Fitzgerald /. New York , c1988. 112 p. : ISBN 1-555-46586-2 DDC 784.5 B 19
ML420.F52 K6 1988 **NYPL [Sc E 88-611]**

Krass, Peter. Sojourner Truth /. New York , c1988. 110 p. : ISBN 1-555-46611-7 DDC 305.5/67/0924 B 92 19
E185.97.T8 K73 1988 **NYPL [Sc E 88-470]**

Lawler, Mary. Marcus Garvey /. New York , c1988. 110 p. : ISBN 1-555-46587-0 DDC 305.8/96073/024 B 92 19
E185.97.G3 L39 1988 **NYPL [Sc E 88-156]**

Preston, Katherine. Scott Joplin /. New York , c1988. 110 p. : ISBN 1-555-46598-6 DDC 780/.92/4 B 92 19
ML3930.J66 P7 1988 **NYPL [Sc E 88-170]**

Rosset, Lisa. James Baldwin /. New York, N.Y. , 1989. 111 p. : ISBN 1-555-46572-2 DDC 818/.5409 B 92 19
PS3552.A45 Z87 1989 **NYPL [Sc E 89-224]**

Rummel, Jack. Langston Hughes /. New York , c1988. 111 p. : ISBN 1-555-46595-1 DDC 818/.5209 B 92 19
PS3515.U274 Z775 1988 **NYPL [Sc E 88-166]**

Rummel, Jack. Muhammad Ali /. New York , c1988. 128 p. : ISBN 1-555-46569-2 DDC 796.8/3/0924 B 92 19
GV1132.A44 R86 1988 **NYPL [Sc E 88-175]**

Russell, Sharman Apt. Frederick Douglass /. New York , c1988. 110 p. : ISBN 1-555-46580-3 DDC 973.8/092/4 B 92 19
E449.D75 R87 1988 **NYPL [Sc E 88-174]**

Scott, Richard, 1956- Jackie Robinson /. New York , 1987. 110 p. : ISBN 1-555-46208-1 : DDC 796.357/092/4 B 92 19
GV865.R6 S36 1987 **NYPL [Sc E 88-168]**

Tanenhaus, Sam. Louis Armstrong /. New York , c1989. 127 p. : ISBN 1-555-46571-4 DDC 785.42/092/4 B 92 19
ML3930.A75 T3 1989 **NYPL [Sc E 89-170]**

Tolbert-Rouchaleau, Jane. James Weldon Johnson /. New York , c1988. 110 p. : ISBN 1-555-46596-X DDC 818/.5209 B 92 19
PS3519.O2625 Z894 1988 **NYPL [Sc E 88-164]**

Urban, Joan, 1950- Richard Wright /. New York, N.Y. [1989] 111 p. : ISBN 1-555-46618-4 DDC 813/.52 19
PS3545.R815 Z85 1989 **NYPL [Sc E 89-196]**

Wilson, M. L. (Matthew Lawrence), 1960- Chester Himes /. New York , c1988. 111 p. : ISBN 1-555-46591-9 DDC 813/.54 B 92 19
PS3515.I713 Z93 1988 **NYPL [Sc E 88-373]**

Black and priceless : the power of black ink. Manchester : Crocus, 1988. xiii, 198 p. : ill. ; 20 cm. ISBN 0-946745-45-5 (pbk) : DDC 821/.914/08 823/.01/08 19
1. English poetry - Black authors. 2. English fiction - Black authors. 3. English poetry - 20th century. 4. Short stories, English. 5. English fiction - 20th century.
PR1225 PR1309.S5 **NYPL [Sc C 89-131]**

BLACK ART (WITCHCRAFT) see **WITCHCRAFT.**

BLACK ARTISTS. see **ARTISTS, BLACK.**

BLACK AUDIO FILM COLLECTIVE.
Fusco, Coco. Young, British, and Black . Buffalo, N.Y. , c1988. 65 p. :
NYPL [Sc D 88-1186]

Black Australia . Stevens, Frank S. Sydney , 1981. xviii, 248 p. : ISBN 0-909188-43-2
NYPL [Sc D 88-1165]

Black Baltimore, 1820-1870 /. Clayton, Ralph. Bowie, MD , 1987. vii, 199 p. : ISBN 1-556-13080-5 (pbk.) : DDC 929/.3/0899607307526 19
F189.B19 N42 1987 **NYPL [APR (Baltimore) 88-868]**

Black book /. Mapplethorpe, Robert. New York , c1986. 91 p. : **NYPL [Sc F 87-42]**

Black Bostonia /. Overbea, Luix V. (Luix Virgil) Boston, Mass. , c1976. 39 p. :
NYPL [Sc C 89-44]

Black British literature . Guptara, Prabhu S. [Sydney] , Berkeley, Calif. [1986] 176 p. : ISBN 87-88213-14-5 (paper) :
NYPL [Sc D 89-20]

Black, brown and red : the movement for freedom among Black, Chicano / Latino and Indian. Detroit, Mich. : News & Letters Committees, 1975. 77 p. : ill., ports. ; 22 cm. (A News & letters pamphlet) Chapter entitled The Chicano/Latino struggle is translated into Spanish. Includes bibliographical references.
1. Afro-Americans - Civil rights. 2. Indians of North America - Civil rights. 3. Mexican Americans - Civil rights. **NYPL [Sc D 84-219]**

Black Catholic protest and the Federated Colored Catholics, 1917-1933 . Nickels, Marilyn Wenzke. New York , 1988. ix, 325 p. : ISBN 0-8240-4098-8 (alk. paper) : DDC 282/.73/08996073 19
BX1407.N4 N5 1988 **NYPL [Sc E 89-85]**

Black characters in the Brazilian novel /. Marotti, Giorgio. [Negro nel romanzo brasiliano. English.] Los Angeles , c1987. ix, 448 p., [18] p. of plates : ISBN 0-934934-24-X : DDC 869.3/093520396 19
PQ9607.B53 M3713 1987 **NYPL [Sc E 87-334]**

Black children and American institutions . Washington, Valora. New York , 1988. xv, 432 p. ; ISBN 0-8240-8517-5 : DDC 305.2/3/08996073 19
Z1361.N39 W34 1988 E185.86 **NYPL [Sc D 89-385]**

Black classics of social science.
Johnson, Charles Spurgeon, 1893-1956. Bitter Canaan . New Brunswick, N.J. , c1987. lxxiii, 256 p. ; ISBN 0-88738-053-0 : DDC 966.6/2 19
DT631 .J59 1987 **NYPL [Sc E 88-351]**

Black colleges and public policy / the National Association for Equal Opportunity in Higher Education ; edited by Andrew Billingsley, Julia C. Elam. Chicago : Follett Press, c1986. 99 p. : ill. ; 22 cm. A selection of papers presented at the National Conference on Blacks in Higher Education, held in Washington, D.C., in 1983. Includes bibliographical references. ISBN 0-695-60050-8
1. Afro-American universities and colleges - Congresses. 2. Afro-American universities and colleges - Finance - Congresses. I. Billingsley, Andrew. II. Elam, Julia C. III. National Association for Equal Opportunity in Higher Education (U. S.). IV. National Conference on Blacks in Higher Education (8th : 1983 : Washington, D.C.). **NYPL [Sc D 88-947]**

Black creatures of destiny /. Law, John, 1900- [New York? , 198-?] 80 p. :
NYPL [Sc D 89-208]

Black culture and the Harlem Renaissance /. Wintz, Cary D., 1943- Houston, Tex. , 1988. 277 p. ; ISBN 0-89263-267-4 : DDC 810/.9/896073 19
PS153.N5 W57 1988 **NYPL [Sc E 89-106]**

Black culture in America . Becknell, Charles Edward, 1941- Albuquerque, New Mexico , c1987. iii, 85, A-J p. ; ISBN 0-913945-50-1
NYPL [Sc F 88-156]

Black, David R. (David Ross), 1960- Foreign policy in small states : Botswana, Lesotho, Swaziland and southern Africa / by David R. Black, Joshua Mugyenyi, Larry A. Swatuk ; with an introduction by Timothy M. Shaw. Halifax, N.S. : Centre for Foreign Policy Studies, Dalhousie University, 1988. viii, 83 p. : maps ; 22 cm. Includes bibliographical references. ISBN 0-7703-0736-1 : DDC 327.681068 19
1. Botswana - Foreign relations - Africa, Southern. 2. Lesotho - Foreign relations - Africa, Southern. 3. Swaziland - Foreign relations - Africa, Southern. 4. Africa, Southern - Foreign relations - Botswana. 5. Africa, Southern - Foreign relations - Lesotho. 6. Africa, Southern - Foreign relations - Swaziland. I. Mugyenyi, Joshua, 1947-. II. Swatuk, Larry A. (Larry Anthony), 1957-. III. Dalhousie University. Centre for Foreign Policy Studies. IV. Title.
NYPL [Sc D 89-564]

BLACK DRAMA. see **DRAMA - BLACK AUTHORS.**

BLACK DRAMA (AMERICAN) see **AMERICAN DRAMA - AFRO-AMERICAN AUTHORS.**

Black Eagle, General Daniel "Chappie" James, Jr. /. McGovern, James R. University, AL , c1985. 204 p. : ISBN 0-8173-0179-8 DDC 355/.0092/4 B 19
UG626.2.J36 M34 1985
NYPL [JFD 85-7082]

Black economic progress : an agenda for the 1990s : a statement / by the Economic Policy Task Force of the Joint Center for Political Studies ; Marcus Alexis ... [et al.] ; edited by Margaret C. Simms. Washington, D.C. : The Center ; Lanham, Md. : Distributed by arrangement with UPA, 1988. xi, 52 p. : ill. ; 24 cm. Bibliography: p. 41-42. ISBN 0-941410-69-2 (alk. paper) DDC 330.973/008996073 19
1. Afro-Americans - Economic conditions. 2. United States - Economic conditions - 1981-. I. Alexis, Marcus. II. Simms, Margaret C. III. Joint Center for Political Studies (U. S.). Economic Policy Task Force.
E185.8 .B496 1988   **NYPL [Sc E 89-154]**

BLACK ENGLISH.
Schneider, Edgar W. (Edgar Werner), 1954- [Morphologische und syntaktische Variablen im amerikanischen early black English. English.] American earlier Black English . Tuscaloosa , 1989. xiv, 314 p. : ISBN 0-8173-0436-3 DDC 427/.973/08996 19
PE3102.N43 S3613 1989
NYPL [Sc E 89-210]

Twum-Akwaboah, Edward. From pidginization to creolization of Africanisms in Black American English /. [Los Angeles , 1973] 46 leaves ;   **NYPL [Sc F 88-210]**

Black executives in white-owned businesses and industries in the Chicago metropolitan area [microform] /. Salmon, Jaslin U. 1977. 197 leaves.   **NYPL [Sc Micro R-4703]**

The Black experience in Wyoming Valley /. Patterson, Christine. [Pennsylvania] [1987?] 9 p. :   **NYPL [Sc D 89-148]**

The Black explosion in British schools /. Dohndy, Farrukh. London , 1985. 64 p. ; ISBN 0-9503498-6-0   **NYPL [Sc D 88-1030]**

Black face, maligned race . Barthelemy, Anthony Gerard, 1949- Baton Rouge , c1987. xi, 215 p. ; ISBN 0-8071-1331-X DDC 822/.3/093520396 19
PR678.A4 B37 1987
NYPL [MWET 87-5064]

Black faces, white faces /. Gardam, Jane. London , 1975. 133 p. ; ISBN 0-241-89250-3 :
PZ4.G218 Bl PR6057.A623
NYPL [JFD 77-1786]

Black families / edited by Harriette Pipes McAdoo. 2nd ed. Newbury Park, Calif. : Sage Publications, c1988. 323 p. ; 23 cm. (Sage focus editions. 41) Includes bibliographies. ISBN 0-8039-3179-4 : DDC 305.8/96073 19
1. McAdoo, Harriette Pipes.
E185.86 .B525 1988   **NYPL [Sc D 89-338]**

Black families in crisis : the middle class / edited by Alice F. Coner-Edwards and Jeanne Spurlock. New York : Brunner/Mazel, c1988. xiv, 305 p. ; 24 cm. Includes bibliographies and index. ISBN 0-87630-524-9 DDC 305.8/96073 19
1. Afro-Americans - Social conditions - 1975-. 2. Middle classes - United States. 3. United States - Social conditions - 1980-. I. Coner-Edwards, Alice F. II. Spurlock, Jeanne.
E185.86 .B5254 1988   **NYPL [Sc E 89-155]**

Black families in therapy . Boyd-Franklin, Nancy. New York, N.Y. , c1989. xiv, 274 p. : ISBN 0-89862-735-4 DDC 616.89/156/08996073 19
RC451.5.N4 B69 1988 **NYPL [Sc E 89-242]**

Black feminist criticism and critical theory / edited by Joe Weixlmann and Houston A. Baker, Jr. Greenwood, Fla. : Penkevill, c1988. iii, 202 p. ; 23 cm. (Studies in Black American literature . v. 3) Includes bibliographical references. ISBN 0-913283-25-8
1. American literature - Afro-American authors - History and criticism. 2. Feminism and literature - United States. I. Weixlmann, Joseph. II. Baker, Houston A. III. Series.   **NYPL [Sc D 88-1394]**

Black fugitive slaves in early Canada /. Bramble, Linda. St. Catharines, Ont. , c1988. 93 p. : ISBN 0-920277-16-0 DDC 973.7/115 19
NYPL [Sc E 89-121]

The Black gestalt . Coleman, Mel. Minneapolis,

Minnesota , 1987. 118 p. :
NYPL [Sc D 88-292]

Black gods and kings . Thompson, Robert Farris. Bloomington , 1976, c1971. 94 p. in various pagings : ISBN 0-253-31204-3 : DDC 732/.2
N7399.N52 Y66 1976   **NYPL [Sc F 77-167]**

Black gold of Chepkube /. Gateria, Wamugunda. Nairobi , 1985. 139 p. ;
NYPL [Sc C 88-284]

The Black gourmet . Stafford, Joseph. Detroit , 1988. 256 p., [6] leaves of plates : ISBN 0-9617123-0-9 :   **NYPL [Sc D 88-1199]**

The Black gourmet cookbook : a unique collection of easy-to-prepare, appetizing, Black American, Creole, Caribbean, and African cuisine. 1st ed. Westland, Mich. : Mademoiselles Noires, 1987. 76 p. : ill. ;c28 cm.
1. Cookery, African. 2. Cookery, Caribbean.
NYPL [Sc F 88-292]

The Black heritage of Western North Carolina /. Davis, Lenwood G. [Asheville, North Carolina , 1986?] 78 leaves ;   **NYPL [Sc F 88-265]**

Black history, black vision. Adele, Lynne. [Austin] , 1989. 93 p. : ISBN 0-935213-15-5
NYPL [Sc F 89-155]

Black Homelands, South Africa. see Homelands, South Africa.

BLACK HUMOR (AFRO-AMERICAN) see AFRO-AMERICAN WIT AND HUMOR.

Black in Colombia /. Paz Gómez, Enelia. Mexico , c1985. 173 p. :
NYPL [Sc D 89-66]

Black Indians . Katz, William Loren. New York , c1986. 198 p. : ISBN 0-689-31196-6
NYPL [IEC 87-411]

The Black laborer, the Black legal experience and the United States Supreme Court with emphasis on the neo-concept of equal employment [microform] /. Simba, Malik. 1977. 357 leaves.   **NYPL [Sc Micro R-4706]**

Black leaders of the nineteenth century / edited by Leon Litwack and August Meier. Urbana : University of Illinois Press, c1988. xii, 344 p. : ill. ; 24 cm. (Blacks in the new world) Includes index. ISBN 0-252-01506-1 (alk. paper) DDC 920/.009296073 19
1. Afro-Americans - Biography. 2. Afro-Americans - History - 19th century. I. Litwack, Leon F. II. Meier, August, 1923-. III. Series.
E185.96 .B535 1988   **NYPL [Sc E 88-365]**

BLACK LITERATURE. see LITERATURE - BLACK AUTHORS.

BLACK LITERATURE (AFRICAN) see AFRICAN LITERATURE.

BLACK LITERATURE (AMERICAN) see AMERICAN LITERATURE - AFRO-AMERICAN AUTHORS.

Black literature and humanism in Latin America /. Jackson, Richard L., 1937- Athens , c1988. xvii, 166 p. ; ISBN 0-8203-0979-6 (alk. paper) DDC 860/.9/896 19
PQ7081 .J263 1988   **NYPL [Sc E 88-359]**

BLACK LITERATURE - BRAZIL. see BRAZILIAN LITERATURE - BLACK AUTHORS.

BLACK LITERATURE (BRAZILIAN) see BRAZILIAN LITERATURE - BLACK AUTHORS.

BLACK LITERATURE (ENGLISH) see ENGLISH LITERATURE - BLACK AUTHORS.

Black lives, white lives . Blauner, Bob. Berkeley , c1989. xii, 347 p. ; ISBN 0-520-06261-2 (alk. paper) DDC 305.8/00973 19
E185.615 .B556 1989   **NYPL [Sc E 89-219]**

Black male entrepreneurs and adult development /. Herbert, James I. New York , 1989. xviii, 235 p. ; ISBN 0-275-93023-8 (alk. paper) : DDC 155.8/496073 19
E185.625 .H44 1989   **NYPL [Sc E 89-256]**

Black mass revolt [microform]. Detroit : News & letters, 1967. 23 p. ; 28 cm. Microfilm. New York: New York Public Library, 1982. 1 microfilm reel; 35 mm. (MN *ZZ-22890)
1. Afro-Americans - Civil rights.
NYPL [Sc Micro R-4202 no.14]

The Black Mennonite Church in North America, 1886-1986 /. Bechler, Le Roy, 1925- Scottdale, Pa. , 1986. 196 p. : ISBN 0-8361-1287-3 : DDC 289.7/08996073 19
BX8116.3.A37 B43 1986
NYPL [Sc E 89-134]

Black ministers and laity in the urban church . Harris, James H., 1952- Lanham, MD , c1987. xi, 133 p. : ISBN 0-8191-5823-2 (alk. paper) : DDC 253/.2/08996073 19
BR563.N4 B575 1987   **NYPL [Sc D 89-127]**

Black Mondays . Joseph, Joel D. Bethesda, MD , c1987. 286 p. : ISBN 0-915765-44-6 : DDC 347.73/26 347.30735 19
KF4549 .J67 1987   **NYPL [Sc D 88-963]**

Black mosaic . Quarles, Benjamin. Amherst, Mass. , 1988. 213 p. : ISBN 0-87023-604-0 (alk. paper) DDC 973/.0496073 19
E185 .Q19 1988   **NYPL [Sc E 88-330]**

Black musical theatre . Woll, Allen. Baton Rouge , 1989. xiv, 301 p. : ISBN 0-8071-1469-3 DDC 782.81/08996073 19
ML1711 .W64 1989   **NYPL [Sc E 89-198]**

BLACK MUSLIMS.
Farrakhan, Louis. [Speeches. Selections.] 7 speeches. New York, 1974. 151 p.
NYPL [Sc D 88-1441]

Jones, Oliver, 1947- The constitutional politics of the Black Muslim movement in America [microform] /. 1978. 297 leaves.
NYPL [Sc Micro R-4227]

BLACK NATIONALISM - HISTORY.
Lewis, Rupert. Marcus Gavey, anti-colonial champion /. Trenton, New Jersey , 1988. 301 p. : ISBN 0-86543-061-6 (hard)
NYPL [Sc D 88-516]

Mackie, Liz. The great Marcus Garvey /. London , 1987. 157 p. : ISBN 1-87051-850-0
NYPL [Sc D 88-999]

BLACK NATIONALISM - PENNSYLVANIA - PHILADELPHIA.
Anderson, John, 1954 Mar. 27- Burning down the house . New York , c1987. xv, 409 p. : ISBN 0-393-02460-1 : DDC 974.8/1104 19
F158.9.N4 A53 1987   **NYPL [Sc E 88-332]**

BLACK NATIONALISM - SOUTH AFRICA.
The National question in South Africa /. London , Atlantic Highlands, N.J. , 1988. 154 p. ; ISBN 0-86232-794-6 DDC 320.5/4/0968 19
DT763 .N35 1988   **NYPL [JLD 88-4552]**

BLACK NATIONALISM - UNITED STATES.
Farrakhan, Louis. [Speeches. Selections.] 7 speeches. New York, 1974. 151 p.
NYPL [Sc D 88-1441]

Kitabu [microform] . Los Angeles [1972?] 13 p. ;   **NYPL [Sc Micro F-10979]**

Shakur, Assata. Assata, an autobiography /. Westport, CT , 1987. xiv, 274 p. ; ISBN 0-88208-221-3 : DDC 973/.0496073024 19
E185.97.S53 A3 1987   **NYPL [Sc E 88-21]**

BLACK NATIONALISM - UNITED STATES - BIBLIOGRAPHY.
Herod, Agustina. Afro-American nationalism . New York , 1986. xvi, 272 p. ; ISBN 0-8240-9813-7 (alk. paper) DDC 016.3058/96073 19
Z1361.N39 H47 1986 E185.625
NYPL [Sc D 87-1338]

BLACK NATIONALISM - UNITED STATES - HISTORY.
Lewis, Rupert. Marcus Garvey . Trenton, N.J. , 1988. 301 p. : ISBN 0-86543-061-6
NYPL [Sc D 88-1454]

Black networks of care [microform] . Maida, Carl Albert. 1981. xiii, 276 leaves ;
NYPL [Sc Micro R-4803]

Black on Red . Robinson, Robert, ca. 1902- Washington, D.C. , 1988. 436 p. : ISBN 0-87491-885-5 DDC 947.084 19
DK34.B53 R63 1988   **NYPL [Sc E 88-377]**

Black Orpheus . Sartre, Jean Paul, 1905-1980. [Orphée noir. English.] [Paris, 1963?] 65 p. ;
NYPL [Sc C 88-110]

BLACK ORPHEUS.
Benson, Peter. Black Orpheus, Transition, and modern cultural awakening in Africa /. Berkeley , c1986. xiii, 320 p. : ISBN

0-520-05418-0 DDC 820/.8 19
PL8000.B63 B4 1986   NYPL [Sc E 88-354]

Black Orpheus, Transition, and modern cultural awakening in Africa /. Benson, Peter. Berkeley , c1986. xiii, 320 p. : ISBN 0-520-05418-0 DDC 820/.8 19
PL8000.B63 B4 1986   NYPL [Sc E 88-354]

BLACK PANTHER PARTY - BIOGRAPHY. Shakur, Assata. Assata, an autobiography /. Westport, CT , 1987. xiv, 274 p. : ISBN 0-88208-221-3 : DDC 973/.0496073024 19
E185.97.S53 A3 1987   NYPL [Sc E 88-21]

Black pearls . Harrison, Daphne Duval, 1932- New Brunswick [N.J.] , c1988. xv, 295 p. : ISBN 0-8135-1279-4 : DDC 784.5/3/0922 19
ML3521 .H38 1988   NYPL [JNE 88-21]

Black people in Brent : explorations in coping strategies / a pilot study / conducted for the Black Workers Support Group (Brent). London : Black Workers Support Group, c1987. 159 p. : ill. ; 21 cm. Includes bibliographies. ISBN 0-9512463-1-3 (pbk.)
1. Blacks - England - London. 2. Brent (London, England) - Social conditions. I. Black Workers Support Group (Brent).   NYPL [Sc D 89-5]

BLACK PEOPLE (U. S.) see AFRO-AMERICANS.

Black philosophy. Frye, Charles A. From Egypt to Don Juan . Lanham, MD , c1988. xiii, 129 p. : ISBN 0-8191-7120-4 (alk. paper) DDC 100 19
BF1999 .F77 1988   NYPL [Sc D 88-1421]

Black plays / selected and introduced by Yvonne Brewster. London : Methuen London ; New York, NY : Methuen, 1987. 139 p. ; 21 cm. (A Methuen theatrefile) "A Methuen paperback." CONTENTS. - Chameleon / by Michael Ellis -- Lonely cowboy / by Alfred Fagon -- The lower depths : an East End story / by Tunde Ikoli -- Basin / by Jacqueline Rudet. ISBN 0-413-15710-5
1. English drama - Black authors. 2. English drama - 20th century. I. Brewster, Yvonne.
NYPL [JFD 88-8329]

BLACK POETRY (AMERICAN) see AMERICAN POETRY - AFRO-AMERICAN AUTHORS.

BLACK POETRY (ENGLISH) see ENGLISH POETRY - BLACK AUTHORS.

BLACK POETRY - FRANCE. see FRENCH POETRY - BLACK AUTHORS.

BLACK POETRY (FRENCH) see FRENCH POETRY - BLACK AUTHORS.

Black political orientation, political activism, and positive mental health [microform] /. Maish, Kemba Asili. 1977. 220 leaves.
NYPL [Sc Micro R-4228]

Black positivism through character growth and development in the short stories of Richard Wright [microform] /. Liston, Carolyn Olivia. 1982. xii, 207 p.   *NYPL [Sc Micro R-4819]*

BLACK POWER - GREAT BRITAIN. From where I stand /. London , 1987. 94 p. : ISBN 0-9956664-9-1   *NYPL [Sc C 88-30]*

BLACK POWER IN LITERATURE. Harris, Norman, 1951- Connecting times . Jackson , c1988. 197 p. ; ISBN 0-87805-335-2 (alk. paper) DDC 813/.54/093520396073 19
PS153.N5 H27 1988   NYPL [Sc E 88-288]

BLACK POWER - JAMAICA. Rodney, Walter. The groundings with my brothers. London, 1969. 68 p. ISBN 0-9501546-0-1
F1896.N4 R6   NYPL [Sc 323.2-R]

BLACK POWER - UNITED STATES. Farrakhan, Louis. [Speeches. Selections.] 7 speeches. New York, 1974. 151 p.
NYPL [Sc D 88-1441]

Black presence in multi-ethnic Canada : abridged / edited by Vincent D'Oyley. Vancouver : Centre for the Study of Curriculum & Instruction Faculty of Education, University of British Columbia, c1982. xvii, 304 p. : ill. ; 28 cm. Papers presented at a symposium in Windsor, Ontario. Contains papers in English with abstracts in French, and one paper in French. Includes bibliographies.
1. Blacks - Canada - Congresses. I. D'Oyley, Vincent.
NYPL [Sc F 88-104]

Black presidential politics in America . Walters,

Ronald W. Albany , c1988. xvii, 255 p. ISBN 0-88706-546-5 DDC 324.6/2/08996073 19
JK1924 .W34 1987   NYPL [Sc E 88-283]

The Black press in Mississippi, 1865-1985 . Thompson, Julius Eric. West Cornwall, CT , 1988. xxiv, 144 p. : ISBN 0-933951-16-7 (alk. paper) : DDC 015.762035 19
Z1361.N39 T52 1988 PN4882.5
NYPL [Sc D 89-34]

BLACK RACE. Johnson, Edward A. (Edward Augustus), 1860-1944. A school history of the Negro race in America from 1619 to 1890 . Chicago , 1894. 200 p. :   *NYPL [Sc Rare F 88-9]*

Théodore, Oriol, 1942- L'idéologie blanche et l'aliénation des noirs /. Montréal [1983] 54 p. : ISBN 2-89270-001-9   *NYPL [Sc C 89-103]*

Black racial attitude change in Detroit, 1968-1976 [microform] /. Hatchett, Shirley. 1982. 171 leaves.   *NYPL [Sc Micro R-4682]*

Black radicals and the civil rights mainstream, 1954-1970 /. Haines, Herbert H. Knoxville , c19. xii, 231 p. : ISBN 0-87049-563-1 (alk. paper) : DDC 305.8/96073 19
E185.615 .H25 1988   NYPL [Sc E 88-511]

Black robes, white justice /. Wright, Bruce, 1918- Secaucus, N.J. , c1987. 214 p. : ISBN 0-8184-0422-1 : DDC 345.73/05/08996073 347.305508996073 19
KF373.W67 A33 1987   NYPL [JLE 87-2842]

The Black roots and white racism of early Pentecostalism in the USA /. MacRobert, Iain, 1949- Basingstoke , 1988. xv, 142 p. : ISBN 0-333-43997-X : DDC 277.3/082 19
BR1644.5.U6   NYPL [Sc D 89-131]

Black Saint Maurice. Suckale-Redlefsen, Gude. Mauritius, der heilige Mohr /. Houston , München , c1987. 295 p. : ISBN 0-939594-03-X DDC 704.9/4863/094 19
N8080.M38 S9 1987   NYPL [Sc D 88-1357]

The Black Saturnalia . Dirks, Robert, 1942- Gainesville , c1987. xvii, 228 p., [7] p. of plates : ISBN 0-8130-0843-3 (pbk. : alk. paper) : DDC 394.2/68282/09729 19
GT4987.23 .D57 1987
NYPL [L-10 5328 no.72]

Black sexual power /. Brown, Leroy. Cleveland, Ohio , c1970. 220 p. ;   *NYPL [Sc C 88-274]*

Black slaveowners . Koger, Larry, 1958- Jefferson, N.C. , 1985. xiii, 286 p. ; ISBN 0-89950-160-5 : DDC 975.7/00496073 19
E445.S7 K64 1985   NYPL [Sc E 88-473]

Black song . Lovell, John, 1907- New York , 1986, c1972. xviii, 686 p. : ISBN 0-913729-53-1 (pbk.) DDC 783.6/7/09 19
ML3556 .L69 1986   NYPL [Sc D 88-421]

Black student retention in higher education / edited by Marvel Lang and Clinita A. Ford. Springfield, Ill., U. S.A. : C.C. Thomas, c1988. xvi, 111 p. : ill. ; 27 cm. Based on papers presented at Conference on Black Student Retention in Higher Education, held in Orlando, Fla., 1985; in Atlanta, Ga., 1986 and organized by the Florida A&M University. Includes bibliographies and index. ISBN 0-398-05477-0 DDC 378/.198/2 19
1. Afro-American college students - Congresses. 2. College attendance - United States - Congresses. 3. College dropouts - United States - Congresses. I. Lang, Marvel. II. Ford, Clinita A. III. Florida Agricultural and Mechanical University. IV. Conference on Black Student Retention in Higher Education (1985 : Orlando, Fla.). V. Conference on Black Student Retention in Higher Education (1986 : Atlanta, Ga.).
LC2781 .B465 1988   NYPL [Sc F 89-139]

Black studies. New York (N.Y.). Bureau of Curriculum Development. New York [c1970] vii, 227 p. DDC 375/.0097471 s
LB1563 .N57 1970-71, no. 3
NYPL [Sc G 87-32]

Black stylization and implications for child welfare . Dodson, Jualynne E. Atlanta, Georgia , 1975. 1 v. (various pagings) ;
NYPL [Sc F 88-223]

The Black Swan. LaBrew, Arthur R. Detroit , 1969. 86 p. :   *NYPL [JND 82-30]*

Black theology . Evans, James H., 1950- New York , c1987. xii, 205 p. ; ISBN 0-313-24822-2 (lib. bdg. : alk. paper) DDC 016.23/008996073

19
Z7774 .E9 1987 BT82.7
NYPL [Sc E 87-426]

BLACK THEOLOGY. Biehl, João Guilherme. De igual pra igual . Petrópolis , São Leopoldo, RS, Brasil , 1987. 155 p. ;
BT83.57 .B54 1987   NYPL [Sc D 88-1016]

Bosch Navarro, Juan. La Iglesia negra . Valencia , 1986 (Valencia : Imprenta Nácher). 57 p. :   *NYPL [Sc D 87-1154]*

Ecumenical Association of Third World Theologians. Identidade negra e religião . Rio de Janeiro , 1986. 201 p. ;
NYPL [Sc D 88-485]

BLACK THEOLOGY - BIBLIOGRAPHY. Evans, James H., 1950- Black theology . New York , c1987. xii, 205 p. ; ISBN 0-313-24822-2 (lib. bdg. : alk. paper) DDC 016.23/008996073 19
Z7774 .E9 1987 BT82.7
NYPL [Sc E 87-426]

Black Think Tank. Hare, Nathan. The endangered Black family . San Francisco, CA , c1984. 192 p. ; ISBN 0-9613086-0-5
NYPL [Sc C 88-307]

Black Untouchables of India. Rajshekar Shetty, V. T., 1932- Dalit, the black Untouchables of India /. Atlanta, Ga. , c1987. 89 p. ; ISBN 0-932863-05-1 (pbk.).
NYPL [Sc D 89-356]

Black urban public road transport . Human Awareness Programme (South Africa) Grant Park [South Africa] [1982] 64 p. : ISBN 0-620-05750-5 (pbk.) : DDC 388.4/1322/089968 19
HE5704.4.A6 H86 1982
NYPL [Sc F 88-150]

The black Valentino . Grupenhoff, Richard, 1941- Metuchen, N.J. , 1988. xi, 188 p. : ISBN 0-8108-2078-1 DDC 790.2/092/4 B 19
PN2287.T78 G78 1988
NYPL [Sc D 88-1029]

Black visions '87 : a salute to the Black filmmaker, February 1-28, 1987 / [James Briggs Murray, exhibition curator]. New York : Mayor's Office of Minority Affairs, 1987. 32 p. : ill. ; 28 cm. Bibliography: p. 31.
1. Afro-American motion picture producers and directors - Interviews. 2. Afro-American motion picture producers and directors - Exhibitions. I. Murray, James Briggs. II. Tweed Gallery (New York (N.Y)).
NYPL [Sc F 88-258]

Black visions '88 : lady legends in jazz, February 1-March 11, 1988 / [James Briggs Murray, exhibition curator]. New York : [Mayor's Office of Minority Affairs, 1988] 44 p. : ill. ; ports. ; 22 x 29 cm. "Reflections and Projections: interviews by James Briggs Murray": p. 26-39. Bibliography: p. 43.
1. Women jazz musicians - United States - Exhibitions. 2. Afro-American women musicians - Exhibitions. I. Murray, James Briggs. II. Tweed Gallery (New York (N.Y). III. Title.   NYPL [Sc D 88-1200]

The Black West /. Katz, William Loren. Seattle, WA , c1987. xiii, 348 p. : ISBN 0-940880-17-2 DDC 978/.00496073 19
E185.925 .K37 1987   NYPL [Sc E 89-86]

The Black/white colleges : dismantling the dual system of higher education. Washington, D.C. : U. S. Commission on Civil Rights, 1981. v, 46 p. : ill. ; 26 cm. (Clearinghouse publication . 66) Written by Carole A. Williams. "April 1981."--Cover. Includes bibliographical references.
1. Universities and colleges - United States. 2. Segregation in higher education - United States. 3. Afro-Americans - Education (Higher) - United States. 4. Afro-American universities and colleges. I. Williams, Carole A. II. Series.   NYPL [Sc F 89-48]

Black-woman-Jew . Eckardt, A. Roy (Arthur Roy), 1918- Bloomington , c1989. 229 p. ; ISBN 0-253-31221-3 DDC 305.4/8896073 19
E185.86 .E28 1989   NYPL [Sc E 89-209]

A Black woman's Civil War memoirs /. Taylor, Susie King, b. 1848. [Reminiscences of my life in camp.] New York , 1988. 154 p. : ISBN 0-910129-85-1 (pbk.) : DDC 973.7/415 B 19
E492.94 33rd .T3 1988
NYPL [Sc D 88-1473]

Black women in antiquity / editor, Ivan Van Sertima. New ed. New Brunswick, [N.J.] ;

London : Transaction Books, 1988. 192 p. :
ill. ; 23 cm. Issued as: Journal of African
civilizations ; v. 6, no. 1. Includes bibliographies.
ISBN 0-87855-982-5
1. Women, Black - Africa - History. 2. Women, Black -
Ethiopia - History. 3. Women, Black - Egypt - History.
4. Civilization, Ancient. 5. Africa - Civilization. I. Van
Sertima, Ivan. II. Journal of African civilizations.
NYPL [Sc D 89-351]

The Black women in the Middle West Project : a
comprehensive resource guide, Illinois and
Indiana : historical essays, oral histories,
biographical profiles, and document collections
/ by Darlene Clark Hine, project director ;
Patrick Kay Bidelman, general editor and
co-director for administration ; Shirley M.
Herd, Donald West, consulting editors.
Indianapolis, Ind. (140 N. Senate Ave., Room
408, Indianapolis 46204) : Indiana Historial
Bureau, 1986. xi, 238 p. : ill. ; 28 cm. Includes
indexes. Bibliography: p. 237-238. DDC
977/.00496073 19
1. Afro-American women - Middle West. 2.
Afro-American women - Middle West - Archival
resources - Middle West. 3. Afro-American women -
Middle West - Research - Middle West - Handbooks,
manuals, etc. 4. Afro-American women - Middle West -
Biography. 5. Middle West - History - Archival
resources - Middle West. 6. Middle West - Biography.
I. Hine, Darlene Clark. II. Bidelman, Patrick Kay.
E185.915 .B52 1986 *NYPL [Sc F 88-141]*

Black women writers series.
Bonner, Marita, 1899-1971. Frye Street &
environs . Boston , c1987. xxix, 286 p. ; ISBN
0-8070-6300-2 DDC 810/.8/0896073 19
PS3503 .O439 1987 *NYPL [Sc D 88-683]*

Black workers : a documentary history from
colonial times to the present / edited by Philip
S. Foner and Ronald L. Lewis. Philadelphia :
Temple University Press, 1989. xv, 733 p. ; 24
cm. Abridged ed. of: The Black worker. Includes index.
Bibliography: p. 708-711. ISBN 0-87722-592-3
1. Afro-Americans - Employment - History. 2.
Afro-Americans - Economic conditions. 3.
Trade-unions - United - United States - Afro-American
membership - History. 4. Afro-American women -
Employment - History. 5. United States - Race
relations. I. Foner, Philip Sheldon, 1910-. II. Lewis,
Ronald L., 1940-. *NYPL [Sc E 89-206]*

Black Workers Support Group (Brent) Black
people in Brent . London , c1987. 159 p. :
ISBN 0-9512463-1-3 (pbk.)
NYPL [Sc D 89-5]

Black working women : debunking the myths : a
multidisciplinary approach : proceedings of a
research conference to examine the status of
black working women in the United States.
Berkeley, Calif. : Center for the Study,
Education and Advancement of Women,
University of California, [1981?] vii, 222 p. :
ill. ; 28 cm. Conference held May 1981 and
sponsored by the Center for the Study, Education and
Advancement of Women, University of California,
Berkeley. "A selected bibliography for multidisciplinary
research on Black women and work / compiled by
Gleoria Bradley-Sapp" : p. 211-222.
1. Afro-American women - Congresses. 2.
Afro-Americans - Employment - Congresses. 3.
Women - Employment - United States - Congresses. 4.
American literature - Afro-American authors -
Congresses. *NYPL [Sc F 89-33]*

Black writers : a selection of sketches from
Contemporary authors ; contains more than
four hundred entries on twentieth-century Black
writers, all updated or originally written for this
volume / Linda Metzger, senior editor. Detroit,
Mi. : Gale Research Inc., c1989. xxiv, 619 p. ;
29 cm. Contains bibliographic information. ISBN
0-8103-2772-4
1. Authors, Black - 20th century - Biography. 2.
Afro-American authors - 20th century - Biography. I.
Metzger, Linda. II. Gale Research Inc. III.
Contemporary authors. *NYPL [Sc F 89-57]*

Black Yankees . Piersen, William Dillon, 1942-
Amherst , 1988. Xii,237 p. ; ISBN 0-87023-586-9
(alk. paper) : DDC 974/.00496073 19
E185.917 .P54 1988 *NYPL [Sc E 88-213]*

Black youth futures : ethnic minorities and the
Youth Training Scheme / edited by Malcolm
Cross and Douglas I. Smith. Leicester :
National Youth Bureau, 1987. ii, 113 p. : ill.,
forms ; 21 cm. (Studies in research) Bibliography: p.
105-108. ISBN 0-86155-106-0 (pbk) DDC

331.3/46/0941 19
1. Youth Training Scheme (Great Britain). 2.
Minorities - Training of - Great Britain. I. Cross,
Malcolm. II. Smith, Douglas I. III. Series.
HD8398 *NYPL [Sc D 89-175]*

Black youth, racism and the state . Solomos,
John. Cambridge [Cambridgeshire] , New
York , 1988. 284 p. ; ISBN 0-521-36019-6 DDC
305.8/96041 19
DA125.N4 S65 1988 *NYPL [Sc E 88-606]*

Blackball stars . Holway, John. Westport, CT ,
c1988. xvi, 400 p. : ISBN 0-88736-094-7 (alk.
paper) : DDC 796.357/08996073/0922 B 19
GV865.A1 H614 1988 *NYPL [JFE 88-6437]*

Blackburn, Dougal. Drama festival plays /.
London , Baltimore, Md. , 1986. iv, 92 p. ;
ISBN 0-7131-8446-9 *NYPL [Sc D 88-638]*

Blackburn, Robin. The overthrow of colonial
slavery, 1776-1848 / Robin Blackburn.
London ; New York : Verso, 1988. 560 p. : ill.,
maps ; 24 cm. Includes bibliographies and index.
ISBN 0-86091-188-8 DDC 326/.0973 19
1. Slavery - America - Anti-slavery movements -
History. 2. Slavery - America - Emancipation - History.
I. Title.
HT1050 .B54 1988 *NYPL [IIR 88-1551]*

Blacke-Bragg, Norma. Flights and dancers :
poems / by Norma Blacke-Bragg. South
Windsor, Conn. : Blue Spruce Press, 1978. vii,
101 p. ; 26 cm.
I. Title. *NYPL [Sc F 89-11]*

The Blacker the berry : a forty day ritual drama
in the State of Hope at a place called
Providence, Feb.-Mar., 1980 / presented by the
Afro-American Studies Program at Brown
University, Rites and Reason, and Rhode Island
Committee for the Humanities. [Providence,
R.I.] : Brown University, [1980?] 20 p. : ill. ; 26
cm.
1. Afro-Americans - History - Drama. I. Brown
University. Afro-American Studies Program. II. Rhode
Island Committee for the Humanities.
NYPL [Sc F 89-80]

Blacks /. Pachai, Bridglal. Tantallon, Nova
Scotia , 1987. 60 p. : ISBN 0-920427-11-1
NYPL [Sc D 88-1022]

Blacks and American government . Smith, J.
Owens. Dubuque, Iowa , c1987. xiii, 148 p. :
ISBN 0-8403-4407-4 (pbk.) DDC 323.1/196073
19
E185.615 .S576 1987 *NYPL [Sc E 89-193]*

Blacks and Jews . National Conference on
African American/Jewish American Relations
(1983 : Savannah State College) [Savannah,
Ga.] [1983] iii, 58 p. ; *NYPL [Sc D 88-335]*

Blacks and the 1984 Republican National
Convention : a guide. Washington, D.C. (1301
Pennsylvania Ave., N.W., Suite 400,
Washington 20004) : Joint Center for Political
Studies, 1984. v, 25 p. ; 28 cm. (Election '84
report . #4) ISBN 0-941410-51-X (pbk.) DDC
324.2734 19
1. Republican National Convention (33rd : 1984 :
Dallas, Tex.). 2. Afro-Americans - Politics and
government. 3. Afro-Americans - Suffrage. I. Joint
Center for Political Studies (U. S.). II. Series.
JK2353 1984 *NYPL [Sc F 87-172 rept. 4]*

BLACKS - BAHAMAS.
Defries, Amelia Dorothy, 1882- The Fortunate
Islands. London [1929] xxiii, 160 p. DDC
917.296
F1651 .D31 *NYPL [Sc D 88-936]*

BLACKS - BERMUDA ISLANDS - HISTORY.
Blacks in Bermuda . [Hamilton? , 1980?] 82 p. :
NYPL [Sc F 88-251]

BLACKS - BIOGRAPHY - JUVENILE
LITERATURE.
Their contribution ignored. London , c1988. 16
p. : *NYPL [Sc F 89-165]*

BLACKS - BRAZIL.
Bastide, Roger, 1898-1974. [Religions africaines
au Brésil. Portuguese.] As religiões africanas no
Brasil . São Paulo , 1985. 567 p. ;
NYPL [Sc D 88-542]

Lopes, Helena Theodoro. Negro e cultura no
Brasil . Rio de Janeiro , 1987. 136 p. ; ISBN
85-85108-02-9 DDC 981/.00496 19
F2659.N4 L67 1987 *NYPL [Sc D 88-1291]*

BLACKS - BRAZIL - CONGRESSES.
Race, class, and power in Brazil / Los
Angeles , c1985. xi, 160 p. : ISBN
0-934934-22-3 : DDC 305.8/96/081 19
F2659.N4 R24 1985 *NYPL [JLE 88-2671]*

BLACKS - BRAZIL - FICTION.
Cunha Junior, H., 1952- Negros na noite /. São
Paulo , 1987. 79 p. : *NYPL [Sc D 88-71]*

BLACKS - BRAZIL - HISTORY.
Freyre, Gilberto, 1900- [Casa-grande & senzala.
English.] The masters and the slaves =.
Berkeley , c1986. xc, 537 xliv p., [3] p. of
plates : ISBN 0-520-05665-5 (pbk. : alk. paper)
DDC 981 19
F2510 .F7522 1986 *NYPL [HFB 87-2095]*

BLACKS - BRAZIL - HISTORY - 19TH
CENTURY.
Azevedo, Celia Maria Marinho de. Onda negra,
medo branco . Rio de Janeiro , c1987. 267 p. ;
NYPL [Sc D 88-469]

BLACKS - BRAZIL - RIO GRANDE DO SUL -
INTERVIEWS.
Histórias de operários negros /. Porto Alegre,
RS, Brazil , c1987. 100 p. ;
NYPL [Sc D 88-823]

BLACKS - BRAZIL - SÃO PAULO.
Ferrara, Miriam Nicolau. A imprensa negra
paulista (1915-1963) /. São Paulo , 1986. 279
p. : *NYPL [Sc B 88-6]*

BLACKS - BRAZIL - SOCIAL CONDITIONS.
Maestri Filho, Mário José. Depoimentos de
escravos brasileiros /. São Paulo , c1988. 88 p. :
ISBN 85-27-40039-1
NYPL [Sc D 88-1379]

Valente, Ana Lúcia E. F. (Ana Lúcia Eduardo
Farah) Ser negro no Brasil hoje /. São Paulo,
SP, Brasil , 1987. 64 p. : DDC 305.8/96/081 19
F2659.N4 V35 1987 *NYPL [HFB 88-2561]*

BLACKS - BRAZIL - SOCIAL LIFE AND
CUSTOMS.
Lody, Raul. Coleção Arthur Ramos /.
[Fortaleza] , 1987. 78 p. : ISBN 85-24-60035-7
NYPL [Sc D 89-479]

BLACKS - CANADA.
Bramble, Linda. Black fugitive slaves in early
Canada /. St. Catharines, Ont. , c1988. 93 p. :
ISBN 0-920277-16-0 DDC 973.7/115 19
NYPL [Sc E 89-121]

BLACKS - CANADA - CONGRESSES.
Black presence in multi-ethnic Canada .
Vancouver , c1982. xvii, 304 p. :
NYPL [Sc F 88-104]

BLACKS - CANADA - RELIGION.
Shreve, Dorothy Shadd. The AfriCanadian
church . Jordan Station, Ontario, Canada ,
c1983. 118 p. : ISBN 0-88815-072-5 (pbk.) DDC
277.1/008996 19
BR570 .S53 1983 *NYPL [Sc D 86-305]*

BLACKS - CARIBBEAN AREA - FICTION.
Morrison, Toni. Tar baby /. New York , 1981.
305 p. ; ISBN 0-452-26012-4
NYPL [Sc D 88-1105]

BLACKS - CUBA.
Ortiz Fernández, Fernando, 1881-1969. Los
bailes y el teatro de los negros en el folklore de
Cuba /. Habana, Cuba , 1981. 602 p. ;
NYPL [JME 82-163]

BLACKS - CUBA - BIBLIOGRAPHY.
Bibliografia de temas afrocubanos /. La
Habana , 1985. 581 p. ;
NYPL [Sc D 89-510]

BLACKS - CUBA - FOLKLORE.
Valdés-Cruz, Rosa. Lo ancestral africano en la
narrativa de Lydia Cabrera /. Barcelona , 1974.
113 p. ; *NYPL [Sc D 89-36]*
PQ7389.C22 Z94

BLACKS - CUBA - HISTORY.
Castellanos, Jorge. Cultura afrocubana /.
Miami, Fla., U.S.A. , 1988- v. ; ISBN
0-89729-462-9 (set) DDC 972.91/00496 20
F1789.N3 C33 1988 *NYPL [Sc D 89-592]*

Soledad, Rosalía de la. Ibo . Miami, Fla. , 1988.
278 p. ; ISBN 0-89729-468-8
NYPL [Sc D 89-436]

BLACKS - CUBA - SOCIAL CONDITIONS.
Cole, Johnnetta B. Race toward equality /.
Havana, Cuba (P.O. Box 4208, Havana) ,

c1986. 99 p. : DDC 305.8/0097291 19
F1789.N3 C65 1986 **NYPL [Sc D 89-359]**

BLACKS - CUBA - SOCIAL LIFE AND CUSTOMS.
Cabrera, Lydia. La lengua sagrada de los Náñigos /. Miami, Fla. , c1988. 530 p. ;
NYPL [Sc D 89-585]

BLACKS - DISEASES - AMERICA - HISTORY.
The African exchange . Durham N.C. , 1987, c1988. vi, 280 p. : ISBN 0-8223-0731-6 DDC 614.4/273/08996073 19
RA442 .A37 1988 **NYPL [Sc D 88-541]**

BLACKS - DRAMA.
Totem voices . New York , 1989. lxiii, 523 p. ; ISBN 0-8021-1053-3 : DDC 812/.54/080896 19
PS628.N4 T68 1988 **NYPL [Sc D 89-381]**

BLACKS - EDUCATION - GREAT BRITAIN.
Dohndy, Farrukh. The Black explosion in British schools /. London , 1985. 64 p. ; ISBN 0-9503498-6-0 **NYPL [Sc D 88-1030]**

BLACKS - EMPLOYMENT - ENGLAND.
Stares, Rodney. Ethnic minorities . [London] , 1982. 62 p. ; ISBN 0-905932-32-3
NYPL [Sc F 88-96]

BLACKS - EMPLOYMENT - LAW AND LEGISLATION - SOUTH AFRICA.
Haarløv, Jens. Labour regulation and black workers' struggles in South Africa /. Uppsala , 1983. 80 p. ; ISBN 91-7106-213-0 (pbk.) DDC 960 s 331.6/9/968 19
DT1 .N64 no. 68 HD6870.5
NYPL [JLD 87-1037]

BLACKS - EMPLOYMENT - NAMIBIA.
Working under South African occupation . London , 1987. 56 p. ; ISBN 0-904759-73-3 (pbk.) : DDC 968 s 331.6/9/9688 19
DT746 .F3 no. 14 HD8808
NYPL [Sc D 89-525]

BLACKS - ENGLAND - LONDON.
Black people in Brent . London , c1987. 159 p. : ISBN 0-9512463-1-3 (pbk.)
NYPL [Sc D 89-5]

Owusu, Kwesi. Behind the masquerade . Edgware , 1988. 90 p. ; ISBN 0-9512770-0-6 (pbk) : DDC 394.2/5/0942134 19
NYPL [Sc E 88-497]

BLACKS - ENGLAND - LONDON - COMMUNICATION.
Hewitt, Roger. White talk, black talk . Cambridge [Cambridgeshire] , New York , 1986. x, 253 p. ; ISBN 0-521-26239-9 DDC 401/.9/094216 19
P40.45.G7 H48 1986 **NYPL [JFE 87-279]**

BLACKS - GREAT BRITAIN.
Bryan, Beverley, 1949- The heart of the race . London , 1985. vi, 250 p. ; ISBN 0-86068-361-3 (pbk.) : DDC 305.4/8896041 19
DA125.N4 B78 1985 **NYPL [Sc C 88-178]**

Demuth, Clare. 'Sus', a report on the Vagrancy Act 1824 /. London , 1978. 62 p. :
NYPL [Sc D 88-1174]

Haynes, Aaron, 1927- The state of Black Britain /. London , 1983. 160 p. ; ISBN 0-946455-01-5 **NYPL [Sc D 88-348]**

BLACKS - GREAT BRITAIN - BIOGRAPHY.
Trill, Carol. Dispossessed daughter of Africa /. London , 1988. 190 p. : ISBN 0-946918-42-2 (pbk) **NYPL [sc C 88-228]**

BLACKS - GREAT BRITAIN - EDUCATION.
Towards the decolonization of the British educational system /. London, England , 19. 128 p. : ISBN 0-907015-32-8
NYPL [Sc D 88-1346]

BLACKS - GREAT BRITAIN - PICTORIAL WORKS.
Race Today Collective. The arrivants . London, England , 1987. 112 p. : ISBN 0-947716-10-6 (pbk.) **NYPL [Sc D 88-1206]**

BLACKS - GREAT BRITAIN - POLITICS AND GOVERNMENT.
Solomos, John. Black youth, racism and the state . Cambridge [Cambridgeshire] , New York , 1988. 284 p. ; ISBN 0-521-36019-6 DDC 305.8/96041 19
DA125.N4 S65 1988 **NYPL [Sc E 88-606]**

BLACKS - GREAT BRITAIN - SOCIAL CONDITIONS.

Britain's Black population . Aldershot, Hants, England , Brookfield, Vt., USA , c1988. xv, 298 p. ; ISBN 0-566-05179-6 : DDC 305.8/96/041 19
DA125.N4 B75 1988 **NYPL [Sc E 89-100]**

Dennis, Ferdinand, 1956- Behind the frontlines . London , 1988. xv, 216 p. ; ISBN 0-575-04098-X **NYPL [JLD 89-210]**

BLACKS - GUADELOUPE - BIOGRAPHY.
Lara, Oruno D. Le commandant Mortenol . Epinay, France , c1985. 275 p. : ISBN 2-905787-00-7 **NYPL [Sc D 88-1085]**

BLACKS - HEALTH AND HYGIENE - ENGLAND - LONDON.
Donovan, Jenny, 1960- We don't buy sickness, it just comes . Aldershot, Hants, England , Brookfield, Vt., USA , c1986. xv, 294 p. ; ISBN 0-566-05201-6 : DDC 362.1/08996/0421 19
RA488.L8 D65 1986 **NYPL [Sc D 86-844]**

Blacks in ancient Cypriot art /. Karageorghis, Vassos. Houston, Tex. , 1988. 62 p. : ISBN 0-939594-13-7 (pbk.) : DDC 704.9/42/093937074 19
N8232 .K37 1988 **NYPL [3-MAE 89-1038]**

BLACKS IN ART.
Suckale-Redlefsen, Gude. Mauritius, der heilige Mohr /. Houston , München , c1987. 295 p. : ISBN 0-939594-03-X DDC 704.9/4863/094 19
N8080.M38 S9 1987 **NYPL [Sc D 88-1357]**

BLACKS IN ART - CATALOGS.
Karageorghis, Vassos. Blacks in ancient Cypriot art /. Houston, Tex. , 1988. 62 p. : ISBN 0-939594-13-7 (pbk.) : DDC 704.9/42/093937074 19
N8232 .K37 1988 **NYPL [3-MAE 89-1038]**

BLACKS IN ART - EXHIBITIONS.
Negripub . [Paris] [1987] 157 p. : ISBN 2-7012-0580-8 **NYPL [Sc E 88-234]**

Blacks in Bermuda : historical perspectives / co-ordinator and editor, W. Michael Brooke . [Hamilton? : Bermuda College, 1980?] 82 p. : ill. ; 28 cm. (A Bermuda College publication) "A lecture series of the Bermuda College extension programme, February-May 1980." Includes bibliographical references.
1. Blacks - Bermuda Islands - History. I. Brooke, W. Michael. **NYPL [Sc F 88-251]**

Blacks in Detroit : a reprint of articles from the Detroit free press / edited by Scott McGehee and Susan Watson. Detroit : Detroit Free Press, 1980. 111 p. : ill. ; 31 cm.
1. Afro-Americans - Michigan - Detroit. I. McGehee, Scott. II. Watson, Susan. III. Detroit Free Press.
NYPL [Sc G 88-15]

Blacks in Ohio, 1880 in the counties of ... /. Nitchman, Paul E. [Decorah? Iowa] , c1985- v. ; DDC 929/.3/089960730771 19
E185.93.O2 N57 1985
NYPL [APR (Ohio) 86-2025]

Blacks in Rhode Island. Stewart, Rowena. A heritage discovered . Providence, R.I. [1975] 39 p. : **NYPL [Sc E 89-110]**

Blacks in southern politics / edited by Laurence W. Moreland, Robert P. Steed, Tod A. Baker. New York : Praeger, 1987. vii, 305 p. : ill. ; 25 cm. Based on papers presented at the 1984 and 1986 Citadel symposia on southern politics. Includes bibliographies and index. ISBN 0-275-92655-9 (alk. paper) : DDC 323.1/196073/075 19
1. Afro-Americans - Southern States - Politics and government - Congresses. 2. Presidents - United States - Election - 1984 - Congresses. 3. Southern States - Politics and government - 1951- - Congresses. I. Moreland, Laurence W. II. Baker, Tod A. III. Steed, Robert P. IV. Citadel Military College of South Carolina.
E185.92 .B58 1987 **NYPL [Sc E 88-196]**

BLACKS IN THE MOTION PICTURE INDUSTRY - GREAT BRITAIN.
Fusco, Coco. Young, British, and Black . Buffalo, N.Y. , c1988. 65 p. :
NYPL [Sc D 88-1186]

Blacks in the new world.
Black leaders of the nineteenth century /. Urbana , c1988. xii, 344 p. : ISBN 0-252-01506-1 (alk. paper) DDC 920/.009296073 19
E185.96 .B535 1988 **NYPL [Sc E 88-365]**

Cheek, William F., 1933- John Mercer Langston and the fight for Black freedom, 1829-65 /. Urbana , c1989. 478 p. ; ISBN

0-252-01550-9 (alk. paper) DDC 973/.0496073/0924 B 19
E185.97.L27 C48 1989 **NYPL [Sc E 89-255]**

Wynes, Charles E. Charles Richard Drew . Urbana , c1988. xvi, 132 p., [14] p. of plates : ISBN 0-252-01551-7 DDC 610/.92/4 B 19
R154.D75 W96 1988 **NYPL [Sc E 89-65]**

Blacks in the workforce . Becknell, Charles Edward, 1941- Albuquerque, New Mexico , c1987. iii, 85 p., A-D leaves ; ISBN 0-913945-52-8 **NYPL [Sc F 88-157]**

Blacks in U. S. foreign policy. Transafrica Forum (Organization) A retrospective . [Washington, D.C.] , c1987. 32 p. : **NYPL [Sc E 88-163]**

BLACKS - INDEXES.
Stevenson, Rosemary M. Index to Afro-American reference resources /. New York , 1988. xxvi, 315 p. ; ISBN 0-313-24580-0 (lib. bdg. : alk. paper) DDC 973/.0496073 19
Z1361.N39 S77 1988 E185
NYPL [Sc E 88-220]

BLACKS - JAMAICA.
Dallas, Robert Charles, 1754-1824. The history of the Maroons, from their origin to the establishment of their chief tribe at Sierra Leone. London, 1803. 2 v. :
F1881 .D14 **NYPL [Sc Rare F 88-76]**

Rodney, Walter. The groundings with my brothers. London, 1969. 68 p. ISBN 0-9501546-0-1
F1896.N4 R6 **NYPL [Sc 323.2-R]**

BLACKS - JAMAICA - BIOGRAPHY.
Seacole, Mary, 1805-1881. Wonderful adventures of Mrs. Seacole in many lands /. New York , 1988. xxxiv, xii, 200 p., [2] p. of plates : ISBN 0-19-505249-8 (alk. paper) DDC 947/.073 19
DK215 .S43 1988 **NYPL [JFC 88-2150]**

BLACKS - JAMAICA - PORTRAITS.
Jaja, Janhoi M. Profile . Kingston, Jamaica , c1984. 48 p. : **NYPL [Sc D 88-932]**

BLACKS - LATIN AMERICA - RELIGION.
Ecumenical Association of Third World Theologians. Identidade negra e religião . Rio de Janeiro , 1986. 201 p. ;
NYPL [Sc D 88-485]

Gallardo, Jorge Emilio. Presencia africana en la cultura de América Latina . Buenos Aires, Argentina , c1986. 123 p. ; ISBN 950-643-006-3 DDC 299/.6 19
BL2490 .G33 1986 **NYPL [Sc D 89-358]**

BLACKS - LEGAL STATUS, LAWS, ETC. - SOUTH AFRICA.
South Africa . London , New York , 1988. 159 p. : ISBN 0-86187-979-1 : DDC 323.4/0968 19
NYPL [JLE 88-4543]

South Africa. [Laws, etc.] Native Land Act, 1913. Amendment Bill, 1927 [microform]. Representation of Natives in Parliament Bill. Union Native Council Bill. Coloured Persons Rights Bill, 1927. [S.l. [1927?] 47 p. ;
NYPL [Sc Micro F-10937]

BLACKS - LIBYA - TRIPOLI - RELIGION - HISTORY.
Sarnelli, Tommaso. Costumi e credenze coloniali [microform] . Napoli , 1925. 39 p. :
NYPL [Sc Micro F-11058]

BLACKS - LITERARY COLLECTIONS.
Littérature négro-africaine francophone . [Pau] , 1986. 137 p. ; DDC 840/.9/896 19
PQ3980.5 .L56 1986 **NYPL [Sc D 89-316]**

BLACKS - MARITIME PROVINCES - CIVIL RIGHTS.
Pachai, Bridglal. Blacks /. Tantallon, Nova Scotia , 1987. 60 p. : ISBN 0-920427-11-1
NYPL [Sc D 88-1022]

BLACKS - MARITIME PROVINCES - HISTORY.
Pachai, Bridglal. Blacks /. Tantallon, Nova Scotia , 1987. 60 p. : ISBN 0-920427-11-1
NYPL [Sc D 88-1022]

BLACKS - MEDICAL CARE - ENGLAND - LONDON.
Donovan, Jenny, 1960- We don't buy sickness, it just comes . Aldershot, Hants, England , Brookfield, Vt., USA , c1986. xv, 294 p. ; ISBN 0-566-05201-6 : DDC 362.1/08996/0421 19
RA488.L8 D65 1986 **NYPL [Sc D 86-844]**

BLACKS - NICARAGUA.
Congress, Rick. The Afro-Nicaraguans .
[Atlanta, Georgia] , c1987. 88 p. :
NYPL [Sc D 88-1280]

BLACKS - NOVA SCOTIA.
Thomson, Colin A., 1938- Born with a call .
Dartmouth, Nova Scotia , 1986. 157 p., [8] p.
of plates : *NYPL [Sc F 88-63]*

BLACKS - NOVA SCOTIA - SOCIAL
CONDITIONS.
Abucar, Mohamed. Struggle for development .
[S.l.] 1988 (Halifax, Nova Scotia: McCurdy
Print. & Typesetting) xiv, 103 p. : ISBN
0-921201-04-4 *NYPL [Sc D 89-138]*

**The Blacks of Pickaway County, Ohio in the
nineteenth century /.** Buchanan, James. Bowie,
Maryland , 1988. iv, 142 p. ; ISBN
1-556-13129-1 *NYPL [Sc D 89-154]*

**Blacks on white campuses, whites on black
campuses** / the National Association for Equal
Opportunity in Higher Education ; edited by
Andrew Billingsley, Ada M. Elam. Chicago :
Follett Press, c1986. 177 p. ; 22 cm. A selection
of papers presented to the National Conference on
Blacks in Higher Education in 1983 and 1984. Includes
bibliographical references. ISBN 0-695-60052-4
*1. College integration - United States - Congresses. I.
Billingsley, Andrew. II. Elam, Ada M. III. National
Association for Equal Opportunity in Higher Education
(U. S.). IV. National Conference on Blacks in Higher
Education.* *NYPL [Sc D 88-949]*

BLACKS - ONTARIO - TORONTO -
BIOGRAPHY.
Hubbard, Stephen, 1961- Against all odds .
Toronto , 1987. 140 p. : ISBN 1-550-02013-7
(bound) *NYPL [Sc D 88-985]*

BLACKS - PERU - LANGUAGE.
Romero, Fernando. El negro en el Perú y su
transculturación lingüística /. [Lima?] , 1987.
176 p. : *NYPL [Sc F 88-20]*

BLACKS - POETRY.
Clarke, A. M. Verses for emancipation . [Port
of Spain , 1986] 41 p. ; DDC 811 19
PR9272.9.C53 V4 1986
NYPL [Sc D 88-981]

Gurus and griots . Brooklyn, N.Y. [1987],
c1985. 108 p. : ISBN 0-9618755-0-X (pbk.) DDC
811/.008/0896 19
PS591.N4 G87 1987 *NYPL [Sc E 89-230]*

BLACKS - PSYCHOLOGY.
Nobles, Wade W. African psychology .
Oakland, California , 1986. 133 p. ; ISBN
0-939205-02-5 *NYPL [Sc D 88-696]*

BLACKS - RACE IDENTITY -
BIBLIOGRAPHY.
Michael, Colette Verger, 1937- Negritude .
West Cornwall, CT , 1988. xvii, 315 p. ; ISBN
0-933951-15-9 (lib. bdg.: alk. paper) : DDC
016.909/04924 19
Z6520.N44 M53 1988 PN56.N36
NYPL [Sc D 88-1470]

BLACKS - RACE IDENTITY -
MISCELLANEA.
Frye, Charles A. From Egypt to Don Juan .
Lanham, MD , c1988. xiii, 129 p. : ISBN
0-8191-7120-4 (alk. paper) DDC 100 19
BF1999 .F77 1988 *NYPL [Sc D 88-1421]*

BLACKS - RELIGION.
Bastide, Roger, 1898-1974. [Religions africaines
au Brésil. Portuguese] As religiões africanas no
Brasil . São Paulo , 1985. 567 p. ;
NYPL [Sc D 88-542]

BLACKS - ROME.
Thompson, L. A. Rome and race . [Ibadan]
1987. iii, 114 p. ; *NYPL [Sc F 88-173]*

BLACKS - SOUTH AFRICA.
Alexander, Neville. Sow the wind .
Johannesburg , c1985 (1987 printing) xi, 180
p. ; ISBN 0-947009-07-8 *NYPL [Sc D 88-196]*

Brickley, Carol. South Africa . London , 1985.
50 p. : ISBN 0-905400-06-2 :
NYPL [Sc D 89-361]

BLACKS - SOUTH AFRICA - ATTITUDES.
Hoile, David. Understanding sanctions /.
London , 1988. 80 p. : ISBN 1-87111-700-3
(pbk.) : DDC 337.68 19
HF1613.4 .H654 1988 NYPL [Sc D 89-317]

BLACKS - SOUTH AFRICA - DRAMA.
Manaka, Matsemela. Egoli, city of gold
[microform] . Johannesburg [198-?] 28 p. ;
NYPL [Sc Micro F-11049]

BLACKS - SOUTH AFRICA - ECONOMIC
CONDITIONS.
Cole, Josette. Crossroads . Johannesburg, South
Africa , 1987. xii, 175 p., [25] p. of plates :
ISBN 0-86975-318-5 *NYPL [Sc D 88-957]*

Harsch, Ernest. South Africa . New York ,
1980. 352 p., [8] leaves of plates : ISBN
0-913460-78-8
DT763 .H29

Keegan, Timothy J. Rural transformations in
industrializing South Africa . Basingstoke ;
London , 1987. xviii, 302 p. : ISBN
0-333-41746-1 *NYPL [Sc D 88-1228]*

A People's history of South Africa .
Johannesburg , c1980- v. : ISBN 0-86975-119-0
(pbk. : v. 1) DDC 968 19
DT766 .P43 *NYPL [JLM 85-439]*

Tsotsi, W. M. From chattel to wage slavery .
Maseru , 1981. 136 p., [2] folded leaves of
plates : DDC 306/.0968 19
DT763.6 .T76 1981 *NYPL [Sc D 89-22]*

BLACKS - SOUTH AFRICA - FICTION.
Tlali, Miriam. Soweto stories /. London , 1989.
xx, 162 p. ; *NYPL [Sc C 89-140]*

BLACKS - SOUTH AFRICA -
GRAHAMSTOWN - ATTITUDES.
Roux, Andre, 1954- Voices from Rini .
Grahamstown, South Africa , 1986. 107 p. ;
ISBN 0-86810-131-1 *NYPL [Sc F 88-216]*

BLACKS - SOUTH AFRICA - HISTORY.
Tsotsi, W. M. From chattel to wage slavery .
Maseru , 1981. 136 p., [2] folded leaves of
plates : DDC 306/.0968 19
DT763.6 .T76 1981 *NYPL [Sc D 89-22]*

BLACKS - SOUTH AFRICA -
JOHANNESBURG - BIOGRAPHY.
Moloi, Godfrey, 1934- My life /.
Johannesburg , 1987- v. : ISBN 0-86975-324-X
(v. 1) DDC 968.2/21/0924 B 19
DT944.J653 M65 1987 NYPL [Sc C 89-113]

BLACKS - SOUTH AFRICA - NATAL - CIVIL
RIGHTS.
Kline, Benjamin. Genesis of apartheid .
Lanham, MD , c1988. xxii, 283 p. ; ISBN
0-8191-6494-1 (alk. paper) : DDC 968.4/04 19
DT872 .K56 1988 NYPL [JLD 88-4097]

BLACKS - SOUTH AFRICA - NATAL -
POLITICS AND GOVERNMENT.
Kline, Benjamin. Genesis of apartheid .
Lanham, MD , c1988. xxii, 283 p. ; ISBN
0-8191-6494-1 (alk. paper) : DDC 968.4/04 19
DT872 .K56 1988 NYPL [JLD 88-4097]

BLACKS - SOUTH AFRICA - POLITICAL
ACTIVITY.
El Mahmud-Okereke, N. O. E. (Noel Olufemi
Enuma), 1948- Beyond the Botha/Buthelezi
political debate . London , c1987. v, 177 p. :
ISBN 978-242-309-2 (pbk) : DDC 346.802/3 19
NYPL [Sc C 88-180]

BLACKS - SOUTH AFRICA - POLITICS AND
GOVERNMENT.
Atkinson, Doreen. The search for power and
legitimacy in Black urban areas . Grahamstown
[South Africa] [1984] 38, xix, v, [1] p. ; ISBN
0-86810-114-1 (pbk.) : DDC 320.8/0968 19
JS7533.A8 A85 1984 *NYPL [Sc F 88-355]*

Bernstein, Hilda (Watts) No. 46 Steve Biko /.
London , 1978. 150 p., [4] p. of plates : ISBN
0-904759-21-0 :
DT779.8.B48 B47 *NYPL [JFD 79-52]*

Harsch, Ernest. South Africa . New York ,
1980. 352 p., [8] leaves of plates : ISBN
0-913460-78-8
DT763 .H29

Meli, Francis, 1942- South Africa belongs to
us . Harare , 1988. xx, 258, [8] p. of plates :
NYPL [Sc D 89-308]

Resistance and ideology in settler societies /.
Johannesburg, Athens, Ohio , 1986. viii, 222
p. ; ISBN 0-86975-304-5
NYPL [Sc D 88-1093]

BLACKS - SOUTH AFRICA - SOCIAL
CONDITIONS.
Cole, Josette. Crossroads . Johannesburg, South

Africa , 1987. xii, 175 p., [25] p. of plates :
ISBN 0-86975-318-5 *NYPL [Sc D 88-957]*

Kuzwayo, Ellen. [Call me woman. French.]
Femme et noire en Afrique du Sud /. Paris ,
c1985. 296, [8] p. of plates : ISBN 2-221-05157-2
NYPL [Sc E 88-315]

Tsotsi, W. M. From chattel to wage slavery .
Maseru , 1981. 136 p., [2] folded leaves of
plates : DDC 306/.0968 19
DT763.6 .T76 1981 *NYPL [Sc D 89-22]*

Two dogs and freedom . Johannesburg , 1986.
55 p. : ISBN 0-86975-301-0 (pbk.)
NYPL [Sc D 88-151]

Two dogs and freedom . New York , 1987. 55
p. : ISBN 0-8050-0637-0 (pbk.) : DDC
323.1/196/068 19
DT763.6 .T96 1987 *NYPL [Sc D 88-422]*

BLACKS - SOUTH AFRICA - SOCIAL
CONDITIONS - CASE STUDIES.
Keegan, Timothy J. Facing the storm .
London , Athens , 1988. vi, 169 p. : ISBN
0-8214-0924-7 DDC 305.8/96068 19
HN801.A8 K44 1989 *NYPL [Sc D 89-233]*

BLACKS - SOUTH AFRICA -
TRANSPORTATION.
Human Awareness Programme (South Africa)
Black urban public road transport . Grant Park
[South Africa] [1982] 64 p. : ISBN
0-620-05750-5 (pbk.) : DDC 388.4/1322/089968
19
HE5704.4.A6 H86 1982
NYPL [Sc F 88-150]

BLACKS - SOUTH AMERICA.
Sandoval, Alonso dc, 1576-1652. Naturaleza,
policia sagrada i profana, costumbres i ritos,
disciplina i catechismo evangelico de todos
etiopes /. En Sevilla , 1627. [23], 334 p., 81
leaves ; *NYPL [Sc Rare F 82-70]*

BLACKS - WEST INDIES.
Carlyle, Thomas, 1795-1881. Occasional
discourse on the Nigger question. London,
1853. 48 p.
HT1091 .C47 *NYPL [Sc C 89-7]*

BLACKS - WEST INDIES - FAMILY
RELATIONSHIPS.
André, Jacques. L'inceste focal dans la famille
noire antillaise . Paris : Presses universitaires de
France, 1987. 396 p. ; ISBN 2-13-040101-5
NYPL [Sc D 88-129]

Blacks who died for Jesus. Hyman, Mark.
Philadelphia , 1983. iv, 107 p. : ISBN
0-915515-00-8 (pbk.) DDC 270/.08996 B 19
BR1702 .H9 1983 *NYPL [Sc D 89-263]*

BLACKSMITHS - MALI.
McNaughton, Patrick R. The Mande
blacksmiths . Bloomington , c1988. xxiv, 241 p.,
[4] p. of plates : ISBN 0-253-33683-X DDC
306/.089963 19
DT551.45.M36 M38 1988
NYPL [Sc E 88-393]

Blackwell, Lee. Wilson, Mary, 1938- To Benji,
with love /. Chicago , c1987. p. cm. ISBN
0-910671-07-9 : DDC 977.3/11043/0924 B 19
F548.9.N4 W559 1987
NYPL [Sc D 88-1219]

Blake, Roger. Brown, Leroy. Black sexual power
/. Cleveland, Ohio , c1970. 220 p. ;
NYPL [Sc C 88-274]

Blaming others : prejudice, race and worldwide
AIDS / Renée Sabatier ... [et al.] London :
Panos Institute ; Philadelphia, PA : New
Society Publishers, 1988. [120] p. ; 22 cm.
Includes bibliography. ISBN 0-86571-146-1 (pbk.)
DDC 362.1/042 19
1. AIDS (Disease) - Social aspects. I. Sabatier, Renée.
RC607.A26 *NYPL [Sc D 88-1215]*

Blanc-Pattin, Charles. Martinique guidebook /
Charles & Christine Blanc-Pattin.
Roquefort-Les-Pins, France : Editions Photoguy,
1988. 48 p. : col. ill., map ; 22 cm.
1. Martinique. I. Title. *NYPL [Sc D 88-1282]*

Blanc, Paul. Le prince et le griot : expériences et
espérances africaines / Paul Blanc. Paris :
Berger-Levrault, c1987. 250 p., [4] p. of plates :
ill. ; 24 cm. (Collection Mondes en devenir. Série
Bâtisseurs d'avenir) ISBN 2-7013-0719-8
1. Africa, Sub-Saharan - Politics and government -

1960-. 2. Africa, Sub-Saharan - History - 1960-. 3. Africa, Sub-Saharan - Social conditions - 1960-. I. Title.
      NYPL [Sc E 88-345]

Blanchard, Joshua Pollard, 1782-1868. Principles of the Revolution: showing the perversion of them and the consequent failure of their accomplishment. By J.P. Blanchard. Boston, Press of Damrell and Moore, 1855. 24 p. 23cm.
1. United States - Politics and government - 1783-1865. I. Title.
JK216 .B63   *NYPL [Sc Rare F 88-40]*

Blanchard, Teódulo. Creole haitiano : vocabulario clasificado y avance gramatical / Teódulo Blanchard. Santo Domingo, D.N. : T. Blanchard, 1983. 117 p. ; 28 cm. Haitian French Creole and Spanish. Bibliography: p. 117. DDC 447/.97294 19
1. Creole dialects, French - Haiti - Glossaries, vocabularies, etc. I. Title.
PM7854.H34 B58 1983   *NYPL [Sc F 87-422]*

Bland, Joy. Teddy the toucan : a story for children / by Joy Bland. Bridgetown, Barbados : s.n., 1987 ; (Barbados : Caribbean Graphic Production) 20 p. : ill. ; 24 cm. SCHOMBURG CHILDREN'S COLLECTION.
1. Tales - Guyana. I. Schomburg Children's Collection. II. Title.   *NYPL [Sc E 88-478]*

Blast at noon . Mbaba, Ita G. Calabar, Nigeria , c1987. x, 40 p. ; ISBN 978-231-602-2
      NYPL [Sc C 89-63]

Blatti, Jo. Past meets present . Washington, D.C. , 1987. x, 169 p. : ISBN 0-87474-272-2 DDC 069/.9973 19
D16.163 .P37 1987   *NYPL [Sc E 88-577]*

Blauner, Bob. Black lives, white lives : three decades of race relations in America / Bob Blauner. Berkeley : University of California Press, c1989. xii, 347 p. ; 24 cm. Includes bibliographical references. ISBN 0-520-06261-2 (alk. paper) DDC 305.8/00973 19
1. Racism - United States - History - 20th century. 2. Afro-Americans - Civil rights. 3. United States - Race relations. I. Title.
E185.615 .B556 1989   *NYPL [Sc E 89-219]*

Bleek, Dorothea Frances, d. 1948. Comparative vocabularies of Bushman languages / by D. F. Bleek. Cambridge [Eng.] : University Press, 1929. 94 p., 1 leaf of plates : map ; 24 cm. (University of Cape Town. Publications of the School of African Life and Language) DDC 496.232
1. English language - Dictionaries - San languages. I. Series: University of Cape Town. School of African Life and Language. Publications. II. Title.
PL8101 .B6   *NYPL [Sc E 88-89]*

Bleeker, Sonia. The Ibo of Biafra. Illustrated by Edith C. Singer. New York, Morrow [1969] 160 p. illus., maps. 20 cm. Describes the way of life of the Ibo, a tribe of southeastern Nigeria, as it was in 1925. SCHOMBURG CHILDREN'S COLLECTION. DDC 916.69/4
1. Igbo (African people) - Juvenile literature. I. Singer, Edith G., illus. II. Schomburg Children's Collection. III. Title.
DT515 .B54   *NYPL [Sc C 88-361]*

Bleser, Carol K. Rothrock. Hammond, James Henry, 1807-1864. Secret and sacred . New York , 1988. xxix, 342 p., [2] leaves of plates : ISBN 0-19-505308-7 DDC 975.7/03/0924 B 19
F273 .H24 1988   *NYPL [Sc E 88-513]*

Blijf even staan! . Helman, Albert. [Netherlands?] c1987. 41 p. :
      NYPL [Sc D 88-1039]

Bliksoldate bloei nie /. De Vries, Abraham H. Kaapstad , 1975. 80 p. ; ISBN 0-7981-0640-9
PT6592.14.E9 B56   *NYPL [Sc D 88-673]*

Blind Tom . Southall, Geneva H. Minneapolis , 1979- v. : DDC 786.1/092/4 B
ML417.B78 S7 1979
      NYPL [Sc Ser.-L .S674]

BLIND TOM, 1849-1908. Southall, Geneva H. Blind Tom . Minneapolis , 1979- v. : DDC 786.1/092/4 B
ML417.B78 S7 1979
      NYPL [Sc Ser.-L .S674]

Block, Arthur R. Rebell, Michael A. Equality and education . Princeton, N.J. , c1985. x, 340 p. ; ISBN 0-691-07692-8 : DDC 344.747/0798 347.4704798 19
KFX2065 .R43 1985   *NYPL [JLD 85-3778]*

Blomfield, Geoffrey. Baal Belbora, the end of the dancing : the agony of the British invasion of the ancient people of Three Rivers : the Hastings, the Manning & the Macleay, in New South Wales / Geoffrey Blomfield. Chippendale, N.S.W. [New South Wales] : APCOL, 1981. 148 p. : ill., maps ; 23 cm. Includes bibliographical references. ISBN 0-909188-57-2
1. Australian aborigines - Australia - New South Wales. 2. New South Wales - History. I. Title.
      NYPL [Sc D 82-242]

Blondé, Jacques. Inventaire des particularités lexicales du français en Afrique noire /. Montréal , Paris [1983] lxi, 550 p. : ISBN 2-920021-15-X *NYPL [Sc E 88-235]*

Blondel, Eaulin. Credit unions, co-operatives, trade unions, and friendly societies in Barbados : a directory / Eaulin A. Blondel. St. Augustine, Trinidad, Trinidad and Tobago : E.A. Blondel, [1986] v, 102 p. ; 28 cm. "April 1986." Includes index. DDC 334/.025/72981 19
1. Cooperative societies - Barbados - Directories. 2. Credit unions - Barbados - Directories. 3. Friendly societies - Barbados - Directories. 4. Trade-unions - Barbados - Directories. I. Title.
HD3464.9.A6 B353 1986
      NYPL [Sc F 88-361]

BLOOD DONORS - SOUTH AFRICA. Palmer, Robin. Blood donation in the Border region. Grahamstown [South Africa] , 1984. 183 p. : ISBN 0-86810-112-5
      NYPL [Sc F 87-432]

Blood on the forge /. Attaway, William. New York , c1987. 315 p. ; ISBN 0-85345-722-0 (pbk.) : DDC 813/.52 19
PS3501.T59 B55 1987
      NYPL [Sc D 88-1438]

Bloodsong and other stories of South Africa /. Havemann, Ernst. Boston , 1987. 134 p. ; ISBN 0-395-43296-0 : DDC 813/.54 19
PR9199.3.H3642 B56 1987
      NYPL [Sc D 88-209]

Bloom, Harold.
Zora Neale Hurston /. New York , 1986. viii, 192 p. ; ISBN 0-87754-627-4 (alk. paper) : DDC 813/.52 19
PS3515.U789 Z96 1986
      NYPL [JFE 87-1592]

Zora Neale Hurston's Their eyes were watching God /. New York , 1987. vii, 130 p. ; ISBN 1-555-46054-2 (alk. paper) : DDC 813/.52 19
PS3515.U789 T639 1987
      NYPL [JFE 87-5315]

Blow the fire /. Ofoegbu, Leslie Jean. Enugu, Nigeria , 1986, c1985. 167 p. ;
      NYPL [Sc C 88-288]

Blue, Adrianne. Faster, higher, further : women's triumphs and disasters at the Olympics / Adrianne Blue. London : Virago, 1988. ix, 182 p. : ill., ports. ; 25 cm. Includes index. Bibliography: p. 177-178. ISBN 0-86068-648-5 (pbk.) :
1. Olympics - History - 20th century. 2. Women athletes - History - 20th century. 3. Afro-American women athletes - History - 20th century. I. Title.
GV721.5 .B58x 1988   *NYPL [Sc E 89-82]*

Blue tights /. Williams-Garcia, Rita. New York , c1987. 138 p. ; ISBN 0-525-67234-6 DDC [Fic] 19
PZ7.W6713 Bl 1987   *NYPL [Sc D 88-939]*

BLUES (MUSIC) - TO 1931 - HISTORY AND CRITICISM. Harrison, Daphne Duval, 1932- Black pearls . New Brunswick [N.J.] , c1988. xv, 295 p. : ISBN 0-8135-1279-4 : DDC 784.5/3/0922 19
ML3521 .H38 1988 *NYPL [JNE 88-21]*

BLUES (MUSIC) - DISCOGRAPHY. Escott, Colin. Sun records . Vollersode, W. Germany , c1987. 240 p. : ISBN 3-924787-09-3 (pbk.)   *NYPL [Sc D 89-243]*

Leadbitter, Mike. Blues records 1943-1970 . London, England , 1987- v. ; ISBN 0-907872-07-7 *NYPL [*R-Phono. 89-790]*

BLUES (MUSIC) - HISTORY AND CRITICISM. Govenar, Alan B., 1952- Meeting the blues /. Dallas, Tex. , c1988. 239 p. : ISBN 0-87833-623-0 : DDC 784.5/3/00922 19
ML3521 .G68 1988   *NYPL [Sc G 89-4]*

BLUES MUSICIANS - PORTRAITS. Klaasse, Piet. Jam session . Newton Abbot [Devon] , 1985. 192 p. : ISBN 0-7153-8710-3 DDC 785.42/092/2 19
ML3506 .K58 1985   *NYPL [Sc G 88-13]*

BLUES MUSICIANS - UNITED STATES - BIOGRAPHY. Harrison, Daphne Duval, 1932- Black pearls . New Brunswick [N.J.] , c1988. xv, 295 p. : ISBN 0-8135-1279-4 : DDC 784.5/3/0922 19
ML3521 .H38 1988   *NYPL [JNE 88-21]*

BLUES MUSICIANS - UNITED STATES - INTERVIEWS. Govenar, Alan B., 1952- Meeting the blues /. Dallas, Tex. , c1988. 239 p. : ISBN 0-87833-623-0 : DDC 784.5/3/00922 19
ML3521 .G68 1988   *NYPL [Sc G 89-4]*

BLUES (MUSIC)ZUNITED STATESXHISTORY AND CRITICISM. Oliver, Paul. The New Grove gospel, blues and jazz . New York , 1986. 395 p. [16] p. of plates : ISBN 0-393-01696-X
      NYPL [JND 88-16]

Blues records 1943-1970 . Leadbitter, Mike. London, England , 1987- v. ; ISBN 0-907872-07-7 *NYPL [*R-Phono. 89-790]*

BLUES (SONGS, ETC.) - HISTORY AND CRITICISM. Finn, Julio. The bluesman . London , New York , 1986. 256 p., [8] p. of plates : ISBN 0-7043-2523-3 *NYPL [Sc E 88-181]*

BLUES (SONGS, ETC.) - UNITED STATES - HISTORY AND CRITICISM. Tracy, Steven C. (Steven Carl), 1954- Langston Hughes & the blues /. Urbana , c1988. xiii, 305 p. ; ISBN 0-252-01457-X (alk. paper) DDC 818/.5209 19
PS3515.U274 Z8 1988 *NYPL [Sc E 88-506]*

The bluesman . Finn, Julio. London , New York , 1986. 256 p., [8] p. of plates : ISBN 0-7043-2523-3 *NYPL [Sc E 88-181]*

Blume, Helmut. Berney, Henri-Maurice. Les Antillles . Paris , 1977, c1972. 128 p. : ISBN 3-405-11035-1   *NYPL [Sc F 89-34]*

Blustein, Ellen. (joint author) Glasser, Barbara. Bongo Bradley. New York [1973] 153 p. DDC [Fic]
PZ7.G48143 Bo   *NYPL [Sc D 89-99]*

Bo Jackson . Devaney, John. New York , 1988. 110 p. : ISBN 0-8027-6818-0 DDC 796.332/092/4 B 92 19
GV865.J28 D48 1988   *NYPL [Sc E 89-12]*

B'ó ti gb` /. Ọlabimtan, Afọlabi. Ibàdàn, Nigeria , 1987, c1980. v. 83 p. : ISBN 978-16-7487-3
      NYPL [Sc D 88-953]

BOARDING-HOUSES. see HOTELS, TAVERNS, ETC.

Boardman, Henry Augustus, 1808-1880. What Christianity demands of us at the present crisis : a sermon preached on Thanksgiving Day, Nov. 29, 1860 / by Henry A. Boardman. Philadelphia : J.B. Lippincott, 1860. 28 p. ; 24 cm. On cover: Dr. Boardman's sermon on the present crisis.
1. Slavery - United States - Sermons. 2. United States - Politics and government - 1857-1861. 3. United States - History - Civil War, 1861-1865 - Sermons. I. Title.
      NYPL [Sc Rare F 88-52]

Bob Marley /. May, Chris. London , 1985. 60 p. : ISBN 0-241-11476-4 : DDC 784.5 B 19
ML420.M3313 M4 1985
      NYPL [Sc D 88-308]

The Bob Marley story /. Sotheby, Madeline. London , 1985. 64 p. ; ISBN 0-09-160031-6 (pbk) : DDC 428.6/2 19
PE1121   *NYPL [Sc C 88-141]*

Bobongo . Vengroenweghe, Daniel. Berlin , c1988. xv, 332 p. : ISBN 3-496-00963-2
      NYPL [Sc E 88-343]

Bocquené, Henri. Moi, un Mbororo : autobiographie de Oumarou Ndoudi, peul nomade du Cameroun / Henri Bocquené. Paris : Editions Karthala, c1986. 387 p., [12] p. of plates : ill. ; 24 cm. (Hommes et sociétés) ISBN 2-86537-164-6
1. Ndoudi, Oumarou, 1945-. 2. Fulahs - Biography. 3. Nomads - Cameroon - Biography. I. Ndoudi, Oumarou, 1945-. II. Series. III. Series: Hommes et sociétés

Bodecker, N. M.

(Editions Karthala). IV. Title.
NYPL *[Sc E 89-66]*

Bodecker, N. M. (ill) Eager, Edward. The well-wishers /. New York , c1960. 191 p. :
NYPL *[Sc D 88-429]*

BODY, HUMAN - SOCIAL ASPECTS - ROME.
Thompson, L. A. Rome and race . [Ibadan] 1987. iii, 114 p. ; **NYPL** *[Sc F 88-173]*

BODY-MARKING - NIGERIA.
Aisien, Ekhaguosa. IWU . Benin City, Nigeria , c1986. 64 p. : **NYPL** *[Sc D 88-728]*

Boesen, Jannik. Tanzania . Uppsala [Stockholm, Sweden] 1986. 325 p. : ISBN 91-7106-257-2 (pbk.) DDC 330.9678/04 19
HD2128.5 .T36 1986 **NYPL** *[Sc E 88-450]*

Bogdon, Klaus. Comics für Afrika . Dormagen [West Germany] [1986] 96 p. :
NYPL *[Sc G 88-27]*

Bogus, SDiane. Dyke hands & sutras erotic & lyric / by SDiane Bogus. San Francisco, Calif. : WIM Publications, 1988. vii, 91 p. ; 22 cm.
ISBN 0-934172-21-8 :
I. Title. **NYPL** *[Sc D 89-536]*

BOHEMIANISM - NEW YORK (N.Y.)
Delany, Samuel R. The motion of light in water . New York , c1988. xviii, 302 p. : ISBN 0-87795-947-1 : DDC 813/.54 19
PS3554.E437 Z475 1988
NYPL *[JFD 88-7818]*

Böhm, Gerhard.
Khoe-kowap : Einführung in die Sprache der Hottentotten, Nama-Dialekt / Gerhard Böhm. Wien : AFRO-Pub, 1985. 406 p. ; 21 cm. (Veröffentlichungen der Institute für Afrikanistik und Ägyptologie der Universität Wien . Nr. 36) Beiträge zur Afrikanistik ; Bd. 25 Bibliography: p. 403-406.
ISBN 3-85043-036-7
1. Nama language. 2. Mythology, African. 3. Nama (African people) - Folklore. I. Title. II. Series.
PL8541 .B6 1985 **NYPL** *[Sc D 89-365]*

Die Sprache der Aithiopen im Lande Kusch / Gerhard Böhm. Wien : AFRO-Pub, 1988. 206 p. : ill. ; 21 cm. (Beiträge zur Afrikanistik. Bd. 34) Veröffentlichungen der Institute für Afrikanistik und Ägyptologie der Universität Wien ; Nr. 47 Bibliography: p. 181-187. ISBN 3-85043-047-2
1. Ethiopia - Language - Grammar. 2. Cushitic languages - Grammar. I. Title.
NYPL *[Sc D 88-1339]*

Bohrer, Dick. John Newton, letters of a slave trader / paraphrased by Dick Bohrer. Chicago : Moody Press, c1983. viii, 130 p. ; 18 cm. Adaptation of: An authentic narrative of some remarkable and interesting particulars in the life of ********, originally published 1764. ISBN 0-8024-0158-9 (pbk.) DDC 283/.3 19
*1. Newton, John, 1725-1807. 2. Church of England - England - Clergy - Biography. I. Newton, John, 1725-1807. An authentic narrative of some remarkable and interesting particulars in the life of ********. II. Title. III. Title: Letters of a slave trader.*
BX5199.N55 B64 1983 **NYPL** *[Sc C 88-235]*

BOKASSA I, EMPEROR OF THE CENTRAL AFRICAN EMPIRE, 1921-
Baccard, André. Les martyrs de Bokassa /. Paris , c1987. 349 p., [16] p. of plates : ISBN 2-02-009669-2 : DDC 967/.4105/0924 B 19
DT546.382.B64 B33 1987
NYPL *[Sc D 88-636]*

Shoumatoff, Alex. African madness /. New York , 1988. xviii, 202 p. ; ISBN 0-394-56914-8 : DDC 967/.0328 19
DT352.2 .S48 1988 **NYPL** *[Sc D 89-160]*

Bola and the Oba's drummer. Schatz, Letta. New York [1967]. 156 p. DDC [Fic] 19
PZ7.S337 Bo **NYPL** *[Sc E 89-26]*

Bolcom, William. Oliver, Paul. The New Grove gospel, blues and jazz . New York , 1986. 395 p. [16] p. of plates : ISBN 0-393-01696-X
NYPL *[JND 88-16]*

Bolin, Robert C. Race, religion, and ethnicity in disaster recovery / Robert Bolin and Patricia Bolton. [Boulder. Colo.] : Institute of Behavioral Science, University of Colorado, 1986. ix, 265 p. : ill. ; 23 cm. (Program on environment and behavior . monograph #42) Bibliography: p. 254-265.
1. Disaster relief - United States. 2. Disasters - United States - Psychological aspects. 3. Disasters - United

States - Social aspects. 4. Ethnic attitudes - United States. I. Bolton, Patricia. II. Title. III. Series.
NYPL *[Sc D 88-904]*

Bolognese, Don. (illus) Rinkoff, Barbara. Headed for trouble /. New York [1970] 119 p. : ISBN 0-394-90494-X **NYPL** *[Sc E 88-227]*

Boloji and Old Hippo /. Shacklett, Juanita Purvis. New York , c1959. 121 p. :
NYPL *[Sc D 88-1166]*

BOLSHEVISM. see COMMUNISM.

Bolton, Patricia. Bolin, Robert C. Race, religion, and ethnicity in disaster recovery /. [Boulder. Colo.] , 1986. ix, 265 p. :
NYPL *[Sc D 88-904]*

Bolton, Shelly. Beauty care for today's woman / By Shelly Bolton. Harare : Books for Africa, 1983. 48 p. : ill. ; 21 cm. Includes index.
I. Title. **NYPL** *[Sc D 88-1444]*

BOMVANA (AFRICAN PEOPLE) - RELIGIOUS LIFE AND CUSTOMS.
Cook, Peter Alan Wilson, 1905- Social organisation and ceremonial institutions of the Bomvana /. Cape Town [1931?] xi, 171 p., [16] p. of plates : **NYPL** *[Sc C 88-31]*

BOMVANA (AFRICAN PEOPLE) - SOCIAL LIFE AND CUSTOMS.
Cook, Peter Alan Wilson, 1905- Social organisation and ceremonial institutions of the Bomvana /. Cape Town [1931?] xi, 171 p., [16] p. of plates : **NYPL** *[Sc C 88-31]*

BOND, JULIAN, 1940-
Ball, Thomas E. Julian Bond vs John Lewis . Atlanta, Ga. , 1988. ix, 144 p. : ISBN 0-9621362-0-4 **NYPL** *[Sc E 88-582]*

Bond-Stewart, Kathy.
Education / by Kathy Bond-Stewart ; illustrated by Chris Hodzi. [Gweru, Zimbabwe] : Mambo Press, 1986. 102 p. : ill. ; 30 cm. "For the Foundation for Education with Production." Bibliography: p. 98-100. ISBN 0-86922-371-2
1. Education - Africa, Southern. 2. Education - Developing countries. I. Foundation for Education with Production (Gaborone, Botswana). II. Title.
NYPL *[Sc F 88-201]*

Independence is not only for one sex / Kathy Bond-Stewart ; photographs by Biddy Partridge and Kate Truscott. Harare, Zimbabwe : Zimbabwe Pub. House, 1987. 128 p. : ports. ; 24 cm. Bibliography: p. 104. ISBN 0-949225-50-9
1. Women - Zimbabwe - Social conditions. 2. Women - Zimbabwe - Biography. I. Title.
NYPL *[Sc E 89-146]*

Bonde, Donatus. A Guide to Zimbabwe /. Gweru, [Zimbabwe] , 1986. 63 p. : ISBN 91-7810-685-0
NYPL *[Sc C 88-371]*

Bonelli Rubio, Juan María. El problema de la colonización [microform] : conferencia pronunciada el día 18 de diciembre de 1944 en el Consejo Superior de Investigaciones Científicas / por Juan Bonelli Rubio. Madrid : Dirección General de Marruecos y Colonias, 1945. 15 p. ; 25 cm. (Curso sobre Africa Española) Cover title. Microfiche. New York: New York Public Library, 198 . 1 microfiche: negative; 11 x 15 cm. (FSN Sc 019,119)
1. Guinea, Gulf of - Colonization. 2. Spain - Colonies - Africa. I. Title. **NYPL** *[Sc Micro F-11057]*

The bonfire of the vanities /. Wolfe, Tom. New York , 1987. 659 p. ; ISBN 0-374-11534-6 : DDC 813/.54 19
PS3573.O526 B6 1987 **NYPL** *[Sc E 88-389]*

Bongo Bradley. Glasser, Barbara. New York [1973] 153 p. DDC [Fic]
PZ7.G48143 Bo **NYPL** *[Sc D 89-99]*

Boni, S. Tanella. Labyrinthe : poèmes / S. Tanella Boni ; préface de Madeleine Borgomano.Ed. originale. [Paris] : Editions Akganon, c1984. 76 p. ; 21 cm. ISBN 2-86427-023-4
I. Title.
MLCS 86/6645 (P) **NYPL** *[Sc D 88-488]*

Bonifácio, José. see Silva, José Bonifácio de Andrada e, 1763-1838.

BONIS (AFRICAN PEOPLE)
Stiles, Daniel. Ethnoarchaeology, a case-study with the Boni of Kenya [microform] /. [Nairobi] [1979] 20 p. ;
NYPL *[Sc Micro R-4108 no. 36]*

Bonjour monsieur le ministre . Bakel, Elimane. Paris , c1983. 75 p. ; ISBN 2-903871-21-3
MLCS 86/6370 (P) **NYPL** *[Sc D 88-1036]*

Bonnafé, Pierre. Afrique plurielle, Afrique actuelle . Paris , c1986. 272 p. ; ISBN 2-86537-151-4 **NYPL** *[Sc E 88-349]*

Bonnardel, Régine. Vitalité de la petite pêche tropicale : pêcheurs de Saint-Louis du Sénégal / par Régine Bonnardel. Paris : Editions du Centre national de la recherche scientifique, 1985. 104 p. : ill., maps ; 27 cm. (Mémoires et documents de géographie) On spine: Pêcheurs de Saint-Louis de Sénégal. Bibliography: p. 97-98. ISBN 2-222-03678-X
1. Fisheries - Senegal - Saint-Louis. 2. Fish trade - Senegal - Saint-Louis. 3. Guet Ndar (Saint-Louis Senegal) - Economic conditions. 4. Saint Louis, Senegal - Economic conditions. I. Title. II. Title: Pêcheurs de Saint-Louis du Sénégal. III. Series.
NYPL *[Sc F 88-329]*

Bonnassieux, Alain. L'autre Abidjan : histoire d'un quartier oublié / Alain Bonnassieux. Abidjan : Inadès Edition ; Paris : Editions Karthala, c1987. 220 p. : maps ; 20 cm. Bibliography: p. [215]-217. ISBN 0-86537-191-3
1. Abidjan, Ivory Coast - Description. I. Title.
NYPL *[Sc C 88-212]*

Bonner, Marita, 1899-1971. Frye Street & environs : the collected works of Marita Bonner / edited and introduced by Joyce Flynn and Joyce Occomy Stricklin. Boston : Beacon Press, c1987. xxix, 286 p. ; 22 cm. (Black women writers series) ISBN 0-8070-6300-2 DDC 810/.8/0896073 19
1. Afro-Americans - Literary collections. I. Flynn, Joyce.. II. Stricklin, Joyce Occomy. III. Title. IV. Title: Frye Street and environs. V. Series.
PS3503 .O439 1987 **NYPL** *[Sc D 88-683]*

Bontemps, Arna Wendell, 1902- Mr. Kelso's lion [by] Arna Bontemps. Illustrated by Len Ebert. [1st ed.] Philadelphia, Lippincott [1970] 48 p. illus. 23 cm. Twelve-year-old Percy and his grandfather arrive at Aunt Clothilde's expecting a quiet visit until they discover the old man next door is boarding a lion in his backyard. SCHOMBURG CHILDREN'S COLLECTION. DDC [Fic]
1. Lions - Juvenile fiction. I. Ebert, Len, illus. II. Schomburg Children's Collection. III. Title.
PZ7.B6443 Mi **NYPL** *[Sc D 88-1493]*

Bonvin, Jean. Changements sociaux et productivité agricole en Afrique Centrale / par Jean Bonvin. Paris : Centre de développement de l'orgnisation de coopértion et de développement économiques, c1986. 140 p. : ill., maps ; 23 cm. (Etudes du Centre de développement) Published in English under title: Social attitudes and agricultural productivity in Central Africa. Includes bibliographical references. ISBN 92-64-22803-9
1. Agriculture - Economic aspects - Burundi. 2. Burundi - Rural conditions. 3. Burundi - Social conditions. I. Organisation for Economic Co-operation and Development. Development Centre. II. Title. III. Series. **NYPL** *[Sc D 88-803]*

BOOK CENSORSHIP. see CENSORSHIP.

BOOK INDUSTRIES. see BOOK INDUSTRIES AND TRADE.

BOOK INDUSTRIES AND TRADE - PUERTO RICO - EXHIBITIONS.
Feria del Libro (9th: 1967: San Juan, Puerto Rico) Programa [microform] . [San Juan , 1967] 37 p. : **NYPL** *[Sc Micro F-11056]*

A book of religious and general poems /. Ming, Richard E. New York, N.Y. , 1986. 113 p. ;
NYPL *[Sc D 89-141]*

BOOK REPAIRING. see BOOKS - CONSERVATION AND RESTORATION.

BOOK TRADE. see BOOK INDUSTRIES AND TRADE; PUBLISHERS AND PUBLISHING.

Booker T. Washington . Harlan, Louis R. New York , 1983. xiv, 548 p. : ISBN 0-19-503202-0 : DDC 378/.111 B 19
E185.97.W4 H373 1983
NYPL *[Sc E 83-233]*

Booker T. Washington and the "Atlanta compromise" / with Louis Harlan. Sharpsburg, Md. : Allen Telecomunication, c1987. 13 p. : ill., ports. ; 28 cm. "Washington's ... speech given at the Cotton States and International Exposition, held in

Atlanta in 1895 ... has become known as the "Atlanta compromise." Bibliography: p. 12.
1. Washington, Booker T. 1856-1915. 2. United States - Race relations. I. Harlan, Louis R. II. Washington, Booker T. 1856-1915. **NYPL [Sc F 88-386]**

Booker T. Washington gives facts and condemns lynching in a statement telegraphed to the New York world. Washington, Booker T. 1856-1915. Baltimore , 1908. [3] p. ;
NYPL [Sc Rare C 89-25]

Booker T. Washington in perspective . Harlan, Louis R. Jackson, c1988. xii, 210 p., [8] p. of plates : ISBN 0-87805-374-3 (alk. paper) DDC 378/.111 B 19
E185.97.W4 H36 1988 **NYPL [Sc E 89-217]**

The Booker T. Washington papers. Washington, Booker T. 1856-1915. Urbana [1972- v.
NYPL [Sc B-Washington, B.]

BOOKS - APPRAISAL. see CRITICISM.

BOOKS - CARE. see BOOKS - CONSERVATION AND RESTORATION.

BOOKS - CENSORSHIP. see CENSORSHIP.

BOOKS - CONSERVATION AND RESTORATION - UNITED STATES.
Organizing for preservation in ARL libraries /. Washington, D.C. , 1985. 131 p. :
NYPL [Sc F 88-327]

BOOKS FOR CHILDREN. see CHILDREN'S LITERATURE.

Books on race and race relations held in the Richard B. Moore Library, Barbados /. Moss, S. G. Barbados , 1987. 133 leaves ;
NYPL [Sc F 89-105]

BOOKS - PRESERVATION. see BOOKS - CONSERVATION AND RESTORATION.

BOOKS, REFERENCE. see REFERENCE BOOKS.

BOOKS - REPAIRING. see BOOKS - CONSERVATION AND RESTORATION.

BOOKS - RESTORATION. see BOOKS - CONSERVATION AND RESTORATION.

Boon, Rudolf. Over vijf jaar in Johannesburg-- : generaties van verzet / Rudi Boon. Amsterdam : J. Mets ; 's-Gravenhage [Netherlands] : NOVIB, 1986. 223 p. ; 22 cm. Includes index. Bibliography: p. 215-216. ISBN 90-70509-53-9
1. Apartheid - South Africa. 2. South Africa - Social conditions - 1961-. 3. South Africa - Politics and government - 1961-. I. Title.
NYPL [Sc D 89-167]

Booth, Esma (Rideout) Kalena and Sana / by Esma Rideout Booth ; illustrated by Robert Pious. New York : D. McKay, 1962. 152 p. : ill. ; 21 cm.
1. Zaire - Juvenile fiction. I. Title.
NYPL [Sc D 88-506]

BOPHUTHATSWANA (SOUTH AFRICA)
Mangope, Lucas. Mandatory sanctions . Lagos, Nigeria , 1988. v. 110, a-t p. of plates : ISBN 978-242-313-0 **NYPL [Sc C 88-181]**

BORDER LIFE. see FRONTIER AND PIONEER LIFE.

Borders, William Holmes, 1905- Seven minutes at the 'mike' in the Deep South / by William Holmes Borders. [Atlanta?] : Logan Press, 1949, c1943. 104 p. : port. ; 22 cm. "These Radio Sermonets originated in the Main Auditorium of Wheat Street Baptist Church over Stations WAGA and WGST. They deal with contemporary problems, seen from the Christian view." ---Foreword. With autograph of author.
1. Sermons, American - Afro-American authors. I. Title.
NYPL [Sc D 87-1426]

Bordes, Ary. Manuel d'hygiène [microform] / Ary Bordes ; ill., Edith Hollant. [Port-au-Prince, : Editions H. Deschamps, 1975. 130 p. : ill. ; 21 cm. "Revisé par une commission fermée du Déjarte,emt de l'education nationale, MM. André Dartiguenave et Montès Philippe du Département de l'agriculture, des ressources naturelles et du developpement rural," On cover: Manuel d'hygiène, cours moyen. Microfilm. New York : New York Public Library, 198 . 1 microfiln rees ; 35 mm. (MN *ZZ-28635)
1. Health education (Secondary) - Haiti - Handbooks, manuals, etc. I. Title.
NYPL [Sc Micro R-4840 no.9]

Manuel d'hygiène [microform] : cours élémentaires I et II / Ary Bordes ; photographie, Jean Guéry. [Port-au-Prince?] : Impr. H. Deschamps, 1976. 78 p. : ill. ; 21 cm. "Ecrit en collaboration avec une commission formée de Mnce Luc Hector et Mr. Max Joseph du Département de l'education nationale, MM. Mont
1. Health education (Elementary) - Haiti - Handbooks, manuels,etc. I. Title.
NYPL [Sc Micro R-4840 no.7]

Born here /. Sekou, Lasana M., 1959- St. Maarten, Caribbean , Staten Island, N.Y. , c1986. xvii, 148 p. : ISBN 0-913441-05-8 (pbk.)
MLCS 86/13366 (P) **NYPL [Sc D 88-491]**

Born with a call . Thomson, Colin A., 1938- Dartmouth, Nova Scotia , 1986. 157 p., [8] p. of plates : **NYPL [Sc F 88-63]**

Bornia, Ligia de. Comidas tipicas dominicanas = Dominican typical meals / Ligia de Bornia ; traducido por Virginia de Vega.3. ed. Santo Domingo Republica Dominicana : Editora Taller, 1987. 132 p. ; 21 cm. In Spanish and English. Imperfect Copy: p. 5-36 in wrong order.
1. Cookery, Dominican. I. Title. II. Title: Dominican typical meals. **NYPL [Sc D 89-157]**

Borno State (Nigeria)
Government white paper on the report of Panel on Eduction Review in Borno State / [Bulama Gana, chairman] Maiduguri : The Govt. Printer, [1984] 56 p. : ill. ; 25 cm.
1. Borno State (Nigeria). Panel on Education Review in Borno State. Report. 2. Education - Nigeria - Borno State. I. Gana, Bulama. II. Title.
NYPL [Sc E 88-424]

BORNO STATE (NIGERIA) - CHURCH HISTORY.
Hickey, Raymond. Christianity in Borno State and Northern Gongola /. [Nigeria , 1984?] (Ibadan : Claverianum Press) vi, 108 p. :
NYPL [Sc D 88-882]

Borno State (Nigeria). Panel on Education Review in Borno State. REPORT.
Borno State (Nigeria) Government white paper on the report of Panel on Eduction Review in Borno State /. Maiduguri [1984] 56 p. : **NYPL [Sc E 88-424]**

Boro, Isaac. The twelve-day revolution / by Isaac Boro ; edited by Tony Tebekaemi. Benin City, Nigeria : Ibodo Umeh Publishers, 1982. 158 p., [8] p. of plates : ill. ; 18 cm. ISBN 978-234-040-5
1. Boro, Isaac. 2. Nigeria - Politics and government - 1960-1975. 3. Nigeria - Ethnic relations. 4. Rivers State, Nigeria - Politics and government. I. Title.
NYPL [Sc C 88-109]

BORO, ISAAC.
Boro, Isaac. The twelve-day revolution /. Benin City, Nigeria , 1982. 158 p., [8] p. of plates : ISBN 978-234-040-5 **NYPL [Sc C 88-109]**

Bosch, Juan, 1909- Composición social dominicana : historia e interpretación / Juan Bosch.3a. ed. Santo Domingo, República Dominicana : Alfa y Omega, 1983. 272 p. ; 22 cm. Includes bibliographical references.
1. Dominican Republic - Social conditions. I. Title.
NYPL [Sc D 88-1065]

Bosch Navarro, Juan. La Iglesia negra : eclesiología militante de James H. Cone / Juan Bosch Navarro. Valencia : [s.n.], 1986 (Valencia : Imprenta Nácher). 57 p. ; 23 cm. At head of title: Facultad de teología San Vicente Ferrer de Valencia. "Escritos del vedat, vol. XV, año 1986". Bibliography: p. 7-8.
1. Cone, James H. - Contributions in Black theology. 2. Afro-American churches. 3. Black theology. I. Title.
NYPL [Sc D 87-1154]

BOSJESMEN. see SAN (AFRICAN PEOPLE)

BOSS RULE. see CORRUPTION (IN POLITICS)

Bossart, Johann Jakob. Oldendorp, C. G. A. (Christian Georg Andreas), 1721-1787. [Geschichte der Mission der Evangelischen Brüder auf den caraibischen Inseln S. Thomas, S. Croix und S. Jan.] C.G.A. Oldendorps Geschichte der Mission der Evangelischen Brüder auf den caraibischen Inseln S. Thomas, S. Croix und S. Jan /. Barby , 1777. 2 v. in 1

(1068 p.) : DDC 266/.46729722 19
BV2848.V5 O42 1777
NYPL [Sc Rare C 89-33]

The bossy wife /. Gbomba, Lele. Freetown , 1987. 91 p. : **NYPL [Sc D 89-429]**

BOSTON CELTICS (BASKETBALL TEAM)
Ryan, Bob. Forty-eight minutes . New York , London , c1987. x, 356 p. ; ISBN 0-02-597770-9 DDC 796.32/364/0973 19
GV885.515.N37 R9 1988
NYPL [JFD 87-10809]

BOSTON - FICTION.
West, Dorothy, 1909- The living is easy /. London , 1987, c1982. 362 p. ; ISBN 0-86068-753-8 **NYPL [Sc C 88-165]**

Boston, L. M. (Lucy Maria), 1892- Treasure of Green Knowe. Drawings by Peter Boston. [1st American ed.] New York, Harcourt, Brace [1958] 185 p. illus. 21 cm. London ed. (Faber) has title: The chimneys of Green Knowe. A young boy listens to his great-grandmother's tales of Green Knowe as it used to be and, gradually, as past and present blend, he shares the strange adventures of the former inhabitants. SCHOMBURG CHILDREN'S COLLECTION. DDC [Fic]
1. Space and time - Juvenile fiction. 2. Children, Black - England - Juvenile fiction. I. Boston, Peter. II. Schomburg Children's Collection. III. Title.
PZ7.B6497 Tr **NYPL [Sc D 88-1497]**

BOSTON (MASS.) - CHURCH HISTORY.
Hayden, Robert C. Faith, culture, and leadership . [Boston, MA , c1983] iv, 56 p. : DDC 280/.08996073074461 19
BR560.B73 H39 1983 **NYPL [Sc F 88-269]**

BOSTON (MASS.) - GARRISON MOB, 1835.
Anti-Slavery Meeting (1855 : Boston) The Boston mob of "gentlemen of property and standing." . Boston , 1855 (Boston : J.B. Yerrinton and Son, printers) 76 p. :
E450.B74 **NYPL [Sc Rare F 88-44]**

BOSTON (MASS.) - HISTORY - ANTI-SLAVERY MOVEMENT, 1830-1863.
Anti-Slavery Meeting (1855 : Boston) The Boston mob of "gentlemen of property and standing." . Boston , 1855 (Boston : J.B. Yerrinton and Son, printers) 76 p. ;
E450.B74 **NYPL [Sc Rare F 88-44]**

The Boston mob of "gentlemen of property and standing." . Anti-Slavery Meeting (1855 : Boston) Boston , 1855 (Boston : J.B. Yerrinton and Son, printers) 76 p. ;
E450.B74 **NYPL [Sc Rare F 88-44]**

Boston, Peter. Boston, L. M. (Lucy Maria), 1892- Treasure of Green Knowe. New York [1958] 185 p. DDC [Fic]
PZ7.B6497 Tr **NYPL [Sc D 88-1497]**

Boston, Thomas D. Race, class, and conservatism / Thomas D. Boston. Boston : Unwin Hyman, 1988. xix, 172 p. : ill. ; 23 cm. Includes bibliography: p. 161-167. ISBN 0-04-330368-4 (alk. paper) DDC 305.5/0973 19
1. Social classes - United States. 2. Afro-Americans - Social conditions. 3. Conservatism - United States. 4. United States - Race relations. I. Title.
HN90.S6 B67 1988 **NYPL [Sc D 89-107]**

Bot, Monica. Training on separate tracks : segregated technical education and prospects for its erosion / Monica Bot. Braamfontein, Johannesburg : South African Institute of Race Relations, 1988. iv, 21 p. ; 21 cm. Bibliography: p. 67-71. ISBN 0-86982-346-9
1. Apartheid - South Africa. 2. Technical education - South Africa. I. Title. **NYPL [Sc D 89-81]**

BOTANY, MEDICAL - NIGERIA - CONGRESSES.
The State of medicinal plants research in Nigeria . [Ibadan?] , c1986. vi, 404 p. : ISBN 978-302-850-2 **NYPL [Sc E 88-305]**

BOTANY - PHYTOGRAPHY. see BOTANY.

BOTANY - SEYCHELLES.
Lionnet, Guy. Coco de mer . Bell Village, Ile Maurice , c1986. 95 p. :
QK495.P17 L56 1986 **NYPL [Sc D 88-572]**

Bothwell, Jean. By sail and wind : the story of the Bahamas / by Jean Bothwell ; illustrated with photographs and drawings by Omar Davis. London ; New York : Abelard-Schuman, c1964. 152 p. : ill., maps ; 21 cm. Includes index. Story of the development of the islands known as the Bahamas. Bibliography: 147-148. SCHOMBURG CHILDREN'S

COLLECTION.
*1. Bahamas. 2. Bahamas - History. I. Schomburg
Children's Collection. II. Title.*
NYPL [Sc D 89-103]

Boto, Eza. see Beti, Mongo, 1932-
BOTSWANA - BIBLIOGRAPHY.
Henderson, Francine I. A guide to periodical
articles about Botswana, 1965-80 /. Gaborone,
Botswana , 1982. v, 147, 6 p. ; DDC 016.96811
19
Z3559 .H46 1982 DT791
NYPL [Sc F 88-161]

**BOTSWANA - FOREIGN RELATIONS -
AFRICA, SOUTHERN.**
Black, David R. (David Ross), 1960- Foreign
policy in small states . Halifax, N.S. , 1988. viii,
83 p. : ISBN 0-7703-0736-1 : DDC 327.681068 19
NYPL [Sc D 89-564]

BOTSWANA - HISTORY - TO 1966.
Crowder, Michael, 1934- The flogging of
Phinehas McIntosh . New Haven , 1988. xii,
248 p. : ISBN 0-300-04098-9 DDC 968/.1103 19
DT791 .C76 1988 *NYPL [Sc E 88-289]*

BOTSWANA - RACE RELATIONS.
Crowder, Michael, 1934- The flogging of
Phinehas McIntosh . New Haven , 1988. xii,
248 p. : ISBN 0-300-04098-9 DDC 968/.1103 19
DT791 .C76 1988 *NYPL [Sc E 88-289]*

**Botte, Theodorico César de Sande Pacheco de
Sacadura.** Memórias e autobiografia : (24
anos em Portugal et 60 em Africa) / de
Theodorico César de Sande Pacheco de
Sacadura Botte. Maputo, República Popular de
Moçambique : Minerva Central, 1985-1986 [i.e.
1987]. 3 v. : ill., ports. ; 23 cm. Includes indexes.
*1. Botte, Theodorico César de Sande Pacheco de
Sacadura, 1902-. 2. Colonial administrators - Portugal -
Biography. 3. Colonial administrators - Mozambique -
Biography. 4. Mozambique - Politics and government -
To 1975.* *NYPL [Sc D 88-130]*

**BOTTE, THEODORICO CÉSAR DE SANDE
PACHECO DE SACADURA, 1902-**
Botte, Theodorico César de Sande Pacheco de
Sacadura. Memórias e autobiografia . Maputo,
República Popular de Moçambique , 1985-1986
[i.e. 1987]. 3 v. : *NYPL [Sc D 88-130]*

Bouedillon, M. F. C. Studies of fishing on Lake
Kariba / by M.F.C. Bourdillon, A. P. Cheater,
M.W. Murphree. [Harare] : Mambo Press,
1985. 185 p. : maps ; 21 cm. (Mambo occasional
papers : social-economic series . no.20)
*1. Fishing - Zimbabwe. 2. Fish trade - Zimbabwe. I.
Cheater, Angela P. II. Murphree, Marshall W. III. Title.
IV. Series.* *NYPL [Sc D 88-875]*

Bouelet, Rémy Sylvestre. Espaces et dialectique
du héros césairien / Rémy Sylvestre Bouelet.
Paris : Harmattan, c1987. 219 p. ; 22 cm.
Bibliography: p. 211-217. ISBN 2-85802-774-9
1. Césaire, Aimé - Criticism and interpretation. I. Title.
NYPL [Sc D 87-1286]

Bouillon, Jo, 1908- Baker, Josephine, 1906-1975.
Josephine /. New York , 1988, c1977. xiii, 302
p., [16] p. of plates : ISBN 1-557-78108-7 (pbk.)
DDC 793.3/2/0924 B 19
GV1785.B3 A3 1988 *NYPL [Sc D 88-1476]*

Boukman, Daniel, 1936- Et jusqu'à la dernière
pulsation de nos veines ... / Daniel Boukman.
Paris : L'Harmattan, [1976] 164 p. ; 22 cm. A
play. Includes bibliographical references. ISBN
2-85802-017-5 :
I. Title.
PQ2662.O758 E8 *NYPL [JFD 80-7874]*

BOURGEOISIE. see MIDDLE CLASSES.

Bourriau, Janine. Pharaohs and mortals :
Egyptian art in the Middle Kingdom /
catalogue by Janine Bourriau ; with a
contribution by Stephen Quirke. Cambridge
[Cambridgeshire] ; New York : Cambridge
University Press ; vi, 167 p. : ill. (some col.) ;
29 cm. (Fitzwilliam Museum publications) "Exhibition
organised by the Fitzwilliam Museum, Cambridge 19
April to 26 June, Liverpool, 18 July to 4 September
1988"--T.p. verso. Includes index.
0-521-35319-X DDC 709/.32/07402659 19
*1. Art, Egyptian - Exhibitions. 2. Art, Ancient -
Egypt - Exhibitions. 3. Egypt - Civilization - To 332
B.C. - Exhibitions. I. Quirke, Stephen. II. Fitzwilliam
Museum. III. Title. IV. Series.*
N5336.G7 C3634 1988
NYPL [3-MAE 88-2748]

Bouzar, Wadi, 1938- La culture en question /
Wadi Bouzar. Alger : SNED ; Paris : Silex
éditions, c1982. 187 p. ; 18 cm. Includes
bibliographical references. ISBN 2-903871-11-6
(pbk.) : DDC 306/.0965 19
*1. Developing countries - Social conditions. 2. Social
history - 1970-. 3. Algeria - Social conditions. I. Title.*
HN980 .B68 1982 *NYPL [JLC 84-337]*

Bowden, Bertram Vivian, Baron Bowden, 1910-
The role of universities in the modern world /
Lord Bowden. Kumasi, Ghana : University of
Science and Technology, [1978?] 81 p. ; 22 cm.
(R.P. Baffour annual lectures) Cover title. On cover:
R.P. Baffour inaugural lectures.
*1. Community and college. 2. Community and college -
Ghana. 3. Education, Higher - Ghana - Aims and
objectives. I. Title.* *NYPL [Sc D 88-465]*

Bowen, David Warren, 1944- Andrew Johnson
and the Negro / David Warren Bowen. 1st ed.
Knoxville : University of Tennessee Press,
c1989. xvi, 206 p. ; 23 cm. Includes index.
Bibliography: p. 191-197. ISBN 0-87049-584-4 (alk.
paper) DDC 973/.0496073 19
*1. Johnson, Andrew, 1808-1875 - Views on
Afro-Americans. 2. Afro-Americans - History - To
1863. 3. Afro-Americans - History - 1863-1877. 4.
Racism - United States - History - 19th century. 5.
United States - Race relations. I. Title.*
E667 .B65 1989 *NYPL [Sc D 89-508]*

**BOXERS (SPORTS) - UNITED STATES -
BIOGRAPHY.**
Barrow, Joe Louis. Joe Louis . New York ,
c1988. xvii, 270 p., [8] leaves of plates : ISBN
0-07-003955-0 : DDC 796.8/3/0924 B 19
GV1132.L6 B37 1988 *NYPL [Sc E 88-566]*

**BOXERS (SPORTS) - UNITED STATES -
BIOGRAPHY - JUVENILE LITERATURE.**
Rummel, Jack. Muhammad Ali /. New York ,
c1988. 128 p. : ISBN 1-555-46569-2 DDC
796.8/3/0924 B 92 19
GV1132.A44 R86 1988
NYPL [Sc E 88-175]

BOXING - HISTORY.
Reading the fights /. New York , c1988. viii,
305 p. : ISBN 0-8050-0510-2 : DDC 796.8/3 19
GV1121 .R4 1988 *NYPL [Sc D 88-899]*

BOXING - MATCHES.
Reading the fights /. New York , c1988. viii,
305 p. : ISBN 0-8050-0510-2 : DDC 796.8/3 19
GV1121 .R4 1988 *NYPL [Sc D 88-899]*

**BOYCOTT - SOUTH AFRICA -
GRAHAMSTOWN.**
Roux, Andre, 1954- Voices from Rini .
Grahamstown, South Africa , 1986. 107 p. ;
ISBN 0-86810-131-1 *NYPL [Sc F 88-216]*

BOYCOTTING. see BOYCOTT.

Boyd-Franklin, Nancy. Black families in therapy :
a multisystems approach / Nancy
Boyd-Franklin ; foreword by Monica
McGoldrick and Paulette Moore Hines. New
York, N.Y. : Guilford Press, c1989. xiv, 274
p. : ill. ; 24 cm. Includes index. Bibliography: p.
261-267. ISBN 0-89862-735-4 DDC
616.89/156/08996073 19
*1. Afro-Americans families - Mental health. 2.
Afro-Americans - Social conditions. I. Title.*
RC451.5.N4 B69 1988 *NYPL [Sc E 89-242]*

Boyeldieu, Pascal.
Les langues fer ("Kara") et yulu du Nord
centrafricain : esquisses descriptives et lexiques
/ Pascal Boyeldieu. Paris : Laboratoire de
langues et civilisations à tradition orale
(LACITO), Département "Langues et parole en
Afrique centrale" (LAPAC) : P. Geuthner,
1987. 280 p. ; 24 cm. Bibliography: p. 273-275.
ISBN 2-7053-0342-1
1. Kara language. 2. Yulu language. I. Title.
NYPL [Sc E 88-124]

La maison du chef et la tête du cabri . Paris ,
c1987. 125 p. : ISBN 2-7053-0339-1
NYPL [Sc E 88-292]

Boyer, Pascal. Barricades mystérieuses & pièges à
pensée : introduction à l'analyse des épopées
fang / par Pascal Boyer. Paris : Société
d'ethnologie, 1988. 190 p. : ill., music ; 25 cm.
(Sociétés africaines . 8) Bibliography: p. 185-187.
ISBN 2-901161-31-6
*1. Epic poetry, Fang. I. Title. II. Title: Barricades
mystérieuses et pièges à pensée. III. Series.*
NYPL [Sc E 88-500]

Boyke, Roy. Patterns of progress: Trinidad &
Tobago 10 years of independence, designed and
edited by Roy Boyke. [Port-of-Spain, Trinidad]
Key Caribbean Publications [c1972] 128 p. illus.
31 cm. Bibliography: p. 118-128. DDC 972.98/304
I. Title.
F2119 .B69 *NYPL [Sc F 89-23]*

Boykin, Yogi Rudolph. [Discovering my "AA"
family roots : passport of my roots land / Yogi
Rudolph Boykin]. Winthorp, Wash. : Universal
Truth Workshop, c1978. 106 p. : ill., map,
music ; 29 cm. Bibliography: p. [107]
*1. Afro-Americans - Genealogy - Handbooks, manuals,
etc. I. Title.* *NYPL [Sc F 89-91]*

Boyles, Denis. African lives : white lies, tropical
truth, darkest gossip, and rumblings of
rumor--from Chinese Gordon to Beryl
Markham, and beyond / Denis Boyles.1st ed.
New York : Weidenfeld & Nicolson, c1988. xi,
225 p., [8] p. of plates : ill. ; 25 cm. "A brief
portion ... first appeared in a different form in GEO
magazine"--T.p. verso. Includes bibliographical
references and index. ISBN 1-555-84034-5 DDC
960/.04034 19
*1. Whites - Africa - Biography. 2. Whites - Africa -
Social life and customs. I. Title.*
DT16.W45 B69 1988 *NYPL [Sc E 88-503]*

BOYS - EMPLOYMENT. see YOUTH -
EMPLOYMENT; CHILDREN -
EMPLOYMENT.

Braceros haitianos en la República Dominicana
/. Báez Evertsz, Franc, 1948- [Santo
Domingo] , c1986. 354 p. : DDC
331.6/2/729407293 19
HD8218.5 .B34 1986 *NYPL [JLE 88-5011]*

Bradman, Tony. Wait and see / Tony Bradman
and Eileen Browne. New York, NY : Oxford
University Press, 1988. [28] p. : col. ill. ; 22
cm. Jo must decide on how to spend her allowance
when she and her mother go on a shopping trip and
leave Dad at home to prepare the midday meal.
SCHOMBURG CHILDREN'S COLLECTION. ISBN
0-19-520644-4 DDC [E] 19
*1. Shopping - Juvenile fiction. 2. Interracial marriage -
Juvenile fiction. 3. Afro-American children - Juvenile
fiction. I. Browne, Eileen. II. Schomburg Children's
Collection. III. Title.*
PZ7.B7275 Wai 1988 *NYPL [Sc D 89-255]*

Bramble, Linda. Black fugitive slaves in early
Canada / Linda Bramble. St. Catharines, Ont. :
Vanwell Pub. Co., c1988. 93 p. : ill. ; 25 cm.
(Vanwell history project series) Includes index.
Bibliography: p. 87. ISBN 0-920277-16-0 DDC
973.7/115 19
*1. Fugitive slaves - Canada. 2. Underground Railroad.
3. Slavery - Canada. 4. Slavery - United States -
Anti-slavery movements. 5. Blacks - Canada. I. Title. II.
Series.* *NYPL [Sc E 89-121]*

Branagan, Thomas, b. 1774. The guardian genius
of the Federal Union, or, Patriotic admonitions
on the signs of the times : in relation to the
evil spirit of party, arising from the root of all
our evils, human slavery : being the first part of
The beauties of philanthropy / by a
philanthropist. New York : The Author, 1839.
104 p. ; 18 cm. Also ascribed to Julius R.
Ames.
*1. Slavery in the United States - Controversial
literature - 1839. I. Ames, Julius Rubens, 1801-1850. II.
Title. III. Title: Beauties of philanthropy.*
NYPL [Sc Rare G 86-18]

Branch, Taylor. Parting the waters : America in
the King years, 1954-63 / Taylor Branch. New
York : Simon and Schuster, c1988- v. : ill. ; 25
cm. Includes index. Bibliography: v. 1, p. [1005]-1009.
ISBN 0-671-46097-8 (v. 1) DDC 973/.0496073
19
*1. King, Martin Luther, Jr., 1929-1968. 2.
Afro-Americans - Civil rights. 3. Civil rights
movements - United States - History - 20th century. 4.
United States - History - 1953-1961. I. Title.*
E185.61 .B7914 1988 *NYPL [IEC 88-122]*

Branchcomb, Sylvia Woingust. Son, never give up
/ written by Sylvia Woingust Branchcomb.
[Yonkers, N.Y.?] : Musical Chords, 1979. 36
p. : ill., facsims., ports. ; 23 cm. First person
memoir of Cecil James Morgan, "the first Black
mechanic and trouble shooter in the history of the Long
Island Railroad." Cover.
*1. Morgan, Cecil James. 2. Long Island Rail Road -
Employees - Biography. 3. Afro-Americans - Biography.*

I. Morgan, Cecil James. II. Title.
NYPL [Sc D 88-568]

Brand, Dionne, 1953-
Chronicles of the hostile sun / Dionne Brand.
Toronto, Ont., Canada : Williams-Wallace
Publishers, 1984. 75 p. ; 22 cm. ISBN
0-88795-033-7 (pbk.) : DDC 811/.54 19
*1. Revolutionary poetry, Canadian. 2. Grenada -
History - American invasion, 1983 - Poetry. I. Title.*
PR9199.3.B683 C48 1984
NYPL [Sc D 88-1227]

Winter epigrams & Epigrams to Ernesto
Cardinal in defense of Claudia / Dionne
Brand ; [edited by Roger McTair]. Toronto :
Williams-Wallace, 1983. 38 p. ; 22 cm. ISBN
0-88795-022-1 :
*I. McTair, Roger. II. Brand, Dionne, 1953- Epigrams to
Ernesto Cardenal in defense of Claudia. III. Title. IV.
Title: Epigrams to Ernesto Cardenal in defense of
Claudia.* **NYPL [Sc D 88-1207]**

**Epigrams to Ernesto Cardenal in defense of
Claudia.** Brand, Dionne, 1953- Winter
epigrams & Epigrams to Ernesto Cardinal in
defense of Claudia / Dionne Brand ; [edited
by Roger McTair]. Toronto , 1983. 38 p. ;
ISBN 0-88795-022-1 :
NYPL [Sc D 88-1207]

**Brandenburg sources for West African history,
1680-1700 /.** Jones, Adam. Stuttgart , 1985.
xiv, 348 p., [14] p. of plates : ISBN
3-515-04315-2   **NYPL [Sc E 88-84]**

Brandon, Brumsic. Outta sight, Luther! New
York, P. S. Eriksson [c1971] 1 v. (chiefly illus.)
17 cm. Cartoons. SCHOMBURG CHILDREN'S
COLLECTION. ISBN 0-8397-6481-2 DDC
741.5/973
*1. Comic books, strips, etc. - United States. I.
Schomburg Children's Collection. II. Title.*
PN6728.L8 B7   **NYPL [Sc B 88-54]**

Brandt, Godfrey L. The realization of anti-racist
teaching / Godfrey L. Brandt. London ; New
York : Falmer Press, 1986. x, 210 p. : ill. ; 25
cm. Includes index. Bibliography: p. 196-200. ISBN
1-85000-126-X : DDC 370.19/0941 19
*1. Educational sociology - Great Britain. 2. Education -
Great Britain - Aims and objectives. 3. Racism - Study
and teaching - Great Britain. I. Title.*
LC192.2 .B73 1986   **NYPL [Sc E 89-77]**

Brandt, Hartmut. Perspectives of independent
development in Southern Africa . Berlin , 1980.
xiv, 183 p. : DDC 338.9688 19
HC910 .P47   **NYPL [JLE 82-36]**

Branley, Franklyn Mansfield, 1915- Eclipse :
darkness in daytime / by Franklyn M. Branley ;
illustrated by Donald Crews.Rev. ed. New
York : Crowell, c1988. 32 p. : col. ill. ; 19 x 24
cm. (Let's-read-and-find-out science book) Explains in
simple terms what happens during a solar eclipse.
SCHOMBURG CHILDREN'S COLLECTION. ISBN
0-690-04619-7 (lib. bdg.) : DDC 523.7/8 19
*1. Eclipses, Solar - Juvenile literature. I. Crews, Donald,
ill. II. Schomburg Children's Collection. III. Title. IV.
Series.*
QB541.5 .B73 1988   **NYPL [Sc E 88-591]**

Branner, John Casper, 1850-1922. How and why
stories / recorded by John C. Branner. New
York : H. Holt, 1921. xi, 104 p. : ill. ; 22 cm.
SCHOMBURG CHILDREN'S COLLECTION.
*1. Afro-Americans - Folklore. I. Schomburg Children's
Collection. II. Title.*   **NYPL [Sc D 89-104]**

Brasileiros na África /. Olinto, Antônio. São
Paulo, S.P. (rua Topázio 478/41, CEP 04105,
São Paulo, S.P.) , 1980. 324 p., [16] pages of
plates : DDC 966.9/004698 19
DT515.42 .O43 1980   **NYPL [Sc D 89-216]**

Brasio, Antonio Duarte, 1906- Monumenta
missionaria africana: Africa ocidental. Lisboa,
Agência Geral do Ultramar, Divisao de
Publicações e Biblioteca, 1952- v. illus., port.,
fold. map. coat of arms, facsims. 25 cm.
Bibliographical footnotes. CONTENTS. - - [For
additional listing of contents see Old Catalog] - v. 11.
1651-1655.--v. 14. 1686-1699.
*1. Missions - Africa - History - Sources. 2. Catholic
Church - Africa - History - Sources. I. Title.*
**NYPL [ZKVX (Brásio, A.D. Monumenta
missionaria africana)]**

Brathwaite, Doris Monica, d.1986. A descriptive
and chronological bibliography (1950-1982) of
the work of Edward Kamau Brathwaite / by
Doris Monica Brathwaite. London : New

Beacon Books, 1988. ix, 97 p. ; 23 cm. Includes
index. ISBN 0-901241-84-9 (cased) : DDC 016.810
19
1. Brathwaite, Edward, 1930- - Bibliography. I. Title.
NYPL [Sc D 89-402]

Brathwaite, Edward. X/self / Edward Kamau
Brathwaite. Oxford [Oxfordshire] ; New York :
Oxford University Press, 1987. vi, 131 p. ; 22
cm. Includes bibliographical references. ISBN
0-19-281987-9 (pbk.) : DDC 811 19
I. Title.
PR9230.9.B68 X7 1987
NYPL [JFD 87-5776]

**BRATHWAITE, EDWARD, 1930- -
BIBLIOGRAPHY.**
Brathwaite, Doris Monica, d.1986. A
descriptive and chronological bibliography
(1950-1982) of the work of Edward Kamau
Brathwaite /. London , 1988. ix, 97 p. ; ISBN
0-901241-84-9 (cased) : DDC 016.810 19
NYPL [Sc D 89-402]

Brathwaite, Farley. Emmanuel, Patrick. Political
change and public opinion in Grenada
1979-1984 /. Cave Hill, Barbados , c1986. xii,
173 p. :   **NYPL [JLM 79-1223 no.19]**

Bratton, Michael. Beyond community
development : the political economy of rural
administration in Zimbabwe / [by] Michael
Bratton. London : Catholic Institute for
International Relations, 1978. 62 p. : 1 ill. ; 22
cm. (From Rhodesia to Zimbabwe. 6) Includes
bibliographical references.
*1. Rural development - Zimbabwe. 2. Local
government - Zimbabwe. I. Title. II. Series.*
HN802.Z9 C62   **NYPL [JLD 81-437]**

Bräuer, Hans-Dieter. Babing, Alfred. Wo die
Sonne wohnt /. Berlin , 1985. 368 p. :
NYPL [Sc D 89-72]

**BRAZIL - CIVILIZATION - AFRICAN
INFLUENCES.**
Crowley, Daniel J., 1921- African myth and
black reality in Bahian Carnaval /. [Los
Angeles, Calif.] [1984] 47 p. :
NYPL [Sc F 86-281]

Freyre, Gilberto, 1900- [Casa-grande & senzala.
English.] The masters and the slaves =.
Berkeley , c1986. xc, 537 xliv p., [3] p. of
plates : ISBN 0-520-05665-5 (pbk. : alk. paper)
DDC 981 19
F2510 .F7522 1986   **NYPL [HFB 87-2095]**

Lopes, Helena Theodoro. Negro e cultura no
Brasil /. Rio de Janeiro , 1987. 136 p. ; ISBN
85-85108-02-9 DDC 981/.00496 19
F2659.N4 L67 1987   **NYPL [Sc D 88-1291]**

BRAZIL - COMMERCE - HISTORY.
Miller, Joseph Calder. Way of death . Madison,
Wis. , c1988. xxx, 770 p. : ISBN 0-299-11560-7 :
DDC 382/.44/09469 19
HT1221 .M55 1988   **NYPL [Sc E 89-105]**

BRAZIL - ECONOMIC CONDITIONS.
Renault, Delso. A vida brasileira no final do
século XIX . Rio de Janeiro ; Brasília : xi, 315
p. : ISBN 85-03-00181-0
NYPL [HFB 87-2508]

BRAZIL - FICTION.
Barbareschi Fino, Maria Antonietta. Il samba .
Milano , 1979. 63 p. ; **NYPL [Sc D 89-187]**

Coelho, Abílio. As hortênsias morrem na
primavera /. Rio de Janeiro , 1987. 271 p. ;
NYPL [Sc D 88-709]

Cunha Junior, H., 1952- Negros na noite /. São
Paulo , 1987. 79 p. :   **NYPL [Sc D 88-71]**

Rodrigues, Eustáquio José. Cauterizai o meu
umbigo /. Rio de Janeiro-RJ , 1986. 181 p. ;
DDC 869.3 19
PQ9280.O269 C3 1986
NYPL [JFD 88-6700]

**Brazil - Government. see Brazil - Politics and
government.**

BRAZIL - HISTORY - 1763-1821.
Algranti, Leila Mezan. D. Joao VI . São Paulo ,
1987. 78 p. ; ISBN 85-08-01870-3
NYPL [Sc C 88-15]

Lara, Silvia Hunold. Campos da violência . Rio
de Janeiro , c1988. 389 p. ;
NYPL [Sc D 89-13]

BRAZIL - HISTORY - 1822-1889.
Kowarick, Lúcio. Trabalho e vadiagem . São
Paulo , 1987. 133 p. ;   **NYPL [Sc D 88-784]**

BRAZIL - HISTORY - 1889-1930.
Renault, Delso. A vida brasileira no final do
século XIX . Rio de Janeiro ; Brasília : xi, 315
p. : ISBN 85-03-00181-0
NYPL [HFB 87-2508]

BRAZIL - HISTORY - HISTORIOGRAPHY.
Lopes, Luis Carlos. O espelho e a imagem . Rio
de Janeiro , 1987. 126 p. ;
NYPL [Sc D 88-350]

**Brazil. Instituto Joaquim Nabuco de Pesquisas
Sociais.**
Série documentos.
(22) Casa-grande & senzala e a crítica
brasileira de 1933 a 1944 /. Recife , 1985.
309 p. ; ISBN 85-7019-079-4 (pbk.) DDC
981/.00498 19
F2510.F7524 C37 1985
NYPL [HFB 86-2252]

**BRAZIL - POLITICS AND GOVERNMENT -
1822-**
Hahner, June Edith, 1940- Poverty and
politics . Albuquerque , 1986. xvi, 415 p. :
ISBN 0-8263-0878-3 : DDC 305.5/69/0981 19
HC190.P6 H34 1986   **NYPL [JLE 86-4407]**

**BRAZIL - POLITICS AND GOVERNMENT -
1822-1889.**
Nabuco, Joaquim, 1849-1910. Minha formação
/. Rio de Janeiro , 1957. 258 p. :
F2536 .N1425 1957   **NYPL [Sc D 87-1353]**

**BRAZIL - POLITICS AND GOVERNMENT -
1889-1930.**
Renault, Delso. A vida brasileira no final do
século XIX . Rio de Janeiro ; Brasília : xi, 315
p. : ISBN 85-03-00181-0
NYPL [HFB 87-2508]

BRAZIL - RACE RELATIONS.
Azevedo, Celia Maria Marinho de. Onda negra,
medo branco . Rio de Janeiro , c1987. 267 p. ;
NYPL [Sc D 88-469]

Azevêdo, Eliane. Raça . São Paulo , 1987. 62
p. ; ISBN 85-08-01878-9   **NYPL [Sc C 88-14]**

Valente, Ana Lúcia E. F. (Ana Lúcia Eduardo
Farah) Ser negro no Brasil hoje /. São Paulo,
SP, Brasil , 1987. 64 p. : DDC 305.8/96/081 19
F2659.N4 V35 1987   **NYPL [HFB 88-2561]**

BRAZIL - RELIGION.
Bastide, Roger, 1898-1974. [Religions africaines
au Brésil. Portuguese.] As religiões africanas no
Brasil . São Paulo , 1985. 567 p. ;
NYPL [Sc D 88-542]

**BRAZIL - RELIGIOUS LIFE AND
CUSTOMS.**
Candomblé . São Paulo , 1987. 168 p. ;
NYPL [Sc D 88-177]

Lody, Raul Giovanni da Motta. Candomblé .
São Paulo , 1987. 85 p. ; ISBN 85-08-01877-0
NYPL [Sc C 88-62]

BRAZIL - SOCIAL CONDITIONS.
Hahner, June Edith, 1940- Poverty and
politics . Albuquerque , 1986. xvi, 415 p. :
ISBN 0-8263-0878-3 : DDC 305.5/69/0981 19
HC190.P6 H34 1986   **NYPL [JLE 86-4407]**

BRAZIL - SOCIAL LIFE AND CUSTOMS.
Freyre, Gilberto, 1900- [Casa-grande & senzala.
English.] The masters and the slaves =.
Berkeley , c1986. xc, 537 xliv p., [3] p. of
plates : ISBN 0-520-05665-5 (pbk. : alk. paper)
DDC 981 19
F2510 .F7522 1986   **NYPL [HFB 87-2095]**

Lopes, Helena Theodoro. Negro e cultura no
Brasil /. Rio de Janeiro , 1987. 136 p. ; ISBN
85-85108-02-9 DDC 981/.00496 19
F2659.N4 L67 1987   **NYPL [Sc D 88-1291]**

Meihy, José Carlos Sebe Bom, 1943- Carnaval,
carnavais /. São Paulo , 1986. 96 p. ; ISBN
85-08-01168-7 : DDC 394.2/5/0981 19
GT4180 .M45 1986   **NYPL [HFB 88-1339]**

Brazilian cinema / edited by Randal Johnson and
Robert Stam. Austin : University of Texas
Press, 1988. 373 p. : ill. ; 25 cm. Includes
bibliographical references and index. ISBN
0-292-70767-3
*1. Moving-pictures - Brazil - Collected works. I.
Johnson, Randal, 1948-. II. Stam, Robert, 1941-.*
NYPL [Sc E 89-59]

BRAZILIAN FICTION - HISTORY AND CRITICISM.
Marotti, Giorgio. [Negro nel romanzo brasiliano. English.] Black characters in the Brazilian novel /. Los Angeles , c1987. ix, 448 p., [18] p. of plates ; ISBN 0-934934-24-X : DDC 869.3/093520396 19
PQ9607.B53 M3713 1987
NYPL [Sc E 87-334]

BRAZILIAN LITERATURE - 19TH CENTURY - HISTORY AND CRITICISM.
Gomes, Heloisa Toller. O negro e o romantismo brasileiro /. São Paulo [1988] 113 p. ;   **NYPL [Sc D 89-515]**

BRAZILIAN LITERATURE - BLACK AUTHORS - HISTORY AND CRITICISM.
Bernd, Zilá, 1944- Introdução à literatura negra /. Sao Paulo , 1988. 101 p. ;
NYPL [Sc D 89-188]
Camargo, Oswaldo de, 1936- O negro escrito . [São Paulo] 1987. 214 p. : DDC 869/.09/896081 19
PQ9523.B57 C36 1987   **NYPL [Sc D 89-608]**

Brazilian pamphlet on the abolition of the slave trade, and the gradual emancipation of slaves. Silva, José Bonifácio de Andrada e, 1763-1838. Memoir addressed to the general, constituent and legislative Assembly of the empire of Brazil, on slavery! London , 1826 London : Printed by A. Redford and W. Robins) 60 p. ;
NYPL [Sc Rare G 86-14]

BRAZILIAN POETRY - BLACK AUTHORS.
A Razão da chama . São Paulo , 1986. xii, 122 p. ;   **NYPL [Sc D 89-462]**

BRAZILIAN POETRY - BLACK AUTHORS - HISTORY AND CRITICISM.
Damasceno, Benedita Gouveia. Poesia negra no modernismo brasileiro /. Campinas, SP [Brasil] , 1988. 142 p. ; ISBN 85-7113-003-5
NYPL [Sc D 88-1290]

BRAZILIANS - NIGERIA.
Olinto, Antônio. Brasileiros na África /. São Paulo, S.P. (rua Topázio 478/41, CEP 04105, São Paulo, S.P.) , 1980. 324 p., [16] pages of plates : DDC 966.9/004698 19
DT515.42 .O43 1980   **NYPL [Sc D 89-216]**

BRAZZAVILLE (CONGO) - FICTION.
Sony Lab'Ou Tansi. Les yeux du volcan . Paris , c1988. 191 p. ; ISBN 2-02-010082-7
NYPL [Sc D 89-237]

Breakfast of sjamboks / Lukas Mkuti. Harare : Zimbabwe Pub. House, 1987. viii, 71 p. : ill. ; 19 cm. ISBN 0-949225-35-5
1. Children's writings, Mozambican (English). I. Mkuti, Lukas.   **NYPL [Sc C 88-299]**

Breaking the ice . Pennington, Richard, 1952- Jefferson, N.C. , c1987. ix, 182 p. : ISBN 0-89950-295-4 : DDC 796.332/72/0973 19
GV939.A1 P46 1987   **NYPL [Sc E 88-35]**

Bref aperçu sur l'évolution de la prostitution en Haïti. Honoré, Narénia François. [Port-au-Prince] , 1981. 49 p., [1] leaf of plates : DDC 306.7/4 19
HQ162.A5 H66   **NYPL [Sc D 88-318]**

Brehme, Gerhard.
African studies. Berlin, 1973. xi, 400 p.
NYPL [JLK 73-249 Bd. 15]
Afrika . Berlin , 1985. 520 p. :
NYPL [Sc C 88-144]

Bréjaut, Alain. see **Brezault, Alain.**

Brenowitz, Ruth. A study of the portrayal of Black Americans in the dramatic literature of the United States [microform] / by Ruth Brenowitz. 1969. 92 leaves. Thesis (M.S.)--Palmer Graduate Library School, 1969. Bibliography: leaves 90-92. Microfilm of typescript. Ann Arbor, Mich.: University Microfilms International, 1971. 1 microfilm reel; 35 mm.
1. Afro-Americans in literature. 2. American drama - 20th century - History and criticism. I. Title.
NYPL [Sc Micro R-4691]

BRENT (LONDON, ENGLAND) - SOCIAL CONDITIONS.
Black people in Brent . London , c1987. 159 p. : ISBN 0-9512463-1-3 (pbk).
NYPL [Sc D 89-5]

Brenthurst Collection. De Meillon, Henry Clifford. Cape views and costumes . Johannesburg , 1978. 134 p. : ISBN

0-909079-05-6 :   DDC 759.968
ND2088.6.S6 D452 1978
NYPL [Sc F 85-112]

BRENTHURST COLLECTION.
De Meillon, Henry Clifford. Cape views and costumes . Johannesburg , 1978. 134 p. : ISBN 0-909079-05-6 :   DDC 759.968
ND2088.6.S6 D452 1978
NYPL [Sc F 85-112]

Brer Rabbit and his tricks. Rees, Ennis. New York [1967] 1 v. (unpaged)
PZ8.3.R254 Br   **NYPL [Sc E 88-530]**

Brereton, Bridget. Social life in the Caribbean, 1838-1938 / Bridget Brereton. London : Heinemann Educational, 1985. 65 p. : ill., 1 map, ports. ; 22 cm. (Heinemann CXC history) Bibliography: p. 62-65. ISBN 0-435-98305-9 (pbk)
 : DDC 909/.09821 19
1. Caribbean area - Social life and customs. I. Title.
F2169   **NYPL [Sc D 88-1307]**

Bret, René-Joseph, d. 1940. Vie du sultan Mohamed Bakhit, 1856-1916 : la pénétration française au Dar Sila, Tchad / René-Joseph Bret. Paris : Editions du Centre national de la recherche scientifique, 1987. [xvi], 258 p. : maps ; 22 cm (Contributions à la connaissance des élites africaines. fasc. 5e) Includes index. Bibliography: p. [xv]-[xvi] ISBN 2-222-03901-0
1. Mohamed Bakhit, sultan of Dar Sila, 1856-1916. 2. Chad - Kings and rulers - Biography. 3. Chad - Relations - France - History - 20th century. 4. France - Relations - Chad - History - 20th century. I. Title.
NYPL [Sc D 89-364]

Brewster, Yvonne. Black plays /. London , New York, NY , 1987. 139 p. ; ISBN 0-413-15710-5
NYPL [JFD 88-8329]

Brezault, Alain. Missions en Afrique : les catholiques face à l'Islam, aux sectes, au Vatican / Alain Brézault et Gérard Clavreuil. Paris : Autrement, c1987. 193 p. : maps ; 24 cm. Title on spine: Missions. Includes bibliographical references. ISBN 2-86260-209-4 : DDC 266/.267 19
1. Missions - Africa, Sub-Saharan. 2. Africa, Sub-Saharan - Religion. I. Clavreuil, Gérard. II. Title. III. Title: Missions.
BV3520 .B74 1987   **NYPL [Sc E 89-163]**

Brickley, Carol. South Africa : Britain out of apartheid, apartheid out of Britain / Carol Brickley, Terry O'Halloran, David Reed. London : Larkin Publications, 1985. 50 p. : ill. ; 21 cm. "An FRFI pamphlet." ISBN 0-905400-06-2 :
1. Segregation - South Africa. 2. Blacks - South Africa. I. O'Halloran, Terry. II. Reed, David. III. Title. IV. Title: Britain out of apartheid, apartheid out of Britain.
NYPL [Sc D 89-361]

A bridge in time /. Odaga, Asenath. Kisumu, Kenya , 1987. 167 p. :
MLCS 88/07442 (P)   **NYPL [Sc C 88-374]**

Bridges, Barbara A. Nunley, John W. (John Wallace), 1945- Caribbean festival arts . [Saint Louis] , 1988. 218 p. : ISBN 0-295-96702-1 : DDC 394.2/5/07409729 19
GT4823 .N85 1988   **NYPL [Sc F 89-89]**

A brief conversion and other stories /. Lovelace, Earl. Oxford [Eng.] , 1988. 141 p. ; ISBN 0-435-98882-4   **NYPL [Sc C 89-43]**

BRIGANDS AND ROBBERS - NIGERIA.
Idowu, Sina, 1947- Armed robbery in Nigeria /. Lagos, Nigeria , c1980. 121 p. : ISBN 978-231-900-7 (pbk) DDC 364.1/552/09669 19
HV6665.N6 I36 1980   **NYPL [Sc D 89-264]**

Brillon, Yves.
[Ethnocriminologie de l'Afrique noire. English] Crime, justice and culture in black Africa : an ethno-criminological study / Yves Brillon ; translated by Dorothy Crelinsten. [Montreal] : Centre international de criminologie comparée, Université de Montréal, [1985] xi, 289 p. : 1 ill. ; 28 cm. (Cahiers de recherches criminologiques . cahier no. 3) Translation of: Ethnocriminologie de l'Afrique noire. Bibliography: p. 273-289.
1. Criminal justice, Administration of - Africa. I. Centre international de criminologie comparée. II. Title. III. Series.   **NYPL [JLF 87-694]**

Brimoh, Peregrino. Saro-Wiwa, Ken. Mr. B /. Port Harcourt , Ewell , 1987. 154 p. : ISBN 1-87071-601-9 (pbk) : DDC 823 19
PZ7   **NYPL [Sc C 88-300]**

Brink, André Philippus, 1935- An instant in the wind / André Brink. New York, N.Y., U. S.A. : Penguin Books, 1985, c1976. 250 p. ; 20 cm. ISBN 0-14-008014-7 (pbk.) : DDC 823 19
1. Larsson, Elisabeth Maria, b. 1727 - Fiction. 2. South Africa - History - To 1836 - Fiction. I. Title.
PR9369.3.B7 I5 1985   **NYPL [Sc C 88-281]**

Brisbane, William Henry, ca. 1803-1878. Speech of the Rev. Wm. H. Brisbane : lately a slaveholder in South Carolina : containing an account of the change in his views on the subject of slavery ... Hartford : published by S. S. Cowles, 1840. 12 p. ; 23 cm. "Delivered before the Ladies' Anti-Slavery Society of Cincinnati, Feb. 12, 1840."
1. Slavery - United States - Controversial literature - 1840. I. Ladies' Anti-Slavery Society of Cincinnati. II. Title.   **NYPL [Sc Rare C 89-26]**

Britain out of apartheid, apartheid out of Britain. Brickley, Carol. South Africa . London , 1985. 50 p. : ISBN 0-905400-06-2 :
NYPL [Sc D 89-361]

Britain's Black population : a new perspective. 2nd ed. / edited by Ashok Bhat, Roy Carr-Hill, Sushel Ohri (The Radical Statistics Race Group). Aldershot, Hants, England ; Brookfield, Vt., USA : Gower Pub. Co., c1988. xv, 298 p. ; 24 cm. Rev. ed. of: Britain's Black population /Runnymede Trust and the Radical Statistics Race Group. 1980. Includes index. Includes references.
  ISBN 0-566-05179-6 :   DDC 305.8/96/041 19
1. Blacks - Great Britain - Social conditions. 2. South Asians - Great Britain - Social conditions. 3. West Indians - Great Britain - Social conditions. 4. Great Britain - Race relations. I. Bhat, Ashok. II. Carr-Hill, R. A. (Roy A.), 1943-. III. Ohri, Sushel, 1951-. IV. Radical Statistics (Association). Race Group.
DA125.N4 B75 1988   **NYPL [Sc E 89-100]**

British Agencies for Adoption and Fostering. Social work with Black children and their families /. London , 1986. 207 p. ; ISBN 0-7134-4888-1 (cased)
NYPL [Sc D 89-281]

British colonial objectives and policies in Nigeria . Ejimofor, Cornelius Ogu, 1940- Onitsha, Nigeria , 1987. viii, 216 p., 1 folded leaf ; ISBN 978-17-5142-8
NYPL [Sc D 88-820]

British imperial policy and decolonization, 1938-64 /. Porter, A. N. (Andrew N.) New York , 1987- v. ; ISBN 0-312-00554-7 (v. 1) : DDC 325/.31/41 19
JV1018 .P66 1987   **NYPL [Sc D 88-219]**

British Institute in Eastern Africa.
Memoir.
(no. 6) Phillipson, D. W. The prehistory of eastern Zambia /. Nairobi , 1976. xi, 229 p., [21] leaves of plates (5 fold.) : ISBN 0-500-97003-3 :
GN865.Z3 P48   **NYPL [JFF 79-1585]**

BRITISH LITERATURE. see **ENGLISH LITERATURE.**

The British massacre of the Gusii freedom defenders /. Nyasani, J. M. (Joseph Major), 1938- Nairobi, Kenya , 1984. v, 85 p. :
NYPL [Sc D 88-1133]

BRITISH POETRY. see **ENGLISH POETRY.**

British Psychological Society. Division of Educational and Child Psychology. Committee. Educational attainments . London , New York , 1988. vii, 180 p. : ISBN 1-85000-308-4 : DDC 370.19/34/0941 19
LC3736.G6 E336 1988   **NYPL [Sc E 89-52]**

British Virgin Islands. Public Library.
A cultural experience . Road Town, Tortola, British Virgin Islands , 1980. viii, 55 p. :
MLCS 81/1586   **NYPL [Sc D 88-1398]**
Reminiscences . Road Town, Tortola, British Virgin Islands , c1981. xii, 94 p. : DDC 700/.97297/25 19
NX430.G72 B757 1981 **NYPL [Sc F 88-331]**

British West Indian slavery, 1750-1834 . Ward, J. R. Oxford [Oxfordshire] , New York , 1988. x, 320 p. : ISBN 0-19-820144-3 (Oxford University Press) : DDC 306/.362/09729 19
HT1092 .W37 1988   **NYPL [Sc D 88-1355]**

British West Indies. see **West Indies, British.**

Brittain, Victoria.
Children of resistance . London , 1988. vii, 146 p. ; *NYPL [Sc D 88-1286]*

Hidden lives, hidden deaths : South Africa's crippling of a continent / Victoria Brittain. London : Faber and Faber, 1988. xvii, 189 p. : maps ; 22 cm. Includes index. ISBN 0-571-13907-8 : DDC 355/.0335/68 19
1. South Africa - Military policy. I. Title.
UA856   NYPL [JLD 88-4608]

Brizan, George I. Thomson, Robert. Green gold . London , 1987. vii, 93 p. : ISBN 0-906156-26-2 *NYPL [Sc D 88-66]*

BROADCASTERS - NIGERIA.
Amadi, John Osinachi. The ethics of the Nigerian broadcaster /. Rome , 1986. 155 p. [6] p. of plates : *NYPL [Sc E 89-138]*

Brockton Art Museum. Belcher, Max. A land and life remembered . Athens , Brockton, Mass. , c1988. [xii], 176 p. : ISBN 0-8203-1085-9 (alk. paper) DDC 720/.9666/2074014482 19
NA1599.L4 B4 1988   NYPL [Sc F 89-90]

Brodwin, Stanley. The Harlem renaissance . New York , 1989. xv, 342 p. ; ISBN 0-8240-5739-2 (alk. paper) DDC 810/.9/896073 19
PS153.N5 H264 1989   NYPL [Sc D 89-591]

Broken alliance . Kaufman, Jonathan. New York , c1988. 311 p. ; ISBN 0-684-18699-3 : DDC 305.8/00973 19
*E185.615 .K33 1988   NYPL [*PXY 88-4777]*

Broken graduate /. Agburum, Ezenwa. Orlu, Imo State, Nigeria , 1986. 96 p. ;
NYPL [Sc C 88-193]

Broken ribs /. Kehinde-Adeniyi, Kehinde. [S.l. , 198-?] (Ibara, Abeokuta : Alayande Printing Press) viii, 48 p. ; *NYPL [Sc C 88-354]*

Bronze booklet.
(no. 7) Brown, Sterling Allen, 1901- Negro poetry and drama /. Washington, D.C. , c1937. 142 p. ; *NYPL [Sc D 89-105]*

The bronze zoo. Rieger, Shay. New York [1970] [48] p. DDC 731.4/56
NB1143 .R5   NYPL [Sc F 88-340]

Broodhagen, Karl R. The National Cultural Foundation presents Tribute, an exhibition of the sculpture of Karl Broodhagen : at the Queen's Park Gallery, Feb. 24-Mar. 17, 1985. [Barbados] : The Foundation, [1985?] 16 p. : ill. ; 23 x 28 cm.
1. Broodhagen, Karl R. I. National Cultural Foundation (Barbados). II. Title. III. Title: Tribute.
MLCM 87/08440 (N)   NYPL [Sc D 88-570]

BROODHAGEN, KARL R.
Broodhagen, Karl R. The National Cultural Foundation presents Tribute, an exhibition of the sculpture of Karl Broodhagen . [Barbados] [1985?] 16 p. :
MLCM 87/08440 (N)   NYPL [Sc D 88-570]

Brooke, Samuel. The slave-holder's religion. By Samuel Brooke. Cincinnati, Sparhawk and Lytle, printers, 1845. 47 p. 19 cm. Published 1846, with other title: Slavery and the slave holders religion. Schomburg Center copy imperfect: Everything after p.24 lacking.
1. Slavery - United States - Controversial literature - 1845. 2. Slavery - United States - Condition of slaves. I. Title. II. Title: Slavery and the slave holder's religion.
E449 .B87   NYPL [Sc Rare F 88-53]

Brooke-Smith, Robin. The scramble for Africa / Robin Brooke-Smith. Basingstoke, Hampshire : Macmillan Education, 1987. viii, 134 p. ; 22 cm. (Documents and debates) ISBN 0-333-42491-3
1. Africa - Colonization - History. I. Title.
NYPL [Sc D 88-98]

Brooke, W. Michael. Blacks in Bermuda . [Hamilton? , 1980?] 82 p. :
NYPL [Sc F 88-251]

Brooklyn Children's Museum. see Brooklyn Institute of Arts and Sciences. Children's Museum.

Brooklyn College. Institute for Studies in American Music.
I. S. A. M. monographs.
(24) Berlin, Edward A. Reflections and research on ragtime /. Brooklyn, N.Y. , c1987. xii, 99 p. : ISBN 0-914678-27-2 (pbk.) DDC 781/.572 19
ML3530 .B5 1987   NYPL [Sc D 88-410]

Brooklyn Institute of Arts and Sciences. Children's Museum. Muse presents Jazz in the first person . [Brooklyn, N.Y. , c1972] 31 p. : *NYPL [JNF 85-14]*

BROOKLYN (NEW YORK, N.Y.) - BIOGRAPHY.
Buckley, Gail Lumet, 1937- The Hornes . New York , 1986. 262 p. : ISBN 0-394-51306-1 : DDC 974.7/2300496073/00922 B 19
F129.B7 B83 1986   NYPL [Sc E 86-286]

BROOKLYN (NEW YORK, N.Y.) - FICTION.
Mason, Clifford. Jamaica run . New York , 1987. 359 p. ; ISBN 0-312-00611-X : DDC 813/.54 19
PS3563.A7878 J3 1987
NYPL [JFD 88-9447]

Brooks, Evelyn, 1945- The women's movement in the Black Baptist church, 1880-1920 / by Evelyn Brooks. [Rochester, N.Y. : s.n.], c1984. viii, 342 leaves ; 28 cm. Thesis (Ph. D.)--University of Rochester, 1984. Abstract. Vita. Bibliography: leaves 320-342. Photocopy. Ann Arbor, Mich. : University Microfilms International, 1987. 22 cm.
1. Afro-American Baptists - History. 2. Afro-American women - History. 3. Feminism - Religious aspects - Baptists. I. Title.   NYPL [Sc D 88-938]

Bross, William, 1813-1890. Illinois and the thirteenth amendment to the constitution of the United States. A paper read before the Chicago historical society, Jan. 15, 1884, by William Bross. Chicago, Jansen, McClurg & co., 1884. 8 p. 23 cm.
1. United States - Constitution - Amendments - 13th. 2. Illinois - Politics and government - Civil War, 1861-1865. I. Chicago Historical Society. II. Title.
NYPL [Sc Rare F 88-43]

Brother Resistance. Rapso explosion / Brother Resistance. London : Karia Press, 1986. 84 p. : ill., ports. ; 21 cm. Poems. ISBN 0-496-91834-1
I. Title.   NYPL [Sc D 88-500]

Brothers . Monroe, Sylvester. New York, N.Y. , c1988. 284 p. : ISBN 0-688-07622-X DDC 977.3/1100496073 19
F548.9.N4 M66 1988   NYPL [Sc E 88-356]

Brothers, Aileen. Just one me / Aileen Brothers and Cora Holsclaw ; illustrated by Jan Balet. Chicago : Follett Pub. Co. c1967. 32 p. : ill. (part col.) ; 23 cm. A youngster speculates on things he would like to be. SCHOMBURG CHILDREN'S COLLECTION.
1. Afro-American children - Juvenile fiction. I. Holsclaw, Cora, joint author. II. Balet, Jan B., 1913- illus. III. Schomburg Children's Collection. IV. Title.
NYPL [Sc D 88-376]

[Broughton, Virginia W] Twenty year's [!] experience of a missionary [microform]. Chicago, Pony press, 1907. 140 p. Black author. Preface signed: V. W. Broughton, authoress. Author's portrait on cover. Microfilm. New York : New York Public Library, [197-] 1 microfilm reel ; 35 mm.
1. Women missionaries - Biography. 2. Afro-American missionaries - Biography. I. Title.
NYPL [Sc Micro R-1445]

Brouillerie . Vincent, Occélus. Port-au-Prince [1964] 54 p. ;
NYPL [Sc Micro R-4840 no.6]

Brown, Alex. Southern Africa; some questions for Canadians / by Alex Brown, Peter Bunting [and] Clyde Sanger. Ottawa, Canadian Council for International Cooperation [1973] 43 p. 22 cm. (Window series. 1) Bibliography: p. 38-41.
1. Nationalism - Africa, Southern. 2. Africa, Southern - Race relations. 3. Africa, Southern - Relations (general) with Canada. 4. Canada - Relations (general) with Southern Africa. I. Bunting, Peter, joint author. II. Sanger, Clyde, joint author. III. Title. IV. Series.
DT746 .B76   NYPL [JLD 75-1128]

Brown, Comical. see Brown, William B.

Brown, Earl Louis, 1900- Why race riots [microform]? Lessons from Detroit, by Earl Brown... [New York, Public affairs committee, inc.] 1944. cover-title, 31, [1] p. illus., diagrs. 21cm. (Public affairs pamphlets. no. 87) Black author. "First edition, January, 1944." "For further reading": p. 31. Microfilm. New York : New York Public Library, [197-] 1 microfilm reel ; 35 mm.
1. Afro-Americans - Michigan - Detroit. 2. Detroit - Riot, 1943. I. Title.
F574.D4 B58   NYPL [Sc Micro R-3541]

Brown, Frank London. The myth maker; a novel. Published posthumously with a remembrance by Sterling Stuckey. Chicago, Path Press [1969] 179 p. 23 cm. DDC 813/.5/4
1. Afro-American - Illinois - Chicago - Fiction. I. Title.
PZ4.B8774 My PS3552.R6855
NYPL [Sc D 88-1118]

Brown, Hallie Q. (Hallie Quinn) Homespun heroines and other women of distinction /. New York , 1988. xxxv, viii, 248 p., [25] leaves of plates : ISBN 0-19-505237-4 (alk. paper) DDC 920.72/08996073 19
E185.96 .H65 1988   NYPL [JFC 88-2157]

BROWN, JIM, 1936-
Terzian, James P. The Jimmy Brown story /. New York , c1964. 190 p. :
NYPL [Sc D 89-432]

BROWN, JOHN, 1800-1859 - JUVENILE LITERATURE.
Nolan, Jeanette Covert, 1896- John Brown /. New York , 1968, c1950. 181 p. :
NYPL [Sc D 88-665]

Brown, Judith E. Brown, Richard Coleman, 1936- The family planning clinic in Africa . London , 1987. ix, 102 p. : ISBN 0-333-43658-X *NYPL [Sc D 88-630]*

Brown, Larissa V. Africans in the New World, 1493-1834 : an exhibition at the John Carter Brown Library / by Larissa V. Brown. Providence, Rhode Island : The Library, 1988. 61 p. : ill. ; 28 cm. "Acknowledgments and sources": p. 59-61. ISBN 0-916617-31-9
1. Slavery - America - Exhibitions. 2. Slavery - America - History. I. John Carter Brown Library. II. Title.   NYPL [Sc D 88-624]

Brown, Leroy. Black sexual power / by Leroy Brown, as told to Roger Blake. Cleveland, Ohio : K.D.S., c1970. 220 p. ; 18 cm. "An original Century book."
1. Brown, Leroy. 2. Afro-American men - Sexual behavior. 3. Sex customs - United States. I. Blake, Roger. II. Title.   NYPL [Sc C 88-274]

BROWN, LEROY.
Brown, Leroy. Black sexual power /. Cleveland, Ohio , c1970. 220 p. ; *NYPL [Sc C 88-274]*

Brown, Marion, 1935- Faces and places : the music and travels of a contemporary jazz musician / Marion Brown. 1976. 2 v. (289 leaves) : facsims., music ; 30 cm. Photocopy of typescript. Thesis (M.A.)-- Wesleyan University, 1976. Bibliography: p. 246-248. Discography: 1. [249]-258. Schomburg Center copy lacks 1. 249.
1. Jazz musicians - United States - Biography. 2. Jazz musicians - Europe - Biography. 3. Afro-American musicians - Biography. 4. Jazz - History and criticism. I. Title.   NYPL [Sc F 88-101]

Brown Rabbit: her story. Morse, Evangeline. Chicago [1967] 191 p.
PZ7.M84586 Br   NYPL [Sc D 89-89]

Brown, Richard Coleman, 1936- The family planning clinic in Africa : a practical guide for contraception clinic professionals / Richard C. Brown and Judith E. Brown. London : Macmillan, 1987. ix, 102 p. : ill. ; 22 cm. Published in conjunction with Teaching aids at low cost, St. Albans, England. Includes index. ISBN 0-333-43658-X
1. Birth control clinics - Africa - Administration. I. Brown, Judith E. II. Title.   NYPL [Sc D 88-630]

Brown, Russell S. African Methodist Episcopal Church. General Conference. Combined minutes of the general conferences 1948-1952-1956 /. [Nashville, Tenn. , 1956?] 503 p. ;   *NYPL [Sc D 87-1381]*

Brown, Scott E., 1960- James P. Johnson : a case of mistaken identity / Scott E. Brown ; a James P. Johnson discography, 1917-1950 [by] Robert Hilbert. Metuchen, N.J. : Scarecrow Press and the Institute of Jazz Studies, Rutgers University, 1986. viii, 500 p., [12] p. of plates : ill. ; 23 cm. (Studies in jazz . no. 4) Includes lists of compositions and indexes. Bibliography: p. [299]-314. ISBN 0-8108-1887-6 DDC 786.1/092/4 B 19
1. Johnson, James P. (James Price), 1894-1955. 2. Johnson, James P. (James Price), 1894-1955 - Discography. 3. Jazz musicians - United States - Biography. 4. Afro-American musicians - Biography. I. Hilbert, Robert, 1939- James P. Johnson discography, 1917-1950. 1986. II. Title. III. Series.
ML417.J62 B76 1986   NYPL [Sc D 88-1435]

Brown sky . Covin, David, 1940- Chicago , c1987. 274 p. ;   ISBN 0-910671-11-7 :   DDC 813/.54 19
PS3553.O875 B7 1987   NYPL [JFD 88-427]

Brown, Sterling Allen, 1901- Negro poetry and drama / by Sterling A. Brown. Washington, D.C. : Associates in Negro Folk Education, c1937. 142 p. ; 21 cm. (Bronze booklet. no. 7) Includes Bibliographical references.
1. Afro-Americans in literature. 2. American poetry - Afro-American authors - History and criticism. 3. American drama - Afro-American authors - History and criticism. I. Title. II. Series.
NYPL [Sc D 89-105]

Brown University. Afro-American Studies Program. The Blacker the berry . [Providence, R.I.] [1980?] 20 p. :
NYPL [Sc F 89-80]

Brown, Valerie Parks. Seven shades / Valerie Parks Brown. 1st ed. New York : Vantage, 1986. 106 p. ; 21 cm. Poems.   ISBN 0-533-06678-6
I. Title.   NYPL [Sc D 88-185]

Brown, Virginia. Out jumped Abraham / Virginia Brown ... [et al.] : illustrators, Don Kueker ... [et al.] St. Louis : Webster Division, McGraw-Hill Book Co., c1967. 94 p. : ill. ; 23 cm. (Shyline series, primer) SCHOMBURG CHILDREN'S COLLECTION.
1. Primers. I. Schomburg Children's Collection. II. Title.
NYPL [Sc D 89-542]

Brown, William B. Religious organizations, and slavery. By Rev. Wm. B. Brown. Oberlin, J.M. Fitch, 1850. 32 p. 22 cm. Cover title. "Extract from a Scriptural argument, in favor of withdrawing fellowship from churches ... tolerating slaveholding ...by Rev. Silas M'Keen": p.[30]-32.
1. Slavery - United States - Controversial literature - 1850. I. McKeen, Silas. Scriptural argument in favor of withdrawing fellwoship from churches and ecclesiastical bodies tolerating slaveholding among them. II. Title.
E449 .B882   NYPL [Sc Rare F 88-45]

Brown, Winifred. Marriage, divorce and inheritance : the Uganda Council of Women's movement for legislative reform / Winifred Brown. Cambridge : African Studies Centre, 1988. vii,91 p. ; 21 cm. (Cambridge African monographs . 10)   ISBN 0-902993-23-2 (pbk) :   DDC 346.76/106134/0880655 19
I. University of Cambridge. African Studies Centre. II. Series: Cambridge African monograph , io. III. Title.
NYPL [Sc D 88-1350]

Browne, Eileen. Bradman, Tony. Wait and see /. New York, NY , 1988. [28] p. :   ISBN 0-19-520644-4   DDC [E] 19
PZ7.B7275 Wai 1988   NYPL [Sc D 89-255]

Brownfoot, Janice. Africa in world politics . Houndmills, Basingstoke, Hampshire , 1987. xvi, 214 p. :   ISBN 0-333-39630-8
NYPL [Sc D 88-220]

Bruce, Dickson D., 1946- Black American writing from the nadir : the evolution of a literary tradition, 1877-1915 / Dickson D. Bruce, Jr. Baton Rouge : Louisiana State University Press, c1989. xiii, 272 p. : ports. ; 24 cm. Includes index.   ISBN 0-8071-1450-2 (alk. paper)   DDC 810/.9/896073 19
1. American literature - Afro-American authors - History and criticism. 2. American literature - 19th century - History and criticism. 3. American literature - 20th century - History and criticism. 4. Afro-Americans - Intellectual life. I. Title.
PS153.N5 B77 1989   NYPL [Sc E 89-197]

Bruce Onobrakpeya--Symbols of ancestral groves . Onobrakpeya, Bruce. [Mushin [Nigeria] , 1985. 252 p. :   ISBN 978-250-900-0
NYPL [Sc F 88-169]

Brueria di henter mundo =. Garmers, Sonia. Curaçao [1986?] 58 p. :   DDC 133.4/3 19
BF1618.D8 G37 1986   NYPL [Sc E 89-237]

Brüggemann, Anne. Amagdala und Akawuruk : das Zwillingsmotiv in westafrikanischen Erzählungen der Bulsa, Mossi und Bambara / Anne Brüggemann. Hohenschäftlarn bei München : K. Renner, 1986. 264 p. : ill. ; 21 cm. (Kulturanthropologische Studien . Bd. 13) Bibliography: p. 257-264.   ISBN 3-87673-106-2
1. Twins. 2. Ethnology - Africa, West. 3. Builsa (African people). 4. Bambara (African people). 5. Mossi (African people). I. Title. II. Series.
NYPL [Sc D 88-652]

Brugger, Eva Maria. Fries, Marianne. Südafrika, SWA/Namibia. Frankfurt [am Main] , 1987. 550 p. :   ISBN 3-87936-153-3
NYPL [Sc B 88-18]

Brüne, Michael. Südafrikas schwieriger Weg . Krefeld , c1988. 167 p., [8] p. of plates :   ISBN 3-88289-803-8   *NYPL [Sc D 89-548]*

Brüne, Stefan. Äthiopien -- Unterentwicklung und radikale Militärherrschaft : zur Ambivalenz einer scheinheiligen Revolution / Stefan Brüne. Hamburg : Institut für Afrika-Kunde, 1986. viii, 372 p. : ill. ; 21 cm. (Hamburger Beiträge zur Afrika-Kunde. 26) Some texts in Ethiopic (sources) Bibliography: p. 211-240.   ISBN 3-923519-63-X
1. Ethiopia - Politics and government. I. Title. II. Series.   NYPL [L-11 2640 Bd. 26]

BRUNTON, NICHOLAS WILLIAM, 1836-1891.
De Verteuil, Anthony. A history of Diego Martin 1784-1884 /. Port of Spain, Trinidad , c1987. viii, 174 p., [96] p. of plates :   ISBN 976-8054-10-7   *NYPL [Sc F 88-192]*

Bryan, Ashley. Sh-ko and his eight wicked brothers / retold by Ashley Bryan ; illustrated by Fumio Yoshimura. 1st ed. New York : Atheneum, 1988. [22] p. : ill. ; 20 x 24 cm. When his handsome older brothers set off to woo the beautiful Princess Yakami, ugly Sh-ko must carry their bags, but his luck changes after meeting a rabbit who lost his fur coat.   ISBN 0-689-31446-9   DDC 398.2/1/0952 E 19
1. Tales - Japan. I. Yoshimura, Fumio, ill. II. Title.
PZ8.B842 Sh 1988   NYPL [Sc E 88-569]

Bryan, Beverley, 1949- The heart of the race : Black women's lives in Britain / Beverley Bryan, Stella Dadzie, and Suzanne Scafe. London : Virago, 1985. vi, 250 p. ; 20 cm. Bibliography: p. 240-243.   ISBN 0-86068-361-3 (pbk.) :   DDC 305.4/8896041 19
1. Women, Black - Great Britain - History. 2. Women, Black - Great Britain - Social life and customs. 3. Blacks - Great Britain. I. Dadzie, Stella, 1952-. II. Scafe, Suzanne, 1954-. III. Title.
DA125.N4 B78 1985   NYPL [Sc C 88-178]

BRYAN COUNTY (GA.) - BIOGRAPHY.
Hoffmann, Charles. North by South . Athens , c1988. xxii, 318 p., [8] p. of plates :   ISBN 0-8203-0976-1 (alk. paper)   DDC 975.8/73203/0924 19
F292.B85 A753 1988   NYPL [Sc E 89-35]

Bryan, Patrick E. The Haitian revolution and its effects / Patrick E. Bryan. Kingston, Jamaica ; Exeter, N.H., USA : Heinemann, 1984. 56 p. : ill. ; 22 cm. (Heinemann CXC history. Theme) Bibliography: p. 55-56.   ISBN 0-435-98301-6 (U. S. : pbk.)   DDC 972.94/03 19
1. Haiti - History - Revolution, 1791-1804. 2. Haiti - History. I. Title. II. Series.
F1923 .B83 1984   NYPL [Sc D 89-299]

Bryant, Coralie. Poverty, policy, and food security in southern Africa /. Boulder , 1988. xii, 291 p. :   ISBN 1-555-87092-9 (lib. bdg.) :   DDC 363.8/56/0968 19
HD9017.A26 P68 1988 NYPL [Sc E 88-355]

Buccau, Quamino. Allinson, William J. Memoir of Quamino Buccau . Philadelphia , London , 1851. 30 p. :   *NYPL [Sc Rare G 86-28]*

Buchanan, James. The Blacks of Pickaway County, Ohio in the nineteenth century / compiled by James Buchanan. Bowie, Maryland : Heritage Books, 1988. iv, 142 p. ; 21 cm.   ISBN 1-556-13129-1
1. Afro-Americans - Ohio - Pickaway County - Genealogy. I. Title.   NYPL [Sc D 89-154]

Buchanan, John, 1855-1896. The Shirè highlands. New illustrated ed. Blantyre [Malawi] : Blantyre Printing and Publishing Co., 1982. xii, 260 p., [8] p. of plates : ill., folded map ; 20 cm. Contains title page of original edition: The Shirè Highlands (East Central Africa) as colony and mission / by John Buchanan. Ed. by James Rankin. Preface to the new edition / John McCracken. Reprint. Originally published: Edinburgh and London : William Blackwood and Sons, 1885.
1. Agricultural resources - Malawi. 2. Malawi - Description and travel. 3. Malawi - History. 4. Shire Highlands (Malawi) - Description and travel. I. Rankin, James, 1831-. II. McCraken, John 1938-. III. Title.
NYPL [Sc C 87-434]

Buckley, Gail Lumet, 1937- The Hornes : an American family / Gail Lumet Buckley.1st ed.

New York : Knopf, 1986. 262 p. : ill., ports. ; 25 cm.   DDC 974.7/2300496073/00922 B 19
1. Horn family. 2. Horne, Lena - Family. 3. Afro-Americans - New York (N.Y.) - Biography. 4. Afro-American entertainers - New York (N.Y.) - Biography. 5. Women singers - United States - Biography. 6. Brooklyn (New York, N.Y.) - Biography. 7. New York (N.Y.) - Biography. I. Title.
F129.B7 B83 1986   NYPL [Sc E 86-286]

Buckley, Peter.
Five friends at school / by Peter Buckley and Hortense Jones. New York : Holt, Rinehart and Winston, c1966. 96 p. : ill. ; 24 cm. (Holt urban social studies) SCHOMBURG CHILDREN'S COLLECTION.
1. City children - Pictorial works. I. Jones, Hortense, joint author. II. Schomburg Children's Collection. III. Schomburg Children's Collection. IV. Title.
NYPL [Sc E 88-590]

William, Andy and Ramón, by Peter Buckley and Hortense Jones. Holt, Rinehart & Winston, 1966. 70 p. illus. 23 cm. (Holt urban social studies) Grades preschool-grade 1. SCHOMBURG CHILDREN'S COLLECTION.
I. Schomburg Children's Collection. II. Title.
NYPL [Sc E 89-41]

BUDGETS, PERSONAL - KENYA - STATISTICS.
Narayan-Parker, Deepa. Women's interest and involvement in income generating activities . Gaborone, Botswana [1983] vi, 143, 3 p. ;   DDC 331.4/09676/2 19
HD6210.5 .N37 1983   NYPL [Sc F 88-312]

Budurwar zuciya /. Yakubu, Balaraba Ramat. Zaria , 1987. 87 p. ;   *NYPL [Sc C 88-301]*

Bueno, Salvador. El negro en la novela hispanoamericana / Salvador Bueno. La Habana, Cuba : Editorial Letras Cubanas, 1986. 294 p. ; 18 cm. (Giraldilla) Cover subtitle: Ensayo. Originally presented as the author's thesis (doctoral)--Academia de Ciencias de Hungría, 1978. Includes bibliographies.   DDC 863/.009/3520396 19
1. Spanish American fiction - 19th century - History and criticism. 2. Spanish American fiction - 20th century - History and criticism. I. Title.
PQ7082.N7 B84 1986   NYPL [Sc C 89-124]

Büttner, Thea.
African studies. Berlin, 1973. xi, 400 p.
NYPL [JLK 73-249 Bd. 15]

Buhle, Paul, 1944- C.L.R. James : the artist as revolutionary / Paul Buhle. London ; New York : Verso, 1988. 197 p. ; 25 cm. Includes index. Bibliography: p. 177-189.   ISBN 0-86091-221-3 :   DDC 818 B 19
1. James, C. L. R. (Cyril Lionel Robert), 1901-. 2. Authors, Trinidadian - 20th century - Biography. 3. Revolutionists - Trinidad - Biography. 4. Historians - Trinidad - Biography. 5. Marxist criticism. I. Title.
PR9272.9.J35 Z59 1988
NYPL [Sc E 89-171]

Buijtenhuijs, Robert. Le Frolinat et les guerres civiles du Tchad (1977-1984) : la révolution introuvable / Robert Buijtenhuijs. Paris, France : Éditions Karthala, c1987. 479 p. : maps ; 24 cm. (Hommes et sociétés) Includes index. Bibliography: p. [442]-458.   ISBN 2-86537-196-4
1. Front de libération nationale du Tchad. 2. Nationalism - Chad. I. Title. II. Series.
NYPL [Sc E 88-426]

BUILDING DESIGN. see ARCHITECTURE.

Building Lagos/. Akinsemoyin, Kunle. Jersey, 1977, c1906. 76 p.:
NYPL [3-MQWW 79-2215]

Building up African Christian families /. Mba, Cyriacus S. Nwosu. Enugu , 1985 (Enugu : (ECTA) 58 p. ;   *NYPL [Sc C 88-355]*

BUILDINGS - MODELS. see ARCHITECTURAL MODELS.

BUILSA (AFRICAN PEOPLE)
Brüggemann, Anne. Amagdala und Akawuruk . Hohenschäftlarn bei München , 1986. 264 p. :   ISBN 3-87673-106-2   *NYPL [Sc D 88-652]*

Bulcha, Mekuria. Flight and integration : causes of mass exodus from Ethiopia and problems of integration in the Sudan / Mekuria Bulcha. Uppsala, Sweden : Scandinavian Institute of African Studies, c1988. 256 p. : ill., maps ; 24 cm.   ISBN 91-7106-279-3
1. Refugees - Ethiopia. 2. Ethiopia - Politics and

government. 3. Ethiopia - Social conditions. 4. Sudan - Emigration and immigration. I. Title.
NYPL [Sc E 88-581]

Bulletin de l'Afrique noire. L'Afrique noire de A à Z. Paris, 1971. 317 p. *NYPL [Sc F 88-75]*

Bullivant, Brian Milton. The ethnic encounter in the secondary school : ethnocultural reproduction and resistance : theory and case studies / Brian M. Bullivant. London ; New York : Falmer Press, 1987. x, 214 p. ; 24 cm. Includes index. Bibliography: p. 193-201. ISBN 1-85000-255-X : DDC 371.97/0994 19
1. Minority youth - Education - Australia - Case studies. 2. High schools - Australia - Case studies. 3. Discrimination in education - Australia - Case studies. 4. Academic achievement - Case studies. I. Title.
LC3739 .B84 1987 *NYPL [JLE 88-2088]*

Bullwhip days : the slaves remember / edited with an introduction by James Mellon.1st ed. New York : Weidenfeld & Nicolson, c1988. xviii, 460 p. : ill., ports., plan ; 24 cm. ISBN 1-555-84210-0 DDC 973/.0496073022 B 19
1. Slaves - United States - Biography. 2. Slavery - United States - Condition of slaves. 3. Afro-Americans - History - To 1863. I. Mellon, James.
E444 .B95 1988 *NYPL [IEC 89-3083]*

Bullwinkle, Davis. African women, a general bibliography, 1976-1985 / compiled by Davis A. Bullwinkle. New York : Greenwood Press, 1989. xx, 334 p. ; 25 cm. (African special bibliographic series, 0749-2308 . no. 9) Includes bibliographies and index. ISBN 0-313-26607-7 (lib. bdg. : alk. paper) DDC 016.3054/096 19
1. Women - Africa - Bibliography. I. Title. II. Series.
Z7964.A3 B84 1989 HQ1787
NYPL [Sc E 89-173]

Bundy, Colin. The rise and fall of the South African peasantry / Colin Bundy. 2nd ed. Cape Town : D. Philip, 1988. [21], 276 p. ; 23 cm. Includes index. Bibliography: p. 253-268. ISBN 0-520-03754-5
1. Peasantry - South Africa. 2. Agriculture - Economic aspects - South Africa. 3. South Africa - Rural conditions. I. Title. *NYPL [Sc D 89-533]*

Bundy, Mary Lee, 1927- Activism in American librarianship, 1962-1973 /. New York , 1987. x, 207 p. ; ISBN 0-313-24602-5 (lib. bdg. : alk. paper) DDC 021 19
Z716.4 .A27 1987 *NYPL [JFE 87-6266]*

Bunge la jamhuri ya muungano /. Halimoja, Yusuf J. Dar es Salaam , 1981. 64 p. ;
NYPL [Sc C 89-61]

Bunker, Stephen G., 1944- Double dependency and constraints on class formation in Bugisu, Uganda / Stephen G. Bunker. Urbana, Ill. : African Studies Program, University of Illinois at Urbana-Champaign, 1983. v, 88 p. : ill. ; 22 cm. (Occasional paper series / African Studies Program, University of Illinois at Urbana-Champaign . no. 2) Bibliography: p. 79-88. DDC 303.3/09676/1 19
1. Peasantry - Uganda - Bugisu (District) - Political activity. 2. Peasantry - Uganda - Bugisu (District) - Societies, etc. - Political activity. 3. Agriculture and state - Uganda - Bugisu (District). 4. Community power - Uganda - Bugisu (District). 5. Central-local government relations - Uganda. I. Series: Occasional papers series (University of Illinois at Urbana-Champaign. African Studies Program) , no. 2. II. Title.
HD1538.U43 B86 1983
NYPL [Sc D 88-1054]

Bunting, Peter. (joint author) Brown, Alex. Southern Africa. Ottawa [1973] 43 p.
DT746 .B76 *NYPL [JLD 75-1128]*

Burchard, Peter, ill. Shotwell, Louisa Rossiter. Roosevelt Grady /. Cleveland, Ohio , c1963. 151 p. : *NYPL [Sc D 88-1425]*

Burchardt, Nellie. Project cat / by Nellie Burchardt ; ill. by Fermin Rocker. New York, N.Y. : F. Watts, c1966. 66 p. : ill. ; 21 cm. SCHOMBURG CHILDREN'S COLLECTION.
1. Cats - Juvenile fiction. 2. Afro-American children - Juvenile fiction. I. Schomburg Children's Collection. II. Title. *NYPL [Sc D 89-435]*

Burdette, Marcia M. (Marcia Muldrow) Zambia : between two worlds / Marcia M. Burdette. Boulder, Colo. : Westview Press, 1988. xiv, 210 p. : ill. ; 24 cm. (Profiles. Nations of contemporary Africa) Includes index. Bibliography: p. 174-196. ISBN 0-86531-617-1 (alk. paper) DDC

968.94/04 19
1. Zambia. I. Title. II. Series.
DT963 .B87 1988 *NYPL [Sc E 89-103]*

Bureau International du Travail. see International Labor Office.

Burford, Barbara. A Dangerous knowing . London [1984] ix, 67 p. ; ISBN 0-907179-28-2
NYPL [Sc D 88-338]

Burgin, Norma. Chukwuka, J. I. N. Zandi and the wonderful pillow /. Lagos, Nigeria , 1977. 48 p. ; ISBN 0-410-80099-6 *NYPL [Sc C 88-76]*

Burgoyne, Elizabeth. Race and politics /. New York , 1985. 174 p. ; ISBN 0-8242-0700-9 (pbk.) : DDC 305.8/00973 19
E184.A1 R25 1985 *NYPL [8-SAD (Reference shelf. v.56, no.6)]*

Burgwyn, Mebane (Holoman)
Lucky mischief / by Mebane Holoman Burgwyn ; pictures by Gertrude Howe. New York : Oxford University Press, 1949. 246 p. : ill. ; 21 cm. SCHOMBURG CHILDREN'S COLLECTION.
1. Afro-American children - North Carolina - Fiction. I. Schomburg Children's Collection. II. Title.
NYPL [Sc D 88-1513]

River treasure, by Mebane Holoman Burgwyn; illustrations by Ralph Ray. New York, Oxford University Press, 1947. 159 p. incl. front., illus. 21 cm. SCHOMBURG CHILDREN'S COLLECTION.
1. Afro-Americans - North Carolina - Juvenile fiction. I. Schomburg Children's Collection. II. Title.
PZ7.B9177 Ri *NYPL [Sc D 89-512]*

Burhani, Z. Mwisho wa kosa / Z. Burhani. Nairobi : Longman Kenya, c1987. 269 p. ; 18 cm. ISBN 996-649-731-5
1. Swahili language - Texts. I. Title.
NYPL [Sc C 89-3]

"Buri" dei negri tripolini. Sarnelli, Tommaso. Costumi e credenze coloniali [microform] . Napoli , 1925. 39 p. :
NYPL [Sc Micro F-11058]

BURIAL STATISTICS. see MORTALITY.

Burji, Konso-Gidole, Dullay . Minker, Gunter. Bremen , 1986. vi, 275 p. : ISBN 3-88299-051-1
NYPL [Sc E 88-236]

BURKINA FASO - BIOGRAPHY.
Traore, Fathié. Mémoires d'autres temps /. Ouagadougou, Burkina Faso? , 1984- (Ouagadougou : Presses africaines) v. ; DDC 966/.25 19
CT2478.T73 A3 1984 *NYPL [Sc D 88-386]*

BURKINA FASO - COLONIZATION.
Traore, Fathié. Mémoires d'autres temps /. Ouagadougou, Burkina Faso? , 1984- (Ouagadougou : Presses africaines) v. ; DDC 966/.25 19
CT2478.T73 A3 1984 *NYPL [Sc D 88-386]*

BURKINA FASO - FICTION.
Ilboudo, Pierre Claver, 1948- Adama, ou, La force des choses . Paris , 1987. 154 p. ; ISBN 2-7087-0484-2
PQ3989.2.I43 A65x 1987
NYPL [Sc C 88-316]

N'Djehoya, Blaise. Le nègre Potemkine /. [Paris] , c1988. 268 p. ; ISBN 2-86705-099-5
NYPL [Sc D 88-996]

BURKINA FASO - POLITICS AND GOVERNMENT.
Front populaire (Burkina Faso) Statuts et programme d'action /. Ouagadougou [1988]. 47 p. ; *NYPL [Sc D 88-1452]*

BURKINA FASO - SOCIAL LIFE AND CUSTOMS - 20TH CENTURY.
Traore, Fathié. Mémoires d'autres temps /. Ouagadougou, Burkina Faso? , 1984- (Ouagadougou : Presses africaines) v. ; DDC 966/.25 19
CT2478.T73 A3 1984 *NYPL [Sc D 88-386]*

Burnet, Mireille. La chienne du quimboiseur / Mireille Burnet. Paris : Editions Caribéennes, c1986. 126 p. ; 20 cm. (Série Tropicalia) ISBN 2-903033-81-1
1. West Indies, French - Fiction. I. Title. II. Series.
NYPL [Sc D 89-168]

Burnett, Michael. Jamaican Music / Michael Burnett. Oxford [England] : Oxford University Press, 1982. 48 p. : ill., music ; 19 x 25 cm.

(Oxford topics in music) Bibliography: p. 48. ISBN 0-19-321333-8 (pbk.)
1. Music - Jamaica - History and criticism. I. Title. II. Series. *NYPL [Sc C 84-99]*

Burnham, Forbes, 1923- To build a new world [microform] : speech / by L. F. S. Burnham, prime minister of the co-operative republic of Guyana, at the sixth conference of Non-aligned Countries, in Havana, Cuba, on Tuesday 4th September, 1979. [Georgetown, Guyana] : Ministry of Information, 1980. 20 p. : ill. ; 23 cm. Microfiche. New York: New York Public Library, 198. 1 microfiche: negative; 11 x 15 cm. (FSN Sc 019,006)
1. Conference of Heads of State or Government of Non-aligned Countries (6th: 1979: Havana, Cuba). II. Title. *NYPL [Sc Micro F-11021]*

Burnham, L. F. S. see Burnham, Forbes, 1923-

Burnham, Linden Forbes Sampson. see Burnham, Forbes, 1923-

A burning desire /. Adzei, Morgan. New York N.Y. , 1984. 145 p. ; ISBN 0-910437-01-7
NYPL [Sc D 89-192]

Burning down the house. Anderson, John, 1954 Mar. 27- New York , c1987. xv, 409 p. : ISBN 0-393-02460-1 : DDC 974.8/1104 19
F158.9.N4 A53 1987 *NYPL [Sc E 88-332]*

Burnley, William Hardin. Observations on the present condition of the island of Trinidad : and the actual state of the experiment of Negro emancipation / by William Hardin Burnley. London : Longman, Brown, Green, and Longmans, 1842. 177 p. ; 22 cm.
1. Slavery - Trinidad - Emancipation. I. Title.
NYPL [Sc Rare F 88-74]

BURNS, ANTHONY, 1834-1862 - JUVENILE LITERATURE.
Hamilton, Virginia. Anthony Burns . New York , c1988. xiii, 193 p. ; ISBN 0-394-88185-0 DDC 973.6/6/0924 B 92 19
E450.B93 H36 1988 *NYPL [Sc D 88-1157]*

Burns, Robert. Nolan, Jeanette Covert, 1896- John Brown /. New York , 1968, c1950. 181 p. : *NYPL [Sc D 88-665]*

BURNT OFFERING. see SACRIFICE.

Burrell, Evelyn Patterson. Of flesh and the spirit / by Evelyn Patterson Burrell ; illustrated by Laurence Hurst ; introductory commentary by Thomas J. Wilcox. Bryn Mawr, Pennsylvania : Dorrance, 1986. 101 p. : ill. ; 23 cm. Poems. ISBN 0-8059-3039-6
1. Hurst, Laurence. II. Wilcox, Thomas J. III. Title.
NYPL [Sc D 88-300]

Burroughs, Margaret Taylor, 1917- (comp) Did you feed my cow? Street games, chants, and rhymes. Compiled by Margaret Taylor Burroughs. Illustrated by Joe E. De Velasco.Rev. ed. Chicago, Follett Pub. Co. [1969] 96 p. illus. 22 cm. Seventy-six chants and rhymes used and adapted by American children for jumping rope, bouncing balls, or just for fun. SCHOMBURG CHILDREN'S COLLECTION. ISBN 0-695-81960-7 DDC 398.8
1. Singing games. I. De Velasco, Joe E., illus. II. Schomburg Children's Collection. III. Title.
PZ8.3.B958 Di5 *NYPL [Sc D 89-57]*

Burrowes, Carl Patrick. The Americo-Liberian ruling class and other myths : a critique of political science in the Liberian context / by Carl Patrick Burrowes. Philadelphia : Temple University, Dept. of African Studies, 1989. 77 leaves ; 28 cm. (Occasional paper series . no. 3) Bibliography: p. 96-97.
1. Social classes - Liberia. 2. Liberia - Politics and government - 1944-1971. 3. Liberia - Politics and government - 1971-1980. I. Series: Occasional paper (Temple University. Institute of African and Afro-American Affairs) , no. 3. II. Title.
NYPL [Sc F 89-128]

Burrowes, Reynold A. Revolution and rescue in Grenada : an account of the U. S.-Caribbean invasion / Reynold A. Burrowes. New York : Greenwood Press, 1988. xiv, 180 p. ; 22 cm. (Contributions in political science. no. 203) Includes index. Bibliography: p. [171]-173. ISBN 0-313-26066-4
1. Grenada - History - American invasion, 1983. I. Title.
F2056.8 .B87 1988 *NYPL [HRG 88-1153]*

Burstein, Paul. Discrimination, jobs, and politics :
the struggle for equal employment opportunity
in the United States since the New Deal / Paul
Burstein. Chicago : University of Chicago Press,
c1985. x, 247 p. : ill. ; 23 cm. Includes index.
Bibliography: p. 225-239. ISBN 0-226-08134-6 DDC
344.73/01133/0262 347.3041133/0262 19
*1. Discrimination in employment - Law and legislation -
United States - History. I. Title.*
KF3464 .B83 1985   **NYPL [JLD 86-132]**

Burt, Al. Diederich, Bernard. [Papa Doc.
Spanish.] Papa Doc y los tontons Macoutes .
Santo Domingo, República Dominicana , 1986.
393 p., [16] p. of plates :
                                NYPL [Sc D 88-452]

Burt, Nancy V. Critical essays on James Baldwin
/. Boston, Mass. , 1988. ix, 312 p. ; ISBN
0-8161-8879-3 DDC 818/.5409 19
PS3552.A45 Z88 1988   **NYPL [JFE 88-2203]**

Burton, William L., 1928- Melting pot soldiers :
the Union's ethnic regiments / William L.
Burton.1st ed. Ames, Iowa : Iowa State
University Press, 1988. x, 282 p. ; 24 cm.
Includes index. Bibliography: p. 257-273. ISBN
0-8138-1115-5 DDC 973.7/4 19
*1. United States. Army - Minorities - History - 19th
century. 2. United States. Army - History - Civil War,
1861-1865. 3. Immigrants - United States - History -
19th century. 4. United States - History - Civil War,
1861-1865 - Participation, Immigrant. I. Title.*
E540.F6 B87 1988   **NYPL [IKC 88-730]**

Le Burundi /. Acquier, Jean-Louis, 1946-
Marseille, France , c1986. 129 p. : ISBN
2-86364-030-5 : DDC 728/.67/0967572 19
GT377.B94 A27 1986 **NYPL [Sc E 88-568]**

**BURUNDI - GOVERNMENT
PUBLICATIONS - BIBLIOGRAPHY -
UNION LISTS.**
Witherell, Julian W. French-speaking central
Africa. Washington, 1973. xiv, 314 p. ISBN
0-8444-0033-5
Z3692 .W5   **NYPL [JLF 74-197]**

BURUNDI - HISTORY.
Histoire rurale. Bujumbura , Paris , 1984. v.,
236 p. :   **NYPL [Sc F 88-217]**

Burundi. President (1976- : Bagaza) Bagaza,
Jean-Baptiste. Discours de son Excellence le
colonel Jean-Baptiste Bagaza, président de la
République du Burundi. Bujumbura , 1980. 167
p. :
DT450.853.B34 A5 1980
                          NYPL [Sc E 88-122]

BURUNDI - RELIGION.
Bigangara, Jean-Baptiste. Le fondement de
l'imanisme, ou, Religion traditionnelle au
Burundi . Bujumbura, Burundi , 1984. 140 p. ;
BL2470.B94 B54 1984 **NYPL [Sc E 88-459]**

BURUNDI - RURAL CONDITIONS.
Bonvin, Jean. Changements sociaux et
productivité agricole en Afrique Centrale /.
Paris : Centre de développement de
l'orgnisation de coopértion et de développement
économiques, c1986. 140 p. : ISBN
92-64-22803-9 **NYPL [Sc D 88-803]**
Histoire rurale. Bujumbura , Paris , 1984. v.,
236 p. :   **NYPL [Sc F 88-217]**

BURUNDI - SOCIAL CONDITIONS.
Bonvin, Jean. Changements sociaux et
productivité agricole en Afrique Centrale /.
Paris : Centre de développement de
l'orgnisation de coopértion et de développement
économiques, c1986. 140 p. : ISBN
92-64-22803-9 **NYPL [Sc D 88-803]**

BURUNDI TALES. see TALES, BURUNDI.

Bury me at the marketplace. Mphahlele,
Ezekiel. Johannesburg , c1984. 202 p. ; ISBN
0-620-06779-9   **NYPL [Sc D 89-117]**

BURYING-GROUNDS. see CEMETERIES.

**BUS DRIVERS - JAMAICA - KINGSTON
METROPOLITAN AREA.**
Anderson, Patricia, Dr. Mini bus ride . Mona,
Kingston, Jamaica , 1987. vii, 179 p. : ISBN
976-400-006-1
HE5647.K56 A53x 1987
                          NYPL [Sc D 89-312]

**BUS LINES - JAMAICA - KINGSTON
METROPOLITAN AREA.**
Anderson, Patricia, Dr. Mini bus ride . Mona,
Kingston, Jamaica , 1987. vii, 179 p. : ISBN

976-400-006-1
HE5647.K56 A53x 1987
                          NYPL [Sc D 89-312]

BUSES - SOUTH AFRICA.
Human Awareness Programme (South Africa)
Black urban public road transport . Grant Park
[South Africa] [1982] 64 p. : ISBN
0-620-05750-5 (pbk.) : DDC 388.4/1322/089968
19
HE5704.4.A6 H86 1982
                          NYPL [Sc F 88-150]

**BUSHMEN (AFRICAN TRIBE) see SAN
(AFRICAN PEOPLE)**

BUSHWHACKERS. see GUERRILLAS.

**BUSINESS ADMINISTRATION. see
BUSINESS.**

**BUSINESS, CHOICE OF. see VOCATIONAL
GUIDANCE.**

**BUSINESS DISTRICTS, CENTRAL. see
CENTRAL BUSINESS DISTRICTS.**

**BUSINESS EDUCATION - NIGERIA -
CONGRESSES.**
Development of management education in
Nigeria /. Ikeja, Nigeria , 1985. 555 p. : ISBN
978-14-0017-X   **NYPL [Sc E 89-161]**

**BUSINESS ENTERPRISES - AFRICA -
CONGRESSES.**
L'Entreprise et ses dirigeants dans le
développement économique de l'Afrique noire .
Kinshasa [1969?] 89 p. :
                          NYPL [Sc F 88-100]

**BUSINESS ENTERPRISES - BURKINA
FASO.**
Labazée, Pascal. Entreprises et entrepreneurs du
Burkina Faso . Paris , c1988. 273 p. ;
                          NYPL [Sc D 89-288]

**BUSINESS ENTERPRISES,
INTERNATIONAL. see
INTERNATIONAL BUSINESS
ENTERPRISES.**

BUSINESS EXECUTIVES. see EXECUTIVES.

BUSINESS - JUVENILE LITERATURE.
Haskins, James, 1941- Jobs in business and
office. New York [1974] 96 p. ISBN
0-688-75011-7 DDC 651/.023
HF5381.2 .H38   **NYPL [Sc E 89-16]**

BUSINESS MEN. see BUSINESSMEN.

**BUSINESS PATRONAGE OF THE ARTS. see
ART PATRONAGE.**

**BUSINESS - SEASONAL VARIATIONS. see
SEASONAL VARIATIONS
(ECONOMICS)**

**BUSINESS - STUDY AND TEACHING. see
BUSINESS EDUCATION.**

BUSINESSMEN - BURKINA FASO.
Labazée, Pascal. Entreprises et entrepreneurs du
Burkina Faso . Paris , c1988. 273 p. ;
                          NYPL [Sc D 89-288]

**BUSINESSMEN - GREAT BRITAIN -
BIOGRAPHY.**
Hall, Richard, 1925- My life with Tiny .
London , Boston , 1987. 256, [4] p. of plates :
ISBN 0-571-14737-2 **NYPL [Sc D 88-515]**

**BUSINESSMEN - HAITI - ATTITUDES -
HISTORY - 20TH CENTURY.**
Plummer, Brenda Gayle. Haiti and the great
powers, 1902-1915 /. Baton Rouge , c1988. xix,
255 p. : ISBN 0-8071-1409-X (alk. paper) DDC
972.94/04 19
F1926 .P68 1988   **NYPL [HPE 88-2374]**

**BUSINESSMEN - RHODE ISLAND -
DIARIES.**
Hoffman, Charles. North by South . Athens ,
c1988. xxii, 318 p., [8] p. of plates : ISBN
0-8203-0976-1 (alk. paper) DDC
975.8/73203/0924 19
F292.B85 A753 1988   **NYPL [Sc E 89-35]**

**BUSINESSMEN - ZIMBABWE -
BIOGRAPHY.**
Hall, Richard, 1925- My life with Tiny .
London , Boston , 1987. 256, [4] p. of plates :
ISBN 0-571-14737-2 **NYPL [Sc D 88-515]**

**BUSING FOR SCHOOL INTEGRATION -
NORTH CAROLINA - CHARLOTTE -
HISTORY.**
Gaillard, Frye, 1946- The dream long deferred
/. Chapel Hill , c1988. xxi, 192 p. ; ISBN

0-8078-1794-5 (alk. paper) DDC 370.19/342 19
LC214.523.C48 G35 1988
                          NYPL [Sc E 88-527]

**BUSOGA - SOCIAL CONDITIONS -
HISTORY.**
Cohen, David William. Misangós song
[microform] . [Nairobi] [1979] 24 p. ;
            NYPL [Sc Micro R-4108 no. 38]

Busoni, Rafaello, 1900- Mary Marguerite, Sister,
1895- Martin's mice. Chicago [1954] 32 p.
PZ8.1.M38 Mar   **NYPL [Sc G 88-28]**

**Bustamante Institute of Public and International
Affairs.** Trotman, Donald A. B. Report on
human rights in Grenada . [Bustamante?]
[198-] viii, 54 p. : DDC 323.4/9/09729845 19
JC599.G76 T76 1980z **NYPL [Sc D 88-816]**

Buthelezi, Gatsha. South Africa : anatomy of
Black-white power sharing : collected speeches
in Europe of Chief M. Gatsha Buthelezi /
Mangosuthu G. Buthelezi. Lagos, Nigeria :
Emmcon (TWORF) Books Nigeria Ltd., c1986.
xxxvii, 143 p. : ill. ; 20 cm. On cover: Sequel to
Mission to South Africa. ISBN 978-242-308-4
*1. Apartheid. 2. South Africa - Politics and
government - 1978-. I. Title.*
                          NYPL [Sc C 88-269]

BUTHELEZI, GATSHA.
Mzala. Gatsha Buthelezi . London , Atlantic
Highlands, N.J. , 1988. ix, 240 p. ; ISBN
0-86232-792-X DDC 968.4/9106/0924 B 19
DT878.Z9 B856 1988 NYPL **[Sc D 88-1324]**

Butler, Ernest W. Neighbors of the 2100 block :
a Philadelphia story / by Ernest W. & Helen
M. Butler. Pitman, N.J. : Webb Press, c1986.
466 p. : ill. ; 22 cm.
*1. Philadelphia (Pa.) - Social life and customs. 2.
Philadelphia (Pa.) - Race relations. I. Title.*
                          NYPL [Sc D 88-940]

Butler, Octavia E. Adulthood rites : xenogenesis
/ Octavia E. Butler. New York, NY Warner
Books, c1988. 277 p. ; 24 cm. (Xenogenesis . [2])
ISBN 0-446-51422-5 : DDC 813/.54 19
I. Title.
PS3552.U827 A65 1988
                          NYPL [JFE 88-6322]

**BUTTERFLIES - AFRICA, SOUTHERN -
GEOGRAPHICAL DISTRIBUTION.**
Cottrell, C. B. Aspects of the biogeography of
southern African butterflies . Salisbury
[Zimbabwe] , c1978. viii, 100 p. ;
QL557.S65 C68 1978 **NYPL [Sc E 88-555]**

**BUTTERFLIES - AFRICA, SOUTHERN -
HOST PLANTS.**
Cottrell, C. B. Aspects of the biogeography of
southern African butterflies . Salisbury
[Zimbabwe] , c1978. viii, 100 p. ;
QL557.S65 C68 1978 **NYPL [Sc E 88-555]**

**Butterworths series in conservation and
museology.**
Horie, C. V. (Charles Velson) Materials for
conservation . London , Boston , 1987. xi, 281
p. : ISBN 0-408-01531-4 : DDC 667/.9 19
TP156.C57 H67 1987 **NYPL [Sc D 88-558]**

**Afrika von den Anfängen bis zur territorialen
Aufteilung Afrikas durch die
imperialistischen Kolonialmächte.**
Geschichte Afrikas. Afrika : Geschichte von
den Anfängen bis zur Gegenwart. Köln ,
1979- v. : ISBN 3-7609-0433-5 (v. 1) : DDC
960 19
DT20 .G47 1979   **NYPL [JFK 82-28]**

Bwengye, Francis Aloysius Wazarwahi. The
agony of Uganda from Idi Amin to Obote :
repressive rule and bloodshed : causes, effects
and the cure / Francis Aloysius Wazarwahi
Bwengye ; foreword by Grace Stuart Ibingira.
London : Regency Press, 1985. xxii, 379 p. :
ill., maps ; 22 cm. Includes index. Bibliography: p.
374-379. ISBN 0-7212-0717-0 :
*1. Democratic Party (Uganda). 2. Elections - Uganda. I.
Title.*   **NYPL [Sc D 88-873]**

By sail and wind . Bothwell, Jean. London , New
York , c1964. 152 p. : **NYPL [Sc D 89-103]**

Bye Bye Umaskini ... /. Maganga, Dotto B. Dar
es Salaam , 1986. 90 p. ;
                          NYPL [Sc C 88-232]

Byrne, Francis. Grammatical relations in a radical
Creole : verb complementation in Saramaccan /
by Francis Byrne. Amsterdam ; Philadelphia : J.
Benjamins, 1987. xiv, 293 p. : ill. ; 23 cm.

(Creole language library . v. 3) Revision of author's thesis (Universidad de Oriente, Venezuela) originally titled: Predicate complementation and verb serialization in Saramaccan. Bibliography: p.277-293. ISBN 0-915027-96-8 (U. S. : alk. paper) : DDC 427/.9883 19
1. Saramaccan language - Syntax. 2. Saramaccan language - Complement. I. Title. II. Series.
PM7875.S27 B97 1987
NYPL [JFD 88-7020]

Byrt, W. J. (William John) Management education . London , New York , 1989. viii, 229 p. ; ISBN 0-415-00423-3 DDC 658/.007 19
HD30.4 .M33 1988 **NYPL [Sc D 89-325]**

C. C. I. C. window series. see Window series.

C.G.A. Oldendorps Geschichte der Mission der Evangelischen Brüder auf den caraibischen Inseln S. Thomas, S. Croix und S. Jan /. Oldendorp, C. G. A. (Christian Georg Andreas), 1721-1787. [Geschichte der Mission der Evangelischen Brüder auf den caraibischen Inseln S. Thomas, S. Croix und S. Jan.] Barby , 1777. 2 v. in 1 (1068 p.) : DDC 266/.46729722 19
BV2848.V5 O42 1777
NYPL [Sc Rare C 89-33]

C. I. C. C. see Centre international de criminologie comparée.

C.L.R. James . Buhle, Paul, 1944- London , New York , 1988. 197 p. ; ISBN 0-86091-221-3 : DDC 818 B 19
PR9272.9.J35 Z59 1988
NYPL [Sc E 89-171]

C. M. R. see Church Missionary Society.

CAAS special publication series, 0882-5300 . (v. 7) Race, class, and power in Brazil /. Los Angeles , c1985. xi, 160 p. : ISBN 0-934934-22-3 : DDC 305.8/96/081 19
F2659.N4 R24 1985 **NYPL [JLE 88-2671]**

Caballero, Armando O. Antonio Maceo, la protesta de Baraguá / Armando O. Caballero. La Habana : Gente Nueva, 1977. 30, [1] p. : col. ports. ; 29 cm. "Nivel juvenil"--T.p. verso. Bibliography: p. [31] SCHOMBURG CHILDREN'S COLLECTION.
1. Maceo, Antonio, 1845-1896 - Juvenile literature. 2. Revolutionists - Cuba - Biography - Juvenile literature. 3. Generals - Cuba - Biography - Juvenile literature. 4. Cuba - History - 1810-1899 - Juvenile literature. I. Schomburg Children's Collection. II. Title.
NYPL [Sc F 88-281]

CABIMAS (VENEZUELA) - FICTION. Díaz Sánchez, Ramón. [Mene. English.] Mene /. Trinidad [193-?] (Trinidad : Multimedia Production Center, Faculty of Education, U.W.I.) 141 p. : **NYPL [Sc D 89-544]**

CABO DELGADO (MOZAMBIQUE) - POLITICS AND GOVERNMENT. Machel, Samora, 1933- A nossa força está na unidade /. [Maputo] [1983] 98 p. : DDC 967/.9803 19
DT465.C32 M32 1983 **NYPL [Sc D 89-531]**

Cabort-Masson, Guy, 1937- La mangrove mulâtre / Guy Cabort-Masson. Saint-Joseph, Martinique : La Voix du peuple, c1986. 282 p. ; 22 cm. On cover: Roman historique martiniquais.
1. Slavery - Martinique - Fiction. 2. Martinque - Fiction. I. Title.
MLCS 87/3007 (P) **NYPL [Sc D 88-571]**

Pourrir, ou, Martyr un peu / Guy Cabort-Masson ; illustrations de René Corail. [Martinique] : Voix du peuple, c1987. 252 p. : ill. ; 22 cm. DDC 843/.914 19
1. Martinique - Fiction. I. Title. II. Title: Pourrir. III. Title: Martyr un peu.
PQ3949.2.C27 P68 1987
NYPL [Sc D 89-527]

CABRAL, AMILCAR - CONGRESSES. Symposium Amilcar Cabral (1983 : Praia, Cape Verde) Pour Cabral . Paris , 1987. 486 p. ; ISBN 2-7087-0482-6
NYPL [Sc D 87-1429]

Cabral, Amílcar, 1921-1973. Unité et lutte / Amílcar Cabral. Paris : F. Maspero, 1980. 329 p. ; 19 cm. (Petite collection Maspéro. 241) ISBN 2-7071-1171-6
1. Partido africano de Independéncia da Guinée Cabo Verde - Collected works. 2. National liberation movement - Guinea-Bissau - Colleted works. 3.

National liberation movement - Cape Verde - Collected works. 4. Guinea-Bissau - Politics and government - Collected works. 5. Cape Verde - Politics and government - To 1975 - Collected works. 6. Guinea-Bissau - History - Revolution, 1963-1974 - Collected works. I. Title. **NYPL [Sc C 88-125]**

Cabrera, Lydia.
Colección del chicherekú en el exilio. Cabrera, Lydia. Supersticiones y buenos consejos /. Miami, Fla. , 1987. 62 p. ; ISBN 0-89729-433-5 **NYPL [Sc D 89-522]**

La lengua sagrada de los Ñáñigos / Lydia Cabrera. Miami, Fla. : V & L Graphics, c1988. 530 p. ; 22 cm. (Colección del chicherekú en el exilio) Includes bibliographical references.
1. Abacuá language. 2. Blacks - Cuba - Social life and customs. I. Title. II. Series. **NYPL [Sc D 89-585]**

Supersticiones y buenos consejos / Lydia Cabrera. Miami, Fla. : Ediciones Universal, 1987. 62 p. ; 22 cm. (Colección del chicherekú) ISBN 0-89729-433-5
1. Folklore - Cuba. I. Series: Cabrera, Lydia. Colección del chicherekú en el exilio. II. Title.
NYPL [Sc D 89-522]

CABRERA, LYDIA. Valdés-Cruz, Rosa. Lo ancestral africano en la narrativa de Lydia Cabrera /. Barcelona , 1974. 113 p. ; ISBN 84-346-0082-X :
PQ7389.C22 Z94 **NYPL [Sc D 89-36]**

CABRERA, LYDIA - CRITICISM AND INTERPRETATION. Gutiérrez, Mariela. Los cuentos negros de Lydia Cabrera . Miami, Fla. , 1986. 148 p. ; ISBN 0-89729-389-4 **NYPL [Sc D 88-370]**

Soto, Sara. Magia e historia en los "Cuentos negros," "Por qué" y "Ayapá" de Lydia Cabrera /. Miami, Fla., U. S.A. , 1988. 162 p. ; ISBN 0-89729-444-0 DDC 863 20
PQ7389.C22 Z87 1988 **NYPL [Sc D 89-601]**

Cabrera, Lydia - Interpretation and criticism. see Cabrera, Lydia - Criticism and interpretation.

Cabrera, M. A. Africa en armas / Miguel Angel Cabrera. Madrid : IEPALA : Fundamentos, [1986] 163 p. ; 21 cm. (Estrategia y paz . [9]) Includes bibliographical footnotes. ISBN 84-85436-37-7
1. Africa - History, Military. 2. Coups d'état - Africa. 3. Africa - National security. 4. Africa - Military relations - Foreign countries. I. Title. II. Series.
NYPL [Sc D 88-757]

CADASTRAL SURVEYS. see REAL PROPERTY.

CADICEC (Association) L'Entreprise et ses dirigeants dans le développement économique de l'Afrique noire . Kinshasa [1969?] 89 p. :
NYPL [Sc F 88-100]

Cadres et dirigeants au Zaïre . Mabi Mulumba. Kinshasa , 1986. 541 p. :
NYPL [Sc E 88-322]

CAFÉS. see HOTELS, TAVERNS, ETC; RESTAURANTS, LUNCH ROOMS, ETC.

CAFETERIAS. see RESTAURANTS, LUNCH ROOMS, ETC.

Cahier (Centre national de la recherche scientifique (France). Groupe de recherches ("Afrique noire") . (no. 11) L'Histoire des femmes en Afrique /. Paris , c1987. 164 p. : ISBN 2-7384-0172-4
NYPL [Sc E 89-226]

(no. 4) Mutations économiques et sociales à la campagne et à la ville . Paris , 1980. 258 p. ;
NYPL [Sc F 87-437]

Cahiers de l'IPD. III, Collection Pédagogie et méthodologie du développement . (1983-no. 2) Langley, Ph. Managing the Botswana brigades . Douala, U.R.C. [1983] 93 p. : DDC 658.3/12404/096811 19
HD5715.5.B55 L36 1983
NYPL [Sc E 88-483]

Cahiers de recherches criminologiques . (cahier no. 3) Brillon, Yves. [Ethnocriminologie de l'Afrique noire. English.] Crime, justice and culture in black Africa . [Montreal] [1985] xi, 289 p. ; **NYPL [JLF 87-694]**

Cahiers d'histoire. (3 (1985)) Pouvoirs et sociétés dans l'Afrique des grands lacs /. Bujumbura , 1986. 146 p. ;
NYPL [Sc F 89-62]

Cahiers d'histoire (Université du Burundi. Dép. d'histoire) . (3 (1985)) Pouvoirs et sociétés dans l'Afrique des grands lacs /. Bujumbura , 1986. 146 p. ;
NYPL [Sc F 89-62]

Caines, Jeannette Franklin. I need a lunch box / by Jeannette Caines ; pictures by Pat Cummings. 1st ed. New York : Harper & Row, c1988. [32] p. : col. ill. ; 21 cm. A little boy yearns for a lunch box, even though he hasn't started school yet. SCHOMBURG CHILDREN'S COLLECTION. ISBN 0-06-020984-4 : DDC [E] 19
1. Afro-American children - Juvenile fiction. I. Cummings, Pat, ill. II. Schomburg Children's Collection. III. Title.
PZ7.C12 Iaan 1988 **NYPL [Sc D 88-1504]**

CALABAR, NIGERIA - HISTORY. The story of the old Calabar . [Lagos?] , c1986. 228 p. : **NYPL [Sc D 89-253]**

Calame-Griaule, Geneviève. Des cauris au marché : essais sur des contes africains / Geneviève Calame-Griaule. [Paris] : Société de africanistes, c1987. 293 p., [12] p. of plates : ill. (some col.) ; 24 cm. Bibliography: p. 285-[292]
1. Tales - Africa, West - Structural analysis. 2. Tales - Africa - Structural analysis. I. Title.
NYPL [Sc E 88-327]

CALAMITIES. see DISASTERS.

Calderon, Agostina. Evasions Antilles / Asostina Calderon. [Pointe-à-Pitre : Office de tourisme de Guadeloupe ; Paris : Office inter-régional Antilles-Guyane, 1987] 223 p. : col. ill., maps ; 21 cm. (Collections "Evasions")
1. West Indies, French - Description and travel - Guide-books. I. Title. **NYPL [Sc D 88-998]**

Caldwell, John C. Let's visit the West Indies John C. Caldwell. 4th rev. ed. London, Eng. : Burke, c1983. 96 p. : ill., map ; 21 cm. Includes index. SCHOMBURG CHILDREN'S COLLECTION. ISBN 0-222-00920-9
1. West Indies - Social life and customs. I. Schomburg Children's Collection. II. Title.
NYPL [Sc D 89-19]

Caldwell, John C. (John Cope), 1913- Let's visit middle Africa: East Africa, Central Africa, the Congo. New York, J. Day Co. [1961] 96 p. illus. 21 cm. SCHOMBURG CHILDREN'S COLLECTION. DDC 916.7
1. Africa, Sub-Saharan - Description and travel - Juvenile literature. I. Schomburg Children's Collection. II. Title.
DT352 .C3 **NYPL [Sc D 88-507]**

CALIFORNIA - IMPRINTS. Equiano, Olaudah, b. 1745. I saw a slave ship /. Sacramento, Calif. , 1983. 42 p. :
NYPL [Sc Rare C 88-1]

CALIFORNIA. LEGISLATURE. HOUSE - BIOGRAPHY. Hayden, Tom. Reunion . New York , c1988. xix, 539 p., [16] p. of plates : ISBN 0-394-56533-9 : DDC 328.794/092/4 B 19
F866.4.H39 A3 1988 **NYPL [JFE 88-6231]**

California. State Dept. of Education. Gray, Mattie Evans. Images . Sacramento, Calif. , c1988. 185 p. : ISBN 0-8011-0782-2
NYPL [Sc F 89-134]

California State Polytechnic University, Pomona. School of Arts. Which path to freedom? . Pomona, Calif. , c1986. iv, 60 p. ; DDC 973.7/114 19
E449 .W565 1986 **NYPL [Sc D 88-1154]**

Call that George /. Odlum, George. [Castries, St. Lucia] , 1979. 44 p. :
F2100 .O35 1979 **NYPL [Sc E 89-2]**

Callahan, John F. In the African-American grain : the pursuit of voice in twentieth-century Black fiction / John F. Callahan. Urbana : University of Illinois Press, c1988. 280 p. ; 24 cm. Includes bibliographies and index. ISBN 0-252-01459-6 (alk. paper) DDC 813/.009/896073 19
1. American fiction - Afro-American authors - History and criticism. 2. Afro-Americans in literature. 3. American fiction - 20th century - History and criticism. I. Title.
PS153.N5 C34 1988 **NYPL [Sc E 88-144]**

Callahan, Nancy. The Freedom Quilting Bee / by Nancy Callahan. Tuscaloosa, Ala. : University of Alabama Press, c1987. xi, 255 p., [8] p. of plates : ill. (some col.) ; 24 cm. Includes index. ISBN 0-8173-0310-3 DDC 976.0/3800496073 19
1. Freedom Quilting Bee (Organization : Alabama) - History. 2. Quilting - Alabama - History - 20th century. 3. Afro-American quiltmakers - Alabama - History. 4. Civil rights in art. I. Title.
NK9112 .C34 1987 **NYPL** *[3-MOT 88-1171]*

Callaloo : a Grenada anthology / Jacob Ross ... [et al.] ; illustrated by Dan Jones. London : Young World Books, 1984. 108 p. : ill., 1 maps ; 21 cm. Ill on inside covers. ISBN 0-905405-09-9 (pbk) : DDC 810.8/09729845 19
1. Grenadan literature (English). I. Ross, Jacob.
PR9275.G **NYPL** *[Sc D 88-702]*

Callaloo poetry series .
(v.5) Weaver, Michael S, 1951- Water song /. Lexington, Kentucky , 1985. 73 p. : ISBN 0-912759-05-4 **NYPL** *[Sc D 88-175]*

Callender, Timothy. The watchman / story, layout and lettering by Timothy Callender ; [photographs by Tony Lynch, Roosevelt "Ty" King, Timothy Callender]. [St. Michael, Barbados? : Callender?, 1978?] [28] p. : chiefly ill. ; 29 cm. Caption title. "A photo-novel".
1. Barbados - Fiction. I. Lynch, Tony. II. King, Roosevelt Ty. III. Title. **NYPL** *[Sc F 89-52]*

Callinicos, Alex. South Africa between reform and revolution / Alex Callinicos. London ; Chicago : Bookmarks, 1988. 231 p. : map ; 20 cm. Includes bibliographical references and index. ISBN 0-906224-46-2
1. Marxist criticism - South Africa. 2. South Africa - Politics and government - 1978-. I. Title.
NYPL *[JLD 89-489]*

Callinicos, Luli. A People's history of South Africa. Johannesburg , c1980- v. : ISBN 0-86975-119-0 (pbk : v. 1) DDC 968 19
DT766 .P43 **NYPL** *[JLM 85-439]*

Caloc, Ray. Secrets dévoilés de la magie caraïbe : tradition de connaissance cachée / Ray Caloc. [Lamentin, Martinique] : Editions France-Caraïbes, [1986] 71 p. : ill. ; 21 cm. (Collection Esotérisme et magie) ISBN 2-905317-02-7
1. Magic - West Indies. 2. Medicine, Magic, mystic and spagiric - West Indies. I. Title.
NYPL *[Sc D 89-274]*

CALUMNY. see LIBEL AND SLANDER.

Calvaire de Canaan. Sala-Molins, Louis. Le Code noir, ou, Le calvaire de Canaan /. Paris , c1987. 292 p. ; ISBN 2-13-039970-3 : DDC 346.4401/3 344.40613 19
KJV4534 .S25 1987 **NYPL** *[Sc D 88-136]*

Calvin, James. Greenfield, Eloise. Talk about a family /. New York , c1978. 60 p. : ISBN 0-590-42247-2 **NYPL** *[Sc C 89-79]*

Calypso from France to Trinidad . Roaring Lion (Musician) San Juan [Trinidad and Tobago?] [between 1985 and 1988] 249 p. :
NYPL *[Sc D 88-894]*

CALYPSO (MUSIC) - HISTORY AND CRITICISM.
Roaring Lion (Musician) Calypso from France to Trinidad . San Juan [Trinidad and Tobago?] [between 1985 and 1988] 249 p. :
NYPL *[Sc D 88-894]*

Camargo, Oswaldo de, 1936-
O negro escrito : apontamentos sobre a presença do negro na literatura brasileira / Oswaldo de Camargo. [São Paulo : Secretaria de Estado da Cultura, Assessoria de Cultura Afro-Brasileira], 1987. 214 p. : ill., ports. 24 cm. Includes bibliographies and index. DDC 869/.09/896081 19
1. Brazilian literature - Black authors - History and criticism. I. Title.
PQ9523.B57 C36 1987 **NYPL** *[Sc D 89-608]*

A Razão da chama . São Paulo , 1986. xii, 122 p. ; **NYPL** *[Sc D 89-462]*

Cambridge African monograph .
(io) Brown, Winifred. Marriage, divorce and inheritance . Cambridge , 1988. vii,91 p. ; ISBN 0-902993-23-2 (pbk) : DDC 346.76/106134/0880655 19
NYPL *[Sc D 88-1350]*

(no. 11) Fox, Christine. Asante brass casting .

Cambridge , 1988. xii, 112 p. : ISBN 0-902993-24-0 (pbk) DDC 739.2/27667 19
NYPL *[Sc D 88-1434]*

The Cambridge encyclopedia of the Middle East and North Africa / executive editor, Trevor Mostyn ; advisory editor, Albert Hourani. Cambridge [England] ; New York : Cambridge University Press, 1988. 504 p. : ill. (some col.), maps ; 27 cm. Map on lining papers. Includes bibliographies and index. ISBN 0-521-32190-5 DDC 956 19
1. Middle East - Dictionaries and encyclopedias. 2. Africa, North - Dictionaries and encyclopedias. I. Mostyn, Trevor. II. Hourani, Albert Habib.
DS44 .C37 1988 **NYPL** *[*R-BCF 89-551]*

Cambridge, Mass. Harvard University. see Harvard University.

Cameron, Ann, 1943-
Julian, secret agent / by Ann Cameron ; illustrated by Diane Allison. New York : Random House, 1988. 62 p. : ill. ; 20 cm. (A Stepping stone book) When Julian, his little brother Huey, and their friend Gloria decide to "crime busters," they find themselves in one adventure after another. SCHOMBURG CHILDREN'S COLLECTION. ISBN 0-394-91949-1 (lib. bdg.) : DDC [Fic] 19
1. Afro-American children - Juvenile fiction. I. Allison, Diane Worfolk, ill. II. Schomburg Children's Collection. III. Title.
PZ7.C1427 Jt 1988 **NYPL** *[Sc C 89-123]*

Julian's glorious summer / by Ann Cameron ; illustrated by Dora Leder. New York : Random House, c1987. 62 p. : ill. ; 20 cm. (A Stepping stone book) When his best friend, Gloria, receives a new bike, seven-year-old Julian spends the summer avoiding her because of his fear of bikes. SCHOMBURG CHILDREN'S COLLECTION. ISBN 0-394-89117-1 (pbk.) : DDC [Fic] 19
1. Afro-American children - Juvenile fiction. I. Leder, Dora, ill. II. Schomburg Children's Collection. III. Title.
PZ7.C1427 Ju 1987 **NYPL** *[Sc C 89-99]*

The stories Julian tells / by Ann Cameron ; illustrated by Ann Strugnell. 1st ed. New York : A.A. Knopf, c1987, c1981. 71 p. : ill. ; 22 cm. (Bullseye books) Relates episodes in seven-year-old Julian's life which include getting into trouble with his younger brother Huey, planting a garden, what he did to try to grow taller, losing a tooth, and finding a new friend. SCHOMBURG CHILDREN'S COLLECTION. ISBN 0-394-82892-5
1. Afro-American children - Juvenile fiction. I. Strugnell, Ann. II. Schomburg Children's Collection. III. Title. **NYPL** *[Sc C 89-93]*

CAMEROON - BIBLIOGRAPHY.
Irele, Modupe. Nigeria and Cameroun . Lagos, Nigeria , c1984. viii, 67 p. : ISBN 978-237-205-6 (pbk.) DDC 016.327669067/11 19
Z3597 .I73 1984 DT515.63.C17 **NYPL** *[Sc E 87-30]*

CAMEROON - COURT AND COURTIERS - PICTORIAL WORKS.
Geary, Christraud M. Images from Bamum . Washington, D.C. , 1988. 151 p. : ISBN 0-87474-455-5 (pbk. : alk. paper) DDC 967/.1102/0880621 19
DT574 .G43 1988 **NYPL** *[Sc F 89-55]*

Cameroon. Dept. of Statistics and National Accounts. Enquête nationale sur la fécondité du Cameroun, 1978 . [Yaoundé] , 1983. 2 v. in 3 : DDC 304.6/32/0967113 19
HB1075.4.A3 E66 1983 **NYPL** *[Sc F 89-51]*

CAMEROON - DESCRIPTION AND TRAVEL.
Aarhaug, Aksel, 1921- Mitt Afrika /. Oslo , 1985. 104 p., [17] p. of plates : ISBN 82-531-4177-7 **NYPL** *[Sc E 88-149]*

Damay, Jean. Lettres du Nord-Cameroun /. Paris , c1985. 231 p. : ISBN 2-86537-121-2 **NYPL** *[Sc D 88-274]*

Cameroon. Direction de la statistique et de la comptabilité nationale. see Cameroon. Dept. of Statistics and National Accounts.

CAMEROON - FICTION.
Mokoso, Ndeley. Man pass man, and other stories /. Harlow, Essex , 1987. 108 p. : ISBN 0-582-01681-9 **NYPL** *[Sc C 88-225]*

Ngongwikwo, Joseph A. The lost child /. Limbé, S.W. Province, Cameroon [1986?] 76 p. : ISBN 978-250-304-5 **NYPL** *[Sc D 88-496]*

CAMEROON - HISTORY - COUP D'ÉTAT, 1984.
Gwellem, Jerome F. (Jerome Fultang) Paul Biya, hero of the New Deal /. Limbe, Cameroon [1984]. 68 p. :
NYPL *[Sc D 88-1255]*

CAMEROON - HISTORY - PICTORIAL WORKS.
Geary, Christraud M. Images from Bamum . Washington, D.C. , 1988. 151 p. : ISBN 0-87474-455-5 (pbk. : alk. paper) DDC 967/.1102/0880621 19
DT574 .G43 1988 **NYPL** *[Sc F 89-55]*

CAMEROON - LANGUAGES.
Situation linguistique en Afrique centrale . Paris , Yaoundé , 1983. 475 p. :
NYPL *[Sc F 88-153]*

CAMEROON - LANGUAGES - MAPS.
Situation linguistique en Afrique centrale . Paris , Yaoundé , 1983. 475 p. :
NYPL *[Sc F 88-153]*

CAMEROON LITERATURE (FRENCH) - HISTORY AND CRITICISM.
John, Elerius Edet. Topics in African literature /. Lagos , 1986. 3 v. ; ISBN 978-244-610-6 (v. 1)
NYPL *[Sc D 89-370]*

Cameroon National Union. Paul Biya . Bamenda , 1985. 103 leaves : **NYPL** *[Sc D 89-278]*

CAMEROON - POLITICS AND GOVERNMENT - 1960-
Eteki-Otabela, Marie-Louise, 1947- Misère et grandeur de la démocratie au Cameroun /. Paris , c1987. 143 p. ; ISBN 2-85802-929-6
NYPL *[Sc D 88-910]*

CAMEROON - POLITICS AND GOVERNMENT - 1982-
Gwellem, Jerome F. (Jerome Fultang) Paul Biya, hero of the New Deal /. Limbe, Cameroon [1984]. 68 p. :
NYPL *[Sc D 88-1255]*

Paul Biya . Bamenda , 1985. 103 leaves :
NYPL *[Sc D 89-278]*

CAMEROON - PRESIDENTS - BIOGRAPHY.
Paul Biya . Bamenda , 1985. 103 leaves :
NYPL *[Sc D 89-278]*

Cameroon. Regional Statistical Service. Dept. of Statistics and National Accounts. see Cameroon. Dept. of Statistics and National Accounts.

CAMEROON - RELATIONS (GENERAL) WITH FRANCE.
Makanda Duc d'Ikoga, André. Non, Monsieur Giscard [microform] /. Paris [1980] 23 p. ;
NYPL *[Sc Micro F-11014]*

CAMEROON - RELATIONS - NIGERIA - BIBLIOGRAPHY.
Irele, Modupe. Nigeria and Cameroun . Lagos, Nigeria , c1984. viii, 67 p. : ISBN 978-237-205-6 (pbk.) DDC 016.327669067/11 19
Z3597 .I73 1984 DT515.63.C17 **NYPL** *[Sc E 87-30]*

CAMEROON - SOCIAL CONDITIONS.
Franqueville, André. Une Afrique entre le village et la ville . Paris . 646 p. : ISBN 2-7099-0805-0 **NYPL** *[Sc E 88-325]*

CAMEROON - SOCIAL LIFE AND CUSTOMS.
Aarhaug, Aksel, 1921- Mitt Afrika /. Oslo , 1985. 104 p., [17] p. of plates : ISBN 82-531-4177-7 **NYPL** *[Sc E 88-149]*

Cameroon. Statistics and National Accounts, Dept. of. see Cameroon. Dept. of Statistics and National Accounts.

Cameroon. Statistique et de la comptabilité nationale, Direction de la. see Cameroon. Dept. of Statistics and National Accounts.

CAMEROUN - FICTION.
Kayo, Patrice. Les sauterelles . Yaoundé , 1986. 79 p. ; **NYPL** *[Sc D 88-180]*

Mongo, Pabe, 1948- L'Homme de la rue . Paris , 1987. 168 p. ; ISBN 2-218-07767-1
NYPL *[Sc C 88-5]*

Camourade . Laraque, Paul, 1920- Willimantic, CT , New York, NY , 1988. 124 p. ; ISBN 0-915306-71-9 **NYPL** *[Sc D 88-629]*

Campaign Against the Namibian Uranium Contracts (Group) Namibia -- a contract to kill : the story of stolen uranium and the British nuclear programme / the Campaign Against the Namibian Uranium Contracts. London : AON Publications, 1986. 80 p. : ill. ; 21 cm. Bibliography: p. 80. ISBN 0-947905-02-2
1. Uranium industry - Namibia. 2. Uranium industry - Great Britain. I. Title. *NYPL [Sc D 88-795]*

CAMPAIGN FUNDS - NIGERIA.
Labode, Sakirudeen Tunji. Party power . Abeokuta, Nigeria , 1988. 244 p. ; ISBN 978-18-3008-5 *NYPL [Sc C 88-376]*

CAMPAIGN LITERATURE, 1860 - REPUBLICAN.
Bingham, John Armor, 1815-1900. Bill and report of John A. Bingham. [Washington, D.C. , 1860] 7, [1] p. ; *NYPL [Sc Rare C 89-2]*

CAMPAIGNS, PRESIDENTIAL. see PRESIDENTS - UNITED STATES - ELECTION.

CAMPBELL, BERTHA PITTS.
Hill, Pauline Anderson Simmons. Too young to be old . Seattle, Washington , c1981. xiv, 58 p. : ISBN 0-89716-098-3 *NYPL [Sc D 88-1214]*

Campbell, James, 1951- New Edinburgh review anthology /. Edinburgh , 1982. 203 p. ; ISBN 0-904919-56-0 : DDC 082 19
AC5 .N37 1982 *NYPL [Sc D 88-1056]*

Campbell, Paul. America needs an ideology / by Paul Campbell and Peter Howard. London : F. Muller, 1957. 184 p. ; 20 cm.650 DDC 179 170
1. Moral rearmament. I. Title.
BJlo.Mb C29 *NYPL [Sc C 87-467]*

Campos da violência . Lara, Silvia Hunold. Rio de Janeiro , c1988. 389 p. ; *NYPL [Sc D 89-13]*

CAMPUS DISORDERS. see STUDENT MOVEMENTS.

CANADA - CHURCH HISTORY.
Shreve, Dorothy Shadd. The AfriCanadian church . Jordan Station, Ontario, Canada , c1983. 138 p. : ISBN 0-88815-072-5 (pbk.) DDC 277.1/008996 19
BR570 .S53 1983 *NYPL [Sc D 86-305]*

CANADA - RELATIONS (GENERAL) WITH SOUTHERN AFRICA.
Brown, Alex. Southern Africa. Ottawa [1973] 43 p.
DT746 .B76 *NYPL [JLD 75-1128]*

Window series. see Window series.

CANADIAN LITERATURE - BLACK AUTHORS.
A Shapely fire . Oakville, Ont. , c1987. 175 p. : ISBN 0-88962-345-7 *NYPL [Sc E 88-263]*

Canadian review of studies in nationalism . (v. 6) Herod, Agustina. Afro-American nationalism . New York , 1986. xvi, 272 p. ; ISBN 0-8240-9813-7 (alk. paper) DDC 016.3058/96073 19
Z1361.N39 H47 1986 E185.625 *NYPL [Sc D 87-1338]*

(vol. 6) Herod, Agustina. Afro-American nationalism . New York , 1986. xvi, 272 p. ; ISBN 0-8240-9813-7 (alk. paper) DDC 016.3058/96073 19
Z1361.N39 H47 1986 E185.625 *NYPL [Sc D 87-1338]*

Canadian Sickle Cell Society. Huntsman, Richard G. (Richard George) Sickle-cell anemia and thalassemia . [St. John's, Newfoundland, Canada , c1987] xv, 223 p. : ISBN 0-921037-00-7 (pbk.) : *NYPL [Sc C 88-84]*

Canale, Jean Suret- see **Suret-Canale, Jean.**

CANCER - PSYCHOLOGICAL ASPECTS.
EVAXX. Black Americans' attitudes toward cancer and cancer tests /. [New York], 1981. 1 v. (various pagings) ; *NYPL [Sc F 88-293]*

Candelario Obeso y la iniciación de la poesía negra en Colombia /. Prescott, Laurence E. (Laurence Emmanuel) Bogota , 1985. 228 p., [17] leaves of plates : *NYPL [JFE 87-5694]*

Candomblé : desvendando identidades : novos escritos sobre a religião dos orixás / Carlos Eugênio Marcondes de Moura, organizador ; Beatriz Góis Dantas ... [et al.]1a edição. São Paulo : EMW Editores, 1987. 168 p. ; 21 cm.

Bibliography: p. 152-168.
1. Brazil - Religious life and customs. I. Moura, Carlos Eugênio Marcondes de. *NYPL [Sc D 88-177]*

Candomblé . Lody, Raul Giovanni da Motta. São Paulo , 1987. 85 p. ; ISBN 85-08-01877-0 *NYPL [Sc C 88-62]*

Canny, Nicholas P. Colonial identity in the Atlantic world, 1500-1800 /. Princeton, N.J. , c1987. xi, 290 p. ; ISBN 0-691-05372-3 (alk. paper) : DDC 909/.09812 19
E18.82 .C64 1987 *NYPL [HAB 87-3215]*

CANON (LITERATURE)
Bishop, Rand. African literature, African critics . New York , 1988. xii, 213 p. ; ISBN 0-313-25918-6 (lib. bdg. : alk. paper) DDC 820/.9/96 19
PR9340 .B5 1988 *NYPL [Sc E 89-129]*

A Gift of tongues . Athens , c1987. xii, 342 p. ; ISBN 0-8203-0952-4 (alk. paper) DDC 811/.5/09920693 19
PS153.M56 G54 1987 *NYPL [Sc E 88-364]*

Cant, Bob. Radical records . London , New York , 1988. xi, 266 p. ; ISBN 0-415-00200-1 DDC 306.7/66/0941 19
HQ76.8.G7 R33 1988 *NYPL [JLD 88-1427]*

Can't quit you, baby /. Douglas, Ellen, 1921- New York , 1988. 256 p. ; ISBN 0-689-11793-0 DDC 813/.54 19
PS3554.O825 C3 1988 *NYPL [JFD 88-11335]*

Cantico barroco /. Abranches, Henrique. Lisboa, Portugal , c1987. 53 p. : *NYPL [Sc C 88-322]*

Canto do amor natural /. Santos, Marcelino dos. [Maputo?] [1987?] 160 p. ; *NYPL [Sc D 88-518]*

A cantomeric analysis of three Afro-American songs recorded in the Commerce, Texas, area [microform] /. Pearson, Boyce Neal. 1978. 47 leaves. *NYPL [Sc Micro R-4701]*

CAP-HAÏTIEN, HAITI - HISTORY.
Péan, Marc. L'échec du firminisme /. Port-au-Prince, Haiti , 1987. 181 p. : *NYPL [Sc D 88-625]*

CAPE TOWN IN ART.
De Meillon, Henry Clifford. Cape views and costumes . Johannesburg , 1978. 134 p. : ISBN 0-909079-05-6 : DDC 759.968
ND2088.6.S6 D452 1978 *NYPL [Sc F 85-112]*

CAPE TOWN (SOUTH AFRICA) - FICTION.
Wicomb, Zoë. You can't get lost in Cape Town /. New York , c1987. 185 p. ; ISBN 0-394-56030-2 : DDC 823 19
PR9369.3.W53 Y6 1987 *NYPL [Sc D 88-341]*

Cape Town. University of Cape Town. School of African Studies. Communications, new ser.
(no. 23) Bernardi, Bernardo. The social structure of the kraal among the Zezuru in Musami (Southern Rhodesia) [Cape Town] 1950. [2], 60, [1] . DDC 572.9689
GN490 .B4 *NYPL [Sc F 88-349]*

CAPE VERDE - BIBLIOGRAPHY.
Lobban, Richard. Historical dictionary of the Republic of Cape Verde /. Metuchen, N.J. , 1988. xix, 171 p. ; ISBN 0-8108-2087-0 DDC 966/.57/00321 19
DT613.5 .L62 1988b *NYPL [Sc D 88-1311]*

CAPE VERDE - ECONOMIC CONDITIONS.
Pina, Marie-Paule de. Les Iles du Cap-Vert /. Paris , c1987. 216, [1] p., [12] p. of plates ; ISBN 2-86507-182-4 *NYPL [Sc D 88-510]*

CAPE VERDE - FICTION.
Lopes da Silva, Baltasar, 1907- Os trabalhos e os dias /. Praia, Cabo Verde , 1987. 83 p. : *NYPL [Sc D 88-1500]*

Lopes, Manuel. Os flagelados do vento leste /. Lisboa , c1985. 216 p. ; *NYPL [Sc D 88-1387]*

Veiga, Manuel. Oju d'agu /. Praia , c1987. 229 p. ; *NYPL [Sc D 88-1413]*

CAPE VERDE - HISTORY - 20TH CENTURY.
Romero, Vicente, 1947- Guinea-Bissau y Cabo Verde . Madrid , 1981. 109 p. ; ISBN 84-85761-09-X DDC 966/.5702 19
DT613.78 .R66 1981 *NYPL [Sc C 89-1]*

CAPE VERDE - HISTORY - DICTIONARIES.
Lobban, Richard. Historical dictionary of the Republic of Cape Verde /. Metuchen, N.J. , 1988. xix, 171 p. ; ISBN 0-8108-2087-0 DDC 966/.57/00321 19
DT613.5 .L62 1988b *NYPL [Sc D 88-1311]*

CAPE VERDE - POLITICS AND GOVERNMENT - TO 1975 - COLLECTED WORKS.
Cabral, Amílcar, 1921-1973. Unité et lutte /. Paris , 1980. 329 p. ; ISBN 2-7071-1171-6 *NYPL [Sc C 88-125]*

CAPE VERDE - POLITICS AND GOVERNMENT - 1975-
Pina, Marie-Paule de. Les Iles du Cap-Vert /. Paris , c1987. 216, [1] p., [12] of plates ; ISBN 2-86507-182-4 *NYPL [Sc D 88-510]*

CAPE VERDE - SOCIAL CONDITIONS.
Pina, Marie-Paule de. Les Iles du Cap-Vert /. Paris , c1987. 216, [1] p., [12] p. of plates ; ISBN 2-86507-182-4 *NYPL [Sc D 88-510]*

Cape views and costumes . De Meillon, Henry Clifford. Johannesburg , 1978. 134 p. : ISBN 0-909079-05-6 : DDC 759.968
ND2088.6.S6 D452 1978 *NYPL [Sc F 85-112]*

CAPITAL ACCUMULATION. see SAVING AND INVESTMENT.

CAPITAL AND LABOR. see INDUSTRIAL RELATIONS.

CAPITAL EXPORTS. see INVESTMENTS, FOREIGN.

CAPITAL FORMATION. see SAVING AND INVESTMENT.

CAPITAL IMPORTS. see INVESTMENTS, FOREIGN.

CAPITAL PUNISHMENT - UNITED STATES.
Gross, Samuel R. Death & discrimination . Boston , c1989. xvi, 268 p. ; ISBN 1-555-53040-0 (alk. paper) : DDC 364.6/6/0973 19
HV8699.U5 G76 1989 *NYPL [Sc D 89-493]*

White, Welsh S., 1940- The death penalty in the eighties . Ann Arbor , c1987. 198 p. ; ISBN 0-472-10088-2 (alk. paper) : DDC 345.73/0773 347.305773 19
KF9227.C2 W44 1987 *NYPL [Sc E 88-129]*

CAPITALISM.
Harris, Abram Lincoln, 1899-1963. Race, radicalism, and reform . New Brunswick, U.S.A. , c1989. viii, 521 p. ; ISBN 0-88738-210-X DDC 305.8/96073 19
E185.8 .H27 1989 *NYPL [Sc E 89-166]*

CAPITALISM - AFRICA.
Kennedy, Paul M., 1945- African capitalism . Cambridge, Cambridgeshire , New York , 1988. x, 233 p. ; ISBN 0-521-26599-1 DDC 332/.041/096 19
HC800 .K46 1988 *NYPL [Sc E 88-520]*

Capitalism and antislavery . Drescher, Seymour. New York , 1987, c1986. xv, 300 p. ; ISBN 0-19-520534-0 (alk. paper) DDC 326/.0941 19
HT1163 .D74 1987 *NYPL [Sc D 89-29]*

CAPITALISM - BRAZIL.
Kowarick, Lúcio. Trabalho e vadiagem . São Paulo , 1987. 133 p. ; *NYPL [Sc D 88-784]*

CAPITALISM - GREAT BRITAIN.
Drescher, Seymour. Capitalism and antislavery . New York , 1987, c1986. xv, 300 p. ; ISBN 0-19-520534-0 (alk. paper) DDC 326/.0941 19
HT1163 .D74 1987 *NYPL [Sc D 89-29]*

CAPITOL PUNISHMENT - JAMAICA.
Jamaica, the death penalty. London , 1989. iii, 85 p. ; *NYPL [Sc F 89-164]*

Caplan, Patricia. The Cultural construction of sexuality /. London , New York , 1987. xi, 304 p. : ISBN 0-416-60870-X DDC 306.7 19
GN484.3 .C85 1987 *NYPL [Sc D 87-1198]*

Caprile, Jean Pierre. Préalables à la reconstruction du proto-tchadique . Paris , 1978. 210 p. ; ISBN 2-85297-022-8 DDC 493/.7 19
PL8026.C53 P73 1978 *NYPL [Sc E 88-418]*

Captains of the sands /. Amado, Jorge, 1912- [Capitães da areia. English.] New York, N.Y. , c1988. 248 p. ; ISBN 0-380-89718-0 (pbk.) :

DDC 869.3 19
PQ9697.A647 C373 1988
                    NYPL [Sc D 89-198]

CARAF books.
Bhêly-Quénum, Olympe. [Piège sans fin.
English.] Snares without end /. Charlottesville ,
1988. xxvi, 204 p. ; ISBN 0-8139-1189-3 (pbk.)
DDC 843 19
PQ3989.2.B5 P513 1988
                    NYPL [Sc D 89-434]

Faces of African independence .
Charlottesville , 1988. xxxvi, 127 p. ; ISBN
0-8139-1186-9 DDC 842 19
PQ3987.5.E5 F33 1988   NYPL [Sc D 89-32]

Card, Orson Scott.
Prentice Alvin / Orson Scott Card. 1st ed. New
York, NY : TOR, 1989. x, 342 p. : maps ; 25
cm. (The Tales of Alvin Maker . 3) "A Tor book"--T.p.
verso. "A Tom Doherty Associates book." Maps on
lining papers. ISBN 0-312-93141-7 : DDC 813/.54
19
*1. Slavery - United States - Fiction. I. Series: Card,
Orson Scott. Tales of Alvin Maker , bk. 3. II. Title.*
PS3553.A655 P74 1989
                    NYPL [JFE 88-3128]

Tales of Alvin Maker .
(bk. 3) Card, Orson Scott. Prentice Alvin /.
New York, NY , 1989. x, 342 p. : ISBN
0-312-93141-7 : DDC 813/.54 19
PS3553.A655 P74 1989
                    NYPL [JFE 88-3128]

Cardoso, Ciro Flamarion Santana. Escravo ou
Camponês? : O protocampesinato negro nas
Américas / Ciro Flamarion S. Cardoso. São
Paulo : Editora Brasiliense, 1987. 125 p. ; 21
cm. Includes bibliographical footnotes.
1. Slavery - America - Condition of slaves. I. Title.
                    NYPL [Sc D 88-793]

**CARE OF SOULS. see PASTORAL
    COUNSELING.**

A career in medical research. Colman, Hila.
Cleveland [1968] 175 p. DDC 610.7
R690 .C65   *NYPL [Sc D 88-425]*

**CAREERS. see PROFESSIONS;
    VOCATIONAL GUIDANCE.**

Careers in the making series.
Colman, Hila. A career in medical research.
Cleveland [1968] 175 p. DDC 610.7
R690 .C65   *NYPL [Sc D 88-425]*

**CARIB INDIANS - SOCIAL LIFE AND
    CUSTOMS.**
Un Flibustier français dans la mer des Antilles
en 1618-1620 /. Clamart [France] , c1987. 263
p. : ISBN 2-9502053-0-5 *NYPL [Sc E 88-247]*

The Caribbean /. James, Winston. London , 1984.
46 p. : ISBN 0-356-07105-7 : DDC 972.9 19
F2175   *NYPL [Sc F 88-128]*

CARIBBEAN AREA.
The Modern Caribbean /. Chapel Hill , c1989.
x, 382 p. : ISBN 0-8078-1825-9 (alk. paper) DDC
972.9 19
F2156 .M63 1989   *NYPL [Sc E 89-253]*

CARIBBEAN AREA - BIBLIOGRAPHY.
Baa, Enid M. Theses on Caribbean topics,
1778-1968. San Juan, 1970. v, 146 p.
Z1501 .C33 no. 1 NYPL [JFL 74-576 no. 1]

**CARIBBEAN AREA - BIBLIOGRAPHY -
    CATALOGS.**
Miami, University of, Coral Gables, Fla. Cuban
and Caribbean Library. Catalog of the Cuban
and Caribbean Library, University of Miami,
Coral Gables, Florida. Boston , 1977. 6 v. ;
DDC 016.9729
Z1595 .M5 1977 F2161
                    NYPL [Pub. Cat. 78-1036]

**CARIBBEAN AREA - CIVILIZATION -
    AFRICAN INFLUENCES.**
Ifill, Max B. The African diaspora .
Port-of-Spain, Trinidad , 1986. vii, 118 p. :
ISBN 976-8008-00-8 (pbk) DDC 382/.44/09729
19
HT1072 .I35 1986   NYPL [Sc D 88-934]

**CARIBBEAN AREA - DESCRIPTION AND
    TRAVEL - 1981-**
Johnson, Amryl. Sequins for a ragged hem. /.
London , c1988. 272 p. ; ISBN 0-86068-971-9
                    NYPL [Sc D 88-612]

**CARIBBEAN AREA - DESCRIPTION AND
    TRAVEL - 1981- - GUIDE-BOOKS.**

Runge, Jonathan. Rum and reggae . New
York , c1988. ix, 227 p. : ISBN 0-312-01509-7
(pbk.) : DDC 917.29/0452 19
F1613 .R86 1988   NYPL [Sc D 88-1217]
Showker, Kay. Caribbean ports of call . Chester,
Conn. , 1987. xviii, 505 p. : ISBN 0-87106-776-5
(pbk.) DDC 917.29/0452 19
F2171.3 .S455 1987   NYPL [Sc D 89-323]

**CARIBBEAN AREA - ECONOMIC
    CONDITIONS.**
Rural development in the Caribbean /.
London , 1985. xxi, 246 p. : ISBN 0-312-69599-3
                    NYPL [Sc D 88-1309]
Ward, J. R. Poverty and progress in the
Caribbean, 1800-1960 /. Houndmills,
Basingstoke, Hampshire , 1985. 82 p. : ISBN
0-333-37212-3 (pbk.) DDC 330.9729 19
HC151 .W37 1985   NYPL [JLD 86-2144]

**CARIBBEAN AREA - ECONOMIC
    CONDITIONS - 1945- - CONGRESSES.**
Crises in the Caribbean basin . Beverly Hills
[Calif.] , c1987. 263 p. ; ISBN 0-8039-2808-4
DDC 330.9729 19
HC151 .C75 1986   NYPL [JLD 87-3555]

**CARIBBEAN AREA - ECONOMIC POLICY -
    CASE STUDIES.**
Thomas, Clive Yolande. The poor and the
powerless . New York , 1988. xv, 396 p. ;
ISBN 0-85345-743-3 : DDC 338.9/009729 19
HC151 .T56 1988   NYPL [Sc D 88-763]

**CARIBBEAN AREA - EMIGRATION AND
    IMMIGRATION.**
The Caribbean exodus /. New York , 1987. vii,
293 p. ; ISBN 0-275-92182-4 (alk. paper) : DDC
325.729 19
JV7321 .C37 1986   NYPL [JLE 87-1789]

**CARIBBEAN AREA - EMIGRATION AND
    IMMIGRATION - ADDRESSES, ESSAYS,
    LECTURES.**
Contemporary Caribbean . [St. Augustine,
Trinidad and Tobago?] , 1981-<1982 >
(Maracas, Trinidad and Tobago, West Indies :
College Press) v. : DDC 304.6/09729 19
HB3545 .C66 1981   NYPL [Sc D 89-499]

CARIBBEAN AREA - FICTION.
Duncan, Jane. My friend the swallow. London,
New York, 1970. 255 p. ISBN 0-333-11677-1
DDC 823/.9/14
PZ4.D9116 Mwk PR6054.U46
                    NYPL [Sc D 88-1115]

**CARIBBEAN AREA - FOREIGN
    RELATIONS - 1945-**
Ashby, Timothy. The bear in the back yard .
Lexington, Mass. , c1987. xii, 240 p. : ISBN
0-669-14768-0 (alk. paper) DDC 327.470729 19
F2178.S65 A84 1987   NYPL [HNB 87-1399]

**CARIBBEAN AREA - FOREIGN
    RELATIONS - SOVIET UNION.**
Ashby, Timothy. The bear in the back yard .
Lexington, Mass. , c1987. xii, 240 p. : ISBN
0-669-14768-0 (alk. paper) DDC 327.470729 19
F2178.S65 A84 1987   NYPL [HNB 87-1399]

Caribbean area - Government. see Caribbean
    Area - Politics and government.

**CARIBBEAN AREA - HISTORY -
    TEXTBOOKS.**
Hall, Douglas. The Caribbean experience .
Kingston , 1982. xi, 146 p. : ISBN 0-435-98300-8
                    NYPL [Sc E 87-670]

Caribbean area - Immigration. see Caribbean
    area - Emigration and immigration.

CARIBBEAN AREA - JUVENILE FICTION.
Owen, Ruth Bryan, 1885- Caribbean caravel.
New York, 1949. viii, 222 p.
PZ7.O972 Car   NYPL [Sc D 88-426]

**CARIBBEAN AREA - POLITICS AND
    GOVERNMENT - 1945-**
Moore, Richard B. (Richard Benjamin) Richard
B. Moore, Caribbean militant in Harlem .
Bloomington, London , 1988. ix, 324 p. :
ISBN 0-253-31299-0 DDC 970.004/96 19
F2183 .M66 1988   NYPL [Sc E 89-148]

**CARIBBEAN AREA - POLITICS AND
    GOVERNMENT - 1945- - CONGRESSES.**
Crises in the Caribbean basin . Beverly Hills
[Calif.] , c1987. 263 p. ; ISBN 0-8039-2808-4
DDC 330.9729 19
HC151 .C75 1986   NYPL [JLD 87-3555]

**CARIBBEAN AREA - POPULATION -
    ADDRESSES, ESSAYS, LECTURES.**
Contemporary Caribbean . [St. Augustine,
Trinidad and Tobago?] , 1981-<1982 >
(Maracas, Trinidad and Tobago, West Indies :
College Press) v. : DDC 304.6/09729 19
HB3545 .C66 1981   NYPL [Sc D 89-499]

**CARIBBEAN AREA - RACE RELATIONS -
    CASE STUDIES.**
Smith, M. G. (Michael Garfield) Culture race
and class in the commonwealth Caribbean /.
Mona, Jamaica , 1984. xiv, 163 p. ; ISBN
976-616-000-7   *NYPL [Sc D 88-454]*

**CARIBBEAN AREA - SOCIAL LIFE AND
    CUSTOMS.**
Brereton, Bridget. Social life in the Caribbean,
1838-1938 /. London , 1985. 65 p. : ISBN
0-435-98305-9 (pbk) DDC 909/.09821 19
F2169   *NYPL [Sc D 88-1307]*

Caribbean bibliographic series.
(no. 1 1) Baa, Enid M. Theses on Caribbean
topics, 1778-1968. San Juan, 1970. v, 146 p.
Z1501 .C33 no. 1   NYPL [JFL 74-576 no. 1]

Caribbean caravel. Owen, Ruth Bryan, 1885-
New York, 1949. viii, 222 p.
PZ7.O972 Car   NYPL [Sc D 88-426]

Caribbean certificate history .
(2) Greenwood, R. (Robert) Emancipation to
emigration /. London , New York , 1980 (1985
printing) viii, 152 p. : ISBN 0-333-28148-9 (pbk.)
DDC 972.9 19
F1621 .G74 1984   NYPL [Sc E 88-526]

The Caribbean connection . Ho, Christine G. T.
c1985. xvi, 290 leaves : *NYPL [Sc F 88-234]*

The Caribbean exodus / edited by Barry B.
Levine. New York : Praeger, 1987. vii, 293 p. ;
25 cm. Includes bibliographical references and index.
ISBN 0-275-92182-4 (alk. paper) : DDC 325.729
19
*1. Caribbean area - Emigration and immigration. 2.
United States - Emigration and immigration -
Government policy. I. Levine, Barry B., 1941-.*
JV7321 .C37 1986   NYPL [JLE 87-1789]

The Caribbean experience . Hall, Douglas.
Kingston , 1982. xi, 146 p. : ISBN 0-435-98300-8
                    NYPL [Sc E 87-670]

Caribbean festival arts . Nunley, John W. (John
Wallace), 1945- [Saint Louis] , 1988. 218 p. :
ISBN 0-295-96702-1 : DDC 394.2/5/07409729
19
GT4823 .N85 1988   NYPL [Sc F 89-89]

Caribbean focus series.
Kirby, Richard, 1958. Ewto' . London , c1985.
27 p. : ISBN 0-946140-24-3 (pbk) : DDC 307.7/72
19
F2380   *NYPL [Sc F 89-104]*

Caribbean guides.
Taylor, Jeremy, 1943- Masquerade . London ,
1986. v, 135 p. : ISBN 0-333-41985-5 (pbk) :
DDC 917.298/3044 19
F2122   *NYPL [Sc D 88-837]*

Caribbean Islands. see West Indies.

**CARIBBEAN LITERATURE (ENGLISH) -
    HISTORY AND CRITICISM.**
Birbalsingh, Frank. Passion and exile . London ,
1988. 186 p. ; ISBN 1-87051-816-0 (pbk) : DDC
810.9/91821 19   *NYPL [JFD 89-183]*

**CARIBBEAN LITERATURE - HISTORY AND
    CRITICISM.**
Saakana, Amon Saba, 1948- The colonial legacy
in Caribbean literature, Vol. I /. London , 1987.
128 p., [7] p. of plates : ISBN 0-907015-34-4
(pbk.) :   *NYPL [Sc D 88-1150]*

Caribbean man's blues /. Douglas, J. D., 1956-
London , 1985. 62 p. : ISBN 0-947638-04-0
(pbk) DDC 821/.914 19
PR6054.O83   NYPL [Sc E 88-462]

**Caribbean minorities in Britain and the
    Netherlands.** Lost illusions . London , 1988. x,
316 p. : ISBN 0-415-00628-7
                    NYPL [Sc D 88-1300]

Caribbean monograph series.
(no. 14) Agosto de Muñoz, Nélida. El
fenómeno de la posesión en la religión Vudú .
Río Piedras, P.R. , 1975, c1974. 119 p. ; DDC
299/.64 19
*BL2490 .A33 1975   NYPL [TB (Caribbean
                    monograph series no. 14)]*

Caribbean pirates /. Alleyne, Warren, 1924-
London , 1986. v, 113 p. : ISBN 0-333-40570-6
(cased) : DDC 910.4/53 19
F2161   *NYPL [Sc D 88-448]*

CARIBBEAN POETRY (ENGLISH)
Flowers blooming late . Montserrat , 1984. 72
p. ; ISBN 976-8018-00-3 *NYPL [Sc D 89-559]*

Caribbean ports of call . Showker, Kay. Chester,
Conn. , 1987. xviii, 505 p. : ISBN 0-87106-776-5
(pbk.) DDC 917.29/0452 19
F2171.3 .S455 1987   *NYPL [Sc D 89-323]*

Caribbean recipes for schools /. Rigby, Alison.
Basingstoke , 1987. 100 p. ; ISBN 0-333-44682-8
(spiral) : DDC 641.59/1821 19
TX716.A1   *NYPL [Sc D 88-1013]*

Caribbean Technology Policy Studies Project.
Girvan, Norman, 1941- Technology policies for
small developing economies . Mona, Jamaica ,
c1983. 224 p. : DDC 338.9729 19
T24.A1 G57 1983   *NYPL [Sc E 88-260]*

**CARIBEAN LITERATURE (FRENCH) -
HISTORY AND CRITICISM.**
Oralitures et littératures africaines et
caribéennes. [Fort-de-France] [1985] 56 p. :
                NYPL [Sc F 89-93]

CARICATURE AND COMIC ART. see
CARICATURES AND CARTOONS.

**CARICATURES AND CARTOONS -
NIGERIA.**
Ajiboye, Josy. Romance of life /. Lagos,
Nigeria , 1985. 108 p. :
MLCS 87/7906 (P)   *NYPL [Sc C 89-85]*

Carlon, S. Jabaru. Ferns, George W. Secondary
level teachers: supply and demand in Liberia.
[East Lansing, c1970] xii, 116 p.
LB2833.4.L7 F4   *NYPL [JFM 72-62 no. 6]*

Carlos, Christopher. see **Charles, Christophe,
1951-**

Carlyle, Thomas, 1795-1881. Occasional discourse
on the Nigger question. Communicated by T.
Carlyle. London, T. Bosworth, 1853. 48 p. 18
cm. "First printed in Fraser's magazine (December,
1849); reprinted here, with some additions, and no
other change."
*1. Blacks - West Indies. 2. Slavery - West Indies. I.
Title.*
HT1091 .C47   *NYPL [Sc C 89-7]*

Carma, Jemel. Happy birthday everybody : a
nursery rhyme coloring book, for children,
teens & adults / [Pretty Fresh Pearlee Winkle ;
character created by Jemel Carma ; illus. by
Franco the Great and Jemel Carma]. New
York, N. Y. : Sole Power Publications, [1988]
[24] p. : ill. ; 44 cm. Cover title. SCHOMBURG
CHILDREN'S COLLECTION.
*1. Afro-American children - Juvenile poetry. 2.
Coloring books. I. Schomburg Children's Collection. II.
Title.*   *NYPL [Sc H 89-1]*

Carmines, Edward G. Issue evolution : race and
the transformation of American politics /
Edward G. Carmines, James A. Stimson.
Princeton, N.J. : Princeton University Press,
c1989. xvii, 217 p. : ill. ; 24 cm. Includes index.
Bibliography: p. 199-207. ISBN 0-691-07802-5 :
DDC 323.1/196073 19
*1. Afro-Americans - Politics and government. 2.
Voting - United States - History - 20th century. 3.
United States - Race relations - Political aspects. 4.
United States - Politics and government - 1945-. I.
Stimson, James A. II. Title.*
E185.615 .C35 1989   *NYPL [Sc E 89-214]*

Carmo, João C. (Kpāo Clodomiro) O que é
cadomblé / João C. Carmo. Sao Paulo : Editora
Brasiliense, 1987. 84, [1] p. : ill. ; 16 cm.
(Coleçõ Primeiros passos . 200) Author's name on
cover: João Clodomiro do Carmo. Bibliography: p. [85]
I. Title. II. Series.   *NYPL [Sc B 88-12]*

Carn, John, 1947- Stressed out : a novel / by
John Benjamin Carn. Indianapolis, Ind. :
African American Visions Small Press, c1988.
vii, 148 p. ; 22 cm. ISBN 0-916967-03-4 :
1. Afro-Americans - Fiction. I. Title.
                NYPL [Sc D 89-423]

Carnaval, carnavais /. Meihy, José Carlos Sebe
Bom, 1943- São Paulo , 1986. 96 p. ; ISBN
85-08-01168-7 : DDC 394.2/5/0981 19
GT4180 .M45 1986   *NYPL [HFB 88-1339]*

Les carnets secrets d'une fille de joie . Ilboudo,
Patrick G. Burkina Faso , c1988. 189 p. ;
                NYPL [Sc C 88-356]

CARNIVAL.
Meihy, José Carlos Sebe Bom, 1943- Carnaval,
carnavais /. São Paulo , 1986. 96 p. ; ISBN
85-08-01168-7 : DDC 394.2/5/0981 19
GT4180 .M45 1986   *NYPL [HFB 88-1339]*

CARNIVAL - BRAZIL.
Meihy, José Carlos Sebe Bom, 1943- Carnaval,
carnavais /. São Paulo , 1986. 96 p. ; ISBN
85-08-01168-7 : DDC 394.2/5/0981 19
GT4180 .M45 1986   *NYPL [HFB 88-1339]*

CARNIVAL - BRAZIL - RIO DE JANEIRO.
Gonzalez, Lélia. Festas populares no Brasil =.
Rio de Janeiro, Brasil , c1987. 144 p. : ISBN
85-7083-015-7
GT4833.A2 G66x 1987 *NYPL [Sc F 89-116]*

**CARNIVAL - BRAZIL - RIO DE JANEIRO -
HISTORY.**
Eneida, 1903-1971. História do carnaval carioca
/. Rio de Janeiro , c1987. 259 p. : ISBN
85-10-29900-5
GT4233.R5 E53 1987   *NYPL [Sc D 89-313]*

**CARNIVAL - BRAZIL - RIO DE JANEIRO -
PICTORIAL WORKS.**
Gonzalez, Lélia. Festas populares no Brasil =.
Rio de Janeiro, Brasil , c1987. 144 p. : ISBN
85-7083-015-7
GT4833.A2 G66x 1987 *NYPL [Sc F 89-116]*

CARNIVAL - ENGLAND - LONDON.
Owusu, Kwesi. Behind the masquerade .
Edgware , 1988. 90 p. : ISBN 0-9512770-0-6
(pbk) : DDC 394.2/5/0942134 19
                NYPL [Sc E 88-497]

Caro, Edythe Quinn. "The Hills" in the
mid-nineteenth century : the history of a rural
Afro-American community in Westchester
County, New York / Edythe Quinn Caro.
Valhalla, New York : Westchester County
Historical Society, c1988. iii, 184 p. : ill.,
maps ; 28 cm. Bibliography: p. 179-184.
*1. Afro-Americans - New York (State) - Westchester
County - History. I. Westchester County Historical
Society. II. Title.*   *NYPL [Sc F 89-71]*

A Carolrhoda creative minds book.
Ferris, Jeri. Go free or die . Minneapolis ,
1987. 63 p. : ISBN 0-87614-317-6 (lib. bdg.) :
DDC 305.5/67/0924 B 92 19
E444.T82 F47 1987   *NYPL [Sc D 88-620]*

Ferris, Jeri. Walking the road to freedom .
Minneapolis , 1987. 64 p. : ISBN 0-87614-318-4
(lib. bdg.) : DDC 305.5/67/0924 B 92 19
E185.97.T8 F47 1987   *NYPL [Sc D 88-1046]*

Ferris, Jeri. What are you figuring now? .
Minneapolis , c1988. 64 p. : ISBN 0-87614-331-1
(lib. bdg.) : DDC 520.92/4 B 92 19
QB36.B22 F47 1988   *NYPL [Sc D 89-120]*

CARPETBAG RULE. see **RECONSTRUCTION.**

Carr-Hill, R. A. (Roy A.), 1943- Britain's Black
population . Aldershot, Hants, England ,
Brookfield, Vt., USA , c1988. xv, 298 p. ;
ISBN 0-566-05179-6 : DDC 305.8/96/041 19
DA125.N4 B75 1988   *NYPL [Sc E 89-100]*

Carroll, Vinnette. Grant, Micki. Croesus and the
witch /. New York, N.Y. , 1984. 67, [119] p. :
ISBN 0-88145-024-3   *NYPL [Sc F 88-205]*

**Cartas de Vindex ao Dr. Luiz Alvares dos
Santos.** Guimarães, Augusto Alvares.
Propaganda abolicionista . Bahia , 1875. 86 p. ;
                NYPL [Sc Rare G 86-33]

Carter, Dorothy Sharp. His Majesty, Queen
Hatshepsut / Dorothy Sharp Carter ; illustrated
by Michele Chessare. 1st ed. New York : J.B.
Lippincott, c1987. viii, 248 p. : ill. ; 22 cm. A
fictionalized account of the life of Hatshepsut, a queen
in ancient Egypt who declared herself king and ruled as
such for more than twenty years. ISBN
0-397-32178-3 : DDC [Fic] 19
*1. Hatshepsut, Queen of Egypt - Juvenile fiction. 2.
Egypt - Civilization - To 332 B.C. - Juvenile fiction. I.
Chessare, Michele. II. Title.*
PZ7.C2434 Hi 1987   *NYPL [Sc D 88-877]*

Carter, Judy. Malaŵi : wildlife, parks and
reserves / Judy Carter. London : Macmillan,
1987. 176 p. : ill. (some col.), maps ; 29 cm.
Includes index. Bibliography: p. 171-172. ISBN
0-333-43987-2 (cased) : DDC 916.897/044 19
1. National parks and reserves - Malawi. 2. Malawi -

Description and travel - Guide-books. I. Title.
DT858.2   *NYPL [Sc F 88-183]*

Cartey, Tom. Two women on the Hudson River /
by Tom Cartey. New York City : The Printed
Word, c1986. 414 p. ; 22 cm. Plays and poems.
Author's autographed presentation copy to the
Schomburg Center.
I. Title.   *NYPL [Sc D 88-754]*

Cartiér, Xam Wilson. Be-bop, re-bop / Xam
Wilson Cartiér. 1st ed. New York : Ballantine
Books, c1987. 147 p. ; 21 cm. ISBN
0-345-34833-8 (pbk.) :
1. Afro-Americans - Fiction. I. Title.
                NYPL [Sc D 88-716]

CARTOONS. see **CARICATURES AND
CARTOONS.**

Carty, Leo. (illus) Clymer, Eleanor (Lowenton)
1906- The house on the mountain. New York
[1971] 39 p. ISBN 0-525-32365-1 DDC [Fic]
PZ7.C6272 Ho   *NYPL [Sc D 88-445]*

Carty, Michel. Sous le masque de l'animal .
Paris , c1987. 380 p. : ISBN 2-13-039831-6
                NYPL [Sc E 88-314]

Carvalho, José Geraldo Vigidal de.
Igreja e a escravidão no Brasil. Balmes, Jaime
Luciano, 1810-1848. [Protestantismo
comparado con el catolicismo en sus
relaciones con la civilización europea.
Selections. Portuguese.] A Igreja católica em
face da escravidão / Jaime Balmes ; tradução
de José G. M. Orsini. São Paulo , 1988. 141
p. ;   *NYPL [Sc D 89-554]*

Casa de las Américas. Galería Latinoamericana.
Juan, Adalaida de. En la Galería
Latinoamericana /. La Habana , 1979. 203 p. :
                NYPL [3-MAM 88-2546]

**Casa-grande & senzala e a crítica brasileira de
1933 a 1944** / artigos reunidos e comentados
por Edson Nery da Fonseca. Recife :
Companhia Editora de Pernambuco, 1985. 309
p. ; 22 cm. (Serie Documentos. 22) Includes
bibliographical references and index. ISBN
85-7019-079-4 (pbk.) DDC 981/.00498 19
*1. Freyre, Gilberto, 1900- Casa-grande & senzala. 2.
Slavery - Brazil. 3. Indians of South America - Brazil.
4. Brazil - Social life and customs. I. Fonseca, Edson
Nery da. II. Title: Casa-grande e senzala e a crítica
brasileira de 1933 a 1944. III. Series: Brazil. Instituto
Joaquim Nabuco de Pesquisas Sociais. Série
documentos, 22.*
F2510.F7524 C37 1985
                NYPL [HFB 86-2252]

Casa-grande & sensala. Freyre, Gilberto, 1900-
[Casa-grande & senzala. English.] The masters
and the slaves =. Berkeley , c1986. xc, 537
xliv p., [3] p. of plates : ISBN 0-520-05665-5
(pbk. : alk. paper) DDC 981 19
F2510 .F7522 1986   *NYPL [HFB 87-2095]*

Casa-grande e senzala. Freyre, Gilberto, 1900-
[Casa-grande & senzala. English.] The masters
and the slaves =. Berkeley , c1986. xc, 537
xliv p., [3] p. of plates : ISBN 0-520-05665-5
(pbk. : alk. paper) DDC 981 19
F2510 .F7522 1986   *NYPL [HFB 87-2095]*

**Casa-grande e senzala e a crítica brasileira de
1933 a 1944.** Casa-grande & senzala e a crítica
brasileira de 1933 a 1944 /. Recife , 1985. 309
p. ; 85-7019-079-4 (pbk.) DDC 981/.00498
19
F2510.F7524 C37 1985
                NYPL [HFB 86-2252]

La Casamance ouvre ses cases . Scibilia, Muriel.
Paris , c1986. 171, [1] p., [8] p. of plates :
ISBN 2-85802-676-9 *NYPL [Sc D 89-170]*

**CASAMANCE (SENEGAL) - DESCRIPTION
AND TRAVEL.**
Scibilia, Muriel. La Casamance ouvre ses cases .
Paris , c1986. 171, [1] p., [8] p. of plates :
ISBN 2-85802-676-9 *NYPL [Sc D 89-170]*

Cascudo, Luís de Câmara, 1898- Locuções
tradicionais no Brasil : coisas que o povo diz /
Luís da Câmara Cascudo. Belo Horizonte :
Editora Itatiaia ; São Paulo : Editora da
Universidade de São Paulo, 1986. 314 p. :
port. ; 23 cm. (Coleção Reconquista do Brasil. 2a.
sér., vol. 93)
*1. Portuguese language - Idioms, corrections, errors. I.
Title. II. Title: Coisas que o povo diz. III. Series:
Coleção Reconquista do Brasil, nova sér., vol. 93.*
                NYPL [Sc D 87-923]

The casebook of Dr. O.P. Asem /. Wosornu,
Lade. Accra , 1985- v, ;   ISBN 996-472-044-0
NYPL [Sc C 89-91]

Casebook on Kenya customary law /. Cotran,
Eugene. Abingdon, Oxon. , 1987. xxviii, 348
p. ;   ISBN 0-86205-255-6   *NYPL [Sc E 89-179]*

The cashier and his rubber stamp /. Omobuarie,
D. O. Benin City, Nigeria , 1987. 79 p. ;   ISBN
978-300-321-6   *NYPL [Sc D 88-738]*

Casilla, Robert.
(ill) Adler, David A. Jackie Robinson . New
York , c1989. 48 p. :   ISBN 0-8234-0734-9 DDC
796.357/092/4 B 19
GV865 .A37 1989   *NYPL [Sc F 89-137]*

(ill) Howard, Elizabeth Fitzgerald. The train to
Lulu's /. New York , c1988. [32] p. :   ISBN
0-02-744620-4 :   DDC [E] 19
PZ7.H8327 Tr 1988   *NYPL [Sc F 88-219]*

Cassin-Scott, Jack. Watson, Philip J. Costume of
ancient Egypt /. New York , 1987. 64 p., [8] p.
of plates :   ISBN 1-555-46771-7 :   DDC 391/.00932
19
GT533 .W38 1987   *NYPL [Sc F 88-228]*

The cast-off restored. Fitts, Hervey. Abraham
Vest, or, The cast-off restored. Boston, 1847.
142 p.
T275.V55 F5 1847   NYPL [Sc Rare C 88-12]

CASTE - INDIA.
Rajshekar Shetty, V. T., 1932- Dalit, the black
Untouchables of India /. Atlanta, Ga. , c1987.
89 p. ;   ISBN 0-932863-05-1 (pbk.) :
NYPL [Sc D 89-356]

CASTE - NIGERIA.
Okeke, Igwebuike Romeo. The "Osu" concept in
Igboland . Enugu. [Nigeria] , 1986. xi, 167 p. :
ISBN 978-248-100-9   *NYPL [Sc E 88-302]*

Castellanos, Isabel, 1939-
Castellanos, Jorge. Cultura afrocubana /.
Miami, Fla. , U. S.A. , 1988- v. ;   ISBN
0-89729-462-9 (set)   DDC 972.91/00496 20
F1789.N3 C33 1988   *NYPL [Sc D 89-592]*

Elegua quiere tambó : cosmovisión religiosa
afrocubana en las canciones populares / Isabel
Castellanos. Cali, Colombia : Universidad del
Valle, 1983. 84 p. ; 22 cm. (Pliegos . 12)
Bibliography: p. 78-79. Discography: p. 80.
*1. Popular music - Cuba - Religious aspects. 2. Africa -
Religion - Influence. I. Title. II. Series.*
NYPL [Sc D 88-534]

Castellanos, Jorge. Cultura afrocubana / Jorge
Castellanos & Isabel Castellanos. Miami, Fla.,
U. S.A. : Ediciones Universal, 1988- v. ; 21 cm.
(Colección Ébano y canela) Includes index.
Bibliography: v. 1, p. 339-360. CONTENTS. - 1. El
negro en Cuba, 1492-1844   ISBN 0-89729-462-9 (set)
DDC 972.91/00496 20
*1. Blacks - Cuba - History. 2. Cuba - Civilization -
African influences. I. Castellanos, Isabel, 1939-. II.
Title.*
F1789.N3 C33 1988   *NYPL [Sc D 89-592]*

CASTILIAN LANGUAGE. see SPANISH
LANGUAGE.

Castillo, Rafael del. Al África, españoles! :
episodios de la guerra contra las tribus del Riff
/ escritos sobre las notas de un testigo ocular
por Álvaro Carrillo ; e ilustrados por el
reputado artista D. León Comelerán.
Barcelona-Gracia : Establecimiento
Tipografico-Editorial de Juan Pons, [1895?]- v.
ill., facsims. ; 22 cm. Schomburg's copy lacks t. 1, p.
489-498.
1. Morocco - History - 19th century. I. Title.
NYPL [Sc D 88-1097]

Castor, Elie, 1943- La Guyane, les grands
problèmes, les solutions possibles / Elie Castor,
Georges Othily. Paris : Éditions caribéennes,
c1984. 337 p., [8] p. of plates : ill. ; 23 cm.
Bibliography: p. 333-[335]   ISBN 2-903033-58-7 :
DDC 988/.203 19
*1. French Guiana - Politics and government - 1947-. 2.
French Guiana - Economic conditions. 3. French
Guiana - Social conditions. I. Othily, Georges, 1944-.
II. Title.*
JL812 .C36 1984   *NYPL [Sc D 89-389]*

CAT. see CATS.

Cat o' nine tales. Linton, W. J. (William James),
1812-1897. Catoninetales . [Hamden, Conn.]
[188-?]. [8], 100 p. :   *NYPL [Sc Rare F 88-4]*

Catalog of the Cuban and Caribbean Library,
University of Miami, Coral Gables, Florida.
Miami, University of, Coral Gables, Fla. Cuban
and Caribbean Library. Boston , 1977. 6 v. ;
DDC 016.9729
Z1595 .M5 1977 F2161
NYPL [Pub. Cat. 78-1036]

CATALOGS, PUBLISHERS' - ZAMBIA.
Multimedia Publications catalogue [microform]
Lusaka, Zambia , 1974. 8 p. ;
NYPL [Sc Micro F-11,053]

CATALOGS, UNION - MISSISSIPPI.
Thompson, Julius Eric. The Black press in
Mississippi, 1865-1985 . West Cornwall, CT ,
1988. xxiv, 144 p. :   ISBN 0-933951-16-7 (alk.
paper) :   DDC 015.762035 19
Z1361.N39 T52 1988 PN4882.5
NYPL [Sc D 89-34]

CATALOGS, UNION - UNITED STATES.
Witherell, Julian W. French-speaking central
Africa. Washington, 1973. xiv, 314 p.   ISBN
0-8444-0033-5
Z3621 .W5   *NYPL [JLF 74-197]*

Catalogue of the papers of the missions of the
Africa (Group 3) Committee /. Church
Missionary Society. Africa (Group 3)
Committee. London , 1981. 8 v. ;   DDC 266/.3
19
CD1069.L715 C47 1981   NYPL [Sc F 88-78]

CATASTRAL SURVEYS. see REAL
PROPERTY.

CATASTROPHES. see DISASTERS.

Cathedral of the August heat /. Clitandre, Pierre.
[Cathédrale du mois d'août. English.] London ,
c1987. 159 p. ;   ISBN 0-930523-31-8 (pbk.) :
NYPL [Sc D 87-1048]

Catholic Church.
[Treaties, etc. Haiti, 1860 Mar. 25]
Concordat signé à Rome le 25 mars 1860 :
Convention du 6 février 1861 avec le
Saint-Siège : Loi sur l'organisation et
l'administration des fabriques [microform].
Port-au-Prince : Impr. nationale, 1918. 31 p. ;
25 cm. Cover title. Microfiche. New York: New
York Public Library, 198 . 1 microfiche: negative; 11
x 15 cm. (FSN Sc 019,028)
*1. Catholic Church in Haiti. I. Haiti (Republic).
Treaties, etc. Catholic Church, 1860 Mar. 25. II. Title.*
NYPL [Sc Micro F-10,892]

CATHOLIC CHURCH - AFRICA.
Luneau, René. Laisse aller mon peuple! . Paris ,
c1987. 193 p. ;   ISBN 2-86537-173-5 DDC 282/.6
19
BX1675 .L86 1987   *NYPL [Sc D 88-315]*

Schultheis, Michael J. Catholic social teaching
and the Church in Africa /. Gweru, Zimbabwe ,
c1984. 56 p. ;   *NYPL [Sc D 88-1198]*

CATHOLIC CHURCH - AFRICA - HISTORY -
SOURCES.
Brasio, Antonio Duarte, 1906- Monumenta
missionaria africana: Africa ocidental. Lisboa,
1952- v.   *NYPL [ZKVX (Brásio, A.D.*
Monumenta missionaria africana)]

CATHOLIC CHURCH - AFRICA, SUB-
SAHARAN.
Christianisme en Afrique noire . Dakar , 1979.
162 p. ;   *NYPL [Sc F 89-17]*

CATHOLIC CHURCH - AFRICA, SUB-
SAHARAN - PASTORAL LETTERS AND
CHARGES.
Die Bischofskonferenzen Angolas und
Südafrikas zu Frieden und Gerechtigkeit in
ihren Länder. Bonn , 1986. 54 p. ;
NYPL [Sc D 88-929]

The Catholic church and Zimbabwe, 1879-1979 /.
Dachs, Anthony J. Gwelo , 1979. xiii, 260 p.,
[26] p. of plates :   DDC 282/.6891 19
BX1682.Z55 D33 1979 NYPL [Sc D 88-900]

CATHOLIC CHURCH. ARCHDIOCESE OF
ONITSHA (NIGERIA) - HISTORY.
The Catholic Church in Onitsha . Onitsha ,
1985. xvii, 341 p. :   DDC 282/.6694 19
BX1682.N5 C36 1985   *NYPL [Sc D 88-891]*

Catholic Church. Archdiocese of Yaoundé
(Cameroon). Synod. Une Eglise africaine
s'interroge [microform] : comment m'interpelle
Jésus-Christ en ce temps de synode? /
Archidiocèse de Yaoundé, Synode diocésain.
Yaoundé, Cameroun : The Archidiocese, [1982?]

36 p. ; 21 cm. Cover title. Microfiche. New York:
New York Public Library, 198. 1 microfiche: negative;
11 x 15 cm. (FSN Sc 019,005)
1. Catholic Church in Cameroon.
NYPL [Sc Micro F-11025]

CATHOLIC CHURCH - BRAZIL.
Balmes, Jaime Luciano, 1810-1848.
[Protestantismo comparado con el catolicismo
en sus relaciones con la civilización europea.
Selections. Portuguese.] A Igreja católica em
face da escravidão /. São Paulo , 1988. 141 p. ;
NYPL [Sc D 89-554]

CATHOLIC CHURCH - CLERGY -
BIOGRAPHY.
Ford, George Barry. A degree of difference.
New York [1969] 271 p.   DDC 282/.0924 B 19
BX4705.F635 A3   *NYPL [Sc D 88-406]*

CATHOLIC CHURCH - CLERGY -
RELIGIOUS LIFE.
Onyeocha, Anthony Ekendu. These hi-fi
priests . Owerri [Nigeria] , 1985. 208 p. :
NYPL [Sc D 88-926]

CATHOLIC CHURCH - CLERGY -
TRAINING OF - AFRICA.
Waliggo, John Mary, 1942- A history of
African priests . Masaka, Uganda , 1988. xi,
236 p., [16] p. of plates :
NYPL [Sc D 89-15]

Catholic Church. Deutsche Bischofskonferenz.
Sekretariat. Die Bischofkonferenzen Angolas
und Südafrikas zu Frieden und Gerechtigkeit in
ihren Länder. Bonn , 1986. 54 p. ;
NYPL [Sc D 88-929]

CATHOLIC CHURCH. DIOCESE OF
MARSABIT - CONGRESSES.
Marsabit Diocesan Pastoral Conference (1987 :
Nyeri Kenya) The Church we want to be .
Marsabit, Kenya , 1988. 42 p. :
NYPL [Sc D 89-463]

Catholic Church. Diocese of Nyeri (Kenya) A
living church : Diocese of Nyeri, 1902-1986.
[Nyeri, Kenya] : The Diocese, [1986] 28 p. :
ports. (some col.), map ; 30 cm. Cover title.
"Issued on the occasion of the celebration of the silver
jubilee of the episcopate of the Rt. Rev. Caesar Maria
Gatimu, bishop of the diocese of Nyeri."
*1. Gatimu, Caesar Maria. 2. Catholic Church - Kenya -
Nyeri - History. I. Title.   NYPL [Sc G 89-16]*

Catholic Church. Diocese of Owerri (Nigeria)
Onyeocha, Anthony Ekendu. These hi-fi
priests . Owerri [Nigeria] , 1985. 208 p. :
NYPL [Sc D 88-926]

CATHOLIC CHURCH - EDUCATION.
Faith and culture . Washington, D.C. , c1987.
111 p. :   ISBN 1-555-86994-7 (pbk.) DDC 268/.82
19
BX1968 .F24 1987   *NYPL [Sc D 88-1059]*

CATHOLIC CHURCH IN CAMEROON.
Catholic Church. Archdiocese of Yaoundé
(Cameroon). Synod. Une Eglise africaine
s'interroge [microform] . Yaoundé, Cameroon
[1982?] 36 p. ;   *NYPL [Sc Micro F-11025]*

CATHOLIC CHURCH IN HAITI.
Catholic Church. [Treaties, etc. Haiti, 1860
Mar. 25.] Concordat signé à Rome le 25 mars
1860 . Port-au-Prince, 1918. 31 p. ;
NYPL [Sc Micro F-10,892]

CATHOLIC CHURCH IN KISANTU, ZAIRE -
HISTORY.
Mayala ma Mpangu. L'église de·Kisantu, hier et
aujourd'hui [microform] /. [Kisantu?] 1982. 40
p. ;   *NYPL [Sc Micro F-11,000]*

The Catholic Church in Onitsha : people, places,
and events, 1885-1985 / edited by V.A. Nwosu.
Onitsha : Etukokwu Press, 1985. xvii, 341 p. :
ill. ; 21 cm. Bibliography: p. 341. DDC 282/.6694
19
*1. Catholic Church. Archdiocese of Onitsha (Nigeria) -
History. 2. Onitsha (Nigeria) - Church history. I.
Nwosu, V. A. (Vincent A.).*
BX1682.N5 C36 1985   *NYPL [Sc D 88-891]*

CATHOLIC CHURCH - JAMAICA -
HISTORY.
Osborne, Francis J. History of the Catholic
church in Jamaica /. Aylesbury, Bucks, U.K. ,
c1977. vii, 210, [8] p. of plates :   ISBN
0-85474-070-8 (pbk.)   DDC 282/.7292 19
BX1455.2 .O84 1977   *NYPL [Sc F 88-290]*

CATHOLIC CHURCH - KENYA.
Marsabit Diocesan Pastoral Conference (1987 :

Nyeri Kenya) The Church we want to be .
Marsabit, Kenya , 1988. 42 p. :
NYPL [Sc D 89-463]

CATHOLIC CHURCH - KENYA - NYERI - HISTORY.
Catholic Church. Diocese of Nyeri (Kenya) A living church . [Nyeri, Kenya] [1986] 28 p. :
NYPL [Sc G 89-16]

CATHOLIC CHURCH - MISSIONS - AFRICA.
Laverdière, Lucien, 1940- L'africain et le missionnaire . Montréal , 1987. 608 p. : ISBN 2-89007-640-7   *NYPL [Sc D 88-343]*

CATHOLIC CHURCH - MISSIONS - NIGERIA, EASTERN - HISTORY.
A Hundred years of the Catholic Church in Eastern Nigeria, 1885-1985 . Onitsha, Nigeria , 1985. 432 p. : ISBN 978-17-5103-7
NYPL [Sc D 88-830]

CATHOLIC CHURCH - MISSIONS - RWANDA - HISTORY.
Rutayisire, Paul. La christianisation du Rwanda (1900-1945) . Fribourg, Suisse , 1987. 571 p. : ISBN 2-8271-0371-0 (pbk.)
NYPL [Sc D 88-1510]

CATHOLIC CHURCH - MISSIONS - SOUTH AFRICA - HISTORY - 19TH CENTURY - SOURCES.
Records from Natal, Lesotho, the Orange Free State, and Mozambique concerning the history of the Catholic Church in southern Africa . Roma, Lesotho [1974] 2 v. : DDC 282/.68 19
BV3625.S67 R43 1974   *NYPL [Sc E 89-47]*

CATHOLIC CHURCH - MISSOURI - PERRY COUNTY - HISTORY - 19TH CENTURY.
Poole, Stafford. Church and slave in Perry County, Missouri, 1818-1865 /. Lewiston, N.Y., USA , c1986. xvii, 251 p. : ISBN 0-88946-666-1 (alk. paper) : DDC 306/.362/09778694 19
E445.M67 P66 1986   *NYPL [Sc E 89-102]*

CATHOLIC CHURCH - NIGERIA.
Asuzu, Boniface Ntomchukwu. Communications strategy in the new era of evangelization . Roma , 1987. xxi, 343 p. :
NYPL [Sc E 88-276]

Eze, Sylvester Omumeka. Steps for socio-political and religious change . [Nsukka?] 1987 (Nsukka : Chinedu Printers) 52 p. ;
NYPL [Sc C 89-53]

Idigo, Peter Meze. Archbishop Heerey . Enugu, Nigeria , 1987. 261 p. : ISBN 978-239-602-8
NYPL [Sc C 89-77]

CATHOLIC CHURCH - NIGERIA, EASTERN - HISTORY.
A Hundred years of the Catholic Church in Eastern Nigeria, 1885-1985 . Onitsha, Nigeria , 1985. 432 p. : ISBN 978-17-5103-7
NYPL [Sc D 88-830]

Catholic Church, Roman. see **Catholic Church.**

CATHOLIC CHURCH - RWANDA - HISTORY.
Rutayisire, Paul. La christianisation du Rwanda (1900-1945) . Fribourg, Suisse , 1987. 571 p. : ISBN 2-8271-0371-0 (pbk.)
NYPL [Sc D 88-1510]

CATHOLIC CHURCH - SOUTH AFRICA.
Torkington, Percy Anthony Thomas, 1931- Love with no regrets . Liverpool , 1988. 232 p. ;
NYPL [Sc D 89-368]

CATHOLIC CHURCH - SOUTH AMERICA.
Pons, François Raymond Joseph de, 1751-1812. Voyage à la partie orientale de la Terre-Ferme, dans l'Amérique Méridionale, fait pendant les années 1801, 1802, 1803 et 1804: contenant la description de la capitainerie générale de Caracas, composée des provinces de Vénézuéla, Maracaïbo, Varinas, la Guiane Espagnole, Cumana, et de l'île de la Marguerite ... Paris, 1806. 3 v.
F2311 .P79   *NYPL [Sc Rare F 88-77]*

CATHOLIC CHURCH - ZAIRE - BANZA-LUTE - HISTORY.
Banza-Lute . Bandundu, République du Zaïre , 1983. 251 p. : DDC 282/.67513 19
BX1682.C6 B36 1983   *NYPL [Sc F 89-38]*

CATHOLIC CHURCH - ZIMBABWE - HISTORY.
Dachs, Anthony J. The Catholic church and Zimbabwe, 1879-1979 /. Gwelo , 1979. xiii,

260 p., [26] p. of plates : DDC 282/.6891 19
BX1682.Z55 D33 1979   *NYPL [Sc D 88-900]*

CATHOLIC HIGH SCHOOLS - ILLINOIS - CHICAGO - ADMINISTRATION.
Moses, James Charles. Desegregation in Catholic schools in the archdiocese of Chicago, 1964-1974, including a case study of a Catholic high school [microform] /. 1977 288 leaves.
NYPL [Sc Micro R-4699]

From Rhodesia to Zimbabwe. see **From Rhodesia to Zimbabwe.**

Catholic social teaching and the Church in Africa /. Schultheis, Michael J. Gweru, Zimbabwe , c1984. 56 p. ;   *NYPL [Sc D 88-1198]*

Catoninetales . Linton, W. J. (William James), 1812-1897. [Hamden, Conn.] [188-?]. [8], 100 p. :   *NYPL [Sc Rare F 88-4]*

CATS - JUVENILE FICTION.
Burchardt, Nellie. Project cat /. New York, N.Y. , c1966. 66 p. :   *NYPL [Sc D 89-435]*

CATS - POETRY.
Linton, W. J. (William James), 1812-1897. Catoninetales . [Hamden, Conn.] [188-?]. [8], 100 p. :   *NYPL [Sc Rare F 88-4]*

Cattell, Raymond B. (Raymond Bernard), 1905-
Intelligence and national achievement /. Washington, D.C. , c1983. 176 p. : ISBN 0-941694-14-3 DDC 153.9 19
BF433.S63 I57 1983   *NYPL [Sc E 89-236]*

CATTLE - SOMALIA.
Massey, Garth. Subsistence and change . Boulder , 1987. xvii, 238 p. : ISBN 0-8133-7294-1 (alk. paper) : DDC 338.1/0967/73 19
DT402.4.R35 M37 1987
NYPL [Sc D 88-298]

Caudill, Rebecca, 1899- Au certain small shepherd / by Rebecca Caudill ; with illustrations by William Pène Du Bois. New York : Holt, Rinehart and Winston, 1965. 48 p. : col. ill. ; 22 cm. SCHOMBURG CHILDREN'S COLLECTION.
1. Christmas stories. I. DuBois, William Pène, 1916-. II. Schomburg Children's Collection. III. Title.
NYPL [Sc D 88-433]

Cauna, Jacques, 1948- Au temps des isles à sucre : histoire d'une plantation de Saint-Domingue au XVIIIe siècle / Jacques Cauna ; préface de Jean Fouchard. Paris : A.C.C.T. : Editions Karthala, c1987. 285 p., [16] p. of plates : ill., maps ; 24 cm. (Hommes et sociétés) Bibliography: p. [265]-282. ISBN 2-86537-186-5
1. Sugar trade - Haiti - History. 2. Plantations - Haiti - History. 3. Haiti - History - To 1791. I. Title. II. Series.
NYPL [Sc E 88-492]

The causes of the American civil war. Motley, John Lothrop, 1814-1877. New York, 1861. 36 p.
E459 .M92   *NYPL [Sc Rare C 89-14]*

Cauterizai o meu umbigo /. Rodrigues, Eustáquio José. Rio de Janeiro-RJ , 1986. 181 p. ; DDC 869.3 19
PQ9280.O269 C3 1986
NYPL [JFD 88-6700]

Cavanagh, Thomas E.
The impact of the Black electorate [microform] / Thomas E. Cavanagh. Washington, D.C. (1301 Pennsylvania Ave., N.W., Suite 400, Washington 20004) : Joint Center for Political Studies, 1984. v, 28 p. ; 28 cm. (Election '84 report . #1) Microfilm. New York : New York Public Library, 1988. 1 microfilm reel ; 35 mm. (MN *ZZ-29,401) DDC 324.973/008996073 19
1. Afro-Americans - Politics and government. 2. Afro-Americans - Suffrage. 3. Presidents - United States - Election - 1984. 4. United States - Politics and government - 1981-. I. Joint Center for Political Studies (U. S.). II. Title. III. Series.
E185.615 .C364 1984   *NYPL [*Z-4913 no.8]*

Jesse Jackson's campaign : the primaries and caucuses / Thomas E. Cavanagh, Lorn S. Foster. Washington, D.C. : Joint Center for Political Studies, 1984. 27 p., [1] ; 28 cm. (Election '84 report . #2) Bibliography: p. [28] ISBN 0-941410-45-5 (pbk.) DDC 324.973 19
1. Jackson, Jesse, 1941-. 2. Presidents - United States - Election - 1984. 3. Primaries - United States. 4. Afro-Americans - Suffrage. I. Foster, Lorn S. II. Title.

III. Series.
JK526 1984c   *NYPL [Sc F 87-172 rept. 2]*

CAVE-DRAWINGS - ZIMBABWE.
Garlake, Peter S. The painted caves . Harare, Zimbabwe , c1987. iv, 100 p., [8] p. of plates :
ISBN 0-908309-00-7   *NYPL [Sc D 89-411]*

Cave, Hugh B. (Hugh Barnett), 1910-
Conquering Kilmarnie / Hugh B. Cave. 1st ed. New York : Macmillan ; London : Collier Macmillan, c1989. 176 p. ; 22 cm. The lives of twelve-year-old Peter and his father, both still grieving for the death of Peter's mother and brother, change dramatically with the arrival of an uneducated but fiercely determined young black boy on their Jamaican coffee plantation. ISBN 0-02-717781-5 DDC [Fic] 19
1. Jamaica - Juvenile fiction. I. Title.
PZ7.C29 Co 1989   *NYPL [Sc D 89-611]*

Cavil, William E. Nobles, Wade W. The KM ebit husia . Oakland, California , 1985. 201 p. ; ISBN 0-939205-03-3   *NYPL [Sc F 88-159]*

CAYMAN ISLANDS - DESCRIPTION AND TRAVEL - GUIDE-BOOKS.
McLeod, Catherine. Jamaika /. Lausanne, Switzerland [1985], c1981. 128 p. :
NYPL [Sc B 88-57]

Cayton, Leonard Bernard. A history of Black public education in Oklahoma [microform] / by Leonard B. Cayton. 1976. 170 leaves. Thesis (Ed. D.)--University of Oklahoma, 1976. Bibliography: leaves 164-170. Microfilm of typescript. Ann Arbor, Mich.: University Microfilms International, 1977. 1 microfilm reel; 35 mm.
1. Afro-Americans - Education - Oklahoma - History. 2. School integration - Oklahoma. I. Title.
NYPL [Sc Micro R-4692]

Cazadores invisibles. Rohmer, Harriet. The invisible hunters . San Francisco , c1987. 32 p. : ISBN 0-89239-031-X : DDC 398.2/08998 19
F1529.M9 R64 1987   *NYPL [Sc E 88-241]*

Cazanove, Michèle. Présumée Solitude, ou, Histoire d'une paysanne haïtienne : roman / Michèle Cazanove. Paris : Julliard, c1988. 178 p. ; 21 cm. ISBN 2-260-00546-2
1. Women - Haiti - Fiction. 2. Haiti - Fiction. I. Title. II. Title: Histoire d'une paysanne haïtienne.
NYPL [Sc D 88-1406]

The CCM guidelines, 1981. Chama Cha Mapinduzi. [Dar es Salaam , 1981?]. iii, 59 p. ;
NYPL [Sc D 88-1260]

Ce que je crois . Senghor, Léopold Sédar, 1906- Paris , c1988. 234 p. ; ISBN 2-246-24941-4
NYPL [Sc D 89-76]

Cecil Rhodes /. Plomer, William, 1903-1973. Cape Town , 1984. xvii, 179 p. ; ISBN 0-86486-018-8   *NYPL [Sc C 88-64]*

CEHILA. see **Comisión de Estudios de Historia de la Iglesia en Latinoamerica.**

Célébration du soixante-dixième anniversaire du président Léopold Sédar Senghor. Sène, Alioune. Célébration du 7oe anniversaire du président Léopold Sédar Senghor (9 Oct. 1906-9 Oct. 1976) [microform] . Dakar , 1976. [4] p.   *NYPL [Sc Micro F-11026]*

Célébration du 7oe anniversaire du président Léopold Sédar Senghor (9 Oct. 1906-9 Oct. 1976) [microform] . Sène, Alioune. Dakar , 1976. [4] p. :   *NYPL [Sc Micro F-11026]*

Celenko, Theodore. A treasury of African art from the Harrison Eiteljorg Collection / Theodore Celenko ; foreword by Roy Sieber ; with commentaries by Harrison Eiteljorg. Bloomington : Indiana University Press, c1983. 239 p. : ill. (some col.) ; 31 cm. Bibliography: p. 232-239. ISBN 0-253-11057-2 DDC 730/.0967/074013 19
1. Eiteljorg, Harrison - Art collections - Catalogs. 2. Art, Black - Africa, Sub-Saharan - Catalogs. 3. Art, Primitive - Africa, Sub-Saharan - Catalogs. I. Eiteljorg, Harrison. II. Title.
NB1091.65 .C46 1983
NYPL [3-MADF+ 88-2098]

CEMETERIES - WASHINGTON (D.C.)
Sluby, Paul E. Selected small cemeteries of Washington, DC /. [Washington] , c1987. 84 p. :   *NYPL [Sc D 88-780]*

CENSORSHIP - NIGERIA.
Tell it as it is /. Enugu [Nigeria] [1985?]- v. ; ISBN 978-247-202-6   *NYPL [Sc C 88-183]*

CENSORSHIP OF THE PRESS. see LIBERTY OF THE PRESS.

Cent ans d'architecture à Kingston. Mattie, Joan. 100 years of architecture in Kingston . [Ottawa] , c1986. 30 p. : ISBN 0-662-54396-3 (pbk.) DDC 720/.9713/72074011384 19
NA747.K56 M38 1986 *NYPL [Sc F 88-195]*

Centenaire de la Conférence de Berlin (1884-1885) . Centenaire de la Conférénce de Berlin (1884-1885) (1985 : Brazzaville, Congo) Paris , 1987. 469 p. ; ISBN 2-7087-0481-8
NYPL [Sc E 88-101]

Centenaire de la Conférénce de Berlin (1884-1885) (1985 : Brazzaville, Congo) Centenaire de la Conférence de Berlin (1884-1885) : Brazzaville, avril 1985 : actes du colloque international. Paris : Présence africaine, 1987. 469 p. ; 24 cm. Includes bibliographical footnotes. ISBN 2-7087-0481-8
1. Berlin West Africa Conference (1884-1885) - Congresses. 2. Africa - Colonization - Congresses. I. Title. *NYPL [Sc E 88-101]*

Center for African Art (New York, N.Y.) Art/artifact . New York , Munich , c1988. 195 p. : ISBN 0-9614587-7-1 DDC 730/.0967/074 19
GN36.A35 A78 1988 *NYPL [Sc G 88-25]*

The Art of collecting African art /. New York , c1988. 64 p. : DDC 730/.0967/07401471 19
N7391.65 .A78 1988 *NYPL [Sc G 88-36]*

Bassani, Ezio. Africa and the Renaissance . New York City , c1988. 255 p. : ISBN 0-945802-00-5 : DDC 736/.62/096607401471 19
NK5989 .B37 1988 *NYPL [Sc F 89-30]*

Center for Cuban Studies. Cuba, a view from inside . New York [1985?] 2 v. :
TR646.U6 N4853x 1985
NYPL [Sc D 88-1511]

Center for Migration Studies (U. S.) A Directory of international migration study centers, research programs, and library resources /. Staten Island, N.Y. , 1987. ix, 299 p. ; ISBN 0-934733-18-X (pbk.) : DDC 325/.07 19
JV6033 .C45 1987 *NYPL [JLF 88-1452]*

Refugees : holdings of the Center for Migration Studies Library/Archives / compiled by Diana Zimmerman, with the assistance of Maria Del Giudice.1st ed. Staten Island, N.Y. : The Center, 1987. ix, 423 p. ; 29 cm. (Bibliographies and documentation series) Includes indexes. ISBN 0-934733-34-1 (pbk.)
1. Center for Migration Studies (U. S.). Library/Archives. 2. Emigration and immigration - Bibliography - Catalogs. 3. Migration, Internal - Bibliography - Catalogs. 4. Emigration and immigration - Library resources. 5. Migration, Internal - Library resources. I. Zimmerman, Diana. II. Del Giudice, Maria. III. Center for Migration Studies (U. S.). Library/Archives. IV. Series: CMS bibliographies and documentation series. V. Title.
NYPL [Sc F 89-60]

Center for Migration Studies (U. S.). Library/Archives. Center for Migration Studies (U. S.) Refugees . Staten Island, N.Y. , 1987. ix, 423 p. ; ISBN 0-934733-34-1 (pbk.) *NYPL [Sc F 89-60]*

CENTER FOR MIGRATION STUDIES (U. S.). LIBRARY/ARCHIVES - CATALOGS. Center for Migration Studies (U. S.) Refugees . Staten Island, N.Y. , 1987. ix, 423 p. ; ISBN 0-934733-34-1 (pbk.) *NYPL [Sc F 89-60]*

Center for the Fine Arts (Miami, Fla.) Museum voor Volkenkunde (Rotterdam, Netherlands) Expressions of belief . New York , 1988. 248 p. : ISBN 0-8478-0959-5 : DDC 730 19
N5310.75.H68 M876 1988
NYPL [Sc G 88-37]

Center for the Study of Southern Culture series. Mississippi writers . Jackson , c1985- v. ; ISBN 0-87805-232-1 (pbk.) DDC 813/.008/09762 19
PS558.M7 M55 1985 *NYPL [Sc E 88-316]*

The Central African journal of Lovell J. Procter, 1860-1864. Procter, Lovell James. [Boston] 1971. xvii, 501 p. DDC 916.8
DT731 .P75 *NYPL [Sc D 88-977]*

CENTRAL AFRICAN REPUBLIC - HISTORY - 1960- Bamboté, Makombo, 1932- Coup d'état nègre . [Montréal] , 1987. 117 p. ; ISBN 2-9800950-7-9 : DDC 843 19
NYPL [Sc D 89-114]

CENTRAL AFRICAN REPUBLIC - POLITICS AND GOVERNMENT - 1966-1979. Baccard, André. Les martyrs de Bokassa /. Paris , c1987. 349 p., [16] p. of plates : ISBN 2-02-009669-2 : DDC 967/.4105/0924 B 19
DT546.382.B64 B33 1987
NYPL [Sc D 88-636]

CENTRAL AMERICA - ECONOMIC CONDITIONS - 1979- - CONGRESSES. Crises in the Caribbean basin . Beverly Hills [Calif.] , c1987. 263 p. ; ISBN 0-8039-2808-4 DDC 330.9729 19
HC151 .C75 1986 *NYPL [JLD 87-3555]*

Central America - Government. see Central America - Politics and government.

CENTRAL AMERICA - POLITICS AND GOVERNMENT - 1979- - CONGRESSES. Crises in the Caribbean basin . Beverly Hills [Calif.] , c1987. 263 p. ; ISBN 0-8039-2808-4 DDC 330.9729 19
HC151 .C75 1986 *NYPL [JLD 87-3555]*

CENTRAL AMERICAN INDIANS. see INDIANS OF CENTRAL AMERICA.

CENTRAL BUSINESS DISTRICTS - WASHINGTON D. C. Williams, Brett. Upscaling downtown . Ithaca [N.Y.] , 1988. xi, 157 p. : ISBN 0-8014-2106-3 (alk. paper) DDC 307.3/42/09753 19
HT177.W3 W55 1988 *NYPL [Sc E 88-387]*

CENTRAL-LOCAL GOVERNMENT RELATIONS - UGANDA. Bunker, Stephen G., 1944- Double dependency and constraints on class formation in Bugisu, Uganda /. Urbana, Ill. , 1983. v, 88 p. : DDC 303.3/09676/1 19
HD1538.U43 B86 1983
NYPL [Sc D 88-1054]

Central State University . Goggins, Lathardus. Wilberforce, Ohio , c1987. xii, 181 p. : ISBN 0-87338-349-4 (alk. paper) DDC 378.771/74 19
LD881.C44 G64 1987 *NYPL [Sc E 88-477]*

CENTRAL STATE UNIVERSITY (WILBERFORCE, OHIO) - HISTORY. Goggins, Lathardus. Central State University . Wilberforce, Ohio , c1987. xii, 181 p. : ISBN 0-87338-349-4 (alk. paper) DDC 378.771/74 19
LD881.C44 G64 1987 *NYPL [Sc E 88-477]*

CENTRALIZATION IN GOVERNMENT. see DECENTRALIZATION IN GOVERNMENT.

Centre de linguistique appliqué de Dakar. Morin, Melle. Les retards scolaires et les échecs au niveau de l'ecole primaire du Sénégal /. [Dakar] [1966?] 143 leaves ; *NYPL [Sc F 87-439]*

Centre de linguistique appliquée de Dakar. Bathily, Abdoulaye. Lexique soninke (sarakole)-français /. [Dakar] , 1975. xx, 191 p. ; *NYPL [Sc F 86-166]*

Dialo, Amadou. Une phonologie du wolof /. [Dakar] , 1981. 60 leaves ;
NYPL [Sc F 86-167]

Faye, Suleymane. Aqatoor a seereer /. Kampala, Ouganda , 1986. 67 p. :
NYPL [Sc F 88-263]

Faye, Waly Coly. Précis grammatical de sérère /. [Dakar] , 1980. 80 leaves ;
NYPL [Sc F 86-168]

Sylla, Yèro, 1942- Récit initiatique peul du Macina . [Dakar] , 1975. vi, 113 p. ;
NYPL [Sc F 87-257]

Centre for Ethnic Minorities Health Studies. Pearson, Maggie. Racial equality and good practice maternity care . London , 1985. 37 p. : ISBN 0-86082-610-4 (pbk) : DDC 362.1/982 19
RG964.G7 *NYPL [Sc F 88-393]*

Centre for Foreign Policy Studies, Halifax, N. S. see Dalhousie University. Centre for Foreign Policy Studies.

Centre for Management Development, Lagos. Development of management education in Nigeria /. Ikeja, Nigeria , 1985. 555 p. : ISBN 978-14-0017-X *NYPL [Sc E 89-161]*

Centre international de criminologie comparée. Brillon, Yves. [Ethnocriminologie de l'Afrique noire. English] Crime, justice and culture in black Africa . [Montreal] [1985] xi, 289 p. :
NYPL [JLF 87-694]

Centre international de hautes études agronomiques méditerranéennes. Debouvry, Pierre. Contribution à la définition d'une méthodologie de transfert de populations paysannes . [Montpellier] [1985] 294 p. : ISBN 0-85352-039-0 *NYPL [Sc F 88-302]*

Centre national de la recherche scientifique (France) Hāj̱j 'Umar ibn Sa'īd al-Fūtī, 1794?-1864. [Bayān mā waqa'a. French & Arabic.] Voilà ce qui est arrivé . Paris , 1983. 261 p., [57] p. of plates : ISBN 2-222-03216-4
NYPL [Sc F 88-211]

Centre national de la recherche scientifique (France). Centre regional de publications de Paris. Hāj̱j 'Umar ibn Sa'īd al-Fūtī, 1794?-1864. [Bayān mā waqa'a. French & Arabic.] Voilà ce qui est arrivé . Paris , 1983. 261 p., [57] p. of plates : ISBN 2-222-03216-4
NYPL [Sc F 88-211]

Centre régional de recherche et de documentation sur les traditions orales et pour le développement des langues africaines (Yaoundé, Cameroon). Equipe nationale du Cameroun. Situation linguistique en Afrique centrale . Paris , Yaoundé , 1983. 475 p. :
NYPL [Sc F 88-153]

Centro Africa . Bardelli, Raimondo. Bologna , 1979. 258 p. : *NYPL [Sc C 87-359]*

A Century of Black surgeons : the U. S.A. experience / edited by Claude H. Organ, Jr. and Margaret M. Kosiba.1st ed. Norman, Okla. : Transcript Press, c1987. 2 v. (xx, 973 p.) : ill., facsims., ports. ; 24 cm. Includes index. Bibliography: v. 2, p. 943-946. ISBN 0-9617380-0-6 (set) DDC 617/.092/2 B 19
1. Afro-American surgeons - United States - Biography. 2. Afro-American surgeons - United States - Directories. I. Organ, Claude H., 1928-. II. Kosiba, Margaret M.
RD27.34 .C46 1987 *NYPL [Sc E 88-216]*

CEREMONIAL EXCHANGE - MARADI RIVER VALLEY (NIGERIA AND NIGER) Nicolas, Guy. Don rituel et échange marchand dans une société sahélienne /. Paris , 1986. 282 p. : ISBN 2-85265-117-3 *NYPL [JFF 87-660]*

CEREMONIES. see RITES AND CEREMONIES.

A certain small shepherd /. Caudill, Rebecca, 1899- New York , 1965. 48 p. :
NYPL [Sc D 88-433]

Ces fruits si doux de l'arbre à pain . Tchicaya U Tam'si, 1931- Paris , c1987. 327 p. ; ISBN 2-221-05172-6 :
MLCS 87/5379 (P) *NYPL [Sc D 88-581]*

CÉSAIRE, AIMÉ. Séphocle, Marie-Line. The reception of negritude writers in the Federal Republic of Germany . Ann Arbor, Mich. , c1987. vi, 121 p. ; *NYPL [Sc D 89-293]*

CÉSAIRE, AIMÉ - CRITICISM AND INTERPRETATION. Boulet, Rémy Sylvestre. Espaces et dialectique du héros césairien /. Paris , c1987. 219 p. ; ISBN 2-85802-774-9
NYPL [Sc D 87-1286]

Iyay Kimoni, 1938- Poésie de la négritude . Kikwit , 1985. vi, 168 p. ; DDC 841/.009/896 19
PQ3897 .I93 1985 *NYPL [Sc B 89-18]*

O cesto de Katandu e outros contos /. Santos, Arnaldo, 1935- Lisboa , c1986. 101 p. :
NYPL [Sc C 88-267]

CHAD - DESCRIPTION AND TRAVEL. Baar, Marius. Tschad--Land ohne Hoffnung? . Bad Liebenzell , c1985. 190 p., [6] p. of plates : ISBN 3-88002-270-4 *NYPL [Sc D 88-892]*

CHAD - HISTORY. Berre, Henri, 1911-1984. Sultans dadjo du Sila, Tchad /. Paris , 1985. xiv, 119 p. : ISBN 2-222-03641-0 : DDC 967/.4302/0922 B 19
DT546.472 .B47 1985 *NYPL [Sc D 88-1421]*

Tourneux, Henry. Les Mbara et leur langue (Tchad) /. Paris , 1986. 319 p. : ISBN 2-85297-188-7 *NYPL [Sc E 88-162]*

Zeltner, J. C. Les pays du Tchad dans la tourmente, 1880-1903 /. Paris , c1988. 285 p. : ISBN 2-85802-914-8
NYPL [Sc D 88-1408]

CHAD - HISTORY - 19TH CENTURY.
Ciammaichella, Glauco. Libyens et Français au
Tchad (1897-1914) . Paris , 1987. 187 p. :
    ISBN 2-222-04067-1   *NYPL [Sc E 89-182]*

CHAD - HISTORY - 1960-
Lisette, Yeyon. Le RDA et le Tchad . Paris ,
Abidjan , 1986. 351 p. ; ISBN 2-7087-0472-9
(Présence africaine)   *NYPL [Sc E 87-627]*

**CHAD - KINGS AND RULERS -
BIOGRAPHY.**
Bret, René-Joseph, d. 1940. Vie du sultan
Mohamed Bakhit, 1856-1916 . Paris , 1987.
[xvi], 258 p. : ISBN 2-222-03901-0
                    NYPL [Sc D 89-364]

CHAD - RELATIONS - FRANCE.
Ciammaichella, Glauco. Libyens et Français au
Tchad (1897-1914) . Paris , 1987. 187 p. :
    ISBN 2-222-04067-1   *NYPL [Sc E 89-182]*

**CHAD - RELATIONS - FRANCE - HISTORY -
20TH CENTURY.**
Bret, René-Joseph, d. 1940. Vie du sultan
Mohamed Bakhit, 1856-1916 . Paris , 1987.
[xvi], 258 p. : ISBN 2-222-03901-0
                    NYPL [Sc D 89-364]

CHAD - RELATIONS - LIBYA.
Ciammaichella, Glauco. Libyens et Français au
Tchad (1897-1914) . Paris , 1987. 187 p. :
    ISBN 2-222-04067-1   *NYPL [Sc E 89-182]*

CHADIC LANGUAGES.
Tourneux, Henry. Les Mbara et leur langue
(Tchad) /. Paris , 1986. 319 p. : ISBN
2-85297-188-7   *NYPL [Sc E 88-162]*

CHADIC LANGUAGES - CONGRESSES.
Préalables à la reconstruction du
proto-tchadique . Paris , 1978. 210 p. ; ISBN
2-85297-022-8 DDC 493/.7 19
PL8026.C53 P73 1978 *NYPL [Sc E 88-418]*

CHADIC LANGUAGES - VERB.
Etudes tchadiques . Paris , c1987. 121 p. ;
    ISBN 2-7053-0341-3   *NYPL [Sc E 88-293]*

Chain of days /. Berry, James. Oxford
[Oxfordshire] , New York , 1985. viii, 94 p. ;
    ISBN 0-19-211964-8 (pbk.) : DDC 821/.914 19
PR9265.9.B47 C5 1985 *NYPL [Sc D 89-45]*

CHAKA, ZULU CHIEF, 1787?-1828 - DRAMA.
Faces of African independence .
Charlottesville , 1988. xxxvi, 127 p. ; ISBN
0-8139-1186-9 DDC 842 19
PQ3987.5.E5 F33 1988 *NYPL [Sc D 89-32]*

**CHAKA, ZULU CHIEF, 1787?-1828 -
JUVENILE LITERATURE.**
Stanley, Diane. Shaka, king of the Zulus /.
New York , c1988. [40] p. : ISBN 0-688-07342-5
DDC 968.04/092/4 B 92 19
DT878.Z9 C565 1988 *NYPL [Sc F 88-358]*

Chakarira chindunduma : nhetembo dzehondo /
dzakakokorodzwa nokupepetwa naMusaemura
Zimunya. Gweru, Zimbabwe : Mambo Press,
1985. x, 78 p. ; 22 cm. (Mambo writers series.
Shona section . v. 21) "A selection from poems written
by Zimbabweans expressing their experiences during the
war of liberation." ISBN 0-86922-365-8
*1. Shona language - Texts. 2. Zimbabwe - Poetry. I.
Zimunya, Musaemura. II. Series. III. Series: Mambo
writers series. v. 21.*   *NYPL [Sc D 88-439]*

Chakrabarti, S. Great Britain. Overseas
Development Administration. Review of UK
manpower and training aid to Nigeria /.
[London? , 1984 or 1985] v, 72 p. ;
                    NYPL [Sc F 88-185]

The chalk doll /. Pomerantz, Charlotte. New
York , c1989. 30 p. : ISBN 0-397-32318-2 :
DDC [E] 19
PZ7.P77 Ch 1989   *NYPL [Sc F 89-175]*

**The Challenge of employment and basic needs in
Africa :** essays in honour of Shyam B.L. Nigam
and to mark the tenth anniversary of JASPA.
Nairobi ; New York : Oxford University Press,
1986. xii, 379 p. ; 25 cm. At head of title: Jobs and
Skills Programme for Africa (JASPA) of the
International Labour Organisation. Includes
bibliographical references. ISBN 0-19-572559-X
*1. Jobs and Skills Programme for Africa. 2. Manpower
policy - Africa. 3. Basic needs - Africa. 4. Rural
development - Africa. 5. Africa - Economic conditions -
1960-. I. Nigam, S. B. L. (Shyam Behari Lal).*
                    NYPL [Sc E 88-419]

The challenge of industrialization in Nigeria .

Kalu, Onwuka O. Lagos, Nigeria , 1986. xviii,
84 p. ;   *NYPL [Sc D 88-1245]*

Challenge to apartheid . Motlhabi, Mokgethi B.
G. (Mokgethi Buti George), 1944- Grand
Rapids, Mich. , c1988. xii, 243 p. ; ISBN
0-8028-0347-4 : DDC 305.8/00968 19
DT763 .M69 1988   *NYPL [JFD 88-11473]*

Chama Cha Mapinduzi. The CCM guidelines,
1981. [Dar es Salaam : Chama cha Mapinduzi,
1981?]. iii, 59 p. ; 21 cm. Published also in Swahili
under title: Mwongozo wa Chama cha Mapinduzi, 1981.
1. Chama Cha Mapinduzi. I. Title.
                    NYPL [Sc D 88-1260]

CHAMA CHA MAPINDUZI.
Chama Cha Mapinduzi. The CCM guidelines,
1981. [Dar es Salaam , 1981?]. iii, 59 p. ;
                    NYPL [Sc D 88-1260]

Chambers, Frances. Trinidad and Tobago /
Frances Chambers, compiler ; edited by Sheila
Herstein. Oxford, England ; Santa Barbara,
Calif. : Clio Press, c1986. xv, 213 p. : map ; 22
cm. (World bibliographical series. v. 74) ISBN
1-8150-9020-7
*1. Trinidad and Tobago - Bibliography. I. Herstein,
Sheila R. II. Title.*   *NYPL [Sc D 89-33]*

Chamoiseau, Patrick.
Manman Dlo contre la fée Carabosse : théâtre
conté / P. Chamoiseau. Paris : Editions
caribéennes, c1982. 143 p. : ill. ; 21 cm.
(Collection veillées vivantes) ISBN 2-903033-33-1
I. Title.
MLCS 82/8314 (P)   *NYPL [JAY B-3918]*

Solibo Magnifique : roman / Patrick
Chamoiseau. [Paris] : Gallimard, c1988. 226 p. ;
21 cm. ISBN 2-07-070990-6
1. Martinique - Fiction. I. Title.
                    NYPL [Sc D 88-1103]

Chan, Stephen. Issues in international relations : a
view from Africa / Stephen Chan. London :
Macmillan, 1987. viii, 206 p. ; 22 cm.
(Macmillan international college editions) Includes
index. Bibliography: p. 199-200. ISBN 0-333-44102-8
(pbk.)
*1. Africa - Foreign relations - 1960-. 2. Africa - Foreign
relations. I. Title.*   *NYPL [Sc D 88-371]*

Chandler, Ruth Forbes. Ladder to the sky / Ruth
Forbes Chandler ; illustrated by Harper
Johnson. London ; New York :
Abelard-Schuman, c1959. 189 p. : ill. ; 21 cm.
SCHOMBURG CHILDREN'S COLLECTION.
*1. Afro-American children - Juvenile fiction. I.
Schomburg Children's Collection. II. Title.*
                    NYPL [Sc D 88-1107]

**CHANGE OF ATTITUDE. see ATTITUDE
CHANGE.**

**Changements sociaux et productivité agricole en
Afrique Centrale /.** Bonvin, Jean. Paris : Centre
de développement de orgnisation de
coopértion et de développement économiques,
c1986. 140 p. : ISBN 92-64-22803-9
                    NYPL [Sc D 88-803]

**Changing and Contemporary Role of Women in
Society, African Seminar on the. see African
Seminar on the Changing and Contemporary
Role of Women in Society, Addis Ababa,
1975.**

La Chanson populaire en Côte-d'Ivoire : essai sur
l'art de Gabriel Srolou / publié sous la direction
de Ch. Wondji ; avec la collaboration de B.
Kotchy, F. Dédy Séri, A. Kouakou et A. Tapé
Gozé. Paris : Présence africaine, c1986. 342 p.,
[12] p. of plates : ill., ports. ; 21 cm.
Bibliography: p. 341-342. ISBN 2-7087-0470-2
*1. Srolou, Gabriel. 2. Popular music - Ivory Coast -
History and criticism. 3. Folk music - Ivory Coast. I.
Wondji, Christophe.*   *NYPL [Sc D 88-1099]*

Chant pour Manou. Akin, Louis. Chants d'aurore
pour Manou . [Abidjan] , c1983. 68 p. ; ISBN
2-86394-013-9   *NYPL [Sc C 88-121]*

Chants d'aurore pour Manou . Akin, Louis.
[Abidjan] , c1983. 68 p. ; ISBN 2-86394-013-9
                    NYPL [Sc C 88-121]

Chapelle des Jésuites (Nîmes, France) Ndiaye,
Iba, 1928- Iba N'Diaye, Gemälde, Lavierungen,
Zeichnungen =. München , c1987. 71 p. :
    ISBN 3-7774-4650-5 *NYPL [Sc C 88-297]*

Chaphole, Sol. Dihaeya / Sol Chaphole. [Cape
Town] : Centre for African Studies, University
of Cape Town, c1986. xiii, 68 p. ; 21 cm.

(Communications. 11) Bibliography: p. 63-68. ISBN
0-7992-1048-X
*1. Sotho language - Texts. 2. Sotho literature - History
and criticism. I. Series. II. Series: Communications
(University of Cape Town. Centre for African Studies) ,
11. III. Title.*   *NYPL [Sc D 88-1123]*

Chappell, Neena L. Driedger, Leo, 1928- Aging
and ethnicity . Toronto , 1987. xv, 131 p. :
    ISBN 0-409-81187-4   *NYPL [Sc E 88-127]*

**CHARACTERISTICS. see NATIONAL
CHARACTERISTICS.**

**CHARISMATIC MOVEMENT. see
PENTECOSTALISM.**

**CHARITIES, FOOD PRODUCING. see FOOD
RELIEF.**

Charles, Christophe, 1951- Obsessions : poèmes
impressionnistes et métaréalistes / Christophe
Philippe Charles. Port-au-Prince, Haiti, W.I. :
Editions Choucoune, c1985. 83 p. ; 18 cm.
(Série Poésie . 27e)
I. Title. II. Series.
MLCS 86/2028 (P)   *NYPL [Sc C 88-122]*

CHARLES ET GEORGES (SHIP)
Documentos relativos ao apresamento,
julgamento e entrega da barca franceza Charles
et Georges . Lisboa , 1858. 249, 16 p. ;
                    NYPL [Sc Rare G 86-1]

Charles Ethan Porter,1847?-1923. Marlborough,
CT : Connecticut Gallery, 1987. 113 p. : ill.
(some col.), facsims., ports. ; 26 cm. Compiled by
Helen K. Fusscas, president of the Connecticut Gallery,
as a preliminary to a projected catalogue raisonné.
Includes bibliographical references. ISBN
0-9619196-0-4
*1. Porter, Charles Ethan, 1847?-1923. 2. Painting,
Modern - 19th century - United States. I. Fusscas,
Helen K. II. Connecticut Gallery. III. Title.*
                    NYPL [Sc F 88-26]

**Charles, Gérard Pierre- see Pierre-Charles,
Gérard.**

Charles Richard Drew . Wynes, Charles E.
Urbana , c1988. xvi, 132 p., [14] p. of plates :
    ISBN 0-252-01551-7 DDC 610/.92/4 B 19
R154.D75 W96 1988   *NYPL [Sc E 89-65]*

**Charles W. Chesnutt and his literary crusade
[microform] /.** Gecau, Kimani. 1975. 187
leaves.   *NYPL [Sc Micro R-4218]*

Charsley, Simon R. The princes of Nyakyusa [by]
S. R. Charsley. With a foreword by P. H.
Gulliver. [Nairobi] Published for the Makerere
Institute of Social Research [by] East African
Pub. House [1969] xii, 125 p. illus., maps. 22
cm. (East African studies. 32) Based on the author's
thesis (M.A.), University of Manchester. Bibliography:
p. [117]-120. DDC 301.29/678
*1. Nyakyusa (African people). 2. Tanganyika - Politics
and government. I. Title. II. Series.*
DT443 .C5   *NYPL [Sc D 88-975]*

Chase-Riboud, Barbara. Portrait of a nude woman
as Cleopatra / Barbara Chase-Riboud. 1st Quill
ed. New York : Morrow, c1987. 110 p. : port. ;
22 cm. ISBN 0-688-06403-5 : DDC 811/.54 19
*1. Cleopatra, Queen of Egypt, d. 30 B.C. - Poetry. 2.
Antonius, Marcus, 83?-30 B.C. - Poetry. I. Title.*
PS3553.H336 P6 1987 *NYPL [Sc D 88-329]*

Chase, Salmon Portland, 1808-1873. The Address
and reply on the presentation of a testimonial
to S.P. Chase by the colored people of
Cincinnati. Cincinnati , 1845. 35 p. ;
                    NYPL [Sc Rare G 86-15]

CHASE, THE. see HUNTING.

Chasing the shadow /. Fakunle, Funmilayo.
Oshogbo [Nigeria] , 1980. 151 p. ;
                    NYPL [Sc C 87-462]

Chavaillon, Jean. Chavaillon, Nicole. Gotera, un
site paléolithique récent d'Ethiopie . Paris ,
1985. 58 p., 25 leaves of plates :
                    NYPL [Sc F 88-359]

Chavaillon, Nicole. Gotera, un site paléolithique
récent d'Ethiopie / Nicole et Jean Chavaillon ;
avec la collaboration de Denis Geraads et
Claude Guillemot. Paris : Editions Recherche
sur les civilisations, 1985. 58 p., 25 leaves of
plates : ill., maps ; 30 cm. (Mémoire / Editions
Recherche sur les civilisations, 0291-1655 . no 59)
Bibliography: p. 53-54.
*1. Paleolithic period - Ethiopia. 2. Ethiopia -
Antiquities. I. Chavaillon, Jean. II. Series: Mémoire*

(Editions Recherche sur les civilisations) , no 59. III.
Title.   *NYPL [Sc F 88-359]*

Chazan, Naomi, 1946- Coping with Africa's food crisis /. Boulder , c1988. xi, 250 p. : ISBN 0-931477-84-0 (lib. bdg.) : DDC 338.1/9/6 19
HD9017.A2 C65 1988   *NYPL [Sc E 88-287]*

Cheater, Angela P.
Bouedillon, M. F. C. Studies of fishing on Lake Kariba /. [Harare] , 1985. 185 p. :
    NYPL [Sc D 88-875]

The politics of factory organization : a case study in independent Zimbabwe / by Angela P. Cheater. Gweru, Zimbabwe : Mambo Press, c1986. xix, 156, [1] p. : ill. ; 22 cm. (Zambeziana. 18) Errata slip inserted. Bibliography: p. 155-[157] ISBN 0-86922-374-7
1. Labor and laboring classes - Zimbabwe. 2. Zimbabwe - Industries. I. Title. II. Series.
    NYPL [Sc D 88-671]

Cheek, Aimee Lee, 1936- Cheek, William F., 1933- John Mercer Langston and the fight for Black freedom, 1829-65 /. Urbana , c1989. 478 p. ; ISBN 0-252-01550-9 (alk. paper) DDC 973/.0496073/0924 B 19
E185.97.L27 C48 1989   *NYPL [Sc E 89-255]*

Cheek, William F., 1933- John Mercer Langston and the fight for Black freedom, 1829-65 / William and Aimee Lee Cheek. Urbana : University of Illinois Press, c1989. 478 p. ; 24 cm. (Blacks in the new world) Includes index. ISBN 0-252-01550-9 (alk. paper) DDC 973/.0496073/0924 B 19
1. Langston, John Mercer, 1829-1897. 2. Afro-Americans - Biography. 3. Afro-Americans - History - To 1863. 4. Slavery - United States - Anti-slavery movements. 5. United States - Race relations. I. Cheek, Aimee Lee, 1936-. II. Title. III. Series.
E185.97.L27 C48 1989   *NYPL [Sc E 89-255]*

Cheetham, Juliet. Social work with Black children and their families /. London , 1986. 207 p. ; ISBN 0-7134-4888-1 (cased)
    NYPL [Sc D 89-281]

Chefs-d'oeuvre inédits de l'Afrique noire / [textes, Bernard de Grunne et Robert Farris Thompson ; plus de la moitié des photographies, Gérald Berjonneau] Paris : Bordas, 1987. 320 p. : ill. (some col.) ; 32 cm. (Chefs-d'oeuvre inédits) Also published in limited edition of 600 copies. Bibliography: p. 313-316. ISBN 2-04-012941-3
I. Berjonneau, Gerald. II. Grunne, Bernard de. III. Thompson, Robert Farris.   *NYPL [Sc G 88-10]*

Chembe cha moyo /. Mazrui, Alamin. Nairobi , 1988. xiv, 73 p. ; ISBN 996-646-366-6
    NYPL [Sc C 89-75]

Chemins de chrétiens africains .
(1) Jeunes intellectuels en recherche . Abidjan , c1982. 67 p. :   *NYPL [Sc D 88-925]*

Chemins d'identité.
Laleye, Barnabé. Une femme dans la lumière de l'aube . Paris , c1988. 228 p. ;
    NYPL [Sc D 88-1407]

Tchicaya U Tam'si, 1931- Ces fruits si doux de l'arbre à pain . Paris , c1987. 327 p. ; ISBN 2-221-05172-6 :
MLCS 87/5379 (P)   *NYPL [Sc D 88-581]*

Cheney, Winifred Green. Cooking for company / Winifred Green Cheney. Birmingham, Ala. : Oxmoor House, c1985. 279 p., [2] p. of plates : col. ill. ; 26 cm. Includes index. ISBN 0-8487-0632-3 : DDC 641.5 19
1. Cookery, American - Southern style. I. Title.
TX715 .C5216 1985   *NYPL [Sc F 87-378]*

Chenfeld, Mimi Brodsky. The house at 12 Rose Street, by Mimi Brodsky. Illustrated by David Hodges. London, New York, Abelard-Schuman 1966. 157 p. illus. 22 cm. When a black family moves into a white neighborhood, their twelve-year-old neighbor learns about mob violence, property values, and the importance of scouting honor. SCHOMBURG CHILDREN'S COLLECTION. DDC [Fic]
1. United States - Race relations - Juvenile fiction. I. Hodges, David, illus. II. Schomburg Children's Collection. III. Title.
PZ7.C4183 Ho   *NYPL [Sc D 88-509]*

Cherchez la femme. Whisson, Michael G., 1937- Grahamstown [South Africa] , 1985. 90 p. [3] leaves of plates : ISBN 0-86810-125-7
    NYPL [Sc F 87-433]

The Cherokee ghost dance . McLoughlin, William Gerald. [Macon, Ga.] , c1984. xxiv, 512 p. : ISBN 0-86554-128-0 : DDC 975/.00497 19
E78.S65 M37 1984   *NYPL [HBC 85-263]*

CHEROKEE INDIANS - SOCIAL CONDITIONS - ADDRESSES, ESSAYS, LECTURES.
McLoughlin, William Gerald. The Cherokee ghost dance . [Macon, Ga.] , c1984. xxiv, 512 p. : ISBN 0-86554-128-0 : DDC 975/.00497 19
E78.S65 M37 1984   *NYPL [HBC 85-263]*

CHERUBIM AND SERAPHIM (SOCIETY)
Oguntomilade, Jacob I. D. Father E. Olu Coker . Lagos , 1987. 313 p. : ISBN 978-248-001-0   *NYPL [Sc D 89-572]*

Cheska, Alyce Taylor. Traditional games and dances in West African nations / Alyce Taylor Cheska. 1st ed. Schorndorf : K. Hofmann, 1987. 136 p. : ill., map ; 24 cm. (Sport science studies . 1) Map on p. [2] of cover. Bibliography: p. 131-135. ISBN 3-7780-6411-8 (pbk.)   DDC 793.3/1966 19
1. Folk dancing - Africa, West. 2. Games - Africa, West. I. Title. II. Series.
GV1713.A358 C48 1987
    NYPL [JFE 87-5517]

Chesler, Mark A. Social science in court : mobilizing experts in the school desegregation cases / Mark A. Chesler, Joseph A. Sanders, and Debra S. Kalmuss. Madison, Wis. : University of Wisconsin Press, 1988. xiv, 286 p. ; 24 cm. Includes index. Bibliography: p. 261-278. ISBN 0-299-11620-4 : DDC 344.73/0798 347.304798 19
1. Discrimination in education - Law and legislation - United States - Trial practice. 2. Segregation in education - Law and legislation - United States - Trial practice. 3. Evidence, Expert - United States. 4. Social scientists - Legal status, laws, etc. - United States. 5. Trial practice - United States. I. Sanders, Joseph A., 1944-. II. Kalmuss, Debra S., 1953-. III. Title.
KF8925.D5 C48 1988   *NYPL [Sc E 89-187]*

CHESNUTT, CHARLES WADDELL, 1858-1932.
Gecau, Kimani. Charles W. Chesnutt and his literary crusade [microform] /. 1975. 187 leaves.   *NYPL [Sc Micro R-4218]*

Chess, Victoria. (ill) Aardema, Verna. Princess Gorilla and a new kind of water . New York , 1988. [32] p. : ISBN 0-8037-0412-7 : DDC 398.2/0966 E 19
PZ8.1.A213 Pr 1987   *NYPL [Sc F 88-133]*

Chessare, Michele. Carter, Dorothy Sharp. His Majesty, Queen Hatshepsut /. New York , c1987. viii, 248 p. : ISBN 0-397-32178-3 : DDC [Fic] 19
PZ7.C2434 Hi 1987   *NYPL [Sc D 88-877]*

Chester, Galina. The silenced voice : hidden music of the kora / by Galina Chester and Tunde Jegede. London : Diabaté Kora Arts, 1987. 47 p. : ill. ; 22 cm. Bibliography: p. 38-39. ISBN 0-9512093-0-2 :
1. Kora (Musical instrument). 2. Folk music - Africa, West - History and criticism. I. Jegede, Tunde. II. Title.
    NYPL [Sc D 89-519]

Chester Himes /. Wilson, M. L. (Matthew Lawrence), 1960- New York , c1988. 111 p. : ISBN 1-555-46591-9 DDC 813/.54 B 92 19
PS3515.I713 Z93 1988   *NYPL [Sc E 88-373]*

Chester, Laura. Deep down . Boston , c1988. xii, 330 p. ; ISBN 0-571-12957-9 : DDC 810/.8/03538 19
PS509.E7 D44 1988   *NYPL [Sc D 88-1080]*

Chevannes, Barry. Social origins of the Rastafari movement / by Barry Chevannes. Mona, Kingston : Institute of Social and Economic Research, UWI, c1978. xii, 323 p. ; 28 cm. Bibliography: p. 318-323.
1. Ras Tafari movement - Jamaica. 2. Jamaica - Religion. I. Title.
BL2532.R37 C48 1978   *NYPL [Sc F 88-368]*

Chevrier, Jacques, fl. 1974- Anthologie africaine d'expression française /. Paris , c1981- v. ; ISBN 2-218-05648-8 (v. 1) :
    NYPL [Sc C 89-80]

CHEWA DIALECT - GRAMMAR.
Salaün, N. Cinyanja/Ciceŵa . Ndola, Zambia , 1979. 146 p. ;   *NYPL [Sc D 88-1178]*

CHEWA DIALECT - TEXTBOOKS FOR FOREIGN SPEAKERS - ENGLISH.
Salaün, N. Cinyanja/Ciceŵa . Ndola, Zambia , 1979. 146 p. ;   *NYPL [Sc D 88-1178]*

Chez Helene . Leslie, Austin. New Orleans, La. , c1984. 64 p. :   *NYPL [Sc B 89-26]*

Chi, the true god in Igbo religion /. Ezekwugo, Christopher U. M. Alwaye, Kerala, India , 1987. xvi, 310 p. :   *NYPL [Sc D 88-881]*

Chiaka, Ralph C. Morality of development aid to the Third World : a descriptive, socio-economic analysis / Ralph C. Chiaka. Rome : [s.n.], 1985. ix, 215 p. : map ; 24 cm. Bibliography: p. 197-211.
1. Economic assistance - Developing countries. 2. Economic assistance - Developing countries - Moral and ethical aspects. 3. Economic assistance - Moral and ethical aspects. 4. Developing countries - Economic conditions. I. Title.   *NYPL [Sc E 88-96]*

Chicago divided . Kleppner, Paul. DeKalb, Ill. , c1985. xviii, 313 p. : ISBN 0-87580-106-4 : DDC 324.9773/11043 19
F548.52.W36 K54 1984
    NYPL [JFE 85-2533]

Chicago Historical Society. Bross, William, 1813-1890. Illinois and the thirteenth amendment to the constitution of the United States. Chicago, 1884. 8 p.
    NYPL [Sc Rare F 88-43]

CHICAGO (ILL.) - BIOGRAPHY.
Wilson, Mary, 1938- To Benji, with love /. Chicago , c1987. p. cm. ISBN 0-910671-07-9 : DDC 977.3/11043/0924 B 19
F548.9.N4 W559 1987
    NYPL [Sc D 88-1219]

CHICAGO (ILL.) - POLITICS AND GOVERNMENT - 1951- - JUVENILE LITERATURE.
Roberts, Naurice. Harold Washington . Chicago , 1988. 30 p. : ISBN 0-516-03657-2 DDC 977.3/1100496073024 B 92 19
F548.52.W36 R63 1988
    NYPL [Sc E 88-501]

CHICAGO - MAYORS - ELECTION.
Kleppner, Paul. Chicago divided . DeKalb, Ill. , c1985. xviii, 313 p. : ISBN 0-87580-106-4 : DDC 324.9773/11043 19
F548.52.W36 K54 1984
    NYPL [JFE 85-2533]

CHICAGO - POLITICS AND GOVERNMENT - 1951-
Kleppner, Paul. Chicago divided . DeKalb, Ill. , c1985. xviii, 313 p. : ISBN 0-87580-106-4 : DDC 324.9773/11043 19
F548.52.W36 K54 1984
    NYPL [JFE 85-2533]

CHICAGO - RACE RELATIONS.
Kleppner, Paul. Chicago divided . DeKalb, Ill. , c1985. xviii, 313 p. : ISBN 0-87580-106-4 : DDC 324.9773/11043 19
F548.52.W36 K54 1984
    NYPL [JFE 85-2533]

CHICAGO SCHOOL OF SOCIOLOGY.
Persons, Stow, 1913- Ethnic studies at Chicago, 1905-45 /. Urbana , c1987. 159 p. ; ISBN 0-252-01344-1 (alk. paper) DDC 305.8/007/1077311 19
HT1506 .P47 1987   *NYPL [JLE 87-1776]*

CHICANOS. see MEXICAN AMERICANS.

CHICKENS - JUVENILE FICTION.
McCall, Virginia, 1909- Adassa and her hen. [New York, 1971] 79 p. DDC [Fic]
PZ7.M12295 Ad   *NYPL [Sc D 89-100]*

Chidester, David. Salvation and suicide : an interpretation of Jim Jones, the Peoples Temple, and Jonestown / by David Chidester. Bloomington : Indiana University Press, c1988. xv, 190 p. ; 25 cm. (Religion in North America) Includes bibliographical references and index. ISBN 0-253-30556-5 DDC 289.9 19
1. Jones, Jim, 1931-1978. I. Title. II. Series.
BP605.P46 C48 1988   *NYPL [JFE 88-4624]*

La chienne du quimboiseur /. Burnet, Mireille. Paris , c1986. 126 p. ; ISBN 2-903033-81-1
    NYPL [Sc D 89-168]

Chigidi, Willie L. Imwe chanzi ichabvepi? : mutambo weChiShona / wakanyorusa naWillie L. Chigidi. Gweru : Mambo Press, 1986. 60 p. ; 19 cm. (Mambo writers series. Shona section . v. 22)
1. Shona language - Texts. I. Title. II. Series.
    NYPL [Sc C 89-114]

CHILD CARE - GAMBIA.
Dixon, Joan. Jaata kendeyaa /. [Amherst, Ma.? , 198-?] 91 p. :   *NYPL [Sc F 89-135]*

Child care policy and practice.
Social work with Black children and their families /. London , 1986. 207 p. ;   ISBN 0-7134-4888-1 (cased)
      NYPL [Sc D 89-281]

CHILD LABOR. see YOUTH - EMPLOYMENT; CHILDREN - EMPLOYMENT.

Child labour series .
(no. 8) Moorehead, Caroline. School age workers in Britain today /. [London] [1987] 60 p. : ISBN 0-900918-24-1   *NYPL [Sc D 89-7]*

CHILD PLACING. see ADOPTION.

CHILD REARING - MIDDLE WEST - CROSS-CULTURAL STUDIES.
Lubeck, Sally. Sandbox society . London , Philadelphia , 1985. xv, 177 p. : ISBN 1-85000-051-4 DDC 372/.21/0977 19
LB1140.24.M53 L8 1985
      NYPL [Sc E 89-80]

CHILD WELFARE - LAW AND LEGISLATION. see CHILDREN - LEGAL STATUS, LAWS, ETC.

CHILDREN, AFRO-AMERICAN. see AFRO-AMERICAN CHILDREN.

CHILDREN AND ANIMALS - JUVENILE POETRY.
Sullivan, Sarah A. The animals talk to Gussie /. [S.l. , c1951 (wilmington, N.C. : Garey-Mintz Print.) 28 p. :   *NYPL [Sc F 89-2]*

Children and prejudice /. Aboud, Frances E. Oxford [Oxfordshire] , New York, NY , 1988. x, 149 p. : ISBN 0-631-14939-2 : DDC 305.2/3 19
BF723.P75 A24 1988   *NYPL [Sc E 89-57]*

CHILDREN AND STRANGERS - JUVENILE LITERATURE.
Duczman, Linda. The baby-sitter /. Milwaukee , Chicago , c1977. 30 p. : ISBN 0-8172-0065-7 (lib. bdg.) : DDC 649/.1
ɪ *HQ772.5 .D8*   *NYPL [Sc E 88-588]*

CHILDREN AS AUTHORS - BIOGRAPHY - JUVENILE LITERATURE.
Sealy, Adrienne V. Mama--watch out, I'm growingup! /. Brooklyn, New York , 1976. [45] p. :   *NYPL [Sc F 88-135]*

CHILDREN - BAHAMAS - JUVENILE FICTION.
Holdridge, Betty. Island boy /. New York , c1942. 110 p. :   *NYPL [Sc D 88-1181]*

CHILDREN, BLACK - ENGLAND - JUVENILE FICTION.
Boston, L. M. (Lucy Maria), 1892- Treasure of Green Knowe. New York [1958] 185 p. DDC [Fic]
PZ7.B6497 Tr   *NYPL [Sc D 88-1497]*

CHILDREN, BLACK - HUNGARY - JUVENILE FICTION.
Gedö, Leopold. [Janiból Jonny lesz. English.] Who is Johnny? /. New York , 1939. 242 p. :   *NYPL [Sc D 88-1512]*

CHILDREN, BLACK - SOUTH AFRICA.
Grosse-Oetringhaus, Hans-Martin. Noxolos Geheimnis . Berlin , 1988. 96 p. : ISBN 3-88520-289-1   *NYPL [Sc C 89-120]*

CHILDREN, BLIND - EDUCATION - NIGERIA.
Abosi, Okechukwu C. Educating the blind . Ibadan , c1985. xiv, 106 p. : ISBN 978-226-553-5 (pbk.) DDC 371.91/1/09669 19
HV2165.5 .A65 1985   *NYPL [Sc D 89-209]*

CHILDREN - EMPLOYMENT - GREAT BRITAIN.
Moorehead, Caroline. School age workers in Britain today /. [London] [1987] 60 p. : ISBN 0-900918-24-1   *NYPL [Sc D 89-7]*

CHILDREN - ETHIOPIA - JUVENILE FICTION.
Kindred, Wendy. Negatu in the garden. New York [1971] [38] p. ISBN 0-07-034585-6 DDC [E]
PZ7.K567 Ne   *NYPL [Sc F 88-246]*

CHILDREN IN AFRICA, SUB-SAHARAN.
Children, youth, women and development plans

in West and Central Africa . Abidjan [1972?] 152 p. ;   *NYPL [Sc E 88-105]*

CHILDREN - JURISPRUDENCE. see CHILDREN - LEGAL STATUS, LAWS, ETC.

CHILDREN - KENYA - JUVENILE FICTION.
Van Stockum, Hilda, 1908- Mogo's flute /. New York , 1966. 88 p. :
PZ7.V36 Mo   *NYPL [Sc E 88-176]*

CHILDREN - LEGAL STATUS, LAWS, ETC. - SOUTH AFRICA - CONGRESSES.
Children of resistance . London , 1988. vii, 146 p. ;   *NYPL [Sc D 88-1286]*

CHILDREN - LITERARY COLLECTIONS.
Mississippi writers . Jackson , c1985- v. ; ISBN 0-87805-232-1 (pbk.) DDC 813/.008/09762 19
PS558.M7 M55 1985   *NYPL [Sc E 88-316]*

CHILDREN - MOZAMBIQUE - MAPUTO - NUTRITION.
Santos, Norberto Teixeira. Avaliação nutricional da população infantil banto (0-5 anos) de uma zona suburbana da cidade Lourenço Marques . [Lourenço Marques, Moçambique] 1974. 400 p., [40] p. of plates :   *NYPL [Sc E 88-143]*

CHILDREN - NAMIBIA.
Moorehead, Caroline. Namibia . Oxford [1988] 50 p. : ISBN 0-85598-111-3 :
      NYPL [Sc F 89-120]

CHILDREN - NEW YORK (N.Y.) - JUVENILE FICTION.
Greene, Roberta. Two and me makes three. New York [1970] [36] p.
PZ7.G843 Tw   *NYPL [Sc F 88-375]*

CHILDREN - NEW YORK (N.Y.) - JUVENILE LITERATURE.
Gross, Mary Anne. (comp) Ah, man, you found me again. Boston [1972] x, 84 p. ISBN 0-8070-1532-6 DDC 810/.8/09282
HQ792.U53 N53 1972   *NYPL [Sc F 88-336]*

CHILDREN - NIGERIA - FICTION.
Okogba, Andrew. When a child is motherless /. Benin City, Nigeria , 1987. v, 326 p. 19 cm. ISBN 978-234-045-6   *NYPL [Sc C 88-206]*

Children of long ago . Little, Lessie Jones. New York , 1988. [32] p. : ISBN 0-399-21473-9 DDC 811/.54 19
PS3562.I78288 C5 1988
      NYPL [Sc F 88-276]

CHILDREN OF MIGRANT LABORERS - UNITED STATES - JUVENILE FICTION.
Shotwell, Louisa Rossiter. Roosevelt Grady /. Cleveland, Ohio , c1963. 151 p. :
      NYPL [Sc D 88-1425]

Children of resistance : statements from the Harare Conference on Children, Repression and the Law in Apartheid South Africa / edited by Victoria Brittain & Abdul S. Minty. London : Kliptown Books, 1988. vii, 146 p. ; 21 cm. Bibliography: p. 144-146.
1. Children - South Africa - Congresses. 2. Children - Legal status, laws, etc. - South Africa - Congresses. 3. Apartheid - South Africa - Congresses. 4. Detention of persons - South Africa - Congresses. I. Brittain, Victoria. II. Minty, Abdul S. III. International Conference on Children, Repression and the Law in Apartheid South Africa (1987 : Harare, Zimbabwe).
      NYPL [Sc D 88-1286]

CHILDREN - PSYCHOLOGICAL TESTING. see PSYCHOLOGICAL TESTS FOR CHILDREN.

CHILDREN - RECREATION. see GAMES.

CHILDREN - SOCIETIES AND CLUBS - JUVENILE FICTION.
Horvath, Betty F. Not enough Indians. New York [1971] [47] p. ISBN 0-531-01968-3 DDC [Fic]
PZ7.H7922 No   *NYPL [Sc F 88-341]*

CHILDREN - SOUTH AFRICA.
Two dogs and freedom . Johannesburg , 1986. 55 p. : ISBN 0-86975-301-0 (pbk.)
      NYPL [Sc D 88-151]

Two dogs and freedom . New York , 1987. 55 p. : ISBN 0-8050-0637-0 (pbk.) : DDC 323.1/196/068 19
DT763.6 .T96 1987   *NYPL [Sc D 88-422]*

CHILDREN - SOUTH AFRICA - CONGRESSES.

Children of resistance . London , 1988. vii, 146 p. ;   *NYPL [Sc D 88-1286]*

CHILDREN - SOUTH AFRICA - JUVENILE FICTION.
Linde, Freda. Toto and the aardvark. Garden City, N.Y. [1969] 59 p.
PZ7.L6574 To   *NYPL [JFE 72-633]*

CHILDREN, VAGRANT - KENYA - NAIROBI.
Dallape, Fabio. "You are a thief". Nairobi, Kenya , 1987. 151 p. : *NYPL [Sc E 88-538]*

CHILDREN - WEST INDIES.
Sylvie-Line. Ti Dolfine et le filibo vert /. Paris , c1985. 123 p. : ISBN 2-903033-72-2
      NYPL [Sc E 88-358]

Children, youth, women and development plans in West and Central Africa : Cameroon, Chad, Gabon, Ivory Coast, Mali, Mauritania, Niger, Togo : report of the conference of ministers held in Lomé, Togo - May 1972. Abidjan : Unicef Regional Office for West and Central Africa [1972?] 152 p. ; 24 cm. "This volume was originally published in French."
1. Children in Africa, Sub-Saharan. 2. Women - Africa, Sub-Saharan. 3. Youth - Africa, Sub-Saharan. I. UNICEF.   *NYPL [Sc E 88-105]*

CHILDREN'S BOOKS. see CHILDREN'S LITERATURE.

CHILDREN'S GAMES. see GAMES.

CHILDREN'S LITERATURE, CUBAN - HISTORY AND CRITICISM.
Piñeiro de Rivera, Flor, 1922- Literatura infantil caribeña . Hato Rey, P.R. (O'Neill 159, Hato Rey) , c1983. 123 p. : DDC 860/.9/9282 19
PQ7361 .P5 1983   *NYPL [Sc D 88-1143]*

CHILDREN'S LITERATURE, DOMINICAN - HISTORY AND CRITICISM.
Piñeiro de Rivera, Flor, 1922- Literatura infantil caribeña . Hato Rey, P.R. (O'Neill 159, Hato Rey) , c1983. 123 p. ; DDC 860/.9/9282 19
PQ7361 .P5 1983   *NYPL [Sc D 88-1143]*

CHILDREN'S LITERATURE - HISTORY AND CRITICISM.
Racism and sexism in children's books. New York , c1978. 72 p. : ISBN 0-930040-29-5
      NYPL [Sc D 89-259]

CHILDREN'S LITERATURE, PUERTO RICAN - HISTORY AND CRITICISM.
Piñeiro de Rivera, Flor, 1922- Literatura infantil caribeña . Hato Rey, P.R. (O'Neill 159, Hato Rey) , c1983. 123 p. ; DDC 860/.9/9282 19
PQ7361 .P5 1983   *NYPL [Sc D 88-1143]*

Children's Museum, Brooklyn. see Brooklyn Institute of Arts and Sciences. Children's Museum.

CHILDREN'S POETRY, AMERICAN.
Giovanni, Nikki. Vacation time . New York , 1980. 59 p. : ISBN 0-688-03657-0 DDC 811/.54
PS3557.I55 V3   *NYPL [Sc D 89-69]*

Little, Lessie Jones. Children of long ago . New York , 1988. [32] p. : ISBN 0-399-21473-9 DDC 811/.54 19
PS3562.I78288 C5 1988
      NYPL [Sc F 88-276]

CHILDREN'S POETRY, BARBADIAN.
Worrell, Vernon, 1952- Under the flambo . Bridgetown, Barbados , 1986. ix, 84 p. : DDC 811 19
PR9230.9.W67 U5 1986
      NYPL [Sc D 88-945]

CHILDREN'S POETRY, ENGLISH.
A Junior secondary poetry anthology /. [Limbe, c1984- v. : DDC 428.6/4 19
PE1126.A44 J86 1984 *NYPL [Sc D 88-384]*

CHILDREN'S STORIES, AMERICAN.
Hearn, Michael Patrick. The porcelain cat /. Boston [1987?]. [32] p. : ISBN 0-316-35330-2 (pbk.) :   *NYPL [Sc F 88-220]*

Jensen, Virginia Allen. Sara and the door /. Reading, Mass. , c1977. [32] p. : ISBN 0-201-03446-8 DDC [E]
PZ8.3.J425 Sar   *NYPL [Sc B 89-17]*

Lexau, Joan M. Don't be my valentine /. New York, N.Y. , c1985. 64 p. : ISBN 0-06-023872-0 : DDC [E] 19
PZ7.L5895 Dp 1985   *NYPL [Sc D 89-58]*

CHILDREN'S STORIES, JAMAICAN.
Berry, James. A thief in the village /. New York , 1988, c1987. 148 p. ; ISBN

0-531-05745-3　DDC [Fic] 19
PZ7.B46173 Th 1988　*NYPL [Sc D 88-1252]*

CHILDREN'S WRITINGS.
Gross, Mary Anne. (comp) Ah, man, you found
me again. Boston [1972] x, 84 p.　ISBN
0-8070-1532-6　DDC 810/.8/09282
HQ792.U53 N53 1972　*NYPL [Sc F 88-336]*

**CHILDREN'S WRITINGS, MOZAMBICAN
(ENGLISH)**
Breakfast of sjamboks /. Harare , 1987. viii, 71
p. :　ISBN 0-949225-35-5　*NYPL [Sc C 88-299]*

CHILDREN'S WRITINGS, SAINT MARTIN.
Nature, I love you . [St. Martin] , c1983. 36
p. :
MLCS 86/1723 (P)　　*NYPL [Sc D 88-626]*

**CHILDREN'S WRITINGS, SOUTH AFRICAN
(ENGLISH)**
Two dogs and freedom . Johannesburg , 1986.
55 p. :　ISBN 0-86975-301-0 (pbk.)
NYPL [Sc D 88-151]

Two dogs and freedom . New York , 1987. 55
p. :　ISBN 0-8050-0637-0 (pbk.) :　DDC
323.1/196/068 19
DT763.6 .T96 1987　*NYPL [Sc D 88-422]*

Childress, Alice. Those other people / Alice
Childress. New York : Putnam, c1988. 186 p. ;
22 cm. Bigotry surfaces at Minitown High when a
popular male teacher sexually assaults a delinquent
fifteen-year-old girl and the only witnesses are a black
boy and a gay student teacher.　ISBN 0-399-21510-7
DDC [Fic] 19
*1. Homosexuality - Juvenile fiction. 2. Afro-Americans -
Juvenile fiction. 3. High schools - Juvenile fiction. I.
Title.*
PZ7.C4412 Th 1988　*NYPL [Sc D 89-327]*

Childs, John Brown. Leadership, conflict, and
cooperation in Afro-American social thought /
John Brown Childs. Philadelphia : Temple
University Press, 1989. xii, 172 p. ; 22 cm.
Includes index. Bibliography: p. 149-162.　ISBN
0-87722-581-8 (alk. paper) :　DDC
303.3/4/08996073 19
*1. Afro-Americans - Intellectual life. 2. Sociology -
United States - History - 20th century. 3. Social
action - United States - History - 20th century. 4.
United States - Intellectual life - 20th century. I. Title.*
E185.6 .C534 1989　*NYPL [Sc D 89-497]*

Chilton, John, 1931 or 2-
McKinney's music : a bio-discography of
McKinney's Cotton Pickers / by John Chilton.
London : Bloomsbury Book Shop, 1978. 68 p. :
ill. ; 21 cm. Includes bibliographical references.
ISBN 0-9501290-1-1 (pbk.)　DDC 785.42/092/2
B 19
*1. McKinney, William, 1895-1969. 2. McKinney's
Cotton Pickers. 3. Jazz musicians - United States -
Biography. I. Title. II. Title: McKinney's Cotton
Pickers.*
ML394 .C55 1978　*NYPL [Sc D 82-387]*

Sidney Bechet, the wizard of jazz / by John
Chilton. Basingstoke : Macmillan, 1987. xiii,
331 p., [32] p. of plates : ill., facsims, ports. ;
25 cm. Includes index. Bibliography: p. 308-310.
Discography: p. 311-314.　ISBN 0-333-44386-1
*1. Bechet, Sidney, 1897-1959. 2. Jazz musicians -
United States - Biography. 3. Afro-American
musicians - Biography. I. Title.*
NYPL [Sc E 88-33]

Chimombo, Steve Bernard Miles. Napolo poems
/ Steve Chimombo. Zomba, Malawi :
Manchichi Publishers, 1987. ix, 55 p. ; 21 cm.
I. Title.　　*NYPL [Sc D 88-788]*

CHIMPANZEES - BEHAVIOR.
Lawick-Goodall, Jane, Barones van. In the
shadow of man. Boston, 1971. xx, 297 p.　ISBN
0-395-12726-2
QL737.P96 L37　　*NYPL [SC 599.8-L]*

CHIMPANZEES - JUVENILE FICTION.
Wassermann, Selma. Moonbeam and Dan Starr.
Westchester, Ill., c1966. 64 p.
NYPL [Sc D 89-398]

Wassermann, Selma. Moonbeam and the rocket
ride. Chicago [c1965] 64 p.
PE1119 .W363　　*NYPL [Sc D 89-92]*

Wassermann, Selma. Moonbeam finds a moon
stone. Chicago [1967] 96 p.　DDC [Fic]
PE1119 .W3636　*NYPL [Sc D 88-1423]*

CHINAWARE. see POTTERY.

**CHINO LANGUAGE. see SHONA
LANGUAGE.**

Chinua Achebe, Things fall apart /. Wren, Robert
M. London , 1980. vi, 56 p. ;　ISBN
0-582-60109-6　　*NYPL [Sc C 88-88]*

Chinweizu. Voices from twentieth-century Africa .
London , Boston , 1988. xl, 424 p. ;　ISBN
0-571-14929-4 (cased) :　DDC 808.8/9896 19
NYPL [Sc D 89-174]

Chirenje, J. Mutero, 1935- Ethiopianism and
Afro-Americans in southern Africa, 1883-1916
/ J. Mutero Chirenje. Baton Rouge : Louisiana
State University Press, c1987. xii, 231 p. : ill.,
map, ports. ; 24 cm. Includes index. Bibliography: p.
[199]-223. ISBN 0-8071-1319-0　DDC 276.8/08 19
*1. African Methodist Episcopal Church - Missions -
Africa, Southern. 2. Ethiopian movement (South
Africa). 3. Africa, Southern - Church history. I. Title.*
BR1450 .C45 1987　*NYPL [Sc E 88-336]*

Chirmuuta, Richard C. Aids, Africa and racism /
Richard C. Chirimuuta, Rosalind J. Chirmuuta.
Bretby [England] : R. Chirmuuta, 1987. 160
p. ; 22 cm. Includes bibliographical references and
index.　ISBN 0-9512804-0-6 hardback
*1. AIDS (Disease) - Africa. 2. AIDS (Disease). I.
Chirmuuta, Rosalind J. II. Title.*
NYPL [Sc D 88-1185]

Chirmuuta, Rosalind J. Chirimuuta, Richard C.
Aids, Africa and racism /. Bretby [England] ,
1987. 160 p. ;　ISBN 0-9512804-0-6 hardback
NYPL [Sc D 88-1185]

Chiromo, Obediah C. Shona folk tales /. Gweru,
Zimbabwe , 1987. 151 p. ;
NYPL [Sc C 88-317]

CHISHOLM, SHIRLEY, 1924-
Chisolm, Shirley, 1924- The good fight /. New
York , c1973. 206 p. ;　*NYPL [Sc C 88-43]*

**CHISHOLM, SHIRLEY, 1924- -
BIBLIOGRAPHY.**
Duffy, Susan, 1951- Shirley Chisholm .
Metuchen, N.J. , 1988. vii, p. ;　ISBN
0-8108-2105-2　DDC 016.32873/092/4 19
Z8167.47 .D83 1988 E840.8.C48
NYPL [Sc D 88-1270]

Chisiya, 1960- Afrikan lullaby : folk tales from
Zambabwe [i.e. Zimbabwe] / by Chisiya ;
illustrations by pupils from Sheffield. London :
Karia, 1986. 60 p. : ill., 1 port. ; 20 cm.　ISBN
0-946918-45-7 (pbk)　DDC 398.2/1/096891 19
1. Tales - Zimbabwe. I. Title.
PZ8.1　　　*NYPL [Sc D 88-436]*

Chisolm, Shirley, 1924- The good fight / Shirley
Chisholm. [Special limited ed.] New York :
[s.n.], c1973. 206 p. ; 16 cm. Reprint.
*1. Chisholm, Shirley, 1924-. 2. Presidents - United
States - Election - 1972. 3. United States - Politics and
government - 1969-1974. I. Title.*
NYPL [Sc C 88-43]

**CHISWINA LANGUAGE. see SHONA
LANGUAGE.**

Chitala, Derrick. SADCC . Tokyo, Japan :
London ; xi, 256 p. ;　ISBN 0-86232-748-2 :
DDC 337.1/68 19
HC900 .S23 1987　　*NYPL [Sc D 89-50]*

The Chitepo assassination /. Martin, David,
1936- Harare, Zimbabwe , 1985. 134 p., [8] p.
of plates :　ISBN 0-949225-04-5
NYPL [Sc D 88-1244]

**CHITEPO, HERBERT WILTSHIRE, 1923-
1975 - ASSASSINATION.**
Martin, David, 1936- The Chitepo assassination
/. Harare, Zimbabwe , 1985. 134 p., [8] p. of
plates :　ISBN 0-949225-04-5
NYPL [Sc D 88-1244]

Chittick, H. Neville. Relations historiques à
travers l'océan Indien. Spanish, Relaciones
históricas a través del océano Índico .
Barcelona , Paris , 1983. 224 p. ;　ISBN
84-85800-51-6　　*NYPL [Sc D 88-593]*

Chiu, Ann. Which path to freedom? . Pomona,
Calif. , c1986. iv, 60 p. ;　DDC 973.7/114 19
E449 .W565 1986　*NYPL [Sc D 88-1154]*

**Chocolate Dandies. see McKinney's Cotton
Pickers.**

A chocolate soldier . Colter, Cyrus. New York ,
c1988. 278 p. ;　ISBN 0-938410-42-3 :　DDC

813/.54 19
PS3553.O477 C5 1988
NYPL [Sc D 88-1396]

**CHOICE OF PROFESSION. see
VOCATIONAL GUIDANCE.**

Choose the sex of your baby . Dada, Victor B. N.
Y. , c1983. xiv, 96 p. ;　ISBN 0-533-05256-4
NYPL [Sc D 88-1180]

Chow, Octavio. Rohmer, Harriet. The invisible
hunters . San Francisco , c1987. 32 p. :　ISBN
0-89239-031-X :　DDC 398.2/08998 19
F1529.M9 R64 1987　*NYPL [Sc E 88-241]*

**Le chrétien, les dons et la mission dans l'église
africaine indépendante .** Wonyu, Eugène, 1933-
Douala , 1979. 68 p. ;　DDC 285 19
BX9162.C35 W66　*NYPL [Sc D 88-1399]*

Christ as our ancestor . Nyamiti, Charles. Gweru
[Zimbabwe] , 1984. 151 p. ;　DDC 232 19
BT205 .N82 1984　*NYPL [Sc D 88-986]*

Christ or Devil? . Obianyido, Anene. Enugu,
Anambra State, Nigeria , 1988. 136 p. ;　ISBN
978-233-544-4　　*NYPL [Sc C 88-194]*

**CHRISTIAN ART AND SYMBOLISM -
MOZAMBIQUE - EXHIBITIONS.**
Museu de Arte Sacra (Mozambique Island)
Museu de Arte Sacra, anexo à Igreja da
Misericórdia, Ilha de Moçambique [microform]
[Lourenço Marques?] , 1969. [16] p. :
NYPL [Sc Micro F-10928]

**CHRISTIAN COMMUNICATION. see
COMMUNICATION (THEOLOGY)**

Christian counselling for students /. Kiriswa,
Benjamin. Eldoret, Kenya , 1988. vi, 81 p. :
NYPL [Sc D 89-350]

**CHRISTIAN DOCTRINE. see THEOLOGY,
DOCTRINAL.**

CHRISTIAN EDUCATION - NIGERIA.
Noibi, D. O. S. Yoruba Muslim youth and
Christian-sponsored education /. Ijebu-Ode,
Nigeria , 1987. 44 p. ;　ISBN 978-253-020-4
NYPL [Sc D 89-537]

CHRISTIAN LIFE.
The Zulu blind boy's story. New York [185-?]
16 p. ;　　*NYPL [Sc Rare C 89-29]*

**CHRISTIAN MARTYRS - KENYA -
MACHAKOS.**
Somba, John Ndeti, 1930- Wananchi mashujaa
wa imani, Kangundo, Machakos /. Kijabe,
Kenya , 1985. 68 p. :　*NYPL [Sc D 89-345]*

**CHRISTIAN NAMES. see NAMES,
PERSONAL.**

**CHRISTIAN SAINTS - PERU - BIOGRAPHY -
JUVENILE LITERATURE.**
Windeatt, Mary Fabyan, 1910- Lad of Lima .
New York , 1942. 152 p. ;
NYPL [Sc D 88-1170]

CHRISTIAN SAINTS - UGANDA.
Uganda saints . [Kampala? , 1969?] 39 p. :
NYPL [Sc F 87-314]

CHRISTIAN SECTS - AFRICA.
Daneel, M. L. (Marthinus L.) Quest for
belonging . Gweru, Zimbabwe , 1987. 310 p.,
[17] p. of plates　ISBN 0-86922-426-3
NYPL [Sc D 88-1007]

CHRISTIAN SECTS - NIGERIA.
Akeredolu, J. L. The Church and its
denominations in Nigeria /. Ibadan , 1986. viii,
68 p. ;　ISBN 978-12-2193-3 (pbk.)　DDC
280/.09669 19
BR1463.N5 A39 1986　*NYPL [Sc C 89-71]*

CHRISTIAN SECTS - SOUTH AFRICA.
Oosthuizen, G. C. (Gerhardus Cornelis) The
birth of Christian Zionism in South Africa /.
KwaDlangezwa, South Africa , 1987. ii, 56 p. ;
ISBN 0-09-079580-2　DDC 289.9 19
BR1450 .O55 1987　*NYPL [Sc D 88-693]*

**CHRISTIAN SYMBOLISM. see CHRISTIAN
ART AND SYMBOLISM.**

CHRISTIAN THEOLOGY. see THEOLOGY.

CHRISTIAN UNION - NIGERIA.
Anaele, Justin Uchechukwu. The role of the
laity in ecumenism with reference to the church
in Nigeria /. Rome , 1985 (Rome : R.
Ambrosini) 146 p.　*NYPL [Sc E 88-608]*

Christiani, Joan. (joint author) Merriman, Stella E. Commonwealth Caribbean writers. Georgetown, Guyana, 1970. iv, 98 p.　*NYPL [JFF 72-67]*

La christianisation du Rwanda (1900-1945) . Rutayisire, Paul. Fribourg, Suisse , 1987. 571 p. : ISBN 2-8271-0371-0 (pbk.)
NYPL [Sc D 88-1510]

Christianisme africain . Agossou, Jacob-Mèdéwalé Jacob. Paris , 1987. 217 p. ; ISBN 2-86537-184-0
NYPL [Sc D 88-552]

Christianisme au miroir de l'Islam . Sanson, Henri. Paris , 1984. 195 p. ; ISBN 2-204-02278-0 :　*NYPL [*OGC 85-2762]*

Christianisme en Afrique noire : points de vue sur les rapports entre catholicisme et religions traditionnelles / [Bénédicta Adotevi ... et al.]. Dakar : Centre culturel L.-J. Lebret, 1979. 162 p. ; 30 cm.
1. Catholic Church - Africa, Sub-Saharan. 2. Africa, Sub-Saharan - Religion. I. Adotevi, Bénédicta. II. Rapports entre catholicisme et religions traditionnelles.
NYPL [Sc F 89-17]

CHRISTIANITY - AFRICA.
Adasu, Moses Orshio. Understanding African traditional religion /. Sherborne, Dorset, England , 1985- v. ; ISBN 0-902129-68-6
NYPL [Sc D 88-856]

Daneel, M. L. (Marthinus L.) Quest for belonging . Gweru, Zimbabwe , 1987. 310 p., [17] p. of plates : ISBN 0-86922-426-3
NYPL [Sc D 88-1007]

Hickey, Raymond. Two thousand years of African Christianity /. Ibadan, Nigeria , 1987. viii, 54 p. :　*NYPL [Sc C 88-207]*

Mbiti, John S. Bible and theology in African Christianity /. Nairobi , 1986. xiv, 248 p., [16] p. of plates : ISBN 0-19-572593-X
NYPL [Sc D 89-296]

Obianyido, Anene. Christ or Devil? . Enugu, Anambra State, Nigeria , 1988. 136 p. ; ISBN 978-233-544-4　*NYPL [Sc C 88-194]*

Salvoldi, Valentino. [Africa, il vangelo ci appartiene. English.] Africa, the gospel belongs to us . Ndola [Zambia] , 1986. 187 p ;
NYPL [Sc D 89-568]

Spiritualité et libération en Afrique /. Paris , c1987. 123 p. ;　*NYPL [Sc D 88-1416]*

CHRISTIANITY - AFRICA, CENTRAL.
Bardelli, Raimondo. Centro Africa . Bologna , 1979. 258 p. :　*NYPL [Sc C 87-359]*

CHRISTIANITY - AFRICA, SUB-SAHARAN.
Agossou, Jacob-Mèdéwalé Jacob. Christianisme africain . Paris , 1987. 217 p. ; ISBN 2-86537-184-0　*NYPL [Sc D 88-552]*

Balling, Adalbert Ludwig. Wo Menschen lachen und sich freuen . Freiburg im Breisgau , c1986. 126 p. ; ISBN 3-451-08297-7
NYPL [Sc C 89-125]

CHRISTIANITY - ALGERIA.
Sanson, Henri. Christianisme au miroir de l'Islam . Paris , 1984. 195 p. ; ISBN 2-204-02278-0 :　*NYPL [*OGC 85-2762]*

CHRISTIANITY AND COMMUNICATION. see **COMMUNICATION (THEOLOGY)**

CHRISTIANITY AND JUSTICE - AFRICA.
Schultheis, Michael J. Catholic social teaching and the Church in Africa /. Gweru, Zimbabwe , c1984. 56 p. ;　*NYPL [Sc D 88-1198]*

CHRISTIANITY AND OTHER RELIGIONS - AFRICA.
Ecumenical Association of Third World Theologians. Identidade negra e religião . Rio de Janeiro , 1986. 201 p. ;
NYPL [Sc D 88-485]

CHRISTIANITY AND OTHER RELIGIONS - AFRICAN.
Ilogu, Edmund. Igbo life and thought /. [Nigeria] , c1985. 42 p. : ISBN 978-16-0344-5
NYPL [Sc D 88-741]

CHRISTIANITY AND OTHER RELIGIONS - ISLAM.
Chukwulozie, Victor. Muslim-Christian dialogue in Nigeria /. Ibadan , 1986. xviii, 201 p. : ISBN 978-12-2192-5　*NYPL [Sc D 88-890]*

Sanni, Ishaq Kunle. Why you should never be a Christian /. Ibadan, Nigeria , 1987. ix, 125 p. :
NYPL [Sc C 88-157]

Sanson, Henri. Christianisme au miroir de l'Islam . Paris , 1984. 195 p. ; ISBN 2-204-02278-0 :　*NYPL [*OGC 85-2762]*

CHRISTIANITY - BRAZIL.
Balling, Adalbert Ludwig. Wo Menschen lachen und sich frauen . Freiburg im Breisgau , c1986. 126 p. ; ISBN 3-451-08297-7
NYPL [Sc C 89-125]

CHRISTIANITY - CONTROVERSIAL LITERATURE.
Obianyido, Anene. Christ or Devil? . Enugu, Anambra State, Nigeria , 1988. 136 p. ; ISBN 978-233-544-4　*NYPL [Sc C 88-194]*

Sanni, Ishaq Kunle. Why you should never be a Christian /. Ibadan, Nigeria , 1987. ix, 125 p. :
NYPL [Sc C 88-157]

Christianity in Borno State and Northern Gongola /. Hickey, Raymond. [Nigeria , 1984?] (Ibadan : Claverianum Press) vi, 108 p. :
NYPL [Sc D 88-882]

CHRISTIANITY IN LITERATURE.
Laverdière, Lucien, 1940- L'africain et le missionnaire . Montr´eal , 1987. 608 p. : ISBN 2-89007-640-7　*NYPL [Sc D 88-343]*

CHRISTIANITY - IVORY COAST.
Jeunes intellectuels en recherche . Abidjan , c1982. 67 p. :　*NYPL [Sc D 88-925]*

CHRISTIANITY - NIGERIA - BORNO STATE.
Hickey, Raymond. Christianity in Borno State and Northern Gongola /. [Nigeria , 1984?] (Ibadan : Claverianum Press) vi, 108 p. :
NYPL [Sc D 88-882]

CHRISTIANITY - NIGERIA - GONGOLA STATE.
Hickey, Raymond. Christianity in Borno State and Northern Gongola /. [Nigeria , 1984?] (Ibadan : Claverianum Press) vi, 108 p. :
NYPL [Sc D 88-882]

CHRISTIANITY - NIGERIA - HISTORY.
Eriwvo, Samuel U. The Urhobo, the Isoko and the Itsekiri /. Ibadan , 1979. vii, 144 p. :
NYPL [Sc D 88-769]

Ikpe, Eno Benjamin. Qua ibo Church of Nigeria . [Uyo? , 1987] (Uyo : Confidence) 31 p. :　*NYPL [Sc D 89-28]*

CHRISTIANITY - RELATIONS - ISLAM.
Sanson, Henri. Christianisme au miroir de l'Islam . Paris , 1984. 195 p. ; ISBN 2-204-02278-0 :　*NYPL [*OGC 85-2762]*

CHRISTIANITY - UNION BETWEEN CHURCHES. see **CHRISTIAN UNION.**

CHRISTIANS, BLACK - BIOGRAPHY.
Hyman, Mark. Blacks who died for Jesus . Philadelphia , 1983. iv, 107 p. : ISBN 0-915515-00-8 (pbk.) DDC 270/.08996 B 19
BR1702 .H9 1983　*NYPL [Sc D 89-263]*

CHRISTMAS - AFRICA.
An African Chris[t]mas? /. Eldoret, Kenya , 1983. 53 p. ; DDC 263/.91/096 19
BS2575.2 .A37 1983　*NYPL [Sc D 88-195]*

CHRISTMAS BOOKS. see **CHRISTMAS STORIES; CHRISTMAS.**

CHRISTMAS - FICTION. see **CHRISTMAS STORIES.**

CHRISTMAS STORIES.
Babcock, Bernie Smade, 1868-1962. Halleroogy's ride with Santa Claus. Perry, Ark., c1943. 48 p.
PZ7.B12 Hal　*NYPL [Sc D 88-1285]*

Caudill, Rebecca, 1899- A certain small shepherd /. New York , 1965. 48 p. :
NYPL [Sc D 88-433]

Colimon, Marie-Thérèse. La source [microform] : conte de Noel /. [Port-au-Prince? , 1973?] (Port-au-Prine : Atelier Fardin) 17 p. :
NYPL [Sc Micro F-10983]

CHRISTMAS STORIES, AMERICAN.
Haley, Alex. A different kind of Christmas /. New York , 1988. 101 p. ; ISBN 0-385-26043-1 : DDC 813/.54 19
PS3558.A3575 D54 1988
NYPL [Sc C 89-38]

CHRISTMAS - WEST INDIES, BRITISH.
Dirks, Robert, 1942- The Black Saturnalia . Gainesville , c1987. xvii, 228 p., [7] p. of

---

plates : ISBN 0-8130-0843-3 (pbk. : alk. paper) : DDC 394.2/68282/09729 19
GT4987.23 .D57 1987
NYPL [L-10 5328 no.72]

Christophe Colomb raconté par son fils /. Colón, Fernando, 1488-1539. [Historie. English.] Paris , 1986. xviii, 265 p., [8] p. of plates : ISBN 2-262-00387-4　*NYPL [Sc D 88-504]*

Christopher, Matt. The basket counts, by Matt Christopher. Illustrated by George Guzzi. [1st ed.] Boston, Little, Brown [1968] 125 p. illus. 20 cm. Long practice improves Mel's value as a basketball player, but how does he surmount the prejudice of a teammate? DDC [Fic] 19
1. Basketball - Stories. 2. Afro-American youth - Juvenile fiction. I. Guzzi, George, ill. II. Title.
PZ7.C458 Bash　*NYPL [Sc C 89-15]*

Chronicle . Greenly, Mike, 1944- New York , c1986. 422 p. ; ISBN 0-8290-1800-X : DDC 616.97/92/00922 19
RC607.A26 G73 1986
NYPL [Sc D 88-1087]

Chronicles of the hostile sun /. Brand, Dionne, 1953- Toronto, Ont., Canada , 1984. 75 p. ; ISBN 0-88795-033-7 (pbk.) : DDC 811/.54 19
PR9199.3.B683 C48 1984
NYPL [Sc D 88-1227]

Chronique d'une journée de répression /. Konaté, Moussa, 1951- Paris , c1988. 143 p. ;
NYPL [Sc D 88-846]

Chuck, Delroy H. Understanding crime : an introduction / by Delroy H. Chuck ; edited by Derrick McKoy. Bridgetown, Barbados : Caribbean Law Publishers, [c1986] xi, 171 p. ; 22 cm. Includes bibliographical references. ISBN 976-8043-00-8 (pbk.) DDC 364 19
1. Crime and criminals - Caribbean Area. I. McKoy, Derrick. II. Title.
HV6025 .C48 1986　*NYPL [Sc D 89-195]*

Chukwuemeka Ike, Vincent. see **Ike, Vincent Chukwuemeka, 1931-**

Chukwuka, J. I. N. Zandi and the wonderful pillow / J.I.N. Chukwuka ; illustrated by Norman Burgin. Lagos, Nigeria : African Universities Press, 1977. 48 p. : ill. ; 19 cm. (African junior library. 13) SCHOMBURG CHILDREN'S COLLECTION. ISBN 0-410-80099-6
1. Demonology - Africa - Juvenile fiction. I. Burgin, Norma. II. Schomburg Children's Collection. III. Title. IV. Series.　*NYPL [Sc C 88-76]*

Chukwulozie, Victor. Muslim-Christian dialogue in Nigeria / Victor Chukwulozie Ibadan : Daystar Press, 1986. xviii, 201 p. : maps ; 21 cm. Includes index. Bibliography: p. 186-199. ISBN 978-12-2192-5
1. Christianity and other religions - Islam. 2. Islam - Relations - Christianity. 3. Nigeria - Religion. I. Title.
NYPL [Sc D 88-890]

The Church and its denominations in Nigeria . Akeredolu, J. L. Ibadan , 1986. viii, 68 p. ; ISBN 978-12-2193-3 (pbk.) DDC 280/.09669 19
BR1463.N5 A39 1986　*NYPL [Sc C 89-71]*

Church and politics in Eastern Nigeria, 1945-66 . Amucheazi, E. C. (Elochukwu C.) Yaba Lagos , 1986. xvii, 256 p. : ISBN 978-13-2786-3 (pbk.) DDC 322/.1/096694 19
DT515.9.E3 A66 1986　*NYPL [Sc D 88-992]*

CHURCH AND RACE RELATION - SOUTH AFRICA.
De Gruchy, John W. Theology and ministry in context and crisis . London , 1987, c1986. 183 p. ; ISBN 0-00-599969-3　*NYPL [Sc C 88-73]*

CHURCH AND RACE RELATIONS - SOUTH AFRICA.
Turner, Richard, 1941- The eye of the needle . Maryknoll, N.Y. , 1978, c1972. xxiv, 173 p. ; ISBN 0-88344-121-7. DDC 309.1/68/06
DT763 .T85 1978　*NYPL [JLD 84-744]*

Church and slave in Perry County, Missouri, 1818-1865 /. Poole, Stafford. Lewiston, N.Y., USA , c1986. xvii, 251 p. : ISBN 0-88946-666-1 (alk. paper) : DDC 306/.362/09778694 19
E445.M67 P66 1986　*NYPL [Sc E 89-102]*

CHURCH AND SOCIAL PROBLEMS - AFRICA.
Schultheis, Michael J. Catholic social teaching and the Church in Africa /. Gweru, Zimbabwe , c1984. 56 p. ;　*NYPL [Sc D 88-1198]*

CHURCH AND SOCIAL PROBLEMS - AFRICA, SOUTHERN.
Die Bischofskonferenzen Angolas und Südafrikas zu Frieden und Gerechtigkeit in ihren Länder. Bonn , 1986. 54 p. ;
NYPL [Sc D 88-929]

CHURCH AND STATE - CAMEROON.
Kengne Pokam, E (Emmanuel), 1941- Les Églises chrétiennes face à la montée du nationalisme camerounais /. Paris [1987] 202 p. ; ISBN 2-85802-823-0 *NYPL [Sc D 88-437]*

CHURCH AND STATE - NIGERIA, EASTERN.
Amucheazi, E. C. (Elochukwu C.) Church and politics in Eastern Nigeria, 1945-66 . Yaba Lagos , 1986. xvii, 256 p. : ISBN 978-13-2786-3 (pbk.) DDC 322/.1/096694 19
DT515.9.E3 A66 1986 NYPL [Sc D 88-992]

Church Missionary Society. Africa (Group 3) Committee.
Catalogue of the papers of the missions of the Africa (Group 3) Committee / catalogued by Rosemary A. Keen. 2nd ed. London : Church Missionary Society, 1981. 8 v. ; 30 cm. Cover title (all v.): Africa (Group 3) missions. Includes other editions of some volumes. CONTENTS.- v. 1. West Africa (Sierra Leone) Mission, 1803-1934 -- v. 2. Nigeria missions, 1844-1934 -- v. 3. South and east Africa missions (South Africa, Kenya, and Tanzania), 1836-1934 -- v. 4. East Africa missions (Nyanza, Uganda, and Ruanda), 1875-1934 -- v. 5. Egypt and Sudanese missions (including Upper Nile), 1889-1934 -- v. 6. Mediterranean and Palestine missions, 1811-1934 -- v. 7. New Zealand Mission, 1809-1914 -- v. 8. West Indies Mission, 1819-1861. DDC 266/.3 19
1. Church Missionary Society. Africa (Group 3) Committee - Archives - Catalogs. 2. University of Birmingham. Library - Catalogs. 3. Missions - Africa - History - Sources - Bibliography - Catalogs. 4. Missions - Palestine - History - Sources - Bibliography - Catalogs. 5. Missions - New Zealand - History - Sources - Bibliography - Catalogs. 6. Missions - Caribbean Area - History - Sources - Bibliography - Catalogs. I. Keen, Rosemary A. II. Title. III. Title: Africa (Group 3) missions.
CD1069.L715 C47 1981 NYPL [Sc F 88-78]

CHURCH MISSIONARY SOCIETY. AFRICA (GROUP 3) COMMITTEE - ARCHIVES - CATALOGS.
Church Missionary Society. Africa (Group 3) Committee. Catalogue of the papers of the missions of the Africa (Group 3) Committee /. London , 1981. 8 v. ; DDC 266/.3 19
CD1069.L715 C47 1981 NYPL [Sc F 88-78]

Church Missionary Society for Africa and the East. see Church Missionary Society.

CHURCH OF ENGLAND - ENGLAND - CLERGY - BIOGRAPHY.
Bohrer, Dick. John Newton, letters of a slave trader /. Chicago , c1983. viii, 130 p. ; ISBN 0-8024-0158-9 (pbk.) DDC 283/.3 19
BX5199.N55 B64 1983 NYPL [Sc C 88-235]

CHURCH OF ENGLAND. PROVINCE OF SOUTH AFRICA - BISHOPS - BIOGRAPHY.
Du Boulay, Shirley. Tutu . London , 1988. 286 p., [8] p. of plates : ISBN 0-340-41614-9 : DDC 283/.68/0924 19
*BX5700.6.Z8T87 NYPL [*R-ZPZ 88-3127]*

The Church of Ethiopia. Ya'Ityoṗy a 'ortodks taw aḥedo béta kerestiy an. Addis Ababa, 1970. iv, 97 p. *NYPL [Sc D 89-386]*

CHURCH OF NIGERIA - SERMONS.
Odunuga, S. A. F. (Samuel Adedoyin Folafunmi), 1902- [Sermons. Selections.] The life of Venerable Archdeacon S.A.F. Odunuga /. [Nigeria] , 1982. xiii, 175 p., [2] p. of plates : DDC 252/.03 19
BX5700.7.Z6 O28 1982
NYPL [Sc E 89-142]

CHURCH OF THE NAZARITES - GOVERNMENT.
Oosthuizen, G. C. (Gerhardus Cornelis) Succession conflict within the Church of the Nazarites, iBandla zamaNazaretha /. Durban [South Africa] [1981] 71 p. ; ISBN 0-949947-43-1 (pbk.) DDC 289.9 19
BX7068.7.Z5 O56 1981
NYPL [Sc F 87-351]

CHURCH OF THE PROVINCE OF CENTRAL AFRICA - CLERGY - BIOGRAPHY.
Walker, David A. C. Paterson of Cyrene . Gweru, Zimbabwe , 1985. xi, 85 p. : ISBN 0-86922-340-2 DDC 283/.3 B 19
BX5700.4.Z8 P378 1985
NYPL [Sc D 88-229]

CHURCH OF THE PROVINCE OF SOUTH AFRICA. DIOCESE OF LESOTHO - HISTORY.
Dove, R. (Reginald) Anglican pioneers in Lesotho . [s.l. , 1975?] (s.l. : Mazenod Institute) 216 p., [1] fold. leaf of plates : DDC 283/.68/6
BX5700.6.A44 L473 NYPL [JXD 84-17]

Church, Ronald James Harrison. Africa and the islands /. London , 1966. xiv, 494 p. :
NYPL [Sc D 88-352]

The Church we want to be . Marsabit Diocesan Pastoral Conference (1987 : Nyeri Kenya) Marsabit, Kenya , 1988. 42 p. :
NYPL [Sc D 89-463]

CHURCH WORK, SOCIAL. see CHURCH AND SOCIAL PROBLEMS.

CHURCH WORK WITH MINORITIES - CATHOLIC CHURCH.
Faith and culture . Washington, D.C. , c1987. 111 p. : ISBN 1-555-86994-7 (pbk.) DDC 268/.82 19
BX1968 .F24 1987 NYPL [Sc D 88-1059]

CHURCH WORK WITH REFUGEES - AFRICA.
All Africa Conference of Churches. Special Agency for EPEAA. Ecumenical Programme for Emergency Action in Africa . Nairobi , 1967. [193] p. ; *NYPL [Sc F 88-74]*

CHURCHES, AFRO-AMERICAN. see AFRO-AMERICAN CHURCHES.

CHURCHES, CITY. see CITY CHURCHES.

CHURCHES, TOWN. see CITY CHURCHES.

CHURCHES, URBAN. see CITY CHURCHES.

CHURCHYARDS. see CEMETERIES.

Chuta, Enyinna. Rural small-scale industries and employment in Africa and Asia . Geneva , 1984. x, 159 p. ; ISBN 92-2-103513-1 (pbk.) : DDC 338.6/42/095 19
HD2346.A55 R87 1984
NYPL [JLE 84-3222]

Ciammaichella, Glauco. Libyens et Français au Tchad (1897-1914) : la confrérie senoussie et le commerce transsaharien / Glauco Ciammaichella ; préface de J.-L. Miège. Paris : Editions du Centre national de la recherche scientifique, 1987. 187 p. : ill., maps ; 24 cm. Bibliography: p. 133-147. ISBN 2-222-04067-1
1. Senussites. 2. Chad - History - 19th century. 3. Chad - Relations - France. 4. France - Relations - Chad. 5. Chad - Relations - Libya. 6. Libya - Relations - Chad. I. Title.
NYPL [Sc E 89-182]

Los cimarrones del maniel de Neiba . Deive, Carlos Esteban, 1935- Santo Domingo, República Dominicana , 1985. 199 p. :
NYPL [Sc D 89-173]

Ciné-rituel de femmes dogon /. Wanono, Nadine. Paris , 1987. 138 p. : ISBN 2-222-03961-4 (pbk)
NYPL [Sc E 88-177]

The cinema of apartheid . Tomaselli, Keyan G., 1948- New York , c1988. 300 p. ; ISBN 0-918266-19-X (pbk.) DDC 384/.8/0968 19
PN1993.5.S6 T58 1988
NYPL [Sc D 88-1242]

Cinyanja/Ciceŵa . Salaün, N. Ndola, Zambia , 1979. 146 p. ; *NYPL [Sc D 88-1178]*

CIRCLE Project. Gray, Mattie Evans. Images . Sacramento, Calif. , c1988. 185 p. : ISBN 0-8011-0782-2 *NYPL [Sc F 89-134]*

CISKEI (SOUTH AFRICA) - ECONOMIC CONDITIONS.
Bekker, S. B. Socio-economic survey of the Amatola Basin . Grahamstown [South Africa] Institute of Social and Economic Rrsearch, 1981. 58, xxxxiv p. : ISBN 0-86810-073-0
NYPL [Sc F 87-430]

CISKEI (SOUTH AFRICA) - SOCIAL CONDITIONS.
Bekker, S. B. Socio-economic survey of the Amatola Basin . Grahamstown [South Africa]

Institute of Social and Economic Rrsearch, 1981. 58, xxxxiv p. : ISBN 0-86810-073-0
NYPL [Sc F 87-430]

Cissé, Ahmed-Tidjani.
Quand les graines éclosent... / Ahmed Tidjani Cissé. Paris : Nubia, 1984. 78 p. ; 18 cm. Poems. ISBN 2-85586-028-8
I. Title. NYPL [Sc C 88-192]

Le tana de Soumangourou / Ahmed-Tidjani Cissé. Paris : Nubia, 1988. 77 p. ; 18 cm. ISBN 2-85586-036-9
1. Kanté, Soumangouru - Drama. I. Title.
NYPL [Sc C 89-73]

Citadel Military College of South Carolina.
Blacks in southern politics /. New York , 1987. vii, 305 p. : ISBN 0-275-92655-9 (alk. paper) : DDC 323.1/196073/075 19
E185.92 .B58 1987 NYPL [Sc E 88-196]

CITIES AND STATE. see URBAN POLICY.

CITIES AND TOWNS - ANGOLA.
Amaral, Ilidio do. Ensaio de um estudo geográfico da rede urbana de Angola. Lisboa, 1962. 99 p.
HT148.A5 A7 NYPL [Sc E 98-118]

CITIES AND TOWNS - ARAB COUNTRIES - CONGRESSES.
Islamic city. Spanish. La ciudad islámica . Barcelona [Paris] , 1982. 260 p. : ISBN 92-3-301665-X (Unesco)
NYPL [Sc D 88-596]

CITIES AND TOWNS - ETHIOPIA - BAGEMDER - CASE STUDIES.
Baker, Jonathan. The rural-urban dichotomy in the developing world . Oslo . 372 p. : ISBN 82-00-07412-9
HC845.Z7 B343 1986 NYPL [JFD 87-3176]

CITIES AND TOWNS, ISLAMIC - ARAB COUNTRIES - CONGRESSES.
Islamic city. Spanish. La ciudad islámica . Barcelona [Paris] , 1982. 260 p. : ISBN 92-3-301665-X (Unesco)
NYPL [Sc D 88-596]

CITIES AND TOWNS, MOVEMENT TO. see URBANIZATION.

Cities and towns, Muslim. see Cities and towns, Islamic.

CITIES AND TOWNS - PLANNING. see CITY PLANNING.

CITIES AND TOWNS - SENEGAL - GROWTH.
Nicolas, Pierre. Naissance d'une ville au Sénégal . Paris , c1988. 193 p., [8] p. of plates ; ISBN 2-86537-195-6 *NYPL [Sc F 89-131]*

CITIES AND TOWNS - TRINIDAD AND TOBAGO.
Anthony, Michael. Towns and villages of Trinidad and Tobago /. St. James, Port of Spain , 1988. v., 342 p. :
NYPL [Sc D 89-404]

Citizen. Parker, Aida. Secret U. S. war against South Africa /. Johannesburg , c1977. 79 p. ;
NYPL [Sc D 88-277]

Citizen of New-York. An address on slavery, and against immediate emancipation : with a plan of their being gradually emancipated & colonized, in 32 years / by a citizen of New-York. New-York : Printed and sold by S.B. White, 1834. 16 p. ; 21 cm. Schomburg's copy imperfect: p. 9-16 wanting.
1. Slavery - United States - Controversial literature - 1834. 2. Slavery - United States - Colonization. I. Title.
NYPL [Sc Rare G 86-19]

CITY AND TOWN LIFE - FICTION.
Williams-Garcia, Rita. Blue tights /. New York , c1987. 138 p. ; ISBN 0-525-67234-6 DDC [Fic] 19
PZ7.W6713 Bl 1987 NYPL [Sc D 88-939]

CITY AND TOWN LIFE - JUVENILE FICTION.
Dean, Leigh. The looking down game. New York [1968] 34 p. DDC [Fic]
PZ7.D3446 Lo NYPL [Sc D 89-111]

Lynch, Lorenzo, 1932- The hot dog man. Indianapolis [1970] [24] p. DDC [Fic]
PZ7.L97977 Ho NYPL [Sc F 88-253]

Weil, Lisl. The funny old bag. New York [1974] [40] p. ISBN 0-8193-0717-3 DDC [E]
PZ7.W433 Fu NYPL [Sc E 88-529]

CITY AND TOWN LIFE - JUVENILE LITERATURE.
Gross, Mary Anne. (comp) Ah, man, you found me again. Boston [1972] x, 84 p. ISBN 0-8070-1532-6 DDC 810/.8/09282
HQ792.U53 N53 1972   **NYPL** *[Sc F 88-336]*

CITY AND TOWN LIFE - UNITED STATES - JUVENILE LITERATURE.
In the city /. New York , c1965. 32 p.
   NYPL *[Sc D 89-82]*

CITY CHILDREN - PICTORIAL WORKS.
Buckley, Peter. Five friends at school /. New York , c1966. 96 p. :   **NYPL** *[Sc E 88-590]*

CITY CHILDREN - UNITED STATES - JUVENILE FICTION.
Around the city /. New York , c1965. 127 p. :
   NYPL *[Sc E 89-17]*

CITY CHURCHES.
Harris, James H., 1952- Black ministers and laity in the urban church. Lanham, MD , c1987. xi, 133 p. : ISBN 0-8191-5823-2 (alk. paper) : DDC 253/.2/08996073 19
BR563.N4 B575 1987   **NYPL** *[Sc D 89-127]*

CITY LIFE. see CITY AND TOWN LIFE.

A city on a hill /. Redhead, Wilfred. Barbados, West Indies , 1985 (Barbados, West Indies : Letchworth Press) 120 p. :
   NYPL *[Sc D 87-1423]*

CITY PLANNING - SENEGAL.
Nicolas, Pierre. Naissance d'une ville au Sénégal . Paris , c1988. 193 p., [8] p. of plates ; ISBN 2-86537-195-6   **NYPL** *[Sc F 89-131]*

CITY PLANNING - SOUTH AFRICA - GRAHAMSTOWN.
Davies, W. J. A review of issues related to planning and development in Grahamstown . Grahamstown [South Africa] , 1986. 114 p. : ISBN 0-86810-130-3   **NYPL** *[Sc F 87-431]*

CITY PLANNING - TANZANIA - DODOMA.
10 years of CDA. Dodoma [Tanzania] [1983] [2], 29 p. : DDC 307.1/4/0967826 19
HT169.T332 D6213 1983
   NYPL *[Sc F 89-61]*

City University of New York. Center for the Study of Women and Society. Library and information sources on women . New York , c1988. ix, 254 p. ; ISBN 0-935312-88-9 (pbk.) : DDC 305.4/025/7471 19
HQ1181.U5 L52 1987
   NYPL *[*R-Econ. 88-4682]*

The city where no one dies /. Dadié, Bernard Binlin, 1916- Washington, D.C. , c1986. 139 p. ; ISBN 0-89410-499-3
   NYPL *[Sc D 88-1468]*

La ciudad islámica . Islamic city. Spanish. Barcelona [Paris] , 1982. 260 p. : ISBN 92-3-301665-X (Unesco)
   NYPL *[Sc D 88-596]*

CIVIC PLANNING. see CITY PLANNING.

CIVIL DISOBEDIENCE. see GOVERNMENT, RESISTANCE TO.

CIVIL DISORDERS. see RIOTS.

CIVIL GOVERNMENT. see POLITICAL SCIENCE.

CIVIL LAW (ISLAMIC LAW) see ISLAMIC LAW.

CIVIL LIBERTY. see LIBERTY.

CIVIL-MILITARY RELATIONS - LIBERIA.
Liberia . Hamburg , 1986. vi, 292 p., [1] folded leaf of plates : ISBN 3-923519-65-6 (pbk.) DDC 322/.5/096662 19
JQ3923.5.C58 L53 1986
   NYPL *[Sc D 88-1320]*

CIVIL-MILITARY RELATIONS - NIGERIA.
The impact of military rule on Nigeria's administration /. Ile-Ife, Nigeria , c1987. vi, 344 p. ; ISBN 978-266-601-7
   NYPL *[Sc D 88-733]*

CIVIL-MILITARY RELATIONS - NIGERIA - CONGRESSES.
Proceedings of the colloquium on Why army rule? . [Lagos? , 1986 or 19. 338 p. ;
   NYPL *[Sc G 88-23]*

CIVIL-MILITARY RELATIONS - UGANDA - HISTORY.
Omara-Otunnu, Amii, 1952- Politics and the military in Uganda, 1890-1985 /. Basingstoke,

Hampshire , 1987. xx, 218 p. : ISBN 0-333-41980-4   **NYPL** *[JFD 87-8644]*

CIVIL OBEDIENCE. see GOVERNMENT, RESISTANCE TO.

CIVIL RIGHTS - AFRICA.
Zimba, L. S. (Lawrence S.) The Zambian Bill of Rights . Nairobi, Kenya , 1984. x, 288 p. ; DDC 342.6894/085 346.8940285 19
LAW   **NYPL** *[Sc E 88-392]*

CIVIL RIGHTS - BERMUDA.
Philip, Ira. Freedom fighters . London , 1987. 275 p., [8] p. of plates : ISBN 0-947638-42-3 (cased) : DDC 323.1/196/07299 19
   NYPL *[Sc D 88-1137]*

CIVIL RIGHTS - BOTSWANA.
Maope, Kelebone A. Human rights in Botswana, Lesotho and Swaziland . Roma, Lesotho , 1986. iii, 155 p. ;
   NYPL *[Sc D 88-855]*

CIVIL RIGHTS CONGRESS (U. S.)
Horne, Gerald. Communist front? . Rutherford [N.J.] , London , c1988. 454 p. ; ISBN 0-8386-3285-8 (alk. paper) DDC 323.1/196073/073 19
E185.61 .H8 1988   **NYPL** *[Sc E 88-147]*

CIVIL RIGHTS - GRENADA.
Trotman, Donald A. B. Report on human rights in Grenada . [Bustamante?] [198-] viii, 54 p. : DDC 323.4/9/09729845 19
JC599.G76 T76 1980z   **NYPL** *[Sc D 88-816]*

CIVIL RIGHTS IN ART.
Callahan, Nancy. The Freedom Quilting Bee /. Tuscaloosa, Ala. , c1987. xi, 255 p., [8] p. of plates : ISBN 0-8173-0310-3 DDC 976.0/3800496073 19
NK9112 .C34 1987   **NYPL** *[3-MOT 88-1171]*

CIVIL RIGHTS - JAMAICA.
The Jamaica Council for Human Rights speaks [microform] [Kingston, Jamaica , 1981] 45 p. ;
   NYPL *[Sc Micro R-4132 no. 22]*

CIVIL RIGHTS - LESOTHO.
Maope, Kelebone A. Human rights in Botswana, Lesotho and Swaziland . Roma, Lesotho , 1986. iii, 155 p. ;
   NYPL *[Sc D 88-855]*

CIVIL RIGHTS - MADAGASCAR.
Deleris, Ferdinand. Ratsiraka . Paris , c1986. 135 p. ; ISBN 2-85802-697-1
   NYPL *[Sc D 88-777]*

CIVIL RIGHTS - MISSISSIPPI - JUVENILE FICTION.
Kelley, Sally. Summer growing time. New York [1971] 125 p. ISBN 0-670-68172-5 DDC [Fic]
PZ7.K2818 Su   **NYPL** *[Sc D 89-88]*

The Civil rights movement in America : essays / by David Levering Lewis ... [et al.] ; edited by Charles W. Eagles. Jackson : University Press of Mississippi, c1986. xii, 188 p. ; 23 cm. Includes index. Bibliography: p. 173-177. ISBN 0-87805-297-6 (alk. paper) DDC 323.1/196073 19
1. Afro-Americans - Civil rights. 2. United States - Race relations. I. Lewis, David L. II. Eagles, Charles W.
E185.615 .C585 1986   **NYPL** *[IEC 87-273]*

CIVIL RIGHTS MOVEMENTS - CANADA.
Thomson, Colin A., 1938- Born with a call . Dartmouth, Nova Scotia , 1986. 157 p., [8] p. of plates :   **NYPL** *[Sc F 88-63]*

CIVIL RIGHTS MOVEMENTS - UNITED STATES.
Eckardt, A. Roy (Arthur Roy), 1918- Black-woman-Jew. Bloomington , c1989. 229 p. ; ISBN 0-253-31221-3 DDC 305.4/8896073 19
E185.86 .E28 1989   **NYPL** *[Sc E 89-209]*

CIVIL RIGHTS MOVEMENTS - UNITED STATES - HISTORY - 20TH CENTURY.
Branch, Taylor. Parting the waters . New York , c1988- v. : ISBN 0-671-46097-8 (v. 1) DDC 973/.0496073 19
E185.61 .B7914 1988   **NYPL** *[IEC 88-122]*

Lipsitz, George. A life in the struggle . Philadelphia , 1988. viii, 292 p. : ISBN 0-87722-550-8 (alk. paper) DDC 973/.0496073.3024 B 19
E185.97.P49 L57 1988   **NYPL** *[Sc E 89-43]*

CIVIL RIGHTS MOVEMENTS - VIRGINIA - NORFOLK.
Suggs, Henry Lewis. P.B. Young,

newspaperman . Charlottesville , 1988. xxii, 254 p. : ISBN 0-8139-1178-8 DDC 070.4/1/0924 B 19
PN4874.Y59 S84 1988   **NYPL** *[JFE 89-97]*

CIVIL RIGHTS - NAMIBIA.
Khalifa, Ahmad M. Adverse consequences for the enjoyment of human rights of political, military, economic, and other forms of assistance given to the racist and colonialist régime of South Africa /. New York , 1985. ii, 164, [30] p. ; ISBN 92-1-154046-1 (pbk.) DDC 332.6/73/0968 19
HG5851.A3 K45 1985   **NYPL** *[Sc F 88-273]*

Menschenrechte im Konflikt um Südwestafrika/Namibia . Frankfurt a.M. , 1985. 56 p. :   **NYPL** *[Sc F 88-162]*

CIVIL RIGHTS - SOUTH AFRICA.
Khalifa, Ahmad M. Adverse consequences for the enjoyment of human rights of political, military, economic, and other forms of assistance given to the racist and colonialist régime of South Africa /. New York , 1985. ii, 164, [30] p. ; ISBN 92-1-154046-1 (pbk.) DDC 332.6/73/0968 19
HG5851.A3 K45 1985   **NYPL** *[Sc F 88-273]*

Mathews, Anthony S., 1930- Freedom, state security and the rule of law . London , c1988. xxx, 312 p. ; ISBN 0-421-39640-7
   NYPL *[Sc F 89-102]*

South Africa . London , New York , 1988. 159 p. : ISBN 0-86187-979-1 : DDC 323.4/0968 19
   NYPL *[JLE 88-4543]*

CIVIL RIGHTS - SWAZILAND.
Maope, Kelebone A. Human rights in Botswana, Lesotho and Swaziland . Roma, Lesotho , 1986. iii, 155 p. ;
   NYPL *[Sc D 88-855]*

CIVIL RIGHTS - UNITED STATES.
Antieau, Chester James. Federal civil rights acts . Rochester, N.Y. , San Francisco, Calif. , 1980. 2 v. ; DDC 342.73/085 19
KF4749 .A745 1980   **NYPL** *[Sc F 83-46]*

A Less than perfect union . New York , 1988. vii, 424 p. ; ISBN 0-85345-738-7 : DDC 342.73/029 347.30229 19
KF4550.A2 L47 1987   **NYPL** *[Sc D 88-724]*

Walton, Hanes, 1941- When the marching stopped . Albany , c1988. xxiv, 263 p. : ISBN 0-88706-687-9 DDC 353.0081/1 19
E185.615 .W325 1988   **NYPL** *[Sc E 89-10]*

CIVIL RIGHTS - UNITED STATES - CASES.
Joseph, Joel D. Black Mondays . Bethesda, MD , c1987. 286 p. : ISBN 0-915765-44-6 : DDC 347.73/26 347.30735 19
KF4549 .J67 1987   **NYPL** *[Sc D 88-963]*

CIVIL RIGHTS - UNITED STATES - HISTORY.
Swinney, Everette, 1923- Suppressing the Ku Klux Klan . New York , 1987. ix, 360 p. ; ISBN 0-8240-8297-4 (alk. paper) : DDC 342.73/0873 347.302873 19
KF4757 .S93 1987   **NYPL** *[Sc D 88-653]*

CIVIL RIGHTS WORKERS IN LITERATURE.
Harris, Norman, 1951- Connecting times . Jackson , c1988. 197 p. ; ISBN 0-87805-335-2 (alk. paper) DDC 813/.54/093520396073 19
PS153.N5 H27 1988   **NYPL** *[Sc E 88-288]*

CIVIL RIGHTS WORKERS - KENTUCKY - BIOGRAPHY.
Johnson, Lyman T., 1906- The rest of the dream . Lexington, Ky. , c1988. xiv, 230 p., [8] p. of plates : ISBN 0-8131-1674-0 (alk. paper) : DDC 976.9/00496073024 B 19
E185.97.J693 A3 1988   **NYPL** *[Sc E 89-211]*

CIVIL RIGHTS WORKERS - MISSISSIPPI - HISTORY - 20TH CENTURY.
McAdam, Doug. Freedom Summer /. New York , c1988. [xiii], 333 p., [14] p. of plates : ISBN 0-19-504367-7 (alk. paper) DDC 976.2/00496073 19
E185.93.M6 M28 1988   **NYPL** *[Sc E 88-563]*

CIVIL RIGHTS WORKERS - SOUTH AFRICA - BIOGRAPHY.
Levine, Janet, 1945- Inside apartheid . Chicago , c1988. xvi, 287 p., [16] p. of plates : ISBN 0-8092-4544-2 : DDC 968.06/3/0924 B 19
DT779.955.L48 A3 1989
   NYPL *[JLE 89-122]*

Ramusi, Molapatene Collins. Soweto, my love

/. New York , c1988. viii, 262 p. ; ISBN
0-8050-0263-4 DDC 968.06/092/4 B 19
DT779.955.R36 A3 1988

NYPL [Sc E 89-95]

**CIVIL RIGHTS WORKERS - SOUTH
AFRICA - BIOGRAPHY - JUVENILE
LITERATURE.**
Haskins, James, 1941- Winnie Mandela . New
York , c1988. 179 p., [12] p. of plates : ISBN
0-399-21515-8 DDC 968.06/092/4 B 92 19
DT779.955.M36 H38 1988

NYPL [Sc D 88-1138]

**CIVIL RIGHTS WORKERS - UNITED
STATES - BIOGRAPHY.**
Johnson, James Weldon, 1871-1938. Along this
way . New York , 1933. 418 p., [16] leaves of
plates :   *NYPL [Sc Rare F 89-9]*

Lipsitz, George. A life in the struggle .
Philadelphia , 1988. viii, 292 p. : ISBN
0-87722-550-8 (alk. paper)   DDC
973/.0496073024 B 19
E185.97.P49 L57 1988   *NYPL [Sc E 89-43]*

**CIVIL RIGHTS WORKERS - UNITED
STATES - BIOGRAPHY - JUVENILE
LITERATURE.**
Rosset, Lisa. James Baldwin /. New York,
N.Y. , 1989. 111 p. : ISBN 1-555-46572-2 DDC
818/.5409 B 92 19
PS3552.A45 Z87 1989   *NYPL [Sc E 89-224]*

Tolbert-Rouchaleau, Jane. James Weldon
Johnson /. New York , c1988. 110 p. : ISBN
1-555-46596-X DDC 818/.5209 B 92 19
PS3519.O2625 Z894 1988

NYPL [Sc E 88-164]

CIVIL RIGHTS - ZAMBIA.
Zimba, L. S. (Lawrence S.) The Zambian Bill of
Rights . Nairobi, Kenya , 1984. x, 288 p. ;
DDC 342.6894/085 346.8940285 19
LAW   *NYPL [Sc E 88-392]*

CIVIL SERVICE - NIGERIA.
Adedeji, Adebayo. The political class, the
higher civil service and the challenge of
nation-building [microform] /. Addis Ababa,
Ethiopia [1981?] 24 p. ;
NYPL [Sc Micro F-11062]

CIVIL SERVICE - ZAMBIA.
Lungu, Gatian F. Administrative
decentralisation in the Zambian bureaucracy .
Gweru, Zimbabwe , c1985. 85 p. :
NYPL [Sc D 89-318]

**CIVIL WAR - UNITED STATES. see UNITED
STATES - HISTORY - CIVIL WAR, 1861-
1865.**

**Civilization, American. see Latin America -
Civilization.**

CIVILIZATION, ANCIENT.
Black women in antiquity /. New Brunswick,
[N.J.] , London , 1988. 192 p. : ISBN
0-87855-982-5   *NYPL [Sc D 89-351]*

Clapham, Christopher S. Transformation and
continuity in revolutionary Ethiopia /
Christopher Clapham. Cambridge
[Cambridgeshire] ; New York : Cambridge
University Press, 1988. xviii, 284 p. : map. ; 24
cm. (African studies series. 61) Includes index.
Bibliography: p. 262-275. ISBN 0-521-33441-1 DDC
963.07 19
1. Ethiopia - Politics and government - 1974-. I. Title.
II. Series.
JQ3752 .C55 1988   *NYPL [Sc E 88-446]*

Clarence and Corinne. Johnson, A. E. (Amelia
E.), b. 1859. Clarence and Corinne, or, God's
way /. New York , 1988. xxxviii, 187 p. :
ISBN 0-19-505264-1 (alk. paper) DDC 813/.4
19
PS2134.J515 C5 1988   *NYPL [JFC 88-2145]*

Clarence and Corinne, or, God's way /. Johnson,
A. E. (Amelia E.), b. 1859. New York , 1988.
xxxviii, 187 p. : ISBN 0-19-505264-1 (alk. paper)
DDC 813/.4 19
PS2134.J515 C5 1988   *NYPL [JFC 88-2145]*

Clark, John Pepper, 1935- Mandela and other
poems / J P Clark. Ikeja : Longman Nigeria,
1988. vi, 37 p. ; 18 cm. (Drumbeat poetry) ISBN
978-13-9633-4
I. Title.   *NYPL [Sc C 89-154]*

Clark, Margaret Goff. Freedom crossing.
Illustrated by Ernest Kurt Barth. New York,
Funk & Wagnalls [1969] 128 p. illus. 21 cm.

After spending four years with relatives in the South, a
fifteen-year-old girl accepts the idea that slaves are
property and is horrified to learn when she returns
North that her home is a station on the underground
railroad. SCHOMBURG CHILDREN'S
COLLECTION.   DDC [Fic]
1. Underground Railroad - Juvenile fiction. I. Barth,
Ernest Kurt, illus. II. Schomburg Children's Collection.
III. Title.
PZ7.C5487 Fr   *NYPL [Sc D 88-1121]*

Clarke, A. M. Verses for emancipation : a tribute
to Dr. Eric Williams / by A.M. Clarke. [Port of
Spain : Printex, 1986] 41 p. ; 21 cm. DDC 811
19
1. Williams, Eric Eustace, 1911-. 2. Blacks - Poetry. 3.
Slavery - Emancipation - Poetry. 4. Folk-songs - West
Indies - Texts. I. Williams, Eric Eustace, 1911-. II.
Title.
PR9272.9.C53 V4 1986

NYPL [Sc D 88-981]

Clarke, Austin, 1934- Nine men who laughed /
Austin Clarke. Markham, Ontario, Canada :
Penguin Books, 1986. 225 p. ; 20 cm. (Penguin
short fiction) ISBN 0-14-008560-2
1. West Indians - Ontario - Toronto - Fiction. I. Title.
NYPL [JFD 87-7697]

Clarke, John Henrik, 1915- The image of Africa
in the mind of the Afro-American : African
identity in the literature of struggle / by John
Henrik Clarke. New York : Phelps-Stokes
Fund, 1973. 32 leaves ; 28 cm. (Phelps-Stokes
seminars on African-American relations) Microfiche
(negative). New York : New York Public Library, 1981.
1 sheet ; 11 x 15 cm. Cover title. "The Afro-American
connection, Moton Conference Center, Capahosic,
Gloucester, Virginia, 5-7 October 1973." Includes
bibliographical references.
1. Afro-Americans - Relations with Africans. I. Title. II.
Series.   *NYPL [Sc Micro F-9664]*

Clarke, Sonia. Zululand at war, 1879 . Houghton,
South Africa , c1984. 299 p. : ISBN
0-909079-23-4   *NYPL [Sc F 85-153]*

Clarkson, Thomas, 1760-1846. Hammond, James
Henry, 1807-1864. Gov. Hammond's letters on
southern slavery . Charleston , 1845. 32 p. ;
NYPL [Sc Rare C 89-24]

CLASS CONFLICT. see SOCIAL CONFLICT.

**CLASS DISTINCTION. see SOCIAL
CLASSES.**

Class, ethnicity and democracy in Nigeria .
Diamond, Larry. Basingstoke , c1988. xiii, 376
p. : ISBN 0-333-39435-6 : DDC 966.9/05 19
DT515.832   *NYPL [Sc D 88-1310]*

Class formation and class struggle : selected
proceedings of the fourth annual conference :
National University of Lesotho, 20-23 June
1981 / edited by John E. Bardill. [Roma?]
Lesotho] : Southern African Universities Social
Science Conference, [1982] 211 p. ; 21 cm. "26
May 1982"--P. 2. Includes bibliographies.
1. Social conflict - Africa, Southern - Congresses. 2.
Social classes - Africa, Southern - Congresses. 3. Africa,
Southern - Social conditions - Congresses. I. Bardill,
John E. II. Southern African Universities Social Science
Conference. Conference (4th : 1981 : National
University of Lesotho). III. Southern African
Universities Social Science Conference.
NYPL [Sc D 89-25]

CLASS STRUGGLE. see SOCIAL CONFLICT.

CLASSE, LÉON-PAUL, 1874-1945.
Rutayisire, Paul. La christianisation du Rwanda
(1900-1945) . Fribourg, Suisse , 1987. 571 p. :
ISBN 2-8271-0371-0 (pbk.)
NYPL [Sc D 88-1510]

CLASSES, SOCIAL. see SOCIAL CLASSES.

Classic baseball cards . Slocum, Frank. New
York, N.Y. , c1987. ca 600 p. : ISBN
0-446-51392-X DDC 769/.49796357/0973 19
GV875.3 .S57 1987 *NYPL [8-*ISGB 89-500]*

Classic reprint series.
Ai, 1947- [Cruelty.] Cruelty ; Killing floor .
New York , c1987. xi, 99 p. ; ISBN
0-938410-38-5 (pbk.) : DDC 811/.54 19
PS3551.I2 A6 1987   *NYPL [JFD 88-417]*

Himes, Chester B., 1909- Lonely crusade . New
York , c1986. x, 398 p. ; ISBN 0-938410-37-7
(pbk.) : DDC 813/.54 19
PS3515.I713 L6 1986 *NYPL [Sc D 88-1362]*

**Classifications raciales populaires et métissage
[microform]** Crépeau, Pierre, 1927- [[Montréal,
1973] 44 p.   *NYPL [*XM-8441]*

Classiques africains.
(no. 860) Vincileoni, Nicole. Comprendre
l'oeuvre de Bernard B. Dadié /. Issy les
Moulineaux , c1986. 319 p.,[12] p. of plates :
ISBN 2-85049-368-6 *NYPL [Sc D 88-721]*

(no 862) Kesteloot, Lilyan. Comprendre les
Poèmes de Léopold Sédar Senghor /. Issy les
Moulineaux , 1986. 143 p. : ISBN 2-85049-376-7
NYPL [Sc D 88-978]

(23) Lamadani, 1893-1972. Satires de Lamadani
/. [Paris] , 1987. 155 p., [9] p. of plates :
NYPL [Sc E 88-223]

Classiques africains (Issy-les-Moulineaux, France)
(no. 831) Grésillon, Marie. Une si longue lettre
de Mariama Bâ . Issy les Moulineux [France] ,
c1986. 94 p. : ISBN 2-85049-344-9
NYPL [Sc D 88-824]

Claudia Jones, 1915-1964 . Tyson, Jennifer.
London , c1988. 16 p. :
NYPL [Sc D 89-553]

Clausson, L. J. Précis historique de la révolution
de Saint-Domingue [microform] . Réfutation de
certains ouvrages publiés sur les causes de cette
révolution. De l'état actuel de cette colonie, et
de la nécessité d'en recouvrer la possession. Par
L. J. Clausson. Paris, Pillet aîné,
imprimeur-libraire, 1819. xij, 155 p. Microfilm.
New York : New York Public Library, [197-] 1
microfilm reel ; 35 mm.
1. Haiti - History - Revolution, 1791-1804. I. Title.
NYPL [Sc Micro R-3541]

La clave xilofónica de la música cubana . Ortiz,
Fernando, 1881-1969. Ciudad de la Habana,
Cuba , 1984. 105 p. ; DDC 789/.6 19
ML1049 .O77 1984   *NYPL [Sc C 87-373]*

CLAVES - HISTORY AND CRITICISM.
Ortiz, Fernando, 1881-1969. La clave xilofónica
de la música cubana . Ciudad de la Habana,
Cuba , 1984. 105 p. ; DDC 789/.6 19
ML1049 .O77 1984   *NYPL [Sc C 87-373]*

Clavreuil, Gérard.
Brezault, Alain. Missions en Afrique . Paris ,
c1987. 193 p. : ISBN 2-86260-209-4 : DDC
266/.267 19
BV3520 .B74 1987   *NYPL [Sc E 89-163]*

Erotisme et littératures . Paris , c1987. 274 p. ;
ISBN 2-7357-0062-3 *NYPL [Sc E 88-184]*

CLAY, CASSIUS, 1944-
Ali/Frazier III /. [S.l.] , 1975. [32] p. :
NYPL [Sc F 89-46]

Clayton, Al, 1934- Egerton, John. Southern food .
New York , c1987. v, 408 p. : ISBN
0-394-54494-3 DDC 641.5975 19
TX715 .E28 1987   *NYPL [JSE 87-1598]*

Clayton, Anthony, 1923- France, soldiers, and
Africa / by Anthony Clayton. 1st ed. London ;
New York : Brassey's Defence Publishers, 1988.
xxv, 444 p., [16] p. of plates : ill., maps ; 23
cm. Includes index. ISBN 0-08-034748-7 : DDC
355.3/52/0944 19
1. France - Colonies - Africa - Defenses. I. Title.
UA855 .C575 1988   *NYPL [Sc E 88-445]*

Clayton, Ralph.
Black Baltimore, 1820-1870 / by Ralph
Clayton. Bowie, MD : Heritage Books, 1987.
vii, 199 p. : ill., port. ; 23 cm. A collection of
articles most of which were published between 1984
and 1986. Includes bibliographical references.
CONTENTS. - The effect of immigration on the Negro
in Baltimore, 1850-1860 -- Baltimore free Black
households with slaves, 1820-1840 -- Slaves by name --
Laurel Cemetery, 1852-1958 -- Slaveholders of
Baltimore, 1860 -- Black families of East Baltimore,
1870. ISBN 1-556-13080-5 (pbk.) : DDC
929/.3/0899607307526 19
1. Afro-Americans - Maryland - Baltimore - Genealogy.
2. Slaves - Maryland - Baltimore - Registers. 3.
Baltimore (Md.) - Genealogy. 4. Baltimore (Md.) -
Population. I. Title.
F189.B19 N42 1987

NYPL [APR (Baltimore) 88-868]

Free Blacks of Anne Arundel County,
Maryland 1850 / by Ralph Clayton. Bowie,
MD. : Heritage Books, 1987. xiv, 51 p. ; 21
cm. ISBN 1-556-13069-4
1. Afro-Americans - Maryland - Anne Arundel County.

2. Ann Arundel County (Maryland) - Census, 7th, 1850 - Indexes. I. Title. **NYPL [Sc D 88-64]**

Cleaned the crocodile's teeth : Nuer song / translated by Terese Svoboda.1st ed. Greenfield Center, N.Y. : Greenfield Review Press, c1985. ix, 104 p. : ill. ; 22 cm. ISBN 0-912678-63-1 (pbk.) : DDC 784.4/9669 19
1. Folk-songs, Nuer - Sudan - Texts. 2. Folk-songs, Nuer - Sudan - History and criticism. I. Svoboda, Terese.
PL8576.N47 C54 1985 **NYPL [Sc D 88-743]**

Clearinghouse publication .
(66) The Black/white colleges . Washington, D.C. , 1981. v, 46 p. : **NYPL [Sc F 89-48]**

Cleavage . Bissundyal, Churaumanie. East Coast Demerara, Guyana , c1986. 64 p. ;
MLCS 87/7682 (P) **NYPL [Sc D 88-714]**

Cleghorn, Sarah Norcliffe, 1876-1959. The true ballad of glorious Harriet Tubman / by Sarah N. Cleghorn. [Manchester, Vt. : s.n. Cleghorn, c1933] 12 p. ; 16 cm. Cover title.
1. Tubman, Harriet, 1820?-1913 - Poetry. I. Title.
NYPL [Sc Rare C 89-6]

CLEMENTE, ROBERTO, 1934-1972 - JUVENILE LITERATURE.
Walker, Paul Robert. Pride of Puerto Rico . San Diego , c1988. 135 p. ; ISBN 0-15-200562-5 DDC 796.357/092/4 B 92 19
GV865.C45 W35 1988 **NYPL [Sc E 88-452]**

Clementine Hunter, American folk artist /.
Wilson, James L. (James Lynwood) Gretna , 1988. 160 p. : ISBN 0-88289-658-X DDC 759.13 B 19
ND237.H915 A4 1988 **NYPL [Sc F 89-94]**

Clemons, Rosemary. Detroit public sites named for Blacks /. [[Detroit, Mich.] , c1987. xii, 62 p. ; **NYPL [Sc D 88-1183]**

CLEOPATRA, QUEEN OF EGYPT, D. 30 B.C. - POETRY.
Chase-Riboud, Barbara. Portrait of a nude woman as Cleopatra /. New York , c1987. 110 p. : ISBN 0-688-06403-5 : DDC 811/.54 19
PS3553.H336 P6 1987 **NYPL [Sc D 88-329]**

Clerfeuille, Sylvie. Seck, Nago. Musiciens africains des années 80 . Paris , c1986. 167 p. : ISBN 2-85802-715-3 **NYPL [JMD 87-441]**

CLERGY - CANADA - BIOGRAPHY.
Thomson, Colin A., 1938- Born with a call . Dartmouth, Nova Scotia , 1986. 157 p., [8] p. of plates : **NYPL [Sc F 88-63]**

CLERGY - NEW YORK (N.Y.) - BIOGRAPHY.
Ford, George Barry. A degree of difference. New York [1969] 271 p. DDC 282/.0924 19
BX4705.F635 A3 **NYPL [Sc D 88-406]**

CLERGY - NIGERIA - BIOGRAPHY.
Oguntomilade, Jacob I. D. Father E. Olu Coker . Lagos , 1987. 313 p. : ISBN 978-248-001-0 **NYPL [Sc D 89-572]**

CLERGYMEN'S WIVES - GREAT BRITAIN - BIOGRAPHY.
Trill, Carol. Dispossessed daughter of Africa /. London , 1988. 190 p. : ISBN 0-946918-42-2 (pbk.) **NYPL [sc C 88-228]**

Clerical and technical workers' strike at Yale University. On strike for respect . Chicago , 1988. 94 p. : **NYPL [Sc C 89-101]**

Clerical & technical workers' strike at Yale University (1984-85). On strike for respect . Chicago , 1988. 94 p. : **NYPL [Sc C 89-101]**

CLEVELAND CAVALIERS (BASKETBALL TEAM)
Ryan, Bob. Forty-eight minutes . New York , London , c1987. x, 356 p. ; ISBN 0-02-597770-9 DDC 796.32/364/0973 19
GV885.515.N37 R9 1988
NYPL [JFD 87-10809]

CLEVELAND REGION (OHIO) - SOCIAL LIFE AND CUSTOMS.
Watson, Wilbur H. The village . Atlanta, Ga. , c1989. xxii, 204 p. : ISBN 0-9621460-0-5 DDC 977.1/3200496073 20
F499.C69 N38 1989 **NYPL [Sc D 89-609]**

!Click song . Williams, John Alfred, 1925- New York , c1987. 430 p. ; ISBN 0-938410-43-1 : DDC 813/.54 19
PS3573.I4495 C5 1987
NYPL [Sc D 88-1344]

Cliffe, Lionel.
(ed) One party democracy. [Nairobi, 1967] 470 p. DDC 324/.678
JQ3519.A55 O5 **NYPL [Sc D 88-976]**

(ed) Selections from One party democracy. [Nairobi, 1967] 143 p. DDC 324/.678
JQ3519.A55 O53 **NYPL [Sc D 87-1320]**

Stoneman, Colin. Zimbabwe . London , New York , 1989. xxi, 210 p. : ISBN 0-86187-454-4 : DDC 968.91 19
JQ2929.A15 S76 1989 **NYPL [Sc D 89-307]**

Clifton, Lucille, 1936-
Everett Anderson's friend / Lucille Clifton ; ill. by Ann Grifalconi. 1st ed. New York : Holt, Rinehart and Winston, c1976. [25] p. : ill. ; 21 x 23 cm. Having eagerly anticipated the new neighbors, a boy is disappointed to get a whole family of girls. SCHOMBURG CHILDREN'S COLLECTION. ISBN 0-03-015161-9 (lib. bdg.) DDC [E]
I. Grifalconi, Ann. II. Schomburg Children's Collection. III. Title.
PZ8.3.C573 Evg **NYPL [Sc D 88-1505]**

Everett Anderson's nine month long / by Lucille Clifton ; ill. by Ann Grifalconi. New York : Holt, Rinehart, and Winston, c1978. [31] p. : ill. ; 21 x 22 cm. A small boy and his family anticipate the birth of their newest member. SCHOMBURG CHILDREN'S COLLECTION. ISBN 0-03-043536-6 DDC [E]
1. Afro-American families - Juvenile fiction. I. Grifalconi, Ann. II. Schomburg Children's Collection. III. Title.
PZ8.3.C573 Evk **NYPL [Sc D 89-30]**

Good woman : poems and a memoir, 1969-1980 / Lucile Clifton.1st ed. Brockport, NY : BoA ; St. Paul, Minnesota : Distributed by Bookslinger, 1987. 276 p. : ill. ; 24 cm. (American poets contunuum series . v. 14) ISBN 0-918526-59-0 (pbk.)
1. Clifton, Lucille, 1936-. I. Title. II. Series.
NYPL [Sc E 88-232]

My friend Jacob / by Lucille Clifton ; illustrated by Thomas Di Grazia. 1st ed. New York : Dutton, c1980. [32] p. : ill. ; 26 cm. A young boy tells about Jacob, who, though older and mentally slower, helps him a lot and is his very best friend. SCHOMBURG CHILDREN'S COLLECTION. ISBN 0-525-35487-5 DDC [E]
1. Mentally handicapped - Juvenile fiction. I. Di Grazia, Thomas. II. Schomburg Children's Collection. III. Title.
PZ7.C6224 Myk 1980 **NYPL [Sc F 88-376]**

Next : new poems / Lucille Clifton.1st ed. Brockport, NY : BOA Editions ; St. Paul, Minnesota : Distributed by Bookslinger, 1987. 85 p. ; 24 cm. (American poets continuum series . v.5) ISBN 0-918526-60-4
I. Title. **NYPL [Sc E 88-413]**

CLIFTON, LUCILLE, 1936-
Clifton, Lucille, 1936- Good woman . Brockport, NY , St. Paul, Minnesota , 1987. 276 p. : ISBN 0-918526-59-0 (pbk.)
NYPL [Sc E 88-232]

Climbing Jacob's ladder . Smith, Edward D. City of Washington , 1988. 143 p. : ISBN 0-87474-829-1 **NYPL [Sc E 88-505]**

Clio Browne . Komo, Dolores. Freedom, Calif. , c1988. 193 p. ; ISBN 0-89594-320-4 (pbk.) : DDC 813/.54 19
PS3561.O4545 C55 1988
NYPL [Sc C 89-50]

Clitandre, Pierre.
[Cathédrale du mois d'août. English]
Cathedral of the August heat / Pierre Clitandre ; translated by Bridget Jones. London : Readers International c1987. 159 p. ; 21 cm. Translation of: Cathédrale du mois d'août. ISBN 0-930523-31-8 (pbk.)
1. Haiti - Fiction. I. Title. **NYPL [Sc D 87-1048]**

CLITORIDECTOMY - BIBLIOGRAPHY.
Sanderson, Lilian Passmore. Female genital mutilation, excision and infibulation . London [1986?] 72 p. ; DDC 016.392 19
Z5118.C57 S26 1986 GN484
NYPL [Sc D 88-1152]

CLOTH. see TEXTILE FABRICS.

CLOTHING FACTORIES - UNITED STATES - JUVENILE LITERATURE.
Meshover, Leonard. You visit a dairy [and a] clothing factory /. Chicago , c1965. 48 p. :
NYPL [Sc D 89-545]

CLS speaks . Committee for Labour Solidarity. [Trinidad and Tobago] [1987] iii, 80 p. :
NYPL [Sc D 88-969]

Clymer, Eleanor (Lowenton) 1906- The house on the mountain, by Eleanor Clymer. Illustrated by Leo Carty. [1st ed.] New York, Dutton [1971] 39 p. illus. 23 cm. When they see the little house on the mountain side, several black city children can almost believe it is the house their mother is always talking about. SCHOMBURG CHILDREN'S COLLECTION. ISBN 0-525-32365-1 DDC [Fic]
1. Afro-American children - Juvenile fiction. I. Carty, Leo, illus. II. Schomburg Children's Collection. III. Title.
PZ7.C6272 Ho **NYPL [Sc D 88-445]**

CMS bibliographies and documentation series. Center for Migration Studies (U. S.) Refugees . Staten Island, N.Y. , 1987. ix, 423 p. ; ISBN 0-934733-34-1 (pbk.) **NYPL [Sc F 89-60]**

Cnockaert, A. Littérature négro-africaine francophone . [Pau] , 1986. 137 p. ; DDC 840/.9/896 19
PQ3980.5 .L56 1986 **NYPL [Sc D 89-316]**

COALITION (SOCIAL SCIENCES)
Libraries, coalitions, & the public good /. New York, NY , c1987. xiv, 174 p. ; ISBN 1-555-70017-9 : DDC 021 19
Z716.4 .L47 1987 **NYPL [JFE 87-6338]**

COATINGS.
Horie, C. V. (Charles Velson) Materials for conservation . London , Boston , 1987. xi, 281 p. : ISBN 0-408-01531-4 : DDC 667/.9 19
TP156.C57 H67 1987 **NYPL [Sc D 88-558]**

Coatsworth, Elizabeth Jane, 1893- Ronnie and the Chief's son. Illustrated by Stefan Martin. New York, Macmillan, 1962. 38 p. ill. 24 cm. SCHOMBURG CHILDREN'S COLLECTION.
1. Africa - Juvenile fiction. I. Schomburg Children's Collection. II. Title.
PZ7.C6294 Ro **NYPL [Sc E 89-23]**

Coco de mer . Lionnet, Guy. Bell Village, Ile Maurice , c1986. 95 p. :
QK495.P17 L56 1986 **NYPL [Sc D 88-572]**

Cocoltchos, Christopher Nickolas, 1949- The invisible government and the viable community : the Ku Klux Klan in Orange County, California during the 1920's. 1979. 2 v. (xv, 774 leaves) : ill. ; 28 cm. Thesis (PH. D.)--University of California, Los Angeles, 1979. Bibliography: leaves 732-774.
1. Ku Klux Klan (1915-) - California - Orange County - History. 2. Orange County (Calif.) - Social conditions. I. Title. **NYPL [Sc F 88-285]**

Coconis, Constantinos. Quigg, Jane. Ted and Bobby look for something special. New York [1969] 42, [3] p. DDC [Fic]
PZ7.Q333 Te3 **NYPL [Sc E 88-543]**

Code noir. Sala-Molins, Louis. Le Code noir, ou, Le calvaire de Canaan /. Paris , c1987. 292 p. ; ISBN 2-13-039970-3 : DDC 346.4401/3 344.40613 19
KJV4534 .S25 1987 **NYPL [Sc D 88-136]**

Le Code noir, ou, Le calvaire de Canaan /. Sala-Molins, Louis. Paris , c1987. 292 p. ; ISBN 2-13-039970-3 : DDC 346.4401/3 344.40613 19
KJV4534 .S25 1987 **NYPL [Sc D 88-136]**

Coelho, Abílio. As hortênsias morrem na primavera / Abílio Coelho. Rio de Janeiro : Codecri, 1987. 271 p. ; 21 cm. (CODECRI/Pasquim . v.3)
1. Slavery - Brazil - Fiction. 2. Brazil - Fiction. I. Title.
NYPL [Sc D 88-709]

Coffin & Co. /. Simon, Njami. [Cercueil & Cie. English.] Berkeley, CA , c1987. 195 p. ; ISBN 0-88739-049-8 (pbk.) **NYPL [Sc C 89-144]**

Coffin and company. Simon, Njami. [Cercueil & Cie. English.] Coffin & Co. /. Berkeley, CA , c1987. 195 p. ; ISBN 0-88739-049-8 (pbk.)
NYPL [Sc C 89-144]

Cognac & collard greens /. Reynolds, A. H. (Alfrieda H.) Bronx, N.Y. , c1985. 138 p. : ISBN 0-938887-00-9
NYPL [Sc D 88-1211]

Cognac and collard greens. Reynolds, A. H. (Alfrieda H.) Cognac & collard greens /. Bronx, N.Y. , c1985. 138 p. : ISBN 0-938887-00-9
NYPL [Sc D 88-1211]

COGNITION AND CULTURE - AFRICA.
Explorations in African systems of thought /.
Washington, D.C. , c1987. xvi, 337 p. : ISBN
0-87474-591-8 (pbk.) *NYPL [Sc D 88-566]*

Cohen, David William.
Misangós song [microform] : adventure and
structure in the precolonial African past / by
D. W. Cohen. [Nairobi] : University of Nairobi,
Dept. of History, [1979] 24 p. ; 33 cm. (Staff
seminar paper / University of Nairobi, Department of
History. no. 10, 1978/79) Cover title. Includes
bibliographical references. Microfilm. New York: New
York Public Library, 1982. 1 microfilm reel; 35 mm.
(MN *ZZ-23051)
*1. Busoga - Social conditions - History. I. Series:
Nairobi. University. Dept. of History. Staff seminar
paper, no. 10. II. Title.*
NYPL [Sc Micro R-4108 no. 38]

Siaya, a historical anthropology of an African
landscape / David William Cohen, E.S. Atieno
Odhiambo. London : J. Currey ; Athens : Ohio
University Press, 1989. viii, 152 p., [8] p. of
plates : ill.(some col.), maps ; 23 cm. Includes
index. Bibliography: p. 141-149. ISBN 0-8214-0901-8
DDC 967.6/2 19
*1. Luo (African people). 2. Land settlement patterns -
Kenya - Siaya District. 3. Rural-urban migration -
Kenya - Siaya District (Kenya) -
Social life and customs. I. Atieno Odhiambo, E. S.,
1946-. II. Title.*
DT433.545.L85 C64 1988
NYPL [Sc D 89-354]

Cohen, Esther. A life without Christ and a new
life in Christ [microform] / by Esther
Clementina Cohen. Miami, Fla. : E. C. Cohen,
1980. [23] p. ; 16 cm. Cover title: A new life in
Christ. Microfiche. New York: New York Public
Library, 198 . 1 microfiche: negative; 11 x 15 cm. (FSN
Sc 019,018)
I. Title. II. Title: A new life in Christ.
NYPL [Sc Micro F-11022]

Cohen, John M. Integrated rural development :
the Ethiopian experience and the debate / John
M. Cohen. Uppsala : Scandinavian Institute of
African Studies, 1987. 267 p. ; 23 cm.
Bibliography: p. 263-267. ISBN 91-7106-267-X
*1. Rural development - Ethiopia. 2. Rural
development - Developing countries. I. Title.*
NYPL [Sc D 88-1100]

Cohen, Robin. Endgame in South Africa? : the
changing structures & ideology of apartheid /
Robin Cohen. London : J. Currey ; Paris :
Unesco Press ; x, 108 p. ; 22 cm. Includes index.
Bibliography: p. [97]-105. ISBN 0-85255-308-0
(pbk.) : DDC 323.1/68 19
1. Apartheid - South Africa. I. Title.
DT763 .C64 1986 **NYPL [Sc D 88-770]**

Coisas que o povo diz. Cascudo, Luís de Câmara,
1898- Locuções tradicionais no Brasil . Belo
Horizonte , São Paulo , 1986. 314 p. :
NYPL [Sc D 87-923]

COKER, E. OLU.
Oguntomilade, Jacob I. D. Father E. Olu
Coker . Lagos , 1987. 313 p. : ISBN
978-248-001-0 **NYPL [Sc D 89-572]**

Colaiaco, James A., 1945- Martin Luther King,
Jr. : apostle of militant nonviolence / James A.
Colaiaco. New York : St. Martin's Press, 1988.
x, 238 p. ; 23 cm. Includes index. Bibliography: p.
219-228. ISBN 0-312-02365-0 : DDC 323.4/092/4
B 19
*1. King, Martin Luther, Jr., 1929-1968. 2.
Afro-Americans - Biography. 3. Baptists - United
States - Clergy - Biography. 4. Afro-Americans - Civil
rights. 5. United States - Race relations. I. Title.*
E185.97.K5 C65 1988 **NYPL [Sc D 89-231]**

Cole, Herbert M.
The mother and child in African sculpture.
Mother and child in African Sculpture : the
African-American Institute, October
21-February 28, 1987. New York , 1987. [16]
p. : **NYPL [Sc F 88-3]**

Cole, Johnnetta B.
Anthropology for the nineties . New York ,
London , c1988. xxvii, 561 p. : ISBN
0-02-906441-4 (pbk.) DDC 306 19
GN316 .A574 1988 **NYPL [Sc E 88-488]**

Race toward equality / Johnnetta Cole. Havana,
Cuba (P.O. Box 4208, Havana) : J. Marti Pub.
House, c1986. 99 p. : ill. ; 21 cm. DDC
305.8/0097291 19

*1. Blacks - Cuba - Social conditions. 2. Racism - Cuba -
History. 3. Cuba - History - Revolution, 1959 -
Influence. 4. Cuba - Race relations - History. I. Title.*
F1789.N3 C65 1986 **NYPL [Sc D 89-359]**

Cole, Josette. Crossroads : the politics of reform
and repression, 1976-1986 / Josette Cole.
Johannesburg, South Africa : Ravan Press,
1987. xii, 175 p., [25] p. of plates : ill. ; 21 cm.
Includes bibliography. Bibliography: p. [165]-169. ISBN
0-86975-318-5
*1. Squatters - South Africa - Cape Town. 2. Blacks -
South Africa - Economic conditions. 3. Blacks - South
Africa - Social conditions. 4. Cross Roads (Cape Town,
South Africa) - History. I. Title.*
NYPL [Sc D 88-957]

Cole, Olivia H. H. (illus) Hopkins, Marjorie. And
the jackal played the masinko. New York
[1969] [41] p. ISBN 0-8193-0271-6
PZ7.H7756 An **NYPL [JFF 72-292]**

Coleção afro-brasiliana .
(6) Histórias de operários negros /. Porto
Alegre, RS, Brazil , c1987. 100 p. ;
NYPL [Sc D 88-823]

Coleção Arthur Ramos /. Lody, Raul.
[Fortaleza] , 1987. 78 p. : ISBN 85-24-60035-7
NYPL [Sc D 89-479]

Coleção Cabala .
(7) Farelli, Maria Helena. Oxóssi e Ossãe . Rio
de Janeiro , 1987. 71 p. :
NYPL [Sc C 88-65]

Coleção Ciências sociais. Série Questão agrária .
(3) Arcangeli, Alberto. O mito da terra . São
Luís , 1987. 302 p. : **NYPL [Sc D 89-579]**

Coleção Documentos brasileiros.
(no. 204) Renault, Delso. A vida brasileira no
final do século XIX . Rio de Janeiro ; Brasília :
xi, 315 p. : ISBN 85-03-00181-0
NYPL [HFB 87-2508]

Coleção História popular .
(no. 4) Peregalli, Enrique, 1950- Escravidão no
Brasil /. São Paulo , c1988. 80 p. : ISBN
85-26-00192-2 **NYPL [Sc D 89-421]**

Coleção Negros em libertação .
(4) Giacomini, Sonia Maria. Mulher e escrava .
Petrópolis , 1988. 95 p., [7] p. of plates :
HT1126 .G49 1988 **NYPL [Sc D 88-1283]**

Coleção Oficinas da história.
(v.6) Azevedo, Celia Maria Marinho de. Onda
negra, medo branco . Rio de Janeiro , c1987.
267 p. : **NYPL [Sc D 88-469]**

(vol. 3) Decca, Maria Auxiliadora Guzzo. A
vida fora das fábricas . Rio de Janeiro, RJ ,
1987. 135 p. ; DDC 305.5/62/098161 19
HD8290.S32 D4 1987
NYPL [Sc D 88-1367]

Lara, Silvia Hunold. Campos da violência . Rio
de Janeiro , c1988. 389 p. ;
NYPL [Sc D 89-13]

Coleção Orixás .
(v.2) Linares, Ronaldo Antonio. Xangô e inhaçã
/. [São Paulo] , c1987. 85 p. :
NYPL [Sc D 88-553]

Coleção Temas Brasileiros .
(no. 62) Morais, Evaristo de, 1871-1939. A
escravidão africana no Brasil . Brasília, Distrito
Federal , c1986. 140 p. ; ISBN 85-23-00070-4
NYPL [Sc D 88-922]

**Coleção Temas brasileiros (Universidade de
Brasília. Editora) .**
(62) Morais, Evaristo de, 1871-1939. A
escravidão africana no Brasil . Brasília, Distrito
Federal , c1986. 140 p. ; ISBN 85-23-00070-4
NYPL [Sc D 88-922]

Colecção Início .
(5) Artur, Armando, 1962- Espelho dos dias /.
[Maputo?] Associação dos Escritores
Mozambicanos, [1986?] 52 p. ;
NYPL [Sc D 88-536]

(7) Muianga, Aldino, 1950- Xitala Mati /.
[Maputo?] [1987?] 87 p. :
NYPL [Sc D 88-531]

**Colecção Para a história das literaturas africanas
de expressão portuguesa .**
(6) Lopes da Silva, Baltasar, 1907- Os trabalhos
e os dias /. Praia, Cabo Verde , 1987. 83 p. :
NYPL [Sc D 88-1500]

Colecção Unidade nacional .
(4) Machel, Samora, 1933- A nossa força está

na unidade /. [Maputo] [1983] 98 p. : DDC
967/.9803 19
DT465.C32 M32 1983 **NYPL [Sc D 89-531]**

Colección Arte y sociedad. [Santo Domingo] see
**Santo Domingo. Universidad Autónoma.
Publicaciones.**

Colección de temas africanos .
(5) Moerdijk, Donald. [Anti-development,
South Africa and its Bantustans. Spanish.]
Antidesarrollo, Suráfrica y sus bantustanes /.
Barcelona , Paris , 1982. 222 p. : ISBN
92-3-301888-1 (Unesco)
NYPL [Sc D 88-595]

(7) Islamic city. Spanish. La ciudad islámica .
Barcelona [Paris] , 1982. 260 p. : ISBN
92-3-301665-X (Unesco)
NYPL [Sc D 88-596]

(10) Concept de pouvoir en Afrique. Spanish.
El concepto del poder en Africa /. Barcelona ,
París , 1983. 178 p. ; ISBN 92-3-301887-3
(Unesco) **NYPL [Sc D 88-604]**

(11) Relations historiques à travers l'océan
Indien. Spanish. Relaciones históricas a través
del océano Índico . Barcelona , Paris , 1983.
224 p. ; ISBN 84-85800-51-6
NYPL [Sc D 88-593]

(12) Décolonisation de l'Afrique. Spanish. La
Descolonización de Africa : Africa austral y el
Cuerno de Africa . Barcelona , Paris , 1983.
197 p. ; ISBN 92-3-301834-2 (Unesco)
NYPL [Sc D 88-590]

(13) Affirmation de l'identité culturelle et la
formation de la conscience nationale dans
l'Afrique contemporaine. Spanish. La
Afrimación de la identidad cultural y la
formación de la coniencia nacional en el África
contemporánea . Barcelona , Paris , 1983. 220
p. ; ISBN 84-85800-57-5 **NYPL [Sc D 88-597]**

(14) Historiographie de l'Afrique australe.
Spanish. La historiografía del Africa austral .
Barcelona , Paris , 1983. 128 p. ; ISBN
92-3-301775-3 (Unesco)
NYPL [Sc D 88-598]

(16) Symposium on the Peopling of Ancient
Egypt and the deciphering of Meroitic Script
(1974 : Cairo, Egypt) [Peuplement de l'Egipte
ancianne et la déchiffrement de l'écriture
méroïtique. Spanish.] Poblamiento del antiguo
Egipto y desciframiento de la escritura
meroítica /. Barcelona , Paris , 1983. 155 p. :
ISBN 0-923301-60-5 (Unesco)
NYPL [Sc D 88-603]

(17) Weinrich, A. K. H., 1933- [Women and
racial discrimination in Rhodesia. Spanish.] La
situación de la mujer en Zimbabue antes de la
independencia /. Barcelona , Paris , 1984. 198
p. ; ISBN 92-3-301621-8 (Unesco)
NYPL [Sc D 88-615]

(18) Dean, Elizabeth. [History in black and
white. Spanish.] Historia en blanco y negro .
Barcelona , Paris , 1984. 196 p. ; ISBN
92-3-302092-4 (Unesco)
NYPL [Sc D 88-594]

(19) Harris, Phil. [Reporting southern Africa.
Spanish.] La información sobre África austral .
Barcelona , Paris , 1984. 188 p. ; ISBN
92-3-301700-1 (Unesco)
NYPL [Sc D 88-614]

(2) Introduction à la culture africaine. Spanish.
Introducción a la cultura africana . Barcelona ,
Paris , 1982. 176 p. ; ISBN 92-3-301478-9
(Unesco) **NYPL [Sc D 88-600]**

(20) Teaching and research in philosophy in
Africa. Spanish. Enseñanza de la filosofía e
investigación filosófica en Africa /. Barcelona ,
París , 1984. 339 p. ; ISBN 92-3-302126-6
(Unesco) **NYPL [Sc D 88-616]**

(21) Mort dans la vie africaine. Spanish. La
Muerte en la vida africana. Barcelona , París ,
1984. 314 p. : ISBN 84-85800-81-8
NYPL [Sc D 88-601]

(3) Socio-political aspects of the palaver in
some African countries. Spanish. Aspectos
sociopolíticos del parlamento tradicional en
algunos países africanos /. Barcelona , Paris ,
1979. 95 p. ; ISBN 84-85800-24-9
NYPL [Sc D 88-599]

(4) Jeunesse, tradition et développement en
Afrique. Spanish. Juventud, tradición y

desarrollo en Africa . Barcelona , Paris , 1982.
148 p. ;   ISBN 84-85800-29-X
NYPL [Sc D 88-592]

(6) Pala, Achola O. [Femme africaine dans la
société précoloniale. Spanish.] La mujer africana
en la sociedad precolonial /. Barcelona
[Paris?] , 1982. 238 p. ;   ISBN 84-85800-35-4
(Serbal)   **NYPL [Sc D 88-833]**

(8) Deux études sur les relations entre groupes
ethniques. Spanish. Dos estudios sobre las
relaciones entre grupos étnicos en Africa .
Barcelona [Paris] , 1982. 174 p. ;   ISBN
84-85000-41-9
DT549.42 .D4818 1982
NYPL [Sc D 88-651]

(9) Pierson-Mathy, Paulette. [Naissance de
l'Etat par la guerre de libération nationale.
Spanish.] El nacimiento del estado por la guerra
de liberación nacional . Barcelona : [Paris] :
1983. 178 p. ;   ISBN 92-3-301794-X (Unesco)
NYPL [Sc D 88-602]

Traite négrière du XVe au XIXe siècle. Spanish.
La trata negrera del siglo XV al XIX .
Barcelona , 1981. 379 p. ;   ISBN 92-3-301672-2
NYPL [Sc D 88-650]

Colección del chicherekú en el exilio.
Cabrera, Lydia. La lengua sagrada de los
Ñáñigos /. Miami, Fla. , c1988. 530 p. ;
NYPL [Sc D 89-585]

Colección Historia y sociedad. [Santo Domingo]
see **Santo Domingo. Universidad Autónoma.
Publicaciones.**

Colección Nuestro continente .
([5]) Haití bajo la opresión de los Duvalier .
Santo Domingo , 1981. 93 p. ;   ISBN
968-590-021-3   DDC 972.94/06 19
F1928 .H33 1981   **NYPL [Sc D 89-457]**

Colección Universidad y planificación. see **Santo
Domingo. Universidad Autónoma.
Publicaciones.**

Coleçõ Primeiros passos .
(200) Carmo, João C. (Kpão Clodomiro) O que
é cadomblé /. Sao Paulo , 1987. 84, [1] p. :
NYPL [Sc B 88-12]

Coleman, James Smoot. African crisis areas and
U. S. foreign policy /. Berkeley , c1985. xiv,
374 p. ;   ISBN 0-520-05548-9 (alk. paper) DDC
327.7306 19
DT38.7 .A39 1986   **NYPL [JLE 85-4182]**

Coleman, Mel. The Black gestalt : an Afro-centric
perspective / Mel Coleman. Minneapolis,
Minnesota : Gestalt Publications, 1987. 118 p. :
ill. ; 23 cm. Includes bibliographical references and
index.
*1. Afro-Americans - Mental health. 2. Afro-Americans -
Conduct of life. I. Title.*   **NYPL [Sc D 88-292]**

Coleman Young and Detroit politics /. Rich,
Wilbur C. Detroit, Mich. , 1989. 298 p. :   ISBN
0-8143-2093-7   DDC 977.4/34043/0924 B 19
F474.D453 Y677 1989   **NYPL [Sc E 89-208]**

Colescott, Robert, 1925-
Sims, Lowery Stokes. Robert Colescott, a
retrospective, 1975-1986 /. San Jose, Calif. ,
c1987. 34 p. :   ISBN 0-938175-01-7 (pbk.) DDC
759.13 19
ND237.C66 A4 1987   **NYPL [Sc F 88-317]**

**COLESCOTT, ROBERT, 1925- -
EXHIBITIONS.**
Sims, Lowery Stokes. Robert Colescott, a
retrospective, 1975-1986 /. San Jose, Calif. ,
c1987. 34 p. :   ISBN 0-938175-01-7 (pbk.) DDC
759.13 19
ND237.C66 A4 1987   **NYPL [Sc F 88-317]**

Colimon, Marie-Thérèse. La source [microform] :
conte de Noel / Marie Thérèse Colimon ;
illustrations de J. R. H. [Port-au-Prince? : s.n.,
1973?] (Port-au-Prine : Atelier Fardin) 17 p. :
ill. ; 21 cm. Microfiche. New York: New York Public
Library, 198 . 1 microfiche: negative; 11 x 15 cm. (FSN
Sc 019,075)
1. Christmas stories. I. Title.
NYPL [Sc Micro F-10983]

Colina, Paulo, 1950- A Razão da chama . São
Paulo , 1986. xii, 122 p. ;
NYPL [Sc D 89-462]

Collected Black women's poetry / edited by Joan
R. Sherman. New York : Oxford University
Press, 1988. 4 v. : ill. ; 17 cm. (The Schomburg
library of nineteenth-century Black women writers)

Reprinted from various sources.   ISBN 0-19-505253-6
(v. 1)   DDC 811/.008/09287 19
*1. American poetry - Women authors. 2. American
poetry - 19th century. 3. Afro-American women -
Poetry. I. Sherman, Joan Rita. II. Series.*
PS591.N4 C57 1988   **NYPL [JFC 88-2144]**

The collected poems of Elma Stuckey /. Stuckey,
Elma, 1907- [Poems.] Chicago , 1987. iv, 187
p. ;   ISBN 0-913750-49-2   DDC 811/.54 19
PS3569.T83 A17 1987   **NYPL [Sc E 89-104]**

The collected poems of Jean Toomer /. Toomer,
Jean, 1894-1967. [Poems. 1988.] Chapel Hill ,
c1988. xxxv, 111 p. ;   ISBN 0-8078-1773-2 (hard) :
DDC 811/.52 19
PS3539.O478 A17 1988   **NYPL [Sc E 88-282]**

Collected speeches of the president /. Babangida,
Ibrahim Badamasi. Lagos [1986?] 280 p. :
NYPL [Sc E 88-303]

The collected works of Phillis Wheatley /.
Wheatley, Phillis, 1753-1784. [Works. 1988.]
New York , 1988. xl, 339 p. :   ISBN
0-19-505241-2 (alk. paper)   DDC 811/.1 19
PS866 .W5 1988   **NYPL [JFC 88-2142]**

Collecting Black Americana /. Reno, Dawn E.
New York , c1986. vii, 150 p. :   ISBN
0-517-56095-X   DDC 700/.8996073/075 19
NK839.3.A35 R46 1986   **NYPL [Sc F 87-6]**

Collection Alternatives paysannes.
Systèmes fonciers à la ville et au village .
Paris , c1986. 296 p. ;   ISBN 2-85802-719-6
DDC 346.6704/32 346.706432 19
LAW   **NYPL [Sc D 89-367]**

Collection Alternatives paysannes, 0757-8091.
Magnant, Jean-Pierre, 1946- La terre sara, terre
tchadienne /. Paris , c1986. 380 p. :   ISBN
2-85802-691-2
DT546.445.S27 M34 1986
NYPL [Sc D 89-101]

**Collection "Appui au monde rural". Série
"Santé" .**
(no 2) Guide pédagogique pour la mise en
œuvre des soins de santé primaires au niveau
villageois /. Bobo-Dioulasso, Burkina Faso ,
1986. 79 p. :
RA771 .G85 1986   **NYPL [Sc D 89-265]**

Collection Architectures traditionnelles .
(3e v) Acquier, Jean-Louis, 1946- Le Burundi /.
Marseille, France , c1986. 129 p. :   ISBN
2-86364-030-5 :   DDC 728/.67/0967572 19
GT377.B94 A27 1986   **NYPL [Sc E 88-568]**

Collection Boboto.
Littérature négro-africaine francophone . [Pau] ,
1986. 137 p. ;   DDC 840/.9/896 19
PQ3980.5 .L56 1986   **NYPL [Sc D 89-316]**

Collection CETIM.
Konare Ba, Adam. L'´epop´ee de Segu . Paris ,
c1987. 201 p. :   ISBN 2-8289-0250-1
NYPL [Sc E 88-180]

Collection des "sans-voix"
Cris intérieurs . Kinshasa/Gombe, Zaïre , 1986.
62 p. ;
MLCS 86/6102 (P)   **NYPL [Sc C 88-124]**

Collection Destins.
Kaké, Ibrahima Baba. Sékou Touré, le héros et
le tyran /. Paris , 1987. 254 p. :
NYPL [Sc D 88-468]

**Collection d'histoire maritime et d'archéologie
sous-marine.**
Un Flibustier français dans la mer des Antilles
en 1618-1620 /. Clamart [France] , c1987. 263
p. :   ISBN 2-9502053-0-5   **NYPL [Sc E 88-247]**

Collection Diasporama. Essai.
Théodore, Oriol, 1942- L'idéologie blanche et
l'aliénation des noirs /. Montréal [1983] 54 p. :
ISBN 2-89270-001-9   **NYPL [Sc C 89-103]**

Collection Economie et développement. Essais.
Nicolas, Pierre. Naissance d'une ville au
Sénégal . Paris , c1988. 193 p., [8] p. of plates :
ISBN 2-86537-195-6   **NYPL [Sc F 89-131]**

Collection Ecrits (Presence africaine (Firm))
Konaté, Moussa, 1951- Une aube incertaine .
Paris , c1985. 217 p. ;   ISBN 2-7087-0459-1
MLCS 86/6414 (P)   **NYPL [Sc C 89-105]**

Collection Encres noires 0223-9930 .
(27) Doumbi-Fakoly. La retraite anticipée du
Guide suprême /. Paris , c1984. 209 p. ;   ISBN

2-85802-382-1   DDC 843 19
PQ3989.2.D639 R48 1984
NYPL [Sc C 88-78]

(43) Fall, Aminata Sow. Ex-père de la nation .
Paris , 1987. 189 p. ;   ISBN 2-85802-875-3
NYPL [Sc D 88-1360]

Collection "Essais" (Sainte-Foy, Québec).
(n. 3) Laroche, Maximilien. L'avènement de la
littérature haïtienne /. Sainte-Foy, Québec ,
1987. 219 p. ;   **NYPL [Sc D 88-1462]**

**Collection "Etudes, guides et inventaires", 0761-
3385 .**
(no 2) France. Bibliothèque nationale.
Département des livres imprimés. Les auteurs
afro-américains, 1965-1982 . Paris , 1985. 28 p.,
[4] leaves of plates :   ISBN 2-7177-1709-9 :
Z1229.N39 F7 1985 PS153.N5
NYPL [Sc F 89-5]

**Collection Expression et valeurs africaines
burundaises .**
(1) Bigangara, Jean-Baptiste. Eléments de
linguistique burundaise /. Bujumbura , 1982.
138 p. ;   DDC 496/.39 19
PL8611.1 .B54 1982   **NYPL [Sc E 88-403]**

(2) Bigangara, Jean-Baptiste. Le fondement de
l'imanisme, ou, Religion traditionnelle au
Burundi . Bujumbura, Burundi , 1984. 140 p. ;
BL2470.B94 B54 1984   **NYPL [Sc E 88-459]**

Collection Histoire romanesque.
Condé, Maryse. Moi, Tituba, sorcière-- . Paris ,
c1986. 276 p. ;   ISBN 2-7152-1440-5
NYPL [Sc E 88-97]

Collection "La Légende des mondes".
Kounta, Albakaye. Contes de Tombouctou et
du Macina /. Paris , c1987- v. :   ISBN
2-85802-853-2 (v. 1)   DDC 843 19
PQ3989.2.K577 C6 1987
NYPL [Sc D 88-1027]

Collection Les Afriques.
Diakité, Tidiane. L'Afrique malade d'elle-même
/. Paris , c1986. 162 p. ;   ISBN 2-86537-158-1
DDC 960/.32 19
DT31 .D5 1986   **NYPL [Sc D 88-1351]**

Freud, Claude. Quelle coopération? . Paris ,
c1988. 270 p. ;   ISBN 2-86537-203-0
HC800 .F74 1988   **NYPL [Sc D 89-602]**

Labazée, Pascal. Entreprises et entrepreneurs du
Burkina Faso . Paris , c1988. 273 p. ;
NYPL [Sc D 89-288]

Toulabor, Comi M. Le Togo sous Éyadéma /.
Paris , c1986. 332 p. ;   ISBN 2-86537-150-6
NYPL [Sc D 88-261]

Yachir, F. Enjeux miniers en Afrique /. Paris ,
c1987. 180 p. ;   ISBN 2-86537-170-0
HD9506.A382 Y34 1987
NYPL [Sc D 89-194]

**Collection "Les Grands romans des Antilles-
Guyane"**
Mattioni, Mario D. Emamori . Fort-de-France ,
1986. 156 p. ;   ISBN 2-85275-108-9   DDC 843 19
PQ3949.2.M36 E4 1986
NYPL [Sc E 88-615]

Mattioni, Mario D. Ma Nou l'esclave .
Fort-de-France [Martinique] , 1986. 157 p. ;
ISBN 2-85275-111-9   DDC 843 19
PQ3949.2.M38 M3 1986
NYPL [Sc E 88-614]

Collection Manuscrits anciens .
(v. 1) Résumés de vieux manuscrits arabes .
Zanzibar [Tanzania] , 1981. x, 50 leaves ;
NYPL [Sc B 88-10]

Collection Monde noir jeunesse.
(3) Gbanfou. Kaméléfata . [Abidjan] [Paris] ,
c1987. 143 p. :   ISBN 2-218-07833-3
NYPL [Sc C 88-161]

(4) Rémy, Mylène. Le masque volé /. Paris ,
1987. 126 p. ;   ISBN 2-218-07832-5
NYPL [Sc C 88-311]

Collection Monde noir poche.
(33) Métellus, Jean, 1937- Voyance . Paris ,
c1985. 124 p. ;   ISBN 2-218-07137-1
NYPL [Sc C 88-100]

(40) Diabaté, Massa M. Le Lion à l'arc . Paris ,
1986. 128 p. ;   ISBN 2-218-07616-0
NYPL [Sc C 89-155]

Collection Monde noir poche. (cont.)

(9-) Anthologie africaine d'expression française
/. Paris , c1981- v. ; ISBN 2-218-05648-8 (v. 1) :
NYPL [Sc C 89-80]

(9, etc) Anthologie africaine d'expression
française /. Paris , c1981- v. ; ISBN
2-218-05648-8 (v. 1) : *NYPL [Sc C 89-80]*

Métellus, Jean, 1937- Anacaona . Paris , 1986.
159 p. : ISBN 2-218-07538-5
NYPL [Sc C 88-6]

Parsemain, Roger, 1944- L'Hidalgo des
campêches . Paris , 1987. 126 p. ; ISBN
2-218-07812-0 *NYPL [Sc C 88-7]*

Pliya, Jean, 1931- Les tresseurs de corde .
Paris , 1987. 239 p. ; ISBN 2-218-07841-X
NYPL [Sc C 88-9]

Timité, Bassori, 1933- Les eaux claires de ma
source /Timité bassori ; et six autres nouvelles.
Paris , 1986. 127 p. ; ISBN 2-218-07813-9
NYPL [Sc C 88-11]

Yoka Lye Mudaba, 1947- Le fossoyeur /.
Paris , 1986. 127 p. ; ISBN 2-218-07830-9
NYPL [Sc C 88-10]

Zinsou, Sénouvo Agbota, 1946- La tortue qui
chante . Paris , 1987. 127 p. ; ISBN
2-218-07842-3 *NYPL [Sc C 88-8]*

A collection of poems and short stories /.
Hammond, Steven T. New York , c1987. ix, 32
p. ; ISBN 0-533-07287-5
NYPL [Sc D 88-1175]

Collection orale.
Ba, Amadou Hampaté. Njeddo Dewal . Abidjan
[Ivory Coast] , c1985. 156 p. ; ISBN
2-7236-0732-1 *NYPL [Sc E 88-417]*

Collection "Points de vue"
Amondji, Marcel, 1934- Côte-d'Ivoire . Paris ,
c1986. 207 p. ; ISBN 2-85802-631-6 DDC
324.2666/806 19
DT545.75 .A46 1986 *NYPL [Sc D 88-297]*

Elungu, P. E. A. Tradition africaine et
rationalité moderne /. Paris , c1987. 187 p. ;
NYPL [Sc D 88-1101]

Eteki-Otabela, Marie-Louise, 1947- Misère et
grandeur de la démocratie au Cameroun /.
Paris , c1987. 143 p. ; ISBN 2-85802-929-6
NYPL [Sc D 88-910]

Hazoumé, Alain T. Afrique, un avenir en sursis
/. Paris , c1988. 214 p. ; ISBN 2-7384-0068-X
NYPL [Sc D 89-290]

Ndebi Biya, Robert, 1946- Etre, pouvoir et
génération . Paris , c1987. 134 p. ;
NYPL [Sc D 88-909]

Sawadogo, Abdoulaye. Un plan Marshall pour
l'Afrique? /. Paris , c1987. 119 p. ; ISBN
2-85802-816-8 *NYPL [Sc D 88-911]*

Songue, Paulette, 1960- Prostitution en
Afrique . Paris , c1986. 154 p. ; ISBN
2-85802-684-X *NYPL [Sc D 88-1164]*

Collection Points de vue, 0761-5248.
Front populaire ivoirien. Propositions pour
gouverner la Côte-d'Ivoire /. Paris , c1987- v. ;
ISBN 2-85802-882-6 (v. 1) DDC
361.6/1/096668 19
JQ3386.A2 F76 1987 *NYPL [Sc D 88-1142]*

Collection "Pour nos enfants"
Mille, Pierre, 1864-1931. Line en Nouvelle
Calédonie /. Paris , c1934. 32, 1 p. ;
NYPL [Sc F 89-20]

Mille, Pierre, 1864-1931. Line en Nouvelle
Calédonie /. Paris , c1934. 32, 1 p. :
NYPL [Sc F 89-20]

**Collection Recherches et documents monde
antillais.**
Rosemain, Jacqueline, 1930- La musique dans
la société antillaise . Paris , c1986. 183 p. :
ISBN 2-85802-685-8 (pbk.)
NYPL [Sc E 88-394]

Collection "Terre des hommes"
Paternostre de La Mairieu, Baudouin. A la
source du Nil . Paris [1985] 108 p., [12] p. of
plates : ISBN 2-85244-730-4 : DDC 967/.571 19
DT450.2 .P38 1985 *NYPL [Sc C 88-308]*

Collection "thèses M.Sc."
Debouvry, Pierre. Contribution à la définition
d'une méthodologie de transfert de populations
paysannes . [Montpellier] [1985] 294 p. ;
ISBN 0-85352-039-0 *NYPL [Sc F 88-302]*

Collection "Villes et enterprises"
Cordonnier, Rita. Femmes africaines et
commerce . Paris , 1987. 190 p. ; ISBN
2-85802-901-6 *NYPL [Sc E 88-368]*

Collection "Vivre dans le monde"
Antilles Caraïbes /. Paris , c1982. 157 p. :
ISBN 2-7191-0177-0 *NYPL [Sc F 88-347]*

**COLLEGE AND COMMUNITY. see
COMMUNITY AND COLLEGE.**

**COLLEGE AND SCHOOL DRAMA,
NIGERIAN (ENGLISH)**
Onadipe, Kola. Halima must not die .
Ijebu-Ode, Nigeria , c1980. 71 p. : ISBN
978-17-8026-6 *NYPL [Sc D 88-1368]*

**COLLEGE ATTENDANCE - UNITED
STATES - CONGRESSES.**
Black student retention in higher education /.
Springfield, Ill., U. S. A. , c1988. xvi, 111 p. :
ISBN 0-398-05477-0 DDC 378/.198/2 19
LC2781 .B465 1988 *NYPL [Sc F 89-139]*

COLLEGE DROPOUTS - UNITED STATES.
Recruitment and retention of Black students in
higher education /. Lanham, MD , c1989. viii,
135 p. : ISBN 0-8191-7292-8 (alk. paper) DDC
378/.1982 19
LC2781 .R43 1989 *NYPL [Sc D 89-590]*

**COLLEGE DROPOUTS - UNITED STATES -
CONGRESSES.**
Black student retention in higher education /.
Springfield, Ill., U. S. A. , c1988. xvi, 111 p. :
ISBN 0-398-05477-0 DDC 378/.198/2 19
LC2781 .B465 1988 *NYPL [Sc F 89-139]*

COLLEGE INTEGRATION - SOUTH AFRICA.
Gaydon, Vanessa. Race against the ratios .
Johannesburg, South Africa , 1987. 70 p ;
ISBN 0-86982-321-3 *NYPL [Sc F 88-322]*

**COLLEGE INTEGRATION - UNITED
STATES - CONGRESSES.**
Blacks on white campuses, whites on black
campuses . Chicago , c1986. 177 p. ; ISBN
0-695-60052-4 *NYPL [Sc D 88-949]*

**COLLEGE PRESSES. see UNIVERSITY
PRESSES.**

**COLLEGE STUDENTS, AFRO-AMERICAN.
see AFRO-AMERICAN COLLEGE
STUDENTS.**

**COLLEGE STUDENTS - ETHIOPIA -
POLITICAL ACTIVITY - HISTORY.**
Balsvik, Randi Rønning. Haile Sellassie's
students . East Lansing, Mich. , c1985. xix, 363
p. ; ISBN 0-87013-262-6 DDC
378/.198/0963 19
LA1518.7 .B35 1985 *NYPL [Sc D 88-1403]*

**COLLEGE STUDENTS - UNITED STATES -
RECRUITING.**
Recruitment and retention of Black students in
higher education /. Lanham, MD , c1989. viii,
135 p. : ISBN 0-8191-7292-8 (alk. paper) DDC
378/.1982 19
LC2781 .R43 1989 *NYPL [Sc D 89-590]*

**COLLEGE THEATER - UNITED STATES -
PRODUCTION AND DIRECTION.**
Marshall, Alex C. (Alexander Charles)
Representative directors, Black theatre
productions, and practices at historically Black
colleges and universities, 1968-1978
[microform] /. 1980. ix, 141 leaves.
NYPL [Sc Micro R-4807]

**COLLEGES, AFRO-AMERICAN. see AFRO-
AMERICAN UNIVERSITIES AND
COLLEGES.**

Collier, James Lincoln, 1928-
Duke Ellington / James Lincoln Collier. New
York : Oxford University Press, 1987. viii, 340
p., [16] p. of plates : ill. ; 24 cm. Includes index.
Discography: p. 323-324. ISBN 0-19-503770-7 (alk.
paper) DDC 785.42/092/4 B 19
*1. Jazz musicians - United States - Biography. 2.
Afro-American musicians - Biography. I. Title.*
ML410.E44 C6 1987 *NYPL [JNE 87-49]*

Louis Armstrong : an American success story /
James Lincoln Collier. New York : Macmillan
Pub. Co., c1985. 165 p. : ill., ports. I. Title.
Includes index. A biography of one of America's most
important musicians, who was born in extreme poverty
and never had a real music lesson, but became world
famous for his singing and trumpet playing. "If you
want to know more about Louis Armstrong-- ": p.
155-157. ISBN 0-02-722830-4 DDC 785.42/092/4
B 92 19

*1. Armstrong, Louis, 1900-1971 - Juvenile literature. 2.
Jazz musicians - United States - Biography - Juvenile
literature. 3. Afro-American musicians - Biography -
Juvenile literature. I. Title.*
ML3930.A75 C67 1985
NYPL [Sc D 86-229]

Outside looking in / James Lincoln Collier. 1st
ed. New York : Macmillan ; London : Collier
Macmillan, c1987. 179 p. ; 22 cm. Ashamed of
his parents' way of life traveling around the country
peddling honey for medicinal purposes and stealing,
Fergy takes his young sister and runs away to find his
mother's wealthy parents and a better way to live.
ISBN 0-02-723100-3 : DDC [Fic] 19
I. Title.
PZ7.C678 Ou 1987 *NYPL [Sc D 88-990]*

Collins, John. Musicmakers of West Africa /
John Collins. 1st ed. Washington, DC : Three
Continents Press, c1985. 177 p. : ports. ; 24 cm.
Principally interviews with West African Pop musicians.
Includes index. Bibliography: p. 161-162. ISBN
0-89410-075-0
*1. Music, Popular (Songs, etc.) - Africa, West - History
and criticism. 2. Musicians - Africa, West - Interviews.
I. Title.*
NYPL [Sc E 87-59]

Collister, Edward A. Harrison, Alice W., 1929-
The conservation of archival and library
materials . Metuchen, N.J. , 1982. xi, 190 p. ;
ISBN 0-8108-1523-0 DDC 025.8/4 19
Z701 .H28 *NYPL [Cons. Div. 84-252]*

**COLLOQUE SUR LE THÈME "CULTURE ET
DÉVELOPPEMENT" (1976: DAKAR,
SENEGAL)**
Sène, Alioune. Célébration du 7oe anniversaire
du président Léopold Sédar Senghor (9 Oct.
1906-9 Oct. 1976) [microform] . Dakar , 1976.
[4] p. ; *NYPL [Sc Micro F-11026]*

**Colloquium on the Islamic City (1976 :
University of Cambridge)** Islamic city.
Spanish. La ciudad islámica . Barcelona
[Paris] , 1982. 260 p. : ISBN 92-3-301665-X
(Unesco) *NYPL [Sc D 88-596]*

Colman, Hila. A career in medical research.
Illustrated by Edna Mason Kaula. Cleveland,
World Pub. Co. [1968] 175 p. illus. 21 cm.
(Careers in the making series) Describes public and
private organizations involved in medical research;
presents a complete profile of Dr. J. Spencer Munroe
who does cancer detection work for the Lenox Hill
Hospital in New York City, describing his education,
training experiences, and the work of his fellow staff;
and finally briefly examines job preparation and career
opportunities for men and women. DDC 610.7
*1. Munroe, J. Spencer. 2. Medicine - Research -
Vocational guidance. I. Kaula, Edna Mason, illus. II.
Title. III. Series.*
R690 .C65 *NYPL [Sc D 88-425]*

Colombel, Véronique de.
Les Ouldémés du Nord-Cameroun :
introduction géographique, historique et
ethnologique / Véronique de Colombel. Paris :
SELAF, 1987. [13]-74 p., [61] p. of plates : ill.,
ports. ; 24 cm. (Langues et cultures Africaines . 9)
Accompanied by cassette entitled: Musique Ouldémé.
Cassette located in Moving Images and Recorded
Sounds, with classification: Sc E 89-244. ISBN
2-85297-199-2
*1. Uldeme language. 2. Uldeme (African people). 3.
Folk music - Cameroon. 4. Uldeme (African people) -
Music. I. Title. II. Series.* *NYPL [Sc E 89-244]*

Phonologie quantitative et synthématique :
propositions méthodologiques et descriptives avec
application à l'ouldémé (langue tchadique du
Nord-Cameroun) : introducion géographique,
historique et ethnologique / Véronique de
Colombel. Paris : SELAF, 1986. 375 p., [31] p.
of plates : ill. ; 24 cm. (Langues et cultures
Africaines, 0755-9305 . 7) French and Uldeme.
Summary in English, French, German, and Spanish.
Bibliography: p. 357-365. ISBN 2-85297-192-5 :
DDC 493/.7 19
1. Uldeme language - Phonology. I. Title.
PL8753.5 .C65 1986 *NYPL [Sc E 89-72]*

**Colombia. Instituto Caro y Cuervo.
Publicaciones.**
(70) Prescott, Laurence E. (Laurence
Emmanuel) Candelario Obeso y la iniciación
de la poesía negra en Colombia /. Bogota ,
1985. 228 p., [17] leaves of plates :
NYPL [JFE 87-5694]

**COLOMBIAN FICTION - 20TH CENTURY -
HISTORY AND CRITICISM.**

Lewis, Marvin A. Treading the ebony path .
Columbia , 1987. 142 p. ; ISBN 0-8262-0638-7
(alk. paper)   DDC 863 19
*PQ8172 .L49 1987	NYPL [Sc D 88-443]*

**COLOMBIAN FICTION - BLACK AUTHORS -
HISTORY AND CRITICISM.**
Lewis, Marvin A. Treading the ebony path .
Columbia , 1987. 142 p. ; ISBN 0-8262-0638-7
(alk. paper)   DDC 863 19
*PQ8172 .L49 1987	NYPL [Sc D 88-443]*

Colón, Fernando, 1488-1539.
[Historie. English]
Christophe Colomb raconté par son fils /
Fernando Colomb ; traduction et notes
d'Eugenè Muller ; préface de Jacques Heers.
Paris : Librairie acadé,mique Perrin, 1986.
xviii, 265 p., [8] p. of plates : ill., ports. ; 23
cm. Origininal title of translation: Histoire de la vie
et des découvertes de Christophe Colomb par
Fernand Colomb, son fils.   ISBN 2-262-00387-4
*1. Columbus, Christopher. 2. Indians of the West
Indies - History. 3. Explorers - Spain - Biography. 4.
West Indies - Discovery and exploration. I. Muller,
Eugène. II. Title. III. Title: Histoire de la vie et des
découvertes de Christophe Colomb par Fernand
Colomb, son fils.	NYPL [Sc D 88-504]*

**COLONIAL ADMINISTRATORS -
MOZAMBIQUE - BIOGRAPHY.**
Botte, Theodorico César de Sande Pacheco de
Sacadura. Memórias e autobiografia . Maputo,
República Popular de Moçambique , 1985-1986
[i.e. 1987]. 3 v. :	*NYPL [Sc D 88-130]*

**COLONIAL ADMINISTRATORS -
PORTUGAL - BIOGRAPHY.**
Botte, Theodorico César de Sande Pacheco de
Sacadura. Memórias e autobiografia . Maputo,
República Popular de Moçambique , 1985-1986
[i.e. 1987]. 3 v. :	*NYPL [Sc D 88-130]*

COLONIAL AFFAIRS. see COLONIES.

**Colonial identity in the Atlantic world,
1500-1800** / edited by Nicholas Canny and
Anthony Pagden. Princeton, N.J. : Princeton
University Press, c1987. xi, 290 p. ; 25 cm.
Chiefly revised versions of essays presented at a
seminar held in 1982 at the Institute for Advanced
Study, Princeton, N.J. Includes bibliographical
references and index. CONTENTS. - Introduction:
colonial identity in the Atlantic world / John H.
Elliott -- The formation of a colonial identity in Brazil
/ Stuart B. Schwartz -- Identity formation in Spanish
America / Anthony Pagden --
Nouvelle-France/Québec/Canada / Gilles Paquet and
Jean-Pierre Wallot -- Identity in British America /
Michael Zuckerman -- Identity formation in Ireland /
Nicholas Canny -- Changing identity in the British
Caribbean / Jack P. Greene -- Afterword : from
identity to independence / Anthony Pagden and
Nicholas Canny.   ISBN 0-691-05372-3 (alk. paper) :
DDC 909/.09812 19
*1. America - History - To 1810 - Congresses. 2.
Europe - Colonies - America - Congresses. 3. Ireland -
Civilization - Congresses. I. Canny, Nicholas P. II.
Pagden, Anthony. III. Institute for Advanced Study
(Princeton, N.J.).*
*E18.82 .C64 1987	NYPL [HAB 87-3215]*

**The colonial legacy in Caribbean literature, Vol.
I** /. Saakana, Amon Saba, 1948- London ,
1987. 128 p., [7] p. of plates : ISBN
0-907015-34-4 (pbk.) :
NYPL [Sc D 88-1150]

The colonial legal heritage in Nigeria /.
Esiemokhai, Emmanuel Omoh. Akure, Nigeria ,
1986. xii, 82 p. ; ISBN 978-16-4248-3
NYPL [Sc D 88-640]

**COLONIALISM. see COLONIES;
IMPERIALISM.**

**COLONIES AND COLONIZATION. see
COLONIES.**

**COLONIES AND COLONIZATION,
BRITISH. see GREAT BRITAIN -
COLONIES.**

**COLONIES AND COLONIZATION,
GERMAN. see GERMANY - COLONIES.**

COLONIES - ECONOMIC CONDITIONS.
Africa, America, and central Asia . [Exeter,
Devon] [Atlantic Highlands, N.J.] 1984. 107
p. : ISBN 0-85989-295-6 (pbk.) : DDC 330.9/034
19
*HC53 .A35 1984	NYPL [Sc D 88-1315]*

La Colonisation, rupture ou parenthèse / sous la

direction de Marc H. Piault ; publié avec le
concours du Centre national des lettres. Paris :
Editions L'Harmattan, c1987. 326 p. : maps ;
22 cm. (Racines du présent, 0757-6366) Includes
indexes. Bibliography: p. 301-303. CONTENTS. -
Avant-propos : L'effet colonial : pour une révision des
faits / Marc H. Piault - Au-delà de la colonisation /
M.H. Piault - Conscommer la rupture / C. Meillassoux -
La colonisation "appropriée" / J.-P. Chauveau - Le futur
antérieur / E. de Latour - La production d'arachide au
Nord-Togo (1935-1949) / P.P. Rey - Le royaume abron
du Gyaman de 1875 à 1910 / E. Terray.
*1. Africa, West - Colonization. 2. Africa, West -
Colonial influence. 3. Africa, West - History -
1884-1960. I. Piault, Marc Henri. II. Series.*
NYPL [Sc D 88-727]

COLONIZATION - HISTORY.
Raynal, Guillaume Thomas François,
1713-1796. Histoire philosophique et politique
des établissemens & du commerce des
Européens dans les deux Indes. A Amsterdam ,
1770. 6 v. ;	*NYPL [Sc Rare C 86-2]*

Colonization Society of the County of Oneida.
To the inhabitants of Oneida County. [Utica,
N.Y. : The Society, 1838?] 8 p. ; 21 cm. Address
reported to a meeting of the Society in Utica, Nov. 20,
1838, by a committee appointed for that purpose.
1. Afro-Americans - Colonization - Africa. I. Title.
NYPL [Sc Rare G 86-40]

COLOR IN THE TEXTILE INDUSTRIES.
Errington, Leah. Natural dyes of Zambia /.
[Zambia? , between 1986 and 1988] (Ndola,
Zambia : Mission Press) 35 p. :
NYPL [Sc B 89-23]

The color purple . Walker, Alice, 1944- New
York , c1982. 245 p. ; ISBN 0-15-119153-0 :
DDC 813/.54 19
PS3573.A425 C6 1982
NYPL [Sc Rare F 88-3]

The color purple /. Walker, Alice, 1944-
London , 1983 (1986 [printing]) 245 p. : ISBN
0-7043-3905-6 (pbk)   DDC 813/.54 19
NYPL [Sc C 88-143]

Color, sex, and poetry . Hull, Gloria T.
Bloomington , c1987. xi, 240 p. : ISBN
0-253-34974-5   DDC 811/.52/099287 19
*PS153.N5 H84 1987	NYPL [Sc E 88-72]*

The color your way into Black history book /.
Sealy, Adrienne V. Brooklyn, N.Y. , c1980. 51
p. : ISBN 0-9602670-6-9   *NYPL [Sc F 89-36]*

Colored mariners in ports of South Carolina.
United States. President, 1841-1845 (Tyler)
[Washington, D. C.] 18. 18 p.;
NYPL [Sc Rare F 88-23]

**COLORED PEOPLE (SOUTH AFRICA) -
ATLANTIS.**
Atlantis a utopian nightmare /. Cape Town ,
1986. 114 p. : ISBN 0-7992-1070-6
NYPL [Sc D 89-17]

**COLORED PEOPLE (SOUTH AFRICA) -
FICTION.**
Wicomb, Zoë. You can't get lost in Cape Town
/. New York , c1987. 185 p. ; ISBN
0-394-56030-2 : DDC 823 19
PR9369.3.W53 Y6 1987
NYPL [Sc D 88-341]

**COLORED PEOPLE (UNITED STATES) see
AFRO-AMERICANS.**

COLORING BOOKS.
Carma, Jemel. Happy birthday everybody .
New York, N. Y. [1988] [24] p. :
NYPL [Sc H 89-1]

Sealy, Adrienne V. The color your way into
Black history book /. Brooklyn, N.Y. , c1980.
51 p. : ISBN 0-9602670-6-9
NYPL [Sc F 89-36]

COLORS (FLAGS) see FLAGS.

Coloured Persons Rights Bill, 1927. South Africa.
[Laws, etc.] Native Land Act, 1913.
Amendment Bill, 1927 [microform].
Representation of Natives in Parliament Bill.
Union Native Council Bill. Coloured Persons
Rights Bill, 1927. [S.I. [1927?] 47 p. ;
NYPL [Sc Micro F-10937]

Colson, Elizabeth, 1917- For prayer and profit :
the ritual, economic, and social importance of
beer in Gwembe District, Zambia, 1950-1982 /
Elizabeth Colson and Thayer Scudder. Stanford,
Calif. : Stanford University Press, 1988. vi, 147

p. : ill., map ; 23 cm. Includes index. Bibliography:
p. [133]-140.   ISBN 0-8047-1444-4 (alk. paper) :
DDC 968.94 19
*1. Tonga (Zambian people) - Alcohol use. 2. Beer -
Zambia - Gwembe District. 3. Drinking customs -
Zambia - Gwembe District. 4. Gwembe District,
Zambia - Economic conditions. I. Scudder, Thayer. II.
Title.*
*DT963.42 .C65 1988	NYPL [Sc D 88-1254]*

Colter, Cyrus. A chocolate soldier : a novel / by
Cyrus Colter.1st ed. New York : Thunder's
Mouth, c1988. 278 p. ; 23 cm.   ISBN
0-938410-42-3 : DDC 813/.54 19
1. Afro-Americans - Fiction. I. Title.
PS3553.O477 C5 1988
NYPL [Sc D 88-1396]

COLUMBUS, CHRISTOPHER.
Colón, Fernando, 1488-1539. [Historie.
English.] Christophe Colomb raconté par son
fils /. Paris , 1986. xviii, 265 p., [8] p. of
plates : ISBN 2-262-00387-4
NYPL [Sc D 88-504]

Columbus Memorial Library. Wharton-Lake,
Beverly D. Creative literature of Trinidad and
Tobago . Washington, D.C. , 1988. xi, 102 p. ;
ISBN 0-8270-2709-5   *NYPL [Sc D 88-710]*

COLUMNISTS. see JOURNALISTS.

Colyer, Vincent, 1825-1888. Committee of
Merchants for the Relief of Colored People,
Suffering from the Late Riots in the City of
New York. Report of the Committee of
Merchants for the Relief of Colored People,
Suffering from the Late Riots in the City of
New York. New York , 1863. 48 p. ;
NYPL [Sc Rare F 89-2]

Le combat d'André Aliker /. Nicolas, Armand.
Fort-de-France , 1974. 108 p. :
NYPL [Sc D 88-1189]

Comboio comakovi . Pessoa, Henrique Novais.
[Portugal] , 1987. 147 p. :
NYPL [Sc D 88-1010]

Come home my love /. Oguntoye, Jide. Ibadan ,
1987. 141 p. ; ISBN 978-243-272-5
NYPL [Sc C 88-226]

Come play hide and seek /. Gles, Margaret.
Champaign, Ill. [1975] 32 p. : ISBN
0-8116-6053-2
*PZ7.G4883 Co	NYPL [Sc D 89-119]*

Come to Mecca . Dhondy, Farrukh, 1944-
London , 1978 (1983 [printing]) 125 p. ; ISBN
0-00-672501-5 (pbk) : DDC 823 19
NYPL [Sc C 88-310]

Comer, James P.
Maggie's American dream : the life and times
of a Black family / by James P. Comer ; with a
foreword by Charlayne Hunter-Gault. New
York, N.Y. : New American Library, c1988.
xxiv, 228 p., [4] leaves of plates : ill. ; 23 cm.
"NAL books." ISBN 0-453-00588-8   DDC
973/.0496073022 B 19
*1. Comer, Maggie, 1904-. 2. Comer, James P. - Family.
3. Afro-Americans - Biography. I. Title.*
E185.97.C68 C66 1988 NYPL [Sc D 89-335]

COMER, JAMES P. - FAMILY.
Comer, James P. Maggie's American dream .
New York, N.Y. , c1988. xxiv, 228 p., [4]
leaves of plates : ISBN 0-453-00588-8   DDC
973/.0496073022 B 19
*E185.97.C68 C66 1988	NYPL [Sc D 89-335]*

COMER, MAGGIE, 1904-
Comer, James P. Maggie's American dream .
New York, N.Y. , c1988. xxiv, 228 p., [4]
leaves of plates : ISBN 0-453-00588-8   DDC
973/.0496073022 B 19
*E185.97.C68 C66 1988	NYPL [Sc D 89-335]*

Comhaire-Sylvain, Suzanne. Food and leisure
among the African youth of Leopoldville,
Belgian Congo. [Rondebosch] University of
Cape Town, 1950. 124 p. illus. 32 cm.
(Communications from the School of African Studies,
new ser., no. 25)   DDC 309.1675
*1. Youth - Zaire - Kinshasa. 2. Kinshasa (Zaire) -
Recreational activities. I. Series: Communications
(University of Cape Town, School of African Studies) ,
new ser., no. 25.*
*HQ799.C6 C6	NYPL [Sc G 89-2]*

**COMIC BOOKS, STRIPS, ETC. - UNITED
STATES.**
Brandon, Brumsic. Outta sight, Luther! New
York [c1971] 1 v. (chiefly illus.) ISBN

0-8397-6481-2 DDC 741.5/973
PN6728.L8 B7 *NYPL [Sc B 88-54]*

COMIC STRIPS. see COMIC BOOKS, STRIPS, ETC.

COMICS. see COMIC BOOKS, STRIPS, ETC.

Comics für Afrika : deutschsprachige Comickünstler zeichnen für Afrika. Dormagen [West Germany] : Edition Quasimodo, [1986] 96 p. : chiefly ill. ; 31 cm. Compiled by Klaus Bogdon-p. 7.
1. Imperialism - Comic books, strips, etc. 2. Racism - Comic books, strips, etc. 3. Africa - Colonization - Comic books, strips, etc. I. Bogdon, Klaus.
NYPL [Sc G 88-27]

Comidas tipicas dominicanas =. Bornia, Ligia de. Santo Domingo Republica Dominicana , 1987. 132 p. ; *NYPL [Sc D 89-157]*

Coming home and other stories /. Karodia, Farida. London , 1988. v, 185 p. ; ISBN 0-435-90738-7 (pbk) :
PR9369.3.K3 *NYPL [Sc C 89-88]*

Coming of age [microform] . Hunter, Wilma King. 1982. 343 leaves.
NYPL [Sc Micro R-4688]

The coming of power, and other stories /. Kariara, Jonathan. Nairobi , 1986. 100 p. ; ISBN 0-19-572597-2
NYPL [Sc D 88-1053]

Coming up on the rough side . Johnson, MayLee. South Orange, N.J. , c1988. vii, 88 p. ; ISBN 0-944734-01-4 *NYPL [Sc D 89-190]*

Comisión de Estudios de Historia de la Iglesia en Latinoamerica. Escravidão negra e história da Igreja na América Latina e no Caribe /. Petrópolis , 1987. 237 p. :
NYPL [Sc D 88-75]

Comissão de Estudos de História da Igreja na América Latina. see Comisión de Estudios de Historia de la Iglesia en Latinoamerica.

Comissão Provincial das Comemorações do V Centenário de Vasco da Gama. Museu de Arte Sacra (Mozambique) Museu de Arte Sacra, anexo à Igreja da Misericórdia, Ilha de Moçambique [microform] [Lourenço Marques?] , 1969. [16] p. :
NYPL [Sc Micro F-10928]

Comité Frantz Fanon de Fort-de-France (Martinique) Mémorial international Frantz Fanon (1982 : Fort-de-France, Martinique) Mémorial international Frantz Fanon . Paris , Dakar , c1984. 278 p. : ISBN 2-7087-0431-1
NYPL [Sc D 88-334]

Commager, Henry Steele, 1902- The great proclamation : a book for young Americans / by Henry Steele Commager. Indianapolis : Bobbs-Merrill [1960] 112 p. : ill. ; 24 cm.
1. Emancipation proclamation - Juvenile literature. I. Title. *NYPL [Sc E 88-229]*

Le commandant Mortenol . Lara, Oruno D. Epinay, France , c1985. 275 p. : ISBN 2-905787-00-7 *NYPL [Sc D 88-1085]*

Commandos de brousse /. Ollivier Patrick. Paris , 1985. 275 p., [8] p. of plates : ISBN 2-246-35481-1 *NYPL [Sc E 87-222]*

Comme des gouttes de sang . Stephenson, Elie, 1944- Paris , c1988. 95 p. ; ISBN 2-7087-0509-1
PQ3959.2.S78 C65x 1988
NYPL [Sc C 89-156]

COMMERCE - EDUCATION. see BUSINESS EDUCATION.

COMMERCE - HISTORY.
Raynal, Guillaume Thomas François, 1713-1796. Histoire philosophique et politique des établissemens & du commerce des Européens dans les deux Indes. A Amsterdam , 1770. 6 v. ; *NYPL [Sc Rare C 86-2]*

COMMERCIAL EDUCATION. see BUSINESS EDUCATION.

COMMERCIAL POLICY - TRINIDAD AND TOBAGO.
Oilfields Workers' Trade Union. Memorandum to the Government of Trinidad and Tobago . San F'do [i.e. San Fernando, Trinidad and Tobago] [1987 or 1988] 124 p. [4] p. of plates : *NYPL [Sc D 88-822]*

COMMERCIAL SCHOOLS. see BUSINESS EDUCATION.

COMMERCIALS, RADIO. see RADIO ADVERTISING.

Commey, James Putsch. The missing link poems / by James Putsch Commey ; with introduction and notes by Charles Faibi. Accra : Putsch Publications, c1988. xvii, 92 p. : ill. ; 21 cm.
I. Title. *NYPL [Sc D 89-584]*

Commission on Race and Housing. Where shall we live? report. Berkeley : University of California Press, 1958. ix, 77 p. 24 cm.
1. Discrimination in housing - United States. I. Title.
HD7293 .C6427 *NYPL [Sc E 88-397]*

Commission Pro-Justice Mariel Prisoners. The Mariel injustice . Coral Gables, Fl. , c1987. 204 p. : *NYPL [Sc F 89-64]*

The Commissioners of the Alms-house, vs. Alexander Whistelo, a black man . Whistelo, Alexander. (defendant) New York , 1808. 56 p. ;
NYPL [Sc Rare F 88-21]

Committee for Labour Solidarity. CLS speaks : a collection of statements by the Committee for Labour Solidarity (Preparatory) [Trinidad and Tobago] : Classline Publications, [1987] iii, 80 p. : ill., ports. ; 21 cm. Cover title. CONTENTS. - A statement of intent - Crisis--the way out - This country needs an alternative to barbarism - Election[s] and the working people - On to people's power.
1. Labor and laboring classes - Trinidad and Tobago - Political activity. 2. Trinidad and Tobago - Economic conditions. I. Title. *NYPL [Sc D 88-969]*

Committee of Merchants for the Relief of Colored People, Suffering from the Late Riots in the City of New York. Report of the Committee of Merchants for the Relief of Colored People, Suffering from the Late Riots in the City of New York. New York : George A. Whitehorn, steam printer, 1863. 48 p. ; 24 cm. Cover title: Report of the Merchants' Committee for the Relief of Colored People Suffering from the Riots in the City of New York. July, 1863. Includes report of the secretary of the committee, Vincent Colyer. Schomburg's copy lacks cover title.
1. Afro-Americans - New York (N.Y.). 2. Draft riot, 1863. 3. United States - History - Civil War, 1861-1865 - Hospitals, charities, etc. I. Colyer, Vincent, 1825-1888. II. Title. III. Title: Report of the Merchants' Committee for the Relief of Colored People Suffering from the Riots in the City of New York. July, 1863.
NYPL [Sc Rare F 89-2]

COMMODITY EXCHANGES - NIGERIA.
Osammor, Vincent Osoloka. Introducing commodities (market) exchange in Nigeria /. Surulere, Lagos, Nigeria , 1986. x, 39 p. ;
NYPL [Sc D 88-1293]

COMMONS (SOCIAL ORDER) see LABOR AND LABORING CLASSES; MIDDLE CLASSES.

Commonwealth Caribbean writers. Merriman, Stella E. Georgetown, Guyana, 1970. iv, 98 p.
NYPL [JFF 72-67]

Commonwealth Conference (1971: Singapore) Nyerere, Julius Kambarage, Pres. Tanzania, 1922- South Africa and the Commonwealth [microform] /. [S.l. , 1971] 14 p. ;
NYPL [Sc Micro F-10922]

Commonwealth Group of Eminent Persons. Mission to South Africa : the Commonwealth report / The Commonwealth Group of Eminent Persons ; foreword by Shridath Ramphal. Harmondsworth, Middlesex, Eng. : Penguin Books for the Commonwealth Secretariat ; New York : Viking Penguin, 1986. 176 p. : ill. ; 20 cm. "A Penguin special"--P. 4 of cover. ISBN 0-14-052384-7 :
1. Apartheid - South Africa. 2. South Africa - Politics and government - 1978-. I. Title.
NYPL [Sc C 88-116]

Commonwealth Institute (Great Britain) Kirby, Richard, 1958. Ewto' . London , c1985. 27 p. : ISBN 0-946140-24-3 (pbk) : DDC 307.7/72 19
F2380 *NYPL [Sc F 89-104]*

Commonwealth literature. Walsh, William, 1916- London, New York, 1973. vi, 150 p.
*NYPL [*R-NCB 74-5085]*

COMMONWEALTH, THE. see POLITICAL SCIENCE; STATE, THE.

Communication and media arts . Akpan, Emmanuel D. (Emanuel David), 1938- Uyo [Nigeria] , c1987. 178 p. : ISBN 978-267-600-4
NYPL [Sc D 88-752]

COMMUNICATION IN COMMUNITY DEVELOPMENT - AFRICA.
Rajabu, A. R. M. S. Communication practice in development /. Nairobi, Kenya , 1986. vi, 50 p. : DDC 307.1/4/096 19
HN780.Z9 C6698 1986 *NYPL [Sc F 88-282]*

COMMUNICATION IN COMMUNITY DEVELOPMENT - STUDY AND TEACHING - AFRICA.
Tadi Liben. Planning and conducting training in communication /. Nairobi, Kenya , 1986. viii, 55 p. : DDC 307.1/4/0706 19
HN780.Z9 C679 1986 *NYPL [Sc F 89-171]*

COMMUNICATION IN PUBLIC ADMINISTRATION - TANZANIA.
Sokoïne, Edward Moringe, 1938-1984. Public policy making and implementation in Tanzania /. Pau [1986?] ix, 124 p. :
NYPL [Sc E 88-319]

COMMUNICATION IN RURAL DEVELOPMENT - NIGERIA.
Aboyade, B. Olabimpe. The provision of information for rural development /. Ibadan , 1987. xv, 104 p. : ISBN 978-267-900-3
NYPL [Sc D 88-739]

COMMUNICATION - NIGERIA.
Akpan, Emmanuel D. (Emanuel David), 1938- Communication and media arts . Uyo [Nigeria] , c1987. 178 p. : ISBN 978-267-600-4
NYPL [Sc D 88-752]

Communication practice in development /. Rajabu, A. R. M. S. Nairobi, Kenya , 1986. vi, 50 p. : DDC 307.1/4/096 19
HN780.Z9 C6698 1986 *NYPL [Sc F 88-282]*

COMMUNICATION - RELIGIOUS ASPECTS - CATHOLIC CHURCH.
Asuzu, Boniface Ntomchukwu. Communications media in the Nigerian Church today /. Rome , 1987. 160 p. : *NYPL [Sc E 88-297]*

Asuzu, Boniface Ntomchukwu. Communications strategy in the new era of evangelization . Roma , 1987. xxi, 343 p. :
NYPL [Sc E 88-276]

COMMUNICATION (THEOLOGY)
Dierks, Friedrich. Evangelium im afrikanischen Kontext . Gütersloh , c1986. 206 p. : ISBN 3-579-00239-2 DDC 266/.0089963 19
BL2480.T76 D54 1986 *NYPL [Sc D 88-879]*

Communications.
(11) Chaphole, Sol. Dihaeya /. [Cape Town] , c1986. xiii, 68 p. ; ISBN 0-7992-1048-X
NYPL [Sc D 88-1123]

Communications for Basic Services Regional Training Project. Tadi Liben. Planning and conducting training in communication /. Nairobi, Kenya , 1986. viii, 55 p. : DDC 307.1/4/0706 19
HN780.Z9 C679 1986 *NYPL [Sc F 89-171]*

Communications media in the Nigerian Church today /. Asuzu, Boniface Ntomchukwu. Rome , 1987. 160 p. : *NYPL [Sc E 88-297]*

Communications strategy in the new era of evangelization . Asuzu, Boniface Ntomchukwu. Roma , 1987. xxi, 343 p. :
NYPL [Sc E 88-276]

Communications (University of Cape Town. Centre for African Studies) .
(no. 6) Dubow, Saul. Land, labour and merchant capital in the pre-industrial rural economy of the Cape . [Cape Town] , 1982. ii, 95 p. : ISBN 0-7992-0472-2
NYPL [Sc D 82-611]

(11) Chaphole, Sol. Dihaeya /. [Cape Town] , c1986. xiii, 68 p. ; ISBN 0-7992-1048-X
NYPL [Sc D 88-1123]

Communications (University of Cape Town, School of African Studies) .
(new ser. no. 19) Sheddick, Vernon George John. The morphology of residential associations as found among the Khwakhwa of Basutoland. [Cape Town], University of Cape Town, 1948. 57 p.
DT786 .S5 *NYPL [Sc G 89-1]*

(new ser., no. 25) Comhaire-Sylvain, Suzanne. Food and leisure among the African youth of Leopoldville, Belgian Congo. [Rondebosch] 1950. 124 p. DDC 309.1675
HQ799.C6 C6 *NYPL [Sc G 89-2]*

COMMUNISM - AFRICA.
Africa's struggle for freedom, the USA and the
USSR. New York , 1972. 96 p. : ISBN
0-87898-096-2   *NYPL [Sc C 88-139]*

Ottaway, Marina. Afrocommunism /. New
York , 1986. ix, 270 p. : ISBN 0-8419-1034-0
DDC 335.43/096 19
HX438.5 .O87 1985   NYPL [JLD 86-4056]

COMMUNISM - CAPE VERDE.
Romero, Vicente, 1947- Guinea-Bissau y Cabo
Verde . Madrid , 1981. 109 p. ; ISBN
84-85761-09-X DDC 966/.5702 19
DT613.78 .R66 1981   NYPL [Sc C 89-1]

COMMUNISM - ETHIOPIA.
Proletarian internationalism and the Ethiopian
revolution /. Addis Ababa , 1984. 56 p. :
DT387.95 .P76 1984   NYPL [Sc F 89-85]

COMMUNISM - GUINEA-BISSAU.
Romero, Vicente, 1947- Guinea-Bissau y Cabo
Verde . Madrid , 1981. 109 p. ; ISBN
84-85761-09-X DDC 966/.5702 19
DT613.78 .R66 1981   NYPL [Sc C 89-1]

**COMMUNISM - HISTORY -
BIBLIOGRAPHY - CATALOGS.**
Guide to the Raya Dunayevskaya collection .
Detroit, Mich. [1986?] 84 p. ;
NYPL [Sc F 88-196]

**COMMUNISM - HISTORY -
SOURCES.**
Dunayevskaya, Raya. The Raya Dunayevskaya
collection [microform] Supplement: Raya
Dunayevskaya's last writings, 1986-1987.
1986-1987. ca. 140 items.
NYPL [Sc Micro R-4838]

COMMUNISM - SUDAN - HISTORY.
El-Amin, Mohammed Nuri. The emergence and
development of the leftist movement in the
Sudan during the 1930's and 1940's /.
[Khartoum] , 1984. 159 p. ; DDC 324.2624/07
19
HX443.5.A6 E42 1984
NYPL [Sc D 88-1261]

Communist front? . Horne, Gerald. Rutherford
[N.J.] , London , c1988. 454 p. ; ISBN
0-8386-3285-8 (alk. paper) DDC
323.1/196073/073 19
E185.61 .H8 1988   NYPL [Sc E 88-147]

Les Communistes expliquent : l'autonomie
démocratique et populaire / [edité par le
Comité central du Parti communiste
martiniquais]. [Fort-de-France : Sociéte
d'imprimerie martiniquaise], 1978. 147 p. ; 18 x
24 cm. Cover title.
*1. Parti communiste martiniquais. 2. Political parties -
Martinique. I. Parti communiste martiniquais. Comité
central.   NYPL [Sc E 89-174]*

COMMUNISTS - MARTINIQUE.
Nicolas, Armand. Le combat d'André Aliker /.
Fort-de-France , 1974. 108 p. :
NYPL [Sc D 88-1189]

Communities and development in Guyana .
Matthews, Lear K. [Georgetown, Guyana?]
1980. 94, v. p. :   *NYPL [Sc F 89-65]*

Communities in Britain.
Saunders, Dave. The West Indians in Britain /.
London , 1984. 72 p. : ISBN 0-7134-4427-4
DA125.W4 S28x 1984   NYPL [Sc F 88-68]

Community action in Haiti [microform] .
Honorat, Jean Jacques. New York , 1982. 45
p. ;   *NYPL [Sc Micro F-11008]*

COMMUNITY AND COLLEGE.
Bowden, Bertram Vivian, Baron Bowden, 1910-
The role of universities in the modern world /.
Kumasi, Ghana [1978?] 81 p. ;
NYPL [Sc D 88-465]

COMMUNITY AND COLLEGE - GHANA.
Bowden, Bertram Vivian, Baron Bowden, 1910-
The role of universities in the modern world /.
Kumasi, Ghana [1978?] 81 p. ;
NYPL [Sc D 88-465]

COMMUNITY AND LIBRARIES. see
LIBRARIES AND COMMUNITY.

COMMUNITY-BASED RESIDENCES. see
GROUP HOMES FOR CHILDREN.

**COMMUNITY COLLEGES - UNITED
STATES.**
Richardson, Richard C. Fostering minority
access and achievement in higher education .
San Francisco, Calif. , c1987. xviii, 244 p. ;

ISBN 1-555-42053-2 (alk. paper) DDC 378/.052
19
LC3727 .R53 1987   NYPL [Sc E 88-472]

COMMUNITY COUNCILS. see **COMMUNITY
ORGANIZATION.**

Community development . Oni, Stephen Bola.
[Zaria, Nigeria] , 1987. vii, 128 p. : ISBN
978-19-4120-0   *NYPL [Sc D 88-791]*

Community development efforts in Igboland /.
Egboh, Edmund Onyemeke. Onitsha [Nigeria] ,
1987. 206 p. : ISBN 978-264-348-3
NYPL [Sc E 88-258]

COMMUNITY DEVELOPMENT - GUYANA.
Matthews, Lear K. Communities and
development in Guyana. [Georgetown,
Guyana?] 1980. 94, v. p. :
NYPL [Sc F 89-65]

COMMUNITY DEVELOPMENT - HAITI.
Honorat, Jean Jacques. Community action in
Haiti [microform] . New York , 1982. 45 p. ;
NYPL [Sc Micro F-11008]

**Community development in pre-independence
Zimbabwe** . Mutizwa-Mangiza, N. D. Harare ,
c1985. iv, 79 p. : ISBN 0-86924-090-0 (pbk.)
DDC 307.1/4/096891 19
HN802.Z9 C65 1985   NYPL [JLD 88-3699]

COMMUNITY DEVELOPMENT - NIGERIA.
Egboh, Edmund Onyemeke. Community
development efforts in Igboland /. Onitsha
[Nigeria] , 1987. 206 p. : ISBN 978-264-348-3
NYPL [Sc E 88-258]

Oni, Stephen Bola. Community development .
[Zaria, Nigeria] , 1987. vii, 128 p. : ISBN
978-19-4120-0   *NYPL [Sc D 88-791]*

Perspectives on community and rural
development in Nigeria /. Jos , c1988. 202 p. ;
ISBN 978-282-700-2   *NYPL [Sc E 89-18]*

**Community development workers' training
series** .
(4) Rajabu, A. R. M. S. Communication
practice in development /. Nairobi, Kenya ,
1986. vi, 50 p. : DDC 307.1/4/096 19
HN780.Z9 C6698 1986   NYPL [Sc F 88-282]

(7) Tadi Liben. Planning and conducting
training in communication /. Nairobi, Kenya ,
1986. viii, 55 p. : DDC 307.1/4/0706 19
HN780.Z9 C679 1986   NYPL [Sc F 89-171]

COMMUNITY HEALTH. see **PUBLIC
HEALTH.**

**COMMUNITY HEALTH AIDES -
TANZANIA.**
Community health workers . Oxford , New
York , 1987. xii, 205 p. : ISBN 0-19-261618-8
(pbk.) : DDC 362.1/0425 19
RA552.T34 C67 1987   NYPL [Sc D 88-1301]

**COMMUNITY HEALTH SERVICES -
TANZANIA.**
Community health workers . Oxford , New
York , 1987. xii, 205 p. : ISBN 0-19-261618-8
(pbk.) : DDC 362.1/0425 19
RA552.T34 C67 1987   NYPL [Sc D 88-1301]

**COMMUNITY HEALTH SERVICES -
UNITED STATES.**
Maida, Carl Albert. Black networks of care
[microform] . 1981. xiii, 276 leaves ;
NYPL [Sc Micro R-4803]

Community health workers : the Tanzanian
experience / H.K. Heggenhougen ... [et al.] ;
with special assistance from M.P. Mandara ;
foreword by A. Chiduo. Oxford ; New York :
Oxford University Press, 1987. xii, 205 p. : ill. ;
22 cm. (Oxford medical publications) Bibliography: p.
175-202. ISBN 0-19-261618-8 (pbk.) : DDC
362.1/0425 19
*1. Community health aides - Tanzania. 2. Community
health services - Tanzania. I. Heggenhougen, H. K. (H.
Kris).*
RA552.T34 C67 1987   NYPL [Sc D 88-1301]

**COMMUNITY ORGANIZATION -
WASHINGTON (D.C.)**
Williams, Brett. Upscaling downtown . Ithaca
[N.Y.] , 1988. xi, 157 p. : ISBN 0-8014-2106-3
(alk. paper) DDC 307.3/42/09753 19
HT177.W3 W55 1988   NYPL [Sc E 88-387]

**COMMUNITY POWER - UGANDA - BUGISU
(DISTRICT)**
Bunker, Stephen G., 1944- Double dependency
and constraints on class formation in Bugisu,

Uganda /. Urbana, Ill. , 1983. v, 88 p. : DDC
303.3/09676/1 19
HD1538.U43 B86 1983
NYPL [Sc D 88-1054]

Comores. see Comoro Islands.

COMORO ISLANDS.
Marquardt, Wilhelm. Seychellen, Komoren und
Maskarenen . München , c1976. 346 p. : ISBN
3-8039-0117-0
DT469.S4 M37   NYPL [JFC 77-3948]

Compagnia di Gesù. see Jesuits.

Compagnie de Jésus. see Jesuits.

COMPANHIA DO NYASSA.
Portugal. Laws, statutes etc. Companhia do
Nyassa [microform] . Lisboa, 1897. 89 p.
JV4229.M7C785
NYPL [Sc Micro R-4840 no.10]

Companhia do Nyassa [microform] . Portugal.
Laws, statutes etc. Lisboa, 1897. 89 p.
JV4229.M7C785
NYPL [Sc Micro R-4840 no.10]

Compañia de Jesús. see Jesuits.

Company of Jesus. see Jesuits.

Comparative American cities.
Detroit, race and uneven development /.
Philadelphia , 1987. xii, 317 p. : ISBN
0-87722-485-4 (alk. paper) DDC
305.8/009774/34 19
HC108.D6 D47 1987   NYPL [Sc E 88-205]

**A comparative analysis of three select
populations of Black unmarried adolescent
fathers /.** Hendricks, Leo E. Washington,
D.C. , 1982. ix, 129 p. :
NYPL [Sc F 88-222]

**Comparative dictionary of Ge'ez (Classical
Ethiopic)** . Leslau, Wolf. Wiesbaden , 1987.
xlix, 813 p. ; ISBN 3-447-02592-1 : DDC 492/.8
19
*PJ9087 .L37 1987   NYPL [*OEC 89-3015]*

Comparative ethnic and race relations series.
Solomos, John. Black youth, racism and the
state . Cambridge [Cambridgeshire] , New
York , 1988. 284 p. ; ISBN 0-521-36019-6 DDC
305.8/96041 19
DA125.N4 S65 1988   NYPL [Sc E 88-606]

**Comparative studies of traditional African
religions /.** Metuh, Emefie Ikenga. Onitsha,
Nigeria , 1987. xi, 288 p. ISBN 978-244-208-9
NYPL [Sc D 88-800]

**Comparative vocabularies of Bushman languages
/.** Bleek, Dorothea Frances, d. 1948. Cambridge
[Eng.] , 1929. 94 p., 1 leaf of plates : DDC
496.232
PL8101 .B6   NYPL [Sc E 88-89]

Competition. Competition, a feminist taboo? /.
New York , 1987. xvi, 260 p. ; ISBN
0-935312-74-9 (pbk.) : DDC 305.4/2 19
HQ1206 .C69 1987   NYPL [JFE 88-6669]

Competition, a feminist taboo? / edited by
Valerie Miner and Helen E. Longino ; foreword
by Nell Irvin Painter. New York : The Feminist
Press at the City University of New York,
1987. xvi, 260 p. ; 23 cm. Half title: Competition.
Includes bibliographical references. ISBN
0-935312-74-9 (pbk.) : DDC 305.4/2 19
*1. Women - Psychology. 2. Competition (Psychology).
3. Feminism - Psychological aspects. I. Miner, Valerie.
II. Longino, Helen E. III. Title: Competition.*
HQ1206 .C69 1987   NYPL [JFE 88-6669]

COMPETITION (BIOLOGY)
Evolution, creative intelligence and intergroup
competition /. Washington , 1986. 96 p. :
ISBN 0-941694-30-5   *NYPL [Sc D 89-532]*

COMPETITION (PSYCHOLOGY)
Competition, a feminist taboo? /. New York ,
1987. xvi, 260 p. ; ISBN 0-935312-74-9 (pbk.) :
DDC 305.4/2 19
HQ1206 .C69 1987   NYPL [JFE 88-6669]

**COMPLAINTS (CRIMINAL PROCEDURE) -
NIGERIA.**
Murder of Dele Giwa . Lagos, Nigeria , 1988.
193 p. : ISBN 978-232-523-6
NYPL [Sc F 89-35]

The compleat guide to Nassau /. Dodge, Steve.
Decatur, Ill. , c1987. 116 p. : ISBN
0-932265-04-9 (pbk.)
NYPL [Sc D 88-685]

Complément au Dictionnaire lomóngo-français .
Hulstaert, G. Bamanya- Mbandaka , 1987. 463
p. ; *NYPL [Sc D 89-193]*

Complete poems of Frances E.W. Harper /.
Harper, Frances Ellen Watkins, 1825-1911.
[Poems.] New York , 1988. lx, 232 p. ; ISBN
0-19-505244-7 (alk. paper) DDC 811/.3 19
PS1799.H7 A17 1988 NYPL [JFC 88-2147]

**COMPOSERS - UNITED STATES -
BIOGRAPHY.**
Green, Jeffrey P. Edmund Thornton Jenkins .
Westport, Conn. , 1982. xii, 213 p. : ISBN
0-313-23253-9 (lib. bdg.) DDC 780/.92/4 B 19
ML410.J44 G7 1982 NYPL [Sc D 86-413]

Southall, Geneva H. Blind Tom . Minneapolis ,
1979- v. : DDC 786.1/092/4 B
ML417.B78 S7 1979
NYPL [Sc Ser.-L .S674]

**COMPOSERS - UNITED STATES -
BIOGRAPHY - JUVENILE LITERATURE.**
Preston, Katherine. Scott Joplin /. New York ,
c1988. 110 p. : ISBN 1-555-46598-6 DDC
780/.92/4 B 92 19
ML3930.J66 P7 1988 NYPL [Sc E 88-170]

Composición social dominicana . Bosch, Juan,
1909- Santo Domingo, República Dominicana ,
1983. 272 p. ; *NYPL [Sc D 88-1065]*

Compreender a nossa tarefa [microform]. Machel,
Samora, 1933- [Maputo, Moçambique , 1979]
20 p. ; *NYPL [Sc Micro F-11,163]*

**A comprehensive approach to study and test
taking /.** Spencer, F. Louise. New York, N.Y. ,
c1988. xii ; *NYPL [Sc D 88-1168]*

Comprendre (Classiques africains (Firm))
Kesteloot, Lilyan. Comprendre les Poèmes de
Léopold Sédar Senghor /. Issy les Moulineaux ,
1986. 143 p. : ISBN 2-85049-376-7
NYPL [Sc D 88-978]

Comprendre Haïti . Hurbon, Laënnec. Paris ,
c1987. 174 p. : ISBN 2-86537-192-1
NYPL [Sc D 88-1045]

**Comprendre les Poèmes de Léopold Sédar
Senghor /.** Kesteloot, Lilyan. Issy les
Moulineaux , 1986. 143 p. : ISBN 2-85049-376-7
NYPL [Sc D 88-978]

Comprendre l'oeuvre de Bernard B. Dadié /.
Vincileoni, Nicole. Issy les Moulineaux , c1986.
319 p.,[12] p. of plates : ISBN 2-85049-368-6
NYPL [Sc D 88-721]

COMPROMISE OF 1850.
Hayne, Robert Young, 1791-1839. Speeches of
Hayne and Webster in the United States
Senate, on the resolution of Mr. Foot, January,
1830 . Boston , 1853. 115 p. ;
E381 .H424 1853 NYPL [Sc Rare C 89-20]

Smith, Whiteford. God, the refuge of his
people . Columbia, S.C. , 1850. 16 p. ;
NYPL [Sc Rare C 89-12]

A comrade is as precious as a rice seedling .
Aguilar, Mila D. New York , c1984. xii, 37 p. :
ISBN 0-913175-04-8
NYPL [Sc D 88-1158]

Concept de pouvoir en Afrique. Spanish. El
concepto del poder en Africa / I.A. Akinjogbin
[et al.]. 1a ed. Barcelona : Serbal ; París :
Unesco, 1983. 178 p. ; 21 cm. (Colección de
temas africanos . 10) Translation of: Le Concept de
pouvoir en Afrique, 1981. Includes bibliographies.
ISBN 92-3-301887-3 (Unesco)
*1. Africa - Civilization. 2. Africa - Politics and
government. I. Akinjogbin, I. A. II. Title. III. Series.*
NYPL [Sc D 88-604]

El concepto del poder en África /. Concept de
pouvoir en Afrique. Spanish. Barcelona , París ,
1983. 178 p. ; ISBN 92-3-301887-3 (Unesco)
NYPL [Sc D 88-604]

**Concilio mundial de iglesias. see World Council
of Churches.**

Concord Press of America. Shehu, Emman
Usman. Questions for big brother /. Nigeria ,
1988. 85 p. ; ISBN 978-302-093-5
NYPL [Sc C 89-121]

Concordat signé à Rome le 25 mars 1860 .
Catholic Church. [Treaties, etc. Haiti, 1860
Mar. 25.] Port-au-Prince , 1918. 31 p. ;
NYPL [Sc Micro F-10,892]

**Concours radiophonique de la meilleure nouvelle
de langue française.**
Timité, Bassori, 1933- Les eaux claires de ma
source /Timité bassori ; et six autres nouvelles.
Paris , 1986. 127 p. ; ISBN 2-218-07813-9
NYPL [Sc C 88-11]

Yoka Lye Mudaba, 1947- Le fossoyeur /.
Paris , 1986. 127 p. ; ISBN 2-218-07830-9
NYPL [Sc C 88-10]

Concurso de Teatro, 1987. Santo Domingo,
República Dominicana : Taller, c1988. 177 p. :
ill. ; 21 cm. CONTENTS. - Hagase la mujer / Juan
Carlos Campos.--No quiero ser fuerte / Germana
Quintana.--Ultimo son / Frank Disla.--La trama de San
Miguel / Willia m García.--Un ladron en mi casa /
Angelo Valenzuela.
*1. Dominican drama. I. Concurso de Teatron (2nd :
1987 : Santo Domingo, Dominican Republ ic).*
MLCS 88/09684 (P) NYPL [Sc D 88-1331]

**Concurso de Teatron (2nd : 1987 : Santo
Domingo, Dominican Republ ic)** Concurso de
Teatro, 1987. Santo Domingo, República
Dominicana , c1988. 177 p. :
MLCS 88/09684 (P) NYPL [Sc D 88-1331]

Condé, Maryse.
Moi, Tituba, sorcière-- : noire de Salem : roman
/ Maryse Condé. Paris : Mercure de France,
c1986. 276 p. ; 24 cm. (Collection Histoire
romanesque) ISBN 2-7152-1440-5
*1. Tituba - Fiction. 2. Witchcraft - Massachusetts -
Salem - Fiction. I. Title. II. Title: Noire de Salem. III.
Series.* *NYPL [Sc E 88-97]*

[Une Saison à Rihata. English]
A season in Rihata / Maryse Condé ;
translated from the French by Richard
Philcox. London : Heinemann Educational,
1988. 192 p. ; 20 cm. (Caribbean writers series)
Translation of: Une saison à Rihata. ISBN
0-435-98832-8 (pbk)
1. Africa - Fiction. I. Title.
PQ3949.2.C65 NYPL [Sc C 89-90]

La vie scélérate : roman / Maryse Condé.
Paris : Seghers, c1987. 333 p. ; 22 cm.
1. Guadeloupe - Fiction. I. Title.
NYPL [Sc D 88-1102]

**CONE, JAMES H. - CONTRIBUTIONS IN
BLACK THEOLOGY.**
Bosch Navarro, Juan. La Iglesia negra .
Valencia , 1986 (Valencia : Imprenta Nácher).
57 p. ; *NYPL [Sc D 87-1154]*

Coner-Edwards, Alice F. Black families in crisis .
New York , c1988. xiv, 305 p. ; ISBN
0-87630-524-9 DDC 305.8/96073 19
E185.86 .B5254 1988 NYPL [Sc E 89-155]

Confederación Granadina. see Colombia.

**CONFEDERATE STATES OF AMERICA -
POLITICS AND GOVERNMENT.**
The African slave trade . Philadelphia , 1863.
24 p. ; *NYPL [Sc Rare F 89-5]*

**Conference of Heads of State or Government of
Non-aligned Countries. 1st, Belgrade, 1961.**
Appeal for world peace [microform] . Accra
[1961?] 19 p. : *NYPL [Sc Micro F-10978]*

**Conference of Heads of State or Government of
Non-aligned Countries (6th: 1979: Havana,
Cuba)** Burnham, Forbes, 1923- To build a
new world [microform]. [Georgetown,
Guyana] , 1980. 20 p. :
NYPL [Sc Micro F-11021]

**Conference of International Black Lutherans
(1986 : University of Zimbabwe)** Theology
and the Black experience . Minneapolis , c1988.
272 p. ; ISBN 0-8066-2353-5 DDC 284.1/08996
19
BX8065.2 .T48 1988 NYPL [Sc D 89-353]

**Conference on Black Student Retention in
Higher Education (1985 : Orlando, Fla.)**
Black student retention in higher education /.
Springfield, Ill., U. S.A. , c1988. xvi, 111 p. :
ISBN 0-398-05477-0 DDC 378/.198/2 19
LC2781 .B465 1988 NYPL [Sc F 89-139]

**Conference on Black Student Retention in
Higher Education (1986 : Atlanta, Ga.)**
Black student retention in higher education /.
Springfield, Ill., U. S.A. , c1988. xvi, 111 p. :
ISBN 0-398-05477-0 DDC 378/.198/2 19
LC2781 .B465 1988 NYPL [Sc F 89-139]

**Conference on Conceptual and Terminological
Analysis in the Social Sciences (1981 :**

Bielefeld, Germany) Ethnicity . Honolulu,
Hawaii (2424 Maile Way, Honolulu 96822) ,
c1985. xxix, 205 p. ; DDC 305.8//0072 19
GN495.6 .E89 1985 NYPL [Sc F 87-355]

**Conference on Southern Letters and Modern
Literature (1985 : Louisiana State University,
Baton Rouge)** The Southern review and
modern literature, 1935-1985 /. Baton Rouge ,
c1988. xvi, 238 p.: ISBN 0-8071-1424-3 : DDC
810/.9/975 19
PS267.B3 S68 1987 NYPL [Sc E 88-280]

**Conference on the Development Problems of
Small Island States (1981: Grenada, West
Indies)**
Bishop, Maurice. Address of the Conference on
Development Problems of Small Island States,
July 13, 1981 /. [St. George's, Grenada , 1981]
9 p. ; *NYPL [Sc Micro R-4108 no.26]*

Bishop, Maurice. Imperialism is the real
problem [microform] . [st. George's], Grenada ,
1981. 13 leaves ;
NYPL [Sc Micro R-4108 no.27]

**Conference "To Fulfill These Rights." see White
House Conference "To Fulfill These Rights",
Washington, D. C., 1966.**

Confiant, Raphaël.
Bitako-A / Raphaël Confiant. [Martinique] :
Editions de GERAC, 1985. 77 p. ; 21 cm.
*1. Creole dialects, French - West Indies - Texts. I.
Title.* *NYPL [Sc D 88-1269]*

Jik dèyè do Bondyé / Raphaël Confiant ; photo
couverture, C. Maurice ; photo intérieur, Jean
Popincourt. [Port-au-Prince? : s.n., 1978?] 64
p. : ill. ; 21 cm. "Supplément à Grif an tè, no. 33."
*1. Creole dialects, French - Haiti - Texts. 2. Haiti -
Fiction. I. Title.* *NYPL [Sc D 88-694]*

Le nègre et l'amiral : roman / Raphaël
Confiant. Paris : B. Grasset, c1988. 334 p. ; 23
cm. ISBN 2-246-40991-8
*1. World War, 1939-1945 - Martinique - Fiction. 2.
Martinique - Fiction. I. Title.*
NYPL [Sc D 89-340]

Conflict and other poems /. Segun, Mabel.
Ibadan , 1986. vi, 49 p. ; ISBN 978-226-613-2
NYPL [Sc C 88-286]

**CONFLICT, SOCIAL. see SOCIAL
CONFLICT.**

The confused society /. Kayode, M. O. Ibadan,
Nigeria , 1987. vii, 138 p. : ISBN 978-16-7457-1
NYPL [Sc D 88-786]

**CONGO (BRAZZAVILLE) - DICTIONARIES
AND ENCYCLOPEDIAS.**
Thompson, Virginia McLean, 1903- Historical
dictionary of the People's Republic of the
Congo /. Metuchen, N.J. , 1984. xxi, 239 p. :
ISBN 0-8108-1716-0 DDC 967/.24 19
DT546.215 .T47 1984 NYPL [Sc D 85-104]

CONGO (BRAZZAVILLE) - FICTION.
Lopes, Henri, 1937- Tribaliks . London , 1987.
86 p. ; ISBN 0-435-90762-X
NYPL [Sc C 88-20]

Tchicaya U Tam'si, 1931- Ces fruits si doux de
l'arbre à pain . Paris , c1987. 327 p. ; ISBN
2-221-05172-6
MLCS 87/5379 (P) NYPL [Sc D 88-581]

CONGO (BRAZZAVILLE) - HISTORY - 1960-
Massengo, Moudileno. Procès de Brazzaville .
Paris [1983] 345 p. : *NYPL [Sc D 88-1160]*

**CONGO (BRAZZAVILLE) - POLITICS AND
GOVERNMENT - 1960-**
Massengo, Moudileno. Procès de Brazzaville .
Paris [1983] 345 p. : *NYPL [Sc D 88-1160]*

Congo Republic (1958-) see Congo (Brazzaville)

The Congo, river into central Africa. Lauber,
Patricia. Champaign, Ill. [1964] 96 p. DDC 967
DT639 .L38 NYPL [Sc E 89-24]

CONGO RIVER - JUVENILE LITERATURE.
Lauber, Patricia. The Congo, river into central
Africa. Champaign, Ill. [1964] 96 p. DDC 967
DT639 .L38 NYPL [Sc E 89-24]

**Congrès international de géographie. see
International Geographical Congress.**

**Congreso Internacional de Geografía. see
International Geographical Congress.**

Congress, Rick. The Afro-Nicaraguans : the
revolution and autonomy / by Rick Congress.
[Atlanta, Georgia] : Atlanta Committee on

Latin America, c1987. 88 p. : ill., map ; 22 cm.
Cover title.
1. Blacks - Nicaragua. I. Title.
NYPL [Sc D 88-1280]

**CONGRESSMEN. see LEGISLATORS -
UNITED STATES.**

Connaissance des hommes.
Bastien, Christine. Folies, mythes et magies
d'Afrique noire . Paris , 1988. 230 p. ; ISBN
2-7384-0038-8 **NYPL [Sc D 89-191]**

Jonckers, Danielle. La société Minyanka du
Mali . Paris , c1987. viii, 234 p., [8] p. of
plates : **NYPL [Sc E 88-344]**

Connecticut Gallery. Charles Ethan
Porter,1847?-1923. Marlborough, CT , 1987.
113 p. : ISBN 0-9619196-0-4
NYPL [Sc F 88-26]

Connecting times . Harris, Norman, 1951-
Jackson , c1988. 197 p. ; ISBN 0-87805-335-2
(alk. paper) DDC 813/.54/093520396073 19
PS153.N5 H27 1988 **NYPL [Sc E 88-288]**

Conquering Kilmarnie /. Cave, Hugh B. (Hugh
Barnett), 1910- New York , London , c1989.
176 p. ; ISBN 0-02-717781-5 DDC [Fic] 19
PZ7.C29 Co 1989 **NYPL [Sc D 89-611]**

Conscience de tracteur /. Sony Lab'Ou Tansi.
[Dakar] [Yaoundé] [1979] 115 p. ; ISBN
2-7236-0439-X
MLCS 86/640 (P) **NYPL [Sc C 88-369]**

The conscience of God /Nwankwo Nnabuchi.
Nnabuchi, Nwankwo. Enugu , 1987. xiii, 231
p. ; ISBN 978-270-501-2
NYPL [Sc D 89-241/]

**Conseil oecumenique des eglises. see World
Council of Churches.**

Conser, Walter H. McLoughlin, William Gerald.
The Cherokee ghost dance . [Macon, Ga.] ,
c1984. xxiv, 512 p. : ISBN 0-86554-128-0 :
DDC 975/.00497 19
E78.S65 M37 1984 **NYPL [HBC 85-263]**

Conservation in Africa : people, policies, and
practice / edited by David Anderson and
Richard Grove. Cambridge [Cambridgeshire] ;
New York : Cambridge University Press, 1987.
ix, 355 p. : maps ; 24 cm. Includes bibliographies
and index. ISBN 0-521-34199-X DDC 333.7/2/096
19
1. Nature conservation - Africa. 2. Conservation of
natural resources - Africa. I. Anderson, David, 1957-.
II. Grove, Richard (Richard H.).
QH77.A4 C66 1987 **NYPL [Sc E 88-199]**

**The conservation of archival and library
materials .** Harrison, Alice W., 1929-
Metuchen, N.J. , 1982. xi, 190 p. ; ISBN
0-8108-1523-0 DDC 025.8/4 19
Z701 .H28 **NYPL [Cons. Div. 84-252]**

**CONSERVATION OF BOOKS. see BOOKS -
CONSERVATION AND RESTORATION.**

**Conservation of library and archive materials and
the graphic arts /** edited by Guy Petherbridge.
London ; Boston : Butterworths, 1985. 328 p. :
ill. (some col.) ; 31 cm. On t.p.: Society of
Archivists, Institute of Paper Conservation. Includes
bibliographies and index. ISBN 0-408-01466-0 :
DDC 025.7 19
1. Library materials - Conservation and restoration. 2.
Archival materials - Conservation and restoration. 3.
Graphic arts - Conservation and restoration. 4. Art -
Conservation and restoration. I. Petherbridge, Guy,
1944-. II. Society of Archivists (Great Britain). III.
Institute of Paper Conservation.
Z701 .C5863 1985 **NYPL [MFW+ 88-574]**

**CONSERVATION OF NATURAL
RESOURCES - AFRICA.**
Conservation in Africa . Cambridge
[Cambridgeshire] , New York , 1987. ix, 355
p. : ISBN 0-521-34199-X DDC 333.7/2/096 19
QH77.A4 C66 1987 **NYPL [Sc E 88-199]**

**CONSERVATION OF NATURE. see NATURE
CONSERVATION.**

**CONSERVATION OF RESOURCES. see
CONSERVATION OF NATURAL
RESOURCES.**

CONSERVATISM - UNITED STATES.
Boston, Thomas D. Race, class, and
conservatism /. Boston , 1988. xix, 172 p. :
ISBN 0-04-330368-4 (alk. paper) DDC

305.5/0973 19
HN90.S6 B67 1988 **NYPL [Sc D 89-107]**

**CONSERVATISM - UNITED STATES -
HISTORY - SOURCES -
BIBLIOGRAPHY.**
University of Iowa. Libraries. The right wing
collection of the University of Iowa Libraries,
1918-1977 . Glen Rock, N.J. , 1978. v, 175 p. ;
ISBN 0-667-00520-X DDC 016.3205/0973
Z7163 .U585 1978 JA1 **NYPL [Sc F 86-176]**

The Constitution of the Republic of Uganda.
Uganda. [Constitution (1986)] Kampala , 1986.
121 p. ; **NYPL [Sc G 89-9]**

Constitutional law and military rule in Nigeria /.
Ojo, Abiola. Ibadan , 1987. vii, 316 p. ; ISBN
978-16-7569-1 **NYPL [Sc D 88-804]**

**The constitutional politics of the Black Muslim
movement in America [microform] /.** Jones,
Oliver, 1947- 1978. 297 leaves.
NYPL [Sc Micro R-4227]

Constitutional roots, rights, and responsibilities :
May 18-23, 1987, Charlotteville, Virginia, and
Washington, D.C. / sponsored by the Office of
Interdisciplinary Studies, Smithsonian
Institution in cooperation with the Universtiy of
Virginia and the American Bar Association.
New York : Prepared for the Smithsonian
Institution by Keens Co., 1987. 152 p. ; 28 cm.
Summary of the ninth International Smithsonian
Symposium.
1. United States - Constitutional history. I. Smithsonian
Institution. Office of Interdisciplinary Studies. II.
University of Virginia. **NYPL [Sc F 88-299]**

CONSTRUCTION. see ARCHITECTURE.

Construisons notre société : textes d'études pour
les classes des 4e, 5e et 6e années. Conakry :
Editions Scolaires universitaires populaires,
1970. x, 201 p. ; 24 cm. "1er cycle--1re partie."
1. Socialist ethics - Guinea - Textbooks. 2. Socialism
and education - Guinea. **NYPL [Sc E 88-254]**

**CONSUMER ADVERTISING. see
ADVERTISING.**

The contact /. Mutasa, Garikai. Gweru,
Zimbabwe , 1985. 125 p. ; ISBN 0-86922-355-0
(pbk.)
MLCS 86/13019 (P) **NYPL [JFC 87-1040]**

**CONTACT VERNACULARS. see PIDGIN
LANGUAGES.**

Conte, Carmelo. Ethiopia : introduzione alla
etnologia del diritto / [di] Carmelo Conte,
Guglielmo Gobbi. [Milano] : Giuffrè, 1976. xi,
196 p. ; 21 cm. (Africa ; 3) Bibliography: p.
[193]-196.
1. Ethnology - Ethiopia. 2. Ethiopia - History. 3.
Ethiopia - Religion. I. Gobbi, Guglielmo, joint author.
II. Title.
DT380 .C59 **NYPL [Sc D 88-1064]**

Le conte créole [microform] /. Jardel, Jean
Pierre. [Montréal] [1977] 37 p. ;
GR120 .J37 **NYPL [*XM-12281]**

Conteh, Isatou. A History of the migration and
the settlement of the Baayo family from
Timbuktu to Bijini in Guine Bissau /. [Banjul? ,
1987.] 71 p. ; **NYPL [Sc F 89-146]**

Contemporains (Editions J.A.)
Mobutu, maréchal du Zaïre. Paris , c1985. 237
p. : ISBN 2-85258-389-5 DDC 967.5/103/0924 B
19
DT658.2.M62 M62 1985
NYPL [Sc F 88-371]

Contemporary African poems . Joseph, 'Lai.
Lagos , 1988. 116 p. ; ISBN 978-302-821-9
MLCS 87/08400 (P) **NYPL [Sc D 89-581]**

**CONTEMPORARY ART. see ART, MODERN -
20TH CENTURY.**

Contemporary authors. Black writers . Detroit,
Mi. , c1989. xxiv, 619 p. ; ISBN 0-8103-2772-4
NYPL [Sc F 89-57]

**Contemporary Black American playwrights and
their plays .** Peterson, Bernard L. New York ,
1988. xxvi, 625 p. ; ISBN 0-313-25190-8 (lib.
bdg. : alk. paper) DDC 812/.54/09896 19
PS153.N5 P43 1988 **NYPL [Sc E 88-378]**

Contemporary Black poets.
McClane, Kenneth A., 1951- Take five . New
York , c1988. xviii, 278 p. ; ISBN 0-313-25761-2

(lib. bdg. : alk. paper) DDC 811/.54 19
PS3563.A26119 T35 1987
NYPL [Sc D 88-723]

Contemporary Caribbean : a sociological reader /
edited by Susan Craig. [St. Augustine, Trinidad
and Tobago?] : S. Craig, 1981-<1982 >
(Maracas, Trinidad and Tobago, West Indies :
College Press) v. : ill. ; 22 cm. Includes
bibliographies. DDC 304.6/09729 19
1. Social classes - Caribbean Area - Addresses, essays,
lectures. 2. Peasantry - Caribbean Area - Addresses,
essays, lectures. 3. Caribbean Area - Population -
Addresses, essays, lectures. 4. Caribbean Area -
Emigration and immigration - Addresses, essays,
lectures. I. Craig, Susan.
HB3545 .C66 1981 **NYPL [Sc D 89-499]**

**Contemporary issues in mass media for
development and national security /** edited by
Ralph A. Akinfeleye. Lagos : Unimedia
Publications, 1988. xiv, 235 p. ; 23 cm. Includes
bibliographical references. ISBN 978-228-317-7
1. Mass media - Nigeria. I. Akinfeleye, Ralph A.
NYPL [Sc D 89-573]

Contemporary North Africa : issues of
development and integration / edited by Halim
Barakat. London : Croom Helm, c1985. 271 p. ;
23 cm. Selections based on papers given at the Center
for Contemporary Arab Studies' symposium, "North
Africa Today: Issues of Development and Integration",
held at Georgetown University, 1982. Includes
bibliographies and index. ISBN 0-7099-3435-1 :
DDC 961 19
1. Africa, North - Congresses. I. Barakat, Halim Isber.
II. Georgetown University. Center for Contemporary
Arab Studies.
DT181.5 .C66 1985b **NYPL [Sc D 88-1017]**

**CONTEMPORARY PAINTING. see
PAINTING, MODERN - 20TH CENTURY.**

Contemporary poetry of the Negro /. Kerlin,
Robert Thomas, 1866-1950. Hampton,
Virginia , 1921. 23 p. ;
NYPL [Sc Rare C 89-22]

Contemporary southern politics / edited by
James F. Lea. Baton Rouge : Louisiana State
University Press, c1988. 309 p. ; 24 cm. Includes
bibliographies and index. ISBN 0-8071-1386-7 (alk.
paper) DDC 320.975 19
1. Southern States - Politics and government - 1951-. I.
Lea, James F.
F216.2 .C59 1988 **NYPL [Sc E 88-522]**

Contending forces . Hopkins, Pauline E. (Pauline
Elizabeth) New York , 1988. xlviii, 402 p., [8]
p. of plates : ISBN 0-19-505258-7 (alk. paper)
DDC 813/.4 19
PS1999.H4226 C66 1988
NYPL [JFC 88-2153]

Content analysis of oríkì oríl Babayemi, S. O.
[Ibadan , 198-?] xi, 352 p. ;
NYPL [Sc E 89-229]

Les contes de la forêt atlantique /. Dorsinville,
Roger. Alger , 1986. 84 p. ;
NYPL [Sc D 89-171]

Contes de Tombouctou et du Macina /. Kounta,
Albkaye. Paris , c1987- v. ; ISBN 2-85802-853-2
(v. 1) DDC 843 19
PQ3989.2.K577 C6 1987
NYPL [Sc D 88-1027]

**Contes, devinettes et jeux de mots des Seychelles
= Zistwar ek zedmo Sesel.**
[Le-Mée-sur-Seine] : Editions Akpagnon ;
[Paris] : A.C.C.T., c1983. 157 p. : ill. ; 22 cm.
Seychelles French Creole and French. ISBN
2-86427-018-8 DDC 398.2/0969/6 19
1. Folklore - Seychelles. 2. Folk literature, French -
Seychelles. 3. Creole dialects, French - Seychelles -
Texts. I. Title: Zistwar ek zedmo Sesel.
GR360.S44 C66 1983 **NYPL [Sc D 88-583]**

Contes du pays malinké = (Gambie, Guinée, Mali,
Sénégal) / [recueillis par] Gérard Meyer. Paris :
Karthala, c1987. 238 p. : maps ; 20 cm.
Bibliography: p. [223]-225.
1. Tales - Africa, West. 2. Mandingo (African people) -
Folklore. I. Meyer, Gérard. **NYPL [Sc C 88-151]**

Contes du Rwanda : textes recueillis et présentés
par Cyprien Rugamba ; illustrations de
Dominique Trupin. Paris : Conseil
international de la langue française : Edicef,
1983. 174 p. : ill. ; 18 cm. (Fleuve et flamme)
ISBN 2-85319-119-2

1. Tales - Rwanda. I. Rugamba, Sipiriyani. II. Troupin, Dominique. **NYPL** *[Sc C 88-83]*

Contes et histoires d'Afrique. Dakar : Nouvelles Editions africaines, c1977- v. : col. ill. ; 27 cm.
SCHOMBURG CHILDREN'S COLLECTION.
CONTENTS. - t. 1. Pourquoi le ciel est si loin / par D. Kouassi. Le soleil, la lune, et les étoiles / dessins, Daniel Marteaud. Le palmier et le colibri / par A. Couli Bali. Le lac Tchad / par D. Kouassi -- t. 2. Mame Coumba ; Téré et l'arc-en-ciel ; Gouai ; N'Djema / texte de A. Coulibali ; dessins de D. Kouassi -- t. 3. Le diable et la jeune fille ; Coniyara ; Le lac des sorciers ; Mandjambé / textes, A. Coulibali.
ISBN 2-7236-0159-5 (v. 1) DDC 741.5/967 19
1. Tales - Africa. I. Schomburg Children's Collection.
PZ24.1 .C6328 1977 **NYPL** *[Sc F 87-184]*

Contes et légendes de l'Afrique des grands lacs /. Bernard, Alain. Arudy, France [1984] 79 p. :
ISBN 2-86819-011-1 **NYPL** *[Sc D 88-309]*

CONTINUING EDUCATION - NIGERIA.
Odokara, E. O. Outreach . Nsukka [between 1976 and 1981] 67 p. : **NYPL** *[Sc E 88-275]*

Continuing enslavement of Blind Tom, the Black pianist-composer (1865-1887) Southall, Geneva H. Blind Tom . Minneapolis , 1979- v. : DDC 786.1/092/4 B
ML417.B78 S7 1979
NYPL *[Sc Ser.-L .S674]*

Contout, Auxence. Langues et cultures guyanaises / Auxence Contout. Guyana : s. n., [197-?] 233 p. : ill., port. ; 22 cm. Cover title.
1. Guyana - Languages. 2. Guyana - Social life and customs. I. Title. **NYPL** *[Sc D 88-1279]*

Contribution à la définition d'une méthodologie de transfert de populations paysannes . Debouvry, Pierre. [Montpellier] [1985] 294 p. :
ISBN 0-85352-039-0 **NYPL** *[Sc F 88-302]*

Contribution a l'histoire des populations du sud-est nigérien. Zakari, Maikorema. Niamey , 1985. 246 p. : ISBN 2-85921-053-9
NYPL *[Sc E 88-328]*

Contribution de l'île d'Haïti à l'histoire de la civilisation [microform] /. Mercier, Louis, of Haiti. Port-au-Prince, Haïti , 1985. 83 p. :
DDC 972.94 19
F1911 .M47 1985
NYPL *[Sc Micro R-4840 no.8]*

Contributions in Afro-American and African studies.
(no. 109) McClane, Kenneth A., 1951- Take five . New York , c1988. xviii, 278 p. ; ISBN 0-313-25761-2 (lib. bdg. : alk. paper) DDC 811/.54 19
PS3563.A26119 T35 1987
NYPL *[Sc D 88-723]*

Contributions in Afro-American and African studies, 0069-9624 .
(no. 110) McGuire, Phillip, 1944- He, too, spoke for democracy . New York , c1988. xvii, 154 p. ; ISBN 0-313-26115-6 (lib. bdg. : alk. paper) DDC 355/.008996073 B 19
KF373.H38 M35 1988 **NYPL** *[Sc E 88-347]*

(no. 113) Moore, Joseph Thomas. Pride against prejudice . New York , c1988. 195 p., [8] p. of plates : ISBN 0-313-25995-X (lib. bdg. : alk. paper) DDC 796.357/092/4 B 19
GV865.D58 M66 1988 **NYPL** *[Sc E 88-272]*

(no. 114) Sander, Reinhard. The Trinidad awakening . New York , 1988. xii, 168 p. ; ISBN 0-313-24562-2 (lib. bdg. : alk. paper) DDC 810/.9 19
PR9272 .S24 1988 **NYPL** *[Sc E 89-111]*

(no. 115) Bishop, Rand. African literature, African critics . New York , 1988. xii, 213 p. ; ISBN 0-313-25918-6 (lib. bdg. : alk. paper) DDC 820/.9/96 19
PR9340 .B5 1988 **NYPL** *[Sc E 89-129]*

(no. 116) Visible now . New York , 1988. xvi, 344 p. ; ISBN 0-313-25926-7 (lib. bdg. : alk. paper) DDC 371/.02/0973 19
LC2761 .V57 1988 **NYPL** *[Sc E 98-257]*

Contributions in ethnic studies, 0196-7088 .
(no. 20) Harap, Louis. Dramatic encounters . New York , c1987. xiv, 177 p. ; ISBN 0-313-25388-9 (lib. bdg. : alk. paper) DDC 810/.9/35203924 19
PS173.J4 H294 1987 **NYPL** *[*PZB 87-5243]*

(no. 21) The South African society . New York , c1987. xv, 217 p. : ISBN 0-313-25724-8

(lib. bdg. : alk. paper) DDC 306/.0968 19
HN801.A8 S68 1987 **NYPL** *[JLD 87-2390]*

(no. 24) Religion, intergroup relations, and social change in South Africa /. New York , 1988. xii, 237 p. : ISBN 0-313-26360-4 (lib. bdg. : alk. paper) DDC 306/.6/0968 19
DT763 .R393 1988 **NYPL** *[Sc D 89-305]*

The contributions of expatriate and indigenous manpower to the manufacturing industry in Nigeria . Ukpong, Ignatius I. [Calabar, Cross River State, Nigeria] [c1986] ix, 61 p. : ISBN 978-227-526-3 DDC 331.12/57/09669 19
HD5848.A6 U37 1986 **NYPL** *[Sc C 89-128]*

The contributions of selected African-American women classical singers, 1850-1955 [microform] /. Estill, Ann H. M. 1982, c1981. 3, vi, 133 leaves : **NYPL** *[Sc Micro R-4426]*

Contributions to the study of education, 0196-707X .
(no. 25) Toward Black undergraduate student equality in American higher education . New York , 1988. xvii, 217 p. : ISBN 0-313-25616-0 (lib. bdg. : alk. paper) DDC 378/.1982 19
LC2781 .T69 1988 **NYPL** *[Sc E 88-507]*

Contributions to the study of music and dance, 0193-9041 .
(no. 2) Green, Jeffrey P. Edmund Thornton Jenkins . Westport, Conn. , 1982. xii, 213 p. : ISBN 0-313-23253-9 (lib. bdg.) DDC 780/.92/4 B 19
ML410.J44 G7 1982 **NYPL** *[Sc D 86-413]*

Controls on exports to South Africa . United States. Congress. House. Committee on Foreign Affairs. Subcommittee on International Economic Policy and Trade. Washington , 1983. iv, 321 p. ; DDC 382/.64/0973 19
KF27 .F6465 1982e **NYPL** *[Sc E 88-113]*

Controverse de la France et de l'Italie mussolinienne. Durant, Franck Alphonse. Rétrospectives [microform] . Port-au-Prince, Haiti , 1977. 16 p. ;
NYPL *[Sc Micro F 10,933]*

CONURBATIONS. see METROPOLITAN AREAS.

Conversations with Maya Angelou /. Angelou, Maya. Jackson , c1989. xvi, 246 p. ; ISBN 0-87805-361-1 (alk. paper) DDC 818/.5409 19
PS3551.N464 Z4635 1989
NYPL *[Sc E 89-225]*

CONVERT MAKING. see EVANGELISTIC WORK.

CONVERTS TO JUDAISM. see PROSELYTES AND PROSELYTING, JEWISH.

COOK-BOOKS. see COOKERY.

Cook, Peter Alan Wilson, 1905- Social organisation and ceremonial institutions of the Bomvana / by P.A.W. Cook. Cape Town : Juta, [1931?] xi, 171 p., [16] p. of plates : ill. ; 20 cm. Includes index.
1. Bomvana (African People) - Social life and customs. 2. Bomvana (African people) - Religious life and customs. I. Title. **NYPL** *[Sc C 88-31]*

Cook, Scott. (ill) McKissack, Pat, 1944- Nettie Jo's friends /. New York , 1989. [33] p. : ISBN 0-394-89158-9 DDC [E] 19
PZ7.M478693 Ne 1989 **NYPL** *[Sc F 89-143]*

Cook up Jamaican style /. Jones, Novelette C. Kingston, Jamaica , 1977. 111 leaves :
NYPL *[Sc F 89-132]*

COOKBOOKS. see COOKERY.

Cooke, Anna L. Lane College : its heritage and outreach, 1882-1982 / by Anna L. Cooke. Jackson, Tenn. : The College, c1987. ix, 150 p. : ill. ; 24 cm. Includes bibliographies and index.
DDC 378.768/51 19
1. Lane College - History. I. Title.
LD2935.L23 C66 1987 **NYPL** *[Sc E 88-81]*

COOKERY, AFRICAN.
(1987) The Africa News cookbook . New York, NY , 1987, c1985. xxix, 175 p. : ISBN 0-14-046751-3 (pbk.) DDC 641.596 19
TX725.A4 A35 1986b **NYPL** *[Sc E 88-371]*

(1987) The Black gourmet cookbook . Westland, Mich. , 1987. 76 p. :
NYPL *[Sc F 88-292]*

COOKERY, AMERICAN.
Gordon, Billi. Billi Gordon's You've had worse

---

things in your mouth cookbook /. San Francisco, Calif. , c1985. 96 p. :
NYPL *[Sc F 88-214]*

Hovis, Gene. [Uptown down home cookbook.] Gene Hovis's uptown down home cookbook /. Boston , c1987. xii, 235 p. ; ISBN 0-316-37443-1 : DDC 641.5 19
TX715 .H8385 1987 **NYPL** *[Sc E 88-476]*

COOKERY, AMERICAN - SOUTHERN STYLE.
Cheney, Winifred Green. Cooking for company /. Birmingham, Ala. , c1985. 279 p., [2] p. of plates : ISBN 0-8487-0632-3 : DDC 641.5 19
TX715 .C5216 1985 **NYPL** *[Sc E 87-378]*

Egerton, John. Southern food . New York , c1987. v, 408 p. : ISBN 0-394-54494-3 DDC 641.5975 19
TX715 .E28 1987 **NYPL** *[JSE 87-1598]*

Hovis, Gene. [Uptown down home cookbook.] Gene Hovis's uptown down home cookbook /. Boston , c1987. xii, 235 p. ; ISBN 0-316-37443-1 : DDC 641.5 19
TX715 .H8385 1987 **NYPL** *[Sc E 88-476]*

COOKERY, BRAZILIAN - BAHIAN STYLE.
Papeta. Pratos da Bahia e outras especialidades /. Rio de Janeiro , 1979. 202 p. :
NYPL *[Sc D 88-294]*

COOKERY, CARIBBEAN.
The Black gourmet cookbook . Westland, Mich. , 1987. 76 p. : **NYPL** *[Sc F 88-292]*

Rigby, Alison. Caribbean recipes for schools /. Basingstoke , 1987. 100 p. ; ISBN 0-333-44682-8 (spiral) DDC 641.59/0973 19
TX716.A1 **NYPL** *[Sc D 88-1013]*

COOKERY, CREOLE.
Leslie, Austin. Chez Helene . New Orleans, La. , c1984. 64 p. : **NYPL** *[Sc B 89-26]*

COOKERY, DOMINICAN.
Bornia, Ligia de. Comidas tipicas dominicanas =. Santo Domingo Republica Dominicana , 1987. 132 p. : **NYPL** *[Sc D 89-157]*

COOKERY, JAMAICAN.
A Festival of Jamaican cuisine /. Kingston, Jamaica [1983?] 36 p. : DDC 641.597292 19
TX716.J27 F47 1983 **NYPL** *[Sc D 88-1074]*

Jones, Novelette C. Cook up Jamaican style /. Kingston, Jamaica , 1977. 111 leaves :
NYPL *[Sc F 89-132]*

COOKERY - LESOTHO.
National Teacher-Training College (Lesotho) NTTC cookery book. Maseru , 1976. 100 p. :
NYPL *[Sc B 89-29]*

COOKERY, MAURITIAN.
Sookhee, L. (Lalita) Mauritian delights . Rose-Hill, Mauritius , 1985. 159 p. : DDC 641.5969/82 19
TX725.M34 S66 1985 **NYPL** *[Sc D 88-181]*

Cooking for company /. Cheney, Winifred Green. Birmingham, Ala. , c1985. 279 p., [2] p. of plates : ISBN 0-8487-0632-3 : DDC 641.5 19
TX715 .C5216 1985 **NYPL** *[Sc E 87-378]*

Cool Jazz . Hellhund, Herbert. Mainz , New York , c1985. 302 p. : ISBN 3-7957-1790-6 : DDC 785.42 19
ML3506 .H45 1985 **NYPL** *[JME 87-29]*

Coolie odyssey /. Dabydeen, David. London , Coventry , 1988. 49 p. : ISBN 1-87051-801-2
NYPL *[Sc D 88-666]*

Cooper, Anna J. (Anna Julia), 1858-1964.
[Attitude de la France à l'égard de l'esclavage pendant la révolution. English]
Slavery and the French revolutionists, 1788-1805 / by Anna Julia Cooper ; translated with a foreword and introductory essay by Frances Richardson Keller. Lewiston : E. Mellen Press, 1988. 228 p. : ill. ; 24 cm. (French civilization . v. 1) Originally presented as the author's thesis (doctoral--University of Paris) under the title: L'attitude de la France à l'égard de l'esclavage pendant la révolution. Includes index. Includes bibliographical references. ISBN 0-88946-637-8 DDC 972.94/03 19
1. Slavery - Haiti - History. 2. Revolutionists - France - Attitudes - History - 18th century. 3. Public opinion - France - History - 18th century. 4. Haiti - History - Revolution, 1791-1804. I. Keller, Frances Richardson. II. Title. III. Series.
F1923 .C7213 1988 **NYPL** *[Sc E 88-469]*

A voice from the South / Anna Julia Cooper ; with an introduction by Mary Helen Washington. New York : Oxford University Press, 1988. liv, 304 p. ; 17 cm. (The Schomburg library of nineteenth-century Black women writers) Includes bibliographical references. Reprint. Originally published: Xenia, Ohio : Aldine Printing House, 1892. ISBN 0-19-505246-3 (alk. paper) DDC 975/.00496073 19
1. Afro-American women - Southern States - History - 19th century. 2. Southern States - Race relations. I. Title. II. Series.
E185.86 .C587 1988　　　**NYPL [IEC 88-1201]**

Cooper, Floyd. (ill) Greenfield, Eloise. Grandpa's face /. New York , 1988. [32] p. : ISBN 0-399-21525-5 DDC [E] 19
PZ7.G845 Gs 1988　　　**NYPL [Sc F 88-387]**

Cooper, J. California. Some soul to keep / J. California Cooper. 1st ed. New York : St. Martin's Press, c1987. xi, 211 p. ; 22 cm. ISBN 0-312-00684-5 : DDC 813/.54 19
1. Afro-Americans - Fiction. I. Title.
PS3553.O5874 S6 1987
NYPL [JFD 88-7431]

Cooper, Page. Thunder / by Page Cooper ; illustrated by Edward Shenton. 1st ed. Cleveland : World Pub., 1954. 218 p. ill. ; 22 cm.
1. Afro-American youth - Juvenile fiction. 2. Horses - Juvenile fiction. I. Shenton, Edward. II. Title.
NYPL [Sc D 88-661]

COOPERATION - NIGERIA.
Fifty years of Nigerian cooperative movement /. Nsukka [Nigeria] , 1986. iii, 64 p. ;
NYPL [Sc D 88-859]

COOPERATIVE ASSOCIATIONS. see **COOPERATIVE SOCIETIES.**

COOPERATIVE DISTRIBUTION. see **COOPERATION; COOPERATIVE SOCIETIES.**

COOPERATIVE PRODUCTION. see **COOPERATION; COOPERATIVE SOCIETIES.**

COOPERATIVE SOCIETIES - BARBADOS - DIRECTORIES.
Blondel, Eaulin. Credit unions, co-operatives, trade unions, and friendly societies in Barbados . St. Augustine, Trinidad, Trinidad and Tobago [1986] v, 102 p. ; DDC 334/.025/72981 19
HD3464.9.A6 B353 1986
NYPL [Sc F 88-361]

COOPERATIVE SOCIETIES - NIGERIA.
Fifty years of Nigerian cooperative movement /. Nsukka [Nigeria] , 1986. iii, 64 p. ;
NYPL [Sc D 88-859]

COOPERATIVE STORES. see **COOPERATIVE SOCIETIES.**

Coote, Belinda. The hunger crop : poverty and the suger industry / by Belinda Coote. Oxford [England] : Oxfam, 1987. v, 124 p. : ill., maps ; 21 cm. On cover on cover: Oxfam Public Affairs Unit. Bibliography: p. 117-124. ISBN 0-85598-081-8
1. Developing countries - Industries. I. Title.
NYPL [Sc D 88-1446]

Coping with Africa's food crisis / edited by Naomi Chazan and Timothy M. Shaw. Boulder : L. Rienner, c1988. xi, 250 p. : ill., map ; 24 cm. (Food in Africa series) Includes index. ISBN 0-931477-84-0 (lib. bdg.) : DDC 338.1/9/6 19
1. Food supply - Government policy - Africa - Case studies. 2. Agriculture and state - Africa - Case studies. I. Chazan, Naomi, 1946-. II. Shaw, Timothy M. III. Series.
HD9017.A2 C65 1988　　**NYPL [Sc E 88-287]**

Coquery, Catherine. see Coquery-Vidrovitch, Catherine.

Coquery-Vidrovitch, Catherine.
Africa : endurance and change south of the Sahara / Catherine Coquery-Vidrovitch ; translated by David Maisel. Berkeley : University of California Press, c1988. x, 403 p. : maps ; 24 cm. Translation of: Afrique noire. Includes index. Bibliography: p. 351-376. ISBN 0-520-05679-5 (alk. paper) DDC 967 19
1. Labor and laboring classes - Africa, Sub-Saharan - History. 2. Africa, Sub-Saharan - Economic conditions. 3. Africa, Sub-Saharan - Population - History. 4. Africa, Sub-Saharan - Colonial influence - History. 5. Africa,

Sub-Saharan - Rural conditions. I. Title.
HC800 .C67513 1988　　NYPL [Sc E 89-221]

L'Histoire des femmes en Afrique /. Paris , c1987. 164 p. : ISBN 2-7384-0172-4
NYPL [Sc E 89-226]

A Cor púrpura /. Walker, Alice, 1844- [Color purple. Portuguese.] Lisboa , 1986. 244 p. ;
NYPL [Sc D 88-388]

Coradin, Jean. Histoire diplomatique d'Haïti 1804-1843 / Jean D. Coradin. Port-au-Prince, Haïti : Edition des Antilles, 1988- v. ; 21 cm. Includes index. CONTENTS. - T. 1. Le reconnaisance de l'indépendance.
1. Haiti - History - 1804-1844. 2. Hiati - Foreign relations - 1804-1844. I. Title.
NYPL [Sc D 88-864]

Cordonnier, Rita. Femmes africaines et commerce : les revendeuses de tissu de la ville de Lomé (Togo) / Rita Cordonnier.[2e éd.] Paris : L'Harmattan, 1987. 190 p. : ill., maps ; 24 cm. (Collection "Villes et enterprises") Bibliography: p. 183-188. ISBN 2-85802-901-6
1. Textile fabrics - Togo - Lomé - Marketing. 2. Women - Employment - Togo - Lomé. 3. Lomé (Togo) - Economic conditions. I. Title. II. Series.
NYPL [Sc E 88-368]

CORN AS FOOD - GHANA.
Rocksloh-Papendieck, Barbara. Frauenarbeit am Strassenrand Kenkeyküchen in Ghana /. Hamburg , 1988. iii, 193 p. : ISBN 3-923519-75-3　　NYPL [Sc D 89-575]

Cornish, Dudley Taylor. The sable arm : Black troops in the Union Army, 1861-1865 / Dudley Taylor Cornish ; with a new foreword by Herman Hattaway. Lawrence, Kan. : University Press of Kansas, c1987. xviii, 342 p. ; 22 cm. (Modern war studies) Reprint. Originally published: New York : Longmans, Green, 1956. Includes index. Includes bibliography. ISBN 0-7006-0328-X (pbk.) DDC 973.7/415 19
1. United States. Army - Afro-American troops - History - 19th century. 2. United States - History - Civil War, 1861-1865 - Participation, Afro-American. I. Title. II. Series.
E540.N3 C77 1987　　**NYPL [Sc D 88-850]**

CORPORATION EXECUTIVES. see **EXECUTIVES.**

CORPORATIONS, BRITISH - NAMIBIA - HISTORY.
Voeltz, Richard Andrew. German colonialism and the South West Africa Company, 1884-1914 /. Athens, Ohio , 1988. x, 133 p. : ISBN 0-89680-146-2 (pbk.) : DDC 325/.343/09688 19
JV2029.A5 S689 1988　　NYPL [JLD 88-3416]

CORPORATIONS, FOREIGN - NAMIBIA.
Khalifa, Ahmad M. Adverse consequences for the enjoyment of human rights of political, military, economic, and other forms of assistance given to the racist and colonialist régime of South Africa /. New York , 1985. ii, 164, [30] p. ; ISBN 92-1-154046-1 (pbk.) DDC 332.6/73/0968 19
HG5851.A3 K45 1985　　NYPL [Sc F 88-273]

CORPORATIONS, FOREIGN - SOUTH AFRICA.
Khalifa, Ahmad M. Adverse consequences for the enjoyment of human rights of political, military, economic, and other forms of assistance given to the racist and colonialist régime of South Africa /. New York , 1985. ii, 164, [30] p. ; ISBN 92-1-154046-1 (pbk.) DDC 332.6/73/0968 19
HG5851.A3 K45 1985　　**NYPL [Sc F 88-273]**

CORRECTION INSTITUTIONS - VIRGIN ISLANDS OF THE UNITED STATES.
Potter, Edwin. The history of the penal system in the Virgin Islands /. [Charlotte Amalie? , between 1985 and 1988] 69 leaves :
NYPL [Sc F 88-136]

CORRUPTION (IN POLITICS) - HAITI.
DeWind, Josh. [Aiding migration. French.] Aide à la migration . Montréal, Québec, Canada , 1988. 216 p. :
NYPL [Sc D 89-441]

CORRUPTION (IN POLITICS) - NIGERIA - DRAMA.
Odumosu, Z. O. The leader . Lagos, Nigeria , c1986. xi, 83 p. : ISBN 978-230-916-8
NYPL [Sc C 88-160]

Cortés, José Luis. La economía /. Madrid , c1986. 109, [4] p. ;　　NYPL [Sc C 88-186]

Cortner, Richard C. A mob intent on death : the NAACP and the Arkansas riot cases / Richard C. Cortner.1st ed. Middletown, Conn. : Wesleyan University Press, c1988. xii, 241 p., [24] p. of plates : ill. ; 24 cm. Includes bibliographical references and index. ISBN 0-8195-5161-9 (alk. paper) : DDC 976.7/88052 19
1. Riots - Arkansas - Phillips County - History. 2. Afro-Americans - Arkansas - Phillips County - History. 3. Phillips County (Ark.) - History. 4. Phillips County (Ark.) - Race relations - History. I. Title.
F417.P45 C67 1988　　**NYPL [Sc E 88-362]**

Corwin (Revenue cutter) Healy, M. A. (Michael A.) Report of the cruise of the revenue marine steamer Corwin in the Arctic Ocean in the year 1884 /. Washington , 1889. 128 p., [39] leaves of plates :　　**NYPL [Sc Rare F 88-62]**

CORWIN (REVENUE CUTTER)
Healy, M. A. (Michael A.) Report of the cruise of the revenue marine steamer Corwin in the Arctic Ocean in the year 1884 /. Washington , 1889. 128 p., [39] leaves of plates :
NYPL [Sc Rare F 88-62]

Cory, Hans. Sheria na kawaida za Wanyamwezi. / Zilizotungwa na Hans Cory ; kwa msaadawa watemi na wazee wa nchi. [S.l. : s.n.], [195-?] ix, 91 p. ; 25 cm.
1. Law, Nyamwezi (African people). 2. Swahili language - Texts. I. Title.　**NYPL [Sc E 89-1]**

Cosby, Bill. see Cosby, William H.

COSBY, BILL, 1937- - JUVENILE LITERATURE.
Haskins, James, 1941- Bill Cosby . New York , 1988. 138 p. : ISBN 0-8027-6785-0 DDC 792.7/028/0924 B 92 19
PN2287.C632 H37 1988
NYPL [Sc D 88-1162]

COSBY SHOW (TELEVISION PROGRAM)
Warner, Malcolm-Jamal. Theo and me . New York , c1988. xiv, [16] p. of plates, 208 p. : ISBN 0-525-24694-0 DDC 791.45/028/0924 19
PN2287.W43 A3 1988　　NYPL [Sc D 89-258]

Cosby, William H.
Fat Albert's survival kit / by Bill Cosby ; cartoon characters originated by Filmation. 1st ed. New York : Windmill Books, [1975] [30] p. : col. ill. ; 17 cm. A collection of humorous rules for survival, many consisting of take-offs on old maxims. ISBN 0-525-61532-6
1. Epigrams. I. Filmation (Firm). II. Title.
PN6281 .C758　　　NYPL [JFC 77-191]

The wit and wisdom of Fat Albert, by Bill Cosby. Illus. by Filmation. [1st ed.] New York, Windmill Books [1973] [64] p. col. illus. 18 cm. Ninety-one wise witticisms dispensed by Bill Cosby characters include "Don't take your mother's word that you're good looking," and "Stop crime in the streets, stay home." SCHOMBURG CHILDREN'S COLLECTION. ISBN 0-525-61004-9 DDC 818/.5/407
1. Afro-American wit and humor. I. Schomburg Children's Collection. II. Title.
PZ8.7.C6 Wi　　　NYPL [Sc C 89-26]

COSMOGONY, BIBLICAL. see **CREATION.**

Costa, Antonio Maria Judice da. Aclarações : a proposito da syndicancia que deu pretexto á minha exoneração de inspector de fazenda da provincia de Angola [microform] / Antonio Maria Judice da Costa. Lisboa : A Liberal, 1898. 28 p. ; 24 cm. Microfiche. New York: New York Public Library, 198 . 1 microfiche: negative; 11 x 15 cm. (FSN Sc 019,026)
1. Costa, Antonio Maria Judice da. 2. Embezzlement - Angola Investigation. I. Title.
NYPL [Sc Micro F-10,894]

COSTA, ANTONIO MARIA JUDICE DA.
Costa, Antonio Maria Judice da. Aclarações . Lisboa , 1898. 28 p. ;
NYPL [Sc Micro F-10,894]

Costa, Haroldo. Eneida, 1903-1971. História do carnaval carioca /. Rio de Janeiro , c1987. 259 p. : ISBN 85-10-29900-5
GT4233.R5 E53 1987　NYPL [Sc D 89-313]

COSTUME - EGYPT - HISTORY.
Watson, Philip J. Costume of ancient Egypt /. New York , 1987. 64 p., [8] p. of plates :

ISBN 1-555-46771-7 : DDC 391/.00932 19
GT533 .W38 1987 **NYPL [Sc F 88-228]**

COSTUME - HISTORY - TO 500.
Watson, Philip J. Costume of ancient Egypt /.
New York , 1987. 64 p., [8] p. of plates :
ISBN 1-555-46771-7 : DDC 391/.00932 19
GT533 .W38 1987 **NYPL [Sc F 88-228]**

Costume of ancient Egypt /. Watson, Philip J.
New York , 1987. 64 p., [8] p. of plates :
ISBN 1-555-46771-7 : DDC 391/.00932 19
GT533 .W38 1987 **NYPL [Sc F 88-228]**

COSTUME, THEATRICAL. see COSTUME.

Costumi e credenze coloniali [microform] .
Sarnelli, Tommaso. Napoli , 1925. 39 p. :
NYPL [Sc Micro F-11058]

Côte-d'Ivoire . Amondji, Marcel, 1934- Paris ,
c1986. 207 p. ; ISBN 2-85802-631-6 DDC
324.2666/806 19
DT545.75 .A46 1986 **NYPL [Sc D 88-297]**

Côte-d'Ivoire . Amondji, Marcel, 1934- Paris ,
c1988. 188 p. ; ISBN 2-7384-0072-8
NYPL [Sc D 89-503]

Côte d'Ivoire. see Ivory Coast.

Cotran, Eugene. Casebook on Kenya customary
law / by Eugene Cotran. Abingdon, Oxon. :
Professional Books, 1987. xxviii, 348 p. ; 24
cm. Includes index. ISBN 0-86205-255-6
1. Customary law - Kenya. I. Title.
NYPL [Sc E 89-179]

**COTTON TEXTILE INDUSTRY -
EMPLOYEES - DISEASES AND
HYGIENE - SOUTHERN STATES -
HISTORY - 20TH CENTURY.**
Beardsley, Edward H. A history of neglect .
Knoxville , c1987. xvi, 383 p. : ISBN
0-87049-523-2 (alk. paper) : DDC 362.1/0425
19
RA448.5.N4 B33 1987 **NYPL [Sc E 87-625]**

**COTTON TEXTILE INDUSTRY -
EMPLOYEES - MEDICAL CARE -
SOUTHERN STATES - HISTORY - 20TH
CENTURY.**
Beardsley, Edward H. A history of neglect .
Knoxville , c1987. xvi, 383 p. : ISBN
0-87049-523-2 (alk. paper) : DDC 362.1/0425
19
RA448.5.N4 B33 1987 **NYPL [Sc E 87-625]**

**COTTON TEXTILE INDUSTRY -
SOUTHERN STATES - EMPLOYEES -
HISTORY.**
McHugh, Cathy L. Mill family . New York ,
1988. x, 144 p. ; ISBN 0-19-504299-9 (alk. paper)
DDC 331.7/67721/0975 19
HD8039.T42 U654 1988
NYPL [Sc D 88-1082]

**COTTON TEXTILE INDUSTRY -
SOUTHERN STATES - HISTORY.**
McHugh, Cathy L. Mill family . New York ,
1988. x, 144 p. ; ISBN 0-19-504299-9 (alk. paper)
DDC 331.7/67721/0975 19
HD8039.T42 U654 1988
NYPL [Sc D 88-1082]

**COTTON - TRADE AND STATISTICS. see
COTTON TRADE.**

**COTTON TRADE - GREAT BRITAIN -
FICTION.**
Armstrong, Thomas, 1899- King cotton /.
London , 1947. 928 p. ; **NYPL [Sc D 88-97]**

**COTTON TRADE - MISSISSIPPI -
HISTORY.**
Moore, John Hebron. The emergence of the
cotton kingdom in the Old Southwest .
Baton Rouge , c1988. xii, 323 p. : ISBN 0-8071-1404-9
(pbk.) DDC 330.9762 19
HC107.M7 M66 1988 **NYPL [Sc E 88-279]**

Cottrell, C. B. Aspects of the biogeography of
southern African butterflies : revealed by an
investigation of the nature of the Cape butterfly
fauna / by C.B. Cottrell. Salisbury [Zimbabwe] :
University of Rhodesia, c1978. viii, 100 p. ; 24
cm. Errata sheet pasted on p. [2] of cover.
"Supplement to Zambezia, 1978." Bibliography: p. 88-93.
1. Butterflies - Africa, Southern - Geographical
distribution. 2. Butterflies - Africa, Southern - Host
plants. 3. Insects - Africa, Southern - Geographical
distribution. 4. Insects - Africa, Southern - Host plants.
I. Zambezia. Supplement. II. Title.
QL557.S65 C68 1978 **NYPL [Sc E 88-555]**

**COUCHORO, FÉLIX, 1900-1968 - CRITICISM
AND INTERPRETATION.**
Ricard, Alain. Naissance du roman africain .
Paris , Dakar , c1987. 228 p., [4] p. of plates :
ISBN 2-7087-0494-X **NYPL [Sc D 89-46]**

Les Couleurs du drapeau National, 1803-1986 /.
Saint-Juste, Laurore. [Port-au-Prince, Haiti ?]
1988. 32 p. : **NYPL [Sc D 88-1440]**

Coulson, David. Van der Post, Laurens. The lost
world of the Kalahari . London , 1988. 261 p. :
NYPL [Sc F 88-381]

Council on American Affairs.
Gannon, Edmund J. Sub-Saharan Africa .
Washington , c1978. 185 p. :
NYPL [JFD 84-783]

Gayner, Jeffrey B. Namibia . Washington,
D.C. , c1979. 101 p. : DDC 968.8/03 19
DT714 .G38 1979 **NYPL [Sc D 89-565]**

Rhodesia alone / . Washington [1977?] 95 p. ;
DDC 320.9/689/104
DT962.75 .R53 **NYPL [Sc E 88-95]**

South Africa--the vital link /. Washington ,
c1976. 120 p. ; **NYPL [Sc D 89-129]**

Council on Interracial Books for Children.
Thinking and rethinking U. S. history /. New
York, N.Y. , c1988. 389 p. ;
NYPL [Sc F 89-130]

COUNSELING - MALAWI.
Peltzer, Karl. Some contributions of traditional
healing practices towards psychosocial health
care in Malawi /. Eschborn bei Frankfurt Om
Main , 1987. 341 p. : ISBN 3-88074-174-3
NYPL [Sc D 88-618]

**COUNSELING, PASTORAL. see PASTORAL
COUNSELING.**

**COUNTER CULTURE. see RADICALISM;
SEX CUSTOMS.**

**COUNTERESPIONAGE. see INTELLIGENCE
SERVICE.**

**COUNTERINTELLIGENCE. see
INTELLIGENCE SERVICE.**

COUNTING.
Giganti, Paul. How many snails? . New York ,
c1988. [24] p. : ISBN 0-688-06369-1 : DDC [E]
19
PZ7.G364 Ho 1988 **NYPL [Sc F 88-301]**

**COUNTRY AND WESTERN MUSIC. see
COUNTRY MUSIC.**

COUNTRY LIFE - KENYA.
Dinesen, Isak, 1885-1962. Isak Dinesen's
Africa . London , 1986, c1985. xvii, 142 p. :
ISBN 0-593-01049-3 **NYPL [Sc G 88-26]**

**COUNTRY LIFE - NORTH CAROLINA -
JUVENILE FICTION.**
Forbes, Tom H. Quincy's harvest /.
Philadelphia , c1976. 143 p. ; ISBN
0-397-31688-7 DDC [Fic]
PZ7.F75222 Qi **NYPL [Sc D 89-93]**

COUNTRY LIFE - ZIMBABWE - FICTION.
Motsi, Daniel, 1964- The beast of fame /.
Harare, Zimbabwe , 1987. 59 p. : ISBN
0-949225-61-4 : **NYPL [Sc C 89-100]**

COUNTRY MUSIC - DISCOGRAPHY.
Escott, Colin. Sun records . Vollersode, W.
Germany , c1987. 240 p. : ISBN 3-924787-09-3
(pbk.) **NYPL [Sc D 89-243]**

Le coup de l'etrier . Pierre, Claude. Ottawa ,
1986. 98 p. : ISBN 0-919925-17-0
NYPL [Sc D 88-342]

Coup d'état nègre . Bamboté, Makombo, 1932-
[Montréal] , 1987. 117 p. ; ISBN 2-9800950-7-9 :
DDC 843 19 **NYPL [Sc D 89-114]**

COUPS D'ÉTAT - AFRICA.
Cabrera, M. A. Africa en armas /. Madrid
[1986] 163 p. ; ISBN 84-85436-37-7
NYPL [Sc D 88-757]

Cours de littérature orale . Kam, Sié Alain.
[Ouagadougou] [1988?] 1 v. (various pagings) :
NYPL [Sc F 89-118]

Cours et documents.
(3) Tempels Placide, 1906- Ecrits polémiques et
politiques [microform] /. Kinshasa-Limete ,
1979. 24 p. : **NYPL [Sc Micro F-11131]**

Covin, David, 1940- Brown sky : a novel / by
David Covin. Chicago : Path Press : Distributed
by Chicago Review Press, c1987. 274 p. ; 23

cm. ISBN 0-910671-11-7 : DDC 813/.54 19
1. World War, 1939-1945 - Participation,
Afro-American - Fiction. 2. Afro-American soldiers -
Fiction. I. Title.
PS3553.O875 B7 1987 **NYPL [JFD 88-427]**

COWBOYS - JUVENILE FICTION.
Gipson, Fred. The trail-driving rooster /. New
York : Harper & Row, c1955. 79 p. :
NYPL [Sc D 88-427]

Le crabe noir /. Bassomb, Nouk. Antony , c1987.
91 p. ; ISBN 2-906661-00-7
NYPL [Sc D 89-446]

A crack in the pavement. Howell, Ruth Rea. New
York, 1970. [48] p. DDC 500.9
PZ10.H7958 Cr **NYPL [Sc E 88-154]**

**CRAFTS (HANDICRAFTS) see
HANDICRAFT.**

Craig, Susan.
Contemporary Caribbean . [St. Augustine,
Trinidad and Tobago?] , 1981-<1982 >
(Maracas, Trinidad and Tobago, West Indies :
College Press) v. : DDC 304.6/09729 19
HB3545 .C66 1981 **NYPL [Sc D 89-499]**

Smiles and blood : the ruling class response to
the workers' rebellion of 1937 in Trinidad and
Tobago / by Susan Craig. London : New
Beacon Books, 1988. vii, 70 p., [4] p. of plates :
ill. ; 23 cm. Bibliography: p. 62-68. ISBN
0-901241-81-4 (hard back)
1. Strikes and lockouts - Trinidad. 2. Trinidad - Social
conditions. I. Title. **NYPL [Sc D 89-418]**

Cranmore, Frederick, 1948- The West Indian /
by Frederick Cranmore. 2nd ed. Brooklyn : T.
Gaus, c1978. 122 p., [1] leaf of plates : ill. ; 23
cm. DDC 813/.5/4
1. West Indians - United States - Fiction. 2. Guyana -
Ficton. I. Title.
PZ4.C8893 We PR9320.9.C7
NYPL [Sc D 88-37]

Crazylegs Merrill. Knott, Bill, 1927- Austin
[1969] iv, 155 p. ; **NYPL [Sc D 88-632]**

**CRCOLE DIALECTS, FRENCH - HAITI -
TEXTS.**
Confiant, Raphaël. Jik dèyè do Bondyé /.
[Port-au-Prince? , 1978?] 64 p. :
NYPL [Sc D 88-694]

Creary, Joanne.
Hernandez, Helen. The maroons-- who are
they? /. Kingston , c1983. 28 p. :
NYPL [Sc D 88-378]

Wheatle, Hiliary-Ann. Museums of the Institute
of Jamaica /. Kingston , 1982. 16 p. :
NYPL [Sc D 88-1173]

CREATION IN LITERATURE.
Hamilton, Virginia. In the beginning . San
Diego , c1988. xi, 161 p. : ISBN 0-15-238740-4
DDC 291.2/4 19
BL226 .H35 1988 **NYPL [JFF 89-62]**

CREATION - JUVENILE LITERATURE.
Osahon, Naiwu, 1937- Madam Universe sent
man /. Apapa, Lagos, Nigeria , 1981. [22] p. :
ISBN 978-18-6002-2 **NYPL [Sc D 89-223]**

CREATIONISM.
Berman, Sanford, 1933- Worth noting .
Jefferson, N.C. , c1988. viii, 175 p. ; ISBN
0-89950-304-7 (lib. bdg.) : DDC 081 19
Z674 .B44 1988 **NYPL [JFE 88-5518]**

CREATIVE ABILITY - GENETIC ASPECTS.
Evolution, creative intelligence and intergroup
competition /. Washington , 1986. 96 p. ;
ISBN 0-941694-30-5 **NYPL [Sc D 89-532]**

**Creative Arts Festival (1979 : Road Town,
Tortola, British Virgin Islands)** A cultural
experience . Road Town, Tortola, British Virgin
Islands , 1980. viii, 55 p. :
MLCS 81/1586 **NYPL [Sc D 88-1398]**

Creative literature of Trinidad and Tobago .
Wharton-Lake, Beverly D. Washington, D.C. ,
1988. xi, 102 p. ; ISBN 0-8270-2709-5
NYPL [Sc D 88-710]

**CREATIVE WRITING - STUDY AND
TEACHING.**
Johnson, Rotimi. Perspectives on creative
writing /. Yaba , 1986, c1985. 85 p. ;
NYPL [Sc C 88-241]

CREATIVENESS. see CREATIVE ABILITY.

CREATIVITY. see CREATIVE ABILITY.

CREDIT UNIONS - BARBADOS - DIRECTORIES.
Blondel, Eaulin. Credit unions, co-operatives, trade unions, and friendly societies in Barbados . St. Augustine, Trinidad, Trinidad and Tobago [1986] v, 102 p. ; DDC 334/.025/72981 19
HD3464.9.A6 B353 1986
NYPL [Sc F 88-361]

Credit unions, co-operatives, trade unions, and friendly societies in Barbados . Blondel, Eaulin. St. Augustine, Trinidad, Trinidad and Tobago [1986] v, 102 p. ; DDC 334/.025/72981 19
HD3464.9.A6 B353 1986
NYPL [Sc F 88-361]

CREOKS (SIERRA LEONE) - HISTORY.
Wyse, Akintola. The Krio of Sierra Leone . London , 1989. xiii, 156 p. : ISBN 1-85322-006-X DDC 966.4/04969729 19
NYPL [Sc D 89-566]

CREOLE DIALECTS.
Les Langues de l'Afrique subsaharienne /. Paris , 1981. 2 v : ISBN 2-222-01720-3 :
NYPL [JFN 81-11 v.1]

CREOLE DIALECTS, DUTCH - SURINAM - TEXTS.
Loy, Harry Jong, 1901-1984. Fosten tori /. [Paramaribo] , c1987. v. : ISBN 999-14-1010-4
NYPL [Sc D 88-921]

CREOLE DIALECTS, ENGLISH - CARIBBEAN AREA.
Focus on the Caribbean /. Amsterdam , Philadelphia , 1986. ix, 209 p. : ISBN 90-272-4866-4 (pbk. : alk. paper) : DDC 427/.9729 19
PM7874.C27 F6 1986 ***NYPL [JFD 87-3902]***

CREOLE DIALECTS, ENGLISH - ENGLAND - LONDON.
Hewitt, Roger. White talk, black talk . Cambridge [Cambridgeshire] , New York , 1986. x, 253 p. ; ISBN 0-521-26239-9 DDC 401/.9/094216 19
P40.45.G7 H48 1986 ***NYPL [JFE 87-279]***

CREOLE DIALECTS, ENGLISH - JAMAICA - TEXTS.
Voices in exile . Tuscaloosa , c1989. xiv, 157 p. ; ISBN 0-8173-0382-0 DDC 427/.97292 19
PM7874.J3 V65 1989 ***NYPL [Sc E 89-207]***

CREOLE DIALECTS, ENGLISH - WEST INDIES.
Roberts, Peter A. West Indians and their language /. Cambridge [Cambridgeshire] , New York , 1988. vii, 215 p. : ISBN 0-521-35136-7 DDC 427/.9729 19
P381.W47 R63 1988 ***NYPL [Sc E 88-331]***

CREOLE DIALECTS, FRENCH - CARIBBEAN AREA - GRAMMAR.
Bernabé, Jean. Grammaire Créole (Fondas Kréyol-la) . Paris , 1987. 205 p. ; ISBN 2-85805-734-X ***NYPL [Sc D 88-521]***

CREOLE DIALECTS, FRENCH - GUDELOUPE - TEXTS.
Gaspard, Albert. Les belles paroles d'Albert Gaspard /. Paris , c1987. 128 p. : ISBN 2-903033-91-9 :
MLCM 87/1949 (P) ***NYPL [JFE 88-5765]***

CREOLE DIALECTS - FRENCH GUIANA - TEXTS.
Parépou, Alfred. Atipa . Paris , 1987. viii, 231 p. : ISBN 2-85802-965-2 ***NYPL [Sc E 88-18]***

CREOLE DIALECTS, FRENCH - HAITI.
Trouillot, Hénock. Les lumières du créole dans notre enseignement /. Port-au-Prince , 1980. 85 p. ;
NYPL [Sc D 88-1400]

CREOLE DIALECTS, FRENCH - HAITI - GLOSSARIES, VOCABULARIES, ETC.
Blanchard, Teódulo. Creole haitiano . Santo Domingo, D.N. , 1983. 117 p. ; DDC 447/.97294 19
PM7854.H34 B58 1983 ***NYPL [Sc F 87-422]***

CREOLE DIALECTS, FRENCH - HAITI - TEXTS.
Frankétienne. Adjanoumelezo . [Port-au-Prince?] 1987. 522 p. ;
NYPL [Sc D 88-466]

Jean-Baptiste, Chavannes. Té-a sé kód lonbret nou. Prémie pati / Konnin tè ou /. [Port-au-Prince, Haiti?] [1978?] 63 p. :
NYPL [Sc D 87-1404]

Saint-Natus, Clotaire. Natif-natal=. Port-au-Prince, Haiti , 1987. 48 p. :
NYPL [Sc C 89-54]

CREOLE DIALECTS, FRENCH - MAURITIUS.
L'Histoire d'une trahison . Port Louis, Mauritius , 1987. vi, 192 p.
NYPL [Sc F 88-275]

CREOLE DIALECTS, FRENCH - MAURITIUS - DICTIONARIES - ENGLISH.
Baker, Philip. Morisyen - English - français . Paris , 1987. 365 p. ; ISBN 2-85802-973-3
NYPL [Sc E 88-407]

CREOLE DIALECTS, FRENCH - MAURITIUS - DICTIONARIES - FRENCH.
Baker, Philip. Morisyen - English - français . Paris , 1987. 365 p. ; ISBN 2-85802-973-3
NYPL [Sc E 88-407]

CREOLE DIALECTS, FRENCH - RÉUNION - DICTIONARIES - FRENCH.
Armand, Alain. Dictionnaire kréol réunioné français /. Saint-André [1987?] lxiv, 399, xxxvii p. ; ISBN 2-907094-01-0
NYPL [Sc C 88-345]

CREOLE DIALECTS, FRENCH - SEYCHELLES - TEXTS.
Contes, devinettes et jeux de mots des Seychelles =. [Le-Mée-sur-Seine] [Paris] , c1983. 157 p. : ISBN 2-86427-018-8 DDC 398.2/0969/6 19
GR360.S44 C66 1983 ***NYPL [Sc D 88-583]***

CREOLE DIALECTS, FRENCH - WEST INDIES, FRENCH.
Germain, Robert. Grammaire créole /. Paris [1980] 303 p. ; ISBN 2-85802-165-1 : DDC 447/.972976 19
PM7854.W47 G4 ***NYPL [Sc D 82-456]***

CREOLE DIALECTS, FRENCH - WEST INDIES - TEXTS.
Confiant, Raphaël. Bitako-A /. [Martinique] , 1985. 77 p. ; ***NYPL [Sc D 88-1269]***

CREOLE DIALECTS - MAURITIUS - TEXTS.
Ramdharrysing, Vimal. Gu Margoz [microform] /. [Mauritius? , 198-?] 29 p. :
NYPL [Sc Micro F-11122]

CREOLE DIALECTS - POLITICAL ASPECTS - CARIBBEAN AREA.
Devonish, Hubert. Language and liberation . London , 1986. 157 p. ; ISBN 0-946918-27-9 (pbk) : DDC 417/.2 19
PM7834.C3 ***NYPL [Sc D 88-512]***

CREOLE DIALECTS, PORTUGUESE - CAPE VERDE - TEXTS.
Veiga, Manuel. Oju d'agu /. Praia , c1987. 229 p. ; ***NYPL [Sc D 88-1413]***

CREOLE DIALECTS, PORTUGUESE - GUINEA-BISSAU - TEXTS.
Lubu ku lebri ku mortu . Bissau , 1988. 49 p. :
NYPL [Sc F 88-351]

Creole haitiano . Blanchard, Teódulo. Santo Domingo, D.N. , 1983. 117 p. ; DDC 447/.97294 19
PM7854.H34 B58 1983 ***NYPL [Sc F 87-422]***

Creole language library .
(v. 3) Byrne, Francis. Grammatical relations in a radical Creole . Amsterdam , Philadelphia , 1987. xiv, 293 p. : ISBN 0-915027-96-8 (U. S. : alk. paper) : DDC 427/.9883 19
PM7875.S27 B97 1987
NYPL [JFD 88-7020]

CREOLE LANGUAGES. see CREOLE DIALECTS.

CREOLES - BRAZIL - AMAPÁ (TERRITORY) - SOCIAL LIFE AND CUSTOMS.
Andrade, Julieta de. Cultura creoula e lanc-patuá no norte do Brasil =. São Paulo , 1984. 310 p. :
F2543 .A53 1984 ***NYPL [HFS 86-2895]***

CREOLIZED LANGUAGES. see CREOLE DIALECTS.

Crépeau, Pierre, 1927- Classifications raciales populaires et métissage [microform : essai d'anthropologie cognitive. [Montréal] Centre de recherches caraïbes [1973] 44 p. illus. 22 cm. Bibliography: p. [43]-44. Microfiche. New York : New York Public Library, 1981. 1 microfiche : negative ; 11 x 15 cm. (FSN 24, 250)
1. Race. I. Title. ***NYPL [*XM-8441]***

Le Crépuscule ensanglante . Lodimus, Robert. [Port-au-Prince , 1983?] 64 p. :
NYPL [Sc D 88-67]

Crew, Spencer R. Field to factory : Afro-American migration 1915-1940 / by Spencer R. Crew. Washington, D.C. : National Museum of American History, Smithsonian Institute, 1987. 79 p., [4] p. of plates : ill. (some col.), map, ports. ; 26 cm. "An exhibition at the National Museum of American History, Smithsonian Institution, February 1987 through March 1988."--Title. Bibliography: p. 79.
1. Afro-Americans - Social conditions - History. 2. Rural-urban migration - United States. 3. Afro-Americans - Economic conditions - History. I. Title. ***NYPL [Sc F 88-369]***

Crews, Donald.
(ill) Branley, Franklyn Mansfield, 1915- Eclipse . New York , c1988. 32 p. : ISBN 0-690-04619-7 (lib. bdg.) : DDC 523.7/8 19
QB541.5 .B73 1988 ***NYPL [Sc E 88-591]***

(ill) Giganti, Paul. How many snails? . New York , c1988. [24] p. : ISBN 0-688-06369-1 : DDC [E] 19
PZ7.G364 Ho 1988 ***NYPL [Sc F 88-301]***

CRICKET PLAYERS - WEST INDIES.
Foster, William A. A. A stage for victory . Kingston, Jamaica, W.I. , 1985. 36 p. [32] p. of plates : ISBN 976-8032-00-6
NYPL [Sc D 88-182]

CRICKET PLAYERS - WEST INDIES - BIOLOGY.
Dalrymple, Henderson. 50 great Westindian Test cricketers /. London , 1983. xxi, 281 p. : ISBN 0-9506664-4-0 ***NYPL [Sc D 88-62]***

CRICKET - WEST INDIES.
Foster, William A. A. A stage for victory . Kingston, Jamaica, W.I. , 1985. 36 p. [32] p. of plates : ISBN 976-8032-00-6
NYPL [Sc D 88-182]

CRICKET - WEST INDIES - HISTORY.
Lawrence, Bridgette. 100 great Westindian test cricketers . London , 1988. 231 p. : ISBN 1-87051-865-9 : DDC 796.35/865 19
GV928.W4 ***NYPL [Sc F 88-380]***

CRIME AND CRIMINALS - BRAZIL - RIO DE JANEIRO (STATE) - HISTORY.
Lara, Silvia Hunold. Campos da violência . Rio de Janeiro , c1988. 389 p. ;
NYPL [Sc D 89-13]

CRIME AND CRIMINALS - BRAZIL - SÃO PAULO (STATE) - HISTORY - 19TH CENTURY.
Machado, Maria Helena Pereira Toledo. Crime e escravidão . São Paulo-SP , 1987. 134 p. : DDC 306/.362/098161 19
HT1129.S27 M33 1987
NYPL [Sc D 88-1015]

CRIME AND CRIMINALS - CARIBBEAN AREA.
Chuck, Delroy H. Understanding crime . Bridgetown, Barbados [c1986] xi, 171 p. ; ISBN 976-8043-00-8 (pbk.) DDC 364 19
HV6025 .C48 1986 ***NYPL [Sc D 89-195]***

CRIME AND CRIMINALS - JUVENILE FICTION.
Norton, Browning, 1909- Johnny/Bingo. New York [1971] 185 p. DDC [Fic]
PZ7.N8217 Jo ***NYPL [Sc D 88-1420]***

CRIME AND CRIMINALS - MASSACHUSETTS - HISTORY.
Hindus, Michael Stephen, 1946- Prison and plantation [microform] . 1975. 398 leaves.
NYPL [Sc Micro R-4225]

CRIME AND CRIMINALS - MISSOURI - ST. LOUIS - FICTION.
Komo, Dolores. Clio Browne . Freedom, Calif. , c1988. 193 p. ; ISBN 0-89594-320-4 (pbk.) : DDC 813/.54 19
PS3561.O4545 C55 1988
NYPL [Sc C 89-50]

CRIME AND CRIMINALS - NIGERIA - BENIN CITY.
Enonchong, Charles. The rise and fall of Anini /. Calabar, Nigeria [1988] 73 p. :
NYPL [Sc C 89-8]

CRIME AND CRIMINALS - SOUTH CAROLINA - HISTORY.
Hindus, Michael Stephen, 1946- Prison and plantation [microform] . 1975. 398 leaves.
NYPL [Sc Micro R-4225]

CRIME AND CRIMINALS - VIRGIN ISLANDS OF THE UNITED STATES.
Potter, Edwin. The history of the penal system in the Virgin Islands /. [Charlotte Amalie?, between 1985 and 1988] 69 leaves :
NYPL [Sc F 88-136]

CRIME DETECTION. see CRIMINAL INVESTIGATION.

Crime e escravidão . Machado, Maria Helena Pereira Toledo. São Paulo-SP , 1987. 134 p. :
DDC 306/.362/098161 19
HT1129.S27 M33 1987
NYPL [Sc D 88-1015]

Crime, justice and culture in black Africa .
Brillon, Yves. [Ethnocriminologie de l'Afrique noire. English.] [Montreal] [1985] xi, 289 p. :
NYPL [JLF 87-694]

The crime of apartheid /. Mwaga, D. Z. Dar es Salaam , c1985. xix, 141 p. ; ISBN 997-660-049-6 DDC 342.68/0873 346.802873 19
LAW
NYPL [Sc C 89-117]

A crime of self-defense . Fletcher, George P. New York , London , c1988. xi, 253 p. ; ISBN 0-02-910311-8 DDC 345.73/04 347.3054 19
KF224.G63 F54 1988
NYPL [JLE 88-4737]

CRIMEAN WAR, 1853-1856 - PERSONAL NARRATIVES, JAMAICAN.
Seacole, Mary, 1805-1881. Wonderful adventures of Mrs. Seacole in many lands /.
New York , 1988. xxxiv, xii, 200 p., [2] p. of plates : ISBN 0-19-505249-8 (alk. paper) DDC 947/.073 19
DK215 .S43 1988
NYPL [JFC 88-2150]

CRIMES AND MISDEMEANORS. see CRIMINAL LAW.

CRIMINAL ASSAULT. see RAPE.

CRIMINAL COURTS - NEW YORK (N.Y.)
Wright, Bruce, 1918- Black robes, white justice /. Secaucus, N.J. , c1987. 214 p. ; ISBN 0-8184-0422-1 : DDC 345.73/05/08996073 347.305508996073 19
KF373.W67 A33 1987 NYPL [JLE 87-2842]

CRIMINAL COURTS - SOUTH AFRICA - JOHANNESBURG.
Monama, Ramarumo. Is this justice? .
Johannesburg [1983] xii, 65 p. :
NYPL [Sc D 88-1240]

CRIMINAL INVESTIGATION - GEORGIA - ATLANTA - CASE STUDIES.
Dettlinger, Chet. The list /. Atlanta , c1983. 516 p., [4] p. of plates : ISBN 0-942894-04-9 : DDC 364.1/523/09758231 19
HV6534.A7 D47 1983 NYPL [Sc E 86-40]

CRIMINAL JUSTICE, ADMINISTRATION OF - AFRICA.
Brillon, Yves. [Ethnocriminologie de l'Afrique noire. English.] Crime, justice and culture in black Africa . [Montreal] [1985] xi, 289 p. :
NYPL [JLF 87-694]

CRIMINAL JUSTICE, ADMINISTRATION OF - GEORGIA - ATLANTA - CASE STUDIES.
Dettlinger, Chet. The list /. Atlanta , c1983. 516 p., [4] p. of plates : ISBN 0-942894-04-9 : DDC 364.1/523/09758231 19
HV6534.A7 D47 1983 NYPL [Sc E 86-40]

CRIMINAL JUSTICE, ADMINISTRATION OF - MASSACHUSETTS - HISTORY.
Hindus, Michael Stephen, 1946- Prison and plantation [microform] . 1975. 398 leaves.
NYPL [Sc Micro R-4225]

CRIMINAL JUSTICE, ADMINISTRATION OF - NEW YORK (N.Y.)
Wright, Bruce, 1918- Black robes, white justice /. Secaucus, N.J. , c1987. 214 p. ; ISBN 0-8184-0422-1 : DDC 345.73/05/08996073 347.305508996073 19
KF373.W67 A33 1987 NYPL [JLE 87-2842]

CRIMINAL JUSTICE, ADMINISTRATION OF - NIGERIA.
Karibi-Whyte, A. G. Criminal policy . Lagos, Nigeria , 1988. xvii, 127 p. ; ISBN 978-232-525-2
NYPL [Sc C 89-47]

CRIMINAL JUSTICE, ADMINISTRATION OF - SOUTH AFRICA - JOHANNESBURG.
Monama, Ramarumo. Is this justice? .
Johannesburg [1983] xii, 65 p. :
NYPL [Sc D 88-1240]

CRIMINAL JUSTICE, ADMINISTRATION OF - SOUTH CAROLINA - HISTORY.
Hindus, Michael Stephen, 1946- Prison and plantation [microform] . 1975. 398 leaves.
NYPL [Sc Micro R-4225]

CRIMINAL JUSTICE, ADMINISTRATION OF - SOUTHERN STATES - CASES.
Slave rebels, abolitionists, and southern courts .
New York , 1988. 2 v. : ISBN 0-8240-6721-5 (set : alk. paper) : DDC 342.75/0872 347.502872 19
KF4545.S5 A5 1987b NYPL [Sc D 88-1263]

CRIMINAL JUSTICE, ADMINISTRATION OF - VIRGINIA - CASES.
Schwarz, Philip J., 1940- Twice condemned .
Baton Rouge , c1988. xiv, 353 p. : ISBN 0-8071-1401-4 (alk. paper) DDC 346.75501/3 347.550613 19
KFV2801.6.S55 S39 1988
NYPL [Sc E 89-112]

CRIMINAL LAW - SOUTHERN STATES - CASES.
Slave rebels, abolitionists, and southern courts .
New York , 1988. 2 v. : ISBN 0-8240-6721-5 (set : alk. paper) : DDC 342.75/0872 347.502872 19
KF4545.S5 A5 1987b NYPL [Sc D 88-1263]

CRIMINAL LAW - VIRGINIA - CASES.
Schwarz, Philip J., 1940- Twice condemned .
Baton Rouge , c1988. xiv, 353 p. : ISBN 0-8071-1401-4 (alk. paper) DDC 346.75501/3 347.550613 19
KFV2801.6.S55 S39 1988
NYPL [Sc E 89-112]

Criminal policy . Karibi-Whyte, A. G. Lagos, Nigeria , 1988. xvii, 127 p. ; ISBN 978-232-525-2 *NYPL [Sc C 89-47]*

CRIMINALS, AFRO-AMERICAN. see AFRO-AMERICAN CRIMINALS.

Cris intérieurs : écrits pour ne pas rompre l'attache avec la terre ancestrale / [sélection et présentation des textes, Comité de lecture de l'UEZA]. Kinshasa/Gombe, Zaïre : Editions de l'Union des écrivains zaïrois, 1986. 62 p. ; 20 cm. (Collection des "sans-voix")
1. Zairian literature (French). I. Union des écrivains zaïrois. II. Series.
MLCS 86/6102 (P) NYPL [Sc C 88-124]

Crises in the Caribbean basin : past and present / edited by Richard Tardanico. Beverly Hills [Calif.] : Sage Publications, c1987. 263 p. ; 23 cm. (Political economy of the world-system annuals. v. 9) "Based on papers presented at the ninth annual Conference on the Political Economy of the World-System, Tulane University, March 28-30, 1985"--Pref. ISBN 0-8039-2808-4 DDC 330.9729 19
1. Caribbean Area - Economic conditions - 1945- - Congresses. 2. Central America - Economic conditions - 1979- - Congresses. 3. Caribbean Area - Politics and government - 1945- - Congresses. 4. Central America - Politics and government - 1979- - Congresses. I. Tardanico, Richard. II. Political Economy of the World-System Conference (9th : 1985 : Tulane University).
HC151 .C75 1986 NYPL [JLD 87-3555]

The crisis in Afro-American leadership /.
Haskins, Ethelbert W., 1921- Buffalo, N.Y. , 1988. 196 p. ; ISBN 0-87975-450-8 : DDC 303.3/4/08996073 19
E185.615 .H327 1988 NYPL [Sc E 88-399]

Crisis in Black sexual politics / [edited by Nathan Hare, Julia Hare ; foreword by Congressman Gues Savage]. [San Francisco, Calif. : Black Think Tank?], c1989. iv, 184 p. ; 22 cm. Bibliography: p. 177-184. ISBN 0-9613086-2-1
1. Afro-Americans - Social conditions. 2. Afro-American men. 3. Afro-Americans - Psychology. I. Hare, Nathan. II. Hare, Julia.
NYPL [Sc D 89-152]

The crisis in the social sciences . Nzimiro, Ikenna, 1927- Oguta, Nigeria , 1986. 89 p. ; ISBN 978-215-003-7 *NYPL [Sc C 88-93]*

Critical essays on American literature.
Critical essays on James Baldwin /. Boston, Mass. , 1988. ix, 312 p. ; ISBN 0-8161-8879-3 DDC 818/.5409 19
PS3552.A45 Z88 1988 NYPL [JFE 88-2203]

Critical essays on James Baldwin / [edited by] Fred L. Standley, Nancy V. Burt. Boston, Mass. : G.K. Hall, 1988. ix, 312 p. ; 25 cm. (Critical essays on American literature) Includes bibliographies and index. ISBN 0-8161-8879-3 DDC 818/.5409 19
1. Baldwin, James, 1924- - Criticism and interpretation. I. Standley, Fred L. II. Burt, Nancy V. III. Series.
PS3552.A45 Z88 1988 NYPL [JFE 88-2203]

Critical perspectives on the past.
Lipsitz, George. A life in the struggle .
Philadelphia , 1988. viii, 292 p. : ISBN 0-87722-550-8 (alk. paper) DDC 973/.0496073024 B 19
E185.97.P49 L57 1988 NYPL [Sc E 89-43]

Critical studies on Black life and culture.
(v. 15) Maduakor, Obi. Wole Soyinka . New York , c1987, 1986. xv, 339 p. : ISBN 0-8240-9141-8 (alk. paper) DDC 822 19
PR9387.9.S6 Z77 1987 NYPL [Sc D 88-643]

(v. 17) The Harlem renaissance . New York , 1989. xv, 342 p. ; ISBN 0-8240-5739-2 (alk. paper) DDC 810/.9/896073 19
PS153.N5 H264 1989 NYPL [Sc D 89-591]

CRITICISM - AFRICA - HISTORY - 20TH CENTURY.
Bishop, Rand. African literature, African critics . New York , 1988. xii, 213 p. ; ISBN 0-313-25918-6 (lib. bdg. : alk. paper) DDC 820/.9/96 19
PR9340 .B5 1988 NYPL [Sc E 89-129]

CRITICISM - UNITED STATES.
Gates, Henry Louis. The signifying monkey .
New York , 1988. xxviii, 290 p. : ISBN 0-19-503463-5 (alk. paper) DDC 810/.9/896073 19
PS153.N5 G28 1988 NYPL [Sc E 89-181]

CROCKERY. see POTTERY.

Croesus and the witch /. Grant, Micki. New York, N.Y. , 1984. 67, [119] p. ; ISBN 0-88145-024-3 *NYPL [Sc F 88-205]*

Crogman, William Henry, 1841- (joint author)
Kletzing, Henry F., 1850- Progress of a race.
Atlanta, Ga., 1897. xxiv, 23-663 p.
NYPL [Sc 973-K]

Crooks, Merrise. Rocky, the woodcarver : something to take back / written by Merrise Crooks ; photos. by Derek Bishton ; design by Alan Hughes ; printed and typeset by John Goodman & sons, Birmingham. Brimingham, England : Handprint, 1984[reprinted 1987] 24 p. : ill. ; 21 cm. (Handprint basic reader series . 1)
1. Wood-carving - Jamaica. 2. Readers for new literates. I. Title.
NYPL [Sc D 88-1076]

Crosley, Réginald O. Immanences : poèms / Réginald O. Crosley.1st ed. Montreal, Quebec, Canada : CIDIHCA, 1988. 168 p. ; 22 cm.
I. Title.
NYPL [Sc D 89-440]

Cross, Malcolm.
Black youth futures . Leicester , 1987. ii, 113 p. : ISBN 0-86155-106-0 (pbk) : DDC 331.3/46/0941 19
HD8398 NYPL [Sc D 89-175]

Lost illusions . London , 1988. x, 316 p. : ISBN 0-415-00628-7
NYPL [Sc D 88-1300]

CROSS RIVER STATE (NIGERIA)
Akwa Ibom and Cross River States . Calabar [Nigeria] , 1987. 284 p. : ISBN 978-228-320-7
NYPL [Sc D 88-740]

CROSS RIVER STATE (NIGERIA) - CULTURAL POLICY - CONGRESSES.
Cultural development and nation building .
Ibadan , 1986. xiv, 157 p. : ISBN 978-246-048-6 (pbk.) DDC 338.4/77/0096694 19
NX750.N6 C85 1986 NYPL [Sc D 88-812]

CROSS ROADS (CAPE TOWN, SOUTH AFRICA) - HISTORY.
Cole, Josette. Crossroads . Johannesburg, South Africa , 1987. xii, 175 p., [25] p. of plates : ISBN 0-86975-318-5 *NYPL [Sc D 88-957]*

Crossroads . Cole, Josette. Johannesburg, South Africa , 1987. xii, 175 p., [25] p. of plates : ISBN 0-86975-318-5 *NYPL [Sc D 88-957]*

Crowder, Michael, 1934- The flogging of Phinehas McIntosh : a tale of colonial folly and injustice : Bechuanaland 1933 / Michael Crowder. New Haven : Yale University Press, 1988. xii, 248 p. : ill. maps ; 24 cm. Includes index. Bibliography: p. 236-238.   ISBN 0-300-04098-9 DDC 968/.1103 19
1. McIntosh, Phinehas. 2. Khama, Tshekedi, 1905-1959. 3. Botswana - History - To 1966. 4. Botswana - Race relations. I. Title.
DT791 .C76 1988   *NYPL [Sc E 88-289]*

Crowley, Daniel J., 1921- African myth and black reality in Bahian Carnaval / Daniel J. Crowley. [Los Angeles, Calif.] : Museum of Cultural History, UCLA, [1984] 47 p. : ill. (some col.), maps ; 28 cm. (Museum of Cultural History UCLA monograph series . no. 25) "Published in conjunction with monograph no. 24, From the inside to the outside ... by Mikelle Smith Omari and the exhibition, Afro-Bahian arts of Candomblé and Carnaval, Museum of Cultural History Gallery, Haines Hall, UCLA, April 11-June 10, 1984"--P. [6] Bibliography: p. 46.
1. Mythology, African. 2. Salvador (Brazil) - Festivals, etc. 3. Brazil - Civilization - African influences. I. University of California, Los Angeles. Museum of Cultural History. II. Title. III. Title: Bahian Carnaval. IV. Series: Monograph series (University of California, Los Angeles. Museum of Cultural History) , no. 25.
NYPL [Sc F 86-281]

Crowther, Bruce, 1933-
The big band years / Bruce Crowther, Mike Pinfold ; picture editor Franklin S. Driggs. Newton Abbot : David & Charles, c1988. 208 p. : ill. (some col.) ; 29 cm. Includes index. Bibliography: p. 202-203.   ISBN 0-7153-9137-2 : DDC 785/.06/660973 19
1. Big bands - United States - History. I. Pinfold, Mike. II. Title.
ML3518   *NYPL [JNF 88-254]*

Gene Krupa, his life & times / Bruce Crowther. Tunbridge Wells, Kent : Spellmount Ltd. ; New York : Universe Books, 1987. 144 p. : ill., ports. ; 26 cm. (Jazz life & times) Includes index. Bibliography: p. 139-142.   ISBN 0-87663-670-9 (USA) DDC 789/.1/0924 B 19
1. Krupa, Gene, 1909-1973. 2. Drummers (Musicians) - United States - Biography. I. Title. II. Title: Gene Krupa, his life and times. III. Series.
ML419.K78 C8 1987   *NYPL [JNF 88-89]*

Crowther, Geoff. East Africa : a travel survival kit / Geoff Crowther. South Yarra : Lonely Planet, 1987. 373 p., [16] p. of plates : ill. (some col.), maps ; 19 cm. Includes index.   ISBN 0-86442-005-6
1. Africa, East - Description and travel - Guide-books. I. Title.   *NYPL [Sc C 88-332]*

Cruelty ; Killing floor . Ai, 1947- [Cruelty.] New York , c1987. xi, 99 p. :   ISBN 0-938410-38-5 (pbk.) :   DDC 811/.54 19
PS3551.I2 A6 1987   *NYPL [JFD 88-417]*

Crush, Jonathan Scott, 1953- The struggle for Swazi labour, 1890-1920 / Jonathan Crush. Kingston, Ont. : McGill-Queen's University Press, 1987. xviii, 292 p., [9] p. of plates : ill. ; 24 cm. Includes index. Bibliography: p. [225]-284.   ISBN 0-7735-0569-5
1. Social structure - Swaziland. 2. Swaziland - Economic conditions. 3. Swaziland - Social conditions. 4. Swaziland - Relations - South Africa. 5. South Africa - Relations - Swaziland. I. Title. II. Title: The struggle for Swazi labor, 1890-1920.
NYPL [Sc E 89-150]

CRUZ E SOUSA, JOÃO DE, 1863?-1898 - POETRY.
Maya-Maya, Estevão. Regresso triunfal de Cruz e Sousa ; e, Os segredos de "seu" bita Dá-nó-em-pingo-d'água /. São Paulo , 1982. x, 85 p. :   *NYPL [Sc D 88-1098]*

Cruz, Rosa Valdés- see Valdés-Cruz, Rosa.

Cry freedom (Motion picture) Richard Attenborough's cry freedom . New York , 1987. [128] p. :   ISBN 0-394-75838-2   DDC 791.43/72 19
PN1997.C885 A88 1987   NYPL [Sc G 89-17]

Cry of the Kalahari /. Owens, Mark. Boston, Mass. , 1986, c1984. 535 p., [16] p. of plates :   ISBN 0-8161-3972-5 (lg. print) :   DDC 591.9681/1 19
QL337.K3 O95 1986   NYPL [Sc E 88-183]

Crying in the wilderness . Tutu, Desmond. London , 1986. xix, 124 p., [8] p. of plates :

ISBN 0-264-67119-8 (pbk) :   DDC 261.7 19
DT737   *NYPL [Sc C 89-10]*

Cuadernos de historia (Universidad National de Córdoba. Instituto de Estudios Americanistas)
.
(no. 33) Endrek, Emiliano. El mestizaje en Córdoba. Córdoba [Argentina] 1966. xi, 151 p.
F2821.1.C7 E5   *NYPL [Sc E 88-61]*

CUB SCOUTS - JUVENILE FICTION.
Glendinning, Sally. Jimmy and Joe look for a bear. Champaign, Ill., 1970. 40 p.   ISBN 0-8116-4703-X   DDC [E]
PZ7.G4829 Jo   *NYPL [Sc D 88-1456]*

Cuba . Stubbs, Jean. London , 1989. 142 p. :   ISBN 0-906156-43-2 (cased) :   DDC 972.91/064 19
F1788   *NYPL [Sc D 89-502]*

Cuba, a view from inside : 40 years of Cuban life in the work and words of 20 photographers, photographs, videotapes, movies, a multimedia project of the Center for Cuban Studies ; [opening exhibit, Ledel Gallery, New York City, January 19-February 24, 1985] / Tito Alvarez ... [et al.]. New York : Center for Cuban Studies, [1985?] 2 v. : ill. ; 21 cm. Bibliography: v. [2], p. 9. CONTENTS. - [v. 1. Cuban photography] / Max Kozloff -- [v. 2] The making of the Cuban nationality / Johnnetta B. Cole. Reflections on the Cuban Revolution / Richard R. Fagen. Words of the photographers.
1. Photography - Cuba - Exhibitions. 2. Photographers - Cuba. 3. Cuba - Description and travel - Views - Exhibitions. 4. Cuba - Social conditions. I. Alvarez, Tito, 1916-. II. Kozloff, Max. III. Ledel Gallery. IV. Center for Cuban Studies.
TR646.U6 N4853x 1985
NYPL [Sc D 88-1511]

CUBA - BIBLIOGRAPHY.
Bibliograf'ia cubana : 1921-1936 /. La Habana , 1977-78. [v. 1, 1978] 2 v. ;
NYPL [HO 80-1472]

CUBA - BIBLIOGRAPHY - CATALOGS.
Miami, University of, Coral Gables, Fla. Cuban and Caribbean Library. Catalog of the Cuban and Caribbean Library, University of Miami, Coral Gables, Florida. Boston , 1977. 6 v. ;   DDC 016.9729
Z1595 .M5 1977 F2161
NYPL [Pub. Cat. 78-1036]

CUBA - CIVILIZATION - AFRICAN INFLUENCES.
Castellanos, Jorge. Cultura afrocubana /. Miami, Fla., U. S.A. , 1988- v. ;   ISBN 0-89729-462-9 (set)   DDC 972.91/00496 20
F1789.N3 C33 1988   *NYPL [Sc D 89-592]*

Cuba. Conseil national de la culture. see Cuba. Consejo Nacional de Cultura.

Cuba. Consejo Nacional de Cultura. Bibliograf'ia cubana : 1921-1936 /. La Habana , 1977-78. [v. 1, 1978] 2 v. ;   *NYPL [HO 80-1472]*

CUBA - DESCRIPTION AND TRAVEL - VIEWS - EXHIBITIONS.
Cuba, a view from inside . New York [1985?] 2 v. :
TR646.U6 N4853x 1985
NYPL [Sc D 88-1511]

CUBA - ECONOMIC CONDITIONS.
Besada, Benito. Antecedentes económicos de la guerra de los diez años/. La Habana , 1978. 17 p. ;   *NYPL [Sc C 88-211]*

CUBA - HISTORY - 1810-1899 - JUVENILE LITERATURE.
Caballero, Armando O. Antonio Maceo, la protesta de Baraguá /. La Habana , 1977. 30, [1] p. :   *NYPL [Sc F 88-281]*

CUBA - HISTORY - 1909-1933 - BIBLIOGRAPHY.
Bibliograf'ia cubana : 1921-1936 /. La Habana , 1977-78. [v. 1, 1978] 2 v. ;
NYPL [HO 80-1472]

CUBA - HISTORY - 1933-1959 - BIBLIOGRAPHY.
Bibliograf'ia cubana : 1921-1936 /. La Habana , 1977-78. [v. 1, 1978] 2 v. ;
NYPL [HO 80-1472]

CUBA - HISTORY - 1959-
Stubbs, Jean. Cuba . London , 1989. 142 p. :   ISBN 0-906156-43-2 (cased) :   DDC 972.91/064 19
F1788   *NYPL [Sc D 89-502]*

CUBA - HISTORY - REVOLUTION, 1959 - INFLUENCE.
Cole, Johnnetta B. Race toward equality /. Havana, Cuba (P.O. Box 4208, Havana) , c1986. 99 p. :   DDC 305.8/0097291 19
F1789.N3 C65 1986   *NYPL [Sc D 89-359]*

Cuba. National Council of Culture. see Cuba. Consejo Nacional de Cultura.

CUBA - RACE RELATIONS - HISTORY.
Cole, Johnnetta B. Race toward equality /. Havana, Cuba (P.O. Box 4208, Havana) , c1986. 99 p. :   DDC 305.8/0097291 19
F1789.N3 C65 1986   *NYPL [Sc D 89-359]*

CUBA - SOCIAL CONDITIONS.
Cuba, a view from inside . New York [1985?] 2 v. :
TR646.U6 N4853x 1985
NYPL [Sc D 88-1511]

CUBANS - UNITED STATES.
The Mariel injustice . Coral Gables, Fl. , c1987. 204 p. :   *NYPL [Sc F 89-64]*

Cuello H., José Israel. Documentos del conflicto dominico-haitiano de 1937 /. Santo Domingo, D.N., República Dominicana , 1985. 606 p. ;
NYPL [Sc F 89-173]

Cuello, José Israel [i. e. José Israel Cuello H.] see Cuello H., José Israel.

Cuenod, R. Tsonga-English dictionary / compiled by R. Cuenod. Braamfontein : Sasavona, 1967. 286 p. ; 22 cm.
1. Tsonga language - Dictionaries - English. I. Mission suisse dans l'Afrique du Sud. II. Title.
NYPL [Sc D 88-89]

Los cuentos negros de Lydia Cabrera . Gutiérrez, Mariela. Miami, Fla. , 1986. 148 p. ;   ISBN 0-89729-389-4   *NYPL [Sc D 88-370]*

Cuffari, Richard, 1925-
(illus) Garden, Nancy. What happened in Marston. New York [1971] 190 p.   DDC [Fic]
PZ7.G165 Wh   *NYPL [Sc D 89-98]*

(illus) Martin, Robert, 1929- Yesterday's people. Garden City, N.Y. [1970] 158 p.   DDC 916.8/03
DT764.B8 M35   *NYPL [Sc F 88-248]*

Cukierman, Maurice. Afrique du Sud : cap sur la liberté / Maurice Cukierman ; préface de F. Meli. Paris : Messidor / Editions sociales, c1987. 279 p. : map ; 22 cm. Bibliography: p. 271-273.   ISBN 2-209-05983-6
1. Apartheid - South Africa. 2. Anti-apartheid movements - South Africa. 3. National liberation movements - South Africa. 4. South Africa - History. I. Title.   *NYPL [Sc D 88-756]*

Cultura afrocubana /. Castellanos, Jorge. Miami, Fla., U. S.A. , 1988- v. ;   ISBN 0-89729-462-9 (set)   DDC 972.91/00496 20
F1789.N3 C33 1988   *NYPL [Sc D 89-592]*

Cultura creoula e lanc-patuá no norte do Brasil =. Andrade, Julieta de. São Paulo , 1984. 310 p. :
F2543 .A53 1984   NYPL [HFS 86-2895]

Cultura crioula e lanc-patuá no norte do Brasil. Andrade, Julieta de. Cultura creoula e lanc-patuá no norte do Brasil =. São Paulo , 1984. 310 p. :
F2543 .A53 1984   NYPL [HFS 86-2895]

Cultural adaptation and resistance on St. John . Olwig, Karen Fog, 1948- Gainesville , c1985. xii, 226 p. :   ISBN 0-8130-0818-2 (pbk)   DDC 306/.097297/22 19
HT1071 .O43 1985   NYPL [Sc D 88-1058]

Cultural adaptation & resistance on St. John. Olwig, Karen Fog, 1948- Cultural adaptation and resistance on St. John . Gainesville , c1985. xii, 226 p. :   ISBN 0-8130-0818-2 (pbk)   DDC 306/.097297/22 19
HT1071 .O43 1985   NYPL [Sc D 88-1058]

CULTURAL ANTHROPOLOGY. see ETHNOLOGY.

The Cultural construction of sexuality / edited by Pat Caplan. London ; New York : Tavistock Publications, 1987. xi, 304 p. : ill. ; 23 cm. (Social science paperbacks. SSP 353) Includes bibliographies and indexes.   ISBN 0-422-60870-X DDC 306.7 19
1. Sex - Cross-cultural studies. I. Caplan, Patricia.
GN484.3 .C85 1987   NYPL [Sc D 87-1198]

Cultural development and nation building : the Nigerian scene as perceived from the Cross

River State / edited by S.O. Unoh. Ibadan :
Spectrum Books, 1986. xiv, 157 p. : ill. ; 22 cm.
"Publication of the academic proceedings of the first
cultural week of the University of Cross River State,
Uyo." Includes bibliographies. ISBN 978-246-048-6
(pbk.) DDC 338.4/77/0096694 19
*1. Arts - Nigeria - Congresses. 2. Arts - Nigeria - Cross
River State - Congresses. 3. Nigeria - Cultural policy -
Congresses. 4. Cross River State (Nigeria) - Cultural
policy - Congresses. I. Unoh, Solomon O. II. University
of Cross River State.*
NX750.N6 C85 1986   *NYPL [Sc D 88-812]*

**CULTURAL EXCHANGE PROGRAMS. see
CULTURAL RELATIONS.**

A cultural experience : award winning stories &
poems, Creative Arts Festival, 1979 : with
writers' and performers' profile / edited by V.E.
Penn. Road Town, Tortola, British Virgin
Islands : Public Library, 1980. viii, 55 p. : ill. ;
22 cm.
*1. English literature - British Virgin Islands. I. Penn,
Verna E. II. British Virgin Islands. Public Library. III.
Creative Arts Festival (1979 : Road Town, Tortola,
British Virgin Islands). IV. Title.*
MLCS 81/1586   *NYPL [Sc D 88-1398]*

CULTURAL PSYCHIATRY - NIGERIA.
Achebe, Chinwe. The world of the Ogbanje /.
Enugu, Nigeria , 1986. iv, 68 p. : ISBN
978-15-6239-0 DDC 616.89/1 19
RC455.4.E8 A34 1986
NYPL [Sc D 88-1246]

CULTURAL RELATIONS - CONGRESSES.
The Effects of the Western culture on the
traditional cultures of Lofa County
[microform] . [Monrovia , 1977] 24 p. :
NYPL [Sc Micro F-10952]

CULTURE.
February, V. A. (Vernie A.) And bid him sing .
London , 1988. xvi, 212 p. : ISBN
0-7103-0278-9 : DDC 306 325/.32 19
NYPL [Sc D 88-1363]

**CULTURE AND COGNITION. see
COGNITION AND CULTURE.**

Culture créole et langue patuá au nord du Brésil.
Andrade, Julieta de. Cultura creoula e
lanc-patuá no norte do Brasil =. São Paulo ,
1984. 310 p. :
F2543 .A53 1984   *NYPL [HFS 86-2895]*

La culture en question /. Bouzar, Wadi, 1938-
Alger , Paris , c1982. 187 p. ; ISBN
2-903871-11-6 (pbk.) : DDC 306/.0965 19
HN980 .B68 1982   *NYPL [JLC 84-337]*

**Culture race and class in the commonwealth
Caribbean /.** Smith, M. G. (Michael Garfield)
Mona, Jamaica , 1984. xiv, 163 p. ; ISBN
976-616-000-7   *NYPL [Sc D 88-454]*

Cumali, Necati. Hughes, Langston, 1902-1967.
Mem-Leket özlemi . Istanbul , 1961. 45 p. ;
NYPL [Sc Rare C 86-1]

Cummings, Pat.
(ill) Caines, Jeannette Franklin. I need a lunch
box /. New York , c1988. [32] p. : ISBN
0-06-020984-4 : DDC [E] 19
PZ7.C12 Iaan 1988   *NYPL [Sc D 88-1504]*

Stolz, Mary, 1920- Storm in the night /. New
York , c1988. [32] p. : ISBN 0-06-025912-4 :
DDC [E] 19
PZ7.S875854 St 1988   *NYPL [Sc F 88-181]*

(ill) Warren, Cathy. Springtime bears /. New
York , c1986. [32] p. : ISBN 0-688-05905-8
DDC [E] 19
PZ7.W2514 Sp 1986   *NYPL [Sc D 87-622]*

Cunette, Lou. (illus) Gles, Margaret. Come play
hide and seek /. Champaign, Ill. [1975] 32 p. :
ISBN 0-8116-6053-2
PZ7.G4883 Co   *NYPL [Sc D 89-119]*

Cunha Junior, H., 1952- Negros na noite / H.
Cunha Jr. São Paulo : EDICON, 1987. 79 p. :
ill. ; 22 cm.
1. Blacks - Brazil - Fiction. 2. Brazil - Fiction. I. Title.
NYPL [Sc D 88-71]

Cunha, Marianno Carneiro da, 1926-1980. Da
senzala ao sobrado : arquitetura brasileira na
Nigéria e na República Popular do Benim =
From slave quarters to town houses : Brazilian
architecture in Nigeria and the People's
Republic of Benin / Marianno Carneiro da
Cunha ; fotos de Pierre Verger ; introdução de
Manuela Carneiro da Cunha. São Paulo, SP :

Nobel : EDUSP, c1985. 185 p. : ill. ; 26 cm.
English and Portuguese. Bibliography: p. 114-116.
ISBN 85-21-30173-1 :
*1. Architecture, Brazilian - Nigeria. 2. Architecture -
Nigeria. 3. Architecture, Brazilian - Benin. 4.
Architecture - Benin. I. Verger, Pierre. II. Title. III.
Title: From slave quarters to town houses.*
NA1599.N5 C86 1985   *NYPL [Sc E 88-565]*

Cunningham, Anna M. University of the
Witwatersrand. Library. Guide to the archives
and papers . Johannesburg , 1979. v, 100 p. ;
ISBN 0-85494-593-8   *NYPL [Sc F 89-32]*

Curaçao close-up /. Heiligers-Halabi, Bernadette.
London , 1986. viii, 63 p. : ISBN 0-333-39881-5
(pbk.) DDC 917.298/604 19
F2049 .H5 1986   *NYPL [Sc D 88-1122]*

CURAÇAO - DESCRIPTION AND TRAVEL.
Heiligers-Halabi, Bernadette. Curaçao close-up
/. London , 1986. viii, 63 p. : ISBN
0-333-39881-5 (pbk.) DDC 917.298/604 19
F2049 .H5 1986   *NYPL [Sc D 88-1122]*

CURAÇÃO - FICTION.
Jongh, Edward Arthur de. E dia di mas
histórico /. Aruba , 1970. 158 p. :
NYPL [Sc D 87-1430]

Jongh, Edward Arthur de. De steeg . [S.l.] ,
1976. 148 p. ;
PT5881.2.O58 S7   *NYPL [Sc D 88-1033]*

CURAÇÃO - JUVENILE FICTION.
Diekmann, Miep. Padu is gek /. Den Haag ,
1960. 120 p. ;   *NYPL [Sc D 89-474]*

Regals, Leo. Henco ruimt op /. Curaçao
[1986?] 72 p. : ISBN 90-6435-111-2
MLCS 87/05319 (P)   *NYPL [Sc D 88-490]*

**CURE OF SOULS. see PASTORAL
COUNSELING.**

Currents of health policy : impacts on Black
Americans / [editor, David P. Willis] New
York : Cambridge University Press, 1987. 2 v. :
ill. ; 24 cm. "The Milbank Quarterly, vol. 65, suppl.
1-2, 1987." Includes bibliographies.
*1. Afro-Americans - Health and hygiene. 2.
Afro-Americans - Mortality. I. Willis, David P. II.
Milbank quarterly. Vol. 65 (Supplement 1-2).*
NYPL [Sc D 88-1205]

Curriculum bulletin (New York, N.Y.) .
(1970-71 ser., no. 3) New York (N.Y.). Bureau
of Curriculum Development. Black studies.
New York [c1970] vii, 227 p. DDC
375/.0097471 s
LB1563 .N57 1970-71, no. 3
NYPL [Sc G 87-32]

Curriculum development . Ondiek, Patroba E.
Kisumu, Kenya , 1986. xiii, 139 p. :
NYPL [Sc D 89-153]

**CURRICULUM DEVELOPMENT. see
CURRICULUM PLANNING.**

**Curriculum Organization of Nigeria monograph
series .**
(no. 2) Issues in teacher education and science
curriculum in Nigeria /. [Nigeria , 1986?] vi,
331 p. : DDC 370/.7/309669 19
LB1727.N5 I88 1986   *NYPL [Sc D 88-125]*

CURRICULUM PLANNING - HAITI.
Institut pédagogique national (Haiti). Comité de
curriculum. La réforme éducative .
[Port-au-Prince] [1982] 65 p. : DDC
375/.001/097294
LB1564.H2 I57 1982   *NYPL [Sc D 88-1401]*

CURRICULUM PLANNING - KENYA.
Ondiek, Patroba E. Curriculum development .
Kisumu, Kenya , 1986. xiii, 139 p. :
NYPL [Sc D 89-153]

CURRICULUM PLANNING - NIGERIA.
Issues in teacher education and science
curriculum in Nigeria /. [Nigeria , 1986?] vi,
331 p. : DDC 370/.7/309669 19
LB1727.N5 I88 1986   *NYPL [Sc D 88-125]*

Curriculum-related handouts for teachers .
University of Illinois at Urbana-Champaign.
African Studies Program. Urbana, Illinois
[1981] ca. 500 p. ;   *NYPL [Sc F 88-215]*

Curtis, Arnold. Memories of Kenya . London ,
1986. xvi, 160 p., [16] p. of plates : ISBN
0-237-50919-9   *NYPL [Sc F 88-102]*

Curtis, Benjamin Robbins, 1809-1874.
EXECUTIVE POWER.
Kirkland, Charles Pinckney, 1830-1904- A

letter to the Hon. Benjamin R. Curtis . New
York , 1863. 20 p. ;
NYPL [Sc Rare C 89-23]

Curtis, Donald, 1939- Preventing famine : policies
and prospects for Africa / Donald Curtis,
Michael Hubbard, and Andrew Shepherd ; with
contributions from Edward Clay ... [et al.].
London ; New York : Routledge, 1988. xi, 250
p. ; 23 cm. Includes index. Bibliography: p. [237]-241.
ISBN 0-415-00711-9 DDC 363.8/7/096 19
*1. Famines - Africa - Case studies. 2. Food relief -
Africa - Case studies. 3. Food supply - Africa.
4. Food supply - Africa. I. Hubbard, Michael. II.
Shepherd, Andrew. III. Title.*
HC800.Z9 F326 1988   *NYPL [JLD 88-3825]*

CUSHITIC LANGUAGES.
Haberland, Eike. Ibaaddo ka-Ba'iso .
Heidelberg , 1988. 184 p. ; ISBN 3-533-04014-3
NYPL [Sc D 89-552]

Lamberti, Marcello. Kuliak and Cushitic .
Heidelberg , 1988. 157 p. ;
NYPL [Sc D 89-330]

CUSHITIC LANGUAGES - GRAMMAR.
Böhm, Gerhard. Die Sprache der Aithiopen im
Lande Kusch /. Wien , 1988. 206 p. : ISBN
3-85043-047-2   *NYPL [Sc D 88-1339]*

Custom and conflict on a Bahamian out-island /.
Lurry-Wright, Jerome Wendell, 1941- Lanham,
MD , c1987. xxii, 188 p. ; ISBN 0-8191-6097-0
(alk. paper) : DDC 347.7296 347.29607 19
KGL210 .L87 1987   *NYPL [Sc D 88-218]*

A custom broken /. Armah, E. O. Tema , 1978.
87 p. ;   *NYPL [Sc C 88-223]*

CUSTOMARY LAW - KENYA.
Cotran, Eugene. Casebook on Kenya customary
law /. Abingdon, Oxon. , 1987. xxviii, 348 p. ;
ISBN 0-86205-255-6   *NYPL [Sc E 89-179]*

**The customary law of the Dinka people of
Sudan .** Makec, John Wuol. London, England,
1988. 287 p. ; ISBN 0-948583-03-7 (Hardback)
NYPL [Sc E 88-434]

Custombook, Inc. Reaching out . Tappan, NY ,
c1986. 120 p. : DDC 283/.7471 19
BV5980.N57 R4 1986   *NYPL [Sc F 87-222]*

Cut 'n' mix . Hebdige, Dick. London , 1987. 177
p. : ISBN 1-85178-029-7 *NYPL [Sc D 89-372]*

Cuti, 1951- Flash crioulo sobre o sangue e o
sonho / Cuti. Belo Horizonte, MG : Mazza
Edições, 1987. 57 p. ; 22 cm.
I. Title.   *NYPL [Sc D 88-1289]*

Cuttington University College. Africana Museum.
Rock of the ancestors : Liberian art and
material culture from the collections of the
Africana Museum = Namôa koni / text,
William C. Siegmann with Cynthia E. Schmidt ;
photography, Michael H. Lee. Suakoko,
Liberia : Cuttington University College, c1977.
102 p. : ill. ; 28 cm. Bibliography: p. 99-102. DDC
730/.09666/2074096662 19
*1. Cuttington University College. Africana Museum -
Catalogs. 2. Art, Liberian - Catalogs. I. Siegmann,
William. II. Schmidt, Cynthia E. III. Title. IV. Title:
Namôa koni.*
N7399.L4 C87 1977   *NYPL [Sc F 89-27]*

**CUTTINGTON UNIVERSITY COLLEGE.
AFRICANA MUSEUM - CATALOGS.**
Cuttington University College. Africana
Museum. Rock of the ancestors . Suakoko,
Liberia , c1977. 102 p. : DDC
730/.09666/2074096662 19
N7399.L4 C87 1977   *NYPL [Sc F 89-27]*

**CYCLISTS - UNITED STATES -
BIOGRAPHY.**
Ritchie, Andrew. Major Taylor . San
Francisco , New York , 1988. 304 p., [32] p. of
plates : ISBN 0-933201-14-1 (hardcover)
NYPL [Sc E 88-570]

**D. I. E. see Deutsches Institut für
Entwicklungspolitik.**

**DIE Schriften. see Deutsches Institut für
Entwicklungspolitik. Schriften.**

D. Joao VI . Algranti, Leila Mezan. São Paulo ,
1987. 78 p. ; ISBN 85-08-01870-3
NYPL [Sc C 88-15]

The D.O. /. Ogunyemi, M. A. Ibadan , 1987. v.
126 p. ; ISBN 978-15-4777-4 (Nigeria)
NYPL [Sc C 88-176]

Da senzala ao sobrado . Cunha, Marianno

Carneiro da, 1926-1980. São Paulo, SP , c1985. 185 p. : ISBN 85-21-30173-1 :
NA1599.N5 C86 1985 **NYPL [Sc E 88-565]**

Da Snøen Kom /. Keats, Ezra Jack. [Norway] , 1967. [20] p. : **NYPL [Sc D 88-467]**

DaBreo, D. Sinclair. --of men and politics : the agony of St. Lucia / by D. Sinclair DaBreo. Castries, St. Lucia : Commonwealth Publishers International, c1981. 208 p. : ill. ; 21 cm. "Commonwealth Publishers International Ltd. (C.P.I.) publication." DDC 972.98/43 19
1. Saint Lucia - Politics and government. I. Title. II. Title: Agony of St. Lucia.
F2100 .D32 1981 **NYPL [Sc D 88-815]**

Dabydeen, Cyril, 1945- A Shapely fire . Oakville, Ont. , c1987. 175 p. : ISBN 0-88962-345-7
NYPL [Sc E 88-263]

Dabydeen, David.
Coolie odyssey / David Dabydeen. London : Hansib ; Conventry : Damgaroo, 1988. 49 p. : ill. ; 21 cm. Poems. "A Hansib-Dangaroo publication." ISBN 1-87051-801-2
I. Title. **NYPL [Sc D 88-666]**

India in the Caribbean /. London , 1987. 326 p. : ISBN 1-87051-805-5 (cased) : DDC 909/.09182/1081 19 **NYPL [Sc D 88-997]**

A reader's guide to West Indian and black British literature / David Dabydeen and Nana Wilson-Tague. London : Hansib, 1988. 182 p. ; 20 cm. Includes bibliography and index. ISBN 1-87051-835-7 (pbk) : DDC 810.9/9729 19
1. West Indian literature (English) - History and criticism. I. Wilson-Tagoe, Nana. II. Title.
PR9210 **NYPL [Sc C 88-363]**

Dachs, Anthony J. The Catholic church and Zimbabwe, 1879-1979 / by A.J. Dachs and W.F. Rea. Gwelo : Mambo Press, 1979. xiii, 260 p., [26] p. of plates : ill. ; 22 cm. (Zambeziana. vol. 8) Includes index. Bibliography: p. 231. DDC 282/.6891 19
1. Catholic Church - Zimbabwe - History. 2. Zimbabwe - Church history. I. Rea, A. J. II. Series. III. Series: Zambeziana, v. 8. IV. Title.
BX1682.Z55 D33 1979 **NYPL [Sc D 88-900]**

Dada, Victor B. Choose the sex of your baby : a psychological approach / by Victor B. Dada.1st. ed. N. Y. : Vantage Press, c1983. xiv, 96 p. ; 22 cm. Includes index. ISBN 0-533-05256-4
1. Sex preselection. I. Title.
NYPL [Sc D 88-1180]

Dadié, Bernard Binlin, 1916-
The city where no one dies / Bernard Dadié ; translated by Janis Mayes. Washington, D.C. : Three Continents Press, c1986. 139 p. ; 23 cm. Translation of: La ville où nul ne meurt. Bibliography: p. 32-34. ISBN 0-89410-499-3
1. Rome - Civilization. I. Title.
NYPL [Sc D 88-1468]

DADIÉ, BERNARD BINLIN, 1916- - CRITICISM AND INTERPRETATION.
Vincileoni, Nicole. Comprendre l'oeuvre de Bernard B. Dadié /. Issy les Moulineaux , c1986. 319 p.,[12] p. of plates : ISBN 2-85049-368-6 **NYPL [Sc D 88-721]**

Dadzie, Stella, 1952- Bryan, Beverley, 1949- The heart of the race . London , 1985. vi, 250 p. : ISBN 0-86068-361-3 (pbk.) : DDC 305.4/8896041 19
DA125.N4 B78 1985 **NYPL [Sc C 88-178]**

Dagbert, Anne. Ndiaye, Iba, 1928- Iba N'Diaye, Gemälde, Lavierungen, Zeichnungen =. München , c1987. 71 p. : ISBN 3-7774-4650-5
NYPL [Sc C 88-297]

Daget, Serge. Répertoire des expéditions négrières françaises à la traite illégale (1814-1850) / Serge Daget. Nantes : Centre de recherches sur l'histoire du monde atlantique, Université de Nantes : Comité nantais d'études en sciences humaines, 1988. viii, 603 p. : maps ; 24 cm. Includes indexes. Bibliography: p. 563-564. ISBN 2-900486-01-7
1. Slave-trade - France - History. I. Title.
NYPL [Sc E 89-265]

DAILY TIMES (LAGOS, NIGERIA)
Jose, Babatunde. Walking a tight rope . Ibadan , 1987. xiii, 421 p. : ISBN 978-15-4911-4 (limp)
NYPL [Sc E 88-296]

DAIRY FARMS - UNITED STATES - JUVENILE LITERATURE.
Meshover, Leonard. You visit a dairy [and a] clothing factory /. Chicago , c1965. 48 p. :
NYPL [Sc D 89-545]

Daise, Ronald. Reminiscences of Sea Island heritage / by Ronald Daise. 2nd ed. Orangeburg, S.C. : Sandlapper Pub., c1987, xvi, 103, [13] p. : ill. ; 28 cm.
1. Afro-Americans - South Carolina - Saint Helena Island - Social life and customs. 2. Saint Helena Island (S.C.) - Social life and customs. I. Title.
NYPL [Sc F 88-168]

Dakar. Université. Centre de linguistique appliquée. [Publications].
(no. 54) Labatut, Roger. Interférences du fulfulde sur le français écrit par les élèves peuls du Nord-Cameroun [microform] /. [Dakar] , 1974. iii, 35 p. :
NYPL [Sc Micro R-4137 no.11]

Dakar. Université. Centre de recherches, d'études et de documentation sur les institutions et la législation africaines. Collection .
(10) Gautron, Jean Claude. Droit public du Sénégal /. Paris , 1977. 447 p. ; ISBN 2-233-00036-6 :
LAW **NYPL [Sc E 88-612]**

Dalby, David. Mann, Michael. A thesaurus of African languages . New York , 1987. 325 p. ; ISBN 0-905450-24-8 **NYPL [Sc F 88-142]**

Dale, George Allan, 1900- Education in the Republic of Haiti. [Washington] : U. S. Dept. of Health, Education, and Welfare, Office of Education [1959] x, 180 p., illus., map 23 cm. (United States. Office of Education. Bulletin, 1959. no. 20)
1. Education - Haiti. I. Title. II. Series.
NYPL [Sc E 88-60]

Dalhousie University. Centre for Foreign Policy Studies. Black, David R. (David Ross), 1960- Foreign policy in small states . Halifax, N.S. 1988. viii, 83 p. : ISBN 0-7703-0736-1 : DDC 327.681068 19 **NYPL [Sc D 89-564]**

Dalhousie University. Dept. of Political Science. Centre for Foreign Policy Studies. see Dalhousie University. Centre for Foreign Policy Studies.

Dalhousie University. Foreign Policy Studies, Center for. see Dalhousie University. Centre for Foreign Policy Studies.

Dalit, the black Untouchables of India /. Rajshekar Shetty, V. T., 1932- Atlanta, Ga. , c1987. 89 p. ; ISBN 0-932863-05-1 (pbk.) :
NYPL [Sc D 89-356]

Dallape, Fabio. "You are a thief" : an experience with street children / Fabio Dallape. Nairobi, Kenya : Undugu Society, 1987. 151 p. : ill. ; 25 cm.
1. Children, vagrant - Kenya - Nairobi. I. Undugu Society of Kenya. II. Title. **NYPL [Sc E 88-538]**

Dallas, Robert Charles, 1754-1824. The history of the Maroons, from their origin to the establishment of their chief tribe at Sierra Leone: including the expedition to Cuba, for the purpose of procuring Spanish chasseurs; and the state of the island of Jamaica for the last ten years: with a succinct history of the island previous to that period... By R. C. Dallas, esq. London, T. N. Longman and O. Rees, 1803. 2 v. : ill., maps ; 21 cm. Errata: v. 2, p. [1] at end. With autograph of Melville J. Herskovits.
1. Blacks - Jamaica. 2. Jamaica - History - Maroon War, 1795-1796. I. Title.
F1881 .D14 **NYPL [Sc Rare F 88-76]**

Dalrymple, Henderson. 50 great Westindian Test cricketers / Henderson Dalrymple ; foreword by Clive Lloyd. London : Hansib, 1983. xxi, 281 p. : ports. ; 22 cm. ISBN 0-9506664-4-0
1. Cricket players - West Indies - Biology. I. Title. II. Title: Fifty great Westindian Test criketers.
NYPL [Sc D 88-62]

Dalton, Karen C. C., 1948- Wood, Peter H., 1943- Winslow Homer's images of Blacks . Austin , c1988. 144 p. : ISBN 0-292-79047-3 (University of Texas Press) DDC 759.13 19
ND237.H7 A4 1988a **NYPL [Sc F 89-133]**

DAMAS, LÉON GONTRAN.
Séphocle, Marie-Line. The reception of negritude writers in the Federal Republic of

Germany . Ann Arbor, Mich. , c1987. vi, 121 p. ; **NYPL [Sc D 89-293]**

DAMAS, LÉON-GONTRAN, 1912-1978 - CRITICISM AND INTERPRETATION.
Iyay Kimoni, 1938- Poésie de la négritude . Kikwit , 1985. vi, 168 p. ; DDC 841/.009/896 19
PQ3897 .I93 1985 **NYPL [Sc B 89-18]**

Damasceno, Benedita Gouveia. Poesia negra no modernismo brasileiro / Benedita Gouveia Damasceno. Campinas, SP [Brasil] : Pontes, 1988. 142 p. ; 22 cm. (Coleção Literatura/Crítica) Originally presented as the author's thesis (Mestre -- Universidade de Brasília, 1980). Bibliography: p. 137-142. ISBN 85-7113-003-5
1. Brazilian poetry - Black authors - History and criticism. 2. Modernism (Literature) - Brazil. I. Title.
NYPL [Sc D 88-1290]

Damay, Jean. Lettres du Nord-Cameroun / Jean Damay ; préface de Bernard Holzer. Paris : C.C.F.D. : Karthala, c1985. 231 p. : maps ; 22 cm. Bibliography: p. 223-225. ISBN 2-86537-121-2
1. Masa (African people) - Social life and customs. 2. Cameroon - Description and travel. I. Title.
NYPL [Sc D 88-274]

Dance : a guide for dance instructors and choreographers / compiled and edited by Carlton Francis. Cocorite : Folksay Publications, c1983. 80 p. : ill. ; 28 cm.
1. Dancing - Study and teaching. 2. Dancing - Study and teaching - Trinidad and Tobago. 3. Dancing - Trinidad and Tobago. I. Francis, Carlton.
NYPL [Sc F 89-13]

DANCE MUSIC - AFRICA, WEST - INSTRUCTION AND STUDY.
Locke, David, 1949- Drum gahu . Crown Point, Ind. , c1987. ix, 142 p. : ISBN 0-941677-03-6 : DDC 789/.01 19
MT655 .L6 1987 **NYPL [Sc E 88-391]**

DANCERS - FRANCE - BIOGRAPHY.
Baker, Josephine, 1906-1975. Josephine /. New York , 1988, c1977. xiii, 302 p., [16] p. of plates : ISBN 1-557-78108-7 (pbk.) DDC 793.3/2/0924 B 19
GV1785.B3 A3 1988 **NYPL [Sc D 88-1476]**

DANCERS - UNITED STATES - BIOGRAPHY.
Haskins, James, 1941- Mr. Bojangles . New York , 1988. 336 p. : ISBN 0-688-07203-8 : DDC 793.3/2/0924 B 19
GV1785.R54 H37 1988
NYPL [Sc D 88-851]

DANCING, AFRO-AMERICAN. see AFRO-AMERICANS - DANCING.

DANCING - CUBA - HISTORY.
Ortiz Fernández, Fernando, 1881-1969. Los bailes y el teatro de los negros en el folklore de Cuba /. Habana, Cuba , 1981. 602 p. :
NYPL [JME 82-163]

DANCING - INSTRUCTION. see DANCING - STUDY AND TEACHING.

DANCING - JUVENILE FICTION.
McKissack, Pat, 1944- Mirandy and Brother Wind /. New York , 1988. [32] p. : ISBN 0-394-88765-4 DDC [E] 19
PZ7.M478693 Mi 1988 **NYPL [Sc F 89-58]**

DANCING - KENYA.
Senoga-Zake, George W. Folk music of Kenya /. Nairobi, Kenya , 1986. 185 p. :
NYPL [Sc D 88-368]

DANCING - NEW YORK (N.Y.) - JUVENILE FICTION.
Williams-Garcia, Rita. Blue tights /. New York , c1987. 138 p. ; ISBN 0-525-67234-6 DDC [Fic] 19
PZ7.W6713 Bl 1987 **NYPL [Sc D 88-939]**

DANCING - STUDY AND TEACHING.
Dance . Cocorite , c1983. 80 p. :
NYPL [Sc F 89-13]

DANCING - STUDY AND TEACHING - TRINIDAD AND TOBAGO.
Dance . Cocorite , c1983. 80 p. :
NYPL [Sc F 89-13]

DANCING - TRINIDAD AND TOBAGO.
Dance . Cocorite , c1983. 80 p. :
NYPL [Sc F 89-13]

DANDRIDGE, RAY, 1913-
Riley, James A. Dandy, Day and the Devil /. Cocoa, FL , 1987. xiii, 153 p. : ISBN 0-9614023-2-6 **NYPL [Sc D 88-104]**

Dandy, Day and the Devil /. Riley, James A. Cocoa, FL , 1987. xiii, 153 p. : ISBN 0-9614023-2-6 *NYPL [Sc D 88-104]*

Daneel, M. L. (Marthinus L.) Quest for belonging : introduction to a study of African independent churches / by M.L. Daneel. Gweru, Zimbabwe : Mambo Press, 1987. 310 p., [17] p. of plates : ill., folded map. ; 22 cm. (Mambo occasional papers. Missio-pastoral series . no. 17) Includes indexes. Bibliography: p. 281-288. ISBN 0-86922-426-3
1. Christian sects - Africa. 2. Zionist churches (Africa). 3. Christianity - Africa. I. Title. II. Series.
NYPL [Sc D 88-1007]

DANGALEAT LANGUAGE - DICTIONARIES - FRENCH. Ebobissé, Carl. Les verbaux du dangaléat de l'est (Guera, Tchad) . Berlin , 1987. 104 p. ; ISBN 3-496-00555-6 *NYPL [Sc E 88-231]*

DANGALEAT LANGUAGE - DICTIONARIES - GERMAN. Ebobissé, Carl. Les verbaux du dangaléat de l'est (Guera, Tchad) . Berlin , 1987. 104 p. ; ISBN 3-496-00555-6 *NYPL [Sc E 88-231]*

DANGALEAT LANGUAGE - VERB. Ebobissé, Carl. Les verbaux du dangaléat de l'est (Guera, Tchad) . Berlin , 1987. 104 p. ; ISBN 3-496-00555-6 *NYPL [Sc E 88-231]*

Dangana, Yahaya S. The barber's nine children / Yahaya S. Dangana. Yaba, Lagos : Macmillan Nigeria, 1987. 17 p. ; 19 cm. SCHOMBURG CHILDREN'S COLLECTION. ISBN 978-13-2850-9
I. Schomburg Children's Collection. II. Title.
NYPL [Sc C 89-24]

Dangarembga, Tsitsi. Nervous conditions / Tsitsi Dangarembga. London : Women's Press, 1988. 204 p. ; 20 cm. ISBN 0-7043-4100-X (pbk) : DDC 823 19
1. Zimbabwe - Fiction. I. Title.
PR9390.9.D3 *NYPL [Sc C 88-278]*

A Dangerous knowing : four black women poets / Barbara Burford ... [et al.]. London : Sheba Feminist Publishers, [1984] ix, 67 p. : ports. ; 22 cm. Poems. Imprint date from Whitaker's Cumulative book list ... 1984. CONTENTS. - Barbara Burford -- Gabriela Pearse -- Grace Nichols -- Jackie Kay. ISBN 0-907179-28-2
1. English poetry - Women authors. 2. English poetry - Black authors. 3. English poetry - 20th century. I. Burford, Barbara. *NYPL [Sc D 88-338]*

Daniel, Anita. The story of Albert Schweitzer / by Anita Daniel : illustrated with photos by Erica Anderson, and drawings by W. T. Mars. New York : Random House, 1957. 179 p. : ill. ; 22 cm. (World landmark books. W-33)
1. Schweitzer, Albert, 1875-1965 - Juvenile literature. 2. Missionaries, Medical - Gabon - Biography - Juvenile literature. I. Title. II. Series.
NYPL [Sc D 88-379]

Dann, Graham. Potter, Robert B. Barbados /. Oxford, England , Santa Barbara, Calif. , c1987. xxxix, 356 p., [1] leaf of plates : ISBN 1-85109-022-3 *NYPL [HRG 87-2371]*

Danns, George K. Matthews, Lear K. Communities and development in Guyana . [Georgetown, Guyana?] 1980. 94, v. p. :
NYPL [Sc F 89-65]

Danska, Herbert. (illus) Sadowsky, Ethel S. François and the langouste. Boston [1969] 60 p. DDC [Fic]
PZ7.S127 Fr *NYPL [Sc D 88-1120]*

Danto, Arthur Coleman, 1924- Art/artifact . New York , Munich , c1988. 195 p. : ISBN 0-9614587-7-1 DDC 730/.0967/074 19
GN36.A35 A78 1988 *NYPL [Sc G 88-25]*

Darby, D. S. Verma, Gajendra K. Race, training, and employment /. London , New York , 1987. vi, 134 p. ; ISBN 1-85000-243-6 : DDC 331.3/46/0941 19
HD5715.5.G7 V47 1987
*NYPL [*QT 88-3245]*

Darden, Joe T. Detroit, race and uneven development /. Philadelphia , 1987. xii, 317 p. : ISBN 0-87722-485-4 (alk. paper) DDC 305.8/009774/34 19
HC108.D6 D47 1987 *NYPL [Sc E 88-205]*

Darensbourg, Joe, 1906-1985.
[Telling it like it is]
Jazz odyssey : the autobiography of Joe Darensbourg / as told to Peter Vacher ;

supplementary material compiled by Peter Vacher. Baton Rouge : Louisiana State University Press, 1988, c1987. vi, 231 p., [32] p. of plates : ports. ; 25 cm. Previous ed. published as: Telling it like it is. 1987. Includes index. Discography: p. [197]-207. Bibliography: p. [217]. ISBN 0-8071-1442-1 : DDC 788/.62/0924 B 19
1. Darensbourg, Joe, 1906-1985. 2. Jazz musicians - United States - Biography. I. Vacher, Peter, 1937-. II. Title.
ML419.D35 A3 1988 *NYPL [Sc E 89-28]*

DARENSBOURG, JOE, 1906-1985. Darensbourg, Joe, 1906-1985. [Telling it like it is.] Jazz odyssey . Baton Rouge , 1988, c1987. vi, 231 p., [32] p. of plates : ISBN 0-8071-1442-1 : DDC 788/.62/0924 B 19
ML419.D35 A3 1988 *NYPL [Sc E 89-28]*

Darity, William A., 1953- Harris, Abram Lincoln, 1899-1963. Race, radicalism, and reform . New Brunswick, U. S.A. , c1989. viii, 521 p. ; ISBN 0-88738-210-X DDC 305.8/96073 19
E185.8 .H27 1989 *NYPL [Sc E 89-166]*

Dark journey . McMillen, Neil R., 1939- Urbana, Ill. , c1989. xvii, 430 p., [10] p. of plates, ISBN 0-252-01568-1 (alk. paper) DDC 976.2/00496073 19
E185.93.M6 M33 1989 *NYPL [Sc E 89-213]*

Darkness and dawn in Zimbabwe /. Elliott, Hugh P. London , 1978. [6], 49 p. ; ISBN 0-901269-37-9 :
DT962.42 .E38 *NYPL [JFD 80-115]*

Darmstadt (Germany). That's jazz, der Sound des 20. Jahrhunderts . [Darmstadt , 1988] xv, 723 p. : DDC 781/.57/0740341 19
ML141.D3 I6 1988 *NYPL [JMF 89-297]*

Darsières, Camille. Lagro, ou, Les debuts du socialisme à la Martinique / par Camille Darsiers. [Fort-de-France] : P.P.M., [198-?] 75 p. : ill., ports. ; 21 cm. Cover title.
1. Lagrosillière, Joseph, 1872-1950. 2. Parti progressiste martiniquais. 3. Socialisme - Martinique. I. Title. II. Title: Les debuts du socialisme à la Martinique.
NYPL [Sc D 89-560]

Dash, J. Michael. Haiti and the United States : national stereotypes and the literary imagination / J. Michael Dash. Basingstoke, Hampshire : Macmillan, 1988. xv, 152 p. ; 23 cm. Includes bibliographical references and index. ISBN 0-333-45491-X
1. Haitian literature - History and criticism. 2. Haitian literature - American influences. 3. American literature - History and criticism. 4. Haiti in literature. 5. United States in literature. 6. National characteristics in literature. 7. Haiti - Relations - United States. 8. United States - Relations - Haiti. I. Title.
NYPL [Sc D 88-1358]

Dash, Leon. When children want children : the urban crisis of teenage childbearing / Leon Dash.1st ed. New York : William Morrow, c1989. 270 p. : ill. ; 24 cm. Includes bibliographical references. ISBN 0-688-06957-6 DDC 306.7/088055 19
1. Washington Highlands (Washington, D.C.). 2. Afro-American teenage mothers - Washington (D.C.) - Case studies. 3. Teenage pregnancy - Washington (D.C.) - Case studies. 4. Afro-American teenagers - Washington (D.C.) - Sexual behavior - Case studies. I. Title.
HQ759.4 .D37 1989 *NYPL [Sc E 89-151]*

DATA STORAGE AND RETRIEVAL SYSTEMS. see INFORMATION STORAGE AND RETRIEVAL SYSTEMS.

Dateline Soweto . Finnegan, William. New York , c1988. x. 244 p. : ISBN 0-06-015932-4 : DDC 070/.92/4 B 19
PN4874.F45 A3 1989 *NYPL [JFE 88-2005]*

Daughter of Maa /. Kulet, Henry R. ole, 1946- Nairobi , 1987. 172 p. ; ISBN 0-582-98653-2
NYPL [Sc C 89-42]

Dauntless in Mississippi . Griffith, Helen. Northampton, Mass. , 1965. xii, 173 p. :
NYPL [Sc D 88-1111]

Dauphin, Claude, 1949- Musique du vaudou : fonctions, structures et styles / Claude Dauphin. Sherbrooke, Québec, Canada : Editions Naaman, [1986] 182 p. : ill. (some col.), music ; 22 cm. (Collection Civilisations. 18) "Errata" label on t.p. verso. Bibliography: p. [180] ISBN 2-89040-366-1 (pbk.) DDC 783/.02/9967

19
1. Voodooism - Haiti - Music - History and criticism. 2. Voodooism - Haiti - Music. I. Title.
ML3565 .D34 1986 *NYPL [Sc D 87-315]*

David, A. S. West African Seminar on Population Studies, University of Ghana, 1972. Interdisciplinary approaches to population studies . Legon , 1975. ix, 333 p. :
HB21 .W38 1972 *NYPL [JLD 78-861]*

David Walker's appeal, in four articles, together with a preamble, to the coloured citizens of the world, but in particular, and very expressly, to those of the United States of America. Walker, David, 1785-1830. New York [1965] xii, 78 p. DDC 326.973
E446 .W178 *NYPL [Sc D 89-456]*

Davidson, Michael. Some boys / by Michael Davidson. London : GMP, 1988, c1970. 201 p. ; 20 cm. Originally published: London : David Bruce & Watson Ltd, 1970. ISBN 0-85449-087-6 (pbk) : DDC 070/.92/4 19
1. Journalists - Great Britain - Biography. 2. Gay men - Great Britain - Biography. I. Title.
PN5123.D *NYPL [Sc C 89-87]*

Davies, Miranda. Third World, second sex, vol. 2 /. London, UK , Atlantic Highlands, N.J., USA , 1987. viii, 284 p. : ISBN 0-86232-752-0 (v. 2) : DDC 305.4/2/091724 19
HQ1870.9 .T48 1987 *NYPL [Sc D 88-931]*

Davies, Robert. South African strategy towards Mozambique in the post-Nkomati period : a critical analysis of effects and implications / Robert Davies. Uppsala : Scandinavian Institute of African Studies, 1985. 71 p. ; 25 cm. (Research report, 0080-6714 . no. 73) Bibliography: p. 62-71. ISBN 91-7106-238-6 (pbk.) : DDC 327.68067/9 19
1. South Africa - Foreign relations - Mozambique. 2. Mozambique - Foreign relations - South Africa. I. Series: Research report (Nordiska Afrikainstitutet) , no. 73. II. Title.
DT771.M85 D38 1985 *NYPL [Sc E 88-121]*

Davies, Robert H. The struggle for South Africa : a reference guide to movements, organizations, and institutions / Robert Davies, Dan O'Meara, and Sipho Dlamini.New ed. London ; Atlantic Highlands, N.J. : Zed Books, 1988. 2 v. : ill. ; 23 cm. Includes bibliographical references and index. ISBN 0-86232-760-1 (v. 1) DDC 322/.0968 19
1. Apartheid - South Africa. 2. National liberation movements - South Africa. 3. Associations, institutions, etc. - South Africa. 4. South Africa - Politics and government - 20th century. 5. South Africa - Economic conditions - 1961-. I. O'Meara, Dan, 1948-. II. Dlamini, Sipho. III. Title.
JQ1931 .D38 1988 *NYPL [Sc D 88-1369]*

Davies, W. J. A review of issues related to planning and development in Grahamstown : planning for growth and development in Grahamstown / W.J. Davies. Grahamstown [South Africa] : Institute of Social and Economic Research, Rhodes University, 1986. 114 p. : maps ; 30 cm. (Development studies working paper . no. 22) "February 1986." Bibliography: p. 113-114. ISBN 0-86810-130-3
1. City planning - South Africa - Grahamstown. 2. Grahamstown, South Africa. I. Title. II. Series.
NYPL [Sc F 87-431]

Davies, William J. Fest-quest 87, : a survey of visitors to the 1987 Standard Bank Festival of the Arts / Bill Davies. Grahamstown, South Africa : Institute of Social and Economic Research, Rhodes University, 1988. iv, 161 p. : ill. ; 30 cm. (Development studies working paper . no. 37) "January 1988." Includes bibliographical references. ISBN 0-86810-165-6
1. National Arts Festival (1987 : Grahamstown, South Africa). I. Series. II. Series: Development studies , working paper no. 37. III. Title.
NYPL [Sc F 88-267]

Davis, Allison, 1902- Deep South; a social anthropological study of caste and class, written by Allison Davis, Burleigh B. Gardner and Mary R. Gardner. Los Angeles, CA : Center for Afro-American Studies, University of California, 1988. xxiii, 567 p. : ill. ; 24 cm. (CAAS community classics) Originally published by the University of Chicago Press in 1941. With a new foreword. ISBN 0-934934-26-6
1. Afro-Americans - Southern States. 2. Southern States - Social conditions. 3. Southern States - Economic conditions. I. Gardner, Burleigh B. (Burleigh

Bradford), 1902- joint author. II. Gardner, Mary R., joint author. III. Title. *NYPL [Sc E 89-45]*

Davis, Angela Yvonne, 1944- Women, culture, & politics / Angela Y. Davis. lst ed. New York, NY : Random House, 1989. xv, 238 p. ; 22 cm. Includes bibliographical references. ISBN 0-394-76976-8 : DDC 305.4/8896073 19
1. Afro-Americans - Social conditions - 1975-. 2. Sexism - United States. 3. Racism - United States. 4. United States - Race relations. I. Title.
E185.86 .D382 1989   *NYPL [Sc D 89-275]*

DAVIS, BENJAMIN O., 1880-1970.
Fletcher, Marvin. America's first Black general . Lawrence, Kan. , c1989. xix, 226 p. : ISBN 0-7006-0381-6 (alk. paper) : DDC 355/.008996073 B 19
U53.D38 F57 1989   *NYPL [Sc D 89-276]*

Davis, Lenwood G. The Black heritage of Western North Carolina / Lenwood Davis [Asheville, North Carolina : s-n., 1986?] 78 leaves ; 28 cm. Bibliography: p. 78.
1. Afro-Americans - North Carolina - History. I. Title.
NYPL [Sc F 88-265]

Davis, Levaster. Torture / Levaster Davis. New York : Vantage Press, c1987. 167 p. ; 21 cm. ISBN 0-533-07293-X
1. Afro-Americans - West (U. S.) - Fiction. 2. West (U. S.) - Fiction. I. Title.   *NYPL [Sc D 88-517]*

Davis, Mary Gould. Kalibala, E. Balintuma. Wakaima and the clay man . New York , 1946. 145 p. :   *NYPL [Sc D 89-486]*

Davis, Russell G.
Land in the sun, the story of West Africa, by Russell Davis and Brent Ashabranner. Illustrated by Robert William Hinds. Boston, Little,Brown [1963] 92 p. illus. 27 cm. SCHOMBURG CHILDREN'S COLLECTION.
1. Africa, West - Description and travel - Juvenile literature. I. Ashabranner, Brent K., 1921- joint author. II. Schomburg Children's Collection. III. Title.
NYPL [Sc F 88-365]
Strangers in Africa, by Russell Davis and Brent Ashabranner. New York, McGraw-Hill [1963] 149 p. 21 cm.
1. Nigeria - Juvenile fiction. I. Ashabranner, Brent K., 1921- joint author. II. Title.
PZ7.D2993 St   *NYPL [Sc D 88-505]*

Davis, Scott C., 1948- The world of Patience Gromes : making and unmaking a Black community / Scott C. Davis. [Lexington, Ky.] : University Press of Kentucky, 1988. 222 p. ; 23 cm. Bibliography: p. 213-219. ISBN 0-8131-1644-9 DDC 975.5/45100496073 19
1. Afro-Americans - Virginia - Richmond - Social conditions. 2. Afro-Americans - Virginia - Richmond - Social life and customs. 3. Richmond (Va.) - Social conditions. 4. Richmond (Va.) - Social life and customs. I. Title.
F234.R59 N43 1988   *NYPL [Sc D 88-1302]*

Davis, Wade. Davis, Wade. Passage of darkness . Chapel Hill , c1988. xx, 344 p. : ISBN 0-8078-1776-7 (alk. paper) DDC 299/.65 19
BL2530.H3 D37 1988   *NYPL [Sc E 88-429]*
Passage of darkness : the ethnobiology of the Haitian zombie / by Wade Davis. Chapel Hill : University of North Carolina Press, c1988. xx, 344 p. : ill. ; 24 cm. Includes index. Bibliography: p. 303-326. ISBN 0-8078-1776-7 (alk. paper) DDC 299/.65 19
1. Zombiism - Haiti. 2. Bizango (Cult). 3. Tetrodotoxin - Physiological effect. 4. Haiti - Religious life and customs. 5. Haiti - Social life and customs. I. Davis, Wade. II. Title.
BL2530.H3 D37 1988   *NYPL [Sc E 88-429]*

Day, George Tiffany, 1822-1875. African adventures and adventurers /. Boston , 1880. 393 p. :   *NYPL [Sc C 88-60]*

A day in their lives /. Singhateh, Modu F. Banjul [1984] 87 p :   *NYPL [Sc E 88-98]*

The day Kenyatta died /. Ng'weno, Hilary. Nairobi , 1978. 68 p., [1] leaf of plates : ISBN 0-582-64283-3 DDC 967.6/204/0924 B 19
DT433.576.K46 N45   *NYPL [Sc F 89-28]*

DAY, LEON, 1916-
Riley, James A. Dandy, Day and the Devil /. Cocoa, FL , 1987. xiii, 153 p. : ISBN 0-9614023-2-6   *NYPL [Sc D 88-104]*

A day with Debbie /. Detroit. Great Cities

Program for School Improvement. Writers' Committee. Chicago , c1964. 55 p. :
NYPL [Sc E 89-178]

D'ca Freedom Party government [microform] : 2nd anniversary 1980-1982. [Roseau, Dominica : Printed by Tropical Printers, 1983?] 36 p. ; 28 cm. Cover title. On cover: Hon. M. Eugenia Charles, Prime Minister/DFP political leader. Microfilm. New York: New York Public Library, 1982. 1 microfilm reel; 35 mm. (MN *ZZ-24640)
1. Dominica - Politics and government. 2. Dominica - Social conditions. 3. Dominica - Economic conditions. I. Dominica Freedom Party.
NYPL [Sc Micro R-4137 no.13]

De Angeli, Marguerite, 1899- Thee, Hannah / by Marguerite De Angeli. 1st ed. New York : Doubleday, Doran, 1940. [88] p. : ill. (some col.) ; 22 x 22 cm. SCHOMBURG CHILDREN'S COLLECTION.
1. Fugitive slaves - Pennsylvania - Juvenile fiction. 2. Quakers - Pennsylvania - Philadelphia - Juvenile fiction. I. Schomburg Children's Collection. II. Title.
NYPL [Sc D 88-635]

De Beer, Marlien. SWA Namibia today /. Windhoek , 1988. 128 p. :
NYPL [Sc D 88-1359]

De Cola, Freya D. Three decades of medical research at the College of Medicine, Ibadan, Nigeria, 1948-1980 : a list of the papers published by members of the College of Medicine of the University of Ibadan from its foundation through 1980 / compiled by Freya D. De Cola, Patricia H. Shoyinka. Ibadan, Nigeria : Ibadan University Press, University of Ibadan, for the E. Latunde Odeku Medical Library, 1984. xv, 208 p. ; 24 cm. (Ibadan tropical medicine series . 4) Includes indexes. ISBN 978-12-1157-1 (pbk.) DDC 016.61 19
1. University of Ibadan. College of Medicine - Bibliography. 2. Medicine - Nigeria - Bibliography. 3. Tropical medicine - Nigeria - Bibliography. I. Shoyinka, Patricia H. II. University of Ibadan. College of Medicine. III. Title. IV. Series.
Z6661.N6 D4 1984 R824.N6
NYPL [Sc E 89-160]

De Gruchy, John W. Theology and ministry in context and crisis : a South African perspective / John W. De Gruchy. London : Collins, 1987, c1986. 183 p. ; 20 cm. "Index of names": p. 170-172. Bibliography: p. 173-183. ISBN 0-00-599969-3
1. Theology, Practical. 2. Church and race relation - South Africa. I. Title.   *NYPL [Sc C 88-73]*

De igual pra igual . Biehl, João Guilherme. Petrópolis , São Leopoldo, RS, Brasil , 1987. 155 p. :
BT83.57 .B54 1987   *NYPL [Sc D 88-1016]*

De instauranda aethiopum salute. Sandoval, Alonso dc, 1576-1652. Naturaleza, policia sagrada i profana, costumbres i ritos, disciplina i catechismo evangelico de todos etiopes /. En Sevilla , 1627. [23], 334 p., 81 leaves ;
NYPL [Sc Rare F 82-70]

De l'état actuel de la marine et des colonies /. Le Brasseur, J. A. A Paris , 1792. 48 p. ;
NYPL [Sc Rare C 86-4]

De Meillon, Henry Clifford. Cape views and costumes : water-colours by H. C. de Meillon in the Brenthurst Collection, Johannesburg / [text by] Anna H. Smith. Johannesburg : Brenthurst Press, 1978. 134 p. : chiefly col. ill. ; 27 cm. (Brenthurst series. no. 3) Bibliography: p. 18-19. ISBN 0-909079-05-6 : DDC 759.968
1. De Meillon, Henry Clifford. 2. Brenthurst Collection. 3. Cape Town in art. I. Smith, Anna H. II. Brenthurst Collection. III. Title.
ND2088.6.S6 D452 1978
NYPL [Sc F 85-112]

DE MEILLON, HENRY CLIFFORD.
De Meillon, Henry Clifford. Cape views and costumes . Johannesburg , 1978. 134 p. : ISBN 0-909079-05-6 : DDC 759.968
ND2088.6.S6 D452 1978
NYPL [Sc F 85-112]

De mojo blues . Flowers, A. R. New York , 1986, c1985. 216 p. ; ISBN 0-525-24376-3 : DDC 813/.54 19
PS3556.L598 D4 1986 *NYPL [JFD 86-3984]*

De Paola, Tomie. Rinkoff, Barbara. Rutherford T. finds 21 B. New York [1970] [47] p. DDC [Fic]
PZ7.R477 Ru   *NYPL [Sc D 88-1404]*

De Silva, Hazel, 1947- Sega of Seychelles / Hazel de Silva. Nairobi, Kenya : East African Pub. House, 1983. 314 p. ; 18 cm. (Modern African library. 39) DDC 821 19
1. Seychelles - Poetry. I. Title.
PR9381.9.D42 S4 1983   *NYPL [Sc C 89-9]*

De Stefano, Gildo. Trecento anni di jazz : 1619 - 1919 ; le origini della musica Afro-Americana, tra sociologia ed antropologia / Gildo de Stefano. Milano : SugarCo Edizioni, 1986. 262 p., [16] leaves of plates : ill. ; 21 cm. Includes index and discography.
1. Jazz music - History and criticism. I. Title.
NYPL [Sc D 88-1226]

De Velasco, Joe E. (illus) Burroughs, Margaret Taylor, 1917- (comp) Did you feed my cow? Chicago [1969] 96 p. ISBN 0-695-81960-7 DDC 398.8
PZ8.3.B958 Di5   *NYPL [Sc D 89-57]*

De Verteuil, Anthony. A history of Diego Martin 1784-1884 / Anthony de Verteuil. Port of Spain, Trinidad : Paria Publishing Co., c1987. viii, 174 p., [96] p. of plates : ill., facsims., maps, ports. ; 29cm. At head of title: Bergorrat--Brunton. Bibliography: p. [172]-174. ISBN 976-8054-10-7
1. Begorrat, St. Hilaire, 1759?-1851. 2. Brunton, Nicholas William, 1836-1891. 3. Diego Martin (Trinidad and Tobago) - History. 4. Trinidad and Tobago - History. I. Title. II. Title: Begorrat--Brunton.
NYPL [Sc F 88-192]

De Villiers, Helene. (comp) Die Sprokiesboom en ander verhale uit Midde-Afrika. Kaapstad, Human en Rousseau, 1970. 84 p ; 22 cm. SCHOMBURG CHILDREN'S COLLECTION.
1. Tales - South Africa. 2. Afrikaans language - Texts. I. Schomburg Children's Collection. II. Title.
P214 .D43   *NYPL [Sc D 89-373]*

De Vries, Abraham H. Bliksoldate bloei nie / Abraham H. De Vries. Kaapstad : Human & Rousseau, 1975. 80 p. ; 22 cm. ISBN 0-7981-0640-9
1. South Africa - Fiction. I. Title.
PT6592.14.E9 B56   *NYPL [Sc D 88-673]*

De Wet, C. J. Rural communities in transition : a study of the socio-economic and agricultural implications of agricultural betterment and development / C.J. de Wet & P.A. McAllister. Grahamstown : Dept. of Anthropology in collaboration with the Institute of Social & Economic Research, Rhodes University, [1983] iii, 113 p., [6] leaves of plates : ill. ; 30 cm. (Development studies . working paper no. 16) Bibliography: p. [75]-78. ISBN 0-86810-101-X (pbk.) DDC 307.7/2/0968 19
1. Agriculture - Economic aspects - South Africa - Homelands - Case studies. 2. Agricultural development projects - South Africa - Homelands - Case studies. 3. Rural development - South Africa - Homelands - Case studies. 4. Villages - South Africa - Homelands - Case studies. 5. Homelands (South Africa) - Rural conditions - Case studies. I. McAllister, P. A. II. Title. III. Series.
HD2130.5.Z9 H653 1983
NYPL [Sc F 88-328]

Deacon, Janette. Late Quaternary palaeoenvironments of southern Africa / Janette Deacon and N. Lancaster. Oxford : Clarendon Press ; New York : Oxford University Press, 1988. viii, 225 p. : ill.,maps ; 24 cm. Includes indexes. Bibliography: p. [187]-209. ISBN 0-19-854449-9 : DDC 560/.1/78 19
1. Paleoecology - Africa, Southern. 2. Paleontology - Quaternary. I. Lancaster, N. II. Title.
QE720 .D43 1988   *NYPL [Sc E 88-341]*

The dead among the living . Onyeneke, Augustine O. Nimo , 1987. xii, 142 p. : ISBN 978-244-232-1   *NYPL [Sc C 89-2]*

Dean, Elizabeth.
[History in black and white. Spanish]
Historia en blanco y negro : análisis de los manuales escolares en Suráfrica / Elizabeth Dean, Paul Hartmann, May Katzen.1˚ed. Barcelona : Serbal ; Paris : UNESCO, 1984. 196 p. ; 20 cm. (Colección de temas africanos . 18) Translation of: History in black and white. 1984. Bibliography: p. [192]-196. ISBN 92-3-302092-4 (Unesco)
1. Education - South Africa - History. 2. Text-books - South Africa - Evaluation. 3. Racism in textbooks - South Africa. 4. South Africa - History - Study and teaching. 5. South Africa - Race relations - Study and

teaching. I. Hartmann, Paul. II. Katzen, May. III. Title. IV. Series.					**NYPL [Sc D 88-594]**

Dean, Leigh. The looking down game. Illustrated by Paul Giovanopoulos. New York, Funk & Wagnalls [1968] 34 p. illus. 22 cm. A new neighborhood makes Edgar feel alone and shy so he makes a game of looking down and concentrating on the things he finds on the sidewalk. SCHOMBURG CHILDREN'S COLLECTION. Author's autographed presentation copy to the Countee Cullen Library. DDC [Fic]
1. City and town life - Juvenile fiction. I. Giovanopoulos, Paul, illus. II. Schomburg Children's Collection. III. Title.
PZ7.D3446 Lo					**NYPL [Sc D 89-111]**

Death & discrimination . Gross, Samuel R. Boston, c1989. xvi, 268 p. ; ISBN 1-555-53040-0 (alk. paper) : DDC 364.6/6/0973 19
HV8699.U5 G76 1989					**NYPL [Sc D 89-493]**

Death and discrimination. Gross, Samuel R. Death & discrimination . Boston, c1989. xvi, 268 p. ; ISBN 1-555-53040-0 (alk. paper) : DDC 364.6/6/0973 19
HV8699.U5 G76 1989					**NYPL [Sc D 89-493]**

Death contractor /. Okuofu, Charles O. Nigeria , 1986. 84 p. ; ISBN 978-14-1060-4
					NYPL [Sc C 88-338]

A death in the Delta . Whitfield, Stephen J., 1942- New York , London , c1988. xiv, 193 p., [8] p. of plates : ISBN 0-02-935121-9 : DDC 345.73/02523 347.3052523 19
E185.61 .W63 1989					**NYPL [Sc E 89-140]**

The death of rhythm & blues /. George, Nelson. New York , c1988. xvi, 222 p., [16] p. of plates : ISBN 0-394-55238-5 : DDC 781.7/296073 19
ML3556 .G46 1988					**NYPL [Sc E 88-504]**

DEATH PENALTY. see CAPITAL PUNISHMENT.

The death penalty in the eighties . White, Welsh S., 1940- Ann Arbor , c1987. 198 p. ; ISBN 0-472-10088-2 (alk. paper) : DDC 345.73/0773 347.305773 19
KF9227.C2 W44 1987					**NYPL [Sc E 88-129]**

DEATH RATE. see MORTALITY.

DEATH - RELIGIOUS ASPECTS.
Mort dans la vie africaine. Spanish. La Muerte en la vida africana. Barcelona , París , 1984. 314 p. : ISBN 84-85800-81-8
					NYPL [Sc D 88-601]

Death row /. Hector, Mario. London , Kingston, Jamaica , 1984. v, lll p. ISBN 0-86232-232-4
					NYPL [Sc C 88-221]

DeBerri, Edward P. Schultheis, Michael J. Catholic social teaching and the Church in Africa /. Gweru, Zimbabwe , c1984. 56 p. ;
					NYPL [Sc D 88-1198]

Debouvry, Pierre. Contribution à la définition d'une méthodologie de transfert de populations paysannes : le cas du groupe Baoulé-Ayaon dans l'operation Kossou en République de Côte d'Ivoire / par Pierre Debouvry. [Montpellier] : Institut agronomique méditerranéen de Montpellier, [1985] 294 p. : ill. ; 30 cm. (Collection Thèse M.Sc) At head of title: Centre international de hautes études agronomiques méditerranéennes. Bibliography: p. 110-126. ISBN 0-85352-039-0
1. Baoulé (African people). 2. Relocation (Housing) - Ivory Coast. 3. Land settlement - Ivory Coast. I. Centre international de hautes études agronomiques méditerranéennes. II. Series: Collection "thèses M.Sc". III. Title.					**NYPL [Sc F 88-302]**

DEBTS, EXTERNAL - AFRICA - CONGRESSES.
African debt and financing /. Washington, D.C. , 1986. 223 p. : ISBN 0-88132-044-7 : DDC 336.3/435/096 19
HJ8826 .A36 1986					**NYPL [JLE 87-3261]**

DEBTS, INTERNATIONAL. see DEBTS, EXTERNAL.

Les debuts du socialisme à la Martinique. Darsières, Camille. Lagro, ou, Les debuts du socialisme à la Martinique /. [Fort-de-France] [198-?] 75 p. :					**NYPL [Sc D 89-560]**

Decalo, Samuel.
Historical dictionary of Benin / by Samuel Decalo. 2nd ed. Metuchen, N.J. : Scarecrow

Press, 1987. xxvii, 349 p. : ill. ; 23 cm. (African historical dictionaries. no. 7) Revised ed. of: Historical dictionary of Dahomey (People's Republic of Benin). 1976. Includes bibliographical references. ISBN 0-8108-1924-4 DDC 966/.83 19
1. Benin - History - Dictionaries. I. Decalo, Samuel. Historical dictionary of Dahomey (People's Republic of Benin). II. Title. III. Series.
DT541.5 .D4 1987					**NYPL [Sc D 88-982]**

Historical dictionary of Dahomey (People's Republic of Benin) Decalo, Samuel. Historical dictionary of Benin / by Samuel Decalo. 2nd ed. Metuchen, N.J. , 1987. xxvii, 349 p. : ISBN 0-8108-1924-4 DDC 966/.83 19
DT541.5 .D4 1987					**NYPL [Sc D 88-982]**

Decarnin, Camilla. Worlds apart . Boston, Mass. , 1986. 293 p. ; ISBN 0-932870-87-2 (pbk.) : DDC 813/.0876/08353 19
PS648.H57 W67 1986					**NYPL [JFD 87-7753]**

Decca, Maria Auxiliadora Guzzo. A vida fora das fábricas : cotidiano operário em São Paulo (1920/1934) / Maria Auxiliadora Guzzo Decca. Rio de Janeiro, RJ : Editora Paz e Terra, 1987. 135 p. ; 21 cm. (Coleção Oficinas da história. vol. 3) Originally presented as the author's thesis (mestrado)--Unicamp, 1983. Bibliography: p. 131-135. DDC 305.5/62/098161 19
1. Labor and laboring classes - Brazil - São Paulo - History - 20th century. I. Title. II. Series.
HD8290.S32 D4 1987					**NYPL [Sc D 88-1367]**

DECENTRALIZATION. see DECENTRALIZATION IN GOVERNMENT.

DECENTRALIZATION IN GOVERNMENT - ZAMBIA.
Lungu, Gatian F. Administrative decentralisation in the Zambian bureaucracy . Gweru, Zimbabwe , c1985. 85 p. :					**NYPL [Sc D 89-318]**

Decision-making strategies for international organizations . Lister, Frederick K., 1921- Denver, Colo. , 1984. ix, 142 p. : ISBN 0-87940-075-7 : DDC 332.1/52 19
HG3881.5.I58 L57 1984					**NYPL [Sc D 88-1218]**

Declaro que estou em tormento . Mota, Maria Elisabete Lima. Rio de Janeiro, c1987. 181 p. ; ISBN 85-85114-15-0 :
MLCS 88/08239 (P)					**NYPL [Sc D 88-919]**

Décolonisation de l'Afrique. Spanish. La Descolonización de Africa : Africa austral y el Cuerno de Africa : documentos de trabajo y actas de la reunión de expertos celebrada en Varsovia (Polonia) del 9 al 13 de octubre de 1978 / A.A. Mazrui ... [et al.] Barcelona : Serbal ; Paris : Unesco, 1983. 197 p. ; 20 cm. (Colección de temas africanos . 12) Translation of: La décolonisation de l'Afrique: Afrique australe et Corne de l'Afrique. 1981. Conference organized by Unesco. Original ed. published simultaneously in French and English; English title: The decolonization of Africa. Includes bibliographies. ISBN 92-3-301834-2 (Unesco)
1. Decolonization - Africa, Southern - Congresses. 2. National liberation movements - Africa, Southern - Congresses. 3. Decolonization - Africa, Northeastern - Congresses. 4. National liberation movements - Africa, Northeastern - Congresses. 5. Africa - Politics and government - Congresses. I. Mazrui, Ali Al'Amin. II. Unesco. III. Title. IV. Series.
					NYPL [Sc D 88-590]

DECOLONIZATION - AFRICA.
Decolonization and African independence . New Haven , 1988. xxix, 651 p. ; ISBN 0-300-04070-9 DDC 960/.32 19
DT30.5 .D42 1988					**NYPL [Sc E 88-517]**

Hargreaves, John D. Decolonization in Africa /. London , New York , 1988. xvi, 263 p. : ISBN 0-582-49150-9 DDC 960/.32 19
DT29 .H37 1988					**NYPL [Sc D 89-315]**

Sevillano Castillo, Rosa. Los Orígenes de la descolonización africana a través de la prensa española (1956-1962) /. Madrid , 1986. 158 p. :
					NYPL [Sc E 88-94]

DECOLONIZATION - AFRICA, NORTHEASTERN - CONGRESSES.
Décolonisation de l'Afrique. Spanish. La Descolonización de Africa : Africa austral y el Cuerno de Africa . Barcelona , Paris , 1983. 197 p. ; ISBN 92-3-301834-2 (Unesco)
					NYPL [Sc D 88-590]

DECOLONIZATION - AFRICA, SOUTHERN - CONGRESSES.
Décolonisation de l'Afrique. Spanish. La Descolonización de Africa : Africa austral y el Cuerno de Africa . Barcelona , Paris , 1983. 197 p. ; ISBN 92-3-301834-2 (Unesco)
					NYPL [Sc D 88-590]

Decolonization and African independence : the transfers of power, 1960-1980 / edited by Prosser Gifford and Wm. Roger Louis. New Haven : Yale University Press, 1988. xxix, 651 p. ; 24 cm. Includes index. Bibliography: p. 573-635. ISBN 0-300-04070-9 DDC 960/.32 19
1. Decolonization - Africa. 2. Africa - Politics and government - 1960-. 3. Africa - Politics and government - 1945-1960. I. Gifford, Prosser. II. Louis, William Roger, 1936-.
DT30.5 .D42 1988					**NYPL [Sc E 88-517]**

DECOLONIZATION - HISTORY.
Porter, A. N. (Andrew N.) British imperial policy and decolonization, 1938-64 /. New York , 1987- v. ; ISBN 0-312-00554-7 (v. 1) : DDC 325/.31/41 19
JV1018 .P66 1987					**NYPL [Sc D 88-219]**

Decolonization in Africa /. Hargreaves, John D. London , New York , 1988. xvi, 263 p. : ISBN 0-582-49150-9 DDC 960/.32 19
DT29 .H37 1988					**NYPL [Sc D 89-315]**

DECORATION AND ORNAMENT - BRAZIL - PERNAMBUCO - HISTORY - SOURCES.
Diario de Pernambuco . Recife [1985]. 256 p. : ISBN 85-7019-094-8					**NYPL [Sc D 88-862]**

DECORATIVE ARTS, FULAH.
Adepgba, Cornelius Oyeleke, 1941- Decorative arts of the Fulani nomads /. Ibadan, Nigeria , 1986. 48 p. : ISBN 978-12-1195-4
					NYPL [Sc D 88-735]

Decorative arts of the Fulani nomads /. Adepgba, Cornelius Oyeleke, 1941- Ibadan, Nigeria , 1986. 48 p. : ISBN 978-12-1195-4
					NYPL [Sc D 88-735]

Découverte de la vannerie caraïbe du Morne des Esses à Salybia / élèves e professeurs de la 5e 3, Collège II de Sainte-Marie. Martinique : CRDP, 1984. 60 p. : ill., map ; 20 cm.
1. Basket making - Martinique - Sainte-Marie. 2. Basket making - Dominica - Salybia.
					NYPL [Sc C 88-323]

Dedan Kimathi papers. Kenya's freedom struggle . London ; Atlantic Highlands, N.J. , 1987. xix, 138 p. ;					**NYPL [Sc D 88-775]**

Dee, Ruby. Two ways to count to ten : a Liberian folktale / retold by Ruby Dee ; illustrated by Susan Meddaugh.1st ed. New York : H. Holt., c1988. [32] p. : col. ill. ; 26 cm. A retelling of a traditional Liberian tale in which King Leopard invites all the animals to a spear-throwing contest whose winner will marry his daughter and succeed him as king. SCHOMBURG CHILDREN'S COLLECTION. ISBN 0-8050-0407-6 : DDC 398.2/096 E 19
1. Tales - Liberia. I. Meddaugh, Susan, ill. II. Schomburg Children's Collection. III. Title.
PZ8.1.D378 Tw 1988					**NYPL [Sc F 88-311]**

Deep down : the new sensual writing by women / edited by Laura Chester. Boston : Faber and Faber, c1988. xii, 330 p. ; 22 cm. ISBN 0-571-12957-9 : DDC 810/.8/03538 19
1. Erotic literature, American - Women authors. 2. Erotic literature - Women authors. 3. Women - Sexual behavior - Literary collections. 4. American literature - 20th century. I. Chester, Laura.
PS509.E7 D44 1988					**NYPL [Sc D 88-1080]**

Deep South. Davis, Allison, 1902- Los Angeles, CA , 1988. xxiii, 567 p. : ISBN 0-934934-26-6
					NYPL [Sc E 89-45]

Deeter, Catherine. (ill) Walker, Alice, 1944- To hell with dying /. San Diego , 1987. [32] p. : ISBN 0-15-289075-0 DDC [Fic] 19
PZ7.W15213 To 1987					**NYPL [Sc F 88-182]**

DEFAMATION. see LIBEL AND SLANDER.

Défi à la pauvreté /. Laraque, Franck. Montréal , 1987. 165 p. ;					**NYPL [Sc C 88-107]**

Defize, Stanislas. Histoire de St. Barth / texte et illustrations, Stanislas Defize = History of St. Barth / text and illustrations by Stanislas Defize ; translation by Joan Fenet. [Paris?] : Editions du Latanier, c1987. [60] p. : col. ill. ; 31 cm. Maps on lining papers. ISBN 2-9502284-0-2
1. Saint Barthélemy - History. I. Fenet, Joan. II. Title.
					NYPL [Sc G 88-29]

Defries, Amelia Dorothy, 1882- The Fortunate
Islands, being adventures with the Negro in the
Bahamas, by Amelia Defries ... With a foreword
by Aloysius Horn; a preface by Rosita
Forbes ... London, C. Palmer [1929] xxiii, 160
p. front., illus. (music) plates, double map. 23
cm. "First edition." Negro songs (6) with music: p.
xix-xxi. DDC 917.296
1. Blacks - Bahamas. 2. Bahamas - Description & travel.
I. Title.
F1651 .D31   **NYPL [Sc D 88-936]**

A degree of difference. Ford, George Barry. New
York [1969] 271 p. DDC 282/.0924 B
BX4705.F635 A3   **NYPL [Sc D 88-406]**

DEGREES, ACADEMIC - UNITED STATES.
Richardson, Richard C. Fostering minority
access and achievement in higher education .
San Francisco, Calif. , c1987. xviii, 244 p. ;
   ISBN 1-555-42053-2 (alk. paper) DDC 378/.052
19
LC3727 .R53 1987   **NYPL [Sc E 88-472]**

Deive, Carlos Esteban, 1935- Los cimarrones del
maniel de Neiba : historia y etnografía / Carlos
Esteban Deive. Santo Domingo, República
Dominicana : Banco Central de la República
Dominicana, 1985. 199 p. : ill. ; 22 cm.
1. Fugitive slaves - Dominican Republic. 2. Fugitive
slaves - Haiti. 3. Maroons - Dominican Republic. 4.
Maroons - Haiti. I. Title. **NYPL [Sc D 89-173]**

Déjà vu, suivi de Chutes /. Ebony, N. X. Paris ,
1983. 191 p. ; ISBN 2-86436-005-5
                     NYPL [Sc D 88-1353]

Del Giudice, Maria. Center for Migration Studies
(U. S.) Refugees . Staten Island, N.Y. , 1987.
ix, 423 p. ; ISBN 0-934733-34-1 (pbk.)
                     NYPL [Sc F 89-60]

Delany, Samuel R. The motion of light in water :
sex and science fiction writing in the East
Village, 1957-1965 / Samuel R. Delany. New
York : Arbor House/W. Morrow, c1988. xviii,
302 p. : port. ;c24 cm. ISBN 0-87795-947-1 :
   DDC 813/.54 19
1. Delany, Samuel R. 2. Authors, American - 20th
century - Biography. 3. Science fiction - Authorship. 4.
Bohemianism - New York (N.Y.). 5. Afro-American
authors - Biography. 6. East Village (New York, N.Y.) -
Popular culture. 7. New York (N.Y.) - Popular culture.
I. Title.
PS3554.E437 Z475 1988
                     NYPL [JFD 88-7818]

DELANY, SAMUEL R.
Delany, Samuel R. The motion of light in
water . New York , c1988. xviii, 302 p. : ISBN
0-87795-947-1 : DDC 813/.54 19
PS3554.E437 Z475 1988
                     NYPL [JFD 88-7818]

Dele Giwa /. Magnate, Joseph. Lagos, , 1987. 190
p. : ISBN 978-303-000-0 **NYPL [Sc D 88-742]**

Deleris, Ferdinand. Ratsiraka : socialisme et
misère à Madagascar / Ferdinand Deleris.
Paris : L'Harmattan, c1986. 135 p. ; 22 cm.
(Collection Points de vue, 0761-54248) Bibliography: p.
133-134. ISBN 2-85802-697-1
1. Socialism - Madagascar. 2. Civil rights - Madagascar.
3. Madagascar - Politics and government - 1960-. 4.
Madagascar - Economic conditions. I. Title.
                     NYPL [Sc D 88-777]

Delessert, Étienne. (ill) Angelou, Maya. Mrs.
Flowers . Minneapolis, Minn. , c1986. 32 p. :
   ISBN 1-556-28009-2 (pbk.) : DDC [Fic] 19
PZ7.A5833 Mr 1986
                     NYPL [Sc Rare C 88-28]

**The delivery of mental health services to Black
children .** Gary, Lawrence E. Washington,
D.C. , 1982. vi, 111, 19 p. ;
                     NYPL [Sc F 88-66]

**Delivery of mental health services to black
children.** Gary, Lawrence E. The delivery of
mental health services to Black children .
Washington, D.C. , 1982. vi, 111, 19 p. ;
                     NYPL [Sc F 88-66]

Della Cava, Olha. A Directory of international
migration study centers, research programs, and
library resources /. Staten Island, N.Y. , 1987.
ix, 299 p. ; ISBN 0-934733-18-X (pbk.) : DDC
325/.07 19
JV6033 .C45 1987 **NYPL [JLF 88-1452]**

DELLUMS, RONALD V., 1935-
Fitch, Robert Beck, 1938- Right on Dellums!
Mankato, Minn. [1971] [47] p. ISBN

0-87191-079-9 DDC 329/.023/79405
JK1978 .F53   **NYPL [Sc F 88-338]**

Delord, J. Le Kabiye / J. Delord. Lomé : Institut
national de la recherche scientifique, 1976. xxxi,
465 p. : ill. ; 24 cm. Includes index. Bibliography: p.
423.
1. Kabre dialect. I. Title.
PL8725.15.Z9 K334 1976
                     NYPL [Sc E 89-119]

Delsham, Tony. L'impuissant / Tony Delsham.
Fort-de-France : Editions M.G.G., 1986. 204
p. ; 22 cm. ISBN 2-86823-006-7
1. Impotence - Martinique - Fiction. 2. Martinique -
Fiction. I. Title. **NYPL [Sc D 88-349]**

Delta campus based / City-wide members . Delta
Sigma Theta Sorority. Grand Chapter.
[Washington, D.C.?] , 1977. [63] p. :
                     NYPL [Sc F 88-5]

DELTA SIGMA THETA SORORITY.
Hill, Pauline Anderson Simmons. Too young to
be old . Seattle, Washington , c1981. xiv, 58
p. : ISBN 0-89716-098-3
                     NYPL [Sc D 88-1214]

**DELTA SIGMA THETA SORORITY -
MEMBERSHIP.**
Delta Sigma Theta Sorority. Grand Chapter.
Delta campus based / City-wide members .
[Washington, D.C.?] , 1977. [63] p. :
                     NYPL [Sc F 88-5]

Delta Sigma Theta Sorrority. Grand Chapter.
Delta campus based / City-wide members : a
1977 profile / Delta Sigma Theta, Inc., Grand
Chapter. [Washington, D.C.?] : Delta Sigma
Theta, 1977. [63] p. : maps ; 28 cm.
1. Delta Sigma Theta Sorority - Membership. I. Title.
                     NYPL [Sc F 88-5]

DELUSIONS. see WITCHCRAFT.

Delval, Raymond, 1917- Andovoranto, son passé
prestigieux / par Raymond Delval.
Antananarivo : [Université de Madagascar,
Etablissement d'enseignement supérieur des
lettres], 1985. 106 p. ; 27 cm. (Etudes et
documents / Université de Madagascar, Etablissement
d'enseignement supérieur des lettres . no 2) Cover title:
Andovoranto, son passé prestigieux. "Paris, octobre
1983." Bibliography: p. 103-104. DDC 969.7 19
1. Andevoranto (Madagascar) - Description. 2.
Andevoranto (Madagascar) - History. I. Title. II. Title:
Andovoranto, son passé prestigieux. III. Series: Etudes
et documents / Université de Madagascar,
Etablissement d'enseignement supérieur des lettres , no
2.
DT469.M38 A543 1985
                     NYPL [Sc F 88-321]

**Demain la Guadeloupe unie, la régionalisation
réussie .** Beaujean, Henri. Paris , c1988. 374
p. ;   **NYPL [Sc D 88-972]**

**The demand for skilled labour in the Border,
Ciskei, southern Transkei regional economy /.**
McCartan, P. J. (Patrick John) Grahamstown
[1983] 50, xxii p. : ISBN 0-86810-058-7 (pbk.) :
   DDC 331.12/3/0968792 19
HD5842.A6 M33 1983 **NYPL [Sc F 88-356]**

Un demi-siecle de swing et de Jazz / Guy
Rolland, gérant, directeur de la publication.
[Paris] : Editions de l'Instant/Jazz Hot, 1986.
109 p. : ill., ports. ; 32 cm. French and English.
On cover: Jazz hot hors série. ISBN 2-86929-034-9
1. Jazz musicians - Portraits. I. Rolland, Guy. II. Jazz
Hot.   **NYPL [Sc G 86-35]**

D'Emilio, John. Intimate matters : a history of
sexuality in America / John D'Emilio and
Estelle Freedman.1st ed. New York : Harper &
Row, c1988. xx, 428 p., [16] leaves of plates :
ill. ; 25 cm. Includes index. Bibliography: p.
[401]-413. ISBN 0-06-015855-7 : DDC 306.7/0973
19
1. Sex customs - United States - History. I. Freedman,
Estelle B., 1947-. II. Title.
HQ18.U5 D45 1988 **NYPL [Sc E 88-436]**

Democracy and prebendal politics in Nigeria .
Joseph, Richard A. Cambridge
[Cambridgeshire] , New York , 1987. x, 237
p. : ISBN 0-521-34136-1 DDC 966.9/05 19
DT515.84 .J67 1987 **NYPL [JFE 88-4953]**

Democracy in developing countries / edited by
Larry Diamond, Juan Linz, and Seymour
Martin Lipset. Boulder, Colo. : L. Rienner,
1988- v. : ill., charts, maps ; 23 cm. Includes
index. CONTENTS. - -- v. 2. Africa. ISBN

1-555-87039-2 (v. 2) : DDC 320.9173/4 19
1. Developing countries - Politics and government. 2.
Africa - Politics and government. I. Diamond, Larry
Jay. II. Linz, Juan J. (Juan José), 1926-. III. Lipset,
Seymour Martin.
D883 .D45 1988   **NYPL [Sc E 88-201]**

DEMOCRATIC PARTY (UGANDA)
Bwengye, Francis Aloysius Wazarwahi. The
agony of Uganda from Idi Amin to Obote .
London , 1985. xxii, 379 p. : ISBN
0-7212-0717-0 :   **NYPL [Sc D 88-873]**

The Democratic theory and practice in Africa /
[edited by] W.O. Oyugi, A. Gitonga. Nairobi :
Heinemann Kenya, 1987. vi, 208 p. ; 21 cm.
Bibliography: p. 199-201.
1. Representative government and representation -
Africa. 2. Africa - Politics and government. I. Oyugi,
W. Ouma. II. Gitonga, Africa K.
                     NYPL [Sc D 89-569]

**La démocratie nouvelle, ou, projet pour le Zaïre
/.** Totime Mikeni. Paris [1984?]. iii, 104 p. ;
                     NYPL [Sc D 88-720]

**DEMONOLOGY - AFRICA - JUVENILE
FICTION.**
Chukwuka, J. I. N. Zandi and the wonderful
pillow /. Lagos, Nigeria , 1977. 48 p. : ISBN
0-410-80099-6   **NYPL [Sc C 88-76]**

**DEMONOLOGY, CHRISTIAN. see
DEMONOLOGY.**

**DEMONOLOGY - COMPARATIVE STUDIES.
see DEMONOLOGY.**

Demuth, Clare. 'Sus', a report on the Vagrancy
Act 1824 / by Clare Demuth ; with a
for[e]word by Geoffrey Bindman. London :
Runnymede Trust, 1978. 62 p. : ill. ; 21 cm.
Bibliography: p. 61-62.
1. Vagrancy - Great Britain. 2. Blacks - Great Britain.
3. Arrest - Great Britain. I. Title.
                     NYPL [Sc D 88-1174]

Denby, Charles.
Indignant heart : a black worker's journal / by
Charles Denby (Matthew Ward). Boston :
South End Press, c1978. 295 p. : ill. ; 21 cm.
   ISBN 0-89608-092-7 DDC
331.6/3/960730774340924 B 19
1. Denby, Charles. 2. International Union, United
Automobile, Aerospace and Agricultural Implement
Workers of America - History. 3. Afro-American
automobile industry workers - Biography. 4.
Afro-American communists - Biography. 5. United
States - Race relations - History. I. Title.
HD8039.A82 U633 1978
                     NYPL [Sc D 88-853]

Indignant heart : a Black worker's journal / by
Charles Denby (Matthew Ward). Detroit :
Wayne State University Press, 1989, c1978. xvi,
303 p. : ill., port. ; 23 cm. (African American
life) Includes bibliographical references.
   ISBN 0-8143-2219-0 (alk. paper) DDC 331.6/396073
B 19
1. Afro-American automobile industry workers -
Biography. 2. Afro-American communists - Biography.
3. International Union, United Automobile, Aerospace
and Agricultural Implement Workers of America -
History. 4. United States - Race relations. I. Series. II.
Series: African American life series. III. Title.
HD8039.A82 U633 1989
                     NYPL [Sc D 89-563]

DENBY, CHARLES.
Denby, Charles. Indignant heart . Boston ,
c1978. 295 p. : ISBN 0-89608-092-7 DDC
331.6/3/960730774340924 B 19
HD8039.A82 U633 1978
                     NYPL [Sc D 88-853]

Denga, Daniel I. Guidance and counselling for
the 6-3-3-4 system of education / Daniel I.
Denga. Calabar [Nigeria] : Wusen Press, 1983
(1986 printing) 159 p. : ill. ; 22 cm. Bibliography:
p. 153-159. ISBN 978-228-192-1
1. Personnel service in education - Nigeria. I. Title.
                     NYPL [Sc D 88-6]

Deniel, Raymond. Jeunes intellectuels en
recherche . Abidjan , c1982. 67 p. :
                     NYPL [Sc D 88-925]

Dennis, Ferdinand, 1956- Behind the frontlines :
journey into Afro-Britain / Ferdinand Dennis.
London : V. Gollancz, 1988. xv, 216 p. ; 21
cm. ISBN 0-575-04098-X
1. Blacks - Great Britain - Social conditions. 2. West
Indians - Great Britain - Social conditions. 3. Great

Britain - Race relations. I. Title.
NYPL *[JLD 89-210]*

Dennis, John Alfred. The René Maran story : the life and times of a Black Frenchman, colonial administrator, novelist and social critic, 1887-1960 / by John Alfred Dennis, Jr. Ann Arbor, Mich. : University Microfilms International, c1987. viii, 275 p. : ill., maps, ports. ; 22 cm. Thesis (Ph. D.)-Stanford University, 1986. Bibliography: p. 253-265.
1. Maran, René, 1887-1960. 2. Authors, French - 20th century - Biography. I. Title.
NYPL *[Sc D 89-292]*

Dennis, Wesley. Arundel, Jocelyn, 1930- Mighty Mo . New York , 1961. 124 p. :
NYPL *[Sc E 88-228]*

DEONTOLOGY. see ETHICS.

DEPENDENCIES. see COLONIES.

Dépestre, René. Hadriana dans tous mes rêves : roman / René Dépestre. [Paris] : Galliamrd, c1988. 195 p. ; 21 cm. ISBN 2-07-071255-9
1. Zombiism - Haiti - Jacmel - Fiction. 2. Voodooism - Haiti - Jacmel - Fiction. 3. Jacmel (Haiti) - Fiction. I. Title.
NYPL *[Sc D 88-1004]*

Depoimentos de escravos brasileiros /. Maestri Filho, Mário José. São Paulo , c1988. 88 p. ;
ISBN 85-27-40039-1
NYPL *[Sc D 88-1379]*

Depons, François Raymond Joseph. see Pons, François Raymond Joseph de, 1751-1812.

Des apparitions à Kibeho . Maindron, Gabriel. Paris , c1984. 243 p., [4] p. of plates : ISBN 2-86839-021-8 : DDC 232.91/7/0967571 19
BT660.K52 M35 1984 *NYPL* *[Sc E 88-516]*

Des cauris au marché . Calame-Griaule, Geneviève. [Paris] , c1987. 293 p., [12] p. of plates :
NYPL *[Sc E 88-327]*

Des troupeaux et des femmes . Tubiana, Marie José. Paris , 1985. 390 p., [16] p. of plates :
ISBN 2-85802-554-9 *NYPL* *[Sc E 88-217]*

Deschamps, Hubert Jules, 1900- Ganiage, Jean. L'Afrique au XXe siècle /. Paris , 1966. 908 p. :
NYPL *[Sc D 88-236]*

La Descolonización de Africa : Africa austral y el Cuerno de Africa . Décolonisation de l'Afrique. Spanish. Barcelona , Paris , 1983. 197 p. ;
ISBN 92-3-301834-2 (Unesco)
NYPL *[Sc D 88-590]*

A descriptive and chronological bibliography (1950-1982) of the work of Edward Kamau Brathwaite /. Brathwaite, Doris Monica, d.1986. London , 1988. ix, 97 p. ;
ISBN 0-901241-84-9 (cased) DDC 016.810 19
NYPL *[Sc D 89-402]*

Desegregation in Catholic schools in the archdiocese of Chicago, 1964-1974, including a case study of a Catholic high school [microform] /. Moses, James Charles. 1977 288 leaves. *NYPL* *[Sc Micro R-4699]*

DESERTIFICATION - CONGRESSES.
Desertification in extremely arid environments /. [Stuttgart] , 1980. 203 p., [1] folded leaf of plates : ISBN 3-88028-095-9 (pbk.) DDC 551.4 19
GB611 .D44 *NYPL* *[JFL 74-410 Bd. 95]*

Desertification in extremely arid environments / edited by Wolfgang Meckelein. [Stuttgart] : Geographisches Institut der Universität Stuttgart, 1980. 203 p., [1] folded leaf of plates : ill. ; 24 cm. (Stuttgarter geographische Studien, 0343-7906 . Bd. 95 95) On t.p.: International Geographical Union. Working Group on Desertification In and Around Arid Lands. Subgroup Extremely Arid Environments. "Special issue on the occasion of the 24th International Geographical Congress Japan 1980."--p. opposite T.p. Includes bibliographical references. ISBN 3-88028-095-9 (pbk.) DDC 551.4 19
1. Desertification - Congresses. 2. Arid regions - Congresses. I. Meckelein, Wolfgang. II. International Geographical Congress. III. International Geographical Union. Working Group on Desertification In and Around Arid Lands. Subgroup Extremely Arid Environments. IV. Series.
GB611 .D44 *NYPL* *[JFL 74-410 Bd. 95]*

DESERTIFICATION - NIGERIA, NORTHERN.
Mortimore, M. J., 1937- Adapting to drought . Cambridge , New York , 1989. xxii, 299 p. :

ISBN 0-521-32312-6 DDC 333.73 19
HC1055.Z7 N6755 1988
NYPL *[Sc E 89-191]*

DESIGN, DECORATIVE - EGYPTIAN INFLUENCES.
Menten, Theodore. Ancient Egyptian cut and use stencils /. New York , 1978. [32] leaves :
ISBN 0-486-23626-9 : *NYPL* *[Sc F 88-366]*

Désir, Harlem, 1959- Touche pas à mon pote / Harlem Désir. Paris : B. Grasset, [c1985] 148 p. ; 19 cm. ISBN 2-246-36421-3 : DDC 323.42/3/06044 19
1. Désir, Harlem, 1959-. 2. S.O.S. racisme (Organization : France). 3. Racism - France. 4. France - Race relations. I. Title.
DC34 .D47 1985 *NYPL* *[Sc C 88-305]*

DÉSIR, HARLEM, 1959-
Désir, Harlem, 1959- Touche pas à mon pote /. Paris [c1985] 148 p. ; ISBN 2-246-36421-3 : DDC 323.42/3/06044 19
DC34 .D47 1985 *NYPL* *[Sc C 88-305]*

Desruisseaux, Jacques. La structure foncière de la Martinique [microform] / Jacques Desruisseaux. [Montréal] : Centre de recherches caraïbes, Université de Montréal, [1975] 49 p. : map ; 22 cm. Bibliography: p. [47] Microfiche. New York : New York Public Library, 1981. 1 microfiche : negative ; 11 x 15 cm. (FSN 31,460)
1. Land tenure - Martinique. I. Title.
HD459.Z8 M372 *NYPL* *[*XME-7721]*

Dessa Rose /. Williams, Sherley Anne, 1944- New York , c1986. 236 p. ; ISBN 0-688-05113-8 : DDC 813/.54 19
PS3573.I45546 D47 1986
NYPL *[JFD 86-8841]*

Dessalines. Placoly, Vincent, 1946- Dessalines, ou, La passion de l'indépendance . Ciudad de La Habana , c1983. 96 p. ;
MLCS 86/2062 (P) *NYPL* *[JFC 87-478]*

Dessalines, ou, La passion de l'indépendance . Placoly, Vincent, 1946- Ciudad de La Habana , c1983. 96 p. ;
MLCS 86/2062 (P) *NYPL* *[JFC 87-478]*

Destiny . Ali, Hauwa. Enugu , 1988. 101 p. ;
ISBN 978-233-583-5 *NYPL* *[Sc C 89-151]*

DESTITUTION. see POVERTY.

DETENTION OF PERSONS - SOUTH AFRICA - CONGRESSES.
Children of resistance . London , 1988. vii, 146 p. ; *NYPL* *[Sc D 88-1286]*

Detroit Free Press. Blacks in Detroit . Detroit , 1980. 111 p. : *NYPL* *[Sc G 88-15]*

Detroit. Great Cities Program for School Improvement. Writers' Committee.
A day with Debbie / Writers' Committee of the Great Cities School Improvement Program of the Detroit Public Schools, Gertrude Whipple, chairman ; illustrated by Ruth Ives. Chicago : Follett Educational Corp., c1964. 55 p. : col. ill. ; 24 cm. (City schools reading program) "The fourth preprimer of the City Schools Reading Program."--p. [56] SCHOMBURG CHILDREN'S COLLECTION.
1. Primers - 1950-1975. I. Ives, Ruth. II. Schomburg Children's Collection. III. Title.
NYPL *[Sc E 89-178]*

Laugh with Larry / Writers' Committee of the Great Cities School Improvement Program of the Detroit Public Schools ; illustrated by Ruth Ives. Chicago : Follett, c1962. 47 p. : col. ill. ; 24 cm. (City schools reading program) Preprimer. SCHOMBURG CHILDREN'S COLLECTION.
1. Primers - 1950-1975. I. Ives, Rwth. II. Schomburg Children's Collection. III. Title.
NYPL *[Sc E 87-268]*

Play with Jimmy / Writers' Committee of the Great Cities School Improvement Program of the Detroit Public Schools, Gertrude Whipple, chairman ; illustrated by Ruth Ives. Chicago : Follett, c1962. 23, [1] p. : chiefly col. ill. ; 24 cm. (City schools reading program) Preprimer. "This is the first preprimer of the City Schools Reading Program." --p. [24].
1. Primers - 1950-1975. I. Ives, Ruth. II. Title.
NYPL *[Sc E 88-237]*

Detroit. Great Cities Program for School Improvement. Writes' Committee.
Fun with David / Writers' Committee of the Great Cities School Improvement Program of the Detroit Public Schools ; illustrated by Ruth Ives.

Chicago : Follett, c1962. 31 p.: col. ill. ; 24 cm. (City schools reading program) Preprimer. SCHOMBURG CHILDREN'S COLLECTION.
1. Primers - 1950-1975. I. Ives, Ruth. II. Schomburg Children's Collection. III. Title.
NYPL *[Sc E 89-40]*

DETROIT (MICH.) - ECONOMIC CONDITIONS.
Detroit, race and uneven development /. Philadelphia , 1987. xii, 317 p. : ISBN 0-87722-485-4 (alk. paper) DDC 305.8/009774/34 19
HC108.D6 D47 1987 *NYPL* *[Sc E 88-205]*

DETROIT (MICH.) - GENEALOGY.
Echols, James, 1932- The Echols of Detroit . [S. l.] 1985 [Port Jefferson Sta., N.Y. : McPrint Graphics Center] v. :
NYPL *[Sc F 88-97]*

DETROIT (MICH.) - POLITICS AND GOVERNMENT.
Rich, Wilbur C. Coleman Young and Detroit politics . Detroit, Mich. , 1989. 298 p. : ISBN 0-8143-2093-7 DDC 977.4/34043/0924 B 19
F474.D453 Y677 1989 *NYPL* *[Sc E 89-208]*

DETROIT (MICH.) - RACE RELATIONS.
Detroit, race and uneven development /. Philadelphia , 1987. xii, 317 p. : ISBN 0-87722-485-4 (alk. paper) DDC 305.8/009774/34 19
HC108.D6 D47 1987 *NYPL* *[Sc E 88-205]*

DETROIT (MICH.) - SOCIAL CONDITIONS.
Detroit, race and uneven development /. Philadelphia , 1987. xii, 317 p. : ISBN 0-87722-485-4 (alk. paper) DDC 305.8/009774/34 19
HC108.D6 D47 1987 *NYPL* *[Sc E 88-205]*

Detroit public sites named for Blacks / [compiled by Rosemary Clemons... et al.] ; edited by Sara E. Hunter ... [et al.]. [Detroit, Mich.] : Fred Hart Williams Genealogical Society, c1987. xii, 62 p. ; 22 cm. Bibliography: p. 60-61.
1. Street names - Michigan - Detroit. 2. Public buildings - Michigan - Detroit. 3. Public buildings - Michigan - Detroit - Names. I. Clemons, Rosemary. *NYPL* *[Sc D 88-1183]*

Detroit, race and uneven development / Joe T. Darden ... [et al.]. Philadelphia : Temple University Press, 1987. xii, 317 p. : maps ; 24 cm. (Comparative American cities) Includes bibliographical references and index. ISBN 0-87722-485-4 (alk. paper) DDC 305.8/009774/34 19
1. Afro-Americans - Michigan - Detroit - Economic conditions. 2. Afro-Americans - Housing - Michigan - Detroit. 3. Urban renewal - Michigan - Detroit. 4. Detroit (Mich.) - Economic conditions. 5. Detroit (Mich.) - Race relations. 6. Detroit (Mich.) - Social conditions. I. Darden, Joe T. II. Series.
HC108.D6 D47 1987 *NYPL* *[Sc E 88-205]*

DETROIT - RACE RELATIONS - HISTORY.
Hatchett, Shirley. Black racial attitude change in Detroit, 1968-1976 [microform] /. 1982. 171 leaves. *NYPL* *[Sc Micro R-4682]*

DETROIT - RIOT, 1943.
Brown, Earl Louis, 1900- Why race riots [microform]? [New York] 1944. cover-title, 31, [1] p.
F574.D4 B58 *NYPL* *[Sc Micro R-3541]*

Dettlinger, Chet. The list / by Chet Dettlinger with Jeff Prugh. 1st ed. Atlanta : Philmay Enterprises, c1983. 516 p., [4] p. of plates : ill. ; 24 cm. ISBN 0-942894-04-9 : DDC 364.1/523/09758231 19
1. Murder - Georgia - Atlanta - Case studies. 2. Victims of crimes - Georgia - Atlanta - Case studies. 3. Afro-American children - Georgia - Atlanta - Case studies. 4. Criminal justice, Administration of - Georgia - Atlanta - Case studies. 5. Criminal investigation - Georgia - Atlanta - Case studies. I. Prugh, Jeff. II. Title.
HV6534.A7 D47 1983 *NYPL* *[Sc E 86-40]*

Deutsches Institut für Entwicklungspolitik. Occasional papers. see Deutsches Institut für Entwicklungspolitik. Schriften.

Schriften.
(Nr. 62. 62) Perspectives of independent development in Southern Africa . Berlin , 1980. xiv, 183 p. : DDC 338.9688 19
HC910 .P47 *NYPL* *[JLE 82-36]*

Deutsches Ledermuseum. Afrika / Deutsches Ledermuseum. Offenbach am Main : Das Museum, 1988. 227 p. : ill. (some col.) ; 21 x 22 cm. (Katalog . 3) Bibliography: p. 222-225. ISBN 3-87280-042-6
1. Leather work - Africa - Exhibitions. I. Series: Katalog (Deutsches Ledermuseum) , 3. II. Title.
NYPL [Sc D 89-506]

Deutsches Übersee-Institut. Institut für Afrika-Kunde (Hamburg, Germany). Bibliothek. Verzeichnis der Zeitschriftenbestände . Hamburg , 1986. 100 p. ;
NYPL [Sc F 88-209]

Deux études sur les relations entre groupes ethniques. Spanish. Dos estudios sobre las relaciones entre grupos étnicos en Africa : Senegal, República Unida de Tanzania / F.A. Diarra ... [et al.].1a edición. Barcelona : Serbal ; [Paris] : Unesco, 1982. 174 p. ; 20 cm. (Colección de temas africanos . 8) Translation of: Deux études sur les relations entre groupes ethniques. Includes bibliographical references. "Bibliografía seleccionada": p. 174. ISBN 84-85000-41-9
1. Ethnology - Senegal. 2. Ethnology - Tanzania. 3. Senegal - Race relations. 4. Tanzania - Race relations. I. Diarra, Fatoumata Agnés. II. Unesco. III. Series.
DT549.42 .D4818 1982
NYPL [Sc D 88-651]

Devaney, John. Bo Jackson : a star for all seasons / by John Devaney. New York : Walker and Co., 1988. 110 p. : ill. ; 24 cm. Includes index. A biography of the first major leaguer to play in both pro baseball and football. ISBN 0-8027-6818-0 DDC 796.332/092/4 B 92 19
1. Jackson, Bo - Juvenile literature. 2. Baseball players - United States - Biography - Juvenile literature. 3. Football players - United States - Biography - Juvenile literature. 4. Afro-American baseball players - Biography - Juvenile literature. 5. Afro-American football players - Biography - Juvenile literature. I. Title.
GV865.J28 D48 1988 *NYPL [Sc E 89-12]*

Devaux-Minié, Hélène. Himes, Chester B., 1909- Faut être nègre pour faire ça ... /. [Paris, France] , c1986. 223 p. ; ISBN 2-86705-064-2
NYPL [Sc D 88-1447]

DEVELOPING COUNTRIES.
Kullas, Ulrike. Lernen von der Dritten Welt? . Saarbrücken , Fort Lauderdale , 1982. 174 p. : ISBN 3-88156-233-8 *NYPL [Sc D 89-339]*

DEVELOPING COUNTRIES - DICTIONARIES.
Kurian, George Thomas. The encyclopedia of the Third World /. New York, N.Y. , 1987. 3 v. (xxix-2342 p.) : ISBN 0-8160-1118-4 (set) DDC 909/.09724 19
HC59.7 .K87 1987 *NYPL [Sc F 88-324]*

DEVELOPING COUNTRIES - ECONOMIC CONDITIONS.
Chiaka, Ralph C. Morality of development aid to the Third World . Rome , 1985. ix, 215 p. :
NYPL [Sc E 88-96]

Goffaux, J. Problèmes de développement . [Kinshasa, Zaire?] , 1986. 223 p. ;
HD83 .G65 1986 *NYPL [Sc D 89-593]*

Hoeven, Rolph van der. Planning for basic needs . Aldershot , c1988. xvii, 380 p. : ISBN 0-566-05680-1 : DDC 330.9172/4 19
HC59.7 *NYPL [Sc D 89-37]*

DEVELOPING COUNTRIES - ECONOMIC CONDITIONS - BOOK REVIEWS.
Heinecke, P. Twenty-two reviews /. Kaduna, [Nigeria] [1986?] 69 p. ;
NYPL [Sc E 88-284]

DEVELOPING COUNTRIES - FOREIGN RELATIONS - UNITED STATES.
Lake, Anthony. Third World radical regimes . New York , 1985. 54 p. : ISBN 0-87124-099-8
NYPL [ILH 86-805]

DEVELOPING COUNTRIES - IMPRINTS - BIBLIOGRAPHY.
Gorman, G. E. Guide to current national bibliographies in the Third World /. London , New York , c1987. xx, 372 p. ; ISBN 0-905450-34-5 *NYPL [Sc E 88-474]*

DEVELOPING COUNTRIES - INDUSTRIES.
Coote, Belinda. The hunger crop . Oxford [England] , 1987. v, 124 p. ; ISBN 0-85598-081-8 *NYPL [Sc D 88-1446]*

DEVELOPING COUNTRIES - LITERATURE.
Dorsinville, Max, 1943- Solidarités . Montréal, Québec, Canada , 1988. xv, 196 p. ; ISBN 2-920862-09-X *NYPL [Sc D 89-484]*

DEVELOPING COUNTRIES - POLITICS AND GOVERNMENT.
Democracy in developing countries /. Boulder, Colo. , 1988- v. : ISBN 1-555-87039-2 (v. 2) : DDC 320.9173/4 19
D883 .D45 1988 *NYPL [Sc E 88-201]*

DEVELOPING COUNTRIES - SOCIAL CONDITIONS.
Bouzar, Wadi, 1938- La culture en question /. Alger , Paris , c1982. 187 p. ; ISBN 2-903871-11-6 (pbk.) : DDC 306/.0965 19
HN980 .B68 1982 *NYPL [JLC 84-337]*

Fisher, Maxine P., 1948- Women in the Third World /. New York , 1989. 176 p. : ISBN 0-531-10666-7 DDC 305.4/09172/4 19
HQ1870.9 .F57 1989 *NYPL [Sc E 89-223]*

DEVELOPING COUNTRIES - SOCIAL POLICY.
Women, state, and ideology . Basingstoke, Hampshire , c1987. xii, 245 p. : ISBN 0-333-41389-X *NYPL [JLD 87-2346]*

Developing models/techniques in the teaching of English as a second foreign language in senior secondary schools in the Congo /. Mombod, Josephine Ntinou. Nairobi , 1983. ii, 67 leaves ; DDC 428/.007/126724 19
PE1068.C74 M67 1983 *NYPL [Sc F 88-200]*

Development in college life. Wesley, Charles H., 1891- The history of Alpha Phi Alpha . Chicago , 1981, c1929. xiv, 567 p. :
NYPL [Sc D 89-135]

The development of black theater in America . Sanders, Leslie Catherine, 1944- Baton Rouge , c1988. 252 p. ; ISBN 0-8071-1328-X DDC 812/.009/896073 19
PS338.N4 S26 1987
NYPL [MWED 88-1125]

The development of group identification in Black Americans [microform] /. McCullough, Wayne Regan. 1982. ix, 84 leaves.
NYPL [Sc Micro R-4802]

The development of Jamaican popular music with special reference to the music of Bob Marley . White, Garth. Kingston , 1982. 49 p. ; DDC 016.78/042/097292 19
ML120.J35 5 1982 *NYPL [Sc F 87-61]*

Development of management education in Nigeria / edited by Pita N.O. Ejiofor. Ikeja, Nigeria : Centre for Management Development in collaboration with Nigerian Association of Schools of Management Education and Training (NASMET), 1985. 555 p. : ill. ; 24 cm. "The papers in this book were presented during the Third Annual Conference of the Nigerian Association of Schools of Management Education and Training...held in Enugu in March 1982..."--Preface. Includes bibliographical references.
1. Management - Study and teaching - Nigeria - Congresses. 2. Management - Nigeria - Congresses. 3. Business education - Nigeria - Congresses. 4. Africanization - Nigeria - Congresses. I. Ejiofor, Pita N. O. II. Centre for Management Development, Lagos. III. Nigerian Association of Schools of Management Education and Training. Conference (3rd : 1982 : Enugu, Nigeria). *NYPL [Sc E 89-161]*

Development of special education in Nigeria / edited by Okechukwu C. Abosi. Ibadan : Fountains Books, 1988. ix, 132 p. ; 24 cm. "Papers in honour of Peter O. Mba and Samuel C.Osunkiyesi." Includes bibliographies. ISBN 978-267-703-5
1. Mba, Peter O. 2. Osunkiyesi, Samuel C. 3. Special education - Nigeria. I. Abosi, Okechukwu C.
NYPL [Sc E 89-70]

The development of special education in Tanzania / edited by C. Kalugula ... [et al.] Dar es Salaam, Tanzania : Institute of Education, c1984. 81 p. : ill., map ; 21 cm. Includes bibliographical references. ISBN 997-661-002-5
1. Special education - Tanzania. I. Kalugula, C.
NYPL [Sc C 89-127]

DEVELOPMENT, RURAL. see RURAL DEVELOPMENT.

Development studies .
(working paper no. 15) McCartan, P. J. (Patrick John) The demand for skilled labour in the

Border, Ciskei, southern Transkei regional economy /. Grahamstown [1983] 50, xxii p. : ISBN 0-86810-058-7 (pbk.) : DDC 331.12/3/0968792 19
HD5842.A6 M33 1983 *NYPL [Sc F 88-356]*

(working paper no. 16) De Wet, C. J. Rural communities in transition . Grahamstown [1983] iii, 113 p., [6] leaves of plates : ISBN 0-86810-101-X (pbk.) DDC 307.7/2/0968 19
HD2130.5.Z9 H653 1983
NYPL [Sc F 88-328]

(working paper no. 20) Atkinson, Doreen. The search for power and legitimacy in Black urban areas . Grahamstown [South Africa] [1984] 38, xix, v, [1] p. ; ISBN 0-86810-114-1 (pbk.) : DDC 320.8/0968 19
JS7533.A8 A85 1984 *NYPL [Sc F 88-355]*

(working paper no. 37) Davies, William J. Fest-quest 87, . Grahamstown, South Africa , 1988. iv, 161 p. : ISBN 0-86810-165-6
NYPL [Sc F 88-267]

(working papers no. 20) Atkinson, Doreen. The search for power and legitimacy in Black urban areas . Grahamstown [South Africa] [1984] 38, xix, v, [1] p. ; ISBN 0-86810-114-1 (pbk.) : DDC 320.8/0968 19
JS7533.A8 A85 1984 *NYPL [Sc F 88-355]*

(Working Paper no. 21) Whisson, Michael G., 1937- Cherchez la femme. Grahamstown [South Africa] , 1985. 90 p. [3] leaves of plates : ISBN 0-86810-125-7 *NYPL [Sc F 87-433]*

Development studies working paper .
(no. 14) Gilmour, J. D. The demand for tertiary education in the East London metropolitan area . Grahamstown [South Africa] , 1983. 1 v. (various pagings) ; ISBN 0-86810-056-0
NYPL [Sc F 87-429]

(no. 17) Bekker, S. B. Perspectives on rural development in Ciskei, 1983 /. Grahamstown [1984] 52 p. : ISBN 0-86810-103-6 (pbk.) : DDC 307.1/4/0968792 19
HN801.C57 B45 1984 *NYPL [Sc F 88-325]*

(no. 18) Palmer, Robin. Blood donation in the Border region. Grahamstown [South Africa] , 1984. 183 p. : ISBN 0-86810-112-5
NYPL [Sc F 87-432]

(no. 2) Bekker, S. B. Socio-economic survey of the Amatola Basin . Grahamstown [South Africa] Institute of Social and Economic Rrsearch, 1981. 58, xxxxiv p. : ISBN 0-86810-073-0 *NYPL [Sc F 87-430]*

(no. 22) Davies, W. J. A review of issues related to planning and development in Grahamstown . Grahamstown [South Africa] , 1986. 114 p. : ISBN 0-86810-130-3
NYPL [Sc F 87-431]

(no. 23) Roux, Andre, 1954- Voices from Rini . Grahamstown, South Africa , 1986. 107 p. ; ISBN 0-86810-131-1 *NYPL [Sc F 88-216]*

(no. 37) Davies, William J. Fest-quest 87, . Grahamstown, South Africa , 1988. iv, 161 p. : ISBN 0-86810-165-6 *NYPL [Sc F 88-267]*

Développement économique pour Haïti /. Dominique, Hilaire. [S.l.] 1987. 51 p. ;
NYPL [Sc D 88-187]

Deverre, Christian. Enjeux fonciers dan la Caraibe, en Amérique centrale et à la Réunion. . Paris , c1987. 232 p. : ISBN 2-7380-0003-7 *NYPL [Sc E 88-246]*

The devil is white /. Umukoro, G. Dean. Kaduna, Nigeria , 1985. 161 p. ; *NYPL [Sc C 88-177]*

DEVIL (ISLAM)
Dopamu, P. Adelumo. ÈSÙ . Nigeria , 1986. 99 p. ; ISBN 978-253-014-X
NYPL [Sc D 88-1375]

Le devoir électoral et les prochaines elections législatives [microform] /. Dévot, Justin, 1857-1920. [Port-au-Prince] , 1902. 12 p. ;
NYPL [Sc Micro F-11,001]

Devonish, Hubert. Language and liberation : Creole language politics in the Caribbean / by Hubert Devonish. London : Karia, 1986. 157 p. ; 23 cm. Bibliography: p. 149-157. ISBN 0-946918-27-9 (pbk) DDC 417/.2 19
1. Creole dialects - Political aspects - Caribbean Area. I. Title.
PM7834.C3 *NYPL [Sc D 88-512]*

Dévot, Justin, 1857-1920. Le devoir électoral et les prochaines elections législatives [microform] / [Justin Dérot] [Port-au-Prince] : Impr. Mme F. Smith, 1902. 12 p. ; 21 cm. Microfiche. New York: FISHER COLLECTION.
1. Haiti - Politics and government - 1844-1915. I. Title.
NYPL [Sc Micro F-11,001]

DeWind, Josh.
[Aiding migration. French]
Aide à la migration : l'impact de l'assistance internationale à Haïti / Josh DeWind, David Kinley III.1st ed. Montréal, Québec, Canada : CIDIHCA, 1988. 216 p. : map ; 22 cm.
Translation of: Aiding migration. Bibliography: p. [187]-207.
1. Economic assistance - Haiti. 2. Corruption (in politics) - Haiti. 3. Haiti - Emigration and immigration - Economic aspects. 4. Haiti - Economic policy. I. Kinley, David H. II. Title. **NYPL [Sc D 89-441]**

Dhanjoo N. Ghista. see Ghista, Dhanjoo N.

DHO LUO (AFRICAN PEOPLE) see LUO (AFRICAN PEOPLE)

Dhondy, Farrukh, 1944- Come to Mecca : and other stories / Farrukh Dhondy. London : Fontana Lions, 1978 (1983 [printing]) 125 p. ; 18 cm. Originally published: Collins ; Fontana, 1978.
ISBN 0-00-672501-5 (pbk) : DDC 823 19
1. Minority youth - England - Fiction. I. Title.
NYPL [Sc C 88-310]

Di Chiara, Catherine Eve. Le dossier Haïti : un pays en péril / Catherine Eve di Chiara ; préface de Léopold Sédar Senghor. Paris : Tallandier, c1988. 480 p., xxiv p. of plates : ill., ports. ; 22 cm. (Dossier) Bibliography: p. 461-[475].
ISBN 2-235-01778-9
1. Haiti - History. 2. Haiti - Social conditions. 3. Haiti - Economic conditions. I. Title.
F1938 .D52x 1988 **NYPL [Sc D 89-394]**

Di Grazia, Thomas. Clifton, Lucille, 1936- My friend Jacob /. New York , c1980. [32] p. :
ISBN 0-525-35487-5 DDC [E]
PZ7.C6224 Myk 1980 **NYPL [Sc F 88-376]**

Dia, Malick. L'impossible compromis / Malick Dia. Abidjan : Nouvelles éditions africaines, c1979. 102 p. ; 21 cm. ISBN 2-7236-0447-0
1. Senegal - Fiction. I. Title.
NYPL [Sc D 88-958]

Diabaté, Massa M. Le Lion à l'arc : récit épique / Massa Makan Diabaté. Paris : Hatier, 1986. 128 p. ; 18 cm. (Collection Monde noir poche. 40)
ISBN 2-218-07616-0
1. Keita, Soundiata, 1255. I. Title. II. Series.
NYPL [Sc C 89-155]

Diabaté, Massa Makan. see Diabaté, Massa M.

Diabété, Massa Makan. see Diabaté, Massa M.

Diakité, Tidiane. L'Afrique malade d'elle-même / Tidiane Diakité. Paris : Karthala, c1986. 162 p. ; 22 cm. (Les Afriques) Includes bibliographical references. ISBN 2-86537-158-1 DDC 960/.32 19
1. Africa - Politics and government - 1960-. 2. Africa - Moral conditions. 3. Africa - Economic conditions. I. Series: Collection Les Afriques. II. Title.
DT31 .D5 1986 **NYPL [Sc D 88-1351]**

The dialectics of oppression in Zaire /. Schatzberg, Michael G. Bloomington , c1988. x, 193 p., [1] p. of plates : ISBN 0-253-31703-7 DDC 323.4/9/0967513 19
JC599.Z282 L577 1988 **NYPL [Sc E 88-512]**

DIALECTS. see LANGUAGE AND LANGUAGES; CREOLE DIALECTS.

Dialembonkebi, Diebo Makani-Ma-Nsi. Le droit de l'homme a l'existence : au regard de la métaphysique négro-africaine / Dialembonkebi Diebo Makani-Ma-Nsi. Kinshasa, Zaire : Editions Lokole, c1988. 36 p. ; 21 cm.
I. Title. **NYPL [Sc D 89-220]**

Diallo, Amadou. La mort de Diallo Telli : 1er secrétaire général de l'O.U.A. / Amadou Diallo ; préface de Siradiou Diallo. Paris : Editions Karthala, 1983. 154 p., [8] p. of plates : ill., ports ; 22 cm. Includes: "Une liste de 'disparus' en Guinée" -- p. 139-154. ISBN 2-86537-072-0
1. Telli, Diallo, 1925-1977. 2. Diallo, Amadou. 3. Political prisoners - Guinea. I. Title.
NYPL [Sc D 88-316]

DIALLO, AMADOU.
Diallo, Amadou. La mort de Diallo Telli .

Paris , 1983. 154 p., [8] p. of plates : ISBN 2-86537-072-0 **NYPL [Sc D 88-316]**

Diallo, Nafissatou, 1941- Fary, princess of Tiali / Nafissatou Diallo ; translated by Ann Woollcombe ; edited by Barbara Hetzner Scherer ; design by W.W. Weems. 1st English language ed. Washington, D.C. : Three Continents Press, c1987. xi, 106 p. : ill., port. ; 22 cm. ISBN 0-89410-411-X
1. Wolofs - Fiction. 2. Senegal - Fiction. I. Scherer, Barbara Hetzner. II. Title.
NYPL [Sc D 88-1366]

Dialo, Amadou. Une phonologie du wolof / par Amadou Dialo. [Dakar] : Centre de linguistique appliquée de Dakar, 1981. 60 leaves ; 30 cm. (Les Langues nationales au Sénégal) French and Wolof. "No 78." Bibliography: p. 55-57.
1. Wolof language - Phonology. I. Centre de linguistique appliquée de Dakar. II. Title.
NYPL [Sc F 86-167]

Dialog Dritte Welt .
(42) Mwangi, Meja, 1948- [Carcase for hounds. German.] Wie ein Aas für Hunde . Bornheim-Merten , 1987. 173 p. ; ISBN 3-88977-136-X **NYPL [Sc C 88-148]**

Diamond, Larry. Class, ethnicity and democracy in Nigeria : the failure of the first republic / Larry Diamond. Basingstoke : Macmillan, c1988. xiii, 376 p. : ill. ; 22 cm. Includes bibliography and index. ISBN 0-333-39435-6 : DDC 966.9/05 19
1. Nigeria - Politics and government - 1960-1975. I. Title.
DT515.832 **NYPL [Sc D 88-1310]**

Diamond, Larry Jay. Democracy in developing countries /. Boulder, Colo. , 1988- v. : ISBN 1-555-87039-2 (v. 2) : DDC 320.9173/4 19
D883 .D45 1988 **NYPL [Sc E 88-201]**

Diario de Pernambuco : arte e natureza no. 2° Reinado / José Antônio Gonsalves de Mello. Recife : Editora Massangana, [1985]. 256 p. : ill. ; 23 cm. (Série Documentos (Fundação Joaquim Nabuco) . 26) Includes bibliographical references.
ISBN 85-7019-094-8
1. Diario de Pernambuco. 2. Decoration and ornament - Brazil - Pernambuco - History - Sources. 3. Photography - Brazil - Pernambuco - History - Sources. 4. Horticulture - Brazil - Pernambuco - History - Sources. I. Series. **NYPL [Sc D 88-862]**

DIARIO DE PERNAMBUCO.
Diario de Pernambuco . Recife [1985]. 256 p. :
ISBN 85-7019-094-8 **NYPL [Sc D 88-862]**

Diarra, Fatoumata Agnés. Deux études sur les relations entre groupes ethniques. Spanish. Dos estudios sobre las relaciones entre grupos étnicos en Africa. Barcelona [Paris] , 1982. 174 p. ; ISBN 84-85000-41-9
DT549.42 .D4818 1982
NYPL [Sc D 88-651]

Díaz, Ramón. see Díaz Sánchez, Ramón.

Díaz Sánchez, Ramón.
[Mene. English]
Mene / Ramon Diaz Sanchez. Trinidad : [s.n., 193-?] (Trinidad : Multimedia Production Center, Faculty of Education, U.W.I.) 141 p. : map ; 21 cm. "A Venezuelan novel translated by Jesse Noel."
1. Trinidadians - Venezuela. 2. Cabimas (Venezuela) - Fiction. I. Title. **NYPL [Sc D 89-544]**

Dibeth, Véronique Carton. Manuel de conversation somali-français suivi d'un guide Dijibouti / Véronique Carton Dibeth. Paris : L'Harmattan, c1988. 80 p. : ill., maps ; 24 cm. ISBN 2-7384-0090-6
1. Somali language - Grammar. 2. Somali language - Conversation and phrase books - French. 3. Djibouti. I. Title. **NYPL [Sc E 88-536]**

Dibundu /. Van-Dúnem, Domingos. Lisbon [1988?] 84 p. ; **NYPL [Sc C 89-134]**

Dickens, Nathaniel A. The gospel Singer / Nathaniel A. Dickens. 1st ed. New York : Vantage Press, c1987. 187 p. ; 21 cm. "A Gunther Publications book." ISBN 0-533-07387-1
1. Afro-American Women - Fiction. I. Title.
NYPL [Sc D 88-1450]

DICKEY, SARAH A., 1838-1904.
Griffith, Helen. Dauntless in Mississippi . Northampton, Mass. , 1965. xii, 173 p. :
NYPL [Sc D 88-1111]

Dickson, Mora, 1918-
(ill) Appiah, Peggy. Tales of an Ashanti father /. Boston , 1989, c1967. 156 p. : ISBN 0-8070-8312-7 DDC 398.2/1/09667 19
PZ8.1.A647 Tal 1989 **NYPL [Sc E 89-87]**

The powerful bond : Hannah Kilham, 1774-1832 / by Mora Dickson. London : Dobson, 1980. 5-252 p. : ill., maps, ports. ; 23 cm. Maps on lining papers. Includes index. Bibliography: p. 242-244. ISBN 0-234-72103-0 : DDC 266/.963 B 19
1. Kilham, Hannah, 1774-1832. 2. Missionaries - Sierra Leone - Biography. 3. Missionaries - England - Biography. I. Title.
BV3625.S5 K393 1980 **NYPL [Sc D 87-37]**

The dictionary of contemporary politics of southern Africa /. Williams, Gwyneth, 1953- London , New York , 1988. xi, 339 p. : ISBN 0-415-00245-1 DDC 320.968/03 19
JQ2720.A127 W55 1988 **NYPL [Sc D 89-2]**

A dictionary of Muslim names /. Orie, S. L. Point à Pierre, Trinidad , 1984. 43 p. ;
NYPL [Sc D 88-946]

Dictionnaire français-yansi /. Wendo Nguma. Bandundu, République du Zaïre , 1986. 276 p. ;
NYPL [Sc F 88-318]

Dictionnaire kréol réunionné français /. Armand, Alain. Saint-André [1987?] lxiv, 399, xxxvii p. ; ISBN 2-907064-01-0 **NYPL [Sc C 88-345]**

Did you feed my cow? Burroughs, Margaret Taylor, 1917- (comp) Chicago [1969] 96 p.
ISBN 0-695-81960-7 DDC 398.8
PZ8.3.B958 Di5 **NYPL [Sc D 89-57]**

Die. see Deutsches Institut für Entwicklungspolitik.

Diederich, Bernard.
[Papa Doc. Spanish]
Papa Doc y los tontons Macoutes : la verdad sobre Haití / Bernard Diederich y Al Burt ; prefacio de Graham Greene ; traducción por Justo G. Beramendi.2a ed. Santo Domingo, República Dominicana : Fundación Cultural Dominicana, 1986. 393 p., [16] p. of plates : ill. ; 22 cm. Translation of: Papa Doc, the truth about Haiti today.
1. Duvalier, François, 1907-1971. 2. Haiti - History. I. Burt, Al. II. Title. **NYPL [Sc D 88-452]**

DIEGO MARTIN (TRINIDAD AND TOBAGO) - HISTORY.
De Verteuil, Anthony. A history of Diego Martin 1784-1884 /. Port of Spain, Trinidad , c1987. viii, 174 p., [96] p. of plates : ISBN 976-8054-10-7 **NYPL [Sc F 88-192]**

Diekmann, Miep. Padu is gek / Miep Diekmann ; met tekeningen van Jenny Dalenoord. Den Haag : H.P. Leopold, 1960. 120 p. ; 21 cm. SCHOMBURG CHILDREN'S COLLECTION.
1. Curaçao - Juvenile fiction. I. Schomburg Children's Collection. II. Title. **NYPL [Sc D 89-474]**

Diepen, Maria van. The National question in South Africa /. London , Atlantic Highlands, N.J. , 1988. 154 p. ; ISBN 0-86232-794-6 DDC 320.5/4/0968 19
DT763 .N35 1988 **NYPL [JLD 88-4552]**

Dierks, Friedrich. Evangelium im afrikanischen Kontext : interkulturelle Kommunikation bei den Tswana / Friedrich Dierks. Gütersloh : Gütersloher Verlagshaus G. Mohn, c1986. 206 p. : ill. ; 23 cm. (Missionswissenschaftliche Forschungen, 0076-9428 . Bd. 19) A slight revision of the author's thesis (doctoral--University of Pretoria, 1982) presented under the title: Die interkulturelle Kommunikation der christlichen Botschaft.
Bibliography: p. 196-206. ISBN 3-579-00239-2 DDC 266/.0089963 19
1. Tswana (African people) - Religion. 2. Communication (Theology). I. Title. II. Series.
BL2480.T76 D54 1986 **NYPL [Sc D 88-879]**

DIET - AFRICA - CONGRESSES.
Food for Africa . [Lusaka?] [1985?] 68 p., [3] p. of plates :
TX360.A26 F67 1985 **NYPL [Sc F 89-40]**

DIET - KENYA.
Becker, Barbara. Wildpflanzen in der Ernährung der Bevölkerung afrikanischer Trockengebiete . Göttingen , 1984. iv, 341 p. :
NYPL [Sc D 88-682]

DIET - SENEGAL.
Becker, Barbara. Wildpflanzen in der Ernährung der Bevölkerung afrikanischer Trockengebiete .

Göttingen , 1984. iv, 341 p. :
NYPL [Sc D 88-682]

Dieterlen, H. Mabille, A. (Adolphe), 1836-1894.
Southern Sotho-English dictionary /. Morija,
Lesotho , 1950 (1974 printing) xvi, 445 p. ;
PL8689.4 .M33 1974 NYPL [Sc D 89-289]

DIETING. see REDUCING.

Dieu dans le vaudou haïtien /. Hurbon, Laënnec.
Port-au-Prince, Haïti , 1987. 268 p. ; DDC
299/.67 19
BL2490 .H87 1987 NYPL [Sc D 89-366]

Différence & identité . Fonkoué, Jean. Paris ,
c1985. 202 p. : ISBN 2-903871-46-9 : DDC
301/.096 19
HM22.A4 F66 1985 NYPL [Sc D 88-1151]

Différence et identité. Fonkoué, Jean.
Différence & identité . Paris , c1985. 202 p. :
ISBN 2-903871-46-9 : DDC 301/.096 19
HM22.A4 F66 1985 NYPL [Sc D 88-1151]

A different kind of Christmas /. Haley, Alex.
New York , 1988. 101 p. ; ISBN 0-385-26043-1 :
DDC 813/.54 19
PS3558.A3575 D54 1988
NYPL [Sc C 89-38]

Diggs, Charles C. Report of Special Study
Mission to Southern Africa, August 10-30,
1969/ by Charles C. Diggs, Lester L. Wolff.
Washington : U. S. G.P.O., 1969. vi, 179 p. :
maps ; 24 cm. (91st Congress, 1st session. House
report no. 91-610) "Pursuant to H. Res. 143 authorizing
the Committee on Foreign Affairs to conduct thorough
studies and investigations of all matters coming within
the jurisdiction of the Committee." DDC
301.29'68'073
*1. Africa, Southern - Relations - United States. 2.
United States - Relations - Africa, Southern. I. Wolff,
Lester L. II. United States. Congress. House. Special
Study Mission to Southern Africa. III. Title.*
DT733.D5 NYPL [Sc E 89-39]

Dihaeya /. Chaphole, Sol. [Cape Town] , c1986.
xiii, 68 p. ; ISBN 0-7992-1048-X
NYPL [Sc D 88-1123]

Dijk, Teun Adrianus van, 1943- Discourse and
discrimination /. Detroit , 1988. 269 p. ; ISBN
0-8143-1957-2 (alk. paper) DDC 401/.9 19
P120.R32 D57 1988 NYPL [Sc E 88-451]

Diksyoner kreol morisyen. Baker, Philip.
Morisyen - English - français . Paris , 1987.
365 p. ; ISBN 2-85802-973-3
NYPL [Sc E 88-407]

Dilemmas of the new Black middle class /
edited, with an introduction by Joseph R.
Washington, Jr. ; [contributors, L. Bart
Landry ... et al.]. [Pa.? : s.n.] c1980. v, 100 p. ;
23 cm. "The edited writings in this volume ... were
developed for a two-day symposium in the Spring of
1980, sponsored by the University of Pennsylvania's
Afro-American Studies Program, entitled "New Black
Middle Class Prospects""--P. i. Includes bibliographies.
CONTENTS - The social and economic adequacy of
the Black middle class / L. Bart Landry -- Occupational
trends of new lifestyles / G. Franklin Edwards -- Black
capitalism and economic expansion / Cora B. Marrett --
Ramifications of affirmative action / Loretta J.
Williams -- Recreative and involvement involvement in
culture / Charles H. Nichols -- The new Black political
class / Martin Kilson.
*1. Afro-Americans - Social conditions - 1964-1975. 2.
Middle classes - United States. 3. Afro-Americans -
Social conditions - 1960-. 4. United States - Social
conditions - 1975-. I. Washington, Joseph R. II. Landry,
L. Bart. III. University of Pennsylvania. Afro-American
Studies Program.*
E185.86 .D54x 1980 NYPL [Sc D 89-24]

Dillon, Diane. (ill) Hearn, Michael Patrick. The
porcelain cat /. Boston [1987?]. [32] p. : ISBN
0-316-35330-2 (pbk.) : *NYPL [Sc F 88-220]*

Dillon, Leo. (ill) Hearn, Michael Patrick. The
porcelain cat /. Boston [1987?]. [32] p. : ISBN
0-316-35330-2 (pbk.) : *NYPL [Sc F 88-220]*

Dine, George Uchechukwu. Traditional leadership
as service among the Igbo of Nigeria :
(anthropo-theological approach) / by George
Uchechukwu Dine. Rome : [Pont. Universita
Lateranense], 1983. xvi, 316 p. : ill. ; 24 cm.
Errata slip inserted. Bibliography: p. 307-316. DDC
299/.6 19
*1. Igbo (African people) - Religion. 2. Igbo (African
people) - Social life and customs. I. Title.*
BL2480.I2 D56 1983 NYPL [Sc E 88-329]

Dinesen, Isak, 1885-1962.
Isak Dinesen's Africa : images of the wild
continent from the writer's life and words /
with text chosen from the memoirs and letters
of Isak Dinesen and photographs by Yann
Arthus-Bertrand ... [et al.] ; introduction by
Judith Thurman. London : Bantam, 1986,
c1985. xvii, 142 p. : ill. (some col.) ; 31 cm.
Bibliography: p. 140. ISBN 0-593-01049-3
*1. Dinesen, Isak, 1885-1962 - Homes and haunts -
Kenya. 2. Country life - Kenya. 3. Kenya - Description
and travel - Views. 4. Kenya - Social life and customs -
1895-1963. I. Title. NYPL [Sc G 88-26]*

**DINESEN, ISAK, 1885-1962 - HOMES AND
HAUNTS - KENYA.**
Dinesen, Isak, 1885-1962. Isak Dinesen's
Africa . London , 1986, c1985. xvii, 142 p. :
ISBN 0-593-01049-3 *NYPL [Sc G 88-26]*

Dinham, Barbara. Agribusiness in Africa /
Barbara Dinham & Colin Hines. London :
Earth Resources Research Ltd., 1983. 224 p. :
map ; 21 cm. (An Earth Resources Research
publication) "A study of the impact of big business on
Africa's food and agricultural production"--Cover. "Food
policy." Includes bibliographical references and index.
ISBN 0-946281-00-9 :
*1. Agriculture - Economic aspects - Africa,
Sub-Saharan. I. Hines, Colin. II. Earth Resources
Research Ltd. III. Title. NYPL [Sc D 84-44]*

DINKA (AFRICAN PEOPLE) - RELIGION.
Lienhardt, Godfrey. Divinity and experience .
Oxford , 1961 (1987 printing) 328 p. : ISBN
0-19-823405-8 (pbk) : DDC 299/.683 19
BL2480.D5 NYPL [Sc D 88-1011]

**DINKA (AFRICAN PEOPLE) - RITES AND
CEREMONIES.**
Makec, John Wuol. The customary law of the
Dinka people of Sudan . London, England,
1988. 287 p. ; ISBN 0-948583-03-7 (Hardback)
NYPL [Sc E 88-434]

DINKA LANGUAGE - VOWELS.
Malou, Job. Dinka vowel system /. Dallas, TX ,
Arlington , 1988. x, 89 p. : ISBN 0-88312-008-9
NYPL [Sc D 88-1445]

DINKA (NILOTIC TRIBE)
Abu Sabah, Mohammed Azim. Tribal structure
of the Ngok Dinka of southern Kordofan
Province [microform] /. Khartoum , 1978. 20
leaves ; *NYPL [Sc Micro F-11037]*

Dinka vowel system /. Malou, Job. Dallas, TX ,
Arlington , 1988. x, 89 p. : ISBN 0-88312-008-9
NYPL [Sc D 88-1445]

Dinslage, Sabine. Kinder der Lyela : Kindheit
und Jugend im kulturellen Wandel bei den
Lyela in Burkina Faso / Sabine Dinslage.
Hohenschäftlarn bei München : K. Renner,
1986. 355 p. : ill. ; 21 cm. (Kulturanthropologische
Studien . Bd. 12) Bibliography: p. 340-349. ISBN
3-87673-105-4 DDC 305.2/3/096625 19
1. Lele (African people) - Children. I. Title. II. Series.
DT650.L38 D56 1986 NYPL [Sc D 88-876]

Diop, Abdoulaye Bara. La famille Wolof :
tradition et changement / Abdoulaye-Bara
Diop. Paris : Karthala, c1985. 262 p. : ill.,
maps ; 24 cm. (Hommes et sociétés) Bibliography: p.
[257]-259. ISBN 2-86537-138-7
1. Family - Senegal. I. Title. II. Series.
NYPL [Sc E 89-126]

Diop, Adja Khady, 1922- Le Sénégal d'hier et ses
traditions / Adja Khady Diop et Archives
culturelles. [S.l.] : Imprimerie Vendome Afric,
[198-?] 61, 18 p. : ill., ports. ; 22 cm. Cover title.
In French, Wolof, or Arabic.
*1. Folklore - Senegal. 2. Wolof language - Texts. I.
Title. NYPL [Sc D 88-933]*

Diop, Anta. see Diop, Cheikh Anta.

Diop, Cheikh Anta. Nouvelles recherches sur
l'égyptien ancien et les langues négro-africaines
modernes / Cheikh Anta Diop. Paris : Présence
africaine, c1988. 221 p. ; 22 cm. "Compléments à
Parenté génétique de l'égyptien pharaonique et des
langues négro-africaines." Bibliography: p. 207-209.
ISBN 2-7087-0507-5
*1. African languages. 2. Egyptian language -
Dictionaries - Wolof. 3. Egyptian language. I. Title.*
NYPL [Sc D 89-550]

Diplomatic soldiering . Garba, Joeseph Nanven,
1943- Ibadan , 1987. xviii, 238 p., [9] p. of
plates ; ISBN 978-246-176-8 (limp)
NYPL [Sc D 88-726]

**Directory of electronic data processing experts in
Africa** = Répertoire des experts en traitement
électronique des données en Afrique. [Addis
Ababa?] : United Nations, [1985] iii, 57 p. ; 28
cm. Cover title. "December 1985." "E/ECA/PSD.4/48."
DDC 004/.025/6 19
*1. Electronic data processing consultants - Africa -
Directories. I. Title: Répertoire des experts en
traitement électronique des données en Afrique.*
QA76.215 .D576 1985 NYPL [Sc F 89-42]

**A Directory of international migration study
centers, research programs, and library
resources /** compiled by Diana Zimmerman,
Nancy Avrin and Olha Della Cava. 1st ed.
Staten Island, N.Y. : Center for Migration
Studies of New York, 1987. ix, 299 p. ; 28 cm.
(Bibliographies & documentation series) Includes
indexes. ISBN 0-934733-18-X (pbk.) : DDC 325/.07
19
*1. Emigration and immigration - Study and teaching -
Directories. 2. Migration, Internal - Study and
teaching - Directories. 3. Emigration and immigration -
Research - Directories. 4. Migration, Internal -
Research - Directories. 5. Emigration and immigration -
Library resources - Directories. 6. Migration, Internal -
Library resources - Directories. I. Zimmerman, Diana.
II. Avrin, Nancy. III. Della Cava, Olha. IV. Center for
Migration Studies (U. S.). V. Series.*
JV6033 .C45 1987 NYPL [JLF 88-1452]

Directory of media women in Kenya /
Association of Media Women in Kenya.
[Nairobi] : The Association, [1985] 48 p. :
ports. ; 30 cm. Cover title. DDC 001.51/02552 19
*1. Women in the mass media industry - Media -
Directories. I. Association of Media Women in Kenya.*
P94.5.W652 K43 1985 NYPL [Sc F 88-370]

**Directory of special libraries/information units in
Trinidad and Tobago /** [prepared by the
Working Group on Special
Libraries/Information Network]. Port of Spain,
Trinidad & Tobago : National Library,
Information, and Archives Service, Ministry of
Education, [1986] iv, 59 p. ; 21 cm. "December
1986." Includes indexes. DDC 026/.00025/72983 19
*1. Libraries, Special - Trinidad and Tobago -
Directories. 2. Information services - Trinidad and
Tobago - Directories. I. Trinidad and Tobago. Working
Group on Special Libraries/Information Network.*
Z753.T7 D57 1986 NYPL [Sc D 88-1019]

Dirks, Robert, 1942- The Black Saturnalia :
conflict and its ritual expression on British
West Indian slave plantations / Robert Dirks.
Gainesville : University Presses of Florida,
University of Florida Press, c1987. xvii, 228 p.,
[7] p. of plates : ill. ; 23 cm. (University of Florida
monographs. Social sciences . no. 72) Includes
bibliography: p. 211-221. ISBN 0-8130-0843-3 (pbk. :
alk. paper) : DDC 394.2/68282/09729 19
*1. Christmas - West Indies, British. 2. Slavery - West
Indies, British. 3. Plantation life - West Indies, British.
4. West Indies, British - Social life and customs. I.
Series. II. Series: Florida. University, Gainesville.
University of Florida monographs. Social sciences, no.
72. III. Title.*
GT4987.23 .D57 1987
NYPL [L-10 5328 no.72]

**DISARMAMENT AND ATOMIC WEAPONS.
see ATOMIC WEAPONS AND
DISARMAMENT.**

Disarmament and development : utilization of
resources for military purposes in black Africa /
A.B. Akinyemi ... [et al.]. Lagos, Nigeria :
Nigerian Institute of International Affairs, 1986.
ix, 117 p., 1 folded leaf : map ; 22 cm. Includes
bibliographical references. ISBN 978-13-2828-2
*1. War - Economic aspects - Africa, Sub-Saharan. 2.
Disarmament - Economic aspects - Africa, Sub-Saharan.
3. Africa, Sub-Saharan - Armed Forces - Appropriations
and expenditures. I. Akinyemi, A. B. II. Title.*
NYPL [Sc D 88-783]

**DISARMAMENT - ECONOMIC ASPECTS -
AFRICA, SUB-SAHARAN.**
Disarmament and development . Lagos,
Nigeria , 1986. ix, 117 p., 1 folded leaf : ISBN
978-13-2828-2 *NYPL [Sc D 88-783]*

**DISASTER RELIEF - PLANNING - ST.
LUCIA.**
St. Lucia. Plan for the coordination of
emergency action in the event of a major
disaster [microform] /. St. Lucia [1964] 22 p. ;
NYPL [Sc Micro F-10955]

DISASTER RELIEF - UNITED STATES.
Bolin, Robert C. Race, religion, and ethnicity in disaster recovery /. [Boulder. Colo.] , 1986. ix, 265 p. :   *NYPL [Sc D 88-904]*

DISASTERS - UNITED STATES - PSYCHOLOGICAL ASPECTS.
Bolin, Robert C. Race, religion, and ethnicity in disaster recovery /. [Boulder. Colo.] , 1986. ix, 265 p. :   *NYPL [Sc D 88-904]*

DISASTERS - UNITED STATES - SOCIAL ASPECTS.
Bolin, Robert C. Race, religion, and ethnicity in disaster recovery /. [Boulder. Colo.] , 1986. ix, 265 p. :   *NYPL [Sc D 88-904]*

La discorde aux cent voix . Ollivier, Emile, 1940- Paris , c1986. 269 p. ; ISBN 2-226-02701-7 : DDC 843 19
PQ3949.2.O44 D5 1986
                              NYPL [Sc D 88-372]

Discours de son Excellence le colonel Jean-Baptiste Bagaza, président de la République du Burundi. Bagaza, Jean-Baptiste. Bujumbura , 1980. 167 p. :
DT450.853.B34 A5 1980
                              NYPL [Sc E 88-122]

Discours du général-major Habyarimana Juvénal, président de la République rwandaise et président-fondateur du Mouvement révolutionnaire national pour le développement à l'occasion du 1er juillet, 1987 =.
Habyarimana, Juvénal. [Kigali?] , 1987. 82 p. : *f-rw---*   *NYPL [Sc D 88-1517]*

Discourse and discrimination / edited by Geneva Smitherman-Donaldson and Teun A. van Dijk. Detroit : Wayne State University Press, 1988. 269 p. ; 24 cm. Includes bibliographical references and index. ISBN 0-8143-1957-2 (alk. paper) DDC 401/.9 19
1. Racism in language. 2. Mass media and minorities. I. Smitherman-Donaldson, Geneva, 1940-. II. Dijk, Teun Adrianus van, 1943-.
P120.R32 D57 1988   *NYPL [Sc E 88-451]*

Discourse, delivered in the Old South Church,Reading, Mass. Barrows, William, 1815-1891. The war and slavery; and their relations to each other . Boston , 1863. 18 p. ;
                              NYPL [Sc Rare F 88-51]

DISCOVERERS. see EXPLORERS.

DISCOVERIES (IN SCIENCE) see SCIENCE.

Discovering my "AA" family roots . Boykin, Yogi Rudolph. Winthorp, Wash. , c1978. 106 p. :
                              NYPL [Sc F 89-91]

DISCRIMINATION IN EDUCATION - AUSTRALIA - CASE STUDIES.
Bullivant, Brian Milton. The ethnic encounter in the secondary school . New York , 1987. x, 214 p. ; ISBN 1-85000-255-X ; DDC 371.97/0994 19
LC3739 .B84 1987   *NYPL [JLE 88-2088]*

DISCRIMINATION IN EDUCATION - GREAT BRITAIN.
Towards the decolonization of the British educational system /. London, England , 19. 128 p. : ISBN 0-907015-32-8
                              NYPL [Sc D 88-1346]

DISCRIMINATION IN EDUCATION - LAW AND LEGISLATION - NEW YORK (CITY)
Rebell, Michael A. Equality and education . Princeton, N.J. , c1985. x, 340 p. ; ISBN 0-691-07692-8 : DDC 344.747/0798 347.4704798 19
KFX2065 .R43 1985   *NYPL [JLD 85-3778]*

DISCRIMINATION IN EDUCATION - LAW AND LEGISLATION - UNITED STATES.
Rebell, Michael A. Equality and education . Princeton, N.J. , c1985. x, 340 p. ; ISBN 0-691-07692-8 : DDC 344.747/0798 347.4704798 19
KFX2065 .R43 1985   *NYPL [JLD 85-3778]*

DISCRIMINATION IN EDUCATION - LAW AND LEGISLATION - UNITED STATES - TRIAL PRACTICE.
Chesler, Mark A. Social science in court . Madison, Wis. , 1988. xiv, 286 p. ; ISBN 0-299-11620-4 : DDC 344.73/0798 347.304798 19
KF8925.D5 C48 1988   *NYPL [Sc E 89-187]*

DISCRIMINATION IN EMPLOYMENT - BIBLIOGRAPHY.
Dworaczek, Marian. Affirmative action and minorities . Monticello. Ill., USA [1988] 63 p. ; ISBN 1-555-90638-9 (pbk.) : DDC 016.33113/3 19
Z7164.A26 D87 1988 HF5549.5.A34
                              NYPL [Sc f 89-39]

DISCRIMINATION IN EMPLOYMENT - LAW AND LEGISLATION - UNITED STATES.
Simba, Malik. The Black laborer, the Black legal experience and the United States Supreme Court with emphasis on the neo-concept of equal employment [microform] /. 1977. 357 leaves.   *NYPL [Sc Micro R-4706]*

DISCRIMINATION IN EMPLOYMENT - LAW AND LEGISLATION - UNITED STATES - HISTORY.
Burstein, Paul. Discrimination, jobs, and politics . Chicago , c1985. x, 247 p. : ISBN 0-226-08134-6 DDC 344.73/01133/0262 347.3041133/0262 19
KF3464 .B83 1985   *NYPL [JLD 86-132]*

DISCRIMINATION IN HOUSING - JUVENILE FICTION.
Raferty, Gerald. Twenty-dollar horse /. Eau Claire, Wisconsin , 1967, c1955. 192 p. :
                              NYPL [Sc D 88-664]

DISCRIMINATION IN HOUSING - SOUTH AFRICA.
Pickard-Cambridge, Claire. Sharing the cities . Braamfontein, Johannesburg, South Africa , 1988. ix, 53 p. : ISBN 0-86982-335-3
                              NYPL [Sc D 88-1336]

DISCRIMINATION IN HOUSING - UNITED STATES.
Commission on Race and Housing. Where shall we live? Berkeley , 1958. ix, 77 p.
HD7293 .C6427   *NYPL [Sc E 88-397]*

DISCRIMINATION IN MEDICAL EDUCATION - LAW AND LEGISLATION - CALIFORNIA.
Schwartz, Bernard, 1923- Behind Bakke . New York , c1988. x, 266 p. ; ISBN 0-8147-7878-X : DDC 347.73/0798 347.304798 19
KF228.B34 S39 1988   *NYPL [JLE 88-4158]*

DISCRIMINATION IN SPORTS - SOUTHWESTERN STATES.
Pennington, Richard, 1952- Breaking the ice . Jefferson, N.C. , c1987. ix, 182 p. : ISBN 0-89950-295-4 : DDC 796.332/72/0973 19
GV939.A1 P46 1987   *NYPL [Sc E 88-35]*

DISCRIMINATION IN SPORTS - UNITED STATES.
Robinson, Frank, 1935- Extra innings /. New York , c1988. x, 270, [8] p. of plates. : ISBN 0-07-053183-8 DDC 796.357/08996073 19
GV863.A1 R582 1988   *NYPL [Sc E 88-382]*

Discrimination, jobs, and politics . Burstein, Paul. Chicago , c1985. x, 247 p. : ISBN 0-226-08134-6 DDC 344.73/01133/0262 347.3041133/0262 19
KF3464 .B83 1985   *NYPL [JLD 86-132]*

DISCRIMINATION, RACIAL. see RACE DISCRIMINATION.

DISEASES - AFRICA, EAST - BIBLIOGRAPHY.
A Bibliography of health and disease in East Africa /. Amsterdam ; New York : 282 p. ; ISBN 0-444-80931-7 (U. S.) DDC 016.3621/0967 19
Z6673.6.A353 B53 1988 RA552.A353
                              NYPL [Sc G 89-6]

DISHES. see POTTERY.

DISINVESTMENT - SOUTH AFRICA - PUBLIC OPINION.
Hoile, David. Understanding sanctions /. London , 1988. 80 p. ; ISBN 1-87111-700-3 (pbk.) : DDC 337.68 19
HF1613.4 .H654 1988   *NYPL [Sc D 89-317]*

Dispossessed daughter of Africa /. Trill, Carol. London , 1988. 190 p. : ISBN 0-946918-42-2 (pbk.)   *NYPL [sc C 88-228]*

DISPUTE RESOLUTION (LAW) - BAHAMAS - MAYAGUANA ISLAND.
Lurry-Wright, Jerome Wendell, 1941- Custom and conflict on a Bahamian out-island /. Lanham, MD , c1987. xxii, 188 p. ; ISBN 0-8191-6097-0 (alk. paper) : DDC 347.7296

347.29607 19
KGL210 .L87 1987   *NYPL [Sc D 88-218]*

Dissertationen der Universität Wien, 0379-1424 . (181) Ebermann, Erwin. Die Sprache der Mauka . Wien , 1986. 207 p. ; ISBN 3-85369-656-2
PL8491.95.I9 E24 1986
                              NYPL [Sc D 88-687]

DISSERTATIONS, ACADEMIC - NIGERIA - ABSTRACTS.
Hezekiah Oluwasanmi Library. Abstracts of theses accepted by University of Ife, 1985 /. Ile-Ife , 1986. ii, ii, 95 p. ;
                              NYPL [Sc D 89-580]

DISSERTATIONS, ACADEMIC - UGANDA.
Makerere University. Library. Annotated list of theses submitted to Makerere University and held by Makerere University Library [microform] /. [Kampala?] , 1981. 89 leaves ;
                         NYPL [Sc Micro R-4840 no.13]

DISSERTATIONS, ACADEMIC - UNITED STATES - ABSTRACTS.
Baker's dozen . Washington [1973] 112 p. ;
                              NYPL [Sc F 88-244]

DISSERTATIONS, ACADEMIC - UNITED STATES - BIBLIOGRAPHY.
Haith, Dorothy May. Theses accepted by the Atlanta University Graduate School of Library Service, 1950-1975 /. Huntsville, Al , 1977. v, 45 p. ;
Z666 .H25   *NYPL [Sc D 88-69]*

Distant companions . Hansen, Karen Tranberg. Ithaca , 1989. xv, 321 p. : ISBN 0-8014-2217-5 (alk. paper) DDC 331.7/6164046/096894 19
HD6072.2.Z33 H36 1989
                              NYPL [Sc E 89-215]

DISTRIBUTION, COOPERATIVE. see COOPERATION; COOPERATIVE SOCIETIES.

DISTRIBUTION (ECONOMICS) see COMMERCE.

DISTRIBUTION OF INCOME. see INCOME DISTRIBUTION.

Divided truths . Heinecke, P. Okpella, Bendel State, Nigeria , 1988. 135 p. ; ISBN 978-252-832-3   *NYPL [Sc D 89-134]*

Divinity and experience . Lienhardt, Godfrey. Oxford , 1961 (1987 [printing]) 328 p. ; ISBN 0-19-823405-8 (pbk) : DDC 299/.683 19
BL2480.D5   *NYPL [Sc D 88-1011]*

DIVISION OF POWERS. see FEDERAL GOVERNMENT.

Divorce among the Wa-Embu /. Josiah, Mwaniki, 1933- Nairobi , 1988. 49 p. ;
                              NYPL [Sc D 89-346]

DIVORCE - KENYA.
Josiah, Mwaniki, 1933- Divorce among the Wa-Embu /. Nairobi , 1988. 49 p. ;
                              NYPL [Sc D 89-346]

Dixon, Glen. Hostage / Glen Dixon: as told to Anthony Mockler. London : Columbus, 1986. 189 p., [8] p. of plates : ill., map, ports. ; 24 cm. ISBN 0-86287-271-5
1. Hostages - Angola - History - 20th century. 2. Angola - History - Civil War, 1975-. I. Mockler, Anthony. II. Title.   *NYPL [Sc E 88-406]*

Dixon, Joan. Jaata kendeyaa / by Joan Dixon. [Amherst, Ma.? : s.n., 198-?] 91 p. : ill. ; 29 cm.
1. Child care - Gambia. 2. Mandingo language - Readers for new literates. I. Title.
                              NYPL [Sc F 89-135]

Dizionario italiano-somalo /. Minozzi, Maria Teresa. Milano , 1961. 178 p. ;
                              NYPL [Sc B 88-4]

DJIBOUTI.
Dibeth, Véronique Carton. Manuel de conversation somali-français suivi d'un guide Dijibouti /. Paris , c1988. 80 p. : ISBN 2-7384-0090-6   *NYPL [Sc E 88-536]*

Djungu-Simba Kamatenda, 1953- Autour du feu : contes d'inspiration lega / Djungu-Simba Kamatenda. Kinshasa : Editions Saint Paul Afrique, 1984. 70 p. : ill. ; 20 cm. DDC 398.2/09675/1 19
1. Waregas - Folklore. 2. Tales - Zaire. 3. Legends - Zaire. I. Title.
GR357.82.W35 D48 1984
                              NYPL [Sc C 88-272]

Dlamini, Sipho. Davies, Robert H. The struggle for South Africa . London , Atlantic Highlands, N.J. , 1988. 2 v. :　ISBN 0-86232-760-1 (v. 1)　DDC 322/.0968 19
JQ1931 .D38 1988　　***NYPL [Sc D 88-1369]***

DLI Museum and Arts Centre. Miniature African sculptures from the Herman collection /. London , 1985. 64 p. :　ISBN 0-7287-0454-4
　　　　NYPL [Sc D 89-41]

Dobson, Narda. A history of Belize. [Port of Spain, Trinidad and Tobago] Longman Caribbean [1973] xiv, 362 p. illus. 23 cm. Bibliography: p. 339-342.　ISBN 0-582-76601-X　DDC 972.82
1. Belize - History. I. Title.
F1446 .D56 1973　　***NYPL [Sc D 88-649]***

DOBY, LARRY.
Moore, Joseph Thomas. Pride against prejudice . New York , c1988. 195 p., [8] p. of plates :　ISBN 0-313-25995-X (lib. bdg. : alk. paper)　DDC 796.357/092/4 B 19
GV865.D58 M66 1988　***NYPL [Sc E 88-272]***

Doc's legacy /. Wise, Leonard. New York , c1986. 410 p. ;　ISBN 0-931933-16-1
　　　　NYPL [JFE 86-5265]

DOCTORS. see PHYSICIANS.

DOCTRINAL THEOLOGY. see THEOLOGY, DOCTRINAL.

DOCTRINES. see THEOLOGY, DOCTRINAL.

DOCUMENTARY PHOTOGRAPHY. see PHOTOGRAPHY, DOCUMENTARY.

Documentos da independência. Proclamação da independência da República Popular de Angola, 11 de novembro de 1975 . Luanda , 1975. 166 p., [6] leaves of plates :
　　　　NYPL [Sc D 88-245]

Documentos del conflicto dominico-haitiano de 1937 / recopilación y notas, José Israel Cuello H. 1a ed. Santo Domingo, D.N., República Dominicana : Taller, 1985. 606 p. ; 29 cm. (Biblioteca Taller. no. 175) Includes index. Bibliography: p. [567]-591.
1. Dominican Republic - Foreign relations - Haiti - Sources. 2. Haiti - Foreign relations - Dominican Republic - Sources. 3. Dominican Republic - History - 1930-1961 - Sources. 4. Haiti - History - 1934- - Sources. I. Cuello H., José Israel.
　　　　NYPL [Sc F 89-173]

Documentos relativos ao apresamento, julgamento e entrega da barca franceza Charles et Georges : e em geral ao engajamento de negros, debaixo da denominação de trabalhadores livres, nas possessões da Coroa de Portugal na costa oriental e occidental de Africa para as colonias francezas ; apresentados ás Cortes na sessão legislativa de 1858 . Lisboa : Imprensa National, 1858. 249, 16 p. ; 32 cm. CONTENTS. - Documentos.--Appendice: Documentos relativos a detenção, no porto do Ibo, da barca franceza Alfred.
1. Charles et Georges (Ship). 2. Alfred (Ship). 3. Slave-trade - Africa. I. Portugal. Cortes.
　　　　NYPL [Sc Rare G 86-1]

Documents des Études nigériennes. see Études nigériennes.

Dodge, Steve.
The compleat guide to Nassau / by Steve Dodge ; with ill. by Laurie Jones. Decatur, Ill. : White Sound Press, c1987. 116 p. : ill. ; 23 cm. Cover title.　ISBN 0-932265-04-9 (pbk.) :
1. Nassau (Bahamas) - Description - Tours. 2. Nassau, Bahamas - Description - Guide-books. I. Title.
　　　　NYPL [Sc D 88-685]

A guide and history of Hope Town / by Steve Dodge and Vernon Malone ; illustrations by Laurie Jones. 1st ed. Decatur, Ill., USA : White Sound Press, c1985. [48] p. : ill. ; 23 cm. Cover title. Bibliography: p. [46]　ISBN 0-932265-01-4 (pbk.).　DDC 917.296 19
1. Hope Town (Bahamas) - Description - Tours. 2. Hope Town (Bahamas) - History. I. Malone, Vernon. II. Title.
F1659.H67 D63 1985　***NYPL [Sc D 88-684]***

Dodson, Howard. Thinking and rethinking U. S. history /. New York, N.Y. , c1988. 389 p. ;
　　　　NYPL [Sc F 89-130]

Dodson, Jualynne E.
Black stylization and implications for child welfare : final report / prepared for [the] Office

---

of Child Development under Grant No. OCD-CB-422(CB) by Jualynne Dodson, Susan Ross, Judy Barton Smith. Atlanta, Georgia : School of Social Work, Atlanta University, 1975. 1 v. (various pagings) ; 28 cm. "May, 1975." Includes bibliography. Schomburg Center copy imperfect; 2 pages in first section blank.
1. Afro-American children - Services for. 2. Afro-Americans - Social life and customs. 3. Afro-American arts. 4. Arts and children - United States. 5. Multicultural education - United States. I. Ross, Susan. II. Smith, Judy Barton. III. Atlanta University. School of Social Work. IV. United States. Office of Child Development. V. Title.
　　　　NYPL [Sc F 88-223]

Toward reflective analysis of Black families . [Atlanta] , 1976. ii, 74 l. :
　　　　NYPL [Sc F 88-224]

Training of personnel for services to Black families : final report / Jualynne Dodson, Project director. [Atlanta] : Atlanta University School of Social Work, [1976] 1 v. (various foliations) ; 29 cm. "SRS # 84-p.-95623/4-01 Includes bibliographical references.
1. Afro-Americans - Social work with. 2. Social work education - United States - Curricula. 3. Intercultural education - United States - Curricula. I. Atlanta University. School of Social Work. II. Title.
　　　　NYPL [Sc F 88-130]

Dodwell, Christina, 1951-
Travels with Pegasus : a microlight journey across West Africa / Christina Dodwell. London : Hodder & Stoughton, 1989. 208 p., [16] p. of plates : ill. (some col.), map ; 25 cm.　ISBN 0-340-42502-4 :　DDC 916.6/04 19
1. Dodwell, Christina, 1951- - Journeys - Africa, West. 2. Ultralight aircraft. 3. Africa, West - Description and travel - 1981-. I. Title.　***NYPL [JFE 89-902]***

DODWELL, CHRISTINA, 1951- - JOURNEYS - AFRICA, WEST.
Dodwell, Christina, 1951- Travels with Pegasus . London , 1989. 208 p., [16] p. of plates :　ISBN 0-340-42502-4 :　DDC 916.6/04 19
　　　　NYPL [JFE 89-902]

DOG. see DOGS.

The dog, the bone, and the wind . Slater, Sandra. Ibadan, Nigeria , c1986. 30 p. :　ISBN 0-19-575567-7
MLCS 88/07439 (P)　***NYPL [Sc D 89-116]***

Doghudje, Chris. Advertising in Nigerian perspective / Chris A. Doghudje. Lagos : Zus Bureau, c1985. 85 p. ; 22 cm. Bibliography: p. 85.　ISBN 978-249-700-2
1. Advertising - Nigeria. I. Title.
　　　　NYPL [Sc D 88-785]

DOGONS (AFRICAN PEOPLE) - SOCIAL LIFE AND CUSTOMS.
Wanono, Nadine. Ciné-rituel de femmes dogon /. Paris , 1987. 138 p. :　ISBN 2-222-03961-4 (pbk)　***NYPL [Sc E 88-177]***

DOGS - JUVENILE FICTION.
Durham, John, fl. 1960- Me and Arch and the Pest. New York [1970] 96 p.　DDC [Fic]
PZ7.D9335 Me　***NYPL [Sc D 88-416]***

Elting, Mary, 1909- Patch /. Garden City, N.Y. , 1948. 156 p. :
PZ7.E53Pat　　***NYPL [Sc C 89-14]***

Woody, Regina Llewellyn (Jones) Almena's dogs /. New York , c1954. 240 p. :
　　　　NYPL [Sc D 88-648]

Doherty, Jaiyeola, 1952- Die Satire im nigerianischen Roman : die Rolle der Satire in den Romanwerken vier nigerianischer Schriftsteller, T.M. Aluko, Chinua Achebe, Nkem Nwankwo und Wole Soyinka / Jaiyeola Doherty. Frankfurt am Main ; New York : Lang, c1986. 381 p. : ill. ; 22 cm. (Europäische Hochschulschriften. Reihe XIV, Angelsächsische Sprache und Literatur, 0721-3387 ; Bd. 151 = vol. 151 = vol. 151) Bibliography: p. 374-381.　ISBN 3-8204-8326-8　DDC 823 19
1. Nigerian fiction (English) - History and criticism. 2. Satire, Nigerian (English) - History and criticism. I. Series: Europäische Hochschulschriften. Reihe XIV, Angelsächsische Sprache und Literatur , Bd. 151. II. Title.
PR9387.4 .D64 1986　***NYPL [Sc D 88-991]***

Dohndy, Farrukh. The Black explosion in British schools / By Farrukh Dhondy, Barbara Beese and Leila Hassan. 2nd ed. London : Race

---

Today Publications, 1985. 64 p. ; 21 cm. Articles written between 1974 and 1979 which were originally published in Race today.　ISBN 0-9503498-6-0
1. Blacks - Education - Great Britain. 2. Educational equalization - Great Britain. 3. Education and state - Great Britain. 4. Education - Great Britain - 1965-. 5. Great Britain - Race relations. I. Beese, Barbara. II. Hassan, Leila. III. Title.　***NYPL [Sc D 88-1030]***

Dokumentationsdienst Afrika. Reihe A .
(23) Kersebaum, Andrea. Integrationsbestrebungen in Afrika . Hamburg , 1986-1987. 2 v. ;　ISBN 3-922852-13-0
　　　　NYPL [Sc F 88-33]

DOLLS - JUVENILE FICTION.
Pomerantz, Charlotte. The chalk doll /. New York , c1989. 30 p. :　ISBN 0-397-32318-2 :　DDC [E] 19
PZ7.P77 Ch 1989　***NYPL [Sc F 89-175]***

DOMESTIC ARCHITECTURE. see ARCHITECTURE, DOMESTIC.

DOMESTIC RELATIONS - HAITI.
Haiti (Republic) Laws, statutes, etc. Formules des actes de l'état civil [microform]. Port-Républicain , 1845. 17 p. ;
　　　　NYPL [Sc Micro F-10,893]

Domestic slavery in its relations with wealth . Allo, Lorenzo. New York , 1855. 16 p. :
　　　　NYPL [Sc Rare G 86-32]

DOMESTIC VIOLENCE. see FAMILY VIOLENCE.

Domestic workers and their employers in the segregated South. Telling memories among southern women . Baton Rouge , c1988. xi, 279 p. :　ISBN 0-8071-1440-5 (alk. paper) :　DDC 305.4/3 19
HD6072.2.U52 A137 1988
　　　　NYPL [Sc E 89-124]

DOMESTICS - ZAMBIA - HISTORY - 20TH CENTURY.
Hansen, Karen Tranberg. Distant companions . Ithaca , 1989. xv, 321 p. :　ISBN 0-8014-2217-5 (alk. paper)　DDC 331.7/6164046/096894 19
HD6072.2.Z33 H36 1989
　　　　NYPL [Sc E 89-215]

Dominica.
Aspects of Dominican history /. Dominica, W.I. , 1972. 172 p. ;　***NYPL [HRG 83-1714]***

DOMINICA - ECONOMIC CONDITIONS.
D'ca Freedom Party government [microform] . [Roseau, Dominica , 1983?] 36 p. ;
　　　　NYPL [Sc Micro R-4137 no.13]

DOMINICA - FICTION.
Lazare, Alick. Native laughter /. [Roseau , c1985] 167 p. ;
MLCS 87/7802 (P)　***NYPL [Sc C 88-329]***

Dominica Freedom Party. D'ca Freedom Party government [microform] . [Roseau, Dominica , 1983?] 36 p. ;
　　　　NYPL [Sc Micro R-4137 no.13]

Dominica - Government. see Dominica - Politics and government.

DOMINICA - HISTORY.
Honychurch, Lennox. The Dominica story . Roseau, Dominica , 1984. 225 p. :
　　　　NYPL [Sc D 88-166]

DOMINICA - HISTORY - ADDRESSES, ESSAYS, LECTURES.
Aspects of Dominican history /. Dominica, W.I. , 1972. 172 p. ;　***NYPL [HRG 83-1714]***

DOMINICA - POLITICS AND GOVERNMENT.
D'ca Freedom Party government [microform] . [Roseau, Dominica , 1983?] 36 p. ;
　　　　NYPL [Sc Micro R-4137 no.13]

DOMINICA - SOCIAL CONDITIONS.
D'ca Freedom Party government [microform] . [Roseau, Dominica , 1983?] 36 p. ;
　　　　NYPL [Sc Micro R-4137 no.13]

The Dominica story . Honychurch, Lennox. Roseau, Dominica , 1984. 225 p. :
　　　　NYPL [Sc D 88-166]

DOMINICAN DRAMA.
Concurso de Teatro, 1987. Santo Domingo, República Dominicana , c1988. 177 p. :
MLCS 88/09684 (P)　***NYPL [Sc D 88-1331]***

DOMINICAN REPUBLIC - ADDRESSES, ESSAYS, LECTURES.

Problemas dominico-haitianos y del Caribe /. - México , 1973. 228 p.;
NYPL [JLK 73-145 [no.] 29]

DOMINICAN REPUBLIC - ANNEXATION TO THE UNITED STATES.
Sumner, Charles, 1811-1874. "He, being dead, yet speaketh" . Boston , New York , 1878. 29, 16 p. ;
NYPL [Sc Rare C 89-4]

DOMINICAN REPUBLIC - DESCRIPTION AND TRAVEL - GUIDE-BOOKS.
McLeod, Catherine. Jamaika /. Lausanne, Switzerland [1985], c1981. 128 p. :
NYPL [Sc B 88-57]

DOMINICAN REPUBLIC - FOREIGN RELATIONS - HAITI - SOURCES.
Documentos del conflicto dominico-haitiano de 1937 /. Santo Domingo, D.N., República Dominicana , 1985. 606 p. ;
NYPL [Sc F 89-173]

DOMINICAN REPUBLIC - HISTORY - 1930-
Matteis, Arthur de. Le massacre de 1937, ou Une succession immobilière internationale /. Port-au-Prince, Haiti , 1987. 68 p. ;
NYPL [Sc D 88-520]

DOMINICAN REPUBLIC - HISTORY - 1930-1961 - SOURCES.
Documentos del conflicto dominico-haitiano de 1937 /. Santo Domingo, D.N., República Dominicana , 1985. 606 p. ;
NYPL [Sc F 89-173]

DOMINICAN REPUBLIC - SOCIAL CONDITIONS.
Bosch, Juan, 1909- Composición social dominicana . Santo Domingo, República Dominicana , 1983. 272 p. ;
NYPL [Sc D 88-1065]

Dominican typical meals. Bornia, Ligia de. Comidas típicas dominicanas =. Santo Domingo Republica Dominicana , 1987. 132 p. ;
NYPL [Sc D 89-157]

DOMINICANS (DOMINICAN REPUBLIC) - BIOGRAPHY.
Personajes populares dominicanos. Santo Domingo, República Dominicana , c1986. 94 p. ;
NYPL [Sc D 89-491]

Dominique, Hilaire. Développement économique pour Haïti / Hilaire Dominique. [S.l. : s.n.], 1987. 51 p. ; 21 cm. Cover title.
1. Haiti - Economic conditions. I. Title.
NYPL [Sc D 88-187]

Dominique, Jean L. Auguste, Michel Hector. Haiti, la lucha por la democracia (clase obrera, partidos y sindicatos) /. Puebla [1986]. 244 p. ;
NYPL [Sc D 88-761]

Don rituel et échange marchand dans une société sahélienne /. Nicolas, Guy. Paris , 1986. 282 p. : ISBN 2-85265-117-3 *NYPL [JFF 87-660]*

Donahey, William, 1883- Sampson, Emma Speed, 1868-1947. Miss Minerva's baby /. Chicago , c1920. 320 p. :
PZ7.S16 Mis *NYPL [Sc C 88-71]*

Donald and the fish that walked /. Ricciuti, Edward R. New York [1974] 62 p. : ISBN 0-06-024997-8 : DDC 597/.52
QL638.C6 R52 1974 *NYPL [Sc D 88-447]*

Donders, Joseph G. War and rumours of war : an action report on war and peace in Africa / by J.G. Donders. Eldoret, Kenya : Gaba Publications, 1986. 51 p. : ill., maps ; 21 cm. (Spearhead (Eldoret, Kenya) . no. 94) Includes bibliographical references.
1. War - Religious aspects - Christianity. 2. Africa - Politics and government - 20th century. 3. Africa - History, Military - 20th century. I. Title. II. Series.
NYPL [Sc D 88-1467]

Dongala, Emmanuel B. Le feu des origines : roman / Emmanuel B Dongala. Paris : Albin Michel, 1987. 255 p. ; 23 cm.
1. Africa, Central - Fiction. I. Title.
NYPL [Sc D 87-1396]

La donna nel romanzo africano in lingua inglese . Pifferi, Annisa. Calliano (Trento) , c1985. 143 p. ; ISBN 88-7024-258-7 *NYPL [Sc D 89-102]*

Donovan, Christine, 1951- Simony, Maggy, 1920- Traveler's reading guides . Bayport, N.Y. , c1981-c1984. 3 v. ; ISBN 0-9602050-1-2 (v. 1) : DDC 016.9104 19
Z6016.T7 S54 G151 *NYPL [Sc D 89-343]*

Donovan, Jenny, 1960- We don't buy sickness, it just comes : health, illness, and health care in the lives of Black people in London / Jenny Donovan. Aldershot, Hants, England ; Brookfield, Vt., USA : Gower, c1986. xv, 294 p. ; 23 cm. Bibliography: p. 275-294. ISBN 0-566-05201-6 : DDC 362.1/08996/0421 19
1. Blacks - Health and hygiene - England - London. 2. Blacks - Medical care - England - London. 3. South Asians - Health and hygiene - England - London. 4. South Asians - Medical care - England - London. I. Title.
RA488.L8 D65 1986 *NYPL [Sc D 86-844]*

Don't be my valentine /. Lexau, Joan M. New York, N.Y. , c1985. 64 p. : ISBN 0-06-023872-0 : DDC [E] 19
PZ7.L5895 Dp 1985 *NYPL [Sc D 89-58]*

Dopamu, P. Adelumo. ÈṢÙ : the invisible foe of man : a comparative study of Satan in Christianity, Islam and Yoruba religion / P. Ade Dopamu. Nigeria : Shebiotimo Publications 1986. 99 p. ; 21 cm. Bibliography: p. 98-99. ISBN 978-253-014-X
1. Devil (Islam). 2. Yorubas - Religion. I. Title.
NYPL [Sc D 88-1375]

Dorant, St. Clair Wesley. Panyard / [St. Clair Wesley Dorant]. [Port-of-Spain : Dorant, 1974] 54 p. ; 27 cm. DDC 81.2 19
I. Title.
PR9272.9.D66 P37 *NYPL [Sc F 88-240]*

Dornan, James E. Rhodesia alone /. Washington [1977?] 95 p. ; DDC 320.9/689/104
DT962.75 .R53 *NYPL [Sc E 88-95]*

Dorsinville, Max, 1943-
Dorsinville, Roger. Accords perdus . Montréal, Québec, Canada , c1987. 190 p. ; ISBN 2-920862-07-3 *NYPL [Sc C 88-128]*

Solidarités : Tiers-Monde et littérature comparée / Max Dorsinville. Montréal, Québec, Canada : CIDIHCA, 1988. xv, 196 p. ; 22 cm. In English and French. Includes bibliographical references and index. ISBN 2-920862-09-X
1. Haitian literature - Canada. 2. Literature - Black authors - History and criticism. 3. Developing countries - Literature. I. Title.
NYPL [Sc D 89-484]

Dorsinville, Roger.
Accords perdus : roman / Roger Dorsinville ; édité par Max Dorsinville.1 ère éd. Montréal, Québec, Canada : CIDIHCA, c1987. 190 p. ; 20 cm. ISBN 2-920862-07-3
1. Haiti - Fiction. I. Dorsinville, Max, 1943-. II. Title.
NYPL [Sc D 88-128]

Les contes de la forêt atlantique / Roger Dorsinville. Alger : Entreprise nationale du livre, 1986. 84 p. ; 21 cm. "Origine des récits et bibliographique": p. 83-84.
1. Folklore - Liberia. I. Title.
NYPL [Sc D 89-171]

D'Orso, Michael. Redford, Dorothy Spruill. Somerset homecoming . New York , c1988. xviii, 266 p. : ISBN 0-385-24245-X : DDC 929/.3/089960730756 19
E185.96 .R42 1988 *NYPL [Sc E 88-498]*

Dossier Benin / Rencontres africaines, Association de la Maison de l'Afrique. Paris : ATN Maison de l'Afrique, 1987. 225 p. : ill. ; 30 cm. Bibliography: p. 213-225.
1. Benin - Economic conditions. 2. Benin - Directories. I. Recontres africaines (Association : Paris, France). II. Maison de l'Afrique (Paris, France).
NYPL [Sc F 88-176]

Le dossier Haïti . Di Chiara, Catherine Eve. Paris , c1988. 480 p., xxiv p. of plates : ISBN 2-235-01778-9
F1938 .D52x 1988 *NYPL [Sc D 89-394]*

The double-cross /. Gicheru, Mwangi. Nairobi , 1983. 169 p. ; ISBN 0-582-78544-8
NYPL [Sc C 87-461]

Double dependency and constraints on class formation in Bugisu, Uganda /. Bunker, Stephen G., 1944- Urbana, Ill. , 1983. v, 88 p. : DDC 303.3/09676/1 19
HD1538.U43 B86 1983
NYPL [Sc D 88-1054]

Douglas, Ellen, 1921- Can't quit you, baby / Ellen Douglas. New York : Atheneum, 1988. 256 p. ; 22 cm. ISBN 0-689-11793-0 DDC 813/.54 19

1. Afro-American Women - Fiction. I. Title.
PS3554.O825 C3 1988
NYPL [JFD 88-11335]

Douglas, J. D., 1956- Caribbean man's blues / J.D. Douglas. London : Akira, 1985. 62 p. ; 24 cm. Errata slip pasted in. ISBN 0-947638-04-0 (pbk) : DDC 821/.914 19
I. Title.
PR6054.O83 *NYPL [Sc E 88-462]*

Douglas, Marjory Stoneman. Freedom river: Florida, 1845. Illustrated by Edward Shenton. New York, Scribner [1953] 264 p. : ill. ; 21 cm. (Strength of the Union)
1. Slavery - Florida - Fiction. 2. Florida - History - Fiction. I. Title. *NYPL [Sc D 89-267]*

DOUGLASS, FREDERICK, 1817?-1895 - JUVENILE LITERATURE.
Russell, Sharman Apt. Frederick Douglass /. New York , c1988. 110 p. : ISBN 1-555-46580-3 DDC 973.8/092/4 B 92 19
E449.D75 R87 1988 *NYPL [Sc E 88-174]*

Doumbi-Fakoly.
Morts pour la France / Doumbi-Fakoly. Paris : Karthala, 1983. 150 p. ; c21 cm. ISBN 2-86537-074-7
1. World War, 1939-1945 - Blacks - Fiction. I. Title.
NYPL [Sc C 88-346]

La retraite anticipée du Guide suprême / Doumbi-Fakoly. Paris : L'Harmattan, c1984. 209 p. ; 19 cm. (Collection Encres noires 0223-9930 . 27) ISBN 2-85802-382-1 DDC 843 19
1. Africa - Fiction. I. Title. II. Series.
PQ3989.2.D639 R48 1984
NYPL [Sc C 88-78]

Douze pour une coupe . Kanté, Cheik Oumar. Paris , c1987. 159 p. ; ISBN 2-7087-0490-7
NYPL [Sc D 88920]

Dove, R. (Reginald) Anglican pioneers in Lesotho : some account of the Diocese of Lesotho, 1876-1930 / by R. Dove. [s.l. : s.n., 1975?] (s.l. : Mazenod Institute) 216 p., [1] fold. leaf of plates : ill. ; 21 cm. DDC 283/.68/6
1. Church of the Province of South Africa. Diocese of Lesotho - History. 2. Lesotho - Church history. I. Title.
BX5700.6.A44 L473 *NYPL [JXD 84-17]*

Dover cut & use stencil book series.
Menten, Theodore. Ancient Egyptian cut and use stencils /. New York , 1978. [32] leaves : ISBN 0-486-23626-9 : *NYPL [Sc F 88-366]*

D'Oyley, Vincent. Black presence in multi-ethnic Canada . Vancouver , c1982. xvii, 304 p. :
NYPL [Sc F 88-104]

DRAFT RIOT, 1863.
Committee of Merchants for the Relief of Colored People, Suffering from the Late Riots in the City of New York. Report of the Committee of Merchants for the Relief of Colored People, Suffering from the Late Riots in the City of New York. New York , 1863. 48 p. ; *NYPL [Sc Rare F 89-2]*

DRAFTING OF BILLS. see BILL DRAFTING.

Dragonwagon, Crescent. Strawberry dress escape / by Crescent Dragonwagon ; pictures by Lillian Hoban. New York : Scribner, [1975] [32] p. : col. ill. ; 27 cm. A little girl slips out of her boring, dusty classroom and enjoys the delights of a spring afternoon in the country. SCHOMBURG CHILDREN'S COLLECTION. ISBN 0-684-13912-X :
1. Afro-American children - Juvenile fiction. I. Hoban, Lillian. II. Schomburg Children's Collection. III. Title.
NYPL [Sc F 88-126]

Drake, William. The first wave : women poets in America, 1915-1945 / William Drake. New York : Macmillan ; London : Collier Macmillan, c1987. xxi, 314 p.; [8] p. of plates : ill. ; 22 cm. Includes bibliographical references and index. ISBN 0-02-533490-5 : DDC 811/.52/099287 19
1. American poetry - Women authors - History and criticism. 2. American poetry - 20th century - History and criticism. 3. Women and literature - United States. I. Title.
PS151 .D7 1987 *NYPL [JFD 87-7537]*

DRAMA - BLACK AUTHORS.
Marshall, Alex C. (Alexander Charles) Representative directors, Black theatre productions, and practices at historically Black

colleges and universities, 1968-1978 [microform] /. 1980. ix, 141 leaves.
NYPL [Sc Micro R-4807]

DRAMA, DOMINICAN. see DOMINICAN DRAMA.

DRAMA, ENGLISH. see ENGLISH DRAMA.

Drama festival plays / compiled by Wasambo Were, Dougal Blackburn. London ; Baltimore, Md. : E. Arnold, 1986. iv, 92 p. ; 22 cm. CONTENTS. - The transgressors / Wambugu E.S. Kariuki -- It's only a matter of time / Jeff Koinange -- A challenge to change / J. Mazimhaka and the senior members of the 1985 Drama Club, Loreto High School, Limuru -- The mobile grave / Fred Kayondo. ISBN 0-7131-8446-9
1. Kenyan drama (English). I. Were, Wasambo. II. Blackburn, Dougal.   *NYPL [Sc D 88-638]*

DRAMA, SOUTH AFRICAN (ENGLISH) see ENGLISH DRAMA.

Dramatic encounters . Harap, Louis. New York , c1987. xiv, 177 p. ; ISBN 0-313-25388-9 (lib. bdg. : alk. paper) DDC 810/.9/35203924 19
PS173.J4 H294 1987   *NYPL [*PZB 87-5243]*

DRAMSHOPS. see HOTELS, TAVERNS, ETC.

DRAWING, FIGURE. see FIGURE DRAWING.

DRAWINGS - NIGERIA - EXHIBITIONS - CATALOGS.
Jegede, Dele, 1945- Paradise battered /. Lagos , 1986. 48 p. :   *NYPL [Sc B 88-20]*

Dream land on the Isle of Nassau in the Bahamas /. Gould, Cora Smith. New York City , 1938. 38 p. :   *NYPL [Sc D 88-1297]*

The dream long deferred /. Gaillard, Frye, 1946- Chapel Hill , c1988. xxi, 192 p. ; ISBN 0-8078-1794-5 (alk. paper) DDC 370.19/342 19
LC214.523.C48 G35 1988
NYPL [Sc E 88-527]

Dreams . Orukari, Patrick Idah. Maiduguri , 1987. xi, 41 p. :   *NYPL [Sc D 88-1288]*

Dred . Stowe, Harriet Beecher, 1811-1896. Boston , 1856. 2 v. ;
PZ3.S89 D   *NYPL [Sc Rare C 89-31]*

Dreijmanis, John. The role of the South African government in tertiary education / John Dreijmanis. Johannesburg, South Africa : South African Institute of Race Relations, 1988. xiii, 156 p. : ill. ; 30 cm. Bibliography: p. 137-156. ISBN 0-86982-329-9
1. Higher education and state - South Africa. 2. Education - Economic aspects - South Africa. I. Title.
NYPL [Sc F 88-184]

DREPANOCYTIC ANEMIA. see SICKLE CELL ANEMIA.

Drescher, Seymour. Capitalism and antislavery : British popular mobilization in comparative perspective / by Seymour Drescher. New York : Oxford University Press, 1987, c1986. xv, 300 p. ; 22 cm. Includes index. Bibliography: p. [269]-291. ISBN 0-19-520534-0 (alk. paper) DDC 326/.0941 19
1. Slavery - Great Britain - Anti-slavery movements. 2. Capitalism - Great Britain. 3. Slavery - Great Britain - Emancipation. I. Title.
HT1163 .D74 1987   *NYPL [Sc D 89-29]*

DREW, CHARLES RICHARD, 1904-1950.
Wynes, Charles E. Charles Richard Drew . Urbana , c1988. xvi, 132 p., [14] p. of plates : ISBN 0-252-01551-7 DDC 610/.92/4 B 19
R154.D75 W96 1988   *NYPL [Sc E 89-65]*

Drew, Noble. see Ali, Noble Drew, 1886-

Drew, Timothy. see Ali, Noble Drew, 1886-

Dreyer, Lynette, 1949- The modern African elite of South Africa / Lynette Dreyer. Houndmills, Basingstoke, Hampshire : Macmillan, 1989. xii, 186 p. ; 23 cm. Based on author's thesis (Ph. D.)--University of Stellenbosch, 1987. Includes index. Bibliography: p. 176-183. ISBN 0-333-46410-9
1. Elite (Social sciences) - South Africa. 2. South Africa - Social conditions - 1961-. I. Title.
NYPL [Sc D 89-306]

Dried millet breaking . Stone, Ruth M. Bloomington , c1988. xvi, 150 p., [5] p. of plates : ISBN 0-253-31818-1 DDC 896/.34 19
PL8411.5 .S76 1988   *NYPL [Sc E 88-519]*

Driedger, Leo, 1928- Aging and ethnicity : toward an interface / by Leo Driedger and Neena L. Chappell. Toronto : Butterworths,
1987. xv, 131 p. : ill., map ; 24 cm. Includes index. Bibliography: p. 109-123. ISBN 0-409-81187-4
1. Minority aged - Canada - Social conditions. 2. Ethnic groups - Canada. 3. Aged - Canada - Social conditions. I. Chappell, Neena L. II. Title.
NYPL [Sc E 88-127]

Drimmer, Melvin. Issues in Black history : reflections and commentaries on the Black historical experience / Melvin Drimmer ; foreword by C. Eric Lincoln. Dubuque, Iowa : Kendall/Hunt Pub. Co., c1987. xviii, 308 p. ; 23 cm. Includes bibliographical references. ISBN 0-8403-4174-1 (pbk.) DDC 973/.0496073 19
1. Afro-Americans - History. 2. United States - Race relations. I. Title.
E185 .D715 1987   *NYPL [Sc E 88-107]*

Drinkers, drummers, and decent folk . Stewart, John O. Albany , c1989. xviii, 230 p. ; ISBN 0-88706-829-4 DDC 306/.097298/3 19
GN564.T7 S74 1988   *NYPL [Sc E 89-220]*

DRINKING CUSTOMS - ZAMBIA - GWEMBE DISTRICT.
Colson, Elizabeth, 1917- For prayer and profit . Stanford, Calif. , 1988. vi, 147 p. : ISBN 0-8047-1444-4 (alk. paper) DDC 968.94 19
DT963.42 .C65 1988   *NYPL [Sc D 88-1254]*

Drisko, Carol F. The unfinished march; the Negro in the United States, Reconstruction to World War I / by Carol F. Drisko and Edgar A. Toppin ; illustrated by Tracy Sugarman.[1st ed.] Garden City, N.Y. : Doubleday, 1967. 118 p. : col. ill. ; 22 cm. (Zenith books) SCHOMBURG CHILDREN'S COLLECTION. DDC 973.8 (j)
1. Afro-Americans - History - 1877-1964 - Juvenile literature. I. Toppin, Edgar Allan, 1928- joint author. II. Schomburg Children's Collection. III. Title.
E185.6 .D7   *NYPL [Sc D 88-1429]*

Le droit de l'homme a l'existence . Dialembonkebi, Diebo Makani-Ma-Nsi. Kinshasa, Zaire , c1988. 36 p. ;
NYPL [Sc D 89-220]

Le droit international du travail en Afrique . Missé, Hermann. Paris , 1987. 263 p. ; ISBN 2-85802-839-7   *NYPL [Sc E 88-20]*

Droit public du Sénégal /. Gautron, Jean Claude. Paris , 1977. 447 p. ; ISBN 2-233-00036-6 :
LAW   *NYPL [Sc E 88-612]*

A drop of mercy /. Humphrey, Dibia. Nigeria , 1987. 230 p. ; ISBN 978-13-9603-2
NYPL [Sc C 88-318]

DROPOUTS, AFRO-AMERICAN. see AFRO-AMERICAN DROPOUTS.

DROPOUTS - EMPLOYMENT - BOTSWANA.
Martin, Anthony. Report on the brigades in Botswana. [n.p.a., 1971?] 96 p.
HD6276.B6 M37   *NYPL [JLF 74-1283]*

DROPOUTS - SWAZILAND.
Sullivan, Gerard. From school--to work . Oxford , c1981. xvi, 190 p. : DDC 373.12/913/096813 19
LC145.S78 S94 1981   *NYPL [Sc F 87-331]*

DROUGHT - AFRICA - DIARIES.
Fanfani, Mariapia. [Hayat. English.] Hayat . New York , c1988. 219 p., [16] p. of plates : ISBN 0-671-66414-X DDC 363.8/83/0924 B 19
HV696.F6 F363 1988   *NYPL [JFD 88-3833]*

DROUGHTS - NIGERIA, NORTHERN.
Mortimore, M. J., 1937- Adapting to drought . Cambridge ; New York , 1989. xxii, 299 p. : ISBN 0-521-32312-6 DDC 333.73 19
HC1055.Z7 N6755 1988
NYPL [Sc E 89-191]

Droy, I. Femmes et projets de développement rural en Afrique Sub-Saharienne : essai d'analyse à partir d'études de cas / I. Droy. 1985. 557 p. : ill., maps ; 22 cm. At head of title: Université des sciences sociales de Grenoble, Institut de recherche économoque et de planification du développement. "Décembre 1985." Thesis--Université des sciences sociales de Grenoble. Bibliography: p. 540-557.
1. Women in rural development - Africa. I. Title.
NYPL [Sc D 88-778]

Drum gahu . Locke, David, 1949- Crown Point, Ind. , c1987. ix, 142 p. : ISBN 0-941677-03-6 : DDC 789/.01 19
MT655 .L6 1987   *NYPL [Sc E 88-391]*

DRUMMERS (MUSICIANS) - UNITED STATES - BIOGRAPHY.
Crowther, Bruce, 1933- Gene Krupa, his life & times /. Tunbridge Wells, Kent , New York , 1987. 144 p. : ISBN 0-87663-670-9 (USA) DDC 789/.1/0924 B 19
ML419.K78 C8 1987   *NYPL [JNF 88-89]*

Du Boulay, Shirley. Tutu : voice of the voiceless / Shirley du Boulay. London : Hodder & Stoughton, 1988. 286 p., [8] p. of plates : ill., ports. ; 22 cm. Includes index. Bibliography: p. 275-276. ISBN 0-340-41614-9 : DDC 283/.68/0924 19
1. Tutu, Desmond. 2. Church of England. Province of South Africa - Bishops - Biography. 3. Bishops - South Africa - Biography. I. Title.
BX5700.6.Z8T87   *NYPL [*R-ZPZ 88-3127]*

Du Pry, Ben. [Address to] 1st conference of Caribbean basin journalists and media workers, April 16-20, 1982, Grenada W.I. [microform] / Ben du Pry. [St. George's, Grenada : s.n., 1982] 6 p. ; 35 cm. Caption title. Microfilm. New York: New York Public Library, 1982. 1 microfilm reel; 35 mm. (MN *ZZ-23051)
1. Liberty of the press - Haiti. I. Title: 1st conference of Caribbean basin journalists and media workers.
NYPL [Sc Micro R-4108 no. 44]

Duarte Brasio, Antonio. see Brasio, Antonio Duarte, 1906-

Duberman, Martin B. Paul Robeson / by Martin Bauml Duberman. 1st ed. New York : Knopf, 1988, c1989. xiii, 804 p., [48] p. of plates : ill., ports. ; 25 cm. Includes bibliographical notes and index. ISBN 0-394-52780-1 : DDC 790.2/092/4 B 19
1. Robeson, Paul, 1898-1976. 2. Afro-Americans - Biography. I. Title.
E185.97.R63 D83 1988   *NYPL [Sc E 89-108]*

DUBOIS, SILVIA, 1788 OR 9-1889.
Larison, Cornelius Wilson, 1837-1910. Silvia Dubois . New York , 1988. xxvii, 124 p. ; ISBN 0-19-505239-0 DDC 305.5/67/0924 B 19
E444.D83 L37 1988   *NYPL [JFC 88-2191]*

DuBois, William Pène, 1916- Caudill, Rebecca, 1899- A certain small shepherd /. New York , 1965. 48 p. :   *NYPL [Sc D 88-433]*

Dubow, Saul. Land, labour and merchant capital in the pre-industrial rural economy of the Cape : the experience of the Graaff-Reinet District (1852-72) / by Saul Dubow. [Cape Town] : Centre for African Studies, University of Cape Town, 1982. ii, 95 p. : map ; 21 cm. (Communications / Centre for African Studies, University of Cape Town . no. 6) "Originally submitted in partial fulfilment of the requirements for the B.A. Honors degree in History, at the University of Cape Town." "Source list": p. 90-95. ISBN 0-7992-0472-2
1. Graaff-Reinet (South Africa) - Economic conditions. I. Series: Communications (University of Cape Town. Centre for African Studies) , no. 6. II. Title.
NYPL [Sc D 82-611]

Ducos, Jean François, 1765-1793. Opinion de Jean-François Ducos sur l'exécution provisoire du concordat, & des arrêtes de l'Assemblée coloniale confirmatifs de cet accord : imprimée par ordre de l'Assemblée nationale. A Paris : De l'Impr. nationale, 1791. 12 p. ; 20 cm. "Colonies. No. 10."
1. Haiti - History - Revolution, 1791-1804 - Sources. I. France. Assemblée nationale constituante, 1789-1791. II. Title.   *NYPL [Sc Rare C 86-7]*

Duczman, Linda. The baby-sitter / words by Linda Duczman ; pictures by Brent Jones. Milwaukee : Raintree Editions ; Chicago : distributed by Childrens Press, c1977. 30 p. : ill. (some col.) ; 25 cm. A child describes his first experience with a baby sitter including his prior fears and anxieties. SCHOMBURG CHILDREN'S COLLECTION. ISBN 0-8172-0065-7 (lib. bdg.) : DDC 649/.1
1. Baby sitters - Juvenile literature. 2. Children and strangers - Juvenile literature. I. Jones, Brent. II. Schomburg Children's Collection. III. Title.
HQ772.5 .D8   *NYPL [Sc E 88-588]*

DUE PROCESS OF LAW - SOUTH AFRICA - JOHANNESBURG.
Monama, Ramarumo. Is this justice? . Johannesburg [1983] xii, 65 p. :
NYPL [Sc D 88-1240]

Duffy, Susan, 1951- Shirley Chisholm : a bibliography of writings by and about her / compiled by Susan Duffy. Metuchen, N.J. : Scarecrow Press, 1988. vii, p. ; 23 cm. Includes

indexes. ISBN 0-8108-2105-2 DDC 016.32873/092/4 19
1. Chisholm, Shirley, 1924- - Bibliography. I. Title.
Z8167.47 .D83 1988 E840.8.C48
　　　　　NYPL [Sc D 88-1270]

Duke and other legends . Alexander, Jim. Atlanta, GA. , c1988. 63 p. : ISBN 0-945708-03-3　　*NYPL [Sc E 89-63]*

Duke Ellington /. Collier, James Lincoln, 1928- New York , 1987. viii, 340 p., [16] p. of plates : ISBN 0-19-503770-7 (alk. paper) DDC 785.42/092/4 B 19
ML410.E44 C6 1987　　*NYPL [JNE 87-49]*

Duke Ellington /. Frankl, Ron. New York , c1988. 110 p. : ISBN 1-555-46584-6 DDC 785.42/092/4 B 92 19
ML3930.E44 F7 1988　　*NYPL [Sc E 88-381]*

Duke Ellington /. Gammond, Peter. London , 1987. 127 p. : ISBN 0-948820-00-4 (pbk.) :
　　　　　NYPL [JNC 87-8]

Duke, Hajia Zainab I. (Hajia Zainab Ibitein)
The revolutionary potentials of the Nigerian military, 1886-1986 / by Hajia Zainab I. Duke. [Lagos?] Nigeria : H.Z.I. Duke, c1987. viii, 145 p., [28] p. of plates : ill., ports. ; 22 cm. Bibliography: p. 90-91. ISBN 978-232-008-0 DDC 322/.5/09669 19
1. Military government - Nigeria. 2. Nigeria - Politics and government - 1960-. 3. Nigeria - Armed Forces - Political activity. 4. Nigeria - Colonial influence. I. Title.
DT515.8 .D84 1987　　*NYPL [Sc D 88-1278]*

Dulzaides, Marta. see **Dulzaides Serrate, Marta.**

Dulzaides Serrate, Marta. Bibliograf ia cubana : 1921-1936 /. La Habana , 1977-78. [v. 1, 1978] 2 v. ;　　　　*NYPL [HO 80-1472]*

Dumas, Alexandre, 1824-1895.
[Dame aux camélias (Novel). English]
La dame aux camélias / Alexandre Dumas fils ; translated with an introduction by David Coward. Oxford ; New York : Oxford University Press, 1986. xxv, 215 p. ; 19 cm. (The World's classics) Bibliography: p. [205]-215. ISBN 0-19-281736-1 (pbk.) : DDC 843/.7 19
I. Title.
PQ2231.D2 E5 1986　　*NYPL [Sc C 88-201]*

Dumas, Marc. Lisette, Yeyon. Le RDA et le Tchad . Paris , Abidjan , 1986. 351 p. ; ISBN 2-7087-0472-9 (Présence africaine)
　　　　　NYPL [Sc E 87-627]

Dumba nengue, run for your life . Magaia, Lina. [Dumba nengue. English.] Trenton, N.J. , 1988. 113 p. : ISBN 0-86543-073-X
　　　　　NYPL [Sc D 88-1509]

Dumila, Faraj O., 1937- The Nyayo decade / by Faraj Dumila. [Nairobi? : S.n., 1988?] 2 v. : ill., ports. ; 30 cm. Cover title. In English, with some Swahili. Title on p. [4] of cover: "10" enzi ya nyayo.
1. Moi, Daniel Arap, 1924-. I. Title. II. Title: "10" enzi ya nyayo.　　*NYPL [Sc F 89-122]*

DuMont Kultur-Reiseführer.
Sheikh-Dilthey, Helmtraut, 1944- Kenya . Köln , 1987. 279 p. :　　*NYPL [Sc D 88-935]*

Dumont, René, 1904- Pour l'Afrique, j'accuse : le journal d'un agronome au Sahel en voie de destruction / par René Dumont, en collaboration avec Charlotte Paquet ; postface de Michel Rocard. [Paris] : Plon, c1986. 457 p., [48] p. of plates : ill. ; 21 cm. (Terre humaine : civilisations et sociétés, 0492-7915) Includes index. Bibliography: p. 413-[419] ISBN 2-259-01455-0
1. Economic assistance - Sahel. 2. Sahel - Economic conditions. 3. Sahel - Social conditions. 4. Sahel - Politics and government. I. Paquet, Charlotte. II. Series: Terre humaine. III. Title.
HC1002 .D85 1986　　*NYPL [Sc D 88-642]*

D'un Fouta-Djalloo à l'autre /. Baldé de Labé, Sirah. Paris , c1985- v. ; ISBN 2-214-06108-8 (v. 1) : DDC 843 19
PQ3989.2.B26 D86 1985
　　　　　NYPL [Sc C 88 103]

Dunayevskaya, Raya.
The Raya Dunayevskaya collection [microform] Supplement: Raya Dunayevskaya's last writings, 1986-1987. 1986-1987. ca. 140 items. Target title. Printed guide accompanying the microfilm has subtitle: Marxism-humanism, a half century of its world development ... Volume XIII: Raya Dunayevskaya's last writings toward the dialectics of organization and

philosophy. Guide prepared by Raya Dunayevskaya Memorial Fund. Microfilm. Detroit : Wayne State University Archives of Labor and Urban Affairs 1988. 1 microfilm reel ; 16 mm.
1. Communism - History - Sources. I. Raya Dunayevskaya Memorial Fund. II. Title. III. Title: Marxist-humanism, a half century of its world development.　　*NYPL [Sc Micro R-4838]*

DUNAYEVSKAYA, RAYA - BIBLIOGRAPHY - CATALOGS.
Guide to the Raya Dunayevskaya collection . Detroit, Mich. [1986?] 84 p. ;
　　　　　NYPL [Sc F 88-196]

Dunbar-Nelson, Alice Moore, 1875-1935.
[Works. 1988]
The works of Alice Dunbar-Nelson / edited by Gloria T. Hull. New York : Oxford University Press, 1988. 3 v. : port. ; 17 cm. (Schomburg library of nineteenth-century Black women writers) Reprinted from various sources. Includes bibliographical references. ISBN 0-19-505250-1 (v. 1 : alk. paper) DDC 818/.5209 19
1. Afro-Americans - Literary collections. I. Hull, Gloria T. II. Title. III. Series.
PS3507 .U6228 1988　　*NYPL [JFC 88-2143]*

DUNBAR-NELSON, ALICE MOORE, 1875-1935 - CRITICISM AND INTERPRETATION.
Hull, Gloria T. Color, sex, and poetry . Bloomington , c1987. xi, 240 p. : ISBN 0-253-34974-5 DDC 811/.52/099287 19
PS153.N5 H84 1987　　*NYPL [Sc E 88-72]*

DUNBAR, PAUL LAURENCE, 1872-1906 - BIOGRAPHY - JUVENILE LITERATURE.
Gentry, Tony. Paul Laurence Dunbar /. New York , c1989. 110 p. : ISBN 1-555-46583-8 DDC 811/.4 B 92 19
PS1557 .G46 1989　　*NYPL [Sc E 88-514]*

Duncan, Jane. My friend the swallow. London, Macmillan; New York, St. Martin's Press, 1970. 255 p. 21 cm. ISBN 0-333-11677-1 DDC 823/.9/14
1. Caribbean area - Fiction. I. Title.
PZ4.D9116 Mwk PR6054.U46
　　　　　NYPL [Sc D 88-1115]

Duncan, Malcolm C. Duncan's Masonic ritual and monitor, or, Guide to the three symbolic degrees E.A., F.C., M.M. / by Malcolm C. Duncan. [Rev. ed.] Danbury, Conn. : Behrens Pub. Co., c1922- v. : ill. ; 17 cm.
1. Freemasonry - Rituals. I. Title. II. Title: Guide to the three symbolic degrees. III. Title: Masonic ritual and monitor.　　*NYPL [Sc B 88-65]*

Duncan, Neville C. Women and politics in Barbados, 1948-1981 / Neville Duncan, Kenneth O'Brien ; with an introduction by Billie Miller. Cave Hill, Barbados : Institute of Social and Economic Research (Eastern Caribbean), University of the West Indies, c1983. x, 68 p. ; 24 cm. (Women in the Caribbean project . v. 3) Bibliography: p. 48-49.
1. Women in politics - Barbados. 2. Women in public life - Barbados. I. O'Brien, Kenneth. II. University of the West Indies (Cave Hill, Barbados). nInstitute of Social and Economic Research. III. Title. IV. Series.
　　　　　NYPL [Sc E 84-107]

Duncan's Masonic ritual and monitor, or, Guide to the three symbolic degrees E.A., F.C., M.M. /. Duncan, Malcolm C. Danbury, Conn. , c1922- v. :　　*NYPL [Sc B 88-65]*

Dundurn lives.
Hubbard, Stephen, 1961- Against all odds . Toronto , 1987. 140 p. : ISBN 1-550-02013-7 (bound)　　　　*NYPL [Sc D 88-985]*

DUNGEONS. see PRISONS.

Dunn, D. Elwood.
Historical dictionary of Liberia / by D. Elwood Dunn and Svend E. Holsoe. Metuchen, N.J. : Scarecrow Press, 1985. xx, 274, [7] p. of plates : maps ; 23 cm. (African historical dictionaries. no. 38) Includes index. Bibliography: p. 193-240. ISBN 0-8108-1767-5 DDC 966.6/2/00321 19
1. Liberia - History - Dictionaries. I. Holsoe, Svend E. II. Title. III. Series.
DT631 .D95 1985　　*NYPL [Sc D 86-127]*

Liberia : a national polity in transition / by D. Elwood Dunn and S. Byron Tarr. Metuchen, N.J. : Scarecrow Press, c1988. xii, 259 p. : ill., maps, ports. ; 23 cm. Includes index. Bibliography:

p. 229-241. ISBN 0-8108-2088-9 DDC 966.6/203 19
1. Liberia - History. I. Tarr, S. Byron, 1943-. II. Title.
DT631 .D953 1988　　*NYPL [JFD 88-8633]*

Dunton, C. P. Wole Soyinka, three short plays : The swamp dwellers, The strong breed, The trials of Brother Jero ; notes / by C.P. Dunton. Harlow, Essex : Longman ; Beirut : York Press, 1982. 71 p. ; 21 cm. (York notes . 172) ISBN 0-582-78260-0
I. Soyinka, Wole. Three short plays. II. Title.
　　　　　NYPL [Sc D 88-159]

Duplechan, Larry.
Eight days a week : a novel / by Larry Duplechan.1st ed. Boston : Alyson Publications, Inc., 1985. 260, [4] p. ; 21 cm. ISBN 0-932870-84-8
1. Gay men - Fiction. I. Title.
　　　　　NYPL [Sc D 89-219]

Tangled up in blue / Larry Duplechan. 1st ed. New York : St. Martin's Press, 1989. 264 p. ; 23 cm. ISBN 0-312-02650-1 : DDC 813/.54 19
1. AIDS (Disease) - Fiction. I. Title.
PS3554.U55 T36 1989　NYPL [Sc D 89-250]

Durant, Franck Alphonse. Rétrospectives [microform] : Adolf Hitler les accords de Locarno ; La controverse de la France et de l'Italie mussolinienne / Franck A. Durant. Port-au-Prince, Haiti : [s.n.], 1977. 16 p. ; 21 cm. Cover title. Microfiche. New York: New York Public Library, 198 . 1 microfiche: negative; 11 x 15 cm. (FSN Sc 019,076) Author's autographed presentation copy to the New York Public Library.
1. Locarno, Conference, 1925. 2. France - Foreign relations - Italy - History. 3. Italy - Foreign relations - France - History. 4. Germany - Politics and government - 1933-1945. I. Title. II. Title: Adolf Hitler et les accords de Locarno. III. Title: Controverse de la France et de l'Italie mussolinienne.
　　　　　NYPL [Sc Micro F 10,933]

Durham, John, fl. 1960- Me and Arch and the Pest. Illustrated by Ingrid Fetz. New York, Four Winds Press [1970] 96 p. illus. 24 cm. Two boys acquire a German shepherd whose disappearance involves them in a crime. DDC [Fic]
1. Dogs - Juvenile fiction. 2. Afro-American children - Juvenile fiction. I. Fetz, Ingrid, illus. II. Title.
PZ7.D9335 Me　　*NYPL [Sc E 88-416]*

Durou, Jean Marc. Sahara : désert magique / photograhies, Jean-Marc Durou ; textes, Théodore Monod.2e éd. Marseille, France : Editions AGEP, 1986. 155 p. : chiefly col. ill., map ; 31 cm. ISBN 2-902634-30-7
1. Tuaregs - Pictorial works. 2. Sahara - Description and travel - Views. I. Monod, Théodore, 1902- . II. Title.　　*NYPL [Sc G 88-1]*

Duvalier . Nérée, Bob. Port-au-Prince, Haiti , 1988. 238 p. ;　　*NYPL [Sc E 88-366]*

DUVALIER, FRANÇOIS, 1907-1971.
Abbott, Elizabeth. Haiti . New York, N.Y. , c1988. xii, 381 p., [8] p. of plates : ISBN 0-07-046029-9 : DDC 972.94/06 19
F1928 .A583 1988　　*NYPL [Sc E 88-605]*

Diederich, Bernard. [Papa Doc. Spanish.] Papa Doc y los tontons Macoutes . Santo Domingo, República Dominicana , 1986. 393 p., [16] p. of plates :　　　*NYPL [Sc D 88-452]*

Ferguson, James, 1956- Papa Doc, Baby Doc . Oxford, UK , New York, NY, USA , 1987. x, 171 p., [8] p. of plates : ISBN 0-631-15601-1 : DDC 972.94/07 19
F1928 .F47 1987　　*NYPL [Sc E 88-269]*

Nérée, Bob. Duvalier . Port-au-Prince, Haiti , 1988. 238 p. ;　　*NYPL [Sc E 88-366]*

DUVALIER, JEAN CLAUDE, 1951-
Abbott, Elizabeth. Haiti . New York, N.Y. , c1988. xii, 381 p., [8] p. of plates : ISBN 0-07-046029-9 : DDC 972.94/06 19
F1928 .A583 1988　　*NYPL [Sc E 88-605]*

Ferguson, James, 1956- Papa Doc, Baby Doc . Oxford, UK , New York, NY, USA , 1987. x, 171 p., [8] p. of plates : ISBN 0-631-15601-1 : DDC 972.94/07 19
F1928 .F47 1987　　*NYPL [Sc E 88-269]*

Guerre, Rockefeller. Mon mandat sous Jn-Claude Duvalier . Port-au-Prince, Haiti , 1987. 260 p. ;　　*NYPL [Sc D 87-935]*

Nérée, Bob. Duvalier . Port-au-Prince, Haiti , 1988. 238 p. ;　　*NYPL [Sc E 88-366]*

Duyile, Dayo. Makers of Nigerian press : an historical analysis of newspaper development, the pioneer heroes, the modern press barons and the new publishers, from 1859-1987 / Dayo Duyile. Nigeria : Gong Communications (Nigeria), 1987. xx, 726 p. : ill., ports. ; 27 cm. Bibliography: p. 725-726.
1. Press - Nigeria - History. 2. Mass media - Nigeria. 3. Journalists - Nigeria. I. Title.
NYPL [Sc F 89-167]

DW-Dokumente .
(3) African writers on the air. Köln , c1984. 119 p. : **NYPL [Sc D 88-674]**

DWELLINGS - BURUNDI.
Acquier, Jean-Louis, 1946- Le Burundi /. Marseille, France , c1986. 129 p. : ISBN 2-86364-030-5 : DDC 728/.67/0967572 19
GT377.B94 A27 1986 **NYPL [Sc E 88-568]**

DWELLINGS - CAPE VERDE ISLANDS - SÃO TIAGO.
Lopes Filho, João. Cabo Verde . Lisboa , 1976. 54 p., [5] leaves of plates :
NYPL [Sc D 84-279]

Dworaczek, Marian. Affirmative action and minorities : a bibliography / Marian Dworaczek. Monticello. Ill., USA : Vance Bibliographies, [1988] 63 p. ; 28 cm. (Public administration series--bibliography, 0193-970X . P 2328) Cover title. "January 1988." ISBN 1-555-90638-9 (pbk.) : DDC 016.33113/3 19
1. Affirmative action programs - Bibliography. 2. Discrimination in employment - Bibliography. 3. Minorities - Bibliography. I. Title. II. Series.
Z7164.A26 D87 1988 HF5549.5.A34
NYPL [Sc f 89-39]

DYES AND DYEING, DOMESTIC.
Errington, Leah. Natural dyes of Zambia /. [Zambia? , between 1986 and 1988] (Ndola, Zambia : Mission Press) 35 p. :
NYPL [Sc B 89-23]

Dyke hands & sutras erotic & lyric /. Bogus, SDiane. San Francisco, Calif. , 1988. vii, 91 p. ; ISBN 0-934172-21-8 :
NYPL [Sc D 89-536]

Dzimbava. Makuya, T. N. Pretoria, 1972. 62 p. ISBN 0-627-00110-6 **NYPL [JFD 76-2629]**

E dia di mas históriko /. Jongh, Edward Arthur de. Aruba , 1970. 158 p. :
NYPL [Sc D 87-1430]

E. R. R. see Earth Resources Research Ltd.

Eager, Edward. The well-wishers / Edward Eager ; illustrated by N.M. Bodecker. New York : Harcourt Brace and World, c1960. 191 p. : ill. ; 21 cm. Six children relate their experiences with an unpredictable old wishing well that involves them in some magical adventures during an eventful autumn. SCHOMBURG CHILDREN'S COLLECTION.
1. Magic - Juvenile fiction. I. Bodecker, N. M., ill. II. Schomburg Children's Collection. III. Title.
NYPL [Sc D 88-429]

Eagles, Charles W. The Civil rights movement in America . Jackson , c1986. xii, 188 p. ; ISBN 0-87805-297-6 (alk. paper) DDC 323.1/196073 19
E185.615 .C585 1986 **NYPL [IEC 87-273]**

EAGLES - JUVENILE FICTION.
Glendinning, Sally. Jimmy and Joe fly a kite. Champaign, Ill. [1970] 38 p. ISBN 0-8116-4704-8 DDC [Fic]
PZ7.G4829 Jm **NYPL [Sc D 88-1475]**

Eames, John. Amin, Mohamed, 1943- The last of the Maasai . London , 1987. 185 p. : ISBN 0-370-31097-7 **NYPL [Sc G 88-21]**

Earle, William. Obi, or, The history of Three-fingered Jack : in a series of letters from a resident in Jamaica to his friend in England ... London : Printed for Earle and Hemet ... , 1800. vi, [2], 232 p., [1] leaf of plates : ill. (etching) ; 19 cm. (12mo) Preface signed: W.E.J. Half-title: Obi, or, Three-fingered Jack.
1. Slavery - Jamaica - Fiction. 2. Slave-trade - Fiction. 3. Maroons - Jamaica - Fiction. I. Title. II. Title: Three-fingered Jack. **NYPL [Sc Rare C 88-3]**

The earliest patriots . O'Callaghan, Evelyn. London , 1986. 61 p. ; ISBN 0-946918-53-8pb
NYPL [Sc C 88-104]

Early hominid activities at Olduvai . Potts, Richard, 1953- New York , c1988. xi, 396 p. :

ISBN 0-202-01176-3 (lib. bdg.) DDC 967.8 19
GN772.42.T34 P67 1988
NYPL [Sc E 89-92]

Early Sudanese nationalism, 1919-1925 /. Abdin, Hasan. [Khartoum?] [1985?] iv, 167 p. : DDC 962.4/03 19
DT156.7 .A23 1985 **NYPL [Sc E 88-335]**

Ears and tails and common sense: more stories from the Caribbean. Sherlock, Philip Manderson, Sir. London , 1988. xvii, 121 p.
NYPL [Sc D 88-1220]

EARTH, EFFECT OF MAN ON. see MAN - INFLUENCE ON NATURE.

Earth Resources Research Ltd. Dinham, Barbara. Agribusiness in Africa /. London , 1983. 224 p. : ISBN 0-946281-00-9 : **NYPL [Sc D 84-44]**

EARTHENWARE. see POTTERY.

Earthscan. Harrison, Paul, 1945- The greening of Africa . London , 1987. 380 p. : ISBN 0-586-08642-0 (pbk) : DDC 330.96/0328 19
HC502 **NYPL [Sc C 88-327]**

Easmon, Carol. (ill) Appiah, Sonia. Amoko and Efua bear /. New York, NY , 1989, c1988. [30] p. : ISBN 0-02-705591-4 DDC E 19
PZ7.A647 Am 1989 **NYPL [Sc F 89-138]**

East Africa . Beddow, Tim. New York, N.Y. , 1988. 21 p., [80] p. of plates : ISBN 0-500-24131-7 **NYPL [Sc F 88-291]**

East Africa . Crowther, Geoff. South Yarra , 1987. 373 p., [16] p. of plates : ISBN 0-86442-005-6 **NYPL [Sc C 88-332]**

East Africa . Knappert, Jan. New Delhi , c1987. 383 p. ; ISBN 0-7069-2822-9 : DDC 967.6 19
DT423 .K56 1987 **NYPL [Sc D 88-852]**

The East Africa library movement and its problems [microform] /. Kaungamno, Ezekiel E. Dar es Salaam [197-?] 6 leaves ;
NYPL [Sc Micro R4094 no. 30]

East African Medical Research Council. A Bibliography of health and disease in East Africa /. Amsterdam ; New York : 282 p. ; ISBN 0-444-80931-7 (U. S.) DDC 016.3621/0967 19
Z6673.6.A353 B53 1988 RA552.A353
NYPL [Sc G 89-6]

East African studies.
(32) Charsley, Simon R. The princes of Nyakyusa. [Nairobi, 1969] xii, 125 p. DDC 301.29/678
DT443 .C5 **NYPL [Sc D 88-975]**

EAST INDIANS - CARIBBEAN AREA.
India in the Caribbean /. London , 1987. 326 p. : ISBN 1-87051-805-5 (cased) : DDC 909/.09182/1081 19 **NYPL [Sc D 88-997]**

EAST INDIANS - CARIBBEAN AREA - FOLKLORE.
Parmasad, Kenneth Vidia. Indian folk tales of the Caribbean . Charlieville, Chaguanas, Trinidad and Tobago, West Indies , c1984. xxii, 131 p., [2] p. of plates : ISBN 976-8016-01-9 (pbk.) DDC 398.2/09729 19
GR120 .P37 1984 **NYPL [Sc D 88-400]**

EAST INDIANS - GUADELOUPE - RELIGIOUS LIFE AND CUSTOMS.
Moutoussamy, Ernest, 1941- La Guadeloupe et son indianité /. Paris , c1987. 119 p., [12] p. of plates : ISBN 2-87679-008-4
NYPL [Sc D 88-968]

EAST INDIANS - GUADELOUPE - SOCIAL LIFE AND CUSTOMS.
Moutoussamy, Ernest, 1941- La Guadeloupe et son indianité /. Paris , c1987. 119 p., [12] p. of plates : ISBN 2-87679-008-4
NYPL [Sc D 88-968]

EAST INDIANS - TRINIDAD AND TOBAGO.
Mahabir, Noor Kumar. The still cry . Tacarigua, Trinidad , Ithaca, N.Y. , c1985. 191 p. ; **NYPL [Sc D 88-401]**

EAST INDIES.
Raynal, Guillaume Thomas François, 1713-1796. Histoire philosophique et politique des établissemens & du commerce des Européens dans les deux Indes. A Amsterdam , 1770. 6 v. ; **NYPL [Sc Rare C 86-2]**

EAST VILLAGE (NEW YORK, N.Y.) - POPULAR CULTURE.
Delany, Samuel R. The motion of light in

water . New York, c1988. xviii, 302 p. : ISBN 0-87795-947-1 : DDC 813/.54 19
PS3554.E437 Z475 1988
NYPL [JFD 88-7818]

Eastern Africa studies.
Kanogo, Tabitha M. Squatters and the roots of Mau Mau, 1905-63 /. Athens , London , 1987. xviii, 206 p. : ISBN 0-8214-0873-9 DDC 307.3/36 19
HD1538.K4 K36 1987 **NYPL [Sc D 88-207]**

Eastern and Southern African Universities Research Programme. University capacity in eastern & southern African countries / Eastern & Southern African Universities Research Programme. London : Currey ; Portsmouth, N.H. : Heinemann, c1987. xix, 259 p. : ill. ; 22 cm. ISBN 0-85255-107-X : DDC 378.67 19
1. Universities and colleges - Africa, Eastern. 2. Universities and colleges - Africa, Southern. 3. Education, Higher - Africa, Eastern. 4. Education, Higher - Africa, Southern. I. Title. II. Title: University capacity in eastern and southern African countries.
LA1503 **NYPL [Sc D 89-314]**

EASTERN PROVINCE, ZAMBIA - ANTIQUITIES.
Phillipson, D. W. The prehistory of eastern Zambia /. Nairobi , 1976. xi, 229 p., [21] leaves of plates (5 fold.) : ISBN 0-500-97003-3 :
GN865.Z3 P48 **NYPL [JFF 79-1585]**

Eastern Province, Zambia - Archaeology. see Eastern Province, Zambia - Antiquities.

Easton, Peter A. Functional literacy and cooperative education : development of the Maradi project, 1970-1971 / Peter A. Easton. 1972. v, 87 leaves : ill. ; 30 cm. Typescript.
1. Illiteracy - Niger. 2. Education, Cooperative - Niger. I. Title. **NYPL [Sc F 88-52]**

Eat this book . Gordon, Billi. San Francisco, California , c1987. 96 p. : ISBN 0-9614979-1-2
NYPL [Sc F 88-110]

Eating what we grow. Jones, Novelette C. Cook up Jamaican style /. Kingston, Jamaica , 1977. 111 leaves : **NYPL [Sc F 89-132]**

Eaton, David. James, Winston. The Caribbean /. London , 1984. 46 p. : ISBN 0-356-07105-7 : DDC 972.9 19
F2175 **NYPL [Sc F 88-128]**

Les eaux claires de ma source /Timité bassori ; et six autres nouvelles. Timité, Bassori, 1933- Paris , 1986. 127 p. ; ISBN 2-218-07813-9
NYPL [Sc C 88-11]

Ebermann, Erwin. Die Sprache der Mauka : eine kleine Grammatik der Sprache eines noch kleinen westafrikanischen Volkes im Nordwesten der Elfenbeinküste / Erwin Ebermann. Wien : VWGÖ, 1986. 207 p. ; 21 cm. (Dissertationen der Universität Wien, 0379-1424 . 181) Bibliography: p. 199-201. ISBN 3-85369-656-2
1. Mau dialect (Ivory Coast) - Grammar. 2. Language and culture - Ivory Coast. I. Title. II. Series.
PL8491.95.I9 E24 1986
NYPL [Sc D 88-687]

Ebert, Len. (illus) Bontemps, Arna Wendell, 1902- Mr. Kelso's lion. Philadelphia [1970] 48 p. DDC [Fic]
PZ7.B6443 Mi **NYPL [Sc D 88-1493]**

Ebinne, S. S. Odunze, Don. The marriage killers /. Enugu [Nigeria] [198-?] 104 p. ; **NYPL [Sc C 88-189]**

Ebira names in Nigeria . Ajayi, John Olufemi. Okpella , 1985. 51 p. : ISBN 978-252-800-5 (pbk.) DDC 929.4/089963 19
CS2375.N6 A34 1985 **NYPL [Sc D 88-1256]**

Ebobissé, Carl. Les verbaux du dangaléat de l'est (Guera, Tchad) : lexiques francais-dangaléat et allemand-dangaleat / Carl Ebobisse. Berlin : D. Reimer, 1987. 104 p. ; 24 cm. (Marburger Studien zur Afrika- und Asienkunde: Serie A, Afrika. Bd. 22) Bibliography: p. 103-104. ISBN 3-496-00555-6
1. Dangaleat language - Verb. 2. Dangaleat language - Dictionaries - French. 3. French language - Dictionaries - Dangaleat. 4. Dangaleat language - Dictionaries - German. 5. German language - Dictionaries - Dangaleat. I. Title.
NYPL [Sc E 88-231]

Ebony and topaz : a collectanea / edited by Charles S. Johnson. New York : Opportunity : Nation Urban League, 1927. 164 p. : illus., facsims., ports. ; 30 cm.

1. American literature - 20th century. I. Johnson, Charles Spurgeon, 1893-1956. II. Opportunity; journal of Negro life. **NYPL [Sc Rare F 82-72]**

Ebony, N. X. Déjà vu, suivi de Chutes / N.X. Ebony. Paris : Ouskokata, 1983. 191 p. ; 22 cm. Lacks: "Chutes : supplement unique à Déjà vu." ISBN 2-86436-005-5
I. Title. **NYPL [Sc D 88-1353]**

Ebroïn, Ary. Quimbois, magie noire et sorcellerie aux Antilles : avec 61 pantacles et sceaux magiques / Ary Ebroïn. Paris : J. Grancher, c1977. 239 p., [4] leaves of plates : ill. ; 23 cm. Bibliography: p. [233]-234. DDC 133.4/09729
1. Magic - West Indies. 2. Witchcraft - West Indies. I. Title.
BF1622.W47 E26 **NYPL [Sc D 89-270]**

ECCENTRICS AND ECCENTRICITIES IN ART - EXHIBITIONS.
Baking in the sun . Lafayette , c1987. 146 p. : ISBN 0-295-96606-8 **NYPL [Sc F 88-197]**

ECCLESIASTICAL ART. see CHRISTIAN ART AND SYMBOLISM.

ECCLESIASTICAL RITES AND CEREMONIES. see RITES AND CEREMONIES.

L'échec du firminisme /. Péan, Marc. Port-au-Prince, Haiti , 1987. 181 p. : **NYPL [Sc D 88-625]**

ECHOLS FAMILY.
Echols, James, 1932- The Echols of Detroit . [S. l.] 1985 [Port Jefferson Sta., N.Y. : McPrint Graphics Center] v. :
NYPL [Sc F 88-97]

Echols, James, 1932- The Echols of Detroit : genealogy / James Echols. [S. l. : s.n.], 1985 [Port Jefferson Sta., N.Y. : McPrint Graphics Center] v. : ports. ; 29 cm. Compiled by James Echols, John Lawrence Echols, and Donald Echols -- copyright statement.
1. Echols family. 2. Afro-Americans - Michigan - Detroit - Genealogy. 3. Detroit (Mich.) - Genealogy. I. Title. **NYPL [Sc F 88-97]**

The Echols of Detroit . Echols, James, 1932- [S. l.] 1985 [Port Jefferson Sta., N.Y. : McPrint Graphics Center] v. : **NYPL [Sc F 88-97]**

Echos d'Afrique : livre unique de français : CM2 : livre du maître. [Paris] : F. Nathan, c1984. 159 p. ; 22 cm. (Nathan Afrique) ISBN 2-09-168451-1
1. French language - Text-books for foreign speakers. 2. French language - Study and teaching - Foreign speakers. I. Series. **NYPL [Sc D 88-907]**

Eckardt, A. Roy (Arthur Roy), 1918-
Black-woman-Jew : three wars for human liberation / A. Roy Eckardt. Bloomington : Indiana University Press, c1989. 229 p. ; 25 cm. Includes index. Bibliography: p. [216]-222. ISBN 0-253-31221-3 DDC 305.4/8896073 19
1. Afro-Americans - Social conditions - 1975-. 2. Afro-Americans - Religion. 3. Women, Jewish - United States. 4. Civil rights movements - United States. I. Title.
E185.86 .E28 1989 **NYPL [Sc E 89-209]**

ECLECTICISM IN ART - SOUTH AFRICA - HOMELANDS.
Younge, Gavin. Art of the South African townships /. New York , 1988. 96 p. : ISBN 0-8478-0973-0 (pbk.) DDC 704/.03968 19
N7394.H66 Y68 1988 **NYPL [Sc F 88-364]**

Eclipse . Branley, Franklyn Mansfield, 1915- New York , c1988. 32 p. : ISBN 0-690-04619-7 (lib. bdg.) : DDC 523.7/8 19
QB541.5 .B73 1988 **NYPL [Sc E 88-591]**

ECLIPSES, SOLAR - JUVENILE LITERATURE.
Branley, Franklyn Mansfield, 1915- Eclipse . New York , c1988. 32 p. : ISBN 0-690-04619-7 (lib. bdg.) : DDC 523.7/8 19
QB541.5 .B73 1988 **NYPL [Sc E 88-591]**

L'école sahraouie . Perregaux, Christiane. Paris , c1987. 158 p., [8] p. of plates : ISBN 2-85802-942-3 DDC 372.964/8 19
LA2034.W47 P47 1987
NYPL [Sc D 89-401]

ECOLOGY - AFRICA.
Lewis, Lawrence. African environments and resources /. Boston , 1988. xii, 404 p. : ISBN 0-04-916010-9 (alk. paper) DDC 333.7/096 19
HC800 .L48 1987 **NYPL [Sc E 89-50]**

ECOLOGY, HUMAN. see HUMAN ECOLOGY.

The Ecology of survival : case studies from northeast African history / edited by Douglas H. Johnson and David M. Anderson. London, England : L. Crook Academic Pub. ; Boulder, Colo. : Westview Press, 1988. xii, 339 p. : maps ; 23 cm. This book is the product of 2 meetings: the 1st was held July 8, 1985 at Wolfson College and sponsored by the Oxford University Inter-faculty Committee for African Studies; the 2nd met at the Institute of Social Anthropology on July 7-8, 1986. Includes index. Bibliography: p. 305-322. ISBN 0-8133-0727-9 (Westview) DDC 304.2/096 19
1. Human ecology - Africa, Northeast. I. Johnson, Douglas Hamilton, 1949-. II. Anderson, David M. III. University of Oxford. Inter-faculty Committee on African Studies.
GF720 .E26 1988 **NYPL [Sc D 89-280]**

ECOLOGY, SOCIAL. see HUMAN ECOLOGY.

La economía / José Luis Cortés ... [et al.] Madrid : Iepala : Fundamentos, c1986. 109, [4] p. ; 20 cm. (Africa internacional . 3) Bibliography: p. [111-113]
1. Africa - Economic conditions. I. Cortés, José Luis. II. Series. **NYPL [Sc C 88-186]**

Economic adjustment in oil-based economies /. Jazayeri, Ahmad, 1957- Aldershot, Hants, England , Brookfield, Vt., USA , c1988. xvi, 260 p. : ISBN 0-566-05682-8 : DDC 330.955/054 19
HD9576.I62 J39 1988 **NYPL [JLD 89-202]**

An economic and social history of Zimbabwe, 1890-1948 . Phimister, I. R. (Ian R.) London , New York , 1988. xii, 336 p. : ISBN 0-582-64423-2 DDC 330.96891/02 19
HC910.Z9 S36 1987 **NYPL [Sc D 89-35]**

ECONOMIC AND TECHNICAL ASSISTANCE. see ECONOMIC ASSISTANCE; TECHNICAL ASSISTANCE.

ECONOMIC ASSISTANCE - AFRICA, SOUTHERN - EVALUATION.
Aid & development in southern Africa . Trenton, N.J. [1988] xi, 148 p. : ISBN 0-86543-047-0 (pbk.) : DDC 338.968 19
HC900 .A53 1988 **NYPL [Sc D 88-1455]**

ECONOMIC ASSISTANCE - DEVELOPING COUNTRIES.
Chiaka, Ralph C. Morality of development aid to the Third World . Rome , 1985. ix, 215 p. :
NYPL [Sc E 88-96]

ECONOMIC ASSISTANCE - DEVELOPING COUNTRIES - MORAL AND ETHICAL ASPECTS.
Chiaka, Ralph C. Morality of development aid to the Third World . Rome , 1985. ix, 215 p. :
NYPL [Sc E 88-96]

ECONOMIC ASSISTANCE, FRENCH - AFRICA.
Freud, Claude. Quelle coopération? . Paris , c1988. 270 p. : ISBN 2-86537-203-0
HC800 .F74 1988 **NYPL [Sc D 89-602]**

ECONOMIC ASSISTANCE - HAITI.
DeWind, Josh. [Aiding migration. French.] Aide à la migration . Montréal, Québec, Canada , 1988. 216 p. :
NYPL [Sc D 89-441]

ECONOMIC ASSISTANCE IN UNDERDEVELOPED AREAS. see ECONOMIC ASSISTANCE.

ECONOMIC ASSISTANCE - MORAL AND ETHICAL ASPECTS.
Chiaka, Ralph C. Morality of development aid to the Third World . Rome , 1985. ix, 215 p. :
NYPL [Sc E 88-96]

ECONOMIC ASSISTANCE - NAMIBIA.
Khalifa, Ahmad M. Adverse consequences for the enjoyment of human rights of political, military, economic, and other forms of assistance given to the racist and colonialist régime of South Africa /. New York , 1985. ii, 164, [30] p. ; ISBN 92-1-154046-1 (pbk.) DDC 332.6/73/0968 19
HG5851.A3 K45 1985 **NYPL [Sc F 88-273]**

ECONOMIC ASSISTANCE - SAHEL.
Dumont, René, 1904- Pour l'Afrique, j'accuse . [Paris] , c1986. 457 p., [48] p. of plates : ISBN 2-259-01455-0
HC1002 .D85 1986 **NYPL [Sc D 88-642]**

ECONOMIC ASSISTANCE - SOUTH AFRICA.

Khalifa, Ahmad M. Adverse consequences for the enjoyment of human rights of political, military, economic, and other forms of assistance given to the racist and colonialist régime of South Africa /. New York , 1985. ii, 164, [30] p. ; ISBN 92-1-154046-1 (pbk.) DDC 332.6/73/0968 19
HG5851.A3 K45 1985 **NYPL [Sc F 88-273]**

ECONOMIC ASSISTANCE, SWEDISH - AFRICA.
Jinadu, Adele. Idealism and pragmatism as aspects of Sweden's development policy in Africa /. Lagos [1982?]. 107 p. ; ISBN 978-227-698-7 **NYPL [Sc D 88-355]**

ECONOMIC DEVELOPMENT - CASE STUDIES.
Alschuler, Lawrence R., 1941- Multinationals and maldevelopment . Basingstoke, Hampshire , c1988. xii, 218 p. : ISBN 0-333-41561-2
NYPL [Sc D 88-701]

Thomas, Clive Yolande. The poor and the powerless . New York , 1988. xv, 396 p. : ISBN 0-85345-743-3 : DDC 338.9/009729 19
HC151 .T56 1988 **NYPL [Sc D 88-763]**

The economic development of Kenya, 1895-1929 [microform] . Spencer, Ian R. G. [Nairobi] [1978] 14 p. ;
NYPL [Sc Micro R-4108 no.33]

ECONOMIC DEVELOPMENT PROJECTS - AFRICA.
All Africa Conference of Churches. Special Agency for EPEAA. Ecumenical Programme for Emergency Action in Africa . Nairobi , 1967. [193] p. ; **NYPL [Sc F 88-74]**

ECONOMIC DEVELOPMENT PROJECTS - AFRICA, SOUTHERN - EVALUATION.
Aid & development in southern Africa . Trenton, N.J. [1988] xi, 148 p. : ISBN 0-86543-047-0 (pbk.) : DDC 338.968 19
HC900 .A53 1988 **NYPL [Sc D 88-1455]**

ECONOMIC DEVELOPMENT PROJECTS - DEVELOPING COUNTRIES.
The Role of women in the execution of low-income housing projects . Nairobi, Kenya , 1986. 64 p. : ISBN 92-1-131005-9
NYPL [Sc F 88-225]

ECONOMIC DEVELOPMENT PROJECTS - PLANNING - CASE STUDIES.
Women and economic development . Oxford [England] ; New York : ix, 231 p. ; ISBN 0-85496-091-0 : DDC 305.4/2 19
HQ1240 .W665 1988 **NYPL [JLD 89-559]**

ECONOMIC DEVELOPMENT - SOCIAL ASPECTS - CASE STUDIES.
Women and economic development . Oxford [England] ; New York : ix, 231 p. ; ISBN 0-85496-091-0 : DDC 305.4/2 19
HQ1240 .W665 1988 **NYPL [JLD 89-559]**

ECONOMIC FORECASTING - GHANA - STATISTICS.
Ewusi, Kodwo. Economic trends in Ghana in 1984-85 and prospects for 1986 /. [Legon] [1986] 52 p. : DDC 330.9667/05 19
HC1060 .E975 1986 **NYPL [Sc G 88-31]**

ECONOMIC FORECASTING - NIGERIA.
Nigeria in search of a future /. Nsukka , 1986. vii, 155 p. ; ISBN 978-229-900-6
NYPL [Sc D 88-884]

ECONOMIC GROWTH. see ECONOMIC DEVELOPMENT.

Economic History Society. Ward, J. R. Poverty and progress in the Caribbean, 1800-1960 /. Houndmills, Basingstoke, Hampshire , 1985. 82 p. : ISBN 0-333-37212-3 (pbk.) DDC 330.9729 19
HC151 .W37 1985 **NYPL [JLD 86-2144]**

Economic issues and black colleges / the National Association for Equal Opportunity in Higher Education ; edited by Samuel L. Myers. Chicago : Follett Press, c1986. 59 p. ; 22 cm. A selection of papers presented to the National Conference on Blacks in Higher Education, held annually in Washington, D.C. Includes bibliographical references. ISBN 0-695-60053-2
1. Afro-Americans - Education (Higher) - Congresses. 2. Education, Higher - Economic aspects - United States - Congresses. I. Myers, Samuel L. II. National Association for Equal Opportunity in Higher Education (U. S.). III. National Conference on Blacks in Higher Education. **NYPL [Sc D 88-950]**

ECONOMIC SANCTIONS - SOUTH AFRICA - PUBLIC OPINION.
Hoile, David. Understanding sanctions /.
London , 1988. 80 p. : ISBN 1-87111-700-3
(pbk.) : DDC 337.68 19
HF1613.4 .H654 1988   *NYPL [Sc D 89-317]*

ECONOMIC SURVEYS - KENYA.
Narayan-Parker, Deepa. Women's interest and
involvement in income generating activities .
Gaborone, Botswana [1983] vi, 143, 3 p. ;
DDC 331.4/09676/2 19
HD6210.5 .N37 1983   *NYPL [Sc F 88-312]*

**Economic trends in Ghana in 1984-85 and
prospects for 1986 /.** Ewusi, Kodwo. [Legon]
[1986] 52 p. : DDC 330.9667/05 19
HC1060 .E975 1986   *NYPL [Sc G 88-31]*

**The economics of educational planning in Nigeria
/.** Akangbou, Stephen D. New Delhi , c1985.
150 p. ; ISBN 0-7069-2338-3
     NYPL [Sc D 88-289]

**Economics of the family and farming systems in
sub-Saharan Africa .** Singh, Ram D. Boulder ,
1988. xxiii, 208 p. ; ISBN 0-8133-7624-6 DDC
338.1/0967 19
HD1476.A357 S56 1988
     NYPL [JLD 88-4512]

Ecrits polémiques et politiques [microform] /.
Tempels Placide, 1906- Kinshasa-Limete , 1979.
24 p. ;   *NYPL [Sc Micro F-11131]*

Ecuador - Government. see Ecuador - Politics
and government.

**ECUADOR - POLITICS AND
GOVERNMENT - 1944-**
Hurtado González, Jaime. Luchando por la
patria nueva . Quito , 1987. ii, 178 p. :
     NYPL [Sc D 88-679]

**Ecumenical Association of Third World
Theologians.** Identidade negra e religião :
consulta sobre cultura negra e teologia na
América Latina / Associação Ecumênica de
Teólogos do Terceiro Mundo (ASETT) ;
[organização do texto: Amélia tavares C.
Neves]. Rio de Janeiro : CEDI, 1986. 201 p. ;
22 cm. Bibliographical footnotes.
*1. Black theology. 2. Race - Religious aspects. 3.
Blacks - Latin America - Religion. 4. Christianity and
other religions - Africa. I. Neves, Amelia Tavares C. II.
Title.*   *NYPL [Sc D 88-485]*

ECUMENICAL MOVEMENT.
Anaele, Justin Uchechukwu. The role of the
laity in ecumenism with reference to the church
in Nigeria /. Rome , 1985 (Rome : R.
Ambrosini) 146 p.   *NYPL [Sc E 88-608]*

**Ecumenical Programme for Emergency Action in
Africa .** All Africa Conference of Churches.
Special Agency for EPEAA. Nairobi , 1967.
[193] p. ;   *NYPL [Sc F 88-74]*

Edgar, Robert. Prophets with honour : a
documentary history of Lekhotla la Bafo /
Robert Edgar. Johannesburg : Ravan Press,
[1987?]. 250 p. ; 22 cm. Includes bibliographical
references and index. ISBN 0-86975-312-6
*1. Lekhotla la Bafo - History. 2. Lesotho - Politics and
government - To 1966. 3. Lesotho - Politics and
government - To 1966 - Sources. I. Title.*
     NYPL [Sc D 88-1391]

Ediciones políticas (Havana, Cuba)
González, Carmen, 1940- Sobre los hombros
ajenos /. La Habana , 1985. 119 p. ; DDC 968
19
DT766 .G66 1985   *NYPL [Sc D 88-416]*

Edition C .
(C 188) Baar, Marius. Tschad--Land ohne
Hoffnung?. Bad Liebenzell , c1985. 190 p., [6]
p. of plates : ISBN 3-88002-270-4
     NYPL [Sc D 88-892]

Éditions Berlitz S. A. McLeod, Catherine.
Jamaika /. Lausanne, Switzerland [1985],
c1981. 128 p. :   *NYPL [Sc B 88-57]*

Editions Fraternité-Hebdo.
Le quatrième séminaire des secrétaires
généraux . [Abidjan] , 1985. 55 p. :
     NYPL [Sc E 88-150]

Séminaires d'information et de formation des
secrétaires généraux . [Abidjan] [1985] 72 p. :
DDC 966.6/805 19
DT545.8 .S46 1985   *NYPL [Sc E 88-151]*

Editions SR .
(v. 8) Johnston, Geoffrey. Of God and maxim

---

guns . Waterloo, Ontario, Canada , 1988. 321
p. : ISBN 0-88920-180-3 (pbk.)
     NYPL [Sc D 88-1229]

Edmond, Lez. Sweeting, Earl. African history .
London , 1988. 31 p. :   *NYPL [Sc D 89-505]*

**Edmund Ruffin and the crisis of slavery in the
Old South .** Mathew, William M. Athens ,
c1988. xiv, 286 p. : ISBN 0-8203-1011-5 (alk.
paper) DDC 306/.362/0924 19
F230.R932 M38 1988   *NYPL [JFE 88-3149]*

Edmund Thornton Jenkins . Green, Jeffrey P.
Westport, Conn. , 1982. xii, 213 p. : ISBN
0-313-23253-9 (lib. bdg.) DDC 780/.92/4 B 19
ML410.J44 G7 1982   *NYPL [Sc D 86-413]*

Edmundo, Lygia Pereira. Instituição : escola de
marginalidade? / Lygia Pereira Edmundo. São
Paulo : Cortez, 1987. 141 p. ; 21 cm.
Bibliogrpahy: p. 139-141.
*1. Marginality, Social - Brazil. 2. Socially handicapped
youth - Brazil - Education. I. Title.*
     NYPL [Sc D 89-332]

An Edo-English dictionary /. Agheyisi, Rebecca
N. Benin City, Nigeria , 1986. xxiv, 169 p. :
ISBN 978-12-3293-5 DDC 496/.33 19
PL8077.4 .A44 1986   *NYPL [Sc D 88-847]*

Educação e movimento operário /. Ghiraldelli,
Paulo. São Paulo , 1987. 167 p. ; ISBN
85-24-90081-4   *NYPL [Sc D 88-369]*

**Educating handicapped young people in eastern
and southern Africa in 1981-83 /.** Ross, D. H.
Paris , 1988. 152 p. : ISBN 92-3-102560-0
     NYPL [Sc E 88-534]

Educating the blind . Abosi, Okechukwu C.
Ibadan , c1985. xiv, 106 p. : ISBN 978-226-553-5
(pbk.) DDC 371.91/1/09669 19
HV2165.5 .A65 1985   *NYPL [Sc D 89-209]*

Education /. Bond-Stewart, Kathy. [Gweru,
Zimbabwe] , 1986. 102 p. : ISBN 0-86922-371-2
     NYPL [Sc F 88-201]

EDUCATION, ADULT. see ADULT
EDUCATION.

EDUCATION - AFRICA - CONGRESSES.
Panafrican Conference on Education (1984 :
Yaoundé, Cameroon) What school for Africa in
the year 2000? /. Morges, Switzerland [1984?]
190 p. ;   *NYPL [Sc D 88-611]*

EDUCATION - AFRICA, SOUTHERN.
Bond-Stewart, Kathy. Education /. [Gweru,
Zimbabwe] , 1986. 102 p. : ISBN 0-86922-371-2
     NYPL [Sc F 88-201]

**Education and Black community development in
ante-bellum New York City /.** Rury, John L.
1975. 100 leaves ;   *NYPL [Sc F 89-114]*

EDUCATION AND INDUSTRY. see
INDUSTRY AND EDUCATION.

EDUCATION AND LANGUAGE. see
LANGUAGE AND EDUCATION.

EDUCATION AND POLITICS. see POLITICS
AND EDUCATION.

EDUCATION AND SOCIALISM. see
SOCIALISM AND EDUCATION.

EDUCATION AND SOCIOLOGY. see
EDUCATIONAL SOCIOLOGY.

EDUCATIONAL AND STATE - GHANA.
Agyeman, Dominic Kofi. Ideological education
and nationalism in Ghana under Nkrumah and
Busia /. Accra , 1988. 81 p. ; ISBN
996-430-120-0   *NYPL [Sc D 89-582]*

**EDUCATION AND STATE - GREAT
BRITAIN.**
Dohndy, Farrukh. The Black explosion in
British schools /. London , 1985. 64 p. ; ISBN
0-9503498-6-0   *NYPL [Sc D 88-1030]*

Education and the law in Nigeria . Nwagwu,
N.A. Owerri , 1987. ix, 190 p. ; ISBN
978-267-184-3   *NYPL [Sc D 89-10]*

**EDUCATION, BILINGUAL - UNITED
STATES.**
Valle, Manuel del. Law and bilingual
education . New York , 1978. i, 206 p. ;
     NYPL [Sc F 88-357]

EDUCATION - BRAZIL.
Mattos, Edgar, 1935- Por uma educacão
libertáda e libertadora . Recife , 1986. 89 p. ;
ISBN 85-7019-098-0   *NYPL [Sc D 88-845]*

EDUCATION - BRAZIL - HISTORY.
Ghiraldelli, Paulo. Educação e movimento
operário /. São Paulo , 1987. 167 p. ; ISBN
85-24-90081-4   *NYPL [Sc D 88-369]*

EDUCATION, BUSINESS. see BUSINESS
EDUCATION.

**EDUCATION - CARIBBEAN AREA -
BIBLIOGRAPHY.**
Robertson, Amy. Select bibliography of
education in the Commonwealth Caribbean,
1976-1985 . Mona, Jamaica , 1987. 174 p. ;
     NYPL [Sc F 88-316]

EDUCATION, CHRISTIAN. see CHRISTIAN
EDUCATION.

EDUCATION, COOPERATIVE - NIGER.
Easton, Peter A. Functional literacy and
cooperative education . 1972. v, 87 leaves :
     NYPL [Sc F 88-52]

EDUCATION - DEVELOPING COUNTRIES.
Bond-Stewart, Kathy. Education /. [Gweru,
Zimbabwe] , 1986. 102 p. : ISBN 0-86922-371-2
     NYPL [Sc F 88-201]

**EDUCATION - ECONOMIC ASPECTS -
HAITI.**
Jean, Rodrigue. Haiti, crise de l'education et
crise du développement /. Port-au-prince,
Haiti , 1988. 152 p. ; ISBN 0-948390-00-X
     NYPL [Sc D 88-914]

**EDUCATION - ECONOMIC ASPECTS -
NIGERIA.**
Akangbou, Stephen D. The economics of
educational planning in Nigeria /. New Delhi ,
c1985. 150 p. ; ISBN 0-7069-2338-3
     NYPL [Sc D 88-289]

**EDUCATION - ECONOMIC ASPECTS -
SOUTH AFRICA.**
Dreijmanis, John. The role of the South African
government in tertiary education /.
Johannesburg, South Africa , 1988. xiii, 156 p. :
ISBN 0-86982-329-9   *NYPL [Sc F 88-184]*

**EDUCATION - ECONOMIC ASPECTS -
SWAZILAND.**
Sullivan, Gerard. From school--to work .
Oxford , c1981. xvi, 190 p. : DDC
373.12/913/096813 19
LC145.S78 S94 1981   *NYPL [Sc F 87-331]*

EDUCATION, ELEMENTARY - SENEGAL.
Morin, Melle. Les retards scolaires et les échecs
au niveau de l'ecole primaire du Sénégal /.
[Dakar] [1966?] 143 leaves :
     NYPL [Sc F 87-439]

**EDUCATION, ELEMENTARY - WESTERN
SAHARA - HISTORY.**
Perregaux, Christiane. L'école sahraouie . Paris ,
c1987. 158 p., [8] p. of plates : ISBN
2-85802-942-3 DDC 372.964/8 19
LA2034.W47 P47 1987
     NYPL [Sc D 89-401]

**L'éducation en Haiti sous l'occupation américaine
1915-1934 /.** Pamphile, Léon Dénius.
[Port-au-Prince , 1988] 316 p. ;
     NYPL [Sc D 88-1002]

Education for manhood . Horst, Samuel L., 1919-
Lanham, MD , c1987. viii, 292 p. ; ISBN
0-8191-6662-6 (alk. paper) : DDC
370/.89960730755 19
LC2802.V8 H67 1987   *NYPL [Sc D 88-550]*

EDUCATION - GHANA.
Agyeman, Dominic Kofi. Ideological education
and nationalism in Ghana under Nkrumah and
Busia /. Accra , 1988. 81 p. ; ISBN
996-430-120-0   *NYPL [Sc D 89-582]*

EDUCATION - GREAT BRITAIN - 1965-
Dohndy, Farrukh. The Black explosion in
British schools /. London , 1985. 64 p. ; ISBN
0-9503498-6-0   *NYPL [Sc D 88-1030]*

**EDUCATION - GREAT BRITAIN - AIMS
AND OBJECTIVES.**
Brandt, Godfrey L. The realization of anti-racist
teaching /. London , New York , 1986. x, 210
p. : ISBN 1-85000-126-X : DDC 370.19/0941 19
LC192.2 .B73 1986   *NYPL [Sc E 89-77]*

EDUCATION - GUIDANCE. see PERSONNEL
SERVICE IN EDUCATION.

EDUCATION - GUINEA-BISSAU.
Barbosa, Rogério Andrade. La-le-li-lo-luta . Rio
de Janeiro , 1984. 124 p. ; DDC 371.1/0092/4 B

19
LA2365.B72 B37 1984   NYPL [Sc D 88-284]

EDUCATION - HAITI.
Dale, George Allan, 1900- Education in the
Republic of Haiti. [Washington] [1959] x, 180
p.,   *NYPL [Sc E 88-60]*

**EDUCATION - HAITI - AIMS AND
OBJECTIVES.**
Institut pédagogique national (Haiti). Comité de
curriculum. La réforme éducative .
[Port-au-Prince] [1982] 65 p. :   DDC
375/.001/097294
LB1564.H2 I57 1982   NYPL [Sc D 88-1401]

EDUCATION - HAITI - HISTORY.
Pamphile, Léon Dénius. L'éducation en Haiti
sous l'occupation américaine 1915-1934 /.
[Port-au-Prince , 1988] 316 p. ;
                             NYPL [Sc D 88-1002]

EDUCATION, HIGHER - AFRICA.
Moock, Joyce Lewinger. Higher education and
rural development in Africa [microform] . New
York , c1977. ii, 42 p. ;
                     NYPL [Sc Micro R-4202 no. 1]

EDUCATION, HIGHER - AFRICA, EASTERN.
Eastern and Southern African Universities
Research Programme. University capacity in
eastern & southern African countries /.
London , Portsmouth, N.H. , c1987. xix, 259
p. : ISBN 0-85255-107-X : DDC 378.67 19
LA1503   *NYPL [Sc D 89-314]*

**EDUCATION, HIGHER - AFRICA,
SOUTHERN.**
Eastern and Southern African Universities
Research Programme. University capacity in
eastern & southern African countries /.
London , Portsmouth, N.H. , c1987. xix, 259
p. : ISBN 0-85255-107-X : DDC 378.67 19
LA1503   *NYPL [Sc D 89-314]*

**EDUCATION, HIGHER - ECONOMIC
ASPECTS - UNITED STATES -
CONGRESSES.**
Economic issues and black colleges /. Chicago ,
c1986. 59 p. ; ISBN 0-695-60053-2
                             NYPL [Sc D 88-950]

**EDUCATION, HIGHER - ETHIOPIA -
HISTORY.**
Balsvik, Randi Rønning. Haile Sellassie's
students . East Lansing, Mich. , c1985. xix, 363
p. : DDC 378/.198/0963 19
LA1518.7 .B35 1985   NYPL [Sc D 88-1403]

**EDUCATION, HIGHER - GHANA - AIMS
AND OBJECTIVES.**
Bowden, Bertram Vivian, Baron Bowden, 1910-
The role of universities in the modern world /.
Kumasi, Ghana [1978?] 81 p. ;
                             NYPL [Sc D 88-465]

**EDUCATION, HIGHER - SUPPLY AND
DEMAND - SOUTH AFRICA - EAST
LONDON.**
Gilmour, J. D. The demand for tertiary
education in the East London metropolitan
area . Grahamstown [South Africa] , 1983. 1 v.
(various pagings) ; ISBN 0-86810-056-0
                             NYPL [Sc F 87-429]

Education in Kenya : information handbook /
Ministry of Education. Nairobi, Kenya : Jomo
Kenyatta Foundation, c1987. iv, 128 p., [1]
folded leaf of plates : ports. ; 21 cm.
    1. Education - Kenya. I. Kenya. Ministry of Education.
                             NYPL [Sc D 89-169]

Education in the Republic of Haiti. Dale, George
Allan, 1900- [Washington] [1959] x, 180 p.,
                             NYPL [Sc E 88-60]

**EDUCATION, INDUSTRIAL. see
TECHNICAL EDUCATION.**

**EDUCATION, INTERCULTURAL. see
INTERCULTURAL EDUCATION.**

**EDUCATION, ISLAMIC. see ISLAM -
EDUCATION.**

EDUCATION - IVORY COAST - HISTORY.
Sosoo, Leonard. L'enseignement en Côte
d'Ivoire /. [Abidjan? , 1980-1987] 2 v. :
                             NYPL [Sc E 88-128]

EDUCATION - KENYA.
Education in Kenya . Nairobi, Kenya , c1987.
iv, 128 p., [1] folded leaf of plates :
                             NYPL [Sc D 89-169]

Kenya. Presidential Working Party on

Education and Manpower Training for the Next
Decade and Beyond. Report of the Presidential
Working Party on Education and Manpower
Training for the Next Decade and Beyond /.
Nairobi , 1988. xvii, 174 p. ;
                             NYPL [Sc E 89-232]

EDUCATION - KENYA - BIBLIOGRAPHY.
Eshiwani, George S. Research in education .
Nairobi, Kenya , 1982? 185 leaves ; DDC
016.37/09676/2 19
Z5815.K4 E83 1982 LA1561
                             NYPL [Sc F 89-154]

EDUCATION - LESOTHO.
Lesotho. Ministry of Education. Report on the
views and recommendations of the Basotho
Nation regarding the future of education in
Lesotho =. Maseru, Lesotho , 1978. 167 p. :
                             NYPL [Sc F 88-354]

EDUCATION - NIGERIA.
Aderounmu, Olusola. Managing the Nigerian
education enterprise /. Ikeja, Lagos, Nigeria ,
1986. 230 p. :   *NYPL [Sc F 88-171]*

Adewole, Ayo. A philosophy of education for
Nigeria . Onitsha , 1988, c1987. 131 p. ; ISBN
978-254-972-X   *NYPL [Sc D 89-85]*

Aminu, Jibril M.,1939- Observations /. [Enugu,
Anambra State, Nigeria] [1988] 148 p. ; ISBN
978-233-531-2   *NYPL [Sc D 89-483]*

Nwagwu, N.A. Education and the law in
Nigeria . Owerri , 1987. ix, 190 p. ; ISBN
978-267-184-3   *NYPL [Sc D 89-10]*

Osokoya, Israel O. 6-3-3-4 education in
Nigeria . Lagos, Nigeria , c1987. x, 108 p. ;
      ISBN 978-259-918-2   *NYPL [Sc E 89-162]*

Solarin, Tai. Timeless Tai /. Lagos, Nigeria ,
1985. x, 232 p. ;   *NYPL [Sc D 89-371]*

Ukeje, B. Onyerisara. School and society in
Nigeria /. Enugu, Nigeria , 1986. 129 p. ;
      ISBN 978-15-6245-5
                             NYPL [Sc D 88-1243]

University of Lagos series in education /. Ikeja,
Lagos , 1987- v. :   *NYPL [Sc D 89-149]*

EDUCATION - NIGERIA - HISTORY.
Ejiogu, Aloy M. Landmarks in educational
development in Nigeria . Ikeja, Lagos , c1986.
xi, 156 p. ; ISBN 978-242-716-0
                             NYPL [Sc D 88-782]

EDUCATION - NIGERIA - OGUN STATE.
Ogun State. Advisory Committee in the
Funding of Education. Report of the Advisory
Committee on the Funding of Education in
Ogun State. [Abeokuta , 1985] 51 p. :
                             NYPL [Sc E 89-212]

**EDUCATION - NIGERIA - OGUN STATE -
FINANCE.**
Ogun State. Advisory Committee in the
Funding of Education. Report of the Advisory
Committee on the Funding of Education in
Ogun State. [Abeokuta , 1985] 51 p. :
                             NYPL [Sc E 89-212]

**EDUCATION OF ADULTS. see ADULT
EDUCATION.**

The education of Blacks in the South, 1860-1935
/. Anderson, James D., 1944- Chapel Hill ,
c1988. xiv, 366 p. : ISBN 0-8078-1793-7 (alk.
paper) DDC 370/.0889073075 19
LC2802.S9 A53 1988   NYPL [Sc E 88-457]

**EDUCATION - PERSONNEL SERVICE. see
PERSONNEL SERVICE IN EDUCATION.**

**EDUCATION, PHYSICAL. see PHYSICAL
EDUCATION AND TRAINING.**

**EDUCATION (PRESCHOOL) - AFRICA,
WEST.**
Ampene, Esther C. Focus on the early learner .
Accra-North , 1987. viii, 65 p. ; ISBN
996-490-189-5   *NYPL [Sc D 88-1383]*

**EDUCATION, PRESCHOOL - MIDDLE
WEST - CROSS-CULTURAL STUDIES.**
Lubeck, Sally. Sandbox society . London ,
Philadelphia , 1985. xv, 177 p. ; ISBN
1-85000-051-4 DDC 372/.21/0977 19
LB1140.24.M53 L8 1985
                             NYPL [Sc E 89-80]

EDUCATION - RESEARCH - KENYA.
Eshiwani, George S. Research in education .
Nairobi, Kenya , 1982? 185 leaves ; DDC

016.37/09676/2 19
Z5815.K4 E83 1982 LA1561
                             NYPL [Sc F 89-154]

**EDUCATION, SCIENTIFIC. see SCIENCE -
STUDY AND TEACHING.**

**EDUCATION, SECONDARY - TANZANIA -
CASE STUDIES.**
Oral histories of three secondary school
students in Tanzania /. Lewiston/Queenston ,
1987. 248 p. ; ISBN 0-88946-179-1 (alk. paper) :
DDC 306/.0967/8 19
LA1842 .O73 1987   NYPL [Sc E 88-267]

**EDUCATION - SEGREGATION. see
SEGREGATION IN EDUCATION.**

**EDUCATION - SOCIAL AND ECONOMIC
ASPECTS. see EDUCATION -
ECONOMIC ASPECTS.**

EDUCATION - SOUTH AFRICA - HISTORY.
Dean, Elizabeth. [History in black and white.
Spanish.] Historia en blanco y negro .
Barcelona , Paris , 1984. 196 p. ; ISBN
92-3-302092-4 (Unesco)
                             NYPL [Sc D 88-594]

EDUCATION - STUDY AND TEACHING.
University of Lagos series in education /. Ikeja,
Lagos , 1987- v. :   *NYPL [Sc D 89-149]*

**EDUCATION - STUDY AND TEACHING -
SOUTH AFRICA.**
Gaydon, Vanessa. Race against the ratios .
Johannesburg, South Africa , 1987. 70 p. ;
      ISBN 0-86982-321-3   *NYPL [Sc F 88-322]*

**EDUCATION, TECHNICAL. see TECHNICAL
EDUCATION.**

**EDUCATION - UNITED STATES - AIMS
AND OBJECTIVES.**
Tollett, Kenneth S. The right to education .
Washington, D.C. , 1983. xiii, 77 p. ;
                             NYPL [Sc D 87-1294]

EDUCATION, URBAN - UNITED STATES.
Lewis, Geraldine Fambrough. An analysis of
interviews with urban Black males who dropped
out of high school [microform] /. 1983. iii, 123
leaves :   *NYPL [Sc Micro R-4791]*

EDUCATION - ZIMBABWE.
Gwarinda, Takawira C. Socialism & education .
Harare, Zimbabwe , 1985. 128 p. : ISBN
0-86925-547-9   *NYPL [Sc D 88-1129]*

**EDUCATIONAL ADMINISTRATION. see
SCHOOL MANAGEMENT AND
ORGANIZATION.**

**EDUCATIONAL ASSISTANCE, AMERICAN -
AFRICA.**
Moock, Joyce Lewinger. Higher education and
rural development in Africa [microform] . New
York , c1977. ii, 42 p. ;
                     NYPL [Sc Micro R-4202 no. 1]

Educational attainments : issues and outcomes in
multicultural education / edited by Gajendra
Verma and Peter Pumfrey. London ; New
York : Falmer Press, 1988. vii, 180 p. : ill. ; 25
cm. Papers from four symposia, two which were
sponsored by the Committee of the Division of
Educational and Child Psychology of the British
Psychological Society, one sponsored by the
International Centre for Intercultural Studies of the
University of Bradford, and the other sponsored by the
Centre for Educational Guidance and Special Needs of
the University of Manchester. Includes bibliographies
and index. CONTENTS. - Issues in multicultural
education / Gajendra Verma -- Monitoring the reading
attainments of children from minority ethnic groups /
Peter Pumfrey -- Developing bilingual children's English
in school / Tony Kerr and Martin Desforges -- Racism
awareness / Peter Pumfrey -- The Swann report and the
ethnic minority attainment / Bhikhu Parekh -- Policies
and promising practices in education / Peter Newsam --
West Indian and Asian children's educational
attainment / N.J. Mackintosh, C.G. Mascie-Taylor, and
A.M. West -- Education achievement of ethnic minority
children in a Midlands town / John R. Roberts -- Black
pupil's progress in secondary school / Barbara Maughan
and Graham Dunn -- Inner city adolescents / Ann
Dawson -- Self-esteem and education achievement in
British young South Asians / Gajendra Verma and
Kanka Mallick -- The Brent inquiry / Jocelyn Barrow.
    ISBN 1-85000-308-4 : DDC 370.19/34/0941 19
    *1. Minorities - Education - Great Britain. 2.
Intercultural education - Great Britain. 3. Pluralism
(Social sciences) - Great Britain. I. Verma, Gajendra K.
II. Pumfrey, Peter. III. British Psychological Society.*

Division of Educational and Child Psychology. Committee. IV. University of Bradford. International Centre for Intercultural Studies. V. University of Manchester. Centre for Educational Guidance and Special Needs.
LC3736.G6 E336 1988   NYPL [Sc E 89-52]

EDUCATIONAL EQUALIZATION - GREAT BRITAIN.
Dohndy, Farrukh. The Black explosion in British schools /. London , 1985. 64 p. ; ISBN 0-9503498-6-0   *NYPL [Sc D 88-1030]*

EDUCATIONAL EQUALIZATION - TRINIDAD AND TOBAGO.
Osuji, Rose C. The effect of socio-economic status on the eductional achievement of Form V students in Trinidad /. St. Augustine, Trinidad , 1987. xiv, 229 p. ; 976-618-002-4   *NYPL [Sc E 88-352]*

EDUCATIONAL EQUALIZATION - UNITED STATES.
Tollett, Kenneth S. The right to education . Washington, D.C. , 1983. xiii, 77 p. ;
     NYPL [Sc D 87-1294]

EDUCATIONAL EQUALIZATION - UNITED STATES - HISTORY.
Toward Black undergraduate student equality in American higher education /. New York , 1988. xvii, 217 p. : ISBN 0-313-25616-0 (lib. bdg. : alk. paper) DDC 378/.1982 19
LC2781 .T69 1988   NYPL [Sc E 88-507]

EDUCATIONAL GUIDANCE. see PERSONNEL SERVICE IN EDUCATION.

EDUCATIONAL LAW AND LEGISLATION - NIGERIA.
Ihenacho, Izuka John. Administrators of special education . [Nigeria] , c1986. 208 p. ; ISBN 978-239-609-5 (pbk.) DDC 371.9/09669 19
LC3988.N6 I44 1986   NYPL [Sc C 89-145]

Nwagwu, N.A. Education and the law in Nigeria . Owerri , 1987. ix, 190 p. ; ISBN 978-267-184-3   *NYPL [Sc D 89-10]*

EDUCATIONAL LAW AND LEGISLATION - UNITED STATES.
Valle, Manuel del. Law and bilingual education . New York , 1978. i, 206 p. ;
     NYPL [Sc F 88-357]

EDUCATIONAL MEASUREMENTS. see EDUCATIONAL TESTS AND MEASUREMENTS.

EDUCATIONAL PLANNING - AFRICA, WEST.
African-American Institute. A system approach to the implications of national school-leaver problems in Dahomey, Ivory Coast, Niger, Togo and Upper Volta . Washington , 1970. 1 v. (various pagings), [7] folded leaves :
     NYPL [Sc F 88-84]

EDUCATIONAL PLANNING - GHANA.
Abban, J. B. Prerequisites of manpower and educational planning in Ghana /. Accra , 1986. xii, 144 p. ; ISBN 996-496-307-6
     NYPL [Sc D 89-496]

Educational planning in Ghana. Abban, J. B. Prerequisites of manpower and educational planning in Ghana /. Accra , 1986. xii, 144 p. ; ISBN 996-496-307-6   *NYPL [Sc D 89-496]*

EDUCATIONAL PLANNING - NIGERIA.
Akangbou, Stephen D. The economics of educational planning in Nigeria /. New Delhi , c1985. 150 p. ; ISBN 0-7069-2338-3
     NYPL [Sc D 88-289]

EDUCATIONAL POLICY. see EDUCATION AND STATE.

EDUCATIONAL PROGRAM. see EDUCATIONAL PLANNING.

EDUCATIONAL SOCIOLOGY - GREAT BRITAIN.
Brandt, Godfrey L. The realization of anti-racist teaching /. London , New York , 1986. x, 210 p. ; ISBN 1-85090-126-X ; DDC 370.19/0941 19
LC192.2 .B73 1986   NYPL [Sc E 89-77]

EDUCATIONAL SOCIOLOGY - TRINIDAD AND TOBAGO.
Osuji, Rose C. The effect of socio-economic status on the eductional achievement of Form V students in Trinidad /. St. Augustine, Trinidad , 1987. xiv, 229 p. ; ISBN 976-618-002-4   *NYPL [Sc E 88-352]*

EDUCATIONAL TESTS AND MEASUREMENTS - CASE STUDIES.
Psychoeducational assessment of minority group children . Berkeley, Calif. , c1988. ix, 429 p. : ISBN 0-943539-00-5 (pbk.) :   DDC 155.4/5 19
BF722 .P77 1988   NYPL [Sc D 89-526]

EDUCATORS - INDIANA - BIOGRAPHY.
Mickey, Rosie Cheatham. Russell Adrian Lane, biography of an urban negro school administrator [microform] /. 1983. xiii, 275 leaves :   *NYPL [Sc Micro R-4813]*

EDUCATORS - MISSISSIPPI.
Griffith, Helen. Dauntless in Mississippi . Northampton, Mass. , 1965. xii, 173 p. :
     NYPL [Sc D 88-1111]

EDUCATORS - UNITED STATES - BIOGRAPHY.
Harlan, Louis R. Booker T. Washington . New York , 1983. xiv, 548 p. : ISBN 0-19-503202-0 : DDC 378/.111 B 19
E185.97.W4 H373 1983
     NYPL [Sc E 83-233]

Harlan, Louis R. Booker T. Washington in perspective . Jackson , c1988. xii, 210 p., [8] p. of plates : ISBN 0-87805-374-3 (alk. paper) DDC 378/.111 B 19
E185.97.W4 H36 1988   NYPL [Sc E 89-217]

Edwards, Pat, 1922- Little John and Plutie / Pat Edwards. Boston : Houghton Mifflin, 1988. 172 p. ; 22 cm. Although delighted to have the resourceful and courageous Pluto as his first real friend, nine-year-old John soon begins to realize how their rural South environment discourages a close relationship between blacks and whites. SCHOMBURG CHILDREN'S COLLECTION. ISBN 0-395-48223-2 DDC [Fic] 19
1. Southern States - Juvenile fiction. 2. Southern States - Race relations - Juvenile fiction. I. Schomburg Children's Collection. II. Title.
PZ7.E2637 Li 1988   NYPL [Sc D 89-126]

Edwards, Sally. Isaac and Snow. Illustrated by Michael Hampshire. New York, Coward, McCann & Geoghegan [1973] 123 p. illus. 22 cm. A boy forms a friendship with an albino porpoise, and must eventually decide if entrusting her to the Seaquarium is the best thing for her. ISBN 0-698-20244-9 DDC [Fic]
1. Porpoises - Juvenile fiction. 2. Sea Islands - Juvenile fiction. I. Title.
PZ7.E265 Is3   NYPL [Sc D 88-1419]

Edwards-Yearwood, Grace. In the shadow of the Peacock / Grace Edwards-Yearwood. New York : McGraw-Hill, c1988. 279 p. ; 24 cm. ISBN 0-07-019037-2 DDC 813/.54 19
1. Afro-American Women - Fiction. 2. Harlem (New York, N.Y.) - Fiction. I. Title.
PS3555.D99 I5 1988   NYPL [JFE 88-4421]

The effect of family size, child spacing and family density on stress in low income Black mothers and their preadolescent children [microform] /. Hendricks, Leo E. 1977. 156 leaves ;
     NYPL [Sc Micro R-4684]

The effect of socio-economic status on the eductional achievement of Form V students in Trinidad /. Osuji, Rose C. St. Augustine, Trinidad , 1987. xiv, 229 p. ; ISBN 976-618-002-4   *NYPL [Sc E 88-352]*

The Effects of the Western culture on the traditional cultures of Lofa County [microform] : a cultural symposium / sponsored by the Lofa University Students Association, University of Liberia, Monrovia, Liberia ; compiled by San Philip Joe. [Monrovia : s. n., 1977] 24 p. ; 28 cm. Cover title. Microfiche. New York: New York Public Library, 198 . 1 microfiche: negative; 11 x 15 cm. (FSN Sc 019,048)
1. Cultural relations - Congresses. 2. Lofa County, Liberia - Intellectual life. 3. Liberia - Relations (general) with Europe. 4. Europe - Relations (general) with Liberia. I. Joe, Kingston Saa P. II. Lofa University Students Association.
     NYPL [Sc Micro F-10952]

Egblewogbe, E. Y., 1934- The wizard's pride and other poems / E.Y. Egblewogbe. Tema, Ghana : Ghana Publishing Corp., 1986, c1974. xiii, 40 p. ; 18 cm. ISBN 996-410-128-7
I. Title.
     NYPL [Sc C 88-351]

Egboh, Edmund Onyemeke. Community development efforts in Igboland / Edmund Onyemeke Egboh. Onitsha [Nigeria] : Etukokwu Press, 1987. 206 p. : ill., maps ; 25

cm. Includes index. Bibliography p. 186-196. ISBN 978-264-348-3
1. Community development - Nigeria. 2. Igbo (African people) - Economic conditions. 3. Igbo (African people) - Social conditions. I. Title.
     NYPL [Sc E 88-258]

Egbunu, Emmanuel. Nwosu, I. E. A guide to Christian writing in Africa /. Enugu, Nigeria , 1987. 116 p. ; ISBN 978-262-606-6
     NYPL [Sc C 88-156]

Egerton, Ann Bleidt. Egerton, John. Southern food . New York , c1987. v, 408 p. : ISBN 0-394-54494-3 DDC 641.5975 19
TX715 .E28 1987   NYPL [JSE 87-1598]

Egerton, John. Southern food : at home, on the road, in history / by John Egerton ; with a special assist from Ann Bleidt Egerton ; and with photographs by Al Clayton.1st ed. New York : Knopf, c1987. v, 408 p. : ill. ; 25 cm. Includes indexes. Bibliography: p. 352-382. ISBN 0-394-54494-3 DDC 641.5975 19
1. Cookery, American - Southern style. 2. Restaurants, lunch rooms, etc. - Southern States. I. Egerton, Ann Bleidt. II. Clayton, Al, 1934-. III. Title.
TX715 .E28 1987   NYPL [JSE 87-1598]

Eglin, Colin. Die beginsels en belied van die Suid-Afrikaanse Progressiewe Reformisteparty [microform] / toespraak deur die Leier, mnr. Colin Eglin, L.V., tyden die stigtingskongres in Johannesburg op 26 Julie 1975 = Principles and policy of the South African Progressive Reform Party : address at the inaugural congress of the Party / by the leader, Mr. Colin Eglin, M.P., at Johannesburg on July 26, 1975. [Cape Town : M. Osler, 1975] 12, 12 p. ; 23 cm. On cover: Die Suid-Afrikaanse Progressiewe Reformisteparty, Alternatief vir apartheid / The South African Progressive Reform Party Alternative to apartheid. In English and Afrikaans. Microfilm. New York: New York Public Library, 1982. 1 microfilm reel; 35 mm. (MN *ZZ-22581)
1. South African Progressive Reform Party. I. Title. II. Title: Principles and policy of the South African Progressive Reform Party. III. Title: Alternaties vir apartheid. IV. Title: Alternative to apartheid.
     NYPL [Sc Micro R-4094 no. 4]

L'église de Kisantu, hier et aujourd'hui [microform] /. Mayala ma Mpangu. [Kisantu?] 1982. 40 p. ;   *NYPL [Sc Micro F-11,000]*

Les Églises chrétiennes face à la montée du nationalisme camerounais /. Kengne Pokam, E (Emmanuel), 1941- Paris [1987] 202 p. ; ISBN 2-85802-823-0   *NYPL [Sc D 88-437]*

Egoli, city of gold [microform]. Manaka, Matsemela. Johannesburg [198-?] 28 p. ;
     NYPL [Sc Micro F-11049]

Egret romance & thrillers . (10) Oguntoye, Jide. Come home my love /. Ibadan , 1987. 141 p. ; ISBN 978-243-272-5
     NYPL [Sc C 88-226]

Egúngún among the Oyó Yoruba /. Babayemi, S. O. Ibadan , c1980. ix, 123 p. :
BL2480.Y6 B33 1980   NYPL [Sc D 88-1149]

EGÚNGÚN (CULT)
Babayemi, S. O. Egúngún among the Oyó Yoruba /. Ibadan , c1980. ix, 123 p. :
BL2480.Y6 B33 1980   NYPL [Sc D 88-1149]

Egyesült Allamok. see United States.

Egypt /. Parker, Derek. London , 1986. 160 p. : ISBN 0-224-02419-1   *NYPL [Sc B 89-21]*

EGYPT - CIVILIZATION - TO 332 B.C. - EXHIBITIONS.
Bourriau, Janine. Pharaohs and mortals . Cambridge [Cambridgeshire] ; New York , 1988. vi, 167 p. : ISBN 0-521-35319-X DDC 709/.32/07402659 19
N5336.G7 C3634 1988
     NYPL [3-MAE 88-2748]

EGYPT - CIVILIZATION - TO 332 B.C. - JUVENILE FICTION.
Carter, Dorothy Sharp. His Majesty, Queen Hatshepsut /. New York , c1987. viii, 248 p. : ISBN 0-397-32178-3 : DDC [Fic] 19
PZ7.C2434 Hi 1987   NYPL [Sc D 88-877]

EGYPT - DESCRIPTION AND TRAVEL.
Irby, Charles Leonard, 1789-1845. Travels in Egypt and Nubia, Syria and Asia Minor . London , 1985. xxxiii, 560 p., [6] leaves of plates (3 folded) : ISBN 1-85077-082-4 : DDC

915.6/041 916.2/043 19
DS48 DT53 **NYPL** *[JFD 88-9340]*

EGYPT - DESCRIPTION AND TRAVEL - GUIDE-BOOKS.
Parker, Derek. Egypt /. London , 1986. 160 p. : ISBN 0-224-02419-1 **NYPL** *[Sc B 89-21]*

EGYPT - DESCRIPTION AND TRAVEL - JUVENILE LITERATURE.
Wallace, John A. Getting to know Egypt, U.A.R. /. New York , c1961. 64 p. :
NYPL *[Sc D 88-569]*

EGYPT - FOREIGN RELATIONS - SOVIET UNION.
El Hussini, Mohrez Mahmoud, 1942- Soviet-Egyptian relations, 1945-85 /. New York , 1987. xix, 276 p. : ISBN 0-312-74781-0 : DDC 327.47062 19
DK69.4.E3 E4 1987 **NYPL** *[Sc D 88-1031]*

Egypt - Guidebooks. see **Egypt - Description and travel - Guide-books.**

EGYPT - HISTORY - EIGHTEENTH DYNASTY, CA. 1570-1320 B.C.
Aldred, Cyril. Akhenaten, King of Egypt /. London, N.Y. , 1988. 320 p. : ISBN 0-500-05048-1 DDC 932/.014/0924 B 19
DT87.4 .A24 1988 **NYPL** *[*OBX 88-4161]*

EGYPT - HISTORY - DICTIONARIES.
Wucher King, Joan. Historical dictionary of Egypt /. Metuchen, N.J. , 1984. xiii, 719 p. : ISBN 0-8108-1670-9 DDC 962/.003/21 19
DT45 .W83 1984 **NYPL** *[Sc D 85-101]*

EGYPT - RELIGION.
Myer, Isaac, 1836-1902. Scarabs [microform]. New York, Leipzig, 1894. xxvii, 177 p.
DT62.S3 M8 **NYPL** *[Sc Micro R-3541]*

EGYPT - RELIGION - MISCELLANEA.
Versluis, Arthur, 1959- The Egyptian mysteries /. London , New York , 1988. vi, 169 p. ; ISBN 1-85063-087-9 (pbk.) DDC 133 19
BF1999 .V43 1988 **NYPL** *[Sc C 88-195]*

EGYPTIAN ART. see **ART, EGYPTIAN.**

EGYPTIAN LANGUAGE.
Diop, Cheikh Anta. Nouvelles recherches sur l'égyptien ancien et les langues négro-africaines modernes /. Paris , c1988. 221 p. ; ISBN 2-7087-0507-5 **NYPL** *[Sc D 89-550]*

EGYPTIAN LANGUAGE - DICTIONARIES - WOLOF.
Diop, Cheikh Anta. Nouvelles recherches sur l'égyptien ancien et les langues négro-africaines modernes /. Paris , c1988. 221 p. ; ISBN 2-7087-0507-5 **NYPL** *[Sc D 89-550]*

The Egyptian mysteries /. Versluis, Arthur, 1959- London , New York , 1988. vi, 169 p. ; ISBN 1-85063-087-9 (pbk.) DDC 133 19
BF1999 .V43 1988 **NYPL** *[Sc C 88-195]*

Egyptian pyramids and mastaba tombs of the Old and Middle Kingdoms /. Watson, Philip J. Aylesbury, Bucks , 1987. 64 p. : ISBN 0-85263-853-1 **NYPL** *[Sc D 88-1259]*

EGYPTIANS - ORIGIN - CONGRESSES.
Symposium on the Peopling of Ancient Egypt and the deciphering of Meroitic Script (1974 : Cairo, Egypt) [Peuplement de l'Egipte ancienne et le déchiffrement de l'écriture méroïtique. Spanish.] Poblamiento del antiguo Egipto y desciframiento de la escritura meroítica /. Barcelona , Paris , 1983. 155 p. : ISBN 0-923301-60-5 (Unesco)
NYPL *[Sc D 88-603]*

Ehiametalor, Egbe T. Aderounmu, Olusola W. An introduction to the administration of schools in Nigeria /. Ibadan, Nigeria , 1985. xiii, 271 p. : ISBN 978-16-7241-2 **NYPL** *[Sc D 88-730]*

Ehrlich, Scott. Paul Robeson / Scott Ehrlich ; senior consulting editor, Nathan Irvin Huggins. New York : Chelsea House Publishers, c1988. 111 p. : ill. ; 24 cm. (Black Americans of achievement) Includes index. A biography of the black man who became both a famous singer and a controversial figure in world politics. Bibliography: p. 108. ISBN 1-555-46608-7 DDC 782.1/092/4 B 92 19
1. Robeson, Paul, 1898-1976 - Juvenile literature. 2. Afro-American - Biography - Juvenile literature. 3. Afro-American singers - Biography - Juvenile literature. I. Title. II. Series.
E185.97.R63 E35 1988 **NYPL** *[Sc E 88-167]*

Eicher, Carl K. Michigan State University. Dept. of Agricultural Economics. An analysis of the Eastern ORD rural development project in Upper Volta . East Lansing , 1976. v, 103 p. : DDC 338.1/866/25
HD2135 .U63 1976 **NYPL** *[Sc F 89-170]*

Eight days a week . Duplechan, Larry. Boston , 1985. 260, [4] p. ; ISBN 0-932870-84-8
NYPL *[Sc D 89-219]*

Eight men. Wright, Richard, 1908-1960. Cleveland [1961] 250 p.
PZ3.W9352 Ei **NYPL** *[Sc Rare F 88-59]*

Eight men . Wright, Richard, 1908-1960. New York , c1987. xxv, 250 p. ; ISBN 0-938410-39-3 : DDC 813/.52 19
PS3545.R815 E4 1987 **NYPL** *[Sc D 89-376]*

Eiteljorg, Harrison.
Celenko, Theodore. A treasury of African art from the Harrison Eiteljorg Collection /. Bloomington , c1983. 239 p. : ISBN 0-253-11057-2 DDC 730/.0967/074013 19
NB1091.65 .C46 1983
NYPL *[3-MADF+ 88-2098]*

EITELJORG, HARRISON - ART COLLECTIONS - CATALOGS.
Celenko, Theodore. A treasury of African art from the Harrison Eiteljorg Collection /. Bloomington , c1983. 239 p. : ISBN 0-253-11057-2 DDC 730/.0967/074013 19
NB1091.65 .C46 1983
NYPL *[3-MADF+ 88-2098]*

EIU economic prospects series.
Hodges, Tony. Angola to the 1990s . London , 1987. 145 p. : **NYPL** *[Sc F 88-138]*

EIU political risk series.
Wright, Stephen, 1954- Nigeria, the dilemmas ahead . London , c1986. 88 p. :
NYPL *[Sc F 88-137]*

Ejimofor, Cornelius Ogu, 1940- British colonial objectives and policies in Nigeria : the roots of conflict / Cornelius Ogu Ejimofor. Onitsha, Nigeria : Africana-FEP Publishers, 1987. viii, 216 p., 1 folded leaf ; 21 cm. Includes index. Bibliography: p. 195-210. ISBN 978-17-5142-8
1. Nigeria - History. 2. Nigeria - Colonial influence. 3. Great Britain - Colonies - Africa - History. I. Title.
NYPL *[Sc D 88-820]*

Ejiofor, Pita N. O. Development of management education in Nigeria /. Ikeja, Nigeria , 1985. 555 p. : ISBN 978-14-0017-X
NYPL *[Sc E 89-161]*

Ejiogu, Aloy M. Landmarks in educational development in Nigeria : an appraisal / by Aloy M. Ejiogu. Ikeja, Lagos : Joja Educational Research and Publishers, c1986. xi, 156 p. ; 22 cm. Includes bibliographical references and index. ISBN 978-242-716-0
1. Education - Nigeria - History. I. Title.
NYPL *[Sc D 88-782]*

Ejizu, Christopher I. Ofo : Igbo ritual symbol / Chris Ifeanyi Ejizu. Enugu, Nigeria : Fourth Dimension Publishers, 1986. xxii, 190 p. : ill. (some col.) ; 22 cm. Includes index. Bibliography: p. 178-186. ISBN 978-15-6268-4
1. Igbo (African people) - Religion. I. Title.
NYPL *[Sc D 88-885]*

Ekechi, Felix K., 1934- Tradition and transformation in Eastern Nigeria : a sociopolitical history of Owerri and its hinterland, 1902-1947 / Felix K. Ekechi. Kent, Ohio : Kent State University Press, c1989. xi, 256 p. ; 24 cm. Includes index. Bibliography: p. [239]-245. ISBN 0-87338-368-0 (alk. paper) DDC 966.9/4 19
1. Owerri (Nigeria : Division) - Politics and government. 2. Owerri (Nigeria : Division) - Social conditions. I. Title.
DT515.9.O87 E39 1989
NYPL *[Sc E 89-186]*

Eklou, Akpaka A. Satzstruktur des Deutschen und des Ewe : eine kontrastive Untersuchung im Rahmen der Dependenz-Verbvalenz-Grammatik / Akpaka A. Eklou. Saarbrücken : Institut für Phonetik, Universität des Saarlandes, 1987. 262 p. ; 21 cm. (Africana Saraviensia linguistica, 0724-0937 . nr. 14) In German and Ewe. Bibliography: p. 244-262.
1. German language - Grammar, comparative - Ewe. 2. Ewe language - Grammar, comparative - German. I. Title. II. Series.
NYPL *[Sc D 89-203]*

EKONDA (BANTU PEOPLE)
Vengroenweghe, Daniel. Bobongo . Berlin , c1988. xv, 332 p. : ISBN 3-496-00963-2
NYPL *[Sc E 88-343]*

EKONDA (BANTU PEOPLE) - FUNERAL CUSTOMS AND RITES.
Vengroenweghe, Daniel. Bobongo . Berlin , c1988. xv, 332 p. : ISBN 3-496-00963-2
NYPL *[Sc E 88-343]*

Ekpo, Violetta I. Akpan, Ekwere Otu. The women's war of 1929 . Calabar, Nigeria , 1988. vii, 68 p. : **NYPL** *[Sc E 89-20]*

El-Amin, Mohammed Nuri. The emergence and development of the leftist movement in the Sudan during the 1930's and 1940's / by Mohammed Nuri El-Amin. [Khartoum] : Institute of African and Asian Studies, University of Khartoum, 1984. 159 p. ; 22 cm. (Occasion[a]l paper / University of Khartoum, Institute of African and Asian Studies . no. 20) Bibliography: p. 153-159. DDC 324.2624/07 19
1. Communism - Sudan - History. I. Series: Occasional paper (Jāmi'at al-Kharṭūm. Ma'had al-Dirāsāt al-Afrīqīyah wa-al-Āsiyawīyah) , no. 20. II. Title.
HX443.5.A6 E42 1984
NYPL *[Sc D 88-1261]*

El Hussini, Mohrez Mahmoud, 1942- Soviet-Egyptian relations, 1945-85 / Mohrez Mahmoud el Hussini. New York : St. Martin's Press, 1987. xix, 276 p. : ill. ; 23 cm. Includes index. Bibliography: p. 261-271. ISBN 0-312-74781-0 : DDC 327.47062 19
1. Soviet Union - Foreign relations - Egypt. 2. Egypt - Foreign relations - Soviet Union. 3. Soviet Union - Foreign relations - 1945-. I. Title.
DK69.4.E3 E4 1987 **NYPL** *[Sc D 88-1031]*

El Mahdi, El Tayeb. Le jeu des maitres : pièce en un acte : farce politico-tragique / El Tayeb El Mahdi. Paris : L'Harmattan, 1988. 69 p. ; 22 cm. (Collection Encres noires. 45) ISBN 2-85802-794-3
I. Title. **NYPL** *[Sc D 89-466]*

El Mahmud-Okereke, N. O. E. (Noel Olufemi Enuma), 1948-
Beyond the Botha/Buthelezi political debate : South Africa multi-racial power sharing blueprint / N.O.E. el Mahmud-Okereke. London : Emmcon (TWORF), c1987. v, 177 p. : ill., facsim., ports. ; 20 cm. ISBN 978-242-309-2 (pbk) DDC 346.802/3 19
1. Blacks - South Africa - Political activity. 2. South Africa - Constitutional law. 3. South Africa - Politics and government - 1978-. I. Title.
NYPL *[Sc C 88-180]*

Nancy Reagan's red dress ; Previewing UK's King Charles ; Israel's indigenous black minority : & other poems of Pan-Afrikan expression / N.O.E. el Mahmud-Okereke. 2nd ed. London : Emmcon (TWORF), 1988, c1987. xxi, 179 p. : ill., facsims., ports. ; 20 cm. ISBN 978-242-304-1 (pbk) DDC 821 19
1. Literature and society - Africa. 2. Africa - Poetry. 3. Africa - Politics and government - 1960-. I. Title.
NYPL *[Sc C 88-182]*

El-Solami-Mewis, Catherine. Lehrbuch des Somali / von Catherine El-Solami-Mewis. 1 Aufl. Leipzig : VEB Verlag Enzyklopädie, c1987. 253 p. ; 23 cm. Includes index. ISBN 3-324-00175-7
1. Somali languages - Text-books for foreign speakers - German. I. Title. **NYPL** *[Sc D 88-896]*

Elam, Ada M.
Blacks on white campuses, whites on black campuses /. Chicago , c1986. 177 p. ; ISBN 0-695-60052-4 **NYPL** *[Sc D 88-949]*

The Status of Blacks in higher education /. Lanham, MD [Washington, D.C.] , c1989. ix, 110 p. ; ISBN 0-8191-7286-3 (alk. paper) DDC 378/.008996073 19
LC2781 .S72 1988 **NYPL** *[Sc D 89-589]*

Elam, Julia C.
Black colleges and public policy /. Chicago , c1986. 99 p. : ISBN 0-695-60050-8
NYPL *[Sc D 88-947]*

Inside black colleges and universities /. Chicago , c1986. 153 p. ; ISBN 0-695-60051-6
NYPL *[Sc D 88-951]*

ELDERLY PERSONS. see **AGED.**

Election '84 report .
(#1) Cavanagh, Thomas E. The impact of the

Black electorate [microform] /. Washington,
D.C. (1301 Pennsylvania Ave., N.W., Suite
400, Washington 20004) , 1984. v, 28 p. ;
DDC 324.973/008996073 19
E185.615 .C364 1984   NYPL [*Z-4913 no.8]

(#2) Cavanagh, Thomas E. Jesse Jackson's
campaign . Washington, D.C. , 1984. 27 p.,
[1] ; ISBN 0-941410-45-5 (pbk.). DDC 324.973 19
JK526 1984c   NYPL [Sc F 87-172 rept. 2]

(#4) Blacks and the 1984 Republican National
Convention . Washington, D.C. (1301
Pennsylvania Ave., N.W., Suite 400,
Washington 20004) , 1984. v, 25 p. ; ISBN
0-941410-51-X (pbk.) DDC 324.2734 19
JK2353 1984   NYPL [Sc F 87-172 rept. 4]

Elections in Nigeria . Miles, William F. S.
Boulder, Colo. , c1988. 168 p. : ISBN
1-555-87054-6 : DDC 324.9669/505 19
JQ3099.N66 E546 1987
                    NYPL [JLE 88-3534]

ELECTIONS - KENYA.
Harbeson, John Willis, 1938- The Kenya little
general election [microform] . Nairobi , 1967.
23 p. ;   NYPL [Sc Micro R-4108 no. 31]

ELECTIONS - NIGERIA, NORTHERN -
    CASE STUDIES.
Miles, William F. S. Elections in Nigeria .
Boulder, Colo. , c1988. 168 p. : ISBN
1-555-87054-6 : DDC 324.9669/505 19
JQ3099.N66 E546 1987
                    NYPL [JLE 88-3534]

ELECTIONS - SENEGAL.
Senegal . Hamburg , 1983. xxxix, 392 p. :
    ISBN 3-922887-28-7 (pbk.) DDC 324.266/3 19
JQ3396.A91 S38 1983   NYPL [JLF 85-1341]

ELECTIONS - TANZANIA.
One party democracy. [Nairobi, 1967] 470 p.
DDC 324/.678
JQ3519.A55 O5   NYPL [Sc D 88-976]

Selections from One party democracy. [Nairobi,
1967] 143 p. DDC 324/.678
JQ3519.A55 O53   NYPL [Sc D 87-1320]

ELECTIONS - UGANDA.
Bwengye, Francis Aloysius Wazarwahi. The
agony of Uganda from Idi Amin to Obote .
London , 1985. xxii, 379 p. ; ISBN
0-7212-0717-0 :   NYPL [Sc D 88-873]

ELECTIONS - UNITED STATES.
Epton, William. Electoral politics [microform] .
New York , 1980. 33 p. :
                    NYPL [Sc Micro F-10975]

ELECTIONS - UNITED STATES - JUVENILE
    LITERATURE.
Fitch, Robert Beck, 1938- Right on Dellums!
Mankato, Minn. [1971] [47] p. ISBN
0-87191-079-9 DDC 329/.023/79405
JK1978 .F53   NYPL [Sc F 88-338]

ELECTORAL COLLEGE. see PRESIDENTS -
    UNITED STATES - ELECTION.

Electoral politics [microform] . Epton, William.
New York , 1980. 33 p. :
                    NYPL [Sc Micro F-10975]

ELECTRONIC DATA PROCESSING
    CONSULTANTS - AFRICA -
    DIRECTORIES.
Directory of electronic data processing experts
in Africa =. [Addis Ababa?] [1985] iii, 57 p. ;
DDC 004/.025/6 19
QA76.215 .D576 1985   NYPL [Sc F 89-42]

Elegua quiere tambó . Castellanos, Isabel, 1939-
Cali, Colombia , 1983. 84 p. ;
                    NYPL [Sc D 88-534]

ELEMENTARY SCHOOL STUDENTS' SOCIO-
    ECONOMIC STATUS - NIGERIA -
    WESTERN STATE.
Western State, Nigeria. Ministry of Economic
Planning and Social Development. Statistics
Division. Report of a sample survey of
unemployment among school leavers
[microform /. Ibadan [1966]- v. ;
                    NYPL [Sc Micro F-10938]

Elements de grammaire lingombe avec une
bibliographie exhaustive /. Mangulu, Motingea.
Mbandaka, Zaire *, 1988. 88 p. :
                    NYPL [Sc D 89-40]

Eléments de linguistique burundaise /. Bigangara,
Jean-Baptiste. Bujumbura , 1982. 138 p. ; DDC

496/.39 19
PL8611.1 .B54 1982   NYPL [Sc E 88-403]

The elements of banking /. Adekanye, Femi.
Leighton Buzzard [1984] xxvi, 461 p. : ISBN
0-907721-19-2 (pbk)   NYPL [Sc D 88-1139]

ELEPHANT HUNTING - KENYA -
    JUVENILE FICTION.
Stinetorf, Louise A. Elephant outlaw /.
Philadelphia , c1956. 173 p. :
                    NYPL [Sc D 88-1167]

Elephant outlaw /. Stinetorf, Louise A.
Philadelphia , c1956. 173 p. :
                    NYPL [Sc D 88-1167]

ELEPHANTS - FICTION.
Resnick, Mike. Ivory /. New York , 1988. 374
p. : ISBN 0-312-93093-3 : DDC 813/.54 19
PS3568.E698 I96 1988   NYPL [Sc D 89-163]

ELEPHANTS - JUVENILE FICTION.
Fischer, Erling Gunnar. Peter är barnvakt /.
Stockholm , 1961. [40] p. :
                    NYPL [Sc F 88-261]

Mwenye Hadithi. Tricky Tortoise /. Boston ,
c1988. [32] p. : ISBN 0-316-33724-2 : DDC [E]
19
PZ7.M975 Tr 1988   NYPL [Sc F 88-389]

ELITE (SOCIAL SCIENCES) - AFRICA.
Nafziger, E. Wayne. Inequality in Africa .
Cambridge [Cambridgeshire] , New York ,
c1988. xii, 204 p. : ISBN 0-521-26881-8 DDC
339.2/096 19
HC800.Z9 I5136 1988   NYPL [Sc E 88-521]

ELITE (SOCIAL SCIENCES) - HAITI -
    ANECDOTES, FACETIAE, SATIRE, ETC.
Victor, Gary, 1958- Albert Buron, ou, Profil
d'une "élite" /. [Port-au-Prince , 1988] 230 p. :
                    NYPL [Sc D 88-1005]

ELITE (SOCIAL SCIENCES) - HAITI -
    ATTITUDES - HISTORY - 20TH
    CENTURY.
Plummer, Brenda Gayle. Haiti and the great
powers, 1902-1915 /. Baton Rouge , c1988. xix,
255 p. : ISBN 0-8071-1409-X (alk. paper) DDC
972.94/04 19
F1926 .P68 1988   NYPL [HPE 88-2374]

ELITE (SOCIAL SCIENCES) - KENYA -
    HISTORY - CASE STUDIES.
Harris, Joseph E., 1929- Repatriates and
refugees in a colonial society . Washington,
D.C. , 1987. ix, 201 p. ; ISBN 0-88258-148-1 :
DDC 304.8/676/2 19
HN793.Z9 E44 1987   NYPL [Sc E 87-558]

ELITE (SOCIAL SCIENCES) - NIGERIA.
Takaya, B. J. The Kaduna mafia /. [Jos,
Nigeria] , c1987. viii, 146 p. ; ISBN
978-16-6045-7   NYPL [Sc D 88-736]

ELITE (SOCIAL SCIENCES) -
    PENNSYLVANIA - PHILADELPHIA -
    HISTORY.
Winch, Julie, 1953- Philadelphia's Black elite .
Philadelphia , 1988. x, 240 p. ; ISBN
0-87722-515-X (alk. paper) : DDC
974.8/1100496073 19
F158.9.N4 W56 1988   NYPL [Sc E 88-198]

ELITE (SOCIAL SCIENCES) - SOUTH
    AFRICA.
Dreyer, Lynette, 1949- The modern African
elite of South Africa /. Houndmills,
Basingstoke, Hampshire , 1989. xii, 186 p. ;
    ISBN 0-333-46410-9   NYPL [Sc D 89-306]

ELITE (SOCIAL SCIENCES) - SOUTHERN
    STATES - HISTORY - 19TH CENTURY.
Van Deburg, William L. The slave drivers .
New York , 1988. xvii, 202 p. : ISBN
0-19-505698-1 DDC 305.5/67/0975 19
E443 .V36 1988   NYPL [Sc D 89-424]

ELITES (SOCIAL SCIENCES) see ELITE
    (SOCIAL SCIENCES)

Elkhider, Mohmed Osman. Some aspects of
economic structures [microform] / by Mohmed
Osman Elkhider. Khartoum : Development
Studies and Research Center, Faculty of
Economic & Social Studies, University of
Khartoum, 1978. 27 leaves ; 28 cm. (Working
report/Abyei Project. no.3) Microfiche. New York:
New York Public Library, 198 . 1 microfiche: negative;
11 x 15 cm. (FSN Sc 019,057)
1. Abyei (Sudan) - Economic conditions. I. Title.
                    NYPL [Sc Micro F-11038]

Elkin, Benjamin. Why the sun was late / By
Benjamin Elkin ; illustrated by Jerome Snyder.
New York : Parents' Magazine Press, 1966.
[40] p. : col. ill. ; 27 cm. SCHOMBURG
CHILDREN'S COLLECTION.
1. Africa - Juvenile fiction. I. Snyder, Jerome. II.
Schomburg Children's Collection. III. Title.
PZ7.#426 Wh   NYPL [Sc F 88-105]

Ella Fitzgerald /. Kliment, Bud. New York ,
c1988. 112 p. : ISBN 1-555-46586-2 DDC 784.5
B 19
ML420.F52 K6 1988   NYPL [Sc E 88-611]

ELLINGTON, DUKE, 1899-1974 - JUVENILE
    LITERATURE.
Frankl, Ron. Duke Ellington /. New York ,
c1988. 110 p. : ISBN 1-555-46584-6 DDC
785.42/092/4 B 92 19
ML3930.E44 F7 1988   NYPL [Sc E 88-381]

Ellington, Edward Kennedy. see Ellington, Duke,
    1899-1974.

Elliot, Geraldine. Where the leopard passes : a
book of African folk tales / by Geraldine
Elliot ; Illustrated by Sheila Hawkins ; with a
foreword by Laura Simms. New York,
Schocken Books 1987. x, 125 p. : ill. ; 21 cm.
First published 1949. SCHOMBURG CHILDREN'S
COLLECTION.
1. Tales - Africa, East. 2. Angoni - Folklore. I.
Hawkins, Sheila. II. Schomburg Children's Collection.
III. Title.   NYPL [Sc D 88-840]

Elliot, Jeffrey M.
Angelou, Maya. Conversations with Maya
Angelou /. Jackson , c1989. xvi, 246 p. ; ISBN
0-87805-361-1 (alk. paper) DDC 818/.5409 19
PS3551.N464 Z4635 1989
                    NYPL [Sc E 89-225]

Kindred spirits . Boston , 1984. 262 p. ; ISBN
0-932870-42-2 (pbk.) :
                    NYPL [Sc D 89-269]

Elliott, Hugh P. Darkness and dawn in
Zimbabwe / [by] Hugh P. Elliott. London :
Grosvenor Books, 1978. [6], 49 p. ; 21 cm.
    ISBN 0-901269-37-9 :
1. Moral rearmament. 2. Nationalism - Rhodesia,
Southern. 3. Rhodesia, Southern - Race relations. I.
Title.
DT962.42 .E38   NYPL [JFD 80-115]

Ellis, G. (Guy) Saint Lucia : Helen of the West
Indies / G. Ellis. London : Macmillan
Caribbean, 1986. v, 72 p. : col. ill., 1 map ; 22
cm. ISBN 0-333-40895-0 (pbk) : DDC
917.298/4304 19
1. Saint Lucia - Description and travel - Guide-books. I.
Title.
F2100   NYPL [Sc D 89-71]

Ellison, Ralph.
INVISIBLE MAN.
Nadel, Alan, 1947- Invisible criticism . Iowa
City , 1988. xiii, 181 p. ; ISBN 0-87745-190-7 :
DDC 813/.54 19
PS3555.L625 I5358 1988
                    NYPL [Sc E 88-281]

ELLISON, RALPH - BIOGRAPHY -
    JUVENILE LITERATURE.
Bishop, Jack, 1910- Ralph Ellison /. New
York , c1988. 110 p. : ISBN 1-555-46585-4
DDC 818/.5409 B 19
PS3555.L625 Z59 1988   NYPL [Sc E 88-165]

Elma Francois . Reddock, Rhoda. London , 1988.
vii, 60 p., [8] p. of plates : ISBN 0-901241-80-6
(Pbk.)   NYPL [Sc D 89-77]

ELMORAN. see MASAI.

Eltayab, Shorhabil Ali. Agricultural and natural
resources [microform] : Abyei District, west
region, Southern Kordofan Province / by
Shorhabil Ali Eltayab. Khartoum : Development
Studies and Research Centre, Faculty of
Economic & Social Studies, University of
Khartoum, 1978. 29 leaves ; 29 cm. (Working
report/Abyei Project. no. 6) Microfiche. New York:
New York Public Library, 198 . 1 microfiche: negative;
11 x 15 cm. (FSN Sc 019,060)
1. Natural resources - Sudan - Abyei. 2. Agricultural
resources - Sudan - Abyei. I. Title.
                    NYPL [Sc Micro F-11041]

Elting, Mary, 1909-
A Mongo homecoming, by Mary Elting and
Robin McKown. Illustrated by Moneta Barnett.
New York, M. Evans [1969] 54 p. col. illus.,
col. maps. 24 cm. Describes the life of a young girl

living in a modern city in Africa and a trip she makes up river to meet her grandparents still living as their ancestors lived. SCHOMBURG CHILDREN'S COLLECTION. DDC 309.1/675
1. Zaire - Social life and customs - Juvenile literature. I. McKown, Robin, joint author. II. Barnett, Moneta, illus. III. Schomburg Children's Collection. IV. Title.
DT644 .E4 *NYPL [Sc E 88-578]*

Patch / by Mary Elting and Margaret Gossett ; pictures by Ursula Koering. [1st ed.] Garden City, N.Y. : Doubleday, 1948. 156 p. : ill. ; 20 cm. SCHOMBURG CHILDREN'S COLLECTION.
1. Dogs - Juvenile fiction. 2. Afro-American children - Juvenile fiction. I. Gossett, Margaret, joint author. II. Schomburg Children's Collection. III. Title.
PZ7.E53Pat *NYPL [Sc C 89-14]*

Elungu, P. E. A.
Teaching and research in philosophy in Africa. Spanish. Enseñanza de la filosofía e investigación filosófica en Africa /. Barcelona , París , 1984. 339 p. ; ISBN 92-3-302126-6
(Unesco) *NYPL [Sc D 88-616]*

Tradition africaine et rationalité moderne / Elungu P.E.A. Paris : L'Harmattan, c1987. 187 p. ; 22 cm. (Points de vue). Bibliography: p. 183-185.
1. Rationalism. I. Series: Collection "Points de vue". II. Title.
NYPL [Sc D 88-1101]

Eluyemi, Omotoso. This is Ile-Ife / by Omotoso Eluyemi. [Ile-Ife] : [s.n] 1986 (Ile-Ife : Adesanmi Printing Works) 62 p. : ill. ; 21 cm.
1. Ife (Nigeria) - Description. I. Title.
NYPL [Sc D 89-27]

Emamori . Mattioni, Mario D. Fort-de-France , 1986. 156 p. ; ISBN 2-85275-108-9 DDC 843 19
PQ3949.2.M36 E4 1986
NYPL [Sc E 88-615]

Emancipation I : a series of lectures to commemorate the 150th anniversary of emancipation / edited by Alvin O. Thompson ; sponsored by the National Cultural Foundation and the History Department, University of the West Indies, Barbados, 1984. Barbados : The Department : The Foundation, c1986. vii, 108 p., [1] leaf of plates : ill. ; 22 cm. Includes bibliographies. DDC 306/.362/0972981 19
1. Slavery - Barbados - History. 2. Slave-trade - History. 3. Slavery - Barbados - Emancipation. I. Thompson, Alvin O. II. National Cultural Foundation (Barbados). III. University of the West Indies (Cave Hill, Barbados). History Dept. IV. Title: Emancipation one. V. Title: Emancipation 1.
HT1119.B35 E46 1986 *NYPL [Sc D 88-248]*

Emancipation one. Emancipation I . Barbados , c1986. vii, 108 p., [1] leaf of plates : DDC 306/.362/0972981 19
HT1119.B35 E46 1986 *NYPL [Sc D 88-248]*

EMANCIPATION PROCLAMATION - JUVENILE LITERATURE.
Commager, Henry Steele, 1902- The great proclamation . Indianapolis [1960] 112 p. :
NYPL [Sc E 88-229]

Emancipation to emigration /. Greenwood, R. (Robert) London , New York , 1980 (1985 printing) viii, 152 p. : ISBN 0-333-28148-9 (pbk.) DDC 972.9 19
F1621 .G74 1984 *NYPL [Sc E 88-526]*

Emancipation 1. Emancipation I . Barbados , c1986. vii, 108 p., [1] leaf of plates : DDC 306/.362/0972981 19
HT1119.B35 E46 1986 *NYPL [Sc D 88-248]*

EMBEZZLEMENT - ANGOLA INVESTIGATION.
Costa, Antonio Maria Judice da. Aclarações . Lisboa , 1898. 28 p. ;
NYPL [Sc Micro F-10,894]

EMBU (BANTU PEOPLE)
Josiah, Mwaniki, 1933- Divorce among the Wa-Embu /. Nairobi , 1988. 49 p. ;
NYPL [Sc D 89-346]

Emecheta, Buchi, 1944. A kind of marriage / Buchi Emecheta. London : Macmillan, 1986. iv, 121 p. ; 18 cm. (Pacesetters) ISBN 0-333-42242-2
1. Nigeria - Fiction. I. Title.
NYPL [Sc D 88-613]

Emenyönu, Ernest, 1939- Literature and society . Oguta, Nigeria , 1986. iv, 303 p. ;
NYPL [Sc D 88-639]

The emergence and development of the leftist movement in the Sudan during the 1930's and 1940's /. El-Amin, Mohammed Nuri.

[Khartoum] , 1984. 159 p. ; DDC 324.2624/07 19
HX443.5.A6 E42 1984
NYPL [Sc D 88-1261]

The emergence of the cotton kingdom in the Old Southwest . Moore, John Hebron. Baton Rouge , c1988. xii, 323 p. : ISBN 0-8071-1404-9 (pbk.) DDC 330.9762 19
HC107.M7 M66 1988 *NYPL [Sc E 88-279]*

EMERGENCY POWERS. see WAR AND EMERGENCY POWERS.

EMERGENCY RELIEF. see DISASTER RELIEF.

EMIGRATION AND IMMIGRATION - BIBLIOGRAPHY - CATALOGS.
Center for Migration Studies (U. S.) Refugees . Staten Island, N.Y. , 1987. ix, 423 p. ; ISBN 0-934733-34-1 (pbk.) *NYPL [Sc F 89-60]*

EMIGRATION AND IMMIGRATION - LIBRARY RESOURCES.
Center for Migration Studies (U. S.) Refugees . Staten Island, N.Y. , 1987. ix, 423 p. ; ISBN 0-934733-34-1 (pbk.) *NYPL [Sc F 89-60]*

EMIGRATION AND IMMIGRATION - LIBRARY RESOURCES - DIRECTORIES.
A Directory of international migration study centers, research programs, and library resources /. Staten Island, N.Y. , 1987. ix, 299 p. ; ISBN 0-934733-18-X (pbk.) : DDC 325/.07 19
JV6033 .C45 1987 *NYPL [JLF 88-1452]*

EMIGRATION AND IMMIGRATION - RESEARCH - DIRECTORIES.
A Directory of international migration study centers, research programs, and library resources /. Staten Island, N.Y. , 1987. ix, 299 p. ; ISBN 0-934733-18-X (pbk.) : DDC 325/.07 19
JV6033 .C45 1987 *NYPL [JLF 88-1452]*

EMIGRATION AND IMMIGRATION - SOCIETIES, ETC. - CROSS-CULTURAL STUDIES.
Ethnic associations and the welfare state . New York , 1988. x, 299 p. : ISBN 0-231-05690-7 DDC 362.8 19
HV4005 .E86 1988 *NYPL [JLE 88-3846]*

EMIGRATION AND IMMIGRATION - STUDY AND TEACHING - DIRECTORIES.
A Directory of international migration study centers, research programs, and library resources /. Staten Island, N.Y. , 1987. ix, 299 p. ; ISBN 0-934733-18-X (pbk.) : DDC 325/.07 19
JV6033 .C45 1987 *NYPL [JLF 88-1452]*

Emigration versus assimilation. Kinshasa, Kwando Mbiassi. Emigration vs. assimilation . Jefferson, N.C. , 1988. xiv, 234 p. ; ISBN 0-89950-338-1 (lib. bdg.) DDC 973/.0496073 19
E185 .K49 1988 *NYPL [IEC 88-2401]*

Emigration vs. assimilation . Kinshasa, Kwando Mbiassi. Jefferson, N.C. , 1988. xiv, 234 p. ; ISBN 0-89950-338-1 (lib. bdg.) DDC 973/.0496073 19
E185 .K49 1988 *NYPL [IEC 88-2401]*

Emmanuel, Patrick. Political change and public opinion in Grenada 1979-1984 / Patrick Emmanuel, Farley Brathwaite, Eudine Barriteau. Cave Hill, Barbados : Institute of Social and Economic Research (Eastern Caribbean), University of the West Indies, c1986. xii, 173 p. : ill. ; 24 cm. (Occasional papers / Institute of Social and Economic Research (Eastern Caribbean), University of the West Indies . no. 19) Bibliography: p.169-173.
1. Public opinion - Grenada. 2. Grenada - Politics and government - 1974-. I. Brathwaite, Farley. II. Barriteau, Eudine. III. Series: University of the West Indies, Cave Hill, Barbados. Institute of Social and Economic Research. Occasional papers, no. 19. IV. Title.
NYPL [JLM 79-1223 no.19]

Emo and the Babalawo /. Ajọṣe, Audrie. Ibadan , 1985. 51 p. : ISBN 978-15-5652-2 (Nigeria)
NYPL [Sc C 88-152]

EMPLOYEE-EMPLOYER RELATIONS. see INDUSTRIAL RELATIONS.

EMPLOYER-EMPLOYEE RELATIONS. see INDUSTRIAL RELATIONS.

EMPLOYMENT AGENCIES - UNITED STATES.

Granger, Lester Blackwell, 1896- Toward job adjustment . [New York] [1941] 78 p. :
NYPL [Sc D 88-178]

EMPLOYMENT DISCRIMINATION. see DISCRIMINATION IN EMPLOYMENT.

EMPLOYMENT INTERVIEWING - UNITED STATES.
Granger, Lester Blackwell, 1896- Toward job adjustment . [New York] [1941] 78 p. :
NYPL [Sc D 88-178]

EMPLOYMENT MANAGEMENT. see PERSONNEL MANAGEMENT.

EMPLOYMENT OF CHILDREN. see CHILDREN - EMPLOYMENT.

EMPLOYMENT OF WOMEN. see WOMEN - EMPLOYMENT.

EMPLOYMENT OF YOUTH. see YOUTH - EMPLOYMENT.

Ẹmwẹn Edo na zedu ẹre y'Ebo =. Aigbe, E. I. Lagos [1986?] viii, 62 p. :
NYPL [Sc C 88-174]

En el atascadero /. Matos Moquete, Manuel, 1944- Santo Domingo, República Dominicana , 1985. 266 p. ;
MLCS 85/21777 (P) *NYPL [JFD 86-4017]*

En la Galería Latinoamericana /. Juan, Adalaida de. La Habana , 1979. 203 p. :
NYPL [3-MAM 88-2546]

The encyclopedia of the Third World /. Kurian, George Thomas. New York, N.Y. , 1987. 3 v. (xxix-2342 p.) : ISBN 0-8160-1118-4 (set) DDC 909/.09724 19
HC59.7 .K87 1987 *NYPL [Sc F 88-324]*

Encyclopedia of world literature in the 20th century : based on the first edition edited by Wolfgang Bernard Fleischmann / Leonard S. Klein, general editor.Rev. ed. New York : Ungar, c1981-1984. 4 v. : ports. ; 29 cm. Includes bibliographies. CONTENTS. - Vol. 1: A-D.--v. 2: E-K.--v. 3: L-Q.--v. 4: R-Z. ISBN 0-8044-3135-3 (v. 1) : DDC 803 19
1. Literature, Modern - 20th century - Bio-bibliography. 2. Literature, Modern - 20th century - Dictionaries. I. Klein, Leonard S.
PN771 .E5 1981 *NYPL [Sc Ser.-M .E565]*

Encyclopédie de la Pléade. Benoist, Jean, 1929- Les Antilles /. [Paris , 1976?] p. [1372]-1448 :
NYPL [Sc D 87-1164]

The End of slavery in Africa / edited by Suzanne Miers and Richard Roberts. Madison, Wis. : University of Wisconsin Press, c1988. xx, 524 p. : ill., maps ; 24 cm. Includes bibliography and index. ISBN 0-299-11550-X : DDC 306/.362/096 19
1. Slavery - Africa - History - 19th century. 2. Slavery - Africa - History - 20th century. I. Miers, Suzanne. II. Roberts, Richard L., 1949-.
HT1323 .E53 1988 *NYPL [Sc E 89-222]*

Enda Tiers-Monde. Nicolas, Pierre. Naissance d'une ville au Sénégal . Paris , c1988. 193 p., [8] p. of plates ; ISBN 2-86537-195-6
NYPL [Sc F 89-131]

The endangered Black family . Hare, Nathan. San Francisco, CA , c1984. 192 p. ; ISBN 0-9613086-0-5 *NYPL [Sc C 88-307]*

Endgame in South Africa? . Cohen, Robin. London : Paris : x, 108 p. ; ISBN 0-85255-308-0 (pbk.) : DDC 323.1/68 19
DT763 .C64 1986 *NYPL [Sc D 88-770]*

Endrek, Emiliano. El mestizaje en Córdoba: siglo XVIII y principios del XIX. Córdoba [Argentina] Universidad Nacional de Córdoba. Dirección General de Publicaciones, 1966. xi, 151 p. 24 cm. (Universidad Nacional de Córdoba. Facultad de Filosofía y Humanidades. Instituto de Estudios Americanistas. Cuadernos de historia, no. 33) "Apéndice documental": p. 99-150. Includes bibliographical references.
1. Indians of South America - Argentina - Córdoba. 2. Indians of South America - Mixed bloods. I. Series: Cuadernos de historia (Universidad Nacional de Córdoba. Instituto de Estudios Americanistas) , no. 33. II. Title.
F2821.1.C7 E5 *NYPL [Sc E 88-61]*

Eneida, 1903-1971. História do carnaval carioca / Eneida. Nova ed. / rev. e ampliada por Haroldo Costa. Rio de Janeiro : Editora

Record, c1987. 259 p. : ill. ; 21 cm. Bibliography: p. 256-259. ISBN 85-10-29900-5
1. Carnival - Brazil - Rio de Janeiro - History. 2. Rio de Janeiro (Brazil) - Social life and customs. I. Costa, Haroldo. II. Title.
GT4233.R5 E53 1987 **NYPL** *[Sc D 89-313]*

Enekwe, Onuora Ossie. Igbo masks : the oneness of ritual and the theatre : a Nigeria magazine publication / Onuora Ossie Enekwe. Lagos : Dept. of Culture, Federal Ministry of Information and Culture, c1987. 164 p. : ill., map ; 21 cm. Includes index. Bibliography: p. 146-162. ISBN 978-17-3040-4
1. Igbo (African people) - Social life and customs. 2. Igbo (African people) - Masks. 3. Theatre - Nigeria. I. Title.   **NYPL** *[Sc D 88-1238]*

ENERGY RESOURCES. see POWER RESOURCES.

Energy supply and economic development in East Africa. Amann, Hans. München, (1969). 254 p. with maps, 7 inserts (in pocket) DDC 333
HD9557.A32 A6 **NYPL** *[Sc E 88-226]*

Engel, Albert. Promoting smallholder cropping systems in Sierra Leone. Berlin , 1985. iv, 227 p. :   **NYPL** *[Sc D 88-817]*

ENGLISH DRAMA - EARLY MODERN AND ELIZABETHAN, 1500-1600 - HISTORY AND CRITICISM.
Barthelemy, Anthony Gerard, 1949- Black face, maligned race . Baton Rouge , c1987. xi, 215 p. ; ISBN 0-8071-1331-X DDC 822/.3/093520396 19
PR678.A4 B37 1987
                         NYPL *[MWET 87-5064]*

ENGLISH DRAMA - 17TH CENTURY - HISTORY AND CRITICISM.
Barthelemy, Anthony Gerard, 1949- Black face, maligned race . Baton Rouge , c1987. xi, 215 p. ; ISBN 0-8071-1331-X DDC 822/.3/093520396 19
PR678.A4 B37 1987
                         NYPL *[MWET 87-5064]*

ENGLISH DRAMA - RESTORATION, 1660-1700 - HISTORY AND CRITICISM.
Barthelemy, Anthony Gerard, 1949- Black face, maligned race . Baton Rouge , c1987. xi, 215 p. ; ISBN 0-8071-1331-X DDC 822/.3/093520396 19
PR678.A4 B37 1987
                         NYPL *[MWET 87-5064]*

ENGLISH DRAMA - 20TH CENTURY.
Black plays /. London , New York, NY , 1987. 139 p. ; ISBN 0-413-15710-5
                         NYPL *[JFD 88-8329]*

ENGLISH DRAMA - 20TH CENTURY - HISTORY AND CRITICISM.
Making a spectacle . Ann Arbor , c1989. 347 p. : ISBN 0-472-09389-4 (alk. paper) : DDC 812/.54/099287 19
PS338.W6 M3 1989 **NYPL** *[JFE 89-144]*

ENGLISH DRAMA - BLACK AUTHORS.
Black plays /. London , New York, NY , 1987. 139 p. ; ISBN 0-413-15710-5
                         NYPL *[JFD 88-8329]*
Totem voices . New York , 1989. lxiii, 523 p. ; ISBN 0-8021-1053-3 : DDC 812/.54/080896 19
PS628.N4 T68 1988 **NYPL** *[Sc D 89-381]*

ENGLISH DRAMA - TRANSLATIONS FROM FRENCH.
Faces of African independence . Charlottesville , 1988. xxxvi, 127 p. ; ISBN 0-8139-1186-9 DDC 842 19
PQ3987.5.E5 F33 1988 **NYPL** *[Sc D 89-32]*

ENGLISH DRAMA - WOMEN AUTHORS - HISTORY AND CRITICISM.
Making a spectacle . Ann Arbor , c1989. 347 p. : ISBN 0-472-09389-4 (alk. paper) : DDC 812/.54/099287 19
PS338.W6 M3 1989 **NYPL** *[JFE 89-144]*

ENGLISH DRAMMA - KENYAN AUTHORS. see KENYAN DRAMA (ENGLISH)

ENGLISH FICTION - 20TH CENTURY.
Black and priceless . Manchester , 1988. xiii, 198 p. : ISBN 0-946745-45-5 (pbk) : DDC 821/.914/08 823/.01/08 19
PR1225 PR1309.S5 **NYPL** *[Sc C 89-131]*

ENGLISH FICTION - BLACK AUTHORS.
Black and priceless . Manchester , 1988. xiii, 198 p. : ISBN 0-946745-45-5 (pbk) : DDC

821/.914/08 823/.01/08 19
PR1225 PR1309.S5 **NYPL** *[Sc C 89-131]*

ENGLISH FICTION - SOCIAL ASPECTS.
Agovi, Kofi Ermeleh, 1944- Novels of social change /. Tema, Ghana , 1988. xxviii, 290 p. ; ISBN 996-410-332-8
                         NYPL *[Sc D 88-1410]*

ENGLISH LANGUAGE - CARIBBEAN AREA.
Focus on the Caribbean /. Amsterdam , Philadelphia , 1986. ix, 209 p. : ISBN 90-272-4866-4 (pbk. : alk. paper) : DDC 427/.9729 19
PM7874.C27 F6 1986 **NYPL** *[JFD 87-3902]*

ENGLISH LANGUAGE - DICTIONARIES - ETHIOPIC.
Leslau, Wolf. Comparative dictionary of Ge'ez (Classical Ethiopic) . Wiesbaden , 1987. xlix, 813 p. ; ISBN 3-447-02592-1 : DDC 492/.8 19
PJ9087 .L37 1987 **NYPL** *[*OEC 89-3015]*

ENGLISH LANGUAGE - DICTIONARIES - SAN LANGUAGES.
Bleek, Dorothea Frances, d. 1948. Comparative vocabularies of Bushman languages /. Cambridge [Eng.] , 1929. 94 p., 1 leaf of plates : DDC 496.232
PL8101 .B6 **NYPL** *[Sc E 88-89]*

ENGLISH LANGUAGE - DICTIONARIES - SWAHILI.
Msamiati wa maneno ya kitheologia. Dodoma [Tanzania] , c1979. iv, 47 p. ;
BR95 .M72 1979 **NYPL** *[Sc C 88-149]*
Yahya, Saad, 1939- English-Swahili glossary of technical terms for valuers and land economists /. [Nairobi] [1979] [8] leaves ; DDC 333/.003/21 19
HD107.7 .Y34 1979 **NYPL** *[Sc F 88-77]*

ENGLISH LANGUAGE - DICTIONARIES - TZOTZIL.
Laughlin, Robert M. The great Tzotzil dictionary of Santo Domingo Zinacantán . Washington, D.C. , 1988. 3 v. (xiii, 1119 p.) : DDC 497/.4 301 s 19
GN1 .S54 no. 31a PM4466.Z5
                         NYPL *[HBR 89-17311]*

ENGLISH LANGUAGE - DICTIONARY - TURKANA.
Barrett, Anthony. English-Turkana dictionary /. Nairobi , 1988. xxx, 225 p. ; ISBN 0-333-44577-5 **NYPL** *[Sc D 89-437]*

ENGLISH LANGUAGE - MORPHOLOGY.
Schneider, Edgar W. (Edgar Werner), 1954- [Morphologische und syntaktische Variablen im amerikanischen early black English. English.] American earlier Black English . Tuscaloosa , 1989. xiv, 314 p. : ISBN 0-8173-0436-3 DDC 427/.973/08996 19
PE3102.N43 S3613 1989
                         NYPL *[Sc E 89-210]*

ENGLISH LANGUAGE - NIGERIA.
Odumuh, A. E. Nigerian English (NigE) . [S.l.] 1987 (Zaria: Printed in Nigeria by A.B. University Press.) vi, 125 p. : ISBN 978-12-5061-5 **NYPL** *[Sc D 88-1378]*

ENGLISH LANGUAGE - PHONETIC TRANSCRIPTIONS.
Larison, Cornelius Wilson, 1837-1910. Silvia Dubois . New York , 1988. xxvii, 124 p. : ISBN 0-19-505239-0 DDC 305.5/67/0924 B 19
E444.D83 L37 1988 **NYPL** *[JFC 89-2191]*

ENGLISH LANGUAGE - PRIMERS. see PRIMERS.

ENGLISH LANGUAGE - STUDY AND TEACHING (SECONDARY) - CONGO (BRAZZAVILLE)
Mombod, Josephine Ntinou. Developing models/techniques in the teaching of English as a second foreign language in senior secondary schools in the Congo /. Nairobi , 1983. ii, 67 leaves ; DDC 428/.007/126724 19
PE1068.C74 M67 1983 **NYPL** *[Sc F 88-200]*

ENGLISH LANGUAGE - STUDY AND TEACHING (SECONDARY) - FRENCH SPEAKERS.
Mombod, Josephine Ntinou. Developing models/techniques in the teaching of English as a second foreign language in senior secondary schools in the Congo /. Nairobi , 1983. ii, 67 leaves ; DDC 428/.007/126724 19
PE1068.C74 M67 1983 **NYPL** *[Sc F 88-200]*

ENGLISH LANGUAGE - STUDY AND TEACHING - SENEGAL.
Le Boulch, Pierre. Today's English . [Dakar] , 1968- v. ; **NYPL** *[Sc F 87-274]*

ENGLISH LANGUAGE - SYNTAX.
Schneider, Edgar W. (Edgar Werner), 1954- [Morphologische und syntaktische Variablen im amerikanischen early black English. English.] American earlier Black English . Tuscaloosa , 1989. xiv, 314 p. : ISBN 0-8173-0436-3 DDC 427/.973/08996 19
PE3102.N43 S3613 1989
                         NYPL *[Sc E 89-210]*

ENGLISH LANGUAGE - TEXT-BOOKS FOR FOREIGN SPEAKERS - FRENCH.
Le Boulch, Pierre. Today's English . [Dakar] , 1968- v. ; **NYPL** *[Sc F 87-274]*

ENGLISH LANGUAGE - TEXTBOOKS FOR FOREIGN SPEAKERS - AFRICAN.
A Junior secondary poetry anthology /. [Limbe , c1984- v. : DDC 428.6/4 19
PE1126.A44 J86 1984 **NYPL** *[Sc D 88-384]*

ENGLISH LANGUAGE - TRINIDAD AND TOBAGO - SLANG - DICTIONARIES.
Haynes, Martin De Coursey, 1939. Trinidad and Tobago dialect (plus) /. San Fernando, Trinidad , 1987. 215 p. ;
                         NYPL *[Sc D 88-860]*

ENGLISH LANGUAGE - TRINIDAD AND TOBAGO - TERMS AND PHRASES.
Haynes, Martin De Coursey, 1939. Trinidad and Tobago dialect (plus) /. San Fernando, Trinidad , 1987. 215 p. ;
                         NYPL *[Sc D 88-860]*

ENGLISH LANGUAGE - UNITED STATES.
Schneider, Edgar W. (Edgar Werner), 1954- [Morphologische und syntaktische Variablen im amerikanischen early black English. English.] American earlier Black English . Tuscaloosa , 1989. xiv, 314 p. : ISBN 0-8173-0436-3 DDC 427/.973/08996 19
PE3102.N43 S3613 1989
                         NYPL *[Sc E 89-210]*

ENGLISH LANGUAGE - UNITED STATES - FOREIGN ELEMENTS - AFRICAN.
Twum-Akwaboah, Edward. From pidginization to creolization of Africanisms in Black American English /. [Los Angeles , 1973] 46 leaves ; **NYPL** *[Sc F 88-210]*

ENGLISH LANGUAGE - WEST INDIES.
Roberts, Peter A. West Indians and their language /. Cambridge [Cambridgeshire] , New York , 1988. vii, 215 p. : ISBN 0-521-35136-7 DDC 427/.9729 19
P381.W47 R63 1988 **NYPL** *[Sc E 88-331]*

ENGLISH LITERATURE - AFRICAN AUTHORS. see AFRICAN LITERATURE (ENGLISH)

ENGLISH LITERATURE - BLACK AUTHORS - BIBLIOGRAPHY.
Guptara, Prabhu S. Black British literature . [Sydney] , Berkeley, Calif. [1986] 176 p. : ISBN 87-88213-14-5 (paper) :
                         NYPL *[Sc D 89-20]*

ENGLISH LITERATURE - BLACK AUTHORS - HISTORY AND CRITICISM.
Let it be told . London , 1987. 145, [1] p. ; ISBN 0-7453-0254-8 **NYPL** *[Sc E 88-125]*

ENGLISH LITERATURE - BRITISH VIRGIN ISLANDS.
A cultural experience . Road Town, Tortola, British Virgin Islands , 1980. viii, 55 p. :
MLCS 81/1586 **NYPL** *[Sc D 88-1398]*

ENGLISH LITERATURE - CANADA. see CANADIAN LITERATURE.

ENGLISH LITERATURE - COMMONWEALTH OF NATIONS AUTHORS - HISTORY AND CRITICISM.
Walsh, William, 1916- Commonwealth literature. London, New York, 1973. vi, 150 p.
                         NYPL *[*R-NCB 74-5085]*

ENGLISH LITERATURE - GUYANESE AUTHORS. see GUYANESE LITERATURE.

ENGLISH LITERATURE - STUDY AND TEACHING - AFRICA.
Ngara, Emmanuel. Teaching literature in Africa . Harare, Zimbabwe , 1984. 76 p. ;

ISBN 0-908300-09-3 :
NYPL [Sc D 89-383]

ENGLISH LITERATURE - TRANSLATIONS FROM AFRICAN LITERATURE.
Voices from twentieth-century Africa .
London , Boston , 1988. xl, 424 p. ; ISBN
0-571-14929-4 (cased) : DDC 808.8/9896 19
NYPL [Sc D 89-174]

ENGLISH LITERATURE - WOMEN AUTHORS.
Sojourn /. London , 1988. 215 p. ; ISBN
0-413-16440-3 (pbk) : DDC 823/.914/08 19
NYPL [Sc C 89-81]

ENGLISH LITERATURE - WOMEN AUTHORS - HISTORY AND CRITICISM.
Let it be told . London , 1987. 145, [1] p. ;
ISBN 0-7453-0254-8 *NYPL [Sc E 88-125]*

ENGLISH POETRY - 20TH CENTURY.
Black and priceless . Manchester , 1988. xiii,
198 p. ; ISBN 0-946745-45-5 (pbk) : DDC
821/.914/08 823/.01/08 19
PR1225 PR1309.S5   NYPL [Sc C 89-131]

A Dangerous knowing . London [1984] ix, 67
p. : ISBN 0-907179-28-2 *NYPL [Sc D 88-338]*

Sergeant, Howard, 1914- New voices of the
Commonwealth. London, 1968. 208 p. ISBN
0-237-49815-4 DDC 821/.008
PR9086 .S4   NYPL [Sc D 89-121]

Tongues untied . London , Boston, MA, USA ,
1987. 95 p. ; ISBN 0-85449-053-1 (pbk) : DDC
821/.914/080920664 19
PR1178.H6   NYPL [JFD 88-7561]

ENGLISH POETRY - 20TH CENTURY - TRANSLATIONS FROM SPANISH.
The image of Black women in twentieth-century
South American poetry . Washington, D.C. ,
c1987. 250 p. ; ISBN 0-89410-275-3
NYPL [Sc E 88-321]

ENGLISH POETRY - BLACK AUTHORS.
Black and priceless . Manchester , 1988. xiii,
198 p. ; ISBN 0-946745-45-5 (pbk) : DDC
821/.914/08 823/.01/08 19
PR1225 PR1309.S5   NYPL [Sc C 89-131]

A Dangerous knowing . London [1984] ix, 67
p. : ISBN 0-907179-28-2 *NYPL [Sc D 88-338]*

Gurus and griots . Brooklyn, N.Y. [1987],
c1985. 108 p. ; ISBN 0-9618755-0-X (pbk.) DDC
811/.008/0896 19
PS591.N4 G87 1987   NYPL [Sc E 89-230]

ENGLISH POETRY - COMMONWEALTH OF NATIONS AUTHORS.
Sergeant, Howard, 1914- New voices of the
Commonwealth. London, 1968. 208 p. ISBN
0-237-49815-4 DDC 821/.008
PR9086 .S4   NYPL [Sc D 89-121]

ENGLISH POETRY - JAMAICAN AUTHORS. see JAMAICAN POETRY.

ENGLISH POETRY - TRANSLATIONS FROM AFRICAN LANGUAGES.
Mambo book of Zimbabwean Verse in English
/. Gweru, Zimbabwe , c986. xxix, 417 p. ;
ISBN 0-86922-367-4 (pbk).
NYPL [JFD 88-10986]

ENGLISH POETRY - WEST INDIAN AUTHORS. see WEST INDIAN POETRY (ENGLISH)

ENGLISH POETRY - WOMEN AUTHORS.
A Dangerous knowing . London [1984] ix, 67
p. : ISBN 0-907179-28-2 *NYPL [Sc D 88-338]*

English-Swahili glossary of technical terms for valuers and land economists /. Yahya, Saad,
1939- [Nairobi] [1979] [8] leaves ; DDC
333/.003/21 19
HD107.7 .Y34 1979   NYPL [Sc F 88-77]

English-Turkana dictionary /. Barrett, Anthony.
Nairobi , 1988. xxx, 225 p. ; ISBN
0-333-44577-5 *NYPL [Sc D 89-437]*

Enjeux fonciers dan la Caraibe, en Amérique centrale et à la Réunion : plantations et
paysanneries / études réunies et présentées par
Christian Deverre. Paris : INRA : Karthala,
c1987. 232 p. : ill., maps ; 24 cm. (Hommes et
sociétés) Papers presented at a conference organized by
the INRA and held in Pointed-Pitre, Guadeloupe, 21-24
November 1983. Some contributions translated from
English or Spanish. Bibliography: p. [227]-230. ISBN
2-7380-0003-7
1. Land use, Rural - Caribbean Area. 2. Agriculture and

state - Caribbean Area. 3. Land reform - Caribbean
Area. 4. France - Colonies - Economic conditions. I.
Deverre, Christian. II. Institute nationale de la
recherche agronomique (France). III. Series.
NYPL [Sc D 88-246]

Enjeux miniers en Afrique /. Yachir, F. Paris ,
c1987. 180 p. ; ISBN 2-86537-170-0
HD9506.A382 Y34 1987
NYPL [Sc D 89-194]

Enonchong, Charles.
The Abagana ambush : the greatest battle of the
Nigerian-Biafran War / by Charles Enonchong.
Calabar, Nigeria : Century Books, [197?] 47 p. :
ill. ; 19 cm. Cover title.
1. Nigeria - History - Civil War, 1967-1970. I. Title.
NYPL [Sc C 89-33]

The rise and fall of Anini / by Charles
Enonchong. Calabar, Nigeria : Century Books,
[1988] 73 p. : ill. ; 19 cm. Cover title.
1. Anini, Lawrence. 2. Crime and criminals - Nigeria -
Benin City. 3. Gangs - Nigeria - Benin City. I. Title.
NYPL [Sc C 89-8]

Enquête nationale sur la fécondité du Cameroun, 1978 : rapport principal. [Yaoundé] : Direction
de la statistique et de la comptabilité nationale,
Ministère de l'économie et du plan en
collaboration avec l'Enquête mondiale sur la
fécondité, 1983. 2 v. in 3 : ill. ; 30 cm.
CONTENTS. - v. 1. Analyse des principaux résultats --
v. 2. Tableaux statistiques (2 v.).   DDC
304.6/32/0967113 19
1. Fertility, Human - Cameroon. 2. Fertility, Human -
Cameroon - Statistics. I. Cameroon. Dept. of Statistics
and National Accounts.
HB1075.4.A3 E66 1983   NYPL [Sc F 89-51]

Ensaio de um estudo geogràfico da rede urbana de Angola. Amaral, Ilidio do. Lisboa, 1962. 99
p.
HT148.A5 A7   NYPL [Sc E 98-118]

Enseignement de l'anglais au Sénégal.
(37) Le Boulch, Pierre. Today's English .
[Dakar] , 1968- v. ;   *NYPL [Sc F 87-274]*

Enseignement du Français au Sénégal .
(27) Morin, Melle. Les retards scolaires et les
échecs au niveau de l'ecole primaire du Sénégal
/. [Dakar] [1966?] 143 leaves ;
NYPL [Sc F 87-439]

L'enseignement en Côte d'Ivoire /. Sosoo,
Leonard. [Abidjan? , 1980-1987] 2 v. :
NYPL [Sc E 88-128]

Enseñanza de la filosofía e investigación filosófica en Africa /. Teaching and research in
philosophy in Africa. Spanish. Barcelona ,
París , 1984. 339 p. ; ISBN 92-3-302126-6
(Unesco)   *NYPL [Sc D 88-616]*

ENSIGNS. see FLAGS.

ENTERTAINERS, AFRO-AMERICAN. see AFRO-AMERICAN ENTERTAINERS.

ENTERTAINERS - UNITED STATES - BIOGRAPHY.
Grupenhoff, Richard, 1941- The black
Valentino . Metuchen, N.J. , 1988. xi, 188 p. :
ISBN 0-8108-2078-1 DDC 790.2/092/4 B 19
PN2287.T78 G78 1988
NYPL [Sc D 88-1029]

ENTERTAINERS - UNITED STATES - INTERVIEWS.
Angelou, Maya. Conversations with Maya
Angelou /. Jackson , c1989. xvi, 246 p. ; ISBN
0-87805-361-1 (alk. paper) DDC 818/.5409 19
PS3551.N464 Z4635 1989
NYPL [Sc E 89-225]

ENTHNOLOGY - BENIN - ATAKORA MOUNTAINS REGION.
Maurice, Albert-Marie. Atakora . Paris , 1986.
xxiii, 481 p., clv p. of plates : ISBN
2-900098-11-4   *NYPL [Sc E 88-106]*

Entrepreneurs of profit and pride . Newman,
Mark. New York , 1988. xvi, 186 p., [4] p. of
plates : ISBN 0-275-92888-8 DDC 305.8/96073 19
PN1991.8.A35 N49 1988
NYPL [Sc E 89-88]

ENTREPRENEURSHIP - UNITED STATES.
Newman, Mark. Entrepreneurs of profit and
pride . New York , 1988. xvi, 186 p., [4] p. of
plates : ISBN 0-275-92888-8 DDC 305.8/96073 19
PN1991.8.A35 N49 1988
NYPL [Sc E 89-88]

L'Entreprise et ses dirigeants dans le développement économique de l'Afrique noire :
Première rencontre africaine UNIAPAC,
Kinshasa, 7-9 juillet, 1969. Kinshasa : Editions
CADICEC (UNIAPAC-Congo), [1969?] 89 p. :
ill. ; 27 cm. At head of title: Union internationale
chrétienne des dirigeants d'entreprise (UNIAPAC)
1. Executives - Africa - Congresses. 2. Business
enterprises - Africa - Congresses. 3. Industrial
management - Africa - Congresses. I. International
Christian Union of Business Executives. II. CADICEC
(Association). III. Title: Prèmiere rencontre africaine
UNIAPAC, Kinshasa, 7-9 juillet, 1969.
NYPL [Sc F 88-100]

Entreprises et entrepreneurs du Burkina Faso .
Labazée, Pascal. Paris , c1988. 273 p. ;
NYPL [Sc D 89-288]

Entzinger, H. B., 1947- Lost illusions . London ,
1988. x, 316 p. : ISBN 0-415-00628-7
NYPL [Sc D 88-1300]

ENVIRONMENT. see ECOLOGY; HUMAN ECOLOGY; MAN - INFLUENCE ON NATURE.

ENVIRONMENT AND STATE. see ENVIRONMENTAL POLICY.

ENVIRONMENTAL CONTROL. see ENVIRONMENTAL POLICY.

Environmental issues in African development planning / edited by J.A. Seeley and W.M.
Adams. Cambridge : African Studies Centre,
c1988. v, 84 p. : maps ; 21 cm. (Cambridge
African monographs . 9) Includes bibliographies.
ISBN 0-902993-21-6 (pbk) : DDC 330.96//0328
19
1. Man - Influence on nature - Africa. I. Adams, W. M.
(William Mark), 1955-. II. Seeley, J. A. (Janet Anne).
HC502   NYPL [Sc D 88-1233]

ENVIRONMENTAL MANAGEMENT. see ENVIRONMENTAL POLICY.

ENVIRONMENTAL POLICY - AFRICA.
Lewis, Lawrence. African environments and
resources /. Boston , 1988. xii, 344 p. : ISBN
0-04-916010-9 (alk. paper) DDC 333.7/096 19
HC800 .L48 1987   NYPL [Sc E 89-50]

Ephson, Isaac S., 1923- The episode of the
innocent man in trouble / by Isaac S. Ephson.
Accra, Ghana : Ilen Publications, 1985. 81 p. ;
21 cm.
1. Islands of the Pacific - Fiction. I. Title.
NYPL [Sc D 88-411]

EPIC POETRY, FANG.
Boyer, Pascal. Barricades mystérieuses & pièges
à pensée . Paris , 1988. 190 p. : ISBN
2-901161-31-6   *NYPL [Sc E 88-500]*

EPIC POETRY, KPELLE - HISTORY AND CRITICISM.
Stone, Ruth M. Dried millet breaking .
Bloomington , c1988. xvi, 150 p., [5] p. of
plates : ISBN 0-253-31818-1   DDC 896/.34 19
PL8411.5 .S76 1988   NYPL [Sc E 88-519]

EPIGENESIS. see BIOLOGY.

EPIGRAMS.
Cosby, William H. Fat Albert's survival kit /.
New York [1975] [30] p. : ISBN 0-525-61532-6
PN6281 .C758   NYPL [JFC 77-191]

Epigrams to Ernesto Cardenal in defense of Claudia. Brand, Dionne, 1953- Winter
epigrams & Epigrams to Ernesto Cardinal in
defense of Claudia /. Toronto , 1983. 38 p. ;
ISBN 0-88795-022-1 :
NYPL [Sc D 88-1207]

EPIGRAPHY. see INSCRIPTIONS.

The episode of the innocent man in trouble /.
Ephson, Isaac S., 1923- Accra, Ghana , 1985.
81 p. ;   *NYPL [Sc D 88-411]*

Epistrophy.
Tercinet, Alain, 1935- West Coast jazz /.
Marseille , 1986. 358 p. : ISBN 2-86364-031-3
NYPL [Sc E 88-307]

L'epop'ee de Segu . Konare Ba, Adam. Paris ,
c1987. 201 p. : ISBN 2-8289-0250-1
NYPL [Sc E 88-180]

Epopée Mulombi / contée par Ambroisine Mawiri
et Victor Mbumba ; écrite et arrangée Vincent
de Paul Nyonda. [Libreville : s.n., 1986?] 138
p. ; 21 cm.

1. Tales - Gabon. I. Mbumba, Victor. II. Nyonda, Vincent de Paul. III. Mawiri, Ambroisine. IV. Title.
NYPL [Sc D 88-561]

Epstein, William, 1912- A nuclear-weapon-free zone in Africa? / William Epstein. Nuclear-weapon-free zones : the South Pacific proposal / Roderic Alley. Muscatine, Iowa : Stanley Foundation, 1977. 52 p. ; 22 cm. (Stanley Foundation. Occasional paper. [no.]14) Includes bibliographical references.
1. Atomic weapons and disarmament. I. Alley, Roderic Martin. Nuclear-weapon-free zones. II. Title. III. Series.
JX1974.7 .E553 **NYPL [JLK 75-198 [no.]14]**

Epton, Bill. see Epton, William.

Epton, William. Electoral politics [microform] : its problems and prospects / Bill Epton. New York : Black Liberation Press, 1980. 33 p. : ill. ; 22 cm. (On organizing the masses. 1) Microfiche. New York: New York Public Library, 198. 1 microfiche: negative; 11 x 15 cm. (FSN Sc 019,064)
1. Elections - United States. 2. Afro-Americans - Politics and suffrage. I. Title. II. Series.
NYPL [Sc Micro F-10975]

EQUAL EDUCATIONAL OPPORTUNITY. see EDUCATIONAL EQUALIZATION.

Equality and education . Rebell, Michael A. Princeton, N.J. , c1985. x, 340 p. ;   ISBN 0-691-07692-8 :   DDC 344.747/0798 347.4704798 19
KFX2065 .R43 1985   **NYPL [JLD 85-3778]**

EQUALIZATION, EDUCATIONAL. see EDUCATIONAL EQUALIZATION.

EQUATORIAL GUINEA - HISTORY - DICTIONARIES.
Liniger-Goumaz, Max. Historical dictionary of Equatorial Guinea /. Metuchen, N.J. , 1988. xxx, 238 p. :   ISBN 0-8108-2120-6 DDC 967/.18/00321 19
DT620.15 .L57 1988   **NYPL [Sc D 89-528]**

EQUATORIAL GUINEA - SOCIAL CONDITIONS.
Nze Abuy, R. María. Familia y matrimonio fań /. [Spain?] [1985?] 77 p. ;
NYPL [Sc C 88-285]

Equatorium . N'Debeka, Maxime, 1944- Paris , c1987. 85 p. ;   ISBN 2-7087-0488-5
NYPL [Sc D 88-913]

Equiano, Olaudah, b. 1745. I saw a slave ship / by Gustavus Vassa. Sacramento, Calif. : Press of Arden Park, 1983. 42 p. : ill. ; 71 mm. Excerpt from The interesting narrative of the life of Olaudah Equiano, or Gustavus Vassa, the African, written by himself, 1791. "125 copies printed October, 1983." Schomburg Center has no. 8, signed by Budd Westreich, proprietor of the press of Arden Park.
1. Equiano, Olaudah, b. 1745. 2. Slaves - Biography. 3. Miniature books - Specimens. 4. California - Imprints. I. Title. II. Title: Interesting narrative of the life of Olaudah Equiano. **NYPL [Sc Rare C 88-1]**

EQUIANO, OLAUDAH, B. 1745.
Equiano, Olaudah, b. 1745. I saw a slave ship /. Sacramento, Calif. , 1983. 42 p. :
NYPL [Sc Rare C 88-1]

Equipe du projet IFA. Inventaire des particularités lexicales du français en Afrique noire /. Montréal , Paris [1983] lxi, 550 p. ;   ISBN 2-920021-15-X **NYPL [Sc E 88-235]**

EQUITY - GHANA.
Kludze, A. K. P. Modern principles of equity . Dordrecht, Holland , Providence, R.I. , 1988. xxxix, 482 p. ;   ISBN 90-6765-147-8
NYPL [Sc E 89-233]

Erichsen, Peter. Hoffnung auf Regen : Beobachtungen und Erlebnisse aus Namibia / Peter Erichsen. Frankfurt am Main : Haag & Herchen, 1988. 385 p. : map ; 21 cm.   ISBN 3-89228-235-8
I. Title.   **NYPL [Sc D 89-206]**

Erika. Raharolahy, Elie. Tantara notsongaina /. [Antananarivo?] [1976] v. :
NYPL [Sc C 88-238]

ERITREA (ETHIOPIA) - HISTORY - REVOLUTION - 1962-
Sauldie, Madan M. Super powers in the Horn of Africa /. New York , c1987. ix, 252 p. ;   ISBN 0-86590-092-2 DDC 320.960 19
DT367.8 .S28 1987   **NYPL [Sc D 89-488]**

Erivwo, Samuel U. The Urhobo, the Isoko and the Itsekiri / by Samuel U. Erivwo. Ibadan :

Daystar Press, 1979. vii, 144 p. : map, ports. ; 22 cm. Based on the second pt. of the author's thesis (University of Ibadan) under the title: Christianity in Urhoboland, 1901-1961. At head of title: A history of Christianity in Nigeria. Includes bibliographical references.
1. Christianity - Nigeria - History. 2. Nigeria - Church history. I. Title. **NYPL [Sc D 88-769]**

Eroshima . Laferrière, Dany. Montréal, Québec , 1987. 168 p. :   ISBN 2-89005-277-X
NYPL [Sc D 88-395]

EROTIC LITERATURE, AMERICAN - WOMEN AUTHORS.
Deep down . Boston , c1988. xii, 330 p. ;   ISBN 0-571-12957-9 :   DDC 810/.8/03538 19
PS509.E7 D44 1988   **NYPL [Sc D 88-1080]**

EROTIC LITERATURE, FRENCH - AFRICA.
Erotisme et littératures . Paris , c1987. 274 p. ;   ISBN 2-7357-0062-3   **NYPL [Sc E 88-184]**

EROTIC LITERATURE, FRENCH - CARIBBEAN AREA.
Erotisme et littératures . Paris , c1987. 274 p. ;   ISBN 2-7357-0062-3   **NYPL [Sc E 88-184]**

EROTIC LITERATURE, FRENCH - ISLANDS OF THE INDIAN OCEAN.
Erotisme et littératures . Paris , c1987. 274 p. ;   ISBN 2-7357-0062-3   **NYPL [Sc E 88-184]**

EROTIC LITERATURE - WOMEN AUTHORS.
Deep down . Boston , c1988. xii, 330 p. ;   ISBN 0-571-12957-9 :   DDC 810/.8/03538 19
PS509.E7 D44 1988   **NYPL [Sc D 88-1080]**

EROTIC POETRY, AMERICAN - AFRO-AMERICAN AUTHORS.
Shange, Ntozake. Some men /. [S.l.] c1981. [52] p. :   **NYPL [Sc Rare C 88-2]**

Erotisme et littératures : Afrique noire, Caraïbes, océan Indien : anthologie / Gérard Clavreuil. Paris : Acropole, c1987. 274 p. ; 24 cm. Includes bibliographical references.   ISBN 2-7357-0062-3
1. Erotic literature, French - Africa. 2. Erotic literature, French - Caribbean area. 3. Erotic literature, French - Islands of the Indian Ocean. I. Clavreuil, Gérard.
NYPL [Sc E 88-184]

Errington, Leah. Natural dyes of Zambia / written by Leah Errington and Sylvester M. Chrisumpa ; illustrated by Zulu Elisha Alex. [Zambia? : s.n., between 1986 and 1988] (Ndola, Zambia : Mission Press) 35 p. : ill. ; 15 x 20 cm.
1. Dyes and dyeing, Domestic. 2. Color in the textile industries. 3. Textile industry - Zambia. I. Title.
NYPL [Sc B 89-23]

Escott, Colin. Sun records : the discography / by Colin Escott & Martin Hawkins ; photo research by Colin Escott. Vollersode, W. Germany : Bear Family Records, c1987. 240 p. : ill. ; 22 cm.   ISBN 3-924789-09-3 (pbk.)
1. Sun Records. 2. Blues (Music) - Discography. 3. Country music - Discography. 4. Rock music - Discography. I. Hawkins, Martin. II. Title.
NYPL [Sc D 89-243]

A escravidão africana no Brasil . Morais, Evaristo de, 1871-1939. Brasília, Distrito Federal , c1986. 140 p. ;   ISBN 85-23-00070-4
NYPL [Sc D 88-922]

Escravidão e invenção da liberdade . Reis, João José. São Paulo , 1988. 323 p. [8] leaves of plates :   ISBN 85-11-13084-5
NYPL [Sc D 88-1388]

Escravidão negra e história da Igreja na América Latina e no Caribe / tradução de Luiz Carlos Nishiura. Petrópolis : Vozes, 1988. 237 p. : maps ; 21 cm. At head of title: Comissão de Estudos de História da Igreja na América Latina (CEHILA). Includes bibliographical references.
1. Slavery - Latin America. 2. Slavery - Caribbean Area. 3. Latin America - Church history. I. Nishiura, Luiz Carlos. II. Comisión de Estudios de Historia de la Iglesia en Latinoamerica. **NYPL [Sc D 88-75]**

Escravidão negra no Brasil /. Quieroz, Suely Robles Reis de. São Paulo , 1987. 86 p. ;
NYPL [Sc C 88-2]

Escravidão no Brasil /. Peregalli, Enrique, 1950- São Paulo , c1988. 80 p. :   ISBN 85-26-00192-2
NYPL [Sc D 89-421]

O escravo branco . Albuquerque, L. M. do Couto de. Lisboa , 1854. 4 v. :   **NYPL [Sc F 82-65]**

Escravo ou Camponês? . Cardoso, Ciro Flamarion Santana. São Paulo , 1987. 125 p. ;
NYPL [Sc D 88-793]

Eshiwani, George S. Research in education : the Kenya register 1963-1980 / by G.S. Eshiwani. Nairobi, Kenya : Bureau of Educational Research, Kenyatta University College, 1982? 185 leaves ; 30 cm. (Occasional paper / Bureau of Educational Research, Kenyatta University College . no. 3050)   DDC 016.37/09676/2 19
1. Education - Kenya - Bibliography. 2. Education - Research - Kenya. I. Series: Occasional paper (Kenyatta University College. Bureau of Educational Research) , no. 3050. II. Title.
Z5815.K4 E83 1982 LA1561
NYPL [Sc F 89-154]

Esiemokhai, Emmanuel Omoh. The colonial legal heritage in Nigeria / by Emmanuel Omoh Esiemokhai. Akure, Nigeria : Fagbamigbe, 1986. xii, 82 p. ; 21 cm. Includes index. Bibliography: p. 79.   ISBN 978-16-4248-3
1. Law - Nigeria. 2. Nigeria - Civilization - Occidental influences. I. Title. **NYPL [Sc D 88-640]**

Espaces et dialectique du héros césairien /. Bouelet, Rémy Sylvestre. Paris , c1987. 219 p. ;   ISBN 2-85802-774-9
NYPL [Sc D 87-1286]

España. see Spain.

Espelho dos dias /. Artur, Armando, 1962- [Maputo?] Associação dos Escritores Mozambicanos, [1986?] 52 p. ;
NYPL [Sc D 88-536]

ESPIONAGE STORIES. see SPY STORIES.

Essack, Karrim. The Mathaba International / [by Karrim Essack]. Dar es Salaam : Thakers Printers and Publishers, [1987?] iv, 81 p. : ill., ports. ; 18 cm.   DDC 325/.32 19
1. Mathaba International (Organization). 2. Anti-imperialist movements. 3. Afro-Asian politics. I. Title.
JC359 .E825 1987   **NYPL [Sc C 89-30]**

Essays. Plato, Ann. New York , 1988. liii, 122 p. ;   ISBN 0-19-505247-1 (alk. paper) DDC 814/.3 19
PS2593 .P347 1988   **NYPL [JFC 88-2156]**

Essays in African and European history. Akiri, Chris W.A. Ikeja, Lagos State Nigeria , 1984. 143 p.   **NYPL [Sc D 88-1132]**

Essays on African history . Suret-Canale, Jean. [Essais d'histoire africaine. English.] London , 1988. 242 p. :   ISBN 0-905838-43-2 :   DDC 960/.3 19
DT29   **NYPL [Sc D 88-1314]**

Essays on local government and administration in Nigeria /. Oyediran, Oyeleye. Surulere, Lagos, Nigeria , 1988. x, 286 p. ;   ISBN 978-277-801-001
NYPL [Sc D 88-1365]

Essays on the nature of intelligence and the analysis of racial differences in the performance of IQ tests / editor, J.W.Jamieson. Washington D.C. : Cliveden Press, c1988. 72 p. : ill. ; 23 cm. (Mankind quarterly. Monograph . no. 4) Errata slip inserted. Includes bibliographies.   ISBN 0-941694-32-1
1. Afro-Americans - Intelligence levels. I. Jamieson, J. W. II. Series. **NYPL [Sc D 89-546]**

Essomba, Joseph-Marie. L'art africain et son message / Joseph-Marie Essomba. Yaoundé, Cameroun : Editions CLE, 1985. 73 p. : ill. ; 21 cm. Errata slip inserted. Bibliography: p. 73.   ISBN 2-7235-0049-7
1. Art and society - Africa. 2. Art - Africa. I. Title.
NYPL [Sc D 88-278]

Estabrook, Irene. Gilstrap, Robert. The sultan's fool and other North African tales /. New York , c1958. 95 p. :   ISBN 931-40-0118-0
NYPL [Sc D 88-548]

Estados Unidos de Colombia. see Colombia.

Estill, Ann H. M. The contributions of selected Afro-American women classical singers, 1850-1955 [microform] / Ann H. M. Estill. 1982, c1981. 3, vi, 133 leaves : ill. Typescript. Thesis (D.A.)--New York University, 1982. Bibliography: leaves [50]-54. Microfilm. Ann Arbor, MI : University Microfilms International, 1982. 1 microfilm reel ; 35 mm. PARTIAL CONTENTS. - Elizabeth Taylor-Greenfield -- Sissieretta Jones -- Marie Selika -- Lillian Evanti -- Mattiwilda Dobbs.
I. Title.   **NYPL [Sc Micro R-4426]**

Estrategia y paz .
([9]) Cabrera, M. A. Africa en armas /. Madrid [1986] 163 p. ; ISBN 84-85436-37-7
NYPL [Sc D 88-757]

Estrelas no dedo /. Alves, Miriam. São Paulo , 1985. 58 p. – *NYPL [Sc B 88-8]*

Estudos, ensaios e documentos .
(v. 97) Amaral, Ilidio do. Ensaio de um estudo geográfico da rede urbana de Angola. Lisboa, 1962. 99 p.
HT148.A5 A7 *NYPL [Sc E 98-118]*

ÈṢÙ . Dopamu, P. Adelumo. Nigeria , 1986. 99 p. ; ISBN 978-253-014-X
NYPL [Sc D 88-1375]

Et jusqu'à la dernière pulsation de nos veines ... /. Boukman, Daniel, 1936- Paris [1976] 164 p. ; ISBN 2-85802-017-5 :
PQ2662.O758 E8 *NYPL [JFD 80-7874]*

Eteki-Otabela, Marie-Louise, 1947- Misère et grandeur de la démocratie au Cameroun / Marie-Louise Eteki-Otabela. Paris : Editions L'Harmattan, c1987. 143 p. ; 22 cm. (Collection "Points de vue") Includes bibliographical references. ISBN 2-85802-929-6
1. Cameroon - Politics and government - 1960-. I. Title. II. Series. *NYPL [Sc D 88-910]*

Eternal life after death [microform] /. 'Isá 'Abd Allāh Muḥammad al-Mahdī, 1945- Brooklyn, N.Y. [197-?] 36 p. ;
NYPL [Sc Micro R-4114 no.3]

Ethics and public policy reprint .
(5) Sowell, Thomas, 1930- Patterns of black excellence /. Washington , 1977. [26]-58 p. ; ISBN 0-89633-004-4 *NYPL [Sc D 89-588]*

ETHICS - NIGERIA.
Ali, Sidi H. The WAI as an ideology of moral rectitude /. [Nigeria] 1985 (Lagos : Academy Press) 88 p. : *NYPL [Sc D 88-869]*

The ethics of the Nigerian broadcaster /. Amadi, John Osinachi. Rome , 1986. 155 p. [6] p. of plates : *NYPL [Sc E 89-138]*

ETHICS, PRACTICAL. see ETHICS.

ETHICS, SOCIALIST. see SOCIALIST ETHICS.

Ethiopia . Conte, Carmelo. [Milano] , 1976. xi, 196 p. ;
DT380 .C59 *NYPL [Sc D 88-1064]*

ETHIOPIA - ANTIQUITIES.
Chavaillon, Nicole. Gotera, un site paléolithique récent d'Ethiopie /. Paris , 1985. 58 p., 25 leaves of plates : *NYPL [Sc F 88-359]*

ETHIOPIA - DESCRIPTION AND TRAVEL.
Thesiger, Wilfred, 1910- The life of my choice /. London , 1987. 459 p., [32] p. of plates : ISBN 0-00-216194-X :
G525 .T415x 1987 *NYPL [Sc E 88-222]*

ETHIOPIA - ECONOMIC CONDITIONS.
Minker, Gunter. Burji, Konso-Gidole, Dullay . Bremen , 1986. vi, 275 p. : ISBN 3-88299-051-1
NYPL [Sc E 88-236]

ETHIOPIA - EMIGRATION AND IMMIGRATION - BIOGRAPHY.
Avraham, Shmuel, 1945- Treacherous journey . New York, NY , 1986. xii, 178 p. : ISBN 0-933503-46-6 (jacket); 0-933503-46-5 : DDC 963/.004924 19
DS135.E75 A93 1986 *NYPL [Sc E 87-275]*

ETHIOPIA - ETHNIC RELATIONS.
Avraham, Shmuel, 1945- Treacherous journey . New York, NY , 1986. xii, 178 p. : ISBN 0-933503-46-6 (jacket); 0-933503-46-5 : DDC 963/.004924 19
DS135.E75 A93 1986 *NYPL [Sc E 87-275]*

ETHIOPIA - FOREIGN RELATIONS - TO 1889 - SOURCES.
Letters from Ethiopian rulers (early and mid-nineteenth century) . Oxford , New York , c1985. xvii, 197 p. ; ISBN 0-19-726046-2
NYPL [Sc E 88-262]

ETHIOPIA - FOREIGN RELATIONS - 1974-
Proletarian internationalism and the Ethiopian revolution /. Addis Ababa , 1984. 56 p. :
DT387.95 .P76 1984 *NYPL [Sc F 89-85]*

ETHIOPIA - FOREIGN RELATIONS - GREAT BRITAIN - SOURCES.
Letters from Ethiopian rulers (early and

mid-nineteenth century) . Oxford , New York , c1985. xvii, 197 p. : ISBN 0-19-726046-2
NYPL [Sc E 88-262]

Ethiopia from feudal autocracy to people's democracy / issued by the Preparatory Committee for the Founding of the People's Democratic Republic of Ethiopia. Addis Ababa, Ethiopia : The Committee, 1987. 74 p. : ill. (some col.) ; 24 cm. Includes bibliographical references.
1. Ethiopia - Politics and government - 1974-. 2. Ethiopia - History. I. Ethiopia. Preparatory Committee for the Founding of the People's Democratic Republic of Ethiopia. *NYPL [Sc E 88-435]*

ETHIOPIA - HISTORY.
Conte, Carmelo. Ethiopia . [Milano] , 1976. xi, 196 p. ;
DT380 .C59 *NYPL [Sc D 88-1064]*
Ethiopia from feudal autocracy to people's democracy /. Addis Ababa, Ethiopia , 1987. 74 p. : *NYPL [Sc E 88-435]*

ETHIOPIA - HISTORY - 1889-1974.
Balsvik, Randi Rønning. Haile Sellassie's students . East Lansing, Mich. , c1985. xix, 363 p. : DDC 378/.198/0963 19
LA1518.7 .B35 1985 *NYPL [Sc D 88-1403]*

ETHIOPIA - JUVENILE FICTION.
Hopkins, Marjorie. And the jackal played the masinko. New York [1969] [41] p. ISBN 0-8193-0271-6
PZ7.H7756 An *NYPL [JFF 72-292]*

ETHIOPIA - LANGUAGE - GRAMMAR.
Böhm, Gerhard. Die Sprache der Aithiopen im Lande Kusch /. Wien , 1988. 206 p. : ISBN 3-85043-047-2 *NYPL [Sc D 88-1339]*

ETHIOPIA - LANGUAGES.
The Non-semitic languages of Ethiopia /. East Lansing , c1976. xv, 738 p. : DDC 492
PL8021.E8 N6 *NYPL [Sc D 88-854]*

ETHIOPIA - POLITICS AND GOVERNMENT.
Brüne, Stefan. Äthiopien -- Unterentwicklung und radikale Militärherrschaft . Hamburg , 1986. viii, 372 p. : ISBN 3-923519-63-X
NYPL [L-11 2640 Bd. 26]
Bulcha, Mekuria. Flight and integration . Uppsala, Sweden , c1988. 256 p. : ISBN 91-7106-279-3 *NYPL [Sc E 88-581]*

ETHIOPIA - POLITICS AND GOVERNMENT - 1974-
Clapham, Christopher S. Transformation and continuity in revolutionary Ethiopia /. Cambridge [Cambridgeshire] , New York , 1988. xviii, 284 p. : ISBN 0-521-33441-1 DDC 963.07 19
JQ3752 .C55 1988 *NYPL [Sc E 88-446]*
Ethiopia from feudal autocracy to people's democracy /. Addis Ababa, Ethiopia , 1987. 74 p. : *NYPL [Sc E 88-435]*
Henze, Paul B., 1924- Rebels and separatists in Ethiopia . Santa Monica, CA , 1985. xv, 98 p. ; ISBN 0-8330-0696-7 DDC 963/.07 19
DT387.95 .H46 1986 *NYPL [JFE 86-5101]*

Ethiopia. Preparatory Committee for the Founding of the People's Democratic Republic of Ethiopia. Ethiopia from feudal autocracy to people's democracy /. Addis Ababa, Ethiopia , 1987. 74 p. :
NYPL [Sc E 88-435]

ETHIOPIA - RELIGION.
Conte, Carmelo. Ethiopia . [Milano] , 1976. xi, 196 p. ;
DT380 .C59 *NYPL [Sc D 88-1064]*

ETHIOPIA - SOCIAL CONDITIONS.
Bulcha, Mekuria. Flight and integration . Uppsala, Sweden , c1988. 256 p. : ISBN 91-7106-279-3 *NYPL [Sc E 88-581]*

ETHIOPIA - SOCIAL LIFE AND CUSTOMS.
Haberland, Eike. Ibaaddo ka-Ba'iso . Heidelberg , 1988. 184 p. ; ISBN 3-533-04014-3
NYPL [Sc D 89-552]
Leslau, Wolf. Ethiopians speak. Berkeley, 1965- v.
PJ8998.5 .L4 *NYPL [Sc F 89-19]*

Ethiopia. Sovereign. Letters from Ethiopian rulers (early and mid-nineteenth century) . Oxford , New York , c1985. xvii, 197 p. : ISBN 0-19-726046-2 *NYPL [Sc E 88-262]*

Ethiopian-African theocracy union policy. Royal Ethiopian Judah-Coptic Church. Rastafari manifesto . [Kingston, Jamaica , 1984?] [97] p. ;
NYPL [Sc G 88-20]

Ethiopian Jews and Israel / edited by Michael Ashkenazi and Alex Weingrod. New Brunswick, NJ, U. S.A. : Transaction Books, c1987. 159 p. : ill., maps ; 24 cm. "Most of the articles in this book appeared in a special issue of Israel social science research, vol. 3 (1-2), 1985"--P. 2. Spine title: Ethiopian Jews & Israel. Includes bibliographies. ISBN 0-88738-133-2 DDC 305.8/924/05694 19
1. Falashas - Israel. 2. Israel - Ethnic relations. I. Ashkenazi, Michael. II. Weingrod, Alex. III. Title: Ethiopian Jews & Israel.
DS113.8.F34 E84 1987 *NYPL [Sc E 88-73]*

Ethiopian Jews & Israel. Ethiopian Jews and Israel /. New Brunswick, NJ, U. S.A. , c1987. 159 p. : ISBN 0-88738-133-2 DDC 305.8/924/05694 19
DS113.8.F34 E84 1987 *NYPL [Sc E 88-73]*

ETHIOPIAN LITERATURE.
Leslau, Wolf. Ethiopians speak. Berkeley, 1965- v.
PJ8998.5 .L4 *NYPL [Sc F 89-19]*

ETHIOPIAN MOVEMENT (SOUTH AFRICA)
Chirenje, J. Mutero, 1935- Ethiopianism and Afro-Americans in southern Africa, 1883-1916 /. Baton Rouge , c1987. xii, 231 p. : ISBN 0-8071-1319-0 DDC 276.8/08 19
BR1450 .C45 1987 *NYPL [Sc E 88-336]*

ETHIOPIAN PHILOSOPHY. see PHILOSOPHY, ETHIOPIAN.

Ethiopianism and Afro-Americans in southern Africa, 1883-1916 /. Chirenje, J. Mutero, 1935- Baton Rouge , c1987. xii, 231 p. : ISBN 0-8071-1319-0 DDC 276.8/08 19
BR1450 .C45 1987 *NYPL [Sc E 88-336]*

Ethiopians speak. Leslau, Wolf. Berkeley, 1965- v.
PJ8998.5 .L4 *NYPL [Sc F 89-19]*

ETHIOPIC LANGUAGE - DICTIONARIES - ENGLISH.
Leslau, Wolf. Comparative dictionary of Ge'ez (Classical Ethiopic) . Wiesbaden , 1987. xlix, 813 p. ; ISBN 3-447-02592-1 : DDC 492/.8 19
PJ9087 .L37 1987 *NYPL [*OEC 89-3015]*

Ethiopie, la face cachée /. Franey, Jean-Pierre. Paris , c1986. 127 p. : ISBN 2-209-05848-1 :
HC845.Z9 F34 1986 *NYPL [Sc F 88-204]*

Ethnic and racial images in American film and television . Woll, Allen L. New York , 1987. xv, 408 p. ; ISBN 0-8240-8733-X (alk. paper) DDC 016.79143/09/093520693 19
Z5784.M9 W65 1987 PN1995.9.M56
NYPL [MFL 87-3104]

Ethnic associations and the welfare state : services to immigrants in five countries / Shirley Jenkins, editor. New York : Columbia University Press, 1988. x, 299 p. : ill. ; 24 cm. (Social work and social issues) Includes bibliographies and index. ISBN 0-231-05690-7 DDC 362.8 19
1. Social work with immigrants - Cross-cultural studies. 2. Emigration and immigration - Societies, etc. - Cross-cultural studies. 3. Immigrants - Cross-cultural studies. 4. Welfare state - Cross-cultural studies. I. Jenkins, Shirley.
HV4005 .E86 1988 *NYPL [JLE 88-3846]*

ETHNIC ATTITUDES - UNITED STATES.
Bolin, Robert C. Race, religion, and ethnicity in disaster recovery /. [Boulder. Colo.] , 1986. ix, 265 p. : *NYPL [Sc D 88-904]*

The ethnic encounter in the secondary school .
Bullivant, Brian Milton. London , New York , 1987. x, 214 p. ; ISBN 1-85000-255-X : DDC 371.97/0994 19
LC3739 .B84 1987 *NYPL [JLE 88-2088]*

ETHNIC GROUPS - CANADA.
Driedger, Leo, 1928- Aging and ethnicity . Toronto , 1987. xv, 131 p. : ISBN 0-409-81187-4
NYPL [Sc E 88-127]

ETHNIC GROUPS IN LITERATURE.
The Invention of ethnicity /. New York , 1989. xx, 294 p. ; ISBN 0-19-504589-0 DDC 810/.9/920692 19
PS153.M56 I58 1988 *NYPL [Sc D 89-374]*

Ethnic groups of the Senegambia .
Sonko-Godwin, Patience. Banjul, Gambia , 1985. viii, 38 p. : ISBN 998-386-001-X (pbk.)

DDC 306/.0966/3 19
GN655.S3 S65 1985   *NYPL [Sc F 88-129]*

Ethnic minorities . Stares, Rodney. [London] ,
1982. 62 p. ;   ISBN 0-905932-32-3
     NYPL [Sc F 88-96]

Ethnic minority broadcasting . Anwar,
Muhammad. London , 1983. 80 p. ;   ISBN
0-907920-39-X   *NYPL [Sc D 88-573]*

ETHNIC PRESS - BRAZIL - SÃO PAULO.
Ferrara, Miriam Nicolau. A imprensa negra
paulista (1915-1963) /. São Paulo , 1986. 279
p. :   *NYPL [Sc B 88-6]*

**ETHNIC RADIO BROADCASTING - GREAT
BRITAIN.**
Anwar, Muhammad. Ethnic minority
broadcasting . London , 1983. 80 p. ;   ISBN
0-907920-39-X   *NYPL [Sc D 88-573]*

Ethnic studies at Chicago, 1905-45 /. Persons,
Stow, 1913- Urbana , c1987. 159 p. ;   ISBN
0-252-01344-1 (alk. paper)   DDC
305.8/007/1077311 19
HT1506 .P47 1987   *NYPL [JLE 87-1776]*

Ethnicity : INTERCOCTA glossary : concepts
and terms used in ethnicity research / edited
by Fred W. Riggs.Pilot ed. Honolulu, Hawaii
(2424 Maile Way, Honolulu 96822) : University
of Hawaii, c1985. xxix, 205 p. ; 28 cm.
(International conceptual encyclopedia for the social
sciences . vol. 1) "Papers and data presented at the
Conference on Conceptual and Terminological Analysis
in the Social Sciences, held in Bielefeld, FRG, during
May 1981"--P. vii. Includes indexes. Bibliography: p.
165-174.   DDC 305.8/0072 19
1. Ethnicity - Terminology. 2. Ethnicity - Research. I.
Riggs, Fred Warren. II. Conference on Conceptual and
Terminological Analysis in the Social Sciences (1981 :
Bielefeld, Germany). III. Series.
GN495.6 .E89 1985   *NYPL [Sc F 87-355]*

ETHNICITY IN CHILDREN.
Aboud, Frances E. Children and prejudice /.
Oxford [Oxfordshire] , New York, NY , 1988.
x, 149 p. ;   ISBN 0-631-14939-2 :   DDC 305.2/3
19
BF723.P75 A24 1988   *NYPL [Sc E 89-57]*

ETHNICITY IN LITERATURE.
The Invention of ethnicity /. New York , 1989.
xx, 294 p. ;   ISBN 0-19-504589-0   DDC
810/.9/920692 19
PS153.M56 I58 1988   *NYPL [Sc D 89-374]*

ETHNICITY - RESEARCH.
Ethnicity . Honolulu, Hawaii (2424 Maile Way,
Honolulu 96822) , c1985. xxix, 205 p. ;   DDC
305.8/0072 19
GN495.6 .E89 1985   *NYPL [Sc F 87-355]*

ETHNICITY - TERMINOLOGY.
Ethnicity . Honolulu, Hawaii (2424 Maile Way,
Honolulu 96822) , c1985. xxix, 205 p. ;   DDC
305.8/0072 19
GN495.6 .E89 1985   *NYPL [Sc F 87-355]*

ETHNOARCHAEOLOGY.
Stiles, Daniel. Ethnoarchaeology, a case-study
with the Boni of Kenya [microform] /.
[Nairobi] [1979] 20 p. ;
     NYPL [Sc Micro R-4108 no. 36]

**Ethnoarchaeology, a case-study with the Boni of
Kenya** [microform] /. Stiles, Daniel. [Nairobi]
[1979] 20 p. ;
     NYPL [Sc Micro R-4108 no. 36]

ETHNOGRAPHY. see ETHNOLOGY.

Ethnologie régionale. Benoist, Jean, 1929- Les
Antilles /. [Paris , 1976?] p. [1372]-1448 :
     NYPL [Sc D 87-1164]

Ethnologiques : hommages à Marcel Griaule /
textes réunis par Solange de Ganay, Annie et
Jean-Paul Lebeuf, Dominique Zahan ; préface
de Léopold Sédar Senghor ; Témoignage de
Georges Henri Riviére. Paris : Hermann, 1987.
xxxvi, 430 p. : ill., facsims., ports. ; 25 cm.
"Bibliographie de Marcel Griaule": p. [xxix]-xxxvi.
ISBN 2-7056-6025-9
1. Griaule, Marcel, 1898-1956. I. Ganay, Solange de. II.
Senghor, Léopold Sédar, 1906-.
     NYPL [Sc E 88-39]

ETHNOLOGY - AFRICA, SUB-SAHARAN.
Afrique plurielle, Afrique actuelle . Paris ,
c1986. 272 p. ;   ISBN 2-86537-151-4
     NYPL [Sc E 88-349]

ETHNOLOGY - AFRICA, WEST.
Brüggemann, Anne. Amagdala und Akawuruk .

Hohenschäftlarn bei München , 1986. 264 p. :
   ISBN 3-87673-106-2   *NYPL [Sc D 88-652]*

Person, Yves. Samori: une révolution dyula.
Dakar, 1968- v. (2377 p.)   DDC 966/.2601/0924
B
DT475.5.S3 P47 1968   *NYPL [Sc F 87-398]*

**ETHNOLOGY - AFRICA, WEST -
CONGRESSES.**
Peuples du golfe du Bénin . Paris , c1984. 328
p. :   ISBN 2-86537-092-5   DDC 966/.8004963 19
DT510.43.E94 P48 1984
     NYPL [Sc E 88-449]

ETHNOLOGY - ETHIOPIA.
Conte, Carmelo. Ethiopia . [Milano] , 1976. xi,
196 p. ;
DT380 .C59   *NYPL [Sc D 88-1064]*

Haberland, Eike. Ibaaddo ka-Ba'iso .
Heidelberg , 1988. 184 p. ;   ISBN 3-533-04014-3
     NYPL [Sc D 89-552]

Minker, Gunter. Burji, Konso-Gidole, Dullay .
Bremen , 1986. vi, 275 p. ;   ISBN 3-88299-051-1
     NYPL [Sc E 88-236]

ETHNOLOGY - GAMBIA.
Sonko-Godwin, Patience. Ethnic groups of the
Senegambia . Banjul, Gambia , 1985. viii, 38
p. :   ISBN 998-386-001-X (pbk.)   DDC 306/.0966/3
19
GN655.S3 S65 1985   *NYPL [Sc F 88-129]*

ETHNOLOGY - KENYA - MERU.
Rimita, David Maitai, 1946- The Njuri-Noheke
of Meru /. [Meru, Kenya?] , c1988. 81 p. :
     NYPL [Sc D 89-310]

ETHNOLOGY - MADAGASCAR.
Patrice, Tongasolo. Fomban-drazana Tsimihety
/. Fianarantsoa [Madagascar] , 1985. 383 p., [8]
p. of plates :
     NYPL [Sc C 88-292]

ETHNOLOGY - MALI.
Jonckers, Danielle. La société Minyanka du
Mali . Paris , c1987. viii, 234 p., [8] p. of
plates :
     NYPL [Sc E 88-344]

ETHNOLOGY - NIGER.
Zakari, Maikorema. Contribution a l'histoire des
populations du sud-est nigérien . Niamey ,
1985. 246 p. ;   ISBN 2-85921-053-9
     NYPL [Sc E 88-328]

**ETHNOLOGY - NIGERIA - BASSA NGE
DISTRICT.**
Habi, Ya'akub H. The people called Bassa-Nge
/. Zaria , c1987. 86 p. ;   ISBN 978-12-5057-7
     NYPL [Sc C 88-372]

ETHNOLOGY - RHODESIA, SOUTHERN.
Bernardi, Bernardo. The social structure of the
kraal among the Zezuru in Musami (Southern
Rhodesia) [Cape Town] 1950. [2], 60, [1] .
   DDC 572.9689
GN490 .B4   *NYPL [Sc F 88-349]*

ETHNOLOGY - SENEGAL.
Deux études sur les relations entre groupes
ethniques. Spanish. Dos estudios sobre las
relaciones entre grupos étnicos en África .
Barcelona [Paris] , 1982. 174 p. ;   ISBN
84-85000-41-9
DT549.42 .D4818 1982
     NYPL [Sc D 88-651]

Sonko-Godwin, Patience. Ethnic groups of the
Senegambia . Banjul, Gambia , 1985. viii, 38
p. :   ISBN 998-386-001-X (pbk.)   DDC 306/.0966/3
19
GN655.S3 S65 1985   *NYPL [Sc F 88-129]*

ETHNOLOGY - TANZANIA.
Deux études sur les relations entre groupes
ethniques. Spanish. Dos estudios sobre las
relaciones entre grupos étnicos en África .
Barcelona [Paris] , 1982. 174 p. ;   ISBN
84-85000-41-9
DT549.42 .D4818 1982
     NYPL [Sc D 88-651]

ETHNOLOGY - TOGO.
Mignot, Alain. La terre et le pouvoir chez les
Guin du sud-est du Togo /. Paris , 1985. 288
p. :   ISBN 2-85944-087-9   *NYPL [Sc E 88-383]*

Textes et documents sur l'histoire des
populations du nord Togo . Lomé [1978] iii,
70 p. :   *NYPL [Sc F 88-332]*

ETHNOLOGY - TRINIDAD.
Stewart, John O. Drinkers, drummers, and
decent folk . Albany , c1989. xviii, 230 p. ;

ISBN 0-88706-829-4   DDC 306/.097298/3 19
GN564.T7 S74 1988   *NYPL [Sc E 89-220]*

ETHNOLOGY - WEST INDIES.
Benoist, Jean, 1929- Les Antilles /. [Paris ,
1976?] p. [1372]-1448 :
     NYPL [Sc D 87-1164]

ETHNOLOGY - ZAIRE.
Kabengele Munanga. Os Basanga de Shaba .
Sao Palulo , 1986. 334 p. :
     NYPL [Sc B 88-7]

Vengroenweghe, Daniel. Bobongo . Berlin ,
c1988. xv, 332 p. ;   ISBN 3-496-00963-2
     NYPL [Sc E 88-343]

**ETHNOLOGY - ZAIRE - KOLOKOSO
(COLLECTIVITY)**
Kitondo Mangombo. Kolokoso . Bandundu,
République du Zaïre , 1983. 172 p. :
     NYPL [Sc F 88-304]

ETHNOLOGY - ZIMBABWE.
Samkange, Stanlake John Thompson, 1922-
Oral history . Harare, Zimbabwe , c1986. ii, 93
p. :   *NYPL [Sc D 89-586]*

Weinrich, A. K. H., 1933- [Women and racial
discrimination in Rhodesia. Spanish.] La
situación de la mujer en Zimbabue antes de la
independencia /. Barcelona , Paris , 1984. 198
p. ;   ISBN 92-3-301621-8 (Unesco)
     NYPL [Sc D 88-615]

ETHNOMUSICOLOGY.
Worlds of music . New York , c1984. xviii, 325
p. :   ISBN 0-02-872600-6   DDC 781.7 19
ML3798 .W67 1984   *NYPL [Sc E 85-247]*

ETHNOPHILOSOPHY - CAMEROON.
Ndebi Biya, Robert, 1946- Etre, pouvoir et
génération . Paris , c1987. 134 p. ;
     NYPL [Sc D 88-909]

ETHS Community history series.
A School for freedom . [Knoxville] , 1986. xiii,
60 p. :   *NYPL [Sc D 88-417]*

Étienne, Gérard, 1936- La reine Soleil Levée :
récit / Gérard Étienne. Montréal : Guérin,
1988, c1987. 195 p. ; 23 cm. (Guérin littérature)
Collection/Roman   ISBN 2-7601-1974-2 :   DDC
C843/.54 19
C843 .E54 19
1. Haiti - Fiction. I. Title.   *NYPL [Sc D 88-1179]*

Etrange héritage . Ami, Gad, 1958- Lomé , 1986,
c1985. 155 p. ;   ISBN 2-7236-0931-6
     NYPL [Sc E 88-427]

L'étrangère intime . Ottino, Paul. Paris, France ,
c1986. 2 v. (xxvii, 630 p.) :   ISBN 2-88124-095-X
(set)   DDC 398/.0969/1 19
GR357 .O88 1986   *NYPL [Sc D 88-1203]*

Etre patriote sous les tropiques . Pérotin-Dumon,
Anne. Basse-Terre , 1985. 339 p. ;   ISBN
2-900339-21-9   *NYPL [Sc E 88-256]*

Etre, pouvoir et génération . Ndebi Biya, Robert,
1946- Paris , c1987. 134 p. ;
     NYPL [Sc D 88-909]

Etudes aequatoria .
(2) Hulstaert, G. Complément au Dictionnaire
lomóngo-français . Bamanya- Mbandaka , 1987.
463 p. ;   *NYPL [Sc D 89-193]*

(3) Mangulu, Motingea. Elements de grammaire
lingombe avec une bibliographie exhaustive /.
Mbandaka, Zaire *, 1988. 88 p. :
     NYPL [Sc D 89-40]

(4) Hulstaert, G. Supplement à la grammaire
lomongo /. Mbandaka, Zaire , 1988. 127 p. ;
     NYPL [Sc D 89-39]

Etudes africaines. Baker, Philip. International
guide to African studies research /. London ,
New York , 1987. 264 p. ;   ISBN 0-905450-25-6
     NYPL [Sc E 88-218]

Etudes du Centre de développement.
Bonvin, Jean. Changements sociaux et
productivité agricole en Afrique Centrale /.
Paris : Centre de développement de
l'orgnisation de coopértion et de développement
économiques, c1986. 140 p. :   ISBN
92-64-22803-9   *NYPL [Sc D 88-803]*

Études nigériennes.
(no 53) Zakari, Maikorema. Contribution a
l'histoire des populations du sud-est nigérien .
Niamey , 1985. 246 p. ;   ISBN 2-85921-053-9
     NYPL [Sc E 88-328]

Etudes sur le bantu oriental : Comores, Tanzanie,
Somalie et Kenya : dialectologie et classification

/ Marie-Françoise Rombi, éditeur. Paris :
SELAF, 1982 [i.e. 1983] 158 p. : ill. ; 24 cm.
(LACITO-documents. Afrique . 9) Bantu, English, and
French; with summaries in German and Spanish.
Includes bibliographies. ISBN 2-85297-144-5 : DDC
496/.39 19
1. *Bantu languages - Addresses, essays, lectures. 2.
Africa, Eastern - Languages. I. Rombi, M.-F.
(Marie-Françoise). II. Series.*
PL8025 .E84 1983   *NYPL [Sc E 88-357]*

Etudes tchadiques : classes et extensions verbales.
Paris : Geuthner, c1987. 121 p. ; 24 cm.
(Publications du Groupe d'études tchadiques (GET))
Includes bibliographical references. ISBN
2-7053-0341-3
1. *Chadic languages - Verb.*   *NYPL [Sc E 88-293]*

Les eunuques /. Sessi, Kpanlingan. Paris , c1984.
71 p. ; ISBN 2-903871-56-6
    NYPL [Sc D 88-1231]

**Europäische Hochschulschriften. Reihe XIV,
Angelsächsische Sprache und Literatur .**
(Bd. 151) Doherty, Jaiyeola, 1952- Die Satire
im nigerianischen Roman . Frankfurt am Main ,
New York , c1986. 381 p. : ISBN 3-8204-8326-8
DDC 823 19
PR9387.4 .D64 1986   *NYPL [Sc D 88-991]*

EUROPE - CIVILIZATION - 1945-
Bizimana, Nsekuye. Müssen die Afrikaner den
Weissen alles nachmachen? /. Berlin , c1985.
271 p. ; ISBN 3-88726-014-7 DDC 940 19
D1055 .B57 1985   *NYPL [Sc D 88-995]*

**EUROPE - COLONIES - AMERICA -
CONGRESSES.**
Colonial identity in the Atlantic world,
1500-1800 /. Princeton, N.J. , c1987. xi, 290
p. ; ISBN 0-691-05372-3 (alk. paper) : DDC
909/.09812 19
E18.82 .C64 1987   *NYPL [HAB 87-3215]*

**EUROPE - EMIGRATION AND
IMMIGRATION.**
Power, Jonathan, 1941- Western Europe's
migrant workers /. London , 1984. 35 p. :
ISBN 0-08-030831-7 *NYPL [Sc F 88-231]*

**EUROPE - RELATIONS (GENERAL) WITH
LIBERIA.**
The Effects of the Western culture on the
traditional cultures of Lofa County
[microform] . [Monrovia , 1977] 24 p. ;
    NYPL [Sc Micro F-10952]

EUROPEAN ART. see ART, EUROPEAN.

**EUROPEAN WAR, 1939-1945. see WORLD
WAR, 1939-1945.**

**EVALUATION OF LITERATURE. see
CRITICISM.**

Evangelische Akademie Hofgeismar. Der Sudan .
Hofgeismar [1985?] 112 p. ;
    NYPL [Sc D 88-737]

EVANGELISM. see EVANGELISTIC WORK.

EVANGELISTIC WORK - NIGERIA.
Asuzu, Boniface Ntomchukwu. Communications
media in the Nigerian Church today /. Rome ,
1987. 160 p. : *NYPL [Sc E 88-297]*

Asuzu, Boniface Ntomchukwu. Communications
strategy in the new era of evangelization .
Roma , 1987. xxi, 343 p. ;
    NYPL [Sc E 88-276]

Evangelium im afrikanischen Kontext . Dierks,
Friedrich. Gütersloh , 1986. 206 p. : ISBN
3-579-00239-2 DDC 266/.0089963 19
BL2480.T76 D54 1986 NYPL [Sc D 88-879]

**L'Evangile en Afrique, vécu et commenté par des
Bayaka /.** Beken, Alain van der, 1935- Nettetal
[Germany] , 1986. 328 p. ; ISBN 3-87787-204-2 :
BV3630.B69 B45 1986 NYPL [Sc E 88-339]

Evans, James H., 1950-
Black theology : a critical assessment and
annotated bibliography / compiled by James H.
Evans, Jr., G.E. Gorman. New York :
Greenwood Press, c1987. xii, 205 p. ; 25 cm.
(Bibliographies and indexes in religious studies,
0742-6836 . no. 10) Includes indexes. ISBN
0-313-24822-2 (lib. bdg. : alk. paper) DDC
016.23/008996073 19
1. *Black theology - Bibliography. I. Gorman, G. E. II.
Title. III. Series.*
Z7774 .E9 1987 BT82.7
    NYPL [Sc E 87-426]
Spiritual empowerment in Afro-American

literature : Frederick Douglass, Rebecca
Jackson, Booker T. Washington, Richard
Wright, Toni Morrison / James H. Evans, Jr.
Lewiston, NY : E. Mellen Press, 1987. 174 p. ;
24 cm. (Studies in art and religious interpretation . v.
6) Includes bibliographies and index. ISBN
0-88946-560-6 DDC 810/.9/896073 19
1. *American literature - Afro-American authors -
History and criticism. 2. Afro-Americans in literature.
3. Afro-Americans - Religion. 4. Religion in literature.
I. Title.*
PS153.N5 E92 1987   *NYPL [Sc E 88-265]*

Evasions Antilles /. Calderon, Agostina.
[Pointe-à-Pitre , Paris , 1987] 223 p. :
    NYPL [Sc D 88-998]

EVAXX. Black Americans' attitudes toward
cancer and cancer tests / conducted for [the]
American Cancer Society [by] EVAXX, Inc.
[New York], 1981. 1 v. (various pagings) ; 29
cm. "January 1981." Presented to the Schomburg
Center by the American Cancer Society.
1. *Cancer - Psychological aspects. 2. Afro-Americans -
Diseases. I. American Cancer Society. II. Title.*
    NYPL [Sc F 88-293]

**Events that marked the first decade of ADPs in
Nigeria.** [Ibadan : Development Communication
Center FACW, Dept. of Rural Development,
Federal Ministry of Agriculture, Water
Resources and Rural Development, 1986] 34
p. : ill. ; 27 cm. Cover title.
1. *Agricultural development projects - Nigeria -
Anniversaries,etc. I. Nigeria. Federal ministry of
Agriculture, Water Resources and Rural Development.*
    NYPL [Sc F 89-74]

Everett Anderson's friend /. Clifton, Lucille,
1936- New York , c1976. [25] p. : ISBN
0-03-015161-9 (lib. bdg.) DDC [E]
PZ8.3.C573 Evg   *NYPL [Sc D 88-1505]*

Everett Anderson's nine month long /. Clifton,
Lucille, 1936- New York , c1978. [31] p. ;
ISBN 0-03-043536-6 DDC [E]
PZ8.3.C573 Evk   *NYPL [Sc D 89-30]*

Everywoman.
Hull, Gloria T. Color, sex, and poetry .
Bloomington , c1987. xi, 240 p. : ISBN
0-253-34974-5 DDC 811/.52/099287 19
PS153.N5 H84 1987   *NYPL [Sc E 88-72]*

EVIDENCE, EXPERT - UNITED STATES.
Chesler, Mark A. Social science in court .
Madison, Wis. , 1988. xiv, 286 p. ; ISBN
0-299-11620-4 : DDC 344.73/0798 347.304798
19
KF8925.D5 C48 1988 NYPL [Sc E 89-187]

EVIL SPIRITS. see DEMONOLOGY.

**Evolution, creative intelligence and intergroup
competition /** edited by Alan McGregor.
Washington : Cliveden Press, 1986. 96 p. ; 23
cm. (The Mankind quarterly . monograph no. 3)
Errata slip inserted. Includes bibliographical references.
ISBN 0-941694-30-5
1. *Creative ability - Genetic aspects. 2. Competition
(Biology). I. Series.*   *NYPL [Sc D 89-532]*

Evolution in Nigerian art. Eze, Okpu. Timeless
search /. [Lagos] [1985?] 51 p. :
    NYPL [Sc C 88-170]

**The evolution of the West Indian's image in the
Afro-American novel /.** Rahming, Melvin B.,
1943- Millwood, N.Y. , c1986. xix, 160 p. ;
ISBN 0-8046-9339-0 DDC
813/.009/35203969729 19
PS153.N5 R3 1985   *NYPL [JFD 86-6569]*

EWE (AFRICAN PEOPLE) - CONGRESSES.
Peuples du golfe du Bénin . Paris , c1984. 328
p. : ISBN 2-86537-092-5 DDC 966/.8004963 19
DT510.43.E94 P48 1984
    NYPL [Sc E 88-449]

**EWE (AFRICAN PEOPLE) - MUSIC -
INSTRUCTION AND STUDY.**
Locke, David, 1949- Drum gahu . Crown Point,
Ind. , c1987. ix, 142 p. : ISBN 0-941677-03-6 :
DDC 789/.01 19
MT655 .L6 1987   *NYPL [Sc E 88-391]*

**EWE (AFRICAN PEOPLE) - RELIGIOUS
LIFE AND CUSTOMS.**
Agbetiafa, Komla. Les ancêtres et nous .
Dakar , 1985. 95 p. : ISBN 2-7236-0929-4
    NYPL [Sc D 88-7]

**EWE LANGUAGE - GRAMMAR,
COMPARATIVE - GERMAN.**

Eklou, Akpaka A. Satzstruktur des Deutschen
und des Ewe . Saarbrücken , 1987. 262 p. ;
    NYPL [Sc D 89-203]

Ewto' . Kirby, Richard, 1958. London , c1985. 27
p. : ISBN 0-946140-24-3 (pbk) : DDC 307.7/72 19
F2380   *NYPL [Sc F 89-104]*

Ewumewu omenala ofufe na nkwenye ndi Igbo /.
Ezeuko, R. O. [Nigeria] , c1986. vi, 70 p. ;
ISBN 978-264-300-9   *NYPL [Sc D 88-970]*

Ewusi, Kodwo. Economic trends in Ghana in
1984-85 and prospects for 1986 / by Kodwo
Ewusi. [Legon] : Institute of Statistical, Social,
and Economic Research, University of Ghana,
[1986] 52 p. : ill. ; 33 cm. "December 1986."
DDC 330.9667/05 19
1. *Economic forecasting - Ghana - Statistics. 2. Ghana -
Economic conditions - 1979- - Statistics. 3. Ghana -
Economic policy - Statistics. I. Title.*
HC1060 .E975 1986   *NYPL [Sc G 88-31]*

Ex-père de la nation . Fall, Aminata Sow. Paris ,
1987. 189 p. ; ISBN 2-85802-875-3
    NYPL [Sc D 88-1360]

**Examination of the decision of the Supreme
Court of the United States, in the case of
Strader, Gorman and Armstrong vs.
Christopher Graham .** Birney, James Gillespie,
1792-1857. Cincinnati , 1852. iv, [1], 6-46, [1]
p. ;
E450 .B57   *NYPL [Sc Rare F 88-37]*

EXAMINATIONS - NIGERIA - QUESTIONS.
Past questions and answers for secondary
modern schools, 1964-1969 /. Ado-Ekiti
[197-?] 301 p. ;   *NYPL [Sc C 86-206]*

EXAMINATIONS - ZAIRE - QUESTIONS.
Kipasaman, Mikalukalu. Philosophie . Kinshasa
[1984?] 61 p. :   *NYPL [Sc G 87-49]*

Kipasman, Mikalukalu. Biologie . Kinshasa
[1984?] 70 p. :   *NYPL [Sc G 87-46]*

Exbrayat, André. Martinique / photographie,
André Exbrayat ; texte, Christine Lemaître.
Fort de France : Editions Exbrayat, c1986. 154,
[2] p. : col. ill. ; 25 cm. Bibliography: p. [155]
ISBN 2-905873-02-7 DDC 972.98/2 19
1. *Martinique - Description and travel - Views. I.
Lemaître, Christine. II. Title.*
F2081.2 .E9 1986   *NYPL [Sc E 88-346]*

**EXCHANGES, COMMODITY. see
COMMODITY EXCHANGES.**

**EXCHANGES, PRODUCE. see COMMODITY
EXCHANGES.**

**EXECUTIVE AGENCIES. see
ADMINISTRATIVE AGENCIES.**

EXECUTIVES - AFRICA - CONGRESSES.
L'Entreprise et ses dirigeants dans le
développement économique de l'Afrique noire .
Kinshasa [1969?] 89 p. :
    NYPL [Sc F 88-100]

EXECUTIVES - AFRICA - TRAINING OF.
Rwegasira, Kami S. P. Administering
management development institutions in Africa
/. Aldershot, England , Brookfield, Vt. , 1988.
vi, 112 p. ; ISBN 0-566-05501-5 DDC
658.4/07124/096 19
HF5549.5.A78 R94 1988
    NYPL [Sc D 88-458]

Exeter studies in history, 0260-8626 .
(no. 9) Africa, America, and central Asia .
[Exeter, Devon] [Atlantic Highlands, N.J.]
1984. 107 p. ; ISBN 0-85969-295-6 (pbk.) : DDC
330.9/034 19
HC53 .A35 1984   *NYPL [Sc D 88-1315]*

**Exigencias de un cimarrón (en suenos) versos del
negro Blas III /.** Jiménez, Blas R. Santo
Domingo, Republica Dominicana , 1987. 113
p. ;   *NYPL [Sc D 87-1395]*

L'exil, ou, La tombe . Tchichellé Tchivéla, 1940-
Paris , c1986. 239 p. ; ISBN 2-7087-0473-7
    NYPL [Sc C 88-289]

The exiles of Florida. Giddings, Joshua Reed,
1795-1864. Columbus, Ohio, 1858. viii, 338 p.
E83.817 .G46   *NYPL [Sc Rare F 88-68]*

**EXPANSION (U. S. POLITICS) see
IMPERIALISM.**

Expatriate and indigenous manpower. Ukpong,
Ignatius I. The contributions of expatriate and
indigenous manpower to the manufacturing
industry in Nigeria . [Calabar, Cross River

State, Nigeria] [c1986] ix, 61 p. ; ISBN
978-227-526-3 DDC 331.12/57/09669 19
HD5848.A6 U37 1986 NYPL [Sc C 89-128]

**EXPEDITIONS, ARCHAEOLOGICAL. see
ARCHAEOLOGICAL EXPEDITIONS.**

**EXPEDITIONS, ARCTIC. see ARCTIC
REGIONS.**

**EXPERT EVIDENCE. see EVIDENCE,
EXPERT.**

Explanation in reply to an assault. Sumner,
Charles, 1811-1874. "He, being dead, yet
speaketh" . Boston , New York , 1878. 29, 16
p. ;   *NYPL [Sc Rare C 89-4]*

Explorations in African systems of thought /
edited by Ivan Karp & Charles S. Bird.
Washington, D.C. : Smithsonian Institution
Press, c1987. xvi, 337 p. : ill. ; 24 cm. (African
systems of thought) "Papers given at a seminar
organized for the African Studies Program at Indiana
University in 1977."-- verso t.p. Includes bibliographies
and index. ISBN 0-87474-591-8 (pbk.)
*1. Philosophy, Primitive - Africa. 2. Cognition and
culture - Africa. 3. Religion, Primitive - Africa. I. Karp,
Ivan. II. Bird, Charles S. III. Indiana University,
Bloomington. African Studies Program.*
NYPL [Sc D 88-566]

**EXPLORERS - AFRICA, EAST - JUVENILE
LITERATURE.**
African adventures and adventurers /. Boston ,
1880. 393 p. :   *NYPL [Sc C 88-60]*

EXPLORERS - SPAIN - BIOGRAPHY.
Colón, Fernando, 1488-1539. [Historie.
English.] Christophe Colomb raconté par son
fils ./. Paris , 1986. xviii, 265 p., [8] p. of
plates : ISBN 2-262-00387-4
NYPL [Sc D 88-504]

**EXPLORERS - UNITED STATES -
BIOGRAPHY - JUVENILE LITERATURE.**
Gilman, Michael. Matthew Henson /. New
York , c1988. 110 p. : ISBN 1-555-46590-0 :
DDC 919.8/04 B 92 19
G635.H4 G55 1988   NYPL [Sc E 88-169]

Exploring Zimbabwe .
(1) Garlake, Peter S. Life at Great Zimbabwe /.
Gweru, Zimbabwe , 1983, c1982. [36] p. :
ISBN 0-86922-180-9 (pbk) DDC 968.91 19
DT962.9.G73 G374 1983
NYPL [Sc F 88-175]
(2) Rushworth, David. The wonders of Hwange
/. Gweru, Zimbabwe , 1986. 35 p. : ISBN
0-86922-389-5   *NYPL [Sc F 89-43]*

EXPORT CONTROLS - UNITED STATES.
United States. Congress. House. Committee on
Foreign Affairs. Subcommittee on International
Economic Policy and Trade. Controls on
exports to South Africa . Washington , 1983. iv,
321 p. ; DDC 382/.64/0973 19
KF27 .F6465 1982e   NYPL [Sc E 88-113]

Expressions of belief . Museum voor
Volkenkunde (Rotterdam, Netherlands) New
York , 1988. 248 p. : ISBN 0-8478-0955-5 :
DDC 730 19
N5310.75.H68 M876 1988
NYPL [Sc G 88-37]

Expresso 2222. Gilberto Gil Expresso 2222 /.
[Salvador, Brasil?] , 1982. 287 p. ;
NYPL [JMD 83-309]

**Expulsion. see United States - Emigration and
immigration.**

EXTERNAL DEBTS. see DEBTS, EXTERNAL.

Extra innings /. Robinson, Frank, 1935- New
York , c1988. x, 270, [8] p. ; ISBN
0-07-053183-8 DDC 796.357/08996073 19
GV863.A1 R582 1988 NYPL [Sc E 88-382]

EXTRADITION - CANADA.
Teatero, William, 1953- John Anderson .
[Kingston, Ont.] , c1986. 183 p. : ISBN
0-9692685-0-5 : DDC 345.71/056/0924 19
NYPL [Sc E 89-113]

**Extraordinary Black Americans from colonial to
contemporary times /.** Altman, Susan R.
Chicago , 1988. 240 p. : ISBN 0-516-00581-2
DDC 973/.0496073022 B 920 19
E185.96 .A56 1988   NYPL [Sc E 89-177]

EYADÉMA, GNASSINGBÉ.
Toulabor, Comi M. Le Togo sous Éyadéma /.
Paris , c1986. 332 p. ; ISBN 2-86537-150-6
NYPL [Sc D 88-261]

The eye of the needle . Turner, Richard, 1941-
Maryknoll, N.Y. , 1978, c1972. xxiv, 173 p. ;
ISBN 0-88344-121-7. DDC 309.1/68/06
DT763 .T85 1978   NYPL [JLD 84-744]

Eze, Okpu. Timeless search / Okpu Eze.
[Lagos] : National Council for Arts and
Culture, [1985?] 51 p. : chiefly ill. ; 20 x 26
cm. Catalog of an exhibition. Cover title. At head of
title: Evolution in Nigerian art.
*1. Sculpture, Modern - Nigeria - Exhibitions. 2. Art,
Modern - Nigeria - Exhibitions. I. Title. II. Title:
Evolution in Nigerian art.* *NYPL [Sc C 88-170]*

Eze, Sylvester Omumeka. Steps for socio-political
and religious change : a case study / by S.
Omumeka Eze. [Nsukka? : s.n], 1987 (Nsukka :
Chinedu Printers) 52 p. ; 20 cm. Cover title.
*1. Catholic Church - Nigeria. 2. Nigeria - Social
conditions. I. Title.*   *NYPL [Sc C 89-53]*

Ezeani, Geo'Ben. Redeeming Nigeria through
Massist ideology : Massism / Geo'Ben Ezeani.
Yola : Juddy Best Publishers, 1987. 226 p. :
ports. ; 20 cm. Includes bibliographical references.
I. Title.   *NYPL [Sc C 89-49]*

Ezekwugo, Christopher U. M. Chi, the true god
in Igbo religion / [Christopher U.M.
Ezekwugo]. Alwaye, Kerala, India : Pontifical
Institute of Philosophy and Theology, 1987. xvi,
310 p. : ill. ; 22 cm. Thesis (doctoral)--University of
Innsbruck, Austria, 1973. Bibliography: p. 295-300.
1. Igbo (African people) - Religion. I. Title.
NYPL [Sc D 88-881]

Ezeuko, R. O. Ewumewu omenala ofufe na
nkwenye ndi Igbo / nke R.O. Ezeuko.
[Nigeria] : Etukokwu Publishers, c1986. vi, 70
p. ; 21 cm. ISBN 978-264-300-9
*1. Igbo (African people). 2. Igbo language - Texts. I.
Title.*   *NYPL [Sc D 88-970]*

Eziokwu bụ ndụ /. Anukwu, Martin. Enugu,
Nigeria , 1986. 110 p. ; ISBN 978-239-649-4
NYPL [Sc C 89-12]

Ezra, Kate. Art of the Dogon : selections from
the Lester Wunderman collection / by Kate
Ezra. New York : Metropolitan Museum of
Art : Distributed by H.N. Abrams, 1988. 116
p. : ill. ; 29 cm. Bibliography: p. 112-116. ISBN
0-87099-507-3 : DDC 730/.089963 19
*1. Wunderman, Lester - Art collections - Exhibitions. 2.
Art, Dogon - Exhibitions. 3. Art, Primitive - Mali -
Exhibitions. I. Title.*
N7399.M3 E97 1988   NYPL [Sc F 88-160]

**F. A. S. see American University, Washington, D.
C. Foreign Area Studies.**

**F. R. O. L. I. Z. I. see Front for the Liberation
of Zimbabwe.**

FABLES, RWANDAN.
Imigani "tima-ngiro" y'u Rwanda =. Butare ,
1987. 267, [1] p. ;   *NYPL [Sc D 88-865]*

FABRICS. see TEXTILE FABRICS.

The face of Black music ; photographs /. Wilmer,
Valerie. New York , 1976. [118] p. : ISBN
0-306-70756-X. DDC 780/.92/2 B
ML87 .W655   NYPL [Sc F 88-207]

Faces and places . Brown, Marion, 1935- 1976. 2
v. (289 leaves) :   *NYPL [Sc F 88-101]*

Faces of African independence : three plays /
translated by Clive Wake ; introduction by
Richard Bjornson. Charlottesville : University
Press of Virginia, 1988. xxxvi, 127 p. ; 23 cm.
(CARAF books) CONTENTS. - Three suitors, one
husband / by Guillaume Oyono-Mbia -- Until further
notice / by Guillaume Oyonô-Mbia -- The death of
Chaka / by Seydou Badian. ISBN 0-8139-1186-9
DDC 842 19
*1. Chaka, Zulu chief, 1787?-1828 - Drama. 2.
Oyono-Mbia, Guillaume, 1939- - Translations, English.
3. African drama (French) - 20th century - Translations
into English. 4. English drama - Translations from
French. 5. Africa - History - Autonomy and
independence movements - Drama. I. Oyono-Mbia,
Guillaume, 1939- Trois prétendants, un mari. English.
1988. II. Oyono-Mbia, Guillaume, 1939- Until further
notice. 1988. III. Badian, Seydou, 1928- Mort de
Chaka. English. 1988. IV. Series.*
PQ3987.5.E5 F33 1988 NYPL [Sc D 89-32]

Facing the storm . Keegan, Timothy J. London ,
Athens , 1986. vii, 169 p. ; ISBN 0-8214-0924-7
DDC 305.8/96068 19
HN801.A8 K44 1989   NYPL [Sc D 89-233]

Fact paper on Southern Africa .
(no. 14) Working under South African
occupation . London , 1987. 56 p. ; ISBN
0-904759-73-3 (pbk.) : DDC 968 s 331.6/9/9688
19
DT746 .F3 no. 14 HD8808
NYPL [Sc D 89-525]

**Facts or fantasy about Virgin Islands history
[microform] /.** Moolenaar, Ruth. [Charlotte
Amalie] , 1978. 22, [1] p. ;
NYPL [Sc Micro F-10966]

FACULTY (EDUCATION) see EDUCATORS.

Fagbamiye, E. O. University of Lagos series in
education /. Ikeja, Lagos , 1987- v. :
NYPL [Sc D 89-149]

Fagg, William Butler. Bassani, Ezio. Africa and
the Renaissance . New York City , c1988. 255
p. : ISBN 0-945802-00-5 : DDC
736/.62/096607401471 19
NK5989 .B37 1988   NYPL [Sc F 89-30]

**FAIR EMPLOYMENT PRACTICE. see
DISCRIMINATION IN EMPLOYMENT.**

Fairbairn, Bill, 1935- Run for freedom / Bill
Fairbairn. [Lusaka, Zambia] : Neczam, 1984.
181 p. ; 19 cm. (NECZAM library series. E5)
1. Zimbabwe - Fiction. I. Title.
NYPL [Sc C 88-227]

Fairclough, Chris. Obadiah. I am a Rastafarian /.
London , New York , c1986. 32 p. : ISBN
0-86313-260-X :
BL2532.R37   NYPL [Sc F 89-12]

FAIRY TALES.
Baker, Augusta. (comp) The golden lynx and
other tales. Philadelphia [1960] 160 p.
PZ8.1.B172 Go   NYPL [Sc D 88-1492]

Faith and culture : a multicultural catechetical
resource / Department of Education, United
States Catholic Conference. Washington, D.C. :
The Conference, c1987. 111 p. : ill. ; 23 cm.
(Publication / Office of Publishing and Promotion
Services, United States Catholic Conference. no. 994-7)
Bibliography: p. [89]-107. ISBN 1-555-86994-7 (pbk.)
DDC 268/.82 19
*1. Catholic Church - Education. 2. Church work with
minorities - Catholic Church. I. United States Catholic
Conference. Dept. of Education.*
BX1968 .F24 1987   NYPL [Sc D 88-1059]

Faith, culture, and leadership . Hayden, Robert
C. [Boston, MA , c1983] iv, 56 p. : DDC
280/.08996073074461 19
BR560.B73 H39 1983 NYPL [Sc F 88-269]

Fakunle, Funmilayo. Chasing the shadow /
written by Funmilayo Fakunle. Oshogbo
[Nigeria] : Fakunle Major Press, 1980. 151 p. ;
19 cm.
1. Nigeria - Fiction. I. Title.
NYPL [Sc C 87-462]

Fakunle, Victor. Tentacles of the gods / by Victor
Fakunle. Oshogbo : Fakunle Major Press, 1984.
111 p. ; 18 cm.
1. Nigeria - Fiction. I. Title.
NYPL [Sc C 88-280]

Falasha no more . Kushner, Arlene. New York ,
c1986. 58 p. ; ISBN 0-933503-55-5
NYPL [Sc F 88-107]

FALASHAS - BIOGRAPHY.
Avraham, Shmuel, 1945- Treacherous journey .
New York, NY , 1986. xii, 178 p. : ISBN
0-933503-46-6 (jacket); 0-933503-46-5 : DDC
963/.004924 19
DS135.E75 A93 1986 NYPL [Sc E 87-275]

FALASHAS - FICTION.
Kushner, Arlene. Falasha no more . New
York , c1986. 58 p. ; ISBN 0-933503-55-5
NYPL [Sc F 88-107]

FALASHAS - ISRAEL.
Ethiopian Jews and Israel /. New Brunswick,
NJ, U. S.A. , c1987. 159 p. : ISBN
0-88738-133-2 DDC 305.8/924/05694 19
DS113.8.F34 E84 1987 NYPL [Sc E 88-73]

Falconbridge, Alexander, d. 1792. An account of
the slave trade on the coast of Africa / by
Alexander Falconbridge. London : Printed by J.
Phillips, 1788. 55 p. ; 21 cm.
*1. Slave-trade - Africa. 2. Slave-trade - West Indies,
British. I. Title.*   *NYPL [Sc Rare F 88-63]*

Falgayrettes, Christiane. Art et mythologie .
Paris , 1988. 117 p. :　ISBN 2-906067-06-7
　　　　　　　　　NYPL [Sc E 89-96]

Falk, Rainer. Südafrika - Widerstand und
Befreiungskampf . Köln , 1987, c1986. 286 p. :
　ISBN 3-7609-1023-8　*NYPL [Sc C 88-190]*

Fall, Aminata Sow. Ex-père de la nation : roman
/ Aminata Sow Fall. Paris : L'Harmattan, 1987.
189 p. ; 22 cm. (Collection Encres noires
0223-9930 . 43)　ISBN 2-85802-875-3
1. Africa - Fiction. I. Title. II. Series.
　　　　　　　　　NYPL [Sc D 88-1360]

Fallen angels /. Myers, Walter Dean, 1937- New
York , c1988. 309 p. :　ISBN 0-590-40942-5 :
DDC [Fic] 19
PZ7.M992 Fal 1988　　*NYPL [Sc D 88-1136]*

Falola, Toyin.
The military in nineteenth century Yoruba
politics / Toyin Falola and Dare Oguntomisin.
Ile-Ife [Nigeria] : University of Ife Press, c1984.
127 p. ; 22 cm. Bibliography: p. 119-127.　ISBN
978-13-6064-X (pbk.)　DDC 966.9/004963 19
1. Yoruba (African people) - Politics and government.
2. Yoruba (African people) - Warfare. 3. Yoruba
(African people) - History - 19th century. I.
Oguntomisin, Dare. II. Title.
DT515.45.Y67 F35 1984
　　　　　　　　　NYPL [Sc D 88-227]
Nigeria and the international capitalist system
/. Boulder, Colo. , 1988. v, 154 p. ;　ISBN
1-555-87087-2 (alk. paper)　DDC 337.669 19
HF1616.7 .N54 1988　*NYPL [JLE 88-3615]*

Familia y matrimonio fań /. Nze Abuy, R. María.
[Spain?] [1985?] 77 p. ;
　　　　　　　　　NYPL [Sc C 88-285]

**FAMILIES, AFRO-AMERICAN. see AFRO-
AMERICAN FAMILIES.**

Families around the world.
Jacobsen, Peter Otto. A family in West Africa
/. Hove , 1985. 32 p. :　ISBN 0-85078-434-4 :
DDC 966/.305 19
DA588　　　　　*NYPL [Sc D 88-1499]*

Families the world over.
Griffin, Michael. A family in Kenya /.
Minneapolis , 1988, c1987. 31 p. :　ISBN
0-8225-1680-2 (lib. bdg.) :　DDC 306.8/5/096762
19
HQ692.5 .G75 1988　*NYPL [Sc C 89-6]*

La famille Wolof . Diop, Abdoulaye Bara. Paris ,
c1985. 262 p. :　ISBN 2-86537-138-7
　　　　　　　　　NYPL [Sc E 89-126]

Family and social change : essays in sociology &
social welfare administration / S.A. Adebagbo,
T.U. Obinyan, 'Lai Olurode. Lagos, Nigeria :
Tap Printing Co., 1986. vi, 96 p. ; 22 cm.
Publication date stamped on tip. Includes bibliographies.
CONTENTS. - Modernization and the dependency
approaches considered /[by Lai Olurode] - Marxism,
articulation of modes of production, family & change
/[byT.U. Obinyan] - Adoption system & practice in
Nigeria : the case of Lagos State /[by S.A Adebagbo]
1. Family - Nigeria. 2. Nigeria - Social conditions. I.
Adebagbo, S. A. II. Obinyan, T. U. III. Olurode, Lai.
　　　　　　　　　NYPL [Sc D 88-794]

FAMILY AND STATE. see FAMILY POLICY.

FAMILY - BRAZIL - HISTORY.
Freyre, Gilberto, 1900- [Casa-grande & senzala.
English.] The masters and the slaves =.
Berkeley , c1986. xc, 537 xliv p., [3] p. of
plates :　ISBN 0-520-05665-5 (pbk. : alk. paper)
　DDC 981 19
F2510 .F7522 1986　*NYPL [HFB 87-2095]*

FAMILY - EQUATORIAL GUINEA.
Nze Abuy, R. María. Familia y matrimonio fań
/. [Spain?] [1985?] 77 p. ;
　　　　　　　　　NYPL [Sc C 88-285]

FAMILY FARMS - AFRICA, SUB-SAHARAN.
Singh, Ram D. Economics of the family and
farming systems in sub-Saharan Africa .
Boulder , 1988. xxiii, 208 p. ;　ISBN
0-8133-7624-6　DDC 338.1/0967 19
HD1476.A357 S56 1988
　　　　　　　　　NYPL [JLD 88-4512]

**FAMILY - HEALTH AND HYGIENE -
NIGERIA.**
Odunze, Don. The marriage killers /. Enugu
[Nigeria] [198-?] 104 p. ;
　　　　　　　　　NYPL [Sc C 88-189]

A family in Kenya /. Griffin, Michael.

Minneapolis , 1988, c1987. 31 p. :　ISBN
0-8225-1680-2 (lib. bdg.) :　DDC 306.8/5/096762
19
HQ692.5 .G75 1988　　*NYPL [Sc C 89-6]*

A family in West Africa /. Jacobsen, Peter Otto.
Hove , 1985. 32 p. :　ISBN 0-85078-434-4 :　DDC
966/.305 19
DA588　　　　　*NYPL [Sc D 88-1499]*

**FAMILY - KENYA - JUVENILE
LITERATURE.**
Griffin, Michael. A family in Kenya /.
Minneapolis , 1988, c1987. 31 p. :　ISBN
0-8225-1680-2 (lib. bdg.) :　DDC 306.8/5/096762
19
HQ692.5 .G75 1988　　*NYPL [Sc C 89-6]*

**FAMILY - LAW. see DOMESTIC
RELATIONS.**

FAMILY LIFE EDUCATION - JAMAICA.
Somerville, Trixie. Family stories . Jamaica
[1950-] 68 p. :　　　　*NYPL [Sc D 89-156]*

FAMILY - NIGERIA.
Family and social change . Lagos, Nigeria ,
1986. vi, 96 p. ;　　　*NYPL [Sc D 88-794]*

A family outing in Africa /. Hampton, Charles.
London , 1988. 267 p., [16] p. of plates :　ISBN
0-333-44190-7 :　DDC 916/.04328 19
DT12.25　　　　*NYPL [Sc D 88-1274]*

FAMILY PLANNING. see BIRTH CONTROL.

The family planning clinic in Africa . Brown,
Richard Coleman, 1936- London , 1987. ix, 102
p. :　ISBN 0-333-43658-X
　　　　　　　　　NYPL [Sc D 88-630]

FAMILY POLICY - UNITED STATES.
Jewell, K. Sue. Survival of the Black family .
New York , 1988. x, 197 p. :　ISBN
0-275-92985-X (alk. paper)　DDC
306.8/5/08996073 19
HQ536 .J48 1988　　*NYPL [Sc E 89-153]*

FAMILY - PROBLEMS, EXERCISES, ETC.
Nobles, Wade W. The KM ebit husia .
Oakland, California , 1985. 201 p. ;　ISBN
0-939205-03-3　　　*NYPL [Sc F 88-159]*

FAMILY REUNIONS - NORTH CAROLINA.
Redford, Dorothy Spruill. Somerset
homecoming . New York , c1988. xviii, 266 p. :
　ISBN 0-385-24245-X :　DDC
929/.3/089960730756 19
E185.96 .R42 1988　　*NYPL [Sc E 88-498]*

FAMILY - SENEGAL.
Diop, Abdoulaye Bara. La famille Wolof .
Paris , c1985. 262 p. :　ISBN 2-86537-138-7
　　　　　　　　　NYPL [Sc E 89-126]

FAMILY - SOUTHERN STATES - HISTORY.
McHugh, Cathy L. Mill family . New York ,
1988. x, 144 p. ;　ISBN 0-19-504299-9 (alk. paper)
　DDC 331.7/67721/0975 19
HD8039.T42 U654 1988
　　　　　　　　　NYPL [Sc D 88-1082]

Family stories . Somerville, Trixie. Jamaica
[1950-] 68 p. :　　　　*NYPL [Sc D 89-156]*

FAMILY VIOLENCE - WEST INDIES.
André, Jacques. L'inceste focal dans la famille
noire antillaise . Paris : Presses universitaires de
France, 1987. 396 p. ;　ISBN 2-13-040101-5
　　　　　　　　　NYPL [Sc D 88-129]

FAMINES - AFRICA - CASE STUDIES.
Curtis, Donald, 1939- Preventing famine .
London , New York , 1988. xi, 250 p. ;　ISBN
0-415-00711-9　DDC 363.8/7/096 19
HC800.Z9 F326 1988　*NYPL [JLD 88-3825]*

FAMINES - ETHIOPIA.
Franey, Jean-Pierre. Ethiopie, la face cachée /.
Paris , c1986. 127 p. :　ISBN 2-209-05848-1 :
HC845.Z9 F34 1986　*NYPL [Sc F 88-204]*

**FAMINES - ETHIOPIA - PICTORIAL
WORKS.**
Franey, Jean-Pierre. Ethiopie, la face cachée /.
Paris , c1986. 127 p. :　ISBN 2-209-05848-1 :
HC845.Z9 F34 1986　*NYPL [Sc F 88-204]*

FAMINES - NIGERIA, NORTHERN.
Mortimore, M. J., 1937- Adapting to drought .
Cambridge , New York , 1989. xxii, 299 p. ;
　ISBN 0-521-32312-6　DDC 333.73 19
HC1055.Z7 N6755 1988
　　　　　　　　　NYPL [Sc E 89-191]

Famous horse stories.
Lang, Don. Strawberry roan /. New York ,
1946. 218 p. :　　　*NYPL [Sc D 88-646]*

Famous women /. Ibuje, Joan, 1941- [Benin City,
Nigeria] [1982] 60 p. :　DDC 305.4/09669/3 19
HQ1815.5.Z8 B465 1982
　　　　　　　　　NYPL [Sc D 88-1144]

FANCY DRESS. see COSTUME.

Fanfani, Mariapia.
[Hayat. English]
Hayat : on the side of life / Mariapia
Fanfani. New York : Simon and Schuster,
c1988. 219 p., [16] p. of plates : ill., ports. ;
22 cm. Translated from the Italian. ISBN
0-671-66414-X　DDC 363.8/83/0924 B 19
1. Fanfani, Mariapia - Diaries. 2. Food relief - Africa -
Diaries. 3. Drought - Africa - Diaries. 4. Missionaries -
Africa - Diaries. I. Title.
HV696.F6 F363 1988　*NYPL [JFD 88-3833]*

FANFANI, MARIAPIA - DIARIES.
Fanfani, Mariapia. [Hayat. English.] Hayat .
New York , c1988. 219 p., [16] p. of plates :
　ISBN 0-671-66414-X　DDC 363.8/83/0924 B 19
HV696.F6 F363 1988　*NYPL [JFD 88-3833]*

**FANG (WEST AFRICAN PEOPLE) - SOCIAL
LIFE AND CUSTOMS.**
Nze Abuy, R. María. Familia y matrimonio fań
/. [Spain?] [1985?] 77 p. ;
　　　　　　　　　NYPL [Sc C 88-285]

Fanks, Russell, 1940- Terminus floride : roman /
Russell banks ; traduit de l'américain par Marc
Chênetier. Paris : Acropole, 1987. 346 p. ; 24
cm. Translation of: Continental drift.　ISBN
2-7357-0059-3
1. Haiti - Emigration and immigration - Fiction. 2.
United States - Emigration and immigration - Fiction. I.
Title.　　　　　*NYPL [Sc E 88-126]*

**FANON, FRANTZ, 1925-1961 - POLITICAL
AND SOCIAL VIEWS - CONGRESSES.**
Mémorial international Frantz Fanon (1982 :
Fort-de-France, Martinique) Mémorial
international Frantz Fanon . Paris , Dakar ,
c1984. 278 p. :　ISBN 2-7087-0431-1
　　　　　　　　　NYPL [Sc D 88-334]

**FANON, FRANTZ, 1925-1961 - INFLUENCE -
CONGRESSES.**
Mémorial international Frantz Fanon (1982 :
Fort-de-France, Martinique) Mémorial
international Frantz Fanon . Paris , Dakar ,
c1984. 278 p. :　ISBN 2-7087-0431-1
　　　　　　　　　NYPL [Sc D 88-334]

Fantaisie, Charles. Archives de la Martinique.
Bibliographie relative aux Antilles .
Fort-de-France , 1978- v. ;　DDC 016.97298/2 19
Z1502.F5 A72 1978 F2151
　　　　　　　　　NYPL [Sc F 88-286]

Fantaro ny fitampoha. Antananarivo : Foibe
Fanolokoloana, 1985. 47 p. : ill. ; 27 cm. On
cover: Repoblika Demokratika Malagasy, Ninisiteran'ny
Fanolokoloana sy ny Zava-Kanto Revolisionera.
Bibliography: p. 47.
1. Menabe (Malagasy people) - Rites and ceremonies. 2.
Malagasy language - Texts.　*NYPL [Sc F 89-121]*

FANTASTIC FICTION, AMERICAN.
Worlds apart . Boston, Mass. , 1986. 293 p. ;
　ISBN 0-932870-87-2 (pbk.)　DDC
813/.0876/08353 19
PS648.H57 W67 1986　*NYPL [JFD 87-7753]*

Fapohunda, Eleanor R. Women in the modern
sector labour force in Nigeria /. Lagos , 1985.
viii, 254 p. ;　ISBN 978-301-560-5
　　　　　　　　　NYPL [Sc D 89-538]

Farelli, Maria Helena. Oxóssi e Ossãe : os dois
senhores da floresta (magias e milagres de
plantas e ervas) / Maria Helena Farelli. Rio de
Janeiro : Editora Cátedra, 1987. 71 p. : ill. ; 20
cm. (Coleção Cabala . 7)
1. Herbs - Religious aspects. 2. Materia medica,
Vegetable. I. Title. II. Series.　*NYPL [Sc C 88-65]*

Farewell to a cannibal rage /. Osofisan, Femi.
Ibadan, Nigeria , 1986. 76 p. ;　ISBN
978-16-7507-1　　　*NYPL [Sc D 89-14]*

Farley, Carol J. The most important thing in the
world / by Carol Farley. New York : F. Watts,
1974. vi, 133 p., front. ; 22 cm. A boy and girl
travel across the country looking for the answer to the
question, "What is the most important thing in the
world?"　ISBN 0-531-02663-9
1. Afro-American youth - Juvenile fiction. I. Title.
　　　　　　　　　NYPL [Sc D 88-431]

FARM LABORERS. see AGRICULTURAL LABORERS.

FARM TENANCY - ECONOMIC ASPECTS - SOUTHERN STATES - HISTORY.
Mitchell, H. L. (Harry Leland), 1906- Roll the union on . Chicago , 1987. 96 p. :
NYPL [Sc F 88-187]

FARM WORKERS. see AGRICULTURAL LABORERS.

FARMING. see AGRICULTURE.

Farquhar, June. Jairos Jiri : the man and his work / by June Farquhar. Gweru : Mambo Press, 1987. 92 p. : ill. ; 22 cm. (Makers of Zimbabwe . 4.) ISBN 0-86922-416-6
1. Jiri, Jairos Dambgwa. 2. Rehabilitation - Zimbabwe. 3. Handicapped - Zimbabwe. 4. Zimbabwe - Biography. I. Title. II. Series. *NYPL [Sc D 89-38]*

Farrakhan, Louis.
[Speeches. Selections]
7 speeches, by Minister Louis Farrakhan, national representative of the Honorable Elijah Muhammad. New York, Published by Ministry Class, Muhammad's Temple No. 7, 1974. 151 p. 22 cm.
1. Black Muslims. 2. Black power - United States. 3. Black nationalism - United States. I. Title. II. Title: Seven speeches. *NYPL [Sc D 88-1441]*

FARRIERY. see HORSES.

Farwell, Byron. The Great War in Africa 1914-1918 / Byron Farwell. Harmondsworth : Viking, 1987. 382 p. : ill., maps ; 22 cm. Includes index. Bibliography: p. [362]-369. ISBN 0-670-80244-1 : DDC 940.4/16 19
1. World War, 1914-1918 - Campaigns - Africa. I. Title.
D575 *NYPL [Sc D 88-834]*

Fary, princess of Tiali /. Diallo, Nafissatou, 1941- Washington, D.C. , c1987. xi, 106 p. : ISBN 0-89410-411-X
NYPL [Sc D 88-1366]

Fasehun, Orobola. Sesay, Amadu. The OAU after twenty years /. Boulder , 1984. ix, 133 p. ; ISBN 0-8133-0112-2 : *NYPL [JLD 85-633]*

Fashagba, S. O. Winds against my people / by S.O. Fashagba. Ilorin : Matanmi, [198-] 57 p. : ill. ; 19 cm.
1. Nigeria - Fiction. I. Title.
NYPL [Sc C 88-353]

Fashoyin, Tayo.
Manpower development and utilization in Nigeria . Lagos, Nigeria , 1986. xiii, 240 p. ; ISBN 978-226-441-5
NYPL [Sc D 88-1077]
Women in the modern sector labour force in Nigeria /. Lagos , 1985. viii, 254 p. ; ISBN 978-301-560-5 *NYPL [Sc D 89-538]*

Fāsī, Muhammad. Africa from the seventh to the eleventh century /. London : Berkeley : xxv, 869 p. : ISBN 0-435-94809-1
NYPL [Sc E 88-384]

FASS, a quarter of a century : a publication of the Faculty of Arts and Social Sciences, Abu, Zaria. Zaria : Ahmadu Bello University Press, 1988. vi, 82 p. ; 25 cm. Includes bibliographical references. ISBN 978-272-500-5
1. Ahmadu Bello University. Faculty of Arts and Social Sciences. *NYPL [Sc E 88-609]*

Fass, Simon M. Political economy in Haiti : the drama of survival / Simon M. Fass. New Brunswick, N.J., U. S.A. : Transaction Books, c1988. xxxi, 369 p. ; 24 cm. Includes index. Bibliography: p. 349-363. ISBN 0-88738-158-8 DDC 338.97294 19
1. Haiti - Economic policy. 2. Haiti - Economic conditions - 1971-. I. Title.
HC153 .F37 1988 *NYPL [Sc E 88-423]*

Faster, higher, further . Blue, Adrianne. London , 1988. ix, 182 p. : ISBN 0-86068-648-5 (pbk.) :
GV721.5 .B58x 1988 *NYPL [Sc E 89-82]*

Fat Albert's survival kit /. Cosby, William H. New York [1975] [30] p. ISBN 0-525-61532-6
PN6281 .C758 *NYPL [JFC 77-191]*

Fate unearthed! . Adeniran, Tunde. [Poems. Selections.] Ibadan , 1982. 71 p. ;
NYPL [Sc C 88-56]

Father E. Olu Coker . Oguntomilade, Jacob I. D. Lagos , 1987. 313 p. : ISBN 978-248-001-0
NYPL [Sc D 89-572]

Father is big. Radlauer, Ruth Shaw. Glendale, Calif. [1967] 1 v. (unpaged)
PZ7.R122 Fat *NYPL [Sc E 88-589]*

FATHERS AND SONS - JUVENILE FICTION.
Radlauer, Ruth Shaw. Father is big. Glendale, Calif. [1967] 1 v. (unpaged)
PZ7.R122 Fat *NYPL [Sc E 88-589]*

FATHERS AND SONS - UNITED STATES.
Teague, Bob. The flip side of soul . New York , c1989. 201 p. ; ISBN 0-688-08260-2 DDC 305.8/96073 19
PS3570.E2 Z495 1989 *NYPL [Sc D 89-303]*

Fatunde, Tunde.
No food, no country / Tunde Fatunde. Benin City, Nigeria : Adena Publishers, 1985. xv, 81 p. ; 19 cm. ISBN 978-249-804-1
1. Land tenure - Nigeria - Drama. I. Title.
NYPL [Sc C 88-342]
Oga na tief-man : a play / Tunde Fatunde. Benin City, Nigeria : Adena Publishers, 1986. xv, 57 p. ; 18 cm. ISBN 978-249-805-X
I. Title. *NYPL [Sc C 88-340]*

FAUNA, PREHISTORIC. see PALEONTOLOGY.

Fauquenoy, Marguerite Saint Jacques. see Saint Jacques Fauquenoy, Marguerite.

Fauset, Jessie Redmon. There is confusion, by Jessie Redmon Fauset. London : Chapman and Hall, 1924. 297 p. 20 cm.
1. Afro-Americans - Fiction. I. Title.
PZ3 .F276.Th *NYPL [Sc Rare C 88-20]*

Faut être nègre pour faire ça ... /. Himes, Chester B., 1909- [Paris, France] , c1986. 223 p. ; ISBN 2-86705-064-2
NYPL [Sc D 88-1447]

Faux-soleils . Runte, Roseann. Sherbrooke, Québec, Canada , 1984. 59 p. ; ISBN 2-89040-312-2 *NYPL [Sc D 88-501]*

Fax,Elton.
Schatz, Letta. Taiwo and her twin /. New York , c1964- 128 p. : *NYPL [Sc E 88-430]*
(illus) Woody, Regina Llewellyn (Jones) Almena's dogs /. New York , c1954. 240 p. :
NYPL [Sc D 88-648]

Faye, Suleymane. Aqatoor a seereer / Suleymaan Fay. Kampala, Ouganda : Bureau linguistique inter-africain de l'OUA, 1986. 67 p. : ill. ; 28 cm. (Publication Bil Oua . no.7) Introduction in Serer and French.
1. Serer language - Orthography and spelling - Glossaries, vocabularies, etc. I. Centre de linguistique appliquée de Dakar. II. Title.
NYPL [Sc F 88-263]

Faye, Waly Coly. Précis grammatical de sérère / Waly Coly Faye. [Dakar] : Centre de linguistique appliquée de Dakar, 1980. 80 leaves ; 30 cm. (Les Langues nationale au Sénégal) Errata slip inserted. Cover title. "No 75." French and Serer.
1. Serer language - Grammar. I. Centre de linguistique appliquée de Dakar. II. Title. III. Series.
NYPL [Sc F 86-168]

FAYETTE COUNTY (TENN.) - SCHOOLS.
Hunt, Frankie L. Cunningham. A history of the desegregation of the Fayette County school system [microform] . 1981. 351 leaves.
NYPL [Sc Micro R-4687]

Fayó, Néstor A. 3333 proverbs in Haitian Creole : the 11th Romance language / Fayo. Port-au-Prince, Haiti : Editions Fardin, [1980?] 428 p. : ill. ; 23 cm. Creole and English.
1. Proverbs, Haitian. 2. Proverbs, Creole - Haiti. I. Title. II. Title: Three thousand three hundred thirty-three proverbs in Haitian Creole.
NYPL [Sc D 86-839]

Fear of the unknown. Kagwema, Prince, 1931- Quo vadis Tanzania . Dar-es-Salaam , c1985. vii, 119 p. ; ISBN 997-691-804-6
NYPL [Sc D 89-11]

February, V. A. (Vernie A.) And bid him sing : essays in literature and cultural domination / Vernon February. London : Kegan Paul International, 1988. xvi, 212 p. : ill., maps ; 23 cm. Includes bibliographies and index. ISBN 0-7103-0278-9 : DDC 306 325/.32 19
1. Culture. 2. African literature. I. Title.
NYPL [Sc D 88-1363]

Federal civil rights acts . Antieau, Chester James. Rochester, N.Y. , San Francisco, Calif. , 1980. 2 v. ; DDC 342.73/085 19
KF4749 .A745 1980 *NYPL [Sc F 83-46]*

FEDERAL GOVERNMENT - AFRICA, EAST.
Rothchild, Donald S. From federalism to neo-federalism in East Africa [microform] /. Nairobi, 1966. 19 leaves.
NYPL [Sc Micro R-4108 no.30]

Federal Republic of Cameroon. see Cameroon.

Federal Republic of Nigeria. see Nigeria.

FEDERAL-STATE RELATIONS. see FEDERAL GOVERNMENT.

FEDERALISM. see FEDERAL GOVERNMENT.

FEDERATED COLORED CATHOLICS OF THE UNITED STATES - HISTORY.
Nickels, Marilyn Wenzke. Black Catholic protest and the Federated Colored Catholics, 1917-1933 . New York , 1988. ix, 325 p. ; ISBN 0-8240-4098-8 (alk. paper) : DDC 282/.73/08996073 19
BX1407.N4 N5 1988 *NYPL [Sc E 89-85]*

Federation of Nigeria. see Nigeria.

FEDERATION OF UNIVERSITY EMPLOYEES.
On strike for respect . Chicago , 1988. 94 p. ;
NYPL [Sc C 89-101]

FEEBLE-MINDED. see MENTALLY HANDICAPPED.

Feelings, Tom. (illus) Schatz, Letta. Bola and the Oba's drummer. New York [1967]. 156 p. DDC [Fic] 19
PZ7.S337 Bo *NYPL [Sc E 89-26]*

FELATA. see FULAHS.

Felber, Monika. Stundenblätter Hansberry " A raisin in the sun" / Monika Felber, Christine Kissker ; [mit] 41 Seiter Beilage. 1. Aufl. Stuttgard : Klett, 1986. 85 p. : ill. ; 23 cm. (Stundenblätter Englisch) A teacher's manual. 41 unbound pages in pocket. Bibliography: p. 85. ISBN 3-12-925163-4
1. Hansberry, Lorraine, 1930-1965. Raisin in the sun. 2. Hansberry, Lorraine, 1930-1965 - Criticism and interpretation. I. Kössler, Christine. II. Title.
NYPL [Sc D 88-631]

FELLANS. see FULAHS.

FELONY. see CRIMINAL LAW.

FEMALE. see WOMEN.

Female genital mutilation, excision and infibulation . Sanderson, Lilian Passmore. London [1986?] 72 p. ; DDC 016.392 19
Z5118.C57 S26 1986 GN484 *NYPL [Sc D 88-1152]*

FEMININITY (PSYCHOLOGY)
Gleason, Judith Illsley. Oya . Boston , 1987. viii, 304 p. : ISBN 0-87773-430-5 (pbk.) : DDC 299/.63 19
BL2480.Y6 G58 1987 *NYPL [Sc D 88-101]*

FEMINISM - AFRICA, SOUTHERN - HISTORY - SOURCES.
Women in development . Gaborone , 1984. 49, 4 p. : *NYPL [Sc F 88-116]*

FEMINISM AND LITERATURE - UNITED STATES.
Black feminist criticism and critical theory /. Greenwood, Fla. , c1988. iii, 202 p. ; ISBN 0-913283-25-8 *NYPL [Sc D 88-1394]*

FEMINISM - DEVELOPING COUNTRIES.
Third World, second sex, vol. 2 /. London, UK , Atlantic Highlands, N.J., USA , 1987. viii, 284 p. ; ISBN 0-86232-752-0 (v. 2) : DDC 305.4/2/091724 19
HQ1870.9 .T48 1987 *NYPL [Sc D 88-931]*

FEMINISM - PSYCHOLOGICAL ASPECTS.
Competition, a feminist taboo? /. New York , 1987. xvi, 260 p. ; ISBN 0-935312-74-9 (pbk.) : DDC 305.4/2 19
HQ1206 .C69 1987 *NYPL [JFE 88-6669]*

FEMINISM - RELIGIOUS ASPECTS - BAPTISTS.
Brooks, Evelyn, 1945- The women's movement in the Black Baptist church, 1880-1920 /. [Rochester, N.Y.] c1984. viii, 342 leaves ;
NYPL [Sc D 88-938]

FEMINISM - RELIGIOUS ASPECTS - CHRISTIANITY.
Biehl, João Guilherme. De igual pra igual .
Petrópolis , São Leopoldo, RS, Brasil , 1987.
155 p. ;
BT83.57 .B54 1987 *NYPL [Sc D 88-1016]*

FEMINIST THEATER.
Making a spectacle . Ann Arbor , c1989. 347
p. : ISBN 0-472-09389-4 (alk. paper) : DDC
812/.54/099287 19
PS338.W6 M3 1989 *NYPL [JFE 89-144]*

FEMINIST THERAPY.
The Psychopathology of everyday racism and
sexism /. New York , c1988. xix, 120 p. ;
ISBN 0-918393-51-5 (pbk.) DDC 305.4/2 19
RC451.4.M58 P79 1988
NYPL [Sc D 89-449]

Une femme dans la lumiére de l'aube . Laleye,
Barnabé. Paris , c1988. 228 p. ;
NYPL [Sc D 88-1407]

Femme du blanchisseur. Zinsou, Sénouvo Agbota,
1946- La tortue qui chante . Paris , 1987. 127
p. ; ISBN 2-218-07842-3 *NYPL [Sc C 88-8]*

Femme et noire en Afrique du Sud /. Kuzwayo,
Ellen. [Call me woman. French.] Paris , c1985.
296, [8] p. of plates : ISBN 2-221-05157-2
NYPL [Sc E 88-315]

Femmes africaines et commerce . Cordonnier,
Rita. Paris , 1987. 190 p. : ISBN 2-85802-901-6
NYPL [Sc E 88-368]

**Femmes et projets de développement rural en
Afrique Sub-Saharienne** . Droy, I. 1985. 557
p. : *NYPL [Sc D 88-778]*

Fenet, Joan. Defize, Stanislas. Histoire de St.
Barth /. [Paris?] , c1987. [60] p. : ISBN
2-9502284-0-2 *NYPL [Sc G 88-29]*

El fenómeno de la posesión en la religión Vudú .
Agosto de Muñoz, Nélida. Río Piedras, P.R. ,
1975, c1974. 119 p. ; DDC 299/.64 19
BL2490 .A33 1975 *NYPL [TB (Caribbean
monograph series no. 14)]*

Fenton, Thomas P. Africa : a directory of
resources / compiled and edited by Thomas P.
Fenton and Mary J. Heffron. Maryknoll, N.Y. :
Orbis Books, c1987. xiv, 144 p. ; 22 cm.
Includes indexes. ISBN 0-88344-542-8
*1. Africa - Bibliography. 2. Africa - Audio-visual aids -
Catalogs. 3. Africa - Societies, etc. - Directories. I.
Heffron, Mary J. II. Title.* *NYPL [Sc D 88-398]*

Fergus, Howard A. Flowers blooming late .
Montserrat , 1984. 72 p. ; ISBN 976-8018-00-3
NYPL [Sc D 89-559]

Ferguson, James, 1956- Papa Doc, Baby Doc :
Haiti and the Duvaliers / James Ferguson.
Oxford, UK ; New York, NY, USA : B.
Blackwell, 1987. x, 171 p., [8] p. of plates : ill.,
map, ; 24 cm. Includes index. Bibliography: p.
[162]-163. ISBN 0-631-15601-1 : DDC 972.94/07
19
*1. Duvalier, François, 1907-1971. 2. Duvalier, Jean
Claude, 1951-. 3. Haiti - History - 1934-1986. I. Title.*
F1928 .F47 1987 *NYPL [Sc E 88-269]*

Ferguson, Moira. Prince, Mary. The history of
Mary Prince, a West Indian slave, related by
herself /. London , New York , 1987. xvi, 124
p. ; ISBN 0-86358-192-7 DDC 305.5/67/0924 B 19
HT869.P6 A3 1987 *NYPL [Sc C 89-31]*

**Feria del Libro (9th: 1967: San Juan, Puerto
Rico)** Programa [microform] : Feria del
Libro, 28 de abril al 14 de mayo de 1967 /
Asociación de Graduadas de la Universidad de
Puerto Rico, Asociación de Maestros de Puerto
Rico. [San Juan : Universidad de Puerto Rico,
1967] 37 p. : ports. ; 22 cm. Cover title.
Microfiche. New York: New York Public Library, 198 .
1 microfiche: negative; 11 x 15 cm. (FSN Sc 019,104)
*1. Book industries and trade - Puerto Rico -
Exhibitions. I. Asociación de Graduadas de la
Universidad de Puerto Rico. II. Asociación de Maestros
de Puerto Rico.* *NYPL [Sc Micro F-11056]*

Fernandes de Oliveira, Mário António. see
Oliveira, Mário António Fernandes de, 1934-

Fernández, Fernando Ortiz. see **Ortiz Fernández,
Fernando, 1881-1969.**

Ferns, George W.
Secondary level teachers: supply and demand in
Liberia [by] George W. Ferns and John W.
Hanson. With a report on a field survey by
Igolima T. D. Amachree and S. Jabaru Carlon.

[East Lansing, Institute for International Studies
in Education, Michigan State University, c1970]
xii, 116 p. 28 cm. (Report on the supply of
secondary level teachers in English-speaking Africa. no.
6) Bibliography: p. 116.
*1. High school teachers - Supply and demand - Liberia.
I. Hanson, John Wagner, joint author. II. Amachree,
Igolima T. D. III. Carlon, S. Jabaru. IV. Title. V. Series.*
LB2833.4.L7 F4 *NYPL [JFM 72-62 no. 6]*

Secondary level teachers: supply and demand in
the Gambia [by] George W. Ferns. [East
Lansing, Institute for International Studies in
Education, Michigan State University, 1969] xi,
78 p. illus. 28 cm. (Report on the supply of
secondary level teachers in English-speaking Africa. no.
2) On cover: Overseas Liaison Committee of the
American Council on Education. Bibliography: p.
[77]-78.
*1. High school teachers - Supply and demand - Gambia.
I. American Council on Education. Overseas Liaison
Committee. II. Title. III. Series.*
LB2833.4.G3 F4 *NYPL [JFM 72-62 no. 2]*

Ferns, George W. (joint author) Hanson, John
Wagner. Secondary level teachers: supply and
demand in Sierra Leone. [East Lansing, c1970]
viii, 85 p. *NYPL [JFM 72-62 no. 11]*

Ferrara, Miriam Nicolau. A imprensa negra
paulista (1915-1963) / Miriam Nicolau Ferrara.
São Paulo : FFLCH-USP, 1986. 279 p. : ill.,
facsims. ; 17 cm. (Antropología. 13) Originally
presented as the author's thesis (master's-- Universidade
de São Paulo, 1981). Bibliography: p. 207-231.
*1. Ethnic press - Brazil - São Paulo. 2. Blacks - Brazil -
São Paulo. I. Series: Antropologia (São Paulo, Brazil) ;
13. II. Title.* *NYPL [Sc B 88-6]*

Ferris, Jeri.
Go free or die : a story about Harriet Tubman
/ by Jeri Ferris ; illustrations by Karen Ritz.
Minneapolis : Carolrhoda House, 1987. 63 p. :
ill. ; 23 cm. (A Carolrhoda creative minds book) A
biography of the black woman whose cruel experiences
as a slave in the South led her to seek freedom in the
North for herself and for others through the
Underground Railroad. SCHOMBURG CHILDREN'S
COLLECTION. ISBN 0-87614-317-6 (lib. bdg.) :
DDC 305.5/67/0924 B 92 19
*1. Tubman, Harriet, 1815?-1913 - Juvenile literature. 2.
Slaves - United States - Biography - Juvenile literature.
3. Afro-Americans - Biography - Juvenile literature. 4.
Underground Railroad - Juvenile literature. I. Ritz,
Karen, ill. II. Schomburg Children's Collection. III.
Title. IV. Series.*
E444.T82 F47 1987 *NYPL [Sc D 88-620]*

Walking the road to freedom : a story about
Sojourner Truth / by Jeri Ferris ; illustrations
by Peter E. Hanson. Minneapolis : Carolrhoda
Books, 1987. 64 p. : ill. ; 23 cm. (A Carolrhoda
creative minds book) Traces the life of the Black
woman orator who spoke out against slavery throughout
New England and the Midwest. SCHOMBURG
CHILDREN'S COLLECTION. ISBN 0-87614-318-4
(lib. bdg.) : DDC 305.5/67/0924 B 92 19
*1. Truth, Sojourner, d. 1883 - Juvenile literature. 2.
Afro-Americans - Biography - Juvenile literature. 3.
Abolitionists - United States - Biography - Juvenile
literature. 4. Social reformers - United States -
Biography - Juvenile literature. I. Hanson, Peter E., ill.
II. Schomburg Children's Collection. III. Title. IV.
Series.*
E185.97.T8 F47 1987 *NYPL [Sc D 88-1046]*

What are you figuring now? : a story about
Benjamin Banneker / by Jeri Ferris ;
illustrations by Amy Johnson. Minneapolis :
Carolrhoda Books, c1988. 64 p. : ill. ; 23 cm.
(A Carolrhoda creative minds book) A biography of the
Afro-American farmer and self-taught mathematician,
astronomer, and surveyor for the new capital city of the
United States in 1791, who also calculated a successful
almanac notable for its preciseness. SCHOMBURG
CHILDREN'S COLLECTION. ISBN 0-87614-331-1
(lib. bdg.) : DDC 520.92/4 B 92 19
*1. Banneker, Benjamin, 1731-1806 - Juvenile literature.
2. Astronomers - United States - Biography - Juvenile
literature. 3. Afro-Americans - United States -
Biography - Juvenile literature. I. Johnson, Amy, ill. II.
Schomburg Children's Collection. III. Title. IV. Series.*
QB36.B22 F47 1988 *NYPL [Sc D 89-120]*

FERROUS METAL INDUSTRIES. see **IRON
INDUSTRY AND TRADE.**

**FERTILITY, HUMAN - AFRICA -
BIBLIOGRAPHY.**
Régulation des naissances en Afrique . Abidjan,

Côte d'Ivoire [1987] 74 p. ;
NYPL [Sc F 88-392]

**FERTILITY, HUMAN - AFRICA, WEST -
CASE STUDIES.**
Sex roles, population and development in West
Africa . London , Portsmouth, N.H. , 1987. xiii,
242 p. ; ISBN 0-435-08022-9 DDC 304.6/0966 19
HB3665.5.A3 S49 1988
NYPL [Sc E 88-318]

FERTILITY, HUMAN - CAMEROON.
Enquête nationale sur la fécondité du
Cameroun, 1978 . [Yaoundé] , 1983. 2 v. in 3 :
DDC 304.6/32/0967113 19
HB1075.4.A3 E66 1983 *NYPL [Sc F 89-51]*

**FERTILITY, HUMAN - CAMEROON -
STATISTICS.**
Enquête nationale sur la fécondité du
Cameroun, 1978 . [Yaoundé] , 1983. 2 v. in 3 :
DDC 304.6/32/0967113 19
HB1075.4.A3 E66 1983 *NYPL [Sc F 89-51]*

FERTILITY, HUMAN - GHANA.
Oppong, Christine. Seven roles of women .
Geneva , 1987. xi, 127 p. :
NYPL [Sc E 89-143]

**FERTILITY, HUMAN - TRINIDAD -
HISTORY - 18TH CENTURY.**
John, A. Meredith. The plantation slaves of
Trinidad, 1783-1816 . Cambridge [Eng.] , New
York , 1988. xvi, 259 p. ; ISBN 0-521-36166-4
DDC 306/.362/0972983 19
HT1105.T6 J65 1988 *NYPL [Sc E 89-235]*

Fest-quest 87, . Davies, William J. Grahamstown,
South Africa , 1988. iv, 161 p. : ISBN
0-86810-165-6 *NYPL [Sc F 88-267]*

Festas populares no Brasil =. Gonzalez, Lélia.
Rio de Janeiro, Brasil, c1987. 144 p. : ISBN
85-7083-015-7
GT4833.A2 G66x 1987 NYPL [Sc F 89-116]

A Festival of Jamaican cuisine / [prepared by
Jamaica Cultural Development's Culinary Arts
Department]. Kingston, Jamaica : The
Department, [1983?] 36 p. : ill. (some col.) ; 22
cm. Cover title. DDC 641.597292 19
*1. Cookery, Jamaican. I. Jamaica Cultural Development
Commission. Culinary Arts Dept.*
TX716.J27 F47 1983 *NYPL [Sc D 88-1074]*

FESTIVALS - BRAZIL.
Gonzalez, Lélia. Festas populares no Brasil =.
Rio de Janeiro, Brasil , c1987. 144 p. : ISBN
85-7083-015-7
GT4833.A2 G66x 1987 *NYPL [Sc F 89-116]*

**FESTIVALS - BRAZIL - PICTORIAL
WORKS.**
Gonzalez, Lélia. Festas populares no Brasil =.
Rio de Janeiro, Brasil , c1987. 144 p. : ISBN
85-7083-015-7
GT4833.A2 G66x 1987 *NYPL [Sc F 89-116]*

**FESTIVALS - CARIBBEAN AREA -
EXHIBITIONS.**
Nunley, John W. (John Wallace), 1945-
Caribbean festival arts . [Saint Louis] , 1988.
218 p. : ISBN 0-295-96702-1 : DDC
394.2/5/07409729 19
GT4823 .N85 1988 *NYPL [Sc F 89-89]*

FESTIVALS - ZAIRE.
Vengroenweghe, Daniel. Bobongo . Berlin ,
c1988. xv, 332 p. : ISBN 3-496-00963-2
NYPL [Sc E 88-343]

FETICIDE. see **ABORTION.**

Fetterman, Marilyn Harer. Ngok Dinka marriage
and cattle transferals [microform] / by Marilyn
Harer Fetterman. Khartoum : Development
Studies and Research Centre, Faculty of
Economic & Social Studies, University of
Khartoum, 1978. 23 leaves ; 28 cm. (Working
report/Abyei Project. no. 5) Microfiche. New York:
New York Public Library, 198 . 1 microfiche: negative;
11 x 15 cm. (FSN Sc 019,058)
*1. Marriage customs and rites - Sudan - Abyei. 2.
Marriage customs and rites, Dinka (Nilotic tribe). I.
Title.* *NYPL [Sc Micro F-11040]*

Fetz, Ingrid.
(illus) Durham, John, fl. 1960- Me and Arch
and the Pest. New York [1970] 96 p. DDC
[Fic]
PZ7.D9335 Me *NYPL [Sc E 88-416]*

Lovelace, Maud Hart, 1892- The valentine box
/. New York , 1966. [48] p. :
PZ7.L9561 Val *NYPL [Sc D 89-115]*

(illus) Molarsky, Osmond. Where the good luck was. New York [1970] 63 p. ISBN 0-8098-1158-8 DDC [Fic]
PZ7.M7317 Wh **NYPL [Sc E 88-552]**

Le feu des origines . Dongala, Emmanuel B. Paris , 1987. 255 p. ; **NYPL [Sc D 87-1396]**

FEUDAL TENURE. see LAND TENURE.

Fiammenghi, Gioia. (illus) Sherlock, Philip Manderson, Sir. The iguana's tail. New York [1969] 97 p. DDC 823 398.2
PZ8.1.S54 Ig **NYPL [Sc D 89-59]**

Fichte, Hubert. Xango / Hubert Fichte. 2. Aufl. Frankfurt am Main : S. Fischer, 1981. 353 p. ; 21 cm. (Die Afroamerikanischen Religionen ; 2 : Bahia, Haiti, Trinidad) Includes bibliographical references. ISBN 3-10-020701-7
I. Series: Afroamerikanischen Religionen , 2. II. Title.
NYPL [Sc D 88-1481]

FIELD SPORTS. see HUNTING; SPORTS.

Field to factory . Crew, Spencer R. Washington, D.C. , 1987. 79 p., [4] p. of plates :
NYPL [Sc F 88-369]

Fielding's literary Africa /. Taylor, Jane. New York, N.Y. , 1988. xv, 506 p. : ISBN 0-688-05071-9 DDC 960 19
DT12.25 .T39 1988 **NYPL [Sc D 88-1361]**

Fields, Julia. The green lion of Zion Street / Julia Fields ; illustrated by Jerry Pinkney. 1st ed. New York : McElderry Books, c1988. [32] p. : col. ill. ; 26 cm. The stone lion on Zion Street, proud and fierce, instills fear and admiration in those who see it in the cold city fog. SCHOMBURG CHILDREN'S COLLECTION. ISBN 0-689-50414-4 DDC [E] 19
1. Lions - Juvenile fiction. 2. Afro-American children - Juvenile fiction. I. Pinkney, Jerry, ill. II. Schomburg Children's Collection. III. Title.
PZ8.3.F458 Gr 1988 **NYPL [Sc F 88-186]**

Fifty great Westindian Test criketers. Dalrymple, Henderson. 50 great Westindian Test cricketers /. London , 1983. xxi, 281 p. : ISBN 0-9506664-4-0 **NYPL [Sc D 88-62]**

Fifty years of Nigerian cooperative movement / edited by M.O. Ijere and Aja Okorie. Nsukka [Nigeria] : Centre for Rural Development and Cooperatives, University of Nigeria, 1986. iii, 64 p. ; 23 cm. Includes bibliographical references.
1. Cooperative societies - Nigeria. 2. Cooperation - Nigeria. I. Ijere, Martin Ohaeri, 1929-. II. Okorie, Aja, 1947-. III. University of Nigeria, Nsukka. Centre for Rural Development and cooperatives. IV. Title.
NYPL [Sc D 88-859]

A fight for honey /. Iroaganachi, John. Lagos, Nigeria , 1977. 30 p. : ISBN 0-410-80181-X
NYPL [Sc C 88-77]

FIGHTING. see WAR; BOXING.

Fighting apartheid : a cartoon history. London : International Defence and Aid Fund for Southern Africa and UNESCO, 1988. 76 p. : ill., ports. ; 21 cm. Includes index. ISBN 0-904759-84-9 (pbk) : DDC 323.1/68 19
1. Apartheid - South Africa - History - Caricatures and cartoons. I. International Defence and Aid Fund. II. Unesco.
DT763 **NYPL [Sc D 88-1092]**

Fighting their own war . Grunlingh, A. M., 1948- Johannesburg , 1987. x, 200 p. ; ISBN 0-86975-321-5 **NYPL [Sc D 88-897]**

The Fighting 99th Air Squadron, 1941-45 /. Johnson, Hayden C. New York , c1987. 49 p. : ISBN 0-533-06879-7 : DDC 940.54/4973 19
D790 .J57 1987 **NYPL [Sc D 88-1192]**

Fignolé, Jean Claude. Les possédés de la pleine lune / Jean-Claude Fignolé. Paris : Seuil, c1987. 220 p. ; 21 cm. Includes glossary of Haitian terms. ISBN 2-02-009535-1
1. Haiti - Fiction. I. Title. **NYPL [JFD 88-532]**

FIGURE DRAWING - STUDY AND TEACHING.
Yajima, Isao, 1945- Mode drawing /. Tokyo, Japan , 1986. 105 p. : ISBN 4-7661-0394-7
NYPL [Sc F 88-238]

Filibert, Elizabeth. Haití bajo la opresión de los Duvalier . Santo Domingo , 1981. 93 p. ; ISBN 968-590-021-3 DDC 972.94/06 19
F1928 .H33 1981 **NYPL [Sc D 89-457]**

Les filles du président . Kimbidima, Julien Omer, 1961- Paris , c1986. 138 p. ; ISBN

2-85802-769-2
MLCS 87/2312 (P) **NYPL [Sc D 88-1083]**

Film and video resources about Africa available from the University of Illinois Film Center /. University of Illinois Film Center. Champaign, Ill. [c1985] 34 p. : DDC 016.96 19
Z3501 .U64 1985 DT3 **NYPL [Sc F 88-335]**

Filmation (Firm) Cosby, William H. Fat Albert's survival kit /. New York [1975] [30] p. : ISBN 0-525-61532-6
PN6281 .C758 **NYPL [JFC 77-191]**

FINANCE, PUBLIC - ST. LUCIA.
St. Lucia. Ministry of Finance. Financial instructions [microform] . St. Lucia [1962?] 24 p. : **NYPL [Sc Micro F-10956]**

Financial instructions [microform] . St. Lucia. Ministry of Finance. St. Lucia [1962?] 24 p. : **NYPL [Sc Micro F-10956]**

FINE ARTS. see ART; ARTS.

Fine Arts Museums of San Francisco. Forms and forces . San Francisco , c1988. 53 p. : ISBN 0-88401-057-0 (pbk) **NYPL [Sc F 88-330]**

Finkelman, Paul, 1949- Slave rebels, abolitionists, and southern courts . New York , 1988. 2 v. : ISBN 0-8240-6721-5 (set : alk. paper) : DDC 342.75/0872 347.502872 19
KF4545.S5 A5 1987b **NYPL [Sc D 88-1263]**

Finn, Julio.
The bluesman : the musical heritage of Black men and women in the Americas / Julio Finn ; illustrations by Willa Woolston. London ; New York : Quartet Books, 1986. 256 p., [8] p. of plates : ill. ; 24 cm. Includes index. Bibliography: p. 239-246. ISBN 0-7043-2523-3
1. Blues (Songs, etc.) - History and criticism. 2. Spirituals (Songs) - History and criticism. 3. Afro-Americans - Music - History and criticism. I. Title. **NYPL [Sc E 88-181]**

Voices of négritude : with an anthology of négritude poems translated from the French, Portuguese and Spanish / Julio Finn. London ; NewYork : Quartet, 1988. 246 p. ; 24 cm. Includes bibliographical references and index.
1. Literature - Black authors - History and criticism. 2. Literature - Black authors. I. Title.
NYPL [Sc E 88-494]

Finnegan, William.
Dateline Soweto : travels with black South African reporters / William Finnegan.1st ed. New York : Harper & Row, c1988. x. 244 p. : maps ; 25 cm. Includes index. ISBN 0-06-015932-4 : DDC 070/.92/4 B 19
1. Finnegan, William - Journeys - South Africa - Soweto. 2. Journalists - United States - Biography. 3. Journalists - South Africa - Biography. 4. Apartheid - South Africa - Soweto. 5. Riots - South Africa - Soweto. 6. Soweto (Africa) - Social conditions. I. Title.
PN4874.F45 A3 1989 **NYPL [JFE 88-2005]**

FINNEGAN, WILLIAM - JOURNEYS - SOUTH AFRICA - SOWETO.
Finnegan, William. Dateline Soweto . New York , c1988. x. 244 p. : ISBN 0-06-015932-4 : DDC 070/.92/4 B 19
PN4874.F45 A3 1989 **NYPL [JFE 88-2005]**

Fino, Maria Antonietta Barbareschi. see Barbareschi Fino, Maria Antonietta.

Fire came to the earth people . Roth, Susan L. New York , 1988, c1987. [32] p. ; ISBN 0-312-01723-5 : DDC 398.2/0966/83 E 19
PZ8.1.R73 Fi 1987 **NYPL [Sc F 89-140]**

Fire music . Backus, Rob, 1946- Chicago, Ill. , 1976. vii, 104 p. : ISBN 0-917702-00-X
NYPL [Sc D 88-337]

FIRMIN, ANTÉNOR, 1851-1911.
Péan, Marc. L'échec du firminisme /. Port-au-Prince, Haiti , 1987. 181 p. :
NYPL [Sc D 88-625]

First five year plan, 1963-1967. Somalia. Planning and Coordinating Committee for Economic and Social Development. Mogadiscio, 1963. xi, 162 p.
HC567.S7 A5 **NYPL [Sc E 88-70]**

The First five years of Dr. Samuel Kanyon Doe : a catalog of achievements. Monrovia, Liberia : Ministry of Information, Capital Hill, [1985] v, 72 p. : port. ; 21 cm. Addendum-appendix B, A brief historical diary (2 p.) inserted at end. DDC 966.6/203 19

1. Liberia - Politics and government - 1980-.
JQ3922 .F57 1985 **NYPL [Sc D 88-872]**

First National City Bank. Economics Dept.
Profile of a city. Prepared by members of the Economics Dept. Introd. by Nathan Glazer. New York, McGraw Hill [1972] x, 273 p. illus. 25 cm. Includes bibliographical references. ISBN 0-07-021066-7
1. Afro-Americans - New York (City). 2. New York (City) - Economic conditions. 3. New York (City) - Social conditions. I. Title.
HC108.N7 F57 **NYPL [Sc 309.174-F]**

First pink light /. Greenfield, Eloise. New York , c1976. [39] p. : ISBN 0-690-01087-7 DDC [E]
PZ7.G845 Fi **NYPL [Sc D 89-60]**

The first shall be last [microform] . Reilly, John Terrence, 1945. 1977. 198 leaves.
NYPL [Sc Micro R-4702]

The first Walter Rodney memorial lecture, 1985 /. Ngugi Wa Thiong'o, 1938- London , 1987. 12 p. : **NYPL [Sc Rare C 88-67]**

The first wave . Drake, William. New York , London , c1987. xxi, 314 p., [8] p. of plates : ISBN 0-02-533490-5 : DDC 811/.52/099287 19
PS151 .D7 1987 **NYPL [JFD 87-7537]**

Fischer, Erling Gunnar. Peter är barnvakt / [av Erling Gunnar Fischer]. Stockholm : Nordisk Rotogravyr, 1961. [40] p. : col. ill. ; 30 cm. SCHOMBURG CHILDREN'S COLLECTION.
1. Elephants - Juvenile fiction. I. Schomburg Children's Collection. II. Title. **NYPL [Sc F 88-261]**

Fischer, Howard E. Johnson, Glenderlyn. Black American pioneers . New York, N.Y. , c1987. ii, 22 p. : **NYPL [Sc D 88-1284]**

FISH, HAMILTON, 1808-1893.
Sumner, Charles, 1811-1874. "He, being dead, yet speaketh" . Boston , New York , 1878. 29, 16 p. ; **NYPL [Sc Rare C 89-4]**

FISH TRADE - SENEGAL - SAINT-LOUIS.
Bonnardel, Régine. Vitalité de la petite pêche tropicale . Paris , 1985. 104 p. : ISBN 2-222-03678-X **NYPL [Sc F 88-329]**

FISH TRADE - ZIMBABWE.
Bouedillon, M. F. C. Studies of fishing on Lake Kariba /. [Harare] , 1985. 185 p. :
NYPL [Sc D 88-875]

Fisher, Aileen Lucia, 1906-
Animal jackets, by Aileen Fisher. Designed and illustrated by Muriel Wood. Lettering by Paul Taylor. [Glendale, Calif.] Bowmar [1973] 43 p. col. illus. 29 cm. (Bowmar nature series) Compares in rhyme the coats people wear to the coverings of a variety of animals. SCHOMBURG CHILDREN'S COLLECTION. ISBN 0-8372-0861-0 DDC [E]
1. Animals - Juvenile poetry. I. Wood, Muriel, illus. II. Schomburg Children's Collection. III. Title.
PZ8.3.F634 Ap **NYPL [Sc F 88-87]**

A lantern in the window / by Aileen Fisher ; illustrated by Harper Johnson. 1st Cadmus ed. Eau Claire, Wisconsin : E.M. Hale, [1962] 126 p. : ill. ; 23 cm. Twelve-year-old Peter goes to live with his Quaker uncle whose farm on the bank of the Ohio River gives him a view of the steamboats he loves and a role in the Underground Railroad. SCHOMBURG CHILDREN'S COLLECTION.
I. Johnson, E. Harper, illus. II. Schomburg Children's Collection. III. Title. **NYPL [Sc D 88-434]**

Seeds on the go / by Aileen Fisher ; designed and illustrated by Hans Zander ; lettering by Paul Taylor. [Los Angeles] : Bowmar, c1977. 43 p. : col. ill. ; 29 cm. (Bowmar nature series) Rhyming text and illustrations describe how seeds travel. SCHOMBURG CHILDREN'S COLLECTION. ISBN 0-8372-2400-4 DDC 582/.01/6
1. Seeds - Dispersal - Juvenile literature. I. Zander, Hans, 1937-. II. Schomburg Children's Collection. III. Title.
QK929 .F57 **NYPL [Sc F 88-344]**

Fisher, Maxine P., 1948- Women in the Third World / by Maxine P. Fisher. New York : F. Watts, 1989. 176 p. : ill. ; 24 cm. Includes index. Examines the lifestyles of women born and raised in developing nations, focusing on their education, employment, marriage, and family life. Bibliography: p. 171-172. ISBN 0-531-10666-7 DDC 305.4/09172/4 19
1. Women - Developing countries - Social conditions - Juvenile literature. 2. Poor women - Developing countries - Juvenile literature. 3. Women - Developing countries - Social conditions. 4. Developing countries -

Social conditions. I. Title.
HQ1870.9 .F57 1989   *NYPL [Sc E 89-223]*

Fisher, Walter. Ideas for Black studies; the
Morgan State College program. Baltimore,
Morgan State College Press, 1971. vii, 51 p.
illus. 23 cm.
*1. Afro-Americans - Study and teaching - Maryland -
Baltimore. I. Maryland. Morgan State College,
Baltimore. II. Title.*
E184.7 .F53   *NYPL [Sc 917.306-F]*

FISHERIES - SENEGAL - SAINT-LOUIS.
Bonnardel, Régine. Vitalité de la petite pêche
tropicale . Paris , 1985. 104 p. : ISBN
2-222-03678-X   *NYPL [Sc F 88-329]*

FISHING - ZIMBABWE.
Bouedillon, M. F. C. Studies of fishing on Lake
Kariba /. [Harare] , 1985. 185 p. :
NYPL [Sc D 88-875]

Fitch, Lynne. (joint author) Fitch, Robert Beck,
1938- Right on Dellums! Mankato, Minn.
[1971] [47] p. ISBN 0-87191-079-9 DDC
329/.023/79405
JK1978 .F53   *NYPL [Sc F 88-338]*

Fitch, Robert Beck, 1938- Right on Dellums! My
dad goes to Congress. Photos and text by Bob
and Lynne Fitch. Edited by Paul J. Deegan.
Mankato, Minn., Creative Educational Society
[1971] [47] p. illus. 28 cm. "An Amecus Street
book." After a long campaign, eight-year-old Brandy
Dellums' father is elected as the first black
Congressman from Berkeley, California, and the family
moves to Washington, D.C. SCHOMBURG
CHILDREN'S COLLECTION. ISBN 0-87191-079-9
DDC 329/.023/79405
*1. Dellums, Ronald V., 1935-. 2. Elections - United
States - Juvenile literature. I. Fitch, Lynne, joint author.
II. Schomburg Children's Collection. III. Title.*
JK1978 .F53   *NYPL [Sc F 88-338]*

Fitts, Hervey. Abraham Vest, or, The cast-off
restored. A true narrative. Boston, J. Putnam,
1847. 142 p. illus. 16 cm. Preface signed: Hervey
Fitts, Wm. C. Richards. Identified in 1847 as the lost
child, John Negus Wilson, b.1813. Includes description
of the Kindness of a black prostitute.
*1. Vest, Abraham, b.1813. 2. Abandoned children -
United States - Biography. I. Richards, William C., joint
author. II. Title. III. Title: The cast-off restored.*
T275.V55 F5 1847 *NYPL [Sc Rare C 88-12]*

FITZGERALD, ELLA.
Kliment, Bud. Ella Fitzgerald /. New York ,
c1988. 112 p. : ISBN 1-555-46586-2 DDC 784.5
B 19
ML420.F52 K6 1988   *NYPL [Sc E 88-611]*

Fitzwilliam Museum. Bourriau, Janine. Pharaohs
and mortals . Cambridge [Cambridgeshire] ;
New York : vi, 167 p. : ISBN 0-521-35319-X
DDC 709/.32/07402659 19
N5336.G7 C3634 1988
NYPL [3-MAE 88-2748]

Fitzwilliam Museum publications.
Bourriau, Janine. Pharaohs and mortals .
Cambridge [Cambridgeshire] ; New York : vi,
167 p. : ISBN 0-521-35319-X DDC
709/.32/07402659 19
N5336.G7 C3634 1988
NYPL [3-MAE 88-2748]

Five friends at school /. Buckley, Peter. New
York , c1966. 96 p. :   *NYPL [Sc E 88-590]*

The five prayers step by step /. Karim, Darnell.
[Chicago] [1987] vi, 202 p. :
NYPL [Sc F 89-160]

Os flagelados do vento leste /. Lopes, Manuel.
Lisboa , c1985. 216 p. ;
NYPL [Sc D 88-1387]

FLAGS - HAITI - HISTORY.
Saint-Juste, Laurore. Les Couleurs du drapeau
National, 1803-1986 /. [Port-au-Prince, Haiti?]
1988. 32 p. :   *NYPL [Sc D 88-1440]*

Flamingo and other plays /. Sowande, Bode.
Harlow, Essex , 1986. 183 p. ; ISBN
0-582-78630-4   *NYPL [Sc C 88-89]*

Flash crioulo sobre o sangue e o sonho /. Cuti,
1951- Belo Horizonte, MG , 1987. 57 p. ;
NYPL [Sc D 88-1289]

Fleming, Elizabeth P. The Takula tree. Illustrated
by Robert Jefferson. Philadelphia, Westminster
Press, 1964. 175 p. ill. 22 cm. SCHOMBURG
CHILDREN'S COLLECTION.
1. Missionaries - Africa - Juvenile fiction. 2. Africa -

Juvenile fiction. I. Schomburg Children's Collection. II.
Title.
PZ7.F5995 Tak   *NYPL [Sc D 88-508]*

Fleming, Josianne. Nature, I love you . [St.
Martin] , c1983. 36 p. :
MLCS 86/1723 (P)   *NYPL [Sc D 88-626]*

Fletcher, George P. A crime of self-defense :
Bernhard Goetz and the law on trial / George
P. Fletcher. New York : Free Press ; London :
Collier Macmillan, c1988. xi, 253 p. ; 25 cm.
Includes bibliographical references and index. ISBN
0-02-910311-8 DDC 345.73/04 347.3054 19
*1. Goetz, Bernhard Hugo, 1947- - Trials, litigation, etc.
2. Trials (Assault and battery) - New York (N.Y.). 3.
Self-defense (Law) - United States. I. Title.*
KF224.G63 F54 1988   *NYPL [JLE 88-4737]*

Fletcher, Marvin. America's first Black general :
Benjamin O. Davis, Sr., 1880-1970 / Marvin E.
Fletcher ; with a foreword by Benjamin O.
Davis, Jr. Lawrence, Kan. : University Press of
Kansas, c1989. xix, 226 p. : ill. ; 23 cm. Includes
index. Bibliography: p. 211-218. ISBN 0-7006-0381-6
(alk. paper) DDC 355/.008996073 B 19
*1. Davis, Benjamin O., 1880-1970. 2. United States.
Army - Biography. 3. United States. Army -
Afro-American troops. 4. Afro-American generals -
Biography. I. Title.*
U53.D38 F57 1988   *NYPL [Sc D 89-276]*

**Un Flibustier français dans la mer des Antilles
en 1618-1620 /** manuscrit inédit du début du
XVIIe siècle / publiée par Jean-Pierre Moreau.
Clamart [France] : Editions J.-P. Moreau,
c1987. 263 p. : map ; 24 cm. (Collection d'histoire
maritime et d'archéologie sous-marine) "Manuscrit
inédit de la Bibliothèque Inguimbertine de Carpentras, n°
590 (L. 595)." T.p. verso. Original title of manuscript:
Relation d'un voyage infortuné fait aux Indes
Occidentales par le capitaine Fleury avec la description
de quelques îles qu'on rencontre, recueilie par l'un de
ceux de la compagnie qui fit le voyage, 1618-1620.
Bibliography: p. [257]-259. ISBN 2-9502053-0-5
*1. Carib Indians - Social life and customs. 2. West
Indies - Description and travel - Early works to 1800.
3. West Indies - Discovery and exploration. I. Moreau,
Jean-Pierre. II. Bibliothèque inguimbertine de
Carpentras. III. Title: Relation d'un voyage infortuné
fait aux Indes Occidentales par le capitaine Fleury. IV.
Series.*
NYPL [Sc E 88-247]

Flight and integration . Bulcha, Mekuria.
Uppsala, Sweden , c1988. 256 p. : ISBN
91-7106-279-3   *NYPL [Sc E 88-581]*

**FLIGHT TO THE MOON. see SPACE
FLIGHT TO THE MOON.**

Flights and dancers . Blacke-Bragg, Norma. South
Windsor, Conn. , 1978. vii, 101 p. ;
NYPL [Sc F 89-11]

The flip side of soul . Teague, Bob. New York ,
c1989. 201 p. ; ISBN 0-688-08260-2 DDC
305.8/96073 19
PS3570.E2 Z495 1989   *NYPL [Sc D 89-303]*

The flogging of Phinehas McIntosh . Crowder,
Michael, 1934- New Haven , 1988. xii, 248 p. :
ISBN 0-300-04098-9 DDC 968/.1103 19
DT791 .C76 1988   *NYPL [Sc E 88-289]*

**Floraison d'or ; Raisins amers ; Raison de croire
/.** Sachy. [Haiti? , 1987] (Port-au-Prince, Haïti :
Impr. II) 160 p. ;
MLCS 88/02114 (P) *NYPL [Sc D 88-1108]*

Florida Agricultural and Mechanical University.
Black student retention in higher education /.
Springfield, Ill., U. S.A. , 1988. xvi, 111 p. :
ISBN 0-398-05477-0 DDC 378/.198/2 19
LC2781 .B465 1988   *NYPL [Sc F 89-139]*

**FLORIDA - EMIGRATION AND
IMMIGRATION.**
Icart, Jean-Claude. Négriers d'eux-mêmes .
Montréal, Québec, Canada , 1987. 188 p. :
ISBN 2-920862-06-5   *NYPL [Sc D 88-396]*

**Florida - History - Seminole Wars, 1817-1858.
see Seminole War, 2d, 1835-1842.**

FLORIDA - HISTORY - FICTION.
Douglas, Marjory Stoneman. Freedom river:
Florida, 1845. New York [1953] 264 p. :
NYPL [Sc D 89-267]

FLORIDA - JUVENILE FICTION.
Ball, Dorothy Whitney. Hurricane. Indianapolis
[c1964] 147 p. :   *NYPL [Sc D 88-486]*

Kendall, Lace. Rain boat /. New York , 1965.
159 p. :   *NYPL [Sc D 88-472]*

**Florida. University, Gainesville.
University of Florida monographs. Social
sciences.**
(no. 72) Dirks, Robert, 1942- The Black
Saturnalia . Gainesville , c1987. xvii, 228 p.,
[7] p. of plates : ISBN 0-8130-0843-3 (pbk. : alk.
paper) : DDC 394.2/68282/09729 19
GT4987.23 .D57 1987
NYPL [L-10 5328 no.72]

**FLORIDA WAR, 1835-1842. see SEMINOLE
WAR, 2D, 1835-1842.**

Flower, Ken.
Serving secretly : an intelligence chief on
record : Rhodesia into Zimbabwe, 1964 to 1981
/ Ken Flower. London : J. Murray, c1987. xxii,
330 p., [12] p. of plates : ill., maps, ports. ; 24
cm. Includes bibliographical references and index.
ISBN 0-7195-4438-6
*1. Flower, Ken. 2. Intelligence service -
Zimbabwe - History. 3. Zimbabwe - Politics and
government - 1965-1979. 4. Zimbabwe - History -
1965-1980. I. Title.*   *NYPL [JFE 88-5776]*

FLOWER, KEN - BIOGRAPHY.
Flower, Ken. Serving secretly . London , c1987.
xxii, 330 p., [12] p. of plates : ISBN
0-7195-4438-6   *NYPL [JFE 88-5776]*

Flowers, A. R. De mojo blues : de quest of
HighJohn de conqueror / A.R. Flowers.1st ed.
New York : E.P. Dutton, 1986, c1985. 216 p. ;
22 cm. ISBN 0-525-24376-3 : DDC 813/.54 19
*1. Afro-Americans - Fiction. 2. Vietnamese Conflict,
1961-1975 - Fiction. I. Title.*
PS3556.L598 D4 1986   *NYPL [JFD 86-3984]*

Flowers blooming late : poems from Montserrat /
edited with an introduction by Howard A.
Fergus. Montserrat : University Centre,
University of the West Indies, 1984. 72 p. ; 23
cm. "Published to celebrate the one hundred and
fiftieth anniversary of emancipation 1834-1984." ISBN
976-8018-00-3
*1. Caribbean poetry (English). I. Fergus, Howard A. II.
Title: Poems from Montserrat.*
NYPL [Sc D 89-559]

Fluchere, Henri André, 1914- (illus) Watson, Jane
(Werner) 1915- The Niger: Africa's river of
mystery. Champaign, Ill. [1971] 96 p. ISBN
0-8116-6374-4 DDC 916.6/2
DT360 .W38   *NYPL [Sc E 88-415]*

Fluker, Walter E., 1951- They looked for a city :
a comparative analysis of the ideal of
community in the thought of Howard Thurman
and Martin Luther King, Jr. / Walter E. Fluker.
Lanham, MD : University Press of America,
c1989. xiv, 281 p. ; 22 cm. Bibliography: p.
261-281. ISBN 0-8191-7262-6 (alk. paper) DDC
307/.092/2 19
*1. Thurman, Howard, 1900-1981 - Views on
community. 2. King, Martin Luther, Jr., 1929-1968 -
Views on community. 3. Sociology, Christian (Baptist) -
History of doctrines - 20th century. 4. Afro-American
Baptists - Doctrines - History - 20th century. I. Title.*
BX6447 .F57 1988   *NYPL [Sc D 89-492]*

Flying high /. Webb, Spud. New York , c1988.
xv, 208 p., [16] p. of plates : ISBN
0-06-015820-4 : DDC 796.32/3/0924 B 19
GV884.W35 A3 1988   *NYPL [Sc D 89-375]*

Flynn, Joyce. Bonner, Marita, 1899-1971. Frye
Street & environs . Boston , c1987. xxix, 286
p. ; ISBN 0-8070-6300-2 DDC 810/.8/0896073 19
PS3503 .O439 1987   *NYPL [Sc D 88-683]*

Fock, Georg, 1867- Taschenbuch für
Südwestafrika, 1909 /. Berlin , 1909. xviii, 495,
60 p., [4] fold. leaves of plates :
NYPL [Sc B 89-24]

Focus on the Caribbean / edited by Manfred
Görlach and John A. Holm. Amsterdam ;
Philadelphia : J. Benjamins Pub. Co., 1986. ix,
209 p. : ill. ; 22 cm. (Varieties of English around the
world, 0172-7362. General series ; v. 8) Includes
bibliographies. ISBN 90-272-4866-4 (pbk. : alk.
paper) : DDC 427/.9729 19
*1. Creole dialects, English - Caribbean Area. 2. English
language - Caribbean Area. I. Görlach, Manfred. II.
Holm, John A. III. Series.*
PM7874.C27 F6 1986   *NYPL [JFD 87-3902]*

Focus on the early learner. Ampene, Esther C.
Accra-North , 1987. viii, 65 p. : ISBN
996-490-189-5   *NYPL [Sc D 88-1383]*

Folies, mythes et magies d'Afrique noire .

Bastien, Christine. Paris , 1988. 230 p. ; ISBN 2-7384-0038-8 *NYPL [Sc D 89-191]*

FOLK ART - CATALOGS.
Volkstümliche Künste . Reinbek , c1986/87. 135 p. : *NYPL [Sc D 89-238]*

FOLK ART - SOUTHERN STATES - EXHIBITIONS.
Baking in the sun . Lafayette , c1987. 146 p. : ISBN 0-295-96606-8 *NYPL [Sc F 88-197]*

FOLK COSTUME. see COSTUME.

FOLK DANCING - AFRICA, WEST.
Cheska, Alyce Taylor. Traditional games and dances in West African nations /. Schorndorf , 1987. 136 p. : ISBN 3-7780-6411-8 (pbk.) DDC 793.3/1966 19
GV1713.A358 C48 1987
NYPL [JFE 87-5517]

FOLK LITERATURE, AFRICAN.
Kam, Sié Alain. Cours de littérature orale . [Ouagadougou] [1988?] 1 v. (various pagings) : *NYPL [Sc F 89-118]*

FOLK LITERATURE, AFRICAN - AFRICA, WEST.
Afrikanische Fabeln und Mythen /. Frankfurt am Main , New York , c1987. vi, 233 p. ; ISBN 3-8204-8641-0 DDC 398.2/0966 19
GR350.3 .A35 1987 *NYPL [JFD 88-8333]*

FOLK LITERATURE, AFRICAN - CONGRESSES.
La Tradition orale, source de la littérature contemporaine en Afrique . Dakar , c1984. 201 p. : ISBN 2-7236-0899-9 *NYPL [Sc E 89-55]*

FOLK LITERATURE, FRENCH - SEYCHELLES.
Contes, devinettes et jeux de mots des Seychelles =. [Le-Mée-sur-Seine] [Paris] , c1983. 157 p. : ISBN 2-86427-018-8 DDC 398.2/0969/6 19
GR360.S44 C66 1983 *NYPL [Sc D 88-583]*

FOLK LITERATURE, GANDA (AFRICAN PEOPLE)
Kalibala, E. Balintuma. Wakaima and the clay man . New York , 1946. 145 p. : *NYPL [Sc D 89-486]*

FOLK LITERATURE - MADAGASCAR.
Ottino, Paul. L'étrangère intime . Paris, France c1986. 2 v. (xxvii, 630 p.) : ISBN 2-88124-095-X (set) DDC 398/.0969/1 19
GR357 .O88 1986 *NYPL [Sc D 88-1203]*

FOLK LITERATURE, SHONA.
Shona folk tales . Gweru, Zimbabwe , 1987. 151 p. ; *NYPL [Sc C 88-317]*

FOLK-LORE, BLACK - BRAZIL.
Sales, Niveo Ramos. Receitas de feitiços e encantos afro-brasileiros /. Rio de Janeiro , 1982. 75 p. ; *NYPL [JFD 84-750]*

FOLK-LORE - MADAGASCAR.
Ireny lovantsofina ireny [microform] /. Tananarive [1978] iv, 48 p. ; *NYPL [Sc Micro F-10987]*

FOLK-LORE, MEDICAL. see FOLK MEDICINE.

FOLK MEDICINE - NIGERIA - FORMULAE, RECEIPTS, PRESCRIPTIONS.
Warren, Dennis M. Yoruba medicines /. Legon , 1971 [i.e. 1973] iii, 93, xii, p. ; DDC 615.8/99 19
DT515.45.Y67 W37 1973
NYPL [Sc G 88-34]

FOLK MUSIC - AFRICA - HISTORY AND CRITICISM.
Muzyka narodov Azii i Afriki /. Moskva , 1969- v. :
ML3740 .M9 *NYPL [Sc D 89-470]*

FOLK MUSIC - AFRICA, WEST - HISTORY AND CRITICISM.
Chester, Galina. The silenced voice . London , 1987. 47 p. : ISBN 0-9512093-0-2 : *NYPL [Sc D 89-519]*

FOLK MUSIC - ASIA - HISTORY AND CRITICISM.
Muzyka narodov Azii i Afriki /. Moskva , 1969- v. :
ML3740 .M9 *NYPL [Sc D 89-470]*

FOLK MUSIC - CAMEROON.
Colombel, Véronique. Les Ouldémés du Nord-Cameroun . Paris , 1987. [13]-74 p., [61]

p. of plates : ISBN 2-85297-199-2
NYPL [Sc E 89-244]

FOLK MUSIC - CUBA - HISTORY AND CRITICISM.
Ortiz Fernández, Fernando, 1881-1969. Los bailes y el teatro de los negros en el folklore de Cuba /. Habana, Cuba , 1981. 602 p. : *NYPL [JME 82-163]*

FOLK MUSIC - IVORY COAST.
La Chanson populaire en Côte-d'Ivoire . Paris , c1986. 342 p., [12] p. of plates : ISBN 2-7087-0470-2 *NYPL [Sc D 88-1099]*

Folk music of Kenya /. Senoga-Zake, George W. Nairobi, Kenya , 1986. 185 p. : *NYPL [Sc D 88-368]*

FOLK MUSIC - UNITED STATES - HISTORY AND CRITICISM.
Lovell, John, 1907- Black song . New York , 1986, c1972. xviii, 686 p. : ISBN 0-913729-53-1 (pbk.) DDC 783.6/7/09 19
ML3556 .L69 1986 *NYPL [Sc D 88-421]*

FOLK POETRY, AMERICAN - AFRO-AMERICAN AUTHORS - HISTORY AND CRITICISM.
Tracy, Steven C. (Steven Carl), 1954- Langston Hughes & the blues /. Urbana , c1988. xiii, 305 p. ; ISBN 0-252-01457-X (alk. paper) DDC 818/.5209 19
PS3515.U274 Z8 1988 *NYPL [Sc E 88-506]*

FOLK-SONGS, ENGLISH - TEXAS - COMMERCE - HISTORY AND CRITICISM.
Pearson, Boyce Neal. A cantometric analysis of three Afro-American songs recorded in the Commerce, Texas, area [microform] /. 1978. 47 leaves. *NYPL [Sc Micro R-4701]*

FOLK-SONGS, ENGLISH - UNITED STATES - HISTORY AND CRITICISM.
Lovell, John, 1907- Black song . New York , 1986, c1972. xviii, 686 p. : ISBN 0-913729-53-1 (pbk.) DDC 783.6/7/09 19
ML3556 .L69 1986 *NYPL [Sc D 88-421]*

FOLK-SONGS - KENYA - HISTORY AND CRITICISM.
Senoga-Zake, George W. Folk music of Kenya /. Nairobi, Kenya , 1986. 185 p. : *NYPL [Sc D 88-368]*

FOLK-SONGS, KISSI.
Kissi stories and songs /. Freetown , 1987. 95 p. : *NYPL [Sc D 89-459]*

FOLK-SONGS, NUER - SUDAN - HISTORY AND CRITICISM.
Cleaned the crocodile's teeth . Greenfield Center, N.Y. , c1985. ix, 104 p. : ISBN 0-912678-63-1 (pbk.) DDC 784.4/9669 19
PL8576.N47 C54 1985 *NYPL [Sc D 88-743]*

FOLK-SONGS, NUER - SUDAN - TEXTS.
Cleaned the crocodile's teeth . Greenfield Center, N.Y. , c1985. ix, 104 p. : ISBN 0-912678-63-1 (pbk.) DDC 784.4/9669 19
PL8576.N47 C54 1985 *NYPL [Sc D 88-743]*

FOLK-SONGS - WEST INDIES - TEXTS.
Clarke, A. M. Verses for emancipation . [Port of Spain , 1986] 41 p. ; DDC 811 19
PR9272.9.C53 V4 1986
NYPL [Sc D 88-981]

FOLK-TALES. see FOLK LITERATURE; LEGENDS; TALES.

Folk-tales from Igboland / collected and translated by Priscilla Ngozi Oguine. Ibadan, Nigeria : Evans Bros., 1986. 90 p. ; 22 cm. ISBN 978-16-7467-9
1. Tales - Nigeria. 2. Igbo (African people) - Folklore. I. Oguine, Priscilla Ngozi. *NYPL [Sc D 88-758]*

Folk tales of East Africa /. Sharma, Veena. New Delhi , c1987. vii, 113 p. : ISBN 81-207-0228-X *NYPL [Sc D 88-781]*

FOLKLORE - AFRICA, WEST.
Aardema, Verna. Princess Gorilla and a new kind of water . New York , 1988. [32] p. : ISBN 0-8037-0412-7 : DDC 398.2/0966 E 19
PZ8.1.A213 Pr 1987 *NYPL [Sc F 88-133]*

Folklore and development in the Sudan .
Folklore and National Development Symposium (1981 : Khartoum, Sudan) Khartoum, 1985. 272 p. :
GR355.8 .F65 1981 *NYPL [Sc E 88-333]*

Folklore and National Development Symposium (1981 : Khartoum, Sudan) Folklore and development in the Sudan : part of the proceedings of the Folklore and National Development Symposium held by the Department of Folklore in Khartoum, 2-5 Feb., 1981 / edited by Aḥmad 'Abd al-Raḥīm Naṣr. Khartoum : Institute of African and Asian Studies, University of Khartoum, 1985. 272 p. : ill., map ; 24 cm. (Sudan library series . 13) English and Arabic. Includes bibliographies and index.
1. Folklore - Sudan. 2. Applied folklore - Sudan. 3. Rural development - Sudan. 4. Sudan - Social life and customs. 5. Sudan - Social conditions. I. Naṣr, Aḥmad 'Abd al-Raḥīm. II. Jāmi'at al-Kharṭūm. Shu'bat al-Fūlklūr. III. Series: Sudanese library series ; no. 13. IV. Title.
GR355.8 .F65 1981 *NYPL [Sc E 88-333]*

FOLKLORE - BAHAMAS.
McCartney, Timothy O. Ten, ten the Bible ten . Nassau, Bahamas , c1976. 192 p. : *NYPL [Sc E 88-425]*

FOLKLORE - BURUNDI.
Vansina, Jan. La légende du passé . Tervuren, Belgique , 1972. ix, 257 p. : *NYPL [Sc F 88-193]*

FOLKLORE - CUBA.
Cabrera, Lydia. Supersticiones y buenos consejos . Miami, Fla. , 1987. 62 p. ; ISBN 0-89729-433-5 *NYPL [Sc D 89-522]*

Valdés-Cruz, Rosa. Lo ancestral africano en la narrativa de Lydia Cabrera /. Barcelona , 1974. 113 p. : ISBN 84-346-0082-X :
PQ7389.C22 Z94 *NYPL [Sc D 89-36]*

FOLKLORE - GHANA.
Appiah, Peggy. Tales of an Ashanti father /. Boston , 1989, c1967. 156 p. : ISBN 0-8070-8312-7 DDC 398.2/1/09667 19
PZ8.1.A647 Tal 1989 *NYPL [Sc E 89-87]*

FOLKLORE IN LITERATURE.
Tracy, Steven C. (Steven Carl), 1954- Langston Hughes & the blues /. Urbana , c1988. xiii, 305 p. ; ISBN 0-252-01457-X (alk. paper) DDC 818/.5209 19
PS3515.U274 Z8 1988 *NYPL [Sc E 88-506]*

FOLKLORE - LIBERIA.
Dorsinville, Roger. Les contes de la forêt atlantique /. Alger , 1986. 84 p. ; *NYPL [Sc D 89-171]*

FOLKLORE - SENEGAL.
Diop, Adja Khady, 1922- Le Sénégal d'hier et ses traditions /. [S.l.] [198-?] 61, 18 p. : *NYPL [Sc D 88-933]*

FOLKLORE - SEYCHELLES.
Contes, devinettes et jeux de mots des Seychelles =. [Le-Mée-sur-Seine] [Paris] , c1983. 157 p. : ISBN 2-86427-018-8 DDC 398.2/0969/6 19
GR360.S44 C66 1983 *NYPL [Sc D 88-583]*

FOLKLORE - SIERRA LEONE.
Hinzen, Heribert. Koranko riddles, songs and stories /. Freetown , 1987. 69 p. : *NYPL [Sc D 89-416]*

FOLKLORE - SUDAN.
Folklore and National Development Symposium (1981 : Khartoum, Sudan) Folklore and development in the Sudan . Khartoum , 1985. 272 p. :
GR355.8 .F65 1981 *NYPL [Sc E 88-333]*

Folktales from Freetown /. Smith, Arthur E. E. Freetown , 1987. 69 p. ; *NYPL [Sc D 89-413]*

Follow the drinking gourd /. Winter, Jeanette. New York , c1988. [48] p. : ISBN 0-394-89694-7 : DDC [E] 19
PZ7.W7547 Fo 1988 *NYPL [Sc F 89-59]*

Fomban-drazana Tsimihety /. Patrice, Tongasolo. Fianarantsoa [Madagascar] , 1985. 383 p., [8] p. of plates : *NYPL [Sc C 88-292]*

Fondas Kréyol-la. Bernabé, Jean. Grammaire Créole (Fondas Kréyol-la) . Paris , 1987. 205 p. ; ISBN 2-85805-734-X *NYPL [Sc D 88-521]*

Fondation Léopold Sédar Senghor. Sène, Alioune. Célébration du 7oe anniversaire du président Léopold Sédar Senghor (9 Oct. 1906-9 Oct. 1976) [microform] /. Dakar , 1976. [4] p. : *NYPL [Sc Micro F-11026]*

Fondement de l'imanisme. Bigangara,

Jean-Baptiste. Le fondement de l'imanisme, ou,
Religion traditionnelle au Burundi . Bujumbura,
Burundi , 1984. 140 p. ;
BL2470.B94 B54 1984 NYPL [Sc E 88-459]

**Le fondement de l'imanisme, ou, Religion
traditionnelle au Burundi** , Jean-Baptiste.
Bujumbura, Burundi , 1984. 140
p. ;
BL2470.B94 B54 1984 NYPL [Sc E 88-459]

Foner, Eric. Reconstruction, America's unfinished
revolution, 1863-1877 / Eric Foner. 1st ed.
New York : Harper & Row, c1988. xxvii, 690
p., [8] p. of plates : ill. ; 25 cm. (New American
nation series) Includes index. Spine title:
Reconstruction, 1863-1877. Bibliography: p. 615-641.
ISBN 0-06-015851-4 : DDC 973.8 19
*1. Afro-Americans - History - 1863-1877. 2. United
States - Politics and government - 1865-1877. I. Title.
II. Title: Reconstruction, 1863-1877. III. Series.*
*E668 .F66 1988 NYPL [*R-IKR 88-5216]*

Foner, Philip Sheldon, 1910- Black workers .
Philadelphia , 1989. xv, 733 p. ; ISBN
0-87722-592-3 *NYPL [Sc E 89-206]*

Fonkoué, Jean. Différence & identité : les
sociologues africains face à la sociologie / Jean
Fonkoué. Paris : Silex, c1985. 202 p. : ill. ; 22
cm. Bibliography: p. 195-202. ISBN 2-903871-46-9 :
DDC 301/.096 19
*1. Sociology - Africa - History. 2. Africa - Social
conditions. 3. Africa - Economic conditions. I. Title. II.
Title: Différence et identité.*
HM22.A4 F66 1985 NYPL [Sc D 88-1151]

Fonseca, Edson Nery da. Casa-grande & senzala e
a crítica brasileira de 1933 a 1944 /. Recife ,
1985. 309 p. ; ISBN 85-7019-079-4 (pbk.) DDC
981/.00498 19
F2510.F7524 C37 1985
NYPL [HFB 86-2252]

Fontaine, Pierre Michel, 1938- Race, class, and
power in Brazil /. Los Angeles , c1985. xi, 160
p. : ISBN 0-934934-22-3 : DDC 305.8/96/081 19
F2659.N4 R24 1985 NYPL [JLE 88-2671]

Fontes historiae africanae. Series arabica .
(8) Ḥājj 'Umar ibn Saʿīd al-Fūtī, 1794?-1864.
[Bayān mā waqaʿa. French & Arabic.] Voilà ce
qui est arrivé . Paris , 1983. 261 p., [57] p. of
plates : ISBN 2-222-03216-4
NYPL [Sc F 88-211]

Fontinelle, Michael. Pierre, K. D. Jn. (Kentry D.
Jn.) Lamentation /. [St. Lucia] , 1987. 62 p. :
NYPL [Sc D 88-908]

FOOD AID PROGRAMS. see FOOD RELIEF.

**FOOD CONSUMPTION - KENYA -
MATHEMATICAL MODELS.**
Greer, Joel William, 1948- Food poverty and
consumption patterns in Kenya /. Geneva ,
1986. xii, 170 p. : ISBN 92-2-105374-1 (pbk.) :
DDC 338.1/9/6762 19
HD9017.K42 G74 1986
NYPL [JLE 87-3435]

FOOD CONTROL. see FOOD SUPPLY.

FOOD CROPS - AFRICA - CONGRESSES.
Food for Africa . [Lusaka?] [1985?] 68 p., [3]
p. of plates :
TX360.A26 F67 1985 NYPL [Sc F 89-40]

Food for Africa : the promotion of traditional and
under-utilized foodstuffs : report of a regional
workshop / organised by the Zambia Alliance
of Women in collaboration with FAO of the
United Nations, Lusaka, 12-19 May, 1985.
[Lusaka?] : The Alliance, [1985?] 68 p., [3] p.
of plates : ill. ; 30 cm. Includes bibliographies.
*1. Diet - Africa - Congresses. 2. Food crops - Africa -
Congresses. 3. Food habits - Africa - Congresses. I.
Zambia Alliance of Women.*
TX360.A26 F67 1985 NYPL [Sc F 89-40]

FOOD HABITS - AFRICA - CONGRESSES.
Food for Africa . [Lusaka?] [1985?] 68 p., [3]
p. of plates :
TX360.A26 F67 1985 NYPL [Sc F 89-40]

Food in Africa series.
Coping with Africa's food crisis /. Boulder ,
c1988. xi, 250 p. : ISBN 0-931477-84-0 (lib. bdg.) :
DDC 338.1/9/6 19
HD9017.A2 C65 1988 NYPL [Sc E 88-287]

Lofchie, Michael F. The policy factor . Boulder,
Colo. , Nairobi , c1989. xii, 235 p. : ISBN
1-555-87136-4 (alk. paper) : DDC 338.1/86762

19
HD2126.5.Z8 L64 1989
NYPL [Sc E 89-123]

**FOOD INDUSTRY AND TRADE - AFRICA,
WEST.**
Improved village technology for women's
activities . Geneva , 1984. vi, 292 p. : ISBN
92-2-103818-1 *NYPL [JLF 85-625]*

Food poverty and consumption patterns in Kenya
/. Greer, Joel William, 1948- Geneva , 1986.
xii, 170 p. : ISBN 92-2-105374-1 (pbk.) : DDC
338.1/9/6762 19
HD9017.K42 G74 1986
NYPL [JLE 87-3435]

The food problem /. Tickner, Vincent. London ,
1979. 78 p. ; *NYPL [Sc D 88-188]*

FOOD RELIEF - AFRICA - CASE STUDIES.
Curtis, Donald, 1939- Preventing famine .
London , New York , 1988. xi, 250 p. ; ISBN
0-415-00711-9 DDC 363.8/7/096 19
HC800.Z9 F326 1988 NYPL [JLD 88-3825]

FOOD RELIEF - AFRICA - DIARIES.
Fanfani, Mariapia. [Hayat. English.] Hayat .
New York , c1988. 219 p., [16] p. of plates :
ISBN 0-671-66414-X DDC 363.8/83/0924 B 19
HV696.F6 F363 1988 NYPL [JFD 88-3833]

FOOD RELIEF - SOMALIA.
Baez, Joan, 1913- One bowl of porridge . Santa
Barbara, Calif. , 1986, c1985. 94 p. : ISBN
0-936784-12-1 (pbk.) : DDC 363.8/83/096773
19
HV696.F6 B34 1986 NYPL [Sc D 89-333]

FOOD SUPPLY - AFRICA.
Curtis, Donald, 1939- Preventing famine .
London , New York , 1988. xi, 250 p. ; ISBN
0-415-00711-9 DDC 363.8/7/096 19
HC800.Z9 F326 1988 NYPL [JLD 88-3825]

FOOD SUPPLY - AFRICA, SOUTHERN.
Poverty, policy, and food security in southern
Africa /. Boulder , 1988. xii, 291 p. : ISBN
1-555-87092-9 (lib. bdg.) : DDC 363.8/56/0968
19
HD9017.A26 P68 1988 NYPL [Sc E 88-355]

**FOOD SUPPLY - GOVERNMENT POLICY -
AFRICA - CASE STUDIES.**
Coping with Africa's food crisis /. Boulder ,
c1988. xi, 250 p. : ISBN 0-931477-84-0 (lib. bdg.) :
DDC 338.1/9/6 19
HD9017.A2 C65 1988 NYPL [Sc E 88-287]

**FOOD SUPPLY - KENYA - MATHEMATICAL
MODELS.**
Greer, Joel William, 1948- Food poverty and
consumption patterns in Kenya /. Geneva ,
1986. xii, 170 p. : ISBN 92-2-105374-1 (pbk.) :
DDC 338.1/9/6762 19
HD9017.K42 G74 1986
NYPL [JLE 87-3435]

FOOD SUPPLY - NIGERIA.
Iyegha, David A., 1949- Agricultural crisis in
Africa . Lanham, MD , c1988. xx, 246 p. :
ISBN 0-8191-7080-1 (alk. paper) DDC
338.1/09669 19
HD2145.5.Z8 I94 1988
NYPL [JLE 88-5390]

FOOD SUPPLY - ZAIRE - BANDUNDU.
Mbo-Ikamba, Iyeti. L'approvisionnement
alimentaire de la ville de Bandundu (Rép. du
Zaïre) /. Bandundu, République du Zaïre ,
1987. 58 p. : *NYPL [Sc F 89-63]*

FOOD SUPPLY - ZIMBABWE.
Tickner, Vincent. The food problem /.
London , 1979. 78 p. ; *NYPL [Sc D 88-188]*

**FOOD - TRADE AND STATISTICS. see
FOOD INDUSTRY AND TRADE; FOOD
SUPPLY.**

Fool's paradise /. Walker, Dale. New York ,
1988. 242 p. ; ISBN 0-394-75818-8 (pbk.) : DDC
915.3/80453 19
DS208 .W35 1988 NYPL [Sc D 88-1463]

FOOT-BALL. see FOOTBALL.

FOOTBALL - JUVENILE FICTION.
Knott, Bill, 1927- Crazylegs Merrill. Austin
[1969] iv, 155 p. ; *NYPL [Sc D 88-632]*

**FOOTBALL PLAYERS - JUVENILE
BIOGRAPHY.**
Terzian, James P. The Jimmy Brown story /.
New York , c1964. 190 p. :
NYPL [Sc D 89-432]

**FOOTBALL PLAYERS - UNITED STATES -
BIOGRAPHY - JUVENILE LITERATURE.**
Devaney, John. Bo Jackson . New York , 1988.
110 p. : ISBN 0-8027-6818-0 DDC 796.332/092/4
B 92 19
GV865.J28 D48 1988 NYPL [Sc E 89-12]

**FOOTBALL - UNITED STATES -
BIOGRAPHY - DICTIONARIES.**
Biographical dictionary of American sports.
Football /. New York , 1987. xvii, 763 p. ;
ISBN 0-313-25771-X (lib. bdg. : alk. paper)
DDC 796.332/092/2 B 19
GV939.A1 B56 1987
*NYPL [*R-MVFF 88-6690]*

FOOTBALL - UNITED STATES - HISTORY.
Biographical dictionary of American sports.
Football /. New York , 1987. xvii, 763 p. ;
ISBN 0-313-25771-X (lib. bdg. : alk. paper)
DDC 796.332/092/2 B 19
GV939.A1 B56 1987
*NYPL [*R-MVFF 88-6690]*

FOOT'S RESOLUTION, 1829.
Hayne, Robert Young, 1791-1839. Speeches of
Hayne and Webster in the United States
Senate, on the resolution of Mr. Foot, January,
1830 . Boston , 1853. 115 p. ;
E381 .H424 1853 NYPL [Sc Rare C 89-20]

Footsteps . Norman, Bruce. London , 1987. 279
p. : ISBN 0-563-20552-0 *NYPL [Sc F 88-18]*

For bread justice and freedom . Kambon, Khafra.
London , 1988. xi, 353 p., [16] p. of plates :
NYPL [Sc D 89-294]

For prayer and profit . Colson, Elizabeth, 1917-
Stanford, Calif. , 1988. vi, 147 p. : ISBN
0-8047-1444-4 (alk. paper) : DDC 968.94 19
DT963.42 .C65 1988 NYPL [Sc D 88-1254]

For the mighty gods-- . Sekou, Lasana M. New
York , 1982. 95 p. : *NYPL [Sc D 88-1405]*

Forbes, Jack D. Black Africans and native
Americans : color, race, and caste in the
evolution of red-black peoples / Jack D.
Forbes. Oxford, UK ; New York, NY, USA :
Blackwell, 1988. 345 p. ; 24 cm. Includes index.
Bibliography: p. [315]-334. ISBN 0-631-15665-8 :
DDC 973/.0496073 19
*1. Indians - Mixed bloods. 2. Miscegenation - America.
3. Afro-Americans - Relations with Indians. I. Title.*
E59.M66 F67 1988 NYPL [HBC 88-2172]

Forbes, Tom H. Quincy's harvest / Tom H.
Forbes. 1st ed. Philadelphia : Lippincott, c1976.
143 p. ; 21 cm. Life for a sharecropper's family is
not easy, but young Quincy finds joy in his friendship
with an elderly black man. ISBN 0-397-31688-7
DDC [Fic]
*1. Country life - North Carolina - Juvenile fiction. 2.
Share-cropping - Juvenile fiction. I. Title.*
PZ7.F75222 Qi NYPL [Sc D 89-93]

Forbes, Vernon Siegfried. Paterson, William,
1755-1810. Paterson's Cape travels, 1777 to
1779 /. Johannesburg, [South Africa] , c1980.
202 p. : ISBN 0-909079-12-9 (standard edition)
NYPL [Sc F 85-110]

Force des choses. Ilboudo, Pierre Claver, 1948-
Adama, ou, La force des choses . Paris , 1987.
154 p. ; ISBN 2-7087-0484-2
PQ3989.2.I43 A65x 1987
NYPL [Sc C 88-316]

**FORCE (POLITICAL AND SOCIAL SCIENCE,
ETC.) see PASSIVE RESISTANCE;
POWER (SOCIAL SCIENCES);
VIOLENCE.**

FORCED LABOR - DOMINICAN REPUBLIC.
Plant, Roger. Sugar and modern slavery .
London , Atlantic Highlands, N.J. , c1987. xiv,
177 p. : ISBN 0-86232-572-2 : DDC
331.7/6/097293 19
HD8039.S852 D657 1987
NYPL [Sc D 87-1240]

FORCED LABOR - ZAIRE - HISTORY.
Northrup, David. Beyond the bend in the
river . Athens, Ohio , 1988. xvii, 264 p. :
ISBN 0-89680-151-9 DDC 331.11/73/0967517
19
HD8811.Z8 K586 1988
NYPL [Sc D 88-960]

Forces littéraires d'Afrique : points de repères et
témoignages / Jean-Pierre Jacquemin et
Monkasa-Bitumba, ed. Bruxelles : C.E.C. : De
Boeck Université, c1987. 238 p. ; 24 cm. Chiefly
papers presented at a symposium "Ecrivains d'Afrique

Noire, écrivains méconnus?" held May 1986 in Brussels sponsored by the Coopération par l'Education et la Culture. Includes bibliographies. ISBN 2-8041-0965-8
1. African literature - Congresses. I. Jacquemin, Jean Pierre. II. Monkasa-Bitumba.
NYPL [Sc E 88-442]

Ford, Clinita A. Black student retention in higher education /. Springfield, Ill., U. S. A., c1988. xvi, 111 p.: ISBN 0-398-05477-0 DDC 378/.198/2 19
LC2781 .B465 1988 *NYPL [Sc F 89-139]*

Ford, George Barry. A degree of difference. New York, Farrar, Straus & Giroux [1969] 271 p. 22 cm. DDC 282/.0924 B
1. Clergy - New York (N.Y.) - Biography. 2. Catholic Church - Clergy - Biography. I. Title.
BX4705.F635 A3 *NYPL [Sc D 88-406]*

Ford, George Cephas. (illus) Napjus, Alice James. Freddie found a frog. New York [1969] [29] p. DDC [Fic]
PZ7.N148 Fr *NYPL [Sc C 89-27]*

FORECASTING, ECONOMIC. see ECONOMIC FORECASTING.

FOREIGN AID PROGRAM. see ECONOMIC ASSISTANCE.

FOREIGN ASSISTANCE. see TECHNICAL ASSISTANCE.

FOREIGN EXCHANGE PROBLEM - NIGERIA.
Ogundipe, S. O. Second-tier foreign exchange market in Nigeria. Ibadan, 1987. xii, 96 p.; ISBN 979-12-9534-1
NYPL [Sc D 88-1248]

Foreign interests and Nigerian trade unions /. Otobo, Dafe. Ibadan [Nigeria], 1986. xxviii, 190 p.: ISBN 978-12-9532-5 (pbk.) DDC 331.88/09669 19
HD6885.5 .O87 1986 *NYPL [Sc E 88-557]*

FOREIGN INVESTMENTS. see INVESTMENTS, FOREIGN.

FOREIGN LABOR. see ALIEN LABOR.

FOREIGN LOANS. see LOANS, FOREIGN.

FOREIGN OPINION OF AFRICA. see AFRICA - FOREIGN OPINION.

Foreign policy in small states . Black, David R. (David Ross), 1960- Halifax, N.S., 1988. viii, 83 p.: ISBN 0-7703-0736-1: DDC 327.681068 19
NYPL [Sc D 89-564]

FOREIGN POPULATION. see EMIGRATION AND IMMIGRATION.

FOREIGN TRADE. see COMMERCE.

FOREIGN TRADE POLICY. see COMMERCIAL POLICY.

FOREIGN WORKERS. see ALIEN LABOR.

FORENAMES. see NAMES, PERSONAL.

Forente stater. see United States.

Forget-me-not, pseud. see Kelley, Emma Dunham.

Forging freedom . Nash, Gary B. Cambridge, Mass., c1988. xii, 354 p.: ISBN 0-674-30934-0 (alk. paper) DDC 974.8/1100496073 19
F158.9.N4 N37 1988 *NYPL [Sc E 88-594]*

Forms and forces : dynamics of African figurative sculpture. San Francisco : Fine Arts Museums of San Francisco, c1988. 53 p. : ill. ; 28 cm.
"...published on the occasion of an exhibition at the M. H. de Young Memorial Museum, 4 May-10 July, 1988."--T.p. verso. ISBN 0-88401-057-0 (pbk)
1. Sculpture, African - Africa, Sub-Saharan - Exhibitions. 2. Sculpture, Primitive - Africa, Sub-Saharan - Exhibitions. I. M.H. De Young Memorial Museum. II. Fine Arts Museums of San Francisco.
NYPL [Sc F 88-330]

Formules des actes de l'état civil [microform]. Haiti (Republic) Laws, statutes, etc. Port-Républicain, 1845. 17 p. :
NYPL [Sc Micro F-10,893]

Forrest, Joshua. Lobban, Richard. Historical dictionary of the Republic of Guinea-Bissau /. Metuchen, N.J., 1988. xx, 210 p. : ISBN 0-8108-2086-2 DDC 966/.57 19
DT613.5 .L62 1988
*NYPL [*R-BMP 88-5080]*

Forten, Charlotte L.
[Journals]
The journals of Charlotte Forten Grimké /

edited by Brenda Stevenson. New York : Oxford University Press, 1988. xlix, 609 p. ; 17 cm. (The Schomburg library of nineteenth-century Black women writers) Bibliography: p. 539-609. ISBN 0-19-505238-2 (alk. paper) DDC 371.1/0092/4 B 19
1. Forten, Charlotte L. - Diaries. 2. Afro-American teachers - Diaries. I. Stevenson, Brenda. II. Title. III. Series.
LA2317.F67 A3 1988 *NYPL [JFC 88-2152]*

FORTEN, CHARLOTTE L. - DIARIES.
Forten, Charlotte L. [Journals.] The journals of Charlotte Forten Grimké /. New York, 1988. xlix, 609 p. ; ISBN 0-19-505238-2 (alk. paper) DDC 371.1/0092/4 B 19
LA2317.F67 A3 1988 *NYPL [JFC 88-2152]*

The Fortunate Islands. Defries, Amelia Dorothy, 1882- London [1929] xxiii, 160 p. DDC 917.296
F1651 .D31 *NYPL [Sc D 88-936]*

Fortune, G. (George), 1915-
A guide to Shona spelling / George Fortune. Harare : Longman Zimbabwe, 1972. 64 p. ; 19 cm. ISBN 0-528-64019-2 DDC 496/.39
1. Shona language - Orthography and spelling. I. Title.
PL8681.2 .F6 *NYPL [Sc C 88-328]*

Ngano. Harare, Zimbabwe, 1980- v. ; ISBN 0-7974-0478-3 (pbk.) :
GR358.62.M3 N47 1980
NYPL [Sc F 87-416]

Fortune, George. Hodza, Aaron C. Shona registers [microform] /. Harare, Zimbabwe, 1977-1984. 3 v. ; ISBN 0-7974-0482-1
NYPL [Sc Micro R-4820 no.12]

FORTUNES. see INCOME.

Forty-eight minutes . Ryan, Bob. New York, London, c1987. x, 356 p. ; ISBN 0-02-597770-9 DDC 796.32/364/0973 19
GV885.515.N37 R9 1988
NYPL [JFD 87-10809]

Forty winters on : memories of Britain's post war Caribbean immigrants. [London] : Lambeth Council, [1988?] 47 p. : ill., ports. ; 21 cm.
1. West Indians - Great Britain. I. Lambeth Council.
NYPL [Sc D 88-1202]

"Forward to 1982--the year of Economic construction" [microform] . Bishop, Maurice. [st. George's], Grenada, 1982. 22 leaves ;
NYPL [Sc Micro R-4108 no. 28]

FOSSEY, DIAN.
Shoumatoff, Alex. African madness /. New York, 1988. xviii, 202 p. ; ISBN 0-394-56914-8 : DDC 967/.0328 19
DT352.2 .S48 1988 *NYPL [Sc D 89-160]*

FOSSILS. see PALEONTOLOGY.

Le fossoyeur /. Yoka Lye Mudaba, 1947- Paris, 1986. 127 p. ; ISBN 2-218-07830-9
NYPL [Sc C 88-10]

Foster, Lorn S. Cavanagh, Thomas E. Jesse Jackson's campaign. Washington, D.C., 1984. 27 p., [1] ; ISBN 0-941410-45-5 (pbk.) DDC 324.973 19
JK526 1984c *NYPL [Sc F 87-172 rept. 2]*

Foster, Mamie Marie Booth. Southern Black creative writers, 1829-1953 : biobibliographies / compiled by M. Marie Booth Foster. New York : Greenwood Press, 1988. xvii, 113 p. ; 25 cm. (Bibliographies and indexes in Afro-American and African studies. no. 22) Bibliography: p. [84]-102. ISBN 0-313-26207-1 (lib. bdg. : alk. paper) DDC 016.81/09/896073 19
1. American literature - Afro-American authors - Bio-bibliography. 2. American literature - Southern States - Bio-bibliography. 3. Afro-American authors - Southern States - Biography - Dictionaries. I. Title. II. Series.
Z1229.N39 F67 1988 PS153.N5 *NYPL [Sc E 88-495]*

Foster, Stephen Collins, 1826-1864.
SONGS.
Austin, William W. "Susanna," "Jeanie," and "The old folks at home". Urbana [Ill.], 1987. xxiv, 422 p. ; ISBN 0-252-01476-6 DDC 784.5/0092/4 19
ML410.F78 A9 1987 *NYPL [Sc E 88-465]*

Foster, William A. A. A stage for victory : drama at Sabina / William A.A. Foster. Kingston, Jamaica, W.I. : Zodiac Worldwide, 1985. 36 p. [32] p. of plates : ill. ; 22 cm. ISBN 976-8032-00-6

1. Cricket - West Indies. 2. Cricket players - West Indies. I. Title. *NYPL [Sc D 88-182]*

Fostering minority access and achievement in higher education . Richardson, Richard C. San Francisco, Calif. , c1987. xviii, 244 p.; ISBN 1-555-42053-2 (alk. paper) DDC 378/.052 19
LC3727 .R53 1987 *NYPL [Sc E 88-472]*

Fouchard, Jean.
Artistes et répertoire des scènes de Saint-Domingue / Jean Fouchard. Port-au-Prince, Haiti : Editions H. Deschamps, 1988. 195 p. ; 22 cm. (Fouchard, Jean. Regards sur le temps passé) Includes bibliographical references. CONTENTS - 1. Dictionnaire des comédiens de Saint-Dominingue---2. Répertoire des spectacles de Saint-Domingue de 1764 à 1797.
1. Actors - Haiti - Biography. 2. Theater - Haiti. 3. Theater - Haiti - Tables. I. Title. II. Series.
NYPL [Sc D 89-410]

Regards sur le temps passé.
Fouchard, Jean. Artistes et répertoire des scènes de Saint-Domingue /. Port-au-Prince, Haiti, 1988. 195 p. ;
NYPL [Sc D 89-410]

Fouchard, Jean, 1912- Plaisirs de Saint-Domingue. Port-au-Prince, Haiti, 1988. 125 p. *NYPL [Sc D 89-407]*

Fouchard, Jean, 1912- Regards sur l'histoire /. Port-au-Prince, Haiti, 1988. 222 p. :
NYPL [Sc D 89-409]

Fouchard, Jean, 1912- Le théâtre à Saint-Domingue /. Port-au-Prince, Haiti, 1988. 294 p. : *NYPL [Sc D 89-419]*

Fouchard, Jean, 1912-
Plaisirs de Saint-Domingue : notes sur sa vie sociale, littéraire et artistique / Jean Fouchard. Port-au-Prince, Haiti : Impr. H. Deschamps, 1988. 125 p. 22cm. (Fouchard, Jean. Regards sur le temps passé) Includes bibliographical references.
1. Haiti - Social life and customs. 2. Haiti - Intellectual life. I. Title. II. Series. *NYPL [Sc D 89-407]*

Regards sur l'histoire / Jean Fouchard. Port-au-Prince, Haiti : Editions H. Deschamps, 1988. 222 p. : ill. ; 22 cm. (Fouchard, Jean. Regards sur le temps passé) Includes bibliographical references.
1. Toussaint Louverture, 1743?-1803. 2. Haiti - History. 3. Haiti - History - To 1791. I. Title. II. Series.
NYPL [Sc D 89-409]

Le théâtre à Saint-Domingue / Jean Fouchard. Port-au-Prince, Haiti : Editions H. Deschamps, 1988. 294 p. : ill. ; 22 cm. (Fouchard, Jean. Regards sur le temps passé) Includes bibliographical references.
1. Theater - Haiti. I. Title. II. Series.
NYPL [Sc D 89-419]

FOULAHS. see FULAHS.

Foundation for Education with Production (Gaborone, Botswana) Bond-Stewart, Kathy. Education /. [Gweru, Zimbabwe] , 1986. 102 p. : ISBN 0-86922-371-2 *NYPL [Sc F 88-201]*

Foundations of human behavior.
Potts, Richard, 1953- Early hominid activities at Olduvai /. New York, c1988. xi, 396 p. : ISBN 0-202-01176-3 (lib. bdg.) DDC 967.8 19
GN772.42.T34 P67 1988
NYPL [Sc E 89-92]

Founding Congress of the Workers' Party of Ethiopia & 10th Anniversary of the Revolution. Propaganda and Culture Committee. Proletarian internationalism and the Ethiopian revolution /. Addis Ababa , 1984. 56 p. ;
DT387.95 .P76 1984 *NYPL [Sc F 89-85]*

Four contrasting world views /. Onuoha, Enyeribe. Enugu , 1987. 70 p. : ISBN 978-302-351-9 : *NYPL [Sc D 88-759]*

Four girls at Cottage City /. Kelley, Emma Dunham. New York , 1988. xxxviii, 379 p. ; ISBN 0-19-505242-0 DDC 813/.4 19
PS2159.K13 F6 1988 *NYPL [JFC 88-2149]*

Four-leaf clover /. Lipkind, William, 1904- New York , 1959. [32] p. : *NYPL [Sc F 89-22]*

Fox, Christine. Asante brass casting : lost wax casting of gold-weights, ritual vessels and sculptures, with handmade equipment / Christine Fox. Cambridge : African Studies Centre, 1988. xii, 112 p. : ill. ; 21 cm. (Cambridge African monographs. no. 11) Bibliography:

p. 110-111. ISBN 0-902993-24-0 (pbk) : DDC
739.2/27667 19
1. Goldweights, Ashanti. I. University of Cambridge.
African Studies Centre. II. Series: Cambridge African
monograph , no. 11. III. Title.
NYPL [Sc D 88-1434]

Fox-Genovese, Elizabeth, 1941- Within the
plantation household : Black and White women
of the Old South / Elizabeth Fox-Genovese.
Chapel Hill : University of North Carolina
Press, c1988. xvii, 544 p. : ill. ; 25 cm.
(Gender & American culture) Includes index.
Bibliography: p. 463-529. ISBN 0-8078-1808-9 (alk.
paper) DDC 305.4/0975 19
1. Women - Southern States - History. 2. Plantation
life - Southern States - History. 3. Slavery - Southern
States - History. 4. Afro-American women - Southern
States - History. I. Title. II. Series.
HQ1438.A13 F69 1988 NYPL [JLE 89-21]

Frame, Paul, 1913-
(illus) Glendinning, Sally. Jimmy and Joe fly a
kite. Champaign, Ill. [1970] 38 p. ISBN
0-8116-4704-8 DDC [Fic]
PZ7.G4829 Jm NYPL [Sc D 88-1475]

(illus) Glendinning, Sally. Jimmy and Joe look
for a bear. Champaign, Ill., 1970. 40 p. ISBN
0-8116-4703-X DDC [E]
PZ7.G4829 Jo NYPL [Sc D 88-1456]

(illus) Glendinning, Sally. Jimmy and Joe meet a
Halloween witch. Champaign, Ill. [1971] 40 p.
ISBN 0-8116-4705-6 DDC [E]
PZ7.G4829 Jq NYPL [Sc D 88-1474]

Les Français en Afrique noire, de Richélieu à
Mitterand . Biarnès, Pierre. Paris , 1987. 447
p. :bill., maps, ports. ; ISBN 2-200-37115-2
NYPL [Sc D 88-562]

France.
CODE NOIR.
Sala-Molins, Louis. Le Code noir, ou, Le
calvaire de Canaan /. Paris , c1987. 292 p. ;
ISBN 2-13-039970-3 : DDC 346.4401/3
344.40613 19
KJV4534 .S25 1987 NYPL [Sc D 88-136]

Code noir. 1987. Sala-Molins, Louis. Le Code
noir, ou, Le calvaire de Canaan / Louis
Sala-Molins. Paris , c1987. 292 p. ; ISBN
2-13-039970-3 : DDC 346.4401/3 344.40613 19
KJV4534 .S25 1987 NYPL [Sc D 88-136]

France and Islam in West Africa, 1860-1960 /.
Harrison, Christopher, 1958- Cambridge
[Cambridgeshire] , New York , 1988. xi, 242
p. : ISBN 0-521-35230-4 DDC 966/.0097451 19
DT530.5.M88 H37 1988
NYPL [Sc E 88-484]

France. Assemblée nationale constituante, 1789-
1791. Ducos, Jean François, 1765-1793.
Opinion de Jean-François Ducos sur l'exécution
provisoire du concordat, & des arrêtés de
l'Assemblée coloniale confirmatifs de cet
accord . A Paris , 1791. 12 p. ;
NYPL [Sc Rare C 86-7]

France. Assemblée nationale legislative, 1791-
1792.
Loi relative aux colonies, & aux moyens d'y
appaiser les troubles : donnée à Paris, le 4 avril
1792. A Niort : Chez Jean-Baptiste
Lefranc-Elies, imprimeur de Dép. des Deux
Sèvres, 1792. 6 p. ; 27 cm. "No. 1606."
1. Haiti - History - Revolution, 1791-1804 - Sources. I.
Title. NYPL [Sc Rare F 82-68]

Santo Domingo (French colony). Assemblée
générale. Commissaires. Pétition faite à
l'Assemblée nationale par MM. les
Commissaires de l'Assemblée générale de la
partie française de St.-Domingue . [Paris?]
[1791?] 7 p. ; *NYPL [Sc Rare C 86-3]*

Tarbé, Charles. Rapport sur les troubles de
Saint-Domingue. Paris, 1791-[1792] 4 v.
F1921 .T17 NYPL [Sc Rare F 88-17]

France. Bibliothèque nationale. Département des
entrées. France. Bibliothèque nationale.
Département des livres imprimés. Les auteurs
afro-américains, 1965-1982 . Paris , 1985. 28 p.,
[4] leaves of plates : ISBN 2-7177-1709-9 :
Z1229.N39 F7 1985 PS153.N5
NYPL [Sc F 89-5]

France. Bibliothèque nationale. Département des
livres imprimés.
Les auteurs afro-américains, 1965-1982 :
inventaire du fonds imprimé conservé à la

Bibliothèque nationale / par Andrée
Paolantonacci. Paris : Bibliothèque nationale,
1985. 28 p., [4] leaves of plates : ill. ; 29 cm.
(Collection "Etudes, guides et inventaires", 0761-3385 .
no 2) At head of title: Bibliothèque nationale,
Département des livres imprimés, Département des
entrées. ISBN 2-7177-1709-9 :
1. France. Bibliothèque nationale. Département des
livres imprimés - Catalogs. 2. American literature -
Afro-American authors - Bibliography - Catalogs. 3.
American literature - 20th century - Bibliography -
Catalogs. 4. Afro-Americans in literature -
Bibliography - Catalogs. I. Paolantonacci, Andrée. II.
France. Bibliothèque nationale. Département des
entrées. III. Title. IV. Series.
Z1229.N39 F7 1985 PS153.N5
NYPL [Sc F 89-5]

FRANCE. BIBLIOTHÈQUE NATIONALE.
DÉPARTEMENT DES LIVRES
IMPRIMÉS - CATALOGS.
France. Bibliothèque nationale. Département
des livres imprimés. Les auteurs afro-américains,
1965-1982 . Paris , 1985. 28 p., [4] leaves of
plates : ISBN 2-7177-1709-9 :
Z1229.N39 F7 1985 PS153.N5
NYPL [Sc F 89-5]

FRANCE - CIVILIZATION.
Senghor, Léopold Sédar, 1906- Ce que je crois .
Paris , c1988. 234 p. ; ISBN 2-246-24941-4
NYPL [Sc D 89-76]

FRANCE - COLONIES - AFRICA.
Biarnès, Pierre. Les Français en Afrique noire,
de Richélieu à Mitterand . Paris , 1987. 447
p. :bill., maps, ports. ; ISBN 2-200-37115-2
NYPL [Sc D 88-562]

Hama, Boubou, 1906- Kotia-Nima . [Niamey?] .
3 v. ; *NYPL [Sc D 88-210]*

FRANCE - COLONIES - AFRICA -
ADMINISTRATION.
Harrison, Christopher, 1958- France and Islam
in West Africa, 1860-1960 /. Cambridge
[Cambridgeshire] , New York , 1988. xi, 242
p. : ISBN 0-521-35230-4 DDC 966/.0097451 19
DT530.5.M88 H37 1988
NYPL [Sc E 88-484]

FRANCE - COLONIES - AFRICA -
DEFENSES.
Clayton, Anthony, 1923- France, soldiers, and
Africa /. London , New York , 1988. xxv, 444
p., [16] p. of plates : ISBN 0-08-034748-7 :
DDC 355.3/52/0944 19
UA855 .C575 1988 NYPL [Sc E 88-445]

FRANCE - COLONIES - ECONOMIC
CONDITIONS.
Enjeux fonciers dan la Caraibe, en Amérique
centrale et à la Réunion. . Paris , c1987. 232
p. : ISBN 2-7380-0003-7 *NYPL [Sc E 88-246]*

FRANCE - FOREIGN RELATIONS - AFRICA.
Biarnès, Pierre. Les Français en Afrique noire,
de Richélieu à Mitterand . Paris , 1987. 447
p. :bill., maps, ports. ; ISBN 2-200-37115-2
NYPL [Sc D 88-562]

FRANCE - FOREIGN RELATIONS -
FRANCE.
Biarnès, Pierre. Les Français en Afrique noire,
de Richélieu à Mitterand . Paris , 1987. 447
p. :bill., maps, ports. ; ISBN 2-200-37115-2
NYPL [Sc D 88-562]

FRANCE - FOREIGN RELATIONS - ITALY -
HISTORY.
Durant, Franck Alphonse. Rétrospectives
[microform] . Port-au-Prince, Haiti , 1977. 16
p. ; *NYPL [Sc Micro F 10,933]*

France. France d'outre-mer, Ministère de la. see
France. Ministère de la France d'outre-mer.

France - History - Crimean War, 1853-1856. see
Crimean War, 1853-1856.

FRANCE. MARINE.
Le Brasseur, J. A. De l'état actuel de la marine
et des colonies /. A Paris , 1792. 48 p. ;
NYPL [Sc Rare C 86-4]

FRANCE. MARINE - OFFICERS -
BIOGRAPHY.
Lara, Oruno D. Le commandant Mortenol .
Epinay, France , c1985. 275 p. : ISBN
2-905787-00-7 *NYPL [Sc D 88-1085]*

France. Ministère de la France d'outre-mer.
Affaires économiques et du plan, Direction
des. see France. Ministère de la France
d'outre-mer. Direction des affaires

économiques et du plan.

France. Ministère de la France d'outre-mer.
Direction des affaires économiques et du
plan. Madagascar [microform]. [Paris, La
Documentation française, 1953?] cover-title, [4]
p., 12 plates, map. Issued in portfolio. Text in
English; captions in French. Published also as la
Documentation photographique, année 1953, hors série.
Microfilm. New York : New York Public Library,
[197-] 1 microfilm reel ; 35 mm.
1. Madagascar. 2. Madagascar - Economic conditions.
3. Madagascar - Description and travel - Views. I. Title.
NYPL [Sc Micro R-3545]

France. Outre-mer, Ministère de la France d'. see
France. Ministère de la France d'outre-mer.

FRANCE - RACE RELATIONS.
Désir, Harlem, 1959- Touche pas à mon pote /.
Paris [c1985] 148 p. ; ISBN 2-246-36421-3 :
DDC 323.42/3/06044 19
DC34 .D47 1985 NYPL [Sc C 88-305]

FRANCE - RELATIONS - AFRICA.
Aurillac, Michel. L'Afrique à coeur . Paris ,
1987. 264 p., [8] p. of plates : ISBN
2-7013-0739-2 *NYPL [Sc E 88-203]*

Vingt questions sur l'Afrique . Paris , 1988. 238
p. ; ISBN 2-7384-0048-5
NYPL [Sc D 88-1390]

FRANCE - RELATIONS - AFRICA -
CONGRESSES.
Francophonie & géopolitique africaine . Paris ,
c1987. 156 p. ; ISBN 2-906861-01-4
NYPL [Sc D 88-1448]

FRANCE - RELATIONS - CHAD.
Ciammaichella, Glauco. Libyens et Français au
Tchad (1897-1914) . Paris , 1987. 187 p. :
ISBN 2-222-04067-1 *NYPL [Sc E 89-182]*

FRANCE - RELATIONS - CHAD - HISTORY -
20TH CENTURY.
Bret, René-Joseph, d. 1940. Vie du sultan
Mohamed Bakhit, 1856-1916 . Paris , 1987.
[xvi], 258 p. : ISBN 2-222-03901-0
NYPL [Sc D 89-364]

FRANCE - RELATIONS (GENERAL) WITH
CAMEROON.
Makanda Duc d'Ikoga, André. Non, Monsieur
Giscard [microform] /. Paris [1980] 23 p. ;
NYPL [Sc Micro F-11014]

France, soldiers, and Africa /. Clayton, Anthony,
1923- London , New York , 1988. xxv, 444 p.,
[16] p. of plates : ISBN 0-08-034748-7 : DDC
355.3/52/0944 19
UA855 .C575 1988 NYPL [Sc E 88-445]

FRANCHISE. see ELECTIONS.

Francis, Carlton. Dance . Cocorite , c1983. 80
p. : *NYPL [Sc F 89-13]*

Francis, Charles E. The Tuskegee airmen : the
men who changed a nation / by Charles E.
Francis. Boston, MA : Branden Pub. Co.,
c1988. 300, [33] p. : ill. ; 24 cm. Includes index.
Bibliography: p. 297-300. ISBN 0-8283-1386-5 :
DDC 940.54/4973 19
1. World War, 1939-1945 - Aerial operations,
American. 2. World War, 1939-1945 - Participation,
Afro-American. 3. Afro-American air pilots - History. I.
Title.
D790 .F637 1988 NYPL [Sc E 89-164]

Franco, Rubén. (joint author) Valle, Manuel del.
Law and bilingual education . New York ,
1978. i, 206 p. ; *NYPL [Sc F 88-357]*

François and the langouste. Sadowsky, Ethel S.
Boston [1969] 60 p. DDC [Fic]
PZ7.S127 Fr NYPL [Sc D 88-1120]

François de Neufchâteau, Nicolas Louis, comte,
1752-1828. Mémoire en forme de discours
sur la disette du numéraire à Saint-Domingue,
et sur les moyens d'y remédier. Lu à la
Chambre de commerce du Cap François, le 19
mars 1787. Nouv. éd. Suivie de lettres et de
pièces relatives à des objets intéressans pour la
France et les colonies. Metz, impr. de C.
Lamort, 1788. 178 p. fold. table. 20 cm. Bound
with miscellaneous works by the same author. FISHER
COLLECTION.
1. Haiti - Economic conditions. I. Title.
*NYPL [Sc *F330.9729-F]*

FRANCOIS, ELMA.
Reddock, Rhoda. Elma Francois . London ,
1988. vii, 60 p., [8] p. of plates : ISBN
0-901241-80-6 (Pbk.) *NYPL [Sc D 89-77]*

Francophonie & géopolitique africaine : colloque des 23, 24, 25 avril 1987, Sorbonne, Paris / sous la direction du pr. Tshiyembe Mwayila. Paris : Editions OKEM, c1987. 156 p. ; 23 cm. Includes bibliographical references.   ISBN 2-906861-01-4
1. Geopolitics - Africa - Congresses. 2. France - Relations - Africa - Congresses. 3. Africa - Relations - France - Congresses. I. Tshiyembe Mwayila. II. Institut panafricain de géopolitique. III. Title: Francophonie et géopolitique africaine.   *NYPL [Sc D 88-1448]*

Francophonie et géopolitique africaine.
Francophonie & géopolitique africaine . Paris , c1987. 156 p. ;   ISBN 2-906861-01-4
                    NYPL [Sc D 88-1448]

FRANCS-TIREURS. see GUERRILLAS.

Franey, Jean-Pierre. Ethiopie, la face cachée / texte, Jean-Pierre Franey ; photos, Lily Franey. Paris : Messidor, c1986. 127 p. : ill. (some col.) ; 29 cm.   ISBN 2-209-05848-1 :
1. Famines - Ethiopia. 2. Famines - Ethiopia - Pictorial works. I. Franey, Lily. II. Title.
HC845.Z9 F34 1986   *NYPL [Sc F 88-204]*

Franey, Lily. Franey, Jean-Pierre. Ethiopie, la face cachée /. Paris , c1986. 127 p. :   ISBN 2-209-05848-1 :
HC845.Z9 F34 1986   *NYPL [Sc F 88-204]*

Frankétienne. Adjanoumelezo : espiral / Frankétienne. [Port-au-Prince? : Imprimerie des Antilles], 1987. 522 p. ; 21 cm. Publisher from spine.
1. Creole dialects, French - Haiti - Texts. I. Title.
                    NYPL [Sc D 88-466]

Frankl, Ron. Duke Ellington / Ron Frankl. New York : Chelsea House, c1988. 110 p. : ill. ; 25 cm. (Black Americans of achievement) Includes index. Chronicles the life of internationally-acclaimed jazz musician Duke Ellington, from the Harlem Renaissance through his later years. Bibliography: p. 108.   ISBN 1-555-46584-6   DDC 785.42/092/4 B 92 19
1. Ellington, Duke, 1899-1974 - Juvenile literature. 2. Jazz musicians - United States - Biography - Juvenile literature. 3. Afro-American musicians - Juvenile biography. I. Title. II. Series.
ML3930.E44 F7 1988   *NYPL [Sc E 88-381]*

Franklin, James. The present state of Hayti (Saint Domingo) with remarks on its agriculture, commerce, laws, religion, finances, and population, etc. etc microform]. London, J. Murray, 1828. viii, 411 p. Microfilm. New York : New York Public Library, [197-] 1 microfilm reel ; 35 mm.
1. Haiti - History. 2. Haiti - Economic conditions. 3. Haiti - Description and travel. I. Title.
                    NYPL [Sc Micro R-1455]

Franqueville, André. Une Afrique entre le village et la ville : les migrations dans le sud du Cameroun / André Franqueville. Paris : Editions de l'ORSTOM : Institut français de recherche scientifique pour le développement en coopération : 646 p. : ill., maps ; 24 cm. (Collection Mémoires . no 109) Bibliography: p. 620-624.   ISBN 2-7099-0805-0
1. Rural-urban migration - Cameroon. 2. Cameroon - Social conditions. I. Series: Mémoires ORSTOM , no 109. II. Title.   *NYPL [Sc E 88-325]*

Fraser, Robert, 1947- West African poetry : a critical history / Robert Fraser. Cambridge [Cambridgeshire] ; New York : Cambridge University Press, 1986. vii, 351 p. : map, music ; 24 cm. Includes index. Bibliography: p. 341-345.   ISBN 0-521-30993-X   DDC 809.1/00966 19
1. West African poetry - History and criticism. I. Title.
PL8014.W37 F73 1986
                    NYPL [JFE 86-4349]

FRATERNITIES. see SECRET SOCIETIES.

Frauenarbeit am Strassenrand Kenkeyküchen in Ghana /. Rocksloh-Papendieck, Barbara. Hamburg , 1988. iii, 193 p. :   ISBN 3-923519-75-3   *NYPL [Sc D 89-575]*

Frazier, Thomas R. Afro-American history . Chicago, Ill. , c1988. xv, 464 p. ;   ISBN 0-256-06306-0 (pbk)   DDC 973/.0496073 19
E184.6 .A35 1988   *NYPL [Sc E 89-44]*

Freddie found a frog. Napjus, Alice James. New York [1969] [29] p.   DDC [Fic]
PZ7.N148 Fr   *NYPL [Sc C 89-27]*

Frederica Charlotte Ulrica Catherina, Duchess of York, 1767-1820. An Address to Her Royal Highness the Dutchess of York, against the use of sugar. [London?] 1792. 20 p. ;
                    NYPL [Sc Rare G 86-31]

Frederick Douglass /. Russell, Sharman Apt. New York , c1988. 110 p. :   ISBN 1-555-46580-3   DDC 973.8/092/4 B 92 19
E449.D75 R87 1988   *NYPL [Sc E 88-174]*

Fredrickson, George M., 1934- The arrogance of race : historical perspectives on slavery, racism, and social inequality / George M. Fredrickson.1st ed. Middletown, Conn. : Wesleyan University Press, c1988. viii, 310 p. ; 24 cm. Essays, most of which were published originally in somewhat different form in various publications from 1966 through 1987. Includes index. Bibliography: p. 271-294.   ISBN 0-8195-5177-5   DDC 973/.0496 19
1. Slavery - United States - History - 19th century. 2. Slavery - United States - Historiography. 3. Racism - United States - History - 19th century. 4. Slavery - History - 19th century. 5. Southern States - History - 1775-1865. 6. United States - Race relations. I. Title.
E441 .F77 1988   *NYPL [Sc E 88-487]*

Free as a frog. Hodges, Elizabeth Jamison. [Reading, Mass., c1969] [32] p.   DDC [Fic]
PZ7.H6634 Fr   *NYPL [Sc D 88-1126]*

Free Blacks of Anne Arundel County, Maryland 1850 /. Clayton, Ralph. Bowie, MD. , 1987. xiv, 51 p. ;   ISBN 1-556-13069-4
                    NYPL [Sc D 88-64]

Free jazz. Jost, Ekkehard. Mainz [1975] 256 p.
                    NYPL [Sc E 77-158]

Free throw. Neigoff, Mike. Chicago [1968] 128 p. DDC [Fic]
PZ7.N427 Fr   *NYPL [Sc D 88-1427]*

Freed, Arthur. Games / Arthur Freed, Leonard J. Simon ; Linda Kosarin, design consultant and typographical designer. [N.J.] : Rutgers-The state University and the Newark Board of Education, 1968. [32] p. : ill. ; 23 x 16 cm. (Camden Street School immediate readers) SCHOMBURG CHILDREN'S COLLECTION.
1. Readers (Elementary). 2. Games - Juvenile literature. I. Simon, Leonard J. II. Schomburg Children's Collection. III. Title.   *NYPL [Sc B 89-25]*

Freedman, Estelle B., 1947- D'Emilio, John. Intimate matters . New York , c1988. xx, 428 p., [16] leaves of plates :   ISBN 0-06-015855-7 : DDC 306.7/0973 19
HQ18.U5 D45 1988   *NYPL [Sc E 88-436]*

FREEDMEN IN ARKANSAS - SOURCES.
United States. Bureau of Refugees, Freedmen and Abandoned Lands. Records of the Assistant Commissioner for the State of Arkansas, Bureau of Refugees, Freedmen, and Abandoned Lands, 1865-1869 [microform] 1865-1869. 24 v.   *NYPL [Sc Micro R-4642]*

United States. Bureau of Refugees, Freedmen and Abandoned Lands. Records of the Superintendent of Education for the State of Arkansas, Bureau of Refugees, Freedmen, and Abandoned Lands, 1865-1871 [microform] 1865-1871. 10 v.   *NYPL [Sc Micro R-4643]*

FREEDMEN IN DISTRICT OF COLUMBIA - SOURCES.
United States. Bureau of Refugees, Freedmen and Abandoned Lands. Records of the Superintendent of Education for the District of Columbia, Bureau of Refugees, Freedmen, and Abandoned Lands, 1865-1872 [microform] 1865-1872. 11 bound v., 15 ft. of unbound doc.
                    NYPL [Sc Micro R-4645]

FREEDMEN IN NORTH CAROLINA - SOURCES.
United States. Bureau of Refugees, Freedmen and Abandoned Lands. Records of the Assistant Commissioner for the state of North Carolina, Bureau of Refugees, Freedmen, and Abandoned Lands, 1865-1870 [microform] 1865-1870. 20 ft. (32 v.)
                    NYPL [Sc Micro R-4646]

United States. Bureau of Refugees, Freedmen and Abandoned Lands. Records of the Superintendent of Education for the State of North Carolina, Bureau of Refugees, Freedmen, and Abandoned Lands, 1865-1870 [microform] 1865-1870. 7 ft. (24 v.)
                    NYPL [Sc Micro R-4647]

FREEDMEN IN THE SOUTHERN STATES - SOURCES.
United States. Bureau of Refugees, Freedmen and Abandoned Lands. Education Division. Records of the Education Division of the Bureau of Refugees, Freedmen, and Abandoned Lands, 1865-1871 [microform] 1865-1871. 23 v.
                    NYPL [Sc Micro R-4641]

FREEDMEN IN VIRGINIA - SOURCES.
United States. Bureau of Refugees, Freedmen and Abandoned Lands. Records of the Assistant Commissioner for the State of Virginia, Bureau of Refugees, Freedmen and Abandoned Lands, 1865-1869 [microform] 1865-1869. 40 bound v., 51 ft. of unbound doc.
                    NYPL [Sc Micro R-4648]

FREEDMEN - KENYA - HISTORY - CASE STUDIES.
Harris, Joseph E., 1929- Repatriates and refugees in a colonial society . Washington, D.C. , 1987. ix, 201 p. ;   ISBN 0-88258-148-1 : DDC 304.8/676/2 19
HN793.Z9 E44 1987   *NYPL [Sc E 87-558]*

FREEDMEN - LEGAL STATUS, LAWS, ETC. - VIRGINIA.
Rutherfoord, John Coles 1825-1866. Speech of John C. Rutherfoord, of Goochland, in the House of Delegates of Virginia, on the removal from the Commonwealth of the free colored population . Richmond , 1853. 20 p. ;
                    NYPL [Sc Rare C 89-10]

Freedmen's Bureau. see United States. Bureau of Refugees, Freedmen and Abandoned Lands.

FREEDOM. see LIBERTY; SLAVERY.

Freedom crossing. Clark, Margaret Goff. New York [1969] 128 p.   DDC [Fic]
PZ7.C5487 Fr   *NYPL [Sc D 88-1121]*

Freedom fighters . Philip, Ira. London , 1987. 275 p., [8] p. of plates :   ISBN 0-947638-42-3 (cased) : DDC 323.1/196/07299 19
                    NYPL [Sc D 88-1137]

FREEDOM OF SPEECH - NIGERIA.
Udoakah, Nkereuwem. Government and the media in Nigeria /. Calabar, Nigeria , c1988. x, 88 p. ;   ISBN 978-231-603-2
                    NYPL [Sc C 89-51]

FREEDOM OF THE PRESS - NIGERIA.
Tell it as it is /. Enugu [Nigeria] [1985?]- v. ;
ISBN 978-247-202-6   *NYPL [Sc C 88-183]*

FREEDOM OF THE PRESS - SOUTH AFRICA.
Phelan, John M. Apartheid media . Westport, Conn. , c1987. xi, 220 p. ;   ISBN 0-88208-244-2 : DDC 323.44/5 19
PN4748.S58 P4 1987   *NYPL [JLD 87-4698]*

The Freedom Quilting Bee /. Callahan, Nancy. Tuscaloosa, Ala. , c1987. xi, 255 p., [8] p. of plates :   ISBN 0-8173-0310-3   DDC 976.0/3800496073 19
NK9112 .C34 1987   *NYPL [3-MOT 88-1171]*

FREEDOM QUILTING BEE (ORGANIZATION : ALABAMA) - HISTORY.
Callahan, Nancy. The Freedom Quilting Bee /. Tuscaloosa, Ala. , c1987. xi, 255 p., [8] p. of plates :   ISBN 0-8173-0310-3   DDC 976.0/3800496073 19
NK9112 .C34 1987   *NYPL [3-MOT 88-1171]*

Freedom river: Florida, 1845. Douglas, Marjory Stoneman. New York [1953] 264 p. :
                    NYPL [Sc D 89-267]

Freedom, state security and the rule of law . Mathews, Anthony S., 1930- London , c1988. xxx, 312 p. ;   ISBN 0-421-39640-7
                    NYPL [Sc F 89-102]

Freedom Summer /. McAdam, Doug. New York , c1988. [xiii], 333 p., [14] p. of plates : ISBN 0-19-504367-7 (alk. paper)   DDC 976.2/00496073 19
E185.93.M6 M28 1988   *NYPL [Sc E 88-563]*

FREEHOLD. see LAND TENURE; REAL PROPERTY.

FREEMASONRY - RITUALS.
Duncan, Malcolm C. Duncan's Masonic ritual and monitor, or, Guide to the three symbolic degrees E.A., F.C., M.M. /. Danbury, Conn. , c1922- v. :   *NYPL [Sc B 88-65]*

Freemasons. Prince Hall Grand Lodge (N.J.)
Masonic monitor / the Most Worshipful Prince
Hall Grand Lodge, Free and Accepted Masons,
State of New Jersey. [Newark, N.J.] : The
Lodge, 1959. 109 p. ; 16 cm.
1. *Freemasons. Prince Hall Grand Lodge (N.J.) -
Handbooks, manuals, etc.*
HS455.N5 F74 1959   *NYPL [Sc C 89-13]*

**FREEMASONS. PRINCE HALL GRAND
LODGE (N.J.) - HANDBOOKS,
MANUALS, ETC.**
Freemasons. Prince Hall Grand Lodge (N.J.)
Masonic monitor /. [Newark, N.J.] , 1959. 109
p. ;
HS455.N5 F74 1959   *NYPL [Sc C 89-13]*

**Freemasons. Prince Hall Grand Lodge, No. 38
(New York, N.Y.)** Prince Hall Lodge No.
38 : Free and Accepted Masons (Prince Hall),
1881-1981. New York, N.Y. : The Lodge,
[1981]. [120] p. : facsims, ports. ; 28 cm.
Presentation copy to the Schomburg Center, signed by
Amos Richmond, Worshipful Master, and by Past
Master Bernard M. Holley, Secretary.
I. Title.   *NYPL [Sc F 88-158]*

Frehn, Beatrice, 1948- Afrikanische Frisuren :
Symbolik und Formenvielfalt traditioneller und
moderner Haartrachten im westafrikanischen
Sahel und Sudan / Beatrice Frehn und Thomas
Krings.Erstveröffentlichung. Köln : Du Mont,
c1986. 147 p. : ill. (some col.) ; 18 cm. (DuMont
Taschenbücher . Bd. 175) Bibliography: p. 144-146.
ISBN 3-7701-1619-4 DDC 391/.5/0966 19
1. *Hairstyles - Africa, West.* I. Krings, Thomas, 1949-.
II. Title.
GT2295.A358 F74 1986
NYPL [Sc C 88-153]

Freire de Matos, Isabel. Piñeiro de Rivera, Flor,
1922- Literatura infantil caribeña . Hato Rey,
P.R. (O'Neill 159, Hato Rey) , c1983. 123 p. ;
DDC 860/.9/9282 19
PQ7361 .P5 1983   *NYPL [Sc D 88-1143]*

Freire, Gilberto. see Freyre, Gilberto, 1900-

Freise, Reinhilde, 1941- Ghana . Stuttgart , 1986.
71, [1] p. :   *NYPL [Sc E 88-274]*

FRELIMO.
Machel, Samora, 1933- A nossa força está na
unidade /. [Maputo] [1983] 98 p. : DDC
967/.9803 19
DT465.C32 M32 1983 NYPL [Sc D 89-531]

**FRELIMO - HISTORY - COMIC BOOKS,
STRIPS, ETC.**
Motta, Helena. Moçambique por Eduardo
Mondlane /. [Maputo?] [1984] 86 p. : DDC
967/.903/0222 19
DT463 .M64 1984   *NYPL [Sc F 89-172]*

FRENCH - AFRICA.
Biarnès, Pierre. Les Français en Afrique noire,
de Richélieu à Mitterand . Paris , 1987. 447
p. :bill., maps, ports. ; ISBN 2-200-37115-2
NYPL [Sc D 88-562]

FRENCH AUTHORS. see AUTHORS,
FRENCH.

French civilization .
(v. 1) Cooper, Anna J. (Anna Julia), 1858-1964.
[Attitude de la France à l'égard de l'esclavage
pendant la révolution. English.] Slavery and the
French revolutionists, 1788-1805 /. Lewiston ,
1988. 228 p. : ISBN 0-88946-637-8 DDC
972.94/04 19
F1923 .C7213 1988   *NYPL [Sc E 88-469]*

FRENCH CREOLE LANGUAGES. see
CREOLE DIALECTS, FRENCH.

**FRENCH FICTION - 20TH CENTURY -
HISTORY AND CRITICISM.**
Ormerod, Beverley, 1937- An introduction to
the French Caribbean novel /. London ,
Portsmouth, N.H., USA , 1985. 152 p. ; ISBN
0-435-91839-7 (pbk.) DDC 843 19
PQ3944 .O76 1985   *NYPL [Sc D 88-1267]*

**FRENCH GUIANA - ECONOMIC
CONDITIONS.**
Castor, Elie, 1943- La Guyane, les grands
problèmes, les solutions possibles /. Paris ,
c1984. 337 p., [8] p. of plates : ISBN
2-903033-58-7 : DDC 988/.203 19
JL812 .C36 1984   *NYPL [Sc D 89-389]*

FRENCH GUIANA - FICTION.
Parépou, Alfred. Atipa . Paris , 1987. viii, 231
p. ; ISBN 2-85802-965-2 *NYPL [Sc E 88-18]*

FRENCH GUIANA - HISTORY.
Petot, Jean. L'or de Guyane . Paris , c1986.
248 p. [8] pages of plates ; ISBN 2-903033-84-6
NYPL [Sc D 88-1395]

**FRENCH GUIANA - POLITICS AND
GOVERNMENT - 1947-**
Castor, Elie, 1943- La Guyane, les grands
problèmes, les solutions possibles /. Paris ,
c1984. 337 p., [8] p. of plates : ISBN
2-903033-58-7 : DDC 988/.203 19
JL812 .C36 1984   *NYPL [Sc D 89-389]*

FRENCH GUIANA - SOCIAL CONDITIONS.
Castor, Elie, 1943- La Guyane, les grands
problèmes, les solutions possibles /. Paris ,
c1984. 337 p., [8] p. of plates : ISBN
2-903033-58-7 : DDC 988/.203 19
JL812 .C36 1984   *NYPL [Sc D 89-389]*

FRENCH LANGUAGE - AFRICA.
Inventaire des particularités lexicales du français
en Afrique noire /. Montréal , Paris [1983] lxi,
550 p. : ISBN 2-920021-15-X
NYPL [Sc E 88-235]

**FRENCH LANGUAGE - DICTIONARIES -
DANGALEAT.**
Ebobissé, Carl. Les verbaux du dangaléat de
l'est (Guera, Tchad) . Berlin , 1987. 104 p. ;
ISBN 3-496-00555-6 *NYPL [Sc E 88-231]*

**FRENCH LANGUAGE - DICTIONARIES -
YANZI.**
Wendo Nguma. Dictionnaire français-yansi /.
Bandundu, République du Zaïre , 1986. 276 p. ;
NYPL [Sc F 88-318]

**FRENCH LANGUAGE - GLOSSARIES,
VOCABULARIES, ETC.**
Inventaire des particularités lexicales du français
en Afrique noire /. Montréal , Paris [1983] lxi,
550 p. : ISBN 2-920021-15-X
NYPL [Sc E 88-235]

FRENCH LANGUAGE - HAITI.
Trouillot, Hénock. Les limites du créole dans
notre enseignement /. Port-au-Prince , 1980. 85
p. ;   *NYPL [Sc D 88-1400]*

**FRENCH LANGUAGE - STUDY AND
TEACHING - CAMEROON.**
Labatut, Roger. Interférences du fulfulde sur le
français écrit par les élèves peuls du
Nord-Cameroun [microform] /. [Dakar] , 1974.
iii, 35 p. ; *NYPL [Sc Micro R-4137 no.11]*

**FRENCH LANGUAGE - STUDY AND
TEACHING - FOREIGN SPEAKERS.**
Echos d'Afrique . [Paris] , c1984. 159 p. ;
ISBN 2-09-168451-1 *NYPL [Sc D 88-907]*

**FRENCH LANGUAGE - STUDY AND
TEACHING - FULAH STUDENTS.**
Labatut, Roger. Interférences du fulfulde sur le
français écrit par les élèves peuls du
Nord-Cameroun [microform] /. [Dakar] , 1974.
iii, 35 p. ; *NYPL [Sc Micro R-4137 no.11]*

**FRENCH LANGUAGE - STUDY AND
TEACHING - SENEGAL.**
Morin, Melle. Les retards scolaires et les échecs
au niveau de l'ecole primaire du Sénégal /.
[Dakar] [1966?] 143 leaves ;
NYPL [Sc F 87-439]

**FRENCH LANGUAGE - TEXT-BOOKS FOR
FOREIGN SPEAKERS.**
Echos d'Afrique . [Paris] , c1984. 159 p. ;
ISBN 2-09-168451-1 *NYPL [Sc D 88-907]*

**FRENCH LITERATURE - AFRICAN
AUTHORS.** see AFRICAN LITERATURE
(FRENCH)

**FRENCH LITERATURE - ZAIRIAN
AUTHORS.** see ZAIRIAN LITERATURE
(FRENCH)

FRENCH POETRY - AFRICAN AUTHORS.
see AFRICAN POETRY (FRENCH)

**FRENCH POETRY - BLACK AUTHORS -
HISTORY AND CRITICISM.**
Iyay Kimoni, 1938- Poésie de la négritude .
Kikwit , 1985. vi, 168 p. ; DDC 841/.009/896 19
PQ3897 .I93 1985   *NYPL [Sc B 89-18]*

Sartre, Jean Paul, 1905-1980. [Orphée noir.
English.] Black Orpheus. [Paris, 1963?] 65 p. ;
NYPL [Sc C 88-110]

**FRENCH POETRY - FOREIGN COUNTRIES -
HISTORY AND CRITICISM.**
Iyay Kimoni, 1938- Poésie de la négritude .

Kikwit , 1985. vi, 168 p. ; DDC 841/.009/896 19
PQ3897 .I93 1985   *NYPL [Sc B 89-18]*

French reaction to British slave emancipation /.
Jennings, Lawrence C. Baton Rouge , c1988. ix,
228 p. ; ISBN 0-8071-1429-4 (alk. paper) DDC
306/.362/0942 19
HT1163 .J46 1988   *NYPL [Sc E 89-139]*

French-speaking central Africa. Witherell, Julian
W. Washington, 1973. xiv, 314 p. ISBN
0-8444-0033-5
Z3692 .W5   *NYPL [JLF 74-197]*

**FRENTE DE LIBERTAÇÃO DE
MOÇAMBIQUE.**
Machel, Samora, 1933- Compreender a nossa
tarefa [microform]. [Maputo, Moçambique ,
1979] 20 p. ; *NYPL [Sc Micro F-11,163]*

Freud, Claude. Quelle coopération? : un bilan de
l'aide au développement / Claude Freud. Paris :
Karthala, c1988. 270 p. : maps ; 22 cm. (Les
Afriques) Bibliography: p. [263]-268. ISBN
2-86537-203-0
1. *Economic assistance, French - Africa.* 2. *Technical
assistance, French - Africa.* I. Series: Collection Les
Afriques. II. Title.
HC800 .F74 1988   *NYPL [Sc D 89-602]*

Freund, Bill. The African worker / Bill Freund.
Cambridge [Cambridgeshire] ; New York :
Cambridge University Press, 1988. viii, 200 p. ;
20 cm. (African society today) Includes index.
Bibliography: p. 166-194. ISBN 0-521-30758-9 DDC
305.5/62/096 19
1. *Labor and laboring classes - Africa.* I. Title. II.
Series.
HD8776.5 .F74 1988   *NYPL [Sc C 88-334]*

**Freyre, Gilberto, 1900-
CASA-GRANDE & SENZALA.**
Casa-grande & senzala e a crítica brasileira de
1933 a 1944 . Recife , 1985. 309 p. ; ISBN
85-7019-079-4 (pbk.) DDC 981/.00498 19
F2510.F7524 C37 1985
NYPL [HFB 86-2252]

[Casa-grande & senzala. English]
The masters and the slaves = Casa-grande &
senzala : a study in the development of
Brazilian civilization / by Gilberto Freyre ;
translated from the Portuguese by Samuel
Putnam ; introduction to the paperback
edition by David H.P. Maybury-Lewis.2nd
English-language ed., rev. Berkeley :
University of California Press, c1986. xc, 537
xliv p., [3] of plates : ill., plans ; 23 cm.
Includes indexes. Bibliography: p. 501-537. ISBN
0-520-05665-5 (pbk. : alk. paper) DDC 981 19
1. *Slavery - Brazil - History.* 2. *Blacks - Brazil -
History.* 3. *Indians of South America - Brazil - History.*
4. *Family - Brazil - History.* 5. *Brazil - Social life and
customs.* 6. *Brazil - Civilization - African influences.* I.
Title. II. Title: Casa-grande & sensala. III. Title:
Casa-grande e senzala.
F2510 .F7522 1986   *NYPL [HFB 87-2095]*

Friday, Keith (Keith Hudson Wellington), 1954-
Trotman, Donald A. B. Report on human rights
in Grenada . [Bustamante?] [198-] viii, 54 p. :
DDC 323.4/9/09729845 19
JC599.G76 T76 1980z NYPL [Sc D 88-816]

Friend to the Union. Remarks upon the
controversy between the Commonwealth of
Massachusetts and the State of South Carolina.
Boston, 1845. 21 p.
F273 .R38   *NYPL [Sc Rare C 89-9]*

**FRIENDLY SOCIETIES - BARBADOS -
DIRECTORIES.**
Blondel, Eaulin. Credit unions, co-operatives,
trade unions, and friendly societies in
Barbados . St. Augustine, Trinidad, Trinidad
and Tobago [1986] v, 102 p. ; DDC
334/.025/72981 19
HD3464.9.A6 B353 1986
NYPL [Sc F 88-361]

Friends of Adire. Okuboyejo, Betti. Adire, a living
craft /. [Nigeria] , c1987. 55 p. :
NYPL [Sc C 89-16]

The friendship /. Taylor, Mildred D. New York ,
1987. 53 p. : ISBN 0-8037-0418-6 (lib. bdg.) :
DDC [Fic] 19
PZ7.T21723 Fr 1987   *NYPL [Sc D 88-126]*

Fries, Marianne. Südafrika, SWA/Namibia :
Reiseführer mit Landeskunde / von Marianne
Fries und Eva Maria Brugger.6., völlig
neubearbeitete und erweuterte Aufl. Frankfurt

[am Main] : Mai's Reiseführer Verlag, 1987. 550 p. : ill., maps ; 17 cm. (Mai's Weltführer. Nr. 43) Folded maps inside covers. Includes index. Bibliography: p. 527-535. ISBN 3-87936-153-3
1. South Africa - Description and travel - 1966- - Guide-books. 2. Namibia - Description and travel - 1981- - Guide-books. I. Brugger, Eva Maria. II. Title.
NYPL [Sc B 88-18]

FRISSELL, HOLLIS BURKE, 1851-1917.
Hunter, Wilma King. Coming of age [microform] . 1982. 343 leaves.
NYPL [Sc Micro R-4688]

FROGS - JUVENILE FICTION.
Napjus, Alice James. Freddie found a frog. New York [1969] [29] p. DDC [Fic]
PZ7.N148 Fr   *NYPL [Sc C 89-27]*

Le Frolinat et les guerres civiles au Tchad (1977-1984) . Buijtenhuijs, Robert. Paris, France , c1987. 479 p. : ISBN 2-86537-196-4
NYPL [Sc E 88-426]

Frolizi. see Front for the Liberation of Zimbabwe.

From African symbols to physics . Umezinwa, Willy A. [Nigeria] c1988. 71 p. :
NYPL [Sc E 89-36]

From chattel to wage slavery. Tsotsi, W. M. Maseru , 1981. 136 p., [2] folded leaves of plates : DDC 306/.0968 19
DT763.6 .T76 1981   *NYPL [Sc D 89-22]*

From Colonial to Republic . Republic Bank (Trinidad and Tobago) Port-of-Spain, Trinidad, W.I. [1987] xxii, 206 p. : ISBN 976-8054-05-0
NYPL [Sc F 89-119]

From Egypt to Don Juan . Frye, Charles A. Lanham, MD , c1988. xiii, 129 p. : ISBN 0-8191-7120-4 (alk. paper) DDC 100 19
BF1999 .F77 1988   *NYPL [Sc D 88-1421]*

From federalism to neo-federalism in East Africa [microform] /. Rothchild, Donald S. Nairobi , 1966. 19 leaves ;
NYPL [Sc Micro R-4108 no.30]

From our yard : Jamaican poetry since independence / edited by Pamela Mordecai. Kingston, Jamaica : Institute of Jamaica Publications, 1987. xxviii, 235 p. ; 21 cm. (Jamaica 21 anthology series : no. 2) Bibliography: p. xxvii-xxviii.
1. Jamaican poetry. I. Mordecai, Pamela. II. Series.
NYPL [Sc D 89-412]

From pidginization to creolization of Africanisms in Black American English /. Twum-Akwaboah, Edward. [Los Angeles , 1973] 46 leaves ;   *NYPL [Sc F 88-210]*

From Rhodesia to Zimbabwe.
(2 2) Riddell, Roger. The land question [microform] /. London [1978?] 40 p. :
HD992.Z63 R52   *NYPL [*XME-13841]*

(6) Bratton, Michael. Beyond community development . London , 1978. 62 p. :
HN802.Z9 C62   *NYPL [JLD 81-437]*

(8) Tickner, Vincent. The food problem /. London , 1979. 78 p. ;   *NYPL [Sc D 88-188]*

From school--to work . Sullivan, Gerard. Oxford , c1981. xvi, 190 p. : DDC 373.12/913/096813 19
LC145.S78 S94 1981   *NYPL [Sc F 87-331]*

From slave boy to bishop . Milsome, John, 1924- Cambridge , 1987. [96] p. : ISBN 0-7188-2678-7 (pbk) DDC 283/.092/4 19
BV3625.N6C7   *NYPL [Sc C 88-106]*

From slave quarters to town houses. Cunha, Marianno Carneiro da, 1926-1980. Da senzala ao sobrado . São Paulo, SP , c1985. 185 p. : ISBN 85-21-30173-1 :
NA1599.N5 C86 1985   *NYPL [Sc E 88-565]*

From slavery to jouvert, 1975 /. Jackman, Randolph, 1932- [Port of Spain?] [1975] 68 p. ; DDC 972.98/3 19
F2119 .J32   *NYPL [Sc C 89-5]*

From the ground of hope /. Kalyegira, Junda. Nairobi , 1980. vii, 53 p. ;
NYPL [Sc C 88-298]

From where I sit . Wanjui, J. B. Nairobi, Kenya , 1986. xi, 88 p. ;   *NYPL [Sc C 88-90]*

From where I stand / Roy Sawh. London : Hasib, 1987. 94 p. : ill., facsims., ports. ; 1987.
CONTENTS. - Introduction / by Rudy Mohammed.--Roy Sawh : a profile / by Lionel

Morrison.--From where I stand / by Roy Sawh.--Black power in Britain / Roy Sawh.--Epilogue / David Dabydeen. ISBN 0-9956664-9-1
1. West Indians - Great Britain - Biography. 2. Black power - Great Britain. I. Sawh, Roy, 1934-. II. Morrison, Lionel.   *NYPL [Sc C 88-30]*

FRONT DE LIBÉRATION NATIONALE DU TCHAD.
Buijtenhuijs, Robert. Le Frolinat et les guerres civiles du Tchad (1977-1984) . Paris, France , c1987. 479 p. : ISBN 2-86537-196-4
NYPL [Sc E 88-426]

Front for the Liberation of Mozambique. see Frente de Libertação de Moçambique.

Front for the Liberation of Zimbabwe.
Resolutions adopted by the inaugural congress of the Front for the Liberation of Zimbabwe, held from August 21 to September 5, 1972 [microform]. [S.l] : The Front, [1972?] 3 leaves ; 33 cm. Microfilm. New York: Imperfect copy: leaf 2 wanting.
1. Zimbabwe - Politics and government - 1965-1979. I. Title.   *NYPL [Sc Micro R-4137 no.15]*

Front populaire (Burkina Faso) Statuts et programme d'action / Front populaire. Ouagadougou : Impr. nationale, [1988]. 47 p. ; 22 cm. Cover title. "Mars 1988."
1. Front populaire (Burkina Faso). 2. Burkina Faso - Politics and government. I. Title.
NYPL [Sc D 88-1452]

FRONT POPULAIRE (BURKINA FASO)
Front populaire (Burkina Faso) Statuts et programme d'action /. Ouagadougou [1988]. 47 p. ;   *NYPL [Sc D 88-1452]*

Front populaire ivoirien. Propositions pour gouverner la Côte-d'Ivoire / Front populaire ivoirien (F.P.I.) ; introduction de Laurent Gbagbo. Paris : L'Harmattan, c1987- v. : ill. ; 22 cm. (Collection Points de vue, 0761-5248) Includes bibliographical references. ISBN 2-85802-882-6 (v. 1) DDC 361.6/1/096668 19
1. Ivory Coast - Politics and government - 1960-. 2. Ivory Coast - Economic policy. 3. Ivory Coast - Social policy. I. Series.
JQ3386.A2 F76 1987   *NYPL [Sc D 88-1142]*

FRONTIER AND PIONEER LIFE - KENYA.
Memories of Kenya . London , 1986. xvi, 160 p., [16] p. of plates : ISBN 0-237-50919-9
NYPL [Sc F 88-102]

FRONTIER AND PIONEER LIFE - WEST (U. S.)
Katz, William Loren. The Black West /. Seattle, WA , c1987. xiii, 348 p. : ISBN 0-940880-17-2 DDC 978/.00496073 19
E185.925 .K37 1987   *NYPL [Sc E 89-86]*

Le frontiere in Africa. Bono, Salvatore. [Milano], 1972. xix, 284 p.   *NYPL [JFD 75-1056]*

Les frontières du refus . Aquarone, Marie-Christine. Paris , 1987. 133 p. : ISBN 2-222-03962-2   *NYPL [Sc F 89-112]*

Frontline Journal. Towards the decolonization of the British educational system /. London, England , 19. 128 p. : ISBN 0-907015-32-8
NYPL [Sc D 88-1346]

Frontline Southern Africa : destructive engagement / edited by Phyllis Johnson and David Martin. New York : Four Walls Eight Windows, 1988. xxxv, 530 p., [16] p. of leaves : ill., maps ; 24 cm. Includes index. Bibliography: p. 467-510. ISBN 0-941423-08-5 : DDC 322/.5/0968 19
1. Apartheid - South Africa. 2. Africa, Southern - Military relations - South Africa. 3. South Africa - Military relations - Africa, Southern. I. Johnson, Phyllis. II. Martin, David, 1956-. III. Gift of J.P. Morgan and Co., Inc.
DT747.S6 F76 1988   *NYPL [JLE 89-595]*

Frontline Southern Africa /. Bernstein, Keith. London , c1988. x, 117 p. : ISBN 0-7470-3012-X (pbk) DDC 968.06/3 19
HN800.A8   *NYPL [Sc E 89-122]*

The fruits of victory . Benedict, Michael Les. Lanham, MD , c1986. xiii, 159 p. ; ISBN 0-8191-5557-8 (pbk. : alk. paper) : DDC 973.8 19
E668 .B462 1986   *NYPL [IKR 87-1888]*

Fry, Jacqueline, 1923- Visual variations : African sculpture from the Justin and Elisabeth Lang collection : 1 March-3 May 1987, Agnes Etherington Art Centre, Queen's University,

Kingston, Canada / Jacqueline Fry. Kingston, Canada : The Centre, c1987. vii, 63 p. : ill. (some col.) ; 23 x 29 cm. English and French. Title on added t.p.: Variations plastiques. Includes bibliographies. DDC 730/.0966/074011372 19
1. Lang, Justin - Art collections - Exhibitions. 2. Lang, Elisabeth - Art collections - Exhibitions. 3. Agnes Etherington Art Centre - Exhibitions. 4. Sculpture, Black - Africa, West - Exhibitions. 5. Sculpture, Primitive - Africa, West - Exhibitions. 6. Sculpture - Private collections - Canada - Kingston - Exhibitions. I. Agnes Etherington Art Centre. II. Title. III. Title: Variations plastiques.
NB1098 .F79 1987   *NYPL [Sc F 88-189]*

Frye, Charles A. From Egypt to Don Juan : the anatomy of Black philosophy / by Charles A. Frye with a preface by August Coppola. Lanham, MD : University Press of America, c1988. xiii, 129 p. : ill. ; 23 cm. Includes bibliographical references. ISBN 0-8191-7120-4 (alk. paper) DDC 100 19
1. Blacks - Race identity - Miscellanea. 2. Philosophy - Miscellanea. I. Title. II. Title: Black philosophy.
BF1999 .F77 1988   *NYPL [Sc D 88-1421]*

Frye Street & environs . Bonner, Marita, 1899-1971. Boston , c1987. xxix, 286 p. ; ISBN 0-8070-6300-2 DDC 810/.8/0896073 19
PS3503 .O439 1987   *NYPL [Sc D 88-683]*

Frye Street and environs. Bonner, Marita, 1899-1971. Frye Street & environs . Boston , c1987. xxix, 286 p. ; ISBN 0-8070-6300-2 DDC 810/.8/0896073 19
PS3503 .O439 1987   *NYPL [Sc D 88-683]*

Fugitive slave notices, Illinois. Tregillis, Helen Cox. River roads to freedom . Bowie, Md. , 1988. 122 p. : ISBN 1-556-13120-8 DDC 929/.3/089960773 19
F540 .T7 1988   *NYPL [Sc D 88-1442]*

FUGITIVE SLAVES - BRAZIL.
Moura, Clovis. Quilombos . São Paulo , 1987. 94 p. ; ISBN 85-08-01858-4
NYPL [Sc C 88-3]

FUGITIVE SLAVES - CANADA.
Bramble, Linda. Black fugitive slaves in early Canada /. St. Catharines, Ont. , c1988. 93 p. : ISBN 0-920277-16-0 DDC 973.7/115 19
NYPL [Sc E 89-121]

Teatero, William, 1953- John Anderson . [Kingston, Ont.] , c1986. 183 p. : ISBN 0-9692685-0-5 : DDC 345.71/056/0924 19
NYPL [Sc E 89-113]

FUGITIVE SLAVES - DOMINICAN REPUBLIC.
Deive, Carlos Esteban, 1935- Los cimarrones del maniel de Neiba . Santo Domingo, República Dominicana , 1985. 199 p. :
NYPL [Sc D 89-173]

FUGITIVE SLAVES - HAITI.
Deive, Carlos Esteban, 1935- Los cimarrones del maniel de Neiba . Santo Domingo, República Dominicana , 1985. 199 p. :
NYPL [Sc D 89-173]

FUGITIVE SLAVES - ILLINOIS - REGISTERS.
Tregillis, Helen Cox. River roads to freedom . Bowie, Md. , 1988. 122 p. : ISBN 1-556-13120-8 DDC 929/.3/089960773 19
F540 .T7 1988   *NYPL [Sc D 88-1442]*

FUGITIVE SLAVES - IOWA - JUVENILE FICTION.
May, Charles Paul. Stranger in the storm. London, New York [1972] 92 p. ISBN 0-200-71821-5 DDC [Fic]
PZ7.M4505 St   *NYPL [Sc D 88-1430]*

FUGITIVE SLAVES - PENNSYLVANIA - JUVENILE FICTION.
De Angeli, Marguerite, 1899- Thee, Hannah /. New York , 1940. [88] p. :
NYPL [Sc D 88-635]

FUGITIVE SLAVES - UNITED STATES - BIOGRAPHY - JUVENILE LITERATURE.
Hamilton, Virginia. Anthony Burns . New York , c1988. xiii, 193 p. ; ISBN 0-394-88185-0 DDC 973.6/6/0924 B 92 19
E450.B93 H36 1988   *NYPL [Sc D 88-1157]*

FUGITIVE SLAVES - UNITED STATES - JUVENILE FICTION.
Winter, Jeanette. Follow the drinking gourd /. New York , c1988. [48] p. : ISBN

0-394-89694-7 :   DDC [E] 19
PZ7.W7547 Fo 1988   NYPL [Sc F 89-59]

FUGITIVE SLAVES - WEST INDIES - BIOGRAPHY.
Prince, Mary. The history of Mary Prince, a West Indian slave, related by herself /.
London , New York , 1987. xvi, 124 p. ;   ISBN 0-86358-192-7 DDC 305.5/67/0924 B 19
HT869.P6 A3 1987   NYPL [Sc C 89-31]

Fuglestad, Finn, 1942- Norwegian missions in African history /. Oslo : Oxford [Oxfordshire] ; 2 v. :   ISBN 82-00-07418-8 (v. 1)   DDC 266/.023/48106 19
BV3625.M2 N67 1986   NYPL [Sc D 89-26]

FUL LANGUAGE. see FULAH LANGUAGE.

FULAH LANGUAGE - TEXTS.
Sylla, Yèro, 1942- Récit initiatique peul du Maciña . [Dakar] , 1975. vi, 113 p. ;
NYPL [Sc F 87-257]

FULAHS.
Adepegba, Cornelius Oyeleke, 1941- Decorative arts of the Fulani nomads /. Ibadan, Nigeria , 1986. 48 p. :   ISBN 978-12-1195-4
NYPL [Sc D 88-735]

FULAHS - BIOGRAPHY.
Bocquené, Henri. Moi, un Mbororo . Paris , c1986. 387 p., [12] p. of plates :   ISBN 2-86537-164-6   *NYPL [Sc E 89-66]*

FULANI. see FULAHS.

Fulani, Dan. Sauna and the drug pedlars. London : Hodder and Stoughton, 1986. 109 p. : ill. ; 21 cm.   ISBN 0-340-32789-8 (pbk)
1. Nigeria - Fiction. I. Title.   *NYPL [Sc C 88-74]*

Fulani, Lenora. The Psychopathology of everyday racism and sexism /. New York , c1988. xix, 120 p. ;   ISBN 0-918393-51-5 (pbk.)   DDC 305.4/2 19
RC451.4.M58 P79 1988
NYPL [Sc D 89-449]

FULBE. see FULAHS.

FULBE LANGUAGE. see FULAH LANGUAGE.

FULDE LANGUAGE. see FULAH LANGUAGE.

FULFULDE. see FULAHS.

FULFULDE LANGUAGE. see FULAH LANGUAGE.

The Full fruits of freedom. Chester County, Pa. : Lincoln University, [1935?] 47 p. : ill., ports. ; 26 cm.
1. Lincoln University (Pa.). I. Lincoln University (Pa.).
NYPL [Sc F 89-69]

Fuller, Louisia. The risks of Ro : episode one : Beginning of no end / Louisia Fuller. Teaneck, N.J. : Ethnic Role Model Productions, c1988. 105 p ; 22 cm.   ISBN 0-945779-00-3
1. Afro-Americans - Fiction. I. Title. II. Title: Beginning of no end.   *NYPL [Sc D 88-1172]*

Fun for Chris /. Randall, Blossom E. Chicago , c1956. 26 p. :   *NYPL [Sc E 88-238]*

Fun with David /. Detroit. Great Cities Program for School Improvement. Writes' Committee. Chicago , c1962. 31 p.:   *NYPL [Sc E 89-40]*

Functional literacy and cooperative education . Easton, Peter A. 1972. v, 87 leaves :
NYPL [Sc F 88-52]

Fundação Joaquim Nabuco. Gilberto Freyre entre nós /. Recife , 1988. 115 p. ;   ISBN 85-7019-140-5 *NYPL [Sc D 89-320]*

Orçamento : 1982 / Fundação Joaquim Nabuco. Recife : Editora Massangana, 1982. 92 p. ; 17 x 22 cm. (Série Documentos (Fundação Joaquim Nabuco) . 18)   ISBN 85-7019-046-8
1. Fundação Joaquim Nabuco - Appropriations and expenditures. I. Title. II. Series.
NYPL [Sc B 88-49]

Plano diretor de informática, 82-84 / Fundação Joaquim Nabuco. Recife : Editora Massangana, 1982. 101 p., 1 folded leaf : ill. ; 22 cm. (Série Documentos (Fundação Joaquim Nabuco) . 20)
1. Fundação Joaquim Nabuco - Data processing. 2. Information storage and retrieval systems - Social sciences. I. Title. II. Series.   NYPL [Sc D 88-924]

30 anos do Instituto Joaquim Nabuco de Pesquisas Sociais /. Recife , 1981. 343 p. :   ISBN 85-7019-008-5   DDC 300.72081 19
H67.R44 A13 1981   NYPL [Sc D 88-871]

FUNDAÇÃO JOAQUIM NABUCO - DATA PROCESSING.
Fundação Joaquim Nabuco. Plano diretor de informática, 82-84 /. Recife , 1982. 101 p., 1 folded leaf :   *NYPL [Sc D 88-924]*

FUNDAÇÃO JOAQUIM NABUCO - APPROPRIATIONS AND EXPENDITURES.
Fundação Joaquim Nabuco. Orçamento . Recife , 1982. 92 p. ;   ISBN 85-7019-046-8
NYPL [Sc B 88-49]

FUNDAMENTAL EDUCATION (COMMUNITY DEVELOPMENT) see COMMUNITY DEVELOPMENT.

FUNERAL RITES AND CEREMONIES, EWE (AFRICAN PEOPLE)
Agbetiafa, Komla. Les ancêtres et nous . Dakar , 1985. 95 p. :   ISBN 2-7236-0929-4
NYPL [Sc D 88-7]

FUNNIES. see COMIC BOOKS, STRIPS, ETC.

The funny old bag. Weil, Lisl. New York [1974] [40] p.   ISBN 0-8193-0717-3   DDC [E]
PZ7.W433 Fu   NYPL [Sc E 88-529]

Fusco, Coco. Young, British, and Black : the work of Sankofa and Black Audio Film Collective / by Coco Fusco. Buffalo, N.Y. : Hallwalls /Contemporary Arts Center, c1988. 65 p. : ill. ; 23 cm. Filmography: p. 61. Includes bibliographical references. With autograph of Martina Attille.
1. Sankofa Film/Video Collective. 2. Black Audio Film Collective. 3. Moving pictures - Great Britain - Production and direction. 4. Blacks in the motion picture industry - Great Britain. I. Title.
NYPL [Sc D 88-1186]

Fusscas, Helen K. Charles Ethan Porter,1847?-1923. Marlborough, CT , 1987. 113 p. :   ISBN 0-9619196-0-4
NYPL [Sc F 88-26]

FUTURE LIFE (ISLAM)
'Isá 'Abd Allāh Muḥammad al-Mahdī, 1945- Eternal life after death [microform] /. Brooklyn, N.Y. [197-?] 36 p. ;
NYPL [Sc Micro R-4114 no.3]

Futures studies for African planners. Reclaiming the future . Oxford , Riverton, N.J. , c1986. xvi, 197 p. ;   ISBN 1-85148-010-2 (pbk.) :   DDC 303.4/96 19
DT4 .R43 1986   NYPL [Sc D 88-584]

Fyfe, Christopher.
African medicine in the modern world . Edinburgh [1987] 222 p. :   DDC 615.8/82/096 19
GR350   NYPL [Sc D 87-1283]

Sierra Leone, 1787-1987 . Manchester ; New York : 577 p., [8] p. of plates :   ISBN 0-7190-2791-8 (pbk.) :   DDC 966/.4 19
DT516.7 .S54 1988   NYPL [Sc E 88-461]

GÃ LANGUAGE - TEXTS.
Nyonmo wiemo, Kanemo hefatalo . London, 1963. v, 154 p. ;   *NYPL [Sc C 87-395]*

GAHU - INSTRUCTION AND STUDY.
Locke, David, 1949- Drum gahu . Crown Point, Ind. , c1987. ix, 142 p. :   ISBN 0-941677-03-6 :   DDC 789/.01 19
MT655 .L6 1987   NYPL [Sc E 88-391]

Gai saber monograph .
(5) Male homosexuality in Central and South America /. New York , 1987. 199 p. ;
NYPL [Sc D 88-557]

Gaillard, Frye, 1946- The dream long deferred / by Frye Gaillard. Chapel Hill : University of North Carolina Press, c1988. xxi, 192 p. ; 24 cm. Includes index.   ISBN 0-8078-1794-5 (alk. paper) DDC 370.19/342 19
1. Busing for school integration - North Carolina - Charlotte - History. 2. School integration - North Carolina - Charlotte - History. I. Title.
LC214.523.C48 G35 1988
NYPL [Sc E 88-527]

Gaither, Edmund B. Massachusetts masters : Afro-American artists : a survey exhibition of the works of Afro-American artists working in Massachusetts in the twentieth century with particular highlights on the careers of Ellen Banks, Calvin Burnett, Allan R. Crite, Milton Derr, Lois Mailou Jones, John Wilson / Edmund Barry Gaither. Boston : Museum of the National Center of Afro-American Artists :

Museum of Fine Arts, [1988] 48 p. : ill. (some col.) ; 29 cm. "Museum of Fine Arts, Boston, in cooperation with the Museum of the National Center of Afro-American Artists, January 16-March 6, 1988, celebrating 350 years of the black presence in Massachusetts."
1. Afro-American art - Massachusetts - Exhibitions. 2. Art, Modern - 20th century - Massachusetts - Exhibitions. 3. Afro-American artists - Massachusetts - Biography. I. National Center of Afro-American Artists. Museum. II. Museum of Fine Arts, Boston. III. Title.
NYPL [Sc F 89-159]

Gakaara wa Wanjaũ.
Mwandĩki wa Mau Mau ithaamĩrio-inĩ / rĩandĩkĩitwo nĩ Gakaara wa Wanjaũ. Nairobi [Kenya] : Heinemann Educational Books, 1983. xvii, 189 p. : ill. ; 21 cm. In Kikuyu.
1. Gakaara wa Wanjaũ. 2. Mau Mau. 3. Kikuyu language - Texts. 4. Political prisoners - Kenya - Diaries. 5. Kenya - History - To 1963. I. Title.
NYPL [Sc D 87-156]

[Mwandĩki wa Mau Mau ithaamĩrio-inĩ. English]
Mau Mau author in detention / Gakaara wa Wanjau ; translated from the Gĩkũyũ by Paul Ngigi Njoroge. Nairobi : Heinemann Kenya, 1988. xix, 252 p. ; 21 cm. "First published in the Gikuyu language, in 1983"--T.p. verso.   ISBN 996-646-354-2
1. Gakaara wa Wanjaũ. 2. Mau Mau. 3. Political prisoners - Kenya - Diaries. 4. Kenya - History - To 1963. I. Title.   *NYPL [Sc D 89-444]*

GAKAARA WA WANJAŨ.
Gakaara wa Wanjaũ. Mwandĩki wa Mau Mau ithaamĩrio-inĩ /. Nairobi [Kenya] , 1983. xvii, 189 p. :   *NYPL [Sc D 87-156]*

Gakaara wa Wanjaũ. [Mwandĩki wa Mau Mau ithaamĩrio-inĩ. English.] Mau Mau author in detention /. Nairobi , 1988. xix, 252 p. ;   ISBN 996-646-354-2   *NYPL [Sc D 89-444]*

Galdone, Paul. (illus) Greene, Roberta. Two and me makes three. New York [1970] [36] p.
PZ7.G843 Tw   NYPL [Sc F 88-375]

Gale Research Inc. Black writers . Detroit, Mi. , c1989. xxiv, 619 p. ;   ISBN 0-8103-2772-4
NYPL [Sc F 89-57]

Galgut, Damon, 1963- Small circle of beings / Damon Galgut. London : Constable, 1988. 221 p. ; 23 cm. CONTENTS. - Small circle of beings.--Lovers.--Shadows.--The clay ox.--Rick.
1. South Africa - Fiction. I. Title.
NYPL [Sc D 88-1342]

Gallardo, Jorge Emilio. Presencia africana en la cultura de América Latina : vigencia de los cultos afroamericanos / Jorge Emilio Gallardo. Buenos Aires, Argentina : F. García Cambeiro, c1986. 123 p. ; 22 cm. (Colección Estudios latinoamericanos. 31) Bibliography: p. 73-82.   ISBN 950-643-006-3   DDC 299/.69 19
1. Blacks - Latin America - Religion. 2. Africa, Sub-Saharan - Religion. 3. Latin America - Religion. I. Title.
BL2490 .G33 1986   NYPL [Sc D 89-358]

Galle, Etienne. L'homme vivant de Wole Soyinka / Etienne Galle. Paris : Silex Éditions, c1987. 270 p. ; 22 cm. Includes bibliographical references and index.   ISBN 2-903871-88-4
1. Soyinka, Wole - Criticism and interpretation. I. Title.
NYPL [Sc D 88-1128]

Gamba la nyoka /. Kezilahabi, Euphrase. Arusha [Tanzania] , 1979, 1981 printing. 151 p. ;
NYPL [Sc C 88-167]

The Gambia : the land and the people : Senegalo-Gambian tourist guide. [Dakar, Senegal] : Nouvelles éditions africaines, [1983?] 80 p. : col. ill., maps ; 27 cm. English and French. With: Le Sénégal. [Dakar, Senegal] : Nouvelles éditions africaines, [1983?]. Colored map of folded leaf of plates inserted.   ISBN 2-7236-0911-1
1. Gambia - Description and travel - Guide-books.
DT509.2 .G36 1967   NYPL [Sc F 88-202]

Gambia. Amersham : Hulton Educational, 1984. 16 p. : ill. (some col.), maps ; 21 cm. (Our world. Around the world) Cover title. Text, maps on inside covers. SCHOMBURG CHILDREN'S COLLECTION.   ISBN 0-7175-1046-8 (pbk)   DDC 966/.5103 19
1. Gambia - Juvenile literature. I. Schomburg Children's Collection. II. Series.
DT509.22   NYPL [Sc D 88-1182]

GAMBIA - DESCRIPTION AND TRAVEL - GUIDE-BOOKS.
The Gambia . [Dakar, Senegal] [1983?] 80 p. :
ISBN 2-7236-0911-1
DT509.2 .G36 1967　　　**NYPL [Sc F 88-202]**

GAMBIA - JUVENILE LITERATURE.
Gambia. Amersham , 1984. 16 p. : ISBN
0-7175-1046-8 (pbk) : DDC 966/.5103 19
DT509.22　　　**NYPL [Sc D 88-1182]**

GAMBIA - OCCUPATIONS.
Singhateh, Modu F. A day in their lives /.
Banjul [1984] 87 p :　　　**NYPL [Sc E 88-98]**

GAMBIA - SOCIAL LIFE AND CUSTOMS.
Wilkins, Frances. Let's visit The Gambia /.
London , 1985. 94 p. : ISBN 0-222-01129-7
　　　　　　　NYPL [Sc D 88-405]

G'amèrakano . Rawiri, Ntyugwetondo. Paris ,
c1988. 197 p. ; ISBN 2-87693-021-8
　　　　　　　NYPL [Sc D 89-202]

Games /. Freed, Arthur. [N.J.] , 1968. [32] p. :
　　　　　　　NYPL [Sc B 89-25]

GAMES - AFRICA, WEST.
Cheska, Alyce Taylor. Traditional games and
dances in West African nations /. Schorndorf ,
1987. 136 p. : ISBN 3-7780-6411-8 (pbk). DDC
793.3/1966 19
GV1713.A358 C48 1987
　　　　　　　NYPL [JFE 87-5517]

Games against nature . Harms, Robert.
Cambridge [Cambridgeshire] , New York ,
1987. xi, 276 p. ; ISBN 0-521-34373-9 DDC
967/.24 19
DT546.245.N86 H37 1987
　　　　　　　NYPL [Sc E 88-192]

GAMES, CHILDREN. see GAMES.

GAMES - JUVENILE LITERATURE.
Freed, Arthur. Games /. [N.J.] , 1968. [32] p. :
　　　　　　　NYPL [Sc B 89-25]

Gammond, Peter. Duke Ellington / Peter
Gammond. London : Apollo, 1987. 127 p. :
ill. ; 20 cm. (Jazz masters series. 10) Bibliography: p.
81-84. Discography: p. 85-127. ISBN 0-948820-00-4
(pbk.) :
*1. Jazz musicians - United States - Biography. 2.
Afro-American musicians - Biography. I. Title. II.
Series.*　　　　**NYPL [JNC 87-8]**

Gana, Bulama. Borno State (Nigeria) Government
white paper on the report of Panel on Eduction
Review in Borno State /. Maiduguri [1984] 56
p. :　　　　　　**NYPL [Sc E 88-424]**

Ganay, Solange de. Ethnologiques . Paris , 1987.
xxxvi, 430 p. : ISBN 2-7056-6025-9
　　　　　　　NYPL [Sc E 88-39]

GANGS - NIGERIA - BENIN CITY.
Enonchong, Charles. The rise and fall of Anini
/. Calabar, Nigeria [1988] 73 p. :
　　　　　　　NYPL [Sc C 89-8]

GANGSTERS. see GANGS.

Ganiage, Jean. L'Afrique au XXe siècle / par
Jean Ganiage et Hubert Deschamps et Odette
Guitard ; avec la collaboration de André
Martel. Paris : Sirey, 1966. 908 p. : maps (some
col.) ; 23 cm. Includes bibliographies.
*1. Africa - History - 20th century. I. Guitard, Odette.
II. Deschamps, Hubert Jules, 1900-. III. Title.*
　　　　　　　NYPL [Sc D 88-236]

Gannon, Edmund J. Sub-Saharan Africa : an
introduction / Edmund J. Gannon.
Washington : Council on American Affairs,
c1978. 185 p. : map ; 23 cm. Includes
bibliographical references.
I. Council on American Affairs. II. Title.
　　　　　　　NYPL [JFD 84-783]

Ganzel, Edi, 1946- Kitanzi / Edi Ganzel. Dar es
Salaam : Utamaduni Publishers, [1984] 80 p. ;
18 cm. In Swahili.
1. Swahili language - Texts. I. Title.
PL8704.G35 K57 1984　　**NYPL [Sc C 88-120]**

Garang, John, 1945- John Garang speaks / by
John Garang ; edited and introduced by
Mansour Khalid. London ; New York : KPI,
1987. xii, 147 p. ; 22 cm. Speeches, letters and
public statements written or delivered between 1984
and 1986. ISBN 0-7103-0268-1
*1. Sudan People's Liberation Movement. I. Kh alid,
Mansour, 1931-. II. Title.*　**NYPL [Sc D 88-418]**

Garba, Joeseph Nanven, 1943- Diplomatic
soldiering : Nigerian foreign policy 1975-1979 /

Joe Garba. Ibadan : Spectrum Books, 1987.
xviii, 238 p., [9] p. of plates : ill. ; 22 cm.
Includes index. ISBN 978-246-176-8 (limp)
*1. Nigeria - Foreign relations - 1960-. 2. Africa -
Politics and government - 1960-. 3. Nigeria - Politics
and government - 1975-1979. I. Title.*
　　　　　　　NYPL [Sc D 88-726]

Garber, Eric. Worlds apart . Boston, Mass. ,
1986. 293 p. ; ISBN 0-932870-87-2 (pbk.) : DDC
813/.0876/08353 19
PS648.H57 W67 1986　　**NYPL [JFD 87-7753]**

García Caturla, Alejandro Evelio, 1906-1940.
Guillén, Nicolás, 1902- Motivos de son /. La
Habana , 1980. 32, [88] p. :
　　　　　　　NYPL [Sc E 87-151]

Garcia, Luc, 1937- Le royaume du Dahomé face à
la pénétration coloniale : affrontements et
incompréhension (1875-1894) / Luc Garcia.
Paris : Karthala. c1988. 284 p., [8] p. of plates :
ill, maps, ports. ; 24 cm. Includes bibliographical
references and index.
1. Benin - History - to 1894. I. Title.
　　　　　　　NYPL [Sc E 89-145]

Gardam, Jane. Black faces, white faces / Jane
Gardam. London : Hamilton, 1975. 133 p. ; 21
cm. ISBN 0-241-89250-3 :
1. Jamaica - Fiction. I. Title.
PZ4.G218 Bl PR6057.A623
　　　　　　　NYPL [JFD 77-1786]

**GARDEN ARCHITECTURE. see
ARCHITECTURE, DOMESTIC.**

Garden, Nancy. What happened in Marston.
Illustrated by Richard Cuffari. New York, Four
Winds Press [1971] 190 p. illus. 22 cm. Because
of their close friendship, a middle class white boy and a
black boy from the slums have a hard time sorting out
their feelings when a race war breaks out in their city.
SCHOMBURG CHILDREN'S COLLECTION. DDC
[Fic]
*1. United States - Race relations - Juvenile fiction. I.
Cuffari, Richard, 1925- illus. II. Schomburg Children's
Collection. III. Title.*
PZ7.G165 Wh　　　**NYPL [Sc D 89-98]**

Gardi, Bernhard. Ein Markt wie Mopti :
Handwerkerkasten und traditionelle Techniken
in Mali / Bernhard Gardi. Basel :
Ethnologisches Seminar der Universität und
Museum für Völkerkunde : In Kommission bei
Wepf, 1985. 387 p. : 104 ill. (some col.) ; 24
cm. (Basler Beiträge zur Ethnologie. Bd. 25) Summary
in English and French. Originally presented as the
author's thesis (doctoral)--Universität Basel, 1983.
Includes index. Bibliography: p. 381-387. ISBN
3-85977-175-2 DDC 745/.0966/23 19
*1. Handicraft - Mali - Mopti Region. 2. Artisans -
Mali - Mopti Region. I. Title. II. Series.*
TT119.M34 G37 1985　　**NYPL [Sc E 87-494]**

Gardner, Burleigh B. (Burleigh Bradford), 1902-
(joint author) Davis, Allison, 1902- Deep South.
Los Angeles, CA , 1988. xxiii, 567 p. :
ISBN 0-934934-26-6　　**NYPL [Sc E 89-45]**

Gardner, Lillian, 1907- Sal Fisher at Girl Scout
camp. New York, F. Watts [1959] 217 p. illus.
21 cm. SCHOMBURG CHILDREN'S
COLLECTION.
*1. Girl Scouts - Juvenile fiction. I. Schomburg
Children's Collection. II. Title.*
PZ7.G1793 Saj　　　**NYPL [Sc D 88-1494]**

Gardner, Mark, 1939- Klaasse, Piet. Jam session .
Newton Abbot [Devon] , 1985. 192 p. : ISBN
0-7153-8710-3 DDC 785.42/092/2 19
ML3506 .K58 1985　　　**NYPL [Sc G 88-13]**

Gardner, Mary R. (joint author) Davis, Allison,
1902- Deep South. Los Angeles, CA , 1988.
xxiii, 567 p. : ISBN 0-934934-26-6
　　　　　　　NYPL [Sc E 89-45]

Garlake, Peter S.
Great Zimbabwe / described and explained by
Peter Garlake. Rev. 1985. Harare, Zimbabwe :
Zimbabwe Pub. House, 1985, 64 p. : ill. ; 21
cm. ISBN 0-949225-24-X
*1. Great Zimbabwe (City). 2. Mashona - Antiquities. I.
Title.*　　　　**NYPL [Sc D 87-1002]**

Life at Great Zimbabwe / devised and written
by Peter Garlake ; illustrated by Zimbabwe
Cooperative Craft Workshop Ltd ; [illustrated
by Michael White, handscripted by Barbara
Strachan]. Gweru, Zimbabwe : Mambo Press,
1983, c1982. [36] p. : ill. ; 30 cm. (Exploring
Zimbabwe. 1) Discusses life at Great Zimbabwe, a city

of stone whose height of power was in the fourteenth
century and whose structure is typical of other
community dwellings at that time. Cover title.
SCHOMBURG CHILDREN'S COLLECTION. ISBN
0-86922-180-9 (pbk.) DDC 968.91 19
*1. Great Zimbabwe (City) - Juvenile literature. I. White,
Michael, ill. II. Zimbabwe Cooperative Craft Workshop.
III. Schomburg Children's Collection. IV. Title. V.
Series.*
DT962.9.G73 G374 1983
　　　　　　　NYPL [Sc F 88-175]

The painted caves : an introduction to the
prehistoric art of Zimbabwe / Peter Garlake.
Harare, Zimbabwe : Modus Publications, c1987.
iv, 100 p., [8] p. of plates : ill. (some col.) ; 24
x 21 cm. Bibliography: p. 96-97. ISBN
0-908309-00-7
*1. Art, Prehistoric - Zimbabwe. 2. Cave-drawings -
Zimbabwe. 3. Zimbabwe - Antiquities. I. Title.*
　　　　　　　NYPL [Sc D 89-411]

**Garland reference library of social science.
Source books on education.**
(vol. 16) Washington, Valora. Black children
and American institutions . New York , 1988.
xv, 432 p. ; ISBN 0-8240-8517-5 : DDC
305.2/3/08996073 19
Z1361.N39 W34 1988 E185.86
　　　　　　　NYPL [Sc D 89-385]

Garmers, Sonia. Brueria di henter mundo =
Magie uit alle landen / Sonia Garmers, Hanny
Lim.3e, geheel herziene en uitgebreide druk.
Curaçao : Augustinus, [1986?] 58 p. : ill. ; 24
cm. Dutch, Papiamento, and Spanish. DDC 133.4/3
19
1. Papiamento - Occultism. I. Lim, Hanny. II. Title.
BF1618.D8 G37 1986　　**NYPL [Sc E 89-237]**

Garnett, Ruth (Ruth Miriam) A move further
south / by Ruth Garnett. Chicago, Ill. : Third
World Press, 1987. 63 p. ; 23 cm. ISBN
0-88378-113-1 (pbk.)
I. Title.　　　　**NYPL [Sc D 88-691]**

GARRISON, WILLIAM LLOYD, 1805-1879.
Anti-Slavery Meeting (1855 : Boston) The
Boston mob of "gentlemen of property and
standing." . Boston , 1855 (Boston : J.B.
Yerrinton and Son, printers) 76 p. ;
E450.B74　　　**NYPL [Sc Rare F 88-44]**

Garvey--Africa, Europe, the Americas / edited by
Rupert Lewis & Maureen Warner-Lewis.
Kingston, Jamaica : Institute of Social and
Economic Research, University of the West
Indies, 1986. xi, 208 p., [4] p. of plates : ill. ;
21 cm. Papers originally presented at the International
Seminar on Marcus Garvey, Mona, Jamaica, January
2-6, 1973. Includes bibliographies.
*1. Garvey, Marcus, 1887-1940 - Congresses. I. Lewis,
Rupert. II. Warner-Lewis, Maureen. III. International
Seminar on Marcus Garvey (1973 : Mona, Jamaica).*
　　　　　　　NYPL [Sc D 88-1131]

GARVEY, AMY ASHWOOD, 1895-1969.
Yard, Lionel M. Biography of Amy Ashwood
Garvey, 1897-1969 . [S.l.] [198-?] vii, 233 p. :
　　　　　　　NYPL [Sc E 88-541]

Garvey, Joan B. Beautiful crescent : a history of
New Orleans / by Joan B. Garvey and Mary
Lou Widmer.3rd ed. New Orleans, LA :
Garmer Pr., c1988. 249 p. : ill. ; 23 cm. Includes
index. Bibliography: p. 209-210. ISBN 0-9612960-0-3
*1. New Orleans (La.) - History. I. Widmer, Mary Lou.
II. Title.*　　　　**NYPL [Sc E 89-189]**

Garvey, Marcus, 1887-1940.
Mackie, Liz. The great Marcus Garvey /.
London , 1987. 157 p. : ISBN 1-87051-850-0
　　　　　　　NYPL [Sc D 88-999]

GARVEY, MARCUS, 1887-1940.
Barron, Charles. Look for me in the whirlwind .
[Brooklyn, NY] , c1987. v, 60 p. : DDC
305.8/96073 19
E185.97.G3 B37 1987
　　　　　　　NYPL [Sc D 88-1501]

Huntley, Eric L. Marcus Garvey . Ealing,
London , 1988. 41 p. : ISBN 0-904521-41-9
　　　　　　　NYPL [Sc E 88-499]

'Isá 'Abd Allāh Muḥammad al-Mahdī, 1945-
Who was Marcus Garvey? . [Brooklyn, N.Y.]
c1988. 101 p. :　　　**NYPL [Sc D 89-139]**

Lewis, Rupert. Marcus Garvey . Trenton, N.J. ,
1988. 301 p. : ISBN 0-86543-061-6
　　　　　　　NYPL [Sc D 88-1454]

Lewis, Rupert. Marcus Gavey, anti-colonial

champion /. Trenton, New Jersey , 1988. 301
p. : ISBN 0-86543-061-6 (hard)
NYPL [Sc D 88-516]

Mackie, Liz. The great Marcus Garvey /.
London , 1987. 157 p. : ISBN 1-87051-850-0
NYPL [Sc D 88-999]

**GARVEY, MARCUS, 1887-1940 -
CONGRESSES.**
Garvey--Africa, Europe, the Americas /.
Kingston, Jamaica , 1986. xi, 208 p., [4] p. of
plates : *NYPL [Sc D 88-1131]*

**GARVEY, MARCUS, 1887-1940 - JUVENILE
LITERATURE.**
Lawler, Mary. Marcus Garvey /. New York ,
c1988. 110 p. : ISBN 1-555-46587-0 DDC
305.8/96073/024 B 92 19
E185.97.G3 L39 1988   NYPL [Sc E 88-156]

GARVEY, MARCUS, 1887-1940 - DRAMA.
Atkinson, Dermot. The meeting /. [Jamaica?] ,
c1985. 68 p. ; *NYPL [Sc C 88-108]*

Gary, Lawrence E. The delivery of mental health
services to Black children : final report /
Lawrence E. Gary, Lula A. Beatty, John H.
West. Washington, D.C. : Mental Health
Research and Development Center, Institute for
Urban Affairs and Research, Howard
University, 1982. vi, 111, 19 p. ; 29 cm. Cover
title: The delivery of mental health services to Black
children. Bibliography: p. 103-111.
*1. Mental health personnel - United States. 2.
Afro-American children - Mental health services. 3.
School psychologists - United States. 4. Student
counselors - United States. I. Beatty, Lula A. II. West,
John Hamilton. III. Title. IV. Title: Delivery of mental
health services to black children.*
NYPL [Sc F 88-66]

Gaspard, Albert. Les belles paroles d'Albert
Gaspard / [recueillis par] Alain Rutil. Paris :
Editions caribéennes, c1987. 128 p. : ill. ; 24
cm. Antilles French Creole and French. ISBN
2-903033-91-9 :
*1. Tales - Guadeloupe. 2. Creole dialects, French -
Gudeloupe - Texts. I. Rutil, Alain. II. Title.*
MLCM 87/1949 (P)   NYPL [JFE 88-5765]

Gastrow, Shelagh. Who's who in South African
politics / by Shelagh Gastrow ; introduced by
Tom Lodge. Johannesburg : Ravan Press, 1985.
xiv, 347 p. : ports. ; 21 cm. Includes bibliography.
ISBN 0-86975-280-4 (pbk) DDC 968.06/092/2
B 19
*1. Politicians - South Africa - Biography. 2. Statesmen -
South Africa - Biography. 3. South Africa - Biography.
4. South Africa - Politics and government - 1978-. I.
Title. II. Title: Who is who in South African politics.*
DT779.954 .G37 1985
NYPL [Sc D 87-1109]

Gateria, Wamugunda. Black gold of Chepkube /
Wamugunda Gateria. Nairobi : Heinemann
Educational Books, 1985. 139 p. ; 18 cm. "Spear
books."
1. Kenya - Fiction. I. Title.   NYPL [Sc C 88-284]

Gates, Doris, 1901- Little Vic / Doris Gates ;
illustrated by Kate Seredy. New York : Viking
Press, 1951. 160 p. : ill. ; 22 cm. Illustrated
lining-papers. Issued with various printing dates.
1. Jockeys - United States - Juvenile fiction. I. Title.
NYPL [Sc D 88-430]

Gates, Henry Louis. The signifying monkey : a
theory of Afro-American literary criticism /
Henry Louis Gates, Jr. New York : Oxford
University Press, 1988. xxviii, 290 p. : ill. ; 24
cm. Includes index. Bibliography: p. 259-280. ISBN
0-19-503463-5 (alk. paper) DDC 810/.9/896073
19
*1. American literature - Afro-American authors -
History and criticism - Theory, etc. 2. Afro-Americans -
Intellectual life. 3. Afro-Americans in literature. 4.
Criticism - United States. 5. Oral tradition - United
States. 6. Mythology, African, in literature. 7.
Afro-Americans - Folklore. 8. American literature -
African influences. I. Title.*
PS153.N5 G28 1988   NYPL [Sc E 89-181]

GATIMU, CAESAR MARIA.
Catholic Church. Diocese of Nyeri (Kenya) A
living church. [Nyeri, Kenya] [1986] 28 p. :
NYPL [Sc G 89-16]

Gatsha Buthelezi . Mzala. London , Atlantic
Highlands, N.J. , 1988. ix, 240 p. ; ISBN
0-86232-792-X DDC 968.4/9106/0924 B 19
DT878.Z9 B856 1988 NYPL [Sc D 88-1324]

Gatti, Attilio. Adventure in black and white / by
Attilio Gatti ; illustrated by Kurt Wiese. New
York : C. Scribner, 1943. 172 p. : ill. ; 21 cm.
1. Zaire - Juvenile fiction. I. Title.
NYPL [Sc D 88-1169]

Gaudio, Attilio, 1930- Le Mali / Attilio Gaudio.
Paris : Karthala, c1988. 267 p., [8] p. of plates :
ill., maps ; 22 cm. (Méridiens) Bibliography: p.
[261]-263. ISBN 2-86537-208-1
1. Mali. I. Title. II. Series.
NYPL [Sc D 88-1412]

Gautron, Jean Claude. Droit public du Sénégal /
par Jean-Claude Gautron, Michel
Rougevin-Baville. 2. éd. entièrement refondue.
Paris : A. Pedone, 1977. 447 p. ; 24 cm.
(Collection du Centre de recherches, d'études et de
documentation sur les institutions et la législation
africaines ; 10) "Constitution de la République du
Sénégal": p. [425]-440. Includes bibliographical
references. ISBN 2-233-00036-6 :
*1. Public law - Senegal. I. Rougevin-Baville, Michel,
joint author. II. Series: Dakar. Université. Centre de
recherches, d'études et de documentation sur les
institutions et la législation africaines. Collection , 10.
III. Title.*
LAW   NYPL [Sc E 88-612]

Gay & lesbian poetry in our time : an anthology
/ edited by Carl Morse & Joan Larkin.1st ed.
New York : St. Martin's Press, c1988. xxviii,
401 p. : ports. ; 24 cm. Includes index.
Bibliography: p. 387-392. ISBN 0-312-02213-1 :
DDC 811/.54/080353 19
*1. Homosexuality - Poetry. 2. American poetry - 20th
century. 3. Gays' writings, American. 4. Lesbians'
writings, American. 5. Lesbianism - Poetry. I. Morse,
Carl. II. Larkin, Joan. III. Title: Gay and lesbian poetry
in our time.*
PS595.H65 G39 1988   NYPL [JFE 89-277]

Gay and lesbian poetry in our time. Gay &
lesbian poetry in our time . New York , c1988.
xxviii, 401 p. : ISBN 0-312-02213-1 : DDC
811/.54/080353 19
PS595.H65 G39 1988   NYPL [JFE 89-277]

Gay, John. Mathematics and logic in the Kpelle
language, by John Gay and William Welmers;
and, A first course in Kpelle, by William
Welmers. Ibadan, Institute of African Studies,
1971. 152, 184 p. 28 cm. (Ibadan, Nigeria.
University. Institute of African Studies. Occasional
publication. no. 21) Bibliography: p. 151-152 (1st
group)
*1. Kpelle language - Grammar. 2. Kpelle language -
Semantics. I. Welmers, William Everett, 1916- joint
author. II. Welmers, William Everett, 1916- First course
in Kpelle. III. Title. IV. Series.*
PL8411.1 .G35   NYPL [JFF 74-877]

Gay, Judith S. Women and development in
Lesotho / by Judith S. Gay. [Maseru, Lesotho :
USAID/Maseru], 1982. 84, xxii p. : ill. ; 29 cm.
Bibliogrpahy: p. i-ix.
1. Women in rural development - Lesotho. I. Title.
NYPL [Sc F 89-136]

GAY LIB. see **GAY LIBERATION
MOVEMENT.**

**GAY LIBERATION MOVEMENT - GREAT
BRITAIN - HISTORY - 20TH CENTURY.**
Radical records . London , New York , 1988.
xi, 266 p. ; ISBN 0-415-00200-1 DDC
306.7/66/0941 19
HQ76.8.G7 R33 1988   NYPL [JLD 88-1427]

**GAY LIBERATION MOVEMENT - UNITED
STATES - HISTORY - 20TH CENTURY.**
Weiss, Andrea. Before Stonewall . Tallahassee,
FL , 1988. 86 p. : ISBN 0-941483-20-7 : DDC
306.7/66/0973 19
HQ76.8.U5 W43 1988
NYPL [Sc D 88-1125]

GAY MEN - CALIFORNIA - FICTION.
Hansen, Joseph, 1923- Pretty boy dead . San
Francisco , 1984. 203 p. ; ISBN 0-917342-48-8 :
DDC 813/.54 19
PS3558.A513 P7 1984 NYPL [JFD 87-9537]

GAY MEN - FICTION.
Duplechan, Larry. Eight days a week . Boston ,
1985. 260, [4] p. ; ISBN 0-932870-84-8
NYPL [Sc D 89-219]

**GAY MEN - GREAT BRITAIN -
BIOGRAPHY.**
Davidson, Michael. Some boys /. London ,
1988, c1970. 201 p. ; ISBN 0-85449-087-6 (pbk) :

DDC 070/.92/4 19
PN5123.D   NYPL [Sc C 89-87]

GAY MEN - NEW YORK (N.Y.) - FICTION.
Baxt, George. A queer kind of death /. New
York , 1986, c1966. 249 p. ; ISBN
0-930330-46-3 (pbk.) : *NYPL [Sc C 88-132]*

Gay verse.
Tongues untied . London , Boston, MA, USA ,
1987. 95 p. ; ISBN 0-85449-053-1 (pbk) : DDC
821/.914/080920664 19
PR1178.H6   NYPL [JFD 88-7561]

Gaydon, Vanessa. Race against the ratios : the
why and how of desegregating teacher training
/ Vanessa Gaydon. Johannesburg, South
Africa : South African Institute of Race
Relations, 1987. 70 p. ; 30 cm. Includes
bibliographical references. ISBN 0-86982-321-3
*1. Teachers - Training of - South Africa. 2. College
integration - South Africa. 3. Education - Study and
teaching - South Africa. 4. Race discrimination - South
Africa. 5. Segregation - South Africa. I. South African
Institute of Race Relations. II. Title.*
NYPL [Sc F 88-322]

Gaye, Malick. Nicolas, Pierre. Naissance d'une
ville au Sénégal . Paris , c1988. 193 p., [8] p. of
plates ; ISBN 2-86537-195-6
NYPL [Sc F 89-131]

Gayibor, N. L. (Nicoué Lodjou) Textes et
documents sur l'histoire des populations du
nord Togo /. Lomé [1978] iii, 70 p. :
NYPL [Sc F 88-332]

Gayle, Lois. Wheatle, Hiliary-Ann. Museums of
the Institute of Jamaica /. Kingston , 1982. 16
p. : *NYPL [Sc D 88-1173]*

Gayner, Jeffrey B. Namibia : the road to
self-government / Jeffrey B. Gayner.
Washington, D.C. : Council on American
Affairs, c1979. 101 p. : maps ; 23 cm. Includes
bibliographies. DDC 968.8/03 19
*1. Namibia - Politics and government - 1946-. I.
Council on American Affairs. II. Title.*
DT714 .G38 1979   NYPL [Sc D 89-565]

Gaynor, Petra, 1977- Obadiah. I am a Rastafarian
/. London , New York , c1986. 32 p. : ISBN
0-86313-260-X :
BL2532.R37   NYPL [Sc F 89-12]

**GAYS - GREAT BRITAIN - POLITICAL
ACTIVITY.**
Radical records . London , New York , 1988.
xi, 266 p. ; ISBN 0-415-00200-1 DDC
306.7/66/0941 19
HQ76.8.G7 R33 1988 NYPL [JLD 88-1427]

**GAYS - UNITED STATES - HISTORY - 20TH
CENTURY.**
Weiss, Andrea. Before Stonewall . Tallahassee,
FL , 1988. 86 p. : ISBN 0-941483-20-7 : DDC
306.7/66/0973 19
HQ76.8.U5 W43 1988
NYPL [Sc D 88-1125]

GAYS' WRITINGS, AMERICAN.
Gay & lesbian poetry in our time . New York ,
c1988. xxviii, 401 p. : ISBN 0-312-02213-1 :
DDC 811/.54/080353 19
PS595.H65 G39 1988   NYPL [JFE 89-277]

**GAZETTES - AFRICA - BIBLIOGRAPHY -
CATALOGS.**
Institut für Afrika-Kunde (Hamburg, Germany).
Bibliothek. Verzeichnis der
Zeitschriftenbestände . Hamburg , 1986. 100
p. ; *NYPL [Sc F 88-209]*

Gbadamosi, T. G. O. A History of the University
of Lagos, 1962-1987 /. Lagos, Nigeria , 1987.
xiii, 600 p. : *NYPL [Sc F 89-82]*

GBANDE (LIBERIAN PEOPLE) see **GBANDI
(LIBERIAN PEOPLE)**

GBANDI (LIBERIAN PEOPLE)
Akpan, Monday B. African resistance in
Liberia . Bremen , 1988. 68 p. : ISBN
3-926771-01-1 *NYPL [Sc D 89-347]*

Gbanfou. Kaméléfata : l'ennemi de la Traite /
Gbanfou ; illustrations de Nguyen Ngoc My.
[Abidjan] : CEDA ; [Paris] : Hatier, c1987. 143
p. : ill. ; 18 cm. (Collection Monde noir jeunesse . 3)
"A partir de 10 ans." -- Back cover. ISBN
2-218-07833-3
1. Slave-trade - Africa - Juvenile fiction. I. Series.
NYPL [Sc C 88-161]

GBASSI (LIBERIAN PEOPLE) see **GBANDI
(LIBERIAN PEOPLE)**

Gbomba, Lele. The bossy wife / by Lele Gbomba. Freetown : People's Educational Association of Sierra Leone, 1987. 91 p. : ill. ; 21 cm. (Stories and songs from Sierra Leone . 23) "These stories of Lele Ghomba ... were collected ... preliminary arrangements for the collection were made by Frederick Bobor James who later translated the stories" --verso of t.p.
1. Sierra Leone - Fiction. I. Title. II. Series.
NYPL [Sc D 89-429]

Gboyega, Alex. Political values and local government in Nigeria / Alex Gboyega. lagos : Malthouse Press, 1987. xii, 200 p. ; 23 cm. Includes index. Bibliography: p. [190]-193. ISBN 978-260-103-9
1. Local government - Nigeria. I. Title.
NYPL [Sc D 88-1372]

GBUNDEE (LIBERIAN PEOPLE) see GBANDI (LIBERIAN PEOPLE)

Geary, Christraud M.
Images from Bamum : German colonial photography at the court of King Njoya, Cameroon, West Africa, 1902-1915 / Christraud M. Geary. Washington, D.C. : Published for the National Museum of African Art by the Smithsonian Institute Press, 1988. 151 p. : ill. ; 26 cm. "Conjunction with the exhibition ... organized by the National Museum of African Art, June 15, 1988-September 6, 1988"--T.p. verso. Bibliography: p. 146-151. ISBN 0-87474-455-5 (pbk. : alk. paper) DDC 967/.1102/0880621 19
1. Njoya, Sultan of Bamoun, 1876?-1933 - Pictorial works. 2. Cameroon - History - Pictorial works. 3. Cameroon - Court and courtiers - Pictorial works. 4. Bamoun (Cameroon) - Court and courtiers - Pictorial works. I. National Museum of African Art (U. S.). II. Title.
DT574 .G43 1988   **NYPL [Sc F 89-55]**

Mandou Yénou : photographies du pays Bamoum, royaume ouest-africain, 1902-1915 / Christraud Geary et Adamou Ndam Njoya. München : Trickster Verlag, c1985. 223 p. : chiefly ill., ports. ; 24 cm. Bibliography: p. 219-221. ISBN 3-923804-08-3
1. Bamum (African people) - Pictorial works. 2. Bamum (African people). I. Ndam Njoya, Adamou, 1942-. II. Title.   **NYPL [Sc E 88-178]**

Gecau, Kimani. Charles W. Chesnutt and his literary crusade [microform] / by Kimani Gecau. 1975. 187 leaves. Thesis (Ph. D.)--University of New York at Buffalo, 1975. Bibliography: leaves 184-187. Microfilm of typescript. Ann Arbor, Mich.: University Microfilms International, 1976. 1 microfilm reel; 35 mm.
1. Chesnutt, Charles Waddell, 1858-1932. I. Title.
NYPL [Sc Micro R-4218]

Gedö, Leopold.
[Janiból Jonny lesz. English]
Who is Johnny? / written and illustrated by Leopold Gedö ; translated from the Hungarian by Kate Seredy. New York : Viking Press, 1939. 242 p. : ill. ; 22 cm. Translation of: Janiból Jonny lesz. SCHOMBURG CHILDREN'S COLLECTION.
1. Children, Black - Hungary - Juvenile fiction. I. Seredy, Kate. II. Schomburg Children's Collection. III. Title.   **NYPL [Sc D 88-1512]**

Geechies . Millard, Gregory, 1947-1984. New York , 1985. 69 p. ; ISBN 0-934378-42-8 :
NYPL [Sc D 88-617]

GEESE - JUVENILE FICTION.
Hays, Wilma Pitchford. The goose that was a watchdog. Boston [1967] 41 p. DDC [Fic]
PZ7.H31493 Go   **NYPL [Sc D 88-1426]**

GENDARMES. see POLICE.

Gender & American culture.
Fox-Genovese, Elizabeth, 1941- Within the plantation household . Chapel Hill , c1988. xvii, 544 p. : ISBN 0-8078-1808-9 (alk. paper) DDC 305.4/0975 19
HQ1438.A13 F69 1988   **NYPL [JLE 89-21]**

Gender and culture.
Awkward, Michael. Inspiriting influences . New York , 1989. x, 178 p. ; ISBN 0-231-06806-9 DDC 813/.5/099287 19
PS153.N5 A94 1989   **NYPL [Sc E 89-188]**

Gene Hovis's uptown down home cookbook /.
Hovis, Gene. [Uptown down home cookbook.] Boston , c1987. xii, 235 p. ; ISBN 0-316-37443-1 : DDC 641.5 19
TX715 .H8385 1987   **NYPL [Sc E 88-476]**

Gene Krupa, his life & times /. Crowther, Bruce, 1933- Tunbridge Wells, Kent , New York , 1987. 144 p. : ill. ; ISBN 0-87663-670-9 (USA) DDC 789/.1/0924 B 19
ML419.K78 C8 1987   **NYPL [JNF 88-89]**

Gene Krupa, his life and times. Crowther, Bruce, 1933- Gene Krupa, his life & times /. Tunbridge Wells, Kent , New York , 1987. 144 p. : ISBN 0-87663-670-9 (USA) DDC 789/.1/0924 B 19
ML419.K78 C8 1987   **NYPL [JNF 88-89]**

General history of Africa .
(3) Africa from the seventh to the eleventh century /. London : Berkeley : xxv, 869 p. :
ISBN 0-435-94809-1   **NYPL [Sc E 88-384]**

GENERALS - CUBA - BIOGRAPHY - JUVENILE LITERATURE.
Caballero, Armando O. Antonio Maceo, la protesta de Baraguá /. La Habana , 1977. 30, [1] p. :   **NYPL [Sc F 88-281]**

GENERALS - UNITED STATES - BIOGRAPHY.
McGovern, James R. Black Eagle, General Daniel "Chappie" James, Jr. /. University, AL , c1985. 204 p. : ISBN 0-8173-0179-8 DDC 355/.0092/4 B 19
UG626.2.J36 M34 1985
NYPL [JFD 85-7082]

Generation gap . Pearce, Daniel. [Credibility gap.] Gweru, Zimbabwe , 1983. xiv, 138 p., [4] p. of plates : ISBN 0-86922-217-1 (pbk.) DDC 822 19
PR9390.9.P37 C7 1983
NYPL [JFC 85-1777]

Generations past . Lawson, Sandra M. Washington , 1988. 101 p. : ISBN 0-8444-0604-X DDC 016.929/1/08996073 19
Z1361.N39 L34 1988 E185.96
NYPL [Sc D 89-360]

Genesis of apartheid . Kline, Benjamin. Lanham, MD , c1988. xxii, 283 p. : ISBN 0-8191-6494-1 (alk. paper) : DDC 968.4/04 19
DT872 .K56 1988   **NYPL [JLD 88-4097]**

Geneva. International Labor Office. see International Labor Office.

Genfi, Nana Kofi. Poems at leisure / Nana Kofi Genfi II. Nurom Kumasi, Ghana : [s.n.], 1983. vii, 46 p. ; 20 cm.
I. Title.
MLCS 85/13012 (P)   **NYPL [Sc C 89-64]**

Les Génies du fleuve /. Gibbal, Jean Marie. Paris , c1988. 257 p. : ISBN 2-85616-467-6
NYPL [Sc D 88-1287]

Genovese, Elizabeth Fox- see Fox-Genovese, Elizabeth, 1941-

Gentrification and distressed cities . Nelson, Kathryn P. Madison, Wis. , 1988. xiii, 187 p. ; ISBN 0-299-11160-1 : DDC 307.2 19
HT175 .N398 1987   **NYPL [JLE 88-3486]**

GENTRIFICATION - UNITED STATES.
Nelson, Kathryn P. Gentrification and distressed cities . Madison, Wis. , 1988. xiii, 187 p. ; ISBN 0-299-11160-1 : DDC 307.2 19
HT175 .N398 1987   **NYPL [JLE 88-3486]**

Gentry, Tony. Paul Laurence Dunbar / Tony Gentry. New York : Chelsea House, c1989. 110 p. : ill., ports. ; 24 cm. (Black Americans of achievement) Includes index. Examines the life of the poet and novelist who battled racism and accepted the challenge of depicting the black experience in America. Bibliography: p. 108 p. ISBN 1-555-46583-8 DDC 811/.4 B 92 19
1. Dunbar, Paul Laurence, 1872-1906 - Biography - Juvenile literature. 2. Poets, American - 19th century - Biography - Juvenile literature. 3. Afro-American poets - Biography - Juvenile literature. I. Title. II. Series.
PS1557 .G46 1989   **NYPL [Sc E 88-514]**

GEOGRAPHERS - TANZANIA - BIOGRAPHY.
Hoyle, B. S. Gillman of Tanganyika, 1882-1946 . Aldershot, Hants. , Brookfield, Vt , 1987. xvii, 448 p. : ISBN 0-566-05028-5
NYPL [Sc D 89-86]

GEOGRAPHICAL DISTRIBUTION OF MAN. see ETHNOLOGY.

Geography, history and civics . Ochieng', William Robert, 1943- London , 1987. 170 p. :
NYPL [Sc F 88-190]

Geography of Kenya and the East African region /. Waters, Grahame H. C. (Grahame Hugh Clement), 1923- London , 1986. 252 p. : ISBN 0-333-41564-7 (pbk) : DDC 916.76 19
DT427   **NYPL [Sc E 88-370]**

GEOPOLITICS - AFRICA - CONGRESSES.
Francophonie & géopolitique africaine . Paris , c1987. 156 p. ; ISBN 2-906861-01-4
NYPL [Sc D 88-1448]

GEOPOLITICS - CARIBBEAN AREA.
Ashby, Timothy. The bear in the back yard . Lexington, Mass. , c1987. xii, 240 p. : ISBN 0-669-14768-0 (alk. paper) DDC 327.470729 19
F2178.S65 A84 1987   **NYPL [HNB 87-1399]**

George III, King of Great Britain, 1738-1820. Jamaica. Assembly. To the King's most Excellent Majesty in Council, the humble petition and memorial of the Assembly of Jamaica . Philadelphia: , 1775. 8 p. ;
NYPL [Sc Rare F 88-14]

George, Nelson.
The death of rhythm & blues / Nelson George. 1st ed. New York : Pantheon Books, c1988. xvi, 222 p., [16] p. of plates : ill. ; 24 cm. Includes index. Bibliographic notes p. 203- 206. ISBN 0-394-55238-5 : DDC 781.7/296073 19
1. Afro-Americans - Music - History and criticism. 2. Music - United States - 20th century - History and criticism. 3. Music trade - United States. I. Title.
ML3556 .G46 1988   **NYPL [Sc E 88-504]**

Where did our love go? : the rise & fall of the Motown sound / Nelson George.1st ed. New York : St. Martin's Press, c1985. xviii, 250 p., [32] p. of plates : ill., ports. ; 25 cm. Includes index. Bibliography: p. 239-240. Discography: p. 203-237. ISBN 0-312-86698-4 : DDC 784.5/0973 19
1. Motown Record Corporation. 2. Soul music - History and criticism. I. Title.
ML3537 .G46 1985   **NYPL [*LE 86-1451]**

Georgetown, Guyana. Public Library. Merriman, Stella E. Commonwealth Caribbean writers. Georgetown, Guyana, 1970. iv, 98 p.
NYPL [JFF 72-67]

Georgetown University. Center for Contemporary Arab Studies. Contemporary North Africa . London , c1985. 271 p. ; ISBN 0-7099-3435-1 : DDC 961 19
DT181.5 .C66 1985b   **NYPL [Sc D 88-1017]**

Georgetown University. Center for Strategic and International Studies. Underwood, David C. West African oil, will it matter? /. Washington, D.C. , c1983. vi, 57 p. : ISBN 0-89206-046-8 (pbk.) DDC 333.8/232/0966 19
HD9577.A3582 U52 1983
NYPL [Sc D 88-888]

Georgetown University, Washington, D. C. Ethics and Public Policy Center. Sowell, Thomas, 1930- Patterns of black excellence /. Washington , 1977. [26]-58 p. ; ISBN 0-89633-004-4   **NYPL [Sc D 89-588]**

GEORGIA - RACE RELATIONS - JUVENILE FICTION.
Herlihy, Dirlie. Ludie's song /. New York , c1988. 212 p. ; ISBN 0-8037-0533-6 : DDC [Fic] 19
PZ7.H43126 Lu 1988   **NYPL [Sc D 89-132]**

Gerber, Will. Gooseberry Jones / by Will Gerber ; illustrated by Dudley Morris. New York : G.P. Putnam, c1947. 96 p. : ill. ; 22 cm. SCHOMBURG CHILDREN'S COLLECTION.
1. Afro-American children - Juvenile fiction. 2. Pets - Juvenile fiction. I. Schomburg Children's Collection. II. Title.   **NYPL [Sc D 89-442]**

Germain, Robert. Grammaire créole / Robert Germain. Paris : L'Harmattan, [1980] 303 p. ; 22 cm. Creole-French lexicon: p. 207-302. Bibliography: p. 164-166. ISBN 2-85802-165-1 : DDC 447/.972976 19
1. Creole dialects, French - West Indies, French. I. Title.
PM7854.W47 G4   **NYPL [Sc D 82-456]**

German colonialism and the South West Africa Company, 1884-1914 /. Voeltz, Richard Andrew. Athens, Ohio , 1988. x, 133 p. : ISBN 0-89680-146-2 (pbk.) : DDC 325/.343/09688 19
JV2029.A5 S689 1988   **NYPL [JLD 88-3416]**

German Development Institute. see Deutsches Institut für Entwicklungspolitik.

GERMAN LANGUAGE - DICTIONARIES - DANGALEAT.
Ebobissé, Carl. Les verbaux du dangaléat de l'est (Guera, Tchad) . Berlin , 1987. 104 p. ;
ISBN 3-496-00555-6 *NYPL [Sc E 88-231]*

GERMAN LANGUAGE - GRAMMAR, COMPARATIVE - EWE.
Eklou, Akpaka A. Satzstruktur des Deutschen und des Ewe . Saarbrücken , 1987. 262 p. ;
NYPL [Sc D 89-203]

German Southwest Africa. see Namibia.

GERMANY - COLONIES - AFRICA - HISTORY.
Voeltz, Richard Andrew. German colonialism and the South West Africa Company, 1884-1914 /. Athens, Ohio , 1988. x, 133 p. :
ISBN 0-89680-146-2 (pbk.) : DDC 325/.343/09688 19
JV2029.A5 S689 1988 NYPL [JLD 88-3416]

GERMANY - COMMERCE - TOGO - HISTORY.
Ahadji, A. Relations commerciales entre l'Allemagne et le Togo, 1680-1914 /. Lomé [1984] 71 leaves :
HF3568.T64 A42 1984 NYPL [Sc F 88-164]

GERMANY - FOREIGN ECONOMIC RELATIONS - AFRICA, WEST.
Jones, Adam. Brandenburg sources for West African history, 1680-1700 /. Stuttgart , 1985. xiv, 348 p., [14] p. of plates : ISBN 3-515-04315-2 *NYPL [Sc E 88-84]*

Germany - Government. see Germany - Politics and government.

GERMANY - POLITICS AND GOVERNMENT - 1933-1945.
Durant, Franck Alphonse. Rétrospectives [microform] . Port-au-Prince, Haiti , 1977. 16 p. ; *NYPL [Sc Micro F 10,933]*

Germeil, Castel. La valse des chandelles / Castel Germeil. [Haiti? : s.n., 198-?] 52 p. ; 19 cm.
I. Title. *NYPL [Sc C 88-295]*

Gersovitz, Mark. The Political economy of risk and choice in Senegal /. London , Totowa, N.J. , 1987. xv, 363 p. : ISBN 0-7146-3297-X : DDC 338.966/3 19
HC1045 .P65 1987 NYPL [Sc E 87-360]

Geschichte Afrikas. Afrika : Geschichte von den Anfängen bis zur Gegenwart. Köln : Pahl-Rugenstein, 1979- v. : maps ; 19 cm.
(Kleine Bibliothek: Politik, Wissenschaft, Zukunft. 155, 156) Originally published: Geschichte Afrikas. Berlin : Akademie-Verlag, 1976- Includes bibliographies and indexes. CONTENTS. - T. 1. Afrika von den Anfängen bis zur territorialen Aufteilung Afrikas durch die imperialistischen Kolonialmächte / Thea Büttner -- T. 2. Afrika unter imperialistischer Kolonialherrschaft und die Formierung der antikolonialen Kräfte, 1884-1945 / Heinrich Loth. ISBN 3-7609-0433-5 (v. 1) : DDC 960 19
1. Africa - History - Collected works. I. Büttner, Thea. Afrika von den Anfängen bis zur territorialen Aufteilung Afrikas durch die imperialistischen Kolonialmächte. II. Loth, Heinrich. Afrika unter imperialistischer Kolonialherrschaft und die Formierung der antikolonialen Kräfte, 1884-1945. III. Title.
DT20 .G47 1979 NYPL [JFK 82-28]

Geschichte der Mission der Evangelischen Brüder auf den caraibischen Inseln S. Thomas, S. Croix und S. Jan. Oldendorp, C. G. A. (Christian Georg Andreas), 1721-1787. [Geschichte der Mission der Evangelischen Brüder auf den caraibischen Inseln S. Thomas, S. Croix und S. Jan.] C.G.A. Oldendorps Geschichte der Mission der Evangelischen Brüder auf den caraibischen Inseln S. Thomas, S. Croix und S. Jan /. Barby , 1777. 2 v. in 1 (1068 p.) : DDC 266/.46729722 19
BV2848.V5 O42 1777
NYPL [Sc Rare C 89-33]

Gesellschaft Jesu. see Jesuits.

Getting to know Egypt, U.A.R. /. Wallace, John A. New York , c1961. 64 p. :
NYPL [Sc D 88-569]

Ghan, A. (Ayicoé), 1945- Semences nouvelles . Lomé, Togo , 1986. 96 p. :
NYPL [Sc C 88-123]

Ghana : Fakten, Bilder, Aspekte / [Redaktion: Reinhilde Freise]. Stuttgart : Evangelisches Missionswerk in Südwestdeutschland, 1986. 71, [1] p. : ill. (some col.), maps, ports. ; 24 cm.

Cover title. "Januar 1986." Bibliogrpahy: p. [72].
1. Ghana - Civilization. 2. Ghana - Social conditions. 3. Ghana - Religious life and customs. I. Freise, Reinhilde, 1941-. *NYPL [Sc E 88-274]*

GHANA - ARMED FORCES - POLITICAL ACTIVITY.
Baynham, Simon, 1950- The military and politics in Nkrumah's Ghana /. Boulder , 1988. xvi, 294 p. ; ISBN 0-8133-7063-9 : DDC 966.7/05 19
DT512 .B39 1986 NYPL [JFD 88-10630]

GHANA - CIVILIZATION.
Ghana . Stuttgart , 1986. 71, [1] p. :
NYPL [Sc E 88-274]

GHANA - COMMERCE.
Tropical Africa Advisory Group trade mission to the Republic of Ghana, 16-22 March 1985. [London] ([1 Victoria Street, SW1H OET]) [1985] iii, 64 p. : DDC 330.9667/05 19
HC1060 NYPL [Sc F 88-88]

GHANA - ECONOMIC CONDITIONS - 1979-
The IMF and Ghana . London , New Jersey , 1987. 298 p. ; ISBN 0-86232-614-1
NYPL [Sc D 88-1095]

Tropical Africa Advisory Group trade mission to the Republic of Ghana, 16-22 March 1985. [London] ([1 Victoria Street, SW1H OET]) [1985] iii, 64 p. : DDC 330.9667/05 19
HC1060 NYPL [Sc F 88-88]

GHANA - ECONOMIC CONDITIONS - 1979- - STATISTICS.
Ewusi, Kodwo. Economic trends in Ghana in 1984-85 and prospects for 1986 /. [Legon] [1986] 52 p. : DDC 330.9667/05 19
HC1060 .E975 1986 NYPL [Sc G 88-31]

GHANA - ECONOMIC POLICY - STATISTICS.
Ewusi, Kodwo. Economic trends in Ghana in 1984-85 and prospects for 1986 /. [Legon] [1986] 52 p. : DDC 330.9667/05 19
HC1060 .E975 1986 NYPL [Sc G 88-31]

GHANA - FICTION.
Adzei, Morgan. A burning desire /. New York N.Y. , 1984. 145 p. ; ISBN 0-910437-01-7
NYPL [Sc D 89-192]

Armah, E. O. A custom broken /. Tema , 1978. 87 p. ; *NYPL [Sc C 88-223]*

Laing, B. Kojo. Woman of the aeroplanes. London , 1988. 196 p. ; ISBN 0-434-40218-4 : DDC 823 19 *NYPL [Sc E 89-120]*

Sebuava, Joseph, 1934- The inevitable hour . Accra , 1987,c1979. 141 p. ;
NYPL [Sc D 88-1384]

Yeboah-Afari, Ajoa. The sound of pestles and other stories /. Accra , 1986. 72 p. ; ISBN 996-470-046-6 *NYPL [Sc C 88-352]*

Ghana, guide to hotels and restaurants. [Ghana] : Ghana Tourist Board, 1986. 71 p. : ill. ; 22 cm.
1. Hotels, taverns, etc. - Ghana - Guide-books. I. Ghana Tourist Board. *NYPL [Sc D 88-1385]*

GHANA - HISTORY - COUP D'ÉTAT, 1966.
Baynham, Simon, 1950- The military and politics in Nkrumah's Ghana /. Boulder , 1988. xvi, 294 p. ; ISBN 0-8133-7063-9 : DDC 966.7/05 19
DT512 .B39 1986 NYPL [JFD 88-10630]

GHANA - HISTORY - DICTIONARIES.
McFarland, Daniel Miles. Historical dictionary of Ghana /. Metuchen, N.J. , 1985. lxxx, 296 p. : ISBN 0-8108-1761-6 DDC 966.7/003/21 19
DT510.5 .M38 1985
*NYPL [*R-BMK 89-3348]*

GHANA - JUVENILE FICTION.
Appiah, Sonia. Amoko and Efua bear /. New York, NY , 1989, c1988. [30] p. : ISBN 0-02-705591-4 DDC E 19
PZ7.A647 Am 1989 NYPL [Sc F 89-138]

Kaye, Geraldine, 1925- Koto and the lagoon. New York [1969, c1967] 128 p. DDC [Fic]
PZ7.K212 Ko3 NYPL [Sc D 89-159]

GHANA - POLITICS AND GOVERNMENT.
Hadjor, Kofi Buenor. Nkrumah and Ghana . London , New York , 1988. ix, 114 p., [8] p. of plates : *NYPL [JFD 88-4445]*

GHANA - POLITICS AND GOVERNMENT - 1957-1979.
Baynham, Simon, 1950- The military and politics in Nkrumah's Ghana /. Boulder , 1988.

xvi, 294 p. ; ISBN 0-8133-7063-9 : DDC 966.7/05 19
DT512 .B39 1986 NYPL [JFD 88-10630]

Rooney, David. Kwame Nkrumah . London , 1988. viii, 292 p. ; *NYPL [Sc D 89-44]*

GHANA - POPULATION - CONGRESSES.
West African Seminar on Population Studies, University of Ghana, 1972. Interdisciplinary approaches to population studies . Legon , 1975. ix, 333 p. :
HB21 .W38 1972 NYPL [JLD 78-861]

GHANA - PRESIDENTS - BIOGRAPHY.
Rooney, David. Kwame Nkrumah . London , 1988. viii, 292 p. ; *NYPL [Sc D 89-44]*

GHANA - RELIGIOUS LIFE AND CUSTOMS.
Belcher, Wendy Laura. Honey from the lion . New York , c1988. xiv, 188 p. : ISBN 0-525-24596-0 : DDC 966.7/05 19
DT510.4 .B38 1988 NYPL [Sc D 88-842]

Ghana . Stuttgart , 1986. 71, [1] p. :
NYPL [Sc E 88-274]

GHANA - SOCIAL CONDITIONS.
Ghana . Stuttgart , 1986. 71, [1] p. :
NYPL [Sc E 88-274]

GHANA - SOCIAL LIFE AND CUSTOMS.
Belcher, Wendy Laura. Honey from the lion . New York , c1988. xiv, 188 p. : ISBN 0-525-24596-0 : DDC 966.7/05 19
DT510.4 .B38 1988 NYPL [Sc D 88-842]

Ghana Tourist Board. Ghana, guide to hotels and restaurants. [Ghana] , 1986. 71 p. :
NYPL [Sc D 88-1385]

Ghana. University, Legon. Population Dynamics Programme. West African Seminar on Population Studies, University of Ghana, 1972. Interdisciplinary approaches to population studies . Legon , 1975. ix, 333 p. :
HB21 .W38 1972 NYPL [JLD 78-861]

The Ghanaian factory worker. Peil, Margaret. [Cambridge, Eng.] 1972. ix, 254 p.
NYPL [Sc 331.7-P]

The Ghanaian revolution /. Amamoo, Joseph G. London , 1988. 234 p. ; ISBN 1-85421-016-5 : DDC 966.7/05 19
DT512.32 NYPL [Sc D 89-392]

GHETTOS. see AFRO-AMERICANS - HOUSING.

Ghiraldelli, Paulo. Educação e movimento operário / Paulo Ghiraldelli, Jr. São Paulo : Cortez : Autores Associados, 1987. 167 p. ; 21 cm. (Educação contemporânea) Bibliography: p. 160-167. ISBN 85-24-90081-4
1. Education - Brazil - History. 2. Labor and laboring classes - Education - Brazil. 3. Labor and laboring classes - Brazil - History. I. Title.
NYPL [Sc D 88-369]

Ghista, Dhanjoo N. African development . Lawrenceville, Va., U.S.A. , c1985. 241 p. : ISBN 0-931494-57-5 (pbk.) DDC 337.1/6 19
HC800 .A565 1985 NYPL [Sc F 87-376]

The ghost walks . Sampson, Henry T., 1934- Metuchen, N.J. , 1988. xix, 570 p. : ISBN 0-8108-2070-6 DDC 792/.08996073 19
PN2270.A35 S25 1988
NYPL [Sc D 88-1145]

Giacomini, Sonia Maria. Mulher e escrava : uma introdução histórica ao estudo da mulher negra no Brasil / Sonia Maria Giacomini. Petrópolis : Vozes, 1988. 95 p., [7] p. of plates ; 21 cm. (Coleção Negros em libertação. 4) Bibliography: p. 91-95.
1. Women slaves - Brazil - History. 2. Slavery - Brazil - History. I. Title. II. Series.
HT1126 .G49 1988 NYPL [Sc D 88-1283]

Gibbal, Jean Marie. Les Génies du fleuve / Jean-Marie Gibbal. Paris : Presses de la Renaissance, c1988. 257 p. : maps ; 23 cm. Bibliography: p. 257. ISBN 2-85616-467-6
1. Water spirits - Mali. 2. Niger River. I. Title.
NYPL [Sc D 88-1287]

Gibbs, C. Jeanean. Gurus and griots . Brooklyn, N.Y. [1987], c1985. 108 p. : ISBN 0-9618755-0-X (pbk.) DDC 811/.008/0896 19
PS591.N4 G87 1987 NYPL [Sc E 89-230]

Gicheru, Mwangi. The double-cross / Mwangi Gicheru. Nairobi : Longman Kenya, 1983. 169

p. ; 18 cm. ISBN 0-582-78544-8
1. Kenya - Fiction. I. Title. **NYPL** *[Sc C 87-461]*

Giddens, Gary. Satchmo / Gary Giddens ;
produced by Toby Byron / Multiprises. 1st ed.
New York : Doubleday, 1988. 239 p. : ill.
(some col.) ; 29 cm. "A Dolphin book."
Discography: p. 224-228. Bibliography: p. 229-231.
    ISBN 0-385-24428-2 :   DDC 785.42/092/4 B 19
1. Armstrong, Louis, 1900-1971 - Pictorial works. 2.
Jazz musicians - United States - Biography - Pictorial
works. 3. Afro-American musicians - Biography -
Pictorial works. I. Title.
ML410.A75 G5 1988   **NYPL** *[Sc F 89-73]*

Giddings, Joshua Reed, 1795-1864. The exiles of
Florida; or,The crimes committed by our
government against the maroons, who fled from
South Carolina and the other slave states,
seeking protection under Spanish laws. By
Joshua R. Giddings. Columbus, Ohio, Follett,
Foster and company, 1858. viii, 338 p. front.,
ports. 21 cm.
1. Seminole War, 2d, 1835-1842. I. Title.
E83.817 .G46   **NYPL** *[Sc Rare F 88-68]*

Gifford, Prosser. Decolonization and African
independence . New Haven , 1988. xxix, 651
p. ; ISBN 0-300-04070-9   DDC 960/.32 19
DT30.5 .D42 1988   **NYPL** *[Sc E 88-517]*

Gift of J.P. Morgan and Co., Inc.
Frontline Southern Africa . New York , 1988.
xxxv, 530 p., [16] p. of leaves : ISBN
0-941423-08-5 :   DDC 322/.5/0968 19
DT747.S6 F76 1988   **NYPL** *[JLE 89-595]*

Graf, William D. The Nigerian state . London ,
Portsmouth, N.H. , 1988. xvi, 281 p. : ISBN
0-85255-313-7 (cased) :   DDC 320.1/09669 19
                    NYPL *[Sc E 89-195]*

A Gift of tongues : critical challenges in
contemporary American poetry / edited by
Marie Harris and Kathleen Aguero. Athens :
University of Georgia Press, c1987. xii, 342 p. ;
24 cm. Bibliography: p. 331-338. ISBN
0-8203-0952-4 (alk. paper)   DDC
811/.5/09920693 19
1. Canon (Literature). 2. American poetry - Minority
authors - History and criticism. 3. American poetry -
20th century - History and criticism. I. Harris, Marie.
II. Aguero, Kathleen.
PS153.M56 G54 1987   **NYPL** *[Sc E 88-364]*

Giganti, Paul. How many snails? : a counting
book / by Paul Giganti, Jr. ; pictures by
Donald Crews.1st ed. New York : Greenwillow
Books, c1988. [24] p. : col. ill. ; 21 cm. A young
child takes walks to different places and wonders about
the amount and variety of things seen on the way.
    ISBN 0-688-06369-1 :   DDC [E] 19
1. Counting. I. Crews, Donald, ill. II. Title.
PZ7.G364 Ho 1988   **NYPL** *[Sc F 88-301]*

Gil, Gilberto. Gilberto Gil Expresso 2222 /.
[Salvador, Brasil?] , 1982. 287 p. ;
                    NYPL *[JMD 83-309]*

GIL, GILBERTO.
Gilberto Gil Expresso 2222 /. [Salvador,
Brasil?] , 1982. 287 p. ;
                    NYPL *[JMD 83-309]*

Gilbert, Herman Cromwell. The uncertain sound;
a novel. Chicago, Path Press [1969] 349 p. 23
cm.   DDC 813/.5/4
1. Afro-American - Illinois - Fiction. I. Title.
PZ4.G4647 Un PS3557.I342
                    NYPL *[Sc D 88-1117]*

Gilbert, Kevin. Inside Black Australia . Ringwood,
Victoria , 1988. xxiv, 213 p. ; ISBN
0-14-011126-3   **NYPL** *[Sc D 89-547]*

Gilbert, Marcel, 1938-
La patrie haïtienne : de Boyer Bazelais à
l'unité historique du peuple haïtien / Marcel
Gilbert.1er éd. Brazzaville : [s.n.], 1984. 60 p. ;
20 cm. Inclus his: Reveil en retrait de deuil ("publié
dans Poésie contemporaine, Edition A.L.C. 1983")
1. Bazelais, Boyer. 2. Haiti - Politics and government -
1804-. I. Gilbert, Marcel, 1938- Reveil en retrait de
deuil. II. Title. **NYPL** *[Sc D 89-629]*

    Reveil en retrait de deuil. Gilbert, Marcel,
    1938- La patrie haïtienne : de Boyer Bazelais
    à l'unité historique du peuple haïtien /
    Marcel Gilbert.1er éd. Brazzaville , 1984. 60
    p. ;   **NYPL** *[Sc D 89-629]*

Gilberto Freyre entre nós / testemunhos de
companheiros de Fundação Joaquim Nabuco ;
apresentação de Clovis Cavalcanti. Recife :

Fundação Joaquim Nabuco, Editora
Massangana, 1988. 115 p. ; 22 cm. (Serie
Documentos. 33)   ISBN 85-7019-140-5
1. Fundação Joaquim Nabuco. II. Series: Série
Documentos (Fundação Joaquim Nabuco) , 33.
                    NYPL *[Sc D 89-320]*

Gilberto Gil Expresso 2222 / organizado por
Antonio Risério. [Salvador, Brasil?] : Corrupio,
1982. 287 p. ; 21 cm. (Baianada . 3) Includes essays
by Gilberto Gil.
1. Gil, Gilberto. 2. Music, Popular (Songs, etc.) -
Brazil - History and criticism. I. Gil, Gilberto. II.
Risério, Antonio. III. Title: Expresso 2222. IV. Series.
                    NYPL *[JMD 83-309]*

Gilchrist, Jan Spivey. (ill) Little, Lessie Jones.
Children of long ago . New York , 1988. [32]
p. :   ISBN 0-399-21473-9   DDC 811/.54 19
PS3562.I78288 C5 1988
                    NYPL *[Sc F 88-276]*

Gilfoy, Peggy Stoltz. Patterns of life : West
African strip-weaving traditions / Peggy Stoltz
Gilfoy. Washington, D.C. : Published for the
National Museum of African Art by the
Smithsonian Institution Press, c1987. 95 p. :
ill. ; 26 cm. Catalog of an exhibition, organized by
the National Museum of African Art and held
September 28, 1987-February 29, 1988. Bibliography: p.
92-95.   ISBN 0-87474-475-X (alk. paper) :   DDC
746.1/4/088042 19
1. Textile fabrics - Africa, West - Exhibitions. 2. Hand
weaving - Africa, West - Exhibitions. 3. Men weavers -
Africa, West - Exhibitions. I. National Museum of
African Art (U. S.). II. Title. III. Title: Strip-weaving
traditions.
NK8989 .G55 1987   **NYPL** *[Sc F 88-166]*

Gill, Margaret. Women, work, and development /
Margaret Gill, Joycelin Massiah ; with an
introduction by Patricia Anderson. Cave Hill,
Barbados : Institute of Social and Economic
Research (Eastern Caribbean), University of the
West Indies, 1984. xviii, 129 p. ; 24 cm.
(Women in the Caribbean project . v. 6) Cover title:
Women and work. Includes bibliographies.
1. Women - Employment - Barbados. 2. Women -
Employment - Caribbean area. 3. Women - Caribbean
area - Economic conditions. I. Massiah, Joycelin. II.
Title: Women and work. III. Series.
                    NYPL *[Sc E 85-274]*

GILLMAN, CLEMENT, 1882-1946.
Hoyle, B. S. Gillman of Tanganyika,
1882-1946 . Aldershot, Hants. , Brookfield, Vt ,
1987. xvii, 448 p. :   ISBN 0-566-05028-5
                    NYPL *[Sc D 89-86]*

Gillman of Tanganyika, 1882-1946 . Hoyle, B. S.
Aldershot, Hants. , Brookfield, Vt , 1987. xvii,
448 p. :   ISBN 0-566-05028-5
                    NYPL *[Sc D 89-86]*

Gilman, Michael. Matthew Henson / Michael
Gilman. New York : Chelsea House Publishers,
c1988. 110 p. : ill. maps ; 25 cm. (Black
Americans of achievement) Includes index. Follows the
life of the black explorer who accompanied Robert
Peary on the expedition to the North Pole.
Bibliography: p. 108.   ISBN 1-555-46590-0 :   DDC
919.8/04 B 92 19
1. Henson, Matthew Alexander, 1866-1955 - Juvenile
literature. 2. Explorers - United States - Biography -
Juvenile literature. 3. North Pole - Juvenile literature. I.
Title. II. Series.
G635.H4 G55 1988   **NYPL** *[Sc E 88-169]*

Gilmour, J. D. The demand for tertiary education
in the East London metropolitan area : a survey
carried out on behalf of Rhodes University to
estimate the demand for non-laboratory and
non-B.Com. courses at the East London
Division of Rhodes / J.D. Gilmour.
Grahamstown [South Africa] : Institute of
Social and Economic Research, Rhodes
University, 1983. 1 v. (various pagings) ; 30 cm.
(Development studies working paper . no. 14)
"February 1983." Includes bibliography.   ISBN
0-86810-056-0
1. Education, Higher - Supply and demand - South
Africa - East London. I. Series.
                    NYPL *[Sc F 87-429]*

Gilpin, Toni. On strike for respect . Chicago ,
1988. 94 p. ;   **NYPL** *[Sc C 89-101]*

Gilstrap, Robert. The sultan's fool and other
North African tales / by Robert Gilstrap and
Irene Estabrook ; illustrated by Robert Greco.
1st ed. New York : Holt, c1958. 95 p. : ill. ; 25
cm. SCHOMBURG CHILDREN'S COLLECTION.

    ISBN 931-40-0118-0
1. Tales - Africa, North. I. Estabrook, Irene. II. Greco,
Robert. III. Schomburg Children's Collection. IV. Title.
                    NYPL *[Sc E 88-548]*

Gimba, Abubakar. Witnesses to tears : a novel /
by Abubakar Gimba. Enugu : Delta
Publications, 1986. 170 p. ; 18 cm.   ISBN
978-233-521-5
1. Nigeria - Fiction. I. Title.
                    NYPL *[Sc C 88-208]*

GIMI LANGUAGE - TEXTS.
Smith, Pat. Soko rareupe harutagaibag namosux
amik kaina [microform] Health and mothercraft
/. Ukarumpa, Papua New Guinea , 1973. 12
p. ;   **NYPL** *[Sc Micro F-10977]*

Ginsburg, Max. (ill) Taylor, Mildred D. The
friendship . New York , 1987. 53 p. :   ISBN
0-8037-0418-6 (lib. bdg.) :   DDC [Fic] 19
PZ7.T21723 Fr 1987   **NYPL** *[Sc D 88-126]*

Gioia, Ted. The imperfect art : reflections on jazz
and modern culture / Ted Gioia. New York :
Oxford University Press, 1988. vi, 152 p. ; 22
cm. Includes bibliographical references and index.
    ISBN 0-19-505343-5 (alk. paper)   DDC
785.42/09 19
1. Jazz music - History and criticism. I. Title.
ML3506 .G56 1988   **NYPL** *[JMD 88-274]*

Giovanni, Nikki.
Sacred cows-- and other edibles / Nikki
Giovanni. 1st ed. New York : W. Morrow,
c1988. 167 p. ; 24 cm.   ISBN 0-688-04333-X:
    DDC 814/.54 19
I. Title.
PS3557.I55 S23 1988   **NYPL** *[Sc E 88-146]*

Vacation time : poems for children / by Nikki
Giovanni ; illustrated by Marisabina Russo.1st
ed. New York : Morrow, 1980. 59 p. : ill. ; 22
cm. Includes 22 poems on a variety of topics.
SCHOMBURG CHILDREN'S COLLECTION.   ISBN
0-688-03657-0   DDC 811/.54
1. Children's poetry, American. I. Russo, Marisabina. II.
Schomburg Children's Collection. III. Title.
PS3557.I55 V3   **NYPL** *[Sc D 89-69]*

Giovanopoulos, Paul.
(illus) Dean, Leigh. The looking down game.
New York [1968] 34 p.   DDC [Fic]
PZ7.D3446 Lo   **NYPL** *[Sc D 89-111]*

(illus) Hodges, Elizabeth Jamison. Free as a frog.
[Reading, Mass.,1969] [32] p.   DDC [Fic]
PZ7.H6634 Fr   **NYPL** *[Sc D 88-1126]*

(illus) Linde, Freda. Toto and the aardvark.
Garden City, N.Y. [1969] 59 p.
PZ7.L6574 To   **NYPL** *[JFE 72-633]*

Gipson, Fred. The trail-driving rooster / by Fred
Gipson. New York : Harper & Row, c1955. 79
p. : ill. ; 23 cm. SCHOMBURG CHILDREN'S
COLLECTION.
1. Roosters - Juvenile fiction. 2. Cowboys - Juvenile
fiction. I. Schomburg Children's Collection. II. Title.
                    NYPL *[Sc D 88-427]*

The Girl Guide movement in Kenya . Khimulu,
Mary M. [Nairob] , c1987. 57 p. :
                    NYPL *[Sc D 89-12]*

GIRL SCOUTS - JUVENILE FICTION.
Gardner, Lillian, 1907- Sal Fisher at Girl Scout
camp. New York [1959] 217 p.
PZ7.G1793 Saj   **NYPL** *[Sc D 88-1494]*

GIRL SCOUTS - KENYA.
Khimulu, Mary M. The Girl Guide movement
in Kenya . [Nairob] , c1987. 57 p. :
                    NYPL *[Sc D 89-12]*

**GIRLS - EMPLOYMENT. see YOUTH -
EMPLOYMENT; CHILDREN -
EMPLOYMENT.**

Girvan, Norman, 1941- Technology policies for
small developing economies : a study of the
Caribbean / Norman P. Girvan, with the
collaboration of P.I. Gomes and Donald B.
Sangster. Mona, Jamaica : Institute of Social
and Economic Research, University of the West
Indies, c1983. 224 p. : ill. ; 25 cm. At head of
title: Caribbean Technology Policy Studies Project.
Bibliography: p. 181-188.   DDC 338.9729 19
1. Technology and state - Caribbean area. 2.
Technology and state - Developing countries. I. Gomes,
P. I. II. Sangster, Donald B. III. Caribbean Technology
Policy Studies Project. IV. Title.
T24.A1 G57 1983   **NYPL** *[Sc E 88-260]*

Gitari, David M.
Let the Bfin id 89b21342/updd M. Gitari.
Nairobi, Kenya : Uzima, 1988. 90 p. : map ; 21
cm. Bibliography: p. 89-90.
1. Gitari, David M. - Sermons. 2. Kenya - Politics and government - 1978-. I. Title.
         NYPL [Sc D 89-400]

GITARI, DAVID M. - SERMONS.
Gitari, David M. Let the Bfin id
89b21342/updd M. Gitari. Nairobi, Kenya ,
1988. 90 p. :   **NYPL [Sc D 89-400]**

Gitonga, Africa K. The Democratic theory and
practice in Africa /. Nairobi , 1987. vi, 208 p. ;
         NYPL [Sc D 89-569]

Gittins, Anthony J. Heart of prayer . London ,
1985. 175 p. : ISBN 0-00-599841-7
         NYPL [Sc C 88-29]

Give birth to brightness. Williams, Sherley Anne,
1944- New York, 1972. 252 p.
PS153.N5 W54   **NYPL [JFD 72-6307]**

Give me some more sense . Lee, Jacintha A.
(Jacintha Anius) Basingstoke , 1983. 40 p. :
ISBN 0-333-46121-5 (pbk)   DDC 813 19
PZ8.1   **NYPL [Sc D 89-284]**

GIWA, DELE.
Murder of Dele Giwa . Lagos, Nigeria , 1988.
193 p. : ISBN 978-232-523-6
         NYPL [Sc F 89-35]

GIWA, DELE, 1947-1986.
Magnate, Joseph. Dele Giwa /. Lagos, , 1987.
190 p. : ISBN 978-303-000-0
         NYPL [Sc D 88-742]

GIWA, DELE, 1947-1986 - ASSASSINATION.
Magnate, Joseph. Dele Giwa /. Lagos, , 1987.
190 p. : ISBN 978-303-000-0
         NYPL [Sc D 88-742]

Giza limeingia /. Mbogo, Emmanuel. Dar es
Salaam , 1980. 98 p. ; ISBN 997-610-022-1
         NYPL [Sc C 89-23]

Glantz, Stephan Hamilton. Spirit heads : the
sculpture of Black Africa / Stephan Hamilton
Glantz. New York : Star Enterprises, 1987. 133
p. : ill., map, port. ; 26 cm. Includes index.
Bibliography: p. 131.
1. Art - Africa. 2. Africa, Sub-Saharan - Religious life and customs. I. Title.   **NYPL [Sc F 88-103]**

**GLASGOW EMANCIPATION SOCIETY
(STRATHCLYDE)**
The William Smeal collection [microform].
1833-1908. ca. 100 items.
         NYPL [Sc Micro R-4837]

Glasser, Barbara. Bongo Bradley [by] Barbara
Glasser and Ellen Blustein. Drawings by Bonnie
Johnson. New York, Hawthorn Books [1973]
153 p. illus. 22 cm. The summer Bradley spends in
North Carolina teaches him many things he couldn't
have learned at home in New York City, especially
about his family heritage and love of music.
SCHOMBURG CHILDREN'S COLLECTION.   DDC
[Fic]
*1. Afro-Americans - Southern States - Juvenile fiction.
I. Blustein, Ellen, joint author. II. Johnson, Bonnie
Helene, illus. III. Schomburg Children's Collection. IV.
Title.*
PZ7.G48143 Bo   **NYPL [Sc D 89-99]**

Gleason, Judith Illsley. Oya : in praise of the
goddess / Judith Gleason. Boston : Shambhala,
1987. viii, 304 p. : ill. ; 23 cm. Includes index.
Bibliography: p. 281-297. ISBN 0-87773-430-5 (pbk.) :
DDC 299/.63 19
*1. Oya (Yoruba deity). 2. Femininity (Psychology). 3.
Yorubas - Religion. I. Title.*
BL2480.Y6 G58 1987   **NYPL [Sc D 88-101]**

Glendinning, Sally.
Jimmy and Joe fly a kite. Paintings by Paul
Frame. Champaign, Ill., Garrard Pub. Co.
[1970] 38 p. col. illus. 23 cm. Because of a mishap
while flying their kite, two boys learn about the
conservation of eagles. SCHOMBURG CHILDREN'S
COLLECTION. ISBN 0-8116-4704-8
*1. Eagles - Juvenile fiction. I. Frame, Paul, 1913- illus.
II. Schomburg Children's Collection. III. Title.*
PZ7.G4829 Jm   **NYPL [Sc D 88-1475]**

Jimmy and Joe look for a bear. Paintings by
Paul Frame. Champaign, Ill., Garrard Pub. Co.,
1970. 40 p. col. illus. 23 cm. (Her A Jimmy and
Joe book) An easy-to-read account of a Cub Scout
outing and who wound up with one Scout's birthday
cake. SCHOMBURG CHILDREN'S COLLECTION.
ISBN 0-8116-4703-X   DDC [E]

*1. Cub Scouts - Juvenile fiction. I. Frame, Paul, 1913-
illus. II. Schomburg Children's Collection. III. Title.*
PZ7.G4829 Jo   **NYPL [Sc D 88-1456]**

Jimmy and Joe meet a Halloween witch.
Paintings by Paul Frame. Champaign, Ill.,
Garrard Pub. Co. [1971] 40 p. col. illus. 23 cm.
Two boys trick-or-treating at a spooky house get a
scare and a surprise. SCHOMBURG CHILDREN'S
COLLECTION. ISBN 0-8116-4705-6   DDC [E]
*1. Halloween - Juvenile fiction. I. Frame, Paul, 1913-
illus. II. Schomburg Children's Collection. III. Title.*
PZ7.G4829 Jq   **NYPL [Sc D 88-1474]**

Gles, Margaret. Come play hide and seek /
Margaret Gles ; drawings by Lou Cunette.
Champaign, Ill. : Garrard Pub. Co. [1975] 32
p. : col. ill. ; 23 cm. The reader is invited to play
hide and seek with Jerry and Jake. SCHOMBURG
CHILDREN'S COLLECTION. ISBN 0-8116-6053-2
*1. Afro-American children - Juvenile fiction. I. Cunette,
Lou, illus. II. Schomburg Children's Collection. III.
Title.*
PZ7.G4883 Co   **NYPL [Sc D 89-119]**

Glimpse at the Paramaribo Zoo. Moonen, Joep.
'n Kijkje in de Paramaribo Zoo /. Paramaribo
[1987] 275 p. :
QL76.5.S752 P375 1987
         NYPL [Sc D 88-690]

Glimpses of old Barbados /. Stoute, Edward.
[Barbados] , 1986. 156 p. ;
         NYPL [Sc D 88-394]

Go free or die . Ferris, Jeri. Minneapolis , 1987.
63 p. : ISBN 0-87614-317-6 (lib. bdg.) : DDC
305.5/67/0924 B 92 19
E444.T82 F47 1987   **NYPL [Sc D 88-620]**

GOALS. see PRISONS.

Gobbi, Guglielmo. (joint author) Conte, Carmelo.
Ethiopia . [Milano] , 1976. xi, 196 p. ;
DT380 .C59   **NYPL [Sc D 88-1064]**

Gobotswang, Z. Pilot evaluation report on
Mahalapye Development Trust / by Z.
Gobotswang, K. Rakorong & M. Segale.
Gaborone, Botswana : National Institute of
Development & Cultural Research, Educational
Research Programme, University College of
Botswana, University of Botswana and
Swaziland, [1982] v leaves, 61, 3 p. ; 30 cm.
(NIR-research notes . no. 7) "February 1982."
*1. Mahalpye Development Trust. 2. Manpower policy,
Rural - Botswana. 3. Rural development - Botswana. I.
Rakorong, K. II. Segale, M. III. Series: Research notes
(National Institute of Development and Cultural
Research (Botswana)) , no. 7. IV. Title.*
HD5710.85.B59 G63 1982
         NYPL [Sc F 89-108]

GOD.
Hurbon, Laënnec. Dieu dans le vaudou haïtien
/. Port-au-Prince, Haïti , 1987. 268 p. ; DDC
299/.67 19
BL2490 .H87 1987   **NYPL [Sc D 89-366]**

God, the refuge of his people . Smith, Whitefoord.
Columbia, S.C. , 1850. 16 p. ;
         NYPL [Sc Rare C 89-12]

Godart, Jacques. Pourquoi les campêches
saignent-ils? / Jacques G. Godart.
Port-au-Prince : H. Deschamps, 1987. 199 p. ;
21 cm. "Prix Deschamps 1987."
1. Haiti - Fiction. I. Title.   **NYPL [Sc D 88-514]**

Goddard, Lawford L. Nobles, Wade W.
Understanding the Black family . Oakland,
California , 1984. 137 p. ; ISBN 0-939205-00-9
         NYPL [Sc D 88-697]

Goddard, Lawford Lawrence. Nobles, Wade W.
The KM ebit husia . Oakland, California , 1985.
201 p. ; ISBN 0-939205-03-3
         NYPL [Sc F 88-159]

Godfrey, E. M. Technical and vocational training
in Kenya and the harambee institutes of
technology [microform] / by E. M. Godfrey.
[Nairobi] : Institute for Development Studies,
University of Nairobi, 1973. 58 p. ; 30 cm.
(Discussion paper / Institute for Development Studies,
University of Nairobi . no. 169) "Revised version of
I.D.S. Working paper no. 40." Microfilm. New York:
New York Public Library, 1982. 1 microfilm reel; 35
mm. (MN *ZZ-23051)
*1. Vocational education - Kenya. 2. Technical
education - Kenya. I. Series: Nairobi. University.
Institute for Development Studies. Discussion paper, no.
169. II. Title.* **NYPL [Sc Micro R-4108 no. 24]**

Godfrey, Martin. Kenya to 1990 : prospects for
growth / by Martin Godfrey. London :
Economist Intelligence Unit, 1986. 105 p. : ill. ;
30 cm. (EIU special report. no. 1052) EIU economic
prospects series Bibliography: p. 98-99.
*1. Kenya - Economic conditions. 2. Kenya - Economic
policy. I. Title.*   **NYPL [Sc F 88-118]**

GODS, UMBANDA.
Linares, Ronaldo Antonio. Xangô e inhaçã /.
[São Paulo] , c1987. 85 p. :
         NYPL [Sc D 88-553]

God's way. Johnson, A. E. (Amelia E.), b. 1859.
Clarence and Corinne, or, God's way /. New
York , 1988. xxxviii, 187 p. : ISBN
0-19-505264-1 (alk. paper)   DDC 813/.4 19
PS2134.J515 C5 1988   **NYPL [JFC 88-2145]**

Görlach, Manfred. Focus on the Caribbean /.
Amsterdam , Philadelphia , 1986. ix, 209 p. :
ISBN 90-272-4866-4 (pbk. : alk. paper) : DDC
427/.9729 19
PM7874.C27 F6 1986   **NYPL [JFD 87-3902]**

**GOETZ, BERNHARD HUGO, 1947- - TRIALS,
LITIGATION, ETC.**
Fletcher, George P. A crime of self-defense.
New York , London , c1988. xi, 253 p. ; ISBN
0-02-910311-8   DDC 345.73/04 347.3054 19
KF224.G63 F54 1988   **NYPL [JLE 88-4737]**

Goffaux, J. Problèmes de développement : quêtes
de chimères, voies de lucidité / J. Goffaux.
[Kinshasa, Zaire?] : C.R.P., 1986. 223 p. ; 21
cm. At head of title: U20. Bibliography: p. 217-219.
1. Developing countries - Economic conditions. I. Title.
HD83 .G65 1986   **NYPL [Sc D 89-593]**

Goggins, Lathardus. Central State University : the
first one hundred years, 1887-1987 / by
Lathardus Goggins. Wilberforce, Ohio : Central
State University, c1987. xii, 181 p. : ill., ports. ;
24 cm. Includes index. Bibliography: p.[162]-170.
ISBN 0-87338-349-4 (alk. paper)   DDC
378.771/74 19
*1. Central State University (Wilberforce, Ohio) -
History. I. Title.*
LD881.C44 G64 1987   **NYPL [Sc E 88-477]**

GOLD - FRENCH GUIANA.
Petot, Jean. L'or de Guyane . Paris , c1986.
248 p. [8] pages of plates : ISBN 2-903033-84-6
         NYPL [Sc D 88-1395]

**GOLD MINES AND MINING - SOUTH
AFRICA - HISTORY.**
A People's history of South Africa.
Johannesburg , c1980- v. ; ISBN 0-86975-119-0
(pbk. : v. 1)   DDC 968 19
DT766 .P43   **NYPL [JLM 85-439]**

Goldberg, Alvin H. Rust, Art, 1927- The Art
Rust Jr. baseball quiz book /. New York,
N.Y. , c1985. 184 p., [16] p. of plates : ISBN
0-8160-1147-4 (pbk.)   DDC 796.357/0973 19
GV867.3 .R87 1985   **NYPL [JFE 85-2627]**

The golden lynx and other tales. Baker, Augusta.
(comp) Philadelphia [1960] 160 p.
PZ8.1.B172 Go   **NYPL [Sc D 88-1492]**

Goldman, Peter Louis, 1933- Monroe, Sylvester.
Brothers . New York, N.Y. , c1988. 284 p. :
ISBN 0-688-07622-X   DDC 977.3/1100496073 B
19
F548.9.N4 M66 1988   **NYPL [Sc E 88-356]**

Goldsborough, June. (illus) Johnson, Eric W. The
stolen ruler. Philadelphia [1970] 64 p.   DDC
[Fic]
PZ7.J631765 St   **NYPL [Sc D 88-1114]**

Goldschmidt, Walter Rochs, 1913- The Sebei : a
study in adaptation / by Walter Goldschmidt.
New York : Holt, Rinehart, and Winston,
c1986. xii, 162 p. : ill. ; 24 cm. (Case studies in
cultural anthropology) Includes index. Bibliography: p.
155. ISBN 0-03-008922-0 : DDC 305/.09676/1 19
1. Sapiny (African people). I. Title.
DT433.245.S24 G65 1986
         NYPL [Sc E 88-225]

GOLDWEIGHTS, ASHANTI.
Fox, Christine. Asante brass casting .
Cambridge , 1988. xii, 112 p. : ISBN
0-902993-24-0 (pbk) : DDC 739.2/27667 19
         NYPL [Sc D 88-1434]

Golliwogg in the African jungle /. Upton, Bertha,
1849-1912. London , New York , 1909. 62, [2]
p. :   **NYPL [Sc Rare F 89-16]**

The Golliwogg's bicycle club. Upton, Florence

Kate, 1873-1922. London, 1967. [1] 62 p.
PZ8.3.U74 Go2   *NYPL [Sc D 88-252]*

Gombo comes to Philadelphia /. Tinker, Edward
Larocque, 1881- Worcester, Mass. , 1957. [10],
22 p. :   *NYPL [Sc E 89-9]*

Gomes, Heloisa Toller. O negro e o romantismo
brasileiro / Heloisa Toller Gomes. São Paulo :
Atual Editora, [1988] 113 p. ; 21 cm. (Série
Lendo) Bibliography: p. 109-113.
*1. Brazilian literature - 19th century - History and
criticism. 2. Romanticism - Brazil. I. Title.*
                         NYPL [Sc D 89-515]

Gomes, P. I.
Girvan, Norman, 1941- Technology policies for
small developing economies . Mona, Jamaica ,
c1983. 224 p. : DDC 338.9729 19
T24.A1 G57 1983   *NYPL [Sc E 88-260]*
Rural development in the Caribbean /.
London , 1985. xxi, 246 p. : ISBN 0-312-69599-3
                         NYPL [Sc D 88-1309]

Gomez, Koffi, 1941- Opération Marigot : roman /
Koffi Gomez. Lomé : Les Nouvelles éditions
africaines, 1982. 146 p. ; 21 cm. ISBN
2-7236-0849-2
1. togo - Fiction. I. Title. *NYPL [Sc D 88-1306]*

GONAÏVES (HAITI) - HISTORY.
Luc, Napoléon Serge. Histoire du déchoukage
/. [Port-au-Prince, Haiti, W.I] [1987?] 124 p. :
                         NYPL [Sc D 87-1419]

GONGA (AFRICAN PEOPLE) - HISTORY.
Lange, Werner J., 1946- History of the
Southern Gonga (Southwestern Ethiopia) /.
Wiesbaden , 1982. xvi, 348 p., [12] p. of
plates : ISBN 3-515-03399-8 (pbk.) : DDC
306/.08996 19
DT380.4.G66 L36 1982
                         NYPL [Sc E 88-379]

**GONGOLA STATE (NIGERIA) - CHURCH
HISTORY.**
Hickey, Raymond. Christianity in Borno State
and Northern Gongola /. [Nigeria , 1984?]
(Ibadan : Claverianum Press) vi, 108 p. :
                         NYPL [Sc D 88-882]

González, Carmen, 1940- Sobre los hombros
ajenos / Carmen González. La Habana :
Editorial de Ciencias Sociales, 1985. 119 p. ; 21
cm. (Ediciones políticas) Includes 12 tables. No. 9 and
10 in pocket. Bibliography: p. 118-119. DDC 968 19
*1. Apartheid - South Africa. 2. South Africa - History.
I. Series: Ediciones políticas (Havana, Cuba). II. Title.*
DT766 .G66 1985   *NYPL [Sc D 88-416]*

Gonzalez, Lélia. Festas populares no Brasil =
Popular festivals in Brazil / texto de Lélia
Gonzalez ; fotografias de A. Hamdan ... [et al.].
Rio de Janeiro, Brasil : Editora Index, c1987.
144 p. : col. ill. ; 30 cm. Portuguese and English.
ISBN 85-7083-015-7
*1. Festivals - Brazil. 2. Festivals - Brazil - Pictorial
works. 3. Carnival - Brazil - Rio de Janeiro. 4.
Carnival - Brazil - Rio de Janeiro - Pictorial works. 5.
Rio de Janeiro (Brazil) - Religious life and customs. I.
Title. II. Title: Popular festivals in Brazil.*
GT4833.A2 G66x 1987 *NYPL [Sc F 89-116]*

The good fight /. Chisolm, Shirley, 1924- New
York , c1973. 206 p. ; *NYPL [Sc C 88-43]*

Good woman . Clifton, Lucille, 1936- Brockport,
NY , St. Paul, Minnesota , 1987. 276 p. :
ISBN 0-918526-59-0 (pbk.)
                         NYPL [Sc E 88-232]

Goodall, Jane van Lawick- see Lawick-Goodall,
Jane, Barones van.

Goodison, Lorna. I am becoming my mother /
Lorna Goodison. London : New Beacon Books,
1986. 50 p. ; 23 cm. Poems. ISBN 0-901241-67-9
I. Title.   *NYPL [Sc D 88-275]*

The goose that was a watchdog. Hays, Wilma
Pitchford. Boston [1967] 41 p. DDC [Fic]
PZ7.H31493 Go   *NYPL [Sc D 88-1426]*

Gooseberry Jones /. Gerber, Will. New York ,
c1947. 96 p. :   *NYPL [Sc D 89-442]*

Gordon, Billi.
Billi Gordon's You've had worse things in your
mouth cookbook / [Billi Gordon]. San
Francisco, Calif. : West Graphics, c1985. 96 p. :
ill. (some col.) ; 26 cm. Includes index.
1. Cookery, American. I. Title.
                         NYPL [Sc F 88-214]
Eat this book : the last diet book / Billi

Gordon. San Francisco, California : West
Graphics, c1987. 96 p. : col. ill. ; 26 cm. ISBN
0-9614979-1-2
*1. Reducing - Anecdotes, facetiae, satire, etc. 2.
Reducing - Psychological aspects. I. Title.*
                         NYPL [Sc F 88-110]

GORDON, EDWARD FITZGERALD.
Philip, Ira. Freedom fighters . London , 1987.
275 p., [8] p. of plates : ISBN 0-947638-42-3
(cased) : DDC 323.1/196/07299 19
                         NYPL [Sc D 88-1137]

Gorey, Edward, 1925- (illus) Rees, Ennis. Brer
Rabbit and his tricks. New York [1967] 1 v.
(unpaged)
PZ8.3.R254 Br   *NYPL [Sc E 88-530]*

Gorman, G. E.
Evans, James H., 1950- Black theology . New
York , c1987. xii, 205 p. ; ISBN 0-313-24822-2
(lib. bdg. : alk. paper) DDC 016.23/008996073
19
Z7774 .E9 1987 BT82.7
                         NYPL [Sc E 87-426]
Guide to current national bibliographies in the
Third World / G.E. Gorman and J.J. Mills. 2nd
rev. ed. London ; New York : H. Zell , c1987.
xx, 372 p. ; 25 cm. Includes index. ISBN
0-905450-34-5
*1. Bibliography - Bibliography - Developing countries.
2. Bibliography, National - Bibliography. 3. Developing
countries - Imprints - Bibliography. I. Mills, J. J. II.
Title.*   *NYPL [Sc E 88-474]*

Gorman, James. Birney, James Gillespie,
1792-1857. Examination of the decision of the
Supreme Court of the United States, in the case
of Strader, Gorman and Armstrong vs.
Christopher Graham . Cincinnati , 1852. iv, [1],
6-46, [1] p. ;
E450 .B57   *NYPL [Sc Rare F 88-37]*

Gorschenek, Margareta, 1946- Neue Kunst aus
Afrika . [Hamburg] , c1984. 111 p. :
                         NYPL [Sc G 88-17]

Gorsline, Douglas W., 1913- Steinman, Beatrice.
This railroad disappears. New York [1958] 181
p.
PZ7.S8266 Th   *NYPL [Sc D 89-391]*

Gort, Enid. Aging in cross-cultural perspective .
New York , c1988. vii, 138 p. ; ISBN
0-940605-51-1   *NYPL [Sc D 89-431]*

Gospel, blues and jazz. Oliver, Paul. The New
Grove gospel, blues and jazz. New York ,
1986. 395 p. [16] p. of plates : ISBN
0-393-01696-X   *NYPL [JND 88-16]*

GOSPEL MUSIC - NEW YORK (N.Y.)
Allen, Robert Raymond. Singing in the spirit .
Ann Arbor, Mich , c1987. xii, 424 p. ;
                         NYPL [Sc D 88-1212]

**GOSPEL MUSIC - TENNESSEE -
MEMPHIS - HISTORY AND
CRITICISM.**
Lornell, Kip, 1953- Happy in the service of the
Lord . Urbana , c1988. x, 171 p., [30] p. of
plates : ISBN 0-252-01523-1 (alk. paper) DDC
783.7/08996073/0976819 19
ML3187 .L67 1988   *NYPL [Sc E 89-101]*

**GOSPEL MUSIC - UNITED STATES -
HISTORY AND CRITICISM.**
Oliver, Paul. The New Grove gospel, blues and
jazz . New York , 1986. 395 p. [16] p. of
plates : ISBN 0-393-01696-X
                         NYPL [JND 88-16]

Gospel parables in African context / edited by
Justin S. Ukpong. Port Harcourt, Nigeria :
CIWA Press, 1988. 68 p. ; 21 cm. Includes
bibliographical references. ISBN 978-272-801-2
I. Likpong, Justin S. *NYPL [Sc D 89-133]*

Gospel pearls : edited and compiled for special
use in the Sunday School, church, evangelistic
meetings, conventions, and all religious services
by the Music Committee of the Sunday School
Publishing Board / Willa A. Townsend, director.
Nashville, Tenn. : Sunday School Publishing
Board, National Baptist Convention, U. S.A.,
c1921. [152] p. : music ; 20 cm. Includes index.
"Printed in both round and shaped notes."
*1. Baptists - Hymns. I. Townsend, Willa A. II. National
Baptist Convention of the United States of America.
Sunday School Publishing Board.*
                         NYPL [Sc C 86-222]

The gospel Singer /. Dickens, Nathaniel A. New
York , c1987. 187 p. ; ISBN 0-533-07387-1
                         NYPL [Sc D 88-1450]

Goss, Bernard, d. 1966. Self portrait -- Bernard
Goss. [S.l. , 1967?] 28 p. :
                         NYPL [Sc D 88-503]

GOSS, BERNARD, D. 1966.
Self portrait -- Bernard Goss. [S.l. , 1967?] 28
p. :   *NYPL [Sc D 88-503]*

Gossett, Hattie, 1942- Presenting-- Sister Noblues
/ by Hattie Gossett. Ithaca, N.Y. : Firebrand
Books, c1988. 143 p. ; 22 cm. ISBN
0-932379-50-8 (alk. paper) DDC 811/.54 19
I. Title. II. Title: Sister Noblues.
PS3557.O785 P7 1988 *NYPL [JFD 89-457]*

Gossett, Margaret. (joint author) Elting, Mary,
1909- Patch /. Garden City, N.Y. , 1948. 156
p. :
PZ7.E53Pat   *NYPL [Sc C 89-14]*

Gotera, un site paléolithique récent d'Ethiopie /.
Chavaillon, Nicole. Paris , 1985. 58 p., 25
leaves of plates :   *NYPL [Sc F 88-359]*

**Göttinger Beiträge Zur Land- und
Forstwirtschaft in den Tropen und
Subtropen .**
(Heft 6) Becker, Barbara. Wildpflanzen in der
Ernährung der Bevölkerung afrikanischer
Trockengebiete . Göttingen , 1984. iv, 341 p. :
                         NYPL [Sc D 88-682]

GOUIN (AFRICAN PEOPLE)
Mignot, Alain. La terre et le pouvoir chez les
Guin du sud-est du Togo /. Paris , 1985. 288
p. ; ISBN 2-85944-087-9 *NYPL [Sc E 88-383]*

Gould, Cora Smith. Dream land on the Isle of
Nassau in the Bahamas / by Cora Smith Gould.
New York City : C. Gould, 1938. 38 p. : ill. ;
22 cm. With autograph of author.
1. Nassau (Bahamas) - Poetry. I. Title.
                         NYPL [Sc D 89-1297]

Goulphin, Fred. Les Veillées de chase d'Henri
Guizard / Fred Goulphin. [Paris] : Fammarion,
1987. 235 p. ; 23 cm. Cover title: Philippe de
Baleine présente les veillés de chasse d'Henri Guizard.
ISBN 2-08-065054-8
*1. Guizard, Henri. 2. Guides for hunters, fishermen,
etc - Gabon. 3. National parks and reserves - Gabon. I.
Baleine, Philippe de. II. Title.*
                         NYPL [Sc D 88-28]

Goumaz, Max Liniger- see Liniger-Goumaz, Max.

Gousse, Edgard Js. Th. Non à une intervention
américaine en Haïti / E. Js. Th. Gousse ;
postface de Paul Laraque. Montréal : Les
Éditions du progrès, 1988. 74 p. ; 21 cm.
Bibliography: p. [73]-74.
*1. Haiti - Dependency on the United States. 2. Haiti -
Foreign relations - United States. 3. United States -
Foreign relations - Haiti. 4. Haiti - History - American
occupation, 1915-1934. I. Title.*
                         NYPL [Sc D 88-861]

Gov. Hammond's letters on southern slavery .
Hammond, James Henry, 1807-1864.
Charleston , 1845. 32 p. ;
                         NYPL [Sc Rare C 89-24]

Govenar, Alan B., 1952- Meeting the blues /
Alan Govenar. Dallas, Tex. : Taylor Pub. Co.,
c1988. 239 p. : ill., ports. ; 31 cm. Includes index.
Discography: p. 234-236. Bibliography: p. 237. ISBN
0-87833-623-0 : DDC 784.5/3/00922 19
*1. Blues musicians - United States - Interviews. 2.
Afro-Americans - United States - Interviews. 3. Blues
(Music) - History and criticism. I. Title.*
ML3521 .G68 1988   *NYPL [Sc G 89-4]*

GOVERNMENT. see POLITICAL SCIENCE.

**GOVERNMENT AGENCIES. see
ADMINISTRATIVE AGENCIES.**

Government and development in rural Lesotho /.
Van de Geer, Roeland. Roma, Lesotho , 1982,
1984 printing. 159 p. ; *NYPL [Sc D 89-52]*

Government and the media in Nigeria /.
Udoakah, Nkereuwem. Calabar, Nigeria ,
c1988. x, 88 p. ; ISBN 978-231-603-2
                         NYPL [Sc C 89-51]

**GOVERNMENT AND THE PRESS - SOUTH
AFRICA.**
Harris, Phil. [Reporting southern, Africa.
Spanish.] La información sobre África austral .
Barcelona , Paris , 1984. 188 p. : ISBN

Government and the press - South Africa. (cont.)

92-3-301700-1 (Unesco)
NYPL [Sc D 88-614]

Phelan, John M. Apartheid media . Westport, Conn. , c1987. xi, 220 p. ; ISBN 0-88208-244-2 : DDC 323.44/5 19
PN4748.S58 P4 1987 *NYPL [JLD 87-4698]*

GOVERNMENT AND THE PRESS - ZIMBABWE.
Harris, Phil. [Reporting southern Africa. Spanish.] La información sobre África austral . Barcelona , Paris , 1984. 188 p. : ISBN 92-3-301700-1 (Unesco)
NYPL [Sc D 88-614]

GOVERNMENT CENTRALIZATION. see DECENTRALIZATION IN GOVERNMENT.

GOVERNMENT DECENTRALIZATION. see DECENTRALIZATION IN GOVERNMENT.

GOVERNMENT DEPARTMENTS. see ADMINISTRATIVE AGENCIES.

GOVERNMENT EMPLOYEES. see CIVIL SERVICE.

GOVERNMENT, FEDERAL. see FEDERAL GOVERNMENT.

GOVERNMENT, LOCAL. see LOCAL GOVERNMENT.

GOVERNMENT REGULATION OF COMMERCE. see COMMERCIAL POLICY.

GOVERNMENT, RESISTANCE TO - SOUTH AFRICA.
Motlhabi, Mokgethi B. G. (Mokgethi Buti George), 1944- Challenge to apartheid . Grand Rapids, Mich. , c1988. xii, 243 p. ; ISBN 0-8028-0347-4 : DDC 305.8/00968 19
DT763 .M69 1988 *NYPL [JFD 88-11473]*

Government white paper on the report of Panel on Eduction Review in Borno State /. Borno State (Nigeria) Maiduguri [1984] 56 p. :
NYPL [Sc E 88-424]

GRAAFF-REINET (SOUTH AFRICE) - ECONOMIC CONDITIONS.
Dubow, Saul. Land, labour and merchant capital in the pre-industrial rural economy of the Cape . [Cape Town] , 1982. ii, 95 p. : ISBN 0-7992-0472-2 *NYPL [Sc D 82-611]*

Graf, William D. The Nigerian state : political economy, state class and political system in the post-colonial era / William D. Graf. London : Currey ; Portsmouth, N.H. : Heinemann, 1988. xvi, 281 p. : ill., maps ; 24 cm. Includes index. Bibliography: p. 248-275. ISBN 0-85255-313-7 (cased) : DDC 320.1/09669 19
1. Nigeria - History - 1960-. I. Gift of J.P. Morgan and Co., Inc. II. Title. *NYPL [Sc E 89-195]*

GRAFT (IN POLITICS) see CORRUPTION (IN POLITICS)

Graham, Christopher. Birney, James Gillespie, 1792-1857. Examination of the decision of the Supreme Court of the United States, in the case of Strader, Gorman and Armstrong vs. Christopher Graham . Cincinnati , 1852. iv, [1], 6-46, [1] p. ;
E450 .B57 *NYPL [Sc Rare F 88-37]*

Graham, Lorenz B.
[North Town. German]
Stadt im Norden / Lorenz Graham. Stuttgart : Union Verlag, 1973, c1965. 157 p. ; 21 cm. Translation of: North Town. ISBN 3-8002-5087-X
1. Afro-American youth - Fiction. I. Title.
NYPL [Sc D 88-1171]

Graham, Maryemma. Harper, Frances Ellen Watkins, 1825-1911. [Poems.] Complete poems of Frances E.W. Harper /. New York , 1988. lx, 232 p. ; ISBN 0-19-505244-7 (alk. paper) DDC 811/.3 19
PS1799.H7 A17 1988 *NYPL [JFC 88-2147]*

GRAHAMSTOWN, SOUTH AFRICA.
Davies, W. J. A review of issues related to planning and development in Grahamstown . Grahamstown [South Africa] , 1986. 114 p. : ISBN 0-86810-130-3 *NYPL [Sc F 87-431]*

GRAHAMSTOWN (SOUTH AFRICA) - RACE RELATIONS.
Roux, Andre, 1954- Voices from Rini .

Grahamstown, South Africa , 1986. 107 p. ; ISBN 0-86810-131-1 *NYPL [Sc F 88-216]*

Grammaire créole /. Germain, Robert. Paris [1980] 303 p. ; ISBN 2-85802-165-1 : DDC 447/.972976 19
PM7854.W47 G4 *NYPL [Sc D 82-456]*

Grammaire Créole (Fondas Kréyol-la) . Bernabé, Jean. Paris , 1987. 205 p. ; ISBN 2-85805-734-X
NYPL [Sc D 88-521]

A grammar of Harar Oromo (Northeastern Ethiopia) . Owens, Jonathan. Hamburg , c1985. 282 p. ; ISBN 3-87118-717-8 (pbk.) DDC 493/.7 19
PJ2476 .O94 1985 *NYPL [Sc D 88-751]*

Grammatical relations in a radical Creole . Byrne, Francis. Amsterdam ; Philadelphia , 1987. xiv, 293 p. : ISBN 0-915027-96-8 (U. S. : alk. paper) : DDC 427/.9883 19
PM7875.S27 B97 1987
NYPL [JFD 88-7020]

Gran Colombia. see Colombia.

GRANADA - HISTORY - AMERICAN INVASION, 1983.
Hopkin, Gerry R. S. Grenada topples the balance in West Indian history . [Grenada] c1984. 76 p. : *NYPL [Sc C 88-147]*

GRANADA - POLITICS AND GOVERNMENT - 1974-
Hopkin, Gerry R. S. Grenada topples the balance in West Indian history . [Grenada] c1984. 76 p. : *NYPL [Sc C 88-147]*

Granadine Confederation. see Colombia.

Grand Palais (Paris, France) Haïti . Paris , 1988. 276 p. : *NYPL [Sc E 89-227]*

Grandpa's face /. Greenfield, Eloise. New York , 1988. [32] p. : ISBN 0-399-21525-5 DDC [E] 19
PZ7.G845 Gs 1988 *NYPL [Sc F 88-387]*

Grandy, Moses, b. 1786? Le récit de Moses Grandy, esclave en Caroline du Nord [microform] / traduit de l'anglais et présenté par Jean Benoist. [Montréal] : Centre de recherches caraïbes, Université de Montréal, [1977] 45 p. ; 22 cm. Translation of Narrative of the life of Moses Grandy. Microfiche. New York : New York Public Library, 1979. 1 microfiche : negative ; 11 x 15 cm. (FSN34,237)
1. Grandy, Moses, b. 1786?. 2. Slavery in the United States - North Carolina. 3. Slaves - North Carolina - Biography. I. Benoist, Jean, 1929-. II. Title.
E444 .G7514 *NYPL [*XM-12976]*

GRANDY, MOSES, B. 1786?
Grandy, Moses, b. 1786? Le récit de Moses Grandy, esclave en Caroline du Nord [microform] /. [Montréal] [1977] 45 p. ;
E444 .G7514 *NYPL [*XM-12976]*

Granger, Lester Blackwell, 1896- Toward job adjustment : with specific reference to the vocational problems of racial, religious and cultural minority groups / by Lester B. Granger, Louis H. Sobel, William H. H. Wilkinson ; prepared under the direction of [the] Committee on Minority Groups. Section on Employment and Vocational guidance, Welfare Council of New York City. [New York] : Welfare Council of New York City, [1941] 78 p. : ill. ; 22 cm. Bibliography: p. 76-78.
1. Employment interviewing - United States. 2. Employment agencies - United States. 3. Minorities - Employment - United States. I. Sobel, Louis H. (Louis Harry), 1904-1955. II. Wilkinson, William H. H. III. Welfare Council of New York City. Section on Employment and Vocational Guidance. IV. Title.
NYPL [Sc D 88-178]

Grant, Micki. Croesus and the witch / adapted from a century-old Black fable by Vinnette Carroll ; music and lyrics by Micki Grant. Hansel and Gretel (in the 1980s) / by Marie Thomas ; music and lyrics by Micki Grant. New York, N.Y. : Broadway Play Publishing, 1984. 67, [119] p. : music ; 28 cm. ISBN 0-88145-024-3
1. Carroll, Vinnette. II. Thomas, Marie. Hansel and Gretel (in the 1980's). 1984. III. Hansel and Gretel (in the 1980's). IV. Title. *NYPL [Sc F 88-205]*

GRANT, ULYSSES S. (ULYSSES SIMPSON), 1822-1885.
Sumner, Charles, 1811-1874. "He, being dead, yet speaketh" . Boston , New York , 1878. 29, 16 p. ; *NYPL [Sc Rare C 89-4]*

GRANTS-IN-AID, INTERNATIONAL. see ECONOMIC ASSISTANCE.

GRAPHIC ARTS - CONSERVATION AND RESTORATION.
Conservation of library and archive materials and the graphic arts /. London , Boston , 1985. 328 p. : ISBN 0-408-01466-0 : DDC 025.7 19
Z701 .C5863 1985 *NYPL [MFW+ 88-574]*

GRAVES. see CEMETERIES; TOMBS.

GRAVEYARDS. see CEMETERIES.

Gray, Genevieve. A kite for Bennie, by Genevieve Gray. Pictures by Floyd Sowell. Designed by Dorothy E. Hayes. New York, McGraw-Hill, 1972. [40] p. illus. 26 cm. Bennie's family doesn't have the money to spare for a kite so he collects the materials and builds one. SCHOMBURG CHILDREN'S COLLECTION. ISBN 0-07-024197-X DDC [Fic]
1. Afro-American children - Juvenile fiction. I. Sowell, Floyd, illus. II. Schomburg Children's Collection. III. Title.
PZ7.G7774 Ki *NYPL [Sc E 88-422]*

Gray, John, 1866-1934. Park : a fantastic story / John Gray ; edited by Philip Healy. Manchester, [Greater Manchester] : Carcanet Press, 1984. 128 p. : 20 cm. Bibliography: p. 128. ISBN 0-85635-538-0
I. Healy, Philip. II. Title. *NYPL [JFD 85-1419]*

Gray, Mattie Evans. Images : a workbook for enhancing self-esteem and promoting career preparation, especially for Black girls / by Mattie Evans Gray. Sacramento, Calif. : California State Dept. of Education, c1988. 185 p. : ill. ; 28 cm. "Developed by the CIRCLE Project, California State University, Sacramento for the California State Department of Education." ISBN 0-8011-0782-2
1. Afro-American women - California. 2. Vocational guidance for women - California. 3. Vocational guidance for minorities - California. I. California. State Dept. of Education. II. CIRCLE Project. III. Title.
NYPL [Sc F 89-134]

Gray, Nigel. A balloon for grandad / Nigel Gray ; pictures by Jane Ray. 1st American ed. London ; New York : Orchard Books, 1988. [30] p. : col. ill. ;27 cm. Unhappy when he loses his silver and red balloon, Sam is comforted by imagining it on its way to visit his grandfather in Egypt. SCHOMBURG CHILDREN'S COLLECTION. ISBN 0-531-05755-0 : DDC [E] 19
1. Balloons - Juvenile fiction. I. Ray, Jane, ill. II. Schomburg Children's Collection. III. Title.
PZ7.G7813 Bal 1988 *NYPL [Sc F 88-345]*

Gray, Stephen, 1941- The Penguin book of Southern African stories /. Harmondsworth, Middlesex, England , New York, N.Y., U. S.A. , 1985. 328 p. ; ISBN 0-14-007239-X (pbk.) : DDC 808.83/1 19
PL8014.S62 P46 1985 *NYPL [Sc C 88-270]*

GREAT BRITAIN. ARMY. WEST AFRICAN FRONTIER FORCE.
Ukpabi, Sam C. The origins of the Nigerian army . Zaria, Nigeria , 1987. 194 p. : ISBN 978-19-4128-6 *NYPL [Sc D 88-1489]*

Great Britain. Central Criminal Court. see London. Central Criminal Court.

Great Britain. Colonial Office. Introducing the Colonies. London, H. M. Stationery Off.; 1949. 87 p. illus., ports., maps (1 fold. col.) 18 cm.
1. Great Britain - Colonies. I. Title.
JV1027 .A473 1949a *NYPL [Sc C 88-231]*

Papers relative to the West Indies. Part I-(5.). Jamaica - British Guiana ... [London] : Ordered by the House of Commons to be printed, 1839. iv, 317 p. ; 34 cm. Running title: "Papers on the condition of the labouring population, West Indies." Continuation of Parliamentary paper no. 272.
1. Labor and laboring classes - Jamaica. 2. Labor and laboring classes - Guyana. I. Title. II. Title: Papers on the condition of the labouring population, West Indies.
NYPL [Sc Rare G 86-3]

GREAT BRITAIN - COLONIES.
Great Britain. Colonial Office. Introducing the Colonies. London, 1949. 87 p.
JV1027 .A473 1949a *NYPL [Sc C 88-231]*

GREAT BRITAIN - COLONIES - ADMINISTRATION - HISTORY.
Porter, A. N. (Andrew N.) British imperial policy and decolonization, 1938-64 /. New

York , 1987- v. ; ISBN 0-312-00554-7 (v. 1) :
DDC 325/.31/41 19
JV1018 .P66 1987   ***NYPL [Sc D 88-219]***

GREAT BRITAIN - COLONIES - AFRICA.
Terrell, Richard. West African interlude .
Salisbury, Wiltshire , 1988. 175 p. :
    NYPL [Sc D 88-1371]

**GREAT BRITAIN - COLONIES - AFRICA -
HISTORY.**
Ejimofor, Cornelius Ogu, 1940- British colonial
objectives and policies in Nigeria . Onitsha,
Nigeria , 1987. viii, 216 p., 1 folded leaf ;
  ISBN 978-17-5142-8   ***NYPL [Sc D 88-820]***

**Great Britain. Committee of Inquiry into the
Education of Children from Ethnic Minority
Groups.
REPORT.**
Swann and the global dimension . Clifton,
Bristol , c1987. 104 p. ;
    NYPL [Sc F 88-257]

Great Britain. Courts. Central Criminal Court.
see London. Central Criminal Court.

**GREAT BRITAIN - FOREIGN RELATIONS -
ETHIOPIA - SOURCES.**
Letters from Ethiopian rulers (early and
mid-nineteenth century) . Oxford , New York ,
c1985. xvii, 197 p. : ISBN 0-19-726046-2
    NYPL [Sc E 88-262]

**GREAT BRITAIN - HISTORY - 19TH
CENTURY.**
Allison, Philip. Life in the white man's grave .
London , 1988. 192 p. : ISBN 0-670-81020-7 :
DDC 966 19
DT476.2   ***NYPL [Sc F 88-174]***

**Great Britain - History - Crimean War, 1853-
1856.** see **Crimean War, 1853-1856.**

**GREAT BRITAIN - HISTORY - 20TH
CENTURY.**
Allison, Philip. Life in the white man's grave .
London , 1988. 192 p. : ISBN 0-670-81020-7 :
DDC 966 19
DT476.2   ***NYPL [Sc F 88-174]***

**GREAT BRITAIN - HISTORY - GEORGE VI,
1936-1952.**
Smith, Graham. When Jim Crow met John
Bull . London , c1987. 265 p. ; ISBN
1-85043-039-X   ***NYPL [Sc D 88-55]***

Great Britain. Manpower Services Commission.
Stares, Rodney. Ethnic minorities . [London] ,
1982. 62 p. ; ISBN 0-905932-32-3
    NYPL [Sc F 88-96]

**Great Britain. Overseas Development
Administration.** Review of UK manpower
and training aid to Nigeria / by B. Steele, J.M.
White. S. Chakrabarti. [London? : s.n., 1984 or
1985] v, 72 p. ; 30 cm.
*1. Technical assistance, British - Nigeria. I. Steele, B. II.
White, J. M. III. Chakrabarti, S.*
    NYPL [Sc F 88-185]

**Great Britain. Parliament. House of Commons.
Select Committee on the Slave Trade.
REPORT.**
Barrister. Analysis of the evidence given
before the select committees upon the slave
trade /. London , 1850. 121 p. ;
    NYPL [Sc Rare G 86-11]

GREAT BRITAIN - RACE RELATIONS.
Britain's Black population . Aldershot, Hants,
England , Brookfield, Vt., USA , c1988. xv, 298
p. ; ISBN 0-566-05179-6 : DDC 305.8/96/041 19
DA125.N4 B75 1988   ***NYPL [Sc E 89-100]***

Dennis, Ferdinand, 1956- Behind the
frontlines . London , 1988. xv, 216 p. ; ISBN
0-575-04098-X   ***NYPL [JLD 89-210]***

Dohndy, Farrukh. The Black explosion in
British schools / . London , 1985. 64 p. ; ISBN
0-9503498-6-0   ***NYPL [Sc D 88-1030]***

Haynes, Aaron, 1927- The state of Black
Britain / . London , 1983. 160 p. ; ISBN
0-946455-01-5   ***NYPL [Sc D 88-348]***

Leech, Kenneth, 1939- Struggle in Babylon .
London , 1988. 253 p. ; ISBN 0-85969-577-8
(pbk) DDC 261.8/348/0941 19
    NYPL [Sc D 89-176]

Solomos, John. Black youth, racism and the
state . Cambridge [Cambridgeshire] , New
York , 1988. 284 p. ; ISBN 0-521-36019-6 DDC

305.8/96041 19
DA125.N4 S65 1988   ***NYPL [Sc E 88-606]***

Third world impact / . London , 1986. 272 p. :
  ISBN 0-9506664-8-3   ***NYPL [Sc F 88-19]***

Widgery, David. Beating time . London ,
1986. 126 p. : ISBN 0-7011-2985-9
    NYPL [JMD 88-112]

Williams, Lincoln Octavious. Partial surrender .
London , New York , 1988. viii, 194 p. ; ISBN
1-85000-289-4 DDC 361.7/97/009421 19
HV1441.G8 L78 1988   ***NYPL [Sc E 89-73]***

**GREAT BRITAIN - RELATIONS SOUTH
AFRICA.**
Nyerere, Julius Kambarage, Pres. Tanzania,
1922- South Africa and the Commonwealth
[microform] /. [S.l. , 1971] 14 p. ;
    NYPL [Sc Micro F-10922]

**GREAT BRITAIN - SOCIAL CONDITIONS -
20TH CENTURY.**
Saunders, Dave. The West Indians in Britain /.
London , 1984. 72 p. : ISBN 0-7134-4427-4
DA125.W4 S28x 1984   ***NYPL [Sc F 88-68]***

The great debate . Okonkwo, Ifeanyichukwu E.
R. Onitsha, Anambra State, Nigeria , 1986. 138
p. ; ISBN 978-264-308-4   ***NYPL [Sc C 89-58]***

The great Marcus Garvey /. Mackie, Liz.
London , 1987. 157 p. ; ISBN 1-87051-850-0
    NYPL [Sc D 88-999]

The great proclamation . Commager, Henry
Steele, 1902- Indianapolis [1960] 112 p. :
    NYPL [Sc E 88-229]

Great tales of the Yorubas / [compiled by Mike
Omoleye. 2d impression (rev. and enl.) Ibadan,
Oyo State, Nigeria : Omoleye Publishing Co.,
1987. 92 p. : ill. ; 21 cm.
*1. Yorubas - Folklore. 2. Tales - Nigeria. I. Omoleye,
Mike. II. Title.*   ***NYPL [Sc D 88-712]***

**The great Tzotzil dictionary of Santo Domingo
Zinacantán .** Laughlin, Robert M. Washington,
D.C. , 1988. 3 v. (xiii, 1119 p.) : DDC 497/.4
301 s 19
GN1 .S54 no. 31a PM4466.Z5
    NYPL [HBR 89-17311]

The Great War in Africa 1914-1918 /. Farwell,
Byron. Harmondsworth , 1987. 382 p. : ISBN
0-670-80244-1 : DDC 940.4/16 19
D575   ***NYPL [Sc D 88-834]***

Great Zimbabwe /. Garlake, Peter S. Harare,
Zimbabwe , 1985. 64 p. : ISBN 0-949225-24-X
    NYPL [Sc D 87-1002]

GREAT ZIMBABWE (CITY)
Garlake, Peter S. Great Zimbabwe /. Harare,
Zimbabwe , 1985. 64 p. : ISBN 0-949225-24-X
    NYPL [Sc D 87-1002]

**GREAT ZIMBABWE (CITY) - JUVENILE
LITERATURE.**
Garlake, Peter S. Life at Great Zimbabwe /.
Gweru, Zimbabwe , 1983, c1982. [36] p. :
  ISBN 0-86922-180-9 (pbk.) DDC 968.91 19
DT962.9.G73 G374 1983
    NYPL [Sc F 88-175]

Grébénart, Danilo. Les origines de la métallurgie
en Afrique occidentale / Danilo Grébénart ;
préface du professeur Gabriel Camps. Paris :
Éditions Errance, c1988. 290 p. : ill., map ; 24
cm. Includes indexes. Bibliography: p. 269-284. ISBN
2-903442-65-7
1. Metallurgy - Africa, West - History. I. Title.
    NYPL [Sc E 88-600]

Greco, Robert. Gilstrap, Robert. The sultan's fool
and other North African tales . New York ,
c1958. 95 p. : ISBN 931-40-0118-0
    NYPL [Sc E 88-548]

Green, Carroll. American visions Afro-American
art, 1986 / . Washington, D.C. , 1987. 57 p. :
    NYPL [Sc F 87-438]

Green, Charles (Charles St. Clair) The struggle
for black empowerment in New York City :
beyond the politics of pigmentation / Charles
Green and Basil Wilson. New York : Praeger,
1989. xvi, 183 p. : ill. ; 25 cm. Includes index.
Bibliography: p. [169]-175. ISBN 0-275-92614-1 (alk.
paper) DDC 974.7/100496073 19
*1. Afro-Americans - New York (N.Y.) - Politics and
government. 2. New York (N.Y.) - Politics and
government. I. Wilson, Basil, 1943-. II. Title.*
F128.9.N3 G74 1989   ***NYPL [Sc E 89-203]***

Green, Ernest Davis. The King, Belshazzar / by
Ernest Davis Green. 1st ed. New York :
Vantage Press, 1962. 178 p. ; 21 cm.
1. Belshazzar - Drama. I. Title.
    NYPL [Sc D 88-839]

Green gold . Thomson, Robert. London , 1987.
vii, 93 p. : ISBN 0-906156-26-2
    NYPL [Sc D 88-66]

Green, Jeffrey P. Edmund Thornton Jenkins : the
life and times of an American Black composer,
1894-1926 / Jeffrey P. Green. Westport,
Conn. : Greenwood Press, 1982. xii, 213 p. :
ill. ; 22 cm. (Contributions to the study of music and
dance, 0193-9041 . no. 2) Includes indexes.
Bibliography: p. [187]-188. ISBN 0-313-23253-9 (lib.
bdg.) DDC 780/.92/4 B 19
*1. Jenkins, Edmund Thornton, 1894-1926. 2.
Composers - United States - Biography. 3.
Afro-American composers - Biography. I. Title. II.
Series.*
ML410.J44 G7 1982   ***NYPL [Sc D 86-413]***

The green lion of Zion Street /. Fields, Julia.
New York , c1988. [32] p. : ISBN 0-689-50414-4
DDC [E] 19
PZ8.3.F458 Gr 1988   ***NYPL [Sc F 88-186]***

Greenberg, Keith Elliot. Whitney Houston /
Keith Elliot Greenberg. Minneapolis : Lerner
Publications, c1988. 32 p. : ill. (some col.) ; 23
cm. Traces the life and career of the popular black
singer who has been called the "prom queen of soul."
SCHOMBURG CHILDREN'S COLLECTION. ISBN
0-8225-1619-5 (lib. bdg.) : DDC 784.5/0092/4 B
92 19
*1. Houston, Whitney - Juvenile literature. 2. Singers -
United States - Biography - Juvenile literature. 3.
Afro-American singers - Biography - Juvenile literature.
I. Schomburg Children's Collection. II. Title.*
ML3930.H7 G7 1988   ***NYPL [Sc D 88-1459]***

Greene, Ellin, 1927- Baker, Augusta. Storytelling .
New York , 1987. xvii, 182 p. : ISBN
0-8352-2336-1 DDC 808.06/8543 19
LB1042 .B34 1987   ***NYPL [Sc E 89-46]***

Greene, Roberta. Two and me makes three. Paul
Galdone drew the pictures. New York,
Coward-McCann [1970] [36] p. col. illus. 27
cm. After a fight it takes three friends a week to
apologize to each other. SCHOMBURG CHILDREN'S
COLLECTION.
*1. Children - New York (N.Y.) - Juvenile fiction. I.
Galdone, Paul, illus. II. Schomburg Children's
Collection. III. Title.*
PZ7.G843 Tw   ***NYPL [Sc F 88-375]***

**GREENFIELD, ELIZABETH T. (ELIZABETH
TAYLOR), D.1876.**
LaBrew, Arthur R. The Black Swan . Detroit ,
1969. 86 p. :   ***NYPL [JND 82-30]***

Greenfield, Eloise.
First pink light / by Eloise Greenfield ;
illustrated by Moneta Barnett. New York :
Crowell, c1976. [39] p. : col. ill. ; 24 cm. A little
black boy determines to stay up all night so he can
welcome his father home in the morning.
SCHOMBURG CHILDREN'S COLLECTION. ISBN
0-690-01087-7 DDC [E]
*1. Afro-American children - Juvenile fiction. I. Barnett,
Moneta. II. Schomburg Children's Collection. III. Title.*
PZ7.G845 Fi   ***NYPL [Sc D 89-60]***

Grandpa's face / Eloise Greenfield ; illustrated
by Floyd Cooper. New York : Philomel Books,
1988. [32] p. : col. ill. ; 27 cm. Seeing her beloved
grandfather making a mean face while he rehearses for
one of his plays, Tamika becomes afraid that someday
she will lose his love and he will make that mean face
at her. SCHOMBURG CHILDREN'S COLLECTION.
  ISBN 0-399-21525-5 DDC [E] 19
*1. Afro-American children - Juvenile fiction. I. Cooper,
Floyd, ill. II. Schomburg Children's Collection. III.
Title.*
PZ7.G845 Gs 1988   ***NYPL [Sc F 88-387]***

Honey, I love, and other love poems / by
Eloise Greenfield ; pictures by Diane and Leo
Dillon. New York : Crowell, c1978. [48] p. :
ill. ; 19 cm. Titles include "I Look Pretty," "Fun,"
"Riding on the Train," "Harriet Tubman," and "By
Myself." SCHOMBURG CHILDREN'S
COLLECTION. With autograph of author. ISBN
0-690-01334-5 (lib. bdg.) DDC 811./5/4
I. Schomburg Children's Collection. II. Title.
PS3557.R39416 H66 1978
    NYPL [Sc C 89-22]

Talk about a family / Eloise Greenfield ;

illustrated by James Calvin. New York :
Scholastic, c1978. 60 p. : ill. ; 20 cm. "An Apple
paperback." SCHOMBURG CHILDREN'S
COLLECTION. ISBN 0-590-42247-2
*1. Afro-American children - Juvenile fiction. 2.
Afro-American families - Juvenile fiction. I. Calvin,
James. II. Schomburg Children's Collection. III. Title.*
NYPL [Sc C 89-79]

The greening of Africa . Harrison, Paul, 1945-
London , 1987. 380 p. : ISBN 0-586-08642-0
(pbk) DDC 330.96/0328 19
HC502 **NYPL [Sc C 88-327]**

Greenly, Mike, 1944- Chronicle : the human side
of AIDS / by Mike Greenly. New York :
Irvington, c1986. 422 p. ; 22 cm. ISBN
0-8290-1800-X : DDC 616.97/92/00922 19
*1. AIDS (Disease) - Popular works. 2. AIDS (Disease) -
Case studies. I. Title.*
RC607.A26 G73 1986
NYPL [Sc D 88-1087]

Greenwood, R. (Robert) Emancipation to
emigration / R. Greenwood, S. Hamber.
London ; New York : Macmillan Caribbean,
1980 (1985 printing) viii, 152 p. : ill. ; 25 cm.
(Caribbean certificate history . 2) Includes index.
Bibliography: p. 145-146. ISBN 0-333-28148-9 (pbk.)
DDC 972.9 19
*1. Slavery - West Indies - History. 2. West Indies -
History. 3. West Indies - Economic conditions. I.
Hamber, S. II. Title. III. Series.*
F1621 .G74 1984 **NYPL [Sc E 88-526]**

Greer, Joel William, 1948- Food poverty and
consumption patterns in Kenya / Joel Greer
and Erik Thorbecke. Geneva : International
Labour Office, 1986. xii, 170 p. : ill. ; 24 cm.
Bibliography: p. 167-170. ISBN 92-2-105374-1 (pbk.) :
DDC 338.1/9/6762 19
*1. Food supply - Kenya - Mathematical models. 2.
Food consumption - Kenya - Mathematical models. 3.
Poverty - Mathematical models. I. Thorbecke, Erik,
1929-. II. Title.*
HD9017.K42 G74 1986
NYPL [JLE 87-3435]

**Gregory, J. Dennis. see Williams, John Alfred,
1925-**

GRENADA - BIOGRAPHY.
Sheppard, Jill. Marryshow of Grenada .
Barbados, West Indies , 1987. 56 p. :
NYPL [Sc D 88-658]

**GRENADA - HISTORY - AMERICAN
INVASION, 1983.**
Burrowes, Reynold A. Revolution and rescue in
Grenada . New York , 1988. xiv, 180 p. ;
ISBN 0-313-26066-4
F2056.8 .B87 1988 **NYPL [HRG 88-1153]**

**GRENADA - HISTORY - AMERICAN
INVASION, 1983 - POETRY.**
Brand, Dionne, 1953- Chronicles of the hostile
sun /. Toronto, Ont., Canada , 1984. 75 p. ;
ISBN 0-88795-033-7 (pbk.) : DDC 811/.54 19
PR9199.3.B683 C48 1984
NYPL [Sc D 88-1227]

**GRENADA - HISTORY - COUP D'ÉTAT,
1979.**
Morizot, Frédéric. Grenade, épices et poudre .
Paris , c1988. 385 p., [8] leaves of plates :
ISBN 2-7384-0082-5 **NYPL [Sc E 89-49]**

**GRENADA - POLITICS AND
GOVERNMENT.**
Morizot, Frédéric. Grenade, épices et poudre .
Paris , c1988. 385 p., [8] leaves of plates :
ISBN 2-7384-0082-5 **NYPL [Sc E 89-49]**

**GRENADA - POLITICS AND
GOVERNMENT - 1974-**
Emmanuel, Patrick. Political change and public
opinion in Grenada 1979-1984 /. Cave Hill,
Barbados , c1986. xii, 173 p. :
NYPL [JLM 79-1223 no.19]

Maurice Bishop Patriotic Movement. Manifesto
of the Maurice Bishop Patriotic Movement. St.
George's, Grenada [1984] 60 p. :
NYPL [Sc D 88-676]

Wagner, Geoffrey. Red calypso . Washington,
D.C. , c1988. 264 p. ; ISBN 0-89526-773-X
NYPL [Sc D 89-301]

**Grenada topples the balance in West Indian
history** . Hopkin, Gerry R. S. [Grenada]
c1984. 76 p. : **NYPL [Sc C 88-147]**

**GRENADA, WEST INDIES - ECONOMIC
CONDITIONS.**

Bishop, Maurice. "Forward to 1982--the year of
Economic construction" [microform] . [st.
George's], Grenada , 1982. 22 leaves ;
NYPL [Sc Micro R-4108 no. 28]

**GRENADA, WEST INDIES - ECONOMIC
POLICY.**
Bishop, Maurice. "Forward to 1982--the year of
Economic construction" [microform] . [st.
George's], Grenada , 1982. 22 leaves ;
NYPL [Sc Micro R-4108 no. 28]

GRENADAN LITERATURE (ENGLISH)
Callaloo . London , 1984. 108 p. : ISBN
0-905405-09-9 (pbk) : DDC 810.8/09729845 19
PR9275.G **NYPL [Sc D 88-702]**

Grenade, épices et poudre . Morizot, Frédéric.
Paris , c1988. 385 p., [8] leaves of plates :
ISBN 2-7384-0082-5 **NYPL [Sc E 89-49]**

Grenet, Eliseo. Guillén, Nicolás, 1902- Motivos
de son /. La Habana , 1980. 32, [88] p. :
NYPL [Sc E 87-151]

Grenet, Emilio. Guillén, Nicolás, 1902- Motivos
de son /. La Habana , 1980. 32, [88] p. :
NYPL [Sc E 87-151]

Grésillon, Marie. Une si longue lettre de
Mariama Bâ : étude / Marie Grésillon. Issy les
Moulineux [France] : Classiques africains,
c1986. 94 p. : ill. ; 21 cm. (Classiques africains
(Issy-les-Moulineaux, France) . no. 831) Approche de
l'oeuvre complète Includes bibliographical references.
ISBN 2-85049-344-9
1. Bâ, Mariama. Si longue lettre. I. Title. II. Series.
NYPL [Sc D 88-824]

Greub, Suzanne. Museum voor Volkenkunde
(Rotterdam, Netherlands) Expressions of belief .
New York , 1988. 248 p. : ISBN 0-8478-0959-5 :
DDC 730 19
N5310.75.H68 M876 1988
NYPL [Sc G 88-37]

**Griaule, Geneviève Calame- see Calame-Griaule,
Geneviève.**

GRIAULE, MARCEL, 1898-1956.
Ethnologiques . Paris , 1987. xxxvi, 430 p. :
ISBN 2-7056-6025-9 **NYPL [Sc E 88-39]**

Gridley, Mark C., 1947- Jazz styles : history &
analysis / Mark C. Gridley.3rd ed. Englewood
Cliffs, N.J. : Prentice-Hall, 1988. xviii, 445 p. :
ill., music, ports. ; 24 cm. + 1 sound cassette.
Includes index. Bibliography: p. 406-411. Discography:
p. 432. ISBN 0-13-509217-5 DDC 785.42 19
1. Jazz musicians. I. Title.
ML3506 .G74 1987 **NYPL [Sc E 88-159]**

Grifalconi, Ann.
Clifton, Lucille, 1936- Everett Anderson's
friend /. New York , c1976. [25] p. : ISBN
0-03-015161-9 (lib. bdg.) DDC [E]
PZ8.3.C573 Evg **NYPL [Sc D 88-1505]**

Clifton, Lucille, 1936- Everett Anderson's nine
month long /. New York , c1978. [31] p. :
ISBN 0-03-043536-6 DDC [E]
PZ8.3.C573 Evk **NYPL [Sc D 89-30]**

(illus) Hopkins, Lee Bennett. This street's for
me! New York [1970] [38] p. ;
PZ8.3.H776 Th **NYPL [JFE 72-966]**

Grifalconi, Ann. Bacmeister, Rhoda Warner,
1893- Voices in the night /. Indianapolis ,
1965. 117 p. : **NYPL [Sc D 88-382]**

Griffin, Michael. A family in Kenya / Michael
Griffin ; photographs by Liba Taylor.
Minneapolis : Lerner Publications Co., 1988,
c1987. 31 p. : col. ill. ; 22 cm. (Families the world
over) Previously published as: Salaama in Kenya.
Describes the home, school, work, customs, and day-to
day life of a young girl living with her family in a
suburb of Mombasa, Kenya's second largest city.
SCHOMBURG CHILDREN'S COLLECTION. ISBN
0-8225-1680-2 (lib. bdg.) : DDC 306.8/5/096762
19
*1. Family - Kenya - Juvenile literature. I. Taylor, Liba,
ill. II. Schomburg Children's Collection. III. Title. IV.
Series.*
HQ692.5 .G75 1988 **NYPL [Sc C 89-6]**

Griffith, Helen. Dauntless in Mississippi : the life
of Sarah A. Dickey, 1838-1904 / by Helen
Griffith. Northampton, Mass. : Metcalf Printing
Co., 1965. xii, 173 p. : port. ; 23 cm. Includes
index. With author's autograph.
*1. Dickey, Sarah A., 1838-1904. 2. Mount Hermon
Female Seminary. 3. Educators - Mississippi. I. Title.*
NYPL [Sc D 88-1111]

GRILLO, DOMINGO, FL. 1663-1674.
Vega Franco, Marisa. El tráfico de esclavos con
América . Sevilla , 1984. x, 220 p. : ISBN
84-00-05675-2 DDC 382/.44/09729 19
HT985 .V44 1984 **NYPL [Sc C 89-132]**

**GRIMKÉ, ANGELINA WELD, 1880-1958 -
CRITICISM AND INTERPRETATION.**
Hull, Gloria T. Color, sex, and poetry .
Bloomington , c1987. xi, 240 p. : ISBN
0-253-34974-5 DDC 811/.52/099287 19
PS153.N5 H84 1987 **NYPL [Sc E 88-72]**

Groenendijk, Paul. Adolf Loos : huis voor
Josephine Baker = Adolf Loos : house for
Josephine Baker / Paul Groenendijk, Piet
Vollaard. Rotterdam : Uitgeverij 010, 1985. 39
p., [6] leaves of plates : ill., plans ; 30 cm.
(Architectuurmodellen = Architectural models . 7)
Dutch, English, French, and German. Bibliography: p.
36. ISBN 90-6450-027-4 DDC 728.3/72/0228 19
*1. Loos, Adolf, 1870-1933 - Criticism and
interpretation. 2. Baker, Josephine, 1906-1975 - Homes
and haunts. 3. Architectural models - Austria. 4.
Architecture, Domestic - 20th century - Designs and
plans. I. Vollaard, Piet. II. Loos, Adolf, 1870-1933. III.
Title. IV. Title: Adolf Loos : house for Josephine Baker.
V. Series: Architectuurmodellen . 7.*
NA1011.5.L6 G76 1985 **NYPL [Sc F 89-67]**

Gross, Mary Anne. (comp) Ah, man, you found
me again. With photos. by Mike Levins and
Jon Stevens. Boston, Beacon Press [1972] x, 84
p. illus. 27 cm. Dialectal stories and poems by New
York City Black and Spanish-speaking children edited
from tape recordings taken in the classroom.
SCHOMBURG CHILDREN'S COLLECTION. ISBN
0-8070-1532-6 DDC 810/.8/09282
*1. Children - New York (N.Y.) - Juvenile literature. 2.
City and town life - Juvenile literature. 3. Children's
writings. I. Levins, Mike, illus. II. Stevens, Jon Ellis,
illus. III. Schomburg Children's Collection. IV. Title.*
HQ792.U53 N53 1972 **NYPL [Sc F 88-336]**

Gross, Samuel R. Death & discrimination : racial
disparities in capital sentencing / Samuel R.
Gross & Robert Mauro. Boston : Northeastern
University Press, c1989. xvi, 268 p. ; 21 cm.
Includes bibliographical references and indexes. ISBN
1-555-53040-0 (alk. paper) : DDC 364.6/6/0973
19
*1. Capital punishment - United States. 2. Race
discrimination - United States. 3. Afro-American
criminals - Civil rights. 4. United States - Race
relations. I. Mauro, Robert. II. Title. III. Title: Death
and discrimination.*
HV8699.U5 G76 1989 **NYPL [Sc D 89-493]**

Grosse-Oetringhaus, Hans-Martin. Noxolos
Geheimnis : Geschichten und informationen
über das Leben Schwarzer Kinder in Südafrika
/ Hans-Martin Grosse-Oetringhaus.1. Aufl.
Berlin : Elefanten Press, 1988. 96 p. : ill. ; 20
cm. (Ein Terre des Hommes Buch) ISBN
3-88520-289-1
1. Children, Black - South Africa. I. Title.
NYPL [Sc C 89-120]

Grottanelli, Vinigi L. The python killer : stories
of Nzema life / Vinigi L. Grottanelli. Chicago :
University of Chicago Press, 1988. xi, 223 p. :
ill. ; 23 cm. Includes index. Bibliography: p. 217-219.
ISBN 0-226-31004-3 : DDC 306/.089963 19
*1. Nzima (African people) - Folklore. 2. Nzima
(African people) - Social life and customs. I. Title.*
DT510.43.N95 G76 1988
NYPL [Sc D 88-1458]

The groundings with my brothers. Rodney,
Walter. London, 1969. 68 p. ISBN 0-9501546-0-1
F1896.N4 R6 **NYPL [Sc 323.2-R]**

**GROUP HOMES FOR CHILDREN - UNITED
STATES - JUVENILE FICTION.**
Rinkoff, Barbara. Headed for trouble /. New
York [1970] 119 p. : ISBN 0-394-90494-X
NYPL [Sc E 88-227]

**Groupe de travail sur les langues tchadiques
(France)** Préalables à la reconstruction du
proto-tchadique . Paris , 1978. 210 p. ; ISBN
2-85297-022-8 DDC 493/.7 19
PL8026.C53 P73 1978 **NYPL [Sc E 88-418]**

GROUPS, ETHNIC. see ETHNIC GROUPS.

Grove, Richard (Richard H.) Conservation in
Africa . Cambridge [Cambridgeshire] ; New
York , 1987. ix, 355 p. : ISBN 0-521-34199-X
DDC 333.7/2/096 19
QH77.A4 C66 1987 **NYPL [Sc E 88-199]**

Growing up with Miss Milly /. Seaforth, Sybil.

Ithaca, N.Y. , 1988. 129 p. ; ISBN
0-911565-04-3   *NYPL [Sc D 89-439]*

Grunlingh, A. M., 1948- Fighting their own war :
South African blacks and the First World War
/ Albert Grundlingh. Johannesburg : Raven
Press, 1987. x, 200 p. ; 22 cm. (New history of
southern Africa series) Includes index. Bibliography: p.
[173]-195. ISBN 0-86975-321-5
*1. World War, 1914-1918 - Blacks - South Africa. 2.
World War, 1914-1918 - South Africa. 3. World War,
1914-1918 - Participation, Black. I. Title. II. Series.*
NYPL [Sc D 88-897]

Grunne, Bernard de. Chefs-d'ouevre inédits de
l'Afrique noire /. Paris , 1987. 320 p. : ISBN
2-04-012941-3   *NYPL [Sc G 88-10]*

Grunwald, John.
Pelrine, Diane. African art from the Rita and
John Grunwald collection /. Bloomington ,
c1988. 159 p. : ISBN 0-253-21061-5 (I.U. Press :
pbk.) : DDC 730/.0966/0740172255 19
N7398 .P44 1988   *NYPL [Sc F 89-158]*

**GRUNWALD, JOHN - ART COLLECTIONS -
EXHIBITIONS.**
Pelrine, Diane. African art from the Rita and
John Grunwald collection /. Bloomington ,
c1988. 159 p. : ISBN 0-253-21061-5 (I.U. Press :
pbk.) : DDC 730/.0966/0740172255 19
N7398 .P44 1988   *NYPL [Sc F 89-158]*

Grunwald, Rita.
Pelrine, Diane. African art from the Rita and
John Grunwald collection /. Bloomington ,
c1988. 159 p. : ISBN 0-253-21061-5 (I.U. Press :
pbk.) : DDC 730/.0966/0740172255 19
N7398 .P44 1988   *NYPL [Sc F 89-158]*

**GRUNWALD, RITA - ART COLLECTIONS -
EXHIBITIONS.**
Pelrine, Diane. African art from the Rita and
John Grunwald collection /. Bloomington ,
c1988. 159 p. : ISBN 0-253-21061-5 (I.U. Press :
pbk.) : DDC 730/.0966/0740172255 19
N7398 .P44 1988   *NYPL [Sc F 89-158]*

Grupenhoff, Richard, 1941- The black Valentino :
the stage and screen career of Lorenzo Tucker
/ by Richard Grupenhoff. Metuchen, N.J. :
Scarecrow Press, 1988. xi, 188 p. : ill., ports. ;
23 cm. Includes indexes. Filmography: p. 162.
Bibliography: p. 163-171. ISBN 0-8108-2078-1 DDC
790.2/092/4 B 19
*1. Tucker, Lorenzo. 2. Entertainers - United States -
Biography. 3. Afro-American theater. 4. Afro-American
entertainers - Biography. I. Title.*
PN2287.T78 G78 1988
NYPL [Sc D 88-1029]

GSIS monograph series in world affairs.
Nigeria and the international capitalist system
/. Boulder, Colo. , 1988. v, 154 p. ; ISBN
1-555-87087-2 (alk. paper) DDC 337.669 19
HF1616.7 .N54 1988   *NYPL [JLE 88-3615]*

Gu Margoz [microform] /. Ramdharrysing, Vimal.
[Mauritius? , 198-?] 29 p. ;
NYPL [Sc Micro F-11122]

La Guadeloupe . Lasserre, Guy. Fort-de-France,
Martinique , 1978. 3 v. (1132 p.) :
NYPL [Sc F 88-112]

La Guadeloupe de 1671 à 1759 . Abénon, Lucien
René, 1937- Paris , c1987. 2 v. : ISBN
2-85802-752-8 (v. 1)   *NYPL [Sc E 88-248]*

**GUADELOUPE - DESCRIPTION AND
TRAVEL.**
Lasserre, Guy. La Guadeloupe . Fort-de-France,
Martinique , 1978. 3 v. (1132 p.) :
NYPL [Sc F 88-112]

GUADELOUPE - ECONOMIC CONDITIONS.
Bangou, Henri. Les voies de la souveraineté .
Paris , c1988. 144 p. ; ISBN 2-87679-021-1
NYPL [Sc D 88-1001]

Beaujean, Henri. Demain la Guadeloupe unie, la
régionalisation réussie . Paris , c1988. 374 p. ;
NYPL [Sc D 88-972]

Lasserre, Guy. La Guadeloupe . Fort-de-France,
Martinique , 1978. 3 v. (1132 p.) :
NYPL [Sc F 88-112]

La Guadeloupe et son indianité /. Moutoussamy,
Ernest, 1941- Paris , c1987. 119 p., [12] p. of
plates : ISBN 2-87679-008-4
NYPL [Sc D 88-968]

GUADELOUPE - FICTION.
Condé, Maryse. La vie scélérate . Paris , c1987.
333 p. ;   *NYPL [Sc D 88-1102]*

**Guadeloupe - Government. see Guadeloupe -
Politics and government.**

GUADELOUPE - HISTORY.
Abénon, Lucien René, 1937- La Guadeloupe de
1671 à 1759 . Paris , c1987. 2 v. : ISBN
2-85802-752-8 (v. 1)   *NYPL [Sc E 88-248]*

Bangou, Henri. Les voies de la souveraineté .
Paris , c1988. 144 p. ; ISBN 2-87679-021-1
NYPL [Sc D 88-1001]

Guadeloupe, 1635-1971 . Tours [1982] 109 p. :
DDC 306/.362/0972976 19
HT1108.G83 G8 1982   *NYPL [Sc F 89-141]*

Nègre, André. La rébellion de la Guadeloupe .
Paris , c1987. 163 p., [4] p. of plates : ISBN
2-87679-006-8   *NYPL [Sc D 88-1333]*

Pérotin-Dumon, Anne. Etre patriote sous les
tropiques . Basse-Terre , 1985. 339 p. : ISBN
2-900339-21-9   *NYPL [Sc E 88-256]*

**GUADELOUPE - POLITICS AND
GOVERNMENT.**
Bangou, Henri. Les voies de la souveraineté .
Paris , c1988. 144 p. ; ISBN 2-87679-021-1
NYPL [Sc D 88-1001]

Beaujean, Henri. Demain la Guadeloupe unie, la
régionalisation réussie . Paris , c1988. 374 p. ;
NYPL [Sc D 88-972]

Nègre, André. La rébellion de la Guadeloupe .
Paris , c1987. 163 p., [4] p. of plates : ISBN
2-87679-006-8   *NYPL [Sc D 88-1333]*

**GUADELOUPE - POLITICS AND
GOVERNMENT - FICTION.**
Plumasseau, Eugène, 1926- Savinien et
Monique . Pointe-à-Pitre , c1986. 188 p. ;
MLCS 86/7257 (P)   *NYPL [Sc D 88-176]*

GUADELOUPE - RACE RELATIONS.
Bangou, Henri. Les voies de la souveraineté .
Paris , c1988. 144 p. ; ISBN 2-87679-021-1
NYPL [Sc D 88-1001]

**GUADELOUPE - RELIGIOUS LIFE AND
CUSTOMS.**
Moutoussamy, Ernest, 1941- La Guadeloupe et
son indianité /. Paris , c1987. 119 p., [12] p. of
plates : ISBN 2-87679-008-4
NYPL [Sc D 88-968]

**GUADELOUPE - SOCIAL LIFE AND
CUSTOMS.**
Moutoussamy, Ernest, 1941- La Guadeloupe et
son indianité /. Paris , c1987. 119 p., [12] p. of
plates : ISBN 2-87679-008-4
NYPL [Sc D 88-968]

Guadeloupe, 1635-1971 : éléments d'histoire : nou
toujou doubout! / A.G.E.G. Tours : Association
générale des étudiants guadeloupéens, [1982]
109 p. : ill. ; 30 cm. "Extraits de: 'Le Patriote
guadeloupéen' et de 'Ja ka ta' 1970-1981." "Supplément
à 'Le Patriote guadeloupéen' no 69, 1982"--P. [3] of
cover. DDC 306/.362/0972976 19
*1. Slavery - Guadeloupe - History. 2. Guadeloupe -
History. I. Association générale des étudiants
guadeloupéens. II. Patriote guadeloupéen. III. Ja ka ta.
IV. Patriote guadeloupéen. No 69, 1982 (Supplement).
V. Title: Nou toujou doubout!.*
HT1108.G83 G8 1982   *NYPL [Sc F 89-141]*

Guannu, Joseph Saye. A short history of the first
Liberian republic / Joseph Saye Guannu . 1st
ed. Pompano Beach, FL : Exposition Press of
Florida, c1985. viii, 152 p. : ill., ports. ; 20 cm.
Sequel to: Liberian history up to 1847. Bibliogrpahy: p.
150-152. ISBN 0-682-40267-2
1. Liberia - History. I. Title.
NYPL [Sc D 88-1023]

**The guardian genius of the Federal Union, or,
Patriotic admonitions on the signs of the
times .** Branagan, Thomas, b. 1774. New York ,
1839. 104 p. ;   *NYPL [Sc Rare G 86-18]*

Guardino, Leonard J. Barrett, William M., 1900-
Ain't you got no shame? /. Washington, D.C. ,
1965. iii, 98 p. :   *NYPL [Sc D 88-483]*

Guarisma, Gladys. La méthode dialectometrique
appliquée aux langues africaines /. Berlin ,
1986. 431 p. : ISBN 3-496-00856-3
NYPL [Sc E 88-46]

Gudykunst, William B. Language and ethnic
identity /. Clevedon , Philadelphia , c1988. 170
p. ; ISBN 1-85359-021-5 DDC 401/.9 19
P35 .L267 1988   *NYPL [Sc F 88-323]*

Guéido /. Leloup, Jacqueline. Yaoundé , 1986.

110 p. :
MLCS 87/6780 (P)   *NYPL [Sc C 88-210]*

**GUEN (AFRICAN PEOPLE) see GOUIN
(AFRICAN PEOPLE)**

GUERILLA WARFARE.
Ollivier Patrick. Commandos de brousse /.
Paris , 1985. 275 p., [8] p. of plates : ISBN
2-246-35481-1   *NYPL [Sc E 87-222]*

Guerre, Rockefeller. Mon mandat sous Jn-Claude
Duvalier : témoignage pour l'histoire /
Rockefeller Guerre. Port-au-Prince, Haiti :
Impri. Henri Deschamps, 1987. 260 p. : ill. ;
21cm.
*1. Duvalier, Jean Claude, 1951-. 2. Haiti - Politics and
government - 1971-. I. Title.*
NYPL [Sc D 87-935]

La guerre sainte d'al-Hajj Umar . Robinson,
David, 1938- [Holy war of Umar Tal. French.]
Paris , c1988. 413 p. : ISBN 2-86537-211-1
NYPL [Sc E 89-258]

GUERRILLAS - SURINAM.
Helman, Albert. Blijf even staan! .
[Netherlands?] c1987. 41 p. :
NYPL [Sc D 88-1039]

**GUET NDAR (SAINT-LOUIS SENEGAL) -
ECONOMIC CONDITIONS.**
Bonnardel, Régine. Vitalité de la petite pêche
tropicale . Paris , 1985. 104 p. : ISBN
2-222-03678-X   *NYPL [Sc F 88-329]*

Guiana, Dutch. see Surinam.

**Guidance and counselling for the 6-3-3-4 system
of education /.** Denga, Daniel I. Calabar
[Nigeria] , 1983 (1986 printing) 159 p. : ISBN
978-228-192-1   *NYPL [Sc D 88-6]*

**GUIDANCE, STUDENT. see PERSONNEL
SERVICE IN EDUCATION;
VOCATIONAL GUIDANCE.**

**GUIDANCE, VOCATIONAL. see
VOCATIONAL GUIDANCE.**

A guide and history of Hope Town /. Dodge,
Steve. Decatur, Ill., USA , c1985. [48] p. :
ISBN 0-932265-01-4 (pbk.) : DDC 917.296 19
F1659.H67 D63 1985   *NYPL [Sc D 88-684]*

Guide de la santé au village . Sillonville, Frank.
Douala, Cameroun , Paris, France , c1985. 204
p. : ISBN 2-86537-126-3 : DDC 614/.0967 19
RA771.7.A357 S56 1985
NYPL [Sc E 88-547]

**Guide pédagogique pour la mise en œuvre des
soins de santé primaires au niveau villageois /**
rédaction ... Bernard Nébila Bassolet ... [et al.] ;
dessins ... de Jean-Pierre Bicaba ; photos de
Prosper Bado. Bobo-Dioulasso, Burkina Faso :
Centre d'études économiques et sociales
d'Afrique occidentale, 1986. 79 p. : ill. ; 21 cm.
(Collection "Appui au monde rural". Série "Santé" . no
2) "Janvier 1986."
*1. Rural health services - Planning - Handbooks,
manuals, etc. 2. Rural health services - Administration -
Handbooks, manuals, etc. I. Bassolet, Bernard Nébila.
II. Series.*
RA771 .G85 1986   *NYPL [Sc D 89-265]*

A guide to Christian writing in Africa /. Nwosu,
I. E. Enugu, Nigeria , 1987. 116 p. ; ISBN
978-262-606-6   *NYPL [Sc D 88-156]*

**Guide to current national bibliographies in the
Third World /.** Gorman, G. E. London , New
York , c1987. xx, 372 p. ; ISBN 0-905450-34-5
NYPL [Sc E 88-474]

Guide to multicultural resources /. Taylor,
Charles A. (Charles Andrew), 1950- Madison,
WI , c1987. ix, 512 p. : ISBN 0-935483-07-1
(pbk.)   *NYPL [Sc D 88-530]*

**Guide to National Museum of Colonial History,
Aba /.** Obiozor, May. [Lagos, Nigeria , 1985]
32 p. :   *NYPL [Sc F 88-259]*

**A guide to periodical articles about Botswana,
1965-80 /.** Henderson, Francine I. Gaborone,
Botswana , 1982. v, 147, 6 p. ; DDC 016.96811
19
Z3559 .H46 1982 DT791
NYPL [Sc F 88-161]

A guide to Shona spelling /. Fortune, G.
(George), 1915- Harare , 1972. 64 p. ; ISBN
0-528-64019-2 DDC 496/.39
PL8681.2 .F6   *NYPL [Sc C 88-328]*

Guide to the archives and papers . University of

the Witwatersrand. Library. Johannesburg , 1979. v, 100 p. ;   ISBN 0-85494-593-8
NYPL [*Sc F 89-32*]

Guide to the Raya Dunayevskaya collection : Marxist-Humanism : a half-century of its world development / Prepared by News & Letters ... Chicago. Il. Detroit, Mich. : Wayne State University Archives of Labor and Urban Affairs, [1986?] 84 p. ; 28 cm. Cover title. Newly added: Volume XI, 1981-1985--Dialectics of revolution, American roots and world humanist concepts.--Volume XII. Retrospective and perspective, The Raya Dunayevskaya collection, 1924-1986. Inserted: Raya Dunayevskaya, return to The source (7 p.) by Lou Turner, including an article from News & letters.
1. Dunayevskaya, Raya - Bibliography - Catalogs. 2. Communism - History - Bibliography - Catalogs. I. Wayne State University. Archives of Labor and Urban Affairs. II. News & letters. III. Title. IV. Title: Marxist-Humanism.   *NYPL* [*Sc F 88-196*]

Guide to the three symbolic degrees. Duncan, Malcolm C. Duncan's Masonic ritual and monitor, or, Guide to the three symbolic degrees E.A., F.C., M.M. /. Danbury, Conn. , c1922- v. :   *NYPL* [*Sc B 88-65*]

A Guide to Zimbabwe / [editors, Donatus Bonde, Gunnar Rydström]. Gweru, [Zimbabwe] : Mambo Press, 1986. 63 p. : ill. (some col.) ; 18 cm. Cover title. ISBN 91-7810-685-0
1. Zimbabwe. I. Bonde, Donatus. II. Rydström, Gunnar.   *NYPL* [*Sc C 88-371*]

Guide touristique de Saint-Louis du Senegal / [préface, Jean Vast] [Saint-Louis, Senegal : s.n., 197-?] 53 p. : ill. ; 23 cm. "Le Guide touristique est l'oeuvre de l'équipe qui réalise le bulletin trimestriel, "L'Echo de Saint-Louis, UNIR"- p. 4. Bibliography: p. 53.
1. St. Louis (Senegal) - Description - Guide-books. I. Vast, Jean.   *NYPL* [*Sc D 89-420*]

Guides bleus visà. Planche, Bernard. A Madagascar /. [Paris] , c1987. 158 p. :   *NYPL* [*Sc D 88-254*]

GUIDES FOR HUNTERS, FISHERMEN, ETC - GABON. Goulphin, Fred. Les Veillées de chase d'Henri Guizard /. [Paris] , 1987. 235 p. ;   ISBN 2-08-065054-8   *NYPL* [*Sc D 88-28*]

Guignard, Henri. La Martinique : histoire et économie : les 24 glorieuses, 1959-1985 / Henri Guignard. Fort de France : Association pour l'information des problèmes antillais, 1985. 172 p., [36] p. of plates : ill. (some col.) ; 25 cm. Bibliography: p. 6.   ISBN 2-9501249-0-9
1. Martinique - Economic conditions - 1918-. I. Title.
HC158.6 .G85 1985   *NYPL* [*Sc E 89-127*]

Guillén, Nicolás, 1902- Motivos de son / Nicolás Guillén ; música de Amadeo Roldán, Alejandro García Caturla, Eliseo Grenet, Emilio Grenet. Edición especial 50 aniversario. La Habana : Editorial Letras Cubanas, 1980. 32, [88] p. : facsim., music ; 24 cm.
I. Roldán, Amadeo, 1900-1939. II. García Caturla, Alejandro Evelio, 1906-1940. III. Grenet, Eliseo. IV. Grenet, Emilio. V. Title.   *NYPL* [*Sc E 87-151*]

Sóngoro Cosongo, y otros poemas / Nicolás Guillén; con una carta de Miguel de Unamuno. 2. ed. La Habana : Editorial Páginas, 1943. 123 p. ; 17 cm. Black author.
I. Title.   *NYPL* [*Sc B 79-31*]

Guillet, Claude. Légendes historiques du Burundi . Paris , Bujumbura , c1987. 286 p. :   ISBN 2-86507-178-6   *NYPL* [*Sc E 88-324*]

Guillobel, Joaquim Cândido, 1787-1859. Usos e costumes do Rio de Janeiro nas figurinhas de Guillobel = Life and manners in Rio de Janeiro as seen in Guillobel's small drawings. [Curitiba?] : C. Guinle de Paula Machado, [1978] [19] p., [25] leaves of plates : col. ill. ; 26 x 27 cm. "For this edition 525 bound copies were printed, 25 of them for privat e circulation." Includes bibliographical references. Schomburg has no. 382.   DDC 967/.5/5
1. Rio de Janeiro (Brazil) - Social life and customs - Pictorial works. I. Title. II. Title: Life and manners in Rio de Janeiro as seen in Guillobel's small drawings.
F2646.2 .G84 1978   *NYPL* [*Sc F 88-188*]

Guimarães, Augusto Alvares. Propaganda abolicionista : cartas de Vindex ao Dr. Luiz Alvares dos Santos, publicadas no Diario da Bahia. Bahia : Typ. do Diario, 1875. 86 p. ; 21

cm.
1. Slavery - Brazil - Emancipation. I. Santos, Luiz Alvares dos, 1825-1886. II. Title. III. Title: Cartas de Vindex ao Dr. Luiz Alvares dos Santos.
NYPL [*Sc Rare G 86-33*]

GUIN (AFRICAN PEOPLE) see GOUIN (AFRICAN PEOPLE)

GUINEA. ARMÉE. Journée nationale du premier novembre 1961 [microform] Conakry [1961?] 38 p. ;
NYPL [*Sc Micro F-11002*]

GUINEA-BISSAU - BIBLIOGRAPHY. Lobban, Richard. Historical dictionary of the Republic of Cape Verde /. Metuchen, N.J. , 1988. xix, 171 p. ;   ISBN 0-8108-2087-0   DDC 966/.57/00321 19
DT613.5 .L62 1988b   *NYPL* [*Sc D 88-1311*]

Lobban, Richard. Historical dictionary of the Republic of Guinea-Bissau /. Metuchen, N.J. , 1988. xx, 210 p. :   ISBN 0-8108-2086-2   DDC 966/.57 19
DT613.5 .L62 1988   *NYPL* [**R-BMP 88-5080*]

Guinea-Bissau - Government. see Guinea-Bissau - Politics and government.

GUINEA-BISSAU - HISTORY - REVOLUTION, 1963-1974. Pierson-Mathy, Paulette. [Naissance de l'Etat par la guerre de libération nationale. Spanish.] El nacimiento del estado por la guerra de liberación nacional . Barcelona : [Paris] : 1983. 178 p. ;   ISBN 92-3-301794-X (Unesco)
NYPL [*Sc D 88-602*]

Romero, Vicente, 1947- Guinea-Bissau y Cabo Verde . Madrid , 1981. 109 p. ;   ISBN 84-85761-09-X   DDC 966/.5702 19
DT613.78 .R66 1981   *NYPL* [*Sc C 89-1*]

GUINEA-BISSAU - HISTORY - REVOLUTION, 1963-1974 - COLLECTED WORKS. Cabral, Amílcar, 1921-1973. Unité et lutte /. Paris , 1980. 329 p. ;   ISBN 2-7071-1171-6
NYPL [*Sc C 88-125*]

GUINEA-BISSAU - HISTORY - REVOLUTION, 1963-1974 - CONGRESSES. Symposium Amilcar Cabral (1983 : Praia, Cape Verde) Pour Cabral . Paris , 1987. 486 p. ;   ISBN 2-7087-0482-6
NYPL [*Sc D 87-1429*]

GUINEA-BISSAU - HISTORY - DICTIONARIES. Lobban, Richard. Historical dictionary of the Republic of Cape Verde /. Metuchen, N.J. , 1988. xix, 171 p. ;   ISBN 0-8108-2087-0   DDC 966/.57/00321 19
DT613.5 .L62 1988b   *NYPL* [*Sc D 88-1311*]

Lobban, Richard. Historical dictionary of the Republic of Guinea-Bissau /. Metuchen, N.J. , 1988. xx, 210 p. :   ISBN 0-8108-2086-2   DDC 966/.57 19
DT613.5 .L62 1988   *NYPL* [**R-BMP 88-5080*]

GUINEA-BISSAU - POLITICS AND GOVERNMENT - COLLECTED WORKS. Cabral, Amílcar, 1921-1973. Unité et lutte /. Paris , 1980. 329 p. ;   ISBN 2-7071-1171-6
NYPL [*Sc C 88-125*]

GUINEA-BISSAU - SOCIAL CONDITIONS. Barbosa, Rogério Andrade. La-le-li-lo-luta . Rio de Janeiro , 1984. 124 p. ;   DDC 371.1/0092/4 B 19
LA2365.B72 B37 1984   *NYPL* [*Sc D 88-284*]

Guinea-Bissau y Cabo Verde . Romero, Vicente, 1947- Madrid , 1981. 109 p. ;   ISBN 84-85761-09-X   DDC 966/.5702 19
DT613.78 .R66 1981   *NYPL* [*Sc C 89-1*]

Guinea. Comité militaire de redressement national. Les orientations de la Deuxième République. 2ème éd. [Conakry : Bureau de presse de la Présidence de la République de Guinée, 1984] 76 p. : map ; 24 cm. Cover title. "Novembre 1984." DDC 967/.1803 19
1. Guinea - History - Coup d'état, 1984. 2. Guinea - Politics and government - 1984-. I. Title.
DT543.825 .G85 1984   *NYPL* [*Sc E 88-310*]

Premières mesures de mise en application du programme du CMRN. 1ère éd. [Conakry,

R.G. : Comité militaire de redressement national, 1984] 84 p. ; 24 cm. "Octobre 84"--Cover.
1. Agriculture and state - Guinea. 2. Rural development - Guinea. 3. Guinea - Social policy. I. Title.
HD2143.Z8 G85 1984   *NYPL* [*Sc E 88-306*]

GUINEA - ECONOMIC CONDITIONS - 1984- Où allons nous?. [Conakry] [1986?] 92 p. ;
HC1030 .O89 1986   *NYPL* [*Sc B 88-58*]

GUINEA, GULF OF - COLONIZATION. Bonelli Rubio, Juan María. El problema de la colonización [microform] . Madrid , 1945. 15 p. ;   *NYPL* [*Sc Micro F-11057*]

GUINEA - HISTORY - COUP D'ÉTAT, 1984. Guinea. Comité militaire de redressement national. Les orientations de la Deuxième République. [Conakry , 1984] 76 p. :   DDC 967/.1803 19
DT543.825 .G85 1984   *NYPL* [*Sc E 88-310*]

GUINEA - POLITICS AND GOVERNMENT - 1958- Où allons nous?. [Conakry] [1986?] 92 p. ;
HC1030 .O89 1986   *NYPL* [*Sc B 88-58*]

GUINEA - POLITICS AND GOVERNMENT - 1958-1984. Bari, Nadine. Noces d'absence /. Paris , c1986. 119 p., [8] p. of plates :   ISBN 2-227-12607-8
NYPL [*Sc D 89-61*]

Kaké, Ibrahima Baba. Sékou Touré, le héros et le tyran /. Paris , 1987. 254 p. :
NYPL [*Sc D 88-468*]

Touré, Ahmed Sékou, 1922- [Conférences, discours, et rapports] Conakry [1958?]- v.
NYPL [*Sc F966.52-T*]

GUINEA - POLITICS AND GOVERNMENT - 1984- Guinea. Comité militaire de redressement national. Les orientations de la Deuxième République. [Conakry , 1984] 76 p. :   DDC 967/.1803 19
DT543.825 .G85 1984   *NYPL* [*Sc E 88-310*]

GUINEA - SOCIAL POLICY. Guinea. Comité militaire de redressement national. Premières mesures de mise en application du programme du CMRN. [Conakry, R.G. , 1984] 84 p. ;
HD2143.Z8 G85 1984   *NYPL* [*Sc E 88-306*]

La Guinée /. Lewin, André. Paris , 1984. 127 p. :   ISBN 2-13-038503-6   *NYPL* [*Sc C 88-23*]

Guinée, où allons nous? Où allons nous?. [Conakry] [1986?] 92 p. ;
HC1030 .O89 1986   *NYPL* [*Sc B 88-58*]

Guitard, Odette. Ganiage, Jean. L'Afrique au XXe siècle /. Paris , 1966. 908 p. :
NYPL [*Sc D 88-236*]

GUITARISTS - UNITED STATES - BIOGRAPHY. Ingram, Adrian. Wes Montgomery /. Gateshead, Tyne and Wear, England , 1985. 127 p. :   ISBN 0-9506224-9-4
NYPL [*Sc F 88-61*]

GUIZARD, HENRI. Goulphin, Fred. Les Veillées de chase d'Henri Guizard /. [Paris] , 1987. 235 p. ;   ISBN 2-08-065054-8   *NYPL* [*Sc D 88-28*]

Gulledge, Jo. The Southern review and modern literature, 1935-1985 /. Baton Rouge , c1988. xvi, 238 p. :   ISBN 0-8071-1424-3 :   DDC 810/.9/975 19
PS267.B3 S68 1987   *NYPL* [*Sc E 88-280*]

Gulmancéba du Bénin. Bene gulmanceba =. Cotonou, R.P. du Bénin , 1983. 101 p., [1] leaf of plates :   DDC 305.8/963 19
DT541.45.G87 B46 1983
NYPL [*Sc D 88-202*]

Gumbs, Bob. Bailey, A. Peter. Harlem today . New York , c1986. viii, 55 p. :   ISBN 0-936073-01-2 (pbk.).   DDC 917.47/1 19
F128.68.H3 B3 1986   *NYPL* [*Sc D 88-1402*]

Gundu, Gabriel A. Tiv bibliography / Gabriel A. Gundu and Heinz Jockers. Makurdi, Nigeria : Govt. Printer, 1985. xxvii, 72 p. : ill. ; 24 cm.
1. Tivi language - Bibliography. 2. Tiv (African people) - Bibliography. I. Jockers, Heinz. II. Title.
NYPL [*Sc E 88-537*]

GUNNING. see HUNTING.

Guptara, Prabhu S. Black British literature : an annotated bibliography / Prahbu [sic] Guptara. [Sydney] : Dangaroo Press ; Berkeley, Calif. : Bookpeople [distributor, U. S.], [1986] 176 p. : 1 port. ; 22 cm. "List of small publishers ... listed in bibliography": p. 169-176. ISBN 87-88213-14-5 (paper) :
1. English literature - Black authors - Bibliography. I. Title. **NYPL [Sc D 89-20]**

GURMA (AFRICAN PEOPLE) - FOLKLORE.
Bene gulmanceba =. Cotonou, R.P. du Bénin , 1983. 101 p., [1] leaf of plates : DDC 305.8/963 19
DT541.45.G87 B46 1983
NYPL [Sc D 88-202]

GURMA (AFRICAN PEOPLE) - SOCIAL LIFE AND CUSTOMS.
Bene gulmanceba =. Cotonou, R.P. du Bénin , 1983. 101 p., [1] leaf of plates : DDC 305.8/963 19
DT541.45.G87 B46 1983
NYPL [Sc D 88-202]

GURMA LANGUAGE - TEXTS.
Bene gulmanceba =. Cotonou, R.P. du Bénin , 1983. 101 p., [1] leaf of plates : DDC 305.8/963 19
DT541.45.G87 B46 1983
NYPL [Sc D 88-202]

Gurney, William Brodie, 1777-1855. Zulueta, Pedro de, Jr. Trial of Pedro de Zulueta, Jun. . London , 1844. lxxiv, 410 p. ;
NYPL [Sc Rare F 88-1]

Gurus and griots : poems from poets of Africa, of America, and of the Caribbean / edited by C. Jeanean Gibbs.1st ed. Brooklyn, N.Y. : Palm Tree Enterprises, [1987], c1985. 108 p. : ill. ; 24 cm. ISBN 0-9618755-0-X (pbk.) DDC 811/.008/0896 19
1. American poetry - 20th century. 2. American poetry - Washington Metropolitan Area. 3. English poetry - Black authors. 4. Afro-Americans - Poetry. 5. Blacks - Poetry. I. Gibbs, C. Jeanean.
PS591.N4 G87 1987 **NYPL [Sc E 89-230]**

GUSII (AFRICAN PEOPLE) - HISTORY.
Nyasani, J. M. (Joseph Major), 1938- The British massacre of the Gusii freedom defenders /. Nairobi, Kenya , 1984. v, 85 p. :
NYPL [Sc D 88-1133]

Gutiérrez, Mariela. Los cuentos negros de Lydia Cabrera : estudio morfológico esquemático / Mariela Gutiérrez. Miami, Fla. : Ediciones Universal, 1986. 148 p. ; 22 cm. (Colección Ébano y canela) Bibliography: p. 129-148. ISBN 0-89729-389-4
1. Cabrera, Lydia - Criticism and interpretation. I. Title.
NYPL [Sc D 88-370]

GUYANA - FICTION.
Salkey, Andrew. The one . London , 1985. 48 p. ; **NYPL [Sc D 88-1238]**

GUYANA - FICTON.
Cranmore, Frederick, 1948- The West Indian /. Brooklyn , c1978. 122 p., [1] leaf of plates : DDC 813/.5/4
PZ4.C8893 We PR9320.9.C7
NYPL [Sc D 88-37]

GUYANA - FOREIGN RELATIONS.
Jackson, Rashleigh E. The right to a peaceful world . [Guyana] 1985. 77 p. :
NYPL [Sc D 89-140]

GUYANA - LANGUAGES.
Contout, Auxence. Langues et cultures guyanaises /. Guyana [197-?] 233 p. :
NYPL [Sc D 88-1279]

GUYANA - SOCIAL LIFE AND CUSTOMS.
Contout, Auxence. Langues et cultures guyanaises /. Guyana [197-?] 233 p. :
NYPL [Sc D 88-1279]

La Guyane, les grands problèmes, les solutions possibles /. Castor, Elie, 1943- Paris , c1984. 337 p., [8] p. of plates : ISBN 2-903033-58-7 : DDC 988/.203 19
JL812 .C36 1984 **NYPL [Sc D 89-389]**

GUYANESE LITERATURE.
Independence 10 . Georgetown, Guyana [introd. 1976] 222 p. ; DDC 810
PR9320.5 .I5 **NYPL [Sc F 89-101]**

Guzzi, George. (ill) Christopher, Matt. The basket counts. Boston [1968] 125 p. DDC [Fic] 19
PZ7.C458 Bash **NYPL [Sc C 89-15]**

Gwarinda, Takawira C. Socialism & education : an introduction / Takawira C. Gwarinda. Harare, Zimbabwe : College Press, 1985. 128 p. : ill. ; 21 cm. "Approved by the Ministry of Education 9th August 1984"--P. 4 of coveer. Includes bibliographical references and index. ISBN 0-86925-547-9
1. Socialism and education - Zimbabwe. 2. Socialism - Zimbabwe. 3. Education - Zimbabwe. I. Title. II. Title: Socialism and education. **NYPL [Sc D 88-1129]**

Gwellem, Jerome F. (Jerome Fultang) Paul Biya, hero of the New Deal / by Jerome F. Gwellem. Limbe, Cameroon : Gwellem Publications, [1984]. 68 p. : ill. ; 22 cm.
1. Biya, Paul, 1933-. 2. Cameroon - Politics and government - 1982-. 3. Cameroon - History - Coup d'état, 1984. I. Title. **NYPL [Sc D 88-1255]**

GWEMBE DISTRICT, ZAMBIA - ECONOMIC CONDITIONS.
Colson, Elizabeth, 1917- For prayer and profit . Stanford, Calif. , 1988. vi, 147 p. : ISBN 0-8047-1444-4 (alk. paper) : DDC 968.94 19
DT963.42 .C65 1988 **NYPL [Sc D 88-1254]**

GWIN (AFRICAN PEOPLE) see GOUIN (AFRICAN PEOPLE)

GYAMAN - HISTORY.
Princes & serviteurs du royaume . Paris , 1987. 225 p. : ISBN 2-901161-29-4
NYPL [Sc E 88-409]

Gyekye, Kwame. the unexamined life : philosophy and the African experience / Kwame Gyekye. Accra : Ghana University Press, 1988. 36 p. ; 21 cm. "An inaugural lecture delivered at the University of Ghana on Thursday, May 7, 1987." ISBN 996-430-147-2
I. Title. **NYPL [Sc D 89-521]**

GYNECOCRACY. see MATRIARCHY.

Haarløv, Jens. Labour regulation and black workers' struggles in South Africa / Jens Haarløv. Uppsala : Scandinavian Institute of African Studies, 1983. 80 p. ; 22 cm. (Research report, 0080-6714 . no. 68) Bibliography: p. 75-80. ISBN 91-7106-213-0 (pbk.) DDC 960 s 331.6/9/968 19
1. Trade-unions - South Africa. 2. Strikes and lockouts - South Africa. 3. Blacks - Employment - Law and legislation - South Africa. I. Series: Nordiska Afrikainstitutet. Research report, no. 68. II. Title.
DT1 .N64 no. 68 HD6870.5
NYPL [JLD 87-1037]

HABEAS CORPUS - CANADA.
Teatero, William, 1953- John Anderson . [Kingston, Ont.] , c1986. 183 p. : ISBN 0-9692685-0-5 : DDC 345.71/056/0924 19
NYPL [Sc E 89-113]

Haberland, Eike. Ibaaddo ka-Ba'iso : culture and language of the Ba'iso / Eike Haberland, Marcello Lamberti. Heidelberg : C. Winter, 1988. 184 p. ; 22 cm. (Studia linguarum Africae orientalis . Bd. 2) Includes index. Bibliography: p. 181-184. ISBN 3-533-04014-3
1. Cushitic languages. 2. Ethnology - Ethiopia. 3. Ethiopia - Social life and customs. I. Lamberti, Marcello. II. Title. III. Series.
NYPL [Sc D 89-552]

Habi, Ya'akub H. The people called Bassa-Nge / Ya'akub H. Habi. Zaria : Y. H. Habi, c1987. 86 p. : ill., maps ; 19 cm. Bibliography: p. 83-86. ISBN 978-12-5057-7
1. Nupe (African people). 2. Ethnology - Nigeria - Bassa Nge District. I. Title. **NYPL [Sc C 88-372]**

Habitant d'Hayti.
IDYLLES ET CHANSONS, OU, ESSAIS DE POÉSIE CRÉOLE.
Tinker, Edward Larocque, 1881- Gombo comes to Philadelphia /. Worcester, Mass. , 1957. [10], 22 p. : **NYPL [Sc E 89-9]**

Idylles et chansons, ou, Essais de poésie créole. 1957. Tinker, Edward Larocque, 1881- Gombo comes to Philadelphia / Edward Larocque Tinker. Worcester, Mass. , 1957. [10], 22 p. — **NYPL [Sc E 89-9]**

L'habitation Saint-Ybars. Mercier, Alfred, 1816-1894. Nouvelle-Orléans, 1881. 234 p.
PQ3939.M5 H3 1881
NYPL [Sc Rare C 88-19]

Hable Selassie, Sergew. see Sergew Hable Selassie, 1929-

Habyarimana, Juvénal. Discours du général-major Habyarimana Juvénal, président de la République rwandaise et président-fondateur du Mouvement révolutionnaire national pour le développement à l'occasion du 1er juillet, 1987 = Disikuru ya nyakubahwa général-major Habyarimana Yuvenali, perezida wa Repubulika yú Rwanda na perezida-fondateri wa Mouvement Révolutionnaire Ihasanira Amajyambere yú Rwanda kuwa 1 Nyakanga, 1987. [Kigali?] : Présidence de la République rwandaise, Service de línformation et des archives nationale, 1987. 82 p. : ill. ; 21 cm. Cover title. In French and Kinyarwanda. Errata slip inserted.
1. Mouvement révolutionnaire national pour le développement (Rwanda) - Anniversaries, etc. 2. Rwanda - Politics and government. 3. Rwanda - Anniversaries, etc. I. Title.
f-rw--- **NYPL [Sc D 88-1517]**

Hackett, Rosalind I. J. New religious movements in Nigeria /. Lewiston, N.Y. , c1987. xvi, 245 p. ; ISBN 0-88946-180-5 (alk. paper) DDC 291.9/09669 19
BL2470.N5 N49 1987 **NYPL [Sc E 88-266]**

Hackland, Brian, 1951- Williams, Gwyneth, 1953- The dictionary of contemporary politics of southern Africa /. London , New York , 1988. xi, 339 p. : ISBN 0-415-00245-1 DDC 320.968/03 19
JQ2720.A127 W55 1988 **NYPL [Sc D 89-2]**

Hackney, Claudius T. How ends the day / by Claudius T. Hackney. Bryn Mawr, Penn. : Dorrance, 1986. 80 p. ; 23 cm. Poems. ISBN 0-8059-3019-1
I. Title. **NYPL [Sc D 88-186]**

Hadjor, Kofi Buenor. Nkrumah and Ghana ; the dilemma of post-colonial power / Kofi Buenor Hadjor. London ; New York : Kegan Paul International, 1988. ix, 114 p., [8] p. of plates : ill., ports., maps ; 23 cm. Includes index. Bibliography: p. 106-108.
1. Nkrumah, Kwame, 1909-1972. 2. Ghana - Politics and government. I. Title. **NYPL [JFD 88-4445]**

Hadriana dans tous mes rêves . Dépestre, René. [Paris] , c1988. 195 p. ; ISBN 2-07-071255-9
NYPL [Sc D 88-1004]

Haeger, Barbara. Africa : on her schedule is written a change / Barbara Haeger ; illustrated by Bruce Onobrakpeya. Ibadan, Nigeria : African Universities Press, 1982. xiii, 105 p. : ill. ; 22 cm.
I. Onobrakpeya, Bruce. II. Title.
NYPL [Sc D 87-759]

Hagher, Iyorwuese H. Aishatu, and other plays / [Iyorwuese H. Hagher] Benin City [Nigeria] : Victory Tutorial Press, c1987. 136 p. ; 21 cm. CONTENTS. - Aishatu.--Swem Karagbe : a parable on leadership.--Antipeople. ISBN 978-235-603-4
1. Nigeria - Drama. I. Hagher, Iyorwuese H. Swem Karagbe. II. Hagher, Iyorwuese H. Antipeople. III. Title. **NYPL [Sc D 88-797]**

Antipeople. Hagher, Iyorwuese H. Aishatu, and other plays / [Iyorwuese H. Hagher] Benin City [Nigeria] , c1987. 136 p. ; ISBN 978-235-603-4 **NYPL [Sc D 88-797]**

Swem Karagbe. Hagher, Iyorwuese H. Aishatu, and other plays / [Iyorwuese H. Hagher] Benin City [Nigeria] , c1987. 136 p. ; ISBN 978-235-603-4 **NYPL [Sc D 88-797]**

Hahner, June Edith, 1940- Poverty and politics : the urban poor in Brazil, 1870-1920 / June E. Hahner. Albuquerque : University of New Mexico Press, 1986. xvi, 415 p. : ill. ; 24 cm. Includes index. Bibliography: p. 373-402. ISBN 0-8263-0878-3 : DDC 305.5/69/0981 19
1. Urban poor - Brazil - History. 2. Urbanization - Brazil - History. 3. Laboring and laboring classes - Brazil - Political activity - History. 4. Brazil - Social conditions. 5. Brazil - Politics and government - 1822-. I. Title.
HC190.P6 H34 1986 **NYPL [JLE 86-4407]**

HAILE SELASSIE I UNIVERSITY - STUDENTS - HISTORY.
Balsvik, Randi Rønning. Haile Sellassie's students . East Lansing, Mich. , c1985. xix, 363 p. : DDC 378/.198/0963 19
LA1518.7 .B35 1985 **NYPL [Sc D 88-1403]**

Haile Sellassie's students . Balsvik, Randi Rønning. East Lansing, Mich. , c1985. xix, 363 p. : DDC 378/.198/0963 19
LA1518.7 .B35 1985 **NYPL [Sc D 88-1403]**

Haines, Herbert H. Black radicals and the civil rights mainstream, 1954-1970 / Herbert H. Haines. Knoxville : University of Tennessee Press, c1988 xii, 231 p. : ill. ; 24 cm. Includes index. Bibliography: p. [207]-216. ISBN 0-87049-563-1 (alk. paper) : DDC 305.8/96073 19
1. Afro-Americans - Civil rights. 2. Afro-Americans - Politics and government. 3. Radicalism - United States - History - 20th century. 4. United States - Politics and government - 1945-. 5. United States - Race relations. I. Title.
E185.615 .H25 1988 ***NYPL [Sc E 88-511]***

HAIRSTYLES - AFRICA, WEST.
Frehn, Beatrice, 1948- Afrimanische Frisuren . Köln , c1986. 147 p. : ISBN 3-7701-1619-4 DDC 391./5/0966 19
GT2295.A358 F74 1986
NYPL [Sc C 88-153]

Haith, Dorothy May.
State of Georgia v. Vincent Derek Mallory M.D. : a select bibliography / by Dorothy M. Haith. Washington : D.M. Haith, 1988. 12 leaves ; 29 cm. Cover title.
1. Mallory, Vincent Derek - Trials, litigation etc. - Bibliography. 2. Afro-American criminals - Georgia - Bibliography. I. Title. ***NYPL [Sc F 88-131]***

Theses accepted by the Atlanta University Graduate School of Library Service, 1950-1975 / by Dorothy M. Haith. Huntsville, Al : Information Exchange System for Minority Personnel, 1977. v, 45 p. ; 23 cm. Includes index.
1. Atlanta University. School of Library Service - Dissertations. 2. Library science - Bibliography. 3. Dissertations, Academic - United States - Bibliography. I. Atlantic University. School of Library Service. II. Title.
Z666 .H25 ***NYPL [Sc D 88-69]***

Haïti : art naïf, art vaudou. Paris : Galeries Nationales du Grand Palais, 1988. 276 p. : ill. (some col.), ports. ; 24 cm. Catalog of an exhibition held at the Galeries Nationales du Grand Palais.
1. Voodooism in art - Haiti - Exhibitions. 2. Haiti - Art - Exhibitions. 3. Primitivism in art - Haiti - Exhibitions. I. Grand Palais (Paris, France).
NYPL [Sc E 89-227]

Haiti . Abbott, Elizabeth. New York, N.Y. , c1988. xii, 381 p., [8] p. of plates : ISBN 0-07-046029-9 : DDC 972.94/06 19
F1928 .A583 1988 ***NYPL [Sc E 88-605]***

HAITI.
Bellegarde, Dantès, 1877-1966. La nación haitiana / . Santo Domingo , 1984. 429 p. :
NYPL [Sc E 88-103]
Hurbon, Laënnec. Comprendre Haïti . Paris , c1987. 174 p. : ISBN 2-86537-192-1
NYPL [Sc D 88-1045]

HAITI - ADDRESSES, ESSAYS, LECTURES.
Problemas dominico-haitianos y del Caribe / . - México , 1973. 228 p.;
NYPL [JLK 73-145 [no.] 29]

Haiti and the great powers, 1902-1915 /.
Plummer, Brenda Gayle. Baton Rouge , c1988. xix, 255 p. : ISBN 0-8071-1409-X (alk. paper) DDC 972.94/04 19
F1926 .P68 1988 ***NYPL [HPE 88-2374]***

Haiti and the United States . Dash, J. Michael. Basingstoke, Hampshire , 1988. xv, 152 p. ; ISBN 0-333-45491-X
NYPL [Sc D 88-1358]

HAITI - ART - EXHIBITIONS.
Haïti . Paris , 1988. 276 p. :
NYPL [Sc E 89-227]

Haïti bajo la opresión de los Duvalier : textos de diversas organizaciones y personalidades de Haití / Elizabeth Filibert ... [et al.] ; coordinador, Gérard Pierre-Charles.2a ed. Santo Domingo : Editora Taller, 1981. 93 p. ; 21 cm. (Colección Nuestro continente . [5]) Includes bibliographical references. ISBN 968-590-021-3 DDC 972.94/06 19
1. Haiti - Politics and government - 1934-1971. 2. Haiti - Politics and government - 1971-. I. Filibert, Elizabeth. II. Pierre-Charles, Gérard. III. Series.
F1928 .H33 1981 ***NYPL [Sc D 89-457]***

HAITI - CIVILIZATION.
Ans, André Marcel d'. Haiti, Paysage et Société / . Paris , 1987. 337 p. : ISBN 2-86537-190-5
NYPL [Sc E 88-251]

Haiti, crise de l'education et crise du développement /. Jean, Rodrigue. Port-au-Prince, Haiti , 1988. 152 p. ; ISBN 0-948390-00-X ***NYPL [Sc D 88-914]***

Haiti. Département de l'éducation nationale. Direction de la planification. Institut pédagogique national (Haiti). Comité de curriculum. La réforme éducative . [Port-au-Prince] [1982] 65 p. : DDC 375/.001/097294
LB1564.H2 I57 1982 ***NYPL [Sc D 88-1401]***

HAITI - DEPENDENCY ON THE UNITED STATES.
Gousse, Edgard Js. Th. Non à une intervention américaine en Haïti / . Montréal , 1988. 74 p. ;
NYPL [Sc D 88-861]
Laraque, Franck. Défi à la pauvreté / . Montréal , 1987. 165 p. ;
NYPL [Sc C 88-107]

HAITI - DESCRIPTION AND TRAVEL.
Franklin, James. The present state of Hayti (Saint Domingo)] London, 1828. viii, 411 p.
NYPL [Sc Micro R-1455]
Wimpffen, François Alexandre Stanislaus, baron de. A voyage to Saint Domingo, in the years 1788, 1789, and 1790. London, 1817 [i. e. 1797] 371 p. ***NYPL [Sc 917.294-W]***

HAITI - DESCRIPTION AND TRAVEL - GUIDE-BOOKS.
McLeod, Catherine. Jamaika / . Lausanne, Switzerland [1985], c1981. 128 p. :
NYPL [Sc B 88-57]

HAITI - DRAMA.
Vincent, Occélus. Brouillerie . Port-au-Prince [1964] 54 p. ;
NYPL [Sc Micro R-4840 no.6]

HAITI - ECONOMIC CONDITIONS.
Di Chiara, Catherine Eve. Le dossier Haïti . Paris , c1988. 480 p., xxiv p. of plates : ISBN 2-235-01778-9
F1938 .D52x 1988 ***NYPL [Sc D 89-394]***
Dominique, Hilaire. Développement économique pour Haïti / . [S.l.] 1987. 51 p. ;
NYPL [Sc D 88-187]
François de Neufchâteau, Nicolas Louis, comte, 1752-1828. Mémoire en forme de discours sur la disette du numéraire à Saint-Domingue, et sur les moyens d'y remédier. Metz, 1788. 178 p. ***NYPL [Sc *F330.9729-F]***
Franklin, James. The present state of Hayti (Saint Domingo)] London, 1828. viii, 411 p.
NYPL [Sc Micro R-1455]
Plummer, Brenda Gayle. Haiti and the great powers, 1902-1915 . Baton Rouge , c1988. xix, 255 p. : ISBN 0-8071-1409-X (alk. paper) DDC 972.94/04 19
F1926 .P68 1988 ***NYPL [HPE 88-2374]***

HAITI - ECONOMIC CONDITIONS - 1971-
Fass, Simon M. Political economy in Haiti . New Brunswick, N.J., U. S.A. , c1988. xxxi, 369 p. : ISBN 0-88738-158-8 DDC 338.97294 19
HC153 .F37 1988 ***NYPL [Sc E 88-423]***
Laraque, Franck. Défi à la pauvreté / . Montréal , 1987. 165 p. ;
NYPL [Sc C 88-107]

HAITI - ECONOMIC POLICY.
DeWind, Josh. [Aiding migration. French.] Aide à la migration . Montréal, Québec, Canada , 1988. 216 p. :
NYPL [Sc D 89-441]
Fass, Simon M. Political economy in Haiti . New Brunswick, N.J., U. S.A. , c1988. xxxi, 369 p. : ISBN 0-88738-158-8 DDC 338.97294 19
HC153 .F37 1988 ***NYPL [Sc E 88-423]***
Laraque, Franck. Défi à la pauvreté / . Montréal , 1987. 165 p. ;
NYPL [Sc C 88-107]

HAITI - EMIGRATION AND IMMIGRATION.
Icart, Jean-Claude. Négriers d'eux-mêmes . Montréal, Québec, Canada , 1987. 188 p. ; ISBN 2-920862-06-5 ***NYPL [Sc D 88-396]***

HAITI - EMIGRATION AND IMMIGRATION - ECONOMIC ASPECTS.
DeWind, Josh. [Aiding migration. French.] Aide à la migration . Montréal, Québec, Canada , 1988. 216 p. :
NYPL [Sc D 89-441]

HAITI - EMIGRATION AND IMMIGRATION - FICTION.
Fanks, Russell, 1940- Terminus floride . Paris , 1987. 346 p. ; ISBN 2-7357-0059-3
NYPL [Sc E 88-126]

HAITI - FICTION.
Cazanove, Michèle. Présumée Solitude, ou, Histoire d'une paysanne haïtienne . Paris , c1988. 178 p. ; ISBN 2-260-00546-2
NYPL [Sc D 88-1406]
Clitandre, Pierre. [Cathédrale du mois d'août. English.] Cathedral of the August heat / . London , c1987. 159 p. ; ISBN 0-930523-31-8 (pbk.) : ***NYPL [Sc D 87-1048]***
Confiant, Raphaël. Jik dèyè do Bondyé / . [Port-au-Prince? , 1978?] 64 p. :
NYPL [Sc D 88-694]
Dorsinville, Roger. Accords perdus . Montréal, Québec, Canada , c1987. 190 p. ; ISBN 2-920862-07-3 ***NYPL [Sc C 88-128]***
Étienne, Gérard, 1936- La reine Soleil Levée . Montréal , 1988, c1987. 195 p. ; ISBN 2-7601-1974-2 : DDC C843/.54 19
NYPL [Sc D 88-1179]
Fignolé, Jean Claude. Les possédés de la pleine lune / . Paris , c1987. 220 p. ; ISBN 2-02-009535-1 ***NYPL [JFD 88-532]***
Godart, Jacques. Pourquoi les campêches saignent-ils? / . Port-au-Prince , 1987. 199 p. ;
NYPL [Sc D 88-514]
Mucci, Floren's. Tu aurais pu lui dire je t'aime / . Port-au-Prince, Haiti [betweem 1985 and 1988] 85 p. ; ***NYPL [Sc C 88-233]***
Novastar, Charles. Le Macho et la fille du macoute / . Port-au-Prince, , 1987. 181 p. ;
NYPL [Sc C 88-101]
Ollivier, Emile, 1940- La discorde aux cent voix . Paris , c1986. 269 p. ; ISBN 2-226-02701-7 : DDC 843 19
PQ3949.2.O44 D5 1986
NYPL [Sc D 88-372]
Thoby-Marcelin, Philippe, 1904-1975. [Bête du Musseau. English.] The beast of the Haitian hills / . San Francisco , 1986. 179 p. ; ISBN 0-87286-189-9 (pbk.) DDC 843 19
PQ3949.T45 B413 1986
NYPL [Sc D 88-199]

HAITI - FOREIGN PUBLIC OPINION, AMERICAN - HISTORY - 19TH CENTURY.
Hunt, Alfred N., 1941- Haiti's influence on antebellum America . Baton Rouge , c1988. xiv, 196 p. : ISBN 0-8071-1370-0 DDC 973/.049697294 19
E184.H27 H86 1987 ***NYPL [Sc E 88-131]***

HAITI - FOREIGN RELATIONS.
Plummer, Brenda Gayle. Haiti and the great powers, 1902-1915 . Baton Rouge , c1988. xix, 255 p. : ISBN 0-8071-1409-X (alk. paper) DDC 972.94/04 19
F1926 .P68 1988 ***NYPL [HPE 88-2374]***

HAITI - FOREIGN RELATIONS - DOMINICAN REPUBLIC - SOURCES.
Documentos del conflicto dominico-haitiano de 1937 / . Santo Domingo, D.N., República Dominicana , 1985. 606 p. ;
NYPL [Sc F 89-173]

HAITI - FOREIGN RELATIONS - UNITED STATES.
Gousse, Edgard Js. Th. Non à une intervention américaine en Haïti / . Montréal , 1988. 74 p. ;
NYPL [Sc D 88-861]

Haiti - Government. see Haiti - Politics and government.

HAITI - HISTORY.
Ans, André Marcel d'. Haiti, Paysage et Société / . Paris , 1987. 337 p. : ISBN 2-86537-190-5
NYPL [Sc E 88-251]
Bellegarde, Dantès, 1877-1966. La nación haitiana / . Santo Domingo , 1984. 429 p. :
NYPL [Sc E 88-103]
Bryan, Patrick E. The Haitian revolution and its effects / . Kingston, Jamaica , Exeter, N.H., USA , 1984. 56 p. : ISBN 0-435-98301-6 (U. S. : pbk.) DDC 972.94/03 19
F1923 .B83 1984 ***NYPL [Sc D 89-299]***
Di Chiara, Catherine Eve. Le dossier Haïti .

Paris , c1988. 480 p., xxiv p. of plates : ISBN
2-235-01778-9
F1938 .D52x 1988   NYPL [Sc D 89-394]

Diederich, Bernard. [Papa Doc. Spanish.] Papa
Doc y los tontons Macoutes . Santo Domingo,
República Dominicana , 1986. 393 p., [16] p. of
plates :   *NYPL [Sc D 88-452]*

Fouchard, Jean, 1912- Regards sur l'histoire /.
Port-au-Prince, Haiti , 1988. 222 p. :
                            NYPL [Sc D 89-409]

Franklin, James. The present state of Hayti
(Saint Domingo)] London, 1828. viii, 411 p.
                            NYPL [Sc Micro R-1455]

Madiou, Thomas, 1814-1884. Histoire d'Haïti /.
Port-au-Prince, Haiti , 1981- v. :
                            NYPL [Sc Ser.-L .M227]

Mercier, Louis, of Haiti. Contribution de l'île
d'Haïti à l'histoire de la civilisation [microform]
/. Port-au-Prince, Haïti , 1985. 83 p. ; DDC
972.94 19
F1911 .M47 1985
                    NYPL [Sc Micro R-4840 no.8]

HAITI - HISTORY - TO 1791.
Cauna, Jacques, 1948- Au temps des isles à
sucre . Paris , c1987. 285 p., [16] p. of plates :
ISBN 2-86537-186-5 *NYPL [Sc E 88-492]*

Fouchard, Jean, 1912- Regards sur l'histoire /.
Port-au-Prince, Haiti , 1988. 222 p. :
                            NYPL [Sc D 89-409]

HAITI - HISTORY - REVOLUTION, 1791-
1804.
Bryan, Patrick E. The Haitian revolution and its
effects /. Kingston, Jamaica , Exeter, N.H.,
USA , 1984. 56 p. : ISBN 0-435-98301-6 (U. S. :
pbk.) DDC 972.94/03 19
F1923 .B83 1984   NYPL [Sc D 89-299]

Clausson, L. J. Précis historique de la
révolution de Saint-Domingue [microform].
Paris, 1819. xij, 155 p.
                            NYPL [Sc Micro R-3541]

Cooper, Anna J. (Anna Julia), 1858-1964.
[Attitude de la France à l'égard de l'esclavage
pendant la révolution. English.] Slavery and the
French revolutionists, 1788-1805 /. Lewiston,
1988. 228 p. : ISBN 0-88946-637-8 DDC
972.94/03 19
F1923 .C7213 1988   NYPL [Sc E 88-469]

HAITI - HISTORY - REVOLUTION, 1791-
1804 - INFLUENCE.
Hunt, Alfred N., 1941- Haiti's influence on
antebellum America . Baton Rouge , c1988. xiv,
196 p. : ISBN 0-8071-1370-0 DDC
973/.049697294 19
E184.H27 H86 1987   NYPL [Sc E 88-131]

HAITI - HISTORY - REVOLUTION, 1791-
1804 - JUVENILE FICTION.
Icenhower, Joseph B. Mr. Murdock takes
command . Philadelphia , c1958. xii, 173 p. :
                            NYPL [Sc D 88-1507]

Lindquist, Willis. The red drum's warning /.
New York , 1958. 128 p. :
                            NYPL [Sc D 88-662]

HAITI - HISTORY - REVOLUTION, 1791-
1804 - SOURCES.
Ducos, Jean François, 1765-1793. Opinion de
Jean-François Ducos sur l'exécution provisoire
du concordat, & des arrêtés de l'Assemblée
coloniale confirmatifs de cet accord . A Paris ,
1791. 12 p. ;   *NYPL [Sc Rare C 86-7]*

France. Assemblée nationale legislative,
1791-1792. Loi relative aux colonies, & aux
moyens d'y appaiser les troubles . A Niort ,
1792. 6 p. ;   *NYPL [Sc Rare F 82-68]*

Le Brasseur, J. A. De l'état actuel de la marine
et des colonies /. A Paris , 1792. 48 p. ;
                            NYPL [Sc Rare C 86-4]

Santo Domingo (French colony). Assemblée
générale. Commissaires. Pétition faite à
l'Assemblée nationale par MM. les
Commissaires de l'Assemblée générale de la
partie française de St.-Domingue . [Paris?]
[1791?] 7 p. ;   *NYPL [Sc Rare C 86-3]*

Tarbé, Charles. Rapport sur les troubles de
Saint-Domingue. Paris, 1791-[1792] 4 v.
F1921 .T17   NYPL [Sc Rare F 88-17]

HAITI - HISTORY - 1804-1844.
Coradin, Jean. Histoire diplomatique d'Haïti
1804-1843 /. Port-au-Prince, Haïti , 1988- v. ;
                            NYPL [Sc D 88-864]

HAITI - HISTORY - 1844-1915.
Péan, Marc. L'échec du firminisme /.
Port-au-Prince, Haiti , 1987. 181 p. :
                            NYPL [Sc D 88-625]

HAITI - HISTORY - AMERICAN
OCCUPATION, 1915-1934.
Gousse, Edgard Js. Th. Non à une intervention
américaine en Haïti /. Montréal , 1988. 74 p. ;
                            NYPL [Sc D 88-861]

Pamphile, Léon Dénius. L'éducation en Haiti
sous l'occupation américaine 1915-1934 /.
[Port-au-Prince , 1988] 316 p. ;
                            NYPL [Sc D 88-1002]

HAITI - HISTORY - 1934- - SOURCES.
Documentos del conflicto dominico-haitiano de
1937 /. Santo Domingo, D.N., República
Dominicana , 1985. 606 p. ;
                            NYPL [Sc F 89-173]

HAITI - HISTORY - 1934-1986.
Ferguson, James, 1956- Papa Doc, Baby Doc .
Oxford, UK , New York, NY, USA , 1987. x,
171 p., [8] p. of plates : ISBN 0-631-15601-1 :
DDC 972.94/07 19
F1928 .F47 1987   NYPL [Sc E 88-269]

HAITI - HISTORY - 1971-
Luc, Napoléon Serge. Histoire du déchoukage
/. [Port-au-Prince, Haiti, W.I] [1987?] 124 p. :
                            NYPL [Sc D 87-1419]

HAITI - HISTORY - DRAMA.
Leconte, Vergniaud. Théâtre [microform]. [n. p.,
1919] xi, 291 p.   *NYPL [Sc Micro R-3541]*

Haiti - Immigration. see Haiti - Emigration and
immigration.

HAITI IN LITERATURE.
Dash, J. Michael. Haiti and the United States .
Basingstoke, Hampshire , 1988. xv, 152 p. :
ISBN 0-333-45491-X
                            NYPL [Sc D 88-1358]

HAITI - INTELLECTUAL LIFE.
Fouchard, Jean, 1912- Plaisirs de
Saint-Domingue . Port-au-Prince, Haiti , 1988.
125 p.   *NYPL [Sc D 89-407]*

Haiti, la lucha por la democracia (clase obrera,
partidos y sindicatos) /. Auguste, Michel
Hector. Puebla [1986]. 244 p. ;
                            NYPL [Sc D 88-761]

HAITI - OFFICIALS AND EMPLOYEES -
ANECDOTES, FACETIAE, SATIRE, ETC.
Victor, Gary, 1958- Albert Buron, ou, Profil
d'une "élite" /. [Port-au-Prince , 1988] 230 p. ;
                            NYPL [Sc D 88-1005]

Haiti, Paysage et Société /. Ans, André Marcel
d'. Paris , 1987. 337 p. : ISBN 2-86537-190-5
                            NYPL [Sc E 88-251]

HAITI - POLITICS AND GOVERNMENT -
1804-
Gilbert, Marcel, 1938- La patrie haïtienne .
Brazzaville , 1984. 60 p. :
                            NYPL [Sc D 89-629]

HAITI - POLITICS AND GOVERNMENT -
1844-1934.
Péan, Marc. L'échec du firminisme /.
Port-au-Prince, Haiti , 1987. 181 p. :
                            NYPL [Sc D 88-625]

Plummer, Brenda Gayle. Haiti and the great
powers, 1902-1915 /. Baton Rouge , c1988. xix,
255 p. : ISBN 0-8071-1409-X (alk. paper) DDC
972.94/04 19
F1926 .P68 1988   NYPL [HPE 88-2374]

HAITI - POLITICS AND GOVERNMENT -
1844-1915.
Dévot, Justin, 1857-1920. Le devoir électoral et
les prochaines elections législatives [microform]
/. [Port-au-Prince] , 1902. 12 p. ;
                            NYPL [Sc Micro F-11,001]

HAITI - POLITICS AND GOVERNMENT -
1934-1971.
Abbott, Elizabeth. Haiti . New York, N.Y. ,
c1988. xii, 381 p., [8] p. of plates : ISBN
0-07-046029-9 : DDC 972.94/06 19
F1928 .A583 1988   NYPL [Sc E 88-605]

Haití bajo la opresión de los Duvalier . Santo
Domingo , 1981. 93 p. ; ISBN 968-590-021-3

DDC 972.94/06 19
F1928 .H33 1981   NYPL [Sc D 89-457]

Pouvoir noir en Haiti . Québec , 1988. 393 p.,
7 p. of plates : ISBN 2-920862-11-1
                            NYPL [Sc D 89-482]

HAITI - POLITICS AND GOVERNMENT -
1934-1971 - PHILOSOPHY.
Nérée, Bob. Duvalier . Port-au-Prince, Haiti ,
1988. 238 p. ;   *NYPL [Sc E 88-366]*

HAITI - POLITICS AND GOVERNMENT -
1971-
Guerre, Rockefeller. Mon mandat sous
Jn-Claude Duvalier . Port-au-Prince, Haiti ,
1987. 260 p. :   *NYPL [Sc D 87-935]*

Haití bajo la opresión de los Duvalier . Santo
Domingo , 1981. 93 p. ; ISBN 968-590-021-3
DDC 972.94/06 19
F1928 .H33 1981   NYPL [Sc D 89-457]

Soukar, Michel. Seize ans de lutte pour un pays
normal /. Port-au-Prince, Haïti . iv, 60 p. ;
                            NYPL [Sc D 88-511]

HAITI - POLITICS AND GOVERNMENT -
1971- - PHILOSOPHY.
Nérée, Bob. Duvalier . Port-au-Prince, Haiti ,
1988. 238 p. ;   *NYPL [Sc E 88-366]*

HAITI - POLITICS AND GOVERNMENT -
1971-1986.
Abbott, Elizabeth. Haiti . New York, N.Y. ,
c1988. xii, 381 p., [8] p. of plates : ISBN
0-07-046029-9 : DDC 972.94/06 19
F1928 .A583 1988   NYPL [Sc E 88-605]

HAITI - RELATIONS - UNITED STATES.
Dash, J. Michael. Haiti and the United States .
Basingstoke, Hampshire , 1988. xv, 152 p. ;
ISBN 0-333-45491-X
                            NYPL [Sc D 88-1358]

HAITI - RELIGION.
Hurbon, Laënnec. Dieu dans le vaudou haïtien
/. Port-au-Prince, Haïti , 1987. 268 p. ; DDC
299/.67 19
BL2490 .H87 1987   NYPL [Sc D 89-366]

HAITI - RELIGIOUS LIFE AND CUSTOMS.
Davis, Wade. Passage of darkness . Chapel
Hill , c1988. xx, 344 p. : ISBN 0-8078-1776-7
(alk. paper) DDC 299/.65 19
BL2530.H3 D37 1988   NYPL [Sc E 88-429]

Haiti (Republic)
Treaties, etc. Catholic Church, 1860 Mar. 25.
Catholic Church. [Treaties, etc. Haiti, 1860
Mar. 25.] Concordat signé le 25
mars 1860 : Convention du 6 février 1861
avec le Saint-Siège : Loi sur l'organisation et
l'administration des fabriques [microform].
Port-au-Prince , 1918. 31 p. ;
                            NYPL [Sc Micro F-10,892]

Haiti (Republic) Laws, statutes, etc. Formules
des actes de l'état civil [microform].
Port-Républicain : Impr. nationale, 1845. 17 p. ;
21 cm. Cover title. Microfiche. New York: New York
Public Library, 198 . 1 microfiche: negative; 11 x 15
cm. (FSN Sc 019,027).
1. Domestic relations - Haiti. I. Title.
                            NYPL [Sc Micro F-10,893]

Haiti (Republic) Statutes. see Haiti (Republic)
Laws, statutes, etc.

HAITI - SOCIAL CONDITIONS.
Di Chiara, Catherine Eve. Le dossier Haïti .
Paris , c1988. 480 p. xxiv p. of plates : ISBN
2-235-01778-9
F1938 .D52x 1988   NYPL [Sc D 89-394]

Plummer, Brenda Gayle. Haiti and the great
powers, 1902-1915 /. Baton Rouge , c1988. xix,
255 p. : ISBN 0-8071-1409-X (alk. paper) DDC
972.94/04 19
F1926 .P68 1988   NYPL [HPE 88-2374]

HAITI - SOCIAL LIFE AND CUSTOMS.
Benoit, Marie. Let's visit Haiti. 1988. 96 p. :
ISBN 0-333-45692-0 : DDC 972.94/07 19
F1916   NYPL [Sc D 89-73]

Davis, Wade. Passage of darkness . Chapel
Hill , c1988. xx, 344 p. : ISBN 0-8078-1776-7
(alk. paper) DDC 299/.65 19
BL2530.H3 D37 1988   NYPL [Sc E 88-429]

Fouchard, Jean, 1912- Plaisirs de
Saint-Domingue . Port-au-Prince, Haiti , 1988.
125 p.   *NYPL [Sc D 89-407]*

HAITIAN ART. see ART, HAITIAN.

HAITIAN FICTION - HISTORY AND CRITICISM.
Shelton, Marie Denise. L'image de la société dans le roman haitien /. 1979 ix,241 p. ;
NYPL [Sc F 88-212]

HAITIAN LITERATURE - AMERICAN INFLUENCES.
Dash, J. Michael. Haiti and the United States . Basingstoke, Hampshire , 1988. xv, 152 p. ; ISBN 0-333-45491-X
NYPL [Sc D 88-1358]

HAITIAN LITERATURE - CANADA.
Dorsinville, Max, 1943- Solidarités . Montréal, Québec, Canada , 1988. xv, 196 p. ; ISBN 2-920862-09-X   *NYPL [Sc D 89-484]*

HAITIAN LITERATURE (FRENCH CREOLE) - HISTORY AND CRITICISM.
Laroche, Maximilien. L'avènement de la littérature haïtienne /. Sainte-Foy, Québec , 1987. 219 p. ;   *NYPL [Sc D 88-1462]*

HAITIAN LITERATURE - HISTORY AND CRITICISM.
Dash, J. Michael. Haiti and the United States . Basingstoke, Hampshire , 1988. xv, 152 p. ; ISBN 0-333-45491-X
NYPL [Sc D 88-1358]

Laroche, Maximilien. L'avènement de la littérature haïtienne /. Sainte-Foy, Québec , 1987. 219 p. ;   *NYPL [Sc D 88-1462]*

Haitian painting : the naives and the moderns : a traveling exhibition for the New York City schools, 1987/88 / curated by Eva Pataki. [New York : School of Education, Queens College, City University of New York : Board of Education of New York City], c1987. 71 p. : chiefly ill. ; 23 cm. At head of title: The School of Education, Queens College, City Univeresity of New York, and the Board of Education of New York City present.
1. Painting, Haitian - Exhibitions. 2. Primitivism in art - Haiti - Exhibitions. I. Pataki, Eva. II. Queens College (New York, N.Y.). School of Education.
NYPL [Sc D 88-451]

HAITIAN PROVERBS. see PROVERBS, HAITIAN.

The Haitian revolution and its effects /. Bryan, Patrick E. Kingston, Jamaica , Exeter, N.H., USA , 1984. 56 p. ; ISBN 0-435-98301-6 (U. S. : pbk.) DDC 972.94/03 19
F1923 .B83 1984   *NYPL [Sc D 89-299]*

HAITIANS - DOMINICAN REPUBLIC.
Báez Evertsz, Franc, 1948- Braceros haitianos en la República Dominicana /. [Santo Domingo] , c1986. 354 p. : DDC 331.6/2/729407293 19
HD8218.5 .B34 1986   *NYPL [JLE 88-5011]*

Matteis, Arthur de. Le massacre de 1937, ou Une succession immobilière internationale /. Port-au-Prince, Haiti , 1987. 68 p. ;
NYPL [Sc D 88-520]

HAITIANS - EMPLOYMENT - DOMINICAN REPUBLIC.
Plant, Roger. Sugar and modern slavery . London , Atlantic Highlands, N.J. , c1987. xiv, 177 p. : ISBN 0-86232-572-2 : DDC 331.7/6361/097293 19
HD8039.S852 D657 1987
NYPL [Sc D 87-1240]

HAITIANS - FLORIDA.
Icart, Jean-Claude. Négriers d'eux-mêmes . Montréal, Québec, Canada , 1987. 188 p. ; ISBN 2-920862-06-5   *NYPL [Sc D 88-396]*

HAITIANS - UNITED STATES - HISTORY - 19TH CENTURY.
Hunt, Alfred N., 1941- Haiti's influence on antebellum America . Baton Rouge , c1988. xiv, 196 p. : ISBN 0-8071-1370-0 DDC 973/.049697294 19
E184.H27 H86 1987   *NYPL [Sc E 88-131]*

Haiti's influence on antebellum America . Hunt, Alfred N., 1941- Baton Rouge , c1988. xiv, 196 p. : ISBN 0-8071-1370-0 DDC 973/.049697294 19
E184.H27 H86 1987   *NYPL [Sc E 88-131]*

Ḥājj 'Umar ibn Sa'īd al-Fūti, 1794?-1864.
[Bayān mā waqa'a. French & Arabic]
Voilà ce qui est arrivé : Bayān mā waqa'a d'al Ḥāǧǧ 'Umar al-Fūti : plaidoyer pour une guerre sainte en Afrique de l'Ouest au XIXe siècle / Sidi Mohamed Mahibou, Jean-Louis Triaud. Paris : Editions du Centre national de la recherche scientifique, 1983. 261 p., [57] p. of plates : facsims., map ; 27 cm. (Fontes historiae africanae. Series arabica . 8) At head of title: Centre régional de publication de Paris. Translation of: Bayān mā waqa'a. Arabic text (57 p.) in facsimile. "Publié avec le concours de la Maison des sciences de l'homme-Paris." Bibliography: p. 239-250. ISBN 2-222-03216-4
1. Ḥājj 'Umar ibn Sa'id al-Fūti, 1794?-1864. 2. Mali empire - History - 19th century. 3. Jihad. 4. Islam - Mali Empire. I. Mahibou, Sidi Mohamed. II. Triaud, Jean Louis. III. Centre national de la recherche scientifique (France). IV. Centre national de la recherche scientifique (France). Centre regional de publications de Paris. V. Title. VI. Title: Bayān mā waqa'a. VII. Series.   *NYPL [Sc F 88-211]*

ḤĀJJ 'UMAR IBN SA'ĪD AL-FŪTĪ, 1794?-1864.
Ḥājj 'Umar ibn Sa'īd al-Fūtī, 1794?-1864. [Bayān mā waqa'a. French & Arabic.] Voilà ce qui est arrivé . Paris , 1983. 261 p., [57] p. of plates : ISBN 2-222-03216-4
NYPL [Sc F 88-211]

Halasa, Malu. Mary McLeod Bethune / Malu Halasa. New York : Chelsea House Publishers, c1989. 111 p. : ill ; 25 cm. (Black Americans of achievement) Includes index. Traces the life and achievements of the black eduacator who fought bigotry and racial injustice and sought equality for blacks in the areas of education and political rights. Bibliography: p. 108. ISBN 1-555-46574-9 DDC 370/.92/4 B 92 19
1. Bethune, Mary McLeod, 1875-1955 - Juvenile literature. 2. Afro-Americans - Biography - Juvenile literature. 3. Teachers - United States - Biography - Juvenile literature. I. Title. II. Series.
E185.97.B34 H35 1989 NYPL [Sc E 88-616]

Halderman, John M. An analysis of continued semi-nomadism of the Kaputiei Maasai group ranches [microform] : sociological and ecological factors / by John M. Halderman. [Nairobi] : Institute for Development Studies, University of Nairobi, [between 1972 and 1974]. 35 p. ; 30 cm. (Discussion paper / Institute for Development Studies, University of Nairobi . no. 152) "Revised version of I.D.S. working paper no. 28 issued in March 1972." Bibliography: p.33. Microfilm. New York: New York Public Library, 1982. 1 microfilm reel; 35 mm. (MN *ZZ-23051) DDC 307.7/2/0967627
1. Masai. 2. Migration, Internal - Kenya. I. Series: Nairobi. University. Institute for Development Studies. Discussion paper, no. 152. II. Title.
DT433.542 .H34
NYPL [Sc Micro R-4108 no.25]

Haley, Alex. A different kind of Christmas / Alex Haley. 1st ed. New York : Doubleday, 1988. 101 p. ; 20 cm. ISBN 0-385-26043-1 : DDC 813/.54 19
1. Slavery - United States - Anti-slavery movements - Fiction. 2. Underground railroad - Fiction. 3. Christmas stories, American. I. Title.
PS3558.A3575 D54 1988
NYPL [Sc C 89-38]

HALF-BREED INDIANS. see INDIANS - MIXED BLOODS.

A half century of freedom of the Negro in Ohio. Joiner, William A., 1868- Xenia, Ohio [1915] 134 p.   *NYPL [Sc Rare F 89-7]*

HALIFAX (NORTH CAROLINA) - GENEALOGY.
Stephenson, Anne N. Informal history of the Black people I have known in Halifax /. [Halifax] c1978. 99 p. :
NYPL [Sc D 88-1209]

Ḥalim Barakāt. see Barakat, Halim Isber.

Halima must not die . Onadipe, Kola. Ijebu-Ode, Nigeria , c1980. 71 p. : ISBN 978-17-8026-6
NYPL [Sc D 88-1368]

Halimoja, Yusuf J.
Bunge la jamhuri ya muungano / kimeandikwa na Yusuf Halimoja. Dar es Salaam : Mwangaza Publishers, 1985. 64 p. : ill., ports. ; 18 cm. (Tanzania inavyojitawala . 18)
1. Legislative bodies - Tanzania. 2. Swahili language - Texts. I. Title. II. Series.   *NYPL [Sc C 89-61]*

Nchi yetu Tanzania / kimeandikwa na Yusuf Halimoja. Dar es Salaam : Mwangaza Publishers, 1981. 70 p. : ill. ; 20 cm. (Tanzania inavyojitawala . 1)
1. Swahili language - Texts. I. Title. II. Series.
NYPL [Sc C 89-55]

Uhusiano na nchi za nje / kimeandikwa na Yusuf Halimoja. Dar es Salaam : Mwangaza Publishers, 1981. 60 p. : ill., ports. ; 20 cm. (Tanzania inavyojitawala . 16)
1. Swahili language - Texts. 2. Tanzania - Foreign relations. I. Title. II. Series.   *NYPL [Sc C 89-60]*

Halisi, Clyde. Kitabu [microform] . Los Angeles [1972?] 13 p. ;   *NYPL [Sc Micro F-10979]*

Hall & Company. see Hall (G. K.) & Company.

Hall, Douglas. The Caribbean experience : an historical survey, 1450-1960 / Douglas Hall. Kingston : Heinemann Educational Books, 1982. xi, 146 p. : ill., maps ; 25 cm. (Heineman CXRC history) Includes index. Bibliography: p. 138-141. ISBN 0-435-98300-8
1. Caribbean area - History - Textbooks. I. Title. II. Series.   *NYPL [Sc E 87-670]*

Hall (G. K.) & Company. Miami, University of, Coral Gables, Fla. Cuban and Caribbean Library. Catalog of the Cuban and Caribbean Library, University of Miami, Coral Gables, Florida. Boston , 1977. 6 v. ; DDC 016.9729 Z1595 .M5 1977 F2161
NYPL [Pub. Cat. 78-1036]

Hall, H. Tom. (illus) Scott, Ann Herbert. Let's catch a monster. New York [1967] 1 v. (unpaged)
PZ7.S415 Le   *NYPL [Sc F 88-342]*

Hall, James. Makeba, Miriam. Makeba . New York , c1987. 249 p., [16] p. of plates : ISBN 0-453-00561-6 : DDC 784.5/0092/4 B 19
ML420.M16 A3 1987   *NYPL [Sc E 88-193]*

Hall, Richard, 1925- My life with Tiny : a biography of Tiny Rowland / Richard Hall. London ; Boston : Faber and Faber, 1987. 256, [4] p. of plates : ill., facsim., ports. ; 22 cm. Includes index. ISBN 0-571-14737-2
1. Rowland, Tiny. 2. Businessmen - Great Britain - Biography. 3. Businessmen - Zimbabwe - Biography. I. Title.   *NYPL [Sc D 88-515]*

Hall, Susan J. Africa in U. S. schools, K-12 [microform] : a survey / Susan J. Hall. New York : African-American Institute, c1978. 39 p. ; 22 cm. Includes bibliographical references. Microfilm. New York: New York Public Library, 1982. 1 microfilm reel; 35 mm. (MN *ZZ-22890)
1. Africa - Study and teaching - United States. I. Title.
NYPL [Sc Micro R-4202 no. 2]

Hall, Wade H. Johnson, Lyman T., 1906- The rest of the dream . Lexington, Ky. , c1988. xiv, 230 p., [8] p. of plates : ISBN 0-8131-1674-0 (alk. paper) : DDC 976.9/00496073024 B 19
E185.97.J693 A3 1988 NYPL [Sc E 89-211]

Hallerloogy's ride with Santa Claus. Babcock, Bernie Smade, 1868-1962. Perry, Ark., c1943. 48 p.
PZ7.B12 Hal   *NYPL [Sc D 88-1285]*

Hallett, George.
The photographs of George Hallett. Amsterdam : Aschenbach Galerie, c1988. [20] p. : ill. ; 30 cm. Text in English, German and Dutch. ISBN 90-72422-01-5
1. Hallett, George - Exhibitions. 2. Photography, Artistic - Exhibitions. I. Title.
NYPL [Sc F 89-70]

HALLETT, GEORGE - EXHIBITIONS.
Hallett, George. The photographs of George Hallett. Amsterdam , c1988. [20] p. : ISBN 90-72422-01-5   *NYPL [Sc F 89-70]*

HALLOWEEN - JUVENILE FICTION.
Glendinning, Sally. Jimmy and Joe meet a Halloween witch. Champaign, Ill. [1971] 40 p. ISBN 0-8116-4705-6 DDC [E]
PZ7.G4829 Jq   *NYPL [Sc D 88-1474]*

Scott, Ann Herbert. Let's catch a monster. New York [1967] 1 v. (unpaged)
PZ7.S415 Le   *NYPL [Sc F 88-342]*

Halpern, Daniel, 1945- Reading the fights /. New York , c1988. viii, 305 p. : ISBN 0-8050-0510-2 : DDC 796.8/3 19
GV1121 .R4 1988   *NYPL [Sc D 88-899]*

Halter, Marilyn. Lobban, Richard. Historical dictionary of the Republic of Cape Verde /. Metuchen, N.J. , 1988. xix, 171 p. ; ISBN 0-8108-2087-0 DDC 966/.57/00321 19
DT613.5 .L62 1988b NYPL [Sc D 88-1311]

Hama, Boubou, 1906- Kotia-Nima : rencontre avec l'Europe / Boubou Hama. [Niamey?] : République du Niger,c1969, c1968. 3 v. ; 21

cm. "Publication de la République du Niger." Vol. 3
has sub-title: Dialogue avec l'Occident.
*1. France - Colonies - Africa. 2. Niger - Politics and
government. I. Title.*   ***NYPL [Sc D 88-210]***

Hamandishe, Nicholas Phinias. Nyoka huru
haizvirumi / N. Ph. Hamandishe ; mufananidzo
naHassam Musa. Harare : Longman Zimbabwe,
1984. 91 p. ; 19 cm.   ISBN 0-582-61173-3
1. Shona language - Texts. I. Title.
NYPL [Sc C 88-365]

Hamber, S. Greenwood, R. (Robert)
Emancipation to emigration /. London , New
York , 1980 (1985 printing) viii, 152 p. :   ISBN
0-333-28148-9 (pbk.)   DDC 972.9 19
F1621 .G74 1984   ***NYPL [Sc E 88-526]***

Hambone's meditations. Alley, J. P. The
meditations of "Hambone". Memphis, Tenn.
[1918] 104 p.   ***NYPL [Sc Rare C 89-28]***

Hamburger Beiträge zur Afrika-Kunde.
(26) Brüne, Stefan. Athiopien --
Unterentwicklung und radikale
Militärherrschaft . Hamburg , 1986. viii, 372
p. :   ISBN 3-923519-63-X
NYPL [L-11 2640 Bd. 26]

Hamidou, Sidikou A. Atlas du Niger /. Paris ,
c1980. 64 p. :   ISBN 2-85258-151-5 :   DDC
912/.6626 19
G2660 .A8 1980   ***NYPL [Sc F 84-232]***

Hamilton, Virginia.
Anthony Burns : the defeat and triumph of a
fugitive slave / by Virginia Hamilton. New
York : A.A. Knopf, c1988. xiii, 193 p. ; 22 cm.
Includes index. A biography of the slave who escaped
to Boston in 1854, was arrested at the instigation of his
owner, and whose trial caused a furor between
abolitionists and those determined to enforce the
Fugitive Slave Acts. Bibliography: p. 187-189.   ISBN
0-394-88185-0   DDC 973.6/6/0924 B 92 19
*1. Burns, Anthony, 1834-1862 - Juvenile literature. 2.
Fugitive slaves - United States - Biography - Juvenile
literature. 3. Slavery - United States - Anti-slavery
movements - Juvenile literature. I. Title.*
E450.B93 H36 1988   ***NYPL [Sc D 88-1157]***

In the beginning : creation stories from around
the world / told by Virginia Hamilton ;
illustrated by Barry Moser.1st ed. San Diego :
Harcourt Brace Jovanovich, c1988. xi, 161 p. :
col. ill. ; 27 cm. An illustrated collection of
twenty-five myths from various parts of the world
explaining the creation of the world. Bibliography: p.
159-161.   ISBN 0-15-238740-4   DDC 291.2/4 19
1. Creation in literature. I. Moser, Barry. II. Title.
BL226 .H35 1988   ***NYPL [JFF 89-62]***

A white romance / Virginia Hamilton. New
York : Philomel Books, 1987. 191 p. ; 22 cm.
As her all-black high school becomes more racially
mixed, Talley befriends a white girl who shares her
passion for running and becomes romantically involved
with a drug dealer.   ISBN 0-399-21213-2 :   DDC
[Fic] 19
1. Afro-American youth - Fiction. I. Title.
PZ7.H1828 Wh 1987   ***NYPL [Sc D 88-221]***

**HAMITO-SEMITIC LANGUAGES -
GRAMMAR, COMPARATIVE - NILO-
HAMITIC.**
Hohenberger, Johannes. Semitische und
hamitische Wortst"amme im Nilo-Hamitischen .
Berlin , 1988. xxii, 310 p. ;   ISBN 3-496-00960-8
NYPL [Sc E 88-542]

Hammond, James Henry, 1807-1864.
Gov. Hammond's letters on southern slavery :
addressed to Thomas Clarkson, the English
abolitionist. Charleston : Walker & Burke, 1845.
32 p. ; 26 cm.
*1. Slavery - United States - Controversial literature -
1845. 2. Slavery - Justification. I. Clarkson, Thomas,
1760-1846. II. Title. III. Title: Letters on southern
slavery.*   ***NYPL [Sc Rare C 89-24]***

Secret and sacred : the diaries of James Henry
Hammond, a southern slaveholder / edited by
Carol Bleser. New York : Oxford University
Press, 1988. xxix, 342 p., [2] leaves of plates :
ill. ; 24 cm. Includes index. Bibliography: p. 328-330.
ISBN 0-19-505308-7   DDC 975.7/03/0924 B 19
*1. Hammond, James Henry, 1807-1864 - Diaries. 2.
Slaveholders - South Carolina - Diaries. 3. Plantation
life - South Carolina - History - 19th century. 4.
Slavery - South Carolina - History - 19th century. 5.
South Carolina - Race relations. I. Bleser, Carol K.
Rothrock. II. Title.*
F273 .H24 1988   ***NYPL [Sc E 88-513]***

**HAMMOND, JAMES HENRY, 1807-1864 -
DIARIES.**
Hammond, James Henry, 1807-1864. Secret
and sacred . New York , 1988. xxix, 342 p., [2]
leaves of plates :   ISBN 0-19-505308-7   DDC
975.7/03/0924 B 19
F273 .H24 1988   ***NYPL [Sc E 88-513]***

Hammond, Steven T. A collection of poems and
short stories / Steven T. Hammond. 1st ed.
New York : Vantage Press, c1987. ix, 32 p. ;
21 cm.   ISBN 0-533-07287-5
I. Title.   ***NYPL [Sc D 88-1175]***

Hampaté Ba, Amadou. see Ba, Amadou
Hampaté.

Hampson, Joe. Social development and rural
fieldwork . Zimbabwe [1986]. 96 p. :
NYPL [Sc D 88-1153]

Hampton, Charles. A family outing in Africa /
[by] Charles and Janie Hampton and their
children. London : Macmillan, 1988. 267 p.,
[16] p. of plates : col. ill. ; 23 cm. Includes
bibliography.   ISBN 0-333-44190-7 :   DDC
916/.04328 19
*1. Africa - Description and travel - 1977-. I. Hampton,
Janie. II. Title.*
DT12.25   ***NYPL [Sc D 88-1274]***

HAMPTON INSTITUTE - HISTORY.
Hunter, Wilma King. Coming of age
[microform] . 1982. 343 leaves.
NYPL [Sc Micro R-4688]

Hampton, Janie. Hampton, Charles. A family
outing in Africa /. London , 1988. 267 p., [16]
p. of plates :   ISBN 0-333-44190-7 :   DDC
916/.04328 19
DT12.25   ***NYPL [Sc D 88-1274]***

**HAND WEAVING - AFRICA, WEST -
EXHIBITIONS.**
Gilfoy, Peggy Stoltz. Patterns of life .
Washington, D.C. , c1987. 95 p. :   ISBN
0-87474-475-X (alk. paper) :   DDC
746.1/4/088042 19
NK8989 .G55 1987   ***NYPL [Sc F 88-166]***

Handbook for research in American history .
Prucha, Francis Paul. Lincoln , c19. xiii, 289
p. ;   ISBN 0-8032-3682-4 (alk. paper)   DDC 016.973
19
Z1236 .P78 1987 E178   ***NYPL [Sc D 88-545]***

**A handbook of vocational-technical education for
Nigeria /.** Osuala, Esogwa C. Oruowulu-Obosi,
Anambra State, Nigeria , 1987. x, 173 p. ;
ISBN 0-9782341-9-1   ***NYPL [Sc D 88-729]***

Handbook to British Central Africa /. Johnston,
Harry Hamilton, Sir, 1858-1927. Blantyre
[Malawi] , 1985. viii, 111 p. :
NYPL [Sc D 88-1006]

**Handbuch der Nama-Sprache in
Deutsch-Südwestafrika /.** Planert, Wilhelm,
1882- Berlin , 1905. 104 p. ;
NYPL [Sc F 89-147]

**HANDICAPPED - SERVICES FOR -
ZIMBABWE.**
Addison, Joan. A historical survey of facilities
for handicapped people in Zimbabwe /. Harare,
Zimbabwe [1986] 36 p. :
NYPL [Sc F 88-266]

HANDICAPPED - ZIMBABWE.
Farquhar, June. Jairos Jiri . Gweru , 1987. 92
p. :   ISBN 0-86922-416-6   ***NYPL [Sc D 89-38]***

**HANDICRAFT - BOTSWANA - RESEARCH -
METHODOLOGY.**
Mackenzie, Bob. A survey of handicrafts in
North East District, 1980 . Gaborone , 1980.
61 p. :   ***NYPL [Sc F 88-2]***

HANDICRAFT - MALI - MOPTI REGION.
Gardi, Bernhard. Ein Markt wie Mopti . Basel ,
1985. 387 p. :   ISBN 3-85977-175-2   DDC
745/.0966/23 19
TT119.M34 G37 1985   ***NYPL [Sc E 87-494]***

HANDICRAFT - NIGERIA - EXHIBITIONS.
Okuboyejo, Betti. Adire, a living craft /.
[Nigeria] , c1987. 55 p. :
NYPL [Sc C 89-16]

Hanks, Robert, 1923- Southern Africa and
Western security / Robert J. Hanks. 1st ed.
Cambridge, Mass. : Institute for Foreign Policy
Analysis, c1983. vii, 74 p. : ill. ; 23 cm. (Foreign
policy report) Includes bibliographical references.
ISBN 0-89549-055-2 :   DDC 355/.033268 19
1. Africa, Southern - Strategic aspects. 2. Africa,

*Southern - Politics and government - 1975-. 3. Africa,
Southern - Foreign relations - 1975-. I. Title.*
UA855.6 .H36 1983   ***NYPL [Sc D 85-489]***

Hanley, Sally. A. Philip Randolph / Sally
Hanley. New York : Chelsea House, [1988],
c1989. 110 p. : ill. ; 25 cm. (Black Americans of
achievement) Includes index. A biography of the civil
rights activist who organized the Brotherhood of
Sleeping Car Porters, which acted as a labor union for
Pullman car porters. Bibliography: p. 108.   ISBN
1-555-46607-9   DDC 323.4/092/4 92 19
*1. Randolph, A. Philip (Asa Philip), 1889- - Juvenile
literature. 2. Afro-Americans - Biography - Juvenile
literature. 3. Afro-Americans - Civil rights - Juvenile
literature. I. Title. II. Series.*
E185.97.R27 H36 1989   ***NYPL [Sc E 88-617]***

**Hansberry, Lorraine, 1930-1965.
RAISIN IN THE SUN.**
Felber, Monika. Stundenblätter Hansberry "
A raisin in the sun" /. Stuttgard , 1986. 85
p. :   ISBN 3-12-925163-4
NYPL [Sc D 88-631]

Hansel and Gretel (in the 1980's) Grant, Micki.
Croesus and the witch /. New York, N.Y. ,
1984. 67, [119] p. :   ISBN 0-88145-024-3
NYPL [Sc F 88-205]

Hansen, Holger Bernt. Uganda now . Athens ,
London , 1988. 376 p. :   ISBN 0-85255-315-3
(cased)   DDC 967.6/104 19
HN800.U35   ***NYPL [Sc D 88-1436]***

Hansen, Joseph, 1923- Pretty boy dead : a novel
/ by Joseph Hansen.1st ed. San Francisco :
Gay Sunshine Press, 1984. 203 p. ; 22 cm.
Previously published in 1968 as: known homosexual,
and in 1977 as: St ranger to himself.   ISBN
0-917342-48-8 :   DDC 813/.54 19
*1. Gay men - California - Fiction. 2. Afro-American
gays - California - Fiction. I. Title. II. Title: Known
homosexual. III. Title: Stranger to himself.*
PS3558.A513 P7 1984   ***NYPL [JFD 87-9537]***

Hansen, Joyce. Out from this place / Joyce
Hansen. New York : Walker, 1988. vi, 135 p. ;
22 cm. (Walker's American history series for young
people) Sequel to: Which way freedom? A
fourteen-year-old black girl tries to find a fellow
ex-slave, who had joined the Union army during the
Civil War, during the confusing times after the
emancipation of the slaves.   ISBN 0-8027-6816-4
DDC [Fic] 19
*1. Afro-Americans - History - 1863-1877 - Juvenile
Fiction. 2. Reconstruction - Juvenile fiction. I. Title. II.
Series.*
PZ7.H19825 Ou 1988   ***NYPL [Sc D 88-1321]***

Hansen, Karen Tranberg. Distant companions :
servants and employers in Zambia, 1900-1985 /
Karen Tranberg Hansen. Ithaca : Cornell
University Press, 1989. xv, 321 p. : ill. ; 24 cm.
Includes bibliographical references and index.   ISBN
0-8014-2217-5 (alk. paper)   DDC
331.7/6164046/096894 19
*1. Domestics - Zambia - History - 20th century. 2.
Sexual division of labor - Zambia - History - 20th
century. 3. Master and servant - Zambia - History -
20th century. 4. Zambia - Social conditions. 5. Zambia -
Colonial influence. I. Title.*
HD6072.2.Z33 H36 1989
NYPL [Sc E 89-215]

Hanson, John Wagner.
(joint author) Ferns, George W. Secondary level
teachers: supply and demand in Liberia. [East
Lansing, c1970] xii, 116 p.
LB2833.4.L7 F4   ***NYPL [JFM 72-62 no. 6]***

Secondary level teachers: supply and demand in
Botswana [by] John W. Hanson. [East Lansing,
Institute for International Studies in Education,
Michigan State University, 1969, c1968] x, 97,
[2] p. illus. 28 cm. (Report on the supply of
secondary level teachers in English-speaking Africa. no.
1) On cover: Overseas Liaison Committee of the
American Council on Education. Bibliography: p. [98]
*1. High school teachers - Supply and demand -
Botswana. I. American Council on Education. Overseas
Liaison Committee. II. Title. III. Series.*
LB2833.4.B55 H3   ***NYPL [JFM 72-62 no. 1]***

Secondary level teachers: supply and demand in
Ghana [by] John W. Hanson. [East Lansing,
Institute for International Studies in Education
and the African Studies Center, Michigan State
University, 1971] xv, 130 p. 28 cm. (Report on
the supply of secondary level teachers in
English-speaking Africa. no. 12) On cover: Overseas
Liaison Committee of American Council on Education.

Hanson, John Wagner. *(cont.)*

Bibliography: p. 129-130.
*1. High school teachers - Supply and demand - Ghana.
I. American Council on Education. Overseas Liaison
Committee. II. Title. III. Series.*
NYPL [JFM 72-62 no. 12]

Secondary level teachers: supply and demand in
Malawi [by] John W. Hanson. [East Lansing,
Institute for International Studies in Education
and the African Studies Center, Michigan State
University, 1969] xi, 73, [2] p. 28 cm. (Report on
the supply of secondary level teachers in
English-speaking Africa. no. 33) Bibliography: p. [75]
*1. Teachers - Supply and demand - Malawi. I.
Michigan. State University, East Lansing. Institute for
International Studies in Education. II. Michigan. State
University, East Lansing. African Studies Center. III.
Title. IV. Series.*
LB2833.4.M3 H3 **NYPL [JFM 72-62 no. 3]**

Secondary level teachers: supply and demand in
Nigeria [by] Segun Adesina [and others] John
W. Hanson, contributor and editor. [East
Lansing, Institute for International Studies in
Education, Michigan State University, c1973] 1
v. (various pagings) 28 cm. (Report on the supply
of secondary level teachers in English-speaking Africa.
country study no. 15) Includes bibliography. DDC
331.1/26
*1. High school teachers - Nigeria - Supply and demand.
I. Adesina, Segun. II. Title. III. Series.*
LB2833.4.N6 H36 **NYPL [Sc F 88-151]**

Secondary level teachers: supply and demand in
Sierra Leone [by] John W. Hanson, George W.
Ferns [and] Victor E. King. [East Lansing,
Institute for International Studies in Education,
Michigan State University, c1970] viii, 85 p. 28
cm. (Report on the supply of secondary level teachers
in English-speaking Africa. no. 11) Bibliography: p. 83.
*1. High school teachers - Supply and demand - Sierra
Leone. I. Ferns, Geroge W., joint author. II. King,
Victor E., joint author. III. Title. IV. Series.*
NYPL [JFM 72-62 no. 11]

Hanson, Peter E. (ill) Ferris, Jeri. Walking the
road to freedom . Minneapolis , 1987. 64 p. :
ISBN 0-87614-318-4 (lib. bdg.) : DDC
305.5/67/0924 B 92 19
E185.97.T8 F47 1987 **NYPL [Sc D 88-1046]**

Happy birthday everybody . Carma, Jemel. New
York, N. Y. [1988] [24] p. :
NYPL [Sc H 89-1]

Happy in the service of the Lord . Lornell, Kip,
1953- Urbana , c1988. x, 171 p., [30] p. of
plates : ISBN 0-252-01523-1 (alk. paper) DDC
783.7/08996073/0976819 19
ML3187 .L67 1988 **NYPL [Sc E 89-101]**

Harap, Louis. Dramatic encounters : the Jewish
presence in twentieth-century American drama,
poetry, and humor and the Black-Jewish literary
relationship / Louis Harap ; foreword by Jacob
Rader Marcus. New York : Greenwood Press,
c1987. xiv, 177 p. ; 25 cm. (Contributions in ethnic
studies, 0196-7088 . no. 20) "Published in cooperation
with the American Jewish Archives." Includes index.
Bibliography: p. [147]-162. ISBN 0-313-25388-9 (lib.
bdg. : alk. paper) DDC 810/.9/35203924 19
*1. Jews in literature - United States. 2. American
literature - 20th century - History and criticism. 3.
American drama - Jewish authors - History and
criticism. 4. American fiction - Jewish authors -
History and criticism. 5. Jewish wit and humor -
History and criticism. 6. United States - Race relations.
I. American Jewish Archives. II. Title. III. Series.*
PS173.J4 H294 1987 **NYPL [*PZB 87-5243]**

**HARARE (ZIMBABWE) - BUILDINGS,
STRUCTURES, ETC. - CATALOGS.**
Jackson, Peter, 1949- Historic buildings of
Harare, 1890-1940 /. Harare, Zimbabwe , 1986.
x, 134 p. : ISBN 0-908306-03-2 (pbk.) DDC
720/.96891 19
NA1596.6.R52 H375 1986
NYPL [Sc D 89-467]

Harbeson, John Willis, 1938- The Kenya little
general election [microform] : a study in
problems of urban political integration / John
W. Harbeson. Nairobi : Institute for
Development Studies, University College, 1967.
23 p. ; 33 cm. (Discussion paper/Institute for
Development Studies, University College, Nairobi. no.
52) Includes bibliographical references. Microform. New
York: New York Public Library, 1982. 1 microfilm reel;
35 mm. (MN *ZZ-23051)
*1. Elections - Kenya. 2. Kenya - Politics and
government. I. Series: Nairobi. University College.*

*Institute for Development Studies. Discussion paper, no.
52. II. Title.* **NYPL [Sc Micro R-4108 no. 31]**

Harbinson, Denis. Silvester, Peter J. A left hand
like God . London , c1988. 324 p. : ISBN
0-7043-2685-X : DDC 785.4 19
NYPL [JNE 89-16]

A hard road to glory . Ashe, Arthur. New York,
NY , 1988. 3 v. : ISBN 0-446-71006-7 DDC
796/.08996073 19
GV583 .A75 1988 **NYPL [IEC 89-1295]**

**HARDING, WARREN G. (WARREN
GAMALIEL), 1865-1923.**
Russell, Francis, 1910- The shadow of
Blooming Grove. New York [1968] xvi, 691 p.
DDC 973.91/4/0924 B
E786 .R95 **NYPL [Sc E 88-579]**

Hardman, Anna. Power, Jonathan, 1941- Western
Europe's migrant workers /. London , 1984. 35
p. : ISBN 0-08-030831-7 **NYPL [Sc F 88-231]**

Hare, Julia.
Crisis in Black sexual politics /. [San Francisco,
Calif.] c1989. iv, 184 p. ; ISBN 0-9613086-2-1
NYPL [Sc D 89-152]

Hare, Nathan. The endangered Black family .
San Francisco, CA , c1984. 192 p. ; ISBN
0-9613086-0-5 **NYPL [Sc C 88-307]**

Hare, Nathan.
Crisis in Black sexual politics /. [San Francisco,
Calif.] c1989. iv, 184 p. ; ISBN 0-9613086-2-1
NYPL [Sc D 89-152]

The endangered Black family : coping with the
unisexualization and coming extinction of the
Black race / by Nathan Hare and Julia Hare.
San Francisco, CA ; Black Think Tank, c1984.
192 p. ; 18 cm. (A Black male/female relationships
book ; no. 1) Includes bibliographical references.
ISBN 0-9613086-0-5
*1. Afro-Americans - Social life and customs. 2.
Afro-Americans - Marriage. 3. Afro-Americans -
Domestic relations. I. Hare, Julia. II. Black Think Tank.
III. Title.* **NYPL [Sc C 88-307]**

Hargreaves, John D. Decolonization in Africa /
John D. Hargreaves. London ; New York :
Longman, 1988. xvi, 263 p. : maps ; 22 cm.
(The Postwar world) Errata slip inserted. Includes
bibliographies and index. ISBN 0-582-49150-9 DDC
960/.32 19
*1. Decolonization - Africa. 2. Africa - History - 20th
century. I. Title. II. Series.*
DT29 .H37 1988 **NYPL [Sc D 89-315]**

Harlan, Louis R.
Booker T. Washington : the wizard of
Tuskegee, 1901-1915 / Louis R. Harlan. New
York : Oxford University Press, 1983. xiv, 548
p. : port. ; 24 cm. Includes bibliographical references
and index. ISBN 0-19-503202-0 : DDC 378/.111 B
19
*1. Washington, Booker T. 1856-1915. 2.
Afro-Americans - Biography. 3. Educators - United
States - Biography. I. Title.*
E185.97.W4 H373 1983
NYPL [Sc E 83-233]

Booker T. Washington and the "Atlanta
compromise" /. Sharpsburg, Md. , c1987. 13
p. : **NYPL [Sc F 88-386]**

Booker T. Washington in perspective : essays of
Louis R. Harlan / edited by Raymond W.
Smock. Jackson : University Press of
Mississippi, c1988. xii, 210 p., [8] p. of plates :
ill. ; 24 cm. Includes bibliographies and index. ISBN
0-87805-374-3 (alk. paper) DDC 378/.111 B 19
*1. Washington, Booker T. 1856-1915. 2.
Afro-Americans - Civil rights. 3. Afro-Americans -
Biography. 4. Educators - United States - Biography. I.
Smock, Raymond. II. Title.*
E185.97.W4 H36 1988 **NYPL [Sc E 89-217]**

(ed) Washington, Booker T. 1856-1915. The
Booker T. Washington papers. Urbana [1972- v.
NYPL [Sc B-Washington, B.]

The Harlem Fox . Walter, John C. (John
Christopher), 1933- Albany, N.Y. , c1989. xv,
287 p. : ISBN 0-88706-756-5 DDC
974.7/1043/0924 B 19
F128.5.J72 W35 1988 **NYPL [Sc E 89-107]**

HARLEM, NEW YORK (CITY)
New York (City). Housing Authority. Harlem,
1934. [New York, 1934] 20 p.
HD268.N5 N27 **NYPL [Sc G 88-30]**

**HARLEM, NEW YORK (CITY) - RELIGIOUS
LIFE AND CUSTOMS.**
Orsi, Robert A. The Madonna of 115th Street .
New Haven , c1985. xxiii, 287 p. : ISBN
0-300-03262-5 (alk. paper) DDC
263/.98/0895107471 19
BT660.N44 O77 1985
NYPL [IEE (Italians) 86-89]

**HARLEM, NEW YORK (CITY) - SOCIAL
CONDITIONS.**
Orsi, Robert A. The Madonna of 115th Street .
New Haven , c1985. xxiii, 287 p. : ISBN
0-300-03262-5 (alk. paper) DDC
263/.98/0895107471 19
BT660.N44 O77 1985
NYPL [IEE (Italians) 86-89]

The People of East Harlem [microform] . New
York , c1974. 90 p. :
NYPL [Sc Micro R-4137 no.12]

HARLEM (NEW YORK, N.Y.)
Howard-Howard, Margo, 1935- I was a white
slave in Harlem /. New York , c1988. vii, 177
p., [8] p. of plates : ISBN 0-941423-14-X (pbk.) :
DDC 306.7/43/0924 19
HQ77.8.H68 A3 1988 **NYPL [JFE 89-340]**

**HARLEM (NEW YORK, N.Y.) -
DESCRIPTION - GUIDE-BOOKS.**
Bailey, A. Peter. Harlem today . New York ,
c1986. viii, 55 p. : ISBN 0-936073-01-2 (pbk.) :
DDC 917.47/1 19
F128.68.H3 B3 1986 **NYPL [Sc D 88-1402]**

HARLEM (NEW YORK, N.Y.) - FICTION.
Edwards-Yearwood, Grace. In the shadow of
the Peacock /. New York , c1988. 279 p. ;
ISBN 0-07-019037-2 DDC 813/.54 19
PS3555.D99 I5 1988 **NYPL [JFE 88-4421]**

Himes, Chester B., 1909- A rage in Harlem /.
London , New York , 1985, c1957. 159 p. ;
ISBN 0-85031-618-9 **NYPL [Sc D 88-692]**

Himes, Chester B., 1909- The real cool killers/.
London , New York , 1985, c1958. 159 p. ;
ISBN 0-85031-615-4 **NYPL [Sc D 88-280]**

McKay, Claude, 1890-1948. Home to Harlem /.
Boston , 1987, c1928. xxvi, 340 p. ; ISBN
1-555-53023-0 (alk. paper) : DDC 813/.52 19
PS3525.A24785 H6 1987
NYPL [Sc D 88-544]

**HARLEM (NEW YORK, N.Y.) - JUVENILE
FICTION.**
Myers, Walter Dean, 1937- Scorpions /. New
York , c1988. 216 p. ; ISBN 0-06-024364-3 :
DDC [Fic] 19
PZ7.M992 Sc 1988 **NYPL [Sc D 88-1146]**

The Harlem renaissance : revaluations / [edited
by] Amritjit Singh, William S. Shiver, Stanley
Brodwin. New York : Garland, 1989. xv, 342
p. ; 22 cm. (Garland reference library of the
humanities. vol. 837) Critical studies on Black life and
culture ; vol. 17 Papers presented at a conference held
May 2-4, 1985, and sponsored by the Hofstra Cultural
Center. Includes bibliographical references and index.
ISBN 0-8240-5739-2 (alk. paper) DDC
810/.9/896073 19
*1. American literature - Afro-American authors -
History and criticism - Congresses. 2. American
literature - New York (N.Y.) - History and criticism -
Congresses. 3. American literature - 20th century -
History and criticism - Congresses. 4. Harlem
Renaissance - Congresses. 5. Afro-American arts - New
York (N.Y.) - Congresses. I. Singh, Amritjit. II. Shiver,
William S. III. Brodwin, Stanley. IV. Hofstra Cultural
Center. V. Series: Critical studies on Black life and
culture, v. 17.*
PS153.N5 H264 1989 **NYPL [Sc D 89-591]**

HARLEM RENAISSANCE.
Achode, Codjo. The Negro renaissance from
America back to Africa . Ann Arbor, Mich. ,
1986. viii, 306 p. : **NYPL [Sc D 89-291]**

Baker, Houston A. Afro-American poetics .
Madison, Wis. , c1988. x, 201 p. : ISBN
0-299-11500-3 : DDC 810/.9/896073 19
PS153.N5 B22 1988 **NYPL [Sc D 88-1356]**

Hull, Gloria T. Color, sex, and poetry .
Bloomington , c1987. xi, 240 p. : ISBN
0-253-34974-5 DDC 811/.52/099287 19
PS153.N5 H84 1987 **NYPL [Sc E 88-72]**

Reid, Margaret Ann, 1940- A rhetorical
analysis of selected Black protest poetry of the
Harlem Renaissance and of the sixties /. , 1981.
284 p. [i.e. 216] p. **NYPL [Sc D 88-264]**

Rollwagen, Elsa. La Renaissance noire . 1978.
iii, 149 leaves ;   *NYPL [Sc F 88-280]*

Wintz, Cary D., 1943- Black culture and the
Harlem Renaissance /. Houston, Tex. , 1988.
277 p. ;   ISBN 0-89263-267-4 :   DDC
810/.9/896073 19
PS153.N5 W57 1988   NYPL [Sc E 89-106]

HARLEM RENAISSANCE - CONGRESSES.
The Harlem renaissance . New York , 1989. xv,
342 p. ;   ISBN 0-8240-5739-2 (alk. paper)   DDC
810/.9/896073 19
PS153.N5 H264 1989   NYPL [Sc D 89-591]

Harlem today /. Bailey, A. Peter. New York,
c1986. viii, 55 p. :   ISBN 0-936073-01-2 (pbk.) :
DDC 917.47/1 19
F128.68.H3 B3 1986   NYPL [Sc D 88-1402]

Harlem, 1934. New York (City). Housing
Authority. [New York, 1934] 20 p.
HD268.N5 N27   NYPL [Sc G 88-30]

Harms, Robert. Games against nature : an
eco-cultural history of the Nunu of equatorial
Africa / Robert Harms. Cambridge
[Cambridgeshire] ; New York : Cambridge
University Press, 1987. xi, 276 p. : ill. ; 24 cm.
(Studies in environment and history) Bibliography: p.
259-265.   ISBN 0-521-34373-9   DDC 967/.24 19
1. Nunu (African people). 2. Human ecology - Congo
(Brazzaville). I. Title. II. Series.
DT546.245.N86 H37 1987
NYPL [Sc E 88-192]

Harold Washington . Roberts, Naurice. Chicago ,
1988. 30 p. :   ISBN 0-516-03657-2   DDC
977.3/1100496073024 B 92 19
F548.52.W36 R63 1988
NYPL [Sc E 88-501]

Harper, Frances Ellen Watkins, 1825-1911.
Iola Leroy, or, Shadows uplifted / Frances
E.W. Harper ; with an introduction by Frances
Smith Foster. New York : Oxford University
Press, 1988. xxxix, 281 p. : port. ; 17 cm. (The
Schomburg library of nineteenth-century Black women
writers) Bibliography: xxxviii-xxxix. Reprint. Originally
published: 2nd ed. Philadelphia : Garrigues, 1893.
ISBN 0-19-505240-4 (alk. paper)   DDC 813/.3
19
1. Afro-Americans - Fiction. I. Title. II. Title: Shadows
uplifted. III. Series.
PS1799.H7 I6 1988   NYPL [JFC 88-2190]

[Poems]
Complete poems of Frances E.W. Harper /
edited by Maryemma Graham. New York :
Oxford University Press, 1988. lx, 232 p. ; 17
cm. (The Schomburg library of nineteenth-century
Black women writers) Reprinted from various
sources. Bibliography: p. 229-232.   ISBN
0-19-505244-7 (alk. paper)   DDC 811/.3 19
I. Graham, Maryemma. II. Title. III. Series.
PS1799.H7 A17 1988   NYPL [JFC 88-2147]

Harper's family library .
(35-36) Lander, Richard, 1804-1834. Journal of
an expedition to explore the course and
termination of the Niger . New York , 1832. 2
v. :   *NYPL [Sc Rare C 89-35]*

**HARPERS FERRY (W. VA.) - HISTORY -
JOHN BROWN'S RAID, 1859.**
Nolan, Jeanette Covert, 1896- John Brown /.
New York , 1968, c1950. 181 p. :
NYPL [Sc D 88-665]

Harriet Beecher Stowe /. Jakoubek, Robert E.
New York , c1989. 111 p. :   ISBN 1-555-46680-X
DDC 813/.3 B 92 19
PS2956.J35 1989   NYPL [Sc E 89-144]

Harriet's daughter /. Philip, Marlene Nourbese.
Toronto, Ontario , 1988. 150 p. ;
NYPL [Sc C 89-109]

Harris, Abram Lincoln, 1899-1963. Race,
radicalism, and reform : selected papers /
Abram L. Harris ; edited with an introduction
by William Darity, Jr. New Brunswick, U.
S.A. : Transaction Publishers, c1989. viii, 521
p. ; 24 cm. "Bibliography of the works of Abram
Lincoln Harris, Jr."--P. 509-513. Includes bibliographies
and index.   ISBN 0-88738-210-X   DDC 305.8/96073
19
1. Mill, John Stuart, 1806-1873. 2. Harris, Abram
Lincoln, 1899-1963. 3. Afro-Americans - Economic
conditions. 4. Marxian economics. 5. Capitalism. 6.
United States - Race relations. I. Darity, William A.,
1953-. II. Title.
E185.8 .H27 1989   NYPL [Sc E 89-166]

HARRIS, ABRAM LINCOLN, 1899-1963.
Harris, Abram Lincoln, 1899-1963. Race,
radicalism, and reform . New Brunswick, U.
S.A., c1989. viii, 521 p. ;   ISBN 0-88738-210-X
DDC 305.8/96073 19
E185.8 .H27 1989   NYPL [Sc E 89-166]

Harris, Fred R. United States. Kerner
Commission. The Kerner report . New York,
N.Y. , 1988. xxvi, 513 p. ;
NYPL [Sc D 89-604]

Harris, Fred R., 1930- Quiet riots . New York ,
1988. xiii, 223 p. ;   ISBN 0-394-57473-7 :   DDC
305.5/69/0973 19
HV4045 .Q54 1988   NYPL [JLD 89-239]

Harris, James H., 1952- Black ministers and laity
in the urban church : an analysis of political
and social expectations / James H. Harris.
Lanham, MD : University Press of America,
c1987. xi, 133 p. : ill. ; 23 cm. Includes index.
Bibliography: p. 97-104.   ISBN 0-8191-5823-2 (alk.
paper) :   DDC 253/.2/08996073 19
1. City churches. 2. Afro-American churches. 3.
Afro-American clergy. I. Title.
BR563.N4 B575 1987   NYPL [Sc D 89-127]

Harris, Joel Chandler, 1848-1908. Rees, Ennis.
Brer Rabbit and his tricks. New York [1967] 1
v. (unpaged)
PZ8.3.R254 Br   NYPL [Sc E 88-530]

Harris, John, librarian. Rapport sur la
coopération inter-universitaire dans le domaine
de l'impression et l'édition [microform] / par
John Harris. 1961. 12 p. ; 30 cm. At head of title:
La coopération inter-universitaire en Afrique
occidentale, séminaire international sous les auspices de
l'University College de Sierra Leone, Fourah Bay
College et du Congrès pour la liberté de la culture.
Freetown, 11-16 décembre 1961. Microfilm. New York:
New York Public Library, 1982. 1 microfilm reel; 35
mm. (MN *ZZ-24640)
1. University presses - Africa, West - Addresses, essays,
lectures. I. International Seminar on Inter-university
Co-operation in West Africa, Freetown, Sierra Leone,
1961. II. Title.
NYPL [Sc Micro R-4137 no. 44]

Harris, Joseph E., 1929- Repatriates and refugees
in a colonial society : the case of Kenya /
Joseph E. Harris. Washington, D.C. : Howard
University Press, 1987. ix, 201 p. ; 25 cm.
Includes index. Bibliography: p. 185-190.   ISBN
0-88258-148-1 :   DDC 304.8/676/2 19
1. Elite (Social sciences) - Kenya - History - Case
studies. 2. Freedmen - Kenya - History - Case studies.
3. Return migration - Kenya - History - Case studies. 4.
Refugees - Kenya - History - Case studies. 5. Kenya -
Colonization - History. I. Title.
HN793.Z9 E44 1987   NYPL [Sc E 87-558]

Harris, Leonard, 1948- The Philosophy of Alain
Locke . Philadelphia , 1989. x, 332 p. :   ISBN
0-87722-584-2 (alk. paper)   DDC 191 19
E185.97.L79 P48 1989   NYPL [Sc D 89-494]

Harris, Marie. A Gift of tongues . Athens ,
c1987. xii, 342 p. :   ISBN 0-8203-0952-4 (alk.
paper)   DDC 811/.5/09920693 19
PS153.M56 G54 1987   NYPL [Sc E 88-364]

Harris, Norman, 1951-
Connecting times : the sixties in Afro-American
fiction / Norman Harris. Jackson : University
Press of Mississippi, c1988. 197 p. ; 24 cm.
Includes bibliographies and index.   ISBN
0-87805-335-2 (alk. paper)   DDC
813/.54/093520396073 19
1. American fiction - Afro-American authors - History
and criticism. 2. American fiction - 20th century -
History and criticism. 3. Afro-Americans in literature.
4. Vietnamese Conflict, 1961-1975 - Literature and the
war. 5. Civil rights workers in literature. 6. Black power
in literature. I. Title.
PS153.N5 H27 1988   NYPL [Sc E 88-288]

Understanding the sixties [microform] : a study
of character development and theme in seven
recent Afro-American novels / by Norman
Harris. 1980. 202 leaves ; Thesis (Ph. D.)--Indiana
University, 1980. Bibliography: leaves 197-202.
Microfilm of typescript. Ann Arbor, Mich.: University
Microfilms International, 1981. 1 microfilm reel; 35
mm.
1. American fiction - Afro-American authors - History
and criticism. 2. American fiction - 20th century -
History and criticism. 3. Afro-Americans in literature.
4. Race relations in literature. I. Title.
NYPL [Sc Micro R-4680]

Harris, Phil.
[Reporting southern Africa. Spanish]
La información sobre Africa austral : cómo
informan desde el sur de Africa las agencias
occidentales de noticias / Phil Harris.1a ed.
Barcelona : Serbal ; Paris : Unesco, 1984. 188
p. : map ; 20 cm. (Colección de temas africanos .
19) Translation of: Reporting southern Africa.
Bibliography: p. [187]-188.   ISBN 92-3-301700-1
(Unesco)
1. News agencies. 2. Government and the press - South
Africa. 3. Government and the press - Zimbabwe. 4.
Zimbabwe - Politics and government. I. Title. II. Series.
NYPL [Sc D 88-614]

Harris, Wilson, 1921- The infinite rehearsal /
Wilson Harris. London : Faber and Faber,
1987. 88 p. ; 20 cm.   ISBN 0-571-14885-9 (pbk) :
DDC 823/.914 19
I. Title.
PR6058.A692   NYPL [Sc D 88-749]

Harrison, Alice W., 1929- The conservation of
archival and library materials : a resource guide
to audiovisual aids / by Alice W. Harrison,
Edward A. Collister, R. Ellen Willis. Metuchen,
N.J. : Scarecrow Press, 1982. xi, 190 p. ; 22
cm. Includes index.   ISBN 0-8108-1523-0   DDC
025.8/4 19
1. Library materials - Conservation and restoration -
Audio-visual aids - Handbooks, manuals, etc. 2.
Archival resources - Conservation and restoration -
Audio-visual aids - Handbooks, manuals, etc. I.
Collister, Edward A. II. Willis, R. Ellen. III. Title.
Z701 .H28   NYPL [Cons. Div. 84-252]

Harrison, Christopher, 1958- France and Islam in
West Africa, 1860-1960 / Christopher Harrison.
Cambridge [Cambridgeshire] ; New York :
Cambridge University Press, 1988. xi, 242 p. :
map ; 23 cm. (African studies series. 60) Revision of
the author's thesis (doctoral--University of London).
Includes index. Bibliography: p. 229-236.   ISBN
0-521-35230-4   DDC 966/.0097451 19
1. Muslims - Africa, French-speaking West - Politics
and government. 2. Islam and politics - Africa,
French-speaking West. 3. France - Colonies - Africa -
Administration. 4. Africa, French-speaking West -
Politics and government - 1884-1960. I. Title. II. Series.
DT530.5.M88 H37 1988
NYPL [Sc E 88-484]

Harrison, Daphne Duval, 1932- Black pearls :
blues queens of the 1920s / Daphne Duval
Harrison. New Brunswick [N.J.] : Rutgers
University Press, c1988. xv, 295 p. : ill., ports. ;
24 cm. Includes indexes. Bibliography: p. [281]-285.
ISBN 0-8135-1279-4 :   DDC 784.5/3/0922 19
1. Blues (Music) - To 1931 - History and criticism. 2.
Blues musicians - United States - Biography. 3.
Afro-American women musicians - Biography. I. Title.
ML3521 .H38 1988   NYPL [JNE 88-21]

Harrison, Max. Oliver, Paul. The New Grove
gospel, blues and jazz . New York , 1986. 395
p. [16] p. of plates :   ISBN 0-393-01696-X
NYPL [JND 88-16]

Harrison, Michael. Miniature African sculptures
from the Herman collection /. London , 1985.
64 p. :   ISBN 0-7287-0454-4
NYPL [Sc D 89-41]

Harrison, Paul Carter, 1931- Totem voices . New
York , 1989. lxiii, 523 p. ;   ISBN 0-8021-1053-3 :
DDC 812/.54/080896 19
PS628.N4 T68 1988   NYPL [Sc D 89-381]

Harrison, Paul, 1945- The greening of Africa :
breaking through in the battle for land and food
/ Paul Harrison. London : Paladin [for]
International Institute for Environment and
Development-Earthscan, 1987. 380 p. : ill.,
maps ; 20 cm. Includes index. Bibliography: p.
359-371.   ISBN 0-586-08642-0 (pbk) :   DDC
330.96/0328 19
1. Man - Influence on nature - Africa. 2. Africa -
Economic conditions - 1945-. I. Earthscan. II. Title.
HC502   NYPL [Sc C 88-327]

Harsch, Ernest. South Africa : white rule, black
revolt / Ernest Harsch. 1st ed. New York :
Monad Press : distributed by Pathfinder Press,
1980. 352 p., [8] leaves of plates : ill. ; 23 cm.
Bibliography: p. 331-341. Includes index.   ISBN
0-913460-78-8
1. Blacks - South Africa - Politics and government. 2.
Blacks - South Africa - Economic conditions. I. Title.
DT763 .H29

Hart, Lynda, 1953- Making a spectacle . Ann
Arbor , c1989. 347 p. :   ISBN 0-472-09389-4 (alk.

paper) : DDC 812/.54/099287 19
PS338.W6 M3 1989 **NYPL** *[JFE 89-144]*

Hartmann, Paul. Dean, Elizabeth. [History in black and white. Spanish.] Historia en blanco y negro . Barcelona , Paris , 1984. 196 p. ; ISBN 92-3-302092-4 (Unesco)
NYPL *[Sc D 88-594]*

Harurwa . Maredza, Claude. Harare , 1987. 52 p. : ISBN 0-908308-13-2 **NYPL** *[Sc C 88-150]*

Harusi /. Saffari, A. J. Dar es Salaam , c1984. 100 p. ; ISBN 997-693-203-0
NYPL *[Sc C 89-89]*

Harvard College. see Harvard University.

HARVARD UNIVERSITY - HISTORY.
Varieties of black experience at Harvard . Cambridge [Mass.] , 1986. v, 180 p. ;
LD2160 .V37x 1986 **NYPL** *[Sc D 88-672]*

HARVARD UNIVERSITY - STUDENTS.
Varieties of black experience at Harvard . Cambridge [Mass.] , 1986. v, 180 p. ;
LD2160 .V37x 1986 **NYPL** *[Sc D 88-672]*

Harvest time stories /. Tucker, Musu Margaret. Freetown , 1985. 55 p. : **NYPL** *[Sc D 89-9]*

Haskins, Ethelbert W., 1921- The crisis in Afro-American leadership / Ethelbert W. Haskins. Buffalo, N.Y. : Prometheus Books, 1988. 196 p. ; 24 cm. Bibliography: p. [197] ISBN 0-87975-450-8 : DDC 303.3/4/08996073 19
I. Title.
E185.615 .H327 1988 **NYPL** *[Sc E 88-399]*

Haskins, James, 1941-
Bill Cosby : America's most famous father / by Jim Haskins. New York : Walker, 1988. 138 p. : ill. ; 22 cm. Includes index. Describes Bill Cosby's meteoric rise to the top of the entertainment world. Bibliography: p. [131]-133. ISBN 0-8027-6785-0 DDC 792.7/028/0924 B 92 19
1. Cosby, Bill, 1937- - Juvenile literature. 2. Afro-American entertainers - Biography - Juvenile literature. I. Title.
PN2287.C632 H37 1988
NYPL *[Sc D 88-1162]*

Jobs in business and office. Consultants: Merle W. Wood [and] Carl M. Tausig. New York, Lothrop, Lee & Shepard [1974] 96 p. illus. 24 cm. (Exploring careers) Discusses career opportunities in business spotlighting six people with varied backgrounds who found interesting jobs. SCHOMBURG CHILDREN'S COLLECTION. ISBN 0-688-75011-7 DDC 651/.023
1. Vocational guidance - Juvenile literature. 2. Business - Juvenile literature. 3. Office practice - Juvenile literature. I. Schomburg Children's Collection. II. Title.
HF5381.2 .H38 **NYPL** *[Sc E 89-16]*

Mr. Bojangles : the biography of Bill Robinson / Jim Haskins and N.R. Mitgang.1st ed. New York : W. Morrow, 1988. 336 p. : ill., ports. ; 22 cm. Includes bibliographical references and index. ISBN 0-688-07203-8 : DDC 793.3/2/0924 B 19
1. Robinson, Bill, 1878-1949. 2. Dancers - United States - Biography. 3. Tap dancing. 4. Afro-Americans - Dancing. I. Mitgang, N. R. II. Title.
GV1785.R54 H37 1988
NYPL *[Sc D 88-851]*

Winnie Mandela : life of struggle / Jim Haskins. New York : Putnam, c1988. 179 p., [12] p. of plates : ill., map, ports. ; 22 cm. Includes index. Follows the life of the woman who married a prominent leader for racial equality in South Africa and then became an activist in that field herself. Bibliography: p. [172]-173. ISBN 0-399-21515-8 DDC 968.06/092/4 B 92 19
1. Mandela, Winnie - Juvenile literature. 2. Mandela, Nelson, 1918- - Juvenile literature. 3. Banned persons (South Africa) - Biography - Juvenile literature. 4. Civil rights workers - South Africa - Biography - Juvenile literature. 5. Anti-apartheid movements - South Africa - Juvenile literature. I. Title.
DT779.955.M36 H38 1988
NYPL *[Sc D 88-1138]*

Hassan, Leila. Dohndy, Farrukh. The Black explosion in British schools /. London , 1985. 64 p. ; ISBN 0-9503498-6-0
NYPL *[Sc D 88-1030]*

Hasson, Gail Snowden. The medical activities of the Freedmen's Bureau in Reconstruction Alabama, 1865-1868 [microform] / by Gail Snowden Hasson. 1982. 252 leaves. Thesis (Ph. D.)--University of Alabama, 1982. Bibliography: leaves

239-252. Microfilm of typescript. Ann Arbor, Mich.: University Microfilms International, 1982. 1 microfilm reel; 35 mm.
1. United States. Bureau of Refugees, Freedmen and Abandoned Lands, Medical Department. 2. Afro-Americans - Medical care - Alabama - History. 3. Reconstruction - Alabama. I. Title.
NYPL *[Sc Micro R-4681]*

HASTIE, WILLIAM.
McGuire, Phillip, 1944- He, too, spoke for democracy . New York , c1988. xvii, 154 p. ; ISBN 0-313-26115-6 (lib. bdg. : alk. paper) DDC 355/.008996073 B 19
KF373.H38 M35 1988 **NYPL** *[Sc E 88-347]*

The hatchet's blood . Schloss, Marc R. Tucson , c1988. xv, 178 p. : ISBN 0-8165-1042-3 (alk. paper) DDC 966/.3 19
DT549.45.B39 S35 1988
NYPL *[Sc E 88-443]*

Hatchett, John F. Notes from the mind of a Black philosopher / by John F. Hatchett. [New York?] : J. Hatchett, c1979. iv, 112 p. : charts ; 28 cm. Bibliography: p. 62-72.
1. Afro-American philosophy. I. Title.
NYPL *[Sc F 89-21]*

Hatchett, Shirley. Black racial attitude change in Detroit, 1968-1976 [microform] / by Shirley Jean Hatchett. 1982. 171 leaves. Thesis (Ph. D.)--University of Michigan, 1982. Bibliography: leaves 168-171. Microfilm of typescript. Ann Arbor, Mich.: University Microfilms International, 1982. 1 microfilm reel; 35 mm.
1. Afro-Americans - Michigan - Detroit - Attitudes. 2. Attitude change. 3. Detroit - Race relations - History. I. Title. **NYPL** *[Sc Micro R-4682]*

HATSHEPSUT, QUEEN OF EGYPT - JUVENILE FICTION.
Carter, Dorothy Sharp. His Majesty, Queen Hatshepsut . New York , c1987. viii, 248 p. : ISBN 0-397-32178-3 : DDC [Fic] 19
PZ7.C2434 Hi 1987 **NYPL** *[Sc D 88-877]*

Hauber, Annette. That's jazz, der Sound des 20. Jahrhunderts . [Darmstadt , 1988] xv, 723 p. : DDC 781/.57/0740341 19
ML141.D3 I6 1988 **NYPL** *[JMF 89-297]*

Hauke, Kathleen Armstrong. A self-portrait of Langston Hughes [microform] / by Kathleen Armstrong Hauke. 1981. 228 leaves. Thesis (Ph. D.)--University of Rhode Island, 1981 Bibliography: leaves [216]-228. Microfilm of typescript. Ann Arbor, Mich.: University Microfilms International, 1983. 1 microfilm reel; 35 mm.
1. Hughes, Langston, 1902-1967. I. Title.
NYPL *[Sc Micro R-4683]*

Haupt, W. Norman. Secondary level teachers: supply and demand in West Cameroon [by] W. Norman Haupt. [East Lansing, Institute for International Studies in Education and African Studies Center, Michigan State University 1971] xii, 45, [20] p. 28 cm. (Report on the supply of secondary level teachers in English-speaking Africa. no. 13) On cover: Overseas Liaison Committee on the American Council on Education. Bibliography: p. [65]
1. High school teachers - Supply and demand - Cameroon - West Cameroon. I. American Council on Education. Overseas Liaison Committee. II. Title. III. Series. **NYPL** *[JFM 72-62 no. 13]*

HAUSA (AFRICAN PEOPLE) - MEDICINE.
Wall, L. Lewis, 1950- Hausa medicine . Durham, N.C. , 1988. xxvii, 369 p. : ISBN 0-8223-0777-4 DDC 306 19
DT515.45.H38 W35 1988
NYPL *[Sc E 88-363]*

HAUSA (AFRICAN PEOPLE) - SOCIAL LIFE AND CUSTOMS.
Wall, L. Lewis, 1950- Hausa medicine . Durham, N.C. , 1988. xxvii, 369 p. : ISBN 0-8223-0777-4 DDC 306 19
DT515.45.H38 W35 1988
NYPL *[Sc E 88-363]*

HAUSA LANGUAGE - TEXTS.
Muhammed, Mairo. Shawara ga mata don aikin Hajji /. [Kano, Nigeria] . 85 p. :
NYPL *[Sc D 88-1042]*

Sudawa, Adamu Sandalo. Zuma (ga zaki, ga harbi) /. Kano , 1987. 56 p. : ISBN 978-18-8000-7 **NYPL** *[Sc D 88-1292]*

Yakubu, Balaraba Ramat. Budurwar zuciya /. Zaria , 1987. 87 p. ; **NYPL** *[Sc C 88-301]*

Hausa medicine . Wall, L. Lewis, 1950- Durham,

N.C. , 1988. xxvii, 369 p. : ISBN 0-8223-0777-4 DDC 306 19
DT515.45.H38 W35 1988
NYPL *[Sc E 88-363]*

Hausa performing arts and music /. Kofoworola, Ziky. Lagos , c1987. viii, 330 p. : ISBN 978-17-3041-2 **NYPL** *[Sc E 89-116]*

HAUSA POETRY.
Wakokin Hausa /. [[Zaria] 1963. 32 p. :
NYPL *[Sc D 89-473]*

HAUSAS - JUVENILE POETRY.
Powe, Edward L. (Edward Llewellyn), 1941- The adventures of Dan Aiki /. Paterson, N.J. , c1987. 32 p. : **NYPL** *[Sc D 88-489]*

HAUSAS - MUSIC.
Kofoworola, Ziky. Hausa performing arts and music /. Lagos , c1987. viii, 330 p. : ISBN 978-17-3041-2 **NYPL** *[Sc E 89-116]*

HAUSAS - POLITICAL ACTIVITY - CASE STUDIES.
Miles, William F. S. Elections in Nigeria . Boulder, Colo. , c1988. 168 p. : ISBN 1-555-87054-6 : DDC 324.9669/505 19
JQ3099.N66 E546 1987
NYPL *[JLE 88-3534]*

HAUSAS - SOCIAL LIFE AND CUSTOMS.
Nicolas, Guy. Don rituel et échange marchand dans une société sahélienne /. Paris , 1986. 282 p. : ISBN 2-85265-117-3 **NYPL** *[JFF 87-660]*

HAUSSAS. see HAUSAS.

Havana. Biblioteca Nacional "José Martí". Colección Cubana, Departamento. see Havana. Biblioteca Nacional "José Martí". Departamento Colección Cubana.

Havana. Biblioteca Nacional "José Martí". Departamento Colección Cubana.
Bibliograf ia cubana : 1921-1936 /. La Habana , 1977-78. [v. 1, 1978] 2 v. ;
NYPL *[HO 80-1472]*

Have you got it? . Banner, Warren M. New York , c1987. x, 371 p. ; ISBN 0-533-07057-0
NYPL *[Sc E 89-68]*

Havemann, Ernst. Bloodsong and other stories of South Africa / Ernst Havemann. Boston : Houghton Mifflin, 1987. 134 p. ; 22 cm. "A Richard Todd book"--T.p. verso. ISBN 0-395-43296-0 : DDC 813/.54 19
1. South Africa - Fiction. I. Title.
PR9199.3.H3642 B56 1987
NYPL *[Sc D 88-209]*

Haviland, John B. Laughlin, Robert M. The great Tzotzil dictionary of Santo Domingo Zinacantán . Washington, D.C. , 1988. 3 v. (xiii, 1119 p.) : DDC 497/.4 301 s 19
GN1 .S54 no. 31a PM4466.Z5
NYPL *[HBR 89-17311]*

The hawk and the eagle /. Osahon, Naiwu. Apapa, Lagos, Nigeria , 1981. [22] p. : ISBN 978-18-6007-3 **NYPL** *[Sc D 89-225]*

Hawkins, Kathleen. Barbados 1900-1950 : the olden days in pictures and verse / by Kathleen Hawkins.1st ed. [S.l. : s.n.], 1986 (Barbados : Letchworth Press) 23 p. : ill., map ; 21 cm.
1. Barbados - Poetry. I. Title.
NYPL *[Sc D 88-1184]*

Hawkins, Martin. Escott, Colin. Sun records . Vollersode, W. Germany , c1987. 240 p. : ISBN 3-924787-09-3 (pbk.)
NYPL *[Sc D 89-243]*

Hawkins, Sheila. Elliot, Geraldine. Where the leopard passes . New York, 1987. x, 125 p. :
NYPL *[Sc D 88-840]*

Hawkinson, Lucy (Ozone) 1924- That new river train. Pictured by Lucy Hawkinson. Chicago, A. Whitman [c1970] [32] p. col. illus., music. 19 cm. "Adapted from More songs to grow on by Beatrice Landeck." Illustrated version of the traditional song about loving everything and everyone. SCHOMBURG CHILDREN'S COLLECTION. ISBN 0-8075-7823-1 DDC 781/.96
I. Schomburg Children's Collection. II. Title.
PZ8.3.H315 Th **NYPL** *[Sc C 89-59]*

Hayat . Fanfani, Mariapia. [Hayat. English.] New York , c1988. 219 p., [16] p. of plates : ISBN 0-671-66414-X DDC 363.8/83/0924 B 19
HV696.F6 F363 1988 **NYPL** *[JFD 88-3833]*

Hayden, Robert C. Faith, culture, and leadership : a history of the Black church in

Boston / Robert C. Hayden.[1st ed.]. [Boston, MA : Boston Branch NAACP, c1983] iv, 56 p. : ill. ; 28 cm. "This historical booklet was prepared for the 24th annual awards banquet of the Boston Branch, National Association for the Advancement of Colored People in its 'Tribute to the Black church in Boston,' October 15, 1983"--P. [i]. DDC 280/.08996073074461 19
1. Afro-American churches - Massachusetts - Boston - History. 2. Boston (Mass.) - Church history. I. National Association for the Advancement of Colored People. Boston Branch. II. Title.
BR560.B73 H39 1983 **NYPL [Sc F 88-269]**

Hayden, Tom. Reunion : a memoir / by Tom Hayden.1st ed. New York : Random House, c1988. xix, 539 p., [16] p. of plates ; 24 cm. Includes index. ISBN 0-394-56533-9 : DDC 328.794/092/4 B 19
1. Hayden, Tom. 2. California. Legislature. House - Biography. 3. Legislators - California - Biography. 4. United States - History - 1961-1969. 5. United States - Social conditions - 1960-1980. I. Title.
F866.4.H39 A3 1988 **NYPL [JFE 88-6231]**

HAYDEN, TOM.
Hayden, Tom. Reunion . New York , c1988. xix, 539 p., [16] p. of plates ; ISBN 0-394-56533-9 : DDC 328.794/092/4 B 19
F866.4.H39 A3 1988 **NYPL [JFE 88-6231]**

Hayne, Robert Young, 1791-1839. Speeches of Hayne and Webster in the United States Senate, on the resolution of Mr. Foot, January, 1830 : also Mr. Webster's celebrated speech on the Slavery compromise bill, Mar. 7, 1850. Boston : A. T. Hotchkiss & W. P. Fetridge, 1853. 115 p. ; 24 cm.
1. Compromise of 1850. 2. Foot's resolution, 1829. 3. Nullification. 4. United States - Politics and government - 1829-1837. I. Webster, Daniel, 1782-1852. II. Title.
E381 .H424 1853 **NYPL [Sc Rare C 89-20]**

Haynes, Aaron, 1927- The state of Black Britain / by Aaron Haynes. London : Root, 1983. 160 p. ; 22 cm. Bibliography: p. 153-160. ISBN 0-946455-01-5
1. Minorities - Great Britain. 2. Blacks - Great Britain. 3. Racism - Great Britain. 4. Great Britain - Race relations. I. Title.
NYPL [Sc D 88-348]

Haynes, John. African poetry and the English language / John Haynes. Basingstoke : Macmillan Education, 1987. 165 p. : ill. ; 22 cm. Includes index. Bibliography: p. [156]-160. ISBN 0-333-44928-2 (pbk) : DDC 821 19
1. African poetry (English) - History and criticism. I. Title.
PR9342 **NYPL [Sc D 88-717]**

Haynes, Martin De Coursey, 1939. Trinidad and Tobago dialect (plus) / Martin Haynes. San Fernando, Trinidad : M. Haynes, 1987. 215 p. ; 22 cm.
1. English language - Trinidad and Tobago - Terms and phrases. 2. English language - Trinidad and Tobago - Slang - Dictionaries. I. Title.
NYPL [Sc D 88-860]

Hays, Wilma Pitchford. The goose that was a watchdog. Illustrated by Nelson McClary. [1st ed.] Boston, Little, Brown [1967] 41 p. illus. 21 cm. A weeder-goose befriends a little boy, helps catch chicken thieves, and earns her keep on the farm. SCHOMBURG CHILDREN'S COLLECTION. DDC [Fic]
1. Geese - Juvenile fiction. 2. Afro-American children - Southern States - Juvenile fiction. I. McClary, Nelson, illus. II. Schomburg Children's Collection. III. Title.
PZ7.H31493 Go **NYPL [Sc D 88-1426]**

Haywood, Carolyn, 1898- Away went the balloons, written and illustrated by Carolyn Haywood. New York, Morrow, 1973. 189 p. illus. 24 cm. Some of the balloons released on Balloon Day by the Blue Bell School first graders go to very special people and places. SCHOMBURG CHILDREN'S COLLECTION. ISBN 0-688-20057-5 DDC [Fic]
1. Balloons - Juvenile fiction. I. Schomburg Children's Collection. II. Title.
PZ7.H31496 Aw **NYPL [Sc D 89-113]**

HAZARDOUS WASTE SITES - ENVIRONMENTAL ASPECTS - UNITED STATES.
Toxic wastes and race in the United States . New York, N.Y. , 1987. xvi, 69 p. : DDC 363.7/28 19
TD811.5 .T695 1987 **NYPL [JLF 88-1607]**

HAZARDOUS WASTES - ENVIRONMENTAL ASPECTS - UNITED STATES.
Toxic wastes and race in the United States . New York, N.Y. , 1987. xvi, 69 p. : DDC 363.7/28 19
TD811.5 .T695 1987 **NYPL [JLF 88-1607]**

HAZARDOUS WASTES - UNITED STATES - MORAL AND ETHICAL ASPECTS.
Toxic wastes and race in the United States . New York, N.Y. , 1987. xvi, 69 p. : DDC 363.7/28 19
TD811.5 .T695 1987 **NYPL [JLF 88-1607]**

The Hazeley family /. Johnson, A. E. (Amelia E.), b. 1859. New York , 1988. xxxvii, 191 p. : ISBN 0-19-505257-9 (alk. paper) DDC 813/.4 19
PS2134.J515 H39 1988
NYPL [JFC 88-2196]

Hazoumé, Alain T. Afrique, un avenir en sursis / Alain et Edgard Hazoumé. Paris : L'Harmattan, c1988. 214 p. ; 22 cm. (Collection "Points de vue") Includes bibliographical references. ISBN 2-7384-0068-X
1. Africa - Economic conditions. 2. Africa - Politics and government. I. Hazoumé, Edgard G. II. Title. III. Series. **NYPL [Sc D 89-290]**

Hazoumé, Edgard G. Hazoumé, Alain T. Afrique, un avenir en sursis /. Paris , c1988. 214 p. ; ISBN 2-7384-0068-X **NYPL [Sc D 89-290]**

"He, being dead, yet speaketh" . Sumner, Charles, 1811-1874. Boston , New York , 1878. 29, 16 p. ; **NYPL [Sc Rare C 89-4]**

He, too, spoke for democracy . McGuire, Phillip, 1944- New York , c1988. xvii, 154 p. ; ISBN 0-313-26115-6 (lib. bdg. : alk. paper) DDC 355/.008996073 B 19
KF373.H38 M35 1988 **NYPL [Sc E 88-347]**

HEAD START PROGRAMS - MIDDLE WEST - CROSS-CULTURAL STUDIES.
Lubeck, Sally. Sandbox society . London , Philadelphia , 1985. xv, 177 p. : ISBN 1-85000-051-4 DDC 372/.21/0977 19
LB1140.24.M53 L8 1985
NYPL [Sc E 89-80]

Headed for trouble /. Rinkoff, Barbara. New York [1970] 119 p. : ISBN 0-394-90494-X
NYPL [Sc E 88-227]

HEADS OF STATE - ANGOLA - BIOGRAPHY.
Khazanov, A. M. (Anatoliĭ Mikhaĭlovich), 1932- [Agostinó Neto. English.] Agostinho Neto /. Moscow , 1986. 301 p. ; DDC 967/.304/0924 B 19
DT611.76.A38 K4213 1986
NYPL [Sc B 88-47]

HEADS OF STATE - CENTRAL AFRICAN REPUBLIC - BIOGRAPHY.
Baccard, André. Les martyrs de Bokassa /. Paris , c1987. 349 p., [16] p. of plates : ISBN 2-02-009669-2 : DDC 967/.4105/0924 B 19
DT546.382.B64 B33 1987
NYPL [Sc D 88-636]

HEALERS - MALI.
Bastien, Christine. Folies, mythes et magies d'Afrique noire . Paris , 1988. 230 p. ; ISBN 2-7384-0038-8 **NYPL [Sc D 89-191]**

Health and mothercraft. Smith, Pat. Soko rareupe harutagaibag namosux amik kaina [microform] Health and mothercraft /. Ukarumpa, Papua New Guinea , 1973. 12 p. ;
NYPL [Sc Micro F-10977]

HEALTH AND RACE - AMERICA - HISTORY.
The African exchange . Durham N.C. , 1987, c1988. vi, 280 p. : ISBN 0-8223-0731-6 DDC 614.4/273/08996073 19
RA442 .A37 1988 **NYPL [Sc D 88-541]**

Health care for blacks and mill workers in the twentieth-century South. Beardsley, Edward H. A history of neglect . Knoxville , c1987. xvi, 383 p. : ISBN 0-87049-523-2 (alk. paper) : DDC 362.1/0425 19
RA448.5.N4 B33 1987 **NYPL [Sc E 87-625]**

HEALTH CARE PLANNING. see HEALTH PLANNING.

HEALTH, COMMUNITY. see PUBLIC HEALTH.

HEALTH EDUCATION (ELEMENTARY) - HAITI - HANDBOOKS, MANUELS,ETC.

Bordes, Ary. Manuel d'hygiène [microform] . [Port-au-Prince?] , 1976. 78 p. :
NYPL [Sc Micro R-4840 no.7]

HEALTH EDUCATION - NIGERIA - DRAMA.
Wosornu, Lade. The casebook of Dr. O.P. Asem /. Accra , 1985- v, ; ISBN 996-472-044-0
NYPL [Sc C 89-91]

HEALTH EDUCATION (SECONDARY) - HAITI - HANDBOOKS, MANUALS, ETC.
Bordes, Ary. Manuel d'hygiène [microform] /. [Port-au-Prince, , 1975. 130 p. :
NYPL [Sc Micro R-4840 no.9]

HEALTH PLANNING - SIERRA LEONE.
Sierra Leone. Ministry of Health. National health plan, 1965-1975 /. Freetown , 1965. 167 p. : **NYPL [Sc E 88-104]**

HEALTH, PUBLIC. see PUBLIC HEALTH.

HEALTH SERVICES. see PUBLIC HEALTH.

HEALTH SERVICES PLANNING. see HEALTH PLANNING.

Healy, M. A. (Michael A.) Report of the cruise of the revenue marine steamer Corwin in the Arctic Ocean in the year 1884 / by M.A. Healy, commander. Washington : G.P.O., 1889. 128 p., [39] leaves of plates : ill., ports. ; 30 cm. Issued also as 50th Congress, 1st session. House. Misc. doc., no. 602.
1. Corwin (Revenue cutter). 2. Indians of North America - Alaska. 3. Natural history - Alaska. 4. Alaska - Description and travel - 1867-1896. 5. Kowak River (Alaska). 6. Arctic regions - Description and travel. I. Corwin (Revenue cutter). II. Title.
NYPL [Sc Rare F 88-62]

Healy, Philip. Gray, John, 1866-1934. Park . Manchester, [Greater Manchester] , 1984. 128 p. : ISBN 0-85635-538-0
NYPL [JFD 85-1419]

Hearn, Michael Patrick. The porcelain cat / by Michael Patrick Hearn ; illustrated by Leo and Diane Dillon. 1st ed. Boston : Little, Brown, [1987?]. [32] p. : col. ill. ; 20 x 27 cm. Text of the book originally appeared in Cricket magazine, February 1977. SCHOMBURG CHILDREN'S COLLECTION. ISBN 0-316-35330-2 (pbk.) :
1. Children's stories, American. I. Dillon, Leo, ill. II. Dillon, Diane, ill. III. Schomburg Children's Collection. IV. Title. **NYPL [Sc F 88-220]**

Hearne, Brian, 1939- An African Chris[t]mas? /. Eldoret, Kenya , 1983. 53 p. ; DDC 263/.91/096 19
BS2575.2 .A37 1983 **NYPL [Sc D 88-195]**

Heart of prayer : African, Jewish and Biblical prayers / [compiled by] Anthony J. Gittins. London : Collins Liturgical Publications, 1985. 175 p. : map ; 18 cm. Includes index. Bibliography: p. 171-172. ISBN 0-00-599841-7
1. Bible - Prayers. I. Gittins, Anthony J.
NYPL [Sc C 88-29]

The heart of the race . Bryan, Beverley, 1949- London , 1985. vi, 250 p. ; ISBN 0-86068-361-3 (pbk.) : DDC 305.4/8896041 19
DA125.N4 B78 1985 **NYPL [Sc C 88-178]**

Hearts and minds . Ashmore, Harry S. Cabin John, Md. , c1988. xviii, 513 p. ; ISBN 0-932020-58-5 (pbk. : alk. paper) DDC 305.8/96073 19
E185.615 .A83 1988 **NYPL [Sc D 89-382]**

Hebdige, Dick. Cut 'n' mix : culture, identity and Caribbean music / by Dick Hebdige. London : New York : Methuen, 1987. 177 p. : ill. ; 23 cm. "A Comedia book." Includes bibliographical references and index. ISBN 1-85178-029-7
1. Music - Caribbean Area - History and criticism. I. Title. **NYPL [Sc D 89-372]**

HEBREWS. see JEWS.

Hector, Mario. Death row / Mario Hector. London : Zed Books ; Kingston, Jamaica : Jamaica Council for Human Rights, 1984. v, 111 p. 21 cm. ISBN 0-86232-232-4
1. Prisons - Jamaica. 2. Prisoners - Jamaica - Biography. I. Jamaica Council for Human Rights. II. Title.
NYPL [Sc C 88-221]

Hedlund, Hans G. B. Migration and change in rural Zambia / Hans Hedlund, Mats Lundahl. Uppsala : Scandinavian Institute of African Studies, 1983. 107 p. : ill. ; 21 cm. (Research report, 0080-6714 . no. 70) Bibliography: p. [99]-107. ISBN 91-7106-220-3 (pbk.) DDC 960 s 307/.2 19

1. Rural-urban migration - Zambia. 2. Zambia - Rural conditions. I. Lundahl, Mats, 1946-. II. Series: Nordiska Afrikainstitutet. Research report, no. 70. III. Title.
DT1 .N64 no. 70 HB1955
NYPL [JLD 85-587]

HEEREY, BERNARD.
Idigo, Peter Meze. Archbishop Heerey . Enugu, Nigeria , 1987. 261 p. : ISBN 978-239-602-8
NYPL [Sc C 89-77]

Heffron, Mary J. Fenton, Thomas P. Africa . Maryknoll, N.Y. , c1987. xiv, 144 p. ; ISBN 0-88344-542-8 **NYPL [Sc D 88-398]**

Heggenhougen, H. K. (H. Kris) Community health workers . Oxford , New York , 1987. xii, 205 p. : ISBN 0-19-261618-8 (pbk.) : DDC 362.1/0425 19
RA552.T34 C67 1987 **NYPL [Sc D 88-1301]**

Heiligers-Halabi, Bernadette. Curaçao close-up / Bernadette Heiligers-Halabi. London : Macmillan Caribbean, 1986. viii, 63 p. : ill. (some col.) ; 22 cm. Bibliography: p. 63. ISBN 0-333-39881-5 (pbk.) DDC 917.298/604 19
1. Curaçao - Description and travel. I. Title.
F2049 .H5 1986 **NYPL [Sc D 88-1122]**

Heinecke, P.
Divided truths : a probe into myths and fallacies of Nigerian social science / by P. Heinecke. Okpella, Bendel State, Nigeria : S. Asekome, 1988. 135 p. ; 21 cm. Bibliography: p. 124-132. ISBN 978-252-832-3
1. Social sciences - Nigeria. 2. Historiography - Nigeria. I. Title. **NYPL [Sc D 89-134]**

The rebel and other stories / by P. Heinecke. Okpella, Bendel State, Nigeria : S. Asekome, 1987. 84 p. ; 24 cm. ISBN 978-252-824-2
1. Nigeria - Fiction. I. Title.
NYPL [Sc E 88-601]

Twenty-two reviews / by P. Heinecke. Kaduna, [Nigeria] : Hotline Pub. Co.; [1986?] 69 p. ; 25 cm. Reviews originally published between 1981 and 1986. Includes bibliographical footnotes.
1. Public administration - Nigeria - Book reviews. 2. Nigeria - Economic conditions - Book reviews. 3. Developing countries - Economic conditions - Book reviews. 4. Africa - Colonial influence - Book reviews. I. Title. **NYPL [Sc E 88-284]**

Heineman CXC history.
Hall, Douglas. The Caribbean experience . Kingston , 1982. xi, 146 p. : ISBN 0-435-98300-8
NYPL [Sc E 87-670]

Heinemann CXC history. Theme.
Bryan, Patrick E. The Haitian revolution and its effects /. Kingston, Jamaica , Exeter, N.H., USA , 1984. 56 p. : ISBN 0-435-98301-6 (U. S. : pbk.) DDC 972.94/03 19
F1923 .B83 1984 **NYPL [Sc D 89-299]**

Heinrichs, Hans-Jürgen, 1945- Afrika /. Frankfurt am Main , New York , c1986. 413 p. : ISBN 3-88655-212-8 DDC 960 19
DT14 .A3747 1986 **NYPL [Sc D 89-311]**

Hellhund, Herbert. Cool Jazz : Grundzüge seiner Entstehung und Entwicklung / Herbert Hellhund. Mainz ; New York : Schott, c1985. 302 p. : ill., music ; 24 cm. (Schott Musikwissenschaft) Originally presented as the author's thesis (doctoral--Universität Giessen) Bibliography: p. 301-302. ISBN 3-7957-1790-6 : DDC 785.42 19
1. Jazz music - History and criticism. I. Title.
ML3506 .H45 1985 **NYPL [JME 87-29]**

Helliker, Kirk. Roux, Andre, 1954- Voices from Rini . Grahamstown, South Africa , 1986. 107 p. ; ISBN 0-86810-131-1 **NYPL [Sc F 88-216]**

Helman, Albert. Blijf even staan! : de situatie in Oost-Suriname = Just a momnet! : report from East-Surinam / [Albert Helman] [Netherlands? : s.n.], c1987. 41 p. : ill., map ; 21 x 28 cm. In Dutch and English.
1. Surinaams Nationaal Bevrijdingsleger. 2. Maroons - Surinam. 3. Guerrillas - Surinam. 4. Surinam - Politics and government - 1950-. I. Title.
NYPL [Sc D 88-1039]

HELP SEEKING BEHAVIOR - UNITED STATES.
Milburn, Norweeta G. Social support . Washington, D.C. , 1986. iii, 67 p. ;
NYPL [Sc F 87-428]

HELVETAS, SCHWEIZER AUFBAUWERT FÜR ENTWICKLUNGS LÄNDER.
Müller, Hans-Peter. Die Helvetas-Wasserversorgungen in Kamerun .

[Zürich , 1978] 94, 45 leaves ;
NYPL [Sc F 88-122]

Die Helvetas-Wasserversorgungen in Kamerun .
Müller, Hans-Peter. [Zürich , 1978] 94, 45 leaves ; **NYPL [Sc F 88-122]**

HEMINGS FAMILY.
Woodson, Minnie Shumate. The Sable curtain /. Washington, D.C. , 1987, c1985. 380, 12 p. : ISBN 0-943153-00-X **NYPL [Sc D 88-68]**

Hemmings, Susan. Radical records . London , New York , 1988. xi, 266 p. ; ISBN 0-415-00200-1 DDC 306.7/66/0941 19
HQ76.8.G7 R33 1988 **NYPL [Sc D 88-1427]**

Hemstedt, Klaus. Die UNO-Sondersitzung über Afrika 1986 in der afrikanischen Presse /. Hamburg , 1986. ii, 104 p. : ISBN 3-923519-66-4
NYPL [Sc F 88-229]

Henco, een jongen van Curacao .
(3) Regals, Leo. Henco ruimt op /. Curaçao [1986?] 72 p. : ISBN 90-6435-111-2
MLCS 87/05319 (P) **NYPL [Sc D 88-490]**

Henco ruimt op /. Regals, Leo. Curaçao [1986?] 72 p. : ISBN 90-6435-111-2
MLCS 87/05319 (P) **NYPL [Sc D 88-490]**

Henderson, David, 1942- 'Scuse me while I kiss the sky : the life of Jimi Hendrix / David Henderson.Rev. ed. Toronto ; New York : Bantam Books, 1981. xi, 411 p. : ill. ; 18 cm. Condensed and rev. from: Jimi Hendrix : voodoo child of the Aquarian age. Garden City, N.Y. : Doubleday, 1978. Discography: p. 406-411. ISBN 0-553-01334-3 (tr. pbk.) : DDC 784.5/4/00924
1. Hendrix, Jimi. 2. Rock musicians - United States - Biography. I. Title.
ML410.H476 H46 1981
NYPL [Sc C 82-243]

Henderson, Francine I. A guide to periodical articles about Botswana, 1965-80 / edited and compiled by Francine Henderson and Tiny Modisakeng. Gaborone, Botswana : National Institute of Development and Cultural Research, Documentation Unit, University College of Botswana, 1982. v, 147, 6 p. ; 30 cm. (Working bibliography . no. 9) Includes index. DDC 016.96811 19
1. Botswana - Bibliography. I. Modisakeng, Tiny. II. Title. III. Series.
Z3559 .H46 1982 DT791
NYPL [Sc F 88-161]

Henderson, H. Michael. Sex, racism and other reflective tidbits / by H. Michael Henderson. A collector's ed. [Chamblee, Georgia : H. M. Henderson, 1987] 63 p. ; 22 cm. Cover title.
I. Title. **NYPL [Sc D 88-265]**

Hendricks, Leo E.
A comparative analysis of three select populations of Black unmarried adolescent fathers / Leo E. Hendricks. Washington, D.C. : Mental Health Research and Development Center, Institute for Urban Affairs and Research, Howard University, 1982. ix, 129 p. : forms ; 28 cm. "Volume II, Final Report." Bibliography: p. 126-128.
1. Unmarried fathers - United States. 2. Adolescent parents - United States. I. Howard University. Mental Health Research and Development Center. II. Title.
NYPL [Sc D 88-222]

The effect of family size, child spacing and family density on stress in low income Black mothers and their preadolescent children [microform] / by Leo Edward Hendricks. 1977. 156 leaves. Thesis (Ph. D.)--University of North Carolina at Chapel Hill, 1977. Bibliography: leaves [131]-136. Microfilm of typescript. Ann Arbor, Mich.: University Microfilms International, 1978. 1 microfilm reel; 35 mm.
1. Stress in children. 2. Poor - Health and hygiene. I. Title. **NYPL [Sc Micro R-4684]**

HENDRIX, JIMI.
Henderson, David, 1942- 'Scuse me while I kiss the sky . Toronto , New York , 1983, 1981. xi, 411 p. : ISBN 0-553-01334-3 (tr. pbk.) : DDC 784.5/4/00924
ML410.H476 H46 1981
NYPL [Sc C 82-243]

HENRI CHRISTOPHE, KING OF HAITI, 1767-1820 - DRAMA.
Leconte, Vergniaud. Théâtre [microform]. [n. p., 1919] xi, 291 p. **NYPL [Sc Micro R-3541]**

Henri Lopes et l'impératif romanesque /.

Malanda, Ange-Séverin. Paris , c1987. 142 p. : ISBN 2-09-387190-6 **NYPL [Sc D 89-207]**

HENSHAW, DAVID, 1791-1852.
A Refutation of the charge of abolitionism. Boston, 1845. 32 p.
F69 .M455 **NYPL [Sc Rare C 89-21]**

HENSON, MATTHEW ALEXANDER, 1866-1955 - JUVENILE LITERATURE.
Gilman, Michael. Matthew Henson /. New York , c1988. 110 p. : ISBN 1-555-46590-0 : DDC 919.8/04 B 92 19
G635.H4 G55 1988 **NYPL [Sc E 88-169]**

Henze, Paul B., 1924- Rebels and separatists in Ethiopia : regional resistance to a Marxist regime / Paul Henze. Santa Monica, CA : Rand, 1985. xv, 98 p. ; 23 cm. "Prepared for the Office of the Under Secretary of Defense for Policy." "R-3347-USDP." "December 1985." Bibliography: p. 95-98. ISBN 0-8330-0696-7 DDC 963/.07 19
1. National liberation movements - Ethiopia. 2. Ethiopia - Politics and government - 1974-. I. United States. Office of the Under Secretary of Defense for Policy. II. Rand Corporation. III. Title.
DT387.95 .H46 1986 **NYPL [JFE 86-5101]**

L'herbe sous les pieds /. Madede-Tsotsa, Simon, 1957- Paris , c1986. 28 p. ; ISBN 2-243-02813-1
NYPL [Sc D 88-498]

Herbert, James I. Black male entrepreneurs and adult development / James I. Herbert. New York : Praeger, 1989. xviii, 235 p. ; 24 cm. Includes index. Bibliography: p. 229-232. ISBN 0-275-93023-8 (alk. paper) : DDC 155.8/496073 19
1. Afro-American men - Psychology. I. Title.
E185.625 .H44 1989 **NYPL [Sc E 89-256]**

HERBS - RELIGIOUS ASPECTS.
Farelli, Maria Helena. Oxóssi e Ossãe . Rio de Janeiro , 1987. 71 p. : **NYPL [Sc C 88-65]**

HERDERS - AFRICA, EAST.
Rigby, Peter. Persistent pastoralists . London , Totowa, N.J. , 1985. x, 198 p. : ISBN 0-86232-226-X : DDC 305.8/9676 19
DT443.3.M37 R54 1985
NYPL [JLD 86-2309]

A heritage discovered . Stewart, Rowena. Providence, R.I. [1975] 39 p. :
NYPL [Sc E 89-110]

The Heritage of American Catholicism.
Nickels, Marilyn Wenzke. Black Catholic protest and the Federated Colored Catholics, 1917-1933 . New York , 1988. ix, 325 p. ; ISBN 0-8240-4098-8 (alk. paper) DDC 282/.73/08996073 19
BX1407.N4 N5 1988 **NYPL [Sc E 89-85]**

Herlihy, Dirlie. Ludie's song / by Dirlie Herlihy. 1st ed. New York : Dial Books, c1988. 212 p. ; 22 cm. In rural Georgia in the 1950's, a young white girl's secret friendship with a black family exposes them all to unforeseen dangers. ISBN 0-8037-0533-6 : DDC [Fic] 19
1. Afro-Americans - Georgia - Juvenile fiction. 2. Georgia - Race relations - Juvenile fiction. I. Title.
PZ7.H43126 Lu 1988 **NYPL [Sc D 89-132]**

Herman, Bernard L., 1951- Belcher, Max. A land and life remembered . Athens , Brockton, Mass. , c1988. [xii], 176 p. : ISBN 0-8203-1085-9 (alk. paper) DDC 720/.9666/2074014482 19
NA1599.L4 B4 1988 **NYPL [Sc F 89-90]**

HERMAN, JOSEPH, 1911- - ART COLLECTIONS - EXHIBITIONS.
Miniature African sculptures from the Herman collection /. London , 1985. 64 p. : ISBN 0-7287-0454-4 **NYPL [Sc D 89-41]**

HERMETIC ART AND PHILOSOPHY. see MAGIC; OCCULT SCIENCES.

Hernandez, Helen. The maroons-- who are they? / prepared by Helen Hernandez ; edited by Joanne Creary. 1st ed. Kingston : JAMAL Foundation, c1983. 28 p. : ill. ; 21 cm. SCHOMBURG CHILDREN'S COLLECTION.
1. Maroons - Jamaica - Juvenile literature. I. Creary, Joanne. II. Schomburg Children's Collection. III. Title.
NYPL [Sc D 88-378]

Herod, Agustina. Afro-American nationalism : an annotated bibliography of militant separatist and nationalist literature / Agustina and Charles C. Herod. New York : Garland, 1986. xvi, 272 p. ; 23 cm. (Canadian review of studies in nationalism . vol. 6) Garland reference library of social science ; vol. 336 Includes index. ISBN 0-8240-9813-7 (alk. paper)

DDC 016.3058/96073 19
*1. Black nationalism - United States - Bibliography. 2.
Afro-Americans - Race identity - Bibliography. I.
Herod, Charles C. II. Series. III. Series: Canadian
review of studies in nationalism , v. 6. IV. Title.*
Z1361.N39 H47 1986 E185.625
                          NYPL [Sc D 87-1338]

Herod, Charles C. Herod, Agustina.
Afro-American nationalism . New York , 1986.
xvi, 272 p. ; ISBN 0-8240-9813-7 (alk. paper)
DDC 016.3058/96073 19
Z1361.N39 H47 1986 E185.625
                          NYPL [Sc D 87-1338]

Heroes & heroines of Onitsha /. Akosa, Chike.
Onitsha, Nigeria , 1987 (Etukokwu Press) viii,
344 p. : ISBN 978-303-730-7
                          NYPL [Sc D 88-1109]

Heroes and heroines of Onitsha. Akosa, Chike.
Heroes & heroines of Onitsha /. Onitsha,
Nigeria , 1987 (Etukokwu Press) viii, 344 p. :
ISBN 978-303-730-7
                          NYPL [Sc D 88-1109]

Heroes of West African nationalism /. Okonkwo,
Rina. Enugu, Nigeria , 1985. x, 128 p. ; ISBN
978-233-596-7   ***NYPL [Sc C 88-95]***

HEROINES. see WOMEN.

HEROINES - KENYA - FOLKLORE.
Njau, Rebeka. Kenya women heroes and their
mystical power /. Nairobi , 1984- v. ; DDC
398/.09676/2 19
GR356.4 .N43 1984   ***NYPL [Sc D 88-1052]***

Hero's welcome /. Anigbedu, Laide. Yaba-Lagos,
Nigeria , 1986. 141 p. ; ISBN 978-256-400-1
                          NYPL [Sc C 88-283]

Herron, Matt. Ruskin, Cindy. The quilt . New
York , 1988. 160 p. : ISBN 0-671-66597-9 :
                          NYPL [Sc F 88-237]

Herstein, Sheila R. Chambers, Frances. Trinidad
and Tobago /. Oxford, England , Santa Barbara,
Calif. , c1986. xv, 213 p. : ISBN 1-8150-9020-7
                          NYPL [Sc D 89-33]

Herzog, Elizabeth. About the poor : some facts
and some fictions. [Washington] : U. S. Dept.
of Health, Education, and Welfare, Children's
Bureau; [for sale by the Supt. of Docs., U. S.
Govt. Print. Off.] 1967 [i.e. 1968] 85 p. illus.
24 cm. (United States. Children's Bureau. Publication
no. 451) Bibliography: p. 78-85. DDC 362.5/0973
1. Poor - United States. I. Title. II. Series.
HC110.P6 H47   ***NYPL [Sc E 88-67]***

Hesselberg, J. (Jan) The Third World in
transition : the case of the peasantry in
Botswana / Jan Hesselberg. Uppsala :
Scandinavian Institute of African Studies ;
Stockholm, Sweden : Distributed by,
Almqvist & Wiksell International, 1985. 256
p. : ill. ; 25 cm. Bibliography: p. 231-256. ISBN
91-7106-243-2 (pbk) DDC 305.5/63 19
*1. Peasantry - Botswana - Case studies. 2. Agriculture -
Economic aspects - Botswana - Cases studies. 3. Land
settlement patterns - Botswana - Case studies. I. Title.*
HD1538.B55 H47 1985
                          NYPL [Sc E 88-290]

Hesseling, Gerti.
[Senegal, staatsrechtelijke en politieke
ontwikkelingen. French]
Histoire politique du Sénégal : institutions,
droit et société / Gerti Hesseling ; préface de
Abd-El Kader Boye ; traduction du
néerlandais, Catherine Miginiac. Paris,
France : Editions Karthala ; Leiden,
Pays-Bas : Afrika-Studiecentrum, c1985. 437
p. : ill. ; 24 cm. (Hommes et sociétés, 0290-6600)
Translation of: Senegal, staatsrechtelijke en politieke
ontwikkelingen. Includes index. Bibliography: p.
[381]-407. ISBN 2-86537-118-2 DDC
342.66/3029 346.630229 19
*1. Law - Senegal - History and criticism. 2. Senegal -
Constitutional history. I. Title. II. Series.*
LAW   ***NYPL [JLE 88-3233]***

Hessou, Henri D.
Le masque de Dakodonou : nouvelles suivies
d'une postface sur "Les vipères de Kétou") /
Henri D. Hessou. Cotonou [Benin] : Office
national d'édition, de presse, de publicité, et
d'imprimerie, 1986. 65 p. : port. ; 19 cm.
Includes the author's Poisson d'avril.
*1. Hessou, Henri D. Vipères de Ketou. 2. Benin -
Fiction. I. Hessou, Henri D. Poisson d'avril. 1986. II.
Title.*   ***NYPL [Sc C 88-370]***

Poisson d'avril. 1986. Hessou, Henri D. Le
masque de Dakodonou : nouvelles suivies
d'une postface sur "Les vipères de Kétou") /
Henri D. Hessou. Cotonou [Benin] , 1986. 65
p. :   ***NYPL [Sc C 88-370]***

VIPÈRES DE KETOU.
Hessou, Henri D. Le masque de Dakodonou .
Cotonou [Benin] , 1986. 65 p. :
                          NYPL [Sc C 88-370]

Heusch, Luc de. Le sacrifice dans les religions
africaines / Luc de Heusch. Paris : Gallimard,
1986. 354 p. : map ; 23 cm. (Bibliothèque des
sciences humaines) Includes index. Bibliography: p.
[345]-354.
*1. Sacrifice. 2. Africa, Sub-Saharan - Religious life and
customs. I. Title.*   ***NYPL [Sc D 88-941]***

Hevenor, Hilary, 1957- Anderson, John, 1954
Mar. 27- Burning down the house . New York ,
c1987. xv, 409 p. : ISBN 0-393-02460-1 : DDC
974.8/1104 19
F158.9.N4 A53 1987   ***NYPL [Sc E 88-332]***

Hewitt, Lawrence L. Port Hudson, Confederate
bastion on the Mississippi / Lawrence Lee
Hewitt. Baton Rouge : Louisiana State
University Press, c1987. xvi, 221 p. : ill.,
ports. ; 24 cm. Includes bibliography: p.
[195]-211. ISBN 0-8071-1351-4 DDC 973.7/33 19
1. Port Hudson (La.) - History - Siege, 1863. I. Title.
E475.42 .H49 1987   ***NYPL [IKE 88-1592]***

Hewitt, Roger. White talk, black talk : inter-racial
friendship and communication amongst
adolescents / Roger Hewitt. Cambridge
[Cambridgeshire] ; New York : Cambridge
University Press, 1986. x, 253 p. ; 24 cm.
(Comparative ethnic and race relations) Includes index.
Bibliography: p. 240-246. ISBN 0-521-26239-9 DDC
401/.9/094216 19
*1. Sociolinguistics - England - London. 2. Creole
dialects, English - England - London. 3. Youth -
England - London - Language. 4. Blacks - England -
London - Communication. 5. London (England) - Race
relations series. I. Series: Comparative ethnic and race
relations. II. Title.*
P40.45.G7 H48 1986   ***NYPL [JFE 87-279]***

Hexham, Irving. Texts on Zulu religion .
Lewiston, NY , Queenston, Ont. , 1987. 488
p. ; ISBN 0-88946-181-3 : DDC 299/.683 19
BL2480.Z8 T48 1987   ***NYPL [Sc E 88-463]***

Hezekiah Oluwasanmi Library. Abstracts of
theses accepted by University of Ife, 1985 /
compiled and edited by Lynda
Quamina-Aiyejina ... [et al.]. Ile-Ife : University
of Ife, Hezekiah Oluwasanmi Library, 1986. ii,
ii, 95 p. ; 20 cm. Includes indexes.
*1. Dissertations, Academic - Nigeria - Abstracts. 2.
University of Ife - Dissertations - Abstracts. I.
Quamina-Aiyejina, Lynda. II. Title.*
                          NYPL [Sc D 89-580]

A hi hlomeni /. Mashele, B. H. M.
Braamfontein , 1982. 52 p. :
                          NYPL [Sc C 88-222]

HIATI - FOREIGN RELATIONS - 1804-1844.
Coradin, Jean. Histoire diplomatique d'Haïti
1804-1843 /. Port-au-Prince, Haïti , 1988- v. ;
                          NYPL [Sc D 88-864]

Hickey, Raymond.
Christianity in Borno State and Northern
Gongola / [Raymond Hickey]. [Nigeria : s.n.,
1984?] (Ibadan : Claverianum Press) vi, 108 p. :
maps ; 23 cm. "Published with the aid of the Institute
of Missiology (MISSIO), Aachen." Bibliography: p. 108.
*1. Christianity - Nigeria - Borno State. 2. Missions -
Nigeria - Borno State. 3. Missions - Nigeria - Gongola
State. 4. Christianity - Nigeria - Gongola State. 5.
Borno State (Nigeria) - Church history. 6. Gongola
State (Nigeria) - Church history. I. Institute of
Missiology (MISSIO). II. Title.*
                          NYPL [Sc D 88-882]

Two thousand years of African Christianity /
Raymond Hickey. Ibadan, Nigeria : Daystar
Press, 1987. viii, 54 p. : maps ; 19 cm. Includes
bibliographical references.
*1. Christianity - Africa. 2. Africa - Church history. I.
Title.*   ***NYPL [Sc C 88-207]***

L'Hidalgo des campèches . Parsemain, Roger,
1944- Paris , 1987. 126 p. ; ISBN 2-218-07812-0
                          NYPL [Sc C 88-7]

Hidden lives, hidden deaths . Brittain, Victoria.
London , Boston , 1988. xvii, 189 p. : ISBN

0-571-13907-8 : DDC 355/.0335/68 19
UA856   ***NYPL [JLD 88-4608]***

High, Egyirba. Scott, Kesho. Tight Spaces /. San
Francisco , 1987. 182 p. ; ISBN 0-933216-27-0
                          NYPL [Sc D 88-12]

**HIGH SCHOOL GRADUATES -
EMPLOYMENT - NIGERIA - WESTERN
STATE.**
Western State, Nigeria. Ministry of Economic
Planning and Social Development. Statistics
Division. Report of a sample survey of
unemployment among school leavers
[microform /. Ibadan [1966]- v. ;
                          NYPL [Sc Micro F-10938]

**HIGH SCHOOL TEACHERS - NIGERIA -
SUPPLY AND DEMAND.**
Hanson, John Wagner. Secondary level
teachers: supply and demand in Nigeria. [East
Lansing, 1971] 1 v. (various pagings) DDC
331.1/26
LB2833.4.N6 H36   ***NYPL [Sc F 88-151]***

**HIGH SCHOOL TEACHERS - SUPPLY AND
DEMAND - BOTSWANA.**
Hanson, John Wagner. Secondary level
teachers: supply and demand in Botswana. [East
Lansing, 1969, c1968] x, 97, [2] p.
LB2833.4.B55 H3   ***NYPL [JFM 72-62 no. 1]***

**HIGH SCHOOL TEACHERS - SUPPLY AND
DEMAND - CAMEROON - WEST
CAMEROON.**
Haupt, W. Norman. Secondary level teachers:
supply and demand in West Cameroon. [East
Lansing, 1971] xii, 45, [20] p.
                     NYPL [JFM 72-62 no. 13]

**HIGH SCHOOL TEACHERS - SUPPLY AND
DEMAND - GAMBIA.**
Ferns, George W. Secondary level teachers:
supply and demand in the Gambia. [East
Lansing, 1969] xi, 78 p.
LB2833.4.G3 F4   ***NYPL [JFM 72-62 no. 2]***

**HIGH SCHOOL TEACHERS - SUPPLY AND
DEMAND - GHANA.**
Hanson, John Wagner. Secondary level
teachers: supply and demand in Ghana. [East
Lansing, 1971] xv, 130 p.
                     NYPL [JFM 72-62 no. 12]

**HIGH SCHOOL TEACHERS - SUPPLY AND
DEMAND - LIBERIA.**
Ferns, George W. Secondary level teachers:
supply and demand in Liberia. [East Lansing,
c1970] xii, 116 p.
LB2833.4.L7 F4   ***NYPL [JFM 72-62 no. 6]***

**HIGH SCHOOL TEACHERS - SUPPLY AND
DEMAND - SIERRA LEONE.**
Hanson, John Wagner. Secondary level
teachers: supply and demand in Sierra Leone.
[East Lansing, c1970] viii, 85 p.
                     NYPL [JFM 72-62 no. 11]

**HIGH SCHOOL TEACHERS - SUPPLY AND
DEMAND - TANZANIA.**
Pratt, Simon. Secondary level teachers: supply
and demand in tanzania. [East Lansing, 1969]
xii, 79 p.   ***NYPL [JFM 72-62 no. 8]***

**HIGH SCHOOLS - AUSTRALIA - CASE
STUDIES.**
Bullivant, Brian Milton. The ethnic encounter
in the secondary school . London , New York ,
1987. x, 214 p. ; ISBN 1-85000-255-X : DDC
371.97/0994 19
LC3739 .B84 1987   ***NYPL [JLE 88-2088]***

HIGH SCHOOLS - JUVENILE FICTION.
Childress, Alice. Those other people /. New
York , c1988. 186 p. ; ISBN 0-399-21510-7
DDC [Fic] 19
PZ7.C4412 Th 1988   ***NYPL [Sc D 89-327]***

**Higher education and rural development in
Africa [microform] .** Moock, Joyce Lewinger.
New York , c1977. ii, 42 p. ;
                          NYPL [Sc Micro R-4202 no. 1]

**HIGHER EDUCATION AND STATE -
MALAWI.**
Kimble, David. The University and the nation
[microform] d. [Zomba, Malawi , 1978] 16 p. ;
                          NYPL [Sc Micro F-11018]

**HIGHER EDUCATION AND STATE -
NIGERIA.**
Achebe, Chinua. The university and the
leadership factor in Nigerian politics /. Enugu,
Nigeria , c1988. 22 p. ; ISBN 978-226-907-7
                          NYPL [Sc D 89-28]

HIGHER EDUCATION AND STATE - SOUTH AFRICA.
Dreijmanis, John. The role of the South African government in tertiary education /. Johannesburg, South Africa , 1988. xiii, 156 p. : ISBN 0-86982-329-9 *NYPL [Sc F 88-184]*

HIGHER LAW. see GOVERNMENT, RESISTANCE TO.

Hilbert, Robert, 1939-
James P. Johnson discography, 1917-1950.
1986. Brown, Scott E., 1960- James P. Johnson : a case of mistaken identity / Scott E. Brown ; a James P. Johnson discography, 1917-1950 [by] Robert Hilbert. Metuchen, N.J. , 1986. viii, 500 p., [12] p. of plates : ISBN 0-8108-1887-6 DDC 786.1/092/4 B 19
ML417.J62 B76 1986 NYPL [Sc D 88-1435]

Hildreth, Richard, 1807-1865.
The white slave. Albuquerque, L. M. do Couto de. O escravo branco : companheiro do tio Thomaz, ou A vida de um fugitivo na Virginia : romance de Hildreth / traducção livre de L.M. do Couto de Albuquerque. Lisboa , 1854. 4 v. : *NYPL [Sc F 82-65]*

Hill, Arthur Cyrus. The history of the Black people of Franklin County, Tennessee [microform] / by Arthur Cyrus Hill. 1981. 408 leaves. Thesis (Ph. D.)--University of Minnesota, 1982. Bibliography: leaves 394-408. Microfilm of typescript. Ann Arbor, Mich.: University Microfilms International, 1982. 1 microfilm reel; 35 mm.
1. Afro-Americans - Tennessee - Franklin County - History. I. Title. *NYPL [Sc Micro R-4685]*

Hill, Carol M. Bailey, A. Peter. Harlem today . New York , c1986. viii, 55 p. : ISBN 0-936073-01-2 (pbk.) DDC 917.47/1 19
F128.68.H3 B3 1986 NYPL [Sc D 88-1402]

Hill, Pauline Anderson Simmons. Too young to be old : the story of Bertha Pitts Campbell / written by Pauline Anderson Simmons Hill ; in collaboration with Sherrilyn Johnson Jordan. Seattle, Washington : Peanut Butter Pub., c1981. xiv, 58 p. : ill., ports. ; 22 cm. ISBN 0-89716-098-3
1. Campbell, Bertha Pitts. 2. Delta Sigma Theta Sorority. 3. Afro-American women - Biography. I. Jordan, Sherrilyn Johnson. II. Title.
NYPL [Sc D 88-1214]

HILLBILLY MUSIC. see COUNTRY MUSIC.

Hillman, Chrisanthia. The relationship between self-esteem and academic achievement among Black students in remedial reading instruction at a community college [microform] / by Chrisanthia Hillman. 1981. 60 leaves. Thesis (M.S.)--California State University, Long Beach, 1981. Bibliography: leaves 55-60. Microfilm of typescript. Ann Arbor, Mich.: University Microfilms International, 19 . 1 microfilm reel; 35 mm.
1. Afro-Americans - Education - Reading. 2. Afro-American college students - Psychology. I. Title.
NYPL [Sc Micro R-4686]

"The Hills" in the mid-nineteenth century . Caro, Edythe Quinn. Valhalla, New York , c1988. 184 p. : *NYPL [Sc F 89-71]*

Himes, Chester B., 1909-
Faut être nègre pour faire ça ... / Chester Himes ; nouvelles traduites de l'américain par Hélène Devaux-Minié. [Paris, France] : Lieu Commun, c1986. 223 p. ; 23 cm. French translations of periodical articles and unedited English writings. ISBN 2-86705-064-2
I. Devaux-Minié, Hélène. II. Title.
NYPL [Sc D 88-1447]

Lonely crusade : a novel / by Chester Himes ; foreword by Graham Hodges. New York : Thunder's Mouth Press, c1986. x, 398 p. ; 22 cm. (Classic reprint series) ISBN 0-938410-37-7 (pbk.) : DDC 813/.54 19
1. Afro-Americans - California - Los Angeles - Fiction. 2. Trade-unions - United States - Fiction. I. Title. II. Series.
PS3515.I713 L6 1986 NYPL [Sc D 88-1362]

A rage in Harlem / Chester Himes. London ; New York : Allison & Busby, 1985, c1957. 159 p. ; 21 cm. "Previously published in the USA as For love of Imabelle." ISBN 0-85031-618-9
1. Harlem (New York, N.Y.) - Fiction. I. Title.
NYPL [Sc D 88-692]

The real cool killers/ Chester Himes. London ;

New York : Allison & Busby, 1985, c1958. 159 p. ; 21 cm. Published in France as:Il pleut des coups dur. ISBN 0-85031-615-4
1. Afro-Americans - New York (N.Y.) - Fiction. 2. Harlem (New York, N.Y.) - Fiction. I. Title.
NYPL [Sc D 88-280]

HIMES, CHESTER B., 1909- - BIOGRAPHY - JUVENILE LITERATURE.
Wilson, M. L. (Matthew Lawrence), 1960- Chester Himes /. New York , c1988. 111 p. : ISBN 1-555-46591-9 DDC 813/.54 B 92 19
PS3515.I713 Z93 1988 NYPL [Sc E 88-373]

Hinderink, J. (Jan) Agricultural commercialization and government policy in Africa / J. Hinderink and J.J. Sterkenburg. London ; New York : KPI, 1987. xii, 328 p. : maps ; 23 cm. (Monographs from the African Studies Centre, Leiden) Includes indexes. Bibliography: p. 281-307. ISBN 0-7103-0205-3
1. Agriculture - Economic aspects - Africa, Sub-Saharan. 2. Agriculture and state - Africa, Sub-Saharan. 3. Rural development - Government policy - Africa, Sub-saharan. I. Sterkenburg, J.J. II. Title. III. Series. *NYPL [Sc D 88-580]*

Hindson, D. Pass controls and the urban African proletariat in South Africa / Doug Hindson. Johannesburg, South Africa : Ravan Press, 1987. xii, 121 p. ; 21 cm. Originally presented as the author's thesis (doctoral--University of Sussex, 1983) Includes index. Bibliography: p. [101]-110. ISBN 0-86975-311-8
1. Occupations and race. 2. South Africa - Occupations. I. Title. *NYPL [Sc D 88-956]*

Hindus, Michael Stephen, 1946- Prison and plantation [microform] : criminal justice in nineteenth-century Massachusetts and South Carolina / by Michael Stephen Hindus. 1975. 398 leaves. Thesis (Ph. D.)--University of California, Berkeley, 1975. Bibliography: leaves 375-398. Microfilm of typescript. Ann Arbor, Mich.: University Microfilms International, 1976. 1 microfilm reel; 35 mm.
1. Criminal justice, Administration of - Massachusetts - History. 2. Criminal justice, Administration of - South Carolina - History. 3. Crime and criminals - Massachusetts - History. 4. Crime and criminals - South Carolina - History. I. Title.
NYPL [Sc Micro R-4225]

Hine, Darlene Clark. The Black women in the Middle West Project . Indianapolis, Ind. (140 N. Senate Ave., Room 408, Indianapolis 46204) , 1986. xi, 238 p. : DDC 977/.00496073 19
E185.915 .B52 1986 NYPL [Sc F 88-141]

Hines, Colin. Dinham, Barbara. Agribusiness in Africa /. London , 1983. 224 p. : ISBN 0-946281-00-9 : *NYPL [Sc D 84-44]*

Hinzen, Heribert.
Koranko riddles, songs and stories / collected by Heribert Hinzen, Jim M. Sorie, Robert F. Jawara. Freetown : Published by People's Educational Association of Sierra Leone, 1987. 69 p. : ill. ; 21 cm. (Stories and songs from Sierra Leone . 28)
1. Kuranko (African people) - Folklore. 2. Folklore - Sierra Leone. I. Sorie, Jim M. II. Jawara, Robert F. III. Title. IV. Series. *NYPL [Sc D 89-416]*

Koroma, Salia. The spider's web /. Freetown , 1986. 134 p. : *NYPL [Sc D 89-403]*

Temne stories and songs /. Freetown, Sierra Leone , 1986. 96 p. : *NYPL [Sc D 89-427]*

Hipólito Unanue bibliographic series .
(4) Wharton-Lake, Beverly D. Creative literature of Trinidad and Tobago . Washington, D.C. , 1988. xi, 102 p. ; ISBN 0-8270-2709-5
NYPL [Sc D 88-710]

HIPPOLOGY. see HORSES.

Hippolyte, Kendel.
Bearings / by Kendel Hippolyte. [St. Lucia? : s.n.], c1986. ii, 52 p. : ill. ; 22 cm. Poems. ISBN 976-8036-00-1
I. Title. *NYPL [Sc D 88-802]*

Island in the sun-side 2 [microform] / Kendel Hippolyte. St. Lucia : U.W.I. Extra Mural Department, [197-?] 50 p. ; 25 cm. (Iouanaloa series. no. 4) Poems. Microfiche. New York: New York Public Library, 198 . 1 microfiche: negative; 11 x 15 cm. (FSN Sc 019,045)
I. Title. *NYPL [Sc Micro F-11023]*

Hirsch, E. D. (Eric Donald), 1928- Stuckey, Elma, 1907- [Poems.] The collected poems of

Elma Stuckey /. Chicago , 1987. iv, 187 p. ; ISBN 0-913750-49-2 DDC 811/.54 19
PS3569.T83 A17 1987 NYPL [Sc E 89-104]

His Majesty, Queen Hatshepsut /. Carter, Dorothy Sharp. New York , c1987. viii, 248 p. : ISBN 0-397-32178-3 : DDC [Fic] 19
PZ7.C2434 Hi 1987 NYPL [Sc D 88-877]

HISPANIC AMERICAN CHILDREN - JUVENILE FICTION.
Talbot, Toby. I am Maria. New York [1969] 28 p. ISBN 0-402-14031-1 DDC [Fic]
PZ7.T148 I NYPL [Sc E 88-531]

HISPANIOLA - COLONIZATION - DRAMA.
Métellus, Jean, 1937- Anacaona . Paris , 1986. 159 p. : ISBN 2-218-07538-5
NYPL [Sc C 88-6]

HISPANOS. see MEXICAN AMERICANS.

Histoire de la vie et des dècouvertes de Christophe Colomb par Fernand Colomb, son fils. Colón, Fernando, 1488-1539. [Historie. English.] Christophe Colomb raconté par son fils /. Paris , 1986. xviii, 265 p., [8] p. of plates : ISBN 2-262-00387-4
NYPL [Sc D 88-504]

Histoire de St. Barth /. Defize, Stanislas. [Paris?] , c1987. [60] p. : ISBN 2-9502284-0-2
NYPL [Sc G 88-29]

Histoire des communes : Antilles-Guyane / collection dirigée par Jacques Adélaïde-Merlande. [S.l.] : Pressplay, c1986. 6 v. : ill. (some col.) ; 28 cm. Includes bibliographical references. CONTENTS. - 1. Les Abymes - Bellefontaine -- 2. Bouillante - Fort-de-France -- 3. Le François - Macouba -- 4. Macouria - Pointe-à-Pitre -- 5. Port-Louis - Saint-François -- 6. Saint-Georges - Vieux-Habitants. ISBN 2-88218-800-4 (set) DDC 972.97/6 19
1. West Indies, French - History. 2. West Indies, French - History, Local. I. Adélaïde-Merlande, Jacques.
F2151 .H575 1986 NYPL [Sc F 88-98]

L'Histoire des femmes en Afrique / enseignement de recherche 1985-1986, sous la direction de Mme Catherine Coquery-Vidrovitch ... Paris : L'Harmattan, c1987. 164 p. : ill. ; 24 cm. (Groupe Afrique noire . cahier no. 11) Includes bibliographical references. ISBN 2-7384-0172-4
1. Women - Africa, Sub-Saharan - History. I. Coquery-Vidrovitch, Catherine. II. Series: Cahier (Centre national de la recherche scientifique (France). Groupe de recherches ("Afrique noire") , no. 11.
NYPL [Sc E 89-226]

Histoire d'Haïti /. Madiou, Thomas, 1814-1884. Port-au-Prince, Haiti , 1981- v. :
NYPL [Sc Ser.-L .M227]

Histoire diplomatique d'Haïti 1804-1843 /. Coradin, Jean. Port-au-Prince, Haïti , 1988- v. ;
NYPL [Sc D 88-864]

Histoire du déchoukage /. Luc, Napoléon Serge. [Port-au-Prince, Haiti, W.I] [1987?] 124 p. :
NYPL [Sc D 87-1419]

Histoire d'une paysanne haïtienne. Cazanove, Michèle. Présumée Solitude, ou, Histoire d'une paysanne haïtienne . Paris , c1988. 178 p. ; ISBN 2-260-00546-2
NYPL [Sc D 88-1406]

Histoire immédiate.
Baccard, André. Les martyrs de Bokassa /. Paris , c1987. 349 p., [16] p. of plates : ISBN 2-02-009669-2 : DDC 967/.4105/0924 B 19
DT546.382.B64 B33 1987
NYPL [Sc D 88-636]

Histoire philosophique et politique des établissemens & du commerce dans les deux Indes. Raynal, Guillaume Thomas François, 1713-1796. A Amsterdam , 1770. 6 v. : *NYPL [Sc Rare C 86-2]*

Histoire politique du Sénégal . Hesseling, Gerti. [Senegal, staatsrechtelijke en politieke ontwikkelingen. French.] Paris, France , Leiden, Pays-Bas , c1985. 437 p. : ISBN 2-86537-118-2 DDC 342.66/3029 346.630229 19
LAW NYPL [JLE 88-3233]

Histoire rurale. Bujumbura : Dép. d'histoire, Faculté des lettres et sciences humaines, Université du Burundi ; Paris : Centre de recherches africaines, Université de Paris, 1984. v., 236 p. : ill., maps ; 30 cm. (Cahiers du Burundi ; no. 4) Cahiers d'histoire / Département d'histoire, Université du Burundi ; no. 2 Includes bibliographies.

1. Burundi - History. 2. Burundi - Rural conditions. I. Université du Burundi. Faculté des lettres et sciences humaines. II. Université de Paris I: Panthéon-Sorbonne. Centre de recherches africaines.
NYPL [Sc F 88-217]

Histoires d'immigrées : itinéraires d'ouvrières colombiennes, grecques, haïtiennes et portugaises de Montréal / Micheline Labelle ... [et al.] Montréal : Boréal, 1987. 275 p. ; 23 cm. Bibliography: p. 263-271. ISBN 2-89052-170-2
1. Alien labor - Québec - Montréal. 2. Women immigrants - Québec - Montréal. 3. Immigrants - Quebec - Montreal. I. Labelle, Micheline, 1940-.
NYPL [Sc D 88-346]

Historia del Estado Miranda /. Ramos Guédez, José Marcial. Caracas , 1981. 222 p. : DDC 987/.35 19
F2331.M6 R36 1981   *NYPL [Sc D 89-390]*

História do carnaval carioca /. Eneida, 1903-1971. Rio de Janeiro , c1987. 259 p. : ISBN 85-10-29900-5
GT4233.R5 E53 1987   *NYPL [Sc D 89-313]*

Historia en blanco y negro . Dean, Elizabeth. [History in black and white. Spanish.] Barcelona , Paris , 1984. 196 p. ; ISBN 92-3-302092-4 (Unesco)
NYPL [Sc D 88-594]

Historia y sociedad. [Santo Domingo] see Santo Domingo. Universidad Autónoma. Publicaciones.

HISTORIANS - TRINIDAD - BIOGRAPHY.
Buhle, Paul, 1944- C.L.R. James . London , New York , 1988. 197 p. ; ISBN 0-86091-221-3 : DDC 818 B 19
PR9272.9.J35 Z59 1988
NYPL [Sc E 89-171]

Histórias de operários negros / contribuição para o estudo do operàrio negro no Rio Grande do Sul / Petronilha Beatriz Gonçalves e Silva. Porto Alegre, RS, Brazil : Escola Superior de Teologia e Espiritualidade Franciscana : Nova Dimensão, c1987. 100 p. ; 23 cm. (Coleção afro-brasiliana . 6) Bibliography: p. 98-100.
1. Labor and laboring classes - Brazil - Rio Grande do Sul - Interviews. 2. Blacks - Brazil - Rio Grande do Sul - Interviews. I. Silva, Petronilha Beatriz Gonçalves e. II. Series. *NYPL [Sc D 88-823]*

Historic Basseterre . Inniss, Probyn, Sir. Basseterre, St. Kitts , c1985. 84 p. :
NYPL [Sc D 88-266]

Historic buildings of Harare, 1890-1940 /. Jackson, Peter, 1949- Harare, Zimbabwe , 1986. x, 134 p. : ISBN 0-908306-03-2 (pbk.) DDC 720/.96891 19
NA1596.6.R52 H375 1986
NYPL [Sc D 89-467]

HISTORIC SITES - UNITED STATES.
Past meets present . Washington, D.C. , 1987. x, 169 p. : ISBN 0-87474-272-2 DDC 069/.9973 19
D16.163 .P37 1987   *NYPL [Sc E 88-577]*

HISTORICAL CRITICISM. see HISTORIOGRAPHY.

Historical dictionary of Benin /. Decalo, Samuel. Metuchen, N.J. , 1987. xxvii, 349 p. : ISBN 0-8108-1924-4 DDC 966/.83 19
DT541.5 .D4 1987   *NYPL [Sc D 88-982]*

Historical dictionary of Egypt /. Wucher King, Joan. Metuchen, N.J. , 1984. xiii, 719 p. : ISBN 0-8108-1670-9 DDC 962/.003/21 19
DT45 .W83 1984   *NYPL [Sc D 85-101]*

Historical dictionary of Equatorial Guinea /. Liniger-Goumaz, Max. Metuchen, N.J. , 1988. xxx, 238 p. : ISBN 0-8108-2120-6 DDC 967/.18/00321 19
DT620.15 .L57 1988   *NYPL [Sc D 89-528]*

Historical dictionary of Ghana /. McFarland, Daniel Miles. Metuchen, N.J. , 1985. lxxx, 296 p. : ISBN 0-8108-1761-6 DDC 966.7/003/21 19
DT510.5 .M38 1985
*NYPL [*R-BMK 89-3348]*

Historical dictionary of Liberia /. Dunn, D. Elwood. Metuchen, N.J. , 1985. xx, 274, [7] p. of plates : ISBN 0-8108-1767-5 DDC 966.6/2/00321 19
DT631 .D95 1985   *NYPL [Sc D 86-127]*

Historical dictionary of Mali /. Imperato, Pascal James. Metuchen, N.J. , 1986. xvii, 359 p. ;

ISBN 0-8108-1885-X   DDC 966/.23 19
DT551.5 .I46 1986   *NYPL [Sc D 87-5]*

Historical dictionary of Nigeria /. Oyewole, A. Metuchen, N.J. , c1987. xvii, 391 p. : ISBN 0-8108-1787-X DDC 966.9/003/21 19
DT515.15 .O94 1987
*NYPL [*R-BMM 89-3341]*

Historical dictionary of South Africa /. Saunders, Christopher C. Metuchen, N.J. , 1983. xxviii, 241 p. ; ISBN 0-8108-1629-6 DDC 968/.003/21 19
DT766 .S23 1983   *NYPL [*R-BN 89-3347]*

Historical dictionary of the People's Republic of the Congo /. Thompson, Virginia McLean, 1903- Metuchen, N.J. , 1984. xxi, 239 p. : ISBN 0-8108-1716-0 DDC 967/.24 19
DT546.215 .T47 1984   *NYPL [Sc D 85-104]*

Historical dictionary of the Republic of Cape Verde /. Lobban, Richard. Metuchen, N.J. , 1988. xix, 171 p. ; ISBN 0-8108-2087-0 DDC 966/.57/00321 19
DT613.5 .L62 1988b   *NYPL [Sc D 88-1311]*

Historical dictionary of the Republic of Guinea-Bissau /. Lobban, Richard. Metuchen, N.J. , 1988. xx, 210 p. : ISBN 0-8108-2086-2 DDC 966/.57 19
DT613.5 .L62 1988
*NYPL [*R-BMP 88-5080]*

HISTORICAL MUSEUMS - UNITED STATES.
Past meets present . Washington, D.C. , 1987. x, 169 p. : ISBN 0-87474-272-2 DDC 069/.9973 19
D16.163 .P37 1987   *NYPL [Sc E 88-577]*

A historical survey of facilities for handicapped people in Zimbabwe /. Addison, Joan. Harare, Zimbabwe [1986] 36 p. :
NYPL [Sc F 88-266]

La historiografía del África austral . Historiographie de l'Afrique austral. Spanish. Barcelona , Paris , 1983. 128 p. ; ISBN 92-3-301775-3 (Unesco)
NYPL [Sc D 88-598]

Historiographie de l'Afrique austral. Spanish. La historiografía del África austral : documentos de trabajo e informe de la reunión de expertos, celebrada en Gaborone, Botswana, del 7 al 11 de marzo de 1977 / L.D. Ngcongco ... [et al.]1a ed. Barcelona : Serbal ; Paris : Unesco, 1983. 128 p. ; 20 cm. (Colección de temas africanos . 14) Translation of: L'Histoiriographie de l'Afrique austral. 1980. Original ed. published simultaneously in English as: The Historiography of southern Africa. Conference organized by Unesco. Bibliography: p. [125]-128. ISBN 92-3-301775-3 (Unesco)
1. Historiography - Africa, Southern - Congresses. 2. Africa, Southern - Historiography - Congresses. I. Ngcongco, L. D. (Leonard D.). II. Unesco. III. Title. IV. Series. *NYPL [Sc D 88-598]*

HISTORIOGRAPHY - AFRICA, SOUTHERN - CONGRESSES.
Historiographie de l'Afrique austral. Spanish. La historiografía del África austral . Barcelona , Paris , 1983. 128 p. ; ISBN 92-3-301775-3 (Unesco) *NYPL [Sc D 88-598]*

HISTORIOGRAPHY - NIGERIA.
Heinecke, P. Divided truths . Okpella, Bendel State, Nigeria , 1988. 135 p. ; ISBN 978-252-832-3 *NYPL [Sc D 89-134]*

HISTORY - CRITICISM. see HISTORIOGRAPHY.

HISTORY, NATURAL. see NATURAL HISTORY.

A history of Africa in the 19th century /. Njiro, Esther I. Nairobi , 1985. viii, 291 p. : DDC 960/.23 19
DT28 .N55 1985   *NYPL [Sc D 88-322]*

A history of African priests /. Waligo, John Mary, 1942- Masaka, Uganda , 1988. xi, 236 p., [16] p. of plates : *NYPL [Sc D 89-15]*

The history of Alpha Phi Alpha . Wesley, Charles H., 1891- Chicago , 1981, c1929. xiv, 567 p. : *NYPL [Sc D 89-135]*

The history of aviation in Trinidad & Tobago 1913-1962 /. Airports Authority of Trinidad and Tobago. Port-of-Spain, Trinidad , 1987. xxv, 159 p., [77] p. of plates : ISBN 976-8054-24-2 *NYPL [Sc D 87-1398]*

A history of Belize. Dobson, Narda. [Port of Spain, Trinidad and Tobago, 1973] xiv, 362 p. ISBN 0-582-76601-X DDC 972.82
F1446 .D56 1973   *NYPL [Sc D 88-649]*

A history of Black public education in Oklahoma [microform] /. Cayton, Leonard Bernard. 1976. 170 leaves.   *NYPL [Sc Micro R-4692]*

A history of Diego Martin 1784-1884 /. De Verteuil, Anthony. Port of Spain, Trinidad , c1987. viii, 174 p., [96] p. of plates : ISBN 976-8054-10-7   *NYPL [Sc F 88-192]*

The history of jazz. Schuller, Gunther. New York, 1968- v. DDC 785.42/09 19
ML3506 .S36 1968   *NYPL [JNL 89-2]*

The history of Mary Prince, a West Indian slave, related by herself /. Prince, Mary. London , New York , 1987. xiv, 124 p. ; ISBN 0-86358-192-7 DDC 305.5/67/0924 B 19
HT869.P6 A3 1987   *NYPL [Sc C 89-31]*

A history of neglect . Beardsley, Edward H. Knoxville , c1987. xvi, 383 p. : ISBN 0-87049-523-2 (alk. paper) : DDC 362.1/0425 19
RA448.5.N4 B33 1987   *NYPL [Sc E 87-625]*

A history of resistance in Namibia /. Katjavivi, Peter H. London , 1988. xvi, 152 p. : ISBN 0-85255-320-X; 0-231-02000-0 (pbk) : DDC 968.8 19
DT714   *NYPL [Sc D 88-1304]*

History of the Black people I have known in Halifax. Stephenson, Anne N. Informal history of the Black people I have known in Halifax /. [Halifax] c1978. 99 p. :
NYPL [Sc D 88-1209]

The history of the Black people of Franklin County, Tennessee [microform] /. Hill, Arthur Cyrus. 1981. 408 leaves.
NYPL [Sc Micro R-4685]

History of the Catholic church in Jamaica /. Osborne, Francis J. Aylesbury, Bucks, U.K. , c1977. vii, 210, [8] p. of plates : ISBN 0-85474-070-8 (pbk.) DDC 282/.7292 19
BX1455.2 .O84 1977   *NYPL [Sc F 88-290]*

A history of the desegregation of the Fayette County school system [microform] . Hunt, Frankie L. Cunningham. 1981. 351 leaves.
NYPL [Sc Micro R-4687]

The history of the Maroons, from their origin to the establishment of their chief tribe at Sierra Leone. Dallas, Robert Charles, 1754-1824. London, 1803. 2 v. :
F1881 .D14   *NYPL [Sc Rare F 88-76]*

A History of the migration and the settlement of the Baayo family from Timbuktu to Bijini in Guine Bissau / edited by Isatou Conteh ... [et al.] [Banjul? : s.n., 1987.] 71 p. : ill., maps ; 28 cm. Includes bibliographical references.
1. Islamic learning and scholarship - Guinea-Bissau - Bijini. 2. Baayo family. 3. Tambouctou (Mali) - History. I. Conteh, Isatou. II. Title. *NYPL [Sc F 89-146]*

The history of the National Association of Colored Women's Clubs . Wesley, Charles H. (Charles Harris), 1891- Washington, D.C. (5808 16th St., N.W., Washington) , 1984. viii, 562 p. : DDC 369/.1 19
E185.86.N36 W47 1984
NYPL [Sc D 88-725]

History of the Nigerian Army in pictures. Nigerian Army Museum. A pictorial history of the Nigerian Army /. Nigeria , c1987. 49 p. :
NYPL [Sc F 89-81]

The history of the penal system in the Virgin Islands /. Potter, Edwin. [Charlotte Amalie? , between 1985 and 1988] 69 leaves :
NYPL [Sc F 88-136]

History of the peoples of Lagos State / edited by Ade Adefuye, Babatunde Agiri, Jide Osuntokun. Ikeja, Lagos : Lantern Books, 1987. xii, 378 p. ; 22 cm. Includes index. Bibliography: p. 364-372. ISBN 978-228-148-4
1. Lagos State (Nigeria) - History. I. Adefuye, Ade. II. Agiri, Babatunde Aremu. III. Osuntokun, Akinjide.
NYPL [Sc D 88-731]

History of the Southern Gonga (Southwestern Ethiopia) /. Lange, Werner J. (1946- Wiesbaden , 1982. xvi, 348 p., [12] p. of plates : ISBN 3-515-03399-8 (pbk.) : DDC

306/.08996 19
DT380.4.G66 L36 1982
NYPL [Sc E 88-379]

A History of the University of Lagos, 1962-1987 / edited by A.B. Aderibigbe and T.G.O. Gbadamosi. Lagos, Nigeria : University of Lagos Press, 1987. xiii, 600 p. : ill., ports. ; 27 cm. Includes bibliographical references and index.
1. University of Lagos - History. I. Aderibigbe, A. B. II. Gbadamosi, T. G. O. **NYPL [Sc F 89-82]**

A history of Warri /. Ayomike, J. O. S. Benin City , 1988. xiii, 198 p. :
NYPL [Sc D 88-1370]

HISTRIONICS. see THEATER.

Hiwsisayin Amerikayi Miats'eal Tĕrut'iwnk'. see United States.

Ho, Christine G. T. The Caribbean connection : transnational social networks, non-assimilation and the structure of group life among Afro-Trinidadian immigrants in Los Angelos / by Christine G.T. Ho. c1985. xvi, 290 leaves : ill. Thesis (Ph. D.)--University of California, Los Angeles, 1985. Bibliography: leaves 282-290.
1. Trinidad and Tobago - Emigration and immigration. I. Title. **NYPL [Sc F 88-234]**

Hoban, Lillian. Dragonwagon, Crescent. Strawberry dress escape /. New York [1975] [32] p. : ISBN 0-684-13912-X :
NYPL [Sc F 88-126]

Hodd, Michael. Tanzania after Nyerere /. London , New York , c1988. ix, 197 p. ; ISBN 0-86187-916-3 : DDC 967.8/04 19
DT448.2 .T29 1988 **NYPL [Sc D 88-838]**

Hodge, Blanca. Nature, I love you . [St. Martin] , c1983. 36 p. :
MLCS 86/1723 (P) **NYPL [Sc D 88-626]**

Hodges, Carl G. Benjie Ream / by Carl G. Hodges. 1st ed. Indianapolis : Bobbs-Merrill, c1964. 153 p. ; 22 cm.
1. Slavery - Kansas - Juvenile fiction. 2. Kansas - History - 1854-1861 - Juvenile fiction. I. Title.
NYPL [Sc D 89-433]

Hodges, David. (illus) Chenfeld, Mimi Brodsky. The house at 12 Rose Street. London, New York, 1966. 157 p. DDC [Fic]
PZ7.C4183 Ho **NYPL [Sc D 88-509]**

Hodges, Elizabeth Jamison. Free as a frog. Drawings by Paul Giovanopoulos. [Reading, Mass.] Addison-Wesley [c1969] [32] p. illus. 23 cm. "An Addisonian Press book." A shy six-year-old feels he never has anything special to do or say until the day he finds a frog in the park. SCHOMBURG CHILDREN'S COLLECTION. DDC [Fic]
1. Afro-American children - Juvenile fiction. I. Giovanopoulos, Paul, illus. II. Schomburg Children's Collection. III. Title.
PZ7.H6634 Fr **NYPL [Sc D 88-1126]**

Hodges, Tony. Angola to the 1990s : the potential for recovery / by Tony Hodges. London : Economist Publications, 1987. 145 p. : ill., col. maps ; 30 cm. (EIU economic prospects series) Special report / Economist Intelligence Unit ; no. 1079 "January 1987."
1. Natural resources - Angola. 2. Angola - Economic conditions. 3. Angola - Industries. 4. Angola - Foreign economic relations. I. Series. II. Series: EIU special report, no. 1079. III. Title. **NYPL [Sc F 88-138]**

Hodza, Aaron C. Shona folk tales /. Gweru, Zimbabwe , 1987. 151 p. ; **NYPL [Sc C 88-317]**

Shona registers [microform] / composed by A.C. Hodza ; foreward and introduction by G. Fortune. 3rd ed. with minor revisions. Harare, Zimbabwe : Mercury Press, 1977-1984. 3 v. ; 30 cm. Text in Shona; introductory material in English. Vol. 1 published in 1984. "Originally published by The Department of African Languages, University of Rhodesia 1975." Microfilm. New York : New York Public Library, 198 . 1 microfilm reel ; 35 mm. (MN *ZZ-28635) CONTENTS. - v. 1. Institutions and relationships -- v. 2. Courtship and marriage -- v. 3. Ancestors, death and witchcraft. ISBN 0-7974-0482-1
1. Shona language. 2. Shona language - Style. 3. Mashona - Social life and customs. I. Fortune, George.
NYPL [Sc Micro R-4820 no.12]

Hoefer, Hans. Bahamas /. Singapore , 1987. 305 p. : ISBN 0-13-056276-9 (pbk.)
NYPL [Sc D 88-477]

Hoeven, Rolph van der. Planning for basic needs : a soft option or a social policy? : a basic needs simulation model applied to Kenya / Rolph van der Hoeven. Aldershot : Gower, c1988. xvii, 380 p. : ill. ; 22 cm. Prepared for the International Labour Office. Includes bibliography and index. ISBN 0-566-05680-1 : DDC 330.9172/4 19
1. Developing countries - Economic conditions. I. International Labour Office. II. Title.
HC59.7 **NYPL [Sc D 89-37]**

Hoey, William, 1930- (illus) Weir, LaVada. Howdy! Austin, Tex. [1972] 32 p. ISBN 0-8114-7735-5 DDC [E]
PZ7.W4415 Ho **NYPL [Sc E 88-613]**

Hoff, Syd, 1912-
(ill) Lexau, Joan M. Don't be my valentine /. New York, N.Y. , c1985. 64 p. : ISBN 0-06-023872-0 : DDC [E] 19
PZ7.L5895 Dp 1985 **NYPL [Sc D 89-58]**

(ill) Ricciuti, Edward R. Donald and the fish that walked /. New York [1974] 62 p. : ISBN 0-06-024997-8 : DDC 597/.52
QL638.C6 R52 1974 **NYPL [Sc D 88-447]**

Hoffmann, Charles. North by South : the two lives of Richard James Arnold / Charles Hoffmann and Tess Hoffmann. Athens : University of Georgia Press, c1988. xxii, 318 p., [8] p. of plates : ill. ; 25 cm. Includes index. Bibliography: p. [273]-308. ISBN 0-8203-0976-1 (alk. paper) DDC 975.8/73203/0924 19
1. Arnold, Richard James, 1796-1873 - Diaries. 2. Slaveholders - Georgia - Bryan County - Diaries. 3. Businessmen - Rhode Island - Diaries. 4. Plantation life - Georgia - Bryan County - History - 19th century. 5. Bryan County (Ga.) - Biography. I. Hoffmann, Tess. II. Title.
F292.B85 A753 1988 **NYPL [Sc E 89-35]**

Hoffmann, Eve. Meshover, Leonard. You visit a dairy [and a] clothing factory /. Chicago , c1965. 48 p. : **NYPL [Sc D 89-545]**

Hoffmann, Tess. Hoffmann, Charles. North by South . Athens , c1988. xxii, 318 p., [8] p. of plates : ISBN 0-8203-0976-1 (alk. paper) DDC 975.8/73203/0924 19
F292.B85 A753 1988 **NYPL [Sc E 89-35]**

Hoffnung auf Regen . Erichsen, Peter. Frankfurt am Main , 1988. 385 p. : ISBN 3-89228-235-8
NYPL [Sc D 89-206]

Hofstra Cultural Center. The Harlem renaissance . New York , 1989. xv, 342 p. : ISBN 0-8240-5739-2 (alk. paper) DDC 810/.9/896073 19
PS153.N5 H264 1989 **NYPL [Sc D 89-591]**

Hohenberger, Johannes. Semitische und hamitische Wortst"amme im Nilo-Hamitischen : mit phonetischen Analysen / Johannes Hohenberger. Berlin : D. Reimer, 1988. xxii, 310 p. ; 24 cm. (Marburger Studien zur Afrika- und Asienkunde: Serie A, Afrika. Bd. 42) Bibliography: p. [xv]-xviii. ISBN 3-496-00960-8
1. Nilo-Hamitic languages - Grammar, Comparative - Hamito-Semitic. 2. Hamito-Semitic languages - Grammar, Comparative - Nilo-Hamitic. I. Title.
NYPL [Sc E 88-542]

Hoile, David. Understanding sanctions / [David Hoile]. London : International Freedom Foundation (UK), 1988. 80 p. : ill. ; 21 cm. Bibliography: p. 73-76. ISBN 1-87111-700-3 (pbk.) : DDC 337.68 19
1. Economic sanctions - South Africa - Public opinion. 2. Disinvestment - South Africa - Public opinion. 3. Blacks - South Africa - Attitudes. 4. Public opinion - South Africa. I. Title.
HF1613.4 .H654 1988 **NYPL [Sc D 89-317]**

Holas, B. (Bohumil), 1909-1979. Image de la mère dans l'art ivoirien / B. Holas ; préf. de Thérèse Houphouët-Boigny. Abidjan : Nouvelles Éditions africaines, [1975] 122 p. : ill. ; 21 cm. DDC 732/.2/096668
1. Sculpture, Primitive - Ivory Coast. 2. Sculpture, African - Ivory Coast. 3. Mothers in art. I. Title.
NB1099.I8 H59 **NYPL [Sc D 88-476]**

Holdridge, Betty. Island boy / by Betty Holdridge ; illustrated with original lithographs by Paul Lantz. New York : Holiday House, c1942. 110 p. : ill. ; 21 cm. SCHOMBURG CHILDREN'S COLLECTION.
1. Children - Bahamas - Juvenile fiction. 2. Bahamas - Juvenile fiction. I. Schomburg Children's Collection. II. Title. **NYPL [Sc D 88-1181]**

HOLIDAY, BILLIE, 1915-1959.
White, John, 1939- Billie Holiday, her life & times /. Tunbridge Wells, Kent , New York , 1987. 144 p. : ISBN 0-87663-668-7 (USA) DDC 784.5/3/00924 B 19
ML420.H58 W5 1987 **NYPL [JNF 88-88]**

Hollings, Jill. African nationalism. Maps by Colin Judge. [1st American ed.] New York, John Day Co. [1972, c1971] 128 p. illus. 23 cm. (The Young historian books) Describes European and British control in Africa and how African countries gained their independence. Includes bibliographical references. DDC 320.5/4/096
1. Nationalism - Africa - Juvenile literature. 2. Africa - Politics and government - Juvenile literature. I. Judge, C. W. (Colin Walter), 1938- illus. II. Title.
DT31 .H577 1972 **NYPL [Sc D 88-1496]**

Holm, John A. Focus on the Caribbean /. Amsterdam , Philadelphia , 1986. ix, 209 p. : ISBN 90-272-4866-4 (pbk. : alk. paper) : DDC 427/.9729 19
PM7874.C27 F6 1986 **NYPL [JFD 87-3902]**

HOLMEAD'S CEMETERY (WASHINGTON, D.C.)
Sluby, Paul E. Holmead's Cemetery (Western Burial Ground), Washington, D.C. /. Washington, D.C. , 1985. iv, 68 leaves : DDC 929.5/09753 19
F193 .S582 1985 **NYPL [Sc D 88-109]**

Holmead's Cemetery (Western Burial Ground), Washington, D.C. /. Sluby, Paul E. Washington, D.C. , 1985. iv, 68 leaves : DDC 929.5/09753 19
F193 .S582 1985 **NYPL [Sc D 88-109]**

Holmes, Peter. Nigeria : giant of Africa / Peter Holmes. Lagos, Nigeria : National Oil and Chemical Marketing Co. of Nigeria, 1985. 206 p. : ill. (some col.) ; 31 cm. Includes index. Bibliography: p. [207]. ISBN 0-9508498-1-2 DDC 966.9/05 19
1. Nigeria - Description and travel - 1981- - Views. I. Title.
DT515.24 .H64 1985 **NYPL [Sc G 88-14]**

Holsclaw, Cora. (joint author) Brothers, Aileen. Just one me /. Chicago , c1967. 32 p. :
NYPL [Sc D 88-376]

Holsoe, Svend E.
Belcher, Max. A land and life remembered . Athens , Brockton, Mass. , c1988. [xii], 176 p. : ISBN 0-8203-1085-9 (alk. paper) DDC 720/.9666/2074014482 19
NA1599.L4 B4 1988 **NYPL [Sc F 89-90]**

Dunn, D. Elwood. Historical dictionary of Liberia /. Metuchen, N.J. , 1985. xx, 274, [7] p. of plates : ISBN 0-8108-1767-5 DDC 966.6/2/00321 19
DT631 .D95 1985 **NYPL [Sc D 86-127]**

Holup, Wopo. Shange, Ntozake. Some men /. [S.l.] c1981. [52] p. :
NYPL [Sc Rare C 88-2]

Holway, John. Blackball stars : Negro League pioneers / John B. Holway. Westport, CT : Meckler Books, c1988. xvi, 400 p. : ill., ports. ; 24 cm. Bibliography: p. 387. ISBN 0-88736-094-7 (alk. paper) : DDC 796.357/08996073/0922 B 19
1. Afro-American baseball players - Biography. 2. Baseball - United States - Records. I. Title.
GV865.A1 H614 1988 **NYPL [JFE 88-6437]**

Holy war [microform] /. 'Isá 'Abd Allāh Muḥammad al-Mahdī, 1945- Brooklyn, N.Y. , c1979. 68 p. :
NYPL [Sc Micro R-4114 no. 8]

HOME DESIGN. see ARCHITECTURE, DOMESTIC.

Home, sweet, sweet home /. Ojo-Ade, Femi. Ibadan , 1987. ix, 123 p. ; ISBN 978-15-4663-8 (Nigeria) **NYPL [Sc C 88-209]**

Home to Harlem /. McKay, Claude, 1890-1948. Boston , 1987, c1928. xxvi, 340 p. ; ISBN 1-555-53023-0 (alk. paper) : DDC 813/.52 19
PS3525.A24785 H6 1987 **NYPL [Sc D 88-544]**

HOMELANDS, SOUTH AFRICA - ECONOMIC CONDITIONS.
Moerdijk, Donald. [Anti-development, South Africa and its Bantustans. Spanish.] Antidesarrollo, Suráfrica y sus bantustanes /. Barcelona , Paris , 1982. 222 p. : ISBN

92-3-301888-1 (Unesco)
NYPL [Sc D 88-595]

HOMELANDS, SOUTH AFRICA - GOVERNMENT PUBLICATIONS - BIBLIOGRAPHY.
Kotzé, D. A. Bibliography of official publications of the Black South African homelands /. Pretoria , 1979. xix, 80 p. : ISBN 0-86981-137-1 DDC 015.68
Z3607.H65 K67 J705.T3;
NYPL [Sc D 88-1197]

HOMELANDS (SOUTH AFRICA) - POLITICS AND GOVERNMENT.
Moerdijk, Donald. [Anti-development, South Africa and its Bantustans. Spanish.] Antidesarrollo, Suráfrica y sus bantustanes /. Barcelona , Paris , 1982. 222 p. : ISBN 92-3-301888-1 (Unesco)
NYPL [Sc D 88-595]

Rural development administration in South Africa /. Pretoria , 1987. 70 p. : ISBN 0-7983-0100-7   *NYPL [Sc F 88-309]*

HOMELANDS (SOUTH AFRICA) - RURAL CONDITIONS - CASE STUDIES.
De Wet, C. J. Rural communities in transition . Grahamstown [1983] iii, 113 p., [6] leaves of plates : ISBN 0-86810-101-X (pbk.) DDC 307.7/2/0968 19
HD2130.5.Z9 H653 1983
NYPL [Sc F 88-328]

HOMELANDS (SOUTH AFRICA) - SOCIAL CONDITIONS.
Moerdijk, Donald. [Anti-development, South Africa and its Bantustans. Spanish.] Antidesarrollo, Suráfrica y sus bantustanes /. Barcelona , Paris , 1982. 222 p. : ISBN 92-3-301888-1 (Unesco)
NYPL [Sc D 88-595]

HOMELESSNESS - NEW YORK (N.Y.)
Manhattan (New York, N.Y.). President's Task Force on Housing for Homeless Families. A shelter is not a home . New York, NY , 1987. iv, 139, [19] p. ;   *NYPL [JLF 87-1294]*

HOMEMAKERS. see HOUSEWIVES.

Homer, Winslow, 1836-1910.
Wood, Peter H., 1943- Winslow Homer's images of Blacks . Austin, c1988. 144 p. : ISBN 0-292-79047-3 (University of Texas Press) DDC 759.13 19
ND237.H7 A4 1988a   NYPL [Sc F 89-133]

HOMER, WINSLOW, 1836-1910 - EXHIBITIONS.
Wood, Peter H., 1943- Winslow Homer's images of Blacks . Austin, c1988. 144 p. : ISBN 0-292-79047-3 (University of Texas Press) DDC 759.13 19
ND237.H7 A4 1988a   NYPL [Sc F 89-133]

HOMES. see DWELLINGS.

Homespun heroines and other women of distinction / Hallie Q. Brown ; with an introduction by Randall K. Burkett. New York : Oxford University Press, 1988. xxxv, viii, 248 p., [25] leaves of plates : ill., ports. ; 17 cm. (The Schomburg library of nineteenth-century Black women writers) Reprint. Originally published: Xenia, Ohio : Aldine Pub. Co., 1926. ISBN 0-19-505237-4 (alk. paper) DDC 920.72/08996073 19
1. Afro-American women - Biography. I. Brown, Hallie Q. (Hallie Quinn). II. Series.
E185.96 .H65 1988   NYPL [JFC 88-2157]

L'Homme de la rue . Mongo, Pabe, 1948- Paris , 1987. 168 p. ; ISBN 2-218-07767-1
NYPL [Sc C 88-5]

Homme, sociétés et développement /. Morel, Yves. Douala , 1980- v. : DDC 338.9 19
HD83 .M59   NYPL [Sc F 87-415]

L'homme vivant de Wole Soyinka /. Galle, Etienne. Paris , c1987. 270 p. ; ISBN 2-903871-88-4   *NYPL [Sc D 88-1128]*

Hommes et sociétés.
Afrique plurielle, Afrique actuelle . Paris , c1986. 272 p. ; ISBN 2-86537-151-4
NYPL [Sc E 88-349]

Ans, André Marcel d'. Haiti, Paysage et Société /. Paris , 1987. 337 p. : ISBN 2-86537-190-5
NYPL [Sc E 88-251]

Bocquené, Henri. Moi, un Mbororo . Paris , c1986. 387 p., [12] p. of plates : ISBN 2-86537-164-6   *NYPL [Sc E 89-66]*

Buijtenhuijs, Robert. Le Frolinat et les guerres civiles du Tchad (1977-1984) . Paris, France , c1987. 479 p. : ISBN 2-86537-196-4
NYPL [Sc E 88-426]

Cauna, Jacques, 1948- Au temps des isles à sucre . Paris , c1987. 285 p., [16] p. of plates : ISBN 2-86537-186-5   *NYPL [Sc E 88-492]*

Diop, Abdoulaye Bara. La famille Wolof . Paris , c1985. 262 p. : ISBN 2-86537-138-7
NYPL [Sc E 89-126]

Enjeux fonciers dan la Caraibe, en Amérique centrale et à la Réunion. . Paris , c1987. 232 p. : ISBN 2-7380-0003-7 *NYPL [Sc E 88-246]*

Légendes historiques du Burundi . Paris , Bujumbura , c1987. 286 p. : ISBN 2-86507-178-6
NYPL [Sc E 88-324]

Robinson, David, 1938- [Holy war of Umar Tal. French.] La guerre sainte d'al-Hajj Umar . Paris , c1988. 413 p. : ISBN 2-86537-211-1
NYPL [Sc E 89-258]

Hommes et sociétés (Editions Karthala)
(7) Peuples du golfe du Bénin . Paris , c1984. 328 p. : ISBN 2-86537-092-5 DDC 966/.8004963 19
DT510.43.E94 P48 1984
NYPL [Sc E 88-449]

Bocquené, Henri. Moi, un Mbororo . Paris , c1986. 387 p., [12] p. of plates : ISBN 2-86537-164-6   *NYPL [Sc E 89-66]*

Robinson, David, 1938- [Holy war of Umar Tal. French.] La guerre sainte d'al-Hajj Umar . Paris , c1988. 413 p. : ISBN 2-86537-211-1
NYPL [Sc E 89-258]

Hommes et sociétés, 0290-6600.
(7) Peuples du golfe du Bénin . Paris , c1984. 328 p. : ISBN 2-86537-092-5 DDC 966/.8004963 19
DT510.43.E94 P48 1984
NYPL [Sc E 88-449]

Hesseling, Gerti. [Senegal, staatsrechtelijke en politieke ontwikkelingen. French.] Histoire politique du Sénégal . Paris, France , Leiden, Pays-Bas , c1985. 437 p. : ISBN 2-86537-118-2 DDC 342.66/3029 346.630229 19
LAW   NYPL [JLE 88-3233]

HOMOPHILE MOVEMENT. see GAY LIBERATION MOVEMENT.

HOMOSEXUAL LIBERATION MOVEMENT. see GAY LIBERATION MOVEMENT.

HOMOSEXUALITY - FICTION.
Kindred spirits . Boston , 1984. 262 p. ; ISBN 0-932870-42-2 (pbk.) :
NYPL [Sc D 89-269]

Worlds apart . Boston, Mass. , 1986. 293 p. ; ISBN 0-932870-87-2 (pbk.) : DDC 813/.0876/08353 19
PS648.H57 W67 1986   NYPL [JFD 87-7753]

HOMOSEXUALITY - JUVENILE FICTION.
Childress, Alice. Those other people /. New York , c1988. 186 p. ; ISBN 0-399-21510-7 DDC [Fic] 19
PZ7.C4412 Th 1988   NYPL [Sc D 89-327]

HOMOSEXUALITY, MALE - CENTRAL AMERICA.
Male homosexuality in Central and South America /. New York , 1987. 199 p. ;
NYPL [Sc D 88-557]

HOMOSEXUALITY, MALE - SOUTH AMERICA.
Male homosexuality in Central and South America /. New York , 1987. 199 p. ;
NYPL [Sc D 88-557]

HOMOSEXUALITY - POETRY.
Gay & lesbian poetry in our time . New York , c1988. xxviii, 401 p. ; ISBN 0-312-02213-1 : DDC 811/.54/080353 19
PS595.H65 G39 1988   NYPL [JFE 89-277]

HOMOSEXUALS, MALE - UNITED STATES - FICTION.
Preston, John. Stolen moments /. Boston , 1985. 125 p. ; ISBN 0-932870-71-6
NYPL [Sc D 88-3]

HOMOSEXUALS' WRITINGS.
Tongues untied . London , Boston, MA, USA , 1987. 95 p. ; ISBN 0-85449-053-1 (pbk) : DDC 821/.914/080920664 19
PR1178.H6   NYPL [JFD 88-7561]

Hondo yeChimurenga : nyaya dzeHondo / mufananidzo naHassam Musa. Gweru : Mambo Press, in association with the Literature Bureau, 1984. 230 p. ; 19 cm. ISBN 0-86922-284-8
1. Shona language - Texts. 2. Zimbabwe - History - Chimurenga War, 1966-1980 - Fiction. I. Musa, Hassam.   NYPL [Sc C 89-110]

HONDURAS - HISTORY.
Lapper, Richard. Honduras, state for sale /. London , 1985. iv, 132 p. : ISBN 0-906156-23-8
NYPL [HML 87-1562]

Honduras, state for sale /. Lapper, Richard. London , 1985. iv, 132 p. : ISBN 0-906156-23-8
NYPL [HML 87-1562]

Honey from the lion . Belcher, Wendy Laura. New York , c1988. xiv, 188 p. : ISBN 0-525-24596-0 : DDC 966.7/05 19
DT510.4 .B38 1988   NYPL [Sc D 88-842]

Honey, I love, and other love poems /. Greenfield, Eloise. New York , c1978. [48] p. : ISBN 0-690-01334-5 (lib. bdg.) DDC 811/.5/4
PS3557.R39416 H66 1978
NYPL [Sc C 89-22]

HONEY - JUVENILE FICTION.
Iroaganachi, John. A fight for honey /. Lagos, Nigeria , 1977. 30 p. : ISBN 0-410-80181-X
NYPL [Sc C 88-77]

Honig, Donald.
Baseball in the '50s : a decade of transition : an illustrated history / by Donald Honig.1st ed. New York : Crown Publishers, 1987. 238 p. : ill. ; 29 cm. Includes index. ISBN 0-517-56578-1 DDC 796.357/0973 19
1. Baseball - United States - History. I. Title. II. Title: Baseball in the fifties.
GV863.A1 H67 1987   NYPL [JFF 88-794]

Mays, Mantle, Snider : a celebration / Donald Honig. New York, N.Y. : Macmillan ; London : Collier Macmillan, c1987. vii, 151 p. : ill. ; 29 cm. Includes index. ISBN 0-02-551200-5 DDC 796.357/092/2 B 19
1. Mays, Willie, 1931-. 2. Mantle, Mickey, 1931-. 3. Snider, Duke. 4. Baseball players - United States - Biography. 5. Afro-American baseball players - Biography. I. Title.
GV865.A1 H6192 1987
NYPL [JFF 87-1461]

Honorat, Jean Jacques. Community action in Haiti [microform] : a case study of social control through charity and illusion / Jean Jacques Honorat. New York : Institute of Haitian Studies, 1982. 45 p. ; 28 cm. Cover title. Bibliography: p. 43-45. Microfiche. New York: New York Public Library, 198. 1 microfiche: negative; 11 x 15 cm. (FSN Sc 019,097).
1. Rural development - Haiti. 2. Community development - Haiti. I. Title.
NYPL [Sc Micro F-11008]

Honoré, Narénia François. Bref aperçu sur l'évolution de la prostitution en Haïti. 1ère éd. [Port-au-Prince] : Imp. Haïti-Presse, 1981. 49 p., [1] leaf of plates : port. ; 21 cm. DDC 306.7/4 19
1. Prostitution - Haiti. I. Title.
HQ162.A5 H66   NYPL [Sc D 88-318]

Honwana, Luís Bernardo, 1942-
[Nós matámos o Cão-Tinhoso. English]
We killed Mangy-Dog, & other stories / Luis Bernardo Honwana ; translated from the Portuguese by Dorothy Guedes. Harare, Zimbabwe : Zimbabwe Pub. House, 1987. 117 p. ; 19 cm. (ZPH writers series. 35) Translation of Nós matamos o Cão-Tinhoso. ISBN 0-9792256-2-2 :
1. Mozambique - Fiction. I. Title. II. Series.
NYPL [Sc C 89-106]

Honwana, Raúl Bernardo Manuel, 1905-
[Histórias ouvidas e vividas dos homens e da terra. English]
The life history of Raúl Honwana : an inside view of Mozambique from colonialism to independence, 1905-1975 / edited and with an introduction by Allen F. Isaacman ; translated by Tamara Bender. Boulder : L. Rienner Publishers, 1988. ix, 181 p. : maps, ports. ; 24 cm. Translation of: Histórias ouvidas e vividas dos homens e da terra. ISBN 1-555-87114-3 (lib. bdg.) : DDC 967/.903/0924 B 19
1. Honwana, Raúl Bernardo Manuel, 1905-. 2. Mozambique - History - 1891-1975. 3. Mozambique -

Biography. I. Isaacman, Allen F. II. Title.
DT463 .H6613 1988   *NYPL [Sc E 88-367]*

**HONWANA, RAÚL BERNARDO MANUEL,
1905-**
Honwana, Raúl Bernardo Manuel, 1905-
[Histórias ouvidas e vividas dos homens e da
terra. English] The life history of Raúl
Honwana . Boulder , 1988. ix, 181 p. : ISBN
1-555-87114-3 (lib. bdg.) : DDC 967/.903/0924
B 19
DT463 .H6613 1988   *NYPL [Sc E 88-367]*

Honychurch, Lennox. The Dominica story : a
history of the island / by Lennox Honychurch ;
the cover painting and all maps and drawings
by Lennox Honychurch. Roseau, Dominica :
Dominica Institute, 1984. 225 p. : ill. ; 22 cm.
Bibliography: p. 224.
1. Dominica - History. I. Title.
   NYPL [Sc D 88-166]

Hookoomsing, Vinesh Y. Baker, Philip.
Morisyeñ - English - français . Paris , 1987.
365 p. ; ISBN 2-85802-973-3
   NYPL [Sc E 88-407]

Hooray for Jasper. Horvath, Betty F. New York
[1966] 1 v. (unpaged)
PZ7.H7922 Ho   *NYPL [Sc F 88-252]*

Hope born out of despair : managing the African
crisis / edited [by] Thomas R. Odhiambo with
Peter Anyang' Nyong'o ... [et al.]. Nairobi :
Heinemann Kenya, 1988. xv, 123 p. ; 21 cm.
Includes bibliographical references. ISBN
996-646-456-5
*1. Africa - Politics and government. 2. Africa -
Economic conditions. I. Odhiambo, Thomas R. II.
Nyong'o, Anyang'.* *NYPL [Sc D 89-477]*

HOPE, LUGENIA BURNS.
Rouse, Jacqueline Anne. Lugenia Burns Hope,
Black southern reformer /. Athens , c1989. xi,
182 p., [8] p. of plates : ISBN 0-8203-1082-4 (alk.
paper) DDC 973/.0496073024 B 19
E185.97.H717 R68 1989
   NYPL [Sc D 89-469]

**HOPE TOWN (BAHAMAS) - DESCRIPTION -
TOURS.**
Dodge, Steve. A guide and history of Hope
Town /. Decatur, Ill., USA , c1985. [48] p. :
ISBN 0-932265-01-4 (pbk) : DDC 917.296 19
F1659.H67 D63 1985   *NYPL [Sc D 88-684]*

HOPE TOWN (BAHAMAS) - HISTORY.
Dodge, Steve. A guide and history of Hope
Town /. Decatur, Ill., USA , c1985. [48] p. :
ISBN 0-932265-01-4 (pbk) : DDC 917.296 19
F1659.H67 D63 1985   *NYPL [Sc D 88-684]*

Hopes and impediments . Achebe, Chinua.
London , 1988. x, 130 p. ; ISBN 0-435-91000-0
(cased) : DDC 823/.914/09 19
PR881   *NYPL [Sc D 88-1265]*

Hopes of the living dead . Rotimi, Ola. Ibadan ,
c1988. xii, 112 p. ; ISBN 978-246-013-3
   NYPL [Sc C 89-138]

Hopkin, Gerry R. S. Grenada topples the balance
in West Indian history : a day to day report of
the Grenada episode / by Gerry R.S. Hopkin.
[Grenada : s.n.], c1984. 76 p. : ill. ; 18 cm.
*1. Granada - Politics and government - 1974-. 2.
Granada - History - American invasion, 1983. I. Title.*
   NYPL [Sc C 88-147]

Hopkins, David, 1936- African comedy / David
Hopkins. London : Collins, 1988. 224 p. ; 22
cm. ISBN 0-00-223235-9 : DDC 823/.914 19
1. Africa - Fiction. I. Title. *NYPL [Sc D 89-162]*

Hopkins, Lee Bennett. This street's for me!
Poems by Lee Bennett Hopkins. Pictures by
Ann Grifalconi. New York, Crown Publishers
[1970] [38] p. col. illus. 25 cm. Seventeen poems
about subways, shoeshines, water fountains, hydrants,
and other elements of city life. SCHOMBURG
CHILDREN'S COLLECTION.
*I. Grifalconi, Ann, illus. II. Schomburg Children's
Collection. III. Title.*
PZ8.3.H776 Th   *NYPL [JFE 72-966]*

Hopkins, Marjorie. And the jackal played the
masinko. Pictures by Olivia H. H. Cole. New
York, Parents' Magazine Press [1969] [41] p.
col. illus. 20 x 26 cm. A young boy devises a way
to make a request of the King of Ethiopia without
appearing greedy. SCHOMBURG CHILDREN'S
COLLECTION. ISBN 0-8193-0271-6
1. Ethiopia - Juvenile fiction. I. Cole, Olivia H. H.,

illus. II. Schomburg Children's Collection. III. Title.
PZ7.H7756 An   *NYPL [JFF 72-292]*

Hopkins, Pauline E. (Pauline Elizabeth)
Contending forces : a romance illustrative of
negro life north and south / Pauline Hopkins ;
with an introduction by Richard Yarborough.
New York : Oxford University Press, 1988.
xlviii, 402 p., [8] p. of plates : ill. ; 17 cm. (The
Schomburg library of nineteenth-century Black women
writers) Bibliography: p. xlvi-xlviii. Reprint.
Originally published: Boston, Mass. : Colored Co-operative Pub.
Co., 1900. ISBN 0-19-505258-7 (alk. paper) DDC
813/.4 19
1. Afro-Americans - Fiction. I. Title. II. Series.
PS1999.H4226 C66 1988
   NYPL [JFC 88-2153]

[Novels. Selections]
The magazine novels of Pauline Hopkins /
with an introduction by Hazel V. Carby. New
York ; Oxford : Oxford University Press,
1988. l, 621 p. ; 17 cm. (The Schomburg library
of nineteenth-century Black women writers)
Reprinted from various sources. Bibliography: xlviii-l.
CONTENTS. - Hagar's daughter -- Winona -- Of
one blood. ISBN 0-19-505248-X (alk. paper) DDC
813/.4 19
1. Afro-Americans - Fiction. I. Title. II. Series.
PS1999.H4226 A6 1988
   NYPL [JFC 88-2195]

Horie, C. V. (Charles Velson) Materials for
conservation : organic consolidants, adhesives
and coatings / C.V. Horie. London ; Boston :
Butterworths, 1987. xi, 281 p. : ill. ; 21 cm.
(Butterworths series in conservation and museology)
Includes index. Bibliography: p. 229-252. ISBN
0-408-01531-4 : DDC 667/.9 19
*1. Coatings. 2. Art - Conservation and restoration. I.
Title. II. Series.*
TP156.C57 H67 1987   *NYPL [Sc D 88-558]*

HORN FAMILY.
Buckley, Gail Lumet, 1937- The Hornes . New
York , 1986. 262 p. : ISBN 0-394-51306-1 :
DDC 974.7/2300496073/00922 B 19
F129.B7 B83 1986   *NYPL [Sc E 86-286]*

Horne, Gerald.
Communist front? : the Civil Rights Congress,
1946-1956 / Gerald Horne. Rutherford [N.J.] :
Fairleigh Dickinson University Press ; London :
Associated University Presses, c1988. 454 p. ;
25 cm. Includes index. Bibliography: p. 359-422.
ISBN 0-8386-3285-8 (alk. paper) DDC
323.1/196073/073 19
*1. Civil Rights Congress (U. S.). 2. Afro-Americans -
Civil rights. 3. Anti-communist movements - United
States - History - 20th century. 4. United States - Race
relations. I. Title.*
E185.61 .H8 1988   *NYPL [Sc E 88-147]*

Thinking and rethinking U. S. history /. New
York, N.Y. , c1988. 389 p. ;
   NYPL [Sc F 89-130]

HORNE, LENA - FAMILY.
Buckley, Gail Lumet, 1937- The Hornes . New
York , 1986. 262 p. : ISBN 0-394-51306-1 :
DDC 974.7/2300496073/00922 B 19
F129.B7 B83 1986   *NYPL [Sc E 86-286]*

The Hornes . Buckley, Gail Lumet, 1937- New
York , 1986. 262 p. : ISBN 0-394-51306-1 :
DDC 974.7/2300496073/00922 B 19
F129.B7 B83 1986   *NYPL [Sc E 86-286]*

Horricks, Raymond, 1933- Quincy Jones /
Raymond Horricks ; selected discography by
Tony Middleton. Tunbridge Wells, Kent :
Spellmount ; New York : Hippocrene Books,
1985. 127 p., [8] p. of plates : ill. ; 24 cm.
"Popular musicians, 2"--Brit. CIP. Errata slip tipped in.
Discography: p. 111-127. ISBN 0-87052-215-9
(Hippocrene Books) : DDC 785.42/092/4 B 19
*1. Jones, Quincy, 1933-. 2. Jazz musicians - United
States - Biography. 3. Afro-American musicians -
Biography. I. Middleton, Tony. II. Title. III. Title:
Popular musicians.*
ML419.J7 H67 1985   *NYPL [Sc E 87-36]*

HORROR STORIES, AMERICAN.
Thomas, Joyce Carol. Journey /. New York ,
c1988. 153 p. ; ISBN 0-590-40627-2 : DDC [Fic]
19
PZ7.T36696 Jo 1988   *NYPL [Sc D 89-235]*

HORSE. see HORSES.

HORSES - JUVENILE FICTION.
Cooper, Page. Thunder /. Cleveland , 1954. 218
p.   *NYPL [Sc D 88-661]*

Lang, Don. Strawberry roan /. New York ,
1946. 218 p. :   *NYPL [Sc D 88-646]*

Raferty, Gerald. Twenty-dollar horse /. Eau
Claire, Wisconsin , 1967, c1955. 192 p. :
   NYPL [Sc D 88-664]

Springer, Nancy. They're all named Wildfire /.
New York , 1989. 103 p. ; ISBN 0-689-31450-7
DDC [Fic] 19
PZ7.S76846 Th 1989   *NYPL [Sc D 89-498]*

Horst, Samuel L., 1919- Education for manhood :
the education of Blacks in Virginia during the
Civil War / Samuel L. Horst. Lanham, MD :
University Press of America, c1987. viii, 292
p. ; 23 cm. Includes index. Bibliography: p. 263-275.
ISBN 0-8191-6662-6 (alk. paper) : DDC
370/.89960730755 19
*1. Afro-Americans - Education - Virginia - History -
19th century. I. Title.*
LC2802.V8 H67 1987   *NYPL [Sc D 88-550]*

Horta, Elisabeth Vorcaro. A mulher na cultura
brasileira / Elisabeth Vorcaro Horta. Belo
Horizonte : [s.n.], 1975. 122 p. ; 23 cm.
Thesis--Universidade Federal de Minas Gerais, 1973.
Bibliography: p. [115]-122.
*1. Women - Brazil - Social conditions. 2. Women -
Employment - Brazil. I. Title.*
HQ1542 .H66   *NYPL [Sc D 86-811]*

As hortênsias morrem na primavera /. Coelho,
Abílio. Rio de Janeiro , 1987. 271 p. ;
   NYPL [Sc D 88-709]

**HORTICULTURE - BRAZIL -
PERNAMBUCO - HISTORY - SOURCES.**
Diario de Pernambuco . Recife [1985]. 256 p. :
ISBN 85-7019-094-8   *NYPL [Sc D 88-862]*

Horvath, Betty F.
Hooray for Jasper, by Betty Horvath. Pictures
by Fermin Rocker. New York, F. Watts [1966]
1 v. (unpaged) col. illus. 27 cm. SCHOMBURG
CHILDREN'S COLLECTION.
*1. Afro-American children - Juvenile fiction. I. Rocker,
Fermin, illus. II. Schomburg Children's Collection. III.
Title.*
PZ7.H7922 Ho   *NYPL [Sc F 88-252]*

Jasper makes music, by Betty Horvath. Pictures
by Fermin Rocker. New York, F. Watts [1967]
[38] p. illus. 27 cm. An eight-year-old boy who
yearns for a guitar finds a snow shovel which he hopes
to put to good use over the winter earning the money
to buy what he wants and needs. SCHOMBURG
CHILDREN'S COLLECTION. DDC [E]
*1. Afro-American children - Juvenile fiction. I. Rocker,
Fermin, illus. II. Schomburg Children's Collection. III.
Title.*
PZ7.H7922 Jas   *NYPL [Sc F 88-343]*

Not enough Indians, by Betty Horvath. Pictures
by Ted Lewin. New York, F. Watts [1971] [47]
p. illus. (part col.) 26 cm. When the Maple Street
Gang becomes the Maple Street Indians they oust the
only girl. After all, who wants a squaw? SCHOMBURG
CHILDREN'S COLLECTION. ISBN 0-531-01968-3
DDC [Fic]
*1. Children - Societies and clubs - Juvenile fiction. I.
Lewin, Ted, illus. II. Schomburg Children's Collection.
III. Title.*
PZ7.H7922 No   *NYPL [Sc F 88-341]*

Hoskins, Robert L. Background characteristics
and selected perceptions of Black administrators
working at Black and white land-grant
institutions of higher education [microform] /
by Robert L. Hoskins. 1977. 213 leaves. Thesis
(Ph. D.)--University of Wisconsin, Milwaukee, 1977.
Bibliography: leaves 210-213. Microfilm of typescript.
Ann Arbor, Mich.: University Microfilms International,
1978. 1 microfilm reel; 35 mm.
*1. Afro-American universities and colleges -
Administration. I. Title.*
   NYPL [Sc Micro R-4226]

HOSPITAL PATIENTS - GREAT BRITAIN.
Pearson, Maggie. Racial equality and good
practice maternity care . London , 1985. 37 p. :
ISBN 0-86082-610-4 (pbk) : DDC 362.1/982 19
RG964.G7   *NYPL [Sc F 88-393]*

**HOSPITALS - GABON - LAMBARÉNÉ
(MOYEN-OGOOUÉ)**
Oswald, Suzanne. Im Urwaldspital von
Lambarene /. Bern , c1986. 31 p. : ISBN
3-258-03594-6   *NYPL [Sc D 87-1076]*

Hostage /. Dixon, Glen. London , 1986. 189 p.,
[8] p. of plates : ISBN 0-86287-271-5
   NYPL [Sc E 88-406]

HOSTAGES - ANGOLA - HISTORY - 20TH CENTURY.
Dixon, Glen. Hostage /. London , 1986. 189 p., [8] p. of plates : ISBN 0-86287-271-5
    NYPL [Sc E 88-406]

HOSTILITIES. see WAR.

The hot dog man. Lynch, Lorenzo, 1932- Indianapolis [1970] [24] p. DDC [Fic]
PZ7.L97977 Ho   *NYPL [Sc F 88-253]*

Hot light/half-made worlds . Webb, Alex. New York, N.Y. , 1986. 91 p. : ISBN 0-500-54116-7 : DDC 779/.99090913 19
TR820.5 .W43 1986   *NYPL [Sc G 87-23]*

Hot sauces . Bergman, Billy. New York , c1985. 144 p. : ISBN 0-688-02193-X (pbk.) : DDC 780/.42/09729 19
ML3475 .B47 1985   *NYPL [Sc F 87-19]*

Hotel boy /. Kaufman, Curt. New York , c1987. 40 p. : ISBN 0-689-31287-3 : DDC 307.3/36 19
HV4046.N6 K38 1987   *NYPL [Sc F 88-362]*

HOTELS, TAVERNS, ETC. - GHANA - GUIDE-BOOKS.
Ghana, guide to hotels and restaurants. [Ghana] , 1986. 71 p. :
    NYPL [Sc D 88-1385]

HOTELS, TAVERNS, ETC. - NEW YORK (N. Y.) - CASE STUDIES - JUVENILE LITERATURE.
Kaufman, Curt. Hotel boy /. New York , c1987. 40 p. : ISBN 0-689-31287-3 : DDC 307.3/36 19
HV4046.N6 K38 1987   *NYPL [Sc F 88-362]*

Houchins, Susan. Spiritual narratives /. New York , 1988. 489 p. in various pagings : ISBN 0-19-505266-8 (alk. paper) DDC 209/.22 B 19
BR1713 .S65 1988   *NYPL [JFC 88-2189]*

Houghton Library. Pushkin and his friends . Cambridge , 1987. xii, 95 p. :
    NYPL [Sc F 88-236]

HOUPHOUET-BOIGNY, FÉLIX, 1905- - CONGRESSES.
Séminaires d'information et de formation des secrétaires généraux . [Abidjan] [1985] 72 p. : DDC 966.6/805 19
DT545.8 .S46 1985   *NYPL [Sc E 88-151]*

Hourani, Albert Habib. The Cambridge encyclopedia of the Middle East and North Africa /. Cambridge [England] , New York , 1988. 504 p. : ISBN 0-521-32190-5 DDC 956 19
DS44 .C37 1988   *NYPL [*R-BCF 89-551]*

The house at 12 Rose Street. Chenfeld, Mimi Brodsky. London, New York, 1966. 157 p. DDC [Fic]
PZ7.C4183 Ho   *NYPL [Sc D 88-509]*

House, Ernest R. Jesse Jackson & the politics of charisma : the rise and fall of the PUSH/Excel program / Ernest R. House. Boulder : Westview Press, 1988. xi, 196 p. ; 24 cm. Includes index. Bibliography: p. 183-190. ISBN 0-8133-0767-8 (alk. paper) DDC 973.92/092/4 19
1. Jackson, Jesse, 1941-. 2. Operation Push. I. Title. II. Title: Jesse Jackson and the politics of charisma.
E840.8.J35 H68 1988   *NYPL [JFE 88-7205]*

House of Representatives (U. S.) see United States. Congress. House.

The house on the mountain. Clymer, Eleanor (Lowenton) 1906- New York [1971] 39 p. ISBN 0-525-32365-1 DDC [Fic]
PZ7.C6272 Ho   *NYPL [Sc D 88-445]*

HOUSEHOLD VIOLENCE. see FAMILY VIOLENCE.

HOUSES. see ARCHITECTURE, DOMESTIC; DWELLINGS.

HOUSEWIVES - SOUTHERN STATES - INTERVIEWS.
Telling memories among southern women . Baton Rouge , c1988. xi, 279 p. : ISBN 0-8071-1440-5 (alk. paper) : DDC 305.4/3 19
HD6072.2.U52 A137 1988   *NYPL [Sc E 89-124]*

HOUSING, AFRO-AMERICAN. see AFRO-AMERICANS - HOUSING.

HOUSING MANAGEMENT - DEVELOPING COUNTRIES.
The Role of women in the execution of low-income housing projects . Nairobi, Kenya ,

1986. 64 p. : ISBN 92-1-131005-9
    NYPL [Sc F 88-225]

HOUSING - SOUTH AFRICA.
Mashabela, Harry. Townships of the PWV /. Braamfontein, Johannesburg , 1988. 184 p. : ISBN 0-86982-343-4   *NYPL [Sc D 89-155]*

HOUSTON, WHITNEY - JUVENILE LITERATURE.
Greenberg, Keith Elliot. Whitney Houston /. Minneapolis , c1988. 32 p. : ISBN 0-8225-1619-5 (lib. bdg.) : DDC 784.5/0092/4 B 92 19
ML3930.H7 G7 1988   *NYPL [Sc D 88-1459]*

Hove, Chenjerai, 1956- Red hills of home / Chenjerai Hove. Gweru, Zimbabwe : Mambo Press, 1985. 68 p. ; 18 cm. (Mambo writers series. English section. vol. 21) ISBN 0-86922-368-2 (pbk.) DDC 821 19
I. Title.
PR9390.9.H68 R4 1985
    NYPL [Sc C 88-314]

Hovis, Gene.
[Uptown down home cookbook]
Gene Hovis's uptown down home cookbook / by Gene Hovis with Sylvia Rosenthal. 1st ed. Boston : Little, Brown, c1987. xii, 235 p. ; 25 cm. Includes index. ISBN 0-316-37443-1 : DDC 641.5 19
1. Cookery, American - Southern style. 2. Cookery, American. I. Rosenthal, Sylvia Dworsky, 1911-. II. Title. III. Title: Uptown down home cookbook.
TX715 .H8385 1987   *NYPL [Sc E 88-476]*

How a little girl went to Africa . Bicknell, Leona Mildred. Boston , 1904. 172 p. :
    NYPL [Sc C 88-368]

How and why stories /. Branner, John Casper, 1850-1922. New York , 1921. xi, 104 p. :
    NYPL [Sc D 89-104]

How ends the day /. Hackney, Claudius T. Bryn Mawr, Penn. , 1986. 80 p. ; ISBN 0-8059-3019-1
    NYPL [Sc D 88-186]

How many snails? . Giganti, Paul. New York , c1988. [24] p. : ISBN 0-688-06369-1 : DDC [E] 19
PZ7.G364 Ho 1988   *NYPL [Sc F 88-301]*

How to survive when you're the only Black in the office . McClenney, Earl H. Richmond, Va. , c1987. 212 p. ; ISBN 0-9618835-0-2 (pbk.) : DDC 650.1/3/0240396073 19
HF5386 .M473 1987   *NYPL [Sc D 89-242]*

Howard, Elizabeth. North winds blow free. New York : Morrow, 1949. 192 p. : ill. ; 22 cm.
1. Underground railroad - Fiction. I. Title.
    NYPL [Sc D 88-1498]

Howard, Elizabeth Fitzgerald. The train to Lulu's / by Elizabeth Fitzgerald Howard ; illustrated by Robert Casilla. New York : Bradbury Press, c1988. [32] p. : col. ill. ; 22 x 27. The experiences of two young sisters traveling alone on the train to their grandmother's house. SCHOMBURG CHILDREN'S COLLECTION. 0-02-744620-4 : DDC [E] 19
1. Afro-American children - Juvenile fiction. I. Casilla, Robert, ill. II. Schomburg Children's Collection. III. Title.
PZ7.H8327 Tr 1988   *NYPL [Sc F 88-219]*

Howard-Howard, Margo, 1935- I was a white slave in Harlem / by Margo Howard-Howard, with Abbe Michaels. 1st ed. New York : Four Walls Eight Windows, c1988. vii, 177 p., [8] p. of plates : ill. ; 23 cm. ISBN 0-941423-14-X (pbk.) : DDC 306.7/43/0924 19
1. Howard-Howard, Margo, 1935-. 2. Impersonators, Female - New York (N.Y.) - Biography. 3. Harlem (New York, N.Y.). I. Michaels, Abbe. II. Title.
HQ77.8.H68 A3 1988   *NYPL [JFE 89-340]*

HOWARD-HOWARD, MARGO, 1935-
Howard-Howard, Margo, 1935- I was a white slave in Harlem /. New York , c1988. vii, 177 p., [8] p. of plates : ISBN 0-941423-14-X (pbk.) : DDC 306.7/43/0924 19
HQ77.8.H68 A3 1988   *NYPL [JFE 89-340]*

Howard, John Tasker, 1890-1964. Arvey, Verna, 1910- William Grant Still. New York, 1939. 48 p.
ML410.S855 A8   *NYPL [Sc D 89-3]*

Howard, Moses L., 1928- The ostrich chase / [by] Moses L. Howard ; illustrated by Barbara Seuling. [1st ed.] New York : Holt, Rinehart and Winston [1974] 118 p. : ill. ; 22 cm.
Although the women are forbidden to participate in the hunt, a young Bushman girl determines to realize her

dream of hunting an ostrich. SCHOMBURG CHILDREN'S COLLECTION. ISBN 0-03-012096-9
1. San (African people) - Juvenile fiction. 2. Kalahari Desert - Juvenile Fiction. I. Seuling, Barbara, illus. II. Schomburg Children's Collection. III. Title.
    NYPL [Sc D 88-374]

Howard University. Institute for the study of Educational Policy. Tollett, Kenneth S. The right to education . Washington, D.C. , 1983. xiii, 77 p. ;   *NYPL [Sc D 87-1294]*

Howard University. Mental Health Research and Development Center. Hendricks, Leo E. A comparative analysis of three select populations of Black unmarried adolescent fathers /. Washington, D.C. , 1982. ix, 129 p. :
    NYPL [Sc F 88-222]

Howard University Press library of contemporary literature.
Marshall, Paule, 1929- Soul clap hands and sing /. Washington, D.C. , 1988, 1961. xlviii, 105 p. ; ISBN 0-88258-155-4
    NYPL [Sc D 88-1451]

Howardena Pindell . Pindell, Howardena, 1943- New York, NY (144 W. 125th St., New York 10027) , c1986. 24 p. : DDC 709/.2/4 19
N6537.P49 A4 1986   *NYPL [Sc F 88-270]*

Howdy! Weir, LaVada. Austin, Tex. [1972] 32 p. ISBN 0-8114-7735-5 DDC [E]
PZ7.W4415 Ho   *NYPL [Sc E 88-613]*

Howe, Gertrude. Lang, Don. Strawberry roan /. New York , 1946. 218 p. :
    NYPL [Sc D 88-646]

Howell, Ruth Rea. A crack in the pavement. Photos. by Arline Strong. [1st ed.] New York, Atheneum, 1970. [48] p. illus. 25 cm. Describes natura! things which still manage to grow in spite of the crowded conditions in cities. SCHOMBURG CHILDREN'S COLLECTION. DDC 500.9
1. Natural history - Juvenile literature. I. Strong, Arline, illus. II. Schomburg Children's Collection. III. Title.
PZ10.H7958 Cr   *NYPL [Sc E 88-154]*

Hoyle, B. S. Gillman of Tanganyika, 1882-1946 : the life and work of a pioneer geographer / B.S. Hoyle. Aldershot, Hants. ; Brookfield, Vt : Avebury, 1987. xvii, 448 p. : ill., maps, ports. ; 23 cm. Includes index. Bibliography: p. 424-439. ISBN 0-566-05028-5
1. Gillman, Clement, 1882-1946. 2. Geographers - Tanzania - Biography. 3. Tanzania - Biography. I. Title.
    NYPL [Sc D 89-86]

Hoyos, Alexander, Sir. Barbados comes of age : from early strivings to happy fulfilment / F.A. Hoyos / ; with a foreword by Sir Hugh Springer. London : Macmillan Caribbean, 1987. ix, 70 p. : ill., map, ports. ; 25 cm. Includes bibliographies ISBN 0-333-43819-1 (pbk) DDC 972.98/1 19
1. Barbados - History. I. Title.
F2041   *NYPL [Sc E 88-326]*

Hoyos, F. A. Tom Adams : a biography / F.A. Hoyos. Basingstoke : Macmillan Caribbean, 1988. x, 198 p., [32] p. of plates : ill. ; 22 cm. Includes index. ISBN 0-333-46332-3 (pbk) : DDC 972.98/1/00994 19
1. Adams, Tom, 1931-1985. 2. Prime ministers - Barbados - Biography. I. Title.
    NYPL [Sc D 88-1275]

Hrbek, Ivan. Africa from the seventh to the eleventh century / . London : Berkeley : xxv, 869 p. : ISBN 0-435-94809-1
    NYPL [Sc E 88-384]

HSRC Investigation into Intergroup Relations. Main Committee. The South African society . New York , c1987. xv, 217 p. : ISBN 0-313-25724-8 (lib. bdg : alk. paper) DDC 306/.0968 19
HN801.A8 S68 1987   *NYPL [JLD 87-2390]*

HSRC Investigation into Intergroup Relations. Work Committee: Religion. Religion, intergroup relations, and social change in South Africa /. New York , 1988. xii, 237 p. : ISBN 0-313-26360-4 (lib. bdg : alk. paper) DDC 306/.6/0968 19
DT763 .R393 1988   *NYPL [Sc D 89-305]*

Hubbard, Michael. Curtis, Donald, 1939- Preventing famine . London , New York , 1988. xi, 250 p. ; ISBN 0-415-00711-9 DDC 363.8/7/096 19
HC800.Z9 F326 1988   *NYPL [JLD 88-3825]*

Hubbard, Stephen, 1961- Against all odds : the story of William Peyton Hubbard, black leader and municipal reformer / by Stephen L. Hubbard ; with a foreword by Daniel G. Hill. Toronto : Dundurn Press, 1987. 140 p. : ill., ports. ; 23 cm. (Dundurn lives) Includes bibliographical references and index.   ISBN 1-550-02013-7 (bound)
1. Hubbard, William Peyton, 1842-1935. 2. Politicians - Ontario - Toronto - Biography. 3. Social reformers - Ontario - Toronto - Biography. 4. Blacks - Ontario - Toronto - Biography. 5. Toronto, Ont. - Politics and government. I. Title. II. Series.
NYPL [Sc D 88-985]

HUBBARD, WILLIAM PEYTON, 1842-1935. Hubbard, Stephen, 1961- Against all odds . Toronto , 1987. 140 p. : ISBN 1-550-02013-7 (bound)   *NYPL [Sc D 88-985]*

Hubbard, Wynant Davis. Wild animal hunter / by Wynant Davis Hubbard ; pictures by Albert Orbaan. [1st ed.] New York : Harper [1958] 148 p. : ill. ; 22 cm. SCHOMBURG CHILDREN'S COLLECTION.
1. Hunting - Africa, South. I. Schomburg Children's Collection. II. Title.   *NYPL [Sc D 88-1130]*

Huggins, Nathan Irvin, 1927- Kliment, Bud. Ella Fitzgerald /. New York , c1988. 112 p. : ISBN 1-555-46586-2 DDC 784.5 B 19
ML420.F52 K6 1988   *NYPL [Sc E 88-611]*

L'odyssée noire / Nathan Irvin Huggins ; préface et épilogue de Roger Garaudy ; [traduit de l'américain par Maud Sissung et adapté par Mathilde Rieussec] Paris : Editions J.A., c1979. 221 p. : ill., map, ports. ; 28 cm. (Collection L'Epopée humaine) Abridged and translated from: Bleck odyssey. "Avec la collaboration de Nicole Marohand." With autograph of N. Marchand. ISBN 1-85258-150-7
1. Slavery - United States - History. 2. Slavery - United States - Condition of slaves. I. Sissung, Maud. II. Rieussec, Mathilde. III. Title.
NYPL [Sc F 88-383]

Russell, Sharman Apt. Frederick Douglass /. New York , c1988. 110 p. : ISBN 1-555-46580-3 DDC 973.8/092/4 B 92 19
E449.D75 R87 1988   *NYPL [Sc E 88-174]*

Hughes, C. E. B. (Christopher E. B.) Bekker, S. B. Perspectives on rural development in Ciskei, 1983 /. Grahamstown [1984] 52 p. : ISBN 0-86810-103-6 (pbk.) : DDC 307.1/4/0968792 19
HN801.C57 B45 1984   *NYPL [Sc F 88-325]*

Hughes, James Langston. see Hughes, Langston, 1902-1967.

Hughes, James Mercer Langston. see Hughes, Langston, 1902-1967.

Hughes, Langston, 1902-1967. Mem-Leket özlemi : şiirler / Langston Hughes ; türkçesi, Necati Cumali. Istanbul : Ataç Kitabevi, 1961. 45 p. ; 17 cm. Translator's autographed presentation copy to the author.
I. Cumali, Necati. II. Title.
NYPL [Sc Rare C 86-1]

Simple speaks his mind / Langston Hughes. New York : Simon and Schuster, c1950. 231 p. ; 21 cm. Author's autographed presentation copy to Patricia Cory.
1. Afro-Americans - New York (City) - Harlem - Fiction. I. Title.   *NYPL [Sc Rare C 82-2]*

The weary blues, by Langston Hughes; with an introduction by Carl Van Vechten. New York, A. A. Knopf, 1935, c1926. 109 p. 20 cm. Poems. Author's autographed presentation copy to Joy Lindsey Blair.
I. Title.   *NYPL [Sc Rare C 88-18]*

HUGHES, LANGSTON, 1902-1967. Hauke, Kathleen Armstrong. A self-portrait of Langston Hughes [microform] /. 1981. 228 leaves.   *NYPL [Sc Micro R-4683]*

Meltzer, Milton, 1915- Langston Hughes . New York [1968] xiii, 281 p. DDC 811./5/2 B
PS3515.U274 Z68   *NYPL [Sc D 89-329]*

HUGHES, LANGSTON, 1902-1967 - BIOGRAPHY. Rampersad, Arnold. The life of Langston Hughes /. New York , 1986-1988. 2 v. : ISBN 0-19-504011-2 (v. 1) DDC 818/.5209 B 19
PS3515.U274 Z698 1986
NYPL [Sc E 87-44]

HUGHES, LANGSTON, 1902-1967 - BIOGRAPHY - JUVENILE LITERATURE. Rummel, Jack. Langston Hughes /. New York , c1988. 111 p. : ISBN 1-555-46595-1 DDC 818/.5209 B 92 19
PS3515.U274 Z775 1988
NYPL [Sc E 88-166]

HUGHES, LANGSTON, 1902-1967 - KNOWLEDGE - FOLKLORE, MYTHOLOGY. Tracy, Steven C. (Steven Carl), 1954- Langston Hughes & the blues /. Urbana , c1988. xiii, 305 p. ; ISBN 0-252-01457-X (alk. paper) DDC 818/.5209 19
PS3515.U274 Z8 1988   *NYPL [Sc E 88-506]*

HUGHES, LANGSTON, 1902-1967- XBIOGRAPHY. Huntley, Jobe. I remember Langston Hughes . [New York] , 1983. 105 p. :
NYPL [Sc D 88-4]

Hughie Lee-Smith . Lee-Smith, Hughie. [Trenton] , c1988. 36 p. :
NYPL [Sc D 89-247]

Hull, Gloria T. Color, sex, and poetry : three women writers of the Harlem Renaissance / Gloria T. Hull. Bloomington : Indiana University Press, c1987. xi, 240 p. : ill. ; 24 cm. (Blacks in the diaspora) Everywoman : studies in history, literature, and culture Includes bibliographical references and index.   ISBN 0-253-34974-5 DDC 811./52/099287 19
1. Dunbar-Nelson, Alice Moore, 1875-1935 - Criticism and interpretation. 2. Grimké, Angelina Weld, 1880-1958 - Criticism and interpretation. 3. Johnson, Georgia Douglas Camp, 1886-1966 - Criticism and interpretation. 4. American poetry - Afro-American authors - History and criticism. 5. American poetry - Women authors - History and criticism. 6. American poetry - 20th century - History and criticism. 7. Harlem Renaissance. 8. Women and literature - United States. 9. Afro-Americans in literature. 10. Afro-American women poets - New York (N.Y.) - Biography. 11. Poets, American - 20th century - Biography. I. Series: Everywoman. II. Title.
PS153.N5 H84 1987   *NYPL [Sc E 88-72]*

Dunbar-Nelson, Alice Moore, 1875-1935. [Works. 1988.] The works of Alice Dunbar-Nelson /. New York , 1988. 3 v. : ISBN 0-19-505250-1 (v. 1 : alk. paper) DDC 818/.5209 19
PS3507 .U6228 1988   *NYPL [JFC 88-2143]*

Hulstaert, G. Complément au Dictionnaire lomóngo-français : additions et corrections / Gustaaf Hulstaert. Bamanya- Mbandaka : Centre aequatoria, 1987. 463 p. ; 20 cm. (Etudes aequatoria . 2) "Corrigenda et addenda": 10 p. inserted.
1. Mongo language - Dictionaries - French. I. Hulstaert, G. Dictionnaire lomóngo-français. II. Title. III. Series.
NYPL [Sc D 89-193]

Dictionnaire lomóngo-français. Hulstaert, G. Complément au Dictionnaire lomóngo-français : additions et corrections / Gustaaf Hulstaert. Bamanya- Mbandaka , 1987. 463 p. ;   *NYPL [Sc D 89-193]*

Grammaire du lomongo. Hulstaert, G. Supplement à la grammaire lomongo / Gustaaf Hulstaert. Mbandaka, Zaire , 1988. 127 p. ;   *NYPL [Sc D 89-39]*

Supplément à la grammaire lomongo / Gustaaf Hulstaert. Mbandaka, Zaire : Centre aequatoria, 1988. 127 p. ; 21 cm. (Etudes aequatoria . 4)
1. Mongo language - Grammar. I. Hulstaert, G. Grammaire du lomongo. II. Title. III. Series.
NYPL [Sc D 89-39]

Hultman, Tami. The Africa News cookbook . New York, NY , 1987, c1985. xxix, 175 p. : ISBN 0-14-046751-3 (pbk.) DDC 641.596 19
TX725.A4 A35 1986b   *NYPL [Sc E 88-371]*

Human and people's rights monograph series . (no. 1) Maope, Kelebone A. Human rights in Botswana, Lesotho and Swaziland . Roma, Lesotho , 1986. iii, 155 p. :
NYPL [Sc D 88-855]

Human Awareness Programme (South Africa) Black urban public road transport : an assessment / Human Awareness Programme. Grant Park [South Africa] : The Programme, [1982] 64 p. : ill. ; 31 cm. (Special report . no. 3 (Aug. 1982)) Cover title. Bibliography: p. 63. ISBN 0-620-05750-5 (pbk.) : DDC 388.4/1322/089968

19
1. Buses - South Africa. 2. Blacks - South Africa - Transportation. I. Series: Special report (Human Awareness Programme (South Africa)) , no. 3. II. Title.
HE5704.4.A6 H86 1982
NYPL [Sc F 88-150]

HUMAN BODY. see BODY, HUMAN.

HUMAN ECOLOGY - AFRICA. Rosenblum, Mort. Squandering Eden . San Diego , c1987. x, 326 p., [32] p. of plates : ISBN 0-15-184860-2 : DDC 960/.3 19
GF701 .R67 1987   *NYPL [Sc E 88-24]*

HUMAN ECOLOGY - AFRICA, NORTHEAST. The Ecology of survival . London, England , Boulder, Colo. , 1988. xii, 339 p. : ISBN 0-8133-0727-9 (Westview) DDC 304.2/096 19
GF720 .E26 1988   *NYPL [Sc D 89-280]*

HUMAN ECOLOGY - CONGO (BRAZZAVILLE) Harms, Robert. Games against nature . Cambridge [Cambridgeshire] , New York , 1987. xi, 276 p. : ISBN 0-521-34373-9 DDC 967/.24 19
DT546.245.N86 H37 1987
NYPL [Sc E 88-192]

HUMAN RESOURCE DEVELOPMENT. see MANPOWER POLICY.

Human resources development and utilization in Africa / edited by Kwesi Prah and Anthony Sets'abi. Maseru [Lesotho] : African Association for Training and Development, 1988. vi, 160 p. ; 21 cm. "Selected proceedings of the 6th biennial Conference of the African Association for Training and Development, Badagry, Nigeria, 8-12 September, 1986." ISBN 0-620-12102-5
1. Manpower policy - Africa - Congresses. 2. Labor supply - Africa - Congresses. I. Kwesi Prah. II. Sets'abi, Anthony. III. African Association for Training and Development. Conference (6th : 1986 : Badagry, Nigeria).   *NYPL [Sc D 89-558]*

HUMAN RIGHTS. Mwaga, D. Z. The crime of apartheid /. Dar es Salaam , c1985. xix, 141 p. ; ISBN 997-660-049-6 DDC 342.68/0873 346.802873 19
LAW   *NYPL [Sc C 89-117]*

Human rights in Botswana, Lesotho and Swaziland . Maope, Kelebone A. Roma, Lesotho , 1986. iii, 155 p. ;
NYPL [Sc D 88-855]

HUMAN RIGHTS - SOUTH AFRICA. Mwaga, D. Z. The crime of apartheid /. Dar es Salaam , c1985. xix, 141 p. ; ISBN 997-660-049-6 DDC 342.68/0873 346.802873 19
LAW   *NYPL [Sc C 89-117]*

HUMAN RIGHTS - ZAIRE - LISALA (EQUATEUR) Schatzberg, Michael G. The dialectics of oppression in Zaire /. Bloomington , c1988. x, 193 p., [1] p. of plates : ISBN 0-253-31703-7 DDC 323.4/9/0967513 19
JC599.Z282 L577 1988   *NYPL [Sc E 88-512]*

HUMANISM IN LITERATURE. Jackson, Richard L., 1937- Black literature and humanism in Latin America /. Athens , c1988. xvii, 166 p. ; ISBN 0-8203-0979-6 (alk. paper) DDC 860/.9/896 19
PQ7081 .J263 1988   *NYPL [Sc E 88-359]*

Humfrey, Michael. No tears for Massa's day / Michael Humfrey. London : Murray, 1987. 192 p. ; 22 cm. ISBN 0-7195-4442-4 : DDC 813 19
1. West Indies - Fiction. I. Title.
PR9265.9.H8   *NYPL [Sc D 88-623]*

HUMOROUS ILLUSTRATIONS. see CARICATURES AND CARTOONS.

Humphrey, Dibia. A drop of mercy / Dibia Humphrey. Nigeria : Longman Nigeria, 1987. 230 p. ; 19 cm. ISBN 978-13-9603-2
1. Nigeria - Fiction. I. Title.
NYPL [Sc C 88-318]

Humphrey, Kathryn Long. Satchel Paige / by Kathryn Long Humphrey. New York : Watts, 1988. 110 p. : ill. ; 24 cm. (An Impact biography) Includes index. Surveys the life and career of the Negro League's pitching phenomenon, the first baseball player in the Negro Leagues to be inducted in the National Baseball Hall of Fame. Bibliography: p. 105-106. ISBN 0-531-10513-X DDC 796.357/092/4 B 92 19
1. Paige, Leroy, 1906-1982. 2. Baseball players - United States - Biography - Juvenile literature. 3. Pitching

(Baseball) - Juvenile literature. 4. *Afro-American baseball players - Biography - Juvenile literature.* I. Title.
GV865.P3 H86 1988   *NYPL [Sc E 88-481]*

A Hundred years of the Catholic Church in Eastern Nigeria, 1885-1985 : a history published to mark the first centenary of the Catholic Church in Onitsha Ecclesiastical Province within the former Lower Niger Mission / produced under the auspices of the Onitsha Ecclesiastical Province Centenary History Commission ; edited by Celestine A. Obi. Onitsha, Nigeria : Africana-FEP Publishers, 1985. 432 p. : ill., maps, ports. ; 21 cm. Includes index. Includes bibliographical footnotes.
ISBN 978-17-5103-7
1. Catholic Church - Nigeria, Eastern - History. 2. *Catholic Church - Missions - Nigeria, Eastern - History.* 3. *Missions - Nigeria, Eastern - History.* 4. *Nigeria, Eastern - Church history.* I. *Obi, Celestine A.* II. *Onitsha Ecclesiastical Province Centenary History Commission.*   *NYPL [Sc D 88-830]*

The hunger crop . Coote, Belinda. Oxford [England] , 1987. v, 124 p. :   ISBN 0-85598-081-8   *NYPL [Sc D 88-1446]*

Hunt, Alfred N., 1941- Haiti's influence on antebellum America : slumbering volcano in the Caribbean / Alfred N. Hunt. Baton Rouge : Louisiana State University Press, c1988. xiv, 196 p. : ill. ; 24 cm. Includes index.   ISBN 0-8071-1370-0   DDC 973/.049697294 19
1. Haitians - United States - History - 19th century. 2. *Public opinion - United States - History - 19th century.* 3. *Immigrants - United States - History - 19th century.* 4. *Haiti - History - Revolution, 1791-1804 - Influence.* 5. *Haiti - Foreign public opinion, American - History - 19th century.* I. Title.
E184.H27 H86 1987   *NYPL [Sc E 88-131]*

Hunt, Frankie L. Cunningham. A history of the desegregation of the Fayette County school system [microform] : Fayette County, Tennessee, 1954-1980 / by Frankie C. Hunt. 1981. 351 leaves. Thesis (Ed. D.)--University of Mississippi, 1981. Bibliography: leaves 278-291. Microfilm of typescript. Ann Arbor, Mich.: University Microfilms International, 1982. 1 microfilm reel; 35 mm.
1. School integration - Tennessee - Fayette County - History. 2. *Fayette County (Tenn.) - Schools.* I. Title.
NYPL [Sc Micro R-4687]

The hunter /. Nyankume, Manty. Freetown , 1987. 68 p. :   *NYPL [Sc D 89-414]*

HUNTER, CLEMENTINE.
Wilson, James L. (James Lynwood) Clementine Hunter, American folk artist /. Gretna , 1988. 160 p. :   ISBN 0-88289-658-X   DDC 759.13 B 19
ND237.H915 A4 1988   *NYPL [Sc F 89-94]*

Hunter, Wilma King. Coming of age [microform] : Hollis B. Frissell and the emergence of Hampton Institute 1893-1917 / by Wilma King Hunter. 1982. 343 leaves. Thesis (Ph. D.)--Indiana University, 1982. Bibliography: leaves 333-343. Microfilm of typescript. Ann Arbor, Mich.: University Microfilms International, 1983. 1 microfilm reel; 35 mm.
1. Frissell, Hollis Burke, 1851-1917. 2. *Hampton Institute - History.* I. Title.
NYPL [Sc Micro R-4688]

HUNTERS - ZAMBIA - BIOGRAPHY.
Sampson, Richard, 1922- [Man with a toothbrush in his hat.] The struggle for British interests in Barotseland, 1871-88 /. Lusaka [198-?] v, 158 p. :   DDC 968.94/01 19
DT963.72.W47 S25 1980z
NYPL [Sc D 88-381]

HUNTING - AFRICA, SOUTH.
Hubbard, Wynant Davis. Wild animal hunter /. New York [1958] 148 p. :
NYPL [Sc D 88-1130]

Huntley, Eric L. Marcus Garvey : a centenary 1887 - 1987 / Eric L. Huntley. Ealing, London : Frinds of Bogle, 1988. 41 p. : ill., maps ; 24 cm.   ISBN 0-904521-41-9
1. Garvey, Marcus, 1887-1940. 2. *Intellectuals - United States - Biography.* 3. *Jamaica - Biography.* I. Title.
NYPL [Sc E 88-499]

Huntley, Jobe.
I remember Langston Hughes : an autobiography / by Jobe Huntley. [New York] : J. Huntley, 1983. 105 p. : facsims, music, ports. ; 22 cm. Includes index.

1. Huntley, Jobe. 2. *Hughes, Langston, 1902-1967.-xBiography.* 3. *Huntley, Jobe. Tambourines to glory.* 4. *Afro-American composers - Biography.* 5. *Afro-American authors - Biography.* 6. *Composers - United States - Biography.* I. Title.
NYPL [Sc D 88-4]

TAMBOURINES TO GLORY.
Huntley, Jobe. I remember Langston Hughes . [New York] , 1983. 105 p. :
NYPL [Sc D 88-4]

HUNTLEY, JOBE.
Huntley, Jobe. I remember Langston Hughes . [New York] , 1983. 105 p. :
NYPL [Sc D 88-4]

Huntsman, Richard G. (Richard George)
Sickle-cell anemia and thalassemia : a primer for health care professionals / [R.G. Huntsman]. [St. John's, Newfoundland, Canada : Canadian Sickle Cell Society, c1987] xv, 223 p. : ill., map ; 20 cm. Cover title. Includes index. Bibliography: p. 204.   ISBN 0-921037-00-7 (pbk.) :
I. Canadian Sickle Cell Society. II. Title.
NYPL [Sc C 88-84]

Hurbon, Laënnec.
Comprendre Haïti : essai sur l'état, la nation, la culture / Laënnec Hurbon. Paris : Karthala, c1987. 174 p. : map ; 22 cm. Bibliography: p. [171]-172.   ISBN 2-86537-192-1
1. Haiti. I. Title.   *NYPL [Sc D 88-1045]*

Dieu dans le vaudou haïtien / Laënnec Hurbon ; préface de Geneviève Calame-Griaule. Port-au-Prince, Haïti : Deschamps, 1987. 268 p. ; 22 cm. Bibliography: p. [259]-268.   DDC 299/.67 19
1. Voodooism. 2. *God.* 3. *Haiti - Religion.* I. Title.
BL2490 .H87 1987   *NYPL [Sc D 89-366]*

Hurmence, Belinda. My folks don't want me to talk about slavery . Winston-Salem, N.C. , c1984. xiv, 103 p. ;   ISBN 0-89587-038-X   DDC 975.6/00496073/0922 B 19
E445.N8 M9 1984   *NYPL [JFD 85-1549]*

Hurricane . Ball, Dorothy Whitney. Indianapolis [c1964] 147 p. ;   *NYPL [Sc D 88-486]*

Hurricane precautionary measures [microform] . St. Lucia. St. Lucia [1957] 18 p. ;
NYPL [Sc Micro F-10954]

HURRICANE PROTECTION - ST. LUCIA.
St. Lucia. Hurricane precautionary measures [microform] . St. Lucia [1957] 18 p. :
NYPL [Sc Micro F-10954]

Hurst, Laurence. Burrell, Evelyn Patterson. Of flesh and the spirit /. Bryn Mawr, Pennsylvania , 1986. 101 p. :   ISBN 0-8059-3039-6   *NYPL [Sc D 88-300]*

Hurston, Zora Neale.
THEIR EYES WERE WATCHING GOD.
Zora Neale Hurston's Their eyes were watching God /. New York , 1987. vii, 130 p. :   ISBN 1-555-46054-2 (alk. paper) :   DDC 813/.52 19
PS3515.U789 T639 1987
NYPL [JFE 87-5315]

HURSTON, ZORA NEALE - CRITICISM AND INTERPRETATION.
Zora Neale Hurston /. New York , 1986. viii, 192 p. ;   ISBN 0-87754-627-4 (alk. paper) :   DDC 813/.52 19
PS3515.U789 Z96 1986
NYPL [JFE 87-1592]

Hurtado González, Jaime. Luchando por la patria nueva : selección de discursos del abogado Jaime Hurtado González. 1a ed. Quito : Editora Eugenio Espejo, 1987. ii, 178 p. : ill. ; 21 cm. (Ediciones "Patria nueva")
1. Movimiento Popular Democrático. 2. *Political parties - Ecuador.* 3. *Ecuador - Politics and government - 1944-.* I. Title.
NYPL [Sc D 88-679]

HUSBANDRY. see AGRICULTURE.

Hust, Mildred Hudgins. The positions, roles, and perceptions of Black elected public school board members in Mississippi [microform] / by Mildred H. Hust. 1977. 144 leaves. Thesis (Ed. D.)--North Texas State University, 1977. Bibliography: leaves 140-144. Microfilm of typescript. Ann Arbor, Mich.: University Microfilms International, 1977. 1 microfilm reel; 35 mm.
1. School boards - Mississippi - Membership,

Afro-American. I. Title.
NYPL [Sc Micro R-4215]

Huston, Anne. Ollie's go-kart. Drawings by Harold James. New York, Seabury Press [1971] 143 p. illus. 22 cm. A Manhattan boy spends much of his time designing go-karts but never tries to build one until he meets an older black boy. SCHOMBURG CHILDREN'S COLLECTION.   DDC [Fic]
1. Afro-American children - New York (N.Y.) - Juvenile fiction. I. *James, Harold Laymont, 1929- illus.* II. *Schomburg Children's Collection.* III. Title.
PZ7.H959 Ol   *NYPL [Sc D 88-1472]*

Hutchful, Eboe. The IMF and Ghana . London , New Jersey , 1987. 298 p. :   ISBN 0-86232-614-1
NYPL [Sc D 88-1095]

Huxley, Elspeth Joscelin Grant. Amin, Mohamed, 1943- The last of the Maasai /. London , 1987. 185 p. :   ISBN 0-370-31097-7
NYPL [Sc G 88-21]

Huxley, Elspeth Joscelin (Grant) 1907-
Memories of Kenya . London , 1986. xvi, 160 p., [16] p. of plates :   ISBN 0-237-50919-9
NYPL [Sc F 88-102]

HWANGE NATIONAL PARK (ZIMBABWE)
Rushworth, David. The wonders of Hwange /. Gweru, Zimbabwe , 1986. 35 p. :   ISBN 0-86922-389-5   *NYPL [Sc F 89-43]*

HYBRID LANGUAGES. see PIDGIN LANGUAGES.

HYBRIDITY OF RACES. see MISCEGENATION.

HYGIENE, PUBLIC. see PUBLIC HEALTH.

HYGIENE, SOCIAL. see PUBLIC HEALTH.

HYGIENE - STUDY AND TEACHING. see HEALTH EDUCATION.

Hyman, Mark. Blacks who died for Jesus : a history book / by Mark Hyman. Philadelphia : Corrective Black History Books, 1983. iv, 107 p. : ill. ; 23 cm. Bibliography: p. 105-107.   ISBN 0-915515-00-8 (pbk.)   DDC 270/.08996 B 19
1. Christians, Black - Biography. I. Title.
BR1702 .H9 1983   *NYPL [Sc D 89-263]*

I am a Rastafarian /. Obadiah. Obadiah, London , New York , c1986. 32 p. :   ISBN 0-86313-260-X :
BL2532.R37   *NYPL [Sc F 89-12]*

I am becoming my mother /. Goodison, Lorna. London , 1986. 50 p. ;   ISBN 0-901241-67-9
NYPL [Sc D 88-275]

I am Maria. Talbot, Toby. New York [1969] 28 p.   ISBN 0-402-14031-1   DDC [Fic]
PZ7.C12 I   *NYPL [Sc E 88-531]*

I did so swear, but -- /. Jikong, Stephen Yeriwa. Yaoundé , 1985. 48 p. ;   *NYPL [Sc B 88-56]*

I. L. O. see International Labor Organization.

ILO. see International Labor Office.

I need a lunch box /. Caines, Jeannette Franklin. New York , c1988. [32] p. :   ISBN 0-06-020984-4 :   DDC [E] 19
PZ7.C12 Iaan 1988   *NYPL [Sc D 88-1504]*

I never scream . Lane, Pinkie Gordon, 1923- Detroit , 1985. 104 p. ;   ISBN 0-916418-58-8 (pbk.)   *NYPL [JFD 87-4790]*

I remember Langston Hughes . Huntley, Jobe. [New York] , 1983. 105 p. :
NYPL [Sc D 88-4]

I saw a slave ship /. Equiano, Olaudah, b. 1745. Sacramento, Calif. , 1983. 42 p. :
NYPL [Sc Rare C 88-1]

I.W.A.R.U. talks (1974-1984) / compiled by John E. Nwanze. [Gusau, Sokoto State, Nigeria : IWARU-Nigeria, 1985] 97 p. ; 25 cm.   DDC 255/.006/06 19
1. I.W.A.R.U. (Organization). 2. *Monasticism and religious orders - Africa.* I. *Nwanze, John E.* II. *I.W.A.R.U. (Organization).* III. *Title: IWARU talks (1974-1984).*
BX2740.A435 I18 1985
NYPL [Sc E 88-120]

I was a white slave in Harlem /. Howard-Howard, Margo, 1935- New York , c1988. vii, 177 p., [8] p. of plates :   ISBN 0-941423-14-X (pbk.) :   DDC 306.7/43/0924 19
HQ77.8.H68 A3 1988   *NYPL [JFE 89-340]*

I will kill you and get away with it /. Onyeneke, Onyewuotu. [Nigeria] 122 p. ;
NYPL [Sc C 89-153]

IAE techinical paper .
(no. 4/80) Mackenzie, Bob. A survey of handicrafts in North East District, 1980 . Gaborone , 1980. 61 p. :   *NYPL [Sc F 88-2]*

Iba N'Diaye, Gemälde, Lavierungen, Zeichnungen =. Ndiaye, Iba, 1928- München , c1987. 71 p. :   ISBN 3-7774-4650-5   *NYPL [Sc C 88-297]*

Ibaaddo ka-Ba'iso . Haberland, Eike. Heidelberg , 1988. 184 p. ;   ISBN 3-533-04014-3
                                    NYPL [Sc D 89-552]

Ibadan, Nigeria. University. Institute of African Studies.
Occasional publication.
(no. 21) Gay, John. Mathematics and logic in the Kpelle language. Ibadan, 1971. 152, 184 p.
PL8411.1 .G35   *NYPL [JFF 74-877]*

Ibadan tropical medicine series .
(4) De Cola, Freya D. Three decades of medical research at the College of Medicine, Ibadan, Nigeria, 1948-1980 . Ibadan, Nigeria , 1984. xv, 208 p. ;   ISBN 978-12-1157-1 (pbk.)   DDC 016.61 19
Z6661.N6 D4 1984 R824.N6
                                    NYPL [Sc E 89-160]

IBIBIO STATE UNION.
Udoma, Egbert Udo, Sir, 1917- The story of the Ibibio Union . Ibadan, Nigeria , 1987. xv, 590 p., [12] leaves of plates :   ISBN 978-246-128-8   *NYPL [Sc D 89-4]*

IBIBIO UNION.
Udoma, Egbert Udo, Sir, 1917- The story of the Ibibio Union . Ibadan, Nigeria , 1987. xv, 590 p., [12] leaves of plates :   ISBN 978-246-128-8   *NYPL [Sc D 89-4]*

IBIBIOS - HISTORY.
Udoma, Egbert Udo, Sir, 1917- The story of the Ibibio Union . Ibadan, Nigeria , 1987. xv, 590 p., [12] leaves of plates :   ISBN 978-246-128-8   *NYPL [Sc D 89-4]*

Ibie, Cromwell Osamaro. Ifism : the Complete work of Orunmila / by C. Osamaro Ibie.1st ed. Lagos, Nigeria : C.O. Ibie, 1986. 251 p., [10] p. of plates : ill., port. ; 26 cm. Cover title.
1. Ifa. 2. Yorubas - Religion. I. Title.
                                    NYPL [Sc E 89-19]

Ibo . Soledad, Rosalía de la. Miami, Fla. , 1988. 278 p. ;   ISBN 0-89729-468-8
                                    NYPL [Sc D 89-436]

IBO (AFRICAN PEOPLE) see IGBO (AFRICAN PEOPLE)

The Ibo of Biafra. Bleeker, Sonia. New York [1969] 160 p.   DDC 916.69/4
DT515 .B54   *NYPL [Sc C 88-361]*

Les Ibos de l'Amélie . Thésée, Françoise. Paris , c1986. 134 p., [8] p. of plates :   ISBN 2-903033-86-2   *NYPL [Sc E 88-560]*

Ibuje, Joan, 1941-
Famous women / Joan Ibuje. [Benin City, Nigeria] : J. Ibuje, [1982] 60 p. : ill., ports. ; 21 cm. Cover title.   DDC 305.4/09669/3 19
1. Women - Nigeria - Bendel State - Biography. 2. Women social reformers - Nigeria - Bendel State - Biography. 3. Women in the professions - Nigeria - Bendel State - Biography. I. Title.
HQ1815.5.Z8 B465 1982
                                    NYPL [Sc D 88-1144]

Memoirs of a great bureaucrat / Joan Ibuje. Benin City [Nigeria] : Bendel Newspapers Corporation, [1985?] 60 p. : ill., ports. ; 21 cm. Cover title.
1. Ibuje, John Otojareri, 1928-1975. 2. Nigeria - Officials and employees - Biography. I. Title.
                                    NYPL [Sc D 88-805]

IBUJE, JOHN OTOJARERI, 1928-1975.
Ibuje, Joan, 1941- Memoirs of a great bureaucrat /. Benin City [Nigeria] [1985?] 60 p. :   *NYPL [Sc D 88-805]*

Ibyemezo, amabwiliza, ibyifuzo mu myaka cumi ya Muvoma /. M.R.N.D. 10ème anniversaire : 1975-1985 : d'un congrès à l'autre. Kigali : Service de la documentation et de la propaganda à la Présidence du MRND, 1985. 424 p. : ill. ; 22 cm. (Irango = Guide du militant . no 2) Cover title. Title on added t.p.: Les résolutions, les instructions, les recommandations dans les 10 ans du M.R.N.D. Kinyarwanda and French.
1. Mouvement révolutionnaire national pour le développement. 2. Rwanda - Politics and government. I.

Mouvement révolutionnaire national pour le développement. II. Title: Résolutions, les instructions, les recommandations dans les 10 ans du M.R.N.D.
                                    NYPL [Sc D 88-807]

Icart, Jean-Claude. Négriers d'eux-mêmes : essai sur les boat people haïtiens de Floride / Jean-Claude Icart. Montréal, Québec, Canada : CIDIHCA, 1987. 188 p. : ill., maps ; 22 cm. Includes index. Bibliography: p. 171-182.   ISBN 2-920862-06-5
1. Haitians - Florida. 2. Haiti - Emigration and immigration. 3. Florida - Emigration and immigration. I. Title.   *NYPL [Sc D 88-396]*

Icenhower, Joseph B. Mr. Murdock takes command : a story of pirates and rebellion in Haiti / by Joseph B. Icenhower ; illustrated by Norman Guthrie Rudolph.1st ed. Philadelphia : J. C. Winston, c1958. xii, 173 p. : ill., map ; 22 cm.
1. Haiti - History - Revolution, 1791-1804 - Juvenile fiction. I. Title.   *NYPL [Sc D 88-1507]*

ICONOGRAPHY. see ART; CHRISTIAN ART AND SYMBOLISM.

The id, the ego, and equal protection . Lawrence Charles R. [San Francisco, Calif.] , 1987. 317-388 p. ;   *NYPL [Sc F 89-47]*

Idealism and pragmatism as aspects of Sweden's development policy in Africa /. Jinadu, Adele. Lagos [1982?]. 107 p. ;   ISBN 978-227-698-7
                                    NYPL [Sc D 88-355]

Ideas for Black studies. Fisher, Walter. Baltimore, 1971. vii, 51 p.
E184.7 .F53   *NYPL [Sc 917.306-F]*

Identidade negra e religião . Ecumenical Association of Third World Theologians. Rio de Janeiro , 1986. 201 p. ;   *NYPL [Sc D 88-485]*

Ideological education and nationalism in Ghana under Nkrumah and Busia /. Agyeman, Dominic Kofi. Accra , 1988. 81 p. ;   ISBN 996-430-120-0   *NYPL [Sc D 89-582]*

L'idéologie blanche et l'aliénation des noirs /. Théodore, Oriol, 1942- Montréal [1983] 54 p. :   ISBN 2-89270-001-9   *NYPL [Sc C 89-103]*

IDEOLOGY.
Ideology and American experience . Washington, DC , c1986. vi, 264 p. ;   ISBN 0-88702-015-1 ;   DDC 320.5/0973 19
E169.12 .I34 1986   *NYPL [Sc E 89-74]*

Ideology and American experience : essays on theory and practice in the United States / edited by John K. Roth and Robert C. Whittemore. Washington, DC : Washington Institute Press, c1986. vi, 264 p. ; 24 cm. Includes bibliographies and index.   ISBN 0-88702-015-1 ;   DDC 320.5/0973 19
1. Ideology. 2. United States - Politics and government - Philosophy. 3. United States - Economic conditions - Philosophy. 4. United States - Foreign relations - Philosophy. I. Roth, John K. II. Whittemore, Robert C. (Robert Clifton), 1921-.
E169.12 .I34 1986   *NYPL [Sc E 89-74]*

Idigo, Peter Meze. Archbishop Heerey : an apostle of Eastern Nigeria / Peter Meze Idigo. Enugu, Nigeria : Cecta (Nigeria), 1987. 261 p. : ill., ports. ; 20 cm. Includes index. Bibliography: p. 254-257.   ISBN 978-239-602-8
1. Heerey, Bernard. 2. Catholic Church - Nigeria. 3. Bishops - Nigeria - Biography. I. Title.
                                    NYPL [Sc C 89-77]

Idowu, Sina, 1947- Armed robbery in Nigeria / by Sina Idowu. Lagos, Nigeria : Jacob & Johnson Books, c1980. 121 p. : ill. ; 21 cm.   ISBN 978-231-900-7 (pbk.)   DDC 364.1/552/09669 19
1. Robbery - Nigeria. 2. Brigands and robbers - Nigeria. I. Title.
HV6665.N6 I36 1980   *NYPL [Sc D 89-264]*

Idylles et chansons. Tinker, Edward Larocque, 1881- Gombo comes to Philadelphia /. Worcester, Mass. , 1957. [10], 22 p. :   *NYPL [Sc E 89-9]*

Idylles et chansons, ou, Essais de poësie créole . Tinker, Edward Larocque, 1881- Gombo comes to Philadelphia /. Worcester, Mass. , 1957. [10], 22 p. :   *NYPL [Sc E 89-9]*

IFA.
Ibie, Cromwell Osamaro. Ifism . Lagos, Nigeria , 1986. 251 p., [10] p. of plates :
                                    NYPL [Sc E 89-19]

IFE (NIGERIA) - DESCRIPTION.
Eluyemi, Omotoso. This is Ile-Ife /. [Ile-Ife]] 1986 (Ile-Ife : Adesanmi Printing Works) 62 p. :   *NYPL [Sc D 89-27]*

Ifill, Max B. The African diaspora : a drama of human exploitation / Max B. Ifill. Port-of-Spain, Trinidad : Economic and Business Research, 1986. vii, 118 p. : ill. (some col.) ; 24 cm. Bibliography: p. 111-118. With autograph of author.   ISBN 976-8008-00-8 (pbk.)   DDC 382/.44/09729 19
1. Slave trade - Caribbean Area - History. 2. Slave-trade - History. 3. Caribbean area - Civilization - African influences. I. Title.
HT1072 .I35 1986   *NYPL [Sc D 88-934]*

Ifism . Ibie, Cromwell Osamaro. Lagos, Nigeria , 1986. 251 p., [10] p. of plates :
                                    NYPL [Sc E 89-19]

IFO-Institut für Wirtschaftsforschung, Munich. Afrika-Studienstelle.
see Afrika-Studien.

Afrika-Studien. Amann, Hans. Energy supply and economic development in East Africa. München, (1969). 254 p. with maps, 7 inserts (in pocket)   DDC 333
HD9557.A32 A6   *NYPL [Sc E 88-226]*

Marquardt, Wilhelm. Seychellen, Komoren und Maskarenen . München , c1976. 346 p. :   ISBN 3-8039-0117-0
DT469.S4 M37   *NYPL [JFC 77-3948]*

IGBO (AFRICAN PEOPLE)
Amadi, L. E. Igbo heritage . Owerri , 1987. iii, 128 p. ;   ISBN 978-259-801-1
                                    NYPL [Sc D 89-252]

Ezeuko, R. O. Ewumewu omenala ofufe na nkwenye ndi Igbo /. Nigeria , c1986. vi, 70 p. ;   ISBN 978-264-300-9   *NYPL [Sc D 88-970]*

Martin, Susan M. Palm oil and protest . Cambridge [Cambridgeshire] , New York , 1988. xi, 209 p. :   ISBN 0-521-34376-3   DDC 338.4/76643 19
HD9490.5.P343 N66 1988
                                    NYPL [JLE 88-3417]

Onyia, Nathaniel Maduabuchi. Pre-colonial history of Amokwe /. Enugu, Nigeria , 1987. 95 p. :   ISBN 978-239-618-4
                                    NYPL [Sc D 89-53]

Thésée, Françoise. Les Ibos de l'Amélie . Paris , c1986. 134 p., [8] p. of plates :   ISBN 2-903033-86-2   *NYPL [Sc E 88-560]*

IGBO (AFRICAN PEOPLE) - ECONOMIC CONDITIONS.
Egboh, Edmund Onyemeke. Community development efforts in Igboland /. Onitsha [Nigeria] , 1987. 206 p. :   ISBN 978-264-348-3   *NYPL [Sc E 88-258]*

IGBO (AFRICAN PEOPLE) - FICTION.
Achebe, Chinua. [Things fall apart. German.] Okonkwo, oder, Das Alte stürzt . Stuttgart , c1958. 230 p. ;   *NYPL [Sc C 88-357]*

Achebe, Chinua. [Things fall apart. Spanish.] Todo se derrumba /. Madrid , 1986. 198 p. ;   ISBN 84-204-2323-8
                                    NYPL [Sc D 88-1415]

IGBO (AFRICAN PEOPLE) - FOLKLORE.
Folk-tales from Igboland /. Ibadan, Nigeria , 1986. 90 p. ;   ISBN 978-16-7467-9
                                    NYPL [Sc D 88-758]

IGBO (AFRICAN PEOPLE) - JUVENILE LITERATURE.
Bleeker, Sonia. The Ibo of Biafra. New York [1969] 160 p.   DDC 916.69/4
DT515 .B54   *NYPL [Sc C 88-361]*

IGBO (AFRICAN PEOPLE) - MASKS.
Enekwe, Onuora Ossie. Igbo masks . Lagos , c1987. 164 p. :   ISBN 978-17-3040-4
                                    NYPL [Sc D 88-1238]

IGBO (AFRICAN PEOPLE) - NIGERIA.
Amadiume, Ifi. Afrikan matriarchal foundations . London , 1987. [120] p. :   ISBN 0-907015-27-1 (pbk)   DDC 966.9/004963 19
DT515.45.I33   *NYPL [Sc D 89-112]*

IGBO (AFRICAN PEOPLE) - PSYCHOLOGY.
Achebe, Chinwe. The world of the Ogbanje /. Enugu, Nigeria , 1986. iv, 68 p. :   ISBN 978-15-6239-0   DDC 616.89/1 19
RC455.4.E8 A34 1986
                                    NYPL [Sc D 88-1246]

IGBO (AFRICAN PEOPLE) - RELIGION.
Dine, George Uchechukwu. Traditional
leadership as service among the Igbo of
Nigeria . Rome , 1983. xvi, 316 p. : DDC
299/.6 19
BL2480.I2 D56 1983   ***NYPL [Sc E 88-329]***

Ejizu, Christopher I. Ofo . Enugu, Nigeria ,
1986. xxii, 190 p. : ISBN 978-15-6268-4
NYPL [Sc D 88-885]

Ezekwugo, Christopher U. M. Chi, the true god
in Igbo religion /. Alwaye, Kerala, India , 1987.
xvi, 310 p. :   ***NYPL [Sc D 88-881]***

Ilogu, Edmund. Igbo life and thought /.
[Nigeria] , c1985. 42 p. ; ISBN 978-16-0344-5
NYPL [Sc D 88-741]

Nnabuchi, Nwankwo. In defence of Igbo belief
system . Enugu, Nigera , 1987. xiii, 216 p. ;
ISBN 978-270-500-4   ***NYPL [Sc D 89-84]***

**IGBO (AFRICAN PEOPLE) - SOCIAL
CONDITIONS.**
Egboh, Edmund Onyemeke. Community
development efforts in Igboland /. Onitsha
[Nigeria] , 1987. 206 p. : ISBN 978-264-348-3
NYPL [Sc E 88-258]

**IGBO (AFRICAN PEOPLE) - SOCIAL LIFE
AND CUSTOMS.**
Dine, George Uchechukwu. Traditional
leadership as service among the Igbo of
Nigeria . Rome , 1983. xvi, 316 p. : DDC
299/.6 19
BL2480.I2 D56 1983   ***NYPL [Sc E 88-329]***

Enekwe, Onuora Ossie. Igbo masks . Lagos ,
c1987. 164 p. : ISBN 978-17-3040-4
NYPL [Sc D 88-1238]

Nwosu, Obiekezie Vic. Our roots . Lagos ,
1986. 55 p. :   ***NYPL [Sc D 88-713]***

Okeke, Igwebuike Romeo. The "Osu" concept in
Igboland . Enugu. [Nigeria] , 1986. xi, 167 p. :
ISBN 978-248-100-9 ***NYPL [Sc E 88-302]***

Olisah, Okenwah. The Ibo native law and
custom [microform] /. Onitsha [196-] 40 p. :
NYPL [Sc Micro F-11,165]

Onyeneke, Augustine O. The dead among the
living . Nimo , 1987. xii, 142 p. : ISBN
978-244-232-1   ***NYPL [Sc C 89-2]***

Ugwu, D. C. This is Obukpa . Enugu, Nigeria,
1987. xii, 76 p. ; ISBN 978-15-6288-9
NYPL [Sc D 88-801]

Igbo heritage . Amadi, L. E. Owerri , 1987. iii,
128 p. ; ISBN 978-259-801-1
NYPL [Sc D 89-252]

IGBO LANGUAGE - TEXTS.
Anukwu, Martin. Eziokwu bụ ndụ /. Enugu,
Nigeria , 1986. 110 p. : ISBN 978-239-649-4
NYPL [Sc C 89-12]

Ezeuko, R. O. Ewumewu omenala ofufe na
nkwenye ndi Igbo /. [Nigeria] , c1986. vi, 70
p. ; ISBN 978-264-300-9 ***NYPL [Sc D 88-970]***

Ihentuge, F. Azoma. Ikenga /. Oshodi, Lagos ,
1985. 140 p. ; ISBN 978-243-256-3
NYPL [Sc C 89-76]

Madubuike, Ihechukwu. Igh Ibadan , 1981. 79
p. ; ISBN 978-15-4603-4   ***NYPL [Sc C 88-96]***

Ugwoke, Oliva Obinna. Onye ije awele /.
[Ihiala, Nigeria , 198-?] iv, 77 p. ;
NYPL [Sc D 88-1040]

Igbo life and thought /. Ilogu, Edmund.
[Nigeria] , c1985. 42 p. ; ISBN 978-16-0344-5
NYPL [Sc D 88-741]

Igbo masks . Enekwe, Onuora Ossie. Lagos ,
c1987. 164 p. : ISBN 978-17-3040-4
NYPL [Sc D 88-1238]

Igh Madubuike, Ihechukwu. Ibadan , 1981. 79
p. ; ISBN 978-15-4603-4   ***NYPL [Sc C 88-96]***

La Iglesia negra . Bosch Navarro, Juan.
Valencia , 1986 (Valencia : Imprenta Nácher).
57 p. ;   ***NYPL [Sc D 87-1154]***

Ignace de Loyola, Saint. see Loyola, Ignacio de,
Saint, 1491-1556.

Ignacio de Loyola, Saint. see Loyola, Ignacio de,
Saint, 1491-1556.

Ignatius de Loyola, Saint. see Loyola, Ignacio de,
Saint, 1491-1556.

Ignatius Lopez de Recalde de Loyola, Saint. see
Loyola, Ignacio de, Saint, 1491-1556.

Ignatius Loyola, Saint. see Loyola, Ignacio de,
Saint, 1491-1556.

A Igreja católica em face da escravidão /.
Balmes, Jaime Luciano, 1810-1848.
[Protestantismo comparado con el catolicismo
en sus relaciones con la civilización europea.
Selections. Portuguese.] São Paulo , 1986. 141
p. ;   ***NYPL [Sc D 89-554]***

The iguana's tail. Sherlock, Philip Manderson, Sir.
New York [1969] 97 p. DDC 823 398.2
PZ8.1.S54 Ig   ***NYPL [Sc D 89-59]***

Ihenacho, Izuka John. Administrators of special
education : organizational issues in Nigeria /
Izuka John Iheanacho [sic]. [Nigeria] : I.J.
Ihenacho, c1986. 208 p. ; 19 cm. Bibliography: p.
207-208. ISBN 978-239-609-5 (pbk.) DDC
371.9/09669 19
*1. Special education - Nigeria - Administration. 2.
Educational law and legislation - Nigeria. I. Title. II.
Title: Organizational issues in Nigeria.*
LC3988.N6 I44 1986   ***NYPL [Sc C 89-145]***

Ihentuge, F. Azoma. Ikenga / F. Azoma
Ihentuge. Oshodi, Lagos : Paperback Publishers,
1985. 140 p. ; 18 cm. (Egret romance & thriller .
no. 8) ISBN 978-243-256-3
1. Igbo language - Texts. I. Title.
NYPL [Sc C 89-76]

Ihonvbere, Julius Omozuanvbo.
Nigeria and the international capitalist system
/. Boulder, Colo. , 1988. v, 154 p. ; ISBN
1-555-87087-2 (alk. paper)   DDC 337.669 19
HF1616.7 .N54 1988   ***NYPL [JLE 88-3615]***

Towards a political economy of Nigeria :
petroleum and politics at the (semi)-periphery /
Julius O. Ihonvbere, Timothy M. Shaw.
Aldershot, [England] ; Brookfield, [Vt.], USA :
Avebury,cc1988. xi, 213 p. : map ; 23 cm.
Includes note. Bibliography: p. 195-204. ISBN
0-566-05422-1 : DDC 338.9669 19
*1. Petroleum industry and trade - Nigeria. 2. Nigeria -
Economic policy. 3. Nigeria - Commercial policy. I.
Shaw, Timothy M. II. Title.*
HC1055 .I38 1988   ***NYPL [Sc D 89-47]***

Ija Ọr Owolabi, Olu. Ibadan, Nigeria , 1986,
c1983. vi, 84 p. : ISBN 978-16-7245-5
NYPL [Sc D 88-954]

Ijere, Martin Ohaeri, 1929- Fifty years of
Nigerian cooperative movement /. Nsukka
[Nigeria] , 1986. iii, 64 p. ;
NYPL [Sc D 88-859]

Ìjìnlè èdè àti lítíréṣ ìwé k Ibadan, Nigeria :
Evans, 1986. vi, 109 p. : ill. ; 22 cm. ISBN
978-16-7525-X
1. Yoruba language - Grammar. I. Owolabi, Olu.
NYPL [Sc D 89-248]

Ike, Chukwumeka. see Ike, Vincent
Chukwuemeka, 1931-

Ike, Vincent Chukwuemeka, 1931- The University
of Nigeria, 1960-1985 . Nsukka, Nigeria , 1986.
xviii, 657 p. : ISBN 978-229-913-8
NYPL [Sc F 88-198]

Ikenga /. Ihentuge, F. Azoma. Oshodi, Lagos ,
1985. 140 p. ; ISBN 978-243-256-3
NYPL [Sc C 89-76]

Ikonné, Chidi, 1940- Unborn child / Chidi
Ikonne. Owerri, Imo State KayBeeCee
Publications, 1987. v. 137 p. ; 18 cm. ISBN
PZ8-267-124-X
1. Nigeria - Fiction. I. Title.
NYPL [Sc C 88-359]

Ikpe, Eno Benjamin. Qua ibo Church of Nigeria :
the first hundred years : the next jubilee / by
Eno Benjamin Ikpe. [Uyo? : s.n., 1987] (Uyo :
Confidence) 31 p. : ports. ; 22 cm.
*1. Qua Iboe Church of Nigeria - History. 2.
Christianity - Nigeria - History. I. Title.*
NYPL [Sc D 89-28]

Ikpeze, N. I. Austerity and the Nigerian society
/. Nsukka , 1987. vi, 240 p. ; ISBN
978-264-356-4   ***NYPL [Sc D 89-205]***

Ilboudo, Patrick G. Les carnets secrets d'une fille
de joie : roman / Patrick G. Ilboudo. Burkina
Faso : La Mante, c1988. 189 p. ; 19 cm.
1. Prostitution - Africa - Fiction. I. Title.
NYPL [Sc C 88-356]

Ilboudo, Pierre Claver, 1948- Adama, ou, La
force des choses : roman / Ilboudo
Pierre-Claver. Paris : Présence africaine, 1987.
154 p. ; 20 cm. (Collection Ecrits) ISBN

2-7087-0484-2
*1. Burkina Faso - Fiction. I. Title. II. Title: Adama. III.
Title: Force des choses.*
PQ3989.2.143 A65x 1987
NYPL [Sc C 88-316]

L'île de braise et de pluie . Soukar, Michel.
[Port-au-Prince?] , 1984. 30 leaves ;
NYPL [Sc E 88-161]

Les Iles du Cap-Vert /. Pina, Marie-Paule de.
Paris , c1987. 216, [1] p., [12] p. of plates ;
ISBN 2-86507-182-4   ***NYPL [Sc D 88-510]***

Ilifa lidliwa ngumninilo /. Ngwenya, M. N.
Zimbabwe , c1982. 94 p. ;
NYPL [Sc C 89-67]

Illegitimacy in Kentucky /. Thompson, Kenneth,
1937- Frankfurt, Ky. , 1961. 52 p. :
NYPL [Sc F 88-36]

ILLEGITIMACY - KENTUCKY.
Thompson, Kenneth, 1937- Illegitimacy in
Kentucky /. Frankfurt, Ky. , 1961. 52 p. :
NYPL [Sc F 88-36]

ILLEGITIMACY - NEW YORK (N.Y.)
Whistelo, Alexander. (defendant) The
Commissioners of the Alms-house, vs.
Alexander Whistelo, a black man . New York ,
1808. 56 p. ;   ***NYPL [Sc Rare F 88-21]***

**Illinois and the thirteenth amendment to the
constitution of the United States.** Bross,
William, 1813-1890. Chicago, 1884. 8 p.
NYPL [Sc Rare F 88-43]

ILLINOIS - GENEALOGY.
Tregillis, Helen Cox. River roads to freedom .
Bowie, Md. , 1988. 122 p. : ISBN 1-556-13120-8
DDC 929/.3/089960773 19
F540 .T7 1988   ***NYPL [Sc D 88-1442]***

**ILLINOIS - POLITICS AND GOVERNMENT -
CIVIL WAR, 1861-1865.**
Bross, William, 1813-1890. Illinois and the
thirteenth amendment to the constitution of the
United States. Chicago, 1884. 8 p.
NYPL [Sc Rare F 88-43]

ILLITERACY - NIGER.
Easton, Peter A. Functional literacy and
cooperative education . 1972. v, 87 leaves :
NYPL [Sc F 88-52]

**An illustrated bio-bibliography of Black
photographers, 1940-1988 /.** Willis-Thomas,
Deborah, 1948- New York , 1989. xiv, 483 p. :
ISBN 0-8240-8389-X (alk. paper)   DDC
770/.92/2 19
TR139 .W55 1988   ***NYPL [Sc F 89-156]***

**ILLUSTRATIONS, HUMOROUS. see
CARICATURES AND CARTOONS.**

Ilogu, Edmund. Igbo life and thought / Edmund
Ilogu. [Nigeria] : University Publishing
Company, c1985. 42 p. ; 22 cm. Bibliography: p.
41-42. ISBN 978-16-0344-5
*1. Igbo (African people) - Religion. 2. Christianity and
other religions - African. 3. Nigeria - Religious life and
customs. I. Title.*   ***NYPL [Sc D 88-741]***

Ilouno, Chukwuemeka. Up from polygamy / by
Chukwuemeka Ilouno. [Nigeria : s.n.], c1985
(Enugu, Nigeria : Bema Press) 68 p. ; 19 cm.
1. Nigeria - Fiction. I. Title.
NYPL [Sc C 88-294]

Im Land der dreizehn Monate . Wenzel, Jürgen.
[Rudolstadt] , 1985. 200 p. :
NYPL [Sc E 88-286]

Im Urwaldspital von Lambarene /. Oswald,
Suzanne. Bern , c1986. 31 p. : ISBN
3-258-03594-6   ***NYPL [Sc D 87-1076]***

Image de la mère dans l'art ivoirien /. Holas, B.
(Bohumil), 1909-1979. Abidjan [1975] 122 p. :
DDC 732/.2/096668
NB1099.I8 H59   ***NYPL [Sc D 88-476]***

L'image de la société dans le roman haïtien /.
Shelton, Marie Denise. 1979 ix,241 p. ;
NYPL [Sc F 88-212]

**The image of Africa in the mind of the
Afro-American** . Clarke, John Henrik, 1915-
New York , 1973. 32 leaves ;
NYPL [Sc Micro F-9664]

**The image of Black women in twentieth-century
South American poetry** : a bilingual anthology
/ edited and translated by Ann Venture Young.
Washington, D.C. : Three Continents Press,
c1987. 250 p. ; 23 cm. Spanish with English

translations on facing pages. Bibliography: p. 245-250.
ISBN 0-89410-275-3
1. Women, Black - South America - Poetry. 2. Spanish American poetry - 20th century. 3. Spanish American poetry - 20th century - Translations into English. 4. English poetry - 20th century - Translations from Spanish. I. Young, Ann Venture.
NYPL [Sc E 88-321]

Images . Gray, Mattie Evans. Sacramento, Calif. , c1988. 185 p. : ISBN 0-8011-0782-2
NYPL [Sc F 89-134]

Images from Bamum . Geary, Christraud M. Washington, D.C. , 1988. 151 p. : ISBN 0-87474-455-5 (pbk. : alk. paper) DDC 967/.1102/0880621 19
DT574 .G43 1988 *NYPL [Sc F 89-55]*

Images of Blacks in American culture : a reference guide to information sources / edited by Jessie Carney Smith ; foreword by Nikki Giovanni. New York : Greenwood Press, 1988. xvii, 390 p. : ill. ; 25 cm. Includes bibliographies and index. ISBN 0-313-24844-3 (lib. bdg. : alk. paper) DDC 700 19
1. Afro-Americans in art. I. Smith, Jessie Carney.
NX652.A37 I43 1988 *NYPL [Sc E 88-466]*

IMANA (RUNDI DEITY)
Bigangara, Jean-Baptiste. Le fondement de l'imanisme, ou, Religion traditionnelle au Burundi . Bujumbura, Burundi , 1984. 140 p. ;
BL2470.B94 B54 1984 *NYPL [Sc E 88-459]*

IMBECILITY. see MENTALLY HANDICAPPED.

Imberg, David. Stares, Rodney. Ethnic minorities . [London] , 1982. 62 p. ; ISBN 0-905932-32-3 *NYPL [Sc F 88-96]*

The IMF and Ghana : the confidential record / [edited by] Eboe Hutchful. London ; New Jersey : Zed Books Ltd, 1987. 298 p. ; 23 cm. Includes bibliographical references. ISBN 0-86232-614-1
1. Ghana - Economic conditions - 1979-. I. Hutchful, Eboe. *NYPL [Sc D 88-1095]*

Imigani "tima-ngiro" y'u Rwanda = les Contes moraux du Rwanda / collection de Aloys Bigirumwami ; présentation et traduction, Bernardin Muzumgu. Butare : Editions de l'Université nationale du Rwanda, 1987. 267, [1] p. ; 21 cm. In French and Kinyarwanda. Rev., bilingual ed. of the author's Imgani miremire. Bibliography: p. [268]
1. Fables, Rwandan. 2. Tales - Rwanda. I. Bigirumwami, Aloys. II. Muzungu, Bernardin.
NYPL [Sc D 88-865]

Immanences . Crosley, Réginald O. Montreal, Quebec, Canada , 1988. 168 p. ;
NYPL [Sc D 89-440]

IMMIGRANT LABOR. see ALIEN LABOR.

IMMIGRANTS - CROSS-CULTURAL STUDIES.
Ethnic associations and the welfare state . New York , 1988. x, 299 p. : ISBN 0-231-05690-7 DDC 362.8 19
HV4005 .E86 1988 *NYPL [JLE 88-3846]*

IMMIGRANTS - QUEBEC - MONTREAL.
Histoires d'immigrées . Montréal , 1987. 275 p. ; ISBN 2-89052-170-2 *NYPL [Sc D 88-346]*

IMMIGRANTS - UNITED STATES - HISTORY - 19TH CENTURY.
Burton, William L., 1928- Melting pot soldiers . Ames, Iowa , 1988. x, 282 p. ; ISBN 0-8138-1115-5 DDC 973.7/4 19
E540.F6 B87 1988 *NYPL [IKC 88-730]*

Hunt, Alfred N., 1941- Haiti's influence on antebellum America . Baton Rouge , c1988. xiv, 196 p. : ISBN 0-8071-1370-0 DDC 973/.049697294 19
E184.H27 H86 1987 *NYPL [Sc E 88-131]*

IMMIGRATION. see EMIGRATION AND IMMIGRATION.

Imobighe, Thomas A. Nigerian defence and security . Bukuru, Plateau State , 1987. xii, 208 p. ; ISBN 978-19-8019-2
NYPL [Sc D 88-1377]

The impact of military rule on Nigeria's administration / edited by A.O. Sanda, Olusola Ojo & Victor Ayeni. Ile-Ife, Nigeria : Faculty of Administration University of Ife, Ile-Ife, c1987. vi, 344 p. ; 21 cm. Bibliography: p. 327-344. ISBN 978-266-601-7

1. Military government - Nigeria. 2. Civil-military relations - Nigeria. 3. Nigeria - Politics and government - 1960-. I. Sanda, A. O. II. Olusola, Ojo. III. Ayeni, Victor. IV. Title.
NYPL [Sc D 88-733]

The impact of the Black electorate [microform] /. Cavanagh, Thomas E. Washington, D.C. (1301 Pennsylvania Ave., N.W., Suite 400, Washington 20004) , 1984. v, 28 p. ; DDC 324.973/008996073 19
E185.615 .C364 1984 *NYPL [*Z-4913 no.8]*

Imperato, Pascal James. Historical dictionary of Mali / by Pascal James Imperato. 2nd ed. Metuchen, N.J. : Scarecrow Press, 1986. xvii, 359 p. ; 23 cm. (African historical dictionaries. no. 11) Bibliography: p. 256-359. ISBN 0-8108-1885-X DDC 966/.23 19
1. Mali - History - Dictionaries. I. Title. II. Series.
DT551.5 .I46 1986 *NYPL [Sc D 87-5]*

The imperfect art . Gioia, Ted. New York , 1988. vi, 152 p. ; ISBN 0-19-505343-5 (alk. paper) DDC 785.42/09 19
ML3506 .G56 1988 *NYPL [JMD 88-274]*

IMPERIALISM - COMIC BOOKS, STRIPS, ETC.
Comics für Afrika . Dormagen [West Germany] [1986] 96 p. ; *NYPL [Sc G 88-27]*

IMPERIALISM - CONGRESSES.
Bishop, Maurice. Imperialism is the real problem [microform] . [st. George's], Grenada , 1981. 13 leaves ;
NYPL [Sc Micro R-4108 no.27]

Imperialism in East Africa /. Nabudere, D. Wadada. London , Westport, Conn. , 1981- v. ;
NYPL [Sc Ser.-L .N238]

Imperialism is the real problem [microform] .
Bishop, Maurice. [st. George's], Grenada , 1981. 13 leaves ;
NYPL [Sc Micro R-4108 no.27]

IMPERSONATORS, FEMALE - NEW YORK (N.Y.) - BIOGRAPHY.
Howard-Howard, Margo, 1935- I was a white slave in Harlem /. New York , c1988. vii, 177 p., [8] p. of plates : ISBN 0-941423-14-X (pbk.) : DDC 306.7/43/0924 19
HQ77.8.H68 A3 1988 *NYPL [JFE 89-340]*

L'impossible compromis /. Dia, Malick. Abidjan , c1979. 102 p. ; ISBN 2-7236-0447-0
NYPL [Sc D 88-958]

IMPOTENCE - MARTINIQUE - FICTION.
Delsham, Tony. L'impuissant /. Fort-de-France , 1986. 204 p. ; ISBN 2-86823-006-7 *NYPL [Sc D 88-349]*

A imprensa negra paulista (1915-1963) /.
Ferrara, Miriam Nicolau. São Paulo , 1986. 279 p. : *NYPL [Sc B 88-6]*

IMPRESSMENT.
Massachusetts. General Court. House of Representatives. Committee on Impressed Seamen. Report of the Committee of the House of Representatives of Massachusetts on the subject of impressed seamen. Boston , 1813. 84, 4 p. ; *NYPL [Sc Rare C 89-13]*

Improved village technology for women's activities : a manual for West Africa / prepared under the auspices of the International Labour Office and the Government of Norway joint Africa Regional Project on Technological Change, Basic Needs and the Condition of Rural Women. Geneva : International Labour Office, 1984. vi, 292 p. : ill. ; 30 cm. (A WEP study) Bibliography: p. 277-282. ISBN 92-2-103818-1
1. Women in rural development - Africa, West. 2. Women - Africa, West - Economic conditions. 3. Technological innovations - Africa, West. 4. Food industry and trade - Africa, West. I. International Labor Office. II. International Labor Organization. World Employment Programme. III. Africa Regional Project on Technological Change, Basic Needs and the Condition of Rural Women. IV. Series.
NYPL [JLF 85-625]

L'impuissant /. Delsham, Tony. Fort-de-France , 1986. 204 p. ; ISBN 2-86823-006-7
NYPL [Sc D 88-349]

Impundu kwa Rusango /. Karengera, Pawulini. [Kigali? , 1983] (Kigali : Imprimerie Scolaire) 319 p. : *NYPL [Sc D 89-447]*

Imwe chanzi ichabvepi? . Chigidi, Willie L. Gweru , 1986. 60 p. ; *NYPL [Sc C 89-114]*

In America in search of gold /. Appiah-Kubi, Kofi. Bloomfield, Conn. , 1985. 103 p. : ISBN 0-9614573-0-9 *NYPL [Sc D 89-583]*

In bondage and freedom . McGraw, Marie Tyler. Richmond, VA. [Chapel Hill, N.C.] , 1988. 71 p. : *NYPL [Sc F 89-107]*

In defence of Igbo belief system . Nnabuchi, Nwankwo. Enugu, Nigeria , 1987. xiii, 216 p. ; ISBN 978-270-500-4 *NYPL [Sc D 89-84]*

In Simbabwe /. Klöppel, Eberhard. Leipzig , c1985. 160 p. : ISBN 0-325-00113-0
NYPL [Sc D 88-627]

In the African-American grain . Callahan, John F. Urbana , c1988. 280 p. ; ISBN 0-252-01459-6 (alk. paper) DDC 813/.009/896073 19
PS153.N5 C34 1988 *NYPL [Sc E 88-144]*

In the beginning . Hamilton, Virginia. San Diego , c1988. xi, 161 p. : ISBN 0-15-238740-4 DDC 291.2/4 19
BL226 .H35 1988 *NYPL [JFF 89-62]*

In the city / prepared by the Bank Street College of Education ; illustrated by Dan Dickas. New York : Macmillan, c1965. 32 p. col. ill. ; 22 cm. (The Bank Street readers) SCHOMBURG CHILDREN'S COLLECTION.
1. City and town life - United States - Juvenile literature. 2. Primers. I. Schomburg Children's Collection. *NYPL [Sc D 89-82]*

In the image of Christ crucified and risen, in the service of the community . Meili, Josef. Gweru, Zimbabwe , 1986. 127 p. ;
NYPL [Sc D 88-1332]

In the shadow of man . Lawick-Goodall, Jane, Barones van. Boston, 1971. xx, 297 p. ISBN 0-395-12726-2
QL737.P96 L37 *NYPL [SC 599.8-L]*

In the shadow of the Peacock /. Edwards-Yearwood, Grace. New York , c1988. 279 p. ; ISBN 0-07-019037-2 DDC 813/.54 19
PS3555.D99 I5 1988 *NYPL [JFE 88-4421]*

In this evening light /. Jackson, Clyde Owen. Hicksville, N. Y. , c1980. xiii, 113 p. ; ISBN 0-682-49479-8 *NYPL [Sc D 88-1213]*

INADES-documentation (Institution) Régulation des naissances en Afrique . Abidjan, Côte d'Ivoire [1987] 74 p. ; *NYPL [Sc F 88-392]*

INADES-documentation (Institution) Les réfugiés en Afrique : bibliographie commentée. Abidjan, Côte d'Ivoire : INADES-documentation, [1986] 55 p. : ill. ; 30 cm. "Novembre 1986." Errata slip inserted. Includes indexes.
1. Refugees - Africa - Bibliography. I. Title.
Z7164.R32 I5 1986 HV640.4.A35
NYPL [Sc F 88-391]

Inaugural addresses [microform] / His Excellency President Kenneth D. Kaunda ... [et al.]. [Lusaka] : University of Zambia, Institute of Human Relations, 1982. [39] p. ; 30 cm. (Occasional paper/University of Zambia, Institute of Human Relations. 82/1) Cover title. "Inauguration of the Institute of Human Relations, February 23rd, 1982."--p. 1. Mimeographed. Microfilm. New York : New York Public Library, 1982. 1 microfilm reel; 35 mm. (MN *ZZ-23207)
1. University of Zambia. Institute of Human Relations. I. Kaunda, Kenneth David, Pres. Zambia, 1924-. II. Series: University of Zambia. Institute of Human Relations. Occasional paper, 82/1 82/1.
NYPL [Sc Micro R-4132 no. 23]

INCANTATIONS.
Sales, Niveo Ramos. Receitas de feitiços e encantos afro-brasileiros /. Rio de Janeiro , 1982. 75 p. ; *NYPL [JFD 84-750]*

L'inceste focal dans la famille noire antillaise . André, Jacques. Paris : Presses universitaires de France, 1987. 396 p. ; ISBN 2-13-040101-5
NYPL [Sc D 88-129]

Incidents at the shrine . Okri, Ben. London , 1986. 135 p. ; ISBN 0-434-53230-4
NYPL [JFD 87-7171]

Incidents in the life of a slave girl /. Jacobs, Harriet A. (Harriet Ann), 1813-1897. New York , 1988. xl, 306 p. ; ISBN 0-19-505243-9 (alk. paper) DDC 973/.0496024 B 19
E444.J17 A3 1988 *NYPL [JFC 88-2193]*

INCOME DISTRIBUTION - AFRICA.
Nafziger, E. Wayne. Inequality in Africa .

Cambridge [Cambridgeshire] , New York ,
c1988. xii, 204 p. : ISBN 0-521-26881-8 DDC
339.2/096 19
HC800.Z9 I5136 1988 NYPL [Sc E 88-521]

INCOME - KENYA - STATISTICS.
Narayan-Parker, Deepa. Women's interest and
involvement in income generating activities .
Gaborone, Botswana [1983] vi, 143, 3 p. ;
DDC 331.4/09676/2 19
HD6210.5 .N37 1983 NYPL [Sc F 88-312]

Independence is not only for one sex /.
Bond-Stewart, Kathy. Harare, Zimbabwe , 1987.
128 p. : ISBN 0-949225-50-9
NYPL [Sc E 89-146]

Independence ten. Independence 10 .
Georgetown, Guyana [introd. 1976] 222 p. ;
DDC 810
PR9320.5 .I5
NYPL [Sc F 89-101]

Independence 10 : Guyanese writing, 1966-1976.
Georgetown, Guyana : National History and
Arts Council, Ministry of Information &
Culture, [introd. 1976] 222 p. ; 28 cm. Errata
slip inserted. DDC 810
*1. Guyanese literature. I. National History and Arts
Council. II. Title: Independence ten.*
PR9320.5 .I5 NYPL [Sc F 89-101]

The Independent trade unions, 1974-1984 : ten
years of the South African Labour Bulletin /
edited by Johann Maree. Johannesburg : Ravan
Press, 1987. xvi, 355 p. ; 21 cm. (Ravan labour
studies . 2) Includes index to v.1-10 of the South
African labour bulletin: p. 280-355. Includes
bibliographical references. ISBN 0-86975-307-X
*1. South African labour bulletin - Indexes. 2.
Trade-unions - South Africa. 3. Labor and laboring
classes - South Africa. I. Maree, Johann. II. South
African labour bulletin.* *NYPL [Sc E 88-1329]*

**Index of subjects, proverbs, and themes in the
writings of Wole Soyinka /.** Avery-Coger,
Greta Margaret Kay McCormick. New York ,
c1988. xxii, 311 p. ; ISBN 0-313-25712-4 (lib.
bdg. : alk. paper) DDC 822 19
PR9387.9.S6 Z54 1988 NYPL [Sc E 88-496]

Index to Afro-American reference resources /.
Stevenson, Rosemary M. New York , 1988.
xxvi, 315 p. ; ISBN 0-313-24580-0 (lib. bdg. : alk.
paper) DDC 973/.0496073 19
Z1361.N39 S77 1988 E185
NYPL [Sc E 88-220]

**Index to livestock literature microfiched in
Zimbabwe /** compiled by Tesfai Berhane and
Negussie Akalework. Addis Ababa :
Documentation Services, International
Livestock Center for Africa, [1986?] viii, 235
p. ; 25 cm. "February 1986."
"IDRC-MP/RH-1542/83." Includes indexes. ISBN
92-9053-064-2
*1. International Livestock Centre for Africa -
Microform catalogs. 2. Livestock - Zimbabwe -
Bibliography - Microform catalogs. 3. Livestock -
Bibliography - Microform catalogs. 4. Livestock -
Zimbabwe - Indexes. 5. Livestock - Indexes. I. Berhane
Tesfay. II. Negussie Akalework. III. International
Livestock Centre for Africa. Documentation Services.
IV. International Development Research Centre
(Canada). V. Title.* *NYPL [Sc E 89-204]*

India and Africa. Indian Council for Africa. [New
Delhi, 1967] 57 p.
HF1590.15.A3 I5 NYPL [JLE 72-1609]

**INDIA - FOREIGN ECONOMIC
RELATIONS - AFRICA - ADDRESSES,
ESSAYS, LECTURES.**
Indian Council for Africa. India and Africa.
[New Delhi, 1967] 57 p.
HF1590.15.A3 I5 NYPL [JLE 72-1609]

INDIA IN ART - EXHIBITIONS.
Pindell, Howardena, 1943- Howardena Pindell .
New York, NY (144 W. 125th St., New York
10027) , c1986. 24 p. : DDC 709/.2/4 19
N6537.P49 A4 1986 NYPL [Sc F 88-270]

India in the Caribbean / edited by David
Dabydeen, Brinsley Samaroo. London : Hansib,
1987. 326 p. : ill. ; 21 cm. Includes index. "A
Hansib/University of Warwick, Centre for Caribbean
Studies publication in cooperation with the London
Strategic Policy Unit". Bibliography: p. 318. ISBN
1-87051-805-5 (cased) : DDC 909/.09182/1081
19
*1. East Indians - Caribbean Area. I. Dabydeen, David.
II. Samaroo, Brinsley. III. University of Warwick.*

*Centre for Caribbean Studies. IV. London Strategic
Policy Unit.* *NYPL [Sc D 88-997]*

**INDIAN-AFRO-AMERICAN RELATIONS. see
AFRO-AMERICANS - RELATIONS WITH
INDIANS.**

Indian Council for Africa. India and Africa:
perspectives of cooperation. [New Delhi, 1967]
57 p. 24 cm. PARTIAL CONTENTS. - Development
problems in Africa, by R. K. A.
Gardiner.--Demographic problems in Africa, by Asok
Mitra.--Economic and social development of Africa: the
role of the Economic Commission for Africa, by
Pravakar Sen.--Economic development in India and
Africa: points of contact, by Asoka Mehta.--India-Africa
Development Association, by Bharat Ram.
*1. India - Foreign economic relations - Africa -
Addresses, essays, lectures. 2. Africa - Foreign
economic relations - India - Addresses, essays, lectures.
3. Africa - Economic conditions - 1945- - Addresses,
essays, lectures. I. Title.*
HF1590.15.A3 I5 NYPL [JLE 72-1609]

Indian folk tales of the Caribbean . Parmasad,
Kenneth Vidia. Charlieville, Chaguanas,
Trinidad and Tobago, West Indies , c1984. xxii,
131 p., [2] p. of plates : ISBN 976-8016-01-9
(pbk.) DDC 398.2/09729 19
GR120 .P37 1984 NYPL [Sc D 88-400]

**Indiana University, Bloomington. African Studies
Program.** Explorations in African systems of
thought /. Washington, D.C. , c1987. xvi, 337
p. : ISBN 0-87474-591-8 (pbk.)
NYPL [Sc D 88-566]

Indiana University, Bloomington. Art Museum.
Pelrine, Diane. African art from the Rita and
John Grunwald collection /. Bloomington ,
c1988. 159 p. : ISBN 0-253-21061-5 (I.U. Press :
pbk.) DDC 730/.0966/0740172255 19
N7398 .P44 1988 NYPL [Sc F 89-158]

**INDIANS, CENTRAL AMERICAN. see
INDIANS OF CENTRAL AMERICA.**

**INDIANS - ETHNOLOGY. see INDIANS OF
NORTH AMERICA; INDIANS OF
SOUTH AMERICA.**

INDIANS - MIXED BLOODS.
Forbes, Jack D. Black Africans and native
Americans . Oxford, UK , New York, NY,
USA , 1988. 345 p. ; ISBN 0-631-15665-8 :
DDC 973/.0496073 19
E59.M66 F67 1988 NYPL [HBC 88-2172]

**INDIANS, NORTH AMERICAN. see
INDIANS OF NORTH AMERICA.**

**INDIANS OF CENTRAL AMERICA -
ETHNOLOGY. see INDIANS OF
CENTRAL AMERICA.**

**INDIANS OF CENTRAL AMERICA -
NICARAGUA - LEGENDS.**
Rohmer, Harriet. The invisible hunters . San
Francisco , c1987. 32 p. : ISBN 0-89239-031-X :
DDC 398.2/08998 19
F1529.M9 R64 1987 NYPL [Sc E 88-241]

**INDIANS OF CENTRAL AMERICA -
TRIBES.** See individual tribes, e.g. Cuna
Indians. For list of tribes, see under:
INDIANS OF CENTRAL AMERICA.

INDIANS OF NORTH AMERICA - ALASKA.
Healy, M. A. (Michael A.) Report of the cruise
of the revenue marine steamer Corwin in the
Arctic Ocean in the year 1884 . Washington ,
1889. 128 p., [39] leaves of plates :
NYPL [Sc Rare F 88-62]

**INDIANS OF NORTH AMERICA - CIVIL
RIGHTS.**
Black, brown and red . Detroit, Mich. , 1975.
77 p. : *NYPL [Sc D 84-219]*

**INDIANS OF NORTH AMERICA -
ETHNOLOGY. see INDIANS OF NORTH
AMERICA.**

**INDIANS OF NORTH AMERICA -
RELATIONS WITH AFRO-AMERICANS.
see AFRO-AMERICANS - RELATIONS
WITH INDIANS.**

**INDIANS OF NORTH AMERICA -
SOUTHERN STATES - MISSIONS -
ADDRESSES, ESSAYS, LECTURES.**
McLoughlin, William Gerald. The Cherokee
ghost dance . [Macon, Ga.] , c1984. xxiv, 512
p. : ISBN 0-86554-128-0 : DDC 975/.00497 19
E78.S65 M37 1984 NYPL [HBC 85-263]

**INDIANS OF NORTH AMERICA -
SOUTHERN STATES - SLAVES,
OWNERSHIP OF - ADDRESSES,
ESSAYS, LECTURES.**
McLoughlin, William Gerald. The Cherokee
ghost dance . [Macon, Ga.] , c1984. xxiv, 512
p. : ISBN 0-86554-128-0 : DDC 975/.00497 19
E78.S65 M37 1984 NYPL [HBC 85-263]

**INDIANS OF NORTH AMERICA -
SOUTHERN STATES - SOCIAL
CONDITIONS - ADDRESSES, ESSAYS,
LECTURES.**
McLoughlin, William Gerald. The Cherokee
ghost dance . [Macon, Ga.] , c1984. xxiv, 512
p. : ISBN 0-86554-128-0 : DDC 975/.00497 19
E78.S65 M37 1984 NYPL [HBC 85-263]

INDIANS OF NORTH AMERICA - TRIBES.
See individual tribes, e.g. Apache Indians.
For list of tribes, see under: **INDIANS OF
NORTH AMERICA.**

**INDIANS OF NORTH AMERICA - UNITED
STATES. see INDIANS OF NORTH
AMERICA.**

**INDIANS OF SOUTH AMERICA -
ARGENTINA - CÓRDOBA.**
Endrek, Emiliano. El mestizaje en Córdoba.
Córdoba [Argentina] 1966. xi, 151 p.
F2821.1.C7 E5 NYPL [Sc E 88-61]

**INDIANS OF SOUTH AMERICA - BRAZIL -
HISTORY.**
Freyre, Gilberto, 1900- [Casa-grande & senzala.
English.] The masters and the slaves =.
Berkeley , c1986. xc, 537 xliv p., [3] p. of
plates : ISBN 0-520-05665-5 (pbk. : alk. paper)
DDC 981 19
F2510 .F7522 1986 NYPL [HFB 87-2095]

**INDIANS OF SOUTH AMERICA -
ETHNOLOGY. see INDIANS OF SOUTH
AMERICA.**

INDIANS OF SOUTH AMERICA - GUYANA.
Kirby, Richard, 1958. Ewto' . London , c1985.
27 p. : ISBN 0-946140-24-3 (pbk) DDC 307.7/72
19
F2380 NYPL [Sc F 89-104]

**INDIANS OF SOUTH AMERICA - MIXED
BLOODS.**
Endrek, Emiliano. El mestizaje en Córdoba.
Córdoba [Argentina] 1966. xi, 151 p.
F2821.1.C7 E5 NYPL [Sc E 88-61]

INDIANS OF SOUTH AMERICA - TRIBES.
See individual tribes, e.g. Carib Indians. For
list of tribes, see under: **INDIANS OF
SOUTH AMERICA.**

**INDIANS OF SOUTH AMERICA -
VENEZUELA.**
Pons, François Raymond Joseph de, 1751-1812.
Voyage à la partie orientale de la Terre-Ferme,
dans l'Amérique Méridionale, fait pendant les
années 1801, 1802, 1803 et 1804: contenant la
description de la capitainerie générale de
Carácas, composée des provinces de Vénézuéla,
Maracaïbo, Varinas, la Guiane Espagnole,
Cumana, et de l'île de la Marguerite ... Paris,
1806. 3 v.
F2311 .P79 NYPL [Sc Rare F 88-77]

**INDIANS OF THE UNITED STATES. see
INDIANS OF NORTH AMERICA.**

**INDIANS OF THE WEST INDIES -
HISTORY.**
Colón, Fernando, 1488-1539. [Historie.
English.] Christophe Colomb raconté par son
fils /. Paris , 1986. xviii, 265 p., [8] p. of
plates : ISBN 2-262-00387-4
NYPL [Sc D 88-504]

**INDIANS, SOUTH AMERICAN. see
INDIANS OF SOUTH AMERICA.**

Indies, East. see East Indies.

Indies, West. see West Indies.

**INDIGENOUS CHURCH
ADMINISTRATION - AFRICA.**
Salvoldi, Valentino. [Africa, il vangelo ci
appartiene. English.] Africa, the gospel belongs
to us . Ndola [Zambia] , 1986. 187 p ;
NYPL [Sc D 89-568]

Indignant heart . Denby, Charles. Boston , c1978.
295 p. : ISBN 0-89608-092-7 DDC
331.6/3/960730774340924 B 19
HD8039.A82 U633 1978
NYPL [Sc D 88-853]

Indignant heart . Denby, Charles. Detroit , 1989, c1978. xvi, 303 p. : ISBN 0-8143-2219-0 (alk. paper) DDC 331.6/396073 B 19
HD8039.A82 U633 1989
NYPL [Sc D 89-563]

Indigo Hill. Lattimore, Eleanor Frances, 1904-New York, 1950. 128 p. DDC [Fic]
PZ7.L37 In   **NYPL [Sc D 88-1428]**

INDUSTRIAL ADMINISTRATION. see INDUSTRIAL MANAGEMENT.

Industrial Development Corporation (Trinidad and Tobago) Trinidad & Tobago investment opportunities in industry. Port-of-Spain, Trinidad , 1985. 40 p. ;   **NYPL [Sc F 88-94]**

INDUSTRIAL EDUCATION. see TECHNICAL EDUCATION.

INDUSTRIAL MANAGEMENT - AFRICA - CONGRESSES.
L'Entreprise et ses dirigeants dans le développement économique de l'Afrique noire . Kinshasa [1969?] 89 p. :
NYPL [Sc F 88-100]

INDUSTRIAL PROMOTION - AFRICA - ADDRESSES, ESSAYS, LECTURES.
Rural small-scale industries and employment in Africa and Asia . Geneva , 1984. x, 159 p. ; ISBN 92-2-103513-1 (pbk.) : DDC 338.6/42/095 19
HD2346.A55 R87 1984
NYPL [JLE 84-3222]

INDUSTRIAL PROMOTION - ASIA - ADDRESSES, ESSAYS, LECTURES.
Rural small-scale industries and employment in Africa and Asia . Geneva , 1984. x, 159 p. ; ISBN 92-2-103513-1 (pbk.) : DDC 338.6/42/095 19
HD2346.A55 R87 1984
NYPL [JLE 84-3222]

INDUSTRIAL RELATIONS - NIGERIA - HISTORY.
Otobo, Dafe. Foreign interests and Nigerian trade unions /. Ibadan [Nigeria] , 1986. xxviii, 190 p. : ISBN 978-12-9532-5 (pbk.) DDC 331.88/09669 19
HD6885.5 .O87 1986   **NYPL [Sc E 88-557]**
Otobo, Dafe. State and industrial relations in Nigeria /. Lagos , 1988. 192 p. ISBN 978-260-104-7   **NYPL [Sc D 89-523]**

INDUSTRIAL UNIONS. see TRADE-UNIONS.

INDUSTRY AND COLLEGES. see INDUSTRY AND EDUCATION.

INDUSTRY AND EDUCATION - SWAZILAND.
Sullivan, Gerard. From school--to work . Oxford , c1981. xvi, 190 p. : DDC 373.12/913/096813 19
LC145.S78 S94 1981   **NYPL [Sc F 87-331]**

INDUSTRY - VOCATIONAL GUIDANCE. see VOCATIONAL GUIDANCE.

Inequality in Africa . Nafziger, E. Wayne. Cambridge [Cambridgeshire] , New York , c1988. xii, 204 p. : ISBN 0-521-26881-8 DDC 339.2/096 19
HC800.Z9 I5136 1988   **NYPL [Sc E 88-521]**

INEQUALITY OF INCOME. see INCOME DISTRIBUTION.

The inevitable hour . Sebuava, Joseph, 1934-Accra , 1987,c1979. 141 p. ;
NYPL [Sc D 88-1384]

INFANTS - LEGAL STATUS, LAWS, ETC. see CHILDREN - LEGAL STATUS, LAWS, ETC.

INFIBULATION - BIBLIOGRAPHY.
Sanderson, Lilian Passmore. Female genital mutilation, excision and infibulation . London [1986?] 72 p. ; DDC 016.392 19
Z5118.C57 S26 1986 GN484
NYPL [Sc D 88-1152]

The infinite rehearsal /. Harris, Wilson, 1921-London , 1987. 88 p. ; ISBN 0-571-14885-9 (pbk) DDC 823/.914 19
PR6058.A692   **NYPL [Sc D 88-749]**

INFLUENCE (LITERARY, ARTISTIC, ETC.)
Awkward, Michael. Inspiriting influences . New York , 1989. x, 178 p. ; ISBN 0-231-06806-9

DDC 813/.5/099287 19
PS153.N5 A94 1989   **NYPL [Sc E 89-188]**

La información sobre África austral. Harris, Phil. [Reporting southern Africa. Spanish.] Barcelona , Paris , 1984. 188 p. : ISBN 92-3-301700-1 (Unesco)
NYPL [Sc D 88-614]

Informal credit for integrated rural development in Sierra Leone /. Johnny, Michael. Hamburg , 1985. xviii, 212 p. : ISBN 3-87895-274-X (pbk.)
HG2146.5.S5 J63x 1985
NYPL [Sc D 88-766]

Informal history of the Black people I have known in Halifax /. Stephenson, Anne N. [Halifax] c1978. 99 p. :
NYPL [Sc D 88-1209]

INFORMAL SECTOR (ECONOMICS) - JAMAICA - KINGSTON METROPOLITAN AREA.
Anderson, Patricia, Dr. Mini bus ride . Mona, Kingston, Jamaica , 1987. vii, 179 p. : ISBN 976-400-006-1
HE5647.K56 A53x 1987
NYPL [Sc D 89-312]

INFORMATION CENTERS. see INFORMATION SERVICES.

INFORMATION PROCESSING SYSTEMS. see INFORMATION STORAGE AND RETRIEVAL SYSTEMS.

INFORMATION RETRIEVAL SYSTEMS. see INFORMATION STORAGE AND RETRIEVAL SYSTEMS.

INFORMATION SERVICES - NEW YORK (N. Y.)
Library and information sources on women . New York , c1988. ix, 254 p. ; ISBN 0-935312-88-9 (pbk.) DDC 305.4/025/7471 19
HQ1181.U5 L52 1987
NYPL [*R-Econ. 88-4682]

INFORMATION SERVICES - TRINIDAD AND TOBAGO - DIRECTORIES.
Directory of special libraries/information units in Trinidad and Tobago /. Port of Spain, Trinidad & Tobago [1986] iv, 59 p. ; DDC 026/.00025/72983 19
Z753.T7 D57 1986   **NYPL [Sc D 88-1019]**

INFORMATION STORAGE AND RETRIEVAL SYSTEMS - SOCIAL SCIENCES.
Fundação Joaquim Nabuco. Plano diretor de informática, 82-84 /. Recife , 1982. 101 p., 1 folded leaf :   **NYPL [Sc D 88-924]**

Informationsstelle Südliches Afrika.
ISSA Wissenschaftliche Reihe .
(7) Martin, Michael. Malawi, ein entwicklungspolitisches Musterland? . Bonn , 1984. 95 p. : ISBN 3-921614-17-1
NYPL [Sc D 88-681]

Ingalls, Robert P., 1941- Urban vigilantes in the New South : Tampa, 1882-1936 / Robert P. Ingalls.1st ed. Knoxville : University of Tennessee Press, c1988. xx, 286 p. : ill. ; 25 cm. Includes index. Bibliography: p. 263-276. ISBN 0-87049-571-2 (alk. paper) DDC 305.8/009759/65 19
1. Vigilantes - Florida - Tampa - History. 2. Violence - Florida - Tampa - History. 3. Tampa, Fla. - Social conditions. 4. Tampa (Fla.) - Race relations. I. Title.
F319.T2 I64 1988   **NYPL [Sc E 88-518]**

Ingram, Adrian. Wes Montgomery / Adrian Ingram. Gateshead, Tyne and Wear, England : Ashley Mark Pub. Co., 1985. 127 p. : ill. ; 29 cm. Bibliography: p. 123-126. Discography: p. 73-109. ISBN 0-9506224-9-4
1. Montgomery, Wes, 1923-1968. 2. Guitarists - United States - Biography. 3. Jazz musicians - United States - Biography. 4. Afro-American musicians - Biography. I. Title.   **NYPL [Sc F 88-61]**

The inmates . Adawaisi, Linus C. [Maiduguri?] 1987 (Maiduguri : Uncle Oguns Press) 72 p. ;
NYPL [Sc C 89-104]

The inna thought and feelings of the poet /. Parchment, Michael. [Jamaica? , 1984?] 46 p. ;
MLCM 84/5607 (P)   **NYPL [Sc F 88-134]**

Inniss, Diana. A selected bibliography of materials and resources on women in the Caribbean available at WAND's Research and Documentation Centre / prepared for women in development ; prepared by Diana Inniss.

Pinelands, St. Michael [Barbados] : Women and Development Unit, Extra Mural Dept., [1987] 119 p. ; 28 cm. Cover title. "June 1987." "To be updated bi-annually."
1. University of the West Indies (Cave Hill, Barbados). Women and Development Unit. Research and Documentation Centre - Catalogs. 2. Women in development - Caribbean Area - Bibliography - Catalogs. I. University of the West Indies (Cave Hill, Barbados). Women and Development Unit. Research and Documentation Centre. II. Title.
NYPL [Sc F 88-218]

Inniss, Probyn, Sir. Historic Basseterre : the story of a West Indian Town / by Sir Probyn Inniss. Basseterre, St. Kitts : P. Inniss, c1985. 84 p. : ill. ; 21 cm. Bibliography: p. 84.
1. Basseterre (Saint Kitts) - History. I. Title.
NYPL [Sc D 88-266]

INNOVATIONS, TECHNOLOGICAL. see TECHNOLOGICAL INNOVATIONS.

INNS. see HOTELS, TAVERNS, ETC.

Innsbrucker theologische Studien .
(Bd. 14) Rücker, Heribert. "Afrikanische Theologie" . Innsbruck , 1985. 271 p. ; ISBN 3-7022-1548-4
BT30.A438 R83 1985   **NYPL [Sc D 88-868]**

INSCRIPTIONS, MEROITIC - CONGRESSES.
Symposium on the Peopling of Ancient Egypt and the deciphering of Meroitic Script (1974 : Cairo, Egypt) [Peuplement de l'Egipte ancienne et la déchiffrement de l'écriture méroïtique. Spanish.] Poblamiento del antiguo Egipto y desciframiento de la escritura meroítica /. Barcelona , Paris , 1983. 155 p. : ISBN 0-923301-60-5 (Unesco)
NYPL [Sc D 88-603]

INSCRIPTIONS - WASHINGTON (D.C.)
Sluby, Paul E. Holmead's Cemetery (Western Burial Ground), Washington, D.C. /. Washington, D.C. , 1985. iv, 68 leaves : DDC 929.5/09753 19
F193 .S582 1985   **NYPL [Sc D 88-109]**

INSECTS - AFRICA, SOUTHERN - GEOGRAPHICAL DISTRIBUTION.
Cottrell, C. B. Aspects of the biogeography of southern African butterflies . Salisbury [Zimbabwe] , c1978. viii, 100 p. ;
QL557.S65 C68 1978   **NYPL [Sc E 88-555]**

INSECTS - AFRICA, SOUTHERN - HOST PLANTS.
Cottrell, C. B. Aspects of the biogeography of southern African butterflies . Salisbury [Zimbabwe] , c1978. viii, 100 p. ;
QL557.S65 C68 1978   **NYPL [Sc E 88-555]**

Inside apartheid . Levine, Janet, 1945- Chicago , c1988. xvi, 287 p., [16] p. of plates : ISBN 0-8092-4544-2 : DDC 968.06/3/0924 B 19
DT779.955.L48 A3 1989
NYPL [JLE 89-122]

Inside Black Australia : an anthology of aboriginal poetry / edited by Kevin Gilbert. Ringwood, Victoria : Penguin Books Australia, 1988. xxiv, 213 p. ; 21 cm. Includes indexes. ISBN 0-14-011126-3
1. Australian aboriginal poetry. I. Gilbert, Kevin.
NYPL [Sc D 89-547]

Inside black colleges and universities / the National Association for Equal Opportunity in Higher Education ; edited by Andrew Billingsley, Julia C. Elam. Chicago : Follett Press, c1986. 153 p. ; 22 cm. A selection of papers presented to the National Conference on Blacks in Higher Education, in Washington, D.C., in 1983. Includes bibliographical references. ISBN 0-695-60051-6
1. Afro-American universites and colleges - Congresses. I. Elam, Julia C. II. Billingsley, Andrew. III. National Association for Equal Opportunity in Higher Education (U. S.). IV. National Conference on Blacks in Higher Education (8th ; 1983 : Washington, DC).
NYPL [Sc D 88-951]

Insight guides.
Bahamas . Singapore , 1987. 305 p. : ISBN 0-13-056276-9 (pbk.) **NYPL [Sc D 88-477]**

INSPECTION OF SCHOOLS. see SCHOOL MANAGEMENT AND ORGANIZATION.

Inspiriting influences . Awkward, Michael. New York , 1989. x, 178 p. ; ISBN 0-231-06806-9

DDC 813/.5/099287 19
PS153.N5 A94 1989   NYPL [Sc E 89-188]

An instant in the wind /. Brink, André Philippus, 1935- New York, N.Y., U. S.A. , 1985, c1976. 250 p. ; ISBN 0-14-008014-7 (pbk.) : DDC 823 19
PR9369.3.B7 I5 1985   NYPL [Sc C 88-281]

Instituição . Edmundo, Lygia Pereira. São Paulo , 1987. 141 p. ;   *NYPL [Sc D 89-332]*

Institut Afriki (Akademiíã nauk SSSR) Potekhin, I. I. (Ivan Izosimovich), 1903-1964. African problems: analysis of eminent Soviet scientist. Moscow, 1968. 141 p. DDC 320.9/6
DT30 .P59   NYPL [Sc C 88-86]

Institut culturel africain. La Tradition orale, source de la littérature contemporaine en Afrique . Dakar , c1984. 201 p. : ISBN 2-7236-0899-9   *NYPL [Sc E 89-55]*

Études nigériennes. see Études nigériennes.

Institut für Afrika-Kunde (Hamburg, Germany). Bibliothek. Verzeichnis der Zeitschriftenbestände : Stand Oktober 1985 / Institut für Afrika-Kunde im Verbund der Stiftung Deutsches Übersee-Institut Biliothek. Hamburg : Die Bibliothek, 1986. 100 p. ; 30 cm.
1. Gazettes - Africa - Bibliography - Catalogs. 2. Africa - Periodicals - Bibliography - Catalogs. I. Deutsches Übersee-Institut. II. Title.
NYPL [Sc F 88-209]

Institut Mathildenhöhe (Stadtmuseum Darmstadt) That's jazz, der Sound des 20. Jahrhunderts . [Darmstadt , 1988] xv, 723 p. : DDC 781/.57/0740341 19
ML141.D3 I6 1988   NYPL [JMF 89-297]

Institut panafricain de géopolitique. Francophonie & géopolitique africaine . Paris , c1987. 156 p. ; ISBN 2-906861-01-4
NYPL [Sc D 88-1448]

Institut pédagogique national (Haiti). Comité de curriculum. La réforme éducative : éléments d'information / Comité de curriculum, Institut pédagogique national [et] Direction de la planification. [Port-au-Prince] : Département de l'éducation nationale, [1982] 65 p. : ill. ; 21 cm. Cover title. At head of title: Département de l'éducation nationale. DDC 375/.001/097294
1. Curriculum planning - Haiti. 2. Education - Haiti - Aims and objectives. I. Haiti. Département de l'éducation nationale. Direction de la planification. II. Title.
LB1564.H2 I57 1982   NYPL [Sc D 88-1401]

Institute for Advanced Study (Princeton, N.J.) Colonial identity in the Atlantic world, 1500-1800 /. Princeton, N.J. , c1987. xi, 290 p. ; ISBN 0-691-05372-3 (alk. paper) : DDC 909/.09812 19
E18.82 .C64 1987   NYPL [HAB 87-3215]

Institute for Independent Education. Start your own school! . Washington, D.C. , 1988. vi, 68 p. : ISBN 0-941001-08-3   *NYPL [Sc D 89-406]*

Institute for International Economics (U. S.) African debt and financing /. Washington, D.C. , 1986. 223 p. : ISBN 0-88132-044-7 : DDC 336.3/435/096 19
HJ8826 .A36 1986   NYPL [JLE 87-3261]

Institute nationale de la recherche agronomique (France) Enjeux fonciers dan la Caraibe, en Amérique centrale et à la Réunion. . Paris , c1987. 232 p. : ISBN 2-7380-0003-7
NYPL [Sc E 88-246]

Institute of African-American Relations. see African-American Institute.

INSTITUTE OF JAMAICA - MUSEUMS. Wheatle, Hiliary-Ann. Museums of the Institute of Jamaica /. Kingston , 1982. 16 p. :
NYPL [Sc D 88-1173]

Institute of Missiology (MISSIO) Hickey, Raymond. Christianity in Borno State and Northern Gongola /. [Nigeria , 1984?] (Ibadan : Claverianum Press) vi, 108 p. :
NYPL [Sc D 88-882]

Institute of Paper Conservation. Conservation of library and archive materials and the graphic arts /. London , Boston , 1985. 328 p. : ISBN 0-408-01466-0 : DDC 025.7 19
Z701 .C5863 1985   NYPL [MFW+ 88-574]

Institute of Texas Cultures at San Antonio. University of Texas. Adele, Lynne. Black history, black vision . [Austin] , 1989. 93 p. : ISBN 0-935213-15-5   *NYPL [Sc F 89-155]*

INSTITUTIONS, ASSOCIATIONS, ETC. see ASSOCIATIONS, INSTITUTIONS, ETC.

INSTITUTIONS, INTERNATIONAL. see INTERNATIONAL AGENCIES.

Institutions politiques et organisation administrative du Togo /. Agbodjan, Combévi. [S.l. , between 1980 and 1984] 134 leaves, [1] folded leaf of plates : DDC 320.966/81 19
JQ3532 .A37 1981   NYPL [Sc D 88-224]

INSTITUTO JOAQUIM NABUCO DE PESQUISAS SOCIAIS. 30 anos do Instituto Joaquim Nabuco de Pesquisas Sociais /. Recife , 1981. 343 p. : ISBN 85-7019-008-5 DDC 300.72081 19
H67.R44 A13 1981   NYPL [Sc D 88-871]

Instituto Lingüístico de Verano. see Summer Institute of Linguistics.

INSTRUCTION. see EDUCATION.

INSTRUMENTS, MUSICAL. see MUSICAL INSTRUMENTS.

INSURRECTIONS. see REVOLUTIONS.

Integración cultural de América Latina . Rasco y Bermudez, José Ignacio. Medellín, [Colombia , 1975] 188 p. ;
F1408.3 .R37   NYPL [HCB 78-2271]

Integrated rural development . Cohen, John M. Uppsala , 1987. 267 p. ; ISBN 91-7106-267-X
NYPL [Sc D 88-1100]

Integration efforts in Africa. Kersebaum, Andrea. Integrationsbestrebungen in Afrika . Hamburg , 1986-1987. 2 v. ; ISBN 3-922852-13-0
NYPL [Sc F 88-33]

INTEGRATION, RACIAL. see RACE RELATIONS.

Integrationsbestrebungen in Afrika . Kersebaum, Andrea. Hamburg , 1986-1987. 2 v. ; ISBN 3-922852-13-0   *NYPL [Sc F 88-33]*

INTELLECTUAL FREEDOM. see CENSORSHIP.

INTELLECTUALS - AFRICA. N'Da, Jean, 1945- Pouvoir, lutte de classes, idéologie et milieu intellectuel africain. /. Paris , c1987. 107 p. ; ISBN 2-7087-0485-0
NYPL [Sc D 88-918]

INTELLECTUALS - BURKINA FASO - BIOGRAPHY. Traore, Fathié. Mémoires d'autres temps /. Ouagadougou, Burkina Faso? , 1984- (Ouagadougou : Presses africaines) v. ; DDC 966/.25 19
CT2478.T73 A3 1984   NYPL [Sc D 88-386]

INTELLECTUALS - HAITI - ANECDOTES, FACETIAE, SATIRE, ETC. Victor, Gary, 1958- Albert Buron, ou, Profil d'une "élite" /. [Port-au-Prince , 1988] 230 p. ;
NYPL [Sc D 88-1005]

INTELLECTUALS - UNITED STATES - BIOGRAPHY. Huntley, Eric L. Marcus Garvey . Ealing, London , 1988. 41 p. : ISBN 0-904521-41-9
NYPL [Sc E 88-499]

INTELLECTUALS - UNITED STATES - BIOGRAPHY - JUVENILE LITERATURE. Lawler, Mary. Marcus Garvey /. New York , c1988. 110 p. : ISBN 1-555-46587-0 DDC 305.8/96073/024 B 92 19
E185.97.G3 L39 1988   NYPL [Sc E 88-156]

Intelligence and national achievement / editor, Raymond B. Cattell. Washington, D.C. : Institute for the Study of Man, c1983. 176 p. : ill. ; 24 cm. Includes bibliographies. ISBN 0-941694-14-3 DDC 153.9 19
1. Intelligence levels. 2. National characteristics. I. Cattell, Raymond B. (Raymond Bernard), 1905-.
BF433.S63 I57 1983   NYPL [Sc E 89-236]

INTELLIGENCE LEVELS. Intelligence and national achievement /. Washington, D.C. , c1983. 176 p. : ISBN 0-941694-14-3 DDC 153.9 19
BF433.S63 I57 1983   NYPL [Sc E 89-236]

INTELLIGENCE LEVELS - AFRO-AMERICANS. Sowell, Thomas, 1930- Patterns of black

excellence /. Washington , 1977. [26]-58 p. ; ISBN 0-89633-004-4   *NYPL [Sc D 89-588]*

INTELLIGENCE SERVICE - ZIMBABWE - HISTORY. Flower, Ken. Serving secretly . London , c1987. xxii, 330 p., [12] p. of plates : ISBN 0-7195-4438-6   *NYPL [JFE 88-5776]*

INTELLIGENTSIA. see INTELLECTUALS.

INTERCULTURAL EDUCATION - GREAT BRITAIN. Educational attainments . London , New York , 1988. vii, 180 p. : ISBN 1-85000-308-4 : DDC 370.19/34/0941 19
LC3736.G6 E336 1988   NYPL [Sc E 89-52]

INTERCULTURAL EDUCATION - UNITED STATES - CURRICULA. Dodson, Jualynne E. Training of personnel for services to Black families . [Atlanta] [1976] 1 v. (various foliations) ;   *NYPL [Sc F 88-130]*

INTERCULTURAL RELATIONS. see CULTURAL RELATIONS.

Interdisciplinary approaches to population studies . West African Seminar on Population Studies, University of Ghana, 1972. Legon , 1975. ix, 333 p. :
HB21 .W38 1972   NYPL [JLD 78-861]

Interesting narrative of the life of Olaudah Equiano. Equiano, Olaudah, b. 1745. I saw a slave ship /. Sacramento, Calif. , 1983. 42 p. :
NYPL [Sc Rare C 88-1]

Interesting people . Lee, George L. Jefferson, N.C. , London , c1989. xiii, 210 p. : ISBN 0-89950-403-5 : DDC 973/.0496073022 19
E185.96   NYPL [Sc E 89-240]

Interférences du fulfulde sur le français écrit par les élèves peuls du Nord-Cameroun [microform] /. Labatut, Roger. [Dakar] , 1974. iii, 35 p. ;   *NYPL [Sc Micro R-4137 no.11]*

Internal migration in Nigeria . Seminar on Internal Migration in Nigeria (1975 : University of Ife) [Ife] , 1976. iii, 300 p. :
NYPL [Sc E 88-489]

INTERNAL SECURITY - SOUTH AFRICA. Mathews, Anthony S., 1930- Freedom, state security and the rule of law . London , c1988. xxx, 312 p. ; ISBN 0-421-39640-7
NYPL [Sc F 89-102]

INTERNATIONAL ADMINISTRATION. see INTERNATIONAL AGENCIES.

International affairs series. Ogunsanwo, Alaba. Our friends, their friends . Yaba , 1986, c1985. 145 p. ; ISBN 978-301-700-4   *NYPL [Sc D 89-137]*

International affairs series (Yaba, Nigeria) Ogunsanwo, Alaba. Our friends, their friends . Yaba , 1986, c1985. 145 p. ; ISBN 978-301-700-4   *NYPL [Sc D 89-137]*

International African library. Spencer, Paul, 1932- The Maasai of Matapato . Bloomington , c1988. xii, 296 p. : ISBN 0-253-33625-2 DDC 306/.08996 19
DT433.545.M33 S64 1988
NYPL [JFE 88-7115]

INTERNATIONAL AGENCIES - DECISION MAKING - CASE STUDIES. Lister, Frederick K., 1921- Decision-making strategies for international organizations . Denver, Colo. , 1984. ix, 142 p. : ISBN 0-87940-075-7 : DDC 332.1/52 19
HG3881.5.I58 L57 1984
NYPL [Sc D 88-1218]

International Association Futuribles. Reclaiming the future . Oxford , Riverton, N.J. , c1986. xvi, 197 p. : ISBN 1-85148-010-2 (pbk.) : DDC 303.4/96 19
DT4 .R43 1986   NYPL [Sc D 88-584]

INTERNATIONAL ASSOCIATION OF THE CONGO. Roark, J. L. American expansionism vs. European colonialism [microform] . [Nairobi] , 1976. 16 leaves :
NYPL [Sc Micro R-4108 no. 34]

INTERNATIONAL ASSOCIATIONS. see INTERNATIONAL AGENCIES.

INTERNATIONAL BUSINESS ENTERPRISES - CASE STUDIES. Alschuler, Lawrence R., 1941- Multinationals

and maldevelopment . Basingstoke, Hampshire , c1988. xii, 218 p. : ISBN 0-333-41561-2
NYPL [Sc D 88-701]

International Centre for Comparative Criminology. see **Centre international de criminologie comparée.**

International Christian Union of Business Executives. L'Entreprise et ses dirigeants dans le développement économique de l'Afrique noire . Kinshasa [1969?] 89 p. :
NYPL [Sc F 88-100]

International Commission of Jurists (1952-) South Africa . London , New York , 1988. 159 p. : ISBN 0-86187-979-1 : DDC 323.4/0968 19
NYPL [JLE 88-4543]

International conceptual encyclopedia for the social sciences . (vol. 1) Ethnicity . Honolulu, Hawaii (2424 Maile Way, Honolulu 96822) , c1985. xxix, 205 p. ; DDC 305.8/0072 19
GN495.6 .E89 1985   *NYPL [Sc F 87-355]*

International Conference on Children, Repression and the Law in Apartheid South Africa (1987 : Harare, Zimbabwe) Children of resistance . London , 1988. vii, 146 p. ;
NYPL [Sc D 88-1286]

International Conference on the Central Bilad al-Sudan Tradition and Adaptation (3rd : 1977 : Khartum, Sudan) Third International Conference on the Central Bilad al-Sudan Tradition and Adaptation [microform] [Khartum] : Institute of African and Asian Studies, University of Khartoum, [1977] 25, 13 p. ; 22 cm. English, French and Arabi. Microfiche. New York: New York Public Library, 198 . 1 microfiche: negative; 11 x 15 cm. (FSN Sc 019,098)
1. Sudan (Region) - Congresses. I. Khartum. University. Institute of African and Asian Studies. II. Title.
NYPL [Sc Micro F-10980]

International Congress of Africanists, 3d, Addis Abeba, 1973. African studies. Berlin, 1973. xi, 400 p.   *NYPL [JLK 73-249 Bd. 15]*

International Congress of Anthropological and Ethnological Sciences (10th : 1978 : New Delhi, India) Social anthropology of peasantry /. Ikeja, Nigeria , 1983. xii, 351 p. ; DDC 305.5/63 19
HT407 .S53 1983   *NYPL [Sc E 87-179]*

INTERNATIONAL DEBTS. see DEBTS, EXTERNAL.

International Defence and Aid Fund. Fighting apartheid . London , 1988. 76 p. : ISBN 0-904759-84-9 (pbk) : DDC 323.1/68 19
DT763   *NYPL [Sc D 88-1092]*

Namibia . London , 1989. 112 p. : ISBN 0-904759-94-6 (pbk) : DDC 968.8/03 19
DT714   *NYPL [Sc F 89-123]*

Working under South African occupation . London , 1987. 56 p. ; ISBN 0-904759-73-3 (pbk.) : DDC 968 s 331.6/9/9688 19
DT746 .F3 no. 14 HD8808
NYPL [Sc D 89-525]

International Development Research Centre (Canada) Index to livestock literature microfiched in Zimbabwe /. Addis Ababa [1986?] viii, 235 p. ; ISBN 92-9053-064-2
NYPL [Sc E 89-204]

International Geographical Congress. Desertification in extremely arid environments /. [Stuttgart] , 1980. 203 p., [1] folded leaf of plates : ISBN 3-88028-095-9 (pbk.) DDC 551.4 19
GB611 .D44   *NYPL [JFL 74-410 Bd. 95]*

International Geographical Union. International Geographical Congress. see **International Geographical Congress.**

International Geographical Union. Working Group on Desertification In and Around Arid Lands. Subgroup Extremely Arid Environments. Desertification in extremely arid environments /. [Stuttgart] , 1980. 203 p., [1] folded leaf of plates : ISBN 3-88028-095-9 (pbk.) DDC 551.4 19
GB611 .D44   *NYPL [JFL 74-410 Bd. 95]*

INTERNATIONAL GRANTS-IN-AID. see ECONOMIC ASSISTANCE.

International guide to African studies research =. Baker, Philip. London , New York , 1987.

264 p. ; ISBN 0-905450-25-6
NYPL [Sc E 88-218]

International handbook on race and race relations / edited by Jay A. Sigler. New York : Greenwood Press, 1987. xviii, 483 p. ; 24 cm. Includes index. Bibliography: p. [449]-454. ISBN 0-313-24770-6 (lib. bdg. : alk. paper) DDC 305.8 19
1. Race - Handbooks, manuals, etc. 2. Race relations - Handbooks, manuals, etc. I. Sigler, Jay A.
HT1521 .I485 1987   *NYPL [Sc E 88-75]*

INTERNATIONAL INSTITUTIONS. see INTERNATIONAL AGENCIES.

International Labor Office. Improved village technology for women's activities . Geneva , 1984. vi, 292 p. : ISBN 92-2-103818-1
NYPL [JLF 85-625]

International Labor Organization. International Labor Office. see **International Labor Office.**

International Labor Organization. Secretariat. see **International Labor Office.**

International Labor Organization. World Employment Programme. Improved village technology for women's activities . Geneva , 1984. vi, 292 p. : ISBN 92-2-103818-1
NYPL [JLF 85-625]

International Labour Conference (72nd : 1986 : Geneva, Switzerland) Special report of the Director-General on the application of the declaration concerning the policy of apartheid in South Africa. Geneva , 1986. 186 p. : ISBN 92-2-105167-6 (pbk.) : *NYPL [Sc E 88-179]*

International Labour Office. Hoeven, Rolph van der. Planning for basic needs . Aldershot , c1988. xvii, 380 p. : ISBN 0-566-05680-1 : DDC 330.9172/4 19
HC59.7   *NYPL [Sc D 89-37]*

Oppong, Christine. Seven roles of women . Geneva , 1987. xi, 127 p. :
NYPL [Sc E 89-143]

Special report of the Director-General on the application of the declaration concerning the policy of apartheid in South Africa. Geneva , 1986. 186 p. : ISBN 92-2-105167-6 (pbk.) :
NYPL [Sc E 88-179]

International Livestock Centre for Africa. Documentation Services. Index to livestock literature microfiched in Zimbabwe /. Addis Ababa [1986?] viii, 235 p. ; ISBN 92-9053-064-2
NYPL [Sc E 89-204]

INTERNATIONAL LIVESTOCK CENTRE FOR AFRICA - MICROFORM CATALOGS. Index to livestock literature microfiched in Zimbabwe /. Addis Ababa [1986?] viii, 235 p. ; ISBN 92-9053-064-2   *NYPL [Sc E 89-204]*

INTERNATIONAL LOANS. see LOANS, FOREIGN.

INTERNATIONAL MONETARY FUND. Lister, Frederick K., 1921- Decision-making strategies for international organizations . Denver, Colo. , 1984. ix, 142 p. : ISBN 0-87940-075-7 : DDC 332.1/52 19
HG3881.5.I58 L57 1984
NYPL [Sc D 88-1218]

INTERNATIONAL ORGANIZATIONS. see INTERNATIONAL AGENCIES.

International Seminar on Internal Conflict (1987 : Makerere, Uganda) Seminar papers on internal conflicts in Uganda : September 20-25, 1987 / sponsored by Makerere Institute of Social Research ... [et al.] [Makerere, Uganda : The Seminar, 1987]. 1 v. ; 29 cm. Includes bibliographies.
1. Social conflict - Uganda - Congresses. 2. Uganda - Politics and government - Congresses. I. Title.
NYPL [Sc F 89-86]

International Seminar on Inter-university Co-operation in West Africa, Freetown, Sierra Leone, 1961. Harris, John, librarian. Rapport sur la coopération inter-universitaire dans le domaine de l'impression et l'édition [microform] /. 1961. 12 p. ;   *NYPL [Sc Micro R-4137 no. 44]*

Lévy, Denis. Problems of co-operation between the English- and French-speaking universities of West Africa [microform] . Freetown [Sierra

Leone] [1961] 7 p. ;
NYPL [Sc Micro R-4094 no. 23]

International Seminar on Marcus Garvey (1973 : Mona, Jamaica) Garvey--Africa, Europe, the Americas /. Kingston, Jamaica , 1986. xi, 208 p., [4] p. of plates : *NYPL [Sc D 88-1131]*

International standard book numbering in Tanzania : a manual. Dar es Salaam : Tanzania Library Services Board, 1982. 17 leaves ; 30 cm. ISBN 997-665-006-X (pbk.) DDC 025.4/2 19
1. International Standard Book Numbers - Tanzania - Handbooks, manuals, etc. I. Tanzania Library Services Board.
Z467.T36 I57 1982   *NYPL [Sc F 88-76]*

INTERNATIONAL STANDARD BOOK NUMBERS - TANZANIA - HANDBOOKS, MANUALS, ETC. International standard book numbering in Tanzania . Dar es Salaam , 1982. 17 leaves ; ISBN 997-665-006-X (pbk.) DDC 025.4/2 19
Z467.T36 I57 1982   *NYPL [Sc F 88-76]*

International Union of Catholic Employers' Associations. see **International Christian Union of Business Executives.**

International Union of Christian Associations of Employers and Managers. see **International Christian Union of Business Executives.**

INTERNATIONAL UNION, UNITED AUTOMOBILE, AEROSPACE AND AGRICULTURAL IMPLEMENT WORKERS OF AMERICA - HISTORY. Denby, Charles. Indignant heart . Boston , c1978. 295 p. : ISBN 0-89608-092-7 DDC 331.6/3/960730774340924 B 19
HD8039.A82 U633 1978
NYPL [Sc D 88-853]

Denby, Charles. Indignant heart . Detroit , 1989, c1978. xvi, 303 p : ISBN 0-8143-2219-0 (alk. paper) DDC 331.6/396073 B 19
HD8039.A82 U633 1989
NYPL [Sc D 89-563]

INTERNATIONAL UNIONS. see INTERNATIONAL AGENCIES.

INTERNATIONAL WOMEN'S YEAR, 1975 - CONGRESSES. Regional Seminar for Africa (Mogadishu : 1975) On African women's equality, role in national liberation, development and peace . [Mogadishu] , 1975. 123 p. :
NYPL [Sc E 88-138]

Internationale Geographische Union. see **International Geographical Union.**

Internationale Gesellschaft für Menschenrechte. Menschenrechte im Konflikt um Südwestafrika/Namibia . Frankfurt a.M. , 1985. 56 p. :   *NYPL [Sc F 88-162]*

Internationale Solidarität und Kommunikation. Amakuru ki? . Frankfurt [1987] 447 p., 1 folded leaf. [8] p. of plates :
NYPL [Sc D 88-898]

Internationaler Geographen-Kongress. see **International Geographical Congress.**

Internationales Musikinstitut Darmstadt. That's jazz, der Sound des 20. Jahrhunderts . [Darmstadt , 1988] xv, 723 p. : DDC 781/.57/0740341 19
ML141.D3 I6 1988   *NYPL [JMF 89-297]*

Interracial books for children bulletin. Racism and sexism in children's books. New York , c1978. 72 p. : ISBN 0-930040-29-5
NYPL [Sc D 89-259]

Interracial digest . (no. 2) Racism and sexism in children's books. New York , c1978. 72 p. : ISBN 0-930040-29-5
NYPL [Sc D 89-259]

Interracial justice . La Farge, John, 1880-1963. New York , 1937. xii, 226 p. ; DDC 325.260973
E185.61 .L25   *NYPL [Sc C 88-146]*

INTERRACIAL MARRIAGE - FICTION. Okpalaeze, Inno-Pat Chuba. Oriental passion /. Onitsha, Nigeria , 1987. 89 p. ;
NYPL [Sc C 89-72]

INTERRACIAL MARRIAGE - JUVENILE FICTION. Bradman, Tony. Wait and see /. New York, NY , 1988. [28] p. : ISBN 0-19-520644-4 DDC [E] 19
PZ7.B7275 Wai 1988   *NYPL [Sc D 89-255]*

INTERTEXTUALITY.
Awkward, Michael. Inspiriting influences . New York , 1989. x, 178 p. ; ISBN 0-231-06806-9 DDC 813/.5/099287 19
PS153.N5 A94 1989 *NYPL [Sc E 89-188]*

Interviews avec des écrivains africains francophones / [guest editor for this issue, Günter Bielemeier. Bayreuth, W. Germany : Bayreuth University, c1986. 95 p. ; 21 cm. (Bayreuth African studies series, 0178-0034 . 8) Contains interviews with René Philombe, Dono Ly Sangaré, Jean-Marie Adiaffi, Amadou Koné, and Bernard Zadi Zourou. Includes bibliographies.
1. African literature (French) - 20th century - History and criticism. 2. Authors, African - Interviews. I. Bielemeier, Günter. II. Series.
NYPL [Sc D 88-906]

Intimate matters . D'Emilio, John. New York , c1988. xx, 428 p., [16] leaves of plates : ISBN 0-06-015855-7 : DDC 306.7/0973 19
HQ18.U5 D45 1988 *NYPL [Sc E 88-436]*

Into the heart of Biafra /. Acholonu, Catherine Obianuju. Owerri, Nigeria , c1985. 86 p. ; ISBN 978-244-914-8 *NYPL [Sc C 88-337]*

L'Intrigue raciale . Salazar, Philippe Joseph. Paris , 1989. 230 p. : ISBN 2-86563-211-3
NYPL [Sc D 89-504]

Introdução à literatura negra /. Bernd, Zilá, 1944- Sao Paulo , 1988. 101 p. :
NYPL [Sc D 89-188]

Introducción a la cultura africana . Introduction à la culture africaine. Spanish. Barcelona , Paris , 1982. 176 p. ; ISBN 92-3-301478-9 (Unesco)
NYPL [Sc D 88-600]

Introducing commodities (market) exchange in Nigeria /. Osammor, Vincent Osoloka. Surulere, Lagos, Nigeria , 1986. x, 39 p. ;
NYPL [Sc D 88-1293]

Introducing the Colonies. Great Britain. Colonial Office. London, 1949. 87 p.
JV1027 .A473 1949a *NYPL [Sc C 88-231]*

Introduction à la culture africaine. Spanish. Introducción a la cultura africana : aspectos generales / Alpha I. Sow ... [et al.] Barcelona : Serbal ; Paris : Unesco, 1982. 176 p. ; 21 cm. (Colección de temas africanos . 2) Essays commissioned by Unesco. Translation of: Introduction à la culture africaine: aspects généraus. Includes bibliographies. ISBN 92-3-301478-9 (Unesco)
1. Africa - Civilization. I. Sow, Alfâ Ibrâhîm. II. Unesco. III. Title. IV. Series.
NYPL [Sc D 88-600]

Introduction aux problèmes de santé des peuples d'Afrique tropicale . Monekosso, G L. Yaoundé , 1978. 241 p. :
NYPL [Sc E 86-437]

Introduction to population analysis /. Orubuloye, I. O. (Israel Olatunji), 1947- Ibadan , 1986. 106 p. : ISBN 978-224-111-3
NYPL [Sc D 88-1417]

An introduction to the administration of schools in Nigeria /. Aderounmu, Olusola W. Ibadan, Nigeria , 1985. xiii, 271 p. : ISBN 978-16-7241-2
NYPL [Sc D 88-730]

An introduction to the French Caribbean novel /. Ormerod, Beverley, 1937- London , Portsmouth, N.H., USA , 1985. 152 p. ; ISBN 0-435-91839-7 (pbk.) DDC 843 19
PQ3944 .O76 1985 *NYPL [Sc D 88-1267]*

Introduction to the health problems of tropical African peoples. Monekosso, G L. Introduction aux problèmes de santé des peuples d'Afrique tropicale . Yaoundé , 1978. 241 p. :
NYPL [Sc E 86-437]

An introduction to the history of central Africa . Wills, A. J. (Alfred John) Oxford [Oxfordshire] , New York , 1985. xiii, 556 p. : ISBN 0-19-873075-6 : DDC 968.9 19
DT963.5 .W54 1985 *NYPL [Sc D 88-656]*

Inventaire des particularités lexicales du français en Afrique noire / Equipe IFA ; [collaborateurs] J. Blondé ... [et al.]. Montréal : AUPELF ; Paris : Agence de coopération culturelle et technique, [1983] lxi, 550 p. : ill. ; 24 cm. Bibliography: p. 510-550. ISBN 2-920021-15-X
1. French language - Africa. 2. French language - Glossaries, vocabularies, etc. I. Blondé, Jacques. II. Equipe du projet IFA. *NYPL [Sc E 88-235]*

L'invention du théâtre . Ricard, Alain. Lausanne , c1986. 134 p. : *NYPL [Sc D 88-707]*

The Invention of ethnicity / edited by Werner Sollors. New York : Oxford University Press, 1989. xx, 294 p. ; 22 cm. Includes index. Bibliography: p. 237-286. ISBN 0-19-504589-0 DDC 810/.9/920692 19
1. American literature - Minority authors - History and criticism. 2. Ethnicity in literature. 3. Ethnic groups in literature. 4. Minorities in literature. I. Sollors, Werner.
PS153.M56 I58 1988 *NYPL [Sc D 89-374]*

INVENTORS - UNITED STATES - BIOGRAPHY - JUVENILE LITERATURE.
Sweet, Dovie Davis. Red light, green light . Smithtown, N.Y. , 1978 (1980 printing) 39 p. : ISBN 0-682-49088-1 *NYPL [Sc D 89-70]*

INVESTMENT AND SAVING. see **SAVING AND INVESTMENT.**

Investment demand in a developing country . Osuagwu, Harold G. O. Washington, D.C. , c1982. xvii, 411 p. : ISBN 0-8191-2048-0 : DDC 332.6/72/09669 19
HG5881.A3 O84 1982 *NYPL [Sc D 88-478]*

INVESTMENTS, AMERICAN - SOUTH AFRICA.
United States. Congress. House. Committee on International Relations. Subcommittee on Africa. United States private investment in South Africa . Washington , 1978. iv, 641 p. ; DDC 332.6/7373/068
KF27 .I54914 1978d *NYPL [Sc E 88-92]*

INVESTMENTS, BRITISH - GHANA.
Tropical Africa Advisory Group trade mission to the Republic of Ghana, 16-22 March 1985. [London] ([1 Victoria Street, SW1H OET]) [1985] iii, 64 p. : DDC 330.9667/05 19
HC1060 *NYPL [Sc F 88-88]*

INVESTMENTS, FOREIGN - NAMIBIA.
Khalifa, Ahmad M. Adverse consequences for the enjoyment of human rights of political, military, economic, and other forms of assistance given to the racist and colonialist régime of South Africa /. New York , 1985. ii, 164, [30] p. ; ISBN 92-1-154046-1 (pbk.) DDC 332.6/73/0968 19
HG5851.A3 K45 1985 *NYPL [Sc F 88-273]*

INVESTMENTS, FOREIGN - SOUTH AFRICA.
Khalifa, Ahmad M. Adverse consequences for the enjoyment of human rights of political, military, economic, and other forms of assistance given to the racist and colonialist régime of South Africa /. New York , 1985. ii, 164, [30] p. ; ISBN 92-1-154046-1 (pbk.) DDC 332.6/73/0968 19
HG5851.A3 K45 1985 *NYPL [Sc F 88-273]*

INVESTMENTS - NIGERIA.
Osuagwu, Harold G. O. Investment demand in a developing country . Washington, D.C. , c1982. xvii, 411 p. : ISBN 0-8191-2048-0 : DDC 332.6/72/09669 19
HG5881.A3 O84 1982 *NYPL [Sc D 88-478]*

INVESTMENTS - TRINIDAD AND TOBAGO.
Trinidad & Tobago investment opportunities in industry. Port-of-Spain, Trinidad , 1985. 40 p. :
NYPL [Sc F 88-94]

Invisible criticism . Nadel, Alan, 1947- Iowa City , 1988. xiii, 181 p. ; ISBN 0-87745-190-7 : DDC 813/.54 19
PS3555.L625 I5358 1988 *NYPL [Sc E 88-281]*

The invisible government and the viable community . Cocoltchos, Christopher Nickolas, 1949- 1979. 2 v. (xv, 774 leaves) :
NYPL [Sc F 88-285]

The invisible hunters . Rohmer, Harriet. San Francisco , c1987. 32 p. : ISBN 0-89239-031-X : DDC 398.2/08998 19
F1529.M9 R64 1987 *NYPL [Sc E 88-241]*

Invisible poets . Sherman, Joan R. Urbana , c1989. xxxii, 288 p. : ISBN 0-252-01620-3 (alk. paper) DDC 811/.009/896073 19
PS153.N5 S48 1989 *NYPL [Sc E 89-216]*

Inzondo engela mkhawulo /. Mabuza, Vivian R. N. Gweru , 1988. 120 p. ; ISBN 0-86922-430-1
NYPL [Sc C 89-7]

Iola Leroy, or, Shadows uplifted /. Harper, Frances Ellen Watkins, 1825-1911. New York , 1988. xxxix, 281 p. : ISBN 0-19-505240-4 (alk.

paper) DDC 813/.3 19
PS1799.H7 I6 1988 *NYPL [JFC 88-2190]*

IOWA - FICTION.
Wise, Leonard. Doc's legacy /. New York , c1986. 410 p. ; ISBN 0-931933-16-1
NYPL [JFE 86-5265]

IRAN - MANUFACTURES.
Jazayeri, Ahmad, 1957- Economic adjustment in oil-based economies /. Aldershot, Hants, England , Brookfield, Vt., USA , c1988. xvi, 260 p. : ISBN 0-566-05682-8 : DDC 330.955/054 19
HD9576.I62 J39 1988 *NYPL [JLD 89-202]*

Iray, Olana. Ranomasina Indiana / Olana Iray ; fomba fijery samy hafa. Antananarivo : Agence de presse Novosti, [1983] 98 p. ; 19 cm.
1. Malagasy language - Texts. I. Title.
NYPL [Sc C 88-239]

Irby, Charles Leonard, 1789-1845. Travels in Egypt and Nubia, Syria and Asia Minor : during the years 1817 & 1818 / by Charles Leonard Irby and James Mangles. London : Darf, 1985. xxxiii, 560 p., [6] leaves of plates (3 folded) : ill., maps, 1 plan ; 22 cm. Includes index. Reprint. Originally published: London : T. White, 1823. ISBN 1-85077-082-4 : DDC 915.6/041 916.2/043 19
1. Near East - Description and travel. 2. Egypt - Description and travel. I. Mangles, James, 1786-1867. II. Title.
DS48 DT53 *NYPL [JFD 88-9340]*

IRELAND - CIVILIZATION - CONGRESSES.
Colonial identity in the Atlantic world, 1500-1800 /. Princeton, N.J. , c1987. xi, 290 p. ; ISBN 0-691-05372-3 (alk. paper) : DDC 909/.09812 19
E18.82 .C64 1987 *NYPL [HAB 87-3215]*

Irele, Modupe. Nigeria and Cameroun : an annotated bibliography / by Modupe Irele. Lagos, Nigeria : Libriservice, c1984. viii, 67 p. : ill. ; 23 cm. Includes index. ISBN 978-237-205-6 (pbk.) DDC 016.327669067/11 19
1. Nigeria - Relations - Cameroon - Bibliography. 2. Cameroon - Relations - Nigeria - Bibliography. 3. Nigeria - Bibliography. 4. Cameroon - Bibliography. I. Title.
Z3597 .I73 1984 DT515.63.C17
NYPL [Sc E 87-30]

Iremonger, Lucille. West Indian folk-tales; Anansi stories, tales from West Indian folk-lore retold for English children. London, G. G. Harrap [1956] 64 p. illus. 19 cm. SCHOMBURG CHILDREN'S COLLECTION.
1. Tales, West Indian. 2. Anansi (Legendary character). I. Schomburg Children's Collection. II. Title.
GR120 .I7 *NYPL [Sc C 89-157]*

IRENICS. see CHRISTIAN UNION.

Ireny lovantsofina ireny [microform] / Rakoto Andrianasolo ... [et al.] ; Karakarain'ny Foibe Filan-Kevitry ny Mpampianatra. Tananarive : Foibe Ara-Tsaina Malagasy, [1978] iv, 48 p. ; 27 cm. (Boky lovanjanahary . 1) In Malagasy. Microfiche. New York: New York Public Library, 198 . 1 microfiche: negative; 11 x 15 cm. (FSN Sc 019,088)
1. Folk-lore - Madagascar. 2. Malagasy language - Texts. I. Rakoto, Andrianasolo.
NYPL [Sc Micro F-10987]

Iroaganachi, John. A fight for honey / John Iroaganachi ; illustrated by I. Onwukwe. Lagos, Nigeria : African Universities Press, 1977. 30 p. : ill. ; 19 cm. (African junior library . 14) SCHOMBURG CHILDREN'S COLLECTION. ISBN 0-410-80181-X
1. Honey - Juvenile fiction. I. Onwukwe, I. II. Schomburg Children's Collection. III. Title. IV. Series.
NYPL [Sc C 88-77]

IRON INDUSTRY AND TRADE - ANGOLA.
Lopes, Francisco Antonio, 1882- Alvares Maciel no degrêdo de Angola. [Rio de Janeiro] , 1958. 104 p. :
HD9527.A22 L6 *NYPL [Sc D 88-419]*

IRON - TRADE AND STATISTICS. see IRON INDUSTRY AND TRADE.

Irvin, Fred M. (illus) Neigoff, Mike. Free throw. Chicago [1968] 128 p. DDC [Fic]
PZ7.N427 Fr *NYPL [Sc D 88-1427]*

Irvine, A. K. Letters from Ethiopian rulers (early and mid-nineteenth century) . Oxford , New York , c1985. xvii, 197 p. : ISBN 0-19-726046-2
NYPL [Sc E 88-262]

Is this justice? . Monama, Ramarumo.
Johannesburg [1983] xii, 65 p. :
NYPL [Sc D 88-1240]

'Isá 'Abd Allāh Muḥammad al-Mahdī, 1945-
Arabic made easy [microform] / [Al Hajj Imam
Isa Abdullah Muhammad al Mahdi] [Brooklyn,
N.Y. : Ansar Publications, 197-?] 2 v. : ill. ; 21
cm. (Edition / Ansaru Allah Community . 48) Cover
title. Title also in Arabic. Paging in reverse. Microfilm.
New York: New York Public Library, 1982. 1
microfilm reel; 35 mm. (MN *ZZ-23673)
*1. Arabic language - Text-books for foreigners - English.
I. Series: Ansaru Allah Community. Edition, 48. II.
Title.*   *NYPL [Sc Micro R-4114 no.2]*

Eternal life after death [microform] / [Al Hajj
Imam Isa Abdullah Muhammad al Mahdi]
Brooklyn, N.Y. : Ansaru Allah Community,
[197-?] 36 p. ; ill. ; 22 cm. (Edition / Ansaru Allah
Community . 30) Cover title. Title also in Arabic;
portions of text in Arabic. Paging in reverse. Microfilm.
New York: New York Public Library, 1982. 1
microfilm reel; 35 mm. (MN *ZZ-23673)
*1. Future life (Islam). I. Series: Ansaru Allah
Community. Edition, no. 30. II. Title.*
NYPL [Sc Micro R-4114 no.3]

Holy war [microform] / Al Hajj Al Imam Isa
Abd'Allah Muhammad Al Mahdi. Brooklyn,
N.Y. : Ansaru Allah Community, c1979. 68 p. :
ill. ; 27 cm. (Edition / Ansaru Allah Community .
no. 92) Title also in Arabic; portions of text in Arabic.
Paging in reverse. Microfilm. New York: New York
Public Library, 1982. 1 microfilm reel; 35 mm. (MN
*ZZ-23673)
*1. Jihad. I. Series: Ansaru Allah Community. Edition,
no. 92. II. Title.*
NYPL [Sc Micro R-4114 no. 8]

Islamic cookery [microform] / [Al Hajj Imam
Isa Abd'Allah Muhammad Al Mahdi]
Brooklyn : Ansaru Allah Community, c1976. 31
p. : ill. ; 27 cm. (Edition / Ansaru Allah
Community . 52) Cover title. Title also in Arabic.
Paging in reverse. Microfilm. New York: New York
Public Library, 1982. 1 microfilm reel; 35 mm. (MN
*ZZ-23673)
*1. Series: Ansaru Allah Community. Edition, 52. II.
Title.*   *NYPL [Sc Micro R-4114 no. 14]*

Islamic marriage ceremony and polygamy
[microform] / [Al Hajj Al Imam Isa Abd 'Allah
Muhammad Al Mahdi] Brooklyn : Ansaru
Allah Community, c1977. 30 p. : ill, port ; 20
cm. (Edition / Ansaru Allah Community . 49) Cover
title. Title also in Arabic; portions of text in Arabic.
Paging in reverse. Microfilm. New York: New York
Public Library, 1982. 1 microfilm reel; 35 mm. (MN
*ZZ-23673)
*1. Polygamy. 2. Marriage - Islam. I. Series: Ansaru
Allah Community. Edition, 49. II. Title.*
NYPL [Sc Micro R-4114 no.1]

Khutbat's of Al Hajj Al Imam Isa Abd'Allah
Muhammad Al Mahdi [microform]. Brooklyn :
Ansaru Allah Community, [1978?] 2 v. : ill. ;
27 cm. (Edition / Ansaru Allah Community . 77)
Cover title. Paging in reverse. Microfilm. New York:
New York Public library, 1982. 1 microfilm reel;35
mm. (MM *ZZ-23673)
*1. Islamic sermons. I. Series: Ansaru Allah Community.
Edition, 77. II. Title.*
NYPL [Sc Micro R-4114 no. 17]

The tribe Israel is no more [microform] / [Al
Hajj Al Imam Isa Abd'Allah Muhammad Al
Mahdi] Brooklyn : Ansaru Allah Community,
[197-?] 62 p. : ill. ; 27 cm. (Edition / Ansaru Allah
Community . 18) Cover title. Title also in Arabic;
portions of text in Arabic. Paging in reverse. Microfilm.
New York: New York Public Library, 1984. 1
microfilm reel; 35 mm. (MN *ZZ-23673) Schomburg's
copy imperfect: p. 47-58 lacking.
*1. Lost tribes of Israel - Miscellanea. I. Series: Ansaru
Allah Community. Edition, 18. II. Title.*
NYPL [Sc Micro R-4114 no. 13]

The true story of Noah (Pbuh) [microform] /
Al Hajj al Imam Isa Abd'Allah Muhammad al
Mahdi. Brooklyn, N.Y. : Ansaru Allah
Community, [1978] 62 p. : ill. ; 28 cm. (Edition
/ Ansaru Allah Community . no. 83) Cover title. Title
also in Arabic; portions of text in Arabic. Paging in
reverse. Microfilm. New York: New York Public
Library, 1982. 1 microfilm reel; 35 mm. (MN
*ZZ-23673)
*1. Series: Ansaru Allah Community. Edition, 83. II.
Title.*   *NYPL [Sc Micro R-4114 no. 9]*

The true story of the Prophet Abraham (Pbuh)

[microform] / [Al Hajj al Imam Isa Abd'Allah
Muhammad al Mahdi]. Brooklyn, N.Y. :
Ansaru Allah Community, [1980?] 96 p. : ill. ;
28 cm. (Edition / Ansaru Allah Community . no. 91)
Cover title. Title also in Arabic; portions of text in
Arabic. Paging in reverse. Microfilm. New York: New
York Public Library, 1982. 1 microfilm reel; 35 mm.
(MN *ZZ-23673)
*1. Abraham, the patriarch - Islamic interpretations. I.
Series: Ansaru Allah Community. Edition, no. 91. II.
Title.*   *NYPL [Sc Micro R-4114 no. 7]*

?Vino el puerco para la humanidad?
[microform] : (clase de hombre) / [Al Hajj Al
Imam Isa Abd'Allah Muhammad Al Mahdi]
[Brooklyn : Comunidad Ansaru Alá, 197-?] 40
p. : ill. ; 27 cm. (Edicíon / Ansaru Allah
Community. 16) Cover title. Title also in Arabic;
portions of text in Arabic. Paging in reverse.
Translation of: Did the hog come for mankind?
Microfilm. New York: New York Public Library, 1982.
1 microfilm reel; 35 mm. (MN *ZZ-23673)
*1. Swine (in religion, folk-lore, etc.). I. Series: Ansaru
Allah Community. Edition, 16. II. Title.*
NYPL [Sc Micro R-4114 no. 12]

Was Christ really crucified? [microform] / Al
Hajj al Imam Isa Abd'Allah Muhammad al
Mahdi. Rev. ed. Brooklyn, N.Y. : Ansaru Allah
Community, [1980] 72 p. : ill. ; 28 cm. (Edition
/ Ansaru Allah Community . no. 3) Cover title. Title
also in Arabic; portions of text in Arabic. Paging in
reverse. Microfilm. New York: New York Public
Library, 1982. 1 microfilm reel; 35 mm. (MN
*ZZ-23673)
*1. Jesus Christ - Islamic interpretations. I. Series:
Ansaru Allah Community. Edition, no. 3. II. Title.*
NYPL [Sc Micro R-4114 no. 6]

Who was Marcus Garvey? : 1887 A.D.-1940
A.D. / by the pen of As Sayyid Al Imaam Isa
Al Haadi Al Mahdi. [Brooklyn, N.Y. : Original
Tents of Kedar], c1988. 101 p. : ill., ports. ; 22
cm. (Edition / Ansaru Allah Community . no. 177)
Portions of text in Arabic.
*1. Garvey, Marcus, 1887-1940. 2. Muslims, Black. I.
Series: Ansaru Allah Community. Edition, no. 177. II.
Title.*   *NYPL [Sc D 89-139]*

Who was Noble Drew Ali? [microform] / [Al
Hajj al Imam Isa Abd'Allah Muhammad al
Mahdi] Brooklyn, N.Y. : Ansaru Allah
Community, [1980] 56 p. : ill. ; 27 cm. (Edition
/ Ansaru Allah Community . no. 109) Cover title. Title
also in Arabic; portions of text in Arabic. Paging in
reverse. Microfilm. New York: New York Public
Library, 1982. 1 microfilm reel; 35 mm. (MN
*ZZ-23673)
*1. Ali, Noble Drew, 1886-. 2. Muslims, Black. I.
Moorish Science Temple of America. II. Series: Ansaru
Allah Community. Edition, no. 109. III. Title.*
NYPL [Sc Micro R-4114 no. 10]

Who was the prophet Muhammad? [microform]
/ [Al Hajj al Imam Isa Abd'Allah Muhammad
al Mahdi] Rev. ed. Brooklyn, N.Y. : Ansaru
Allah Community, [1980] 96 p. : 28 cm. (Edition
/ Ansaru Allah Community . no. 11) Cover title. Title
also in Arabic; portions of text in Arabic. Paging in
reverse. Microfilm. New York: New York Public
Library, 1982. 1 microfilm reel; 35 mm. (MN
*ZZ-23673)
*1. Muḥammad, the prophet. I. Series: Ansaru Allah
Community. Edition, no. 11. II. Title.*
NYPL [Sc Micro R-4114 no. 11]

**Isa Muhammad. see 'Isá 'Abd Allāh Muḥammad
al-Mahdī, 1945-**

Isaac and Snow. Edwards, Sally. New York
[1973] 123 p. ISBN 0-698-20244-9 DDC [Fic]
PZ7.E265 Is3   *NYPL [Sc D 88-1419]*

Isaacman, Allen F. Honwana, Raúl Bernardo
Manuel, 1905- [Histórias ouvidas e vividas dos
homens e da terra. English.] The life history of
Raúl Honwana . Boulder , 1988. ix, 181 p. :
ISBN 1-555-87114-3 (lib. bdg.) : DDC
967/.903/0924 B 19
DT463 .H6613 1988   *NYPL [Sc E 88-367]*

Isadora, Rachel. Willaby / by Rachel Isadora.
New York : Macmillan, c1977. [32] p. : ill.
(some col.) ; 21 x 26 cm. A first grader gets into
trouble when her love of drawing keeps her from doing
something important. SCHOMBURG CHILDREN'S
COLLECTION. ISBN 0-02-747746-0 DDC [E]
*1. Afro-American children - Juvenile fiction. I.
Schomburg Children's Collection. II. Title.*
PZ7.I763 Wi   *NYPL [Sc F 88-374]*

Isak Dinesen's Africa . Dinesen, Isak, 1885-1962.

London , 1986, c1985. xvii, 142 p. : ISBN
0-593-01049-3   *NYPL [Sc G 88-26]*

I.S.A.M. monographs .
(no. 24) Berlin, Edward A. Reflections and
research on ragtime /. Brooklyn, N.Y. , c1987.
xii, 99 p. : ISBN 0-914678-27-2 (pbk.) DDC
781/.572 19
ML3530 .B5 1987   *NYPL [Sc D 88-410]*

I.S.E.R. (Series) .
(no. 13) Oosthuizen, G. C. (Gerhardus
Cornelis) Succession conflict within the Church
of the Nazarites, iBandla zamaNazaretha /.
Durban [South Africa] [1981] 71 p. ; ISBN
0-949947-43-1 (pbk.) DDC 289.9 19
BX7068.7.Z5 O56 1981
NYPL [Sc F 87-351]

Islam. Williams, John Alden. (ed) New York,
1961. 256 p. DDC 297.082
BP161.2 .W5   *NYPL [Sc D 88-1044]*

ISLAM - ALGERIA.
Sanson, Henri. Christianisme au miroir de
l'Islam . Paris , 1984. 195 p. ; ISBN
2-204-02278-0 :   *NYPL [*OGC 85-2762]*

**ISLAM AND POLITICS - AFRICA, FRENCH-
SPEAKING WEST.**
Harrison, Christopher, 1958- France and Islam
in West Africa, 1860-1960 /. Cambridge
[Cambridgeshire] , New York , 1988. xi, 242
p. : ISBN 0-521-35230-4 DDC 966/.0097451 19
DT530.5.M88 H37 1988
NYPL [Sc E 88-484]

ISLAM - EDUCATION - NIGERIA.
Noibi, D. O. S. Yoruba Muslim youth and
Christian-sponsored education /. Ijebu-Ode,
Nigeria , 1987. 44 p. ; ISBN 978-253-020-4
NYPL [Sc D 89-537]

ISLAM - MALI EMPIRE.
Hājj 'Umar ibn Sa'īd al-Fūtī, 1794?-1864.
[Bayān mā waqa'a. French & Arabic.] Voilà ce
qui est arrivé . Paris , 1983. 261 p., [57] p. of
plates : ISBN 2-222-03216-4
NYPL [Sc F 88-211]

**ISLAM - NIGERIA - RELATIONS -
CHRISTIANITY.**
Noibi, D. O. S. Yoruba Muslim youth and
Christian-sponsored education /. Ijebu-Ode,
Nigeria , 1987. 44 p. ; ISBN 978-253-020-4
NYPL [Sc D 89-537]

**ISLAM - PRAYER-BOOKS AND
DEVOTIONS.**
Karim, Darnell. The five prayers step by step /.
[Chicago] [1987] vi, 202 p. :
NYPL [Sc F 89-160]

ISLAM - RELATIONS - CHRISTIANITY.
Chukwulozie, Victor. Muslim-Christian dialogue
in Nigeria /. Ibadan , 1986. xviii, 201 p. :
ISBN 978-12-2192-5   *NYPL [Sc D 88-890]*

Sanni, Ishaq Kunle. Why you should never be a
Christian /. Ibadan, Nigeria , 1987. ix, 125 p. :
NYPL [Sc C 88-157]

Sanson, Henri. Christianisme au miroir de
l'Islam . Paris , 1984. 195 p. ; ISBN
2-204-02278-0 :   *NYPL [*OGC 85-2762]*

ISLAM - UGANDA - HISTORY.
Kasozi, A. B. K. (Abdu Basajabaka Kawalya),
1942- The spread of Islam in Uganda /.
Nairobi, Kenya , 1986. vi, 136 p., [4] p. of
plates : ISBN 0-19-572596-4
NYPL [Sc E 89-109]

**Islamic cities and towns. see Cities and towns,
Islamic.**

Islamic city. Spanish. La ciudad islámica :
comunicaciones científicas seleccionadas del
coloquio celebrado en el Middle East Centre,
Faculty of Oriental Studies, Cambridge, Gran
Bretaña, del 19 al 23 de Julio de 1976 / R.B.
Serjeant (ed.) ; traducción y transcripción de
términos árabes: Pedro Balaña Abadía.
Barcelona : Serbal ; [Paris] : Unesco, 1982. 260
p. : ill. ; 20 cm. (Colección de temas africanos . 7)
Translation of: The Islamic city. 1980. Includes
bibliographies. ISBN 92-3-301665-X (Unesco)
*1. Cities and towns, Islamic - Arab countries -
Congresses. 2. Cities and towns Islamic - Arab countries -
Congresses. I. Setjeant, R. B. (Robert Bertram). II.
Colloquium on the Islamic City (1976 : University of
Cambridge). III. Title. IV. Series.*
NYPL [Sc D 88-596]

Islamic cookery [microform] /. 'Isá 'Abd Allāh

Muḥammad al-Mahdī, 1945- Brooklyn , c1976.
31 p. :   *NYPL [Sc Micro R-4114 no. 14]*

**ISLAMIC EDUCATION. see ISLAM -
EDUCATION.**

Islamic law in Nigeria : application and teaching
/ edited by S. Khalid Rashid. Lagos : Islamic
Publications Bureau, 1986. 309 p. ; 22 cm.
Includes bibliographical references and index.   ISBN
978-247-037-6
1. Islamic law - Nigeria - Study and teaching. I. Rashid,
S. Khalid.   *NYPL [Sc D 89-417]*

**ISLAMIC LAW - NIGERIA - STUDY AND
TEACHING.**
Islamic law in Nigeria . Lagos , 1986. 309 p. ;
ISBN 978-247-037-6   *NYPL [Sc D 89-417]*

**ISLAMIC LEARNING AND SCHOLARSHIP -
GUINEA-BISSAU - BIJINI.**
A History of the migration and the settlement
of the Baayo family from Timbuktu to Bijini in
Guine Bissau /. [Banjul? , 1987.] 71 p. :
NYPL [Sc F 89-146]

Islamic marriage ceremony and polygamy
[microform] /. 'Isá 'Abd Allāh Muḥammad
al-Mahdī, 1945- Brooklyn , c1977. 30 p. :
NYPL [Sc Micro R-4114 no.1]

ISLAMIC SERMONS.
'Isá 'Abd Allāh Muḥammad al-Mahdī, 1945-
Khutbat's of Al Hajj Al Imam Isa Abd'Allah
Muhammad Al Mahdi [microform]. Brooklyn
[1978?] 2 v. :
NYPL [Sc Micro R-4114 no. 17]

ISLAMIC WOMEN. see WOMEN, MUSLIM.

ISLAMISM. see ISLAM.

Island boy /. Holdridge, Betty. New York ,
c1942. 110 p. :   *NYPL [Sc D 88-1181]*

Island in the sun-side 2 [microform] /.
Hippolyte, Kendel. St. Lucia [197-?] 50 p. ;
NYPL [Sc Micro F-11023]

**ISLANDS OF THE INDIAN OCEAN -
CONGRESSES.**
Relations historiques à travers l'océan Indien.
Spanish. Relaciones históricas a través del
océano Índico . Barcelona , Paris , 1983. 224
p. ;   ISBN 84-85800-51-6 *NYPL [Sc D 88-593]*

ISLANDS OF THE PACIFIC - FICTION.
Ephson, Isaac S., 1923- The episode of the
innocent man in trouble /. Accra, Ghana ,
1985. 81 p. ;   *NYPL [Sc D 88-411]*

Israel and Black Africa . Mahmud-Okereke, N.
Enuma el, 1948- Lagos, Nigeria , 1986. xxxiv,
211 p. ;   ISBN 978-242-301-7
NYPL [Sc C 88-205]

**ISRAEL - EMIGRATION AND
IMMIGRATION - BIOGRAPHY.**
Avraham, Shmuel, 1945- Treacherous journey .
New York, NY , 1986. xii, 178 p. :   ISBN
0-933503-46-6 (jacket); 0-933503-46-5 :   DDC
963/.004924 19
DS135.E75 A93 1986   *NYPL [Sc E 87-275]*

ISRAEL - ETHNIC RELATIONS.
Ethiopian Jews and Israel /. New Brunswick,
NJ, U. S. A. , c1987. 159 p. :   ISBN
0-88738-133-2   DDC 305.8/924/05694 19
DS113.8.F34 E84 1987   *NYPL [Sc E 88-73]*

**ISRAEL - FOREIGN RELATIONS - AFRICA,
SUB-SAHARAN.**
Mahmud-Okereke, N. Enuma el, 1948- Israel
and Black Africa . Lagos, Nigeria , 1986. xxxiv,
211 p. ;   ISBN 978-242-301-7
NYPL [Sc C 88-205]

Israel (State) see Israel.

**ISRAEL, TEN LOST TRIBES. see LOST
TRIBES OF ISRAEL.**

ISRAELITES. see JEWS.

Issue evolution . Carmines, Edward G. Princeton,
N.J. , c1989. xvii, 217 p. :   ISBN 0-691-07802-5 :
DDC 323.1/196073 19
E185.615 .C35 1989   *NYPL [Sc E 89-214]*

Issues in Black history . Drimmer, Melvin.
Dubuque, Iowa , c1987. xviii, 308 p. ;   ISBN
0-8403-4174-1 (pbk.)   DDC 973/.0496073 19
E185 .D715 1987   *NYPL [Sc E 88-107]*

Issues in education and training series .
(10) Williams, Lincoln Octavious. Partial
surrender . London , New York , 1988. viii,
194 p. ;   ISBN 1-85000-289-4   DDC

361.7/97/009421 19
HV1441.G8 L78 1988   *NYPL [Sc E 89-73]*

Issues in international relations . Chan, Stephen.
London , 1987. viii, 206 p. ;   ISBN 0-333-44102-8
(pbk.)   *NYPL [Sc D 88-371]*

Issues in Nigerian development.
(ser. no. 1) Nwankwo, Arthur A. Thoughts on
Nigeria /. Enugu, Nigeria , 1986. xxii, 198 p. ;
ISBN 987-15-6264-1   *NYPL [Sc E 88-448]*

Okongwu, Chu S. P., 1934- The Nigerian
economy . Enugu, Nigeria , 1986. vi, 453 p. :
ISBN 978-15-6038-X (pbk.) :   DDC 330.9669/05
19
HC1055 .O39 1986   *NYPL [Sc D 88-1250]*

**Issues in teacher education and science
curriculum in Nigeria** / edited by T.O.
Mgbodile ... [et al.]. [Nigeria : The
Organization, 1986?] vi, 331 p. : ill. ; 21 cm.
(Curriculum Organization of Nigeria monograph series .
no. 2) Includes bibliographies.   DDC 370/.7/309669
19
1. Teachers, Training of - Nigeria. 2. Science - Study
and teaching - Nigeria. 3. Curriculum planning -
Nigeria. I. Mgbodile, T. O. II. Series.
LB1727.N5 I88 1986   *NYPL [Sc D 88-125]*

Istituto geografico De Agostini. World Book, Inc.
The World Book atlas. Chicago , c1988. 1 atlas
(432 p.) : ill. (some col.), col. maps ; 38 cm.
ISBN 0-7166-3181-4 :   DDC 912 19
G1021 .W6735 1986   *NYPL [Sc Ref 89-1]*

Ita, Bassey. Jazz in Nigeria : an outline cultural
history / [Bassey Ita]. Ikoyi : Atiaya
Communications Co., c1984. 99 p. : ports. ; 21
cm. "A Radical House publication."   DDC
785.42/09669 19
1. Jazz music - Nigeria - History and criticism. I. Title.
ML3509.N6 I8 1984   *NYPL [Sc D 88-435]*

**ITALIAANDER, ROLF, 1913- - ART
COLLECTIONS - CATALOGS.**
Volkstümliche Künste . Reinbek , c1986/87.
135 p. :   *NYPL [Sc D 89-238]*

**ITALIAN AMERICANS - NEW YORK (CITY) -
RELIGIOUS LIFE.**
Orsi, Robert A. The Madonna of 115th Street .
New Haven , c1985. xxiii, 287 p. :   ISBN
0-300-03262-5 (alk. paper)   DDC
263/.98/0895107471 19
BT660.N44 O77 1985
NYPL [IEE (Italians) 86-89]

**ITALIAN AMERICANS - NEW YORK (CITY) -
SOCIAL CONDITIONS.**
Orsi, Robert A. The Madonna of 115th Street .
New Haven , c1985. xxiii, 287 p. :   ISBN
0-300-03262-5 (alk. paper)   DDC
263/.98/0895107471 19
BT660.N44 O77 1985
NYPL [IEE (Italians) 86-89]

**ITALIAN AMERICANS - UNITED STATES.
see ITALIAN AMERICANS.**

**ITALIAN LANGUAGE - DICTIONARIES -
SOMALI.**
Minozzi, Maria Teresa. Dizionario
italiano-somalo /. Milano , 1961. 178 p. ;
NYPL [Sc B 88-4]

**ITALY - FOREIGN RELATIONS - FRANCE -
HISTORY.**
Durant, Franck Alphonse. Rétrospectives
[microform] . Port-au-Prince, Haiti , 1977. 16
p. ;   *NYPL [Sc Micro F 10,933]*

I've been a woman . Sanchez, Sonia, 1935-
Chicago , c1985. 101 p. ;   ISBN 0-88378-112-1
NYPL [Sc D 88-205]

Ives, Ruth.
Detroit. Great Cities Program for School
Improvement. Writers' Committee. A day with
Debbie /. Chicago , c1964. 55 p. :
NYPL [Sc E 89-178]

Detroit. Great Cities Program for School
Improvement. Writers' Committee. Play with
Jimmy /. Chicago , c1962. 23, [1] p. :
NYPL [Sc E 88-237]

Detroit. Great Cities Program for School
Improvement. Writes' Committee. Fun with
David /. Chicago , c1962. 31 p.:
NYPL [Sc E 89-40]

Ives, Rwth. Detroit. Great Cities Program for
School Improvement. Writers' Committee.
Laugh with Larry /. Chicago , c1962. 47 p. :
NYPL [Sc E 87-268]

**IVORIES - AFRICA, WEST - HISTORY -
16TH CENTURY - EXHIBITIONS.**
Bassani, Ezio. Africa and the Renaissance .
New York City , c1988. 255 p. :   ISBN
0-945802-00-5 :   DDC 736/.62/096607401471 19
NK5989 .B37 1988   *NYPL [Sc F 89-30]*

Ivory /. Resnick, Mike. New York , 1988. 374
p. :   ISBN 0-312-93093-3 :   DDC 813/.54 19
PS3568.E698 I96 1988   *NYPL [Sc D 89-163]*

**IVORY COAST - COMMERCE - UNITED
STATES.**
United States. Bureau of International
Commerce. A market for U. S. products in the
Ivory Coast /. Washington, D.C. [1966] viii,
87 p. :   *NYPL [Sc F 89-79]*

IVORY COAST - ECONOMIC CONDITIONS.
United States. Bureau of International
Commerce. A market for U. S. products in the
Ivory Coast /. Washington, D.C. [1966] viii,
87 p. :   *NYPL [Sc F 89-79]*

IVORY COAST - ECONOMIC POLICY.
Alschuler, Lawrence R., 1941- Multinationals
and maldevelopment . Basingstoke, Hampshire ,
c1988. xii, 218 p. :   ISBN 0-333-41561-2
NYPL [Sc D 88-701]

Front populaire ivoirien. Propositions pour
gouverner la Côte-d'Ivoire /. Paris , c1987- v. :
ISBN 2-85802-882-6 (v. 1)   DDC
361.6/1/096668 19
JQ3386.A2 F76 1987   *NYPL [Sc D 88-1142]*

**Ivory Coast - Government. see Ivory Coast -
Politics and government.**

IVORY COAST - JUVENILE FICTION.
Rémy, Mylène. Le masque volé /. Paris , 1987.
126 p. :   ISBN 2-218-07832-5
NYPL [Sc C 88-311]

**IVORY COAST - POLITICS AND
GOVERNMENT.**
Amondji, Marcel, 1934- Côte-d'Ivoire . Paris ,
c1986. 207 p. ;   ISBN 2-85802-631-6   DDC
324.2666/806 19
DT545.75 .A46 1986   *NYPL [Sc D 88-297]*

**IVORY COAST - POLITICS AND
GOVERNMENT - 1960-**
Amondji, Marcel, 1934- Côte-d'Ivoire . Paris ,
c1988. 188 p. ;   ISBN 2-7384-0072-8
NYPL [Sc D 89-503]

Front populaire ivoirien. Propositions pour
gouverner la Côte-d'Ivoire /. Paris , c1987- v. :
ISBN 2-85802-882-6 (v. 1)   DDC
361.6/1/096668 19
JQ3386.A2 F76 1987   *NYPL [Sc D 88-1142]*

**IVORY COAST - POLITICS AND
GOVERNMENT - 1960- - CONGRESSES.**
Le quatrième séminaire des secrétaires
généraux . [Abidjan] , 1985. 55 p. :
NYPL [Sc E 88-150]

Séminaires d'information et de formation des
secrétaires généraux . [Abidjan] [1985] 72 p. :
DDC 966.6/805 19
DT545.8 .S46 1985   *NYPL [Sc E 88-151]*

IVORY COAST - SOCIAL POLICY.
Front populaire ivoirien. Propositions pour
gouverner la Côte-d'Ivoire /. Paris , c1987- v. :
ISBN 2-85802-882-6 (v. 1)   DDC
361.6/1/096668 19
JQ3386.A2 F76 1987   *NYPL [Sc D 88-1142]*

Iwalewa-Haus Bayreuth.
Zementskulpturen aus Nigeria . Stuttgart ,
c1988. 70 p. :   *NYPL [Sc F 89-44]*

Zementskulpturen aus Nigeria . Stuttgart ,
c1988. 70 p. :   *NYPL [Sc F 89-44]*

I.W.A.R.U. (Organization) I.W.A.R.U. talks
(1974-1984) /. [Gusau, Sokoto State, Nigeria ,
1985] 97 p. ;   DDC 255/.006/06 19
BX2740.A435 I18 1985
NYPL [Sc E 88-120]

I.W.A.R.U. (ORGANIZATION)
I.W.A.R.U. talks (1974-1984) /. [Gusau, Sokoto
State, Nigeria , 1985] 97 p. ;   DDC 255/.006/06
19
BX2740.A435 I18 1985
NYPL [Sc E 88-120]

IWARU talks (1974-1984) I.W.A.R.U. talks
(1974-1984) /. [Gusau, Sokoto State, Nigeria ,
1985] 97 p. ;   DDC 255/.006/06 19
BX2740.A435 I18 1985
NYPL [Sc E 88-120]

Iwe ede yoruba . Babalọlá, Adébóyè. [Ikeja] [1968] 139 p. :   *NYPL [Sc C 88-127]*

IWU . Aisien, Ekhaguosa. Benin City, Nigeria , c1986. 64 p. :   *NYPL [Sc D 88-728]*

Iyay Kimoni, 1938- Poésie de la négritude : une manière de lire / Iyay Kimoni. Kikwit : Bibliothèque africaine, 1985. vi, 168 p. ; 17 cm. Bibliography: p. [160]-165.   DDC 841/.009/896 19
1. Damas, Léon-Gontran, 1912-1978 - Criticism and interpretation. 2. Senghor, Léopold Sédar, - Criticism and interpretation. 3. Césaire, Aimé - Criticism and interpretation. 4. French poetry - Foreign countries - History and criticism. 5. French poetry - Black authors - History and criticism. 6. Negritude (Literary movement). 7. Race awareness in literature. I. Title.
PQ3897 .I93 1985   *NYPL [Sc B 89-18]*

Iyegha, David A., 1949- Agricultural crisis in Africa : the Nigerian experience / David A. Iyegha. Lanham, MD : University Press of America, c1988. xx, 246 p. : ill. ; 24 cm. Includes index. Bibliography: p. 225-239.   ISBN 0-8191-7080-1 (alk. paper)   DDC 338.1/09669 19
1. Agriculture and state - Nigeria. 2. Agriculture - Economic aspects - Nigeria. 3. Agriculture - Nigeria. 4. Food supply - Nigeria. I. Title.
HD2145.5.Z8 I94 1988
    NYPL [JLE 88-5390]

Izainahary [microform] /. Rakoto, Andrianasolo. Tananarive [1978] 36 p. ;
    NYPL [Sc Micro F-10989]

Izdatel'stvo nauka. Redaktsiia "Obshchestvennye nauki i souvremennost'." The USSR and Africa. Moscow , 1983. 205 p. ;   DDC 303.4/8247/06 19
DT38.9.S65 U86 1983   *NYPL [Sc D 88-980]*

Ja ka ta. Guadeloupe, 1635-1971 . Tours [1982] 109 p. ;   DDC 306/.362/0972976 19
HT1108.G83 G8 1982   *NYPL [Sc F 89-141]*

Jaamac Cumar Ciise. Taariikhdii daraawiishta iyo Sayid Maxamed Cabdulle Xasan, 1895-1921 / waxaa qoray Jaamac Cumar Ciise. Muqdisho : Wasaaradda Hiddaha iyo Tacliinta Sare, Akadeemiyaha Dhaqanka, 1976. vii, 320 p., [2] leaves of plates : ill. ; 24 cm. Includes bibliographical references.
1. Maxamad Cabdulle Xasan, 1864-1920. 2. Muslims - Somalia - Biography. 3. Nationalists - Somalia - Biography. 4. Maxamad Cabdulle Xasan's Rebellion, British Somaliland, 1900-1920. 5. Somalia - History. I. Title.
DT404.3.M38 C55   *NYPL [Sc E 87-435]*

Jaata kendeyaa /. Dixon, Joan. [Amherst, Ma.? , 198-?] 91 p. :   *NYPL [Sc F 89-135]*

Jackie Robinson . Adler, David A. New York , c1989. 48 p. :   ISBN 0-8234-0734-9   DDC 796.357/092/4 B 19
GV865 .A37 1989   *NYPL [Sc F 89-137]*

Jackie Robinson . Robinson, Jackie, 1919-1972. New York , 1948. 170 p. :
    NYPL [Sc C 88-61]

Jackie Robinson /. Scott, Richard, 1956- New York , 1987. 110 p. :   ISBN 1-555-46208-1 :   DDC 796.357/092/4 B 92 19
GV865.R6 S36 1987   *NYPL [Sc E 88-168]*

Jackie Robinson's Little League baseball book. Robinson, John Roosevelt, 1919-1972. Englewood Cliffs, N.J. [1972] 135 p.   ISBN 0-13-509232-9
GV867.5 .R6   *NYPL [JFD 72-7423]*

Jackman, Randolph, 1932- From slavery to jouvert, 1975 / by Randolph Jackman. [Port of Spain?] : Jackman, [1975] 68 p. ; 19 cm.   DDC 972.98/3 19
1. Trinidad - Miscellanea. I. Title.
F2119 .J32   *NYPL [Sc C 89-5]*

Jackson, Angela, 1951- The man with the white liver : poems / by Angela Jackson ; art by Melora Walters. New York City : Contact II Publications, 1987. [12] p. : col. ill. ; 28 cm. "Originally published in the fall 1985 issue of Contact/II magazine, as a special chapbook. Reprinted with additional drawings by Melora Walters"--T.p. verso.   ISBN 0-936556-16-1   DDC 811/.54 19
I. Walters, Melora. II. Title.
PS3560.A179 M3 1987   *NYPL [Sc F 89-14]*

JACKSON, BO - JUVENILE LITERATURE.
Devaney, John. Bo Jackson . New York , 1988. 110 p. :   ISBN 0-8027-6818-0   DDC 796.332/092/4

B 92 19
GV865.J28 D48 1988   *NYPL [Sc E 89-12]*

Jackson, Clyde Owen. In this evening light / Clyde Owen Jackson. 1st ed. Hicksville, N. Y. : Exposition Press, c1980. xiii, 113 p. ; 22 cm.   ISBN 0-682-49479-8
1. Jackson, Clyde Owen. 2. Afro-Americans - Biography. I. Title.   *NYPL [Sc D 88-1213]*

JACKSON, CLYDE OWEN.
Jackson, Clyde Owen. In this evening light /. Hicksville, N. Y. , c1980. xiii, 113 p. ;   ISBN 0-682-49479-8   *NYPL [Sc D 88-1213]*

Jackson College for Negro Teachers. Africana, an exhibit of West African art . [Jackson, Miss. , 1950] 23 p. :   *NYPL [Sc F 85-236]*

Jackson, James S. (James Sidney), 1944- The Black American elderly . New York , c1988. xvi, 383 p. ;   ISBN 0-8261-5810-2   DDC 362.1/9897/00973 19
RA448.5.N4 B56 1988   *NYPL [JLE 88-5391]*

JACKSON, JANET, 1966- - JUVENILE LITERATURE.
Mabery, D. L. Janet Jackson /. Minneapolis , c1988. 32 p. :   ISBN 0-8225-1618-7 (lib bdg.) :   DDC 784.5/4/00924 B 920 19
ML3930.J15 M3 1988
    NYPL [Sc D 88-1460]

JACKSON, JESSE, 1941-
Cavanagh, Thomas E. Jesse Jackson's campaign . Washington, D.C. , 1984. 27 p., [1] ;   ISBN 0-941410-45-5 (pbk)   DDC 324.973 19
JK526 1984c   *NYPL [Sc F 87-172 rept. 2]*
House, Ernest R. Jesse Jackson & the politics of charisma . Boulder , 1988. xi, 196 p. ;   ISBN 0-8133-0767-8 (alk. paper)   DDC 973.92/092/4 19
E840.8.J35 H68 1988   *NYPL [JFE 88-7205]*

JACKSON, MISS. - RACE RELATIONS.
Spofford, Tim. Lynch Street . Kent, Ohio , c1988. 219 p., [1] leaf of plates :   ISBN 0-87338-355-9 (alk. paper)   DDC 976.2/51 19
F349.J13 S66 1988   *NYPL [Sc E 89-27]*

Jackson, Peter, 1949- Historic buildings of Harare, 1890-1940 / Peter Jackson ; photographs by Neils Lassen. Harare, Zimbabwe : Quest Pub., 1986. x, 134 p. : ill. ; 22 cm. Includes index. Bibliography: p. 130.   ISBN 0-908306-03-2 (pbk.)   DDC 720/.96891 19
1. Architecture - Zimbabwe - Harare - Catalogs. 2. Architecture, Modern - 19th century - Zimbabwe - Harare - Catalogs. 3. Architecture, Modern - 20th century - Zimbabwe - Harare - Catalogs. 4. Architecture, Colonial - Zimbabwe - Harare - Catalogs. 5. Architecture, Tropical - Zimbabwe - Harare - Catalogs. 6. Harare (Zimbabwe) - Buildings, structures, etc. - Catalogs. I. Title.
NA1596.6.R52 H375 1986
    NYPL [Sc D 89-467]

Jackson, Rashleigh E. The right to a peaceful world : text of statements by the Minister of Foreign Affairs of the Co-operative Republic of Guyana during the year 1985. [Guyana : Ministry of Foreign Affairs], 1985. 77 p. : ill. ; 22 cm.
1. Guyana - Foreign relations. I. Title.
    NYPL [Sc D 89-140]

Jackson, Richard L., 1937- Black literature and humanism in Latin America / Richard L. Jackson. Athens : University of Georgia Press, c1988. xvii, 166 p. ; 24 cm. Includes index. Bibliography: p. [147]-163.   ISBN 0-8203-0979-6 (alk. paper)   DDC 860/.9/896 19
1. Latin American literature - Black authors - History and criticism. 2. Latin American literature - 20th century - History and criticism. 3. Humanism in literature. I. Title.
PQ7081 .J263 1988   *NYPL [Sc E 88-359]*

JACKSON STATE COLLEGE.
Spofford, Tim. Lynch Street . Kent, Ohio , c1988. 219 p., [1] leaf of plates :   ISBN 0-87338-355-9 (alk. paper)   DDC 976.2/51 19
F349.J13 S66 1988   *NYPL [Sc E 89-27]*

JACMEL (HAITI) - FICTION.
Depestre, René. Hadriana dans tous mes rêves . [Paris] , c1988. 195 p. ;   ISBN 2-07-071255-9
    NYPL [Sc D 88-1004]

JACOB AND HIS SONS, OR THE SECOND PART OF A CONVERSATION BETWEEN MARY AND HER MOTHER.
Tappan, Lewis, 1788-1873. Letters respecting a

book "dropped from the catalogue" of the American Sunday School Union in compliance with the dictation of the slave power. New York , 1848. 36 p. ;
    NYPL [Sc Rare C 89-11]

Jacobs, Harriet A. (Harriet Ann), 1813-1897. Incidents in the life of a slave girl / Harriet Jacobs ; with an introduction by Valerie Smith. New York : Oxford University Press, 1988. xl, 306 p. ; 17 cm. (The Schomburg library of nineteenth-century Black women writers) Bibliography: xxxviii-xl. Reprint. Originally published : Boston, Mass. : for the author, 1861.   ISBN 0-19-505243-9 (alk. paper)   DDC 973/.0496024 B 19
1. Jacobs, Harriet A. (Harriet Ann), 1813-1897. 2. Slaves - United States - Biography. 3. Women slaves - United States - Biography. I. Title. II. Series.
E444.J17 A3 1988   *NYPL [JFC 88-2193]*

JACOBS, HARRIET A. (HARRIET ANN), 1813-1897.
Jacobs, Harriet A. (Harriet Ann), 1813-1897. Incidents in the life of a slave girl /. New York , 1988. xl, 306 p. ;   ISBN 0-19-505243-9 (alk. paper)   DDC 973/.0496024 B 19
E444.J17 A3 1988   *NYPL [JFC 88-2193]*

Jacobsen, Peter Otto. A family in West Africa / Peter Otto Jacobsen, Preben Sejer Kristensen. Hove : Wayland, 1985. 32 p. : col. ill. ; 20 x 22 cm. (Families around the world) Includes index.   SCHOMBURG CHILDREN'S COLLECTION.   ISBN 0-85078-434-4 :   DDC 966/.305 19
1. Senegal - Social life and customs - Juvenile literature. I. Kristensen, Preben Sejer. II. Schomburg Children's Collection. III. Title. IV. Series.
DA588   *NYPL [Sc D 88-1499]*

Jacquemin, Jean Pierre. Forces littéraires d'Afrique . Bruxelles , c1987. 238 p. ;   ISBN 2-8041-0965-8   *NYPL [Sc E 88-442]*

Jacques, Robin. Van Stockum, Hilda, 1908- Mogo's flute /. New York , 1966. 88 p. :
PZ7.V36 Mo   *NYPL [Sc E 88-176]*

Jahannes, Ja A. National Conference on African American/Jewish American Relations (1983 : Savannah State College) Blacks and Jews . [Savannah, Ga.] [1983] iii, 58 p. ;
    NYPL [Sc D 88-335]

Jahn, Wolfgang. Afrika anders erlebt / Jahn. Hannover : Landbuch, 1986. 207 p. : ill. ; 22 cm.   ISBN 3-7842-0336-1
1. Africa - Description and travel - 1977-. I. Title.
    NYPL [Sc D 88-806]

Jairos Jiri . Farquhar, June. Gweru , 1987. 92 p. :   ISBN 0-86922-416-6   *NYPL [Sc D 89-38]*

Jaja, Janhoi M. Profile / by Janhoi M. Jaja. 1st ed. Kingston, Jamaica : Published by Invincible Rases International Enterprises in association with Kingston Publishers, c1984. 48 p. : chiefly ill. ; 21 cm.
1. Blacks - Jamaica - Portraits. 2. Photography - Portraits. I. Title.   *NYPL [Sc D 88-932]*

Jaja, S. O. Women in development . Calabar , 1988. 153 p. :   *NYPL [Sc D 89-79]*

Jakoubek, Robert E.
Adam Clayton Powell, Jr. / Robert E. Jakoubek. New York : Chelsea House, c1988. xiv, 252 p. ; 22 cm. (Black Americans of achievement) Includes index. Follows the life of the Black politician who rose to great power in the House of Representatives during the post-Depression era and became an influential Black leader.   ISBN 1-555-46606-0   DDC 973/.0496073024 B 92 19
1. Powell, Adam Clayton, 1908-1972 - Juvenile literature. 2. United States. Congress. House - Biography - Juvenile literature. 3. Legislators - United States - Biography - Juvenile literature. 4. Afro-Americans - Biography - Juvenile literature. 5. Afro-American legislators - Biography - Juvenile literature. I. Title. II. Series.
E748.P86 J35 1988   *NYPL [Sc E 88-372]*

Harriet Beecher Stowe / Robert E. Jakoubek. New York : Chelsea House, c1989. 111 p. : ill., ports. ; 25 cm. (American women of achievement) Includes index. A biography of the author famous for the antislavery novel, "Uncle Tom's Cabin," but who wrote other works presenting a clear picture of nineteenth-century New England. Bibliography: p. 106.   ISBN 1-555-46680-X   DDC 813/.3 B 92 19
1. Stowe, Harriet Beecher, 1811-1896 - Biography - Juvenile literature. 2. Authors, American - 19th century - Biography - Juvenile literature. 3. Abolitionists - United States - Biography - Juvenile

literature. I. Title. II. Series.
PS2956 .J35 1989   *NYPL [Sc E 89-144]*

Jallier, Maurice. Musique aux Antilles = Mizik bô kay / Maurice Jallier, Yollen Lossen. Paris : Editions caribéennes, c1985. 145 p., [16] p. of plates : ill. ; 21 cm.   ISBN 2-903033-65-X :   DDC 780/.42/09729 19
1. Music, Popular (Songs, etc.) - Guadeloupe - History and criticism. 2. Music, Popular (Songs, etc.) - Martinique - History and criticism. 3. Music, Popular (Songs, etc.) - French Guiana - History and criticism. I. Lossen, Yollen. II. Title. III. Title: Mizik bô kay.
ML3486.G8 J3 1985   *NYPL [Sc D 87-576]*

JALUO (AFRICAN PEOPLE) see LUO (AFRICAN PEOPLE)

Jam session . Klaasse, Piet. Newton Abbot [Devon] , 1985. 192 p. :   ISBN 0-7153-8710-3   DDC 785.42/092/2 19
ML3506 .K58 1985   *NYPL [Sc G 88-13]*

al-Jamāhīrīyah al-'Arabīyah al-Lībīyah al-Sha'bīyah al-Ishtirākiyah. see Libya.

al-Jamāhøriyah al-'Arabīyas al-Lībīyah al-sha'biyah al-Ishtirāktyah. see Libya.

Jamaica /. Salkey, Andrew. London , 1983. 106 p. ;   ISBN 0-904521-26-5
NYPL [Sc D 88-1156]

Jamaica.
EMERGENCY POWERS REGULATIONS 1976.
Allegations of corrupt use of powers of detention during 1976 state of emergency [microform]. [Kingston , 1979?] 70.2 p. ;
NYPL [Sc Micro R-4108 no.13]

Jamaica. Assembly. To the King's most Excellent Majesty in Council, the humble petition and memorial of the Assembly of Jamaica : (voted in Assembly, on the 28th of December, 1774.) Philadelphia: : Printed by William and Thomas Bradford, at the London Coffee-House., 1775. 8 p. ; 19 cm.
1. Jamaica - Politics and government - To 1962. 2. United States - History - Revolution, 1775-1783. I. George III, King of Great Britain, 1738-1820.
NYPL [Sc Rare F 88-14]

JAMAICA - BIOGRAPHY.
Huntley, Eric L. Marcus Garvey . Ealing, London , 1988. 41 p. :   ISBN 0-904521-41-9
NYPL [Sc E 88-499]
Lewis, Rupert. Marcus Garvey . Trenton, N.J. , 1988. 301 p. :   ISBN 0-86543-061-6
NYPL [Sc D 88-1454]

JAMAICA - CHURCH HISTORY.
Osborne, Francis J. History of the Catholic church in Jamaica /. Aylesbury, Bucks, U.K. , c1977. vii, 210, [8] p. of plates :   ISBN 0-85474-070-8 (pbk.)   DDC 282/.7292 19
BX1455.2 .O84 1977   *NYPL [Sc F 88-290]*

JAMAICA - CIVILIZATION.
Alleyne, Mervyn. Roots of Jamaican culture /. London , 1988. xii, 186 p. ;   ISBN 0-7453-0245-9   DDC 972.92 19
F1874   *NYPL [Sc D 88-1190]*

Jamaica Council for Human Rights.
Hector, Mario. Death row /. London , Kingston, Jamaica , 1984. v, lll p.   ISBN 0-86232-232-4   *NYPL [Sc C 88-221]*

The Jamaica Council for Human Rights speaks [microform] [Kingston, Jamaica , 1981] 45 p. ;
NYPL [Sc Micro R-4132 no. 22]

The Jamaica Council for Human Rights speaks [microform] [Kingston, Jamaica : The Council, 1981] 45 p. ; 28 cm. Cover title. News releases issued between 1976 and 1981. Microfilm. New York : New York Public Library, 198. 1 microfilm reel; 35 mm. (MN *ZZ-23207)
1. Civil rights - Jamaica. 2. Police - Jamaica - Complaints against. 3. Violence - Jamaica. I. Jamaica Council for Human Rights.
NYPL [Sc Micro R-4132 no. 22]

Jamaica Cultural Development Commission. Speech anthology, 1986-1987 /. [Kingston] [1986] 183 p. ;   DDC 820/.8 19
PN4228.J25 S6 1986   *NYPL [Sc F 88-303]*

Jamaica Cultural Development Commission. Culinary Arts Dept. A Festival of Jamaican cuisine /. Kingston, Jamaica [1983?] 36 p. :   DDC 641.597292 19
TX716.J27 F47 1983   *NYPL [Sc D 88-1074]*

JAMAICA - DESCRIPTION AND TRAVEL - 1981- - GUIDE-BOOKS.
Morris, Margaret. Tour Jamaica /. Kingston, Jamaica , 1985. 125 p. :   ISBN 976-612-001-3
NYPL [Sc F 88-283]
Sherlock, Philip M. (Philip Manderson) Keeping company with Jamaica /. London , 1984. vii, 211 p. :   ISBN 0-333-37419-3 (pbk) :   DDC 917.292/046 19
F1869   *NYPL [Sc D 88-1466]*

JAMAICA - DESCRIPTION AND TRAVEL - GUIDE-BOOKS.
McLeod, Catherine. Jamaika /. Lausanne, Switzerland [1985], c1981. 128 p. :
NYPL [Sc B 88-57]

JAMAICA - ECONOMIC POLICY.
Pathways to progress . Morant Bay, Jamaica, W.I. , 1985. vii, 128 p. ;   DDC 338.97292 19
HC154 .P38 1985   *NYPL [Sc D 88-1239]*

JAMAICA - FICTION.
Gardam, Jane. Black faces, white faces /. London , 1975. 133 p. ;   ISBN 0-241-89250-3 :
PZ4.G218 Bl PR6057.A623
NYPL [JFD 77-1786]
Mason, Clifford. Jamaica run . New York , 1987. 359 p. ;   ISBN 0-312-00611-X :   DDC 813/.54 19
PS3563.A7878 J3 1987
NYPL [JFD 88-9447]

JAMAICA - HISTORY - TO 1962 - JUVENILE FICTION.
Thompson, Roydon, 1911- Stella, the princess /. Kingston, Jamaica, West Indies (9 Roselle Ave., Kingston 6) , 1984. 255 p. :   ISBN 976-8024-00-3 (pbk.)   DDC [Fic] 19
PZ7.T37199 St 1984   *NYPL [Sc D 88-317]*

JAMAICA - HISTORY - MAROON WAR, 1795-1796.
Dallas, Robert Charles, 1754-1824. The history of the Maroons, from their origin to the establishment of their chief tribe at Sierra Leone. London, 1803. 2 v. :
F1881 .D14   *NYPL [Sc Rare F 88-76]*

JAMAICA - HISTORY - DRAMA.
Atkinson, Dermot. The meeting /. [Jamaica?] , c1985. 68 p. ;   *NYPL [Sc C 88-108]*

JAMAICA - JUVENILE FICTION.
Berry, James. A thief in the village /. New York , 1988, c1987. 148 p. ;   ISBN 0-531-05745-3   DDC [Fic] 19
PZ7.B46173 Th 1988   *NYPL [Sc D 88-1252]*
Cave, Hugh B. (Hugh Barnett), 1910- Conquering Kilmarnie /. New York , London , c1989. 176 p. ;   ISBN 0-02-717781-5   DDC [Fic] 19
PZ7.C29 Co 1989   *NYPL [Sc D 89-611]*
Kirkpatrick, Oliver. Naja the snake and Mangus the mongoose. Garden City, N.Y. [1970] 40 p.   DDC [Fic]
PZ7.K6358 Naj   *NYPL [Sc F 88-339]*
McCall, Virginia, 1909- Adassa and her hen. [New York, 1971] 79 p.   DDC [Fic]
PZ7.M12295 Ad   *NYPL [Sc D 89-100]*
Persaud, Pat. Tipsy /. Kingston, Jamaica , c1986. [28] p. :
MLCS 87/7926 (P)   *NYPL [Sc F 88-255]*
Pomerantz, Charlotte. The chalk doll /. New York , c1989. 30 p. :   ISBN 0-397-32318-2 :   DDC [E] 19
PZ7.P77 Ch 1989   *NYPL [Sc F 89-175]*

JAMAICA - MAPS.
(1971) Jamaica. Town Planning Dept. National atlas of Jamaica. Kingston, 1971. viii, 79 p.
NYPL [Map Div 73-738]

Jamaica. Ministry of Development and Welfare. Town Planning Dept. Jamaica. Ministry of Finance and Planning. Town Planning Dept. see Jamaica. Town Planning Dept.

JAMAICA - POETRY.
Salkey, Andrew. Jamaica /. London , 1983. 106 p. ;   ISBN 0-904521-26-5
NYPL [Sc D 88-1156]

JAMAICA - POLITICS AND GOVERNMENT - TO 1962.
Jamaica. Assembly. To the King's most Excellent Majesty in Council, the humble

petition and memorial of the Assembly of Jamaica . Philadelphia: , 1775. 8 p. ;
NYPL [Sc Rare F 88-14]

JAMAICA - POLITICS AND GOVERNMENT - 1962-
Payne, Anthony, 1952- Politics in Jamaica /. London , New York, N.Y. , 1988. xii, 196 p. :   ISBN 0-312-01869-X (St. Martin's)   DDC 972.92 19
F1887 .P39 1988   *NYPL [Sc D 88-1230]*

JAMAICA - RELIGION.
Chevannes, Barry. Social origins of the Rastafari movement /. Mona, Kingston , c1978. xii, 323 p. :
BL2532.R37 C48 1978   *NYPL [Sc F 88-368]*

Jamaica run . Mason, Clifford. New York , 1987. 359 p. ;   ISBN 0-312-00611-X :   DDC 813/.54 19
PS3563.A7878 J3 1987
NYPL [JFD 88-9447]

Jamaica, the death penalty. London : Amnesty International Publications, 1989. iii, 85 p. : map ; 27 cm.
1. Capitol punishment - Jamaica.
NYPL [Sc F 89-164]

Jamaica. Town Planning Dept.
National atlas of Jamaica. Kingston, 1971. viii, 79 p. col. illus., maps (part col.) 28 x 46 cm. "United Nations special fund project, 'Assistance in physical development planning.'" Scale of principal maps 1:500,000. Planned as v. 2 of A national physical plan for Jamaica by the Town Planning Department's Physical Planning Unit.
1. Jamaica - Maps. I. Jamaica. Town Planning Dept. Physical Planning Unit. A national physical plan for Jamaica. II. Title.   *NYPL [Map Div 73-738]*

Jamaica. Town Planning Dept. Physical Planning Unit.
A national physical plan for Jamaica. Jamaica. Town Planning Dept. National atlas of Jamaica. Kingston, 1971. viii, 79 p.
NYPL [Map Div 73-738]

Jamaica 21 anthology series .
(no. 2) From our yard . Kingston, Jamaica , 1987. xxviii, 235 p. ;   *NYPL [Sc D 89-412]*

Jamaican Music /. Burnett, Michael. Oxford [England] , 1982. 48 p. :   ISBN 0-19-321333-8 (pbk)   *NYPL [Sc C 84-99]*

JAMAICAN POETRY.
From our yard . Kingston, Jamaica , 1987. xxviii, 235 p. ;   *NYPL [Sc D 89-412]*

Jamaika /. McLeod, Catherine. Lausanne, Switzerland [1985], c1981. 128 p. :
NYPL [Sc B 88-57]

James Baldwin /. Rosset, Lisa. New York, N.Y. , 1989. 111 p. :   ISBN 1-555-46572-2   DDC 818/.5409 B 92 19
PS3552.A45 Z87 1989   *NYPL [Sc E 89-224]*

JAMES, C. L. R. (CYRIL LIONEL ROBERT), 1901-
Buhle, Paul, 1944- C.L.R. James . London , New York , 1988. 197 p. :   ISBN 0-86091-221-3 :   DDC 818 B 19
PR9272.9.J35 Z59 1988
NYPL [Sc E 89-171]

JAMES, DANIEL, 1920-1978.
McGovern, James R. Black Eagle, General Daniel "Chappie" James, Jr. /. University, AL , c1985. 204 p. :   ISBN 0-8173-0179-8   DDC 355/.0092/4 B 19
UG626.2.J36 M34 1985
NYPL [JFD 85-7082]

James, Frederick Bobor. The weaver birds / written by Frederick Bobor James. Freetown [Sierra Leone] : People's Educational Association of Sierra Leone, 1986. 79 p. ; 21 cm. (Stories and songs from Sierra Leone . 15)   DDC 822 19
I. Title. II. Series.
PR9393.9.J36 W4 1986
NYPL [Sc D 89-517]

James, Harold Laymont, 1929- (illus) Huston, Anne. Ollie's go-kart. New York [1971] 143 p.   DDC [Fic]
PZ7.H959 Ol   *NYPL [Sc D 88-1472]*

James P. Johnson . Brown, Scott E., 1960- Metuchen, N.J. , 1986. viii, 500 p., [12] p. of plates :   ISBN 0-8108-1887-6   DDC 786.1/092/4 B 19
ML417.J62 B76 1986   *NYPL [Sc D 88-1435]*

James, Selma. The ladies and the mammies : Jane Austen & Jean Rhys / by Selma James. Bristol, England : Falling Wall Press, 1983. 96 p. ; 23 cm. ISBN 0-905046-24-2 :
1. Austen, Jane, 1775-1817 - Criticism and interpretation. 2. Rhys, Jean. Wide Sargasso sea - Criticism and interpretation. I. Title.
NYPL [JFD 84-4049]

James, W. Martin. Vanneman, Peter. Soviet foreign policy in Southern Africa . Pretoria, Republic of South Africa , 1982. 57 p. ; ISBN 0-7983-0078-7 (pbk.) DDC 327.68047 19
DT747.S65 V36 1982 NYPL [Sc D 88-1155]

James Weldon Johnson /. Tolbert-Rouchaleau, Jane. New York , c1988. 110 p. : ISBN 1-555-46596-X DDC 818/.5209 B 92 19
PS3519.O2625 Z894 1988
NYPL [Sc E 88-164]

James, Winston. The Caribbean / Winston James ; [illustrators Dave Eaton, Kevin Maddison and Maggie Raynor] London : Macdonald Educational, 1984. 46 p. : ill. (some col.), col. maps ; 29 cm. (Looking at lands) Includes index. Spine title: Looking at the Caribbean. SCHOMBURG CHILDREN'S COLLECTION. ISBN 0-356-07105-7 : DDC 972.9 19
1. West Indies - Juvenile literature. I. Eaton, David. II. Maddison, Kevin W., 1946-. III. Raynor, Maggie. IV. Schomburg Children's Collection. V. Title. VI. Title: Looking at the Caribbean. VII. Series.
F2175 NYPL [Sc F 88-128]

Jāmi'at al-Kharṭūm. Shu'bat al-Fūlklūr. Folklore and National Development Symposium (1981 : Khartoum, Sudan) Folklore and development in the Sudan . Khartoum , 1985. 272 p. :
GR355.8 .F65 1981 NYPL [Sc E 88-333]

Jamieson, J. W. Essays on the nature of intelligence and the analysis of racial differences in the performance of IQ tests /. Washington D.C. , c1988. 72 p. : ISBN 0-941694-32-1
NYPL [Sc D 89-546]

Janet Jackson /. Mabery, D. L. Minneapolis , c1988. 32 p. : ISBN 0-8225-1618-7 (lib bdg.) : DDC 784.5/4/00924 B 920 19
ML3930.J15 M3 1988
NYPL [Sc D 88-1460]

JAPAN IN ART - EXHIBITIONS.
Pindell, Howardena, 1943- Howardena Pindell . New York, NY (144 W. 125th St., New York 10027) , c1986. 24 p. : DDC 709/.2/4 19
N6537.P49 A4 1986 NYPL [Sc F 88-270]

Jardel, Jean Pierre. Le conte créole [microform] / Jean-Pierre Jardel. [Montréal] : Centre de recherches caraïbes, Université de Montréal, [1977] 37 p. ; 22 cm. Includes indexes. Bibliography: p. [23]-37. Microfiche. New York : New York Public Library, 1981. 1 microfiche : negative ; 11 x 15 cm. (FSN 32,795).
1. Tales, West Indian. 2. Tales, French - Bibliography. 3. Tales, West Indian - Bibliography. I. Title.
*GR120 .J37 NYPL [*XM-12281]*

JARGONS. see PIDGIN LANGUAGES.

Jasen, David A. Tin Pan Alley : the composers, the songs, the performers, and their times : the golden age of American popular music from 1886 to 1956 / David A. Jasen. New York : D.I. Fine, c1988. xxiv, 312 p., [32] p. of plates : ill., ports. ; 24 cm. Includes index. Bibliography: p. 293-296. ISBN 1-556-11099-5 : DDC 784.5/00973 19
1. Popular music - United States - History and criticism. I. Title.
ML3477 .J34 1988 NYPL [Sc E 88-562]

Jasper makes music. Horvath, Betty F. New York [1967] [38] p. DDC [E]
PZ7.H7922 Jas NYPL [Sc F 88-343]

Jawara, Robert F. Hinzen, Heribert. Koranko riddles, songs and stories /. Freetown , 1987. 69 p. :
NYPL [Sc D 89-416]

Jay, John, 1817-1894. Thoughts on the duty of the Episcopal Church, in relation to slavery : being a speech delivered in N.Y.A.S. convention, February 12, 1839 / by John Jay. New York : Piercy & Reed, 1839. 11 p. ; 18 cm.
1. Slavery and the church - Episcopal Church. 2. Slavery - United States - Controversial literature. I. Title. *NYPL [Sc Rare F 88-25]*

Jazayeri, Ahmad, 1957- Economic adjustment in oil-based economies / Ahmad Jazayeri.

Aldershot, Hants, England ; Brookfield, Vt., USA : Avebury, c1988. xvi, 260 p. : ill. ; 23 cm. Includes index. Bibliography: p. 248-254. ISBN 0-566-05682-8 : DDC 330.955/054 19
1. Petroleum industry and trade - Iran. 2. Agriculture - Economic aspects - Iran. 3. Petroleum industry and trade - Nigeria. 4. Agriculture - Economic aspects - Nigeria. 5. Iran - Manufactures. I. Title.
HD9576.I62 J39 1988 NYPL [JLD 89-202]

Jazz . Sandner, Wolfgang. [Laaber] , 1982. 152 p. : ISBN 3-921518-75-X DDC 785.42/09 19
ML3506 .S26 1982 NYPL [Sc D 89-161]

JAZZ. see JAZZ MUSIC.

Jazz giants: a visual retrospective / compiled and designed by K. Abé. New York : Billboard Publications, 1988,c1986. 280 p. : chiefly ill., (some col.) ; 33 cm. Includes index. ISBN 0-8230-7536-2 : DDC 779/.978542 19
1. Jazz music - Pictorial works. 2. Jazz musicians - Portraits. 3. Afro-American musicians - Portraits. I. Abé, K. (Katsuji).
ML3506 .J43 1988 NYPL [Sc G 89-14]

The jazz handbook /. McRae, Barry. Harlow, Essex, England , 1987. 272 p. : ISBN 0-582-00092-0 NYPL [Sc D 87-940]

JAZZ - HISTORY AND CRITICISM.
Brown, Marion, 1935- Faces and places . 1976. 2 v. (289 leaves) : *NYPL [Sc F 88-101]*

Jazz Hot . Un demi-siecle de swing et de Jazz /. [Paris] , 1986. 109 p. : ISBN 2-86929-034-9
NYPL [Sc G 86-35]

Jazz in Nigeria . Ita, Bassey. Ikoyi , c1984. 99 p. : DDC 785.42/09669 19
ML3509.N6 I8 1984 NYPL [Sc D 88-435]

Jazz in the first person. Muse presents Jazz in the first person . [Brooklyn, N.Y. , c1972] 31 p. : *NYPL [JNF 85-14]*

Jazz in Willisau : hundertmal Jazz live / Fotos von Andreas Raggenbass ; Plakate von Niklaus Troxler ; Texte von Peter Rüedi und Margrit Staber. Luzern : Raeber, c1978. 206 p. : ill. (some col.) ; 30 cm. ISBN 3-7239-0051-8 DDC 785.42/09494/5 19
1. Jazz music - Switzerland - Willisau. 2. Jazz music - Switzerland - Willisau - Pictorial works. I. Raggenbass, Andreas, 1942-. II. Troxler, Niklaus. III. Rüedi, Peter. IV. Staber, Margrit.
ML3509.S9 J4 1978 NYPL [Sc F 89-24]

Jazz life & times.
Crowther, Bruce, 1933- Gene Krupa, his life & times /. Tunbridge Wells, Kent , New York , 1987. 144 p. : ISBN 0-87663-670-9 (USA) DDC 789/.1/0924 B 19
ML419.K78 C8 1987 NYPL [JNF 88-89]

White, John, 1939- Billie Holiday, her life & times /. Tunbridge Wells, Kent , New York , 1987. 144 p. : ISBN 0-87663-668-7 (USA) DDC 784.5/3/0924 B 19
ML420.H58 W5 1987 NYPL [JNF 88-88]

Jazz masters series.
(10) Gammond, Peter. Duke Ellington /. London , 1987. 127 p. : ISBN 0-948820-00-4 (pbk.) : *NYPL [JNC 87-8]*

Palmer, Richard (Richard Hilary), 1947- Oscar Peterson /. Tunbridge Wells , New York , 1984. c. 93 p. : ISBN 0-87052-011-3 (Hippocrene Books) : DDC 785.42/092/4 B 19
ML417.P46 P3 1984 NYPL [Sc C 88-142]

JAZZ MUSIC - COLLECTED WORKS.
Keepnews, Orrin. The view from within . New York , 1988. x, 238 p. ; ISBN 0-19-505284-6 DDC 785.42 19
ML3507 .K43 1988 NYPL [Sc D 88-1453]

JAZZ MUSIC - DISCOGRAPHY.
Rust, Brian A. L., 1922- Jazz records, 1897-1942 /. Chigwell, Essex [1982?] 2 v. ; ISBN 0-902391-04-6 (set)
*NYPL [*R-Phono 84-254]*

JAZZ MUSIC - EXHIBITIONS.
Muse presents Jazz in the first person . [Brooklyn, N.Y. , c1972] 31 p. :
NYPL [JNF 85-14]

That's jazz, der Sound des 20. Jahrhunderts . [Darmstadt , 1988] xv, 723 p. : DDC 781/.57/0740341 19
ML141.D3 I6 1988 NYPL [JMF 89-297]

JAZZ MUSIC - HISTORY.
Priestley, Brian, 1946- Jazz on record .

London , 1988. xii, 225 p., [8] leaves of plates : ISBN 0-241-12440-9
NYPL [Sc D 88-1335]

JAZZ MUSIC - HISTORY AND CRITICISM.
Backus, Rob, 1946- Fire music . Chicago, Ill. , 1976. vii, 104 p. : ISBN 0-917702-00-X
NYPL [Sc D 88-337]

De Stefano, Gildo. Trecento anni di jazz . Milano , 1986. 262 p., [16] leaves of plates :
NYPL [Sc D 88-1226]

Gioia, Ted. The imperfect art . New York , 1988. vi, 152 p. ; ISBN 0-19-505343-5 (alk. paper) DDC 785.42/09 19
ML3506 .G56 1988 NYPL [JMD 88-274]

Hellhund, Herbert. Cool Jazz . Mainz , New York , c1985. 302 p. : ISBN 3-7957-1790-6 : DDC 785.42 19
ML3506 .H45 1985 NYPL [JME 87-29]

McRae, Barry. The jazz handbook /. Harlow, Essex, England , 1987. 272 p. : ISBN 0-582-00092-0 NYPL [Sc D 87-940]

Sandner, Wolfgang. Jazz . [Laaber] , 1982. 152 p. : ISBN 3-921518-75-X DDC 785.42/09 19
ML3506 .S26 1982 NYPL [Sc D 89-161]

Schuller, Gunther. The history of jazz. New York , 1968- v. DDC 785.42/09 19
ML3506 .S36 1968 NYPL [JNL 89-2]

JAZZ MUSIC - LOUISIANA - NEW ORLEANS.
Armstrong, Louis, 1900-1971. Satchmo . New York, N.Y. , 1986, c1954. xiii, p. 7-240 : ISBN 0-306-80276-7 (pbk.) : DDC 785.42/092/4 B 19
ML419.A75 A3 1986 NYPL [Sc D 88-339]

JAZZ MUSIC - NEW YORK (N.Y.)
Such, David Glen. Music, metaphor and values among avant-garde jazz musicians living in New York City /. 1985. ix, 307 leaves. :
NYPL [Sc F 88-284]

JAZZ MUSIC - NIGERIA - HISTORY AND CRITICISM.
Ita, Bassey. Jazz in Nigeria . Ikoyi , c1984. 99 p. : DDC 785.42/09669 19
ML3509.N6 I8 1984 NYPL [Sc D 88-435]

JAZZ MUSIC - PACIFIC STATES.
Tercinet, Alain, 1935- West Coast jazz /. Marseille , 1986. 358 p. : ISBN 2-86364-031-3
NYPL [Sc E 88-307]

JAZZ MUSIC - PICTORIAL WORKS.
Jazz giants. New York , 1988,c1986. 280 p. : ISBN 0-8230-7536-2 : DDC 779/.978542 19
ML3506 .J43 1988 NYPL [Sc G 89-14]

Longstreet, Stephen, 1907- Storyville to Harlem . New Brunswick, N.J. , c1986. 211 p. : ISBN 0-8135-1174-7 : DDC 785.42/09 19
ML87 .L66 1986 NYPL [Sc G 87-4]

JAZZ MUSIC - SWITZERLAND - WILLISAU.
Jazz in Willisau . Luzern , c1978. 206 p. : ISBN 3-7239-0051-8 DDC 785.42/09494/5 19
ML3509.S9 J4 1978 NYPL [Sc F 89-24]

JAZZ MUSIC - SWITZERLAND - WILLISAU - PICTORIAL WORKS.
Jazz in Willisau . Luzern , c1978. 206 p. : ISBN 3-7239-0051-8 DDC 785.42/09494/5 19
ML3509.S9 J4 1978 NYPL [Sc F 89-24]

JAZZ MUSIC - UNITED STATES.
Ogren, Kathy J. The jazz revolution . New York , 1989. vii, 221 p., [8] p. of plates : ISBN 0-19-505153-X (alk. paper) DDC 781/.57/0973 19
ML3508 .O37 1987 NYPL [Sc D 89-451]

JAZZ MUSIC - UNITED STATES - HISTORY AND CRITICISM.
Lees, Gene. Meet me at Jim & Andy's . New York, N.Y. , c1988. xviii, 265 p. ; ISBN 0-19-504611-0 (alk. paper) DDC 785.42/092/2 19
ML394 .L4 1988 NYPL [JND 89-5]

Oliver, Paul. The New Grove gospel, blues and jazz . New York , 1986. 395 p. [16] p. of plates : ISBN 0-393-01696-X
NYPL [JND 88-16]

Young, Al, 1939- Things ain't what they used to be . Berkeley , 1987. xvii, 233 p. : ISBN 0-88739-024-2 NYPL [Sc D 88-704]

JAZZ MUSICIANS.
Gridley, Mark C., 1947- Jazz styles .

Englewood Cliffs, N.J. , 1988. xviii, 445 p. :
ISBN 0-13-509217-5 DDC 785.42 19
ML3506 .G74 1987   **NYPL [Sc E 88-159]**

Jost, Ekkehard. Free jazz. Mainz [1975] 256 p.
NYPL [Sc E 77-158]

JAZZ MUSICIANS - BIOGRAPHY.
Lyons, Leonard. Jazz portraits . New York ,
c1989. 610 p. : ISBN 0-688-04946-X DDC
785.42/092/2 B 19
ML394 .L97 1989   **NYPL [Sc E 89-91]**

McRae, Barry. The jazz handbook /. Harlow,
Essex, England , 1987. 272 p. : ISBN
0-582-00092-0   **NYPL [Sc D 87-940]**

Palmer, Richard (Richard Hilary), 1947- Oscar
Peterson /. Tunbridge Wells , New York ,
1984. c. 93 p. : ISBN 0-87052-011-3 (Hippocrene
Books) :   DDC 785.42/092/4 B 19
ML417.P46 P3 1984   **NYPL [Sc C 88-142]**

**JAZZ MUSICIANS - EUROPE -
BIOGRAPHY.**
Brown, Marion, 1935- Faces and places . 1976.
2 v. (289 leaves) :   **NYPL [Sc F 88-101]**

JAZZ MUSICIANS - JUVENILE FICTION.
Thomas, Ianthe, 1951- Willie blows a mean
horn /. New York , c1981. 22 p. : ISBN
0-06-026106-4 : DDC [E]
PZ7.T36693 Wi   **NYPL [Sc E 89-22]**

**JAZZ MUSICIANS - LOUISIANA - NEW
ORLEANS.**
Martinez, Raymond J. (Raymond Joseph),
1889- Portraits of New Orleans jazz. New
Orleans [1971] 63 p. DDC 785.4/2/0976335
ML200.8.N48 M4   **NYPL [Sc E 87-69]**

JAZZ MUSICIANS - NEW YORK (N.Y.)
Such, David Glen. Music, metaphor and values
among avant-garde jazz musicians living in New
York City /. 1985. ix, 307 leaves. :
NYPL [Sc F 88-284]

JAZZ MUSICIANS - PACIFIC STATES.
Tercinet, Alain, 1935- West Coast jazz /.
Marseille , 1986. 358 p. : ISBN 2-86364-031-3
NYPL [Sc E 88-307]

JAZZ MUSICIANS - PORTRAITS.
Un demi-siecle de swing et de Jazz /. [Paris] ,
1986. 109 p. : ISBN 2-86929-034-9
NYPL [Sc G 86-35]

Jazz giants. New York , 1988,c1986. 280 p. :
ISBN 0-8230-7536-2 : DDC 779/.978542 19
ML3506 .J43 1988   **NYPL [Sc G 89-14]**

Klaasse, Piet. Jam session . Newton Abbot
[Devon] , 1985. 192 p. : ISBN 0-7153-8710-3
DDC 785.42/092/2 19
ML3506 .K58 1985   **NYPL [Sc G 88-13]**

Longstreet, Stephen, 1907- Storyville to
Harlem . New Brunswick, N.J. , c1986. 211 p. :
ISBN 0-8135-1174-7 : DDC 785.42/09 19
ML87 .L66 1986   **NYPL [Sc G 87-4]**

Wilmer, Valerie. The face of Black music ;
photographs /. New York , 1976. [118] p. :
ISBN 0-306-70756-X. DDC 780/.92/2 B
ML87 .W655   **NYPL [Sc F 88-207]**

JAZZ MUSICIANS - UNITED STATES.
Young, Al, 1939- Things ain't what they used
to be . Berkeley , 1987. xvii, 233 p. : ISBN
0-88739-024-2   **NYPL [Sc D 88-704]**

**JAZZ MUSICIANS - UNITED STATES -
BIOGRAPHY.**
Armstrong, Louis, 1900-1971. Satchmo . New
York, N.Y. , 1986, c1954. xiii, p. 7-240 : ISBN
0-306-80276-7 (pbk.) DDC 785.42/092/4 B 19
ML419.A75 A3 1986   **NYPL [Sc D 88-339]**

Backus, Rob, 1946- Fire music. Chicago, Ill. ,
1976. vii, 104 p. : ISBN 0-917702-00-X
NYPL [Sc D 88-337]

Balliett, Whitney. American singers . New
York , 1988. x, 244 p. : ISBN 0-19-504610-2 (alk.
paper) *ML400 .B25 1988* DDC 784.5 B 19
ML400 .B25 1988   **NYPL [JNE 88-46]**

Brown, Marion, 1935- Faces and places . 1976.
2 v. (289 leaves) :   **NYPL [Sc F 88-101]**

Brown, Scott E., 1960- James P. Johnson .
Metuchen, N.J. , 1986. viii, 500 p., [12] p. of
plates : ISBN 0-8108-1887-6 DDC 786.1/092/4 B
19
ML417.J62 B76 1986   **NYPL [Sc D 88-1435]**

Chilton, John, 1931 or 2- McKinney's music .
London , 1978. 68 p. : ISBN 0-9501290-1-1 (pbk.)

DDC 785.42/092/2 B 19
ML394 .C55 1978   **NYPL [Sc D 82-387]**

Chilton, John, 1931 or 2- Sidney Bechet, the
wizard of jazz /. Basingstoke , 1987. xiii, 331
p., [32] p. of plates : ISBN 0-333-44386-1
NYPL [Sc E 88-33]

Collier, James Lincoln, 1928- Duke Ellington /.
New York , 1987. viii, 340 p., [16] p. of
plates : ISBN 0-19-503770-7 (alk. paper) DDC
785.42/092/4 B 19
ML410.E44 C6 1987   **NYPL [JNE 87-49]**

Darensbourg, Joe, 1906-1985. [Telling it like it
is.] Jazz odyssey . Baton Rouge , 1988, c1987.
vi, 231 p., [32] p. of plates : ISBN
0-8071-1442-1 : DDC 788/.62/0924 B 19
ML419.D35 A3 1988   **NYPL [Sc E 89-28]**

Gammond, Peter. Duke Ellington /. London ,
1987. 127 p. : ISBN 0-948820-00-4 (pbk.) :
NYPL [JNC 87-8]

Horricks, Raymond, 1933- Quincy Jones /.
Tunbridge Wells, Kent , New York , 1985. 127
p., [8] p. of plates : ISBN 0-87052-215-9
(Hippocrene Books) : DDC 785.42/092/4 B 19
ML419.J7 H67 1985   **NYPL [Sc E 87-36]**

Ingram, Adrian. Wes Montgomery /.
Gateshead, Tyne and Wear, England , 1985.
127 p. : ISBN 0-9506224-9-4
NYPL [Sc F 88-61]

Koch, Lawrence O. Yardbird suite . Bowling
Green, Ohio , c1988. 336 p. : ISBN
0-87972-259-2 (clothbound)
NYPL [Sc E 89-48]

Lees, Gene. Meet me at Jim & Andy's . New
York, N.Y. , c1988. xviii, 265 p. : ISBN
0-19-504611-0 (alk. paper) DDC 785.42/092/2
B 19
ML394 .L4 1988   **NYPL [JND 89-5]**

Pinfold, Mike. Louis Armstrong, his life and
times /. New York , c1987. 143 p. : ISBN
0-87663-667-9 DDC 785.42/092/4 B 19
ML419.A75 P55 1987   **NYPL [Sc F 88-65]**

Wilber, Bob, 1928- Music was not enough /.
New York , 1988. 216 p. [8] p. of plates :
ISBN 0-19-520629-0   **NYPL [Sc E 89-6]**

**JAZZ MUSICIANS - UNITED STATES -
BIOGRAPHY - JUVENILE LITERATURE.**
Collier, James Lincoln, 1928- Louis
Armstrong . New York , c1985. 165 p. : ISBN
0-02-722830-4 DDC 785.42/092/4 B 92 19
ML3930.A75 C67 1985
NYPL [Sc D 86-229]

Frankl, Ron. Duke Ellington /. New York ,
c1988. 110 p. : ISBN 1-555-46584-6 DDC
785.42/092/4 B 92 19
ML410.E44 F7 1988   **NYPL [Sc E 88-381]**

Tanenhaus, Sam. Louis Armstrong /. New
York , c1989. 127 p. : ISBN 1-555-46571-4
DDC 785.42/092/4 B 92 19
ML3930.A75 T3 1989   **NYPL [Sc E 89-170]**

**JAZZ MUSICIANS - UNITED STATES -
BIOGRAPHY - PICTORIAL WORKS.**
Giddens, Gary. Satchmo /. New York , 1988.
239 p. : ISBN 0-385-24428-2 : DDC 785.42/092/4
B 19
ML410.A75 G5 1988   **NYPL [Sc F 89-73]**

**JAZZ MUSICIANS - UNITED STATES -
PORTRAITS.**
Alexander, Jim. Duke and other legends .
Atlanta, GA. , c1988. 63 p. : ISBN
0-945708-03-3   **NYPL [Sc E 89-63]**

Jazz odyssey . Darensbourg, Joe, 1906-1985.
[Telling it like it was.] Baton Rouge , 1988,
c1987. vi, 231 p., [32] p. of plates : ISBN
0-8071-1442-1 : DDC 788/.62/0924 B 19
ML419.D35 A3 1988   **NYPL [Sc E 89-28]**

Jazz on record . Priestley, Brian, 1946- London ,
1988. vi, 225 p., [8] leaves of plates : ISBN
0-241-12440-9   **NYPL [Sc D 88-1335]**

Jazz photographs. Alexander, Jim. Duke and
other legends . Atlanta, GA. , c1988. 63 p. :
ISBN 0-945708-03-3   **NYPL [Sc E 89-63]**

Jazz portraits . Lyons, Leonard. New York ,
c1989. 610 p. : ISBN 0-688-04946-X DDC
785.42/092/2 B 19
ML394 .L97 1989   **NYPL [Sc E 89-91]**

Jazz records, 1897-1942 /. Rust, Brian A. L.,
1922- Chigwell, Essex [1982?] 2 v. ; ISBN

0-902391-04-6 (set)
NYPL [*R-Phono 84-254]

The jazz revolution . Ogren, Kathy J. New
York , 1989. vii, 221 p., [8] p. of plates : ISBN
0-19-505153-X (alk. paper) DDC 781/.57/0973
19
ML3508 .O37 1987   **NYPL [Sc D 89-451]**

Jazz styles . Gridley, Mark C., 1947- Englewood
Cliffs, N.J. , 1988. xviii, 445 p. : ISBN
0-13-509217-5 DDC 785.42 19
ML3506 .G74 1987   **NYPL [Sc E 88-159]**

Jean-Baptiste, Chavannes. Té-a sé kód lonbret
nou. Prémie pati : Konnin tè ou / Chavannes
Jean-Baptiste. 2e éd. [Port-au-Prince, Haiti?] :
Bon nouvel, [1978?] 63 p. : ill. ; 22 cm.
*1. Creole dialects, French - Haiti - Texts. I. Title. II.
Title: Konnin tè ou.*   **NYPL [Sc D 87-1404]**

Jean, Rodrigue. Haiti, crise de l'education et crise
du développement / Rodrigue Jean.
Port-au-Prince, Haiti : Imprimerie des Antilles,
1988. 152 p. ; 21 cm. Bibliography: p. 149-[154]
ISBN 0-948390-00-X
*1. Education - Economic aspects - Haiti. 2. Politics and
education - Haiti. I. Title.*   **NYPL [Sc D 88-914]**

Jean Toomer : a critical evaluation / edited by
Therman B. O'Daniel. Washington, D.C. :
Howard University Press, c1988. xxi, 557 p. :
port. ; 25 cm. Includes index. Bibliography: p.
505-528. ISBN 0-88258-111-2 : DDC 813/.52 19
*1. Toomer, Jean, 1894-1967 - Criticism and
interpretation. I. O'Daniel, Therman B., 1908-.*
PS3539.O478 Z68 1988
NYPL [Sc E 89-231]

**Jean Toomer's life search for identity as realized
in Cane [microform]** /. Shaw, Brenda Joyce.
1975. 169 leaves. **NYPL [Sc Micro R-4219]**

The Jeep. Leicester [Eng.] : Brown Watson ;
Montreal Canada : Montbec, [195-?] [8] p. :
col. ill. ; 16 x 23 cm. ("Wheely" Collection) Cover
consists of a picture of a jeep, with two plastic wheels
attached. SCHOMBURG CHILDREN'S
COLLECTION.
*1. Africa - Juvenile fiction. I. Schomburg Children's
Collection. II. Title.*   **NYPL [Sc C 88-325]**

Jegede, Dele, 1945- Paradise battered / Dele
Jegede. Lagos : Federal Department of Culture
and Archives : Centre for Cultural Studies
University of Lagos, 1986. 48 p. : hiefly ill. ;
"Catalogue of an exhibition of paintings and drawings
co-sponsored by the Federal Department of Culture and
Archives, and the centre for Cultural Studies,
University of Lagos, July 4-18, 1986.
*1. Drawings - Nigeria - Exhibitions - Catalogs. 2.
Painting - Nigeria - Exhibitions - Catalogs. I. Title.*
NYPL [Sc B 88-20]

Jegede, Tunde. Chester, Galina. The silenced
voice . London , 1987. 47 p. : ISBN
0-9512093-0-2 :   **NYPL [Sc D 89-519]**

JEKRI (AFRICAN PEOPLE) - HISTORY.
Ayomike, J. O. S. A history of Warri /. Benin
City , 1988. xiii, 198 p. :
NYPL [Sc D 88-1370]

Jenkins, Adelbert H. The psychology of the
Afro-American : a humanistic approach /
Adelbert H. Jenkins. New York : Pergamon
Press, 1982. xix, 213 p. ; 24 cm. (Pergamon
general psychology series. v. 103) Includes index.
Bibliography: p. 187-198. ISBN 0-08-027206-1 DDC
155.8/496073 19
1. Afro-Americans - Psychology. I. Title.
E185.625 .J47 1982   **NYPL [Sc D 88-718]**

**JENKINS, EDMUND THORNTON, 1894-
1926.**
Green, Jeffrey P. Edmund Thornton Jenkins .
Westport, Conn. , 1982. xii, 213 p. : ISBN
0-313-23253-9 (lib. bdg.) DDC 780/.92/4 B 19
ML410.J44 G7 1982   **NYPL [Sc D 86-413]**

Jenkins, Shirley. Ethnic associations and the
welfare state . New York , 1988. x, 299 p. :
ISBN 0-231-05690-7 DDC 362.8 19
HV4005 .E86 1988   **NYPL [JLE 88-3846]**

Jennings, Chris, 1954- Understanding and
preventing AIDS : a book for everyone / by
Chris Jennings.2nd ed. Cambridge, MA (P.O.
Box 2060, Cambridge 02238-2060) : Health
Alert Press, c1988. 230 p. : ill. ; 26 cm. Includes
index. ISBN 0-936571-01-2
1. AIDS (Disease) - Popular works. I. Title.
NYPL [Sc F 88-239]

Jennings, Jerry E. (joint author) Allen, William
Dangaix, 1904- Africa. Grand Rapids [c1972]
172, 20 p. DDC 916
DT5 .A53 1972 *NYPL [Sc F 88-377]*

Jennings, Lawrence C. French reaction to British
slave emancipation / Lawrence C. Jennings.
Baton Rouge : Louisiana State University Press,
c1988. ix, 228 p. ; 24 cm. Includes index.
Bibliography: p. 209-220. ISBN 0-8071-1429-4 (alk.
paper) DDC 306/.362/0942 19
*1. Slavery - Great Britain - Emancipation - Public
opinion. 2. Public opinion - France. I. Title.*
HT1163 .J46 1988 *NYPL [Sc E 89-139]*

Jensen, Virginia Allen. Sara and the door /
Virginia Allen Jensen ; drawings by Ann
Strugnell. Reading, Mass. : Addison-Wesley,
c1977. [32] p. : ill. ; 16 x 16 cm. While trying to
free herself from the front door, Sara learns about
buttons. SCHOMBURG CHILDREN'S
COLLECTION. ISBN 0-201-03446-8 DDC [E]
*1. Children's stories, American. 2. Afro-American
children - Juvenile fiction. I. Strugnell, Ann. II.
Schomburg Children's Collection. III. Title.*
PZ8.3.J425 Sar *NYPL [Sc B 89-17]*

Jesse, Charles. Peeps into St. Lucia's past / by
Charles Jesse ; broadcast by Winville King,
Radio St. Lucia, February 1979 ; prepared for
broadcast by the Extra-Mural Department of
the University of the West Indies, St. Lucia. St.
Lucia : The Art Printery, 1979. 100 p. :
facsims. ; 24 cm.
1. Saint Lucia - History. I. King, C. Winville. II. Title.
NYPL [Sc E 88-311]

Jesse Jackson & the politics of charisma . House,
Ernest R. Boulder , 1988. xi, 196 p. ; ISBN
0-8133-0767-8 (alk. paper) DDC 973.92/092/4
19
E840.8.J35 H68 1988 *NYPL [JFE 88-7205]*

Jesse Jackson and the politics of charisma.
House, Ernest R. Jesse Jackson & the politics
of charisma . Boulder , 1988. xi, 196 p. ;
0-8133-0767-8 (alk. paper) DDC 973.92/092/4
19
E840.8.J35 H68 1988 *NYPL [JFE 88-7205]*

Jesse Jackson's campaign . Cavanagh, Thomas E.
Washington, D.C. , 1984. 27 p., [1] ; ISBN
0-941410-45-5 (pbk.) DDC 324.973 19
JK526 1984c *NYPL [Sc F 87-172 rept. 2]*

Jésuite en Afrique [microform] : pour dieu et les
hommes. Douala [Cameroon] : Collège
Libermann, 1982 43 p. : ill., maps ; 21 cm.
Cover title. Microfilm. New York: New York Public
Library, 1984. 1 microfilm reel; 35 mm. (MN
*ZZ-24498)
*1. Loyola, Ignacio de, Saint, 1491-1556. 2. Jesuits -
Africa. 3. Jesuits - History.*
NYPL [Sc Micro R-4135 no.10]

JESUITS - AFRICA.
Jésuite en Afrique [microform] . Douala
[Cameroon] , 19. 43 p. :
NYPL [Sc Micro R-4135 no.10]

JESUITS - HISTORY.
Jésuite en Afrique [microform] . Douala
[Cameroon] , 19. 43 p. :
NYPL [Sc Micro R-4135 no.10]

JESUITS - MISSIONS.
Sandoval, Alonso dc, 1576-1652. Naturaleza,
policia sagrada i profana, costumbres i ritos,
disciplina i catechismo evangelico de todos
etiopes /. En Sevilla , 1627. [23], 334 p., 81
leaves ; *NYPL [Sc Rare F 82-70]*

Jesus and Fat Tuesday. McElroy, Colleen J.
Berkeley, Calif. , c1987. 202 p. ; ISBN
0-88739-023-4 (pbk.) *NYPL [Sc D 88-586]*

Jesus Christ - Biography - Drama. see Jesus
Christ - Drama.

JESUS CHRIST - DRAMA.
Lee, Easton. The rope and the cross . Kingston,
Jamaica , 1985. 48 p., [4] p. of plates :
NYPL [Sc D 89-458]

JESUS CHRIST IN ISLAM. see JESUS
CHRIST - ISLAMIC
INTERPRETATIONS.

Jesus Christ - Interpretations, Islamic. see Jesus
Christ - Islamic interpretations.

**JESUS CHRIST - ISLAMIC
INTERPRETATIONS.**
'Isá 'Abd Allāh Muḥammad al-Mahdī, 1945-
Was Christ really crucified? [microform] /.

Brooklyn, N.Y. [1980] 72 p. :
NYPL [Sc Micro R-4114 no. 6]
People call him the Son of God [microform]
Brooklyn [197-?] 11 p. :
NYPL [Sc Micro R-4114 no. 20]

Jesus Christ - Mohammedan interpretations. see
Jesus Christ - Islamic interpretations.

Jesus Christ - Muslim interpretations. see Jesus
Christ - Islamic interpretations.

Jesus Christ - Nativity - Drama. see Jesus
Christ - Drama.

Jesus Christ - Passion - Drama. see Jesus Christ -
Drama; Passion-plays.

JESUS CHRIST - PERSON AND OFFICES.
Nyamiti, Charles. Christ as our ancestor .
Gweru [Zimbabwe] , 1984. 151 p. ; DDC 232
19
BT205 .N82 1984 *NYPL [Sc D 88-986]*

Jesus, Society of. see Jesuits.

Le jeu des maitres . El Mahdi, El Tayeb. Paris ,
1988. 69 p. ; ISBN 2-85802-794-3
NYPL [Sc D 89-466]

Jeunes intellectuels en recherche : propos /
recueillis par Raymond Deniel.2e éd. Abidjan :
INADES-edition, c1982. 67 p. : maps ; 21 cm.
(Chemins de chrétiens africains . 1)
*1. Christianity - Ivory Coast. 2. Youth - Religious life.
I. Deniel, Raymond. II. Series.*
NYPL [Sc D 88-925]

**Jeunesse, tradition et développement en Afrique.
Spanish.** Juventud, tradición y desarrollo en
Africa : reunión regional africana sobre la
juventud, Nairobi (Kenya), 17-22 de diciembre
de 1979. 1a ed. Barcelona : Serbal ; Paris :
Unesco, 1982. 148 p. ; 21 cm. (Colección de
temas africanos . 4) Translation of: Jeunesse, tradition
et développement en Afrique. Conference organized by
Unesco. Includes bibliographies. ISBN 84-85800-29-X
*1. Youth - Africa, Sub-Saharan - Congresses. I. Unesco.
II. Title. III. Series.* *NYPL [Sc D 88-592]*

Jewell, K. Sue. Survival of the Black family : the
institutional impact of U. S. social policy / K.
Sue Jewell. New York : Praeger, 1988. x, 197
p. : ill. ; 25 cm. Includes index. Bibliography: p.
[181]-188. ISBN 0-275-92985-X (alk. paper) DDC
306.8/5/08996073 19
1. Family policy - United States. I. Title.
HQ536 .J48 1988 *NYPL [Sc E 89-153]*

JEWISH-AFRO-AMERICAN RELATIONS. see
AFRO-AMERICANS - RELATIONS WITH
JEWS.

JEWISH CONVERTS. see PROSELYTES AND
PROSELYTING, JEWISH.

**JEWISH PROSELYTES AND
PROSELYTING.** see PROSELYTES AND
PROSELYTING, JEWISH.

**JEWISH WIT AND HUMOR - HISTORY
AND CRITICISM.**
Harap, Louis. Dramatic encounters . New
York , c1987. xiv, 177 p. ; ISBN 0-313-25388-9
(lib. bdg. : alk. paper) DDC 810/.9/35203924 19
PS173.J4 H294 1987 *NYPL [*PZB 87-5243]*

JEWISH WOMEN. see WOMEN, JEWISH.

JEWS - ETHIOPIA - PERSECUTIONS.
Avraham, Shmuel, 1945- Treacherous journey .
New York, NY , 1986. xii, 178 p. : ISBN
0-933503-46-6 (jacket); 0-933503-46-5 : DDC
963/.004924 19
DS135.E75 A93 1986 *NYPL [Sc E 87-275]*

JEWS IN LITERATURE - UNITED STATES.
Harap, Louis. Dramatic encounters . New
York , c1987. xiv, 177 p. ; ISBN 0-313-25388-9
(lib. bdg. : alk. paper) DDC 810/.9/35203924 19
PS173.J4 H294 1987 *NYPL [*PZB 87-5243]*

JEWS - LOST TRIBES. see LOST TRIBES OF
ISRAEL.

JEWS - MISSIONS. see PROSELYTES AND
PROSELYTING, JEWISH.

**JEWS - RELATIONS WITH AFRO-
AMERICANS.** see AFRO-AMERICANS -
RELATIONS WITH JEWS.

**JEWS - SOUTH AFRICA -
JOHANNESBURG - FICTION.**
Zwi, Rose. Another year in Africa /.
Johannesburg , c1980. 172 p. ; ISBN
0-86975-316-9 *NYPL [Sc D 88-1328]*

JEWS - TEN LOST TRIBES. see LOST
TRIBES OF ISRAEL.

JEWS - UNITED STATES - CONGRESSES.
National Conference on African
American/Jewish American Relations (1983 :
Savannah State College) Blacks and Jews .
[Savannah, Ga.] [1983] iii, 192 p. ;
NYPL [Sc D 88-335]

JEWS - WOMEN. see WOMEN, JEWISH.

JEWS - ZIMBABWE - HISTORY.
Kosmin, Barry Alexander. Majuta . Gwelo,
Zimbabwe , c1980. xii, 223 p., [32] p. of
plates : *NYPL [Sc D 82-130]*

J.F. Odunjo memorial lectures series .
(no. 1) Bamgbose, Ayo. Yoruba . Lagos,
Nigeria , 1986. xvii, 83 p. ;
NYPL [Sc D 88-1091]

Jibrin, Sani A. Africa must be free / by Sani A.
Jibrin. Kano State, Nigeria : ASAJ Educational
Pub. Co., 1987. x, 48 p. : ill. ; 21 cm.
*1. National liberation movements - South Africa -
Poetry. I. Title.* *NYPL [Sc C 88-302]*

JIHAD.
Ḥājj 'Umar ibn Sa'īd al-Fūtī, 1794?-1864.
[Bayān mā waqa'a. French & Arabic.] Voilà ce
qui est arrivé . Paris , 1983. 261 p., [57] p. of
plates ; ISBN 2-222-03216-4
NYPL [Sc F 88-211]
'Isá 'Abd Allāh Muḥammad al-Mahdī, 1945-
Holy war [microform] /. Brooklyn, N.Y. ,
c1979. 68 p. :
NYPL [Sc Micro R-4114 no. 8]

Jik dèyè do Bondyé /. Confiant, Raphaël.
[Port-au-Prince? , 1978?] 64 p. :
NYPL [Sc D 88-694]

Jikong, Stephen Yeriwa. I did so swear, but -- /
by Jikong Stephen Yeriwa. Yaoundé : CEPER,
1985. 48 p. ; 17 cm. A play. Cover title.
I. Title. *NYPL [Sc B 88-56]*

Jiménez, Blas R.
Caribe africano en despertar : versos del negro
Blas III / no escritor: Blas R. Jiménez. Santo
Domingo, R.D. : Nuevas Rutas, 1984. 89. ; 21
cm. (Colección Cimarrones . no. 1) Poems.
NYPL [Sc D 88-502]
Exigencias de un cimarrón (en suenos) versos
del negro Blas III / Blas R. Jiménez. Santo
Domingo, Republica Dominicana : Taller, 1987.
113 p. : ill. ; 21 cm. (Colección Cimarrones . no. 2)
I. Title. *NYPL [Sc D 87-1395]*

Jimerson, Randall C. The private Civil War :
popular feeling during the sectional conflict /
Randall C. Jimerson. Baton Rouge, LA :
Louisiana State University Press, 1988. xiv, 270
p., [8] p. of plates : ill. ; 24 cm. Includes index.
Bibliography: p. [253]-263. ISBN 0-8071-1454-5 (alk.
paper) : DDC 973.7 19
*1. United States - History - Civil War, 1861-1865 -
Public opinion. 2. United States - History - Civil War,
1861-1865 - Social aspects. I. Title.*
E468.9 .J55 1988 *NYPL [IKI 89-2276]*

Jimmy and Joe fly a kite. Glendinning, Sally.
Champaign, Ill. [1970] 38 p. ISBN 0-8116-4704-8
DDC [Fic]
PZ7.G4829 Jm *NYPL [Sc D 88-1475]*

Jimmy and Joe look for a bear. Glendinning,
Sally. Champaign, Ill., 1970. 40 p. ISBN
0-8116-4703-X DDC [E]
PZ7.G4829 Jo *NYPL [Sc D 88-1456]*

Jimmy and Joe meet a Halloween witch.
Glendinning, Sally. Champaign, Ill. [1971] 40 p.
ISBN 0-8116-4705-6 DDC [E]
PZ7.G4829 Jq *NYPL [Sc D 88-1474]*

The Jimmy Brown story /. Terzian, James P.
New York , c1964. 190 p. :
NYPL [Sc D 89-432]

Jinadu, Adele. Idealism and pragmatism as
aspects of Sweden's development policy in
Africa / L. Adele Jinadu. Lagos : Nigerian
Institute of International Affairs, [1982?]. 107
p. ; 22 cm. (Monograph series) Includes
bibliographical references. ISBN 978-227-698-7
*1. Economic assistance, Swedish - Africa. 2. Sweden -
Relations - Africa. 3. Africa - Relations - Sweden. I.
Series: NIIA monograph series. II. Title.*
NYPL [Sc D 88-355]

JIRI, JAIROS DAMBGWA.
Farquhar, June. Jairos Jiri . Gweru , 1987. 92
p. : ISBN 0-86922-416-6 *NYPL [Sc D 89-38]*

JO LUO (AFRICAN PEOPLE) see **LUO
(AFRICAN PEOPLE)**

JOB DISCRIMINATION. see
DISCRIMINATION IN EMPLOYMENT.

JOB SATISFACTION.
Malone, Beverly Louise. Relationship of Black
female administrators' mentoring experience and
career satisfaction [Microform] /. 1982. 165
leaves.   *NYPL [Sc Micro R-4804]*

JOB TRAINING. see **OCCUPATIONAL
TRAINING.**

JOBS. see **PROFESSIONS.**

Jobs and Skills Programme for Africa.
Livingstone, Ian. Youth employment & youth
employment programmes in Africa . Addis
Ababa , 1986. 9 v. : ISBN 92-2-105527-2 (pbk. :
v. 1) DDC 331.3/4/096 19
HD6276.A32 L58 1986 *NYPL [Sc F 88-313]*

**JOBS AND SKILLS PROGRAMME FOR
AFRICA.**
The Challenge of employment and basic needs
in Africa . Nairobi , New York , 1986. xii, 379
p. ; ISBN 0-19-572559-X *NYPL [Sc E 88-419]*

Jobs in business and office. Haskins, James, 1941-
New York [1974] 96 p. ISBN 0-688-75011-7
DDC 651/.023
HF5381.2 .H38   *NYPL [Sc E 89-16]*

Jockers, Heinz. Gundu, Gabriel A. Tiv
bibliography /. Makurdi, Nigeria , 1985. xxvii,
72 p. :   *NYPL [Sc E 88-537]*

**JOCKEYS - UNITED STATES - JUVENILE
FICTION.**
Gates, Doris, 1901- Little Vic /. New York ,
1951. 160 p. :   *NYPL [Sc D 88-430]*

Joe, Kingston Saa P. The Effects of the Western
culture on the traditional cultures of Lofa
County [microform] . [Monrovia , 1977] 24 p. ;
          NYPL [Sc Micro F-10952]

Joe Louis . Barrow, Joe Louis. New York ,
c1988. xvii, 270 p., [8] leaves of plates : ISBN
0-07-003955-0 : DDC 796.8/3/0924 B 19
GV1132.L6 B37 1988 *NYPL [Sc E 88-566]*

**Johannesburg. South African Institute of Race
Relations.** see **South African Institute of
Race Relations.**

John, A. Meredith. The plantation slaves of
Trinidad, 1783-1816 : a mathematical and
demographic enquiry / A. Meredith John.
Cambridge [Eng.] ; New York : Cambridge
University Press, 1988. xvi, 259 p. : ill. ; 24 cm.
Includes index. Bibliography: p. 243-254. ISBN
0-521-36166-4 DDC 306/.362/0972983 19
1. Slavery - Trinidad - History - 18th century. 2.
Fertility, Human - Trinidad - History - 18th century. 3.
Mortality - Trinidad - History - 18th century. 4.
Trinidad - Population - History - 18th century. 5.
Trinidad - Statistics, Vital - History - 18th century. I.
Title.
HT1105.T6 J65 1988 *NYPL [Sc E 89-235]*

John Anderson . Teatero, William, 1953-
[Kingston, Ont.] , c1986. 183 p. : ISBN
0-9692685-0-5 : DDC 345.71/056/0924 19
          NYPL [Sc E 89-113]

John Brown /. Nolan, Jeanette Covert, 1896-
New York , 1968, c1950. 181 p. :
          NYPL [Sc D 88-665]

John Carter Brown Library. Brown, Larissa V.
Africans in the New World, 1493-1834 .
Providence, Rhode Island , 1988. 61 p. : ISBN
0-916617-31-9 *NYPL [Sc D 88-624]*

John, Elerius Edet. Topics in African literature /
by Elerius Edet John. Lagos : Paico, 1986. 3
v. ; 21 cm. Includes bibliographies. CONTENTS. - v.
1. Creative responses of Mongo Beti and Ferdinand
Oyono to historical realities in Cameroun -- v. 2. The
rise of the Camerounian novel in French -- v. 3.
Literature and development, the West African
experience. ISBN 978-244-610-6 (v. 1)
1. Beti, Mongo, 1932-. 2. Oyono, Ferdinand, 1929-. 3.
African literature - History and criticism. 4. Cameroon
literature (French) - History and criticism. I. Title.
          NYPL [Sc D 89-370]

John Garang speaks /. Garang, John, 1945-
London , New York , 1987. xii, 147 p. ; ISBN
0-7103-0268-1 *NYPL [Sc D 88-418]*

**John Mercer Langston and the fight for Black
freedom, 1829-65 /.** Cheek, William F., 1933-
Urbana , c1989. 478 p. ; ISBN 0-252-01550-9
(alk. paper) DDC 973/.0496073/0924 B 19
E185.97.L27 C48 1989 *NYPL [Sc E 89-255]*

John Newton, letters of a slave trader /. Bohrer,
Dick. Chicago , c1983. viii, 130 p. ; ISBN
0-8024-0158-9 (pbk.) DDC 283/.3 19
BX5199.N55 B64 1983 *NYPL [Sc C 88-235]*

Johnny/Bingo. Norton, Browning, 1909- New
York [1971] 185 p. DDC [Fic]
PZ7.N8217 Jo   *NYPL [Sc D 88-1420]*

Johnny, Michael. Informal credit for integrated
rural development in Sierra Leone / Michael
Johnny. Hamburg : Verlag Weltarchiv, 1985.
xviii, 212 p. : ill. ; 21 cm. (Studien zur integrierten
ländlichen Entwicklung, 0177-2503 . 6) Bibliography: p.
199-212. ISBN 3-87895-274-X (pbk.)
1. Agricultural credit - Sierra Leone. 2. Rural
development projects - Sierra Leone. 3. Sierra Leone -
Economic conditions. I. Title. II. Series.
HG2146.5.S5 J63x 1985
          NYPL [Sc D 88-766]

Johnson, A. E. (Amelia E.), b. 1859.
Clarence and Corinne, or, God's way / Mrs.
A.E. Johnson ; with an introduction by
Hortense J. Spillers. New York : Oxford
University Press, 1988. xxxviii, 187 p. : ill. ; 17
cm. (The Schomburg library of nineteenth-century
Black women writers) Includes bibliographical
references. Reprint. Originally published : Philadelphia :
American Baptist Publication Society, c1890. ISBN
0-19-505264-1 (alk. paper) DDC 813/.4 19
1. Title. II. Title: Clarence and Corinne. III. Title: God's
way. IV. Series.
PS2134.J515 C5 1988 *NYPL [JFC 88-2145]*

The Hazeley family / Mrs. A.E. Johnson ; with
an introduction by Barbara Christian. New
York : Oxford University Press, 1988. xxxvii,
191 p. : ill. ; 17 cm. (The Schomburg library of
nineteenth-century Black women writers) Reprint.
Originally published: Philadelphia : American Babtist
Publication Society, c1894. ISBN 0-19-505257-9 (alk.
paper) DDC 813/.4 19
1. Title. II. Series.
PS2134.J515 H39 1988
          NYPL [JFC 88-2196]

Johnson, Amryl. Sequins for a ragged hem. / by
Amril Johnson. London : Virago, c1988. 272
p. ; 20 cm. ISBN 0-86068-971-9
1. Caribbean Area - Description and travel - 1981-. I.
Title.   *NYPL [Sc D 88-612]*

Johnson, Amy. (ill) Ferris, Jeri. What are you
figuring now? . Minneapolis , c1988. 64 p. :
ISBN 0-87614-331-1 (lib. bdg.) : DDC 520.92/4
B 92 19
QB36.B22 F47 1988 *NYPL [Sc D 89-120]*

**JOHNSON, ANDREW, 1808-1875 - VIEWS
ON AFRO-AMERICANS.**
Bowen, David Warren, 1944- Andrew Johnson
and the Negro /. Knoxville , c1989. xvi, 206
p. ; ISBN 0-87049-584-4 (alk. paper) DDC
973/.0496073 19
E667 .B65 1989 *NYPL [Sc D 89-508]*

Johnson, Angela. Tell me a story, Mama / by
Angela Johnson ; pictures by David Soman.
New York : Orchard Books, c1989. [32] p. :
col. ill. ; 24 cm. "A Richard Jackson book." A young
girl and her mother remember together all the girl's
favorite stories about her mother's childhood.
SCHOMBURG CHILDREN'S COLLECTION. ISBN
0-531-05794-1 : DDC [E] 19
1. Mothers and daughters - Juvenile fiction. I. Soman,
David, ill. II. Schomburg Children's Collection. III.
Title.
PZ7.J629 Te 1988 *NYPL [Sc F 89-109]*

Johnson, Avery F. Kalibala, E. Balintuma.
Wakaima and the clay man . New York , 1946.
145 p. :   *NYPL [Sc D 89-486]*

Johnson, Bonnie Helene.
(illus) Glasser, Barbara. Bongo Bradley. New
York [1973] 153 p. DDC [Fic]
PZ7.G48143 Bo   *NYPL [Sc D 89-99]*

(illus) Walter, Mildred Pitts. Lillie of Watts
takes a giant step. Garden City, N.Y. [1971]
187 p. DDC [Fic]
PZ7.W17125 Lk   *NYPL [Sc D 88-1119]*

Johnson, Charles Spurgeon, 1893-1956.
Bitter Canaan : the story of the Negro republic
/ Charles S. Johnson ; introductory essay by

John Stanfield. New Brunswick, N.J. :
Transaction Books, c1987. lxxiii, 256 p. ; 24
cm. (Black classics of social science) Includes index.
Bibliography: p. 243-247. ISBN 0-88738-053-0 :
DDC 966.6/2 19
1. Afro-Americans - Colonization - Liberia. 2. Liberia -
History. 3. Liberia - Relations - United States. 4.
United States - Relations - Liberia. 5. Liberia -
Economic conditions. 6. Liberia - Social conditions. I.
Title. II. Series.
DT631 .J59 1987 *NYPL [Sc E 88-351]*

Ebony and topaz . New York , 1927. 164 p. :
          NYPL [Sc Rare F 82-72]

Johnson, Deborah J. (Deborah Jean), 1958-
Visible now . New York , 1988. xvi, 344 p. ;
ISBN 0-313-25926-7 (lib. bdg. : alk. paper) DDC
371/.02/0973 19
LC2761 .V57 1988 *NYPL [Sc E 98-257]*

Johnson, Douglas Hamilton, 1949- The Ecology
of survival . London, England , Boulder, Colo. ,
1988. xii, 339 p. ; ISBN 0-8133-0727-9 (Westview)
DDC 304.2/096 19
GF720 .E26 1988 *NYPL [Sc D 89-280]*

Johnson, E. Harper.
(illus) Fisher, Aileen Lucia, 1906- A lantern in
the window /. Eau Claire, Wisconsin [1962]
126 p. :   *NYPL [Sc D 88-434]*

Lindquist, Willis. The red drum's warning /.
New York , 1958. 128 p. :
          NYPL [Sc D 88-662]

**Johnson, Edward A. (Edward Augustus), 1860-
1944.** A school history of the Negro race in
America from 1619 to 1890 : with a short
introduction as to the origin of the race : also a
short sketch of Liberia / by Edward A.
Johnson.Rev.ed. Chicago : W.B. Conkey , 1894.
200 p. : ill., ports. ; 21 cm. Includes index.
1. Afro-Americans - History. 2. Black race. I. Title.
          NYPL [Sc Rare F 88-9]

Johnson, Edward Augustus, 1860-1944. Light
ahead for the Negro / by E. A. Johnson. New
York : Grafton Press, 1904. vi, 132 p. ; 20 cm.
1. United States - Race relations. I. Title.
          NYPL [Sc Rare C 88-6]

Johnson, Eric W. The stolen ruler, by Eric W.
Johnson. Illustrated by June Goldsborough. [1st
ed.] Philadelphia, Lippincott [1970] 64 p. illus.
21 cm. When Claude is accused of stealing his own
ruler, he collects testimony and evidence to prove his
innocence. SCHOMBURG CHILDREN'S
COLLECTION. DDC [Fic]
1. Afro-American children - Juvenile fiction. I.
Goldsborough, June, illus. II. Schomburg Children's
Collection. III. Title.
PZ7.J631765 St   *NYPL [Sc D 88-1114]*

**JOHNSON, GEORGIA DOUGLAS CAMP,
1886-1966 - CRITICISM AND
INTERPRETATION.**
Hull, Gloria T. Color, sex, and poetry .
Bloomington , c1987. xi, 240 p. : ISBN
0-253-34974-5 DDC 811/.52/099287 19
PS153.N5 H84 1987 *NYPL [Sc E 88-72]*

Johnson, Glenderlyn. Black American pioneers :
stamped on history / Glenderlyn Johnson and
Howard E. Fischer. New York, N.Y. : Venture
Pub. Co., c1987. ii, 22 p. : ill. ; 22 cm. On cover:
Profiles of twenty Black Americans on United States
postage stamps. Includes bibliographical references.
1. Postage-stamps - United States. 2. Postage-stamps -
Topics - Afro-Americans. I. Fischer, Howard E. II.
Title.   *NYPL [Sc D 88-1284]*

Johnson, Hayden C. The Fighting 99th Air
Squadron, 1941-45 / Hayden C.Johnson. 1st ed.
New York : Vantage Press, c1987. 49 p. : ill. ;
21 cm. ISBN 0-533-06879-7 : DDC 940.54/4973
19
1. Johnson, Hayden C. 2. United States. Army Air
Forces. Fighter Squadron, 99th - History. 3. United
States. Army Air Forces - Biography. 4. World War,
1939-1945 - Aerial operations, American. 5.
Afro-American pilots - Biography. I. Title.
D790 .J57 1987 *NYPL [Sc D 88-1192]*

JOHNSON, HAYDEN C.
Johnson, Hayden C. The Fighting 99th Air
Squadron, 1941-45 /. New York , c1987. 49
p. : ISBN 0-533-06879-7 : DDC 940.54/4973 19
D790 .J57 1987 *NYPL [Sc D 88-1192]*

**JOHNSON, JAMES P. (JAMES PRICE), 1894-
1955.**
Brown, Scott E., 1960- James P. Johnson .

Metuchen, N.J. , 1986. viii, 500 p., [12] p. of plates : ISBN 0-8108-1887-6 DDC 786.1/092/4 B 19
ML417.J62 B76 1986 NYPL [Sc D 88-1435]

JOHNSON, JAMES P. (JAMES PRICE), 1894-1955 - DISCOGRAPHY.
Brown, Scott E., 1960- James P. Johnson . Metuchen, N.J. , 1986. viii, 500 p., [12] p. of plates : ISBN 0-8108-1887-6 DDC 786.1/092/4 B 19
ML417.J62 B76 1986 NYPL [Sc D 88-1435]

Johnson, James Weldon, 1871-1938.
Along this way : the autobiography of James Weldon Johnson. New York : Viking Press, 1933. 418 p., [16] leaves of plates : ill., ports., 25 cm. Includes bibliographical references and index. Author's autographed presentation copy to Regina M. Anderson Andrews.
1. Johnson, James Weldon, 1871-1938. 2. Authors, American - 20th century - Biography. 3. Afro-American authors - Biography. 4. Civil rights workers - United States - Biography. I. Title.
NYPL [Sc Rare F 89-9]

JOHNSON, JAMES WELDON, 1871-1938.
Johnson, James Weldon, 1871-1938. Along this way . New York , 1933. 418 p., [16] leaves of plates : *NYPL [Sc Rare F 89-9]*

JOHNSON, JAMES WELDON, 1871-1938 - BIOGRAPHY - JUVENILE LITERATURE.
Tolbert-Rouchaleau, Jane. James Weldon Johnson /. New York , c1988. 110 p. : ISBN 1-555-46596-X DDC 818/.5209 B 92 19
PS3519.O2625 Z894 1988
NYPL [Sc E 88-164]

Johnson, Louise A. (ed) The People of East Harlem [microform] . New York , c1974. 90 p. : *NYPL [Sc Micro R-4137 no.12]*

Johnson, Lyman T., 1906- The rest of the dream : the Black odyssey of Lyman Johnson / [edited by] Wade Hall. Lexington, Ky. : University Press of Kentucky, c1988. xiv, 230 p., [8] p. of plates : ill., ports. ; 24 cm. Oral autobiography based on interviews from 1979 to 1987. Includes index. ISBN 0-8131-1674-0 (alk. paper) : DDC 976.9/00496073024 B 19
1. Johnson, Lyman T., 1906-. 2. Afro-Americans - Kentucky - Biography. 3. Civil rights workers - Kentucky - Biography. 4. Afro-Americans - Civil rights - Kentucky. 5. Kentucky - Race relations. I. Hall, Wade H. II. Title.
E185.97.J693 A3 1988 NYPL [Sc E 89-211]

JOHNSON, LYMAN T., 1906-
Johnson, Lyman T., 1906- The rest of the dream . Lexington, Ky. , c1988. xiv, 230 p., [8] p. of plates : ISBN 0-8131-1674-0 (alk. paper) : DDC 976.9/00496073024 B 19
E185.97.J693 A3 1988 NYPL [Sc E 89-211]

Johnson, MayLee. Coming up on the rough side : a Black Catholic story / Maylee Johnson with Anne Barsanti. South Orange, N.J. : PILLAR Books, c1988. vii, 88 p. ; 22 cm. ISBN 0-944734-01-4
1. Johnson, MayLee. 2. Afro-American women - Biography. 3. Afro-American Catholics - Biography. I. Barsanti, Anne. II. Title. NYPL [Sc D 89-190]

JOHNSON, MAYLEE.
Johnson, MayLee. Coming up on the rough side . South Orange, N.J. , c1988. vii, 88 p. ; ISBN 0-944734-01-4 *NYPL [Sc D 89-190]*

Johnson, Phyllis. Frontline Southern Africa . New York , 1988. xxxv, 530 p., [16] p. of leaves : ISBN 0-941423-08-5 : DDC 322/.5/0968 19
DT747.S6 F76 1988 NYPL [JLE 89-595]

Martin, David, 1936- The Chitepo assassination /. Harare, Zimbabwe , 1985. 134 p., [8] p. of plates : ISBN 0-949225-04-5
NYPL [Sc D 88-1244]

Johnson, Randal, 1948- Brazilian cinema /. Austin , 1988. 373 p. : ISBN 0-292-70767-3
NYPL [Sc E 89-59]

Johnson, Rotimi. Perspectives on creative writing / Rotimi Johnson. Yaba : Dominion, 1986, c1985. 85 p. ; 20 cm. Includes bibliographical references.
1. Creative writing - Study and teaching. I. Title.
NYPL [Sc C 88-241]

Johnson, Shaun. South Africa . Basingstoke, Hampshire , 1988. xxiii, 390 p. : ISBN

0-333-47095-8 (hardcover)
NYPL [Sc D 89-257]

Johnston, Geoffrey. Of God and maxim guns : Presbyterianism in Nigeria, 1846-1966 / Geoffrey Johnston. Waterloo, Ontario, Canada : published for the Canadian Corp. for Studies in Religion ... by Wilfrid Laurier University Press, 1988. 321 p. : map ; 23 cm. (Editions SR . v. 8.) Includes bibliographies and index. ISBN 0-88920-180-3 (pbk.)
1. Presbyterian Church - Nigeria - History. 2. Presbyterian Church - Missions - Nigeria. 3. Nigeria - Church history. I. Title. II. Series.
NYPL [Sc D 88-1229]

Johnston, Harry Hamilton, Sir, 1858-1927. Handbook to British Central Africa / [by Sir Harry Johnston]. Blantyre [Malawi] : [Rotary International], 1985. viii, 111 p. : ill. ; 22 cm. Reprint. Originally published: London : British Central Africa Co., 1905. With new introd. limited ed. of 1,000 numbered copies. Includes index. Schomburg Center has no. 641.
1. Malawi - Description and travel - Guide-books. 2. Malawi - Commerce - Handbooks, manuals, etc. I. Title.
NYPL [Sc D 88-1006]

Joiner, William A., 1868- A half century of freedom of the Negro in Ohio. Xenia, Ohio, Press of Smith Adv. Co. [1915] 134 p. illus. 23 cm. Cover title: The Ohio book for the Lincoln jubilee. Includes a history of Wilberforce University and a description of courses offered (p.41-134)
1. Wilberforce University. 2. Afro-Americans - Ohio. I. Title. II. Title: Ohio book for the Lincoln jubilee.
NYPL [Sc Rare F 89-7]

Joint Center for Political Studies (U. S.). Blacks and the 1984 Republican National Convention . Washington, D.C. (1301 Pennsylvania Ave., N.W., Suite 400, Washington 20004) , 1984. v, 25 p. ; ISBN 0-941410-51-X (pbk.) DDC 324.2734 19
JK2353 1984 NYPL [Sc F 87-172 rept. 4]

Cavanagh, Thomas E. The impact of the Black electorate [microform] /. Washington, D.C. (1301 Pennsylvania Ave., N.W., Suite 400, Washington 20004) , 1984. v, 28 p. ; DDC 324.973/008996073 19
*E185.615 .C364 1984 NYPL [*Z-4913 no.8]*

Joint Center for Political Studies (U. S.). **Economic Policy Task Force.** Black economic progress . Washington, D.C. , Lanham, Md. , 1988. xi, 52 p. ; ISBN 0-941410-69-2 (alk. paper) DDC 330.973/008996073 19
E185.8 .B496 1988 NYPL [Sc E 89-154]

Jonckers, Danielle. La société Minyanka du Mali : traditions communautaires et développement cotonnier / Danielle Jonckers. Paris : L'Harmattan, c1987. viii, 234 p., [8] p. of plates : ill., map ; 25 cm. (Connaissance des hommes) Bibliography: p. 209-231.
1. Minianka (African people). 2. Ethnology - Mali. I. Title. II. Series. NYPL [Sc E 88-344]

Jones, Adam. Brandenburg sources for West African history, 1680-1700 / Adam Jones. Stuttgart : F. Steiner Verlag Wiesbaden, 1985. xiv, 348 p., [14] p. of plates : maps, plates ; 24 cm. (Studien zur Kulturkunde. Bd. 77) "Veröffentlichungen des Frobenius-Instituts an der Johann Wolfgang Goethe-Universität zu Frankfurt/Main." Sequel to author's 'German sources for West African history, 1599-1669', published in 1983. Includes indexes. Bibliography: p. [322]-330. ISBN 3-515-04315-2
1. Africa, West - Bibliography. 2. Germany - Foreign economic relations - Africa, West. 3. Africa, West - Foreign economic relations - Germany. I. Title. II. Series. NYPL [Sc E 88-84]

Jones, Brent. Duczman, Linda. The baby-sitter /. Milwaukee , Chicago , c1977. 30 p. : ISBN 0-8172-0065-7 (lib. bdg.) : DDC 649/.1
HQ772.5 .D8 NYPL [Sc E 88-588]

JONES CLAUDIA, 1915-1964.
Tyson, Jennifer. Claudia Jones, 1915-1964 . London , c1988. 16 p. :
NYPL [Sc D 89-553]

Jones, Eldred D. Women in African literature today . London , Trenton, N.J. , 1987. vi, 162 p. ; ISBN 0-85255-500-8 (pbk) : DDC 809/.89287 19
PL8010 NYPL [Sc D 88-984]

The writing of Wole Soyinka / Eldred Durosimi Jones. 3rd ed. London : J. Currey ;

Portsmouth, N.H. : Heinemann, 1988. xiv, 242 p. ; 22 cm. Includes index. Bibliography: p. [235]-237. ISBN 0-435-08021-0 (pbk. : U. S.) DDC 822 19
1. Soyinka, Wole - Criticism and interpretation. I. Title.
PR9387.9.S6 Z7 1988 NYPL [Sc D 88-1134]

Jones, Hortense. (joint author) Buckley, Peter. Five friends at school /. New York , c1966. 96 p. :
NYPL [Sc E 88-590]

JONES, J. RAYMOND (JOHN RAYMOND), 1899-
Walter, John C. (John Christopher), 1933- The Harlem Fox . Albany, N.Y. , c1989. xv, 287 p. : ISBN 0-88706-756-5 DDC 974.7/1043/0924 B 19
F128.5.J72 W35 1988 NYPL [Sc E 89-107]

JONES, JIM, 1931-1978.
Chidester, David. Salvation and suicide . Bloomington , c1988. xv, 190 p. ; ISBN 0-253-35056-5 DDC 289.9 19
BP605.P46 C48 1988 NYPL [JFE 88-4624]

Jones, Marjorie. Women in African literature today . London , Trenton, N.J. , 1987. vi, 162 p. ; ISBN 0-85255-500-8 (pbk) : DDC 809/.89287 19
PL8010 NYPL [Sc D 88-984]

Jones, Novelette C. Cook up Jamaican style / by Novelette C. Jones. 1st ed. Kingston, Jamaica : Extension Division, Ministry of Agriculture, 1977. 111 leaves : ill., port. ; 28 cm. Includes index. On cover: Eating what we grow. Photocopy.
1. Cookery, Jamaican. I. Title. II. Title: Eating what we grow. NYPL [Sc F 89-132]

Jones, Oliver, 1947- The constitutional politics of the Black Muslim movement in America [microform] / by Oliver Jones, Jr. 1978. 297 leaves. Thesis (Ph. D.)--University of Illinois at Urbana-Champaign, 1978. Bibliography: leaves 289-296. Microfilm of typescript. Ann Arbor, Mich.: University Microfilms International, 1979. 1 microfilm reel; 35 mm.
1. Black Muslims. I. Title.
NYPL [Sc Micro R-4227]

JONES, QUINCY, 1933-
Horricks, Raymond, 1933- Quincy Jones /. Tunbridge Wells, Kent , New York , 1985. 127 p., [8] p. of plates : ISBN 0-87052-215-9 (Hippocrene Books) : DDC 785.42/092/4 B 19
ML419.J7 H67 1985 NYPL [Sc E 87-36]

Jones, Reginald Lanier, 1931- Psychoeducational assessment of minority group children . Berkeley, Calif. , c1988. ix, 429 p. : ISBN 0-943539-00-5 (pbk.) : DDC 155.4/5 19
BF722 .P77 1988 NYPL [Sc D 89-526]

Jones, Robert B. Toomer, Jean, 1894-1967. [Poems. 1988.] The collected poems of Jean Toomer /. Chapel Hill , c1988. xxxv, 111 p. ; ISBN 0-8078-1773-2 (hard) : DDC 811/.52 19
PS3539.O478 A17 1988
NYPL [Sc E 88-282]

Jones, Woodrow. Smith, J. Owens. Blacks and American government . Dubuque, Iowa , c1987. xii, 148 p. : ISBN 0-8403-4407-4 (pbk.) DDC 323.1/196073 19
E185.615 .S576 1987 NYPL [Sc E 89-193]

Jongh, Edward Arthur de. E dia di mas histórico / Edward A. de Jongh. Aruba : VAD, 1970. 158 p. : ill., facsims, ports ; 21 cm. A fictional treatment of the labor protest and riot of May 30, 1969.
1. Riots - Curaçao - Fiction. 2. Papiamento - Texts. 3. Curaçao - Fiction. I. Title.
NYPL [Sc D 87-1430]

De steeg : (met de dood op de lippen) / Edward A. de Jongh. [S.l.] : Bartolomé, 1976. 148 p. ; 21 cm.
1. Curaçao - Fiction. I. Title.
PT5881.2.O58 S7 NYPL [Sc D 88-1033]

JOPLIN, SCOTT, 1868-1917 - JUVENILE LITERATURE.
Preston, Katherine. Scott Joplin /. New York , c1988. 110 p. : ISBN 1-555-46598-6 DDC 780/.92/4 B 92 19
ML3930.J66 P7 1988 NYPL [Sc E 88-170]

Jordan, Lawrence V. Publications of the faculty and staff of West Virginia State College [microform] / [Lawrence V. Jordan and Robert A. Anglin] Institute : West Virginia State College, 1960. 23 p. ; 24 cm. (West Virginia State College bulletin. series 47, no.5) Microfiche. New York: Compilers' autographed presentation copy to the

Schomburg Collection.
1. West Virginia. State College, Institute - Faculty. I. Anglin, Robert Alton, 1910-. II. Title.
NYPL *[Sc Micro F-11,160]*

JORDAN, MICHAEL, 1963- - JUVENILE LITERATURE.
Martin, Gene L. Michael Jordan, gentleman superstar /. Greensboro, N.C. , c1987. 69 p. : ISBN 0-936389-02-8 : DDC 796.32/3/0924 B 19
GV884.J67 M37 1987   **NYPL** *[Sc E 88-320]*

Jordan, Sherrilyn Johnson. Hill, Pauline Anderson Simmons. Too young to be old . Seattle, Washington , c1981. xiv, 58 p. : ISBN 0-89716-098-3   **NYPL** *[Sc D 88-1214]*

JOS (NIGERIA) - HISTORY.
Bingel, Anthony Dung. Jos, origins and growth of the town, 1900 to 1972 /. Jos, Nigeria , 1978. v, 22 p. : ISBN 978-16-6000-7
MLCM 83/4794 (D)   **NYPL** *[Sc F 88-249]*

Jos, origins and growth of the town, 1900 to 1972 /. Bingel, Anthony Dung. Jos, Nigeria , 1978. v, 22 p. : ISBN 978-16-6000-7
MLCM 83/4794 (D)   **NYPL** *[Sc F 88-249]*

Jose, Babatunde. Walking a tight rope : power play in Daily Times / Isma'il Babatunde Jose. Ibadan : University Press, 1987. xiii, 421 p. : ill., ports. ; 24 cm. Includes index. ISBN 978-15-4911-4 (limp)
1. Daily times (Lagos, Nigeria). I. Title.
NYPL *[Sc E 88-296]*

José Martí, revolutionary democrat / edited by Christopher Abel and Nissa Torrents. London : Athlone Press, 1986. xviii, 238 p. ; 23 cm. Includes index. Bibliography: p. 229-233. ISBN 0-485-15018-2
I. Abel, Christopher. II. Torrents, Nissa.
NYPL *[JFD 86-9243]*

Joseph, Joel D. Black Mondays : worst decisions of the Supreme Court / Joel D. Joseph.1st ed. Bethesda, MD : National Press, 1987. 286 p. : ill. ; 23 cm. (A Zenith ed) Includes bibliographical references and index. ISBN 0-915765-44-6 : DDC 347.73/26 347.30735 19
1. Civil rights - United States - Cases. 2. United States - Constitutional law - Cases. I. Title.
KF4549 .J67 1987   **NYPL** *[Sc D 88-963]*

Joseph, 'Lai. Contemporary African poems : universe in focus / by Lai Joseph. Lagos : Dubeo Press, 1987. 116 p. ; 23 cm. Includes index. ISBN 978-302-821-9
I. Title.
MLCS 87/08400 (P)   **NYPL** *[Sc D 89-581]*

Joseph, Richard A. Democracy and prebendal politics in Nigeria : the rise and fall of the Second Republic / Richard A. Joseph. Cambridge [Cambridgeshire] ; New York : Cambridge University Press, 1987. x, 237 p. : ill., maps ; 24 cm. (African studies series. 56) Includes index. Bibliography: p. 224-232. ISBN 0-521-34136-1 DDC 966.9/05 19
1. Nigeria - Politics and governmen - 1979-1983. I. Title. II. Series.
DT515.84 .J67 1987   **NYPL** *[JFE 88-4953]*

Josephine /. Baker, Josephine, 1906-1975. New York , 1988, c1977. xiii, 302 p., [16] p. of plates : ISBN 1-557-78108-7 (pbk.) DDC 793.3/2/0924 B 19
GV1785.B3 A3 1988   **NYPL** *[Sc D 88-1476]*

Josey, Charles Conant, 1893-
[Race and national solidarity]
The philosophy of nationalism / by Charles Conant Josey. Washington, D.C. : Cliveden Press, c1983. xi, 227 p. ; 22 cm. Reprint. Originally published: Race and national solidarity. New York : Scribner, 1923. ISBN 0-941694-16-X
I. Title.
JC311 .J66 1983   **NYPL** *[Sc D 89-514]*

Josey, E. J. Libraries, coalitions, & the public good /. New York, NY , c1987. xiv, 174 p. ; ISBN 1-555-70017-9 : DDC 021 19
Z716.4 .L47 1987   **NYPL** *[JFE 87-6338]*

Josiah, Mwaniki, 1933- Divorce among the Wa-Embu / Mwaniki Josiah. Nairobi : Uzima Press, 1988. 49 p. ; 21 cm.
1. Divorce - Kenya. 2. Embu (Bantu people). 3. Marriage customs and rites, Embu (Bantu people). I. Title.
NYPL *[Sc D 89-346]*

Jospin, Lionel. Vingt questions sur l'Afrique . Paris , 1988. 238 p. ; ISBN 2-7384-0048-5
NYPL *[Sc D 88-1390]*

The Jossey-Bass higher education series.
Richardson, Richard C. Fostering minority access and achievement in higher education . San Francisco, Calif. , c1987. xviii, 244 p. ; ISBN 1-555-42053-2 (alk. paper) DDC 378/.052 19
LC3727 .R53 1987   **NYPL** *[Sc E 88-472]*

Jost, Ekkehard.
Free jazz; stilkritische Untersuchungen zum Jazz der 60er Jahre. Mainz, B. Schott [1975] 256 p. music. 24 cm. "Diskographische Anmerkungen": p. 230-238. Bibliography: p. 239-243. Includes index.
1. Jazz musicians. I. Title.   **NYPL** *[Sc E 77-158]*

That's jazz, der Sound des 20. Jahrhunderts . [Darmstadt , 1988] xv, 723 p. : DDC 781.57/0740341 19
ML141.D3 I6 1988   **NYPL** *[JMF 89-297]*

Jouanny, Robert A. Les voies du lyrisme dans les "Poèmes" de Léopold Sédar Senghor (Chants d'ombre, Hosties noires, Ethiopiques, Nocturnes) : étude critique suivie d'un lexique. Paris : Librairie Honoré Champion, 1986. 161 p. ; 22 cm. (Collection Unichamp . 15) Bibliography: p.[137]-138. ISBN 2-85203-026-8
1. Senghor, Léopold Sédar, 1906- - Criticism and interpretation. 2. Senghor, Léopold Sédar, 1906- Poems. I. Title.   **NYPL** *[Sc D 88-1026]*

JOURNAL AND GUIDE - HISTORY.
Suggs, Henry Lewis. P.B. Young, newspaperman . Charlottesville , 1988. xxii, 254 p. : ISBN 0-8139-1178-8 DDC 070.4/1/0924 B 19
PN4874.Y59 S84 1988   **NYPL** *[JFE 89-97]*

Journal of African civilizations. Black women in antiquity /. New Brunswick, [N.J.] , London , 1988. 192 p. : ISBN 0-87855-982-5
NYPL *[Sc D 89-351]*

Journal of an expedition to explore the course and termination of the Niger . Lander, Richard, 1804-1834. New York , 1832. 2 v. :
NYPL *[Sc Rare C 89-35]*

JOURNALISM - PRESS ASSOCIATIONS. see NEWS AGENCIES.

JOURNALISTS - GREAT BRITAIN - BIOGRAPHY.
Davidson, Michael. Some boys /. London , 1988, c1970. 201 p. ; ISBN 0-85449-087-6 (pbk) : DDC 070/.92/4 19
PN5123.D   **NYPL** *[Sc C 89-87]*

JOURNALISTS - NIGERIA.
Duyile, Dayo. Makers of Nigerian press . Nigeria , 1987. xx, 726 p. :
NYPL *[Sc F 89-167]*

JOURNALISTS - NIGERIA - BIOGRAPHY.
Magnate, Joseph. Dele Giwa /. Lagos, , 1987. 190 p. : ISBN 978-303-000-0
NYPL *[Sc D 88-742]*

JOURNALISTS - SOUTH AFRICA - SOCIAL CONDITIONS.
Finnegan, William. Dateline Soweto . New York , c1988. x. 244 p. : ISBN 0-06-015932-4 : DDC 070/.92/4 B 19
PN4874.F45 A3 1989   **NYPL** *[JFE 88-2005]*

JOURNALISTS - UNITED STATES - BIOGRAPHY.
Finnegan, William. Dateline Soweto . New York , c1988. x. 244 p. : ISBN 0-06-015932-4 : DDC 070/.92/4 B 19
PN4874.F45 A3 1989   **NYPL** *[JFE 88-2005]*

Waters, Enoch P., 1909- American diary . Chicago , c1987. xxiii, 520 p. ; ISBN 0-910671-01-X : DDC 070.4/1/0924 B 19
PN4874.W293 A33 1987   **NYPL** *[Sc E 88-270]*

JOURNALISTS - UNITED STATES - CORRESPONDENCE.
Teague, Bob. The flip side of soul . New York , c1989. 201 p. ; ISBN 0-688-08260-2 DDC 305.8/96073 19
PS3570.E2 Z495 1989   **NYPL** *[Sc D 89-303]*

The journals of Charlotte Forten Grimké /. Forten, Charlotte L. [Journals]. New York , 1988. xlix, 609 p. : ISBN 0-19-505238-2 (alk. paper) DDC 371.1/0092/4 B 19
LA2317.F67 A3 1988   **NYPL** *[JFC 88-2152]*

Journée nationale du premier novembre 1961 [microform] Conakry : Impr. Patrice Lumumba, [1961?] 38 p. ; 24 cm. Microfiche. New York: New York Public Library, 198 . 1 microfiche: negative; 11 x 15 cm. (FSN Sc 019,015) CONTENTS. - Discours à l'occasion de manifestations de solidarité en faveur de l'indépendance de l'Algérie et des cérémonies anniversaires de la création de l'Armée nationale guinéenne/le président Sékou Touré.--Discours au 3e anniversaire de la création de l'Armée de la République de Guinée/Ministre de la défense nationale et de la sécurité.--Discours pour la commémoration du 3e anniversaire de la création de l'Armée guinéenne/Sékou Touré.
1. Guinea. Armée. 2. Algeria - Politics and government - 1945-1962. I. Touré, Sékou, Pres. Guinea, 1922-.   **NYPL** *[Sc Micro F-11002]*

Journey /. Thomas, Joyce Carol. New York , c1988. 153 p. ; ISBN 0-590-40627-2 : DDC [Fic] 19
PZ7.T36996 Jo 1988   **NYPL** *[Sc D 89-235]*

Joy, Charles Rhind, 1885- Young people of East and South Africa . New York , c1962. vii, 211 p. ;   **NYPL** *[Sc D 88-660]*

Joyce, Joyce Ann, 1949- Richard Wright's art of tragedy / by Joyce Ann Joyce. 1st ed. Iowa City : University of Iowa Press, 1986. xvii, 129 p. ; 23 cm. Includes index. Bibliography: p. [121]-125. ISBN 0-87745-148-6 DDC 813/.52 19
1. Wright, Richard, 1908-1960. Native son. 2. Afro-Americans in literature. 3. Tragic, The, in literature. I. Title.
PS3545.R815 N34 1986
NYPL *[JFD 87-289]*

Juan, Adalaida de. En la Galería Latinoamericana / Adalaida de Juan. La Habana : Casa de las Américas, 1979. 203 p. : ill. ; 23 cm. (Colección nuestros países, Serie galeria) Includes bibliographical references.
1. Art - Latin America. 2. Art - Caribbean area. 3. Art, Modern - 20th century - Latin America. 4. Art, Modern - 20th century - Caribbean area. I. Casa de las Américas. Galería Latinoamericana. II. Title.
NYPL *[3-MAM 88-2546]*

Jubiabá /. Amado, Jorge, 1912- [Jubiabá. English.] New York , c1984. 294 p. ; ISBN 0-380-58567-0 (pbk.) : DDC 869.3 19
PQ9697.A647 J813 1984
NYPL *[JFC 85-368]*

JUDAICA. see JEWS.

Judge, C. W. (Colin Walter), 1938- (illus) Hollings, Jill. African nationalism. New York [1972, c1971] 128 p. DDC 320.5/4/096
DT31 .H577 1972   **NYPL** *[Sc D 88-1496]*

JUDGES - NIGERIA - BIOGRAPHY.
Udo-Inyang, D. S. (Denis S.) The man--Sir Justice Udo Udoma /. Calabar [Nigeria] [1985] 72 p. : ISBN 978-228-168-9 (pbk) DDC 347.669/03534 B 346.69073534 B 19
LAW   **NYPL** *[Sc D 88-776]*

JUDGES - UGANDA - BIOGRAPHY.
Udo-Inyang, D. S. (Denis S.) The man--Sir Justice Udo Udoma /. Calabar [Nigeria] [1985] 72 p. : ISBN 978-228-168-9 (pbk) DDC 347.669/03534 B 346.69073534 B 19
LAW   **NYPL** *[Sc D 88-776]*

Julian Bond vs John Lewis . Ball, Thomas E. Atlanta, Ga. , 1988. ix, 144 p. : ISBN 0-9621362-0-4   **NYPL** *[Sc E 88-582]*

Julian, secret agent /. Cameron, Ann, 1943- New York , 1988. 62 p. : ISBN 0-394-91949-1 (lib. bdg.) : DDC [Fic] 19
PZ7.C1427 Jt 1988   **NYPL** *[Sc C 89-123]*

Julian's glorious summer /. Cameron, Ann, 1943- New York , c1987. 62 p. : ISBN 0-394-89117-1 (pbk.) : DDC [Fic] 19
PZ7.C1427 Ju 1987   **NYPL** *[Sc C 89-99]*

Juncker, Clara. Black roses : Afro-American women writers / Clara Juncker, Inger Juncker. København : Kaleidoscope, c1985. 158 p. : ports. ; 24 cm. Bibliography: p. 152-158. ISBN 87-7565-316-8 (styksalg)
1. Afro-American women authors. I. Juncker, Inger.
NYPL *[Sc E 88-441]*

Juncker, Inger. Juncker, Clara. Black roses . København , c1985. 158 p. : ISBN 87-7565-316-8 (styksalg)   **NYPL** *[Sc E 88-441]*

June 16 . Magubane, Peter. Johannesburg , c1986. [85] p. : ISBN 0-947009-13-2 (pbk.) DDC

968.2/21 19
DT944.J66 S674 1986   *NYPL [Sc G 88-12]*

Jungraithmayr, Herrmann. Préalables à la reconstruction du proto-tchadique . Paris , 1978. 210 p. ; ISBN 2-85297-022-8 DDC 493/.7 19
PL8026.C53 P73 1978   *NYPL [Sc E 88-418]*

A Junior secondary poetry anthology / compiled by Comfort Eneke Ashu. [Limbe : Nooremac Press, c1984- v. : ill. ; 22 cm. Includes index. A collection of poems for African students learning English by well-known English poets and secondary school students from Cameroon. DDC 428.6/4 19
1. English language - Textbooks for foreign speakers - African. 2. Readers (Secondary) - Poetry. 3. Children's poetry, English. I. Ashu, Comfort Eneke.
PE1126.A44 J86 1984   *NYPL [Sc D 88-384]*

Junta de investigações do Ultramar. Estudos, ensaios e documentos.
(v. 97) Amaral, Ilidio do. Ensaio de um estudo geográfico da rede urbana de Angola. Lisboa, 1962. 99 p.
HT148.A5 A7   *NYPL [Sc E 98-118]*

Just before dawn . Omotoso, Kole. Ibadan , 1988. xi, 345 p. ; ISBN 978-246-007-9
NYPL [Sc D 88-1485]

Just being Black . Patrick, Herbert R. Petersburg, Va. (3406 Union Branch Rd., Petersburg 23805) , c1984. 50 p. : DDC 811/.54 19
PS3566.A778 J87 1984   *NYPL [Sc D 88-668]*

Just one me /. Brothers, Aileen. Chicago , c1967. 32 p. :   *NYPL [Sc D 88-376]*

JUSTICE - ADMINISTRATION. see JUSTICE, ADMINISTRATION OF.

JUSTICE, ADMINISTRATION OF - BAHAMAS - MAYAGUANA ISLAND.
Lurry-Wright, Jerome Wendell, 1941- Custom and conflict on a Bahamian out-island /. Lanham, MD , c1987. xxii, 188 p. ; ISBN 0-8191-6097-0 (alk. paper) : DDC 347.7296 347.29607 19
KGL210 .L87 1987   *NYPL [Sc D 88-218]*

JUSTICE, ADMINISTRATION OF - ZAMBIA - BIBLIOGRAPHY.
Msiska, Augustine W. C. Law and justice in Zambia . Lusaka, Zambia , 1986. iii, 75 p. ; DDC 016.3476894 016.34689407 19
LAW   *NYPL [Sc F 89-9]*

JUSTICE AND CHRISTIANITY. see CHRISTIANITY AND JUSTICE.

Justice and expediency. Whittier, John Greenleaf, 1807-1892. New-York, 1833. [49]-63 p.
E449 .A624   *NYPL [Sc Rare F 98-1]*

Justin, Augustus. Odlum, George. Call that George /. [Castries, St. Lucia] , 1979. 44 p. :
F2100 .O35 1979   *NYPL [Sc E 89-2]*

Justus, May, 1898- New boy in school. Illustrated by Joan Balfour Payne. New York, Hastings House [1963] 56 p. illus. 24 cm. When his family moves from Louisiana to Tennessee, seven-year-old Lennie discovers he is the only black person in his classroom. SCHOMBURG CHILDREN'S COLLECTION. DDC [Fic]
1. Afro-American children - Juvenile fiction. I. Payne, Joan Balfour. II. Schomburg Children's Collection. III. Title.
PZ7.J986 Ng   *NYPL [Sc E 89-25]*

Juta, Jan. Look out for the ostriches! Tales of South Africa; [1st ed.] New York, Knopf, 1949. xii, 177 p. illus. 22 cm.
1. South Africa - Description and travel. I. Title.
DT757 .J8   *NYPL [Sc D 89-90]*

JUVENILE LITERATURE. see CHILDREN'S LITERATURE.

Juventud, tradición y desarrollo en Africa . Jeunesse, tradition et développement en Afrique. Spanish. Barcelona , Paris , 1982. 148 p. ; ISBN 84-85800-29-X
NYPL [Sc D 88-592]

K. A. N. U. see Kenya African National Union.

Kabarin'ny Filoham-pirenena /. Ratsiraka, Didier, 1936- [Antananarivo? , 1985] 487 p. ;
NYPL [Sc F 88-268]

Kabary tatitra nataon' Andriamatoa Didier Ratsiraka, filohan' ny Repoblika Demokratika Malagasy. Ratsiraka, Didier. Antananarivo , 1985. 93 p. :   *NYPL [Sc D 88-1295]*

Kabengele Munanga.
Os Basanga de Shaba : um grupo étnico do Zaire : ensaio de antropologia geral. Sao Palulo : FFLCH-USP, 1986. 334 p. : ill., map ; 17 cm. (Antropología. 7) Originally presented as the author's thesis (doctoral-- Universidade de São Paulo, 1977). Bibliography: p. 327-334.
1. Luba (African people). 2. Ethnology - Zaire. I. Series: Antropologia (São Paulo, Brazil) , 7. II. Title.
NYPL [Sc B 88-7]

Negritude : usos e sentidos / Kabengele Munanga. São Paulo : Editora Atica, 1986. 88 p. ; 18 cm. (Série Princípios . 40) Bibliography: p. 86-88. ISBN 85-08-00686-1
I. Title. II. Series.   *NYPL [Sc C 88-105]*

Le Kabiye /. Delord, J. Lomé , 1976. xxxi, 465 p. :
PL8725.15.Z9 K334 1976
NYPL [Sc E 89-119]

KABRE DIALECT.
Delord, J. Le Kabiye /. Lomé , 1976. xxxi, 465 p. :
PL8725.15.Z9 K334 1976
NYPL [Sc E 89-119]

The Kaduna mafia /. Takaya, B. J. [Jos, Nigeria] , c1987. viii, 146 p. ; ISBN 978-16-6045-7
NYPL [Sc D 88-736]

Kämpfe im Süden Afrikas . Neffe, Dieter. Berlin , 1987. 64 p. : ISBN 3-327-00283-5
NYPL [Sc D 88-680]

Kagwema, Prince, 1931-
Quo vadis Tanzania : fear of the unknown / by Prince Kagwma. Dar-es-Salaam : Three Stars Publications, c1985. vii, 119 p. ; 21 cm. Bibliography: p. 119. ISBN 997-691-804-6
1. Tanzania - Politics and government - 1964-. I. Title. II. Title: Fear of the unknown.
NYPL [Sc D 89-11]

Society in the dock : a novel / by Prince Kagwema. Dar es Salaam : Three Stars Publications, c1984. viii, 147 p. ; 21 cm. ISBN 997-691-803-8
1. Tanzania - Fiction. I. Title.
NYPL [Sc D 88-1515]

Kahan, Mitchell Douglas, 1951- Sims, Lowery Stokes. Robert Colescott, a retrospective, 1975-1986 /. San Jose, Calif. , c1987. 34 p. : ISBN 0-938175-01-7 (pbk.) DDC 759.13 19
ND237.C66 A4 1987   *NYPL [Sc F 88-317]*

Kaké, Ibrahima Baba. Sékou Touré, le héros et le tyran / Ibrahima Baba Kaké. Paris : Jeune Afrique Livres, 1987. 254 p. : ill., ports. ; 21 cm. (Collection Destins) Bibliography: p. 252-253.
1. Touré, Ahmed Sékou, 1922-. 2. Statesmen - Guinea - Biography. 3. Guinea - Politics and government - 1958-1984. I. Title. II. Series.
NYPL [Sc D 88-468]

Kakooza, Teresa. The problems of the university's role in adult education in Uganda / by Teresa Kakooza. [Kampala?] : Centre for continuing Education, Makerere University, 1987. 20 p. ; 29 cm. Bibliography: p. 19-20.
1. Adult education - Uganda. 2. University extension - Uganda. I. Title.   *NYPL [Sc F 89-92]*

KALAHARI DESERT.
Martin, Robert, 1929- Yesterday's people. Garden City, N.Y. [1970] 158 p. DDC 916.8/03
DT764.B8 M35   *NYPL [Sc F 88-248]*

Owens, Mark. Cry of the Kalahari /. Boston, Mass. , 1986, c1984. 535 p., [16] p. of plates : ISBN 0-8161-3972-5 (lg. print) : DDC 591.9681/1 19
QL337.K3 O95 1986   *NYPL [Sc E 88-183]*

Van der Post, Laurens. The lost world of the Kalahari . London , 1988. 261 p. :
NYPL [Sc F 88-381]

KALAHARI DESERT - JUVENILE FICTION.
Howard, Moses L., 1928- The ostrich chase /. New York [1974] 118 p. : ISBN 0-03-012096-9
NYPL [Sc D 88-374]

Kalb, Marion. Women as food producers in developing countries /. Los Angeles, CA , c1985. ix, 118 p. : ISBN 0-918456-56-8 : DDC 331.4/83/091724 19
HD6073.A292 D4485 1985
NYPL [JLE 88-2659]

Kalejaiye, Dipo. Polygyny and Polyandry : two plays about marriage / Dipo Kalejaiye. London : Macmillan, 1985. 55 p. ; 22 cm. (Open

stage) ISBN 0-333-35822-8
I. Title. II. Series.   *NYPL [Sc D 88-1049]*

Kalena and Sana /. Booth, Esma (Rideout) New York , 1962. 152 p. :   *NYPL [Sc D 88-506]*

Kalibala, E. Balintuma. Wakaima and the clay man : and other African folktales / by E. Balintuma Kalibala and Mary Gould Davis ; illustrated by Avery Johnson.1st ed. New York : Longmans Green, 1946. 145 p. : ill. ; 21 cm. SCHOMBURG CHILDREN'S COLLECTION.
1. Tales - Uganda. 2. Folk literature, Ganda (African people). I. Davis, Mary Gould. II. Johnson, Avery F. III. Schomburg Children's Collection. IV. Title.
NYPL [Sc D 89-486]

Kalina, Amy. Kushner, Arlene. Falasha no more . New York , c1986. 58 p. : ISBN 0-933503-55-5
NYPL [Sc F 88-107]

Kalmuss, Debra S., 1953- Chesler, Mark A. Social science in court . Madison, Wis. , 1988. xiv, 286 p. ; ISBN 0-299-11620-4 : DDC 344.73/0798 347.304798 19
KF8925.D5 C48 1988   *NYPL [Sc E 89-187]*

Kalu, Onwuka O. The challenge of industrialization in Nigeria : a personal insight / Onwuka O. Kalu. Lagos, Nigeria : Basic Trust Ltd., 1986. xviii, 84 p. ; 22 cm.
1. Small business - Nigeria. 2. Nigeria - Industries. 3. Nigeria - Economic policy. I. Title.
NYPL [Sc D 88-1245]

Kalugula, C. The development of special education in Tanzania /. Dar es Salaam, Tanzania , c1984. 81 p. : ISBN 997-661-002-5
NYPL [Sc C 89-127]

Kalyalya, Denny. Aid & development in southern Africa . Trenton, N.J. [1988] xi, 148 p. : ISBN 0-86543-047-0 (pbk.) : DDC 338.968 19
HC900 .A53 1988   *NYPL [Sc D 88-1455]*

Kalyegira, Junda. From the ground of hope / by Junda Kalyegira. Nairobi : Kenya Literature Bureau, 1980. vii, 53 p. ; 19 cm.
I. Title.   *NYPL [Sc C 88-298]*

Kam, Sié Alain. Cours de littérature orale : généralités / Kam Sié Alain. [Ouagadougou] : Université de Ouagadougou, Institut supérieur des langues, des lettres et des arts, [1988?] 1 v. (various pagings) : ill. ; 30 cm. Includes bibliographical references. With autograph of author.
1. Folk literature, African. I. Université de Ouagadougou. Institut supérieur des langues, des lettres et des arts. II. Title.   *NYPL [Sc F 89-118]*

Kamara, Lansana. Temne stories and songs /. Freetown, Sierra Leone , 1986. 96 p. :
NYPL [Sc D 89-427]

Kambon, Khafra. For bread justice and freedom : a political biography of George Weekes / by Khafra Kambon. London : New Beacon Books, 1988. xi, 353 p., [16] p. of plates : ill. ; 23 cm. Includes bibliographical references and index.
1. Weekes, George. 2. Oilfields Workers' Trade Union. 3. Trade-unions - Trinidad and Tobago. I. Title.
NYPL [Sc D 89-294]

Kamkondo, Dede. The children of the lake / by Dede Kamkondo. Limbe Malaŵi : Popular Publications, c1987. 103 p. ; 18 cm. (Malaŵian writers series)
1. Malawi - Fiction.   *NYPL [Sc C 89-108]*

East African studies. see East African studies.

Kampala, Uganda. Makerere University College. Makerere Institute of Social Research. see Makerere Institute of Social Research.

Kamunge, James Mwangi. Kenya. Presidential Working Party on Education and Manpower Training for the Next Decade and Beyond. Report of the Presidential Working Party on Education and Manpower Training for the Next Decade and Beyond /. Nairobi , 1988. xvii, 174 p. ;   *NYPL [Sc E 89-232]*

Kamusi ya kwanza . Attas, Ali. Nairobi , 1986. 169 p. : ISBN 0-333-42702-5
NYPL [Sc E 89-125]

Kamwa, Joseph. L'orphelin et son destin [microform] : comédie en 4 actes / Sagesse Noire. Bafoussam, [Cameroon] : Librairie populaire, 1981. 27 p. ; 27 cm. Microfilm. New York: New York Public Library, 198. 1 microfilm reel; 35 mm. (MN *ZZ-24640)
I. Title.   *NYPL [Sc Micro R-4137 no.17]*

Kane, Mohamadou K. Literature and African identity. Bayreuth , c1986. 125 p. ;
NYPL [Sc D 89-369]

Kano State : 20 years of progress / editor, Mohammed Mousa-Booth. [Kano] : Kano State Ministry of Home Affairs, Information and Culture, [1987]. 192 p. : ill., maps ; 27 cm. Cover title: This is Kano State.
1. Kano State (Nigeria). I. Mousa-Booth, Mohammed.
II. Title: This is Kano State.   *NYPL [Sc F 89-37]*

KANO STATE (NIGERIA)
Kano State . [Kano] [1987]. 192 p. :
NYPL [Sc F 89-37]

Kanogo, Tabitha M. Squatters and the roots of Mau Mau, 1905-63 / Tabitha Kanogo. Athens : Ohio University Press ; London : J. Currey, 1987. xviii, 206 p. : maps ; 23 cm. (Eastern Africa studies) Includes index. Bibliography: p. [188]-197.   ISBN 0-8214-0873-9   DDC 307.3/36 19
1. Mau Mau - History. 2. Migrant agricultural laborers - Kenya - History - 20th century. 3. Squatters - Kenya - History - 20th century. 4. Kikuyu (Africa people) - History. I. Title. II. Series.
HD1538.K4 K36 1987   *NYPL [Sc D 88-207]*

KANSAS - HISTORY - 1854-1861 - JUVENILE FICTION.
Hodges, Carl G. Benjie Ream /. Indianapolis , c1964. 153 p. ;   *NYPL [Sc D 89-433]*

Kanté, Cheik Oumar. Douze pour une coupe : roman / Cheick Oumar Kanté. Paris : Présence africaine, c1987. 159 p. ; 20 cm. (Collection Ecrits)   ISBN 2-7087-0490-7
1. Africa, West - Fiction. I. Title.
NYPL [Sc D 88920]

KANTÉ, SOUMANGOURU - DRAMA.
Cissé, Ahmed-Tidjani. Le tana de Soumangourou /. Paris , 1988. 77 p. ;   ISBN 2-85586-036-9   *NYPL [Sc C 89-73]*

KANU. see Kenya African National Union.

Kappel, Robert. Liberia . Hamburg , 1986. vi, 292 p., [1] folded leaf of plates :   ISBN 3-923519-65-6 (pbk.)   DDC 322/.5/096662 19
JQ3923.5.C58 L53 1986
NYPL [Sc D 88-1320]

Kaptue, Léon. Travail et main-d'oeuvre au Cameroun sous régime français, 1916-1952 / Léon Kaptue. Paris : Éditions L'Harmattan, [c1986] 282 p. : maps ; 22 cm. (Mémoires africaines) Bibliography: p. 271-280.   ISBN 2-85802-655-6
1. Labor and laboring classes - Cameroon - History. 2. Labor supply - Cameroon - History. I. Title. II. Series.
NYPL [Sc D 88-1237]

KARA LANGUAGE.
Boyeldieu, Pascal. Les langues fer ("Kara") et yulu du Nord centrafricain . Paris , 1987. 280 p. ;   ISBN 2-7053-0342-1 *NYPL [Sc E 88-124]*

Karageorges, Basos. see Karageorghis, Vassos.

Karageorghis, Vassos. Blacks in ancient Cypriot art / Vassos Karageorghis. Houston, Tex. : Menil Foundation, 1988. 62 p. : ill. ; 22 cm. Bibliography: p. 58-62.   ISBN 0-939594-13-7 (pbk.) : DDC 704.9/42/093937074 19
1. Blacks in art - Catalogs. 2. Art, Cypriote - Catalogs. 3. Art, Ancient - Cyprus - Catalogs. I. Title.
N8232 .K37 1988   *NYPL [3-MAE 89-1038]*

Karageorgis, Vassos. see Karageorghis, Vassos.

KARANGA (AFRICAN PEOPLE)
Aschwanden, Herbert, 1933- Symbols of death . Gweru, Zimbabwe , 1987. 389 p. ;   ISBN 0-86922-390-9   *NYPL [Sc D 88-979]*

KARENGA, MAULANA.
Kitabu [microform] . Los Angeles [1972?] 13 p. ;   *NYPL [Sc Micro F-10979]*

Karengera, Pawulini. Impundu kwa Rusango / Pawulini Karengera. [Kigali? : s.n., 1983] (Kigali : Imprimerie Scolaire) 319 p. : ill., ports. ; 21 cm. On cover: 1973-1983, 10e anniversaire.
1. Ruanda language - Texts. I. Title.
NYPL [Sc D 89-447]

Kariara, Jonathan. The coming of power, and other stories / Jonathan Kariara. Nairobi : Oxford University Press, 1986. 100 p. ; 21 cm.   ISBN 0-19-572597-2
1. Kenya - Fiction. I. Title.
NYPL [Sc D 88-1053]

Karibi-Whyte, A. G. Criminal policy : traditional & modern trends / by A.G. Karibi-Whyte. Lagos, Nigeria : Nigerian Law Publications, 1988. xvii, 127 p. ; 20 cm. (Judges' series) Includes bibliographical references.   ISBN 978-232-525-2
1. Criminal justice, Administration of - Nigeria. I. Title.
NYPL [Sc C 89-47]

Karim, Darnell. The five prayers step by step / Darnell Karim. [Chicago] : W.D.M. Publications, [1987] vi, 202 p. : ill. ; 28 cm. + 2 sound cassettes. Cover title. English and Arabic. Cassettes located in Moving Images and Recorded Sounds, with classification : Sc F 89-160.
1. Prayer (Islam). 2. Islam - Prayer-books and devotions. I. Title.   *NYPL [Sc F 89-160]*

Karima /. McLoughlin, T. O. Gweru, Zimbabwe , 1985. 211 p. ;   ISBN 0-86922-319-4 (pbk.)   DDC 823 19
PR9390.9.M35 K37 1985
NYPL [JFC 86-1652]

KARIPUNA CREOLE DIALECT - BRAZIL - AMAPA (TERRITORY)
Andrade, Julieta de. Cultura creoula e lanc-patuá no norte do Brasil =. São Paulo , 1984. 310 p. :
F2543 .A53 1984   *NYPL [HFS 86-2895]*

Karnak literary criticism.
Saakana, Amon Saba, 1948- The colonial legacy in Caribbean literature, Vol. I /. London , 1987. 128 p., [7] p. of plates :   ISBN 0-907015-34-4 (pbk.) :   *NYPL [Sc D 88-1150]*

Karodia, Farida. Coming home and other stories / Farida Karodia. London : Heinemann Educational, 1988. v, 185 p. ; 20 cm. (African witers series)   ISBN 0-435-90738-7 (pbk) :
1. South Africa - Fiction. I. Title. II. Series.
PR9369.3.K3   *NYPL [Sc C 89-88]*

Karp, Ivan. Explorations in African systems of thought /. Washington, D.C. , c1987. xvi, 337 p. :   ISBN 0-87474-591-8 (pbk.)
NYPL [Sc D 88-566]

Kasajja, Jane. Makerere University. Library. Annotated list of theses submitted to Makerere University and held by Makerere University Library [microform] /. [Kampala?] , 1981. 89 leaves ;   *NYPL [Sc Micro R-4840 no.13]*

Kasalama, Mark M. Kila mtu na wake / Kimetungwa na Mark M. Kasalama. Peramiho, Tanzania : Benedictine Publications Ndanda, 1983. 55 p. : ill. ; 21 cm.   ISBN 997-663-006-9
1. Swahili language - Texts. I. Title.
NYPL [Sc D 89-1]

Kasozi, A. B. K. (Abdu Basajabaka Kawalya), 1942- The spread of Islam in Uganda / Abdu B. Kasozi. Nairobi, Kenya : Oxford University Press, in association with the Islamic African Centre, Khartoum, 1986. vi, 136 p., [4] p. of plates : ill., map, ports. ; 25 cm. Revised version of thesis (Ph. D.)--University of California, Santa Cruz, 1974. Includes bibliographical references.   ISBN 0-19-572596-4
1. Islam - Uganda - History. 2. Uganda - History. I. Title.   *NYPL [Sc E 89-109]*

Kassam, Kassim Mussa. Shuga dedi / kimetungwa Kassim Mussa Kassam. Dar es Salaam, Tanzania : International Publishers Agencies, c1984. 60 p. ; 18 cm. In Swahili.   ISBN 997-692-101-2
1. Swahili language - Texts. I. Title.
NYPL [Sc C 88-69]

Katalog (Deutsches Ledermuseum) .
(3) Deutsches Ledermuseum. Afrika /. Offenbach am Main , 1988. 227 p. :   ISBN 3-87280-042-6   *NYPL [Sc D 89-506]*

Katapu, Agbeko. Workable strategies to end Africa's poverty : some aspects of nation management economics / Agbeko Katapu. Syracuse, N.Y. : Center for Nation Management Economics, c1986. xxiv, 288 p. ; 23 cm.   ISBN 0-944338-00-3   DDC 338.96 19
1. Poor - Africa. 2. Africa - Economic policy. I. Title.
HC800 .K37 1988   *NYPL [Sc D 89-610]*

Katiba ya Jamhuri ya Muungano wa Tanzania, ya mwaka 1977. Tanzania. [Katiba (1977)] Dar es Salaam, Tanzania , 1985. 100 p. ;
NYPL [Sc E 89-156]

KATIGONDO NATIONAL MAJOR SEMINARY - HISTORY.
Waliggo, John Mary, 1942- A history of

African priests . Masaka, Uganda , 1988. xi, 236 p., [16] p. of plates :
NYPL [Sc D 89-15]

Katjavivi, Peter H. A history of resistance in Namibia / Peter H. Katjavivi. London : Currey, 1988. xvi, 152 p. : ill., maps ; 22 cm. (Apartheid & society) Includes index. Includes bibliographical references.   ISBN 0-85255-320-X; 0-231-02000-0 (pbk)   DDC 968.8 19
I. Title.
DT714   *NYPL [Sc D 88-1304]*

Katz, Elaine N. Baines, Thomas, 1820-1875. Baines on the Zambezi 1858 to 1859 /. Johannesburg , c1982. 251 p. ;   ISBN 0-909079-17-X (Standard ed.)
NYPL [Sc F 83-34]

Katz, William Loren.
Black Indians : a hidden heritage / William Loren Katz.1st ed. New York : Atheneum, c1986. 198 p. : ill. ; 25 cm. Includes index. Bibliography: p. 191-193.   ISBN 0-689-31196-6
1. Afro-Americans - Relations with Indians. I. Title.
NYPL [IEC 87-411]

The Black West / by William Loren Katz. 3rd ed., rev. and expanded. Seattle, WA : Open Hand Pub., c1987. xiii, 348 p. : ill., ports. ; 24 cm. Includes index. A history of the black people who participated in the development of the Western frontier in the United States, in such categories as the explorers, fur traders, early settlers, slaves, cowboys, and soldiers. Bibliography: p. [334]-344.   ISBN 0-940880-17-2 DDC 978/.00496073 19
1. Afro-Americans - West (U. S.) - History. 2. Afro-Americans - West (U. S.) - Biography. 3. Frontier and pioneer life - West (U. S.). 4. West (U. S.) - History. 5. West (U. S.) - Biography. I. Title.
E185.925 .K37 1987   *NYPL [Sc E 89-86]*

Katzen, May. Dean, Elizabeth. [History in black and white. Spanish.] Historia en blanco y negro . Barcelona , Paris , 1984. 196 p. ;   ISBN 92-3-302092-4 (Unesco)
NYPL [Sc D 88-594]

Kaufman, Curt. Hotel boy / by Curt & Gita Kaufman ; with photographs by Curt Kaufman. 1st ed. New York : Atheneum, c1987. 40 p. : ill. ; 26 cm. A boy describes what it is like living in a hotel in New York City with his brother and his mother while she waits to find a job and an apartment. SCHOMBURG CHILDREN'S COLLECTION.   ISBN 0-689-31287-3 :   DDC 307.3/36 19
1. Poor children - New York (N.Y.) - Case studies - Juvenile literature. 2. Welfare recipients - Housing - New York (N.Y.) - Case studies - Juvenile literature. 3. Hotels, taverns, etc. - New York (N.Y.) - Case studies - Juvenile literature. I. Kaufman, Gita. II. Schomburg Children's Collection. III. Title.
HV4046.N6 K38 1987   *NYPL [Sc F 88-362]*

Kaufman, Gita. Kaufman, Curt. Hotel boy /. New York , c1987. 40 p. :   ISBN 0-689-31287-3 : DDC 307.3/36 19
HV4046.N6 K38 1987   *NYPL [Sc F 88-362]*

Kaufman, Jonathan. Broken alliance : the turbulent times between Blacks and Jews in America / Jonathan Kaufman. New York : Scribner, c1988. 311 p. ; 24 cm. Includes index. Bibliography: p. 285-300.   ISBN 0-684-18699-3 : DDC 305.8/00973 19
1. United States - Race relations. I. Title.
E185.615 .K33 1988   *NYPL [*PXY 88-4777]*

Kaula, Edna Mason.
(illus) Colman, Hila. A career in medical research. Cleveland [1968] 175 p.   DDC 610.7 R690 .C65   *NYPL [Sc D 88-425]*

The land and people of Tanzania. [1st ed.] Philadelphia, Lippincott [1972] 139 p. illus. 21 cm. (Portraits of the nations series) An introduction to the geography, history, people, industries, culture, and social progress of the largest country in East Africa. SCHOMBURG CHILDREN'S COLLECTION.   ISBN 0-397-31270-9   DDC 916.78
1. Tanzania - Juvenile literature. I. Schomburg Children's Collection. II. Title.
DT438 .K33   *NYPL [Sc D 88-1112]*

Kaunda, Kenneth David, Pres. Zambia, 1924- Inaugural addresses [microform] /. [Lusaka] , 1982. [39] p. ;
NYPL [Sc Micro R-4132 no. 23]

Kaungamno, E. E. see Kaungamno, Ezekiel E.

Kaungamno, Ezekiel E. The East Africa library movement and its problems [microform] / by

E.E. Kaungamno. Dar es Salaam : National Central Library, [197-?] 6 leaves ; 33 cm. (Occasional paper/Tanzania Library Service; no. 27) Cover title. "Paper appeared in the East African Journal, vol. VI no. 6, June 1969, pp. 36-39." Includes bibliographical references. Microfilm. New York: New York Public Library, 1982. 1 microfilm reel; 35 mm. (MN *ZZ-22581)
1. Libraries - Africa, East. I. Series: Tanzania Library Service. Occasional paper, no. 27. II. Title.
NYPL [Sc Micro R4094 no. 30]

KAVIRONDO (NILOTIC PEOPLE) see LUO (AFRICAN PEOPLE)

Kawara, James. Sajeni Chimedza / James Kawara. Gweru, [Zimbabwe] : Mambo Press, 1984. 174 p. ; 19 cm. (Mambo writers series. Shona section . vol. 18) ISBN 0-86922-327-5
1. Shona language - Texts. 2. Zimbabwe - Fiction. I. Title. II. Series. *NYPL [Sc C 88-97]*

Kaye, Geraldine, 1925- Koto and the lagoon. Illus. by Joanna Stubbs. New York, Funk & Wagnalls [1969, c1967] 128 p. illus. 22 cm. When the runaway slave girl from north Ghana comes to live near the sacred lagoon with no respect for the customs of Koto and his people, Koto can not betray their friendship even though he blames her for the tragic times befalling his people. SCHOMBURG CHILDREN'S COLLECTION. DDC [Fic]
1. Ghana - Juvenile fiction. I. Stubbs, Joanna, illus. II. Schomburg Children's Collection. III. Title.
PZ7.K212 Ko3   *NYPL [Sc D 89-159]*

Kayo, Patrice. Les sauterelles : (nouvelles) / Patrice Kayo. Yaoundé : Éditions CLE, 1986. 79 p. ; 21 cm.
1. Cameroun - Fiction. I. Title.
NYPL [Sc D 88-180]

Kayode, M. O. The confused society / Femi Kayode. Ibadan, Nigeria : Evans Brothers (Nigeria Publishers), 1987. vii, 138 p. : ill. ; 22 cm. ISBN 978-16-7457-1
1. Nigeria - Social conditions - 1960-. 2. Nigeria - Politics and government - 1960-. I. Title.
NYPL [Sc D 88-786]

Kayongo, Kabunda. Reciprocity and interdependence : the rise and fall of the Kololo Empire in Southern Africa in the 19th century / Kabunda Kayongo. [Stockholm] : Almqvist & Wiksell International, 1987. 189 p. : ill., maps, ports. ; 23 cm. (Lund studies in sociology. 78.) Bibliography: p. 157-189. ISBN 91-22-00891-8
1. Zambia - History - To 1890. I. Title.
NYPL [Sc D 88-863]

Keats, Ezra Jack. Da Snøen Kom / Ezra Jack Keats ; norsk text: Jo Tenfjord. [Norway] : Tiden Norsk Forlag, 1967. [20] p. : col ill. ; 21 x 24 cm. Translation of: The snowy day. SCHOMBURG CHILDREN'S COLLECTION.
1. Snow - Juvenile fiction. 2. Afro-American children - Juvenile fiction. I. Schomburg Children's Collection. II. Title. *NYPL [Sc D 88-467]*

Keckley, Elizabeth, 1824-1907. Behind the scenes, or, Thirty years a slave, and four years in the White House / Elizabeth Keckley ; with an introduction by James Olney. New York : Oxford University Press, 1988. xxxvi, xvi, 371 p. : port. ; 17 cm. (The Schomburg library of nineteenth-century Black women writers) Reprint. Originally published: New York : G.W. Carlton, 1868. ISBN 0-19-505255-5 DDC 973.7/092/2 19
1. Lincoln, Abraham, 1809-1865. 2. Lincoln, Mary (Todd) 1818-1882. 3. Keckley, Elizabeth, 1824-1907. 4. Slaves - United States - Biography. I. Title. II. Title: Thirty years a slave and four years in the White House. III. Title: Behind the scenes. IV. Series.
E457.15 .K26 1988   *NYPL [JFC 88-2194]*

KECKLEY, ELIZABETH, 1824-1907.
Keckley, Elizabeth, 1824-1907. Behind the scenes, or, Thirty years a slave, and four years in the White House /. New York , 1988. xxxvi, xvi, 371 p. : ISBN 0-19-505259-5 DDC 973.7/092/2 19
E457.15 .K26 1988   *NYPL [JFC 88-2194]*

Keegan, Timothy J.
Facing the storm : portraits of Black lives in rural South Africa / Tim Keegan. London : Zed Books ; Athens : Ohio University Press, 1988. vi, 169 p. : ill., ports. ; 23 cm. ISBN 0-8214-0924-7 DDC 305.8/96068 19
1. Blacks - South Africa - Social conditions - Case studies. 2. South Africa - Rural conditions - Case studies. I. Title.
HN801.A8 K44 1989   *NYPL [Sc D 89-233]*

Rural transformations in industrializing South Africa : the southern highveld to 1914 / Timothy J. Keegan. Basingstoke ; London : Macmillan, 1987. xviii, 302 p. : map ; 23 cm. Includes index. Bibliography: p. 272-291. ISBN 0-333-41746-1
1. Agriculture - Economic aspects - South Africa - History. 2. Agriculture and state - South Africa. 3. Land tenure - South Africa. 4. Blacks - South Africa - Economic conditions. 5. Afrikaners - Economic conditions. 6. South Africa - Economic conditions - To 1918. I. Title. *NYPL [Sc D 88-1228]*

Keen, Ian. Being Black . Canberra , 1988. xiv, 273 p. : ISBN 0-85575-185-1
NYPL [Sc E 88-515]

Keen, Rosemary A. Church Missionary Society. Africa (Group 3) Committee. Catalogue of the papers of the missions of the Africa (Group 3) Committee /. London , 1981. 8 v. ; DDC 266/.3 19
CD1069.L715 C47 1981   *NYPL [Sc F 88-78]*

Keeping company with Jamaica /. Sherlock, Philip M. (Philip Manderson) London , 1984. vii, 211 p. : ISBN 0-333-37419-3 (pbk) : DDC 917.292/046 19
F1869   *NYPL [Sc D 88-1466]*

Keeping the dream alive . Peake, Thomas R., 1939- New York , 1987. xiv, 492 p. : ISBN 0-8204-0397-0 : DDC 323.42/3/06073 19
E185.61 .P4 1987   *NYPL [Sc D 88-444]*

Keepnews, Orrin. The view from within : jazz writings, 1948-1987 / Orrin Keepnews. New York : Oxford University Press, 1988. x, 238 p. ; 22 cm. ISBN 0-19-505284-6 DDC 785.42 19
1. Jazz music - Collected works. I. Title.
ML3507 .K43 1988   *NYPL [Sc D 88-1453]*

Kehinde-Adeniyi, Kehinde. Broken ribs / by Kehinde Kehinde-Adeniyi. [S.l. : s.n., 198-?] (Ibara, Abeokuta : Alayande Printing Press) viii, 48 p. ; 19 cm.
1. Title. *NYPL [Sc C 88-354]*

Keita, Djigui. Le rôle socio-religieux de la cola dans la société malinké : exemple de Kaaba / présenté par Keita Djigui ; sous la direction de M. Koume N'Guessan. [Abidjan? : s.n., 1985] 72 leaves : maps ; 28 cm. Thesis (Master's)--Université d'Abidjan, 1985. At head of title: Faculté des lettres et sciences humaines, Institut d'ethno-sociologie. "Septembre 1985." Bibliography: leaves 71-72.
1. Mandingo (African people) - Social life and customs. 2. Kola nuts - Africa, West. I. Title.
NYPL [Sc F 88-307]

KEITA, SOUNDIATA, 1255.
Diabaté, Massa M. Le Lion à l'arc . Paris , 1986. 128 p. ; ISBN 2-218-07616-0
NYPL [Sc C 89-155]

Keller, Frances Richardson. Cooper, Anna J. (Anna Julia), 1858-1964. [Attitude de la France à l'égard de l'esclavage pendant la révolution. English] Slavery and the French revolutionists, 1788-1805 /. Lewiston , 1988. 228 p. : ISBN 0-88946-637-8 DDC 972.94/03 19
F1923 .C7213 1988   *NYPL [Sc E 88-469]*

Kelley, Emma Dunham.
Four girls at Cottage City / Emma D. Kelley-Hawkins ; with an introduction by Deborah E. McDowell. New York : Oxford University Press, 1988. xxxviii, 379 p. ; 17 cm. (The Schomburg library of nineteenth-century Black women writers) Bibliography: xxxvii-xxxviii. Reprint. Originally published: Boston : James H. Earle, 1898. ISBN 0-19-505242-0 DDC 813/.4 19
1. Title. II. Series.
PS2159.K13 F6 1988   *NYPL [JFC 88-2149]*

Megda / Emma Dunham Kelley ; with an introduction by Molly Hite. New York : Oxford University Press, 1988. xxxvii, 394 p. : port. ; 17 cm. (The Schomburg library of nineteenth-century Black women writers) Reprint. Originally published: Boston : James H. Earle, 1891. ISBN 0-19-505245-5 (alk. paper) DDC 813/.4 19
1. Title. II. Series.
PS2159.K13 M44 1988
NYPL [JFC 88-2146]

Kelley, Sally. Summer growing time. Illustrated by Donald A. Mackay. [1st ed.] New York, Viking Press [1971] 125 p. illus. 22 cm. June and her grandmother live in their own world absorbed in gardening until growing racial unrest in the town intrudes on their lives. SCHOMBURG CHILDREN'S

COLLECTION. ISBN 0-670-68172-5 DDC [Fic]
1. Civil rights - Mississippi - Juvenile fiction. I. Mackay, Donald A., illus. II. Schomburg Children's Collection. III. Title.
PZ7.K2818 Su   *NYPL [Sc D 89-88]*

Kelshall, Gaylord. Airports Authority of Trinidad and Tobago. The history of aviation in Trinidad & Tobago 1913-1962 /. Port-of-Spain, Trinidad , 1987. xxv, 159 p., [77] p. of plates : ISBN 976-8054-24-2
NYPL [Sc D 87-1398]

Kendall, Lace. Rain boat / by Lace Kendall ; pictures by John Kaufmann. New York : Coward-McCann 1965. 159 p. : ill. ; 23 cm.
1. Florida - Juvenile fiction. I. Title.
NYPL [Sc D 88-472]

Kengne Pokam, E (Emmanuel), 1941- Les Églises chrétiennes face à la montée du nationalisme camerounais / Kengne Pakam. Paris : L'Harmattan, [1987] 202 p. ; 22 cm. (Points de vue) Bibliography: p. 199-200. ISBN 2-85802-823-0
1. Union des populations du Cameroun. 2. Church and state - Cameroon. 3. Nationalism - Cameroon. I. Title.
NYPL [Sc D 88-437]

KENNEDY, JOHN FITZGERALD, PRES. U. S., 1917-1963.
Saunders, Doris E. The Kennedy years and the Negro . Chicago , 1964. xiii, 143 p. :
NYPL [Sc F 89-75]

Kennedy, Paul M., 1945- African capitalism : the struggle for ascendency / Paul Kennedy. Cambridge, Cambridgeshire ; New York : Cambridge University Press, 1988. x, 233 p. ; 24 cm. (African society today) Includes index. Bibliography: p. 192-225. ISBN 0-521-26599-1 DDC 332/.041/096 19
1. Capitalism - Africa. 2. Africa - Economic conditions - 1960-. I. Title. II. Series.
HC800 .K46 1988   *NYPL [Sc E 88-520]*

KENTUCKY - RACE RELATIONS.
Johnson, Lyman T., 1906- The rest of the dream . Lexington, Ky. , c1988. xiv, 230 p., [8] p. of plates : ISBN 0-8131-1674-0 (alk. paper) : DDC 976.9/00496073024 B 19
E185.97.J693 A3 1988   *NYPL [Sc E 89-211]*

Kenworthy, Leonard Stout, 1912- Profile of Nigeria / by Leonard S. Kenworthy. Garden City, New York : Doubleday, c1960. 96 p. : ill. ; 25 cm. Includes index. SCHOMBURG CHILDREN'S COLLECTION.
1. Nigeria - Juvenile literature. I. Schomburg Children's Collection. II. Title. *NYPL [Sc E 88-240]*

Kenya . Amin, Mohamed, 1943- London , 1988. 191 p. : ISBN 0-370-31225-2 : DDC 967.6/204/0222 19
DT433.52   *NYPL [Sc G 88-33]*

Kenya . Sheikh-Dilthey, Helmtraut, 1944- Köln , 1987. 279 p. : *NYPL [Sc D 88-935]*

Kenya African National Union. A Tribute to president Daniel T. Arap Moi. Nairobi , 1988. 52 p. : *NYPL [Sc F 89-113]*

KENYA - BIOGRAPHY.
Memories of Kenya . London , 1986. xvi, 160 p., [16] p. of plates : ISBN 0-237-50919-9
NYPL [Sc F 88-102]

KENYA - COLONIZATION - HISTORY.
Harris, Joseph E., 1929- Repatriates and refugees in a colonial society . Washington, D.C. , 1987. ix, 201 p. ; ISBN 0-88258-148-1 : DDC 304.8/676/2 19
HN793.Z9 E44 1987   *NYPL [Sc E 87-558]*

KENYA - DESCRIPTION AND TRAVEL.
Sheikh-Dilthey, Helmtraut, 1944- Kenya . Köln , 1987. 279 p. : *NYPL [Sc D 88-935]*

KENYA - DESCRIPTION AND TRAVEL - 1981-
Amin, Mohamed, 1943- Kenya . London , 1988. 191 p. : ISBN 0-370-31225-2 : DDC 967.6/204/0222 19
DT433.52   *NYPL [Sc G 88-33]*

KENYA - DESCRIPTION AND TRAVEL - 1981- - GUIDE-BOOKS.
Trillo, Richard. The rough guide to Kenya /. London , New York , 1987. 374 p. : ISBN 0-7102-0616-X (pbk.) DDC 916.76/2044 19
DT433.52 .T75 1986   *NYPL [Sc C 88-145]*

KENYA - DESCRIPTION AND TRAVEL - VIEWS.
Amin, Mohamed, 1943- Kenya . London ,

1988. 191 p. : ISBN 0-370-31225-2 : DDC
967.6/204/0222 19
DT433.52   *NYPL [Sc G 88-33]*

Dinesen, Isak, 1885-1962. Isak Dinesen's
Africa . London , 1986, c1985. xvii, 142 p. :
ISBN 0-593-01049-3   *NYPL [Sc G 88-26]*

KENYA - ECONOMIC CONDITIONS.
Godfrey, Martin. Kenya to 1990 . London ,
1986. 105 p. :   *NYPL [Sc F 88-118]*

Spencer, Ian R. G. The economic development
of Kenya, 1895-1929 [microform] . [Nairobi]
[1978] 14 p. ;
    NYPL [Sc Micro R-4108 no.33]

KENYA - ECONOMIC CONDITIONS - 1963-
A Tribute to president Daniel T. Arap Moi.
Nairobi , 1988. 52 p. :   *NYPL [Sc F 89-113]*

Wanjui, J. B. From where I sit . Nairobi,
Kenya , 1986. xi, 88 p. ;   *NYPL [Sc C 88-90]*

**KENYA - ECONOMIC CONDITIONS - 1963- -
CONGRESSES.**
The Political economy of Kenya /. New York ,
1987. viii, 245 p., [1] leaf of plates : ISBN
0-275-92672-9 (alk. paper) : DDC 330.9676/204
19
HC865 .P65 1987   *NYPL [Sc E 88-157]*

KENYA - ECONOMIC POLICY.
Godfrey, Martin. Kenya to 1990 . London ,
1986. 105 p. :   *NYPL [Sc F 88-118]*

Kenya. Education, Ministry of. see Kenya.
Ministry of Education.

KENYA - FICTION.
Gateria, Wamugunda. Black gold of Chepkube
/. Nairobi , 1985. 139 p. ;
    NYPL [Sc C 88-284]

Gicheru, Mwangi. The double-cross /. Nairobi ,
1983. 169 p. ; ISBN 0-582-78544-8
    NYPL [Sc C 87-461]

Kariara, Jonathan. The coming of power, and
other stories /. Nairobi , 1986. 100 p. ; ISBN
0-19-572597-2   *NYPL [Sc D 88-1053]*

Kulet, Henry R. ole, 1946- Daughter of Maa /.
Nairobi , 1987. 172 p. ; ISBN 0-582-98653-2
    NYPL [Sc C 89-42]

Macgoye, Marjorie Oludhe. Street life /.
Nairobi , 1987. 102 p. ; ISBN 996-646-362-3
    NYPL [Sc C 89-4]

Maillu, David G., 1939- The ayah /. Nairobi ,
1986. 178 p. ;
MLCS 89/131165 (P)   *NYPL [Sc C 89-158]*

Mumba, Maurice Kambishera. The wrath of
Koma /. Nairobi , 1987. 153 p. ; ISBN
996-646-342-6   *NYPL [Sc C 89-45]*

Odaga, Asenath. A bridge in time /. Kisumu,
Kenya , 1987. 167 p. ;
MLCS 88/07442 (P)   *NYPL [Sc C 88-374]*

Odaga, Asenath. The shade changes /. [Kisumu,
Kenya] [c1984] 175 p. ;
MLCS 87/7892 (P)   *NYPL [Sc 88-214]*

Saisi, Frank. The bhang syndicate /. Nairobi ,
1984. 180 p. ;
MLCS 84/916 (P)   *NYPL [Sc C 88-282]*

Kenya - Government. see Kenya - Politics and
government.

KENYA - HISTORY.
Sheikh-Dilthey, Helmtraut, 1944- Kenya .
Köln , 1987. 279 p. :   *NYPL [Sc D 88-935]*

KENYA - HISTORY - TO 1963.
Gakaara wa Wanjaū. Mwandĩki wa Mau Mau
ithaamĩrio-inĩ /. Nairobi [Kenya] , 1983. xvii,
189 p. :   *NYPL [Sc D 87-156]*

Gakaara wa Wanjaū. [Mwandĩki wa Mau Mau
ithaamĩrio-inĩ. English.] Mau Mau author in
detention /. Nairobi , 1988. xix, 252 p. ; ISBN
996-646-354-2   *NYPL [Sc D 89-444]*

Kenya's freedom struggle . London ; Atlantic
Highlands, N.J. , 1987. xix, 138 p. :
    NYPL [Sc D 88-775]

Nyasani, J. M. (Joseph Major), 1938- The
British massacre of the Gusii freedom defenders
/. Nairobi, Kenya , 1984. v, 85 p. :
    NYPL [Sc D 88-1133]

KENYA - HISTORY - 1895-1963 - FICTION.
Mwangi, Meja, 1948- [Carcase for hounds.
German.] Wie ein Aas für Hunde .

Bornheim-Merten , 1987. 173 p. ; ISBN
3-88977-136-X   *NYPL [Sc C 88-148]*

Kenya is my country /. Moon, Bernice. Hove ,
1985. 60 p. : ISBN 0-85078-489-1 : DDC
967.6/204 19   *NYPL [Sc F 88-379]*

KENYA - JUVENILE FICTION.
Stinetorf, Louise A. Elephant outlaw /.
Philadelphia , c1956. 173 p. :
    NYPL [Sc D 88-1167]

KENYA - JUVENILE LITERATURE.
Moon, Bernice. Kenya is my country /. Hove ,
1985. 60 p. : ISBN 0-85078-489-1 : DDC
967.6/204 19   *NYPL [Sc F 88-379]*

Ochieng', William Robert, 1943- Geography,
history and civics . London , 1987. 170 p. :
    NYPL [Sc F 88-190]

The Kenya little general election [microform] .
Harbeson, John Willis, 1938- Nairobi , 1967. 23
p. ;   *NYPL [Sc Micro R-4108 no. 31]*

Kenya Medical Research Institute. A
Bibliography of health and disease in East
Africa /. Amsterdam ; New York : 282 p. ;
ISBN 0-444-80931-7 (U. S.) DDC
016.3621/0967 19
Z6673.6.A353 B53 1988 RA552.A353
    NYPL [Sc G 89-6]

Kenya. Ministry of Education. Education in
Kenya . Nairobi, Kenya , c1987. iv, 128 p., [1]
folded leaf of plates ;   *NYPL [Sc D 89-169]*

**Kenya. Ministry of Planning and National
Development.** Socio-cultural profiles, Baringo
District . [Nairobi?] , 1986. xviii, 268 p. : DDC
967.6/27 19
DT434.B36 S63 1986   *NYPL [Sc F 88-230]*

Kenya NGO Organising Committee--Forum '85.
Women and population . [Nairobi?] [1985] 73
p. ; DDC 363.9/6/096762 19
HQ766.5.K4 W65 1985   *NYPL [Sc F 88-191]*

KENYA - POLITICS AND GOVERNMENT.
Harbeson, John Willis, 1938- The Kenya little
general election [microform] . Nairobi , 1967.
23 p. ;   *NYPL [Sc Micro R-4108 no. 31]*

**KENYA - POLITICS AND GOVERNMENT -
TO 1963.**
Teubert-Seiwert, Bärbel, 1951- Parteipolitik in
Kenya 1960-1969 /. Frankfurt am Main , New
York , c1987. 428 p. ; ISBN 3-8204-0151-2
DDC 324.2676/2 19
JQ2947.A979 .T48 1987
    NYPL [Sc D 88-1141]

**KENYA - POLITICS AND GOVERNMENT -
1963-1978.**
Teubert-Seiwert, Bärbel, 1951- Parteipolitik in
Kenya 1960-1969 /. Frankfurt am Main , New
York , c1987. 428 p. ; ISBN 3-8204-0151-2
DDC 324.2676/2 19
JQ2947.A979 .T48 1987
    NYPL [Sc D 88-1141]

**KENYA - POLITICS AND GOVERNMENT -
1978-**
Dumila, Faraj O., 1937- The Nyayo decade /.
[Nairobi? , 1988?] 2 v. :
    NYPL [Sc F 89-122]

Gitari, David M. Let the Bfin id
89b21342/updd M. Gitari. Nairobi, Kenya ,
1988. 90 p. :   *NYPL [Sc D 89-400]*

Moi's reign of terror . London , 1989. 88 p. :
ISBN 1-87188-601-5   *NYPL [Sc D 89-524]*

A Tribute to president Daniel T. Arap Moi.
Nairobi , 1988. 52 p. :   *NYPL [Sc F 89-113]*

**KENYA - POPULATION POLICY -
CONGRESSES.**
Women and population . [Nairobi?] [1985] 73
p. ; DDC 363.9/6/096762 19
HQ766.5.K4 W65 1985   *NYPL [Sc F 88-191]*

**Kenya. Presidential Working Party on Education
and Manpower Training for the Next Decade
and Beyond.** Report of the Presidential
Working Party on Education and Manpower
Training for the Next Decade and Beyond /
Chairman, James Mwangi Kamunge. Nairobi :
[s.n.], 1988. xvii, 174 p. ; 25 cm. "March, 1988."
*1. Education - Kenya. 2. Manpower - Kenya. I.
Kamunge, James Mwangi. II. Title.*
    NYPL [Sc E 89-232]

KENYA - PRESIDENTS - BIOGRAPHY.
Ng'weno, Hilary. The day Kenyatta died /.
Nairobi , 1978. 68 p., [1] leaf of plates : ISBN

0-582-64283-3 DDC 967.6/204/0924 B 19
DT433.576.K46 N45   *NYPL [Sc F 89-28]*

KENYA - RURAL CONDITIONS.
Narayan-Parker, Deepa. Women's interest and
involvement in income generating activities .
Gaborone, Botswana [1983] vi, 143, 3 p. ;
DDC 331.4/09676/2 19
HD6210.5 .N37 1983   *NYPL [Sc F 88-312]*

**KENYA - SOCIAL CONDITIONS - 1963- -
CONGRESSES.**
The Political economy of Kenya /. New York ,
1987. viii, 245 p., [1] leaf of plates : ISBN
0-275-92672-9 (alk. paper) : DDC 330.9676/204
19
HC865 .P65 1987   *NYPL [Sc E 88-157]*

**KENYA - SOCIAL LIFE AND CUSTOMS -
1895-1963.**
Dinesen, Isak, 1885-1962. Isak Dinesen's
Africa . London , 1986, c1985. xvii, 142 p. :
ISBN 0-593-01049-3   *NYPL [Sc G 88-26]*

KENYA TALES. see TALES, KENYA.

Kenya to 1990 . Godfrey, Martin. London , 1986.
105 p. :   *NYPL [Sc F 88-118]*

Kenya women heroes and their mystical power /.
Njau, Rebeka. Nairobi , 1984- v. ; DDC
398/.09676/2 19
GR356.4 .N43 1984   *NYPL [Sc D 88-1052]*

KENYAN DRAMA (ENGLISH)
Drama festival plays /. London , Baltimore,
Md. , 1986. iv, 92 p. ; ISBN 0-7131-8446-9
    NYPL [Sc D 88-638]

Kenya's freedom struggle : the Dedan Kimathi
papers / edited by Maina wa Kinyatti ;
foreword by Ngugi wa Thiong'o. London ;
Atlantic Highlands, N.J. : Zed Books, 1987. xix,
138 p. ; 22 cm. Consists chiefly of documents of the
Mau Mau movement, some translated from Kikuyu or
Swahili.
*1. Kimathi, Dedan, 1920-1957. 2. Mau Mau - Archives.
3. Kenya - History - To 1963. I. Maina-wa-Kinyatti. II.
Title. III. Title: Dedan Kimathi papers.*
    NYPL [Sc D 88-775]

KENYATTA, JOMO - DEATH AND BURIAL.
Ng'weno, Hilary. The day Kenyatta died /.
Nairobi , 1978. 68 p., [1] leaf of plates : ISBN
0-582-64283-3 DDC 967.6/204/0924 B 19
DT433.576.K46 N45   *NYPL [Sc F 89-28]*

Kenyo, Elisha Alademomi. Awon olori Yoruba ati
isedale won / lati owo E. Alademomi Kenyo.
Lagos, Nigeria : Yoruba Historical Research
Co., 1952. 96 p. : ports. ; 22cm.
*1. Yorubas - History. 2. Yorubas - Social life and
customs. 3. Yoruba language - Texts. 4. Nigeria - Kings
and rulers - History. I. Title.*
    NYPL [Sc D 88-818]

Kerlin, Robert Thomas, 1866-1950. Contemporary
poetry of the Negro / by Robert Thomas
Kerlin. Hampton, Virginia : Press of the
Hampton Normal and Agricultural Institute,
1921. 23 p. ; 23 cm.
*1. American poetry - Afro-American authors - History
and criticism. 2. American poetry - 20th century -
History and criticism. I. Title.*
    NYPL [Sc Rare C 89-22]

The Kerner report . United States. Kerner
Commission. New York, N.Y. , 1988. xxvi, 513
p. ; ISBN 0-679-72078-2   *NYPL [Sc D 89-604]*

Kersebaum, Andrea. Integrationsbestrebungen in
Afrika : zwischenstaatliche Organisationen und
regionale Zusammenarbeit : eine
Auswahlbibliographie = Integration efforts in
Africa : international organizations and regional
co-operation : a selected bibliography / Andrea
Kersebaum. Hamburg : Deutsches
Ubersee-Institut, Ubersee-Dokumentation,
Referat Afrika, 1986-1987. 2 v. ; 30 cm.
(Dokumentationsdienst Afrika. Reihe A . 23) Includes
indexes. CONTENTS. - v. 1. Afrika = Africa --- v. 2.
Nord-, West-, Zentral- Südliches und Ostafrika =
North, West, Central, Southern and East Africa.
ISBN 3-922852-13-0
*1. African cooperation - Bibliography. 2. Africa -
Economic integration - Bibliography. I. Title. II. Title:
Integration efforts in Africa. III. Series.*
    NYPL [Sc F 88-33]

Kessler, Leonard P., 1920- (illus) Lawrence, James
Duncan, 1918- Binky brothers, detectives. New
York [1968] 60 p. DDC [Fic]
PZ7.L4359 Bi   *NYPL [Sc D 89-118]*

Kesteloot, Lilyan. Comprendre les Poèmes de Léopold Sédar Senghor / Lilyan Kesteloot. Issy les Moulineaux : Classiques africains, 1986. 143 p. : ill., maps, ports. ; 21 cm. (Classiques africains. no 862) Comprendre Bibliography: p. 120-121. ISBN 2-85049-376-7
1. Senghor, Léopold Sédar, 1906- - Criticism and interpretation. 2. Senghor, Léopold Sédar, 1906- . Poèmes. I. Series. II. Series: Comprendre (Classiques africains (Firm)). III. Title. **NYPL [Sc D 88-978]**

Ketchum, Jean, 1926- Stick-in-the-mud : a tale of a village, a custom and a little boy / story by Jean Ketchum ; illustrated by Fred Ketchum. New York : W.R. Scott, [c1953] unpaged : ill. ; 20 cm. SCHOMBURG CHILDREN'S COLLECTION.
I. Schomburg Childrn's Collection. II. Title.
NYPL [Sc C 88-375]

Kezilahabi, Euphrase. Gamba la nyoka / Euphrase Kezilahabi. Arusha [Tanzania] : Eastern Africa Publications Limited, 1979, 1981 printing. 151 p. ; 19 cm.
1. Swahili language - Texts. 2. Tanzania - Fiction. I. Title. **NYPL [Sc C 88-167]**

Kh alid, Mansour, 1931- Garang, John, 1945- John Garang speaks /. London , New York , 1987. xii, 147 p. ; ISBN 0-7103-0268-1
NYPL [Sc D 88-418]

Khalifa, Ahmad M. Adverse consequences for the enjoyment of human rights of political, military, economic, and other forms of assistance given to the racist and colonialist régime of South Africa / by Ahmad M. Khalifa. New York : United Nations, 1985. ii, 164, [30] p. ; 30 cm. "E/CN.4/Sub.2/1984/8/Rev.1"--Cover. Presented to the Sub-commission on Prevention of Discrimination and Protection of Minorities. "United Nations publication sales no. E.85.XIV.4"--Verso t.p. ISBN 92-1-154046-1 (pbk.) DDC 332.6/73/0968 19
1. Investments, Foreign - South Africa. 2. Investments, Foreign - Namibia. 3. Corporations, Foreign - South Africa. 4. Corporations, Foreign - Namibia. 5. Economic assistance - South Africa. 6. Economic assistance - Namibia. 7. Civil rights - South Africa. 8. Civil rights - Namibia. I. United Nations. Sub-commission on Prevention of Discrimination and Protection of Minorities.
HG5851.A3 K45 1985 **NYPL [Sc F 88-273]**

KHAMA, TSHEKEDI, 1905-1959. Crowder, Michael, 1934- The flogging of Phinehas McIntosh . New Haven , 1988. xii, 248 p. : ISBN 0-300-04098-9 DDC 968/.1103 19
DT791 .C76 1988 **NYPL [Sc E 88-289]**

Khan, Lurey. One day, Levin ... he be free; William Still and the underground railroad. [1st ed.] New York, E. P. Dutton [1972] 231 p. illus. 22 cm. Chronicles the efforts of William Still, son of an escaped slave, to help his people through his work with Philadelphia's Anti-slavery Society and the Underground Railroad. Bibliography: p. 231. ISBN 0-525-36415-3 DDC 973.7/115 B 92
1. Still, William, 1821-1902. 2. Underground Railroad. I. Title.
E450.S852 K45 1972 **NYPL [Sc D 88-1116]**

Khartum. University. Institute of African and Asian Studies. International Conference on the Central Bilad al-Sudan Tradition and Adaptation (3rd : 1977 : Khartum, Sudan) Third International Conference on the Central Bilad al-Sudan Tradition and Adaptation [microform] [Khartum] [1977] 25, 13 p. ;
NYPL [Sc Micro F-10980]

Khayundi, Festus E. A survey of preservation of library collections in Kenya / by Festus E. Khayundi. [Nairobi? : s.n.,], 1988. iii, 36 leaves ; 30 cm. Bibliography: leaves 21-22.
1. Library materials - Conservation and restoration. 2. Library administration - Kenya. I. Title.
NYPL [Sc F 89-142]

Khazanov, A. M. (Anatoliĭ Mikhaĭlovich), 1932- [Agostinó Neto. English]
Agostinho Neto / A.M. Khazanov ; [translated from the Russian by Cynthia Carlile]. Moscow : Progress Publishers, 1986. 301 p. ; 17 cm. Translation of: Agostinó Neto. Includes bibliographical references. DDC 967/.304/0924 B 19
1. Agostinho Neto, António, 1922-. 2. Movimento Popular de Liberta ção de Angola. 3. Heads of state - Angola - Biography. 4. Revolutionists - Angola -

Biography. I. Title.
DT611.76.A38 K4213 1986
NYPL [Sc B 88-47]

Khimulu, Mary M. The Girl Guide movement in Kenya : role, evaluation and impact, binding strong characters and personality / Mary M. Khimulu. [Nairob] : Kenya Girl Guide Publication, c1987. 57 p. : ill. ; 21 cm.
1. Girl Scouts - Kenya. I. Title.
NYPL [Sc D 89-12]

Khoe-kowap . Böhm, Gerhard. Wien , 1985. 406 p. ; ISBN 3-85043-036-7
PL8541 .B6 1985 **NYPL [Sc D 89-365]**

Khutbat's of Al Hajj Al Imam Isa Abd'Allah Muhammad Al Mahdi [microform]. 'Isá 'Abd Allāh Muḥammad al-Mahdī, 1945- Brooklyn [1978?] 2 v. :
NYPL [Sc Micro R-4114 no. 17]

KHWAKHWA (AFRICAN PEOPLE) Sheddick, Vernon George John. The morphology of residential associations as found among the Khwakhwa of Basutoland. [Cape Town], University of Cape Town, 1948. 57 p.
DT786 .S5 **NYPL [Sc G 89-1]**

A Kì í . Owomoyela, Oyekan. Lanham , c1988. x, 388 p. ; ISBN 0-8191-6502-6 (alk. paper) : DDC 398/.9/96333 19
PN6519.Y6 O96 1987 **NYPL [Sc E 88-278]**

KIBEHO (RWANDA) - RELIGIOUS LIFE AND CUSTOMS. Maindron, Gabriel. Des apparitions à Kibeho . Paris , c1984. 243 p., [4] p. of plates : ISBN 2-86839-021-8 : DDC 232.91/7/0967571 19
BT660.K52 M35 1984 **NYPL [Sc E 88-516]**

Kibreab, Gaim. Refugees and development in Africa : the case of Eritrea / Gaim Kibreab. Trenton, N.J. : Red Sea Press, [1987] xii, 304 p. : ill. ; 22 cm. Revision of the author's thesis (doctoral) Bibliography: p. 293-304. ISBN 0-932415-27-X (pbk.) DDC 325/.21/09624 19
1. Refugees - Sudan - Economic conditions. 2. Refugees - Ethiopia - Eritea. 3. Refugees - Sudan - Social conditions. I. Title.
JV9025.S73 K53 1987 **NYPL [Sc D 89-534]**

Kichenapanaïdou, Marc. Ma terre / Marc Kichenapanaïdou, Hamed Mortouza. Saint-Louis, Réunion : [S.n., 1978?] 43 p. ; 21 cm. French and Réunion creole.
1. Political poetry - Réunion. 2. Réunion - Poetry. I. Mortouza, Hamed. II. Title.
NYPL [Sc D 88-484]

Kidron, Michael. The new state of the world atlas / Michael Kidron & Ronald Segal. [2nd ed.], rev. and updated. New York : Simon and Schuster, 1987. 1 atlas ([54] p., 57 [i.e. 114] p.) : col. maps. ; 25 cm. "A Pluto Press Project." "A Touchstone book." ISBN 0-671-64554-4 (hard) : DDC 912/.132 19
I. Segal, Ronald, 1932-. II. Title.
G1021 .K46 1987
NYPL [Map Div. 87-1075]

Kiel. Universität. Museum für Völkerkunde. Arbeiten.
(7) Schlosser, Katesa. Medizinen des Blitzzauberers Laduma Madela . Kiel , 1984. 186 p., 64, [1] p. of plates : ISBN 3-88312-106-1 DDC 615.8/99/089963 19
DT878.Z9 S32 1984 **NYPL [Sc E 87-271]**

KIKUYU (AFRICA PEOPLE) - HISTORY. Kanogo, Tabitha M. Squatters and the roots of Mau Mau, 1905-63 . Athens , London , 1987. xviii, 206 p. ; ISBN 0-8214-0873-9 DDC 307.3/36 19
HD1538.K4 K36 1987 **NYPL [Sc D 88-207]**

KIKUYU LANGUAGE - TEXTS. Gakaara wa Wanjaū. Mwandĩki wa Mau Mau ithaamĩrio-inĩ /. Nairobi [Kenya] , 1983. xvii, 189 p. : **NYPL [Sc D 87-156]**

Kila mtu na wake /. Kasalama, Mark M. Peramiho, Tanzania , 1983. 55 p. : ISBN 997-663-006-9 **NYPL [Sc D 89-1]**

Kileff, Clive. Shona folk tales /. Gweru, Zimbabwe , 1987. 151 p. ;
NYPL [Sc C 88-317]

Kilgour, Bayard L., Jr., 1904-1984. Pushkin and his friends . Cambridge , 1987. xii, 95 p. :
NYPL [Sc F 88-236]

KILHAM, HANNAH, 1774-1832. Dickson, Mora, 1918- The powerful bond .

London , 1980. 5-252 p. : ISBN 0-234-72103-0 : DDC 266/.963 B 19
BV3625.S5 K393 1980 **NYPL [Sc D 87-37]**

Killing floor. Ai, 1947- [Cruelty.] Cruelty ; Killing floor . New York , c1987. xi, 99 p. ; ISBN 0-938410-38-5 (pbk.) : DDC 811/.54 19
PS3551.I2 A6 1987 **NYPL [JFD 88-417]**

Kimani, John Kiggia. Life and times of a bank robber / John Kiggia Kimani. Nairobi : Spear Books, 1988. 133 p. ; 18 cm. (Spear book) ISBN 996-646-376-3
1. Kimani, John Kiggia. 2. Bank robberies - Kenya. I. Title. **NYPL [Sc C 89-97]**

KIMANI, JOHN KIGGIA. Kimani, John Kiggia. Life and times of a bank robber /. Nairobi , 1988. 133 p. ; ISBN 996-646-376-3 **NYPL [Sc C 89-97]**

KIMATHI, DEDAN, 1920-1957. Kenya's freedom struggle . London ; Atlantic Highlands, N.J. , 1987. xix, 138 p. :
NYPL [Sc D 88-775]

Kimball, Gregg D. McGraw, Marie Tyler. In bondage and freedom . Richmond, VA. [Chapel Hill, N.C.] , 1988. 71 p. :
NYPL [Sc F 89-107]

Kimbidima, Julien Omer, 1961- Les filles du président : roman / Julien Omer Kimbidima. Paris : L'Harmattan, c1986. 138 p. ; 22 cm. (Collection Encres noires. 41) ISBN 2-85802-769-2
1. Africa - Fiction. I. Title.
MLCS 87/2312 (P) **NYPL [Sc D 88-1083]**

Kimble, David.
The University and the Great Hall complex [microform] : address / by David Kimble to the congregation held in Zamba on 11 December 1982. [Zomba, Malawi : University of Malawi, 1982] 17 p., [2] leaves of plates : ill. ; 19 cm. Cover title. Microfiche. New York: New York Public Library, 198 . 1 microfiche: negative; 11 x 15 cm. (FSN Sc 019,083)
I. Title. **NYPL [Sc Micro F-11020]**

The University and the nation [microform] d address / by David Kimble to the congregation held in Zomba on 29 July 1978. [Zomba, Malawi : University of Malawi, 1978] 16 p. ; 19 cm. Cover title. Microfiche. New Yorkd New York Public Library, 198 . 1 microfiche: negative; 11 x 15 cm. (FSN Sc 019,084)
1. Higher education and state - Malawi. I. Title.
NYPL [Sc Micro F-11018]

The University community in Malawi [microform] : address / by David Kimble to the congregation held in Zomba on 25 October 1980. [Zomba, Malawi : University of Malawi, between 1980 and 1983] 19 p. ; 19 cm. Cover title. Microfiche. New York: New York Public Library, 198 . 1 microfiche: negative; 11 x 15 cm. (FSN Sc 019,083)
I. Title. **NYPL [Sc Micro F-11019]**

Kimmelman, Judith. Miniature African sculptures from the Herman collection /. London , 1985. 64 p. : ISBN 0-7287-0454-4
NYPL [Sc D 89-41]

Kincaid, Jamaica.
Annie John / Jamaica Kincaid. New York : Farrar, Straus, Giroux, 1985. 148 p. ; 21 cm. ISBN 0-374-10521-9 : DDC 813/.54 19
1. Antigua - Fiction. I. Title.
PS3561.I425 A55 1985
NYPL [JFD 85-2648]

A small place / Jamaica Kincaid. 1st ed. New York : Farrar, Straus, Giroux, 1988. 81 p. : ill. ; 21 cm. ISBN 0-374-26638-7 : DDC 813 19
1. Antigua - Fiction. I. Title.
PR9275.A583 K5637 1988
NYPL [Sc D 88-1061]

A kind of marriage /. Emecheta, Buchi, 1944. London , 1986. iv, 121 p. ; ISBN 0-333-42242-2
NYPL [Sc D 88-613]

Kinder der Lyela . Dinslage, Sabine. Hohenschäftlarn bei München , 1986. 355 p. : ISBN 3-87673-105-4 DDC 305.2/3/096625 19
DT650.L38 D56 1986 **NYPL [Sc D 88-876]**

Kindred spirits : an anthology of gay and Lesbian science fiction stories / Jeffrey M. Elliot, editor.1st ed. Boston : Alyson, 1984. 262 p. ; 21 cm. ISBN 0-932870-42-2 (pbk.)
1. Science fiction, American. 2. Homosexuality - Fiction. 3. American fiction - 20th century. I. Elliot, Jeffrey M. **NYPL [Sc D 89-269]**

Kindred, Wendy. Negatu in the garden, story and woodcuts by Wendy Kindred. New York, McGraw-Hill [1971] [38] p. illus. 27 cm. A six-year-old boy finds himself left out of the games his sister plays with two new friends. SCHOMBURG CHILDREN'S COLLECTION ISBN 0-07-034585-6 DDC [E]
1. Children - Ethiopia - Juvenile fiction. I. Schomburg Children's Collection. II. Title.
PZ7.K567 Ne   **NYPL [Sc F 88-246]**

The King, Belshazzar /. Green, Ernest Davis. New York , 1962. 178 p. ;
NYPL [Sc D 88-839]

King, Bruce Alvin. Literature and African identity. Bayreuth , c1986. 125 p. ;
NYPL [Sc D 89-369]

King, C. Winville. Jesse, Charles. Peeps into St. Lucia's past /. St. Lucia , 1979. 100 p. :
NYPL [Sc E 88-311]

King, Coretta Scott, 1927- Rummel, Jack. Langston Hughes /. New York , c1988. 111 p. : ISBN 1-555-46595-1 DDC 818/.5209 B 92 19
PS3515.U274 Z775 1988
NYPL [Sc E 88-166]

King cotton /. Armstrong, Thomas, 1899- London , 1947. 928 p. ;   **NYPL [Sc D 88-97]**

King, Don. Ali/Frazier III /. [S.l.] , 1975. [32] p. :   **NYPL [Sc F 89-46]**

King, Martin Luther, Jr., 1929-1968.
The measure of a man / Martin Luther King, Jr. Philadelphia : Fortress Press, c1988. 59 p. : ill., ports. ; 19 cm. ISBN 0-8006-2088-7 DDC 233 19
I. Title.
BT703 .K5 1988   **NYPL [Sc C 88-326]**

KING, MARTIN LUTHER, JR., 1929-1968.
Assensoh, A. B. Rev Dr Martin Luther King, Jr. and America's quest for racial integration . Ilfracombe, Devon , 1987. 104 p. ;
0-7223-2084-1   **NYPL [Sc D 88-100]**

Branch, Taylor. Parting the waters . New York , c1988- v. : ISBN 0-671-46097-8 (v. 1) DDC 973/.0496073 19
E185.61 .B7914 1988   **NYPL [IEC 88-122]**

Colaiaco, James A., 1945- Martin Luther King, Jr. . New York , 1988. x, 238 p. ; ISBN 0-312-02365-0 : DDC 323.4/092/4 B 19
E185.97.K5 C65 1988   **NYPL [Sc D 89-231]**

KING, MARTIN LUTHER, JR., 1929-1968 - VIEWS ON COMMUNITY.
Fluker, Walter E., 1951- They looked for a city . Lanham, MD , c1989. xiv, 281 p. ; ISBN 0-8191-7262-6 (alk. paper) DDC 307/.092/2 19
BX6447 .F57 1988   **NYPL [Sc D 89-492]**

King, Roosevelt Ty. Callender, Timothy. The watchman /. [St. Michael, Barbados? , 1978?] [28] p. :   **NYPL [Sc F 89-52]**

King, Victor E. (joint author) Hanson, John Wagner. Secondary level teachers: supply and demand in Sierra Leone. [East Lansing, c1970] viii, 85 p.   **NYPL [JFM 72-62 no. 11]**

Kingdoms of the Yoruba /. Smith, Robert, 1919- London , 1988. xii, 174 p. ; ISBN 0-85255-028-6 (cased) : DDC 966/.004963 19
DT513   **NYPL [Sc E 88-482]**

King's College (Lagos, Nigeria) 75 years of King's College / King's College, Lagos. [Lagos? : s.n.], 1987. vi, 89 p. : ports., facsim. ; 25 cm. Cover title.
1. Preparatory schools - Nigeria. I. Title. II. Title: Seventy-five years of King's College.
NYPL [Sc E 88-257]

KINGSTON METROPOLITAN AREA (JAMAICA) - ECONOMIC CONDITIONS.
Anderson, Patricia, Dr. Mini bus ride . Mona, Kingston, Jamaica , 1987. vii, 179 p. : ISBN 976-400-006-1
HE5647.K56 A53x 1987
NYPL [Sc D 89-312]

KINGSTON (ONT.) - BUILDINGS, STRUCTURES, ETC. - EXHIBITIONS.
Mattie, Joan. 100 years of architecture in Kingston . [Ottawa] , c1986. 30 p. : ISBN 0-662-54396-3 (pbk.) DDC 720/.9713/07074011384 19
NA747.K56 M38 1986 **NYPL [Sc F 88-195]**

Kinley, David H. DeWind, Josh. [Aiding migration. French.] Aide à la migration . Montréal, Québec, Canada , 1988. 216 p. :
NYPL [Sc D 89-441]

Kinshasa, Kwando Mbiassi. Emigration vs. assimilation : the debate in the African-American press, 1827-1861 / by Kwando M. Kinshasa. Jefferson, N.C. : McFarland, 1988. xiv, 234 p. ; 24 cm. Includes index. Bibliography: p. 225-230. Author's autographed presentation to the Schomburg Center. ISBN 0-89950-338-1 (lib. bdg.) DDC 973/.0496073 19
1. Afro-Americans - History - To 1863. 2. Afro-Americans - Colonization - Africa - History - 19th century. 3. Afro-Americans - Cultural assimilation - History - 19th century. 4. Afro-American press - History - 19th century. I. Title. II. Title: Emigration versus assimilation.
E185 .K49 1988   **NYPL [IEC 88-2401]**

KINSHASA (ZAIRE) - RECREATIONAL ACTIVITIES.
Comhaire-Sylvain, Suzanne. Food and leisure among the African youth of Leopoldville, Belgian Congo. [Rondebosch] 1950. 124 p. DDC 309.1675
HQ799.C6 C6   **NYPL [Sc G 89-2]**

Kinyatti, Maina-wa- see **Maina-wa-Kinyatti.**

Kipasaman, Mikalukalu. Philosophie : avec items : á l'usage des candidats aux examens d'Etat / por Mikalukalu Kipasaman. Kinshasa : Institut de la Victoire, [1984?] 61 p. ; 34 cm.
1. Philosophy - Outlines, syllabi, etc. 2. Philosophy - Examinations, questions, etc. 3. Examinations - Zaire - Questions. I. Title.   **NYPL [Sc G 87-49]**

Kipasman, Mikalukalu. Biologie : (avec exercices et items résolus), á l'usage des candidats aux examens d'Etat / par Mikalukalu Kipasman.2 ème éd. Kinshasa : Institut de Victoire, [1984?] 70 p. : ill. ; 34 cm. Bibliography: p. 70.
1. Biology - Outlines, syllabi, etc. 2. Biology - Examinations, questions, etc. 3. Examinations - Zaire - Questions. I. Title.   **NYPL [Sc G 87-46]**

Kiple, Kenneth F., 1939- The African exchange . Durham N.C. , 1987, c1988. vi, 280 p. ; ISBN 0-8223-0731-6 DDC 614.4/273/08996073 19
RA442 .A37 1988   **NYPL [Sc D 88-541]**

Kirby, Richard, 1958. Ewto' : an introduction to Amerindian village life in Guyana / [written by Richard Kirby ; illustrations by Richard Berridge] London : Commonwealth Institute, c1985. 27 p. : ill., 1 map ; 30 cm. (Caribbean focus series) Cover title. Bibliography: p. 27. ISBN 0-946140-24-3 (pbk) DDC 307.7/72 19
1. Indians of South America - Guyana. I. Commonwealth Institute (Great Britain). II. Title. III. Series.
F2380   **NYPL [Sc F 89-104]**

Kirchherr, Eugene C.
Abyssinia to Zimbabwe. Kirchherr, Eugene C. Place names of Africa, 1935-1986 : a political gazetteer / by Eugene C. Kirchherr.Rev., enl., and updated ed. Metuchen, N.J. , c1987. viii, 136 p. ; ISBN 0-8108-2061-7 DDC 911/.6 19
DT31 .K53 1987   **NYPL [Sc D 88-813]**

Place names of Africa, 1935-1986 : a political gazetteer / by Eugene C. Kirchherr.Rev., enl., and updated ed. Metuchen, N.J. : Scarecrow Press, c1987. viii, 136 p. : maps ; 23 cm. Rev. enl., and updated ed. of: Abyssinia to Zimbabwe. 3rd. ed. c1979. Bibliography: p. [125]-136. ISBN 0-8108-2061-7 DDC 911/.6 19
1. Africa - Politics and government - 1945-1960. 2. Africa - Politics and government - 1960-. 3. Africa - Gazetteers. I. Kirchherr, Eugene C. Abyssinia to Zimbabwe. II. Title.
DT31 .K53 1987   **NYPL [Sc D 88-813]**

Kiriswa, Benjamin. Christian counselling for students / Benjamin Kiriswa. Eldoret, Kenya : AMECEA Gaba Publications, 1988. vi, 81 p. : ill. ; 22 cm. (Spearhead. no. 102) Bibliography: p. [80]-81.
1. Students - Pastoral counseling of. 2. Pastoral counseling. I. Title.   **NYPL [Sc D 89-350]**

Kirkenes verdensråd. see **World Council of Churches.**

Kirkland, Charles Pinckney, 1830-1904- A letter to the Hon. Benjamin R. Curtis : late judge of the Supreme Court of the United States, in review of his recently published pamphlet on the "Emancipation proclamation" of the President / by Charles P. Kirkland, of New

York.2nd ed. New York : A.D.F. Randolph, 1863. 20 p. ; 23 cm.
1. Curtis, Benjamin Robbins, 1809-1874. Executive power. 2. United States. President (1861-1865 : Lincoln). Emancipation Proclamation. I. Title.
NYPL [Sc Rare C 89-23]

Kirkpatrick, Oliver. Naja the snake and Mangus the mongoose; a Jamaican folktale. Illustrated by Enid Richardson.1st ed. Garden City, N.Y. , Doubleday, [1970] 40 p. illus. (part col.) 21 x 28 cm. Mangus the Mongoose is supposed to kill Naja, the last living snake in Jamaica, but complications arise when the two begin to like each other. SCHOMBURG CHILDREN'S COLLECTION. DDC [Fic]
1. Snakes - Juvenile fiction. 2. Mongooses - Juvenile fiction. 3. Jamaica - Juvenile fiction. I. Richardson, Enid, illus. II. Schomburg Children's Collection. III. Title.
PZ7.K6358 Naj   **NYPL [Sc F 88-339]**

Kisseloff, Jeff. You must remember this : an oral history of Manhattan from the 1890s to World War II / Jeff Kisseloff.1st ed. San Diego : Harcourt Brace Jovanovich, c1989. xvii, 622 p., [16] p. of plates : ill., ports. ; 25 cm. Bibliography: p. [601]-605. ISBN 0-15-187988-5 : DDC 974.7/1042 19
1. Oral history. 2. New York (N.Y.) - History - 1898-1951. 3. New York (N.Y.) - Social life and customs. I. Title.
F128.5 .K55 1988   **NYPL [Sc E 89-54]**

Kissi stories and songs / collected by Charles Manga ... [et al.] Freetown : People's Educational Association of Sierra Leone, 1987. 95 p. : ill. ; 21 cm. (Stories and songs from Sierra Leone . 31)
1. Tales - Sierra Leone. 2. Folk-songs, Kissi. I. Manga, Charles. II. Series.   **NYPL [Sc D 89-459]**

Kiswahili . Adam, Hassan. Hamburg , 1987. 208 p. : ISBN 3-87118-843-3   **NYPL [Sc E 88-433]**

Kitabu [microform] : beginning concepts in Kawaida : Temple of Kawaida, US inc., Maulana Karenga, founder-emeritus / edited by Imamu Halisi. Los Angeles : US organization : Saidi Publications, [1972?] 13 p. ; 21 cm. Microfiche. New York: New York Public Library, 198 . 1 microfiche: negative; 11 x 15 cm. (FSN Sc 019,019)
1. Karenga, Maulana. 2. Black nationalism - United States. I. Halisi, Clyde.
NYPL [Sc Micro F-10979]

Kitanzi /. Ganzel, Edi, 1946- Dar es Salaam [1984] 80 p. ;
PL8704.G35 K57 1984 **NYPL [Sc C 88-120]**

Kitchen, Helen A. South Africa, in transition to what? /. New York , Washington, D.C. , 1988. xii, 201 p. ; ISBN 0-275-92975-2 (alk. paper) DDC 968.06/3 19
DT779.952 .S654 1988   **NYPL [Sc E 88-510]**

A kite for Bennie. Gray, Genevieve. New York, 1972. [40] p. ; ISBN 0-07-024197-X DDC [Fic]
PZ7.G7774 Ki   **NYPL [Sc E 88-422]**

Kitondo Mangombo. Kolokoso : histoire, tradition et changements (Rép. du Zaïre) / Kitondo Mangombo. Bandundu, République du Zaïre : Ceeba, 1983. 172 p. : ill., maps ; 27 cm. (Publications (Ceeba). Série II . vol. 87) Bibliography: p. 164-168.
1. Ethnology - Zaire - Kolokoso (Collectivity). I. Series. II. Series: Publications (Ceeba). Série II , vol. 87. III. Title.   **NYPL [Sc F 88-304]**

Kittler, Glenn D. Let's travel in the Congo / by Glen D. Kittler ; edited by Darlene Geis. Chicago : Children's Press, 1965, c1961. 85 p. : col. ill., map ; 29 cm. Includes index. "A Travel press book."
1. Zaire - Description and travel - Juvenile literature. I. Title.   **NYPL [Sc F 89-7]**

Kiwanuka, M. S. M. Semakula.
Amin and the tragedy of Uganda / by Semakula Kiwanuka. München : Weltforum Verlag, 1979. ix, 201 p. : port. ; 21 cm. (Afrika-Studien. nr. 104 104) Bibliography: p. 199-201. ISBN 3-8039-0177-4
1. Amin, Idi, 1925-. 2. Uganda - History - 1971-1979. 3. Uganda - Tanzania War, 1978-1979. 4. Uganda - History - 1979-. I. Title. II. Series.
DT433.283 .K58 **NYPL [L-10 9005 nr. 104]**

Muteesa of Uganda, by M. S. M. Kiwanuka. Nairobi, East African Literature Bureau [1967] viii, 89 p. illus. 19 cm. (Uganda's famous men series) Bibliography: p. 82. DDC 967.6/101/0924 B

1. Mutesa, King of Buganda, d. 1884.
DT433.26.M88 K58 **NYPL** *[Sc C 88-87]*

Kizito Sesana, Renato. Salvoldi, Valentino. [Africa, il vangelo ci appartiene. English.] Africa, the gospel belongs to us . Ndola [Zambia] , 1986. 187 p ;
NYPL *[Sc D 89-568]*

Klaasse, Piet. Jam session : portraits of jazz and blues musicians drawn on the scene / Piet Klaasse ; Mark Gardner, J. Bernlef, text. Newton Abbot [Devon] : David & Charles, 1985. 192 p. : ill. (some col.) ; 35 cm. Includes index. ISBN 0-7153-8710-3 DDC 785.42/092/2 19
1. Jazz musicians - Portraits. 2. Blues musicians - Portraits. I. Gardner, Mark, 1939-. II. Bernlef, J. III. Title.
ML3506 .K58 1985 **NYPL** *[Sc G 88-13]*

Klein, Leonard S. Encyclopedia of world literature in the 20th century . New York , c1981-1984. 4 v. : ISBN 0-8044-3135-3 (v. 1) : DDC 803 19
PN771 .E5 1981 **NYPL** *[Sc Ser.-M .E565]*

Kleppner, Paul. Chicago divided : the making of a Black mayor / Paul Kleppner. DeKalb, Ill. : Northern Illinois University Press, c1985. xviii, 313 p. : ill. ; 24 cm. Includes index. Bibliography: p. [255]-300. ISBN 0-87580-106-4 : DDC 324.9773/11043 19
1. Washington, Harold, 1922-. 2. Chicago - Mayors - Election. 3. Chicago - Politics and government - 1951-. 4. Chicago - Race relations. I. Title.
F548.52.W36 K54 1984
NYPL *[JFE 85-2533]*

Kletzing, Henry F., 1850- Progress of a race; or, The remarkable advancement of the American Negro from the bondage of slavery, ignorance and poverty to the freedom of citizenship, intelligence, affluence, honor and trust, by H. F. Kletzing and W. H. Crogman. With an introd. by Booker T. Washington. Atlanta, Ga., J. L. Nichols, 1897. xxiv, 23-663 p. illus. 20 cm. Negro authors.
1. Afro-Americans - History. 2. Afro-Americans - Biography. I. Crogman, William Henry, 1841- joint author. II. Title. **NYPL** *[Sc 973-K]*

Kliment, Bud. Ella Fitzgerald / Bud Kliment ; senior consulting editor, Nathan Irvin Huggins. New York : Chelsea House Publishers, c1988. 112 p. : ill. (ports.) ; 25 cm. (Black Americans of achievement) Includes index. Discography: p. 106. Bibliography: p. 108. ISBN 1-555-46586-2 DDC 784.5 B 19
1. Fitzgerald, Ella. 2. Singers - United States - Biography. 3. Afro-American singers - Biography. I. Huggins, Nathan Irvin, 1927-. II. Title. III. Series.
ML420.F52 K6 1988 **NYPL** *[Sc E 88-611]*

Kline, Benjamin. Genesis of apartheid : British African policy in the colony of Natal, 1845-1893 / Benjamin Kline. Lanham, MD : University Press of America, c1988. xxii, 283 p. ; 23 cm. Includes index. Bibliography: p. 265-276. ISBN 0-8191-6494-1 (alk. paper) : DDC 968.4/04 19
1. Apartheid - South Africa - Natal - History - 19th century. 2. Blacks - South Africa - Natal - Politics and government. 3. Blacks - South Africa - Natal - Civil rights. 4. Natal (South Africa) - Politics and government - 1843-1893. I. Title.
DT872 .K56 1988 **NYPL** *[JLD 88-4097]*

Klöppel, Eberhard. In Simbabwe / Fotos: Eberhard Klöpper ; Text: Christa Schaffmann. 2. Aufl. Leipzig : F.A. Brockhaus, c1985. 160 p. : chiefly ill. (some col), map ; 23 cm. ISBN 0-325-00113-0
1. Zimbabwe - Description and travel - Views. I. Schaffmann, Christa. II. Title.
NYPL *[Sc D 88-627]*

Kludze, A. K. P. Modern principles of equity : an exposition with particular reference to Ghana / A.K.P. Kludze. Dordrecht, Holland ; Providence, R.I. : Foris Publications, 1988. xxxix, 482 p. ; 24 cm. Includes bibliographical references and index. ISBN 90-6765-147-8
1. Equity - Ghana. I. Title. **NYPL** *[Sc E 89-233]*

The KM ebit husia . Nobles, Wade W. Oakland, California , 1985. 201 p. ; ISBN 0-939205-03-3
NYPL *[Sc F 88-159]*

Knappert, Jan. East Africa : Kenya, Tanzania & Uganda / Jan Knappert. New Delhi : Vikas Pub. House, c1987. 383 p. ; 23 cm. (Afro-Asian nations: history and culture) Includes index. Bibliography: p. [343]-356. ISBN 0-7069-2822-9 : DDC 967.6 19
1. Africa, East. I. Title. II. Series.
DT423 .K56 1987 **NYPL** *[Sc D 88-852]*

Knight, Franklin W. The Modern Caribbean /. Chapel Hill , c1989. x, 382 p. : ISBN 0-8078-1825-9 (alk. paper) DDC 972.9 19
F2156 .M63 1989 **NYPL** *[Sc E 89-253]*

Knights, Ian E.
The Bahamas [microform] : an outline guide for expatriate contract employees / Ian E. Knights.[15th ed.] London : Royal Commonwealth Society, 1979. 18 p. : maps ; 30 cm. (Notes on conditions) Cover title. Includes index. Bibliography: p.16-17. Microfilm. New York: New York Public Library, 1982. 1 microfilm reel; 35 mm. (MN *ZZ-23051)
1. Bahamas. I. Royal Commonwealth Society.
NYPL *[Sc Micro R-4108 no.16]*

Bermuda [microform] : an outline guide for expatriate contract employees. [15th ed.] London : Royal Commonwealth Society, 1979. 18 p. : maps ; 30 cm. (Notes on conditions) Cover title. Includes index. Bibliography: p. 16-18. Microfilm. New York: New York Public Library, 1982. 1 microfilm reel; 35 mm. (MN *ZZ-23051)
I. Royal Commonwealth Society.
NYPL *[Sc Micro R-4108 no.19]*

The British Virgin Islands [microform] : an outline guide for expatriate contract employees / Ian E. Knights.2nd rev. ed. London : Royal Commonwealth Society, 1979. 17p. : maps ; 30 cm. (Notes on conditions) Cover title. Includes index. Bibliography: p.16-17. Microfilm. New York: New York Public Library, 1982. 1 microfilm reel; 35 mm. (MN *ZZ-23051)
I. Royal Commonwealth Society.
NYPL *[Sc Micro R-4108 no.22]*

The British Virgin Islands [microform] : an outline guide for expatriate contract employees. [4th ed.] London : Royal Commonwealth Society, 1982. 15 p. : maps ; 30 cm. (Notes on conditions) Cover title. Includes index. Bibliography: p.14-15. Microfilm. New York: New York Public Library, 1982. 1 microfilm reel; 35 mm. (MN *ZZ-23051)
I. Royal Commonwealth Society.
NYPL *[Sc Micro R-4108 no.18]*

Malawi [microform] : an outline guide for expatriate contract employees. London : Royal Commonwealth Society, 1980. 19 p. : maps ; 30 cm. (Notes on conditions) Cover title. Includes index. Bibliography: p.18-19. Microfilm. New York: New York Public Library, 1982. 1 microfilm reel; 35 mm. (MN *ZZ-23051)
1. Malawi. I. Royal Commonwealth Society.
NYPL *[Sc Micro R-4108 no.21]*

Nigeria [microform] : an outline guide for expatriate contract employees. [15th ed.] London : Royal Commonwealth Society, 1980. 19 p. : maps ; 30 cm. (Notes on conditions) Cover title. Includes index. Bibliography: p.17-19. Microfilm. New York: New York Public Library, 1982. 1 microfilm reel; 35 mm. (MN *ZZ-23051) ISBN 0-905067-80-0
I. Royal Commonwealth Society.
NYPL *[Sc Micro R-4108 no.17]*

The Seychelles [Microform] : an outline guide for expatriate contract employees. [16th ed.] London : Royal Commonwealth Society, 1982. 16 p. : maps ; 30 cm. (Notes on conditions) Cover title. Includes index. Bibliography: p.14-15. Microfilm. New York: New York Public Library, 1982. 1 microfilm reel; 35 mm. (MN *ZZ-23051)
1. Seychelles. I. Royal Commonwealth Society.
NYPL *[Sc Micro R-4108 no.15]*

Tanzania [microform] : an outline guide for expatriate contract employees. 15th rev. ed. London : The Royal Commonwealth Society, 1979. 20 p. : maps ; 30 cm. (Notes on conditions) Cover title. Includes index. Bibliography: p.18-19. Microfilm. New York: New York Public Library, 1982. 1 microfilm reel; 35 mm. (MN *ZZ-23051)
I. Royal Commonwealth Society.
NYPL *[Sc Micro R-4108 no.20]*

Knott, Bill, 1927- Crazylegs Merrill, by Bill J. Carol. Austin : Steck-Vaughn Co. [1969] iv, 155 p. ; 22 cm. As he gains football experience as end on the varsity team, a high school boy crippled by polio conquers the shyness caused by his handicap.
1. Football - Juvenile fiction. 2. Afro-Americans - Juvenile fiction. I. Title. **NYPL** *[Sc D 88-632]*

Knott, William C. see Knott, Bill, 1927-

Know what I mean? . Turkie, Alan. Leicester , 1982. 82 p. : ISBN 0-86155-062-5 :
NYPL *[Sc D 89-464]*

Known homosexual. Hansen, Joseph, 1923- Pretty boy dead . San Francisco , 1984. 203 p. ; ISBN 0-917342-48-8 : DDC 813/.54 19
PS3558.A513 P7 1984 **NYPL** *[JFD 87-9537]*

Knox, Ellis Oneal. A study of Negro periodicals in the United States / by Ellis Oneal Knox. 1928. 77 leaves ; 28 cm. Typescript (photocopy) Thesis (M.A)-University of Southern California, 1928. Bibliography: leaves 74-77.
1. Afro-American periodicals - United States. I. Title.
NYPL *[Sc F 88-264]*

Koch, Lawrence O. Yardbird suite : a compendium of the music and life of Charlie Parker / Lawrence O. Koch. Bowling Green, Ohio : Bowling Green State University Popular Press, c1988. 336 p. : music ; 24 cm. Bibliography: p. 333-336. ISBN 0-87972-259-2 (clothbound)
1. Parker, Charlie, 1920-1955. 2. Jazz musicians - United States - Biography. 3. Afro-American musicians - Biography. I. Title.
NYPL *[Sc E 89-48]*

Kód yanm.
Thésée, Françoise. Les Ibos de l'Amélie . Paris , c1986. 134 p., [8] p. of plates : ISBN 2-903033-86-2 **NYPL** *[Sc E 88-560]*

Koering, Ursula. (illus) McCall, Virginia, 1909- Adassa and her hen. [New York, 1971] 79 p. DDC [Fic]
PZ7.M12295 Ad **NYPL** *[Sc D 89-100]*

Kofoworola, Ziky. Hausa performing arts and music / by Ziky Kofoworola and Yusef Lateef. Lagos : Dept. of Culture, Federal Ministry of Information and culture c1987. viii, 330 p. : ill., music ; 25 cm. "A Nigeria magazine publication" -t. p. Bibliography: p. 317-330. ISBN 978-17-3041-2
1. Hausas - Music. 2. Music - Nigeria - History and criticism. 3. Performing arts - Nigeria. I. Lateef, Yusef. II. Title. **NYPL** *[Sc E 89-116]*

Koger, Larry, 1958- Black slaveowners : free Black slave masters in South Carolina, 1790-1860 / by Larry Koger. Jefferson, N.C. : McFarland, 1985. xiii, 286 p. ; 24 cm. Includes bibliographical references and index. ISBN 0-89950-160-5 : DDC 975.7/00496073 19
1. Afro-American slaveholders - South Carolina - History. 2. Slavery - South Carolina - History. 3. Slavery - South Carolina - Conditions of slaves. 4. Afro-Americans - Employment - South Carolina - History - 19th century. 5. South Carolina - Race relations. I. Title.
E445.S7 K64 1985 **NYPL** *[Sc E 88-473]*

KOLA NUTS - AFRICA, WEST.
Keita, Djigui. Le rôle socio-religieux de la cola dans la société malinké . [Abidjan? , 1985] 72 leaves : **NYPL** *[Sc F 88-307]*

KOLANKO (AFRICAN PEOPLE) see KURANKO (AFRICAN PEOPLE)

Kolokoso . Kitondo Mangombo. Bandundu, République du Zaïre , 1983. 172 p. :
NYPL *[Sc F 88-304]*

Komo, Dolores. Clio Browne : private investigator / by Dolores Komo. Freedom, Calif. : Crossing Press, c1988. 193 p. ; 18 cm. (A WomanSleuth mystery) ISBN 0-89594-320-4 (pbk.) : DDC 813/.54 19
1. Afro-American Women - Fiction. 2. Crime and criminals - Missouri - St. Louis - Fiction. I. Title. II. Series.
PS3561.O4545 C55 1988
NYPL *[Sc C 89-50]*

Konare Ba, Adam. L'´epop´ee de Segu : Da Monson :un pouvoir guerrier / Adam Konare Ba. Paris : Favre, c1987. 201 p. : maps ; 24 cm. (Collection CETIM) Bibliography: p. 183-186. ISBN 2-8289-0250-1
1. Segou (Mali : Region) - History. 2. Segou (Mali : Region) - Politics and government. I. Title. II. Series.
NYPL *[Sc E 88-180]*

Konaté, Moussa, 1951-
Une aube incertaine : roman / Moussa Konaté. Paris : Présence africaine, c1985. 217 p. ; 20 cm. (Collection Ecrits) ISBN 2-7087-0459-1
1. Mali - Fiction. I. Series: Collection Ecrits (Presence africaine (Firm)). II. Title.
MLCS 86/6414 (P) **NYPL** *[Sc C 89-105]*

Chronique d'une journée de répression / Moussa Konaté. Paris : Edition L'Harmattan, c1988. 143 p. ; 22 cm. (Collection Encres noires. 47.)
1. Mali - Fiction. I. Title. **NYPL** *[Sc D 88-846]*

KONGO LANGUAGE - TEXTS.
Matondo kwa Nzambi. Biso banso lisanga totonga eklezya ya biso . Kinshasa [1988] 72 p. : **NYPL** *[Sc D 89-221]*

Koninklijk Instituut voor de Tropen. A Bibliography of health and disease in East Africa /. Amsterdam ; New York : 282 p. ; ISBN 0-444-80931-7 (U. S.) DDC 016.3621/0967 19
Z6673.6.A353 B53 1988 RA552.A353
NYPL *[Sc G 89-6]*

Konnin tè ou. Jean-Baptiste, Chavannes. Té-a sé kòd lonbret nou. Prémie pati : Konnin tè ou /. [Port-au-Prince, Haiti?] [1978?] 63 p. :
NYPL *[Sc D 87-1404]*

KORA (MUSICAL INSTRUMENT)
Chester, Galina. The silenced voice . London , 1987. 47 p. : ISBN 0-9512093-0-2 : **NYPL** *[Sc D 89-519]*

Koran - Law. see Islamic law.

Koranko riddles, songs and stories /. Hinzen, Heribert. Freetown , 1987. 69 p. :
NYPL *[Sc D 89-416]*

KOREA (SOUTH) - ECONOMIC POLICY - 1960-
Alschuler, Lawrence R., 1941- Multinationals and maldevelopment . Basingstoke, Hampshire , c1988. xii, 218 p. : ISBN 0-333-41561-2
NYPL *[Sc D 88-701]*

Koroma, Salia. The spider's web / by Salia Koroma ; collected by M.B. Lamin and Heribert Hinzen. Freetown : Published by People's Educational Association of Sierra Leone, 1986. 134 p. : ill. ; 21 cm. (Stories and songs from Sierra Leone. 14)
1. Sierra Leone - Fiction. I. Lamin, M. B. II. Hinzen, Heribert. III. Title. IV. Series.
NYPL *[Sc D 89-403]*

Korte, Werner. Liberia . Hamburg , 1986. vi, 292 p., [1] folded leaf of plates : ISBN 3-923519-65-6 (pbk.) DDC 322/.5/096662 19
JQ3923.5.C58 L53 1986
NYPL *[Sc D 88-1320]*

Kosiba, Margaret M. A Century of Black surgeons . Norman, Okla. , c1987. 2 v. (xx, 973 p.) : ISBN 0-9617380-0-6 (set) DDC 617./092/2 B 19
RD27.34 .C46 1987 **NYPL** *[Sc E 88-216]*

Kosmin, Barry Alexander. Majuta : a history of the Jewish community of Zimbabwe / by B.A. Kosmin ; with a foreword by M. Gelfand. Gwelo, Zimbabwe : Mambo Press, c1980. xii, 223 p., [32] p. of plates : ill., ports. ; 22 cm. (Zambeziana. v. 10 10) Includes index. Bibliography: p. 207-211.
1. Jews - Zimbabwe - History. I. Title. II. Series.
NYPL *[Sc D 82-130]*

Kössler, Christine. Felber, Monika. Stundenblätter Hansberry " A raisin in the sun" /. Stuttgard , 1986. 85 p. : ISBN 3-12-925163-4
NYPL *[Sc D 88-631]*

Kotia-Nima . Hama, Boubou, 1906- [Niamey?] . 3 v. ; **NYPL** *[Sc D 88-210]*

Koto and the lagoon. Kaye, Geraldine, 1925- New York [1969, c1967] 128 p. DDC [Fic]
PZ7.K212 Ko3 **NYPL** *[Sc D 89-159]*

Kotzé, D. A.
Bibliography of official publications of the Black South African homelands / D. A. Kotzé. Pretoria : University of South Africa, 1979. xix, 80 p. : map ; 21 cm. (Documenta - University of South Africa ; 19) ISBN 0-86981-137-1 DDC 015.68
1. Homelands, South Africa - Government publications - Bibliography. I. Series: South Africa. University. Documenta, 19. II. Title.
Z3607.H65 K67 J705.T3;
NYPL *[Sc D 88-1197]*

Rural development administration in South Africa /. Pretoria , 1987. 70 p. : ISBN 0-7983-0100-7 **NYPL** *[Sc F 88-309]*

Kounta, Albakaye. Contes de Tombouctou et du Macina / Albakaye Ousmane Kounta. Paris : L'Harmattan, c1987- v. ; 22 cm. (Collection "La Légende des mondes") ISBN 2-85802-853-2 (v. 1) DDC 843 19
1. Tales - Mali. I. Title. II. Series.
PQ3989.2.K577 C6 1987
NYPL *[Sc D 88-1027]*

KOWAK RIVER (ALASKA)
Healy, M. A. (Michael A.) Report of the cruise of the revenue marine steamer Corwin in the Arctic Ocean in the year 1884 /. Washington , 1889. 128 p., [39] leaves of plates :
NYPL *[Sc Rare F 88-62]*

Kowarick, Lúcio. Trabalho e vadiagem : a origem do trabalho livre no Brasil / Lúcio Kowarick. São Paulo : Editora Brasiliense, 1987. 133 p. ; 21 cm. Bibliography: p. 130-133.
1. Labor and laboring classes - Brazil - History. 2. Capitalism - Brazil. 3. Brazil - History - 1822-1889. I. Title. **NYPL** *[Sc D 88-784]*

Kozloff, Max. Cuba, a view from inside . New York [1985?] 2 v. :
TR646.U6 N4853x 1985
NYPL *[Sc D 88-1511]*

KPELLE LANGUAGE - GRAMMAR.
Gay, John. Mathematics and logic in the Kpelle language. Ibadan, 1971. 152, 184 p.
PL8411.1 .G35 **NYPL** *[JFF 74-877]*

KPELLE LANGUAGE - SEMANTICS.
Gay, John. Mathematics and logic in the Kpelle language. Ibadan, 1971. 152, 184 p.
PL8411.1 .G35 **NYPL** *[JFF 74-877]*

Krafona, Kwesi. Organization of African Unity 25 years on . London , 1988. vii, 175 p. : ISBN 0-948583-05-3 (Hardback)
NYPL *[Sc D 89-556]*

Kramer, Hans. Afrika . Berlin , 1985. 520 p. :
NYPL *[Sc C 88-144]*

Krass, Peter. Sojourner Truth / Peter Krass. New York : Chelsea House, c1988. 110 p. : ill. ; 23 cm. (Black Americans of achievement) Includes index. Traces the life of the former slave who could neither read nor write, yet earned a reputation as one of the most articulate and outspoken antislavery and women's rights activists in the United States. Bibliography: p. 108. ISBN 1-555-46611-7 DDC 305.5/67/0924 B 92 19
1. Truth, Sojourner, d. 1883 - Juvenile literature. 2. Afro-Americans - Biography - Juvenile literature. 3. Abolitionists - United States - Biography - Juvenile literature. 4. Social reformers - United States - Biography - Juvenile literature. 5. Afro-American women - Biography - Juvenile literature. I. Title. II. Series.
E185.97.T8 K73 1988 **NYPL** *[Sc E 88-470]*

Krieger, Nancy. The politics of AIDS / by Nancy Krieger and Rose Applemna. Oakland, CA : Frontline Pamphlets, 1986 60 p. : ill. ; 22 cm. Includes bibliographical references. ISBN 0-913781-06-1
1. AIDS (Disease) - United States. 2. AIDS (Disease) - Political aspects - United States. I. Appleman, Rose. II. Title. **NYPL** *[Sc D 88-1299]*

Krings, Thomas, 1949- Frehn, Beatrice, 1948- Afrikanische Frisuren . Köln , c1986. 147 p. : ISBN 3-7701-1619-4 DDC 391/.5/0966 19
GT2295.A358 F74 1986
NYPL *[Sc C 88-153]*

Krinsky, Norman. Art for city children. New York, Van Nostrand Reinhold [1970] 96 p. illus. 22 x 27 cm. SCHOMBURG CHILDREN'S COLLECTION. DDC 372.5/2
1. Art - Study and teaching (Elementary). I. Schomburg Children's Collection. II. Title.
N350 .K7 **NYPL** *[Sc F 88-378]*

The Krio of Sierra Leone . Wyse, Akintola. London , 1989. xiii, 156 p. : ISBN 1-85322-006-X DDC 966.4/04969729 19
NYPL *[Sc D 89-566]*

Kristensen, Preben Sejer. Jacobsen, Peter Otto. A family in West Africa. Hove , 1985. 32 p. : ISBN 0-85078-434-4 : DDC 966/.305 19
DA588 **NYPL** *[Sc D 88-1499]*

KRUPA, GENE, 1909-1973.
Crowther, Bruce, 1933- Gene Krupa, his life & times /. Tunbridge Wells, Kent , New York , 1987. 144 p. : ISBN 0-87663-670-9 (USA) DDC 789/.1/0924 B 19
ML419.K78 C8 1987 **NYPL** *[JNF 88-89]*

Krush, Beth. Weiss, Edna S. Truly Elizabeth /. Boston , 1957. 178 p. **NYPL** *[Sc D 88-663]*

KU-KLUX KLAN - HISTORY.
Swinney, Everette, 1923- Suppressing the Ku Klux Klan . New York , 1987. ix, 360 p. : ISBN 0-8240-8297-4 (alk. paper) : DDC 342.73/0873 347.302873 19
KF4757 .S93 1987 **NYPL** *[Sc D 88-653]*

KU KLUX KLAN (1915-) - CALIFORNIA - ORANGE COUNTY - HISTORY.
Cocoltchos, Christopher Nickolas, 1949- The invisible government and the viable community . 1979. 2 v. (xv, 774 leaves) :
NYPL *[Sc F 88-285]*

KU KLUX KLAN (1915-) - CALIFORNIA, SOUTHERN - HISTORY.
Salley, Robert Lee. Activities of the Knights of the Ku Klux Klan in Southern California, 1921-1925 /. 1963. v, 199 leaves ;
NYPL *[Sc F 88-119]*

Kuhn, Philalethes, 1870- Taschenbuch für Südwestafrika, 1909 /. Berlin , 1909. xviii, 495, 60 p., [4] fold. leaves of plates :
NYPL *[Sc B 89-24]*

KULANKO (AFRICAN PEOPLE) see KURANKO (AFRICAN PEOPLE)

Kulet, Henry R. ole, 1946- Daughter of Maa / H.R. Ole Kulet. Nairobi : Longman Kenya, 1987. 172 p. ; 19 cm. ISBN 0-582-98653-2
1. Kenya - Fiction. I. Title. **NYPL** *[Sc C 89-42]*

Kuliak and Cushitic . Lamberti, Marcello. Heidelberg , 1988. 157 p. :
NYPL *[Sc D 89-330]*

Kullas, Ulrike. Lernen von der Dritten Welt? : Chancen und Probleme am Beispiel eines work-camps in Tanzania / Ulrike Kullas. Saarbrücken ; Fort Lauderdale : Breitenbach, 1982. 174 p. : ill. ; 21 cm. (Schriften des Instituts für Internationale Begegnungen e. V. . 8) Bibliography: 167-174. ISBN 3-88156-233-8
1. Work camps - Tanzania. 2. Developing countries. 3. Students, Interchange of. I. Title. II. Series.
NYPL *[Sc D 89-339]*

Kulturanthropologische Studien .
(Bd. 12) Dinslage, Sabine. Kinder der Lyela . Hohenschäftlarn bei München , 1986. 355 p. : ISBN 3-87673-105-4 DDC 305.2/3/096625 19
DT650.L38 D56 1986 **NYPL** *[Sc D 88-876]*

(Bd. 13) Brüggemann, Anne. Amagdala und Akawuruk . Hohenschäftlarn bei München , 1986. 264 p. : ISBN 3-87673-106-2
NYPL *[Sc D 88-652]*

Kulturbehörde Hamburg. Neue Kunst aus Afrika . [Hamburg] , c1984. 111 p. :
NYPL *[Sc G 88-17]*

Kuluka /. Van-Dúnem, Domingos, 1925- Lisboa [1988?] 87 p. ; **NYPL** *[Sc C 89-129]*

!KUNG (AFRICAN PEOPLE)
Bateman, Walter L. The Kung of the Kalahari. Boston [1970] 128 p. ISBN 0-8070-1898-8 DDC 301.2
DT764.B8 B3 **NYPL** *[Sc E 88-550]*

The Past and future of !Kung ethnography . Hamburg , 1986. 423 p. : ISBN 3-87118-780-1
NYPL *[Sc D 88-234]*

The Kung of the Kalahari. Bateman, Walter L. Boston [1970] 128 p. ISBN 0-8070-1898-8 DDC 301.2
DT764.B8 B3 **NYPL** *[Sc E 88-550]*

KURANKO (AFRICAN PEOPLE) - FOLKLORE.
Hinzen, Heribert. Koranko riddles, songs and stories /. Freetown , 1987. 69 p. :
NYPL *[Sc D 89-416]*

Nyankume, Manty. The hunter /. Freetown , 1987. 68 p. : **NYPL** *[Sc D 89-414]*

Kurian, George Thomas. The encyclopedia of the Third World / by George Thomas Kurian. 3rd ed. New York, N.Y. : Facts on File, 1987. 3 v. (xxix-2342 p.) : ill., maps ; 29 cm. Includes bibliographies and index. CONTENTS. - v. 1. Afghanistan to Guinea -- v. 2. Guinea-Bissau to Peru -- v. 3. Philippines to Zimbabwe. ISBN 0-8160-1118-4 (set) DDC 909/.09724 19
1. Developing countries - Dictionaries. I. Title.
HC59.7 .K87 1987 **NYPL** *[Sc F 88-324]*

Kuschitische Sprachstudien .
(Bd. 4) Owens, Jonathan. A grammar of Harar Oromo (Northeastern Ethiopia) . Hamburg , c1985. 282 p. ; ISBN 3-87118-717-8 (pbk.) DDC

493/.7 19
PJ2476 .O94 1985   *NYPL [Sc D 88-751]*

Kushner, Arlene.
Avraham, Shmuel, 1945- Treacherous journey .
New York, NY , 1986. xii, 178 p. : ISBN
0-933503-46-6 (jacket); 0-933503-46-5 : DDC
963/.004924 19

DS135.E75 A93 1986   *NYPL [Sc E 87-275]*

Falasha no more : an Ethiopian Jewish child
comes home / by Arlene Kushner ; illustrations
by Amy Kalina. New York : Shapolsky Books,
c1986. 58 p. : ill. ; 23 x 29 cm. Avraham and his
Falasha family, Jews suffering from discrimination in
Ethiopia, finally flee the country and resettle in Israel.
SCHOMBURG CHILDREN'S COLLECTION. ISBN
0-933503-55-5
*1. Falashas - Fiction. I. Kalina, Amy. II. Schomburg
Children's Collection. III. Title.*
    NYPL [Sc F 88-107]

Kuus, Juhan. South Africa in black and white /
Juhan Kuus ; text by Trevor McDonald.
London : Harrap, c1987. [190] p. : chiefly ill. ;
27 cm. ISBN 0-245-54543-3 (pbk.).
*1. South Africa. - Race relations - Pictorial works. 2.
South Africa - Social conditions - Pictorial works. I.
McDonald, Trevor. II. Title.*
    NYPL [MFX (Kuus) 89-1313]

Kuzenzama, K. P. M. La structure bipartite de Jn
6, 26-71 : nouvelle approche / par Kuzenzama
K.P.M. Kinshasa : Faculté de théologie
catholique, 1987. 124 p. ; 24 cm. (Recherches
africaines de théologie. 9) Bibliography: p. 111-115.
*1. Bible. N. T. John - Criticism, interpretation, etc. I.
Title.*   *NYPL [Sc E 88-374]*

Kuziva mbuya huudzwa /. Matindike, Gabriel A.
Harare, Zimbabwe , 1982- v. : ISBN
0-908300-01-8 (v. 1)
PL8681.2 .M37 1982   *NYPL [Sc D 88-385]*

Kuzwayo, Ellen.
[Call me woman. French]
Femme et noire en Afrique du Sud / Ellen
Kuzwayo ; traduit de l'anglais par
Marie-Hélène Dumas ; préface de Nadine
Gordimer. Paris : Editions Robert Laffont,
c1985. 296, [8] p. of plates : ill., ports. ; 24
cm. (Collection Vécu) Translation of: Call me
woman. ISBN 2-221-05157-2
*1. Kuzwayo, Ellen. 2. Women, Black - South Africa -
Social conditions. 3. Women - South Africa - Social
conditions. 4. Blacks - South Africa - Social conditions.
I. Title.*   *NYPL [Sc E 88-315]*

KUZWAYO, ELLEN.
Kuzwayo, Ellen. [Call me woman. French.]
Femme et noire en Afrique du Sud /. Paris ,
c1985. 296, [8] p. of plates : ISBN 2-221-05157-2
    NYPL [Sc E 88-315]

Kwame Nkrumah . Rooney, David. London ,
1988. viii, 292 p. ;   *NYPL [Sc D 89-44]*

**KWAZULU, SOUTH AFRICA - POLITICS
AND GOVERNMENT.**
Mzala. Gatsha Buthelezi . London , Atlantic
Highlands, N.J. , 1988. ix, 240 p. : ISBN
0-86232-792-X DDC 968.4/9106/0924 B 19
DT878.Z9 B856 1988 *NYPL [Sc D 88-1324]*

Kwesi Prah. Human resources development and
utilization in Africa /. Maseru [Lesotho] , 1988.
vi, 160 p. ; ISBN 0-620-12102-5
    NYPL [Sc D 89-558]

La dame aux camélias /. Dumas, Alexandre,
1824-1895. [Dame aux camélias (Novel).
English.] Oxford , New York , 1986. xxv, 215
p. ; ISBN 0-19-281736-1 (pbk.) : DDC 843/.7 19
PQ2231.D2 E5 1986   *NYPL [Sc C 88-201]*

La Farge, John, 1880-1963. Interracial justice : a
study of the Catholic doctrine of race relations
/ by John LaFarge. New York : America Press,
1937. xii, 226 p. ; 20 cm. Includes index.
Bibliography: p. 195-198. DDC 325.260973
*1. Sociology, Christian (Catholic). 2. United States -
Race relations. I. Title.*
E185.61 .L25   *NYPL [Sc C 88-146]*

La-le-li-lo-luta . Barbosa, Rogério Andrade. Rio
de Janeiro , 1984. 124 p. ; DDC 371.1/0092/4 B
19
LA2365.B72 B37 1984   *NYPL [Sc D 88-284]*

**La Mairieu, Baudouin Paternostre de. see
Paternostre de La Mairieu, Baudouin.**

La Point, Velma. Washington, Valora. Black
children and American institutions . New
York , 1988. xv, 432 p. ; ISBN 0-8240-8517-5 :

DDC 305.2/3/08996073 19
Z1361.N39 W34 1988 E185.86
    NYPL [Sc D 89-385]

Labatut, Roger. Interférences du fulfulde sur le
français écrit par les élèves peuls du
Nord-Cameroun [microform] / par R. Labatut.
[Dakar] : Centre de linpuistique appliquée de
Dakar, 1974. iii, 35 p. ; 27 cm.
([Publications]/Centre de linguistique appliquée de
Dakar. no. 54) Microfilm. New York: New York Public
Library, 198. 1 microfilm reel; 35 mm. (MN
*ZZ-24640)
*1. French language - Study and teaching - Cameroon. 2.
French language - Study and teaching - Fulah students.
I. Series: Dakar. Université. Centre de linguistique
appliquée. [Publications], no. 54. II. Title.*
    NYPL [Sc Micro R-4137 no.11]

Labazée, Pascal. Entreprises et entrepreneurs du
Burkina Faso : vers une lecture anthropologique
de l'entreprise africaine / Pascal Labazée.
Paris : Karthala, c1988. 273 p. ; 22 cm.
(Collection Les Afriques) Includes index. Bibliography:
p. [261]-267.
*1. Business enterprises - Burkina Faso. 2. Businessmen -
Burkina Faso. I. Title. II. Series.*
    NYPL [Sc D 89-288]

Labelle, Micheline, 1940- Histoires d'immigrées .
Montréal , 1987. 275 p. ; ISBN 2-89052-170-2
    NYPL [Sc D 88-346]

Labode, Sakirudeen Tunji. Party power : the
experience of an accountant / S.T. Labode.
Abeokuta, Nigeria : Gbemi Sodipo Press, 1988.
244 p. ; 20 cm. ISBN 978-18-3008-5
*1. Unity Party of Nigeria - Accounting. 2. Campaign
funds - Nigeria. 3. Nigeria - Politics and government -
1979-1983. I. Title.*   *NYPL [Sc C 88-376]*

**LABOR, AGRICULTURAL. see
AGRICULTURAL LABORERS.**

**LABOR AND CAPITAL. see INDUSTRIAL
RELATIONS.**

**LABOR AND LABORING CLASSES -
AFRICA.**
Freund, Bill. The African worker /. Cambridge
[Cambridgeshire] , New York , 1988. viii, 200
p. ; ISBN 0-521-30758-9 DDC 305.5/62/096 19
HD8776.5 .F74 1988   *NYPL [Sc C 88-334]*

**LABOR AND LABORING CLASSES -
AFRICA, SUB-SAHARAN - HISTORY.**
Coquery-Vidrovitch, Catherine. Africa .
Berkeley , c1988. x, 403 p. : ISBN
0-520-05679-5 (alk. paper) DDC 967 19
HC800 .C67513 1988 *NYPL [Sc E 89-221]*

**LABOR AND LABORING CLASSES -
BRAZIL - HISTORY.**
Ghiraldelli, Paulo. Educação e movimento
operário /. São Paulo , 1987. 167 p. ; ISBN
85-24-90081-4   *NYPL [Sc D 88-369]*

Kowarick, Lúcio. Trabalho e vadiagem . São
Paulo , 1987. 133 p. ;   *NYPL [Sc D 88-784]*

**LABOR AND LABORING CLASSES -
BRAZIL - RIO GRANDE DO SUL -
INTERVIEWS.**
Histórias de operários negros /. Porto Alegre,
RS, Brazil , c1987. 100 p. ;
    NYPL [Sc D 88-823]

**LABOR AND LABORING CLASSES -
BRAZIL - SÃO PAULO - HISTORY -
20TH CENTURY.**
Decca, Maria Auxiliadora Guzzo. A vida fora
das fábricas . Rio de Janeiro, RJ , 1987. 135
p. ; DDC 305.5/62/098161 19
HD8290.S32 D4 1987
    NYPL [Sc D 88-1367]

**LABOR AND LABORING CLASSES -
CAMEROON - HISTORY.**
Kaptue, Léon. Travail et main-d'oeuvre au
Cameroun sous régime français, 1916-1952 /.
Paris [c1986] 282 p. ; ISBN 2-85802-655-6
    NYPL [Sc D 88-1237]

**LABOR AND LABORING CLASSES - CHILD
LABOR. see CHILDREN -
EMPLOYMENT.**

**LABOR AND LABORING CLASSES -
EDUCATION - BRAZIL.**
Ghiraldelli, Paulo. Educação e movimento
operário /. São Paulo , 1987. 167 p. ; ISBN
85-24-90081-4   *NYPL [Sc D 88-369]*

**LABOR AND LABORING CLASSES -
GHANA.**

Peil, Margaret. The Ghanaian factory worker.
[Cambridge, Eng.] 1972. ix, 254 p.
    NYPL [Sc 331.7-P]

**LABOR AND LABORING CLASSES -
GUYANA.**
Great Britain. Colonial Office. Papers relative
to the West Indies. Part I-(5.). Jamaica - British
Guiana ... [London] , 1839. iv, 317 p. ;
    NYPL [Sc Rare G 86-3]

**LABOR AND LABORING CLASSES - HAITI -
HISTORY.**
Auguste, Michel Hector. Haiti, la lucha por la
democracia (clase obrera, partidos y sindicatos)
/. Puebla [1986]. 244 p. ;
    NYPL [Sc D 88-761]

**LABOR AND LABORING CLASSES - HAITI -
POLITICAL ACTIVITY.**
Auguste, Michel Hector. Haiti, la lucha por la
democracia (clase obrera, partidos y sindicatos)
/. Puebla [1986]. 244 p. ;
    NYPL [Sc D 88-761]

**LABOR AND LABORING CLASSES -
JAMAICA.**
Great Britain. Colonial Office. Papers relative
to the West Indies. Part I-(5.). Jamaica - British
Guiana ... [London] , 1839. iv, 317 p. ;
    NYPL [Sc Rare G 86-3]

**LABOR AND LABORING CLASSES -
NAMIBIA.**
Working under South African occupation .
London , 1987. 56 p. ; ISBN 0-904759-73-3
(pbk.) : DDC 968 s 331.6/9/9688 19
DT746 .F3 no. 14 HD8808
    NYPL [Sc D 89-525]

**LABOR AND LABORING CLASSES - SOUTH
AFRICA.**
The Independent trade unions, 1974-1984 .
Johannesburg , 1987. xvi, 355 p. ; ISBN
0-86975-307-X   *NYPL [Sc D 88-1329]*

A People's history of South Africa.
Johannesburg , c1980- v. : ISBN 0-86975-119-0
(pbk. : v. 1) DDC 968 19
DT766 .P43   *NYPL [JLM 85-439]*

**LABOR AND LABORING CLASSES -
TRINIDAD AND TOBAGO - POLITICAL
ACTIVITY.**
Committee for Labour Solidarity. CLS speaks .
[Trinidad and Tobago] [1987] iii, 80 p. :
    NYPL [Sc D 88-969]

**LABOR AND LABORING CLASSES - ZAIRE -
HAUT-ZAIRE - HISTORY.**
Northrup, David. Beyond the bend in the
river . Athens, Ohio , 1988. xvii, 264 p. :
    ISBN 0-89680-151-9 DDC 331.11/73/0967517
19
HD8811.Z8 K586 1988
    NYPL [Sc D 88-960]

**LABOR AND LABORING CLASSES - ZAIRE -
KIVU - HISTORY.**
Northrup, David. Beyond the bend in the
river . Athens, Ohio , 1988. xvii, 264 p. :
    ISBN 0-89680-151-9 DDC 331.11/73/0967517
19
HD8811.Z8 K586 1988
    NYPL [Sc D 88-960]

**LABOR AND LABORING CLASSES -
ZIMBABWE.**
Cheater, Angela P. The politics of factory
organization . Gweru, Zimbabwe , c1986. xix,
156, [1] p. : ISBN 0-86922-374-7
    NYPL [Sc D 88-671]

LABOR AND STATE. see LABOR POLICY.

**LABOR DISPUTES - TRINIDAD AND
TOBAGO.**
Reddock, Rhoda. Elma Francois . London ,
1988. vii, 60 p., [8] p. of plates : ISBN
0-901241-80-6 (Pbk.)   *NYPL [Sc D 89-77]*

LABOR FORCE. see LABOR SUPPLY.

**LABOR FORCE PARTICIPATION. see
LABOR SUPPLY.**

LABOR, FOREIGN. see ALIEN LABOR.

**LABOR - JURISPRUDENCE. see LABOR
LAWS AND LEGISLATION.**

**LABOR LAW, MARITIME. see MERCHANT
SEAMEN - LEGAL STATUS, LAWS, ETC.**

**LABOR LAWS AND LEGISLATION -
CAMEROON.**
Missé, Hermann. Le droit international du

travail en Afrique . Paris , 1987. 263 p. ;　ISBN
2-85802-839-7　　*NYPL [Sc E 88-20]*

**LABOR LAWS AND LEGISLATION,
INTERNATIOANL.**
Missé, Hermann. Le droit international du
travail en Afrique . Paris , 1987. 263 p. ;　ISBN
2-85802-839-7　　*NYPL [Sc E 88-20]*

**LABOR LAWS AND LEGISLATION -
PORTUGAL - COLONIES.**
Portugal. Regulamento do trabalho dos
indigenas, approvado por decreto de 9 de
novembro de 1899 [microform] Lisboa , 1899.
27 p. ;　　　*NYPL [Sc Micro F-10926]*

**LABOR-MANAGEMENT RELATIONS. see
INDUSTRIAL RELATIONS.**

**LABOR ORGANIZATIONS. see TRADE-
UNIONS.**

LABOR, ORGANIZED. see TRADE-UNIONS.

LABOR POLICY - NIGERIA - HISTORY.
Otobo, Dafe. State and industrial relations in
Nigeria /. Lagos , 1988. 192 p.　ISBN
978-260-104-7　　*NYPL [Sc D 89-523]*

**LABOR POLICY - TRINIDAD AND
TOBAGO.**
Oilfields Workers' Trade Union. Memorandum
to the Government of Trinidad and Tobago .
San F'do [i.e. San Fernando, Trinidad and
Tobago] [1987 or 1988] 124 p. [4] p. of
plates :　　*NYPL [Sc D 88-822]*

**LABOR RELATIONS. see INDUSTRIAL
RELATIONS.**

LABOR SUPPLY - AFRICA - CONGRESSES.
Human resources development and utilization
in Africa . Maseru [Lesotho] , 1988. vi, 160
p. ;　ISBN 0-620-12102-5　*NYPL [Sc D 89-558]*

LABOR SUPPLY - CAMEROON - HISTORY.
Kaptue, Léon. Travail et main-d'oeuvre au
Cameroun sous régime français, 1916-1952 /.
Paris [c1986] 282 p. :　ISBN 2-85802-655-6
　　　　NYPL [Sc D 88-1237]

LABOR SUPPLY - NIGERIA.
Manpower development and utilization in
Nigeria . Lagos, Nigeria , 1986. xiii, 240 p. ;
ISBN 978-226-441-5
　　　　NYPL [Sc D 88-1077]

LABOR SUPPLY - UNITED STATES.
Baker's dozen . Washington [1973] 112 p. ;
　　　　NYPL [Sc F 88-244]

LABOR UNIONS. see TRADE-UNIONS.

**LABORERS. see LABOR AND LABORING
CLASSES.**

**LABORING AND LABORING CLASSES -
BRAZIL - POLITICAL ACTIVITY -
HISTORY.**
Hahner, June Edith, 1940- Poverty and
politics . Albuquerque , 1986. xvi, 415 p. :
　　ISBN 0-8263-0878-3 :　DDC 305.5/69/0981 19
HC190.P6 H34 1986　*NYPL [JLE 86-4407]*

Labour and unions in Asia and Africa :
contemporary issues / edited by Roger Southall.
New York : St. Martin's Press, 1988. x, 258
p. ; 22 cm. Includes index. Includes bibliographies.
　　ISBN 0-312-01362-0 :　DDC 331.88/095 19
*1. Trade-unions - Asia. 2. Trade-unions - Africa. I.
Southall, Roger.*
HD6796 .L3 1988　　*NYPL [Sc D 88-1393]*

**Labour regulation and black workers' struggles in
South Africa /.** Haarløv, Jens. Uppsala , 1983.
80 p. ;　ISBN 91-7106-213-0 (pbk.)　DDC 960 s
331.6/9/968 19
DT1 .N64 no. 68 HD6870.5
　　　　NYPL [JLD 87-1037]

LaBrew, Arthur R. The Black Swan : Elizabeth T.
Greenfield, songstress : biographical study /
annotated and compiled by Arthur R. LaBrew.
Detroit : [s.n.], 1969. 86 p. : facsims., ports. ;
22 cm.
*1. Greenfield, Elizabeth T. (Elizabeth Taylor), d.1876.
2. Afro-American singers - Biography. I. Title.*
　　　　NYPL [JND 82-30]

Labyrinthe . Boni, S. Tanella. [Paris] , c1984. 76
p. ;　ISBN 2-86427-023-4
MLCS 86/6645 (P)　　*NYPL [Sc D 88-488]*

Labyrinths of the delta /. Ojaide, Tanure, 1948-
Greenfield Center, NY , c1986. 103 p. ;　ISBN
0-912678-67-4　　　*NYPL [Sc D 88-1191]*

LACITO-documents. Afrique .
(2) Préalables à la reconstruction du
proto-tchadique . Paris , 1978. 210 p. ;　ISBN
2-85297-022-8　DDC 493/.7 19
PL8026.C53 P73 1978　*NYPL [Sc E 88-418]*

(9) Etudes sur le bantu oriental . Paris , 1982
[i.e. 1983] 158 p. ;　ISBN 2-85297-144-5 :　DDC
496/.39 19
PL8025 .E84 1983　　*NYPL [Sc E 88-357]*

Lad of Lima . Windeatt, Mary Fabyan, 1910-
New York , 1942. 152 p. :
　　　　NYPL [Sc D 88-1170]

Ladder to the sky /. Chandler, Ruth Forbes.
London , New York , c1959. 189 p. :
　　　　NYPL [Sc D 88-1107]

Ladele, T. A. A. Akójop Lagos , 1986. xi, 324 p.,
map, ports. ;　ISBN 978-13-2563-1
　　　　NYPL [Sc D 88-955]

The ladies and the mammies . James, Selma.
Bristol, England , 1983. 96 p. ;　ISBN
0-905046-24-2 :　*NYPL [JFD 84-4049]*

Ladies' Anti-Slavery Society of Cincinnati.
Brisbane, William Henry, ca. 1803-1878. Speech
of the Rev. Wm. H. Brisbane . Hartford , 1840.
12 p. ;　　　*NYPL [Sc Rare C 89-26]*

Lafarge, Francine. Tourneux, Henry. Les Mbara
et leur langue (Tchad) /. Paris , 1986. 319 p. :
　　ISBN 2-85297-188-7　*NYPL [Sc E 88-162]*

LAFARGE, JOHN, 1880-1963.
Nickels, Marilyn Wenzke. Black Catholic
protest and the Federated Colored Catholics,
1917-1933 . New York , 1988. ix, 325 p. ;
　　ISBN 0-8240-4098-8 (alk. paper) :　DDC
282/.73/08996073 19
BX1407.N4 N5 1988　　*NYPL [Sc E 89-85]*

Laferrière, Dany. Eroshima : roman / Dany
Laferrière. Montréal, Québec : VLB Editeur,
1987. 168 p. : port. ; 22 cm.　ISBN
2-89005-277-X
I. Title.　　　*NYPL [Sc D 88-395]*

LAGOS (CITY) - HISTORY.
Akinsemoyin, Kunle. Building Lagos/. Jersey,
1977, c1906. 76 p.:
　　　　NYPL [3-MQWW 79-2215]

Akinsemoyin, Kunle. Who are Lagosians?
[microform] /. [Lagos] 23 p. ;
　　　　NYPL [Sc Micro F-11129]

LAGOS PLAN OF ACTION - CONGRESSES.
African development . Lawrenceville, Va., U.
S.A. , c1985. 241 p. :　ISBN 0-931494-57-5 (pbk.)
DDC 337.1/6 19
HC800 .A565 1985　　*NYPL [Sc F 87-376]*

LAGOS STATE (NIGERIA) - HISTORY.
History of the peoples of Lagos State /. Ikeja,
Lagos , 1987. xii, 378 p. ;　ISBN 978-228-148-4
　　　　NYPL [Sc D 88-731]

**Lagro, ou, Les debuts du socialisme à la
Martinique /.** Darsières, Camille.
[Fort-de-France] [198-?] 75 p. :
　　　　NYPL [Sc D 89-560]

LAGROSILLIÈRE, JOSEPH, 1872-1950.
Darsières, Camille. Lagro, ou, Les debuts du
socialisme à la Martinique /. [Fort-de-France]
[198-?] 75 p. :　　*NYPL [Sc D 89-560]*

Laing, B. Kojo. Woman of the aeroplanes.
London : Heinemann, 1988. 196 p. ; 24 cm.
　　ISBN 0-434-40218-4 :　DDC 823 19
1. Ghana - Fiction. I. Title.　NYPL [Sc E 89-120]

Laing, E., 1931- West African Seminar on
Population Studies, University of Ghana, 1972.
Interdisciplinary approaches to population
studies . Legon , 1975. ix, 333 p. :
HB21 .W38 1972　　*NYPL [JLD 78-861]*

Laisse aller mon peuple! . Luneau, René. Paris ,
c1987. 193 p. ;　ISBN 2-86537-173-5　DDC 282/.6
19
BX1675 .L86 1987　　*NYPL [Sc D 88-315]*

LAITY - CATHOLIC CHURCH.
Anaele, Justin Uchechukwu. The role of the
laity in ecumenism with reference to the church
in Nigeria /. Rome , 1985 (Rome : R.
Ambrosini) 146 p.　　*NYPL [Sc E 88-608]*

LAITY - NIGERIA.
Anaele, Justin Uchechukwu. The role of the
laity in ecumenism with reference to the church
in Nigeria /. Rome , 1985 (Rome : R.
Ambrosini) 146 p.　　*NYPL [Sc E 88-608]*

Lake, Anthony. Third World radical regimes : U.
S. policy under Carter and Reagan / by
Anthony Lake. New York : Foreign Policy
Association, 1985. 54 p. : ill., maps, ports. ; 20
cm. (Headline series, 0017-8780 . no. 272)
Bibliography: p. 53-54.　ISBN 0-87124-099-8
*1. United States - Foreign relations - Developing
countries. 2. Developing countries - Foreign relations -
United States. 3. United States - Foreign relations -
1977-. I. Title.*　　*NYPL [ILH 86-805]*

Laleye, Barnabé. Une femme dans la lumiére de
l'aube : roman / Barnabé Laye. Paris : Seghers,
c1988. 228 p. ; 22 cm. (Chemins d'identité)
1. Africa - Fiction. I. Title. II. Series.
　　　　NYPL [Sc D 88-1407]

Lalit. L'Histoire d'une trahison . Port Louis,
Mauritius , 1987. vi, 192 p.
　　　　NYPL [Sc F 88-275]

Lalla, Barbara, 1949- Voices in exile .
Tuscaloosa , c1989. xiv, 157 p. :　ISBN
0-8173-0382-0　DDC 427/.97292 19
PM7874.J3 V65 1989　　*NYPL [Sc E 89-207]*

Lamadani, 1893-1972. Satires de Lamadani /
publiées par Éric de Dampierre. [Paris] : A.
Colin, 1987. 155 p., [9] p. of plates : ill.,
ports. ; 25 cm. + 1 sound cassette. (Classiques
africains. 23) Nzakara and French on opposite pages.
Cassette located in Moving Images and Recorded
Sound, with same classification. CONTENTS. - v. 1.
[Texts].--v. 2. [Cassette]: chant et harpe.
1. Nzakara dialect - Texts. I. Title. II. Series.
　　　　NYPL [Sc E 88-223]

**Lamar, Lucius Q. C. (Lucius Quintus
Cincinnatus), 1825-1893.** The African slave
trade . Philadelphia , 1863. 24 p. ;
　　　　NYPL [Sc Rare F 89-5]

Lamberti, Marcello.
Haberland, Eike. Ibaaddo ka-Ba'iso .
Heidelberg , 1988. 184 p. ;　ISBN 3-533-04014-3
　　　　NYPL [Sc D 89-552]

Kuliak and Cushitic : a comparative study /
Marcello Lamberti. Heidelberg : Carl Winter
Universitätsverlag, 1988. 157 p. ; 21 cm. (Studia
linguarum Africae orientalis. Bd. 3) Bibliography: p.
155-157.
*1. Teuso languages. 2. Cushitic languages. I. Title. II.
Series.*　　　*NYPL [Sc D 89-330]*

Lambeth Council. Forty winters on . [London]
[1988?] 47 p. :　　*NYPL [Sc D 88-1202]*

Lamentation /. Pierre, K. D. Jn. (Kentry D. Jn.)
[St. Lucia] , 1987. 62 p. :
　　　　NYPL [Sc D 88-908]

Lamentos só lamentos /. Bélsiva. [São Paulo?]
1973 (São Paulo : Empresa Gráfica da Revista
dos Tribunais). vii, 48 p. ;
　　　　NYPL [Sc D 88-1104]

Lamin, M. B. Koroma, Salia. The spider's web /.
Freetown , 1986. 134 p. :
　　　　NYPL [Sc D 89-403]

Lamur, H. E. The production of sugar and the
reproduction of slaves at Vossenburg
(Suriname), 1705-1863 / [Humphrey E. Lamur]
Amsterdam, The Netherlands : Amsterdam
Centre for Caribbean Studies, c1987. 164 p. :
ill., facsims., maps ; 21 cm. (Caribbean culture
studies . 1) Author's name from cover; imprint from
label on verso of t.p. Bibliography: p. 158-164.　ISBN
90-70313-19-7
*1. Sugar trade - Surinam - History. 2. Slavery -
Economic aspects - Surinam. I. Title.*
　　　　NYPL [Sc D 88-555]

Lancaster, Carol. African debt and financing /.
Washington, D.C. , 1986. 223 p. :　ISBN
0-88132-044-7 :　DDC 336.3/435/096 19
HJ8826 .A36 1986　　*NYPL [JLE 87-3261]*

Lancaster, N. Deacon, Janette. Late Quaternary
palaeoenvironments of southern Africa /.
Oxford , New York , 1988. viii, 225 p. :　ISBN
0-19-854449-9 :　DDC 560/.1/78 19
QE720 .D43 1988　　*NYPL [Sc E 88-341]*

Lancaster pamphlets.
MacKenzie, John M. The partition of Africa,
1880-1900 and European imperialism in the
nineteenth century / . London , New York ,
1983. x, 48 p. :　ISBN 0-416-35050-X　DDC
960/.23 19
DT29 .M33 1983　　*NYPL [Sc D 88-268]*

A land and life remembered . Belcher, Max.
Athens , Brockton, Mass. , c1988. [xii], 176 p. :

ISBN 0-8203-1085-9 (alk. paper)   DDC
720/.9666/2074014482 19
NA1599.L4 B4 1988   *NYPL [Sc F 89-90]*

The land and people of Tanzania. Kaula, Edna
Mason. Philadelphia [1972] 139 p.   ISBN
0-397-31270-9   DDC 916.78
DT438 .K33   *NYPL [Sc D 88-1112]*

Land in the sun. Davis, Russell G. Boston [1963]
92 p.   *NYPL [Sc F 88-365]*

**Land, labour and merchant capital in the
pre-industrial rural economy of the Cape** .
Dubow, Saul. [Cape Town] , 1982. ii, 95 p. :
ISBN 0-7992-0472-2   *NYPL [Sc D 82-611]*

Land of the hummingbird. Trinidad . Port of
Spain, Trinidad [193-?] [28] p. :
NYPL [Sc B 88-2]

The land of the spirits /. Osahon, Naiwu, 1937-
Apapa, Lagos, Nigeria , 1981. [30] p. :   ISBN
978-18-6008-1   *NYPL [Sc D 89-226]*

LAND QUESTION. see LAND TENURE.

The land question [microform] /. Riddell, Roger.
London [1978?] 40 p. :
HD992.Z63 R52   *NYPL [*XME-13841]*

**LAND, RECLAMATION OF. see
RECLAMATION OF LAND.**

LAND REFORM - CARIBBEAN AREA.
Enjeux fonciers dan la Caraïbe, en Amérique
centrale et à la Réunion. . Paris , c1987. 232
p. :   ISBN 2-7380-0003-7   *NYPL [Sc E 88-246]*

LAND REFORM - ZIMBABWE.
Riddell, Roger. The land question [microform]
/. London [1978?] 40 p. :
HD992.Z63 R52   *NYPL [*XME-13841]*

**LAND REFORM - ZIMBABWE - HISTORY -
20TH CENTURY.**
Mutizwa-Mangiza, N. D. Community
development in pre-independence Zimbabwe .
Harare , c1985. iv, 79 p. :   ISBN 0-86924-090-0
(pbk.)   DDC 307.1/4/096891 19
HN802.Z9 C65 1985   *NYPL [JLD 88-3699]*

**LAND SETTLEMENT - BRAZIL -
MARANHÃO.**
Arcangeli, Alberto. O mito da terra . São Luís ,
1987. 302 p. :   *NYPL [Sc D 89-579]*

LAND SETTLEMENT - IVORY COAST.
Debouvry, Pierre. Contribution à la définition
d'une méthodologie de transfert de populations
paysannes . [Montpellier] [1985] 294 p. :
ISBN 0-85352-039-0   *NYPL [Sc F 88-302]*

**LAND SETTLEMENT PATTERNS -
BOTSWANA - CASE STUDIES.**
Hesselberg, J. (Jan) The Third World in
transition . Uppsala , Stockholm, Sweden ,
1985. 256 p. :   ISBN 91-7106-243-2 (pbk.)   DDC
305.5/63 19
HD1538.B55 H47 1985
NYPL [Sc E 88-290]

**LAND SETTLEMENT PATTERNS - KENYA -
SIAYA DISTRICT.**
Cohen, David William. Siaya, a historical
anthropology of an African landscape /.
London , Athens , 1989. viii, 152 p., [8] p. of
plates :   ISBN 0-8214-0901-8   DDC 967.6/2 19
DT433.545.L85 C64 1988
NYPL [Sc D 89-354]

**LAND TENURE - LAW AND LEGISLATION -
AFRICA, SUB-SAHARAN.**
Systèmes fonciers à la ville et au village .
Paris , c1986. 296 p. ;   ISBN 2-85802-719-6
DDC 346.6704/32 346.706432 19
LAW   *NYPL [Sc D 89-367]*

LAND TENURE - MARTINIQUE.
Desruisseaux, Jacques. La structure foncière de
la Martinique [microform] /. [Montréal] [1975]
49 p. :
HD459.Z8 M372   *NYPL [*XME-7721]*

LAND TENURE - NIGERIA - DRAMA.
Fatunde, Tunde. No food, no country /. Benin
City, Nigeria , 1985. xv, 81 p. :   ISBN
978-249-804-1   *NYPL [Sc C 88-342]*

LAND TENURE - SOUTH AFRICA.
Keegan, Timothy J. Rural transformations in
industrializing South Africa . Basingstoke ;
London , 1987. xviii, 302 p. :   ISBN
0-333-41746-1   *NYPL [Sc D 88-1228]*

LAND TENURE - ZIMBABWE.
Riddell, Roger. The land question [microform]

/. London [1978?] 40 p. :
HD992.Z63 R52   *NYPL [*XME-13841]*

LAND USE - DICTIONARIES.
Yahya, Saad, 1939- English-Swahili glossary of
technical terms for valuers and land economists
/. [Nairobi] [1979] [8] leaves ;   DDC
333/.003/21 19
HD107.7 .Y34 1979   *NYPL [Sc F 88-77]*

LAND USE - NIGERIA.
Uduehi, Godfrey O. Public lands acquisition
and compensation practice in Nigeria /. Ogba,
Ikeja , 1987. xviii, 162 p. :   ISBN 978-16-3064-7
NYPL [Sc D 89-480]

LAND USE, RURAL - CARIBBEAN AREA.
Enjeux fonciers dan la Caraïbe, en Amérique
centrale et à la Réunion. . Paris , c1987. 232
p. :   ISBN 2-7380-0003-7   *NYPL [Sc E 88-246]*

**LAND USE, URBAN - PLANNING. see CITY
PLANNING.**

**LAND VALUATION. see REAL PROPERTY -
VALUATION.**

**LAND VALUES. see REAL PROPERTY -
VALUATION.**

Lander, John, 1807-1839. Lander, Richard,
1804-1834. Journal of an expedition to explore
the course and termination of the Niger . New
York , 1832. 2 v. :   *NYPL [Sc Rare C 89-35]*

Lander, Richard, 1804-1834. Journal of an
expedition to explore the course and
termination of the Niger : with a narrative of a
voyage down that river to its termination / by
Richard and John Lander.Harper's stereotype
ed. New York : Harper, 1832. 2 v. : ill., maps
(1 fold.), port ; 14 cm. (Harper's family library .
35-36) Cover title: Landers' discovery of the
termination of the Niger.
1. Niger River. I. Lander, John, 1807-1839. II. Title.
III. Title: Landers' discovery of the termination of the
Niger. IV. Series.   *NYPL [Sc Rare C 89-35]*

**Landers' discovery of the termination of the
Niger.** Lander, Richard, 1804-1834. Journal of
an expedition to explore the course and
termination of the Niger . New York , 1832. 2
v. :   *NYPL [Sc Rare C 89-35]*

**Der l"andliche Arbeitskalender in der
Regionalplanung Burundis** /. Stremplat, Axel
V., 1941- Giessen , 1984. 130 p. :   ISBN
3-924840-08-3   *NYPL [Sc D 88-556]*

**Landmarks in educational development in
Nigeria** . Ejiogu, Aloy M. Ikeja, Lagos, c1986.
xi, 156 p. ;   ISBN 978-242-716-0
NYPL [Sc D 88-782]

**LANDMARKS, LITERARY. see LITERARY
LANDMARKS.**

Landry, Bart. The new Black middle class / by
Bart Landry. Berkeley : University of California
Press, 1987. xi, 250 p. ; 22 cm. Includes
bibliographical references and index.   ISBN
0-520-05942-5 (alk. paper)   DDC 305.8/96073 19
1. Afro-Americans - Social conditions - 1975-. 2.
Middle classes - United States. 3. United States - Race
relations. I. Title.
E185.86 .L35 1987   *NYPL [Sc D 87-1006]*

Landry, L. Bart. Dilemmas of the new Black
middle class /. [Pa.?] c1980. v, 100 p. ;
E185.86 .D54x 1980   *NYPL [Sc D 89-24]*

The lands and peoples of West Africa /. Niven,
Cecil Rex, 1898- London [1961] vii, 84 p. :
NYPL [Sc D 88-669]

Lands and peoples series.
Niven, Cecil Rex, 1898- The lands and peoples
of West Africa /. London [1961] vii, 84 p. :
NYPL [Sc D 88-669]

Lane College . Cooke, Anna L. Jackson, Tenn. ,
c1987. ix, 150 p. :   DDC 378.768/51 19
LD2935.L23 C66 1987   *NYPL [Sc E 88-81]*

LANE COLLEGE - HISTORY.
Cooke, Anna L. Lane College . Jackson, Tenn. ,
c1987. ix, 150 p. :   DDC 378.768/51 19
LD2935.L23 C66 1987   *NYPL [Sc E 88-81]*

Lane, Pinkie Gordon, 1923- I never scream : new
and selected poems / by Pinkie Gordon
Lane.1st ed. Detroit : Lotus Press, 1985. 104
p. ; 22 cm.   ISBN 0-916418-58-8 (pbk.)
I. Title.   *NYPL [JFD 87-4790]*

LANE, RUSSELL A., 1897-
Mickey, Rosie Cheatham. Russell Adrian Lane,

biography of an urban negro school
administrator [microform] /. 1983. xiii, 275
leaves :   *NYPL [Sc Micro R-4813]*

Lang, Don. Strawberry roan / Don Lang ;
illustrated by Gertrude Howe. New York :
Grosset & Dunlap, 1946. 218 p. : ill. ; 22 cm.
(Famous horse stories) SCHOMBURG CHILDREN'S
COLLECTION.
1. Horses - Juvenile fiction. 2. Afro-American children -
Juvenile fiction. I. Howe, Gertrude. II. Schomburg
Children's Collection. III. Title. IV. Series.
NYPL [Sc D 88-646]

**LANG, ELISABETH - ART COLLECTIONS -
EXHIBITIONS.**
Fry, Jacqueline, 1923- Visual variations .
Kingston, Canada , c1987. vii, 63 p. :   DDC
730/.0966/074011372 19
NB1098 .F79 1987   *NYPL [Sc F 88-189]*

**LANG, JUSTIN - ART COLLECTIONS -
EXHIBITIONS.**
Fry, Jacqueline, 1923- Visual variations .
Kingston, Canada , c1987. vii, 63 p. :   DDC
730/.0966/074011372 19
NB1098 .F79 1987   *NYPL [Sc F 88-189]*

Lang, Marvel. Black student retention in higher
education /. Springfield, Ill., U. S. A. , c1988.
xvi, 111 p. :   ISBN 0-398-05477-0   DDC
378/.198/2 19
LC2781 .B465 1988   *NYPL [Sc F 89-139]*

Langa, Mandla, 1950- Tenderness of blood /
Mandla Langa. Harare : Zimbabwe Pub. House,
1987. 427 p. ; 19 cm. (ZPH writers series. 31)
ISBN 0-949225-30-4
1. South Africa - Fiction. I. Title. II. Series.
NYPL [Sc C 89-102]

Lange, Werner J., 1946- History of the Southern
Gonga (Southwestern Ethiopia) / Werner J.
Lange. Wiesbaden : Steiner, 1982. xvi, 348 p.,
[12] p. of plates : ill. ; 24 cm. (Studien zur
Kulturkunde. Bd. 61) Bibliography: p. [330]-348.
ISBN 3-515-03399-8 (pbk.) :   DDC 306/.08996
19
1. Gonga (African people) - History. I. Title. II. Series.
DT380.4.G66 L36 1982
NYPL [Sc E 88-379]

Langley, Ph. Managing the Botswana brigades :
an experience in training development staff /
based on the training programme designed and
implemented by PAID-ESA staff, G.K.
Addai ... [et al.] ; in collaboration with Philip
Langley. Douala, U.R.C. : Panafrican Institute
for Development, [1983] 93 p. : ill. ; 24 cm.
(Cahiers de l'IPD . no 6. n 2-1983 =) Summary in
French. Bibliography: p. 88-90.   DDC
658.3/12404/096811 19
1. Occupational training - Botswana - Management. 2.
Youth - Employment - Botswana. I. Addai, G. K. II.
Series: Cahiers de l'IPD , no 6. III. Title.
HD5715.5.B55 L36 1983
NYPL [Sc E 88-483]

Langston Hughes /. Rummel, Jack. New York ,
c1988. 111 p. :   ISBN 1-555-46595-1   DDC
818/.5209 B 92 19
PS3515.U274 Z775 1988
NYPL [Sc E 88-166]

Langston Hughes & the blues /. Tracy, Steven C.
(Steven Carl), 1954- Urbana , c1988. xiii, 305
p. ;   ISBN 0-252-01457-X (alk. paper)   DDC
818/.5209 19
PS3515.U274 Z8 1988   *NYPL [Sc E 88-506]*

Langston Hughes and the blues. Tracy, Steven C.
(Steven Carl), 1954- Langston Hughes & the
blues /. Urbana , c1988. xiii, 305 p. ;   ISBN
0-252-01457-X (alk. paper)   DDC 818/.5209 19
PS3515.U274 Z8 1988   NYPL [Sc E 88-506]

LANGSTON, JOHN MERCER, 1829-1897.
Cheek, William F., 1933- John Mercer
Langston and the fight for Black freedom,
1829-65 /. Urbana , c1989. 478 p. ;   ISBN
0-252-01550-9 (alk. paper)   DDC
973/.0496073/0924 B 19
E185.97.L27 C48 1989   NYPL [Sc E 89-255]

**LANGUAGE AND CULTURE - IVORY
COAST.**
Ebermann, Erwin. Die Sprache der Mauka .
Wien , 1986. 207 p. ;   ISBN 3-85369-656-2
PL8491.95.I9 E24 1986
NYPL [Sc D 88-687]

**LANGUAGE AND CULTURE - WEST
INDIES.**

Roberts, Peter A. West Indians and their language /. Cambridge [Cambridgeshire] , New York , 1988. vii, 215 p. : ISBN 0-521-35136-7 DDC 427/.9729 19
P381.W47 R63 1988   *NYPL [Sc E 88-331]*

LANGUAGE AND EDUCATION - AFRICA, SUB-SAHARAN.
Richmond, Edmun B. New directions in language teaching in Sub-Saharan Africa . Washington, D.C. , c1983. viii, 65 p. ; ISBN 0-8191-2980-1 (pbk.) : DDC 418/.007/067 19
P57.A37 R5 1983   *NYPL [Sc D 88-479]*

LANGUAGE AND EDUCATION - WEST INDIES.
Roberts, Peter A. West Indians and their language /. Cambridge [Cambridgeshire] , New York , 1988. vii, 215 p. : ISBN 0-521-35136-7 DDC 427/.9729 19
P381.W47 R63 1988   *NYPL [Sc E 88-331]*

Language and ethnic identity / edited by William B. Gudykunst. Clevedon ; Philadelphia : Multilingual Matters, c1988. 170 p. ; 26 cm. Includes bibliographies and index. ISBN 1-85359-021-5 DDC 401/.9 19
I. Gudykunst, William B.
P35 .L267 1988   *NYPL [Sc F 88-323]*

LANGUAGE AND LANGUAGES - STUDY AND TEACHING - AFRICA, SUB-SAHARAN.
Richmond, Edmun B. New directions in language teaching in Sub-Saharan Africa . Washington, D.C. , c1983. viii, 65 p. ; ISBN 0-8191-2980-1 (pbk.) : DDC 418/.007/067 19
P57.A37 R5 1983   *NYPL [Sc D 88-479]*

Language and liberation . Devonish, Hubert. London , 1986. 157 p. ; ISBN 0-946918-27-9 (pbk) : DDC 417/.2 19
PM7834.C3   *NYPL [Sc D 88-512]*

LANGUAGE AND SOCIETY. see SOCIOLINGUISTICS.

LANGUAGE POLICY - AFRICA, SUB-SAHARAN.
Richmond, Edmun B. New directions in language teaching in Sub-Saharan Africa . Washington, D.C. , c1983. viii, 65 p. ; ISBN 0-8191-2980-1 (pbk.) : DDC 418/.007/067 19
P57.A37 R5 1983   *NYPL [Sc D 88-479]*

LANGUAGES - SOCIOLOGICAL ASPECTS. see SOCIOLINGUISTICS.

LANGUE D'OÏL. see FRENCH LANGUAGE.

Langues dans le monde ancien et moderne .
(1) Les Langues de l'Afrique subsaharienne /. Paris , 1981. 2 v : ISBN 2-222-01720-3 :
   NYPL [JFN 81-11 v.1]

Les Langues de l'Afrique subsaharienne / textes réunis par Gabriel Manessy. Pidgins et créoles / textes réunis par Albert Valdman. Paris : Editions du Centre national de la recherche scientifique, 1981. 2 v : ill., maps (some folded, col.) ; 31 cm. (Les Langues dans le monde ancien et moderne / ouvrage publié sous la direction de Jean Perrot . 1) Includes bibliographies and index. CONTENTS. - [1.] Texte -- [2.] Cartes. ISBN 2-222-01720-3 :
1. African languages. 2. Pidgin languages. 3. Creole dialects. 4. Africa, Sub-Saharan - Languages. I. Manessy, Gabriel. II. Valdman, Albert. III. Series: Langues dans le monde ancien et moderne , 1.
   NYPL [JFN 81-11 v.1]

Langues et cultures Africaines .
(9) Colombel, Véronique de. Les Ouldémés du Nord-Cameroun . Paris , 1987. [13]-74 p., [61] p. of plates : ISBN 2-85297-199-2
   NYPL [Sc E 89-244]
(6) Tourneux, Henry. Les Mbara et leur langue (Tchad) /. Paris , 1986. 319 p. : ISBN 2-85297-188-7   *NYPL [Sc E 88-162]*

Langues et cultures guyanaises /. Contout, Auxence. Guyana [197-?] 233 p. :
   NYPL [Sc D 88-1279]

Les langues fer ("Kara") et yulu du Nord centrafricain . Boyeldieu, Pascal. Paris , 1987. 280 p. ; ISBN 2-7053-0342-1
   NYPL [Sc E 88-124]

A lantern in the window /. Fisher, Aileen Lucia, 1906- Eau Claire, Wisconsin [1962] 126 p. :
   NYPL [Sc D 88-434]

Lapper, Richard. Honduras, state for sale / [written by Richard Lapper and James Painter].

London : Latin America Bureau, 1985. iv, 132 p. : ill. ; 21 cm. (Latin America Bureau special brief) Erratum slip inserted. Bibliography: p. 132. ISBN 0-906156-23-8
1. Honduras - History. I. Painter, James. II. Title.
   NYPL [HML 87-1562]

Lara, Oruno D. Le commandant Mortenol : un officier guadeloupéen dans la "Royale" / Oruno D. Lara. Epinay, France : Centre de recherches Caraïbes-Amériques, Université Paris X-Nanterre, c1985. 275 p. : ill., maps ; 24 cm. (Série biographies, hommes et femmes des Caraïbes) Includes index. Bibliography: p. 265-266. ISBN 2-905787-00-7
1. Mortenol, Sosthème Héliodore Camille, 1859-1930. 2. France. Marine - Officers - Biography. 3. Blacks - Guadeloupe - Biography. I. Université de Paris X: Nanterre. Centre de recherches Caraïbes-Amériques. II. Title. III. Series.   *NYPL [Sc D 88-1085]*

Lara, Silvia Hunold. Campos da violência : escravos e senhores na Capitania do Rio de Janeiro, 1750-1808 / Silvia Hunold Lara. Rio de Janeiro : Paz e Terra, c1988. 389 p. ; 21 cm. (Coleção Oficinas da história) Bibliography: p. [383]-389.
1. Slavery - Brazil - Rio de Janeiro (State) - History. 2. Crime and criminals - Brazil - Rio de Janeiro (State) - History. 3. Rio de Janeiro (Brazil : State) - Social conditions. 4. Rio de Janeiro (Brazil : State) - History. 5. Brazil - History - 1763-1821. I. Title. II. Series.
   NYPL [Sc D 89-13]

Laraque, Franck. Défi à la pauvreté / Franck Loraque. Montréal : Les Editions du CIDIHCA, 1987. 165 p. ; 20 cm. Bibliography: p. 159-165.
1. Haiti - Economic conditions - 1971-. 2. Haiti - Economic policy. 3. Haiti - Dependency on the United States. I. Title.   *NYPL [Sc C 88-107]*

Laraque, Paul, 1920- Camourade : selected poems of Paul Laraque / translated by Rosemary Manno. Willimantic, CT : Curbstone Press ; New York, NY : Distributed in the United States by the Talman Co., 1988. 124 p. ; 22 cm. French and English on opposite pages. ISBN 0-915306-71-9
I. Manno, Rosemary. II. Title.
   NYPL [Sc D 88-629]

Larison, Cornelius Wilson, 1837-1910. Silvia Dubois : a biografy of the slav who whipt her mistres and gand her fredom / C.W. Larison ; edited with a translation and introduction by Jared C. Lobdell. New York : Oxford University Press, 1988. xxvii, 124 p. : ill., port. ; 17 cm. (The Schomburg library of nineteenth-century Black women writers) Reprint. Originally published: Ringos, N. J. : Larison, c1883. ISBN 0-19-505239-0 DDC 305.5/67/0924 B 19
1. Dubois, Silvia, 1788 or 9-1889. 2. Slaves - United States - Biography. 3. Afro-Americans - Biography. 4. English language - Phonetic transcriptions. I. Lobdell, Jared, 1937-. II. Title. III. Series.
E444.D83 L37 1988   *NYPL [JFC 88-2191]*

Larkin, Joan. Gay & lesbian poetry in our time . New York , c1988. xxviii, 401 p. : ISBN 0-312-02213-1 : DDC 811/.54/080353 19
PS595.H65 G39 1988   *NYPL [JFE 89-277]*

Laroche, Maximilien. L'avènement de la littérature haïtienne / Maximilien Laroche. Sainte-Foy, Québec : Groupe de recherche sur les littératures de la Caraïbe, Université Laval, 1987. 219 p. ; 21 cm. (Collection "Essais" (Sainte-Foy, Québec) . n. 3) Bibliographical references contained in "Notes": p. 193-217.
1. Haitian literature - History and criticism. 2. Haitian literature (French Creole) - History and criticism. I. Title. II. Series.   *NYPL [Sc D 88-1462]*

LARSSON, ELISABETH MARIA, B. 1727 - FICTION.
Brink, André Philippus, 1935- An instant in the wind /. New York, N.Y., U. S. A. , 1985, c1976. 250 p. : ISBN 0-14-008014-7 (pbk.) : DDC 823 19
PR9369.3.B7 I5 1985   *NYPL [Sc C 88-281]*

Laruba and the two wicked men /. Osahon, Naiwu, 1937- Apapa, Lagos, Nigeria , 1981. [22] p. ; ISBN 978-18-6004-9
   NYPL [Sc D 89-224]

Lasserre, Guy. La Guadeloupe : étude géographique / Guy Lasserre. Fort-de-France, Martinique : E. Kolodziej, 1978. 3 v. (1132 p.) : ill. ; 29 cm. Originally presented as the author's thesis, Bordeaux. Originally published: Bordeaux :

Union française d'impression, 1961. Bibliography: v.3, p. [1069]-1112. CONTENTS. - t. 1. La nature et les hommes.--t. 2-3. Les îles et leurs problèmes.
1. Guadeloupe - Description and travel. 2. Guadeloupe - Economic conditions. I. Title.
   NYPL [Sc F 88-112]

The last Don out /. Serrano, Jumoke. Ibadan, Nigeria , 1986. 106 p. ; ISBN 978-14-1062-0
   NYPL [Sc C 88-341]

The last laugh and other stories /. Achebe, Chinelo. Ibadan , 1988. 79 p. ; ISBN 978-12-9853-7   *NYPL [Sc C 89-152]*

Last, Murray. Sierra Leone, 1787-1987 . Manchester ; New York : 577 p., [8] p. of plates : ISBN 0-7190-2791-8 (pbk.) : DDC 966/.4 19
DT516.7 .S54 1988   *NYPL [Sc E 88-461]*

The last of the Maasai /. Amin, Mohamed, 1943- London , 1987. 185 p. : ISBN 0-370-31097-7
   NYPL [Sc G 88-21]

Late Quaternary palaeoenvironments of southern Africa /. Deacon, Janette. Oxford , New York , 1988. viii, 225 p. : ISBN 0-19-854449-9 : DDC 560/.1/78 19
QE720 .D43 1988   *NYPL [Sc E 88-341]*

Lateef, Yusef. Kofoworola, Ziky. Hausa performing arts and music /. Lagos , c1987. viii, 330 p. : ISBN 978-17-3041-2
   NYPL [Sc E 89-116]

Latimer, Margery Toomer. Toomer, Jean, 1894-1967. [Poems. 1988.] The collected poems of Jean Toomer /. Chapel Hill , c1988. xxxv, 111 p. ; ISBN 0-8078-1773-2 (hard) : DDC 811/.52 19
PS3539.O478 A17 1988
   NYPL [Sc E 88-282]

LATIN AMERICA - CHURCH HISTORY.
Escravidão negra e história da Igreja na América Latina e no Caribe /. Petrópolis , 1987. 237 p. :   *NYPL [Sc D 88-75]*

LATIN AMERICA - CIVILIZATION - HISTORY - ADDRESSES, ESSAYS, LECTURES.
Rasco y Bermudez, José Ignacio. Integración cultural de América Latina . Medellín, [Colombia , 1975] 188 p. ;
F1408.3 .R37   *NYPL [HCB 78-2271]*

LATIN AMERICA - ECONOMIC CONDITIONS.
Africa, America, and central Asia . [Exeter, Devon] [Atlantic Highlands, N.J.] 1984. 107 p. : ISBN 0-85989-295-6 (pbk.) : DDC 330.9/034 19
HC53 .A35 1984   *NYPL [Sc D 88-1315]*

LATIN AMERICA - FOREIGN RELATIONS - UNITED STATES.
The Politics of Latin American liberation theology . Washington, D.C. , c1988. xxi, 360 p. ; ISBN 0-88702-039-9 : DDC 261.7/09181/2 19
BT83.57 .P643 1988   *NYPL [Sc E 89-75]*

LATIN AMERICA - RELIGION.
Gallardo, Jorge Emilio. Presencia africana en la cultura de América Latina . Buenos Aires, Argentina , c1986. 123 p. ; ISBN 950-643-006-3 DDC 299/.69 19
BL2490 .G33 1986   *NYPL [Sc D 89-358]*

LATIN AMERICAN LITERATURE - 20TH CENTURY - HISTORY AND CRITICISM.
Jackson, Richard L., 1937- Black literature and humanism in Latin America /. Athens , c1988. xvii, 166 p. ; ISBN 0-8203-0979-6 (alk. paper) DDC 860/.9/896 19
PQ7081 .J263 1988   *NYPL [Sc E 88-359]*

LATIN AMERICAN LITERATURE - BLACK AUTHORS - HISTORY AND CRITICISM.
Jackson, Richard L., 1937- Black literature and humanism in Latin America /. Athens , c1988. xvii, 166 p. ; ISBN 0-8203-0979-6 (alk. paper) DDC 860/.9/896 19
PQ7081 .J263 1988   *NYPL [Sc E 88-359]*

LATTER RAIN MOVEMENT. see PENTECOSTALISM.

Lattimore, Eleanor Frances, 1904- Indigo Hill; written and illustrated by Eleanor Frances Lattimore. New York, Morrow, 1950. 128 p. illus. 21 cm. The everyday experiences of the children of Indigo Hill in South Carolina, especially eight-year-old Lydia, as she goes to church and school, minds her younger brothers, and helps her aunt.

SCHOMBURG CHILDREN'S COLLECTION. DDC
[Fic]
*1. Afro-American children - South Carolina - Juvenile
fiction. I. Schomburg Children's Collection. II. Title.*
PZ7.L37 In   **NYPL** *[Sc D 88-1428]*

Lauber, Patricia. The Congo, river into central
Africa. Illus. by Ted Schroeder. Maps by Fred
Kliem. Champaign, Ill., Garrard Pub. Co. [1964]
96 p. illus., ports. 24 cm. (Rivers of the world.
W-10) A history of exploration, travel, and trade on the
Congo River. Describes the journeys of Henry M.
Stanley, the animal and mineral riches of the river, and
the life of its peoples today. SCHOMBURG
CHILDREN'S COLLECTION. DDC 967
*1. Congo River - Juvenile literature. I. Schroeder, Ted,
illus. II. Schomburg Children's Collection. III. Series:
Rivers of the world (Champaign, Ill.), W-10. IV. Title.*
DT639 .L38   **NYPL** *[Sc E 89-24]*

LAUDATORY POETRY, YORUBA.
Babayemi, S. O. Content analysis of oríkì oríl
[Ibadan , 198-?] xi, 352 p. ;
     NYPL *[Sc E 89-229]*

Laugh with Larry /. Detroit. Great Cities
Program for School Improvement. Writers'
Committee. Chicago , c1962. 47 p. ;
     NYPL *[Sc E 87-268]*

Laughlin, Robert M. The great Tzotzil dictionary
of Santo Domingo Zinacantán : with
grammatical analysis and historical commentary
/ Robert M. Laughlin with John B. Haviland.
Washington, D.C. : Smithsonian Institution
Press, 1988. 3 v. (xiii, 1119 p.) : ill., facsims. ;
28 cm. (Smithsonian contributions to anthropology.
no. 31) Bibliography: v. 1, p. 346-356. CONTENTS. -
v. 1. Tzotzil-English -- v. 2. English-Tzotzil -- v. 3.
Spanish-Tzotzil. DDC 497/.4 301 s 19
*1. Tzotzil language - Dictionaries - English. 2. English
language - Dictionaries - Tzotzil. 3. Spanish language -
Dictionaries - Tzotzil. I. Haviland, John B. II. Title. III.
Series.*
GN1 .S54 no. 31a PM4466.Z5
     NYPL *[HBR 89-17311]*

Launko, Okinba. Minted coins : (Poems) /
Okinba Launko. Ibadan : Heinemann
Educational Books, 1987. vii, 72 p. : ill. ; 19
cm. ISBN 978-12-9847-2
I. Title.   **NYPL** *[Sc C 88-158]*

Lauture, Denize.
[Cactus legend. Selections]
When the denizen weeps : poems / by
Denize Lauture, Sambas' nephew. Bronx,
N.Y. : Denizenism Editions, c1988. vi, 98
p. ; 21 cm.
I. Title.   **NYPL** *[Sc D 89-80]*

Laverdière, Lucien, 1940- L'africain et le
missionnaire : l'image du missionnaire dans la
litt´erature africaine d'expression française :
essai de sociologie littéraire / Lucien
Laverdière. Montr´eal : Bellarmin, 1987. 608
p. : ill. ; 23 cm. Includes indexes. Bibliography: p.
571-590. ISBN 2-89007-640-7
*1. Missionaries in literature. 2. African literature
(French) - History and criticism. 3. Christianity in
literature. 4. Catholic Church - Missions - Africa. I.
Title.*   **NYPL** *[Sc D 88-343]*

**LAW - AFRICA - HISTORY AND
CRITICISM.**
African and western legal systems in contact
Bayreuth, W. Germany , c1989. 89 p. ; ISBN
3-927510-01-7 :   **NYPL** *[Sc D 89-465]*

LAW AND ANTHROPOLOGY.
Lurry-Wright, Jerome Wendell, 1941- Custom
and conflict on a Bahamian out-island /.
Lanham, MD , c1987. xxii, 188 p. ; ISBN
0-8191-6097-0 (alk. paper) : DDC 347.7296
347.29607 19
KGL210 .L87 1987   **NYPL** *[Sc D 88-218]*

Law and bilingual education . Valle, Manuel del.
New York , 1978. i, 206 p. ;
     NYPL *[Sc F 88-357]*

Law and justice in Zambia . Msiska, Augustine
W. C. Lusaka, Zambia , 1986. iii, 75 p. ; DDC
016.3476894 016.34689407 19
LAW   **NYPL** *[Sc F 89-9]*

Law and the status of women in Ghana. Addis
Ababa : United Nations, Economic Commission
for Africa, 1984. iii, 75 p. ; 28 cm. (Research
series / African Training and Research Centre for
Women) "E/ECA/ATRCW/84/26." Includes
bibliographies. DDC 342.669/0878 346.6902878 19
1. Women - Legal status, laws, etc. - Ghana. I. Series:

*Research series / African Training and Research Centre
for Women.*
LAW   **NYPL** *[Sc F 88-274]*

LAW, ARAB. see ISLAMIC LAW.

LAW, CRIMINAL. see CRIMINAL LAW.

LAW, DINKA (AFRICAN PEOPLE)
Makec, John Wuol. The customary law of the
Dinka people of Sudan . London, England,
1988. 287 p. ; ISBN 0-948583-03-7 (Hardback)
     NYPL *[Sc E 88-434]*

LAW IN THE KORAN. see ISLAMIC LAW.

**LAW, INDUSTRIAL. see LABOR LAWS AND
LEGISLATION.**

LAW, ISLAMIC. see ISLAMIC LAW.

Law, John, 1900- Black creatures of destiny / by
John Law. [New York? : s.n., 198-?] 80 p. :
ill. ; 21 cm. Cover title.
*1. Law, John, 1900-. 2. United States - Race relationas.
I. Title.*   **NYPL** *[Sc D 89-208]*

LAW, JOHN, 1900-
Law, John, 1900- Black creatures of destiny /.
[New York? , 198-?] 80 p. :
     NYPL *[Sc D 89-208]*

**LAW, LABOR. see LABOR LAWS AND
LEGISLATION.**

LAW - NIGERIA.
African and western legal systems in contact
Bayreuth, W. Germany , c1989. 89 p. ; ISBN
3-927510-01-7 :   **NYPL** *[Sc D 89-465]*

Esiemokhai, Emmanuel Omoh. The colonial
legal heritage in Nigeria /. Akure, Nigeria ,
1986. xii, 82 p. ; ISBN 978-16-4248-3
     NYPL *[Sc D 88-640]*

LAW, NYAMWEZI (AFRICAN PEOPLE)
Cory, Hans. Sheria na kawaida za
Wanyamwezi. /. [S.l. , 195-?] ix, 91 p. ;
     NYPL *[Sc E 89-1]*

**LAW - SENEGAL - HISTORY AND
CRITICISM.**
Hesseling, Gerti. [Senegal, staatsrechtelijke en
politieke ontwikkelingen. French.] Histoire
politique du Sénégal . Paris, France , Leiden,
Pays-Bas , c1985. 437 p. ; ISBN 2-86537-118-2
DDC 342.66/3029 346.630229 19
LAW   **NYPL** *[JLE 88-3233]*

LAW - ZAMBIA - BIBLIOGRAPHY.
Msiska, Augustine W. C. Law and justice in
Zambia . Lusaka, Zambia , 1986. iii, 75 p. ;
DDC 016.3476894 016.34689407 19
LAW   **NYPL** *[Sc F 89-9]*

Lawal, Ayo. A Nigerian story in Shareent/ful
Ayo Lawal]. Nigeria : s.n., 198-?] (Ilorin :
Govt. Printer) 132 p. ; 21 cm. Cover title.
1. Nigeria - Fiction. I. Title.
     NYPL *[Sc D 88-1386]*

Lawick-Goodall, Jane, Barones van. In the
shadow of man. Photos. by Hugo van Lawick.
Boston, Houghton Mifflin, 1971. xx, 297 p.
illus. 24 cm. Bibliography: p. [287]-289. ISBN
0-395-12726-2
1. Chimpanzees - Behavior. I. Title.
QL737.P96 L37   **NYPL** *[SC 599.8-L]*

Lawler, Mary. Marcus Garvey / Mary Lawler ;
senior consulting editor, Nathan Irvin Huggins.
New York : Chelsea House, c1988. 110 p. :
ill. ; 24 cm. (Black Americans of achievement)
Includes index. A biography of the black leader who
started a "Back-to-Africa" movement in the United
States, believing blacks would never receive justice in
countries with a white majority. Bibliography: p. 108.
ISBN 1-555-46587-0 DDC 305.8/96073/024 B
92 19
*1. Garvey, Marcus, 1887-1940 - Juvenile literature. 2.
Universal Negro Improvement Association - Juvenile
literature. 3. Afro-Americans - Biography - Juvenile
literature. 4. Intellectuals - United States - Biography -
Juvenile literature. I. Title. II. Series.*
E185.97.G3 L39 1988   **NYPL** *[Sc E 88-156]*

Lawrence, Bridgette. 100 great Westindian test
cricketers : from Challenor to Richards / by
Bridgette Lawrence with Reg Scarlett. London :
Hansib, 1988. 231 p. : ports. ; 26 cm. ISBN
1-87051-865-9 : DDC 796.35/865 19
*1. Test matches (Cricket). 2. Cricket - West Indies -
History. I. Scarlett, Reg, 1934-. II. Title. III. Title: One
hundred great Westindian test cricketers.*
GV928.W4   **NYPL** *[Sc F 88-380]*

Lawrence Charles R. The id, the ego, and equal
protection : reckoning with unconscious racisim
/ Charles R. Lawrence III. [San Francisco,
Calif.] : Leland Stanford Junior University,
1987. 317-388 p. ; 26 cm. "Reprinted from the
Stanford Law Review, vol. 39, no. 2, Jan. 1987."
Includes bibliographical references.
I. Title.   **NYPL** *[Sc F 89-47]*

Lawrence, James Duncan, 1918- Binky brothers,
detectives, by James Lawrence. Pictures by
Leonard Kessler. New York, Harper & Row
[1968] 60 p. illus. (part col.) 23 cm. (An I can
read mystery) When the Binky brothers get a case
involving a missing catcher's mitt, the younger brother
proves the better detective and establishes his right to
be a full partner in the agency. SCHOMBURG
CHILDREN'S COLLECTION. DDC [Fic]
*1. Afro-American children - Juvenile fiction. I. Kessler,
Leonard P., 1920- illus. II. Schomburg Children's
Collection. III. Title.*
PZ7.L4359 Bi   **NYPL** *[Sc D 89-118]*

Lawson, Sandra M. Generations past : a selected
list of sources for Afro-American genealogical
research / compiled by Sandra M. Lawson.
Washington : Library of Congress : For sale by
the Supt. of Docs., U. S. G.P.O., 1988. 101 p. :
ill. ; 23 cm. Includes index. ISBN 0-8444-0604-X
DDC 016.929/1/08996073 19
1. Afro-Americans - Genealogy - Bibliography. I. Title.
Z1361.N39 L34 1988 E185.96
     NYPL *[Sc D 89-360]*

Laycock, Muriel. Paz Gómez, Enelia. Black in
Colombia /. Mexico , c1985. 173 p. :
     NYPL *[Sc D 89-66]*

LAYMEN. see LAITY.

Lazare, Alick. Native laughter / Alick Lazare.
[Roseau : Tropical Printers, c1985] 167 p. ; 19
cm. Short stories and poems.
1. Dominica - Fiction. I. Title.
MLCS 87/7802 (P)   **NYPL** *[Sc C 88-329]*

Lazzaro, Victor. (illus) Warren, Ruth. The Nile.
New York [1968] 127 p. DDC 916.2
DT115 .W33   **NYPL** *[Sc E 89-21]*

Le Boulch, Pierre. Today's English : ready!
steady! go! : méthode d'anglais à l'usage des
classes de sixième du Sénégal / par P. Le
Boulche, J. Ailloud, C. Ben Said ; avec la
collaboration de C. Rudigoz ; figurines
exécutées par G. Niang. [Dakar] : Centre de
linguistique appliquée de Dakar, 1968- v. ; 27
cm. (Enseignement de l'anglais au Sénégal. 37)
CONTENTS. - t.1. Dossiers 1 à 12.
*1. English language - Study and teaching - Senegal. 2.
English language - Text-books for foreign speakers -
French. I. Ailloud, Jean. II. Ben Said, Christine. III.
Title. IV. Series.*   **NYPL** *[Sc F 87-274]*

Le Brasseur, J. A. De l'état actuel de la marine
et des colonies / par M. Le Brasseur. A Paris :
Impr. de L. P. Couret, 1792. 48 p. ; 20 cm.
*1. France. Marine. 2. Haiti - History - Revolution,
1791-1804 - Sources. I. Title.*
     NYPL *[Sc Rare C 86-4]*

Le Pensec, Louis. Vingt questions sur l'Afrique .
Paris , 1988. 238 p. ; ISBN 2-7384-0048-5
     NYPL *[Sc D 88-1390]*

Le Riverend, Julio. Temas acerca de la
esclavitud . [La Habana, Cuba , 1988. 288 p. ;
     NYPL *[Sc C 89-118]*

Le Roy, Alexandre, abp., 1854-1938. Sur terre et
sur l'eau : voyage d'exploration dans l'Afrique
orientale / par Mgr. Le Roy. Tours : A. Mame,
1894. 350 p. : ill., maps ; 28 cm. (Bibliothèque
des familles)
1. Africa, East - Description and travel. I. Title.
     NYPL *[Sc F 88-13]*

Lea, James F. Contemporary southern politics /.
Baton Rouge , c1988. 309 p. ; ISBN
0-8071-1386-7 (alk. paper) DDC 320.975 19
F216.2 .C59 1988   **NYPL** *[Sc E 88-522]*

Leach, Gerald. Beyond the woodfuel crisis :
people, land and trees in Africa / by Gerry
Leach and Robin Mearns. London : Earthscan,
1988. [x], 309 p. : ill., maps ; 22 cm. Includes
index. ISBN 1-85383-031-3 (pbk) DDC 333.75 19
*1. Woodfuel consumption - Africa. I. Mearns, Robin. II.
Title.*   **NYPL** *[Sc D 89-397]*

Leadbitter, Mike. Blues records 1943-1970 : a
selective discography / Mike Leadbitter, Neil
Slaven. London, England : Record Information
Services, 1987- v. ; 22 cm. CONTENTS. - v. 1.

A-K -- v. 2. L-Z. ISBN 0-907872-07-7
1. Blues (Music) - Discography. I. Slaven, Neil. II.
Title.   **NYPL [*R-Phono. 89-790]**

The leader . Odumosu, Z. O. Lagos, Nigeria ,
c1986. xi, 83 p. : ISBN 978-230-916-8
                    NYPL [Sc C 88-160]

**Leadership, conflict, and cooperation in
Afro-American social thought** /. Childs, John
Brown. Philadelphia , 1989. xii, 172 p. ; ISBN
0-87722-581-8 (alk. paper) : DDC
303.3/4/08996073 19
E185.6 .C534 1989   **NYPL [Sc D 89-497]**

**A leaf of honey and the proverbs of the rain
forest** /. Sheppherd, Joseph. c1988.
xii, 319 p. : ISBN 1-87098-902-3 (pbk.) : DDC
305.8/966 19   **NYPL [Sc D 89-453]**

LEAGUE OF NATIONS.
Pienaar, Sara. South Africa and international
relations between the two World Wars .
Johannesburg , 1987. 207 p. ; ISBN
0-85494-936-4   **NYPL [Sc D 88-1026]**

League of Nations. International Labor Office.
see International Labor Office.

LEAGUE OF NATIONS - SOUTH AFRICA.
Pienaar, Sara. South Africa and international
relations between the two World Wars .
Johannesburg , 1987. 207 p. ; ISBN
0-85494-936-4   **NYPL [Sc D 88-1026]**

Leakey, Louis Seymour Bazett, 1903-1972. YllA,
1910-1955. Animals in Africa /. New York ,
1953. 146 p. :   **NYPL [Sc F 88-127]**

**LEARNING AND SCHOLARSHIP -
MUSLIMS. see ISLAMIC LEARNING
AND SCHOLARSHIP.**

**LEASES, USUFRUCTUARY. see FARM
TENANCY.**

**LEATHER WORK - AFRICA -
EXHIBITIONS.**
Deutsches Ledermuseum. Afrika /. Offenbach
am Main , 1988. 227 p. : ISBN 3-87280-042-6
                    NYPL [Sc D 89-506]

Leber, Gisela. Agrarstrukturen und Landflucht im
Senegal : historische Entwicklung und
sozio-ökonomische Konsequenzen / Gisela
Leber. Saarbrücken ; Fort Lauderdale : Verlag
Breitenbach, 1979. vii, 142 p. : ill. ; 21 cm.
(Sozialwissenschaftliche Studien zu internationalen
Problemen. Heft 44 0584-603X) Bibliography: p.
133-142. ISBN 3-88156-125-0
*1. Agriculture - Economic aspects - Senegal. 2.
Rural-urban migration - Senegal. 3. Senegal - Rural
conditions. I. Title.*
HD2144.5 .L42   **NYPL [JLD 80-2814]**

Leconte, Vergniaud. Théâtre [microform]. Drame:
Le roi Christophe, Coulou, Une princesse
aborigène ... [n. p., 1919] xi, 291 p. Black author.
Microfilm. New York : New York Public Library,
[197-] 1 microfilm reel ; 35 mm.
*1. Henri Christophe, King of Haiti, 1767-1820 - Drama.
2. Haiti - History - Drama. I. Title.*
                    NYPL [Sc Micro R-3541]

Ledel Gallery. Cuba, a view from inside . New
York [1985?] 2 v. :
TR646.U6 N4853x 1985
                    NYPL [Sc D 88-1511]

Leder, Dora. (ill) Cameron, Ann, 1943- Julian's
glorious summer /. New York , c1987. 62 p. :
ISBN 0-394-89117-1 (pbk.) : DDC [Fic] 19
PZ7.C1427 Ju 1987   **NYPL [Sc C 89-99]**

Ledwaba, John Moalusi. Manaka, Matsemela.
Egoli, city of gold [microform] . Johannesburg
[198-?] 28 p. : **NYPL [Sc Micro F-11049]**

Lee, Easton. The rope and the cross : a
dramatization of the Passion specially written
for performance in churches / Easton Lee.
Kingston, Jamaica : Creative Projects Ltd, 1985.
48 p., [4] p. of plates : ill. ; 23 cm.
1. Jesus Christ - Drama. 2. Passion-plays. I. Title.
                    NYPL [Sc D 89-458]

Lee, George L. Interesting people : Black
American history makers / by George L. Lee.
Jefferson, N.C. ; London : McFarland, c1989.
xiii, 210 p. : ports. ; 24 cm. Includes index. ISBN
0-89950-403-5 : DDC 973/.0496073022 19
1. Afro-Americans - Biography. I. Title.
E185.96   **NYPL [Sc E 89-240]**

Lee, Hannah Farnham Sawyer, 1780-1865.
Memoir of Pierre Toussaint, born a slave in St.

Domingo. By the author of "Three experiments
in living,"etc.3rd ed. Boston, Crosby, Nichols,
and company, 1854. 124 p. front. (port.) 18 cm.
1. Toussaint, Pierre, 1766-1853?. I. Title.
E189.97 T732   **NYPL [Sc Rare C 88-23]**

Lee, Jacintha A. (Jacintha Anius) Give me some
more sense : a collection of St. Lucian folk
tales / Jacintha A. Lee. Illustrations Alwin St.
Omer.2nd ed. Basingstoke : Macmillan, 1983.
40 p. : ill. ; 22 cm. ISBN 0-333-46121-5 (pbk) :
DDC 813 19
1. Tales - Saint Lucia. I. Title.
PZ8.1   **NYPL [Sc D 89-284]**

Lee, Leslie. Between now and then : a drama /
by Leslie Lee. New York : S. French, c1984.
108 p. ; [4] p. of plates : ill. ; 19 cm. ISBN
0-573-61911-5 (pbk.) DDC 812/.54 19
I. Title.
PS3562.E35435 B4 1984 **NYPL [Sc C 88-55]**

Lee-Smith, Hughie.
Hughie Lee-Smith : retrospective exhibition ... /
organized by the New Jersey State Museum.
[Trenton] : The Museum, c1988. 36 p. : ill.
(some col.) ; 22 x 28 cm. "Exhibition schedule:
New Jersey State Museum, Trenton Nov. 5, 1987-Jan.
2, 1988. The Cultural Center, Chicago, Ill., Feb. 4,
1988-Mar. 18, 1989." Bibliography: p. 10.
*1. Lee-Smith, Hughie - Exhibitions. I. New Jersey State
Museum. II. Title.*   **NYPL [Sc D 89-247]**

LEE-SMITH, HUGHIE - EXHIBITIONS.
Lee-Smith, Hughie. Hughie Lee-Smith .
[Trenton] , c1988. 36 p. :
                    NYPL [Sc D 89-247]

Leech, Kenneth, 1939- Struggle in Babylon :
racism in the cities and churches of Britain.
London : Sheldon, 1988. 253 p. ; 22 cm.
Includes bibliographical references and index. ISBN
0-85969-577-8 (pbk) DDC 261.8/348/0941 19
*1. Racism - Great Britain. 2. Great Britain - Race
relations. I. Title.*   **NYPL [Sc D 89-176]**

Lees, Gene. Meet me at Jim & Andy's : jazz
musicians and their world / Gene Lees. New
York, N.Y. : Oxford University Press, c1988.
xviii, 265 p. ; 22 cm. ISBN 0-19-504611-0 (alk.
paper) DDC 785.42/092/2 B 19
*1. Jazz musicians - United States - Biography. 2. Jazz
music - United States - History and criticism. 3.
Afro-American musicians - Biography. I. Title. II. Title:
Meet me at Jim and Andy's.*
ML394 .L4 1988   **NYPL [JND 89-5]**

A left hand like God . Silvester, Peter J. London ,
c1988. 324 p. : ISBN 0-7043-2685-X : DDC
785.4 19   **NYPL [JNE 89-16]**

**LEGAL STATUS OF WOMEN. see WOMEN -
LEGAL STATUS, LAWS, ETC.**

La légende du passé . Vansina, Jan. Tervuren,
Belgique , 1972. ix, 257 p. :
                    NYPL [Sc F 88-193]

Légendes historiques du Burundi : les multiples
visages du roi Ntáre / récits présentés par
Claude Guillet et Pascal Ndayishinguje ;
postface de Jean-Pierre Chrétien. Paris :
Editions Karthala ; Bujumbura : Centre de
civilisation burundaise, c1987. 286 p. : maps ;
24 cm. (Hommes et sociétés) Text in French and
Kirundi. Bibliography: p. [283] ISBN 2-86507-178-6
*1. Legends - Burundi. 2. Tales, Burundi. I. Guillet,
Claude. II. Ndayishinguje, Pascal. III. Series.*
                    NYPL [Sc E 88-324]

LEGENDS - BURUNDI.
Légendes historiques du Burundi . Paris ,
Bujumbura , c1987. 286 p. : ISBN 2-86507-178-6
                    NYPL [Sc E 88-324]

Vansina, Jan. La légende du passé . Tervuren,
Belgique , 1972. ix, 257 p. :
                    NYPL [Sc F 88-193]

Legends from Yorubaland /. Morgan, Kemi.
Ibadan, Nigeria , 1988. iii, 100 p. : ISBN
978-246-003-6   **NYPL [Sc C 88-344]**

LEGENDS - MADAGASCAR.
Ottino, Paul. L'étrangère intime . Paris,
France , c1986. 2 v. (xxvii, 630 p.) : ISBN
2-88124-095-X (set) DDC 398/.0969/1 19
GR357 .O88 1986   **NYPL [Sc D 88-1203]**

LEGENDS - ZAIRE.
Djungu-Simba Kamatenda, 1953- Autour du
feu . Kinshasa , 1984. 70 p. : DDC
398.2/09675/1 19
GR357.82.W35 D48 1984
                    NYPL [Sc C 88-272]

LEGENDS - ZIMBABWE.
Maredza, Claude. Harurwa . Harare , 1987. 52
p. : ISBN 0-908308-13-2 **NYPL [Sc C 88-150]**

LEGERDEMAIN. see MAGIC.

**LEGISLATION DRAFTING. see BILL
DRAFTING.**

LEGISLATIVE BODIES - TANZANIA.
Halimoja, Yusuf J. Bunge la jamhuri ya
muungano /. Dar es Salaam , 1981. 64 p. :
                    NYPL [Sc C 89-61]

**LEGISLATORS - CALIFORNIA -
BIOGRAPHY.**
Hayden, Tom. Reunion . New York , c1988.
xix, 539 p., [16] p. of plates ; ISBN
0-394-56533-9 : DDC 328.794/092/4 B 19
F866.4.H39 A3 1988   **NYPL [JFE 88-6231]**

**LEGISLATORS - UNITED STATES -
BIOGRAPHY - JUVENILE LITERATURE.**
Jakoubek, Robert E. Adam Clayton Powell, Jr.
/. New York , c1988. xiv, 252 p. ; ISBN
1-555-46606-0 DDC 973/.0496073024 B 92 19
E748.P86 J35 1988   **NYPL [Sc E 88-372]**

Legum, Colin. The battlefronts of Southern Africa
/ Colin Legum. New York : Africana Pub. Co.,
c1988. xxix, 451 p. : map ; 24 cm. Includes
bibliographies and indexes. ISBN 0-8419-1135-5 (alk.
paper) DDC 327.68 19
*1. Apartheid - South Africa. 2. Africa, Southern -
Foreign relations - 1975-. 3. Africa, Southern - Politics
and government - 1975-. I. Title.*
DT746 .L425 1987   **NYPL [Sc E 88-468]**

Lehrbuch des Somali. El-Solami-Mewis,
Catherine. Leipzig , c1987. 253 p. ; ISBN
3-324-00175-7   **NYPL [Sc D 88-896]**

Lei de treze de maio. Amaral, Angelo Thomaz
do. Lei de 13 de maio /. [Fortaleza, Brazil]
[1907] p. [331]-336 ;
                    NYPL [Sc Rare G 86-30]

Lei de 13 de maio /. Amaral, Angelo Thomaz do.
[Fortaleza, Brazil] [1907] p. [331]-336 ;
                    NYPL [Sc Rare G 86-30]

Leite, Glacyra Lazzari. Pernambuco 1817 :
estrutura e comportamento sociais / Glacyra
Lazzari Leite ; prefácio de Manuel Correia de
Andrade. Recife : Fundação Joaquim Nabuco,
Editora Massangana, 1988. 275 p. ; 23 cm.
(Série Estudos e pesquisas. 52) Originally presented as
the author's thesis (doutor em ciências). Bibliography: p.
259-273. ISBN 85-7019-122-7 DDC 981/.3403 20
*1. Pernambuco (Brazil) - History - Revolution, 1817. 2.
Pernambuco (Brazil) - Social conditions. 3. Pernambuco
(Brazil) - Economic conditions. I. Series: Série Estudos
e pesquisas (Fundação Joaquim Nabuco) , 52. II. Title.*
F2534 .L45 1988   **NYPL [Sc D 89-605]**

LEKHOTLA LA BAFO - HISTORY.
Edgar, Robert. Prophets with honour .
Johannesburg [1987?]. 250 p. ; ISBN
0-86975-312-6   **NYPL [Sc D 88-1391]**

LELE (AFRICAN PEOPLE) - CHILDREN.
Dinslage, Sabine. Kinder der Lyela .
Hohenschäftlarn bei München , 1986. 355 p. :
ISBN 3-87673-105-4 DDC 305.2/3/096625 19
DT650.L38 D56 1986   **NYPL [Sc D 88-876]**

Leloup, Jacqueline. Guéido / Jacqueline Leloup.
Yaoundé : Editions CLE, 1986. 110 p. : ill. ; 18
cm. Adaptation of: Oedipus Rex / Sophocles.
I. Sophocles. Oedipus Rex. II. Title.
MLCS 87/6780 (P)   **NYPL [Sc C 88-210]**

Lemaître, Christine. Exbrayat, André. Martinique
/. Fort de France , c1986. 154, [2] p. : ISBN
2-905873-02-7 DDC 972.98/2 19
F2081.2 .E9 1986   **NYPL [Sc E 88-346]**

Lemon, Anthony. Apartheid in transition /
Anthony Lemon. Aldershot, Hants ; Brookfield,
Vt. : Gower, c1987. xi, 414 p. : ill. ; 23 cm.
Includes index. Bibliography: p. 371-398. ISBN
0-566-00635-9
*1. Apartheid - South Africa. 2. South Africa -
Economic conditions - 1961-. 3. South Africa - Social
conditions - 1961-. I. Title.* **NYPL [Sc D 88-644]**

Lengelo Guyigisa. Les Maitresses du feu et de la
cuisine . Bandundu, République du Zaïre ,
1983. 164 p. :   **NYPL [Sc F 88-308]**

La lengua sagrada de los Ñáñigos /. Cabrera,
Lydia. Miami, Fla. , c1988. 530 p. ;
                    NYPL [Sc D 89-585]

Leon, Eli. Who'd a thought it : improvisation in
African-American quiltmaking / Eli Leon. San

Francisco, CA : San Francisco Craft & Folk Art Museum, c1987. 87 p. : (col.) ill. ; 28 cm. Bibliography: p. 85-87.
1. *Afro-American quilts.* 2. *Quilts and quilting.* 3. *Quilts - United States.* I. *San Francisco Craft & Folk Art Museum.* II. *Title.*   **NYPL** *[Sc F 88-235]*

Leonard, Robert. Swahili phrasebook / Robert Leonard. Yarra Vic, Australia ; Berkeley, CA : Lonely Planet, 1988, c1987. 101 p. : ill. ; 13 cm. (Language survival kit) ISBN 0-86442-025-0
1. *Swahili language - Conversation and phrase books - English.* I. *Title.*   **NYPL** *[Sc B 88-62]*

Leratosello /. Rafapa, J. R. L. Pretoria , 1979, c1983 printing. 115 p. ;
   NYPL *[Sc D 88-647]*

Lernen von der Dritten Welt? . Kullas, Ulrike. Saarbrücken , Fort Lauderdale , 1982. 174 p. : ISBN 3-88156-233-8   **NYPL** *[Sc D 89-339]*

Les belles paroles d'Albert Gaspard /. Gaspard, Albert. Paris , c1987. 128 p. : ISBN 2-903033-91-9 :
MLCM 87/1949 (P)   **NYPL** *[JFE 88-5765]*

Les Languages nationales au Sénégal. Sylla, Yèro, 1942- Récit initiatique peul du Macĩna . [Dakar] , 1975. vi, 113 p. ;
   NYPL *[Sc F 87-257]*

Les Langues africaines au Sénégal. Bathily, Abdoulaye. Lexique soninke (sarakole)-français /. [Dakar] , 1975. xx, 191 p. ;   **NYPL** *[Sc F 86-166]*

Les Langues nationale au Sénégal. Faye, Waly Coly. Précis grammatical de sérère /. [Dakar] , 1980. 80 leaves ;
   NYPL *[Sc F 86-168]*

Les verbaux du dangaléat de l'est (Guera, Tchad) . Ebobissé, Carl. Berlin , 1987. 104 p. ; ISBN 3-496-00555-6   **NYPL** *[Sc E 88-231]*

LESBIAN LOVE. see LESBIANISM.

LESBIANISM - POETRY.
Gay & lesbian poetry in our time . New York , c1988. xxviii, 401 p. : ISBN 0-312-02213-1 : DDC 811/.54/080353 19
PS595.H65 G39 1988   **NYPL** *[JFE 89-277]*

LESBIANS - GREAT BRITAIN - POLITICAL ACTIVITY.
Radical records . London , New York , 1988. xi, 266 p. ; ISBN 0-415-00200-1 DDC 306.7/66/0941 19
HQ76.8.G7 R33 1988 **NYPL** *[JLD 88-1427]*

LESBIANS' WRITINGS, AMERICAN.
Gay & lesbian poetry in our time . New York , c1988. xxviii, 401 p. : ISBN 0-312-02213-1 : DDC 811/.54/080353 19
PS595.H65 G39 1988   **NYPL** *[JFE 89-277]*

Leslau, Wolf.
Comparative dictionary of Ge'ez (Classical Ethiopic) : Ge'ez-English, English-Ge'ez, with an index of the Semitic roots / by Wolf Leslau. Wiesbaden : O. Harrassowitz, 1987. xlix, 813 p. ; 27 cm. Bibliography: p. [xxvii]-xlix. ISBN 3-447-02592-1 : DDC 492/.8 19
1. *Ethiopic language - Dictionaries - English.* 2. *English language - Dictionaries - Ethiopic.* I. *Title.*
PJ9087 .L37 1987   **NYPL** *[*OEC 89-3015]*

Ethiopians speak; studies in cultural background. Berkeley, University of California Press, 1965- v. 26 cm. (University of California publications. Near Eastern studies . v. 7, 9, 11,) Vol. 2 includes Chaha text in characters, in transliteration, and in English translation. "A free translation of [v. 2] was published in 1964 ... under the title of Shinega's village; scenes of Ethiopian life." Vol. 4- has imprint: Wiesbaden, Steiner. Vol. 4- issued in series Äthiopistische Forschungen, Bd. 11, 16 CONTENTS. - 1. Harari.--2. Chaha.--3. Soddo.--4. Muher.--5. Chaha-Ennemor.
1. *Ethiopian literature.* 2. *Ethiopia - Social life and customs.* I. *Series.* II. *Series: University of California publications. v.7, etc.* III. *Title.*
PJ8998.5 .L4   **NYPL** *[Sc F 89-19]*

Leslie, Austin. Chez Helene : house of good food / Austin Leslie. New Orleans, La. : De Simonin Publications, c1984. 64 p. : ill. ; 15 cm.
1. *Cookery, Creole.* I. *Title.* **NYPL** *[Sc B 89-26]*

LESOTHO - CHURCH HISTORY.
Dove, R. (Reginald) Anglican pioneers in Lesotho . [s.l. , 1975?] (s.l. : Mazenod Institute) 216 p., [1] fold. leaf of plates : DDC 283/.68/6
BX5700.6.A44 L473   **NYPL** *[JXD 84-17]*

Lesotho. Education, Ministry of. see **Lesotho. Ministry of Education.**

LESOTHO - FOREIGN RELATIONS - AFRICA, SOUTHERN.
Black, David R. (David Ross), 1960- Foreign policy in small states . Halifax, N.S. , 1988. viii, 83 p. : ISBN 0-7703-0736-1 :
   NYPL *[Sc D 89-564]*

Lesotho - Government. see **Lesotho - Politics and government.**

Lesotho. Ministry of Education. Report on the views and recommendations of the Basotho Nation regarding the future of education in Lesotho = Tlaleho ea maikutlo le likhothaletso tsa sechaba ka bokamoso ba thuto Lesotho / the Kingdom of Lesotho, Ministry of Education. Maseru, Lesotho : Govt. Printer, 1978. 167 p. : map ; 30 cm. Title page and conclusions in English and Sesotho.
1. *Education - Lesotho.* I. *Title.* II. *Title: Tlaleho ea maikutlo le likhothaletso tsa sechaba ka bokamoso ba thuto Lesotho.*   **NYPL** *[Sc F 88-354]*

LESOTHO - POLITICS AND GOVERNMENT - TO 1966.
Edgar, Robert. Prophets with honour . Johannesburg [1987?]. 250 p. ; ISBN 0-86975-312-6   **NYPL** *[Sc D 88-1391]*

LESOTHO - POLITICS AND GOVERNMENT - TO 1966 - SOURCES.
Edgar, Robert. Prophets with honour . Johannesburg [1987?]. 250 p. ; ISBN 0-86975-312-6   **NYPL** *[Sc D 88-1391]*

A Less than perfect union : alternative perspectives on the U. S. Constitution / edited by Jules Lobel. New York : Monthly Review Press, 1988. vii, 424 p. ; 22 cm. Includes bibliographical references. ISBN 0-85345-738-7 : DDC 342.73/029 347.30229 19
1. *Civil rights - United States.* 2. *United States - Constitutional law.* I. *Lobel, Jules.*
KF4550.A2 L47 1987   **NYPL** *[Sc D 88-724]*

Lessac, Frané. (ill) Pomerantz, Charlotte. The chalk doll /. New York , c1989. 30 p. : ISBN 0-397-32318-2 : DDC [E] 19
PZ7.P77 Ch 1989   **NYPL** *[Sc F 89-175]*

Lesser Antilles. see **West Indies.**

Lester, Julius.
Lovesong : becoming a Jew / by Julius Lester.1st ed. New York, N.Y. : H. Holt, c1988. 248 p., [4] leaves of plates : ill. ; 24 cm. ISBN 0-8050-0588-9 DDC 296.8/346/0924 B 19
1. *Lester, Julius.* 2. *Proselytes and proselyting,Jewish - Converts from Christianity - Biography.* 3. *Authors, American - 20th century - Biography.* I. *Title.*
BM755.L425 A3 1988   **NYPL** *[Sc E 88-317]*

More tales of Uncle Remus : further adventures of Brer Rabbit, his friends, enemies, and others / as told by Julius Lester ; illustrated by Jerry Pinkney.1st ed. New York : Dial Books, c1988. xvi, 143 p. : ill. (some col.) ; 24 cm. A continuation of The tales of Uncle Remus: the adventures of Brer Rabbit. On spine: The author retells the classic Afro-American tales. Bibliography: p. 143. ISBN 0-8037-0419-4 DDC 398.2/08996073 19
1. *Afro-Americans - Folklore.* 2. *Tales - United States.* I. *Pinkney, Jerry, ill.* II. *Title.*
PZ8.1.L434 Mo 1988   **NYPL** *[Sc E 88-458]*

LESTER, JULIUS.
Lester, Julius. Lovesong . New York, N.Y. , c1988. 248 p., [4] leaves of plates : ISBN 0-8050-0588-9 DDC 296.8/346/0924 B 19
BM755.L425 A3 1988   **NYPL** *[Sc E 88-317]*

Let it be told : essays by Black women in Britain / edited by Lauretta Ngcobo. London : Pluto Press, 1987. 145, [1] p. ; 23 cm. Bibliography: p. 144-[146] CONTENTS. - Introduction -- Amryl Johnson -- Maud Sulter -- Agnes Sam -- Valerie Bloom -- Grace Nichols -- Marsha Prescod -- The Collective: Beverley Bryan, Stella Dadzie and Suzanne Scafe -- Lauretta Ngcobo. ISBN 0-7453-0254-8
1. *Women authors, Blacks - Great Britain.* 2. *Authors, Black - Great Britain.* 3. *English literature - Black authors - History and criticism.* 4. *English literature - Women authors - History and criticism.* I. *Ngcobo, Lauretta G.*   **NYPL** *[Sc E 88-125]*

Let the Bfin id 89b21342/updd M. Gitari. Gitari, David M. Nairobi, Kenya , 1988. 90 p. :
   NYPL *[Sc D 89-400]*

Let's catch a monster. Scott, Ann Herbert. New

York [1967] 1 v. (unpaged)
PZ7.S415 Le   **NYPL** *[Sc F 88-342]*

Let's-read-and-find-out science book.
Branley, Franklyn Mansfield, 1915- Eclipse . New York , c1988. 32 p. : ISBN 0-690-04619-7 (lib. bdg.) : DDC 523.7/8 19
QB541.5 .B73 1988   **NYPL** *[Sc E 88-591]*

Let's travel in the Congo /. Kittler, Glenn D. Chicago , 1965, c1961. 85 p. :
   NYPL *[Sc F 89-7]*

Let's visit Haiti. Benoit, Marie. 1988. 96 p. : ISBN 0-333-45692-0 : DDC 972.94/07 19
F1916   **NYPL** *[Sc D 89-73]*

Let's visit Mali. /. Naylor, Kim. Basingstoke , 1987. 96 p. : ISBN 0-333-44988-6
   NYPL *[Sc D 89-397]*

Let's visit middle Africa. Caldwell, John C. (John Cope), 1913- New York [1961] 96 p. DDC 916.7
DT352 .C3   **NYPL** *[Sc D 88-507]*

Let's visit The Gambia /. Wilkins, Frances. London , 1985. 94 p. : ISBN 0-222-01129-7
   NYPL *[Sc D 88-405]*

Let's visit the West Indies. Caldwell, John C. London, Eng. , c1983. 96 p. : ISBN 0-222-00920-9   **NYPL** *[Sc D 89-19]*

A letter to the Hon. Benjamin R. Curtis . Kirkland, Charles Pinckney, 1830-1904- New York , 1863. 20 p. ;
   NYPL *[Sc Rare C 89-23]*

La Letteratura della negritudine / C. Bartocci ... [et al.]. Roma : Bulzoni, 1986. 243 p. ; 21 cm. (Argomenti (letterature d'America) . 1)
1. *America - Literatures - Black authors - History and criticism.* I. *Bartocci, Clara.*
   NYPL *[Sc D 87-1377]*

Letters from Ethiopian rulers (early and mid-nineteenth century) : preserved in the British Library, the Public Record Office, Lambeth Palace, the National Army Museum, India Office Library and Records / translated by David L. Appleyard from Gi'iz and Amharic and by A.K. Irvine from Arabic ; and annoted by Richard K.P. Pankhurst ; with an appendix by Bairu Tafla. Oxford ; New York : Published for the British Academy by Oxford University Press, c1985. xvii, 197 p. : facsims. ; 24 cm. (Oriental documents . 9) "Intended to precede, and supplement, the ... earlier volume The Amharic letters of Emperor Theodore of Ethiopia to Queen Victoria and her special envoy by Girma-Selassie Asfaw and David L. Appleyard ..."--Introd. Includes index. Bibliography: p. 185-189. ISBN 0-19-726046-2
1. *Ethiopia - Foreign relations - Great Britain - Sources.* 2. *Great Britain - Foreign relations - Ethiopia - Sources.* 3. *Ethiopia - Foreign relations - To 1889 - Sources.* I. *Appleyard, David L.* II. *Irvine, A. K.* III. *Pankhurst, Richard Keir Pethick, 1927-.* IV. *Theodore II, Negus of Ethiopia, d. 1868. Correspondence. English & Arabic. Selections. 1979.* V. *Ethiopia. Sovereign.* VI. *Series.*   **NYPL** *[Sc E 88-262]*

Letters of a slave trader. Bohrer, Dick. John Newton, letters of a slave trader /. Chicago , c1983. viii, 130 p. ; ISBN 0-8024-0158-9 (pbk.) DDC 283/.3 19
BX5199.N55 B64 1983   **NYPL** *[Sc C 88-235]*

Letters on southern slavery. Hammond, James Henry, 1807-1864. Gov. Hammond's letters on southern slavery. Charleston , 1845. 32 p. ;
   NYPL *[Sc Rare C 89-24]*

Letters respecting a book "dropped from the catalogue" of the American Sunday School Union in compliance with the dictation of the slave power. Tappan, Lewis, 1788-1873. New York , 1848. 36 p. ;
   NYPL *[Sc Rare C 89-11]*

Lettres du Nord-Cameroun /. Damay, Jean. Paris , c1985. 231 p. : ISBN 2-86537-121-2
   NYPL *[Sc D 88-274]*

LEVIAS, JERRY.
Pennington, Richard, 1952- Breaking the ice . Jefferson, N.C. , c1987. ix, 182 p. : ISBN 0-89950-295-4 : DDC 796.332/72/0973 19
GV939.A1 P46 1987   **NYPL** *[Sc E 88-35]*

Levine, Barry B., 1941- The Caribbean exodus /. New York , 1987. vii, 293 p. ; ISBN 0-275-92182-4 (alk. paper) : DDC 325.729 19
JV7321 .C37 1986   **NYPL** *[JLE 87-1789]*

Levine, Janet, 1945- Inside apartheid : one woman's struggle in South Africa / Janet Levine. Chicago : Contemporary Books, c1988. xvi, 287 p., [16] p. of plates : ill. ; 24 cm. ISBN 0-8092-4544-2 : DDC 968.06/3/0924 B 19
1. Levine, Janet, 1945-. 2. Anti-apartheid movements - Biography. 3. Civil rights workers - South Africa - Biography. 4. Apartheid - South Africa. I. Title.
DT779.955.L48 A3 1989
                              NYPL [JLE 89-122]

LEVINE, JANET, 1945-
Levine, Janet, 1945- Inside apartheid .
Chicago , c1988. xvi, 287 p., [16] p. of plates :
ISBN 0-8092-4544-2 : DDC 968.06/3/0924 B 19
DT779.955.L48 A3 1989
                              NYPL [JLE 89-122]

Levins, Mike. (illus) Gross, Mary Anne. (comp) Ah, man, you found me again. Boston [1972] x, 84 p. ISBN 0-8070-1532-6 DDC 810/.8/09282
HQ792.U53 N53 1972 *NYPL [Sc F 88-336]*

Levy, Cathi. Persaud, Pat. Tipsy /. Kingston, Jamaica , c1986. [28] p. :
MLCS 87/7926 (P) *NYPL [Sc F 88-255]*

Lévy, Denis. Problems of co-operation between the English- and French-speaking universities of West Africa [microform] : discussion paper / by Denis Lévy. Freetown [Sierra Leone] : [s.n., 1961] 7 p. ; 31 cm. At head of title: Inter-University Co-operation in West Africa, an International Seminar sponsored by the University College of Sierra Leone, Fourah Bay College, and the Congress for Cultural Freedom. "SL/XII (E)". Microfilm. New York: New York Public Library, 1982. 1 microfilm reel; 35 mm. (MN *ZZ-22581)
1. University cooperation - Africa, West. 2. Universities and colleges - Africa, West - Administration. I. International Seminar on Inter-university Co-operation in West Africa, Freetown, Sierra Leone, 1961. II. Title.
  NYPL [Sc Micro R-4094 no. 23]

Lewin, André. La Guinée / André Lewin. 1re éd. Paris : Presses Universitaires de France, 1984. 127 p. : maps ; 18 cm. (Que sais-je? 2184) Bibliography: p. 127. ISBN 2-13-038503-6
I. Title. *NYPL [Sc C 88-23]*

Lewin, Ted. (illus) Horvath, Betty F. Not enough Indians. New York [1971] [47] p. ISBN 0-531-01968-3 DDC [Fic]
PZ7.H7922 No *NYPL [Sc F 88-341]*

Lewis, David L. The Civil rights movement in America . Jackson , c1986. xii, 188 p. ; ISBN 0-87805-297-6 (alk. paper) DDC 323.1/196073 19
E185.615 .C585 1986 *NYPL [IEC 87-273]*

Lewis, Geraldine Fambrough. An analysis of interviews with urban Black males who dropped out of high school [microform] / by Geraldine F. Lewis. 1983. iii, 123 leaves : ill. ; 28 cm. Thesis (Ed.D.)--Temple University, 1983. Bibliography: leaves 111-119. Microfilm of typescript. Ann Arbor, Mich. : University Microfilms International, 1983. 1 reel ; 35 mm.
1. Afro-American dropouts. 2. Education, Urban - United States. I. Title.
  NYPL [Sc Micro R-4791]

Lewis, I. M. A modern history of Somalia : nation and state in the horn of Africa / by Ioan M. Lewis. Rev. ed. Boulder : Westview Press, 1988. xiii, 297 p. : maps ; 22 cm. (Westview special studies on Africa) Includes index. Bibliography: p. 270-288. ISBN 0-8133-7402-2 : DDC 967/.73 19
1. Somalia - History. I. Title.
DT403 .L395 1988 *NYPL [Sc D 88-1347]*

Lewis, Ioan. see Lewis, I. M.

LEWIS, JOHN.
Ball, Thomas E. Julian Bond vs John Lewis .
Atlanta, Ga. , 1988. ix, 144 p. : ISBN 0-9621362-0-4 *NYPL [Sc E 88-582]*

Lewis, Lawrence. African environments and resources / L.A. Lewis and L. Berry. Boston : Hyman & Unwin, 1988. xii, 404 p. : ill. ; 25 cm. Includes index. Bibliography: p. 394-400. ISBN 0-04-916010-9 (alk. paper) DDC 333.7/096 19
1. Natural resources - Africa. 2. Ecology - Africa. 3. Natural resources - Government policy - Africa. 4. Environmental policy - Africa. I. Berry, Leonard, 1930-. II. Title.
HC800 .L48 1987 *NYPL [Sc E 89-50]*

Lewis, Marvin A. Treading the ebony path : ideology and violence in contemporary Afro-Colombian prose fiction / Marvin A. Lewis. Columbia : University of Missouri Press, 1987. 142 p. ; 23 cm. Includes index. Bibliography: p. 131-138. ISBN 0-8262-0638-7 (alk. paper) DDC 863 19
1. Colombian fiction - 20th century - History and criticism. 2. Colombian fiction - Black authors - History and criticism. 3. Alienation (Social psychology) in literature. 4. Violence in literature. I. Title.
PQ8172 .L49 1987 *NYPL [Sc D 88-443]*

Lewis, Richard W. A summer adventure / story and pictures by Richard W. Lewis. New York : Harper & Row, c1962. 105 p. : ill. ; 23 cm. SCHOMBURG CHILDREN'S COLLECTION. With autograph of author.
1. Afro-American children - Juvenile fiction. I. Schomburg Children's Collection. II. Title.
  NYPL [Sc D 89-405]

Lewis, Ronald L., 1940- Black workers .
Philadelphia , 1989. xv, 733 p. ; ISBN 0-87722-592-3 *NYPL [Sc E 89-206]*

Lewis, Rupert.
Garvey--Africa, Europe, the Americas /.
Kingston, Jamaica , 1986. xi, 208 p., [4] p. of plates : *NYPL [Sc D 88-1131]*

Marcus Garvey : anti-colonial champion / by Rupert Lewis. 1st American ed. Trenton, N.J. : Africa World Press, 1988. 301 p. : ill., ports. ; 22 cm. Includes index. Bibliography: p. [287]-298. ISBN 0-86543-061-6
1. Garvey, Marcus, 1887-1940. 2. Black nationalism - United States - History. 3. Jamaica - Biography. I. Title.
  NYPL [Sc D 88-1454]

Marcus Gavey, anti-colonial champion / Rupert Lewis. 1st American ed. Trenton, New Jersey : Africa World Press, 1988. 301 p. : ill., facsims., ports. ; 22 cm. Includes index. Bibliography: p. 288-301. ISBN 0-86543-061-6 (hard)
1. Garvey, Marcus, 1887-1940. 2. Universal Negro Improvement Association - History. 3. Black nationalism - History. I. Title.
  NYPL [Sc D 88-516]

Lewis, Vashti Crutcher. The mulatto woman as major female character in novels by Black women, 1892-1937 [microform] / by Vashti Crutcher Lewis. [Iowa City, Ia. : s.n.], 1981. iv, 182 leaves ; 28 cm. Thesis (Ph.D.)--University of Iowa, 1981. Bibliography: leaves 174-182. Microfilm. Ann Arbor, Mich. : University Microfilms International, 1986. 1 reel ; 35 mm.
1. Afro-American women authors. 2. American fiction - Afro-American authors - History and criticism. 3. Mulattoes in literature. 4. Afro-Americans in literature. I. Title. *NYPL [Sc Micro R-4792]*

LEWISHAM (LONDON, ENGLAND)
Turkie, Alan. Know what I mean? . Leicester , 1982. 82 p. : ISBN 0-86155-062-5 :
  NYPL [Sc D 89-464]

Lexau, Joan M. Don't be my valentine / by Joan M. Lexau ; pictures by Syd Hoff. New York, N.Y. : Harper & Row, c1985. 64 p. : col. ill. ; 23 cm. (An I can read book) Sam's mean valentine for Amy Lou goes astray at school and almost ruins the day for him and his friends. SCHOMBURG CHILDREN'S COLLECTION. ISBN 0-06-023872-0 : DDC [E] 19
1. Children's stories, American. 2. Valentines - Juvenile fiction. 3. Afro-American children - Juvenile fiction. I. Hoff, Syd, 1912- ill. II. Schomburg Children's Collection. III. Title.
PZ7.L5895 Dp 1985 *NYPL [Sc D 89-58]*

Lexique soninke (sarakole)-français /. Bathily, Abdoulaye. [Dakar] , 1975. xx, 191 p. ;
  NYPL [Sc F 86-166]

L'Histoire d'une trahison : MMM so sosyalism / [finn ekrir par Lalit ; bann mam responsab pu redaksyon se Alain Ah-Vee...et al.]. Port Louis, Mauritius : Lalit, 1987. vi, 192 p. ill. ; 29 cm. In Kreol (Mauritian French creole), French and English.
1. Mouvement militant mauricien. 2. Socialism - Mauritius. 3. Creole dialects, French - Mauritius. 4. Mauritius - Politics and government - 1968-. I. Lalit.
  NYPL [Sc F 88-275]

LIBEL AND SLANDER - TANZANIA.
Mwakasungula, N. E. R. Sheria ya kashfa /.
Tabora, Tanzania , c1985. x, 77 p. ;
  NYPL [Sc C 88-191]

Liberation Support Movement. Information Center. Road to liberation . Richmond, B. C. , pref. 1976. viii, 53 p. :
  NYPL [JFD 80-10236]

Liberia : underdevelopment and political rule in a peripheral society = unterentwicklung und politische Herrschaft in einer peripheren Gesellschaft / Robert Kappel, Werner Korte, R. Friedegund Mascher (Hrsg.). Hamburg : Institut für Afrika-Kunde, 1986. vi, 292 p., [1] folded leaf of plates : ill. ; 21 cm. (Arbeiten aus dem Institut für Afrika-Kunde . 50) English and German. Includes bibliographies. CONTENTS. - Samuel K. Doe, der People's Redemption Council und die Macht / Günter Schröder, Werner Korte -- Liberia under military rule (1980-1985) / J. Pal Chaudhuri -- Zwischen "primärem" Widerstand und den sozialen Bewegungen, 1970-1980 in Liberia / Werner Korte -- The role of the Putu Development Corporation (PUDECO) in rural conscientization and mobilization in the 1970's / Siapha Kamara -- The role of the military in the history of Liberia / Monday B. Akpan -- The Open Door Policy / Fred van der Kraaij -- Strukturelle Abhängigkeit und Unterentwicklung in Liberia / Robert Kappel -- The IMF and Liberia / Claudia Dziobek -- USA und Liberia / Robert Kappel -- Regionale Disparitäten und Entwicklungsplanung in Liberia / R. Friedegund Mascher -- Das Schulwesen Liberias / Renate Bosch, Horst Waskow. ISBN 3-923519-65-6 (pbk.) DDC 322/.5/096662 19
1. Civil-military relations - Liberia. 2. Liberia - Politics and government - 1980-. 3. Liberia - Economic conditions - 1980- - Regional disparities. I. Kappel, Robert. II. Korte, Werner. III. Mascher, R. Friedegund. IV. Series.
JQ3923.5.C58 L53 1986
                              NYPL [Sc D 88-1320]

Liberia . Dunn, D. Elwood. Metuchen, N.J. , c1988. xii, 259 p. : ISBN 0-8108-2088-9 DDC 966.6/203 19
DT631 .D953 1988 *NYPL [JFD 88-8633]*

LIBERIA - CIVILIZATION - HISTORY - 19TH CENTURY - EXHIBITIONS.
Belcher, Max. A land and life remembered .
Athens , Brockton, Mass. , c1988. [xii], 176 p. : ISBN 0-8203-1085-9 (alk. paper) DDC 720/.9666/2074014482 19
NA1599.L4 B4 1988 *NYPL [Sc F 89-90]*

LIBERIA - DESCRIPTION AND TRAVEL.
Williams, Alfred Brockenbrough, 1856-1930.
The Liberian exodus. Charleston, S.C., 1878. 62 p.
E448 .W53 *NYPL [Sc Rare F 88-58]*

LIBERIA - ECONOMIC CONDITIONS.
Johnson, Charles Spurgeon, 1893-1956. Bitter Canaan . New Brunswick, N.J. , c1987. lxxiii, 256 p. ; ISBN 0-88738-053-0 : DDC 966.6/2 19
DT631 .J59 1987 *NYPL [Sc E 88-351]*

LIBERIA - ECONOMIC CONDITIONS - 1980- - REGIONAL DISPARITIES.
Liberia . Hamburg , 1986. vi, 292 p., [1] folded leaf of plates : ISBN 3-923519-65-6 (pbk.) DDC 322/.5/096662 19
JQ3923.5.C58 L53 1986
                              NYPL [Sc D 88-1320]

LIBERIA - HISTORY.
Dunn, D. Elwood. Liberia . Metuchen, N.J. , c1988. xii, 259 p. : ISBN 0-8108-2088-9 DDC 966.6/203 19
DT631 .D953 1988 *NYPL [JFD 88-8633]*

Guannu, Joseph Saye. A short history of the first Liberian republic /. Pompano Beach, FL , c1985. viii, 152 p. : ISBN 0-682-40267-2
  NYPL [Sc D 88-1023]

Johnson, Charles Spurgeon, 1893-1956. Bitter Canaan . New Brunswick, N.J. , c1987. lxxiii, 256 p. ; ISBN 0-88738-053-0 : DDC 966.6/2 19
DT631 .J59 1987 *NYPL [Sc E 88-351]*

LIBERIA - HISTORY - TO 1847.
Akpan, Monday B. African resistance in Liberia . Bremen , 1988. 68 p. : ISBN 3-926771-01-1 *NYPL [Sc D 89-347]*

LIBERIA - HISTORY - 1847-1944.
Akpan, Monday B. African resistance in Liberia . Bremen , 1988. 68 p. : ISBN 3-926771-01-1 *NYPL [Sc D 89-347]*

LIBERIA - HISTORY - DICTIONARIES.
Dunn, D. Elwood. Historical dictionary of Liberia /. Metuchen, N.J. , 1985. xx, 274, [7] p. of plates : ISBN 0-8108-1767-5 DDC

966.6/2/00321 19
DT631 .D95 1985   *NYPL [Sc D 86-127]*

**LIBERIA - POLITICS AND GOVERNMENT -
1944-1971.**
Burrowes, Carl Patrick. The Americo-Liberian
ruling class and other myths . Philadelphia ,
1989. 77 leaves ;   *NYPL [Sc F 89-128]*

**LIBERIA - POLITICS AND GOVERNMENT -
1971-1980.**
Burrowes, Carl Patrick. The Americo-Liberian
ruling class and other myths . Philadelphia ,
1989. 77 leaves ;   *NYPL [Sc F 89-128]*

**LIBERIA - POLITICS AND GOVERNMENT -
1980-.**
The First five years of Dr. Samuel Kanyon
Doe . Monrovia, Liberia [1985] v, 72 p. :
      DDC 966.6/203 19
JQ3922 .F57 1985   *NYPL [Sc D 88-872]*
Liberia . Hamburg , 1986. vi, 292 p., [1] folded
leaf of plates : ISBN 3-923519-65-6 (pbk.) DDC
322/.5/096662 19
JQ3923.5.C58 L53 1986
                          NYPL [Sc D 88-1320]

**LIBERIA - RELATIONS (GENERAL) WITH
EUROPE.**
The Effects of the Western culture on the
traditional cultures of Lofa County
[microform] . [Monrovia , 1977] 24 p. ;
                NYPL [Sc Micro F-10952]

LIBERIA - RELATIONS - UNITED STATES.
Johnson, Charles Spurgeon, 1893-1956. Bitter
Canaan . New Brunswick, N.J. , c1987. lxxiii,
256 p. ; ISBN 0-88738-053-0 : DDC 966.6/2 19
DT631 .J59 1987   *NYPL [Sc E 88-351]*

LIBERIA - SOCIAL CONDITIONS.
Johnson, Charles Spurgeon, 1893-1956. Bitter
Canaan . New Brunswick, N.J. , c1987. lxxiii,
256 p. ; ISBN 0-88738-053-0 : DDC 966.6/2 19
DT631 .J59 1987   *NYPL [Sc E 88-351]*

Liberia Working Group papers, 0932-1896 .
(no. 2) Akpan, Monday B. African resistance in
Liberia . Bremen , 1988. 68 p. : ISBN
     3-926771-01-1   *NYPL [Sc D 89-347]*

The Liberian exodus. Williams, Alfred
Brockenbrough, 1856-1930. Charleston, S.C.,
1878. 62 p.
E448 .W53   *NYPL [Sc Rare F 88-58]*

LIBERTY OF THE PRESS - HAITI.
Du Pry, Ben. [Address to] 1st conference of
Caribbean basin journalists and media workers,
April 16-20, 1982, Grenada W.I. [microform] /.
[St. George's, Grenada , 1982] 6 p. ;
                NYPL [Sc Micro R-4108 no. 44]

LIBERTY - SOUTH AFRICA.
Mathews, Anthony S., 1930- Freedom, state
security and the rule of law . London , c1988.
xxx, 312 p. ; ISBN 0-421-39640-7
                         NYPL [Sc F 89-102]

Libia. see Libya.

**LIBRARIANS - PROFESSIONAL ETHICS -
UNITED STATES - HISTORY - 20TH
CENTURY.**
Activism in American librarianship, 1962-1973
/. New York , 1987. x, 207 p. : ISBN
0-313-24602-5 (lib. bdg. : alk. paper) DDC 021
19
Z716.4 .A27 1987   *NYPL [JFE 87-6266]*

LIBRARIANSHIP. see LIBRARY SCIENCE.

**LIBRARIES - ADMINISTRATION. see
LIBRARY ADMINISTRATION; LIBRARY
SCIENCE.**

LIBRARIES - AFRICA, EAST.
Kaungamno, Ezekiel E. The East Africa library
movement and its problems [microform] /. Dar
es Salaam [197-?] 6 leaves ;
              NYPL [Sc Micro R4094 no. 30]

**LIBRARIES - AFRICA - PERIODICALS -
BIBLIOGRAPHY.**
Prichard, R. J. African librarianship .
Aberystwyth, Dyfed, Great Britain , 1987. 35
p. ; ISBN 0-904020-21-5 (pbk.) DDC 016.02706 19
Z857.A1 P75 1987   *NYPL [Sc D 88-1518]*

LIBRARIES AND COMMUNITY.
Libraries, coalitions, & the public good /. New
York, NY , c1987. xiv, 174 p. ; ISBN
1-555-70017-9 : DDC 021 19
Z716.4 .L47 1987   *NYPL [JFE 87-6338]*

**LIBRARIES AND SOCIETY - UNITED
STATES - HISTORY - 20TH CENTURY.**
Activism in American librarianship, 1962-1973
/. New York , 1987. x, 207 p. : ISBN
0-313-24602-5 (lib. bdg. : alk. paper) DDC 021
19
Z716.4 .A27 1987   *NYPL [JFE 87-6266]*

Libraries, coalitions, & the public good / edited
with a preface and introduction by E.J. Josey.
New York, NY : Neal-Schuman, c1987. xiv,
174 p. ; 23 cm. Includes index. Includes
bibliographies. ISBN 1-555-70017-9 : DDC 021 19
*1. Libraries and community. 2. Coalition (Social
sciences). I. Josey, E. J. II. Title: Libraries, coalitions,
and the public good.*
Z716.4 .L47 1987   *NYPL [JFE 87-6338]*

Libraries, coalitions, and the public good.
Libraries, coalitions, & the public good /. New
York, NY , c1987. xiv, 174 p. ; ISBN
     1-555-70017-9 : DDC 021 19
Z716.4 .L47 1987   *NYPL [JFE 87-6338]*

**LIBRARIES - GHANA - JUVENILE
LITERATURE.**
Ntrakwah, Abena. Ama goes to the library /.
Accra , 1987. 16 p. :   *NYPL [Sc F 88-352]*

**LIBRARIES - ORGANIZATION. see
LIBRARIES; LIBRARY
ADMINISTRATION; LIBRARY
SCIENCE.**

**LIBRARIES - REFERENCE BOOKS. see
REFERENCE BOOKS.**

**LIBRARIES, SOCIAL SCIENCE. see SOCIAL
SCIENCE LIBRARIES.**

**LIBRARIES, SPECIAL - TRINIDAD AND
TOBAGO - DIRECTORIES.**
Directory of special libraries/information units
in Trinidad and Tobago /. Port of Spain,
Trinidad & Tobago [1986] iv, 59 p. ; DDC
026/.00025/72983 19
Z753.T7 D57 1986   *NYPL [Sc D 88-1019]*

LIBRARY ADMINISTRATION - KENYA.
Khayundi, Festus E. A survey of preservation
of library collections in Kenya /. [Nairobi?]
1988. iii, 36 leaves ;   *NYPL [Sc F 89-142]*

Library and information sources on women : a
guide to collections in the Greater New York
area / compiled and edited by the Women's
Resources Group of the Greater New York
Metropolitan Area Chapter of the Association
of College and Research Libraries and the
Center for the Study of Women and Society of
the Graduate School and University Center of
the City University of New York. New York :
Feminist Press at the City University of New
York, c1988. ix, 254 p. ; 23 cm. Includes index.
     ISBN 0-935312-88-9 (pbk.) : DDC
305.4/025/7471 19
*1. Women - Information services - New York (N.Y.) -
Directories. 2. Women - Research - New York (N.Y.) -
Information services - Directories. 3. Information
services - New York (N.Y.). I. Association of College
and Research Libraries. Greater New York
Metropolitan Area Chapter. Women's Resources Group.
II. City University of New York. Center for the Study
of Women and Society.*
HQ1181.U5 L52 1987
                      *NYPL [*R-Econ. 88-4682]*

**LIBRARY CATALOGS - UNION. see
CATALOGS, UNION.**

**LIBRARY ECONOMY. see LIBRARY
SCIENCE.**

LIBRARY EDUCATION - BIBLIOGRAPHY.
Ajayi, John Olufemi. Library education in
Nigeria, 1948-1986 /. Zaria , 1987. ii, 81 p. ;
                       NYPL [Sc D 88-1376]

Library education in Nigeria, 1948-1986 /. Ajayi,
John Olufemi. Zaria , 1987. ii, 81 p. ;
                       NYPL [Sc D 88-1376]

**LIBRARY EDUCATION - NIGERIA -
BIBLIOGRAPHY.**
Ajayi, John Olufemi. Library education in
Nigeria, 1948-1986 /. Zaria , 1987. ii, 81 p. ;
                       NYPL [Sc D 88-1376]

**LIBRARY ETHICS. see LIBRARIANS -
PROFESSIONAL ETHICS.**

Library handbook, 1982-1983 [microform] /.
Ralph M. Paiewonsky Library. [St. Thomas]
[1982?] 10 p. :   *NYPL [Sc Micro F-10939]*

**LIBRARY MATERIALS - CONSERVATION
AND RESTORATION.**
Conservation of library and archive materials
and the graphic arts /. London , Boston , 1985.
328 p. : ISBN 0-408-01466-0 : DDC 025.7 19
Z701 .C5863 1985   *NYPL [MFW+ 88-574]*
Khayundi, Festus E. A survey of preservation
of library collections in Kenya /. [Nairobi?]
1988. iii, 36 leaves ;   *NYPL [Sc F 89-142]*

**LIBRARY MATERIALS - CONSERVATION
AND RESTORATION - AUDIO-VISUAL
AIDS - HANDBOOKS, MANUALS, ETC.**
Harrison, Alice W., 1929- The conservation of
archival and library materials . Metuchen, N.J. ,
1982. xi, 190 p. ; ISBN 0-8108-1523-0 DDC
025.8/4 19
Z701 .H28   *NYPL [Cons. Div. 84-252]*

**LIBRARY SCIENCE - AFRICA -
PERIODICALS - BIBLIOGRAPHY.**
Prichard, R. J. African librarianship .
Aberystwyth, Dyfed, Great Britain , 1987. 35
p. ; ISBN 0-904020-21-5 (pbk.) DDC 016.02706 19
Z857.A1 P75 1987   *NYPL [Sc D 88-1518]*

LIBRARY SCIENCE - BIBLIOGRAPHY.
Haith, Dorothy May. Theses accepted by the
Atlanta University Graduate School of Library
Service, 1950-1975 /. Huntsville, Al , 1977. v,
45 p. ;
Z666 .H25   *NYPL [Sc D 88-69]*

**LIBRARY SCIENCE - POLITICAL ASPECTS -
UNITED STATES - HISTORY - 20TH
CENTURY.**
Activism in American librarianship, 1962-1973
/. New York , 1987. x, 207 p. : ISBN
0-313-24602-5 (lib. bdg. : alk. paper) DDC 021
19
Z716.4 .A27 1987   *NYPL [JFE 87-6266]*

**LIBRARY SCIENCE - SOCIAL ASPECTS -
UNITED STATES - HISTORY - 20TH
CENTURY.**
Activism in American librarianship, 1962-1973
/. New York , 1987. x, 207 p. : ISBN
0-313-24602-5 (lib. bdg. : alk. paper) DDC 021
19
Z716.4 .A27 1987   *NYPL [JFE 87-6266]*

LIBYA - RELATIONS - CHAD.
Ciammaichella, Glauco. Libyens et Français au
Tchad (1897-1914) . Paris , 1987. 187 p. :
     ISBN 2-222-04067-1 *NYPL [Sc E 89-182]*

Libyan Arab Republic. see Libya.

Libyens et Français au Tchad (1897-1914) .
Ciammaichella, Glauco. Paris , 1987. 187 p. :
     ISBN 2-222-04067-1 *NYPL [Sc E 89-182]*

Lienhardt, Godfrey. Divinity and experience : the
religion of the Dinka / Godfrey Lienhardt.
Oxford : Clarendon, 1961 (1987 [printing]) 328
p. : ill., 2 maps ; 22 cm. Includes index. Includes
bibliographical footnotes. ISBN 0-19-823405-8 (pbk) :
     DDC 299/.683 19
1. Dinka (African people) - Religion. I. Title.
BL2480.D5   *NYPL [Sc D 88-1011]*

**Life and manners in Rio de Janeiro as seen in
Guillobel's small drawings.** Guillobel, Joaquim
Cândido, 1787-1859. Usos e costumes do Rio
de Janeiro nas figurinhas de Guillobel =.
[Curitiba?] [1978] [19] p., [25] leaves of
plates : DDC 981/.5
F2646.2 .G84 1978   *NYPL [Sc F 88-188]*

Life and times of a bank robber /. Kimani, John
Kiggia. Nairobi , 1988. 133 p. : ISBN
     996-646-376-3   *NYPL [Sc C 89-97]*

Life at Great Zimbabwe /. Garlake, Peter S.
Gweru, Zimbabwe , 1983, c1982. [36] p. :
     ISBN 0-86922-180-9 (pbk.) DDC 968.91 19
DT962.9.G73 G374 1983
                          NYPL [Sc F 88-175]

Life histories of African women / edited by
Patricia W. Romero. London ; Atlantic
Highlands, NJ : Ashfield Press, 1988. 200 p. :
ill. ; 22 cm. Includes bibliographies and index. ISBN
0-948660-04-X DDC 305.4/0967 19
*1. Women - Africa, Sub-Saharan - Biography. 2.
Women - Africa, Sub-Saharan - Social conditions - Case
studies. 3. Women, Muslim - Africa, Sub-Saharan -
Social conditions - Case studies. I. Romero, Patricia W.*
HQ1787.A3 L54 1988
                          NYPL [Sc D 88-1469]

The life history of Raúl Honwana . Honwana,
Raúl Bernardo Manuel, 1905- [Histórias ouvidas
e vividas dos homens e da terra. English.]

Boulder , 1988. ix, 181 p. : ISBN 1-555-87114-3 (lib. bdg.) : DDC 967/.903/0924 B 19
DT463 .H6613 1988 **NYPL [Sc E 88-367]**

A life in the struggle . Lipsitz, George. Philadelphia , 1988. viii, 292 p. : ISBN 0-87722-550-8 (alk. paper) DDC 973/.0496073024 B 19
E185.97.P49 L57 1988 **NYPL [Sc E 89-43]**

Life in the white man's grave . Allison, Philip. London , 1988. 192 p. : ISBN 0-670-81020-7 : DDC 966 19
DT476.2 **NYPL [Sc F 88-174]**

The life of Langston Hughes /. Rampersad, Arnold. New York , 1986-1988. 2 v. : ISBN 0-19-504011-2 (v. 1) DDC 818/.5209 B 19
PS3515.U274 Z698 1986
NYPL [Sc E 87-44]

The life of my choice /. Thesiger, Wilfred, 1910- London , 1987. 459 p., [32] p. of plates : ISBN 0-00-216194-X :
G525 .T415x 1987 **NYPL [Sc E 88-222]**

The life of Venerable Archdeacon S.A.F. Odunuga /. Odunuga, S. A. F. (Samuel Adedoyin Folafunmi), 1902- [Sermons. Selections.] [Nigeria] , 1982. xiii, 175 p., [2] p. of plates : DDC 252/.03 19
BX5700.7.Z6 O28 1982
NYPL [Sc E 89-142]

Life on old St. David's, Bermuda /. McCallan, E. A. (Ernest Albert), 1874- Hamilton, Bermuda , 1986. 258 p., [26] p. of plates :
F1639.S26 M35x 1986 **NYPL [Sc E 88-539]**

A life without Christ and a new life in Christ [microform] /. Cohen, Esther. Miami, Fla. , 1980. [23] p. ; **NYPL [Sc Micro F-11022]**

LIFELONG EDUCATION. see CONTINUING EDUCATION.

Lifschitz, Edward, 1945- The Art of West African kingdoms /. Washington, D.C. , 1987. 48 p., [4] folded leaves : ISBN 0-87474-611-6 DDC 709/.01/10966 19
N7398 .A75 1987 **NYPL [Sc F 89-26]**

Light ahead for the Negro /. Johnson, Edward Augustus, 1860-1944. New York , 1904. vi, 132 p. ; **NYPL [Sc Rare C 88-6]**

A light rising from the west /. Rétout, Marie Thérèse. Trinidad , 1985. xiii, 268 p. : DDC 378.7298/3 19
LE15.S7 R48 1985 **NYPL [Sc C 88-67]**

Likpong, Justin S. Gospel parables in African context /. Port Harcourt, Nigeria , 1988. 68 p. ; ISBN 978-272-801-2 **NYPL [Sc D 89-133]**

Lillie of Watts takes a giant step. Walter, Mildred Pitts. Garden City, N.Y. [1971] 187 p. DDC [Fic]
PZ7.W17125 Lk **NYPL [Sc D 88-1119]**

Lim, Hanny. Garmers, Sonia. Brueria di henter mundo =. Curaçao [1986?] 58 p. : DDC 133.4/3 19
BF1618.D8 G37 1986 **NYPL [Sc E 89-237]**

Lima antigua. [Lima, Imprenta Universal de C. Prince, 1890] 3 v. illus. 23 cm. (Biblioteca popular) CONTENTS. - I. Tipos de antaño.--II. Fiestas religiosas y profanas.--III. La limeña, y más tipos de antaño.
1. Lima (Peru) - Social life and customs.
NYPL [Sc Rare F 89-15]

LIMA (PERU) - SOCIAL LIFE AND CUSTOMS.
Lima antigua. [Lima, 1890] 3 v.
NYPL [Sc Rare F 89-15]

Limeira, José Carlos. Atabaques / José Carlos Limeira,Éle Semog. [Rio de Janeiro? : Limeira : Semog, 1983] 171 p. ; 21 cm.
I. Semog, Éle. II. Title. **NYPL [Sc D 88-1096]**

LIMITATION OF ARMAMENT. see DISARMAMENT.

LIMITATIONS (LAW) see REAL PROPERTY.

Les limites du créole dans notre enseignement /. Trouillot, Hénock. Port-au-Prince , 1980. 85 p. : **NYPL [Sc D 88-1400]**

Limota. Ogunyẹmi, Diipọ. A needle in the haystack ; [and] Limota. Ibandan, Nigeria , 1987. iv, 88 p. ; **NYPL [Sc C 88-166]**

Linares, Ronaldo Antonio. Xangô e inhaçá / Ronaldo Antonio Linares, Diamantino Fernandes Trindade. [São Paulo] : Tríade,

c1987. 85 p. : ill, music ; 21 cm. (Coleção Orixás . v.2)
1. Gods, Umbanda. 2. Shango. I. Trindade, Diamantino Fernandes. II. Title. III. Series.
NYPL [Sc D 88-553]

LINCOLN, ABRAHAM, 1809-1865.
Keckley, Elizabeth, 1824-1907. Behind the scenes, or, Thirty years a slave, and four years in the White House /. New York , 1988. xxxvi, xvi, 371 p. : ISBN 0-19-505259-5 DDC 973.7/092/2 19
E457.15 .K26 1988 **NYPL [JFC 88-2194]**

Lincoln, C. Eric (Charles Eric), 1924- The Avenue, Clayton City / C. Eric Lincoln. New York : Morrow, c1988. 288 p. ; 25 cm. ISBN 0-688-07702-1 DDC 813/.54 19
1. Afro-Americans - Southern States - Fiction. I. Title.
PS3562.I472 A94 1988
NYPL [JFE 88-5108]

LINCOLN, MARY (TODD) 1818-1882.
Keckley, Elizabeth, 1824-1907. Behind the scenes, or, Thirty years a slave, and four years in the White House /. New York , 1988. xxxvi, xvi, 371 p. : ISBN 0-19-505259-5 DDC 973.7/092/2 19
E457.15 .K26 1988 **NYPL [JFC 88-2194]**

Lincoln University (Pa.) The Full fruits of freedom. Chester County, Pa. [1935?] 47 p. : **NYPL [Sc F 89-69]**

LINCOLN UNIVERSITY (PA.)
The Full fruits of freedom. Chester County, Pa. [1935?] 47 p. : **NYPL [Sc F 89-69]**

Linde, Freda. Toto and the aardvark. Translated from the Afrikaans by Jan and Polly Berends. Illustrated by Paul Giovanopoulos. [1st ed.] Garden City, N.Y., Doubleday [1969] 59 p. col. illus. 25 cm. When his brother announces he is going to hunt down an aardvark, young Toto objects and tries to warn the animal. SCHOMBURG CHILDREN'S COLLECTION.
1. Children - South Africa - Juvenile fiction. I. Giovanopoulos, Paul, illus. II. Schomburg Children's Collection. III. Title.
PZ7.L6574 To **NYPL [JFE 72-633]**

Lindfors, Bernth. Literature and African identity. Bayreuth , c1986. 125 p. ;
NYPL [Sc D 89-369]

Lindquist, Willis. The red drum's warning / by Willis Lindquist ; illustrated by Harper Johnson. New York : Whittlesey House, McGraw-Hill, 1958. 128 p. : ill. ; 22 cm. SCHOMBURG CHILDREN'S COLLECTION.
1. Haiti - History - Revolution, 1791-1804 - Juvenile fiction. I. Johnson, E. Harper. II. Schomburg Children's Collection. III. Title. **NYPL [Sc D 88-662]**

Line en Nouvelle Calédonie /. Mille, Pierre, 1864-1931. Paris , c1934. 32, 1 p. :
NYPL [Sc F 89-20]

Liniger-Goumaz, Max. Historical dictionary of Equatorial Guinea / by Max Liniger-Goumaz. 2nd ed. Metuchen, N.J. : Scarecrow Press, 1988. xxx, 238 p. : map ; 23 cm. (African historical dictionaries. no. 21) Bibliography: p. 193-238. ISBN 0-8108-2120-6 DDC 967/.18/00321 19
1. Equatorial Guinea - History - Dictionaries. I. Title. II. Series.
DT620.15 .L57 1988 **NYPL [Sc D 89-528]**

Liniger, Max [i.e. Max Liniger-Goumaz] see Liniger-Goumaz, Max.

Linton, W. J. (William James), 1812-1897.
Catoninetales : a domestic epic / by Hattie Brown, a young lady of colour lately deceased at the age of 14. [Hamden, Conn.] : Printed at the Appledore U. S. Press, [188-?]. [8], 100 p. : ill. ; 22 cm. Poems. Hattie Brown is a pseudonym of W.J. Linton. Title vignette. "Twenty-five copies"
1. Cats - Poetry. I. Title. II. Title: Cat o' nine tales.
NYPL [Sc Rare F 88-4]

Linz, Juan J. (Juan José), 1926- Democracy in developing countries /. Boulder, Colo. , 1988-v. : ISBN 1-555-87039-2 (v. 2) DDC 320.9173/4 19
D883 .D45 1988 **NYPL [Sc E 88-201]**

Le Lion à l'arc . Diabaté, Massa M. Paris , 1986. 128 p. ; ISBN 2-218-07616-0
NYPL [Sc C 89-155]

The lion and the jewel /. Soyinka, Wole. Harare, Zimbabwe , 1986. 64 p. ; ISBN 0-949225-41-X :
NYPL [Sc C 89-107]

Lionnet, Guy. Coco de mer : le roman d'un palmier = the romance of a palm / Guy Lionnet. Bell Village, Ile Maurice : L'Ile aux images, c1986. 95 p. : ill.(some col.) ; 22 cm. English and French. Bibliography: p. 93.
1. Sea coconut - Seychelles. 2. Botany - Seychelles. I. Title.
QK495.P17 L56 1986 **NYPL [Sc D 88-572]**

LIONS - JUVENILE FICTION.
Bontemps, Arna Wendell, 1902- Mr. Kelso's lion. Philadelphia [1970] 48 p. DDC [Fic]
PZ7.B6443 Mi **NYPL [Sc D 88-1493]**

Fields, Julia. The green lion of Zion Street /. New York , c1988. [32] p. : ISBN 0-689-50414-4 DDC [E] 19
PZ8.3.F458 Gr 1988 **NYPL [Sc F 88-186]**

Lipkind, William, 1904- Four-leaf clover / By Will [i.e. Lipkind] and Nicolas [i.e. N. Mordvinoff] 1st ed. New York : Harcourt, Brace, 1959. [32] p. : col. ill, ; 29 cm. SCHOMBURG CHILDREN'S COLLECTION.
1. Afro-American children - Juvenile fiction. I. Mordvinoff, Nicolas, 1911- joint author. II. Schomburg Children's Collection. III. Title.
NYPL [Sc F 89-22]

Lipset, Seymour Martin. Democracy in developing countries /. Boulder, Colo. , 1988-v. : ISBN 1-555-87039-2 (v. 2) DDC 320.9173/4 19
D883 .D45 1988 **NYPL [Sc E 88-201]**

Lipsitz, George. A life in the struggle : Ivory Perry and the culture of opposition / by George Lipsitz. Philadelphia : Temple University Press, 1988. viii, 292 p. : ill. ; 24 cm. (Critical perspectives on the past) Includes bibliographical references and index. ISBN 0-87722-550-8 (alk. paper) DDC 973/.0496073024 B 19
1. Perry, Ivory. 2. Afro-Americans - Biography. 3. Civil rights workers - United States - Biography. 4. Civil rights movements - United States - History - 20th century. 5. Afro-Americans - Civil rights. 6. Afro-Americans - Civil rights - Missouri - Saint Louis. 7. Saint Louis (Mo.) - Race relations. I. Title. II. Series.
E185.97.P49 L57 1988 **NYPL [Sc E 89-43]**

LISALA (EQUATEUR, ZAIRE) - HISTORY.
Schatzberg, Michael G. The dialectics of oppression in Zaire /. Bloomington , c1988. x, 193 p., [1] p. of plates : ISBN 0-253-31703-7 DDC 323.4/9/0967513 19
JC599.Z282 L577 1988 **NYPL [Sc E 88-512]**

Lisette, Yeyon. Le RDA et le Tchad : histoire d'une décolonisation / Yeyon Lisette, Marc Dumas. Paris : Présence africaine ; Abidjan : Nouvelles Éditions africaines, 1986. 351 p. ; 24 cm. Includes index. ISBN 2-7087-0472-9 (Présence africaine)
1. Rassemblement démocratique africain. 2. Chad - History - 1960-. I. Dumas, Marc. II. Title.
NYPL [Sc E 87-627]

The list /. Dettlinger, Chet. Atlanta , c1983. 516 p., [4] p. of plates : ISBN 0-942894-04-9 : DDC 364.1/523/09758231 19
HV6534.A7 D47 1983 **NYPL [Sc E 86-40]**

A list of books, articles and government publications on the economy of Nigeria, 1963 and 1964. Visser, Johanna, 1898- Ibadan, 1965. x, 81 p. **NYPL [Sc F 78-58]**

Lister, Frederick K., 1921- Decision-making strategies for international organizations : the IMF model / Frederick K. Lister ; foreword by Seymour Maxwell Finger. Denver, Colo. : Graduate School of International Studies, University of Denver, 1984. ix, 142 p. : ill. ; 22 cm. (Monograph series in world affairs . v. 20, bk. 4) Bibliography: p. 127-129. ISBN 0-87940-075-7 : DDC 332.1/52 19
1. International Monetary Fund. 2. International agencies - Decision making - Case studies. I. Title. II. Series.
HG3881.5.I58 L57 1984
NYPL [Sc D 88-1218]

Liston, Carolyn Olivia. Black positivism through character growth and development in the short stories of Richard Wright [microform] / by Carolyn Olivia Liston. 1982. xii, 207 p. Thesis (Ph.D.)--University of Colorado, 1982. Bibliography: p. [188]-207. Microfilm. Ann Arbor, Mich. : University Microfilms International, 1983. 1 reel ; 35 mm.
1. Wright, Richard, 1908-1960 - Criticism and

interpretation. I. Title.
NYPL [Sc Micro R-4819]

LITERACY - AFRICA, SUB-SAHARAN.
Richmond, Edmun B. New directions in
language teaching in Sub-Saharan Africa .
Washington, D.C. , c1983. viii, 65 p. ; ISBN
0-8191-2980-1 (pbk.) : DDC 418/.007/067 19
P57.A37 R5 1983 *NYPL [Sc D 88-479]*

Literary Africa. Taylor, Jane. Fielding's literary
Africa /. New York, N.Y. , 1988. xv, 506 p. :
ISBN 0-688-05071-9 DDC 960 19
DT12.25 .T39 1988 *NYPL [Sc D 88-1361]*

Literary conversations series.
Angelou, Maya. Conversations with Maya
Angelou /. Jackson , c1989. xvi, 246 p. ; ISBN
0-87805-361-1 (alk. paper) DDC 818/.5409 19
PS3551.N464 Z4635 1989
NYPL [Sc E 89-225]

LITERARY CRITICISM. see CRITICISM.

**LITERARY INFLUENCE. see INFLUENCE
(LITERARY, ARTISTIC, ETC.)**

LITERARY LANDMARKS - AFRICA.
Taylor, Jane. Fielding's literary Africa /. New
York, N.Y. , 1988. xv, 506 p. : ISBN
0-688-05071-9 DDC 960 19
DT12.25 .T39 1988 *NYPL [Sc D 88-1361]*

**LITERARY TRADITION. see INFLUENCE
(LITERARY, ARTISTIC, ETC.)**

Literatura infantil caribeña . Piñeiro de Rivera,
Flor, 1922- Hato Rey, P.R. (O'Neill 159, Hato
Rey) , c1983. 123 p. ; DDC 860/.9/9282 19
PQ7361 .P5 1983 *NYPL [Sc D 88-1143]*

Literatura puertorriqueña. Martinez Masdeu,
Edgar. Río Piedras [P.R.] 1983. 2 v.
NYPL [Sc D 87-1020]

Literature and African identity. Bayreuth :
Bayreuth University, c1986. 125 p. ; 21 cm.
(Bayreuth African studies series, 0178-0034 . 6) In
English or French. Includes bibliographical references.
CONTENTS. - Xenophobia and class consciousness in
recent African literature / B. Lindfors -- Literature and
African identity, the example of Ayi Kwei Armah / K.
Anyidoho -- Is there a Nigerian literature? / B. King --
The changing identity of the Igbo in literature / D.I.
Nwoga -- Le thème de l'identité culturelle et ses
variations dans le roman africain francophone / M.
Kane.
*1. African literature - History and criticism. 2. African
literature (French) - History and criticism. I. Lindfors,
Bernth. II. King, Bruce Alvin. III. Nwoga, Donatus Ibe.
IV. Kane, Mohamadou K. V. Series. VI. Series:
Bayreuth African studies series , 6.*
NYPL [Sc D 89-369]

**LITERATURE AND FOLKLORE - UNITED
STATES - HISTORY - 20TH CENTURY.**
Tracy, Steven C. (Steven Carl), 1954- Langston
Hughes & the blues /. Urbana , c1988. xiii, 305
p. ; ISBN 0-252-01457-X (alk. paper) DDC
818/.5209 19
PS3515.U274 Z8 1988 *NYPL [Sc E 88-506]*

Literature and society : selected essays on
African literature / edited by Prof. Ernest N.
Emenyonu. Oguta, Nigeria : Zim Pan-African,
1986. iv, 303 p. ; 22 cm. "A publication of the
Department of English and Literary Studies,University
of Calabar, Calabar, Nigeria". Includes bibliographical
references.
*1. African literature (English) - Collected works. I.
Emenyōnu, Ernest, 1939-.* *NYPL [Sc D 88-639]*

LITERATURE AND SOCIETY - AFRICA.
El Mahmud-Okereke, N. O. E. (Noel Olufemi
Enuma), 1948- Nancy Reagan's red dress ;
Previewing UK's King Charles / Israel's
indigenous black minority : & other poems of
Pan-Afrikan expression /. London , 1988,
c1987. xxi, 179 p. : ISBN 978-242-304-1 (pbk)
: DDC 821 19 *NYPL [Sc C 88-182]*

Ogidan, Anna. Thememschwerpunkte im Werk
Ayi Kwei Armahs /. Wien , 1988. ii, 202 p. :
ISBN 3-85043-046-4
NYPL [Sc D 88-1035]

**LITERATURE AND SOCIETY - AFRICA -
HISTORY - 20TH CENTURY.**
Bishop, Rand. African literature, African
critics . New York , 1988. xii, 213 p. ; ISBN
0-313-25918-6 (lib. bdg. : alk. paper) DDC
820/.9/96 19
PR9340 .B5 1988 *NYPL [Sc E 89-129]*

**LITERATURE AND SOCIOLOGY. see
LITERATURE AND SOCIETY.**

**LITERATURE AND WOMEN. see WOMEN
AND LITERATURE.**

LITERATURE - BLACK AUTHORS.
Finn, Julio. Voices of négritude . London ,
NewYork , 1988. 246 p. ;
NYPL [Sc E 88-494]

**LITERATURE - BLACK AUTHORS -
HISTORY AND CRITICISM.**
Dorsinville, Max, 1943- Solidarités . Montréal,
Québec, Canada , 1988. xv, 196 p. ; ISBN
2-920862-09-X *NYPL [Sc D 89-484]*

Finn, Julio. Voices of négritude . London ,
NewYork , 1988. 246 p. ;
NYPL [Sc E 88-494]

**LITERATURE - BLACK AUTHORS - STUDY
AND TEACHING.**
Towards the decolonization of the British
educational system /. London, England , 19.
128 p. ; ISBN 0-907015-32-8
NYPL [Sc D 88-1346]

**LITERATURE, EROTIC. see EROTIC
LITERATURE.**

**LITERATURE - EVALUATION. see
CRITICISM.**

**LITERATURE, MODERN - 20TH CENTURY -
BIO-BIBLIOGRAPHY.**
Encyclopedia of world literature in the 20th
century . New York , c1981-1984. 4 v. : ISBN
0-8044-3135-3 (v. 1) : DDC 803 19
PN771 .E5 1981 *NYPL [Sc Ser.-M .E565]*

**LITERATURE, MODERN - 20TH CENTURY -
DICTIONARIES.**
Encyclopedia of world literature in the 20th
century . New York , c1981-1984. 4 v. : ISBN
0-8044-3135-3 (v. 1) : DDC 803 19
PN771 .E5 1981 *NYPL [Sc Ser.-M .E565]*

**LITERATURE, MODERN - BLACK
AUTHORS. COLLETTE Verger, 1937- Négritude .
West Cornwall, CT , 1988. xvii, 315 p. ; ISBN
0-933951-15-9 (lib. bdg. : alk. paper) : DDC
016.909/04924 19
Z6520.N44 M53 1988 PN56.N36
NYPL [Sc D 88-1470]

**LITERATURE, PRIMITIVE. see FOLK
LITERATURE.**

**LITERATURE PUBLISHING - SOUTHERN
STATES - HISTORY - 20TH CENTURY -
CONGRESSES.**
The Southern review and modern literature,
1935-1985 /. Baton Rouge , c1988. xvi, 238 p.:
ISBN 0-8071-1424-3 : DDC 810/.9/975 19
PS267.B3 S68 1987 *NYPL [Sc E 88-280]*

Littérature africaine et antillaise. Réception
critique de la littérature africaine et antillaise
d'expression française. Paris , 1979. 272 p. ;
NYPL [Sc E 87-557]

Littérature africaine et sa critique /. Locha
Mateso. Paris , c1986. 399 p. ; ISBN
2-86537-153-0 DDC 840/.9/896 19
PQ3981 .L6 1986 *NYPL [Sc D 88-1392]*

Littérature négro-africaine francophone :
panorama historique et choix de textes / A.
Cnockaert. [Pau] : C.R.P., 1986. 137 p. ; 21
cm. (Collection Boboto) Bibliography: p. 133-135.
DDC 840/.9/896 19
*1. African literature (French) - Black authors - History
and criticism. 2. African literature (French) - Black
authors. 3. Blacks - Literary collections. I. Cnockaert,
A. II. Series.*
PQ3980.5 .L56 1986 *NYPL [Sc D 89-316]*

The little black book of business inspirations /.
Adams, Robert Hugo. Hempstead, NY , 1987.
vi, 74 p. : *NYPL [Sc D 88-440]*

Little Black Sambo. Picture parade. Akron
[Ohio] , c1942. [36] p. :
NYPL [Sc F 88-262]

The little brown hen. Martin, Patricia Miles. New
York [1960] 23 p.
PZ7 .M36418 Li *NYPL [Sc D 88-1495]*

Little John and Plutie /. Edwards, Pat, 1922-
Boston , 1988. 172 p. ; ISBN 0-395-48223-2
DDC [Fic] 19
PZ7.E2637 Li 1988 *NYPL [Sc D 89-126]*

Little League baseball book. Robinson, John

Roosevelt, 1919-1972. Jackie Robinson's Little
League baseball book. Englewood Cliffs, N.J.
[1972] 135 p. ISBN 0-13-509232-9
GV867.5 .R6 *NYPL [JFD 72-7423]*

Little, Lessie Jones. Children of long ago : poems
/ by Lessie Jones Little ; pictures by Jan Spivey
Gilchrist. New York : Philomel Books, 1988.
[32] p. : col. ill. ; 27 cm. Poems reflecting simpler
days, with grandmothers who read aloud and children
who walk barefoot on damp earth and pick blackberries
for their paper dolls to eat. SCHOMBURG
CHILDREN'S COLLECTION. ISBN 0-399-21473-9
DDC 811/.54 19
*1. Children's poetry, American. 2. Afro-American
children - Poetry. I. Gilchrist, Jan Spivey, ill. II.
Schomburg Children's Collection. III. Title.*
PS3562.I78288 C5 1988
NYPL [Sc F 88-276]

A little new light . Smith, Abdullahi, 1920-1984.
Zaria , 1987- v. : *NYPL [Sc D 88-708]*

Little Vic /. Gates, Doris, 1901- New York ,
1951. 160 p. : *NYPL [Sc D 88-430]*

**LITURGICAL ADAPTATION - CATHOLIC
CHURCH - CONGRESSES.**
Amecea Liturgical Colloquium (1985 : Catholic
Higher Institute of Eastern Africa) Liturgy .
Eldoret, Kenya , 1986. viii, 78 p. ;
NYPL [Sc D 88-901]

**LITURGICS - AFRICA, EASTERN -
CONGRESSES.**
Amecea Liturgical Colloquium (1985 : Catholic
Higher Institute of Eastern Africa) Liturgy .
Eldoret, Kenya , 1986. viii, 78 p. ;
NYPL [Sc D 88-901]

Liturgy . Amecea Liturgical Colloquium (1985 :
Catholic Higher Institute of Eastern Africa)
Eldoret, Kenya , 1986. viii, 78 p. ;
NYPL [Sc D 88-901]

LITURGY. see LITURGICS.

Litwack, Leon F. Black leaders of the nineteenth
century /. Urbana , c1988. xii, 344 p. : ISBN
0-252-01506-1 (alk. paper) DDC
920/.009296073 19
E185.96 .B535 1988 *NYPL [Sc E 88-365]*

The lives of celebrated travellers [microform]. St.
John, James Augustus, 1801-1875. New York,
1859-68. 3 v. *NYPL [Sc Micro R-3541]*

**LIVESTOCK - BIBLIOGRAPHY -
MICROFORM CATALOGS.**
Index to livestock literature microfiched in
Zimbabwe /. Addis Ababa [1986?] viii, 235 p. ;
ISBN 92-9053-064-2 *NYPL [Sc E 89-204]*

LIVESTOCK - INDEXES.
Index to livestock literature microfiched in
Zimbabwe /. Addis Ababa [1986?] viii, 235 p. ;
ISBN 92-9053-064-2 *NYPL [Sc E 89-204]*

**LIVESTOCK - ZIMBABWE -
BIBLIOGRAPHY - MICROFORM
CATALOGS.**
Index to livestock literature microfiched in
Zimbabwe /. Addis Ababa [1986?] viii, 235 p. ;
ISBN 92-9053-064-2 *NYPL [Sc E 89-204]*

LIVESTOCK - ZIMBABWE - INDEXES.
Index to livestock literature microfiched in
Zimbabwe /. Addis Ababa [1986?] viii, 235 p. ;
ISBN 92-9053-064-2 *NYPL [Sc E 89-204]*

Living by the word . Walker, Alice, 1944- San
Diego , c1988. xxi, 196 p. ; ISBN
0-15-152900-0 : DDC 813/.54 19
PS3573.A425 A6 1988
NYPL [Sc D 88-1014]

A living church . Catholic Church. Diocese of
Nyeri (Kenya) [Nyeri, Kenya] [1986] 28 p. :
NYPL [Sc G 89-16]

The living is easy /. West, Dorothy, 1909-
London , 1987, c1982. 362 p. ; ISBN
0-86068-753-8 *NYPL [Sc C 88-165]*

Livingstone, David, 1813-1873.
[Missionary travels and researches in South
Africa. Danish]
Livingstones Reise : Syd-Adrika / oversat
efter den engelske original af M. Th.
Wøldike. Kjøbenhavn : Fr. Wøldike,
1858-1859. 2 v. : ill., map, port. ; 24 cm.
*1. Missions - South Africa. 2. South Africa -
Description and travel - 1801-1900. I. Title. II. Title:
Reise ; Syd-Afrika.* *NYPL [Sc E 88-47]*

**LIVINGSTONE, DAVID, 1813-1873 -
JOURNEYS - AFRICA, EAST -
JUVENILE LITERATURE.**
African adventures and adventurers /. Boston ,
1880. 393 p. :   *NYPL [Sc C 88-60]*

Livingstone, Ian. Youth employment & youth
employment programmes in Africa : a
comparative sub-regional study : the case of
[name of country] Nigeria. Addis Ababa :
International Labour Organisation, Jobs & Skills
Programme for Africa, 1986. 9 v. : ill. ; 29 cm.
Cover title: Youth employment and youth employment
programmes in Africa. Includes bibliographies.
CONTENTS. - [1] Botswana -- [2] Ethiopia -- [3]
Kenya -- [4] Malawi -- [5] Mauritius -- [6] Somalia --
[7] Zambia. -- [8] Nigeria -- [9] Synthesis report.
    ISBN 92-2-105527-2 (pbk. : v. 1) DDC
331.3/4/096 19
*1. Youth - Employment - Africa. 2. Youth -
Government policy - Africa. 3. Occupational training -
Africa. I. Jobs and Skills Programme for Africa. II.
Title. III. Title: Youth employment and youth
employment programmes in Africa.*
HD6276.A32 L58 1986 *NYPL [Sc F 88-313]*

Livingstones Reise : Syd-Adrika /. Livingstone,
David, 1813-1873. [Missionary travels and
researches in South Africa. Danish.]
Kjøbenhavn , 1858-1859. 2 v. :
                                        NYPL [Sc E 88-47]

Livre d'or de la République Malgache.
[Tananarive? : bS.n., 1960] 176 p. : ill., maps,
ports. ; 33 cm. "Romuald Bigaignon, journaliste à
Tananarive, a assuré l'édition, les maquettes et la mise
en pages de ce livre d'or."-- Colophon.
1. Madagascar. I. Bigaignon, Romuald.
                                        NYPL [Sc G 88-18]

Lo, Magatte, 1925- Syndicalisme et participation
responsable / Magatte Lo ; préface de
Mamadou Seyni Mbengue. Paris : L'Harmattan,
[1987] 151 p. : ill. ; 22 cm. (Mémoires africaines)
At head of title: Sénégal. ISBN 2-85802-885-0
*1. Syndicalism - Senegal. I. Title. II. Title:
Syndicalisme et participation responsable. III. Series.*
                                        NYPL [Sc D 88-915]

**LOANS, FOREIGN - AFRICA -
CONGRESSES.**
African debt and financing /. Washington,
D.C. , 1986. 223 p. : ISBN 0-88132-044-7 :
DDC 336.3/435/096 19
HJ8826 .A36 1986   *NYPL [JLE 87-3261]*

LOANS, INTERNATIONAL. see **LOANS,
FOREIGN.**

Lobban, Richard.
Historical dictionary of the Republic of Cape
Verde / by Richard Lobban and Marilyn
Halter. 2nd ed. Metuchen, N.J. : Scarecrow
Press, 1988. xix, 171 p. ; 23 cm. (African
historical dictionaries. no. 42) Rev. ed. of: Historical
dictionary of the Republics of Guinea-Bissau and Cape
Verde. 1979. Bibliography: p. 122-165. ISBN
0-8108-2087-0 DDC 966/.57/00321 19
*1. Guinea-Bissau - History - Dictionaries. 2. Cape
Verde - History - Dictionaries. 3. Guinea-Bissau -
Bibliography. 4. Cape Verde - Bibliography. I. Halter,
Marilyn. II. Lobban, Richard. Historical dictionary of
the Republics of Guinea-Bissau and Cape Verde. III.
Title. IV. Series.*
DT613.5 .L62 1988b   *NYPL [Sc D 88-1311]*

Historical dictionary of the Republic of
Guinea-Bissau / by Richard Lobban and Joshua
Forrest. 2nd ed. Metuchen, N.J. : Scarecrow
Press, 1988. xx, 210 p. ; 23 cm. (African
historical dictionaries. no. 22) Rev. ed. of: Historical
dictionary of the Republics of Guinea-Bissau and Cape
Verde. 1979. Bibliography: p. 138-203 ISBN
0-8108-2086-2 DDC 966/.57 19
*1. Guinea-Bissau - History - Dictionaries. 2.
Guinea-Bissau - Bibliography. I. Forrest, Joshua. II.
Lobban, Richard. Historical dictionary of the Republics
of Guinea-Bissau and Cape Verde. III. Title. IV. Series.*
DT613.5 .L62 1988
                                        *NYPL [*R-BMP 88-5080]*

**Historical dictionary of the Republics of
Guinea-Bissau and Cape Verde.**
Lobban, Richard. Historical dictionary of the
Republic of Cape Verde / by Richard Lobban
and Marilyn Halter. 2nd ed. Metuchen, N.J. ,
1988. xix, 171 p. ; ISBN 0-8108-2087-0 DDC
966/.57/00321 19
DT613.5 .L62 1988b   *NYPL [Sc D 88-1311]*

Lobban, Richard. Historical dictionary of the
Republic of Guinea-Bissau / by Richard

Lobban and Joshua Forrest. 2nd ed.
Metuchen, N.J. , 1988. xx, 210 p. : ISBN
0-8108-2086-2 DDC 966/.57 19
DT613.5 .L62 1988
                                        *NYPL [*R-BMP 88-5080]*

Lobdell, Jared, 1937- Larison, Cornelius Wilson,
1837-1910. Silvia Dubois . New York , 1988.
xxvii, 124 p. : ISBN 0-19-505239-0 DDC
305.5/67/0924 B 19
E444.D83 L37 1988   *NYPL [JFC 88-2191]*

Lobel, Jules. A Less than perfect union . New
York , 1988. vii, 424 p. ; ISBN 0-85345-738-7 :
DDC 342.73/029 347.30229 19
KF4550.A2 L47 1987   *NYPL [Sc D 88-724]*

LOCAL ADMINISTRATION. see **LOCAL
GOVERNMENT.**

LOCAL GOVERNMENT - LESOTHO.
Van de Geer, Roeland. Government and
development in rural Lesotho /. Roma,
Lesotho , 1982, 1984 printing. 159 p. ;
                                        NYPL [Sc D 89-52]

LOCAL GOVERNMENT - NIGERIA.
Gboyega, Alex. Political values and local
government in Nigeria /. lagos , 1987. xii, 200
p. ; ISBN 978-260-103-9
                                        NYPL [Sc D 88-1372]

Oyediran, Oyeleye. Essays on local government
and administration in Nigeria /. Surulere,
Lagos, Nigeria , 1988. x, 286 p. ; ISBN
978-277-801-001   *NYPL [Sc D 88-1365]*

Readings in Nigerian local government /. Ile-Ife
[1986?] 274 p. ;   *NYPL [Sc D 89-501]*

LOCAL GOVERNMENT - SOUTH AFRICA.
Mashabela, Harry. Townships of the PWV /.
Braamfontein, Johannesburg , 1988. 184 p. ;
    ISBN 0-86982-343-4 *NYPL [Sc D 89-155]*

**LOCAL GOVERNMENT - SOUTH AFRICA -
HOMELANDS.**
Rural development administration in South
Africa /. Pretoria , 1987. 70 p. : ISBN
0-7983-0100-7   *NYPL [Sc F 88-309]*

LOCAL GOVERNMENT - SUDAN - ABYEI.
Salih, Mohamed Abdel Rahim M. Abeyi,
administration and public services [microform]
/. Khartoum , 1978. 27 leaves ;
                                        NYPL [Sc Micro F-11039]

LOCAL GOVERNMENT - TOGO.
Agbodjan, Combévi. Institutions politiques et
organisation administrative du Togo /. [S.l. ,
between 1981 and 1984] 134 leaves, [1] folded
leaf of plates ; DDC 320.966/81 19
JQ3532 .A37 1981   *NYPL [Sc D 88-224]*

LOCAL GOVERNMENT - ZIMBABWE.
Bratton, Michael. Beyond community
development . London , 1978. 62 p. :
HN802.Z9 C62   *NYPL [JLD 81-437]*

**LOCAL OFFICIALS AND EMPLOYEES -
NIGERIA - FICTION.**
Ogunyemi, M. A. The D.O. /. Ibadan , 1987. v.
126 p. ; ISBN 978-15-4777-4 (Nigeria)
                                        NYPL [Sc C 88-176]

LOCARNO. CONFERENCE, 1925.
Durant, Franck Alphonse. Rétrospectives
[microform] . Port-au-Prince, Haiti , 1977. 16
p. ;   *NYPL [Sc Micro F 10,933]*

Locha Mateso. Littérature africaine et sa critique
/ Locha Mateso. Paris : A.C.C.T. ; Karthala,
c1986. 399 p. ; 22 cm. Bibliography: p. [369]-394.
    ISBN 2-86537-153-0 DDC 840/.9/896 19
*1. African literature (French) and criticism. 2.
African literature (French) - 20th century - History and
criticism. I. Title.*
PQ3981 .L6 1986   *NYPL [Sc D 88-1392]*

**LOCKE, ALAIN LEROY, 1886-1954 -
PHILOSOPHY.**
The Philosophy of Alain Locke . Philadelphia ,
1989. x, 332 p. : ISBN 0-87722-584-2 (alk. paper)
DDC 191 19
E185.97.L79 P48 1989 *NYPL [Sc D 89-494]*

Locke, David, 1949- Drum gahu : a systematic
method for an African percussion piece / by
David Locke ; [illustrations by Steve Leicach].
Crown Point, Ind. : White Cliffs Media Co.,
c1987. ix, 142 p. : ill., music ; 24 cm.
(Performance in world music series . no. 1) Includes
index. Bibliography: p. 134-135. ISBN
0-941677-03-6 :   DDC 789/.01 19
*1. Gahu - Instruction and study. 2. Dance music -
Africa, West - Instruction and study. 3. Ewe (African

people) - Music - Instruction and study. I. Title. II.
Series.*
MT655 .L6 1987   *NYPL [Sc E 88-391]*

Locuções tradicionais no Brasil . Cascudo, Luís
de Câmara, 1898- Belo Horizonte , São Paulo ,
1986. 314 p. :   *NYPL [Sc D 87-923]*

Lodge, Tom, fl. 1979- Resistance and ideology in
settler societies /. Johannesburg, Athens, Ohio ,
1986. viii, 222 p. ; ISBN 0-86975-304-5
                                        NYPL [Sc D 88-1093]

Lodimus, Robert. Le Crépuscule ensanglante :
Poèmes / Robert Lodimus ; illustrations par
l'auteur. [Port-au-Prince : Imprimerie M.
Nemours, 1983?] 64 p. : ill. ; 22 cm.
I. Title.   *NYPL [Sc D 88-67]*

Lody, Raul. Coleção Arthur Ramos / Raul Lody.
[Fortaleza] : Universidade Federal do Ceará,
1987. 78 p. : ill. ; 22 cm. Bibliography: p. 77-78.
    ISBN 85-24-60035-7
*1. Ramos, Arthur, 1903-1949. 2. Blacks - Brazil - Social
life and customs. 3. Museums - Brazil. I. Title.*
                                        NYPL [Sc D 89-479]

Lody, Raul Giovanni da Motta. Candomblé :
religião e resistência cultural / Raul Lody. São
Paulo : Editora Atica, 1987. 85 p. ; 18 cm.
(Série Princípios . 108) Bibliography: p. 82-85. ISBN
85-08-01877-0
1. Brazil - Religious life and customs. I. Title. II. Series.
                                        NYPL [Sc C 88-62]

**LOFA COUNTY, LIBERIA - INTELLECTUAL
LIFE.**
The Effects of the Western culture on the
traditional cultures of Lofa County
[microform] . [Monrovia , 1977] 24 p. ;
                                        NYPL [Sc Micro F-10952]

Lofa University Students Association. The Effects
of the Western culture on the traditional
cultures of Lofa County [microform] .
[Monrovia , 1977] 24 p. ;
                                        NYPL [Sc Micro F-10952]

Lofchie, Michael F. The policy factor :
agricultural performance in Kenya and Tanzania
/ Michael F. Lofchie. Boulder, Colo. : L.
Rienner Publishers ; Nairobi : Heinemann
Kenya, c1989. xii, 235 p. : ill. ; 24 cm. (Food in
Africa series) Includes index. Bibliography: p. 224-229.
    ISBN 1-555-87136-4 (alk. paper) : DDC
338.1/86762 19
*1. Agriculture and state - Kenya. 2. Agriculture and
state - Tanzania. I. Title. II. Series.*
HD2126.5.Z8 L64 1989
                                        NYPL [Sc E 89-123]

Logan, Harold G. A study of the inclusion of
Black administrators in American medical
schools, 1968-78, and their perception of their
roles [microform] / Harold G. Logan. 1982. v,
90 leaves : ill., forms ; 29 cm. "Graduate School of
Education." Thesis (Ed. D.)--Rutgers University, 1982.
Bibliography: leaves 79-80. Microfilm. Ann Arbor,
Mich. : University Microfilms International, 1982. 1
reel ; 35 mm.
*1. Afro-American executives - United States. 2. Medical
colleges - United States - Administration. I. Title.*
                                        NYPL [Sc Micro R-4793]

**Loi relative aux colonies, & aux moyens d'y
appaiser les troubles .** France. Assemblée
nationale legislative, 1791-1792. A Niort , 1792.
6 p. ;   *NYPL [Sc Rare F 82-68]*

Loiola, Ignazio di, Saint. see **Loyola, Ignacio de,
Saint, 1491-1556.**

Lola frontline drama series.
Aderinlewo, 'Dele. Youths in revolt . Ibadan,
Oyo State, Nigeria , 1985. 63 p. : ISBN
978-18-0006-2   *NYPL [Sc C 88-293]*

LOMÉ (TOGO) - ECONOMIC CONDITIONS.
Cordonnier, Rita. Femmes africaines et
commerce . Paris , 1987. 190 p. ; ISBN
2-85802-901-6   *NYPL [Sc E 88-368]*

LOMELÍN, AMBROSIO, FL. 1663-1674.
Vega Franco, Marisa. El tráfico de esclavos con
América . Sevilla , 1984. x, 220 p. : ISBN
84-00-05675-2 DDC 382/.44/09729 19
HT985 .V44 1984   *NYPL [Sc C 89-132]*

London. African Institution. see **African
Institution, London.**

London. Central Criminal Court. Zulueta, Pedro
de, Jr. Trial of Pedro de Zulueta, Jun. .
London , 1844. lxxiv, 410 p. ;
                                        NYPL [Sc Rare F 88-1]

London. Courts. Central Criminal Court. see
London. Central Criminal Court.

LONDON (ENGLAND) - RACE RELATIONS.
Pilkington, Edward. Beyond the mother
country . London , 1988. 182 p. ; ISBN
1-85043-113-2 DDC 305.8/96/041 19
NYPL [Sc D 89-122]

**LONDON (ENGLAND) - RACE RELATIONS
SERIES.**
Hewitt, Roger. White talk, black talk .
Cambridge [Cambridgeshire] , New York ,
1986. x, 253 p. ; ISBN 0-521-26239-9 DDC
401/.9/094216 19
P40.45.G7 H48 1986   *NYPL [JFE 87-279]*

London. Old Bailey. see **London. Central
Criminal Court.**

London Strategic Policy Unit. India in the
Caribbean /. London , 1987. 326 p. : ISBN
1-87051-805-5 (cased) : DDC 909/.09182/1081
19   *NYPL [Sc D 88-997]*

Lone Ranger in Pakistan /. Samuel, Julian.
Peterborough, Ontario , 1986. 51 p. : ISBN
0-919740-01-4   *NYPL [Sc D 88-70]*

Lonely crusade . Himes, Chester B., 1909- New
York , c1986. x, 398 p. ; ISBN 0-938410-37-7
(pbk.) : DDC 813/.54 19
PS3515.I713 L6 1986   *NYPL [Sc D 88-1362]*

Lonely men /. Olugbile, Femi. Nigeria , 1987.
183 p. ; ISBN 978-13-9605-9
NYPL [Sc C 88-336]

**LONG ISLAND RAIL ROAD - EMPLOYEES -
BIOGRAPHY.**
Branchcomb, Sylvia Woingust. Son, never give
up /. [Yonkers, N.Y.?] , 1979. 36 p. :
NYPL [Sc D 88-568]

Longino, Helen E. Competition, a feminist taboo?
/. New York , 1987. xvi, 260 p. ; ISBN
0-935312-74-9 (pbk.) : DDC 305.4/2 19
HQ1206 .C69 1987   *NYPL [JFE 88-6669]*

Longman guides to literature.
Wren, Robert M. Chinua Achebe, Things fall
apart /. London , 1980. vi, 56 p. ; ISBN
0-582-60109-6   *NYPL [Sc C 88-88]*

Longman social studies : a junior secondary
course. Nigeria : Longman Nigeria, [1984?]- v. :
ill., maps ; 30 cm. ISBN 0-582-65043-7
*1. Social sciences - Study and teaching (Secondary) -
Nigeria.*   *NYPL [Sc F 88-350]*

Longstreet, Stephen, 1907- Storyville to Harlem :
fifty years in the jazz scene / Stephen
Longstreet. New Brunswick, N.J. : Rutgers
University Press, c1986. 211 p. : chiefly ill. ; 31
cm. ISBN 0-8135-1174-7 : DDC 785.42/09 19
*1. Jazz music - Pictorial works. 2. Jazz musicians -
Portraits. I. Title.*
ML87 .L66 1986   *NYPL [Sc G 87-4]*

Lonsdale, John. South Africa in question /.
Cambridge, Cambridgeshire , Portsmouth, NH ,
c1988. x, 244 p. : ISBN 0-85255-325-0 DDC
305.8/00968 19
DT763 .S6428 1988   *NYPL [Sc D 88-841]*

Look for me in the whirlwind . Barron, Charles.
[Brooklyn, NY] , c1987. v, 60 p. : DDC
305.8/96073 19
E185.97.G3 B37 1987
NYPL [Sc D 88-1501]

Look out for the ostriches! Juta, Jan. New York ,
1949. xii, 177 p.
DT757 .J8   *NYPL [Sc D 89-90]*

Looking at lands.
James, Winston. The Caribbean /. London ,
1984. 46 p. : ISBN 0-356-07105-7 : DDC 972.9
19
F2175   *NYPL [Sc F 88-128]*

Looking at the Caribbean. James, Winston. The
Caribbean /. London , 1984. 46 p. : ISBN
0-356-07105-7 : DDC 972.9 19
F2175   *NYPL [Sc F 88-128]*

The looking down game. Dean, Leigh. New York
[1968] 34 p. DDC [Fic]
PZ7.D3446 Lo   *NYPL [Sc D 89-111]*

Looman, Theodorus Matthijs, 1816-1900. Tucker,
Charlotte Maria, 1821-1893. Abbeokoeta.
Amsterdam, 1860. viii, 330 p.
NYPL [Sc Rare C 88-25]

Loos, Adolf, 1870-1933.
Groenendijk, Paul. Adolf Loos . Rotterdam ,

1985. 39 p., [6] leaves of plates : ISBN
90-6450-027-4 DDC 728.3/72/0228 19
NA1011.5.L6 G76 1985   *NYPL [Sc F 89-67]*

**LOOS, ADOLF, 1870-1933 - CRITICISM AND
INTERPRETATION.**
Groenendijk, Paul. Adolf Loos . Rotterdam ,
1985. 39 p., [6] leaves of plates : ISBN
90-6450-027-4 DDC 728.3/72/0228 19
NA1011.5.L6 G76 1985   *NYPL [Sc F 89-67]*

Lopes da Silva, Baltasar, 1907- Os trabalhos e os
dias / Baltazar Lopes. Praia, Cabo Verde :
Instituto Caboverdiano do Livro, 1987. 83 p. :
port ; 23 cm. (Colecção Para a história das literaturas
africanas de expressão portuguesa . 6) Short stories.
1. Cape Verde - Fiction. I. Title. II. Series.
NYPL [Sc D 88-1500]

Lopes Filho, João. Cabo Verde : apontamentos
etnográficos / João Lopes Filho. Lisboa : [s.n.],
1976. 54 p., [5] leaves of plates : ill. ; 21 cm.
Bibliography: p. 39-40. CONTENTS. - Contribuição
para o estudo da habitação rural em Santiago de Cabo
Verde.--Berimbau e cimbó, dois intrumentos musicais
em vias de desaparecimento no Arquipélago de Cabo
Verde.
*1. Dwellings - Cape Verde Islands - São Tiago. 2.
Musical instruments - Cape Verde Islands.*
NYPL [Sc D 84-279]

Lopes, Francisco Antonio, 1882- Alvares Maciel
no degrêdo de Angola. [Rio de Janeiro] :
Ministerio da Educação e Cultura, Serviço de
Documentação, 1958. 104 p. ; 22 cm. (Coleção
Aspectos. [36])
*1. Maciel, José Alvares, 1761-1804. 2. Iron industry
and trade - Angola. 3. Minas Gerais, Brazil - History. I.
Title.*
HD9527.A22 L6   *NYPL [Sc D 88-419]*

Lopes, Helena Theodoro. Negro e cultura no
Brasil / Helena Theodoro Lopes, José Jorge
Siqueira, Maria Beatriz Nascimento. Rio de
Janeiro : UNIBRADE-Centro de Cultura :
UNESCO, 1987. 136 p. ; 22 cm. (Pequena
enciclopédia da cultura brasileira) Includes
bibliographies. ISBN 85-85108-02-9 DDC
981/.00496 19
*1. Blacks - Brazil. 2. Brazil - Civilization - African
influences. 3. Brazil - Social life and customs. I.
Siqueira, José Jorge. II. Nascimento, Maria Beatriz. III.
Title. IV. Series.*
F2659.N4 L67 1987   *NYPL [Sc D 88-1291]*

Lopes, Henri, 1937-
Tribaliks : contemporary Congolese stories /
Henri Lopes ; translated by Andrea Leskes.
London : Heinemann, 1987. 86 p. ; 20 cm.
(African writers series) Translation of: Tribaliques.
Includes bibliographical references. ISBN
0-435-90762-X
1. Congo (Brazzaville) - Fiction. I. Title.
NYPL [Sc C 88-20]

**LOPES, HENRI, 1937- - CRITICISM AND
INTERPRETATION.**
Malanda, Ange-Séverin. Henri Lopes et
l'impératif romanesque /. Paris , c1987. 142 p. ;
ISBN 2-09-387190-6   *NYPL [Sc D 89-207]*

Lopes, Luis Carlos. O espelho e a imagem : o
escravo na historiografia brasileira (1808-1920)
/ Luís Carlos Lopes. Rio de Janeiro : Achiamé,
1987. 126 p. ; 21 cm. Bibliography: p. 115-126.
*1. Slavery - Brazil - History. 2. Brazil - History -
Historiography.*   *NYPL [Sc D 88-350]*

Lopes, Manuel. Os flagelados do vento leste /
Manuel Lopes. 2a. ed. Lisboa : Edições 70,
c1985. 216 p. ; 22 cm. (Autores de Cabo Verde)
1. Cape Verde - Fiction. I. Title. II. Series.
NYPL [Sc D 88-1387]

Lorenz, Bente. Traditional Zambian pottery / text
by Bente Lorenz ; photography by Margaret
plesner. London : Ethnographica ; 1989. 47 p. :
ill. ; 19 x 20 cm. ISBN 0-905788-75-3
1. Pottery - Zambia. I. Plesner, Margaret. II. Title.
NYPL [Sc C 89-141]

Loring, Ellis Gray. Massachusetts Anti-Slavery
Society. Board of Managers. An address to the
abolitionists of Massachusetts, on the subject of
political action /. [Boston , 1838] 20 p. ;
NYPL [Sc Rare G 86-10]

Lornell, Kip, 1953- Happy in the service of the
Lord : Afro-American gospel quartets in
Memphis / Kip Lornell. Urbana : University of
Illinois Press, c1988. x, 171 p. ; [30] p. of
plates : ill. ; 24 cm. (Music in American life)
Includes index. Bibliography: p. [159]-164. ISBN

0-252-01523-1 (alk. paper) DDC
783.7/08996073/0976819 19
*1. Gospel music - Tennessee - Memphis - History and
criticism. I. Title.*
ML3187 .L67 1988   *NYPL [Sc E 89-101]*

**Los Angeles. Basketball Team (National
Basketball Association)** see **Los Angeles
Lakers (Basketball team)**

**LOS ANGELES LAKERS (BASKETBALL
TEAM) - HISTORY.**
Ostler, Scott. Winnin' times . New York ,
c1988. 304 p. ; ISBN 0-02-029591-X (pbk.) DDC
796.32/364/0979494 19
GV885.52.L67 O87 1986
NYPL [Sc D 89-106]

Lossen, Yollen. Jallier, Maurice. Musique aux
Antilles =. Paris , c1985. 145 p., [16] p. of
plates : ISBN 2-903033-65-X : DDC
780/.42/09729 19
ML3486.G8 J3 1985   *NYPL [Sc D 87-576]*

The lost child /. Ngongwikuo, Joseph A. Limbé,
S.W. Province, Cameroon [1986?] 76 p. :
ISBN 978-250-304-5   *NYPL [Sc D 88-496]*

Lost illusions : Caribbean minorities in Britain
and the Netherlands / edited by Malcolm Cross
and Han Entzinger. London : Routledge, 1988.
x, 316 p. : maps ; 23 cm. Includes indexes.
Bibliography: p. [285]-301. CONTENTS. - Caribbean
minorities in Britain and the Netherlands / Malcolm
Cross and Han Entzinger -- Workers of the night /
Alistair Hennessy -- Caribbean migration to the
Netherlands / Gert J. Oostindie -- Mobility denied /
Malcolm Cross and Mark Johnson -- On the way
up?-Surinamese and Antilleans in the Dutch labour
market / Theo Reubsaet -- Race, class, and residence /
Peter Ratcliffe -- Surinamese settlement in Amsterdam,
1973-83 / Leo de Klerk and Hans van Amersfoort --
British schooling and the reproduction of racial
inequality / Barry Troyna -- Education, the way up for
the Surinamese in the Netherlands? / William Koot and
Petrien Uniken Venema -- Caribbean business enterprise
in Britain / Robin Ward -- Culture, structure, and
ethnic enterprise / Jeremy Boissevain and Hanneke
Grotenbreg -- Afro-Caribbean involvement in British
politics / Marian FitzGerald -- Mobilization of ethnicity
in Dutch politics / Jan Rath. ISBN 0-415-00628-7
*1. West Indians - Great Britain - Social conditions. 2.
West Indians - Netherlands - Social conditions. 3.
Surinamese - Netherlands - Social conditions. I. Cross,
Malcolm. II. Entzinger, H. B., 1947-. III. Title:
Caribbean minorities in Britain and the Netherlands.*
NYPL [Sc D 88-1300]

LOST TRIBES OF ISRAEL - MISCELLANEA.
'Isā 'Abd Allāh Muḥammad al-Mahdī, 1945-
The tribe Israel is no more [microform] /.
Brooklyn [197-?] 62 p. :
NYPL [Sc Micro R-4114 no. 13]

The lost world of the Kalahari . Van der Post,
Laurens. London , 1988. 261 p. :
NYPL [Sc F 88-381]

Loth, Heinrich.
**Afrika unter imperialistischer
Kolonialherrschaft und die Formierung der
antikolonialen Kräfte, 1884-1945.**
Geschichte Afrikas. Afrika : Geschichte von
den Anfängen bis zur Gegenwart. Köln ,
1979- v. : ISBN 3-7609-0433-5 (v. 1) : DDC
960 19
DT20 .G47 1979   *NYPL [JFK 82-28]*

[Frau im Alten Afrika. English]
Woman in ancient Africa / by Heinrich
Loth ; translated from the German by Sheila
Marnie. Westport, Conn. : L. Hill & Co.,
c1987. 189 p. : ill. (some col.) ; 28 cm.
Translation of: Die Frau im Alten Afrika. Includes
index. Bibliography: p. [183]-186. ISBN
0-88208-218-3 DDC 305.4/096 19
*1. Women - Africa - History. 2. Africa - Social life and
customs. I. Title.*
HQ1137.A35 L6813 1987
NYPL [Sc F 88-132]

Woman of ancient Africa / by Heinrich
Loth ; translated from the German by Sheila
Marnie. Westport, Conn. : L. Hill & Co.,
c1987. 189 p. : ill. (some col.) ; 28 cm.
Translation of: Die Frau im Alten Afrika. Includes
index. Bibliography: p. [183]-186. ISBN
0-88208-218-3 DDC 305.4/096 19
*1. Women - Africa - History. 2. Africa - Social life and
customs. I. Title.*
HQ1137.A35 L6813 1987
NYPL [Sc F 88-114]

Louis Armstrong . Collier, James Lincoln, 1928-
New York , c1985. 165 p. : ISBN 0-02-722830-4
DDC 785.42/092/4 B 92 19
ML3930.A75 C67 1985
NYPL [Sc D 86-229]

Louis Armstrong /. Tanenhaus, Sam. New York ,
c1989. 127 p. : ISBN 1-555-46571-4 DDC
785.42/092/4 B 92 19
ML3930.A75 T3 1989   **NYPL [Sc E 89-170]**

Louis Armstrong, his life and times /. Pinfold,
Mike. New York , c1987. 143 p. : ISBN
0-87663-667-9 DDC 785.42/092/4 B 19
ML419.A75 P55 1987   **NYPL [Sc F 88-65]**

LOUIS, JOE, 1914-1981.
Barrow, Joe Louis. Joe Louis . New York ,
c1988. xvii, 270 p., [8] leaves of plates : ISBN
0-07-003955-0 : DDC 796.8/3/0924 B 19
GV1132.L6 B37 1988   **NYPL [Sc E 88-566]**

Louis, William Roger, 1936- Decolonization and
African independence . New Haven , 1988.
xxix, 651 p. ; ISBN 0-300-04070-9 DDC 960/.32
19
DT30.5 .D42 1988   **NYPL [Sc E 88-517]**

LOUISIANA - FICTION.
Shaik, Fatima, 1952- The mayor of New
Orleans . Berkeley , 1987. 143 p. ; ISBN
0-88739-050-1 : DDC 813/.54 19
PS3569.H316 M39 1987
NYPL [JFD 88-11303]

Loutard, J. B. Tati- see Tati-Loutard, J. B.

Loutfi, Martha Fetherolf. Rural women : unequal
partners in development / Martha Fetherolf
Loutfi.5th impression with modifications.
Geneva : International Labour Office, c1980
(1985 printing) v, 81 p., [4] p. of plates : ill. ;
24 cm. (A WEP study) Bibliography: p. [75]-81.
ISBN 92-2-102389-3 (pbk).
*1. Women in rural development. 2. Rural women -
Developing countries - Economic conditions. 3. Rural
women - Developing countries - Social conditions. I.
Title. II. Series.*   **NYPL [Sc E 89-67]**

Louw, Leon. South Africa : the solution / Leon
Louw & Frances Kendall. Bisho, Ciskei : Amagi
Publications, 1986. xvi, 238 p. : ill. ; 22 cm.
Bibliography: p. 235-237. ISBN 0-620-09371-4 (pbk.)
DDC 306/.0968 19
*1. Social predictions - South Africa. 2. South Africa -
Social conditions. 3. South Africa - Economic
conditions. I. Title.*
HN801.A8 L68 1986   **NYPL [Sc D 88-197]**

Love at first flight /. Abejo, Bisi. Ibadan,
Nigeria , 1986. 241 p. ;
MLCS 87/7911 (P)   **NYPL [Sc C 88-367]**

Love with no regrets . Torkington, Percy
Anthony Thomas, 1931- Liverpool , 1988. 232
p. ;   **NYPL [Sc D 89-368]**

Love without questions /. Rogers, Braima.
Freetown , 1986. 86 p. ;
NYPL [Sc D 89-415]

Lovelace, Earl. A brief conversion and other
stories / Earl Lovelace. Oxford [Eng.] :
Heinemann International, 1988. 141 p. ; 20 cm.
(Caribbean writers series) ISBN 0-435-98882-4
1. Trinidad - Fiction. I. Title.
NYPL [Sc C 89-43]

Lovelace, Maud Hart, 1892- The valentine box /
by Maud Hart Lovelace ; illustrated by Ingrid
Fetz. New York : Crowell, 1966. [48] p. : ill. ;
22 cm. SCHOMBURG CHILDREN'S
COLLECTION.
*1. Afro-American children - Juvenile fiction. I. Fetz,
Ingrid. II. Schomburg Children's Collection. III. Title.*
PZ7.L9561 Val   **NYPL [Sc D 89-115]**

Lovell, John, 1907- Black song : the forge and
the flame : the story of how the Afro-American
spiritual was hammered out / John Lovell,
Jr.1st U. S. pbk. ed. New York : Paragon
House, 1986, c1972. xviii, 686 p. : ill. ; 23 cm.
Includes indexes. Bibliography: p. 587-635. Reprint.
Originally published: New York : Macmillan, 1972.
ISBN 0-913729-53-1 (pbk.) DDC 783.6/7/09 19
*1. Spirituals (Songs) - History and criticism. 2.
Afro-Americans - Music - History and criticism. 3. Folk
music - United States - History and criticism. 4.
Folk-songs, English - United States - History and
criticism. I. Title.*
ML3556 .L69 1986   **NYPL [Sc D 88-421]**

Lovesong . Lester, Julius. New York, N.Y. ,
c1988. 248 p., [4] leaves of plates : ISBN

0-8050-0588-9 DDC 296.8/346/0924 B 19
BM755.L425 A3 1988   NYPL [Sc E 88-317]

LOW INCOME HOUSING. see HOUSING.

LOWE, SYLVIA - ART COLLECTIONS.
Baking in the sun . Lafayette , c1987. 146 p. :
ISBN 0-295-96606-8   **NYPL [Sc F 88-197]**

LOWE, WARREN - ART COLLECTIONS.
Baking in the sun . Lafayette , c1987. 146 p. :
ISBN 0-295-96606-8   **NYPL [Sc F 88-197]**

Loy, Harry Jong, 1901-1984. Fosten tori / Harry
Jong Loy. [Paramaribo] : Afdeling Cultuur
Studies, Ministerie van Onderwijs,
Wentenschappen en Cultuur, c1987. v. : ill. ; 22
cm. ISBN 999-14-1010-4
*1. Creole dialects, Dutch - Surinam - Texts. 2.
Surinam - Fiction.*   **NYPL [Sc D 88-921]**

Loyalties /. Maja-Pearce, Adewale. Harlow ,
1986. 152 p. ; ISBN 0-582-78628-2 (pbk) : DDC
823 19   **NYPL [Sc C 89-56]**

LOYOLA, IGNACIO DE, SAINT, 1491-1556.
Jésuite en Afrique [microform] . Douala
[Cameroon] , 19. 43 p. :
NYPL [Sc Micro R-4135 no.10]

LOZI LANGUAGE - TEXTS.
Mukuni, R. M., 1929- U zibe mutu /.
[Lusaka] , c1976. 54 p. :
PL8460.9.M77 U2 1976   **NYPL [Sc C 89-37]**

Lu, Georzef. Woman of my uncle / Georzef Lu.
Lusaka : NECZAM, 1985. iv, 236 p. ; 19 cm.
(NECZAM library series. E6)
1. Zambia - Fiction. I. Title.
MLCS 87/7908 (P)   **NYPL [Sc C 89-94]**

LUBA (AFRICAN PEOPLE)
Kabengele Munanga. Os Basanga de Shaba .
Sao Palulo , 1986. 334 p. :
NYPL [Sc B 88-7]

Lubeck, Sally. Sandbox society : early education
in black and white America / Sally Lubeck.
London ; Philadelphia : Falmer Press, 1985. xv,
177 p. : ill. ; 24 cm. Includes indexes. Bibliography:
p. 153-165. ISBN 1-85000-051-4 DDC
372/.21/0977 19
*1. Education, Preschool - Middle West - Cross-cultural
studies. 2. Head start programs - Middle West -
Cross-cultural studies. 3. Child rearing - Middle West -
Cross-cultural studies. I. Title.*
LB1140.24.M53 L8 1985
NYPL [Sc E 89-80]

Lubu ku lebri ku mortu : i utrus storya di
Guiné-Bissau / seleson i Adaptason Augusto
Pereira ; Illustrason, Paulo dos Santos.Ed.
bilingue. Bissau : Editora Nimba, da Direcção
Geral da Cultura, 1988. 49 p. : ill. ; 29 cm. In
Portuguese and Creole.
*1. Tales - Guinea-Bissau. 2. Creole dialects,
Portuguese - Guinea-Bissau - Texts. I. Pereira, Augusto.
II. Santos, Paulo dos. III. Title.*
NYPL [Sc F 88-351]

Luc, Napoléon Serge. Histoire du déchoukage /
de Napoléon Serge Luc. [Port-au-Prince, Haiti,
W.I.] . N. S. Luc, [1987?] 124 p. : ill., ports. ;
22 cm. Imprint from p. 104.
*1. Gonaïves (Haiti) - History. 2. Haiti - History -
1971-. I. Title.*   **NYPL [Sc D 87-1419]**

Luchando por la patria nueva . Hurtado
González, Jaime. Quito , 1987. ii, 178 p. :
NYPL [Sc D 88-679]

Luck, love and life : a book of experience / by
adults learning to read. [Ft. Lauderdale, Fla. :
Broward County Library, Special Services
Dept., "Read Campaign", 1987] 50 p. ill. ; 22
cm.   **NYPL [Sc D 88-1465]**

Lucky mischief /. Burgwin, Mebane (Holoman)
New York , 1949. 246 p. :
NYPL [Sc D 88-1513]

**LUCUMÍ (CULTUS) see SANTERIA
(CULTUS)**

Ludie's song /. Herlihy, Dirlie. New York ,
c1988. 212 p. ; ISBN 0-8037-0533-6 : DDC [Fic]
19
PZ7.H43126 Lu 1988   **NYPL [Sc D 89-132]**

Lugenia Burns Hope, Black southern reformer /.
Rouse, Jacqueline Anne. Athens , c1989. xi,
182 p., [8] p. of plates : ISBN 0-8203-1082-4 (alk.
paper) DDC 973/.0496073024 B 19
E185.97.H717 R68 1989
NYPL [Sc D 89-469]

LUMUMBA, PATRICE, 1925-1961.
Manya K'Omalowete a Djonga, 1950- Patrice
Lumumba, le Sankuru et l'Afrique . Lutry
[1985] 166 p. :   **NYPL [Sc D 88-1490]**

**LUNAR EXPEDITIONS. see SPACE FLIGHT
TO THE MOON.**

**LUNCH ROOMS. see RESTAURANTS,
LUNCH ROOMS, ETC.**

Lundahl, Mats, 1946- Hedlund, Hans G. B.
Migration and change in rural Zambia /.
Uppsala , 1983. 107 p. : ISBN 91-7106-220-3
(pbk.) DDC 960 s 307/.2 19
DT1 .N64 no. 70 HB1955
NYPL [JLD 85-587]

Lundy, Harold Wayne. A study of the transition
from white to Black presidents at three selected
schools founded by the American Missionary
Association [microform] / by Harold W. Lundy.
1978. 676 leaves. Thesis (Ph. D.)--University of
Wisconsin, Madison, 1978. Bibliography: leaves
671-673. Microfilm of typescript. Ann Arbor, Mich.:
University Microfilms International, 1979. 1 microfilm
reel ; 35 mm.
*1. American Missionary Association. 2. Afro-American
universities and colleges - Administration. I. Title.*
NYPL [Sc Micro R-4216]

Luneau, René. Laisse aller mon peuple! : églises
africaines au-delà des modèles? / René
Luneau ; préface du P. Boka di Mpasi Londi.
Paris : Karthala, c1987. 193 p. ; 22 cm. Includes
bibliographical references. ISBN 2-86537-173-5
DDC 282/.6 19
*1. Catholic Church - Africa. 2. Africa - Church history.
I. Title.*
BX1675 .L86 1987   **NYPL [Sc D 88-315]**

Lunemann, Evelyn. Tip off. Illus. by Tony Paul.
Westchester, Ill., Benefic Press [1969] 70 p. col.
illus. 24 cm. (Sports mystery series) After he injures
his foot and unknowingly causes his replacement to be
removed from the team, Center City's star basketball
player hurt he must spur his team on to victory.
DDC [Fic]
*1. Basketball - Juvenile fiction. I. Paul, Tony, illus. II.
Title.*
PZ7.L979115 Ti   **NYPL [Sc E 88-533]**

Lungu, Gatian F. Administrative decentralisation
in the Zambian bureaucracy : an analysis of
environmental constraints / by Gatian F.
Lungu. Gweru, Zimbabwe : published on behalf
of the Institute for African Studies, University
of Zambia, Lusaka, by Mambo Press, c1985. 85
p. : ill. ; 23 cm. (Zambian papers. no.' 18) Originally
written as part of the M.P.A. thesis submitted to the
University of Massachusetts in 1980. Bibliography: p.
81-85.
*1. Decentralization in government - Zambia. 2. Civil
service - Zambia. 3. Zambia - Politics and government -
1964-. I. Title. II. Series.*   **NYPL [Sc D 89-318]**

LUO (AFRICAN PEOPLE)
Cohen, David William. Siaya, a historical
anthropology of an African landscape .
London , Athens , 1989. viii, 152 p., [8] p. of
plates : ISBN 0-8214-0901-8 DDC 967.6/2 19
DT433.545.L85 C64 1988
NYPL [Sc D 89-354]

Lurry-Wright, Jerome Wendell, 1941- Custom
and conflict on a Bahamian out-island / Jerome
Wendell Lurry-Wright. Lanham, MD :
University Press of America, c1987. xxii, 188
p. ; 22 cm. Includes indexes. Bibliography: p.
171-180. ISBN 0-8191-6097-0 (alk. paper) : DDC
347.7296 347.29607 19
*1. Justice, Administration of - Bahamas - Mayaguana
Island. 2. Dispute resolution (Law) - Bahamas -
Mayaguana Island. 3. Law and anthropology. 4.
Mayaguana Island (Bahamas) - Social life and customs.
I. Title.*
KGL210 .L87 1987   **NYPL [Sc D 88-218]**

Lusambu Kauy Mutombo. Les Maitresses du feu
et de la cuisine . Bandundu, République du
Zaïre , 1983. 164 p. ;   **NYPL [Sc F 88-308]**

**LUTHERAN CHURCH - DOCTRINES -
CONGRESSES.**
Theology and the Black experience .
Minneapolis , c1988. 272 p. ; ISBN
0-8066-2353-5 DDC 284.1/08996 19
BX8065.2 .T48 1988   **NYPL [Sc D 89-353]**

Ly, Ibrahima. Les noctuelles vivent de larmes /
Ibrahima Ly. Paris : L'Harmattan, c1988- v. ;
22 cm. (Encres noires. 50) CONTENTS. - [V.] 1.
Ténèbres blanches. ISBN 2-7384-0066-3

*1. Africa - Fiction. I. Series: Collection Encres noires,
50. II. Title.* **NYPL [Sc D 88-1338]**

Ly, Madina. Pala, Achola O. [Femme africaine
dans la société précoloniale. Spanish.] La mujer
africana en la sociedad precolonial / . Barcelona
[Paris?] , 1982. 238 p. ; ISBN 84-85800-35-4
(Serbal) **NYPL [Sc D 88-833]**

Lynch, Lorenzo, 1932- The hot dog man. [1st ed.]
Indianapolis, Bobbs-Merrill [1970] [24] p. col.
illus. 23 x 29 cm. A trip with the Hot Dog Man
around the city. SCHOMBURG CHILDREN'S
COLLECTION. DDC [Fic]
*1. City and town life - Juvenile fiction. I. Schomburg
Children's Collection. II. Title.*
PZ7.L97977 Ho **NYPL [Sc F 88-253]**

Lynch Street . Spofford, Tim. Kent, Ohio ,
c1988. 219 p., [1] leaf of plates : ISBN
0-87338-355-9 (alk. paper) DDC 976.2/51 19
F349.J13 S66 1988 **NYPL [Sc E 89-27]**

Lynch, Tony. Callender, Timothy. The watchman
/ . [St. Michael, Barbados? , 1978?] [28] p. :
NYPL [Sc F 89-52]

The lynchers /. Wideman, John Edgar. New
York , 1986. 264 p. ; ISBN 0-8050-0118-2 (pbk.) :
DDC 813/.54 19
PS3573.I26 L9 1986 **NYPL [Sc D 88-306]**

LYNCHING - UNITED STATES.
Washington, Booker T. 1856-1915. Booker T.
Washington gives facts and condemns lynching
in a statement telegraphed to the New York
world. Baltimore , 1908. [3] p. ;
NYPL [Sc Rare C 89-25]

Lyons, Leonard. Jazz portraits : the lives and
music of the jazz masters / Len Lyons and
Don Perlo. New York : Morrow, c1989. 610
p. : ill., ports. ; 25 cm. Includes index. Bibliography:
p. 595-598. ISBN 0-688-04946-X DDC
785.42/092/2 B 19
*1. Jazz musicians - Biography. 2. Afro-American
musicians - Biography. I. Perlo, Don. II. Title.*
ML394 .L97 1989 **NYPL [Sc E 89-91]**

M. I. S. R. For corporate body represented by
these initials see: **Makerere Institute of
Social Research.**

M. P. L. A. see **Movimento Popular de
Libertação de Angola.**

M. R. A. see **Moral rearmament.**

Ma Nou l'esclave . Mattioni, Mario D.
Fort-de-France [Martinique] , 1986. 157 p. ;
ISBN 2-85275-111-9 DDC 843 19
PQ3949.2.M38 M3 1986
NYPL [Sc E 88-614]

Ma terre /. Kichenapanaïdou, Marc. Saint-Louis,
Réunion [1978?] 43 p. ;
NYPL [Sc D 88-484]

Maasai-Frauen . Mitzlaff, Ulrike von. München ,
1988. 181 p. : ISBN 3-923804-23-7
NYPL [Sc D 89-551]

The Maasai of Matapato . Spencer, Paul, 1932-
Bloomington , c1988. xii, 296 p. : ISBN
0-253-33625-2 DDC 306/.08996 19
DT433.545.M33 S64 1988
NYPL [JFE 88-7115]

Mabery, D. L. Janet Jackson / by D.L. Mabery.
Minneapolis : Lerner Publications Co., c1988.
32 p. : ill. (some col.) ; 23 cm. A biography of
Janet Jackson, "baby" in a famous family, who is not
only Michael Jackson's sister, but a strong singing
talent who has also worked in television.
SCHOMBURG CHILDREN'S COLLECTION. ISBN
0-8225-1618-7 (lib bdg.) : DDC 784.5/4/00924
B 920 19
*1. Jackson, Janet, 1966- - Juvenile literature. 2.
Singers - United States - Biography - Juvenile literature.
3. Afro-American singers - Biography - Juvenile
literature. I. Schomburg Children's Collection. II. Title.*
ML3930.J15 M3 1988
NYPL [Sc D 88-1460]

Mabi Mulumba. Cadres et dirigeants au Zaïre :
qui sont-ils? : dictionnaire biographique / Mabi
Mulumba, Mutamba Makombo. Kinshasa :
Editions du Centre de recherches pédagogiques,
1986. 541 p. : col. port. ; 25 cm. Includes index.
Bibliography: p. 511-513.
*1. Zaire - Biography. I. Mutamba Makombo, 1945-. II.
Title.* **NYPL [Sc E 88-322]**

Mabille, A. (Adolphe), 1836-1894. Southern
Sotho-English dictionary / by A. Mabille and
H. Dieterlen. Reclassified, rev. and enl. / by

R.A. Paroz. Morija, Lesotho : Morija Sesuto
Book Depot, 1950 (1974 printing) xvi, 445 p. ;
23 cm. "Seventh edition"--P. v. Rev. ed. of:
Sesuto-English dictionary. 6th ed. 1937.
*1. Sotho language - Dictionaries - English. I. Dieterlen,
H. II. Paroz, R. A. III. Title.*
PL8689.4 .M33 1974 **NYPL [Sc D 89-289]**

Mabuza, Vivian R. N. Inzondo engela mkhawulo
/ V.R.N. Mabuza. Gweru : Mambo Press, 1988.
120 p. ; 18 cm. (Mambo writers series. Ndebele
section ; v. 5) Title translated into English: Hatred
without limits. ISBN 0-86922-430-1
*1. Ndebele language (Zimbabwe) - Texts. I. Title. II.
Series.* **NYPL [Sc C 89-7]**

McAdam, Doug. Freedom Summer / by Doug
McAdam. New York : Oxford University Press,
c1988. [xiii], 333 p., [14] p. of plates : ill. ; 25
cm. Includes index. Bibliography: p. 311-322. ISBN
0-19-504367-7 (alk. paper) DDC
976.2/00496073 19
*1. Mississippi Freedom Project. 2. Afro-Americans -
Suffrage - Mississippi. 3. Civil rights workers -
Mississippi - History - 20th century. 4.
Afro-Americans - Civil rights - Mississippi. 5.
Mississippi - Race relations. I. Title.*
E185.93.M6 M28 1988 **NYPL [Sc E 88-563]**

McAdoo, Harriette Pipes. Black families / .
Newbury Park, Calif. , c1988. 323 p. ; ISBN
0-8039-3179-4 : DDC 305.8/96073 19
E185.86 .B525 1988 **NYPL [Sc D 89-338]**

McAllister, P. A. De Wet, C. J. Rural
communities in transition . Grahamstown
[1983] iii, 113 p., [6] leaves of plates : ISBN
0-86810-101-X (pbk.) DDC 307.7/2/0968 19
HD2130.5.Z9 H653 1983
NYPL [Sc F 88-328]

McCain, W. Calvin. Pieces of peace; concepts of
a poet. 1st ed. Jericho, N. Y., Exposition Press
[1974] 80 p. 21 cm. Poems.
I. Title. **NYPL [Sc D 78-61]**

McCall, Virginia, 1909- Adassa and her hen, by
Virginia Nielsen. Illustrated by Ursula Koering.
[New York] D. McKay Co. [1971] 79 p. illus.
22 cm. Except for a chance meeting with the Prime
Minister, a young Jamaican girl's troublesome pet hen
would have been sold at market. SCHOMBURG
CHILDREN'S COLLECTION. DDC [Fic]
*1. Chickens - Juvenile fiction. 2. Jamaica - Juvenile
fiction. I. Koering, Ursula, illus. II. Schomburg
Children's Collection. III. Title.*
PZ7.M12295 Ad **NYPL [Sc D 89-100]**

McCallan, E. A. (Ernest Albert), 1874- Life on
old St. David's, Bermuda / by E.A. McCallan.
2nd ed. Hamilton, Bermuda : Bermuda
Historical Society, 1986. 258 p., [26] p. of
plates : ill. ; c24 cm. Reprint. Previously published:
Hamilton : Bermuda Historical Monuments Trust, 1948.
Includes index. Bibliography: p. 246-248.
*1. McCallan, E. A. (Ernest Albert), 1874-. 2. Saint
David's Island (Bermuda Islands) - History. 3. Bermuda
Islands - Social life and customs. 4. Saint David's Island
(Bermuda Islands) - Biography. I. Title.*
F1639.S26 M35x 1986 **NYPL [Sc E 88-539]**

MCCALLAN, E. A. (ERNEST ALBERT), 1874-
McCallan, E. A. (Ernest Albert), 1874- Life on
old St. David's, Bermuda /. Hamilton,
Bermuda , 1986. 258 p., [26] p. of plates :
F1639.S26 M35x 1986 **NYPL [Sc E 88-539]**

McCartan, P. J. (Patrick John) The demand for
skilled labour in the Border, Ciskei, southern
Transkei regional economy / P.J. McCartan.
Grahamstown : Institute of Social and
Economic Research, Rhodes University, [1983]
50, xxii p. : ill. ; 30 cm. (Development studies .
working paper no. 15) Bibliography: p. 48-50. ISBN
0-86810-058-7 (pbk.) : DDC 331.12/3/0968792
19
*1. Skilled labor - South Africa - Supply and demand. 2.
South Africa - Economic conditions - 1961-. I. Title. II.
Series.*
HD5842.A6 M33 1983 **NYPL [Sc F 88-356]**

McCartney, Timothy O. Ten, ten the Bible ten :
Obeah in the Bahamas / Timothy McCartney.
Nassau, Bahamas : Timpaul Pub. Co., c1976.
192 p. : ill., maps ; 24 cm. Maps on lining papers.
Bibliography: p. 188-189.
*1. Obeah (Cult) - Bahamas. 2. Folklore - Bahamas. I.
Title. II. Title: Obeah in the Bahamas.*
NYPL [Sc E 88-425]

McClane, Kenneth A., 1951- Take five : collected
poems, 1971-1986 / Kenneth A. McClane. New

York : Greenwood Press, c1988. xviii, 278 p. ;
22 cm. (Contemporary Black poets) Contributions in
Afro-American studies, 0069-9624 ; no. 109 ISBN
0-313-25761-2 (lib. bdg. : alk. paper) DDC
811/.54 19
*I. Series. II. Series: Contributions in Afro-American and
African studies, no. 109. III. Title.*
PS3563.A26119 T35 1987
NYPL [Sc D 88-723]

McClary, Nelson. (illus) Hays, Wilma Pitchford.
The goose that was a watchdog. Boston [1967]
41 p. DDC [Fic]
PZ7.H31493 Go **NYPL [Sc D 88-1426]**

McClenney, Earl H. How to survive when you're
the only Black in the office : what they can't
teach you at white business schools: an attitude
manual for Black men! / by Earl H.
McClenney, Jr. Richmond, Va. : First
Associates Pub., c1987. 212 p. ; 21 cm. Cover
title. ISBN 0-9618835-0-2 (pbk.) : DDC
650.1/3/0240396073 19
*1. Office politics. 2. Afro-Americans - Life skill guides.
I. Title.*
HF5386 .M473 1987 **NYPL [Sc D 89-242]**

McClure, James, 1939- The artful egg / James
McClure. London ; New York : Macmillan,
1984. 283 p. ; 21 cm. ISBN 0-333-37103-8 :
DDC 823 19
I. Title.
PR9369.3.M394 A87 1984
NYPL [JFD 88-7714]

McCraken, John 1938- Buchanan, John,
1855-1896. The Shirè highlands. Blantyre
[Malawi] , 1982. xii, 260 p., [8] p. of plates :
NYPL [Sc C 87-434]

McCullough, Wayne Regan. The development of
group identification in Black Americans
[microform] / by Wayne Regan McCullough.
1982. ix, 84 leaves. Thesis (Ph. D.)--University of
Michigan, 1982. Bibliography: leaves 76-84. Microfilm.
Ann Arbor, Mich. : University Microfilms International,
1982. 1 reel ; 35 mm.
I. Title. **NYPL [Sc Micro R-4802]**

McDonald, Trevor. Kuus, Juhan. South Africa in
black and white / . London , c1987. [190] p. :
ISBN 0-245-54543-3 (pbk.)
NYPL [MFX (Kuus) 89-1313]

McElroy, Colleen J. Jesus and Fat Tuesday : and
other short stories / by Colleen J. McElroy.
Berkeley, Calif. : Creative Arts Book Co.,
c1987. 202 p. ; 23 cm. ISBN 0-88739-023-4 (pbk.)
I. Afro-Americans - Fiction. I. Title.
NYPL [Sc D 88-586]

**MACEO, ANTONIO, 1845-1896 - JUVENILE
LITERATURE.**
Caballero, Armando O. Antonio Maceo, la
protesta de Baraguá / . La Habana , 1977. 30,
[1] p. : **NYPL [Sc F 88-281]**

McEvedy, Colin. Atlas of African history / Colin
McEvedy. New York : Facts on File, c1980.
142 p. : maps ; 22 cm. Includes index. ISBN
0-87196-480-5 : DDC 911/.6
1. Africa - Historical geography - Maps. I. Title.
G2446.S1 M3 1980 **NYPL [Sc D 89-395]**

McFarland, Daniel Miles. Historical dictionary of
Ghana / by Daniel Miles McFarland.
Metuchen, N.J. : Scarecrow Press, 1985. lxxx,
296 p. : maps ; 23 cm. (African historical
dictionaries. no. 39) Bibliography: p. 199-289. ISBN
0-8108-1761-6 DDC 966.7/003/21 19
1. Ghana - History - Dictionaries. I. Title. II. Series.
DT510.5 .M38 1985
NYPL [*R-BMK 89-3348]

McGehee, Scott. Blacks in Detroit . Detroit ,
1980. 111 p. : **NYPL [Sc G 88-15]**

McGovern, James R. Black Eagle, General Daniel
"Chappie" James, Jr. / James R. McGovern.
University, AL : University of Alabama Press,
c1985. 204 p. : ill., ports. ; 23 cm. Includes index.
Bibliography: p. [187]- 194. ISBN 0-8173-0179-8
DDC 355/.0092/4 B 19
*1. James, Daniel, 1920-1978. 2. United States. Air
Force - Biography. 3. Generals - United States -
Biography. 4. Afro-American generals - Biography. I.
Title.*
UG626.2.J36 M34 1985
NYPL [JFD 85-7082]

Macgoye, Marjorie Oludhe. Street life / Marjorie
Oludhe Macgoye. Nairobi : Heinemann Kenya,

1987. 102 p. ; 19 cm. ISBN 996-646-362-3
1. Kenya - Fiction. I. Title. *NYPL [Sc C 89-4]*

McGraw, Marie Tyler. In bondage and freedom :
antebellum Black life in Richmond, Virginia :
an exhibition at the Valentine Museum,
Richmond, Virginia, February 11,
1988-September 13, 1988 / Marie
Tyler-McGraw and Gregg D. Kimball.
Richmond, VA. : Valentine Museum ; [Chapel
Hill, N.C.] : Distributed by the University of
North Carolina Press, 1988. 71 p. : ill. ; 28 cm.
Catalog. Includes bibliographical references.
*1. Afro-Americans - Virginia - Richmond - History - To
1863 - Exhibitions. 2. Afro-Americans - Virginia -
Richmond - Social conditions - To 1964 - Exhibitions.
3. Slavery - Virginia - Richmond - History -
Exhibitions. 4. Richmond (Va.) - History - Exhibitions.
5. Richmond (Va.) - Social conditions - Exhibitions. I.
Kimball, Gregg D. II. Valentine Museum. III. Title.*
NYPL [Sc F 89-107]

McGuire, Phillip, 1944- He, too, spoke for
democracy : Judge Hastie, World War II, and
the black soldier / Phillip McGuire. New
York : Greenwood Press, c1988. xvii, 154 p. ;
25 cm. (Contributions in Afro-American and African
studies, 0069-9624 . no. 110) Includes index.
Bibliography: p. [131]-148. ISBN 0-313-26115-6 (lib.
bdg. : alk. paper) DDC 355/.008996073 B 19
*1. Hastie, William. 2. Afro-American judges -
Biography. 3. Afro-American soldiers - Civil rights. 4.
Race discrimination - United States. 5. World War,
1939-1945 - Participation, Afro-American. 6. United
States - Armed Forces - Afro-Americans. I. Title. II.
Series.*
KF373.H38 M35 1988 NYPL [Sc E 88-347]

Machado, Maria Helena Pereira Toledo. Crime e
escravidão : trabalho, luta e resistência nas
lavouras paulistas, 1830-1888 / Maria Helena
Pereira Toledo Machado. São Paulo-SP :
Editora Brasiliense, 1987. 134 p. : port. ; 21
cm. Bibliography: p. [127]-134. DDC
306/.362/098161 19
*1. Slavery - Brazil - São Paulo (State) - Conditions of
slaves. 2. Crime and criminals - Brazil - São Paulo
(State) - History - 19th century. I. Title.*
HT1129.S27 M33 1987
NYPL [Sc D 88-1015]

Machel, Samora, 1933-
Compreender a nossa tarefa [microform]: notas
de estudo para os instrutores / Samora Moisés
Machel. [Maputo, Moçambique : Depart. do
Trabalho Idealógico do Partido FRELIMO,
1979] 20 p. ; 21 cm. (Colecção "Estudos e
orientações". 13) Cover title. Microfiche. New York:
New York Public Library, 198 . 1 microfiche: negative;
11 x 15 cm. (FSN Sc 019,125)
*1. Frente de Libertação de Moçambique. 2.
Mozambique - Politics and government - 1975-. I. Title.*
NYPL [Sc Micro F-11,163]

A nossa força está na unidade / Samora Moisés
Machel. [Maputo] : Instituto Nacional do Livro
e do Disco, [1983] 98 p. : ports. ; 21 cm.
(Colecção Unidade nacional . 4) DDC 967/.9803 19
*1. FRELIMO. 2. Cabo Delgado (Mozambique) -
Politics and government. 3. Mozambique - Politics and
government - 1975-. I. Title. II. Series.*
DT465.C32 M32 1983 NYPL [Sc D 89-531]

**MACHINE DATA STORAGE AND
RETRIEVAL. see INFORMATION
STORAGE AND RETRIEVAL SYSTEMS.**

Le Macho et la fille du macoute /. Novastar,
Charles. Port-au-Prince, , 1987. 181 p. ;
NYPL [Sc C 88-101]

McHugh, Cathy L. Mill family : the labor system
in the Southern cotton textile industry,
1880-1915 / Cathy L. McHugh. New York :
Oxford University Press, 1988. x, 144 p. ; 22
cm. Includes index. Bibliography: p. 129-133. ISBN
0-19-504299-9 (alk. paper) DDC
331.7/67721/0975 19
*1. Cotton textile industry - Southern States -
Employees - History. 2. Cotton textile industry -
Southern States - History. 3. Family - Southern States -
History. I. Title.*
HD8039.T42 U654 1988
NYPL [Sc D 88-1082]

MACIEL, JOSÉ ALVARES, 1761-1804.
Lopes, Francisco Antonio, 1882- Alvares
Maciel no degrêdo de Angola. [Rio de
Janeiro] , 1958. 104 p. ;
HD9527.A22 L6 NYPL [Sc D 88-419]

MCINTOSH, PHINEHAS.
Crowder, Michael, 1934- The flogging of
Phinehas McIntosh . New Haven , 1988. xii,
248 p. : ISBN 0-300-04098-9 DDC 968/.1103 19
DT791 .C76 1988 NYPL [Sc E 88-289]

MacIntyre, Kate. The Nairobi guide / Kate
Macintyre. London : Macmillan, 1986. 154 p.,
[8] p. of plates : ill., maps ; 22 cm. Includes
index. Bibliography: p. 147-148. ISBN 0-333-41987-1
*1. Nairobi (Kenya) - Description - Guide-books. I.
Title.*
NYPL [Sc D 88-287]

McKay, Claude, 1890-1948. Home to Harlem /
by Claude McKay. 1st Northeastern University
Press ed. Boston : Northeastern University
Press, 1987, c1928. xxvi, 340 p. ; 22 cm.
Reprint. Originally published: New York : Harper,
1928. With new introd. ISBN 1-555-53023-0 (alk.
paper) DDC 813/.52 19
*1. Afro-Americans - Harlem (New York, N.Y.) -
Fiction. 2. Harlem (New York, N.Y.) - Fiction. I. Title.*
PS3525.A24785 H6 1987
NYPL [Sc D 88-544]

Mackay, Donald A. (illus) Kelley, Sally. Summer
growing time. New York [1971] 125 p. ISBN
0-670-68172-5 DDC [Fic]
PZ7.K2818 Su NYPL [Sc D 89-88]

McKeen, Silas.
**Scriptural argument in favor of withdrawing
fellwoship from churches and ecclesiastical
bodies tolerating slaveholding among them.**
Brown, William B. Religious organizations,
and slavery. By Rev. Wm. B. Brown. Oberlin,
1850. 32 p.
E449 .B882 NYPL [Sc Rare F 88-45]

Mackenzie, Bob. A survey of handicrafts in
North East District, 1980 : survey design and
methdology / by Bob MacKenzie. Gaborone :
University College of Botswana, Institute of
Adult Education, 1980. 61 p. : map, port. ; 30
cm. (IAE techinical paper . no. 4/80) "June 1981."
*1. Handicraft - Botswana - Research - Methodology. I.
University College of Botswana. Institute of Adult
Education. II. Title. III. Series.*
NYPL [Sc F 88-2]

MacKenzie, John M. The partition of Africa,
1880-1900 and European imperialism in the
nineteenth century / John M. MacKenzie.
London ; New York : Methuen, 1983. x, 48 p. :
ill. ; 22 cm. (Lancaster pamphlets) Bibliography: p.
47-48. ISBN 0-416-35050-X DDC 960/.23 19
*1. Africa - History - 1884-1918. 2. Africa -
Colonization. I. Title. II. Series.*
DT29 .M33 1983 NYPL [Sc D 88-268]

Mackie, Liz. The great Marcus Garvey / Liz
Mackie. London : Hansib, 1987. 157 p. : ill. ;
21 cm. "A Hansib educational book." Pt. 2 consists of
articles and speeches by Garvey. Bibliography: p. 69.
ISBN 1-87051-850-0
*1. Garvey, Marcus, 1887-1940. 2. Black nationalism -
History. I. Garvey, Marcus, 1887-1940. II. Title.*
NYPL [Sc D 88-999]

McKinney-Ludd, S. L. Poetic privilege / S.L.
McKinney-Ludd. New York : Vantage Press,
1986. 52 p. ; 21 cm. Poems. ISBN 0-533-06838-X
I. Title.
NYPL [Sc D 88-184]

MCKINNEY, WILLIAM, 1895-1969.
Chilton, John, 1931 or 2- McKinney's music .
London , 1978. 68 p. : ISBN 0-9501290-1-1 (pbk.)
DDC 785.42/092/2 B 19
ML394 .C55 1978 NYPL [Sc D 82-387]

McKinney's Cotton Pickers. Chilton, John, 1931
or 2- McKinney's music . London , 1978. 68
p. : ISBN 0-9501290-1-1 (pbk.) DDC 785.42/092/2
B 19
ML394 .C55 1978 NYPL [Sc D 82-387]

MCKINNEY'S COTTON PICKERS.
Chilton, John, 1931 or 2- McKinney's music .
London , 1978. 68 p. : ISBN 0-9501290-1-1 (pbk.)
DDC 785.42/092/2 B 19
ML394 .C55 1978 NYPL [Sc D 82-387]

McKinney's music . Chilton, John, 1931 or 2-
London , 1978. 68 p. : ISBN 0-9501290-1-1 (pbk.)
DDC 785.42/092/2 B 19
ML394 .C55 1978 NYPL [Sc D 82-387]

McKissack, Pat, 1944-
Mirandy and Brother Wind / by Patricia C.
McKissack ; pictures by Jerry Pinkney. New
York : Knopf : Distributed by Random House,
1988. [32] p. : col. ill. ; 29 cm. To win first prize
in the Junior Cakewalk, Mirandy tries to capture the

wind for her partner. ISBN 0-394-88765-4 DDC [E]
19
*1. Dancing - Juvenile fiction. 2. Afro-Americans -
Juvenile fiction. I. Pinkney, Jerry, ill. II. Title.*
PZ7.M478693 Mi 1988 NYPL [Sc F 89-58]

Nettie Jo's friends / by Patricia C. McKissack ;
illustrated by Scott Cook. New York : Knopf,
1989. [33] p. : col. ill. ; 28 cm. Nettie Jo
desperately needs a needle to sew a new wedding dress
for her beloved doll, but the three animals she helps
during her search do not seem inclined to give her their
assistance in return. SCHOMBURG CHILDREN'S
COLLECTION. ISBN 0-394-89158-9 DDC [E] 19
*1. Afro-American children - Juvenile fiction. I. Cook,
Scott, ill. II. Schomburg Children's Collection. III. Title.*
PZ7.M478693 Ne 1989 NYPL [Sc F 89-143]

McKown, Robin. (joint author) Elting, Mary, 1909-
A Mongo homecoming. New York [1969] 54 p.
DDC 309.1/675
DT644 .E4 NYPL [Sc E 88-578]

McKoy, Derrick. Chuck, Delroy H.
Understanding crime . Bridgetown, Barbados
[c1986] xi, 171 p. ; ISBN 976-8043-00-8 (pbk.)
DDC 364 19
HV6025 .C48 1986 NYPL [Sc D 89-195]

Maclean, Una. African medicine in the modern
world . Edinburgh [1987] 222 p. : DDC
615.8/82/096 19
GR350 NYPL [Sc D 87-1283]

McLeod, Catherine. Jamaika / [text, Catherine
McLeod] 4. Aufl. Lausanne, Switzerland :
Editions Berlitz, [1985], c1981. 128 p. : col. ill.,
maps ; 15 cm. (Berlitz Reiseführer)
*1. Jamaica - Description and travel - Guide-books. 2.
Haiti - Description and travel - Guide-books. 3.
Dominican Republic - Description and travel -
Guide-books. 4. Cayman Islands - Description and
travel - Guide-books. I. Éditions Berlitz S. A. II. Title.
III. Series. NYPL [Sc B 88-57]*

McLoughlin, T. O. Karima / T.O. McLoughlin.
Gweru, Zimbabwe : Mambo Press, 1985. 211
p. ; 18 cm. (Mambo writers series. English section.
vol. 18) ISBN 0-86922-319-4 (pbk.) DDC 823 19
1. Zimbabwe - History - 1965-1980 - Fiction. I. Title.
PR9390.9.M35 K37 1985
NYPL [JFC 86-1652]

McLoughlin, Virginia Duffy. McLoughlin, William
Gerald. The Cherokee ghost dance . [Macon,
Ga.] , c1984. xxiv, 512 p. : ISBN 0-86554-128-0 :
DDC 975/.00497 19
E78.S65 M37 1984 NYPL [HBC 85-263]

McLoughlin, William Gerald. The Cherokee ghost
dance : essays on the Southeastern Indians,
1789-1861 / by William G. McLoughlin with
Walter H. Conser, Jr. and Virginia Duffy
McLoughlin. [Macon, Ga.] : Mercer, c1984.
xxiv, 512 p. : ill., ports. ; 24 cm. Includes
bibliographical references and index. ISBN
0-86554-128-0 : DDC 975/.00497 19
*1. Indians of North America - Southern States - Social
conditions - Addresses, essays, lectures. 2. Cherokee
Indians - Social conditions - Addresses, essays, lectures.
3. Indians of North America - Southern States -
Missions - Addresses, essays, lectures. 4. Indians of
North America - Southern States - Slaves, Ownership
of - Addresses, essays, lectures. 5. Afro-Americans -
Relations with Indians - Addresses, essays, lectures. I.
Conser, Walter H. II. McLoughlin, Virginia Duffy. III.
Title.*
E78.S65 M37 1984 NYPL [HBC 85-263]

McMillen, Neil R., 1939- Dark journey : black
Mississippians in the age of Jim Crow / Neil R.
McMillen. Urbana, Ill. : University of Illinois,
c1989. xvii, 430 p., [10] p. of plates, ill. ; 24
cm. Includes index. Bibliography: p. [319]-417. ISBN
0-252-01568-1 (alk. paper) DDC
976.2/00496073 19
*1. Afro-Americans - Mississippi - History. 2.
Afro-Americans - Mississippi - Segregation - History. 3.
Mississippi - Race relations. I. Title.*
E185.93.M6 M33 1989 NYPL [Sc E 89-213]

McNaughton, Patrick R.
The Mande blacksmiths : knowledge, power,
and art in West Africa / Patrick R.
McNaughton. Bloomington : Indiana University
Press, c1988. xxiv, 241 p., [4] p. of plates : ill.
(some col.), maps ; 25 cm. (Traditional arts of
Africa) Includes index. Bibliography: p. [217]-235.
ISBN 0-253-33683-X DDC 306/.089963 19
1. Blacksmiths - Mali. 2. Sculpture, Mandingo (African

BIBLIOGRAPHIC GUIDE
224

McNaughton, Patrick R. (cont.)

people). 3. Witchcraft - Mali. I. Title. II. Series.
DT551.45.M36 M38 1988
NYPL [Sc E 88-393]

Pelrine, Diane. African art from the Rita and
John Grunwald collection /. Bloomington ,
c1988. 159 p. : ISBN 0-253-21061-5 (I.U. Press :
pbk.) DDC 730/.0966/0740172255 19
N7398 .P44 1988
NYPL [Sc F 89-158]

McRae, Barry. The jazz handbook / Barry
McRae. Harlow, Essex, England : Longman,
1987. 272 p. : ill., ports. ; 22 cm. Includes
bibliographical references and index. ISBN
0-582-00092-0
1. Jazz music - History and criticism. 2. Jazz
musicians - Biography. I. Title.
NYPL [Sc D 87-940]

MacRobert, Iain, 1949- The Black roots and
white racism of early Pentecostalism in the
USA / Iain MacRobert ; foreword by Walter J.
Hollenweger. Basingstoke : Macmillan, 1988.
xv, 142 p. ; 22 cm. Includes index. Bibliography: p.
131-138. ISBN 0-333-43997-X DDC 277.3/082 19
1. Pentecostalism - United States - History. 2.
Afro-American Pentecostalism - History. 3.
Afro-American - Religion. I. Title.
BR1644.5.U6 *NYPL [Sc D 89-131]*

McRobie, John. Stares, Rodney. Ethnic
minorities . [London] , 1982. 62 p. ; ISBN
0-905932-32-3 *NYPL [Sc F 88-96]*

McTair, Dionyse. Notes toward an escape from
death / by Dionyse McTair. London ;
Port-of-Spain, Trinidad : New Beacon Books,
c1987. 66 p. ; 22 cm. Poems. ISBN 0-901241-77-6
I. Title. *NYPL [Sc D 89-215]*

McTair, Roger. Brand, Dionne, 1953- Winter
epigrams & Epigrams to Ernesto Cardinal in
defense of Claudia /. Toronto , 1983. 38 p. ;
ISBN 0-88795-022-1 :
NYPL [Sc D 88-1207]

MCVEA, WARREN.
Pennington, Richard, 1952- Breaking the ice .
Jefferson, N.C. , c1987. ix, 182 p. : ISBN
0-89950-295-4 : DDC 796.332/72/0973 19
GV939.A1 P46 1987 *NYPL [Sc E 88-35]*

MADAGASCAR.
France. Ministère de la France d'outre-mer.
Direction des affaires économiques et du plan.
Madagascar [microform]. [Paris, 1953?]
cover-title, [4] p., 12 plates, map.
NYPL [Sc Micro R-3545]
Livre d'or de la République Malgache.
[Tananarive? , 1960] 176 p. :
NYPL [Sc G 88-18]

MADAGASCAR - ANTIQUITIES.
Rasamuel, David. Traditions orales et
archéologie de la basse Sahatorendrika .
[Antananarivo] , 1979. 287 p., [33] leaves of
plates :
DT469.M37 S247 1979 *NYPL [Sc F 88-79]*

Madagascar - Archaeology. see Madagascar -
Antiquities.

MADAGASCAR - CIVILIZATION.
Ottino, Paul. L'étrangère intime . Paris,
France , c1986. 2 v. (xxvii, 630 p.) : ISBN
2-88124-095-X (set) DDC 398/.0969/1 19
GR357 .O88 1986 *NYPL [Sc D 88-1203]*

MADAGASCAR - DESCRIPTION AND
TRAVEL - 1981- - GUIDE-BOOKS.
Planche, Bernard. A Madagascar /. [Paris] ,
c1987. 158 p. : *NYPL [Sc D 88-254]*

MADAGASCAR - DESCRIPTION AND
TRAVEL - VIEWS.
France. Ministère de la France d'outre-mer.
Direction des affaires économiques et du plan.
Madagascar [microform]. [Paris, 1953?]
cover-title, [4] p., 12 plates, map.
NYPL [Sc Micro R-3545]

MADAGASCAR - ECONOMIC CONDITIONS.
Deleris, Ferdinand. Ratsiraka . Paris , c1986.
135 p. ; ISBN 2-85802-697-1
NYPL [Sc D 88-777]
France. Ministère de la France d'outre-mer.
Direction des affaires économiques et du plan.
Madagascar [microform]. [Paris, 1953?]
cover-title, [4] p., 12 plates, map.
NYPL [Sc Micro R-3545]

MADAGASCAR - ECONOMIC POLICY.
Ratsiraka, Didier, 1936- Kabarin'ny

Filoham-pirenena /. [Antananarivo? , 1985] 487
p. ; *NYPL [Sc F 88-268]*

MADAGASCAR - FICTION.
Rakotoson, Michèle. Le bain des reliques .
Paris , c1988. 146 p. ; ISBN 2-86537-218-9
NYPL [Sc D 89-245]

Madagascar - Government. see Madagascar -
Politics and government.

MADAGASCAR - HISTORY.
Norwegian missions in African history /. Oslo :
Oxford [Oxfordshire] ; 2 v. : ISBN
82-00-07418-8 (v. 1) DDC 266/.023/48106 19
BV3625.M2 N67 1986 *NYPL [Sc D 89-26]*
Prou, Michel, 1934- Malagasy . Paris , 1987-
v. : ISBN 2-85802-513-1 *NYPL [Sc D 88-102]*

MADAGASCAR - HISTORY - CONGRESSES.
Relations historiques à travers l'océan Indien.
Spanish. Relaciones históricas a través del
océano Índico . Barcelona , Paris , 1983. 224
p. ; ISBN 84-85800-51-6 *NYPL [Sc D 88-593]*

MADAGASCAR - KINGS AND RULERS.
Ottino, Paul. L'étrangère intime . Paris,
France , c1986. 2 v. (xxvii, 630 p.) : ISBN
2-88124-095-X (set) DDC 398/.0969/1 19
GR357 .O88 1986 *NYPL [Sc D 88-1203]*

Madagascar [microform]. France. Ministère de la
France d'outre-mer. Direction des affaires
économiques et du plan. [Paris, 1953?]
cover-title, [4] p., 12 plates, map.
NYPL [Sc Micro R-3545]

MADAGASCAR - POLITICS AND
GOVERNMENT - 1947-1960.
Rajoelina, Patrick. Quarante années de la vie
politique de Madagascar, 1947-1987 /. Paris ,
c1988. 176 p. : ISBN 2-85802-915-6
NYPL [Sc D 89-254]

MADAGASCAR - POLITICS AND
GOVERNMENT - 1960-.
Deleris, Ferdinand. Ratsiraka . Paris , c1986.
135 p. ; ISBN 2-85802-697-1
NYPL [Sc D 88-777]
Rajoelina, Patrick. Quarante années de la vie
politique de Madagascar, 1947-1987 /. Paris ,
c1988. 176 p. : ISBN 2-85802-915-6
NYPL [Sc D 89-254]
Ratsiraka, Didier. Kabary tatitra nataon'
Andriamatoa Didier Ratsiraka, filohan' ny
Repoblika Demokratika Malagasy.
Antananarivo , 1985. 93 p. :
NYPL [Sc D 88-1295]

MADAGASCAR - RELIGION.
Rakoto, Andrianasolo. Izinahary [microform]
/. Tananarive [1978] 36 p. ;
NYPL [Sc Micro F-10989]

MADAGASCAR - SOCIAL LIFE AND
CUSTOMS.
Ny djoutche Malagasy [microform] /.
Tananarive [1978] 28 p. ;
NYPL [Sc Micro F-10988]

MADAGASCAR - SOCIAL POLICY.
Ratsiraka, Didier, 1936- Kabarin'ny
Filoham-pirenena /. [Antananarivo? , 1985] 487
p. ; *NYPL [Sc F 88-268]*

Madam Universe sent man /. Osahon, Naiwu,
1937- Apapa, Lagos, Nigeria , 1981. [22] p. :
ISBN 978-18-6002-2 *NYPL [Sc D 89-223]*

Madame Tinubu . Yemitan, Oladipo. Ibadan ,
1987. x, 85 p. : ISBN 978-15-4985-9
NYPL [Sc D 88-1382]

Madden, Betsy. The All-America Coeds / by
Betsy Madden. New York, Criterion Books
[1971] 143 p. ; 22 cm. Determined to prove that a
girls' basketball team can be as good as a boys', Joyce
organizes a team that becomes so successful it defeats
several male teams. ISBN 0-200-71785-5
1. Basketball - Juvenile fiction. 2. Afro-American
youth - Juvenile fiction. I. Title.
NYPL [Sc D 88-432]

Maddison, Kevin W., 1946- James, Winston. The
Caribbean /. London , 1984. 46 p. : ISBN
0-356-07105-7 : DDC 972.9 19
F2175 *NYPL [Sc F 88-128]*

Madede-Tsotsa, Simon, 1957- L'herbe sous les
pieds / Simon Madede-Tsotsa. Ed. originale.
Paris : Editions Saint-Germain-des-Prés, c1986.
28 p. ; 21 cm. (Collection A l'écoute des sources)
ISBN 2-243-02813-1
I. Title. *NYPL [Sc D 88-498]*

MADELA, LADUMA.
Schlosser, Katesa. Medizinen des Blitzzauberers
Laduma Madela . Kiel , 1984. 186 p., 64, [1] p.
of plates : ISBN 3-88312-106-1 DDC
615.8/99/089963 19
DT878.Z9 S32 1984 *NYPL [Sc E 87-271]*

Madgett, Naomi Cornelia (Long) Octavia and
other poems / by Naomi Long Madgett ;
illustrated by Leisia Duskin. 1st ed. Chicago :
Third World Press, 1988. 117 p. : ill., ports. ;
22 cm. ISBN 0-88378-121-2 :
I. Title.
MLCS 88/07430 (P) *NYPL [Sc D 89-430]*

Madgett, Naomi Cornelia Long, 1923- Songs to a
phantom nightingale / by Naomi Cornelia
Long. 1st ed. New York : Fortuny's, 1941. 30
p., [1] p. of plates : ill. ; 19 cm. With autograph of
author.
I. Title. *NYPL [Sc C 89-136]*

Madiou, Thomas, 1814-1884. Histoire d'Haïti /
Thomas Madiou. Port-au-Prince, Haiti : Les
Éditions Fardin, 1981- v. : 20 cm. Vols. 4-
published by H. Deschamps. Facsim. of: 2e éd.
Port-au-Prince : Impr. E. Chenet, 1922-23.
CONTENTS. - t. 1. 1492-1799 -- t. 2. 1799-1803. -- t.
3. 1804-1807. -- t. 4. 1807-1811. -- t. 5. 1811-1818.
1. Haiti - History. I. Title.
NYPL [Sc Ser.-L .M227]

The Madonna of 115th Street . Orsi, Robert A.
New Haven , c1985. xxiii, 287 p. : ISBN
0-300-03262-5 (alk. paper) DDC
263/.98/0895107471 19
BT660.N44 O77 1985
NYPL [IEE (Italians) 86-89]

Madu, Oliver V. Models of class domination in
plural societies of Central Africa / Oliver V.
Madu. Washington : University Press of
America, c1978. vi, 510 p. ; 22 cm. Includes
index. Bibliography: p. 457-506.
1. Social classes - Africa, Central. 2. Zambia - Social
conditions. 3. Malawi - Social conditions. 4. Malawi -
Politics and government. I. Title.
NYPL [Sc D 88-1067]

Maduakor, Obi. Wole Soyinka : an introduction
to his writing / Obi Maduakor. New York :
Garland, c1987, 1986. xv, 339 p. : ill. ; 23 cm.
(Critical studies on Black life and culture. v. 15)
Bibliography: p. 333-339. ISBN 0-8240-9141-8 (alk.
paper) DDC 822 19
1. Soyinka, Wole - Criticism and interpretation. I. Title.
II. Series.
PR9387.9.S6 Z77 1987 *NYPL [Sc D 88-643]*

Madubuike, Ihechukwu. Igh nke Ihechukwu
Madubuike, dere. Ibadan : University Press,
1981. 79 p. ; 18 cm. ISBN 978-15-4603-4
1. Igbo language - Texts. I. Title.
NYPL [Sc C 88-96]

Madunagu, Edwin. Nigeria, the economy and the
people [microform] : the political economy of
state robbery and its popular-democratic
negation / Edwin Madunagu. London : New
Beacon Books, 1983. 38 p. ; 22 cm. Microfiche.
New York: New York Public Library, 198 . 1
microfiche: negative; 11 x 15 cm. (FSN Sc 019,100)
ISBN 0-901241-54-7
1. Nigeria - Economic conditions. 2. Nigeria - Politics
and government - 1960-. I. Title.
NYPL [Sc Micro F-11069]

Maestri Filho, Mário José. Depoimentos de
escravos brasileiros / Mário José Maestri Filho.
São Paulo : Icone, c1988. 88 p. ; 21 cm.
(Coleção Malungo-Memória) Bibliography: p. 71-88.
ISBN 85-27-40039-1
1. Slavery - Brazil - History. 2. Slaves - Brazil -
Biography. 3. Blacks - Brazil - Social conditions. I.
Title. *NYPL [Sc D 88-1379]*

Mafuta /. Mkangi, Katama G. C. Nairobi , 1984.
92 p. : *NYPL [Sc C 88-198]*

Magaia, Lina.
[Dumba nengue. English]
Dumba nengue, run for your life : peasant
tales of tragedy in Mozambique / Lina
Magaia ; translated by Michael Wolfers ;
historical introduction by Allen Isaacman.
Trenton, N.J. : Africa World Press, 1988. 113
p. : ill. ; 22 cm. Translation of: Dumba nengue.
Includes bibliographical references. ISBN
0-86543-073-X
1. RENAMO (Organization). 2. Atrocities -
Mozambique. 3. Political refugees - Mozambique. 4.
Mozambique - Politics and government - 1975-. 5.

South Africa - Foreign relations - Mozambique. 6. Mozambique - Foreign relations - South Africa. I. Title.
NYPL [Sc D 88-1509]

Maganga, Dotto B. Bye Bye Umaskini ... / Dotto B. Maganga. Dar es Salaam : Heko publishers, 1986. 90 p. ; 20 cm. In Swahili.
1. Swahili language - Texts. I. Title.
NYPL [Sc C 88-232]

The magazine novels of Pauline Hopkins /.
Hopkins, Pauline E. (Pauline Elizabeth) [Novels. Selections.] New York , Oxford , 1988. l, 621 p. ; ISBN 0-19-505248-X (alk. paper) DDC 813/.4 19
PS1999.H4226 A6 1988
NYPL [JFC 88-2195]

Maggie's American dream . Comer, James P. New York, N.Y. , c1988. xxiv, 228 p., [4] leaves of plates : ISBN 0-453-00588-8 DDC 973/.0496073022 B 19
E185.97.C68 C66 1988 **NYPL [Sc D 89-335]**

Magia e historia en los "Cuentos negros," "Por qué" y "Ayapá" de Lydia Cabrera /. Soto, Sara. Miami, Fla., U. S.A. , 1988. 162 p. ; ISBN 0-89729-444-0 DDC 863 20
PQ7389.C22 Z87 1988 **NYPL [Sc D 89-601]**

MAGIC IN LITERATURE.
Soto, Sara. Magia e historia en los "Cuentos negros," "Por qué" y "Ayapá" de Lydia Cabrera /. Miami, Fla., U. S.A. , 1988. 162 p. ; ISBN 0-89729-444-0 DDC 863 20
PQ7389.C22 Z87 1988 **NYPL [Sc D 89-601]**

MAGIC - JUVENILE FICTION.
Eager, Edward. The well-wishers /. New York , c1960. 191 p. : **NYPL [Sc D 88-429]**

MAGIC - WEST INDIES.
Caloc, Ray. Secrets dévoilés de la magie caraïbe . [Lamentin, Martinique] [1986] 71 p. : ISBN 2-905317-02-7 **NYPL [Sc D 89-274]**

Ebroïn, Ary. Quimbois, magie noire et sorcellerie aux Antilles . Paris , c1977. 239 p., [4] leaves of plates : DDC 133.4/09729
BF1622.W47 E26 **NYPL [Sc D 89-270]**

Mességué, Maurice. Tu as rendez-vous avec le Diable /. Paris , c1987. 219 p. ; ISBN 2-87679-008-4 **NYPL [Sc E 88-540]**

Magid, Alvin, 1937- Urban nationalism : a study of political development in Trinidad / Alvin Magid. Gainesville : University Presses of Florida : University of Florida Press, 1988. x, 294 p. : ill. ; 24 cm. Includes index. Bibliography: p. 281-287. ISBN 0-8130-0853-0 DDC 972.98/3 19
1. Nationalism - Trinidad - History. 2. Trinidad - Ethnic relations. I. Title.
F2119 .M34 1988 **NYPL [HRG 88-1040]**

Magnant, Jean-Pierre, 1946- La terre sara, terre tchadienne / Jean-Pierre Magnant. Paris : L'Harmattan, c1986. 380 p. : ill., maps ; 22 cm. (Collection Alternatives paysannes, 0757-8091) Bibliography: p. 353-374. Cartography: p. [375] ISBN 2-85802-691-2
1. Sara (African people). I. Title. II. Series.
DT546.445.S27 M34 1986
NYPL [Sc D 89-101]

Magnate, Joseph. Dele Giwa / by Joseph Magnate. Lagos, : New Academy Publications, 1987. 190 p. : ill. ; 21 cm. "October, 1987." ISBN 978-303-000-0
1. Giwa, Dele, 1947-1986. 2. Giwa, Dele, 1947-1986 - Assassination. 3. Journalists - Nigeria - Biography. I. Title. **NYPL [Sc D 88-742]**

Magubane, Bernard. The ties that bind : African-American consciousness of Africa / by Bernard Makhosezwe Magubane. Trenton, N.J. : Africa World Press, [1987] xi, 251 p. ; 22 cm. Includes bibliographies and index. ISBN 0-86543-037-3 (pbk.) DDC 305.8/96073 19
1. Afro-Americans - Relations with Africans. 2. Afro-Americans - Attitudes. 3. Public opinion - United States. 4. Africa - Foreign public opinion, American. I. Title.
E185.625 .M83 1987 **NYPL [Sc D 88-1348]**

Magubane, Peter. June 16 : the fruit of fear / Peter Magubane. Johannesburg : Skotaville, c1986. [85] p. : chiefly ill. ; 31 cm. ISBN 0-947009-13-2 (pbk.) DDC 968.2/21 19
1. Riots - South Africa - Soweto - Pictorial works. 2. Soweto (South Africa) - History - Pictorial works. I. Title.
DT944.J66 S674 1986 **NYPL [Sc G 88-12]**

Mahabir, Noor Kumar. The still cry : personal accounts of East Indians in Trinidad and Tobago during indentureship (1845-1917) / Noor Kumar Mahabir ; with a foreword by Selwyn R. Cudjoe. Tacarigua, Trinidad ; Ithaca, N.Y. : Calaloux Publications, c1985. 191 p. ; 21 cm. Bibliography: p. 32-33.
1. West Indian poetry (English). 2. Trinidad and Tobago literature (English). 3. East Indians - Trinidad and Tobago. I. Title. **NYPL [Sc D 88-401]**

MAHALPYE DEVELOPMENT TRUST.
Gobotswang, Z. Pilot evaluation report on Mahalapye Development Trust /. Gaborone, Botswana [1982] v leaves, 61, 3 p. ;
HD5710.85.B59 G63 1982
NYPL [Sc F 89-108]

Mahibou, Sidi Mohamed. Ḥājj 'Umar ibn Sa'īd al-Fūtī, 1794?-1864. [Bayān mā waqa'a. French & Arabic.] Voilà ce qui est arrivé . Paris , 1983. 261 p., [57] p. of plates ; ISBN 2-222-03216-4 **NYPL [Sc F 88-211]**

Mahmud-Okereke, N. Enuma el, 1948- Israel and Black Africa : time to normalise / N.O.E. el Mahmud-Okereke. Lagos, Nigeria : Emmcon (TWORF) Books Nigeria, 1986. xxxiv, 211 p. : facsims. ; 20 cm. ISBN 978-242-301-7
1. Africa, Sub-Saharan - Foreign relations - Israel. 2. Israel - Foreign relations - Africa, Sub-Saharan. I. Title.
NYPL [Sc C 88-205]

Mahmud-Okereke, N. Enuma, 1948- OAU--time to admit South Africa / N.O.E. el Mahmud-Okereke. 2d ed. Lagos, Nigeria : Emmcon (TWORF) Books Nigeria, 1986. xxvi, 57, 190 p. : ill., facsims., ports. ; 20 cm. At head of title: Beyond a Kennedy-backed J. Jackson 1988 ticket. ISBN 978-242-302-5
1. South Africa - Foreign relations. 2. South Africa - Politics and government - 1978-. 3. Africa - Politics and government - 1960-. I. Title. II. Title: Beyond a Kennedy-backed J. Jackson 1988 ticket.
NYPL [Sc C 88-204]

Mahomet. see **Muḥammad, the prophet.**

Maida, Carl Albert. Black networks of care [microform] : culture, health and learning in an urban community / by Carl Albert Maida. 1981. xiii, 276 leaves ; 28 cm. Typescript. Thesis (Ph. D.)--University of California, Los Angeles, 1981. Bibliography: leaves 269-276. Microfilm. Ann Arbor, Mich. : University Microfilms International, 1981. 1 reel ; 35 mm.
1. Afro-Americans - Medical care. 2. Community health services - United States. 3. Medical personnel and patient - United States. I. Title.
NYPL [Sc Micro R-4803]

Maids, blessing or blight? /. Ndegwa, Rosemary. Nairobi, Kenya , c1987. x, 141 p. ;
NYPL [Sc D 89-399]

Maillu, David G., 1939-
After 4.30 / David G. Maillu. 2nd ed. Nairobi, Kenya : Maillu Pub. House, 1987. 249 p. ; 18 cm. (MPH novels)
I. Title. **NYPL [Sc C 89-143]**

The ayah / David G. Maillu. Nairobi : Heinemann Kenya, 1986. 178 p. ; 18 cm.
1. Kenya - Fiction. I. Title.
MLCS 89/131165 (P) **NYPL [Sc C 89-158]**

Maina-wa-Kinyatti. Kenya's freedom struggle . London ; Atlantic Highlands, N.J. , 1987. xix, 138 p. ; **NYPL [Sc D 88-775]**

Maindron, Gabriel. Des apparitions à Kibeho : annonce de Marie au cœur de l'Afrique / Gabriel Maindron. Paris : O.E.I.L., c1984. 243 p., [4] p. of plates : ill. (some col.) ; 24 cm. (Pèlerinages, sanctuaires, apparitions) Bibliography: p. 243. ISBN 2-86839-021-8 : DDC 232.91/7/0967571 19
1. Mary, Blessed Virgin, Saint - Apparitions and miracles - Rwanda - Kibeho. 2. Kibeho (Rwanda) - Religious life and customs. I. Title. II. Series.
BT660.K52 M35 1984 **NYPL [Sc E 88-516]**

Mainguy, Christine. Thomas, Michel. [Histoire d'un art. English.] Textile art . Geneva, Switzerland , New York, NY , 1985. 279 p. : ISBN 0-8478-0640-5 (Rizzoli) : DDC 746 19
NK8806 .T4813 1985
NYPL [3-MON+ 86-527]

Maish, Kemba Asili. Black political orientation, political activism, and positive mental health [microform] / by Kemba Asili Maish. 1977. 220 leaves. Thesis (Ph. D.)--University of Maryland, 1977.

Bibliography: leaves 212-220. Microfilm of typescript. Ann Arbor, Mich.: University Microfilms International, 1978. 1 microfilm reel; 35 mm.
1. Afro-Americans - Political activity. 2. Afro-Americans - Psychology. I. Title.
NYPL [Sc Micro R-4228]

Maison de l'Afrique (Paris, France) Dossier Benin /. Paris , 1987. 225 p. :
NYPL [Sc F 88-176]

La maison du chef et la tête du cabri : des degrés de la détermination nominale dans les langues d'Afrique centrale / collectif édité par Pascal Boyeldieu. Paris : Laboratoire de langues et civilisations à tradition orale (LACITO) Département Langues et parole en Afrique centrale : Geuthner, c1987. 125 p. : map ; 24 cm. (Publications du Département Langues et parole en Afrique centrale, LAPAC) Includes bibliographical references. ISBN 2-7053-0339-1
1. Africa, Central - Languages - Determiners. I. Boyeldieu, Pascal. **NYPL [Sc E 88-292]**

Les Maitresses du feu et de la cuisine : mythes pende (Rép. du Zaïre). Bandundu, République du Zaïre : Ceeba, 1983. 164 p. : ill., map ; 27 cm. (Publications (Ceeba). Série II . vol. 88) Pende text and translation into French on facing pages. At head of title: Lengelo & Lusambu. Lusambu Kauy Mutombo wrote the introductory description of the Pende people; Lengelo Guyigisa compiled, transcribed and translated the tales. Bibliography: p. 163-164.
1. Pende (African people) - Folklore. 2. Tales - Zaire. I. Lengelo Guyigisa. II. Lusambu Kauy Mutombo. III. Series. IV. Series: Publications (Ceeba). Série II , vol. 88. **NYPL [Sc F 88-308]**

Maja-Pearce, Adewale. Loyalties / Adewale Maja-Pearce. Harlow : Longman, 1986. 152 p. ; 20 cm. (Longman African writers) ISBN 0-582-78628-2 (pbk) DDC 823 19
1. Nigeria - Fiction. 2. Nigeria - History - Civil War, 1967-1970 - Fiction. I. Title. **NYPL [Sc C 89-56]**

Major, Clarence. Such was the season : a novel / by Clarence Major. San Francisco : Mercury House, c1987. 213 p. ; 23 cm. ISBN 0-916515-20-6 : DDC 813/.54 19
1. Afro-Americans - Georgia - Fiction. I. Title.
PS3563.A39 S8 1987 **NYPL [Sc D 88-744]**

Major Taylor . Ritchie, Andrew. San Francisco , New York , 1988. 304 p., [32] p. of plates : ISBN 0-933201-14-1 (hardcover)
NYPL [Sc E 88-570]

Majuta . Kosmin, Barry Alexander. Gwelo, Zimbabwe , c1980. xii, 223 p., [32] p. of plates : **NYPL [Sc D 82-130]**

Makanda Duc d'Ikoga, André. Non, Monsieur Giscard [microform] / par le colonel Makanda Duc d'Ikoga. Paris : Cédex, [1980] 23 p. ; 28 cm. Microfiche. New York: New York Public Library, 198 . 1 microfiche: negative; 11 x 15 cm. (FSN Sc 019,055)
1. Africans in France. 2. Cameroon - Relations (general) with France. 3. France - Relations (general) with Cameroon. I. Title.
NYPL [Sc Micro F-11014]

Makarfi, M. Shu'aibu. Zamanin Nan Namu : wasanni biyu / na M. Shu'aibu Makarfi. Zariya : Norla, 1959. 88 p. ; 22 cm.
I. Title. **NYPL [Sc D 89-481]**

Makeba . Makeba, Miriam. New York , c1987. 249 p., [16] p. of plates : ISBN 0-453-00561-6 : DDC 784.5/0092/4 B 19
ML420.M16 A3 1987 **NYPL [Sc E 88-193]**

Makeba, Miriam. Makeba : my story / by Miriam Makeba with James Hall. New York : New American Library, c1987. 249 p., [16] p. of plates : ill. ; 24 cm. "NAL books." ISBN 0-453-00561-6 : DDC 784.5/0092/4 B 19
1. Makeba, Miriam. 2. Singers - South Africa - Biography. I. Hall, James. II. Title.
ML420.M16 A3 1987 **NYPL [Sc E 88-193]**

MAKEBA, MIRIAM.
Makeba, Miriam. Makeba . New York , c1987. 249 p., [16] p. of plates : ISBN 0-453-00561-6 : DDC 784.5/0092/4 B 19
ML420.M16 A3 1987 **NYPL [Sc E 88-193]**

Makec, John Wuol. The customary law of the Dinka people of Sudan : in comparison with aspects of Western and Islamic laws / by John Wuol Makec. London, England Afroworld Pub. Co., 1988. 287 p. ; 25 cm. (African traditional law) Includes bibliographical references and index. ISBN

0-948583-03-7 (Hardback)
1. Dinka (African people) - Rites and ceremonies. 2.
Law, Dinka (African people). I. Title.
NYPL [Sc E 88-434]

East African studies. see East African studies.

Makerere Institute of Social Research. Political
Science Research Programme. One party
democracy. [Nairobi, 1967] 470 p. DDC
324/.678
JQ3519.A55 O5   *NYPL [Sc D 88-976]*

MAKERERE UNIVERSITY -
DISSERTATIONS - BIBLIOGRAPHY
CATALOGS.
Makerere University. Library. Annotated list of
theses submitted to Makerere University and
held by Makerere University Library
[microform] /. [Kampala?] , 1981. 89 leaves ;
NYPL [Sc Micro R-4840 no.13]

Makerere University. Library. Annotated list of
theses submitted to Makerere University and
held by Makerere University Library
[microform] / compiled by Elizabeth Wamala
and Jane Kasajja. [Kampala?] : The Library,
1981. 89 leaves ; 33 cm. Includes index. Microfilm.
New York : New York Public Library, 198 . 1
microfilm reel ; 35 mm. (MN *ZZ-28635)
1. Makerere University - Dissertations - Bibliography
Catalogs. 2. Dissertations, Academic - Uganda. I.
Wamala, Elizabeth. II. Kasajja, Jane. III. Title.
NYPL [Sc Micro R-4840 no.13]

Makers of Nigerian press . Duyile, Dayo.
Nigeria , 1987. xx, 726 p. ;
NYPL [Sc F 89-167]

Makers of Zimbabwe .
(4) Farquhar, June. Jairos Jiri . Gweru , 1987.
92 p. : ISBN 0-86922-416-6
NYPL [Sc D 89-38]

Makhanya, Sibusisiwe, 1894-
Moya, Lily Patience. Not either an
experimental doll . Bloomington , c1987. xv,
217 p., [18] p. of plates : ISBN 0-253-34843-9
DDC 968.05/6 19
HQ1800 .M69 1988   *NYPL [Sc D 89-282]*

MAKHANYA, SIBUSISIWE, 1894- -
CORRESPONDENCE.
Moya, Lily Patience. Not either an
experimental doll . Bloomington , c1987. xv,
217 p., [18] p. of plates : ISBN 0-253-34843-9
DDC 968.05/6 19
HQ1800 .M69 1988   *NYPL [Sc D 89-282]*

Makhoere, Caesarina Khana. No child's play : in
prison under apartheid / Caesarina Kona
Makhoere. London : Women's Press, 1988. 121
p. ; 20 cm. ISBN 0-7043-4111-5 :
1. Makhoere, Caesarina Khana. 2. Political prisioners -
South Africa - Biography. 3. Apartheid - South Africa.
4. Women - South AFrica - Political activity. I. Title.
NYPL [Sc C 88-333]

MAKHOERE, CAESARINA KHANA.
Makhoere, Caesarina Khana. No child's play .
London , 1988. 121 p. ; ISBN 0-7043-4111-5 :
NYPL [Sc C 88-333]

Makinde, M. Akin. African philosophy, culture,
and traditional medicine / by M. Akin
Makinde. Athens, Ohio : Ohio University
Center for International Studies, 1988. xvii, 154
p., [2] leaves of plates : ill. ; 22 cm. (Monographs
in international studies. Africa series . no. 53) Includes
index. Bibliography: p. 141-149. ISBN 0-89680-152-7
DDC 199/.6 19
1. Medicine, Primitive - Africa, Sub-Saharan. 2. Africa,
Sub-Saharan - Civilization. I. Title. II. Series.
B5375 .M35 1988   *NYPL [Sc D 88-1273]*

Makinde, Olu. Profile of career education / Olu
Makinde & Kayode Alao. Ibadan, Oyo State,
Nigeria : Signal Educational Services, 1987. xv,
308 p. ; 22 cm. Bibliography: p. 308-309. ISBN
978-254-605-4
1. Vocational education - Nigeria. I. Alao, Kayode. II.
Title.   *NYPL [Sc D 89-177]*

Making a spectacle : feminist essays on
contemporary women's theatre / edited and
with an introduction by Lynda Hart. Ann
Arbor : University of Michigan Press, c1989.
347 p. : ill. ; 24 cm. (Women and culture series)
Includes bibliographies. ISBN 0-472-09389-4 (alk.
paper) : DDC 812/.54/099287 19
1. American drama - Women authors - History and
criticism. 2. American drama - 20th century - History
and criticism. 3. English drama - Women authors -

History and criticism. 4. English drama - 20th century -
History and criticism. 5. Feminist theater. I. Hart,
Lynda, 1953-.
PS338.W6 M3 1989   *NYPL [JFE 89-144]*

Making it happen. Naylor, Phyllis Reynolds.
Chicago [1970] 128 p. ISBN 0-695-80144-9
DDC [Fic]
PZ7.N24 Mak   *NYPL [Sc D 88-446]*

Makinwa, P. Kofo. The Urban poor in Nigeria /.
Ibadan, Nigeria , 1987. xvi, 413 p. : ISBN
978-16-7489-4   *NYPL [Sc D 88-779]*

Makuya, T. N. Dzimbava [by] T. N. Makuya. 1st
ed. Pretoria, Van Schaik, 1972. 62 p. 22 cm.
ISBN 0-627-00110-6
1. Venda language - Texts. I. Title.
NYPL [JFD 76-2629]

Malabí Maticulambí . Alvarez, Alexandra, 1946-
Montevideo, Uruguay? , c1987. 191 p. ;
NYPL [Sc D 88-1012]

Malagasy . Prou, Michel, 1934- Paris , 1987- v. :
ISBN 2-85802-513-1   *NYPL [Sc D 88-102]*

MALAGASY LANGUAGE - TEXTS.
Fantaro ny fitampoha. Antananarivo , 1985. 47
p. :   *NYPL [Sc F 89-121]*

Iray, Olana. Ranomasina Indiana /.
Antananarivo [1983] 98 p. ;
NYPL [Sc C 88-239]

Ireny lovantsofina ireny [microform] /.
Tananarive [1978] iv, 48 p. ;
NYPL [Sc Micro F-10987]

Ny djoutche Malagasy [microform] /.
Tananarive [1978] 28 p. ;
NYPL [Sc Micro F-10988]

Raharolahy, Elie. Tantara notsongaina /.
[Antananarivo?] [1976] v. :
NYPL [Sc C 88-238]

Ratsiraka, Didier. Kabary tatitra nataon'
Andriamatoa Didier Ratsiraka, filohan' ny
Repoblika Demokratika Malagasy.
Antananarivo , 1985. 93 p. :
NYPL [Sc D 88-1295]

Malami, Shehu, Alhaji. Nigerian memories /
Alhaji Shehu Malami ; edited and introduced
by David Williams. London : Cass ; Ibadan :
Evans, 1985. xii, [139] p., [12] p. of plates : ill.,
col. port. ; 25 cm. ISBN 978-16-7526-8 (Nigeria)
1. Nigeria - Civilization. 2. Nigeria - Politics and
government - 1960-. I. Williams, David, 1913-. II. Title.
NYPL [Sc D 88-532]

Malanda, Ange-Séverin. Henri Lopes et
l'impératif romanesque / Ange-Séverin
Malanda. éd. originale Paris : Silex, c1987. 142
p. ; 22 cm. Includes bibliographical references. ISBN
2-09-387190-6
1. Lopes, Henri, 1937- - Criticism and interpretation. I.
Title.   *NYPL [Sc D 89-207]*

Malaŵi . Carter, Judy. London , 1987. 176 p. ;
ISBN 0-333-43987-2 (cased) : DDC 916.897/044
19
DT858.2   *NYPL [Sc F 88-183]*

MALAWI.
Knights, Ian E. Malawi [microform] . London ,
1980. 19 p. :
NYPL [Sc Micro R-4108 no.21]

MALAWI - COMMERCE - HANDBOOKS,
MANUALS, ETC.
Johnston, Harry Hamilton, Sir, 1858-1927.
Handbook to British Central Africa /. Blantyre
[Malawi] , 1985. viii, 111 p. :
NYPL [Sc D 88-1006]

Malawi Congress Party. Banda, Hastings
Kamuzu, 1905- Address by His Excellency the
Life President, Ngwazi Dr. H. Kamuzu Banda,
to open the 1978 convention of the Malaŵi
Congress Party, Zomba Catholic Secondary
School, September 24, 1978 [microform]
Blantyre [1978] 16 p. ;
NYPL [Sc Micro F-11123]

MALAWI - DESCRIPTION AND TRAVEL.
Buchanan, John, 1855-1896. The Shirè
highlands. Blantyre [Malawi] , 1982. xii, 260 p.,
[8] p. of plates :   *NYPL [Sc C 87-434]*

MALAWI - DESCRIPTION AND TRAVEL -
GUIDE-BOOKS.
Carter, Judy. Malaŵi . London , 1987. 176 p. :
ISBN 0-333-43987-2 (cased) : DDC 916.897/044
19
DT858.2   *NYPL [Sc F 88-183]*

Johnston, Harry Hamilton, Sir, 1858-1927.
Handbook to British Central Africa /. Blantyre
[Malawi] , 1985. viii, 111 p. :
NYPL [Sc D 88-1006]

MALAWI - ECONOMIC CONDITIONS.
Martin, Michael. Malawi, ein
entwicklungspolitisches Musterland? . Bonn ,
1984. 95 p. : ISBN 3-921614-17-1
NYPL [Sc D 88-681]

Malawi, ein entwicklungspolitisches
Musterland? . Martin, Michael. Bonn , 1984.
95 p. : ISBN 3-921614-17-1
NYPL [Sc D 88-681]

MALAWI - FICTION.
Kamkondo, Dede. The children of the lake /.
Limbe Malaŵi , c1987. 103 p. ;
NYPL [Sc C 89-108]

MALAWI - HISTORY.
Buchanan, John, 1855-1896. The Shirè
highlands. Blantyre [Malawi] , 1982. xii, 260 p.,
[8] p. of plates :   *NYPL [Sc C 87-434]*

Wills, A. J. (Alfred John) An introduction to
the history of central Africa . Oxford
[Oxfordshire] , New York , 1985. xiii, 556 p. :
ISBN 0-19-873075-6 : DDC 968.9 19
DT963.5 .W54 1985   *NYPL [Sc D 88-656]*

MALAWI - POLITICS AND GOVERNMENT.
Madu, Oliver V. Models of class domination in
plural societies of Central Africa /.
Washington , c1978. vi, 510 p. ;
NYPL [Sc D 88-1067]

MALAWI - POLITICS AND GOVERNMENT -
1964-
Banda, Hastings Kamuzu, 1905- Address by His
Excellency the Life President, Ngwazi Dr. H.
Kamuzu Banda, to open the 1978 convention of
the Malaŵi Congress Party, Zomba Catholic
Secondary School, September 24, 1978
[microform] Blantyre [1978] 16 p. ;
NYPL [Sc Micro F-11123]

MALAWI - SOCIAL CONDITIONS.
Madu, Oliver V. Models of class domination in
plural societies of Central Africa /.
Washington , c1978. vi, 510 p. ;
NYPL [Sc D 88-1067]

MALAWI - SOCIAL LIFE AND CUSTOMS.
Peltzer, Karl. Some contributions of traditional
healing practices towards psychosocial health
care in Malawi /. Eschborn bei Frankfurt Om
Main , 1987. 341 p. : ISBN 3-88074-174-3
NYPL [Sc D 88-618]

MALE HOMOSEXUALITY. see
HOMOSEXUALITY, MALE.

Male homosexuality in Central and South
America / edited by Stephen O. Murray. New
York : GAU-NY, 1987. 199 p. ; 22 cm. (Gai
saber monograph . 5) Includes bibliographies.
1. Homosexuality, Male - Central America. 2.
Homosexuality, Male - South America. I. Murray,
Stephen O. II. Series.   *NYPL [Sc D 88-557]*

Maleyana, Nwagumana J. Schnorr von Carolsfeld,
Julius, 1794-1872. [Bibel in Bildern. Selections.]
Bibele hi swifaniso . Kensington, Tvl. , 1970. 64
p. :   *NYPL [Sc E 89-180]*

Le Mali /. Gaudio, Attilio, 1930- Paris , c1988.
267 p., [8] p. of plates : ISBN 2-86537-208-1
NYPL [Sc D 88-1412]

MALI.
Gaudio, Attilio, 1930- Le Mali /. Paris , c1988.
267 p., [8] p. of plates : ISBN 2-86537-208-1
NYPL [Sc D 88-1412]

Naylor, Kim. Let's visit Mali. /. Basingstoke ,
1987. 96 p. : ISBN 0-333-44988-6
NYPL [Sc D 88-397]

MALI EMPIRE - HISTORY - 19TH
CENTURY.
Hājj 'Umar ibn Sa'īd al-Fūtī, 1794?-1864.
[Bayān mā waqa'a. French & Arabic.] Voilà ce
qui est arrivé . Paris , 1983. 261 p., [57] p. of
plates : ISBN 2-222-03216-4
NYPL [Sc F 88-211]

MALI - FICTION.
Konaté, Moussa, 1951- Une aube incertaine .
Paris , c1985. 217 p. ; ISBN 2-7087-0459-1
MLCS 86/6414 (P)   *NYPL [Sc C 89-105]*

Konaté, Moussa, 1951- Chronique d'une
journée de répression /. Paris , c1988. 143 p. ;
NYPL [Sc D 88-846]

MALI - HISTORY - DICTIONARIES.
Imperato, Pascal James. Historical dictionary of
Mali /. Metuchen, N.J. , 1986. xvii, 359 p. ;
   ISBN 0-8108-1885-X   DDC 966/.23 19
DT551.5 .I46 1986   *NYPL [Sc D 87-5]*

**MALLORY, VINCENT DEREK - TRIALS,
   LITIGATION ETC. - BIBLIOGRAPHY.**
Haith, Dorothy May. State of Georgia v.
Vincent Derek Mallory M.D. . Washington ,
1988. 12 leaves ;   *NYPL [Sc F 88-131]*

Malmstad, John E. Pushkin and his friends .
Cambridge , 1987. xii, 95 p. :
                        NYPL [Sc F 88-236]

**MALNUTRITION IN CHILDREN -
   MOZAMBIQUE - MAPUTO.**
Santos, Norberto Teixeira. Avaliação nutricional
da população infantil banto (0-5 anos) de uma
zona suburbana da cidade Lourenço Marques .
[Lourenço Marques, Moçambique] 1974. 400
p., [40] p. of plates :   *NYPL [Sc E 88-143]*

Malone, Beverly Louise. Relationship of Black
female administrators' mentoring experience and
career satisfaction [Microform] / by Beverly
Louise Malone. 1982. 165 leaves. Thesis (Ph.
D.)-- University of Cincinnati, 1982. Bibliography:
leaves [105]-116. Microfilm of typescript. Ann Arbor,
Mich. : University Microfilms International, 1982. 1
microfilm reel ; 35 mm.
*1. Afro-American women executives. 2. Job satisfaction.
I. Title.*   *NYPL [Sc Micro R-4804]*

Malone, Vernon. Dodge, Steve. A guide and
history of Hope Town /. Decatur, Ill., USA ,
c1985. [48] p. :   ISBN 0-932265-01-4 (pbk.) :
   DDC 917.296 19
F1659.H67 D63 1985   NYPL [Sc D 88-684]

Malou, Job. Dinka vowel system / Job Malou.
Dallas, TX : Summer Institute of Linguistics ;
Arlington : University of Texas at Arlington,
1988. x, 89 p. : ill. ; 23 cm. (Summer Institute of
Linguistics. Publications in linguistics. publication no.
82) Bibliography: p. 85-89.   ISBN 0-88312-008-9
1. Dinka language - Vowels. I. Title. II. Series.
                        NYPL [Sc D 88-1445]

Malveaux, Julianne. Slipping through the cracks .
New Brunswick, N.J. , 1986. 302 p. ;   ISBN
0-88738-662-8   *NYPL [Sc D 88-767]*

Mama--watch out, I'm growingup! /. Sealy,
Adrienne V. Brooklyn, New York , 1976. [45]
p. :   *NYPL [Sc F 88-135]*

Mambo book of Zimbabwean Verse in English /
editors: Colin & O-lan Style. Gweru,
Zimbabwe : Mambo Press, c986. xxix, 417 p. ;
22 cm. (Mambo writers series. English section. vol.
23) Includes bibliographical references and indexes.
   ISBN 0-86922-367-4 (pbk.)
*1. Zimbabwean poetry (English). 2. Zimbabwean
poetry - Translation into English. 3. English poetry -
Translations from African languages. 4. African
literature (English). I. Style, Colin. II. Style, O-lan.*
                        NYPL [JFD 88-10986]

**Mambo occasional papers : social-economic
   series .**
(no.20) Bouedillon, M. F. C. Studies of fishing
on Lake Kariba /. [Harare] , 1985. 185 p. :
                        NYPL [Sc D 88-875]

**Mambo occasional papers. Missio-pastoral
   series .**
(no. 11) Nyamiti, Charles. Christ as our
ancestor . Gweru [Zimbabwe] , 1984. 151 p. ;
   DDC 232 19
BT205 .N82 1984   *NYPL [Sc D 88-986]*

(no. 14) Schultheis, Michael J. Catholic social
teaching and the Church in Africa /. Gweru,
Zimbabwe , c1984. 56 p. ;
                        NYPL [Sc D 88-1198]

(no. 15) Meili, Josef. In the image of Christ
crucified and risen, in the service of the
community . Gweru, Zimbabwe , 1986. 127 p. ;
                        NYPL [Sc D 88-1332]

(no. 17) Daneel, M. L. (Marthinus L.) Quest
for belonging . Gweru, Zimbabwe , 1987. 310
p., [17] p. of plates :   ISBN 0-86922-426-3
                        NYPL [Sc D 88-1007]

Mambo writers. English section .
(v. 27) Parwada, Batisai B., 1966- Shreds of
darkness /. Gweru, Zimbabwe , 1987. 111 p. ;
                        NYPL [Sc C 89-96]

Mambo writers series. Ndebele section .
(v. 5) Mabuza, Vivian R. N. Inzondo engela

mkhawulo /. Gweru , 1988. 120 p. ;   ISBN
                        NYPL [Sc C 89-7]

Mambo writers series. Shona section .
(v. 21) Chakarira chindunduma . Gweru,
Zimbabwe , 1985. x, 78 p. ;   ISBN 0-86922-365-8
                        NYPL [Sc D 88-439]

(v. 21) Chakarira chindunduma . Gweru,
Zimbabwe , 1985. x, 78 p. ;   ISBN 0-86922-365-8
                        NYPL [Sc D 88-439]

(v. 22) Chigidi, Willie L. Imwe chanzi
ichabvepi? . Gweru , 1986. 60 p. ;
                        NYPL [Sc C 89-114]

(v. 24) Mzemba, C. (Charles), 1955- Aita twake
/. Zimbabwe , 1987. 135 p. ;   ISBN
0-86922-418-2   *NYPL [Sc C 89-119]*

(vol. 18) Kawara, James. Sajeni Chimedza /.
Gweru, [Zimbabwe] , 1984. 174 p. ;   ISBN
0-86922-327-5   *NYPL [Sc C 88-97]*

**al-Mamlakah al-'Arabīyah al-Sa'ūdīyah. see Saudi
Arabia.**

Mamma Decemba /. Moffatt, Nigel D. London ,
1987. 34 p. ;   ISBN 0-571-14775-5 :
                        NYPL [Sc C 87-465]

MAN - FOOD HABITS. see FOOD HABITS.

MAN - INFLUENCE ON NATURE - AFRICA.
Environmental issues in African development
planning /. Cambridge , c1988. v, 84 p. :   ISBN
0-902993-21-6 (pbk) :   DDC 330.96/0328 19
HC502   *NYPL [Sc D 88-1233]*

Harrison, Paul, 1945- The greening of Africa .
London , 1987. 380 p. :   ISBN 0-586-08642-0
(pbk) :   DDC 330.96/0328 19
HC502   *NYPL [Sc C 88-327]*

Man pass man, and other stories /. Mokoso,
Ndeley. Harlow, Essex , 1987. 108 p. ;   ISBN
0-582-01681-9   *NYPL [Sc C 88-225]*

MAN POWER. see MANPOWER.

**MAN, PREHISTORIC - EGYPT -
   CONGRESSES.**
Symposium on the Peopling of Ancient Egypt
and the deciphering of Meroitic Script (1974 :
Cairo, Egypt) [Peuplement de l'Egipte ancienne
et la déchiffrement de l'écriture méroïtique.
Spanish.] Poblamiento del antiguo Egipto y
desciframiento de la escritura meroítica /.
Barcelona , Paris , 1983. 155 p. :   ISBN
0-923301-60-5 (Unesco)
                        NYPL [Sc D 88-603]

MAN, PREHISTORIC - TANGANYIKA.
Perkins, Carol Morse. The shattered skull .
New York, 1965. 59 p.,
DT440 .P4   *NYPL [Sc E 88-145]*

**MAN, PREHISTORIC - ZAMBIA - EASTERN
   PROVINCE.**
Phillipson, D. W. The prehistory of eastern
Zambia /. Nairobi , 1976. xii, 229 p., [21] leaves
of plates (5 fold.) :   ISBN 0-500-97003-3 :
GN865.Z3 P48   *NYPL [JFF 79-1585]*

The man--Sir Justice Udo Udoma /. Udo-Inyang,
D. S. (Denis S.) Calabar [Nigeria] [1985] 72
p. :   ISBN 978-228-168-9 (pbk.)   DDC
347.669/03534 B 346.69073534 B 19
LAW   *NYPL [Sc D 88-776]*

The man who died . Acquah, Kobena Eyi. Accra ,
1984. 94 p. :   ISBN 996-478-065-6 (pbk.)   DDC
821 19
PR9379.9.A27 M3 1984
                        NYPL [Sc D 88-247]

The man with the white liver . Jackson, Angela,
1951- New York City , 1987. [12] p. :   ISBN
0-936556-16-1   DDC 811/.54 19
PS3560.A179 M3 1987   *NYPL [Sc F 89-14]*

Management education : an international survey /
edited by William Byrt. London ; New York :
Routledge, 1989. viii, 229 p. ; 23 cm. Includes
index.   ISBN 0-415-00423-3   DDC 658/.007 19
*1. Management - Study and teaching. I. Byrt, W. J.
(William John).*
HD30.4 .M33 1988   *NYPL [Sc D 89-325]*

**MANAGEMENT, INDUSTRIAL. see
   INDUSTRIAL MANAGEMENT.**

MANAGEMENT - NIGERIA - CONGRESSES.
Development of management education in
Nigeria /. Ikeja, Nigeria , 1985. 555 p. :   ISBN
978-14-0017-X   *NYPL [Sc E 89-161]*

MANAGEMENT - STUDY AND TEACHING.
Management education . London , New York ,

1989. viii, 229 p. ;   ISBN 0-415-00423-3   DDC
658/.007 19
HD30.4 .M33 1988   *NYPL [Sc D 89-325]*

**MANAGEMENT - STUDY AND TEACHING -
   NIGERIA - CONGRESSES.**
Development of management education in
Nigeria /. Ikeja, Nigeria , 1985. 555 p. :   ISBN
978-14-0017-X   *NYPL [Sc E 89-161]*

Managing the Botswana brigades . Langley, Ph.
Douala, U.R.C. [1983] 93 p. :   DDC
658.3/12404/096811 19
HD5715.5.B55 L36 1983
                        NYPL [Sc E 88-483]

Managing the Nigerian education enterprise /.
Aderounmu, Olusola. Ikeja, Lagos, Nigeria ,
1986. 230 p. :   *NYPL [Sc F 88-171]*

Manaka, Matsemela. Egoli, city of gold
[microform] : a Soyikwa Black Theatre
production / written by Matsemela Manaka ;
acted and developed by John Moalusi Ledwaba,
Hamilton Mahonga Silwane. Johannesburg :
Ravan Press, [198-?] 28 p. ; 20 cm.
(Soyikwa-Ravan publication) Microfiche. New York:
New York Public Library, 198 . 1 microfiche: negative;
11 x 15 cm. (FSN Sc 019,004)
*1. Blacks - South Africa - Drama. I. Ledwaba, John
Moalusi. II. Silwane, Hamilton Mahonga. III. Title.*
                        NYPL [Sc Micro F-11049]

Mandatory sanctions . Mangope, Lucas. Lagos,
Nigeria , 1988. v. 110, a-t p. of plates :   ISBN
978-242-313-0   *NYPL [Sc C 88-181]*

Mandaza, Ibbo. SADCC . Tokyo, Japan :
London ; xi, 256 p. ;   ISBN 0-86232-748-2 :
   DDC 337.1/68 19
HC900 .S23 1987   *NYPL [Sc D 89-50]*

**MANDÉ (AFRICAN PEOPLE) see
   MANDINGO (AFRICAN PEOPLE)**

The Mande blacksmiths . McNaughton, Patrick
R. Bloomington , c1988. xxiv, 241 p., [4] p. of
plates :   ISBN 0-253-33683-X   DDC 306/.089963
19
DT551.45.M36 M38 1988
                        NYPL [Sc E 88-393]

Mandela and other poems /. Clark, John Pepper,
1935- Ikeja , 1988. vi, 37 p. ;   ISBN
978-13-9633-4   *NYPL [Sc C 89-154]*

MANDELA, NELSON, 1918-
Nelson Mandela . [London , 1988] 61 p. :
                        NYPL [Sc G 89-3]

**MANDELA, NELSON, 1918- - JUVENILE
   LITERATURE.**
Haskins, James, 1941- Winnie Mandela . New
York , c1988. 179 p., [12] p. of plates :   ISBN
0-399-21515-8   DDC 968.06/092/4 B 92 19
DT779.955.M36 H38 1988
                        NYPL [Sc D 88-1138]

**MANDELA, WINNIE - JUVENILE
   LITERATURE.**
Haskins, James, 1941- Winnie Mandela . New
York , c1988. 179 p., [12] p. of plates :   ISBN
0-399-21515-8   DDC 968.06/092/4 B 92 19
DT779.955.M36 H38 1988
                        NYPL [Sc D 88-1138]

Mandela's earth and other poems /. Soyinka,
Wole. New York, N.Y. , 1988. 70 p. ;   ISBN
0-394-57021-9 :   DDC 821 19
PR9387.9.S6 M36 1988
                        NYPL [Sc D 88-1480]

**MANDINGO (AFRICAN PEOPLE) -
   FOLKLORE.**
Contes du pays malinké . Paris , c1987. 238 p. :
   ISBN 2-86537-188-3   *NYPL [Sc C 88-151]*

**MANDINGO (AFRICAN PEOPLE) - SOCIAL
   LIFE AND CUSTOMS.**
Keita, Djigui. Le rôle socio-religieux de la cola
dans la société malinké . [Abidjan? , 1985] 72
leaves :   *NYPL [Sc F 88-307]*

**MANDINGO LANGUAGE - READERS FOR
   NEW LITERATES.**
Dixon, Joan. Jaata kendeyaa /. [Amherst,
Ma.? , 198-?] 91 p. :   *NYPL [Sc F 89-135]*

Mandou Yénou . Geary, Christraud M.
München , c1985. 223 p. :   ISBN 3-923804-08-3
                        NYPL [Sc E 88-178]

Maneno yanayotatiza /. Zani, Zachariah M.
Nairobi , c1983. xi, 112 ;
                        NYPL [Sc C 89-57]

Manessy, Gabriel. Les Langues de l'Afrique subsaharienne /. Paris , 1981. 2 v : ISBN 2-222-01720-3 : *NYPL [JFN 81-11 v.1]*

Manga, Charles. Kissi stories and songs /. Freetown , 1987. 95 p. :
NYPL [Sc D 89-459]

Mangan, J. A. Pleasure, profit, proselytism . London, England , Totowa, NJ , 1988. 284 p. [8] p. ofplates : ISBN 0-7146-3289-9 : DDC 796/.0941 19
GV605 .P58 1988 *NYPL [JLE 88-1312]*

Manganyi, N. C. Mphahlele, Ezekiel. Bury me at the marketplace . Johannesburg , c1984. 202 p. ; ISBN 0-620-06779-9 *NYPL [Sc D 89-117]*

Mangles, James, 1786-1867. Irby, Charles Leonard, 1789-1845. Travels in Egypt and Nubia, Syria and Asia Minor . London , 1985. xxxiii, 560 p., [6] leaves of plates (3 folded) : ISBN 1-85077-082-4 : DDC 915.6/041 916.2/043 19
DS48 DT53 *NYPL [JFD 88-9340]*

Mangope, Lucas. Mandatory sanctions : Bophuthatswana and frontline OAU nations (vintage speeches) / Lucas Mangope. Lagos, Nigeria : Emmcon (TWORF), 1988. v. 110, a-t p. of plates : ill., ports. ; 20 cm. ISBN 978-242-313-0
1. Bophuthatswana (South Africa). 2. Africa, Southern - Politics and government - 1975-. I. Title.
NYPL [Sc C 88-181]

La mangrove mulâtre /. Cabort-Masson, Guy, 1937- Saint-Joseph, Martinique , c1986. 282 p. ;
MLCS 87/3007 (P) *NYPL [Sc D 88-571]*

Mangua, Charles. Son of woman in Mombasa / Charles Mangua. Nairobi : Heinemann, 1986. 211 p. ; 18 cm. (Spear book)
1. Mombasa (Kenya) - Fiction. I. Title.
NYPL [Sc C 88-303]

Mangulu, Motingea. Elements de grammaire lingombe avec une bibliographie exhaustive / Motingea Mangulu. Mbandaka, Zaire * Centre aequatoria, 1988. 88 p. : fold map ; 21 cm. (Etudes aequatoria . 3)
1. Ngombe language - Grammar. I. Title. II. Series.
NYPL [Sc D 89-40]

Manhattan (New York, N.Y.). President's Task Force on Housing for Homeless Families. A shelter is not a home : report / of the Manhattan Borough President's Task Force on Housing for Homeless Families. New York, NY : Task Force, 1987. iv, 139, [19] p. ; 28 cm. "March 1987." Bibliography: p. 134-139.
1. Homelessness - New York (N.Y.). I. Title.
NYPL [JLF 87-1294]

Manifesto of the Maurice Bishop Patriotic Movement. Maurice Bishop Patriotic Movement. St. George's, Grenada [1984] 60 p. : *NYPL [Sc D 88-676]*

Manigat, Sabine. Auguste, Michel Hector. Haiti, la lucha por la democracia (clase obrera, partidos y sindicatos) /. Puebla [1986]. 244 p. ;
NYPL [Sc D 88-761]

The manipulation of religion in Nigeria, 1977-1987 /. Usman, Yusufu Bala, 1945- Kaduna, Nigeria , 1987. 153 p. ; ISBN 978-255-708-0 *NYPL [Sc C 88-220]*

The Mankind quarterly .
(monograph no. 3) Evolution, creative intelligence and intergroup competition /. Washington , 1986. 96 p. ; ISBN 0-941694-30-5
NYPL [Sc D 89-532]

Mankind quarterly. Monograph .
(no. 4) Essays on the nature of intelligence and the analysis of racial differences in the performance of IQ tests /. Washington D.C. , c1988. 72 p. : ISBN 0-941694-32-1
NYPL [Sc D 89-546]

Manman Dlo contre la fée Carabosse . Chamoiseau, Patrick. Paris , c1982. 143 p. : ISBN 2-903033-33-1
MLCS 82/8314 (P) *NYPL [JAY B-3918]*

Mann, Horace, 1796-1859.
Speech of Horace Mann, of Massachusetts, in the House of Representatives, Feb. 23, 1849; on slavery in the United States, and the slave trade in the District of Columbia. Boston : Published by Wm. B. Fowle 138 1/2 Washington Street, [1849]. [15] p. ; 26 cm.

1. Slavery - United States - Speeches in Congress - 1849. 2. Slavery - Washington (D.C.). I. Title. II. Title: Slavery in the United States, and the slave trade in the District of Columbia.
E416 .M28 *NYPL [Sc Rare C 89-3]*
Speech of Mr. Horace Mann, of Massachusetts, in the House of Representatives of the United States, June 30, 1848 : on the right of Congress to legislate for the territories of the United States, and its duty to exclude slavery therefrom. [Rev. ed.] [Boston] : Wm. B. Fowle, 1848. 31 p. ; 25 cm. Caption title.
1. Slavery - United States - Extension to the territories. 2. Slavery - United States - Speeches in Congress - 1848. I. Title. *NYPL [Sc Rare C 89-30]*

Mann, Michael. A thesaurus of African languages : a classified and annotated inventory of the spoken languages of Africa with an appendix on their written representation / by Michael Mann and David Dalby with Philip Baker ... [et al.]. New York : H. Zell, 1987. 325 p. ; 31 cm. Includes bibliographical references and index. ISBN 0-905450-24-8
1. African languages. I. Dalby, David. II. Baker, Philip. III. Title. *NYPL [Sc F 88-142]*

Manno, Rosemary. Laraque, Paul, 1920- Camourade . Willimantic, CT , New York, NY , 1988. 124 p. ; ISBN 0-915306-71-9
NYPL [Sc D 88-629]

Manona, C. W.
Bekker, S. B. Socio-economic survey of the Amatola Basin . Grahamstown [South Africa] Institute of Social and Economic Rrsearch, 1981. 58, xxxxiv p. : ISBN 0-86810-073-0
NYPL [Sc F 87-430]
Whisson, Michael G., 1937- Cherchez la femme. Grahamstown [South Africa] , 1985. 90 p. [3] leaves of plates : ISBN 0-86810-125-7
NYPL [Sc F 87-433]

Manpower and educational planning in Ghana. Abban, J. B. Prerequisites of manpower and educational planning in Ghana /. Accra , 1986. xii, 144 p. ; ISBN 996-496-307-6
NYPL [Sc D 89-496]

MANPOWER DEVELOPMENT AND TRAINING. see OCCUPATIONAL TRAINING.

Manpower development and utilization in Nigeria : problems and policies / edited by Folayan Ojo, Adeyemo Aderinto and Tayo Fashoyin. Lagos, Nigeria : Lagos University Press, 1986. xiii, 240 p. ; 23 cm. Includes bibliographical references and index. ISBN 978-226-441-5
1. Manpower policy - Nigeria. 2. Labor supply - Nigeria. I. Ojo, Folayan. II. Aderinto, Adeyemo. III. Fashoyin, Tayo. *NYPL [Sc D 88-1077]*

MANPOWER - KENYA.
Kenya. Presidential Working Party on Education and Manpower Training for the Next Decade and Beyond. Report of the Presidential Working Party on Education and Manpower Training for the Next Decade and Beyond /. Nairobi , 1988. xvii, 174 p. ;
NYPL [Sc E 89-232]

MANPOWER PLANNING - GHANA.
Abban, J. B. Prerequisites of manpower and educational planning in Ghana /. Accra , 1986. xii, 144 p. ; ISBN 996-496-307-6
NYPL [Sc D 89-496]

MANPOWER POLICY - AFRICA.
The Challenge of employment and basic needs in Africa . Nairobi , New York , 1986. xii, 379 p. ; ISBN 0-19-572559-X *NYPL [Sc E 88-419]*

MANPOWER POLICY - AFRICA - CONGRESSES.
Human resources development and utilization in Africa . Maseru [Lesotho] , 1988. vi, 160 p. ; ISBN 0-620-12102-5 *NYPL [Sc D 89-558]*

MANPOWER POLICY - AFRICA, WEST - CASE STUDIES.
Sex roles, population and development in West Africa . London , Portsmouth, N.H. , 1987. xiii, 242 p. ; ISBN 0-435-08022-9 DDC 304.6/0966 19
HB3665.5.A3 S49 1988
NYPL [Sc E 88-318]

MANPOWER POLICY - NIGERIA.
Manpower development and utilization in Nigeria . Lagos, Nigeria , 1986. xiii, 240 p. ;

ISBN 978-226-441-5
NYPL [Sc D 88-1077]
Ukpong, Ignatius I. The contributions of expatriate and indigenous manpower to the manufacturing industry in Nigeria . [Calabar, Cross River State, Nigeria [c1986] ix, 61 p. ; ISBN 978-227-526-3 DDC 331.12/57/09669 19
HD5848.A6 U37 1986 *NYPL [Sc C 89-128]*

MANPOWER POLICY, RURAL - BOTSWANA.
Gobotswang, Z. Pilot evaluation report on Mahalapye Development Trust /. Gaborone, Botswana [1982] v leaves, 61, 3 p. ;
HD5710.85.B59 G63 1982
NYPL [Sc F 89-108]

Manpower research monograph .
(no. 27) Baker's dozen . Washington [1973] 112 p. ; *NYPL [Sc F 88-244]*

MANPOWER UTILIZATION. see MANPOWER POLICY; PERSONNEL MANAGEMENT.

MANPOWER UTILIZATION PLANNING. see MANPOWER PLANNING.

MANSLAUGHTER. see MURDER.

MANTLE, MICKEY, 1931-
Honig, Donald. Mays, Mantle, Snider . New York, N.Y. , London , c1987. vii, 151 p. : ISBN 0-02-551200-5 DDC 796.357/092/2 B 19
GV865.A1 H6192 1987
NYPL [JFF 87-1461]

Manuel de conversation somali-français suivi d'un guide Dijibouti /. Dibeth, Véronique Carton. Paris , c1988. 80 p. : ISBN 2-7384-0090-6
NYPL [Sc E 88-536]

Manuel d'hygiène [microform] /. Bordes, Ary. [Port-au-Prince, , 1975. 130 p. :
NYPL [Sc Micro R-4840 no.9]

Manuel d'hygiène [microform] . Bordes, Ary. [Port-au-Prince?] , 1976. 78 p. :
NYPL [Sc Micro R-4840 no.7]

MANUSCRIPTS, ARABIC - TANZANIA - ZANZIBAR - CATALOGS.
Résumés de vieux manuscrits arabes . Zanzibar [Tanzania] , 1981. x, 50 leaves ;
NYPL [Sc B 88-10]

MANUSCRIPTS - SOUTH AFRICA - TRANSVAAL - CATALOGS.
University of the Witwatersrand. Library. Guide to the archives and papers . Johannesburg , 1979. v, 100 p. ; ISBN 0-85494-593-8
NYPL [Sc F 89-32]

Manya K'Omalowete a Djonga, 1950- Patrice Lumumba, le Sankuru et l'Afrique : essai / Manya K'Omalowete a Djonga. Lutry : Jean-Marie Bouchain, [1985] 166 p. : maps ; 21 cm. Bibliography: p. 53-54.
1. Lumumba, Patrice, 1925-1961. 2. Zaire - Politics and government - 1960-. 3. Sankuru (Zaire) - Politics and government. I. Title. *NYPL [Sc D 88-1490]*

MAOISM. see COMMUNISM.

Maope, Kelebone A. Human rights in Botswana, Lesotho and Swaziland : survey / by K.A. Maope. Roma, Lesotho : Institute of Southern African Studies, National University of Lesotho, 1986. iii, 155 p. ; 21 cm. (Human Rights Project. Monograph series . no. 1)
1. Civil rights - Botswana. 2. Civil rights - Lesotho. 3. Civil rights - Swaziland. I. Series: Human and people's rights monograph series , no. 1. II. Title.
NYPL [Sc D 88-855]

Mapplethorpe, Robert. Black book / photographs by Robert Mapplethorpe ; foreword by Ntozake Shange. 1st ed. New York : St. Martin's Press, c1986. 91 p. : chiefly ill. ; 30 cm.
1. Afro-American men - Pictorial works. 2. Photography of men. 3. Photography - Portraits. I. Shange, Ntozake. II. Title. III. Title: Robert Mapplethorpe black book. *NYPL [Sc F 87-42]*

MARADI RIVER VALLEY (NIGERIA AND NIGER) - ECONOMIC CONDITIONS.
Nicolas, Guy. Don rituel et échange marchand dans une société sahélienne /. Paris , 1986. 282 p. : ISBN 2-85265-117-3 *NYPL [JFF 87-660]*

MARADI RIVER VALLEY (NIGERIA AND NIGER) - SOCIAL LIFE AND CUSTOMS.
Nicolas, Guy. Don rituel et échange marchand dans une société sahélienne /. Paris , 1986. 282 p. : ISBN 2-85265-117-3 *NYPL [JFF 87-660]*

MARAN, RENÉ, 1887-1960.
Dennis, John Alfred. The René Maran story .
Ann Arbor, Mich. , c1987. viii, 275 p. :
NYPL [Sc D 89-292]

Marcelin, Pierre, 1908- Thoby-Marcelin, Philippe,
1904-1975. [Bête du Musseau. English.] The
beast of the Haitian hills /. San Francisco ,
1986. 179 p. ; ISBN 0-87286-189-9 (pbk.) DDC
843 19
PQ3949.T45 B413 1986
NYPL [Sc D 88-199]

The march of faith . Baldwin, Lindley. J. Bronx,
N.Y. , 1944. 94 p. : *NYPL [Sc C 88-13]*

Marcus Garvey . Huntley, Eric L. Ealing,
London , 1988. 41 p. : ISBN 0-904521-41-9
NYPL [Sc E 88-499]

Marcus Garvey /. Lawler, Mary. New York ,
c1988. 110 p. : ISBN 1-555-46587-0 DDC
305.8/96073/024 B 92 19
E185.97.G3 L39 1988 *NYPL [Sc E 88-156]*

Marcus Garvey . Lewis, Rupert. Trenton, N.J. ,
1988. 301 p. : ISBN 0-86543-061-6
NYPL [Sc D 88-1454]

Marcus Gavey, anti-colonial champion /. Lewis,
Rupert. Trenton, New Jersey , 1988. 301 p. :
ISBN 0-86543-061-6 (hard)
NYPL [Sc D 88-516]

Maredza, Claude. Harurwa : the amazing but true
mystery of Norumedzo in Zimbabwe / Claude
Maredza. Harare : Longman Zimbabwe, 1987.
52 p. : ill. ; 20 cm. (Storylines) ISBN
0-908308-13-2
1. Legends - Zimbabwe. I. Title.
NYPL [Sc C 88-150]

Maree, Johann. The Independent trade unions,
1974-1984 . Johannesburg , 1987. xvi, 355 p. ;
ISBN 0-86975-307-X
NYPL [Sc D 88-1329]

MARGINAL PEOPLES. see MARGINALITY,
SOCIAL.

MARGINALITY, SOCIAL - BRAZIL.
Edmundo, Lygia Pereira. Instituição . São
Paulo , 1987. 141 p. ; *NYPL [Sc D 89-332]*

Mariah loves rock /. Walter, Mildred Pitts. New
York , c1988. 117 p. : ISBN 0-02-792511-0
DDC [Fic] 19
PZ7.W17125 Mar 1988 *NYPL [Sc C 89-29]*

Marian Anderson /. Patterson, Charles. New
York , 1988. 154 p. : ISBN 0-531-10568-7 DDC
782.1/092/4 B 92 19
ML420.A6 P4 1988 *NYPL [Sc E 89-4]*

Marian Anderson /. Stevenson, Janet. Chicago
[1963] 189 p. : *NYPL [Sc D 88-377]*

MARIEL BOATLIFT, 1980.
The Mariel injustice . Coral Gables, Fl. , c1987.
204 p. : *NYPL [Sc F 89-64]*

The Mariel injustice : in the bicentennial of the
United States constitution / by the Commission
Pro-Justice Mariel Prisoners. Coral Gables, Fl. :
The Commission, c1987. 204 p. : ill. ; 27 cm.
1. Cubans - United States. 2. Refugees - Government
policy - United States. 3. Mariel Boatlift, 1980. 4.
United States - Emigration and immigration -
Government policy. I. Commission Pro-Justice Mariel
Prisoners. *NYPL [Sc F 89-64]*

MARITIME LABOR LAW. see MERCHANT
SEAMEN - LEGAL STATUS, LAWS, ETC.

Mark Antony. see Antonius, Marcus, 83?-30 B.
C.

Markakis, John. National and class conflict in
the Horn of Africa / John Markakis.
Cambridge ; New York : Cambridge University
Press, 1987. xvii, 314 p. : maps ; 23 cm. (African
studies series. 55) "Published in collaboration with the
African Studies Centre, Cambridge"--Ser. t.p. Includes
index. Bibliography: p. 298-306. ISBN 0-521-33362-8
DDC 960/.3 19
1. Nationalism - Africa, Northeast - History - 20th
century. 2. National liberation movements - Africa,
Northeast - History - 20th century. 3. Revolutions -
Africa, Northeast - History - 20th century. 4. Africa,
Northeast - Politics and government. I. Title. II. Series.
DT367.75 .M37 1987 *NYPL [JFE 88-364]*

Markaz Dirāsāt al-Waḥdah al-ʿArabīyah (Beirut,
Lebanon) Arabs & Africa. French. Les arabes
et l'Afrique . Paris , 1986. 2 v. ; ISBN
2-85802-589-1 *NYPL [Sc E 88-390]*

A market for U. S. products in the Ivory Coast
/. United States. Bureau of International
Commerce. Washington, D.C. [1966] viii, 87
p. : *NYPL [Sc F 89-79]*

MARKETING OF MANUSCRIPTS. see
AUTHORSHIP.

MARKOE, WILLIAM MORGAN.
Nickels, Marilyn Wenzke. Black Catholic
protest and the Federated Colored Catholics,
1917-1933 . New York , 1988. ix, 325 p. ;
ISBN 0-8240-4098-8 (alk. paper) : DDC
282/.73/08996073 19
BX1407.N4 N5 1988 *NYPL [Sc E 89-85]*

Marks, Shula. Moya, Lily Patience. Not either an
experimental doll . Bloomington , c1987. xv,
217 p., [18] p. of plates : ISBN 0-253-34843-9
DDC 968.05/6 19
HQ1800 .M69 1988 *NYPL [Sc D 89-282]*

Ein Markt wie Mopti . Gardi, Bernhard. Basel ,
1985. 387 p. ; ISBN 3-85977-175-2 DDC
745/.0966/23 19
TT119.M34 G37 1985 *NYPL [Sc E 87-494]*

MARLEY, BOB - BIBLIOGRAPHY.
White, Garth. The development of Jamaican
popular music with special reference to the
music of Bob Marley . Kingston , 1982. 49 p. ;
DDC 016.78/042/097292 19
ML120.J35 5 1982 *NYPL [Sc F 87-61]*

MARLEY, BOB - JUVENILE LITERATURE.
May, Chris. Bob Marley /. London , 1985. 60
p. : ISBN 0-241-11476-4 : DDC 784.5 B 19
ML420.M3313 M4 1985
NYPL [Sc D 88-308]

Sotheby, Madeline. The Bob Marley story /.
London , 1985. 64 p. ; ISBN 0-09-160031-6
(pbk) : DDC 428.6/2 19
PE1121 *NYPL [Sc C 88-141]*

MAROONS - DOMINICAN REPUBLIC.
Deive, Carlos Esteban, 1935- Los cimarrones
del maniel de Neiba . Santo Domingo,
República Dominicana , 1985. 199 p. :
NYPL [Sc D 89-173]

MAROONS - HAITI.
Deive, Carlos Esteban, 1935- Los cimarrones
del maniel de Neiba . Santo Domingo,
República Dominicana , 1985. 199 p. :
NYPL [Sc D 89-173]

MAROONS - JAMAICA - FICTION.
Earle, William. Obi, or, The history of
Three-fingered Jack . London , 1800. vi, [2],
232 p., [1] leaf of plates :
NYPL [Sc Rare C 88-3]

MAROONS - JAMAICA - JUVENILE
LITERATURE.
Hernandez, Helen. The maroons-- who are
they? /. Kingston , c1983. 28 p. :
NYPL [Sc D 88-378]

MAROONS - SURINAM.
Helman, Albert. Blijf even staan! .
[Netherlands?] c1987. 41 p. :
NYPL [Sc D 88-1039]

The maroons-- who are they? /. Hernandez,
Helen. Kingston , c1983. 28 p. :
NYPL [Sc D 88-378]

Marotti, Giorgio.
[Negro nel romanzo brasiliano. English]
Black characters in the Brazilian novel /
Giorgio Marotti ; translated by Maria O.
Marotti and Harry Lawton. Los Angeles :
Center for Afro-American Studies, University
of California, c1987. ix, 448 p., [18] p. of
plates ; 24 cm. (Afro-American culture and
society, 0882-5297 . v. 6) Translation of: Il negro nel
romanzo brasiliano. Includes index. Bibliography: p.
435-441. ISBN 0-934934-24-X : DDC
869.3/093520396 19
1. Brazilian fiction - History and criticism. I. Title. II.
Series.
PQ9607.B53 M3713 1987
NYPL [Sc E 87-334]

Marowitz, Roberta Lee. Psychosocial dynamics of
Black rapists [microform] : a case study / by
Roberta Lee Marowitz. 1982. x, 216 leaves ; 28
cm. Typescript. Abstract and vita inserted. Thesis
(Ed.D.)--George Washington University, 1982.
Bibliography: leaves 201-216. Microfilm. Ann Arbor,
Mich. : University Microfilms International, 1982. 1
microfilm reel ; 35 mm.
1. Afro-American criminals. 2. Rape - United States. I.
Title. *NYPL [Sc Micro R-4806]*

Marquardt, Wilhelm. Seychellen, Komoren und
Maskarenen : Handbuch der ostafrikanischen
Inselwelt / von Wilhelm Marquardt. München :
Weltforum Verlag, c1976. 346 p. : ill. ; 20 cm.
(Afrika-Studien. Sonderreihe Information und
Dokumentation. no. 5 5) At head of title: IFO-Institut
für Wirtschaftsforschung München, Afrika-Studienstelle.
Erratum slip inserted. Bibliography: p. 306-318.
Includes indexes. ISBN 3-8039-0117-0
1. Mascarene Islands. 2. Seychelles. 3. Comoro Islands.
I. IFO-Institut für Wirtschaftsforschung, Munich.
Afrika-Studienstelle. II. Title. III. Series.
DT469.S4 M37 *NYPL [JFC 77-3948]*

MARRIAGE - AFRICA.
Mba, Cyriacus S. Nwosu. Building up African
Christian families /. Enugu , 1985 (Enugu :
(ECTA) 58 p. ; *NYPL [Sc C 88-355]*

MARRIAGE - CHAD.
Tubiana, Marie José. Des troupeaux et des
femmes . Paris , 1985. 390 p., [16] p. of plates :
ISBN 2-85802-554-9 *NYPL [Sc E 88-217]*

MARRIAGE CUSTOMS AND RITES, DINKA
(NILOTIC TRIBE)
Fetterman, Marilyn Harer. Ngok Dinka
marriage and cattle transferals [microform] /.
Khartoum , 1978. 23 leaves ;
NYPL [Sc Micro F-11040]

MARRIAGE CUSTOMS AND RITES, EMBU
(BANTU PEOPLE)
Josiah, Mwaniki, 1933- Divorce among the
Wa-Embu /. Nairobi , 1988. 49 p. ;
NYPL [Sc D 89-346]

MARRIAGE CUSTOMS AND RITES -
SUDAN - ABYEI.
Fetterman, Marilyn Harer. Ngok Dinka
marriage and cattle transferals [microform] /.
Khartoum , 1978. 23 leaves ;
NYPL [Sc Micro F-11040]

Marriage, divorce and inheritance . Brown,
Winifred. Cambridge , 1988. vii,91 p. ; ISBN
0-902993-23-2 (pbk) : DDC
346.76/106134/0880655 19
NYPL [Sc D 88-1350]

MARRIAGE - EQUATORIAL GUINEA.
Nze Abuy, R. María. Familia y matrimonio faṅ
/. [Spain?] [1985?] 77 p. ;
NYPL [Sc C 88-285]

MARRIAGE - ISLAM.
ʿIsá ʿAbd Allāh Muḥammad al-Mahdī, 1945-
Islamic marriage ceremony and polygamy
[microform] /. Brooklyn , c1977. 30 p. :
NYPL [Sc Micro R-4114 no.1]

The marriage killers /. Odunze, Don. Enugu
[Nigeria] [198-?] 104 p. ;
NYPL [Sc C 88-189]

MARRIAGE - NIGERIA.
Uku, Patience Essie Urutajirinere Blankson. 25
years of partnership /. [Benin City, Nigeria ,
1981?] 114 p. ; *NYPL [Sc D 88-380]*

MARRIAGE - RELIGIOUS ASPECTS -
CHRISTIANITY.
Odunze, Don. The marriage killers /. Enugu
[Nigeria] [198-?] 104 p. ;
NYPL [Sc C 88-189]

MARRIAGE - RELIGIOUS ASPECTS -
CHRISTIANITY - AFRICA.
Mba, Cyriacus S. Nwosu. Building up African
Christian families /. Enugu , 1985 (Enugu :
(ECTA) 58 p. ; *NYPL [Sc C 88-355]*

Marryshow of Grenada . Sheppard, Jill. Barbados,
West Indies , 1987. 56 p. :
NYPL [Sc D 88-658]

MARRYSHOW, THEOPHILUS ALBERT.
Sheppard, Jill. Marryshow of Grenada .
Barbados, West Indies , 1987. 56 p. :
NYPL [Sc D 88-658]

Marsabit Diocesan Pastoral Conference (1987 :
Nyeri Kenya) The Church we want to be : a
profession of faith and a programme for action
by the Catholic communities of Marsabit and
Samburu districts : proceedings and declarations
of the Plenary Assembly of the Marsabit
Diocesan Pastoral Conference (31st August-4th
September 1987) Marsabit, Kenya : The
Diocese, 1988. 42 p. : col. ports. ; 21 x 30 cm.
At head of title: The pastoral plan of the Diocese of
Marsabit, Kenya.
1. Catholic Church. Diocese of Marsabit - Congresses.
2. Catholic Church - Kenya. I. Title.
NYPL [Sc D 89-463]

Marshall, Alex C. (Alexander Charles)
Representative directors, Black theatre productions, and practices at historically Black colleges and universities, 1968-1978 [microform] / Alex C. Marshall. 1980. ix, 141 leaves. Thesis (Ph.D.)--Bowling Green State University, 1980. Bibliography: leaves [84]-91. Microfilm. Ann Arbor Mich. : University Microfilms International, 1980. 1 reel ; 35 mm.
1. Afro-American theater. 2. Theater management - United States. 3. College theater - United States - Production and direction. 4. Drama - Black authors. I. Title. **NYPL [Sc Micro R-4807]**

Marshall, Lorna. The Past and future of !Kung ethnography . Hamburg , 1986. 423 p. : ISBN 3-87118-780-1 **NYPL [Sc D 88-234]**

MARSHALL, LORNA.
The Past and future of !Kung ethnography . Hamburg , 1986. 423 p. : ISBN 3-87118-780-1 **NYPL [Sc D 88-234]**

Marshall, Paule, 1929- Soul clap hands and sing / Paule Marshall. Washington, D.C. : Howard Univ. Press 1988, 1961. xlviii, 105 p. ; 21 cm. (Howard University Press library of contemporary literature) Introductaion by Darwin T. Turner. ISBN 0-88258-155-4
I. Turner, Darwin T., 1981. II. Title. III. Series. **NYPL [Sc D 88-1451]**

Marshall, Thurgood, 1908- White House Conference "To Fulfill These Rights", Washington, D. C., 1966. Major addresses at the White House Conference to Fulfill These Rights, June 1-2, 1966. [Washington, 1966] 66 p. DDC 323.4/09174/96
E185.615 .W45 1966c **NYPL [Sc E 88-386]**

Martin, Anthony. Report on the brigades in Botswana. [n.p., 1971?] 96 p. illus. 30 cm. Cover title.
1. Occupational training - Botswana. 2. Dropouts - Employment - Botswana. 3. Youth - Employment - Botswana. I. Title.
HD6276.B6 M37 **NYPL [JLF 74-1283]**

Martin, David, 1936- The Chitepo assassination / David Martin & Phyllis Johnson. Harare, Zimbabwe : Zimbabwe Pub. House, 1985. 134 p., [8] p. of plates : ill. ; 21 cm. Includes bibliographical references. ISBN 0-949225-04-5
1. Chitepo, Herbert Wiltshire, 1923-1975 - Assassination. 2. Zimbabwe African National Union. 3. Zimbabwe - Politics and government. 4. Zimbabwe - History - 1965-1980. I. Johnson, Phyllis. II. Title.
NYPL [Sc D 88-1244]

Martin, David, 1956- Frontline Southern Africa . New York , 1988. xxxv, 530 p., [16] p. of leaves : ISBN 0-941423-08-5 : DDC 322/.5/0968 19
DT747.S6 F76 1988 **NYPL [JLE 89-595]**

MARTÍN DE PORRES, SAINT, 1579-1639 - JUVENILE FICTION.
Mary Marguerite, Sister, 1895- Martin's mice. Chicago [1954] 32 p.
PZ8.1.M38 Mar **NYPL [Sc G 88-28]**

MARTIN DE PORRES, SAINT, 1579-1639 - JUVENILE LITERATURE.
Windeatt, Mary Fabyan, 1910- Lad of Lima . New York , 1942. 152 p. :
NYPL [Sc D 88-1170]

Martin, Denis-Constant. Tanzanie : l'invention d'une culture politique / Denis-Constant Martin. Paris : Presses de la Fondation nationale des sciences politiques : Karthala, c1988. 318 p. : maps ; 22 cm. Includes index. Bibliography: p. [293]-313. ISBN 2-7246-0550-0 (Presses de la fondation nationale des sciences politiques)
1. Tanzania - Politics and government - 1964-. 2. Tanzania - Social conditions - 1964-. 3. Tanzania - History. I. Title. **NYPL [Sc D 89-603]**

Martin, Gene L. Michael Jordan, gentleman superstar / Gene L. Martin. Greensboro, N.C. : Tudor Publishers, c1987. 69 p. : ill. ; 24 cm. ISBN 0-936389-02-8 : DDC 796.32/3/0924 B 19
1. Jordan, Michael, 1963- - Juvenile literature. 2. National Basketball Association - Juvenile literature. 3. Basketball players - United States - Biography - Juvenile literature. I. Title.
GV884.J67 M37 1987 **NYPL [Sc E 88-320]**

Martin Luther King, Jr. Colaiaco, James A., 1945- New York , 1988. x, 238 p. ; ISBN

0-312-02365-0 : DDC 323.4/092/4 B 19
E185.97.K5 C65 1988 **NYPL [Sc D 89-231]**

Martin, Michael. Malawi, ein entwicklungspolitisches Musterland? : eine Untersuchung / von Michael Martin. Bonn : Informationsstelle Südliches Afrika, 1984. 95 p. : ill., maps ; 21 cm. (ISSA Wissenschaftliche Reihe . 19) Bibliography: p. 94-95. ISBN 3-921614-17-1
1. Agriculture - Economic aspects - Malawi. 2. Malawi - Economic conditions. I. Series: Informationsstelle Südliches Afrika. ISSA Wissenschaftliche Reihe , 7. II. Title.
NYPL [Sc D 88-681]

Martin, Patricia Miles. The little brown hen. Illustrated by Harper Johnson. New York, Crowell [1960] 23 p. illus. 21 cm. SCHOMBURG CHILDREN'S COLLECTION.
1. Afro-American children - Juvenile fiction. I. Schomburg Children's Collection. II. Title.
PZ7 .M36418 Li **NYPL [Sc D 88-1495]**

Martin, Priscilla Clark. Taylor, James Lumpkin, 1892- A Portuguese-English dictionary. Stanford, Calif., 1970 [c1958] xx, 655 p. ISBN 0-8047-0480-5 DDC 469/.3/21
PC5333 .T3 1970 **NYPL [Sc E 81-99]**

Martin, Robert, 1929- Yesterday's people. With an introd. by Marlin Perkins. Illustrated by Richard Cuffari. [1st ed.] Garden City, N.Y., Doubleday [1970] 158 p. col. illus., col. maps. 27 cm. At head of title: Marlin Perkins' Wild kingdom. Describes the characteristics of the Bushmen, their customs, homes, families, and methods of survival in the Kalahari Desert. SCHOMBURG CHILDREN'S COLLECTION. DDC 916.8/03
1. San (African people) - Juvenile literature. 2. San (African people). 3. Kalahari Desert. I. Perkins, Marlin. II. Cuffari, Richard, 1925- illus. III. Schomburg Children's Collection. IV. Title.
DT764.B8 M35 **NYPL [Sc F 88-248]**

Martin, Susan M. Palm oil and protest : an economic history of the Ngwa region, south-eastern Nigeria, 1800-1980 / Susan M. Martin. Cambridge [Cambridgeshire] ; New York : Cambridge University Press, 1988. xi, 209 p. : maps ; 24 cm. (African studies series. 59) Includes index. Bibliography: p. 193-203. ISBN 0-521-34376-3 DDC 338.4/76643 19
1. Palm-oil industry - Nigeria - History - 20th century. 2. Igbo (African people). I. Title. II. Series.
HD9490.5.P343 N66 1988 **NYPL [JLE 88-3417]**

Martinez, Edgar. see **Martinez Masdeu, Edgar.**

Martinez Masdeu, Edgar. Literatura puertorriqueña; antología general [por] Edgar Martínez Masdeu [y] Esther M. Melón.2. ed. rev. y aumentada. Río Piedras [P.R.] : Editorial Edil, 1983. 2 v. 22 cm. Includes bibliographies. CONTENTS. - t. 1. Siglo XIX.--t. 2. Siglo XX.
1. Puerto Rican literature. I. Melón de Díaz, Esther, 1933-. II. Title. **NYPL [Sc D 87-1020]**

Martinez, Raymond J. (Raymond Joseph), 1889- Portraits of New Orleans jazz; its peoples and places. Miscellaneous notes compiled and edited by Raymond J. Martinez. New Orleans, Hope Publications [1971] 63 p. illus., ports. 24 cm. DDC 785.4/2/0976335
1. Music - Louisiana - New Orleans. 2. Jazz musicians - Louisiana - New Orleans. I. Title.
ML200.8.N48 M4 **NYPL [Sc D 87-69]**

Martinique /. Exbrayat, André. Fort de France , c1986. 154, [2] p. : ISBN 2-905873-02-7 DDC 972.98/2 19
F2081.2 .E9 1986 **NYPL [Sc E 88-346]**

La Martinique . Guignard, Henri. Fort de France , 1985. 172 p., [36] p. of plates : ISBN 2-9501249-0-9 :
HC158.6 .G85 1985 **NYPL [Sc E 89-127]**

MARTINIQUE.
Blanc-Pattin, Charles. Martinique guidebook /. Roquefort-Les-Pins, France , 1988. 48 p. :
NYPL [Sc D 88-1282]

MARTINIQUE - BIBLIOGRAPHY - CATALOGS.
Archives de la Martinique. Bibliographie relative aux Antilles . Fort-de-France , 1978- v. ; DDC 016.97298/2 19
Z1502.F5 A72 1978 F2151
NYPL [Sc F 88-286]

MARTINIQUE - DESCRIPTION AND TRAVEL - VIEWS.
Exbrayat, André. Martinique /. Fort de France , c1986. 154, [2] p. : ISBN 2-905873-02-7 DDC 972.98/2 19
F2081.2 .E9 1986 **NYPL [Sc E 88-346]**

MARTINIQUE - ECONOMIC CONDITIONS - 1918-
Guignard, Henri. La Martinique . Fort de France , 1985. 172 p., [36] p. of plates : ISBN 2-9501249-0-9 :
HC158.6 .G85 1985 **NYPL [Sc E 89-127]**

MARTINIQUE - FICTION.
Cabort-Masson, Guy, 1937- Pourrir, ou, Martyr un peu / [Martinique] , c1987. 252 p. : DDC 843/.914 19
PQ3949.2.C27 P68 1987
NYPL [Sc D 89-527]

Chamoiseau, Patrick. Solibo Magnifique . [Paris] , c1988. 226 p. ; ISBN 2-07-070990-6
NYPL [Sc D 88-1103]

Confiant, Raphaël. Le nègre et l'amiral . Paris , c1988. 334 p. ; ISBN 2-246-40991-8
NYPL [Sc D 89-340]

Delsham, Tony. L'impuissant /. Fort-de-France , 1986. 204 p. ; ISBN 2-86823-006-7 **NYPL [Sc D 88-349]**

Martinique guidebook /. Blanc-Pattin, Charles. Roquefort-Les-Pins, France , 1988. 48 p. :
NYPL [Sc D 88-1282]

MARTINIQUE - HISTORY.
Nicolas, Armand. Le combat d'André Aliker /. Fort-de-France , 1974. 108 p. :
NYPL [Sc D 88-1189]

MARTINIQUE - HISTORY - FICTION.
Mattioni, Mario D. Emamori . Fort-de-France , 1986. 156 p. ; ISBN 2-85275-108-9 DDC 843 19
PQ3949.2.M36 E4 1986
NYPL [Sc E 88-615]

Mattioni, Mario D. Ma Nou l'esclave . Fort-de-France [Martinique] , 1986. 157 p. ; ISBN 2-85275-111-9 DDC 843 19
PQ3949.2.M38 M3 1986
NYPL [Sc E 88-614]

MARTINIQUE - JUVENILE FICTION.
Sadowsky, Ethel S. François and the langouste. Boston [1969] 60 p. DDC [Fic]
PZ7.S127 Fr **NYPL [Sc D 88-1120]**

MARTINIQUE - FICTION.
Cabort-Masson, Guy, 1937- La mangrove mulâtre /. Saint-Joseph, Martinique , c1986. 282 p. ;
MLCS 87/3007 (P) **NYPL [Sc D 88-571]**

Martin's mice. Mary Marguerite, Sister, 1895- Chicago [1954] 32 p.
PZ8.1.M38 Mar **NYPL [Sc G 88-28]**

Martyr un peu. Cabort-Masson, Guy, 1937- Pourrir, ou, Martyr un peu /. [Martinique] , c1987. 252 p. : DDC 843/.914 19
PQ3949.2.C27 P68 1987
NYPL [Sc D 89-527]

Les martyrs de Bokassa /. Baccard, André. Paris , c1987. 349 p., [16] p. of plates : ISBN 2-02-009669-2 : DDC 967/.4105/0924 B 19
DT546.382.B64 B33 1987
NYPL [Sc D 88-636]

MARTYRS - UGANDA.
Uganda saints . [Kampala? , 1969?] 39 p. :
NYPL [Sc F 87-314]

MARXIAN ECONOMICS.
Harris, Abram Lincoln, 1899-1963. Race, radicalism, and reform . New Brunswick, U. S.A. , c1989. viii, 521 p. ; ISBN 0-88738-210-X DDC 305.8/96073 19
E185.8 .H27 1989 **NYPL [Sc E 89-166]**

MARXIST CRITICISM.
Buhle, Paul, 1944- C.L.R. James . London , New York , 1988. 197 p. ; ISBN 0-86091-221-3 : DDC 818 B 19
PR9272.9.J35 Z59 1988
NYPL [Sc E 89-171]

MARXIST CRITICISM - SOUTH AFRICA.
Callinicos, Alex. South Africa between reform and revolution /. London , Chicago , 1988. 231 p. ; ISBN 0-906224-46-2 **NYPL [JLD 89-489]**

Marxist-Humanism. Guide to the Raya Dunayevskaya collection . Detroit, Mich. [1986?] 84 p. ;
NYPL [Sc F 88-196]

Marxist-humanism, a half century of its world development. Dunayevskaya, Raya. The Raya Dunayevskaya collection [microform] Supplement: Raya Dunayevskaya's last writings, 1986-1987. 1986-1987. ca. 140 items.
NYPL [Sc Micro R-4838]

Marxist regimes series. Stoneman, Colin. Zimbabwe . London , New York , 1989. xxi, 210 p. : ISBN 0-86187-454-4 : DDC 968.91 19
JQ2929.A15 S76 1989   NYPL [Sc D 89-307]

MARY, BLESSED VIRGIN, SAINT - APPARITIONS AND MIRACLES - RWANDA - KIBEHO. Maindron, Gabriel. Des apparitions à Kibeho . Paris , c1984. 243 p., [4] p. of plates : ISBN 2-86839-021-8 : DDC 232.91/7/0967571 19
BT660.K52 M35 1984   NYPL [Sc E 88-516]

MARY - CULT - NEW YORK (CITY) Orsi, Robert A. The Madonna of 115th Street . New Haven , c1985. xxiii, 287 p. : ISBN 0-300-03262-5 (alk. paper) DDC 263/.98/0895107471 19
BT660.N44 O77 1985
NYPL [IEE (Italians) 86-89]

Mary Marguerite, Sister, 1895- Martin's mice. Illustrations by Rafaello Busoni. Chicago, Follett Pub. Co. [1954] 32 p. illus. 32 cm. SCHOMBURG CHILDREN'S COLLECTION.
1. Martín de Porres, Saint, 1579-1639 - Juvenile Fiction. I. Busoni, Rafaello, 1900-. II. Schomburg Children's Collection. III. Title.
PZ8.1.M38 Mar   NYPL [Sc G 88-28]

Mary McLeod Bethune /. Halasa, Malu. New York , c1989. 111 p. : ISBN 1-555-46574-9 DDC 370/.92/4 B 92 19
E185.97.B34 H35 1989   NYPL [Sc E 88-616]

Maryland. Morgan State College, Baltimore. Fisher, Walter. Ideas for Black studies. Baltimore, 1971. vii, 51 p.
E184.7 .F53   NYPL [Sc 917.306-F]

MASA (AFRICAN PEOPLE) - SOCIAL LIFE AND CUSTOMS. Damay, Jean. Lettres du Nord-Cameroun /. Paris , c1985. 231 p. : ISBN 2-86537-121-2
NYPL [Sc D 88-274]

MASAI. Amin, Mohamed, 1943- The last of the Maasai /. London , 1987. 185 p. : ISBN 0-370-31097-7
NYPL [Sc G 88-21]

Halderman, John M. An analysis of continued semi-nomadism of the Kaputiei Maasai group ranches [microform] . [Nairobi] [between 1972 and 1974]. 35 p. ; DDC 307.7/2/0967627
DT433.542 .H34
NYPL [Sc Micro R-4108 no.25]

MASAI (AFRICAN PEOPLE) - RITES AND CEREMONIES. Spencer, Paul, 1932- The Maasai of Matapato . Bloomington , c1988. xii, 296 p. : ISBN 0-253-33625-2 DDC 306/.08996 19
DT433.545.M33 S64 1988
NYPL [JFE 88-7115]

MASAI (AFRICAN PEOPLE) - SOCIAL LIFE AND CUSTOMS. Spencer, Paul, 1932- The Maasai of Matapato . Bloomington , c1988. xii, 296 p. : ISBN 0-253-33625-2 DDC 306/.08996 19
DT433.545.M33 S64 1988
NYPL [JFE 88-7115]

MASAI - ECONOMIC CONDITIONS. Rigby, Peter. Persistent pastoralists . London , Totowa, N.J. , 1985. x, 198 p. : ISBN 0-86232-226-X : DDC 305.8/9676 19
DT443.3.M37 R54 1985
NYPL [JLD 86-2309]

MASAI - FICTION. Resnick, Mike. Ivory /. New York , 1988. 374 p. : ISBN 0-312-93093-3 : DDC 813/.54 19
PS3568.E698 I96 1988   NYPL [Sc D 89-163]

MASAI - SOCIAL LIFE AND CUSTOMS. Mitzlaff, Ulrike von. Maasai-Frauen . München , 1988. 181 p. : ISBN 3-923804-23-7
NYPL [Sc D 89-551]

Mascareignes, Îles. see Mascarene Islands.

MASCARENE ISLANDS. Marquardt, Wilhelm. Seychellen, Komoren und Maskarenen . München , c1976. 346 p. : ISBN

3-8039-0117-0
DT469.S4 M37   NYPL [JFC 77-3948]

Mascher, R. Friedegund. Liberia . Hamburg , 1986. vi, 292 p., [1] folded leaf of plates : ISBN 3-923519-65-6 (pbk.) DDC 322/.5/096662 19
JQ3923.5.C58 L53 1986
NYPL [Sc D 88-1320]

Masdeu, Edgar Martinez. see Martinez Masdeu, Edgar.

Mashabela, Harry. Townships of the PWV / Harry Mashabela. Braamfontein, Johannesburg : South African Institute of Race Relations, 1988. 184 p. : ill. ; 21 cm. Includes bibliographies. ISBN 0-86982-343-4
1. Housing - South Africa. 2. Local government - South Africa. I. Title.   NYPL [Sc D 89-155]

Mashele, B. H. M. A hi hlomeni / hi B.H.M. Mashele. Braamfontein : Sasavona, 1982. 52 p. ; 20 cm. Poems.
I. Title.   NYPL [Sc C 88-222]

MASHONA - ANTIQUITIES. Garlake, Peter S. Great Zimbabwe /. Harare, Zimbabwe , 1985. 64 p. : ISBN 0-949225-24-X
NYPL [Sc D 87-1002]

MASHONA - FOLKLORE - COLLECTED WORKS. Ngano /. Harare, Zimbabwe , 1980- v. ; ISBN 0-7974-0478-3 (pbk.) :
GR358.62.M3 N47 1980
NYPL [Sc F 87-416]

MASHONA - SOCIAL LIFE AND CUSTOMS. Hodza, Aaron C. Shona registers [microform] /. Harare, Zimbabwe , 1977-1984. 3 v. ; ISBN 0-7974-0482-1
NYPL [Sc Micro R-4820 no.12]

Mason, Clifford. Jamaica run : a Joe Cinquez mystery / Clifford Mason.1st ed. New York : St. Martin's Press, 1987. 359 p. ; 22 cm. "A Thomas Dunne book." ISBN 0-312-00611-X : DDC 813/.54 19
1. Brooklyn (New York, N.Y.) - Fiction. 2. Jamaica - Fiction. I. Title.
PS3563.A7878 J3 1987
NYPL [JFD 88-9447]

Mason, Julian D. (Julian Dewey), 1931- Wheatley, Phillis, 1753-1784. [Poems.] The poems of Phillis Wheatley /. Chapel Hill , c1989. xvi, 235 p. ; ISBN 0-8078-1835-6 (alk. paper) DDC 811/.1 19
PS866 .W5 1989   NYPL [Sc E 89-205]

Masonic orders. see Freemasons.

Masonic ritual and monitor. Duncan, Malcolm C. Duncan's Masonic ritual and monitor, or, Guide to the three symbolic degrees E.A., F.C., M.M. /. Danbury, Conn. , c1922- v. :
NYPL [Sc B 88-65]

Masons (Secret order) see Freemasons.

Le masque de Dakodonou . Hessou, Henri D. Cotonou [Benin] , 1986. 65 p. :
NYPL [Sc C 88-370]

Le masque volé /. Rémy, Mylène. Paris , 1987. 126 p. : ISBN 2-218-07832-5
NYPL [Sc C 88-311]

Masquerade . Taylor, Jeremy, 1943- London , 1986. v, 135 p. : ISBN 0-333-41985-5 (pbk) : DDC 917.298/3044 19
F2122   NYPL [Sc D 88-837]

MASQUERADES - NIGERIA. Onyeneke, Augustine O. The dead among the living . Nimo , 1987. xii, 142 p. : ISBN 978-244-232-1   *NYPL [Sc C 89-2]*

MASS COMMUNICATION. see COMMUNICATION; MASS MEDIA.

MASS MEDIA AND MINORITIES. Discourse and discrimination /. Detroit , 1988. 269 p. ; ISBN 0-8143-1957-2 (alk. paper) DDC 401/.9 19
P120.R32 D57 1988   NYPL [Sc E 88-451]

MASS MEDIA AND STATE. see MASS MEDIA POLICY.

MASS MEDIA IN RELIGION - NIGERIA. Asuzu, Boniface Ntomchukwu. Communications media in the Nigerian Church today /. Rome , 1987. 160 p. :   *NYPL [Sc E 88-297]*

MASS MEDIA - NIGERIA. Akpan, Emmanuel D. (Emanuel David), 1938-

Communication and media arts . Uyo [Nigeria] , c1987. 178 p. : ISBN 978-267-600-4
NYPL [Sc D 88-752]

Contemporary issues in mass media for development and national security /. Lagos , 1988. xiv, 235 p. ; ISBN 978-228-317-7
NYPL [Sc D 89-573]

Duyile, Dayo. Makers of Nigerian press . Nigeria , 1987. xx, 726 p. :
NYPL [Sc F 89-167]

MASS MEDIA - NIGERIA - MORAL AND RELIGIOUS ASPECTS. Amadi, John Osinachi. The ethics of the Nigerian broadcaster /. Rome , 1986. 155 p. [6] p. of plates :   *NYPL [Sc E 89-138]*

MASS MEDIA POLICY - NIGERIA. Udoakah, Nkereuwem. Government and the media in Nigeria /. Calabar, Nigeria , c1988. x, 88 p. ; ISBN 978-231-603-2
NYPL [Sc C 89-51]

MASS MEDIA - RELIGIOUS ASPECTS - CATHOLIC CHURCH. Asuzu, Boniface Ntomchukwu. Communications media in the Nigerian Church today /. Rome , 1987. 160 p. :   *NYPL [Sc E 88-297]*

Massachusetts Anti-Slavery Society. Board of Managers. An address to the abolitionists of Massachusetts, on the subject of political action / by the Board of Managers of the Mass. A.S. Society. [Boston : The Society, 1838] 20 p. ; 17 cm. Written by Ellis Gray Loring.
1. Abolitionists - Massachusetts. I. Loring, Ellis Gray. II. Title.   NYPL [Sc Rare G 86-10]

Massachusetts. General Court. House of Representatives. Committee on Impressed Seamen. Report of the Committee of the House of Representatives of Massachusetts on the subject of impressed seamen, with the evidence and documents accompanying it. Boston : Russell and Cutler, 1813. 84, 4 p. ; 21 cm. "Published by the order of the House of Representatives."
1. Impressment. I. Title.
NYPL [Sc Rare C 89-13]

MASSACHUSETTS INFANTRY. 54TH REGT., 1863-1865. Smith, Marion Whitney. Beacon Hill's Colonel Robert Gould Shaw /. New York , 1986. 512 p. : ISBN 0-8062-2732-X
NYPL [Sc D 88-414]

Massachusetts. Legislature. see Massachusetts. General Court.

Massachusetts masters . Gaither, Edmund B. Boston [1988] 48 p. :   *NYPL [Sc F 89-159]*

MASSACHUSETTS - POLITICS AND GOVERNMENT - 1775-1865. Remarks upon the controversy between the Commonwealth of Massachusetts and the State of South Carolina. Boston, 1845. 21 p.
F273 .R38   NYPL [Sc Rare C 89-9]

Le massacre de 1937, ou Une succession immobilière internationale /. Matteis, Arthur de. Port-au-Prince, Haiti , 1987. 68 p. ;
NYPL [Sc D 88-520]

MASSACRES - DOMINICAN REPUBLIC. Matteis, Arthur de. Le massacre de 1937, ou Une succession immobilière internationale /. Port-au-Prince, Haiti , 1987. 68 p. ;
NYPL [Sc D 88-520]

MASSACRES - KENYA. Nyasani, J. M. (Joseph Major), 1938- The British massacre of the Gusii freedom defenders /. Nairobi, Kenya , 1984. v, 85 p. :
NYPL [Sc D 88-1133]

MASSAI. see MASAI.

Massengo, Moudileno. Procès de Brazzaville : le requisitoire / [Moudileno Massengo]. Paris : L'Harmattan, [1983] 345 p. : facsims. ; 21 cm.
1. N'Gouabi, Marien, 1938-1977 - Assassination. 2. Congo (Brazzaville) - History - 1960-. 3. Congo (Brazzaville) - Politics and government - 1960-. I. Title. II. Title: Requisitoire.   NYPL [Sc D 88-1160]

Massey, Garth. Subsistence and change : lessons of agropastoralism in Somalia / Garth Massey. Boulder : Westview Press, 1987. xvii, 238 p. : ill. ; 23 cm. (Westview special studies in social, political and economic development) Includes index. Bibliography: p. 226-233. ISBN 0-8133-7294-1 (alk. paper) : DDC 338.1/0967/73 19

1. Rahanweyn (African people) - Economic conditions. 2. Agriculture - Somalia. 3. Cattle - Somalia. 4. Rural development - Somalia. 5. Subsistence economy - Somalia. 6. Somalia - Economic conditions. I. Title.
DT402.4.R35 M37 1987
NYPL [Sc D 88-298]

Massiah, Joycelin. Gill, Margaret. Women, work, and development /. Cave Hill, Barbados , 1984. xviii, 129 p. ; *NYPL [Sc E 85-274]*

MASTER AND SERVANT - ZAMBIA - HISTORY - 20TH CENTURY.
Hansen, Karen Tranberg. Distant companions . Ithaca , 1989. xv, 321 p. : ISBN 0-8014-2217-5 (alk. paper) DDC 331.7/6164046/096894 19
HD6072.2.Z33 H36 1989
NYPL [Sc E 89-215]

The masters and the slaves =. Freyre, Gilberto, 1900- [Casa-grande & senzala. English.] Berkeley , c1986. xc, 537 xliv p., [3] p. of plates : ISBN 0-520-05665-5 (pbk. : alk. paper) DDC 981 19
F2510 .F7522 1986
NYPL [HFB 87-2095]

Mataka, Laini. Never as strangers / Laini Mataka. Baltimore : W.M. DuForcelf, c1988. x, 65 p. ; 22 cm.
I. Title.
NYPL [Sc D 89-445]

MATAPATU (KENYA) - SOCIAL LIFE AND CUSTOMS.
Spencer, Paul, 1932- The Maasai of Matapato . Bloomington , c1988. xii, 296 p. : ISBN 0-253-33625-2 DDC 306/.08996 19
DT433.545.M33 S64 1988
NYPL [JFE 88-7115]

MATERIA MEDICA, VEGETABLE.
Farelli, Maria Helena. Oxóssi e Ossãe . Rio de Janeiro , 1987. 71 p. : *NYPL [Sc C 88-65]*

Materialien des Zentrums für regionale Entwicklungsforschung der Justus-Liebig-Universität Giessen .
(Bd. 8) Stremplat, Axel V., 1941- Der l"andliche Arbeitskalender in der Regionalplanung Burundis /. Giessen , 1984. 130 p. : ISBN 3-924840-08-3
NYPL [Sc D 88-556]

Materials for conservation . Horie, C. V. (Charles Velson) London , Boston , 1987. xi, 281 p. : ISBN 0-408-01531-4 : DDC 667/.9 19
TP156.C57 H67 1987
NYPL [Sc D 88-558]

MATERNAL HEALTH SERVICES - GREAT BRITAIN.
Pearson, Maggie. Racial equality and good practice maternity care . London , 1985. 37 p. : ISBN 0-86082-610-4 (pbk) : DDC 362.1/982 19
RG964.G7
NYPL [Sc F 88-393]

The Mathaba International . Essack, Karrim. Dar es Salaam [1987?] iv, 81 p. : DDC 325/.32 19
JC359 .E825 1987
NYPL [Sc C 89-30]

MATHABA INTERNATIONAL (ORGANIZATION)
Essack, Karrim. The Mathaba International /. Dar es Salaam [1987?] iv, 81 p. : DDC 325/.32 19
JC359 .E825 1987
NYPL [Sc C 89-30]

Mathematics and logic in the Kpelle language.
Gay, John. Ibadan, 1971. 152, 184 p.
PL8411.1 .G35
NYPL [JFF 74-877]

Mathew, William M. Edmund Ruffin and the crisis of slavery in the Old South : the failure of agricultural reform / William M. Mathew. Athens : University of Georgia Press, c1988. xiv, 286 p. : ill. ; 24 cm. Includes index. Bibliography: p. 257-270. ISBN 0-8203-1011-5 (alk. paper) DDC 306/.362/0924 19
1. Ruffin, Edmund, 1794-1865. 2. Slavery - Southern States. 3. Agriculture - Southern States - History - 19th century. 4. Southern States - History - 1775-1865. I. Title.
F230.R932 M38 1988
NYPL [JFE 88-3149]

Mathews, Anthony S., 1930- Freedom, state security and the rule of law : dilemmas of the apartheid society / Anthony S. Mathews. London : Sweet & Maxwell, c1988. xxx, 312 p. ; 26 cm. Includes index. Bibliography: p. xi-xiv. ISBN 0-421-39640-7
1. Rule of law - South Africa. 2. Internal security - South Africa. 3. Civil rights - South Africa. 4. Liberty - South Africa. I. Title.
NYPL [Sc F 89-102]

Matindike, Gabriel A. Kuziva mbuya huudzwa / Gabriel A. Matindike. Harare, Zimbabwe :

Zimbabwe Educational Books, 1982- v. : ill. ; 21 cm. (ZEB secondary school Shona series) In Shona. Issued with various printing dates. ISBN 0-908300-01-8 (v. 1)
1. Shona language - Readers. I. Title. II. Series.
PL8681.2 .M37 1982
NYPL [Sc D 88-385]

Mating in Islam! [microform] : the Ansars present an educational guide to a real Islamic marriage. Brooklyn : Ansaru Allah Publications, [197-?] 11 p. : ill. ; 43 cm. Cover title. Title also in Arabic; portions of text in Arabic. Paging in reverse. Microfilm. New York: New York Public Library, 1982. 1 microfilm reel; 35 mm. (MN *ZZ-23673)
I. Ansaru Allah Community.
NYPL [Sc Micro R-4114 no. 21]

Matondo kwa Nzambi. Biso banso lisanga totonga eklezya ya biso : monkanda mwa episkopo / Matondo kwa Nzambi. Kinshasa : L'Epiphanie, [1988] 72 p. : ill. ; 21 cm.
1. Kongo language - Texts. I. Title.
NYPL [Sc D 89-221]

Matos, Isabel Freire de. see Freire de Matos, Isabel.

Matos Moquete, Manuel, 1944- En el atascadero / Manuel Matos Moquete. Santo Domingo, República Dominicana : Editora Universitaria-UASD, 1985. 266 p. ; 21 cm. (Publicaciones de la Universidad Autónoma de Santo Domingo. Colección Arte y sociedad . no. 21) Publicaciones de la Universidad Autónoma de Santo Domingo ; v. 390
I. Series. II. Series: Santo Domingo. Universidad Autónoma. Publicaciones, 390. III. Title.
MLCS 85/21777 (P)
NYPL [JFD 86-4017]

MATRIARCHY - NIGERIA.
Amadiume, Ifi. Afrikan matriarchal foundations . London , 1987. [120] p. : ISBN 0-907015-27-1 (pbk) : DDC 966.9/004963 19
DT515.45.I33
NYPL [Sc D 89-112]

MATRIMONY. see MARRIAGE.

Matsepe, O. K. Todi ya dinose / O. K. Matsepe. 1st ed. Pretoria : Van Schaik, 1968, 1982 printing. 50 p. ; 21 cm. ISBN 0-627-00818-6
1. Northern Sotho language - Texts. I. Title.
PL8690.9.M36 T6
NYPL [Sc D 89-607]

Matteis, Arthur de. Le massacre de 1937, ou Une succession immobilière internationale / Arthur de Matteis. Port-au-Prince, Haiti : L'Imprimeur II, 1987. 68 p. ; 21 cm. Bibliography: p. 41-50.
1. Haitians - Dominican Republic. 2. Massacres - Dominican Republic. 3. Dominican Republic - History - 1930-. I. Title.
NYPL [Sc D 88-520]

A matter of upbringing /. Popoola, Dimeji. Ibadan , c1987. v. 133 p. ; ISBN 0-19-575759-9 (Outside Nigeria)
NYPL [Sc c 88-173]

Matthew Henson /. Gilman, Michael. New York , c1988. 110 p. ; ISBN 1-555-46590-0 : DDC 919.8/04 B 92 19
G635.H4 G55 1988
NYPL [Sc E 88-169]

Matthews, Lear K. Communities and development in Guyana : a neglected dimension in nation building / Lear K. Matthews, George K. Danns. [Georgetown, Guyana? : University of Guyana?], 1980. 94, v. p. : ill. ; 28 cm. Bibliography: p. [i]-v.
1. Community development - Guyana. I. Danns, George K. II. Title.
NYPL [Sc F 89-65]

Mattie, Joan. 100 years of architecture in Kingston : John Power to Drever & Smith = 100 ans d'architecture à Kingston : de John Power à Drever & Smith / Joan Mattie. [Ottawa] : Public Archives Canada, c1986. 30 p. : ill. ; 28 cm. English and French. Catalog of an exhibition of drawings owned by the Archives since 1981. Bibliography: p. 29-30. ISBN 0-662-54396-3 (pbk.) DDC 720/.9713/72074011384 19
1. Architecture - Ontario - Kingston - Exhibitions. 2. Architecture, Modern - 19th century - Ontario - Kingston - Exhibitions. 3. Architecture, Modern - 20th century - Ontario - Kingston - Exhibitions. 4. Kingston (Ont.) - Buildings, structures, etc. - Exhibitions. I. Public Archives Canada. II. Title. III. Title: One hundred years of architecture in Kingston. IV. Title: 100 ans d'architecture à Kingston. V. Title: Cent ans d'architecture à Kingston.
NA747.K56 M38 1986
NYPL [Sc F 88-195]

Mattioni, Mario D. Emamori : les premières années de la colonisation en Martinique / Mario Mattioni. Fort-de-France : Désormeaux, 1986. 156 p. ; 24

cm. (Collection "Les Grands romans des Antilles-Guyane") ISBN 2-85275-108-9 DDC 843 19
1. Martinique - History - Fiction. I. Title. II. Series.
PQ3949.2.M36 E4 1986
NYPL [Sc E 88-615]

Ma Nou l'esclave : sous l'administration de Du Parquet / Mario Mattioni. Fort-de-France [Martinique] : Désormeaux, 1986. 157 p. ; 24 cm. (Collection "Les Grands romans des Antilles-Guyane") ISBN 2-85275-111-9 DDC 843 19
1. Martinique - History - Fiction. I. Title. II. Series.
PQ3949.2.M38 M3 1986
NYPL [Sc E 88-614]

Mattos, Edgar, 1935- Por uma educacão libertáda e libertadora : verberações de um combatente / Edgar Mattos. Recife : Fundação Joaquim Nabuco : Editora Massangana, 1986. 89 p. ; 22 cm. (Série Documentos (Fundação Joaquim Nabuco) . 30) ISBN 85-7019-098-0
1. Education - Brazil. I. Title. II. Series.
NYPL [Sc D 88-845]

MAU DIALECT (IVORY COAST) - GRAMMAR.
Ebermann, Erwin. Die Sprache der Mauka . Wien , 1986. 207 p. ; ISBN 3-85369-656-2
PL8491.95.I9 E24 1986
NYPL [Sc D 88-687]

MAU MAU.
Gakaara wa Wanjaũ. Mwandĩki wa Mau Mau ithaamĩrio-inĩ /. Nairobi [Kenya] , 1983. xvii, 189 p. : *NYPL [Sc D 87-156]*

Gakaara wa Wanjaũ. [Mwandĩki wa Mau Mau ithaamĩrio-inĩ. English.] Mau Mau author in detention /. Nairobi , 1988. xix, 252 p. ; ISBN 996-646-354-2 *NYPL [Sc D 89-444]*

Resistance and ideology in settler societies /. Johannesburg, Athens, Ohio·, 1986. viii, 222 p. ; ISBN 0-86975-304-5
NYPL [Sc D 88-1093]

MAU MAU - ARCHIVES.
Kenya's freedom struggle . London ; Atlantic Highlands, N.J. , 1987. xix, 138 p. ;
NYPL [Sc D 88-775]

Mau Mau author in detention /. Gakaara wa Wanjaũ. [Mwandĩki wa Mau Mau ithaamĩrio-inĩ. English.] Nairobi , 1988. xix, 252 p. ; ISBN 996-646-354-2 *NYPL [Sc D 89-444]*

MAU MAU - FICTION.
Mwangi, Meja, 1948- [Carcase for hounds. German.] Wie ein Aas für Hunde . Bornheim-Merten , 1987. 173 p. ; ISBN 3-88977-136-X *NYPL [Sc C 88-148]*

MAU MAU - HISTORY.
Kanogo, Tabitha M. Squatters and the roots of Mau Mau, 1905-63 /. Athens , London , 1987. xviii, 206 p. : ISBN 0-8214-0873-9 DDC 307.3/36 19
HD1538.K4 K36 1987 *NYPL [Sc D 88-207]*

Maurice, Albert-Marie. Atakora : Otiau, Otammari, Osuri, peuples du Nord Bénin (1950) / Albert-Marie Maurice. Paris : Académie des sciences d'outre-mer, 1986. xxiii, 481 p., clv p. of plates : ill., maps ; 24 cm. Bibliography: p. [xi]-xiv. ISBN 2-900098-11-4
1. Enthnology - Benin - Atakora Mountains Region. 2. Benin - Social life and customs. I. Title.
NYPL [Sc E 88-106]

Maurice Bishop Patriotic Movement. Manifesto of the Maurice Bishop Patriotic Movement. St. George's, Grenada : The Movement, [1984] 60 p. : ill. ; 21 cm.
1. Political parties - Grenada. 2. Grenada - Politics and government - 1974-. I. Title.
NYPL [Sc D 88-676]

MAURICE, SAINT, D. CA. 287 - ART.
Suckale-Redlefsen, Gude. Mauritius, der heilige Mohr /. Houston , München , c1987. 295 p. : ISBN 0-939594-03-X DDC 704.9/4863/094 19
N8080.M38 S9 1987 *NYPL [Sc D 88-1357]*

MAURICE, SAINT, D. CA. 287 - ART - CATALOGS.
Suckale-Redlefsen, Gude. Mauritius, der heilige Mohr /. Houston , München , c1987. 295 p. : ISBN 0-939594-03-X DDC 704.9/4863/094 19
N8080.M38 S9 1987 *NYPL [Sc D 88-1357]*

MAURICE, SAINT, D. CA. 287 - CULT - EUROPE.
Suckale-Redlefsen, Gude. Mauritius, der heilige

Mohr /. Houston , München , c1987. 295 p. :
ISBN 0-939594-03-X   DDC 704.9/4863/094 19
N8080.M38 S9 1987   *NYPL [Sc D 88-1357]*

Mauritian delights . Sookhee, L. (Lalita)
Rose-Hill, Mauritius , 1985. 159 p. :   DDC
641.5969/82 19
TX725.M34 S66 1985   *NYPL [Sc D 88-181]*

Mauritius, der heilige Mohr /. Suckale-Redlefsen,
Gude. Houston , München , c1987. 295 p. :
ISBN 0-939594-03-X   DDC 704.9/4863/094 19
N8080.M38 S9 1987   *NYPL [Sc D 88-1357]*

Mauritius - Government. see **Mauritius - Politics
and government.**

**MAURITIUS - POLITICS AND
    GOVERNMENT - 1968-**
L'Histoire d'une trahison . Port Louis,
Mauritius , 1987. vi, 192 p.
               NYPL [Sc F 88-275]

Mauro, Robert. Gross, Samuel R. Death &
discrimination . Boston , c1989. xvi, 268 p. ;
ISBN 1-555-53040-0 (alk. paper) :   DDC
364.6/6/0973 19
HV8699.U5 G76 1989   *NYPL [Sc D 89-493]*

**MAURRAS, CHARLES 1868-1952 -
    INFLUENCE.**
Nérée, Bob. Duvalier . Port-au-Prince, Haiti ,
1988. 238 p. ;   *NYPL [Sc E 88-366]*

MAUSOLEUMS. see **TOMBS.**

Mawiri, Ambroisine. Epopée Mulombi /.
[Libreville , 1986?] 138 p. ;
               NYPL [Sc D 88-561]

MAXAMAD CABDULLE XASAN, 1864-1920.
Jaamac Cumar Ciise. Taariikhdii daraawiishta
iyo Sayid Maxamed Cabdulle Xasan, 1895-1921
/. Muqdisho , 1976. vii, 320 p., [2] leaves of
plates :
DT404.3.M38 C55   *NYPL [Sc E 87-435]*

**MAXAMAD CABDULLE XASAN'S
    REBELLION, BRITISH SOMALILAND,
    1900-1920.**
Jaamac Cumar Ciise. Taariikhdii daraawiishta
iyo Sayid Maxamed Cabdulle Xasan, 1895-1921
/. Muqdisho , 1976. vii, 320 p., [2] leaves of
plates :
DT404.3.M38 C55   *NYPL [Sc E 87-435]*

May, Charles Paul. Stranger in the storm.
Illustrated by Victor Ambrus. London, New
York, Abelard-Schuman [1972] 92 p. illus. 22
cm. Although frightened at first by the fugitive slave
they discover in the barn, two Iowa farm girls stranded
in a blizzard soon rely on him for their survival.
SCHOMBURG CHILDREN'S COLLECTION.   ISBN
0-200-71821-5   DDC [Fic]
*1. Fugitive slaves - Iowa - Juvenile fiction. I. Ambrus,
Victor G., illus. II. Schomburg Children's Collection.
III. Title.*
PZ7.M4505 St   *NYPL [Sc D 88-1430]*

May, Chris. Bob Marley / Chris May ; illustrated
by Trevor Parkin. London : H. Hamilton, 1985.
60 p. : ill. ; 22 cm. (Profiles) A biography of the
Jamaican musician who moved reggae into the
international eye and remained phenomenally popular
even after his untimely death. SCHOMBURG
CHILDREN'S COLLECTION.   ISBN 0-241-11476-4 :
DDC 784.5 B 19
*1. Marley, Bob - Juvenile literature. 2. Reggae
musicians - Jamaica - Biography - Juvenile literature. I.
Parkin, Trevor, ill. II. Schomburg Children's Collection.
III. Series: Profiles (London, England). IV. Title.*
ML420.M3313 M4 1985
               NYPL [Sc D 88-308]

May, Cris. Stapleton, Cris. African all-stars .
London , 1987. 373 p., [16] p. of plates :   ISBN
0-7043-2504-7   *NYPL [Sc E 88-137]*

Maya-Maya, Estevão. Regresso triunfal de Cruz e
Sousa ; e, Os segredos de "seu" bita
Dá-nó-em-pingo-d'água / Estevão Maya-Maya.
São Paulo : Editora Kikulakaji, 1982. x, 85 p. :
ill., port. ; 21 cm.
*1. Cruz e Sousa, João de, 1863?-1898 - Poetry. I. Title.
II. Title: Segredos de "seu" bita Dá-nó-em-pingo-d'água.*
               NYPL [Sc D 88-1098]

**MAYAGUANA ISLAND (BAHAMAS) -
    SOCIAL LIFE AND CUSTOMS.**
Lurry-Wright, Jerome Wendell, 1941- Custom
and conflict on a Bahamian out-island /.
Lanham, MD , c1987. xxii, 188 p. ;   ISBN
0-8191-6097-0 (alk. paper) :   DDC 347.7296
347.29607 19
KGL210 .L87 1987   *NYPL [Sc D 88-218]*

Mayala ma Mpangu. L'église de Kisantu, hier et
aujourd'hui [microform] / Mayala ma Mpangu.
[Kisantu? : s.n.], 1982. 40 p. ; 20 cm. Includes
bibliographical references. Microfiche. New York: New
York Public Library, 198 . 1 microfiche: negative; 11 x
15 cm. (FSN Sc 019,115)
1. Catholic Church in Kisantu, Zaire - History. I. Title.
            NYPL [Sc Micro F-11,000]

MAYFLOWER SCHOOL (IKENE, NIGERIA)
Solarin, Tai. To mother with love /. Ibadan ,
c1987. 302 p. :   ISBN 978-19-1050-X
            NYPL [Sc D 88-732]

**MAYFLOWER SCHOOL (IKENE, NIGERIA) -
    DRAMA.**
Omole, Wale, 1960- Tai Solarin's adventure .
Ibadan , 1985. x, 90 p. :   DDC 822 19
PR9387.9.O396 T3 1985
            NYPL [Sc C 88-309]

The mayor of New Orleans . Shaik, Fatima,
1952- Berkeley , 1987. 143 p. ;   ISBN
0-88739-050-1 :   DDC 813/.54 19
PS3569.H316 M39 1987
            NYPL [JFD 88-11303]

**MAYORS - ILLINOIS - CHICAGO -
    BIOGRAPHY - JUVENILE LITERATURE.**
Roberts, Naurice. Harold Washington .
Chicago , 1988. 30 p. :   ISBN 0-516-03657-2
DDC 977.3/1100496073024 B 92 19
F548.52.W36 R63 1988
            NYPL [Sc E 88-501]

**MAYORS - MICHIGAN - DETROIT -
    BIOGRAPHY.**
Rich, Wilbur C. Coleman Young and Detroit
politics . Detroit, Mich. , 1989. 298 p. :   ISBN
0-8143-2093-7   DDC 977.4/34043/0924 B 19
F474.D453 Y677 1989   *NYPL [Sc E 89-208]*

Mays, Mantle, Snider . Honig, Donald. New
York, N.Y. , London , c1987. vii, 151 p. :
ISBN 0-02-551200-5   DDC 796.357/092/2 B 19
GV865.A1 H6192 1987
            NYPL [JFF 87-1461]

MAYS, WILLIE, 1931-
Honig, Donald. Mays, Mantle, Snider . New
York, N.Y. , London , c1987. vii, 151 p. :
ISBN 0-02-551200-5   DDC 796.357/092/2 B 19
GV865.A1 H6192 1987
            NYPL [JFF 87-1461]

Mazrui, Alamin. Chembe cha moyo / Alamin
Mazrui. Nairobi : Heinemann Kenya, 1988. xiv,
73 p. ; 18 cm. In Swahili.   ISBN 996-646-366-6
1. Swahili language - Texts. I. Title.
            NYPL [Sc C 89-75]

Mazrui, Ali Al'Amin. Décolonisation de l'Afrique.
Spanish. La Descolonización de Africa : Africa
austral y el Cuerno de Africa . Barcelona ,
Paris , 1983. 197 p. ;   ISBN 92-3-301834-2
(Unesco)   *NYPL [Sc D 88-590]*

Mba, Cyriacus S. Nwosu. Building up African
Christian families / Cyriacus S. Nwosu Mba.
Enugu : C.S.N. Mba, 1985 (Enugu : (ECTA) 58
p. ; 19 cm. "Bigard Memorial Seminary Enugu" - from
title page. Bibliography: p. 56-58.
*1. Marriage - Africa. 2. Marriage - Religious aspects -
Christianity - Africa. I. Title.*
            NYPL [Sc C 88-355]

MBA, PETER O.
Development of special education in Nigeria /.
Ibadan , 1988. ix, 132 p. ;   ISBN 978-267-703-5
            NYPL [Sc E 89-70]

Mbaabu, Ireri. New horizons in Kiswahili : a
synthesis in developments, research, and
literature / Ireri Mbaabu. Nairobi : Kenya
Literature Bureau, 1985. 229 p. ; 19 cm.
Bibliography: p. [223]-229.   DDC 496/.392 19
1. Swahili philology. I. Title.
PL8701 .M374 1985   *NYPL [Sc C 85-128]*

Mbaba, Ita G. Blast at noon : a collection of
thirty poems in honour of matyrs for humanity
[sic] for humanity / by Ita G. Mbaba. Calabar,
Nigeria : Centaur Publishers, c1987. x, 40 p. :
19 cm.   ISBN 978-231-602-2
1. Nigeria - Social conditions. I. Title.
            NYPL [Sc C 89-63]

MBARA (AFRICAN PEOPLE) - LANGUAGE.
Tourneux, Henry. Les Mbara et leur langue
(Tchad) /. Paris , 1986. 319 p. :   ISBN
2-85297-188-7   *NYPL [Sc E 88-162]*

Les Mbara et leur langue (Tchad) /. Tourneux,
Henry. Paris , 1986. 319 p. :   ISBN
2-85297-188-7   *NYPL [Sc E 88-162]*

Mbiti, John S. Bible and theology in African
Christianity / John S. Mbiti. Nairobi : Oxford
University Press, 1986. xiv, 248 p., [16] p. of
plates : ill. ; 21 cm. Errata slip tipped in. Includes
bibliographies and indexes.   ISBN 0-19-572593-X
*1. Bible - Africa. 2. Christianity - Africa. 3. Theology,
Doctrinal - Africa. 4. Africa - Religion. I. Title.*
            NYPL [Sc D 89-296]

Mbo-Ikamba, Iyeti. L'approvisionnement
alimentaire de la ville de Bandundu (Rép. du
Zaïre) / Mbo-Ikamba Iyeti. Bandundu,
République du Zaïre : Ceeba, 1987. 58 p. :
map ; 27 cm. (Publications (Ceeba). Série II . vol.
97) Bibliography: p. 56-58.
*1. Food supply - Zaire - Bandundu. I. Series. II. Series:
Publications (Ceeba). Série II , v. 97. III. Title.*
            NYPL [Sc F 89-63]

Mbogo, Emmanuel. Giza limeingia / Emmanuel
Mbogo. Dar es Salaam : Tanzania Pub. House,
1980. 98 p. ; 19 cm. (Michezo ya kuigiza. 13) A
play. In Swahili.   ISBN 997-610-022-1
1. Swahili language - Texts. I. Title.
            NYPL [Sc C 89-23]

Mbotela, James. Uhuru wa watumwa / by James
Mbotela. Nairobi : East African Literature
Bureau, 1956. viii, 102 p. : ill. ; 19 cm.
1. Slavery - Africa. 2. Swahili language - Texts. I. Title.
            NYPL [Sc C 89-35]

MBOUIN (AFRICAN PEOPLE) see **GOUIN
    (AFRICAN PEOPLE)**

Mboya, Alakie-Akinyi. Ontongolia /
Alakie-Akinyi Mboya. Nairobi : Oxford
University Press, 1986. xiv, 92 p., [4] p. of
plates ; 18 cm. (New drama from Africa. 12)   ISBN
0-19-572615-4
*1. Africa, Sub-Saharan - Politics and government -
Drama. I. Title. II. Series.*   *NYPL [Sc C 88-138]*

Mbumba, Victor. Epopée Mulombi /. [Libreville ,
1986?] 138 p. ;   *NYPL [Sc D 88-561]*

Me and Arch and the Pest. Durham, John, fl.
1960- New York [1970] 96 p.   DDC [Fic]
PZ7.D9335 Me   *NYPL [Sc E 88-416]*

Me, Mop, and the Moondance Kid /. Myers,
Walter Dean, 1937- New York , 1988. 154 p. :
ISBN 0-440-50065-6   DDC [Fic] 19
PZ7.M992 Me 1988   *NYPL [Sc D 88-1457]*

Meakin, Budgett, 1866-1906. The Moorish
empire, [microform] : a historical epitome,
London, S. Sonnenschein & co., lim; New
York, The Macmillan company, 1899. [xi]-xxiii,
576 p. illus. (incl. ports.) plates, maps (part
fold.) facsims., 2 fold. tab. 23 cm. Includes
bibliographies. Microfilm. New York : New York Public
Library, 1988. 1 microfilm reel ; 35 mm. (MN
*ZZ-29232)
1. Morocco - History. I. Title.
DT314 .M48   *NYPL [Sc Micro R-4844]*

Mearns, Robin. Leach, Gerald. Beyond the
woodfuel crisis . London , 1988. [x], 309 p. :
ISBN 1-85383-031-3 (pbk) :   DDC 333.75 19
            NYPL [Sc D 89-397]

The measure of a man /. King, Martin Luther,
Jr., 1929-1968. Philadelphia , c1988. 59 p. :
ISBN 0-8006-2088-7   DDC 233 19
BT703 .K5 1988   *NYPL [Sc C 88-326]*

Measuring the moment . Sandiford, Keith Albert,
1947- Selinsgrove , c1988. 181 p. ;   ISBN
0-941664-79-1 (alk. paper)   DDC 828 19
PR9340 .S26 1988   *NYPL [Sc E 88-467]*

**MECHANIZED INFORMATION STORAGE
    AND RETRIEVAL SYSTEMS.** see
    **INFORMATION STORAGE AND
    RETRIEVAL SYSTEMS.**

Meckelein, Wolfgang. Desertification in extremely
arid environments /. [Stuttgart] , 1980. 203 p.,
[1] folded leaf of plates :   ISBN 3-88028-095-9
(pbk.)   DDC 551.4 19
GB611 .D44   *NYPL [JFL 74-410 Bd. 95]*

Meddaugh, Susan. (ill) Dee, Ruby. Two ways to
count to ten . New York , c1988. [32] p. :
ISBN 0-8050-0407-6 :   DDC 398.2/096 E 19
PZ8.1.D378 Tw 1988   *NYPL [Sc F 88-311]*

Medeiros, François de. Peuples du golfe du
Bénin . Paris , c1984. 328 p. :   ISBN
2-86537-092-5   DDC 966/.8004963 19
DT510.43.E94 P48 1984
            NYPL [Sc E 88-449]

Medetognon-Benissan, Tétévi. Tourbillons /
Tétévi Medetognon-Benissan. Lomé : Editions

HAHO, 1984, c1985. 116 p. ; 22 cm.
1. togo - Fiction. I. Title.　　*NYPL [Sc D 89-210]*

Media and society series.
Newman, Mark. Entrepreneurs of profit and
pride . New York , 1988. xvi, 186 p., [4] p. of
plates :　ISBN 0-275-92888-8　DDC 305.8/96073 19
PN1991.8.A35 N49 1988
　　　　　　　　　　　NYPL [Sc E 89-88]

The Media and the movement [microform] ; the
role of the press in a changing society : a
conference / sponsored by Birmingfind, the
University of Alabama in Birmingham and the
Birmingham Bar Association. [Birmingham,
Ala. : Birmingfind, 1981?] [12] p. : ill. ; 23 cm.
Cover title. Microfiche. New York: New York Public
Library, 198 . 1 microfiche: negative; 11 x 15 cm. (FSN
Sc 019,073)
*1. Race relations and the press - Alabama -
Birmingham - Congresses. I. Birmingfind.*
　　　　　　　　　　　NYPL [Sc Micro F-10982]

Médiations religieuses.
Spiritualité et libération en Afrique /. Paris ,
c1987. 123 p. ;　　*NYPL [Sc D 88-1416]*

**The medical activities of the Freedmen's Bureau
in Reconstruction Alabama, 1865-1868
[microform]** /. Hasson, Gail Snowden. 1982.
252 leaves.　　*NYPL [Sc Micro R-4681]*

**MEDICAL CARE PLANNING. see HEALTH
PLANNING.**

**MEDICAL COLLEGES - CALIFORNIA -
ADMISSION.**
Schwartz, Bernard, 1923- Behind Bakke . New
York , c1988. x, 266 p. ;　ISBN 0-8147-7878-X :
DDC 347.73/0798 347.304798 19
KF228.B34 S39 1988　*NYPL [JLE 88-4158]*

**MEDICAL COLLEGES - UNITED STATES -
ADMINISTRATION.**
Logan, Harold G. A study of the inclusion of
Black administrators in American medical
schools, 1968-78, and their perception of their
roles [microform] /. 1982. v, 90 leaves :
　　　　　　　　　　NYPL [Sc Micro R-4793]

**MEDICAL FOLK-LORE. see FOLK
MEDICINE.**

**MEDICAL PERSONNEL AND PATIENT -
UNITED STATES.**
Maida, Carl Albert. Black networks of care
[microform] . 1981. xiii, 276 leaves ;
　　　　　　　　　　NYPL [Sc Micro R-4803]

MEDICAL POLICY - ZIMBABWE.
Ushewokunze, H. S. M. (Herbert Sylvester
Masiyiwa), 1938- An agenda for Zimbabwe /.
[Harare, Zimbabwe] c1984. vi, 198 p. ;　ISBN
0-906041-67-8　DDC 361.6/1/096891 19
HX451.A6 U84 1984　*NYPL [Sc D 88-942]*

**MEDICAL PROFESSION. see MEDICINE;
PHYSICIANS.**

Medical Research Centre, Nairobi. A
Bibliography of health and disease in East
Africa /. Amsterdam ; New York : 282 p. ;
ISBN 0-444-80931-7 (U. S.)　DDC
016.3621/0967 19
Z6673.6.A353 B53 1988 RA552.A353
　　　　　　　　　　NYPL [Sc G 89-6]

**MEDICINE AND STATE. see MEDICAL
POLICY.**

**MEDICINE, MAGIC, MYSTIC AND
SPAGIRIC - MALAWI -
PSYCHOLOGICAL ASPECTS.**
Peltzer, Karl. Some contributions of traditional
healing practices towards psychosocial health
care in Malawi /. Eschborn bei Frankfurt Om
Main , 1987. 341 p. :　ISBN 3-88074-174-3
　　　　　　　　　　NYPL [Sc D 88-618]

**MEDICINE, MAGIC, MYSTIC, AND
SPAGIRIC - MALI.**
Bastien, Christine. Folies, mythes et magies
d'Afrique noire . Paris , 1988. 230 p. ;　ISBN
2-7384-0038-8　*NYPL [Sc D 89-191]*

**MEDICINE, MAGIC, MYSTIC AND
SPAGIRIC - WEST INDIES.**
Caloc, Ray. Secrets dévoilés de la magie
caraïbe . [Lamentin, Martinique] [1986] 71 p. :
ISBN 2-905317-02-7　*NYPL [Sc D 89-274]*

MEDICINE - NIGERIA - BIBLIOGRAPHY.
De Cola, Freya D. Three decades of medical
research at the College of Medicine, Ibadan,
Nigeria, 1948-1980 . Ibadan, Nigeria , 1984. xv,
208 p. ;　ISBN 978-12-1157-1 (pbk.)　DDC 016.61

19
Z6661.N6 D4 1984 R824.N6
　　　　　　　　　　NYPL [Sc E 89-160]

**MEDICINE, OCCULT. see MEDICINE,
MAGIC, MYSTIC AND SPAGIRIC.**

**MEDICINE, PRIMITIVE - AFRICA, SUB-
SAHARAN.**
Makinde, M. Akin. African philosophy, culture,
and traditional medicine /. Athens, Ohio ,
1988. xvii, 154 p., [2] leaves of plates :　ISBN
0-89680-152-7　DDC 199/.6 19
B5375 .M35 1988　*NYPL [Sc D 88-1273]*

**MEDICINE, PRIMITIVE - MALAWI -
PSYCHOLOGICAL ASPECTS.**
Peltzer, Karl. Some contributions of traditional
healing practices towards psychosocial health
care in Malawi /. Eschborn bei Frankfurt Om
Main , 1987. 341 p. :　ISBN 3-88074-174-3
　　　　　　　　　　NYPL [Sc D 88-618]

**MEDICINE - RESEARCH - VOCATIONAL
GUIDANCE.**
Colman, Hila. A career in medical research.
Cleveland [1968] 175 p.　DDC 610.7
R690 .C65　　*NYPL [Sc D 88-425]*

Medina, Pablo. Pork rind and Cuban songs / by
Pablo Medina. 1st ed. Washington : Nuclassics
and Science Pub. Co., [1975] 69 p. ; 22 cm.
DDC 811/.5/4
I. Title.
PS3563.E24 P6　　*NYPL [Sc D 88-327]*

The meditations of "Hambone". Alley, J. P.
Memphis, Tenn. [1918] 104 p.
　　　　　　　　　　NYPL [Sc Rare C 89-28]

Meditations on the rainbow. New
York , 1987. 71 p. ;　ISBN 0-931885-00-0
　　　　　　　　　　NYPL [Sc D 88-72]

Medizinen des Blitzzauberers Laduma Madela .
Schlosser, Katesa. Kiel , 1984. 186 p., 64, [1] p.
of plates :　ISBN 3-88312-106-1　DDC
615.8/99/089963 19
DT878.Z9 S32 1984　*NYPL [Sc E 87-271]*

Meet me at Jim & Andy's . Lees, Gene. New
York, N.Y., c1988. xviii, 265 p. ;　ISBN
0-19-504611-0 (alk. paper)　DDC 785.42/092/2
B 19
ML394 .L4 1988　　*NYPL [JND 89-5]*

Meet me at Jim and Andy's. Lees, Gene. Meet
me at Jim & Andy's . New York, N.Y. , c1988.
xviii, 265 p. ;　ISBN 0-19-504611-0 (alk. paper)
DDC 785.42/092/2 B 19
ML394 .L4 1988　　*NYPL [JND 89-5]*

The meeting /. Atkinson, Dermot. [Jamaica?] ,
c1985. 68 p. ;　　*NYPL [Sc C 88-108]*

Meeting the blues /. Govenar, Alan B., 1952-
Dallas, Tex. , c1988. 239 p. :　ISBN
0-87833-623-0 :　DDC 784.5/3/00922 19
ML3521 .G68 1988　*NYPL [Sc G 89-4]*

**MEETINGS, PUBLIC. see PUBLIC
MEETINGS.**

Megda /. Kelley, Emma Dunham. New York ,
1988. xxxvii, 394 p. :　ISBN 0-19-505245-5 (alk.
paper)　DDC 813/.4 19
PS2159.K13 M44 1988
　　　　　　　　　　NYPL [JFC 88-2146]

Meghji, Zakia. The woman co-operator &
development : experiences from eastern, central
and southern Africa / Zakia Meghji, Ramadhan
Meghji, Clement Kwayu. Nairobi : Maarifa
Publishers, 1985. iv, 127 p. ; 19 cm. Bibliography:
p. 126-127.　DDC 334/.088042 19
*1. Women in cooperative societies - Africa, Southern. 2.
Women in development - Africa, Southern. I. Title. II.
Title: Woman co-operator and development.*
HD3561.9.A4 M44 1985
　　　　　　　　　　NYPL [Sc C 88-92]

Meier, August, 1923-
Black leaders of the nineteenth century /.
Urbana , c1988. xii, 344 p. :　ISBN 0-252-01506-1
(alk. paper)　DDC 920/.009296073 19
E185.96 .B535 1988　*NYPL [Sc E 88-365]*

Negro thought in America, 1880-1915 : racial
ideologies in the age of Booker T. Washington :
with a new introduction / by August Meier.
Ann Arbor : University of Michigan Press,
1988, c1963. xii, 336 p. ; 22 cm. (Ann Arbor
paperbacks. AA118) Includes index. Bibliography: p.
280-316.　ISBN 0-472-64230-8　DDC 973/.0496073
19
1. Washington, Booker T., 1856-1915 - Influence. 2.

*Afro-Americans - Intellectual life. 3. Afro-Americans -
History - 1877-1964. 4. United States - Intellectual
life - 1865-1918. I. Title.*
E185.6 .M5 1988　　*NYPL [Sc D 89-509]*

Meihy, José Carlos Sebe Bom, 1943- Carnaval,
carnavais / José Carlos Sebe. São Paulo :
Editora Atica, 1986. 96 p. ; 19 cm. (Série
Princípios . 65) Bibliography: p. [93]-96.　ISBN
85-08-01168-7 :　DDC 394.2/5/0981 19
*1. Carnival. 2. Carnival - Brazil. 3. Brazil - Social life
and customs. I. Title. II. Series.*
GT4180 .M45 1986　*NYPL [HFB 88-1339]*

Meili, Josef. In the image of Christ crucified and
risen, in the service of the community :
elements for a spirituality of church ministry /
Josef Meili. Gweru, Zimbabwe : Mambo Press,
1986. 127 p. ; 21 cm. (Mambo occasional papers.
Missio-pastoral series . no. 15) Bibliography: p.
118-127.
1. Paul, the Apostle, Saint. I. Title. II. Series.
　　　　　　　　　　NYPL [Sc D 88-1332]

Meillassoux, Claude.
Anthropologie de l'esclavage : le ventre de fer
et d'argent / Claude Meillassoux.le ´ed. Paris :
Presses Universitaires de France, c1986. 375
p. ; 23 cm. (Pratiques th´eoretiques) Bibliography: p.
333-357.　ISBN 2-13-039480-9
I. Title. II. Series.　*NYPL [Sc D 88-768]*

Bathily, Abdoulaye. Lexique soninke
(sarakole)-français /. [Dakar] , 1975. xx, 191
p. ;　　　　　　　*NYPL [Sc F 86-166]*

Meli, Francis, 1942- South Africa belongs to us :
a history of the ANC / Francis Meli. Harare :
Zimbabwe Publishing House, 1988. xx, 258, [8]
p. of plates : ill. ; 21 cm. Includes index.
Bibliography: p.246-249.
*1. African National Congress - History. 2. Blacks -
South Africa - Politics and government. 3. Apartheid -
South Africa - History. 4. South Africa - Politics and
government - 20th century. I. Title.*
　　　　　　　　　　NYPL [Sc D 89-308]

Melissa & Smith /. Shange, Ntozake. St. Paul,
Mn. , 1976. [13] p. ;　ISBN 0-09-377807-6
　　　　　　　　　　NYPL [Sc Rare C 86-6]

Melissa and Smith. Shange, Ntozake. Melissa &
Smith /. St. Paul, Mn. , 1976. [13] p. ;　ISBN
0-09-377807-6　*NYPL [Sc Rare C 86-6]*

**Mello Freyre, Gilberto de. see Freyre, Gilberto,
1900-**

Mellon, James. Bullwhip days . New York ,
c1988. xviii, 460 p. :　ISBN 1-555-84210-0　DDC
973/.0496073022 B 19
E444 .B95 1988　　*NYPL [IEC 89-3083]*

Melón de Díaz, Esther, 1933- Martinez Masdeu,
Edgar. Literatura puertorriqueña. Río Piedras
[P.R.] 1983. 2 v.　　*NYPL [Sc D 87-1020]*

Melting pot soldiers . Burton, William L., 1928-
Ames, Iowa , 1988. x, 282 p. ;　ISBN
0-8138-1115-5　DDC 973.7/4 19
E540.F6 B87 1988　*NYPL [IKC 88-730]*

Meltzer, Milton, 1915- Langston Hughes : a
biography. New York, Crowell [1968] xiii, 281
p. 21 cm. Bibliography: p. 269-274.　DDC 811/.5/2
B
*1. Hughes, Langston, 1902-1967. 2. Poets, American -
20th century - Biography. 3. Afro-American poets -
Biography.*
PS3515.U274 Z68　*NYPL [Sc D 89-329]*

Mem-Leket özlemi . Hughes, Langston,
1902-1967. Istanbul , 1961. 45 p. ;
　　　　　　　　　　NYPL [Sc Rare C 86-1]

**MEMBERS OF CONGRESS (UNITED
STATES) see LEGISLATORS - UNITED
STATES.**

**MEMBERS OF CONGRESS (UNITED
STATES HOUSE OF
REPRESENTATIVES) see
LEGISLATORS - UNITED STATES.**

**MEMBERS OF CONGRESS (UNITED
STATES SENATE) see LEGISLATORS -
UNITED STATES.**

**Memoir addressed to the general, constituent and
legislative Assembly of the empire of Brazil,
on slavery!** Silva, José Bonifácio de Andrada e,
1763-1838. London , 1826 London : Printed by
A. Redford and W. Robins) 60 p. ;
　　　　　　　　　　NYPL [Sc Rare G 86-14]

Memoir of Pierre Toussaint. Lee, Hannah

Farnham Sawyer, 1780-1865. Boston, 1854. 124 p.
E189.97 T732   **NYPL [Sc Rare C 88-23]**

Memoir of Quamino Buccau . Allinson, William J. Philadelphia , London , 1851. 30 p. ;
NYPL [Sc Rare G 86-28]

Mémoire (Editions Recherche sur les civilisations)
.
(no 59) Chavaillon, Nicole. Gotera, un site paléolithique récent d'Ethiopie /. Paris , 1985. 58 p., 25 leaves of plates :
NYPL [Sc F 88-359]

Mémoire en forme de discours sur la disette du numéraire à Saint-Domingue, et sur les moyens d'y remédier. François de Neufchâteau, Nicolas Louis, comte, 1752-1828. Metz, 1788. 178 p.
NYPL [Sc *F330.9729-F]

Mémoires africaines.
Kaptue, Léon. Travail et main-d'oeuvre au Cameroun sous régime français, 1916-1952 /. Paris [c1986] 282 p. : ISBN 2-85802-655-6
NYPL [Sc D 88-1237]

Lo, Magatte, 1925- Syndicalisme et participation responsable /. Paris [1987] 151 p. : ISBN 2-85802-885-0   **NYPL [Sc D 88-915]**

Mémoires d'autres temps /. Traore, Fathié. Ouagadougou, Burkina Faso? , 1984- (Ouagadougou : Presses africaines) v. ;   DDC 966/.25 19
CT2478.T73 A3 1984   **NYPL [Sc D 88-386]**

Mémoires de lI'nstitut fondamental d'Afrique noire .
(no 80) Person, Yves. Samori: une révolution dyula. Dakar, 1968- v. (2377 p.) DDC 966/.2601/0924 B
DT475.5.S3 P47 1968   **NYPL [Sc F 87-398]**

Mémoires et documents de géographie.
Aquarone, Marie-Christine. Les frontières du refus . Paris , 1987. 133 p. : ISBN 2-222-03962-2
NYPL [Sc F 89-112]

Bonnardel, Régine. Vitalité de la petite pêche tropicale . Paris , 1985. 104 p. : ISBN 2-222-03678-X   **NYPL [Sc F 88-329]**

Mémoires ORSTOM .
(no 109) Franqueville, André. Une Afrique entre le village et la ville . Paris . 646 p. :
ISBN 2-7099-0805-0   **NYPL [Sc E 88-325]**

Memoirs of a great bureaucrat /. Ibuje, Joan, 1941- Benin City [Nigeria] [1985?] 60 p. :
NYPL [Sc D 88-805]

Memoirs of the reign of Bossa Ahádee. Norris, Robert, d. 1791. London, 1789. xvi, 184 p. ;
DT541 .N85   **NYPL [Sc Rare F 88-64]**

Memorandum to the Government of Trinidad and Tobago . Oilfields Workers' Trade Union. San F'do [i.e. San Fernando, Trinidad and Tobago] [1987 or 1988] 124 p. [4] p. of plates :
NYPL [Sc D 88-822]

Mémorial international Frantz Fanon . Mémorial international Frantz Fanon (1982 : Fort-de-France, Martinique) Paris , Dakar , c1984. 278 p. : ISBN 2-7087-0431-1
NYPL [Sc D 88-334]

Mémorial international Frantz Fanon (1982 : Fort-de-France, Martinique) Mémorial international Frantz Fanon : interventions et communications prononcées à l'occasion du Mémorial international Frantz Fanon de Fort-de-France (Martinique) du 31 mars - 3 avril 1982. Paris ; Dakar : Présence africaine, c1984. 278 p. : port. ; 22 cm. "L'édition de cet ouvrage a été rendue possible grâce à l'aide du Comité Frantz Fanon de Fort-de-France (Martinique)." Includes bibliographical references. ISBN 2-7087-0431-1
1. Fanon, Frantz, 1925-1961 - Political and social views - Congresses. 2. Fanon, Frantz, 1925-1961 - Influence - Congresses. I. Comité Frantz Fanon de Fort-de-France (Martinique). II. Title.
NYPL [Sc D 88-334]

Memórias de um projecto /. Vera, Maité, 1930- [Memorias de un proyecto. Portuguese.] Maputo , c1980] 86 p. ;
NYPL [Sc D 88-628]

Memories and records of St. Jude's Chapel [microform] : on the occasion of the 175th anniversary of the founding of St. Michael's Church New York City : the feast of St. Simon & St. Jude. [New York : s.n., 1982] [18] p. ; 22 cm. Cover title. Microfiche. New York: New

York Public Library, 198 . 1 microfiche: negative; 11 x 15 cm. (FSN Sc 019,016)
1. St. Jude's Chapel (Manhattan: Episcopal). 2. St. Michael's Church (Manhattan: Episcopal). 3. Afro-American Episcopalians - New York (N.Y.).
NYPL [Sc Micro F-11024]

Memories of Kenya : stories from the pioneers / edited by Arnold Curtis ; with an introduction by Elspeth Huxley. London : Evans Brothers, 1986. xvi, 160 p., [16] p. of plates : ill. (some col.), maps ; 29 cm. Includes index. ISBN 0-237-50919-9
1. Frontier and pioneer life - Kenya. 2. Pioneers - Kenya - Biography. 3. Kenya - Biography. I. Curtis, Arnold. II. Huxley, Elspeth Joscelin (Grant) 1907-.
NYPL [Sc F 88-102]

MEN, AFRO-AMERICAN. see AFRO-AMERICAN MEN.

Men behind bars . Wooden, Wayne S. New York , c1982. x, 264 p. : ISBN 0-306-41074-5
NYPL [Sc D 89-249]

MEN, NEGRO. see AFRO-AMERICAN MEN.

MEN WEAVERS - AFRICA, WEST - EXHIBITIONS.
Gilfoy, Peggy Stoltz. Patterns of life . Washington, D.C. , c1987. 95 p. : ISBN 0-87474-475-X (alk. paper) : DDC 746.1/4/088042 19
NK8989 .G55 1987   **NYPL [Sc F 88-166]**

MENABE (MALAGASY PEOPLE) - RITES AND CEREMONIES.
Fantaro ny fitamphoa. Antananarivo , 1985. 47 p. :   **NYPL [Sc F 89-121]**

Mencher, Joan P., 1930- Social anthropology of peasantry /. Ikeja, Nigeria , 1983. xii, 351 p. ; DDC 305.5/63 19
HT407 .S53 1983   **NYPL [Sc E 87-179]**

Mendizábal, Horacio. Primeros versos / de Horacio Mendizábal. Buenos Aires : Imp. de Buenos Aires, 1865. 187 p. ; 21 cm.
I. Title.   **NYPL [Sc Rare F 88-75]**

Mene /. Díaz Sánchez, Ramón. [Mene. English.] Trinidad [193-?] (Trinidad : Multimedia Production Center, Faculty of Education, U.W.I.) 141 p. :   **NYPL [Sc D 89-544]**

Menil Collection (Houston, Tex.) Wood, Peter H., 1943- Winslow Homer's images of Blacks . Austin , c1988. 144 p. : ISBN 0-292-79047-3 (University of Texas Press) DDC 759.13 19
ND237.H7 A4 1988a   **NYPL [Sc F 89-133]**

MENISCOCYTOSIS. see SICKLE CELL ANEMIA.

Menschenrechte im Konflikt um Südwestafrika/Namibia : Dokumentation. Frankfurt a.M. : Internationale Gesellschaft für Menschenrechte, 1985. 56 p. : ill., maps ; 30 cm. Cover title.
1. SWAPO. 2. Civil rights - Namibia. 3. National liberation movements - Namibia. I. Internationale Gesellschaft für Menschenrechte.
NYPL [Sc F 88-162]

MENTAL HEALTH PERSONNEL - UNITED STATES.
Gary, Lawrence E. The delivery of mental health services to Black children . Washington, D.C. , 1982. vi, 111, 19 p. ;
NYPL [Sc F 88-66]

MENTAL PHILOSOPHY. see PHILOSOPHY; PSYCHOLOGY.

MENTAL TESTS. see EDUCATIONAL TESTS AND MEASUREMENTS.

MENTALLY HANDICAPPED - JUVENILE FICTION.
Clifton, Lucille, 1936- My friend Jacob /. New York , c1980. [32] p. : ISBN 0-525-35487-5 DDC [E]
PZ7.C6224 Myk 1980   **NYPL [Sc 88-376]**

MENTALLY RETARDED. see MENTALLY HANDICAPPED.

Menten, Theodore. Ancient Egyptian cut and use stencils / Theodore Menten. New York : Dover, 1978. [32] leaves : chiefly ill. ; 28 cm. (Dover cut & use stencil book series) ISBN 0-486-23626-9 :
1. Stencil work. 2. Design, Decorative - Egyptian influences. I. Title. II. Series.
NYPL [Sc F 88-366]

MERCANTILE SYSTEM - HAITI - HISTORY - 20TH CENTURY.
Plummer, Brenda Gayle. Haiti and the great powers, 1902-1915 /. Baton Rouge , c1988. xix, 255 p. : ISBN 0-8071-1409-X (alk. paper) DDC 972.94/04 19
F1926 .P68 1988   **NYPL [HPE 88-2374]**

MERCENARIES (SOLDIERS) see MERCENARY TROOPS.

Mercenary activity in Africa since 1960 /. Reed, John Neville. 1982. vi, 342 leaves ;
NYPL [Sc F 88-121]

MERCENARY TROOPS - AFRICA.
Reed, John Neville. Mercenary activity in Africa since 1960 /. 1982. vi, 342 leaves ;
NYPL [Sc F 88-121]

Merchant. An attempt to strip Negro emancipation of its difficulties as well as its terrors : by shewing that the country has the means of accomplishing it with ease, and doing justice to all parties ... / by a merchant. London : Printed for J.M. Richardson, 1824. 48 p. ; 21 cm.
1. Slavery - British West Indies - Emancipation. I. Title.
NYPL [Sc Rare G 86-13]

MERCHANT BANKS - NIGERIA - HISTORY.
Adewunmi, Wole. Twenty five years of merchant banking in Nigeria /. Akoka , 1985. xvi, 136 p. ; ISBN 978-226-475-X : DDC 332.66//09669 19
HG1971.N6 A34 1985
NYPL [Sc D 88-1020]

MERCHANT SEAMEN - LEGAL STATUS, LAWS, ETC. - SOUTH CAROLINA.
United States. President, 1841-1845 (Tyler) Colored mariners in ports of South Carolina. [Washington, D. C.] 18. 18 p.;
NYPL [Sc Rare F 88-23]

MERCHANTS - ZAMBIA - BIOGRAPHY.
Sampson, Richard, 1922- [Man with a toothbrush in his hat.] The struggle for British interests in Barotseland, 1871-88 /. Lusaka [198-?] v, 158 p. : DDC 968.94/01 19
DT963.72.W47 S25 1980z
NYPL [Sc D 88-381]

Mercier, Alfred, 1816-1894. L'habitation Saint-Ybars; ou, Maîtres et esclaves en Louisiane, récit social. Par Alfred Mercier. Nouvelle-Orléans, Imprimerie franco-américaine (E. Antoine) 1881. 234 p. 20 cm.
1. Slavery - Louisiana - Fiction. I. Title.
PQ3939.M5 H3 1881
NYPL [Sc Rare C 88-19]

Mercier, Louis, of Haiti. Contribution de l'île d'Haïti à l'histoire de la civilisation [microform] / par Louis Mercier. 2e éd. Port-au-Prince, Haïti : Editions Fardin, 1985. 83 p. ; 20 cm. Cover title. Microfilm. New York : New York Public Library, 198 . 1 microfilm reel ; 35 mm. (MN *ZZ28635) DDC 972.94 19
1. Haiti - History. I. Title.
F1911 .M47 1985
NYPL [Sc Micro R-4840 no.8]

Méridiens.
Gaudio, Attilio, 1930- Le Mali /. Paris , c1988. 267 p., [8] p. of plates : ISBN 2-86537-208-1
NYPL [Sc D 88-1412]

Pina, Marie-Paule de. Les Iles du Cap-Vert /. Paris , c1987. 216, [1] p., [12] p. of plates ; ISBN 2-86507-182-4   **NYPL [Sc D 88-510]**

Merlat-Guitard, Odette. see Guitard, Odette.

Merriman, Stella E. Commonwealth Caribbean writers; a bibliography / compiled by Stella E. Merriman and Joan Christiani. Georgetown, Guyana [Public Library] 1970. iv, 98 p. 28 cm. CONTENTS. - Lawson Edward Brathwaite. - Ian Alwyn Carew (Jan Carew). - Theodore Wilson Harris. - John Hearne - George Lamming. - Victor Stafford Reid. - Philip Manderson Sherlock. - Sylvia Wynter-Carew. - Commonwealth Caribbean literature.
1. West Indian literature (English) - Bibliography. I. Christiani, Joan, joint author. II. Georgetown, Guyana. Public Library. III. Title.   **NYPL [JFF 72-67]**

MERU (AFRICAN PEOPLE)
Rimita, David Maitai, 1946- The Njuri-Noheke of Meru /. [Meru, Kenya?] , c1988. 81 p. :
NYPL [Sc D 89-310]

Meshover, Leonard. You visit a dairy [and a] clothing factory / by Leonard Meshover ; photographs, Eve Hoffmann. Chicago : Benefic

Press, c1965. 48 p. : ill. ; 21 cm. (Urban living
series) SCHOMBURG CHILDREN'S COLLECTION.
*1. Dairy farms - United States - Juvenile literature. 2.
Clothing factories - United States - Juvenile literature.
3. Readers - 1950-. I. Hoffmann, Eve. II. Schomburg
Children's Collection. III. Title.*
NYPL [Sc D 89-545]

**Message from the President of the United
States, stating the interpretation which has
been given to the act entitled An Act in
Addition to the Acts Prohibiting the Slave
Trade.** United States. President (1817-1825 :
Monroe) Washington , 1819. 4 p. :
NYPL [Sc Rare F 89-25]

Messaoud, Jir, 1938- Soudan : trente ans
d'indépendance : mutations et obstacles au
développement socio-économique / Messaoud
Jir. Paris : Présence africaine, c1987. 160 p.,
[12] p. of plates : ill., maps. ; 23 cm.
Bibliography: p. [150]-156. ISBN 2-7087-0491-5
*1. Sudan - History. 2. Sudan - Economic conditions. I.
Title.* **NYPL [Sc D 88-1008]**

Mességué, Maurice. Tu as rendez-vous avec le
Diable / Maurice Mességué et Pierre Poiret.
Paris : Editions caribéennes, c1987. 219 p. ; 24
cm. ISBN 2-87679-008-4
1. Magic - West Indies. I. Poiret, Pierre. II. Title.
NYPL [Sc E 88-540]

El mestizaje en Córdoba. Endrek, Emiliano.
Córdoba [Argentina] 1966. xi, 151 p.
F2821.1.C7 E5 **NYPL [Sc E 88-61]**

**METAL INDUSTRIES. see MINERAL
INDUSTRIES.**

METALLURGY - AFRICA, WEST - HISTORY.
Grébénart, Danilo. Les origines de la
métallurgie en Afrique occidentale /. Paris ,
c1988. 290 p. : ISBN 2-903442-65-7
NYPL [Sc E 88-600]

The metaphor lays barren /. Watson, Norbert.
[Toronto?] , c1986. 86 p. ;
NYPL [Sc D 88-493]

Métellus, Jean, 1937-
Anacaona : théâtre / Jean Métellus. Paris :
Hatier, 1986. 159 p. : map ; 18 cm. (Collection
Monde noir poche) ISBN 2-218-07538-5
*1. Arawak Indians - Drama. 2. Hispaniola -
Colonization - Drama. I. Title. II. Series.*
NYPL [Sc C 88-6]

La parole prisonnière : roman / Jean Métellus.
[Paris] : Gallimard, c1986. 234 p. ; 21 cm.
ISBN 2-07-070698-2 :
I. Title.
MLCS 86/6890 (P) **NYPL [JFD 88-7194]**

Voyance : poèmes / Jean Métellus. Paris :
Hatier, c1985. 124 p. ; 18 cm. (Collection Monde
noir poche. 33) ISBN 2-218-07137-1
I. Title. II. Series. **NYPL [Sc C 88-100]**

La méthode dialectometrique appliquée aux
langues africaines / Gladys Guarisma, Wilhelm
J.G. Möhlig (éditeurs). Berlin : D. Reimer,
1986. 431 p. : maps ; 25 cm. French and English.
"Résumés" in French, German, English and Spanish: p.
7-9. Includes bibliographies. ISBN 3-496-00856-3
*1. African languages - Classification. 2. African
languages - Dialectology. I. Guarisma, Gladys. II.
Möhlig, Wilhelm J. G., 1934-.*
NYPL [Sc E 88-46]

**METROPOLITAN AREAS - UNITED
STATES.**
Nelson, Kathryn P. Gentrification and
distressed cities . Madison, Wis. , 1988. xiii,
187 p. : ISBN 0-299-11160-1 : DDC 307.2 19
HT175 .N398 1987 **NYPL [JLE 88-3486]**

Metuh, Emefie Ikenga. Comparative studies of
traditional African religions / by Emefie
Ikenga-Metuh. Onitsha, Nigeria : IMICO
Publishers, 1987. xi, 288 p. ill., ; 22 cm. Includes
bibliographical references. ISBN 978-244-208-9
1. Africa - Religion. I. Title.
NYPL [Sc D 88-800]

Metzger, Linda. Black writers . Detroit, Mi. ,
c1989. xxiv, 619 p. ; ISBN 0-8103-2772-4
NYPL [Sc F 89-57]

Meu amor da Rua Onze /. Santos, Aires de
Almeida. Lisboa , 1987. 72 p. :
NYPL [Sc C 88-129]

MEXICAN AMERICANS - CIVIL RIGHTS.
Black, brown and red . Detroit, Mich. , 1975.
77 p. : **NYPL [Sc D 84-219]**

**Mexico (City). Universidad Nacional. Facultad
de Ciencias Políticas y Sociales.
Serie estudios.**
([no.] 29) Problemas dominico-haitianos y del
Caribe /. - México , 1973. 228 p.;
NYPL [JLK 73-145 [no.] 29]

Meyer, Gérard. Contes du pays malinké . Paris ,
c1987. 238 p. : ISBN 2-86537-188-3
NYPL [Sc C 88-151]

**Mezhdunarodnaĭa organizatsiĭa truda. see
International Labor Organization.**

**Mezhdunarodnyĭ geograficheskiĭ kongress. see
International Geographical Congress.**

Mfoulou, Jean, 1938- L'O.U.A. triomphe de
l'unité ou des nationalités? : essai d'une
sociologie politique de l'Organisation de l'unité
africaine / Jean Mfoulu. Paris : L'Harmattan,
1986. 88 p. ; 22 cm. (Points de vue) Includes
bibliographical references. ISBN 2-85802-832-X
I. Title. **NYPL [Sc D 88-688]**

Mgbodile, T. O. Issues in teacher education and
science curriculum in Nigeria /. [Nigeria ,
1986?] vi, 331 p. : DDC 370./7/309669 19
LB1727.N5 I88 1986 **NYPL [Sc D 88-125]**

M.H. De Young Memorial Museum. Forms and
forces . San Francisco , c1988. 53 p. : ISBN
0-88401-057-0 (pbk) **NYPL [Sc F 88-330]**

Mhire, Herman. Baking in the sun . Lafayette ,
c1987. 146 p. : ISBN 0-295-96606-8
NYPL [Sc F 88-197]

**Miami, University of, Coral Gables, Fla. Cuban
and Caribbean Library.** Catalog of the Cuban
and Caribbean Library, University of Miami,
Coral Gables, Florida. Boston : G. K. Hall,
1977. 6 v. ; 36 cm. DDC 016.9729
*1. Miami, University of, Coral Gables, Fla. Cuban and
Caribbean Library. 2. Caribbean area - Bibliography -
Catalogs. 3. Cuba - Bibliography - Catalogs. I. Hall (G.
K.) & Company. II. Title.*
Z1595 .M5 1977 F2161
NYPL [Pub. Cat. 78-1036]

**MIAMI, UNIVERSITY OF, CORAL GABLES,
FLA. CUBAN AND CARIBBEAN
LIBRARY.**
Miami, University of, Coral Gables, Fla. Cuban
and Caribbean Library. Catalog of the Cuban
and Caribbean Library, University of Miami,
Coral Gables, Florida. Boston , 1977. 6 v. :
DDC 016.9729
Z1595 .M5 1977 F2161
NYPL [Pub. Cat. 78-1036]

Michael, Colette Verger, 1937- Negritude : an
annotated bibliography / by Colette V. Michael.
West Cornwall, CT : Locust Hill Press, 1988.
xvii, 315 p. ; 23 cm. Includes indexes. ISBN
0-933951-15-9 (lib. bdg. : alk. paper) : DDC
016.909/04924 19
*1. Negritude (Literary movement) - Bibliography. 2.
Literature, Modern - Black authors - Bibliography. 3.
Blacks - Race identity - Bibliography. 4. African
literature - Bibliography. I. Title.*
Z6520.N44 M53 1988 PN56.N36
NYPL [Sc D 88-1470]

Michael Jordan, gentleman superstar /. Martin,
Gene L. Greensboro, N.C. , c1987. 69 p. :
ISBN 0-936389-02-8 : DDC 796.32/3/0924 B
19
GV884.J67 M37 1987 **NYPL [Sc E 88-320]**

Michaels, Abbe. Howard-Howard, Margo, 1935- I
was a white slave in Harlem /. New York ,
c1988. vii, 177 p., [8] p. of plates : ISBN
0-941423-14-X (pbk.) : DDC 306.7/43/0924 19
HQ77.8.H68 A3 1988 **NYPL [JFE 89-340]**

**Michigan State University. Dept. of Agricultural
Economics.** An analysis of the Eastern ORD
rural development project in Upper Volta :
report of the M.S.U. mission / by Carl K.
Eicher ... [et al.]. East Lansing : Dept. of
Agricultural Economics, Michigan State
University, 1976. v, 103 p. : ill. ; 28 cm.
(Working paper - African Rural Economy Program ; no.
9) "AID/afr-C-1182." Bibliography: p. 92-95. DDC
338.1/866/25
*1. Agriculture and state - Burkina Faso. 2. Agriculture -
Economic aspects - Burkina Faso. 3. Rural development
projects - Burkina Faso. I. Eicher, Carl K. II. Series:
African Rural Economy Program. Working paper -
African Rural Economy Program , no. 9. III. Title.*
HD2135 .U63 1976 **NYPL [Sc F 89-170]**

**Michigan. State University, East Lansing.
African Studies Center.** Hanson, John
Wagner. Secondary level teachers: supply and
demand in Malawi. [East Lansing 1969] xi, 73,
[2] p.
LB2833.4.M3 H3 **NYPL [JFM 72-62 no. 3]**

**Michigan. State University, East Lansing.
Committee on Ethiopian Studies.
Occasional papers series .**
(monograph no. 5) The Non-semitic
languages of Ethiopia /. East Lansing ,
c1976. xv, 738 p. : DDC 492
PL8021.E8 N6 **NYPL [Sc D 88-854]**

**Michigan. State University, East Lansing.
Institute for International Studies in
Education.** Hanson, John Wagner. Secondary
level teachers: supply and demand in Malawi.
[East Lansing 1969] xi, 73, [2] p.
LB2833.4.M3 H3 **NYPL [JFM 72-62 no. 3]**

Mickey, Rosie Cheatham. Russell Adrian Lane,
biography of an urban negro school
administrator [microform] / Rosie Cheatham
Mickey. 1983. xiii, 275 leaves : port. ; 29 cm.
Thesis (Ph.D.)--University of Akron, 1983.
Bibliography: leaves 265-275. Microfilm. Ann Arbor
Mich. : University Microfilms International, 1983. 1
reel ; 35 mm.
*1. Lane, Russell A., 1897-. 2. Educators - Indiana -
Biography. 3. Afro-Americans - Biography. I. Title.*
NYPL [Sc Micro R-4813]

MIDDLE CLASSES - UNITED STATES.
Black families in crisis . New York , c1988. xiv,
305 p. ; ISBN 0-87630-524-9 DDC 305.8/96073
19
E185.86 .B5254 1988 **NYPL [Sc E 89-155]**

Dilemmas of the new Black middle class /.
[Pa.?] c1980. v, 100 p. ;
E185.86 .D54x 1980 **NYPL [Sc D 89-24]**

Landry, Bart. The new Black middle class /.
Berkeley , 1987. xi, 250 p. ; ISBN 0-520-05942-5
(alk. paper) DDC 305.8/96073 19
E185.86 .L35 1987 **NYPL [Sc D 87-1006]**

**MIDDLE EAST - DICTIONARIES AND
ENCYCLOPEDIAS.**
The Cambridge encyclopedia of the Middle
East and North Africa /. Cambridge
[England] , New York , 1988. 504 p. : ISBN
0-521-32190-5 DDC 956 19
DS44 .C37 1988 **NYPL [*R-BCF 89-551]**

MIDDLE WEST - BIOGRAPHY.
The Black women in the Middle West Project .
Indianapolis, Ind. (140 N. Senate Ave., Room
408, Indianapolis 46204) , 1986. xi, 238 p. ;
DDC 977/.00496073 19
E185.915 .B52 1986 **NYPL [Sc F 88-141]**

**MIDDLE WEST - HISTORY - ARCHIVAL
RESOURCES - MIDDLE WEST.**
The Black women in the Middle West Project .
Indianapolis, Ind. (140 N. Senate Ave., Room
408, Indianapolis 46204) , 1986. xi, 238 p. ;
DDC 977/.00496073 19
E185.915 .B52 1986 **NYPL [Sc F 88-141]**

Middleton, Tony. Horricks, Raymond, 1933-
Quincy Jones /. Tunbridge Wells, Kent , New
York , 1985. 127 p., [8] p. of plates : ISBN
0-87052-215-9 (Hippocrene Books) : DDC
785.42/092/4 B 19
ML419.J7 H67 1985 **NYPL [Sc E 87-36]**

Midiohouan, Guy Ossito, 1952. Nouvelle poésie
du Bénin . Avignon , 1986. 78 p. :
NYPL [Sc C 88-70]

Midnight hotel /. Osofisan, Femi. Ibadan,
Nigeria , 1986. 65 p. ; ISBN 978-16-7508-X
NYPL [Sc D 88-1050]

Midsummer /. Walcott, Derek. London , Boston ,
1984. 79 p. ; ISBN 0-571-13180-8 (pbk.) : DDC
811 19
PR9272.9.W3 M5 1984b
NYPL [Sc C 88-306]

Miers, Suzanne. The End of slavery in Africa /.
Madison, Wis. , c1988. xx, 524 p. : ISBN
0-299-11550-X : DDC 306/.362/096 19
HT1323 .E53 1988 **NYPL [Sc E 89-222]**

Mighty Mo . Arundel, Jocelyn, 1930- New
York , 1961. 124 p. : **NYPL [Sc E 88-228]**

Mignot, Alain. La terre et le pouvoir chez les
Guin du sud-est du Togo / par Alain Mignot ;
préface de Claude Rivière. Paris : Publications
de la Sorbonne, 1985. 288 p. : map ; 24 cm.

(Série "Afrique". no 8) Includes bibliographical references. ISBN 2-85944-087-9
1. *Gouin (African people). 2. Ethnology - Togo. I. Series: Publications de la Sorbonne. Série "Afrique", no 8. II. Title.*   **NYPL [Sc E 88-383]**

MIGRANT AGRICULTURAL LABORERS - KENYA - HISTORY - 20TH CENTURY.
Kanogo, Tabitha M. Squatters and the roots of Mau Mau, 1905-63 /. Athens , London , 1987. xviii, 206 p. : ISBN 0-8214-0873-9 DDC 307.3/36 19
HD1538.K4 K36 1987   **NYPL [Sc D 88-207]**

MIGRANT LABOR - EUROPE.
Power, Jonathan, 1941- Western Europe's migrant workers /. London , 1984. 35 p. :
ISBN 0-08-030831-7   **NYPL [Sc F 88-231]**

MIGRATION. see MIGRATION, INTERNAL.

Migration and change in rural Zambia /.
Hedlund, Hans G. B. Uppsala , 1983. 107 p. :
ISBN 91-7106-220-3 (pbk.) DDC 960 s 307/.2 19
DT1 .N64 no. 70 HB1955
                        NYPL [JLD 85-587]

MIGRATION, INTERNAL - BIBLIOGRAPHY - CATALOGS.
Center for Migration Studies (U. S.) Refugees . Staten Island, N.Y. , 1987. ix, 423 p. ; ISBN 0-934733-34-1 (pbk.)   **NYPL [Sc F 89-60]**

MIGRATION, INTERNAL - GHANA.
Oppong, Christine. Seven roles of women . Geneva , 1987. xi, 127 p. :
                        NYPL [Sc E 89-143]

MIGRATION, INTERNAL - KENYA.
Halderman, John M. An analysis of continued semi-nomadism of the Kaputiei Maasai group ranches [microform] . [Nairobi] [between 1972 and 1974]. 35 p. ; DDC 307.7/2/0967627
DT433.542 .H34
                NYPL [Sc Micro R-4108 no.25]

MIGRATION, INTERNAL - LIBRARY RESOURCES.
Center for Migration Studies (U. S.) Refugees . Staten Island, N.Y. , 1987. ix, 423 p. ; ISBN 0-934733-34-1 (pbk.)   **NYPL [Sc F 89-60]**

MIGRATION, INTERNAL - LIBRARY RESOURCES - DIRECTORIES.
A Directory of international migration study centers, research programs, and library resources /. Staten Island, N.Y. , 1987. ix, 299 p. ; ISBN 0-934733-18-X (pbk.) : DDC 325/.07 19
JV6033 .C45 1987   **NYPL [JLF 88-1452]**

MIGRATION, INTERNAL - NIGERIA - CONGRESSES.
Seminar on Internal Migration in Nigeria (1975 : University of Ife) Internal migration in Nigeria . [Ife] , 1976. iii, 300 p. :
                        NYPL [Sc E 88-489]

MIGRATION, INTERNAL - RESEARCH - DIRECTORIES.
A Directory of international migration study centers, research programs, and library resources /. Staten Island, N.Y. , 1987. ix, 299 p. ; ISBN 0-934733-18-X (pbk.) : DDC 325/.07 19
JV6033 .C45 1987   **NYPL [JLF 88-1452]**

MIGRATION, INTERNAL - STUDY AND TEACHING - DIRECTORIES.
A Directory of international migration study centers, research programs, and library resources /. Staten Island, N.Y. , 1987. ix, 299 p. ; ISBN 0-934733-18-X (pbk.) : DDC 325/.07 19
JV6033 .C45 1987   **NYPL [JLF 88-1452]**

Miguel, Brother. Rastaman chant / by Brother Miguel. Castries, St. Lucia, W.I. : African Children Unlimited, c1983. 151 p. : ill., ports. ; 21 cm.
1. *Ras Tafari movement - Poetry. I. Title.*
MLCS 84/17323 (P)   **NYPL [Sc D 88-621]**

MILAM, J. W. - TRIALS, LITIGATION, ETC.
Whitfield, Stephen J., 1942- A death in the Delta . New York , London , c1988. xiv, 193 p., [8] p. of plates : ISBN 0-02-935121-9 : DDC 345.73/02523 347.3052523 19
E185.61 .W63 1989   **NYPL [Sc E 89-140]**

Milbank quarterly. Vol. 65 (Supplement 1-2)
Currents of health policy . New York , 1987. 2 v. :   **NYPL [Sc D 88-1205]**

Milburn, Norweeta G. Social support : a critical review of the literature as it applies to Black Americans / by Norweeta G. Milburn.

Washington, D.C. : Institute for Urban Affairs and Research, Howard University, 1986. iii, 67 p. ; 28 cm. (Occasional paper. no. 26) On cover: Mental Health Research and Development Center, Institute for Urban Affairs and Research, Howard University. Bibliography: p. 61-67.
1. *Afro-Americans - Social life and customs. 2. Help seeking behavior - United States. 3. Afro-Americans - Psychology. 4. Afro-Americans - Mental health. I. Series: Occasional paper (Howard University. Mental Health Research and Development Center), no. 26. II. Title.*   **NYPL [Sc F 87-428]**

Miles, William F. S. Elections in Nigeria : a grassroots perspective / William Miles. Boulder, Colo. : L. Rienner Publishers, c1988. 168 p. : ill., maps, charts ; 24 cm. Includes index. Bibliography: p. 162-165 ISBN 1-555-87054-6 : DDC 324.9669/505 19
1. *Elections - Nigeria, Northern - Case studies. 2. Political participation - Nigeria, Northern - Case studies. 3. Hausas - Political activity - Case studies. I. Title.*
JQ3099.N66 E546 1987
                        NYPL [JLE 88-3534]

Militärgeschichtliche Skizzen.
Neffe, Dieter. Kämpfe im Süden Afrikas . Berlin , 1987. 64 p. : ISBN 3-327-00283-5
                        NYPL [Sc D 88-680]

The military and politics in Nkrumah's Ghana /.
Baynham, Simon, 1950- Boulder , 1988. xvi, 294 p. ; ISBN 0-8133-7063-9 : DDC 966.7/05 19
DT512 .B39 1986   **NYPL [JFD 88-10630]**

MILITARY BALLOONS. see BALLOONS.

MILITARY GOVERNMENT - NIGERIA.
Duke, Hajia Zainab I. (Hajia Zainab Ibitein) The revolutionary potentials of the Nigerian military, 1886-1986 /. [Lagos?] Nigeria , c1987. viii, 145 p., [28] p. of plates : ISBN 978-232-008-0 DDC 322/.5/09669 19
DT515.8 .D84 1987   **NYPL [Sc D 88-1278]**

The impact of military rule on Nigeria's administration /. Ile-Ife, Nigeria , c1987. vi, 344 p. ; ISBN 978-266-601-7
                        NYPL [Sc D 88-733]

Ojo, Abiola. Constitutional law and military rule in Nigeria /. Ibadan , 1987. vii, 316 p. ; ISBN 978-16-7569-1   **NYPL [Sc D 88-804]**

MILITARY GOVERNMENT - NIGERIA - CONGRESSES.
Proceedings of the colloquium on Why army rule? . [Lagos? , 1986 or 19. 338 p. ;
                        NYPL [Sc G 88-23]

The military in nineteenth century Yoruba politics /. Falola, Toyin. Ile-Ife [Nigeria] , c1984. 127 p. ; ISBN 978-13-6064-X (pbk.) DDC 966.9/004963 19
DT515.45.Y67 F35 1984
                        NYPL [Sc D 88-227]

MILITARY POWER. see DISARMAMENT.

Mill, Eleanor. (illus) Talbot, Toby. I am Maria. New York [1969] 28 p. ISBN 0-402-14031-1 DDC [Fic]
PZ7.T148 I   **NYPL [Sc E 88-531]**

Mill family . McHugh, Cathy L. New York , 1988. x, 144 p. ; ISBN 0-19-504299-9 (alk. paper) DDC 331.7/67721/0975 19
HD8039.T42 U654 1988
                        NYPL [Sc D 88-1082]

MILL, JOHN STUART, 1806-1873.
Harris, Abram Lincoln, 1899-1963. Race, radicalism, and reform . New Brunswick, U. S.A. , c1989. viii, 521 p. ; ISBN 0-88738-210-X DDC 305.8/96073 19
E185.8 .H27 1989   **NYPL [Sc E 89-166]**

Millar, Margaret. Spider webs / Margaret Millar. New York : International Polygonics, c1986. 323 p. ; 19 cm. ISBN 0-930330-76-5
1. *Afro-Americans - Fiction. I. Title.*
                        NYPL [Sc C 88-350]

Millard, Gregory, 1947-1984. Geechies : poems 1972-1982 / Gregory Millard. New York : Tanam Press, 1985. 69 p. ; 23 cm. ISBN 0-934378-42-8 :
1. *Title.*   **NYPL [Sc D 88-617]**

Mille, Pierre, 1864-1931. Line en Nouvelle Calédonie / images d'Edy Legrand. Paris : Calmann-Lévy, c1934. 32, 1 p. : ill. ; 26 cm. (Collection "Pour nos enfants") SCHOMBURG CHILDREN'S COLLECTION.

1. *New Caledonia - Juvenile fiction. I. Schomburg Children's Collection. II. Series. III. Series: Collection "Pour nos enfants". IV. Title.*   **NYPL [Sc F 89-20]**

Miller, E. Ethelbert. Where are the love poems for dictators? / by E. Ethelbert Miller ; with illustrations by Carlos Arrien. Washington, DC : Open Hand Pub., c1986. 91 p. : ill. ; 22 cm. ISBN 0-940880-16-4 (pbk.) : DDC 811/.54 19
1. *Title.*
PS3563.I3768 W45 1986
                        NYPL [Sc D 88-383]

Miller, Heather G. AIDS . Washington, DC , 1989. xiii, 589 p. : ISBN 0-309-03976-2; 0-309-03976-2 (pbk.)   **NYPL [Sc D 89-342]**

Miller, Joseph Calder. Way of death : merchant capitalism and the Angolan slave trade, 1730-1830 / Joseph C. Miller. Madison, Wis. : University of Wisconsin Press, c1988. xxx, 770 p. : ill., maps ; 24 cm. Includes index. Bibliography: p. 717-745. ISBN 0-299-11560-7 : DDC 382/.44/09469 19
1. *Slave-trade - Portugal - History. 2. Slave trade - Angola - History. 3. Slave-trade - Brazil - History. 4. Slave traders - Angola - History. 5. Portugal - Commercial policy - History. 6. Brazil - Commerce - History. I. Title.*
HT1221 .M55 1988   **NYPL [Sc E 89-105]**

Miller, Marion Clinton. The anti-slavery movement in Indiana [microform] / by Marion Clinton Miller. 1938. 290 leaves. Thesis (Ph. D.)--University of Michigan, 1938. Bibliography: leaves 261-290. Microfilm of typescript. Ann Arbor, Mich. : University of Michigan, 1961. 1 microfilm reel ; 35 mm.
1. *Slavery - Indiana - Anti-slavery movemants. I. Title.*
                        NYPL [Sc Micro R-4836]

Miller, Randall M. Woll, Allen L. Ethnic and racial images in American film and television . New York , 1987. xv, 408 p. ; ISBN 0-8240-8733-X (alk. paper) DDC 016.79143/09/093520693 19
Z5784.M9 W65 1987 PN1995.9.M56
                        NYPL [MFL 87-3104]

Mills, J. J. Gorman, G. E. Guide to current national bibliographies in the Third World /. London , New York , c1987. xx, 372 p. ; ISBN 0-905450-34-5   **NYPL [Sc E 88-474]**

Milsome, John, 1924- From slave boy to bishop : the story of Samuel Adjai Crowther / by John Milsome. Cambridge : Lutterworth, 1987. [96] p. ; 19 cm. (Stories of faith and fame) SCHOMBURG CHILDREN'S COLLECTION. ISBN 0-7188-2678-7 (pbk) DDC 283/.092/4 19
1. *Missionaries - Nigeria - Biography - Juvenile literature. 2. Bishops - Nigeria - Biography - Juvenile literature. I. Schomburg Children's Collection. II. Title.*
BV3625.N6C7   **NYPL [Sc C 88-106]**

MINAS GERAIS, BRAZIL - HISTORY.
Lopes, Francisco Antonio, 1882- Alvares Maciel no degrêdo de Angola. [Rio de Janeiro] , 1958. 104 p. ;
HD9527.A22 L6   **NYPL [Sc D 88-419]**

MIND. see PSYCHOLOGY.

Miner, Valerie. Competition, a feminist taboo? /. New York , 1987. xvi, 260 p. ; ISBN 0-935312-74-9 (pbk.) : DDC 305.4/2 19
HQ1206 .C69 1987   **NYPL [JFE 88-6669]**

MINERAL INDUSTRIES - AFRICA.
Yachir, F. Enjeux miniers en Afrique /. Paris , c1987. 180 p. ; ISBN 2-86537-170-0
HD9506.A382 Y34 1987
                        NYPL [Sc D 89-194]

MINERAL RESOURCES. see MINES AND MINERAL RESOURCES.

MINERALS. see MINES AND MINERAL RESOURCES.

MINES AND MINERAL RESOURCES - AFRICA.
Yachir, F. Enjeux miniers en Afrique /. Paris , c1987. 180 p. ; ISBN 2-86537-170-0
HD9506.A382 Y34 1987
                        NYPL [Sc D 89-194]

MINES AND MINING. see MINERAL INDUSTRIES; MINES AND MINERAL RESOURCES.

Ming, Richard E. A book of religious and general poems / by Richard E. Ming. New York, N.Y. : R. E. Ming, 1986. 113 p. ; 22 cm. Cover

title.
I. Title. *NYPL [Sc D 89-141]*

Minha formação /. Nabuco, Joaquim, 1849-1910.
Rio de Janeiro , 1957. 258 p. :
F2536 .N1425 1957 NYPL [Sc D 87-1353]

Mini bus ride . Anderson, Patricia, Dr. Mona,
Kingston, Jamaica , 1987. vii, 179 p. : ISBN
976-400-006-1
HE5647.K56 A53x 1987
NYPL [Sc D 89-312]

MINIANKA (AFRICAN PEOPLE)
Jonckers, Danielle. La société Minyanka du
Mali . Paris , c1987. viii, 234 p., [8] p. of
plates : *NYPL [Sc E 88-344]*

**Miniature African sculptures from the Herman
collection /** [introduction by David
Attenborough; exhibition organised by Michael
Harrison with Judith Kimmelman]. London :
Arts Council of Great Britain, 1985. 64 p. : ill.,
port. ; 20 x 22 cm. Catalog of an exhibition held at
DLI Museum and Arts Centre, Durham, May 11-June
6, 1985 and other British museums. Catalog notes by
Hermione Waterfield. Map on inside back cover.
Bibliography: p. 64. ISBN 0-7287-0454-4
1. Herman, Joseph, 1911- - Art collections -
Exhibitions. 2. Sculpture, African - Exhibitions. I.
Harrison, Michael. II. Kimmelman, Judith. III.
Waterfield, Hermione. IV. DLI Museum and Arts
Centre. *NYPL [Sc D 89-41]*

MINIATURE BOOKS - SPECIMENS.
Equiano, Olaudah, b. 1745. I saw a slave ship
/. Sacramento, Calif. , 1983. 42 p. :
NYPL [Sc Rare C 88-1]

**MINING. see MINERAL INDUSTRIES;
MINES AND MINERAL RESOURCES.**

**MINORITIES AS A THEME IN
LITERATURE. see MINORITIES IN
LITERATURE.**

MINORITIES - BIBLIOGRAPHY.
Dworaczek, Marian. Affirmative action and
minorities . Monticello. Ill., USA [1988] 63
p. ; ISBN 1-555-90638-9 (pbk.) : DDC 016.33113/3
19
Z7164.A26 D87 1988 HF5549.5.A34
NYPL [Sc f 89-39]

MINORITIES - DEVELOPING COUNTRIES.
Third world impact /. London , 1986. 272 p. :
ISBN 0-9506664-8-3 *NYPL [Sc F 88-19]*

**MINORITIES - EDUCATION - GREAT
BRITAIN.**
Educational attainments . London , New York ,
1988. vii, 180 p. : ISBN 1-85000-308-4 : DDC
370.19/34/0941 19
LC3736.G6 E336 1988 NYPL [Sc E 89-52]

**MINORITIES - EDUCATION (HIGHER) -
UNITED STATES.**
Minority student enrollments in higher
education. Garrett Park, Md [1987] [73] p. ;
ISBN 0-912048-49-2 *NYPL [Sc F 88-39]*

Richardson, Richard C. Fostering minority
access and achievement in higher education .
San Francisco, Calif. , c1987. xviii, 244 p. ;
ISBN 1-555-42053-2 (alk. paper) DDC 378/.052
19
LC3727 .R53 1987 NYPL [Sc E 88-472]

MINORITIES - EMPLOYMENT - ENGLAND.
Stares, Rodney. Ethnic minorities . [London] ,
1982. 62 p. ; ISBN 0-905932-32-3
NYPL [Sc F 88-96]

**MINORITIES - EMPLOYMENT - GREAT
BRITAIN.**
Verma, Gajendra K. Race, training, and
employment /. London , New York , 1987. vi,
134 p. ; ISBN 1-85000-243-6 : DDC
331.73/46/0941 19
HD5715.5.G7 V47 1987
*NYPL [*QT 88-3245]*

**MINORITIES - EMPLOYMENT - UNITED
STATES.**
Baker's dozen . Washington [1973] 112 p. ;
NYPL [Sc F 88-244]

Granger, Lester Blackwell, 1896- Toward job
adjustment . [New York] [1941] 78 p. :
NYPL [Sc D 88-178]

MINORITIES - GREAT BRITAIN.
Haynes, Aaron, 1927- The state of Black
Britain /. London , 1983. 160 p. ; ISBN
0-946455-01-5 *NYPL [Sc D 88-348]*

Third world impact /. London , 1986. 272 p. :
ISBN 0-9506664-8-3 *NYPL [Sc F 88-19]*

**MINORITIES - GREAT BRITAIN -
PICTORIAL WORKS.**
Race Today Collective. The arrivants . London,
England , 1987. 112 p. : ISBN 0-947716-10-6
(pbk.) *NYPL [Sc D 88-1206]*

**MINORITIES - HEALTH AND HYGIENE -
UNITED STATES.**
Toxic wastes and race in the United States .
New York, N.Y. , 1987. xvi, 69 p. : DDC
363.7/28 19
TD811.5 .T695 1987 NYPL [JLF 88-1607]

United States. Dept. of Health and Human
Services. Task Force on Black and Minority
Health. Report of the Secretary's Task Force on
Black & Minority Health. Washington, D.C. ,
1985-1986. 8 v. in 9 : DDC 362.1/08996073 19
RA448.5.N4 U55 1985 NYPL [JLM 86-589]

**MINORITIES - HEALTH AND HYGIENE -
UNITED STATES - STATISTICS.**
United States. Dept. of Health and Human
Services. Task Force on Black and Minority
Health. Report of the Secretary's Task Force on
Black & Minority Health. Washington, D.C. ,
1985-1986. 8 v. in 9 : DDC 362.1/08996073 19
RA448.5.N4 U55 1985 NYPL [JLM 86-589]

MINORITIES IN LITERATURE.
The Invention of ethnicity /. New York , 1989.
xx, 294 p. ; ISBN 0-19-504589-0 DDC
810/.9/920692 19
PS153.M56 I58 1988 NYPL [Sc D 89-374]

**MINORITIES IN MOTION PICTURES -
UNITED STATES.**
Woll, Allen L. Ethnic and racial images in
American film and television . New York ,
1987. xv, 408 p. ; ISBN 0-8240-8733-X (alk.
paper) DDC 016.79143/09/093520693 19
Z5784.M9 W65 1987 PN1995.9.M56
NYPL [MFL 87-3104]

**MINORITIES IN MOTION PICTURES -
UNITED STATES - BIBLIOGRAPHY.**
Woll, Allen L. Ethnic and racial images in
American film and television . New York ,
1987. xv, 408 p. ; ISBN 0-8240-8733-X (alk.
paper) DDC 016.79143/09/093520693 19
Z5784.M9 W65 1987 PN1995.9.M56
NYPL [MFL 87-3104]

**MINORITIES IN TELEVISION - UNITED
STATES.**
Woll, Allen L. Ethnic and racial images in
American film and television . New York ,
1987. xv, 408 p. ; ISBN 0-8240-8733-X (alk.
paper) DDC 016.79143/09/093520693 19
Z5784.M9 W65 1987 PN1995.9.M56
NYPL [MFL 87-3104]

**MINORITIES IN TELEVISION - UNITED
STATES - BIBLIOGRAPHY.**
Woll, Allen L. Ethnic and racial images in
American film and television . New York ,
1987. xv, 408 p. ; ISBN 0-8240-8733-X (alk.
paper) DDC 016.79143/09/093520693 19
Z5784.M9 W65 1987 PN1995.9.M56
NYPL [MFL 87-3104]

**MINORITIES - MEDICAL CARE - GREAT
BRITAIN.**
Pearson, Maggie. Racial equality and good
practice maternity care . London , 1985. 37 p. :
ISBN 0-86082-610-4 (pbk) : DDC 362.1/982 19
RG964.G7 NYPL [Sc F 88-393]

**MINORITIES - STUDY AND TEACHING
(HIGHER) - ILLINOIS - CHICAGO.**
Persons, Stow, 1913- Ethnic studies at Chicago,
1905-45 /. Urbana , c1987. 159 p. ; ISBN
0-252-01344-1 (alk. paper) DDC
305.8/007/1077311 19
HT1506 .P47 1987 NYPL [JLE 87-1776]

**MINORITIES - TRAINING OF - GREAT
BRITAIN.**
Black youth futures . Leicester , 1987. ii, 113
p. : ISBN 0-86155-106-0 (pbk) : DDC
331.3/46/0941 19
HD8398 NYPL [Sc D 89-175]

**MINORITIES - UNITED STATES -
BIBLIOGRAPHY.**
Taylor, Charles A. (Charles Andrew), 1950-
Guide to multicultural resources /. Madison,
WI , c1987. ix, 512 p. : ISBN 0-935483-07-1
(pbk.) *NYPL [Sc D 88-530]*

**MINORITIES - UNITED STATES -
POLITICAL ACTIVITY.**
Race and politics /. New York , 1985. 174 p. ;
ISBN 0-8242-0700-9 (pbk.) : DDC 305.8/00973
19
*E184.A1 R25 1985 NYPL [8-SAD
(Reference shelf. v.56, no.6)]*

**MINORITIES - UNITED STATES -
SOCIETIES, ETC. - DIRECTORIES.**
Taylor, Charles A. (Charles Andrew), 1950-
Guide to multicultural resources /. Madison,
WI , c1987. ix, 512 p. : ISBN 0-935483-07-1
(pbk.) *NYPL [Sc D 88-530]*

**MINORITY AGED - CANADA - SOCIAL
CONDITIONS.**
Driedger, Leo, 1928- Aging and ethnicity .
Toronto , 1987. xv, 131 p. : ISBN 0-409-81187-4
NYPL [Sc E 88-127]

**MINORITY BUSINESS ENTERPRISES -
UNITED STATES.**
Adams, Robert Hugo. The little black book of
business inspirations /. Hempstead, NY , 1987.
vi, 74 p. : *NYPL [Sc D 88-440]*

MINORITY GROUPS. see MINORITIES.

**Minority student enrollments in higher
education:** a guide to institutions with highest
persent of Asian, Black, Hispanic, and Native
America students. Garrett Park, Md. Garrett
Park Press, [1987] [73] ; 28 cm. Includes
index. Bibliography: p. [72-73] ISBN 0-912048-49-2
1. Minorities - Education (Higher) - United States. 2.
Universities and colleges - United States - Directories.
NYPL [Sc F 88-39]

**MINORITY WOMEN - MENTAL HEALTH -
UNITED STATES.**
The Psychopathology of everyday racism and
sexism /. New York , c1988. xix, 120 p. ;
ISBN 0-918393-51-5 (pbk.) DDC 305.4/2 19
RC451.4.M58 P79 1988
NYPL [Sc D 89-449]

**MINORITY WOMEN - UNITED STATES -
BIBLIOGRAPHY.**
Redfern, Bernice, 1947- Women of color in the
United States . New York , 1989. vii, 156 p. ;
ISBN 0-8240-5849-6 (alk. paper) DDC
016.3054/8/0973 19
Z7964.U49 R4 1989 HQ1410
NYPL [Sc D 89-562]

**MINORITY WOMEN - UNITED STATES -
PSYCHOLOGY.**
The Psychopathology of everyday racism and
sexism /. New York , c1988. xix, 120 p. ;
ISBN 0-918393-51-5 (pbk.) DDC 305.4/2 19
RC451.4.M58 P79 1988
NYPL [Sc D 89-449]

**MINORITY YOUTH - EDUCATION -
AUSTRALIA - CASE STUDIES.**
Bullivant, Brian Milton. The ethnic encounter
in the secondary school . London , New York ,
1987. x, 214 p. ; ISBN 1-85000-255-X : DDC
371.97/0994 19
LC3739 .B84 1987 NYPL [JLE 88-2088]

MINORITY YOUTH - ENGLAND - FICTION.
Dhondy, Farrukh, 1944- Come to Mecca .
London , 1978 (1983 [printing]) 125 p. ; ISBN
0-00-672501-5 (pbk) : DDC 823 19
NYPL [Sc C 88-310]

MINORITY YOUTH - ENGLAND - LONDON.
Turkie, Alan. Know what I mean? . Leicester ,
1982. 82 p. : ISBN 0-86155-062-5 :
NYPL [Sc D 89-464]

**MINORS (LAW) see CHILDREN - LEGAL
STATUS, LAWS, ETC.**

Minozzi, Maria Teresa. Dizionario
italiano-somalo / Maria Teresa Minozzi,
Cinzica Poletti Turrin. Milano : A. Carcano,
1961. 178 p. ; 17 cm.
1. Italian language - Dictionaries - Somali. I. Poletti
Turrin, Cinzica. II. Title. *NYPL [Sc B 88-4]*

Minted coins . Launko, Okinba. Ibadan , 1987.
vii, 72 p. : ISBN 978-12-9847-2
NYPL [Sc C 88-158]

Minty, Abdul S. Children of resistance . London ,
1988. vii, 146 p. ; *NYPL [Sc D 88-1286]*

**MIRANDA (VENEZUELA : STATE) -
HISTORY.**
Ramos Guédez, José Marcial. Historia del
Estado Miranda /. Caracas , 1981. 222 p. :

DDC 987/.35 19
F2331.M6 R36 1981 NYPL *[Sc D 89-390]*

Mirandy and Brother Wind /. McKissack, Pat, 1944- New York , 1988. [32] p. : ISBN 0-394-88765-4 DDC [E] 19
PZ7.M478693 Mi 1988 NYPL *[Sc F 89-58]*

Mirror for campus /. Onwueme, Tess Akaeke. Owerri , 1987. iii leaves, 76 p. ;
NYPL *[Sc C 88-159]*

Mirsky, Reba Paeff. Nomusa and the new magic. Illustrated by W. T. Mars. Chicago, Follett, 1962. 190 p. ill. 24 cm. SCHOMBURG CHILDREN'S COLLECTION.
1. Zulus - Juvenile fiction. I. Schomburg Children's Collection. II. Title.
PZ7.M675 No NYPL *[Sc E 89-175]*

Misangós song [microform] . Cohen, David William. [Nairobi] [1979] 24 p. ;
NYPL *[Sc Micro R-4108 no. 38]*

MISCARRIAGE. see ABORTION.

MISCEGENATION - AMERICA.
Forbes, Jack D. Black Africans and native Americans . Oxford, UK , New York, NY, USA , 1988. 345 p. ; ISBN 0-631-15665-8 : DDC 973/.0496073 19
E59.M66 F67 1988 NYPL *[HBC 88-2172]*

MISDEMEANORS (LAW) see CRIMINAL LAW.

Misère et grandeur de la démocratie au Cameroun /. Eteki-Otabela, Marie-Louise, 1947- Paris , c1987. 143 p. ; ISBN 2-85802-929-6 NYPL *[Sc D 88-910]*

Misr. see Egypt.

Miss Minerva's baby /. Sampson, Emma Speed, 1868-1947. Chicago , c1920. 320 p. :
PZ7.S16 Mis NYPL *[Sc C 88-71]*

Missé, Hermann. Le droit international du travail en Afrique : le cas du Cameroun / Hermann Missé ; préface de Francis Blanchard. Paris : L'harmattan, 1987. 263 p. ; 24 cm. (Collection Droits et sociétés) Bibliography: p. 257-260. ISBN 2-85802-839-7
1. Labor laws and legislation, Internatioanl. 2. Labor laws and legislation - Cameroun. I. Title.
NYPL *[Sc E 88-20]*

The missing gold ring /. Osahon, Naiwu, 1937- Apapa, Lagos, Nigeria , c1981. [24] p. : ISBN 978-18-6000-6
MLCS 85/698 (P) NYPL *[Sc D 89-222]*

The missing link poems /. Commey, James Putsch. Accra , c1988. xvii, 92 p. :
NYPL *[Sc D 89-584]*

Mission suisse dans l'Afrique du Sud. Cuenod, R. Tsonga-English dictionary /. Braamfontein , 1967. 286 p. : NYPL *[Sc D 88-89]*

Mission to South Africa . Commonwealth Group of Eminent Persons. Harmondsworth, Middlesex, Eng. , New York , 1986. 176 p. : ISBN 0-14-052384-7 : NYPL *[Sc C 88-116]*

MISSIONARIES - AFRICA - DIARIES.
Fanfani, Mariapia. [Hayat. English.] Hayat . New York , c1988. 219 p., [16] p. of plates : ISBN 0-671-66414-X DDC 363.8/83/0924 B 19
HV696.F6 F363 1988 NYPL *[JFD 88-3833]*

MISSIONARIES - AFRICA - JUVENILE FICTION.
Fleming, Elizabeth P. The Takula tree. Philadelphia, 1964. 175 p.
PZ7.F5995 Tak NYPL *[Sc D 88-508]*

MISSIONARIES - ENGLAND - BIOGRAPHY.
Dickson, Mora, 1918- The powerful bond . London , 1980. 5-252 p. : ISBN 0-234-72103-0 : DDC 266/.963 B 19
BV3625.S5 K393 1980 NYPL *[Sc D 87-37]*

MISSIONARIES - FRANCE - BIOGRAPHY.
Rutayisire, Paul. La christianisation du Rwanda (1900-1945) . Fribourg, Suisse , 1987. 571 p. : ISBN 2-8271-0371-0 (pbk.)
NYPL *[Sc D 88-1510]*

MISSIONARIES IN LITERATURE.
Laverdière, Lucien, 1940- L'africain et le missionnaire . Montr´eal , 1987. 608 p. : ISBN 2-89007-640-7 NYPL *[Sc D 88-343]*

MISSIONARIES, MEDICAL - GABON - BIOGRAPHY - JUVENILE LITERATURE.
Daniel, Anita. The story of Albert Schweitzer

/. New York , 1957. 179 p. :
NYPL *[Sc D 88-379]*

MISSIONARIES - NIGERIA - BIOGRAPHY - JUVENILE LITERATURE.
Milsome, John, 1924- From slave boy to bishop . Cambridge , 1987. [96] p. ; ISBN 0-7188-2678-7 (pbk) : DDC 283/.092/4 19
BV3625.N6C7 NYPL *[Sc C 88-106]*

MISSIONARIES - RWANDA - BIOGRAPHY.
Rutayisire, Paul. La christianisation du Rwanda (1900-1945) . Fribourg, Suisse , 1987. 571 p. : ISBN 2-8271-0371-0 (pbk.)
NYPL *[Sc D 88-1510]*

MISSIONARIES - SIERRA LEONE - BIOGRAPHY.
Dickson, Mora, 1918- The powerful bond . London , 1980. 5-252 p. : ISBN 0-234-72103-0 : DDC 266/.963 B 19
BV3625.S5 K393 1980 NYPL *[Sc D 87-37]*

Missions. Brezault, Alain. Missions en Afrique . Paris , c1987. 193 p. : ISBN 2-86260-209-4 : DDC 266/.267 19
BV3520 .B74 1987 NYPL *[Sc E 89-163]*

MISSIONS - AFRICA.
Salvoldi, Valentino. [Africa, il vangelo ci appartiene. English.] Africa, the gospel belongs to us . Ndola [Zambia] , 1986. 187 p ;
NYPL *[Sc D 89-568]*

MISSIONS - AFRICA, EAST.
Pruen, Septimus Tristram (Septimus Tristam) The Arab and the African . London , 1896. vii, 338 p. [8] p. of plates : NYPL *[Sc D 88-387]*

MISSIONS - AFRICA - HISTORY - SOURCES.
Brasio, Antonio Duarte, 1906- Monumenta missionaria africana: Africa ocidental. Lisboa, 1952- v. NYPL *[ZKVX (Brásio, A.D. Monumenta missionaria africana)]*

MISSIONS - AFRICA - HISTORY - SOURCES - BIBLIOGRAPHY - CATALOGS.
Church Missionary Society. Africa (Group 3) Committee. Catalogue of the papers of the missions of the Africa (Group 3) Committee /. London , 1981. 8 v. ; DDC 266/.3 19
CD1069.L715 C47 1981 NYPL *[Sc F 88-78]*

MISSIONS - AFRICA, SUB-SAHARAN.
Brezault, Alain. Missions en Afrique . Paris , c1987. 193 p. : ISBN 2-86260-209-4 : DDC 266/.267 19
BV3520 .B74 1987 NYPL *[Sc E 89-163]*

MISSIONS - CAMEROON.
Aarhaug, Aksel, 1921- Mitt Afrika /. Oslo , 1985. 104 p., [17] p. of plates : ISBN 82-531-4177-7 NYPL *[Sc E 88-149]*

MISSIONS - CARIBBEAN AREA - HISTORY - SOURCES - BIBLIOGRAPHY - CATALOGS.
Church Missionary Society. Africa (Group 3) Committee. Catalogue of the papers of the missions of the Africa (Group 3) Committee /. London , 1981. 8 v. ; DDC 266/.3 19
CD1069.L715 C47 1981 NYPL *[Sc F 88-78]*

MISSIONS - CHAD.
Baar, Marius. Tschad--Land ohne Hoffnung? . Bad Liebenzell , c1985. 190 p., [6] p. of plates : ISBN 3-88002-270-4 NYPL *[Sc D 88-892]*

Missions de la Congrégation des missionaires oblats de Marie immaculée. Records from Natal, Lesotho, the Orange Free State, and Mozambique concerning the history of the Catholic Church in southern Africa /. Roma, Lesotho [1974] 2 v. : DDC 282/.68 19
BV3625S67 R43 1974 NYPL *[Sc E 89-47]*

Missions en Afrique. Brezault, Alain. Paris , c1987. 193 p. : ISBN 2-86260-209-4 : DDC 266/.267 19
BV3520 .B74 1987 NYPL *[Sc E 89-163]*

MISSIONS - INDIVIDUAL DENOMINATIONS. See subdivision Missions under names of churches, denominations, religious orders, etc., e.g.: **CATHOLIC CHURCH - MISSIONS.**

MISSIONS - NEW ZEALAND - HISTORY - SOURCES - BIBLIOGRAPHY - CATALOGS.
Church Missionary Society. Africa (Group 3) Committee. Catalogue of the papers of the missions of the Africa (Group 3) Committee /.

London , 1981. 8 v. ; DDC 266/.3 19
CD1069.L715 C47 1981 NYPL *[Sc F 88-78]*

MISSIONS - NIGERIA - BORNO STATE.
Hickey, Raymond. Christianity in Borno State and Northern Gongola /. [Nigeria , 1984?] (Ibadan : Claverianum Press) vi, 108 p. :
NYPL *[Sc D 88-882]*

MISSIONS - NIGERIA, EASTERN - HISTORY.
A Hundred years of the Catholic Church in Eastern Nigeria, 1885-1985 . Onitsha, Nigeria , 1985. 432 p. : ISBN 978-17-5103-7
NYPL *[Sc D 88-830]*

MISSIONS - NIGERIA - GONGOLA STATE.
Hickey, Raymond. Christianity in Borno State and Northern Gongola /. [Nigeria , 1984?] (Ibadan : Claverianum Press) vi, 108 p. :
NYPL *[Sc D 88-882]*

MISSIONS, NORWEGIAN - MADAGASCAR - HISTORY - 19TH CENTURY.
Norwegian missions in African history /. Oslo : Oxford [Oxfordshire] ; 2 v. : ISBN 82-00-07418-8 (v. 1) DDC 266/.023/48106 19
BV3625.M2 N67 1986 NYPL *[Sc D 89-26]*

MISSIONS - PALESTINE - HISTORY - SOURCES - BIBLIOGRAPHY - CATALOGS.
Church Missionary Society. Africa (Group 3) Committee. Catalogue of the papers of the missions of the Africa (Group 3) Committee /. London , 1981. 8 v. ; DDC 266/.3 19
CD1069.L715 C47 1981 NYPL *[Sc F 88-78]*

MISSIONS - RWANDA - HISTORY.
Rutayisire, Paul. La christianisation du Rwanda (1900-1945) . Fribourg, Suisse , 1987. 571 p. : ISBN 2-8271-0371-0 (pbk.)
NYPL *[Sc D 88-1510]*

MISSIONS - SOUTH AFRICA.
Livingstone, David, 1813-1873. [Missionary travels and researches in South Africa. Danish.] Livingstones Reise : Syd-Adrika /. Kjøbenhavn , 1858-1859. 2 v. :
NYPL *[Sc E 88-47]*

The Zulu blind boy's story. New York [185-?] 16 p. ; NYPL *[Sc Rare C 89-29]*

MISSIONS TO BAYAKA (AFRICAN PEOPLE)
Beken, Alain van der, 1935- L'Evangile en Afrique, vécu et commenté par des Bayaka /. Nettetal [Germany] , 1986. 328 p. ; ISBN 3-87787-204-2 :
BV3630.B69 B45 1986 NYPL *[Sc E 88-339]*

MISSIONS TO BLACKS.
Sandoval, Alonso dc, 1576-1652. Naturaleza, policia sagrada i profana, costumbres i ritos, disciplina i catechismo evangelico de todos etiopes /. En Sevilla , 1627. [23], 334 p., 81 leaves ; NYPL *[Sc Rare F 82-70]*

MISSIONS TO YORUBAS.
Tucker, Charlotte Maria, 1821-1893. Abbeokoeta. Amsterdam, 1860. viii, 330 p.
NYPL *[Sc Rare C 88-25]*

MISSIONS - VIRGIN ISLANDS OF THE UNITED STATES.
Oldendorp, C. G. A. (Christian Georg Andreas), 1721-1787. [Geschichte der Mission der Evangelischen Brüder auf den caraibischen Inseln S. Thomas, S. Croix an Jan.] C.G.A. Oldendorps Geschichte der Mission der Evangelischen Brüder auf den caraibischen Inseln S. Thomas, S. Croix and S. Jan /. Barby , 1777. 2 v. in 1 (1068 p.) : DDC 266/.46729722 19
BV2848.V5 O42 1777
NYPL *[Sc Rare C 89-33]*

Missionsjahrbuch der Schweiz . (1974, Jahrg. 41) Afrika sucht sein Menschenbild . Freiburg, Basel , 1974. 112 p. : *DT351 .A38* NYPL *[Sc D 87-1433]*

Missionswissenschaftliche Forschungen, 0076-9428 . (Bd. 19) Dierks, Friedrich. Evangelium im afrikanischen Kontext . Gütersloh , c1986. 206 p. : ISBN 3-579-00239-2 DDC 266/.0089963 19
BL2480.T76 D54 1986 NYPL *[Sc D 88-879]*

MISSISSIPPI - ECONOMIC CONDITIONS.
Moore, John Hebron. The emergence of the cotton kingdom in the Old Southwest . Baton Rouge , c1988. xii, 323 p. : ISBN 0-8071-1404-9

(pbk.) DDC 330.9762 19
HC107.M7 M66 1988   NYPL [Sc E 88-279]

MISSISSIPPI FREEDOM PROJECT.
McAdam, Doug. Freedom Summer /. New
York , c1988. [xiii], 333 p., [14] p. of plates :
ISBN 0-19-504367-7 (alk. paper) DDC
976.2/00496073 19
E185.93.M6 M28 1988   NYPL [Sc E 88-563]

MISSISSIPPI - LITERARY COLLECTIONS.
Mississippi writers . Jackson , c1985- v. ; ISBN
0-87805-232-1 (pbk). DDC 813/.008/09762 19
PS558.M7 M55 1985   NYPL [Sc E 88-316]

MISSISSIPPI - RACE RELATIONS.
McAdam, Doug. Freedom Summer /. New
York , c1988. [xiii], 333 p., [14] p. of plates :
ISBN 0-19-504367-7 (alk. paper) DDC
976.2/00496073 19
E185.93.M6 M28 1988   NYPL [Sc E 88-563]

McMillen, Neil R., 1939- Dark journey .
Urbana, Ill. , c1989. xvii, 430 p., [10] p. of
plates, ISBN 0-252-01568-1 (alk. paper) DDC
976.2/00496073 19
E185.93.M6 M33 1989   NYPL [Sc E 89-213]

Mississippi writers : reflections of childhood and
youth / edited by Dorothy Abbott. Jackson :
University Press of Mississippi, c1985- v. ; 23
cm. (Center for the Study of Southern Culture series)
CONTENTS. - v. 1. Fiction. ISBN 0-87805-232-1
(pbk). DDC 813/.008/09762 19
1. American literature - Mississippi. 2. American
literature - 20th century. 3. Children - Literary
collections. 4. Youth - Literary collections. 5.
Mississippi - Literary collections. I. Abbott, Dorothy,
1944-. II. Series.
PS558.M7 M55 1985   NYPL [Sc E 88-316]

Mr. B /. Saro-Wiwa, Ken. Port Harcourt , Ewell ,
1987. 154 p. : ISBN 1-87071-601-9 (pbk) : DDC
823 19
PZ7   NYPL [Sc C 88-300]

Mr. Bojangles . Haskins, James, 1941- New
York , 1988. 336 p. : ISBN 0-688-07203-8 :
DDC 793.3/2/0924 B 19
GV1785.R54 H37 1988
NYPL [Sc D 88-851]

Mr. Kelso's lion. Bontemps, Arna Wendell, 1902-
Philadelphia [1970] 48 p. DDC [Fic]
PZ7.B6443 Mi   NYPL [Sc D 88-1493]

Mr. Murdock takes command . Icenhower,
Joseph B. Philadelphia , c1958. xii, 173 p. :
NYPL [Sc D 88-1507]

Mitchell, H. L. (Harry Leland), 1906- Roll the
union on : a pictorial history of the Southern
Tenant Farmers' Union / as told by its
co-founder, H.L. Mitchell ; with an introduction
by Orville Vernon Burton. Chicago : C.H. Kerr
Pub. Co., 1987. 96 p. : ill. ; 21 x 28 cm.
1. Southern Tenant Farmers' Union - History. 2. Farm
tenancy - Economic aspects - Southern States - History.
I. Title. II. Title: Pictorial history of the Southern
Tenant Farmers' Union.   *NYPL [Sc F 88-187]*

Mitchell, Loften. Tell Pharaoh / Loften Mitchell.
N.Y., N.Y. : Broadway play Pub., c1986. viii,
60 p. ; 22 cm. "A concert drama." ISBN
0-88145-048-0
I. Title.   *NYPL [Sc D 88-1187]*

Mitgang, N. R. Haskins, James, 1941- Mr.
Bojangles . New York , 1988. 336 p. : ISBN
0-688-07203-8 : DDC 793.3/2/0924 B 19
GV1785.R54 H37 1988
NYPL [Sc D 88-851]

Miti Katabaro. Sokoïne, Edward Moringe,
1938-1984. Public policy making and
implementation in Tanzania / Pau [1986?] ix,
124 p. :   *NYPL [Sc E 88-319]*

O mito da terra . Arcangeli, Alberto. São Luís ,
1987. 302 p. :   *NYPL [Sc D 89-579]*

Mitt Afrika /. Aarhaug, Aksel, 1921- Oslo ,
1985. 104 p., [17] p. of plates : ISBN
82-531-4177-7   *NYPL [Sc E 88-149]*

Mitzlaff, Ulrike von. Maasai-Frauen : Leben in
einer patriarchalischen Gesellschaft :
Feldforschung bei den Parakuyo, Tansania /
Ulrike von Mitzlaff. München : Trickster, 1988.
181 p. : ill., map ; 22 cm. (Rites de passages . Bd.
1) Summary in English: p. 181. Bibliography: p.
178-180. ISBN 3-923804-23-7
1. Women, Masai. 2. Masai - Social life and customs. I.
Title.   *NYPL [Sc D 89-551]*

MIXED BLOODS (AMERICAN INDIANS)
see **INDIANS - MIXED BLOODS.**

Mizik bô kay. Jallier, Maurice. Musique aux
Antilles =. Paris , c1985. 145 p., [16] p. of
plates : ISBN 2-903033-65-X : DDC
780/.42/09729 19
ML3486.G8 J3 1985   NYPL [Sc D 87-576]

Mkangi, Katama G. C. Mafuta / Katama G.
Mkangi. Nairobi : Heinemann [i.e. Heinemann]
Educational Books, 1984. 92 p. ; 18 cm.
(Waandishi wa Kiafrika. S30)
1. Swahili language - Texts. I. Title.
NYPL [Sc C 88-198]

Mkelle, M. B. (Mohamed Burhan) Résumés de
vieux manuscrits arabes . Zanzibar [Tanzania] ,
1981. x, 50 leaves ;   *NYPL [Sc B 88-10]*

Mkuti, Lukas. Breakfast of sjamboks /. Harare ,
1987. viii, 71 p. : ISBN 0-949225-35-5
NYPL [Sc C 88-299]

A mob intent on death . Cortner, Richard C.
Middletown, Conn. , c1988. xii, 241 p., [24] p.
of plates : ISBN 0-8195-5161-9 (alk. paper) : DDC
976.7/88052 19
F417.P45 C67 1988   NYPL [Sc E 88-362]

MOBILITY. see MIGRATION, INTERNAL.

Mobutu. Mobutu, maréchal du Zaïre. Paris ,
c1985. 237 p. : ISBN 2-85258-389-5 DDC
967.5/103/0924 B 19
DT658.2.M62 M62 1985
NYPL [Sc F 88-371]

Mobutu, maréchal du Zaïre. Paris : Editions J.A.,
c1985. 237 p. : ports. ; 30 cm. (Les
Contemporains) Cover title: Mobutu. ISBN
2-85258-389-5 DDC 967.5/103/0924 B 19
1. Mobutu Sese Seko, 1930- - Pictorial works. 2. Zaire -
Presidents - Pictorial works. 3. Zaire - Politics and
government - 1960- - Pictorial works. I. Title: Mobutu.
II. Series: Contemporains (Editions J.A.).
DT658.2.M62 M62 1985
NYPL [Sc F 88-371]

MOBUTU SESE SEKO, 1930- - PICTORIAL
WORKS.
Mobutu, maréchal du Zaïre. Paris , c1985. 237
p. : ISBN 2-85258-389-5 DDC 967.5/103/0924 B
19
DT658.2.M62 M62 1985
NYPL [Sc F 88-371]

Moçambique. see Mozambique.

Moçambique por Eduardo Mondlane /. Motta,
Helena. [Maputo?] [1984] 86 p. : DDC
967/.903/0222 19
DT463 .M64 1984   NYPL [Sc F 89-172]

Mockler, Anthony. Dixon, Glen. Hostage /.
London , 1986. 189 p., [8] p. of plates : ISBN
0-86287-271-5   *NYPL [Sc E 88-406]*

Mode drawing /. Yajima, Isao, 1945- Tokyo,
Japan , 1986. 105 p. : ISBN 4-7661-0394-7
NYPL [Sc F 88-238]

Mode drawing, nude. Yajima, Isao, 1945- Mode
drawing /. Tokyo, Japan , 1986. 105 p. : ISBN
4-7661-0394-7   *NYPL [Sc F 88-238]*

MODEL CITIES. see CITY PLANNING.

MODELS, ARCHITECTURAL. see
ARCHITECTURAL MODELS.

Models of class domination in plural societies of
Central Africa /. Madu, Oliver V. Washington ,
c1978. vi, 510 p. :   *NYPL [Sc D 88-1067]*

The modern African elite of South Africa /.
Dreyer, Lynette, 1949- Houndmills,
Basingstoke, Hampshire , 1989. xii, 186 p. ;
ISBN 0-333-46410-9   *NYPL [Sc D 89-306]*

MODERN ART. see ART, MODERN.

The Modern Caribbean / edited by Franklin W.
Knight and Colin A. Palmer. Chapel Hill :
University of North Carolina Press, c1989. x,
382 p. : map ; 24 cm. Includes index. Bibliography:
p. [341]-361. ISBN 0-8078-1825-9 (alk. paper) DDC
972.9 19
1. Caribbean Area. I. Knight, Franklin W. II. Palmer,
Colin A., 1942-.
F2156 .M63 1989   NYPL [Sc E 89-253]

Modern critical interpretations.
Zora Neale Hurston's Their eyes were watching
God /. New York , 1987. vii, 130 p. ; ISBN
1-555-46054-2 (alk. paper) : DDC 813/.52 19
PS3515.U789 T639 1987
NYPL [JFE 87-5315]

Modern critical views.
Zora Neale Hurston /. New York , 1986. viii,
192 p. ; ISBN 0-87754-627-4 (alk. paper) : DDC
813/.52 19
PS3515.U789 Z96 1986
NYPL [JFE 87-1592]

Modern essays on African literature .
(v. 1) Studies in the African novel /. [Ibadan]
[1985?] viii, 258 p. ;   *NYPL [Sc D 88-1316]*

A modern history of Somalia . Lewis, I. M.
Boulder , 1988. xiii, 297 p. : ISBN
0-8133-7402-2 : DDC 967/.73 19
DT403 .L395 1988   NYPL [Sc D 88-1347]

MODERN LITERATURE. see LITERATURE,
MODERN.

MODERN PAINTING. see PAINTING,
MODERN.

Modern principles of equity . Kludze, A. K. P.
Dordrecht, Holland , Providence, R.I. , 1988.
xxxix, 482 p. ; ISBN 90-6765-147-8
NYPL [Sc E 89-233]

Modern war studies.
Cornish, Dudley Taylor. The sable arm .
Lawrence, Kan. , c1987. xviii, 342 p. ; ISBN
0-7006-0328-X (pbk.) DDC 973.7/415 19
E540.N3 C77 1987   NYPL [Sc D 88-850]

MODERNISM (LITERATURE) - BRAZIL.
Damasceno, Benedita Gouveia. Poesia negra no
modernismo brasileiro /. Campinas, SP [Brasil] ,
1988. 142 p. ; ISBN 85-7113-003-5
NYPL [Sc D 88-1290]

Modisakeng, Tiny. Henderson, Francine I. A
guide to periodical articles about Botswana,
1965-80 /. Gaborone, Botswana , 1982. v, 147,
6 p. ; DDC 016.96811 19
Z3559 .H46 1982 DT791
NYPL [Sc F 88-161]

Möhlig, Wilhelm J. G., 1934- La méthode
dialectométrique appliquée aux langues
africaines /. Berlin , 1986. 431 p. : ISBN
3-496-00856-3   *NYPL [Sc E 88-46]*

Moerdijk, Donald.
[Anti-development, South Africa and its
Bantustans. Spanish]
Antidesarrollo, Suráfrica y sus bantustanes /
Donald Moedijk. Barcelona : Serbal ; Paris :
Unesco, 1982. 222 p. : ill., maps ; 21 cm.
(Colección de temas africanos . 5) Translation of:
Anti-development: South Africa and its Bantustans.
1981. Bibliography: p. 217-222. ISBN
92-3-301888-1 (Unesco)
1. Apartheid - South Africa. 2. Homelands (South
Africa) - Politics and government. 3. Homelands, South
Africa - Economic conditions. 4. Homelands (South
Africa) - Social conditions. I. Title. II. Series.
NYPL [Sc D 88-595]

Moffatt, Nigel D. Mamma Decemba / Nigel D.
Moffatt. London : Boston and Faber, 1987. 34
p. ; 20 cm. ISBN 0-571-14775-5 :
1. West Indians - England - Drama. I. Title.
NYPL [Sc C 87-465]

Mogo's flute /. Van Stockum, Hilda, 1908- New
York , 1966. 88 p. :
PZ7.V36 Mo   NYPL [Sc E 88-176]

MOHAMED BAKHIT, SULTAN OF DAR
SILA, 1856-1916.
Bret, René-Joseph, d. 1940. Vie du sultan
Mohamed Bakhit, 1856-1916 . Paris , 1987.
[xvi], 258 p. : ISBN 2-222-03901-0
NYPL [Sc D 89-364]

Mohammad. see Muḥammad, the prophet.

MOHAMMEDANISM. see ISLAM.

MOI, DANIEL ARAP, 1924-
Dumila, Faraj O., 1937- The Nyayo decade /.
[Nairobi? , 1988?] 2 v. :   *NYPL [Sc F 89-122]*

Moi's reign of terror . London , 1989. 88 p. :
ISBN 1-87188-601-5   *NYPL [Sc D 89-524]*

A Tribute to president Daniel T. Arap Moi.
Nairobi , 1988. 52 p. :   *NYPL [Sc F 89-113]*

Moi, Tituba, sorcière-- . Condé, Maryse. Paris ,
c1986. 276 p. ; ISBN 2-7152-1440-5
NYPL [Sc E 88-97]

Moi, un Mfoforo . Bocquené, Henri. Paris ,
c1986. 387 p., [12] p. of plates : ISBN
2-86537-164-6   *NYPL [Sc E 89-66]*

Moi's reign of terror : a decade of nyayo crimes

against the people of Kenya / UMOJA. London : UMOJA, 1989. 88 p. : ill. ; 21 cm. "January 1989." "UMOJA, Umoja wa Kupigania Demokrasia Kenya, United Movement for Democracy in Kenya." ISBN 1-87188-601-5
1. Moi, Daniel Arap, 1924-. 2. Kenya - Politics and government - 1978-. I. UMOJA.
NYPL [Sc D 89-524]

Mokoso, Ndeley. Man pass man, and other stories / Ndeley Mokoso. Harlow, Essex : Longman, 1987. 108 p. ; 20 cm. (Longman African writers) ISBN 0-582-01681-9
1. Cameroon - Fiction. I. Title.
NYPL [Sc C 88-225]

Molarsky, Osmond. Where the good luck was. Illustrated by Ingrid Fetz. New York, H. Z. Walck [1970] 63 p. illus. 24 cm. When Arnold breaks his ankle and needs crutches, his friends try to earn money for a shiny aluminum pair. SCHOMBURG CHILDREN'S COLLECTION. ISBN 0-8098-1158-8 DDC [Fic]
1. Afro-American children - Juvenile fiction. I. Fetz, Ingrid, illus. II. Schomburg Children's Collection. III. Title.
PZ7.M7317 Wh   *NYPL [Sc E 88-552]*

Molins, Louis Sala- see Sala-Molins, Louis.

Moll, V. P. (Verna P.) Reminiscences . Road Town, Tortola, British Virgin Islands , c1981. xii, 94 p. : ill. ; 20 cm.
NX430.G72 B757 1981   *NYPL [Sc F 88-331]*

Moloi, Godfrey, 1934- My life / Godfrey Moloi. Johannesburg : Ravan Press, 1987. v. : ill. ; 18 cm. ISBN 0-86975-324-X (v. 1) DDC 968.2/21/0924 B 19
1. Moloi, Godfrey, 1934-. 2. Blacks - South Africa - Johannesburg - Biography. I. Title.
DT944.J653 M65 1987 *NYPL [Sc C 89-113]*

MOLOI, GODFREY, 1934-
Moloi, Godfrey, 1934- My life /. Johannesburg , 1987- v. : ISBN 0-86975-324-X (v. 1) DDC 968.2/21/0924 B 19
DT944.J653 M65 1987   *NYPL [Sc C 89-113]*

Molony, Rowland. Themba and the crocodile / Rowland Molony. Harare : Longman Zimbabwe, 1984. 74 p. : ill. ; 21 cm. ISBN 0-582-58741-7
1. Zimbabwe - Juvenile fiction. I. Title.
NYPL [Sc D 88-347]

MOMBASA (KENYA) - FICTION.
Mangua, Charles. Son of woman in Mombasa /. Nairobi , 1986. 211 p. ;
NYPL [Sc C 88-303]

Mombod, Josephine Ntinou. Developing models/techniques in the teaching of English as a second foreign language in senior secondary schools in the Congo / Josephine Ntinou Mombod. Nairobi : ACO [African Curriculum Organization] Project, 1983. ii, 67 leaves ; 30 cm. (African studies in curriculum development & evaluation . no. 133) Thesis (post graduate diploma)--University of Nairobi, 1983. Bibliography: leaf 60. DDC 428/.007/126724 19
1. English language - Study and teaching (Secondary) - Congo (Brazzaville). 2. English language - Study and teaching (Secondary) - French speakers. I. Title. II. Series.
PE1068.C74 M67 1983 *NYPL [Sc F 88-200]*

Mon mandat sous Jn-Claude Duvalier . Guerre, Rockefeller. Port-au-Prince, Haiti , 1987. 260 p. :
NYPL [Sc D 87-935]

MONACHISM. see MONASTICISM AND RELIGIOUS ORDERS.

Monama, Ramarumo. Is this justice? : a study of the Johannesburg commissioners' ('pass') courts / by Ramarumo Monama. Johannesburg : Centre for Applied Legal Studies, University of the Witwatersrand, [1983] xii, 65 p. : forms ; 21 cm. (Occasional papers / Centre for Applied Legal Studies, University of the Witwatersrand . 4) "June 1983"--P. [1] of cover.
1. Criminal justice, Administration of - South Africa - Johannesburg. 2. Criminal courts - South Africa - Johannesburg. 3. Due process of law - South Africa - Johannesburg. I. Series: Occasional papers (University of the Witwatersrand. Centre for Applied Legal Studies) , 4. II. Title.   *NYPL [Sc D 88-1240]*

MONASTIC ORDERS. see MONASTICISM AND RELIGIOUS ORDERS.

MONASTICISM AND RELIGIOUS ORDERS - AFRICA.

I.W.A.R.U. talks (1974-1984) /. [Gusau, Sokoto State, Nigeria , 1985] 97 p. ; DDC 255/.006/06 19
BX2740.A435 I18 1985
NYPL [Sc E 88-120]

MONASTICISM AND RELIGIOUS ORDERS OF MEN. see MONASTICISM AND RELIGIOUS ORDERS.

Monday, Hannatu. Nwosu, I. E. A guide to Christian writing in Africa /. Enugu, Nigeria , 1987. 116 p. ; ISBN 978-262-606-6
NYPL [Sc C 88-156]

Mondes en devenir. Série Bâtisseurs d'avenir. Aurillac, Michel. L'Afrique à coeur . Paris , 1987. 264 p., [8] p. of plates : ISBN 2-7013-0739-2   *NYPL [Sc E 88-203]*

MONDLANE, EDUARDO, 1920-1969 - COMIC BOOKS, STRIPS, ETC.
Motta, Helena. Moçambique por Eduardo Mondlane /. [Maputo?] [1984] 86 p. : DDC 967/.903/0222 19
DT463 .M64 1984   *NYPL [Sc F 89-172]*

Monekosso, G L. Introduction aux problèmes de santé des peuples d'Afrique tropicale : Introduction to the health problems of tropical African Peoples / G.L. Monekosso.[Ed. bilingue] Yaoundé : Université de Yaoundé, Centre universitaire des sciences de la santé, 1978. 241 p. : ill. ; 24 cm. French and English.
1. Tropical medicine - Africa. I. Title. II. Title: Introduction to the health problems of tropical African peoples.   *NYPL [Sc E 86-437]*

A Mongo homecoming. Elting, Mary, 1909- New York [1969] 54 p. DDC 309.1/675
DT644 .E4   *NYPL [Sc E 88-578]*

MONGO LANGUAGE - DICTIONARIES - FRENCH.
Hulstaert, G. Complément au Dictionnaire lomóngo-français . Bamanya- Mbandaka , 1987. 463 p. ;   *NYPL [Sc D 89-193]*

MONGO LANGUAGE - GRAMMAR.
Hulstaert, G. Supplement à la grammaire lomongo /. Mbandaka, Zaire , 1988. 127 p. ;
NYPL [Sc D 89-39]

Mongo, Pabe, 1948- L'Homme de la rue : roman / Pabé Mongo. Paris : Hatier, 1987. 168 p. ; 18 cm. ISBN 2-218-07767-1
1. Cameroun - Fiction. I. Title.
NYPL [Sc C 88-5]

MONGOOSES - JUVENILE FICTION.
Kirkpatrick, Oliver. Naja the snake and Mangus the mongoose. Garden City, N.Y. [1970] 40 p. DDC [Fic]
PZ7.K6358 Naj   *NYPL [Sc F 88-339]*

MONK, CHARLES VINTON.
Philip, Ira. Freedom fighters . London , 1987. 275 p., [8] p. of plates : ISBN 0-947638-42-3 (cased) : DDC 323.1/196/07299 19
NYPL [Sc D 88-1137]

Monkasa-Bitumba. Forces littéraires d'Afrique . Bruxelles , c1987. 238 p. ; ISBN 2-8041-0965-8
NYPL [Sc E 88-442]

Monod, Théodore, 1902- . Durou, Jean Marc. Sahara . Marseille, France , 1986. 155 p. : ISBN 2-902634-30-7   *NYPL [Sc G 88-1]*

Monograph (Michigan State University. Committee on Northeast African Studies) .
(no. 16) Balsvik, Randi Rønning. Haile Sellassie's students . East Lansing, Mich. , c1985. xix, 363 p. ; DDC 378/.198/0963 19
LA1518.7 .B35 1985   *NYPL [Sc D 88-1403]*

Monograph series in world affairs .
(v. 20, bk. 4) Lister, Frederick K., 1921- Decision-making strategies for international organizations . Denver, Colo. , 1984. ix, 142 p. : ISBN 0-87940-075-7 : DDC 332.1/52 19
HG3881.5.I58 L57 1984
NYPL [Sc D 88-1218]

Monograph series (University of California, Los Angeles. Museum of Cultural History) .
(no. 25) Crowley, Daniel J., 1921- African myth and black reality in Bahian Carnaval /. [Los Angeles, Calif.] [1984] 47 p. :
NYPL [Sc F 86-281]

Monographs from the African Studies Centre, Leiden.
Hinderink, J. (Jan) Agricultural commercialization and government policy in

Africa /. London , New York , 1987. xii, 328 p. : ISBN 0-7103-0205-3 *NYPL [Sc D 88-580]*

Monographs in international studies. Africa series .
(no. 52) Northrup, David. Beyond the bend in the river . Athens, Ohio , 1988. xvii, 264 p. : ISBN 0-89680-151-9 DDC 331.11/73/0967517 19
HD8811.Z8 K586 1988
NYPL [Sc D 88-960]
(no. 53) Makinde, M. Akin. African philosophy, culture, and traditional medicine /. Athens, Ohio , 1988. xvii, 154 p., [2] leaves of plates : ISBN 0-89680-152-7 DDC 199/.6 19
B5375 .M35 1988   *NYPL [Sc D 88-1273]*

Monographs in international studies. African series .
(no. 50) Voeltz, Richard Andrew. German colonialism and the South West Africa Company, 1884-1914 /. Athens, Ohio , 1988. x, 133 p. : ISBN 0-89680-146-2 (pbk.) : DDC 325/.343/09688 19
JV2029.A5 S689 1988 *NYPL [JLD 88-3416]*

Monroe, James, 1758-1831. United States. President (1817-1825 : Monroe) Message from the President of the United States, stating the interpretation which has been given to the act entitled An Act in Addition to the Acts Prohibiting the Slave Trade. Washington , 1819. 4 p. ;   *NYPL [Sc Rare F 89-25]*

Monroe, Sylvester. Brothers : black and poor--a true story of courage and survival / Sylvester Monroe and Peter Goldman with Vern E. Smith ... [et al.].1st ed. New York, N.Y. : Morrow, c1988. 284 p. : ill., ports. ; 24 cm. "A Newsweek book." ISBN 0-688-07622-X DDC 977.3/1100496073 B 19
1. Afro-Americans - Illinois - Chicago - Biography. I. Goldman, Peter Louis, 1933-. II. Smith, Vern E. III. Title.
F548.9.N4 M66 1988   *NYPL [Sc E 88-356]*

Monson, Jamie. Women as food producers in developing countries /. Los Angeles, CA , c1985. ix, 118 p. : ISBN 0-918456-56-8 : DDC 331.4/83/091724 19
HD6073.A292 D4485 1985
NYPL [JLE 88-2659]

The monstrous angel [microform] . Alladin, M. P. Maraval, Trinidad [1969] viii, 41 p. ;
PR9272.9.A4 M6   *NYPL [*XM-10236]*

Montgomery, Denis. The reflected face of Africa / Denis Montgomery. Bolton, England : African Insight, 1988. 288 p. : ill., maps ; 25 cm. Bibliography: p. 288. ISBN 1-85421-008-4
1. Africa - Description and travel - 1977-. I. Title.
NYPL [Sc E 88-535]

MONTGOMERY, WES, 1923-1968.
Ingram, Adrian. Wes Montgomery /. Gateshead, Tyne and Wear, England , 1985. 127 p. : ISBN 0-9506224-9-4
NYPL [Sc F 88-61]

MONTRÉAL (QUÉBEC) - CHURCH HISTORY.
Bertley, Leo W. Montreal's oldest black congregation . Pierrefonds, Quebec , c1976. 30 p. :
BX9882.8.M668 B47 1976
NYPL [Sc F 89-49]

Montréal, Québec. Université. Centre international de criminologie comparée. see Centre international de criminologie comparée.

Montreal's oldest black congregation . Bertley, Leo W. Pierrefonds, Quebec , c1976. 30 p. :
BX9882.8.M668 B47 1976
NYPL [Sc F 89-49]

Monumenta missionaria africana: Africa ocidental. Brasio, Antonio Duarte, 1906- Lisboa, 1952- v. *NYPL [ZKVX (Brásio, A.D. Monumenta missionaria africana)]*

Moock, Joyce Lewinger. Higher education and rural development in Africa [microform] : toward a balanced approach for donor assistance / Joyce Lewinger Moock and Peter R. Moock. New York : African-American Institute, c1977. ii, 42 p. ; 22 cm. Bibliography: p. 37-42. Microfilm. New York: New York Public Library, 1982. 1 microfilm reel; 35 mm. (MN *ZZ-22890)
1. Rural development - Africa. 2. Education, Higher - Africa. 3. Educational assistance, American - Africa. I.

Moock, Peter R., joint author. II. Title.
NYPL *[Sc Micro R-4202 no. 1]*

Moock, Peter R. (joint author) Moock, Joyce
Lewinger. Higher education and rural
development in Africa [microform] . New
York , c1977. ii, 42 p. ;
NYPL *[Sc Micro R-4202 no. 1]*

Moolenaar, Ruth. Facts or fantasy about Virgin
Islands history [microform] / researched by
Ruth Moolenaar ; assisted by Keith Fleming.
[Charlotte Amalie] : Project Introspection,
Dept. of Education, 1978. 22, [1] p. ; 28 cm.
"Produced by Project Introspection Department of
Education, funded by Virgin Islands Employment and
Training Administration, 1978." Bibliography: p. [23]
Microfiche. New York: New York Public Library, 198 .
1 microfiche: negative; 11 x 15 cm. (FSN Sc 019,049)
1. Virgin Islands of the United States - History,
Juvenile. I. Title.   **NYPL** *[Sc Micro F-10966]*

Moon, Bernice. Kenya is my country / Bernice
and Cliff Moon. Hove : Wayland, 1985. 60 p. :
col. ill., 1 col. map, col. ports. ; 26 cm. (My
country) Includes index. SCHOMBURG CHILDREN'S
COLLECTION. ISBN 0-85078-489-1 : DDC
967.6/204 19
1. Kenya - Juvenile literature. I. Moon, Cliff. II.
Schomburg Children's Collection. III. Title. IV. Series.
NYPL *[Sc F 88-379]*

Moon, Cliff. Moon, Bernice. Kenya is my country
/. Hove , 1985. 60 p. : ISBN 0-85078-489-1 :
DDC 967.6/204 19   **NYPL** *[Sc F 88-379]*

MOON, FLIGHT TO THE. see SPACE
FLIGHT TO THE MOON.

MOON - JUVENILE FICTION.
Osahon, Naiwu, 1937- Right-on Miss Moon /.
Apapa, Lagos, Nigeria , 1981. [22] p. : ISBN
978-18-6003-0   **NYPL** *[Sc D 89-228]*

Moonbeam and Dan Starr. Wassermann, Selma.
Westchester, Ill., c1966. 64 p.
NYPL *[Sc D 89-398]*

Moonbeam and the rocket ride. Wassermann,
Selma. Chicago [c1965] 64 p.
PE1119 .W363   **NYPL** *[Sc D 89-92]*

Moonbeam finds a moon stone. Wassermann,
Selma. Chicago [1967] 96 p. DDC [Fic]
PE1119 .W3636   **NYPL** *[Sc D 88-1423]*

Moonen, Joep. 'n Kijkje in de Paramaribo Zoo /
door Joep M. Moonen = A glimpse at the
Paramaribo Zoo / by Joep M. Moonen.
Paramaribo : C. Kersten, [1987] 275 p. : ill. ;
17 x 22 cm. Includes indexes.
1. Paramaribo Zoo - Pictorial works. I. Title. II. Title:
Glimpse at the Paramaribo Zoo.
QL76.5.S752 P375 1987
NYPL *[Sc D 88-690]*

Mooney, Elizabeth Comstock. The Sandy Shoes
mystery. Illustrated by Gustave Nebel. [1st ed.]
Philadelphia, Lippincott [1970] 128 p. illus. 21
cm. Eleven-year-old Emily has only a week left on St.
Croix to prove that her friend the waiter is not a jewel
thief. SCHOMBURG CHILDREN'S COLLECTION.
DDC [Fic]
1. Saint Croix (V.I.) - Juvenile fiction. I. Nebel,
Gustave E., illus. II. Schomburg Children's Collection.
III. Title.
PZ7.M78 San   **NYPL** *[Sc D 89-96]*

Moono, Muchimba Simuwana. The ring /
Muchimba Simuwana Moono. 1st ed. Lusaka :
NECZAM, 1985. 121 p. ; 19 cm. (Neczam library
series no. E5)
1. Zambia - Fiction. I. Title. **NYPL** *[Sc C 89-70]*

Moonsongs /. Osundare, Niyi. Ibadan , 1988. viii,
74 p. : ISBN 978-246-017-6
NYPL *[Sc D 88-1380]*

Moore, Adrienne, 1945- (ill) Mwenye Hadithi.
Tricky Tortoise /. Boston , c1988. [32] p. :
ISBN 0-316-33724-2 : DDC [E] 19
PZ7.M975 Tr 1988   **NYPL** *[Sc F 88-389]*

Moore, Emily. Whose side are you on? / Emily
Moore. 1st ed. New York : Farrar Straus
Giroux, 1988. 133 p. ; 22 cm. SCHOMBURG
CHILDREN'S COLLECTION. ISBN 0-374-38409-6
1. Afro-American youth - Harlem (New York, N.Y.) -
Juvenile fiction. I. Schomburg Children's Collection. II.
Title.   **NYPL** *[Sc D 88-1330]*

Moore, J. D. L. (John Davey Lewis) South
Africa and nuclear proliferation : South Africa's
nuclear capabilities and intentions in the
context of international non-proliferation

policies / J.D.L. Moore. New York : St.
Martin's Press, 1987. xvii, 227 p. : ill. ; 21 cm.
Includes index. Bibliography: p. 208-217. ISBN
0-312-74698-9 : DDC 355.8/25119/0968 19
1. Nuclear weapons - South Africa. 2. South Africa -
Military policy. I. Title.
U264 .M66 1987   **NYPL** *[Sc D 88-765]*

Moore, James E. Pelican guide to the Bahamas /
James E. Moore. 2d ed. Gretna, LA : Pelican
Publishing Co., c1988. 322 p. : maps ; 22 cm.
Includes index. ISBN 0-88289-663-6 :
1. Bahamas - Description and travel - 1981- -
Guide-books. I. Title.   **NYPL** *[Sc D 89-272]*

Moore, John Hebron. The emergence of the
cotton kingdom in the Old Southwest :
Mississippi, 1770-1860 / John Hebron Moore.
Baton Rouge : Louisiana State University Press,
c1988. xii, 323 p. : map ; 23 cm. Includes index.
Bibliography: p. 299-313. ISBN 0-8071-1404-9 (pbk.)
DDC 330.9762 19
1. Cotton trade - Mississippi - History. 2. Plantation
life - Mississippi - History. 3. Slavery - Mississippi -
History. 4. Mississippi - Economic conditions. I. Title.
HC107.M7 M66 1988   **NYPL** *[Sc E 88-279]*

Moore, Joseph Thomas. Pride against prejudice :
the biography of Larry Doby / Joseph Thomas
Moore. New York : Greenwood Press, c1988.
195 p., [8] p. of plates : ill. ; 24 cm.
(Contributions in Afro-American and African studies,
0069-9624 . no. 113) Includes index. Bibliography: p.
[183]-185. ISBN 0-313-25995-X (lib. bdg. : alk. paper)
DDC 796.357/092/4 B 19
1. Doby, Larry. 2. Baseball players - United States -
Biography. 3. Segregation in sports - United States. 4.
Afro-American baseball players - Case studies. I. Title.
II. Series.
GV865.D58 M66 1988   **NYPL** *[Sc E 88-272]*

Moore, Richard B. (Richard Benjamin) Richard
B. Moore, Caribbean militant in Harlem :
collected writings, 1920-1972 / edited by W.
Burghardt Turner and Joyce Moore Turner with
biography by Joyce Moore Turner ;
introduction by Franklin W. Knight.
Bloomington : Indiana University Press ;
London : Pluto Press , 1988. ix, 324 p. : ill. ,
ports. ; 25 cm. (Blacks in the diaspora) Includes
index. Bibliography: p. 313-316. ISBN 0-253-31299-0
DDC 970.004/96 19
1. Nationalism - Caribbean area. 2. Afro-Americans -
History. 3. Caribbean Area - Politics and government -
1945-. I. Turner, W. Burghardt, 1915-. II. Turner, Joyce
Moore, 1920-. III. Title.
F2183 .M66 1988   **NYPL** *[Sc E 89-148]*

Moorehead, Caroline.
Namibia : apartheid's forgotten children ; a
report for Oxfam / by Caroline Moorehead.
Oxford : Oxfam, [1988] 50 p. : ill. ; 30 cm.
Bibliography: p. 49. ISBN 0-85598-111-3 :
1. Apartheid - Namibia. 2. Children - Namibia. I.
Oxfam. II. Title.   **NYPL** *[Sc F 89-120]*

School age workers in Britain today / Caroline
Moorehead. [London] : Anti-Slavery Society for
the Protection of Human Rights, [1987] 60 p. :
ill. ; 21 cm. (Child labour series . no. 8) ISBN
0-900918-24-1
1. Children - Employment - Great Britain. I. Title. II.
Series.   **NYPL** *[Sc D 89-7]*

The Moorish empire, [microform] Meakin,
Budgett, 1866-1906. London, New York, 1899.
[xi]-xxiii, 576 p.
DT314 .M48   **NYPL** *[Sc Micro R-4844]*

Moorish Science Temple of America.
Is a Abd All ah Muḥammad al-Hahd i, 1945-
Who was Noble Drew Ali? /. [Brooklyn, N.Y.]
1988, c1980. 122 p. :   **NYPL** *[Sc D 89-74]*

'Isá 'Abd Allāh Muḥammad al-Mahdī, 1945-
Who was Noble Drew Ali? [microform] /.
Brooklyn, N.Y. [1980] 56 p. :
NYPL *[Sc Micro R-4114 no. 10]*

Morais, Evaristo de, 1871-1939. A escravidão
africana no Brasil : (das origens à extinção) /
Evaristo de Moraes.2.a ed / rev. de Evaristo de
los Santos ; pref. de Evaristo de Moraes Filho.
Brasília, Distrito Federal : Editora Universidade
de Brasília, c1986. 140 p. ; 23 cm. (Coleção
Temas Brasileiros . no. 62) First ed. published 1933.
"Notas" : p. 137-140. ISBN 85-223-00070-4
1. Slavery - Brazil. I. Santos, Alberto de los. II. Series.
III. Series: Coleção Temas brasileiros (Universidade de
Brasília. Editora) , 62. IV. Title.
NYPL *[Sc D 88-922]*

MORAL PHILOSOPHY. see ETHICS.

MORAL REARMAMENT.
Campbell, Paul. America needs an ideology /.
London , 1957. 184 p. ; DDC 179 170
BJlo.Mb C29   **NYPL** *[Sc C 87-467]*

Elliott, Hugh P. Darkness and dawn in
Zimbabwe /. London , 1978. [6], 49 p. ; ISBN
0-901269-37-9 :
DT962.42 .E38   **NYPL** *[JFD 80-115]*

Moralische Aufrüstung. see Moral rearmament.

MORALITY. see ETHICS.

Morality of development aid to the Third
World . Chiaka, Ralph C. Rome , 1985. ix, 215
p. :   **NYPL** *[Sc E 88-96]*

MORALS. see ETHICS.

Morán, Fernando, 1926- Nación y alienación en
la literatura negroafricana [por] Fernando
Morán. [Madrid, Taurus, 1964] 90 p. 18 cm.
(Cuadernos Taurus, 61) Bibliographical footnotes.
1. African literature - History and criticism. I. Title.
PL8010 .M65   **NYPL** *[Sc C 88-347]*

MORAVIAN CHURCH - MISSIONS -
VIRGIN ISLANDS OF THE UNITED
STATES.
Oldendorp, C. G. A. (Christian Georg
Andreas), 1721-1787. [Geschichte der Mission
der Evangelischen Brüder auf den caraibischen
Inseln S. Thomas, S. Croix und S. Jan.] C.G.A.
Oldendorps Geschichte der Mission der
Evangelischen Brüder auf den caraibischen
Inseln S. Thomas, S. Croix und S. Jan /.
Barby , 1777. 2 v. in 1 (1068 p.) : DDC
266/.46729722 19
BV2848.V5 O42 1777
NYPL *[Sc Rare C 89-33]*

Mordecai, Pamela. From our yard . Kingston,
Jamaica , 1987. xxviii, 235 p. ;
NYPL *[Sc D 89-412]*

Mordvinoff, Nicolas, 1911- (joint author) Lipkind,
William, 1904- Four-leaf clover /. New York ,
1959. [32] p. ;   **NYPL** *[Sc F 89-22]*

More adventures of Spider . Arkhurst, Joyce
Cooper. New York , c1972. 48 p. :
NYPL *[Sc D 88-1449]*

MORÉ, BENY, 1919-1963.
Naser, Amín E. (Amín Egeraige), 1936- Benny
Moré . Ciudad de La Habana , c1985. 231 p.,
[61] p. of plates : DDC 784.5/0092/4 B 19
ML420.M596 N3 1985   **NYPL** *[Sc C 87-302]*

More tales of Uncle Remus . Lester, Julius. New
York , c1988. xvi, 143 p. : ISBN 0-8037-0419-4
DDC 398.2/08996073 19
PZ8.1.L434 Mo 1988   **NYPL** *[Sc E 88-458]*

Moreau, Jean-Pierre. Un Flibustier français dans
la mer des Antilles en 1618-1620 /. Clamart
[France] , c1987. 263 p. : ISBN 2-9502053-0-5
NYPL *[Sc E 88-247]*

Morel, Yves. Homme, sociétés et développement
/ Yves Morel. Douala : Collège Libermann,
1980- v. : ill. ; 30 cm. CONTENTS. - t. 1. Les
sociétés avancées -- t. 2. Les pays en developpement.
DDC 338.9 19
1. Africa - Economic conditions - 1960-. I. Title.
HD83 .M59   **NYPL** *[Sc F 87-415]*

Moreland, Laurence W. Blacks in southern
politics /. New York , 1987. vii, 305 p. : ISBN
0-275-92655-9 (alk. paper) : DDC
323.1/196073/075 19
E185.92 .B58 1987   **NYPL** *[Sc E 88-196]*

Morgan, Cecil James. Branchcomb, Sylvia
Woingust. Son, never give up /. [Yonkers,
N.Y.?] , 1979. 36 p. : **NYPL** *[Sc D 88-568]*

MORGAN, CECIL JAMES.
Branchcomb, Sylvia Woingust. Son, never give
up /. [Yonkers, N.Y.?] , 1979. 36 p. :
NYPL *[Sc D 88-568]*

MORGAN, GARRETT A., 1877-1963 -
JUVENILE LITERATURE.
Sweet, Dovie Davis. Red light, green light .
Smithtown, N.Y. , 1978 (1980 printing) 39 p. :
ISBN 0-682-49088-1 **NYPL** *[Sc D 89-70]*

Morgan, Kemi. Legends from Yorubaland /
Kemi Morgan. Ibadan, Nigeria : Spectrum
Books, 1988. iii, 100 p. : ill. ; 19 cm.
SCHOMBURG CHILDREN'S COLLECTION. ISBN
978-246-003-6

1. Yorubas - Legends. I. Schomburg Children's Collection. II. Title.   **NYPL** *[Sc C 88-344]*

Morgan State College, Baltimore, Md. see **Maryland. Morgan State College, Baltimore.**

Morin, Melle. Les retards scolaires et les échecs au niveau de l'ecole primaire du Sénégal / par Melle Morin. [Dakar] : Centre de linguistique appliquee de Dakar, [1966?] 143 leaves ; 27 cm. (Enseignement du Français au Sénégal . 27) Cover title. *1. Academic achievement - Senegal. 2. Education, Elementary - Senegal. 3. French language - Study and teaching - Senegal. I. Centre de linguistique appliqué de Dakar. II. Title. III. Series.*   **NYPL** *[Sc F 87-439]*

Morisyen - English - français . Baker, Philip. Paris , 1987. 365 p. ;   ISBN 2-85802-973-3   **NYPL** *[Sc E 88-407]*

Morizot, Frédéric. Grenade, épices et poudre : une épopée caraïbe / Frédéric Morizot ; préface de Jean Ziegler. Paris : L'Harmattan, c1988. 385 p., [8] leaves of plates : ill., maps ; 24 cm. (Collection monde antillais, recherche et documents) "Bibliographie sommaire": p. 339-341.   ISBN 2-7384-0082-5 *1. Grenada - History - Coup d'état, 1979. 2. Grenada - Politics and government. I. Ziégler, Jean. II. Title.*   **NYPL** *[Sc E 89-49]*

MOROCCO - HISTORY.
Meakin, Budgett, 1866-1906. The Moorish empire, [microform] London, New York, 1899. [xi]-xxiii, 576 p.
DT314 .M48   **NYPL** *[Sc Micro R-4844]*

MOROCCO - HISTORY - 19TH CENTURY.
Castillo, Rafael del. Al África, españoles! . Barcelona-Gracia [1895?]- v.
   NYPL *[Sc D 88-1097]*

MORONS. see **MENTALLY HANDICAPPED.**

The morphology of residential associations as found among the Khwakhwa of Basutoland. Sheddick, Vernon George John. [Cape Town], University of Cape Town, 1948. 57 p.
DT786 .S5   **NYPL** *[Sc G 89-1]*

Morris, kenneth M. Powe, Edward L. (Edward Llewellyn), 1941- The adventures of Dan Aiki /. Paterson, N.J. , c1987. 32 p. :
   NYPL *[Sc D 88-489]*

Morris, Margaret. Tour Jamaica / by Margaret Morris. 1st ed. Kingston, Jamaica : Gleaner Co., 1985. 125 p. : ill., maps (some col.) ; 28 cm. Road map of Jamaica folded and tipped-in at end of text. Includes index. ISBN 976-612-001-3 *1. Jamaica - Description and travel - 1981- - Guide-books. I. Title.*   **NYPL** *[Sc F 88-283]*

Morris, Peter. Africa, America, and central Asia . [Exeter, Devon] [Atlantic Highlands, N.J.] 1984. 107 p. ;   ISBN 0-85989-295-6 (pbk.) :   DDC 330.9/034 19
HC53 .A35 1984   **NYPL** *[Sc D 88-1315]*

MORRIS, SAMUEL, 1873-1893.
Baldwin, Lindley. J. The march of faith . Bronx, N.Y. , 1944. 94 p. :   **NYPL** *[Sc C 88-13]*

Morrison, Keith. Art in Washington and its Afro-American presence 1940-1970 / Keith Morrison. Washington, D.C. : Washington Project for the Arts, 1985. 109 p. : ill.(some col.), ports. ; 28 cm. Catalog of an exhibition held April 2-May 11, 1985 sponsored by the Washington Project for the Arts. "Additions to the Exhibition" tipped in. "Checklist" (in pocket) supersedes pages 107-109 of catalog. Bibliography: p. 85-87. Library's copy lacks "Additions" and "Checklists". *1. Afro-American art - Washington (D.C.) - Exhibitions. 2. Art, African - Washington, D.C. - Exhibitions. 3. Art, Modern - 20th century - Washington (D.C.) - Exhibitions. 4. Art, Modern - 20th century - African influences - Exhibitions. I. Washington Project for the Arts. II. Title.*   **NYPL** *[Sc F 88-34]*

Morrison, Lionel. From where I stand /. London , 1987. 94 p. :   ISBN 0-9956664-9-1
   NYPL *[Sc C 88-30]*

Morrison, Toni. Beloved : a novel / by Toni Morrison.1st ed. New York : Knopf : Distributed by Random House, 1987. 275 p. ; 24 cm. ISBN 0-394-53597-9 ;   DDC 813/.54 19 *1. Afro-Americans - Ohio - Cincinnati - Fiction. I. Title.*
PS3563.O8749 B4 1987   **NYPL** *[Sc E 88-188]*

Beloved / Toni Morrison. Large print ed.

Thorndike, Me. : Thorndike Press, 1988. 472 p.; 22 cm. ISBN 0-89621-123-1 (alk. paper) DDC 813/.54 19 *1. Afro-Americans - Ohio - Cincinnati - Fiction. I. Title.*
PS3563.O8749 B4 1988   **NYPL** *[Sc D 88-1503]*

Sula / Toni Morrison. New York : New American Library, [1987], c1973. 174 p. ; 21 cm. "A Plume book." Originally published: New York : Knopf, 1973. "First Plume Printing, April, 1982"--T.p. verso. ISBN 0-452-26010-8 DDC 813/.54 19 *1. Afro-American Women - Fiction. 2. Afro-Americans - Ohio - Fiction. I. Title.*
PS3563.O8749 S8 1987   **NYPL** *[Sc D 88-633]*

Tar baby / Toni Morrison. New York : New American Library, 1981. 305 p. ; 21 cm. "A Plume book." ISBN 0-452-26012-4 *1. Blacks - Caribbean Area - Fiction. 2. Afro-Americans - Fiction. I. Title.*
   NYPL *[Sc D 88-1105]*

MORRISTOWN COLLEGE - HISTORY.
A School for freedom . [Knoxville] , 1986. xiii, 60 p. :   **NYPL** *[Sc D 88-417]*

Morse, Carl. Gay & lesbian poetry in our time . New York , c1988. xxviii, 401 p. :   ISBN 0-312-02213-1 :   DDC 811/.54/080353 19
PS595.H65 G39 1988   **NYPL** *[JFE 89-277]*

Morse, Evangeline. Brown Rabbit: her story. Illustrated by David Stone Martin. Chicago, Follett Pub. Co. [1967] 191 p. illus. 23 cm. SCHOMBURG CHILDREN'S COLLECTION. *1. Afro-American children - Juvenile fiction. I. Schomburg Children's Collection. II. Title.*
PZ7.M84586 Br   **NYPL** *[Sc E 89-89]*

Mort dans la vie africaine. Spanish. La Muerte en la vida africana. 1a ed. Barcelona : Serbal ; París : Unesco, 1984. 314 p. : map ; 20 cm. (Colección de temas africanos . 21) Translation of: La mort dans la vie africaine. "Bibliografía en castellano": p. [313]-314. CONTENTS. - La idea de la muerte en la vida africana / U.K. Bamunoba -- Contribución a una problemática antropológica y religiosa de la muerte en el pensamiento adja-fon / B. Adoukonou. ISBN 84-85800-81-8 *1. Death - Religious aspects. 2. Aja (African people) - Religion. 3. Africa - Religion. I. Bamunoba, Y. K. II. Adoukonou, B. III. Title. IV. Series.*
   NYPL *[Sc D 88-601]*

La mort de Diallo Telli . Diallo, Amadou. Paris , 1983. 154 p., [8] p. of plates :   ISBN 2-86537-072-0   **NYPL** *[Sc D 88-316]*

MORTALITY - TRINIDAD - HISTORY - 18TH CENTURY.
John, A. Meredith. The plantation slaves of Trinidad, 1783-1816 . Cambridge [Eng.] , New York , 1988. xvi, 259 p. :   ISBN 0-521-36166-4   DDC 306/.362/0972983 19
HT1105.T6 J65 1988   **NYPL** *[Sc E 89-235]*

MORTALITY - UNITED STATES - STATISTICS.
United States. Dept. of Health and Human Services. Task Force on Black and Minority Health. Report of the Secretary's Task Force on Black & Minority Health. Washington, D.C. , 1985-1986. 8 v. in 9 :   DDC 362.1/08996073 19
RA448.5.N4 U55 1985   **NYPL** *[JLM 86-589]*

MORTENOL, SOSTHÈME HÉLIODORE CAMILLE, 1859-1930.
Lara, Oruno D. Le commandant Mortenol . Epinay, France , c1985. 275 p. :   ISBN 2-905787-00-7   **NYPL** *[Sc D 88-1085]*

Mortimore, M. J., 1937- Adapting to drought : farmers, famines, and desertification in west Africa / Michael Mortimore. Cambridge ; New York : Cambridge University Press, 1989. xxii, 299 p. : ill., maps ; 24 cm. Includes index. Bibliography: p. [253]-288. ISBN 0-521-32312-6 DDC 333.73 19 *1. Famines - Nigeria, Northern. 2. Agriculture - Economic aspects - Nigeria, Northern. 3. Droughts - Nigeria, Northern. 4. Desertification - Nigeria, Northern. 5. Arid regions farming - Nigeria, Northern. 6. Nigeria, Northern - Rural conditions. I. Title.*
HC1055.Z7 N6755 1988   **NYPL** *[Sc E 89-191]*

MORTON, MARCUS, 1784-1864.
A Refutation of the charge of abolitionism. Boston, 1845. 32 p.
F69 .M455   **NYPL** *[Sc Rare C 89-21]*

Mortouza, Hamed. Kichenapanaïdou, Marc. Ma terre /. Saint-Louis, Réunion [1978?] 43 p. ;
   NYPL *[Sc D 88-484]*

Morts pour la France /. Doumbi-Fakoly. Paris , 1983. 150 p. ;   ISBN 2-86537-074-7
   NYPL *[Sc C 88-346]*

MORTUARY STATISTICS. see **MORTALITY.**

Moser, Barry. Hamilton, Virginia. In the beginning . San Diego , c1988. xi, 161 p. :   ISBN 0-15-238740-4   DDC 291.2/4 19
BL226 .H35 1988   **NYPL** *[JFF 89-62]*

Moses, James Charles. Desegregation in Catholic schools in the archdiocese of Chicago, 1964-1974, including a case study of a Catholic high school [microform] / by James C. Moses. 1977 288 leaves. Thesis (Ph. D.)--Loyola University of Chicago, 1977. Bibliography: leaves 200-206 Microfilm of typescript. Ann Arbor, Mich.: University Microfilms International, 1978. 1 microfilm reel; 35 mm. *1. Catholic high schools - Illinois - Chicago - Administration. 2. School integration - Illinois - Chicago - History. I. Title.*
   NYPL *[Sc Micro R-4699]*

Moses, Lincoln E. AIDS . Washington, DC , 1989. xiii, 589 p. :   ISBN 0-309-03976-2; 0-309-03976-2 (pbk.)   **NYPL** *[Sc D 89-342]*

MOSKITO INDIANS. see **MOSQUITO INDIANS.**

MOSQUITO INDIANS - LEGENDS.
Rohmer, Harriet. The invisible hunters . San Francisco , c1987. 32 p. :   ISBN 0-89239-031-X :   DDC 398.2/08998 19
F1529.M9 R64 1987   **NYPL** *[Sc E 88-241]*

Moss, Geoffrey. (illus) Teague, Bob. Agent K-13. Garden City, N.Y., c1974. 47 p.,   ISBN 0-385-08704-7   DDC [E]
PZ7.T21937 Ag   **NYPL** *[Sc E 88-587]*

Moss, S. G.
Books on race and race relations held in the Richard B. Moore Library, Barbados / compiled by S.G. Moss. Barbados : Richard B. Moore Library, 1987. 133 leaves ; 28 cm. (Richard B. Moore Library printed catalogue . v. 2) *1. Race - Bibliography. 2. Race relations - Bibliography. I. Title. II. Series.*   **NYPL** *[Sc F 89-105]*

Slavery and emancipation : a bibliography of pamphlets published in the 19th century and early 20th century contained in the Richard B. Moore Library / compiled by S. G. Moss. St. Michael, Barbados : S.G. Moss, 1986. 61 l. ; 28 cm. (Richard B. Moore Library printed catalog . v. 1 : supplement) *1. Slavery - United States - Bibliography. 2. Afro-Americans - History - Bibliography. I. Title. II. Series.*   **NYPL** *[Sc F 88-83]*

Mossell, N. F., Mrs., 1855- The work of the Afro-American woman / Mrs. N.F. Mossell ; with an introduction by Joanne Braxton. New York : Oxford University Press, 1988. xlii, 178 p. : ill. ; 17 cm. (The Schomburg library of nineteenth-century Black women writers) Bibliography: p. xlii. Reprint. Originally published: Philadelphia : Geo. S. Ferguson Company, c1908. ISBN 0-19-505265-X (alk. paper) DDC 305.8/96073 19 *1. Afro-American women - Poetry. I. Title. II. Series.*
E185.86 .M65 1988   **NYPL** *[JFC 88-2155]*

MOSSI (AFRICAN PEOPLE)
Brüggemann, Anne. Amagdala und Akawuruk . Hohenschäftlarn bei München , 1986. 264 p. :   ISBN 3-87673-106-2   **NYPL** *[Sc D 88-652]*

MOSSI (AFRICAN PEOPLE) - HISTORY.
Princes & serviteurs du royaume . Paris , 1987. 225 p. :   ISBN 2-901161-29-4
   NYPL *[Sc E 88-409]*

The most important thing in the world /. Farley, Carol J. New York , 1974. vi, 133 p.,   ISBN 0-531-02663-9   **NYPL** *[Sc D 88-431]*

Mostyn, Trevor. The Cambridge encyclopedia of the Middle East and North Africa /. Cambridge [England] , New York , 1988. 504 p. :   ISBN 0-521-32190-5   DDC 956 19
DS44 .C37 1988   **NYPL** *[*R-BCF 89-551]*

Mota, Maria Elisabete Lima. Declaro que estou em tormento : poesias da sarjeta / Maria Elisabete Lima Mota. Rio de Janeiro : Espaço e Tempo, c1987. 181 p. ; 21 cm. (Coleção Ficções deste espaço e tempo . 1) ISBN 85-85114-15-0 :

I. Title.
MLCS 88/08239 (P)   *NYPL [Sc D 88-919]*

Mother and child in African Sculpture : the African-American Institute, October 21-February 28, 1987. New York : The African-American Institute, 1987. [16] p. : ill. ; 27 cm. Cover title. Includes an essay by Herbert M. Cole under the title: The mother and child in African sculpture. Bibliography: p. [14]
1. Sculpture, Black - Africa, Sub-Saharan - Exhibitions. 2. Wood-carving - Africa, Sub-Saharan - Exhibitions. 3. Mothers in art - Exhibitions. I. Cole, Herbert M. The mother and child in African sculpture. II. African-American Institute.   *NYPL [Sc F 88-3]*

MOTHERS AND DAUGHTERS - JUVENILE FICTION.
Johnson, Angela. Tell me a story, Mama /. New York , c1989. [32] p. :   ISBN 0-531-05794-1 :   DDC [E] 19
PZ7.J629 Te 1988   *NYPL [Sc F 89-109]*

Pomerantz, Charlotte. The chalk doll /. New York , c1989. 30 p. :   ISBN 0-397-32318-2 :   DDC [E] 19
PZ7.P77 Ch 1989   *NYPL [Sc F 89-175]*

MOTHERS IN ART.
Holas, B. (Bohumil), 1909-1979. Image de la mère dans l'art ivoirien /. Abidjan [1975] 122 p. :   DDC 732/.2/096668
NB1099.I8 H59   *NYPL [Sc D 88-476]*

MOTHERS IN ART - EXHIBITIONS.
Mother and child in African Sculpture . New York , 1987. [16] p. :   *NYPL [Sc F 88-3]*

Mothers of the novel.
Prince, Mary. The history of Mary Prince, a West Indian slave, related by herself /. London , New York , 1987. xvi, 124 p. ;   ISBN 0-86358-192-7 DDC 305.5/67/0924 B 19
HT869.P6 A3 1987   *NYPL [Sc C 89-31]*

The motion of light in water . Delany, Samuel R. New York , c1988. xviii, 302 p. :   ISBN 0-87795-947-1 :   DDC 813/.54 19
PS3554.E437 Z475 1988
     NYPL [JFD 88-7818]

MOTION PICTURES - SOUTH AFRICA - HISTORY.
Tomaselli, Keyan G., 1948- The cinema of apartheid . New York , c1988. 300 p. ;   ISBN 0-918266-19-X (pbk.) :   DDC 384/.8/0968 19
PN1993.5.S6 T58 1988
     NYPL [Sc D 88-1242]

Motivos de son /. Guillén, Nicolás, 1902- La Habana , 1980. 32, [88] p. :
     NYPL [Sc E 87-151]

Motley, John Lothrop, 1814-1877. The causes of the American civil war. A letter to the London Times. By John Lothrop Motley. New York, James G. Gregory (successor to W.A. Townsend & Co.) No. 46 Walker Street, 1861. 36 p. 20 cm.
I. Title.
E459 .M92   *NYPL [Sc Rare C 89-14]*

Motlhabi, Mokgethi B. G. (Mokgethi Buti George), 1944- Challenge to apartheid : toward a morally defensible strategy / Mokgethi Motlhabi. Grand Rapids, Mich. : William B. Eerdmans Pub. Co., c1988. xii, 243 p. ; 21 cm. Includes index. Bibliography: p. 217-238.   ISBN 0-8028-0347-4 :   DDC 305.8/00968 19
1. Apartheid - South Africa. 2. Government, Resistance to - South Africa. 3. Apartheid - Moral and ethical aspects. I. Title.
DT763 .M69 1988   *NYPL [JFD 88-11473]*

MOTOWN RECORD CORPORATION.
George, Nelson. Where did our love go? . New York , c1985. xviii, 250 p., [32] p. of plates :   ISBN 0-312-86698-4 :   DDC 784.5/5/00973 19
ML3537 .G46 1985   *NYPL [*LE 86-1451]*

Motsi, Daniel, 1964- The beast of fame / Daniel Motsi ; ill. and cover by Mqabuko Mabena. Harare, Zimbabwe : Zimbabwe Pub. House, 1987. 59 p. : ill. ; 19 cm. ISBN 0-949225-61-4 :
1. Country life - Zimbabwe - Fiction. 2. Zimbabwe - Fiction. I. Title.   *NYPL [Sc C 89-100]*

Mott, A. (Abigail Field), 1766-1851.
Narratives of colored Americans. New York , 1877. 276 p. ;   *NYPL [Sc Rare C 88-4]*

Narratives of colored Americans. New York , 1882. 276 p. ;   *NYPL [Sc Rare C 88-26]*

Motta, Helena. Moçambique por Eduardo Mondlane / [texto, capa e ilustrações, Helena Motta]. [Maputo?] : Instituto Nacional do Livro e do Disco, [1984] 86 p. : chiefly ill. ; 30 cm. (Banda desenhada . 3)   DDC 967/.903/0222 19
1. Mondlane, Eduardo, 1920-1969 - Comic books, strips, etc. 2. FRELIMO - History - Comic books, strips, etc. 3. Mozambique - History - Revolution, 1964-1975 - Comic books, strips, etc. I. Title. II. Series.
DT463 .M64 1984   *NYPL [Sc F 89-172]*

Motta Lody, Raul Giovanni da. see Lody, Raul Giovanni da Motta.

Moundjegou-Mangangue, Pierre Edgar. Ainsi parlaient les anciens / Pierre Edgar Moundjegou Mangangue. Paris : Silex, 1987. 87 p. ; 22 cm. Poems. ISBN 2-903871-78-7
I. Title.   *NYPL [Sc D 88-393]*

MOUNT HERMON FEMALE SEMINARY.
Griffith, Helen. Dauntless in Mississippi . Northampton, Mass. , 1965. xii, 173 p. :
     NYPL [Sc D 88-1111]

Mount Sinai School of Medicine. The People of East Harlem [microform] . New York , c1974. 90 p. :   *NYPL [Sc Micro R-4137 no.12]*

Moura, Carlos Eugênio Marcondes de.
Candomblé . São Paulo , 1987. 168 p. ;
     NYPL [Sc D 88-177]

Moura, Clovis. Quilombos : resistência ao escravismo / Clóvis Moura. São Paulo : Editora Atica, 1987. 94 p. ; 18 cm. (Série Princípios . 106.) Bibliography: p. 92-94. ISBN 85-08-01858-4
1. Fugitive slaves - Brazil. 2. Slavery - Brazil - Insurrections, etc. I. Title. II. Series.
     NYPL [Sc C 88-3]

Mouralis, Bernard. V.Y. Mudimbe : ou, Le discours, l'écart et l'écriture / Bernard Mouralis. Paris : Présence africaine, c1988. 143 p., [2] leaves of plates : facsims., port. ; 21 cm. Bibliography: p. [133]-141. ISBN 2-7087-0506-7
1. Mudimbe, V. Y., 1941?- - Criticism and interpretation. I. Title.   *NYPL [Sc D 89-251]*

Mousa-Booth, Mohammed. Kano State . [Kano] [1987]. 192 p. :   *NYPL [Sc F 89-37]*

Moutoussamy, Ernest, 1941- La Guadeloupe et son indianité / Ernest Moutoussamy. Paris : Editions Caribéennees, c1987. 119 p., [12] p. of plates : ill. (some col.) ; 23 cm. (Collection Parti-pris) Bibliography: p. 113. ISBN 2-87679-008-4
1. East Indians - Guadeloupe - Social life and customs. 2. East Indians - Guadeloupe - Religious life and customs. 3. Guadeloupe - Social life and customs. 4. Guadeloupe - Religious life and customs. I. Title.
     NYPL [Sc D 88-968]

MOUVEMENT MILITANT MAURICIEN.
L'Histoire d'une trahison . Port Louis, Mauritius , 1987. vi, 192 p.
     NYPL [Sc F 88-275]

Mouvement national démocratique (Guinea) Où allons nous?. [Conakry] [1986?] 92 p. ;
HC1030 .O89 1986   *NYPL [Sc B 88-58]*

Mouvement révolutionnaire national pour le développement. Ibyemezo, amabwiliza, ibyifuzo mu myaka cumi ya Muvoma . Kigali , 1985. 424 p. :   *NYPL [Sc D 88-807]*

MOUVEMENT RÉVOLUTIONNAIRE NATIONAL POUR LE DÉVELOPPEMENT.
Ibyemezo, amabwiliza, ibyifuzo mu myaka cumi ya Muvoma . Kigali , 1985. 424 p. :
     NYPL [Sc D 88-807]

MOUVEMENT RÉVOLUTIONNAIRE NATIONAL POUR LE DÉVELOPPEMENT (RWANDA) - ANNIVERSARIES, ETC.
Habyarimana, Juvénal. Discours du général-major Habyarimana Juvénal, président de la République rwandaise et président-fondateur du Mouvement révolutionnaire national pour le développement à l'occasion du 1er juillet, 1987 =. [Kigali?] , 1987. 82 p. :
f-rw---   *NYPL [Sc D 88-1517]*

A move further south /. Garnett, Ruth (Ruth Miriam) Chicago, Ill. , 1987. 63 p. ;   ISBN 0-88308-113-1 (pbk.)   *NYPL [Sc D 88-691]*

MOVE (ORGANIZATION)
Anderson, John, 1954 Mar. 27- Burning down the house . New York , c1987. xv, 409 p. ;

ISBN 0-393-02460-1 :   DDC 974.8/1104 19
F158.9.N4 A53 1987   *NYPL [Sc E 88-332]*

MOVEMENT, ECUMENICAL. see ECUMENICAL MOVEMENT.

MOVIES. see MOVING-PICTURES.

MOVIMENTO POPULAR DE LIBERTA ÇÃO DE ANGOLA.
Khazanov, A. M. (Anatoliĭ Mikhaĭlovich), 1932- [Agostinó Neto. English.] Agostinho Neto /. Moscow , 1986. 301 p. ;   DDC 967/.304/0924 B 19
DT611.76.A38 K4213 1986
     NYPL [Sc B 88-47]

Movimento Popular de Libertação de Angola.
Road to liberation . Richmond, B. C. , pref. 1976. viii, 53 p. :   *NYPL [JFD 80-10236]*

MOVIMIENTO POPULAR DEMOCRÁTICO.
Hurtado González, Jaime. Luchando por la patria nueva . Quito , 1987. ii, 178 p. :
     NYPL [Sc D 88-679]

MOVING-PICTURES - AFRICA, SOUTHERN - BIBLIOGRAPHY.
Southern Africa film guide [microform] New York [1982] 12 p. :
     NYPL [Sc Micro F-11052]

MOVING-PICTURES - AFRICA, SUB-SAHARAN - BIBLIOGRAPHY.
Schmidt, Nancy J. Sub-Saharan African films and filmmakers . London , 1988. 401 p. ;   ISBN 0-905450-32-9 :   DDC 016.79143/096 19
     NYPL [Sc D 89-196]

MOVING-PICTURES - BRAZIL - COLLECTED WORKS.
Brazilian cinema /. Austin , 1988. 373 p. :   ISBN 0-292-70767-3   *NYPL [Sc E 89-59]*

MOVING-PICTURES - COSTUME. see COSTUME.

MOVING-PICTURES - GREAT BRITAIN - PRODUCTION AND DIRECTION.
Fusco, Coco. Young, British, and Black . Buffalo, N.Y. , c1988. 65 p. :
     NYPL [Sc D 88-1186]

MOVING-PICTURES IN ETHNOLOGY.
Wanono, Nadine. Ciné-rituel de femmes dogon /. Paris , 1987. 138 p. : ISBN 2-222-03961-4 (pbk)   *NYPL [Sc E 88-177]*

Moya, Lily Patience.
Not either an experimental doll : the separate worlds of three South African women / edited by Shula Marks. Bloomington : Indiana University Press, c1987. xv, 217 p., [18] p. of plates : ill. ; 22 cm. Correspondence of Lily Moya, Mabel Palmer, and Sibusisiwe Makhanya. Includes bibliographical references and index. ISBN 0-253-34843-9 DDC 968.05/6 19
1. Moya, Lily Patience - Correspondence. 2. Palmer, Mabel, b. 1876- - Correspondence. 3. Makhanya, Sibusisiwe, 1894- - Correspondence. 4. Women - South Africa - Correspondence. 5. Women, Black - Education - South Africa. I. Palmer, Mabel, b. 1876. II. Makhanya, Sibusisiwe, 1894-. III. Marks, Shula. IV. Title.
HQ1800 .M69 1988   *NYPL [Sc D 89-282]*

MOYA, LILY PATIENCE - CORRESPONDENCE.
Moya, Lily Patience. Not either an experimental doll . Bloomington , c1987. xv, 217 p., [18] p. of plates : ISBN 0-253-34843-9 DDC 968.05/6 19
HQ1800 .M69 1988   *NYPL [Sc D 89-282]*

Moyo, Ambrose, 1943- Theology and the Black experience . Minneapolis , c1988. 272 p. ;   ISBN 0-8066-2353-5 DDC 284.1/08996 19
BX8065.2 .T48 1988   *NYPL [Sc D 89-353]*

MOZAMBIQUE - BIOGRAPHY.
Honwana, Raúl Bernardo Manuel, 1905- [Histórias ouvidas e vividas dos homens e da terra. English] The life history of Raúl Honwana . Boulder , 1988. ix, 181 p. : ISBN 1-555-87114-3 (lib. bdg.) : DDC 967/.903/0924 B 19
DT463 .H6613 1988   *NYPL [Sc E 88-367]*

Mozambique, dix ans de solitude-- /. Verschuur, Christine. Paris , c1986. 182 p. : ISBN 2-85802-700-5   *NYPL [Sc D 89-285]*

MOZAMBIQUE - ECONOMIC CONDITIONS.
Verschuur, Christine. Mozambique, dix ans de

solitude-- /. Paris , c1986. 182 p. : ISBN 2-85802-700-5 *NYPL [Sc D 89-285]*

MOZAMBIQUE - FICTION.
Honwana, Luís Bernardo, 1942- [Nós matámos o Cão-Tinhoso. English.] We killed Mangy-Dog. Harare, Zimbabwe , 1987. 117 p. ; ISBN 0-9792256-2-2 : *NYPL [Sc C 89-106]*

Muianga, Aldino, 1950- Xitala Mati /. [Maputo?] [1987?] 87 p. :
NYPL [Sc D 88-531]

MOZAMBIQUE - FOREIGN RELATIONS - SOUTH AFRICA.
Davies, Robert. South African strategy towards Mozambique in the post-Nkomati period . Uppsala , 1985. 71 p. ; ISBN 91-7106-238-6 (pbk.) : DDC 327.68067/9 19
DT771.M85 D38 1985 NYPL [Sc E 88-121]

Magaia, Lina. [Dumba nengue. English.] Dumba nengue, run for your life . Trenton, N.J. , 1988. 113 p. : ISBN 0-86543-073-X
NYPL [Sc D 88-1509]

Mozambique - Government. see Mozambique - Politics and government.

MOZAMBIQUE - HISTORY.
Portugal. Laws, statutes etc. Companhia do Nyassa [microform] . Lisboa, 1897. 89 p.
JV4229.M7C785
NYPL [Sc Micro R-4840 no.10]

MOZAMBIQUE - HISTORY - 1891-1975.
Honwana, Raúl Bernardo Manuel, 1905- [Histórias ouvidas e vividas dos homens e da terra. English.] The life history of Raúl Honwana . Boulder , 1988. ix, 181 p. : ISBN 1-555-87114-3 (lib. bdg.) : DDC 967/.903/0924 B 19
DT463 .H6613 1988 NYPL [Sc E 88-367]

MOZAMBIQUE - HISTORY - REVOLUTION, 1964-1975 - COMIC BOOKS, STRIPS, ETC.
Motta, Helena. Moçambique por Eduardo Mondlane /. [Maputo?] [1984] 86 p. : DDC 967/.903/0222 19
DT463 .M64 1984 NYPL [Sc F 89-172]

MOZAMBIQUE - HISTORY - 1975-
Bernstein, Keith. Frontline Southern Africa /. London , c1988. x, 117 p. : ISBN 0-7470-3012-X (pbk) : DDC 968.06/3 19
HN800.A8 NYPL [Sc E 89-122]

Mozambique Liberation Front. see Frente de Libertação de Moçambique.

MOZAMBIQUE - POLITICS AND GOVERNMENT - TO 1975.
Botte, Theodorico César de Sande Pacheco de Sacadura. Memórias e autobiografia . Maputo, República Popular de Moçambique , 1985-1986 [i.e. 1987]. 3 v. : *NYPL [Sc D 88-130]*

MOZAMBIQUE - POLITICS AND GOVERNMENT - 1975-
Machel, Samora, 1933- Compreender a nossa tarefa [microform]. [Maputo, Moçambique , 1979] 20 p. ; *NYPL [Sc Micro F-11,163]*

Machel, Samora, 1933- A nossa força está na unidade /. [Maputo] [1983] 98 p. : DDC 967/.9803 19
DT465.C32 M32 1983 NYPL [Sc D 89-531]

Magaia, Lina. [Dumba nengue. English.] Dumba nengue, run for your life . Trenton, N.J. , 1988. 113 p. : ISBN 0-86543-073-X
NYPL [Sc D 88-1509]

MOZAMBIQUE - SOCIAL CONDITIONS - 1975-
Verschuur, Christine. Mozambique, dix ans de solitude-- /. Paris , c1986. 182 p. : ISBN 2-85802-700-5 *NYPL [Sc D 89-285]*

Mphahlele, Ezekiel.
Bury me at the marketplace : selected letters of Es'kia Mphahlele, 1943-1980 / [edited by] N. Chabani Manganyi. Johannesburg : Skotaville Publishers, c1984. 202 p. ; 21 cm. Includes bibliographical references and index. ISBN 0-620-06779-9
1. Mphahlele, Ezekiel - Correspondence. 2. Authors, South African - 20th century - Correspondence. 3. Authors, Black - South Africa - Correspondence. I. Manganyi, N. C. II. Title. NYPL [Sc D 89-117]

MPHAHLELE, EZEKIEL - CORRESPONDENCE.
Mphahlele, Ezekiel. Bury me at the

marketplace . Johannesburg , c1984. 202 p. ; ISBN 0-620-06779-9 *NYPL [Sc D 89-117]*

MPONGWE (AFRICAN PEOPLE) - FOLKLORE.
Aardema, Verna. Princess Gorilla and a new kind of water . New York , 1988. [32] p. : ISBN 0-8037-0412-7 : DDC 398.2/0966 E 19
PZ8.1.A213 Pr 1987 NYPL [Sc F 88-133]

Mrs. Flowers . Angelou, Maya. Minneapolis, Minn. , c1986. 32 p. : ISBN 1-556-28009-2 (pbk.) : DDC [Fic] 19
PZ7.A5833 Mr 1986
NYPL [Sc Rare C 88-28]

Msamiati wa maneno ya kitheologia. Dodoma [Tanzania] : Central Tanganyika Press, c1979. iv, 47 p. ; 18 cm. English and Swahili. Produced by the Kamati ya Vitabu vya Theologia vya Kiswahili of the Ushirika wa Vyuo vya Afrika ya Mashariki.
1. Theology - Dictionaries - Swahili. 2. Theology - Dictionaries. 3. Swahili language - Dictionaries - English. 4. English language - Dictionaries - Swahili. I. Ushirika wa Vyuo vya Theologia vya Afrika ya Mashariki. Kamati ya Vitabu vya Theologia vya Kiswahili.
BR95 .M72 1979 NYPL [Sc C 88-149]

Msiska, Augustine W. C.
Law and justice in Zambia : a bibliography / compiled by Augustine W.C. Msiska. Lusaka, Zambia : University of Zambia Library, 1986. iii, 75 p. ; 30 cm. (Occasional publications / University of Zambia Library. no. 5) DDC 016.3476894 016.34689407 19
1. Law - Zambia - Bibliography. 2. Justice, Administration of - Zambia - Bibliography. I. Series: Occasional publications / University of Zambia Library , no. 5. II. Title.
LAW NYPL [Sc F 89-9]

University of Zambia. Library. Special Collections Division. Subject guide to research papers held by the University of Zambia Library, Special Collections Division (Lusaka Campus) /. Lusaka, Zambia , 1986. v, 423 p. ; DDC 016.96894 19
Z5055.Z334 U558 1986 AS623.L84
NYPL [Sc F 88-353]

Mucci, Floren's. Tu aurais pu lui dire je t'aime / Floren's Mucci. Port-au-Prince, Haiti : Editions Fardin, [betweem 1985 and 1988] 85 p. ; 20 cm.
1. Haiti - Fiction. I. Title. NYPL [Sc C 88-233]

Mudimbe, V. Y., 1941?-
[Bel immonde. English]
Before the birth of the moon / V.Y. Mudimbe ; with a foreword by Jacques Howlett ; translated from the French by Marjolijn de Jager. New York : Simon & Schuster, c1989. 203 p. ; 22 cm. Translation of: Le bel immonde. "A Fireside book." ISBN 0-671-66840-4 : DDC 843 19
1. Zaire - Fiction. I. Title.
PQ3989.2.M77 B413 1989
NYPL [Sc D 89-236]

MUDIMBE, V. Y., 1941?- - CRITICISM AND INTERPRETATION.
Mouralis, Bernard. V.Y. Mudimbe . Paris , c1988. 143 p., [2] leaves of plates : ISBN 2-7087-0506-7 *NYPL [Sc D 89-251]*

Müller, Hans-Peter. Die Helvetas-Wasserversorgungen in Kamerun : eine ethnologische evaluation / Hans-Peter Müller. [Zürich : s.n., 1978] 94, 45 leaves ; 30 cm. Cover title. German and English. Bibliography: leaf 84 (1st group)
1. Helvetas, Schweizer Aufbauwert für Entwicklungs länder. 2. Water-Supply, rural - Cameroon. I. Title.
NYPL [Sc F 88-122]

La Muerte en la vida africana. Mort dans la vie africaine. Spanish. Barcelona , París , 1984. 314 p. : ISBN 84-85800-81-8 *NYPL [Sc D 88-601]*

Müssen die Afrikaner den Weissen alles nachmachen? /. Bizimana, Nsekuye. Berlin , c1985. 271 p. : ISBN 3-88726-014-7 DDC 940 19
D1055 .B57 1985 NYPL [Sc D 88-995]

Mugyenyi, Joshua, 1947- Black, David R. (David Ross), 1960- Foreign policy in small states . Halifax, N.S. , 1988. viii, 83 p. : ISBN 0-7703-0736-1 : DDC 327.681068 19
NYPL [Sc D 89-564]

Muhammad, Ahmad al-'Awad. Sudan Defence Force : origin and role 1925-1955 / by Ahmad al-'Awad Muhammad. [Khartoum? : s.n., 198-?]. ([Khartoum?] : Military Printing Press) 118 p. : ill. ; 25 cm. (Occasional paper / Institute of African and Asian studies . no. 13) Bibliography: p. 113-118.
1. Sudan. Defence Force - History. 2. Sudan - Armed Forces - History. I. Series: Occasional paper (Jami'at al-Khartūm. Mahad al-Dirāsāt al-Afrīqīyah wa-al-Asiyawīyah) , no. 13. II. Title.
NYPL [Sc E 88-261]

Muhammad Ali /. Rummel, Jack. New York , c1988. 128 p. : ISBN 1-555-46569-2 DDC 796.8/3/0924 B 92 19
GV1132.A44 R86 1988
NYPL [Sc E 88-175]

MUHAMMAD, THE PROPHET.
'Isá 'Abd Allāh Muhammad al-Mahdī, 1945- Who was the prophet Muhammad? [microform] /. Brooklyn, N.Y. [1980] 96 p. :
NYPL [Sc Micro R-4114 no. 11]

MUHAMMADANISM. see ISLAM.

Muhammed, Mairo. Shawara ga mata don aikin Hajji / na Hajiya Mairo Muhammed. [Kano, Nigeria] : M. Mohammed. 85 p. : ill. ; 21 cm.
1. Hausa language - Texts. I. Title.
NYPL [Sc D 88-1042]

Muhanji, Cherry. Scott, Kesho. Tight Spaces /. San Francisco , 1987. 182 p. ; ISBN 0-933216-27-0 *NYPL [Sc D 88-12]*

MUI TSAI. see SLAVERY.

Muianga, Aldino, 1950- Xitala Mati / Aldino Muianga. [Maputo?] : Associação dos Escritores Moçambicanos, [1987?] 87 p. : ill. ; 21 cm. (Colecção Início . 7)
1. Mozambique - Fiction. I. Title. II. Series.
NYPL [Sc D 88-531]

La mujer africana en la sociedad precolonial /. Pala, Achola O. [Femme africaine dans la société précoloniale. Spanish.] Barcelona [Paris?] , 1982. 238 p. ; ISBN 84-85800-35-4 (Serbal) *NYPL [Sc D 88-833]*

Mukuni, R. M., 1929- U zibe mutu / R.M. Mukuni. [Lusaka] : NECZAM, c1976. 54 p. : ill. ; 18 cm. In Lozi.
1. Lozi language - Texts. I. Title.
PL8460.9.M77 U2 1976 NYPL [Sc C 89-37]

Mulaki, Gideon. Njau, Rebeka. Kenya women heroes and their mystical power /. Nairobi , 1984- v. ; DDC 398/.09676/2 19
GR356.4 .N43 1984 NYPL [Sc D 88-1052]

The mulatto woman as major female character in novels by Black women, 1892-1937 [microform] /. Lewis, Vashti Crutcher. [Iowa City, Ia.] 1981. iv, 182 leaves ;
NYPL [Sc Micro R-4792]

MULATTOES IN LITERATURE.
Lewis, Vashti Crutcher. The mulatto woman as major female character in novels by Black women, 1892-1937 [microform] /. [Iowa City, Ia.] 1981. iv, 182 leaves ;
NYPL [Sc Micro R-4792]

Mulher e escrava . Giacomini, Sonia Maria. Petrópolis , 1988. 95 p., [7] p. of plates :
HT1126 .G49 1988 NYPL [Sc D 88-1283]

A mulher na cultura brasileira /. Horta, Elisabeth Vorcaro. Belo Horizonte , 1975. 122 p. ;
HQ1542 .H66 NYPL [Sc D 86-811]

Muller, A. S. (Alexander Samuel), 1930- A Bibliography of health and disease in East Africa /. Amsterdam ; New York : 282 p. ; ISBN 0-444-80931-7 (U. S.) DDC 016.3621/0967 19
Z6673.6.A353 B53 1988 RA552.A353
NYPL [Sc G 89-6]

Muller, Eugène. Colón, Fernando, 1488-1539. [Historie. English] Christophe Colomb raconté par son fils /. Paris , 1986. xviii, 265 p., [8] p. of plates : ISBN 2-262-00387-4
NYPL [Sc D 88-504]

Mullins, Richard T. There's some of me in each day of life / by Richard T. Mullins. [S.l. : Brandon Marcus Publications], c1980. vi, 56 p. : ill. ; 23 cm. Poems.
I. Title. NYPL [Sc D 88-535]

MULTICULTURAL EDUCATION - UNITED STATES.
Dodson, Jualynne E. Black stylization and

implications for child welfare . Atlanta, Georgia , 1975. 1 v. (various pagings) ;
NYPL [Sc F 88-223]

Multimedia Publications catalogue [microform] Lusaka, Zambia : Multimedia Publications, 1974. 8 p. : ill. ; 19 cm. Microfiche. New York: New York Public Library, 198 . 1 microfiche: negative; 11 x 15 cm. (FSN Sc 019,116).
1. Catalogs, Publishers' - Zambia.
NYPL [Sc Micro F-11,053]

MULTINATIONAL CORPORATIONS. see INTERNATIONAL BUSINESS ENTERPRISES.

Multinationals and maldevelopment . Alschuler, Lawrence R., 1941- Basingstoke, Hampshire , c1988. xii, 218 p. : ISBN 0-333-41561-2
NYPL [Sc D 88-701]

Mumba, Maurice Kambishera. The wrath of Koma / Maurice Kambishera Mumba. Nairobi : Heinemann Kenya, 1987. 153 p. ; 18 cm. ISBN 996-646-342-6
1. Kenya - Fiction. I. Title. *NYPL [Sc C 89-45]*

MUNDANG (AFRICAN PEOPLE) Princes & serviteurs du royaume . Paris , 1987. 225 p. : ISBN 2-901161-29-4
NYPL [Sc E 88-409]

Munder, Barbara. Barrow, Joe Louis. Joe Louis . New York , c1988. xvii, 270 p., [8] leaves of plates : ISBN 0-07-003955-0 : DDC 796.8/3/0924 B 19
GV1132.L6 B37 1988 NYPL [Sc E 88-566]

MUNICIPAL UNIVERSITIES AND COLLEGES - UNITED STATES. Richardson, Richard C. Fostering minority access and achievement in higher education . San Francisco, Calif. , c1987. xviii, 244 p. ; ISBN 1-555-42053-2 (alk. paper) DDC 378/.052 19
LC3727 .R53 1987 NYPL [Sc E 88-472]

MUNICIPALITIES. see CITIES AND TOWNS.

MUNROE, J. SPENCER. Colman, Hila. A career in medical research. Cleveland [1968] 175 p. DDC 610.7
R690 .C65 NYPL [Sc D 88-425]

Munroe, Trevor. The working class party : principles and standards / by Trevor Munroe. [Jamaica?] : T. Munroe, 1983. 72 p. ; 22 cm. DDC 324.27292/075 19
1. Workers Party of Jamaica. I. Title.
JL639.A8 W676 1983 NYPL [Sc D 88-1271]

Muraho, Guten Tag : Begegnungen in Rwanda : Bericht einer entwicklungspolitischen Studenreise der Pfadfinderinnenschaft St. Georg / [Redaktion: Uta Richter ... [et al.] ; Mitarbeiter: Christa Altmeyer ... [et al.]. Leverkusen : PSG-Verlag, 1983. 86 p., [16] leaves of plates : ill., maps ; 30 cm.
1. Rwanda - Description and travel.
NYPL [Sc F 88-256]

MURDER - GEORGIA - ATLANTA - CASE STUDIES. Dettlinger, Chet. The list /. Atlanta , c1983. 516 p., [4] p. of plates : ISBN 0-942894-04-9 : DDC 364.1/523/09758231 19
HV6534.A7 D47 1983 NYPL [Sc E 86-40]

MURDER - ILLINOIS - CHICAGO. Wilson, Mary, 1938- To Benji, with love /. Chicago , c1987. p. cm. ISBN 0-910671-07-9 : DDC 977.3/11043/0924 B 19
F548.9.N4 W559 1987
NYPL [Sc D 88-1219]

MURDER - MISSISSIPPI - JACKSON. Spofford, Tim. Lynch Street . Kent, Ohio , c1988. 219 p., [1] leaf of plates : ISBN 0-87338-355-9 (alk. paper) DDC 976.2/51 19
F349.J13 S66 1988 NYPL [Sc E 89-27]

Murder of Dele Giwa : the right of a private prosecutor. Lagos, Nigeria : Nigerian Law Publications, 1988. 193 p. : col. ill., ports. ; 27 cm. ISBN 978-232-523-6
1. Giwa, Dele. 2. Private prosecutors - Nigeria. 3. Complaints (Criminal procedure) - Nigeria. I. Title: Right of a private prosecutor.
NYPL [Sc F 89-35]

MURDER - WEST INDIES. André, Jacques. L'inceste focal dans la famille

noire antillaise . Paris : Presses universitaires de France, 1987. 396 p. ; ISBN 2-13-040101-5
NYPL [Sc D 88-129]

Murphree, Marshall W. Bouedillon, M. F. C. Studies of fishing on Lake Kariba /. [Harare] , 1985. 185 p. : *NYPL [Sc D 88-875]*

Murray, James Briggs. Black visions '87 . New York , 1987. 32 p. :
NYPL [Sc F 88-258]

Black visions '88 . New York [1988] 44 p. :
NYPL [Sc D 88-1200]

Murray, Martin J. South Africa, time of agony, time of destiny : the upsurge of popular protest / Martin Murray. London : Verso, 1987. xii, 496 p.: ill., map ; 23 cm. Includes bibliographical references and index.
1. South Africa - Politics and government - 1978-. 2. South Africa - History - 1961-. I. Title.
NYPL [JFD 87-8776]

Murray, Stephen O. Male homosexuality in Central and South America /. New York , 1987. 199 p. ; *NYPL [Sc D 88-557]*

Musa, Hassam. Hondo yeChimurenga . Gweru , 1984. 230 p. ; ISBN 0-86922-284-8
NYPL [Sc C 89-110]

Musangi Ntemo, 1946- Bamba Ndombasi Kifimba, 1937- Anthologie des sculptuers et peintres zaïrois contemporains /. Paris , 1987. 109 p. : ISBN 2-09-168350-7
NYPL [Sc G 88-11]

Muse presents Jazz in the first person : August through October 1972. [Brooklyn, N.Y. : Brooklyn Children's Museum, c1972] 31 p. : ill. ; 26 cm. Published in conjunction with an exhibit at the Brooklyn Children's Museum. Discography: [7] leaves, inserted. CONTENTS. - Introduction / Doug Harris -- The music is the message / Chris White -- Some of the great ones / George Ford.
1. Jazz music - Exhibitions. 2. Afro-American music - Exhibitions. I. Brooklyn Institute of Arts and Sciences. Children's Museum. II. Title: Jazz in the first person.
NYPL [JNF 85-14]

Museu de Arte Sacra, anexo à Igreja da Misericórdia, Ilha de Moçambique [microform] Museu de Arte Sacra (Mozambique Island) [Lourenço Marques?] , 1969. [16] p. :
NYPL [Sc Micro F-10928]

Museu de Arte Sacra (Mozambique Island) Museu de Arte Sacra, anexo à Igreja da Misericórdia, Ilha de Moçambique [microform] [Lourenço Marques?] : Comissão Provincial das Comemorações Centenárias de Vasco da Gama e Luís de Camões, 1969. [16] p. : ill. ; 21 cm. Text by Alberto Feliciano Marques Pereira. Portuguese and English. Microfiche. New York: New York Public Library, 198 . 1 microfiche: negative; 11 x 15 cm. (FSN Sc 019,043).
1. Museu de Arte Sacra (Mozambique Island). 2. Christian art and symbolism - Mozambique - Exhibitions. I. Pereira, Alberto Feliciano Marques. II. Comissão Provincial das Comemorações do V Centenário de Vasco da Gama. III. Title.
NYPL [Sc Micro F-10928]

MUSEU DE ARTE SACRA (MOZAMBIQUE ISLAND) Museu de Arte Sacra (Mozambique Island) Museu de Arte Sacra, anexo à Igreja da Misericórdia, Ilha de Moçambique [microform] [Lourenço Marques?] , 1969. [16] p. :
NYPL [Sc Micro F-10928]

Museum of Fine Arts, Boston. Gaither, Edmund B. Massachusetts masters . Boston [1988] 48 p. : *NYPL [Sc F 89-159]*

Museum of Fine Arts, Houston. Bassani, Ezio. Africa and the Renaissance . New York City , c1988. 255 p. : ISBN 0-945802-00-5 : DDC 736/.62/096607401471 19
NK5989 .B37 1988 NYPL [Sc F 89-30]

Museum voor Volkenkunde (Rotterdam, Netherlands) Expressions of belief . New York , 1988. 248 p. : ISBN 0-8478-0959-5 : DDC 730 19
N5310.75.H68 M876 1988
NYPL [Sc G 88-37]

Museum of Modern Art (New York, N.Y.) African Negro art : edited by James Johnson Sweeney. New York : The Museum of Modern Art [c1935] 58 p. : plates. ; 26 cm. "Two thousand copies ... printed ... by Plantin Press, New York." A catalog of an exhibition held by the Museum

of Modern Art. CONTENTS. - The art of Negro Africa, by J. J. Sweeney.--Previous exhibitions of African art.--Museums containing collections of African art.--Bibliography (p. 25-29)--Catalog.
1. Art, African - Exhibitions. 2. Sculpture, African - Exhibitions. 3. Art - Africa - Exhibitions. 4. Sculpture, Primitive - Africa - Exhibitions. I. Sweeney, James Johnson. II. Title. *NYPL [Sc F 88-125]*

Museum of the National Center of Afro-American Artists. see National Center of Afro-American Artists. Museum.

Museum Rade am Schloss Reinbek. Volkstümliche Künste . Reinbek , c1986/87. 135 p. : *NYPL [Sc D 89-238]*

MUSEUM RADE AM SCHLOSS REINBEK - CATALOGS. Volkstümliche Künste . Reinbek , c1986/87. 135 p. : *NYPL [Sc D 89-238]*

Museum voor Volkenkunde (Rotterdam, Netherlands) Expressions of belief : masterpieces of African, Oceanic, and Indonesian art from the Museum voor Volkenkunde, Rotterdam / edited by Suzanne Greub. New York : Rizzoli, 1988. 248 p. : ill. (some col.) ; 31 cm. Catalogue of an exhibition at the Museum of Fine Arts, Houston, Tex., Oct. 1-Nov. 27, 1988; Utah Museum of Fine Arts, Salt Lake City, Dec. 18, 1988-Feb. 26, 1989; Toledo Museum of Art, Apr. 2-May 14, 1989; Portland Art Museum, June 14-Aug. 27, 1989; and Center for the Fine Arts, Miami, Sept. 30-Nov. 30, 1989. Includes index. Bibliography: p. 240-244. ISBN 0-8478-0959-5 : DDC 730 19
1. Museum voor Volkenkunde (Rotterdam, Netherlands) - Exhibitions. 2. Art, Primitive - Exhibitions. I. Greub, Suzanne. II. Museum of Fine Arts, Houston. III. Utah Museum of Fine Arts. IV. Portland Art Museum (Or.). V. Center for the Fine Arts (Miami, Fla.). VI. Title.
N5310.75.H68 M876 1988
NYPL [Sc G 88-37]

MUSEUM VOOR VOLKENKUNDE (ROTTERDAM, NETHERLANDS) - EXHIBITIONS. Museum voor Volkenkunde (Rotterdam, Netherlands) Expressions of belief . New York , 1988. 248 p. : ISBN 0-8478-0959-5 : DDC 730 19
N5310.75.H68 M876 1988
NYPL [Sc G 88-37]

MUSEUMS - BRAZIL. Lody, Raul. Coleção Arthur Ramos /. [Fortaleza] , 1987. 78 p. : ISBN 85-24-60035-7
NYPL [Sc D 89-479]

MUSEUMS - JAMAICA. Wheatle, Hiliary-Ann. Museums of the Institute of Jamaica /. Kingston , 1982. 16 p. :
NYPL [Sc D 88-1173]

Museums of the Institute of Jamaica /. Wheatle, Hiliary-Ann. Kingston , 1982. 16 p. :
NYPL [Sc D 88-1173]

MUSIC - AFRICA. Perspectives on African music /. Bayreuth, W. Germany , c1989. 139 p., [8] leaves of plates : ISBN 3-927510-00-9 *NYPL [Sc D 89-448]*

MUSIC - AFRICA - HISTORY AND CRITICISM. Stapleton, Cris. African all-stars . London , 1987. 373 p., [16] p. of plates : ISBN 0-7043-2504-7 *NYPL [Sc E 88-137]*

MUSIC, AFRICAN - CONGRESSES. African music. Paris [c1972] 154 p.
NYPL [JMF 74-320]

MUSIC - CARIBBEAN AREA - HISTORY AND CRITICISM. Hebdige, Dick. Cut 'n' mix . London , 1987. 177 p. : ISBN 1-85178-029-7
NYPL [Sc D 89-372]

MUSIC, DRAMATIC. see MUSICAL REVUE, COMEDY, ETC.

MUSIC - HISTORY AND CRITICISM. Worlds of music . New York , c1984. xviii, 325 p. : ISBN 0-02-872600-6 DDC 781.7 19
ML3798 .W67 1984 NYPL [Sc E 85-247]

MUSIC - JAMAICA - HISTORY AND CRITICISM. Burnett, Michael. Jamaican Music /. Oxford [England] , 1982. 48 p. : ISBN 0-19-321333-8 (pbk.)
NYPL [Sc C 84-99]

MUSIC - LOUISIANA - NEW ORLEANS.
Martinez, Raymond J. (Raymond Joseph), 1889- Portraits of New Orleans jazz. New Orleans [1971] 63 p. DDC 785.4/2/0976335
ML200.8.N48 M4   *NYPL [Sc D 87-69]*

Music, metaphor and values among avant-garde jazz musicians living in New York City /. Such, David Glen. 1985. ix, 307 leaves. :
NYPL [Sc F 88-284]

MUSIC - NIGERIA - HISTORY AND CRITICISM.
Kofoworola, Ziky. Hausa performing arts and music /. Lagos, c1987. viii, 330 p. : ISBN 978-17-3041-2   *NYPL [Sc E 89-116]*

MUSIC - ONTARIO - BUXTON - HISTORY AND CRITICISM.
Robbins, Vivian M. Musical Buxton /. [S.l. , 197-] 44 p. : DDC 780/.9713/1 19
ML205.8.B8 R6   *NYPL [Sc F 88-149]*

MUSIC, POPULAR (SONGS, ETC.) - AFRICA.
Seck, Nago. Musiciens africains des années 80 . Paris , c1986. 167 p. : ISBN 2-85802-715-3
NYPL [JMD 87-441]

MUSIC, POPULAR (SONGS, ETC.) - AFRICA, WEST - HISTORY AND CRITICISM.
Collins, John. Musicmakers of West Africa /. Washington, DC , c1985. 177 p. : ISBN 0-89410-075-0   *NYPL [Sc E 87-59]*

MUSIC, POPULAR (SONGS, ETC.) - BRAZIL - HISTORY AND CRITICISM.
Gilberto Gil Expresso 2222 /. [Salvador, Brasil?] , 1982. 287 p. ;
NYPL [JMD 83-309]

MUSIC, POPULAR (SONGS, ETC.) - FRENCH GUIANA - HISTORY AND CRITICISM.
Jallier, Maurice. Musique aux Antilles =. Paris , c1985. 145 p., [16] p. of plates : ISBN 2-903033-65-X : DDC 780/.42/09729 19
ML3486.G8 J3 1985   *NYPL [Sc D 87-576]*

MUSIC, POPULAR (SONGS, ETC.) - GUADELOUPE - HISTORY AND CRITICISM.
Jallier, Maurice. Musique aux Antilles =. Paris , c1985. 145 p., [16] p. of plates : ISBN 2-903033-65-X : DDC 780/.42/09729 19
ML3486.G8 J3 1985   *NYPL [Sc D 87-576]*

MUSIC, POPULAR (SONGS, ETC.) - JAMAICA - BIBLIOGRAPHY.
White, Garth. The development of Jamaican popular music with special reference to the music of Bob Marley . Kingston , 1982. 49 p. ; DDC 016.78/042/097292 19
ML120.J35 5 1982   *NYPL [Sc F 87-61]*

MUSIC, POPULAR (SONGS, ETC.) - MARTINIQUE - HISTORY AND CRITICISM.
Jallier, Maurice. Musique aux Antilles =. Paris , c1985. 145 p., [16] p. of plates : ISBN 2-903033-65-X : DDC 780/.42/09729 19
ML3486.G8 J3 1985   *NYPL [Sc D 87-576]*

MUSIC, SOUL. see SOUL MUSIC.

MUSIC, THEATRICAL. see MUSICAL REVUE, COMEDY, ETC.

MUSIC TRADE - UNITED STATES.
George, Nelson. The death of rhythm & blues /. New York , c1988. xvi, 222 p., [16] p. of plates : ISBN 0-394-55238-5 : DDC 781.7/296073 19
ML3556 .G46 1988   *NYPL [Sc E 88-504]*

MUSIC - UNITED STATES - 20TH CENTURY - HISTORY AND CRITICISM.
George, Nelson. The death of rhythm & blues /. New York , c1988. xvi, 222 p., [16] p. of plates : ISBN 0-394-55238-5 : DDC 781.7/296073 19
ML3556 .G46 1988   *NYPL [Sc E 88-504]*

MUSIC - UNITED STATES - ADDRESSES, ESSAYS, LECTURES.
Readings in Black American music /. New York , c1983. xii, 338 p. : ISBN 0-393-95280-0 (pbk.) DDC 781.7/296073 19
ML3556 .R34 1983   *NYPL [Sc D 85-30]*

Music was not enough /. Wilber, Bob, 1928- New York , 1988. 216 p. [8] p. of plates : ISBN 0-19-520629-0   *NYPL [Sc E 89-6]*

MUSIC - WEST INDIES, FRENCH - HISTORY AND CRITICISM.

Rosemain, Jacqueline, 1930- La musique dans la société antillaise . Paris , c1986. 183 p. : ISBN 2-85802-685-8 (pbk.)
NYPL [Sc E 88-394]

Musical Buxton /. Robbins, Vivian M. [S.l. , 197-] 44 p. : DDC 780/.9713/1 19
ML205.8.B8 R6   *NYPL [Sc F 88-149]*

MUSICAL COMEDY. see MUSICAL REVUE, COMEDY, ETC.

MUSICAL EXTRAVAGANZA. see MUSICAL REVUE, COMEDY, ETC.

MUSICAL FARCE. see MUSICAL REVUE, COMEDY, ETC.

MUSICAL INSTRUMENTS - CAPE VERDE ISLANDS.
Lopes Filho, João. Cabo Verde . Lisboa , 1976. 54 p., [5] leaves of plates :
NYPL [Sc D 84-279]

MUSICAL INSTRUMENTS - CUBA - HISTORY AND CRITICISM.
Ortiz, Fernando, 1881-1969. La clave xilofónica de la música cubana . Ciudad de la Habana, Cuba , 1984. 105 p. ; DDC 789/.6 19
ML1049 .O77 1984   *NYPL [Sc C 87-373]*

MUSICAL INSTRUMENTS - INDUSTRY AND TRADE. see MUSIC TRADE.

MUSICAL INSTRUMENTS - KENYA.
Senoga-Zake, George W. Folk music of Kenya /. Nairobi, Kenya , 1986. 185 p. :
NYPL [Sc D 88-368]

MUSICAL PLAY. see MUSICAL REVUE, COMEDY, ETC.

MUSICAL REVUE, COMEDY, ETC. - UNITED STATES.
Woll, Allen. Black musical theatre . Baton Rouge , c1989. xiv, 301 p. : ISBN 0-8071-1469-3 DDC 782.81/08996073 19
ML1711 .W64 1989   *NYPL [Sc E 89-198]*

MUSICIANS - AFRICA - BIOGRAPHY.
Seck, Nago. Musiciens africains des années 80 . Paris , c1986. 167 p. : ISBN 2-85802-715-3
NYPL [JMD 87-441]

MUSICIANS - AFRICA, WEST - INTERVIEWS.
Collins, John. Musicmakers of West Africa /. Washington, DC , c1985. 177 p. : ISBN 0-89410-075-0   *NYPL [Sc E 87-59]*

MUSICIANS, AFRO-AMERICAN. see AFRO-AMERICAN MUSICIANS.

MUSICIANS - ONTARIO - BUXTON - BIOGRAPHY.
Robbins, Vivian M. Musical Buxton /. [S.l. , 197-] 44 p. : DDC 780/.9713/1 19
ML205.8.B8 R6   *NYPL [Sc F 88-149]*

MUSICIANS, TOWN. see MUSICIANS.

Musiciens africains de années quatre-vingts. Seck, Nago. Musiciens africains des années 80 . Paris , c1986. 167 p. : ISBN 2-85802-715-3
NYPL [JMD 87-441]

Musiciens africains des années 80 . Seck, Nago. Paris , c1986. 167 p. : ISBN 2-85802-715-3
NYPL [JMD 87-441]

Musicmakers of West Africa /. Collins, John. Washington, DC , c1985. 177 p. : ISBN 0-89410-075-0   *NYPL [Sc E 87-59]*

Musique aux Antilles =. Jallier, Maurice. Paris , c1985. 145 p., [16] p. of plates : ISBN 2-903033-65-X : DDC 780/.42/09729 19
ML3486.G8 J3 1985   *NYPL [Sc D 87-576]*

La musique dans la société antillaise . Rosemain, Jacqueline, 1930- Paris , c1986. 183 p. : ISBN 2-85802-685-8 (pbk.)   *NYPL [Sc E 88-394]*

Musique du vaudou . Dauphin, Claude, 1949- Sherbrooke, Québec, Canada [1986] 182 p. : ISBN 2-89040-366-1 (pbk.) DDC 783/.02/9967 19
ML3565 .D34 1986   *NYPL [Sc D 87-315]*

Muslim-Christian dialogue in Nigeria /. Chukwulozie, Victor. Ibadan , 1986. xviii, 201 p. : ISBN 978-12-2192-5   *NYPL [Sc D 88-890]*

Muslim cities and towns. see Cities and towns, Islamic.

MUSLIM EDUCATION. see ISLAM - EDUCATION.

MUSLIM LEARNING AND SCHOLARSHIP. see ISLAMIC LEARNING AND SCHOLARSHIP.

MUSLIM WOMEN. see WOMEN, MUSLIM.

MUSLIMISM. see ISLAM.

MUSLIMS - AFRICA, FRENCH-SPEAKING WEST - POLITICS AND GOVERNMENT.
Harrison, Christopher, 1958- France and Islam in West Africa, 1860-1960 /. Cambridge [Cambridgeshire] , New York , 1988. xi, 242 p. : ISBN 0-521-35230-4 DDC 966/.0097451 19
DT530.5.M88 H37 1988
NYPL [Sc E 88-484]

MUSLIMS, BLACK.
Is a Abd All ah Muḥammad al-Hahd i, 1945- Who was Noble Drew Ali? /. [Brooklyn, N.Y.] 1988, c1980. 122 p. :   *NYPL [Sc D 89-74]*

'Isá 'Abd Allāh Muḥammad al-Mahdī, 1945- Who was Marcus Garvey? . [Brooklyn, N.Y.] c1988. 101 p. :   *NYPL [Sc D 89-139]*

'Isá 'Abd Allāh Muḥammad al-Mahdī, 1945- Who was Noble Drew Ali? [microform] /. Brooklyn, N.Y. [1980] 56 p. :
NYPL [Sc Micro R-4114 no. 10]

MUSLIMS, BLACK - NEW YORK (N.Y.) - BROOKLYN - SOCIAL LIFE AND CUSTOMS.
Abba island in America [microform] Brooklyn [197-?] 11 p. :
NYPL [Sc Micro R-4114 no. 19]

MUSLIMS - LEARNING AND SCHOLARSHIP. see ISLAMIC LEARNING AND SCHOLARSHIP.

MUSLIMS - SOMALIA - BIOGRAPHY.
Jaamac Cumar Ciise. Taariikhdii daraawiishta iyo Sayid Maxamed Cabdulle Xasan, 1895-1921 /. Muqdisho , 1976. vii, 320 p., [2] leaves of plates :
DT404.3.M38 C55   *NYPL [Sc E 87-435]*

MUSLIMS - WOMEN. see WOMEN, MUSLIM.

MUSSULMANISM. see ISLAM.

Mutahaba, G. R. Sokoïne, Edward Moringe, 1938-1984. Public policy making and implementation in Tanzania /. Pau [1986?] ix, 124 p. :   *NYPL [Sc E 88-319]*

Mutamba Makombo, 1945- Mabi Mulumba. Cadres et dirigeants au Zaïre . Kinshasa , 1986. 541 p. :   *NYPL [Sc E 88-322]*

Mutasa, Garikai. The contact / Garikai Mutasa. Gweru, Zimbabwe : Mambo Press, 1985. 125 p. ; 18 cm. (Mambo writers series. English section. vol. 20) ISBN 0-86922-355-0 (pbk.)
1. Zimbabwe - Fiction. I. Title.
MLCS 86/13019 (P)   *NYPL [JFC 87-1040]*

Mutations économiques et sociales à la campagne et à la ville : transformations du régime foncier : génèse du monde des entreprises. Paris : Laboratoire "Connaissance du Tiers-Monde", Université Paris VII, 1980. 258 p. ; 29 cm. (Cahier / Groupe Afrique noire . no. 4) Includes bibliographies.
1. Africa, Sub-Saharan - Economic conditions - 1918-1960. 2. Africa, Sub-Saharan - Social conditions. I. Series: Cahier (Centre national de la recherche scientifique (France). Groupe de recherches ("Afrique noire") , no. 4.   *NYPL [Sc F 87-437]*

Mutero Chirenje, J. see Chirenje, J. Mutero, 1935-

MUTESA, KING OF BUGANDA, D. 1884.
Kiwanuka, M. S. M. Semakula. Muteesa of Uganda. Nairobi [1967] viii, 89 p. DDC 967.6/101/0924 B
DT433.26.M88 K58   *NYPL [Sc C 88-87]*

Mutizwa-Mangiza, N. D. Community development in pre-independence Zimbabwe : a study of policy with special reference to rural land / by N.D. Mutziwa [i.e. Mutizwa]-Mangiza. Harare : University of Zimbabwe, c1985. iv, 79 p. : ill., maps ; 21 cm. "Supplement to Zambezia, 1985; the journal of the University of Zimbabwe." Bibliography: p. 78-79.
ISBN 0-86924-090-0 (pbk.) DDC 307.1/4/096891 19
1. Rural development - Zimbabwe - History - 20th century. 2. Land reform - Zimbabwe - History - 20th century. I. Zambezia. II. Title.
HN802.Z9 C65 1985   *NYPL [JLD 88-3699]*

Muzungu, Bernardin. Imigani "tima-ngiro" y'u Rwanda =. Butare , 1987. 267, [1] p. ;
NYPL [Sc D 88-865]

Muzyka narodov Azii i Afriki / [sostavlenie i redaktsiiā V.S. Vinogradova]. Moskva : "Sov. kompozitor", 1969- v. : ill., music ; 21 cm. Includes bibliographical references.
1. Folk music - Asia - History and criticism. 2. Folk music - Africa - History and criticism. I. Vinogradov, V. S. (Viktor Sergeevich).
ML3740 .M9   *NYPL [Sc D 89-470]*

Mveng, Engelbert. Spiritualité et libération en Afrique /. Paris , c1987. 123 p. ;
NYPL [Sc D 88-1416]

Mwaga, D. Z. The crime of apartheid / D.Z. Mwaga. Dar es Salaam : Dar es Salaam University Press, c1985. xix, 141 p. ; 20 cm. Bibliography: p. 115-122. ISBN 997-660-049-6 DDC 342.68/0873 346.802873 19
1. Apartheid - South Africa. 2. Race discrimination - Law and legislation - South Africa. 3. Human rights - South Africa. 4. Apartheid. 5. Race discrimination - Law and legislation. 6. Human rights. I. Title.
LAW   *NYPL [Sc C 89-117]*

Mwakasungula, N. E. R. Sheria ya kashfa / Kimeandikwa na N.E.R. Mwakasungula ; hapo mwanzo hakimu mkazi mwandamizi na mwalimu wa sheria Chuo cha Uongozi wa Maendeleo Mzumbe, Morogoro, na sasa wakili Iringa. Tabora, Tanzania : T.M.P. Book Department, c1985. x, 77 p. ; 19 cm. (Sheria za Tanzania . 7) Includes index.
1. Libel and slander - Tanzania. 2. Swahili language - Texts. I. Title. II. Series. *NYPL [Sc C 88-191]*

Mwandīki wa Mau Mau ithaamīrio-inī /. Gakaara wa Wanjaū. Nairobi [Kenya] , 1983. xvii, 189 p. :   *NYPL [Sc D 87-156]*

Mwangi, Meja, 1948-
[Carcase for hounds. German]
Wie ein Aas für Hunde : Roman aus Kenia / Meja Mwangi ; aus dem Englischen und mit einer Nachbemerkung von Gunter Böhnke.1. Aufl. Bornheim-Merten : Lamuv Verlag, 1987. 173 p. ; 19 cm. (Dialog Dritte Welt . 42) Translation of: Carcase for hounds. ISBN 3-88977-136-X
1. Mau Mau - Fiction. 2. Kenya - History - 1895-1963 - Fiction. I. Title. II. Series.
NYPL [Sc C 88-148]

Mwenye Hadithi. Tricky Tortoise / by Mwenye Hadithi ; illustrated by Adrienne Kennaway. 1st ed. Boston : Little, Brown, c1988. [32] p. : ill. ; 22 x 27 cm. Tortoise outsmarts Elephant by proving he can jump right over the elephant's "tiny and stupid" head. SCHOMBURG CHILDREN'S COLLECTION. ISBN 0-316-33724-2 : DDC [E] 19
1. Turtles - Africa - Juvenile fiction. 2. Elephants - Juvenile fiction. 3. Africa - Juvenile fiction. I. Moore, Adrienne, 1945- ill. II. Schomburg Children's Collection. III. Title.
PZ7.M975 Tr 1988   *NYPL [Sc F 88-389]*

Mwisho wa kosa /. Burhani, Z. Nairobi , c1987. 269 p. ; ISBN 996-649-731-5
NYPL [Sc C 89-3]

Mwiwawi, Andrew M., 1952- The act / Andrew M. Mwiwawi. Nairobi, Kenya : Comb Books, 1976. 76 p. ; 14 cm. (CB mini novels ; no. 4) DDC 823
1. Nigeria - Fiction. I. Title.
PZ4.M9933 Ac PR9381.9.M93
NYPL [Sc B 89-22]

My belief.
Obadiah. I am a Rastafarian /. London , New York , c1986. 32 p. : ISBN 0-86313-260-X ;
BL2532.R37   *NYPL [Sc F 89-12]*

My country.
Moon, Bernice. Kenya is my country /. Hove , 1985. 60 p. : ISBN 0-85078-489-1 : DDC 967.6/204 19   *NYPL [Sc F 88-379]*

My folks don't want me to talk about slavery : twenty-one oral histories of former North Carolina Slaves / edited by Belinda Hurmence. Winston-Salem, N.C. : J.F. Blair Publisher, c1984. xiv, 103 p. ; 21 cm. Bibliography: p. 101-103. ISBN 0-89587-038-X DDC 975.6/00496073/0922 B 19
1. Slaves - North Carolina - Biography. 2. Afro-Americans - North Carolina - Biography. 3. Oral history. 4. North Carolina - Biography. I. Hurmence, Belinda.
E445.N8 M9 1984   *NYPL [JFD 85-1549]*

My friend Jacob /. Clifton, Lucille, 1936- New York , c1980. [32] p. : ISBN 0-525-35487-5 DDC [E]
PZ7.C6224 Myk 1980   *NYPL [Sc F 88-376]*

My friend the swallow. Duncan, Jane. London, New York, 1970. 255 p. ISBN 0-333-11677-1 DDC 823/.9/14
PZ4.D9116 Mwk PR6054.U46
NYPL [Sc D 88-1115]

My happy days /. Shackelford, Jane Dabney. Washington, D.C. , c1944. 121 p. :
NYPL [Sc F 88-337]

My life /. Moloi, Godfrey, 1934- Johannesburg , 1987- v. : ISBN 0-86975-324-X (v. 1) DDC 968.2/21/0924 B 19
DT944.J653 M65 1987 *NYPL [Sc C 89-113]*

My life with Tiny . Hall, Richard, 1925- London , Boston , 1987. 256, [4] p. of plates : ISBN 0-571-14737-2 *NYPL [Sc D 88-515]*

My own story. Robinson, Jackie, 1919-1972. Jackie Robinson . New York , 1948. 170 p. :
NYPL [Sc C 88-61]

My role in nationalism /. Onyia, Obi J. I. G. Asaba , 1986. 73 p. : *NYPL [Sc E 89-115]*

Myer, Isaac, 1836-1902. Scarabs [microform]. The history, manufacture and religious symbolism of the scarabæus in ancient Egypt, Phœnicia, Sardinia, Etruria, etc. Also remarks on the learning, philosophy, arts ethics ... etc., of the ancient Egyptians, Phœnicians, etc. ... by Isaac Myer ... New York, E. W. Dayton; Leipzig, O. Harrassowitz; [etc., etc.] 1894. xxvii, 177 p. 19 cm. "Taken in part from an address delivered ... before the American numismatic and archaeological society ... on March 30th, 1893." Includes bibliographical references and index. Microfilm. New York : New York Public Library, [197-]. 1 microfilm reel ; 35 mm.
1. Scarabs. 2. Symbolism. 3. Egypt - Religion. I. Title.
DT62.S3 M8   *NYPL [Sc Micro R-3541]*

Myers, Jonathan. Aron, Janine. Asbestos and asbestos-related disease in South Africa . Cape Town , 1987. 71 p. : ISBN 0-7992-1126-5
NYPL [Sc D 88-1258]

Myers, Samuel L. Economic issues and black colleges /. Chicago , c1986. 59 p. ; ISBN 0-695-60053-2   *NYPL [Sc D 88-950]*

Myers, Walter Dean, 1937-
Fallen angels / Walter Dean Myers. New York : Scholastic Inc., c1988. 309 p. : map ; 22 cm. Seventeen-year-old Richie Perry, just out of his Harlem high school, enlists in the Army in the summer of 1967 and spends a devastating year on active duty in Vietnam. ISBN 0-590-40942-5 : DDC [Fic] 19
1. Vietnamese Conflict, 1961-1975 - Juvenile fiction. I. Title.
PZ7.M992 Fal 1988   *NYPL [Sc D 88-1136]*

Me, Mop, and the Moondance Kid / by Walter Dean Myers ; illustrated by Rodney Pate. New York : Delacorte Press, 1988. 154 p. : ill. ; 22 cm. Although adoption has taken them out of the New Jersey institution where they grew up, eleven-year-old T.J. and his younger brother Moondance remain involved with their friend Mop's relentless attempts to become adopted herself and to wreak revenge on their baseball rivals the obnoxious Eagles. SCHOMBURG CHILDREN'S COLLECTION. ISBN 0-440-50065-6 DDC [Fic] 19
1. Baseball - Juvenile fiction. 2. Adoption - Juvenile fiction. 3. Afro-American children - Fiction. I. Pate, Rodney, ill. II. Schomburg Children's Collection. III. Title.
PZ7.M992 Me 1988   *NYPL [Sc D 88-1457]*

Scorpions / by Walter Dean Myers. 1st ed. New York : Harper & Row, c1988. 216 p. ; 22 cm. After reluctantly taking on the leadership of the Harlem gang, the Scorpions, Jamal finds that his enemies treat him with respect when he acquires a gun until a tragedy occurs. ISBN 0-06-024364-3 : DDC [Fic] 19
1. Afro-American youth - Juvenile fiction. 2. Harlem (New York, N.Y.) - Juvenile fiction. I. Title.
PZ7.M992 Sc 1988   *NYPL [Sc D 88-1146]*

MYSTERIES, RELIGIOUS - MISCELLANEA.
Versluis, Arthur, 1959- The Egyptian mysteries /. London , New York , 1988. vi, 169 p. : ISBN 1-85063-087-9 (pbk.) DDC 133 19
BF1999 .V43 1988   *NYPL [Sc C 88-195]*

MYSTERY STORIES. see ADVENTURE AND ADVENTURERS.

Mystical and sacred uses of the holy book of Psalms /. Ofori-Amankwah, E. H. [S.L. , 1985] Zaria : printed by Gaskiya Corp.) 48 p. ;
NYPL [Sc B 88-61]

MYSTICS - INDIA - BIOGRAPHY.
Wawili, Rafiki. Sadhu Sundar Singh . London , 1949. 48 p. ;   *NYPL [Sc C 89-111]*

The myth maker. Brown, Frank London. Chicago [1969] 179 p. DDC 813/.5/4
PZ4.B8774 My PS3552.R6855
NYPL [Sc D 88-1118]

MYTHOLOGY, AFRICAN.
Böhm, Gerhard. Khoe-kowap . Wien , 1985. 406 p. ; ISBN 3-85043-036-7
PL8541 .B6 1985   *NYPL [Sc D 89-365]*

Crowley, Daniel J., 1921- African myth and black reality in Bahian Carnaval /. [Los Angeles, Calif.] [1984] 47 p. :
NYPL [Sc F 86-281]

MYTHOLOGY, AFRICAN, IN LITERATURE.
Gates, Henry Louis. The signifying monkey . New York , 1988. xxviii, 290 p. : ISBN 0-19-503463-5 (alk. paper) DDC 810/.9/896073 19
PS153.N5 G28 1988   *NYPL [Sc E 89-181]*

Mzala. Gatsha Buthelezi : chief with a double agenda / Mzala. London ; Atlantic Highlands, N.J. : Zed Books, 1988. ix, 240 p. ; 23 cm. Includes bibliographical references and index. ISBN 0-86232-792-X DDC 968.4/9106/0924 B 19
1. Buthelezi, Gatsha. 2. Statesmen - South Africa - Kwazulu - Biography. 3. Zulus - Biography. 4. Kwazulu, South Africa - Politics and government. I. Title.
DT878.Z9 B856 1988 *NYPL [Sc D 88-1324]*

Mzamane, Mbulelo, 1948- Sepamla, Sydney Sipho, 1932- [Poems. Selections.] Selected poems /. Craighall [South Africa] , 1984. 135 p. ; ISBN 0-86852-037-3 DDC 821 19
PR9369.3.S43 A6 1984
NYPL [Sc D 88-988]

Mzemba, C. (Charles), 1955- Aita twake / Charles Mzemba. Zimbabwe : Mambo Press, 1987. 135 p. ; 19 cm. (Mambo writers series. Shona section . v. 24) ISBN 0-86922-418-2
1. Shona language - Texts. I. Title. II. Series.
NYPL [Sc C 89-119]

N. A. A. C. P. see National Association for the Advancement of Colored People.

N. B. A. see National Basketball Association.

N. C. T. E. see National Council of Teachers of English.

'n Kijkje in de Paramaribo Zoo /. Moonen, Joep. Paramaribo [1987] 275 p. :
QL76.5.S752 P375 1987
NYPL [Sc D 88-690]

Nabuco, Joaquim, 1849-1910. Minha formação / Joaquim Nabuco. Rio de Janeiro : J. Olympio, 1957. 258 p. : ill. ; 23 cm. (Coleção Documentos brasileiros ; 90) First published 1901.
1. Nabuco, Joaquim, 1849-1910. 2. Abolitionists - Brazil - Biography. 3. Statesmen - Brazil - Biography. 4. Brazil - Politics and government - 1822-1889. I. Title.
F2536 .N1425 1957   *NYPL [Sc D 87-1353]*

NABUCO, JOAQUIM, 1849-1910.
Nabuco, Joaquim, 1849-1910. Minha formação /. Rio de Janeiro , 1957. 258 p. :
F2536 .N1425 1957   *NYPL [Sc D 87-1353]*

Nabudere, D. Wadada. Imperialism in East Africa / D. Wadada Nabudere. London : Zed Press ; Westport, Conn. : L. Hill [distributor], 1981- v. ; 23 cm. (Africa. [series]) CONTENTS. - v. 1. Imperialism and exploitation.--v. 2. Imperialism and integration.
1. Africa, East - History. 2. Africa, East - Economic conditions. 3. Africa, East - Politics and government. I. Title. *NYPL [Sc Ser.-L .N238]*

El nacimiento del estado por la guerra de liberación nacional . Pierson-Mathy, Paulette. [Naissance de l'Etat par la guerre de libération nationale. Spanish.] Barcelona : [Paris] : 1983. 178 p. ; ISBN 92-3-301794-X (Unesco)
NYPL [Sc D 88-602]

La nación haitiana /. Bellegarde, Dantès, 1877-1966. Santo Domingo , 1984. 429 p. :
NYPL [Sc E 88-103]

Nación y alienación en la literatura negroafricana. Morán, Fernando, 1926-

[Madrid, 1964] 90 p.
PL8010 .M65 **NYPL [Sc C 88-347]**

Naciones Unidas. see United Nations.

Nadel, Alan, 1947- Invisible criticism : Ralph Ellison and the American canon / by Alan Nadel.1st ed. Iowa City : University of Iowa Press, 1988. xiii, 181 p. ; 24 cm. Includes index. Bibliography: p. [163]-172. ISBN 0-87745-190-7 : DDC 813/.54 19
1. Ellison, Ralph. Invisible man. 2. Canon (Literature). I. Title.
PS3555.L625 I5358 1988
NYPL [Sc E 88-281]

NAFEO Research Institute (U. S.)
Recruitment and retention of Black students in higher education /. Lanham, MD , c1989. viii, 135 p. ; ISBN 0-8191-7292-8 (alk. paper) DDC 378/.1982 19
LC2781 .R43 1989 **NYPL [Sc D 89-590]**

The Status of Blacks in higher education /. Lanham, MD [Washington, D.C.] , c1989. ix, 110 p. ; ISBN 0-8191-7286-3 (alk. paper) DDC 378/.008996073 19
LC2781 .S72 1988 **NYPL [Sc D 89-589]**

Nafziger, E. Wayne. Inequality in Africa : political elites, proletariat, peasants, and the poor / E. Wayne Nafziger. Cambridge [Cambridgeshire] ; New York : Cambridge University Press, c1988. xii, 204 p. : map ; 24 cm. (African society today) Includes index. Bibliography: p. 178-192. ISBN 0-521-26881-8 DDC 339.2/096 19
1. Income distribution - Africa. 2. Poor - Africa. 3. Peasantry - Africa. 4. Elite (Social sciences) - Africa. 5. Africa - Economic conditions. I. Title. II. Series.
HC800.Z9 I5136 1988 **NYPL [Sc E 88-521]**

The Nairobi guide /. MacIntyre, Kate. London , 1986. 154 p., [8] p. of plates : ISBN 0-333-41987-1 **NYPL [Sc D 88-287]**

NAIROBI (KENYA) - DESCRIPTION - GUIDE-BOOKS.
MacIntyre, Kate. The Nairobi guide /. London , 1986. 154 p., [8] p. of plates : ISBN 0-333-41987-1 **NYPL [Sc D 88-287]**

Nairobi. University College. Institute for Development Studies.
Discussion paper.
(no. 34) Rothchild, Donald S. From federalism to neo-federalism in East Africa [microform] /. Nairobi , 1966. 19 leaves ;
NYPL [Sc Micro R-4108 no.30]

(no. 52) Harbeson, John Willis, 1938- The Kenya little general election [microform] . Nairobi , 1967. 23 p. ;
NYPL [Sc Micro R-4108 no. 31]

Nairobi. University. Dept. of History.
Staff seminar paper.
(no. 10) Cohen, David William. Misangós song [microform] . [Nairobi] [1979] 24 p. ;
NYPL [Sc Micro R-4108 no. 38]

(no. 16) Stiles, Daniel. Ethnoarchaeology, a case-study with the Boni of Kenya [microform] /. [Nairobi] [1979] 20 p. ;
NYPL [Sc Micro R-4108 no. 36]

(no. 2) Roark, J. L. American expansionism vs. European colonialism [microform] . [Nairobi] , 1976. 16 leaves ;
NYPL [Sc Micro R-4108 no. 34]

(no. 6) Spencer, Ian R. G. The economic development of Kenya, 1895-1929 [microform] . [Nairobi] [1978] 14 p. ;
NYPL [Sc Micro R-4108 no.33]

(no. 7) Amolo, Milcah. Trade unionism and colonial authority [microform] . [Nairobi] [1978] 16 p. ;
NYPL [Sc Micro R-4108 no. 37]

Nairobi. University. Institute for Development Studies.
Discussion paper.
(no. 152) Halderman, John M. An analysis of continued semi-nomadism of the Kaputiei Maasai group ranches [microform] . [Nairobi] [between 1972 and 1974]. 35 p. ; DDC 307.7/2/0967627
DT433.542 .H34
NYPL [Sc Micro R-4108 no.25]

(no. 169) Godfrey, E. M. Technical and vocational training in Kenya and the harambee institutes of technology [microform]

/. [Nairobi] , 1973. 58 p. ;
NYPL [Sc Micro R-4108 no. 24]

Naissance du roman africain . Ricard, Alain. Paris , Dakar , c1987. 228 p., [4] p. of plates : ISBN 2-7087-0494-X **NYPL [Sc D 89-46]**

Naissance d'une ville au Sénégal . Nicolas, Pierre. Paris , 1989. 193 p., [8] p. of plates ; 2-86537-195-6 **NYPL [Sc F 89-131]**

Naja the snake and Mangus the mongoose. Kirkpatrick, Oliver. Garden City, N.Y. [1970] 40 p. DDC [Fic]
PZ7.K6358 Naj **NYPL [Sc F 88-339]**

NAL Merchant Bank.
Adewunmi, Wole. Twenty five years of merchant banking in Nigeria . Akoka , 1985. xvi, 136 p. ; ISBN 978-226-475-X : DDC 332.66/09669 19
HG1971.N6 A34 1985
NYPL [Sc D 88-1020]

NAL MERCHANT BANK - HISTORY.
Adewunmi, Wole. Twenty five years of merchant banking in Nigeria . Akoka , 1985. xvi, 136 p. ; ISBN 978-226-475-X : DDC 332.66/09669 19
HG1971.N6 A34 1985
NYPL [Sc D 88-1020]

NAMA (AFRICAN PEOPLE) - FOLKLORE.
Böhm, Gerhard. Khoe-kowap . Wien , 1985. 406 p. ; ISBN 3-85043-036-7
PL8541 .B6 1985 **NYPL [Sc D 89-365]**

NAMA LANGUAGE.
Böhm, Gerhard. Khoe-kowap . Wien , 1985. 406 p. ; ISBN 3-85043-036-7
PL8541 .B6 1985 **NYPL [Sc D 89-365]**

Planert, Wilhelm, 1882- Handbuch der Nama-Sprache in Deutsch-Südwestafrika . Berlin , 1905. 104 p. ; **NYPL [Sc F 89-147]**

NAMA LANGUAGE - GLOSSARIES, VOCABULARIES, ETC. - GERMAN.
Planert, Wilhelm, 1882- Handbuch der Nama-Sprache in Deutsch-Südwestafrika /. Berlin , 1905. 104 p. ; **NYPL [Sc F 89-147]**

NAMES, CHRISTIAN. see NAMES, PERSONAL.

NAMES, PERSONAL - IGBIRA.
Ajayi, John Olufemi. Ebira names in Nigeria . Okpella , 1985. 51 p. : ISBN 978-252-800-5 (pbk.) DDC 929.4/089963 19
CS2375.N6 A34 1985 **NYPL [Sc D 88-1256]**

NAMES, PERSONAL - NIGERIA.
Ajayi, John Olufemi. Ebira names in Nigeria . Okpella , 1985. 51 p. : ISBN 978-252-800-5 (pbk.) DDC 929.4/089963 19
CS2375.N6 A34 1985 **NYPL [Sc D 88-1256]**

NAMES, PERSONAL - RELIGIOUS ASPECTS - ISLAM - DICTIONARIES.
Orie, S. L. A dictionary of Muslim names /. Point à Pierre, Trinidad , 1984. 43 p. ;
NYPL [Sc D 88-946]

NAMES, PERSONAL - RUNDI.
Bigangara, Jean-Baptiste. Eléments de linguistique burundaise /. Bujumbura , 1982. 138 p. ; DDC 496/.39 19
PL8611.1 .B54 1982 **NYPL [Sc E 88-403]**

Namibia : a direct United Nations responsibility / [prepared by the United Nations Council for Namibia]. Lusaka : United Nations Institute for Namibia, 1987. 408 p. : map ; 24 cm. Includes index. Bibliography: p. [388]-394. ISBN 998-211-001-2
1. United Nations - Namibia. 2. Namibia - International status. I. United Nations Council on Namibia.
NYPL [Sc E 89-132]

Namibia : the facts. London : IDAF Publications, 1989. 112 p. : ill. ; 27 cm. Includes bibliography and index. ISBN 0-904759-94-6 (pbk) : DDC 968.8/03 19
1. Namibia - Politics and government - 1946-. 2. Namibia - Economic conditions. 3. Namibia - Social conditions. 4. Namibia - Race relations. I. International Defence and Aid Fund.
DT714 **NYPL [Sc F 89-123]**

Namibia . Gayner, Jeffrey B. Washington, D.C. , c1979. 101 p. : DDC 968.8/03 19
DT714 .G38 1979 **NYPL [Sc D 89-565]**

Namibia . Moorehead, Caroline. Oxford [1988] 50 p. : ISBN 0-85598-111-3 :
NYPL [Sc F 89-120]

Namibia -- a contract to kill . Campaign Against the Namibian Uranium Contracts (Group) London , 1986. 80 p. : ISBN 0-947905-02-2
NYPL [Sc D 88-795]

NAMIBIA - COLONIAL INFLUENCE - ADDRESSES, ESSAYS, LECTURES.
Perspectives of independent development in Southern Africa . Berlin , 1980. xiv, 183 p. : DDC 338.9688 19
HC910 .P47 **NYPL [JLE 82-36]**

NAMIBIA - DESCRIPTION AND TRAVEL.
Sauerbier, Udo. Auf Pad in Südwest . [Mainz] c1982. 224 p. : **NYPL [Sc D 88-619]**

NAMIBIA - DESCRIPTION AND TRAVEL - 1981- - GUIDE-BOOKS.
Fries, Marianne. Südafrika, SWA/Namibia . Frankfurt [am Main] , 1987. 550 p. : 3-87936-153-3 **NYPL [Sc B 88-18]**

NAMIBIA - DESCRIPTION AND TRAVEL - ADDRESSES, ESSAYS, LECTURES.
Taschenbuch für Südwestafrika, 1909 /. Berlin , 1909. xviii, 495, 60 p., [4] fold. leaves of plates : **NYPL [Sc B 89-24]**

NAMIBIA - ECONOMIC CONDITIONS.
Namibia . London , 1989. 112 p. : ISBN 0-904759-94-6 (pbk) : DDC 968.8/03 19
DT714 **NYPL [Sc F 89-123]**

Namibia the economy /. Windhoek, SWA/Namibia , 1987. 40 p. :
NYPL [Sc F 88-254]

Working under South African occupation . London , 1987. 56 p. ; ISBN 0-904759-73-3 (pbk.) : DDC 968 s 331.6/9/9688 19
DT746 .F3 no. 14 HD8808
NYPL [Sc D 89-525]

NAMIBIA - ECONOMIC CONDITIONS - ADDRESSES, ESSAYS, LECTURES.
Perspectives of independent development in Southern Africa . Berlin , 1980. xiv, 183 p. : DDC 338.9688 19
HC910 .P47 **NYPL [JLE 82-36]**

NAMIBIA - FOREIGN RELATIONS - UNITED STATES.
Pomeroy, William J., 1916- Apartheid, imperialism, and African freedom /. New York , 1986. ix, 259 p. : ISBN 0-7178-0640-5 : DDC 305.8/00968 19
E183.8.S6 P65 1986 **NYPL [Sc D 88-1147]**

Namibia - Government. see Namibia - Politics and government.

NAMIBIA - HISTORY - 1884-1915.
Voeltz, Richard Andrew. German colonialism and the South West Africa Company, 1884-1914 /. Athens, Ohio , 1988. x, 133 p. : ISBN 0-89680-146-2 (pbk.) : DDC 325/.343/09688 19
JV2029.A5 S689 1988 **NYPL [JLD 88-3416]**

NAMIBIA - INTERNATIONAL STATUS.
Namibia . Lusaka , 1987. 408 p. : ISBN 998-211-001-2 **NYPL [Sc E 89-132]**

Namibia News Bureau. Namibia the economy /. Windhoek, SWA/Namibia , 1987. 40 p. :
NYPL [Sc F 88-254]

NAMIBIA - POLITICS AND GOVERNMENT - 20TH CENTURY.
Resistance and ideology in settler societies /. Johannesburg, Athens, Ohio , 1986. viii, 222 p. ; ISBN 0-86975-304-5
NYPL [Sc D 88-1093]

NAMIBIA - POLITICS AND GOVERNMENT - 1946-
Gayner, Jeffrey B. Namibia . Washington, D.C. , c1979. 101 p. : DDC 968.8/03 19
DT714 .G38 1979 **NYPL [Sc D 89-565]**

Namibia . London , 1989. 112 p. : ISBN 0-904759-94-6 (pbk) : DDC 968.8/03 19
DT714 **NYPL [Sc F 89-123]**

NAMIBIA - RACE RELATIONS.
Namibia . London , 1989. 112 p. : ISBN 0-904759-94-6 (pbk) : DDC 968.8/03 19
DT714 **NYPL [Sc F 89-123]**

NAMIBIA - SOCIAL CONDITIONS.
Namibia . London , 1989. 112 p. : ISBN 0-904759-94-6 (pbk) : DDC 968.8/03 19
DT714 **NYPL [Sc F 89-123]**

Namibia the economy / [issued by Namibia News Bureau]. Windhoek, SWA/Namibia : The Information Service, Dept. of Governmental

Affairs, 1987. 40 p. : col. ill. ; 30 cm.
1. Namibia - Economic conditions. I. Namibia News Bureau.   **NYPL [Sc F 88-254]**

Namibia today. SWA Namibia today /.
Windhoek , 1988. 128 p. :
NYPL [Sc D 88-1359]

Namôa koni. Cuttington University College.
Africana Museum. Rock of the ancestors .
Suakoko, Liberia, c1977. 102 p. : DDC
730/.09666/2074096662 19
N7399.L4 C87 1977   **NYPL [Sc F 89-27]**

**Nancy Reagan's red dress ; Previewing UK's
King Charles ; Israel's indigenous black
minority : & other poems of Pan-Afrikan
expression /.** El Mahmud-Okereke, N. O. E.
(Noel Olufemi Enuma), 1948- London , 1988,
c1987. xxi, 179 p. : ISBN 978-242-304-1 (pbk) :
DDC 821 19   **NYPL [Sc C 88-182]**

Los ñáñigos . Sosa, Enrique. Ciudad de La
Habana, Cuba , c1982. 464 p., [44] p. of
plates : DDC 366/.097291 19
HS221.Z6 S66 1982   **NYPL [JLC 84-260]**

Nanterre, France. Université de Paris X. see
Université de Paris X: Nanterre.

Napjus, Alice James. Freddie found a frog.
Illustrated by George Ford. New York, Van
Nostrand Reinhold [1969] [29] p. col. illus. 19
cm. Freddie wants to find a home for the frog he
caught, but they're hard to come by in the city.
SCHOMBURG CHILDREN'S COLLECTION. DDC
[Fic]
*1. Frogs - Juvenile fiction. 2. Afro-American children -
Juvenile fiction. I. Ford, George Cephas, illus. II.
Schomburg Children's Collection. III. Title.*
PZ7.N148 Fr   **NYPL [Sc C 89-27]**

Napolo poems /. Chimombo, Steve Bernard
Miles. Zomba, Malawi , 1987. ix, 55 p. ;
NYPL [Sc D 88-788]

Naranjit, Darryl. The righteous state / Darryl
Naranjit. [Chaguanas? Trinidad] : D. Naranjit,
c1987. ii, 225 p. ; 22 cm. Bibliography: p. 220-225.
DDC 172 19
1. State, The - Moral and ethical aspects. I. Title.
JA79 .N34 1987   **NYPL [Sc D 89-518]**

Naranjo, Carmen. Ondina / Carmen Naranjo. La
Habana, Cuba : Casa de las Américas, c1988.
135 p. ; 19 cm. (Colección La Honda) Short stories.
I. Title.
PQ7489.2.N3 O5x 1988   **NYPL [Sc C 89-84]**

Narayan-Parker, Deepa. Women's interest and
involvement in income generating activities :
implications for extension services / by Deepa
Narayan-Parker. Gaborone, Botswana : National
Institute for [i.e. of] Development Research and
Documentation, University of Botswana, [1983]
vi, 143, 3 p. ; 30 cm. (Working paper / National
Institute of Development Research & Documentation .
no. 44) "December 1983." DDC 331.4/09676/2 19
*1. Rural women - Employment - Kenya. 2. Rural
women - Kenya - Attitudes. 3. Income - Kenya -
Statistics. 4. Budgets, Personal - Kenya - Statistics. 5.
Economic surveys - Kenya. 6. Kenya - Rural
conditions. I. Series: Working paper (National Institute
of Development Research & Documentation
(Botswana)) no. 44. II. Title.*
HD6210.5 .N37 1983   **NYPL [Sc F 88-312]**

**NARCOTICS DEALERS - NIGERIA -
FICTION.**
Serrano, Jumoke. The last Don out /. Ibadan,
Nigeria, 1986. 106 p. ; ISBN 978-14-1062-0
NYPL [Sc C 88-341]

Narni of the desert. Westwood, Gwen. [Chicago,
c1967] 93 p. DDC [Fic]
PZ7.W5275 Nar   **NYPL [Sc D 88-1424]**

Narratives of colored Americans. New York :
William Wood & Co., 1877. 276 p. ; 20 cm.
Compiled by A. Mott and M.S. Wood. "Printed by
order of the trustees of the residuary estate of Lindley
Murray." M.S. Wood's autographed presentation copy
to Arnold Wood.
*1. Afro-Americans - Biography. I. Mott, A. (Abigail
Field), 1766-1851. II. Wood, M. S. (Mary S.),
1805-1894.*   **NYPL [Sc Rare C 88-4]**

Narratives of colored Americans. New York :
Bowne & Co., 1882. 276 p. ; 20 cm. Compiled by
A. Mott and M.S. Wood. "Printed by order of the
trustees of the residuary estate of Lindley Murray."
*1. Afro-Americans - Biography. I. Mott, A. (Abigail
Field), 1766-1851. II. Wood, M. S. (Mary S.),
1805-1894.*   **NYPL [Sc Rare C 88-26]**

Nascimento, Maria Beatriz. Lopes, Helena
Theodoro. Negro e cultura no Brasil /. Rio de
Janeiro , 1987. 136 p. ; ISBN 85-85108-02-9
DDC 981/.00496 19
F2659.N4 L67 1987   **NYPL [Sc D 88-1291]**

Naser, Amín E. (Amín Egeraige), 1936- Benny
Moré : perfil libre / Amín E. Naser. Ciudad de
La Habana : Unión de Escritores y Artistas de
Cuba, c1985. 231 p., [61] p. of plates : ill. ; 19
cm. Bibliography: p. 229. Discography: p. 199-224.
DDC 784.5/0092/4 B 19
*1. Moré, Beny, 1919-1963. 2. Singers - Cuba -
Biography. I. Title.*
ML420.M596 N3 1985   **NYPL [Sc C 87-302]**

Nash, Gary B. Forging freedom : the formation of
Philadelphia's Black community, 1720-1840 /
Gary B. Nash. Cambridge, Mass. : Harvard
University Press, c1988. xii, 354 p. : ill., maps ;
24 cm. Includes bibliographical references and index.
ISBN 0-674-30934-0 (alk. paper) DDC
974.8/1100496073 19
*1. Afro-Americans - Pennsylvania - Philadelphia -
History. 2. Philadelphia (Pa.) - History. 3. Philadelphia
(Pa.) - Race relations. I. Title.*
F158.9.N4 N37 1988   **NYPL [Sc E 88-594]**

Nasisse, Andy. Baking in the sun . Lafayette ,
c1987. 146 p. : ISBN 0-295-96606-8
NYPL [Sc F 88-197]

Naṣr, Aḥmad 'Abd al-Raḥim. Folklore and
National Development Symposium (1981 :
Khartoum, Sudan) Folklore and development in
the Sudan . Khartoum , 1985. 272 p. :
GR355.8 .F65 1981   **NYPL [Sc E 88-333]**

**NASSAU, BAHAMAS - DESCRIPTION -
GUIDE-BOOKS.**
Dodge, Steve. The compleat guide to Nassau /.
Decatur, Ill. , c1987. 116 p. : ISBN
0-932265-04-9 (pbk.) :
NYPL [Sc D 88-685]

**NASSAU (BAHAMAS) - DESCRIPTION -
TOURS.**
Dodge, Steve. The compleat guide to Nassau /.
Decatur, Ill. , c1987. 116 p. : ISBN
0-932265-04-9 (pbk.) :
NYPL [Sc D 88-685]

NASSAU (BAHAMAS) - POETRY.
Gould, Cora Smith. Dream land on the Isle of
Nassau in the Bahamas /. New York City ,
1938. 38 p. :   **NYPL [Sc D 88-1297]**

Nat Turner /. Bisson, Terry. New York , c1988.
111 p. ; ISBN 1-555-46613-3 DDC
975.5/5503/0924 B 92 19
F232.S7 T873 1988   **NYPL [Sc E 88-454]**

Natal. Pretoria : South African Tourist Corp.,
1955. [40] p. : ill. (some col.) ; 19 cm. Cover
title.
1. Natal (South Africa) - Description and travel.
NYPL [Sc C 88-304]

**NATAL (SOUTH AFRICA) - DESCRIPTION
AND TRAVEL.**
Natal. Pretoria , 1955. [40] p. :
NYPL [Sc C 88-304]

**NATAL (SOUTH AFRICA) - POLITICS AND
GOVERNMENT - 1843-1893.**
Kline, Benjamin. Genesis of apartheid .
Lanham, MD , c1988. xxii, 283 p. ; ISBN
0-8191-6494-1 (alk. paper) DDC 968.4/04 19
DT872 .K56 1988   **NYPL [JLD 88-4097]**

Nathan Afrique.
Echos d'Afrique . [Paris] , c1984. 159 p. ;
ISBN 2-09-168451-1   **NYPL [Sc D 88-907]**

Natif-natal=. Saint-Natus, Clotaire.
Port-au-Prince, Haiti , 1987. 48 p. :
NYPL [Sc C 89-54]

Nation of Islam. see Black Muslims.

**National Advisory Commission on Civil
Disorders.** United States. Kerner Commission.
The Kerner report . New York, N.Y. , 1988.
xxvi, 513 p. ; ISBN 0-679-72078-2
NYPL [Sc D 89-604]

**National and class conflict in the Horn of Africa
/.** Markakis, John. Cambridge , New York ,
1987. xvii, 314 p. : ISBN 0-521-33362-8 DDC
960/.3 19
DT367.75 .M37 1987   **NYPL [JFE 88-364]**

**NATIONAL ARTS FESTIVAL (1987 :
GRAHAMSTOWN, SOUTH AFRICA)**
Davies, William J. Fest-quest 87, .

Grahamstown, South Africa , 1988. iv, 161 p. :
ISBN 0-86810-165-6   **NYPL [Sc F 88-267]**

**National Association for Equal Opportunity in
Higher Education (U. S.)**
Black colleges and public policy /. Chicago ,
c1986. 99 p. : ISBN 0-695-60050-8
NYPL [Sc D 88-947]

Blacks on white campuses, whites on black
campuses /. Chicago , c1986. 177 p. ; ISBN
0-695-60052-4   **NYPL [Sc D 88-949]**

Economic issues and black colleges /. Chicago ,
c1986. 59 p. ; ISBN 0-695-60053-2
NYPL [Sc D 88-950]

Inside black colleges and universities /.
Chicago , c1986. 153 p. : ISBN 0-695-60051-6
NYPL [Sc D 88-951]

Recruitment and retention of Black students in
higher education /. Lanham, MD , c1989. viii,
135 p. : ISBN 0-8191-7292-8 (alk. paper) DDC
378/.1982 19
LC2781 .R43 1989   **NYPL [Sc D 89-590]**

**National Association for the Advancement of
Colored People. Boston Branch.** Hayden,
Robert C. Faith, culture, and leadership .
[Boston, MA , c1983] iv, 56 p. : DDC
280/.08996073074461 19
BR560.B73 H39 1983   **NYPL [Sc F 88-269]**

**NATIONAL ASSOCIATION FOR THE
ADVANCEMENT OF COLORED
PEOPLE - HISTORY.**
Watson, Denton L. Reclaiming a heritage .
New York, N.Y. , c1977. 63 p. :
NYPL [Sc F 89-78]

**NATIONAL ASSOCIATION OF COLORED
WOMEN'S CLUBS (U. S.) - HISTORY.**
Wesley, Charles H. (Charles Harris), 1891- The
history of the National Association of Colored
Women's Clubs . Washington, D.C. (5808 16th
St., N.W., Washington) , 1984. viii, 562 p. :
DDC 369/.1 19
E185.86.N36 W47 1984

**National Association of Negro Business and
Professional Women's Club. New York Club.**
Annual founder's day : Sojourner Truth award
luncheon, Sunday, April 23rd, 1961, 1:30 P M.,
Grand Ballroom, Waldorf Astoria Hotel, 50th
St. & Park Ave., NYC / sponsored by the New
York Club of the National Association of
Negro Business and Professional Women's
Clubs. [New York : The Club, 1961] [68] p. :
ports. ; 28 cm. Cover title.
*1. Afro-American women - New York (N.Y.) -
Societies and clubs. I. Title.*   **NYPL [Sc F 87-379]**

National atlas of Jamaica. Jamaica. Town
Planning Dept. Kingston, 1971. viii, 79 p.
NYPL [Map Div 73-738]

**National Baptist Convention of the United
States of America. Sunday School Publishing
Board.** Gospel pearls . Nashville, Tenn. ,
c1921. [152] p. :   **NYPL [Sc F 86-222]**

NATIONAL BASKETBALL ASSOCIATION.
Ryan, Bob. Forty-eight minutes . New York ,
London , c1987. x, 356 p. ; ISBN 0-02-597770-9
DDC 796.32/364/0973 19
GV885.515.N37 R9 1988
NYPL [JFD 87-10809]

**NATIONAL BASKETBALL ASSOCIATION -
JUVENILE LITERATURE.**
Martin, Gene L. Michael Jordan, gentleman
superstar /. Greensboro, N.C. , c1987. 69 p. :
ISBN 0-936389-02-8 : DDC 796.32/3/0924 B
19
GV884.J67 M37 1987   **NYPL [Sc E 88-320]**

**National Center of Afro-American Artists.
Museum.** Gaither, Edmund B. Massachusetts
masters . Boston [1988] 48 p. :
NYPL [Sc F 89-159]

NATIONAL CHARACTERISTICS.
Intelligence and national achievement /.
Washington, D.C. , c1983. 176 p. : ISBN
0-941694-14-3 DDC 153.9 19
BF433.S63 I57 1983   **NYPL [Sc E 89-236]**

**NATIONAL CHARACTERISTICS IN
LITERATURE.**
Dash, J. Michael. Haiti and the United States .
Basingstoke, Hampshire , 1988. xv, 152 p. ; ;
ISBN 0-333-45491-X
NYPL [Sc D 88-1358]

National Committee on Racism in Children's Books (Great Britain) Their contribution ignored. London , c1988. 16 p. :
NYPL [Sc F 89-165]

National Conference of the Urban Poor (1984 : University of Benin) The Urban poor in Nigeria /. Ibadan, Nigeria , 1987. xvi, 413 p. :
ISBN 978-16-7489-4 *NYPL [Sc D 88-779]*

National Conference on African American/Jewish American Relations (1983 : Savannah State College) Blacks and Jews : a new dialogue : selected papers from the proceedings of the National Conference on African American/Jewish American Relations, Savannah State College, Savannah, Georgia / edited by Ja A. Jahannes. [Savannah, Ga.] : Savannah State College Press, [1983] iii, 58 p. ; 23 cm. Includes bibliographical references.
1. Afro-Americans - Relations with Jews - Congresses. 2. Jews - United States - Congresses. 3. United States - Ethnic relations - Congresses. I. Jahannes, Ja A. II. Savannah State College (Ga.). III. Title.
NYPL [Sc D 88-335]

National Conference on Blacks in Higher Education.
Blacks on white campuses, whites on black campuses /. Chicago , c1986. 177 p. ; ISBN 0-695-60052-4 *NYPL [Sc D 88-949]*

Economic issues and black colleges /. Chicago , c1986. 59 p. ; ISBN 0-695-60053-2
NYPL [Sc D 88-950]

National Conference on Blacks in Higher Education (8th ; 1983 : Washington, DC)
Inside black colleges and universities /. Chicago , c1986. 153 p. ; ISBN 0-695-60051-6
NYPL [Sc D 88-951]

National Conference on Blacks in Higher Education (8th : 1983 : Washington, D.C.)
Black colleges and public policy /. Chicago , c1986. 99 p. : ISBN 0-695-60050-8
NYPL [Sc D 88-947]

NATIONAL CONSCIOUSNESS. see NATIONALISM.

National Council of Teachers of English. Rollins, Charlemae Hill. We build together. [Champaign, Ill. , 1967] xxviii, 71 p. ; DDC 016.818
Z1361.N39 R77 1967 *NYPL [Sc D 89-387]*

National Cultural Foundation (Barbados) Broodhagen, Karl R. The National Cultural Foundation presents Tribute, an exhibition of the sculpture of Karl Broodhagen. [Barbados] [1985?] 16 p. :
MLCM 87/08440 (N) *NYPL [Sc D 88-570]*

Emancipation I . Barbados , c1986. vii, 108 p., [1] leaf of plates : DDC 306/.362/0972981 19
HT1119.B35 E46 1986 *NYPL [Sc D 88-248]*

The National Cultural Foundation presents Tribute, an exhibition of the sculpture of Karl Broodhagen . Broodhagen, Karl R. [Barbados] [1985?] 16 p. :
MLCM 87/08440 (N) *NYPL [Sc D 88-570]*

NATIONAL DANCES. see FOLK DANCING.

NATIONAL FRONT (GREAT BRITAIN) Widgery, David. Beating time /. London , 1986. 126 p. : ISBN 0-7011-2985-9
NYPL [JMD 88-112]

National Geographic Society (U. S.). Special Publications Division. Primitive worlds: people lost in time. [Washington, 1973] 211 p.
ISBN 0-87044-127-2
GN400 .P66 *NYPL [Sc 301.2-P]*

National health plan, 1965-1975 /. Sierra Leone. Ministry of Health. Freetown , 1965. 167 p. :
NYPL [Sc E 88-104]

National History and Arts Council. Independence 10 . Georgetown, Guyana [introd. 1976] 222 p. ; DDC 810
PR9320.5 .I5 *NYPL [Sc F 89-101]*

NATIONAL IMAGES. see NATIONAL CHARACTERISTICS.

National Institute for Policy and Strategic Studies (Nigeria). Research Dept. Nigerian defence and security . Bukuru, Plateau State , 1987. xii, 208 p. ; ISBN 978-19-8019-2
NYPL [Sc D 88-1377]

National Institute of Development Research & Documentation (Botswana) Women in development . Gaborone , 1984. 49, 4 p. :
NYPL [Sc F 88-116]

National Institute on Aging. The Black American elderly . New York , c1988. xvi, 308 p. ; ISBN 0-8261-5810-2 DDC 362.1/9897/00973 19
RA448.5.N4 B56 1988 *NYPL [JLE 88-5391]*

National intelligencer. The African slave trade . Philadelphia , 1863. 24 p. :
NYPL [Sc Rare F 89-5]

NATIONAL LIBERATION MOVEMENT - CAPE VERDE - COLLECTED WORKS.
Cabral, Amílcar, 1921-1973. Unité et lutte /. Paris , 1980. 329 p. ; ISBN 2-7071-1171-6
NYPL [Sc C 88-125]

NATIONAL LIBERATION MOVEMENT - GUINEA-BISSAU - COLLECTED WORKS.
Cabral, Amílcar, 1921-1973. Unité et lutte /. Paris , 1980. 329 p. ; ISBN 2-7071-1171-6
NYPL [Sc C 88-125]

NATIONAL LIBERATION MOVEMENTS - AFRICA, NORTHEAST - HISTORY - 20TH CENTURY.
Markakis, John. National and class conflict in the Horn of Africa /. Cambridge , New York , 1987. xvii, 314 p. : ISBN 0-521-33362-8 DDC 960/.3 19
DT367.75 .M37 1987 *NYPL [JFE 88-364]*

NATIONAL LIBERATION MOVEMENTS - AFRICA, NORTHEASTERN - CONGRESSES.
Décolonisation de l'Afrique. Spanish. La Descolonización de Africa : Africa austral y el Cuerno de Africa . Barcelona , Paris , 1983. 197 p. ; ISBN 92-3-301834-2 (Unesco)
NYPL [Sc D 88-590]

NATIONAL LIBERATION MOVEMENTS - AFRICA, SOUTHERN - CONGRESSES.
Décolonisation de l'Afrique. Spanish. La Descolonización de Africa : Africa austral y el Cuerno de Africa . Barcelona , Paris , 1983. 197 p. ; ISBN 92-3-301834-2 (Unesco)
NYPL [Sc D 88-590]

NATIONAL LIBERATION MOVEMENTS - ALGERIA.
Suliman, Hassan Sayed. The nationalist movements in the Maghrib . Uppsala , 1987. 87 p. ; ISBN 91-7106-266-1 *NYPL [Sc E 88-202]*

NATIONAL LIBERATION MOVEMENTS - ANGOLA.
Savimbi, Jonas Malheiro. Por um futuro melhor /. Lisboa , 1986. 192 p. : DDC 967/.304 19
DT611.8 .S28 1986 *NYPL [Sc D 88-771]*

NATIONAL LIBERATION MOVEMENTS - ETHIOPIA.
Henze, Paul B., 1924- Rebels and separatists in Ethiopia . Santa Monica, CA , 1985. xv, 98 p. ; ISBN 0-8330-0696-7 DDC 963/.07 19
DT387.95 .H46 1986 *NYPL [JFE 86-5101]*

NATIONAL LIBERATION MOVEMENTS - MOROCCO.
Suliman, Hassan Sayed. The nationalist movements in the Maghrib . Uppsala , 1987. 87 p. ; ISBN 91-7106-266-1 *NYPL [Sc E 88-202]*

NATIONAL LIBERATION MOVEMENTS - NAMIBIA.
Menschenrechte im Konflikt um Südwestafrika/Namibia . Frankfurt a.M. , 1985. 56 p. :
NYPL [Sc F 88-162]

NATIONAL LIBERATION MOVEMENTS - SOUTH AFRICA.
Cukierman, Maurice. Afrique du Sud . Paris , c1987. 279 p. : ISBN 2-209-05983-6
NYPL [Sc D 88-756]

Davies, Robert H. The struggle for South Africa . London , Atlantic Highlands, N.J. , 1988. 2 v. : ISBN 0-86232-760-1 (v. 1) DDC 322/.0968 19
JQ1931 .D38 1988 *NYPL [Sc D 88-1369]*

Südafrika - Widerstand und Befreiungskampf . Köln , 1987, c1986. 286 p. : ISBN 3-7609-1023-8
NYPL [Sc C 88-190]

NATIONAL LIBERATION MOVEMENTS - SOUTH AFRICA - POETRY.
Jibrin, Sani A. Africa must be free /. Kano State, Nigeria , 1987. x, 48 p. :
NYPL [Sc C 88-302]

NATIONAL LIBERATION MOVEMENTS - TUNISIA.
Suliman, Hassan Sayed. The nationalist movements in the Maghrib . Uppsala , 1987. 87 p. ; ISBN 91-7106-266-1 *NYPL [Sc E 88-202]*

NATIONAL MILITARY PARKS. see NATIONAL PARKS AND RESERVES.

National Museum of African Art (U. S.) The Art of West African kingdoms /. Washington, D.C. , 1987. 48 p., [4] folded leaves : ISBN 0-87474-611-6 DDC 709/.01/10966 19
N7398 .A75 1987 *NYPL [Sc F 89-26]*

Geary, Christraud M. Images from Bamum . Washington, D.C. , 1988. 151 p. : ISBN 0-87474-455-5 (pbk. : alk. paper) DDC 967/.1102/0880621 19
DT574 .G43 1988 *NYPL [Sc F 89-55]*

Gilfoy, Peggy Stoltz. Patterns of life . Washington, D.C. , c1987. 95 p. : ISBN 0-87474-475-X (alk. paper) : DDC 746.1/4/088042 19
NK8989 .G55 1987 *NYPL [Sc F 88-166]*

National Museum of Colonial History (Nigeria) Obiozor, May. Guide to National Museum of Colonial History, Aba /. [Lagos, Nigeria , 1985] 32 p. : *NYPL [Sc F 88-259]*

National Opera Ebony. Opera Ebony's 10th anniversary souvenir journal. Philadelphia, Pa. : Opera Ebony, [1984] 84 p. : chiefly ill., facsims., ports. ; 28 cm.
1. Opera Ebony - Anniversaries, etc. I. Title. II. Title: Opera Ebony's tenth anniversary souvenir journal.
NYPL [Sc F 87-425]

NATIONAL PARKS AND RESERVES - GABON.
Goulphin, Fred. Les Veillées de chase d'Henri Guizard /. [Paris] , 1987. 235 p. ; ISBN 2-08-065054-8 *NYPL [Sc D 88-28]*

NATIONAL PARKS AND RESERVES - MALAWI.
Carter, Judy. Malaŵi . London , 1987. 176 p. : ISBN 0-333-43987-2 (cased) : DDC 916.897/044 19
DT858.2 *NYPL [Sc F 88-183]*

NATIONAL PARKS AND RESERVES - ZIMBABWE.
Rushworth, David. The wonders of Hwange /. Gweru , Zimbabwe , 1986. 35 p. : ISBN 0-86922-389-5 *NYPL [Sc F 89-43]*

NATIONAL PSYCHOLOGY. see NATIONAL CHARACTERISTICS.

National Puerto Rican Task Force on Educational Policy. Valle, Manuel del. Law and bilingual education . New York , 1978. i, 206 p. ; *NYPL [Sc F 88-357]*

The National question in South Africa / edited by Maria van Diepen. London ; Atlantic Highlands, N.J. : Zed Books, 1988. 154 p. ; 23 cm. Includes bibliographical references and index. ISBN 0-86232-794-6 DDC 320.5/4/0968 19
1. Apartheid - South Africa. 2. Nationalism - South Africa. 3. Black nationalism - South Africa. I. Diepen, Maria van.
DT763 .N35 1988 *NYPL [JLD 88-4552]*

National Research Council. Committee on AIDS Research and the Behavioral, Social, and Statistical Sciences. AIDS . Washington, DC , 1989. xiii, 589 p. : ISBN 0-309-03976-2; 0-309-03976-2 (pbk.) *NYPL [Sc D 89-342]*

NATIONAL RESOURCES. see NATURAL RESOURCES.

National Teacher-Training College (Lesotho) NTTC cookery book. Rev. ed. Maseru : NTTC, 1976. 100 p. : ill. ; 17 x 24 cm. Cover title.
1. Cookery - Lesotho. I. Title.
NYPL [Sc B 89-29]

NATIONALISM - AFRICA.
Oshisanya, Samuel Adekoya. The ultimate end of Pan-Africanism /. [Lagos], Nigeria , 1983] 105 p. : *NYPL [Sc E 86-472]*

NATIONALISM - AFRICA - CONGRESSES.
Affirmation de l'identité culturelle et la formation de la conscience nationale dans l'Afrique contemporaine. Spanish. La Afirmación de la identidad cultural y la formación de la coniencia nacional en el África contemporánea /. Barcelona , Paris , 1983. 220 p. ; ISBN 84-85800-57-5 *NYPL [Sc D 88-597]*

NATIONALISM - AFRICA - JUVENILE LITERATURE.
Hollings, Jill. African nationalism. New York [1972, c1971] 128 p.   DDC 320.5/4/096
DT31 .H577 1972   *NYPL [Sc D 88-1496]*

NATIONALISM - AFRICA, NORTHEAST - HISTORY - 20TH CENTURY.
Markakis, John. National and class conflict in the Horn of Africa /. Cambridge , New York , 1987. xvii, 314 p. :   ISBN 0-521-33362-8 DDC 960/.3 19
DT367.75 .M37 1987   *NYPL [JFE 88-364]*

NATIONALISM - AFRICA, SOUTHERN.
Brown, Alex. Southern Africa. Ottawa [1973] 43 p.
DT746 .B76   *NYPL [JLD 75-1128]*

NATIONALISM AND NATIONALITY. see NATIONALISM.

NATIONALISM - CAMEROON.
Kengne Pokam, E (Emmanuel), 1941- Les Églises chrétiennes face à la montée du nationalisme camerounais /. Paris [1987] 202 p. ;   ISBN 2-85802-823-0 *NYPL [Sc D 88-437]*

NATIONALISM - CARIBBEAN AREA.
Moore, Richard B. (Richard Benjamin) Richard B. Moore, Caribbean militant in Harlem . Bloomington , London , 1988. ix, 324 p. :   ISBN 0-253-31299-0 DDC 970.004/96 19
F2183 .M66 1988   *NYPL [Sc E 89-148]*

NATIONALISM - CHAD.
Buijtenhuijs, Robert. Le Frolinat et les guerres civiles du Tchad (1977-1984) . Paris, France , c1987. 479 p. :   ISBN 2-86537-196-4
NYPL [Sc E 88-426]

NATIONALISM - GHANA.
Agyeman, Dominic Kofi. Ideological education and nationalism in Ghana under Nkrumah and Busia /. Accra , 1988. 81 p. ;   ISBN 996-430-120-0 *NYPL [Sc D 89-582]*

NATIONALISM - NIGERIA.
Onyia, Obi J. I. G. My role in nationalism /. Asaba , 1986. 73 p. :   *NYPL [Sc E 89-115]*

NATIONALISM - RHODESIA, SOUTHERN.
Elliott, Hugh P. Darkness and dawn in Zimbabwe /. London , 1978. [6], 49 p. ;   ISBN 0-901269-37-9 :
DT962.42 .E38   *NYPL [JFD 80-115]*

NATIONALISM - SOUTH AFRICA.
The National question in South Africa /. London , Atlantic Highlands, N.J. , 1988. 154 p. ;   ISBN 0-86232-794-6 DDC 320.5/4/0968 19
DT763 .N35 1988   *NYPL [JLD 88-4552]*
Time for Azania [microform] [Toronto] , 1976. 89 p. ;   DDC 320.5/4/0968
DT770 .T55   *NYPL [Sc Micro R-4849 no.1]*

NATIONALISM - SUDAN - HISTORY - 20TH CENTURY.
Abdin, Hasan. Early Sudanese nationalism, 1919-1925 /. [Khartoum?] [1985?] iv, 167 p. :   DDC 962.4/03 19
DT156.7 .A23 1985   *NYPL [Sc E 88-335]*

NATIONALISM - TRINIDAD - HISTORY.
Magid, Alvin, 1937- Urban nationalism . Gainesville , 1988. x, 294 p. :   ISBN 0-8130-0853-0 DDC 972.98/3 19
F2119 .M34 1988   *NYPL [HRG 88-1040]*

The nationalist movements in the Maghrib.
Suliman, Hassan Sayed. Uppsala , 1987. 87 p. ;   ISBN 91-7106-266-1 *NYPL [Sc E 88-202]*

NATIONALISTS - NIGERIA - BIOGRAPHY.
Onyia, Obi J. I. G. My role in nationalism /. Asaba , 1986. 73 p. :   *NYPL [Sc E 89-115]*

NATIONALISTS - SOMALIA - BIOGRAPHY.
Jaamac Cumar Ciise. Taariikhdii daraawiishta iyo Sayid Maxamed Cabdulle Xasan, 1895-1921 /. Muqdisho , 1976. vii, 320 p., [2] leaves of plates :
DT404.3.M38 C55   *NYPL [Sc E 87-435]*

NATIONS, SMALL. see STATES, SMALL.

Nations Unies. see United Nations.

Native Land Act, 1913. Amendment Bill, 1927 [microform]. Representation of Natives in Parliament Bill. Union Native Council Bill. Coloured Persons Rights Bill, 1927. South Africa. [Laws, etc.] [S.I. [1927?] 47 p. :
NYPL [Sc Micro F-10937]

Native laughter /. Lazare, Alick. [Roseau ,

c1985] 167 p. ;
MLCS 87/7802 (P)   *NYPL [Sc C 88-329]*

Natural dyes of Zambia /. Errington, Leah. [Zambia? , between 1986 and 1988] (Ndola, Zambia : Mission Press) 35 p. :
NYPL [Sc B 89-23]

NATURAL HISTORY - ALASKA.
Healy, M. A. (Michael A.) Report of the cruise of the revenue marine steamer Corwin in the Arctic Ocean in the year 1884 /. Washington , 1889. 128 p., [39] leaves of plates :
NYPL [Sc Rare F 88-62]

NATURAL HISTORY - JUVENILE LITERATURE.
Howell, Ruth Rea. A crack in the pavement. New York, 1970. [48] p.   DDC 500.9
PZ10.H7958 Cr   *NYPL [Sc E 88-154]*

NATURAL HISTORY - SOUTH AFRICA.
Paterson, William, 1755-1810. Paterson's Cape travels, 1777 to 1779 /. Johannesburg, [South Africa] , c1980. 202 p. :   ISBN 0-909079-12-9 (standard edition)   *NYPL [Sc F 85-110]*

NATURAL HISTORY - TANZANIA.
Barns, Thomas Alexander, 1880- Across the great craterland to the Congo . London , 1923. 271, [1] p., [64] leaves of plates, 2 folded leaves :   *NYPL [Sc E 88-252]*

NATURAL HISTORY - ZAIRE.
Barns, Thomas Alexander, 1880- Across the great craterland to the Congo . London , 1923. 271, [1] p., [64] leaves of plates, 2 folded leaves :   *NYPL [Sc E 88-252]*

NATURAL RESOURCES - AFRICA.
Baker, Richard St. Barbe, 1889- Sahara conquest. London, 1966. 186 p.   DDC 333.7/3/096
S616.S16 B3   *NYPL [Sc C 88-117]*
Lewis, Lawrence. African environments and resources /. Boston , 1988. xii, 404 p. :   ISBN 0-04-916010-9 (alk. paper) DDC 333.7/096 19
HC800 .L48 1987   *NYPL [Sc E 89-50]*

NATURAL RESOURCES - ANGOLA.
Hodges, Tony. Angola to the 1990s . London , 1987. 145 p. :   *NYPL [Sc F 88-138]*

NATURAL RESOURCES - CONSERVATION. see CONSERVATION OF NATURAL RESOURCES.

NATURAL RESOURCES - GOVERNMENT POLICY - AFRICA.
Lewis, Lawrence. African environments and resources /. Boston , 1988. xii, 404 p. :   ISBN 0-04-916010-9 (alk. paper) DDC 333.7/096 19
HC800 .L48 1987   *NYPL [Sc E 89-50]*

NATURAL RESOURCES - SUDAN - ABYEI.
Eltayab, Shorhabil Ali. Agricultural and natural resources [microform] . Khartoum , 1978. 29 leaves ;   *NYPL [Sc Micro F-11041]*

NATURAL SCIENCE. see NATURAL HISTORY; SCIENCE.

Naturaleza, policia sagrada i profana, costumbres i ritos, disciplina i catechismo evangelico de todos etiopes /. Sandoval, Alonso de, 1576-1652. En Sevilla , 1627. [23], 334 p., 81 leaves ;   *NYPL [Sc Rare F 82-70]*

NATURALISTS - AFRICA - BIOGRAPHY - JUVENILE LITERATURE.
Sutton, Felix. Big game hunter . New York , 1960. 192 p. :   *NYPL [Sc D 88-659]*

NATURALISTS - UNITED STATES - BIOGRAPHY - JUVENILE LITERATURE.
Sutton, Felix. Big game hunter . New York , 1960. 192 p. ;   *NYPL [Sc D 88-659]*

NATURE CONSERVATION - AFRICA.
Conservation in Africa . Cambridge [Cambridgeshire] , New York , 1987. ix, 355 p. :   ISBN 0-521-34199-X DDC 333.7/2/096 19
QH77.A4 C66 1987   *NYPL [Sc E 88-199]*

NATURE, EFFECT OF MAN ON. see MAN - INFLUENCE ON NATURE.

Nature, I love you : Children's Book Week 1980 : poems and stories by children of St. Maarten. [St. Martin : J. Fleming, B. Hodge, and W. Smith, c1983. 36 p. : ill. ; 22 cm. Compiled by Josianne Fleming, Blanca Hodge and Wycliffe Smith.
1. Children's writings, Saint Martin. 2. Saint Martin - Poetry. I. Fleming, Josianne. II. Hodge, Blanca. III. Smith, Wycliffe.
MLCS 86/1723 (P)   *NYPL [Sc D 88-626]*

NATURE IN ORNAMENT. see DECORATION AND ORNAMENT.

NATURE PROTECTION. see NATURE CONSERVATION.

Navarro Azcue, Concepción, 1952- La abolición de la esclavitud negra en la legislación española, 1870-1886 / Concepción Navarro Azcue. Madrid : Instituto de Cooperación Iberoamericana : Ediciones Cultura Hispánica, c1987. 296 p. ; 21 cm. Bibliography: p. 237-247.   ISBN 84-7232-420-6
1. Slavery - Law and legislation - Cuba - History. 2. Slavery - Law and legislation - Puerto Rico - History. I. Title.
KG546 .N38 1987   *NYPL [Sc D 89-574]*

NAVIGATORS. see EXPLORERS.

NAVVIES. see LABOR AND LABORING CLASSES.

Naylor, Kim. Let's visit Mali. / Kim Naylor. Basingstoke : Macmillan, 1987. 96 p. : ill. (some col.), map ; 22 cm. Includes index.   ISBN 0-333-44988-6
1. Mali. I. Title.   *NYPL [Sc D 88-397]*

Naylor, Phyllis Reynolds. Making it happen. Chicago, Follett [1970] 128 p. 23 cm. Three junior high boys perfect the techniques of making a Happening, but only two of them ever understand why.   ISBN 0-695-80144-9 DDC [Fic]
1. Afro-American youth - Juvenile fiction. I. Title.
PZ7.N24 Mak   *NYPL [Sc D 88-446]*

Nchi yetu Tanzania /. Halimoja, Yusuf J. Dar es Salaam , 1981. 70 p. :   *NYPL [Sc C 89-55]*

N'Da, Paul, 1945- Pouvoir, lutte de classes, idéologie et milieu intellectuel africain. / Paul N'Da. Paris : Présence africaine, c1987. 107 p. ; 21 cm. Includes bibliographical footnotes.   ISBN 2-7087-0485-0
1. Intellectuals - Africa. 2. Social classes - Africa. 3. Africa - Intellectual life. I. Title.
NYPL [Sc D 88-918]

Ndam Njoya, Adamou, 1942-
Les Amo : recueil de poèmes / par Adamou Ndam Njoya. Yaoundé : Editions Ndam et Raynier Issa, c1982. 29 p. ; 21 cm. (Collection Poésie. vol. 1)
I. Title.
MLCS 84/860 (P)   *NYPL [Sc D 89-185]*
Geary, Christraud M. Mandou Yénou . München , c1985. 223 p. :   ISBN 3-923804-08-3
NYPL [Sc E 88-178]
Njoya : réformateur du royaume Bamoun / Adamou Ndam Njoya. Paris (9, rue du Château-d'Eau, 75010) : A.B.C. [Afrique biblio-club] ; Dakar ; [116] : map ; 18 cm. (Grandes figures africaines 0338-0882)   ISBN 2-85809-101-3 :   DDC 967/.113 B 19
1. Njoya, Sultan of the Bamun, d. 1933. 2. Bamun (African people) - History. 3. Bamun (African people) - Kings and rulers - Biography.
DT570 .N22   *NYPL [Sc C 88-162]*

Ndayishinguje, Pascal. Légendes historiques du Burundi . Paris , Bujumbura , c1987. 286 p. :   ISBN 2-86507-178-6 *NYPL [Sc E 88-324]*

N'Debeka, Maxime, 1944- Equatorium : pièce de théâtre / maxime N'Debeka. Paris : Présence africaine, c1987. 85 p. ; 21 cm.   ISBN 2-7087-0488-5
I. Title.   *NYPL [Sc D 88-913]*

NDEBELE LANGUAGE - TEXTS.
Ngwenya, M. N. Ilifa lidliwa ngumninilo /. Zimbabwe , c1982. 94 p. ;
NYPL [Sc C 89-67]

NDEBELE LANGUAGE (ZIMBABWE) - TEXTS.
Mabuza, Vivian R. N. Inzondo engela mkhawulo /. Gweru , 1988. 120 p. ;   ISBN 0-86922-430-1 *NYPL [Sc C 89-7]*

Ndebi Biya, Robert, 1946- Etre, pouvoir et génération : le système mbok chez les Basa du Sud-Cameroun / Ndebi Biya. Paris : L'Harmattan, c1987. 134 p. ; 22 cm. (Collection "Points de vue") Bibliography: p. 131-134.
1. Basa language - Terms and phrases. 2. Ethnophilosophy - Cameroon. 3. Basa (Cameroon people). I. Title. II. Series.   *NYPL [Sc D 88-909]*

Ndegwa, Rosemary. Maids, blessing or blight? / Rosemary Ndegwa. Nairobi, Kenya : Uzima, c1987. x, 141 p. ; 21 cm.

1. Women domestics - Kenya. I. Title.
NYPL [Sc D 89-399]

Ndem, E. B. E. Women in development .
Calabar , 1988. 153 p. :   *NYPL [Sc D 89-79]*

Ndiaye, Iba, 1928-
Iba N'Diaye, Gemälde, Lavierungen,
Zeichnungen = peintures, lavis, dessins / mit
einem Beitrag von Anne Dagbert. München :
Hirmer, c1987. 71 p. : ill. (some col.), port. ; 20
cm. Catalog of an exhibition held at Chapelle des
Jésuites, Nîmes, Aug. 19-Sept. 19, 1987 and Staatlichen
Völkerkundemuseum München, May 26-July 26, 1987.
French and German. Bibliography: p. 69-71. ISBN
3-7774-4650-5
1. Ndiaye, Iba, 1928- - Exhibitions. I. Dagbert, Anne.
II. Staatliches Museum für Völkerkunde München. III.
Chapelle des Jésuites (Nîmes, France). IV. Title.
NYPL [Sc C 88-297]

NDIAYE, IBA, 1928- - EXHIBITIONS.
Ndiaye, Iba, 1928- Iba N'Diaye, Gemälde,
Lavierungen, Zeichnungen =. München ,
c1987. 71 p. : ISBN 3-7774-4650-5
NYPL [Sc C 88-297]

N'Djehoya, Blaise. Le nègre Potemkine / Blaise
N'Djehoya. [Paris] : Lieu commun, c1988. 268
p. ; 22 cm. ISBN 2-86705-099-5
1. Burkina Faso - Fiction. I. Title.
NYPL [Sc D 88-996]

Ndoudi, Oumarou, 1945- Bocquené, Henri. Moi,
un Mbororo . Paris , c1986. 387 p., [12] p. of
plates : ISBN 2-86537-164-6
NYPL [Sc E 89-66]

NDOUDI, OUMAROU, 1945-
Bocquené, Henri. Moi, un Mbororo . Paris ,
c1986. 387 p., [12] p. of plates : ISBN
2-86537-164-6   *NYPL [Sc E 89-66]*

NEAR EAST - DESCRIPTION AND TRAVEL.
Irby, Charles Leonard, 1789-1845. Travels in
Egypt and Nubia, Syria and Asia Minor .
London , 1985. xxxiii, 560 p., [6] leaves of
plates (3 folded) : ISBN 1-85077-082-4 : DDC
915.6/041 916.2/043 19
DS48 DT53   *NYPL [JFD 88-9340]*

Nebel, Gustave E. (illus) Mooney, Elizabeth
Comstock. The Sandy Shoes mystery.
Philadelphia [1970] 128 p. DDC [Fic]
PZ7.M78 San   *NYPL [Sc D 89-96]*

NECROMANCY. see MAGIC.

A needle in the haystack ; [and] Limota .
Ogunyẹmi, Diipọ. Ibandan, Nigeria , 1987. iv,
88 p. ;   *NYPL [Sc C 88-166]*

Neffe, Dieter. Kämpfe im Süden Afrikas : 1652
bis 1980 / Dieter Neffe.1. Aufl. Berlin :
Militärverlag der Deutschen Demokratischen
Republik, 1987. 64 p. : ill., maps (some col.),
ports. ; 23 cm. (Militärgeschichtliche Skizzen)
Bibliography: p. 64. ISBN 3-327-00283-5
1. South Africa - History, Military. 2. South Africa -
History. I. Title. II. Series.   *NYPL [Sc D 88-680]*

Negatu in the garden. Kindred, Wendy. New
York [1971] [38] p. ISBN 0-07-034585-6 DDC
[E]
PZ7.K567 Ne   *NYPL [Sc F 88-246]*

Nègre, André. La rébellion de la Guadeloupe :
1801-1802 / André Nègre. Paris : Editions
caribéennes, c1987. 163 p., [4] p. of plates : ill.,
ports. ; 23 cm. ISBN 2-87679-006-8
1. Guadeloupe - History. 2. Guadeloupe - Politics and
government. I. Title.   *NYPL [Sc D 88-1333]*

Le nègre et l'amiral . Confiant, Raphaël. Paris ,
c1988. 334 p. ; ISBN 2-246-40991-8
NYPL [Sc D 89-340]

Le nègre Potemkine /. N'Djehoya, Blaise.
[Paris] , c1988. 268 p. ; ISBN 2-86705-099-5
NYPL [Sc D 88-996]

Négriers d'eux-mêmes . Icart, Jean-Claude.
Montréal, Québec, Canada , 1987. 188 p. ;
ISBN 2-920862-06-5   *NYPL [Sc D 88-396]*

Negripub : l'image des Noirs dans la publicité
depuis un siècle : 14 janvier-28 mars 1987,
Bibliothèque Forney ... . [Paris] : Société des
Amis de la Bibliothèque Forney, [1987] 157 p. :
ill. (some col.) ; 23 cm. At head of title: Ville de
Paris. Bibliography: p. 43. ISBN 2-7012-0580-8
1. Blacks in art - Exhibitions. 2. Advertising -
Exhibitions. I. Bibliothèque Forney.
NYPL [Sc E 88-234]

Negritude . Kabengele Munanga. São Paulo ,

1986. 88 p. ; ISBN 85-08-00686-1
NYPL [Sc C 88-105]

Negritude . Michael, Colette Verger, 1937- West
Cornwall, CT , 1988. xvii, 315 p. ; ISBN
0-933951-15-9 (lib. bdg. : alk. paper) : DDC
016.909/04924 19
Z6520.N44 M53 1988 PN56.N36
NYPL [Sc D 88-1470]

NEGRITUDE (LITERARY MOVEMENT)
Iyay Kimoni, 1938- Poésie de la négritude .
Kikwit , 1985. vi, 168 p. ; DDC 841/.009/896 19
PQ3897 .I93 1985   *NYPL [Sc B 89-18]*

NEGRITUDE (LITERARY MOVEMENT) -
BIBLIOGRAPHY.
Michael, Colette Verger, 1937- Negritude .
West Cornwall, CT , 1988. xvii, 315 p. ; ISBN
0-933951-15-9 (lib. bdg. : alk. paper) : DDC
016.909/04924 19
Z6520.N44 M53 1988 PN56.N36
NYPL [Sc D 88-1470]

Negro e cultura no Brasil /. Lopes, Helena
Theodoro. Rio de Janeiro , 1987. 136 p. ;
ISBN 85-85108-02-9 DDC 981/.00496 19
F2659.N4 L67 1987   *NYPL [Sc D 88-1291]*

O negro e o romantismo brasileiro /. Gomes,
Heloisa Toller. São Paulo [1988] 113 p. ;
NYPL [Sc D 89-515]

El negro en el Perú y su transculturación
lingüística /. Romero, Fernando. [Lima?] ,
1987. 176 p. :   *NYPL [Sc F 88-20]*

El negro en la novela hispanoamericana /. Bueno,
Salvador. La Habana, Cuba , 1986. 294 p. ;
DDC 863/.009/3520396 19
PQ7082.N7 B84 1986   *NYPL [Sc C 89-124]*

O negro escrito . Camargo, Oswaldo de, 1936-
[São Paulo] 1987. 214 p. : DDC 869/.09/896081
19
PQ9523.B57 C36 1987   *NYPL [Sc D 89-608]*

Negro folk tales of the Old South. Short, Sam B.
'Tis so . Baton Rouge, La. , c1972. 114 p. :
NYPL [Sc D 89-63]

The Negro in modern American history
textbooks . Sloan, Irving J. Chicago, Ill. , 1966.
47 p. ;   *NYPL [Sc D 89-262]*

The Negro in the making of America /. Quarles,
Benjamin. New York , London , c1987. 362 p. ;
ISBN 0-02-036140-8 DDC 973/.0496073 19
E185 .Q2 1987   *NYPL [Sc E 88-364]*

NEGRO MUSICIANS. see AFRO-AMERICAN
MUSICIANS.

NEGRO NATIONALISM. see RAS TAFARI
MOVEMENT.

Negro poetry and drama /. Brown, Sterling Allen,
1901- Washington, D.C. , c1937. 142 p. ;
NYPL [Sc D 89-105]

NEGRO RACE. see BLACK RACE.

The Negro renaissance from America back to
Africa . Achode, Codjo. Ann Arbor, Mich. ,
1986. viii, 306 p. ;   *NYPL [Sc D 89-291]*

NEGRO SPIRITUALS. see SPIRITUALS
(SONGS)

Negro thought in America, 1880-1915 . Meier,
August, 1923- Ann Arbor , 1988, c1963. xii,
336 p. ; ISBN 0-472-64230-8 DDC 973/.0496073
19
E185.6 .M5 1988   *NYPL [Sc D 89-509]*

NEGRO WELFARE CULTURAL AND
SOCIAL ASSOCIATION.
Reddock, Rhoda. Elma Francois . London ,
1988. vii, 60 p., [8] p. of plates : ISBN
0-901241-80-6 (Pbk.)   *NYPL [Sc D 89-77]*

Negroes and negro "slavery". Van Evrie, John H.,
1814-1896. New York, 1861. xvi, 339 p.
E449 .V253   *NYPL [Sc Rare C 88-22]*

NEGROES (UNITED STATES) see AFRO-
AMERICANS.

Negros na noite /. Cunha Junior, H., 1952- São
Paulo , 1987. 79 p. :   *NYPL [Sc D 88-71]*

Negussie Akalework. Index to livestock literature
microfiched in Zimbabwe /. Addis Ababa
[1986?] viii, 235 p. ; ISBN 92-9053-064-2
NYPL [Sc E 89-204]

NEIGHBORHOOD GOVERNMENT - SOUTH
AFRICA.
Atkinson, Doreen. The search for power and
legitimacy in Black urban areas . Grahamstown

[South Africa] [1984] 38, xix, v, [1] p. ; ISBN
0-86810-114-1 (pbk.) : DDC 320.8/0968 19
JS7533.A8 A85 1984   *NYPL [Sc F 88-355]*

Neighbors of the 2100 block . Butler, Ernest W.
Pitman, N.J. , c1986. 466 p. :
NYPL [Sc D 88-940]

Neigoff, Mike. Free throw. Pictures by Fred
Irvin. Chicago, A. Whitman [1968] 128 p. illus.
22 cm. A young black student is happy to make the
basketball team in his new school but finds it difficult
to get along with white teammates. DDC [Fic]
1. Basketball - Juvenile fiction. 2. Race relations -
Fiction. I. Irvin, Fred M., illus. II. Title.
PZ7.N427 Fr   *NYPL [Sc D 88-1427]*

Nelson, Harold D. Area handbook for Southern
Rhodesia / coauthors, Harold D. Nelson ... [et
al.]. 250 Washington : American University,
Foreign Area Studies : for sale by the Supt. of
Docs., U. S. Govt. Print. Off., 1975. xiv, 394 p.
maps. 24 cm. "DA Pam 550-171." "One of a series of
handbooks prepared by Foreign Area Studies (FAS) of
the American University." Bibliography: p. 353-372.
Includes index.
1. Zimbabwe. I. American University, Washington, D.
C. Foreign Area Studies. II. Title.
DT962 .N36   *NYPL [JFE 75-2684]*

Nelson, JohnnieRenee. A quest for Kwanzaa :
poems / by JohnnieRenee Nelson. Naitional
City, Calif. : House of Nia, c1988. [36] p. : ill. ;
22 cm.
I. Title.   *NYPL [Sc D 89-540]*

Nelson, Kathryn P. Gentrification and distressed
cities : an assessment of trends in
intrametropolitan migration / Kathryn P.
Nelson. Madison, Wis. : University of
Wisconsin Press, 1988. xiii, 187 p. : ill. ; 24 cm.
(Social demography) Includes index. Bibliography: p.
163-180. ISBN 0-299-11160-1 : DDC 307.2 19
1. Urban renewal - United States. 2. Gentrification -
United States. 3. Residential mobility - United States. 4.
Metropolitan areas - United States. 5. Urban policy -
United States. I. Title. II. Series.
HT175 .N398 1987   *NYPL [JLE 88-3486]*

Nelson Mandela : 70th birthday tribute, with
Artists Against Apartheid in support of the anti
apartheid movement, Wembley Stadium
Saturday 11 June. [London : Anti-apartheid
Movement, 1988] 61 p. : ill. (some col.) ; 31
cm. Cover title.
1. Mandela, Nelson, 1918-. 2. Anti-apartheid
movements - South Africa. I. Anti-Apartheid
Movement. II. Artists Against apartheid.
NYPL [Sc G 89-3]

Nérée, Bob. Duvalier : le pouvoir sur les autres,
de père en fils / Bob Nérée.1ère éd.
Port-au-Prince, Haiti : Impr. H. Deschamps,
1988. 238 p. ; 23 cm. "Cette première édition est
limitée à 1250 exemplaires numérotés" --Added tip.
Includes bibliographical references. Schomburg Center
has copy 834, autographed by the author.
1. Duvalier, François, 1907-1971. 2. Duvalier, Jean
Claude, 1951-. 3. Maurras, Charles 1868-1952 -
Influence. 4. Haiti - Politics and government -
1934-1971 - Philosophy. 5. Haiti - Politics and
government - 1971- - Philosophy. I. Title.
NYPL [Sc E 88-366]

Nervous conditions /. Dangarembga, Tsitsi.
London , 1988. 204 p. ; ISBN 0-7043-4100-X
(pbk) : DDC 823 19
PR9390.9.D3   *NYPL [Sc C 88-278]*

Netherlands Guiana. see Surinam.

Nettie Jo's friends /. McKissack, Pat, 1944- New
York , 1989. [33] p. : ISBN 0-394-89158-9 DDC
[E]
PZ7.M478693 Ne 1989 NYPL [Sc F 89-143]

Nettleford, Rex M., 1933- Nunley, John W.
(John Wallace), 1945- Caribbean festival arts .
[Saint Louis] , 1988. 218 p. : ISBN
0-295-96702-1 : DDC 394.2/5/07409729 19
GT4823 .N85 1988   *NYPL [Sc F 89-89]*

Nettles, Michael T., 1955- Toward Black
undergraduate student equality in American
higher education /. New York , 1988. xvii, 217
p. : ISBN 0-313-25616-0 (lib. bdg. : alk. paper)
DDC 378/.1982 19
LC2781 .T69 1988   *NYPL [Sc E 88-507]*

Neue Kunst aus Afrika : afrikanische
Gegenwartskunst aus der Sammlung Gunter
Péus / [Redaktion, Margareta Gorschenek,
Gunter Péus, Annamaria Rucktäschel ; mit

Beiträgen von Ulli Beier ... et al.]. [Hamburg] : Katholische Akademie Hamburg : Kulturbehörde Hamburg, c1984. 111 p. : ill. (some col.) ; 31 cm. Bibliography: p. 47.
1. Péus, Gunter - Art collections - Exhibitions. 2. Art, African - Exhibitions. 3. Art, Modern - 20th century - Africa - Exhibitions. I. Gorschenek, Margareta, 1946-. II. Péus, Gunter. III. Rucktäschel, Annamaria. IV. Kulturbehörde Hamburg.   *NYPL [Sc G 88-17]*

Neufchâteau, François de. see François de Neufchâteau, Nicolas Louis, comte, 1752-1828.

Neufchâteau, Nicolas Louis François de. see François de Neufchâteau, Nicolas Louis, comte, 1752-1828.

Never as strangers /. Mataka, Laini. Baltimore , c1988. x, 65 p. ;   *NYPL [Sc D 89-445]*

Never too late to love /. Thomas, Veona. Saddle Brook, N. J. , 1987. 69 p. :
NYPL [Sc D 87-1427]

Neverdon-Morton, Cynthia, 1944- Afro-American women of the South and the advancement of the race, 1895-1925 / by Cynthia Neverdon-Morton. 1st ed. Knoxville : University of Tennessee Press, c1989. 272 p. : ill. ; 24 cm. Includes bibliographical references and index. ISBN 0-87049-583-6 (alk. paper) : DDC 305.4/8896073/075 19
1. Afro-American women - Southern States - History. 2. Social service - Southern States - History. 3. Southern States - Race relations. I. Title.
E185.86 .N48 1989   NYPL [Sc E 89-218]

Neves, Amelia Tavares C. Ecumenical Association of Third World Theologians. Identidade negra e religião . Rio de Janeiro , 1986. 201 p. ;
NYPL [Sc D 88-485]

Nevin, Evelyn C. Underground escape / Evelyn C. Nevin. Philadelphia : WESTMINSTER PRESS, c1926. 191 p. : ill. ; 22 cm. SCHOMBURG CHILDREN'S COLLECTION.
1. Slaves - United States - Juvenile fiction. 2. Underground Railroad - Juvenile fiction. I. Schomburg Children's Collection. II. Title.
NYPL [Sc D 88-1506]

New American nation series.
Foner, Eric. Reconstruction, America's unfinished revolution, 1863-1877 /. New York , c1988. xxvii, 690 p., [8] p. of plates : ISBN 0-06-015851-4 : DDC 973.8 19
*E668 .F66 1988   NYPL [*R-IKR 88-5216]*

The new Black middle class /. Landry, Bart. Berkeley , 1987. xi, 250 p. ; ISBN 0-520-05942-5 (alk. paper) DDC 305.8/96073 19
E185.86 .L35 1987   NYPL [Sc D 87-1006]

New boy in school. Justus, May, 1898- New York [1963] 56 p. DDC [Fic]
PZ7.J986 Ng   NYPL [Sc E 89-25]

NEW CALEDONIA - JUVENILE FICTION.
Mille, Pierre, 1864-1931. Line en Nouvelle Calédonie /. Paris , c1934. 32, 1 p. :
NYPL [Sc F 89-20]

New directions in language teaching in Sub-Saharan Africa . Richmond, Edmun B. Washington, D.C. , c1983. viii, 65 p. ; ISBN 0-8191-2980-1 (pbk.) : DDC 418/.007/067 19
P57.A37 R5 1983   NYPL [Sc D 88-479]

New drama from Africa.
(12) Mboya, Alakie-Akinyi. Ontongolia /. Nairobi , 1986. xiv, 92 p., [4] p. of plates ; ISBN 0-19-572615-4 *NYPL [Sc C 88-138]*

New Edinburgh review. New Edinburgh review anthology /. Edinburgh , 1982. 203 p. ; ISBN 0-904919-56-0 : DDC 082 19
AC5 .N37 1982   NYPL [Sc D 88-1056]

New Edinburgh review anthology / edited by James Campbell. Edinburgh : Polygon Books, 1982. 203 p. ; 23 cm. "Of the sorrow songs: the cross of redemption [by] James Baldwin": p. 85-92. ISBN 0-904919-56-0 : DDC 082 19
I. Campbell, James, 1951-. II. Baldwin, James, 1924- Of the sorrow songs. III. New Edinburgh review.
AC5 .N37 1982   NYPL [Sc D 88-1056]

New Granada (Republic, 1842-1858) see Colombia.

New Granada (State, 1831-1842) see Colombia.

New Grove dictionary of music and musicians.
Oliver, Paul. The New Grove gospel, blues and jazz . New York , 1986. 395 p. [16] p. of

plates : ISBN 0-393-01696-X
NYPL [JND 88-16]

The New Grove gospel, blues and jazz . Oliver, Paul. New York , 1986. 395 p. [16] p. of plates : ISBN 0-393-01696-X
NYPL [JND 88-16]

New history of southern Africa series.
Grunlingh, A. M., 1948- Fighting their own war . Johannesburg , 1987. x, 200 p. ; ISBN 0-86975-321-5   *NYPL [Sc D 88-897]*

New horizons in Kiswahili . Mbaabu, Ireri. Nairobi , 1985. 229 p. ; DDC 496/.392 19
PL8701 .M374 1985   NYPL [Sc C 85-128]

NEW JERSEY - RACE RELATIONS.
Wright, Giles R. Afro-Americans in New Jersey . Trenton , c1988. 100 p. : ISBN 0-89743-075-1 DDC 974.9/00496073 19
E185.93.N54 W75 1988
NYPL [Sc D 89-529]

New Jersey State Museum. Lee-Smith, Hughie. Hughie Lee-Smith . [Trenton] , c1988. 36 p. :
NYPL [Sc D 89-247]

A new life in Christ. Cohen, Esther. A life without Christ and a new life in Christ [microform] /. Miami, Fla. , 1980. [23] p. ;
NYPL [Sc Micro F-11022]

A new Negro for a new century. Washington, Booker T. 1856-1915. Miami, Fla., 1969. 428 p. DDC 301.45/22
E185 .W315 1969b   NYPL [Sc D 89-43]

NEW ORLEANS (LA.) - HISTORY.
Garvey, Joan B. Beautiful crescent . New Orleans, LA , c1988. 249 p. : ISBN 0-9612960-0-3   *NYPL [Sc E 89-189]*

New religious movements in Nigeria / edited by Rosalind I.J. Hackett. Lewiston, N.Y. : E. Mellen Press, c1987. xvi, 245 p. ; 24 cm. (African studies . v. 5) Includes bibliographical references. ISBN 0-88946-180-5 (alk. paper) DDC 291.9/09669 19
1. Nigeria - Religion. I. Hackett, Rosalind I. J. II. Series: African studies (Lewiston, N.Y.) , v. 5.
BL2470.N5 N49 1987   NYPL [Sc E 88-266]

NEW SOUTH WALES - HISTORY.
Blomfield, Geoffrey. Baal Belbora, the end of the dancing . Chippendale, N.S.W. [New South Wales] , 1981. 148 p. : ISBN 0-909188-57-2
NYPL [Sc D 82-242]

The new state of the world atlas /. Kidron, Michael. New York , 1987. 1 atlas ([54] p., 57 [i.e. 114] p.) : ISBN 0-671-64554-4 (hard) : DDC 912/.132 19
G1021 .K46 1987
NYPL [Map Div. 87-1075]

New voices of the Commonwealth. Sergeant, Howard, 1914- London, 1968. 208 p. ISBN 0-237-49815-4 DDC 821/.008
PR9086 .S4   NYPL [Sc D 89-121]

New York Building Congress. Land Utilization Committee. New York (City). Housing Authority. Harlem, 1934. [New York, 1934] 20 p.
HD268.N5 N27   NYPL [Sc G 88-30]

NEW YORK (CITY) - AFRO-AMERICANS.
First National City Bank. Economics Dept. Profile of a city. New York [1972] x, 273 p. ISBN 0-07-021066-7
HC108.N7 F57   NYPL [Sc 309.174-F]

New York (City). Housing Authority. Harlem, 1934. [New York, 1934] 20 p.
HD268.N5 N27   NYPL [Sc G 88-30]

New York (City). City University of New York. Mount Sinai School of Medicine. see Mount Sinai School of Medicine.

NEW YORK (CITY) - ECONOMIC CONDITIONS.
First National City Bank. Economics Dept. Profile of a city. New York [1972] x, 273 p. ISBN 0-07-021066-7
HC108.N7 F57   NYPL [Sc 309.174-F]

New York (City). Housing Authority. Harlem, 1934; a study of real property and Negro population, prepared by Real Property Inventory of New York and Land Utilization Committee, New York Building Congress, for the New York City Housing Authority. [New York, Printed by the Polygraphic Company of America, 1934] 20 p. illus. (plans) 31 cm.

Cover-title.
1. Real property - New York (City). 2. Afro-Americans - New York (City). 3. Harlem, New York (City). I. New York Building Congress. Land Utilization Committee. II. Title.
HD268.N5 N27   NYPL [Sc G 88-30]

New York (City). Mount Sinai Hospital. Mount Sinai School of Medicine. see Mount Sinai School of Medicine.

New York (City). Mount Sinai School of Medicine. see Mount Sinai School of Medicine.

NEW YORK (CITY) - REAL PROPERTY.
New York (City). Housing Authority. Harlem, 1934. [New York, 1934] 20 p.
HD268.N5 N27   NYPL [Sc G 88-30]

NEW YORK (CITY) - RELIGIOUS LIFE AND CUSTOMS.
Orsi, Robert A. The Madonna of 115th Street . New Haven , c1985. xxiii, 287 p. : ISBN 0-300-03262-5 (alk. paper) DDC 263/.98/0895107471 19
BT660.N44 O77 1985
NYPL [IEE (Italians) 86-89]

NEW YORK (CITY) - RIOT, 1863.
Committee of Merchants for the Relief of Colored People, Suffering from the Late Riots in the City of New York. Report of the Committee of Merchants for the Relief of Colored People, Suffering from the Late Riots in the City of New York. New York , 1863. 48 p. ;   *NYPL [Sc Rare F 89-2]*

NEW YORK (CITY) - SCHOOLS.
Rebell, Michael A. Equality and education . Princeton, N.J. , c1985. x, 340 p. ; ISBN 0-691-07692-8 : DDC 344.747/0798 347.4704798 19
KFX2065 .R43 1985   NYPL [JLD 85-3778]

NEW YORK (CITY) - SOCIAL CONDITIONS.
First National City Bank. Economics Dept. Profile of a city. New York [1972] x, 273 p. ISBN 0-07-021066-7
HC108.N7 F57   NYPL [Sc 309.174-F]

Orsi, Robert A. The Madonna of 115th Street . New Haven , c1985. xxiii, 287 p. : ISBN 0-300-03262-5 (alk. paper) DDC 263/.98/0895107471 19
BT660.N44 O77 1985
NYPL [IEE (Italians) 86-89]

New York Council for the Humanities. Past meets present . Washington, D.C. , 1987. x, 169 p. : ISBN 0-87474-272-2 DDC 069/.9973 19
D16.163 .P37 1987   NYPL [Sc E 88-577]

New York (N.Y.). Almshouse. Whistelo, Alexander. (defendant) The Commissioners of the Alms-house, vs. Alexander Whistelo, a black man . New York , 1808. 56 p. ;
NYPL [Sc Rare F 88-21]

New York (N.Y.) - BIOGRAPHY.
Buckley, Gail Lumet, 1937- The Hornes . New York , 1986. 262 p. : ISBN 0-394-51306-1 : DDC 974.7/2300496073/00922 B 19
F129.B7 B83 1986   NYPL [Sc E 86-286]

New York (N.Y.). Bureau of Curriculum Development. Black studies: related learning materials and activities in social studies for kindergarten, grade 1 and grade 2. New York [c1970] vii, 227 p. illus. 36 cm. (Curriculum bulletin . 1970-71 ser., no. 3) Includes bibliographies. DDC 375/.0097471 s
1. Social sciences - Study and teaching (Primary) - New York (City). 2. Afro-Americans - Study and teaching - New York (City). I. Series: Curriculum bulletin (New York, N.Y.) , 1970-71 ser., no. 3. II. Title.
LB1563 .N57 1970-71, no. 3
NYPL [Sc G 87-32]

NEW YORK (N.Y.) - CHURCH HISTORY.
Reaching out . Tappan, NY , c1986. 120 p. : DDC 283/.7471 19
BV5980.N57 R4 1986   NYPL [Sc F 87-222]

New York (N.Y.). Commissioners of the Alms-house. Whistelo, Alexander. (defendant) The Commissioners of the Alms-house, vs. Alexander Whistelo, a black man . New York , 1808. 56 p. ;   *NYPL [Sc Rare F 88-21]*

NEW YORK (N.Y.) - DESCRIPTION - 1981- - GUIDE-BOOKS.
Bailey, A. Peter. Harlem today . New York , c1986. viii, 55 p. : ISBN 0-936073-01-2 (pbk.) :

DDC 917.47/1 19
F128.68.H3 B3 1986   NYPL [Sc D 88-1402]

NEW YORK (N.Y.) - FICTION.
Wolfe, Tom. The bonfire of the vanities /. New York , 1987. 659 p. ; ISBN 0-374-11534-6 : DDC 813/.54 19
PS3573.O526 B6 1987   NYPL [Sc E 88-389]

NEW YORK (N.Y.) - HISTORY - 1898-1951.
Kisseloff, Jeff. You must remember this . San Diego , c1989. xvii, 622 p., [16] p. of plates : ISBN 0-15-187988-5 : DDC 974.7/1042 19
F128.5 .K55 1988   NYPL [Sc E 89-54]

New York (N.Y.) Mayor's Commission on Black New Yorkers. The report of the Mayor's Commission on Black New Yorkers. New York : The Commission, 1988. xxi, 315 p. ; 28 cm. Bibliography: p. 299-302.
1. Afro-Americans - New York (N.Y.). 2. Afro-Americans - New York (N.Y.) - Economic conditions.   *NYPL [Sc F 89-96]*

NEW YORK (N.Y.) - POLITICS AND GOVERNMENT.
Green, Charles (Charles St. Clair) The struggle for black empowerment in New York City . New York , 1989. xvi, 183 p. : ISBN 0-275-92614-1 (alk. paper) : DDC 974.7/100496073 19
F128.9.N3 G74 1989   NYPL [Sc E 89-203]

NEW YORK (N.Y.) - POLITICS AND GOVERNMENT - 1898-1951.
Walter, John C. (John Christopher), 1933- The Harlem Fox . Albany, N.Y. , c1989. xv, 287 p. : ISBN 0-88706-756-5 DDC 974.7/1043/0924 B 19
F128.5.J72 W35 1988   NYPL [Sc E 89-107]

NEW YORK (N.Y.) - POLITICS AND GOVERNMENT - 1951-
Walter, John C. (John Christopher), 1933- The Harlem Fox . Albany, N.Y. , c1989. xv, 287 p. : ISBN 0-88706-756-5 DDC 974.7/1043/0924 B 19
F128.5.J72 W35 1988   NYPL [Sc E 89-107]

NEW YORK (N.Y.) - POPULAR CULTURE.
Delany, Samuel R. The motion of light in water . New York, c1988. xviii, 302 p. : ISBN 0-87795-947-1 : DDC 813/.54 19
PS3554.E437 Z475 1988
                         NYPL [JFD 88-7818]

NEW YORK (N.Y.) - SOCIAL LIFE AND CUSTOMS.
Kisseloff, Jeff. You must remember this . San Diego , c1989. xvii, 622 p., [16] p. of plates : ISBN 0-15-187988-5 : DDC 974.7/1042 19
F128.5 .K55 1988   NYPL [Sc E 89-54]

NEW YORK YANKEES (BASEBALL TEAM)
Winfield, Dave, 1951- Winfield . New York , c1988. 314 p., [22] p. of plates : ISBN 0-393-02467-9 : DDC 796.357/092/4 B 19
GV865.W57 A3 1988
                         NYPL [JFD 88-11493]

Newman, Mark. Entrepreneurs of profit and pride : from Black-appeal to radio soul / Mark Newman. New York : Praeger, 1988. xvi, 186 p., [4] p. of plates : ill., port.; 24 cm. (Media and society series) Includes index. Bibliography: p. [171]-180. ISBN 0-275-92888-8 DDC 305.8/96073 19
1. Afro-Americans in radio broadcasting. 2. Afro-Americans - Social life and customs. 3. Radio audiences - United States. 4. Afro-American radio stations. 5. Radio advertising - United States. 6. Entrepreneurship - United States. I. Title. II. Series.
PN1991.8.A35 N49 1988
                         NYPL [Sc E 89-88]

NEWS AGENCIES.
Harris, Phil. [Reporting southern Africa. Spanish.] La información sobre Africa austral . Barcelona , Paris , 1984. 188 p. : ISBN 92-3-301700-1 (Unesco)
                         NYPL [Sc D 88-614]

News & letters. Guide to the Raya Dunayevskaya collection . Detroit, Mich. [1986?] 84 p. ;
                         NYPL [Sc F 88-196]

NEWS-GATHERING ORGANIZATIONS. see NEWS AGENCIES.

NEWS SERVICES. see NEWS AGENCIES.

Newsum, H. E., 1951- The politics of "scholarship" in Black intellectual discourse [microform] : writing as writers / by Horace Estill Newsum. 1977 116 leaves. Thesis (Ph.

D.)--University of Michigan, 1977. Bibliography: leaves 113-116. Microfilm of typescript. Ann Arbor, Mich.: University Microfilms International, 1978. 1 microfilm reel; 35 mm.
1. Afro-American studies. I. Title.
                         NYPL [Sc Micro R-4689]

Newton, John, 1725-1807.
NEWTON, JOHN, 1725-1807.
Bohrer, Dick. John Newton, letters of a slave trader /. Chicago , c1983. viii, 130 p. ; ISBN 0-8024-0158-9 (pbk) DDC 283/.3 19
BX5199.N55 B64 1983   NYPL [Sc C 88-235]

An authentic narrative of some remarkable and interesting particulars in the life of ******.** Bohrer, Dick. John Newton, letters of a slave trader / paraphrased by Dick Bohrer. Chicago , c1983. viii, 130 p. ; ISBN 0-8024-0158-9 (pbk.) DDC 283/.3 19
BX5199.N55 B64 1983   NYPL [Sc C 88-235]

Newton, Velma. The silver men : West Indian labour migration to Panama, 1850-1914 / Velma Newton. Mona, Kingston, Jamaica : Institute of Social and Economic Research, University of the West Indies, 1984. xx, 218 p., [4] p. of plates : ill. ; 22 cm. Based on the author's thesis (M.A.--University of the West Indies, 1973). Includes index. Bibliography: p. 193-201. DDC 325/.2729/07287 19
1. Panama - Emigration and immigration - History. 2. West Indies, British - Emigration and immigration - History. 3. Panama Canal (Panama) - Design and construction - History. 4. Panama Railroad - Design and construction - History. 5. West Indies - Panama - History. I. Title.
JV7429 .N49 1984   NYPL [Sc D 89-478]

Next . Clifton, Lucille, 1936- Brockport, NY , St. Paul, Minnesota , 1987. 85 p. ; ISBN 0-918526-60-4   *NYPL [Sc E 88-413]*

Ngano / [edited by G. Fortune]. Harare, Zimbabwe : Mercury Press, 1980- v. ; 30 cm. In Shona. ISBN 0-7974-0478-3 (pbk.) :
1. Mashona - Folklore - Collected works. 2. Tales - Zimbabwe - Collected works. 3. Shona language - Texts. I. Fortune, G. (George), 1915-.
GR358.62.M3 N47 1980
                         NYPL [Sc F 87-416]

Ngara, Emmanuel. Teaching literature in Africa : principles and techniques / by Emmanuel Ngara. Harare, Zimbabwe : Zimbabwe Educational Books, 1984. 76 p. ; 21 cm. "Intended specifically for the teacher of literature in English in Africa"--P. 1. Bibliography: p. 75-76. ISBN 0-908300-09-3 :
1. English literature - Study and teaching - Africa. I. Title.   *NYPL [Sc D 89-383]*

Ngcobo, Lauretta G. Let it be told . London , 1987. 145, [1] p. ; ISBN 0-7453-0254-8
                         NYPL [Sc E 88-125]

Ngcongco, L. D. (Leonard D.) Historiografía de l'Afrique australe. Spanish. La historiografía del Africa austral . Barcelona , Paris , 1983. 128 p. ; ISBN 92-3-301775-3 (Unesco)
                         NYPL [Sc D 88-598]

Ngok Dinka marriage and cattle transferals [microform] /. Fetterman, Marilyn Harer. Khartoum , 1978. 23 leaves ;
                         NYPL [Sc Micro F-11040]

NGOMBE LANGUAGE - GRAMMAR.
Mangulu, Motingea. Elements de grammaire lingombe avec une bibliographie exhaustive /. Mbandaka, Zaire *, 1988. 88 p. :
                         NYPL [Sc D 89-40]

Ngongwikwo, Joseph A. The lost child / by Joseph A. Ngongwikwo. Limbé, S.W. Province, Cameroon : Nooremac Press, [1986?] 76 p. : ill. ; 21 cm. ISBN 978-250-304-5
1. Cameroon - Fiction. I. Title.
                         NYPL [Sc D 88-496]

N'GOUABI, MARIEN, 1938-1977 - ASSASSINATION.
Massengo, Moudileno. Procès de Brazzaville . Paris [1983] 345 p. :   *NYPL [Sc D 88-1160]*

Ngugi, James. see Ngugi Wa Thiong'o, 1938-

Ngugi Wa Thiong'o, 1938- The first Walter Rodney memorial lecture, 1985 / Ngũgĩ wa Thiong'o. London : Friends of Bogle, 1987. 12 p. : ill. ; 21 cm.
1. Rodney, Walter. I. Title.
                         NYPL [Sc Rare F 88-67]

Ng'weno, Hilary. The day Kenyatta died / Hilary Ng'weno. Nairobi : Longman Kenya, 1978. 68 p., [1] leaf of plates : ill. ; 28 cm. ISBN 0-582-64283-3 DDC 967.6/204/0924 B 19
1. Kenyatta, Jomo - Death and burial. 2. Statesmen - Kenya - Biography. 3. Kenya - Presidents - Biography. I. Title.
DT433.576.K46 N45   NYPL [Sc F 89-28]

Ngwenya, M. N. Ilifa lidliwa ngumninilo / ngu M. N. Ngwenya. Zimbabwe : Mambo Press in association with the Literature Bureau, c1982. 94 p. ; 18 cm.
1. Ndebele language - Texts. I. Title.
                         NYPL [Sc C 89-67]

NIASSA, MOZAMBIQUE (PROVINCE)
Portugal. Laws, statutes etc. Companhia do Nyassa [microform] . Lisboa, 1897. 89 p.
JV4229.M7C785
                         NYPL [Sc Micro R-4840 no.10]

Niba, Johnson N. Recruitment and retention of Black students in higher education /. Lanham, MD , c1989. viii, 135 p. : ISBN 0-8191-7292-8 (alk. paper) DDC 378/.1982 19
LC2781 .R43 1989   NYPL [Sc D 89-590]

Nichele, Franc. Valentin, Christophe. Sierra Leone /. Paris, France , c1985. 128 p. : ISBN 2-901151-16-7 DDC 966/.404/0222 19
DT516.19 .V35 1985   NYPL [Sc G 89-10]

Nickels, Marilyn Wenzke. Black Catholic protest and the Federated Colored Catholics, 1917-1933 : three perspectives on racial justice / Marilyn Wenzke Nickels. New York : Garland, 1988. ix, 325 p. ; 24 cm. (The Heritage of American Catholicism) Originally presented as the author's thesis (Ph. D.--Catholic University of America, 1975) Bibliography: p. 315-325. ISBN 0-8240-4098-8 (alk. paper) : DDC 282/.73/08996073 19
1. Turner, Thomas Wyatt. 2. Markoe, William Morgan. 3. LaFarge, John, 1880-1963. 4. Federated Colored Catholics of the United States - History. 5. Afro-American Catholics - History - 20th century. I. Title. II. Series.
BX1407.N4 N5 1988   NYPL [Sc E 89-85]

Nicolas, Armand. Le combat d'André Aliker / Armand Nicolas. Fort-de-France : [s.n.], 1974. 108 p. : port. ; 21 cm. "Supplément à 'Action' no. 19"
1. Aliker, André, 1894-1934. 2. Communists - Martinique. 3. Martinique - History. I. Action (Parti communiste martiniquais). II. Title.
                         NYPL [Sc D 88-1189]

Nicolas, Guy. Don rituel et échange marchand dans une société sahélienne / Guy Nicolas. Paris : Institut d'Ethnologie, Musée de l'Homme, 1986. 282 p. : ill. ; 27 cm. (Mémoires de l'institut d'ethnologie / Muséum national d'histoire naturelle, 0768-1380 . 25) Bibliography: p. [273]-280. ISBN 2-85265-117-3
1. Hausas - Social life and customs. 2. Ceremonial exchange - Maradi River Valley (Nigeria and Niger). 3. Maradi River Valley (Nigeria and Niger) - Social life and customs. 4. Maradi River Valley (Nigeria and Niger) - Economic conditions. I. Title.
                         NYPL [JFF 87-660]

Nicolas, Pierre. Naissance d'une ville au Sénégal : évolution d'un groupe de six villages de Casamance vers une agglomeration urbaine / Pierre Nicolas et Malick Gaye. Paris : Karthala, c1988. 193 p., [8] p. of plates : ill., maps ; 24 cm. (Collection Economie et développement. Essais) Bibliography: p. [175]-188. ISBN 2-86537-195-6
1. City planning - Senegal. 2. Cities and towns - Senegal - Growth. I. Gaye, Malick. II. Enda Tiers-Monde. III. Title. IV. Series.
                         NYPL [Sc F 89-131]

Nicolas, pseud. see Mordvinoff, Nicolas, 1911-

Nielsen, Aldon Lynn. Reading race : white American poets and the racial discourse in the twentieth century / Aldon Lynn Nielsen. Athens, Ga. : University of Georgia Press, c1988. xii, 178 p. ; 24 cm. (South Atlantic Modern Language Association. Award study) Includes index. Bibliography: p. [163]-173. ISBN 0-8203-1061-1 (alk. paper) DDC 811/.5/09355 19
1. American poetry - 20th century - History and criticism. 2. American poetry - White authors - History and criticism. 3. Race in literature. 4. Race relations in literature. 5. Racism in literature. 6. Afro-Americans in literature. I. Title.
PS310.R34 N54 1988   NYPL [JFE 88-3098]

Nigam, S. B. L. (Shyam Behari Lal) The
Challenge of employment and basic needs in
Africa . Nairobi , New York , 1986. xii, 379
p. ; ISBN 0-19-572559-X *NYPL [Sc E 88-419]*

NIGEARIA - SOCIAL POLICY.
Oshisanya, Samuel Adekoya. Nigeria as a world
power /. [Lagos , 1986] iii, 80 p. :
NYPL [Sc D 88-689]

The Niger: Africa's river of mystery. Watson,
Jane (Werner) 1915- Champaign, Ill. [1971] 96
p. ISBN 0-8116-6374-4 DDC 916.6/2
DT360 .W38 *NYPL [Sc E 88-415]*

Niger - Government. see Niger - Politics and
government.

NIGER - HISTORY.
Zakari, Maikorema. Contribution a l'histoire des
populations du sud-est nigérien . Niamey ,
1985. 246 p. : ISBN 2-85921-053-9
NYPL [Sc E 88-328]

NIGER - MAPS.
(1980) Atlas du Niger /. Paris , c1980. 64 p. :
ISBN 2-85258-151-5 : DDC 912/.6626 19
G2660 .A8 1980 *NYPL [Sc F 84-232]*

NIGER - POLITICS AND GOVERNMENT.
Hama, Boubou, 1906- Kotia-Nima . [Niamey?] .
3 v. ; *NYPL [Sc D 88-210]*

NIGER RIVER.
Gibbal, Jean Marie. Les Génies du fleuve /.
Paris , c1988. 257 p. : ISBN 2-85616-467-6
NYPL [Sc D 88-1287]

Lander, Richard, 1804-1834. Journal of an
expedition to explore the course and
termination of the Niger . New York , 1832. 2
v. : *NYPL [Sc Rare C 89-35]*

NIGER RIVER - JUVENILE LITERATURE.
Watson, Jane (Werner) 1915- The Niger:
Africa's river of mystery. Champaign, Ill. [1971]
96 p. ISBN 0-8116-6374-4 DDC 916.6/2
DT360 .W38 *NYPL [Sc E 88-415]*

Nigeria . Holmes, Peter. Lagos, Nigeria , 1985.
206 p. : ISBN 0-9508498-1-2 DDC 966.9/05 19
DT515.24 .H64 1985 · *NYPL [Sc G 88-14]*

Nigeria and Cameroun . Irele, Modupe. Lagos,
Nigeria , c1984. viii, 67 p. : ISBN 978-237-205-6
(pbk) DDC 016.327669067/11 19
Z3597 .I73 1984 DT515.63.C17
NYPL [Sc E 87-30]

Nigeria and the international capitalist system /
edited by Toyin Falola and Julius O. Ihonvbere.
Boulder, Colo. : L. Rienner Publishers, 1988. v,
154 p. ; 24 cm. (GSIS monograph series in world
affairs) Includes index. Bibliography: p. 129-148.
ISBN 1-555-87087-2 (alk. paper) : DDC 337.669
19
*1. Petroleum industry and trade - Nigeria. 2. Nigeria -
Foreign economic relations. 3. Nigeria - Economic
conditions - 1960-. 4. Nigeria - Foreign relations. 5.
Nigeria - Dependency on foreign countries. I. Falola,
Toyin. II. Ihonvbere, Julius Omozuanvbo. III. Series.*
HF1616.7 .N54 1988 *NYPL [JLE 88-3615]*

**NIGERIA - ANECDOTES, FACETIAE,
SATIRE, ETC.**
Ask the humorist . Enugu, 1986. 104 p. :
ISBN 978-225-808-3 *NYPL [Sc C 88-240]*

NIGERIA - ARMED FORCES.
Nigerian defence and security . Bukuru, Plateau
State , 1987. xii, 208 p. ; ISBN 978-19-8019-2
NYPL [Sc D 88-1377]

**NIGERIA - ARMED FORCES - POLITICAL
ACTIVITY.**
Duke, Hajia Zainab I. (Hajia Zainab Ibitein)
The revolutionary potentials of the Nigerian
military, 1886-1986 /. [Lagos?] Nigeria , c1987.
viii, 145 p., [28] p. of plates : ISBN
978-232-008-0 DDC 322/.5/09669 19
DT515.8 .D84 1987 *NYPL [Sc D 88-1278]*

**NIGERIA - ARMED FORCES - POLITICAL
ACTIVITY - CONGRESSES.**
Proceedings of the colloquium on Why army
rule? . [Lagos? , 1986 or 19. 338 p. ;
NYPL [Sc G 88-23]

NIGERIA. ARMY.
Babangida, Ibrahim Badamasi. Quotes of a
general . Surulere [Nigeria] , 1987. 90 p. :
NYPL [Sc D 88-711]

NIGERIA. ARMY - HISTORY.
Nigerian Army Museum. A pictorial history of
the Nigerian Army /. Nigeria , c1987. 49 p. :
NYPL [Sc F 89-81]

Nigeria as a world power /. Oshisanya, Samuel
Adekoya. [Lagos , 1986] iii, 80 p. :
NYPL [Sc D 88-689]

NIGERIA - BIBLIOGRAPHY.
Irele, Modupe. Nigeria and Cameroun . Lagos,
Nigeria , c1984. viii, 67 p. : ISBN 978-237-205-6
(pbk) DDC 016.327669067/11 19
Z3597 .I73 1984 DT515.63.C17
NYPL [Sc E 87-30]

NIGERIA - CHURCH HISTORY.
Akeredolu, J. L. The Church and its
denominations in Nigeria /. Ibadan , 1986. viii,
68 p. ; ISBN 978-12-2193-3 (pbk.) DDC
280/.09669 19
BR1463.N5 A39 1986 *NYPL [Sc C 89-71]*

Erivwo, Samuel U. The Urhobo, the Isoko and
the Itsekiri . Ibadan , 1979. vii, 144 p. :
NYPL [Sc D 88-769]

Johnston, Geoffrey. Of God and maxim guns .
Waterloo, Ontario, Canada , 1988. 321 p. :
ISBN 0-88920-180-3 (pbk.)
NYPL [Sc D 88-1229]

NIGERIA - CIVILIZATION.
Malami, Shehu, Alhaji. Nigerian memories /.
London , Ibadan , 1985. xii, [139] p., [12] p. of
plates : ISBN 978-16-7526-8 (Nigeria)
NYPL [Sc D 88-532]

Nigeria, the people and their heritage /.
Calabar [Nigeria] , 1987. 339 p. : ISBN
978-228-328-2 *NYPL [Sc D 88-734]*

Tapping Nigeria's limitless cultural treasures /.
Ikeja [1987?] 119 p., [2] leaves of plates :
NYPL [Sc F 89-1]

Udeaja, Philip. The way we are /. [Enugu,
Anambra State, Nigeria] [1987?]. vii, 61 p. ;
NYPL [Sc C 89-36]

**NIGERIA - CIVILIZATION - 20TH
CENTURY.**
Oshisanya, Samuel Adekoya. Nigeria as a world
power /. [Lagos , 1986] iii, 80 p. :
NYPL [Sc D 88-689]

**NIGERIA - CIVILIZATION - OCCIDENTAL
INFLUENCES.**
Esiemokhai, Emmanuel Omoh. The colonial
legal heritage in Nigeria /. Akure, Nigeria ,
1986. xii, 82 p. ; ISBN 978-16-4248-3
NYPL [Sc D 88-640]

NIGERIA - COLONIAL INFLUENCE.
Duke, Hajia Zainab I. (Hajia Zainab Ibitein)
The revolutionary potentials of the Nigerian
military, 1886-1986 /. [Lagos?] Nigeria , c1987.
viii, 145 p., [28] p. of plates : ISBN
978-232-008-0 DDC 322/.5/09669 19
DT515.8 .D84 1987 *NYPL [Sc D 88-1278]*

Ejimofor, Cornelius Ogu, 1940- British colonial
objectives and policies in Nigeria . Onitsha,
Nigeria , 1987. viii, 216 p., 1 folded leaf ;
ISBN 978-17-5142-8 *NYPL [Sc D 88-820]*

NIGERIA - COMMERCE.
Nigeria. Federal Dept. of Information. Saga of
progress: Nigeria 1960-1985. Lagos, 19. 79 p. :
NYPL [Sc F 88-170]

NIGERIA - COMMERCIAL POLICY.
Ihonvbere, Julius Omozuanvbo. Towards a
political economy of Nigeria . Aldershot,
[England] ; Brookfield, [Vt.], USA : xi, 213 p. :
ISBN 0-566-05422-1 : DDC 338.9669 19
HC1055 .I38 1988 *NYPL [Sc D 89-47]*

NIGERIA - CONSTITUTIONAL LAW.
Ojo, Abiola. Constitutional law and military
rule in Nigeria . Ibadan , 1987. vii, 316 p. ;
ISBN 978-16-7569-1 *NYPL [Sc D 88-804]*

**NIGERIA - CULTURAL POLICY -
CONGRESSES.**
Cultural development and nation building .
Ibadan , 1986. xiv, 157 p. : ISBN 978-246-048-6
(pbk.) DDC 338.4/77/0096694 19
NX750.N6 C85 1986 *NYPL [Sc D 88-812]*

NIGERIA - DEFENSES.
Nigerian defence and security . Bukuru, Plateau
State , 1987. xii, 208 p. ; ISBN 978-19-8019-2
NYPL [Sc D 88-1377]

**NIGERIA - DEPENDENCY ON FOREIGN
COUNTRIES.**

Nigeria and the international capitalist system
/. Boulder, Colo. , 1988. v, 154 p. ; ISBN
1-555-87087-2 (alk. paper) : DDC 337.669 19
HF1616.7 .N54 1988 *NYPL [JLE 88-3615]*

**NIGERIA - DESCRIPTION AND TRAVEL -
1981- - VIEWS.**
Holmes, Peter. Nigeria . Lagos, Nigeria , 1985.
206 p. : ISBN 0-9508498-1-2 DDC 966.9/05 19
DT515.24 .H64 1985 *NYPL [Sc G 88-14]*

NIGERIA - DRAMA.
Hagher, Iyorwuese H. Aishatu, and other plays
/. Benin City [Nigeria] , c1987. 136 p. ; ISBN
978-235-603-4 *NYPL [Sc D 88-797]*

Ogunyemi, Diipo. A needle in the haystack ;
[and] Limota . Ibandan, Nigeria , 1987. iv, 88
p. ; *NYPL [Sc C 88-166]*

Onwueme, Tess Akaeke. Ban empty barn .
Owerri, Nigeria , 1986. 145 p. ; ISBN
978-244-909-4 *NYPL [Sc C 88-202]*

Onwueme, Tess Akaeke. Mirror for campus /.
Owerri , 1987. iii leaves, 76 p. ;
NYPL [Sc C 88-159]

Osofisan, Femi. Midnight hotel /. Ibadan,
Nigeria , 1986. 65 p. ; ISBN 978-16-7508-X
NYPL [Sc D 88-1050]

NIGERIA, EASTERN - CHURCH HISTORY.
A Hundred years of the Catholic Church in
Eastern Nigeria, 1885-1985 . Onitsha, Nigeria ,
1985. 432 p. : ISBN 978-17-5103-7
NYPL [Sc D 88-830]

**NIGERIA, EASTERN - POLITICS AND
GOVERNMENT.**
Amucheazi, E. C. (Elochukwu C.) Church and
politics in Eastern Nigeria, 1945-66 . Yaba
Lagos , 1986. xvii, 256 p. : ISBN 978-13-2786-3
(pbk.) DDC 322/.1/096694 19
DT515.9.E3 A66 1986 *NYPL [Sc D 88-992]*

NIGERIA - ECONOMIC CONDITIONS.
Madunagu, Edwin. Nigeria, the economy and
the people [microform] . London , 1983. 38 p. ;
ISBN 0-901241-54-7
NYPL [Sc Micro F-11069]

Nigeria. Federal Dept. of Information. Saga of
progress: Nigeria 1960-1985. Lagos, 19. 79 p. :
NYPL [Sc F 88-170]

**NIGERIA - ECONOMIC CONDITIONS -
1960-**
Ayida, A. A. Reflections on Nigerian
development /. Lagos , Ibadan , 1987. xxiii,
278 p. ; ISBN 978-260-101-2
NYPL [Sc D 88-1078]

Nigeria and the international capitalist system
/. Boulder, Colo. , 1988. v, 154 p. ; ISBN
1-555-87087-2 (alk. paper) : DDC 337.669 19
HF1616.7 .N54 1988 *NYPL [JLE 88-3615]*

Osuagwu, Harold G. O. Investment demand in
a developing country . Washington, D.C. ,
c1982. xvii, 411 p. ; ISBN 0-8191-2048-0 : DDC
332.6/72/09669 19
HG5881.A3 O84 1982 *NYPL [Sc D 88-478]*

Wright, Stephen, 1954- Nigeria, the dilemmas
ahead . London , c1986. 88 p. :
NYPL [Sc F 88-137]

**NIGERIA - ECONOMIC CONDITIONS -
1970-**
Nigeria in search of a future /. Nsukka , 1986.
vii, 155 p. ; ISBN 978-229-900-6
NYPL [Sc D 88-884]

Nigeria, the people and their heritage /.
Calabar [Nigeria] , 1987. 339 p. : ISBN
978-228-328-2 *NYPL [Sc D 88-734]*

Nwankwo, Arthur A. Thoughts on Nigeria /.
Enugu, Nigeria , 1986. xxii, 198 p. ;
987-15-6264-1 *NYPL [Sc E 88-448]*

Obasanjo, Olusegun. Africa embattled . Agodi,
Ibadan , 1988. xi, 118 p. ; ISBN 978-267-924-0
DT30.5 .O23x 1988 *NYPL [Sc E 88-574]*

Ogunbanjo, C. O. (Christopher Oladipo), 1923-
Nigeria, the search for economic stability /.
[S.l.] , 1986. 103 p., [4] p. of plates : ISBN
0-946233-04-7 *NYPL [Sc D 88-883]*

Okongwu, Chu S. P., 1934- The Nigerian
economy . Enugu, Nigeria , 1986. vi, 453 p. :
ISBN 978-15-6038-X (pbk.) : DDC 330.9669/05
19
HC1055 .O39 1986 *NYPL [Sc D 88-1250]*

Osammor, Vincent Osoloka. Introducing

commodities (market) exchange in Nigeria /. Surulere, Lagos, Nigeria , 1986. x, 39 p. ; *NYPL [Sc D 88-1293]*

NIGERIA - ECONOMIC CONDITIONS - BIBLIOGRAPHY.
Visser, Johanna, 1898- A list of books, articles and government publications on the economy of Nigeria, 1963 and 1964. Ibadan, 1965. x, 81 p. *NYPL [Sc F 78-58]*

NIGERIA - ECONOMIC CONDITIONS - BOOK REVIEWS.
Heinecke, P. Twenty-two reviews /. Kaduna, [Nigeria] [1986?] 69 p. ; *NYPL [Sc E 88-284]*

NIGERIA - ECONOMIC CONDITIONS - CONGRESSES.
Alternative political futures for Nigeria /. Nigeria , 1987. xviii, 565 p. ; ISBN 978-303-170-8   *NYPL [Sc D 88-1374]*

Austerity and the Nigerian society /. Nsukka , 1987. vi, 240 p. : ISBN 978-264-356-6 *NYPL [Sc D 89-205]*

NIGERIA - ECONOMIC POLICY.
Ayida, A. A. Reflections on Nigerian development /. Lagos , Ibadan , 1987. xxiii, 278 p. ; ISBN 978-260-101-2 *NYPL [Sc D 88-1078]*

Better life for Nigerians /. Lagos , 1987. 56 p. : *NYPL [Sc D 88-796]*

Ihonvbere, Julius Omozuanvbo. Towards a political economy of Nigeria . Aldershot, [England] ; Brookfield, [Vt.], USA : xi, 213 p. : ISBN 0-566-05422-1 : DDC 338.9669 19 *HC1055 .I38 1988*   *NYPL [Sc D 89-47]*

Kalu, Onwuka O. The challenge of industrialization in Nigeria . Lagos, Nigeria , 1986. xviii, 84 p. ;   *NYPL [Sc D 88-1245]*

Nigerian alternatives /. [Zaria, Nigeria] 1987. 323 p. ; ISBN 978-301-130-11 *NYPL [Sc D 88-698]*

Nwankwo, Uchenna. Strategy for political stability /. Lagos , 1988. ix, 310 p. ; *NYPL [Sc D 89-539]*

Ogunbanjo, C. O. (Christopher Odadipo), 1923- Nigeria, the search for economic stability /. [Nigeria?] 1986. 102 p., [4] p. of plates : ISBN 0-946233-04-7   *NYPL [Sc D 88-519]*

Ogunbanjo, C. O. (Christopher Oladipo), 1923- Nigeria, the search for economic stability /. [S.l.] , 1986. 103 p., [4] p. of plates : ISBN 0-946233-04-7   *NYPL [Sc D 88-883]*

Okongwu, Chu S. P., 1934- The Nigerian economy . Enugu, Nigeria , 1986. vi, 453 p. : ISBN 978-15-6038-X (pbk.) : DDC 330.9669/05 19
HC1055 .O39 1986   NYPL [Sc D 88-1250]

Okonkwo, Ifeanyichukwu E. R. The great debate . Onitsha, Anambra State, Nigeria , 1986. 138 p. : ISBN 978-264-308-4 *NYPL [Sc C 89-58]*

Oshisanya, Samuel Adekoya. Nigeria as a world power /. [Lagos , 1986] iii, 80 p. : *NYPL [Sc D 88-689]*

NIGERIA - ETHNIC RELATIONS.
Boro, Isaac. The twelve-day revolution /. Benin City, Nigeria , 1982. 158 p., [8] p. of plates : ISBN 978-234-040-5 *NYPL [Sc C 88-109]*

Nigeria. Federal Dept. of Information. Saga of progress: Nigeria 1960-1985. Lagos: The Ministry, 1986 79 p. : ill. (some col.) ; 26 cm.
1. Nigeria - Economic conditions. 2. Nigeria - Commerce. 3. Nigeria - Industries. I. Title.
NYPL [Sc F 88-170]

Nigeria. Federal ministry of Agriculture, Water Resources and Rural Development. Events that marked the first decade of ADPs in Nigeria. [Ibadan , 1986] 34 p. : *NYPL [Sc F 89-74]*

Nigeria. Federal Ministry of Information and Culture. Better life for Nigerians /. Lagos , 1987. 56 p. : *NYPL [Sc D 88-796]*

NIGERIA - FICTION.
Abejo, Bisi. Love at first flight /. Ibadan, Nigeria , 1986. 241 p. ;
MLCS 87/7911 (P)   NYPL [Sc C 88-367]

Achebe, Chinelo. The last laugh and other

stories /. Ibadan , 1988. 79 p. ; ISBN 978-12-9853-7   *NYPL [Sc C 89-152]*

Achebe, Chinua. [Things fall apart.] Okonkwo, oder, Das Alte stürzt . Stuttgart , c1958. 230 p. ;   *NYPL [Sc C 88-357]*

Achebe, Chinua. [Things fall apart. Spanish.] Todo se derrumba /. Madrid , 1986. 198 p. ; ISBN 84-204-2323-8
NYPL [Sc D 88-1415]

Adebowale, Bayo. Out of his mind/. Ibadan , 1987. 149 p. ; ISBN 978-246-160-1
NYPL [Sc C 88-168]

Ali, Hauwa. Destiny . Enugu , 1988. 101 p.; ISBN 978-233-583-5   *NYPL [Sc C 89-151]*

Anigbedu, Laide. Hero's welcome /. Yaba-Lagos, Nigeria , 1986. 141 p. ; ISBN 978-256-400-1   *NYPL [Sc C 88-283]*

Awonge, Flora. A year for my nation /. Calabar , c1986. 99 p. ;
MLCS 87/7812 (P)   NYPL [Sc C 88-155]

Emecheta, Buchi, 1944. A kind of marriage /. London , 1986. iv, 121 p. ; ISBN 0-333-42242-2
NYPL [Sc D 88-613]

Fakunle, Funmilayo. Chasing the shadow /. Oshogbo [Nigeria] , 1980. 151 p. ; *NYPL [Sc C 87-462]*

Fakunle, Victor. Tentacles of the gods /. Oshogbo , 1984. 111 p. ;
NYPL [Sc C 88-280]

Fashagba, S. O. Winds against my people /. Ilorin [198-] 57 p. :   *NYPL [Sc C 88-353]*

Fulani, Dan. Sauna and the drug pedlars. London , 1986. 109 p. : ISBN 0-340-32789-8 (pbk) :   *NYPL [Sc C 88-74]*

Gimba, Abubakar. Witnesses to tears . Enugu , 1986. 170 p. ; ISBN 978-233-521-5
NYPL [Sc C 88-208]

Heinecke, P. The rebel and other stories /. Okpella, Bendel State, Nigeria , 1987. 84 p. ; ISBN 978-252-824-2   *NYPL [Sc E 88-601]*

Humphrey, Dibia. A drop of mercy /. Nigeria , 1987. 230 p. ; ISBN 978-13-9603-2
NYPL [Sc C 88-318]

Ikonné, Chidi, 1940- Unborn child /. Owerri, Imo State, 1987. v. 137 p. ; ISBN 978-267-124-X
NYPL [Sc C 88-359]

Ilouno, Chukwuemeka. Up from polygamy /. [Nigeria] c1985 (Enugu, Nigeria : Bema Press) 68 p. ;   *NYPL [Sc C 88-294]*

Lawal, Ayo. A Nigerian story in Shareent/ful Ayo Lawal]. Nigeria , 198-?] (Ilorin : Govt. Printer) 132 p. ;   *NYPL [Sc D 88-1386]*

Maja-Pearce, Adewale. Loyalties /. Harlow , 1986. 152 p. ; ISBN 0-582-78628-2 (pbk) : DDC 823 19   *NYPL [Sc C 89-56]*

Mwiwawi, Andrew M., 1952- The act /. Nairobi, Kenya , 1976. 76 p. ; DDC 823
PZ4.M9933 Ac PR9381.9.M93
NYPL [Sc B 89-22]

Ogbobine, R. A. I. (Rufus A. I.) A post in the military government /. [Benin City, Nigeria] 159 p. ; ISBN 978-300-455-7
NYPL [Sc C 89-48]

Ogunmuyiwa, Adetokunbo. Three days in Nigeria /. [Lagos? , 1988] (Lagos : Remckoye Press) 80 p. ;   *NYPL [Sc D 89-535]*

Oguntoye, Jide. Come home my love /. Ibadan , 1987. 141 p. ; ISBN 978-243-272-5
NYPL [Sc C 88-226]

Ogunyemi, M. A. The D.O. /. Ibadan , 1987. v. 126 p. ; ISBN 978-15-4777-4 (Nigeria)
NYPL [Sc C 88-176]

Ojo-Ade, Femi. Home, sweet, sweet home /. Ibadan , 1987. ix, 123 p. ; ISBN 978-15-4663-8 (Nigeria)   *NYPL [Sc C 88-209]*

Okogba, Andrew. When a child is motherless /. Benin City, Nigeria , 1987. v, 326 p. 19 cm. ISBN 978-234-045-6   *NYPL [Sc C 88-206]*

Okri, Ben. Incidents at the shrine . London , 1986. 135 p. ; ISBN 0-434-53230-4
NYPL [JFD 87-7171]

Okri, Ben. Stars of the new curfew /. London , 1988. 194 p. ; ISBN 0-436-33944-7 :
NYPL [Sc D 89-454]

Okuofu, Charles O. Death contractor /. Nigeria , 1986. 84 p. ; ISBN 978-14-1060-4
NYPL [Sc C 88-338]

Okwechime, Ireneus. The sacrifice /. Benin City, Nigeria , 1987. 136 p. ; ISBN 978-234-047-2   *NYPL [Sc C 88-175]*

Olugbile, Femi. Lonely men /. Nigeria , 1987. 183 p. ; ISBN 978-13-9605-9
NYPL [Sc C 88-336]

Omotoso, Kole, 1943- Sacrifice /. Ibadan, Nigeria , 1978. 123 p. ; *NYPL [Sc C 87-346]*

Onyeneke, Onyewuotu. I will kill you and get away with it /. [Nigeria] 122 p. ; *NYPL [Sc C 89-153]*

Popoola, Dimeji. A matter of upbringing /. Ibadan , c1987. v. 133 p. ; ISBN 0-19-575759-9 (Outside Nigeria)   *NYPL [Sc c 88-173]*

Serrano, Jumoke. The last Don out /. Ibadan, Nigeria , 1986. 106 p. ; ISBN 978-14-1062-0
NYPL [Sc C 88-341]

Soyinka, Wole. [Season of anomy. French.] Une Saison d'anomie /. Paris , c1987. 326 p. ; ISBN 2-7144-1999-2
NYPL [Sc D 88-1000]

Tsaro-Wiwa, Ken. Basi and company . Port Harcourt, Nigeria , Epsom,Surrey , 1987. 216 p. ; ISBN 1-87071-600-0 (pbk) : DDC 823 19
PR9387.9.S3   NYPL [Sc B 88-224]

Umobuarie, D. O. Adventures of a bank inspector /. Nigeria , 1988. 168 p. ; ISBN 978-300-323-2   *NYPL [Sc C 88-339]*

NIGERIA - FOREIGN ECONOMIC RELATIONS.
Nigeria and the international capitalist system /. Boulder, Colo. , 1988. v, 154 p. ; ISBN 1-555-87087-2 (alk. paper) : DDC 337.669 19
HF1616.7 .N54 1988   NYPL [JLE 88-3615]

Otobo, Dafe. Foreign interests and Nigerian trade unions /. Ibadan [Nigeria] , 1986. xxviii, 190 p. : ISBN 978-12-9532-5 (pbk.) DDC 331.88/09669 19
HD6885.5 .O87 1986   NYPL [Sc E 88-557]

NIGERIA - FOREIGN RELATIONS.
Nigeria and the international capitalist system /. Boulder, Colo. , 1988. v, 154 p. ; ISBN 1-555-87087-2 (alk. paper) : DDC 337.669 19
HF1616.7 .N54 1988   NYPL [JLE 88-3615]

Ogunsanwo, Alaba. Our friends, their friends . Yaba , 1986, c1985. 145 p. ; ISBN 978-301-700-4   *NYPL [Sc D 89-137]*

NIGERIA - FOREIGN RELATIONS - 1960-
Garba, Joesph Nanven, 1943- Diplomatic soldiering . Ibadan , 1987. xviii, 238 p., [9] p. of plates : ISBN 978-246-176-8 (limp)
NYPL [Sc D 88-726]

Nigeria - Government. see Nigeria - Politics and government.

The Nigeria handbook : 25 years of progress : a silver jubilee review. Surulere, Lagos : Patike Communications Ltd., c1985. 176 p. : ill. (some col.) ; 28 cm. Errata slip inserted. DDC 966.9/05 19
I. Patike Communications Limited.
DT515.22 .N54 1985   NYPL [Sc F 88-367]

NIGERIA - HISTO - 1851-1899.
Obiozor, May. Guide to National Museum of Colonial History, Aba /. [Lagos, Nigeria , 1985] 32 p. :   *NYPL [Sc F 88-259]*

NIGERIA - HISTORIOGRAPHY.
Smith, Abdullahi, 1920-1984. A little new light . Zaria , 1987- v. :
NYPL [Sc D 88-708]

NIGERIA - HISTORY.
Ejimofor, Cornelius Ogu, 1940- British colonial objectives and policies in Nigeria . Onitsha, Nigeria , 1987. viii, 216 p., 1 folded leaf : ISBN 978-17-5142-8   *NYPL [Sc D 88-820]*

NIGERIA - HISTORY - TO 1851.
Smith, Abdullahi, 1920-1984. A little new light . Zaria , 1987- v. :
NYPL [Sc D 88-708]

NIGERIA - HISTORY - 1900-1960.
Obiozor, May. Guide to National Museum of Colonial History, Aba /. [Lagos, Nigeria , 1985] 32 p. :   *NYPL [Sc F 88-259]*

NIGERIA - HISTORY - 1960-
Graf, William D. The Nigerian state . London ,

Portsmouth, N.H. , 1988. xvi, 281 p. : ISBN 0-85255-313-7 (cased) : DDC 320.1/09669 19
NYPL [Sc E 89-195]

NIGERIA - HISTORY - CIVIL WAR, 1967-1970.
Enonchong, Charles. The Abagana ambush . Calabar, Nigeria [197?] 47 p. :
NYPL [Sc C 89-33]

NIGERIA - HISTORY - CIVIL WAR, 1967-1970 - CIVILIAN RELIEF.
Okpoko, John. The Biafran nightmare . Enugu, Nigeria , 1986. x, 76, [4] p. of plates : ISBN 978-233-504-5 *NYPL [Sc C 88-184]*

NIGERIA - HISTORY - CIVIL WAR, 1967-1970 - DRAMA.
Acholonu, Catherine Obianuju. Into the heart of Biafra /. Owerri, Nigeria , c1985. 86 p. ; ISBN 978-244-914-8 *NYPL [Sc C 88-337]*

NIGERIA - HISTORY - CIVIL WAR, 1967-1970 - FICTION.
Maja-Pearce, Adewale. Loyalties /. Harlow , 1986. 152 p. ; ISBN 0-582-78628-2 (pbk) : DDC 823 19 *NYPL [Sc C 89-56]*

Soyinka, Wole. [Season of anomy. French.] Une Saison d'anomie /. Paris , c1987. 326 p. ; ISBN 2-7144-1999-2
NYPL [Sc D 88-1000]

NIGERIA - HISTORY - CIVIL WAR, 1967-1970 - PERSONAL NARRATIVES.
Ofoegbu, Leslie Jean. Blow the fire /. Enugu, Nigeria , 1986, c1985. 167 p. ;
NYPL [Sc C 88-288]

NIGERIA - HISTORY - DICTIONARIES.
Oyewole, A. Historical dictionary of Nigeria /. Metuchen, N.J. , c1987. xvii, 391 p. : ISBN 0-8108-1787-X DDC 966.9/003/21 19
DT515.15 .O94 1987
NYPL [*R-BMM 89-3341]

NIGERIA - HISTORY - FICTION.
Omotoso, Kole. Just before dawn /. Ibadan , 1988. xi, 345 p. ; ISBN 978-246-007-9
NYPL [Sc D 88-1485]

NIGERIA - HISTORY - PROBLEMS, EXERCISES, ETC.
Thomas, Howell. Practical exercises in Nigerian history /. Ibadan , 1966. 104 p. :
NYPL [Sc E 88-598]

Nigeria in search of a future / edited by G.E.K. Ofomata and C.C. Ukaegbu. Nsukka : Faculty of the Social Sciences, University of Nigeria, 1986. vii, 155 p. ; 21 cm. "[This book] grew out of the 1986 Faculty Week activities... It contains the papers presented at the Week's Symposium and the Faculty Week Lecture"--P. 4 of cover. ISBN 978-229-900-6
1. Economic forecasting - Nigeria. 2. Nigeria - Politics and government - 1984-. 3. Nigeria - Economic conditions - 1970-. I. Ukaegbu, Chikwendu Christian, 1945-. II. Ofomata, G. E. K.
NYPL [Sc D 88-884]

NIGERIA - INDUSTRIES.
Kalu, Onwuka O. The challenge of industrialization in Nigeria . Lagos, Nigeria , 1986. xviii, 84 p. ; *NYPL [Sc D 88-1245]*

Nigeria. Federal Dept. of Information. Saga of progress: Nigeria 1960-1985. Lagos, 19. 79 p. :
NYPL [Sc F 88-170]

NIGERIA - JUVENILE FICTION.
Davis, Russell G. Strangers in Africa. New York [1963] 149 p.
PZ7.D2993 St *NYPL [Sc D 88-505]*

Saro-Wiwa, Ken. Mr. B /. Port Harcourt , Ewell , 1987. 154 p. : ISBN 1-87071-601-9 (pbk) : DDC 823 19
PZ7 *NYPL [Sc C 88-300]*

Schatz, Letta. Bola and the Oba's drummer. New York [1967]. 156 p. DDC [Fic] 19
PZ7.S337 Bo *NYPL [Sc E 89-26]*

Ugochukwu, Françoise, 1949- La source interdite /. Abidjan , Paris , c1984. 63 p. :
NYPL [Sc B 88-33]

Umeh, Rich Enujioke. Why the cock became a sacrificial animal /. Enugu, Nigeria , 1985. 38 p. : ISBN 978-239-648-6 *NYPL [Sc C 89-18]*

NIGERIA - JUVENILE LITERATURE.
Ajoṣe, Audrie. Emo and the Babalawo /. Ibadan , 1985. 51 p. : ISBN 978-15-5652-2 (Nigeria) *NYPL [Sc C 88-152]*

Kenworthy, Leonard Stout, 1912- Profile of Nigeria /. Garden City, New York , c1960. 96 p. :
NYPL [Sc E 88-240]

NIGERIA - KINGS AND RULERS - HISTORY.
Kenyo, Elisha Alademomi. Awon olori Yoruba ati isedale won /. Lagos, Nigeria , 1952. 96 p. :
NYPL [Sc D 88-818]

NIGERIA - MANUFACTURES.
Ukpong, Ignatius I. The contributions of expatriate and indigenous manpower to the manufacturing industry in Nigeria . [Calabar, Cross River State, Nigeria] [c1986] ix, 61 p. : ISBN 978-227-526-3 DDC 331.12/57/09669 19
HD5848.A6 U37 1986 *NYPL [Sc C 89-128]*

NIGERIA - MILITARY POLICY - QUOTATIONS, MAXIMS, ETC.
Babangida, Ibrahim Badamasi. Quotes of a general . Surulere [Nigeria] , 1987. 90 p. :
NYPL [Sc D 88-711]

NIGERIA - MORAL CONDITIONS.
Ali, Sidi H. The WAI as an ideology of moral rectitude /. [Nigeria] 1985 (Lagos : Academy Press) 88 p. : *NYPL [Sc D 88-869]*

Nigeria. National Commission for Museums and Monuments. The story of the old Calabar . [Lagos?] , c1986. 228 p. :
NYPL [Sc D 89-253]

NIGERIA - NATIONAL SECURITY.
Nigerian defence and security . Bukuru, Plateau State , 1987. xii, 208 p. ; ISBN 978-19-8019-2
NYPL [Sc D 88-1377]

NIGERIA, NORTHERN - RURAL CONDITIONS.
Mortimore, M. J., 1937- Adapting to drought . Cambridge , New York , 1989. xxii, 299 p. : ISBN 0-521-32312-6 DDC 333.73 19
HC1055.Z7 N6755 1988
NYPL [Sc E 89-191]

NIGERIA - OFFICIALS AND EMPLOYEES - BIOGRAPHY.
Ibuje, Joan, 1941- Memoirs of a great bureaucrat /. Benin City [Nigeria] [1985?] 60 p. : *NYPL [Sc D 88-805]*

Nigeria on the forward march /. Bisuga, Mike. Ikeja, Nigeria , 1984. v, 119 p. ; ISBN 978-16-3030-2 *NYPL [Sc D 89-65]*

NIGERIA - POLITICS AND GOVERNMEN - 1979-1983.
Joseph, Richard A. Democracy and prebendal politics in Nigeria . Cambridge [Cambridgeshire] , New York , 1987. x, 237 p. : ISBN 0-521-34136-1 DDC 966.9/05 19
DT515.84 .J67 1987 *NYPL [JFE 88-4953]*

NIGERIA - POLITICS AND GOVERNMENT - TO 1960.
Akpan, Ekwere Otu. The women's war of 1929 . Calabar, Nigeria , 1988. vii, 68 p. :
NYPL [Sc E 89-20]

Schärer, Therese, 1946- Das Nigerian Youth Movement . Frankfurt am Main , New York , c1986. xiii, 376, A76 p., 3 leaves of plates : ISBN 3-261-03567-6 *NYPL [Sc D 88-878]*

Terrell, Richard. West African interlude . Salisbury, Wiltshire , 1988. 175 p. :
NYPL [Sc D 88-1371]

NIGERIA - POLITICS AND GOVERNMENT - 1960-.
Babatope, Ebenezer. Awo & Nigeria . Ikeja [Nigeria] , 1984. 97 p. : ISBN 3-7830-0100-0
NYPL [Sc D 88-1397]

Duke, Hajia Zainab I. (Hajia Zainab Ibitein) The revolutionary potentials of the Nigerian military, 1886-1986 /. [Lagos?] Nigeria , c1987. viii, 145 p., [28] p. of plates : ISBN 978-232-008-0 DDC 322/.5/09669 19
DT515.8 .D84 1987 *NYPL [Sc D 88-1278]*

The impact of military rule on Nigeria's administration /. Ile-Ife, Nigeria , c1987. vi, 344 p. ; ISBN 978-266-601-7
NYPL [Sc D 88-733]

Kayode, M. O. The confused society /. Ibadan , Nigeria , 1987. vii, 138 p. : ISBN 978-16-7457-1
NYPL [Sc D 88-786]

Madunagu, Edwin. Nigeria, the economy and the people [microform] . London , 1983. 38 p. : ISBN 0-901241-54-7
NYPL [Sc Micro F-11069]

Malami, Shehu, Alhaji. Nigerian memories /. London , Ibadan , 1985. xii, [139] p., [12] p. of plates : ISBN 978-16-7526-8
NYPL [Sc D 88-532]

Nigerian alternatives /. [Zaria, Nigeria] 1987. 323 p. ; ISBN 978-301-130-11
NYPL [Sc D 88-698]

Nwankwo, Arthur A. Thoughts on Nigeria /. Enugu, Nigeria , 1986. xxii, 198 p. ; ISBN 987-15-6264-1 *NYPL [Sc E 88-448]*

Odunewu, Alade. Winners take all /. [Nigeria?] [1988?] vi, 330 p. ; *NYPL [Sc D 89-543]*

Oyaide, William John, 1936- Presidentialism . Benin City, Nigeria , c1987. xi, 133 p. ; ISBN 978-300-550-2 *NYPL [Sc D 88-917]*

Takaya, B. J. The Kaduna mafia /. [Jos, Nigeria] , c1987. viii, 146 p. ; ISBN 978-16-6045-7 *NYPL [Sc D 88-736]*

Usman, Yusufu Bala, 1945- The manipulation of religion in Nigeria, 1977-1987 /. Kaduna, Nigeria , 1987. 153 p. ; ISBN 978-255-708-0
NYPL [Sc C 88-220]

Wright, Stephen, 1954- Nigeria, the dilemmas ahead . London , c1986. 88 p. :
NYPL [Sc F 88-137]

NIGERIA - POLITICS AND GOVERNMENT - 1960-- CONGRESSES.
Proceedings of the colloquium on Why army rule? . [Lagos? , 1986 or 19. 338 p. ;
NYPL [Sc G 88-23]

NIGERIA - POLITICS AND GOVERNMENT - 1960-- DRAMA.
Odumosu, Z. O. The leader . Lagos, Nigeria , c1986. xi, 83 p. : ISBN 978-230-916-8
NYPL [Sc C 88-160]

NIGERIA - POLITICS AND GOVERNMENT - 1960-1975.
Boro, Isaac. The twelve-day revolution /. Benin City, Nigeria , 1982. 158 p., [8] p. of plates : ISBN 978-234-040-5 *NYPL [Sc C 88-109]*

Diamond, Larry. Class, ethnicity and democracy in Nigeria . Basingstoke , c1988. xiii, 376 p. : ISBN 0-333-39435-6 : DDC 966.9/05 19
DT515.832 *NYPL [Sc D 88-1310]*

NIGERIA - POLITICS AND GOVERNMENT - 1975-1979.
Garba, Joseph Nanven, 1943- Diplomatic soldiering /. Ibadan , 1987. xviii, 238 p., [9] p. of plates : ISBN 978-246-176-8 (limp)
NYPL [Sc D 88-726]

NIGERIA - POLITICS AND GOVERNMENT - 1979-.
Okonkwo, Ifeanyichukwu E. R. The great debate . Onitsha, Anambra State, Nigeria , 1986. 138 p. : ISBN 978-264-308-4
NYPL [Sc C 89-58]

Tell it as it is /. Enugu [Nigeria] [1985?]- v. ; ISBN 978-247-202-6 *NYPL [Sc C 88-183]*

NIGERIA - POLITICS AND GOVERNMENT - 1979-1983.
Labode, Sakirudeen Tunji. Party power . Abeokuta, Nigeria , 1988. 244 p. ; ISBN 978-18-3008-5 *NYPL [Sc C 88-376]*

NIGERIA - POLITICS AND GOVERNMENT - 1984-
Babangida, Ibrahim Badamasi. Collected speeches of the president /. Lagos [1986?] 280 p. : *NYPL [Sc E 88-303]*

Nigeria in search of a future /. Nsukka , 1986. vii, 155 p. ; ISBN 978-229-900-6
NYPL [Sc D 88-884]

Oyediran, Oyeleye. Essays on local government and administration in Nigeria /. Surulere, Lagos, Nigeria , 1988. x, 286 p. ; ISBN 978-277-801-001 *NYPL [Sc D 88-1365]*

NIGERIA - POLITICS AND GOVERNMENT - CONGRESSES.
Alternative political futures for Nigeria /. Nigeria , 1987. xviii, 565 p. ; ISBN 978-303-170-8 *NYPL [Sc D 88-1374]*

NIGERIA - POLITICS AND GOVERNMENT - PHILOSOPHY.
Obi, Chike. Our struggle . Enugu, Nigeria , 1986. 76 p. ; ISBN 978-15-6187-4
NYPL [Sc D 88-753]

Nigeria. President (1985- : Babangida)
Babangida, Ibrahim Badamasi. Collected
speeches of the president /. Lagos [1986?] 280
p. : *NYPL [Sc E 88-303]*

NIGERIA - PRESIDENTS.
Oyaide, William John, 1936- Presidentialism .
Benin City, Nigeria, c1987. xi, 133 p. ; ISBN
978-300-550-2 *NYPL [Sc D 88-917]*

Nigeria Psychological Association. Psychology
and society . [Ife?] , 1986. 212 p. ;
NYPL [Sc E 88-432]

NIGERIA - PUBLIC LANDS.
Uduehi, Godfrey O. Public lands acquisition
and compensation practice in Nigeria /. Ogba,
Ikeja, 1987. xviii, 162 p. : ISBN 978-16-3064-7
NYPL [Sc D 89-480]

NIGERIA - RELATIONS - CAMEROON -
BIBLIOGRAPHY.
Irele, Modupe. Nigeria and Cameroun . Lagos,
Nigeria, c1984. viii, 67 p. : ISBN 978-237-205-6
(pbk.) DDC 016.327669067/11 19
Z3597 .I73 1984 DT515.63.C17
NYPL [Sc E 87-30]

NIGERIA - RELATIONS - FOREIGN
COUNTRIES.
Nigerian alternatives /. [Zaria, Nigeria] 1987.
323 p. ; ISBN 978-301-130-11
NYPL [Sc D 88-698]

NIGERIA - RELIGION.
Chukwulozie, Victor. Muslim-Christian dialogue
in Nigeria /. Ibadan, 1986. xviii, 201 p. :
ISBN 978-12-2192-5 *NYPL [Sc D 88-890]*

New religious movements in Nigeria /.
Lewiston, N.Y., c1987. xvi, 245 p. ; ISBN
0-88946-180-5 (alk. paper) DDC 291.9/09669 19
BL2470.N5 N49 1987 NYPL [Sc E 88-266]

Usman, Yusufu Bala, 1945- The manipulation of
religion in Nigeria, 1977-1987 /. Kaduna,
Nigeria, 1987. 153 p. ; ISBN 978-255-708-0
NYPL [Sc C 88-220]

NIGERIA - RELIGIOUS LIFE AND
CUSTOMS.
Ilogu, Edmund. Igbo life and thought /.
[Nigeria], c1985. 42 p. ; ISBN 978-16-0344-5
NYPL [Sc D 88-741]

NIGERIA - SOCIAL CONDITIONS.
Ali, Sidi H. The WAI as an ideology of moral
rectitude /. [Nigeria] 1985 (Lagos : Academy
Press) 88 p. : *NYPL [Sc D 88-869]*

Eze, Sylvester Omumeka. Steps for
socio-political and religious change . [Nsukka?]
1987 (Nsukka : Chinedu Printers) 52 p. ;
NYPL [Sc C 89-53]

Family and social change . Lagos, Nigeria ,
1986. vi, 96 p. ; *NYPL [Sc D 88-794]*

Mbaba, Ita G. Blast at noon . Calabar, Nigeria ,
c1987. x, 40 p. ; ISBN 978-231-602-2
NYPL [Sc C 89-63]

NIGERIA - SOCIAL CONDITIONS - 1960-
Kayode, M. O. The confused society /. Ibadan,
Nigeria, 1987. vii, 138 p. : ISBN 978-16-7457-1
NYPL [Sc D 88-786]

Nigeria, the people and their heritage /.
Calabar [Nigeria], 1987. 339 p. : ISBN
978-228-328-2 *NYPL [Sc D 88-734]*

Okongwu, Chu S. P., 1934- The Nigerian
economy . Enugu, Nigeria , 1986. vi, 453 p. :
ISBN 978-15-6038-X (pbk.) : DDC 330.9669/05
19
HC1055 .O39 1986 NYPL [Sc D 88-1250]

Social change in Nigeria /. Harlow, Essex,
England, 1984. 261 p. ; ISBN 0-582-64434-8
(pbk.) : DDC 306/.09669 19
HN831.A8 S63 1984 NYPL [Sc D 88-880]

Social change in Nigeria /. London , 1986. 261
p. ; ISBN 0-582-64434-8 (pbk.) : DDC 306/.09669
19
HN831.A8 S63 1986 NYPL [JLE 87-3643]

Ukeje, B. Onyerisara. School and society in
Nigeria /. Enugu, Nigeria , 1986. 129 p. ;
ISBN 978-15-6245-5
NYPL [Sc D 88-1243]

NIGERIA - SOCIAL CONDITIONS -
CONGRESSES.
Austerity and the Nigerian society /. Nsukka ,
1987. vi, 240 p. ; ISBN 978-264-356-4
NYPL [Sc D 89-205]

NIGERIA - SOCIAL LIFE AND CUSTOMS -
JUVENILE LITERATURE.
Barker, Carol. Village in Nigeria /. London ,
c19. 25 p. : ISBN 0-7136-2391-8 : DDC 966.9/05
19
DT515.8 .B29 1984 NYPL [Sc D 88-605]

NIGERIA - SOCIAL POLICY.
Better life for Nigerians /. Lagos , 1987. 56 p. :
NYPL [Sc D 88-796]

Nigerian alternatives /. [Zaria, Nigeria] 1987.
323 p. ; ISBN 978-301-130-11
NYPL [Sc D 88-698]

Okongwu, Chu S. P., 1934- The Nigerian
economy . Enugu, Nigeria , 1986. vi, 453 p. :
ISBN 978-15-6038-X (pbk.) : DDC 330.9669/05
19
HC1055 .O39 1986 NYPL [Sc D 88-1250]

Solarin, Tai. Timeless Tai /. Lagos, Nigeria ,
1985. x, 232 p. ; *NYPL [Sc D 89-371]*

Nigeria teacher education . Okafor, Festus C.
Enugu, Nigeria , 1988. 173 p. : ISBN
978-15-6298-6 *NYPL [Sc D 89-180]*

Nigeria, the dilemmas ahead . Wright, Stephen,
1954- London , c1986. 88 p. :
NYPL [Sc F 88-137]

Nigeria, the economy and the people
[microform] . Madunagu, Edwin. London ,
1983. 38 p. ; ISBN 0-901241-54-7
NYPL [Sc Micro F-11069]

Nigeria, the people and their heritage / edited by
J.U. Obot. Calabar [Nigeria] : Wusen Press,
1987. 339 p. : ill., maps ; 21 cm. Includes
bibliographical references and index. ISBN
978-228-328-2
1. *Nigeria - Civilization.* 2. *Nigeria - Social conditions -*
1960-. 3. *Nigeria - Economic conditions - 1970-.* I.
Obot, J. U. *NYPL [Sc D 88-734]*

Nigeria, the search for economic stability /.
Ogunbanjo, C. O. (Christopher Odadipo), 1923-
[Nigeria?] 1986. 102 p., [4] p. of plates : ISBN
0-946233-04-7 *NYPL [Sc D 88-519]*

Nigeria, the search for economic stability /.
Ogunbanjo, C. O. (Christopher Oladipo), 1923-
[S.l.] , 1986. 103 p., [4] p. of plates : ISBN
0-946233-04-7 *NYPL [Sc D 88-883]*

Nigerian alternatives / edited by Okello Oculi.
[Zaria, Nigeria : Department of Political
Science, Ahmadu Bello University], 1987. 323
p. ; 22 cm. Includes bibliographical references. ISBN
978-301-130-11
1. *Nigeria - Politics and government - 1960-.* 2.
Nigeria - Economic policy. 3. *Nigeria - Social policy.* 4.
Nigeria - Relations - Foreign countries. I. *Oculi, Okello,*
1942-. *NYPL [Sc D 88-698]*

Nigerian Army Museum. A pictorial history of
the Nigerian Army / by Nigerian Army
Museum. Nigeria : Directorate of Army
Education, c1987. 49 p. : ill., ports. ; 26 cm.
Cover title: The history of the Nigerian Army in
pictures.
1. *Nigeria. Army - History.* I. *Title.* II. *Title: History of*
the Nigerian Army in pictures.
NYPL [Sc F 89-81]

Nigerian Association of Schools of Management
Education and Training. Conference (3rd :
1982 : Enugu, Nigeria) Development of
management education in Nigeria /. Ikeja,
Nigeria, 1985. 555 p. : ISBN 978-14-0017-X
NYPL [Sc E 89-161]

Nigerian defence and security : issues and options
for policy / edited by T.A. Imobighe. Bukuru,
Plateau State : Dept. of Research, National
Institute for Policy and Strategic Studies in
cooperation with Macmillan Nigeria, Yaba,
Lagos, 1987. xii, 208 p. ; 23 cm. Includes
bibliographical references and index. ISBN
978-19-8019-2
1. *Nigeria - Defenses.* 2. *Nigeria - National security.* 3.
Nigeria - Armed Forces. I. *Imobighe, Thomas A.* II.
National Institute for Policy and Strategic Studies
(Nigeria). Research Dept. *NYPL [Sc D 88-1377]*

The Nigerian economy . Okongwu, Chu S. P.,
1934- Enugu, Nigeria , 1986. vi, 453 p. : ISBN
978-15-6038-X (pbk.) : DDC 330.9669/05 19
HC1055 .O39 1986 NYPL [Sc D 88-1250]

Nigerian English (NigE) . Odumuh, A. E. [S.l.]
1987 (Zaria: Printed in Nigeria by A.B.
University Press.) vi, 125 p. ; ISBN
978-12-5061-5 *NYPL [Sc D 88-1378]*

NIGERIAN FICTION (ENGLISH) -
HISTORY AND CRITICISM.
Doherty, Jaiyeola, 1952- Die Satire im
nigerianischen Roman . Frankfurt am Main ,
New York , c1986. 381 p. : ISBN 3-8204-8326-8
DDC 823 19
PR9387.4 .D64 1986 NYPL [Sc D 88-991]

Nigerian Institute of Advanced Legal Studies.
Proceedings of the colloquium on Why army
rule? . [Lagos?] , 1986 or 19. 338 p. ;
NYPL [Sc G 88-23]

Nigerian Institute of International Affairs,
1961-1986 . Banjo, A. Olugboyega. Lagos,
1986. iv, 34 p. : *NYPL [Sc E 89-254]*

Nigerian Institute of International Affairs,
1961-1986. Banjo, A. Olugboyega. Nigerian
Institute of International Affairs, 1961-1986 .
Lagos, 1986. iv, 34 p. :
NYPL [Sc E 89-254]

Nigerian Institute of Social and Economic
Research. Visser, Johanna, 1898- A list of
books, articles and government publications on
the economy of Nigeria, 1963 and 1964.
Ibadan, 1965. x, 81 p. *NYPL [Sc F 78-58]*

NIGERIAN LITERATURE - HISTORY.
Perspectives on Nigerian literature, 1700 to the
present /. Oshodi, Lagos, Nigeria , 1988. 2 v. ;
NYPL [Sc E 89-19]

Nigerian memories /. Malami, Shehu, Alhaji.
London , Ibadan , 1985. xii, [139] p., [12] p. of
plates : ISBN 978-16-7526-8 (Nigeria)
NYPL [Sc D 88-532]

Nigerian Political Science Association.
Alternative political futures for Nigeria /.
Nigeria , 1987. xviii, 565 p. ; ISBN
978-303-170-8 *NYPL [Sc D 88-1374]*

The Nigerian state . Graf, William D. London ,
Portsmouth, N.H. , 1988. xvi, 281 p. : ISBN
0-85255-313-7 (cased) : DDC 320.1/09669 19
NYPL [Sc E 89-195]

A Nigerian story in Shareent/ful Ayo Lawal].
Lawal, Ayo. Nigeria , 198-?] (Ilorin : Govt.
Printer) 132 p. ; *NYPL [Sc D 88-1386]*

Nigerian women and development / editors, F.
Adetowun Ogunsheye ... [et al.]. Ibadan,
Nigeria : Ibadan University Press, 1988. xv, 495
p. ; 22 cm. Includes bibliographies and index. ISBN
978-12-1219-5
1. *Women - Nigeria.* 2. *Women in development -*
Nigeria. I. *Ogunsheye, F. Adetowun.*
NYPL [Sc D 89-576]

Das Nigerian Youth Movement . Schärer,
Therese, 1946- Frankfurt am Main , New
York , c1986. xiii, 376, A76 p., 3 leaves of
plates : ISBN 3-261-03567-6
NYPL [Sc D 88-878]

NIGERIAN YOUTH MOVEMENT.
Schärer, Therese, 1946- Das Nigerian Youth
Movement . Frankfurt am Main , New York ,
c1986. xiii, 376, A76 p., 3 leaves of plates :
ISBN 3-261-03567-6 *NYPL [Sc D 88-878]*

NIGERIANS - FICTION.
Okpalaeze, Inno-Pat Chuba. Oriental passion /.
Onitsha, Nigeria , 1987. 89 p. ;
NYPL [Sc C 89-72]

NIGERIANS - GREAT BRITAIN -
BIOGRAPHY.
Trill, Carol. Dispossessed daughter of Africa /.
London , 1988. 190 p. : ISBN 0-946918-42-2
(pbk.) *NYPL [sc C 88-228]*

Nigerija. see Nigeria.

Nights of a mystical beast; and, The new dawn .
Obafemi, Olu, 1945- [Nights of a mystical
beast.] Benin City, Nigeria , c1986. vii,82 p. ;
ISBN 978-249-806-8
MLCS 87/7882 (P) NYPL [Sc C 88-169]

NIIA monograph series.
(no. 13) Banjo, A. O. Social science librairies in
West Africa . Lagos, Nigeria , 1987. iii, 63 p. :
NYPL [Sc D 88-1204]

(no.12) Banjo, A. Olugboyega. Nigerian
Institute of International Affairs, 1961-1986 .
Lagos, 1986. iv, 34 p. :
NYPL [Sc E 89-254]

Jinadu, Adele. Idealism and pragmatism as
aspects of Sweden's development policy in
Africa /. Lagos [1982?]. 107 p. ; ISBN
978-227-698-7 *NYPL [Sc D 88-355]*

Niiwam, suivi de Taaw . Sembene, Ousmane, 1923- Paris , c1987. 189 p. ; ISBN 2-7087-0486-9   *NYPL [Sc C 88-320]*

Nike chieftaincy, 1919-1985 /. Nnamani, Jude Onuchukwu. Enugu [1986?] xvi, 68 p. :
NYPL [Sc D 89-286]

NIKE (NIGERIA) - KINGS AND RULERS - HISTORY.
Nnamani, Jude Onuchukwu. Nike chieftaincy, 1919-1985 /. Enugu [1986?] xvi, 68 p. :
NYPL [Sc D 89-286]

NIKE (NIGERIA - POLITICS AND GOVERNMENT.
Nnamani, Jude Onuchukwu. Nike chieftaincy, 1919-1985 /. Enugu [1986?] xvi, 68 p. :
NYPL [Sc D 89-286]

The Nile. Warren, Ruth. New York [1968] 127 p. DDC 916.2
DT115 .W33   *NYPL [Sc E 89-21]*

NILE RIVER - DISCOVERY AND EXPLORATION - JUVENILE LITERATURE.
African adventures and adventurers /. Boston , 1880. 393 p. :
NYPL [Sc C 88-60]

NILE RIVER VALLEY - JUVENILE LITERATURE.
Warren, Ruth. The Nile. New York [1968] 127 p. DDC 916.2
DT115 .W33   *NYPL [Sc E 89-21]*

NILO-HAMITIC LANGUAGES - GRAMMAR, COMPARATIVE - HAMITO-SEMITIC.
Hohenberger, Johannes. Semitische und hamitische Wortst"amme im Nilo-Hamitischen . Berlin , 1988. xxii, 310 p. ; ISBN 3-496-00960-8
NYPL [Sc E 88-542]

Nine men who laughed /. Clarke, Austin, 1934- Markham, Ontario, Canada , 1986. 225 p. ; ISBN 0-14-008560-2   *NYPL [JFD 87-7697]*

Nishiura, Luiz Carlos. Escravidão negra e história da Igreja na América Latina e no Caribe /. Petrópolis , 1987. 237 p. ;
NYPL [Sc D 88-75]

Nitchman, Paul E. Blacks in Ohio, 1880 in the counties of ... / by Paul E. Nitchman. [Decorah? Iowa] : P.E. Nitchman, c1985- v. ; 29 cm. Vol. 5 has title: Blacks in Ohio, 1880, in the city of Cincinnati. Includes indexes. CONTENTS. - v. 1. Adams-Carroll -- v. 2. Champaign-Clinton -- v. 3. Columbiana-Fayette -- v. 4. Franklin-Geauga -- v. 5. Cincinnati -- v. 6. Greene-Henry -- v. 7. Highland-Lorain. DDC 929/.3/089960730771 19
1. Afro-Americans - Ohio - Genealogy. 2. Registers of births, etc. - Ohio. 3. Ohio - Genealogy. 4. Ohio - Census, 1880. 5. United States - Census, 10th, 1880. I. Title.
E185.93.O2 N57 1985
NYPL [APR (Ohio) 86-2025]

Niven, Cecil Rex, 1898- The lands and peoples of West Africa / by Sir Rex Niven. 2nd ed. London : A and C. Black ; [1961] vii, 84 p. : ill., map. ; 20 cm. (Lands and peoples series)
1. Africa, West - Description and travel. 2. Africa, West - Social life and customs. I. Title. II. Series.
NYPL [Sc D 88-669]

Njai, D. M. (Daniel Michael) Abortion, the way it is / [By D.M. Njai] Nairobi : Catholic Bookshop, [198-] 31 p. ; 21 cm. Bibliography: p. 30-31.
1. Abortion - Religious aspects - Catholic Church. I. Title.   *NYPL [Sc D 89-321]*

Njau, Rebeka. Kenya women heroes and their mystical power / Rebeka Njau, Gideon Mulaki. Nairobi : Risk Publications, 1984- v. ; 21 cm. DDC 398/.09676/2 19
1. Heroines - Kenya - Folklore. 2. Women - Kenya - Folklore. 3. Tales, Kenya. 4. Women - Kenya - Biography. I. Mulaki, Gideon. II. Title.
GR356.4 .N43 1984   NYPL [Sc D 88-1052]

Njeddo Dewal . Ba, Amadou Hampaté. Abidjan [Ivory Coast] , c1985. 156 p. ; ISBN 2-7236-0732-1   *NYPL [Sc E 88-417]*

Njiro, Esther I. A history of Africa in the 19th century / Esther I. Njiro. Nairobi : Kenya Literature Bureau, 1985. viii, 291 p. : ill. ; 21 cm. Includes index. Bibliography: p. 287-288. DDC 960/.23 19
1. Africa - History - 19th century. I. Title.
DT28 .N55 1985   NYPL [Sc D 88-322]

NJOYA, SULTAN OF BAMOUN, 1876?-1933 - PICTORIAL WORKS.
Geary, Christraud M. Images from Bamum . Washington, D.C. , 1988. 151 p. : ISBN 0-87474-455-5 (pbk. : alk. paper) DDC 967/.1102/0880621 19
DT574 .G43 1988   *NYPL [Sc F 89-55]*

NJOYA, SULTAN OF THE BAMUN, D. 1933.
Ndam Njoya, Adamou, 1942- Njoya . Paris (9, rue du Château-d'Eau, 75010) : Dakar ; [116] p. : ISBN 2-85809-101-3 : DDC 967/.113 B 19
DT570 .N22   *NYPL [Sc C 88-162]*

The Njuri-Noheke of Meru /. Rimita, David Maitai, 1946- [Meru, Kenya?] , c1988. 81 p. :
NYPL [Sc D 89-310]

Nkrumah and Ghana . Hadjor, Kofi Buenor. London , New York , 1988. ix, 114 p., [8] p. of plates :   *NYPL [JFD 88-4445]*

NKRUMAH, KWAME, 1909-1972.
Baynham, Simon, 1950- The military and politics in Nkrumah's Ghana /. Boulder , 1988. xvi, 294 p. ; ISBN 0-8133-7063-9 : DDC 966.7/05 19
DT512 .B39 1986   *NYPL [JFD 88-10630]*

Hadjor, Kofi Buenor. Nkrumah and Ghana . London , New York , 1988. ix, 114 p., [8] p. of plates :   *NYPL [JFD 88-4445]*

Organization of African Unity 25 years on . London , 1988. vii, 175 p. : ISBN 0-948583-05-3 (Hardback)   *NYPL [Sc D 89-556]*

Rooney, David. Kwame Nkrumah . London , 1988. viii, 292 p. ;   *NYPL [Sc D 89-44]*

Nkrumah, Kwanie, Pres. Ghana 1909-1972.
Appeal for world peace [microform] . Accra [1961?] 19 p. :   *NYPL [Sc Micro F-10978]*

Nnabuchi, Nwankwo.
The conscience of God /Nwankwo Nnabuchi. Enugu : Life Paths Printing Press, 1987. xiii, 231 p. ; 22 cm. ISBN 978-270-501-2
I. Title.   *NYPL [Sc D 89-241/]*

In defence of Igbo belief system : a dialetical [sic] approach / Nwankwo Nnabuchi. Enugu, Nigera : Life Paths Printing Press, 1987. xiii, 216 p. ; 21 cm. ISBN 978-270-500-4
1. Igbo (African people) - Religion. I. Title.
NYPL [Sc D 89-84]

Nnamani, Jude Onuchukwu. Nike chieftaincy, 1919-1985 / by Jude Onuchukwu Nnamani. Enugu : Govt. Printer, [1986?] xvi, 68 p. : ill., map, ports. ; 21 cm. Bibliography: p. 65.
1. Nike (Nigeria) - Kings and rulers - History. 2. Nike (Nigeria - Politics and government. I. Title.
NYPL [Sc D 89-286]

Nńkan Àṣírí /. Akinlabí, Bánjọ. Ibadan, Oyo State, Nigeria , 1985. 62 p. ; ISBN 978-14-1052-3   *NYPL [Sc D 88-1381]*

No child's play . Makhoere, Caesarina Khana. London , 1988. 121 p. ; ISBN 0-7043-4111-5 :
NYPL [Sc C 88-333]

No food, no country /. Fatunde, Tunde. Benin City, Nigeria , 1985. xv, 81 p. ; ISBN 978-249-804-1   *NYPL [Sc C 88-342]*

No master, no mortgage, no sale . Patel, H. H. Nairobi, Kenya , 1987. 61 p. columns ;
NYPL [Sc F 88-297]

No tears for Massa's day /. Humfrey, Michael. London , 1987. 192 p. ; ISBN 0-7195-4442-4 : DDC 813 19
PR9265.9.H8   *NYPL [Sc D 88-623]*

No. 46 Steve Biko /. Bernstein, Hilda (Watts) London , 1978. 150 p., [4] p. of plates : ISBN 0-904759-21-0 :
DT779.8.B48 B47   *NYPL [JFD 79-52]*

Noble Drew Ali. *see* Ali, Noble Drew, 1886-

Nobles, Wade W.
African psychology : toward its reclamation, reascension and revitalization / [by Wade E. Nobles]. Oakland, California : Institute for the Advanced Study of Black Family Life and Culture, 1986. 133 p. ; 22 cm. Author's name from cover. "A Black Family Institute publication." Bibliography: p.117-133. ISBN 0-939205-02-5
1. Blacks - Psychology. 2. Psychology - Methodology. I. Title.   *NYPL [Sc D 88-696]*

The KM ebit husia : authoritative utterances of exceptional insight for the Black family / [developed by Wade W. Nobles, Lawford L.

Goddard, William E. Cavil]. Oakland, California : Institute for the Advanced Study of Black Family Life and Culture, 1985. 201 p. ; 28 cm. A workbook intended to help the user apply the lessons of Egyptian wisdom literature to Black family life. Authors' names from cover. ISBN 0-939205-03-3
1. Afro-Americans - Families - Problems, exercises, etc. 2. Family - Problems, exercises, etc. I. Goddard, Lawford Lawrence. II. Cavil, William E. III. Title.
NYPL [Sc F 88-159]

Understanding the Black family : a guide for scholarship and research / by Wades W. Nobles and Lawford L. Goddard.Limited edition. Oakland, California : Black Family Institute Publication, 1984. 137 p. ; 22 cm. Bibliography: p. 129-137. ISBN 0-939205-00-9
1. Afro-Americans - Families - Research. I. Goddard, Lawford L. II. Title.   *NYPL [Sc D 88-697]*

Nobles, Wade Winfred, 1945- Africanity and the Black family : the development of a theoretical model / by Wade W. Nobles. Oakland, Calif. : Institute for the Advanced Study of Black Family Life and Culture, 1985. 116 p. ; 21 cm. (A Black Family Institute publication) Cover title. Bibliography: p. 113-116. ISBN 0-939205-01-7
I. Title.   *NYPL [Sc D 88-760]*

Noces d'absence /. Bari, Nadine. Paris , c1986. 119 p., [8] p. of plates : ISBN 2-227-12607-8
NYPL [Sc D 89-61]

Les noctuelles vivent de larmes /. Ly, Ibrahima. Paris , c1988- v. ; ISBN 2-7384-0066-3
NYPL [Sc D 88-1338]

Noibi, D. O. S. Yoruba Muslim youth and Christian-sponsored education / by D.O.S. Noibi. Ijebu-Ode, Nigeria : Shebiotimo Publications, 1987. 44 p. ; 21 cm. Includes bibliographical references. ISBN 978-253-020-4
1. Islam - Education - Nigeria. 2. Islam - Nigeria - Relations - Christianity. 3. Christian education - Nigeria. 4. Yorubas - Religion. I. Title.
NYPL [Sc D 89-537]

Noin nengia, bere nengia = nembe n'akabu = More days, more wisdom : Nembe proverbs / E.J. Alagoa. Port Harcourt, Nigeria : University of Port Harcourt Press, 1986. 137 p. ; 25 cm. (Delta series . no. 5) Nembe and English. ISBN 978-232-110-9
1. Proverbs, Nembe. I. Alagoa, Ebiegberi Joe.
NYPL [Sc E 89-130]

Noire de Salem. Condé, Maryse. Moi, Tituba, sorcière-- . Paris , c1986. 276 p. ; ISBN 2-7152-1440-5   *NYPL [Sc E 88-97]*

Nolan, Jeanette Covert, 1896- John Brown / by Jeannette Covert Nolan ; decorations by Robert Burns. New York : J. Messner, 1968, c1950. 181 p. : ill. ; 22 cm. Bibliography: p. 175-181.
1. Brown, John, 1800-1859 - Juvenile literature. 2. Abolitionists - United States - Biography - Juvenile literature. 3. Harpers Ferry (W. Va.) - History - John Brown's Raid, 1859. I. Burns, Robert. II. Title.
NYPL [Sc D 88-665]

NOMADS - AFRICA, EAST.
Rigby, Peter. Persistent pastoralists . London , Totowa, N.J. , 1985. x, 198 p. : ISBN 0-86232-226-X : DDC 305.8/9676 19
DT443.3.M37 R54 1985
NYPL [JLD 86-2309]

NOMADS - CAMEROON - BIOGRAPHY.
Bocquené, Henri. Moi, un Mbororo . Paris , c1986. 387 p., [12] p. of plates : ISBN 2-86537-164-6   *NYPL [Sc E 89-66]*

Nomusa and the new magic. Mirsky, Reba Paeff. Chicago, 1962. 190 p.
PZ7.M675 No   *NYPL [Sc E 89-175]*

Non à une intervention américaine en Haïti /. Gousse, Edgard Js. Th. Montréal , 1988. 74 p. ;
NYPL [Sc D 88-861]

Non, Monsieur Giscard [microform] /. Makanda Duc d'Ikoga, André. Paris [1980] 23 p. :
NYPL [Sc Micro F-11014]

NON-RESISTANCE TO GOVERNMENT. *see* GOVERNMENT, RESISTANCE TO.

The Non-semitic languages of Ethiopia / edited by M. Lionel Bender. East Lansing : African Studies Center, Michigan State University, c1976. xv, 738 p. : ill. ; 23 cm. (Occasional papers series - Committee on Ethiopian Studies ; monograph no. 5) Includes indexes. Bibliography: p. 659-714. DDC 492

1. Ethiopia - Languages. I. Bender, M. Lionel (Marvin Lionel), 1934-. II. Series: Michigan. State University, East Lansing. Committee on Ethiopian Studies. Occasional papers series , monograph no. 5.
PL8021.E8 N6   ***NYPL [Sc D 88-854]***

NONVIOLENT NONCOOPERATION. see PASSIVE RESISTANCE.

Nordiska Afrikainstitutet.
   Research report.
   (no. 68) Haarløv, Jens. Labour regulation and black workers' struggles in South Africa /. Uppsala , 1983. 80 p. ; ISBN 91-7106-213-0 (pbk.) DDC 960 s 331.6/9/968 19
DT1 .N64 no. 68 HB6870.5
          NYPL [JLD 87-1037]

(no. 70) Hedlund, Hans G. B. Migration and change in rural Zambia /. Uppsala , 1983. 107 p. : ISBN 91-7106-220-3 (pbk.) DDC 960 s 307/.2 19
DT1 .N64 no. 70 HB1955
          NYPL [JLD 85-587]

NORFOLK (VIRGINIA) - BIOGRAPHY.
Suggs, Henry Lewis. P.B. Young, newspaperman . Charlottesville , 1988. xxii, 254 p. : ISBN 0-8139-1178-8 DDC 070.4/1/0924 B 19
PN4874.Y59 S84 1988   ***NYPL [JFE 89-97]***

NORFOLK (VIRGINIA) - RACE RELATIONS.
Suggs, Henry Lewis. P.B. Young, newspaperman . Charlottesville , 1988. xxii, 254 p. : ISBN 0-8139-1178-8 DDC 070.4/1/0924 B 19
PN4874.Y59 S84 1988   ***NYPL [JFE 89-97]***

Norges Røde kors. AIDS and the Third World /. London , Philadelphia , 1989. v, 198 p. : ISBN 0-86571-143-7 (hardcover)
          NYPL [Sc D 89-51]

Norman Bethune Institute. Time for Azania [microform] [Toronto] , 1976. 89 p. : DDC 320.5/4/0968
DT770 .T55   ***NYPL [Sc Micro R-4849 no.1]***

Norman, Bruce. Footsteps : nine archaeological journeys of romance and discovery / by Bruce Norman. London : BBC Books, 1987. 279 p. : ill. (some col.), maps, ports. ; 26 cm. Includes index. Companion volume for the BBC2 television series of the same title. Bibliography: p. 273-274.
ISBN 0-563-20552-0
1. Archaeological expeditions. I. Title.
          NYPL [Sc F 88-18]

Norman, Regina. Recruitment and retention of Black students in higher education /. Lanham, MD , c1989. viii, 135 p. : ISBN 0-8191-7292-8 (alk. paper) DDC 378/.1982 19
LC2781 .R43 1989   ***NYPL [Sc D 89-590]***

Norris, Robert, d. 1791. Memoirs of the reign of Bossa Ahádee, king of Dahomy, an inland country of Guiney. To which are added, the author's journey to Abomey, the capital; and A short account of the African slave trade. By Robert Norris. Illus. with a new map. London, W. Lowndes, 1789. xvi, 184 p. ; 21 cm. Schomburg's copy lacks map. PARTIAL CONTENTS. - "A short account of the African slave trade. Second edition, with additions": p. [149]-184.
1. Slave-trade - Africa. 2. Benin - History - to 1894. I. Title. II. Title: Short account of the African slave trade.
DT541 .N85   ***NYPL [Sc Rare F 88-64]***

North Africa. Ogrizek, Doré, 1899- (ed) New York [1955] 447 p. DDC 916.1
DT165 .O372   ***NYPL [Sc C 88-362]***

NORTH AMERICAN INDIANS. see INDIANS OF NORTH AMERICA.

North by South . Hoffmann, Charles. Athens , c1988. xxii, 318 p., [8] p. of plates : ISBN 0-8203-0976-1 (alk. paper) DDC 975.8/73203/0924 19
F292.B85 A753 1988   ***NYPL [Sc E 89-35]***

NORTH CAROLINA - BIOGRAPHY.
My folks don't want me to talk about slavery . Winston-Salem, N.C. , c1984. xiv, 103 p. ; ISBN 0-89587-038-X DDC 975.6/00496073/0922 B 19
E445.N8 M9 1984   ***NYPL [JFD 85-1549]***

NORTH CAROLINA - GENEALOGY.
Redford, Dorothy Spruill. Somerset homecoming . New York , c1988. xviii, 266 p. : ISBN 0-385-24245-X : DDC 929/.3/089960730756 19
E185.96 .R42 1988   ***NYPL [Sc E 88-498]***

NORTH POLE - JUVENILE LITERATURE.
Gilman, Michael. Matthew Henson /. New York , c1988. 110 p. : ISBN 1-555-46590-0 : DDC 919.8/04 B 92 19
G635.H4 G55 1988   ***NYPL [Sc E 88-169]***

North winds blow free. Howard, Elizabeth. New York , 1949. 192 p. :   ***NYPL [Sc D 88-1498]***

NORTHERN SOTHO LANGUAGE - TEXTS.
Matsepe, O. K. Todi ya dinose /. Pretoria , 1968, 1982 printing. 50 p. : ISBN 0-627-00818-6
PL8690.9.M36 T6   ***NYPL [Sc D 89-607]***

Rafapa, J. R. L. Leratosello /. Pretoria , 1979, c1983 printing. 115 p. ;
          NYPL [Sc D 88-647]

Northrup, David. Beyond the bend in the river : African labor in Eastern Zaire, 1865-1940 / by David Northrup. Athens, Ohio : Ohio University Center for International Studies, 1988. xvii, 264 p. : map ; 22 cm. (Monographs in international studies. Africa series . no. 52) Includes index. Bibliography: p. 233-253. ISBN 0-89680-151-9 DDC 331.11/73/0967517 19
1. Labor and laboring classes - Zaire - Kivu - History. 2. Labor and laboring classes - Zaire - Haut-Zaïre - History. 3. Slavery - Zaire - History. 4. Forced labor - Zaire - History. I. Title. II. Series.
HD8811.Z8 K586 1988
          NYPL [Sc D 88-960]

Northup, Solomon, b. 1808. Twelve years a slave : narrative of Solomon Northup, a citizen of New York, kidnapped in Washington City in 1841, and rescued in 1853, from a cotton plantation near the Red River, in Louisiana. New York : Miller, Orton & Co., 1857. 336 p. : ill., music, port. ; 20 cm. Editor's preface signed: David Wilson.
1. Northup, Solomon, b. 1808. 2. Plantation life - Louisiana. 3. Slaves - United States - Biography. I. Wilson, David, 1818-1887. II. Title.
          NYPL [Sc Rare C 89-34]

NORTHUP, SOLOMON, B. 1808.
Northup, Solomon, b. 1808. Twelve years a slave . New York , 1857. 336 p. :
          NYPL [Sc Rare C 89-34]

Northwest ordinance. see Ordinance of 1787.

Norton, Browning, 1909- Johnny/Bingo. New York, Coward, McCann & Geoghegan [1971] 185 p. 22 cm. As the only witnesses to a bank robbery, two boys are held hostage with the threat that their families will die if they attempt to escape. SCHOMBURG CHILDREN'S COLLECTION. DDC [Fic]
1. Crime and criminals - Juvenile fiction. I. Schomburg Children's Collection. II. Title.
PZ7.N8217 Jo   ***NYPL [Sc D 88-1420]***

Norwegian missions in African history / edited by Jarle Simensen. Oslo : Norwegian University Press ; Oxford [Oxfordshire] , 1986. 2 v. : ill. ; 23 cm. Vol. 2 edited by Finn Fuglestad and Jarle Simensen. Includes bibliographies and indexes.
CONTENTS. - v. 1. South Africa - v. 2. Madagascar. ISBN 82-00-07418-8 (v. 1) DDC 266/.023/48106 19
1. Missions, Norwegian - Madagascar - History - 19th century. 2. Madagascar - History. I. Simensen, Jarle. II. Fuglestad, Finn, 1942-.
BV3625.M2 N67 1986   ***NYPL [Sc D 89-26]***

A nossa força está na unidade /. Machel, Samora, 1933- [Maputo] [1983] 98 p. : DDC 967/.9803 19
DT465.C32 M32 1983   ***NYPL [Sc D 89-531]***

Not either an experimental doll . Moya, Lily Patience. Bloomington , c1987. xv, 217 p., [18] p. of plates : ISBN 0-253-34843-9 DDC 968.05/6 19
HQ1800 .M69 1988   ***NYPL [Sc D 89-282]***

Not enough Indians. Horvath, Betty F. New York [1971] [47] p. : ISBN 0-531-01968-3 DDC [Fic]
PZ7.H7922 No   ***NYPL [Sc F 88-341]***

Notes and documents (United Nations Center against Apartheid)
Apartheid, South Africa and international law . New York, NY , 1985. iv, 136 p. ;
          NYPL [Sc F 88-289]

Notes from the mind of a Black philosopher /. Hatchett, John F. [New York?] , c1979. iv, 112 p. :   ***NYPL [Sc F 89-21]***

Notes toward an escape from death /. McTair, Dionyse. London , Port-of-Spain, Trinidad ,

c1987. 66 p. ; ISBN 0-901241-77-6
          NYPL [Sc D 89-215]

Notice of the Rev. John B. Adger's article on the slave trade. B. Charleston, S.C. , 1858 (Charleston, S.C. : Steam Power Press of Walker, Evans) 28 p. ;
          NYPL [Sc Rare G 86-8]

Notting Hill Carnival. Owusu, Kwesi. Behind the masquerade . Edgware , 1988. 90 p. : ISBN 0-9512770-0-6 (pbk) : DDC 394.2/6 19
          NYPL [Sc E 88-497]

Nou toujou doubout! Guadeloupe, 1635-1971 . Tours [1982] 109 p. : DDC 306/.362/0972976 19
HT1108.G83 G8 1982   ***NYPL [Sc F 89-141]***

Nouvelle poésie du Bénin : anthologie / textes choisis et présentés par Guy Ossito Midiohouan. Avignon : C.F.N.A., 1986. 78 p. : ill. ; 19 cm.
1. Benin poetry (French). I. Midiohouan, Guy Ossito, 1952.
          NYPL [Sc C 88-70]

Nouvelles recherches sur l'égyptien ancien et les langues négro-africaines modernes /. Diop, Cheikh Anta. Paris , c1988. 221 p. ; ISBN 2-7087-0507-5   ***NYPL [Sc D 89-550]***

Novastar, Charles. Le Macho et la fille du macoute / Charles Novastar. Port-au-Prince, : Choucoune, 1987. 181 p. ; 20 cm.
1. Haiti - Fiction. I. Title.   ***NYPL [Sc C 88-101]***

NOVELISTS, AMERICAN - 20TH CENTURY - BIOGRAPHY.
Walker, Margaret, 1915- Richard Wright, daemonic genius . New York , c1988. xix, 428 p., [8] leaves of plates : ISBN 0-446-71001-6 DDC 813/.52 B 19
PS3545.R815 Z892 1988
          NYPL [Sc E 88-604]

Wilson, M. L. (Matthew Lawrence), 1960- Chester Himes /. New York , c1988. 111 p. : ISBN 1-555-46591-9 DDC 813/.54 B 92 19
PS3515.I713 Z93 1988   ***NYPL [Sc E 88-373]***

NOVELISTS, AMERICAN - 20TH CENTURY - BIOGRAPHY - JUVENILE LITERATURE.
Bishop, Jack, 1910- Ralph Ellison /. New York , c1988. 110 p. : ISBN 1-555-46585-4 DDC 813/.5409 B 19
PS3555.L625 Z59 1988   ***NYPL [Sc E 88-165]***

Wilson, M. L. (Matthew Lawrence), 1960- Chester Himes /. New York , c1988. 111 p. : ISBN 1-555-46591-9 DDC 813/.54 B 92 19
PS3515.I713 Z93 1988   ***NYPL [Sc E 88-373]***

Novels of social change /. Agovi, Kofi Ermeleh, 1944- Tema, Ghana , 1988. xxviii, 290 p. ; ISBN 996-410-332-8
          NYPL [Sc D 88-1410]

Noxolos Geheimnis . Grosse-Oetringhaus, Hans-Martin. Berlin , 1988. 96 p. : ISBN 3-88520-289-1   ***NYPL [Sc C 89-120]***

Ntalaja, Nzongola. see Nzongola, Ntalaja, 1944-

Ntrakwah, Abena. Ama goes to the library / Abena Ntrakwah. Accra : Woeli Pub. Services, 1987. 16 p. : ill. ; 19 x 26 cm. SCHOMBURG CHILDREN'S COLLECTION.
1. Libraries - Ghana - Juvenile literature. I. Schomburg Children's Collection. II. Title.
          NYPL [Sc F 88-352]

NTTC cookery book. National Teacher-Training College (Lesotho) Maseru , 1976. 100 p. :
          NYPL [Sc B 89-29]

NTUMU (AFRICAN PEOPLE)
Shepphard, Joseph. A leaf of honey and the proverbs of the rain forest /. London , c1988. xii, 319 p. : ISBN 1-87098-902-3 (pbk.) : DDC 305.8/966 19   ***NYPL [Sc D 89-453]***

A nuclear-weapon-free zone in Africa? /. Epstein, William, 1912- Muscatine, Iowa , 1977. 52 p. ;
JX1974.7 .E553 NYPL [JLK 75-198 [no.]14]

NUCLEAR WEAPONS - SOUTH AFRICA.
Moore, J. D. L. (John Davey Lewis) South Africa and nuclear proliferation . New York , 1987. xvii, 227 p. : ISBN 0-312-74698-9 : DDC 355.8/25119/0968 19
U264 .M66 1987   ***NYPL [Sc D 88-765]***

Nueva Granada (Republic, 1842-1858) see Colombia.

Nueva Granada (State, 1831-1842) see Colombia.

NULLIFICATION.
Hayne, Robert Young, 1791-1839. Speeches of Hayne and Webster in the United States Senate, on the resolution of Mr. Foot, January, 1830 . Boston , 1853. 115 p. ;
E381 .H424 1853   *NYPL [Sc Rare C 89-20]*

Núñez, Victor Rodriguez. Roca, Juan Manuel. [Poems. Selections.] País secreto /. La Habana , c1987. 115 p. ;   *NYPL [Sc C 89-39]*

Nunley, John W. (John Wallace), 1945-
Caribbean festival arts : each and every bit of difference / John W. Nunley, Judith Bettelheim ; special consultant, Rex Nettleford ; with contributions by Barbara Bridges ... [et al.]. [Saint Louis] : Saint Louis Art Museum in association with University of Washington Press, 1988. 218 p. : ill. (some col.) ; 29 cm. Includes index. "This work began as a doctoral dissertation [of Judith Bettelheim] for the Department of Art History at Yale University"--Acknowledgements. Published on the occasion of the exhibition organized by the Saint Louis Art Museum and shown there, Dec. 11 1988-Feb. 19 1989, and at other locations. Bibliography: p. 214.   ISBN 0-295-96702-1 :   DDC 394.2/5/07409729 19
1. Festivals - Caribbean Area - Exhibitions. 2. West Indians - Social life and customs - Exhibitions. I. Bettelheim, Judith, 1944-. II. Nettleford, Rex M., 1933-. III. Bridges, Barbara A. IV. St. Louis Art Museum. V. Title.
GT4823 .N85 1988   *NYPL [Sc F 89-89]*

NUNU (AFRICAN PEOPLE)
Harms, Robert. Games against nature . Cambridge [Cambridgeshire] , New York , 1987. xi, 276 p. :   ISBN 0-521-34373-9 DDC 967/.24 19
DT546.245.N86 H37 1987
NYPL [Sc E 88-192]

NUPE (AFRICAN PEOPLE)
Habi, Ya'akub H. The people called Bassa-Nge /. Zaria , c1987. 86 p. :   ISBN 978-12-5057-7
NYPL [Sc C 88-372]

NURSES - NIGERIA - BIOGRAPHY.
Akinsanya, Justus A. An African "Florence Nightingale" . Ibadan, Nigeria , 1987. xii, 224 p. :   ISBN 978-245-826-0 (hard back ed.)
NYPL [Sc D 88-895]

NURSES - ZIMBABWE - BIOGRAPHY.
Nzenza, Sekai. Zimbabwean woman . London , 1988. 160 p. ;   *NYPL [Sc C 88-291]*

NURSING - EXAMINATIONS.
Spencer, F. Louise. A comprehensive approach to study and test taking /. New York, N.Y. , c1986. xii ;   *NYPL [Sc D 88-1168]*

NURSING - STUDY AND TEACHING.
Spencer, F. Louise. A comprehensive approach to study and test taking /. New York, N.Y. , c1986. xii ;   *NYPL [Sc D 88-1168]*

Nwagwu, N.A. Education and the law in Nigeria : the rights of teachers and students / by N. A. Nwagwu. Owerri : KayBeeCee Publications, 1987. ix, 190 p. ; 23 cm. Bibliography: p. 189-190.   ISBN 978-267-184-3
1. Education - Nigeria. 2. Educational law and legislation - Nigeria. I. Title. *NYPL [Sc D 89-10]*

Nwamuo, Chris. The prisoners / by Chris Nwamuo. Enugu : Tana Press, 1985. x, 73 p. ; 21 cm.   ISBN 978-250-304-5
1. Prisons - Africa - Drama. 2. Political plays - Nigeria. I. Title.   *NYPL [Sc D 88-495]*

Nwankwo, Arthur A. Thoughts on Nigeria / by Arthur A. Nwankwo. Enugu, Nigeria : Fourth Dimension Pub. Co., 1986. xxii, 198 p. ; 25 cm. (Issues in Nigerian development. ser. no. 1) Includes index.   ISBN 987-15-6264-1
1. Publishers and publishing - Nigeria. 2. Nigeria - Economic conditions - 1970-. 3. Nigeria - Politics and government - 1960-. I. Title. II. Series.
NYPL [Sc E 88-448]

Nwankwo, Chimalum. The trumpet parable : a play / by Chimalum Nwankwo. Enugu, Nigeria : ABIC Publishers, 1987. 126 p. : music ; 17 cm.   ISBN 978-226-931-X
I. Title.   *NYPL [Sc B 89-16]*

Nwankwo, Uchenna. Strategy for political stability / by Uchenna Nwankwo. Lagos : Pathway Communications : Oliver Ibekwe & Associates, 1988. ix, 310 p. ; 22 cm. Includes index. Bibliography: p. 287-300.

1. Political planning - Nigeria. 2. Political socialization - Nigeria. 3. Nigeria - Economic policy. I. Title.
NYPL [Sc D 89-539]

Nwanze, John E. I.W.A.R.U. talks (1974-1984) /. [Gusau, Sokoto State, Nigeria , 1985] 97 p. ;   DDC 255/.006/06 19
BX2740.A435 I18 1985
NYPL [Sc E 88-120]

Nwaze, Amechi. Perspectives on community and rural development in Nigeria /. Jos , c1988. 202 p. ;   ISBN 978-282-700-2
NYPL [Sc E 89-18]

Nwoga, Donatus Ibe. Literature and African identity. Bayreuth , c1986. 125 p. ;
NYPL [Sc D 89-369]

Nwosu, I. E. A guide to Christian writing in Africa / Ikechukwu E. Nwosu ; with contributions by Emmanuel Egbunu, Jacob Tsado, Hannatu Monday. 1st ed. Enugu, Nigeria : Christian Communication International, 1987. 116 p. ; 20 cm. Includes bibliographical references.   ISBN 978-262-606-6
1. Religious literature - Authorship - Handbooks, manuels, etc. 2. Authorship - Handbooks, manuals, etc. I. Egbunu, Emmanuel. II. Tsado, Jacob. III. Monday, Hannatu. IV. Title.   *NYPL [Sc C 88-156]*

Nwosu, Obiekezie Vic. Our roots : Osumenyi in perspective / by Obiekezie Vic Nwosu. Lagos : Markson Nig., 1986. 55 p. : ill., maps ; 21 cm. Bibliography: p. 54.
1. Igbo (African people) - Social life and customs. 2. Osumenyi (Nigeria) - Social life and customs. I. Title.
NYPL [Sc D 88-713]

Nwosu, V. A. (Vincent A.) The Catholic Church in Onitsha . Onitsha , 1985. xvii, 341 p. :   DDC 282/.6694 19
BX1682.N5 C36 1985   *NYPL [Sc D 88-891]*

Ny djoutche Malagasy [microform] / Rakoto Andrianasolo ... [et al.] ; Karakarain'ny Foibe Filan-Kevitry ny Mpampianatra. Tananarive : Foibe Ara-Tsaina Malagasy, [1978] 28 p. ; 27 cm. (Boky lovanjanahary . 5) In Malagasy. Microfiche. New York: New York Public Library, 198 . 1 microfiche: negative; 11 x 15 cm. (FSN Sc 019,089)
1. Madagascar - Social life and customs. 2. Rites and ceremonies - Madagascar. 3. Malagasy language - Texts. I. Rakoto, Andrianasolo.
NYPL [Sc Micro F-10988]

NYAKYUSA (AFRICAN PEOPLE)
Charsley, Simon R. The princes of Nyakyusa. [Nairobi, 1969] xii, 125 p.   DDC 301.29/678
DT443 .C5   *NYPL [Sc D 88-975]*

Nyamiti, Charles. Christ as our ancestor : christology from an African perspective / Charles Nyamiti. Gweru [Zimbabwe] : Mambo Press, 1984. 151 p. ; 21 cm. (Mambo occasional papers. Missio-pastoral series . no. 11) Includes bibliographies.   DDC 232 19
1. Jesus Christ - Person and offices. 2. Ancestor worship - Africa. I. Title. II. Series.
BT205 .N82 1984   *NYPL [Sc D 88-986]*

Nyamubaya, Freedom T. V. On the road again : poems during and after the national liberation of Zimbabwe / Freedom T.V. Nyamubaya. Harare, Zimbabwe : Zimbabwe Pub. House, 1986. 69 p. : ill. ; 19 cm. (ZPH writers . 29)   ISBN 0-949225-00-4
1. Political poetry, Zimbabwean. 2. Zimbabwe - Poetry. I. Title. II. Series.   *NYPL [Sc C 88-136]*

Nyamwaya, David. Socio-cultural profiles, Baringo District . [Nairobi?] , 1986. xviii, 268 p. :   DDC 967.6/27 19
DT434.B36 S63 1986   *NYPL [Sc F 88-230]*

Nyankume, Manty. The hunter / by Manty Nyankume. Freetown : People's Educational Association of Sierra Leone, 1987. 68 p. : ill. ; 21 cm. (Stories and songs from Sierra Leone . 32)
1. Tales - Sierra Leone. 2. Kuranko (African people) - Folklore. I. Title. II. Series.
NYPL [Sc D 89-414]

Nyasa, Mozambique (Province) see Niassa, Mozambique (Province)

Nyasani, J. M. (Joseph Major), 1938- The British massacre of the Gusii freedom defenders / J.M. Nyasani. Nairobi, Kenya : Nairobi Bookmen, 1984. v, 85 p. : ill., maps ; 21 cm. Includes bibliographical references and index.
1. Gusii (African people) - History. 2. Massacres - Kenya. 3. Kenya - History - To 1963. I. Title.
NYPL [Sc D 88-1133]

The Nyayo decade /. Dumila, Faraj O., 1937- [Nairobi? , 1988?] 2 v. :
NYPL [Sc F 89-122]

Nyerere, Julius Kambarage, Pres. Tanzania, 1922-
South Africa and the Commonwealth [microform] / Julius K. Nyerere. [S.l. : s.n., 1971] 14 p. ; 21 cm. Cover title. At head of title: Commonwealth Conference, Singapore, January 1971. Microfiche. New York: New York Public Library, 198. 1 microfiche: negative; 11 x 15 cm. (FSN Sc 019,063)
1. Great Britain - Relations South Africa. 2. South Africa - Relations (general) with Great Britain. I. Commonwealth Conference (1971: Singapore). II. Title.
NYPL [Sc Micro F-10922]

Stability and change in Africa [microform] d address / by President Julius K. Nyerere of the United Republic of Tanzania at the University of Toronto, Canada, on 2nd October, 1969. Dar es Salaam : Govt. Printer, 1969. 15 p. ; 24 cm. Microfiche. New York: New York Public Library, 198 . 1 microfiche: negative; 11 x 15 cm. (FSN Sc 019,094)
I. Title.   *NYPL [Sc Micro F-10986]*

NYIFWA (AFRICAN PEOPLE) see LUO (AFRICAN PEOPLE)

Nyika, Oliver P. Old Mapicha, and other stories / Oliver P. Nyika. Gweru, Zimbabwe : Mambo Press, 1983. 102 p. ; 18 cm. (Mambo writers series. English section. vol. 13) CONTENTS. - Old Mapicha -- The measles -- Going back home -- Makendro -- The condemned wife -- The brave become rich -- Those were the days.   ISBN 0-86922-263-5 (pbk.) :   DDC 823 19
1. Africa - Fiction. I. Title.
PR9390.9.N93 O4 1983
NYPL [JFC 86-1443]

Nyika, Tambayi O., 1961-
[Ndinodawo mwana. English]
A rat on her back : a play / by Tambayi O. Nyika. Gweru : Mambo Press, 1986. 51 p. ; 18 cm. (Mambo writers series. English section. v. 24) "Translated from the Shona Ndinodawo mzsana. ISBN 0-86922-394-1
I. Title.   *NYPL [Sc C 89-20]*

Nyoka huru haizvirumi /. Hamandishe, Nicholas Phinias. Harare , 1984. 91 p. ;   ISBN 0-582-61173-3   *NYPL [Sc C 88-365]*

Nyonda, Vincent de Paul. Epopée Mulombi /. [Libreville , 1986?] 138 p. ;
NYPL [Sc D 88-561]

Nyong'o, Anyang'. Hope born out of despair . Nairobi , 1988. xv, 123 p. ;   ISBN 996-646-456-5
NYPL [Sc D 89-477]

Nyonmo wiemo, Kanemo hefatalo : a short introduction to the Bible in the Ga language / compiled by W. Rottmann. London: Macmillan, 1963. v, 154 p. ; 19 cm. "Basel Mission Book Depot, Kumasi."
1. Gã language - Texts. I. Rottmann, W.
NYPL [Sc C 87-395]

NZAKARA DIALECT - TEXTS.
Lamadani, 1893-1972. Satires de Lamadani /. [Paris] , 1987. 155 p., [9] p. of plates :
NYPL [Sc E 88-223]

Nze Abuy, R. María. Familia y matrimonio fań / Rafael Maréa Nze Abuy. [Spain?] : Ediciones Guinea, [1985?] 77 p. ; 19 cm. Includes bibliographical references.
1. Fang (West African people) - Social life and customs. 2. Marriage - Equatorial Guinea. 3. Family - Equatorial Guinea. 4. Equatorial Guinea - Social conditions. I. Title.   *NYPL [Sc C 88-285]*

Nzenza, Sekai. Zimbabwean woman : my own story / by Sekai Nzenza. London : Karia Press, 1988. 160 p. ; 20 cm.
1. Nzenza, Sekai. 2. Women - Zimbabwe - Biography. 3. Nurses - Zimbabwe - Biography. I. Title.
NYPL [Sc C 88-291]

NZENZA, SEKAI.
Nzenza, Sekai. Zimbabwean woman . London , 1988. 160 p. ;   *NYPL [Sc C 88-291]*

Nzeribe, G. O. Tell it as it is /. Enugu [Nigeria] [1985?]- v. ;   ISBN 978-247-202-6
NYPL [Sc C 88-183]

NZIMA (AFRICAN PEOPLE) - FOLKLORE.
Grottanelli, Vinigi L. The python killer . Chicago , 1988. xi, 223 p. :   ISBN 0-226-31004-3 :   DDC 306/.089963 19
DT510.43.N95 G76 1988
NYPL [Sc D 88-1458]

NZIMA (AFRICAN PEOPLE) - SOCIAL LIFE AND CUSTOMS.
Grottanelli, Vinigi L. The python killer .
Chicago , 1988. xi, 223 p. : ISBN
0-226-31004-3 : DDC 306/.089963 19
DT510.43.N95 G76 1988
                    NYPL [Sc D 88-1458]

Nzimiro, Ikenna, 1927- The crisis in the social
sciences : the Nigerian situation / Ikenna
Nzimiro. Oguta, Nigeria : Zim Pan-African
Publishers, 1986. 89 p. ; 18 cm. First published by
Third World Forum, Mexico, 1977. Includes
bibliographical references and index. ISBN
978-215-003-7
1. Social sciences - Nigeria. I. Title.
                    NYPL [Sc C 88-93]

Nzongola, George. see **Nzongola, Ntalaja, 1944-**

Nzongola, Ntalaja, 1944- Revolution and
counter-revolution in Africa . London , 1987. x,
130 p. ; ISBN 0-86232-750-4 (cased) : DDC
320.96 19
JQ1872   *NYPL [Sc D 88-637]*

O. A. U. For corporate body referred to by these
initials, see: **Organization of African Unity.**

O.A.U. after twenty years. Sesay, Amadu. The
OAU after twenty years /. Boulder , 1984. ix,
133 p. ; ISBN 0-8133-0112-2 :
                    NYPL [JLD 85-633]

O. I. T. see **International Labor Organization.**

O. U. A. For corporate body referred to by these
initials, see: **Organization of African Unity.**

**L'O.U.A. triomphe de l'unité ou des
nationalités?** . Mfoulou, Jean, 1938- Paris ,
1986. 88 p. ; ISBN 2-85802-832-X
                    NYPL [Sc D 88-688]

Oates, Joyce Carol, 1938- Reading the fights /.
New York , c1988. viii, 305 p. : ISBN
0-8050-0510-2 : DDC 796.8/3 19
GV1121 .R4 1988   *NYPL [Sc D 88-899]*

The OAU after twenty years /. Sesay, Amadu.
Boulder , 1984. ix, 133 p. ; ISBN 0-8133-0112-2 :
                    NYPL [JLD 85-633]

OAU--time to admit South Africa /.
Mahmud-Okereke, N. Enuma, 1948- Lagos,
Nigeria , 1986. xxvi, 57, 190 p. : ISBN
978-242-302-5   *NYPL [Sc C 88-204]*

Obadiah. I am a Rastafarian / Obadiah meets
Petra Gaynor ; photography, Chris Fairclough.
London ; New York : F. Watts, c1986. 32 p. :
col. ill. ; 26 cm. (My belief) Includes index.
SCHOMBURG CHILDREN'S COLLECTION. ISBN
0-86313-260-X :
*1. RasTafari movement - Juvenile literature. I. Gaynor,
Petra, 1977-. II. Fairclough, Chris. III. Schomburg
Children's Collection. IV. Title. V. Series.*
BL2532.R37   *NYPL [Sc F 89-12]*

Obafemi, Olu, 1945-
New dawn. Obafemi, Olu, 1945- [Nights of a
mystical beast.] Nights of a mystical beast;
and, The new dawn : plays / Olu Obafemi.
Benin City, Nigeria , c1986. vii,82 p. ; ISBN
978-249-806-8
MLCS 87/7882 (P)   NYPL [Sc C 88-169]

[Nights of a mystical beast]
Nights of a mystical beast; and, The new
dawn : plays / Olu Obafemi. Benin City,
Nigeria : Adena, c1986. vii,82 p. ; 19 cm.
ISBN 978-249-806-8
I. Obafemi, Olu, 1945- New dawn. II. Title.
MLCS 87/7882 (P)   NYPL [Sc C 88-169]

Obasanjo, Olusegun. Africa embattled : selected
essays on contemporary African development /
Olusegun Obasanjo. Agodi, Ibadan : Fountain
Publications, 1988. xi, 118 p. ; 24 cm. ISBN
978-267-924-0
*1. Africa - Politics and government - 1960-. 2. Africa -
Economic conditions - 1960-. 3. Nigeria - Economic
conditions - 1970-. I. Title.*
DT30.5 .O23x 1988   NYPL [Sc E 88-574]

OBEAH (CULT) - BAHAMAS.
McCartney, Timothy O. Ten, ten the Bible
ten . Nassau, Bahamas , c1976. 192 p. :
                    NYPL [Sc E 88-425]

Obeah in the Bahamas. McCartney, Timothy O.
Ten, ten the Bible ten . Nassau, Bahamas ,
c1976. 192 p. :   *NYPL [Sc E 88-425]*

OBEDIENCE, POLITICAL. see
GOVERNMENT, RESISTANCE TO.

Obeng, Ernest E. Ancient Ashanti chieftaincy /
Ernest E. Obeng. Tema, Ghana : Ghana pub.
Corp., 1988. 74 p. : ill. ; 20 cm. ISBN
996-410-329-8
1. Ashanti - Kings and rulers. I. Title.
                    NYPL [Sc C 88-343]

Obenga, Théophile. Astres si longtemps : poèmes
en sept chants / Théophile Obenga. Paris :
Présence Africaine, c1988. 123 p. : 19 cm.
ISBN 2-7087-0500-8
I. Title.   *NYPL [Sc C 89-69]*

OBESITY - CONTROL. see **REDUCING.**

Obeso, Candelario, 1849-1884.
CANTOS POPULARES DE MI TIERRA.
Prescott, Laurence E. (Laurence Emmanuel)
Candelario Obeso y la iniciación de la poesía
negra en Colombia /. Bogota , 1985. 228 p.,
[17] leaves of plates :
                    NYPL [JFE 87-5694]

Obi, Celestine A. A Hundred years of the
Catholic Church in Eastern Nigeria,
1885-1985 . Onitsha, Nigeria , 1985. 432 p. :
     ISBN 978-17-5103-7   *NYPL [Sc D 88-830]*

Obi, Chike. Our struggle : a political analysis of
the problems of peoples struggling for true
freedom / Chike Obi. Enugu, Nigeria : Fourth
Dimension Pub., 1986. 76 p. ; 22 cm. Most of
this work was first issued in 1953. Includes
bibliographical references. ISBN 978-15-6187-4
*1. Africa - Politics and government - Philosophy. 2.
Nigeria - Politics and government - Philosophy. I. Title.*
                    NYPL [Sc D 88-753]

Obi, or, The history of Three-fingered Jack .
Earle, William. London , 1800. vi, [2], 232 p.,
[1] leaf of plates :   *NYPL [Sc Rare C 88-3]*

Obianyido, Anene. Christ or Devil? : the corrupt
face of Christianity in Africa / by Anene
Obianyido. Enugu, Anambra State, Nigeria :
Delta of Nigeria, 1988. 136 p. ; 19 cm. Includes
bibliograpical references. ISBN 978-233-544-4
*1. Christianity - Controversial literature. 2.
Christianity - Africa. I. Title.*
                    NYPL [Sc C 88-194]

Obiechina, Emmanuel N., 1933-
African creations . Enugu, Nigeria , 1985,
c1982. 180 p. ; ISBN 978-15-6181-5
                    NYPL [Sc D 88-436]

The University of Nigeria, 1960-1985 . Nsukka,
Nigeria , 1986. xviii, 657 p. : ISBN
978-229-913-8   *NYPL [Sc F 88-198]*

Obinyan, T. U. Family and social change . Lagos,
Nigeria , 1986. vi, 96 p. ;
                    NYPL [Sc D 88-794]

Obiozor, May. Guide to National Museum of
Colonial History, Aba / [text compiled by May
Obiozor] [Lagos, Nigeria : National
Commission for Museums and Monuments,
1985] 32 p. : ill., ports. ; 20 cm. Text based on
Crowder's The story of Nigeria, illustrated with
photographs from the Museum.
*1. Nigeria - Histo - 1851-1899. 2. Nigeria - History -
1900-1960. I. National Museum of Colonial History
(Nigeria). II. Title.*   *NYPL [Sc F 88-259]*

Obot, J. U. Nigeria, the people and their heritage
/. Calabar [Nigeria] , 1987. 339 p. : ISBN
978-228-328-2   *NYPL [Sc D 88-734]*

O'Brien, Kenneth. Duncan, Neville C. Women
and politics in Barbados, 1948-1981 /. Cave
Hill, Barbados , c1983. x, 68 p. ;
                    NYPL [Sc E 84-107]

Observations /. Aminu, Jibril M.,1939- [Enugu,
Anambra State, Nigeria] [1988] 148 p. ; ISBN
978-233-531-2   *NYPL [Sc D 89-483]*

**Observations of the present condition of the
island of Trinidad** . Burnley, William Hardin.
London , 1842. 177 p. ;
                    NYPL [Sc Rare F 88-74]

Obsessions . Charles, Christophe, 1951-
Port-au-Prince, Haiti, W.I. , c1985. 83 p. ;
MLCS 86/2028 (P)   NYPL [Sc C 88-122]

**OBUKPA (NIGERIA) - SOCIAL LIFE AND
CUSTOMS.**
Ugwu, D. C. This is Obukpa . Enugu, Nigeria,
1987. xii, 76 p. ; ISBN 978-15-6288-9
                    NYPL [Sc D 88-801]

O'Callaghan, Evelyn. The earliest patriots : being
The true adventures of certain survivors of
"Bussa's Rebellion" (1816) in the island of

Barbados and abroad / by Evelyn O'Callaghan ;
introd. by Hilary Beckles. London : Karia Press,
1986. 61 p. ; 20 cm. ISBN 0-946918-53-8pb
*1. Slavery - Barbados - Insurrections, etc. - History. 2.
Barbados - History. I. Title.*
                    NYPL [Sc C 88-104]

Occasional discourse on the Nigger question.
Carlyle, Thomas, 1795-1881. London, 1853. 48
p.
HT1091 .C47   *NYPL [Sc C 89-7]*

**Occasional paper (Howard University. Mental
Health Research and Development Center)** .
(no. 26) Milburn, Norweeta G. Social support .
Washington, D.C. , 1986. iii, 67 p. ;
                    NYPL [Sc F 87-428]

**Occasional paper (Jami'at al-Khartūm. Mahad al-
Dirāsāt al-Afriqīyah wa-al-Asiyawiyah)** .
**Occasional paper (Jāmi'at al-Khartūm. Ma'had al-
Dirāsāt al-Afriqīyah wa-al-Asiyawiyah)** .
(no. 13) Muhammad, Ahmad al-'Awad. Sudan
Defence Force . [Khartoum? , 198-?].
([Khartoum?] : Military Printing Press) 118 p. :
                    NYPL [Sc E 88-261]

(no. 20) El-Amin, Mohammed Nuri. The
emergence and development of the leftist
movement in the Sudan during the 1930's and
1940's /. [Khartoum] , 1984. 159 p. ; DDC
324.2624/07 19
HX443.5.A6 E42 1984
                    NYPL [Sc D 88-1261]

**Occasional paper (Kenyatta University College.
Bureau of Educational Research)** .
(no. 3050) Eshiwani, George S. Research in
education . Nairobi, Kenya , 1982? 185 leaves ;
     DDC 016.37/09676/2 19
Z5815.K4 E83 1982 LA1561
                    NYPL [Sc F 89-154]

**Occasional paper of the Institute for the Study
of Educational Policy** .
(1983, no.5) Tollett, Kenneth S. The right to
education . Washington, D.C. , 1983. xiii, 77
p. ;   *NYPL [Sc D 87-1294]*

**Occasional paper (Temple University. Institute
of African and Afro-American Affairs)** .
(no. 3) Burrowes, Carl Patrick. The
Americo-Liberian ruling class and other myths .
Philadelphia , 1989. 77 leaves ;
                    NYPL [Sc F 89-128]

**Occasional papers series (University of Illinois at
Urbana-Champaign. African Studies Program)**

(no. 2) Bunker, Stephen G., 1944- Double
dependency and constraints on class formation
in Bugisu, Uganda . Urbana, Ill. , 1983. v, 88
p. : DDC 303.3/09676/1 19
HD1538.U43 B86 1983
                    NYPL [Sc D 88-1054]

**Occasional papers (University of the
Witwatersrand. Centre for Applied Legal
Studies)** .
(4) Monama, Ramarumo. Is this justice? .
Johannesburg [1983] xii, 65 p. :
                    NYPL [Sc D 88-1240]

OCCIDENTAL ART. see **ART.**

OCCULT MEDICINE. see **MEDICINE,
MAGIC, MYSTIC AND SPAGIRIC.**

OCCULT SCIENCES - BRAZIL.
Sales, Niveo Ramos. Receitas de feitiços e
encantos afro-brasileiros /. Rio de Janeiro ,
1982. 75 p. :   *NYPL [JFD 84-750]*

OCCULTISM.
Versluis, Arthur, 1959- The Egyptian mysteries
/. London , New York , 1988. vi, 169 p. ;
     ISBN 1-85063-087-9 (pbk.) DDC 133 19
BF1999 .V43 1988   NYPL [Sc C 88-195]

OCCUPATION, CHOICE OF. see
VOCATIONAL GUIDANCE.

OCCUPATIONAL TRAINING - AFRICA.
Livingstone, Ian. Youth employment & youth
employment programmes in Africa . Addis
Ababa , 1986. 9 v. : ISBN 92-2-105527-2 (pbk. :
v. 1) DDC 331.3/4/096 19
HD6276.A32 L58 1986 NYPL [Sc F 88-313]

OCCUPATIONAL TRAINING - BOTSWANA.
Martin, Anthony. Report on the brigades in
Botswana. [n.p., 1971?] 96 p.
HD6276.B6 M37   *NYPL [JLF 74-1283]*

**OCCUPATIONAL TRAINING - BOTSWANA -
MANAGEMENT.**

Langley, Ph. Managing the Botswana brigades .
Douala, U.R.C. [1983] 93 p. : DDC
658.3/12404/096811 19
HD5715.5.B55 L36 1983
NYPL [Sc E 88-483]

**OCCUPATIONAL TRAINING - GREAT
BRITAIN.**
Verma, Gajendra K. Race, training, and
employment /. London , New York , 1987. vi,
134 p. : ISBN 1-85000-243-6 : DDC
331.3/46/0941 19
HD5715.5.G7 V47 1987
*NYPL [*QT 88-3245]*

OCCUPATIONAL TRAINING - NIGERIA.
Osuala, Esogwa C. A handbook of
vocational-technical education for Nigeria /.
Oruowulu-Obosi, Anambra State, Nigeria ,
1987. x, 173 p. ; ISBN 0-9782341-9-1
NYPL [Sc D 88-729]

OCCUPATIONS AND RACE.
Hindson, D. Pass controls and the urban
African proletariat in South Africa /.
Johannesburg, South Africa , 1987. xii, 121 p. ;
ISBN 0-86975-311-8 *NYPL [Sc D 88-956]*

**OCCUPATIONS - CHOICE. see
VOCATIONAL GUIDANCE.**

OCEAN TRAVEL - GUIDE-BOOKS.
Showker, Kay. Caribbean ports of call . Chester,
Conn. , 1987. xviii, 505 p. : ISBN 0-87106-776-5
(pbk.) DDC 917.29/0452 19
F2171.3 .S455 1987 *NYPL [Sc D 89-323]*

Ochieng', William Robert, 1943- Geography,
history and civics : standard eight / W.R.
Ochieng, R.T. Ogonda. London : Arnold
Hodder Africa, 1987. 170 p. : ill. ; 30 cm.
1. Kenya - Juvenile literature. I. Ogonda, R. T. II. Title.
NYPL [Sc F 88-190]

Octavia and other poems /. Madgett, Naomi
Cornelia (Long) Chicago , 1988. 117 p. : ISBN
0-88378-121-2 :
MLCS 88/07430 (P) *NYPL [Sc D 89-430]*

Oculi, Okello, 1942- Nigerian alternatives /.
[Zaria, Nigeria] 1987. 323 p. ; ISBN
978-301-130-11 *NYPL [Sc D 88-698]*

Odaga, Asenath.
A bridge in time / Asenath Bole Odaga.
Kisumu, Kenya : Lake Publishers & Enterprises,
1987. 167 p. ; 20 cm.
1. Kenya - Fiction. I. Title.
MLCS 88/07442 (P) *NYPL [Sc C 88-374]*

The shade changes / Asenath Bole Odaga.
[Kisumu, Kenya] : Lake Publishers &
Enterprises, [c1984] 175 p. ; 19 cm.
1. Kenya - Fiction. I. Title.
MLCS 87/7892 (P) *NYPL [Sc 88-214]*

O'Daniel, Therman B., 1908- Jean Toomer .
Washington, D.C. , c1988. xxi, 557 p. : ISBN
0-88258-111-2 : DDC 813/.52 19
PS3539.O478 Z68 1988
NYPL [Sc E 89-231]

Odear, Godwin N. (Goodwin Nwafor), 1958- 336
hours in the hero cities of Russians :
impressions of the Soviet Union / by Godwin
N. Odear. [Nigeria? : s.n., 1984?] 145, [17] p.
of plates : ill. ; 22 cm.
1. Socialism - Soviet Union. 2. Soviet Union -
Description and travel - 1970. I. Title. II. Title: Three
hundred thirty-six hours in the hero cities of Russians.
NYPL [Sc D 88-790]

Odedeyi, M. B. Yoruba dun ka : apa keta, ni
titun / M.B. Odedeyi. London ; New York :
Nelson, 1965. 75 p. : ill. ; 19 cm. SCHOMBURG
CHILDREN'S COLLECTION.
1. Yoruba language - Readers. I. Schomburg Children's
Collection. II. Title. *NYPL [Sc C 88-275]*

Odero, John. Waters, Grahame H. C. (Grahame
Hugh Clement), 1923- Geography of Kenya and
the East African region /. London , 1986. 252
p. : ISBN 0-333-41564-7 (pbk) : DDC 916.76 19
DT427 *NYPL [Sc E 88-370]*

Odhiambo, Thomas R. Hope born out of despair .
Nairobi , 1988. xv, 123 p. ; ISBN 996-646-456-5
NYPL [Sc D 89-477]

Odife, Dennis O. Privatization in Nigeria :
concepts, issues and modalities / Dennis O.
Odife. Yaba, Lagos : Alkestis Books, c1988. vii,
151 p. ; 21 cm. Includes index. Includes
bibliographical references. ISBN 978-301-672-5 (pbk)

1. Privatization - Nigeria. I. Title.
NYPL [Sc D 88-755]

Odlum, George. Call that George / [compiled by
Augustin Justin. [Castries, St. Lucia] :
Lithographic Press St. Lucia, 1979. 44 p. : ill. ;
24 cm. Cover title. Editorials originally published in
the St. Lucia newspaper Crusader, 1975-1978.
1. Saint Lucia - Politics and government. I. Justin,
Augustus. II. Title.
F2100 .O35 1979 *NYPL [Sc E 89-2]*

Odokara, E. O. Outreach : University's concern
for communities around it / by E.O. Odokara.
Nsukka : University of Nigeria, [between 1976
and 1981] 67 p. : ill. ; 24 cm.
1. University of Nigeria, Nsukka. Division of
Extra-Mural Studies. 2. Adult education - Nigeria. 3.
Continuing education - Nigeria. I. Title.
NYPL [Sc E 88-275]

Odu and Onah /. Osahon, Naiwu, 1937- Apapa,
Lagos, Nigeria , 1981. [22] p. :
NYPL [Sc D 89-227]

Odumosu, Z. O. The leader : a drama in four acts
/ Z.O. Odumosu. Lagos, Nigeria : Concept
Publications, c1988. xi, 83 p. : ill. ; 18 cm.
(Concept Brightstars) ISBN 978-230-916-8
1. Corruption (in politics) - Nigeria - Drama. 2.
Nigeria - Politics and government - 1960- - Drama. I.
Title. *NYPL [Sc C 88-160]*

Odumuh, A. E. Nigerian English (NigE) : selected
essays / by A.E. Odumuh. [S.l. : s.n.], 1987
(Zaria: Printed in Nigeria by A.B. University
Press.) vi, 125 p. ; 21 cm. ISBN 978-12-5061-5
1. English language - Nigeria. I. Title.
NYPL [Sc D 88-1378]

Odunewu, Alade. Winners take all / Alade
Odunewu. [Nigeria?] : West African Book
Publishers, [1988?] vi, 330 p. ; 22 cm. Selections
from the author's weekly newspaper column,
1963-1969.
1. Nigeria - Politics and government - 1960-.
NYPL [Sc D 89-543]

**Odunuga, S. A. F. (Samuel Adedoyin Folafunmi),
1902-
[Sermons. Selections]**
The life of Venerable Archdeacon S.A.F.
Odunuga / compiled by Adebisi Fola
Adenuga (nee Odunuga). [Nigeria] : A.F.
Adenuga, 1982. xiii, 175 p., [2] p. of plates :
ports. ; 24 cm. DDC 252/.03 19
1. Odunuga, S. A. F. (Samuel Adedoyin Folafunmi),
1902-. 2. Church of Nigeria - Sermons. 3. Anglican
Communion - Sermons. 4. Sermons, English - Nigeria.
I. Adenuga, Adebisi Fola. II. Title.
BX5700.7.Z6 O28 1982
NYPL [Sc E 89-142]

**ODUNUGA, S. A. F. (SAMUEL ADEDOYIN
FOLAFUNMI), 1902-**
Odunuga, S. A. F. (Samuel Adedoyin
Folafunmi), 1902- [Sermons. Selections.] The
life of Venerable Archdeacon S.A.F. Odunuga
/. [Nigeria] , 1982. xiii, 175 p., [2] p. of plates :
DDC 252/.03 19
BX5700.7.Z6 O28 1982
NYPL [Sc E 89-142]

Odunze, Don. The marriage killers / Don
Odunze. Enugu [Nigeria] : Donze Family Circle
Publications, [198-?] 104 p. ; 19 cm. "Family and
medication: interview with Dr. S.S. Ebinne": p. 60-87.
1. Marriage - Religious aspects - Christianity. 2.
Family - Health and hygiene - Nigeria. I. Ebinne, S. S.
II. Title. *NYPL [Sc C 88-189]*

Oduyoye, Modupe. The sons of the gods and the
daughters of men : an Afro-Asiatic
interpretation of Genesis 1-11 / Modupe
Oduyoye. Maryknoll, N.Y. : Orbis Books,
c1984. xi, 132 p. : maps ; 21 cm. Includes
bibliographical references and indexes. ISBN
0-88344-467-4 (pbk.) DDC 222/.1106 19
1. Bible. O. T. Genesis I-XI - Criticism, interpretation,
etc. I. Title.
BS1235.2 .O38 1984 *NYPL [Sc D 88-1236]*

L'odyssée noire /. Huggins, Nathan Irvin, 1927-
Paris , c1979. 221 p. : ISBN 1-85258-150-7
NYPL [Sc F 88-383]

Odyssey. Pindell, Howardena, 1943- Howardena
Pindell . New York, NY (144 W. 125th St.,
New York 10027) , c1986. 24 p. : DDC
709/.2/4 19
N6537.P49 A4 1986 *NYPL [Sc F 88-270]*

OECOLOGY. see ECOLOGY.

OEF International. Women as food producers in
developing countries /. Los Angeles, CA ,
c1985. ix, 118 p. : ISBN 0-918456-56-8 : DDC
331.4/83/091724 19
HD6073.A292 D4485 1985
NYPL [JLE 88-2659]

**Ökumenischer Rat der Kirchen. see World
Council of Churches.**

Oeuvres & critiques. Réception critique de la
littérature africaine et antillaise d'expression
française. Paris , 1979. 272 p. :
NYPL [Sc E 87-557]

Of flesh and the spirit /. Burrell, Evelyn
Patterson. Bryn Mawr, Pennsylvania , 1986.
101 p. : ISBN 0-8059-3039-6
NYPL [Sc D 88-300]

Of God and maxim guns . Johnston, Geoffrey.
Waterloo, Ontario, Canada , 1988. 321 p. :
ISBN 0-88920-180-3 (pbk.)
NYPL [Sc D 88-1229]

--of men and politics . DaBreo, D. Sinclair.
Castries, St. Lucia , c1981. 208 p. : DDC
972.98/43 19
F2100 .D32 1981 *NYPL [Sc D 88-815]*

Of poetry of prose /. Providence, Tien. [St.
Vincent? , 198-?] 69 p. ;
MLCS 87/7473 (P) *NYPL [Sc D 88-1322]*

**Offenbach am Main. Deutsches Ledermuseum.
see Deutsches Ledermuseum.**

OFFICE POLITICS.
McClenney, Earl H. How to survive when
you're the only Black in the office . Richmond,
Va. , c1987. 212 p. ; ISBN 0-9618835-0-2 (pbk.) :
DDC 650.1/3/0240396073 19
HF5386 .M473 1987 *NYPL [Sc D 89-242]*

**OFFICE PRACTICE - JUVENILE
LITERATURE.**
Haskins, James, 1941- Jobs in business and
office. New York [1974] 96 p. ISBN
0-688-75011-7 DDC 651/.023
HF5381.2 .H38 *NYPL [Sc E 89-16]*

OFFICE, TENURE OF. see CIVIL SERVICE.

**Oficina Internacional de Trabajo. see
International Labor Office.**

Ofo . Ejizu, Christopher I. Enugu, Nigeria , 1986.
xxii, 190 p. : ISBN 978-15-6268-4
NYPL [Sc D 88-885]

Ofoegbu, Leslie Jean. Blow the fire / Leslie Jean
Ofoegbu. Enugu, Nigeria : Tana Press, 1986,
c1985. 167 p. ; 18 cm.
1. Nigeria - History - Civil War, 1967-1970 - Personal
narratives. I. Title. *NYPL [Sc C 88-288]*

Ofomata, G. E. K.
Austerity and the Nigerian society /. Nsukka ,
1987. vi, 240 p. : ISBN 978-264-356-4
NYPL [Sc D 89-205]

Nigeria in search of a future /. Nsukka , 1986.
vii, 155 p. ; ISBN 978-229-900-6
NYPL [Sc D 88-884]

Ofori-Amankwah, E. H. Mystical and sacred uses
of the holy book of Psalms / by E.H.
Ofori-Amankwah. [S.L. ; s.n., 1985] Zaria :
printed by Gaskiya Corp.) 48 p. ; 17 cm.
1. Bible. O.T. Psalms - Folklore. I. Title.
NYPL [Sc B 88-61]

Oga na tief-man . Fatunde, Tunde. Benin City,
Nigeria , 1986. xv, 57 p. ; ISBN 978-249-805-X
NYPL [Sc C 88-340]

Ogbobine, R. A. I. (Rufus A. I.) A post in the
military government / by Rufus Ogbobine.
[Benin City, Nigeria : Ruf-Bine Pub. Co.,1988?]
159 p. ; 20 cm. (The Assizes) ISBN 978-300-455-7
1. Nigeria - Fiction. I. Title. *NYPL [Sc C 89-48]*

Ogidan, Anna. Thememschwerpunkte im Werk
Ayi Kwei Armahs / Anna Ogidan. Wien :
Afro-Pub, 1988. ii, 202 p. ; 21 cm.
(Veröffentlichungen der Institute für Afrikanistik und
Ägyptologie der Universität Wien. Nr. 46) Beiträge
zur Afrikanistik ; Bd. 33 Bibliography: p. 181-202.
ISBN 3-85043-046-4
1. Armah, Ayi Kwei, 1939- - Criticism and
interpretation. 2. Armah, Ayi Kwei, 1939- - Political
and social views. 3. Race relations in literature. 4.
Literature and society - Africa. 5. African literature -
Social aspects. I. Title. II. Series.
NYPL [Sc D 88-1035]

Ogonda, R. T. Ochieng', William Robert, 1943- Geography, history and civics . London , 1987. 170 p. : *NYPL [Sc F 88-190]*

Ogren, Kathy J. The jazz revolution : twenties America & the meaning of jazz / Kathy J. Ogren. New York : Oxford University Press, 1989. vii, 221 p., [8] p. of plates : ill. ; 22 cm. Includes index. Bibliography: p. 197-212. ISBN 0-19-505153-X (alk. paper) DDC 781/.57/0973 19
1. Jazz music - United States. 2. Afro-Americans - Music. 3. United States - Popular culture - History - 20th century. I. Title.
ML3508 .O37 1987 *NYPL [Sc D 89-451]*

Ogrizek, Doré, 1899- (ed) North Africa. [Translation by David Rowan] New York, McGraw-Hill [1955] 447 p. illus. 20 cm. (The World in color series) DDC 916.1
1. Africa, North - Description and travel. I. Title.
DT165 .O372 *NYPL [Sc C 88-362]*

Oguine, Priscilla Ngozi. Folk-tales from Igboland /. Ibadan, Nigeria , 1986. 90 p. ; ISBN 978-16-7467-9 *NYPL [Sc D 88-758]*

Ogun State. Advisory Committee in the Funding of Education. Report of the Advisory Committee on the Funding of Education in Ogun State. [Abeokuta : Ogun State Print Corp., 1985] 51 p. ; 25 cm.
1. Education - Nigeria - Ogun State. 2. Education - Nigeria - Ogun State - Finance. I. Title.
NYPL [Sc E 89-212]

Ogunbanjo, C. O. (Christopher Odadipo), 1923- Nigeria, the search for economic stability / C.O. Ogunbanjo. [Nigeria? : s.n.], 1986. 102 p., [4] p. of plates : ill., ports. ; 23 cm. Speeches dilivered between 1983 and 1986. Includes bibliographical references. ISBN 0-946233-04-7
1. Public finance - Nigeria. 2. Nigeria - Economic policy. I. Title. *NYPL [Sc D 88-519]*

Ogunbanjo, C. O. (Christopher Oladipo), 1923- Nigeria, the search for economic stability / C.O. Ogunbanjo. [S.l.] : Ogunbanjo, 1986. 103 p., [4] p. of plates : ill. ; 23 cm. Speeches delivered between 1983 and 1986. ISBN 0-946233-04-7
1. Nigeria - Economic policy. 2. Nigeria - Economic conditions - 1970-. I. Title. *NYPL [Sc D 88-883]*

Ogunbiyi, Yemi. Perspectives on Nigerian literature, 1700 to the present /. Oshodi, Lagos, Nigeria , 1988. 2 v. ; *NYPL [Sc C 89-19]*

Ogundipe, S. O. Second-tier foreign exchange market in Nigeria : objectives, operation and policy option / by S.O. Ogundipe. Ibadan : Heinemann Educational Books (Nigeria), 1987. xii, 96 p. ; 23 cm. (Issues in the Nigerian economy) Cover title: SFEM in Nigeria. Includes index. ISBN 979-12-9534-1
1. Foreign exchange problem - Nigeria. I. Title. II. Title: SFEM in Nigeria. *NYPL [Sc D 88-1248]*

Ogunmuyiwa, Adetokunbo. Three days in Nigeria / by Adetokunbo Ogunmuyiwa. [Lagos? : s.n., 1988] (Lagos : Remcoye Press) 80 p. ; 21 cm.
1. Nigeria - Fiction. I. Title.
NYPL [Sc D 89-535]

Ogunsanwo, Alaba. Our friends, their friends : Nigerian external relations 1960-85 / Alaba Ogunsanwo.1st ed. Yaba : ALFA Communications Ltd., 1986, c1985. 145 p. ; 21 cm. (International affairs series) Includes bibliographical references. ISBN 978-301-700-4
1. Nigeria - Foreign relations. I. Series. II. Series: International affairs series (Yaba, Nigeria). III. Title.
NYPL [Sc D 89-137]

Ogunṣhéyé, F. Adetowun. Nigerian women and development /. Ibadan, Nigeria , 1988. xv, 495 p. ; ISBN 978-12-1219-5 *NYPL [Sc D 89-576]*

Oguntomilade, Jacob I. D. Father E. Olu Coker : a charismatic Star of the Cherubims : a biography / Jacob I.D. Oguntomilade. Lagos : Landmark Publications, 1987. 313 p. : ill., ports. ; 22 cm. Bibliography: p. 313. ISBN 978-248-001-0
1. Coker, E. Olu. 2. Cherubim and Seraphim (Society). 3. Clergy - Nigeria - Biography. I. Title.
NYPL [Sc D 89-572]

Oguntomisin, Dare. Falola, Toyin. The military in nineteenth century Yoruba politics /. Ile-Ife [Nigeria] , c1984. 127 p. ; ISBN 978-13-6064-X

(pbk.) DDC 966.9/004963 19
DT515.45.Y67 F35 1984
NYPL [Sc D 88-227]

Oguntoye, Jide. Come home my love / Jide Oguntoye. Ibadan : Paperback Publishers Limited, 1987. 141 p. ; 19 cm. (Egret romance & thrillers . 10) ISBN 978-243-272-5
1. Nigeria - Fiction. I. Title. II. Series.
NYPL [Sc C 88-226]

Ogunyẹmi, Diipọ. A needle in the haystack ; [and] Limota : plays / by Diipọ Ogunyẹmi. Ibandan, Nigeria : Jambros Press & Publishers, 1987. iv, 88 p. ; 19 cm.
1. Nigeria - Drama. I. Title. II. Title: Limota.
NYPL [Sc C 88-166]

Ogunyẹmi, M. A. The D.O. / M.A. Ogunyẹmi. Ibadan : University Press, 1987. v. 126 p. ; 18 cm. ISBN 978-15-4777-4 (Nigeria)
1. Local officials and employees - Nigeria - Fiction. 2. Nigeria - Fiction. I. Title. *NYPL [Sc C 88-176]*

Ogunyẹmi, Wale, 1939- The vow / Wale Ogunyẹmi. London : MacMillan, 1985. vi, 47 p. ; 22 cm. (Open stage) ISBN 0-333-35819-8
I. Title. II. Series. *NYPL [Sc D 88-1210]*

Oh, brother /. Wilson, Johnniece Marshall. New York , c1988. 121 p. ; ISBN 0-590-41363-5 : DDC [Fic] 19
PZ7.W696514 Oh 1988
NYPL [Sc D 88-699]

O'Halloran, Terry. Brickley, Carol. South Africa . London , 1985. 50 p. : ISBN 0-905400-06-2 :
NYPL [Sc D 89-361]

Ohiani, Bello. Oni, Stephen Bola. Community development . [Zaria, Nigeria] , 1987. vii, 128 p. : ISBN 978-19-4120-0 *NYPL [Sc D 88-791]*

Ohio book for the Lincoln jubilee. Joiner, William A., 1868- A half century of freedom of the Negro in Ohio. Xenia, Ohio [1915] 134 p.
NYPL [Sc Rare F 89-7]

OHIO - CENSUS, 1880.
Nitchman, Paul E. Blacks in Ohio, 1880 in the counties of ... /. [Decorah? Iowa] , c1985- v. ;
DDC 929/.3/089960730771 19
E185.93.O2 N57 1985
NYPL [APR (Ohio) 86-2025]

OHIO - GENEALOGY.
Nitchman, Paul E. Blacks in Ohio, 1880 in the counties of ... /. [Decorah? Iowa] , c1985- v. ;
DDC 929/.3/089960730771 19
E185.93.O2 N57 1985
NYPL [APR (Ohio) 86-2025]

Ohri, Sushel, 1951- Britain's Black population . Aldershot, Hants, England , Brookfield, Vt., USA , c1988. xv, 298 p. ; ISBN 0-566-05179-6 : DDC 305.8/96/041 19
DA125.N4 B75 1988 *NYPL [Sc E 89-100]*

OIL INDUSTRIES - GOVERNMENT POLICY - TRINIDAD AND TOBAGO.
Oilfields Workers' Trade Union. Memorandum to the Government of Trinidad and Tobago . San F'do [i.e. San Fernando, Trinidad and Tobago] [1987 or 1988] 124 p. [4] p. of plates : *NYPL [Sc D 88-822]*

OIL INDUSTRY WORKERS - LEGAL STATUS, LAWS, ETC. - TRINIDAD.
Oilfields Workers' Trade Union. Memorandum to the Government of Trinidad and Tobago . San F'do [i.e. San Fernando, Trinidad and Tobago] [1987 or 1988] 124 p. [4] p. of plates : *NYPL [Sc D 88-822]*

OIL-PAINTING. see PAINTING.

Oilfields Workers' Trade Union. Memorandum to the Government of Trinidad and Tobago : November 10th 1987 / Oilfields Workers' Trade Union. San F'do [i.e. San Fernando, Trinidad and Tobago] : Vanguard Pub. Co., [1987 or 1988] 124 p. [4] p. of plates : ill. ; 21 cm. Cover title.
1. Oilfields Workers' Trade Union. 2. Labor policy - Trinidad and Tobago. 3. Commercial policy - Trinidad and Tobago. 4. Oil industry workers - Legal status, laws, etc. - Trinidad. 5. Oil industries - Government policy - Trinidad and Tobago. I. Title.
NYPL [Sc D 88-822]

Our fight for people's ownership and control of the oil industry : memorandum submitted to the government of Trinidad and Tobago by the Oilfields Workers' Trade Union on the nationalisation of the oil industry, September

1982. [San Fernando] : Vanguard, 1982. 80 p. : ill. ; 22 cm. Bibliography: p. 79-80.
1. Petroleum industry and trade - Trinidad and Tobago. 2. Trade-unions - Petroleum workers - Trinidad and Tobago. 3. Petroleum workers - Trinidad and Tobago. I. Title. *NYPL [Sc D 88-1253]*

Towards a new people's order. San Fernando, Trinidad , c1988. 87 p. ;
NYPL [Sc D 88-1516]

OILFIELDS WORKERS' TRADE UNION.
Kambon, Khafra. For bread justice and freedom . London , 1988. xi, 353 p., [16] p. of plates : *NYPL [Sc D 89-294]*

Oilfields Workers' Trade Union. Memorandum to the Government of Trinidad and Tobago . San F'do [i.e. San Fernando, Trinidad and Tobago] [1987 or 1988] 124 p. [4] p. of plates : *NYPL [Sc D 88-822]*

Ojaide, Tanure, 1948- Labyrinths of the delta / by Tanure Ojaide. Greenfield Center, NY : Greenfield Review Press, c1986. 103 p. ; 22 cm. Cover title. Poems. ISBN 0-912678-67-4
I. Title. *NYPL [Sc D 88-1191]*

Ojior, Omoh T. Oyaide, William John, 1936- Presidentialism . Benin City, Nigeria , c1987. xi, 133 p. ; ISBN 978-300-550-2
NYPL [Sc D 88-917]

Ojo, Abiola. Constitutional law and military rule in Nigeria / Abiola Ojo. Ibadan : Evans Brothers, 1987. vii, 316 p. ; 22 cm. Includes bibliographical references. ISBN 978-16-7569-1
1. Military government - Nigeria. 2. Nigeria - Constitutional law. I. Title. *NYPL [Sc D 88-804]*

Ojo-Ade, Femi. Home, sweet, sweet home / Femi Ojo-Ade. Ibadan : University Press Limited, 1987. ix, 123 p. ; 18 cm. ISBN 978-15-4663-8 (Nigeria)
1. Return migration - Nigeria - Fiction. 2. Nigeria - Fiction. I. Title. *NYPL [Sc C 88-209]*

Ojo, Folayan. Manpower development and utilization in Nigeria . Lagos, Nigeria , 1986. xiii, 240 p. ; ISBN 978-226-441-5
NYPL [Sc D 88-1077]

Ojo, Olusola. Sesay, Amadu. The OAU after twenty years /. Boulder , 1984. ix, 133 p. ; ISBN 0-8133-0112-2 : *NYPL [JLD 85-633]*

Oju d'agu /. Veiga, Manuel. Praia , c1987. 229 p. ; *NYPL [Sc D 88-1413]*

Okafor, Festus C. Nigeria teacher education : a search for a new direction / by Festus C. Okafor. Enugu, Nigeria : Fourth Dimension, 1988. 173 p. : map ; 22 cm. (FDP educational series) Includes index. Bibliography: p. 163-166. ISBN 978-15-6298-6
1. Teachers - Training of. 2. Teachers, Training of - Nigeria. I. Title. *NYPL [Sc D 89-180]*

Okeke, Igwebuike Romeo. The "Osu" concept in Igboland : a study of the types of slavery in Igbo-speaking areas of Nigeria / Igwebuike Romeo Okeke. Enugu. [Nigeria] : Access Publishers (Nigeria), 1986. xi, 167 p. : ill., facsims., ports. ; 25 cm. Includes bibliographical references. ISBN 978-248-100-9
1. Caste - Nigeria. 2. Slavery - Nigeria. 3. Igbo (African people) - Social life and customs. I. Title.
NYPL [Sc E 88-302]

Okeke, Okeke Okore, 1954- Self-employment for unemployed Nigerians / Okeke Okore Okeke. Festac Town, Lagos, Nigeria : IPL, Inter-Regional Publishers, 1987. 110 p. ; 23 cm. Includes index. Bibliography: p. 105-106. ISBN 978-333-011-27
1. Self-employed - Nigeria. 2. Small business - Nigeria. I. Title. *NYPL [Sc D 89-298]*

Okike. African creations . Enugu, Nigeria , 1985, c1982. 180 p. ; ISBN 978-15-6181-5
NYPL [Sc D 88-436]

Oklahoma. University. Summer Institute of Linguistics. see Summer Institute of Linguistics.

Okogba, Andrew. When a child is motherless / by Andrew Okogba. Benin City, Nigeria : Idodo Umeh Publishers, 1987. v, 326 p. 19 cm. (Summit writers series) ISBN 978-234-045-6
1. Children - Nigeria - Fiction. 2. Nigeria - Fiction. I. Title. *NYPL [Sc C 88-206]*

Okoko, Kimse A. B. Socialism and self-reliance in Tanzania / Kimse A.B. Okoko. London ; New York : KPI in association with the University of

Okon, Kate. Port Harcourt Press, 1987. xiii, 272 p. : ill., map ; 23 cm. Includes index. Bibliography: p. 240-255. ISBN 0-7103-0269-X
1. Socialism - Tanzania. 2. Tanzania - Politics and government - 1964-. 3. Tanzania - Economic policy. I. Title. *NYPL [Sc D 88-902]*

Okon, Kate. Women in development . Calabar , 1988. 153 p. : *NYPL [Sc D 89-79]*

Okongwu, Chu S. P., 1934- The Nigerian economy : being an anatomy of a traumatized economy with some proposals for stabilization / by Chu S.P. Okongwu. Enugu, Nigeria : Fourth Dimension Pub. Co., 1986. vi, 453 p. : ill. ; 23 cm. (Issues in Nigerian development) Includes index. Bibliography: p. 451-453. ISBN 978-15-6038-X (pbk.) : DDC 330.9669/05 19
1. Nigeria - Economic conditions - 1970-. 2. Nigeria - Social conditions - 1960-. 3. Nigeria - Economic policy. 4. Nigeria - Social policy. I. Title. II. Series.
HC1055 .O39 1986 *NYPL [Sc D 88-1250]*

Okonkwo, Ifeanyichukwu E. R. The great debate : a national challenge / Ifeanyichukwu E.R. Okonkwo. Onitsha, Anambra State, Nigeria : First Edition Publishers, 1986. 138 p. : ill. ; 20 cm. ISBN 978-264-308-4
1. Nigeria - Politics and government - 1979-. 2. Nigeria - Economic policy. I. Title. *NYPL [Sc C 89-58]*

Okonkwo, oder, Das Alte stürzt . Achebe, Chinua. [Things fall apart. German.] Stuttgart , c1958. 230 p. ; *NYPL [Sc D 88-357]*

Okonkwo, Rina. Heroes of West African nationalism / by Rina Okonkwo. Enugu, Nigeria : Delta of Nigeria, 1985. x, 128 p. ; 18 cm. Bibliography: p. 120-128. ISBN 978-233-596-7
1. Africa, West - Biography. I. Title. *NYPL [Sc C 88-95]*

Okorie, Aja, 1947- Fifty years of Nigerian cooperative movement /. Nsukka [Nigeria] , 1986. iii, 64 p. ; *NYPL [Sc D 88-859]*

Okpalaeze, Inno-Pat Chuba. Oriental passion / Inno - Pat Chuba Okpalaeze. Onitsha, Nigeria : Allied Communications Bureau, 1987. 89 p. ; 19 cm.
1. Nigerians - Fiction. 2. Interracial marriage - Fiction. I. Title. *NYPL [Sc C 89-72]*

Okpewho, Isidore. University of Ibadan 1948-88 . Ibadan, Nigeria , 1988. iv, 46 p. : ISBN 978-16-7861-5 *NYPL [Sc E 89-246]*

Okpoko, John. The Biafran nightmare : the controversial role of international relief agencies in a war of genocide / John Okpoko. Enugu, Nigeria : Delta of Nigeria, 1986. x, 76, [4] p. of plates : ill., map ; 18 cm. Bibliography: p. 73-76. ISBN 978-233-504-5
1. Nigeria - History - Civil War, 1967-1970 - Civilian relief. I. Title. *NYPL [Sc C 88-184]*

Okri, Ben. Incidents at the shrine : short stories / Ben Okri. London : Heinemann, 1986. 135 p. ; 22 cm. ISBN 0-434-53230-4
1. Nigeria - Fiction. I. Title.
NYPL [JFD 87-7171]

Stars of the new curfew / Ben Okri. London : Secker & Warburg, 1988. 194 p. ; 23 cm. CONTENTS. - In the shadow of war -- Worlds that flourish -- In the city of red dust -- Stars of the new curfew -- When the lights return -- What the tapster saw. ISBN 0-436-33944-7 :
1. Nigeria - Fiction. I. Title.
NYPL [Sc D 89-454]

Okuboyejo, Betti. Adire, a living craft / Betti Okuboyejo. [Nigeria] : Friends of Adire, c1987. 55 p. : ill. ; 20 x 23 cm. "An exhibition of the indigo-dyed cloth of the Yoruba women of Nigeria organized by Friends of Adire."
1. Handicraft - Nigeria - Exhibitions. 2. Tie-dyeing - Nigeria - Exhibitions. I. Friends of Adire. II. Title. *NYPL [Sc C 89-16]*

Okuofu, Charles O. Death contractor / Charles O. Okuofu. Nigeria : Abiprint Pub Co., 1986. 84 p. ; 18 cm. (Bloom series) ISBN 978-14-1060-4
1. Nigeria - Fiction. I. Title.
NYPL [Sc C 88-338]

Okwechime, Ireneus. The sacrifice / by Ireneus Okwechime. Benin City, Nigeria : Idodo Umeh Publishers, 1987. 136 p. ; 19 cm. ISBN 978-234-047-2
1. Nigeria - Fiction. I. Title.
NYPL [Sc C 88-175]

Ola, Robert F., 1938- Oyaide, William John, 1936- Presidentialism . Benin City, Nigeria , c1987. xi, 133 p. ; ISBN 978-300-550-2
NYPL [Sc D 88-917]

Ọlabimtan, Afọlabi. Akójọp Lagos , 1986. xi, 324 p., map, ports. ; ISBN 978-13-2563-1 *NYPL [Sc D 88-955]*

B'ó ti gb'/ Afọlabi Ọlabimtan. Ibàdàn, Nigeria : Evans, 1987, c1980. v. 83 p. ; 22 cm. (Ojúlówó Yorùbá) ISBN 978-16-7487-3
1. Yoruba languages - Texts. I. Title.
NYPL [Sc D 88-953]

Ọlatúnjí, Ọlatúndé O. Bamgbose, Ayo. Yoruba . Lagos, Nigeria , 1986. xvii, 83 p. ; *NYPL [Sc D 88-1091]*

Olaudah Equiano. see Equiano, Olaudah, b. 1745.

Old Bailey, London. see London. Central Criminal Court.

Old Calabar, Nigeria. see Calabar, Nigeria.

Old Mapicha, and other stories /. Nyika, Oliver P. Gweru, Zimbabwe , 1983. 102 p. ; ISBN 0-86922-263-5 (pbk.) : DDC 823 19
PR9390.9.N93 O4 1983
NYPL [JFC 86-1443]

OLD RESIDENCY MUSEUM (CALABAR, NIGERIA)
The story of the old Calabar . [Lagos?] , c1986. 228 p. : *NYPL [Sc D 89-253]*

OLD STONE AGE. see PALEOLITHIC PERIOD.

Oldendorp, C. G. A. (Christian Georg Andreas), 1721-1787.
[Geschichte der Mission der Evangelischen Brüder auf den caraibischen Inseln S. Thomas, S. Croix und S. Jan]
C.G.A. Oldendorps Geschichte der Mission der Evangelischen Brüder auf den caraibischen Inseln S. Thomas, S. Croix und S. Jan / herausgegeben durch Johann Jakob Bossart. Barby : Bey Christian Friedrich Laux, und in Leipzig in Commission bey Weidmanns Erben und Reich, 1777. 2 v. in 1 (1068 p.) : 4 ill., 3 maps (engravings) ; 19 cm. (8vo) Title page of v. 2 lacks publisher/distributor statement. Signatures: a A-2E chi1 2chi1 3chi1 2F-3Z 4A . Paged continuously: [16], 444, [9], 448-1068, [44] p., [7] folded leaves of plates (+ [2] p. of text on folded leaf inserted after p. 346) With errata/binder's leaf ([2] p.) at end. Includes index. DDC 266/.46729722 19
1. Moravian Church - Missions - Virgin Islands of the United States. 2. Missions - Virgin Islands of the United States. 3. Virgin Islands of the United States - Church history. I. Bossart, Johann Jakob. II. Title. III. Title: Geschichte der Mission der Evangelischen Brüder auf den caraibischen Inseln S. Thomas, S. Croix und S. Jan.
BV2848.V5 O42 1777
NYPL [Sc Rare C 89-33]

OLDUVAI GORGE (TANZANIA) - ANTIQUITIES.
Potts, Richard, 1953- Early hominid activities at Olduvai /. New York , c1988. xi, 396 p. : ISBN 0-202-01176-3 (lib. bdg.) DDC 967.8 19
GN772.42.T34 P67 1988
NYPL [Sc E 89-92]

Olinto, Antônio.
Brasileiros na África / Antonio Olinto ; [capa, Regina Helena Garcia Dorea]. 2.a ed. São Paulo, S.P. (rua Topázio 478/41, CEP 04105, São Paulo, S.P.) : Edições GRD, 1980. 324 p., [16] pages of plates : ill. ; 21 cm. "Em convênio com o Instituto Nacional do Livro." Bibliography: p. 317-324. DDC 966.9/004698 19
1. Brazilians - Nigeria. I. Title.
DT515.42 .O43 1980 *NYPL [Sc D 89-216]*

Trono de vidro : romance / Antônio Olinto. Rio de Janeiro : Editorial Nórdica, 1987. 382 p. ; 21 cm. ISBN 85-7007-110-8
1. Africa, Sub-Saharan - Politics and government - Fiction. I. Title. *NYPL [Sc D 88-76]*

Olisah, Okenwah. The Ibo native law and custom [microform] / by Okenwa Olisah (the Strong Man of the Pen) ; forewoded [sic] by Chukwuno Metuh. Onitsha : New Era Press, [196-] 40 p. : ill. ; 21 cm. Microfiche. New York : New York Public Library, 198 . 1 microfiche: negative; 11 x 15 cm. (FSN Sc 019,134)
1. Igbo (African people) - Social life and customs.
NYPL [Sc Micro F-11,165]

Oliveira, Mário António Fernandes de, 1934-
Afonso, o africano [microform] / M. António. Braga : Editora Pax, 1980. 30 p. ; 21 cm. Poems. Microfiche. New York : New York Public Library, 198 . 1 microfiche: negative; 11 x 15 cm. (FSN Sc 019,038)
I. Title. *NYPL [Sc Micro F-10927]*

Oliver, Paul. The New Grove gospel, blues and jazz : with spirituals and ragtime / Paul Oliver, Max Harrison, William Bolcom.1st American ed. in book form with additions. New York : W.W. Norton, 1986. 395 p. [16] p. of plates : ill., music, ports ; 21 cm. "Parts of this material were first published in The new Grove dictionary of music and musicians ... 1980"--T.p. verso. Includes bibliographies, discographies and indexes. ISBN 0-393-01696-X
1. Gospel music - United States - History and criticism. 2. Blues (Music)zUnited StatesxHistory and criticism. 3. Jazz music - United States - History and criticism. 4. Spirituals (Songs) - History and criticism. 5. Ragtime music - United States - History and criticism. I. Harrison, Max. II. Bolcom, William. III. New Grove dictionary of music and musicians. IV. Title. V. Title: Gospel, blues and jazz. *NYPL [JND 88-16]*

Oliver, Paula, 1962- Sáhara : drama de una descolonización (1960-1987) / Paula Oliver ; prólogo histórico, J.B. Vilar ; prólogo geográfico, B. Barceló Pons.1a ed. Mallorca : M. Font, 1987. 287 p. : ill. ; 21 cm. (Arca de Noé . no. 4) Bibliography: p. 283-286. ISBN 84-86366-56-9 DDC 964/.805 19
1. Western Sahara - History - 1884-1975. 2. Western Sahara - History - 1975-. I. Title.
DT346.S7 O43 1987 *NYPL [Sc D 89-319]*

Oliver Tambo and the struggle against apartheid / edited by E.S. Reddy. New Delhi : Sterling Publishers, in collaboration with Namedia Foundation, c1987. xii, 172 p., [1] leaf of plates : port. ; 22 cm. Festschrift honoring Oliver Tambo, b. 1919, South African freedom fighter; comprises transcript of his speeches and articles by authors on apartheid. ISBN 81-207-0779-6 : DDC 323.1/196/068 19
1. Tambo, Oliver, 1919-. 2. Apartheid - South Africa. 3. Anti-apartheid movement - South Africa. I. Tambo, Oliver, 1919-. II. Reddy, E. S.
DT763 .O57 1987 *NYPL [Sc D 88-1443]*

OLIVER, WILLIAM PEARLY.
Thomson, Colin A., 1938- Born with a call . Dartmouth, Nova Scotia , 1986. 157 p., [8] p. of plates : *NYPL [Sc F 88-63]*

Ollie's go-kart. Huston, Anne. New York [1971] 143 p. DDC [Fic]
PZ7.H959 Ol *NYPL [Sc D 88-1472]*

Ollivier, Emile, 1940- La discorde aux cent voix : roman / Emile Ollivier. Paris : A. Michel, c1986. 269 p. ; 23 cm. ISBN 2-226-02701-7 : DDC 843 19
1. Haiti - Fiction. I. Title.
PQ3949.2.O44 D5 1986
NYPL [Sc D 88-372]

Ollivier Patrick. Commandos de brousse / Patrick Ollivier ; texte revu par Jérôme Sarde. Paris : B. Grasset, 1985. 275 p., [8] p. of plates : ill., map ; 24 cm. ISBN 2-246-35481-1
1. Ollivier Patrick. 2. Zimbabwe. Army - Commando troops - Biography. 3. Guerilla warfare. I. Title.
NYPL [Sc E 87-222]

OLLIVIER PATRICK.
Ollivier Patrick. Commandos de brousse /. Paris , 1985. 275 p., [8] p. of plates : ISBN 2-246-35481-1 *NYPL [Sc E 87-222]*

Olney, James. The Southern review and modern literature, 1935-1985 /. Baton Rouge , c1988. xvi, 238 p.: ISBN 0-8071-1424-3 : DDC 810/.9/975 19
PS267.B3 S68 1987 *NYPL [Sc E 88-280]*

Olorunfemi, J. F. Orubuloye, I. O. (Israel Olatunji), 1947- Introduction to population analysis /. Ibadan , 1986. 106 p. : ISBN 978-224-111-3 *NYPL [Sc D 88-1417]*

Olsen, Aileen. Bernadine and the water bucket / by Aileen Olsen ; pictures by Nola Langner. London ; New York : Abelard-Schuman, 1966. [41] p : ill. ; 27 cm. SCHOMBURG CHILDREN'S COLLECTION.
1. West Indies - Juvenile fiction. I. Schomburg Children's Collection. II. Title.
NYPL [Sc F 88-99]

Olson, Gene. The tall one : a basketball story / Gene Olson. New York : Dodd, Mead, 1957,

c1956. 211 p. ; 21 cm.
1. Basketball - Stories. I. Title.
NYPL [Sc D 89-428]

Olugbemi, Stephen Oluwole, 1940- Alternative political futures for Nigeria /. Nigeria , 1987. xviii, 565 p. ;   ISBN 978-303-170-8
NYPL [Sc D 88-1374]

Olugbile, Femi. Lonely men / Femi Olugbile. Nigeria : Longman Nigeria, 1987. 183 p. ; 19 cm.   ISBN 978-13-9605-9
1. Nigeria - Fiction. I. Title.
NYPL [Sc C 88-336]

Olurode, Lai. Family and social change . Lagos, Nigeria , 1986. vi, 96 p. ;
NYPL [Sc D 88-794]

Olusanya, P. Olufemi. Nursemaids and the pill : a study of household structure, female employment, and the small family ideal in a Nigerian metropolis / P. O. Olusanya. Legon : Population Dynamics Programme, University of Ghana, 1981. xiii, 157 p. : ill. ; 24 cm. (University of Ghana population studies. no. 9)
Bibliography: p. 155-157.
1. Women domestics - Nigeria. 2. Birth control - Nigeria. I. Series.   **NYPL [Sc E 89-249]**

Olusola, Ojo. The impact of military rule on Nigeria's administration /. Ile-Ife, Nigeria , c1987. vi, 344 p. ;   ISBN 978-266-601-7
NYPL [Sc D 88-733]

Olwig, Karen Fog, 1948- Cultural adaptation and resistance on St. John : three centuries of Afro-Caribbean life / Karen Fog Olwig. Gainesville : University of Florida Press, c1985. xii, 226 p. : ill. ; 23 cm. Cover title: Cultural adaptation & resistance on St. John. Includes index. Bibliography: p. [201]-216.   ISBN 0-8130-0818-2 (pbk.)
DDC 306/.097297/22 19
1. Slavery - Virgin Islands of the United States - Saint John - History. 2. Plantation life - Virgin Islands of the United States - Saint John. 3. Saint John (V.I.) - Race relations. I. Title. II. Title: Cultural adaptation & resistance on St. John.
HT1071 .O43 1985   **NYPL [Sc D 88-1058]**

OLYMPICS - HISTORY - 20TH CENTURY.
Blue, Adrianne. Faster, higher, further . London , 1988. ix, 182 p. :   ISBN 0-86068-648-5 (pbk.) :
GV721.5 .B58x 1988   **NYPL [Sc E 89-82]**

Omara-Otunnu, Amii, 1952- Politics and the military in Uganda, 1890-1985 / Amii Omara-Otunnu. Basingstoke, Hampshire : Macmillan Press in association with St. Antony's College, Oxford, 1987. xx, 218 p. : ill. ; 23 cm. ([St. Antony's/Macmillan series]) Includes index. Bibliography: p. 204-209.   ISBN 0-333-41980-4
1. Civil-military relations - Uganda - History. 2. Uganda - Armed Forces - Political activity. I. Title.
NYPL [JFD 87-8644]

O'Meara, Dan, 1948- Davies, Robert H. The struggle for South Africa . London , Atlantic Highlands, N.J. , 1988. 2 v. :   ISBN 0-86232-760-1 (v. 1)   DDC 322/.0968 19
JQ1931 .D38 1988   **NYPL [Sc D 88-1369]**

OMNIBUS BILL, 1850. see COMPROMISE OF 1850.

Omobuarie, D. O. The cashier and his rubber stamp / D.O. Omobuarie. Benin City, Nigeria : King David Writers, 1987. 79 p. ; 21 cm.   ISBN 978-300-321-6
1. Bank employees - Nigeria. 2. Bank tellers. I. Title.
NYPL [Sc D 88-738]

Omole, Wale, 1960- Tai Solarin's adventure : a practised philosophy / Wale Omole. Ibadan : AR-Rauph Commercial Press, 1985. x, 90 p. : ill. ; 18 cm.   DDC 822 19
1. Solarin, Tai - Drama. 2. Mayflower School (Ikene, Nigeria) - Drama. I. Title.
PR9387.9.O396 T3 1985
NYPL [Sc C 88-309]

Omoleye, Mike. Great tales of the Yorubas /. Ibadan, Oyo State, Nigeria , 1987. 92 p. :
NYPL [Sc D 88-712]

Omoniwa, Moses Adekunle. Ajayi, John Olufemi. Library education in Nigeria, 1948-1986 /. Zaria , 1987. ii, 81 p. ;
NYPL [Sc D 88-1376]

Omotoso, Kole. Just before dawn / Kole Omotoso. Ibadan : Spectrum Books, 1988. xi, 345 p. ; 22 cm.   ISBN 978-246-007-9

1. Nigeria - History - Fiction. I. Title.
NYPL [Sc D 88-1485]

Omotoso, Kole, 1943- Sacrifice / by Kole Omotoso. Ibadan, Nigeria : Onibonoje Publishers, 1978. 123 p. ; 18 cm. (African literature series. 6)
1. Nigeria - Fiction. I. Title.
NYPL [Sc C 87-346]

On a plantation in Kenya /. Visram, M. G. Mombasa, Kenya , 1987 (reprinted 1988) 164 p., [4] p. of plates   ISBN 996-698-411-9
NYPL [Sc C 89-92]

On African women's equality, role in national liberation, development and peace . Regional Seminar for Africa (Mogadishu : 1975) [Mogadishu] , 1975. 123 p. ;
NYPL [Sc E 88-138]

On ne guérit pas de son enfance /. Turian Cardozo, Jacqueline. Port-au-Prince , 1987. 220 p., [1] folded leaf plates :
NYPL [Sc D 88-293]

On organizing the masses.
(1) Epton, William. Electoral politics [microform] . New York , 1980. 33 p. :
NYPL [Sc Micro F-10975]

On slavery! Silva, José Bonifácio de Andrada e, 1763-1838. Memoir addressed to the general, constituent and legislative Assembly of the empire of Brazil, on slavery! London , 1826 London : Printed by A. Redford and W. Robins) 60 p. ;   **NYPL [Sc Rare G 86-14]**

On strike for respect : the clerical & technical workers' strike at Yale University (1984-1985) / Toni Gilpin ... [et al.] ; foreward by David Montgomery. Chicago : Charles H. Kerr Pub. Co., 1988. 94 p. ; 18 cm. On cover: The Yale strike of 1984-85.
1. Federation of University Employees. 2. Strikes and lockouts - Connecticut. I. Gilpin, Toni. II. Title: Yale strike of 1984-85. III. Title: Clerical & technical workers' strike at Yale University (1984-1985). IV. Title: Clerical and technical workers' strike at Yale University.   **NYPL [Sc C 89-101]**

On the occasion of the first meeting of the Saint Lucia House of Assembly, dated and March, 1967 [microform] St. Lucia. St. Lucia [1967] [11] p. ;   **NYPL [Sc Micro F-10953]**

On the road again . Nyamubaya, Freedom T. V. Harare, Zimbabwe , 1986. 69 p. :   ISBN 0-949225-00-4   **NYPL [Sc C 88-136]**

Onadipe, Kola. Halima must not die : and other plays for schools / by Kola Onadipe. Ijebu-Ode, Nigeria : Natona, c1980. 71 p. : ill. ; 22 cm.   ISBN 978-17-8026-6
1. College and school drama, Nigerian (English). I. Title.   **NYPL [Sc D 88-1368]**

Onda negra, medo branco . Azevedo, Celia Maria Marinho de. Rio de Janeiro , c1987. 267 p. ;
NYPL [Sc D 88-469]

Ondiek, Patroba E. Curriculum development : alternatives in educational theory & practice / Patroba E. Ondiek. Kisumu, Kenya : Lake Publishers and Enterprises, 1986. xiii, 139 p. : ill. ; 22 cm. Bibliography: p. 137-139.
1. Curriculum planning - Kenya. I. Title.
NYPL [Sc D 89-153]

Ondina /. Naranjo, Carmen. La Habana, Cuba , c1988. 135 p. ;
PQ7489.2.N3 O5x 1988   **NYPL [Sc C 89-84]**

The one . Salkey, Andrew. London , 1985. 48 p. :
NYPL [Sc D 88-1238]

One bad casa. Baku, Shango. 3 plays of our time /. Belmont, Trinidad , 1984. 116 p. ;
NYPL [Sc D 88-971]

One bowl of porridge . Baez, Joan, 1913- Santa Barbara, Calif. , 1986, c1985. 94 p. :   ISBN 0-936784-12-1 (pbk.) :   DDC 363.8/83/096773 19
HV696.F6 B34 1986   **NYPL [Sc D 89-333]**

One day, Levin ... he be free. Khan, Lurey. New York [1972] 231 p.   ISBN 0-525-36415-3   DDC 973.7/115 B 92
E450.S852 K45 1972   **NYPL [Sc D 88-1116]**

One hundred great Westindian test cricketers. Lawrence, Bridgette. 100 great Westindian test cricketers . London , 1988. 231 p. :   ISBN 1-87051-865-9 :   DDC 796.35/865 19
GV928.W4   **NYPL [Sc F 88-380]**

One hundred years of architecture in Kingston. Mattie, Joan. 100 years of architecture in Kingston . [Ottawa] , c1986. 30 p. :   ISBN 0-662-54396-3 (pbk.)   DDC 720/.9713/72074011384 19
NA747.K56 M38 1986   **NYPL [Sc F 88-195]**

One party democracy; the 1965 Tanzania general elections. Lionel Cliffe, editor. Co-authors: Lionel Cliffe [and others] Foreword by Rashidi Kawawa. [Nairobi] East African Pub. House [1967] 470 p. illus. 22 cm. (EAPH political studies, 3) "Written under the auspices of the Political Science Research Programme, Makerere Institute of Social Research, Kampala." Includes bibliographies.   DDC 324/.678
1. Elections - Tanzania. 2. Tanzania - Politics and government - 1964-. I. Cliffe, Lionel, ed. II. Makerere Institute of Social Research. Political Science Research Programme.
JQ3519.A55 O5   **NYPL [Sc D 88-976]**

Oni, Stephen Bola. Community development : the back-bone for promoting socio-economic growth / by Stephen Bola Oni and Bello Ohiani. [Zaria, Nigeria] : Oluseyi Boladeji Co., 1987. vii, 128 p. : ill. ; 22 cm. Bibliography: p. 127-128.   ISBN 978-19-4120-0
1. Community development - Nigeria. I. Ohiani, Bello. II. Title.   **NYPL [Sc D 88-791]**

ONIBONOKUTA, ADEMOLA.
Beier, Ulli. Three Yoruba artists . Bayreuth, W. Germany , c19. 93 p. ;
NYPL [Sc D 88-1325]

Onimode, Bade. A political economy of the African crisis / Bade Onimode. London ; Atlantic Highlands, N.J. : Zed Books with the Institute for African Alternatives, 1988. 333 p. ; 23 cm. Includes index. Bibliography: p. [324]-330.   ISBN 0-86232-373-8   DDC 330.96/0328 19
1. Africa - Economic conditions - 1960-. 2. Africa - Social conditions - 1960-. I. Title.
HC800 .O55 1988   **NYPL [JLD 88-4614]**

Onitsha Ecclesiastical Province Centenary History Commission. A Hundred years of the Catholic Church in Eastern Nigeria, 1885-1985 . Onitsha, Nigeria , 1985. 432 p. :   ISBN 978-17-5103-7   **NYPL [Sc D 88-830]**

ONITSHA (NIGERIA) - BIOGRAPHY.
Akosa, Chike. Heroes & heroines of Onitsha /. Onitsha, Nigeria , 1987 (Etukokwu Press) viii, 344 p. :   ISBN 978-303-730-7
NYPL [Sc D 88-1109]

ONITSHA (NIGERIA) - CHURCH HISTORY.
The Catholic Church in Onitsha . Onitsha , 1985. xvii, 341 p.   DDC 282/.6694 19
BX1682.N5 C36 1985   **NYPL [Sc D 88-891]**

ONITSHA, NIGERIA - HISTORY.
Akosa, Chike. Heroes & heroines of Onitsha /. Onitsha, Nigeria , 1987 (Etukokwu Press) viii, 344 p. :   ISBN 978-303-730-7
NYPL [Sc D 88-1109]

Only the ball was white. Peterson, Robert, 1925- Englewood Cliffs, N.J. [1970] vii, 406 p.   ISBN 0-13-637215-5   DDC 796.357/09
GV863 .P4   **NYPL [Sc 796.357-P]**

Onobrakpeya, Bruce.
Bruce Onobrakpeya--Symbols of ancestral groves : [monograph of prints and paintings, 1978-1985 / Bruce Onobrakpeya. Mushin [Nigeria] : Ovuomaroro Gallery, 1985. 252 p. : ill. (some col.) : 29 cm. Editor: Safy Quel. Bibliography: p. 236-247.   ISBN 978-250-900-0
1. Art, Modern - 20th century - Nigeria. I. Quel, Safy. II. Title. III. Title: Symbols of ancestral groves.
NYPL [Sc F 88-169]

Haeger, Barbara. Africa . Ibadan, Nigeria , 1982. xiii, 105 p. :   **NYPL [Sc D 87-759]**

Sahelian masquerades / Bruce Onobrakpeya ; edited by Safy Quel. Papa Ajao, Mushin : Ovuomaroro Gallery, c1988. xi, 132 p. : ill. (some col.), port. ; 29 cm. "Artistic experiments Nov. 1985 - Aug. 1988" -- t.p.   ISBN 978-250-908-6
1. Onobrakpeya, Bruce - Exhibitions. I. Ovuomaroro Gallery. II. Title.   **NYPL [Sc F 89-16]**

ONOBRAKPEYA, BRUCE - EXHIBITIONS.
Onobrakpeya, Bruce. Sahelian masquerades /. Papa Ajao, Mushin , c1988. xi, 132 p. :   ISBN 978-250-908-6   **NYPL [Sc F 89-16]**

Ontongolia /. Mboya, Alakie-Akinyi. Nairobi , 1986. xiv, 92 p., [4] p. of plates ;   ISBN 0-19-572615-4   **NYPL [Sc C 88-138]**

Onuoha, Enyeribe. Four contrasting world views / by Enyeribe Onuoha. Enugu. : Empress Pub. Co., 1987. 70 p. : ill. ; 21 cm. Bibliography: p. 65. ISBN 978-302-351-9 :
I. Title.   *NYPL [Sc D 88-759]*

Onwueme, Tess Akaeke.
Ban empty barn : [and other plays] / Tess Akaeke Onwueme. Owerri, Nigeria : Totan Publishers, 1986. 145 p. ; 19 cm. Cover title. CONTENTS. - Ban empty barn - The artist's homecoming - Cattle egret versus Nama. ISBN 978-244-909-4
1. Nigeria - Drama. I. Title.
                            NYPL [Sc C 88-202]
Mirror for campus / by Tess Akaede Onwueme. Owerri : Headway Communication Books, 1987. iii leaves, 76 p. ; 20 cm.
1. Universities and colleges - Nigeria - Drama. 2. Nigeria - Drama. I. Title. *NYPL [Sc C 88-159]*

Onwuka, Ralph I. African development . Lawrenceville, Va., U. S. A. , c1985. 241 p. : ISBN 0-931494-57-5 (pbk.) DDC 337.1/6 19
HC800 .A565 1985   *NYPL [Sc F 87-376]*

Onwukwe, I. Iroaganachi, John. A fight for honey /. Lagos, Nigeria , 1977. 30 p. : ISBN 0-410-80181-X   *NYPL [Sc C 88-77]*

Onwumere, S. O. Social research and information gathering /. Lagos [1987?] v. 72 p. :
                            NYPL [Sc E 88-301]

Onye ije awele /. Ugwoke, Oliva Obinna. [Ihiala, Nigeria , 198-?] iv, 77 p. :
        NYPL [Sc D 88-1040]

Onyeneke, Augustine O. The dead among the living : masquerades in Igbo society / by Augustine O. Onyeneke. Nimo : Holy Ghost Congregation, Province of Nigeria and Asele Institute, 1987. xii, 142 p. : ill., map ; 20 cm. Bibliography: p. 140-142. ISBN 978-244-232-1
1. Igbo (African people) - Social life and customs. 2. Masquerades - Nigeria. I. Title.
                               NYPL [Sc C 89-2]

Onyeneke, Onyewuotu. I will kill you and get away with it / Onyewuotu Onyeneke. [Nigeria : s.n.,197-?] (Lagos : Lukab) 122 p. ; 19 cm.
1. Nigeria - Fiction. I. Title.
                            NYPL [Sc C 89-153]

Onyeocha, Anthony Ekendu. These hi-fi priests : spirituality for priests / Anthony Ekendu Onyeocha. Owerri [Nigeria] : Gunson Headway Press, 1985. 208 p. : port. ; 21 cm. At head of title: Retreat talks to priests.
1. Catholic Church - Clergy - Religious life. 2. Retreats for clergy. 3. Retreats - Nigeria. I. Catholic Church. Diocese of Owerri (Nigeria). II. Title. III. Title: Retreat talks to priests.   *NYPL [Sc D 88-926]*

Onyia, Nathaniel Maduabuchi. Pre-colonial history of Amokwe / Nathaniel Maduabuchi Onyia. Enugu, Nigeria : Cecta, 1987. 95 p. : ill. ; 21 cm. Bibliography: p. 90-93. ISBN 978-239-618-4
1. Igbo (African people). 2. Amokwe (Nigeria) - History. I. Title.   *NYPL [Sc D 89-53]*

Onyia, Obi J. I. G. My role in nationalism / by Obi (chief) J.I.G. Onyia, O.F.R. Asaba : Ilojei Odibosa House, 1986. 73 p. : ill., ports. ; 24 cm.
1. Onyia, Obi J. I. G. 2. Nationalism - Nigeria. 3. Nationalists - Nigeria - Biography. I. Title.
                            NYPL [Sc E 89-115]

ONYIA, OBI J. I. G.
Onyia, Obi J. I. G. My role in nationalism /. Asaba , 1986. 73 p. :   *NYPL [Sc E 89-115]*

Ooft, Benny Ch. Suriname, 10 jaar republiek / Benny Ooft. Nieuwegein : Stichting Basispers ; Paramaribo : Art Incorporation, 1985. 145 p. : ill. ; 25 cm. ISBN 90-71138-05-4
1. Surinam - History - 1950-. I. Title. II. Title: Suriname, tien jaar republiek.
                            NYPL [Sc E 88-361]

Oosthuizen, G. C. (Gerhardus Cornelis)
The birth of Christian Zionism in South Africa / G.C. Oosthuizen. KwaDlangezwa, South Africa : University of Zululand, 1987. ii, 56 p. ; 21 cm. (Publication series of the University of Zululand. Series T i.e. F . 4) Bibliography: p. 56. ISBN 0-09-079580-2 DDC 289.9 19
1. Christian sects - South Africa. 2. Zionist churches (Africa). 3. South Africa - Church history. I. Series: Publication series of the University of Zululand. Series

F , 4. II. Title.
BR1450 .O55 1987   *NYPL [Sc D 88-693]*
Religion, intergroup relations, and social change in South Africa /. New York , 1988. xii, 237 p. : ISBN 0-313-26360-4 (lib. bdg. : alk. paper) DDC 306/.6/0968 19
DT763 .R393 1988   *NYPL [Sc D 89-305]*
Succession conflict within the Church of the Nazarites, iBandla zamaNazaretha / by G.C. Oosthuizen. Durban [South Africa] : Institute for Social and Economic Research, University of Durban-Westville, [1981] 71 p. ; 30 cm. (I.S.E.R. - no. 13 (1981)) Bibliography: p. 71. ISBN 0-949947-43-1 (pbk.) DDC 289.7 19
1. Church of the Nazarites - Government. I. Series: I.S.E.R. (Series) ; no. 13. II. Title.
BX7068.7.Z5 O56 1981
                            NYPL [Sc F 87-351]

Opadotun, 'Tunji.
Aròf Ọlátúnjí, Ọpádòtun (Eléwì-Odò) Ibàdàn : Oníbonòjé Press & Book Industries, 1987. v, 82 p. ; 18 cm. ISBN 978-14-5069-X
1. Yoruba language - Texts. I. Title.
                            NYPL [Sc C 88-218]
Arokò : àwọn àmì àti ìró ìbánis Ibadan : Vantage Publishers, 1986. viii, 120 p. : ill. ; 22 cm. Bibliography: p. 120. ISBN 978-245-840-6
1. Yoruba language - Texts. I. Title.
                            NYPL [Sc D 88-948]

The open prison /. Richmond, Angus. London , 1988. 225 p. ; ISBN 1-87051-825-X (pbk.) : DDC 813 19   *NYPL [JFD 89-478]*

Open School (Johannesburg, South Africa)
Two dogs and freedom . Johannesburg , 1986. 55 p. : ISBN 0-86975-301-0 (pbk.)
                            NYPL [Sc D 88-151]
Two dogs and freedom . New York , 1987. 55 p. : ISBN 0-8050-0637-0 (pbk.) : DDC 323.1/196/068 19
DT763.6 .T96 1987   *NYPL [Sc D 88-422]*

Open stage.
Kalejaiye, Dipo. Polygyny and Polyandry . London , 1985. 55 p. ; ISBN 0-333-35822-8
                            NYPL [Sc D 88-1049]
Ogunyẹmi, Wale, 1939- The vow /. London , 1985. vi, 47 p. ; ISBN 0-333-35819-8
                            NYPL [Sc D 88-1210]

OPERA EBONY - ANNIVERSAREES, ETC.
National Opera Ebony. Opera Ebony's 10th anniversary souvenir journal. Philadelphia, Pa. [1984] 84 p. :   *NYPL [Sc F 87-425]*

Opera Ebony's tenth anniversary souvenir journal. National Opera Ebony. Opera Ebony's 10th anniversary souvenir journal. Philadelphia, Pa. [1984] 84 p. :   *NYPL [Sc F 87-425]*

Opera Ebony's 10th anniversary souvenir journal. National Opera Ebony. Philadelphia, Pa. [1984] 84 p. :   *NYPL [Sc F 87-425]*

Opération Marigot . Gomez, Koffi, 1941- Lomé , 1982. 146 p. ; ISBN 2-7236-0849-2
                            NYPL [Sc D 88-1306]

OPERATION PUSH.
House, Ernest R. Jesse Jackson & the politics of charisma . Boulder , 1988. xi, 196 p. ; ISBN 0-8133-0767-8 (alk. paper) DDC 973.92/092/4 19
E840.8.J35 H68 1988   *NYPL [JFE 88-7205]*

Opinion de Jean-François Ducos sur l'exécution provisoire du concordat, & des arrêtés de l'Assemblée coloniale confirmatifs de cet accord . Ducos, Jean François, 1765-1793. A Paris , 1791. 12 p. ; *NYPL [Sc Rare C 86-7]*

OPINION EVIDENCE. see **EVIDENCE, EXPERT.**

OPINION, PUBLIC. see **PUBLIC OPINION.**

Opon Ifa series .
(no. 3) Segun, Mabel. Conflict and other poems /. Ibadan , 1986. vi, 49 p. ; ISBN 978-226-613-2
                            NYPL [Sc C 88-286]

Oppong, Christine.
Seven roles of women : impact of education, migration and employment on Ghanaian mothers / Christine Oppong and Katharine Abu. Geneva : International Labour Office, 1987. xi, 127 p. : ill. ; 24 cm. (Women, work and development, 0253-2042 . 13) "Prepared with the financial support of the United Nations Fund for Population Activities." Bibliography: p. 117-127.

1. Fertility, Human - Ghana. 2. Women - Education - Ghana. 3. Migration, Internal - Ghana. 4. Women - Employment - Ghana. I. Abu, Katharine. II. International Labour Office. III. United Nations Fund for Population Activities. IV. Title. V. Series.
                            NYPL [Sc E 89-143]
Sex roles, population and development in West Africa . London , Portsmouth, N.H. , 1987. xiii, 242 p. ; ISBN 0-435-08022-9 DDC 304.6/0966 19
HB3665.5.A3 S49 1988
                            NYPL [Sc E 88-318]

Opportunity; journal of Negro life. Ebony and topaz . New York , 1927. 164 p. :
                            NYPL [Sc Rare F 82-72]

L'or de Guyane . Petot, Jean. Paris , c1986. 248 p. [8] pages of plates : ISBN 2-903033-84-6
                            NYPL [Sc D 88-1395]

Oral histories of three secondary school students in Tanzania / translated and edited by Sara Joan Talis. Lewiston/Queenston : E. Mellen Press, 1987. 248 p. ; 24 cm. (African studies . v. 2) Includes bibliographical references and index. ISBN 0-88946-179-1 (alk. paper) : DDC 306/.0967/8 19
1. Education, Secondary - Tanzania - Case studies. 2. Tanzania - Social conditions - Case studies. 3. Tanzania - Social life and customs - Case studies. I. Talis, Sara Joan. II. Series: African studies (Lewiston, N.Y.) , v. 2.
LA1842 .O73 1987   *NYPL [Sc E 88-267]*

Oral history . Samkange, Stanlake John Thompson, 1922- Harare, Zimbabwe , c1986. ii, 93 p. :   *NYPL [Sc D 89-586]*

ORAL HISTORY.
Kisseloff, Jeff. You must remember this . San Diego , c1989. xvii, 622 p., [16] p. of plates : ISBN 0-15-187988-5 : DDC 974.7/1042 19
F128.5 .K55 1988   *NYPL [Sc E 89-54]*
My folks don't want me to talk about slavery . Winston-Salem, N.C. , c1984. xiv, 103 p. ; ISBN 0-89587-038-X DDC 975.6/00496073/0922 B 19
E445.N8 M9 1984   *NYPL [JFD 85-1549]*
Watson, Wilbur H. The village . Atlanta, Ga. , c1989. xxii, 204 p. : ISBN 0-9621460-0-5 DDC 977.1/3200496073 20
F499.C69 N38 1989   *NYPL [Sc D 89-609]*

ORAL TRADITION - UNITED STATES.
Gates, Henry Louis. The signifying monkey . New York , 1988. xxviii, 290 p. : ISBN 0-19-503463-5 (alk. paper) DDC 810/.9/896073 19
PS153.N5 G28 1988   *NYPL [Sc E 89-181]*

Oralitures et littératures africaines et caribéennes. [Fort-de-France] : LARIAMEP, [1985] 56 p. : ill. ; 28cm. (Annales martiniquaises. Série sciences humaines . no.3) French and English Title from cover. Includes bibliographies.
1. Caribean literature (French) - History and criticism. I. Series.   *NYPL [Sc F 89-93]*

ORANGE COUNTY (CALIF.) - SOCIAL CONDITIONS.
Cocoltchos, Christopher Nickolas, 1949- The invisible government and the viable community . 1979. 2 v. (xv, 774 leaves) :
                            NYPL [Sc F 88-285]

Orçamento . Fundação Joaquim Nabuco. Recife , 1982. 92 p. ; ISBN 85-7019-046-8
                            NYPL [Sc B 88-49]

ORDERS, MONASTIC. see **MONASTICISM AND RELIGIOUS ORDERS.**

ORDINANCE OF 1787.
Birney, James Gillespie, 1792-1857. Examination of the decision of the Supreme Court of the United States, in the case of Strader, Gorman and Armstrong vs. Christopher Graham . Cincinnati , 1852. iv, [1], 6-46, [1] p. ;
E450 .B57   *NYPL [Sc Rare F 88-37]*

Ordre national de la République démocratique de Madagascar.
Livre d'or de l'Ordre national. Tananarive : Éditions Madprint, [between 1977 and 1979] p. 402-727 : port. ; 24 cm. At head of title: République démocratique malagasy. Contains names of members of the Ordre national de la République démocratique de Madagascar, 1971-1977. DDC 929.8/1691 19
1. Ordre national de la République démocratique de

Madagascar - Registers.
CR6190.M3 O69 1977   NYPL [Sc E 87-526]

ORDRE NATIONAL DE LA RÉPUBLIQUE DÉMOCRATIQUE DE MADAGASCAR - REGISTERS.
Ordre national de la République démocratique de Madagascar. Livre d'or de l'Ordre national. Tananarive [between 1977 and 1979] p. 402-727 :   DDC 929.8/1691 19
CR6190.M3 O69 1977   NYPL [Sc E 87-526]

Organ, Claude H., 1928- A Century of Black surgeons . Norman, Okla. , c1987. 2 v. (xx, 973 p.) :   ISBN 0-9617380-0-6 (set)   DDC 617/.092/2 B 19
RD27.34 .C46 1987   NYPL [Sc E 88-216]

ORGAN TRADE. see MUSIC TRADE.

Organisation de l'unité africaine. see Organization of African Unity.

Organisation des Nations Unies. see United Nations.

Organisation for Economic Co-operation and Development. Development Centre. Bonvin, Jean. Changements sociaux et productivité agricole en Afrique Centrale /. Paris : Centre de développement de l'orgnisation de coopértion et de développement économiques, c1986. 140 p. :   ISBN 92-64-22803-9
NYPL [Sc D 88-803]

Organisation Internationale du Travail. see International Labor Organization.

Organisation of African Unity. Bureau for Placement and Education of African Refugees. Africa and its refugees . [Addis Ababa] [1975] 76 p. :   DDC 362.8/7/096 19
HV640.4.A35 A35 1975
NYPL [Sc D 88-198]

Organizacion Internacional del Trabajo. see International Labor Office.

ORGANIZATION OF AFICAN UNITY.
The pedagogy of a decade of OAU mock-summits at ABU. Zaria [1988] (Zaria : Ahmadu Bello University Press) 64 p. :   ISBN 978-301-130-12   *NYPL [Sc G 88-38]*

The Organization of African Unity and African diplomacy, 1963-1979 /. Agbi, Sunday O. Agodi, Ibadan , 1986. x, 166 p. :   ISBN 978-238-601-4 (pbk.)   DDC 960/.326 19
DT30.5 .A374 1986   NYPL [Sc D 89-124]

ORGANIZATION OF AFRICAN UNITY - HISTORY.
Agbi, Sunday O. The Organization of African Unity and African diplomacy, 1963-1979 /. Agodi, Ibadan , 1986. x, 166 p. :   ISBN 978-238-601-4 (pbk.)   DDC 960/.326 19
DT30.5 .A374 1986   NYPL [Sc D 89-124]

Sesay, Amadu. The OAU after twenty years /. Boulder , 1984. ix, 133 p. ;   ISBN 0-8133-0112-2 :
NYPL [JLD 85-633]

Organization of African Unity 25 years on : essays in honour of Kwame Nkrumah / edited by Kwesi Krafona. London : Afroworld Pub. Co., 1988. vii, 175 p. : ports ; 23 cm. Includes bibliographical references.   ISBN 0-948583-05-3 (Hardback)
1. Nkrumah, Kwame, 1909-1972. 2. Africa - Politics and government - 1960-. 3. Africa - Economic conditions - 1960-. I. Krafona, Kwesi.
NYPL [Sc D 89-556]

Organization of American States. Biblioteca Conmemorativa de Colón. see Columbus Memorial Library.

Organization of American States. Columbus Memorial Library. see Columbus Memorial Library.

Organization of American States. Dept. of Publications. Columbus Memorial Library. see Columbus Memorial Library.

Organization of American States. Dept. of Publicatons. Biblioteca Conmemorativa de Colón. see Columbus Memorial Library.

Organization of American States. General Secretariat. Biblioteca Conmemorativa de Colón. see Columbus Memorial Library.

Organization of American States. General Secretariat. Columbua Memorial Library. see Columbus Memorial Library.

ORGANIZATION, SOCIAL. see SOCIAL STRUCTURE.

Organizational issues in Nigeria. Ihenacho, Izuka John. Administrators of special education . [Nigeria] , c1986. 208 p. ;   ISBN 978-239-609-5 (pbk.)   DDC 371.9/09669 19
LC3988.N6 I44 1986   NYPL [Sc C 89-145]

ORGANIZATIONS. see ASSOCIATIONS, INSTITUTIONS, ETC.

ORGANIZATIONS, INTERNATIONAL. see INTERNATIONAL AGENCIES.

Organizing for preservation in ARL libraries / Systems and Procedures Exchange Center. Washington, D.C. : Association of Research Libraries, Office of Management Studies, 1985. 131 p. : ill. ; 28 cm. (SPEC kit . no. 116) SPEC flyer ; no. 116. Cover title. Accompanied by SPEC flyer ; no. 116. "July-August 1985."
1. Books - Conservation and restoration - United States.
I. Association of Research Libraries. Systems and Procedures Exchange Program.
NYPL [Sc F 88-327]

Organizzazione dell'unità africana. see Organization of African Unity.

Orie, S. L. A dictionary of Muslim names / compiled by S.L. Orie ; edited by Waffie Mohammed & Rehana Mohammed. 1st ed. Point à Pierre, Trinidad : Baitul Maal, 1984. 43 p. ; 21 cm.
1. Names, Personal - Religious aspects - Islam - Dictionaries. I. Title.   NYPL [Sc D 88-946]

Oriental documents .
(9) Letters from Ethiopian rulers (early and mid-nineteenth century) . Oxford , New York , c1985. xvii, 197 p. :   ISBN 0-19-726046-2
NYPL [Sc E 88-262]

Oriental passion /. Okpalaeze, Inno-Pat Chuba. Onitsha, Nigeria , 1987. 89 p. ;
NYPL [Sc C 89-72]

Les orientations de la Deuxième République. Guinea. Comité militaire de redressement national. [Conakry , 1984] 76 p. :   DDC 967/.1803 19
DT543.825 .G85 1984   NYPL [Sc E 88-310]

Los Orígenes de la descolonización africana a través de la prensa española (1956-1962) /. Sevillano Castillo, Rosa. Madrid , 1986. 158 p. ;
NYPL [Sc E 88-94]

Les origines de la métallurgie en Afrique occidentale /. Grébénart, Danilo. Paris , c1988. 290 p. :   ISBN 2-903442-65-7
NYPL [Sc E 88-600]

Origines et évolution du Royaume de l'Arindrano jusqu'au XIXe siècle . Raherisoanjato, Daniel. Antananarivo , 1984. 334 leaves :   DDC 969/.1 19
DT469.M37 A747 1984
NYPL [Sc F 88-390]

The origins of the Nigerian army . Ukpabi, Sam C. Zaria, Nigeria , 1987. 194 p. :   ISBN 978-19-4128-6   *NYPL [Sc D 88-1489]*

Ormerod, Beverley, 1937- An introduction to the French Caribbean novel / Beverley Ormerod. London ; Portsmouth, N.H., USA : Heinemann, 1985. 152 p. ; 22 cm. (Studies in Caribbean literature) Includes index. Bibliography: p. 140-145.   ISBN 0-435-91839-7 (pbk.)   DDC 843 19
1. West Indian fiction (French) - History and criticism. 2. French fiction - 20th century - History and criticism. I. Title. II. Series.
PQ3944 .O76 1985   NYPL [Sc D 88-1267]

ORNAMENT. see DECORATION AND ORNAMENT.

OROMO LANGUAGE - DIALECTS - ETHIOPIA - HARER REGION - GRAMMAR.
Owens, Jonathan. A grammar of Harar Oromo (Northeastern Ethiopia) . Hamburg , c1985. 282 p. ;   ISBN 3-87118-717-8 (pbk.)   DDC 493/.7 19
PJ2476 .O94 1985   NYPL [Sc D 88-751]

L'orphelin et son destin [microform] . Kamwa, Joseph. Bafoussam, [Cameroon] , 1981. 27 p. :
NYPL [Sc Micro R-4137 no.17]

Orsi, Robert A. The Madonna of 115th Street : faith and community in Italian Harlem, 1880-1950 / Robert Anthony Orsi. New Haven : Yale University Press, c1985. xxiii, 287 p. : ill. ; 24 cm. Includes index. Bibliography: p.

235-282.   ISBN 0-300-03262-5 (alk. paper)   DDC 263/.98/0895107471 19
1. Mary - Cult - New York (City). 2. Italian Americans - New York (City) - Religious life. 3. Italian Americans - New York (City) - Social conditions. 4. Harlem, New York (City) - Religious life and customs. 5. New York (City) - Religious life and customs. 6. Harlem, New York (City) - Social conditions. 7. New York (City) - Social conditions. I. Title.
BT660.N44 O77 1985
NYPL [IEE (Italians) 86-89]

Orsini, José G. M. Balmes, Jaime Luciano, 1810-1848. [Protestantismo comparado con el catolicismo en sus relaciones con la civilización europea. Selections. Portuguese.] A Igreja católica em face da escravidão /. São Paulo , 1988. 141 p. ;   *NYPL [Sc D 89-554]*

Ortiz Fernández, Fernando, 1881-1969. Los bailes y el teatro de los negros en el folklore de Cuba / Fernando Ortiz. 2a ed. Habana, Cuba : Editorial Letras Cubanas, 1981. 602 p. : ill., music ; 24 cm. "Este libro es la continuación a modo de segunda parte ... de ... 'La africanía de la música folklórica de Cuba' (Habana, 1950)"--Introd. Bibliography: p. [589]-602.
1. Folk music - Cuba - History and criticism. 2. Blacks - Cuba. 3. Dancing - Cuba - History. 4. Theater - Cuba - History. I. Title.
NYPL [JME 82-163]

Ortiz, Fernando, 1881-1969. La clave xilofónica de la música cubana : ensayo etnográfico / Fernando Ortiz. Ciudad de la Habana, Cuba : Editorial Letras Cubanas, 1984. 105 p. ; 18 cm. (Mínima. Ensayo) Includes bibliographical references.   DDC 789/.6 19
1. Claves - History and criticism. 2. Musical instruments - Cuba - History and criticism. I. Title.
ML1049 .O77 1984   NYPL [Sc C 87-373]

Ortiz, Fernando. see Ortiz Fernández, Fernando, 1881-1969.

Orubuloye, I. O. (Israel Olatunji), 1947- Introduction to population analysis / by Isreal [sic] O. orubuloye and J.F. Olorunfemi. Ibadan : Afrografica Publishers, 1986. 106 p. : ill. ; 21 cm. Includes bibliographies.   ISBN 978-224-111-3
1. Population - Statistics. 2. Population research. I. Olorunfemi, J. F. II. Title.
NYPL [Sc D 88-1417]

Orukari, Patrick Idah. Dreams : a collection of selected poems / Patrick Idah Orukari.1st ed. Maiduguri : Federal Information Centre, 1987. xi, 41 p. : ill. ; 21 cm.
I. Title.   NYPL [Sc D 88-1288]

Osahon, Naiwu.
Alphabets and careers / Naiwu Osahon. Apapa, Lagos, Nigeria : Obobo Books, 1981. [32] p. : ill. ; 29 cm. (Obobo Colouring book Series . 1) SCHOMBURG CHILDREN'S COLLECTION.   ISBN 978-18-6006-5
1. Professions - Juvenile literature. I. Schomburg Children's Collection. II. Title.
NYPL [Sc F 88-295]

The hawk and the eagle / Naiwu Osahon. Apapa, Lagos, Nigeria : Obobo Books, 1981. [22] p. : ill. (some col.) ; 22 cm. (Obobo story series . no. 6) SCHOMBURG CHILDREN'S COLLECTION.   ISBN 978-18-6007-3
1. Africa - Juvenile fiction. I. Schomburg Children's Collection. II. Title.   NYPL [Sc D 89-225]

Osahon, Naiwu, 1937-
The land of the spirits / Naiwu Osahon. Apapa, Lagos, Nigeria : Obobo Books, 1981. [30] p. : ill. (some col.) ; 22 cm. (Obobo story series . no. 7) SCHOMBURG CHILDREN'S COLLECTION.   ISBN 978-18-6008-1
1. Africa - Juvenile fiction. I. Schomburg Children's Collection. II. Title.   NYPL [Sc D 89-226]

Laruba and the two wicked men / Naiwu Osahon. Apapa, Lagos, Nigeria : Obobo Books, 1981. [22] p. : ill. (some col.) ; 22 cm. (Obobo story series . no. 2) SCHOMBURG CHILDREN'S COLLECTION. ISBN 978-18-6004-9
1. Africa - Juvenile fiction. I. Schomburg Children's Collection. II. Title.   NYPL [Sc D 89-224]

Madam Universe sent man / Naiwu Osahon. Apapa, Lagos, Nigeria : Obobo Books, 1981. [22] p. : ill. (some col.) ; 22 cm. (Obobo story series . no. 5) SCHOMBURG CHILDREN'S COLLECTION. ISBN 978-18-6002-2
1. Creation - Juvenile literature. I. Schomburg

Children's Collection. II. Title.
NYPL [Sc D 89-223]

The missing gold ring / Naiwu Osahon. Apapa, Lagos, Nigeria : Obobo Books, c1981. [24] p. : ill. (some col.) ; 22 cm. (Obobo story series . no. 1) SCHOMBURG CHILDREN'S COLLECTION. ISBN 978-18-6000-6
1. Africa - Juvenile fiction. I. Schomburg Children's Collection. II. Title.
MLCS 85/698 (P) **NYPL [Sc D 89-222]**

Odu and Onah / Naiwu Osahon. Apapa, Lagos, Nigeria : Obobo Books, 1981. [22] p. : ill. (some col.) ; 22 cm. (Obobo story series . no.8) SCHOMBURG CHILDREN'S COLLECTION.
1. Africa - Juvenile fiction. I. Schomburg Children's Collection. II. Title. **NYPL [Sc D 89-227]**

Right-on Miss Moon / Naiwu Osahon. Apapa, Lagos, Nigeria : Obobo Books, 1981. [22] p. : ill. (some col.) ; 1981. (Obobo story series . no.4) SCHOMBURG CHILDREN'S COLLECTION. ISBN 978-18-6003-0
1. Moon - Juvenile fiction. I. Schomburg Children's Collection. II. Title. **NYPL [Sc D 89-228]**

Osammor, Vincent Osoloka. Introducing commodities (market) exchange in Nigeria / Vincent Osoloka Osammor. Surulere, Lagos, Nigeria : Voo Industrial and Management Consultants, 1986. x, 39 p. ; 21 cm.
1. Commodity exchanges - Nigeria. 2. Nigeria - Economic conditions - 1970-. I. Title.
NYPL [Sc D 88-1293]

Osborne, Francis J. History of the Catholic church in Jamaica / Francis J. Osborne. Aylesbury, Bucks, U.K. : Caribbean Universities Press, c1977. vii, 210, [8] p. of plates : ill. ; 30 cm. Includes index. Bibliography: p. 201. ISBN 0-85474-070-8 (pbk.) DDC 282/.7292 19
1. Catholic Church - Jamaica - History. 2. Jamaica - Church history. I. Title.
BX1455.2 .O84 1977 **NYPL [Sc F 88-290]**

Oscar Peterson /. Palmer, Richard (Richard Hilary), 1947- Tunbridge Wells , New York , 1984. c. 93 p. : ISBN 0-87052-011-3 (Hippocrene Books) : DDC 785.42/092/4 B 19
ML417.P46 P3 1984 **NYPL [Sc C 88-142]**

Oshisanya, Samuel Adekoya.
Nigeria as a world power / by Samuel Adekoya Oshisanya. [Lagos : Samlab Enterprises, 1986] iii, 80 p. : ill., map, ports ; 23 cm. Cover title.
1. Nigeria - Civilization - 20th century. 2. Nigeria - Social policy. 3. Nigeria - Economic policy. I. Title.
NYPL [Sc D 88-689]

The ultimate end of Pan-Africanism / by Samuel Adekoya Oshisanya. [Lagos], Nigeria : S. Oshisanya?, 1983] 105 p. : ill., map, ports. ; 24 cm. Cover title.
1. Nationalism - Africa. 2. Africa - Politics and government. I. Title. **NYPL [Sc E 86-472]**

Osofisan, Femi.
Farewell to a cannibal rage / Femi Osofisan. Ibadan, Nigeria : Evans Brothers (Nigeria Publishers), 1986. 76 p. ; 22 cm. ISBN 978-16-7507-1
I. Title. **NYPL [Sc D 89-14]**

Midnight hotel / Femi Osofisan. Ibadan, Nigeria : Evans Bros., 1986. 65 p. ; 21 cm. ISBN 978-16-7508-X
1. Nigeria - Drama. I. Title.
NYPL [Sc D 88-1050]

Osokoya, Israel O. 6-3-3-4 education in Nigeria : history, strategies, issues and problems / Israel O Osokoya. Lagos, Nigeria : Bisinaike Educational Publishers and Printers, c1987. x, 108 p. ; 25 cm. Bibliography: p. 100-108. ISBN 978-259-918-2
1. Education - Nigeria. I. Title. II. Title: Six-three-three-four education in Nigeria.
NYPL [Sc E 89-162]

Ostler, Scott. Winnin' times : the magical journey of the Los Angeles Lakers / Scott Ostler & Steve Springer. New York : Collier Books, c1988. 304 p. ; 21 cm. Reprint. Originally published: New York : Macmillan, c1986. With new epilogue. ISBN 0-02-029591-X (pbk.) DDC 796.32/364/0979494 19
1. Los Angeles Lakers (Basketball team) - History. I. Springer, Steve. II. Title.
GV885.52.L67 O87 1986
NYPL [Sc D 89-106]

The ostrich chase /. Howard, Moses L., 1928- New York [1974] 118 p. : ISBN 0-03-012096-9
NYPL [Sc D 88-374]

The "Osu" concept in Igboland . Okeke, Igwebuike Romeo. Enugu. [Nigeria] , 1986. xi, 167 p. : ISBN 978-248-100-9
NYPL [Sc E 88-302]

Osuagwu, Harold G. O. Investment demand in a developing country : the Nigerian case / Harold G.O. Osuagwu. Washington, D.C. : University Press of America, c1982. xvii, 411 p. : ill. ; 22 cm. Includes index. Bibliography: p. 362-391. ISBN 0-8191-2048-0 : DDC 332.6/72/09669 19
1. Investments - Nigeria. 2. Nigeria - Economic conditions - 1960-. I. Title.
HG5881.A3 O84 1982 **NYPL [Sc D 88-478]**

Osuala, Esogwa C. A handbook of vocational-technical education for Nigeria / by Esogwa C. Osuala. Oruowulu-Obosi, Anambra State, Nigeria : Pacific Publishers, 1987. x, 173 p. ; 21 cm. Includes bibliographical references. ISBN 0-9782341-9-1
1. Vocational education - Nigeria. 2. Occupational training - Nigeria. I. Title. **NYPL [Sc D 88-729]**

Osuji, Rose C. The effect of socio-economic status on the eductional achievement of Form V students in Trinidad / by Rose C. Osuji. St. Augustine, Trinidad : Institute of Social and Economic Research. The University of the West Indies, 1987. xiv, 229 p. ; 25 cm. "August, 1987." Bibliography: p. [161]-187. ISBN 976-618-002-4
1. Academic achievement - Social aspects - Trinidad and Tobago. 2. Educational sociology - Trinidad and Tobago. 3. Educational equalization - Trinidad and Tobago. I. Title. **NYPL [Sc E 88-352]**

OSUMENYI (NIGERIA) - SOCIAL LIFE AND CUSTOMS.
Nwosu, Obiekezie Vic. Our roots . Lagos , 1986. 55 p. : **NYPL [Sc D 88-713]**

Osundare, Niyi. Moonsongs / Niyi Osundare. Ibadan : Spectrum Books, 1988. viii, 74 p. : ill. ; 22 cm. ISBN 978-246-017-6
I. Title. **NYPL [Sc D 88-1380]**

OSUNKIYESI, SAMUEL C.
Development of special education in Nigeria /. Ibadan , 1988. ix, 132 p. : ISBN 978-267-703-5
NYPL [Sc E 89-70]

Osuntokun, Akinjide. History of the peoples of Lagos State /. Ikeja, Lagos , 1987. xii, 378 p. ; ISBN 978-228-148-4 **NYPL [Sc D 88-731]**

Oswald, Suzanne. Im Urwaldspital von Lambarene / Suzanne Oswald. Bern : Verlag P. Haupt, c1986. 31 p. : ill. ; 21 cm. ISBN 3-258-03594-6
1. Schweitzer, Albert, 1875-1965. 2. Hospitals - Gabon - Lambaréné (Moyen-Ogooué). I. Title.
NYPL [Sc D 87-1076]

Othily, Georges, 1944- Castor, Elie, 1943- La Guyane, les grands problèmes, les solutions possibles /. Paris , c1984. 337 p., [8] p. of plates : 2-903033-58-7 : DDC 988/.203 19
JL812 .C36 1984 **NYPL [Sc D 89-389]**

Otobo, Dafe.
Foreign interests and Nigerian trade unions / Dafe Otobo. Ibadan [Nigeria] : Heinemann Educational Books, 1986. xxviii, 190 p. : ill. ; 24 cm. Bibliography: p. [177]-190. ISBN 978-12-9532-5 (pbk.) DDC 331.88/09669 19
1. Trade-unions - Nigeria - History. 2. Industrial relations - Nigeria - History. 3. Trade-unions and foreign policy - Nigeria - History. 4. Nigeria - Foreign economic relations. I. Title.
HD6885.5 .O87 1986 **NYPL [Sc E 88-557]**

State and industrial relations in Nigeria / by Dafe Otobo. Lagos : Malthouse Press, 1988. 192 p. 21 cm. Bibliography: p. [174]-181. ISBN 978-260-104-7
1. Industrial relations - Nigeria - History. 2. Labor policy - Nigeria - History. I. Title.
NYPL [Sc D 89-523]

Ottaway, David. Ottaway, Marina. Afrocommunism /. New York , 1986. ix, 270 p. : ISBN 0-8419-1034-0 DDC 335.43/096 19
HX438.5 .O87 1985 **NYPL [JLD 86-4056]**

Ottaway, Marina. Afrocommunism / Marina and David Ottaway. 2nd ed. New York : Africana Pub. Co., 1986. ix, 270 p. : map ; 24 cm. Includes index. Bibliography: p. 244-264. ISBN 0-8419-1034-0 DDC 335.43/096 19

1. Communism - Africa. 2. Socialism - Africa. I. Ottaway, David. II. Title.
HX438.5 .O87 1985 **NYPL [JLD 86-4056]**

Ottino, Paul. L'étrangère intime : essai d'anthropologie de la civilisation de l'ancien Madagascar / Paul Ottino. Paris, France : Editions des archives contemporaines, c1986. 2 v. (xxvii, 630 p.) : ill. ; 23 cm. (Ordres sociaux, 0294-1945) Includes indexes. Bibliography: p. [581]-599. ISBN 2-88124-095-X (set) DDC 398/.0969/1 19
1. Folk literature - Madagascar. 2. Legends - Madagascar. 3. Madagascar - Civilization. 4. Madagascar - Kings and rulers. I. Title.
GR357 .O88 1986 **NYPL [Sc D 88-1203]**

Où allons nous?. [Conakry] : Mouvement national démocratique, [1986?] 92 p. ; 17 cm. Cover title: Guinée, où allons nous?
1. Guinea - Economic conditions - 1984-. 2. Guinea - Politics and government - 1958-. I. Mouvement national démocratique (Guinea). II. Title: Guinée, où allons nous?.
HC1030 .O89 1986 **NYPL [Sc B 88-58]**

Oubliés. Bernard, Patrick, 1956- Les oubliés du temps /. Paris [1984] 160 p. : ISBN 2-902906-09-9 DDC 306 19
GN378 .B45 1984 **NYPL [Sc F 88-69]**

Les oubliés du temps /. Bernard, Patrick, 1956- Paris [1984] 160 p. : ISBN 2-902906-09-9 DDC 306 19
GN378 .B45 1984 **NYPL [Sc F 88-69]**

Les Ouldémés du Nord-Cameroun . Colombel, Véronique de. Paris , 1987. [13]-74 p., [61] p. of plates : ISBN 2-85297-199-2
NYPL [Sc E 89-244]

Our fight for people's ownership and control of the oil industry . Oilfields Workers' Trade Union. [San Fernando] , 1982. 80 p. :
NYPL [Sc D 88-1253]

Our friends, their friends . Ogunsanwo, Alaba. Yaba , 1986, c1985. 145 p. : ISBN 978-301-700-4 **NYPL [Sc D 89-137]**

Our international years /. Adebo, Simeon O., 1913- Ibadan , 1988. xi, 281 p., [10] p. of plates : ISBN 987-246-025-7
NYPL [Sc D 89-75]

Our roots . Nwosu, Obiekezie Vic. Lagos , 1986. 55 p. : **NYPL [Sc D 88-713]**

Our struggle . Obi, Chike. Enugu, Nigeria , 1986. 76 p. ; ISBN 978-15-6187-4
NYPL [Sc D 88-753]

Our world. Around the world.
Gambia. Amersham , 1984. 16 p. : ISBN 0-7175-1046-8 (pbk) DDC 966/.5103 19
DT509.22 **NYPL [Sc D 88-1182]**

Out from this place /. Hansen, Joyce. New York , 1988. vi, 135 p. ; ISBN 0-8027-6816-4 DDC [Fic] 19
PZ7.H19825 Ou 1988 **NYPL [Sc D 88-1321]**

Out jumped Abraham /. Brown, Virginia. St. Louis , c1967. 94 p. : **NYPL [Sc D 89-542]**

Out of his mind/. Adebowale, Bayo. Ibadan , 1987. 149 p. ; ISBN 978-246-160-1
NYPL [Sc C 88-168]

Outreach . Odokara, E. O. Nsukka [between 1976 and 1981] 67 p. : **NYPL [Sc E 88-275]**

Outside looking in /. Collier, James Lincoln, 1928- New York , London , c1987. 179 p. : ISBN 0-02-723100-3 : DDC [Fic] 19
PZ7.C678 Ou 1987 **NYPL [Sc D 88-990]**

Outta sight, Luther! Brandon, Brumsic. New York [c1971] 1 v. (chiefly illus.) ISBN 0-8397-6481-2 DDC 741.5/973
PN6728.L8 B7 **NYPL [Sc B 88-54]**

Over vijf jaar in Johannesburg-- . Boon, Rudolf. Amsterdam , 's-Gravenhage [Netherlands] , 1986. 223 p. ; ISBN 90-70509-53-9
NYPL [Sc D 89-167]

Overbea, Luix V. (Luix Virgil) Black Bostonia / [Luix Overbea, writer] Boston, Mass. : Boston 200 Corp., c1976. 39 p. : ill., ports. ; 20 cm. (Boston 200 neighborhood history series)
1. Afro-Americans - Massachusetts - Boston. 2. Afro-American families - Massachusetts - Boston. I. Title. **NYPL [Sc C 89-44]**

Overseas Development Institute. Prospects for Africa . London , 1988. 97 p. : ISBN

0-340-42909-7 (pbk) : DDC 330.96/0328 19
HC800   NYPL [Sc E 89-34]

The overthrow of colonial slavery, 1776-1848 /.
Blackburn, Robin. London , New York , 1988.
560 p. : ISBN 0-86091-188-8 DDC 326/.0973 19
HT1050 .B54 1988   NYPL [IIR 88-1551]

Ovuomaroro Gallery. Onobrakpeya, Bruce.
Sahelian masquerades /. Papa Ajao, Mushin ,
c1988. xi, 132 p. : ISBN 978-250-908-6
                      NYPL [Sc F 89-16]

Owen, Ruth Bryan, 1885- Caribbean caravel.
New York, Dodd, Mead, 1949. viii, 222 p. illus.
21 cm. SCHOMBURG CHILDREN'S
COLLECTION.
1. Caribbean Area - Juvenile fiction. I. Schomburg
Children's Collection. II. Title.
PZ7.O972 Car   NYPL [Sc D 88-426]

Owens, Delia. Owens, Mark. Cry of the Kalahari
/. Boston, Mass. , 1986, c1984. 535 p., [16] p.
of plates : ISBN 0-8161-3972-5 (lg. print) : DDC
591.9681/1 19
QL337.K3 O95 1986   NYPL [Sc E 88-183]

Owens, Jonathan. A grammar of Harar Oromo
(Northeastern Ethiopia) : including a text and a
glossary / Jonathan Owens. Hamburg : H.
Buske, c1985. 282 p. ; 21 cm. (Kuschitische
Sprachstudien, 0721-4340 . Bd. 4 =) Includes index.
Bibliography: p. 277-278. ISBN 3-87118-717-8 (pbk.)
DDC 493/.7 19
1. Oromo language - Dialects - Ethiopia - Härer
Region - Grammar. I. Series: Kuschitische
Sprachstudien , Bd. 4. II. Title.
PJ2476 .O94 1985   NYPL [Sc D 88-751]

Owens, Mark. Cry of the Kalahari / Mark and
Delia Owens. Large print ed. Boston, Mass. :
G.K. Hall, 1986, c1984. 535 p., [16] p. of
plates : ill. ; 24 cm. (G.K. Hall large print book
series) Bibliography: p. 525. ISBN 0-8161-3972-5 (lg.
print) : DDC 591.9681/1 19
1. Zoology - Kalahari Desert. 2. Zoology - Botswana. 3.
Kalahari Desert. I. Owens, Delia. II. Title.
QL337.K3 O95 1986   NYPL [Sc E 88-183]

OWERRI (NIGERIA : DIVISION) -
POLITICS AND GOVERNMENT.
Ekechi, Felix K., 1934- Tradition and
transformation in Eastern Nigeria . Kent,
Ohio , c1989. xi, 256 p. ; ISBN 0-87338-368-0
(alk. paper) DDC 966.9/4 19
DT515.9.O87 E39 1989
                      NYPL [Sc E 89-186]

OWERRI (NIGERIA : DIVISION) - SOCIAL
CONDITIONS.
Ekechi, Felix K., 1934- Tradition and
transformation in Eastern Nigeria . Kent,
Ohio , c1989. xi, 256 p. ; ISBN 0-87338-368-0
(alk. paper) DDC 966.9/4 19
DT515.9.O87 E39 1989
                      NYPL [Sc E 89-186]

Owolabi, Olu.
Agbà tí ń y Olú Owólabí. Ibàdàn, Nigeria :
Evans, 1985. iii, 117 p. ; 19 cm. (Ojúlówó
Yorùbá) ISBN 978-16-7246-3
1. Yoruba language - Texts. I. Title.
                      NYPL [Sc C 88-219]

Ija Qr Olú Owólabí. Ibadan, Nigeria : Evans,
1986, c1983. vi, 84 p. : ill. ; 22 cm. (Ojúlówó
Yorùbá) ISBN 978-16-7245-5
1. Yoruba language - Texts. I. Title.
                      NYPL [Sc D 88-954]

Ìjìnlè èdè àti lítíréṣ Ibadan, Nigeria , 1986. vi,
109 p. : ISBN 978-16-7525-X
                      NYPL [Sc D 89-248]

Owomoyela, Oyekan. A Kì í : Yorùbá
proscriptive and prescriptive proverbs / Oyekan
Owomoyela. Lanham : University Press of
America, c1988. x, 388 p. ; 23 cm. Includes
indexes. Proverbs in Yoruba, commentary in English.
Bibliography: p. 385-388. ISBN 0-8191-6502-6 (alk.
paper) : DDC 398/.9/96333 19
1. Proverbs, Yoruba. I. Title.
PN6519.Y6 O96 1987   NYPL [Sc E 88-278]

Owusu, Kwesi.
Behind the masquerade : the story of Notting
Hill Carnival / Kwesi Owusu and Jacob Ross ;
photographs by David A. Bailey, Jacob Ross
and Ian Watts. Edgware : Arts Media Group,
1988. 90 p. : ill. (some col.) ; 25 cm. Includes
bibliography. ISBN 0-9512770-0-6 (pbk) : DDC
394.2/5/0942134 19
1. Carnival - England - London. 2. Blacks - England -

London. I. Ross, Jacob. II. Title. III. Title: Notting Hill
Carnival.   NYPL [Sc E 88-497]

Storms of the heart . London , 1988. 308 p. :
ISBN 0-948491-30-2 (pbk) : DDC 700/.8996 19
                      NYPL [Sc D 88-1364]

Oxfam. Moorehead, Caroline. Namibia . Oxford
[1988] 50 p. : ISBN 0-85598-111-3 :
                      NYPL [Sc F 89-120]

Oxford Committee for Famine Relief. see Oxfam.

Oxford topics in music.
Burnett, Michael. Jamaican Music /. Oxford
[England] , 1982. 48 p. : ISBN 0-19-321333-8
(pbk.)   NYPL [Sc C 84-99]

Oxóssi e Ossãe . Farelli, Maria Helena. Rio de
Janeiro , 1987. 71 p. :   NYPL [Sc C 88-65]

Oya . Gleason, Judith Illsley. Boston , 1987. viii,
304 p. : ISBN 0-87773-430-5 (pbk.) : DDC
299/.63 19
BL2480.Y6 G58 1987   NYPL [Sc D 88-101]

OYA (YORUBA DEITY)
Gleason, Judith Illsley. Oya . Boston , 1987.
viii, 304 p. : ISBN 0-87773-430-5 (pbk.) : DDC
299/.63 19
BL2480.Y6 G58 1987   NYPL [Sc D 88-101]

Oyaide, William John, 1936- Presidentialism :
new recipes for Nigeria's political system / by
William J. Oyaide, Omoh T. Ojior, Nwabueze
H. Achime ; [edited by R.F. Ola] Benin City,
Nigeria : Afflatus Publications, c1987. xi, 133
p. ; ill., maps, ports. ; 21 cm. Bibliography: p.
132-133. CONTENTS - Introduction /Omoh T.
Ojior - The presidential political order for Nigeria
/Omoh T. Ojior, William J. Oyaide - Rotational
presidentialism and two political parties for Nigeria /
Nwabueze H. Achime - Revenue allocation under
presidentialism / William J. Oyaide. ISBN
978-300-550-2
1. Nigeria - Politics and government - 1960-. 2.
Nigeria - Presidents. I. Ojior, Omoh T. II. Achime,
Nwafueze H. III. Ola, Robert F., 1938-. IV. Title.
                      NYPL [Sc D 88-917]

Oyedeji, Lekan. Asiedu, Kobina. An adult
functional literacy manual /. Ibadan , 1985. ix,
148 p. : ISBN 978-15-4737-5 (Nigeria)
                      NYPL [Sc D 88-799]

Oyediran, Oyeleye. Essays on local government
and administration in Nigeria / by Oyeleye
Oyediran. Surulere, Lagos, Nigeria : Project
Publications, 1988. x, 286 p. ; 21 cm. Includes
bibliographical references and index. ISBN
978-277-801-001
1. Local government - Nigeria. 2. Nigeria - Politics and
government - 1984-. I. Title.
                      NYPL [Sc D 88-1365]

Oyekammi,Felicia Durojaiye. Women in the
modern sector labour force in Nigeria /.
Lagos , 1985. viii, 254 p. ; ISBN 978-301-560-5
                      NYPL [Sc D 89-538]

OYELAMI, MURAINA.
Beier, Ulli. Three Yoruba artists . Bayreuth, W.
Germany , c19. 93 p. ;   NYPL [Sc D 88-1325]

Oyewole, A. Historical dictionary of Nigeria / by
A. Oyewole. Metuchen, N.J. : Scarecrow Press,
c1987. xvii, 391 p. : maps ; 23 cm. (African
historical dictionaries. no. 40) Bibliography: p.
[347]-384. ISBN 0-8108-1787-X DDC 966.9/003/21
19
1. Nigeria - History - Dictionaries. I. Title. II. Series.
DT515.15 .O94 1987
                      NYPL [*R-BMM 89-3341]

Oyo State Council for Arts and Culture.
Babayemi, S. O. Egúngún among the Oyo
Yoruba /. Ibadan , c1980. ix, 123 p. :
BL2480.Y6 B33 1980   NYPL [Sc D 88-1149]

OYONO, FERDINAND, 1929-
John, Elerius Edet. Topics in African literature
/. Lagos , 1986. 3 v. ; ISBN 978-244-610-6 (v. 1)
                      NYPL [Sc D 89-370]

Oyono-Mbia, Guillaume, 1939-
Trois prétendants, un mari. English. 1988.
Faces of African independence : three plays /
translated by Clive Wake ; introduction by
Richard Bjornson. Charlottesville , 1988.
xxxvi, 127 p. ; ISBN 0-8139-1186-9 DDC 842
19
PQ3987.5.E5 F33 1988 NYPL [Sc D 89-32]

Until further notice. 1988. Faces of African
independence : three plays / translated by

Clive Wake ; introduction by Richard
Bjornson. Charlottesville , 1988. xxxvi, 127
p. ; ISBN 0-8139-1186-9 DDC 842 19
PQ3987.5.E5 F33 1988 NYPL [Sc D 89-32]

OYONO-MBIA, GUILLAUME, 1939- -
TRANSLATIONS, ENGLISH.
Faces of African independence .
Charlottesville , 1988. xxxvi, 127 p. ; ISBN
0-8139-1186-9 DDC 842 19
PQ3987.5.E5 F33 1988 NYPL [Sc D 89-32]

Oyugi, W. Ouma. The Democratic theory and
practice in Africa /. Nairobi , 1987. vi, 208 p. ;
                      NYPL [Sc D 89-569]

Ozo, A. O. The Urban poor in Nigeria /. Ibadan,
Nigeria , 1987. xvi, 413 p. : ISBN 978-16-7489-4
                      NYPL [Sc D 88-779]

Ozoji, Emeka D. Abosi, Okechukwu C.
Educating the blind . Ibadan , c1985. xiv, 106
p. : ISBN 978-226-553-5 (pbk.) DDC
371.91/1/09669 19
HV2165.5 .A65 1985   NYPL [Sc D 89-209]

P.B. Young, newspaperman . Suggs, Henry Lewis.
Charlottesville , 1988. xxii, 254 p. : ISBN
0-8139-1178-8 DDC 070.4/1/0924 B 19
PN4874.Y59 S84 1988   NYPL [JFE 89-97]

Pachai, Bridglal. Blacks / Bridglal Pachai. 1st ed.
Tantallon, Nova Scotia : Four East Publications,
1987. 60 p. : ill., ports. ; 23 cm. (Peoples of the
Maritimes) Errata slip affixed inside back cover.
Bibliogrpahy: p. 59-60. ISBN 0-920427-11-1
1. Blacks - Maritime Provinces - History. 2. Blacks -
Maritime Provinces - Civil rights. I. Title.
                      NYPL [Sc D 88-1022]

PACIFISM - RELIGIOUS ASPECTS -
CHRISTIANITY.
Biehl, João Guilherme. De igual pra igual .
Petrópolis , São Leopoldo, RS, Brasil , 1987.
155 p. ;
BT83.57 .B54 1987   NYPL [Sc D 88-1016]

Packer, George. The village of waiting / George
Packer. 1st ed. New York : Vintage Books,
1988. 316 p. : map ; 21 cm. (Vintage departures)
ISBN 0-394-75754-8 : DDC 966/.81 19
1. Packer, George. 2. Peace Corps (U. S.) - Togo -
Biography. 3. Togo - Description and travel. I. Title.
DT582.27 .P33 1988   NYPL [Sc D 88-1318]

PACKER, GEORGE.
Packer, George. The village of waiting /. New
York , 1988. 316 p. : ISBN 0-394-75754-8 :
DDC 966/.81 19
DT582.27 .P33 1988   NYPL [Sc D 88-1318]

Padu is gek /. Diekmann, Miep. Den Haag ,
1960. 120 p. :   NYPL [Sc D 89-474]

Pagan Spain /. Wright, Richard, 1908-1960.
London , 1960, c1957. 191 p. ;
                      NYPL [Sc Rare F 88-65]

Pagden, Anthony. Colonial identity in the
Atlantic world, 1500-1800 /. Princeton, N.J. ,
c1987. xi, 290 p. ; ISBN 0-691-05372-3 (alk.
paper) : DDC 909/.09812 19
E18.82 .C64 1987   NYPL [HAB 87-3215]

PAIGE, LEROY, 1906-1982.
Humphrey, Kathryn Long. Satchel Paige /.
New York , 1988. 110 p. : ISBN 0-531-10513-X
DDC 796.357/092/4 B 92 19
GV865.P3 H86 1988   NYPL [Sc E 88-481]

Paillière, Madeleine. Saint-Brice en six tableaux
et un dessin / Madeleine Pailliere ;
photographies, Dominique Franck-Simon.
Port-au-Prince, Haiti : H. Deschamps, [1979?]
62, [4] p., [8] leaves of plates : ill. (some col.) ;
21 cm. "Peintre d'Haiti." "Errata": p. [66] Bibliography:
p. [63]
1. Saint-Brice, Robert, 1898-1973. I. Saint-Brice,
Robert, 1898-1973. II. Title.
                      NYPL [Sc D 88-1193]

The painted caves . Garlake, Peter S. Harare,
Zimbabwe , c1987. iv, 100 p., [8] p. of plates :
ISBN 0-908309-00-7 NYPL [Sc D 89-411]

Painter, James. Lapper, Richard. Honduras, state
for sale /. London , 1985. iv, 132 p. : ISBN
0-906156-23-8   NYPL [HML 87-1562]

PAINTING, AMERICAN - EXHIBITIONS.
Sims, Lowery Stokes. Robert Colescott, a
retrospective, 1975-1986 /. San Jose, Calif. ,
c1987. 34 p. : ISBN 0-938175-01-7 (pbk.) DDC
759.13 19
ND237.C66 A4 1987   NYPL [Sc F 88-317]

PAINTING, DECORATIVE. see DECORATION AND ORNAMENT.

PAINTING, HAITIAN - EXHIBITIONS.
Haitian painting . [New York , c1987. 71 p. :
NYPL [Sc D 88-451]

PAINTING, MODERN - 19TH CENTURY - UNITED STATES.
Charles Ethan Porter,1847?-1923. Marlborough, CT , 1987. 113 p. : ISBN 0-9619196-0-4
NYPL [Sc F 88-26]

PAINTING, MODERN - 20TH CENTURY - LOUISIANA - NATCHITOCHES.
Wilson, James L. (James Lynwood) Clementine Hunter, American folk artist /. Gretna , 1988. 160 p. : ISBN 0-88289-658-X DDC 759.13 B 19
ND237.H915 A4 1988 NYPL [Sc F 89-94]

PAINTING, MODERN - 20TH CENTURY - UNITED STATES - EXHIBITIONS.
Sims, Lowery Stokes. Robert Colescott, a retrospective, 1975-1986 /. San Jose, Calif. , c1987. 34 p. : ISBN 0-938175-01-7 (pbk.) DDC 759.13 19
ND237.C66 A4 1987 NYPL [Sc F 88-317]

PAINTING - NIGERIA - EXHIBITIONS - CATALOGS.
Jegede, Dele, 1945- Paradise battered /. Lagos , 1986. 48 p. : *NYPL [Sc B 88-20]*

PAINTING, RELIGIOUS. see CHRISTIAN ART AND SYMBOLISM.

País secreto /. Roca, Juan Manuel. [Poems. Selections.] La Habana , c1987. 115 p. ;
NYPL [Sc C 89-39]

Paisner, Daniel. Warner, Malcolm-Jamal. Theo and me . New York , c1988. xiv, [16] p. of plates, 208 p. : ISBN 0-525-24694-0 DDC 791.45/028/0924 19
PN2287.W43 A3 1988 NYPL [Sc D 89-258]

Pala, Achola O.
[Femme africaine dans la société précoloniale. Spanish]
La mujer africana en la sociedad precolonial / Achola O. Pala, Madina Ly ; [traducción, Pedro L. Gómez]. 1.a ed. Barcelona : Serbal ; [Paris?] : Unesco, 1982. 238 p. ; 20 cm. (Colección de temas africanos . 6) Translation of: La femme africaine dans la société précoloniale. Bibliography: p. [237]-238. ISBN 84-85800-35-4 (Serbal)
1. Women - Kenya - History. 2. Women - Mali - History. 3. Women - Africa - History. I. Ly, Madina. II. Title. III. Series. NYPL [Sc D 88-833]

A preliminary survey of avenues for and constraints on women's involvement in the development process in Kenya [microform] / by Achola O. Pala. [Nairobi? : s.n., 1975] 26 p. ; 28 cm. "M75-2449" "Background paper for the discussion on Women in rural areas: experience from Kenya, presented at WFUNA/ECA/SIDA Seminar on the Changing and Contemporary Role of Women in Society, Africa Hall, Addis Ababa, Ethiopia, 1-10 December 1975." Bibliography: p. 25-26. Microfilm. New York: New York Public Library, 1982. 1 microfilm reel; 35 mm. (MN *ZZ-23051)
1. African Seminar on the Changing and Contemporary Role of Women in Society, Addis Ababa, 1975. 2. Women - Kenya. 3. Women in rural development - Kenya. I. Title. NYPL [Sc Micro R-4108 no.14]

Paleo, Lyn. Worlds apart . Boston, Mass. , 1986. 293 p. ; ISBN 0-932870-87-2 (pbk.) : DDC 813/.0876/08353 19
PS648.H57 W67 1986 NYPL [JFD 87-7753]

PALEOANTHROPOLOGY. see MAN, PREHISTORIC.

PALEOECOLOGY - AFRICA, SOUTHERN.
Deacon, Janette. Late Quaternary palaeoenvironments of southern Africa /. Oxford , New York , 1988. viii, 225 p. : ISBN 0-19-854043-6 DDC 560/.1/78 19
QE720 .D43 1988 NYPL [Sc E 88-341]

PALEOETHNOGRAPHY. see MAN, PREHISTORIC.

PALEOLITHIC PERIOD - ETHIOPIA.
Chavaillon, Nicole. Gotera, un site paléolithique récent d'Ethiopie /. Paris , 1985. 58 p. , 25 leaves of plates : *NYPL [Sc F 88-359]*

PALEOLITHIC PERIOD, LOWER - TANZANIA - OLDUVAI GORGE.
Potts, Richard, 1953- Early hominid activities

at Olduvai /. New York , c1988. xi, 396 p. : ISBN 0-202-01176-3 (lib. bdg.) DDC 967.8 19
GN772.42.T34 P67 1988
NYPL [Sc E 89-92]

PALEONTOLOGY - QUATERNARY.
(1988) Deacon, Janette. Late Quaternary palaeoenvironments of southern Africa /. Oxford , New York , 1988. viii, 225 p. : ISBN 0-19-854043-6 DDC 560/.1/78 19
QE720 .D43 1988 NYPL [Sc E 88-341]

PALEONTOLOGY, ZOOLOGICAL. see PALEONTOLOGY.

PALEOZOOLOGY. see PALEONTOLOGY.

Palm oil and protest . Martin, Susan M. Cambridge [Cambridgeshire] , New York , 1988. xi, 209 p. : ISBN 0-521-34376-3 DDC 338.4/76643 19
HD9490.5.P343 N66 1988
NYPL [JLE 88-3417]

PALM-OIL INDUSTRY - NIGERIA - HISTORY - 20TH CENTURY.
Martin, Susan M. Palm oil and protest . Cambridge [Cambridgeshire] , New York , 1988. xi, 209 p. : ISBN 0-521-34376-3 DDC 338.4/76643 19
HD9490.5.P343 N66 1988
NYPL [JLE 88-3417]

Palmer, Colin A., 1942- The Modern Caribbean /. Chapel Hill , c1989. x, 382 p. : ISBN 0-8078-1825-9 (alk. paper) DDC 972.9 19
F2156 .M63 1989 NYPL [Sc E 89-253]

Palmer, Eustace. Women in African literature today . London , Trenton, N.J. , 1987. vi, 162 p. ; ISBN 0-85255-500-8 (pbk) : DDC 809/.89287 19
PL8010 NYPL [Sc D 88-984]

Palmer, Mabel, b. 1876.
Moya, Lily Patience. Not either an experimental doll . Bloomington , c1987. xv, 217 p., [18] p. of plates : ISBN 0-253-34843-9 DDC 968.05/6 19
HQ1800 .M69 1988 NYPL [Sc D 89-282]

PALMER, MABEL, B. 1876- - CORRESPONDENCE.
Moya, Lily Patience. Not either an experimental doll . Bloomington , c1987. xv, 217 p., [18] p. of plates : ISBN 0-253-34843-9 DDC 968.05/6 19
HQ1800 .M69 1988 NYPL [Sc D 89-282]

Palmer, Richard (Richard Hilary), 1947- Oscar Peterson / Richard Palmer ; selected discography by Richard Palmer. Tunbridge Wells : Spellmount ; New York : Hippocrene Books, 1984. can 93 p. : ports. ; 20 cm. (Jazz masters series) Bibliography: p. 76-77. Discography: p. 79-93. ISBN 0-87052-011-3 (Hippocrene Books) : DDC 785.42/092/4 B 19
1. Peterson, Oscar, 1925-. 2. Jazz musicians - Biography. 3. Afro-American musicians - Biography. I. Title. II. Series.
ML417.P46 P3 1984 NYPL [Sc C 88-142]

Palmer, Robin. Blood donation in the Border region: Black donors, exdonors and nondonors / Robin Palmer. Grahamstown [South Africa] : Institute of Social and Economic Research, Rhodes University, 1984. 183 p. : harts, map ; (Development studies working paper . no. 18) "August 1984." Bibliography: p. 182-183. ISBN 0-86810-112-5
1. Blood donors - South Africa. I. Series.
NYPL [Sc F 87-432]

Pamphile, Léon Dénius. L'éducation en Haiti sous l'occupation américaine 1915-1934 / Léon Dénius Pamphile. [Port-au-Prince : Imprimerie des Antilles, 1988] 316 p. ; 21 cm. Includes index. Bibliography: p. 297-308.
1. Education - Haiti - History. 2. Haiti - History - American occupation, 1915-1934. I. Title.
NYPL [Sc D 88-1002]

Pan American Union. Biblioteca Conmemorativa de Colón. see Columbus Memorial Library.

Pan American Union. Dept. of Cultural Affairs. Biblioteca Conmemorativa de Colón. see Columbus Memorial Library.

Pan American Union. Dept. of Cultural Affairs. Columbus Memorial Library. see Columbus Memorial Library.

Pan American Union. Library. see Columbus Memorial Library.

Panafrican Conference on Education (1984 : Yaoundé, Cameroon) What school for Africa in the year 2000? / Panafrican Conference on Education Yaounde, Cameroon, 2-9 April 1984. Morges, Switzerland : World Confederation of Organizations of the Teaching Profession, [1984?] 190 p. ; 21 cm. Conference organized by the WCOTP.
1. Education - Africa - Congresses. I. World Confederation of Organizations of the Teaching Professions. II. Title. NYPL [Sc D 88-611]

Pan-Africanist Congress. Time for Azania [microform] [Toronto] , 1976. 89 p. : DDC 320.5/4/0968
DT770 .T55 NYPL [Sc Micro R-4849 no.1]

PAN-AFRICANIST CONGRESS.
Time for Azania [microform] [Toronto] , 1976. 89 p. : DDC 320.5/4/0968
DT770 .T55 NYPL [Sc Micro R-4849 no.1]

Pan-Africanist Congress of Azania. see Pan-Africanist Congress.

PANAMA CANAL (PANAMA) - DESIGN AND CONSTRUCTION - HISTORY.
Newton, Velma. The silver men . Mona, Kingston, Jamaica , 1984. xx, 218 p., [4] p. of plates : DDC 325/.2729/07287 19
JV7429 .N49 1984 NYPL [Sc D 89-478]

PANAMA - EMIGRATION AND IMMIGRATION - HISTORY.
Newton, Velma. The silver men . Mona, Kingston, Jamaica , 1984. xx, 218 p., [4] p. of plates : DDC 325/.2729/07287 19
JV7429 .N49 1984 NYPL [Sc D 89-478]

PANAMA RAILROAD - DESIGN AND CONSTRUCTION - HISTORY.
Newton, Velma. The silver men . Mona, Kingston, Jamaica , 1984. xx, 218 p., [4] p. of plates : DDC 325/.2729/07287 19
JV7429 .N49 1984 NYPL [Sc D 89-478]

Panama (Republic) see Panama.

Pankhurst, Richard Keir Pethick, 1927- Letters from Ethiopian rulers (early and mid-nineteenth century) . Oxford , New York , c1985. xvii, 197 p. : ISBN 0-19-726046-2
NYPL [Sc E 88-262]

Panos dossier .
(1) AIDS and the Third World /. London , Philadelphia , 1989. v, 198 p. : ISBN 0-86571-143-7 (hardcover)
NYPL [Sc D 89-51]

Panos Institute. AIDS and the Third World /. London , Philadelphia , 1989. v, 198 p. : ISBN 0-86571-143-7 (hardcover)
NYPL [Sc D 89-51]

A Pantheon modern writers original.
Wicomb, Zoë. You can't get lost in Cape Town /. New York , c1987. 185 p. ; ISBN 0-394-56030-2 : DDC 823 19
PR9369.3.W53 Y6 1987
NYPL [Sc D 88-341]

Panther Party. see Black Panther Party.

Panyard /. Dorant, St. Clair Wesley. [Port-of-Spain , 1974] 54 p. ; DDC 81.2 19
PR9272.9.D66 P37 NYPL [Sc F 88-240]

Paolantonacci, Andrée. France. Bibliothèque nationale. Département des livres imprimés. Les auteurs afro-américains, 1965-1982 . Paris , 1985. 28 p., [4] leaves of plates : ISBN 2-7177-1709-9 :
Z1229.N39 F7 1985 PS153.N5
NYPL [Sc F 89-5]

Papa Doc, Baby Doc . Ferguson, James, 1956- Oxford, UK , New York, NY, USA , 1987. x, 171 p., [8] p. of plates : ISBN 0-631-15601-1 : DDC 972.94/07 19
F1928 .F47 1987 NYPL [Sc E 88-269]

Papa Doc y los tontons Macoutes . Diederich, Bernard. [Papa Doc. Spanish.] Santo Domingo, República Dominicana , 1986. 393 p., [16] p. of plates : *NYPL [Sc D 88-452]*

Papers on the condition of the labouring population, West Indies. Great Britain. Colonial Office. Papers relative to the West Indies. Part I-(5.). Jamaica - British Guiana ... [London] , 1839. iv, 317 p. ; *NYPL [Sc Rare G 86-3]*

**Papers relative to the West Indies. Part I-(5.).
Jamaica - British Guiana ... Great Britain.**
Colonial Office. [London] , 1839. iv, 317 p. ;
NYPL [Sc Rare G 86-3]

Papeta. Pratos da Bahia e outras especialidades /
Papeta. Rio de Janeiro : Edições de Ouro,
1979. 202 p. : ill. ; 21 cm.
1. Cookery, Brazilian - Bahian style. I. Title.
NYPL [Sc D 88-294]

PAPIAMENTO - OCCULTISM.
Garmers, Sonia. Brueria di henter mundo =.
Curaçao [1986?] 58 p. : DDC 133.4/3 19
BF1618.D8 G37 1986   NYPL [Sc E 89-237]

PAPIAMENTO - TEXTS.
Jongh, Edward Arthur de. E dia di mas
histórico /. Aruba , 1970. 158 p. :
NYPL [Sc D 87-1430]

Paquet, Charlotte. Dumont, René, 1904- Pour
l'Afrique, j'accuse. [Paris] , c1986. 457 p., [48]
p. of plates : ISBN 2-259-01455-0
HC1002 .D85 1986   NYPL [Sc D 88-642]

Paradise battered /. Jegede, Dele, 1945- Lagos ,
1986. 48 p. :   *NYPL [Sc B 88-20]*

PARAMARIBO ZOO - PICTORIAL WORKS.
Moonen, Joep. 'n Kijkje in de Paramaribo Zoo
/. Paramaribo [1987] 275 p. :
QL76.5.S752 P375 1987
NYPL [Sc D 88-690]

Parchment, Michael. The inna thought and
feelings of the poet / Michael Parchment.
[Jamaica? : s.n., 1984?] 46 p. ; 28 cm. Poems.
I. Title.
MLCM 84/5607 (P)   NYPL [Sc F 88-134]

PARENTHOOD - AFRICA - BIBLIOGRAPHY.
Régulation des naissances en Afrique . Abidjan,
Côte d'Ivoire [1987] 74 p. ;
NYPL [Sc F 88-392]

PARENTING - AFRICA - BIBLIOGRAPHY.
Régulation des naissances en Afrique . Abidjan,
Côte d'Ivoire [1987] 74 p. ;
NYPL [Sc F 88-392]

Parépou, Alfred. Atipa : roman guyanais / Alfred
Parépou ; traduit et annoté par Marguerite
Fauquenoy. Paris : Editions l'Harmattan, 1987.
viii, 231 p. : ill., maps ; 24 cm. (Testes, études et
documents . nos 4-5) Originally published : Paris : A.
Ghio, 1885. Creole and French on facing pages, with
introduction and footnotes in French. Bibliography: p.
vii-viii. ISBN 2-85802-965-2
*1. Creole dialects - French Guiana - Texts. 2. French
Guiana - Fiction. I. Saint Jacques Fauquenoy,
Marguerite. II. Title. III. Series.*
NYPL [Sc E 88-18]

**Paris. Université de Paris I: Panthéon-Sorbonne.
see Université de Paris I: Panthéon-
Sorbonne.**

Park . Gray, John, 1866-1934. Manchester,
[Greater Manchester] , 1984. 128 p. : ISBN
0-85635-538-0   *NYPL [JFD 85-1419]*

Parker, Aida. Secret U. S. war against South
Africa / by Aida Parker. Johannesburg : S.A.
Today, c1977. 79 p. ; 21 cm. "The articles in this
booklet are reprinted from a series published in the
Citizen, the Johannesburg morning newspaper."--P. 4 of
cover.
*1. United States - Relations - South Africa. 2. South
Africa - Foreign opinion, American. 3. South Africa -
Politics and government - 1961-1978. I. Citizen. II.
Title.   NYPL [Sc D 88-277]*

PARKER, CHARLIE, 1920-1955.
Koch, Lawrence O. Yardbird suite . Bowling
Green, Ohio , c1988. 336 p. : ISBN
0-87972-259-2 (clothbound)
NYPL [Sc E 89-48]

Parker, Derek. Egypt / by Derek and Julia
Parker. London : Jonathan Cape, 1986. 160 p. :
ill., maps ; 17 cm. (Travellers' guide) Includes index.
Bibliography: p. 153-154. ISBN 0-224-02419-1
*1. Egypt - Description and travel - Guide-books. I.
Parker, Julia. II. Title. NYPL [Sc B 89-21]*

Parker, Jay, 1945- Wooden, Wayne S. Men
behind bars . New York , c1982. x, 264 p. :
ISBN 0-306-41074-5 *NYPL [Sc D 89-249]*

Parker, Julia. Parker, Derek. Egypt /. London ,
1986. 160 p. : ISBN 0-224-02419-1
NYPL [Sc B 89-21]

Parker, Marjorie H.
An Alpha Kappa Alpha family album / by

Majorie H. Parker. [Chicago] : Alpha Kappa
Alpha Sorority, 1984. 210 p. : ill., ports ; 29
cm. Presentation copy to the Schomburg Center from
the New York State AKA Connection Committee.
1. Alpha Kappa Alpha. I. Title.
NYPL [Sc F 88-17]

Alpha Kappa Alpha sorority : 1908-1958 / by
Marjorie H. Parker. [Washington, D.C. : Alpha
Kappa Alpha Sorority, 1958] iii, 108 leaves ; 28
cm.
1. Alpha Kappa Alpha - History. I. Title.
NYPL [Sc F 89-66]

Parker, Tom, 1943- Winfield, Dave, 1951-
Winfield . New York , c1988. 314 p., [22] of
plates : ISBN 0-393-02467-9 : DDC
796.357/092/4 B 19
GV865.W57 A3 1988
NYPL [JFD 88-11493]

Parkin, Trevor. (ill) May, Chris. Bob Marley /.
London , 1985. 60 p. : ISBN 0-241-11476-4 :
DDC 784.5 B 19
ML420.M3313 M4 1985
NYPL [Sc D 88-308]

PARKMAN FAMILY.
Smith, Marion Whitney. Beacon Hill's Colonel
Robert Gould Shaw /. New York , 1986. 512
p. : ISBN 0-8062-2732-X
NYPL [Sc D 88-414]

PARKS, NATIONAL. Individual parks are
entered under name of park, e.g. Zion
National Park. For works of a general nature
see: **NATIONAL PARKS AND
RESERVES.**

**PARLIAMENTARY GOVERNMENT. see
REPRESENTATIVE GOVERNMENT AND
REPRESENTATION.**

Parmasad, Kenneth Vidia. Indian folk tales of the
Caribbean : a first collection : salt and roti /
researched, retold, introduced by Kenneth Vidia
Parmasad ; preface by Gordon Rohlehr ;
illustrated by Marquis Gittens. Charlieville,
Chaguanas, Trinidad and Tobago, West Indies :
Sankh Productions, c1984. xxii, 131 p., [2] p. of
plates : ill. ; 21 cm. ISBN 976-8016-01-9 (pbk.)
DDC 398.2/09729 19
*1. Tales - Caribbean Area. 2. East Indians - Caribbean
Area - Folklore. I. Title. II. Title: Salt and roti.*
GR120 .P37 1984   NYPL [Sc D 88-400]

La parole prisonnière . Métellus, Jean, 1937-
[Paris] , c1986. 234 p. ; ISBN 2-07-070698-2 :
MLCS 86/6890 (P)   NYPL [JFD 88-7194]

Paroz, R. A. Mabille, A. (Adolphe), 1836-1894.
Southern Sotho-English dictionary /. Morija,
Lesotho , 1950 (1974 printing) xvi, 445 p. ;
PL8689.4 .M33 1974   NYPL [Sc D 89-289]

Parpart, Jane L. Women and the state in Africa
/. Boulder, Colo. , c1989. ix, 229 p. ; ISBN
1-555-87082-1 (alk. paper) : DDC 305.4/2/096
19
HQ1236.5.A357 W65 1988
NYPL [Sc E 89-159]

Parsemain, Roger, 1944- L'Hidalgo des
campêches : poèmes / Roger Parsemain. Paris :
Hatier, 1987. 126 p. ; 18 cm. (Collection Monde
noir poche) ISBN 2-218-07812-0
I. Title. II. Series.   NYPL [Sc C 88-7]

Parteipolitik in Kenya 1960-1969 /.
Teubert-Seiwert, Bärbel, 1951- Frankfurt am
Main , New York , c1987. 428 p. ; ISBN
3-8204-0151-2 DDC 324.2676/2 19
JQ2947.A979 .T48 1987
NYPL [Sc D 88-1141]

Parti africain de k'indépendance du Cap-Vert.
Symposium Amilcar Cabral (1983 : Praia, Cape
Verde) Pour Cabral . Paris , 1987. 486 p. ;
ISBN 2-7087-0482-6
NYPL [Sc D 87-1429]

PARTI COMMUNISTE MARTINIQUAIS.
Les Communistes expliquent . [Fort-de-France]
1978. 147 p. ;   *NYPL [Sc E 89-174]*

Parti communiste martiniquais. Comité central.
Les Communistes expliquent . [Fort-de-France]
1978. 147 p. ;   *NYPL [Sc E 89-174]*

Parti démocratique de Côte d'Ivoire. Séminaires
d'information et de formation des secrétaires
généraux . [Abidjan] [1985] 72 p. : DDC
966.6/805 19
DT545.8 .S46 1985   NYPL [Sc E 88-151]

**PARTI DÉMOCRATIQUE DE CÔTE
D'IVOIRE.**
Amondji, Marcel, 1934- Côte-d'Ivoire . Paris ,
c1986. 207 p. : ISBN 2-85802-631-6 DDC
324.2666/806 19
DT545.75 .A46 1986   NYPL [Sc D 88-297]

PARTI DÉMOCRATIQUE DE GUINÉE.
Touré, Ahmed Sékou, 1922- [Conférences,
discours, et rapports] Conakry [1958?]- v.
NYPL [Sc F966.52-T]

PARTI PROGRESSISTE MARTINIQUAIS.
Darsières, Camille. Lagro, ou, Les debuts du
socialisme à la Martinique /. [Fort-de-France]
[198-?] 75 p. : *NYPL [Sc D 89-560]*

PARTI SOCIALISTE DU SÉNÉGAL.
Le Parti socialiste du Sénégal de Senghor à
Abdou Diouf /. [Dakar] [1987?] 176 p. ;
ISBN 2-7236-1007-1 DDC 324.266/3072 19
JQ3396.A98 S65 1987   NYPL [Sc D 89-125]

**Le Parti socialiste du Sénégal de Senghor à
Abdou Diouf /** par le Groupe d'études et de
recherches du Parti socialiste du Sénégal ;
préface d'Abdou Diouf. [Dakar] : Nouvelles
Editions africaines, [1987?] 176 p. ; 21 cm.
ISBN 2-7236-1007-1 DDC 324.266/3072 19
*1. Parti socialiste du Sénégal. 2. Socialism - Senegal. I.
Parti socialiste du Sénégal. Groupe d'études et de
recherches.*
JQ3396.A98 S65 1987   NYPL [Sc D 89-125]

**Parti socialiste du Sénégal. Groupe d'études et de
recherches.** Le Parti socialiste du Sénégal de
Senghor à Abdou Diouf /. [Dakar] [1987?] 176
p. ; ISBN 2-7236-1007-1 DDC 324.266/3072 19
JQ3396.A98 S65 1987   NYPL [Sc D 89-125]

Partial surrender . Williams, Lincoln Octavious.
London , New York , 1988. viii, 194 p. ; ISBN
1-85000-289-4 DDC 361.7/97/009421 19
HV1441.G8 L78 1988   NYPL [Sc E 89-73]

**PARTICIPATION, POLITICAL. see
POLITICAL PARTICIPATION.**

**PARTIDO AFRICANO DA INDEPENDÉNCIA
DA GUINÉE E CABO VERDE -
HISTORY.**
Romero, Vicente, 1947- Guinea-Bissau y Cabo
Verde . Madrid , 1981. 109 p. ; ISBN
84-85761-09-X DDC 966/.5702 19
DT613.78 .R66 1981   NYPL [Sc C 89-1]

**PARTIDO AFRICANO DE INDEPÉNDENCIA
DA GUINÉE CABO VERDE -
COLLECTED WORKS.**
Cabral, Amílcar, 1921-1973. Unité et lutte /.
Paris , 1980. 329 p. : ISBN 2-7071-1171-6
NYPL [Sc C 89-125]

**PARTIES, POLITICAL. see POLITICAL
PARTIES.**

Parting the waters . Branch, Taylor. New York ,
c1988- v. : ISBN 0-671-46097-8 (v. 1) DDC
973/.0496073 19
E185.61 .B7914 1988   NYPL [IEC 88-122]

PARTISANS. see GUERRILLAS.

**The partition of Africa, 1880-1900 and European
imperialism in the nineteenth century /.**
MacKenzie, John M. London , New York ,
1983. x, 48 p. : ISBN 0-416-35050-X DDC
960/.23 19
DT29 .M33 1983   NYPL [Sc D 88-268]

Partridge, Nancy. To breathe and wait / Nancy
Partridge. Gweru [Zimbabwe] : Mambo Press,
1986. 242 p. ; 18 cm. (Mambo writers series.
English section. v. 22) ISBN 0-86922-379-8
1. Zimbabwe - Fiction. I. Title.
NYPL [Sc C 88-130]

Party power . Labode, Sakirudeen Tunji.
Abeokuta, Nigeria , 1988. 244 p. ; ISBN
978-18-3008-5   *NYPL [Sc C 88-376]*

Parwada, Batisai B., 1966- Shreds of darkness /
Batisai B. Parwada. Gweru, Zimbabwe : Mambo
Press, 1987. 111 p. ; 18 cm. (Mambo writers.
English section . v. 27)
1. Zimbabwe - Fiction. I. Title. II. Series.
NYPL [Sc C 89-96]

**Pass controls and the urban African proletariat
in South Africa /.** Hindson, D. Johannesburg,
South Africa , 1987. xii, 121 p. ; ISBN
0-86975-311-8   *NYPL [Sc D 88-956]*

Passage of darkness . Davis, Wade. Chapel Hill ,
c1988. xx, 344 p. : ISBN 0-8078-1776-7 (alk.

paper) DDC 299/.65 19
BL2530.H3 D37 1988 **NYPL** *[Sc E 88-429]*

Passion and exile . Birbalsingh, Frank. London ,
1988. 186 p. ; ISBN 1-87051-816-0 (pbk) : DDC
810.9/91821 19
NYPL *[JFD 89-183]*

Passion de l'indépendance. Placoly, Vincent, 1946-
Dessalines, ou, La passion de l'indépendance .
Ciudad de La Habana, c1983. 96 p. ;
MLCS 86/2062 (P) **NYPL** *[JFC 87-478]*

PASSION-PLAYS.
Lee, Easton. The rope and the cross . Kingston,
Jamaica , 1985. 48 p., [4] p. of plates :
NYPL *[Sc D 89-458]*

PASSIVE RESISTANCE - INDIA.
Schechter, Betty. The peaceable revolution.
Boston, 1963. 243 p. DDC 301.24
HM278.S35 **NYPL** *[Sc D 88-1422]*

PASSIVE RESISTANCE - UNITED STATES.
Schechter, Betty. The peaceable revolution.
Boston, 1963. 243 p. DDC 301.24
HM278.S35 **NYPL** *[Sc D 88-1422]*

The Past and future of !Kung ethnography :
critical reflections and symbolic perspectives :
essays in honour of Lorna Marshall / edited by
Megan Biesele with Robert Gordon and
Richard Lee. Hamburg, 1986. 423 p. :
ill., maps ; 21 cm. (Quellen zur Khoisan-Forschung
0176-3369 . Bd.4) Includes bibliography. ISBN
3-87118-780-1
*1. Marshall, Lorna. 2. !Kung (African people). I.
Marshall, Lorna. II. Biesele, Megan.*
NYPL *[Sc D 88-234]*

Past meets present : essays about historic
interpretation and public audiences / Jo Blatti,
editor. Washington, D.C. : Smithsonian
Institution Press, 1987. x, 169 p. : ill. ; 23 cm.
"A Project of the New York Council for the
Humanities." Includes bibliographical references. ISBN
0-87474-272-2 DDC 069/.9973 19
*1. Public history. 2. Historical museums - United States.
3. Public relations - Historical museums. 4. Historic
sites - United States. 5. Audiences. I. Blatti, Jo. II. New
York Council for the Humanities.*
D16.163 .P37 1987 **NYPL** *[Sc E 88-577]*

**Past questions and answers for secondary modern
schools, 1964-1969** / [edited by J. A. Babalola]
Ado-Ekiti : Ilori Print. Service, [197-?] 301 p. ;
18 cm. Cover title.
1. Examinations - Nigeria - Questions. I. Babalola, J. A.
NYPL *[Sc C 86-206]*

PASTIMES. see GAMES; SPORTS.

PASTORAL COUNSELING.
Kiriswa, Benjamin. Christian counselling for
students /. Eldoret, Kenya , 1988. vi, 81 p. :
NYPL *[Sc D 89-350]*

PASTORAL PEOPLES. see NOMADS.

Pataki, Eva. Haitian painting . [New York ,
c1987. 71 p. : **NYPL** *[Sc D 88-451]*

Patch /. Elting, Mary, 1909- Garden City, N.Y. ,
1948. 156 p. :
PZ7.E53Pat **NYPL** *[Sc C 89-14]*

Pate, Rodney. (ill) Myers, Walter Dean, 1937-
Me, Mop, and the Moondance Kid /. New
York , 1988. 154 p. : ISBN 0-440-50065-6 DDC
[Fic] 19
PZ7.M992 Me 1988 **NYPL** *[Sc D 88-1457]*

Patel, H. H. No master, no mortgage, no sale :
the foreign policy of Zimbabwe. / Hasu H.
Patel. Nairobi, Kenya : CREDU, 1987. 61 p.
columns ; 21 x 30 cm. (Workingusing paper . no. 2)
Bibliography: columns 52-61.
*1. Zimbabwe - Foreign policy. I. Series: Working paper
(CREDU (Organization)) , no. 2. II. Title.*
NYPL *[Sc F 88-297]*

PATERNITY - NEW YORK (N.Y.)
Whistelo, Alexander. (defendant) The
Commissioners of the Alms-house, vs.
Alexander Whistelo, a black man . New York ,
1808. 56 p. : **NYPL** *[Sc Rare F 88-21]*

Paternostre de La Mairieu, Baudouin. A la
source du Nil : les mille collines du Rwanda /
Baudouin Paternostre de La Mairieu ; préface
d'Haroun Tazieff. Paris : Téqui, [1985] 108 p.,
[12] p. of plates : ill. ; 18 cm. (Collection "Terre
des hommes") Bibliography: p. 105-107. ISBN
2-85244-730-4
1. Rwanda - Description and travel. I. Title. II. Series.
DT450.2 .P38 1985 **NYPL** *[Sc C 88-308]*

PATERSON, EDWARD GEORGE, 1895-1974.
Walker, David A. C. Paterson of Cyrene .
Gweru, Zimbabwe , 1985. xi, 85 p. : ISBN
0-86922-340-2 DDC 283/.3 B 19
BX5700.4.Z8 P378 1985
NYPL *[Sc D 88-229]*

**PATERSON, EDWARD GEORGE, 1895-1974 -
CONTRIBUTIONS IN SCULPTURE.**
Walker, David A. C. Paterson of Cyrene .
Gweru, Zimbabwe , 1985. xi, 85 p. : ISBN
0-86922-340-2 DDC 283/.3 B 19
BX5700.4.Z8 P378 1985
NYPL *[Sc D 88-229]*

Paterson of Cyrene . Walker, David A. C.
Gweru, Zimbabwe , 1985. xi, 85 p. : ISBN
0-86922-340-2 DDC 283/.3 B 19
BX5700.4.Z8 P378 1985
NYPL *[Sc D 88-229]*

Paterson, William, 1755-1810. Paterson's Cape
travels, 1777 to 1779 / Vernon S. Forbes and
John Rourke. Johannesburg, [South Africa] :
Brenthurst Press, c1980. 202 p. : ill. (some
col.) ; 27 cm. (Brenthurst series. 6) Includes index.
Bibliography: p. 181-184. ISBN 0-909079-12-9
(standard edition)
*1. Natural history - South Africa. 2. South Africa -
Description and travel - To 1800. I. Forbes, Vernon
Siegfried. II. Rourke, John P. III. Title.*
NYPL *[Sc F 85-110]*

Paterson's Cape travels, 1777 to 1779 /.
Paterson, William, 1755-1810. Johannesburg,
[South Africa] , c1980. 202 p. : ISBN
0-909079-12-9 (standard edition)
NYPL *[Sc F 85-110]*

Pathways to progress : the people's plan for
socialist transformation, Jamaica, 1977-78 / by
the Jamaican people with the assistance of
George Beckford ... [et al.]. Morant Bay,
Jamaica, W.I. : Maroon Pub. House, 1985. vii,
128 p. ; 22 cm. Errata slip inserted. DDC
338.97292 19
*1. Socialism - Jamaica. 2. Jamaica - Economic policy. I.
Beckford, George L.*
HC154 .P38 1985 **NYPL** *[Sc D 88-1239]*

Patike Communications Limited. The Nigeria
handbook . Surulere, Lagos , c1985. 176 p. :
DDC 966.9/05 19
DT515.22 .N54 1985 **NYPL** *[Sc F 88-367]*

Patrice Lumumba, le Sankuru et l'Afrique .
Manya K'Omalowete a Djonga, 1950- Lutry
[1985] 166 p. : **NYPL** *[Sc D 88-1490]*

Patrice, Tongasolo. Fomban-drazana Tsimihety /
mpanoratra, Tongasolo Patrice ; mpanamboatra,
Manfred M. Marent ; mpanangona ohabolana,
Gebhard Randel samy Antsakabary.
Fianarantsoa [Madagascar] : Ambozontany,
1985. 383 p., [8] p. of plates : ill., map ; 19 cm.
(Bainga voavadika)
*1. Ethnology - Madagascar. 2. Tsimihety (Madagascan
people). I. Title.* **NYPL** *[Sc C 88-292]*

Patrick, Herbert R. Just being Black : a book of
poems and illustrations / by Herbert R. Patrick,
Sr. ; illustrations by Kenneth Johnson and
Larry Goodwyn. Petersburg, Va. : (3406 Union
Branch Rd., Petersburg 23805) : H.R. Patrick,
c1984. 50 p. : ill. ; 28 cm. DDC 811/.54 19
1. Afro-Americans - Poetry. I. Title.
PS3566.A778 J87 1984 **NYPL** *[Sc D 88-668]*

La patrie haïtienne . Gilbert, Marcel, 1938-
Brazzaville , 1984. 60 p. ;
NYPL *[Sc D 89-629]*

Patriote guadeloupéen. Guadeloupe, 1635-1971 .
Tours [1982] 109 p. : DDC 306/.362/0972976
19
HT1108.G83 G8 1982 **NYPL** *[Sc E 89-141]*

**Patriote guadeloupéen. No 69, 1982
(Supplement)** Guadeloupe, 1635-1971 . Tours
[1982] 109 p. : DDC 306/.362/0972976 19
HT1108.G83 G8 1982 **NYPL** *[Sc E 89-141]*

Patterns of black excellence /. Sowell, Thomas,
1930- Washington , 1977. [26]-58 p. ; ISBN
0-89633-004-4 **NYPL** *[Sc D 89-588]*

Patterns of life . Gilfoy, Peggy Stoltz.
Washington, D.C. , c1987. 95 p. : ISBN
0-87474-475-X (alk. paper) : DDC
746.1/4/088042 19
NK8989 .G55 1987 **NYPL** *[Sc F 88-166]*

**Patterns of progress: Trinidad & Tobago 10 years
of independence.** Boyke, Roy. [Port-of-Spain,

Trinidad, c1972] 128 p. DDC 972.98/304
F2119 .B69 **NYPL** *[Sc F 89-23]*

Patterson, Charles. Marian Anderson / Charles
Patterson. New York : Watts, 1988. 154 p. :
ill., ports. ; 24 cm. (An Impact book) Includes
index. A biography of the opera and concert singer
who, among other achievements, was the first black
soloist to perform with the Metropolitan Opera
Company in 1955. Bibliography: p. 155. ISBN
0-531-10568-7 DDC 782.1/092/4 B 92 19
*1. Singers - United States - Biography. 2.
Afro-American singers - Biography. I. Title.*
ML420.A6 P4 1988 **NYPL** *[Sc E 89-4]*

Patterson, Christine. The Black experience in
Wyoming Valley / by Christine Patterson.
[Pennsylvania] : Family Service Association of
Wyoming Valley, [1987?] 9 p. : ill., ports. ; 22
cm.
*1. Afro-Americans - Pennsylvania - Wyoming Valley. I.
Title.* **NYPL** *[Sc D 89-148]*

Patuelli, Jacques. Antilles Caraïbes /. Paris ,
c1982. 157 p. : ISBN 2-7191-0177-0
NYPL *[Sc F 88-347]*

Paul Biya : the president of all Cameroonians.
Bamenda : Cameroon National Union, 1985.
103 leaves : ill. ; 22 cm.
*1. Biya, Paul, 1933-. 2. Cameroon - Politics and
government - 1982-. 3. Cameroon - Presidents -
Biography. I. Cameroon National Union.*
NYPL *[Sc D 89-278]*

Paul Biya, hero of the New Deal /. Gwellem,
Jerome F. (Jerome Fultang) Limbe, Cameroon
[1984]. 68 p. : **NYPL** *[Sc D 88-1255]*

Paul Laurence Dunbar /. Gentry, Tony. New
York , c1989. 110 p. : ISBN 1-555-46583-8
DDC 811/.4 B 92 19
PS1557 .G46 1989 **NYPL** *[Sc E 88-514]*

Paul Robeson /. Duberman, Martin B. New
York , 1988, c1989. xiii, 804 p., [48] p. of
plates : ISBN 0-394-52780-1 : DDC 790.2/092/4
B 19
E185.97.R63 D83 1988 **NYPL** *[Sc E 89-108]*

Paul Robeson /. Ehrlich, Scott. New York ,
c1988. 111 p. : ISBN 1-555-46608-7 DDC
782.1/092/4 B 92 19
E185.97.R63 E35 1988 **NYPL** *[Sc E 88-167]*

PAUL, THE APOSTLE, SAINT.
Meili, Josef. In the image of Christ crucified
and risen, in the service of the community .
Gweru, Zimbabwe , 1986. 127 p. :
NYPL *[Sc D 88-1332]*

Paul, Tony. (illus) Lunemann, Evelyn. Tip off.
Westchester, Ill. [1969] 70 p. DDC [Fic]
PZ7.L979115 Ti **NYPL** *[Sc E 88-533]*

Paulin, Adjai. La Revolte des esclaves
mercenaires : Douala 1893 / par Adjai Paulin.
Bayreuth, W. Germany : Bayreuth University,
1987. 96 p. : map ; 21 cm. (Bayreuth African
studies series . 10) Bibliography: p. 95-96.
*1. Slavery - Cameroon - Insurrections, etc. I. Title. II.
Series.* **NYPL** *[Sc D 88-1326]*

PAUPERISM. see POOR.

Payne, Anthony, 1952- Politics in Jamaica / by
Anthony Payne. London : C. Hurst ; New
York, N.Y. : St. Martin's Press, 1988. xii, 196
p. : maps ; 23 cm. Includes index. Bibliography: p.
189-191. ISBN 0-312-01869-X (St. Martin's) DDC
972.92 19
1. Jamaica - Politics and government - 1962-. I. Title.
F1887 .P39 1988 **NYPL** *[Sc D 88-1230]*

Payne, Joan Balfour. Justus, May, 1898- New
boy in school. New York [1963] 56 p. DDC
[Fic]
PZ7.J986 Ng **NYPL** *[Sc E 89-25]*

**Les pays du Tchad dans la tourmente, 1880-1903
/.** Zeltner, J. C. Paris , c1988. 285 p. : ISBN
2-85802-914-8 **NYPL** *[Sc D 88-1408]*

Paz Gómez, Enelia. Black in Colombia / by
Enelia Paz Gómez ; English version by Muriel
Laycock in collaboration with the author.
Mexico : Costa-Amic Editores, c1985. 173 p. :
ill. ; 21 cm. (Costa Amic English library)
*1. Paz Gómez, Enelia. 2. Artists, Black - Colombia -
Biography. I. Laycock, Muriel. II. Title.*
NYPL *[Sc D 89-66]*

PAZ GÓMEZ, ENELIA.
Paz Gómez, Enelia. Black in Colombia /.
Mexico , c1985. 173 p. :
NYPL *[Sc D 89-66]*

PEACE - CONGRESSES.
Appeal for world peace [microform] . Accra [1961?] 19 p. :　*NYPL [Sc Micro F-10978]*

PEACE CORPS (U. S.) - TOGO - BIOGRAPHY.
Packer, George. The village of waiting /. New York , 1988. 316 p. :　ISBN 0-394-75754-8 : DDC 966/.81 19
DT582.27 .P33 1988　　NYPL [Sc D 88-1318]

The peaceable revolution. Schechter, Betty. Boston, 1963. 243 p.　DDC 301.24
HM278.S35　　　　　NYPL [Sc D 88-1422]

Peake, Thomas R., 1939- Keeping the dream alive : a history of the Southern Christian Leadership Conference from King to the nineteen eighties / by Thomas R. Peake. New York : P. Lang Pub., 1987. xiv, 492 p. : ill. ; 23 cm. Includes index. Bibliography: p. 425-475.　ISBN 0-8204-0397-0 :　DDC 323.42/3/06073 19
1. Southern Christian Leadership Conference - History. 2. Afro-Americans - Civil rights - Southern States. 3. Southern States - Race relations. I. Title.
E185.61 .P4 1987　　NYPL [Sc D 88-444]

Péan, Marc. L'échec du firminisme / Marc Péan. Port-au-Prince, Haiti : Deschamps, 1987. 181 p. : ill., ports. ; 22 cm. "Ce second volume embrasse pour l'essentiel la période comprise entre mai et décembre 1902." --p. [7]. Bibliography: p. [179]-181.
1. Firmin, Anténor, 1851-1911. 2. Haiti - History - 1844-1915. 3. Haiti - Politics and government - 1844-1934. 4. Cap-Haïtien, Haiti - History. I. Title.
NYPL [Sc D 88-625]

Pearce, Daniel.
[Credibility gap]
Generation gap : a double bill of plays / Daniel Pearce. Gweru, Zimbabwe : Mambo Press, 1983. xiv, 138 p., [4] p. of plates : ill. ; 19 cm. (Mambo writers series. English section. v. 12) CONTENTS. - Credibility gap -- A credit to the family. ISBN 0-86922-217-1 (pbk.)　DDC 822 19
1. Pearce, Daniel. Credit to the family. II. Title.
PR9390.9.P37 C7 1983
NYPL [JFC 85-1777]

Credit to the family. Pearce, Daniel. [Credibility gap.] Generation gap : a double bill of plays / Daniel Pearce. Gweru, Zimbabwe , 1983. xiv, 138 p., [4] p. of plates :　ISBN 0-86922-217-1 (pbk.)　DDC 822 19
PR9390.9.P37 C7 1983
NYPL [JFC 85-1777]

Pearce, Tola Olu.
Social change in Nigeria /. Harlow, Essex, England , 1984. 261 p. :　ISBN 0-582-64434-8 (pbk.) :　DDC 306/.09669 19
HN831.A8 S63 1984　NYPL [Sc D 88-880]

Social change in Nigeria /. London , 1986. 261 p. ;　ISBN 0-582-64434-8 (pbk.) :　DDC 306/.09669 19
HN831.A8 S63 1986　　NYPL [JLE 87-3643]

Pearse, Adetokunbo. Towards the decolonization of the British educational system /. London, England , 19. 128 p. :　ISBN 0-907015-32-8
NYPL [Sc D 88-1346]

Pearson, Boyce Neal. A cantomeric analysis of three Afro-American songs recorded in the Commerce, Texas, area [microform] / by Boyce N. Pearson. 1978. 47 leaves. Thesis (M.S.)--East Texas State University, 1978. Bibliography: leaves 35-41 Microfilm of typescript. Ann Arbor, Mich.: University Microfilms International, 1978. 1 microfilm reel; 35 mm.
1. Afro-Americans - Music - History and criticism. 2. Folk-songs, English - Texas - Commerce - History and criticism. I. Title.　NYPL [Sc Micro R-4701]

Pearson, Maggie. Racial equality and good practice maternity care : a report of two workshops held in Bradford organised by Training in Health and Race and the Centre for Ethnic Minorities Health Studies / compiled by Maggie Pearson. London : Training in Health and Race, 1985. 37 p. : ill. ; 30 cm. Bibliography: p. 36-37.　ISBN 0-86082-610-4 (pbk) :　DDC 362.1/982 19
1. Maternal health services - Great Britain. 2. Hospital patients - Great Britain. 3. Minorities - Medical care - Great Britain. I. Training in Health and Race (Project). II. Centre for Ethnic Minorities Health Studies. III. Title.
RG964.G7　　　　　NYPL [Sc F 88-393]

PEASANT ART. see FOLK ART.

PEASANTRY - AFRICA.
Nafziger, E. Wayne. Inequality in Africa . Cambridge [Cambridgeshire] ; New York , c1988. xii, 204 p. :　ISBN 0-521-26881-8 DDC 339.2/096 19
HC800.Z9 I5136 1988　　NYPL [Sc E 88-521]

PEASANTRY - BOTSWANA - CASE STUDIES.
Hesselberg, J. (Jan) The Third World in transition /. Uppsala , Stockholm, Sweden , 1985. 256 p. :　ISBN 91-7106-243-2 (pbk.)　DDC 305.5/63 19
HD1538.B55 H47 1985
NYPL [Sc E 88-290]

PEASANTRY - CARIBBEAN AREA - ADDRESSES, ESSAYS, LECTURES.
Contemporary Caribbean . [St. Augustine, Trinidad and Tobago?] , 1981-<1982 > (Maracas, Trinidad and Tobago, West Indies : College Press) v. :　DDC 304.6/09729 19
HB3545 .C66 1981　　NYPL [Sc D 89-499]

PEASANTRY - DEVELOPING COUNTRIES - CONGRESSES.
Social anthropology of peasantry /. Ikeja, Nigeria , 1983. xii, 351 p. ;　DDC 305.5/63 19
HT407 .S53 1983　　NYPL [Sc E 87-179]

PEASANTRY - SOUTH AFRICA.
Bundy, Colin. The rise and fall of the South African peasantry /. Cape Town , 1988. [21], 276 p. ;　ISBN 0-520-03754-5
NYPL [Sc D 89-533]

PEASANTRY - UGANDA - BUGISU (DISTRICT) - POLITICAL ACTIVITY.
Bunker, Stephen G., 1944- Double dependency and constraints on class formation in Bugisu, Uganda /. Urbana, Ill. , 1983. v, 88 p. :　DDC 303.3/09676/1 19
HD1538.U43 B86 1983
NYPL [Sc D 88-1054]

Pêcheurs de Saint-Louis du Sénégal. Bonnardel, Régine. Vitalité de la petite pêche tropicale . Paris , 1985. 104 p. :　ISBN 2-222-03678-X
NYPL [Sc F 88-329]

PEDAGOGY. see EDUCATION; EDUCATION - STUDY AND TEACHING.

The pedagogy of a decade of OAU mock-summits at ABU. Zaria : [S.n.], 1988] (Zaria : Ahmadu Bello University Press) 64 p. : ill. ; 31 cm.　ISBN 978-301-130-12
1. Ahmadu Bello University. 2. Organization of Afican Unity. 3. Political science - Study and teaching - Nigeria - Zaria. 4. Political science - Study and teaching - Simulation methods.
NYPL [Sc G 88-38]

PEDOLOGY (CHILD STUDY) see CHILDREN.

Peeps into St. Lucia's past /. Jesse, Charles. St. Lucia , 1979. 100 p. :　*NYPL [Sc E 88-311]*

Peil, Margaret. The Ghanaian factory worker: industrial man in Africa . [Cambridge, Eng.] University Press, 1972. ix, 254 p. maps. 24 cm. (African studies series. no. 5) Bibliography: p. 245-250.
1. Labor and laboring classes - Ghana. I. Title. II. Series.　　　　　NYPL [Sc 331.7-P]

Pèlerinages, sanctuaires, apparitions. Maindron, Gabriel. Des apparitions à Kibeho . Paris , c1984. 243 p., [4] p. of plates :　ISBN 2-86839-021-8 :　DDC 232.91/7/0967571 19
BT660.K52 M35 1984　NYPL [Sc E 88-516]

Pelican guide to the Bahamas /. Moore, James E. Gretna, LA , c1988. 322 p. :　ISBN 0-88289-663-6 :　*NYPL [Sc D 89-272]*

Pelrine, Diane. African art from the Rita and John Grunwald collection / exhibition organized and catalogue by Diane M. Pelrine ; introduction by Diane M. Pelrine and Patrick R. McNaughton. Bloomington : Indiana University Art Museum in association with Indiana University Press, c1988. 159 p. : ill. ; 27 cm. Exhibition held Indiana University Art Museum, Sept. 27-Dec. 16, 1988 and other museums. Bibliography: p. 158-159.　ISBN 0-253-21061-5 (I.U. Press : pbk.)　DDC 730/.0966/0740172255 19
1. Grunwald, Rita - Art collections - Exhibitions. 2. Grunwald, John - Art collections - Exhibitions. 3. Art, Black - West - Exhibitions. 4. Art, Black - Africa, Central - Exhibitions. 5. Art, Primitive - Africa, West - Exhibitions. 6. Art, Primitive - Africa, Central - Exhibitions. 7. Art - Private collections - Indiana - Bloomington - Exhibitions. I. Grunwald, Rita. II.

Grunwald, John. III. McNaughton, Patrick R. IV. Indiana University, Bloomington. Art Museum. V. Title.
N7398 .P44 1988　　NYPL [Sc F 89-158]

Peltzer, Karl. Some contributions of traditional healing practices towards psychosocial health care in Malawi / Karl Peltzer. Eschborn bei Frankfurt Om Main : Fachbuchhandlung für Psychologie, 1987. 341 p. : ill., map ; 21 cm. Bibliography: p. 304-341.　ISBN 3-88074-174-3
1. Medicine, Primitive - Malawi - Psychological aspects. 2. Counseling - Malawi. 3. Medicine, Magic, mystic and spagiric - Malawi - Psychological aspects. 4. Malawi - Social life and customs. I. Title.
NYPL [Sc D 88-618]

PEN. La Tradition orale, source de la littérature contemporaine en Afrique . Dakar , c1984. 201 p. :　ISBN 2-7236-0899-9　*NYPL [Sc E 89-55]*

PENAL CODES. see CRIMINAL LAW.

PENAL INSTITUTIONS. see PRISONS.

PENAL LAW. see CRIMINAL LAW.

PENDE (AFRICAN PEOPLE) - FOLKLORE.
Les Maitresses du feu et de la cuisine . Bandundu, République du Zaïre , 1983. 164 p. :
NYPL [Sc F 88-308]

The Penguin book of Southern African stories / edited by Stephen Gray. Harmondsworth, Middlesex, England ; New York, N.Y., U. S.A. : Penguin Books, 1985. 328 p. ; 20 cm.　ISBN 0-14-007239-X (pbk.) :　DDC 808.83/1 19
1. Short stories, Southern African. 2. Tales - Africa, Southern. I. Gray, Stephen, 1941-. II. Title: Southern African stories.
PL8014.S62 P46 1985　NYPL [Sc C 88-270]

PENITENTIARIES. see PRISONS.

Penn, Verna E. A cultural experience . Road Town, Tortola, British Virgin Islands , 1980. viii, 55 p. :
MLCS 81/1586　　　NYPL [Sc D 88-1398]

Pennington, Richard, 1952- Breaking the ice : the racial integration of Southwest Conference football / by Richard Pennington. Jefferson, N.C. : McFarland, c1987. ix, 182 p. : ill., ports. ; 24 cm. Includes index. Bibliography: p. 165-169.　ISBN 0-89950-295-4 :　DDC 796.332/72/0973 19
1. McVea, Warren. 2. Westbrook, John. 3. LeVias, Jerry. 4. Southwest Conference (U. S.). 5. Afro-American football players - Biography. 6. Discrimination in sports - Southwestern States. 7. Southwestern States - Race relations. I. Title.
GV939.A1 P46 1987　NYPL [Sc E 88-35]

PENOLOGY. see PRISONS.

PENTECOSTAL MOVEMENT. see PENTECOSTALISM.

PENTECOSTALISM - UNITED STATES - HISTORY.
MacRobert, Iain, 1949- The Black roots and white racism of early Pentecostalism in the USA /. Basingstoke , 1988. xv, 142 p. :　ISBN 0-333-43997-X :　DDC 277.3/082 19
BR1644.5.U6　　　NYPL [Sc D 89-131]

People call him the Son of God [microform] Brooklyn : Ansaru Allah Community, [197-?] 11 p. : ill. ; 38 cm. Cover title. Title also in Arabic; portions of text in Arabic. Paging in reverse. Microfilm. New York: New York Public Library, 1982. 1 microfilm reel; 35 mm. (MN *ZZ-23673)
1. Jesus Christ - Islamic interpretations. I. Ansaru Allah Community. NYPL [Sc Micro R-4114 no. 20]

The people called Bassa-Nge /. Habi, Ya'akub H. Zaria , c1987. 86 p. :　ISBN 978-12-5057-7
NYPL [Sc C 88-372]

The People of East Harlem [microform] : the needs of the community and the resources for meeting them / Louise A. Johnson, ed. ; with the assistance of Gloria Booker ... [et al.]. New York : Mount Sinai School of Medicine, c1974. 90 p. : ill., maps ; 28 cm. Bibliography: p. 75. Microfilm. New York: New York Public Library, 198. 1 microfilm reel; 35 mm. (MN *ZZ-24640)
1. Harlem, New York (City) - Social conditions. I. Johnson, Louise A., ed. II. Mount Sinai School of Medicine.　NYPL [Sc Micro R-4137 no.12]

A People's history of South Africa. Johannesburg : Ravan Press, c1980- v. : ill. ; 30 cm. Bibliography: v. 1, p. 112. CONTENTS. - v. 1. Gold and workers / by Luli Callinicos. ISBN 0-86975-119-0 (pbk. : v. 1)　DDC 968 19
1. Blacks - South Africa - Economic conditions. 2.

Labor and laboring classes - South Africa. 3. Gold mines and mining - South Africa - History. 4. South Africa - History. I. Callinicos, Luli.
DT766 .P43   *NYPL [JLM 85-439]*

People's Movement for the Liberation of Angola.
see Movimento Popular de Libertação de Angola.

Pépin, Ernest. Au verso du silence / Ernest Pépin. Paris : L'Harmattan, c1984. 108 p. ; 19 cm. (Collection Encres noires. 28)   ISBN 2-85802-279-8   DDC 841 19
I. Title.
PQ3949.2.P37 A9 1984
    NYPL [Sc C 88-273]

Pequena enciclopédia da cultura brasileira.
Lopes, Helena Theodoro. Negro e cultura no Brasil /. Rio de Janeiro , 1987. 136 p. ;   ISBN 85-85108-02-9   DDC 981/.00496 19
F2659.N4 L67 1987   *NYPL [Sc D 88-1291]*

Peregalli, Enrique, 1950- Escravidão no Brasil / Enrique Peregalli. São Paulo : Global, c1988. 80 p. : ill., maps ; 21 cm. (História popular . 4)   Bibliography: p. 79-80.   ISBN 85-26-00192-2
1. Slavery - Brazil - History. I. Series: Coleção História popular , no. 4. II. Title.   *NYPL [Sc D 89-421]*

Pereira, Alberto Feliciano Marques. Museu de Arte Sacra (Mozambique Island) Museu de Arte Sacra, anexo à Igreja da Misericórdia, Ilha de Moçambique [microform] [Lourenço Marques?] , 1969. [16] p. :
    NYPL [Sc Micro F-10928]

Pereira, Augusto. Lubu ku lebri ku mortu . Bissau , 1988. 49 p. :   *NYPL [Sc F 88-351]*

Performance in world music series .
(no. 1) Locke, David, 1949- Drum gahu . Crown Point, Ind. , c1987. ix, 142 p. :   ISBN 0-941677-03-6 :   DDC 789/.01 19
MT655 .L6 1987   *NYPL [Sc E 88-391]*

PERFORMING ARTS - NIGERIA.
Kofoworola, Ziky. Hausa performing arts and music /. Lagos , c1987. viii, 330 p. :   ISBN 978-17-3041-2   *NYPL [Sc E 89-116]*

Perkins, Carol Morse. The shattered skull ; a safari to man's past / Carol Morse Perkins. New York, Atheneum, 1965. 59 p., ill., map, 25 cm. SCHOMBURG CHILDREN'S COLLECTION.
1. Man, Prehistoric - Tanganyika. 2. Tanganyika - Description & travel. I. Schomburg Children's Collection. II. Title.
DT440 .P4   *NYPL [Sc E 88-145]*

Perkins, Marlin. Martin, Robert, 1929- Yesterday's people. Garden City, N.Y. [1970] 158 p.   DDC 916.8/03
DT764.B8 M35   *NYPL [Sc F 88-248]*

Perlo, Don. Lyons, Leonard. Jazz portraits . New York , c1989. 610 p. :   ISBN 0-688-04946-X   DDC 785.42/092/2 B 19
ML394 .L97 1989   *NYPL [Sc E 89-91]*

PERMANENT EDUCATION. see CONTINUING EDUCATION.

PERNAMBUCO (BRAZIL) - ECONOMIC CONDITIONS.
Leite, Glacyra Lazzari. Pernambuco 1817 . Recife , 1988. 275 p. ;   ISBN 85-7019-122-7   DDC 981/.3403 20
F2534 .L45 1988   *NYPL [Sc D 89-605]*

PERNAMBUCO (BRAZIL) - HISTORY - REVOLUTION, 1817.
Leite, Glacyra Lazzari. Pernambuco 1817 . Recife , 1988. 275 p. ;   ISBN 85-7019-122-7   DDC 981/.3403 20
F2534 .L45 1988   *NYPL [Sc D 89-605]*

PERNAMBUCO (BRAZIL) - SOCIAL CONDITIONS.
Leite, Glacyra Lazzari. Pernambuco 1817 . Recife , 1988. 275 p. ;   ISBN 85-7019-122-7   DDC 981/.3403 20
F2534 .L45 1988   *NYPL [Sc D 89-605]*

Pernambuco 1817 . Leite, Glacyra Lazzari. Recife , 1988. 275 p. ;   ISBN 85-7019-122-7   DDC 981/.3403 20
F2534 .L45 1988   *NYPL [Sc D 89-605]*

Pero, Albert, 1935- Theology and the Black experience . Minneapolis , c1988. 272 p. ;   ISBN 0-8066-2353-5   DDC 284.1/08996 19
BX8065.2 .T48 1988   *NYPL [Sc D 89-353]*

Pérotin-Dumon, Anne. Etre patriote sous les tropiques : la Guadeloupe, la colonisation et la révolution (1789-1794) / Anne Pérotin-Dumon. Basse-Terre : Société d'histoire de la Guadeloupe, 1985. 339 p. : ill. ; 24 cm. (Bibliothèque d'histoire antillaise. 10) Includes index. Bibliography: p. 307-317.   ISBN 2-900339-21-9
1. Guadeloupe - History. I. Title. II. Series.
    NYPL [Sc E 88-256]

Perregaux, Christiane. L'école sahraouie : de la caravane à la guerre de libération / Christiane Perregaux. Paris : L'Harmattan, c1987. 158 p., [8] p. of plates : ill., maps ; 22 cm. Based on the author's thesis (mémoire de licence--Université de Genève). Bibliography: p. 153-156.   ISBN 2-85802-942-3   DDC 372.964/8 19
1. Education, Elementary - Western Sahara - History. 2. Western Sahara - Social life and customs. I. Title.
LA2034.W47 P47 1987
    NYPL [Sc D 89-401]

PERRY COUNTY (MO.) - RACE RELATIONS.
Poole, Stafford. Church and slave in Perry County, Missouri, 1818-1865 /. Lewiston, N.Y., USA , c1986. xvii, 251 p. :   ISBN 0-88946-666-1 (alk. paper) :   DDC 306/.362/09778694 19
E445.M67 P66 1986   *NYPL [Sc E 89-102]*

PERRY, IVORY.
Lipsitz, George. A life in the struggle . Philadelphia , 1988. viii, 292 p. :   ISBN 0-87722-550-8 (alk. paper)   DDC 973/.0496073024 B 19
E185.97.P49 L57 1988   *NYPL [Sc E 89-43]*

Persaud, Pat. Tipsy / written by Pat Persaud ; edited by Elaine Brooks ; illustrated by Cathi Levy. Kingston, Jamaica : Children's Writers Circle, c1986. [28] p. : ill. ; 22 cm. SCHOMBURG CHILDREN'S COLLECTION.
1. Jamaica - Juvenile fiction. I. Levy, Cathi. II. Schomburg Children's Collection. III. Title.
MLCS 87/7926 (P)   *NYPL [Sc F 88-255]*

Persia. see Iran.

Persistent pastoralists . Rigby, Peter. London , Totowa, N.J. , 1985. x, 198 p. :   ISBN 0-86232-226-X :   DDC 305.8/9676 19
DT443.3.M37 R54 1985
    NYPL [JLD 86-2309]

Person, Yves. Samori: une révolution dyula. Dakar, I.F.A.N., 1968- v. (2377 p.) 28 cm. (Mémoires de l'Institut fondamental d'Afrique noire, no 80, 89) Originally presented as the author's thesis, Paris, 1970. "Errata et addenda" (16 p.) inserted in v. 1; errata slip inserted in v. 3. Includes indexes. Bibliography: p. 2165-2192.   DDC 966/.2601/0924 B
1. Samory, ca. 1830-1900. 2. Ethnology - Africa, West. 3. Africa, West - History - 1884-1960. 4. Africa, West - Kings and rulers - Biography. I. Series: Mémoires de ll'nstitut fondamental d'Afrique noire , no 80. II. Title.
DT475.5.S3 P47 1968   *NYPL [Sc F 87-398]*

Personajes populares dominicanos. 1a ed. Santo Domingo, República Dominicana : Taller, c1986. 94 p. : ill. ; 21 cm. (Biblioteca Taller. no. 233)
1. Dominicans (Dominican Republic) - Biography.
    NYPL [Sc D 89-491]

PERSONAL LIBERTY. see LIBERTY.

PERSONAL NAMES. see NAMES, PERSONAL.

Personal relations with the President and Secretary of State. Sumner, Charles, 1811-1874. "He, being dead, yet speaketh" . Boston , New York , 1878. 29, 16 p. ;
    NYPL [Sc Rare C 89-4]

PERSONNEL ADMINISTRATION. see PERSONNEL MANAGEMENT.

PERSONNEL MANAGEMENT - STUDY AND TEACHING - AFRICA.
Rwegasira, Kami S. P. Administering management development institutions in Africa /. Aldershot, England , Brookfield, Vt. , 1988. vi, 112 p. ;   ISBN 0-566-05501-5   DDC 658.4/07124/096 19
HF5549.5.A78 R94 1988
    NYPL [Sc D 88-458]

PERSONNEL SERVICE IN EDUCATION - NIGERIA.
Denga, Daniel I. Guidance and counselling for the 6-3-3-4 system of education /. Calabar [Nigeria] , 1983 (1986 printing) 159 p. :   ISBN 978-228-192-1   *NYPL [Sc D 88-6]*

Persons, Stow, 1913- Ethnic studies at Chicago, 1905-45 / Stow Persons. Urbana : University of Illinois Press, c1987. 159 p. ; 24 cm. Includes index. Bibliography: p. 153-156.   ISBN 0-252-01344-1 (alk. paper).   DDC 305.8/007/1077311 19
1. Race relations - Study and teaching (Higher) - Illinois - Chicago. 2. Minorities - Study and teaching (Higher) - Illinois - Chicago. 3. Chicago school of sociology. I. Title.
HT1506 .P47 1987   *NYPL [JLE 87-1776]*

Perspectives of independent development in Southern Africa : the cases of Zimbabwe and Namibia / Hartmut Brandt ... [et al.] ; [translated from the German by Douglas Ross]. Berlin : German Development Institute, 1980. xiv, 183 p. : maps ; 24 cm. (Occasional papers of the German Development Institute . no. 62) Includes bibliographical references.   DDC 338.9688 19
1. Zimbabwe - Economic conditions - 1965-1980 - Addresses, essays, lectures. 2. Namibia - Economic conditions - Addresses, essays, lectures. 3. Zimbabwe - Colonial influence - Addresses, essays, lectures. 4. Namibia - Colonial influence - Addresses, essays, lectures. I. Brandt, Hartmut. II. Series: Deutsches Institut für Entwicklungspolitik. Schriften, Nr. 62. 62.
HC910 .P47   *NYPL [JLE 82-36]*

Perspectives on African music / Wolfgang Bender, ed. Bayreuth, W. Germany ; Bayreuth University, c1989. 139 p., [8] leaves of plates : ill., music ; 21 cm. (Bayreuth African studies series, 0178-0034 . 9) Includes bibliographies. In English and German.   ISBN 3-927510-00-9
1. Music - Africa. I. Bender, Wolfgang. II. Series.
    NYPL [Sc D 89-448]

Perspectives on community and rural development in Nigeria / edited by Amechi Nweze. Jos : Centre for Development Studies, c1988. 202 p. ; 24 cm. "Collection of papers presented during an international seminary workshop on rural and community development held at the University of Jos in Nov. 1983" -Pref. Includes bibliographies.   ISBN 978-282-700-2
1. Community development - Nigeria. 2. Rural development - Nigeria. I. Nwaze, Amechi.
    NYPL [Sc E 89-18]

Perspectives on creative writing /. Johnson, Rotimi. Yaba , 1986, c1985. 85 p. ;
    NYPL [Sc C 88-241]

Perspectives on Nigerian literature, 1700 to the present / edited by Yemi Ogunbiyi ; with a foreword by Stanley Macebuh. Oshodi, Lagos, Nigeria : Guardian Books Nigeria Limited, 1988. 2 v. ; 20 cm. Includes index. "A critical selection from Guardian Literary Series."
1. Nigerian literature - History. I. Ogunbiyi, Yemi.
    NYPL [Sc C 89-19]

Perspectives on rural development in Ciskei, 1983 /. Bekker, S. B. Grahamstown [1984] 52 p. :   ISBN 0-86810-103-6 (pbk.) :   DDC 307.1/4/0968792 19
HN801.C57 B45 1984   *NYPL [Sc F 88-325]*

PERU - LANGUAGES.
Romero, Fernando. El negro en el Perú y su transculturación lingüística /. [Lima?] , 1987. 176 p. :   *NYPL [Sc F 88-20]*

Pessar, Patricia R. When borders don't divide . Staten Island, N.Y. , c1988. viii, 220 p. :   ISBN 0-934733-26-0 :   DDC 325.8 19
JV7398 .W47 1988   *NYPL [Sc E 89-169]*

Pessoa, Henrique Novais. Comboio comakovi : histórias africanas : (contos da vida real) / Henrique novais Pessoa. [Portugal] : Alhos Vedros, 1987. 147 p. : ill. ; 21 cm.
1. Angola - Fiction. I. Title.
    NYPL [Sc D 88-1010]

Peter är barnvakt /. Fischer, Erling Gunnar. Stockholm , 1961. [40] p. :
    NYPL [Sc F 88-261]

Peter of Mount Ephraim . Reid, Victor Stafford, 1913- Kingston , 1971. 140 p. :
MLCS 83/10255 (P)   *NYPL [Sc C 88-185]*

Peters, Marguerite Andree. Bibliography of the Tswana language : a bibliography of books, periodicals, pamphlets, and manuscripts to the year 1980 / compiled by Marguerite Andrée Peters and Matthew Mathêthê Tabane = Bibliokerafi ya puo ya Setswana : bibiliokerafi ya dibuka, dimakasini, dipamfolêtê, le mayakgatiso go fitlha ka ngwaga wa 1980 / e kokoantswe ke Marguerite Andrée Peters le Matthew Mathêthê Tabane. Pretoria : State Library, 1982. l [i.e. L], 175 p., [3] leaves of plates : ill. ; 26 cm. (Bibliographies / The State

Library, Pretoria . no. 25 = no. 25) Includes index.
ISBN 0-7989-0116-0 DDC 015.68 19
1. Tswana imprints. 2. Tswana language - Bibliography.
3. South Africa - Imprints. I. Tabane, Matthew
Mathêthê. II. South Africa. State Library. III. Title. IV.
Title: Bibiliokerafi ya puo ya Setswana. V. Series:
Bibliographies (South Africa. State Library) , no. 25.
Z3601 .P47 1982   NYPL [Sc E 87-667]

Peterson, Bernard L. Contemporary Black
American playwrights and their plays : a
biographical directory and dramatic index /
Bernard L. Peterson, Jr ; foreword by James V.
Hatch. New York : Greenwood Press, 1988.
xxvi, 625 p. ; 25 cm. Includes indexes. Bibliography:
p. 533-550. ISBN 0-313-25190-8 (lib. bdg. : alk.
paper) DDC 812/.54/09896 19
1. Afro-American dramatists - 20th century -
Biography - Dictionaries. 2. American drama -
Afro-American authors - Bio-bibliography -
Dictionaries. 3. American drama - 20th century -
Bio-bibliography - Dictionaries. 4. Afro-American
theater - Directories. I. Title.
PS153.N5 P43 1988   NYPL [Sc E 88-378]

PETERSON, OSCAR, 1925-
Palmer, Richard (Richard Hilary), 1947- Oscar
Peterson /. Tunbridge Wells , New York ,
1984. c. 93 p. : ISBN 0-87052-011-3 (Hippocrene
Books) : DDC 785.42/092/4 B 19
ML417.P46 P3 1984   NYPL [Sc C 88-142]

Peterson, Robert, 1925- Only the ball was white.
Englewood Cliffs, N.J., Prentice-Hall [1970] vii,
406 p. illus., ports. 24 cm. Includes index. ISBN
0-13-637215-5 DDC 796.357/09
1. Baseball - History. 2. Afro-American baseball
players - Biography. I. Title.
GV863 .P4   NYPL [Sc 796.357-P]

Petherbridge, Guy, 1944- Conservation of library
and archive materials and the graphic arts /.
London , Boston , 1985. 328 p. : ISBN
0-408-01466-0 : DDC 025.7 19
Z701 .C5863 1985   NYPL [MFW+ 88-574]

Petie, Haris. (illus) Wallace, John A. Getting to
know Egypt, U.A.R. /. New York , c1961. 64
p. :   *NYPL [Sc D 88-569]*

Pétition faite à l'Assemblée nationale par MM.
les Commissaires de l'Assemblée générale de la
partie française de St.-Domingue . Santo
Domingo (French colony). Assemblée générale.
Commissaires. [Paris?] [1791?] 7 p. ;
                     NYPL [Sc Rare C 86-3]

Petot, Jean. L'or de Guyane : son histoire, ses
hommes / Jean Petot. Paris : Editions
Caribéennes, c1986. 248 p. [8] pages of plates :
ill. ; 23 cm. Includes bibliography. ISBN
2-903033-84-6
1. Gold - French Guiana. 2. French Guiana - History.
I. Title.   NYPL [Sc D 88-1395]

PETROLEUM INDUSTRY AND TRADE -
AFRICA, WEST.
Underwood, David C. West African oil, will it
matter? /. Washington, D.C. , c1983. vi, 57 p. :
ISBN 0-89206-046-8 (pbk) DDC
333.8/232/0966 19
HD9577.A3582 U52 1983
                     NYPL [Sc D 88-888]

PETROLEUM INDUSTRY AND TRADE -
IRAN.
Jazayeri, Ahmad, 1957- Economic adjustment
in oil-based economies /. Aldershot, Hants,
England , Brookfield, Vt., USA , c1988. xvi,
260 p. : ISBN 0-566-05682-8 : DDC 330.955/054
19
HD9576.I62 J39 1988   NYPL [JLD 89-202]

PETROLEUM INDUSTRY AND TRADE -
NIGERIA.
Ihonvbere, Julius Omozuanvbo. Towards a
political economy of Nigeria. Aldershot,
[England] ; Brookfield, [Vt.], USA : xi, 213 p. :
ISBN 0-566-05422-1 : DDC 338.9669 19
HC1055 .I38 1988   NYPL [Sc D 89-47]

Jazayeri, Ahmad, 1957- Economic adjustment
in oil-based economies /. Aldershot, Hants,
England , Brookfield, Vt., USA , c1988. xvi,
260 p. : ISBN 0-566-05682-8 : DDC 330.955/054
19
HD9576.I62 J39 1988   NYPL [JLD 89-202]

Nigeria and the international capitalist system
/. Boulder, Colo. , 1988. v, 154 p. ; ISBN
1-555-87087-2 (alk. paper) : DDC 337.669 19
HF1616.7 .N54 1988   NYPL [JLE 88-3615]

PETROLEUM INDUSTRY AND TRADE -
TRINIDAD AND TOBAGO.
Oilfields Workers' Trade Union. Our fight for
people's ownership and control of the oil
industry . [San Fernando] , 1982. 80 p. :
                     NYPL [Sc D 88-1253]

PETROLEUM - TRADE AND STATISTICS.
see PETROLEUM INDUSTRY AND
TRADE.

PETROLEUM WORKERS - TRINIDAD AND
TOBAGO.
Oilfields Workers' Trade Union. Our fight for
people's ownership and control of the oil
industry . [San Fernando] , 1982. 80 p. :
                     NYPL [Sc D 88-1253]

PETS - JUVENILE FICTION.
Gerber, Will. Gooseberry Jones /. New York ,
c1947. 96 p. :   *NYPL [Sc D 89-442]*

PEUL LANGUAGE. see FULAH LANGUAGE.

PEULHS. see FULAHS.

Peuples du golfe du Bénin : Aja-Éwé : colloque
de Cotonou / études réunies et présentées par
François de Medeiros. Paris : Editions
Karthala : Centre de recherches africaines,
c1984. 328 p. : ill. ; 24 cm. (Hommes et sociétés,
0290-6600. 7) English and French. Summaries in
English and Spanish. Includes bibliographical references.
ISBN 2-86537-092-5 DDC 966/.8004963 19
1. Ewe (African people) - Congresses. 2. Aja (African
people) - Congresses. 3. Ethnology - Africa, West -
Congresses. 4. Africa, West - Social life and customs -
Congresses. 5. Africa, West - History - Congresses. I.
Medeiros, François de. II. Series. III. Series: Hommes
et sociétés (Editions Karthala) 7.
DT510.43.E94 P48 1984
                     NYPL [Sc E 88-449]

Péus, Gunter. Neue Kunst aus Afrika . [Hamburg] , c1984.
111 p. :   *NYPL [Sc G 88-17]*

PÉUS, GUNTER - ART COLLECTIONS -
EXHIBITIONS.
Neue Kunst aus Afrika . [Hamburg] , c1984.
111 p. :   *NYPL [Sc G 88-17]*

Pharaohs and mortals . Bourriau, Janine.
Cambridge [Cambridgeshire] ; New York : vi,
167 p. : ISBN 0-521-35319-X DDC
709/.32/07402659 19
N5336.G7 C3634 1988
                     NYPL [3-MAE 88-2748]

Phelan, Helene C. And why not every man? : an
account of slavery, the Underground Railroad,
and the road to freedom in New York's
Southern Tier / by Helene C. Phelan.
Interlaken, New York : Heart of the Lakes
Publishing, 1987. 247 p. : ill. ; 23 cm. Includes
index. Bibliography: p. 233-239. ISBN 0-9605836-4-5
1. Slavery - New York (State) - Anti-slavery
movements. 2. Underground railroad - New York
(State). I. Title.   NYPL [Sc D 87-1420]

Phelan, John M. Apartheid media :
disinformation and dissent in South Africa / by
John M. Phelan. Westport, Conn. : Lawrence
Hill, c1987. xi, 220 p. ; 23 cm. Includes index.
Bibliography: p. 210-216. ISBN 0-88208-244-2 :
DDC 323.44/5 19
1. Government and the press - South Africa. 2.
Freedom of the press - South Africa. 3. Apartheid -
South Africa. 4. Anti-apartheid movements. 5. South
Africa - Politics and government - 1978-. I. Title.
PN4748.S58 P4 1987   NYPL [JLD 87-4698]

Phelps-Stokes seminars on African-American
relations.
Clarke, John Henrik, 1915- The image of Africa
in the mind of the Afro-American . New York ,
1973. 32 leaves ;   *NYPL [Sc Micro F-9664]*

PHILADELPHIA (PA.) - HISTORY.
Nash, Gary B. Forging freedom . Cambridge,
Mass. , c1988. xii, 354 p. : ISBN 0-674-30934-0
(alk. paper) DDC 974.8/1100496073 19
F158.9.N4 N37 1988   NYPL [Sc E 88-594]

Winch, Julie, 1953- Philadelphia's Black elite .
Philadelphia , 1988. x, 240 p. ; ISBN
0-87722-515-X (alk. paper) : DDC
974.8/1100496073 19
F158.9.N4 W56 1988   NYPL [Sc E 88-198]

PHILADELPHIA (PA.) - RACE RELATIONS.
Anderson, John, 1954 Mar. 27- Burning down
the house . New York , c1987. xv, 409 p. :
ISBN 0-393-02460-1 : DDC 974.8/1104 19
F158.9.N4 A53 1987   NYPL [Sc E 88-332]

Butler, Ernest W. Neighbors of the 2100 block .
Pitman, N.J. , c1986. 466 p. :
                     NYPL [Sc D 88-940]

Nash, Gary B. Forging freedom . Cambridge,
Mass. , c1988. xii, 354 p. : ISBN 0-674-30934-0
(alk. paper) DDC 974.8/1100496073 19
F158.9.N4 N37 1988   NYPL [Sc E 88-594]

PHILADELPHIA (PA.) - SOCIAL
CONDITIONS.
Rose, Dan. Black American street life .
Philadelphia, Pa. , c1987. x, 278 p. : ISBN
0-8122-8071-7 DDC 974.8/1100496073 19
F158.9.N4 R67 1987   NYPL [Sc E 88-76]

PHILADELPHIA (PA.) - SOCIAL LIFE AND
CUSTOMS.
Butler, Ernest W. Neighbors of the 2100 block .
Pitman, N.J. , c1986. 466 p. :
                     NYPL [Sc D 88-940]

Rose, Dan. Black American street life .
Philadelphia, Pa. , c1987. x, 278 p. : ISBN
0-8122-8071-7 DDC 974.8/1100496073 19
F158.9.N4 R67 1987   NYPL [Sc E 88-76]

Philadelphia's Black elite . Winch, Julie, 1953-
Philadelphia , 1988. x, 240 p. ; ISBN
0-87722-515-X (alk. paper) : DDC
974.8/1100496073 19
F158.9.N4 W56 1988   NYPL [Sc E 88-198]

PHILANTHROPY. see SOCIAL SERVICE.

Philip, Ira. Freedom fighters : from Monk to
Mazumbo / by Ira Philip. London : Akira,
1987. 275 p., [8] p. of plates : ill., ports. ; 21
cm. Includes bibliography and index. ISBN
0-947638-42-3 (cased) DDC 323.1/196/07299
19
1. Monk, Charles Vinton. 2. Gordon, Edward
Fitzgerald. 3. Civil rights - Bermuda. I. Title.
                     NYPL [Sc D 88-1137]

Philip, Marlene.
Salmon courage / Marlene Philip. Toronto :
Williams-Wallace, c1983. 40 p. ; 21 cm. With
autograph of author. ISBN 0-88795-030-2
I. Title.   NYPL [Sc D 88-497]

Thorns / by Marlene Philip. Toronto, Ontario,
Canada : Williams-Wallace International, 1980.
56 p. ; 22 cm. Bibliography: p. 56. With autograph of
author. ISBN 0-88795-008-6
I. Title.   NYPL [Sc D 87-1425]

Philip, Marlene Nourbese. Harriet's daughter /
Marlene Nourbese Philip. Toronto, Ontario :
Women's Press, 1988. 150 p. ; 20 cm. With
autograph of author.
1. West Indians - Canada - Fiction. I. Title.
                     NYPL [Sc C 89-109]

PHILLIPS COUNTY (ARK.) - HISTORY.
Cortner, Richard C. A mob intent on death .
Middletown, Conn. , c1988. xii, 241 p., [24] p.
of plates : ISBN 0-8195-5161-9 (alk. paper) : DDC
976.7/88052 19
F417.P45 C67 1988   NYPL [Sc E 88-362]

PHILLIPS COUNTY (ARK.) - RACE
RELATIONS - HISTORY.
Cortner, Richard C. A mob intent on death .
Middletown, Conn. , c1988. xii, 241 p., [24] p.
of plates : ISBN 0-8195-5161-9 (alk. paper) : DDC
976.7/88052 19
F417.P45 C67 1988   NYPL [Sc E 88-362]

Phillipson, D. W. The prehistory of eastern
Zambia / by D. W. Phillipson. Nairobi : British
Institute in Eastern Africa, 1976. xi, 229 p.,
[21] leaves of plates (5 fold.) : ill. ; 28 cm.
(British Institute in Eastern Africa. Memoir. no. 6)
Includes index. Bibliography: p. 221-226. ISBN
0-500-97003-3 :
1. Man, Prehistoric - Zambia - Eastern Province. 2.
Zambia - Antiquities. 3. Eastern Province, Zambia -
Antiquities. I. Title. II. Series.
GN865.Z3 P48   NYPL [JFF 79-1585]

Phillis Wheatley / . Richmond, M. A. (Merle A.)
New York , 1988. 111 p ISBN 1-555-46683-4
DDC 811/.1 B 92 19
PS866.W5 Z683 1987   NYPL [Sc E 88-173]

Philosophie . Kipasaman, Mikalukalu. Kinshasa
[1984?] 61 p. :   *NYPL [Sc G 87-49]*

PHILOSOPHY - AFRICA - CONGRESSES.
Teaching and research in philosophy in Africa.
Spanish. Enseñanza de la filosofía e
investigación filosófica en Africa /. Barcelona ,
París , 1984. 339 p. : ISBN 92-3-302126-6
(Unesco)   *NYPL [Sc D 88-616]*

PHILOSOPHY, AFRO-AMERICAN. see AFRO-AMERICAN PHILOSOPHY.

PHILOSOPHY, ETHIOPIAN.
Sumner, Claude. The source of African philosophy . Stuttgart , 1986. 153 p. : ISBN 3-515-04438-8 DDC 199/.63 19
B5409.M27 S86 1986 *NYPL [Sc E 89-260]*

PHILOSOPHY - EXAMINATIONS, QUESTIONS, ETC.
Kipasaman, Mikalukalu. Philosophie . Kinshasa [1984?] 61 p. ; *NYPL [Sc G 87-49]*

PHILOSOPHY - MISCELLANEA.
Frye, Charles A. From Egypt to Don Juan . Lanham, MD , c1988. xiii, 129 p. : ISBN 0-8191-7120-4 (alk. paper) DDC 100 19
BF1999 .F77 1988 *NYPL [Sc D 88-1421]*

PHILOSOPHY, MORAL. see ETHICS.

The Philosophy of Alain Locke : Harlem renaissance and beyond / edited by Leonard Harris. Philadelphia : Temple University Press, 1989. x, 332 p. : ill., ports. ; 22 cm. Includes index. Bibliography: p. [301]-325. ISBN 0-87722-584-2 (alk. paper) DDC 191 19
1. Locke, Alain LeRoy, 1886-1954 - Philosophy. I. Harris, Leonard, 1948-.
E185.97.L79 P48 1989 NYPL [Sc D 89-494]

A philosophy of education for Nigeria . Adewole, Ayo. Onitsha , 1988, c1987. 131 p. ; ISBN 978-254-972-X *NYPL [Sc D 89-85]*

The philosophy of nationalism /. Josey, Charles Conant, 1893- [Race and national solidarity.] Washington, D.C. , c1983. xi, 227 p. ; ISBN 0-941694-16-X
JC311 .J66 1983 *NYPL [Sc D 89-514]*

PHILOSOPHY - OUTLINES, SYLLABI, ETC.
Kipasaman, Mikalukalu. Philosophie . Kinshasa [1984?] 61 p. ; *NYPL [Sc G 87-49]*

PHILOSOPHY, PRIMITIVE - AFRICA.
Explorations in African systems of thought /. Washington, D.C. , c1987. xvi, 337 p. : ISBN 0-87474-591-8 (pbk.) *NYPL [Sc D 88-566]*

PHILOSOPHY - STUDY AND TEACHING - AFRICA - CONGRESSES.
Teaching and research in philosophy in Africa. Spanish. Enseñanza de la filosofía e investigación filosófica en África /. Barcelona , París , 1984. 339 p. ; ISBN 92-3-302126-6 (Unesco) *NYPL [Sc D 88-616]*

Phimister, I. R. (Ian R.) An economic and social history of Zimbabwe, 1890-1948 : capital accumulation and class struggle / Ian Phimister. London ; New York : Longman, 1988. xii, 336 p. : maps ; 23 cm. Includes index. Bibliography: p. 301-319. ISBN 0-582-64423-2 DDC 330.96891/02 19
1. Saving and investment - Zimbabwe - History. 2. Social conflict - Zimbabwe - History. 3. Zimbabwe - Economic conditions - To 1965. 4. Zimbabwe - Social conditions - 1890-1965. I. Title.
HC910.Z9 S36 1987 NYPL [Sc D 89-35]

Une phonologie du wolof /. Dialo, Amadou. [Dakar] , 1981. 60 leaves ;
NYPL [Sc F 86-167]

Phonologie quantitative et synthématique . Colombel, Véronique de. Paris , 1986. 375 p., [31] p. of plates : ISBN 2-85297-192-5 : DDC 493/.7 19
PL8753.5 .C65 1986 *NYPL [Sc E 89-72]*

PHOTOGRAPHERS, AFRO-AMERICAN. see AFRO-AMERICAN PHOTOGRAPHERS.

PHOTOGRAPHERS - CUBA.
Cuba, a view from inside . New York [1985?] 2 v. :
TR646.U6 N4853x 1985
NYPL [Sc D 88-1511]

The photographs of George Hallett. Hallett, George. Amsterdam , c1988. [20] p. : ISBN 90-72422-01-5 *NYPL [Sc F 89-70]*

PHOTOGRAPHY - AESTHETICS. see PHOTOGRAPHY, ARTISTIC.

PHOTOGRAPHY - ANIMATED PICTURES. see MOVING-PICTURES.

PHOTOGRAPHY, ARTISTIC - EXHIBITIONS.
Hallett, George. The photographs of George Hallett. Amsterdam , c1988. [20] p. : ISBN 90-72422-01-5 *NYPL [Sc F 89-70]*

PHOTOGRAPHY - BIO-BIBLIOGRAPHY.
Willis-Thomas, Deborah, 1948- An illustrated bio-bibliography of Black photographers, 1940-1988 /. New York , 1989. xiv, 483 p. : ISBN 0-8240-8389-X (alk. paper) DDC 770/.92/2 19
TR139 .W55 1988 *NYPL [Sc F 89-156]*

PHOTOGRAPHY - BRAZIL - PERNAMBUCO - HISTORY - SOURCES.
Diario de Pernambuco . Recife [1985]. 256 p. : ISBN 85-7019-094-8 *NYPL [Sc D 88-862]*

PHOTOGRAPHY - CUBA - EXHIBITIONS.
Cuba, a view from inside . New York [1985?] 2 v. :
TR646.U6 N4853x 1985
NYPL [Sc D 88-1511]

PHOTOGRAPHY, DOCUMENTARY - TROPICS.
Webb, Alex. Hot light/half-made worlds . New York, N.Y. , 1986. 91 p. : ISBN 0-500-54116-7 : DDC 779/.99090913 19
TR820.5 .W43 1986 *NYPL [Sc G 87-23]*

PHOTOGRAPHY - MOVING-PICTURES. see MOVING-PICTURES.

PHOTOGRAPHY OF MEN.
Mapplethorpe, Robert. Black book /. New York, c1986. 91 p. : *NYPL [Sc F 87-42]*

PHOTOGRAPHY, PICTORIAL. see PHOTOGRAPHY, ARTISTIC.

PHOTOGRAPHY - PORTRAITS.
Jaja, Janhoi M. Profile /. Kingston, Jamaica , c1984. 48 p. : *NYPL [Sc D 88-932]*
Mapplethorpe, Robert. Black book /. New York, c1986. 91 p. : *NYPL [Sc F 87-42]*

PHYSICAL CULTURE. see PHYSICAL EDUCATION AND TRAINING.

PHYSICAL EDUCATION AND TRAINING - AFRICA - HISTORY - 19TH CENTURY.
Rummelt, Peter. Sport im Kolonialismus, Kolonialismus im Sport . Köln , 1986. 341 p. : ISBN 3-7609-5213-5 DDC 796/.096 19
GV665 .R85 1986 *NYPL [Sc D 88-973]*

PHYSICAL TRAINING. see PHYSICAL EDUCATION AND TRAINING.

PHYSICIANS - UNITED STATES - BIOGRAPHY.
Wynes, Charles E. Charles Richard Drew . Urbana , c1988. xvi, 132 p., [14] p. of plates : ISBN 0-252-01551-7 DDC 610/.92/4 B 19
R154.D75 W96 1988 *NYPL [Sc E 89-65]*

PHYSIOPHILOSOPHY. see NATURAL HISTORY.

PHYTOGRAPHY. see BOTANY.

PHYTOLOGY. see BOTANY.

PIANISTS - UNITED STATES - BIOGRAPHY.
Southall, Geneva H. Blind Tom . Minneapolis , 1979- v. : DDC 786.1/092/4 B
ML417.B78 S7 1979
NYPL [Sc Ser.-L .S674]

PIANO MUSIC (BOOGIE-WOOGIE) - HISTORY AND CRITICISM.
Silvester, Peter J. A left hand like God . London , c1988. 324 p. : ISBN 0-7043-2685-X : DDC 785.4 19 *NYPL [JNE 89-16]*

PIANO TRADE. see MUSIC TRADE.

Piault, Marc Henri. La Colonisation, rupture ou parenthèse /. Paris , c1987. 326 p. :
NYPL [Sc D 88-727]

Pickard-Cambridge, Claire. Sharing the cities : residential desegregation in Harare, Windhoek and Mafikeng / Claire Pickard-Cambridge. Braamfontein, Johannesburg, South Africa : South African Institute of Race Relations, 1988. ix, 53 p. : ill. ; 21 cm. Bibliography: p. 47-53. ISBN 0-86982-335-3
1. Discrimination in housing - South Africa. I. Title.
NYPL [Sc D 88-1336]

A pictorial history of the Nigerian Army /. Nigerian Army Museum. Nigeria , c1987. 49 p. : *NYPL [Sc F 89-81]*

Pictorial history of the Southern Tenant Farmers' Union. Mitchell, H. L. (Harry Leland), 1906- Roll the union on . Chicago , 1987. 96 p. : *NYPL [Sc F 88-187]*

PICTORIAL PHOTOGRAPHY. see PHOTOGRAPHY, ARTISTIC.

Picture parade. Akron [Ohio] : Saalfield Pub. Co., c1942. [36] p. : col. ill. ; 26 cm. SCHOMBURG CHILDREN'S COLLECTION. CONTENTS. - Picture parade.--[2] Little Black Sambo.--[3] Real animals.
I. Schomburg Children's Collection. II. Title: Little Black Sambo. *NYPL [Sc F 88-262]*

Pictures and stories from Uncle Tom's cabin. Boston: John P. Jewett & Co. [c1853] [5],6-32p. illus. 22cm. "The purpose of the Editor of this little Work, has been to adapt it for the juvenile family circle." Title vignette. Caption and running title: Uncle Tom's picture book. Yellow paper covers, with cover title duplicating title page. Page 32 contains: "Little Eva song. Uncle Tom's guardian angel. Words by John G. Whittier. Music by Manuel Emilio." SCHOMBURG CHILDREN'S COLLECTION.
I. Whittier, John Greenleaf, 1807-1892. II. Stowe, Harriet Beecher, 1811-1896. Uncle Tom's cabin. III. Schomburg Children's Collection. IV. Title. V. Title: Uncle Tom's picture book.
NYPL [Sc Rare C 89-1]

PICTURES, HUMOROUS. see CARICATURES AND CARTOONS.

PIDGIN LANGUAGES.
Les Langues de l'Afrique subsaharienne /. Paris , 1981. 2 v : ISBN 2-222-01720-3 :
NYPL [JFN 81-11 v.1]

Pieces of peace. McCain, W. Calvin. Jericho, N. Y. [1974] 80 p. *NYPL [Sc D 78-61]*

Pieces of wood . Anatsui, El. [Nigeria] , 1987 ; (Enugu : SNAAP Press) 39 p. :
NYPL [Sc B 88--59]

Pienaar, Sara. South Africa and international relations between the two World Wars : the League of Nations dimension / Sara Pienaar. Johannesburg : Witwatersrand University Press, 1987. 207 p ; 21 cm. Originally presented as the author's thesis (Ph. D.)--University of the Witwatersrand) Includes index. Bibliography: p. 184-192. ISBN 0-85494-936-4
1. League of Nations. 2. League of Nations - South Africa. 3. South Africa - Foreign relations. I. Title.
NYPL [Sc D 88-1026]

Pierre-Charles, Gérard.
Haití bajo la opresión de los Duvalier . Santo Domingo , 1981. 93 p. ; ISBN 968-590-021-3 DDC 972.94/06 19
F1928 .H33 1981 *NYPL [Sc D 89-457]*
Problemas dominico-haitianos y del Caribe /. - México , 1973. 320 p.
NYPL [JLK 73-145 [no.] 29]

Pierre, Claude. Le coup de l'étrier : textes poétiques / Claude Pierre. Ottawa : Les Editions du Vermillon, 1986. 98 p. : ill. ; 21 cm. (Collection "Parole vivante". no. 8) ISBN 0-919925-17-0
I. Title. *NYPL [Sc D 88-342]*

Pierre, K. D. Jn. (Kentry D. Jn.) Lamentation / K.D. Jn. Pierre. Michael Fontinelle. [St. Lucia] : Micken Publication, 1987. 62 p. : port. : 22 cm. Poems. Cover title. Errata slip tipped in.
I. Fontinelle, Michael. II. Title.
NYPL [Sc D 88-908]

Piersen, William Dillon, 1942- Black Yankees : the development of an Afro-American subculture in eighteenth-century New England / by William D. Piersen. Amherst : University of Massachusetts Press, 1988. Xii,237 p. ; 23 cm. Includes index. Bibliography: p. [177]-223. ISBN 0-87023-586-9 (alk. paper) DDC 974/.00496073 19
1. Afro-Americans - New England - History - 18th century. I. Title.
E185.917 .P54 1988 *NYPL [Sc E 88-213]*

Pierson-Mathy, Paulette.
[Naissance de l'Etat par la guerre de libération nationale. Spanish]
El nacimiento del estado por la guerra de liberación nacional : el caso de Guinea-Bissau / Paulette Pierson-Mathy. Barcelona : Serbal ; [Paris] : Unesco, 1983. 178 p. ; 20 cm. (Colección de temas africanos . 9) Translation of: L raissance de l'Etat par la guerre de liberation nationale: le cas de la Guinée-Bissau. Includes bibliographical footnotes. ISBN 92-3-301794-X (Unesco)
1. Guinea-Bissau - History - Revolution, 1963-1974. I.

Unesco. II. Title. III. Series.
NYPL [Sc D 88-602]

Pifferi, Annisa. La donna nel romanzo africano in lingua inglese : (letteratura) / Annisa Pifferi. Calliano (Trento) : Manfrini, c1985. 143 p. ; 20 cm. Contains extensive quotations in English with Italian translations. Bibliography: p. 139-143. ISBN 88-7024-258-7
1. African fiction (English) - Criticism and interpretation. I. Title. *NYPL [Sc D 89-102]*

Pilgrimage of two friends. Ray, Walter I. The pilgrimage of 2 friends . Silver Spring, Md. , 1984. v, 80 p. ;
NYPL [Sc F 87-440]

The pilgrimage of 2 friends . Ray, Walter I. Silver Spring, Md. , 1984. v, 80 p. ;
NYPL [Sc F 87-440]

Pilkington, Edward. Beyond the mother country : West Indians and the Notting Hill white riots / Edward Pilkington. London : Tauris, 1988. 182 p. ; 22 cm. Includes bibliographical references and index. ISBN 1-85043-113-2 DDC 305.8/96/041 19
1. West Indians - Great Britain. 2. London (England) - Race relations. I. Title. *NYPL [Sc D 89-122]*

Pilot evaluation report on Mahalapye Development Trust /. Gobotswang, Z. Gaborone, Botswana [1982] v leaves, 61, 3 p. ;
HD5710.85.B59 G63 1982
NYPL [Sc F 89-108]

Pina, Marie-Paule de. Les Iles du Cap-Vert / Marie-Paule de Pina ; préface de Claude Wauthier. Paris : Editions Karthala, c1987. 216, [1] p., [12] p. of plates ; ill., maps ; 22 cm. (Méridiens) Bibliography: p. [217]. ISBN 2-86537-182-4
1. Cape Verde - Social conditions. 2. Cape Verde - Economic conditions. 3. Cape Verde - Politics and government - 1975-. I. Title. II. Series.
NYPL [Sc D 88-510]

Pindell, Howardena, 1943-
Howardena Pindell : Odyssey, February 12-June 12, 1986, an exhibition organized by the Studio Museum in Harlem, 144 West 125th Street, New York, New York 10027. New York, NY (144 W. 125th St., New York 10027) : The Museum, c1986. 24 p. : ill. (some col.) ; 28 cm. Includes bibliographical references. DDC 709/.2/4 19
1. Pindell, Howardena, 1943- - Exhibitions. 2. India in art - Exhibitions. 3. Japan in art - Exhibitions. I. Studio Museum in Harlem. II. Title. III. Title: Odyssey.
N6537.P49 A4 1986 *NYPL [Sc F 88-270]*

PINDELL, HOWARDENA, 1943- - EXHIBITIONS.
Pindell, Howardena, 1943- Howardena Pindell . New York, NY (144 W. 125th St., New York 10027) , c1986. 24 p. : DDC 709/.2/4 19
N6537.P49 A4 1986 *NYPL [Sc F 88-270]*

Piñeiro de Rivera, Flor, 1922- Literatura infantil caribeña : Puerto Rico, República Dominicana y Cuba / Flor Piñeiro de Rivera, Isabel Freire de Matos. Hato Rey, P.R. (O'Neill 159, Hato Rey) : Boriken Libros, c1983. 123 p. ; 21 cm. Includes bibliographies. DDC 860/.9/9282 19
1. Children's literature, Puerto Rican - History and criticism. 2. Children's literature, Dominican - History and criticism. 3. Children's literature, Cuban - History and criticism. I. Freire de Matos, Isabel. II. Title.
PQ7361 .P5 1983 *NYPL [Sc D 88-1143]*

Pinfold, Mike.
Crowther, Bruce, 1933- The big band years /. Newton Abbot , c1988. 208 p. : ISBN 0-7153-9137-2 : DDC 785/.06/660973 19
ML3518 *NYPL [JNF 88-254]*

Louis Armstrong, his life and times / by Mike Pinfold. New York : Universe Books, c1987. 143 p. : ill., ports. ; 25 cm. Bibliography: p. 137-140. "Satchmography": p. 121-135. ISBN 0-87663-667-9 DDC 785.42/092/4 B 19
1. Armstrong, Louis, 1900-1971. 2. Jazz musicians - United States - Biography. 3. Afro-American musicians - Biography. I. Title.
ML419.A75 P55 1987 *NYPL [Sc F 88-65]*

Pinkney, Jerry.
Arkhurst, Joyce Cooper. More adventures of Spider . New York , c1972. 48 p. :
NYPL [Sc D 88-1449]

(ill) Fields, Julia. The green lion of Zion Street /. New York , c1988. [32] p. : ISBN 0-689-50414-4 DDC [E] 19
PZ8.3.F458 Gr 1988 *NYPL [Sc F 88-186]*

(ill) Lester, Julius. More tales of Uncle Remus .

New York , c1988. xvi, 143 p. : ISBN 0-8037-0419-4 DDC 398.2/08996073 19
PZ8.1.L434 Mo 1988 *NYPL [Sc E 88-458]*

(ill) McKissack, Pat, 1944- Mirandy and Brother Wind /. New York , 1988. [32] p. : ISBN 0-394-88765-4 DDC [E] 19
PZ7.M478693 Mi 1988 *NYPL [Sc F 89-58]*

PIONEER LIFE. see FRONTIER AND PIONEER LIFE.

PIONEERS - KENYA - BIOGRAPHY.
Memories of Kenya . London , 1986. xvi, 160 p., [16] p. of plates : ISBN 0-237-50919-9
NYPL [Sc F 88-102]

PIRATES - CARIBBEAN AREA - HISTORY.
Alleyne, Warren, 1924- Caribbean pirates /. London , 1986. v, 113 p. : ISBN 0-333-40570-6 (cased) : DDC 910.4/53 19
F2161 *NYPL [Sc D 88-448]*

Pisani, Edgard. Pour l'Afrique / Edgard Pisani. Paris : Editions Odile Jacob, 1988. 251 p. ; 24 cm.
1. Agriculture - Economic aspects - Africa. 2. Africa - Economic conditions - 1960-. 3. Africa - Politics and government - 1960-. I. Title.
NYPL [Sc E 88-249]

PITCHING (BASEBALL) - JUVENILE LITERATURE.
Humphrey, Kathryn Long. Satchel Paige /. New York , 1988. 110 p. : ISBN 0-531-10513-X DDC 796.357/092/4 B 92 19
GV865.P3 H86 1988 *NYPL [Sc E 88-481]*

PITTSBURGH PIRATES (BASEBALL TEAM) - JUVENILE LITERATURE.
Walker, Paul Robert. Pride of Puerto Rico . San Diego , c1988. 135 p. ; ISBN 0-15-200562-5 DDC 796.357/092/4 B 92 19
GV865.C45 W35 1988 *NYPL [Sc E 88-452]*

Place names of Africa, 1935-1986 . Kirchherr, Eugene C. Metuchen, N.J. , c1987. viii, 136 p. : ISBN 0-8108-2061-7 DDC 911/.6 19
DT31 .K53 1987 *NYPL [Sc D 88-813]*

Placoly, Vincent, 1946- Dessalines, ou, La passion de l'indépendance : théâtre / Vincent Placoly. Ciudad de La Habana : Casa de las Américas, c1983. 96 p. ; 19 cm.
I. Title. II. Title: Dessalines. III. Title: Passion de l'indépendance.
MLCS 86/2062 (P) *NYPL [JFC 87-478]*

Plaisirs de Saint-Domingue . Fouchard, Jean, 1912- Port-au-Prince, Haiti , 1988. 125 p.
NYPL [Sc D 89-407]

Plan for the coordination of emergency action in the event of a major disaster [microform] . St. Lucia. St. Lucia [1964] 22 p. ;
NYPL [Sc Micro F-10955]

Un plan Marshall pour l'Afrique? /. Sawadogo, Abdoulaye. Paris , c1987. 119 p. ; ISBN 2-85802-816-8 *NYPL [Sc D 88-911]*

Planche, Bernard. A Madagascar / [établi par Bernard Planche. [Paris] : Hachette, c1987. 158 p. : ill. (some col.) ; 22 cm. (Hachette guides bleus visa) Includes index. Bibliography: p. 155.
1. Madagascar - Description and travel - 1981- - Guide-books. I. Series: Guides bleus visà. II. Title.
NYPL [Sc D 88-254]

Planert, Wilhelm, 1882- Handbuch der Nama-Sprache in Deutsch-Südwestafrika / von W. Planert. Berlin : D. Reimer (E. Vohson), 1905. 104 p. ; 26 cm.
1. Nama language. 2. Nama language - Glossaries, vocabularies, etc. - German. I. Title.
NYPL [Sc F 89-147]

Planning and conducting training in communication /. Tadi Liben. Nairobi, Kenya , 1986. viii, 55 p. : DDC 307.1/4/0706 19
HN780.Z9 C679 1986 *NYPL [Sc F 89-171]*

PLANNING, CITY. see CITY PLANNING.

PLANNING, CURRICULUM. see CURRICULUM PLANNING.

PLANNING, EDUCATIONAL. see EDUCATIONAL PLANNING.

Planning for basic needs . Hoeven, Rolph van der. Aldershot , c1988. xvii, 380 p. : ISBN 0-566-05680-1 : DDC 330.9172/4 19
HC59.7 *NYPL [Sc D 89-37]*

PLANNING IN POLITICS. see POLITICAL PLANNING.

Plano diretor de informática, 82-84 /. Fundação Joaquim Nabuco. Recife , 1982. 101 p., 1 folded leaf : *NYPL [Sc D 88-924]*

Plant, Roger. Sugar and modern slavery : a tale of two countries / Roger Plant. London ; Atlantic Highlands, N.J. : Zed Books, c1987. xiv, 177 p. : map ; 23 cm. Includes index. Bibliography: p. [168]-172. ISBN 0-86232-572-2 : DDC 331.7/6361/097293 19
1. Sugar workers - Dominican Republic. 2. Sugarcane industry - Dominican Republic. 3. Alien labor, Haitian - Dominican Republic. 4. Haitians - Employment - Dominican Republic. 5. Forced labor - Dominican Republic. I. Title.
HD8039.S852 D657 1987
NYPL [Sc D 87-1240]

PLANTATION LIFE - CARIBBEAN AREA.
Rural development in the Caribbean /. London , 1985. xxi, 246 p. : ISBN 0-312-69599-3
NYPL [Sc D 88-1309]

PLANTATION LIFE - GEORGIA - BRYAN COUNTY - HISTORY - 19TH CENTURY.
Hoffmann, Charles. North by South . Athens , c1988. xxii, 318 p., [8] p. of plates : ISBN 0-8203-0976-1 (alk. paper) DDC 975.8/73203/0924 19
F292.B85 A753 1988 *NYPL [Sc E 89-35]*

PLANTATION LIFE - KENYA - YOI.
Visram, M. G. On a plantation in Kenya /. Mombasa, Kenya , 1987 (reprinted 1988) 164 p., [4] p. of plates : ISBN 996-698-411-9
NYPL [Sc C 89-92]

PLANTATION LIFE - LOUISIANA.
Northup, Solomon, b. 1808. Twelve years a slave . New York , 1857. 336 p. :
NYPL [Sc Rare C 89-34]

PLANTATION LIFE - MISSISSIPPI - HISTORY.
Moore, John Hebron. The emergence of the cotton kingdom in the Old Southwest . Baton Rouge , c1988. xii, 323 p. : ISBN 0-8071-1404-9 (pbk.) DDC 330.9762 19
HC107.M7 M66 1988 *NYPL [Sc E 88-279]*

PLANTATION LIFE - SOUTH CAROLINA - HISTORY - 19TH CENTURY.
Hammond, James Henry, 1807-1864. Secret and sacred . New York , 1988. xxix, 342 p., [2] leaves of plates : ISBN 0-19-505308-7 DDC 975.7/03/0924 B 19
F273 .H24 1988 *NYPL [Sc E 88-513]*

PLANTATION LIFE - SOUTHERN STATES - HISTORY.
Fox-Genovese, Elizabeth, 1941- Within the plantation household . Chapel Hill , c1988. xvii, 544 p. : ISBN 0-8078-1808-9 (alk. paper) DDC 305.4/0975 19
HQ1438.A13 F69 1988 *NYPL [JLE 89-21]*

PLANTATION LIFE - SOUTHERN STATES - HISTORY - 19TH CENTURY.
Van Deburg, William L. The slave drivers . New York , 1988. xvii, 202 p. : ISBN 0-19-505698-1 DDC 305.5/67/0975 19
E443 .V36 1988 *NYPL [Sc D 89-424]*

PLANTATION LIFE - VIRGIN ISLANDS OF THE UNITED STATES - SAINT JOHN.
Olwig, Karen Fog, 1948- Cultural adaptation and resistance on St. John . Gainesville , c1985. xii, 226 p. : ISBN 0-8130-0818-2 (pbk.) DDC 306/.097297/22 19
HT1071 .O43 1985 *NYPL [Sc D 88-1058]*

PLANTATION LIFE - WEST INDIES, BRITISH.
Dirks, Robert, 1942- The Black Saturnalia . Gainesville , c1987. xvii, 228 p., [7] p. of plates : ISBN 0-8130-0843-3 (pbk. : alk. paper) : DDC 394.2/68282/09729 19
GT4987.23 .D57 1987
NYPL [L-10 5328 no.72]

PLANTATION LIFE - WEST INDIES, BRITISH - HISTORY.
Ward, J. R. British West Indian slavery, 1750-1834 . Oxford [Oxfordshire] , New York , 1988. x, 320 p. : ISBN 0-19-820144-3 (Oxford University Press) : DDC 306/.362/09729 19
HT1092 .W37 1988 *NYPL [Sc D 88-1355]*

The plantation slaves of Trinidad, 1783-1816 . John, A. Meredith. Cambridge [Eng.] , New York , 1988. xvi, 259 p. ; ISBN 0-521-36166-4 DDC 306/.362/0972983 19
HT1105.T6 J65 1988 *NYPL [Sc E 89-235]*

PLANTATIONS - HAITI - HISTORY.
Cauna, Jacques, 1948- Au temps des isles à
sucre . Paris , c1987. 285 p., [16] p. of plates :
ISBN 2-86537-186-5   *NYPL [Sc E 88-492]*

PLANTING. see AGRICULTURE.

Plato, Ann. Essays including biographies and
misellaneaus pieces, in prose and poetry / Ann
Plato ; with an introduction by Kenny J.
Williams. New York : Oxford University Press,
1988. liii, 122 p. ; 17 cm. (The Schomburg library
of nineteenth-century Black women writers) Reprint.
Originally published: Hartford : [s.n.], c1841.   ISBN
0-19-505247-1 (alk. paper)   DDC 814/.3 19
1. Afro-Americans - Literary collections. I. Title. II.
Series.
PS2593 .P347 1988   *NYPL [JFC 88-2156]*

Play with Jimmy /. Detroit. Great Cities
Program for School Improvement. Writers'
Committee. Chicago , c1962. 23, [1] p. :
NYPL [Sc E 88-237]

PLAYS. see DRAMA.

PLAYS, MEDIEVAL. see PASSION-PLAYS.

Pleasure, profit, proselytism : British culture and
sport at home and abroad, 1700-1914 / edited
by J.A. Mangan. London, England ; Totowa,
NJ : F. Cass, 1988. 284 p. [8] p. ofplates : ill. ;
24 cm. Includes bibliographical references and index.
ISBN 0-7146-3289-9 :   DDC 796/.0941 19
1. Sports - Social aspects - Great Britain - History. 2.
Sports - Social aspects - Great Britain - History - 19th
century. 3. Sports - Social aspects - Great Britain -
Colonies - History. I. Mangan, J. A.
GV605 .P58 1988   *NYPL [JLE 88-1312]*

Plesner, Margaret. Lorenz, Bente. Traditional
Zambian pottery /. London , 1989. 47 p. :
ISBN 0-905788-75-3   *NYPL [Sc C 89-141]*

Pliegos .
(12) Castellanos, Isabel, 1939- Elegua quiere
también . Cali, Colombia , 1983. 84 p. ;
NYPL [Sc D 88-534]

Pliya, Jean, 1931- Les tresseurs de corde : roman
/ Jean Pliya. Paris : Hatier, 1987. 239 p. ; 18
cm. (Collection Monde noir poche)   ISBN
2-218-07841-X
1. Africa, Sub-Saharan - Fiction. I. Title. II. Series.
NYPL [Sc C 88-9]

Plomer, William, 1903-1973. Cecil Rhodes /
William Plomer. Cape Town : D. Philip, 1984.
xvii, 179 p. ; 19 cm. (Africasouth paperbacks)
"Bibliographical note": p. 173-175.   ISBN
0-86486-018-8
1. Rhodes, Cecil, 1853-1902. 2. Statesmen - South
Africa - Biography. I. Series. II. Series: Africasouth
paperbacks. III. Title.   *NYPL [Sc C 88-64]*

Pluchon, Pierre. Vaudou, sorciers,
empoisonneurs : de Saint-Domingue à Haïti /
Pierre Pluchon. Paris : Editions Karthala,
c1987. 320 p. ; 22 cm. Bibliography: p. [319]-320.
ISBN 2-86537-185-9
1. Voodooism - Haiti. I. Title.
NYPL [Sc D 88-912]

Plumasseau, Eugène, 1926- Savinien et Monique :
les chemins de l'engagement : roman / Eugène
Plumasseau. Pointe-à-Pitre : Société
guadeloupéenne d'édition et de diffusion, c1986.
188 p. ; 21 cm.
1. Guadeloupe - Politics and government - Fiction. I.
Title.
MLCS 86/7257 (P)   *NYPL [Sc D 88-176]*

Plummer, Brenda Gayle. Haiti and the great
powers, 1902-1915 / Brenda Gayle Plummer.
Baton Rouge : Louisiana State University Press,
c1988. xix, 255 p. : ill., maps, ports. ; 24 cm.
Includes bibliographical references and index.   ISBN
0-8071-1409-X (alk. paper)   DDC 972.94/04 19
1. Elite (Social sciences) - Haiti - Attitudes - History -
20th century. 2. Businessmen - Haiti - Attitudes -
History - 20th century. 3. Mercantile system - Haiti -
History - 20th century. 4. Haiti - Politics and
government - 1844-1934. 5. Haiti - Economic
conditions. 6. Haiti - Foreign relations. 7. Haiti - Social
conditions. I. Title.
F1926 .P68 1988   *NYPL [HPE 88-2374]*

**PLURALISM (SOCIAL SCIENCES) -
CARIBBEAN AREA - CASE STUDIES.**
Smith, M. G. (Michael Garfield) Culture race
and class in the commonwealth Caribbean /.
Mona, Jamaica , 1984. xiv, 163 p. ;   ISBN
976-616-000-7   *NYPL [Sc D 88-454]*

**PLURALISM (SOCIAL SCIENCES) - GREAT
BRITAIN.**
Educational attainments . London , New York ,
1988. vii, 180 p. : ISBN 1-85000-308-4 : DDC
370.19/34/0941 19
LC3736.G6 E336 1988   *NYPL [Sc E 89-52]*

Pluto, Terry, 1955- Ryan, Bob. Forty-eight
minutes . New York , London , c1987. x, 356
p. ;   ISBN 0-02-597770-9 DDC 796.32/364/0973 19
GV885.515.N37 R9 1988
NYPL [JFD 87-10809]

**Poblamiento del antiguo Egipto y desciframiento
de la escritura meroítica** /. Symposium on the
Peopling of Ancient Egypt and the deciphering
of Meroitic Script (1974 : Cairo, Egypt)
[Peuplement de l'Egipte ancianne et la
déchiffrement de l'écriture méroïtique. Spanish.]
Barcelona , Paris , 1983. 155 p. :   ISBN
0-923301-60-5 (Unesco)
NYPL [Sc D 88-603]

Poèmes du maquis /. Titus, Hénec.
[Port-au-Prince , 1986?] 60 p. :
NYPL [Sc D 88-499]

Poems at leisure /. Genfi, Nana Kofi. Nurom
Kumasi, Ghana , 1983. vii, 46 p. ;
MLCS 85/13012 (P)   *NYPL [Sc C 89-64]*

Poems for Afrika's children /. Wilson, Joy
Carter. South Framingham, Mass. , c1975. 30
p. :   *NYPL [Sc D 89-183]*

Poems from Montserrat. Flowers blooming late .
Montserrat , 1984. 72 p. ; ISBN 976-8018-00-3
NYPL [Sc D 89-559]

The poems of Phillis Wheatley /. Wheatley,
Phillis, 1753-1784. [Poems.] Chapel Hill ,
c1989. xvi, 235 p. ; ISBN 0-8078-1835-6 (alk.
paper) DDC 811/.1 19
PS866 .W5 1989   *NYPL [Sc E 89-205]*

Poesía /. Bañuelos, Juan. [Poems. Selections.] La
Habana , c1987. 58 p. ;   *NYPL [Sc C 89-41]*

Poesia intermitente /. Abreu, Antero. Lisboa,
Portugal , c1987. 48 p. ;
NYPL [Sc C 88-321]

Poesia negra no modernismo brasileiro /.
Damasceno, Benedita Gouveia. Campinas, SP
[Brasil] , 1988. 142 p. ; ISBN 85-7113-003-5
NYPL [Sc D 88-1290]

Poésie de la négritude /. Iyay Kimoni, 1938-
Kikwit , 1985. vi, 168 p. ; DDC 841/.009/896 19
PQ3897 .I93 1985   *NYPL [Sc B 89-18]*

Poetic privilege /. McKinney-Ludd, S. L. New
York , 1986. 52 p. ;   ISBN 0-533-06838-X
NYPL [Sc D 88-184]

**POETRY, AMERICAN. see AMERICAN
POETRY.**

**POETRY AND SOCIETY. see LITERATURE
AND SOCIETY.**

POETRY, ENGLISH. see ENGLISH POETRY.

POETRY, FRENCH. see FRENCH POETRY.

**POETRY, SPANISH AMERICAN. see
SPANISH AMERICAN POETRY.**

**POETS, AMERICAN - 18TH CENTURY -
BIOGRAPHY - JUVENILE LITERATURE.**
Richmond, M. A. (Merle A.) Phillis Wheatley
/. New York , 1988. 111 p :   ISBN
1-555-46683-4   DDC 811/.1 B 92 19
PS866.W5 Z683 1987   *NYPL [Sc E 88-173]*

**POETS, AMERICAN - 18TH CENTURY -
CORRESPONDENCE.**
Wheatley, Phillis, 1753-1784. [Works. 1988.]
The collected works of Phillis Wheatley /. New
York , 1988. xl, 339 p. ; ISBN 0-19-505241-2
(alk. paper) DDC 811/.1 19
PS866 .W5 1988   *NYPL [JFC 88-2142]*

**POETS, AMERICAN - 19TH CENTURY -
BIOGRAPHY - JUVENILE LITERATURE.**
Gentry, Tony. Paul Laurence Dunbar /. New
York , c1989. 110 p. : ISBN 1-555-46583-8
DDC 811/.4 B 92 19
PS1557 .G46 1989   *NYPL [Sc E 88-514]*

**POETS, AMERICAN - 20TH CENTURY -
BIOGRAPHY.**
Hull, Gloria T. Color, sex, and poetry .
Bloomington , c1987. xi, 240 p. : ISBN
0-253-34974-5 DDC 811/.52/099287 19
PS153.N5 H84 1987   *NYPL [Sc E 88-72]*

Meltzer, Milton, 1915- Langston Hughes . New

York [1968] xiii, 281 p.   DDC 811/.5/2 B
PS3515.U274 Z68   *NYPL [Sc D 89-329]*

Rampersad, Arnold. The life of Langston
Hughes /. New York , 1986-1988. 2 v. : ISBN
0-19-504011-2 (v. 1) DDC 818/.5209 B 19
PS3515.U274 Z698 1986
NYPL [Sc E 87-44]

**POETS, AMERICAN - 20TH CENTURY -
BIOGRAPHY - JUVENILE LITERATURE.**
Rummel, Jack. Langston Hughes /. New York ,
c1988. 111 p. : ISBN 1-555-46595-1 DDC
818/.5209 B 92 19
PS3515.U274 Z775 1988
NYPL [Sc E 88-166]

**POETS, AMERICAN - 20TH CENTURY -
INTERVIEWS.**
American poetry observed . Urbana , c1984. xi,
313 p. : ISBN 0-252-01042-6 DDC 811/.54/09 19
PS129 .A54 1984   *NYPL [JFE 84-3478]*

Poiret, Pierre. Mességué, Maurice. Tu as
rendez-vous avec le Diable /. Paris , c1987. 219
p. ; ISBN 2-87679-008-4   *NYPL [Sc E 88-540]*

**POITIER, SIDNEY - JUVENILE
LITERATURE.**
Bergman, Carol. Sidney Poitier /. New York ,
c1988. 110 p. : ISBN 1-555-46605-2 DDC
791.43/028/0924 B 92 19
PN2287.P57 B47 1988   *NYPL [Sc E 88-171]*

**POLAR EXPEDITIONS. see NORTH POLE;
ARCTIC REGIONS.**

Polaris Research and Development (Firm) A
baseline survey of AIDS risk behaviors and
attitudes in San Francisco's Black communities
/. San Francisco, Calif. [1987] vii, 74, [59]
leaves :   *NYPL [Sc F 88-232]*

Poletti Turrin, Cinzica. Minozzi, Maria Teresa.
Dizionario italiano-somalo /. Milano , 1961.
178 p. ;   *NYPL [Sc B 88-4]*

POLICE CORRUPTION - SOUTH AFRICA.
Bernstein, Hilda (Watts) No. 46 Steve Biko /.
London , 1978. 150 p., [4] p. of plates : ISBN
0-904759-21-0 :
DT779.8.B48 B47   *NYPL [JFD 79-52]*

**POLICE - JAMAICA - COMPLAINTS
AGAINST.**
The Jamaica Council for Human Rights speaks
[microform] [Kingston, Jamaica , 1981] 45 p. ;
NYPL [Sc Micro R-4132 no. 22]

The policy factor . Lofchie, Michael F. Boulder,
Colo. , Nairobi , c1989. xii, 235 p. : ISBN
1-555-87136-4 (alk. paper) : DDC 338.1/86762
19
HD2126.5.Z8 L64 1989
NYPL [Sc E 89-123]

**Political change and public opinion in Grenada
1979-1984** /. Emmanuel, Patrick. Cave Hill,
Barbados , c1986. xii, 173 p. :
NYPL [JLM 79-1223 no.19]

**The political class, the higher civil service and
the challenge of nation-building [microform]** /.
Adedeji, Adebayo. Addis Ababa, Ethiopia
[1981?] 24 p. ;   *NYPL [Sc Micro F-11062]*

Political economy in Haiti . Fass, Simon M. New
Brunswick, N.J., U. S. A. , c1988. xxxi, 369 p. ;
ISBN 0-88738-158-8 DDC 338.97294 19
HC153 .F37 1988   *NYPL [Sc E 88-423]*

The Political economy of Kenya / edited by
Michael G. Schatzberg. New York : Praeger,
1987. xix, 245 p., [1] leaf of plates : map ; 25
cm. (SAIS study on Africa) Papers from a conference
held in Apr. 1986 at the Johns Hopkins University
School of Advanced International Studies. Includes
index. Bibliography: p. [203]-236.   ISBN
0-275-92672-9 (alk. paper) :   DDC 330.9676/204
19
1. Kenya - Economic conditions - 1963- - Congresses.
2. Kenya - Social conditions - 1963- - Congresses. I.
Schatzberg, Michael G. II. Series.
HC865 .P65 1987   *NYPL [Sc E 88-157]*

**The Political economy of risk and choice in
Senegal** / edited by Mark Gersovitz and John
Waterbury. London, England ; Totowa, N.J. :
F. Cass, 1987. xv, 363 p. : ill. ; 24 cm. Includes
index. Bibliography: p. 327-343.   ISBN
0-7146-3297-X :   DDC 338.966/3 19
1. Senegal - Economic conditions. 2. Senegal -
Economic policy. I. Gersovitz, Mark. II. Waterbury,
John.
HC1045 .P65 1987   *NYPL [Sc E 87-360]*

A political economy of the African crisis /.
Onimode, Bade. London , Atlantic Highlands,
N.J. , 1988. 333 p. ; ISBN 0-86232-373-8 DDC
330.96/0328 19
HC800 .O55 1988   *NYPL [JLD 88-4614]*

**Political Economy of the World-System
Conference (9th : 1985 : Tulane University)**
Crises in the Caribbean basin . Beverly Hills
[Calif.] , c1987. 263 p. ; ISBN 0-8039-2808-4
DDC 330.9729 19
HC151 .C75 1986   *NYPL [JLD 87-3555]*

POLITICAL LEADERSHIP - NIGERIA.
Achebe, Chinua. The university and the
leadership factor in Nigerian politics /. Enugu,
Nigeria , c1988. 22 p. ; ISBN 978-226-907-7
     NYPL [Sc D 89-28]

**POLITICAL PARTICIPATION - NIGERIA,
NORTHERN - CASE STUDIES.**
Miles, William F. S. Elections in Nigeria .
Boulder, Colo. , c1988. 168 p. ; ISBN
1-555-87054-6 : DDC 324.9669/505 19
JQ3099.N66 E546 1987
     NYPL [JLE 88-3534]

POLITICAL PARTIES - ECUADOR.
Hurtado González, Jaime. Luchando por la
patria nueva . Quito , 1987. ii, 178 p. :
     NYPL [Sc D 88-679]

POLITICAL PARTIES - GRENADA.
Maurice Bishop Patriotic Movement. Manifesto
of the Maurice Bishop Patriotic Movement. St.
George's, Grenada [1984] 60 p. :
     NYPL [Sc D 88-676]

POLITICAL PARTIES - KENYA.
Teubert-Seiwert, Bärbel, 1951- Parteipolitik in
Kenya 1960-1969 /. Frankfurt am Main , New
York , c1987. 428 p. ; ISBN 3-8204-0151-2
DDC 324.2676/2 19
JQ2947.A979 .T48 1987
     NYPL [Sc D 88-1141]

POLITICAL PARTIES - MARTINIQUE.
Les Communistes expliquent . [Fort-de-France]
1978. 147 p. ;   *NYPL [Sc E 89-174]*

POLITICAL PARTIES - SENEGAL.
Senegal . Hamburg , 1983. xxxix, 392 p. :
ISBN 3-922887-28-7 (pbk.) DDC 324.266/3 19
JQ3396.A91 S38 1983 *NYPL [JLF 85-1341]*

POLITICAL PERSECUTION - GUINEA.
Bari, Nadine. Noces d'absence /. Paris , c1986.
119 p., [8] p. of plates : ISBN 2-227-12607-8
     NYPL [Sc D 89-61]

**POLITICAL PERSECUTION - ZAIRE -
LISALA (EQUATEUR)**
Schatzberg, Michael G. The dialectics of
oppression in Zaire /. Bloomington , c1988. x,
193 p., [1] p. of plates : ISBN 0-253-31703-7
DDC 323.4/9/0967513 19
JC599.Z282 L577 1988 *NYPL [Sc E 88-512]*

POLITICAL PLANNING - NIGERIA.
Nwankwo, Uchenna. Strategy for political
stability /. Lagos , 1988. ix, 310 p. ;
     NYPL [Sc D 89-539]

**POLITICAL PLANNING - NIGERIA -
CONGRESSES.**
Alternative political futures for Nigeria /.
Nigeria , 1987. xviii, 565 p. ; ISBN
978-303-170-8   *NYPL [Sc D 88-1374]*

POLITICAL PLANNING - TANZANIA.
Sokoïne, Edward Moringe, 1938-1984. Public
policy making and implementation in Tanzania
/. Pau [1986?] ix, 124 p. :
     NYPL [Sc E 88-319]

**POLITICAL PLATFORMS. see POLITICAL
PARTIES.**

POLITICAL PLAYS - NIGERIA.
Nwamuo, Chris. The prisoners /. Enugu , 1985.
x, 73 p. ; ISBN 978-250-304-5
     NYPL [Sc D 88-495]

POLITICAL POETRY - RÉUNION.
Kichenapanaïdou, Marc. Ma terre /.
Saint-Louis, Réunion [1978?] 43 p. ;
     NYPL [Sc D 88-484]

POLITICAL POETRY, ZIMBABWEAN.
Nyamubaya, Freedom T. V. On the road
again . Harare, Zimbabwe , 1986. 69 p. ; ISBN
0-949225-00-4 *NYPL [Sc C 88-136]*

**POLITICAL PRISIONERS - SOUTH
AFRICA - BIOGRAPHY.**

Makhoere, Caesarina Khana. No child's play .
London , 1988. 121 p. ; ISBN 0-7043-4111-5 :
     NYPL [Sc C 88-333]

POLITICAL PRISONERS - GUINEA.
Bari, Nadine. Noces d'absence /. Paris , c1986.
119 p., [8] p. of plates : ISBN 2-227-12607-8
     NYPL [Sc D 89-61]

Diallo, Amadou. La mort de Diallo Telli .
Paris , 1983. 154 p., [8] p. of plates : ISBN
2-86537-072-0 *NYPL [Sc D 88-316]*

**POLITICAL PRISONERS - KENYA -
DIARIES.**
Gakaara wa Wanjaũ. Mwandĩki wa Mau Mau
ithaamĩrio-inĩ /. Nairobi [Kenya] , 1983. xvii,
189 p. :   *NYPL [Sc D 87-156]*

Gakaara wa Wanjaũ. [Mwandĩki wa Mau Mau
ithaamĩrio-inĩ. English.] Mau Mau author in
detention /. Nairobi , 1988. xix, 252 p. ; ISBN
996-646-354-2 *NYPL [Sc D 89-444]*

**POLITICAL PRISONERS - SOUTH AFRICA -
BIOGRAPHY.**
Bernstein, Hilda (Watts) No. 46 Steve Biko /.
London , 1978. 150 p., [4] p. of plates : ISBN
0-904759-21-0 :
DT779.8.B48 B47   *NYPL [JFD 79-52]*

POLITICAL REFUGEES - MOZAMBIQUE.
Magaia, Lina. [Dumba nengue. English.] Dumba
nengue, run for your life . Trenton, N.J. , 1988.
113 p. : ISBN 0-86543-073-X
     NYPL [Sc D 88-1509]

**POLITICAL SCIENCE - STUDY AND
TEACHING - NIGERIA - ZARIA.**
The pedagogy of a decade of OAU
mock-summits at ABU. Zaria [1988] (Zaria :
Ahmadu Bello University Press) 64 p. : ISBN
978-301-130-12 *NYPL [Sc G 88-38]*

**POLITICAL SCIENCE - STUDY AND
TEACHING - SIMULATION METHODS.**
The pedagogy of a decade of OAU
mock-summits at ABU. Zaria [1988] (Zaria :
Ahmadu Bello University Press) 64 p. : ISBN
978-301-130-12 *NYPL [Sc G 88-38]*

POLITICAL SOCIALIZATION - NIGERIA.
Nwankwo, Uchenna. Strategy for political
stability /. Lagos , 1988. ix, 310 p. ;
     NYPL [Sc D 89-539]

Political values and local government in Nigeria
/. Gboyega, Alex. lagos , 1987. xii, 200 p. ;
ISBN 978-260-103-9
     NYPL [Sc D 88-1372]

**POLITICIANS - NEW YORK (N.Y.) -
BIOGRAPHY.**
Walter, John C. (John Christopher), 1933- The
Harlem Fox . Albany, N.Y. , c1989. xv, 287
p. : ISBN 0-88706-756-5 DDC 974.7/1043/0924 B
19
F128.5.J72 W35 1988 *NYPL [Sc E 89-107]*

POLITICIANS - NIGERIA - BIOGRAPHY.
Yemitan, Oladipo. Madame Tinubu . Ibadan ,
1987. x, 85 p. : ISBN 978-15-4985-9
     NYPL [Sc D 88-1382]

**POLITICIANS - ONTARIO - TORONTO -
BIOGRAPHY.**
Hubbard, Stephen, 1961- Against all odds .
Toronto , 1987. 140 p. : ISBN 1-550-02013-7
(bound) *NYPL [Sc D 88-985]*

**POLITICIANS - SOUTH AFRICA -
BIOGRAPHY.**
Gastrow, Shelagh. Who's who in South African
politics /. Johannesburg , 1985. xiv, 347 p. :
ISBN 0-86975-280-4 (pbk.) DDC 968.06/092/2
B 19
DT779.954 .G37 1985
     NYPL [Sc D 87-1109]

POLITICS AND EDUCATION - HAITI.
Jean, Rodrigue. Haiti, crise de l'education et
crise du développement /. Port-au-Prince,
Haiti , 1988. 152 p. : ISBN 0-948390-00-X
     NYPL [Sc D 88-914]

**POLITICS AND RELIGION. see RELIGION
AND POLITICS.**

Politics and the military in Uganda, 1890-1985 /.
Omara-Otunnu, Amii, 1952- Basingstoke,
Hampshire , 1987. xx, 218 p. : ISBN
0-333-41980-4 *NYPL [JFD 87-8644]*

Politics in Jamaica /. Payne, Anthony, 1952-
London , New York, N.Y. , 1988. xii, 196 p. :
ISBN 0-312-01869-X (St. Martin's) DDC 972.92

19
F1887 .P39 1988   *NYPL [Sc D 88-1230]*

The politics of AIDS /. Krieger, Nancy. Oakland,
CA , 19. 60 p. : ISBN 0-913781-06-1
     NYPL [Sc D 88-1299]

The politics of factory organization . Cheater,
Angela P. Gweru, Zimbabwe , c1986. xix, 156,
[1] p. : ISBN 0-86922-374-7
     NYPL [Sc D 88-671]

**The Politics of Latin American liberation
theology :** the challenge to U. S. public policy /
edited by Richard L. Rubenstein and John K.
Roth ; foreword by Dave Durenburger.
Washington, D.C. : Washington Institute Press,
c1988. xxi, 360 p. ; 24 cm. Includes index.
Bibliography: p. 325-348. ISBN 0-88702-039-9 :
DDC 261.7/09181/2 19
*1. United States - Economic policy - 1981-. 2. United
States - Foreign relations - Latin America. 3. Latin
America - Foreign relations - United States. I.
Rubenstein, Richard L. II. Roth, John K.*
BT83.57 .P643 1988   *NYPL [Sc E 89-75]*

**The politics of "scholarship" in Black intellectual
discourse [microform] .** Newsum, H. E., 1951-
1977 116 leaves. *NYPL [Sc Micro R-4689]*

POLLS. see ELECTIONS; VOTING.

POLYGAMY.
'Isá 'Abd Allāh Muḥammad al-Mahdī, 1945-
Islamic marriage ceremony and polygamy
[microform] /. Brooklyn , c1977. 30 p. :
     NYPL [Sc Micro R-4114 no.1]

Polygyny and Polyandry . Kalejaiye, Dipo.
London , 1985. 55 p. ; ISBN 0-333-35822-8
     NYPL [Sc D 88-1049]

Pomerance, Alan. Repeal of the blues / by Alan
Pomerance. Secaucus, N.J. : Citadel Press,
c1988. x, 264 p., [16] p. of plates : ill., ports. ;
24 cm. Includes index. Bibliography: p. 252-254
ISBN 0-8065-1105-2 : DDC 792/.08996073 19
*1. Afro-Americans in the performing arts. 2.
Afro-Americans - History - 1877-1964. 3. United
States - Race relations. I. Title.*
PN1590.B53 P6 1988 *NYPL [Sc E 89-90]*

Pomerantz, Charlotte. The chalk doll / by
Charlotte Pomerantz ; pictures by Frané Lessac.
lst ed. New York : Lippincott , c1989. 30 p. :
col. ill. ; 27 cm. Rosy's mother remembers the
pleasures of her childhood in Jamaica and the very
special dolls she used to play with. SCHOMBURG
CHILDREN'S COLLECTION. ISBN 0-397-32318-2 :
DDC [E] 19
*1. Dolls - Juvenile fiction. 2. Mothers and daughters -
Juvenile fiction. 3. Jamaica - Juvenile fiction. I. Lessac,
Frané, ill. II. Schomburg Children's Collection. III.
Title.*
PZ7.P77 Ch 1989   *NYPL [Sc F 89-175]*

Pomeroy, William J., 1916- Apartheid,
imperialism, and African freedom / William J.
Pomeroy. New York : International Publishers,
1986. ix, 259 p. : ill. ; 23 cm. Includes index.
ISBN 0-7178-0640-5 : DDC 305.8/00968 19
*1. Apartheid - South Africa. 2. Apartheid - Namibia. 3.
United States - Foreign relations - South Africa. 4.
South Africa - Foreign relations - United States. 5.
United States - Foreign relations - Namibia. 6.
Namibia - Foreign relations - United States. I. Title.*
E183.8.S6 P65 1986   *NYPL [Sc D 88-1147]*

Pommier, Sophie. Thomas, Michel. [Histoire d'un
art. English.] Textile art /. Geneva,
Switzerland , New York, NY , 1985. 279 p. :
ISBN 0-8478-0640-5 (Rizzoli) : DDC 746 19
NK8806 .T4813 1985
     NYPL [3-MON+ 86-527]

Pons, François Raymond Joseph de, 1751-1812.
Voyage à la partie orientale de la Terre-Ferme,
dans l'Amérique Méridionale, fait pendant les
années 1801, 1802, 1803 et 1804: contenant la
description de la capitainerie générale de
Caráccas, composée des provinces de Vénézuéla,
Maracaíbo, Varinas, la Guiane Espagnole,
Cumana, et de l'île de la Marguerite ... Par F.
Depons ... Avec une carte géographique, et les
plans de la ville capitale et des ports principaux.
Paris, Colnet [etc.] 1806. 3 v. fold. maps. 21
cm.
*1. Catholic Church - South America. 2. Indians of
South America - Venezuela. 3. Venezuela. 4. Spain -
Colonies - South America. 5. Spain - Commercial
policy. I. Title.*
F2311 .P79   *NYPL [Sc Rare F 88-77]*

Poole, Stafford. Church and slave in Perry County, Missouri, 1818-1865 / Stafford Poole and Douglas J. Slawson. Lewiston, N.Y., USA : E. Mellen Press, c1986. xvii, 251 p. : ill. ; 24 cm. (Studies in American religion . v. 22) Includes indexes. Bibliography: p. [223]-228. ISBN 0-88946-666-1 (alk. paper) : DDC 306/.362/09778694 19
1. Catholic Church - Missouri - Perry County - History - 19th century. 2. Slavery - Missouri - Perry County. 3. Slavery and the church - Catholic Church. 4. Perry County (Mo.) - Race relations. I. Slawson, Douglas J. II. Title.
E445.M67 P66 1986   *NYPL [Sc E 89-102]*

POOR - AFRICA.
Katapu, Agbeko. Workable strategies to end Africa's poverty . Syracuse, N.Y. , c1986. xxiv, 288 p. : ISBN 0-944338-00-3 DDC 338.96 19
HC800 .K37 1988   *NYPL [Sc D 89-610]*

Nafziger, E. Wayne. Inequality in Africa . Cambridge [Cambridgeshire] , New York , c1988. xii, 204 p. : ISBN 0-521-26881-8 DDC 339.2/096 19
HC800.Z9 I5136 1988   *NYPL [Sc E 88-521]*

POOR - AFRICA, SOUTHERN.
Poverty, policy, and food security in southern Africa /. Boulder , 1988. xii, 291 p. : ISBN 1-555-87092-9 (lib. bdg.) : DDC 363.8/56/0968 19
HD9017.A26 P68 1988 *NYPL [Sc E 88-355]*

The poor and the powerless . Thomas, Clive Yolande. New York , 1988. xv, 396 p. : ISBN 0-85345-743-3 : DDC 338.9/009729 19
HC151 .T56 1988   *NYPL [Sc D 88-763]*

POOR - CARIBBEAN AREA - HISTORY.
Ward, J. R. Poverty and progress in the Caribbean, 1800-1960 /. Houndmills, Basingstoke, Hampshire , 1985. 82 p. : ISBN 0-333-37212-3 (pbk.) DDC 330.9729 19
HC151 .W37 1985   *NYPL [JLD 86-2144]*

POOR CHILDREN - NEW YORK (N.Y.) - CASE STUDIES - JUVENILE LITERATURE.
Kaufman, Curt. Hotel boy /. New York , c1987. 40 p. : ISBN 0-689-31287-3 : DDC 307.3/36 19
HV4046.N6 K38 1987   *NYPL [Sc F 88-362]*

POOR - HEALTH AND HYGIENE.
Hendricks, Leo E. The effect of family size, child spacing and family density on stress in low income Black mothers and their preadolescent children [microform] /. 1977. 156 leaves.   *NYPL [Sc Micro R-4684]*

POOR - UNITED STATES.
Herzog, Elizabeth. About the poor . [Washington] , 1967 [i.e. 1968] 85 p. DDC 362.5/0973
HC110.P6 H47   *NYPL [Sc E 88-67]*

POOR WOMEN - DEVELOPING COUNTRIES - JUVENILE LITERATURE.
Fisher, Maxine P., 1948- Women in the Third World /. New York , 1989. 176 p. : ISBN 0-531-10666-7 DDC 305.4/09172/4 19
HQ1870.9 .F57 1989   *NYPL [Sc E 89-223]*

Popoola, Dimeji. A matter of upbringing / Dimeji Popoola. Ibadan : University Press Limited, c1987. v. 133 p. ; 18 cm. ISBN 0-19-575759-9 (Outside Nigeria)
1. Nigeria - Fiction. I. Title.
                   NYPL [Sc c 88-173]

Popular festivals in Brazil. Gonzalez, Lélia. Festas populares no Brasil =. Rio de Janeiro, Brasil , c1987. 144 p. : ISBN 85-7083-015-7
GT4833.A2 G66x 1987 *NYPL [Sc F 89-116]*

Popular Movement for the Liberation of Angola. see Movimento Popular de Libertação de Angola.

POPULAR MUSIC - CUBA - RELIGIOUS ASPECTS.
Castellanos, Isabel, 1939- Elegua quiere tambó . Cali, Colombia , 1983. 84 p. ;
                   NYPL [Sc D 88-534]

POPULAR MUSIC - IVORY COAST - HISTORY AND CRITICISM.
La Chanson populaire en Côte-d'Ivoire . Paris , c1986. 342 p., [12] p. of plates : ISBN 2-7087-0470-2 *NYPL [Sc D 88-1099]*

POPULAR MUSIC - LATIN AMERICA - HISTORY AND CRITICISM.
Bergman, Billy. Hot sauces . New York ,

c1985. 144 p. : ISBN 0-688-02193-X (pbk.) : DDC 780/.42/09729 19
ML3475 .B47 1985   *NYPL [Sc F 87-19]*

POPULAR MUSIC - UNITED STATES - HISTORY AND CRITICISM.
Bergman, Billy. Hot sauces . New York , c1985. 144 p. : ISBN 0-688-02193-X (pbk.) : DDC 780/.42/09729 19
ML3475 .B47 1985   *NYPL [Sc F 87-19]*

Jasen, David A. Tin Pan Alley . New York , c1988. xxiv, 312 p., [32] p. of plates : ISBN 1-556-11099-5 : DDC 784.5/00973 19
ML3477 .J34 1988   *NYPL [Sc E 88-562]*

POPULAR MUSIC - WEST INDIES - HISTORY AND CRITICISM.
Bergman, Billy. Hot sauces . New York , c1985. 144 p. : ISBN 0-688-02193-X (pbk.) : DDC 780/.42/09729 19
ML3475 .B47 1985   *NYPL [Sc F 87-19]*

POPULAR MUSIC - ZIMBABWE - HISTORY AND CRITICISM.
Zindi, Fred. Roots rocking in Zimbabwe /. Gweru, Zimbabwe , 1985. viii, 98 p., [32] p. of plates : ISBN 0-86922-360-7
                   NYPL [Sc D 88-1323]

Popular musicians. Horricks, Raymond, 1933- Quincy Jones /. Tunbridge Wells, Kent , New York , 1985. 127 p., [8] p. of plates : ISBN 0-87052-215-9 (Hippocrene Books) : DDC 785.42/092/4 B 19
ML419.J7 H67 1985   *NYPL [Sc E 87-36]*

POPULATION - CONGRESSES.
West African Seminar on Population Studies, University of Ghana, 1972. Interdisciplinary approaches to population studies . Legon , 1975. ix, 333 p. :
HB21 .W38 1972   *NYPL [JLD 78-861]*

POPULATION, FOREIGN. see EMIGRATION AND IMMIGRATION.

POPULATION RESEARCH.
Orubuloye, I. O. (Israel Olatunji), 1947- Introduction to population analysis /. Ibadan , 1986. 106 p. : ISBN 978-224-111-3
                   NYPL [Sc D 88-1417]

POPULATION RESEARCH - AFRICA, WEST - CONGRESSES.
West African Seminar on Population Studies, University of Ghana, 1972. Interdisciplinary approaches to population studies . Legon , 1975. ix, 333 p. :
HB21 .W38 1972   *NYPL [JLD 78-861]*

POPULATION - STATISTICS.
Orubuloye, I. O. (Israel Olatunji), 1947- Introduction to population analysis /. Ibadan , 1986. 106 p. : ISBN 978-224-111-3
                   NYPL [Sc D 88-1417]

Population Studies, West African Seminar on. see West African Seminar on Population Studies, University of Ghana, 1972.

Por um futuro melhor /. Savimbi, Jonas Malheiro. Lisboa , 1986. 192 p. : DDC 967/.304 19
DT611.8 .S28 1986   *NYPL [Sc D 88-771]*

Por uma educacão libertáda e libertadora . Mattos, Edgar, 1935- Recife , 1986. 89 p. : ISBN 85-7019-098-0 *NYPL [Sc D 88-845]*

The porcelain cat /. Hearn, Michael Patrick. Boston [1987?]. [32] p. : ISBN 0-316-35330-2 (pbk.) :   *NYPL [Sc F 88-220]*

Pork rind and Cuban songs /. Medina, Pablo. Washington [1975] 69 p. ; DDC 811/.5/4
PS3563.E24 P6   *NYPL [Sc D 88-327]*

PORPOISES - JUVENILE FICTION.
Edwards, Sally. Isaac and Snow. New York [1973] 123 p. : ISBN 0-698-20244-9 DDC [Fic]
PZ7.E265 Is3   *NYPL [Sc D 88-1419]*

Port Hudson, Confederate bastion on the Mississippi /. Hewitt, Lawrence L. Baton Rouge , c1987. xvi, 221 p. : ISBN 0-8071-1351-4 DDC 973.7/33 19
E475.42 .H49 1987   *NYPL [IKE 88-1592]*

PORT HUDSON (LA.) - HISTORY - SIEGE, 1863.
Hewitt, Lawrence L. Port Hudson, Confederate bastion on the Mississippi /. Baton Rouge , c1987. xvi, 221 p. : ISBN 0-8071-1351-4 DDC 973.7/33 19
E475.42 .H49 1987   *NYPL [IKE 88-1592]*

Porter, A. N. (Andrew N.) British imperial policy and decolonization, 1938-64 / A.N. Porter and A.J. Stockwell. New York : St. Martin's Press, 1987- v. ; 23 cm. Includes index. Bibliography: v. 1, p. 379-393 CONTENTS. - v. 1. 1938-51. ISBN 0-312-00554-7 (v. 1) : DDC 325/.31/41 19
1. Decolonization - History. 2. Great Britain - Colonies - Administration - History. I. Stockwell, A. J. II. Title.
JV1018 .P66 1987   *NYPL [Sc D 88-219]*

PORTER, CHARLES ETHAN, 1847?-1923.
Charles Ethan Porter,1847?-1923. Marlborough, CT , 1987. 113 p. : ISBN 0-9619196-0-4
                   NYPL [Sc F 88-26]

Porter, David L., 1941- Biographical dictionary of American sports. Football /. New York , 1987. xvii, 763 p. ; ISBN 0-313-25771-X (lib. bdg. : alk. paper) DDC 796.332/092/2 B 19
GV939.A1 B56 1987
                   *NYPL [*R-MVFF 88-6690]*

Porter, Horace A., 1950- Stealing the fire : the art and protest of James Baldwin / Horace A. Porter.1st ed. Middletown, Conn. : Wesleyan University Press ; Scranton, Pa. : Distributed by Harper & Row, c1989. xviii, 220 p. ; 23 cm. Includes index. Bibliography: p. 191-212. ISBN 0-8195-5197-X : DDC 818/.5409 19
1. Baldwin, James, 1924- - Criticism and interpretation. I. Title.
PS3552.A45 Z85 1989 *NYPL [Sc D 89-468]*

Portland Art Museum (Or.) Museum voor Volkenkunde (Rotterdam, Netherlands) Expressions of belief . New York , 1988. 248 p. : ISBN 0-8478-0959-5 : DDC 730 19
N5310.75.H68 M876 1988
                   NYPL [Sc G 88-37]

Portrait of a nude woman as Cleopatra /. Chase-Riboud, Barbara. New York , c1987. 110 p. : ISBN 0-688-06403-5 : DDC 811/.54 19
PS3553.H336 P6 1987 *NYPL [Sc D 88-329]*

PORTRAIT SCULPTURE, ANCIENT - EGYPT - EXHIBITIONS.
Spanel, Donald, 1952- Through ancient eyes . Birmingham, AL , 1988. xiii, 159 p. : DDC 732/.8 19
NB1296.2 .S63 1988
                   NYPL [3-MAE 88-3366]

PORTRAIT SCULPTURE, EGYPTIAN - EXHIBITIONS.
Spanel, Donald, 1952- Through ancient eyes . Birmingham, AL , 1988. xiii, 159 p. : DDC 732/.8 19
NB1296.2 .S63 1988
                   NYPL [3-MAE 88-3366]

Portraits of New Orleans jazz. Martinez, Raymond J. (Raymond Joseph), 1889- New Orleans [1971] 63 p. DDC 785.4/2/0976335
ML200.8.N48 M4   *NYPL [Sc D 87-69]*

Portugal.
Regulamento do trabalho dos indigenas, approvado por decreto de 9 de novembro de 1899 [microform] Lisboa : Imprensa Nacional, 1899. 27 p. ; 23 cm. At head of title: Ministério dos Negocios da Marinha e Ultramar. Microfiche. New York: New York Public Library, 198 . 1 microfiche: negative; 11 x 15 cm. (FSN Sc 019,037)
1. Labor laws and legislation - Portugal - Colonies. I. Portugal. Ministerio da Marinha e Ultramar. II. Title.
                  NYPL [Sc Micro F-10926]

PORTUGAL - COMMERCIAL POLICY - HISTORY.
Miller, Joseph Calder. Way of death . Madison, Wis. , c1988. xxx, 770 p. : ISBN 0-299-11560-7 : DDC 382/.44/09469 19
HT1221 .M55 1988   *NYPL [Sc E 89-105]*

Portugal. Cortes. Documentos relativos ao apresamento, julgamento e entrega da barca franceza Charles et Georges . Lisboa , 1858. 249, 16 p. ;   *NYPL [Sc Rare G 86-1]*

Portugal. Laws, statutes etc. Companhia do Nyassa [microform] ; decretos, portarias, regulamentos e mais diplomas relativos a esta companhia. Lisboa, Imprensa Nacional, 1897. 89 p. 24 cm. At head of title: Ministerio da Marinha e Ultramar. Microfilm. New York : New York Public Library, 198 . 1 microfilm reel ; 35 mm. (MN *ZZ-28635)
1. Companhia do Nyassa. 2. Niassa, Mozambique (Province). 3. Mozambique - History. I. Portugal.

Ministerio da Marinha e Ultramar. II. Title.
JV4229.M7C785
                    NYPL [Sc Micro R-4840 no.10]

Portugal. Marinha e Ultramar, Ministerio da. see Portugal. Ministerio da Marinha e Ultramar.

Portugal. Ministerio da Marinha e Ultramar.
Portugal. Regulamento do trabalho dos indigenas, approvado por decreto de 9 de novembro de 1899 [microform] Lisboa , 1899. 27 p. ;   *NYPL [Sc Micro F-10926]*
Portugal. Laws, statutes etc. Companhia do Nyassa [microform] . Lisboa, 1897. 89 p.
JV4229.M7C785
                    NYPL [Sc Micro R-4840 no.10]

Portugal. Ministerio dos Negocios da Marinha e Ultramar. see Portugal. Ministerio da Marinha e Ultramar.

Portugal. Statutes. see Portugal. Laws, statutes etc.

A Portuguese-English dictionary. Taylor, James Lumpkin, 1892- Stanford, Calif., 1970 [c1958] xx, 655 p. ISBN 0-8047-0480-5 DDC 469/.3/21
PC5333 .T3 1970   *NYPL [Sc E 81-99]*

PORTUGUESE LANGUAGE - DICTIONARIES - ENGLISH.
Taylor, James Lumpkin, 1892- A Portuguese-English dictionary. Stanford, Calif., 1970 [c1958] xx, 655 p. ISBN 0-8047-0480-5 DDC 469/.3/21
PC5333 .T3 1970   *NYPL [Sc E 81-99]*

PORTUGUESE LANGUAGE - IDIOMS, CORRECTIONS, ERRORS.
Cascudo, Luís de Câmara, 1898- Locuções tradicionais no Brasil . Belo Horizonte , São Paulo , 1986. 314 p. :   *NYPL [Sc D 87-923]*

PORTUGUESE LITERATURE - BRAZIL. see BRAZILIAN LITERATURE.

The positions, roles, and perceptions of Black elected public school board members in Mississippi [microform] /. Hust, Mildred Hudgins. 1977. 144 leaves.
                    NYPL [Sc Micro R-4215]

Les possédés de la pleine lune /. Fignolé, Jean Claude. Paris , c1987. 220 p. ; ISBN 2-02-009535-1   *NYPL [JFD 88-532]*

A post in the military government /. Ogbobine, R. A. I. (Rufus A. I.) [Benin City, Nigeria] 159 p. ; ISBN 978-300-455-7
                    NYPL [Sc C 89-48]

POSTAGE-STAMPS - TOPICS - AFRO-AMERICANS.
Johnson, Glenderlyn. Black American pioneers . New York, N.Y. , c1987. ii, 22 p. :
                    NYPL [Sc D 88-1284]

POSTAGE-STAMPS - UNITED STATES.
Johnson, Glenderlyn. Black American pioneers . New York, N.Y. , c1987. ii, 22 p. :
                    NYPL [Sc D 88-1284]

The Postwar world.
Hargreaves, John D. Decolonization in Africa /. London , New York , 1988. xvi, 263 p. : ISBN 0-582-49150-9 DDC 960/.32 19
DT29 .H37 1988   *NYPL [Sc D 89-315]*

Potekhin, I. I. (Ivan Izosimovich), 1903-1964.
African problems: analysis of eminent Soviet scientist [by] I. I. Potekhin. Moscow, "Nauka" Publishing House, 1968. 141 p. 20 cm. At head of title: U. S.S. R. Academy of Sciences. Institute of Africa. Bibliographical footnotes. DDC 320.9/6
1. Africa. I. Institut Afriki (Akademiia nauk SSSR). II. Title.
DT30 .P59   *NYPL [Sc C 88-86]*

Potter, Edwin. The history of the penal system in the Virgin Islands / by Edwin Potter. [Charlotte Amalie? : s.n., between 1985 and 1988] 69 leaves : ill., facsims., ports. ; 29 cm. Cover title.
1. Correction institutions - Virgin Islands of the United States. 2. Crime and criminals - Virgin Islands of the United States. I. Title. *NYPL [Sc F 88-136]*

Potter, Robert B. Barbados / Robert B. Potter, Graham M.S. Dann. Oxford, England ; Santa Barbara, Calif. : Clio Press, c1987. xxxix, 356 p., [1] leaf of plates : map ; 23 cm. (World bibliographical series. v. 76) Includes index. ISBN 1-85109-022-3
1. Barbados - Bibliography. I. Dann, Graham. II. Title.
                    NYPL [HRG 87-2371]

POTTERY - AFRICA - EXHIBITIONS.
African heritage . Cape Town , 1987. 24 p. :
                    NYPL [Sc F 89-117]

POTTERY - ZAMBIA.
Lorenz, Bente. Traditional Zambian pottery /. London , 1989. 47 p. : ISBN 0-905788-75-3
                    NYPL [Sc C 89-141]

Potts, Richard, 1953- Early hominid activities at Olduvai / Richard Potts. New York : A. de Gruyter, c1988. xi, 396 p. : ill. ; 24 cm. (Foundations of human behavior) Includes index. Bibliography: p. 313-332. ISBN 0-202-01176-3 (lib. bdg.) DDC 967.8 19
1. Paleolithic period, Lower - Tanzania - Olduvai Gorge. 2. Animal remains (Archaeology) - Tanzania - Olduvai Gorge. 3. Olduvai Gorge (Tanzania) - Antiquities. 4. Tanzania - Antiquities. I. Title. II. Series.
GN772.42.T34 P67 1988
                    NYPL [Sc E 89-92]

POUL LANGUAGE. see FULAH LANGUAGE.

Pour Cabral . Symposium Amilcar Cabral (1983 : Praia, Cape Verde) Paris , 1987. 486 p. ; ISBN 2-7087-0482-6   *NYPL [Sc D 87-1429]*

Pour l'Afrique /. Pisani, Edgard. Paris , 1988. 251 p. ; ISBN 2-7381-0026-0 *NYPL [Sc D 88-249]*

Pour l'Afrique, j'accuse . Dumont, René, 1904- [Paris] , c1986. 457 p., [48] p. of plates : ISBN 2-259-01455-0
HC1002 .D85 1986   *NYPL [Sc D 88-642]*

Pour mon plaisir et pour ma peine /. Bernardin, Antoine. Port-au-Prince, Haiti [19]88. 163 p. ;
                    NYPL [Sc D 88-10003]

Pourquoi les campêches saignent-ils? /. Godart, Jacques. Port-au-Prince , 1987. 199 p. ;
                    NYPL [Sc D 88-514]

Pourrir. Cabort-Masson, Guy, 1937- Pourrir, ou, Martyr un peu /. [Martinique] , c1987. 252 p. : DDC 843/.914 19
PQ3949.2.C27 P68 1987
                    NYPL [Sc D 89-527]

Pourrir, ou, Martyr un peu /. Cabort-Masson, Guy, 1937- [Martinique] , c1987. 252 p. : DDC 843/.914 19
PQ3949.2.C27 P68 1987
                    NYPL [Sc D 89-527]

Pouvoir et droit au Rwanda . Reyntjens, Filip. Tervuren, Belgique , 1985. 584 p. ;
                    NYPL [Sc E 87-668]

Pouvoir, lutte de classes, idéologie et milieu intellectuel africain. /. N'Da, Paul, 1945- Paris , c1987. 107 p. ; ISBN 2-7087-0485-0
                    NYPL [Sc D 88-918]

Pouvoir noir en Haiti : l'explosion de 1946 / [sous la direction de Frantz Voltaire].1e ed. Québec : V & R éditeurs, les éditions du CIDIHCA, 1988. 393 p., 7 p. of plates : ill., ports. ; 22 cm. Includes index. Bibliography: p. [377]-380. ISBN 2-920862-11-1
1. Haiti - Politics and government - 1934-1971. I. Voltaire, Frantz.   *NYPL [Sc D 89-482]*

Pouvoirs et sociétés dans l'Afrique des grands lacs / Université du Burundi, Faculté des lettres et sciences humaines, Département d'histoire. Bujumbura : Le Département, 1986. 146 p. ; 29 cm. (Cahiers d'histoire. 3 (1985)) Cover title: Sociétés et pouvoirs dans l'Afrique des grands lacs. Includes bibliographical references.
1. Africa, Sub-Saharan - History. I. Title: Sociétés et pouvoirs dans l'Afrique des grands lacs. II. Series. III. Series: Cahiers d'histoire (Université du Burundi. Dép. d'histoire) , 3 (1985). *NYPL [Sc F 89-62]*

Poverty and politics . Hahner, June Edith, 1940- Albuquerque , 1986. xvi, 415 p. : ISBN 0-8263-0878-3 : DDC 305.5/69/0981 19
HC190.P6 H34 1986   *NYPL [JLE 86-4407]*

Poverty and progress in the Caribbean, 1800-1960 /. Ward, J. R. Houndmills, Basingstoke, Hampshire , 1985. 82 p. : ISBN 0-333-37212-3 (pbk.) DDC 330.9729 19
HC151 .W37 1985   *NYPL [JLD 86-2144]*

POVERTY - MATHEMATICAL MODELS.
Greer, Joel William, 1948- Food poverty and consumption patterns in Kenya / Geneva , 1986. xii, 170 p. : ISBN 92-2-105374-1 (pbk.) : DDC 338.1/9/6762 19
HD9017.K42 G74 1986
                    NYPL [JLE 87-3435]

Poverty, policy, and food security in southern Africa / edited by Coralie Bryant. Boulder : L. Rienner, 1988. xii, 291 p. : maps ; 24 cm. Includes bibliographical references and index. ISBN 1-555-87092-9 (lib. bdg.) : DDC 363.8/56/0968 19
1. Food supply - Africa, Southern. 2. Poor - Africa, Southern. 3. Apartheid - South Africa. 4. Africa, Southern - Economic policy. 5. South Africa - Foreign relations - Africa, Southern. 6. Africa, Southern - Foreign relations - South Africa. I. Bryant, Coralie.
HD9017.A26 P68 1988 NYPL [Sc E 88-355]

Powe, Edward L. (Edward Llewellyn), 1941- The adventures of Dan Aiki / Edward L. Powe ; illustrated by Kenneth M. Morris. Paterson, N.J. : Dan Aiki Publications, c1987. 32 p. : ill. ; 21 cm. (Adventures of Dan Aiki . bk. 1) With autograph of author. SCHOMBURG CHILDREN'S COLLECTION.
1. Hausas - Juvenile poetry. I. Morris, kenneth M. II. Schomburg Children's Collection. III. Title.
                    NYPL [Sc D 88-489]

POWELL, ADAM CLAYTON, 1908-1972 - JUVENILE LITERATURE.
Jakoubek, Robert E. Adam Clayton Powell, Jr. /. New York , c1988. xiv, 252 p. ; ISBN 1-555-46606-0 DDC 973/.0496073024 B 92 19
E748.P86 J35 1988   *NYPL [Sc E 88-372]*

The power in you . Amos, Wally. New York , c1988. xiii, 217 p. ; ISBN 1-556-11093-6 :
                    NYPL [Sc D 89-266]

Power, Jonathan, 1941- Western Europe's migrant workers / by Jonathan Power in collaboration with Anna Hardman. [Rev. 1984 ed.] London : Minority Rights Group, 1984. 35 p. : ill., map ; 30 cm. (Report - Minority Rights Group ; no. 28 0305-6252) "Revised by Carina Byrne-Varain and Kaye Stearman." Bibliography: p. 34. ISBN 0-08-030831-7
1. Alien labor - Europe. 2. Migrant labor - Europe. 3. Europe - Emigration and immigration. I. Hardman, Anna. II. Series: Report (Minority Rights Group) , no. 28. III. Title.   *NYPL [Sc F 88-231]*

POWER RESOURCES - AFRICA, EAST.
Amann, Hans. Energy supply and economic development in East Africa. München, (1969). 254 p. with maps, 7 inserts (in pocket) DDC 333
HD9557.A32 A6   *NYPL [Sc E 88-226]*

POWER (SOCIAL SCIENCES) - CONGRESSES.
Race, class, and power in Brazil /. Los Angeles , c1985. xi, 160 p. ; ISBN 0-934934-22-3 : DDC 305.8/96/081 19
F2659.N4 R24 1985   *NYPL [JLE 88-2671]*

POWER SUPPLY. see POWER RESOURCES.

The powerful bond . Dickson, Mora, 1918- London , 1980. 5-252 p. : ISBN 0-234-72103-0 : DDC 266/.963 B 19
BV3625.S5 K393 1980   *NYPL [Sc D 87-37]*

Practical exercises in Nigerian history /. Thomas, Howell. Ibadan , 1966. 104 p. :
                    NYPL [Sc E 88-598]

Pratiques th´eoretiques.
Meillassoux, Claude. Anthropologie de l'esclavage . Paris , c1986. 375 p. ; ISBN 2-13-039480-9   *NYPL [Sc D 88-768]*

Pratiques théoriques.
Sala-Molins, Louis. Le Code noir, ou, Le calvaire de Canaan /. Paris , c1987. 292 p. : ISBN 2-13-039970-3 : DDC 346.4401/3 344.40613 19
KJV4534 .S25 1987   *NYPL [Sc D 88-136]*

Pratos da Bahia e outras especialidades /. Papeta. Rio de Janeiro , 1979. 202 p. :
                    NYPL [Sc D 88-294]

PRATT, KOFOWORULA ABENI.
Akinsanya, Justus A. An African "Florence Nightingale" . Ibadan, Nigeria , 1987. xii, 224 p. : ISBN 978-245-826-0 (hard back ed.)
                    NYPL [Sc D 88-895]

Pratt, Simon. Secondary level teachers: supply and demand in tanzania. [Edited by] John W. Hanson. [East Lansing, Institute for International Studies in Education, Michigan State University, 1969] xii, 79 p. 28 cm. (Report on the supply of secondary level teachers in English-speaking Africa. no. 8) Bibliography: p. 79.
1. High school teachers - Supply and demand -

Tanzania. I. Title. II. Series.
NYPL [JFM 72-62 no. 8]

PRAYER (ISLAM)
Karim, Darnell. The five prayers step by step /.
[Chicago] [1987] vi, 202 p. :
NYPL [Sc F 89-160]

**Préalables à la reconstruction du
proto-tchadique** : Groupe de travail sur les
langues tchadiques, Ivry, 22-24 septembre 1977
/ éditeurs, Jean-Pierre Caprile et Herrmann
Jungraithmayr. Paris : SELAF, 1978. 210 p. ;
24 cm. (LACITO-documents. Afrique . 2) English and
French text with pref. in French and German. Title on
spine: Reconstruction du proto-tchadique. "LP 3.121 du
CNRS, Programme Ju 34/19 de la DFG." Includes
bibliographical references. ISBN 2-85297-022-8
DDC 493/.7 19
*1. Chadic languages - Congresses. I. Caprile, Jean
Pierre. II. Jungraithmayr, Herrmann. III. Groupe de
travail sur les langues tchadiques (France). IV. Title:
Reconstruction du proto-tchadique. V. Series.*
PL8026.C53 P73 1978 NYPL [Sc E 88-418]

Précis grammatical de sérère /. Faye, Waly Coly.
[Dakar] , 1980. 80 leaves ;
NYPL [Sc F 86-168]

**Précis historique de la révolution de
Saint-Domingue [microform]**. Clausson, L. J.
Paris, 1819. xij, 155 p.
NYPL [Sc Micro R-3541]

Pre-colonial history of Amokwe /. Onyia,
Nathaniel Maduabuchi. Enugu, Nigeria , 1987.
95 p. : ISBN 978-239-618-4
NYPL [Sc D 89-53]

**PREHISTORIC ANTIQUITIES. see MAN,
PREHISTORIC.**

**PREHISTORIC ART. see ART,
PREHISTORIC.**

**PREHISTORIC FAUNA. see
PALEONTOLOGY.**

**PREHISTORIC MAN. see MAN,
PREHISTORIC.**

The prehistory of eastern Zambia /. Phillipson,
D. W. Nairobi , 1976. xi, 229 p., [21] leaves of
plates (5 fold.) : ISBN 0-500-97003-3 :
GN865.Z3 P48 NYPL [JFF 79-1585]

PREJUDICES IN CHILDREN.
Aboud, Frances E. Children and prejudice /.
Oxford [Oxfordshire] , New York, NY , 1988.
x, 149 p. : ISBN 0-631-14939-2 : DDC 305.2/3
19
BF723.P75 A24 1988 NYPL [Sc E 89-57]

**A preliminary survey of avenues for and
constraints on women's involvement in the
development process in Kenya [microform]** /.
Pala, Achola O. [Nairobi? , 1975] 26 p. ;
NYPL [Sc Micro R-4108 no.14]

**Prèmiere rencontre africaine UNIAPAC,
Kinshasa, 7-9 juillet, 1969.** L'Entreprise et ses
dirigeants dans le développement économique
de l'Afrique noire . Kinshasa [1969?] 89 p. :
NYPL [Sc F 88-100]

**Premières mesures de mise en application du
programme du CMRN.** Guinea. Comité
militaire de redressement national. [Conakry,
R.G. , 1984] 84 p. ;
HD2143.Z8 G85 1984 NYPL [Sc E 88-306]

Prentice Alvin /. Card, Orson Scott. New York,
NY , 1989. x, 342 p. : ISBN 0-312-93141-7 :
DDC 813/.54 19
PS3553.A655 P74 1989
NYPL [JFE 88-3128]

PREPARATORY SCHOOLS - NIGERIA.
King's College (Lagos, Nigeria) 75 years of
King's College /. [Lagos?] 1987. vi, 89 p. :
NYPL [Sc E 88-257]

**Prerequisites of manpower and educational
planning in Ghana** /. Abban, J. B. Accra ,
1986. xii, 144 p. ; ISBN 996-496-307-6
NYPL [Sc D 89-496]

PRESBYTERIAN CHURCH IN CAMEROON.
Wonyu, Eugène, 1933- Le chrétien, les dons et
la mission dans l'église africaine indépendant .
Douala , 1979. 68 p. ; DDC 285 19
BX9162.C35 W66 NYPL [Sc D 88-1399]

**PRESBYTERIAN CHURCH - MISSIONS -
NIGERIA.**
Johnston, Geoffrey. Of God and maxim guns .
Waterloo, Ontario, Canada , 1988. 321 p. :

ISBN 0-88920-180-3 (pbk.)
NYPL [Sc D 88-1229]

**PRESBYTERIAN CHURCH - NIGERIA -
HISTORY.**
Johnston, Geoffrey. Of God and maxim guns .
Waterloo, Ontario, Canada , 1988. 321 p. :
ISBN 0-88920-180-3 (pbk.)
NYPL [Sc D 88-1229]

**PRESBYTERIAN CHURCH - NIGERIA -
MISSIONS - HISTORY.**
Aye, Efiong U. Presbyterianism in Nigeria /.
Calabar, Cross River State , 1987. 175 p. :
ISBN 978-228-288-X *NYPL [Sc C 88-234]*

Presbyterianism in Nigeria /. Aye, Efiong U.
Calabar, Cross River State , 1987. 175 p. :
ISBN 978-228-288-X *NYPL [Sc C 88-234]*

PRESBYTERIANS - NIGERIA - HISTORY.
Aye, Efiong U. Presbyterianism in Nigeria /.
Calabar, Cross River State , 1987. 175 p. :
ISBN 978-228-288-X *NYPL [Sc C 88-234]*

Prescott, Laurence E. (Laurence Emmanuel)
Candelario Obeso y la iniciación de la poesía
negra en Colombia / Laurence E. Prescott.
Bogota : Instituto Caro y Cuervo, 1985. 228 p.,
[17] leaves of plates : ill., port., facsims. ; 24
cm. (Publicaciones del Instituto Caro y Cuervo. 70)
Based on the author's thesis (doctoral--Indiana
University) entitled La poesía negra en Colombia a
través de la obra de Candelario Obeso. "Este libro es un
estudio de los Cantos populares de mi tierra de
Candelario Obeso." Includes index. Bibliography: p.
[207]-221.
*1. Obeso, Candelario, 1849-1884. Cantos populares de
mi tierra. 2. Colombian poetry - Black authors - History
and criticism. I. Series: Colombia. Instituto Caro y
Cuervo. Publicaciones, 70. II. Title.*
NYPL [JFE 87-5694]

**Presencia africana en la cultura de América
Latina** . Gallardo, Jorge Emilio. Buenos Aires,
Argentina , c1986. 123 p. ; ISBN 950-643-006-3
DDC 299/.69 19
BL2490 .G33 1986 NYPL [Sc D 89-358]

The present state of Hayti (Saint Domingo)
Franklin, James. London, 1828. viii, 411 p.
NYPL [Sc Micro R-1455]

Presenting-- Sister Noblues /. Gossett, Hattie,
1942- Ithaca, N.Y. , c1988. 143 p. ; ISBN
0-932379-50-8 (alk. paper) DDC 811/.54 19
PS3557.O785 P7 1988 NYPL [JFD 89-457]

Preservation guidelines in ARL libraries /
Systems and Procedures Exchange Center.
Washington, D.C. : Association of Research
Libraries, Office of Management Studies, [1987]
110 p. : ill. ; 28 cm. (SPEC kit . no. 137) SPEC
flyer ; no. 137
*I. Association of Research Libraries. Systems and
Procedures Exchange Center.*
NYPL [Sc F 88-326]

**PRESERVATION OF BOOKS. see BOOKS -
CONSERVATION AND RESTORATION.**

**PRESERVATION OF FORESTS. see
NATURAL RESOURCES.**

Presidentialism . Oyaide, William John, 1936-
Benin City, Nigeria , c1987. xi, 133 p. ; ISBN
978-300-550-2 *NYPL [Sc D 88-917]*

The president's house . Seale, William.
Washington, D.C. , 1986. 2 v. (xx, 1224 p. [80]
p. of plates : ISBN 0-912308-28-1 (set) DDC 975
19
F204.W5 S43 1986 NYPL [Sc E 89-183]

**PRESIDENTS - UNITED STATES -
DWELLINGS.**
Seale, William. The president's house .
Washington, D.C. , 1986. 2 v. (xx, 1224 p. [80]
p. of plates : ISBN 0-912308-28-1 (set) DDC 975
19
F204.W5 S43 1986 NYPL [Sc E 89-183]

**PRESIDENTS - UNITED STATES -
ELECTION - 1972.**
Chisolm, Shirley, 1924- The good fight /. New
York , c1973. 206 p. ; *NYPL [Sc C 88-43]*

**PRESIDENTS - UNITED STATES -
ELECTION - 1984.**
Cavanagh, Thomas E. The impact of the Black
electorate [microform] /. Washington, D.C.
(1301 Pennsylvania Ave., N.W., Suite 400,
Washington 20004) , 1984. v, 28 p. ; DDC
324.973/008996073 19
*E185.615 .C364 1984 NYPL [*Z-4913 no.8]*

Cavanagh, Thomas E. Jesse Jackson's
campaign . Washington, D.C. , 1984. 27 p.,
[1] ; ISBN 0-941410-45-5 (pbk.) DDC 324.973 19
JK526 1984c NYPL [Sc F 87-172 rept. 2]

**PRESIDENTS - UNITED STATES -
ELECTION - 1984 - CONGRESSES.**
Blacks in southern politics /. New York , 1987.
vii, 305 p. : ISBN 0-275-92655-9 (alk. paper) :
DDC 323.1/196073/075 19
E185.92 .B58 1987 NYPL [Sc E 88-196]

**PRESIDENTS - UNITED STATES -
ELECTION - HISTORY.**
Walters, Ronald W. Black presidential politics
in America . Albany , c1988. xvii, 255 p. ISBN
0-88706-546-5 DDC 324.6/2/08996073 19
JK1924 .W34 1987 NYPL [Sc E 88-283]

**PRESS AND GOVERNMENT. see
GOVERNMENT AND THE PRESS.**

**PRESS CENSORSHIP. see LIBERTY OF THE
PRESS.**

PRESS-GANGS. see IMPRESSMENT.

**PRESS, LIBERTY OF THE. see LIBERTY OF
THE PRESS.**

PRESS - NIGERIA - HISTORY.
Duyile, Dayo. Makers of Nigerian press .
Nigeria , 1987. xx, 726 p. :
NYPL [Sc F 89-167]

**PRESSES, COLLEGE. see UNIVERSITY
PRESSES.**

**PRESSES, UNIVERSITY. see UNIVERSITY
PRESSES.**

PRESTIDIGITATION. see MAGIC.

Preston, John. Stolen moments / by John
Preston. 1st ed. Boston : Alyson Publications,
1985. 125 p. ; 21 cm. (The mission of Alex Kane .
no. 4) ISBN 0-932870-71-6
*1. Afro-American homosexuals - Fiction. 2.
Homosexuals, Male - United States - Fiction. I. Title.*
NYPL [Sc D 88-3]

Preston, Katherine. Scott Joplin / Katherine
Preston ; senior consulting editor, Nathan Irvin
Huggins. New York : Chelsea House Publishers,
c1988. 110 p. : ill. ; 24 cm. (Black Americans of
achievement) Includes index. Traces the life of the
well-known ragtime pianist and composer who wrote
over 500 pieces of music, including a ballet and two
operas. Bibliography: p. 108. ISBN 1-555-46598-6
DDC 780/.92/4 B 92 19
*1. Joplin, Scott, 1868-1917 - Juvenile literature. 2.
Composers - United States - Biography - Juvenile
literature. 3. Afro-American composers - Biography -
Juvenile literature. I. Title. II. Series.*
ML3930.J66 P7 1988 NYPL [Sc 88-170]

**Présumée Solitude, ou, Histoire d'une paysanne
haïtienne** . Cazanove, Michèle. Paris , c1988.
178 p. ; ISBN 2-260-00546-2
NYPL [Sc D 88-1406]

Pretty boy dead . Hansen, Joseph, 1923- San
Francisco , 1984. 203 p. ; ISBN 0-917342-48-8 :
DDC 813/.54 19
PS3558.A513 P7 1984 NYPL [JFD 87-9537]

Preventing famine . Curtis, Donald, 1939-
London , New York , 1988. xi, 250 p. ; ISBN
0-415-00711-9 DDC 363.8/7/096 19
HC800.Z9 F326 1988 NYPL [JLD 88-3825]

Prichard, R. J. African librarianship : a
bibliography of periodicals / by R.J. Prichard.
Aberystwyth, Dyfed, Great Britain : Library,
College of Librarianship Wales, University of
Wales School of Librarianship and Information
Studies, 1987. 35 p. ; 21 cm. Cover title. Includes
indexes. ISBN 0-904020-21-5 (pbk.) DDC
016.02706 19
*1. Library science - Africa - Periodicals - Bibliography.
2. Libraries - Africa - Periodicals - Bibliography. I.
Title.*
Z857.A1 P75 1987 NYPL [Sc D 88-1518]

Pride against prejudice . Moore, Joseph Thomas.
New York , c1988. 195 p., [8] p. of plates :
ISBN 0-313-25995-X (lib. bdg. : alk. paper)
DDC 796.357/092/4 B 19
GV865.D58 M66 1988 NYPL [Sc E 88-272]

Pride of Puerto Rico . Walker, Paul Robert. San
Diego , c1988. 135 p. ; ISBN 0-15-200562-5
DDC 796.357/092/4 B 92 19
GV865.C45 W35 1988 NYPL [Sc E 88-452]

Priestley, Brian, 1946- Jazz on record : a history
/ Brian Priestley. London : Elm Tree, 1988. xii,

225 p., [8] leaves of plates : ill., ports. ; 23 cm.
Includes index. Bibliography: p. 202-203. ISBN
0-241-12440-9
1. Jazz music - History. I. Title.
NYPL [Sc D 88-1335]

PRIMARIES - UNITED STATES.
Cavanagh, Thomas E. Jesse Jackson's
campaign . Washington, D.C. , 1984. 27 p.,
[1] ; ISBN 0-941410-45-5 (pbk.) DDC 324.973 19
JK526 1984c   **NYPL [Sc F 87-172 rept. 2]**

**PRIME MINISTERS - BARBADOS -
    BIOGRAPHY.**
Hoyos, F. A. Tom Adams . Basingstoke , 1988.
x, 198 p., [32] p. of plates : ISBN 0-333-46332-3
(pbk) : DDC 972.98/1/00994 19
                                  NYPL [Sc D 88-1275]

**Primeiro seminário interdisciplinar de
antropologia /.** Seminario Interdisciplinar de
Antropologia (1st : 1982 : Maputo,
Mozambique) Maputo , 1987. 153 p. ;
                                  NYPL [Sc F 88-172]

Primeros versos /. Mendizábal, Horacio. Buenos
Aires , 1865. 187 p. ;
                                  NYPL [Sc Rare F 88-75]

PRIMERS.
Brown, Virginia. Out jumped Abraham /. St.
Louis, c1967. 94 p. :   **NYPL [Sc D 89-542]**
In the city /. New York , c1965. 32 p.
                                  NYPL [Sc D 89-82]

PRIMERS - 1950-1975.
Detroit. Great Cities Program for School
Improvement. Writers' Committee. A day with
Debbie /. Chicago , c1964. 55 p. :
                                  NYPL [Sc E 89-178]
Detroit. Great Cities Program for School
Improvement. Writers' Committee. Laugh with
Larry /. Chicago , c1962. 47 p. :
                                  NYPL [Sc E 87-268]
Detroit. Great Cities Program for School
Improvement. Writers' Committee. Play with
Jimmy /. Chicago , c1962. 23, [1] p. :
                                  NYPL [Sc E 88-237]
Detroit. Great Cities Program for School
Improvement. Writes' Committee. Fun with
David /. Chicago , c1962. 31 p.:
                                  NYPL [Sc E 89-40]

PRIMITIVE ART. see ART, PRIMITIVE.

**PRIMITIVE LITERATURE. see FOLK
    LITERATURE.**

**PRIMITIVE RELIGION. see RELIGION,
    PRIMITIVE.**

Primitive worlds: people lost in time. Prepared
by the Special Publications Division, National
Geographic Society. [Washington, National
Geographic Society, 1973] 211 p. col. illus. 27
cm. Bibliography: p. 210. CONTENTS. - The ghosts of
our ancestors, by E. R. Service. - Mbotgate, by E. R.
Sorenson. - Tifalmin, by W. Wheatcroft. - Turkana, by
N. Dyson-Hudson. - Somba, by V. Englebert. -
Yanomamö, by N. A. Chagnon. - Tarahumara, by T.
Eigeland. ISBN 0-87044-127-2
*1. Society, Primitive. I. National Geographic Society
(U. S.). Special Publications Division.*
GN400 .P66   **NYPL [Sc 301.2-P]**

PRIMITIVISM IN ART - HAITI.
Rodman, Selden, 1909- Where art is joy . New
York , c1988. 236 p. : ISBN 0-938291-01-7 :
DDC 759.97294 19
N6606.5.P74 R64 1988
                            NYPL [3-MAM+ 89-6425]

**PRIMITIVISM IN ART - HAITI -
    EXHIBITIONS.**
Haïti . Paris , 1988. 276 p. :
                                  NYPL [Sc E 89-227]
Haitian painting . [New York , c1987. 71 p. :
                                  NYPL [Sc D 88-451]

**PRIMITIVISM IN ART - LOUISIANA -
    NATCHITOCHES.**
Wilson, James L. (James Lynwood) Clementine
Hunter, American folk artist /. Gretna , 1988.
160 p. : ISBN 0-88289-658-X DDC 759.13 B 19
ND237.H915 A4 1988   **NYPL [Sc F 89-94]**

**PRIMITIVISM IN ART - NIGERIA -
    EXHIBITIONS.**
Zementskulpturen aus Nigeria . Stuttgart ,
c1988. 70 p. :   **NYPL [Sc F 89-44]**

Le prince et le griot . Blanc, Paul. Paris , c1987.
250 p., [4] p. of plates : ISBN 2-7013-0719-8
                                  NYPL [Sc E 88-345]

Prince Hall Lodge No. 38 . Freemasons. Prince
Hall Grand Lodge, No. 38 (New York, N.Y.)
New York, N.Y. [1981]. [120] p. :
                                  NYPL [Sc F 88-158]

Prince, Mary. The history of Mary Prince, a
West Indian slave, related by herself / edited
with an introduction by Moira Ferguson ; with
a preface by Ziggi Alexander. London ; New
York : Pandora Press, 1987. xvi, 124 p. ; 21
cm. (Mothers of the novel) Reprint. Originally
published in 1831. ISBN 0-86358-192-7 DDC
305.5/67/0924 B 19
*1. Prince, Mary. 2. Fugitive slaves - West Indies -
Biography. 3. Slavery - West Indies. I. Ferguson, Moira.
II. Title. III. Series.*
HT869.P6 A3 1987   **NYPL [Sc C 89-31]**

PRINCE, MARY.
Prince, Mary. The history of Mary Prince, a
West Indian slave, related by herself /.
London , New York , 1987. xvi, 124 p. ; ISBN
0-86358-192-7 DDC 305.5/67/0924 B 19
HT869.P6 A3 1987   **NYPL [Sc C 89-31]**

Princes & serviteurs du royaume : cinq études de
monarchies Africaines / par Alfred Adler ... [et
al.] ; présentées par Claude Tardits. Paris :
Société d'ethnographie, 1987. 225 p. : ill., map ;
25 cm. (Sociétés africaines . ?) Bibliography: p.
224-225. ISBN 2-901161-29-4
*1. Abron (African people) - History. 2. Mossi (African
people) - History. 3. Bamum (African tribe). 4.
Mundang (African people). 5. Baguirmi (African
people). 6. Gyaman - History. 7. Yatenga (Kingdom) -
History. I. Tardits, Claude. II. Adler, Alfred. III. Title:
Princes et serviteurs du royaume. IV. Series.*
                                  NYPL [Sc E 88-409]

Princes et serviteurs du royaume. Princes &
serviteurs du royaume . Paris , 1987. 225 p. :
ISBN 2-901161-29-4   **NYPL [Sc E 88-409]**

The princes of Nyakyusa. Charsley, Simon R.
[Nairobi, 1969] xii, 125 p. DDC 301.29/678
DT443 .C5   **NYPL [Sc D 88-975]**

Princess Gorilla and a new kind of water .
Aardema, Verna. New York , 1988. [32] p. :
    ISBN 0-8037-0412-7 : DDC 398.2/0966 E 19
PZ8.1.A213 Pr 1987   **NYPL [Sc F 88-133]**

**Principles and policy of the South African
Progressive Reform Party.** Eglin, Colin. Die
beginsels en belied van die Suid-Afrikaanse
Progressiewe Reformisteparty [microform] /.
[Cape Town , 1975] 12, 12 p. ;
                            NYPL [Sc Micro R-4094 no. 4]

Principles of the Revolution. Blanchard, Joshua
Pollard, 1782-1868. Boston, 1855. 24 p.
JK216 .B63   **NYPL [Sc Rare F 88-40]**

**PRINTING - UNIVERSITY PRESSES. see
    UNIVERSITY PRESSES.**

Prison and plantation [microform] . Hindus,
Michael Stephen, 1946- 1975. 398 leaves.
                                  NYPL [Sc Micro R-4225]

The prisoners /. Nwamuo, Chris. Enugu , 1985.
x, 73 p. ; ISBN 978-250-304-5
                                  NYPL [Sc D 88-495]

PRISONERS - JAMAICA - BIOGRAPHY.
Hector, Mario. Death row /. London ,
Kingston, Jamaica , 1984. v, lll p. ISBN
0-86232-232-4   **NYPL [Sc C 88-221]**

PRISONERS - SEXUAL BEHAVIOR.
Wooden, Wayne S. Men behind bars . New
York , c1982. x, 264 p. : ISBN 0-306-41074-5
                                  NYPL [Sc D 89-249]

PRISONS - AFRICA - DRAMA.
Nwamuo, Chris. The prisoners /. Enugu , 1985.
x, 73 p. ; ISBN 978-250-304-5
                                  NYPL [Sc D 88-495]

PRISONS - JAMAICA.
Hector, Mario. Death row /. London ,
Kingston, Jamaica , 1984. v, lll p. ISBN
0-86232-232-4   **NYPL [Sc C 88-221]**

The private Civil War . Jimerson, Randall C.
Baton Rouge, LA , 1988. xiv, 270 p., [8] p. of
plates : ISBN 0-8071-1454-5 (alk. paper) : DDC
973.7 19
E468.9 .J55 1988   **NYPL [IKI 89-2276]**

PRIVATE PROSECUTORS - NIGERIA.
Murder of Dele Giwa . Lagos, Nigeria , 1988.

193 p. : ISBN 978-232-523-6
                                  NYPL [Sc F 89-35]

PRIVATE SCHOOLS - UNITED STATES.
Start your own school! /. Washington, D.C. ,
1988. vi, 68 p. : ISBN 0-941001-08-3
                                  NYPL [Sc D 89-406]
Visible now . New York , 1988. xvi, 344 p. ;
    ISBN 0-313-25926-7 (lib. bdg. : alk. paper) DDC
371./02/0973 19
LC2761 .V57 1988   **NYPL [Sc E 98-257]**

Privatization in Nigeria . Odife, Dennis O. Yaba,
Lagos , c1988. vii, 151 p. ; ISBN 978-301-672-5
(pbk)   **NYPL [Sc D 88-755]**

PRIVATIZATION - NIGERIA.
Odife, Dennis O. Privatization in Nigeria .
Yaba, Lagos , c1988. vii, 151 p. ; ISBN
978-301-672-5 (pbk)   **NYPL [Sc D 88-755]**

PRIZE-FIGHTING. see BOXING.

El problema de la colonizacón [microform] .
Bonelli Rubio, Juan María. Madrid , 1945. 15
p. ;   **NYPL [Sc Micro F-11057]**

Problemas dominico-haitianos y del Caribe /
Gérard Pierre-Charles ... [et al.]. 1. ed. -
México : Universidad Nacional Autónoma de
México, 1973. 228 p.; 22 cm. (Mexico (City).
Universidad Nacional. Facultad de Ciencias Políticas y
Sociales. Serie estudios. [no.] 29) Includes
bibliographical references. CONTENTS: Pierre-Charles,
G. Interpretacinó socioeconómica de Haití. - Casimir, J.
Los "bosales" y el surgimiento de una cultura oprimida
en Haití. - Franco, F. J. Antihaitianismo e ideología del
trujillato. - Tolentino, H. El fenómeno racial en Haití y
en la República Dominicana. - Mir, p. Acerca de las
tentativas históricas de unificación de la Isla de Santo
Domingo. - Maldonado-Denis, M. Puerto Rico:
sociedad colonial en el Caribe.
*1. Haiti - Addresses, essays, lectures. 2. Dominican
Republic - Addresses, essays, lectures. 3. Puerto Rico -
Addresses, essays, lectures. I. Pierre-Charles, Gérard. II.
Series.*   **NYPL [JLK 73-145 [no.] 29]**

Problèmes de développement . Goffaux, J.
[Kinshasa, Zaire?] , 1986. 223 p. ;
HD83 .G65 1986   **NYPL [Sc D 89-593]**

**Problems of co-operation between the English-
and French-speaking universities of West
Africa [microform] .** Lévy, Denis. Freetown
[Sierra Leone] [1961] 7 p. ;
                            NYPL [Sc Micro R-4094 no. 23]

**The problems of the university's role in adult
education in Uganda /.** Kakooza, Teresa.
[Kampala?] , 1987. 20 p. ;
                                  NYPL [Sc F 89-92]

**Proceedings of the American Anti-slavery
Society, at its third decade .** American
Anti-slavery Society. New York , 1864. 175 p. ;
                                  NYPL [Sc Rare G 86-43]

**Proceedings of the Anti-Slavery Meeting held in
Stacy Hall, Boston.** Anti-Slavery Meeting
(1855 : Boston) The Boston mob of "gentlemen
of property and standing." . Boston , 1855
(Boston : J.B. Yerrinton and Son, printers) 76
p. ;
E450.B74   **NYPL [Sc Rare F 88-44]**

**Proceedings of the colloquium on Why army
rule? :** May 20-22, 1986, under the sponsorship
of Nigerian Institute of Advanced Legal
Studies, Lagos. [Lagos? : The Institute?, 1986 or
1987 338 p. ; 30 cm. Cover title.
*1. Military government - Nigeria - Congresses. 2.
Civil-military relations - Nigeria - Congresses. 3.
Nigeria - Armed forces - Political activity - Congresses.
4. Nigeria - Politics and government - 1960- -
Congresses. I. Nigerian Institute of Advanced Legal
Studies. II. Title: Why army rule?.*
                                  NYPL [Sc G 88-23]

Procès de Brazzaville . Massengo, Moudileno.
Paris [1983] 345 p. :   **NYPL [Sc D 88-1160]**

**Proclamação da independência da República
Popular de Angola, 11 de novembro de 1975 :**
documentos. Luanda : Ministério da
Informação, 1975. 166 p., [2] leaves of plates :
ill. ; 21 cm. Portuguese, French and English; cover
title: Angola, 11 de novembro de 1975 : documentos da
independência = documents de l'indépendance =
documents of independency.
*1. Angola - Politics and government - 1975- - Sources.
I. Angola. Ministério da Informação. II. Title: Angola,
11 de novembro de 1975. III. Title: Documentos da
independência. IV. Title: Angola, onze de novembro de
1975.*   **NYPL [Sc D 88-245]**

Procter, Lovell James. The Central African journal of Lovell J. Procter, 1860-1864. Edited with an introd. by Norman Robert Bennett and Marguerite Ylvisaker. [Boston] African Studies Center, Boston University, 1971. xvii, 501 p. illus. 23 cm. ([African historical documents series. 2]) Includes bibliographical references. DDC 916.8
1. *Africa, Southern - Description and travel.* I. Title. II. Series.
DT731 .P75 **NYPL [Sc D 88-977]**

PRODUCE EXCHANGES. see COMMODITY EXCHANGES.

Producer/User Seminar on Household Statistics and Indicators for Women in Development held at the Conference Centre, University of Lagos, August 11th-13th, 1986 / sponsors, Federal Office of Statistics, United Nations International Research and Training Institute for Advancement of Women. [Lagos : FOS?, 1986?] 2 v. ; 25 cm. CONTENTS. - Vol. 1. Summary of proceedings.--v. 2. Proceedings.
1. *Women in development - Nigeria.* I. University of Lagos. Conference Centre. **NYPL [Sc E 89-158]**

PRODUCTION, COOPERATIVE. see COOPERATION.

The production of sugar and the reproduction of slaves at Vossenburg (Suriname), 1705-1863 /. Lamur, H. E. Amsterdam, The Netherlands. 164 p. : ISBN 90-70313-19-7
NYPL [Sc D 88-555]

PROFESSIONS - CHOICE. see VOCATIONAL GUIDANCE.

PROFESSIONS - JUVENILE LITERATURE.
Osahon, Naiwu. Alphabets and careers /. Apapa, Lagos, Nigeria , 1981. [32] p. : ISBN 978-18-6006-5 **NYPL [Sc F 88-295]**

Profile /. Jaja, Janhoi M. Kingston, Jamaica , c1984. 48 p. : **NYPL [Sc D 88-932]**

Profile of a city. First National City Bank. Economics Dept. New York [1972] x, 273 p. ISBN 0-07-021066-7
HC108.N7 F57 **NYPL [Sc 309.174-F]**

Profile of career education /. Makinde, Olu. Ibadan, Oyo State, Nigeria , 1987. xv, 308 p. ; ISBN 978-254-605-4 **NYPL [Sc D 89-177]**

Profile of Nigeria /. Kenworthy, Leonard Stout, 1912- Garden City, New York , c1960. 96 p. : **NYPL [Sc E 88-240]**

Profiles (London, England)
May, Chris. Bob Marley /. London , 1985. 60 p. : ISBN 0-241-11476-4 : DDC 784.5 B 19
ML420.M3313 M4 1985
NYPL [Sc D 88-308]

Profiles. Nations of contemporary Africa.
Burdette, Marcia M. (Marcia Muldrow) Zambia . Boulder, Colo. , 1988. xiv, 210 p. : ISBN 0-86531-617-1 (alk. paper) DDC 968.94/04 19
DT963 .B87 1988 **NYPL [Sc E 89-103]**

Program on environment and behavior . (monograph #42) Bolin, Robert C. Race, religion, and ethnicity in disaster recovery /. [Boulder. Colo.] , 1986. ix, 265 p. :
NYPL [Sc D 88-904]

PROGRAMS, ACADEMIC. see DISSERTATIONS, ACADEMIC.

Progress of a race. Kletzing, Henry F., 1850- Atlanta, Ga., 1897. xxiv, 23-663 p.
NYPL [Sc 973-K]

Project cat /. Burchardt, Nellie. New York, N.Y. , c1966. 66 p. : **NYPL [Sc D 89-435]**

Projeto Passo à frente. Coleção Polêmica . (11) Valente, Ana Lúcia E. F. (Ana Lúcia Eduardo Farah) Ser negro no Brasil hoje /. São Paulo, SP, Brasil , 1987. 64 p. : DDC 305.8/96/081 19
F2659.N4 V35 1987 **NYPL [HFB 88-2561]**

Proletarian internationalism and the Ethiopian revolution / by the Propaganda and Culture Committee of the Founding Congress of the Workers' Party of Ethiopia & 10th Anniversary of the Revolution. Addis Ababa : The Committee, 1984. 56 p. : ill. ; 28 cm. Includes bibliographies.
1. *Communism - Ethiopia.* 2. *Ethiopia - Foreign relations - 1974-.* I. Founding Congress of the Workers' Party of Ethiopia & 10th Anniversary of the

Revolution. Propaganda and Culture Committee.
DT387.95 .P76 1984 **NYPL [Sc F 89-85]**

Promoting smallholder cropping systems in Sierra Leone : an assessment of traditional cropping systems and recommendations for the Bo-Pujehun Rural Development Project / Albert Engel ... [et. al.] Berlin : Fachbereich Internationale Agrarentwicklung der Technischen Universität Berlin, 1985. xiv, 227 p. : maps ; 21 cm. (Schriftenreihe des Fachbereichs . Nr. IV/86) At head of title: Seminar für Landwirtschaftliche Entwicklung, Institut für Sozialökonomie der Agrarentwicklung, Technische Universität Berlin.
1. *Agriculture - Economic aspects - Sierra Leone.* I. Engel, Albert. II. Technische Universität Berlin. Seminar für Landwirtschaftliche Entwicklung.
NYPL [Sc D 88-817]

Propaganda abolicionista . Guimarães, Augusto Alvares. Bahia , 1875. 86 p. ;
NYPL [Sc Rare G 86-33]

PROPERTY, REAL. see REAL PROPERTY.

Prophetic fragments /. West, Cornel. Grand Rapids, Mich. , Trenton, N.J. , c1988. xi, 294 p. ; ISBN 0-8028-0308-3 : DDC 291/.0973 19
BL2525 .W42 1988 **NYPL [Sc E 88-401]**

Prophets with honour . Edgar, Robert. Johannesburg [1987?]. 250 p. ; ISBN 0-86975-312-6 **NYPL [Sc D 88-1391]**

PROSELYTES AND PROSELYTING, JEWISH - CONVERTS FROM CHRISTIANITY - BIOGRAPHY.
Lester, Julius. Lovesong . New York, N.Y. , c1988. 248 p., [4] leaves of plates : ISBN 0-8050-0588-9 DDC 296.8/346/0924 B 19
BM755.L425 A3 1988 **NYPL [Sc E 88-317]**

Prospects and progress in South Afirca. South Africa. Consulate (New York) New York [1973?] 153 p. : **NYPL [JLD 79-3283]**

Prospects for Africa : a special report for the Save the Children Fund and the Overseas Development Institute for The Africa Review Group / introduction by HRH The Princess Royal. London : Hodder and Stoughton, 1988. 97 p. : ill., maps ; 25 cm. Includes index. ISBN 0-340-42909-7 (pbk) : DDC 330.96/0328 19
1. *Africa - Economic development.* 2. *Africa - Economic conditions - 1960-.* I. Save the Children Fund. II. Overseas Development Institute.
HC800 **NYPL [Sc E 89-34]**

Prosper, Jean Georges, 1933- Les saignées du saigneur / Jean-Georges Prosper. [Ile Maurice? : s.n., 1983?] (Réduit : Institut de Pédagogie) 87 p. ; 20 cm.
I. Title. **NYPL [Sc C 88-118]**

PROSTITUTION - AFRICA - FICTION.
Ilboudo, Patrick G. Les carnets secrets d'une fille de joie . Burkina Faso , c1988. 189 p. ;
NYPL [Sc C 88-356]

PROSTITUTION - CAMEROON - YAOUNDÉ.
Songue, Paulette, 1960- Prostitution en Afrique . Paris , c1986. 154 p. ; ISBN 2-85802-684-X **NYPL [Sc D 88-1164]**

Prostitution en Afrique . Songue, Paulette, 1960- Paris , c1986. 154 p. ; ISBN 2-85802-684-X
NYPL [Sc D 88-1164]

PROSTITUTION - HAITI.
Honoré, Narénia François. Bref aperçu sur l'évolution de la prostitution en Haïti. [Port-au-Prince] , 1981. 49 p., [1] leaf of plates : DDC 306.7/4 19
HQ162.A5 H66 **NYPL [Sc D 88-318]**

PROTECTION OF NATURE. see NATURE CONSERVATION.

PROTEST LITERATURE, AFRICAN (ENGLISH) - HISTORY AND CRITICISM.
Sandiford, Keith Albert, 1947- Measuring the moment . Selinsgrove , c1988. 181 p. ; ISBN 0-941664-79-1 (alk. paper) DDC 828 19
PR9340 .S26 1988 **NYPL [Sc E 88-467]**

PROTEST POETRY, AMERICAN - HISTORY AND CRITICISM.
Reid, Margaret Ann, 1940- A rhetorical analysis of selected Black protest poetry of the Harlem Renaissance and of the sixties /. , 1981. 284 p. [i.e. 216] p. **NYPL [Sc D 88-264]**

Prou, Michel, 1934- Malagasy : "un pas de plus" / Michel Prou. Paris : L'Harmattan, 1987- v. :

ill., maps, ports. ; 22 cm. CONTENTS. - T. 1 : Vers l'histoire du "Royaume de Madagascar" au XIXe siècle. ISBN 2-85802-513-1
1. *Madagascar - History.* I. Title.
NYPL [Sc D 88-102]

PROVERBS, AFRICAN.
Afrika für dich . St. Gallen [1986]. [43] p. :
NYPL [Sc D 88-675]

PROVERBS, BLACK - AFRICA. see PROVERBS, AFRICAN.

PROVERBS, CREOLE - HAITI.
Fayó, Néstor A. 3333 proverbs in Haitian Creole . Port-au-Prince, Haiti [1980?] 428 p. :
NYPL [Sc D 86-839]

PROVERBS, HAITIAN.
Fayó, Néstor A. 3333 proverbs in Haitian Creole . Port-au-Prince, Haiti [1980?] 428 p. :
NYPL [Sc D 86-839]

PROVERBS, NEMBE.
Noin nengia, bere nengia . Port Harcourt, Nigeria , 1986. 137 p. ; ISBN 978-232-110-9
NYPL [Sc E 89-130]

PROVERBS, NTUMU.
Sheppherd, Joseph. A leaf of honey and the proverbs of the rain forest /. London , c1988. xii, 319 p. : ISBN 1-87098-902-3 (pbk.) : DDC 305.8/966 19 **NYPL [Sc D 89-453]**

PROVERBS, TIMNE.
Temne names and proverbs /. Freetown , 1986. 137 p. ; **NYPL [Sc D 89-489]**

PROVERBS, YORUBA.
Owomoyela, Oyekan. A Kì í . Lanham , c1988. x, 388 p. ; ISBN 0-8191-6502-6 (alk. paper) : DDC 398/.9/96333 19
PN6519.Y6 O96 1987 **NYPL [Sc E 88-278]**

Providence, Tien. Of poetry of prose / Tien Providence. [St. Vincent? : s.n., 198-?] 69 p. ; 21 cm. Cover title.
I. Title.
MLCS 87/7473 (P) **NYPL [Sc D 88-1322]**

The provision of information for rural development /. Aboyade, B. Olabimpe. Ibadan , 1987. xv, 104 p. ; ISBN 978-267-900-3
NYPL [Sc D 88-739]

Prti démocratique de Côte d'Ivoire. Le quatrième séminaire des secrétaires généraux. [Abidjan] , 1985. 55 p. : **NYPL [Sc E 88-150]**

Prucha, Francis Paul. Handbook for research in American history : a guide to bibliographies and other reference works / Francis Paul Prucha. Lincoln : University of Nebraska Press, c1987 xiii, 289 p. ; 24 cm. Includes index. ISBN 0-8032-3682-4 (alk. paper) DDC 016.973 19
1. *United States - Bibliography - Bibliography.* 2. *United States - History - Bibliography.* I. Title.
Z1236 .P78 1987 E178 **NYPL [Sc D 88-545]**

Pruen, Septimus Tristram (Septimus Tristam) The Arab and the African : experiences in eastern equatorial Africa during a residence of three years / by S. Tristram Pruen. London : Darf, 1896. vii, 338 p. [8] p. of plates : ill., maps, port. ; 23 cm. Reprint. Originally published : London : Seeley, 1891.
1. *Slavery - Africa, East.* 2. *Missions - Africa, East.* 3. *Africa, East - Description and travel.* 4. *Africa, East - Social life and customs.* I. Title.
NYPL [Sc D 88-387]

Prugh, Jeff. Dettlinger, Chet. The list /. Atlanta , c1983. 516 p., [4] p. of plates : ISBN 0-942894-04-9 : DDC 364.1/523/09758231 19
HV6534.A7 D47 1983 **NYPL [Sc E 86-40]**

PSEUDO-ROMANTICISM. see ROMANTICISM.

PSYCHAGOGY. see PSYCHOTHERAPY.

Psychoeducational assessment of minority group children : a casebook / Reginald L. Jones, editor. Berkeley, Calif. : Cobb & Henry, c1988. ix, 429 p. : ill. ; 23 cm. Includes bibliographies and indexes. ISBN 0-943539-00-5 (pbk.) : DDC 155.4/5 19
1. *Psychological tests for children - Case studies.* 2. *Educational tests and measurements - Case studies.* 3. *Psychological tests for minorities - Case studies.* I. Jones, Reginald Lanier, 1931-.
BF722 .P77 1988 **NYPL [Sc D 89-526]**

PSYCHOLOGICAL TESTING OF CHILDREN. see PSYCHOLOGICAL TESTS FOR CHILDREN.

**PSYCHOLOGICAL TESTS FOR CHILDREN -
    CASE STUDIES.**
Psychoeducational assessment of minority group
children . Berkeley, Calif. , c1988. ix, 429 p. :
    ISBN 0-943539-00-5 (pbk.) : DDC 155.4/5 19
BF722 .P77 1988   *NYPL [Sc D 89-526]*

**PSYCHOLOGICAL TESTS FOR
    MINORITIES - CASE STUDIES.**
Psychoeducational assessment of minority group
children . Berkeley, Calif. , c1988. ix, 429 p. :
    ISBN 0-943539-00-5 (pbk.) : DDC 155.4/5 19
BF722 .P77 1988   *NYPL [Sc D 89-526]*

Psychology and society : selected readings /
edited proceedings by Eileen B. Wilson. [Ife?] :
Nigerian Psychological Association, 1986. 212
p. ; 24 cm. Includes bibliographical references.
    *1. Psychology - Nigeria. I. Wilson, Eileen B. II. Nigeria
    Psychological Association.* *NYPL [Sc E 88-432]*

PSYCHOLOGY - METHODOLOGY.
Nobles, Wade W. African psychology .
Oakland, California , 1986. 133 p. ; ISBN
    0-939205-02-5   *NYPL [Sc D 88-696]*

**PSYCHOLOGY, NATIONAL. see NATIONAL
    CHARACTERISTICS.**

PSYCHOLOGY - NIGERIA.
Psychology and society . [Ife?] , 1986. 212 p. ;
                         NYPL [Sc E 88-432]

The psychology of the Afro-American . Jenkins,
Adelbert H. New York , 1982. xix, 213 p. ;
    ISBN 0-08-027206-1 DDC 155.8/496073 19
E185.625 .J47 1982   *NYPL [Sc D 88-718]*

**The Psychopathology of everyday racism and
sexism** / edited by Lenora Fulani. New York :
Harrington Park Press, c1988. xix, 120 p. ; 22
cm. "Simultaneously issued by the Haworth Press, Inc.,
under the title: The politics of race and gender in
therapy, a special issue of Women and therapy, volume
6, number 4, winter 1987." Includes bibliographies.
    ISBN 0-918393-51-5 (pbk.) DDC 305.4/2 19
    *1. Minority women - Mental health - United States. 2.
    Minority women - United States - Psychology. 3.
    Racism - United States - Psychological aspects. 4.
    Sexism - United States - Psychological aspects. 5.
    Psychotherapy - United States. 6. Feminist therapy. I.
    Fulani, Lenora.*
RC451.4.M58 P79 1988
                         NYPL [Sc D 89-449]

Psychosocial dynamics of Black rapists
[microform] . Marowitz, Roberta Lee. 1982. x,
216 leaves ;   *NYPL [Sc Micro R-4806]*

PSYCHOTHERAPY - UNITED STATES.
The Psychopathology of everyday racism and
sexism / . New York , c1988. xix, 120 p. ;
    ISBN 0-918393-51-5 (pbk.) DDC 305.4/2 19
RC451.4.M58 P79 1988
                         NYPL [Sc D 89-449]

**PUBLIC ADMINISTRATION - NIGERIA -
    BOOK REVIEWS.**
Heinecke, P. Twenty-two reviews / . Kaduna,
[Nigeria] [1986?] 69 p. ;
                         NYPL [Sc E 88-284]

**Public administration series--bibliography, 0193-
    970X .**
(P 2328) Dworaczek, Marian. Affirmative
action and minorities . Monticello. Ill., USA
[1988] 63 p. ; ISBN 1-555-90638-9 (pbk.) : DDC
    016.33113/3 19
Z7164.A26 D87 1988 HF5549.5.A34
                         NYPL [Sc f 89-39]

PUBLIC ADMINISTRATION - TANZANIA.
Sokoïne, Edward Moringe, 1938-1984. Public
policy making and implementation in Tanzania
/ . Pau [1986?] ix, 124 p. :
                         NYPL [Sc E 88-319]

Public Archives Canada. Mattie, Joan. 100 years
of architecture in Kingston . [Ottawa] , c1986.
30 p. : ISBN 0-662-54396-3 (pbk.) DDC
    720/.9713/72074011384 19
NA747.K56 M38 1986 *NYPL [Sc F 88-195]*

**PUBLIC BUILDINGS - MICHIGAN -
    DETROIT - NAMES.**
Detroit public sites named for Blacks / .
[[Detroit, Mich.] , c1987. xii, 62 p. ;
                         NYPL [Sc D 88-1183]

PUBLIC FINANCE. see FINANCE, PUBLIC.

PUBLIC FINANCE - NIGERIA.
Ogunbanjo, C. O. (Christopher Odadipo), 1923-
Nigeria, the search for economic stability / .

[Nigeria?] 1986. 102 p., [4] p. of plates : ISBN
0-946233-04-7   *NYPL [Sc D 88-519]*

**PUBLIC HEALTH - AFRICA, EAST -
    BIBLIOGRAPHY.**
A Bibliography of health and disease in East
Africa / . Amsterdam ; New York : 282 p. ;
    ISBN 0-444-80931-7 (U. S.) DDC
    016.3621/0967 19
Z6673.6.A353 B53 1988 RA552.A353
                         NYPL [Sc G 89-6]

**PUBLIC HEALTH - PLANNING. see
    HEALTH PLANNING.**

**PUBLIC HEALTH SERVICES. see PUBLIC
    HEALTH.**

PUBLIC HISTORY.
Past meets present . Washington, D.C. , 1987.
x, 169 p. : ISBN 0-87474-272-2 DDC 069/.9973
    19
D16.163 .P37 1987   *NYPL [Sc E 88-577]*

**PUBLIC HOUSES. see HOTELS, TAVERNS,
    ETC.**

PUBLIC HYGIENE. see PUBLIC HEALTH.

**PUBLIC LABOR POLICY. see LABOR
    POLICY.**

**Public lands acquisition and compensation
practice in Nigeria /.** Uduehi, Godfrey O.
Ogba, Ikeja , 1987. xviii, 162 p. : ISBN
    978-16-3064-7   *NYPL [Sc D 89-480]*

PUBLIC LAW - RWANDA - HISTORY.
Reyntjens, Filip. Pouvoir et droit au Rwanda .
Tervuren, Belgique , 1985. 584 p. ;
                         NYPL [Sc E 87-668]

PUBLIC LAW - SENEGAL.
Gautron, Jean Claude. Droit public du Sénégal
/ . Paris , 1977. 447 p. ; ISBN 2-233-00036-6 :
LAW   *NYPL [Sc E 88-612]*

The public looks at higher education
[microform] . West Virginia. State College,
Institute. Institute, W. Va. , 1959. 15 p. :
                   NYPL [Sc Micro F-11,161]

PUBLIC MEETINGS - AFRICA.
Socio-political aspects of the palaver in some
African countries. Spanish. Aspectos
sociopolíticos del parlamento tradicional en
algunos países africanos / . Barcelona , Paris ,
1979. 95 p. ; ISBN 84-85800-24-9
                         NYPL [Sc D 88-599]

PUBLIC OPINION - FRANCE.
Jennings, Lawrence C. French reaction to
British slave emancipation / . Baton Rouge ,
c1988. ix, 228 p. ; ISBN 0-8071-1429-4 (alk.
paper) DDC 306/.362/0942 19
HT1163 .J46 1988   *NYPL [Sc E 89-139]*

**PUBLIC OPINION - FRANCE - HISTORY -
    18TH CENTURY.**
Cooper, Anna J. (Anna Julia), 1858-1964.
[Attitude de la France à l'égard de l'esclavage
pendant la révolution. English.] Slavery and the
French revolutionists, 1788-1805 / . Lewiston ,
1988. 228 p. : ISBN 0-88946-637-8 DDC
    972.94/03 19
F1923 .C7213 1988   *NYPL [Sc E 88-469]*

PUBLIC OPINION - GRENADA.
Emmanuel, Patrick. Political change and public
opinion in Grenada 1979-1984 / . Cave Hill,
Barbados , c1986. xii, 173 p. :
                   NYPL [JLM 79-1223 no.19]

PUBLIC OPINION - SOUTH AFRICA.
Hoile, David. Understanding sanctions / .
London , 1988. 80 p. : ISBN 1-87111-700-3
(pbk.) : DDC 337.68 19
HF1613.4 .H654 1988 *NYPL [Sc D 89-317]*

PUBLIC OPINION - UNITED STATES.
Magubane, Bernard. The ties that bind .
Trenton, N.J. [1987] xi, 251 p. ; ISBN
    0-86543-037-3 (pbk.) DDC 305.8/96073 19
E185.625 .M83 1987 *NYPL [Sc D 88-1348]*

**PUBLIC OPINION - UNITED STATES -
    HISTORY - 19TH CENTURY.**
Hunt, Alfred N., 1941- Haiti's influence on
antebellum America . Baton Rouge , c1988. xiv,
196 p. : ISBN 0-8071-1370-0 DDC
    973/.049697294 19
E184.H27 H86 1987   *NYPL [Sc E 88-131]*

**Public policy making and implementation in
Tanzania /.** Sokoïne, Edward Moringe,
1938-1984. Pau [1986?] ix, 124 p. :
                         NYPL [Sc E 88-319]

**PUBLIC RELATIONS - BUSINESS. see
    PUBLIC RELATIONS.**

**PUBLIC RELATIONS - HISTORICAL
    MUSEUMS.**
Past meets present . Washington, D.C. , 1987.
x, 169 p. : ISBN 0-87474-272-2 DDC 069/.9973
    19
D16.163 .P37 1987   *NYPL [Sc E 88-577]*

**PUBLIC RELATIONS - INDUSTRY. see
    PUBLIC RELATIONS.**

**PUBLIC RELATIONS - PENNSYLVANIA -
    PHILADELPHIA - POLICE.**
Anderson, John, 1954 Mar. 27- Burning down
the house . New York , c1987. xv, 409 p. :
    ISBN 0-393-02460-1 : DDC 974.8/1104 19
F158.9.N4 A53 1987   *NYPL [Sc E 88-332]*

**PUBLIC RELATIONS - UNIVERSITIES AND
    COLLEGES - WEST VIRGINIA.**
West Virginia. State College, Institute. The
public looks at higher education [microform] .
Institute, W. Va. , 1959. 15 p. :
                   NYPL [Sc Micro F-11,161]

**Publicaciones de la Universidad Autónoma de
Santo Domingo. Colección Arte y sociedad .**
(no. 21) Matos Moquete, Manuel, 1944- En el
atascadero / . Santo Domingo, República
Dominicana , 1985. 266 p. ;
MLCS 85/21777 (P)   *NYPL [JFD 86-4017]*

**Publication de la Faculté des lettres de
l'Université nationale du Rwanda .**
(fasc. no. 1) Les Réactions africaines à la
colonisation en Afrique Centrale . Ruhengeri ,
1986. 478 p. ;   *NYPL [Sc G 87-9]*

**Publication series of the University of Zululand.
Series F .**
(4) Oosthuizen, G. C. (Gerhardus Cornelis) The
birth of Christian Zionism in South Africa / .
KwaDlangezwa, South Africa , 1987. ii, 56 p. ;
    ISBN 0-09-079580-2 DDC 289.9 19
BR1450 .O55 1987   *NYPL [Sc D 88-693]*

Publications (Ceeba). Série II .
(v. 84) Wymeersch, Patrick. Les Bin Kanyok .
Bandundu, République du Zaïre , 1983. ix, 368
p. :   *NYPL [Sc F 89-41]*

(v. 84) Wymeersch, Patrick. Les Bin Kanyok .
Bandundu, République du Zaïre , 1983. ix, 368
p. :   *NYPL [Sc F 89-41]*

(v. 90) Banza-Lute . Bandundu, République du
Zaïre , 1983. 251 p. : DDC 282/.67513 19
BX1682.C6 B36 1983   *NYPL [Sc F 89-38]*

(v. 97) Mbo-Ikamba, Iyeti. L'approvisionnement
alimentaire de la ville de Bandundu (Rép. du
Zaïre) / . Bandundu, République du Zaïre ,
1987. 58 p. :   *NYPL [Sc F 89-63]*

(vol. 87) Kitondo Mangombo. Kolokoso .
Bandundu, République du Zaïre , 1983. 172 p. :
                         NYPL [Sc F 88-304]

(vol. 87) Kitondo Mangombo. Kolokoso .
Bandundu, République du Zaïre , 1983. 172 p. :
                         NYPL [Sc F 88-304]

(vol. 88) Les Maitresses du feu et de la
cuisine . Bandundu, République du Zaïre ,
1983. 164 p. :   *NYPL [Sc F 88-308]*

(vol. 88) Les Maitresses du feu et de la
cuisine . Bandundu, République du Zaïre ,
1983. 164 p. :   *NYPL [Sc F 88-308]*

(vol. 97) Mbo-Ikamba, Iyeti.
L'approvisionnement alimentaire de la ville de
Bandundu (Rép. du Zaïre) / . Bandundu,
République du Zaïre , 1987. 58 p.--/
                         NYPL [Sc F 89-63]

Publications de la Sorbonne. Série "Afrique" .
(no 8) Mignot, Alain. La terre et le pouvoir
chez les Guin du sud-est du Togo / . Paris ,
1985. 288 p. ; ISBN 2-85944-087-9
                         NYPL [Sc E 88-383]

Publications du CHEAM, 0769-2161.
Zuccarelli, François. La vie politique sénégalaise
(1789 - 1940) / . Paris , c1987. 157 p. ; ISBN
2-903182-23-X   *NYPL [Sc E 88-342]*

**Publications of the faculty and staff of West
Virginia State College [microform]** / . Jordan,
Lawrence V. Institute , 1960. 23 p. /.
                   NYPL [Sc Micro F-11,160]

**Publications series of the University of Zululand.
Series C .**
(no.15) Aspects of legislative drafting / .

KwaDlangezwa, South Africa , 1987. ix, 204 p. ; ISBN 0-907995-73-X *NYPL [Sc C 88-66]*

PUBLICITY, GOVERNMENT. see GOVERNMENT AND THE PRESS.

PUBLISHERS AND PUBLISHING - NIGERIA.
Nwankwo, Arthur A. Thoughts on Nigeria /. Enugu, Nigeria , 1986. xxii, 198 p. ; ISBN 987-15-6264-1 *NYPL [Sc E 88-448]*

PUERTO RICAN LITERATURE.
Martinez Masdeu, Edgar. Literatura puertorriqueña. Río Piedras [P.R.] 1983. 2 v. *NYPL [Sc D 87-1020]*

PUERTO RICAN MEN - NEW YORK (N.Y.) - PHOTOGRAPHS.
Vincent, Alan W. The bangy book . Berlin , 1988. [80] p. : ISBN 3-924040-62-1 *NYPL [Sc F 89-115]*

PUERTO RICANS - UNITED STATES - EDUCATION.
Valle, Manuel del. Law and bilingual education . New York , 1978. i, 206 p. ; *NYPL [Sc F 88-357]*

PUERTO RICO - ADDRESSES, ESSAYS, LECTURES.
Problemas dominico-haitianos y del Caribe /. - México , 1973. 228 p.; *NYPL [JLK 73-145 [no.] 29]*

PUGILISM. see BOXING.

Pumfrey, Peter. Educational attainments . London , New York , 1988. vii, 180 p. : ISBN 1-85000-308-4 : DDC 370.19/34/0941 19 *LC3736.G6 E336 1988 NYPL [Sc E 89-52]*

PUNISHMENT, CAPITAL. see CAPITAL PUNISHMENT.

PUSHKIN, ALEXANDR SERGEEVICH, 1799-1837 - EXHIBITIONS.
Pushkin and his friends . Cambridge , 1987. xii, 95 p. : *NYPL [Sc F 88-236]*

PUSHKIN, ALEXANDR SERGEEVICH, 1799-1837 - FRIENDS AND ASSOCIATES - EXHIBITIONS.
Pushkin and his friends . Cambridge , 1987. xii, 95 p. : *NYPL [Sc F 88-236]*

Pushkin and his friends : the making of a literature and a myth : an exhibition of the Kilgour Collection / selection and commentaries by John E. Malmstad ; with introductory prefaces by William Mills Todd III. Cambridge : The Houghton Library, 1987. xii, 95 p. : ill., facsims., ports. ; 28 cm. P. [i]: Pushkin i ego druz´iā. Includes index. Bibliography: p. xi.
1. Pushkin, Alexandr Sergeevich, 1799-1837 - Exhibitions. 2. Pushkin, Alexandr Sergeevich, 1799-1837 - Friends and associates - Exhibitions. I. Malmstad, John E. II. Todd, William Mills, 1944-. III. Kilgour, Bayard L., Jr., 1904-1984. IV. Houghton Library. *NYPL [Sc F 88-236]*

PYRAMIDS - EGYPT.
Watson, Philip J. Egyptian pyramids and mastaba tombs of the Old and Middle Kingdoms /. Aylesbury, Bucks , 1987. 64 p. : ISBN 0-85263-853-1 *NYPL [Sc D 88-1259]*

The python killer . Grottanelli, Vinigi L. Chicago , 1988. xi, 223 p. : ISBN 0-226-31004-3 : DDC 306/.089963 19 *DT510.43.N95 G76 1988 NYPL [Sc D 88-1458]*

Qua ibo Church of Nigeria . Ikpe, Eno Benjamin. [Uyo? , 1987] (Uyo : Confidence) 31 p. : *NYPL [Sc D 89-28]*

QUA IBOE CHURCH OF NIGERIA - HISTORY.
Ikpe, Eno Benjamin. Qua ibo Church of Nigeria . [Uyo? , 1987] (Uyo : Confidence) 31 p. : *NYPL [Sc D 89-28]*

Quadridge (Presses universitaires de France), 0291-0489 .
(66) Senghor, Léopold Sédar, 1906- Anthologie de la nouvelle poésie nègre et malgache de langue française /. Paris , 1985, c1948. xliv, 227 p. ; ISBN 2-13-038715-2 *NYPL [Sc C 88-134]*

QUAKERS - PENNSYLVANIA - PHILADELPHIA - JUVENILE FICTION.
De Angeli, Marguerite, 1899- Thee, Hannah /.

New York , 1940. [88] p. : *NYPL [Sc D 88-635]*

Quamina-Aiyejina, Lynda. Hezekiah Oluwasanmi Library. Abstracts of theses accepted by University of Ife, 1985 /. Ile-Ife , 1986. ii, ii, 95 p. : *NYPL [Sc D 89-580]*

Quand les graines éclosent... /. Cissé, Ahmed-Tidjani. Paris , 1984. 78 p. ; ISBN 2-85586-028-8 *NYPL [Sc C 88-192]*

Quarante années de la vie politique de Madagascar, 1947-1987 /. Rajoelina, Patrick. Paris , c1988. 176 p. : ISBN 2-85802-915-6 *NYPL [Sc D 89-254]*

Quarcoopome, T. N. O. West African traditional religion / T.N.O. Quarcoopome. Ibadan : African Universities Press, 1987. viii, 200 p. : ill. ; 22 cm. Bibliography: p. 200. ISBN 978-14-8223-8
1. Africa, West - Religion - Text-books. I. Title. *NYPL [Sc D 88-819]*

Quarles, Benjamin.
Black mosaic : essays in Afro-American history and historiography / Benjamin Quarles ; introduction by August Meier. Amherst, Mass. : University of Massachusetts Press, 1988. 213 p. ; 24 cm. Includes bibliographical references. ISBN 0-87023-604-0 (alk. paper) DDC 973/.0496073 19
1. Afro-Americans - History. 2. Afro-Americans - Historiography. 3. United States - Race relations. I. Title.
E185 .Q19 1988 NYPL [Sc E 88-330]

The Negro in the making of America / Benjamin Quarles. 2nd rev. ed. New York : Collier Books ; London : Collier Macmillan, c1987. 362 p. ; 18 cm. Includes index. Bibliography: p. 331-337. ISBN 0-02-036140-8 DDC 973/.0496073 19
1. Afro-Americans - History. I. Title.
E185 .Q2 1987 NYPL [Sc C 88-364]

Quarter-century of Ahmadu Bello University, Zaria. Silver jubilee . Zaria [1987] 76 p. : *NYPL [Sc D 89-6]*

Le quatrième séminaire des secrétaires généraux : Yamoussoukro: 7, 8 et 9 Mars, 1985. [Abidjan] : Fraternité Hebdoéditions, 1985. 55 p. : ill., ports. ; 24 cm. (Documents du Parti) "Documents du parti." On cover: RDA PDCI.
1. Ivory Coast - Politics and government - 1960- - Congresses. I. Editions Fraternité-Hebdo. II. Prti démocratique de Côte d'Ivoire.
NYPL [Sc E 88-150]

O que é cadomblé /. Carmo, João C. (Kpão Clodomiro) Sao Paulo , 1987. 84, [1] p. : *NYPL [Sc B 88-12]*

Queens College (New York, N.Y.). School of Education. Haitian painting . [New York , c1987. 71 p. : *NYPL [Sc D 88-451]*

A queer kind of death /. Baxt, George. New York , 1986, c1966. 249 p. ; ISBN 0-930330-46-3 (pbk.) : *NYPL [Sc C 88-132]*

Quel, Safy. Onobrakpeya, Bruce. Bruce Onobrakpeya--Symbols of ancestral groves . [Mushin [Nigeria] , 1985. 252 p. : ISBN 978-250-900-0 *NYPL [Sc F 88-169]*

Quelle coopération? . Freud, Claude. Paris , c1988. 270 p. : ISBN 2-86537-203-0 *HC800 .F74 1988 NYPL [Sc D 89-602]*

Quest for belonging . Daneel, M. L. (Marthinus L.) Gweru, Zimbabwe , 1987. 310 p., [17] p. of plates : ISBN 0-86922-426-3 *NYPL [Sc D 88-1007]*

A quest for Kwanzaa . Nelson, JohnnnieRenee. Naitional City, Calif. , c1988. [36] p. : *NYPL [Sc D 89-540]*

Questions for big brother /. Shehu, Emman Usman. Nigeria , 1988. 85 p. ; ISBN 978-302-093-5 *NYPL [Sc C 89-121]*

Quieroz, Suely Robles Reis de. Escravidão negra no Brasil / Suely Robles Reis de Queiroz. São Paulo : Editora Atica, 1987. 86 p. ; 18 cm. (Série Princípios . 116) Bibliography: p. 83-86.
1. Slavery - Brazil - History. I. Title. II. Series.
NYPL [Sc C 88-2]

Quiet riots : race and poverty in the United States / edited by Fred R. Harris and Roger W. Wilkins.1st ed. New York : Pantheon Books, 1988. xiii, 223 p. : ill. ; 21 cm. Includes index.

"The Kerner Report twenty years later." Bibliography: p. 185-209. CONTENTS. - The 1967 riots and the Kerner Commission / Fred R. Harris -- The Kerner Report / John Herbers -- Poverty is still with us--and worse / David Hamilton -- Blacks, Hispanics, American Indians, and poverty--and what worked / Gary D. Sandefur -- The persistence of urban poverty / Terry K. Adams, Greg J. Duncan, and Willard L. Rodgers -- Separate societies / Gary Orfield -- The ghetto underclass and the changing structure of urban poverty / William Julius Wilson ... [et al.] -- Thomas Jefferson, the Kerner Commission, and the Retreat of Folly / Lynn A. Curtis -- Race and poverty in the United States--and what should be done / 1988 Commission on the Cities.
ISBN 0-394-57473-7 : DDC 305.5/69/0973 19
1. United States. Kerner Commission. 2. Urban poor - United States. 3. Afro-Americans - Economic conditions. 4. United States - Race relations. I. Harris, Fred R., 1930-. II. Wilkins, Roger W., 1932-.
HV4045 .Q54 1988 NYPL [JLD 89-239]

Quigg, Jane. Ted and Bobby look for something special. Pictures by Ted Coconis. New York, Funk & Wagnalls [1969] 42, [3] p. illus. 24 cm. Blue-butterfly day, by Robert Frost: p. [45] To make up for giving his father the measles, seven-year-old Ted wants to give him a special present and searches all over the neighborhood before finding the perfect gift in his own back yard. SCHOMBURG CHILDREN'S COLLECTION. DDC [Fic]
I. Coconis, Constantinos. II. Schomburg Children's Collection. III. Title.
PZ7.Q333 Te3 NYPL [Sc E 88-543]

Quilombos . Moura, Clovis. São Paulo , 1987. 94 p. ; ISBN 85-08-01858-4 *NYPL [Sc C 88-3]*

The quilt . Ruskin, Cindy. New York , 1988. 160 p. : ISBN 0-671-66597-9 : *NYPL [Sc F 88-237]*

QUILTING - ALABAMA - HISTORY - 20TH CENTURY.
Callahan, Nancy. The Freedom Quilting Bee /. Tuscaloosa, Ala. , c1987. xi, 255 p., [8] p. of plates : ISBN 0-8173-0310-3 DDC 976.0/3800496073 19
NK9112 .C34 1987 NYPL [3-MOT 88-1171]

QUILTS, AMERICAN.
Ruskin, Cindy. The quilt . New York , 1988. 160 p. : ISBN 0-671-66597-9 : *NYPL [Sc F 88-237]*

QUILTS AND QUILTING.
Leon, Eli. Who'd a thought it . San Francisco, CA , c1987. 87 p. : *NYPL [Sc F 88-235]*

QUILTS - UNITED STATES.
Leon, Eli. Who'd a thought it . San Francisco, CA , c1987. 87 p. : *NYPL [Sc F 88-235]*

Quimbois, magie noire et sorcellerie aux Antilles . Ebroïn, Ary. Paris , c1977. 239 p., [4] leaves of plates : DDC 133.4/09729 *BF1622.W47 E26 NYPL [Sc D 89-270]*

Quincy Jones /. Horricks, Raymond, 1933- Tunbridge Wells, Kent , New York , 1985. 127 p., [8] p. of plates : ISBN 0-87052-215-9 (Hippocrene Books) : DDC 785.42/092/4 B 19 *ML419.J7 H67 1985 NYPL [Sc E 87-36]*

Quincy's harvest /. Forbes, Tom H. Philadelphia , c1976. 143 p. : ISBN 0-397-31688-7 DDC [Fic] *PZ7.F75222 Qi NYPL [Sc D 89-93]*

Quintas, Fátima. Sexo e marginalidade : um estudo sobre a sexualidade em camadas de baixa renda / Fátima Quintas. Petrópolis :Vozes, 1986. 191 p. ; 21 cm. Bibliography: p. 184-191.
1. Women - Brazil - Sexual behaviour. 2. Women - Brazil - Sociological aspects. I. Title.
NYPL [Sc D 88-1477]

Quirke, Stephen. Bourriau, Janine. Pharaohs and mortals . Cambridge [Cambridgeshire] ; New York : vi, 167 p. : ISBN 0-521-35319-X DDC 709/.32/07402659 19 *N5336.G7 C3634 1988 NYPL [3-MAE 88-2748]*

Quo vadis Tanzania . Kagwema, Prince, 1931- Dar-es-Salaam , c1985. vii, 119 p. ; ISBN 997-691-804-6 *NYPL [Sc D 89-11]*

Quotes of a general . Babangida, Ibrahim Badamasi. Surulere [Nigeria] , 1987. 90 p. : *NYPL [Sc D 88-711]*

Raça . Azevêdo, Eliane. São Paulo , 1987. 62 p. ; ISBN 85-08-01878-9 *NYPL [Sc C 88-14]*

RACE.
Azevêdo, Eliane. Raça . São Paulo , 1987. 62 p. ; ISBN 85-08-01878-9 *NYPL [Sc C 88-14]*

Banton, Michael P. Racial consciousness /. London , New York , 1988. ix, 153 p. : ISBN 0-582-02385-8 DDC 305.8 19
GN269 .B36 1988 *NYPL [Sc D 89-123]*

Crépeau, Pierre, 1927- Classifications raciales populaires et métissage [microform . [Montréal, 1973] 44 p. *NYPL [*XM-8441]*

Race against the ratios . Gaydon, Vanessa. Johannesburg, South Africa , 1987. 70 p. ; ISBN 0-86982-321-3 *NYPL [Sc F 88-322]*

RACE AND OCCUPATIONS. see OCCUPATIONS AND RACE.

Race and politics / edited by Elizabeth Burgoyne. New York : H.W. Wilson Co., 1985. 174 p. ; 19 cm. (The Reference shelf. v. 56, no. 6) Bibliography: p. 167-174. ISBN 0-8242-0700-9 (pbk.) : DDC 305.8/00973 19
1. Minorities - United States - Political activity. 2. United States - Ethnic relations. 3. United States - Race relations. I. Burgoyne, Elizabeth. II. Series.
E184.A1 R25 1985 *NYPL [8-SAD (Reference shelf. v.56, no.6)]*

RACE AWARENESS.
Banton, Michael P. Racial consciousness /. London , New York , 1988. ix, 153 p. : ISBN 0-582-02385-8 DDC 305.8 19
GN269 .B36 1988 *NYPL [Sc D 89-123]*

RACE AWARENESS IN CHILDREN.
Aboud, Frances E. Children and prejudice /. Oxford [Oxfordshire] , New York, NY , 1988. x, 149 p. : ISBN 0-631-14939-2 : DDC 305.2/3 19
BF723.P75 A24 1988 *NYPL [Sc E 89-57]*

RACE AWARENESS IN LITERATURE.
Iyay Kimoni, 1938- Poésie de la négritude . Kikwit , 1985. vi, 168 p. ; DDC 841/.009/896 19
PQ3897 .I93 1985 *NYPL [Sc B 89-18]*

The race between the flags /. Willis, Priscilla D. New York , 1955. 177 p. :
NYPL [Sc D 88-1508]

RACE - BIBLIOGRAPHY.
Moss, S. G. Books on race and race relations held in the Richard B. Moore Library, Barbados /. Barbados , 1987. 133 leaves ;
NYPL [Sc F 89-105]

Race, class, and conservatism /. Boston, Thomas D. Boston , 1988. xix, 172 p. : ISBN 0-04-330368-4 (alk. paper) DDC 305.5/0973 19
HN90.S6 B67 1988 *NYPL [Sc D 89-107]*

Race, class, and power in Brazil / Pierre-Michel Fontaine, editor. Los Angeles : Center for Afro-American Studies, University of California, c1985. xi, 160 p. : ill. ; 24 cm. (CAAS special publication series, 0882-5300 . v. 7) Papers first presented at a symposium held in 1980. Includes bibliographies. CONTENTS. - Race and class in Brazil / Thomas E. Skidmore -- Race and socioeconomic inequalities in Brazil / Carlos A. Hasenbalg -- Updating the cost of not being white in Brazil / Nelson do Valle Silva -- Blacks and the search for power in Brazil / Pierre-Michel Fontaine -- Brown into Black / J. Michael Turner -- Blacks and the abertura democrática / Michael Mitchell -- The unified Black movement / Lélia Gonzalez -- The African connection and the Afro-Brazilian condition / Anani Dzidzienyo. ISBN 0-934934-22-3 : DDC 305.8/96/081 19
1. Blacks - Brazil - Congresses. 2. Social classes - Brazil - Congresses. 3. Power (Social sciences) - Congresses. I. Fontaine, Pierre Michel, 1938-. II. University of California, Los Angeles. Center for Afro-American Studies. III. Series.
F2659.N4 R24 1985 *NYPL [JLE 88-2671]*

Race, class & the apartheid state /. Wolpe, Harold. London , 1988. viii, 118 p. ; ISBN 0-85255-319-6 (pbk.) DDC 305.8/968 19
DT763 *NYPL [JLD 88-3222]*

Race, class and the apartheid state /. Wolpe, Harold. Race, class & the apartheid state /. London , 1988. viii, 118 p. ; ISBN 0-85255-319-6 (pbk.) DDC 305.8/968 19
DT763 *NYPL [JLD 88-3222]*

RACE DISCRIMINATION - LAW AND LEGISLATION.
Mwaga, D. Z. The crime of apartheid /. Dar es Salaam , c1985. xix, 141 p. ; ISBN 997-660-049-6 DDC 342.68/0873 346.802873 19
LAW *NYPL [Sc C 89-117]*

RACE DISCRIMINATION - LAW AND LEGISLATION - SOUTH AFRICA.
Mwaga, D. Z. The crime of apartheid /. Dar es Salaam , c1985. xix, 141 p. ; ISBN 997-660-049-6 DDC 342.68/0873 346.802873 19
LAW *NYPL [Sc C 89-117]*

RACE DISCRIMINATION - NEW YORK (N. Y.)
Wright, Bruce, 1918- Black robes, white justice /. Secaucus, N.J. , c1987. 214 p. ; ISBN 0-8184-0422-1 : DDC 345.73/05/08996073 347.305508996073 19
KF373.W67 A33 1987 *NYPL [JLE 87-2842]*

RACE DISCRIMINATION - SOUTH AFRICA.
Gaydon, Vanessa. Race against the ratios . Johannesburg, South Africa , 1987. 70 p. ; ISBN 0-86982-321-3 *NYPL [Sc F 88-322]*

RACE DISCRIMINATION - UNITED STATES.
Gross, Samuel R. Death & discrimination . Boston , c1989. xvi, 268 p. ; ISBN 1-555-53040-0 (alk. paper) : DDC 364.6/6/0973 19
HV8699.U5 G76 1989 *NYPL [Sc D 89-493]*

McGuire, Phillip, 1944- He, too, spoke for democracy . New York , c1988. xvii, 154 p. ; ISBN 0-313-26115-6 (lib. bdg. : alk. paper) DDC 355/.008996073 B 19
KF373.H38 M35 1988 *NYPL [Sc E 88-347]*

RACE - HANDBOOKS, MANUALS, ETC.
International handbook on race and race relations /. New York , 1987. xviii, 483 p. ; ISBN 0-313-24770-6 (lib. bdg. : alk. paper) DDC 305.8 19
HT1521 .I485 1987 *NYPL [Sc E 88-75]*

RACE IN LITERATURE.
Nielsen, Aldon Lynn. Reading race . Athens, Ga. , c1988. xii, 178 p. ; ISBN 0-8203-1061-1 (alk. paper) DDC 811/.5/09355 19
PS310.R34 N54 1988 *NYPL [JFE 88-3098]*

RACE - JUVENILE LITERATURE.
Randall, Blossom E. Fun for Chris /. Chicago , c1956. 26 p. : *NYPL [Sc E 88-238]*

RACE PREJUDICE. see RACE DISCRIMINATION; RACISM.

RACE QUESTION. see RACE RELATIONS.

Race, radicalism, and reform . Harris, Abram Lincoln, 1899-1963. New Brunswick, U. S. A. , c1989. viii, 521 p. ; ISBN 0-88738-210-X DDC 305.8/96073 19
E185.8 .H27 1989 *NYPL [Sc E 89-166]*

RACE RELATIONS AND THE PRESS - ALABAMA - BIRMINGHAM - CONGRESSES.
The Media and the movement [microform] . [Birmingham, Ala. , 1981?] [12] p. :
NYPL [Sc Micro F-10982]

RACE RELATIONS - BIBLIOGRAPHY.
Moss, S. G. Books on race and race relations held in the Richard B. Moore Library, Barbados /. Barbados , 1987. 133 leaves ;
NYPL [Sc F 89-105]

RACE RELATIONS - FICTION.
Neigoff, Mike. Free throw. Chicago [1968] 128 p. DDC [Fic]
PZ7.N427 Fr *NYPL [Sc D 88-1427]*

RACE RELATIONS - HANDBOOKS, MANUALS, ETC.
International handbook on race and race relations /. New York , 1987. xviii, 483 p. ; ISBN 0-313-24770-6 (lib. bdg. : alk. paper) DDC 305.8 19
HT1521 .I485 1987 *NYPL [Sc E 88-75]*

RACE RELATIONS IN LITERATURE.
Harris, Norman, 1951- Understanding the sixties [microform] . 1980. 202 leaves ;
NYPL [Sc Micro R-4680]

Nielsen, Aldon Lynn. Reading race . Athens, Ga. , c1988. xii, 178 p. ; ISBN 0-8203-1061-1 (alk. paper) DDC 811/.5/09355 19
PS310.R34 N54 1988 *NYPL [JFE 88-3098]*

Ogidan, Anna. Thememschwerpunkte im Werk Ayi Kwei Armahs /. Wien , 1988. ii, 202 p. : ISBN 3-85043-046-4
NYPL [Sc D 88-1035]

RACE RELATIONS - STUDY AND TEACHING (HIGHER) - ILLINOIS - CHICAGO.
Persons, Stow, 1913- Ethnic studies at Chicago, 1905-45 /. Urbana , c1987. 159 p. ; ISBN 0-252-01344-1 (alk. paper) DDC 305.8/007/1077311 19
HT1506 .P47 1987 *NYPL [JLE 87-1776]*

Race, religion, and ethnicity in disaster recovery /. Bolin, Robert C. [Boulder. Colo.] , 1986. ix, 265 p. : *NYPL [Sc D 88-904]*

RACE - RELIGIOUS ASPECTS.
Ecumenical Association of Third World Theologians. Identidade negra e religião . Rio de Janeiro , 1986. 201 p. ;
NYPL [Sc D 88-485]

Race Today Collective. The arrivants : a pictorial essay on Blacks in Britain / by the Race Today Collective. London, England : Race Today Publications, 1987. 112 p. : ill. ; 21 cm. ISBN 0-947716-10-6 (pbk.)
1. Blacks - Great Britain - Pictorial works. 2. Minorities - Great Britain - Pictorial works. I. Title.
NYPL [Sc D 88-1206]

Race toward equality /. Cole, Johnnetta B. Havana, Cuba (P.O. Box 4208, Havana) , c1986. 99 p. ; DDC 305.8/0097291 19
F1789.N3 C65 1986 *NYPL [Sc D 89-359]*

Race, training, and employment /. Verma, Gajendra K. London , New York , 1987. vi, 134 p. ; ISBN 1-85000-243-6 : DDC 331.3/46/0941 19
HD5715.5.G7 V47 1987
*NYPL [*QT 88-3245]*

RACES OF MAN. see ETHNOLOGY.

RACIAL AMALGAMATION. see MISCEGENATION.

Racial consciousness /. Banton, Michael P. London , New York , 1988. ix, 153 p. : ISBN 0-582-02385-8 DDC 305.8 19
GN269 .B36 1988 *NYPL [Sc D 89-123]*

RACIAL CROSSING. see MISCEGENATION.

RACIAL DISCRIMINATION. see RACE DISCRIMINATION.

Racial equality and good practice maternity care . Pearson, Maggie. London , 1985. 37 p. : ISBN 0-86082-610-4 (pbk) : DDC 362.1/982 19
RG964.G7 *NYPL [Sc F 88-393]*

RACIAL IDENTITY OF AFRO-AMERICANS. see AFRO-AMERICANS - RACE IDENTITY.

RACIAL IDENTITY OF BLACKS. see BLACKS - RACE IDENTITY.

Racines du présent, 0757-6366.
La Colonisation, rupture ou parenthèse /. Paris , c1987. 326 p. : *NYPL [Sc D 88-727]*

Racism and sexism in children's books. New York : Council on Interracial Books for Children, c1978. 72 p. : ill. ; 22 cm. (Interracial digest . no. 2) Title from cover. Includes ten articles originally published by the Council on Interracial Books for Children in its Bulletin (1974-1977). ISBN 0-930040-29-5
1. Children's literature - History and criticism. 2. Racism in literature. 3. Sex role in literature. I. Interracial books for children bulletin. II. Series.
NYPL [Sc D 89-259]

RACISM - COMIC BOOKS, STRIPS, ETC.
Comics für Afrika . Dormagen [West Germany] [1986] 96 p. : *NYPL [Sc G 88-27]*

RACISM - CUBA - HISTORY.
Cole, Johnnetta B. Race toward equality /. Havana, Cuba (P.O. Box 4208, Havana) , c1986. 99 p. ; DDC 305.8/0097291 19
F1789.N3 C65 1986 *NYPL [Sc D 89-359]*

RACISM - FRANCE.
Désir, Harlem, 1959- Touche pas à mon pote /. Paris [c1985] 148 p. ; ISBN 2-246-36421-3 : DDC 323.42/3/06044 19
DC34 .D47 1985 *NYPL [Sc C 88-305]*

RACISM - GREAT BRITAIN.
Haynes, Aaron, 1927- The state of Black Britain /. London , 1983. 160 p. ; ISBN 0-946455-01-5 *NYPL [Sc D 88-348]*

Leech, Kenneth, 1939- Struggle in Babylon . London , 1988. 253 p. : ISBN 0-85969-577-8 (pbk) DDC 261.8/348/0941 19
NYPL [Sc D 89-176]

Smith, Graham. When Jim Crow met John

Bull . London , c1987. 265 p. ; ISBN
1-85043-039-X   *NYPL [Sc D 88-55]*

Solomos, John. Black youth, racism and the
state . Cambridge [Cambridgeshire] , New
York , 1988. 284 p. ; ISBN 0-521-36019-6 DDC
305.8/96041 19
DA125.N4 S65 1988   *NYPL [Sc E 88-606]*

Widgery, David. Beating time /. London ,
1986. 126 p. : ISBN 0-7011-2985-9
            NYPL [JMD 88-112]

RACISM IN LANGUAGE.
Discourse and discrimination /. Detroit , 1988.
269 p. ; ISBN 0-8143-1957-2 (alk. paper) DDC
401/.9 19
P120.R32 D57 1988   *NYPL [Sc E 88-451]*

RACISM IN LITERATURE.
Barthelemy, Anthony Gerard, 1949- Black face,
maligned race . Baton Rouge , c1987. xi, 215
p. ; ISBN 0-8071-1331-X DDC 822/.3/093520396
19
PR678.A4 B37 1987
            NYPL [MWET 87-5064]

Nielsen, Aldon Lynn. Reading race . Athens,
Ga. , c1988. xii, 178 p. ; ISBN 0-8203-1061-1
(alk. paper) DDC 811/.5/09355 19
PS310.R34 N54 1988   *NYPL [JFE 88-3098]*

Racism and sexism in children's books. New
York , c1978. 72 p. : ISBN 0-930040-29-5
            NYPL [Sc D 89-259]

RACISM IN TEXTBOOKS - SOUTH AFRICA.
Dean, Elizabeth. [History in black and white.
Spanish.] Historia en blanco y negro .
Barcelona , Paris , 1984. 196 p. ; ISBN
92-3-302092-4 (Unesco)
            NYPL [Sc D 88-594]

RACISM - SOUTHERN STATES - HISTORY - 20TH CENTURY.
Whitfield, Stephen J., 1942- A death in the
Delta . New York , London , c1988. xiv, 193
p., [8] p. of plates : ISBN 0-02-935121-9 : DDC
345.73/02523 347.3052523 19
E185.61 .W63 1989   *NYPL [Sc E 89-140]*

RACISM - STUDY AND TEACHING - GREAT BRITAIN.
Brandt, Godfrey L. The realization of anti-racist
teaching /. London , New York , 1986. x, 210
p. : ISBN 1-85000-126-X : DDC 370.19/0941 19
LC192.2 .B73 1986   *NYPL [Sc E 89-77]*

RACISM - UNITED STATES.
Davis, Angela Yvonne, 1944- Women,
culture, & politics /. New York, NY , 1989. xv,
238 p. ; ISBN 0-394-76976-8 : DDC
305.4/8896073 19
E185.86 .D382 1989   *NYPL [Sc D 89-275]*

Shakur, Assata. Assata, an autobiography /.
Westport, CT , 1987. xiv, 274 p. ; ISBN
0-88208-221-3 : DDC 973/.0496073024 19
E185.97.S53 A3 1987   *NYPL [Sc E 88-21]*

Staples, Robert. The urban plantation .
Oakland, CA , c1987. 248 p. ; ISBN
0-933296-13-4 (pbk.)
            NYPL [Sc D 88-1021]

RACISM - UNITED STATES - HISTORY - 19TH CENTURY.
Bowen, David Warren, 1944- Andrew Johnson
and the Negro /. Knoxville , c1989. xvi, 206
p. ; ISBN 0-87049-584-4 (alk. paper) DDC
973/.0496073 19
E667 .B65 1989   *NYPL [Sc D 89-508]*

Fredrickson, George M., 1934- The arrogance
of race . Middletown, Conn. , c1988. viii, 310
p. ; ISBN 0-8195-5177-5 DDC 973/.0496 19
E441 .F77 1988   *NYPL [Sc E 88-487]*

Werner, John M., 1941- Reaping the bloody
harvest . New York , 1986. 333 p. ; ISBN
0-8240-8301-6 (alk. paper) : DDC 973.5/6 19
E185 .W44 1986   *NYPL [Sc E 88-242]*

RACISM - UNITED STATES - HISTORY - 20TH CENTURY.
Ashmore, Harry S. Hearts and minds . Cabin
John, Md. , c1988. xviii, 513 p. ; ISBN
0-932020-58-5 (pbk. : alk. paper) DDC
305.8/96073 19
E185.615 .A83 1988   *NYPL [Sc D 89-382]*

Blauner, Bob. Black lives, white lives .
Berkeley , c1989. xii, 347 p. ; ISBN
0-520-06261-2 (alk. paper) DDC 305.8/00973 19
E185.615 .B556 1989   *NYPL [Sc E 89-219]*

RACISM - UNITED STATES - PSYCHOLOGICAL ASPECTS.
The Psychopathology of everyday racism and
sexism /. New York , c1988. xix, 120 p. ;
ISBN 0-918393-51-5 (pbk.) DDC 305.4/2 19
RC451.4.M58 P79 1988
            NYPL [Sc D 89-449]

Radical records : thirty years of lesbian and gay
history, 1957-1987 / edited by Bob Cant and
Susan Hemmings. London ; New York :
Routledge, 1988. xi, 266 p. ; 22 cm. Errata slip
inserted. ISBN 0-415-00200-1 DDC 306.7/66/0941
19
1. Gay liberation movement - Great Britain - History -
20th century. 2. Gays - Great Britain - Political
activity. 3. Lesbians - Great Britain - Political activity.
I. Cant, Bob. II. Hemmings, Susan.
HQ76.8.G7 R33 1988   *NYPL [JLD 88-1427]*

Radical Statistics (Association). Race Group.
Britain's Black population . Aldershot, Hants,
England , Brookfield, Vt., USA , c1988. xv, 298
p. ; ISBN 0-566-05179-6 : DDC 305.8/96/041 19
DA125.N4 B75 1988   *NYPL [Sc E 89-100]*

RADICALISM - UNITED STATES - HISTORY - 20TH CENTURY.
Haines, Herbert H. Black radicals and the civil
rights mainstream, 1954-1970 /. Knoxville ,
c19. xii, 231 p. : ISBN 0-87049-563-1 (alk. paper) :
DDC 305.8/96073 19
E185.615 .H25 1988   *NYPL [Sc E 88-511]*

RADIO ADVERTISING - UNITED STATES.
Newman, Mark. Entrepreneurs of profit and
pride . New York , 1988. xvi, 186 p., [4] p. of
plates : ISBN 0-275-92888-8 DDC 305.8/96073 19
PN1991.8.A35 N49 1988
            NYPL [Sc E 89-88]

RADIO AUDIENCES - GREAT BRITAIN.
Anwar, Muhammad. Ethnic minority
broadcasting . London , 1983. 80 p. ; ISBN
0-907920-39-X   *NYPL [Sc D 88-573]*

RADIO AUDIENCES - UNITED STATES.
Newman, Mark. Entrepreneurs of profit and
pride . New York , 1988. xvi, 186 p., [4] p. of
plates : ISBN 0-275-92888-8 DDC 305.8/96073 19
PN1991.8.A35 N49 1988
            NYPL [Sc E 89-88]

RADIO COMMERCIALS. see RADIO ADVERTISING.

Radlauer, Edward. (joint author) Radlauer, Ruth
Shaw. Father is big. Glendale, Calif. [1967] 1 v.
(unpaged)
PZ7.R122 Fat   *NYPL [Sc E 88-589]*

Radlauer, Ruth Shaw. Father is big. Written by
Ruth and Ed Radlauer. Photographed by
Harvey Mandlin. Glendale, Calif., Bowmar Pub.
Corp. [1967] 1 v. (unpaged) col. illus. 21 x 23
cm. (Bowmar early childhood series) SCHOMBURG
CHILDREN'S COLLECTION.
1. Fathers and sons - Juvenile fiction. I. Radlauer,
Edward, joint author. II. Schomburg Children's
Collection. III. Title.
PZ7.R122 Fat   *NYPL [Sc E 88-589]*

Rafapa, J. R. L. Leratosello / J.R.L. Rafapa. 2nd
rev. ed. Pretoria : Van Schaik, 1979, c1983
printing. 115 p. ; 22 cm.
1. Northern Sotho language - Texts. I. Title.
            NYPL [Sc D 88-647]

Raferty, Gerald. Twenty-dollar horse / bby
Gerald Raferty ; illustions by Bernard Safran.
1st Cadmus ed. Eau Claire, Wisconsin : E.M.
Hale, 1967, c1955. 192 p. : ill. ; cm. Summary:
Jack Leach and Teddy Washington make a handsome
profit from their carnival horse, but racism nearly
prevents the Washingtons from buying a mew house.
SCHOMBURG CHILDREN'S COLLECTION.
1. Horses - Juvenile fiction. 2. Discrimination in
housing - Juvenile fiction. I. Safran, Bernard. II.
Schomburg Children's Collection. III. Title.
            NYPL [Sc D 88-664]

A rage in Harlem /. Himes, Chester B., 1909-
London , New York , 1985, c1957. 159 p. ;
ISBN 0-85031-618-9   *NYPL [Sc D 88-692]*

Raggenbass, Andreas, 1942- Jazz in Willisau .
Luzern , c1978. 206 p. ; ISBN 3-7239-0051-8
DDC 785.42/09494/5 19
ML3509.S9 J4 1978   *NYPL [Sc F 89-24]*

RAGTIME MUSIC - HISTORY AND CRITICISM.
Berlin, Edward A. Reflections and research on
ragtime /. Brooklyn, N.Y. , c1987. xii, 99 p. :

ISBN 0-914678-27-2 (pbk.) DDC 781/.572 19
ML3530 .B5 1987   *NYPL [Sc D 88-410]*

RAGTIME MUSIC - UNITED STATES - HISTORY AND CRITICISM.
Oliver, Paul. The New Grove gospel, blues and
jazz . New York , 1986. 395 p. [16] p. of
plates : ISBN 0-393-01696-X
            NYPL [JND 88-16]

RAHANWEYN (AFRICAN PEOPLE) - ECONOMIC CONDITIONS.
Massey, Garth. Subsistence and change .
Boulder , 1987. xvii, 238 p. : ISBN
0-8133-7294-1 (alk. paper) : DDC
338.1/0967/73 19
DT402.4.R35 M37 1987
            NYPL [Sc D 88-298]

Raharolahy, Elie. Tantara notsongaina / Erika
(Elie Raharolahy) [Antananarivo?] : Librairie
Mixte, [1976] v. : ill., port. ; 17 cm. Title from
t.p. and fascicules; it is lacking on cover.
1. Malagasy language - Texts. I. Title. II. Title: Erika.
            NYPL [Sc C 88-238]

Raherisoanjato, Daniel. Origines et évolution du
Royaume de l'Arindrano jusqu'au XIXe siècle :
contribution à l'histoire régionale de
Madagascar / Daniel Raherisoanjato.
Antananarivo : Musée d'art et d'archéologie,
Université de Madagascar, 1984. 334 leaves :
ill. ; 27 cm. (Travaux et documents / Musée d'art et
d'archéologie, Université de Madagascar . no 22) Thesis
(maîtrise d'histoire)--Université de Madagascar, 1980.
Bibliography: leaves 14-25. DDC 969/.1 19
1. Betsileos - History. 2. Arindrano (Madagascar :
Region) - History. I. Series: Travaux et documents
(Université de Madagascar. Musée d'art et
d'archéologie) , 22. II. Title.
DT469.M37 A747 1984
            NYPL [Sc F 88-390]

Rahming, Melvin B., 1943- The evolution of the
West Indian's image in the Afro-American
novel / Melvin B. Rahming. Millwood, N.Y. :
Associated Faculty Press, c1986. xix, 160 p. ;
23 cm. (Series in modern and contemporary literature)
National university publications Includes index.
Bibliography: p. 150-154. ISBN 0-8046-9339-0 DDC
813/.009/35203969729 19
1. American fiction - Afro-American authors - History
and criticism. 2. West Indians in literature. 3. West
Indian Americans in literature. 4. Afro-Americans -
Relations with West Indians. I. Title. II. Series.
PS153.N5 R3 1985   *NYPL [JFD 86-6569]*

Rain boat /. Kendall, Lace. New York , 1965.
159 p.   *NYPL [Sc D 88-472]*

Rainibe, Dahy. La Vie quotidienne dans un
district, 1913-1935 . Antananarivo , 1984. 53
p., [6] leaves of plates : DDC 969/.1 19
DT469.M37 A758 1984
            NYPL [Sc F 88-241]

Raisins amers. Sachy. Floraison d'or ; Raisins
amers ; Raison de croire /. [Haiti? , 1987]
(Port-au-Prince, Haïti : Impr. II) 160 p. ;
MLCS 88/02114 (P)   *NYPL [Sc D 88-1108]*

Raison de croire. Sachy. Floraison d'or ; Raisins
amers ; Raison de croire /. [Haiti? , 1987]
(Port-au-Prince, Haïti : Impr. II) 160 p. ;
MLCS 88/02114 (P)   *NYPL [Sc D 88-1108]*

Rajab, Hammie.
Roho mkononi / Hammie Rajab. Dar es
Salaam : Busara, c1984. 113 p. : ill. ; 19 cm. In
Swahili. ISBN 997-693-102-6
1. Swahili language - Texts. I. Title.
            NYPL [Sc C 88-94]

Somo kaniponza / Hammie Rajab. Dar es
Salaam : Busara Publications, c1984. 69 p. ; 19
cm. In Swahili. ISBN 997-693-103-4; 997-693-103-04
1. Swahili language - Texts. I. Title.
PL8704.R28 S66 1984   *NYPL [Sc C 88-57]*

Rajabu, A. R. M. S. Communication practice in
development / A.R.M.S. Rajabu. Nairobi,
Kenya : Communications for Basic Services
Regional Training Project, UNICEF Eastern
and Southern Africa Regional Office, 1986. vi,
50 p. : ill. ; 30 cm. (Community development
workers' training series . 4) Bibliography: p. 50. DDC
307.1/4/096 19
1. Communication in community development - Africa.
I. Title. II. Series.
HN780.Z9 C6698 1986 *NYPL [Sc F 88-282]*

Rajoelina, Patrick. Quarante années de la vie
politique de Madagascar, 1947-1987 / Patrick

Rajoelina. Paris : L'Harmattan, c1988. 176 p. : maps ; 22 cm. Includes index. Bibliography: p. 163-169. ISBN 2-85802-915-6
1. Madagascar - Politics and government - 1947-1960. 2. Madagascar - Politics and government - 1960-. I. Title.   NYPL [Sc D 89-254]

Rajshekar Shetty, V. T., 1932-
Dalit, the black Untouchables of India / by V.T. Rajshekar ; [foreword by Y.N. Kly]. Atlanta, Ga. : Clarity Press, c1987. 89 p. ; 22 cm. Originally published under title: Apartheid in India. Includes bibliographical references. ISBN 0-932863-05-1 (pbk.) :
1. Caste - India. I. Rajshekar Shetty, V. T., 1932- Apartheid in India. II. Title. III. Title: Apartheid in India. IV. Title: Black Untouchables of India.
NYPL [Sc D 89-356]

Apartheid in India. Rajshekar Shetty, V. T., 1932- Dalit, the black Untouchables of India / by V.T. Rajshekar ; [foreword by Y.N. Kly]. Atlanta, Ga. , c1987. 89 p. ; ISBN 0-932863-05-1 (pbk.) :
NYPL [Sc D 89-356]

Rakorong, K. Gobotswang, Z. Pilot evaluation report on Mahalapye Development Trust /. Gaborone, Botswana [1982] v leaves, 61, 3 p. ; HD5710.85.B59 G63 1982
NYPL [Sc F 89-108]

Rakoto, Andrianaronosy. Rakoto, Andrianasolo. Izainahary [microform] /. Tananarive [1978] 36 p. ;   NYPL [Sc Micro F-10989]

Rakoto, Andrianasolo.
Ireny lovantsofina ireny [microform] /. Tananarive [1978] iv, 48 p. ;
NYPL [Sc Micro F-10987]

Izainahary [microform] / Rakoto Andrianasolo, Rakoto Andrianaronosy, Tantsaha sy Fokonolona. Tananarive : Foibe Ara-Tsaina Malagasy, [1978] 36 p. ; 27 cm. (Boky lovanjanahary . 8) In Malagasy. On cover: FOFIPA (Foibe Filan-Kevitry ny Mpampianatra) Microfiche. New York: New York Public Library, 198 . 1 microfiche: negative; 11 x 15 cm. (FSN Sc 019,090)
1. Madagascar - Religion. I. Rakoto, Andrianaronosy. II. Title. NYPL [Sc Micro F-10989]

Ny djoutche Malagasy [microform] /. Tananarive [1978] 28 p. ;
NYPL [Sc Micro F-10988]

Rakotoson, Michèle. Le bain des reliques : roman malgache / Michèle Rakotoson. Paris : Karthala, c1988. 146 p. ; 22 cm. ISBN 2-86537-218-9
1. Madagascar - Fiction. I. Title.
NYPL [Sc D 89-245]

Ralph Ellison /. Bishop, Jack, 1910- New York , c1988. 110 p. : ISBN 1-555-46585-4 DDC 818/.5409 B 19
PS3555.L625 Z59 1988 NYPL [Sc E 88-165]

Ralph M. Paiewonsky Library. Library handbook, 1982-1983 [microform] / Ralph M. Paiewonsky Library, College of the Virgin Islands. [St. Thomas] : The Library, [1982?] 10 p. : ill. ; 22 cm. Cover title. Microfiche. New York: New York Public Library, 198 . 1 microfiche: negative; 11 x 15 cm. (FSN Sc 019,072)
I. Title.   NYPL [Sc Micro F-10939]

Ramdharrysing, Vimal. Gu Margoz [microform] / Vimal Ramdharrysing. [Mauritius? : Central Printing, 198-?] 29 p. ; 20 cm. Cover title. Microfiche. New York: New York Public Library, 1986. 1 microfiche: negative; 11 x 15 cm. (FSN Sc, 019,124)
1. Creole dialects - Mauritius - Texts. I. Title.
NYPL [Sc Micro F-11122]

RAMOS, ARTHUR, 1903-1949.
Lody, Raul. Coleção Arthur Ramos /. [Fortaleza] , 1987. 78 p. : ISBN 85-24-60035-7
NYPL [Sc D 89-479]

Ramos Guédez, José Marcial. Historia del Estado Miranda / José Marcial Ramos Guédez. Caracas : Ediciones de la Presidencia de la República, 1981. 222 p. : ill. ; 23 cm. Bibliography: p. 215-219. Author's autographed presentation copy to the Schomburg Center. DDC 987/.35 19
1. Miranda (Venezuela : State) - History. I. Title.
F2331.M6 R36 1981 NYPL [Sc D 89-390]

Ramos, Miguel. Ase omo osayin-- ewe aye / Miguel "Willie" Ramos. 2a. ed. [S.l.] : M. Ramos, 1985, c1982. 113 p. ; 21 cm. In Yoruba and Spanish.

1. Santeria (Cultus) - Songs and music. 2. Yoruba language - Texts. I. Title. NYPL [Sc D 89-487]

Rampersad, Arnold. The life of Langston Hughes / Arnold Rampersad. New York : Oxford University Press, 1986-1988. 2 v. : ill., ports. ; 24 cm. Includes. CONTENTS. - v. 1. 1902-1941, I, too, sing America-- v. 2. 1941-1967, I dream a world. ISBN 0-19-504011-2 (v. 1) DDC 818/.5209 B 19
1. Hughes, Langston, 1902-1967 - Biography. 2. Poets, American - 20th century - Biography. 3. Afro-American poets - Biography. I. Title.
PS3515.U274 Z698 1986
NYPL [Sc E 87-44]

Ramusi, Molapatene Collins. Soweto, my love / by Molapatene Collins Ramusi and Ruth S. Turner. 1st ed. New York : Holt, c1988. viii, 262 p. ; 24 cm. ISBN 0-8050-0263-4 DDC 968.06/092/4 B 19
1. Ramusi, Molapatene Collins. 2. Civil rights workers - South Africa - Biography. 3. Anti-apartheid movements - South Africa. 4. Tlokwa (African people) - Biography. I. Turner, Ruth S. II. Title.
DT779.955.R36 A3 1988
NYPL [Sc E 89-95]

RAMUSI, MOLAPATENE COLLINS.
Ramusi, Molapatene Collins. Soweto, my love /. New York , c1988. viii, 262 p. ; ISBN 0-8050-0263-4 DDC 968.06/092/4 B 19
DT779.955.R36 A3 1988
NYPL [Sc E 89-95]

Rand Corporation. Henze, Paul B., 1924- Rebels and separatists in Ethiopia . Santa Monica, CA , 1985. xv, 98 p. ; ISBN 0-8330-0696-7 DDC 963/.07 19
DT387.95 .H46 1986 NYPL [JFE 86-5101]

Rand McNally and Company. World Book, Inc. The World Book atlas. Chicago , c1988. 1 atlas (432 p.) : ill. (some col.), col. maps ; 38 cm. ISBN 0-7166-3181-4 : DDC 912 19
G1021 .W6735 1986 NYPL [Sc Ref 89-1]

Randall, Blossom E. Fun for Chris / by Blossom E. Randall ; pictures by Eunice Young Smith. Chicago : Albert Whitman, c1956. 26 p. : ill. (chiefly col.) ; 24 cm. SCHOMBURG CHILDREN'S COLLECTION.
1. Race - Juvenile literature. I. Smith, Eunice Young, 1902-. II. Schomburg Children's Colecction. III. Title.
NYPL [Sc E 88-238]

Randolph, A. Philip (Asa Philip), 1889-
White House Conference "To Fulfill These Rights", Washington, D. C., 1966. Major addresses at the White House Conference to Fulfill These Rights, June 1-2, 1966. [Washington, 1966] 66 p. DDC 323.4/09174/96
E185.615 .W45 1966c NYPL [Sc E 88-386]

RANDOLPH, A. PHILIP (ASA PHILIP), 1889- - JUVENILE LITERATURE.
Hanley, Sally. A. Philip Randolph /. New York [1988], 1989. 110 p. : ISBN 1-555-46607-9 DDC 323.4/092/4 92 19
E185.97.R27 H36 1989 NYPL [Sc E 88-617]

RANGE MANAGEMENT - AFRICA, EAST.
Rigby, Peter. Persistent pastoralists . London , Totowa, N.J. , 1985. x, 198 p. : ISBN 0-86232-226-X : DDC 305.8/9676 19
DT443.3.M37 R54 1985
NYPL [JLD 86-2309]

RANK. see SOCIAL CLASSES.

Rankin, James, 1831- Buchanan, John, 1855-1896. The Shiré highlands. Blantyre [Malawi] , 1982. xii, 260 p., [8] p. of plates :
NYPL [Sc C 87-434]

Ranomasina Indiana /. Iray, Olana. Antananarivo [1983] 98 p. ;   NYPL [Sc C 88-239]

RAPE - UNITED STATES.
Marowitz, Roberta Lee. Psychosocial dynamics of Black rapists [microform] . 1982. x, 216 leaves ;   NYPL [Sc Micro R-4806]

RAPPING (MUSIC)
Adler, B. Tougher than leather . New York , c1987. viii, 191 p., [14] p. of plates : ISBN 0-451-15121-6 (pbk.) : NYPL [Sc D 88-271]

Rapport sur la coopération inter-universitaire dans le domaine de l'impression et l'édition [microform] /. Harris, John, librarian. 1961. 12 p. ;   NYPL [Sc Micro R-4137 no. 44]

Rapport sur les troubles de Saint-Domingue.

Tarbé, Charles. Paris, 1791-[1792] 4 v.
F1921 .T17   NYPL [Sc Rare F 88-17]

Rapports entre catholicisme et religions traditionnelles. Christianisme en Afrique noire . Dakar , 1979. 162 p. ;
NYPL [Sc F 89-17]

Rapso explosion /. Brother Resistance. London , 1986. 84 p. : ISBN 0-496-91834-1
NYPL [Sc D 88-500]

RAS TAFARI MOVEMENT.
Royal Ethiopian Judah-Coptic Church. Rastafari manifesto. [Kingston, Jamaica , 1984?] [97] p. ;   NYPL [Sc G 88-20]

RAS TAFARI MOVEMENT - JAMAICA.
Chevannes, Barry. Social origins of the Rastafari movement /. Mona, Kingston , c1978. xii, 323 p. ;
BL2532.R37 C48 1978 NYPL [Sc F 88-368]

RAS TAFARI MOVEMENT - POETRY.
Miguel, Brother. Rastaman chant /. Castries, St. Lucia, W.I. , c1983. 151 p. :
MLCS 84/17323 (P)   NYPL [Sc D 88-621]

Rasamuel, David. Traditions orales et archéologie de la basse Sahatorendrika : étude de sources concernant le peuplement / David Rasamuel. [Antananarivo] : Musée d'art et d'archéologie de l'Université de Madagascar, 1979. 287 p., [33] leaves of plates : ill., maps ; 27 cm. (Travaux et documents / Musée d'art et d'archéologie de l'Université de Madagascar . no. 19) "Mémoire présenté en vue de la maîtrise ès lettres, Centre d'art et d'archéologie." Bibliography: p. 18-29.
1. Sahatorendrika River Valley (Antananarivo, Madagascar) - History. 2. Sahatorendrika River Valley (Antananarivo, Madagascar) - Population. 3. Sahatorendrika River Valley (Antananarivo, Madagascar) - Antiquities. 4. Madagascar - Antiquities. I. Series: Tananarive, Malagasy Republic. Université de Madagascar. Musée d'art et d'archéologie. Travaux et documents, 19. II. Title.
DT469.M37 S247 1979 NYPL [Sc F 88-79]

Rasco, José Ignacio [i. e. Rasco y Bermudez, José Ignacio] see Rasco y Bermudez, José Ignacio.

Rasco y Bermudez, José Ignacio. Integración cultural de América Latina : panorama histórico, ciclo de conferencias / José Ignacio Rasco. Medellín, [Colombia : Editorial Bedout, 1975] 188 p. ; 22 cm. Bibliography: p. 157-176.
1. Latin America - Civilization - History - Addresses, essays, lectures. I. Title.
F1408.3 .R37   NYPL [HCB 78-2271]

Rashid, S. Khalid. Islamic law in Nigeria . Lagos , 1986. 309 p. ; ISBN 978-247-037-6
NYPL [Sc D 89-417]

Raspaid, Jean. Antilles Caraïbes /. Paris , c1982. 157 p. : ISBN 2-7191-0177-0
NYPL [Sc F 88-347]

RASSEMBLEMENT DÉMOCRATIQUE AFRICAIN.
Lisette, Yeyon. Le RDA et le Tchad . Paris , Abidjan , 1986. 351 p. ; ISBN 2-7087-0472-9
(Présence africaine) NYPL [Sc E 87-627]

Rastafari manifesto . Royal Ethiopian Judah-Coptic Church. [Kingston, Jamaica , 1984?] [97] p. ;   NYPL [Sc G 88-20]

RASTAFARI MOVEMENT - JUVENILE LITERATURE.
Obadiah. I am a Rastafarian /. London , New York , c1986. 32 p. : ISBN 0-86313-260-X :
BL2532.R37   NYPL [Sc F 89-12]

Rastaman chant /. Miguel, Brother. Castries, St. Lucia, W.I. , c1983. 151 p. :
MLCS 84/17323 (P) NYPL [Sc D 88-621]

A rat on her back . Nyika, Tambayi O., 1961- [Ndinodawo mwana. English.] Gweru , 1986. 51 p. ; ISBN 0-86922-394-1
NYPL [Sc C 89-20]

RATIONALISM.
Elungu, P. E. A. Tradition africaine et rationalité moderne /. Paris , c1987. 187 p. ;
NYPL [Sc D 88-1101]

RATIONALIZATION OF INDUSTRY. see INDUSTRIAL MANAGEMENT.

Ratsiraka . Deleris, Ferdinand. Paris , c1986. 135 p. ; ISBN 2-85802-697-1 NYPL [Sc D 88-777]

Ratsiraka, Didier. Kabary tatitra nataon' Andriamatoa Didier Ratsiraka, filohan' ny

Repoblika Demokratika Malagasy.
Antananarivo : Impr. national, 1985. 93 p. : ill.,
port. ; 23 cm. Cover title. In Malagasy.
*1. Madagascar - Politics and government - 1960-. 2.
Malagasy language - Texts. I. Title.*
                                        NYPL [Sc D 88-1295]

Ratsiraka, Didier, 1936- Kabarin'ny
Filoham-pirenena / Didier Ratsiraka.
[Antananarivo? : s.n., 1985] 487 p. ; 27 cm.
Cover title : Kabary nation' Andriamatoa Didier
Ratsiraka, filohan' ny Repoblika Demokratika Malagasy.
"Première décennie-Fola taona voalohany" --Cover.
Malagasy and French.
*1. Madagascar - Social policy. 2. Madagascar -
Economic policy. I. Title.*   **NYPL [Sc F 88-268]**

Rawiri, Ntyugwetondo. G'amèrakano : au
carrefour : roman / Ntyugwetondo Rawiri.
Paris : Silex, c1988. 197 p. ; 23 cm. ISBN
2-87693-021-8
*1. Africa - Fiction. I. Title. **NYPL [Sc D 89-202]***

Ray, Jane. (ill) Gray, Nigel. A balloon for
grandad /. London , New York , 1988. [30] p. :
     ISBN 0-531-05755-0 : DDC [E] 19
PZ7.G7813 Bal 1988   **NYPL [Sc F 88-345]**

Ray, Walter I. The pilgrimage of 2 friends :
(selected poems) / Walter I. Ray, and Ernest J.
Wilson. Silver Spring, Md. : Esoray Pub. Co.,
1984. v, 80 p. ; 28 cm.
*I. Wilson, Ernest J. II. Title. III. Title: Pilgrimage of
two friends.*   **NYPL [Sc F 87-440]**

**The Raya Dunayevskaya collection [microform]
Supplement: Raya Dunayevskaya's last
writings, 1986-1987.** Dunayevskaya, Raya.
1986-1987. ca. 140 items.
                            NYPL [Sc Micro R-4838]

Raya Dunayevskaya Memorial Fund.
Dunayevskaya, Raya. The Raya Dunayevskaya
collection [microform] Supplement: Raya
Dunayevskaya's last writings, 1986-1987.
1986-1987. ca. 140 items.
                            NYPL [Sc Micro R-4838]

Raynal, Guillaume Thomas François, 1713-1796.
Histoire philosophique et politique des
établissemens & du commerce des Européens
dans les deux Indes. A Amsterdam : [s.n.],
1770. 6 v. ; 20 cm. Seventeen "books" in six vols.
*1. Colonization - History. 2. Commerce - History. 3.
East Indies. I. Title.*   **NYPL [Sc Rare C 86-2]**

Raynor, Maggie. James, Winston. The Caribbean
/. London , 1984. 46 p. : ISBN 0-356-07105-7 :
DDC 972.9 19
F2175   **NYPL [Sc F 88-128]**

A Razão da chama : antologia de poetas negros
brasileiros / coordenação e seleção, Oswaldo de
Camargo ; colaboradores, Paulo Colina e
Abelardo Rodrigues. São Paulo : GRD, 1986.
xii, 122 p. ; 21 cm.
*1. Brazilian poetry - Black authors. I. Camargo,
Oswaldo de, 1936-. II. Colina, Paulo, 1950-. III.
Rodrigues, Abelardo, 1952-.*
                            NYPL [Sc D 89-462]

Le RDA et le Tchad . Lisette, Yeyon. Paris ,
Abidjan , 1986. 351 p. ; ISBN 2-7087-0472-9
(Présence africaine)   **NYPL [Sc E 87-627]**

Rea, A. J. Dachs, Anthony J. The Catholic
church and Zimbabwe, 1879-1979 /. Gwelo ,
1979. xiii, 260 p., [26] p. of plates : DDC
282/.6891 19
BX1682.Z55 D33 1979 **NYPL [Sc D 88-900]**

Reaching out : an epic of the people of St.
Philip's Church. 1st ed. Tappan, NY :
Custombook, c1986. 120 p. : ill. (some col.),
ports. ; 27 cm. Bibliography: p. 120. DDC
283/.7471 19
*1. St. Philip's Church (New York, N.Y.) - History. 2.
New York (N.Y.) - Church history. I. Custombook, Inc.*
BV5980.N57 R4 1986 **NYPL [Sc F 87-222]**

**Les Réactions africaines à la colonisation en
Afrique Centrale :** actes du colloque
international d'histoire, Kigali, 06-10 mai 1985.
Ruhengeri : Faculté des Lettres de l'Université
Nationale du Rwanda, 1986. 478 p. ; 33 cm.
(Publication de la Faculté des lettres de l'Université
nationale du Rwanda . fasc. no. 1) Cover title. English
title: African reactions to colonization in Central Africa.
In English and French. Includes bibliographical
references.
1. Africa, Central - Colonization - Congresses. 2.

*Africa, Central - History - Congresses. I. Title: African
reactions to colonization in Central Africa. II. Series.*
                            NYPL [Sc G 87-9]

READERS - 1950-
Meshover, Leonard. You visit a dairy [and a]
clothing factory /. Chicago , c1965. 48 p. :
                            NYPL [Sc D 89-545]

Wassermann, Selma. Moonbeam and Dan Starr.
Westchester, Ill., c1966. 64 p.
                            NYPL [Sc D 89-398]

Wassermann, Selma. Moonbeam and the rocket
ride. Chicago [c1965] 64 p.
PE1119 .W363   **NYPL [Sc D 89-92]**

Wassermann, Selma. Moonbeam finds a moon
stone. Chicago [1967] 96 p. DDC [Fic]
PE1119 .W3636   **NYPL [Sc D 88-1423]**

READERS (ELEMENTARY)
Freed, Arthur. Games /. [N.J.] , 1968. [32] p. :
                            NYPL [Sc B 89-25]

READERS FOR NEW LITERATES.
Crooks, Merrise. Rocky, the woodcarver .
Brimingham, England , 1984[reprinted 1987] 24
p. :   **NYPL [Sc D 88-1076]**

**A reader's guide to West Indian and black
British literature /.** Dabydeen, David.
London , 1988. 182 p. ; ISBN 1-87051-835-7
(pbk)   DDC 810.9/9729 19
PR9210   **NYPL [Sc C 88-363]**

READERS, PRESCHOOL. see PRIMERS.

READERS (PRIMARY)
Around the city /. New York , c1965. 127 p. :
                            NYPL [Sc E 89-17]

Simon, Leonard J. Adam and the roof /. [New
Jersey? , 198-?] 36 p. :   **NYPL [Sc B 89-28]**

READERS (SECONDARY) - POETRY.
A Junior secondary poetry anthology /.
[Limbe , c1984- v. : DDC 428.6/4 19
PE1126.A44 J86 1984 **NYPL [Sc D 88-384]**

**READING (ADULT EDUCATION) -
NIGERIA.**
Asiedu, Kobina. An adult functional literacy
manual /. Ibadan , 1985. ix, 148 p. ; ISBN
978-15-4737-5 (Nigeria)
                            NYPL [Sc D 88-799]

Reading race . Nielsen, Aldon Lynn. Athens,
Ga. , c1988. xii, 178 p. ; ISBN 0-8203-1061-1
(alk. paper) DDC 811.5/09355 19
PS310.R34 N54 1988   **NYPL [JFE 88-3098]**

Reading the fights / edited by Joyce Carol Oates
and Daniel Halpern. 1st ed. New York : H.
Holt, c1988. viii, 305 p. : ill. ; 22 cm. ISBN
0-8050-0510-2 : DDC 796.8/3 19
*1. Boxing - History. 2. Boxing - Matches. 3.
Afro-American boxers. I. Oates, Joyce Carol, 1938-. II.
Halpern, Daniel, 1945-.*
GV1121 .R4 1988   **NYPL [Sc D 88-899]**

Readings in Black American music / compiled
and edited by Eileen Southern. 2nd ed. New
York : W.W. Norton, c1983. xii, 338 p. :
music ; 21 cm. Includes bibliographical references
and index. ISBN 0-393-95280-0 (pbk.) DDC
781.7/296073 19
*1. Afro-Americans - Music - Addresses, essays, lectures.
2. Music - United States - Addresses, essays, lectures. I.
Southern, Eileen.*
ML3556 .R34 1983   **NYPL [Sc D 85-30]**

Readings in Nigerian local government / edited
by Oladimeji Aborisade. Ile-Ife : Dept. of Local
Government Studies, Faculty of Administration,
Obafemi Awolowo University, [1986?] 274 p. ;
23 cm. Includes bibliographical references and index.
1. Local government - Nigeria. I. Aborisade, Oladimeji.
                            NYPL [Sc D 89-501]

The real cool killers/. Himes, Chester B., 1909-
London , New York , 1985, c1958. 159 p. ;
     ISBN 0-85031-615-4 **NYPL [Sc D 88-280]**

REAL ESTATE. see REAL PROPERTY.

Real picture of slavery. Bickell, Richard. The
West Indies as they are, or, A real picture of
slavery . London , 1825. xvi, 256 p. ;
                            NYPL [Sc Rare F 88-57]

REAL PROPERTY - NEW YORK (CITY)
New York (City). Housing Authority. Harlem,
1934. [New York, 1934] 20 p.
HD268.N5 N27   **NYPL [Sc G 88-30]**

**REAL PROPERTY - VALUATION -
DICTIONARIES.**

Yahya, Saad, 1939- English-Swahili glossary of
technical terms for valuers and land economists
/. [Nairobi] [1979] [8] leaves ; DDC
333/.003/21 19
HD107.7 .Y34 1979   **NYPL [Sc F 88-77]**

The realization of anti-racist teaching /. Brandt,
Godfrey L. London , New York , 1986. x, 210
p. : ISBN 1-85000-126-X : DDC 370.19/0941 19
LC192.2 .B73 1986   **NYPL [Sc E 89-77]**

REALTY. see REAL PROPERTY.

Reaping the bloody harvest . Werner, John M.,
1941- New York , 1986. 333 p. ; ISBN
0-8240-8301-6 (alk. paper) : DDC 973.5/6 19
E185 .W44 1986   **NYPL [Sc E 88-242]**

Réarmement moral. see Moral rearmament.

**Reasons for establishing a registry of slaves in
the British colonies .** African Institution,
London. London , 1815 (London : Printed by
Ellerton and Henderson) 118 p. ;
                            NYPL [Sc Rare G 86-4]

The rebel and other stories /. Heinecke, P.
Okpella, Bendel State, Nigeria , 1987. 84 p. ;
     ISBN 978-252-824-2 **NYPL [Sc E 88-601]**

Rebell, Michael A. Equality and education :
federal civil rights enforcement in the New
York City school system / Michael A. Rebell
and Arthur R. Block. Princeton, N.J. :
Princeton University Press, c1985. x, 340 p. ;
23 cm. Includes index. ISBN 0-691-07692-8 :
DDC 344.747/0798 347.4704798 19
*1. United States. Dept. of Health, Education, and
Welfare. Office for Civil Rights. 2. Discrimination in
education - Law and legislation - New York (State). 3.
Discrimination in education - Law and legislation -
United States. 4. New York (City) - Schools. I. Block,
Arthur R. II. Title.*
KFX2065 .R43 1985   **NYPL [JLD 85-3778]**

**REBELLION. see GOVERNMENT,
RESISTANCE TO.**

La rébellion de la Guadeloupe . Nègre, André.
Paris , c1987. 163 p., [4] p. of plates : ISBN
2-87679-006-8   **NYPL [Sc D 88-1333]**

REBELLIONS. see REVOLUTIONS.

Rebels and separatists in Ethiopia . Henze, Paul
B., 1924- Santa Monica, CA , 1985. xv, 98 p. ;
     ISBN 0-8330-0696-7 DDC 963/.07 19
DT387.95 .H46 1986   **NYPL [JFE 86-5101]**

Receitas de feitiços e encantos afro-brasileiros /.
Sales, Niveo Ramos. Rio de Janeiro , 1982. 75
p. ;   **NYPL [JFD 84-750]**

**Réception critique de la littérature africaine et
antillaise d'expression française :** J.-M.
Place, 1979. 272 p. ; 24 cm. Cover title:
Littérature africaine et antillaise. Oeuvres & critiques, t.
3, no 2/t.4, no 1 (automne 1979) Includes
bibliographical references.
*1. African literature (French) - History and criticism. 2.
West Indian literature (French) - History and criticism.
I. Oeuvres & critiques. II. Title: Littérature africaine et
antillaise.*   **NYPL [Sc E 87-557]**

**RECHAHECRIAN INDIANS. see CHEROKEE
INDIANS.**

Reciprocity and interdependence . Kayongo,
Kabunda. [Stockholm] , 1987. 189 p. : ISBN
91-22-00891-8   **NYPL [Sc D 88-863]**

Le récit de la mort /. Tati-Loutard, J. B. Paris ,
c1987. 166 p. ; ISBN 2-7087-0492-3
                            NYPL [Sc D 88-923]

**Le récit de Moses Grandy, esclave en Caroline
du Nord [microform] /.** Grandy, Moses, b.
1786? [Montréal] [1977] 45 p. ;
E444 .G7514   **NYPL [*XM-12976]**

Récit initiatique peul du Macina . Sylla, Yèro,
1942- [Dakar] , 1975. vi, 113 p. ;
                            NYPL [Sc F 87-257]

Reclaiming a heritage . Watson, Denton L. New
York, N.Y. , c1977. 63 p. :
                            NYPL [Sc F 89-78]

Reclaiming the future : a manual on futures
studies for African planners / World Futures
Studies Federation, Association internationale
futuribles, Association mondiale de prospective
sociale. Oxford ; Riverton, N.J. : Tycooly
International, c1986. xvi, 197 p. : ill. ; 21 cm.
"Prepared on behalf of the United Nations Development
Programme." Includes index. Bibliography: p. 185-193.
     ISBN 1-85148-010-2 (pbk.) : DDC 303.4/96 19

1. Twentieth century - Forecasts. 2. Twenty-first century - Forecasts. 3. Africa - Forecasting. I. World Future Studies Federation. II. International Association Futuribles. III. World Social Prospects Study Association. IV. Title: Futures studies for African planners.
DT4 .R43 1986 **NYPL [Sc D 88-584]**

RECLAMATION OF LAND - SAHARA.
Baker, Richard St. Barbe, 1889- Sahara conquest. London, 1966. 186 p. DDC 333.7/3/096
S616.S16 B3 **NYPL [Sc C 88-117]**

RECONSTRUCTION - ALABAMA.
Hasson, Gail Snowden. The medical activities of the Freedmen's Bureau in Reconstruction Alabama, 1865-1868 [microform] /. 1982. 252 leaves. **NYPL [Sc Micro R-4681]**

Reconstruction, America's unfinished revolution, 1863-1877 /. Foner, Eric. New York , c1988. xxvii, 690 p., [8] p. of plates : ISBN 0-06-015851-4 : DDC 973.8 19
E668 .F66 1988 **NYPL [*R-IKR 88-5216]**

RECONSTRUCTION - ARKANSAS - SOURCES.
United States. Bureau of Refugees, Freedmen and Abandoned Lands. Records of the Assistant Commissioner for the State of Arkansas, Bureau of Refugees, Freedmen, and Abandoned Lands, 1865-1869 [microform] 1865-1869. 24 v. **NYPL [Sc Micro R-4642]**

United States. Bureau of Refugees, Freedmen and Abandoned Lands. Records of the Superintendent of Education for the State of Arkansas, Bureau of Refugees, Freedmen, and Abandoned Lands, 1865-1871 [microform] 1865-1871. 10 v. **NYPL [Sc Micro R-4643]**

RECONSTRUCTION - DISTRICT OF COLUMBIA - SOURCES.
United States. Bureau of Refugees, Freedmen and Abandoned Lands. Records of the Assistant Commissioner for the District of Columbia, Bureau of Refugees, Freedmen, and Abandoned Lands, 1865-1869 [microform] 1865-1869. 42 bound v., 18 ft. of unbound doc.
NYPL [Sc Micro R-4644]

United States. Bureau of Refugees, Freedmen and Abandoned Lands. Records of the Superintendent of Education for the State of Columbia, Bureau of Refugees, Freedmen, and Abandoned Lands, 1865-1872 [microform] 1865-1872. 11 bound v., 15 ft. of unbound doc.
NYPL [Sc Micro R-4645]

Reconstruction du proto-tchadique. Préalables à la reconstruction du proto-tchadique . Paris , 1978. 210 p. ; ISBN 2-85297-022-8 DDC 493/.7 19
PL8026.C53 P73 1978 **NYPL [Sc E 88-418]**

RECONSTRUCTION - JUVENILE FICTION.
Hansen, Joyce. Out from this place /. New York , 1988. vi, 135 p. ; ISBN 0-8027-6816-4 DDC [Fic] 19
PZ7.H19825 Ou 1988 **NYPL [Sc D 88-1321]**

RECONSTRUCTION - NORTH CAROLINA - SOURCES.
United States. Bureau of Refugees, Freedmen and Abandoned Lands. Records of the Assistant Commissioner for the state of North Carolina, Bureau of Refugees, Freedmen, and Abandoned Lands, 1865-1870 [microform] 1865-1870. 20 ft. (32 v.)
NYPL [Sc Micro R-4646]

United States. Bureau of Refugees, Freedmen and Abandoned Lands. Records of the Superintendent of Education for the State of North Carolina, Bureau of Refugees, Freedmen, and Abandoned Lands, 1865-1870 [microform] 1865-1870. 7 ft. (24 v.)
NYPL [Sc Micro R-4647]

RECONSTRUCTION - SOURCES.
Benedict, Michael Les. The fruits of victory . Lanham, MD , c1986. xiii, 159 p. ; ISBN 0-8191-5557-8 (pbk. : alk. paper) : DDC 973.8 19
E668 .B462 1986 **NYPL [IKR 87-1888]**

RECONSTRUCTION - SOUTHERN STATES - SOURCES.
United States. Bureau of Refugees, Freedmen and Abandoned Lands. Education Division. Records of the Education Division of the

Bureau of Refugees, Freedmen, and Abandoned Lands, 1865-1871 [microform] 1865-1871. 23 v.
NYPL [Sc Micro R-4641]

RECONSTRUCTION - VIRGINIA - SOURCES.
United States. Bureau of Refugees, Freedmen and Abandoned Lands. Records of the Assistant Commissioner for the State of Virginia, Bureau of Refugees, Freedmen, and Abandoned Lands, 1865-1869 [microform] 1865-1869. 40 bound v., 51 ft. of unbound doc.
NYPL [Sc Micro R-4648]

Reconstruction, 1863-1877. Foner, Eric. Reconstruction, America's unfinished revolution, 1863-1877 /. New York , c1988. xxvii, 690 p., [8] p. of plates : ISBN 0-06-015851-4 : DDC 973.8 19
E668 .F66 1988 **NYPL [*R-IKR 88-5216]**

Recontres africaines (Association : Paris, France) Dossier Benin /. Paris , 1987. 225 p. :
NYPL [Sc F 88-176]

Records from Natal, Lesotho, the Orange Free State, and Mozambique concerning the history of the Catholic Church in southern Africa / translated from the original French by Leo Sormany. Roma, Lesotho : Social Centre, [1974] 2 v. : map ; 25 cm. (Lesotho-Documents) "Letters and reports written between 1859 and 1866 by the first Vicar Apostolic of Natal, the Right Reverend Bishop J.F. Allard, O.M.I. and his fellow Oblate missionaries, and published from 1862 to 1867 [in] Missions de la Congrégation des missionnaires oblate de Marie Immaculée." DDC 282/.68 19
1. Catholic Church - Missions - South Africa - History - 19th century - Sources. 2. South Africa - Church history - Sources. I. Allard, Jean-François-Marie, 1806-1889. II. Missions de la Congrégation des missionnaires oblats de Marie immaculée.
BV3625S67 R43 1974 **NYPL [Sc E 89-47]**

Records of the Assistant Commissioner for the District of Columbia, Bureau of Refugees, Freedmen, and Abandoned Lands, 1865-1869 [microform] United States. Bureau of Refugees, Freedmen and Abandoned Lands. 1865-1869. 42 bound v., 18 ft. of unbound doc.
NYPL [Sc Micro R-4644]

Records of the Assistant Commissioner for the State of Arkansas, Bureau of Refugees, Freedmen, and Abandoned Lands, 1865-1869 [microform] United States. Bureau of Refugees, Freedmen and Abandoned Lands. 1865-1869. 24 v. **NYPL [Sc Micro R-4642]**

Records of the Assistant Commissioner for the state of North Carolina, Bureau of Refugees, Freedmen, and Abandoned Lands, 1865-1870 [microform] United States. Bureau of Refugees, Freedmen and Abandoned Lands. 1865-1870. 20 ft. (32 v.) **NYPL [Sc Micro R-4646]**

Records of the Assistant Commissioner for the State of Virginia, Bureau of Refugees, Freedmen, and Abandoned Lands, 1865-1869 [microform] United States. Bureau of Refugees, Freedmen and Abandoned Lands. 1865-1869. 40 bound v., 51 ft. of unbound doc.
NYPL [Sc Micro R-4648]

Records of the Education Division of the Bureau of Refugees, Freedmen, and Abandoned Lands, 1865-1871 [microform] United States. Bureau of Refugees, Freedmen and Abandoned Lands. Education Division. 1865-1871. 23 v.
NYPL [Sc Micro R-4641]

Records of the Superintendent of Education for the District of Columbia, Bureau of Refugees, Freedmen, and Abandoned Lands, 1865-1872 [microform] United States. Bureau of Refugees, Freedmen and Abandoned Lands. 1865-1872. 11 bound v., 15 ft. of unbound doc.
NYPL [Sc Micro R-4645]

Records of the Superintendent of Education for the State of Arkansas, Bureau of Refugees, Freedmen, and Abandoned Lands, 1865-1871 [microform] United States. Bureau of Refugees, Freedmen and Abandoned Lands. 1865-1871. 10 v. **NYPL [Sc Micro R-4643]**

Records of the Superintendent of Education for the State of North Carolina, Bureau of Refugees, Freedmen, and Abandoned Lands, 1865-1870 [microform] United States. Bureau of Refugees, Freedmen and Abandoned Lands.

1865-1870. 7 ft. (24 v.)
NYPL [Sc Micro R-4647]

RECREATIONS. see GAMES; SPORTS.

Recruitment and retention of Black students in higher education / Johnson N. Niba, Regina Norman, editors. Lanham, MD : University Press of America, c1989. viii, 135 p. : ill. ; 22 cm. "A NAFEO Research Institute publication supported by grants from the Carnegie Corporation ... [et al.]." "Co-published by arrangement with the National Association for Equal Opportunity in Higher Education"--T.p. verso. Bibliography: p. 125-129. ISBN 0-8191-7292-8 (alk. paper) DDC 378/.1982 19
1. Afro-Americans - Education (Higher). 2. College students - United States - Recruiting. 3. College dropouts - United States. 4. Student aid - United States. 5. Afro-American college students. I. Niba, Johnson N. II. Norman, Regina. III. NAFEO Research Institute (U. S.). IV. National Association for Equal Opportunity in Higher Education (U. S.).
LC2781 .R43 1989 **NYPL [Sc D 89-590]**

RECURRENT EDUCATION. see CONTINUING EDUCATION.

Red calypso . Wagner, Geoffrey. Washington, D.C. , c1988. 264 p. ; ISBN 0-89526-773-X
NYPL [Sc D 89-301]

The red drum's warning /. Lindquist, Willis. New York , 1958. 128 p. : **NYPL [Sc D 88-662]**

Red hills of home /. Hove, Chenjerai, 1956- Gweru, Zimbabwe , 1985. 68 p. ; ISBN 0-86922-368-2 (pbk.) DDC 821 19
PR9390.9.H68 R4 1985
NYPL [Sc C 88-314]

Red light, green light . Sweet, Ozzie Davis. Smithtown, N.Y. , 1978 (1980 printing) 39 p. : ISBN 0-682-49088-1 **NYPL [Sc D 89-70]**

Redding, J. Saunders (Jay Saunders), 1906- To make a poet Black / J. Saunders Redding ; with an introduction by Henry Louis Gates, Jr. Ithaca : Cornell University Press, 1988. xxxii, 142 p. ; 23 cm. "First published 1939 by the University of North Carolina Press"--T.p. verso. Includes index. "A J. Saunders Redding bibliography": p. [xxv]-xxviii. Bibliography: p. [131]-136. ISBN 0-8014-1982-4 (alk. paper) DDC 811/.009/896073 19
1. American poetry - Afro-American authors - History and criticism. 2. American literature - Afro-American authors - History and criticism. 3. Afro-Americans - Intellectual life. I. Title.
PS153.N5 R4 1988 **NYPL [Sc D 89-388]**

Reddock, Rhoda. Elma Francois : the NWCSA and the worker's struggle for change in the Caribbean / by Rhoda Reddock. London : New Beacon Books, 1988. vii, 60 p., [8] p. of plates : ill., ports. ; 23 cm. Bibliography: p. 59-60. ISBN 0-901241-80-6 (Pbk.)
1. Francois, Elma. 2. Negro Welfare Cultural and Social Association. 3. Women, Black - Trinidad and Tobago - Biography. 4. Labor disputes - Trinidad and Tobago. I. Title. **NYPL [Sc D 89-77]**

Reddy, E. S. Oliver Tambo and the struggle against apartheid /. New Delhi , c1987. xii, 172 p., [1] leaf of plates : ISBN 81-207-0779-6 : DDC 323.1/196/068 19
DT763 .O57 1987 **NYPL [Sc D 88-1443]**

Reddy, Enuga S. Apartheid, South Africa and international law . New York, NY , 1985. iv, 136 p. ; **NYPL [Sc F 88-289]**

Redeeming Nigeria through Massist ideology . Ezeani, Geo'Ben. Yola , 1987. 226 p. :
NYPL [Sc C 89-49]

REDEVELOPMENT, URBAN. see CITY PLANNING.

Redfern, Bernice, 1947- Women of color in the United States : a guide to the literature / Bernice Redfern. New York : Garland, 1989. vii, 156 p. ; 23 cm. (Garland reference library of social science. v. 469) Includes index. ISBN 0-8240-5849-6 (alk. paper) DDC 016.3054/8/0973 19
1. Minority women - United States - Bibliography. 2. Afro-American women - Bibliography. I. Title.
Z7964.U49 R4 1989 HQ1410
NYPL [Sc D 89-562]

Redford, Dorothy Spruill. Somerset homecoming : recovering a lost heritage / Dorothy Spruill Redford with Michael D'Orso ; introduction by Alex Haley.1st ed. New York :

Doubleday, c1988. xviii, 266 p. : ill., ports. ; 24 cm. Geneal. table on lining papers. Bibliography: p. 265-266. ISBN 0-385-24245-X : DDC 929/.3/089960730756 19
1. Redford, Dorothy Spruill. 2. Afro-Americans - North Carolina - History. 3. Slavery - North Carolina - History. 4. Family reunions - North Carolina. 5. Afro-Americans - Genealogy. 6. Somerset Place (N.C.) - History. 7. North Carolina - Genealogy. I. D'Orso, Michael. II. Title.
E185.96 .R42 1988   **NYPL [Sc E 88-498]**

REDFORD, DOROTHY SPRUILL.
Redford, Dorothy Spruill. Somerset homecoming . New York , c1988. xviii, 266 p. : ISBN 0-385-24245-X : DDC 929/.3/089960730756 19
E185.96 .R42 1988   **NYPL [Sc E 88-498]**

Redhead, Wilfred. A city on a hill / by Wilfred A. Redhead. Barbados, West Indies : [s.n.], 1985 (Barbados, West Indies : Letchworth Press) 120 p. : ill. ; 23 cm.
1. Saint George's (Granada). I. Title.
   NYPL [Sc D 87-1423]

REDUCING - ANECDOTES, FACETIAE, SATIRE, ETC.
Gordon, Billi. Eat this book . San Francisco, California , c1987. 96 p. : ISBN 0-9614979-1-2
   NYPL [Sc F 88-110]

REDUCING - PSYCHOLOGICAL ASPECTS.
Gordon, Billi. Eat this book . San Francisco, California , c1987. 96 p. : ISBN 0-9614979-1-2
   NYPL [Sc F 88-110]

Reed, David. Brickley, Carol. South Africa . London , 1985. 50 p. : ISBN 0-905400-06-2 :
   NYPL [Sc D 89-361]

Reed, Ishmael, 1938- The terrible twos / Ishmael Reed. New York : Atheneum, 1988, c1982. 178 p. ; 21 cm. ISBN 0-689-70727-4 (pbk.) : DDC 813/.54 19
I. Title.
PS3568.E365 T4 1988   **NYPL [Sc D 89-362]**

Reed, John Neville. Mercenary activity in Africa since 1960 / by John Neville Read. 1982. vi, 342 leaves ; 28 cm. Thesis (M.A.)-- University of California, Los Angeles, 1982. Bibliography: leaves 337-342.
1. Mercenary troops - Africa. 2. Africa - History, Military. 3. Africa - History - 1960-. I. Title.
   NYPL [Sc F 88-121]

Rees, Ennis. Brer Rabbit and his tricks. Drawings by Edward Gorey. New York, Young Scott Books [1967] 1 v. (unpaged) col. illus. 21 x 25 cm. Rhymed versions of Brer Rabbit and the tar baby, Winnianimus grass, and Hello house, first collected by J. C. Harris. SCHOMBURG CHILDREN'S COLLECTION.
I. Gorey, Edward, 1925- illus. II. Harris, Joel Chandler, 1848-1908. III. Schomburg Children's Collection. IV. Title.
PZ8.3.R254 Br   **NYPL [Sc E 88-530]**

REFERENCE BOOKS - AFRO-AMERICANS - INDEXES.
Stevenson, Rosemary M. Index to Afro-American reference resources /. New York , 1988. xxvi, 315 p. ; ISBN 0-313-24580-0 (lib. bdg. : alk. paper) DDC 973/.0496073 19
Z1361.N39 S77 1988 E185
   NYPL [Sc E 88-220]

REFERENCE BOOKS - BLACKS - INDEXES.
Stevenson, Rosemary M. Index to Afro-American reference resources /. New York , 1988. xxvi, 315 p. ; ISBN 0-313-24580-0 (lib. bdg. : alk. paper) DDC 973/.0496073 19
Z1361.N39 S77 1988 E185
   NYPL [Sc E 88-220]

The Reference shelf.
(v. 56, no. 6) Race and politics /. New York , 1985. 174 p. ; ISBN 0-8242-0700-9 (pbk.) : DDC 305.8/00973 19
E184.A1 R25 1985   **NYPL [8-SAD (Reference shelf. v.56, no.6)]**

The reflected face of Africa /. Montgomery, Denis. Bolton, England , 1988. 288 p. : ISBN 1-85421-008-4   **NYPL [Sc E 88-535]**

Reflections and research on ragtime /. Berlin, Edward A. Brooklyn, N.Y. , c1987. xii, 99 p. : ISBN 0-914678-27-2 (pbk.) DDC 781/.572 19
ML3530 .B5 1987   **NYPL [Sc D 88-410]**

Reflections on Nigerian development /. Ayida, A.

A. Lagos , Ibadan , 1987. xxiii, 278 p. ; ISBN 978-260-101-2   **NYPL [Sc D 88-1078]**

REFORM OF CRIMINALS. see CRIME AND CRIMINALS.

La réforme éducative . Institut pédagogique national (Haiti). Comité de curriculum. [Port-au-Prince] [1982] 65 p. : DDC 375/.001/097294
LB1564.H2 I57 1982   **NYPL [Sc D 88-1401]**

Refugees . Center for Migration Studies (U. S.) Staten Island, N.Y. , 1987. ix, 423 p. ; ISBN 0-934733-34-1 (pbk.)   **NYPL [Sc F 89-60]**

REFUGEES - AFRICA.
Africa and its refugees . [Addis Ababa] [1975] 76 p. ; DDC 362.8/7/096 19
HV640.4.A35 A35 1975
   NYPL [Sc D 88-198]

REFUGEES - AFRICA - BIBLIOGRAPHY.
INADES-documentation (Institution) Les réfugiés en Afrique . Abidjan, Côte d'Ivoire [1986] 55 p. :
Z7164.R32 I5 1986 HV640.4.A35
   NYPL [Sc F 88-391]

REFUGEES - AMERICA.
When borders don't divide . Staten Island, N.Y. , c1988. viii, 220 p. : ISBN 0-934733-26-0 : DDC 325.8 19
JV7398 .W47 1988   **NYPL [Sc E 89-169]**

Refugees and development in Africa . Kibreab, Gaim. Trenton, N.J. [1987] xii, 304 p. : ISBN 0-932415-27-X (pbk.) DDC 325/.21/09624 19
JV9025.S73 K53 1987   **NYPL [Sc D 89-534]**

REFUGEES - CHARITIES - AFRICA.
All Africa Conference of Churches. Special Agency for EPEAA. Ecumenical Programme for Emergency Action in Africa . Nairobi , 1967. [193] p. ;   **NYPL [Sc F 88-74]**

REFUGEES - ETHIOPIA.
Bulcha, Mekuria. Flight and integration . Uppsala, Sweden , c1988. 256 p. : ISBN 91-7106-279-3   **NYPL [Sc E 88-581]**

REFUGEES - ETHIOPIA - ERITEA.
Kibreab, Gaim. Refugees and development in Africa . Trenton, N.J. [1987] xii, 304 p. : ISBN 0-932415-27-X (pbk.) DDC 325/.21/09624 19
JV9025.S73 K53 1987   **NYPL [Sc D 89-534]**

REFUGEES - GOVERNMENT POLICY - UNITED STATES.
The Mariel injustice . Coral Gables, Fl. , c1987. 204 p. :   **NYPL [Sc F 89-64]**

REFUGEES - KENYA - HISTORY - CASE STUDIES.
Harris, Joseph E., 1929- Repatriates and refugees in a colonial society . Washington, D.C. , 1987. ix, 201 p. ; ISBN 0-88258-148-1 : DDC 304.8/676/2 19
HN793.Z9 E44 1987   **NYPL [Sc E 87-558]**

REFUGEES, SOUTHERN - NORTH CAROLINA - SOURCES.
United States. Bureau of Refugees, Freedmen and Abandoned Lands. Records of the Assistant Commissioner for the state of North Carolina, Bureau of Refugees, Freedmen, and Abandoned Lands, 1865-1870 [microform] 1865-1870. 20 ft. (32 v.)
   NYPL [Sc Micro R-4646]

REFUGEES - SUDAN - ECONOMIC CONDITIONS.
Kibreab, Gaim. Refugees and development in Africa . Trenton, N.J. [1987] xii, 304 p. : ISBN 0-932415-27-X (pbk.) DDC 325/.21/09624 19
JV9025.S73 K53 1987   **NYPL [Sc D 89-534]**

REFUGEES - SUDAN - SOCIAL CONDITIONS.
Kibreab, Gaim. Refugees and development in Africa . Trenton, N.J. [1987] xii, 304 p. : ISBN 0-932415-27-X (pbk.) DDC 325/.21/09624 19
JV9025.S73 K53 1987   **NYPL [Sc D 89-534]**

Les réfugiés en Afrique . INADES-documentation (Institution) Abidjan, Côte d'Ivoire [1986] 55 p. :
Z7164.R32 I5 1986 HV640.4.A35
   NYPL [Sc F 88-391]

A Refutation of the charge of abolitionism, brought by David Henshaw and his partizans, against the Hon. Marcus Morton. Boston,

---

Felch's press, 1845. 32 p. 23 cm.
1. Morton, Marcus, 1784-1864. 2. Henshaw, David, 1791-1852. 3. Abolitionists - United States.
F69 .M455   **NYPL [Sc Rare C 89-21]**

Regals, Leo. Henco ruimt op / [Leo Regals] ; illustraties, Wop Sijtsma. Curaçao : R. Jungslager, [1986?] 72 p. : ill. ; 22 cm. (Henco, een jongen van Curacao . 3) SCHOMBURG CHILDREN'S COLLECTION. ISBN 90-6435-111-2
1. Curaçao - Juvenile fiction. I. Schomburg Children's Collection. II. Title. III. Series.
MLCS 87/05319 (P)   **NYPL [Sc D 88-490]**

Regards sur l'histoire /. Fouchard, Jean, 1912- Port-au-Prince, Haiti , 1988. 222 p. :
   NYPL [Sc D 89-409]

REGGAE MUSIC - BIBLIOGRAPHY.
White, Garth. The development of Jamaican popular music with special reference to the music of Bob Marley . Kingston , 1982. 49 p. ; DDC 016.78/042/097292 19
ML120.J35 5 1982   **NYPL [Sc F 87-61]**

REGGAE MUSICIANS - JAMAICA - BIOGRAPHY - JUVENILE LITERATURE.
May, Chris. Bob Marley /. London , 1985. 60 p. : ISBN 0-241-11476-4 : DDC 784.5 B 19
ML420.M3313 M4 1985
   NYPL [Sc D 88-308]

Sotheby, Madeline. The Bob Marley story /. London , 1985. 64 p. ; ISBN 0-09-160031-6 (pbk) : DDC 428.6/2 19
PE1121   **NYPL [Sc C 88-141]**

REGIONAL PLANNING - BURUNDI - MUSSO-BUYOGOMA REGION.
Stremplat, Axel V., 1941- Der l''andliche Arbeitskalender in der Regionalplanung Burundis /. Giessen , 1984. 130 p. : ISBN 3-924840-08-3   **NYPL [Sc D 88-556]**

REGIONAL PLANNING - SOUTH AFRICA.
Regional restructuring under apartheid . Johannesburg , 1987. xxii, 317 p. ; ISBN 0-86975-327-4   **NYPL [Sc D 89-16]**

Regional restructuring under apartheid : urban and regional policies in contemporary South Africa / edited and introduced by Richard Tomlinson and Mark Addleson. Johannesburg : Ravan Press, 1987. xxii, 317 p. : map ; 22 cm. Contains contributions to a workshop on 'South Africa's regional strategy, with special reference to industrial decentralisation', held September 5-6, 1985, at the University of the Witwatersrand. Includes bibliographies and index. ISBN 0-86975-327-4
1. Urbanization - South Africa. 2. Regional planning - South Africa. 3. South Africa - Economic policy. 4. South Africa - Social policy. 5. South Africa - Industries - Location. I. Tomlinson, Richard. II. Addleson, Mark.   **NYPL [Sc D 89-16]**

Regional Seminar for Africa (Mogadishu : 1975)
On African women's equality, role in national liberation, development and peace : report and proceedings of the Regional Seminar for Africa held in connection with International Women's Year, in Mogadishu April 3rd to 5th 1975. [Mogadishu] : Women's Section of the Political Office of the Presidency of the Supreme Revolutionary Council of the Somali Democratic Republic, 1975. 123 p. : ill. ; 24 cm. At head of title: Somali Democratic Republic.
1. International Women's Year, 1975 - Congresses. 2. Women and socialism - Africa - Congresses. 3. Women - Africa - Congresses. 4. Africa - Politics and government - 1960- - Congresses. I. Title.
   NYPL [Sc E 88-138]

REGISTERS OF BIRTHS, ETC. - OHIO.
Nitchman, Paul E. Blacks in Ohio, 1880 in the counties of ... /. [Decorah? Iowa] , c1985- v. ; DDC 929/.3/089960730771 19
E185.93.O2 N57 1985
   NYPL [APR (Ohio) 86-2025]

REGISTERS OF BIRTHS, ETC. - WASHINGTON, D. C.
Sluby, Paul E. Holmead's Cemetery (Western Burial Ground), Washington, D.C. /. Washington, D.C. , 1985. iv, 68 leaves : DDC 929.5/09753 19
F193 .S582 1985   **NYPL [Sc D 88-109]**

Sluby, Paul E. Selected small cemeteries of Washington, DC /. [Washington] , c1987. 84 p. :   **NYPL [Sc D 88-780]**

Regresso triunfal de Cruz e Sousa ; e, Os segredos de "seu" bita Dá-nó-em-pingo-d'água /.

Maya-Maya, Estevão. São Paulo , 1982. x, 85 p. :   *NYPL [Sc D 88-1098]*

Regulamento do trabalho dos indigenas, approvado por decreto de 9 de novembro de 1899 [microform] Portugal. Lisboa , 1899. 27 p. ;   *NYPL [Sc Micro F-10926]*

Régulation des naissances en Afrique : pour une parenté responsable : bibliographie commentée / INADES documentation. Abidjan, Côte d'Ivoire : INADES, [1987] 74 p. ; 30 cm. "Mars 1987." Includes indexes.
1. Birth control - Africa - Bibliography. 2. Parenthood - Africa - Bibliography. 3. Parenting - Africa - Bibliography. 4. Fertility, Human - Africa - Bibliography. I. Title: INADES-documentation (Institution).   *NYPL [Sc F 88-392]*

REHABILITATION - AFRICA, EAST.
Ross, D. H. Educating handicapped young people in eastern and southern Africa in 1981-83 /. Paris , 1988. 152 p. :   ISBN 92-3-102560-0   *NYPL [Sc E 88-534]*

REHABILITATION, RURAL. see RURAL DEVELOPMENT.

REHABILITATION - SOUTH AFRICA.
Ross, D. H. Educating handicapped young people in eastern and southern Africa in 1981-83 /. Paris , 1988. 152 p. :   ISBN 92-3-102560-0   *NYPL [Sc E 88-534]*

REHABILITATION - ZIMBABWE.
Farquhar, June. Jairos Jiri . Gweru , 1987. 92 p. : ISBN 0-86922-416-6   *NYPL [Sc D 89-38]*

Reid, Margaret Ann, 1940- A rhetorical analysis of selected Black protest poetry of the Harlem Renaissance and of the sixties / by Margaret Ann Reid. , 1981. 284 p. [i.e. 216] p. Vita. Includes index Thesis (Ph. D.)-Indiana University of Pennsylvania, 1981. P. 200-230 and 233-270 consist of copyrighted poems, and at the author's request they have not been filmed. Bibliography: p. 271-281. Photocopy. Ann Arbor, Mich. : University Microfilms International, 1987. 21 cm.
1. American poetry - Afro-American authors - History and criticism. 2. American poetry - 20th century - History and criticism. 3. Protest poetry, American - History and criticism. 4. Harlem Renaissance. I. Title.
   NYPL [Sc D 88-264]

Reid, Victor Stafford, 1913- Peter of Mount Ephraim : the Daddy Sharpe rebellion / Vic Reid ; illustrated by Dennis Ranston. Kingston : Jamaica Pub. House, 1971. 140 p. : ill. ; 20 cm. (Mahoe adventure series)
1. Slavery - Jamaica - Insurrections, etc. - Juvenile fiction. I. Title.
MLCS 83/10255 (P)   *NYPL [Sc C 88-185]*

Reilly, John Terrence, 1945. The first shall be last [microform] : a study of the pattern of confrontation between old and young in the Afro-American novel / by John Terrence Reilly. 1977. 198 leaves. Thesis (Ph. D.)--Cornell University, 1977. Bibliography: leaf 198. Microfilm of typescript. Ann Arbor, Mich.: University Microfilms International, 1978. 1 microfilm reel; 35 mm.
1. American fiction - Afro-American authors - History and criticism. I. Title. NYPL [Sc Micro R-4702]

La reine Soleil Levée . Étienne, Gérard, 1936- Montréal , 1988, c1987. 195 p. ; ISBN 2-7601-1974-2 :   DDC C843/.54 19
   NYPL [Sc D 88-1179]

Reis, João José. Escravidão e invenção da liberdade : estudos sobre o negro no Brasil / João José Reis ; fotografias, Holanda Cavalcanti. São Paulo : Editora Brasiliense, 1988. 323 p. [8] leaves of plates : ill. ; 21 cm. Includes bibliographical references. ISBN 85-11-13084-5
1. Slavery - Bahia (Brazil) : State) - History. I. Title.
   NYPL [Sc D 88-1388]

Reise ; Syd-Afrika. Livingstone, David, 1813-1873. [Missionary travels and researches in South Africa. Danish.] Livingstones Reise : Syd-Adrika /. Kjøbenhavn , 1858-1859. 2 v. :
   NYPL [Sc E 88-47]

Relaciones históricas a través del océano Índico . Relations historiques à travers l'océan Indien. Spanish. Barcelona , Paris , 1983. 224 p. : ISBN 84-85800-51-6   *NYPL [Sc D 88-593]*

Relation d'un voyage infortuné fait aux Indes Occidentales par le capitaine Fleury. Un Flibustier français dans la mer des Antilles en 1618-1620 /. Clamart [France] , c1987. 263 p. : ISBN 2-9502053-0-5   *NYPL [Sc E 88-247]*

Relations commerciales entre l'Allemagne et le Togo, 1680-1914 /. Ahadji, A. Lomé [1984] 71 leaves :
HF3568.T64 A42 1984   *NYPL [Sc F 88-164]*

Relations historiques à travers l'océan Indien. Spanish. Relaciones históricas a través del océano Índico ; informe y documentos de trabajo de la reunión de expertos sobre "Los contactos históricos entre Africa oriental por una parte y el sureste asiático por otra, a través del océano Índico," Mauricio, 15-19 de julio de 1974 / N. Chittick ... [et al.]1a ed. Barcelona : Serbal ; Paris : Unesco, 1983. 224 p. ; 21 cm. (Colección de temas africanos . 11) Papers presented at a conference organized by Unesco and held in Port-Louis, Mauritius. Translation of: Relations historiques à travers l'océan Indien. Includes bibliographies. ISBN 84-85800-51-6
1. Islands of the Indian Ocean - Congresses. 2. Madagascar - History - Congresses. 3. Africa, Eastern - History - Congresses. I. Chittick, H. Neville. II. Unesco. III. Title. IV. Series.
   NYPL [Sc D 88-593]

RELATIONS, RACE. see RACE RELATIONS.

The relationship between self-esteem and academic achievement among Black students in remedial reading instruction at a community college [microform] /. Hillman, Chrisanthia. 1981. 60 leaves.   *NYPL [Sc Micro R-4686]*

Relationship of Black female administrators' mentoring experience and career satisfaction [Microform] /. Malone, Beverly Louise. 1982. 165 leaves.   *NYPL [Sc Micro R-4804]*

RELAY RACES - KENYA.
All-Africa Games (4th : 1987 : Nairobi, Kenya) 4th All Africa Games . Lausanne , 1987. 64 p. :   *NYPL [Sc F 88-82]*

RELGIOUS RITES. see RITES AND CEREMONIES.

As religiões africanas no Brasil . Bastide, Roger, 1898-1974. [Religions africaines au Brésil. Portuguese.] São Paulo , 1985. 567 p. ;
   NYPL [Sc D 88-542]

RELIGION AND POLITICS - NIGERIA.
Takaya, B. J. The Kaduna mafia . [Jos, Nigeria] , c1987. viii, 146 p. ; ISBN 978-16-6045-7   *NYPL [Sc D 88-736]*
Usman, Yusufu Bala, 1945- The manipulation of religion in Nigeria, 1977-1987 /. Kaduna, Nigeria , 1987. 153 p. ; ISBN 978-255-708-0
   NYPL [Sc C 88-220]

RELIGION AND SOCIAL PROBLEMS. see CHURCH AND SOCIAL PROBLEMS.

RELIGION IN LITERATURE.
Evans, James H., 1950- Spiritual empowerment in Afro-American literature . Lewiston, NY , 1987. 174 p. ; ISBN 0-88946-560-6 DDC 810/.9/896073 19
PS153.N5 E92 1987   *NYPL [Sc E 88-265]*

Religion in North America.
Chidester, David. Salvation and suicide . Bloomington , c1988. xv, 190 p. ; ISBN 0-253-35056-5 DDC 289.9 19
BP605.P46 C48 1988   *NYPL [JFE 88-4624]*

Religion, intergroup relations, and social change in South Africa / G.C. Oosthuizen ... [et al.] ; Work Committee: Religion, Human Sciences Research Council. New York : Greenwood Press, 1988. xii, 237 p. : ill. ; 24 cm. (Contributions in ethnic studies, 0196-7088 . no. 24) Includes index. Bibliography: p. 193-226. ISBN 0-313-26360-4 (lib. bdg. : alk. paper) DDC 306/.6/0968 19
1. South Africa - Race relations - Religious aspects - Christianity. 2. South Africa - Church history - 20th century. I. Oosthuizen, G. C. (Gerhardus Cornelis). II. HSRC Investigation into Intergroup Relations. Work Committee: Religion. III. Series.
DT763 .R393 1988   *NYPL [Sc D 89-305]*

RELIGION, PRIMITIVE - AFRICA.
Explorations in African systems of thought /. Washington, D.C. , c1987. xvi, 337 p. : ISBN 0-87474-591-8 (pbk.)   *NYPL [Sc D 88-566]*

RELIGIOUS ART. see CHRISTIAN ART AND SYMBOLISM.

RELIGIOUS CEREMONIES. see RITES AND CEREMONIES.

The religious instruction of the colored population . Adger, John Bailey, 1810-1899. Charleston , 1847. 19 p. ;
   NYPL [Sc Rare G 86-6]

RELIGIOUS LITERATURE - AUTHORSHIP - HANDBOOKS, MANUELS, ETC.
Nwosu, I. E. A guide to Christian writing in Africa /. Enugu, Nigeria , 1987. 116 p. ; ISBN 978-262-606-6   *NYPL [Sc C 88-156]*

RELIGIOUS MYSTERIES. see MYSTERIES, RELIGIOUS.

RELIGIOUS ORDERS. see MONASTICISM AND RELIGIOUS ORDERS.

Religious organizations, and slavery. Brown, William B. Oberlin, 1850. 32 p.
E449 .B882   *NYPL [Sc Rare F 88-45]*

RELIGIOUS PAINTING. see CHRISTIAN ART AND SYMBOLISM.

RELIGIOUS SCULPTURE. see CHRISTIAN ART AND SYMBOLISM.

RELOCATION (HOUSING) - IVORY COAST.
Debouvry, Pierre. Contribution à la définition d'une méthodologie de transfert de populations paysannes . [Montpellier] [1985] 294 p. : ISBN 0-85352-039-0   *NYPL [Sc F 88-302]*

Remarks upon the controversy between the Commonwealth of Massachusetts and the State of South Carolina. By a friend to the Union. Boston, W. Crosby & H.P. Nichols, 1845. 21 p. 23 cm. S.D. Ward, supposed author. Inscription on cover: Hon. Joseph Bell with the respects of the writer.
1. Slavery - South Carolina. 2. Massachusetts - Politics and government - 1775-1865. I. Ward, S. D., supposed author. II. Friend to the Union.
F273 .R38   *NYPL [Sc Rare C 89-9]*

Reminiscences : award winning stories & poems, Creative Arts Festival, 1981 / edited by V. Penn (Moll). Road Town, Tortola, British Virgin Islands : Public Library, Ministry of Social Services, c1981. xii, 94 p. : ill. ; 28 cm. DDC 700/.97297/25 19
1. Art festivals - British Virgin Islands. 2. Arts, Black - British Virgin Islands. I. Moll, V. P. (Verna P.). II. British Virgin Islands. Public Library.
NX430.G72 B757 1981 *NYPL [Sc F 88-331]*

Reminiscences of my life in camp with the 33rd U. S. Colored Troops, late 1st South Carolina Volunteers. Taylor, Susie King, b. 1848. [Reminiscences of my life in camp.] A Black woman's Civil War memoirs . New York , 1988. 154 p. : ISBN 0-910129-85-1 (pbk.) : DDC 973.7/415 B 19
E492.94 33rd .T3 1988
   NYPL [Sc D 88-1473]

Reminiscences of Sea Island heritage /. Daise, Ronald. Orangeburg, S.C. , c1987. xvi, 103, [13] p. :   *NYPL [Sc F 88-168]*

Rémy, Mylène. Le masque volé / Mylène Rémy ; illustrations de Sophie Mondésir. Paris : Ceda-Hatier, 1987. 126 p. : ill. ; 16 cm. (Collection Monde noir jeunesse . 4) SCHOMBURG CHILDREN'S COLLECTION. ISBN 2-218-07832-5
1. Ivory Coast - Juvenile fiction. I. Schomburg Children's Collection. II. Title. III. Series.
   NYPL [Sc C 88-311]

La Renaissance noire . Rollwagen, Elsa. 1978. iii, 149 leaves ;   *NYPL [Sc F 88-280]*

RENAMO (ORGANIZATION)
Magaia, Lina. [Dumba nengue. English.] Dumba nengue, run for your life . Trenton, N.J. , 1988. 113 p. : ISBN 0-86543-073-X
   NYPL [Sc D 88-1509]

Renault, Delso. A vida brasileira no final do século XIX : visão sócio-cultural e política de 1890 a 1901 / Delso Renault. Rio de Janeiro ; Brasília : J. Olympio : xi, 315 p. : ill. ; 21 cm. (Coleção Documentos brasileiros. no. 204) Includes index. Bibliography: p. 295-300. ISBN 85-03-00181-0
1. Brazil - History - 1889-1930. 2. Brazil - Politics and government - 1889-1930. 3. Brazil - Economic conditions. I. Title. II. Series.
   NYPL [HFB 87-2508]

The René Maran story . Dennis, John Alfred. Ann Arbor, Mich. , c1987. viii, 275 p. :
   NYPL [Sc D 89-292]

Reno, Dawn E. Collecting Black Americana / Dawn E. Reno ; photographs by Donald Vogt. 1st ed. New York : Crown Publishers, c1986. vii, 150 p. : ill. ; 29 cm. Includes index.

Bibliography: p. 144-145. ISBN 0-517-56095-X
DDC 700/.8996073/075 19
1. Afro-Americans - Collectibles. I. Title. II. Title:
Black Americana.
NK839.3.A35 R46 1986   *NYPL [Sc F 87-6]*

Repatriates and refugees in a colonial society .
Harris, Joseph E., 1929- Washington, D.C. ,
1987. ix, 201 p. ; ISBN 0-88258-148-1 : DDC
304.8/676/2 19
HN793.Z9 E44 1987   *NYPL [Sc E 87-558]*

Repeal of the blues /. Pomerance, Alan.
Secaucus, N.J. , c1988. x, 264 p., [16] p. of
plates : ISBN 0-8065-1105-2 : DDC
792/.08996073 19
PN1590.B53 P6 1988   *NYPL [Sc E 89-90]*

**Répertoire des expéditions négrières françaises à
la traite illégale (1814-1850) /.** Daget, Serge.
Nantes , 1988. viii, 603 p. : ISBN 2-900486-01-7
NYPL [Sc E 89-265]

**Répertoire des experts en traitement électronique
des données en Afrique.** Directory of electronic
data processing experts in Africa =. [Addis
Ababa?] [1985] iii, 57 p. ; DDC 004/.025/6 19
QA76.215 .D576 1985   *NYPL [Sc F 89-42]*

**Report (Kenya NGO Organising Committee--
Forum '85) .**
(no. 15) Women and population . [Nairobi?]
[1985] 73 p. ; DDC 363.9/6/096762 19
HQ766.5.K4 W65 1985   *NYPL [Sc F 88-191]*

**Report made at an adjourned meeting of the
friends of the American Colonization Society,
in Worcester County, held in Worcester, Dec.
8, 1830 /.** Worcester County Colonization
Society. Worcester , 1831. 20 p. ;
NYPL [Sc Rare G 86-29]

Report (Minority Rights Group) .
(no. 28) Power, Jonathan, 1941- Western
Europe's migrant workers /. London , 1984. 35
p. : ISBN 0-08-030831-7   *NYPL [Sc F 88-231]*

**Report of a sample survey of unemployment
among school leavers [microform /]** Western
State, Nigeria. Ministry of Economic Planning
and Social Development. Statistics Division.
[Ibadan [1966]- v. ;
NYPL [Sc Micro F-10938]

**Report of Special Study Mission to Southern
Africa, August 10-30, 1969/.** Diggs, Charles C.
Washington , 1969. vi, 179 p. : DDC
301.29'68'073
DT733.D5   *NYPL [Sc E 89-39]*

**Report of the Advisory Committee on the
Funding of Education in Ogun State.** Ogun
State. Advisory Committee in the Funding of
Education. [Abeokuta , 1985] 51 p. ;
NYPL [Sc E 89-212]

**Report of the Committee of Merchants for the
Relief of Colored People, Suffering from the
Late Riots in the City of New York.**
Committee of Merchants for the Relief of
Colored People, Suffering from the Late Riots
in the City of New York. New York , 1863. 48
p. ;   *NYPL [Sc Rare F 89-2]*

**Report of the Committee of the House of
Representatives of Massachusetts on the
subject of impressed seamen.** Massachusetts.
General Court. House of Representatives.
Committee on Impressed Seamen. Boston ,
1813. 84, 4 p. ;   *NYPL [Sc Rare C 89-13]*

**Report of the cruise of the revenue marine
steamer Corwin in the Arctic Ocean in the
year 1884 /.** Healy, M. A. (Michael A.)
Washington , 1889. 128 p., [39] leaves of
plates :   *NYPL [Sc Rare F 88-62]*

**Report of the Merchants' Committee for the
Relief of Colored People Suffering from the
Riots in the City of New York. July, 1863.**
Committee of Merchants for the Relief of
Colored People, Suffering from the Late Riots
in the City of New York. Report of the
Committee of Merchants for the Relief of
Colored People, Suffering from the Late Riots
in the City of New York. New York , 1863. 48
p. ;   *NYPL [Sc Rare F 89-2]*

**Report of the National Advisory Commission on
Civil Disorders.** United States. Kerner
Commission. The Kerner report . New York,
N.Y. , 1988. xxvi, 513 p. ; ISBN 0-679-72078-2
NYPL [Sc D 89-604]

**Report of the Presidential Working Party on
Education and Manpower Training for the
Next Decade and Beyond /.** Kenya.
Presidential Working Party on Education and
Manpower Training for the Next Decade and
Beyond. Nairobi , 1988. xvii, 174 p. ;
NYPL [Sc E 89-232]

**Report of the Secretary's Task Force on Black &
Minority Health.** United States. Dept. of
Health and Human Services. Task Force on
Black and Minority Health. Washington, D.C. ,
1985-1986. 8 v. in 9 : DDC 362.1/08996073 19
RA448.5.N4 U55 1985 *NYPL [JLM 86-589]*

Report on human rights in Grenada . Trotman,
Donald A. B. [Bustamante?] [198-] viii, 54 p. :
DDC 323.4/9/09729845 19
JC599.G76 T76 1980z   *NYPL [Sc D 88-816]*

Report on the brigades in Botswana. Martin,
Anthony. [n.p., 1971?] 96 p.
HD6276.B6 M37   *NYPL [JLF 74-1283]*

**Report on the sixth census of South Africa, 5th
May, 1936, v. 7 : Occupations and industries
[microform]** South Africa. [Census of
population (1936)] Pretoria , 1941. lx, 119 p.
NYPL [Sc Micro R-4651 no.1]

**Report on the supply of secondary level teachers
in English-speaking Africa.**
(no. 1) Hanson, John Wagner. Secondary level
teachers: supply and demand in Botswana. [East
Lansing, 1969, c1968] x, 97, [2] p.
LB2833.4.B55 H3 *NYPL [JFM 72-62 no. 1]*

(no. 11) Hanson, John Wagner. Secondary
level teachers: supply and demand in Sierra
Leone. [East Lansing, c1970] viii, 85 p.
NYPL [JFM 72-62 no. 11]

(no. 12) Hanson, John Wagner. Secondary
level teachers: supply and demand in Ghana.
[East Lansing, 1971] xv, 130 p.
NYPL [JFM 72-62 no. 12]

(no. 13) Haupt, W. Norman. Secondary level
teachers: supply and demand in West
Cameroon. [East Lansing, 1971] xii, 45, [20] p.
NYPL [JFM 72-62 no. 13]

(no. 2) Ferns, George W. Secondary level
teachers: supply and demand in the Gambia.
[East Lansing, 1969] xi, 78 p.
LB2833.4.G3 F4 *NYPL [JFM 72-62 no. 2]*

(no. 6) Ferns, George W. Secondary level
teachers: supply and demand in Liberia. [East
Lansing, c1970] xii, 116 p.
LB2833.4.L7 F4 *NYPL [JFM 72-62 no. 6]*

(no. 8) Pratt, Simon. Secondary level teachers:
supply and demand in tanzania. [East Lansing,
1969] xii, 79 p. *NYPL [JFM 72-62 no. 8]*

(country study no. 15) Hanson, John Wagner.
Secondary level teachers: supply and demand in
Nigeria. [East Lansing, c1973] 1 v. (various
pagings) DDC 331.1/26
LB2833.4.N6 H36   *NYPL [Sc F 88-151]*

(no. 33) Hanson, John Wagner. Secondary level
teachers: supply and demand in Malawi. [East
Lansing, 1969] xi, 73, [2] p.
LB2833.4.M3 H3 *NYPL [JFM 72-62 no. 3]*

**Report on the views and recommendations of the
Basotho Nation regarding the future of
education in Lesotho =.** Lesotho. Ministry of
Education. Maseru, Lesotho , 1978. 167 p. :
NYPL [Sc F 88-354]

**REPRESENTATION. see REPRESENTATIVE
GOVERNMENT AND
REPRESENTATION.**

Representation of Natives in Parliament Bill.
South Africa. [Laws, etc.] Native Land Act,
1913. Amendment Bill, 1927 [microform].
Representation of Natives in Parliament Bill.
Union Native Council Bill. Coloured Persons
Rights Bill, 1927. [S.l. [1927?] 47 p. ;
NYPL [Sc Micro F-10937]

**Representative directors, Black theatre
productions, and practices at historically Black
colleges and universities, 1968-1978
[microform] /.** Marshall, Alex C. (Alexander
Charles) 1980. ix, 141 leaves.
NYPL [Sc Micro R-4807]

**REPRESENTATIVE GOVERNMENT AND
REPRESENTATION - AFRICA.**
The Democratic theory and practice in Africa

/. Nairobi , 1987. vi, 208 p. ;
NYPL [Sc D 89-569]

**REPRESENTATIVES IN CONGRESS
(UNITED STATES) see LEGISLATORS -
UNITED STATES.**

Republic Bank (Trinidad and Tobago) From
Colonial to Republic : one hundred and fifty
years of business and banking in Trinidad and
Tobago, 1837-1987 / authorized by Republic
Bank. Port-of-Spain, Trinidad, W.I. : Paria Pub.
Co., [1987] xxii, 206 p. : ill. (some col.), map ;
29 x 44 cm. Includes bibliographical references.
ISBN 976-8054-05-0
1. Banks and banking - Trinidad and Tobago - History.
I. Title.   *NYPL [Sc F 89-119]*

Republic of Nigeria. see Nigeria.

Republic of South Africa. see South Africa.

República de Colombia. see Colombia.

República de Nueva Granada. see Colombia.

**REPUBLICAN NATIONAL CONVENTION
(33RD : 1984 : DALLAS, TEX.)**
Blacks and the 1984 Republican National
Convention . Washington, D.C. (1301
Pennsylvania Ave., N.W., Suite 400,
Washington 20004) , 1984. v, 25 p. ; ISBN
0-941410-51-X (pbk.) DDC 324.2734 19
JK2353 1984   *NYPL [Sc F 87-172 rept. 4]*

La République . Sall, Ibrahima. Dakar , c1985. 83
p. ; ISBN 2-7236-0974-X
NYPL [Sc D 88-1161]

République autonome du Togo. see Togo.

**République Centrafricaine. see Central African
Republic.**

République de Guinée. see Guinea.

République du Togo. see Togo.

République fédérale du Cameroun. see Cameroon.

Requiem for a futurologist /. Soyinka, Wole.
London , 1985. [6], 56 p. ; ISBN 0-86036-207-8
NYPL [Sc D 89-355]

Requiem for a village ; Apartheid love /.
Sharlowe. Trinidad , 1982. 78, 70 p. ;
NYPL [Sc C 88-63]

Requisitoire. Massengo, Moudileno. Procès de
Brazzaville . Paris [1983] 345 p. :
NYPL [Sc D 88-1160]

**Research & Decisions Corporation (San
Francisco, Calif.)** A baseline survey of AIDS
risk behaviors and attitudes in San Francisco's
Black communities /. San Francisco, Calif.
[1987] vii, 74, [59] leaves :
NYPL [Sc F 88-232]

Research in education . Eshiwani, George S.
Nairobi, Kenya , 1982? 185 leaves ; DDC
016.37/09676/2 19
Z5815.K4 E83 1982 LA1561
NYPL [Sc F 89-154]

RESEARCH - NIGERIA - METHODOLOGY.
What science? . Ibadan , 1985. xvii, 321 p. :
ISBN 978-12-9118-4 (pbk.) DDC 507/.11669 19
Q183.4.N5 W48 1985 *NYPL [Sc E 88-402]*

**Research notes (National Institute of
Development and Cultural Research
(Botswana)) .**
(no. 7) Gobotswang, Z. Pilot evaluation report
on Mahalapye Development Trust /. Gaborone,
Botswana [1982] v leaves, 61, 3 p. ;
HD5710.85.B59 G63 1982
NYPL [Sc F 89-108]

**Research report (Kentucky. General Assembly.
Legislative Research com mission) .**
(no. 4) Thompson, Kenneth, 1937- Illegitimacy
in Kentucky /. Frankfort, Ky. , 1961. 52 p. ;
NYPL [Sc F 88-36]

Research report (Nordiska Afrikainstitutet) .
(no. 73) Davies, Robert. South African strategy
towards Mozambique in the post-Nkomati
period . Uppsala , 1985. 71 p. ; ISBN
91-7106-238-6 (pbk.) DDC 327.68067/9 19
DT771.M85 D38 1985 *NYPL [Sc E 88-121]*

(no. 78) Suliman, Hassan Sayed. The nationalist
movements in the Maghrib . Uppsala , 1987. 87
p. ; ISBN 91-7106-266-1 *NYPL [Sc E 88-202]*

**RESIDENCES. see ARCHITECTURE,
DOMESTIC; DWELLINGS.**

RESIDENTIAL MOBILITY - UNITED STATES.
Nelson, Kathryn P. Gentrification and distressed cities . Madison, Wis. , 1988. xiii, 187 p. : ISBN 0-299-11160-1 : DDC 307.2 19
HT175 .N398 1987   NYPL [JLE 88-3486]

RESISTANCE TO GOVERNMENT. see GOVERNMENT, RESISTANCE TO.

Resnick, Mike. Ivory / Mike Resnick. 1st ed. New York : Tor/Tom Doherty : Distributed by St. Martin's Pr., 1988. 374 p. : photo. ; 22 cm. "A Tom Doherty Associates book." ISBN 0-312-93093-3 : DDC 813/.54 19
1. Elephants - Fiction. 2. Masai - Fiction. I. Title.
PS3568.E698 I96 1988 NYPL [Sc D 89-163]

Resolutions adopted by the inaugural congress of the Front for the Liberation of Zimbabwe, held from August 21 to September 5, 1972 [microform]. Front for the Liberation of Zimbabwe. [S.1] [1972?] 3 leaves ;
NYPL [Sc Micro R-4137 no.15]

Résolutions, les instructions, les recommandations dans les 10 ans du M.R.N.D. Ibyemezo, amabwiliza, ibyifuzo mu myaka cumi ya Muvoma . Kigali , 1985. 424 p. :
NYPL [Sc D 88-807]

RESOURCES, NATURAL. see NATURAL RESOURCES.

Resources, power and women . African and Asian Inter-regional Workshop on Strategies for Improving the Employment Conditions of Rural Women (1984 : Arusha, Tanzania) Geneva , 1985. ix, 82 p. ; ISBN 92-2-105009-2 (pbk.) : DDC 331.4/83/095 19
HD6207 .A78 1984 NYPL [JLF 87-1038]

The rest of the dream . Johnson, Lyman T., 1906- Lexington, Ky. , c1988. xiv, 230 p., [8] p. of plates ; ISBN 0-8131-1674-0 (alk. paper) : DDC 976.9/00496073024 B 19
E185.97.J693 A3 1988 NYPL [Sc E 89-211]

RESTAURANTS, LUNCH ROOMS, ETC. - SOUTHERN STATES.
Egerton, John. Southern food . New York , c1987. v, 408 p. : ISBN 0-394-54494-3 DDC 641.5975 19
TX715 .E28 1987 NYPL [JSE 87-1598]

RESTORATION OF BOOKS. see BOOKS - CONSERVATION AND RESTORATION.

Résumés de vieux manuscrits arabes : collectés dans l'île de Zanzibar / par M.B. Mkelle = Summary of old Arabic manuscripts : collected in Zanzibar Island / by M.B. Mkelle. Zanzibar [Tanzania] : Centre de recherche sur les traditions orales et les langues nationales africaines en Afrique de l'est, 1981. x, 50 leaves ; 21 x 33 cm. (Collection Manuscrits anciens = Series Ancient manuscripts . v. 1) Arabic, English, and French. Title also in Arabic.
1. Manuscripts, Arabic - Tanzania - Zanzibar - Catalogs. I. Mkelle, M. B. (Mohamed Burhan). II. Title: Summary of old Arabics manuscripts. III. Series: Collection Manuscrits anciens , v. 1.
NYPL [Sc B 88-10]

RETAIL ADVERTISING. see ADVERTISING.

Les retards scolaires et les échecs au niveau de l'ecole primaire du Sénégal /. Morin, Melle. [Dakar] [1966?] 143 leaves ;
NYPL [Sc F 87-439]

Rétout, Marie Thérèse. A light rising from the west / by Marie Thérèse Rétout. Trinidad : Inprint Caribbean, 1985. xiii, 268 p. : ill. ; 20 cm. Includes index. Bibliography: p. 252-254. DDC 378.7298/3 19
1. University of the West Indies (St. Augustine, Trinidad and Tobago) - History. I. Title.
LE15.S7 R48 1985 NYPL [Sc C 88-67]

La retraite anticipée du Guide suprême /. Doumbi-Fakoly. Paris , c1984. 209 p. ; ISBN 2-85802-382-1 DDC 843 19
PQ3989.2.D639 R48 1984
NYPL [Sc C 88-78]

Retreat talks to priests. Onyeocha, Anthony Ekendu. These hi-fi priests . Owerri [Nigeria] , 1985. 208 p. : *NYPL [Sc D 88-926]*

RETREATS FOR CLERGY.
Onyeocha, Anthony Ekendu. These hi-fi priests . Owerri [Nigeria] , 1985. 208 p. :
NYPL [Sc D 88-926]

RETREATS - NIGERIA.
Onyeocha, Anthony Ekendu. These hi-fi priests . Owerri [Nigeria] , 1985. 208 p. :
NYPL [Sc D 88-926]

A retrospective . Transafrica Forum (Organization) [Washington, D.C.] , c1987. 32 p. : *NYPL [Sc E 88-163]*

Rétrospectives [microform] . Durant, Franck Alphonse. Port-au-Prince, Haiti , 1977. 16 p. :
NYPL [Sc Micro F 10,933]

RETURN MIGRATION - KENYA - HISTORY - CASE STUDIES.
Harris, Joseph E., 1929- Repatriates and refugees in a colonial society . Washington, D.C. , 1987. ix, 201 p. ; ISBN 0-88258-148-1 : DDC 304.8/676/2 19
HN793.Z9 E44 1987 NYPL [Sc E 87-558]

RETURN MIGRATION - NIGERIA - FICTION.
Ojo-Ade, Femi. Home, sweet, sweet home /. Ibadan , 1987. ix, 123 p. ; ISBN 978-15-4663-8 (Nigeria) *NYPL [Sc C 88-209]*

Reuben . Wideman, John Edgar. New York , c1987. 215 p. ; ISBN 0-8050-0375-4 DDC 813/.54 19
PS3573.I26 R4 1987 NYPL [JFE 88-3493]

Reunion . Hayden, Tom. New York , c1988. xix, 539 p., [16] p. of plates ; ISBN 0-394-56533-9 : DDC 328.794/092/4 B 19
F866.4.H39 A3 1988 NYPL [JFE 88-6231]

RÉUNION - POETRY.
Kichenapanaïdou, Marc. Ma terre /. Saint-Louis, Réunion [1978?] 43 p. ;
NYPL [Sc D 88-484]

Rev Dr Martin Luther King, Jr. and America's quest for racial integration . Assensoh, A. B. Ilfracombe, Devon , 1987. 104 p. : ISBN 0-7223-2084-1 *NYPL [Sc D 88-100]*

A review of issues related to planning and development in Grahamstown . Davies, W. J. Grahamstown [South Africa] , 1986. 114 p. : ISBN 0-86810-130-3 *NYPL [Sc F 87-431]*

Review of issues related to planning and development in Grahamstown. Roux, Andre, 1954- Voices from Rini . Grahamstown, South Africa , 1986. 107 p. ; ISBN 0-86810-131-1 *NYPL [Sc F 88-216]*

A review of the colonial slave registration acts . African Institution, London. London , 1820. 139, 11 p. ; *NYPL [Sc Rare G 86-24]*

Review of the Remarks on Dr. Channing's Slavery [microform] . [Simmons, George Frederick] 1814-1855. Boston, 1836. 48 p.
E449 .C4562 NYPL [Sc Micro R-4839]

REVIVAL (RELIGION) see EVANGELISTIC WORK.

Revo! Baku, Shango. 3 plays of our time /. Belmont, Trinidad , 1984. 116 p. ;
NYPL [Sc D 88-971]

La Revolte des esclaves mercenaires . Paulin, Adjai. Bayreuth, W. Germany , 1987. 96 p. :
NYPL [Sc D 88-1326]

Revolution and counter-revolution in Africa : essays in contemporary politics / Nzongola-Ntalaja. London : Zed, 1987. x, 130 p. ; 23 cm. Includes bibliographical references and index. ISBN 0-86232-750-4 (cased) : DDC 320.96 19
1. Africa - Politics and government - 1960-. I. Nzongola, Ntalaja, 1944-.
JQ1872 NYPL [Sc D 88-637]

Revolution and rescue in Grenada . Burrowes, Reynold A. New York , 1988. xiv, 180 p. ; ISBN 0-313-26066-4
F2056.8 .B87 1988 NYPL [HRG 88-1153]

REVOLUTIONARY POETRY, CANADIAN.
Brand, Dionne, 1953- Chronicles of the hostile sun /. Toronto, Ont., Canada , 1984. 75 p. ; ISBN 0-88795-033-7 (pbk.) : DDC 811/.54 19
PR9199.3.B683 C48 1984
NYPL [Sc D 88-1227]

The revolutionary potentials of the Nigerian military, 1886-1986 /. Duke, Hajia Zainab I. (Hajia Zainab Ibitein) [Lagos?] Nigeria , c1987. viii, 145 p., [28] p. of plates : ISBN 978-232-008-0 DDC 322/.5/09669 19
DT515.8 .D84 1987 NYPL [Sc D 88-1278]

REVOLUTIONISTS - ANGOLA - BIOGRAPHY.
Khazanov, A. M. (Anatoliĭ Mikhaĭlovich), 1932- [Agostinó Neto. English.] Agostinho Neto /. Moscow , 1986. 301 p. ; DDC 967/.304/0924 B 19
DT611.76.A38 K4213 1986
NYPL [Sc B 88-47]

REVOLUTIONISTS - CUBA - BIOGRAPHY - JUVENILE LITERATURE.
Caballero, Armando O. Antonio Maceo, la protesta de Baraguá /. La Habana , 1977. 30, [1] p. : *NYPL [Sc F 88-281]*

REVOLUTIONISTS - FRANCE - ATTITUDES - HISTORY - 18TH CENTURY.
Cooper, Anna J. (Anna Julia), 1858-1964. [Attitude de la France à l'égard de l'esclavage pendant la révolution. English.] Slavery and the French revolutionists, 1788-1805 /. Lewiston, 1988. 228 p. : ISBN 0-88946-637-8 DDC 972.94/03 19
F1923 .C7213 1988 NYPL [Sc E 88-469]

REVOLUTIONISTS - TRINIDAD - BIOGRAPHY.
Buhle, Paul, 1944- C.L.R. James . London , New York , 1988. 197 p. ; ISBN 0-86091-221-3 : DDC 818 B 19
PR9272.9.J35 Z59 1988
NYPL [Sc E 89-171]

REVOLUTIONS - AFRICA, NORTHEAST - HISTORY - 20TH CENTURY.
Markakis, John. National and class conflict in the Horn of Africa /. Cambridge , New York , 1987. xvii, 314 p. : ISBN 0-521-33362-8 DDC 960/.3 19
DT367.75 .M37 1987 NYPL [JFE 88-364]

Reynolds, A. H. (Alfrieda H.) Cognac & collard greens / A.H. Reynolds. Bronx, N.Y. : Images/Single Action Productions, c1985. 138 p. : ill. ; 22 cm. With autograph of author. ISBN 0-938887-00-9
I. Title. II. Title: Cognac and collard greens.
NYPL [Sc D 88-1211]

Reyntjens, Filip. Pouvoir et droit au Rwanda : droit public et évolution politique, 1916-1973 / par Filip Reyntjens. Tervuren, Belgique : Musée royal de l'Afrique centrale, 1985. 584 p. ; 24 cm. (Annalen / Koninklijk Museum voor Midden-Afrika. Reeks in-8 , Menselijke wetenschappen ; Nr 117 = Annales / Musée royal de l'Afrique centrale. Série in-8 , Sciences humaines . N 117) Slightly modified version of thesis (doctoral)--Université d'Anvers, 1983. Published simultaneously: Butare, Rwanda : Institut national de recherche scientifique. Includes index. Bibliography: p. 531-552.
1. Public law - Rwanda - History. 2. Rwanda - Politics and government. 3. Rwanda - Constitutional history. I. Series: Tervuren, Belgium. Musée royal de l'Afrique centrale. Annals. Serie in -8 . Sciences humaines , no. 117. II. Title.
NYPL [Sc E 87-668]

Rhea, H. W. Rhea's new citizen's directory of Chicago, Ill. and suburban towns . Chicago, Ill. , 1908. 173 p. : *NYPL [Sc Rare F 89-3]*

Rhea's new citizen's directory of Chicago, Ill. and suburban towns : also other towns and cities. Chicago, Ill. : W. S. McCleland, 1908. 173 p. : port. ; 24 cm. "August 1, 1908."
1. Afro-Americans - Illinois - Chicago - Directory. I. Rhea, H. W. *NYPL [Sc Rare F 89-3]*

A rhetorical analysis of selected Black protest poetry of the Harlem Renaissance and of the sixties /. Reid, Margaret Ann, 1940- , 1981. 284 p. [i.e. 216] p. *NYPL [Sc D 88-264]*

Rhode Island Committee for the Humanities. The Blacker the berry . [Providence, R.I.] [1980?] 20 p. : *NYPL [Sc F 89-80]*

RHODE ISLAND - HISTORY.
Stewart, Rowena. A heritage discovered . Providence, R.I. [1975] 39 p. :
NYPL [Sc E 89-110]

RHODES, CECIL, 1853-1902.
Plomer, William, 1903-1973. Cecil Rhodes /. Cape Town , 1984. xvii, 179 p. ; ISBN 0-86486-018-8 *NYPL [Sc C 88-64]*

Rhodesia alone / edited by James E. Dornan, Jr. Washington : Council on American Affairs, [1977?] 95 p. ; 26 cm. "One of a series of monographs produced by the Council on American

Affairs in conjunction with the Council's quarterly Journal of social and political studies." Includes bibliographical references. DDC 320.9/689/104
1. Zimbabwe - Politics and government - 1965-. 2. Zimbabwe - Foreign relations - 1965-. I. Dornan, James E. II. Council on American Affairs.
DT962.75 .R53   NYPL [Sc E 88-95]

RHODESIA, SOUTHERN - RACE RELATIONS.
Elliott, Hugh P. Darkness and dawn in Zimbabwe /. London , 1978. [6], 49 p. ; ISBN 0-901269-37-9 :
DT962.42 .E38   NYPL [JFD 80-115]

Rhys, Jean.
WIDE SARGASSO SEA - CRITICISM AND INTERPRETATION.
James, Selma. The ladies and the mammies . Bristol, England , 1983. 96 p. ; ISBN 0-905046-24-2 :   NYPL [JFD 84-4049]

Ricard, Alain.
L'invention du théâtre : le théâtre et les comédiens en Afrique noire / Alain Ricard . Lausanne : Age D'homme, c1986. 134 p. : ill., maps ; 21 cm. Includes bibliographical references.
1. Theater - Africa, Sub-Saharan. I. Title.
        NYPL [Sc D 88-707]
Naissance du roman africain : Félix Couchoro (1900-1968) / Alain Ricard. Paris ; Dakar : Présence africaine, c1987. 228 p., [4] p. of plates : ill., map, port. ; 22 cm. (Situations et (Présence africaine (Firm)) perspectives) Bibliography: p. [205]-213. ISBN 2-7087-0494-X
1. Couchoro, Félix, 1900-1968 - Criticism and interpretation. 2. African fiction - History and criticism. I. Title.   NYPL [Sc D 89-46]

Ricciuti, Edward R. Donald and the fish that walked / by Edward R. Ricciuti ; pictures by Syd Hoff. 1st ed. New York : Harper & Row, [1974] 62 p. : col. ill. ; 22 cm. (A Science I can read book) Originally brought to Florida as an aquarium pet, the walking catfish soon spread throughout southern Florida threatening the ecological balance. SCHOMBURG CHILDREN'S COLLECTION. ISBN 0-06-024997-8 : DDC 597/.52
1. Walking catfish - Juvenile literature. I. Hoff, Syd, 1912- ill. II. Schomburg Children's Collection. III. Title.
QL638.C6 R52 1974   NYPL [Sc D 88-447]

Rice, Mitchell F. Smith, J. Owens. Blacks and American government . Dubuque, Iowa , c1987. xii, 148 p. : ISBN 0-8403-4407-4 (pbk.) DDC 323.1/196073 19
E185.615 .S576 1987   NYPL [Sc E 89-193]

Rich, Wilbur C. Coleman Young and Detroit politics : from social activist to power broker / Wilbur C. Rich. Detroit, Mich. : Wayne State University Press, 1989. 298 p. : ill., ports. ; 24 cm. (African American life series) Includes index. Bibliography: p. 282-295. ISBN 0-8143-2093-7 DDC 977.4/34043/0924 B 19
1. Young, Coleman A. 2. Mayors - Michigan - Detroit - Biography. 3. Afro-American mayors - Michigan - Detroit - Biography. 4. Detroit (Mich.) - Politics and government. I. Title. II. Series.
F474.D453 Y677 1989   NYPL [Sc E 89-208]

Richard Attenborough's cry freedom : a pictorial record. 1st American ed. New York : Knopf, 1987. [128] p. : col. ill. ; 19 x 24 cm. ISBN 0-394-75838-2 DDC 791.43/72 19
1. Biko, Stephen, 1946-1977 - Drama. 2. Woods, Donald, 1933- - Drama. 3. South Africa - Race relations - Drama. I. Attenborough, Richard. II. Cry freedom (Motion picture).
PN1997.C885 A88 1987 NYPL [Sc G 89-17]

Richard B. Moore, Caribbean militant in Harlem . Moore, Richard B. (Richard Benjamin) Bloomington , London , 1988. ix, 324 p : ISBN 0-253-31299-0 DDC 970.004/96 19
F2183 .M66 1988   NYPL [Sc E 89-148]

Richard B. Moore Library printed catalog . (v. 1 : supplement) Moss, S. G. Slavery and emancipation . St. Michael, Barbados , 1986. 61 l.   NYPL [Sc F 88-83]

Richard B. Moore Library printed catalogue . (v. 2) Moss, S. G. Books on race and race relations held in the Richard B. Moore Library, Barbados /. Barbados , 1987. 133 leaves :
        NYPL [Sc F 89-105]

Richard Wright /. Urban, Joan, 1950- New York, N.Y. [1989] 111 p : ISBN 1-555-46618-4 DDC

813/.52 19
PS3545.R815 Z85 1989
        NYPL [Sc E 89-196]

Richard Wright's art of tragedy /. Joyce, Joyce Ann, 1949- Iowa City , 1986. xvii, 129 p. ; ISBN 0-87745-148-6 DDC 813/.52 19
PS3545.R815 N34 1986
        NYPL [JFD 87-289]

Richards, Alan Vaughan- see Vaughan-Richards, Alan.

Richards, Paul. Sierra Leone, 1787-1987 . Manchester ; New York : 577 p., [8] p. of plates : ISBN 0-7190-2791-8 (pbk.) : DDC 966/.4 19
DT516.7 .S54 1988   NYPL [Sc E 88-461]

Richards, William C. (joint author) Fitts, Hervey. Abraham Vest, or, The cast-off restored. Boston, 1847. 142 p.
T275.V55 F5 1847 NYPL [Sc Rare C 88-12]

Richardson, Diane. Women and AIDS / Diane Richardson. New York : Methuen, 1988. 183 p. ; 20 cm. Includes index. Bibliography: p. [164]-165. ISBN 0-416-01741-X : DDC 616.9/792 19
1. AIDS (Disease) - Popular works. I. Title.
RC607.A26 R53 1988 NYPL [Sc D 88-987]

Richardson, Enid. (illus) Kirkpatrick, Oliver. Naja the snake and Mangus the mongoose. Garden City, N.Y. [1970] 40 p. DDC [Fic]
PZ7.K6358 Naj NYPL [Sc F 88-339]

Richardson, Richard C. Fostering minority access and achievement in higher education : the role of urban community colleges and universities / Richard C. Richardson, Jr., Louis W. Bender.1st ed. San Francisco, Calif. : Jossey-Bass Inc., c1987. xviii, 244 p. ; 24 cm. (The Jossey-Bass higher education series) Includes index. Bibliography: p. 231-235. ISBN 1-555-42053-2 (alk. paper) DDC 378/.052 19
1. Minorities - Education (Higher) - United States. 2. Community colleges - United States. 3. Municipal universities and colleges - United States. 4. Students, Transfer of - United States. 5. Degrees, Academic - United States. I. Bender, Louis W. II. Title. III. Series.
LC3727 .R53 1987   NYPL [Sc E 88-472]

Richmond, Angus. The open prison / Angus Richmond. London : Hansib, 1988. 225 p. ; 21 cm. ISBN 1-87051-825-X (pbk.) : DDC 813 19
I. Title.   NYPL [JFD 89-478]

Richmond, Edmun B. New directions in language teaching in Sub-Saharan Africa : a seven-country study of current policies and programs for teaching official and national languages and adult functional literacy / Edmun B. Richmond. Washington, D.C. : University Press of America, c1983. viii, 65 p. ; 21 cm. Includes bibliographical references and index. ISBN 0-8191-2980-1 (pbk.) : DDC 418/.007/067 19
1. Language and languages - Study and teaching - Africa, Sub-Saharan. 2. Language policy - Africa, Sub-Saharan. 3. Language and education - Africa, Sub-Saharan. 4. Literacy - Africa, Sub-Saharan. I. Title.
P57.A37 R5 1983   NYPL [Sc D 88-479]

Richmond, M. A. (Merle A.) Phillis Wheatley / Merle Richmond. New York : Chelsea House Publishers, 1988. 111 p : ill. ; 25 cm. (American women of achievement) Includes index. Traces the life of the Black American poet who was born in Africa, brought over to New England as a slave, and published her first poem while still a teenager. Bibliography: p. 106. ISBN 1-555-46683-4 DDC 811/.1 B 92 19
1. Wheatley, Phillis, 1753-1784 - Biography - Juvenile literature. 2. Poets, American - 18th century - Biography - Juvenile literature. 3. Afro-American poets - Biography - Juvenile literature. I. Title. II. Series.
PS866.W5 Z683 1987   NYPL [Sc E 88-173]

RICHMOND (VA.) - HISTORY - EXHIBITIONS.
McGraw, Marie Tyler. In bondage and freedom . Richmond, VA. [Chapel Hill, N.C.] , 1988. 71 p. :   NYPL [Sc F 89-107]

RICHMOND (VA.) - SOCIAL CONDITIONS.
Davis, Scott C., 1948- The world of Patience Gromes . [Lexington, Ky.] , 1988. 222 p. ; ISBN 0-8131-1644-9 DDC 975.5/45100496073 19
F234.R59 N43 1988   NYPL [Sc D 88-1302]

RICHMOND (VA.) - SOCIAL CONDITIONS - EXHIBITIONS.
McGraw, Marie Tyler. In bondage and

freedom . Richmond, VA. [Chapel Hill, N.C.] , 1988. 71 p. :   NYPL [Sc F 89-107]

RICHMOND (VA.) - SOCIAL LIFE AND CUSTOMS.
Davis, Scott C., 1948- The world of Patience Gromes . [Lexington, Ky.] , 1988. 222 p. ; ISBN 0-8131-1644-9 DDC 975.5/45100496073 19
F234.R59 N43 1988   NYPL [Sc D 88-1302]

Riddell, Roger. The land question [microform] / Roger Riddell. London : Catholic Institute for International Relations, [1978?] 40 p. : ill. ; 21 cm. (From Rhodesia to Zimbabwe. 2 2) Includes bibliographical references. Microfiche. New York : New York Public library, 1981. 1 microfiche : negative ; 11 x 15 cm. (FSN 35,581)
1. Land reform - Zimbabwe. 2. Land tenure - Zimbabwe. I. Title. II. Series.
HD992.Z63 R52   NYPL [*XME-13841]

Rideout, Esma. see Booth, Esma (Rideout)

Ridin' the moon in Texas . Shange, Ntozake. New York , 1987. xiii, 81 p. : ISBN 0-312-88929-1 : DDC 811/.54 19
PS3569.H3324 R5 1987
        NYPL [Sc D 89-384]

Rieger, Shay. The bronze zoo. New York, Scribner [1970] [48] p. illus. 27 cm. A sculptor describes the sketching, clay and plaster modeling, and casting processes she used in making eight bronze animals for outdoor parks. SCHOMBURG CHILDREN'S COLLECTION. DDC 731.4/56
I. Schomburg Children's Collection. II. Title.
NB1143 .R5   NYPL [Sc F 88-340]

Rieussec, Mathilde. Huggins, Nathan Irvin, 1927- L'odyssée noire /. Paris , c1979. 221 p. : ISBN 1-85258-150-7   NYPL [Sc F 88-383]

Rigby, Alison. Caribbean recipes for schools / Alison Rigby. Basingstoke : Macmillan, 1987. 100 p. ; 22 cm. Includes index. ISBN 0-333-44682-8 (spiral) : DDC 641.59/1821 19
1. Cookery, Caribbean. I. Title.
TX716.A1   NYPL [Sc D 88-1013]

Rigby, Peter. Persistent pastoralists : nomadic societies in transition / Peter Rigby. London : Zed ; Totowa, N.J. : Biblio Distribution Center, 1985. x, 198 p. : ill. ; 23 cm. (Third World books) Includes index. Bibliography: p. 176-190. ISBN 0-86232-226-X : DDC 305.8/9676 19
1. Masai - Economic conditions. 2. Herders - Africa, East. 3. Nomads - Africa, East. 4. Rural development - Africa, East. 5. Range management - Africa, East. I. Title. II. Series.
DT443.3.M37 R54 1985
        NYPL [JLD 86-2309]

Rigby, Reginald. St. Lo, Montague. Ten little nigger boys /. [London] , New York , 1904. [20] leaves, [20] leaves of plates :
        NYPL [Sc Rare C 86-1]

Riggs, Fred Warren. Ethnicity . Honolulu, Hawaii (2424 Maile Way, Honolulu 96822) , c1985. xxix, 205 p. ; DDC 305.8/0072 19
GN495.6 .E89 1985   NYPL [Sc F 87-355]

Right of a private prosecutor. Murder of Dele Giwa . Lagos, Nigeria , 1988. 193 p. : ISBN 978-232-523-6   NYPL [Sc F 89-35]

Right on Dellums! Fitch, Robert Beck, 1938- Mankato, Minn. [1971] [47] p. ISBN 0-87191-079-9 DDC 329/.023/79405
JK1978 .F53   NYPL [Sc F 88-338]

Right-on Miss Moon /. Osahon, Naiwu, 1937- Apapa, Lagos, Nigeria , 1981. [22] p. : ISBN 978-18-6003-0   NYPL [Sc D 89-228]

The right to a peaceful world . Jackson, Rashleigh E. [Guyana] 1985. 77 p. :
        NYPL [Sc D 89-140]

The right to education . Tollett, Kenneth S. Washington, D.C. , 1983. xiii, 77 p. ;
        NYPL [Sc D 87-1294]

RIGHT TO EDUCATION.
Tollett, Kenneth S. The right to education . Washington, D.C. , 1983. xiii, 77 p. ;
        NYPL [Sc D 87-1294]

RIGHT TO LEARN. see RIGHT TO EDUCATION.

The right wing collection of the University of Iowa Libraries, 1918-1977 . University of Iowa. Libraries. Glen Rock, N.J. , 1978. v, 175 p. ;

ISBN 0-667-00520-X   DDC 016.3205/0973
Z7163 .U585 1978 JA1   NYPL [Sc F 86-176]

The righteous state /. Naranjit, Darryl.
[Chaguanas? Trinidad] , c1987. ii, 225 p. ;
DDC 172 19
JA79 .N34 1987   NYPL [Sc D 89-518]

RIGHTS, CIVIL. see CIVIL RIGHTS.

Riley, James A. Dandy, Day and the Devil / by
James A. Riley ; foreword by Monte Irvin ;
original artwork by Jon Houghton. Cocoa, FL :
TK Publishers, 1987. xiii, 153 p. : ill., ports. ;
21 cm. Includes index.   ISBN 0-9614023-2-6
*1. Dandridge, Ray, 1913-. 2. Day, Leon, 1916-. 3.
Wells, Willie, 1905-. 4. Baseball players - United
States - Biography. 5. Afro-American baseball players -
Biography. I. Title.   NYPL [Sc D 88-104]*

Rimita, David Maitai, 1946- The Njuri-Noheke
of Meru / David Maitai Rimita. [Meru,
Kenya?] : D. M. Rimita, c1988. 81 p. : ill. ; 21
cm.
*1. Meru (African people). 2. Ethnology - Kenya -
Meru. I. Title.   NYPL [Sc D 89-310]*

Rimmer, Douglas. Rural transformation in tropical
Africa /. London , 1988. 177 p. :   ISBN
1-85293-012-8 :   DDC 330.96/0328 19
HC800   NYPL [JLE 88-4346]

The ring /. Moono, Muchimba Simuwana.
Lusaka , 1985. 121 p. ;   *NYPL [Sc C 89-70]*

Rinkoff, Barbara.
Headed for trouble / Barbara Rinkoff ;
illustrated by Don Bolognese. [1st ed.] New
York : Knopf, [1970] 119 p. : ill. ; 24 cm.
Deserted by his alcoholic father, a thirteen-year-old boy
refuses to adjust to the welfare home to which he is
sent.   ISBN 0-394-90494-X
*1. Group homes for children - United States - Juvenile
fiction. I. Bolognese, Don, illus. II. Title.
                          NYPL [Sc E 88-227]*
Rutherford T. finds 21 B. Illustrated by Tomie
de Paola. New York, Putnam [1970] [47] p. col.
illus. 23 cm. (A See and read beginning to read
storybook) While looking for his homeroom, a
six-year-old boy makes many new friends on his first
day of school. SCHOMBURG CHILDREN'S
COLLECTION.   DDC [Fic]
*1. Afro-American children - Juvenile fiction. I. De
Paola, Tomie. II. Schomburg Children's Collection. III.
Title.*
PZ7.R477 Ru   NYPL [Sc D 88-1404]

**RIO DE JANEIRO (BRAZIL : STATE) -
HISTORY.**
Lara, Silvia Hunold. Campos da violência . Rio
de Janeiro , c1988. 389 p. ;
                          NYPL [Sc D 89-13]

**RIO DE JANEIRO (BRAZIL : STATE) -
SOCIAL CONDITIONS.**
Lara, Silvia Hunold. Campos da violência . Rio
de Janeiro , c1988. 389 p. ;
                          NYPL [Sc D 89-13]

**RIO DE JANEIRO (BRAZIL) - RELIGIOUS
LIFE AND CUSTOMS.**
Gonzalez, Lélia. Festas populares no Brasil =.
Rio de Janeiro, Brasil , c1987. 144 p. :   ISBN
85-7083-015-7
GT4833.A2 G66x 1987   NYPL [Sc F 89-116]

**RIO DE JANEIRO (BRAZIL) - SOCIAL LIFE
AND CUSTOMS.**
Eneida, 1903-1971. História do carnaval carioca
/. Rio de Janeiro , c1987. 259 p. :   ISBN
85-10-29900-5
GT4233.R5 E53 1987   NYPL [Sc D 89-313]

**RIO DE JANEIRO (BRAZIL) - SOCIAL LIFE
AND CUSTOMS - PICTORIAL WORKS.**
Guillobel, Joaquim Cândido, 1787-1859. Usos e
costumes do Rio de Janeiro nas figurinhas de
Guillobel =. [Curitiba?] [1978] [19] p., [25]
leaves of plates :   DDC 981/.5
F2646.2 .G84 1978   NYPL [Sc F 88-188]

**RIO DE LA PLATA REGION (ARGENTINA
AND URUGUAY) - HISTORY.**
Studer, Elena F. S. de. La trata de negros en el
Río de la Plata durante el siglo XVIII /. Bs.
As. [i.e. Buenos Aires] [1984] 378 p., [27]
leaves of plates (some folded) :   ISBN
950-9138-08-8
HT1123.R5 S78 1984   NYPL [Sc E 87-419]

**RIOTS - ARKANSAS - PHILLIPS COUNTY -
HISTORY.**
Cortner, Richard C. A mob intent on death .
Middletown, Conn. , c1988. xii, 241 p., [24] p.

of plates :   ISBN 0-8195-5161-9 (alk. paper) :   DDC
976.7/88052 19
F417.P45 C67 1988   NYPL [Sc E 88-362]

RIOTS - CURAÇAO - FICTION.
Jongh, Edward Arthur de. E dia di mas
históriko /. Aruba , 1970. 158 p. :
                          NYPL [Sc D 87-1430]

RIOTS - MASSACHUSETTS - BOSTON.
Anti-Slavery Meeting (1855 : Boston) The
Boston mob of "gentlemen of property and
standing." . Boston , 1855 (Boston : J.B.
Yerrinton and Son, printers) 76 p. :
E450.B74   NYPL [Sc Rare F 88-44]

RIOTS - MISSISSIPPI - JACKSON.
Spofford, Tim. Lynch Street . Kent, Ohio ,
c1988. 219 p., [1] leaf of plates :   ISBN
0-87338-355-9 (alk. paper)   DDC 976.2/51 19
F349.J13 S66 1988   NYPL [Sc E 89-27]

**RIOTS - NEW YORK (CITY) - 1863. see
DRAFT RIOT, 1863.**

RIOTS - SOUTH AFRICA - SOWETO.
Finnegan, William. Dateline Soweto . New
York , c1988. x. 244 p. :   ISBN 0-06-015932-4 :
DDC 070/.92/4 B 19
PN4874.F45 A3 1989   NYPL [JFE 88-2005]

**RIOTS - SOUTH AFRICA - SOWETO -
PICTORIAL WORKS.**
Magubane, Peter. June 16 . Johannesburg ,
c1986. [85] p. :   ISBN 0-947009-13-2 (pbk.)   DDC
968.2/21 19
DT944.J66 S674 1986   NYPL [Sc G 88-12]

RIOTS - UNITED STATES.
United States. Kerner Commission. The Kerner
report . New York, N.Y. , 1988. xxvi, 513 p. ;
ISBN 0-679-72078-2   *NYPL [Sc D 89-604]*

**RIOTS - UNITED STATES - HISTORY -
19TH CENTURY.**
Werner, John M., 1941- Reaping the bloody
harvest . New York , 1986. 333 p. ;   ISBN
0-8240-8301-6 (alk. paper) :   DDC 973.5/6 19
E185 .W44 1986   NYPL [Sc E 88-242]

The rise and fall of Anini /. Enonchong, Charles.
Calabar, Nigeria [1988] 73 p. :
                          NYPL [Sc C 89-8]

The rise and fall of the South African peasantry
/. Bundy, Colin. Cape Town , 1988. [21], 276
p. ;   ISBN 0-520-03754-5   *NYPL [Sc D 89-533]*

Risério, Antonio. Gilberto Gil Expresso 2222 /.
[Salvador, Brasil?] , 1982. 287 p. ;
                          NYPL [JMD 83-309]

The risks of Ro . Fuller, Louisia. Teaneck, N.J. ,
c1988. 105 p. ;   ISBN 0-945779-00-3
                          NYPL [Sc D 88-1172]

Ritchie, Andrew. Major Taylor : the extraordinary
career of a champion bicycle racer / Andrew
Ritchie. San Francisco : Bicycle Books ; New
York : Distributed in the USA by
Kampmann & Co., 1988. 304 p., [32] p. of
plates : ill., ports., ; 24 cm. Includes index.
Bibliography: p. [289]-294.   ISBN 0-933201-14-1
(hardcover)
*1. Taylor, Marshall W. (Marshall William), b. 1878. 2.
Cyclists - United States - Biography. 3. Afro-American
athletes - Biography. I. Title.
                          NYPL [Sc E 88-570]*

RITES AND CEREMONIES - MADAGASCAR.
Ny djoutche Malagasy [microform] /.
Tananarive [1978] 73 p. :
                          NYPL [Sc Micro F-10988]

**RITES OF PASSAGE. see RITES AND
CEREMONIES.**

Ritz, Karen. (ill) Ferris, Jeri. Go free or die .
Minneapolis , 1987. 63 p. :   ISBN 0-87614-317-6
(lib. bdg.) :   DDC 305.5/67/0924 B 92 19
E444.T82 F47 1987   NYPL [Sc D 88-620]

River roads to freedom . Tregillis, Helen Cox.
Bowie, Md. , 1988. 122 p. :   ISBN 1-556-13120-8
DDC 929/.3/089960773 19
F540 .T7 1988   NYPL [Sc D 88-1442]

River treasure. Burgwin, Mebane (Holoman)
New York, 1947. 159 p.
PZ7.B9177 Ri   NYPL [Sc D 89-512]

Rivers of the world (Champaign, Ill.) .
(W-10) Lauber, Patricia. The Congo, river into
central Africa. Champaign, Ill. [1964] 96 p.
DDC 967
DT639 .L38   NYPL [Sc E 89-24]

**RIVERS STATE, NIGERIA - POLITICS AND
GOVERNMENT.**
Boro, Isaac. The twelve-day revolution /. Benin
City, Nigeria , 1982. 158 p., [8] p. of plates :
ISBN 978-234-040-5   *NYPL [Sc C 88-109]*

Rives, Claude. Antilles Caraïbes /. Paris , c1982.
157 p. :   ISBN 2-7191-0177-0
                          NYPL [Sc F 88-347]

**ROAD SIGNS. see TRAFFIC SIGNS AND
SIGNALS.**

Road to liberation : MPLA documents on the
founding of the People's Republic of Angola.
Richmond, B. C. : LSM Information Center,
pref. 1976. viii, 53 p. : ill. (some col.) ; 22 cm.
*1. Angola - Politics and government - 1961-1975. I.
Liberation Support Movement. Information Center. II.
Movimento Popular de Libertação de Angola.
                          NYPL [JFD 80-10236]*

The road to Zimbabwe, 1890-1980 /. Verrier,
Anthony. London , 1986. xiv, 364 p., [8] p. of
plates :   ISBN 0-224-02161-3
                          NYPL [Sc D 88-313]

**ROADS - SIGNS. see TRAFFIC SIGNS AND
SIGNALS.**

**ROADS - TRAFFIC SIGNS. see TRAFFIC
SIGNS AND SIGNALS.**

**ROADSIDE TRAFFIC SIGNS. see TRAFFIC
SIGNS AND SIGNALS.**

Roaring Lion (Musician) Calypso from France to
Trinidad : 800 years of history / by the
Roaring Lion. San Juan [Trinidad and
Tobago?] : General Printers of San Juan,
[between 1985 and 1988] 249 p. : ill., ports. ;
21 cm. Cover title. Bibliography: p. 248-249.
*1. Calypso (Music) - History and criticism. I. Title.
                          NYPL [Sc D 88-894]*

Roark, J. L. American expansionism vs. European
colonialism [microform] : the congo episode
1883-1885 / by J. L. Roark. [Nairobi] :
University of Nairobi, Dept. of History, 1976.
16 leaves ; 33 cm. (Staff seminar paper / University
of Nairobi, Department of History. [no. 2]) Cover title.
Includes bibliographical references. Microfilm. New
York: New York Public Library, 1982. 1 microfilm reel;
35 mm. (MN *ZZ-23051)
*1. Sanford, Henry Shelton, 1823-1891. 2. International
Association of the Congo. 3. Zaire - History - To 1908.
4. United States - Relations (general) with Zaire -
History. 5. Zaire - Relations (general) with the United
States. I. Series: Nairobi. University. Dept. of History.
Staff seminar paper, no. 2. II. Title.
                          NYPL [Sc Micro R-4108 no. 34]*

Robaina, Tomás Fernández, 1941- Bibliografía de
temas afrocubanos /. La Habana , 1985. 581
p. ;   *NYPL [Sc D 89-510]*

ROBBERY - NIGERIA.
Idowu, Sina, 1947- Armed robbery in Nigeria /.
Lagos, Nigeria , c1980. 121 p. :   ISBN
978-231-900-7 (pbk.)   DDC 364.1/552/09669 19
HV6665.N6 136 1980   NYPL [Sc D 89-264]

Robbins, Vivian M. Musical Buxton / by Vivian
Robbins. [S.l. : s.n., 197-] 44 p. : ill. ; 28 cm.
Cover title.   DDC 780/.9713/1 19
*1. Music - Ontario - Buxton - History and criticism. 2.
Musicians - Ontario - Buxton - Biography. I. Title.
ML205.8.B8 R6   NYPL [Sc F 88-149]

Robert Colescott, a retrospective, 1975-1986 /.
Sims, Lowery Stokes. San Jose, Calif. , c1987.
34 p. :   ISBN 0-938175-01-7 (pbk.)   DDC 759.13 19
ND237.C66 A4 1987   NYPL [Sc F 88-317]

Robert Mapplethorpe black book. Mapplethorpe,
Robert. Black book /. New York , c1986. 91
p. :   *NYPL [Sc F 87-42]*

Roberts, Naurice. Harold Washington : mayor
with a vision / by Naurice Roberts. Chicago :
Childrens Press, 1988. 30 p. : ill. ; 25 cm.
(Picture-story biographies) Follows the life and career
of Chicago's first black mayor, assessing his impact as
lawyer, state representative, state senator, mayor, and
national leader. SCHOMBURG CHILDREN'S
COLLECTION.   ISBN 0-516-03657-2   DDC
977.3/1100496073024 B 92 19
*1. Washington, Harold, 1922-1987 - Juvenile literature.
2. Washington, Harold, 1922-1987. 3. Mayors -
Illinois - Chicago - Biography - Juvenile literature. 4.
Chicago (Ill.) - Politics and government - 1951- -
Juvenile literature. I. Schomburg Children's Collection.
II. Title.*
F548.52.W36 R63 1988
                          NYPL [Sc E 88-501]

Roberts, Peter A. West Indians and their language / Peter A. Roberts. Cambridge [Cambridgeshire] ; New York : Cambridge University Press, 1988. vii, 215 p. : ill. ; 25 cm. Bibliography: p. 205-210. ISBN 0-521-35136-7 DDC 427/.9729 19
1. Creole dialects, English - West Indies. 2. English language - West Indies. 3. Language and culture - West Indies. 4. Language and education - West Indies. 5. West Indies - Languages. I. Title.
P381.W47 R63 1988   ***NYPL [Sc E 88-331]***

Roberts, Richard L., 1949- The End of slavery in Africa /. Madison, Wis. , c1988. xx, 524 p. :
     ISBN 0-299-11550-X :   DDC 306/.362/096 19
HT1323 .E53 1988   ***NYPL [Sc E 89-222]***

Robertson, Amy. Select bibliography of education in the Commonwealth Caribbean, 1976-1985 : a supplement to Select bibliography of education in the Commonwealth Caribbean 1940-1975 / compiled by Amy Robertson. Mona, Jamaica : Documentation Centre, School of Education, University of the West Indies, 1987. 174 p. ; 28 cm. Includes index.
1. Education - Caribbean area - Bibliography. I. Title.
     NYPL [Sc F 88-316]

ROBESON, PAUL, 1898-1976.
Duberman, Martin B. Paul Robeson /. New York , 1988, c1989. xiii, 804 p., [48] p. of plates :   ISBN 0-394-52780-1 :   DDC 790.2/092/4 B 19
E185.97.R63 D83 1988   ***NYPL [Sc E 89-108]***

ROBESON, PAUL, 1898-1976 - JUVENILE LITERATURE.
Ehrlich, Scott. Paul Robeson /. New York , c1988. 111 p. :   ISBN 1-555-46608-7 DDC 782.1/092/4 B 92 19
E185.97.R63 E35 1988   ***NYPL [Sc E 88-167]***

ROBINSON, BILL, 1878-1949.
Haskins, James, 1941- Mr. Bojangles . New York , 1988. 336 p. :   ISBN 0-688-07203-8 : DDC 793.3/2/0924 B 19
GV1785.R54 H37 1988
     NYPL [Sc D 88-851]

Robinson, David, 1938-
[Holy war of Umar Tal. French]
La guerre sainte d'al-Hajj Umar : le Soudan occidental au milieu du XIXe siècle / David Robinson ; traduit de l'anglais par Henry Tourneux et Jean-Claude Vuillemin. Paris : Karthala, c1988. 413 p. : maps ; 24 cm. (Hommes et sociétés) Translation of: The holy war of Umar Tal. Includes bibliographical references. ISBN 2-86537-211-1
1. Tal, Umar, 1794?-1864. 2. Senegambia - History. I. Series. II. Series: Hommes et sociétés (Editions Karthala). III. Title.   ***NYPL [Sc E 89-258]***

Robinson, Frank, 1935- Extra innings / Frank Robinson and Berry Stainback. New York : McGraw-Hill, c1988. x, 230, [8] p. of plates. : ports. ; 24 cm.   ISBN 0-07-053183-8 DDC 796.357/08996073 19
1. Robinson, Frank - United States - History. 2. Afro-American baseball players. 3. Discrimination in sports - United States. I. Stainback, Berry. II. Title.
GV863.A1 R582 1988   ***NYPL [Sc E 88-382]***

Robinson, Jackie. see **Robinson, John Roosevelt, 1919-1972.**

Robinson, Jackie, 1919-1972.
Jackie Robinson : my own story / as told by Jackie Robinson to Wendell Smith ; foreword by Branch Rickey. New York : Greenberg, 1948. 170 p. : ill., ports. ; 20 cm.
1. Baseball players - United States - Biography. 2. Afro-American baseball players - Biography. I. Smith, Wendell. II. Title. III. Title: My own story.
     NYPL [Sc C 88-61]

ROBINSON, JACKIE, 1919-1972 - JUVENILE LITERATURE.
Adler, David A. Jackie Robinson . New York , c1989. 48 p. :   ISBN 0-8234-0734-9 DDC 796.357/092/4 B 19
GV865 .A37 1989   ***NYPL [Sc F 89-137]***

Scott, Richard, 1956- Jackie Robinson /. New York , 1987. 110 p. :   ISBN 1-555-46208-1 : DDC 796.357/092/4 B 92 19
GV865.R6 S36 1987   ***NYPL [Sc E 88-168]***

Robinson, John Roosevelt, 1919-1972. Jackie Robinson's Little League baseball book, by Jackie Robinson. Englewood Cliffs, N.J., Prentice-Hall [1972] 135 p. illus. 22 cm.
Discusses ways for Little League players to improve their baseball skills.   ISBN 0-13-509232-9
1. Baseball - Juvenile literature. I. Title. II. Title: Little League baseball book.
GV867.5 .R6   ***NYPL [JFD 72-7423]***

Robinson, Robert, ca. 1902- Black on Red : my 44 years inside the Soviet Union ; an autobiography by Black American / Robert Robinson with Jonathan Slevin. Washington, D.C. : Acropolis Books, 1988. 436 p. : ill., maps ; 24 cm. Includes index.   ISBN 0-87491-885-5 DDC 947.084 19
1. Robinson, Robert, ca. 1902-. 2. Afro-Americans - Soviet Union - Biography. I. Slevin, Jonathan. II. Title.
DK34.B53 R63 1988   ***NYPL [Sc E 88-377]***

ROBINSON, ROBERT, CA. 1902-
Robinson, Robert, ca. 1902- Black on Red . Washington, D.C. , 1988. 436 p. :   ISBN 0-87491-885-5   DDC 947.084 19
DK34.B53 R63 1988   ***NYPL [Sc E 88-377]***

Roca, Juan Manuel.
[Poems. Selections]
País secreto / Juan Manuel Roca ; selección de Victor Rodriguez Núñez. La Habana : Casa de las Américas, c1987. 115 p. ; 19 cm. (Cuadernos de la honda) Includes index.
I. Núñez, Victor Rodriguez. II. Title.
     NYPL [Sc C 89-39]

Rochegude, Anne. Systèmes fonciers à la ville et au village . Paris , c1986. 296 p. ;   ISBN 2-85802-719-6   DDC 346.6704/32 346.706432 19
LAW   ***NYPL [Sc D 89-367]***

Rochman, Hazel. Somehow tenderness survives . New York , c1988. 147 p. :   ISBN 0-06-025022-4 :   DDC [Fic] 19
PZ5 .S695 1988   ***NYPL [Sc D 88-1461]***

ROCK AND ROLL MUSIC. see **ROCK MUSIC.**

ROCK MUSIC - DISCOGRAPHY.
Escott, Colin. Sun records . Vollersode, W. Germany , c1987. 240 p. :   ISBN 3-924787-09-3 (pbk.)   ***NYPL [Sc D 89-243]***

ROCK MUSIC - SOCIAL ASPECTS - GREAT BRITAIN.
Widgery, David. Beating time /. London , 1986. 126 p. :   ISBN 0-7011-2985-9
     NYPL [JMD 88-112]

ROCK MUSICIANS - BIOGRAPHY.
Adler, B. Tougher than leather . New York , c1987. viii, 191 p., [14] p. of plates :   ISBN 0-451-15121-6 (pbk.) :   ***NYPL [Sc C 88-271]***

ROCK MUSICIANS - UNITED STATES - BIOGRAPHY.
Henderson, David, 1942- 'Scuse me while I kiss the sky . Toronto , New York , 1983, 1981. xi, 411 p. :   ISBN 0-553-01334-3 (tr. pbk.) :   DDC 784.5/4/00924
ML410.H476 H46 1981
     NYPL [Sc C 82-243]

Swenson, John. Stevie Wonder /. London , c1986. 160 p. :   ISBN 85965-076-6 (pbk.) : DDC 784.5/4/00924 B 19
ML410.W836 S9 1986b
     NYPL [Sc F 88-363]

ROCK-N-ROLL MUSIC. see **ROCK MUSIC.**

Rock of the ancestors . Cuttington University College. Africana Museum. Suakoko, Liberia , c1977. 102 p. :   DDC 730/.09666/2074096662 19
N7399.L4 C87 1977   ***NYPL [Sc F 89-27]***

ROCK-TOMBS. see **TOMBS.**

Rocker, Fermin.
(illus) Horvath, Betty F. Hooray for Jasper. New York [1966] 1 v. (unpaged)
PZ7.H7922 Ho   ***NYPL [Sc F 88-252]***

(illus) Horvath, Betty F. Jasper makes music. New York [1967] [38] p. DDC [E]
PZ7.H7922 Jas   ***NYPL [Sc F 88-343]***

ROCKET FLIGHT. see **SPACE FLIGHT.**

Rocksloh-Papendieck, Barbara. Frauenarbeit am Strassenrand Kenkeyküchen in Ghana / Barbara Rocksloh-Papendieck. Hamburg : Institut für Afrika-kunde, 1988. iii, 193 p. : ill., maps ; 21 cm. (Arbeiten aus dem Institut für Afrika-Kunde . 55) German with English summary. Bibliography: p. 178-190. ISBN 3-923519-75-3
1. Women merchants - Ghana. 2. Women - Ghana. 3. Corn as food - Ghana. I. Title. II. Series.
     NYPL [Sc D 89-575]

Rocky, the woodcarver . Crooks, Merrise.

Brimingham, England , 1984[reprinted 1987] 24 p. :   ***NYPL [Sc D 88-1076]***

Rodman, Selden, 1909- Where art is joy : Haitian art : the first forty years / Selden Rodman.1st ed. New York : Ruggles deLatour, c1988. 236 p. : ill. (some col.) ; 32 cm. Includes indexes.
     ISBN 0-938291-01-7 :   DDC 759.97294 19
1. Art, Haitian. 2. Primitivism in art - Haiti. I. Title.
N6606.5.P74 R64 1988
     NYPL [3-MAM+ 89-6425]

Rodney, Walter.
The groundings with my brothers; with an introduction by Richard Small. London, Bogle-L'Ouverture Publications, 1969. 68 p. map. 22 cm. Negro author.   ISBN 0-9501546-0-1
1. Blacks - Jamaica. 2. Black power - Jamaica. I. Title.
F1896.N4 R6   ***NYPL [Sc 323.2-R]***

RODNEY, WALTER.
Ngugi Wa Thiong'o, 1938- The first Walter Rodney memorial lecture, 1985 /. London , 1987. 12 p. :   ***NYPL [Sc Rare F 88-67]***

RODNEY, WALTER - FICTION.
Salkey, Andrew. The one . London , 1985. 48 p. :   ***NYPL [Sc D 88-1238]***

Rodrigues, Abelardo, 1952- A Razão da chama . São Paulo , 1986. xii, 122 p. ;
     NYPL [Sc D 89-462]

Rodrigues, Eustáquio José. Cauterizai o meu umbigo / Eustáquio José Rodrigues. Rio de Janeiro-RJ : Anima, 1986. 181 p. ; 21 cm.
     DDC 869.3 19
1. Brazil - Fiction. I. Title.
PQ9280.O269 C3 1986
     NYPL [JFD 88-6700]

Rodríguez, Camille. (joint author) Valle, Manuel del. Law and bilingual education . New York , 1978. i, 206 p. ;   ***NYPL [Sc F 88-357]***

Rogers, Braima. Love without questions / by Braima Rogers. Freetown : People's Educational Association of Sierra Leone, 1986. 86 p. ; 22 cm. (Stories and songs from Sierra Leone . 20) CONTENTS. - Love without questions.--The rightful heir.--The jealous hunter.
1. Sierra Leone - Fiction. I. Title. II. Series.
     NYPL [Sc D 89-415]

Rohmer, Harriet. The invisible hunters : a legend from the Miskito Indians of Nicaragua = Los cazadores invisibles : una leyenda de los indios miskitos de Nicaragua / Harriet Rohmer, Octavio Chow, Morris Vidaure ; illustrations/ilustraciones, Joe Sam ; version in Spanish/versión en español, Rosalma Zubizarreta & Alma Flor Ada. San Francisco : Children's Book Press, c1987. 32 p. : col. ill. ; 26 cm. (Stories from Central America = Cuentos de Centroamérica) English and Spanish. This Miskito Indian legend set in seventeenth-century Nicaragua illustrates the impact of the first European traders on traditional life. SCHOMBURG CHILDREN'S COLLECTION.   ISBN 0-89239-031-X :   DDC 398.2/08998 19
1. Mosquito Indians - Legends. 2. Indians of Central America - Nicaragua - Legends. I. Chow, Octavio. II. Vidauro, Morris. III. Sam, Joe, ill. IV. Schomburg Children's Collection. V. Title. VI. Title: Cazadores invisibles. VII. Series: Stories from Central America.
F1529.M9 R64 1987   ***NYPL [Sc E 88-241]***

Roho mkononi /. Rajab, Hammie. Dar es Salaam , c1984. 113 p. :   ISBN 997-693-102-6
     NYPL [Sc C 88-94]

Rohrer, George.
Wassermann, Selma. Moonbeam and Dan Starr. Westchester, Ill., c1966. 64 p.
     NYPL [Sc D 89-398]

(illus) Wassermann, Selma. Moonbeam and the rocket ride. Chicago [c1965] 64 p.
PE1119 .W363   ***NYPL [Sc D 89-92]***

Roldán, Amadeo, 1900-1939. Guillén, Nicolás, 1902- Motivos de son /. La Habana , 1980. 32, [88] p. :   ***NYPL [Sc E 87-151]***

The role of the laity in ecumenism with reference to the church in Nigeria /. Anaele, Justin Uchechukwu. Rome , 1985 (Rome : R. Ambrosini) 146 p.   ***NYPL [Sc E 88-608]***

The role of the South African government in tertiary education /. Dreijmanis, John. Johannesburg, South Africa , 1988. xiii, 156 p. :   ISBN 0-86982-329-9   ***NYPL [Sc F 88-184]***

The role of universities in the modern world /.

Bowden, Bertram Vivian, Baron Bowden, 1910-
Kumasi, Ghana [1978?] 81 p. ;
                                    NYPL [Sc D 88-465]

**The Role of women in the execution of
low-income housing projects** : training module.
Nairobi, Kenya : United Nations Centre for
Human Settlements (Habitat), 1986. 64 p. : ill. ;
30 cm. "This training module has been prepared on
the basis of research carried out by Caroline O. Moser
and Sylvia H. Chant of the Development Planning Unit
of the University of London." -- T.p. verso.
Bibliography: p. 62-64.   ISBN 92-1-131005-9
1. Women in community development - Developing
countries. 2. Economic development projects -
Developing countries. 3. Housing management -
Developing countries. I. University of London.
Development Planning Unit. II. United Nations Centre
for Human Settlements.   **NYPL [Sc F 88-225]**

**Le rôle socio-religieux de la cola dans la société
malinké** . Keita, Djigui. [Abidjan? , 1985] 72
leaves :   **NYPL [Sc F 88-307]**

Roll the union on . Mitchell, H. L. (Harry
Leland), 1906- Chicago , 1987. 96 p. :
                                    NYPL [Sc F 88-187]

Rolland, Guy. Un demi-siecle de swing et de Jazz
/. [Paris] , 1986. 109 p. :   ISBN 2-86929-034-9
                                    NYPL [Sc G 86-35]

Rollins, Charlemae Hill. We build together; a
reader's guide to Negro life and literature for
elementary and high school use [edited by]
Charlemae Rollins. Contributors: Augusta Baker
[and others]3d ed. [Champaign, Ill. : National
Council of Teachers of English, 1967] xxviii, 71
p. ; 21 cm.   DDC 016.818
1. Afro-Americans - Bibliography. 2. Afro-Americans in
literature - Bibliography. I. Baker, Augusta. II. National
Council of Teachers of English. III. Title.
Z1361.N39 R77 1967   **NYPL [Sc D 89-387]**

Rollwagen, Elsa. La Renaissance noire : (Harlem,
New York - 1919/1929) / Elsa Rollwagen.
1978. iii, 149 leaves ; 30 cm. Thesis
(master's)--Université de Paris VIII, 1978. Bibliography:
p. 148-149.
1. Harlem Renaissance. I. Title.
                                    NYPL [Sc F 88-280]

Roman Catholic Church. see Catholic Church.

Romance of life /. Ajiboye, Josy. Lagos, Nigeria ,
1985. 108 p. :
MLCS 87/7906 (P)   **NYPL [Sc C 89-85]**

ROMANTICISM - BRAZIL.
Gomes, Heloisa Toller. O negro e o
romantismo brasileiro /. São Paulo [1988] 113
p. ;   **NYPL [Sc D 89-515]**

**ROMANTICISM IN LITERATURE. see
ROMANTICISM.**

Rombi, M.-F. (Marie-Françoise) Etudes sur le
bantu oriental . Paris , 1982 [i.e. 1983] 158 p. :
ISBN 2-85297-144-5 :   DDC 496/.39 19
PL8025 .E84 1983   **NYPL [Sc E 88-357]**

Rome and race . Thompson, L. A. [Ibadan]
1987. iii, 114 p. :   **NYPL [Sc F 88-173]**

ROME - CIVILIZATION.
Dadié, Bernard Binlin, 1916- The city where no
one dies /. Washington, D.C. , c1986. 139 p. ;
ISBN 0-89410-499-3
                                    NYPL [Sc D 88-1468]

ROME - ETHNIC RELATIONS.
Thompson, L. A. Rome and race . [Ibadan]
1987. iii, 114 p. :   **NYPL [Sc F 88-173]**

ROME - RACE RELATIONS.
Thompson, L. A. Rome and race . [Ibadan]
1987. iii, 114 p. :   **NYPL [Sc F 88-173]**

Romero, Fernando. El negro en el Perú y su
transculturación lingüística / Fernando Romero.
[Lima?] : Editorial Milla Batres, 1987. 176 p. :
ill., maps ; 26 cm.
1. Blacks - Peru - Language. 2. Peru - Languages. I.
Title.   **NYPL [Sc F 88-20]**

Romero, Patricia W. Life histories of African women /. London ,
Atlantic Highlands, NJ , 1988. 200 p. :   ISBN
0-948660-04-X DDC 305.4/0967 19
HQ1787.A3 L54 1988
                                    NYPL [Sc D 88-1469]

Taylor, Susie King, b. 1848. [Reminiscences of
my life in camp.] A Black woman's Civil War
memoirs . New York , 1988. 154 p. :   ISBN

0-910129-85-1 (pbk.) :   DDC 973.7/415 B 19
E492.94 33rd .T3 1988
                                    NYPL [Sc D 88-1473]

Romero, Vicente, 1947- Guinea-Bissau y Cabo
Verde : los "afrocomunistas" / Vicente Romero.
Madrid : Molinos de Agua, 1981. 109 p. ; 20
cm. (Textos del Tercer Mundo) Spine title: Los
afrocomunistas. On cover: Guerra y revolución en
Guinea Bissau y Cabo Verde. Includes bibliographical
references.   ISBN 84-85761-09-X DDC 966/.5702
19
1. Partido Africano da Independéncia da Guinée e
Cabo Verde - History. 2. Communism - Guinea-Bissau.
3. Communism - Cape Verde. 4. Guinea-Bissau -
History - Revolution, 1963-1974. 5. Cape Verde -
History - 20th century. I. Title. II. Title:
Afrocomunistas. III. Series.
DT613.78 .R66 1981   **NYPL [Sc C 89-1]**

Romyn, Conrad. Saint Lucia life and scenes /
Dick Romyn. London : Macmillan, 1985. [92]
p. : all ill. (chiefly col.) ; 31 cm.   ISBN
0-333-40009-7
1. St. Lucia - Description and travel - Views. I. Title.
                                    NYPL [Sc G 88-3]

Ronnie and the Chief's son. Coatsworth,
Elizabeth Jane, 1893- New York, 1962. 38 p.
PZ7.C6294 Ro   **NYPL [Sc E 89-23]**

Ronton, Josef. Analogía de umbanda : ponto
riscado / Josef Ronton. São Paulo : Traíde,
c1985. 389 p. : ill. ; 21 cm.
I. Title.   **NYPL [JFD 87-5626]**

**ROOMING HOUSES. see HOTELS,
TAVERNS, ETC.**

Rooney, David. Kwame Nkrumah : the political
kingdom in the Third World / David Rooney.
London : I.B. Tauris, 1988. viii, 292 p. ; 23 cm.
Includes index. Map on lining papers. Bibliography: p.
279-283.
1. Nkrumah, Kwame, 1909-1972. 2. Ghana - Politics
and government - 1957-1979. 3. Ghana - Presidents -
Biography. I. Title.   **NYPL [Sc D 89-44]**

Roosevelt Grady /. Shotwell, Louisa Rossiter.
Cleveland, Ohio , c1963. 151 p. :
                                    NYPL [Sc D 88-1425]

ROOSTERS - JUVENILE FICTION.
Gipson, Fred. The trail-driving rooster /. New
York : Harper & Row, c1955. 79 p. :
                                    NYPL [Sc D 88-427]

Roots of Jamaican culture /. Alleyne, Mervyn.
London , 1988. xii, 186 p. ;   ISBN 0-7453-0245-9
DDC 972.92 19
F1874   **NYPL [Sc D 88-1190]**

Roots rocking in Zimbabwe /. Zindi, Fred.
Gweru, Zimbabwe , 1985. viii, 98 p., [32] p. of
plates :   ISBN 0-86922-360-7
                                    NYPL [Sc D 88-1323]

The rope and the cross . Lee, Easton. Kingston,
Jamaica , 1985. 48 p., [4] p. of plates :
                                    NYPL [Sc D 89-458]

Rosberg, Carl G. Africa and the world today / by
Carl G. Rosberg ; editor: Martha J. Porter.
[Chicago?] : North Central Association of
Colleges and Secondary Schools, 1960. 66 p. :
ill., maps ; 17 x 22 cm. Bibliography on foldout of
back cover.
1. Africa, Sub-Saharan - Study and teaching. 2. Africa,
Sub-Saharan - History. I. Title.
                                    NYPL [Sc B 88-5]

Rose, Dan. Black American street life : South
Philadelphia, 1969-1971 / Dan Rose.
Philadelphia, Pa. : University of Pennsylvania
Press, c1987. x, 278 p. : ill., ports. ; 23 cm.
(University of Pennsylvania Press conduct and
communication series) Includes index. Bibliography: p.
[271]-275.   ISBN 0-8122-8071-7 DDC
974.8/1100496073 19
1. Rose, Dan. 2. Afro-Americans - Pennsylvania -
Philadelphia - Social life and customs. 3.
Afro-Americans - Pennsylvania - Philadelphia - Social
conditions. 4. South Philadelphia (Philadelphia, Pa.) -
Social life and customs. 5. South Philadelphia
(Philadelphia, Pa.) - Social conditions. 6. Philadelphia
(Pa.) - Social conditions. 7. Philadelphia (Pa.) - Social
life and customs. I. Title.
F158.9.N4 R67 1987   **NYPL [Sc E 88-76]**

ROSE, DAN.
Rose, Dan. Black American street life .
Philadelphia, Pa. , c1987. x, 278 p. :   ISBN
0-8122-8071-7 DDC 974.8/1100496073 19
F158.9.N4 R67 1987   **NYPL [Sc E 88-76]**

Rose, Karen. A single trail. Chicago, Follett
[1969] 158 p. 22 cm. Parallels the lives of a Negro
youth beginning a possible journey into crime and a
white boy uncertain of his self-image in his new
neighborhood. SCHOMBURG CHILDREN'S
COLLECTION. ISBN 0-695-44082-9 DDC [Fic]
1. Afro-American children - Juvenile fiction. I.
Schomburg Children's Collection. II. Title.
PZ7.R717 Si   **NYPL [Sc D 89-91]**

Rosemain, Jacqueline, 1930- La musique dans la
société antillaise : 1635-1902, Martinique
Guadeloupe / Jacqueline Rosemain. Paris :
Éditions L'Harmattan, c1986. 183 p. : music ;
24 cm. (Collection Recherches et documents monde
antillais) Bibliography: p. 177-182.   ISBN
2-85802-685-8 (pbk.).
1. Music - West Indies, French - History and criticism.
2. West Indies, French - Social life and customs. I.
Title. II. Series.   **NYPL [Sc E 88-394]**

Rosenblum, Mort. Squandering Eden : Africa at
the edge / Mort Rosenblum and Doug
Williamson.1st ed. San Diego : Harcourt Brace
Jovanovich, c1987. x, 326 p., [32] p. of plates :
ill., map ; 24 cm. Includes index. Bibliography: p.
[309]-314.   ISBN 0-15-184860-2 :   DDC 960/.3 19
1. Human ecology - Africa. 2. Africa - Economic
conditions. 3. Africa - Social conditions. I. Williamson,
Doug. II. Title.
GF701 .R67 1987   **NYPL [Sc E 88-24]**

Rosenthal, Sylvia Dworsky, 1911- Hovis, Gene.
[Uptown down home cookbook.] Gene Hovis's
uptown down home cookbook /. Boston ,
c1987. xii, 235 p. ;   ISBN 0-316-37443-1 :   DDC
641.5 19
TX715 .H8385 1987   **NYPL [Sc E 88-476]**

Ross, D. H. Educating handicapped young people
in eastern and southern Africa in 1981-83 /
D.H. Ross. Paris : United Nations Educational,
Scientific and Cultural Organization, 1988. 152
p. : ill. ; 25 cm. Bibliography: p. [149]-150.   ISBN
92-3-102560-0
1. Rehabilitation - South Africa. 2. Rehabilitation -
Africa, East. I. Unesco. II. Title.
                                    NYPL [Sc E 88-534]

Ross, Jacob.
Callaloo . London , 1984. 108 p. :   ISBN
0-905405-09-9 (pbk) :   DDC 810.8/09729845 19
PR9275.G   **NYPL [Sc D 88-702]**

Owusu, Kwesi. Behind the masquerade .
Edgware , 1988. 90 p. :   ISBN 0-9512770-0-6
(pbk) :   DDC 394.2/5/0942134 19
                                    NYPL [Sc E 88-497]

Ross, Susan. Dodson, Jualynne E. Black
stylization and implications for child welfare .
Atlanta, Georgia , 1975. 1 v. (various pagings) ;
                                    NYPL [Sc F 88-223]

Rosset, Lisa. James Baldwin / Lisa Rosset. New
York, N.Y. : Chelsea House, 1989. 111 p. : ill.,
ports. ; 25 cm. (Black Americans of achievement)
Includes index. A biography of an American author
noted for his books on racial conflict in the United
States. Bibliography: p. 108.   ISBN 1-555-46572-2
DDC 818/.5409 B 92 19
1. Baldwin, James, 1924- - Biography - Juvenile
literature. 2. Authors, American - 20th century -
Biography - Juvenile literature. 3. Civil rights workers -
United States - Biography - Juvenile literature. 4.
Afro-Americans - Civil rights - History - 20th century -
Juvenile literature. I. Title. II. Series.
PS3552.A45 Z87 1989   **NYPL [Sc E 89-224]**

Rosskam, Edwin, 1903- 12 million Black voices /.
New York , 1988, c1941. xx, 152 p. :   ISBN
0-938410-48-2 :   DDC 973/.0496073 19
E185.86 .A13 1988   **NYPL [Sc F 88-315]**

Rotberg, Robert I. Africa in the 1990s and
beyond /. Algonac, Mich. , 1988. 309 p. :   ISBN
0-917256-44-1 (pbk) :   DDC 303.4/8273/06 19
DT38 .A44 1988   **NYPL [Sc E 89-98]**

Roth, John K.
Ideology and American experience .
Washington, DC , c1986. vi, 264 p. ;   ISBN
0-88702-015-1 :   DDC 320.5/0973 19
E169.12 .I34 1986   **NYPL [Sc E 89-74]**

The Politics of Latin American liberation
theology . Washington, D.C. , c1988. xxi, 360
p. ;   ISBN 0-88702-039-9 :   DDC 261.7/09181/2 19
BT83.57 .P643 1988   **NYPL [Sc E 89-75]**

Roth, Susan L. Fire came to the earth people : a
Dahomean folktale / Susan L. Roth. New
York : St. Martin's Press, 1988, c1987. [32] p. :

col. ill. ; 26 cm. The earth animals fail in every attempt to capture fire from the selfish moon god Mawu, until Chameleon and Tortoise combine their talents and help bring light and warmth to the newly-created earth. SCHOMBURG CHILDREN'S COLLECTION. ISBN 0-312-01723-5 : DDC 398.2/0966/83 E 19
I. Schomburg Children's Collection. II. Title.
PZ8.1.R73 Fi 1987   *NYPL [Sc F 89-140]*

Rothchild, Donald S. From federalism to neo-federalism in East Africa [microform] / Donald Rothchild. Nairobi : Institute for Development Studies, University College, 1966. 19 leaves ; 33 cm. (Discussion paper/Institute for Development Studies, University College, Nairobi. no. 34) Includes bibliographical references. Microfilm. New York: New York Public Library, 1982. 1 microfilm reel ; 35 mm. (MN *ZZ-23051)
1. Federal government - Africa, East. 2. Africa, East - Politics and government. I. Series: Nairobi. University College. Institute for Development Studies. Discussion paper, no. 34. II. Title.
   NYPL [Sc Micro R-4108 no.30]

Rotimi, Ola. Hopes of the living dead : a drama of struggle / Ola Rotimi. Ibadan : Spectrum Books, c1988. xii, 112 p. ; 19 cm. ISBN 978-246-013-3
1. Whyte, Ikoli Harcourt, 1905-1977 - Drama. I. Title.
   NYPL [Sc C 89-138]

Rottmann, W. Nyonmo wiemo, Kanemo hefatalo . London, 1963. v, 154 p. ;
   NYPL [Sc C 87-395]

Rougevin-Baville, Michel. (joint author) Gautron, Jean Claude. Droit public du Sénégal /. Paris , 1977. 447 p. ; ISBN 2-233-00036-6 :
LAW   *NYPL [Sc E 88-612]*

The rough guide to Kenya /. Trillo, Richard. London , New York , 1987. 374 p. : ISBN 0-7102-0616-X (pbk.) DDC 916.76/2044 19
DT433.52 .T75 1986   *NYPL [Sc C 88-145]*

The Rough guides.
Trillo, Richard. The rough guide to Kenya /. London , New York , 1987. 374 p. : ISBN 0-7102-0616-X (pbk.) DDC 916.76/2044 19
DT433.52 .T75 1986   *NYPL [Sc C 88-145]*

Rourke, John P. Paterson, William, 1755-1810. Paterson's Cape travels, 1777 to 1779 /. Johannesburg, [South Africa] , c1980. 202 p. : ISBN 0-909079-12-9 (standard edition)
   NYPL [Sc F 85-110]

Rouse, Jacqueline Anne. Lugenia Burns Hope, Black southern reformer / Jacqueline Anne Rouse. Athens : University of Georgia Press, c1989. xi, 182 p., [8] p. of plates : ill. ; 23 cm. Includes index. Bibliography: p. 157-171. ISBN 0-8203-1082-4 (alk. paper) DDC 973/.0496073024 B 19
1. Hope, Lugenia Burns. 2. Afro-Americans - Southern States - Biography. 3. Social reformers - Southern States - Biography. 4. Southern States - History - 1865-1951. I. Title.
E185.97.H717 R68 1989
   NYPL [Sc D 89-469]

ROUTES OF TRAVEL. see OCEAN TRAVEL.

Roux, Andre, 1954- Voices from Rini : a survey of black attitudes towards a consumer boycott in Grahamstown / Andre Roux and Kirk Helliker. Grahamstown, South Africa : Rhodes University, 1986. 107 p. ; 30 cm. (Development studies working paper . no. 23) "April 1986." At head of title: A review of issues related to planning and development in Grahamstown. ISBN 0-86810-131-1
1. Boycott - South Africa - Grahamstown. 2. Anti-apartheid movement - South Africa - Grahamstown. 3. Blacks - South Africa - Grahamstown - Attitudes. 4. Grahamstown (South Africa) - Race relations. I. Helliker, Kirk. II. Title. III. Title: Review of issues related to planning and development in Grahamstown. IV. Series.
   NYPL [Sc F 88-216]

ROWLAND, TINY.
Hall, Richard, 1925- My life with Tiny . London ; Boston , 1987. 256, [4] p. of plates : ISBN 0-571-14737-2 *NYPL [Sc D 88-515]*

Roy, Lucinda. Wailing the dead to sleep / Lucinda Roy ; with an introduction by Nikki Giovanni. London : Bogle-L'Ouverture Publications, c1988. 75 p. ; 22 cm. ISBN 0-904521-43-3 (pbk.)
I. Title.   *NYPL [Sc D 88-1294]*

Royal Colonial Institute. see Royal Commonwealth Society.

Royal Colonial Society. see Royal Commonwealth Society.

Royal Commonwealth Society.
Knights, Ian E. The Bahamas [microform] . London , 1979. 18 p. :
   NYPL [Sc Micro R-4108 no.16]

Knights, Ian E. Bermuda [microform] . London , 1979. 18 p. :
   NYPL [Sc Micro R-4108 no.19]

Knights, Ian E. The British Virgin Islands [microform] . London , 1979. 17p. :
   NYPL [Sc Micro R-4108 no.22]

Knights, Ian E. The British Virgin Islands [microform] . London , 1982. 15 p. :
   NYPL [Sc Micro R-4108 no.18]

Knights, Ian E. Malawi [microform] . London , 1980. 19 p. :
   NYPL [Sc Micro R-4108 no.21]

Knights, Ian E. Nigeria [microform] . London , 1980. 19 p. : ISBN 0-905067-80-0
   NYPL [Sc Micro R-4108 no.17]

Knights, Ian E. The Seychelles [Microform] . London , 1982. 16 p. :
   NYPL [Sc Micro R-4108 no.15]

Knights, Ian E. Tanzania [microform] . London , 1979. 20 p. :
   NYPL [Sc Micro R-4108 no.20]

Royal Empire Society. see Royal Commonwealth Society.

Royal Ethiopian Judah-Coptic Church. Rastafari manifesto : including new draft constitution proposals. The Ethiopian-African theocracy union policy: EATUP ; true genuine authentic fundamental indigenous [sic] original comprehensive alternative policy: FIOCAP / produced by Jahrastafari Royal Ethiopian Judah-Coptic Church ; drafted by [the] Illect of Jahrastafari, Haila Sillase I theocracy government. [Kingston, Jamaica : Royal Ethiopian Judah Coptic Church, 1984?] [97] p. ; 34 cm.
1. Ras Tafari movement. I. Title. II. Title: Ethiopian-African theocracy union policy.
   NYPL [Sc G 88-20]

Royal Tropical Institute, Amsterdam. see Koninklijk Instituut voor de Tropen.

Le royaume du Dahomé face à la pénétration coloniale . Garcia, Luc, 1937- Paris , c1988. 284 p., [8] p. of plates :
   NYPL [Sc E 89-145]

Ruanda. see Rwanda.

RUANDA LANGUAGE - TEXTS.
Karengera, Pawulini. Impundu kwa Rusango /. [Kigali? , 1983] (Kigali : Imprimerie Scolaire) 319 p. :   *NYPL [Sc D 89-447]*

Rugamba, Sipiriyani. Turirimbane /. Butare, Rwanda, 1987. 289 p. :
   NYPL [Sc D 88-1514]

Rubenstein, Richard L. The Politics of Latin American liberation theology . Washington, D.C. , c1988. xxi, 360 p. ; ISBN 0-88702-039-9 : DDC 261.7/09181/2 19
BT83.57 .P643 1988   *NYPL [Sc E 89-75]*

Ruby my dear. Baku, Shango. 3 plays of our time /. Belmont, Trinidad , 1984. 116 p. ;
   NYPL [Sc D 88-971]

Rücker, Heribert. "Afrikanische Theologie" : Darstellung und Dialog / Heribert Rücker. Innsbruck : Tyrolia, 1985. 271 p. ; 23 cm. (Innsbrucker theologische Studien . Bd. 14) Originally presented as the author's thesis (doctoral--Ruhr-Universität Bochum, 1983) Includes indexes. Bibliography: p. [239]-266. ISBN 3-7022-1548-4
1. Theology, Doctrinal - Africa, Sub-Saharan. I. Title. II. Series.
BT30.A438 R83 1985   *NYPL [Sc D 88-868]*

Rucktäschel, Annamaria. Neue Kunst aus Afrika . [Hamburg] , c1984. 111 p. :
   NYPL [Sc G 88-17]

RUDOLPH, WILMA, 1940- - JUVENILE LITERATURE.
Biracree, Tom, 1947- Wilma Rudolph /. New York , 1988. 111 p. : ISBN 1-555-46675-3 DDC

796.4/2/0924 B 92 19
GV697.R8 B57 1988   *NYPL [Sc E 88-172]*

Rüedi, Peter. Jazz in Willisau . Luzern , c1978. 206 p. : ISBN 3-7239-0051-8 DDC 785.42/09494/5 19
ML3509.S9 J4 1978   *NYPL [Sc F 89-24]*

RUFFIN, EDMUND, 1794-1865.
Mathew, William M. Edmund Ruffin and the crisis of slavery in the Old South . Athens , c1988. xiv, 286 p. : ISBN 0-8203-1011-5 (alk. paper) DDC 306/.362/0924 19
F230.R932 M38 1988   *NYPL [JFE 88-3149]*

Rugamba, Sipiriyani.
Contes du Rwanda . Paris , 1983. 174 p. : ISBN 2-85319-119-2 *NYPL [Sc C 88-83]*

Turirimbane / indirimbo zahimbwe na Sipiriyani Rugamba. Butare, Rwanda : Institut national de recherche scientifique, 1987. 289 p. ; 21 cm. (Publication . no. 38)
1. Ruanda language - Texts. I. Series: Publication / Institut national de recherche scientifique , no. 38. II. Title.   *NYPL [Sc D 88-1514]*

RULE OF LAW - SOUTH AFRICA.
Mathews, Anthony S., 1930- Freedom, state security and the rule of law . London , c1988. xxx, 312 p. ; ISBN 0-421-39640-7
   NYPL [Sc F 89-102]

Rum and reggae . Runge, Jonathan. New York , c1988. ix, 227 p. : ISBN 0-312-01509-7 (pbk.) : DDC 917.29/0452 19
F1613 .R86 1988   *NYPL [Sc D 88-1217]*

Rummel, Jack.
Langston Hughes / Jack Rummel ; [introductory essay by Coretta Scott King]. New York : Chelsea House Publishers, c1988. 111 p. : ill., ports. ; 25 cm. (Black Americans of achievement) Includes index. Examines the life of the Harlem poet who spent his career writing about the black experience in America. Bibliography: p. 108. ISBN 1-555-46595-1 DDC 818/.5209 B 92 19
1. Hughes, Langston, 1902-1967 - Biography - Juvenile literature. 2. Poets, American - 20th century - Biography - Juvenile literature. 3. Afro-American poets - Biography - Juvenile literature. I. King, Coretta Scott, 1927-. II. Title. III. Series.
PS3515.U274 Z775 1988
   NYPL [Sc E 88-166]

Muhammad Ali / Jack Rummel. New York : Chelsea House Publishers, c1988. 128 p. : ill. ; 25 cm. (Black Americans of achievement) Chronicles the life of the heavyweight boxing champion, from his early years to his draft resistance through his astounding boxing career which established him as one of the greatest fighters of all time. Bibliography: p. 124. ISBN 1-555-46569-2 DDC 796.8/3/0924 B 92 19
1. Ali, Muhammad, 1942- - Juvenile literature. 2. Boxers (Sports) - United States - Biography - Juvenile literature. 3. Afro-American boxers - Biography - Juvenile literature. I. Title. II. Series.
GV1132.A44 R86 1988
   NYPL [Sc E 88-175]

Rummelt, Peter. Sport im Kolonialismus, Kolonialismus im Sport : zur Genese und Funktion des Sports in Kolonial-Afrika von 1870 bis 1918 / Peter Rummelt. Köln : Pahl-Rugenstein, 1986. 341 p. : ill. ; 21 cm. (Serie, Dritte Welt) Pahl-Rugenstein Hochschulschriften Gesellschafts- und Naturwissenschaften ; 213 Includes indexes. Bibliography: p. 308-329. ISBN 3-7609-5213-5 DDC 796/.096 19
1. Sports - Africa - History - 19th century. 2. Sports - Europe - History - 19th century. 3. Physical education and training - Africa - History - 19th century. 4. Sports - Africa - History - 20th century. 5. Africa - Colonization. I. Title. II. Series.
GV665 .R85 1986   *NYPL [Sc D 88-973]*

Run for freedom /. Fairbairn, Bill, 1935- [Lusaka, Zambia] , 1984. 181 p. ;
   NYPL [Sc C 88-227]

RUNDI LANGUAGE - GRAMMAR.
Bigangara, Jean-Baptiste. Eléments de linguistique burundaise /. Bujumbura , 1982. 138 p. ; DDC 496/.39 19
PL8611.1 .B54 1982   *NYPL [Sc E 88-403]*

Runge, Jonathan. Rum and reggae : [what's hot and what's not in the Caribbean] / Jonathan Runge.1st ed. New York : St. Martin's Press, c1988. ix, 227 p. : ill. ; 21 cm. ISBN 0-312-01509-7 (pbk.) : DDC 917.29/0452 19
1. West Indies - Description and travel - 1981- -

Guide-books. 2. Caribbean Area - Description and travel - 1981- - Guide-books. I. Title.
F1613 .R86 1988   *NYPL [Sc D 88-1217]*

Runte, Roseann. Faux-soleils : poèmes-pensées / Roseann Runte. Sherbrooke, Québec, Canada : Naaman, 1984. 59 p. ; 22 cm. (Collection Creation. 147) Poems. ISBN 2-89040-312-2
I. Title.   *NYPL [Sc D 88-501]*

Runyowa, Genius T., 1945- Akada wokure / Genius T. Runyowa ; mufananidzo naHassam Musa. Gwelo, Zimbabwe : Mambo Press in association with the Literature Bureau, 1981. 123 p. ; 18 cm. Novel. In Shona.
1. Shona language - Texts. I. Title.
NYPL [Sc C 88-140]

RURAL ARCHITECTURE. see ARCHITECTURE, DOMESTIC.

Rural communities in transition . De Wet, C. J. Grahamstown [1983] iii, 113 p., [6] leaves of plates :   ISBN 0-86810-101-X (pbk.)   DDC 307.7/2/0968 19
HD2130.5.Z9 H653 1983
NYPL [Sc F 88-328]

RURAL COMMUNITY DEVELOPMENT. see RURAL DEVELOPMENT.

Rural development administration in South Africa / D.A. Kotzé ... [et al.] Pretoria : Africa Institute of South Africa, 1987. 70 p. : ill., map ; 30 cm. (Communications of the Africa Institute. no. 49) Bibliography: p. 68-70. ISBN 0-7983-0100-7
1. Rural development - South Africa - Homelands. 2. Local government - South Africa - Homelands. 3. Homelands (South Africa) - Politics and government. I. Kotzé, D. A.   *NYPL [Sc F 88-309]*

RURAL DEVELOPMENT - AFRICA.
The Challenge of employment and basic needs in Africa . Nairobi , New York , 1986. xii, 379 p. ;   ISBN 0-19-572559-X   *NYPL [Sc E 88-419]*

Moock, Joyce Lewinger. Higher education and rural development in Africa [microform] . New York , c1977. ii, 42 p. :
NYPL [Sc Micro R-4202 no. 1]

RURAL DEVELOPMENT - AFRICA - ADDRESSES, ESSAYS, LECTURES.
Rural small-scale industries and employment in Africa and Asia . Geneva , 1984. x, 159 p. ;   ISBN 92-2-103513-1 (pbk.) :   DDC 338.6/42/095 19
HD2346.A55 R87 1984
NYPL [JLE 84-3222]

RURAL DEVELOPMENT - AFRICA - CONGRESSES.
Social development and rural fieldwork . Zimbabwe [1986]. 96 p. ;
NYPL [Sc D 88-1153]

RURAL DEVELOPMENT - AFRICA, EAST.
Rigby, Peter. Persistent pastoralists . London , Totowa, N.J. , 1985. x, 198 p. :   ISBN 0-86232-226-X :   DDC 305.8/9676 19
DT443.3.M37 R54 1985
NYPL [JLD 86-2309]

RURAL DEVELOPMENT - ASIA - ADDRESSES, ESSAYS, LECTURES.
Rural small-scale industries and employment in Africa and Asia . Geneva , 1984. x, 159 p. ;   ISBN 92-2-103513-1 (pbk.) :   DDC 338.6/42/095 19
HD2346.A55 R87 1984
NYPL [JLE 84-3222]

RURAL DEVELOPMENT - BOTSWANA.
Gobotswang, Z. Pilot evaluation report on Mahalapye Development Trust /. Gaborone, Botswana [1982] v leaves, 61, 3 p. ;
HD5710.85.B59 G63 1982
NYPL [Sc F 89-108]

RURAL DEVELOPMENT - CARIBBEAN AREA.
Rural development in the Caribbean /. London , 1985. xxi, 246 p. :   ISBN 0-312-69599-3
NYPL [Sc D 88-1309]

RURAL DEVELOPMENT - DEVELOPING COUNTRIES.
Cohen, John M. Integrated rural development . Uppsala , 1987. 267 p. ;   ISBN 91-7106-267-X
NYPL [Sc D 88-1100]

RURAL DEVELOPMENT - ETHIOPIA.
Cohen, John M. Integrated rural development . Uppsala , 1987. 267 p. ;   ISBN 91-7106-267-X
NYPL [Sc D 88-1100]

RURAL DEVELOPMENT - GOVERNMENT POLICY - AFRICA, SUB-SAHARAN.
Hinderink, J. (Jan) Agricultural commercialization and government policy in Africa /. London , New York , 1987. xii, 328 p. :   ISBN 0-7103-0205-3   *NYPL [Sc D 88-580]*

RURAL DEVELOPMENT - GUINEA.
Guinea. Comité militaire de redressement national. Premières mesures en matière en application du programme du CMRN. [Conakry, R.G. , 1984] 84 p. ;
HD2143.Z8 G85 1984   *NYPL [Sc E 88-306]*

RURAL DEVELOPMENT - HAITI.
Honorat, Jean Jacques. Community action in Haiti [microform] . New York , 1982. 45 p. ;
NYPL [Sc Micro F-11008]

Rural development in the Caribbean / [edited by] P.I. Gomes. London : Heinemann Educational, 1985. xxi, 246 p. : ill., map ; 22 cm. Includes bibliographies and index. ISBN 0-312-69599-3
1. Rural development - Caribbean area. 2. Agriculture - Caribbean area. 3. Plantation life - Caribbean area. 4. Villages - Caribbean area. 5. Caribbean Area - Economic conditions. I. Gomes, P. I.
NYPL [Sc D 88-1309]

RURAL DEVELOPMENT - LESOTHO.
Van de Geer, Roeland. Government and development in rural Lesotho /. Roma, Lesotho , 1982, 1984 printing. 159 p. ;
NYPL [Sc D 89-52]

RURAL DEVELOPMENT - NIGERIA.
Perspectives on community and rural development in Nigeria /. Jos , c1988. 202 p. ;   ISBN 978-282-700-2   *NYPL [Sc E 89-18]*

RURAL DEVELOPMENT - NIGERIA - INFORMATION SERVICES.
Aboyade, B. Olabimpe. The provision of information for rural development /. Ibadan , 1987. xv, 104 p. ;   ISBN 978-267-900-3
NYPL [Sc D 88-739]

RURAL DEVELOPMENT PROJECTS - BURKINA FASO.
Michigan State University. Dept. of Agricultural Economics. An analysis of the Eastern ORD rural development project in Upper Volta . East Lansing , 1976. v, 103 p. :   DDC 338.1/866/25
HD2135 .U63 1976   *NYPL [Sc F 89-170]*

RURAL DEVELOPMENT PROJECTS - SIERRA LEONE.
Johnny, Michael. Informal credit for integrated rural development in Sierra Leone /. Hamburg , 1985. xviii, 212 p. :   ISBN 3-87895-274-X (pbk.)
HG2146.5.S5 J63x 1985   *NYPL [Sc D 88-766]*

RURAL DEVELOPMENT - SOMALIA.
Massey, Garth. Subsistence and change . Boulder , 1987. xvii, 238 p. :   ISBN 0-8133-7294-1 (alk. paper) :   DDC 338.1/0967/73 19
DT402.4.R35 M37 1987
NYPL [Sc D 88-298]

RURAL DEVELOPMENT - SOUTH AFRICA - CISKEI.
Bekker, S. B. Perspectives on rural development in Ciskei, 1983 /. Grahamstown [1984] 52 p. :   ISBN 0-86810-103-6 (pbk.) :   DDC 307.1/4/0968792 19
HN801.C57 B45 1984   *NYPL [Sc F 88-325]*

RURAL DEVELOPMENT - SOUTH AFRICA - HOMELANDS.
Rural development administration in South Africa /. Pretoria , 1987. 70 p. :   ISBN 0-7983-0100-7   *NYPL [Sc F 88-309]*

RURAL DEVELOPMENT - SOUTH AFRICA - HOMELANDS - CASE STUDIES.
De Wet, C. J. Rural communities in transition . Grahamstown [1983] iii, 113 p., [6] leaves of plates :   ISBN 0-86810-101-X (pbk.)   DDC 307.7/2/0968 19
HD2130.5.Z9 H653 1983
NYPL [Sc F 88-328]

RURAL DEVELOPMENT - SUDAN.
Folklore and National Development Symposium (1981 : Khartoum, Sudan) Folklore and development in the Sudan . Khartoum , 1985.

272 p. :
GR355.8 .F65 1981   *NYPL [Sc E 88-333]*

RURAL DEVELOPMENT - ZIMBABWE.
Bratton, Michael. Beyond community development . London , 1978. 62 p. :
HN802.Z9 C62   *NYPL [JLD 81-437]*

RURAL DEVELOPMENT - ZIMBABWE - HISTORY - 20TH CENTURY.
Mutizwa-Mangiza, N. D. Community development in pre-independence Zimbabwe . Harare , c1985. iv, 79 p. :   ISBN 0-86924-090-0 (pbk.)   DDC 307.1/4/096891 19
HN802.Z9 C65 1985   *NYPL [JLD 88-3699]*

RURAL ECONOMIC DEVELOPMENT. see RURAL DEVELOPMENT.

RURAL HEALTH - AFRICA, SUB-SAHARAN - MISCELLANEA.
Sillonville, Frank. Guide de la santé au village . Douala, Cameroun , Paris, France , c1985. 204 p. :   ISBN 2-86537-126-3 :   DDC 614/.0967 19
RA771.7.A357 S56 1985
NYPL [Sc E 88-547]

RURAL HEALTH SERVICES - ADMINISTRATION - HANDBOOKS, MANUALS, ETC.
Guide pédagogique pour la mise en œuvre des soins de santé primaires au niveau villageois /. Bobo-Dioulasso, Burkina Faso , 1986. 79 p. :
RA771 .G85 1986   *NYPL [Sc D 89-265]*

RURAL HEALTH SERVICES - PLANNING - HANDBOOKS, MANUALS, ETC.
Guide pédagogique pour la mise en œuvre des soins de santé primaires au niveau villageois /. Bobo-Dioulasso, Burkina Faso , 1986. 79 p. :
RA771 .G85 1986   *NYPL [Sc D 89-265]*

RURAL LIFE. see COUNTRY LIFE; PEASANTRY.

Rural small-scale industries and employment in Africa and Asia : a review of programmes and policies / edited by Enyinna Chuta and S.V. Sethuraman. Geneva : International Labour Office, 1984. x, 159 p. ; 25 cm. (A WEP study) Bibliography: p. 157-159. ISBN 92-2-103513-1 (pbk.) :   DDC 338.6/42/095 19
1. Small business - Government policy - Africa - Addresses, essays, lectures. 2. Industrial promotion - Africa - Addresses, essays, lectures. 3. Rural development - Africa - Addresses, essays, lectures. 4. Small business - Government policy - Asia - Addresses, essays, lectures. 5. Industrial promotion - Asia - Addresses, essays, lectures. 6. Rural development - Asia - Addresses, essays, lectures. I. Chuta, Enyinna. II. Sethuraman, S. V. III. Series.
HD2346.A55 R87 1984
NYPL [JLE 84-3222]

RURAL SOCIOLOGY. see SOCIOLOGY, RURAL.

Rural transformation in tropical Africa / edited by Douglas Rimmer. London : Belhaven, 1988. 177 p. : ill. ; 24 cm. Includes index. Bibliography: 162-167. ISBN 1-85293-012-8 :   DDC 330.96/0328 19
1. Africa - Economic conditions - 1960-. 2. Africa - Rural conditions. I. Rimmer, Douglas.
HC800   *NYPL [JLE 88-4346]*

Rural transformations in industrializing South Africa . Keegan, Timothy J. Basingstoke ; London , 1987. xviii, 302 p. :   ISBN 0-333-41746-1   *NYPL [Sc D 88-1228]*

The rural-urban dichotomy in the developing world . Baker, Jonathan. Oslo . 372 p. :   ISBN 82-00-07412-9
HC845.Z7 B343 1986   *NYPL [JFD 87-3176]*

RURAL-URBAN MIGRATION - CAMEROON.
Franqueville, André. Une Afrique entre le village et la ville . Paris . 646 p. :   ISBN 2-7099-0805-0   *NYPL [Sc E 88-325]*

RURAL-URBAN MIGRATION - ETHIOPIA - BAGEMDER - CASE STUDIES.
Baker, Jonathan. The rural-urban dichotomy in the developing world . Oslo . 372 p. :   ISBN 82-00-07412-9
HC845.Z7 B343 1986   *NYPL [JFD 87-3176]*

RURAL-URBAN MIGRATION - KENYA - SIAYA DISTRICT.
Cohen, David William. Siaya, a historical anthropology of an African landscape /. London , Athens , 1989. viii, 152 p., [8] p. of

plates : ISBN 0-8214-0901-8 DDC 967.6/2 19
DT433.545.L85 C64 1988
NYPL [Sc D 89-354]

RURAL-URBAN MIGRATION - SENEGAL.
Leber, Gisela. Agrarstrukturen und Landflucht
im Senegal . Saarbrücken , Fort Lauderdale ,
1979. vii, 142 p. : ISBN 3-88156-125-0
HD2144.5 .L42 **NYPL [JLD 80-2814]**

**RURAL-URBAN MIGRATION - UNITED
STATES.**
Crew, Spencer R. Field to factory .
Washington, D.C. , 1987. 79 p., [4] p. of
plates : **NYPL [Sc F 88-369]**

RURAL-URBAN MIGRATION - ZAMBIA.
Hedlund, Hans G. B. Migration and change in
rural Zambia /. Uppsala , 1983. 107 p. : ISBN
91-7106-220-3 (pbk.) DDC 960 s 307/.2 19
DT1 .N64 no. 70 HB1955
NYPL [JLD 85-587]

Rural women . Loutfi, Martha Fetherolf. Geneva ,
c1980 (1985 printing) v, 81 p., [4] p. of plates :
ISBN 92-2-102389-3 (pbk.)
NYPL [Sc E 89-67]

**RURAL WOMEN - DEVELOPING
COUNTRIES - ECONOMIC
CONDITIONS.**
Loutfi, Martha Fetherolf. Rural women .
Geneva , c1980 (1985 printing) v, 81 p., [4] p.
of plates : ISBN 92-2-102389-3 (pbk.)
NYPL [Sc E 89-67]

**RURAL WOMEN - DEVELOPING
COUNTRIES - SOCIAL CONDITIONS.**
Loutfi, Martha Fetherolf. Rural women .
Geneva , c1980 (1985 printing) v, 81 p., [4] p.
of plates : ISBN 92-2-102389-3 (pbk.)
NYPL [Sc E 89-67]

**RURAL WOMEN - EMPLOYMENT -
AFRICA - CONGRESSES.**
African and Asian Inter-regional Workshop on
Strategies for Improving the Employment
Conditions of Rural Women (1984 : Arusha,
Tanzania) Resources, power and women .
Geneva , 1985. ix, 82 p. ; ISBN 92-2-105009-2
(pbk.) : DDC 331.4/83/095 19
HD6207 .A78 1984 **NYPL [JLF 87-1038]**

**RURAL WOMEN - EMPLOYMENT - ASIA -
CONGRESSES.**
African and Asian Inter-regional Workshop on
Strategies for Improving the Employment
Conditions of Rural Women (1984 : Arusha,
Tanzania) Resources, power and women .
Geneva , 1985. ix, 82 p. ; ISBN 92-2-105009-2
(pbk.) : DDC 331.4/83/095 19
HD6207 .A78 1984 **NYPL [JLF 87-1038]**

RURAL WOMEN - EMPLOYMENT - KENYA.
Narayan-Parker, Deepa. Women's interest and
involvement in income generating activities .
Gaborone, Botswana [1983] vi, 143, 3 p. ;
DDC 331.4/09676/2 19
HD6210.5 .N37 1983 **NYPL [Sc F 88-312]**

RURAL WOMEN - KENYA - ATTITUDES.
Narayan-Parker, Deepa. Women's interest and
involvement in income generating activities .
Gaborone, Botswana [1983] vi, 143, 3 p. ;
DDC 331.4/09676/2 19
HD6210.5 .N37 1983 **NYPL [Sc F 88-312]**

Rury, John L. Education and Black community
development in ante-bellum New York City /
by John L. Rury. 1975. 100 leaves ; 30 cm.
Thesis (Ms.C.)--City University of New York, 1975.
Bibliography: p. [92]-100.
*1. Afro-Americans - Education - New York (N.Y.). I.
Title.* **NYPL [Sc F 89-114]**

Rushworth, David. The wonders of Hwange /
devised and written by David Rushworth ;
illustrated by Rosemary Owen. Gweru,
Zimbabwe : Mambo Press, 1986. 35 p. : ill. ; 30
cm. (Exploring Zimbabwe . 2) Cover title. ISBN
0-86922-389-5
*1. Hwange National Park (Zimbabwe). 2. National
parks and reserves - Zimbabwe. I. Title. II. Series.*
NYPL [Sc F 89-43]

Ruskin, Cindy. The quilt : stories from the
NAMES project / written by Cindy Ruskin ;
photographs by Matt Herron ; design by
Deborah Zemke ; with an introduction by
Elizabeth Taylor. New York : Pocket Books,
1988. 160 p. : col. ill. ; 28 x 28 cm. ISBN
0-671-66597-9 :
1. AIDS (Disease) - Patients - Family relationships. 2.

*AIDS (Disease) - Social aspects - United States. 3.
Quilts, American. I. Herron, Matt. II. Title.*
NYPL [Sc F 88-237]

**Russell Adrian Lane, biography of an urban
negro school administrator [microform]** /.
Mickey, Rosie Cheatham. 1983. xiii, 275
leaves : **NYPL [Sc Micro R-4813]**

Russell, Francis, 1910- The shadow of Blooming
Grove; Warren G. Harding in his times. [1st
ed.] New York, McGraw-Hill [1968] xvi, 691 p.
23 cm. Bibliographical references included in "Notes"
(p. 667-672) DDC 973.91/4/0924 B
*1. Harding, Warren G. (Warren Gamaliel), 1865-1923.
I. Title.*
E786 .R95 **NYPL [Sc E 88-579]**

Russell, Sharman Apt. Frederick Douglass /
Sharman Apt Russell ; senior consulting editor,
Nathan Irvin Huggins. New York : Chelsea
House Publishers, c1988. 110 p. : ill. ; 25 cm.
(Black Americans of achievement) Includes index. A
biography of the man who, after escaping slavery,
became an orator, writer, and leader in the anti-slavery
movement of the early nineteenth century.
Bibliography: p. 108. ISBN 1-555-46580-3 DDC
973.8/092/4 B 92 19
*1. Douglass, Frederick, 1817?-1895 - Juvenile literature.
2. Abolitionists - United States - Biography - Juvenile
literature. 3. Afro-Americans - Biography - Juvenile
literature. I. Huggins, Nathan Irvin, 1927-. II. Title. III.
Series.*
E449.D75 R87 1988 **NYPL [Sc E 88-174]**

Russo, Marisabina. Giovanni, Nikki. Vacation
time . New York , 1980. 59 p. : ISBN
0-688-03657-0 DDC 811/.54
PS3557.I55 V3 **NYPL [Sc D 89-69]**

**RUSSO-TURKISH WAR, 1853-1856. see
CRIMEAN WAR, 1853-1856.**

Rust, Art, 1927- The Art Rust Jr. baseball quiz
book / Art Rust, Jr., with Alvin H. Goldberg.
New York, N.Y. : Facts on File, c1985. 184 p.,
[16] p. of plates : ill., ports. ; 24 cm. ISBN
0-8160-1147-4 (pbk.) DDC 796.357/0973 19
*1. Baseball - United States - Miscellanea. I. Goldberg,
Alvin H. II. Title. III. Title: Art Rust Junior baseball
quiz book.*
GV867.3 .R87 1985 **NYPL [JFE 85-2627]**

Rust, Brian A. L., 1922- Jazz records, 1897-1942
/ compiled by Brian Rust. 5th rev. and enl. ed.
Chigwell, Essex : Storyville Publications,
[1982?] 2 v. ; 23 cm. Includes index.
CONTENTS. - v. 1. Irving Aaronson to Abe Lyman --
v. 2. Abe Lyman to Bob Zurke. ISBN 0-902391-04-6
(set)
1. Jazz music - Discography. I. Title.
NYPL [*R-Phono 84-254]

Rutayisire, Paul. La christianisation du Rwanda
(1900-1945) : méthode missionnaire et politique
selon Mgr Léon Classe / Paul Rutayisire.
Fribourg, Suisse : Editions universitaires, 1987.
571 p. : maps ; 22 cm. Includes bibliographical
references. ISBN 2-8271-0371-0 (pbk.)
*1. Classe, Léon-Paul, 1874-1945. 2. White Fathers -
Missions - Rwanda. 3. White Fathers - Rwanda -
Biography. 4. Catholic Church - Missions - Rwanda -
History. 5. Catholic Church - Rwanda - History. 6.
Missionaries - France - Biography. 7. Missionaries -
Rwanda - Biography. 8. Missions - Rwanda - History.
9. Rwanda - Church history. I. Title.*
NYPL [Sc D 88-1510]

Rutherfoord, John Coles 1825-1866. Speech of
John C. Rutherfoord, of Goochland, in the
House of Delegates of Virginia, on the removal
from the Commonwealth of the free colored
population : delivered Feb. 18, 1853.
Richmond : Printed by Pitchies & Dunnavant,
1853. 20 p. ; 24 cm.
*1. Freedmen - Legal status, laws, etc. - Virginia. 2.
Afro-Americans - Colonization - Liberia. I. Title.*
NYPL [Sc Rare C 89-10]

Rutherford T. finds 21 B. Rinkoff, Barbara. New
York [1970] [47] p. DDC [Fic]
PZ7.R477 Ru **NYPL [Sc D 88-1404]**

Rutil, Alain. Gaspard, Albert. Les belles paroles
d'Albert Gaspard /. Paris , c1987. 128 p. :
ISBN 2-903033-91-9 :
MLCM 87/1949 (P) **NYPL [JFE 88-5765]**

RWANDA - ANNIVERSARIES, ETC.
Habyarimana, Juvénal. Discours du
général-major Habyarimana Juvénal, président
de la République rwandaise et
président-fondateur du Mouvement

révolutionnaire national pour le développement
à l'occasion du 1er juillet, 1987 =. [Kigali?] ,
1987. 82 p. :
f-rw--- **NYPL [Sc D 88-1517]**

RWANDA - CHURCH HISTORY.
Rutayisire, Paul. La christianisation du Rwanda
(1900-1945) . Fribourg, Suisse , 1987. 571 p. :
ISBN 2-8271-0371-0 (pbk.)
NYPL [Sc D 88-1510]

RWANDA - CONSTITUTIONAL HISTORY.
Reyntjens, Filip. Pouvoir et droit au Rwanda .
Tervuren, Belgique , 1985. 584 p. ;
NYPL [Sc E 87-668]

RWANDA - DESCRIPTION AND TRAVEL.
Muraho, Guten Tag . [Leverkusen, 1983. 86
p., [16] leaves of plates :
NYPL [Sc F 88-256]

Paternostre de La Mairieu, Baudouin. A la
source du Nil . Paris [1985] 108 p., [12] p. of
plates : ISBN 2-85244-730-4 : DDC 967/.571 19
DT450.2 .P38 1985 **NYPL [Sc C 88-308]**

**Rwanda - Government. see Rwanda - Politics and
government.**

**RWANDA - GOVERNMENT
PUBLICATIONS - BIBLIOGRAPHY -
UNION LISTS.**
Witherell, Julian W. French-speaking central
Africa. Washington, 1973. xiv, 314 p. ISBN
0-8444-0033-5
Z3692 .W5 **NYPL [JLF 74-197]**

RWANDA - POLITICS AND GOVERNMENT.
Habyarimana, Juvénal. Discours du
général-major Habyarimana Juvénal, président
de la République rwandaise et
président-fondateur du Mouvement
révolutionnaire national pour le développement
à l'occasion du 1er juillet, 1987 =. [Kigali?] ,
1987. 82 p. :
f-rw--- **NYPL [Sc D 88-1517]**

Ibyemezo, amabwiliza, ibyifuzo mu myaka cumi
ya Muvoma . Kigali , 1985. 424 p. :
NYPL [Sc D 88-807]

Reyntjens, Filip. Pouvoir et droit au Rwanda .
Tervuren, Belgique , 1985. 584 p. ;
NYPL [Sc E 87-668]

Rwegasira, Kami S. P. Administering
management development institutions in Africa
/ Kami Rwegasira. Aldershot, England : Gower
Pub. Co. Ltd. ; Brookfield, Vt. : Gower Pub.
Co., 1988. vi, 112 p. ; 23 cm. Includes index.
Bibliography: p. 103-106. ISBN 0-566-05501-5 DDC
658.4/07124/096 19
*1. Assessment centers (Personnel management
procedure). 2. Executives - Africa - Training of. 3.
Personnel management - Study and teaching - Africa. I.
Title.*
HF5549.5.A78 R94 1988
NYPL [Sc D 88-458]

Ryan, Bob. Forty-eight minutes : a night in the
life of the NBA / Bob Ryan and Terry Pluto.
New York : Macmillan Pub. Co. ; London :
Collier Macmillan, c1987. x, 356 p. ; 22 cm.
Includes index. ISBN 0-02-597770-9 DDC
796.32/364/0973 19
*1. National Basketball Association. 2. Boston Celtics
(Basketball team). 3. Cleveland Cavaliers (Basketball
team). 4. Basketball - United States. I. Pluto, Terry,
1955-. II. Title. III. Title: 48 minutes.*
GV885.515.N37 R9 1988
NYPL [JFD 87-10809]

Rydström, Gunnar. A Guide to Zimbabwe /.
Gweru, [Zimbabwe] , 1986. 63 p. : ISBN
91-7810-685-0 **NYPL [Sc C 88-371]**

**S. P. E. C. see Association of Research Libraries.
Systems and Procedures Exchange Center.**

Saakana, Amon Saba, 1948-
The colonial legacy in Caribbean literature, Vol.
I / Amon Saba Saakana. London : Karnak
House, 1987. 128 p., [7] p. of plates : ports ; 22
cm. (Karnak literary criticism) "Vol. I: Literature,
liberation & colonial conventions: psycho-dynamics in
the novels of Roy Heath."--T.p. Bibliography: p.
125-128. ISBN 0-907015-34-4 (pbk.)
*1. Caribbean literature - History and criticism. I. Title.
II. Series.* **NYPL [Sc D 88-1150]**

Towards the decolonization of the British
educational system /. London, England , 19.
128 p. : ISBN 0-907015-32-8
NYPL [Sc D 88-1346]

Sabatier, Renée. Blaming others . London , Philadelphia, PA , 1988. [120] p. ; ISBN 0-86571-146-1 (pbk.) DDC 362.1/042 19
RC607.A26   *NYPL [Sc D 88-1215]*

The sable arm . Cornish, Dudley Taylor. Lawrence, Kan. , c1987. xviii, 342 p. ; ISBN 0-7006-0328-X (pbk.) DDC 973.7/415 19
E540.N3 C77 1987   *NYPL [Sc D 88-850]*

The Sable curtain /. Woodson, Minnie Shumate. Washington, D.C. , 1987, c1985. 380, 12 p. : ISBN 0-943153-00-X   *NYPL [Sc D 88-68]*

Sachy. Floraison d'or ; Raisins amers ; Raison de croire / Sachy. [Haiti? : s.n., 1987] (Port-au-Prince, Haïti : Impr. II) 160 p. ; 21 cm. French and Creole.
I. Title. II. Title: Raisins amers. III. Title: Raison de croire.
MLCS 88/02114 (P)   *NYPL [Sc D 88-1108]*

SACRED ART. see CHRISTIAN ART AND SYMBOLISM.

Sacred cows-- and other edibles /. Giovanni, Nikki. New York , c1988. 167 p. ; ISBN 0-688-04333-X: DDC 814/.54 19
PS3557.I55 S23 1988   *NYPL [Sc E 88-146]*

The sacrifice /. Okwechime, Ireneus. Benin City, Nigeria , 1987. 136 p. ; ISBN 978-234-047-2
   NYPL [Sc C 88-175]

Sacrifice /. Omotoso, Kole, 1943- Ibadan, Nigeria , 1978. 123 p. ; *NYPL [Sc C 87-346]*

SACRIFICE.
Heusch, Luc de. Le sacrifice dans les religions africaines /. Paris , 1986. 354 p. :
   NYPL [Sc D 88-941]

SACRIFICE - AFRICA, SUB-SAHARAN.
Sous le masque de l'animal . Paris , c1987. 380 p. : ISBN 2-13-039831-6   *NYPL [Sc E 88-314]*

Le sacrifice dans les religions africaines /. Heusch, Luc de. Paris , 1986. 354 p. :
   NYPL [Sc D 88-941]

SADCC : prospects for disengagement and development in Southern Africa / edited by Samir Amin, Derrick Chitala, Ibbo Mandaza. Tokyo, Japan : United Nations University ; London ; xi, 256 p. ; 23 cm. (Studies in African political economy) Includes index. Bibliography: p. [245]-254. ISBN 0-86232-748-2 : DDC 337.1/68 19
1. Southern African Development Coordination Conference. 2. Africa, Southern - Economic conditions. 3. Africa, Southern - Industries. 4. Africa, Southern - Economic integration. I. Chitala, Derrick. II. Mandaza, Ibbo. III. Series.
HC900 .S23 1987   *NYPL [Sc D 89-50]*

SADCC . Southern African Development Coordination Conference. Gaborone, Botswana , c1984. 24 p. : DDC 338.968 19
HC900 .S66 1984   *NYPL [Sc F 88-394]*

Sadhu Sundar Singh . Wawili, Rafiki. London , 1949. 48 p. ;   *NYPL [Sc C 89-111]*

Sadowsky, Ethel S. François and the langouste; a story of Martinique, by Ethel S. Sadowsky. Illustrated by Herbert Danska.[1st ed.] Boston, Little, Brown [1969] 60 p. col. illus. 22 cm. Late to school for a third time when he had tried so hard to be punctual, François remembered the picture that would prove his excuse was valid. SCHOMBURG CHILDREN'S COLLECTION. DDC [Fic]
1. Martinique - Juvenile fiction. I. Danska, Herbert, illus. II. Schomburg Children's Collection. III. Title.
PZ7.S127 Fr   *NYPL [Sc D 88-1120]*

Saffari, A. J. Harusi / na A.J. Saffari. Dar es Salaam : BCI Publishers, c1984. 100 p. ; 20 cm. In Swahili. ISBN 997-693-203-0
1. Swahili language - Texts. I. Title.
   NYPL [Sc C 89-89]

Safran, Bernard. Raferty, Gerald. Twenty-dollar horse /. Eau Claire, Wisconsin , 1967, c1955. 192 p. :   *NYPL [Sc D 88-664]*

Saga of progress: Nigeria 1960-1985. Nigeria. Federal Dept. of Information. Lagos, 19. 79 p. :
   NYPL [Sc F 88-170]

Sagrada esperança /. Agostinho Neto, António, 1922- São Paulo , 1985. 126 p. ; ISBN 85-08-01056-7   *NYPL [Sc D 89-64]*

Sahara . Durou, Jean Marc. Marseille, France , 1986. 155 p. : ISBN 2-902634-30-7
   NYPL [Sc G 88-1]

Sáhara . Oliver, Paula, 1962- Mallorca , 1987.

287 p. : ISBN 84-86366-56-9 DDC 964/.805 19
DT346.S7 O43 1987   *NYPL [Sc D 89-319]*

Sahara conquest. Baker, Richard St. Barbe, 1889-London, 1966. 186 p. DDC 333.7/3/096
S616.S16 B3   *NYPL [Sc C 88-117]*

SAHARA - DESCRIPTION AND TRAVEL.
Baker, Richard St. Barbe, 1889- Sahara conquest. London, 1966. 186 p. DDC 333.7/3/096
S616.S16 B3   *NYPL [Sc C 88-117]*

SAHARA - DESCRIPTION AND TRAVEL - VIEWS.
Durou, Jean Marc. Sahara . Marseille, France , 1986. 155 p. : ISBN 2-902634-30-7
   NYPL [Sc G 88-1]

SAHATORENDRIKA RIVER VALLEY (ANTANANARIVO, MADAGASCAR) - ANTIQUITIES.
Rasamuel, David. Traditions orales et archéologie de la basse Sahatorendrika . [Antananarivo] , 1979. 287 p., [33] leaves of plates :
DT469.M37 S247 1979   *NYPL [Sc F 88-79]*

SAHATORENDRIKA RIVER VALLEY (ANTANANARIVO, MADAGASCAR) - HISTORY.
Rasamuel, David. Traditions orales et archéologie de la basse Sahatorendrika . [Antananarivo] , 1979. 287 p., [33] leaves of plates :
DT469.M37 S247 1979   *NYPL [Sc F 88-79]*

SAHATORENDRIKA RIVER VALLEY (ANTANANARIVO, MADAGASCAR) - POPULATION.
Rasamuel, David. Traditions orales et archéologie de la basse Sahatorendrika . [Antananarivo] , 1979. 287 p., [33] leaves of plates :
DT469.M37 S247 1979   *NYPL [Sc F 88-79]*

SAHEL - ECONOMIC CONDITIONS.
Dumont, René, 1904- Pour l'Afrique, j'accuse . [Paris] , c1986. 457 p., [48] p. of plates : ISBN 2-259-01455-0
HC1002 .D85 1986   *NYPL [Sc D 88-642]*

SAHEL - POLITICS AND GOVERNMENT.
Dumont, René, 1904- Pour l'Afrique, j'accuse . [Paris] , c1986. 457 p., [48] p. of plates : ISBN 2-259-01455-0
HC1002 .D85 1986   *NYPL [Sc D 88-642]*

SAHEL - SOCIAL CONDITIONS.
Dumont, René, 1904- Pour l'Afrique, j'accuse . [Paris] , c1986. 457 p., [48] p. of plates : ISBN 2-259-01455-0
HC1002 .D85 1986   *NYPL [Sc D 88-642]*

Sahelian masquerades /. Onobrakpeya, Bruce. Papa Ajao, Mushin , c1988. xi, 132 p. : ISBN 978-250-908-6   *NYPL [Sc F 89-16]*

Les saignées du saigneur /. Prosper, Jean Georges, 1933- [Ile Maurice? , 1983?] (Réduit : Institut de Pédagogie) 87 p. ;
   NYPL [Sc C 88-118]

SAINT BARTHÉLEMY - HISTORY.
Defize, Stanislas. Histoire de St. Barth /. [Paris?] , c1987. [60] p. : ISBN 2-9502284-0-2
   NYPL [Sc G 88-29]

Saint-Brice en six tableaux et un dessin /. Paillière, Madeleine. Port-au-Prince, Haiti [1979?] 62, [4] p., [8] leaves of plates :
   NYPL [Sc D 88-1193]

Saint-Brice, Robert, 1898-1973. Paillière, Madeleine. Saint-Brice en six tableaux et un dessin /. Port-au-Prince, Haiti [1979?] 62, [4] p., [8] leaves of plates :
   NYPL [Sc D 88-1193]

SAINT-BRICE, ROBERT, 1898-1973.
Paillière, Madeleine. Saint-Brice en six tableaux et un dessin /. Port-au-Prince, Haiti [1979?] 62, [4] p., [8] leaves of plates :
   NYPL [Sc D 88-1193]

Saint-Cheron, François de. Senghor et la terre / François de Saint-Cheron. Paris : Éditions Sang de la terre, c1988. 138 p. ; 20 cm. (Écrivains et la terre, 0986-4040) "Textes de Léopold Sédar Senghor": p. [107]-128. Bibliography: p. [135] ISBN 2-86985-033-6
1. Senghor, Léopold Sédar, 1906- - Criticism and interpretation. I. Senghor, Léopold Sédar, 1906- Selections. 1988. II. Title.   *NYPL [Sc C 89-137]*

SAINT CROIX (V.I.) - JUVENILE FICTION.
Mooney, Elizabeth Comstock. The Sandy Shoes mystery. Philadelphia [1970] 128 p. DDC [Fic]
PZ7.M78 San   *NYPL [Sc D 89-96]*

ST. CROIX, VIRGIN ISLANDS - DRAMA.
Teytaud, Anton C. Sarah & Addie . [S.l.] c1976 (Christiansted, St. Croix, V.I. : Crown Printing Co.) 68 p. :   *NYPL [Sc D 87-340]*

SAINT DAVID'S ISLAND (BERMUDA ISLANDS) - BIOGRAPHY.
McCallan, E. A. (Ernest Albert), 1874- Life on old St. David's, Bermuda /. Hamilton, Bermuda , 1986. 258 p., [26] p. of plates :
F1639.S26 M35x 1986   *NYPL [Sc E 88-539]*

SAINT DAVID'S ISLAND (BERMUDA ISLANDS) - HISTORY.
McCallan, E. A. (Ernest Albert), 1874- Life on old St. David's, Bermuda /. Hamilton, Bermuda , 1986. 258 p., [26] p. of plates :
F1639.S26 M35x 1986   *NYPL [Sc E 88-539]*

Saint-Domingue. Assembl ee g en erale. Tarbé, Charles. Rapport sur les troubles de Saint-Domingue. Paris, 1791-[1792] 4 v.
F1921 .T17   *NYPL [Sc Rare F 88-17]*

SAINT GEORGE'S (GRANADA)
Redhead, Wilfred. A city on a hill /. Barbados, West Indies , 1985 (Barbados, West Indies : Letchworth Press) 120 p. :
   NYPL [Sc D 87-1423]

SAINT HELENA ISLAND (S.C.) - SOCIAL LIFE AND CUSTOMS.
Daise, Ronald. Reminiscences of Sea Island heritage /. Orangeburg, S.C. , c1987. xvi, 103, [13] p. :   *NYPL [Sc F 88-168]*

Saint Jacques Fauquenoy, Marguerite. Parépou, Alfred. Atipa . Paris , 1987. viii, 231 p. : ISBN 2-85802-965-2   *NYPL [Sc E 88-18]*

St. John, James Augustus, 1801-1875. The lives of celebrated travellers [microform]. By James Augustus St. John ... New York, Harper & brothers, 1859-68. 3 v. 15 1/2cm. [v. 2, '59] "Ibn Batūta": v. 1, p. 69-109. "Leo Africanus": v. 1, p. 109-148. "James Bruce": v. 2, p. 233-301. "Mungo Park": v. 3, p. [13]-65. "John Lewis Burckhardt": v. 3, p. 168-218. "Volney": v. 3, p. [219]-237. "François Le Vaillant": v. 3, p. 262-326. "Belzoni": v. 3, p. 327-345. Microfilm. New York : New York Public Library, [197-] 1 microfilm reel ; 35 mm.
1. Travelers - Biography. I. Title.
   NYPL [Sc Micro R-3541]

SAINT JOHN (V.I.) - RACE RELATIONS.
Olwig, Karen Fog, 1948- Cultural adaptation and resistance on St. John . Gainesville , c1985. xii, 226 p. : ISBN 0-8130-0818-2 (pbk.) DDC 306/.097297/22 19
HT1071 .O43 1985   *NYPL [Sc D 88-1058]*

ST. JUDE'S CHAPEL (MANHATTAN: EPISCOPAL)
Memories and records of St. Jude's Chapel [microform] . [New York , 1982] [18] p. ;
   NYPL [Sc Micro F-11024]

Saint-Juste, Laurore. Les Couleurs du drapeau National, 1803-1986 / Laurore Saint-Juste. [Port-au-Prince, Haiti? : s.n.], 1988. 32 p. : ill. ; 21 cm. Cover title. Bibliography: p. 30-31. Author's autographed presentation copy to the New York Public Library.
1. Flags - Haiti - History. I. Title.
   NYPL [Sc D 88-1440]

Saint Kitts-Nevis. National Youth Council. 1st annual convention, September 1973 [microform] / St. Kitts-Nevis National Youth Council. St. Kitts : Govt. Printery, [1973?] 26 p. ; 21 cm. Cover title. Microfiche. New York: New York Public Library, 198 . 1 microfiche: negative; 11 x 15 cm. (FSN Sc 019,086)
1. Youth - Saint Kitts-Nevis - Congresses.
   NYPL [Sc Micro F-10999]

St. Lo, Montague. Ten little nigger boys / by "The Pilgrims" (Montague St. Lo & Reginald Rigby) [London] : A. Treherne ; New York : H.B. Claflin, 1904. [20] leaves, [20] leaves of plates : col. ill. ; 5 x 16 cm. (The Stump books) Last plate mounted to rear cover. Fastened with bone clasp.
I. Rigby, Reginald. II. Title.
   NYPL [Sc Rare C 86-1]

St. Louis Art Museum. Nunley, John W. (John Wallace), 1945- Caribbean festival arts . [Saint Louis] , 1988. 218 p. : ISBN 0-295-96702-1 :

DDC 394.2/5/07409729 19
GT4823 .N85 1988   *NYPL [Sc F 89-89]*

Saint-Louis du Sénégal . Biondi, Jean Pierre.
Paris , c1987. 234 p., [16] p. of plates : ISBN
2-207-23350-2   *NYPL [Sc D 88-1501]*

SAINT LOUIS (MO.) - RACE RELATIONS.
Lipsitz, George. A life in the struggle .
Philadelphia , 1988. viii, 292 p. : ISBN
0-87722-550-8 (alk. paper) DDC
973/.0496073024 B 19
E185.97.P49 L57 1988   *NYPL [Sc E 89-43]*

**ST. LOUIS (SENEGAL) - DESCRIPTION -
GUIDE-BOOKS.**
Guide touristique de Saint-Louis du Senegal /.
[Saint-Louis, Senegal , 197-?] 53 p. :
NYPL [Sc D 89-420]

**SAINT LOUIS, SENEGAL - ECONOMIC
CONDITIONS.**
Bonnardel, Régine. Vitalité de la petite pêche
tropicale . Paris , 1985. 104 p. : ISBN
2-222-03678-X   *NYPL [Sc F 88-329]*

SAINT LOUIS (SENEGAL) - HISTORY.
Biondi, Jean Pierre. Saint-Louis du Sénégal .
Paris , c1987. 234 p., [16] p. of plates : ISBN
2-207-23350-2   *NYPL [Sc D 88-1501]*

Saint Lucia . Ellis, G. (Guy) London , 1986. v,
72 p. : ISBN 0-333-40895-0 (pbk) : DDC
917.298/4304 19
F2100   *NYPL [Sc D 89-71]*

St. Lucia.
Hurricane precautionary measures [microform] :
to be forewarned is to be forearmed. St. Lucia :
[s.n., 1957] 18 p. ; 24 cm. Cover title. Microfiche.
New York: New York Public Library, 198. 1
microfiche: negative; 11 x 15 cm. (FSN Sc 019,065)
1. Hurricane protection - St. Lucia. I. Title.
NYPL [Sc Micro F-10954]

On the occasion of the first meeting of the
Saint Lucia House of Assembly, dated and
March, 1967 [microform] St. Lucia : [s.n.,
1967] [11] p. ; 25 cm. Cover title. Address/Arthur
Bottomley.--Address/John G.M. Compton.--Throne
Speech/Frederick Clarke. Microfiche. New York: New
York Public Library, 198 . 1 microfiche: negative; 11 x
15 cm. (FSN Sc 019,087)
*1. St. Lucia - Politics and government. I. St. Lucia
House of Assembly. II. Title.*
NYPL [Sc Micro F-10953]

Plan for the coordination of emergency action
in the event of a major disaster [microform] : to
be forewarned is to be forearmed. St. Lucia :
[s.n., 1964] 22 p. ; 25 cm. Cover title. Microfiche.
New York: New York Public Library, 198.1
microfiche: negative; 11 x 15 cm. (FSN Sc 019,066)
1. Disaster relief - Planning - St. Lucia. I. Title.
NYPL [Sc Micro F-10955]

Windward Islands letters patent and additional
instructions [microform] [Saint Lucia? : s.n.,
1955?] [17] p. ; 24 cm. Cover title. Microfiche.
New York: New York Public Library, 198 . 1
microfiche: negative; 11 x 15 cm. (FSN Sc 019,121)
CONTENTS. - Windward Islands letters patent,
1955.--Additional instructions, 1955.--The Saint Lucia
(Legislative Council) (amendment) order in council,
1955.
*1. St. Lucia - Politics and government. 2. Windward
Islands - Politics and government. I. Title.*
NYPL [Sc Micro F-10,886]

**ST. LUCIA - POLITICS AND
GOVERNMENT.**
St. Lucia. On the occasion of the first meeting
of the Saint Lucia House of Assembly, dated
and March, 1967 [microform] St. Lucia [1967]
[11] p. ;   *NYPL [Sc Micro F-10953]*

St. Lucia. Windward Islands letters patent and
additional instructions [microform] [Saint
Lucia? , 1955?] [17] p. ;
NYPL [Sc Micro F-10,886]

**SAINT LUCIA - DESCRIPTION AND
TRAVEL - GUIDE-BOOKS.**
Ellis, G. (Guy) Saint Lucia . London , 1986. v,
72 p. : ISBN 0-333-40895-0 (pbk) : DDC
917.298/4304 19
F2100   *NYPL [Sc D 89-71]*

**ST. LUCIA - DESCRIPTION AND TRAVEL -
VIEWS.**
Romyn, Conrad. Saint Lucia life and scenes /.
London , 1985. [92] p. : ISBN 0-333-40009-7
NYPL [Sc G 88-3]

SAINT LUCIA - HISTORY.
Jesse, Charles. Peeps into St. Lucia's past /. St.
Lucia , 1979. 100 p. :   *NYPL [Sc E 88-311]*

St. Lucia House of Assembly. St. Lucia. On the
occasion of the first meeting of the Saint Lucia
House of Assembly, dated and March, 1967
[microform] St. Lucia [1967] [11] p. ;
NYPL [Sc Micro F-10953]

Saint Lucia life and scenes /. Romyn, Conrad.
London , 1985. [92] p. : ISBN 0-333-40009-7
NYPL [Sc G 88-3]

St. Lucia. Ministry of Finance. Financial
instructions [microform] : for the guidance of
public officers on the preparation and
submission of the annual estimates and the
control of local and colonial development and
welfare expenditure / issued by the Ministry of
Finance. St. Lucia : The Ministry, [1962?] 24
p. : forms ; 25 cm. Cover title. Microfiche. New
York: New York Public Library, 198. 1 microfiche:
negative; 11 x 15 cm. (FSN Sc 019,067)
1. Finance, Public - St. Lucia. I. Title.
NYPL [Sc Micro F-10956]

**SAINT LUCIA - POLITICS AND
GOVERNMENT.**
DaBreo, D. Sinclair. --of men and politics .
Castries , New York , c1981. 208 p. : DDC
972.98/43 19
F2100 .D32 1981   *NYPL [Sc D 88-815]*

Odlum, George. Call that George /. [Castries,
St. Lucia] , 1979. 44 p. :
F2100 .O35 1979   *NYPL [Sc E 89-2]*

SAINT MARTIN - POETRY.
Nature, I love you . [St. Martin] , c1983. 36
p. :
MLCS 86/1723 (P)   *NYPL [Sc D 88-626]*

**ST. MICHAEL'S CHURCH (MANHATTAN:
EPISCOPAL)**
Memories and records of St. Jude's Chapel
[microform] . [New York , 1982] [18] p. ;
NYPL [Sc Micro F-11024]

Saint-Natus, Clotaire. Natif-natal =
Nativos=Natives = Les natif / Clotaire
Saint-Natus. Port-au-Prince, Haiti : Bibliothèque
nationale, 1987. 48 p. : ill. ; 20 x 23 cm. In
Creole. Translations into Spanish, English, French by
Nazaire Nacier, Nirvah Jean-Jacque, Emile Célestin-
Mégie respectively.
1. Creole dialects, French - Haiti - Texts. I. Title.
NYPL [Sc C 89-54]

**ST. PHILIP'S CHURCH (NEW YORK, N.Y.) -
HISTORY.**
Reaching out . Tappan, NY , c1986. 120 p. :
DDC 283/.7471 19
BV5980.N57 R4 1986   *NYPL [Sc F 87-222]*

SAIS study on Africa.
The Political economy of Kenya /. New York ,
1987. viii, 245 p., [1] leaf of plates : ISBN
0-275-92672-9 (alk. paper) : DDC 330.9676/204
19
HC865 .P65 1987   *NYPL [Sc E 88-157]*

Saisi, Frank. The bhang syndicate / Frank Saisi.
Nairobi : Spear Books, 1984. 180 p. ; 17 cm. (A
Spear book)
1. Kenya - Fiction. I. Title.
MLCS 84/916 (P)   *NYPL [Sc C 88-282]*

Une Saison d'anomie /. Soyinka, Wole. [Season
of anomy. French.] Paris , c1987. 326 p. ;
ISBN 2-7144-1999-2
NYPL [Sc D 88-1000]

Sajeni Chimedza /. Kawara, James. Gweru,
[Zimbabwe] , 1984. 174 p. ; ISBN 0-86922-327-5
NYPL [Sc C 88-97]

Sal Fisher at Girl Scout camp. Gardner, Lillian,
1907- New York [1959] 217 p.
PZ7.G1793 Saj   *NYPL [Sc D 88-1494]*

Sala-Molins, Louis. Le Code noir, ou, Le calvaire
de Canaan / Louis Sala-Molins. Paris : Presses
universitaires de France, c1987. 292 p. ; 22 cm.
(Pratiques théoriques) Includes text of the Code noir.
Includes index. Bibliography: p. [281]-287. ISBN
2-13-039970-3 : DDC 346.4401/3 344.40613 19
*1. France. Code noir. 2. Blacks - Legal status, laws,
etc. - France - Colonies. 3. Slavery - Law and
legislation - France - Colonies. I. France. Code noir.
1987. II. Title. III. Title: Code noir. IV. Title: Calvaire
de Canaan. V. Series.*
KJV4534 .S25 1987   *NYPL [Sc D 88-136]*

Salaün, N. Cinyanja/Cicewa : intensive course /
N. Salaün. Ndola, Zambia : Mission Press,
1979. 146 p. ; 21 cm. Includes index. "First ed.
printed and published in 1969 by Likuni Press and Pub.
house, ... Lilongwe, Malawi."
*1. Chewa dialect - Grammar. 2. Chewa dialect -
Textbooks for foreign speakers - English. I. Title.*
NYPL [Sc D 88-1178]

Salazar, Philippe Joseph. L'Intrigue raciale : essai
de critique anthropologique l'Afrique du Sud /
Philippe-Joseph Salazar. Paris : Meridiens
Klincksieck, 1989. 230 p. : ill. ; 21 cm.
(Sociologies au quotidien) Bibliography: p. [207]-209.
ISBN 2-86563-211-3
1. Apartheid - South Africa. I. Title. II. Series.
NYPL [Sc D 89-504]

Saldru working paper .
(no. 66) Atlantis a utopian nightmare /. Cape
Town , 1986. 114 p. : ISBN 0-7992-1070-6
NYPL [Sc D 89-17]

(no. 71) Aron, Janine. Asbestos and
asbestos-related disease in South Africa . Cape
Town , 1987. 71 p. : ISBN 0-7992-1126-5
NYPL [Sc D 88-1258]

Sales, Niveo Ramos. Receitas de feitiços e
encantos afro-brasileiros / Niveo Ramos Sales.
Rio de Janeiro : Achiamé, 1982. 75 p. ; 22 cm.
*1. Occult sciences - Brazil. 2. Incantations. 3. Folk-lore,
Black - Brazil. I. Title.*   *NYPL [JFD 84-750]*

Salih, Mohamed Abdel Rahim M. Abeyi,
administration and public services [microform] /
by Mohamed Abdel Rahim M. Salih.
Khartoum : Development Studies and Research
Centre, Faculty of Economic & Social Studies,
University of Khartoum, 1978. 27 leaves ; 28
cm. (Working report/Abyei Project. no. 4) Microfiche.
New York: New York Public Library, 198 . 1
microfiche: negative; 11 x 15 cm. (FSN Sc 019,059)
*1. Local government - Sudan - Abyei. 2. Villages -
Sudan - Abyei. I. Title.*
NYPL [Sc Micro F-11039]

Salkey, Andrew.
Jamaica / Andrew Salkey. 2nd ed. London :
Bogle-L'Ouverture Publications, 1983. 106 p. ;
22 cm. ISBN 0-904521-26-5
1. Jamaica - Poetry. I. Title.
NYPL [Sc D 88-1156]

The one : the story of how the people of
Guyana avenge the murder of their Pasero with
help from Brother Anancy and Sister Buxton /
by Andre w Salkey. London :
Bogle-L'Ouverture, 1985. 48 p. ; 22 cm.
*1. Rodney, Walter - Fiction. 2. Guyana - Fiction. I.
Title.*   *NYPL [Sc D 88-1238]*

Sall, Ibrahima. La République : farce tragique /
[Ibrahima Sall]. Dakar : Nouvelles Editions
africaines, c1985. 83 p. ; 21 cm. ISBN
2-7236-0974-X
I. Title.   *NYPL [Sc D 88-1161]*

Salley, Robert Lee. Activities of the Knights of
the Ku Klux Klan in Southern California,
1921-1925 / by Robert Lee Salley. 1963. v, 199
leaves ; 28 cm. Thesis (M.A.)--University of
Southern California, 1963. Bibliography: leaves 192-199.
*1. Ku Klux Klan (1915-) - California, Southern -
History. I. Title.*   *NYPL [Sc F 88-119]*

Salmon courage /. Philip, Marlene. Toronto ,
c1983. 40 p. ; ISBN 0-88795-030-2
NYPL [Sc D 88-497]

Salmon, Jaslin U. Black executives in
white-owned businesses and industries in the
Chicago metropolitan area [microform] / by
Jaslin Uriah Salmon. 1977. 197 leaves. Thesis
(Ph. D.)--University of Illinois at Chicago Circle, 1977.
Bibliography: leaves 185-194. Microfilm of typescript.
Ann Arbor, Mich.: University Microfilms International,
1977. 1 microfilm reel; 35 mm.
*1. Afro-American executives - Illinois - Chicago. 2.
Afro-Americans - Employment - Illinois - Chicago. I.
Title.*   *NYPL [Sc Micro R-4703]*

SALOONS. see HOTELS, TAVERNS, ETC.

Salt and roti. Parmasad, Kenneth Vidia. Indian
folk tales of the Caribbean . Charlieville,
Chaguanas, Trinidad and Tobago, West Indies ,
c1984. xxii, 131 p., [2] p. of plates : ISBN
976-8016-01-9 (pbk) DDC 398.2/09729 19
GR120 .P37 1984   *NYPL [Sc D 88-400]*

**Salt Lake City. Utah Museum of Fine Arts. see
Utah Museum of Fine Arts.**

SALVADOR (BRAZIL) - FESTIVALS, ETC.
Crowley, Daniel J., 1921- African myth and black reality in Bahian Carnaval /. [Los Angeles, Calif.] [1984] 47 p. :
NYPL [Sc F 86-281]

SALVADOR (BRAZIL) - FICTION.
Amado, Jorge, 1912- [Capitães da areia. English.] Captains of the sands /. New York, N.Y., c1988. 248 p. ; ISBN 0-380-89718-0 (pbk.) : DDC 869.3 19
PQ9697.A647 C373 1988
NYPL [Sc D 89-198]

Amado, Jorge, 1912- [Jubiabá. English.] Jubiabá /. New York , c1984. 294 p. ; ISBN 0-380-88567-0 (pbk.) : DDC 869.3 19
PQ9697.A647 J813 1984
NYPL [JFC 85-368]

Salvation and suicide . Chidester, David. Bloomington , c1988. xv, 190 p. ; ISBN 0-253-35056-5 DDC 289.9 19
BP605.P46 C48 1988   *NYPL [JFE 88-4624]*

Salvoldi, Valentino.
[Africa, il vangelo ci appartiene. English]
Africa, the gospel belongs to us : problems and prospects for an African Council / Valentino Salvoldi, Renato Kizito Sesana ; [translated by Maire Swift]. Ndola [Zambia] : Mission Press, 1986. 187 p ; 21 cm.
Translation of: Africa, il vangelo ci appartiene. Bibliography: p. 177-184.
1. Christianity - Africa. 2. Indigenous church administration - Africa. 3. Missions - Africa. 4. Theology, Doctrinal - Africa. I. Kizito Sesana, Renato. II. Title.   *NYPL [Sc D 89-568]*

Sam, Joe. (ill) Rohmer, Harriet. The invisible hunters . San Francisco , c1987. 32 p. : ISBN 0-89239-031-X : DDC 398.2/08998 19
F1529.M9 R64 1987   *NYPL [Sc E 88-241]*

Samaroo, Brinsley. India in the Caribbean /. London , 1987. 326 p. : ISBN 1-87051-805-5 (cased) : DDC 909/.09182/1081 19
NYPL [Sc D 88-997]

Samatar, Ahmed I. (Ahmed Ismail) Socialist Somalia : rhetoric and reality / Ahmed I. Samatar. London ; Atlantic Highlands, N.J. : Zed Books, 1988. 186 p. ; 23 cm. Includes index. Bibliography: p. [164]-181. ISBN 0-86232-588-9 DDC 967/.7305 19
1. Socialism - Somalia. 2. Somalia - Politics and government - 1960-. I. Title.
DT407 .S26 1988   *NYPL [JLD 89-340]*

Il samba . Barbareschi Fino, Maria Antonietta. Milano , 1979. 63 p. ;   *NYPL [Sc D 89-187]*

Samba . Tchakoute, Paul, 1945- Bafoussam, Cameroun , 1980. 95 p. ; DDC 842 19
PQ3989.2.T33 S2   *NYPL [Sc C 89-164]*

Samkange, Stanlake John Thompson, 1922- Oral history : the Zvimba people of Zimbabwe / S.J.T. Samkange. Harare, Zimbabwe : Harare Pub. House, c1986. ii, 93 p. : ill., geneal. table ; 21 cm.
1. Ethnology - Zimbabwe. 2. Zezeru (African people). 3. Zimbabwe - History. I. Title. II. Title: Zvimba people of Zimbabwe.   *NYPL [Sc D 89-586]*

Samori: une révolution dyula. Person, Yves. Dakar, 1968- v. (2377 p.) DDC 966/.2601/0924 B
DT475.5.S3 P47 1968   *NYPL [Sc F 87-398]*

SAMORY, CA. 1830-1900.
Person, Yves. Samori: une révolution dyula. Dakar, 1968- v. (2377 p.) DDC 966/.2601/0924 B
DT475.5.S3 P47 1968   *NYPL [Sc F 87-398]*

Sampson, C. Garth (Clavil Garth), 1941- Stylistic boundaries among mobile hunter-foragers / C. Garth Sampson. Washington : Smithsonian Institution Press, c1988. 186 p. : ill. ; 29 cm. (Smithsonian series in archaeological inquiry) Bibliography: p. 182-186. ISBN 0-87474-838-0 DDC 968/.004961 19
1. San (African people) - Pottery. 2. Art, San (African people). I. Title. II. Series.
DT764.B8 S24 1988   *NYPL [Sc F 89-97]*

Sampson, Emma Speed, 1868-1947. Miss Minerva's baby / by Emma Speed Sampson ; illustrated by William Donahey. Chicago : Reilly & Lee, c1920. 320 p. : ill. ; 19 cm.
1. Afro-Americans - Fiction. I. Donahey, William, 1883-. II. Title.
PZ7.S16 Mis
NYPL [Sc C 88-71]

Sampson, Henry T., 1934- The ghost walks : a chronological history of Blacks in show business, 1865-1910 / by Henry T. Sampson. Metuchen, N.J. : Scarecrow Press, 1988. ix, 570 p. : ill. ; 23 cm. Includes index. ISBN 0-8108-2070-6 DDC 792/.08996073 19
1. Afro-American theater - Chronology. 2. Afro-American theater - Reviews. I. Title.
PN2270.A35 S25 1988
NYPL [Sc D 88-1145]

Sampson, Richard, 1922-
[Man with a toothbrush in his hat]
The struggle for British interests in Barotseland, 1871-88 / Richard Sampson. Lusaka : Multimedia Publications, [198-?] v, 158 p. : ill. ; 21 cm. Previously published as: The man with a toothbrush in his hat. 1972. Bibliography: p. 150-158. DDC 968.94/01 19
1. Westbeech, George. 2. Hunters - Zambia - Biography. 3. Merchants - Zambia - Biography. 4. Zambia - History - To 1890. I. Title.
DT963.72.W47 S25 1980z
NYPL [Sc D 88-381]

Samuel, Julian. Lone Ranger in Pakistan / by Julian Samuel. Peterborough, Ontario : Emergency Press, 1986. 51 p. : ill. ; 23 cm. ISBN 0-919740-01-4
I. Title.   *NYPL [Sc D 88-70]*

SAN (AFRICAN PEOPLE)
Martin, Robert, 1929- Yesterday's people. Garden City, N.Y. [1970] 158 p. DDC 916.8/03
DT764.B8 M35   *NYPL [Sc F 88-248]*

Van der Post, Laurens. The lost world of the Kalahari . London , 1988. 261 p. :
NYPL [Sc F 88-381]

SAN (AFRICAN PEOPLE) - JUVENILE FICTION.
Howard, Moses L., 1928- The ostrich chase /. New York [1974] 118 p. : ISBN 0-03-012096-9
NYPL [Sc D 88-374]

Westwood, Gwen. Narni of the desert. [Chicago, c1967] 93 p. DDC [Fic]
PZ7.W5275 Nar   *NYPL [Sc D 88-1424]*

SAN (AFRICAN PEOPLE) - JUVENILE LITERATURE.
Martin, Robert, 1929- Yesterday's people. Garden City, N.Y. [1970] 158 p. DDC 916.8/03
DT764.B8 M35   *NYPL [Sc F 88-248]*

SAN (AFRICAN PEOPLE) - POTTERY.
Sampson, C. Garth (Clavil Garth), 1941- Stylistic boundaries among mobile hunter-foragers /. Washington , c1988. 186 p. : ISBN 0-87474-838-0 DDC 968/.004961 19
DT764.B8 S24 1988   *NYPL [Sc F 89-97]*

San Francisco (Calif.). Dept. of Public Health. AIDS Surveillance Office. A baseline survey of AIDS risk behaviors and attitudes in San Francisco's Black communities /. San Francisco, Calif. [1987] vii, 74, [59] leaves :
NYPL [Sc F 88-232]

San Francisco Craft & Folk Art Museum. Leon, Eli. Who'd a thought it . San Francisco, CA , c1987. 87 p. :   *NYPL [Sc F 88-235]*

San Jose, Calif. Museum of Art. see San Jose Museum of Art.

San Jose Museum of Art. Sims, Lowery Stokes. Robert Colescott, a retrospective, 1975-1986 /. San Jose, Calif. , c1987. 34 p. : ISBN 0-938175-01-7 (pbk.) DDC 759.13 19
ND237.C66 A4 1987   *NYPL [Sc F 88-317]*

Sánchez Ramón, Díaz. see Díaz Sánchez, Ramón.

Sanchez, Sonia, 1935- I've been a woman : new and selected poems / Sonia Sanchez. Chicago : Third World Press, c1985. 101 p. ; 22 cm. ISBN 0-88378-112-1
I. Title.   *NYPL [Sc D 88-205]*

Sanda, A. O. The impact of military rule on Nigeria's administration /. Ile-Ife, Nigeria , c1987. vi, 344 p. ; ISBN 978-266-601-7
NYPL [Sc D 88-733]

Sanda, Akinade Olumuyiwa, 1942- see Sanda, A. O.

Sandbox society . Lubeck, Sally. London , Philadelphia , 1985. xv, 177 p. ; ISBN 1-85000-051-4 DDC 372/.21/0977 19
LB1140.24.M53 L8 1985
NYPL [Sc E 89-80]

Sander, Reinhard. The Trinidad awakening : West Indian literature of the nineteen-thirties / Reinhard W. Sander. New York : Greenwood Press, 1988. xii, 168 p. ; 24 cm. (Contributions in Afro-American and African studies, 0069-9624 . no. 114) Includes index. Bibliography: p. [157]-161. ISBN 0-313-24562-2 (lib. bdg. : alk. paper) DDC 810/.9 19
1. Trinidad and Tobago literature (English) - 20th century - History and criticism. 2. West Indian literature (English) - 20th century - History and criticism. I. Title. II. Series.
PR9272 .S24 1988   *NYPL [Sc E 89-111]*

Sanders, Joseph A., 1944- Chesler, Mark A. Social science in court . Madison, Wis. , 1988. xiv, 286 p. ; ISBN 0-299-11620-4 : DDC 344.73/0798 347.304798 19
KF8925.D5 C48 1988   *NYPL [Sc E 89-187]*

Sanders, Leslie Catherine, 1944- The development of black theater in America : from shadows to selves / Leslie Catherine Sanders. Baton Rouge : Louisiana State University Press, c1988. 252 p. ; 24 cm. Includes index. Bibliography: p. [233]-248. ISBN 0-8071-1328-X DDC 812/.009/896073 19
1. American drama - Afro-American authors - History and criticism. 2. Afro-American theater - History. 3. Afro-Americans in literature. I. Title.
PS338.N4 S26 1987
NYPL [MWED 88-1125]

Sanderson, Lilian Passmore. Female genital mutilation, excision and infibulation : a bibliography / this bibliography has been compiled by Lilian Passmore Sanderson. London : Anti-Slavery Society for the Protection of Human Rights, [1986?] 72 p. ; 21 cm. Cover title. "An Anti-Slavery Society bibliography 1986." DDC 016.392 19
1. Clitoridectomy - Bibliography. 2. Infibulation - Bibliography. I. Title.
Z5118.C57 S26 1986 GN484
NYPL [Sc D 88-1152]

Sandiford, Keith Albert, 1947- Measuring the moment : strategies of protest in eighteenth-century Afro-English writing / Keith A. Sandiford. Selinsgrove : Susquehanna University Press, c1988. 181 p. ; 24 cm. Includes index. Bibliography: p. 167-173. ISBN 0-941664-79-1 (alk. paper) DDC 828 19
1. African prose literature (English) - History and criticism. 2. Protest literature, African (English) - History and criticism. 3. Africans - Great Britain - History - 18th century. 4. Slavery - Anti-slavery movements - History - 18th century. 5. Slavery and slaves in literature. 6. Slave-trade in literature. I. Title.
PR9340 .S26 1988   *NYPL [Sc E 88-467]*

Sandison, Janet. see Duncan, Jane.

Sandner, Wolfgang. Jazz : zur Geschichte und stilistischen Entwicklung afro-amerikanischer Musik / von Wolfgang Sandner.1. Aufl. [Laaber] : Laaber-Verlag, 1982. 152 p. : music ; 21 cm. (Musik-Taschen-Bücher. Theoretica. Bd. 19) Includes index. Bibliography: p. 141-144. Discography: p. 145-146. ISBN 3-921518-75-X DDC 785.42/09 19
1. Jazz music - History and criticism. I. Title.
ML3506 .S26 1982   *NYPL [Sc D 89-161]*

Sandoval, Alonso dc, 1576-1652. Naturaleza, policia sagrada i profana, costumbres i ritos, disciplina i catechismo evangelico de todos etiopes / por el p. Alonso, de Sandoval ... En Sevilla : Por Francisco de Lira, impresor, 1627. [23], 334 p., 81 leaves ; 21 cm. "Suma del privilegio" refers to the book under title: De instauranda aethiopum salute. Running title: Tract[atus] de inst[auranda] ethiop[um] sal[ute] Title page and following two leaves in facsimile.
1. Jesuits - Missions. 2. Missions to Blacks. 3. Blacks - South America. 4. Slave-trade - Africa. 5. Africa - Social life and customs. I. Title. II. Title: De instauranda aethiopum salute. III. Title: Tractatus de instauranda ethiopum salute.
NYPL [Sc Rare F 82-70]

The Sandy Shoes mystery. Mooney, Elizabeth Comstock. Philadelphia [1970] 128 p. DDC [Fic]
PZ7.M78 San   *NYPL [Sc D 89-96]*

SANFORD, HENRY SHELTON, 1823-1891.
Roark, J. L. American expansionism vs. European colonialism [microform] . [Nairobi] , 1976. 16 leaves :
NYPL [Sc Micro R-4108 no. 34]

Sanger, Clyde. (joint author) Brown, Alex. Southern Africa. Ottawa [1973] 43 p.
DT746 .B76 *NYPL [JLD 75-1128]*

SANGO. see SHANGO.

Sangster, Donald B. Girvan, Norman, 1941- Technology policies for small developing economies . Mona, Jamaica , c1983. 224 p. :
DDC 338.9729 19
T24.A1 G57 1983 *NYPL [Sc E 88-260]*

SANITARY AFFAIRS. see PUBLIC HEALTH.

Sanjuán de Novas, María J. Soledad, Rosalía de la. Ibo . Miami, Fla. , 1988. 278 p. ; ISBN 0-89729-468-8 *NYPL [Sc D 89-436]*

SANKOFA FILM/VIDEO COLLECTIVE. Fusco, Coco. Young, British, and Black . Buffalo, N.Y. , c1988. 65 p. :
NYPL [Sc D 88-1186]

SANKURU (ZAIRE) - POLITICS AND GOVERNMENT. Manya K'Omalowete a Djonga, 1950- Patrice Lumumba, le Sankuru et l'Afrique . Lutry [1985] 166 p. : *NYPL [Sc D 88-1490]*

Sanni, Ishaq Kunle. Why you should never be a Christian / by Ishaq 'Kunle Sanni and Dawood Ayodele Amoo. Ibadan, Nigeria : Iman Publications, 1987. ix, 125 p. : facsims. ; 20 cm. (Preacher's guide)
1. Christianity - Controversial literature. 2. Christianity and other religions - Islam. 3. Islam - Relations - Christianity. I. Amoo, Dawood Ayodele. II. Title.
NYPL [Sc C 88-157]

Sanson, Henri. Christianisme au miroir de l'Islam : essai sur la rencontre des cultures en Algérie / Henri Sanson. Paris : Cerf, 1984. 195 p. ; 20 cm. (Rencontres. no. 36) ISBN 2-204-02278-0 :
1. Christianity and other religions - Islam. 2. Islam - Relations - Christianity. 3. Islam - Algeria. 4. Christianity - Algeria. 5. Christianity - Relations - Islam. 6. Algeria - Religious life and customs. I. Title.
*NYPL [*OGC 85-2762]*

Santa Barbara Museum of Art. Antelopes and elephants, hornbills and hyenas; animals in African art. An exhibition organized by Ronald A. Kuchta, curator. [Santa Barbara, 1973] [48] p. illus. 28 cm. Catalog of the exhibition held Oct. 4-Dec. 2, 1973 at the Santa Barbara Museum of Art, Calif. DDC 732/.2/0967
1. Sculpture, African - Exhibitions. 2. Sculpture, Primitive - Africa, West. 3. Animals in art. I. Title.
NB1098 .S27 1973 *NYPL [Sc F 88-165]*

Santana Cardoso, Ciro Flamarion. see Cardoso, Ciro Flamarion Santana.

SANTERIA (CULTUS) - SONGS AND MUSIC. Ramos, Miguel. Ase omo osayin-- ewe aye /. [S.l.] , 1985, c1982. 113 p. ;
NYPL [Sc D 89-487]

Santo Domingo (French colony). Assemblée générale. Commissaires. Pétition faite à l'Assemblée nationale par MM. les Commissaires de l'Assemblée générale de la partie française de St.-Domingue : le 2 décembre 1791, et lue le 3. [Paris?] : De l'Impr. de P.F. Didot le jeune, [1791?] 7 p. ; 20 cm.
1. Haiti - History - Revolution, 1791-1804 - Sources. I. France. Assemblée nationale législative, 1791-1792. II. Title. *NYPL [Sc Rare C 86-3]*

Santo Domingo. Universidad Autónoma. Publicaciones. (390) Matos Moquete, Manuel, 1944- En el atascadero /. Santo Domingo, República Dominicana , 1985. 266 p. ;
MLCS 85/21777 (P) *NYPL [JFD 86-4017]*

Santos, Aires de Almeida. Meu amor da Rua Onze / Aires de Almeida Santos. Lisboa : Edições 70, 1987. 72 p. : ill., port. ; 20 cm. (Autores angolanos. 43) Poems.
I. Title. *NYPL [Sc C 88-129]*

Santos, Alberto de los. Morais, Evaristo de, 1871-1939. A escravidão africana no Brasil . Brasília, Distrito Federal , c1986. 140 p. :
ISBN 85-23-00070-4 *NYPL [Sc D 88-922]*

Santos, Arnaldo, 1935- O cesto de Katandu e outros contos / Arnaldo Santos. Lisboa : Edições 70, c1986. 101 p. ; 20 cm. (Autores angolanos. 42)
1. Angola - Fiction. I. Title.
NYPL [Sc C 88-267]

Santos, Luiz Alvares dos, 1825-1886. Guimarães, Augusto Alvares. Propaganda abolicionista . Bahia , 1875. 86 p. ;
NYPL [Sc Rare G 86-33]

Santos, Marcelino dos. Canto do amor natural / Marcelino dos Santos. [Maputo?] : Associação dos Escritores Moçambicanos, [1987?] 160 p. ; 21 cm. (Colecção Timbila . no. 1) Poems.
I. Title. *NYPL [Sc D 88-518]*

Santos, Norberto Teixeira. Avaliação nutricional da população infantil banto (0-5 anos) de uma zona suburbana da cidade Lourenço Marques : dissertação de doutoramento / Norberto Teixeira Santos. [Lourenço Marques, Moçambique : Universidado de Lourenço Marques], 1974. 400 p., [40] p. of plates : ill. (some col.), maps ; 24 cm. Revista de ciências médicas, v. 17, Série B, 1974. Abstract in Portuguese, French and English. Errata slip inserted. Author's autographed presentation copy to the African-American Institute.
1. Malnutrition in children - Mozambique - Maputo. 2. Children - Mozambique - Maputo - Nutrition. I. Title.
NYPL [Sc E 88-143]

Santos, Paulo dos. Lubu ku lebri ku mortu . Bissau , 1988. 49 p. : *NYPL [Sc F 88-351]*

SAPINY (AFRICAN PEOPLE) Goldschmidt, Walter Rochs, 1913- The Sebei . New York , c1986. xii, 162 p. : ISBN 0-03-008922-0 : DDC 305/.09676/1 19
DT433.245.S24 G65 1986
NYPL [Sc E 88-225]

Sapphire. Meditations on the rainbow : poetry / by Sapphire. New York : Crystal Banana Press, 1987. 71 p. ; 22 cm. ISBN 0-931885-00-0
I. Title. *NYPL [Sc D 88-72]*

SARA (AFRICAN PEOPLE) Magnant, Jean-Pierre, 1946- La terre sara, terre tchadienne /. Paris , c1986. 380 p. : ISBN 2-85802-691-2
DT546.445.S27 M34 1986
NYPL [Sc D 89-101]

Sara and the door /. Jensen, Virginia Allen. Reading, Mass. , c1977. [32] p. : ISBN 0-201-03446-8 DDC [E]
PZ8.3.J425 Sar *NYPL [Sc B 89-17]*

Sarah & Addie . Teytaud, Anton C. [S.l.] c1976 (Christiansted, St. Croix, V.I. : Crown Printing Co.) 68 p. : *NYPL [Sc D 87-340]*

Sarah and Addie. Teytaud, Anton C. Sarah & Addie . [S.l.] c1976 (Christiansted, St. Croix, V.I. : Crown Printing Co.) 68 p. :
NYPL [Sc D 87-340]

SARAMACCAN LAGUAGES - SYNTAX. Studies in Saramaccan language structure /. [Amsterdam] , 1987. viii, 112 p. ; ISBN 976-410-004-X *NYPL [Sc D 88-554]*

SARAMACCAN LANGUAGE - COMPLEMENT. Byrne, Francis. Grammatical relations in a radical Creole . Amsterdam , Philadelphia , 1987. xiv, 293 p. : ISBN 0-915027-96-8 (U. S. : alk. paper) : DDC 427/.9883 19
PM7875.S27 B97 1987
NYPL [JFD 88-7020]

SARAMACCAN LANGUAGE - SYNTAX. Byrne, Francis. Grammatical relations in a radical Creole . Amsterdam , Philadelphia , 1987. xiv, 293 p. : ISBN 0-915027-96-8 (U. S. : alk. paper) : DDC 427/.9883 19
PM7875.S27 B97 1987
NYPL [JFD 88-7020]

SARAMACCAN LANGUAGES - MORPHOPHONEMICS. Studies in Saramaccan language structure /. [Amsterdam] , 1987. viii, 112 p. ; ISBN 976-410-004-X *NYPL [Sc D 88-554]*

Sarnelli, Tommaso. Costumi e credenze coloniali [microform] : il "buri" dei negri tripolini / Tommaso Sarnelli. Napoli : Società africana d'italia, 1925. 39 p. : ill. ; 25 cm. "Dall' 'Africa italiana', boll. della società africana d'Italia, Napoli, 1924-1925." Microfiche. New York: New York Public Library, 198 . 1 microfiche: negative; 11 x 15 cm. (FSN Sc 019,120)
1. Blacks - Libya - Tripoli - Religion - History. I. Società africana d'Italia (Naples). II. Title. III. Title: "Buri" dei negri tripolini.
NYPL [Sc Micro F-11058]

Saro-Wiwa, Ken. Mr. B / Ken Saro-Wiwa ; illustrated by Peregrino Brimoh. Port Harcourt ; Ewell : Saros International, 1987. 154 p. : ill. ; 18 cm. SCHOMBURG CHILDREN'S COLLECTION. ISBN 1-87071-601-9 (pbk) : DDC 823 19
1. Nigeria - Juvenile fiction. I. Brimoh, Peregrino. II. Schomburg Children's Collection. III. Title.
PZ7 *NYPL [Sc C 88-300]*

Sartre, Jean Paul, 1905- Orphée noir. 1985. Senghor, Léopold Sédar, 1906- Anthologie de la nouvelle poésie nègre et malgache de langue française / par Léopold Sédar Senghor, précédée de Orphée noir / par Jean-Paul Sartre. 5. éd. Paris , 1985, c1948. xliv, 227 p. ; ISBN 2-13-038715-2 *NYPL [Sc C 88-134]*

Sartre, Jean Paul, 1905-1980. [Orphée noir. English] Black Orpheus. Translated by S. W. Allen. [Paris, Présence africaine, 1963?] 65 p. ; 18 cm. Translation of Orphée noir.
1. French poetry - Black authors - History and criticism. I. Allen, S. W. II. Title.
NYPL [Sc C 88-110]

Satchel Paige /. Humphrey, Kathryn Long. New York , 1988. 110 p. : ISBN 0-531-10513-X DDC 796.357/092/4 B 92 19
GV865.P3 H86 1988 *NYPL [Sc E 88-481]*

Satchmo . Armstrong, Louis, 1900-1971. New York, N.Y. , 1986, c1954. xiii, p. 7-240 : ISBN 0-306-80276-7 (pbk.) : DDC 785.42/092/4 B 19
ML419.A75 A3 1986 *NYPL [Sc D 88-339]*

Satchmo /. Giddens, Gary. New York , 1988. 239 p. : ISBN 0-385-24428-2 : DDC 785.42/092/4 B 19
ML410.A75 G5 1988 *NYPL [Sc F 89-73]*

Die Satire im nigerianischen Roman . Doherty, Jaiyeola, 1952- Frankfurt am Main , New York , c1986. 381 p. : ISBN 3-8204-8326-8 DDC 823 19
PR9387.4 .D64 1986 *NYPL [Sc D 88-991]*

SATIRE, NIGERIAN (ENGLISH) - HISTORY AND CRITICISM. Doherty, Jaiyeola, 1952- Die Satire im nigerianischen Roman . Frankfurt am Main , New York , c1986. 381 p. : ISBN 3-8204-8326-8 DDC 823 19
PR9387.4 .D64 1986 *NYPL [Sc D 88-991]*

Satires de Lamadani /. Lamadani, 1893-1972. [Paris] , 1987. 155 p., [9] p. of plates :
NYPL [Sc E 88-223]

SATYAGRAHA. see PASSIVE RESISTANCE.

Satzstruktur des Deutschen und des Ewe . Eklou, Akpaka A. Saarbrücken , 1987. 262 p. ;
NYPL [Sc D 89-203]

SAUDI ARABIA - DESCRIPTION AND TRAVEL. Walker, Dale. Fool's paradise /. New York , 1988. 242 p. ; ISBN 0-394-75818-8 (pbk.) : DDC 915.3/80453 19
DS208 .W35 1988 *NYPL [Sc D 88-1463]*

Sauerbier, Udo. Auf Pad in Südwest : eine Reisebegleiter durch Südwestafrika / Udo Sauerbier. [Mainz : s.n.], c1982. 224 p. : ill., facsims., map ; 22 cm.
1. Namibia - Description and travel. I. Title.
NYPL [Sc D 88-619]

Sauldie, Madan M. Super powers in the Horn of Africa / by Madan M. Sauldie. New York : APT Books, c1987. ix, 252 p. ; 23 cm. Includes bibliographies and index. ISBN 0-86590-092-2 DDC 320.960 19
1. Somali-Ethiopian Conflict, 1979-. 2. Africa, Northeast - Politics and government - 1974-. 3. Africa, Northeast - Foreign relations - United States. 4. Africa, Northeast - Foreign relations - Soviet Union. 5. United States - Foreign relations - Africa, Northeast. 6. Soviet Union - Foreign relations - Africa, Northeast. 7. Eritrea (Ethiopia) - History - Revolution - 1962-. I. Title.
DT367.8 .S28 1987 *NYPL [Sc D 89-488]*

Sauna and the drug pedlars. Fulani, Dan. London , 1986. 109 p. : ISBN 0-340-32789-8 (pbk) : *NYPL [Sc C 88-74]*

Saunders, Christopher C. Historical dictionary of South Africa / by Christopher Saunders. Metuchen, N.J. : Scarecrow Press, 1983. xxviii, 241 p. ; 22 cm. (African historical dictionaries. no. 37) Includes indexes. Bibliography: p. 202-234. ISBN 0-8108-1629-6 DDC 968/.003/21 19

1. South Africa - History - Dictionaries. I. Title. II. Series.
DT766 .S23 1983   **NYPL [*R-BN 89-3347]**

Saunders, Dave. The West Indians in Britain / Dave Saunders. London : Batsford Academic and Educational, 1984. 72 p. : ill., maps, ports. ; 26 cm. (Communities in Britain) Includes index. Bibliography: p. 69.   ISBN 0-7134-4427-4
1. West Indians - Great Britain. 2. Great Britain - Social conditions - 20th century. I. Title. II. Series.
DA125.W4 S28x 1984   **NYPL [Sc F 88-68]**

Saunders, Doris E. The Kennedy years and the Negro : a photographic record / edited by Doris E. Saunders ; introduction by Andrew T. Hatcher ... Chicago : Johnson Publishing Co., 1964. xiii, 143 p. : ill., ports. ; 28 cm.
1. Kennedy, John Fitzgerald, Pres. U. S., 1917-1963. 2. Afro-Americans - History - 1877-1964. 3. Afro-Americans - Civil rights.
NYPL [Sc F 89-75]

Les sauterelles . Kayo, Patrice. Yaoundé , 1986. 79 p. ;   **NYPL [Sc D 88-180]**

SAVAGE, AUGUSTA - EXHIBITIONS.
Augusta Savage and the art Schools of Harlem. New York, N.Y. , 1988. 27 p. :
NYPL [Sc F 89-45]

Savannah State College (Ga.) National Conference on African American/Jewish American Relations (1983 : Savannah State College) Blacks and Jews . [Savannah, Ga.] [1983] iii, 58 p. ;   **NYPL [Sc D 88-335]**

SAVATE. see BOXING.

Save the Children Fund. Prospects for Africa . London , 1988. 97 p. :   ISBN 0-340-42909-7 (pbk) :   DDC 330.96/0328 19
HC800   **NYPL [Sc E 89-34]**

Savimbi, Jonas Malheiro. Por um futuro melhor / Jonas Savimbi. Lisboa : Nova Nórdica, 1986. 192 p. : ports. ; 21 cm.   DDC 967/.304 19
1. União Nacional para a Independência Total de Angola. 2. National liberation movements - Angola. 3. Angola - Politics and government - 1975-. 4. Angola - History - Civil War, 1975-. I. Title.
DT611.8 .S28 1986   **NYPL [Sc D 88-771]**

SAVING AND INVESTMENT - ZIMBABWE - HISTORY.
Phimister, I. R. (Ian R.) An economic and social history of Zimbabwe, 1890-1948 . London , New York , 1988. xii, 336 p. :   ISBN 0-582-64423-2   DDC 330.96891/02 19
HC910.Z9 S36 1987   **NYPL [Sc D 89-35]**

Savinien et Monique . Plumasseau, Eugène, 1926- Pointe-à-Pitre , c1986. 188 p. ;
MLCS 86/7257 (P)   **NYPL [Sc D 88-176]**

Sawadogo, Abdoulaye. Un plan Marshall pour l'Afrique? / Abdoulaye Sawadogo. Paris : Editions L'Harmattan, c1987. 119 p. ; 22 cm. (Collection "Points de vue") Includes bibliographical references.   ISBN 2-85802-816-8
1. Africa - Economic policy. I. Title. II. Series.
NYPL [Sc D 88-911]

Sawh, Roy, 1934- From where I stand /. London , 1987. 94 p. :   ISBN 0-9956664-9-1
NYPL [Sc C 88-30]

SAYINGS. see EPIGRAMS.

Scafe, Suzanne, 1954- Bryan, Beverley, 1949- The heart of the race . London , 1985. vi, 250 p. ;   ISBN 0-86068-361-3 (pbk.) :   DDC 305.4/8896041 19
DA125.N4 B78 1985   **NYPL [Sc C 88-178]**

Scandinavian Institute of African Studies. see Nordiska Afrikainstitutet.

SCARABS.
Myer, Isaac, 1836-1902. Scarabs [microform]. New York, Leipzig, 1894. xxvii, 177 p.
DT62.S3 M8   **NYPL [Sc Micro R-3541]**

Scarabs [microform]. Myer, Isaac, 1836-1902. New York, Leipzig, 1894. xxvii, 177 p.
DT62.S3 M8   **NYPL [Sc Micro R-3541]**

Scarlett, Reg, 1934- Lawrence, Bridgette. 100 great Westindian test cricketers . London , 1988. 231 p. :   ISBN 1-87051-865-9 :   DDC 796.35/865 19
GV928.W4   **NYPL [Sc F 88-380]**

Schaffmann, Christa. Klöppel, Eberhard. In Simbabwe /. Leipzig , c1985. 160 p. :   ISBN 0-325-00113-0   **NYPL [Sc D 88-627]**

Schärer, Therese, 1946- Das Nigerian Youth Movement : eine Untersuchung zur Politisierung der afrikanischen Bildungsschicht vor dem Zweiten Weltkrieg / Therese Schärer. Frankfurt am Main ; New York : P. Lang, c1986. xiii, 376, A76 p., 3 leaves of plates : maps ; 21 cm. (Europäische Hochschulschriften. Reihe XXXI, Politikwissenschaft . Bd. 89 = v. 89 = v. 89) Originally presented as the author's thesis (doctoral--Universität Zürich, 1984/85) German and English. Bibliography: p. A67-A76.   ISBN 3-261-03567-6
1. Nigerian Youth Movement. 2. Youth movement - Nigeria. 3. Nigeria - Politics and government - To 1960. I. Series: Europäische Hochschulschriften. Reihe XXXI, Politikwissenschaft , Bd. 89. II. Title.
NYPL [Sc D 88-878]

Schatz, Letta.
Bola and the Oba's drummer. Illustrated by Tom Feelings. New York, McGraw-Hill [1967]. 156 p. illus. 23 cm. A Nigerian youth aspires to become a drummer for the king. SCHOMBURG CHILDREN'S COLLECTION.   DDC [Fic] 19
1. Nigeria - Juvenile fiction. I. Feelings, Tom, illus. II. Schomburg Children's Collection. III. Title.
PZ7.S337 Bo   **NYPL [Sc E 89-26]**

Taiwo and her twin / by Letta Schatz ; illustrated by Elton Fax. New York : McGraw-Hill Book, c1964- 128 p. : ill. ; 24 cm. SCHOMBURG CHILDREN'S COLLECTION.
1. Yorubas - Juvenile fiction. I. Fax,Elton. II. Schomburg Children's Collection. III. Title.
NYPL [Sc E 88-430]

Schatzberg, Michael G.
The dialectics of oppression in Zaire / Michael G. Schatzberg. Bloomington : Indiana University Press, c1988. x, 193 p., [1] p. of plates : 1 map ; 25 cm. Includes index. Bibliography: p. [174]-189.   ISBN 0-253-31703-7   DDC 323.4/9/0967513 19
1. Human rights - Zaire - Lisala (Equateur). 2. Political persecution - Zaire - Lisala (Equateur). 3. Lisala (Equateur, Zaire) - History. I. Title.
JC599.Z282 L577 1988   **NYPL [Sc E 88-512]**

The Political economy of Kenya /. New York , 1987. viii, 245 p., [1] leaf of plates :   ISBN 0-275-92672-9 (alk. paper) :   DDC 330.9676/204 19
HC865 .P65 1987   **NYPL [Sc E 88-157]**

Schechter, Betty. The peaceable revolution. Boston, Houghton Mifflin, 1963. 243 p. illus. 23 cm.   DDC 301.24
1. Passive resistance - United States. 2. Passive resistance - India. I. Title.
HM278.S35   **NYPL [Sc D 88-1422]**

Scherer, Barbara Hetzner. Diallo, Nafissatou, 1941- Fary, princess of Tiali /. Washington, D.C. , c1987. xi, 106 p. :   ISBN 0-89410-411-X
NYPL [Sc D 88-1366]

Scherrer, Christian. Tourismus und selbstbestimmte Entwicklung-ein Widerspruch : das Fallbeispiel Tanzania / Christian Scherrer. Berlin : D. Reimer, c1988. 270 p. : ill. ; 21 cm. (Ethnologie) Bibliography: p. 235-269.   ISBN 3-496-00955-1
1. Tourist trade - Tanzania. I. Title.
NYPL [Sc D 88-1334]

Schiller, Greta. Weiss, Andrea. Before Stonewall . Tallahassee, FL , 1988. 86 p. :   ISBN 0-941483-20-7 :   DDC 306.7/66/0973 19
HQ76.8.U5 W43 1988   **NYPL [Sc D 88-1125]**

Schloss, Marc R. The hatchet's blood : separation, power, and gender in Ehing social life / Marc R. Schloss. Tucson : University of Arizona Press, c1988. xv, 178 p. : ill. ; 24 cm. (The Anthropology of form and meaning) Includes index. Bibliography: p. 171-173.   ISBN 0-8165-1042-3 (alk. paper)   DDC 966/.3 19
1. Bayot (African people). I. Title. II. Series.
DT549.45.B39 S35 1988   **NYPL [Sc E 88-443]**

Schlosser, Katesa. Medizinen des Blitzzauberers Laduma Madela : eine bildliche Dokumentation aus Kwa Zulu/Südafrika / von Katesa Schlosser ; Fotos von Katesa Schlosser und Anders Fogelqvist. Kiel : Schmidt & Klaunig, 1984. 186 p., 64, [1] p. of plates : ill. ; 24 cm. (Arbeiten aus dem Museum für Völkerkunde der Universität Kiel . 7) Includes index. Bibliography: p. 173-175.   ISBN 3-88312-106-1   DDC 615.8/99/089963 19

1. Madela, Laduma. 2. Zulus - Medicine. 3. Shamans - South Africa. 4. Zulus - Religion. I. Fogelqvist, Anders. II. Series: Kiel. Universität. Museum für Völkerkunde. Arbeiten, 7. II. Title.
DT878.Z9 S32 1984   **NYPL [Sc E 87-271]**

Schmidt, Cynthia E. Cuttington University College. Africana Museum. Rock of the ancestors . Suakoko, Liberia , c1977. 102 p. :   DDC 730/.09666/2074096662 19
N7399.L4 C87 1977   **NYPL [Sc F 89-27]**

Schmidt, Nancy J. Sub-Saharan African films and filmmakers : an annotated bibliography / Nancy J. Schmidt. London : Zell, 1988. 401 p. ; 22 cm. Includes index.   ISBN 0-905450-32-9 :   DDC 016.79143/096 19
1. Moving-pictures - Africa, Sub-Saharan - Bibliography. I. Title.
NYPL [Sc D 89-196]

Schneider, Bertrand. L'Afrique face à ses priorités /. Paris , c1987. 144 p. ;   ISBN 2-7178-1296-2   **NYPL [Sc E 88-291]**

Schneider, Edgar W. (Edgar Werner), 1954- [Morphologische und syntaktische Variablen im amerikanischen early black English. English]
American earlier Black English : morphology and syntactic variables / Edgar W. Schneider. Tuscaloosa : University of Alabama Press, 1989. xiv, 314 p. : ill. ; 25 cm. Translation of: Morphologische und syntaktische Variablen im amerikanischen early black English. Bibliography: p. 289-314.   ISBN 0-8173-0436-3   DDC 427/.973/08996 19
1. Black English. 2. English language - Syntax. 3. English language - Morphology. 4. English language - United States. I. Title.
PE3102.N43 S3613 1989
NYPL [Sc E 89-210]

Schnorr von Carolsfeld, Julius, 1794-1872. [Bibel in Bildern. Selections]
Bibele hi swifaniso : ti huma eka testamente ya khale ni ka Testamente Leyintshwa / swifaniso swi lulamisiwile hi Schnorr von Carolsfeld ; xitsonga xi tsariwile hi Nwagumana J. Maleyana. Kensington, Tvl. : Swiss Mission in S.A., 1970. 64 p. : chiefly col. ill. ; 26 cm. Selections from Die Bibel in Bildern, with explanatory text in Tsonga.
1. Tsonga language - Texts. I. Maleyana, Nwagumana J. II. Title.   **NYPL [Sc E 89-180]**

SCHOLASTIC SUCCESS. see ACADEMIC ACHIEVEMENT.

Schomburg Children's Colecction. Randall, Blossom E. Fun for Chris /. Chicago , c1956. 26 p. :   **NYPL [Sc E 88-238]**

Schomburg Children's Colltction. Holdridge, Betty. Island boy /. New York , c1942. 110 p. :
NYPL [Sc D 88-1181]

Schomburg Children's Collection.
Aardema, Verna. Princess Gorilla and a new kind of water . New York , 1988. [32] p. :   ISBN 0-8037-0412-7 :   DDC 398.2/0966 E 19
PZ8.1.A213 Pr 1987   **NYPL [Sc F 88-133]**

Aardema, Verna. The sky-god stories /. New York , c1960. [50] p. :   **NYPL [Sc D 89-83]**

Ajoṣe, Audrie. Emo and the Babalawo /. Ibadan , 1985. 51 p. :   ISBN 978-15-5652-2 (Nigeria)   **NYPL [Sc C 88-152]**

Alcock, Gudrun. Turn the next corner. New York [1969] 160 p.   DDC [Fic]
PZ7.A332 Tu   **NYPL [Sc D 88-1471]**

Allen, William Dangaix, 1904- Africa. Grand Rapids [c1972] 172, 20 p.   DDC 916
DT5 .A53 1972   **NYPL [Sc F 88-377]**

Anderson, Joan. A Williamsburg household /. New York , c1988. [48] p. :   ISBN 0-89919-516-4 :   DDC [Fic] 19
PZ7.A5367 Wi 1988   **NYPL [Sc F 88-242]**

Appiah, Peggy. Why there are so many roads /. Lagos , 1972. 62 p. :   **NYPL [Sc C 88-12]**

Appiah, Sonia. Amoko and Efua bear /. New York, NY , 1989, c1988. [30] p. :   ISBN 0-02-705591-4   DDC E 19
PZ7.A647 Am 1989   **NYPL [Sc F 89-138]**

Arkhurst, Joyce Cooper. More adventures of Spider . New York , c1972. 48 p. :
NYPL [Sc D 88-1449]

Around the city /. New York , c1965. 127 p. :
NYPL [Sc E 89-17]

Arundel, Jocelyn, 1930- Mighty Mo . New York , 1961. 124 p. :   *NYPL [Sc E 88-228]*

Babcock, Bernie Smade, 1868-1962. Hallerloogy's ride with Santa Claus. Perry, Ark., c1943. 48 p. *PZ7.B12 Hal*   *NYPL [Sc D 88-1285]*

Bacmeister, Rhoda Warner, 1893- Voices in the night /. Indianapolis , 1965. 117 p. :   *NYPL [Sc D 88-382]*

Baker, Augusta. (comp) The golden lynx and other tales. Philadelphia [1960] 160 p. *PZ8.1.B172 Go*   *NYPL [Sc D 88-1492]*

Barker, Carol. Village in Nigeria /. London , c19. 25 p. : ISBN 0-7136-2391-8 : DDC 966.9/05 19 *DT515.8 .B29 1984*   *NYPL [Sc D 88-605]*

Bateman, Walter L. The Kung of the Kalahari. Boston [1970] 128 p. ISBN 0-8070-1898-8 DDC 301.2 *DT764.B8 B3*   *NYPL [Sc E 88-550]*

Benedict, Niyi. The tortoise & the dog . Ilupeju, Lagos , 1988. 21 p. :   *NYPL [Sc E 88-599]*

Bland, Joy. Teddy the toucan . Bridgetown, Barbados , 1987 ; (Barbados : Caribbean Graphic Production) 20 p. :   *NYPL [Sc E 88-478]*

Bleeker, Sonia. The Ibo of Biafra. New York [1969] 160 p. DDC 916.69/4 *DT515 .B54*   *NYPL [Sc C 88-361]*

Bontemps, Arna Wendell, 1902- Mr. Kelso's lion. Philadelphia [1970] 48 p. DDC [Fic] *PZ7.B6443 Mi*   *NYPL [Sc D 88-1493]*

Boston, L. M. (Lucy Maria), 1892- Treasure of Green Knowe. New York [1958] 185 p. DDC [Fic] *PZ7.B6497 Tr*   *NYPL [Sc D 88-1497]*

Bothwell, Jean. By sail and wind . London , New York , c1964. 152 p. :   *NYPL [Sc D 89-103]*

Bradman, Tony. Wait and see /. New York, NY , 1988. [28] p. : ISBN 0-19-520644-4 DDC [E] 19 *PZ7.B7275 Wai 1988*   *NYPL [Sc D 89-255]*

Brandon, Brumsic. Outta sight, Luther! New York [c1971] 1 v. (chiefly illus.) ISBN 0-8397-6481-2 DDC 741.5/973 *PN6728.L8 B7*   *NYPL [Sc B 88-54]*

Branley, Franklyn Mansfield, 1915- Eclipse . New York , c1988. 32 p. : ISBN 0-690-04619-7 (lib. bdg.) : DDC 523.7/8 19 *QB541.5 .B73 1988*   *NYPL [Sc E 88-591]*

Branner, John Casper, 1850-1922. How and why stories /. New York , 1921. xi, 104 p. :   *NYPL [Sc D 89-104]*

Brothers, Aileen. Just one me /. Chicago , c1967. 32 p. :   *NYPL [Sc D 88-376]*

Brown, Virginia. Out jumped Abraham /. St. Louis , c1967. 94 p. :   *NYPL [Sc D 89-542]*

Buckley, Peter. Five friends at school /. New York , c1966. 96 p. :   *NYPL [Sc E 88-590]*

Buckley, Peter. Five friends at school /. New York , c1966. 96 p. :   *NYPL [Sc E 88-590]*

Buckley, Peter. William, Andy and Ramón. 1966. 70 p.   *NYPL [Sc E 89-41]*

Burchardt, Nellie. Project cat /. New York, N.Y. , c1966. 66 p. :   *NYPL [Sc D 89-435]*

Burgwyn, Mebane (Holoman) Lucky mischief /. New York , 1949. 246 p. :   *NYPL [Sc D 88-1513]*

Burgwyn, Mebane (Holoman) River treasure. New York, 1947. 159 p. *PZ7.B9177 Ri*   *NYPL [Sc D 89-512]*

Burroughs, Margaret Taylor, 1917- (comp) Did you feed my cow? Chicago [1969] 96 p. ISBN 0-695-81960-7 DDC 398.8 *PZ8.3.B958 Di5*   *NYPL [Sc D 89-57]*

Caballero, Armando O. Antonio Maceo, la protesta de Baraguá . La Habana , 1977. 30, [1] p. :   *NYPL [Sc F 88-281]*

Caines, Jeannette Franklin. I need a lunch box /. New York , c1988. [32] p. : ISBN 0-06-020984-4 : DDC [E] 19 *PZ7.C12 Iaan 1988*   *NYPL [Sc D 88-1504]*

Caldwell, John C. Let's visit the West Indies.

London, Eng. , c1983. 96 p. : ISBN 0-222-00920-9   *NYPL [Sc D 89-19]*

Caldwell, John C. (John Cope), 1913- Let's visit middle Africa. New York [1961] 96 p. DDC 916.7 *DT352 .C3*   *NYPL [Sc D 88-507]*

Cameron, Ann, 1943- Julian, secret agent /. New York , 1988. 62 p. : ISBN 0-394-91949-1 (lib. bdg.) : DDC [Fic] 19 *PZ7.C1427 Jt 1988*   *NYPL [Sc C 89-123]*

Cameron, Ann, 1943- Julian's glorious summer /. New York , c1987. 62 p. : ISBN 0-394-89117-1 (pbk.) : DDC [Fic] 19 *PZ7.C1427 Ju 1987*   *NYPL [Sc C 89-99]*

Cameron, Ann, 1943- The stories Julian tells /. New York : c1987, c1981. 71 p. : ISBN 0-394-82892-5   *NYPL [Sc C 89-93]*

Carma, Jemel. Happy birthday everybody . New York, N. Y. [1988] [24] p. :   *NYPL [Sc H 89-1]*

Caudill, Rebecca, 1899- A certain small shepherd /. New York , 1965. 48 p. :   *NYPL [Sc D 88-433]*

Chandler, Ruth Forbes. Ladder to the sky /. London , New York , c1959. 189 p. :   *NYPL [Sc D 88-1107]*

Chenfeld, Mimi Brodsky. The house at 12 Rose Street. London , New York, 1966. 157 p. DDC [Fic] *PZ7.C4183 Ho*   *NYPL [Sc D 88-509]*

Chukwuka, J. I. N. Zandi and the wonderful pillow /. Lagos, Nigeria , 1977. 48 p. : ISBN 0-410-80099-6   *NYPL [Sc C 88-76]*

Clark, Margaret Goff. Freedom crossing. New York [1969] 128 p. DDC [Fic] *PZ7.C5487 Fr*   *NYPL [Sc D 88-1121]*

Clifton, Lucille, 1936- Everett Anderson's friend /. New York , c1976. [25] p. : ISBN 0-03-015161-9 (lib. bdg.) DDC [E] *PZ8.3.C573 Evg*   *NYPL [Sc D 88-1505]*

Clifton, Lucille, 1936- Everett Anderson's nine month long /. New York , c1978. [31] p. : ISBN 0-03-043536-6 DDC [E] *PZ8.3.C573 Evk*   *NYPL [Sc D 89-30]*

Clifton, Lucille, 1936- My friend Jacob /. New York , c1980. [32] p. : ISBN 0-525-35487-5 DDC [E] *PZ7.C6224 Myk 1980*   *NYPL [Sc F 88-376]*

Clymer, Eleanor (Lowenton) 1906- The house on the mountain. New York [1971] 39 p. ISBN 0-525-32365-1 DDC [Fic] *PZ7.C6272 Ho*   *NYPL [Sc D 88-445]*

Coatsworth, Elizabeth Jane, 1893- Ronnie and the Chief's son. New York, 1962. 38 p. *PZ7.C6294 Ro*   *NYPL [Sc E 89-23]*

Contes et histoires d'Afrique. Dakar , c1977- v. : ISBN 2-7236-0159-5 (v. 1) DDC 741.5/967 19 *PZ24.1 .C6328 1977*   *NYPL [Sc F 87-184]*

Cosby, William H. The wit and wisdom of Fat Albert. New York [1973] [64] p. ISBN 0-525-61004-9 DDC 818/.5/407 *PZ8.7.C6 Wi*   *NYPL [Sc C 89-26]*

Dangana, Yahaya S. The barber's nine children /. Yaba, Lagos , 1987. 17 p. ; ISBN 978-13-2850-9   *NYPL [Sc C 89-24]*

Davis, Russell G. Land in the sun. Boston [1963] 92 p.   *NYPL [Sc F 88-365]*

De Angeli, Marguerite, 1899- Thee, Hannah /. New York , 1940. [88] p. :   *NYPL [Sc D 88-635]*

De Villiers, Helene. (comp) Die Sprokiesboom en ander verhale uit Midde-Afrika. Kaapstad, 1970. 84 p.; *P214 .D43*   *NYPL [Sc D 89-373]*

Dean, Leigh. The looking down game. New York [1968] 34 p. DDC [Fic] *PZ7.D3446 Lo*   *NYPL [Sc D 89-111]*

Dee, Ruby. Two ways to count to ten . New York , c1988. [32] p. : ISBN 0-8050-0407-6 : DDC 398.2/096 E 19 *PZ8.1.D378 Tw 1988*   *NYPL [Sc F 88-311]*

Detroit. Great Cities Program for School Improvement. Writers' Committee. A day with Debbie /. Chicago , c1964. 55 p. :   *NYPL [Sc E 89-178]*

Detroit. Great Cities Program for School Improvement. Writers' Committee. Laugh with Larry /. Chicago , c1962.   *NYPL [Sc E 87-268]*

Detroit. Great Cities Program for School Improvement. Writes' Committee. Fun with David /. Chicago , c1962. 31 p.:   *NYPL [Sc E 89-40]*

Diekmann, Miep. Padu is gek /. Den Haag , 1960. 120 p. ;   *NYPL [Sc D 89-474]*

Dragonwagon, Crescent. Strawberry dress escape /. New York [1975] [32] p. : ISBN 0-684-13912-X :   *NYPL [Sc F 88-126]*

Drisko, Carol F. The unfinished march. Garden City, N.Y. , 1967. 118 p. : DDC 973.8 (j) *E185.6 .D7*   *NYPL [Sc D 88-1429]*

Duczman, Linda. The baby-sitter /. Milwaukee , Chicago , c1977. 30 p. : ISBN 0-8172-0065-7 (lib. bdg.) : DDC 649/.1 *HQ772.5 .D8*   *NYPL [Sc E 88-588]*

Eager, Edward. The well-wishers /. New York , c1960. 191 p. :   *NYPL [Sc D 88-429]*

Edwards, Pat, 1922- Little John and Plutie /. Boston , 1988. 172 p. : ISBN 0-395-48223-2 DDC [Fic] 19 *PZ7.E2637 Li 1988*   *NYPL [Sc D 89-126]*

Elkin, Benjamin. Why the sun was late /. New York , 1966. [40] p. : *PZ7.#426 Wh*   *NYPL [Sc F 88-105]*

Elliot, Geraldine. Where the leopard passes . New York, 1987. x, 125 p. :   *NYPL [Sc D 88-840]*

Elting, Mary, 1909- A Mongo homecoming. New York [1969] 54 p. DDC 309.1/675 *DT644 .E4*   *NYPL [Sc E 88-578]*

Elting, Mary, 1909- Patch /. Garden City, N.Y. , 1948. 156 p. : *PZ7.E53Pat*   *NYPL [Sc C 89-14]*

Ferris, Jeri. Go free or die . Minneapolis , 1987. 63 p. : ISBN 0-87614-317-6 (lib. bdg.) : DDC 305.5/67/0924 B 92 19 *E444.T82 F47 1987*   *NYPL [Sc D 88-620]*

Ferris, Jeri. Walking the road to freedom . Minneapolis, 1987. 64 p. : ISBN 0-87614-318-4 (lib. bdg.) : DDC 305.5/67/0924 B 92 19 *E185.97.T8 F47 1987*   *NYPL [Sc D 88-1046]*

Ferris, Jeri. What are you figuring now? . Minneapolis , c1988. 64 p. : ISBN 0-87614-331-1 (lib. bdg.) : DDC 520.92/4 B 92 19 *QB36.B22 F47 1988*   *NYPL [Sc D 89-120]*

Fields, Julia. The green lion of Zion Street /. New York , c1988. [32] p. : ISBN 0-689-50414-4 DDC [E] 19 *PZ8.3.F458 Gr 1988*   *NYPL [Sc F 88-186]*

Fischer, Erling Gunnar. Peter är barnvakt /. Stockholm , 1961. [40] p. :   *NYPL [Sc F 88-261]*

Fisher, Aileen Lucia, 1906- Animal jackets. [Glendale, Calif., 1973] 43 p. ISBN 0-8372-0861-0 DDC [E] *PZ8.3.F634 Ap*   *NYPL [Sc F 88-87]*

Fisher, Aileen Lucia, 1906- A lantern in the window /. Eau Claire, Wisconsin [1962] 126 p. :   *NYPL [Sc D 88-434]*

Fisher, Aileen Lucia, 1906- Seeds on the go /. [Los Angeles] , c1977. 43 p. : ISBN 0-8372-2400-4 DDC 582/.01/6 *QK929 .F57*   *NYPL [Sc F 88-344]*

Fitch, Robert Beck, 1938- Right on Dellums! Mankato, Minn. [1971] [47] p. ISBN 0-87191-079-9 DDC 329/.023/79405 *JK1978 .F53*   *NYPL [Sc F 88-338]*

Fleming, Elizabeth P. The Takula tree. Philadelphia, 1964. 175 p. *PZ7.F5995 Tak*   *NYPL [Sc D 88-508]*

Freed, Arthur. Games /. [N.J.] , 1968. [32] p. :   *NYPL [Sc B 89-25]*

Gambia. Amersham , 1984. 16 p. : ISBN 0-7175-1046-8 (pbk) DDC 966/.5103 19 *DT509.22*   *NYPL [Sc D 88-1182]*

Garden, Nancy. What happened in Marston. New York [1971] 190 p. DDC [Fic] *PZ7.G165 Wh*   *NYPL [Sc D 89-98]*

Gardner, Lillian, 1907- Sal Fisher at Girl Scout

camp. New York [1959] 217 p.
PZ7.G1793 Saj   **NYPL [Sc D 88-1494]**

Garlake, Peter S. Life at Great Zimbabwe /.
Gweru, Zimbabwe , 1983, c1982. [36] p. :
ISBN 0-86922-180-9 (pbk.)   DDC 968.91 19
DT962.9.G73 G374 1983
                             NYPL [Sc F 88-175]

Gedö, Leopold. [Janiból Jonny lesz. English.]
Who is Johnny? /. New York , 1939. 242 p. :
                             NYPL [Sc D 88-1512]

Gerber, Will. Gooseberry Jones /. New York ,
c1947. 96 p. :   **NYPL [Sc D 89-442]**

Gilstrap, Robert. The sultan's fool and other
North African tales /. New York , c1958. 95
p. : ISBN 931-40-0118-0   **NYPL [Sc E 88-548]**

Giovanni, Nikki. Vacation time . New York ,
1980. 59 p. : ISBN 0-688-03657-0   DDC 811/.54
PS3557.I55 V3   **NYPL [Sc D 89-69]**

Gipson, Fred. The trail-driving rooster /. New
York : Harper & Row, c1955. 79 p. :
                             NYPL [Sc D 88-427]

Glasser, Barbara. Bongo Bradley. New York
[1973] 153 p. DDC [Fic]
PZ7.G48143 Bo   **NYPL [Sc D 89-99]**

Glendinning, Sally. Jimmy and Joe fly a kite.
Champaign, Ill. [1970] 38 p. ISBN 0-8116-4704-8
DDC [Fic]
PZ7.G4829 Jm   **NYPL [Sc D 88-1475]**

Glendinning, Sally. Jimmy and Joe look for a
bear. Champaign, Ill., 1970. 40 p. ISBN
0-8116-4703-X   DDC [E]
PZ7.G4829 Jo   **NYPL [Sc D 88-1456]**

Glendinning, Sally. Jimmy and Joe meet a
Halloween witch. Champaign, Ill. [1971] 40 p.
ISBN 0-8116-4705-6   DDC [E]
PZ7.G4829 Jq   **NYPL [Sc D 88-1474]**

Gles, Margaret. Come play hide and seek /.
Champaign, Ill. [1975] 32 p. : ISBN
0-8116-6053-2
PZ7.G4883 Co   **NYPL [Sc D 89-119]**

Gray, Genevieve. A kite for Bennie. New York,
1972. [40] p. ISBN 0-07-024197-X   DDC [Fic]
PZ7.G7774 Ki   **NYPL [Sc E 88-422]**

Gray, Nigel. A balloon for grandad /. London ,
New York , 1988. [30] p. : ISBN 0-531-05755-0 :
DDC [E] 19
PZ7.G7813 Bal 1988   **NYPL [Sc F 88-345]**

Greenberg, Keith Elliot. Whitney Houston /.
Minneapolis , c1988. 32 p. : ISBN 0-8225-1619-5
(lib. bdg.)   DDC 784.5/0092/4 B 92 19
ML3930.H7 G7 1988   **NYPL [Sc D 88-1459]**

Greene, Roberta. Two and me makes three.
New York [1970] [36] p.
PZ7.G843 Tw   **NYPL [Sc F 88-375]**

Greenfield, Eloise. First pink light /. New
York, c1976. [39] p. : ISBN 0-690-01087-7
DDC [E]
PZ7.G845 Fi   **NYPL [Sc D 89-60]**

Greenfield, Eloise. Grandpa's face /. New
York , 1988. [32] p. : ISBN 0-399-21525-5   DDC
[E] 19
PZ7.G845 Gs 1988   **NYPL [Sc F 88-387]**

Greenfield, Eloise. Honey, I love, and other
love poems /. New York , c1978. [48] p. :
ISBN 0-690-01334-5 (lib. bdg.)   DDC 811/.5/4
PS3557.R39416 H66 1978
                             NYPL [Sc C 89-22]

Greenfield, Eloise. Talk about a family /. New
York , c1978. 60 p. : ISBN 0-590-42247-2
                             NYPL [Sc C 89-79]

Griffin, Michael. A family in Kenya /.
Minneapolis , 1988, c1987. 31 p. : ISBN
0-8225-1680-2 (lib. bdg.) : DDC 306.8/5/096762
19
HQ692.5 .G75 1988   **NYPL [Sc C 89-6]**

Gross, Mary Anne. (comp) Ah, man, you found
me again. Boston [1972] x, 84 p. ISBN
0-8070-1532-6   DDC 810/.8/09282
HQ792.U53 N53 1972   **NYPL [Sc F 88-336]**

Haskins, James, 1941- Jobs in business and
office. New York [1974] 96 p. ISBN
0-688-75011-7   DDC 651/.023
HF5381.2 .H38   **NYPL [Sc E 89-16]**

Hawkinson, Lucy (Ozone) 1924- That new river
train. Chicago [c1970] [32] p. ISBN

0-8075-7823-1   DDC 781/.96
PZ8.3.H315 Th   **NYPL [Sc C 89-59]**

Hays, Wilma Pitchford. The goose that was a
watchdog. Boston [1967] 41 p. DDC [Fic]
PZ7.H31493 Go   **NYPL [Sc D 88-1426]**

Haywood, Carolyn, 1898- Away went the
balloons. New York, 1973. 189 p. ISBN
0-688-20057-5   DDC [Fic]
PZ7.H31496 Aw   **NYPL [Sc D 89-113]**

Hearn, Michael Patrick. The porcelain cat /.
Boston [1987?]. [32] p. : ISBN 0-316-35330-2
(pbk.) :   **NYPL [Sc F 88-220]**

Hernandez, Helen. The maroons-- who are
they? /. Kingston , c1983. 28 p. :
                             NYPL [Sc D 88-378]

Hodges, Elizabeth Jamison. Free as a frog.
[Reading, Mass., c1969] [32] p. DDC [Fic]
PZ7.H6634 Fr   **NYPL [Sc D 88-1126]**

Hopkins, Lee Bennett. This street's for me!
New York [1970] [38] p.
PZ8.3.H776 Th   **NYPL [JFE 72-966]**

Hopkins, Marjorie. And the jackal played the
masinko. New York [1969] [41] p. ISBN
0-8193-0271-6
PZ7.H7756 An   **NYPL [JFF 72-292]**

Horvath, Betty F. Hooray for Jasper. New York
[1966] 1 v. (unpaged)
PZ7.H7922 Ho   **NYPL [Sc F 88-252]**

Horvath, Betty F. Jasper makes music. New
York [1967] [38] p. DDC [E]
PZ7.H7922 Jas   **NYPL [Sc F 88-343]**

Horvath, Betty F. Not enough Indians. New
York [1971] [47] p. ISBN 0-531-01968-3   DDC
[Fic]
PZ7.H7922 No   **NYPL [Sc F 88-341]**

Howard, Elizabeth Fitzgerald. The train to
Lulu's /. New York , c1988. [32] p. : ISBN
0-02-744620-4 : DDC [E] 19
PZ7.H8327 Tr 1988   **NYPL [Sc F 88-219]**

Howard, Moses L., 1928- The ostrich chase /.
New York [1974] 118 p. : ISBN 0-03-012096-9
                             NYPL [Sc D 88-374]

Howell, Ruth Rea. A crack in the pavement.
New York, 1970. [48] p. DDC 500.9
PZ10.H7958 Cr   **NYPL [Sc E 88-154]**

Hubbard, Wynant Davis. Wild animal hunter /.
New York [1958] 148 p. :
                             NYPL [Sc D 88-1130]

Huston, Anne. Ollie's go-kart. New York
[1971] 143 p. DDC [Fic]
PZ7.H959 Ol   **NYPL [Sc D 88-1472]**

In the city /. New York , c1965. 32 p.
                             NYPL [Sc D 89-82]

Iremonger, Lucille. West Indian folk-tales.
London [1956] 64 p.
GR120 .I7   **NYPL [Sc C 89-157]**

Iroaganachi, John. A fight for honey /. Lagos,
Nigeria , 1977. 30 p. : ISBN 0-410-80181-X
                             NYPL [Sc C 88-77]

Isadora, Rachel. Willaby /. New York , c1977.
[32] p. : ISBN 0-02-747746-0   DDC [E]
PZ7.I763 Wi   **NYPL [Sc F 88-374]**

Jacobsen, Peter Otto. A family in West Africa
/. Hove , 1985. 32 p. : ISBN 0-85078-434-4 :
DDC 966/.305 19
DA588   **NYPL [Sc D 88-1499]**

James, Winston. The Caribbean /. London ,
1984. 46 p. : ISBN 0-356-07105-7 : DDC 972.9
19
F2175   **NYPL [Sc F 88-128]**

The Jeep. Leicester [Eng.] , Montreal Canada
[195-?] [8] p. :   **NYPL [Sc C 88-325]**

Jensen, Virginia Allen. Sara and the door /.
Reading, Mass. , c1977. [32] p. : ISBN
0-201-03446-8   DDC [E]
PZ8.3.J425 Sar   **NYPL [Sc B 89-17]**

Johnson, Angela. Tell me a story, Mama /.
New York , c1989. [32] p. : ISBN
0-531-05794-1 : DDC [E] 19
PZ7.J629 Te 1988   **NYPL [Sc F 89-109]**

Johnson, Eric W. The stolen ruler. Philadelphia
[1970] 64 p. DDC [Fic]
PZ7.J631765 St   **NYPL [Sc D 88-1114]**

Justus, May, 1898- New boy in school. New

York [1963] 56 p. DDC [Fic]
PZ7.J986 Ng   **NYPL [Sc E 89-25]**

Kalibala, E. Balintuma. Wakaima and the clay
man . New York , 1946. 145 p. :
                             NYPL [Sc D 89-486]

Kaufman, Curt. Hotel boy /. New York ,
c1987. 40 p. : ISBN 0-689-31287-3 : DDC
307.3/36 19
HV4046.N6 K38 1987   **NYPL [Sc F 88-362]**

Kaula, Edna Mason. The land and people of
Tanzania. Philadelphia [1972] 139 p. ISBN
0-397-31270-9   DDC 916.78
DT438 .K33   **NYPL [Sc D 88-1112]**

Kaye, Geraldine, 1925- Koto and the lagoon.
New York [1969, c1967] 128 p. DDC [Fic]
PZ7.K212 Ko3   **NYPL [Sc D 89-159]**

Keats, Ezra Jack. Da Snøen Kom /. [Norway] ,
1967. [20] p. :   **NYPL [Sc D 88-467]**

Kelley, Sally. Summer growing time. New York
[1971] 125 p. ISBN 0-670-68172-5   DDC [Fic]
PZ7.K2818 Su   **NYPL [Sc D 89-88]**

Kenworthy, Leonard Stout, 1912- Profile of
Nigeria /. Garden City, New York , c1960. 96
p. :   **NYPL [Sc D 88-240]**

Kindred, Wendy. Negatu in the garden. New
York [1971] [38] p. ISBN 0-07-034585-6   DDC
[E]
PZ7.K567 Ne   **NYPL [Sc F 88-246]**

Kirkpatrick, Oliver. Naja the snake and Mangus
the mongoose. Garden City, N.Y. [1970] 40 p.
DDC [Fic]
PZ7.K6358 Naj   **NYPL [Sc F 88-339]**

Krinsky, Norman. Art for city children. New
York [1970] 96 p. DDC 372.5/2
N350 .K7   **NYPL [Sc F 88-378]**

Kushner, Arlene. Falasha no more . New
York , c1986. 58 p. : ISBN 0-933503-55-5
                             NYPL [Sc F 88-107]

Lang, Don. Strawberry roan /. New York ,
1946. 218 p. :   **NYPL [Sc D 88-646]**

Lattimore, Eleanor Frances, 1904- Indigo Hill.
New York, 1950. 128 p. DDC [Fic]
PZ7.L37 In   **NYPL [Sc D 88-1428]**

Lauber, Patricia. The Congo, river into central
Africa. Champaign, Ill. [1964] 96 p. DDC 967
DT639 .L38   **NYPL [Sc E 89-24]**

Lawrence, James Duncan, 1918- Binky
brothers, detectives. New York [1968] 60 p.
DDC [Fic]
PZ7.L4359 Bi   **NYPL [Sc D 89-118]**

Lewis, Richard W. A summer adventure /.
New York , c1962. 105 p. :
                             NYPL [Sc D 89-405]

Lexau, Joan M. Don't be my valentine /. New
York, N.Y. , c1985. 64 p. : ISBN
0-06-023872-0 : DDC [E] 19
PZ7.L5895 Dp 1985   **NYPL [Sc D 89-58]**

Linde, Freda. Toto and the aardvark. Garden
City, N.Y. [1969] 59 p.
PZ7.L6574 To   **NYPL [JFE 72-633]**

Lindquist, Willis. The red drum's warning /.
New York , 1958. 128 p. :
                             NYPL [Sc D 88-662]

Lipkind, William, 1904- Four-leaf clover /.
New York , 1959. [32] p. :
                             NYPL [Sc F 89-22]

Little, Lessie Jones. Children of long ago . New
York , 1988. [32] p. : ISBN 0-399-21473-9   DDC
811/.54 19
PS3562.I78288 C5 1988
                             NYPL [Sc F 88-276]

Lovelace, Maud Hart, 1892- The valentine box
/. New York , 1966. [48] p. :
PZ7.L9561 Val   **NYPL [Sc D 89-115]**

Lynch, Lorenzo, 1932- The hot dog man.
Indianapolis [1970] [24] p. DDC [Fic]
PZ7.L97977 Ho   **NYPL [Sc F 88-253]**

Mabery, D. L. Janet Jackson /. Minneapolis ,
c1988. 32 p. : ISBN 0-8225-1618-7 (lib. bdg.) :
DDC 784.5/4/00924 B 920 19
ML3930.J15 M3 1988
                             NYPL [Sc D 88-1460]

McCall, Virginia, 1909- Adassa and her hen.
[New York, 1971] 79 p. DDC [Fic]
PZ7.M12295 Ad   **NYPL [Sc D 89-100]**

McKissack, Pat, 1944- Nettie Jo's friends /.
New York , 1989. [33] p. : ISBN 0-394-89158-9
DDC [E] 19
PZ7.M478693 Ne 1989 **NYPL [Sc F 89-143]**

Martin, Patricia Miles. The little brown hen.
New York [1960] 23 p.
PZ7 .M36418 Li **NYPL [Sc D 88-1495]**

Martin, Robert, 1929- Yesterday's people.
Garden City, N.Y. [1970] 158 p. DDC 916.8/03
DT764.B8 M35 **NYPL [Sc F 88-248]**

Mary Marguerite, Sister, 1895- Martin's mice.
Chicago [1954] 32 p.
PZ8.1.M38 Mar **NYPL [Sc G 88-28]**

May, Charles Paul. Stranger in the storm.
London, New York [1972] 92 p. ISBN
0-200-71821-5 DDC [Fic]
PZ7.M4505 St **NYPL [Sc D 88-1430]**

May, Chris. Bob Marley /. London , 1985. 60
p. : ISBN 0-241-11476-4 : DDC 784.5 B 19
ML420.M3313 M4 1985
NYPL [Sc D 88-308]

Meshover, Leonard. You visit a dairy [and a]
clothing factory /. Chicago , c1965. 48 p. :
NYPL [Sc D 89-545]

Mille, Pierre, 1864-1931. Line en Nouvelle
Calédonie /. Paris , c1934. 32, 1 p. :
NYPL [Sc F 89-20]

Milsome, John, 1924- From slave boy to
bishop . Cambridge , 1987. [96] p. ; ISBN
0-7188-2678-7 (pbk) : DDC 283/.092/4 19
BV3625.N6C7 **NYPL [Sc C 88-106]**

Mirsky, Reba Paeff. Nomusa and the new
magic. Chicago, 1962. 190 p.
PZ7.M675 No **NYPL [Sc E 89-175]**

Molarsky, Osmond. Where the good luck was.
New York [1970] 63 p. ,ISBN 0-8098-1158-8
DDC [Fic]
PZ7.M7317 Wh **NYPL [Sc E 88-552]**

Moon, Bernice. Kenya is my country /. Hove ,
1985. 60 p. : ISBN 0-85078-489-1 : DDC
967.6/204 19 **NYPL [Sc F 88-379]**

Mooney, Elizabeth Comstock. The Sandy Shoes
mystery. Philadelphia [1970] 128 p. DDC [Fic]
PZ7.M78 San **NYPL [Sc D 89-96]**

Moore, Emily. Whose side are you on? /. New
York , 1988. 133 p. ; ISBN 0-374-38409-6
NYPL [Sc D 88-1330]

Morgan, Kemi. Legends from Yorubaland /.
Ibadan, Nigeria , 1988. iii, 100 p. : ISBN
978-246-003-6 **NYPL [Sc C 88-344]**

Morse, Evangeline. Brown Rabbit: her story.
Chicago [1967] 191 p.
PZ7.M84586 Br **NYPL [Sc D 89-89]**

Mwenye Hadithi. Tricky Tortoise /. Boston ,
c1988. [32] p. : ISBN 0-316-33724-2 : DDC [E]
19
PZ7.M975 Tr 1988 **NYPL [Sc F 88-389]**

Myers, Walter Dean, 1937- Me, Mop, and the
Moondance Kid /. New York , 1988. 154 p. :
ISBN 0-440-50065-6 DDC [Fic] 19
PZ7.M992 Me 1988 **NYPL [Sc D 88-1457]**

Napjus, Alice James. Freddie found a frog.
New York [1969] [29] p. DDC [Fic]
PZ7.N148 Fr **NYPL [Sc C 89-27]**

Nevin, Evelyn C. Underground escape /.
Philadelphia , c1926. 191 p. :
NYPL [Sc D 88-1506]

Norton, Browning, 1909- Johnny/Bingo. New
York [1971] 185 p. DDC [Fic]
PZ7.N8217 Jo **NYPL [Sc D 88-1420]**

Ntrakwah, Abena. Ama goes to the library /.
Accra , 1987. 16 p. : **NYPL [Sc F 88-352]**

Obadiah. I am a Rastafarian /. London , New
York , c1986. 32 p. : ISBN 0-86313-260-X :
BL2532.R37 **NYPL [Sc F 89-12]**

Odedeyi, M. B. Yoruba dun ka . London , New
York , 1965. 75 p. : **NYPL [Sc C 88-275]**

Olsen, Aileen. Bernadine and the water bucket
/. London , New York, 1966. [41] p :
NYPL [Sc F 88-99]

Osahon, Naiwu. Alphabets and careers /.
Apapa, Lagos, Nigeria , 1981. [32] p. : ISBN
978-18-6006-5 **NYPL [Sc F 88-295]**

Osahon, Naiwu. The hawk and the eagle /.

Apapa, Lagos, Nigeria , 1981. [22] p. : ISBN
978-18-6007-3 **NYPL [Sc D 89-225]**

Osahon, Naiwu, 1937- The land of the spirits /.
Apapa, Lagos, Nigeria , 1981. [30] p. : ISBN
978-18-6008-1 **NYPL [Sc D 89-226]**

Osahon, Naiwu, 1937- Laruba and the two
wicked men /. Apapa, Lagos, Nigeria , 1981.
[22] p. : ISBN 978-18-6004-9
NYPL [Sc D 89-224]

Osahon, Naiwu, 1937- Madam Universe sent
man /. Apapa, Lagos, Nigeria , 1981. [22] p. :
ISBN 978-18-6002-2 **NYPL [Sc D 89-223]**

Osahon, Naiwu, 1937- The missing gold ring /.
Apapa, Lagos, Nigeria , c1981. [24] p. : ISBN
978-18-6000-6
MLCS 85/698 (P) **NYPL [Sc D 89-222]**

Osahon, Naiwu, 1937- Odu and Onah /.
Apapa, Lagos, Nigeria , 1981. [22] p. :
NYPL [Sc D 89-227]

Osahon, Naiwu, 1937- Right-on Miss Moon /.
Apapa, Lagos, Nigeria , 1981. [22] p. : ISBN
978-18-6003-0 **NYPL [Sc D 89-228]**

Owen, Ruth Bryan, 1885- Caribbean caravel.
New York, 1949. viii, 222 p.
PZ7.O972 Car **NYPL [Sc D 88-426]**

Perkins, Carol Morse. The shattered skull .
New York, 1965. 59 p.,
DT440 .P4 **NYPL [Sc E 88-145]**

Persaud, Pat. Tipsy /. Kingston, Jamaica ,
c1986. [28] p. :
MLCS 87/7926 (P) **NYPL [Sc F 88-255]**

Picture parade. Akron [Ohio] , c1942. [36] p. :
NYPL [Sc F 88-262]

Pictures and stories from Uncle Tom's cabin.
Boston [c1853] [5],6-32p.
NYPL [Sc Rare C 89-1]

Pomerantz, Charlotte. The chalk doll /. New
York , c1989. 30 p. : ISBN 0-397-32318-2 :
DDC [E] 19
PZ7.P77 Ch 1989 **NYPL [Sc F 89-175]**

Powe, Edward L. (Edward Llewellyn), 1941-
The adventures of Dan Aiki /. Paterson, N.J. ,
c1987. 32 p. : **NYPL [Sc D 88-489]**

Quigg, Jane. Ted and Bobby look for something
special. New York [1969] 42, [3] p. DDC [Fic]
PZ7.Q333 Te3 **NYPL [Sc E 88-543]**

Radlauer, Ruth Shaw. Father is big. Glendale,
Calif. [1967] 1 v. (unpaged)
PZ7.R122 Fat **NYPL [Sc E 88-589]**

Raferty, Gerald. Twenty-dollar horse /. Eau
Claire, Wisconsin , 1967, c1955. 192 p. :
NYPL [Sc D 88-664]

Rees, Ennis. Brer Rabbit and his tricks. New
York [1967] 1 v. (unpaged)
PZ8.3.R254 Br **NYPL [Sc E 88-530]**

Regals, Leo. Henco ruimt op /. Curaçao
[1986?] 72 p. : ISBN 90-6435-111-2
MLCS 87/05319 (P) **NYPL [Sc D 88-490]**

Rémy, Mylène. Le masque volé /. Paris , 1987.
126 p. : ISBN 2-218-07832-5
NYPL [Sc C 88-311]

Ricciuti, Edward R. Donald and the fish that
walked /. New York [1974] 62 p. : ISBN
0-06-024997-8 : DDC 597/.52
QL638.C6 R52 1974 **NYPL [Sc D 88-447]**

Rieger, Shay. The bronze zoo. New York
[1970] [48] p. DDC 731.4/56
NB1143 .R5 **NYPL [Sc F 88-340]**

Rinkoff, Barbara. Rutherford T. finds 21 B.
New York [1970] [47] p. DDC [Fic]
PZ7.R477 Ru **NYPL [Sc D 88-1404]**

Roberts, Naurice. Harold Washington .
Chicago , 1988. 30 p. : ISBN 0-516-03657-2
DDC 977.3/1100496073024 B 92 19
F548.52.W36 R63 1988
NYPL [Sc E 88-501]

Rohmer, Harriet. The invisible hunters . San
Francisco , c1987. 32 p. : ISBN 0-89239-031-X :
DDC 398.2/08998 19
F1529.M9 R64 1987 **NYPL [Sc E 88-241]**

Rose, Karen. A single trail. Chicago [1969] 158
p. ISBN 0-695-44082-9 DDC [Fic]
PZ7.R717 Si **NYPL [Sc D 89-91]**

Roth, Susan L. Fire came to the earth people .
New York , 1988, c1987. [32] p. : ISBN

0-312-01723-5 : DDC 398.2/0966/83 E 19
PZ7.R73 Fi 1987 **NYPL [Sc F 89-140]**

Sadowsky, Ethel S. François and the langouste.
Boston [1969] 60 p. DDC [Fic]
PZ7.S127 Fr **NYPL [Sc D 88-1120]**

Saro-Wiwa, Ken. Mr. B /. Port Harcourt ,
Ewell , 1987. 154 p. : ISBN 1-87071-601-9 (pbk) :
DDC 823 19
PZ7 **NYPL [Sc C 88-300]**

Schatz, Letta. Bola and the Oba's drummer.
New York [1967]. 156 p. DDC [Fic] 19
PZ7.S337 Bo **NYPL [Sc E 89-26]**

Schatz, Letta. Taiwo and her twin /. New
York , c1964- 128 p. : **NYPL [Sc E 88-430]**

Scott, Ann Herbert. Let's catch a monster. New
York [1967] 1 v. (unpaged)
PZ7.S415 Le **NYPL [Sc F 88-342]**

Sealy, Adrienne V. The color your way into
Black history book /. Brooklyn, N.Y. , c1980.
51 p. : ISBN 0-9602670-6-9
NYPL [Sc F 89-36]

Sealy, Adrienne V. Mama--watch out, I'm
growingup! /. Brooklyn, New York , 1976. [45]
p. : **NYPL [Sc F 88-135]**

Shackelford, Jane Dabney. My happy days /.
Washington, D.C. , c1944. 121 p. :
NYPL [Sc F 88-337]

Shacklett, Juanita Purvis. Boloji and Old Hippo
/. New York , c1959. 121 p. :
NYPL [Sc D 88-1166]

Sherlock, Philip Manderson, Sir. Ears and tails
and common sense: more stories from the
Caribbean. London , 1982. xvii, 121 p.
NYPL [Sc D 88-1220]

Sherlock, Philip Manderson, Sir. The iguana's
tail. New York [1969] 97 p. DDC 823 398.2
PZ8.1.S54 Ig **NYPL [Sc D 89-59]**

Shotwell, Louisa Rossiter. Roosevelt Grady /.
Cleveland, Ohio , c1963. 151 p. :
NYPL [Sc D 88-1425]

Simon, Leonard J. Adam and the roof /. [New
Jersey? , 198-?] 36 p. : **NYPL [Sc B 89-28]**

Slater, Sandra. The dog, the bone, and the
wind . Ibadan, Nigeria , c1986. 30 p. : ISBN
0-19-575567-7
MLCS 88/07439 (P) **NYPL [Sc D 89-116]**

Stanley, Diane. Shaka, king of the Zulus /.
New York , c1988. [40] p. : ISBN 0-688-07342-5
DDC 968.04/092/4 B 92 19
DT878.Z9 C565 1988 **NYPL [Sc F 88-358]**

Steinman, Beatrice. This railroad disappears.
New York [1958] 181 p.
PZ7.S8266 Th **NYPL [Sc D 89-391]**

Steptoe, John, 1950- Baby says /. New York ,
1988. [24] p. : ISBN 0-688-07423-5 DDC [E] 19
PZ7.S8367 Bab 1988 **NYPL [Sc D 88-1257]**

Stinetorf, Louise A. Elephant outlaw /.
Philadelphia , c1956. 173 p. :
NYPL [Sc D 88-1167]

Stolz, Mary, 1920- Storm in the night /. New
York , c1988. [32] p. : ISBN 0-06-025912-4 :
DDC [E] 19
PZ7.S875854 St 1988 **NYPL [Sc F 88-181]**

Sullivan, Sarah A. The animals talk to Gussie /.
[S.l. , c1951 (wilmington, N.C. : Garey-Mintz
Print.) 28 p. : **NYPL [Sc F 89-2]**

Sweet, Dovie Davis. Red light, green light .
Smithtown, N.Y. , 1978 (1980 printing) 39 p. :
ISBN 0-682-49088-1 **NYPL [Sc D 89-70]**

Sylvie-Line. Ti Dolfine et le filibo vert /. Paris ,
c1985. 123 p. : ISBN 2-903033-72-2
NYPL [Sc E 88-358]

Talbot, Toby. I am Maria. New York [1969] 28
p. ISBN 0-402-14031-1 DDC [Fic]
PZ7.T148 I **NYPL [Sc E 88-531]**

Taylor, Mildred D. The friendship /. New
York , 1987. 53 p. : ISBN 0-8037-0418-6 (lib.
bdg.) : DDC [Fic] 19
PZ7.T21723 Fr 1987 **NYPL [Sc D 88-126]**

Teague, Bob. Agent K-13. Garden City, N.Y.,
c1974. 47 p., ISBN 0-385-08704-7 DDC [E]
PZ7.T21937 Ag **NYPL [Sc E 88-587]**

Thomas, Ianthe, 1951- Willie blows a mean
horn /. New York , c1981. 22 p. : ISBN

0-06-026106-4 : DDC [E]
PZ7.T36693 Wi **NYPL [Sc E 89-22]**

Ugochukwu, Françoise, 1949- La source
interdite /. Abidjan , Paris , c1984. 63 p. :
NYPL [Sc B 88-33]

Umeh, Rich Enujioke. Why the cock became a
sacrificial animal /. Enugu, Nigeria , 1985. 38
p. : ISBN 978-239-648-6 **NYPL [Sc C 89-18]**

Upton, Bertha, 1849-1912. Golliwogg in the
African jungle /. London , New York , 1909.
62, [2] p. : **NYPL [Sc Rare F 89-16]**

Upton, Florence Kate, 1873-1922. The
Golliwogg's bicycle club. London, 1967. [1] 62
p.
PZ8.3.U74 Go2 **NYPL [Sc D 88-252]**

Van Stockum, Hilda, 1908- Mogo's flute /.
New York , 1966. 88 p. :
PZ7.V36 Mo **NYPL [Sc E 88-176]**

Walker, Alice, 1944- To hell with dying /. San
Diego , 1987. [32] p. : ISBN 0-15-289075-0
DDC [Fic] 19
PZ7.W15213 To 1987 **NYPL [Sc F 88-182]**

Wallace, John A. Getting to know Egypt,
U.A.R. /. New York , c1961. 64 p. :
NYPL [Sc D 88-569]

Walter, Mildred Pitts. Lillie of Watts takes a
giant step. Garden City, N.Y. [1971] 187 p.
DDC [Fic]
PZ7.W17125 Lk **NYPL [Sc D 88-1119]**

Walter, Mildred Pitts. Mariah loves rock /.
New York , c1988. 117 p. : ISBN 0-02-792511-0
DDC [Fic] 19
PZ7.W17125 Mar 1988 **NYPL [Sc C 89-29]**

Warren, Ruth. The Nile. New York [1968] 127
p. DDC 916.2
DT115 .W33 **NYPL [Sc E 89-21]**

Wassermann, Selma. Moonbeam and Dan Starr.
Westchester, Ill., c1966. 64 p.
NYPL [Sc D 89-398]

Wassermann, Selma. Moonbeam and the rocket
ride. Chicago [c1965] 64 p.
PE1119 .W363 **NYPL [Sc D 89-92]**

Wassermann, Selma. Moonbeam finds a moon
stone. Chicago [1967] 96 p. DDC [Fic]
PE1119 .W3636 **NYPL [Sc D 88-1423]**

Watson, Jane (Werner) 1915- The Niger:
Africa's river of mystery. Champaign, Ill. [1971]
96 p. ISBN 0-8116-6374-4 DDC 916.6/2
DT360 .W38 **NYPL [Sc E 88-415]**

Weil, Lisl. The funny old bag. New York
[1974] [40] p. ISBN 0-8193-0717-3 DDC [E]
PZ7.W433 Fu **NYPL [Sc E 88-529]**

Weir, LaVada. Howdy! Austin, Tex. [1972] 32
p. ISBN 0-8114-7735-5 DDC [E]
PZ7.W4415 Ho **NYPL [Sc E 88-613]**

Weiss, Edna S. Truly Elizabeth /. Boston ,
1957. 178 p. **NYPL [Sc D 88-663]**

Westwood, Gwen. Narni of the desert.
[Chicago, c1967] 93 p. DDC [Fic]
PZ7.W5275 Nar **NYPL [Sc D 88-1424]**

Wilson, Joy Carter. Poems for Afrika's children
/. South Framingham, Mass. , c1975. 30 p. :
NYPL [Sc D 89-183]

Windeatt, Mary Fabyan, 1910- Lad of Lima.
New York , 1942. 152 p. :
NYPL [Sc D 88-1170]

Woody, Regina Llewellyn (Jones) Almena's
dogs /. New York , c1954. 240 p. :
NYPL [Sc D 88-648]

Worrell, Vernon, 1952- Under the flambo .
Bridgetown, Barbados , 1986. ix, 84 p. : DDC
811 19
PR9230.9.W67 U5 1986
NYPL [Sc D 88-945]

Yarbrough, Camille. The shimmershine queens
/. New York , c1988. 142 p. ; ISBN
0-399-21465-8 DDC [Fic] 19
PZ7.Y1955 Sh 1988 **NYPL [Sc D 89-283]**

Schomburg Childrn's Collection. Ketchum, Jean,
1926- Stick-in-the-mud . New York [c1953]
unpaged : **NYPL [Sc C 88-375]**

**Schomburg library of nineteenth-century Black
women writers.**
**The Schomburg library of nineteenth-century
Black women writers.**

Collected Black women's poetry /. New York ,
1988. 4 v. : ISBN 0-19-505253-6 (v. 1) DDC
811/.008/09287 19
PS591.N4 C57 1988 **NYPL [JFC 88-2144]**

Cooper, Anna J. (Anna Julia), 1858-1964. A
voice from the South /. New York , 1988. liv,
304 p. ; ISBN 0-19-505246-3 (alk. paper) DDC
975/.00496073 19
E185.86 .C587 1988 **NYPL [IEC 88-1201]**

Dunbar-Nelson, Alice Moore, 1875-1935.
[Works. 1988.] The works of Alice
Dunbar-Nelson /. New York , 1988. 3 v. :
ISBN 0-19-505250-1 (v. 1 : alk. paper) DDC
818/.5209 19
PS3507 .U6228 1988 **NYPL [JFC 88-2143]**

Forten, Charlotte L. [Journals.] The journals of
Charlotte Forten Grimké /. New York , 1988.
xlix, 609 p. ; ISBN 0-19-505238-2 (alk. paper)
DDC 371.1/0092/4 B 19
LA2317.F67 A3 1988 **NYPL [JFC 88-2152]**

Harper, Frances Ellen Watkins, 1825-1911. Iola
Leroy, or, Shadows uplifted /. New York ,
1988. xxxix, 281 p. : ISBN 0-19-505240-4 (alk.
paper) DDC 813/.3 19
PS1799.H7 I6 1988 **NYPL [JFC 88-2190]**

Harper, Frances Ellen Watkins, 1825-1911.
[Poems.] Complete poems of Frances E.W.
Harper /. New York , 1988. lx, 232 p. ; ISBN
0-19-505244-7 (alk. paper) DDC 811/.3 19
PS1799.H7 A17 1988 **NYPL [JFC 88-2147]**

Homespun heroines and other women of
distinction /. New York , 1988. xxxv, viii, 248
p., [25] leaves of plates : ISBN 0-19-505237-4
(alk. paper) DDC 920.72/08996073 19
E185.96 .H65 1988 **NYPL [JFC 88-2157]**

Hopkins, Pauline E. (Pauline Elizabeth)
Contending forces . New York , 1988. xlviii,
402 p., [8] p. of plates : ISBN 0-19-505258-7 (alk.
paper) DDC 813/.4 19
PS1999.H4226 C66 1988
NYPL [JFC 88-2153]

Hopkins, Pauline E. (Pauline Elizabeth)
[Novels. Selections.] The magazine novels of
Pauline Hopkins /. New York , Oxford , 1988.
l, 621 p. ; ISBN 0-19-505248-X (alk. paper) DDC
813/.4 19
PS1999.H4226 A6 1988
NYPL [JFC 88-2195]

Jacobs, Harriet A. (Harriet Ann), 1813-1897.
Incidents in the life of a slave girl /. New
York , 1988. xl, 306 p. ; ISBN 0-19-505243-9
(alk. paper) DDC 973/.0496024 B 19
E444.J17 A3 1988 **NYPL [JFC 88-2193]**

Johnson, A. E. (Amelia E.), b. 1859. Clarence
and Corinne, or, God's way /. New York ,
1988. xxxviii, 187 p. : ISBN 0-19-505264-1 (alk.
paper) DDC 813/.4 19
PS2134.J515 C5 1988 **NYPL [JFC 88-2145]**

Johnson, A. E. (Amelia E.), b. 1859. The
Hazeley family /. New York , 1988. xxxvii, 191
p. : ISBN 0-19-505257-9 (alk. paper) DDC 813/.4
19
PS2134.J515 H39 1988
NYPL [JFC 88-2196]

Keckley, Elizabeth, 1824-1907. Behind the
scenes, or, Thirty years a slave, and four years
in the White House /. New York , 1988. xxxvi,
xvi, 371 p. : ISBN 0-19-505259-5 DDC
973.7/092/2 19
E457.15 .K26 1988 **NYPL [JFC 88-2194]**

Kelley, Emma Dunham. Four girls at Cottage
City /. New York , 1988. xxxviii, 379 p. ;
ISBN 0-19-505242-0 DDC 813/.4 19
PS2159.K13 F6 1988 **NYPL [JFC 88-2149]**

Kelley, Emma Dunham. Megda /. New York ,
1988. xxxvii, 394 p. ; ISBN 0-19-505245-5 (alk.
paper) DDC 813/.4 19
PS2159.K13 M44 1988
NYPL [JFC 88-2146]

Larison, Cornelius Wilson, 1837-1910. Silvia
Dubois /. New York , 1988. xxvii, 124 p. :
ISBN 0-19-505239-0 DDC 305.5/67/0924 B 19
E444.D83 L37 1988 **NYPL [JFC 88-2191]**

Mossell, N. F., Mrs., 1855- The work of the
Afro-American woman /. New York , 1988.
xlii, 178 p. : ISBN 0-19-505265-X (alk. paper)
DDC 305.8/96073 19
E185.86 .M65 1988 **NYPL [JFC 88-2155]**

Plato, Ann. Essays. New York , 1988. liii, 122

p. ; ISBN 0-19-505247-1 (alk. paper) DDC 814/.3
19
PS2593 .P347 1988 **NYPL [JFC 88-2156]**

Seacole, Mary, 1805-1881. Wonderful
adventures of Mrs. Seacole in many lands /.
New York , 1988. xxxiv, xii, 200 p., [2] p. of
plates : ISBN 0-19-505249-8 (alk. paper) DDC
947/.073 19
DK215 .S43 1988 **NYPL [JFC 88-2150]**

Smith, Amanda, 1837-1915. An autobiography .
New York , 1988. xlii, 506 p. [23] p. of plates :
ISBN 0-19-505261-7 (alk. paper) DDC
269/.2/0924 B 19
BV3785.S56 A3 1988 **NYPL [JFC 88-2154]**

Spiritual narratives /. New York , 1988. 489 p.
in various pagings : ISBN 0-19-505266-8 (alk.
paper) DDC 209/.22 B 19
BR1713 .S65 1988 **NYPL [JFC 88-2189]**

Wheatley, Phillis, 1753-1784. [Works. 1988.]
The collected works of Phillis Wheatley /. New
York , 1988. xl, 339 p. : ISBN 0-19-505241-2
(alk. paper) DDC 811/.1 19
PS866 .W5 1988 **NYPL [JFC 88-2142]**

**SCHOOL ADMINISTRATION. see SCHOOL
MANAGEMENT AND ORGANIZATION.**

School age workers in Britain today /.
Moorehead, Caroline. [London] [1987] 60 p. :
ISBN 0-900918-24-1 **NYPL [Sc D 89-7]**

School and society in Nigeria /. Ukeje, B.
Onyerisara. Enugu, Nigeria , 1986. 129 p. ;
ISBN 978-15-6245-5
NYPL [Sc D 88-1243]

**SCHOOL BOARDS - MISSISSIPPI -
MEMBERSHIP, AFRO-AMERICAN.**
Hust, Mildred Hudgins. The positions, roles,
and perceptions of Black elected public school
board members in Mississippi [microform] /.
1977. 144 leaves. **NYPL [Sc Micro R-4215]**

A School for freedom : Morristown College and
five generations of education for Blacks,
1868-1985 / edited by Jovita Wells.
[Knoxville] : East Tennessee Historical Society,
1986. xiii, 60 p. : ill., facsims. ; 22 cm. (ETHS
Community history series) Includes index.
*1. Morristown College - History. 2. Afro-American
universities and colleges - Tennessee - History. I. Wells,
Jovita. II. Title. III. Series.* **NYPL [Sc D 88-417]**

**A school history of the Negro race in America
from 1619 to 1890 /.** Johnson, Edward A.
(Edward Augustus), 1860-1944. Chicago , 1894.
200 p. : **NYPL [Sc Rare F 88-9]**

**SCHOOL INSPECTION. see SCHOOL
MANAGEMENT AND ORGANIZATION.**

**SCHOOL INTEGRATION - ILLINOIS -
CHICAGO - HISTORY.**
Moses, James Charles. Desegregation in
Catholic schools in the archdiocese of Chicago,
1964-1974, including a case study of a Catholic
high school [microform] /. 1977 288 leaves.
NYPL [Sc Micro R-4699]

**SCHOOL INTEGRATION - NORTH
CAROLINA - CHARLOTTE - HISTORY.**
Gaillard, Frye, 1946- The dream long deferred
/. Chapel Hill , c1988. xxi, 192 p. ; ISBN
0-8078-1794-5 (alk. paper) DDC 370.19/342 19
LC214.523.C48 G35 1988
NYPL [Sc E 88-527]

SCHOOL INTEGRATION - OKLAHOMA.
Cayton, Leonard Bernard. A history of Black
public education in Oklahoma [microform] /.
1976. 170 leaves. **NYPL [Sc Micro R-4692]**

**SCHOOL INTEGRATION - TENNESSEE -
FAYETTE COUNTY - HISTORY.**
Hunt, Frankie L. Cunningham. A history of the
desegregation of the Fayette County school
system [microform] . 1981. 351 leaves.
NYPL [Sc Micro R-4687]

**SCHOOL MANAGEMENT AND
ORGANIZATION - NIGERIA.**
Aderounmu, Olusola. Managing the Nigerian
education enterprise /. Ikeja, Lagos, Nigeria ,
1986. 230 p. : **NYPL [Sc F 88-171]**

Aderounmu, Olusola W. An introduction to the
administration of schools in Nigeria /. Ibadan,
Nigeria , 1985. xiii, 271 p. : ISBN 978-16-7241-2
NYPL [Sc D 88-730]

**SCHOOL MANAGEMENT AND
ORGANIZATION - NIGERIA -**

PROBLEMS, EXERCISES, ETC.
Adesua, Adeleye. Administrative problems in Nigerian schools /. Agege-Lagos [Nigeria] , c1987. vii, 136 p. ; ISBN 978-302-711-5
NYPL [Sc D 88-789]

SCHOOL MANAGEMENT AND ORGANIZATION - NIGERIA - TEXTBOOKS.
Udoh, Sunday. Theory and practice of educational administration in Nigeria /. Jos, Nigeria , 1987. x, 347 p. :
NYPL [Sc E 88-295]

SCHOOL OPERATION POLICIES. see SCHOOL MANAGEMENT AND ORGANIZATION.

SCHOOL ORGANIZATION. see SCHOOL MANAGEMENT AND ORGANIZATION.

SCHOOL PSYCHOLOGISTS - UNITED STATES.
Gary, Lawrence E. The delivery of mental health services to Black children . Washington, D.C. , 1982. vi, 111, 19 p. ;
NYPL [Sc F 88-66]

SCHOOL SUPERINTENDENTS AND PRINCIPALS - NIGERIA - BIOGRAPHY.
Solarin, Tai. To mother with love /. Ibadan , c1987. 302 p. : ISBN 978-19-1050-X
NYPL [Sc D 88-732]

SCHOOLS, COMMERCIAL. see BUSINESS EDUCATION.

SCHOOLS - INSPECTION. see SCHOOL MANAGEMENT AND ORGANIZATION.

SCHOOLS - JUVENILE FICTION.
Yarbrough, Camille. The shimmershine queens /. New York , c1988. 142 p. ; ISBN 0-399-21465-8 DDC [Fic] 19
PZ7.Y1955 Sh 1988   *NYPL [Sc D 89-283]*

SCHOOLS - MANAGEMENT AND ORGANIZATION. see SCHOOL MANAGEMENT AND ORGANIZATION.

SCHOOLS - RECREATIONS. see GAMES.

Schriften des Instituts für Internationale Begegnungen e. V. .
(8) Kullas, Ulrike. Lernen von der Dritten Welt? . Saarbrücken , Fort Lauderdale , 1982. 174 p. : ISBN 3-88156-233-8
NYPL [Sc D 89-339]

Schroeder, Ted. (illus) Lauber, Patricia. The Congo, river into central Africa. Champaign, Ill. [1964] 96 p. DDC 967
DT639 .L38   *NYPL [Sc E 89-24]*

Schuettinger, Robert Lindsay, 1936- South Africa--the vital link /. Washington , c1976. 120 p. ;
NYPL [Sc F 89-129]

Schuller, Gunther. The history of jazz. New York, Oxford University Press, 1968- v. map, music. 24 cm. Title other: vol. 2. "A selected discography": v. 1, pts. 385-389. Includes index. CONTENTS. - [v. 1]. Early jazz: its roots and musical development -- v. 2. The swing era : the development of jazz 1930-1945 -- DDC 785.42/09 19
1. Jazz music - History and criticism. I. Title.
ML3506 .S36 1968   *NYPL [JNL 89-2]*

Schultheis, Michael J. Catholic social teaching and the Church in Africa / Michael J. Schultheis, Ed. DeBerri. Gweru, Zimbabwe : Mambo Press, c1984. 56 p. ; 21 cm. (Mambo occasional papers. Missio-pastoral series : no. 14) Bibliography: p. 56.
1. Catholic Church - Africa. 2. Christianity and justice - Africa. 3. Church and social problems - Africa. I. DeBerri, Edward P. II. Title. III. Series.
NYPL [Sc D 88-1198]

Schümer, Martin. Die amerikanische Politik gegenüber dem südlichen Afrika / Martin Schümer. Bonn : Forschungsinstitut der Deutschen Gesellschaft für Auswärtige Politik : Vertrieb, Europa Union Verlag, [1986]. v, 183 p. ; 21 cm. (Arbeitspapiere zur internationalen politik. 39) "Februar 1986." Includes bibliographical references.
ISBN 3-7713-0275-7
1. United States - Foreign relations - Africa, Southern. 2. Africa, Southern - Foreign relations - United States. 3. Foreign relations - South Africa. 4. South Africa - Foreign relations - United States. 5. United States - Foreign relations - 1981-. I. Title. II. Series.   *NYPL [Sc D 88-983]*

Schwabe,Kurd, 1866- Taschenbuch für Südwestafrika, 1909 /. Berlin , 1909. xviii, 495,

60 p., [4] fold. leaves of plates :
NYPL [Sc B 89-24]

Schwartz, Andy. Bergman, Billy. Hot sauces . New York, c1985. 144 p. : ISBN 0-688-02193-X (pbk.) : DDC 780/.42/09729 19
ML3475 .B47 1985   *NYPL [Sc F 87-19]*

Schwartz, Bernard, 1923- Behind Bakke : affirmative action and the Supreme Court / Bernard Schwartz. New York : New York University Press, c1988. x, 266 p. ; 23 cm. Includes index. Bibliography: p. 261-262. ISBN 0-8147-7878-X : DDC 347.73/0798 347.304798 19
1. Bakke, Allan Paul - Trials, litigation, etc. 2. University of California, Berkeley - Trials, litigation, etc. 3. Discrimination in medical education - Law and legislation - California. 4. Medical colleges - California - Admission. 5. Affirmative action programs - Law and legislation - United States. I. Title.
KF228.B34 S39 1988   *NYPL [JLE 88-4158]*

Schwarz-Bart, Simone. Ton beau capitaine : pièce en un acte et quatre tableaux / Simone Schwarz-Bart. Paris : Editions du Seuil, c1987. 57 p. ; 19 cm. ISBN 2-02-009832-6
I. Title.   *NYPL [Sc C 88-112]*

Schwarz, Philip J., 1940- Twice condemned : slaves and the criminal laws of Virginia, 1705-1865 / Philip J. Schwarz. Baton Rouge : Louisiana State University Press, c1988. xiv, 353 p. : maps ; 24 cm. Includes index. Bibliography: p. [337]-345. ISBN 0-8071-1401-4 (alk. paper) DDC 346.75501/3 347.550613 19
1. Slavery - Law and legislation - Virginia - Cases. 2. Criminal law - Virginia - Cases. 3. Criminal justice, Administration of - Virginia - Cases. I. Title.
KFV2801.6.S55 S39 1988
NYPL [Sc E 89-112]

SCHWEITZER, ALBERT, 1875-1965.
Oswald, Suzanne. Im Urwaldspital von Lambarene /. Bern , c1986. 31 p. : ISBN 3-258-03594-6   *NYPL [Sc D 87-1076]*

SCHWEITZER, ALBERT, 1875-1965 - JUVENILE LITERATURE.
Daniel, Anita. The story of Albert Schweitzer /. New York , 1957. 179 p. :
NYPL [Sc D 88-379]

Schweizerischer Evangelischer Missionsrat. Afrika sucht sein Menschenbild . Freiburg , Basel , 1974. 112 p. :
DT351 .A38   *NYPL [Sc D 87-1433]*

Schweizerischer Katholischer Missionsrat. Afrika sucht sein Menschenbild . Freiburg , Basel , 1974. 112 p. :
DT351 .A38   *NYPL [Sc D 87-1433]*

Scibilia, Muriel. La Casamance ouvre ses cases : tourisme au Sénégal / Muriel Scibilia. Paris : L'Harmattan, c1986. 171, [1] p., [8] p. of plates : ill., maps ; 22 cm. Bibliography: p. 171-[172]. ISBN 2-85802-676-9
1. Tourist trade - Senegal - Casamance. 2. Casamance (Senegal) - Description and travel. I. Title.
NYPL [Sc D 89-170]

SCIENCE AND STATE - NIGERIA - ADDRESSES, ESSAYS, LECTURES.
Anya, A. O., 1937- Science, development and the future . [Nsukka] [1982] v, 90 p. ; ISBN 978-229-902-2   *NYPL [Sc E 88-136]*

Science, development and the future . Anya, A. O., 1937- [Nsukka] [1982] v, 90 p. ; ISBN 978-229-902-2   *NYPL [Sc E 88-136]*

SCIENCE FICTION, AMERICAN.
Kindred spirits . Boston , 1984. 262 p. ; ISBN 0-932870-42-2 (pbk.) :
NYPL [Sc D 89-269]

Worlds apart . Boston, Mass. , 1986. 293 p. ; ISBN 0-932870-87-2 (pbk.) : DDC 813/.0876/08353 19
PS648.H57 W67 1986 *NYPL [JFD 87-7753]*

SCIENCE FICTION - AUTHORSHIP.
Delany, Samuel R. The motion of light in water . New York , c1988. xviii, 302 p. : ISBN 0-87795-947-1 : DDC 813/.54 19
PS3554.E437 Z475 1988
NYPL [JFD 88-7818]

SCIENCE, MENTAL. see PSYCHOLOGY.

SCIENCE, MORAL. see ETHICS.

SCIENCE, POLITICAL. see POLITICAL SCIENCE.

SCIENCE - RESEARCH. see RESEARCH.

SCIENCE, SOCIAL. see SOCIOLOGY.

SCIENCE STORIES. see SCIENCE FICTION.

SCIENCE - STUDY AND TEACHING (HIGHER) - NIGERIA.
What science? . Ibadan , 1985. xvii, 321 p. : ISBN 978-12-9118-4 (pbk.) DDC 507/.11669 19
Q183.4.N5 W48 1985   *NYPL [Sc E 88-402]*

SCIENCE - STUDY AND TEACHING - NIGERIA.
Issues in teacher education and science curriculum in Nigeria /. [Nigeria , 1986?] vi, 331 p. : DDC 370/.7/309669 19
LB1727.N5 I88 1986   *NYPL [Sc D 88-125]*

SCIENCES, OCCULT. see OCCULT SCIENCES.

SCIENCES, SOCIAL. see SOCIAL SCIENCES.

SCIENTIFIC EDUCATION. see SCIENCE - STUDY AND TEACHING.

SCIENTIFIC MANAGEMENT. see INDUSTRIAL MANAGEMENT.

SCIENTIFIC RESEARCH. see RESEARCH.

Scorpions /. Myers, Walter Dean, 1937- New York , c1988. 216 p. ; ISBN 0-06-024364-3 : DDC [Fic] 19
PZ7.M992 Sc 1988   *NYPL [Sc D 88-1146]*

Scott, Ann Herbert. Let's catch a monster. Illustrated by H. Tom Hall. New York, Lothrop, Lee & Shepard Co. [1967] 1 v. (unpaged) illus. (part col.) 26 cm. SCHOMBURG CHILDREN'S COLLECTION
1. Halloween - Juvenile fiction. 2. Afro-American children - Juvenile fiction. I. Hall, H. Tom, illus. II. Schomburg Children's Collection. III. Title.
PZ7.S415 Le   *NYPL [Sc F 88-342]*

Scott, Jack Cassin- . see Cassin-Scott, Jack.

Scott Joplin /. Preston, Katherine. New York , c1988. 110 p. : ISBN 1-555-46598-6 DDC 780/.92/4 B 92 19
ML3930.J66 P7 1988   *NYPL [Sc E 88-170]*

Scott, Kesho. Tight Spaces / Kesho Scott, Cherry Muhanji, Egyirba High. 1st ed. San Francisco : Spinsters/Aunt Lute, 1987. 182 p. ; 22 cm. ISBN 0-933216-27-0
1. Afro-American women - Literary collections. I. Muhanji, Cherry. II. High, Egyirba. III. Title.
NYPL [Sc D 88-12]

Scott, Richard, 1956- Jackie Robinson / Richard Scott. New York : Chelsea House, 1987. 110 p. : ill. ; 25 cm. (Black Americans of achievement) Includes index. Traces the life of the athelete who broke the color barrier in major league baseball when he joined the Brooklyn Dodgers in 1947. Bibliography: p. 108. ISBN 1-555-46208-1 : DDC 796.357/092/4 B 92 19
1. Robinson, Jackie, 1919-1972 - Juvenile literature. 2. Baseball players - United States - Biography - Juvenile literature. 3. Afro-American baseball players - Biography - Juvenile literature. I. Title. II. Series.
GV865.R6 S36 1987   *NYPL [Sc E 88-168]*

The scramble for Africa /. Brooke-Smith, Robin. Basingstoke, Hampshire , 1987. viii, 134 p. ; ISBN 0-333-42491-3   *NYPL [Sc D 88-98]*

Scribe sistren . Benji. London , 1987. 72 p. ; ISBN 0-903738-72-4   *NYPL [Sc D 88-686]*

Scudder, Thayer. Colson, Elizabeth, 1917- For prayer and profit . Stanford, Calif. , 1988. vi, 147 p. : ISBN 0-8047-1444-4 (alk. paper) : DDC 968.94 19
DT963.42 .C65 1988   *NYPL [Sc D 88-1254]*

SCULPTURE, AFRICAN - AFRICA, SUB-SAHARAN - EXHIBITIONS.
Forms and forces . San Francisco, c1988. 53 p. : ISBN 0-88401-057-0 (pbk)
NYPL [Sc F 88-330]

SCULPTURE, AFRICAN - EXHIBITIONS.
Miniature African sculptures from the Herman collection /. London , 1985. 64 p. : ISBN 0-7287-0454-4   *NYPL [Sc D 89-41]*

Museum of Modern Art (New York, N.Y.) African Negro art . New York [c1935] 58 p. :
NYPL [Sc F 88-125]

Santa Barbara Museum of Art. Antelopes and elephants, hornbills and hyenas. [Santa Barbara, 1973] [48] p. DDC 732/.2/0967
NB1098 .S27 1973   *NYPL [Sc F 88-165]*

SCULPTURE, AFRICAN - IVORY COAST.
Holas, B. (Bohumil), 1909-1979. Image de la
mère dans l'art ivoirien /. Abidjan [1975] 122
p. : DDC 732/.2/096668
NB1099.I8 H59 **NYPL [Sc D 88-476]**

**SCULPTURE, BLACK - AFRICA, SUB-
SAHARAN - EXHIBITIONS.**
Mother and child in African Sculpture . New
York , 1987. [16] p. : **NYPL [Sc F 88-3]**

**SCULPTURE, BLACK - AFRICA, WEST -
EXHIBITIONS.**
Fry, Jacqueline, 1923- Visual variations .
Kingston, Canada , c1987. vii, 63 p. : DDC
730/.0966/074011372 19
NB1098 .F79 1987 **NYPL [Sc F 88-189]**

SCULPTURE, BLACK - ZIMBABWE.
Arnold, Marion I. Zimbabwean stone sculpture
/. Bulawayo , 1986. xxvi, 234 p. : ISBN
0-7974-0747-2 DDC 730/.96891 19
NB1209.Z55 A76 1986
NYPL [Sc D 89-326]

**SCULPTURE, CHOKWE (AFRICAN PEOPLE)
- EXHIBITIONS.**
Art et mythologie . Paris , 1988. 117 p. : ISBN
2-906067-06-7 **NYPL [Sc E 89-96]**

**SCULPTURE, MANDINGO (AFRICAN
PEOPLE)**
McNaughton, Patrick R. The Mande
blacksmiths . Bloomington , c1988. xxiv, 241 p.,
[4] p. of plates : ISBN 0-253-33683-X DDC
306/.089963 19
DT551.45.M36 M38 1988
NYPL [Sc E 88-393]

**SCULPTURE, MODERN - NIGERIA -
EXHIBITIONS.**
Eze, Okpu. Timeless search /. [Lagos] [1985?]
51 p. : **NYPL [Sc C 88-170]**

SCULPTURE, NIGERIAN - EXHIBITIONS.
Zementskulpturen aus Nigeria . Stuttgart ,
c1988. 70 p. : **NYPL [Sc F 89-44]**

**SCULPTURE, PRIMITIVE - AFRICA -
EXHIBITIONS.**
Museum of Modern Art (New York, N.Y.)
African Negro art . New York [c1935] 58 p. :
NYPL [Sc F 88-125]

**SCULPTURE, PRIMITIVE - AFRICA, SUB-
SAHARAN - EXHIBITIONS.**
Forms and forces . San Francisco , c1988. 53
p. : ISBN 0-88401-057-0 (pbk)
NYPL [Sc F 88-330]

SCULPTURE, PRIMITIVE - AFRICA, WEST.
Santa Barbara Museum of Art. Antelopes and
elephants, hornbills and hyenas. [Santa Barbara,
1973] [48] p. DDC 732/.2/0967
NB1098 .S27 1973 **NYPL [Sc F 88-165]**

**SCULPTURE, PRIMITIVE - AFRICA, WEST -
EXHIBITIONS.**
Fry, Jacqueline, 1923- Visual variations .
Kingston, Canada , c1987. vii, 63 p. : DDC
730/.0966/074011372 19
NB1098 .F79 1987 **NYPL [Sc F 88-189]**

SCULPTURE, PRIMITIVE - IVORY COAST.
Holas, B. (Bohumil), 1909-1979. Image de la
mère dans l'art ivoirien /. Abidjan [1975] 122
p. : DDC 732/.2/096668
NB1099.I8 H59 **NYPL [Sc D 88-476]**

**SCULPTURE - PRIVATE COLLECTIONS -
CANADA - KINGSTON - EXHIBITIONS.**
Fry, Jacqueline, 1923- Visual variations .
Kingston, Canada , c1987. vii, 63 p. : DDC
730/.0966/074011372 19
NB1098 .F79 1987 **NYPL [Sc F 88-189]**

**SCULPTURE, RELIGIOUS. see CHRISTIAN
ART AND SYMBOLISM.**

SCULPTURE, SHONA.
Arnold, Marion I. Zimbabwean stone sculpture
/. Bulawayo , 1986. xxvi, 234 p. : ISBN
0-7974-0747-2 DDC 730/.96891 19
NB1209.Z55 A76 1986
NYPL [Sc D 89-326]

'Scuse me while I kiss the sky . Henderson,
David, 1942- Toronto , New York , 1983,
1981. xi, 411 p. : ISBN 0-553-01334-3 (tr. pbk.) :
DDC 784.5/4/00924
ML410.H476 H46 1981
NYPL [Sc C 82-243]

SEA COCONUT - SEYCHELLES.
Lionnet, Guy. Coco de mer . Bell Village, Ile

Maurice , c1986. 95 p. :
QK495.P17 L56 1986 **NYPL [Sc D 88-572]**

SEA ISLANDS - JUVENILE FICTION.
Edwards, Sally. Isaac and Snow. New York
[1973] 123 p. ISBN 0-698-20244-9 DDC [Fic]
PZ7.E265 Is3 **NYPL [Sc D 88-1419]**

SEA TRAVEL. see OCEAN TRAVEL.

Seacole, Mary, 1805-1881. Wonderful adventures
of Mrs. Seacole in many lands / Mary Seacole ;
with an introduction by William L. Andrews.
New York : Oxford University Press, 1988.
xxxiv, xii, 200 p., [2] p. of plates : ill. ; 17 cm.
(The Schomburg library of nineteenth-century Black
women writers) Reprint. Originally published: London :
J. Blackwood, 1857. ISBN 0-19-505249-8 (alk. paper)
DDC 947/.073 19
*1. Seacole, Mary, 1805-1881. 2. Crimean War,
1853-1856 - Personal narratives, Jamaican. 3. Blacks -
Jamaica - Biography. I. Title. II. Series.*
DK215 .S43 1988 **NYPL [JFC 88-2150]**

SEACOLE, MARY, 1805-1881.
Seacole, Mary, 1805-1881. Wonderful
adventures of Mrs. Seacole in many lands /.
New York , 1988. xxxiv, xii, 200 p., [2] p. of
plates : ISBN 0-19-505249-8 (alk. paper) DDC
947/.073 19
DK215 .S43 1988 **NYPL [JFC 88-2150]**

Seaforth, Sybil. Growing up with Miss Milly /
Sybil Seaforth. Ithaca, N.Y. : Calaloux
Publications, 1988. 129 p. ; 22 cm. ISBN
0-911565-04-3
1. West Indies - Fiction. I. Title.
NYPL [Sc D 89-439]

Seale, William. The president's house : a history
/ by William Seale. Washington, D.C. : White
House Historical Association with the
cooperation of the National Geographic
Society, 1986. 2 v. (xx, 1224 p. [80] p. of
plates : ill. ; 25 cm. Includes index. Bibliography: v.
2, p. 1058-1068. ISBN 0-912308-28-1 (set) DDC
975 19
*1. Presidents - United States - Dwellings. 2. White
House (Washington, D.C.). 3. Washington (D.C.) -
Buildings, structures, etc. I. Title.*
F204.W5 S43 1986 **NYPL [Sc E 89-183]**

Sealy, Adrienne V.
The color your way into Black history book /
by Adrienne V. Sealy. Brooklyn, N.Y. :
Association for the Study of Family Living,
c1980. 51 p. : ill., ports. ; 28 cm. "Black coloring
book for all children." Cover title. Bibliography: p. [52]
SCHOMBURG CHILDREN'S COLLECTION. ISBN
0-9602670-6-9
*1. Afro-Americans - History - Juvenile literature. 2.
Coloring books. I. Schomburg Children's Collection. II.
Title.*
NYPL [Sc F 89-36]

Mama--watch out, I'm growingup! / by
Adrienne V. Sealy. Brooklyn, New York :
Copen Press 1976. [45] p. : ill., ports. ; 28 cm.
SCHOMBURG CHILDREN'S COLLECTION.
*1. Sealy, Adrienne V. - Juvenile literature. 2. Children
as authors - Biography - Juvenile literature. I.
Schomburg Children's Collection. II. Title.*
NYPL [Sc F 88-135]

**SEALY, ADRIENNE V. - JUVENILE
LITERATURE.**
Sealy, Adrienne V. Mama--watch out, I'm
growingup! /. Brooklyn, New York , 1976. [45]
p. : **NYPL [Sc F 88-135]**

**The search for power and legitimacy in Black
urban areas** . Atkinson, Doreen. Grahamstown
[South Africa] [1984] 38, xix, v, [1] p. ; ISBN
0-86810-114-1 (pbk.) DDC 320.8/0968 19
JS7533.A8 A85 1984 **NYPL [Sc F 88-355]**

A season in Rihata /. Condé, Maryse. [Une
Saison à Rihata. English.] London , 1988. 192
p. ; ISBN 0-435-98832-8 (pbk)
PQ3949.2.C65 **NYPL [Sc C 89-90]**

**SEASONAL LABOR - BURUNDI - MUSSO-
BUYOGOMA REGION.**
Stremplat, Axel V., 1941- Der l"andliche
Arbeitskalender in der Regionalplanung
Burundis /. Giessen , 1984. 130 p. : ISBN
3-924840-08-3 **NYPL [Sc D 88-556]**

**SEASONAL VARIATIONS (ECONOMICS) -
BURUNDI - MUSSO-BUYOGOMA.**
Stremplat, Axel V., 1941- Der l"andliche
Arbeitskalender in der Regionalplanung
Burundis /. Giessen , 1984. 130 p. : ISBN
3-924840-08-3 **NYPL [Sc D 88-556]**

The Sebei . Goldschmidt, Walter Rochs, 1913-
New York , c1986. xii, 162 p. : ISBN
0-03-008922-0 : DDC 305/.09676/1 19
DT433.245.S24 G65 1986
NYPL [Sc E 88-225]

Sebuava, Joseph, 1934- The inevitable hour : a
novel / by Joseph Sebuava.2nd ed. Accra :
Woeli Pub. 1987,c1979. 141 p. ; 21 cm.
"Originally published by vantage Press, N.Y."
1. Ghana - Fiction. I. Title.
NYPL [Sc D 88-1384]

Seck, Nago. Musiciens africains des années 80 :
guide / Nago Seck, Sylvie Clerfeuille. Paris :
Éditions L'Harmattan, c1986. 167 p. : ill.,
ports. ; 22 cm. Includes bibliographies and
discographies. ISBN 2-85802-715-3
*1. Musicians - Africa - Biography. 2. Music, Popular
(Songs, etc.) - Africa. I. Clerfeuille, Sylvie. II. Title. III.
Title: Musiciens africains des années quatre-vingts.*
NYPL [JMD 87-441]

Second-tier foreign exchange market in Nigeria .
Ogundipe, S. O. Ibadan , 1987. xii, 96 p. ;
ISBN 979-12-9534-1
NYPL [Sc D 88-1248]

SECONDARY BOYCOTTS. see BOYCOTT.

**Secondary level teachers: supply and demand in
Botswana.** Hanson, John Wagner. [East
Lansing, 1969, c1968] x, 97, [2] p.
LB2833.4.B55 H3 **NYPL [JFM 72-62 no. 1]**

**Secondary level teachers: supply and demand in
Ghana.** Hanson, John Wagner. [East Lansing,
1971] xv, 130 p. **NYPL [JFM 72-62 no. 12]**

**Secondary level teachers: supply and demand in
Liberia.** Ferns, George W. [East Lansing,
c1970] xii, 116 p.
LB2833.4.L7 F4 **NYPL [JFM 72-62 no. 6]**

**Secondary level teachers: supply and demand in
Malawi.** Hanson, John Wagner. [East Lansing,
1969] xu, 73, [2] p.
LB2833.4.M3 H3 **NYPL [JFM 72-62 no. 3]**

**Secondary level teachers: supply and demand in
Nigeria.** Hanson, John Wagner. [East Lansing,
c1973] 1 v. (various pagings) DDC 331.1/26
LB2833.4.N6 H36 **NYPL [Sc F 88-151]**

**Secondary level teachers: supply and demand in
Sierra Leone.** Hanson, John Wagner. [East
Lansing, c1970] viii, 85 p.
NYPL [JFM 72-62 no. 11]

**Secondary level teachers: supply and demand in
tanzania.** Pratt, Simon. [East Lansing, 1969] xii,
79 p. **NYPL [JFM 72-62 no. 8]**

**Secondary level teachers: supply and demand in
the Gambia.** Ferns, George W. [East Lansing,
1969] xi, 78 p. **NYPL [JFM 72-62 no. 2]**

**Secondary level teachers: supply and demand in
West Cameroon.** Haupt, W. Norman. [East
Lansing, 1971] xii, 45, [20] p.
NYPL [JFM 72-62 no. 13]

Secret and sacred . Hammond, James Henry,
1807-1864. New York , 1988. xxix, 342 p., [2]
leaves of plates : ISBN 0-19-505308-7 DDC
975.7/03/0924 B 19
F273 .H24 1988 **NYPL [Sc E 88-513]**

SECRET SOCIETIES - CUBA.
Sosa, Enrique. Los ñáñigos . Ciudad de La
Habana, Cuba , c1982. 464 p., [44] p. of
plates : DDC 366/.097291 19
HS221.Z6 S66 1982 **NYPL [JLC 84-260]**

Secret U. S. war against South Africa /. Parker,
Aida. Johannesburg , c1977. 79 p. ;
NYPL [Sc D 88-277]

**SECRETARIAL PRACTICE. see OFFICE
PRACTICE.**

Secrets dévoilés de la magie caraïbe . Caloc, Ray.
[Lamentin, Martinique] [1986] 71 p. : ISBN
2-905317-02-7 **NYPL [Sc D 89-274]**

**SECURITY, INTERNAL. see INTERNAL
SECURITY.**

**SEEDS - DISPERSAL - JUVENILE
LITERATURE.**
Fisher, Aileen Lucia, 1906- Seeds on the go /.
[Los Angeles] , c1977. 43 p. : ISBN
0-8372-2400-4 DDC 582/.01/6
QK929 .F57 **NYPL [Sc F 88-344]**

Seeds on the go /. Fisher, Aileen Lucia, 1906-
[Los Angeles] , c1977. 43 p. : ISBN

0-8372-2400-4 DDC 582/.01/6
QK929 .F57 **NYPL [Sc F 88-344]**

Seeley, J. A. (Janet Anne) Environmental issues in African development planning /. Cambridge , c1988. v, 84 p. : ISBN 0-902993-21-6 (pbk) : DDC 330.96/0328 19
HC502 **NYPL [Sc D 88-1233]**

Sega of Seychelles /. De Silva, Hazel, 1947- Nairobi, Kenya , 1983. 314 p. ; DDC 821 19
PR9381.9.D42 S4 1983 **NYPL [Sc C 89-9]**

Segal, Ronald, 1932- Kidron, Michael. The new state of the world atlas /. New York , 1987. 1 atlas ([54] p., 57 [i.e. 114] p.) : ISBN 0-671-64554-4 (hard) : DDC 912/.132 19
G1021 .K46 1987
NYPL [Map Div. 87-1075]

Segale, M. Gobotswang, Z. Pilot evaluation report on Mahalapye Development Trust /. Gaborone, Botswana [1982] v leaves, 61, 3 p. ;
HD5710.85.B59 G63 1982
NYPL [Sc F 89-108]

SEGOU (MALI : REGION) - HISTORY.
Konare Ba, Adam. L'épop'ee de Segu . Paris , c1987. 201 p. : ISBN 2-8289-0250-1
NYPL [Sc E 88-180]

SEGOU (MALI : REGION) - POLITICS AND GOVERNMENT.
Konare Ba, Adam. L'épop'ee de Segu . Paris , c1987. 201 p. : ISBN 2-8289-0250-1
NYPL [Sc E 88-180]

Segredos de "seu" bita Dá-nó-em-pingo-d'água.
Maya-Maya, Estevão. Regresso triunfal de Cruz e Sousa ; e, Os segredos de "seu" bita Dá-nó-em-pingo-d'água /. São Paulo , 1982. x, 85 p. : **NYPL [Sc D 88-1098]**

SEGREGATION IN EDUCATION - LAW AND LEGISLATION - UNITED STATES - TRIAL PRACTICE.
Chesler, Mark A. Social science in court . Madison, Wis. , 1988. xiv, 286 p. ; ISBN 0-299-11620-4 : DDC 344.73/0798 347.304798 19
KF8925.D5 C48 1988 **NYPL [Sc E 89-187]**

SEGREGATION IN HIGHER EDUCATION - UNITED STATES.
The Black/white colleges . Washington, D.C. , 1981. v, 46 p. : **NYPL [Sc F 89-48]**

SEGREGATION IN SPORTS - UNITED STATES.
Moore, Joseph Thomas. Pride against prejudice . New York , c1988. 195 p., [8] p. of plates : ISBN 0-313-25995-X (lib. bdg. : alk. paper) DDC 796.357/092/4 B 19
GV865.D58 M66 1988 **NYPL [Sc E 88-272]**

SEGREGATION - SOUTH AFRICA.
Brickley, Carol. South Africa . London , 1985. 50 p. : ISBN 0-905400-06-2 :
NYPL [Sc D 89-361]

Gaydon, Vanessa. Race against the ratios . Johannesburg, South Africa , 1987. 70 p. ; ISBN 0-86982-321-3 **NYPL [Sc F 88-322]**

Segun, Mabel. Conflict and other poems / by Mabel Segun. Ibadan : New Horn Press, 1986. vi, 49 p. ; 18 cm. (Opon Ifa series . no. 3) ISBN 978-226-613-2
I. Title. II. Series. **NYPL [Sc C 88-286]**

Seignobos, Christian. Tourneux, Henry. Les Mbara et leur langue (Tchad) /. Paris , 1986. 319 p. ; ISBN 2-85297-188-7
NYPL [Sc E 88-162]

Seize ans de lutte pour un pays normal /. Soukar, Michel. Port-au-Prince, Haïti . iv, 60 p. ; **NYPL [Sc D 88-511]**

Sekou, Lasana M. For the mighty gods-- : an offering / Lasana Sekou ; Introd. by Amiri Baraka. New York : House of Nehesi, 1982. 95 p. : ill. ; 22 cm.
I. Title. **NYPL [Sc D 88-1405]**

Sekou, Lasana M., 1959- Born here / Lasana M. Sekou ; introduction by Fabian Badejo ; illustrations by Doñanite Cozbi Sanchez ... [et al.]. St. Maarten, Caribbean ; Staten Island, N.Y. : House of Nehesi, c1986. xvii, 148 p. : ill. ; 22 cm. Poems. ISBN 0-913441-05-8 (pbk.)
I. Title.
MLCS 86/13366 (P) **NYPL [Sc D 88-491]**

Sékou Touré, le héros et le tyran /. Kaké, Ibrahima Baba. Paris , 1987. 254 p. :
NYPL [Sc D 88-468]

Selassie, Sergew Hable. see Sergew Hable Selassie, 1929-

Select bibliography of education in the Commonwealth Caribbean, 1976-1985 . Robertson, Amy. Mona, Jamaica , 1987. 174 p. ; **NYPL [Sc F 88-316]**

A selected bibliography of materials and resources on women in the Caribbean available at WAND's Research and Documentation Centre /. Inniss, Diana. Pinelands, St. Michael [Barbados] [1987] 119 p. ;
NYPL [Sc F 88-218]

Selected poems /. Sepamla, Sydney Sipho, 1932- [Poems. Selections.] Craighall [South Africa] , 1984. 135 p. ; ISBN 0-86852-037-3 DDC 821 19
PR9369.3.S43 A6 1984
NYPL [Sc D 88-988]

Selected poems of Jay Wright /. Wright, Jay. Princeton, N.J. , c1987. xv, 197 p. ; ISBN 0-691-06687-6 (alk. paper) : DDC 811/.54 19
PS3573.R5364 A6 1987
NYPL [JFD 87-6880]

Selected small cemeteries of Washington, DC /. Sluby, Paul E. [Washington] , c1987. 84 p. :
NYPL [Sc D 88-780]

Selections from One party democracy: the 1965 Tanzania general elections. Lionel Cliffe, editor. [Nairobi] East African Pub. House [1967] 143 p. 22 cm. Includes bibliographies. CONTENTS. - The political system, by L. Cliffe.--UGOGO: local government changes, by P. Rigby.--Kilimanjaro: localism and nationalism, by B. Mramba.--Voters look at the elections, by K. Prewitt and G. Hyden.--The impact of the elections, by L. Cliffe.--Extracts from the Presidential Commission report. DDC 324/.678
1. Elections - Tanzania. 2. Tanzania - Politics and government - 1964-. I. Cliffe, Lionel, ed.
JQ3519.A55 O53 **NYPL [Sc D 87-1320]**

SELENOLOGY. see MOON.

SELF-DEFENSE (LAW) - UNITED STATES.
Fletcher, George P. A crime of self-defense . New York , London , c1988. xi, 253 p. ; ISBN 0-02-910311-8 DDC 345.73/04 345.7305 4 19
KF224.G63 F54 1988 **NYPL [JLE 88-4737]**

SELF-EMPLOYED - NIGERIA.
Okeke, Okeke Okore, 1954- Self-employment for unemployed Nigerians /. Festac Town, Lagos, Nigeria , 1987. 110 p. ; ISBN 978-333-011-27 **NYPL [Sc D 89-298]**

Self-employment for unemployed Nigerians /. Okeke, Okeke Okore, 1954- Festac Town, Lagos, Nigeria , 1987. 110 p. ; ISBN 978-333-011-27 **NYPL [Sc D 89-298]**

SELF-GOVERNMENT. see REPRESENTATIVE GOVERNMENT AND REPRESENTATION.

SELF-HELP GROUPS - UNITED STATES - CASE STUDIES.
Washington Consulting Group. Uplift . Salt Lake City , c1974. xviii, 465 p. : ISBN 0-913420-38-7
HV547 .W38 1974 **NYPL [JLE 75-1370]**

Self portrait -- Bernard Goss. [S.l. : s.n., 1967?] 28 p. : ill. ; 23 cm. Cover title. CONTENTS. - Form of a woman : a speech symphony / Evangeline Zehmer ; illustrations by B. Goss.--Peace, truth, beauty : selections honoring Bernard Goss, artist.
1. Goss, Bernard, d. 1966. I. Zehmer, Evangeline. II. Goss, Bernard, d. 1966. **NYPL [Sc D 88-503]**

A self-portrait of Langston Hughes [microform] /. Hauke, Kathleen Armstrong. 1981. 228 leaves. **NYPL [Sc Micro R-4683]**

Sellassie, Sergew Hable. see Sergew Hable Selassie, 1929-

Selle, Rianne. SWA Namibia today /. Windhoek , 1988. 128 p. ;
NYPL [Sc D 88-1359]

Sembene, Ousmane, 1923-
Niiwam, suivi de Taaw : nouvelles / Sembene Ousmane. Paris : Presence africaine, c1987. 189 p. ; 18 cm. ISBN 2-7087-0486-9
1. Senegal - Fiction. I. Sembene, Ousmane, 1923- Taaw. II. Title. III. Title: Taaw. **NYPL [Sc C 88-320]**

Taaw. Sembene, Ousmane, 1923- Niiwam, suivi de Taaw : nouvelles / Sembene Ousmane. Paris , c1987. 189 p. ; ISBN 2-7087-0486-9
NYPL [Sc C 88-320]

SEMEIOTIC. see SIGNS AND SYMBOLS.

Semences nouvelles : poèmes / A. Ghan ... [et al.] Lomé, Togo : Éditions HAHO, 1986. 96 p. : ill., ports. ; 18 cm.
1. Togolese poetry (French). I. Ghan, A. (Ayicoé), 1945-. **NYPL [Sc C 88-123]**

SEMIARID REGIONS. see ARID REGIONS.

Séminaires d'information et de formation des secrétaires généraux : Yamoussoukro, 3-7 mai 1982, Abidjan, 10-11 décembre 1982, Yamoussoukro, 27-29 décembre 1983. [Abidjan] : Fraternité-Hebdo éditions, [1985] 72 p. : ill. ; 24 cm. "Documents du parti." On cover: RDA PDCI. DDC 966.6/805 19
1. Houphouet-Boigny, Félix, 1905- - Congresses. 2. Ivory Coast - Politics and government - 1960- - Congresses. I. Editions Fraternité-Hebdo. II. Parti démocratique de Côte d'Ivoire.
DT545.8 .S46 1985 **NYPL [Sc E 88-151]**

Seminar on Internal Migration in Nigeria (1975 : University of Ife) Internal migration in Nigeria : proceedings of the Seminar on Internal Migration in Nigeria, University of Ife, 1975 / edited by Aderanti Adepoju. [Ife] : Dept. of Demography and Social Statistics, University of Ife, 1976. iii, 300 p. : maps, graphs ; 25 cm. Includes bibliographical references.
1. Migration, Internal - Nigeria - Congresses. I. Adepoju, Aderanti. II. University of Ife. Dept. of Demography and Social Statistics. III. Title.
NYPL [Sc E 88-489]

Seminar on Population Studies, West African. see West African Seminar on Population Studies, University of Ghana, 1972.

Seminar on the Changing and Contemporary Role of Women in Society, African. see African Seminar on the Changing and Contemporary Role of Women in Society, Addis Ababa, 1975.

Seminar papers on internal conflicts in Uganda . International Seminar on Internal Conflict (1987 : Makerere, Uganda) [Makerere, Uganda , 1987]. 1 v. ; **NYPL [Sc F 89-86]**

Seminar proceedings (University of Edinburgh. Centre of African Studies. (no. 27) African medicine in the modern world . Edinburgh [1987] 222 p. : DDC 615.8/82/096 19
GR350 **NYPL [Sc D 87-1283]**

Seminario Interdisciplinar de Antropologia (1st : 1982 : Maputo, Mozambique) Primeiro seminário interdisciplinar de antropologia / Departamento de Arqueologia e Antropologia, Universidade Eduardo Mondlane. Maputo : O Departamento, 1987. 153 p. ; 30 cm. (Trabalhos de arqueologia e antropologia . no. 2) Errata slip inserted. Bibliography: p. [125]-130.
1. Anthropology - Mozambique - Congresses. I. Universidade Eduardo Mondlane. Departamento de Arqueologia e Antropologia. II. Title.
NYPL [Sc F 88-172]

SEMINOLE WAR, 2D, 1835-1842.
Giddings, Joshua Reed, 1795-1864. The exiles of Florida. Columbus, Ohio, 1858. viii, 338 p.
E83.817 .G46 **NYPL [Sc Rare F 88-68]**

SEMIOTIC. see SIGNS AND SYMBOLS.

Semitische und hamitische Wortst'amme im Nilo-Hamitischen . Hohenberger, Johannes. Berlin , 1988. xxii, 310 p. ; ISBN 3-496-00960-8
NYPL [Sc D 88-542]

Semog, Éle. Limeira, José Carlos. Atabaques /. [Rio de Janeiro? , 1983] 171 p. ;
NYPL [Sc D 88-1096]

SENATORS (UNITED STATES) see LEGISLATORS - UNITED STATES.

Sène, Alioune. Célébration du 7oe anniversaire du président Léopold Sédar Senghor (9 Oct. 1906-9 Oct. 1976) [microform] : Colloque sur le thème "culture et développement" (2-9 Oct. 1976) : argument / présenté par [le président du] Comité scientifique international Dakar, le 10 févr. 1976. Dakar : Fondation Léopold Sédar Senghor, 1976. [4] p. ; 21 cm. Microfiche. New York: New York Public Library, 198 . 1 microfiche: negative; 11 x 15 cm. (FSN Sc 019,108)

1. Senghor, Léopold Sédar, Pres. Senegal, 1906-. 2. Colloque sur le thème "Culture et développement" (1976: Dakar, Senegal). I. Fondation Léopold Sédar Senghor. II. Title. III. Title: Célébration du soixante-dixième anniversaire du président Léopold Sédar Senghor. **NYPL [Sc Micro F-11026]**

Senegal : Mehrparteiensystem und Wahlen 1983 : Dokumentation zur politischen Entwicklung = Sénégal : multipartisme et élections 1983 : une documentation de l'évolution politique / [Herausgeber], Marianne Weiss, Ernst Stetter, Klaus Voll. Hamburg : Institut für Afrika-Kunde, Dokumentations-Leitstelle Afrika, 1983. xxxix, 392 p. : ill. ; 30 cm. (Aktueller Informationsdienst Afrika, 0720-0471. Sondernummer . 5) Includes texts in French. Bibliography: p. xxvii. ISBN 3-922887-28-7 (pbk.) DDC 324.266/3 19
1. Elections - Senegal. 2. Political parties - Senegal. 3. Senegal - Politics and government - 1960-. I. Weiss, Marianne. II. Stetter, Ernst. III. Voll, Klaus. IV. Series.
JQ3396.A91 S38 1983 **NYPL [JLF 85-1341]**

Le Sénégal : la terre et les hommes : guide touristique sénégalo-gambien. [Dakar, Senegal] : Nouvelles éditions africaines, [1983?] 80 p. : col. ill., maps ; 27 cm. English and French. With: The Gambia. [Dakar, Senegal] : Nouvelles éditions africaines, [1983?] Colored map on folded leaf of plates inserted. ISBN 2-7236-0911-1
1. Senegal - Description and travel - 1981- - Guide-books.
DT509.2 .G36 1967 DT549.2
NYPL [Sc F 88-202]

SENEGAL - CONSTITUTIONAL HISTORY.
Hesseling, Gerti. [Senegal, staatsrechtelijke en politieke ontwikkelingen. French.] Histoire politique du Sénégal . Paris, France , Leiden, Pays-Bas , c1985. 437 p. : ISBN 2-86537-118-2 DDC 342.66/3029 346.630229 19
LAW   **NYPL [JLE 88-3233]**

SENEGAL - DESCRIPTION AND TRAVEL - 1981- - GUIDE-BOOKS.
Le Sénégal . [Dakar, Senegal] [1983?] 80 p. : ISBN 2-7236-0911-1
DT509.2 .G36 1967 DT549.2
NYPL [Sc F 88-202]

Le Sénégal d'hier et ses traditions /. Diop, Adja Khady, 1922- [S.l.] [198-?] 61, 18 p. :
NYPL [Sc D 88-933]

SENEGAL - ECONOMIC CONDITIONS.
The Political economy of risk and choice in Senegal /. London, England , Totowa, N.J. , 1987. xv, 363 p. : ISBN 0-7146-3297-X : DDC 338.966/3 19
HC1045 .P65 1987   **NYPL [Sc E 87-360]**

SENEGAL - ECONOMIC POLICY.
The Political economy of risk and choice in Senegal /. London, England , Totowa, N.J. , 1987. xv, 363 p. : ISBN 0-7146-3297-X : DDC 338.966/3 19
HC1045 .P65 1987   **NYPL [Sc E 87-360]**

SENEGAL - FICTION.
Dia, Malick. L'impossible compromis /. Abidjan , c1979. 102 p. ; ISBN 2-7236-0447-0
NYPL [Sc D 88-958]

Diallo, Nafissatou, 1941- Fary, princess of Tiali /. Washington, D.C. , c1987. xi, 106 p. : ISBN 0-89410-411-X   **NYPL [Sc D 88-1366]**

Sembene, Ousmane, 1923- Niiwam, suivi de Taaw . Paris , c1987. 189 p. ; ISBN 2-7087-0486-9   **NYPL [Sc C 88-320]**

Senegal - Government. see Senegal - Politics and government.

SENEGAL - POLITICS AND GOVERNMENT - TO 1960.
Zuccarelli, François. La vie politique sénégalaise (1789 - 1940) /. Paris , c1987. 157 p. ; ISBN 2-903182-23-X   **NYPL [Sc E 88-342]**

SENEGAL - POLITICS AND GOVERNMENT - 1960-
Senegal . Hamburg , 1983. xxxix, 392 p. : ISBN 3-922887-28-7 (pbk.) DDC 324.266/3 19
JQ3396.A91 S38 1983 **NYPL [JLF 85-1341]**

SENEGAL - RACE RELATIONS.
Deux études sur les relations entre groupes ethniques. Spanish. Dos estudios sobre las relaciones entre grupos étnicos en África . Barcelona [Paris] , 1982. 174 p. ; ISBN

84-85000-41-9
DT549.42 .D4818 1982
NYPL [Sc D 88-651]

SENEGAL - RURAL CONDITIONS.
Leber, Gisela. Agrarstrukturen und Landflucht im Senegal . Saarbrücken , Fort Lauderdale , 1979. vii, 142 p. : ISBN 3-88156-125-0
HD2144.5 .L42   **NYPL [JLD 80-2814]**

SENEGAL - SOCIAL LIFE AND CUSTOMS - JUVENILE LITERATURE.
Jacobsen, Peter Otto. A family in West Africa /. Hove , 1985. 32 p. : ISBN 0-85078-434-4 : DDC 966/.305 19
DA588   **NYPL [Sc D 88-1499]**

Sénégal, Syndicalisme et participation responsable. Lo, Magatte, 1925- Syndicalisme et participation responsable /. Paris [1987] 151 p. : ISBN 2-85802-885-0   **NYPL [Sc D 88-915]**

SENEGAMBIA - HISTORY.
Barry, Boubacar. La Sénégambie du XVe au XIXe siècle . Paris , c1988. 431 p., [8] p. of plates :   **NYPL [Sc D 89-600]**

Robinson, David, 1938- [Holy war of Umar Tal. French.] La guerre sainte d'al-Hajj Umar . Paris , c1988. 413 p. : ISBN 2-86537-211-1
NYPL [Sc E 89-258]

La Sénégambie du XVe au XIXe siècle . Barry, Boubacar. Paris , c1988. 431 p., [8] p. of plates :   **NYPL [Sc D 89-600]**

SENESCENCE. see AGING.

Senghor et la terre /. Saint-Cheron, François de. Paris , c1988. 138 p. ; ISBN 2-86985-033-6
NYPL [Sc C 89-137]

SENGHOR, LÉOPOLD SÉDAR.
Séphocle, Marie-Line. The reception of negritude writers in the Federal Republic of Germany . Ann Arbor, Mich. , c1987. vi, 121 p. ;   **NYPL [Sc D 89-293]**

SENGHOR, LÉOPOLD SÉDAR, PRES. SENEGAL, 1906-
Sène, Alioune. Célébration du 7oe anniversaire du président Léopold Sédar Senghor (9 Oct. 1906-9 Oct. 1976) [microform]. Dakar , 1976. [4] p. ;   **NYPL [Sc Micro F-11026]**

Senghor, Léopold Sédar, 1906-
Anthologie de la nouvelle poésie nègre et malgache de langue française / par Léopold Sédar Senghor, précédée de Orphée noir / par Jean-Paul Sartre. 5. éd. Paris : Presses universitaires de France, 1985, c1948. xliv, 227 p. ; 20 cm. (Quadrige (Presses universitaires de France), 0291-0489 . 66) Includes bibliographical references. ISBN 2-13-038715-2
1. African poetry (French). I. Sartre, Jean Paul, 1905- Orphée noir. 1985. II. Title. III. Series.
NYPL [Sc C 88-134]

Ce que je crois : négritude, francité et civilisation de l'universel / Léopold Sédar Senghor. Paris : B. Grasset, c1988. 234 p. ; 21 cm. (Ce que je crois, 0768-231X) Series statement from p. [9] Includes bibliographical references. ISBN 2-246-24941-4
1. France - Civilization. I. Title.
NYPL [Sc D 89-76]

Ethnologiques . Paris , 1987. xxxvi, 430 p. : ISBN 2-7056-6025-9   **NYPL [Sc E 88-39]**

POÈMES.
Kesteloot, Lilyan. Comprendre les Poèmes de Léopold Sédar Senghor /. Issy les Moulineaux , 1986. 143 p. : ISBN 2-85049-376-7   **NYPL [Sc D 88-978]**

POEMS.
Jouanny, Robert A. Les voies du lyrisme dans les "Poèmes" de Léopold Sédar Senghor (Chants d'ombre, Hosties noires, Ethiopiques, Nocturnes) . Paris , 1986. 161 p. ; ISBN 2-85203-026-8   **NYPL [Sc D 88-1026]**

Selections. 1988. Saint-Cheron, François de. Senghor et la terre / François de Saint-Cheron. Paris , c1988. 138 p. ; ISBN 2-86985-033-6   **NYPL [Sc C 89-137]**

SENGHOR, LÉOPOLD SÉDAR, 1906- - CRITICISM AND INTERPRETATION.
Iyay Kimoni, 1938- Poésie de la négritude . Kikwit , 1985. vi, 168 p. ; DDC 841/.009/896 19
PQ3897 .I93 1985   **NYPL [Sc B 89-18]**

Jouanny, Robert A. Les voies du lyrisme dans les "Poèmes" de Léopold Sédar Senghor (Chants

d'ombre, Hosties noires, Ethiopiques, Nocturnes) . Paris , 1986. 161 p. ; ISBN 2-85203-026-8   **NYPL [Sc D 88-1026]**

Kesteloot, Lilyan. Comprendre les Poèmes de Léopold Sédar Senghor /. Issy les Moulineaux , 1986. 143 p. : ISBN 2-85049-376-7
NYPL [Sc D 88-978]

Saint-Cheron, François de. Senghor et la terre /. Paris , c1988. 138 p. ; ISBN 2-86985-033-6
NYPL [Sc C 89-137]

SENIOR CITIZENS. see AGED.

Senoga-Zake, George W. Folk music of Kenya / George W. Senoga-Zake. Nairobi, Kenya : Uzima Press, 1986. 185 p. : ill., music ; 21 cm.
1. Musical instruments - Kenya. 2. Dancing - Kenya. 3. Folk-songs - Kenya - History and criticism. I. Title.
NYPL [Sc D 88-368]

SENUSSITES.
Ciammaichella, Glauco. Libyens et Français au Tchad (1897-1914) . Paris , 1987. 187 p. : ISBN 2-222-04067-1   **NYPL [Sc E 89-182]**

Sepamla, Sydney Sipho, 1932- [Poems. Selections]
Selected poems / Sipho Sepamla ; edited and introduced by Mbulelo Vizikhungo Mzamane. Craighall [South Africa] : Ad. Donker, 1984. 135 p. ; 21 cm. ISBN 0-86852-037-3 DDC 821 19
I. Mzamane, Mbulelo, 1948-. II. Title.
PR9369.3.S43 A6 1984
NYPL [Sc D 88-988]

Séphocle, Marie-Line. The reception of negritude writers in the Federal Republic of Germany : Aimé Césaire, Léon Gontran Damas, Léopold Sédar Senghor / by Marie-Line Séphocle. Ann Arbor, Mich. : University Microfilms International, c1987. vi, 121 p. ; 22 cm. Thesis (Ph.D.)-New York University, 1987. Bibliography: p. 112-121.
1. Césaire, Aimé. 2. Damas, Léon Gontran. 3. Senghor, Léopold Sédar. I. Title. **NYPL [Sc D 89-293]**

SEPULCHERS. see TOMBS.

Sequins for a ragged hem. /. Johnson, Amryl. London , c1988. 272 p. ; ISBN 0-86068-971-9
NYPL [Sc D 88-612]

Ser negro no Brasil hoje /. Valente, Ana Lúcia E. F. (Ana Lúcia Eduardo Farah) São Paulo, SP, Brasil , 1987. 64 p. : DDC 305.8/96/081 19
F2659.N4 V35 1987   **NYPL [HFB 88-2561]**

Seredy, Kate. Gedö, Leopold. [Janiböl Jonny lesz. English.] Who is Johnny? /. New York , 1939. 242 p. :   **NYPL [Sc D 88-1512]**

SERER LANGUAGE - GRAMMAR.
Faye, Waly Coly. Précis grammatical de sérère /. [Dakar] , 1980. 80 leaves ;
NYPL [Sc F 86-168]

SERER LANGUAGE - ORTHOGRAPHY AND SPELLING - GLOSSARIES, VOCABULARIES, ETC.
Faye, Suleymane. Aqatoor a seereer /. Kampala, Ouganda , 1986. 67 p. :
NYPL [Sc F 88-263]

Sergeant, Howard, 1914- New voices of the Commonwealth. Edited by Howard Sergeant. London, Evans Bros., 1968. 208 p. 23 cm. Poems. ISBN 0-237-49815-4 DDC 821/.008
1. English poetry - 20th century. 2. English poetry - Commonwealth of Nations authors. I. Title.
PR9086 .S4   **NYPL [Sc D 89-121]**

Sergew Hable Selassie, 1929- Ya'Ityoṗ̄a 'ortodoks taw aḥedo béta kerestiy an. The Church of Ethiopia. Addis Ababa, 1970. iv, 97 p.   **NYPL [Sc D 89-386]**

Série biographies, hommes et femmes des Caraïbes.
Lara, Oruno D. Le commandant Mortenol . Epinay, France , c1985. 275 p. : ISBN 2-905787-00-7   **NYPL [Sc D 88-1085]**

Série Documentos (Fundação Joaquim Nabuco).
(15) 30 anos do Instituto Joaquim Nabuco de Pesquisas Sociais /. Recife , 1981. 343 p. : ISBN 85-7019-008-5 DDC 300.72081 19
H67.R44 A13 1981   **NYPL [Sc D 88-871]**

(15) 30 anos do Instituto Joaquim Nabuco de Pesquisas Sociais /. Recife , 1981. 343 p. : ISBN 85-7019-008-5 DDC 300.72081 19
H67.R44 A13 1981   **NYPL [Sc D 88-871]**

(18) Fundação Joaquim Nabuco. Orçamento . Recife , 1982. 92 p. ; ISBN 85-7019-046-8
NYPL [Sc B 88-49]

(20) Fundação Joaquim Nabuco. Plano diretor de informática, 82-84 /. Recife , 1982. 101 p., 1 folded leaf : *NYPL [Sc D 88-924]*

(26) Diario de Pernambuco . Recife [1985]. 256 p. : ISBN 85-7019-094-8
NYPL [Sc D 88-862]

(30) Mattos, Edgar, 1935- Por uma educacão libertáda e libertadora . Recife , 1986. 89 p. ; ISBN 85-7019-098-0 *NYPL [Sc D 88-845]*

(33) Gilberto Freyre entre nós /. Recife , 1988. 115 p. ; ISBN 85-7019-140-5
NYPL [Sc D 89-320]

Serie, Dritte Welt.
Rummelt, Peter. Sport im Kolonialismus, Kolonialismus im Sport . Köln , 1986. 341 p. : ISBN 3-7609-5213-5 DDC 796/.096 19
GV665 .R85 1986 *NYPL [Sc D 88-973]*

Südafrika - Widerstand und Befreiungskampf . Köln , 1987, c1986. 286 p. : ISBN 3-7609-1023-8
NYPL [Sc C 88-190]

Série Estudos e pesquisas (Fundação Joaquim Nabuco) .
(52) Leite, Glacyra Lazzari. Pernambuco 1817 . Recife , 1988. 275 p. ; ISBN 85-7019-122-7 DDC 981/.3403 20
F2534 .L45 1988 *NYPL [Sc D 89-605]*

Série Poésie .
(27e) Charles, Christophe, 1951- Obsessions . Port-au-Prince, Haiti, W.I. , c1985. 83 p. ;
MLCS 86/2028 (P) *NYPL [Sc C 88-122]*

Série Princípios .
(106) Moura, Clovis. Quilombos . São Paulo , 1987. 94 p. ; ISBN 85-08-01858-4
NYPL [Sc C 88-3]

(107) Azevêdo, Eliane. Raça . São Paulo , 1987. 62 p. ; ISBN 85-08-01878-9
NYPL [Sc C 88-14]

(108) Lody, Raul Giovanni da Motta. Candomblé . São Paulo , 1987. 85 p. ; ISBN 85-08-01877-0 *NYPL [Sc C 88-62]*

(115) Algranti, Leila Mezan. D. Joao VI . São Paulo , 1987. 78 p. ; ISBN 85-08-01870-3
NYPL [Sc C 88-15]

(116) Quieroz, Suely Robles Reis de. Escravidão negra no Brasil /. São Paulo , 1987. 86 p. ; *NYPL [Sc C 88-2]*

(40) Kabengele Munanga. Negritude . São Paulo , 1986. 88 p. ; ISBN 85-08-00686-1
NYPL [Sc C 88-105]

(65) Meihy, José Carlos Sebe Bom, 1943- Carnaval, carnavais /. São Paulo , 1986. 96 p. ; ISBN 85-08-01168-7 : DDC 394.2/5/0981 19
GT4180 .M45 1986 *NYPL [HFB 88-1339]*

Série Tropicalia.
Burnet, Mireille. La chienne du quimboiseur /. Paris , c1986. 126 p. ; ISBN 2-903033-81-1
NYPL [Sc D 89-168]

Series in modern and contemporary literature.
Rahming, Melvin B., 1943- The evolution of the West Indian's image in the Afro-American novel /. Millwood, N.Y. , c1986. xix, 160 p. ; ISBN 8046-9339-0 DDC 813/.009/35203969729 19
PS153.N5 R3 1985 *NYPL [JFD 86-6569]*

SERMONS, AMERICAN - AFRO-AMERICAN AUTHORS.
Borders, William Holmes, 1905- Seven minutes at the 'mike' in the Deep South /. [Atlanta?] , 1949, c1943. 104 p. : *NYPL [Sc D 87-1426]*

SERMONS, ENGLISH - NIGERIA.
Odunuga, S. A. F. (Samuel Adedoyin Folafunmi), 1902- [Sermons. Selections.] The life of Venerable Archdeacon S.A.F. Odunuga /. [Nigeria] , 1982. xiii, 175 p., [2] p. of plates : DDC 252/.03 19
BX5700.7.Z6 O28 1982
NYPL [Sc E 89-142]

SERMONS, ISLAMIC. see ISLAMIC SERMONS.

Serote, Mongane, 1944- A tough tale / by Mongane Wally Serote. London : Kliptown, 1987. 48 p. ; 21 cm. ISBN 0-904759-80-6 (pbk) : DDC 821 19

1. South Africa - Poetry. I. Title.
NYPL [Sc D 88-513]

SERPENTS IN LITERATURE.
Umezinwa, Willy A. From African symbols to physics . [Nigeria] c1988. 71 p. :
NYPL [Sc E 89-36]

Serrano, Jumoke. The last Don out / Jumoke Serrano. Ibadan, Nigeria : Abiprint Pub. Co., 1986. 106 p. ; 18 cm. (Bloom series) ISBN 978-14-1062-0
1. Narcotics dealers - Nigeria - Fiction. 2. Nigeria - Fiction. I. Title. *NYPL [Sc C 88-341]*

Serrate, Marta Dulzaides. see Dulzaides Serrate, Marta.

Serving secretly . Flower, Ken. London , c1987. xxii, 330 p., [12] p. of plates : ISBN 0-7195-4438-6 *NYPL [JFE 88-5776]*

SERVITUDE. see SLAVERY.

Sesana, Renato Kizito. see Kizito Sesana, Renato.

Sesay, Amadu. The OAU after twenty years / Amadu Sesay, Olusola Ojo, and Orobola Fasehun. Boulder : Westview Press, 1984. ix, 133 p. ; 23 cm. (Westview special studies on Africa) Includes bibliographical references and index. ISBN 0-8133-0112-2 :
1. Organization of African Unity - History. I. Ojo, Olusola. II. Fasehun, Orobola. III. Title. IV. Title: O.A.U. after twenty years. *NYPL [JLD 85-633]*

Sessi, Kpanlingan. Les eunuques / Kpanlingan Sessi. Paris : Silex, c1984. 71 p. ; 22 cm. ISBN 2-903871-56-6
1. Africa - Fiction. I. Title.
NYPL [Sc D 88-1231]

Sethuraman, S. V. Rural small-scale industries and employment in Africa and Asia. Geneva , 1984. x, 159 p. ; ISBN 92-2-103513-1 (pbk.) : DDC 338.6/42/095 19
HD2346.A55 R87 1984
NYPL [JLE 84-3222]

Setjeant, R. B. (Robert Bertram) Islamic city. Spanish. La ciudad islámica . Barcelona [Paris] , 1982. 260 p. : ISBN 92-3-301665-X (Unesco) *NYPL [Sc D 88-596]*

Sets'abi, Anthony. Human resources development and utilization in Africa /. Maseru [Lesotho] , 1988. vi, 160 p. ; ISBN 0-620-12102-5
NYPL [Sc D 89-558]

Seuling, Barbara. (illus) Howard, Moses L., 1928- The ostrich chase /. New York [1974] 118 p. : ISBN 0-03-012096-9 *NYPL [Sc D 88-374]*

Seven minutes at the 'mike' in the Deep South /. Borders, William Holmes, 1905- [Atlanta?] , 1949, c1943. 104 p. : *NYPL [Sc D 87-1426]*

Seven roles of women . Oppong, Christine. Geneva , 1987. xi, 127 p. :
NYPL [Sc E 89-143]

Seven shades /. Brown, Valerie Parks. New York , 1986. 106 p. ; ISBN 0-533-06678-6
NYPL [Sc D 88-185]

Seven speeches. Farrakhan, Louis. [Speeches. Selections.] 7 speeches. New York, 1974. 151 p. *NYPL [Sc D 88-1441]*

The Seventh Day Adventists in Yorubaland, 1914--1964 . Agboola, David. Ibadan , 1987. ix, 92 p. : ISBN 978-12-2197-6
NYPL [Sc D 88-1043]

SEVENTH-DAY ADVENTISTS - NIGERIA - HISTORY.
Agboola, David. The Seventh Day Adventists in Yorubaland, 1914--1964 . Ibadan , 1987. ix, 92 p. : ISBN 978-12-2197-6
NYPL [Sc D 88-1043]

Seventy-five years of King's College. King's College (Lagos, Nigeria) 75 years of King's College /. [Lagos?] 1987. vi, 89 p. :
NYPL [Sc E 88-257]

Severo-Amerikanskie Shtaty. see United States.

Sevillano Castillo, Rosa. Los Orígenes de la descolonización africana a través de la prensa española (1956-1962) / Rosa Sevillano Castillo. Madrid : Ministerio de Asuntos Exteriores, Secretaría de Estado para la Cooperación Internacional y para Iberoamérica, Dirección General de Relationes Culturales, 1986. 158 p. ; 25 cm. Bibliography: p. [155]-158.
1. Decolonization - Africa. 2. Africa - Politics and government - 1960-. 3. Africa - Politics and government - 1945-1960. I. Title.
NYPL [Sc E 88-94]

SEX BIAS. see SEXISM.

SEX - CROSS-CULTURAL STUDIES.
The Cultural construction of sexuality /. London , New York , 1987. xi, 304 p. : ISBN 0-422-60870-X DDC 306.7 19
GN484.3 .C85 1987 *NYPL [Sc D 87-1198]*

SEX CUSTOMS - UNITED STATES.
Brown, Leroy. Black sexual power /. Cleveland, Ohio , c1970. 220 p. ; *NYPL [Sc C 88-274]*

SEX CUSTOMS - UNITED STATES - HISTORY.
D'Emilio, John. Intimate matters . New York , c1988. xx, 428 p., [16] leaves of plates : ISBN 0-06-015855-7 : DDC 306.7/0973 19
HQ18.U5 D45 1988 *NYPL [Sc E 88-436]*

SEX IN PRISONS. see PRISONERS - SEXUAL BEHAVIOR.

SEX PRESELECTION.
Dada, Victor B. Choose the sex of your baby . N. Y. , c1983. xiv, 96 p. ; ISBN 0-533-05256-4
NYPL [Sc D 88-1180]

Sex, racism and other reflective tidbits /. Henderson, H. Michael. [Chamblee, Georgia , 1987] 63 p. ; *NYPL [Sc D 88-265]*

SEX ROLE - AFRICA, SUB-SAHARAN.
Women and the state in Africa /. Boulder, Colo. , c1989. ix, 229 p. ; ISBN 1-555-87082-1 (alk. paper) : DDC 305.4/2/096 19
HQ1236.5.A357 W65 1988
NYPL [Sc E 89-159]

SEX ROLE IN LITERATURE.
Racism and sexism in children's books. New York , c1978. 72 p. : ISBN 0-930040-29-5
NYPL [Sc D 89-259]

Sex roles, population and development in West Africa : policy-related studies on work and demographic issues / edited by Christine Oppong. London : J. Currey ; Portsmouth, N.H. : Heinemann in association with ILO Publications, Geneva, 1987. xiii, 242 p. ; 24 cm. Includes index. Bibliography: p. [221]-236. ISBN 0-435-08022-9 DDC 304.6/0966 19
1. Women - Employment - Africa, West - Case studies. 2. Women in development - Africa, West - Case studies. 3. Manpower policy - Africa, West - Case studies. 4. Fertility, Human - Africa, West - Case studies. 5. Birth control - Africa, West - Case studies. 6. Africa, West - Population policy - Case studies. I. Oppong, Christine.
HB3665.5.A3 S49 1988
NYPL [Sc E 88-318]

SEXISM - UNITED STATES.
Davis, Angela Yvonne, 1944- Women, culture, & politics /. New York, NY , 1989. xv, 238 p. ; ISBN 0-394-76976-8 : DDC 305.4/8896073 19
E185.86 .D382 1989 *NYPL [Sc D 89-275]*

SEXISM - UNITED STATES - PSYCHOLOGICAL ASPECTS.
The Psychopathology of everyday racism and sexism /. New York , c1988. xix, 120 p. ; ISBN 0-918393-51-5 (pbk.) DDC 305.4/2 19
RC451.4.M58 P79 1988
NYPL [Sc D 89-449]

Sexo e marginalidade . Quintas, Fátima. Petrópolis :Vozes, 1986. 191 p. ;
NYPL [Sc D 88-1477]

SEXUAL BEHAVIOR. see SEX CUSTOMS.

SEXUAL BEHAVIOR SURVEYS - CALIFORNIA - SAN FRANCISCO.
A baseline survey of AIDS risk behaviors and attitudes in San Francisco's Black communities /. San Francisco, Calif. [1987] vii, 74, [59] leaves : *NYPL [Sc F 88-232]*

SEXUAL DIVISION OF LABOR - ZAMBIA - HISTORY - 20TH CENTURY.
Hansen, Karen Tranberg. Distant companions . Ithaca , 1989. xv, 321 p. : ISBN 0-8014-2217-5 (alk. paper) DDC 331.7/6164046/096894 19
HD6072.2.Z33 H36 1989
NYPL [Sc E 89-215]

SEXUAL INVERSION. see HOMOSEXUALITY.

Seychellen, Komoren und Maskarenen . Marquardt, Wilhelm. München , c1976. 346 p. :

ISBN 3-8039-0117-0
DT469.S4 M37 **NYPL [JFC 77-3948]**

SEYCHELLES.
Knights, Ian E. The Seychelles [Microform] .
London , 1982. 16 p. :
NYPL [Sc Micro R-4108 no.15]

Marquardt, Wilhelm. Seychellen, Komoren und
Maskarenen . München , c1976. 346 p. : ISBN
3-8039-0117-0
DT469.S4 M37 **NYPL [JFC 77-3948]**

SEYCHELLES - POETRY.
De Silva, Hazel, 1947- Sega of Seychelles /.
Nairobi, Kenya , 1983. 314 p. ; DDC 821 19
PR9381.9.D42 S4 1983 **NYPL [Sc C 89-9]**

SFEM in Nigeria. Ogundipe, S. O. Second-tier
foreign exchange market in Nigeria . Ibadan ,
1987. xii, 96 p. ; ISBN 979-12-9534-1
NYPL [Sc D 88-1248]

Sh-ko and his eight wicked brothers /. Bryan,
Ashley. New York , 1988. [22] p. : ISBN
0-689-31446-9 DDC 398.2/1/0952 E 19
PZ8.B842 Sh 1988 **NYPL [Sc E 88-569]**

Shackelford, Jane Dabney. My happy days / by
Jane Dabney Shackelford ; photographs by
Cecil Vinson. Washington, D.C. : Associated
Publishers, c1944. 121 p. : ill., ports. ; 28 cm.
SCHOMBURG CHILDREN'S COLLECTION.
*1. Afro-American children - Juvenile literature. 2.
Afro-American families - Juvenile literature. I.
Schomburg Children's Collection. II. Title.*
NYPL [Sc F 88-337]

Shacklett, Juanita Purvis. Boloji and Old Hippo
/ by Juanita Purvis Shacklett ; illustrations by
Brinton Turkle. New York : Friendship Press,
c1959. 121 p. : ill. ; 21 cm. SCHOMBURG
CHILDREN'S COLLECTION.
*1. Zaire - Juvenile fiction. I. Schomburg Children's
Collection. II. Title.* **NYPL [Sc D 88-1166]**

The shade changes /. Odaga, Asenath. [Kisumu,
Kenya] [c1984] 175 p. ;
MLCS 87/7892 (P) **NYPL [Sc 88-214]**

The shadow of Blooming Grove. Russell, Francis,
1910- New York [1968] xvi, 691 p. DDC
973.91/4/0924 B
E786 .R95 **NYPL [Sc E 88-579]**

Shadows uplifted. Harper, Frances Ellen Watkins,
1825-1911. Iola Leroy, or, Shadows uplifted /.
New York , 1988. xxxix, 281 p. : ISBN
0-19-505240-4 (alk. paper) DDC 813/.3 19
PS1799.H7 I6 1988 **NYPL [JFC 88-2190]**

Shaffer, Ralph E. Which path to freedom? .
Pomona, Calif. , c1986. iv, 60 p. ; DDC
973.7/114 19
E449 .W565 1986 **NYPL [Sc D 88-1154]**

Shaik, Fatima, 1952- The mayor of New
Orleans : just talking jazz / by Fatima Shaik.
Berkeley : Creative Arts Book Co., 1987. 143
p. ; 23 cm. CONTENTS. The mayor of New
Orleans -- Climbing Monkey Hill -- Before echo.
ISBN 0-88739-050-1 : DDC 813/.54 19
PS3569.H316 M39 1987
NYPL [JFD 88-11303]

Shaka, king of the Zulus /. Stanley, Diane. New
York , c1988. [40] p. : ISBN 0-688-07342-5
DDC 968.04/092/4 B 92 19
DT878.Z9 C565 1988 **NYPL [Sc F 88-358]**

Shakur, Assata. Assata, an autobiography / by
Assata Shakur. Westport, CT : L. Hill, 1987.
xiv, 274 p. ; 25 cm. ISBN 0-88208-221-3 : DDC
973/.0496073024 19
*1. Shakur, Assata. 2. Black Panther Party - Biography.
3. Afro-American women - Biography. 4. Black
nationalism - United States. 5. Racism - United States.
6. United States - Race relations. I. Title.*
E185.97.S53 A3 1987 **NYPL [Sc E 88-21]**

SHAKUR, ASSATA.
Shakur, Assata. Assata, an autobiography /.
Westport, CT , 1987. xiv, 274 p. ; ISBN
0-88208-221-3 : DDC 973/.0496073024 19
E185.97.S53 A3 1987 **NYPL [Sc E 88-21]**

SHAMANS - SOUTH AFRICA.
Schlosser, Katesa. Medizinen des Blitzzauberers
Laduma Madela . Kiel , 1984. 186 p., 64, [1] p.
of plates : ISBN 3-88312-106-1 DDC
615.8/99/089963 19
DT878.Z9 S32 1984 **NYPL [Sc E 87-271]**

Shange, Ntozake.
Mapplethorpe, Robert. Black book /. New
York , c1986. 91 p. : **NYPL [Sc F 87-42]**

Melissa & Smith / Ntozake Shange. St. Paul,
Mn. : Bookslinger Editions, 1976. [13] p. ; 19
cm. "No. 118 of 300 copies ... signed by the author."
ISBN 0-09-377807-6
*1. Afro-American poets - Fiction. I. Title. II. Title:
Melissa and Smith.* **NYPL [Sc Rare C 86-6]**

Ridin' the moon in Texas : word paintings /
Ntozake Shange.1st ed. New York : St.
Martin's Press, 1987. xiii, 81 p. : ill. ; 25 cm.
ISBN 0-312-88929-1 : DDC 811/.54 19
I. Title.
PS3569.H3324 R5 1987
NYPL [Sc D 89-384]

Some men / Ntozake Shange [poetry] ; Wopo
Holup [images]. [S.l. : s.n.], c1981. [52] p. : ill.
(some col.) ; 11 cm. Cover title. With autograph of
author.
*1. Erotic poetry, American - Afro-American authors. I.
Holup, Wopo. II. Title.* **NYPL [Sc Rare C 88-2]**

SHANGO.
Linares, Ronaldo Antonio. Xangô e inhaçã /.
[São Paulo] , c1987. 85 p. :
NYPL [Sc D 88-553]

A Shapely fire : changing the literary landscape /
edited by Cyril Dabydeen. Oakville, Ont. :
Mosaic Press, c1987. 175 p. : ill. ; 23 cm.
ISBN 0-88962-345-7
*1. West Indians - Canada - Fiction. 2. Canadian
literature - Black authors. I. Dabydeen, Cyril, 1945-.*
NYPL [Sc E 88-263]

SHARE-CROPPING - JUVENILE FICTION.
Forbes, Tom H. Quincy's harvest /.
Philadelphia , c1976. 143 p. ; ISBN
0-397-31688-7 DDC [Fic]
PZ7.F75222 Qi **NYPL [Sc D 89-93]**

**SHARIA (ISLAMIC LAW) see ISLAMIC
LAW.**

Sharing the cities . Pickard-Cambridge, Claire.
Braamfontein, Johannesburg, South Africa ,
1988. ix, 53 p. : ISBN 0-86982-335-3
NYPL [Sc D 88-1336]

Sharlowe.
Apartheid love. 1982. Sharlowe. Requiem for a
village ; Apartheid love / by Sharlowe.
Trinidad , 1982. 78, 70 p. ;
NYPL [Sc C 88-63]

Requiem for a village ; Apartheid love / by
Sharlowe. Trinidad : Inprint Caribbean, 1982.
78, 70 p. ; 20 cm.
*1. Trinidad and Tobago - Fiction. I. Sharlowe.
Apartheid love. 1982. II. Title.*
NYPL [Sc C 88-63]

Sharma, Veena. Folk tales of East Africa / Veena
Sharma. New Delhi : Sterling, c1987. vii, 113
p. : ill. ; 22 cm. (Folk tales of the world. 18) ISBN
81-207-0228-X
1. Tales - Africa, East. I. Title.
NYPL [Sc D 88-781]

The shattered skull . Perkins, Carol Morse. New
York, 1965. 59 p.,
DT440 .P4 **NYPL [Sc E 88-145]**

Shaw, Brenda Joyce. Jean Toomer's life search
for identity as realized in Cane [microform] /
Brenda Joyce Shaw. 1975. 169 leaves. Thesis
(doctoral)--Middle Tennessee State University, 1975.
Bibliography: leaves 165-169. Microfilm of typescript.
Ann Arbor, Mich.: University Microfilms International,
1976. 1 microfilm reel; 35 mm.
*1. Toomer, Jean, 1894-1967. 2. Toomer, Jean,
1894-1967. Care. I. Title.*
NYPL [Sc Micro R-4219]

SHAW FAMILY.
Smith, Marion Whitney. Beacon Hill's Colonel
Robert Gould Shaw /. New York , 1986. 512
p. : ISBN 0-8062-2732-X
NYPL [Sc D 88-414]

SHAW, ROBERT GOULD, 1837-1863.
Smith, Marion Whitney. Beacon Hill's Colonel
Robert Gould Shaw /. New York , 1986. 512
p. : ISBN 0-8062-2732-X
NYPL [Sc D 88-414]

Shaw, Timothy M.
Coping with Africa's food crisis /. Boulder ,
c1988. xi, 250 p. : ISBN 0-931477-84-0 (lib. bdg.) :
DDC 338.1/9/6 19
HD9017.A2 C65 1988 **NYPL [Sc E 88-287]**

Ihonvbere, Julius Omozuanvbo. Towards a
political economy of Nigeria . Aldershot,
[England] ; Brookfield, [Vt.], USA : xi, 213 p. :
ISBN 0-566-05422-1 : DDC 338.9669 19
HC1055 .I38 1988 **NYPL [Sc D 89-47]**

Shawara ga mata don aikin Hajji /. Muhammed,
Mairo. [Kano, Nigeria] . 85 p. :
NYPL [Sc D 88-1042]

Sheddick, Vernon George John. The morphology
of residential associations as found among the
Khwakhwa of Basutoland. [Cape Town],
University of Cape Town, 1948. 57 p. illus.,
maps (1 fold.) 33 cm. (Communications from the
School of African Studies, new ser. no. 19)
*1. Khwakhwa (African people). I. Series:
Communications (University of Cape Town, School of
African Studies) , new ser. no. 19. II. Title.*
DT786 .S5 **NYPL [Sc G 89-1]**

Shehu, Emman Usman. Questions for big brother
/ by Emman Usman Shehu. Nigeria : Update
Communications, 1988. 85 p. ; 18 cm. "A special
publication for the Association of Nigerian Authors
sponsored by Concord Press of America." ISBN
978-302-093-5
*1. Concord Press of America. II. Association of
Nigerian Authors. III. Title.*
NYPL [Sc C 89-121]

Sheikh-Dilthey, Helmtraut, 1944- Kenya : Kunst,
Kultur und Geschichte am Eingangstor zu
Innerafrika / Helmtraut Sheikh-Dilthey.5 Aufl.
Köln : DuMont, 1987. 279 p. : ill. (some col.) ;
21 cm. (DuMont Kultur-Reiseführer)
DuMont-Dokumente Includes indexes. Bibliography: p.
245.
*1. Art, Kenyan. 2. Art, Primitive - Kenya. 3. Kenya -
Description and travel. 4. Kenya - History. I. Title. II.
Series.* **NYPL [Sc D 88-935]**

A shelter is not a home . Manhattan (New York,
N.Y.). President's Task Force on Housing for
Homeless Families. New York, NY , 1987. iv,
139, [19] p. ; **NYPL [JLF 87-1294]**

Shelton, Marie Denise. L'image de la société
dans le roman haïtien / Marie-Denise Shelton.
1979 ix,241 p. ; 28 cm. Thesis
(Doctoral)--University of California, Los Angeles, 1979.
Bibliography: p. 236-241. Photocopy of typescript.
1. Haitian fiction - History and criticism. I. Title.
NYPL [Sc F 88-212]

Shenton, Edward. Cooper, Page. Thunder /.
Cleveland , 1954. 218 p.
NYPL [Sc D 88-661]

Shepherd, Andrew. Curtis, Donald, 1939-
Preventing famine . London , New York , 1988.
xi, 250 p. ; ISBN 0-415-00711-9 DDC
363.8/7/096 19
HC800.Z9 F326 1988 **NYPL [JLD 88-3825]**

Sheppard, Jill. Marryshow of Grenada : an
introduction / by Jill Sheppard ; foreword by
Beveley Steele. Barbados, West Indies : J.
Sheppard, 1987. 56 p. : ill. ; 23 cm. Includes
bibliographical references.
*1. Marryshow, Theophilus Albert. 2. Grenada -
Biography. I. Title.* **NYPL [Sc D 88-658]**

Sheppherd, Joseph. A leaf of honey and the
proverbs of the rain forest / Joseph Sheppherd.
London : Bahá'i Publishing Trust, c1988. xii,
319 p. : ill. ; 22 cm. ISBN 1-87098-902-3 (pbk.) :
DDC 305.8/966 19
*1. Ntumu (African people). 2. Proverbs, Ntumu. I.
Title.* **NYPL [Sc D 89-453]**

Sheria na kawaida za Wanyamwezi. /. Cory,
Hans. [S.l. , 195-?] ix, 91 p. :
NYPL [Sc E 89-1]

Sheria ya kashfa /. Mwakasungula, N. E. R.
Tabora, Tanzania , c1985. x, 77 p. ;
NYPL [Sc C 88-191]

Sheria za Tanzania.
(7) Mwakasungula, N. E. R. Sheria ya kashfa /.
Tabora, Tanzania , c1985. x, 77 p. ;
NYPL [Sc C 88-191]

Sherlock, Hilary. (joint author) Sherlock, Philip
Manderson, Sir. Ears and tails and common
sense: more stories from the Caribbean.
London , 1982. xvii, 121 p.
NYPL [Sc D 88-1220]

Sherlock, Philip M. (Philip Manderson) Keeping
company with Jamaica / Philip Sherlock.
London : Macmillan Caribbean, 1984. vii, 211
p. : col. ill., maps, ports. ; 22 cm. ISBN
0-333-37419-3 (pbk) : DDC 917.292/046 19

*1. Jamaica - Description and travel - 1981- -
Guide-books. I. Title.*
F1869　　　　　*NYPL [Sc D 88-1466]*

Sherlock, Philip Manderson, Sir.
Ears and tails and common sense: more stories
from the Caribbean, by Philip M. Sherlock and
Hilary Sherlock. Illustrated by Aliki. London :
Macmillan Caribbean, 1982. xvii, 121 p. illus.
21 cm. During each evening of their six-day party the
forest animals listen to a story told by the animals who
guess the answers to Chimpanzee's riddles.
SCHOMBURG CHILDREN'S COLLECTION.
*1. Tales - West Indies. I. Sherlock, Hilary, joint author.
II. Aliki, illus. III. Schomburg Children's Collection. IV.
Title.*　　　　　*NYPL [Sc D 88-1220]*

The iguana's tail; crick crack stories from the
Caribbean [by] Sir Philip Sherlock. Illustrated
by Gioia Fiammenghi. New York, Crowell
[1969] 97 p. illus. 23 cm. Six folk tales from the
West Indies which the storyteller begins with the phrase
"Crick Crack" and the audience must answer "Break my
back" before the tale starts. SCHOMBURG
CHILDRN'S COLLECTION. DDC 823 398.2
*1. Tales - West Indies. I. Fiammenghi, Gioia, illus. II.
Schomburg Children's Collection. III. Title.*
PZ8.1.S54 Ig　　　　　*NYPL [Sc D 89-59]*

Sherman, Joan R. Invisible poets :
Afro-Americans of the nineteenth century /
Joan R. Sherman.2nd ed. Urbana : University of
Illinois Press, c1989. xxxii, 288 p. : ill., ports. ;
23 cm. Includes index. Bibliography: p. 211-272.
ISBN 0-252-01620-3 (alk. paper) DDC
811/.009/896073 19
*1. American poetry - Afro-American authors - History
and criticism. 2. American poetry - 19th century -
History and criticism. 3. Afro-Americans - Intellectual
life. 4. Afro-Americans in literature. I. Title.*
PS153.N5 S48 1989　　*NYPL [Sc E 89-216]*

Sherman, Joan Rita. Collected Black women's
poetry /. New York , 1988. 4 v. :　ISBN
0-19-505253-6 (v. 1) DDC 811/.008/09287 19
PS591.N4 C57 1988　　*NYPL [JFC 88-2144]*

Shields, John, 1944- Wheatley, Phillis, 1753-1784.
[Works. 1988.] The collected works of Phillis
Wheatley /. New York , 1988. xl, 339 p. :
ISBN 0-19-505241-2 (alk. paper) DDC 811/.1
19
PS866 .W5 1988　　　*NYPL [JFC 88-2142]*

The shimmershine queens /. Yarbrough, Camille.
New York , c1988. 142 p. ;　ISBN 0-399-21465-8
DDC [Fic] 19
PZ7.Y1955 Sh 1988　　*NYPL [Sc D 89-283]*

Shire Egyptology .
(6) Watson, Philip J. Egyptian pyramids and
mastaba tombs of the Old and Middle
Kingdoms /. Aylesbury, Bucks , 1987. 64 p. :
ISBN 0-85263-853-1
　　　　　NYPL [Sc D 88-1259]

The Shirè highlands. Buchanan, John, 1855-1896.
Blantyre [Malawi] , 1982. xii, 260 p., [8] p. of
plates :　　　　*NYPL [Sc C 87-434]*

**SHIRE HIGHLANDS (MALAWI) -
DESCRIPTION AND TRAVEL.**
Buchanan, John, 1855-1896. The Shirè
highlands. Blantyre [Malawi] , 1982. xii, 260 p.,
[8] p. of plates :　　　*NYPL [Sc C 87-434]*

Shirley Chisholm . Duffy, Susan, 1951-
Metuchen, N.J. , 1988. vii, p. ;　ISBN
0-8108-2105-2 DDC 016.32873/092/4 19
Z8167.47 .D83 1988 E840.8.C48
　　　　　NYPL [Sc D 88-1270]

Shiver, William S. The Harlem renaissance . New
York , 1989. xv, 342 p. ;　ISBN 0-8240-5739-2
(alk. paper) DDC 810/.9/896073 19
PS153.N5 H264 1989　*NYPL [Sc D 89-591]*

Shockley, Ann Allen. Afro-American women
writers, 1746-1933 . Boston , 1988. xxviii, 465
p. ;　ISBN 0-8161-8823-8　*NYPL [Sc E 88-428]*

Shona folk tales / collected by A.C. Hodza ;
translated by O.C. Chiromo ; edited by C.
Kileff. Gweru, Zimbabwe : Mambo Press in
association with the Literature bureau, 1987.
151 p. ; 19 cm. Includes index. "Originally published
in Shona ; Mambo Press, 1983."
*1. Folk literature, Shona. I. Kileff, Clive. II. Hodza,
Aaron C. III. Chiromo, Obediah C. IV. Title.*
　　　　　NYPL [Sc C 88-317]

SHONA LANGUAGE.
Hodza, Aaron C. Shona registers [microform] /.
Harare, Zimbabwe , 1977-1984. 3 v. ;　ISBN

0-7974-0482-1
　　　　　NYPL [Sc Micro R-4820 no.12]

**SHONA LANGUAGE - ORTHOGRAPHY AND
SPELLING.**
Fortune, G. (George), 1915- A guide to Shona
spelling /. Harare , 1972. 64 p. ;　ISBN
0-528-64019-2 DDC 496/.39
PL8681.2 .F6　　　*NYPL [Sc C 88-328]*

SHONA LANGUAGE - READERS.
Matindike, Gabriel A. Kuziva mbuya huudzwa
/. Harare, Zimbabwe , 1982- v. :　ISBN
0-908300-01-8 (v. 1)
PL8681.2 .M37 1982　*NYPL [Sc D 88-385]*

**SHONA LANGUAGE - SPELLING. see
SHONA LANGUAGE - ORTHOGRAPHY
AND SPELLING.**

SHONA LANGUAGE - STYLE.
Hodza, Aaron C. Shona registers [microform] /.
Harare, Zimbabwe , 1977-1984. 3 v. ;　ISBN
0-7974-0482-1
　　　　　NYPL [Sc Micro R-4820 no.12]

SHONA LANGUAGE - TEXTS.
Chakarira chindunduma . Gweru, Zimbabwe ,
1985. x, 78 p. ;　ISBN 0-86922-365-8
　　　　　NYPL [Sc D 88-439]

Chigidi, Willie L. Imwe chanzi ichabvepi? .
Gweru , 1986. 60 p. ;　*NYPL [Sc C 89-114]*

Hamandishe, Nicholas Phinias. Nyoka huru
haizvirumi /. Harare , 1984. 91 p. ;　ISBN
0-582-61173-3　　　*NYPL [Sc C 88-365]*

Hondo yeChimurenga . Gweru , 1984. 230 p. ;
ISBN 0-86922-284-8　*NYPL [Sc C 89-110]*

Kawara, James. Sajeni Chimedza /. Gweru,
[Zimbabwe] , 1984. 174 p. ;　ISBN 0-86922-327-5
　　　　　NYPL [Sc C 88-97]

Mzemba, C. (Charles), 1955- Aita twake /.
Zimbabwe , 1987. 135 p. ;　ISBN 0-86922-418-2
　　　　　NYPL [Sc C 89-119]

Ngano /. Harare, Zimbabwe , 1980- v. ;　ISBN
0-7974-0478-3 (pbk.) :
GR358.62.M3 N47 1980
　　　　　NYPL [Sc F 87-416]

Runyowa, Genius T., 1945- Akada wokure /.
Gwelo, Zimbabwe , 1981. 123 p. ;
　　　　　NYPL [Sc C 88-140]

SHOPPING - JUVENILE FICTION.
Bradman, Tony. Wait and see /. New York,
NY , 1988. [28] p. ;　ISBN 0-19-520644-4 DDC
[E] 19
PZ7.B7275 Wai 1988　*NYPL [Sc D 89-255]*

Short account of the African slave trade. Norris,
Robert, d. 1791. Memoirs of the reign of Bossa
Ahádee. London, 1789. xvi, 184 p. ;
DT541 .N85　　*NYPL [Sc Rare F 88-64]*

The short fiction of Richard Wright [microform]
/. Benson, Brian Joseph. 1972. 266 leaves.
　　　　　NYPL [Sc Micro R-4217]

A short history of the first Liberian republic /.
Guannu, Joseph Saye. Pompano Beach, FL ,
c1985. viii, 152 p. :　ISBN 0-682-40267-2
　　　　　NYPL [Sc D 88-1023]

Short, Sam B. 'Tis so : Negro folk tales of the
Old South, including Negro dialect / by Sam B.
Short. Baton Rouge, La. : Claitor's Pub.
Division, c1972. 114 p. : ill. ; 23 cm.
*1. Afro-Americans - Anecdotes, facetiae, satire, etc. I.
Title. II. Title: Negro folk tales of the Old South.*
　　　　　NYPL [Sc D 89-63]

SHORT STORIES, AFRICAN (ENGLISH)
African creations . Enugu, Nigeria , 1985,
c1982. 180 p. ;　ISBN 978-15-6181-5
　　　　　NYPL [Sc D 88-436]

SHORT STORIES, AFRICAN (FRENCH)
Timité, Bassori, 1933- Les eaux claires de ma
source /Timité bassori ; et six autres nouvelles.
Paris , 1986. 127 p. ;　ISBN 2-218-07813-9
　　　　　NYPL [Sc C 88-11]

Yoka Lye Mudaba, 1947- Le fossoyeur /.
Paris , 1986. 127 p. ;　ISBN 2-218-07830-9
　　　　　NYPL [Sc C 88-10]

SHORT STORIES, ENGLISH.
Black and priceless . Manchester , 1988. xiii,
198 p. :　ISBN 0-946745-45-5 (pbk)　DDC
821/.914/08 823/.01/08 19
PR1225 PR1309.S5　*NYPL [Sc C 89-131]*

**SHORT STORIES, ENGLISH - AFRICAN
AUTHORS. see SHORT STORIES,**

AFRICAN (ENGLISH)

**SHORT STORIES, ENGLISH - SOUTH
AFRICAN AUTHORS. see SHORT
STORIES, SOUTH AFRICAN (ENGLISH)**

**SHORT STORIES, SOUTH AFRICAN
(ENGLISH)**
Somehow tenderness survives . New York ,
c1988. 147 p. ;　ISBN 0-06-025022-4 :　DDC [Fic]
19
PZ5 .S695 1988　　*NYPL [Sc D 88-1461]*

SHORT STORIES, SOUTHERN AFRICAN.
The Penguin book of Southern African stories
/. Harmondsworth, Middlesex, England , New
York, N.Y., U. S. A. , 1985. 328 p. ;　ISBN
0-14-007239-X (pbk.) :　DDC 808.83/1 19
PL8014.S62 P46 1985　*NYPL [Sc C 88-270]*

Shotwell, Louisa Rossiter. Roosevelt Grady /
Louisa R. Shotwell ; illustrated by Peter
Burchard. Cleveland, Ohio : World, c1963. 151
p. : ill. ; 22 cm. SCHOMBURG CHILDREN'S
COLLECTION.
*1. Children of migrant laborers - United States -
Juvenile fiction. I. Burchard, Peter, ill. II. Schomburg
Children's Collection. III. Title.*
　　　　　NYPL [Sc D 88-1425]

Shoumatoff, Alex.
African madness / by Alex Shoumatoff. 1st ed.
New York : A.A. Knopf, 1988. xviii, 202 p. ;
22 cm. ISBN 0-394-56914-8 : DDC 967/.0328 19
*1. Shoumatoff, Alex - Journeys - Africa, Sub-Saharan.
2. Fossey, Dian. 3. Bokassa I, Emperor of the Central
African Empire, 1921-. 4. AIDS (Disease) - Africa,
Sub-Saharan. 5. Africa, Sub-Saharan - Description and
travel - 1981-. I. Title.*
DT352.2 .S48 1988　　*NYPL [Sc D 89-160]*

**SHOUMATOFF, ALEX - JOURNEYS -
AFRICA, SUB-SAHARAN.**
Shoumatoff, Alex. African madness /. New
York , 1988. xviii, 202 p. ;　ISBN 0-394-56914-8 :
DDC 967/.0328 19
DT352.2 .S48 1988　　*NYPL [Sc D 89-160]*

A Shout across the wall /. Ahmad, Idzia. Lagos,
Nigeria , 1988. 115 p. ;　ISBN 978-302-092-7
　　　　　NYPL [Sc C 89-135]

SHOW BUSINESS. see PERFORMING ARTS.

SHOW-MEN. see ENTERTAINERS.

Showker, Kay. Caribbean ports of call : a guide
for today's cruise passenger / Kay Showker.
Chester, Conn. : Globe Pequot Press, 1987.
xviii, 505 p. : ill., maps ; 21 cm. "A Voyager
book." Includes index. ISBN 0-87106-776-5 (pbk.)
DDC 917.29/0452 19
*1. Ocean travel - Guide-books. 2. Caribbean Area -
Description and travel - 1981- - Guide-books. I. Title.*
F2171.3 .S455 1987　　*NYPL [Sc D 89-323]*

Shoyinka, Patricia H. De Cola, Freya D. Three
decades of medical research at the College of
Medicine, Ibadan, Nigeria, 1948-1980 . Ibadan,
Nigeria , 1984. xv, 208 p. ;　ISBN 978-12-1157-1
(pbk.) DDC 016.61 19
Z6661.N6 D4 1984 R824.N6
　　　　　NYPL [Sc E 89-160]

Shreds of darkness /. Parwada, Batisai B., 1966-
Gweru, Zimbabwe , 1987. 111 p. ;
　　　　　NYPL [Sc C 89-96]

Shreve, Dorothy Shadd. The AfriCanadian
church : a stabilizer / by Dorothy Shadd
Shreve. Jordan Station, Ontario, Canada :
Paideia Press, c1983. 138 p. : ill. ; 21 cm.
Includes index. Bibliography: p. 128-131. ISBN
0-88815-072-5 (pbk.) DDC 277.1/08996 19
*1. Blacks - Canada - Religion. 2. Canada - Church
history. I. Title.*
BR570 .S53 1983　　*NYPL [Sc D 86-305]*

Shuga dedi /. Kassam, Kassim Mussa. Dar es
Salaam, Tanzania , c1984. 60 p. ;　ISBN
997-692-101-2　　　*NYPL [Sc C 88-69]*

Une si longue lettre de Mariama Bâ . Grésillon,
Marie. Issy les Moulineux [France] , c1986. 94
p. :　ISBN 2-85049-344-9　*NYPL [Sc D 88-824]*

**Siaya, a historical anthropology of an African
landscape /.** Cohen, David William. London ,
Athens , 1989. viii, 152 p., [8] p. of plates :
ISBN 0-8214-0901-8 DDC 967.6/2 19
DT433.545.L85 C64 1988
　　　　　NYPL [Sc D 89-354]

**SIAYA DISTRICT (KENYA) - SOCIAL LIFE
AND CUSTOMS.**
Cohen, David William. Siaya, a historical

anthropology of an African landscape /.
London , Athens , 1989. viii, 152 p., [8] p. of
plates : ISBN 0-8214-0901-8 DDC 967.6/2 19
DT433.545.L85 C64 1988
NYPL [Sc D 89-354]

Sickle-cell anemia and thalassemia . Huntsman,
Richard G. (Richard George) [St. John's,
Newfoundland, Canada , c1987] xv, 223 p. :
ISBN 0-921037-00-7 (pbk.) :
NYPL [Sc C 88-84]

SICKLE CELL ANEMIA - BIBLIOGRAPHY.
University of the West Indies (Mona, Jamaica)
Medical Library. Sickle cell disease
[microform] . [Mona, Jamaica] , 1978. 24
leaves ; **NYPL [Sc Micro F-10935]**

Sickle cell disease [microform] . University of
the West Indies (Mona, Jamaica) Medical
Library. [Mona, Jamaica] , 1978. 24 leaves ;
NYPL [Sc Micro F-10935]

Sidney Bechet, the wizard of jazz /. Chilton,
John, 1931 or 2- Basingstoke , 1987. xiii, 331
p., [32] p. of plates : ISBN 0-333-44386-1
NYPL [Sc E 88-33]

Sidney Poitier /. Bergman, Carol. New York ,
c1988. 110 p. : ISBN 1-555-46605-2 DDC
791.43/028/0924 B 92 19
PN2287.P57 B47 1988 **NYPL [Sc E 88-171]**

The siege /. Waweru, Mwaura. Nairobi , 1985.
273 p. ; **NYPL [Sc C 88-287]**

Siegmann, William. Cuttington University
College. Africana Museum. Rock of the
ancestors . Suakoko, Liberia , c1977. 102 p. :
DDC 730/.09666/2074096662 19
N7399.L4 C87 1977 **NYPL [Sc F 89-27]**

Sierra Leone /. Valentin, Christophe. Paris,
France , c1985. 128 p. : ISBN 2-901151-16-7
DDC 966/.404/0222 19
DT516.19 .V35 1985 **NYPL [Sc G 89-10]**

**SIERRA LEONE - DESCRIPTION AND
TRAVEL.**
Williams, Alfred Brockenbrough, 1856-1930.
The Liberian exodus. Charleston, S.C., 1878. 62
p.
E448 .W53 **NYPL [Sc Rare F 88-58]**

**SIERRA LEONE - DESCRIPTION AND
TRAVEL - 1981- - VIEWS.**
Valentin, Christophe. Sierra Leone /. Paris,
France , c1985. 128 p. : ISBN 2-901151-16-7
DDC 966/.404/0222 19
DT516.19 .V35 1985 **NYPL [Sc G 89-10]**

**SIERRA LEONE - ECONOMIC
CONDITIONS.**
Johnny, Michael. Informal credit for integrated
rural development in Sierra Leone /. Hamburg ,
1985. xviii, 212 p. : ISBN 3-87895-274-X (pbk.)
HG2146.5.S5 J63x 1985
NYPL [Sc D 88-766]

SIERRA LEONE - FICTION.
Gbomba, Lele. The bossy wife /. Freetown ,
1987. 91 p. : **NYPL [Sc D 89-429]**

Koroma, Salia. The spider's web /. Freetown ,
1986. 134 p. : **NYPL [Sc D 89-403]**

Rogers, Braima. Love without questions /.
Freetown , 1986. 86 p. ;
NYPL [Sc D 89-415]

**SIERRA LEONE - INTELLECTUAL LIFE -
19TH CENTURY.**
Sierra Leone, 1787-1987 . Manchester ; New
York : 577 p., [8] p. of plates : ISBN
0-7190-2791-8 (pbk.) : DDC 966/.4 19
DT516.7 .S54 1988 **NYPL [Sc E 88-461]**

**SIERRA LEONE - INTELLECTUAL LIFE -
20TH CENTURY.**
Sierra Leone, 1787-1987 . Manchester ; New
York : 577 p., [8] p. of plates : ISBN
0-7190-2791-8 (pbk.) : DDC 966/.4 19
DT516.7 .S54 1988 **NYPL [Sc E 88-461]**

Sierra Leone. Ministry of Health. National
health plan, 1965-1975 / Government of Sierra
Leone, Ministry of Health. Freetown : The
Ministry 1965. 167 p. : ill., 1 folded map ; 24
cm.
1. Health planning - Sierra Leone. I. Title.
NYPL [Sc E 88-104]

Sierra Leone, 1787-1987 : two centuries of
intellectual life / edited by Murray Last, Paul
Richards ; consultant editor, Christopher Fife.
Manchester ; New York : Manchester

University Press in association with Africa,
journal of the International African Institute ;
577 p., [8] p. of plates : ill. ; 24 cm. "A special
edition in book form of Africa, the journal of the
International African Institute, vol. 57, no. 4"--T.p.
verso. Includes bibliographies and index. ISBN
0-7190-2791-8 (pbk.) : DDC 966/.4 19
*1. Sierra Leone - Intellectual life - 19th century. 2.
Sierra Leone - Intellectual life - 20th century. I. Last,
Murray. II. Richards, Paul. III. Fyfe, Christopher.*
DT516.7 .S54 1988 **NYPL [Sc E 88-461]**

Sigler, Jay A. International handbook on race and
race relations /. New York , 1987. xviii, 483
p. ; ISBN 0-313-24770-6 (lib. bdg. : alk. paper)
DDC 305.8 19
HT1521 .I485 1987 **NYPL [Sc E 88-75]**

Significant issues series, 0736-7163 .
(v. 5, no. 6) Underwood, David C. West
African oil, will it matter? /. Washington,
D.C. , c1983. vi, 57 p. : ISBN 0-89206-046-8
(pbk.) DDC 333.8/232/0966 19
HD9577.A3582 U52 1983
NYPL [Sc D 88-888]

The signifying monkey . Gates, Henry Louis.
New York , 1988. xxviii, 290 p. : ISBN
0-19-503463-5 (alk. paper) DDC 810/.9/896073
19
PS153.N5 G28 1988 **NYPL [Sc E 89-181]**

SIGNS. see SIGNS AND SYMBOLS.

SIGNS AND SYMBOLS - AFRICA.
Umezinwa, Willy A. From African symbols to
physics . [Nigeria] c1988. 71 p. :
NYPL [Sc E 89-36]

Silamaka fara dikko : ein westafrikanisches Epos
in den Bambara- Versionen von Mamadou Kida
und Almami Bah (Mali) : Text, Übersetzung
und literarischer Kommentar / [redigiert von]
Ousmane Bâ. Berlin : D. Reimer, 1988. xi, 271
p., 1 folded page : map ; 24 cm. (Marburger
Studien zur Afrika- und Asienkunde: Serie A, Afrika.
Bd. 46) Bibliography: p. 266-271. ISBN
3-496-00961-6
*1. Bambara language - Texts. I. Bâ, Ardo Ousmane,
1948-.* **NYPL [Sc E 88-230]**

The silenced voice . Chester, Galina. London ,
1987. 47 p. : ISBN 0-9512093-0-2 :
NYPL [Sc D 89-519]

Sillonville, Frank. Guide de la santé au village :
"Docteur" Maïmcuna parle avec les villageois /
Frank Sillonville. Douala, Cameroun : IPD ;
Paris, France : Karthala, [distributor], c1985.
204 p. : ill. ; 24 cm. (Cahiers de l'IPD . no. 11)
Bibliography: p. 203-204. ISBN 2-86537-126-3 :
DDC 614/.0967 19
*1. Rural health - Africa, Sub-Saharan - Miscellanea. I.
Title.*
RA771.7.A357 S56 1985
NYPL [Sc E 88-547]

Silva, José Bonifácio de Andrada e, 1763-1838.
Memoir addressed to the general, constituent
and legislative Assembly of the empire of
Brazil, on slavery! by Jose Bonifacio d'Andrada
e Silva ; translated from the Portuguese by
William Walton. London : Sold by Butterworth,
Ridgway, Booth, and Wilson, 1826 London :
Printed by A. Redford and W. Robins) 60 p. ;
22 cm. Cover title: Brazilian pamphlet on the abolition
of the slave trade, and the gradual emancipation of
slaves.
*1. Slave-trade - Brazil. 2. Slavery in Brazil -
Emancipation. I. Walton, William, 1784-1857. II. Title.
III. Title: On slavery!. IV. Title: Brazilian pamphlet on
the abolition of the slave trade, and the gradual
emancipation of slaves.*
NYPL [Sc Rare G 86-14]

Silva, Petronilha Beatriz Gonçalves e. Histórias
de operários negros /. Porto Alegre, RS,
Brazil , c1987. 100 p. : **NYPL [Sc D 88-823]**

Silver jubilee : Ahmadu Bello University, Zaria /
compiled by Y.O. Aliu. Zaria : Ahmadu Bello
University, [1987] 76 p. : ill., maps, ports. ; 22
x 30 cm. Cover title: Quarter-century of Ahmadu
Bello University, Zaria : pictorial history.
*1. Ahmadu Bello University - History. I. Aliu, Y. O. II.
Title. III. Title: Quarter-century of Ahmadu Bello
University, Zaria.* **NYPL [Sc D 89-6]**

The silver men . Newton, Velma. Mona,
Kingston, Jamaica , 1984. xx, 218 p., [4] p. of
plates : DDC 325/.2729/07287 19
JV7429 .N49 1984 **NYPL [Sc D 89-478]**

Silvester, Peter J. A left hand like God : a study
of boogie-woogie / Peter J. Silvester with a
special contribution from Denis Harbinson.
London : Quartet Books, c1988. 324 p. : ill. ;
24 cm. Includes bibliographical references and index.
Discography: p. 302-309. ISBN 0-7043-2685-X :
DDC 785.4 19
*1. Piano music (Boogie-woogie) - History and criticism.
I. Harbinson, Denis. II. Title.*
NYPL [JNE 89-16]

Silvia Dubois . Larison, Cornelius Wilson,
1837-1910. New York , 1988. xxvii, 124 p. :
ISBN 0-19-505239-0 DDC 305.5/67/0924 B 19
E444.D83 L37 1988 **NYPL [JFC 88-2191]**

Silwane, Hamilton Mahonga. Manaka,
Matsemela. Egoli, city of gold [microform] .
Johannesburg [198-?] 28 p. ;
NYPL [Sc Micro F-11049]

Simba, Malik. The Black laborer, the Black legal
experience and the United States Supreme
Court with emphasis on the neo-concept of
equal employment [microform] / by Malik
Simba. 1977. 357 leaves. Thesis (Ph.
D.)--University of Minnesota, 1977. Bibliography: leaves
330-357. Microfilm of typescript. Ann Arbor, Mich.:
University Microfilms International, 1978. 1 microfilm
reel ; 35 mm.
*1. Afro-Americans - Employment - Law and
legislation - History. 2. Afro-Americans - Civil rights -
History. 3. Discrimination in employment - Law and
legislation - United States. I. Title.*
NYPL [Sc Micro R-4706]

Simensen, Jarle. Norwegian missions in African
history /. Oslo : Oxford [Oxfordshire] ; 2 v. :
ISBN 82-00-07418-8 (v. 1) DDC
266/.023/48106 19
BV3625.M2 N67 1986 **NYPL [Sc D 89-26]**

[Simmons, George Frederick] 1814-1855. Review
of the Remarks on Dr. Channing's Slavery
[microform] , by a citizen of Massachusetts.
Boston, J. Munroe and Company, 1836. 48 p.
24 cm. Microfilm. New York : New York Public
Library, 198 . 1 microfilm reel ; 35 mm. (MN
*ZZ-28490)
*1. Austin, James Trecothick, 1784-1870. Remarks on
Dr. Channing's Slavery. 2. Slavery - United States -
Controversial literature - 1836. I. Title.*
E449 .C4562 **NYPL [Sc Micro R-4839]**

Simms, Margaret C.
Black economic progress . Washington, D.C. ,
Lanham, Md. , 1988. xi, 52 p. : ISBN
0-941410-69-2 (alk. paper) DDC
330.973/008996073 19
E185.8 .B496 1988 **NYPL [Sc E 89-154]**

Slipping through the cracks . New Brunswick,
N.J. , 1986. 302 p. ; ISBN 0-88738-662-8
NYPL [Sc D 88-767]

Simon, Leonard J.
Adam and the roof / Leonard J. Simon ;
Arthur Freed, photography ; Arthur Freed,
Linda Kosarin, book design. [New Jersey? : s.n.,
198-?] 36 p. : ill. ; 16 x 23 cm. (Camden Street
School immediate readers) SCHOMBURG
CHILDREN'S COLLECTION.
*1. Readers (Primary). I. Schomburg Children's
Collection. II. Title.* **NYPL [Sc B 89-28]**

Freed, Arthur. Games /. [N.J.] , 1968. [32] p. :
NYPL [Sc B 89-25]

Simon, Njami.
[Cerceuil & Cie. English]
Coffin & Co. / Njami Simon ; translated
from the French by Marlene Raderman.
Berkeley, CA : Black Lizard Books, c1987.
195 p. ; 18 cm. ISBN 0-88739-049-8 (pbk.)
*1. Afro-Americans - France - Paris - Fiction. 2.
Africans - France - Paris - Fiction. I. Title. II. Title:
Coffin and company.* **NYPL [Sc C 89-144]**

Simony, Maggy, 1920- Traveler's reading guides :
background books, novels, travel literature, and
articles / Maggy Simony, ed. ; editorial
assistants, Christine Donovan & Maria Simony.
Bayport, N.Y. : Freelance Publications,
c1981-c1984. 3 v. ; 21 cm. Includes indexes.
CONTENTS. - v. 1. Europe -- v. 2. North America --
v. 3. Rest of the world. ISBN 0-9602050-1-2 (v. 1) :
DDC 016.9104 19
*1. Travel - Bibliography. 2. Travel in literature -
Bibliography. I. Donovan, Christine, 1951-. II. Simony,
Maria, 1956-. III. Title.*
Z6016.T7 S54 G151 **NYPL [Sc D 89-343]**

Simony, Maria, 1956- Simony, Maggy, 1920-
Traveler's reading guides . Bayport, N.Y. ,
c1981-c1984. 3 v. ; ISBN 0-9602050-1-2 (v. 1) :
DDC 016.9104 19
Z6016.T7 S54 G151   NYPL [Sc D 89-343]

Simple speaks his mind /. Hughes, Langston,
1902-1967. New York , c1950. 231 p. ;
NYPL [Sc Rare C 82-2]

Simpson, Lewis P. The Southern review and
modern literature, 1935-1985 /. Baton Rouge ,
c1988. xvi, 238 p.: ISBN 0-8071-1424-3 : DDC
810/.9/975 19
PS267.B3 S68 1987   NYPL [Sc E 88-280]

Sims, Edward. Symposium on race and class.
Philadelphia , 1984. 62 p. ;
NYPL [Sc D 88-2]

Sims, Lowery Stokes. Robert Colescott, a
retrospective, 1975-1986 / essays by Lowery S.
Sims and Mitchell D. Kahan ; organized by the
San Jose Museum of Art ; with support from
the Metropolitan Life Foundation, the National
Endowments for the Arts, and the California
Arts Council ; circulated under the auspices of
the Art Museum Association of America. San
Jose, Calif. : The Museum, c1987. 34 p. : ill.
(some col.) ; 28 cm. Includes bibliographies. ISBN
0-938175-01-7 (pbk.) DDC 759.13 19
*1. Colescott, Robert, 1925-- Exhibitions. 2. Painting,
American - Exhibitions. 3. Painting, Modern - 20th
century - United States - Exhibitions. I. Colescott,
Robert, 1925-. II. Kahan, Mitchell Douglas, 1951-. III.
San Jose Museum of Art. IV. Art Museum Association
of America. V. Title.*
ND237.C66 A4 1987   NYPL [Sc F 88-317]

Singer, Edith G. (illus) Bleeker, Sonia. The Ibo of
Biafra. New York [1969] 160 p. DDC 916.69/4
DT515 .B54   NYPL [Sc C 88-361]

**SINGERS, AFRO-AMERICAN. see AFRO-
AMERICAN SINGERS.**

SINGERS - CUBA - BIOGRAPHY.
Naser, Amín E. (Amín Egeraige), 1936- Benny
Moré . Ciudad de La Habana , c1985. 231 p.,
[61] p. of plates : DDC 784.5/0092/4 B 19
ML420.M596 N3 1985 NYPL [Sc C 87-302]

SINGERS - SOUTH AFRICA - BIOGRAPHY.
Makeba, Miriam. Makeba . New York , c1987.
249 p., [16] p. of plates : ISBN 0-453-00561-6 :
DDC 784.5/0092/4 B 19
ML420.M16 A3 1987   NYPL [Sc E 88-193]

SINGERS - UNITED STATES - BIOGRAPHY.
Balliett, Whitney. American singers . New
York , 1988. x, 244 p. ; ISBN 0-19-504610-2 (alk.
paper) DDC 784.5 B 19
ML400 .B25 1988   NYPL [JNE 88-46]

Kliment, Bud. Ella Fitzgerald /. New York ,
c1988. 112 p. : ISBN 1-555-46586-2 DDC 784.5
B 19
ML420.F52 K6 1988   NYPL [Sc E 88-611]

Patterson, Charles. Marian Anderson /. New
York , 1988. 154 p. : ISBN 0-531-10568-7 DDC
782.1/092/4 B 92 19
ML420.A6 P4 1988   NYPL [Sc E 89-4]

White, John, 1939- Billie Holiday, her life &
times /. Tunbridge Wells, Kent , New York ,
1987. 144 p. : ISBN 0-87663-668-7 (USA) DDC
784.5/3/00924 B 19
ML420.H58 W5 1987   NYPL [JNF 88-88]

**SINGERS - UNITED STATES - BIOGRAPHY -
JUVENILE LITERATURE.**
Greenberg, Keith Elliot. Whitney Houston /.
Minneapolis , c1988. 32 p. : ISBN 0-8225-1619-5
(lib. bdg.) DDC 784.5/0092/4 B 92 19
ML3930.H7 G7 1988   NYPL [Sc D 88-1459]

Mabery, D. L. Janet Jackson /. Minneapolis ,
c1988. 32 p. : ISBN 0-8225-1618-7 (lib bdg.) :
DDC 784.5/4/00924 B 920 19
ML3930.J15 M3 1988
NYPL [Sc D 88-1460]

Stevenson, Janet. Marian Anderson /. Chicago
[1963] 189 p. :   *NYPL [Sc D 88-377]*

SINGERS, WOMEN. see WOMEN SINGERS.

Singh, Amritjit. The Harlem renaissance . New
York , 1989. xv, 342 p. ; ISBN 0-8240-5739-2
(alk. paper) DDC 810/.9/896073 19
PS153.N5 H264 1989 NYPL [Sc D 89-591]

Singh, Ram D. Economics of the family and
farming systems in sub-Saharan Africa :
development perspectives / Ram D. Singh.

Boulder : Westview Press, 1988. xxiii, 208 p. ;
23 cm. (Westview special studies in social, political
and economic development) Includes bibliographical
references and index. ISBN 0-8133-7624-6 DDC
338.1/0967 19
1. Family farms - Africa, Sub-Saharan. I. Title.
HD1476.A357 S56 1988
NYPL [JLD 88-4512]

Singhateh, Modu F. A day in their lives / by
Modu F. Singhateh. Banjul : s.n., [1984] 87 p :
ill. ; 25 cm. Cover title.
1. Gambia - Occupations. I. Title.
NYPL [Sc E 88-98]

SINGING GAMES.
Burroughs, Margaret Taylor, 1917- (comp) Did
you feed my cow? Chicago [1969] 96 p. ISBN
0-695-81960-7 DDC 398.8
PZ8.3.B958 Di5   NYPL [Sc D 89-57]

Singing in the spirit . Allen, Robert Raymond.
Ann Arbor, Mich , c1987. xii, 424 p. ;
NYPL [Sc D 88-1212]

A single trail. Rose, Karen. Chicago [1969] 158
p. ISBN 0-695-44082-9 DDC [Fic]
PZ7.R717 Si   NYPL [Sc D 89-91]

Sioen, Gérard. Antilles Caraïbes /. Paris , c1982.
157 p. : ISBN 2-7191-0177-0
NYPL [Sc F 88-347]

Siqueira, José Jorge. Lopes, Helena Theodoro.
Negro e cultura no Brasil /. Rio de Janeiro ,
1987. 136 p. : ISBN 85-85108-02-9 DDC
981/.00496 19
F2659.N4 L67 1987 NYPL [Sc D 88-1291]

Sissung, Maud. Huggins, Nathan Irvin, 1927-
L'odyssée noire /. Paris , c1979. 221 p. : ISBN
1-85258-150-7   *NYPL [Sc F 88-383]*

Sister Nobluee. Gossett, Hattie, 1942-
Presenting-- Sister Nobluee /. Ithaca, N.Y. ,
c1988. 143 p. ; ISBN 0-932379-50-8 (alk. paper)
DDC 811/.54 19
PS3557.O785 P7 1988   NYPL [JFD 89-457]

**La situación de la mujer en Zimbabue antes de la
independencia /.** Weinrich, A. K. H., 1933-
[Women and racial discrimination in Rhodesia.
Spanish.] Barcelona , Paris , 1984. 198 p. ;
ISBN 92-3-301621-8 (Unesco)
NYPL [Sc D 88-615]

Situation linguistique en Afrique centrale :
inventaire préliminaire : le Cameroun. Paris :
Agence de coopération culturelle et technique ;
Yaoundé : Centre regional de recherche et de
documentation sur les traditions orales et pour
le développement des langues Africaines,
Equipe nationale [du Cameroun], 1983. 475 p. :
ill., maps ; 30 cm. (Atlas linguistique du Cameroun)
Atlas linguistique de l'Afrique centrale Ten maps laid
in. Includes index. Bibliography: p. 181-342.
*1. Cameroon - Languages. 2. Cameroon - Languages -
Maps. I. Centre régional de recherche et de
documentation sur les traditions orales et pour le
développement des langues africaines (Yaoundé,
Cameroon). Equipe nationale du Cameroun. II. Series.*
NYPL [Sc F 88-153]

Six-three-three-four education in Nigeria.
Osokoya, Israel O. 6-3-3-4 education in
Nigeria . Lagos, Nigeria , c1987. x, 108 p. ;
ISBN 978-259-918-2 *NYPL [Sc E 89-162]*

Sjedinjene Američke Države. see United States.

**SKELETAL REMAINS. see MAN,
PREHISTORIC.**

**SKILLED LABOR - SOUTH AFRICA -
SUPPLY AND DEMAND.**
McCartan, P. J. (Patrick John) The demand for
skilled labour in the Border, Ciskei, southern
Transkei regional economy /. Grahamstown
[1983] 50, xxii p. : ISBN 0-86810-058-7 (pbk.) :
DDC 331.12/3/0968792 19
HD5842.A6 M33 1983 NYPL [Sc F 88-356]

Sklar, Richard L. African crisis areas and U. S.
foreign policy /. Berkeley , c1985. xiv, 374 p. :
ISBN 0-520-05548-9 (alk. paper) DDC 327.7306
19
DT38.7 .A39 1986   NYPL [JLE 85-4182]

The sky-god stories /. Aardema, Verna. New
York , c1960. [50] p. : *NYPL [Sc D 89-83]*

SLANDER (LAW) see LIBEL AND SLANDER.

Slater, Sandra. The dog, the bone, and the wind :
a story from Nigeria / retold by Sandra Slater ;
illustrated by A.L. Satti. Ibadan, Nigeria :

University Press, c1986. 30 p. : ill. ; 18 x 22
cm. SCHOMBURG CHILDREN'S COLLECTION.
ISBN 0-19-575567-7
*1. Tales - Nigeria. I. Schomburg Children's Collection.
II. Title.*
MLCS 88/07439 (P)   NYPL [Sc D 89-116]

Slaughter, Diana T. Visible now . New York ,
1988. xvi, 344 p. ; ISBN 0-313-25926-7 (lib. bdg. :
alk. paper) DDC 371/.02/0973 19
LC2761 .V57 1988   NYPL [Sc E 98-257]

Slaughter, Reid. Webb, Spud. Flying high /. New
York , c1988. xv, 208 p., [16] p. of plates :
ISBN 0-06-015820-4 : DDC 796.32/3/0924 B
19
GV884.W35 A3 1988   NYPL [Sc D 89-375]

The slave drivers . Van Deburg, William L. New
York , 1988. xvii, 202 p. : ISBN 0-19-505698-1
DDC 305.5/67/0975 19
E443 .V36 1988   NYPL [Sc D 89-424]

The slave-holder's religion. Brooke, Samuel.
Cincinnati, 1845. 47 p.
E449 .B87   NYPL [Sc Rare F 88-53]

SLAVE LABOR - SOUTHERN STATES.
Van Deburg, William L. The slave drivers .
New York , 1988. xvii, 202 p. : ISBN
0-19-505698-1 DDC 305.5/67/0975 19
E443 .V36 1988   NYPL [Sc D 89-424]

The slave narrative . Starling, Marion Wilson,
1907. Washington, D.C. , 1988. xxx, 375 p. ;
ISBN 0-88258-165-1 : DDC 973/.0496073 19
E444 .S8 1988   NYPL [Sc E 89-185]

**SLAVE NARRATIVES. see SLAVES -
BIOGRAPHY.**

Slave rebels, abolitionists, and southern courts :
the pamphlet literature / edited with an
introduction by Paul Finkelman. New York :
Garland, 1988. 2 v. : ill., ports. ; 23 cm.
(Slavery, race and the American legal system,
1700-1872 . ser. 4) Consists of works originally
published 1819-1857. Includes bibliographical
references. ISBN 0-8240-6721-5 (set : alk. paper) :
DDC 342.75/0872 347.502872 19
*1. Slavery - Law and legislation - Southern States -
Cases. 2. Afro-Americans - Legal status, laws, etc. -
Southern States - Cases. 3. Abolitionists - Legal status,
laws, etc. - Southern States - Cases. 4. Criminal law -
Southern States - Cases. 5. Criminal justice,
Administration of - Southern States - Cases. I.
Finkelman, Paul, 1949-. II. Series.*
KF4545.S5 A5 1987b NYPL [Sc D 88-1263]

SLAVE-TRADE.
The African slave trade . Philadelphia , 1863.
24 p. ;   *NYPL [Sc Rare F 89-5]*

SLAVE-TRADE - AFRICA.
Documentos relativos ao apresamento,
julgamento e entrega da barca franceza Charles
et Georges . Lisboa , 1858. 249, 16 p. ;
NYPL [Sc Rare G 86-1]

Falconbridge, Alexander, d. 1792. An account
of the slave trade on the coast of Africa /.
London , 1788. 55 p. ;
NYPL [Sc Rare F 88-63]

Norris, Robert, d. 1791. Memoirs of the reign
of Bossa Ahádee. London, 1789. xvi, 184 p. ;
DT541 .N85   NYPL [Sc Rare F 88-64]

Sandoval, Alonso dc, 1576-1652. Naturaleza,
policia sagrada i profana, costumbres i ritos,
disciplina i catechismo evangelico de todos
etiopes /. En Sevilla , 1627. [23], 334 p., 81
leaves ;   *NYPL [Sc Rare F 82-70]*

Zulueta, Pedro de, Jr. Trial of Pedro de
Zulueta, Jun. . London , 1844. lxxiv, 410 p. ;
NYPL [Sc Rare F 88-1]

**SLAVE TRADE - AFRICA - HISTORY - 17TH
CENTURY.**
Vega Franco, Marisa. El tráfico de esclavos con
América . Sevilla , 1984. x, 220 p. : ISBN
84-00-05675-2 DDC 382/.44/09729 19
HT985 .V44 1984   NYPL [Sc C 89-132]

**SLAVE-TRADE - AFRICA - JUVENILE
FICTION.**
Gbanfou. Kaméléfata . [Abidjan] [Paris] ,
c1987. 143 p. : ISBN 2-218-07833-3
NYPL [Sc C 88-161]

SLAVE TRADE - ANGOLA - HISTORY.
Miller, Joseph Calder. Way of death . Madison,
Wis. , c1988. xxx, 770 p. : ISBN 0-299-11560-7 :
DDC 382/.44/09469 19
HT1221 .M55 1988   NYPL [Sc E 89-105]

SLAVE-TRADE - BRAZIL.
Silva, José Bonifácio de Andrada e, 1763-1838.
Memoir addressed to the general, constituent
and legislative Assembly of the empire of
Brazil, on slavery! London , 1826 London :
Printed by A. Redford and W. Robins) 60 p. ;
           NYPL [Sc Rare G 86-14]

SLAVE-TRADE - BRAZIL - HISTORY.
Miller, Joseph Calder. Way of death . Madison,
Wis. , c1988. xxx, 770 p. :   ISBN 0-299-11560-7 :
DDC 382/.44/09469 19
HT1221 .M55 1988   *NYPL [Sc E 89-105]*

SLAVE TRADE - CARIBBEAN AREA -
HISTORY.
Ifill, Max B. The African diaspora .
Port-of-Spain, Trinidad , 1986. vii, 118 p. :
    ISBN 976-8008-00-8 (pbk.)   DDC 382/.44/09729
19
HT1072 .I35 1986   *NYPL [Sc D 88-934]*

SLAVE TRADE - CARIBBEAN AREA -
HISTORY - 17TH CENTURY.
Vega Franco, Marisa. El tráfico de esclavos con
América . Sevilla , 1984. x, 220 p. :   ISBN
84-00-05675-2   DDC 382/.44/09729 19
HT985 .V44 1984   *NYPL [Sc C 89-132]*

SLAVE TRADE - EUROPE - HISTORY -
17TH CENTURY.
Vega Franco, Marisa. El tráfico de esclavos con
América . Sevilla , 1984. x, 220 p. :   ISBN
84-00-05675-2   DDC 382/.44/09729 19
HT985 .V44 1984   *NYPL [Sc C 89-132]*

SLAVE-TRADE - FICTION.
Earle, William. Obi, or, The history of
Three-fingered Jack . London , 1800. vi, [2],
232 p., [1] leaf of plates :
           NYPL [Sc Rare C 88-3]

SLAVE-TRADE - FRANCE - HISTORY.
Daget, Serge. Répertoire des expéditions
négrières françaises à la traite illégale
(1814-1850) / . Nantes , 1988. viii, 603 p. :
ISBN 2-900486-01-7   *NYPL [Sc E 89-265]*

SLAVE-TRADE - GREAT BRITAIN.
African Institution, London. Reasons for
establishing a registry of slaves in the British
colonies . London , 1815 (London : Printed by
Ellerton and Henderson) 118 p. ;
           NYPL [Sc Rare G 86-4]

SLAVE-TRADE - HISTORY.
Emancipation I . Barbados , c1986. vii, 108 p.,
[1] leaf of plates :   DDC 306/.362/0972981 19
HT1119.B35 E46 1986   *NYPL [Sc D 88-248]*

Ifill, Max B. The African diaspora .
Port-of-Spain, Trinidad , 1986. vii, 118 p. :
    ISBN 976-8008-00-8 (pbk.)   DDC 382/.44/09729
19
HT1072 .I35 1986   *NYPL [Sc D 88-934]*

SLAVE TRADE - HISTORY - 17TH
CENTURY.
Vega Franco, Marisa. El tráfico de esclavos con
América . Sevilla , 1984. x, 220 p. :   ISBN
84-00-05675-2   DDC 382/.44/09729 19
HT985 .V44 1984   *NYPL [Sc C 89-132]*

SLAVE TRADE - HISTORY - CONGRESSES.
Traite négrière du XVe au XIXe siècle. Spanish.
La trata negrera del siglo XV al XIX .
Barcelona , 1981. 379 p. :   ISBN 92-3-301672-2
           NYPL [Sc D 88-650]

SLAVE-TRADE IN LITERATURE.
Sandiford, Keith Albert, 1947- Measuring the
moment . Selinsgrove , c1988. 181 p. ;   ISBN
0-941664-79-1 (alk. paper)   DDC 828 19
PR9340 .S26 1988   *NYPL [Sc E 88-467]*

SLAVE-TRADE - MARTINIQUE - HISTORY.
Thésée, Françoise. Les Ibos de l'Amélie .
Paris , c1986. 134 p., [8] p. of plates :   ISBN
2-903033-86-2   *NYPL [Sc E 88-560]*

SLAVE-TRADE - PORTUGAL - HISTORY.
Miller, Joseph Calder. Way of death . Madison,
Wis. , c1988. xxx, 770 p. :   ISBN 0-299-11560-7 :
DDC 382/.44/09469 19
HT1221 .M55 1988   *NYPL [Sc E 89-105]*

SLAVE-TRADE - RIO DE LA PLATA
REGION (ARGENTINA AND URUGUAY)
- HISTORY - 18TH CENTURY.
Studer, Elena F. S. de. La trata de negros en el
Río de la Plata durante el siglo XVIII / . Bs.
As. [i.e. Buenos Aires]   [1984] 378 p., [27]
leaves of plates (some folded) :   ISBN
950-9138-08-8
HT1123.R5 S78 1984   *NYPL [Sc E 87-419]*

SLAVE-TRADE - WEST INDIES, BRITISH.
Falconbridge, Alexander, d. 1792. An account
of the slave trade on the coast of Africa / .
London , 1788. 55 p. ;
           NYPL [Sc Rare F 88-63]

SLAVE TRADERS - AFRICA.
Zulueta, Pedro de, Jr. Trial of Pedro de
Zulueta, Jun. . London , 1844. lxxiv, 410 p. ;
           NYPL [Sc Rare F 88-1]

SLAVE TRADERS - ANGOLA - HISTORY.
Miller, Joseph Calder. Way of death . Madison,
Wis. , c1988. xxx, 770 p. :   ISBN 0-299-11560-7 :
DDC 382/.44/09469 19
HT1221 .M55 1988   *NYPL [Sc E 89-105]*

SLAVEHOLDERS - GEORGIA - BRYAN
COUNTY - DIARIES.
Hoffmann, Charles. North by South . Athens ,
c1988. xxii, 318 p., [8] of plates :   ISBN
0-8203-0976-1 (alk. paper)   DDC
975.8/73203/0924 19
F292.B85 A753 1988   *NYPL [Sc E 89-35]*

SLAVEHOLDERS - SOUTH CAROLINA -
DIARIES.
Hammond, James Henry, 1807-1864. Secret
and sacred . New York , 1988. xxix, 342 p., [2]
leaves of plates :   ISBN 0-19-505308-7   DDC
975.7/03/0924 B 19
F273 .H24 1988   *NYPL [Sc E 88-513]*

Slaven, Neil. Leadbitter, Mike. Blues records
1943-1970 . London, England , 1987- v. ;
    ISBN 0-907872-07-7
           *NYPL [*R-Phono. 89-790]*

SLAVERY - AFRICA.
Mbotela, James. Uhuru wa watumwa / .
Nairobi , 1956. viii, 102 p. :
           NYPL [Sc C 89-35]

SLAVERY - AFRICA, EAST.
Pruen, Septimus Tristram (Septimus Tristam)
The Arab and the African . London , 1896. vii,
338 p. [8] p. of plates :   *NYPL [Sc D 88-387]*

SLAVERY - AFRICA - HISTORY - 19TH
CENTURY.
The End of slavery in Africa / . Madison, Wis. ,
c1988. xx, 524 p. :   ISBN 0-299-11550-X :   DDC
306/.362/096 19
HT1323 .E53 1988   *NYPL [Sc E 89-222]*

SLAVERY - AFRICA - HISTORY - 20TH
CENTURY.
The End of slavery in Africa / . Madison, Wis. ,
c1988. xx, 524 p. :   ISBN 0-299-11550-X :   DDC
306/.362/096 19
HT1323 .E53 1988   *NYPL [Sc E 89-222]*

SLAVERY - AMERICA - ANTI-SLAVERY
MOVEMENTS - HISTORY.
Blackburn, Robin. The overthrow of colonial
slavery, 1776-1848 / . London , New York ,
1988. 560 p. :   ISBN 0-86091-188-8   DDC
326/.0973 19
HT1050 .B54 1988   *NYPL [IIR 88-1551]*

SLAVERY - AMERICA - CONDITION OF
SLAVES.
Cardoso, Ciro Flamarion Santana. Escravo ou
Camponês? . São Paulo , 1987. 125 p. ;
           NYPL [Sc D 88-793]

SLAVERY - AMERICA - CONDITION OF
SLAVES - HISTORY.
The African exchange . Durham N.C. , 1987,
c1988. vi, 280 p. :   ISBN 0-8223-0731-6   DDC
614.4/273/08996073 19
RA442 .A37 1988   *NYPL [Sc D 88-541]*

SLAVERY - AMERICA - EMANCIPATION -
HISTORY.
Blackburn, Robin. The overthrow of colonial
slavery, 1776-1848 / . London , New York ,
1988. 560 p. :   ISBN 0-86091-188-8   DDC
326/.0973 19
HT1050 .B54 1988   *NYPL [IIR 88-1551]*

SLAVERY - AMERICA - EXHIBITIONS.
Brown, Larissa V. Africans in the New World,
1493-1834 . Providence, Rhode Island , 1988.
61 p. :   ISBN 0-916617-31-9
           NYPL [Sc D 88-624]

SLAVERY - AMERICA - HISTORY.
Brown, Larissa V. Africans in the New World,
1493-1834 . Providence, Rhode Island , 1988.
61 p. :   ISBN 0-916617-31-9
           NYPL [Sc D 88-624]

Slavery and emancipation . Moss, S. G. St.

Michael, Barbados , 1986. 61 l. ;
           NYPL [Sc F 88-83]

Slavery and other forms of unfree labour / edited
by Léonie J. Archer. London ; New York :
Routledge, 1988. xi, 307 p. ; 23 cm. (History
workshop series) Papers from a workshop held in
Oxford. Includes index. Bibliography: p. [280]-297.
    ISBN 0-415-00203-6   DDC 306/.362 19
1. Slavery - Congresses. I. Archer, Leonie.
HT855 .S57 1988   *NYPL [Sc D 89-334]*

SLAVERY AND SLAVES IN LITERATURE.
Sandiford, Keith Albert, 1947- Measuring the
moment . Selinsgrove , c1988. 181 p. ;   ISBN
0-941664-79-1 (alk. paper)   DDC 828 19
PR9340 .S26 1988   *NYPL [Sc E 88-467]*

SLAVERY AND THE CHURCH - CATHOLIC
CHURCH.
Poole, Stafford. Church and slave in Perry
County, Missouri, 1818-1865 / . Lewiston, N.Y.,
USA , c1986. xvii, 251 p. :   ISBN 0-88946-666-1
(alk. paper) :   DDC 306/.362/09778694 19
E445.M67 P66 1986   *NYPL [Sc E 89-102]*

SLAVERY AND THE CHURCH - CATHOLIC
CHURCH - HISTORY.
Balmes, Jaime Luciano, 1810-1848.
[Protestantismo comparado con el catolicismo
en sus relaciones con la civilización europea.
Selections. Portuguese.] A Igreja católica em
face da escravidão / . São Paulo , 1988. 141 p. ;
           NYPL [Sc D 89-554]

SLAVERY AND THE CHURCH - EPISCOPAL
CHURCH.
Jay, John, 1817-1894. Thoughts on the duty of
the Episcopal Church, in relation to slavery .
New York , 1839. 11 p. ;
           NYPL [Sc Rare F 88-25]

Slavery and the French revolutionists, 1788-1805
/ . Cooper, Anna J. (Anna Julia), 1858-1964.
[Attitude de la France à l'égard de l'esclavage
pendant la révolution. English.] Lewiston ,
1988. 228 p. :   ISBN 0-88946-637-8   DDC
972.94/03 19
F1923 .C7213 1988   *NYPL [Sc E 88-469]*

Slavery and the slave holder's religion. Brooke,
Samuel. The slave-holder's religion. Cincinnati,
1845. 47 p.
E449 .B87   *NYPL [Sc Rare F 88-53]*

SLAVERY - ANTI-SLAVERY MOVEMENTS -
HISTORY - 18TH CENTURY.
Sandiford, Keith Albert, 1947- Measuring the
moment . Selinsgrove , c1988. 181 p. ;   ISBN
0-941664-79-1 (alk. paper)   DDC 828 19
PR9340 .S26 1988   *NYPL [Sc E 88-467]*

SLAVERY - BAHAMAS - EMANCIPATION -
EXHIBITION.
Bahamas. Dept. of Archives. Aspects of slavery,
part II . Nassau, Bahamas [1984] 52 p. :   DDC
306/.362/097296 19
HT1119.B34 B35 1984   *NYPL [Sc F 88-346]*

SLAVERY - BAHAMAS - EXHIBITIONS.
Bahamas. Dept. of Archives. Aspects of slavery,
part II . Nassau, Bahamas [1984] 52 p. :   DDC
306/.362/097296 19
HT1119.B34 B35 1984   *NYPL [Sc F 88-346]*

SLAVERY - BAHIA (BRAZIL) : STATE) -
HISTORY.
Reis, João José. Escravidão e invenção da
liberdade . São Paulo , 1988. 323 p. [8] leaves
of plates :   ISBN 85-11-13084-5
           NYPL [Sc D 88-1388]

SLAVERY - BARBADOS - EMANCIPATION.
Emancipation I . Barbados , c1986. vii, 108 p.,
[1] leaf of plates :   DDC 306/.362/0972981 19
HT1119.B35 E46 1986   *NYPL [Sc D 88-248]*

SLAVERY - BARBADOS - HISTORY.
Emancipation I . Barbados , c1986. vii, 108 p.,
[1] leaf of plates :   DDC 306/.362/0972981 19
HT1119.B35 E46 1986   *NYPL [Sc D 88-248]*

SLAVERY - BARBADOS - INSURRECTIONS,
ETC. - HISTORY.
O'Callaghan, Evelyn. The earliest patriots .
London , 1986. 61 p. ;   ISBN 0-946918-53-8pb
           NYPL [Sc C 88-104]

SLAVERY - BRAZIL.
Balmes, Jaime Luciano, 1810-1848.
[Protestantismo comparado con el catolicismo
en sus relaciones con la civilización europea.
Selections. Portuguese.] A Igreja católica em
face da escravidão / . São Paulo , 1988. 141 p. ;
           NYPL [Sc D 89-554]

Morais, Evaristo de, 1871-1939. A escravidão africana no Brasil . Brasília, Distrito Federal , c1986. 140 p. ;   ISBN 85-23-00070-4
NYPL [Sc D 88-922]

SLAVERY - BRAZIL - EMANCIPATION.
Amaral, Angelo Thomaz do. Lei de 13 de maio /. [Fortaleza, Brazil] [1907] p. [331]-336 ;
NYPL [Sc Rare G 86-30]
Guimarães, Augusto Alvares. Propaganda abolicionista . Bahia , 1875. 86 p. ;
NYPL [Sc Rare G 86-33]

SLAVERY - BRAZIL - FICTION.
Coelho, Abílio. As hortênsias morrem na primavera /. Rio de Janeiro , 1987. 271 p. ;
NYPL [Sc D 88-709]

SLAVERY - BRAZIL - HISTORY.
Freyre, Gilberto, 1900- [Casa-grande & senzala. English.] The masters and the slaves =. Berkeley , c1986. xc, 537 xliv p., [3] p. of plates :   ISBN 0-520-05665-5 (pbk. : alk. paper) DDC 981 19
F2510 .F7522 1986   *NYPL [HFB 87-2095]*
Giacomini, Sonia Maria. Mulher e escrava . Petrópolis , 1988. 95 p., [7] p. of plates :
HT1126 .G49 1988   *NYPL [Sc D 88-1283]*
Lopes, Luis Carlos. O espelho e a imagem . Rio de Janeiro , 1987. 126 p. ;
NYPL [Sc D 88-350]
Maestri Filho, Mário José. Depoimentos de escravos brasileiros /. São Paulo , c1988. 88 p. ;   ISBN 85-27-40039-1
NYPL [Sc D 88-1379]
Peregalli, Enrique, 1950- Escravidão no Brasil /. São Paulo , c1988. 80 p. ;   ISBN 85-26-00192-2   *NYPL [Sc D 89-421]*
Quieroz, Suely Robles Reis de. Escravidão negra no Brasil /. São Paulo , 1987. 86 p. ;
NYPL [Sc C 88-2]

SLAVERY - BRAZIL - INSURRECTIONS, ETC.
Moura, Clovis. Quilombos . São Paulo , 1987. 94 p. ;   ISBN 85-08-01858-4
NYPL [Sc C 88-3]

SLAVERY - BRAZIL - RIO DE JANEIRO (STATE) - HISTORY.
Lara, Silvia Hunold. Campos da violência . Rio de Janeiro , c1988. 389 p. ;
NYPL [Sc D 89-13]

SLAVERY - BRAZIL - SÃO PAULO (STATE) - CONDITIONS OF SLAVES.
Machado, Maria Helena Pereira Toledo. Crime e escravidão . São Paulo-SP , 1987. 134 p. :   DDC 306/.362/098161 19
HT1129.S27 M33 1987
NYPL [Sc D 88-1015]

SLAVERY - BRITISH WEST INDIES - EMANCIPATION.
Merchant. An attempt to strip Negro emancipation of its difficulties as well as its terrors . London , 1824. 48 p. ;
NYPL [Sc Rare G 86-13]

SLAVERY - CAMEROON - INSURRECTIONS, ETC.
Paulin, Adjai. La Revolte des esclaves mercenaires . Bayreuth, W. Germany , 1987. 96 p. :   *NYPL [Sc D 88-1326]*

SLAVERY - CANADA.
Bramble, Linda. Black fugitive slaves in early Canada /. St. Catharines, Ont. , c1988. 93 p. :   ISBN 0-920277-16-0 DDC 973.7/115 19
NYPL [Sc E 89-121]

SLAVERY - CARIBBEAN AREA.
Escravidão negra e história da Igreja na América Latina e no Caribe /. Petrópolis , 1987. 237 p. :   *NYPL [Sc D 88-75]*

SLAVERY - CONGRESSES.
Slavery and other forms of unfree labour /. London , New York , 1988. xi, 307 p. ;   ISBN 0-415-00203-6 DDC 306/.362 19
HT855 .S57 1988   *NYPL [Sc D 89-334]*

SLAVERY - CUBA.
Temas acerca de la esclavitud . [La Habana, Cuba , 1988. 288 p. ;   *NYPL [Sc C 89-118]*

SLAVERY - CUBA - EMANCIPATION.
Allo, Lorenzo. Domestic slavery in its relations with wealth . New York , 1855. 16 p. ;
NYPL [Sc Rare G 86-32]

SLAVERY - ECONOMIC ASPECTS.
Allo, Lorenzo. Domestic slavery in its relations with wealth . New York , 1855. 16 p. ;
NYPL [Sc Rare G 86-32]

SLAVERY - ECONOMIC ASPECTS - SURINAM.
Lamur, H. E. The production of sugar and the reproduction of slaves at Vossenburg (Suriname), 1705-1863 /. Amsterdam, The Netherlands . 164 p. :   ISBN 90-70313-19-7
NYPL [Sc D 88-555]

SLAVERY - EMANCIPATION - POETRY.
Clarke, A. M. Verses for emancipation . [Port of Spain , 1986] 41 p. ;   DDC 811 19
PR9272.9.C53 V4 1986
NYPL [Sc D 88-981]

SLAVERY - FLORIDA - FICTION.
Douglas, Marjory Stoneman. Freedom river: Florida, 1845. New York [1953] 264 p. :
NYPL [Sc D 89-267]

SLAVERY - GREAT BRITAIN - ANTI-SLAVERY MOVEMENTS.
Drescher, Seymour. Capitalism and antislavery . New York , 1987, c1986. xv, 300 p. ;   ISBN 0-19-520534-0 (alk. paper) DDC 326/.0941 19
HT1163 .D74 1987   *NYPL [Sc D 89-29]*

SLAVERY - GREAT BRITAIN - ANTI-SLAVERY MOVEMENTS - SOURCES.
The William Smeal collection [microform]. 1833-1908. ca. 100 items.
NYPL [Sc Micro R-4837]

SLAVERY - GREAT BRITAIN - EMANCIPATION.
Drescher, Seymour. Capitalism and antislavery . New York , 1987, c1986. xv, 300 p. ;   ISBN 0-19-520534-0 (alk. paper) DDC 326/.0941 19
HT1163 .D74 1987   *NYPL [Sc D 89-29]*

SLAVERY - GREAT BRITAIN - EMANCIPATION - PUBLIC OPINION.
Jennings, Lawrence C. French reaction to British slave emancipation /. Baton Rouge , c1988. ix, 228 p. ;   ISBN 0-8071-1429-4 (alk. paper) DDC 306/.362/0942 19
HT1163 .J46 1988   *NYPL [Sc E 89-139]*

SLAVERY - GUADELOUPE - HISTORY.
Guadeloupe, 1635-1971 . Tours [1982] 109 p. :   DDC 306/.362/0972976 19
HT1108.G83 G8 1982 *NYPL [Sc F 89-141]*

SLAVERY - HAITI - HISTORY.
Cooper, Anna J. (Anna Julia), 1858-1964. [Attitude de la France à l'égard de l'esclavage pendant la révolution. English.] Slavery and the French revolutionists, 1788-1805 /. Lewiston , 1988. 228 p. :   ISBN 0-88946-637-8 DDC 972.94/03 19
F1923 .C7213 1988   *NYPL [Sc E 88-469]*

SLAVERY - HISTORY - 19TH CENTURY.
Fredrickson, George M., 1934- The arrogance of race . Middletown, Conn. , c1988. viii, 310 p. ;   ISBN 0-8195-5177-5 DDC 973/.0496 19
E441 .F77 1988   *NYPL [Sc E 88-487]*

SLAVERY IN BRAZIL - EMANCIPATION.
Silva, José Bonifácio de Andrada e, 1763-1838. Memoir addressed to the general, constituent and legislative Assembly of the empire of Brazil, on slavery! London , 1826 London : Printed by A. Redford and W. Robins] 60 p. ;
NYPL [Sc Rare G 86-14]

Slavery in the United States, and the slave trade in the District of Columbia. Mann, Horace, 1796-1859. Speech of Horace Mann, of Massachusetts, in the House of Representatives, Feb. 23, 1849; on slavery in the United States, and the slave trade in the District of Columbia. Boston [1849]. [15] p. ;
E416 .M28   *NYPL [Sc Rare C 89-3]*

SLAVERY IN THE UNITED STATES - CONTROVERSIAL LITERATURE - 1833.
Whittier, John Greenleaf, 1807-1892. Justice and expediency. New-York, 1833. [49]-63 p. ;
E449 .A624   *NYPL [Sc Rare F 98-1]*

SLAVERY IN THE UNITED STATES - CONTROVERSIAL LITERATURE - 1839.
Branagan, Thomas, b. 1774. The guardian genius of the Federal Union, or, Patriotic admonitions on the signs of the times . New York , 1839. 104 p. ;
NYPL [Sc Rare G 86-18]

SLAVERY IN THE UNITED STATES - FICTION.

Albuquerque, L. M. do Couto de. O escravo branco . Lisboa , 1854. 4 v. :
NYPL [Sc F 82-65]

SLAVERY IN THE UNITED STATES - NORTH CAROLINA.
Grandy, Moses, b. 1786? Le récit de Moses Grandy, esclave en Caroline du Nord [microform] /. [Montréal] [1977] 45 p. ;
E444 .G7514   *NYPL [*XM-12976]*

SLAVERY - INDIANA - ANTI-SLAVERY MOVEMENTS.
Miller, Marion Clinton. The anti-slavery movement in Indiana [microform] /. 1938. 290 leaves.   *NYPL [Sc Micro R-4836]*

SLAVERY - JAMAICA.
Bickell, Richard. The West Indies as they are, or, A real picture of slavery . London , 1825. xvi, 256 p. ;   *NYPL [Sc Rare F 88-57]*

SLAVERY - JAMAICA - FICTION.
Earle, William. Obi, or, The history of Three-fingered Jack . London , 1800. vi, [2], 232 p., [1] leaf of plates :
NYPL [Sc Rare C 88-3]

SLAVERY - JAMAICA - INSURRECTIONS, ETC. - JUVENILE FICTION.
Reid, Victor Stafford, 1913- Peter of Mount Ephraim . Kingston , 1971. 140 p. :
MLCS 83/10255 (P)   *NYPL [Sc C 88-185]*

SLAVERY - JUSTIFICATION.
Hammond, James Henry, 1807-1864. Gov. Hammond's letters on southern slavery . Charleston , 1845. 32 p. ;
NYPL [Sc Rare C 89-24]
Smith, Whitefoord. God, the refuge of his people . Columbia, S.C. , 1850. 16 p. ;
NYPL [Sc Rare C 89-12]
Van Evrie, John H., 1814-1896. Negroes and negro "slavery". New York, 1861. xvi, 339 p.
E449 .V253   *NYPL [Sc Rare C 88-22]*

SLAVERY - JUVENILE FICTION.
Anderson, Joan. A Williamsburg household /. New York , c1988. [48] p. :   ISBN 0-89919-516-4 :   DDC [Fic] 19
PZ7.A5367 Wi 1988   *NYPL [Sc F 88-242]*

SLAVERY - KANSAS - JUVENILE FICTION.
Hodges, Carl G. Benjie Ream /. Indianapolis , c1964. 153 p. :   *NYPL [Sc D 89-433]*

SLAVERY - LATIN AMERICA.
Escravidão negra e história da Igreja na América Latina e no Caribe /. Petrópolis , 1987. 237 p. :   *NYPL [Sc D 88-75]*

SLAVERY - LAW AND LEGISLATION - CUBA - HISTORY.
Navarro Azcue, Concepción, 1952- La abolición de la esclavitud negra en la legislación española, 1870-1886 /. Madrid , c1987. 296 p. ;   ISBN 84-7232-420-6
KG546 .N38 1987   *NYPL [Sc D 89-574]*

SLAVERY - LAW AND LEGISLATION - PUERTO RICO - HISTORY.
Navarro Azcue, Concepción, 1952- La abolición de la esclavitud negra en la legislación española, 1870-1886 /. Madrid , c1987. 296 p. ;   ISBN 84-7232-420-6
KG546 .N38 1987   *NYPL [Sc D 89-574]*

SLAVERY - LAW AND LEGISLATION - SOUTHERN STATES - CASES.
Slave rebels, abolitionists, and southern courts . New York , 1988. 2 v. :   ISBN 0-8240-6721-5 (set : alk. paper) :   DDC 342.75/0872 347.502872 19
KF4545.S5 A5 1987b *NYPL [Sc D 88-1263]*

SLAVERY - LAW AND LEGISLATION - VIRGINIA - CASES.
Schwarz, Philip J., 1940- Twice condemned . Baton Rouge , c1988. xiv, 353 p. :   ISBN 0-8071-1401-4 (alk. paper) DDC 346.75501/3 347.550613 19
KFV2801.6.S55 S39 1988
NYPL [Sc E 89-112]

SLAVERY - LOUISIANA - FICTION.
Mercier, Alfred, 1816-1894. L'habitation Saint-Ybars. Nouvelle-Orléans, 1881. 234 p.
PQ3939.M5 H3 1881
NYPL [Sc Rare C 88-19]

SLAVERY - MARTINQUE - FICTION.
Cabort-Masson, Guy, 1937- La mangrove mulâtre /. Saint-Joseph, Martinique , c1986.

282 p. ;
MLCS 87/3007 (P)   NYPL [Sc D 88-571]

SLAVERY - MISSISSIPPI - HISTORY.
Moore, John Hebron. The emergence of the
cotton kingdom in the Old Southwest. Baton
Rouge , c1988. xii, 323 p. : ISBN 0-8071-1404-9
(pbk.) DDC 330.9762 19
HC107.M7 M66 1988   NYPL [Sc E 88-279]

SLAVERY - MISSOURI - PERRY COUNTY.
Poole, Stafford. Church and slave in Perry
County, Missouri, 1818-1865 /. Lewiston, N.Y.,
USA , c1986. xvii, 251 p. : ISBN 0-88946-666-1
(alk. paper) : DDC 306/.362/09778694 19
E445.M67 P66 1986   NYPL [Sc E 89-102]

SLAVERY - NEW MEXICO.
Bingham, John Armor, 1815-1900. Bill and
report of John A. Bingham . [Washington,
D.C. , 1860] 7, [1] p. ;
NYPL [Sc Rare C 89-2]

**SLAVERY - NEW YORK (STATE) - ANTI-
SLAVERY MOVEMENTS.**
Phelan, Helene C. And why not every man? .
Interlaken, New York , 1987. 247 p. : ISBN
0-9605836-4-5   *NYPL [Sc D 87-1420]*

SLAVERY - NIGERIA.
Okeke, Igwebuike Romeo. The "Osu" concept in
Igboland . Enugu. [Nigeria] , 1986. xi, 167 p. :
ISBN 978-248-100-9   *NYPL [Sc E 88-302]*

SLAVERY - NORTH CAROLINA - HISTORY.
Redford, Dorothy Spruill. Somerset
homecoming . New York , c1988. xviii, 266 p. :
ISBN 0-385-24245-X : DDC
929/.3/089960730756 19
E185.96 .R42 1988   NYPL [Sc E 88-498]

SLAVERY - OHIO.
The Address and reply on the presentation of a
testimonial to S.P. Chase by the colored people
of Cincinnati. Cincinnati , 1845. 35 p. ;
NYPL [Sc Rare G 86-15]

**Slavery, race and the American legal system,
1700-1872 .**
(ser. 4) Slave rebels, abolitionists, and southern
courts . New York , 1988. 2 v. : ISBN
0-8240-6721-5 (set : alk. paper) : DDC
342.75/0872 347.502872 19
KF4545.S5 A5 1987b   NYPL [Sc D 88-1263]

**SLAVERY - RIO DE LA PLATA REGION
(ARGENTINA AND URUGUAY) -
HISTORY - 18TH CENTURY.**
Studer, Elena F. S. de. La trata de negros en el
Río de la Plata durante el siglo XVIII /. Bs.
As. [i.e. Buenos Aires] [1984] 378 p., [27]
leaves of plates (some folded) : ISBN
950-9138-08-8
HT1123.R5 S78 1984   NYPL [Sc E 87-419]

SLAVERY - SOUTH CAROLINA.
Remarks upon the controversy between the
Commonwealth of Massachusetts and the State
of South Carolina. Boston, 1845. 21 p.
F273 .R38   NYPL [Sc Rare C 89-9]

**SLAVERY - SOUTH CAROLINA -
CHARLESTON - CONDITION OF
SLAVES.**
Adger, John Bailey, 1810-1899. The religious
instruction of the colored population .
Charleston , 1847. 19 p. ;
NYPL [Sc Rare G 86-6]

**SLAVERY - SOUTH CAROLINA -
CONDITIONS OF SLAVES.**
Koger, Larry, 1958- Black slaveowners .
Jefferson, N.C. , 1985. xiii, 286 p. ; ISBN
0-89950-160-5 : DDC 975.7/00496073 19
E445.S7 K64 1985   NYPL [Sc E 88-473]

SLAVERY - SOUTH CAROLINA - HISTORY.
Koger, Larry, 1958- Black slaveowners .
Jefferson, N.C. , 1985. xiii, 286 p. ; ISBN
0-89950-160-5 : DDC 975.7/00496073 19
E445.S7 K64 1985   NYPL [Sc E 88-473]

**SLAVERY - SOUTH CAROLINA - HISTORY -
19TH CENTURY.**
Hammond, James Henry, 1807-1864. Secret
and sacred . New York , 1988. xxix, 342 p., [2]
leaves of plates : ISBN 0-19-505308-7 DDC
975.7/03/0924 B 19
F273 .H24 1988   NYPL [Sc E 88-513]

SLAVERY - SOUTHERN STATES.
Mathew, William M. Edmund Ruffin and the
crisis of slavery in the Old South . Athens ,
c1988. xiv, 286 p. : ISBN 0-8203-1011-5 (alk.

paper) DDC 306/.362/0924 19
F230.R932 M38 1988   NYPL [JFE 88-3149]

**SLAVERY - SOUTHERN STATES -
CONDITION OF SLAVES.**
Van Deburg, William L. The slave drivers .
New York , 1988. xvii, 202 p. : ISBN
0-19-505698-1 DDC 305.5/67/0975 19
E443 .V36 1988   NYPL [Sc D 89-424]

**SLAVERY - SOUTHERN STATES -
HISTORY.**
Fox-Genovese, Elizabeth, 1941- Within the
plantation household . Chapel Hill , c1988. xvii,
544 p. : ISBN 0-8078-1808-9 (alk. paper) DDC
305.4/0975 19
HQ1438.A13 F69 1988   NYPL [JLE 89-21]

SLAVERY - TRINIDAD - EMANCIPATION.
Burnley, William Hardin. Observations of the
present condition of the island of Trinidad .
London , 1842. 177 p. ;
NYPL [Sc Rare F 88-74]

**SLAVERY - TRINIDAD - HISTORY - 18TH
CENTURY.**
John, A. Meredith. The plantation slaves of
Trinidad, 1783-1816 . Cambridge [Eng.] , New
York , 1988. xvi, 259 p. : ISBN 0-521-36166-4
DDC 306/.362/0972983 19
HT1105.T6 J65 1988   NYPL [Sc E 89-235]

**SLAVERY - UNITED STATES - ANTI-
SLAVERY MOVEMENTS.**
Bramble, Linda. Black fugitive slaves in early
Canada /. St. Catharines, Ont. , c1988. 93 p. :
ISBN 0-920277-16-0 DDC 973.7/115 19
NYPL [Sc E 89-121]

Cheek, William F., 1933- John Mercer
Langston and the fight for Black freedom,
1829-65 /. Urbana , c1989. 478 p. : ISBN
0-252-01550-9 (alk. paper) DDC
973/.0496073/0924 B 19
E185.97.L27 C48 1989   NYPL [Sc E 89-255]

Which path to freedom? . Pomona, Calif. ,
c1986. iv, 60 p. ; DDC 973.7/114 19
E449 .W565 1986   NYPL [Sc D 88-1154]

**SLAVERY - UNITED STATES - ANTI-
SLAVERY MOVEMENTS - FICTION.**
Haley, Alex. A different kind of Christmas /.
New York , 1988. 101 p. ; ISBN 0-385-26043-1 :
DDC 813/.54 19
PS3558.A3575 D54 1988
NYPL [Sc C 89-38]

**SLAVERY - UNITED STATES - ANTI-
SLAVERY MOVEMENTS - JUVENILE
LITERATURE.**
Hamilton, Virginia. Anthony Burns . New
York , c1988. xiii, 193 p. ; ISBN 0-394-88185-0
DDC 973.6/6/0924 B 92 19
E450.B93 H36 1988   NYPL [Sc D 88-1157]

**SLAVERY - UNITED STATES -
BIBLIOGRAPHY.**
American Anti-slavery Society. Proceedings of
the American Anti-slavery Society, at its third
decade . New York , 1864. 175 p. ;
NYPL [Sc Rare G 86-43]

Moss, S. G. Slavery and emancipation . St.
Michael, Barbados , 1986. 61 l. ;
NYPL [Sc F 88-83]

**SLAVERY - UNITED STATES -
COLONIZATION.**
Citizen of New-York. An address on slavery,
and against immediate emancipation .
New-York , 1834. 16 p. ;
NYPL [Sc Rare G 86-19]

**SLAVERY - UNITED STATES - CONDITION
OF SLAVES.**
Brooke, Samuel. The slave-holder's religion.
Cincinnati, 1845. 47 p.
E449 .B87   NYPL [Sc Rare F 88-53]

Bullwhip days . New York , c1988. xviii, 460
p. : ISBN 1-555-84210-0 DDC 973/.0496073022 B
19
E444 .B95 1988   NYPL [IEC 89-3083]

Huggins, Nathan Irvin, 1927- L'odyssée noire /.
Paris , c1979. 221 p. : ISBN 1-85258-150-7
NYPL [Sc F 88-383]

**SLAVERY - UNITED STATES -
CONTROVERSIAL LITERATURE.**
Jay, John, 1817-1894. Thoughts on the duty of
the Episcopal Church, in relation to slavery .
New York , 1839. 11 p. ;
NYPL [Sc Rare F 88-25]

**SLAVERY - UNITED STATES -
CONTROVERSIAL LITERATURE - 1830.**
Walker, David, 1785-1830. David Walker's
appeal, in four articles, together with a
preamble, to the coloured citizens of the world,
but in particular, and very expressly, to those of
the United States of America. New York [1965]
xii, 78 p. DDC 326.973
E446 .W178   NYPL [Sc D 89-456]

**SLAVERY - UNITED STATES -
CONTROVERSIAL LITERATURE - 1834.**
Citizen of New-York. An address on slavery,
and against immediate emancipation .
New-York , 1834. 16 p. ;
NYPL [Sc Rare G 86-19]

**SLAVERY - UNITED STATES -
CONTROVERSIAL LITERATURE - 1840.**
Brisbane, William Henry, ca. 1803-1878. Speech
of the Rev. Wm. H. Brisbane . Hartford , 1840.
12 p. ;   *NYPL [Sc Rare C 89-26]*

**SLAVERY - UNITED STATES -
CONTROVERSIAL LITERATURE - 1845.**
Brooke, Samuel. The slave-holder's religion.
Cincinnati, 1845. 47 p.
E449 .B87   NYPL [Sc Rare F 88-53]

Hammond, James Henry, 1807-1864. Gov.
Hammond's letters on southern slavery .
Charleston , 1845. 32 p. ;
NYPL [Sc Rare C 89-24]

**SLAVERY - UNITED STATES -
CONTROVERSIAL LITERATURE - 1848.**
Tappan, Lewis, 1788-1873. Letters respecting a
book "dropped from the catalogue" of the
American Sunday School Union in compliance
with the dictation of the slave power. New
York , 1848. 36 p. ;
NYPL [Sc Rare C 89-11]

**SLAVERY - UNITED STATES -
CONTROVERSIAL LITERATURE - 1850.**
Brown, William B. Religious organizations, and
slavery. Oberlin, 1850. 32 p.
E449 .B882   NYPL [Sc Rare F 88-45]

**SLAVERY - UNITED STATES -
CONTROVERSIAL LITERATURE - 1853.**
Van Evrie, John H., 1814-1896. Negroes and
negro "slavery". New York, 1861. xvi, 339 p.
E449 .V253   NYPL [Sc Rare C 88-22]

**SLAVERY - UNITED STATES - ECONOMIC
ASPECTS - FICTION.**
Armstrong, Thomas, 1899- King cotton /.
London , 1947. 928 p. ; *NYPL [Sc D 88-97]*

**SLAVERY - UNITED STATES -
EMANCIPATION.**
An Address to the citizens of the United States,
on the subject of slavery /. [Philadelphia] ,
1838 ([Philadelphia] : Neall & Shann, printers)
24 p. ;   *NYPL [Sc Rare G 86-12]*

**SLAVERY - UNITED STATES - EXTENSION
TO THE TERRITORIES.**
Mann, Horace, 1796-1859. Speech of Mr.
Horace Mann, of Massachusetts, in the House
of Representatives of the United States, June
30, 1848. [Boston] , 1848. 31 p. ;
NYPL [Sc Rare C 89-30]

SLAVERY - UNITED STATES - FICTION.
Card, Orson Scott. Prentice Alvin /. New
York, NY , 1989. x, 342 p. : ISBN
0-312-93141-7 : DDC 813/.54 19
PS3553.A655 P74 1989
NYPL [JFE 88-3128]

Stowe, Harriet Beecher, 1811-1896. Dred .
Boston , 1856. 2 v. ;
PZ3.S89 D   NYPL [Sc Rare C 89-31]

Texan. The Yankee slave-dealer, or, An
abolitionist down South . Nashville, Tenn. ,
1860. 368 p. ;   *NYPL [Sc Rare C 88-21]*

Williams, Sherley Anne, 1944- Dessa Rose /.
New York , c1986. 236 p. ; ISBN
0-688-05113-8 : DDC 813/.54 19
PS3573.I45546 D47 1986
NYPL [JFD 86-8841]

**SLAVERY - UNITED STATES -
HISTORIOGRAPHY.**
Fredrickson, George M., 1934- The arrogance
of race . Middletown, Conn. , c1988. viii, 310
p. ; ISBN 0-8195-5177-5 DDC 973/.0496 19
E441 .F77 1988   NYPL [Sc E 88-487]

SLAVERY - UNITED STATES - HISTORY.
Huggins, Nathan Irvin, 1927- L'odyssée noire /.
Paris , c1979. 221 p. :
NYPL [Sc F 88-383]

**SLAVERY - UNITED STATES - HISTORY -
19TH CENTURY.**
Fredrickson, George M., 1934- The arrogance
of race . Middletown, Conn. , c1988. viii, 310
p. ; ISBN 0-8195-5177-5 DDC 973/.0496 19
E441 .F77 1988 *NYPL [Sc E 88-487]*

**SLAVERY - UNITED STATES - LEGAL
STATUS, LAWS, ETC.**
Bestor, Arthur. State sovereignty and slavery .
Springfield, IL , 1961. 64 p. ;
NYPL [Sc E 87-669]

**SLAVERY - UNITED STATES - LEGAL
STATUS OF SLAVES IN FREE STATES.**
Birney, James Gillespie, 1792-1857.
Examination of the decision of the Supreme
Court of the United States, in the case of
Strader, Gorman and Armstrong vs.
Christopher Graham . Cincinnati , 1852. iv, [1],
6-46, [1] p. ;
E450 .B57 *NYPL [Sc Rare F 88-37]*

**SLAVERY - UNITED STATES - POLITICAL
ASPECTS.**
Barrows, William, 1815-1891. The war and
slavery; and their relations to each other .
Boston , 1863. 18 p. ;
NYPL [Sc Rare F 88-51]

SLAVERY - UNITED STATES - SERMONS.
Boardman, Henry Augustus, 1808-1880. What
Christianity demands of us at the present
crisis . Philadelphia , 1860. 28 p. ;
NYPL [Sc Rare F 88-52]

Smith, Whitefoord. God, the refuge of his
people . Columbia, S.C. , 1850. 16 p. ;
NYPL [Sc C 89-12]

**SLAVERY - UNITED STATES - SOCIETIES,
ETC.**
American Anti-slavery Society. Proceedings of
the American Anti-slavery Society, at its third
decade . New York , 1864. 175 p. ;
NYPL [Sc Rare G 86-43]

**SLAVERY - UNITED STATES - SPEECHES
IN CONGRESS - 1848.**
Mann, Horace, 1796-1859. Speech of Mr.
Horace Mann, of Massachusetts, in the House
of Representatives of the United States, June
30, 1848. [Boston] , 1848. 31 p. ;
NYPL [Sc Rare C 89-30]

**SLAVERY - UNITED STATES - SPEECHES
IN CONGRESS - 1849.**
Mann, Horace, 1796-1859. Speech of Horace
Mann, of Massachusetts, in the House of
Representatives, Feb. 23, 1849; on slavery in
the United States, and the slave trade in the
District of Columbia. Boston [1849]. [15] p. ;
E416 .M28 *NYPL [Sc Rare C 89-3]*

**SLAVERY - UNITED STATES - SPEECHES
IN CONGRESS - 1860.**
Bingham, John Armor, 1815-1900. Bill and
report of John A. Bingham . [Washington,
D.C. , 1860] 7, [1] p. ;
NYPL [Sc Rare C 89-2]

**SLAVERY - VIRGIN ISLANDS OF THE
UNITED STATES - SAINT JOHN -
HISTORY.**
Olwig, Karen Fog, 1948- Cultural adaptation
and resistance on St. John . Gainesville , c1985.
xii, 226 p. ; ISBN 0-8130-0818-2 (pbk.) DDC
306/.097297/22 19
HT1071 .O43 1985 *NYPL [Sc D 88-1058]*

**SLAVERY - VIRGINIA - RICHMOND -
HISTORY - EXHIBITIONS.**
McGraw, Marie Tyler. In bondage and
freedom . Richmond, VA. [Chapel Hill, N.C.] ,
1988. 71 p. : *NYPL [Sc F 89-107]*

SLAVERY - WASHINGTON (D.C.)
Mann, Horace, 1796-1859. Speech of Horace
Mann, of Massachusetts, in the House of
Representatives, Feb. 23, 1849; on slavery in
the United States, and the slave trade in the
District of Columbia. Boston [1849]. [15] p. ;
E416 .M28 *NYPL [Sc Rare C 89-3]*

SLAVERY - WEST INDIES.
Bickell, Richard. The West Indies as they are,
or, A real picture of slavery . London , 1825.
xvi, 256 p. ; *NYPL [Sc Rare F 88-57]*

Carlyle, Thomas, 1795-1881. Occasional

discourse on the Nigger question. London,
1853. 48 p.
HT1091 .C47 *NYPL [Sc C 89-7]*

Prince, Mary. The history of Mary Prince, a
West Indian slave, related by herself /.
London , New York , 1987. xvi, 124 p. ; ISBN
0-86358-192-7 DDC 305.5/67/0924 B 19
HT869.P6 A3 1987 *NYPL [Sc C 89-31]*

SLAVERY - WEST INDIES, BRITISH.
An Address to Her Royal Highness the
Dutchess of York, against the use of sugar.
[London?] 1792. 20 p. ;
NYPL [Sc Rare G 86-31]

African Institution, London. A review of the
colonial slave registration acts . London , 1820.
139, 11 p. ; *NYPL [Sc Rare G 86-24]*

Antidote to West-Indian sketches, drawn from
authentic sources. London , 1816-1817. 7 nos. ;
NYPL [Sc Rare G 86-16]

Dirks, Robert, 1942- The Black Saturnalia .
Gainesville , c1987. xvii, 228 p., [7] p. of
plates : ISBN 0-8130-0843-3 (pbk. : alk. paper)
DDC 394.2/68282/09729 19
GT4987.23 .D57 1987
NYPL [L-10 5328 no.72]

**SLAVERY - WEST INDIES, BRITISH -
CONDITION OF SLAVES.**
African Institution, London. Reasons for
establishing a registry of slaves in the British
colonies . London , 1815 (London : Printed by
Ellerton and Henderson) 118 p. ;
NYPL [Sc Rare G 86-4]

**SLAVERY - WEST INDIES, BRITISH -
CONDITION OF SLAVES - HISTORY.**
Ward, J. R. British West Indian slavery,
1750-1834 . Oxford [Oxfordshire] , New York ,
1988. x, 320 p. : ISBN 0-19-820144-3 (Oxford
University Press) DDC 380/.362/09729 19
HT1092 .W37 1988 *NYPL [Sc D 88-1355]*

SLAVERY - WEST INDIES - HISTORY.
Greenwood, R. (Robert) Emancipation to
emigration /. London , New York , 1980 (1985
printing) viii, 152 p. : ISBN 0-333-28148-9 (pbk.)
DDC 972.9 19
F1621 .G74 1984 *NYPL [Sc E 88-526]*

SLAVERY - ZAIRE - HISTORY.
Northrup, David. Beyond the bend in the
river . Athens, Ohio , 1988. xvii, 264 p. :
ISBN 0-89680-151-9 DDC 331.11/73/0967517
19
HD8811.Z8 K586 1988
NYPL [Sc D 88-960]

SLAVES - BIOGRAPHY.
Equiano, Olaudah, b. 1745. I saw a slave ship
/. Sacramento, Calif. , 1983. 42 p. :
NYPL [Sc Rare C 88-1]

SLAVES - BRAZIL - BIOGRAPHY.
Maestri Filho, Mário José. Depoimentos de
escravos brasileiros /. São Paulo , c1988. 88 p. ;
ISBN 85-27-40039-1
NYPL [Sc D 88-1379]

**SLAVES - MARYLAND - BALTIMORE -
REGISTERS.**
Clayton, Ralph. Black Baltimore, 1820-1870 /.
Bowie, MD , 1987. vii, 199 p. : ISBN
1-556-13080-5 (pbk.) : DDC
929/.3/0899607307526 19
F189.B19 N42 1987
NYPL [APR (Baltimore) 88-868]

**SLAVES - NORTH CAROLINA -
BIOGRAPHY.**
Grandy, Moses, b. 1786? Le récit de Moses
Grandy, esclave en Caroline du Nord
[microform] /. [Montréal] [1977] 45 p. ;
E444 .G7514 *NYPL [*XM-12976]*

My folks don't want me to talk about slavery .
Winston-Salem, N.C. , c1984. xiv, 103 p. ;
ISBN 0-89587-038-X DDC
975.6/00496073/0922 B 19
E445.N8 M9 1984 *NYPL [JFD 85-1549]*

SLAVES - UNITED STATES - BIOGRAPHY.
Allinson, William J. Memoir of Quamino
Buccau . Philadelphia , London , 1851. 30 p. ;
NYPL [Sc Rare G 86-28]

Bullwhip days . New York , c1988. xviii, 460
p. : ISBN 1-555-84210-0 DDC 973/.0496073022 B
19
E444 .B95 1988 *NYPL [IEC 89-3083]*

Jacobs, Harriet A. (Harriet Ann), 1813-1897.

Incidents in the life of a slave girl /. New
York , 1988. xl, 306 p. ; ISBN 0-19-505243-9
(alk. paper) DDC 973/.0496024 B 19
E444.J17 A3 1988 *NYPL [JFC 88-2193]*

Keckley, Elizabeth, 1824-1907. Behind the
scenes, or, Thirty years a slave, and four years
in the White House /. New York , 1988. xxxvi,
xvi, 371 p. : ISBN 0-19-505259-5 DDC
973.7/092/2 19
E457.15 .K26 1988 *NYPL [JFC 88-2194]*

Larison, Cornelius Wilson, 1837-1910. Silvia
Dubois . New York , 1988. xxxvii, 124 p. :
ISBN 0-19-505239-0 DDC 305.5/67/0924 B 19
E444.D83 L37 1988 *NYPL [JFC 88-2191]*

Northup, Solomon, b. 1808. Twelve years a
slave . New York , 1857. 336 p. :
NYPL [Sc Rare C 89-34]

**SLAVES - UNITED STATES - BIOGRAPHY -
HISTORY AND CRITICISM.**
Starling, Marion Wilson, 1907. The slave
narrative . Washington, D.C. , 1988. xxx, 375
p. ; ISBN 0-88258-165-1 : DDC 973/.0496073 19
E444 .S8 1988 *NYPL [Sc E 89-185]*

**SLAVES - UNITED STATES - BIOGRAPHY -
JUVENILE LITERATURE.**
Ferris, Jeri. Go free or die . Minneapolis ,
1987. 63 p. : ISBN 0-87614-317-6 (lib. bdg.) :
DDC 305.5/67/0924 B 92 19
E444.T82 F47 1987 *NYPL [Sc D 88-620]*

**SLAVES - UNITED STATES - JUVENILE
FICTION.**
Nevin, Evelyn C. Underground escape /.
Philadelphia , c1926. 191 p. :
NYPL [Sc D 88-1506]

**SLAVES - VIRGINIA - BIOGRAPHY -
JUVENILE LITERATURE.**
Bisson, Terry. Nat Turner /. New York ,
c1988. 111 p. : ISBN 1-555-46613-3 DDC
975.5/5503/0924 B 92 19
F232.S7 T873 1988 *NYPL [Sc E 88-454]*

**SLAVES' WRITINGS, AMERICAN -
HISTORY AND CRITICISM.**
Starling, Marion Wilson, 1907. The slave
narrative . Washington, D.C. , 1988. xxx, 375
p. ; ISBN 0-88258-165-1 : DDC 973/.0496073 19
E444 .S8 1988 *NYPL [Sc E 89-185]*

Slawson, Douglas J. Poole, Stafford. Church and
slave in Perry County, Missouri, 1818-1865 /.
Lewiston, N.Y., USA , c1986. xvii, 251 p. :
ISBN 0-88946-666-1 (alk. paper) : DDC
306/.362/09778694 19
E445.M67 P66 1986 *NYPL [Sc E 89-102]*

SLEIGHT OF HAND. see MAGIC.

Slevin, Jonathan. Robinson, Robert, ca. 1902-
Black on Red . Washington, D.C. , 1988. 436
p. : ISBN 0-87491-885-5 DDC 947.084 19
DK34.B53 R63 1988 *NYPL [Sc E 88-377]*

Slipping through the cracks : the status of Black
women / edited by Margaret C. Simms and
Julianne Malveaux. New Brunswick, N.J. :
Transaction Books, 1986. 302 p. ; 23 cm.
Includes bibliographical references. ISBN
0-88738-662-8
*1. Afro-American women - Social conditions. I. Simms,
Margaret C. II. Malveaux, Julianne.*
NYPL [Sc D 88-767]

Slips from grace /. Anderson, Hope. Toronto ,
1987. 82 p. : ISBN 0-88910-352-6
NYPL [Sc D 88-73]

Sloan, Irving J. The Negro in modern American
history textbooks : a study of the Negro in
selected junior and senior high history
textbooks as of September 1966 / Irving Sloan.
Chicago, Ill. : American Federation of Teachers,
AFL-CIO, 1966. 47 p. ; 21 cm. (Curricular
viewpoints series) Author's autographed presentation
copy to the Schomburg Center.
*1. Afro-American studies - Bibliography. 2. United
States - History - Text-books - Bibliography. I. Title.*
NYPL [Sc D 89-262]

Slocum, Frank. Classic baseball cards : the golden
years 1886-1956 / text by Frank Slocum ;
foreword by Yogi Berra. New York, N.Y. :
Warner Books, c1987. ca 800 p. : ill. (some
col.) ; 37 cm. ISBN 0-446-51392-X DDC
769/.49796357/0973 19
*1. Baseball cards - United States - Collectors and
collecting. I. Title.*
GV875.3 .S57 1987 *NYPL [8-*ISGB 89-500]*

Sluby, Paul E.
Holmead's Cemetery (Western Burial Ground), Washington, D.C. / compiled by Paul E. Sluby, Sr. ; edited by Stanton L. Wormley. Washington, D.C. : Columbian Harmony Society, 1985. iv, 68 leaves : ill. ; 24 cm. Bibliography: p. 66-68. DDC 929.5/09753 19
1. Registers of births, etc. - Washington, D. C. 2. Inscriptions - Washington (D.C.). 3. Washington, D. C. - Genealogy. 4. Holmead's Cemetery (Washington, D.C.). I. Wormley, Stanton L. (Stanton Lawrence), 1909-. II. Title.
F193 .S582 1985 **NYPL [Sc D 88-109]**

Selected small cemeteries of Washington, DC / compiled by Paul E. Sluby, Sr. ; edited by Stanton L. Wormley, Sr. [Washington] : Columbian Harmony Society, c1987. 84 p. : ill. ; 23 cm. Includes one Afro-American graveyard, Union Baptist Cemetery.
1. Cemeteries - Washington (D.C.). 2. Registers of births, etc. - Washington, D. C. 3. Washington, D. C. - Genealogy. I. Wormley, Stanton L. (Stanton Lawrence), 1909-. II. Title. **NYPL [Sc D 88-780]**

SLUM CLEARANCE. see CITY PLANNING; HOUSING.

SMALL BUSINESS - GOVERNMENT POLICY - AFRICA - ADDRESSES, ESSAYS, LECTURES.
Rural small-scale industries and employment in Africa and Asia . Geneva , 1984. x, 159 p. ; ISBN 92-2-103513-1 (pbk.) : DDC 338.6/42/095 19
HD2346.A55 R87 1984
NYPL [JLE 84-3222]

SMALL BUSINESS - GOVERNMENT POLICY - ASIA - ADDRESSES, ESSAYS, LECTURES.
Rural small-scale industries and employment in Africa and Asia . Geneva , 1984. x, 159 p. ; ISBN 92-2-103513-1 (pbk.) : DDC 338.6/42/095 19
HD2346.A55 R87 1984
NYPL [JLE 84-3222]

SMALL BUSINESS - NIGERIA.
Kalu, Onwuka O. The challenge of industrialization in Nigeria . Lagos, Nigeria , 1986. xviii, 84 p. ; **NYPL [Sc D 88-1245]**
Okeke, Okeke Okore, 1954- Self-employment for unemployed Nigerians /. Festac Town, Lagos, Nigeria , 1987. 110 p. ; ISBN 978-333-011-27 **NYPL [Sc D 89-298]**

Small circle of beings /. Galgut, Damon, 1963- London , 1988. 221 p. ;
NYPL [Sc D 88-1342]

SMALL COUNTRIES. see STATES, SMALL.

Small, John. Social work with Black children and their families /. London , 1986. 207 p. ; ISBN 0-7134-4888-1 (cased)
NYPL [Sc D 89-281]

SMALL NATIONS. see STATES, SMALL.

A small place /. Kincaid, Jamaica. New York , 1988. 81 p. ; ISBN 0-374-26638-7 : DDC 813 19
PR9275.A583 K5637 1988
NYPL [Sc D 88-1061]

Smet, A.J. Tempels Placide, 1906- Ecrits polémiques et politiques [microform] /. Kinshasa-Limete , 1979. 24 p. ;
NYPL [Sc Micro F-11131]

Smiles and blood . Craig, Susan. London , 1988. vii, 70 p., [4] p. of plates : ISBN 0-901241-81-4 (hard back) **NYPL [Sc D 89-418]**

Smith, Abdullahi, 1920-1984. A little new light : selected historical writings of Professor Abdullahi Smith / The Abdullahi Smith Centre for Historical Research. Zaria : The Abdullahi Smith Centre for Historical Research, 1987- v. : ill. ; 22 cm. Includes bibliographical references.
1. Nigeria - History - To 1851. 2. Nigeria - Historiography. I. Abdullahi Smith Centre for Historical Research. II. Title. **NYPL [Sc D 88-708]**

Smith, Amanda, 1837-1915. An autobiography : the story of the Lord's dealings with Mrs. Amanda Smith, the Colored evangelist / Amanda Smith ; with an introduction by Jualynne E. Dodson. New York : Oxford University Press, 1988. xlii, 506 p. [23] p. of plates : ill., port. ; 17 cm. (The Schomburg library of nineteenth-century Black women writers) Bibliography: p. xxxix-xlii. Reprint. Originally published: Chicago : Meyer, 1893. ISBN 0-19-505261-7 (alk.

paper) DDC 269/.2/0924 B 19
1. Smith, Amanda, 1837-1915. 2. Afro-American evangelists - Biography. 3. Women evangelists - United States - Biography. I. Title. II. Series.
BV3785.S56 A3 1988 **NYPL [JFC 88-2154]**

SMITH, AMANDA, 1837-1915.
Smith, Amanda, 1837-1915. An autobiography . New York , 1988. xlii, 506 p. [23] p. of plates : ISBN 0-19-505261-7 (alk. paper) DDC 269/.2/0924 B 19
BV3785.S56 A3 1988 **NYPL [JFC 88-2154]**

Smith, Anna H. De Meillon, Henry Clifford. Cape views and costumes . Johannesburg , 1978. 134 p. : ISBN 0-909079-05-6 : DDC 759.968
ND2088.6.S6 D452 1978
NYPL [Sc F 85-112]

Smith, Arthur E. E. Folktales from Freetown / by Arthur E.E. Smith. Freetown : People's Educational Association of Sierra Leone, 1987. 69 p. ; 21 cm. (Stories and songs from Sierra Leone . 26) Bibliography: p. [70]
1. Tales - Sierra Leone. I. Title. II. Series.
NYPL [Sc D 89-413]

Smith, Douglas I. Black youth futures . Leicester , 1987. ii, 113 p. ; ISBN 0-86155-106-0 (pbk) : DDC 331.3/46/0941 19
HD8398 **NYPL [Sc D 89-175]**

Smith, Edward D. Climbing Jacob's ladder : the rise of Black churches in Eastern American cities, 1740-1877 / Edward D. Smith. City of Washington : Published for the Anacostia Museum of the Smithsonian Institution by the Smithsonian Institution Press, 1988. 143 p. : ill., ports. ; 25 cm. Includes index. Bibliography: p.127-258. ISBN 0-87474-829-1
1. Afro-American churches - Atlantic States - History. 2. Atlantic States - Church history. I. Anacostia Museum. II. Title. **NYPL [Sc E 88-505]**

Smith, Eunice Young, 1902- Randall, Blossom E. Fun for Chris /. Chicago , c1956. 26 p. :
NYPL [Sc E 88-238]

Smith, Graham. When Jim Crow met John Bull : Black American soldiers in World War II Britain / Graham Smith. London : I.B. Tauris, c1987. 265 p. ; 22 cm. Includes index. Bibliography: p. [247]-258. ISBN 1-85043-039-X
1. United States. Army - Afro-American troops. 2. Afro-American soldiers - Great Britain. 3. World War, 1939-1945 - Participation, Afro-American. 4. Racism - Great Britain. 5. Great Britain - History - George VI, 1936-1952. I. Title. **NYPL [Sc D 88-55]**

Smith, J. Owens. Blacks and American government : politics, policy, and social change / J. Owens Smith, Mitchell F. Rice, Woodrow Jones, Jr. Dubuque, Iowa : Kendall/Hunt Pub. Co., c1987. xii, 148 p. : ill. ; 24 cm. Includes bibliographies. ISBN 0-8403-4407-4 (pbk) DDC 323.1/196073 19
1. Afro-Americans - Politics and government. 2. Afro-Americans - Civil rights. 3. United States - Politics and government - 1981-. I. Rice, Mitchell F. II. Jones, Woodrow. III. Title.
E185.615 .S576 1987 **NYPL [Sc E 89-193]**

Smith, Jessie Carney. Images of Blacks in American culture . New York , 1988. xvii, 390 p. : ISBN 0-313-24844-3 (lib. bdg. : alk. paper) DDC 700 19
NX652.A37 I43 1988 **NYPL [Sc E 88-466]**

Smith, Judy Barton. Dodson, Jualynne E. Black stylization and implications for child welfare . Atlanta, Georgia , 1975. 1 v. (various pagings) ;
NYPL [Sc F 88-223]

Smith, M. G. (Michael Garfield) Culture race and class in the commonwealth Caribbean / by M.G. Smith ; with a foreword by Rex Nettleford. Mona, Jamaica : Department of Extra-Mural Studies,University of the West Indies, 1984. xiv, 163 p. ; 23 cm. Errata slip inserted. Bibliography: p. [143]-163. ISBN 976-616-000-7
1. Social classes - Caribbean Area - Case studies. 2. Social structure - Caribbean area - Case studies. 3. Pluralism (Social sciences) - Caribbean Area - Case studies. 4. Caribbean Area - Race relations - Case studies. I. Title. **NYPL [Sc D 88-454]**

Smith, Marion Whitney. Beacon Hill's Colonel Robert Gould Shaw / by Marion Whitney Smith. New York : Carlton Press, 1986. 512 p. : ill. ; 21 cm. "A Hearthstone Book." ISBN 0-8062-2732-X

1. Shaw, Robert Gould, 1837-1863. 2. Massachusetts Infantry. 54th Regt., 1863-1865. 3. Shaw family. 4. Parkman family. 5. United States - History - Civil War, 1861-1865 - Participation, Afro-American. I. Title.
NYPL [Sc D 88-414]

Smith, Obediah Michael. Acts : a poem / by Obediah Michael Smith. [Nassau? : s.n., c1983] 56 p. ; 22 cm.
I. Title.
MLCS 85/735 (P) **NYPL [Sc D 88-494]**

Smith, Pat. Soko rareupe harutagaibag namosux amik kaina [microform] Health and mothercraft / by Pat Smith Ukarumpa, Papua New Guinea : Summer Institute of Linguistics, 1973. 12 p. ; 21 cm. Microfiche. New York: New York Public Library, 198 . 1 microfiche: negative; 11 x 15 cm. (FSN Sc 019,071)
1. Gimi language - Texts. I. Title. II. Title: Health and mothercraft. **NYPL [Sc Micro F-10977]**

Smith, Robert, 1919- Kingdoms of the Yoruba / Robert Smith. 3rd ed. London : Currey, 1988. xii, 174 p. : ill., maps, plans ; 24 cm. Previous ed.: [London] : Methuen, 1976. Includes bibliography and index. ISBN 0-85255-028-6 (cased) : DDC 966/.004963 19
1. Yorubas - History. I. Title.
DT513 **NYPL [Sc E 88-482]**

Smith, Sid. 10 super Sunday schools in the Black community / Sid Smith. Nashville, Tenn. : Broadman Press, c1986. 178 p. : ill. ; 20 cm. ISBN 0-8054-6252-X : DDC 268/.861/08996073 19
1. Afro-American Sunday schools. 2. Afro-American Baptists. I. Title. II. Title: Ten super Sunday schools in the Black community.
BV1523.A37 S65 1986 **NYPL [Sc C 88-229]**

Smith, Vern E. Monroe, Sylvester. Brothers . New York, N.Y. , c1988. 284 p. : ISBN 0-688-07622-X DDC 977.3/1100496073 B 19
F548.9.N4 M66 1988 **NYPL [Sc E 88-356]**

Smith, Wendell. Robinson, Jackie, 1919-1972. Jackie Robinson . New York , 1948. 170 p. :
NYPL [Sc C 88-61]

Smith, Whiteford. God, the refuge of his people : a sermon delivered before the General Assembly of South Carolina, on Friday, Dec. 6, 1850, being a day of fasting, humiliation, and prayer / by Whiteoford Smith. Columbia, S.C. : Printed by A.S. Johnston, 1850. 16 p. ; 22 cm.
1. Compromise of 1850. 2. Slavery - United States - Sermons. 3. Slavery - Justification. I. Title.
NYPL [Sc Rare C 89-12]

Smith, William Gardner, 1926-1974.
[Return to Black America. Frech]
L'Amérique noire. Traduit de l'américain par Rosine Fitzgerald. [Tournai] Casterman [1972] 149 p. 18 cm. (Politique. Histoire. 3) Translation of Return to Black America.
1. United States - Race relations. I. Title.
NYPL [IEC 79-113]

Smith, Wycliffe. Nature, I love you . [St. Martin] , c1983. 36 p. :
MLCS 86/1723 (P) **NYPL [Sc D 88-626]**

Smitherman-Donaldson, Geneva, 1940- Discourse and discrimination /. Detroit , 1988. 269 p. ; ISBN 0-8143-1957-2 (alk. paper) DDC 401/.9 19
P120.R32 D57 1988 **NYPL [Sc E 88-451]**

Smithsonian contributions to anthropology. (no. 31) Laughlin, Robert M. The great Tzotzil dictionary of Santo Domingo Zinacantán . Washington, D.C. , 1988. 3 v. (xiii, 1119 p.) : DDC 497/.4 301 s 19
GN1 .S54 no. 31a PM4466.Z5
NYPL [HBR 89-17311]

Smithsonian Institution. Office of Interdisciplinary Studies. Constitutional roots, rights, and responsibilities . New York , 1987. 152 p. ; **NYPL [Sc F 88-299]**

Smithsonian series in archaeological inquiry. Sampson, C. Garth (Clavil Garth), 1941- Stylistic boundaries among mobile hunter-foragers /. Washington, c1988. 186 p. : ISBN 0-87474-838-0 DDC 968/.004961 19
DT764.B8 S24 1988 **NYPL [Sc F 89-97]**

Smock, Raymond. Harlan, Louis R. Booker T. Washington in perspective . Jackson , c1988. xii, 210 p., [8] p. of plates : ISBN 0-87805-374-3 (alk. paper) DDC 378/.111 B 19
E185.97.W4 H36 1988 **NYPL [Sc E 89-217]**

SNAKES - JUVENILE FICTION.
Kirkpatrick, Oliver. Naja the snake and Mangus the mongoose. Garden City, N.Y. [1970] 40 p.
DDC [Fic]
PZ7.K6358 Naj   *NYPL [Sc F 88-339]*

Snares without end /. Bhêly-Quénum, Olympe.
[Piège sans fin. English.] Charlottesville , 1988.
xxvi, 204 p. ; ISBN 0-8139-1189-3 (pbk.)   DDC
843 19
PQ3989.2.B5 P513 1988
NYPL [Sc D 89-434]

SNIDER, DUKE.
Honig, Donald. Mays, Mantle, Snider . New
York, N.Y. , London , c1987. vii, 151 p. :
ISBN 0-02-551200-5 DDC 796.357/092/2 B 19
GV865.A1 H6192 1987
NYPL [JFF 87-1461]

SNOW - JUVENILE FICTION.
Keats, Ezra Jack. Da Snøen Kom /. [Norway] ,
1967. [20] p. :   *NYPL [Sc D 88-467]*

Snowden, Thomas Gayle. Symposium on race and
class. Philadelphia , 1984. 62 p. ;
NYPL [Sc D 88-2]

Snyder, Jerome. Elkin, Benjamin. Why the sun
was late /. New York , 1966. [40] p. :
PZ7.#426 Wh   *NYPL [Sc F 88-105]*

Sobel, Louis H. (Louis Harry), 1904-1955.
Granger, Lester Blackwell, n.d.- Toward job
adjustment . [New York] [1941] 78 p. :
NYPL [Sc D 88-178]

Sobre los hombros ajenos /. González, Carmen,
1940- La Habana , 1985. 119 p. ;   DDC 968 19
DT766 .G66 1985   *NYPL [Sc D 88-416]*

**SOCIAL ACTION - UNITED STATES -
HISTORY - 20TH CENTURY.**
Childs, John Brown. Leadership, conflict, and
cooperation in Afro-American social thought /.
Philadelphia , 1989. xii, 172 p. ; ISBN
0-87722-581-8 (alk. paper) :   DDC
303.3/4/08996073 19
E185.6 .C534 1989   *NYPL [Sc D 89-497]*

Social anthropology of peasantry / [edited by]
Joan P. Mencher. 1st ed. Ikeja, Nigeria : John
West Publications, 1983. xii, 351 p. ; 25 cm.
"Papers ... presented at a post-plenary session which
met in Lucknow, India, following the Tenth
International Congress of Anthropological Sciences in
New Delhi, India, in December 1978"--Introd. Includes
bibliographies.   DDC 305.5/63 19
*1. Sociology, Rural - Congresses. 2. Peasantry -
Developing countries - Congresses. I. Mencher, Joan P.,
1930-. II. International Congress of Anthropological and
Ethnological Sciences (10th : 1978 : New Delhi, India).*
HT407 .S53 1983   *NYPL [Sc E 87-179]*

Social change in Nigeria / edited by Simi Afonja
and Tola Olu Pearce. Harlow, Essex, England :
Longman, 1984. 261 p. ; 23 cm. Includes
bibliographies and index.   ISBN 0-582-64434-8 (pbk.) :
DDC 306/.09669 19
*1. Nigeria - Social conditions - 1960-. I. Afonja, Simi.
II. Pearce, Tola Olu.*
HN831.A8 S63 1984   *NYPL [Sc D 88-880]*

Social change in Nigeria / edited by Simi Afonja
and Tola Olu Pearce. London : Longman, 1986.
261 p. ; 23 cm. Includes bibliographical references
and index.   ISBN 0-582-64434-8 (pbk.) :   DDC
306/.09669 19
*1. Nigeria - Social conditions - 1960-. I. Afonja, Simi.
II. Pearce, Tola Olu.*
HN831.A8 S63 1986   *NYPL [JLE 87-3643]*

SOCIAL CLASSES - AFRICA.
N'Da, Paul, 1945- Pouvoir, lutte de classes,
idéologie et milieu intellectuel africain. /. Paris ,
c1987. 107 p. ; ISBN 2-7087-0485-0
NYPL [Sc D 88-918]

SOCIAL CLASSES - AFRICA, CENTRAL.
Madu, Oliver V. Models of class domination in
plural societies of Central Africa /.
Washington , c1978. vi, 510 p. ;
NYPL [Sc D 88-1067]

**SOCIAL CLASSES - AFRICA, SOUTHERN -
CONGRESSES.**
Class formation and class struggle . [Roma?
Lesotho] [1982] 211 p. ;
NYPL [Sc D 89-25]

**SOCIAL CLASSES - BRAZIL -
CONGRESSES.**
Race, class, and power in Brazil /. Los
Angeles , c1985. xi, 160 p. : ISBN
0-934934-22-3 :   DDC 305.8/96/081 19
F2659.N4 R24 1985   *NYPL [JLE 88-2671]*

**SOCIAL CLASSES - CARIBBEAN AREA -
ADDRESSES, ESSAYS, LECTURES.**
Contemporary Caribbean . [St. Augustine,
Trinidad and Tobago?] , 1981-<1982 >
(Maracas, Trinidad and Tobago, West Indies :
College Press) v. :   DDC 304.6/09729 19
HB3545 .C66 1981   *NYPL [Sc D 89-499]*

**SOCIAL CLASSES - CARIBBEAN AREA -
CASE STUDIES.**
Smith, M. G. (Michael Garfield) Culture race
and class in the commonwealth Caribbean /.
Mona, Jamaica , 1984. xiv, 163 p. ;   ISBN
976-616-000-7   *NYPL [Sc D 88-454]*

SOCIAL CLASSES - LIBERIA.
Burrowes, Carl Patrick. The Americo-Liberian
ruling class and other myths . Philadelphia ,
1989. 77 leaves ;   *NYPL [Sc F 89-128]*

SOCIAL CLASSES - UNITED STATES.
Boston, Thomas D. Race, class, and
conservatism /. Boston , 1988. xix, 172 p. :
ISBN 0-04-330368-4 (alk. paper)   DDC
305.5/0973 19
HN90.S6 B67 1988   *NYPL [Sc D 89-107]*

Symposium on race and class. Philadelphia ,
1984. 62 p. ;   *NYPL [Sc D 88-2]*

**SOCIAL CONFLICT - AFRICA, SOUTHERN -
CONGRESSES.**
Class formation and class struggle . [Roma?
Lesotho] [1982] 211 p. ;
NYPL [Sc D 89-25]

**SOCIAL CONFLICT - UGANDA -
CONGRESSES.**
International Seminar on Internal Conflict
(1987 : Makerere, Uganda) Seminar papers on
internal conflicts in Uganda. [Makerere,
Uganda , 1987]. 1 v.   *NYPL [Sc F 89-86]*

**SOCIAL CONFLICT - ZIMBABWE -
HISTORY.**
Phimister, I. R. (Ian R.) An economic and
social history of Zimbabwe, 1890-1948 .
London , New York , 1988. xii, 336 p. :   ISBN
0-582-64423-2 DDC 330.96891/02 19
HC910.Z9 S36 1987   *NYPL [Sc D 89-35]*

SOCIAL DEMOCRACY. see SOCIALISM.

Social demography.
Nelson, Kathryn P. Gentrification and
distressed cities . Madison, Wis. , 1988. xiii,
187 p. : ISBN 0-299-11160-1 : DDC 307.2 19
HT175 .N398 1987   *NYPL [JLE 88-3486]*

Social development and rural fieldwork : edited
proceedings of a workshop entitled Social
Development, Rural Poverty and Fieldwork
Intervention, held in Harare, Zimbabwe, June
1986 / edited by Joe Hampson and Brigid
Willmore. Zimbabwe : Journal of Social
Development in Africa, [1986]. 96 p. ; 21 cm.
Includes bibliographies.
*1. Rural development - Africa - Congresses. 2. Africa -
Social conditions - Congresses. I. Hampson, Joe. II.
Willmore, Brigid. III. Workshop on Social
Development, Rural Poverty, and Fieldwork
Intervention (1986 : Harare, Zimbabwe).*
NYPL [Sc D 88-1153]

SOCIAL ECOLOGY. see HUMAN ECOLOGY.

SOCIAL HISTORY - 1970-
Bouzar, Wadi, 1938- La culture en question /.
Alger , Paris , c1982. 187 p. ; ISBN
2-903871-11-6 (pbk.) :   DDC 306/.0965 19
HN980 .B68 1982   *NYPL [JLC 84-337]*

SOCIAL HYGIENE. see PUBLIC HEALTH.

Social life in the Caribbean, 1838-1938 /.
Brereton, Bridget. London , 1985. 65 p. :   ISBN
0-435-98305-9 (pbk)   DDC 909/.09821 19
F2169   *NYPL [Sc D 88-1307]*

**SOCIAL MARGINALITY. see MARGINALITY,
SOCIAL.**

**Social organisation and ceremonial institutions of
the Bomvana** /. Cook, Peter Alan Wilson,
1905- Cape Town [1931?] xi, 171 p., [16] p. of
plates :   *NYPL [Sc C 88-31]*

**SOCIAL ORGANIZATION. see SOCIAL
STRUCTURE.**

Social origins of the Rastafari movement /.
Chevannes, Barry. Mona, Kingston , c1978. xii,
323 p. ;
BL2532.R37 C48 1978   *NYPL [Sc F 88-368]*

SOCIAL PREDICTIONS - SOUTH AFRICA.
Louw, Leon. South Africa . Bisho, Ciskei ,
1986. xvi, 238 p. :   ISBN 0-620-09371-4 (pbk.)
DDC 306/.0968 19
HN801.A8 L68 1986   *NYPL [Sc D 88-197]*

**SOCIAL PROBLEMS AND THE CHURCH.
see CHURCH AND SOCIAL PROBLEMS.**

**SOCIAL PROBLEMS IN EDUCATION. see
EDUCATIONAL SOCIOLOGY.**

Social psychology and society.
Aboud, Frances E. Children and prejudice /.
Oxford [Oxfordshire] , New York, NY , 1988.
x, 149 p. : ISBN 0-631-14939-2 : DDC 305.2/3
19
BF723.P75 A24 1988   *NYPL [Sc E 89-57]*

**SOCIAL REFORMERS - ONTARIO -
TORONTO - BIOGRAPHY.**
Hubbard, Stephen, 1961- Against all odds .
Toronto , 1987. 140 p. :   ISBN 1-550-02013-7
(bound)   *NYPL [Sc D 88-985]*

**SOCIAL REFORMERS - SOUTHERN
STATES - BIOGRAPHY.**
Rouse, Jacqueline Anne. Lugenia Burns Hope,
Black southern reformer /. Athens , c1989. xi,
182 p., [8] p. of plates :   ISBN 0-8203-1082-4 (alk.
paper)   DDC 973/.0496073024 B 19
E185.97.H717 R68 1989
NYPL [Sc D 89-469]

**SOCIAL REFORMERS - UNITED STATES -
BIOGRAPHY - JUVENILE LITERATURE.**
Ferris, Jeri. Walking the road to freedom .
Minneapolis , 1987. 64 p. :   ISBN 0-87614-318-4
(lib. bdg.) :   DDC 305.5/67/0924 B 92 19
E185.97.T8 F47 1987   *NYPL [Sc D 88-1046]*

Krass, Peter. Sojourner Truth /. New York ,
c1988. 110 p. :   ISBN 1-555-46611-7   DDC
305.5/67/0924 B 92 19
E185.97.T8 K73 1988   *NYPL [Sc E 88-470]*

**SOCIAL REFORMERS - UNITED STATES -
CORRESPONDENCE.**
Washington, Booker T. 1856-1915. The Booker
T. Washington papers. Urbana [1972- v.
NYPL [Sc B-Washington, B.]

Social research and information gathering /
edited by D.C.E. Ugwuegbu and S.O.
Onwumere. Lagos : Federal Govt. Printer,
[1987?] v. 72 p. : ill. ; 24 cm. Cover title.
Outcome of a conference held in Ibadan, 17-21
November 1986. Includes bibliographical references.
*1. Social sciences - Research - Methodology. I.
Ugwuegbu, Denis C. E. II. Onwumere, S. O.*
NYPL [Sc E 88-301]

**SOCIAL SCIENCE. see SOCIAL SCIENCES;
SOCIOLOGY.**

Social science in court . Chesler, Mark A.
Madison, Wis. , 1988. xiv, 286 p. ; ISBN
0-299-11620-4 : DDC 344.73/0798 347.304798
19
KF8925.D5 C48 1988   *NYPL [Sc E 89-187]*

Social science librairies in West Africa . Banjo,
A. O. Lagos, Nigeria , 1987. iii, 63 p. :
NYPL [Sc D 88-1204]

**SOCIAL SCIENCE LIBRARIES - AFRICA,
WEST - DIRECTORIES.**
Banjo, A. O. Social science librairies in West
Africa . Lagos, Nigeria , 1987. iii, 63 p. :
NYPL [Sc D 88-1204]

SOCIAL SCIENCES - NIGERIA.
Heinecke, P. Divided truths . Okpella, Bendel
State, Nigeria , 1988. 135 p. ; ISBN
978-252-832-3   *NYPL [Sc D 89-134]*

Nzimiro, Ikenna, 1927- The crisis in the social
sciences . Oguta, Nigeria , 1986. 89 p. ;   ISBN
978-215-003-7   *NYPL [Sc C 88-93]*

SOCIAL SCIENCES - RESEARCH - BRAZIL.
30 anos do Instituto Joaquim Nabuco de
Pesquisas Sociais /. Recife , 1981. 343 p. :
ISBN 85-7019-008-5 DDC 300.72081 19
H67.R44 A13 1981   *NYPL [Sc D 88-871]*

**SOCIAL SCIENCES - RESEARCH -
METHODOLOGY.**
Social research and information gathering /.
Lagos [1987?] v. 72 p. :
NYPL [Sc E 88-301]

**SOCIAL SCIENCES - STUDY AND
TEACHING (PRIMARY) - NEW YORK
(CITY)**
New York (N.Y.). Bureau of Curriculum

Development. Black studies. New York [c1970]
vii, 227 p. DDC 375/.0097471 s
LB1563 .N57 1970-71, no. 3
NYPL [Sc G 87-32]

**SOCIAL SCIENCES - STUDY AND
TEACHING (SECONDARY) - NIGERIA.**
Longman social studies . Nigeria [1984?]- v. :
ISBN 0-582-65043-7 *NYPL [Sc F 88-350]*

**SOCIAL SCIENTISTS - LEGAL STATUS,
LAWS, ETC. - UNITED STATES.**
Chesler, Mark A. Social science in court .
Madison, Wis. , 1988. xiv, 286 p. ; ISBN
0-299-11620-4 : DDC 344.73/0798 347.304798
19
KF8925.D5 C48 1988 NYPL [Sc E 89-187]

**SOCIAL SERVICE - SOUTHERN STATES -
HISTORY.**
Neverdon-Morton, Cynthia, 1944-
Afro-American women of the South and the
advancement of the race, 1895-1925 /.
Knoxville , c1989. 272 p. : ISBN 0-87049-583-6
(alk. paper) : DDC 305.4/8896073/075 19
E185.86 .N48 1989 NYPL [Sc E 89-218]

**SOCIAL STRATIFICATION. see SOCIAL
CLASSES.**

**SOCIAL STRUCTURE - CARIBBEAN AREA -
CASE STUDIES.**
Smith, M. G. (Michael Garfield) Culture race
and class in the commonwealth Caribbean /.
Mona, Jamaica , 1984. xiv, 163 p. ; ISBN
976-616-000-7 *NYPL [Sc D 88-454]*

**The social structure of the kraal among the
Zezuru in Musami (Southern Rhodesia)**
Bernardi, Bernardo. [Cape Town] 1950. [2], 60,
[1] . DDC 572.9689
GN490 .B4 NYPL [Sc F 88-349]

SOCIAL STRUCTURE - SWAZILAND.
Crush, Jonathan Scott, 1953- The struggle for
Swazi labour, 1890-1920 /. Kingston, Ont. ,
1987. xviii, 292 p., [9] p. of plates : ISBN
0-7735-0569-5 *NYPL [Sc E 89-150]*

SOCIAL STUDIES. see SOCIAL SCIENCES.

Social support . Milburn, Norweeta G.
Washington, D.C. , 1986. iii, 67 p. ;
NYPL [Sc F 87-428]

SOCIAL WELFARE. see SOCIAL SERVICE.

**SOCIAL WORK EDUCATION - UNITED
STATES - CURRICULA.**
Dodson, Jualynne E. Training of personnel for
services to Black families . [Atlanta] [1976] 1
v. (various foliations) ; *NYPL [Sc F 88-130]*

**Social work with Black children and their
families /** edited by Shama Ahmed, Juliet
Cheetham and John Small. London : Batsford
in association with British Agencies for
Adoption and Fostering, 1986. 207 p. ; 22 cm.
(Child care policy and practice) Includes bibliographies
and index. ISBN 0-7134-4888-1 (cased)
*1. Social work with children - Great Britain. 2. Social
work with minorities - Great Britain. I. Ahmed, Shama.
II. Cheetham, Juliet. III. Small, John. IV. British
Agencies for Adoption and Fostering. V. Series.*
NYPL [Sc D 89-281]

**SOCIAL WORK WITH CHILDREN - GREAT
BRITAIN.**
Social work with Black children and their
families /. London , 1986. 207 p. ; ISBN
0-7134-4888-1 (cased)
NYPL [Sc D 89-281]

**SOCIAL WORK WITH IMMIGRANTS -
CROSS-CULTURAL STUDIES.**
Ethnic associations and the welfare state . New
York , 1988. x, 299 p. : ISBN 0-231-05690-7
DDC 362.8 19
HV4005 .E86 1988 NYPL [JLE 88-3846]

**SOCIAL WORK WITH MINORITIES -
GREAT BRITAIN.**
Social work with Black children and their
families /. London , 1986. 207 p. ; ISBN
0-7134-4888-1 (cased)
NYPL [Sc D 89-281]

**SOCIAL WORK WITH YOUTH - ENGLAND -
LONDON.**
Williams, Lincoln Octavious. Partial surrender .
London , New York , 1988. viii, 194 p. ; ISBN
1-85000-289-4 DDC 361.7/97/009421 19
HV1441.G8 L78 1988 NYPL [Sc E 89-73]

SOCIALISM - AFRICA.
Ottaway, Marina. Afrocommunism /. New

York , 1986. ix, 270 p. : ISBN 0-8419-1034-0
DDC 335.43/096 19
HX438.5 .O87 1985 NYPL [JLD 86-4056]

Socialism & education . Gwarinda, Takawira C.
Harare, Zimbabwe , 1985. 128 p. : ISBN
0-86925-547-9 *NYPL [Sc D 88-1129]*

Socialism and education . Gwarinda, Takawira C.
Socialism & education . Harare, Zimbabwe ,
1985. 128 p. : ISBN 0-86925-547-9
NYPL [Sc D 88-1129]

SOCIALISM AND EDUCATION - GUINEA.
Construisons notre société . Conakry , 1970. x,
201 p. ; *NYPL [Sc E 88-254]*

**SOCIALISM AND EDUCATION -
ZIMBABWE.**
Gwarinda, Takawira C. Socialism & education .
Harare, Zimbabwe , 1985. 128 p. : ISBN
0-86925-547-9 *NYPL [Sc D 88-1129]*

Socialism and self-reliance in Tanzania /. Okoko,
Kimse A. B. London , New York , 1987. xiii,
272 p. : ISBN 0-7103-0269-X
NYPL [Sc D 88-902]

**SOCIALISM AND WOMEN. see WOMEN
AND SOCIALISM.**

**SOCIALISM IN LATIN AMERICA -
CONGRESSES.**
Bishop, Maurice. Address by Prime Minister
Maurice Bishop at the opening of the Socialist
International meeting held in Grenada, July
23-24 [microform]. [St. George's, Grenada]
[1981?] 12 leaves ;
NYPL [Sc Micro R-4108 no.29]

**SOCIALISM IN THE CARIBBEAN AREA -
CONGRESSES.**
Bishop, Maurice. Address by Prime Minister
Maurice Bishop at the opening of the Socialist
International meeting held in Grenada, July
23-24 [microform]. [St. George's, Grenada]
[1981?] 12 leaves ;
NYPL [Sc Micro R-4108 no.29]

SOCIALISM - JAMAICA.
Pathways to progress . Morant Bay, Jamaica,
W.I. , 1985. vii, 128 p. ; DDC 338.97292 19
HC154 .P38 1985 NYPL [Sc D 88-1239]

SOCIALISM - MADAGASCAR.
Deleris, Ferdinand. Ratsiraka . Paris , c1986.
135 p. ; ISBN 2-85802-697-1
NYPL [Sc D 88-777]

SOCIALISM - MARTINIQUE.
Darsières, Camille. Lagro, ou, Les debuts du
socialisme à la Martinique /. [Fort-de-France]
[198-?] 75 p. : *NYPL [Sc D 89-560]*

SOCIALISM - MAURITIUS.
L'Histoire d'une trahison . Port Louis,
Mauritius , 1987. vi, 192 p.
NYPL [Sc F 88-275]

SOCIALISM - SENEGAL.
Le Parti socialiste du Sénégal de Senghor à
Abdou Diouf /. [Dakar] [1987?] 176 p. ;
ISBN 2-7236-1007-1 DDC 324.266/3072 19
JQ3396.A98 S65 1987 NYPL [Sc D 89-125]

SOCIALISM - SOMALIA.
Samatar, Ahmed I. (Ahmed Ismail) Socialist
Somalia . London , Atlantic Highlands, N.J. ,
1988. 186 p. ; ISBN 0-86232-588-9 DDC
967/.7305 19
DT407 .S26 1988 NYPL [JLD 89-340]

SOCIALISM - SOVIET UNION.
Odear, Godwin N. (Goodwin Nwafor), 1958-
336 hours in the hero cities of Russians .
[Nigeria? , 1984?] 145, [17] p. of plates ;
NYPL [Sc D 88-790]

SOCIALISM - TANZANIA.
Okoko, Kimse A. B. Socialism and self-reliance
in Tanzania /. London , New York , 1987. xiii,
272 p. : ISBN 0-7103-0269-X
NYPL [Sc D 88-902]

SOCIALISM - ZIMBABWE.
Gwarinda, Takawira C. Socialism & education .
Harare, Zimbabwe , 1985. 128 p. : ISBN
0-86925-547-9 *NYPL [Sc D 88-1129]*

Ushewokunze, H. S. M. (Herbert Sylvester
Masiyiwa), 1938- An agenda for Zimbabwe /.
[Harare, Zimbabwe] c1984. vi, 198 p. ; ISBN
0-906041-67-8 DDC 361.6/1/096891 19
HX451.A6 U84 1984 NYPL [Sc D 88-942]

**SOCIALIST ETHICS - GUINEA -
TEXTBOOKS.**

Construisons notre société . Conakry , 1970. x,
201 p. ; *NYPL [Sc E 88-254]*

**Socialist Peoples Libyan Arab Jamahirya. see
Libya.**

Socialist Somalia . Samatar, Ahmed I. (Ahmed
Ismail) London , Atlantic Highlands, N.J. ,
1988. 186 p. ; ISBN 0-86232-588-9 DDC
967/.7305 19
DT407 .S26 1988 NYPL [JLD 89-340]

**SOCIALIZATION, POLITICAL. see
POLITICAL SOCIALIZATION.**

**SOCIALLY HANDICAPPED YOUTH -
BRAZIL - EDUCATION.**
Edmundo, Lygia Pereira. Instituição . São
Paulo , 1987. 141 p. ; *NYPL [Sc D 89-332]*

Società africana d'Italia (Naples) Sarnelli,
Tommaso. Costumi e credenze coloniali
[microform] . Napoli , 1925. 39 p. :
NYPL [Sc Micro F-11058]

Societas Jesu. see Jesuits.

**Société américaine des écoles du dimanche. see
American Sunday-School Union.**

**Bibliothèque d'histoire antillaise. see
Bibliothèque d'histoire antillaise.**

La société Minyanka du Mali . Jonckers,
Danielle. Paris , c1987. viii, 234 p., [8] p. of
plates : *NYPL [Sc E 88-344]*

Sociétés africaines.
(7) Princes & serviteurs du royaume . Paris ,
1987. 225 p. : ISBN 2-901161-29-4
NYPL [Sc E 88-409]

(8) Boyer, Pascal. Barricades mystérieuses &
pièges à pensée . Paris , 1988. 190 p. : ISBN
2-901161-31-6 *NYPL [Sc E 88-500]*

**Sociétés et pouvoirs dans l'Afrique des grands
lacs.** Pouvoirs et sociétés dans l'Afrique des
grands lacs /. Bujumbura , 1986. 146 p. ;
NYPL [Sc F 89-62]

**SOCIETIES, COOPERATIVE. see
COOPERATIVE SOCIETIES.**

**SOCIETIES, SECRET. SEE SECRET
SOCIETIES.**

SOCIETY AND ART. see ART AND SOCIETY.

**SOCIETY AND EDUCATION. see
EDUCATIONAL SOCIOLOGY.**

**SOCIETY AND LANGUAGE. see
SOCIOLINGUISTICS.**

**SOCIETY AND LIBRARIES. see LIBRARIES
AND SOCIETY.**

**SOCIETY AND LITERATURE. see
LITERATURE AND SOCIETY.**

Society in the dock . Kagwema, Prince, 1931-
Dar es Salaam , c1984. viii, 147 p. ; ISBN
997-691-803-8 *NYPL [Sc D 88-1515]*

Society of Archivists (Great Britain)
Conservation of library and archive materials
and the graphic arts /. London , Boston , 1985.
328 p. : ISBN 0-408-01466-0 : DDC 025.7 19
Z701 .C5863 1985 NYPL [MFW+ 88-574]

Society of Jesus. see Jesuits.

SOCIETY, PRIMITIVE.
Primitive worlds: people lost in time.
[Washington, 1973] 211 p. ISBN 0-87044-127-2
GN400 .P66 NYPL [Sc 301.2-P]

Socio-cultural profiles, Baringo District : a joint
research and training project of the Ministry of
Planning and National Development, and the
Institute of African Studies, University of
Nairobi / project director, Chris L. Wanjala,
project co-ordinator, David Nyamwaya ;
[general editor, Gideon S. Were, assistant
editor, Joshua Akong'a]. [Nairobi?] : The
Ministry : The Institute, 1986. xviii, 268 p. :
ill., maps ; 30 cm. Includes index. Bibliography: p.
[262]-264. DDC 967.6/27 19
*1. Baringo District (Kenya). 2. Baringo District
(Kenya) - Social life and customs. I. Wanjala, Chris. II.
Nyamwaya, David. III. Kenya. Ministry of Planning
and National Development. IV. University of Nairobi.
Institute of African Studies.*
DT434.B36 S63 1986 NYPL [Sc F 88-230]

Socio-economic survey of the Amatola Basin .
Bekker, S. B. Grahamstown [South Africa]

Institute of Social and Economic Rrsearch,
1981. 58, xxxxiv p. : ISBN 0-86810-073-0
NYPL [Sc F 87-430]

**Socio-political aspects of the palaver in some
African countries. Spanish.** Aspectos
sociopolíticos del parlamento tradicional en
algunos países africanos / Robert G.
Armstrong ... [et al.] 1°ed. Barcelona : Serbal ;
Paris : UNESCO, 1979. 95 p. ; 21 cm.
(Colección de temas africanos . 3) Translation of:
Socio-political aspects of the palaver in some African
countries. Includes bibliographies. ISBN
84-85800-24-9
*1. Public meetings - Africa. 2. Africa - Politics and
government. 3. Africa - Social conditions - 1960-. I.
Armstrong, Robert G., 1917-. II. Unesco. III. Title. IV.
Series.* *NYPL [Sc D 88-599]*

**SOCIOLINGUISTICS - ENGLAND -
LONDON.**
Hewitt, Roger. White talk, black talk .
Cambridge [Cambridgeshire] , New York ,
1986. x, 253 p. ; ISBN 0-521-26239-9 DDC
401/.9/094216 19
P40.45.G7 H48 1986 *NYPL [JFE 87-279]*

Sociologies au quotidien .
Salazar, Philippe Joseph. L'Intrigue raciale .
Paris , 1989. 230 p. : ISBN 2-86563-211-3
NYPL [Sc D 89-504]

SOCIOLOGY - AFRICA - HISTORY.
Fonkoué, Jean. Différence & identité . Paris ,
c1985. 202 p. : ISBN 2-903871-46-9 : DDC
301/.096 19
HM22.A4 F66 1985 *NYPL [Sc D 88-1151]*

SOCIOLOGY AND ART. see **ART AND
SOCIETY.**

SOCIOLOGY AND LITERATURE. see
LITERATURE AND SOCIETY.

**SOCIOLOGY, CHRISTIAN (BAPTIST) -
HISTORY OF DOCTRINES - 20TH
CENTURY.**
Fluker, Walter E., 1951- They looked for a
city . Lanham, MD , c1989. xiv, 281 p. ; ISBN
0-8191-7262-6 (alk. paper) DDC 307/.092/2 19
BX6447 .F57 1989 *NYPL [Sc D 89-492]*

SOCIOLOGY, CHRISTIAN (CATHOLIC)
La Farge, John, 1880-1963. Interracial justice .
New York , 1937. xii, 226 p. ; DDC 325.260973
E185.61 .L25 *NYPL [Sc C 88-146]*

SOCIOLOGY, DESCRIPTIVE. see **SOCIAL
HISTORY.**

SOCIOLOGY, EDUCATIONAL. see
EDUCATIONAL SOCIOLOGY.

SOCIOLOGY OF LANGUAGES. see
SOCIOLINGUISTICS.

SOCIOLOGY, RURAL - CONGRESSES.
Social anthropology of peasantry /. Ikeja,
Nigeria , 1983. xii, 351 p. ; DDC 305.5/63 19
HT407 .S53 1983 *NYPL [Sc E 87-179]*

**SOCIOLOGY - UNITED STATES - HISTORY -
20TH CENTURY.**
Childs, John Brown. Leadership, conflict, and
cooperation in Afro-American social thought /.
Philadelphia , 1989. xii, 172 p. ; ISBN
0-87722-581-8 (alk. paper) : DDC
303.3/4/08996073 19
E185.6 .C534 1989 *NYPL [Sc D 89-497]*

Sofowora, Abayomi. The State of medicinal plants
research in Nigeria . [Ibadan?] , c1986. vi, 404
p. : ISBN 978-302-850-2 *NYPL [Sc E 88-305]*

SOFT SCULPTURE - HISTORY.
Thomas, Michel. [Histoire d'un art. English.]
Textile art / . Geneva, Switzerland , New York,
NY , 1985. 279 p. : ISBN 0-8478-0640-5
(Rizzoli) : DDC 746 19
NK8806 .T4813 1985
NYPL [3-MON+ 86-527]

Sojourn / edited by Zhana. London : Methuen,
1988. 215 p. ; 20 cm. ISBN 0-413-16440-3 (pbk) :
DDC 823/.914/08 19
*1. Women, Black - England. 2. English literature -
Women authors. I. Zhana.* *NYPL [Sc C 89-81]*

Sojourner Truth /. Krass, Peter. New York ,
c1988. 110 p. : ISBN 1-555-46611-7 DDC
305.5/67/0924 B 92 19
E185.97.T8 K73 1988 *NYPL [Sc E 88-470]*

**Soko rareupe harutagaibag namosux amik kaina
[microform] Health and mothercraft /.** Smith,

Pat. Ukarumpa, Papua New Guinea , 1973. 12
p. ; *NYPL [Sc Micro F-10977]*

Sokoïne, Edward Moringe, 1938-1984. Public
policy making and implementation in Tanzania
/ by Edward Moringe Sokoïne. Pau : Université
de Pau et des pays de l'Adour, Centre de
recherche et d'étude sur les pays d'Afrique
Orientale, [1986?] ix, 124 p. : ill., map ; 24 cm.
(Cahiers de l'Université . no spécial, 1986) Travau et
documents du CREPAO ; no. 2 "This text was prepared
from a[n] uncompleted manuscript of the late E.M.
Sokoïne by Dr. Katabaro Miti [and] Prof. Gelase
Mutahaba." Prefatory material in French. Includes
bibliographical references.
*1. Public administration - Tanzania. 2. Political
planning - Tanzania. 3. Communication in public
administration - Tanzania. I. Miti Katabaro. II.
Mutahaba, G. R. III. Title.* *NYPL [Sc E 88-319]*

Sokoto State : it's [sic] people & environment /
[designed and produced by the Ministry of
Information, Home Affairs and Culture,
Sokoto]. Sokoto : Govt. Printer, [1987?] 51 p. :
ill., ports. ; 25 cm. Cover title.
*1. Sokoto State (Nigeria). 2. Sokoto State (Nigeria) -
Social conditions.* *NYPL [Sc E 88-610]*

SOKOTO STATE (NIGERIA)
Sokoto State . Sokoto [1987?] 51 p. :
NYPL [Sc E 88-610]

**SOKOTO STATE (NIGERIA) - SOCIAL
CONDITIONS.**
Sokoto State . Sokoto [1987?] 51 p. :
NYPL [Sc E 88-610]

SOLAR ECLIPSES. see **ECLIPSES, SOLAR.**

Solarin, Tai.
Timeless Tai / edited by A. Adenubi. Lagos,
Nigeria : F & A Publishers, 1985. x, 232 p. ; 21
cm. Consists chiefly of articles on education by Tai
Solarin, published between 1958 and 1977.
*1. Education - Nigeria. 2. Nigeria - Social policy. I.
Adenubi, A. II. Title.* *NYPL [Sc D 89-371]*

To mother with love / Tai Solarin. Ibadan :
Board Publications, c1987. 302 p. : ill., ports. ;
21 cm. ISBN 978-19-1050-X
*1. Solarin, Tai. 2. Mayflower School (Ikene, Nigeria). 3.
School superintendents and principals - Nigeria -
Biography. I. Title.* *NYPL [Sc D 88-732]*

SOLARIN, TAI.
Solarin, Tai. To mother with love /. Ibadan ,
c1987. 302 p. : ISBN 978-19-1050-X
NYPL [Sc D 88-732]

SOLARIN, TAI - DRAMA.
Omole, Wale, 1960- Tai Solarin's adventure .
Ibadan , 1985. x, 90 p. : DDC 822 19
PR9387.9.O396 T3 1985
NYPL [Sc C 88-309]

Soledad, Rosalía de la. Ibo : (Yorubas en tierras
cubanas) / Rosalía de la Soledad y María J.
Sanjuán de Novas. Miami, Fla. : E. Universal,
1988. 278 p. ; ill. ; 22 cm. (Colección Ébano y
canela) Includes bibliographical references. ISBN
0-89729-468-8
*1. Yorubas - Cuba. 2. Yorubas - Religion. 3. Blacks -
Cuba - History. I. Sanjuán de Novas, María J. II. Title.*
NYPL [Sc D 89-436]

Solibo Magnifique . Chamoiseau, Patrick. [Paris] ,
c1988. 226 p. ; ISBN 2-07-070990-6
NYPL [Sc D 88-1103]

Solidarités . Dorsinville, Max, 1943- Montréal,
Québec, Canada , 1988. xv, 196 p. ; ISBN
2-920862-09-X *NYPL [Sc D 89-484]*

Sollors, Werner.
The Invention of ethnicity /. New York , 1989.
xx, 294 p. ; ISBN 0-19-504589-0 DDC
810/.9/920692 19
PS153.M56 I58 1988 *NYPL [Sc D 89-374]*

Varieties of black experience at Harvard .
Cambridge [Mass.] , 1986. v, 180 p. ;
LD2160 .V37x 1986 *NYPL [Sc D 88-672]*

Solomos, John. Black youth, racism and the
state : the politics of ideology and policy /
John Solomos. Cambridge [Cambridgeshire] ;
New York : Cambridge University Press, 1988.
284 p. ; 24 cm. (Comparative ethnic and race
relations) Includes index. Bibliography: p. [262]-278.
ISBN 0-521-36019-6 DDC 305.8/96041 19
*1. Blacks - Great Britain - Politics and government. 2.
Youth, Black - Great Britain - Social conditions. 3.
Youth, Black - Great Britain - Economic conditions. 4.
Racism - Great Britain. 5. Great Britain - Race
relations. I. Series: Comparative ethnic and race
relations series. II. Title.*
DA125.N4 S65 1988 *NYPL [Sc E 88-606]*

Somali Democratic Republic. see **Somalia.**

SOMALI-ETHIOPIAN CONFLICT, 1979-
Sauldie, Madan M. Super powers in the Horn
of Africa /. New York , c1987. ix, 252 p. ;
ISBN 0-86590-092-2 DDC 320.960 19
DT367.8 .S28 1987 *NYPL [Sc D 89-488]*

**SOMALI LANGUAGE - CONVERSATION
AND PHRASE BOOKS - FRENCH.**
Dibeth, Véronique Carton. Manuel de
conversation somali-français suivi d'un guide
Dijibouti /. Paris , c1988. 80 p. : ISBN
2-7384-0090-6 *NYPL [Sc E 88-536]*

SOMALI LANGUAGE - GRAMMAR.
Dibeth, Véronique Carton. Manuel de
conversation somali-français suivi d'un guide
Dijibouti /. Paris , c1988. 80 p. : ISBN
2-7384-0090-6 *NYPL [Sc E 88-536]*

**SOMALI LANGUAGES - TEXT-BOOKS FOR
FOREIGN SPEAKERS - GERMAN.**
El-Solami-Mewis, Catherine. Lehrbuch des
Somali /. Leipzig , c1987. 253 p. ; ISBN
3-324-00175-7 *NYPL [Sc D 88-896]*

Somali Republic. see **Somalia.**

Somalia. Constitution. The Constitution [as
amended up to 31 December 1963] Mogadiscio,
Stamperia di Stato [1964?] 48 p. 25 cm.
NYPL [JLE 76-3786]

**Somalia. Economic and Social Development,
Planning and Coordinating Committee for.**
see **Somalia. Planning and Coordinating
Committee for Economic and Social
Development.**

SOMALIA - ECONOMIC CONDITIONS.
Massey, Garth. Subsistence and change .
Boulder , 1987. xvii, 238 p. : ISBN
0-8133-7294-1 (alk. paper) : DDC
338.1/0967/73 19
DT402.4.R35 M37 1987
NYPL [Sc D 88-298]

SOMALIA - ECONOMIC POLICY.
Somalia. Planning and Coordinating Committee
for Economic and Social Development. First
five year plan, 1963-1967. Mogadiscio, 1963. xi,
162 p.
HC567.S7 A5 *NYPL [Sc E 88-70]*

SOMALIA - HISTORY.
Jaamac Cumar Ciise. Taariikhdii daraawiishta
iyo Sayid Maxamed Cabdulle Xasan, 1895-1921
/. Muqdisho , 1976. vii, 320 p., [2] leaves of
plates :
DT404.3.M38 C55 *NYPL [Sc E 87-435]*

Lewis, I. M. A modern history of Somalia .
Boulder , 1988. xiii, 297 p. : ISBN
0-8133-7402-2 : DDC 967/.73 19
DT403 .L395 1988 *NYPL [Sc D 88-1347]*

**Somalia. Planning and Coordinating Committee
for Economic and Social Development.** First
five year plan, 1963-1967. Mogadiscio, 1963. xi,
162 p. 24 cm.
*1. Somalia - Economic policy. 2. Somalia - Social
policy. I. Title.*
HC567.S7 A5 *NYPL [Sc E 88-70]*

**SOMALIA - POLITICS AND GOVERNMENT -
1960-**
Samatar, Ahmed I. (Ahmed Ismail) Socialist
Somalia . London , Atlantic Highlands, N.J. ,
1988. 186 p. ; ISBN 0-86232-588-9 DDC
967/.7305 19
DT407 .S26 1988 *NYPL [JLD 89-340]*

SOMALIA - SOCIAL POLICY.
Somalia. Planning and Coordinating Committee
for Economic and Social Development. First
five year plan, 1963-1967. Mogadiscio, 1963. xi,
162 p.
HC567.S7 A5 *NYPL [Sc E 88-70]*

Soman, David. (ill) Johnson, Angela. Tell me a
story, Mama /. New York , c1989. [32] p. :
ISBN 0-531-05794-1 : DDC [E] 19
PZ7.J629 Te 1988 *NYPL [Sc F 89-109]*

Somba, John Ndeti, 1930- Wananchi mashujaa
wa imani, Kangundo, Machakos / mwandishi
John Ndeti Somba. Kijabe, Kenya : Kesho
Publications, 1985. 68 p. : ill. ; 22 cm.
*1. Christian martyrs - Kenya - Machakos. 2. Swahili
language - Texts. I. Title.* *NYPL [Sc D 89-345]*

Some aspects of economic structures [microform] /. Elkhider, Mohmed Osman. Khartoum , 1978. 27 leaves ;   *NYPL [Sc Micro F-11038]*

Some boys /. Davidson, Michael. London , 1988, c1970. 201 p. ;   ISBN 0-85449-087-6 (pbk) :   DDC 070/.92/4 19
PN5123.D   *NYPL [Sc C 89-87]*

Some contributions of traditional healing practices towards psychosocial health care in Malawi /. Peltzer, Karl. Eschborn bei Frankfurt Om Main , 1987. 341 p. :   ISBN 3-88074-174-3
                                    NYPL [Sc D 88-618]

Some men /. Shange, Ntozake. [S.l.] c1981. [52] p. :   *NYPL [Sc Rare C 88-2]*

Some soul to keep /. Cooper, J. California. New York , c1987. xi, 211 p. ;   ISBN 0-312-00684-5 : DDC 813/.54 19
PS3553.O5874 S6 1987
                          NYPL [JFD 88-7431]

Somehow tenderness survives : stories of southern Africa / selected by Hazel Rochman.1st ed. New York : Harper & Row, c1988. 147 p. ; 22 cm. "A Charlotte Zolotow book." A collection of ten short stories about South Africa--five by black South Africans and five by white South Africans.   ISBN 0-06-025022-4 :   DDC [Fic] 19
1. Short stories, South African (English). 2. South Africa - Fiction. I. Rochman, Hazel.
PZ5 .S695 1988   *NYPL [Sc D 88-1461]*

Someone was here . Whitmore, George, 1945- New York, N.Y. , c1988. 211 p. ;   ISBN 0-453-00601-9 :   DDC 362.1/969792/00924 19
RC607.A26 W495 1988
                          NYPL [JLD 88-4435]

Somers Islands. see Bermuda Islands.

Somerset homecoming . Redford, Dorothy Spruill. New York , c1988. xviii, 266 p. :   ISBN 0-385-24245-X :   DDC 929/.3/089960730756 19
E185.96 .R42 1988   *NYPL [Sc E 88-498]*

SOMERSET PLACE (N.C.) - HISTORY.
Redford, Dorothy Spruill. Somerset homecoming . New York , c1988. xviii, 266 p. : ISBN 0-385-24245-X   DDC 929/.3/089960730756 19
E185.96 .R42 1988   *NYPL [Sc E 88-498]*

Somerville, Trixie. Family stories : a guide to group discussions on home and family life / Trixie Somerville. Jamaica : [S.n.], [1950-] 68 p. : ill. ; 22 cm.
1. Family life education - Jamaica. I. Title.
                          NYPL [Sc D 89-156]

Somo kaniponza /. Rajab, Hammie. Dar es Salaam , c1984. 69 p. ;   ISBN 997-693-103-4; 997-693-103-04
PL8704.R28 S66 1984   *NYPL [Sc C 88-57]*

Son, never give up /. Branchcomb, Sylvia Woingust. [Yonkers, N.Y.?] , 1979. 36 p. :
                          NYPL [Sc D 88-568]

Son of woman in Mombasa /. Mangua, Charles. Nairobi , 1986. 211 p. ;
                          NYPL [Sc C 88-303]

Sóngoro Cosongo, y otros poemas /. Guillén, Nicolás, 1902- La Habana , 1943. 123 p. ;
                          NYPL [Sc B 79-31]

Songs to a phantom nightingale /. Madgett, Naomi Cornelia Long, 1923- New York , 1941. 30 p., [1] p. of plates :   *NYPL [Sc C 89-136]*

Songue, Paulette, 1960- Prostitution en Afrique : l'exemple de Yaoundé / Paulette Songue. Paris : L'Harmattan, c1986. 154 p. ; 22 cm. (Points de vue concrets) Bibliography: p. 143-145.   ISBN 2-85802-684-X
1. Prostitution - Cameroon - Yaoundé. I. Series: Collection "Points de vue". II. Title.
                          NYPL [Sc D 88-1164]

SONINKE LANGUAGE - DICTIONARIES - FRENCH.
Bathily, Abdoulaye. Lexique soninke (sarakole)-français /. [Dakar] , 1975. xx, 191 p. ;   *NYPL [Sc F 86-166]*

Sonko-Godwin, Patience. Ethnic groups of the Senegambia : a brief history / by Patience Sonko-Godwin. Banjul, Gambia : Book Production and Material Resources Unit, 1985. viii, 38 p. : ill., maps ; 30 cm.   ISBN 998-386-001-X (pbk.)   DDC 306/.0966/3 19
1. Ethnology - Senegal. 2. Ethnology - Gambia. I. Title.
GN655.S3 S65 1985   *NYPL [Sc F 88-129]*

The sons of the gods and the daughters of men . Oduyoye, Modupe. Maryknoll, N.Y. , c1984. xi, 132 p. ;   ISBN 0-88344-467-4 (pbk.)   DDC 222/.1106 19
BS1235.2 .O38 1984   *NYPL [Sc D 88-1236]*

Sony Lab'Ou Tansi.
[Anté-peuple. English]
The antipeople : a novel / Sony Labou Tansi ; translated by J.A. Underwood. London ; New York : M. Boyars ; 170 p. ; 23 cm. Translation of: L'anté-peuple.   ISBN 0-7145-2845-5 :   DDC 843 19
1. Zaire - Fiction. I. Title.
PQ3989.2.S64 A813 1987
                          NYPL [Sc D 88-835]

Conscience de tracteur / Sony Lab'Ou Tansi. [Dakar] : Nouvelles Editions africaines ; [Yaoundé] : CLE, [1979] 115 p. ; 18 cm. (Répertoire théâtral africain. 26)   ISBN 2-7236-0439-X
I. Title.
MLCS 86/640 (P)   *NYPL [Sc C 88-369]*

Les yeux du volcan : roman / Sony Labou Tansi. Paris : Éditions du Seuil, c1988. 191 p. ; 21 cm.   ISBN 2-02-010082-7
1. Brazzaville (Congo) - Fiction. I. Title.
                          NYPL [Sc D 89-237]

Sookhee, L. (Lalita) Mauritian delights : over 200 tested recipes depicting a varied Muritian cuisine / L. Sookhee. Rose-Hill, Mauritius : L. Sookhee, 1985. 159 p. : ill. ; 21 cm. Includes index.   DDC 641.5969/82 19
1. Cookery, Mauritian. I. Title.
TX725.M34 S66 1985   *NYPL [Sc D 88-181]*

Sophocles.
Oedipus Rex. Leloup, Jacqueline. Guéido / Jacqueline Leloup. Yaoundé , 1986. 110 p. :
MLCS 87/6780 (P)   *NYPL [Sc C 88-210]*

SORCERY. see MAGIC; WITCHCRAFT.

Sorie, Jim M. Hinzen, Heribert. Koranko riddles, songs and stories /. Freetown , 1987. 69 p. :
                          NYPL [Sc D 89-416]

S.O.S. RACISME (ORGANIZATION : FRANCE)
Désir, Harlem, 1959- Touche pas à mon pote /. Paris [c1985] 148 p. ;   ISBN 2-246-36421-3 : DDC 323.42/3/06044 19
DC34 .D47 1985   *NYPL [Sc C 88-305]*

Sosa, Enrique. Los ñáñigos : ensayo / Enrique Sosa Rodríguez. Ciudad de La Habana, Cuba : Casa de Las Américas, c1982. 464 p., [44] p. of plates : ill. ; 19 cm. Bibliography: p. 453-464. DDC 366/.097291 19
1. Secret societies - Cuba. I. Title.
HS221.Z6 S66 1982   *NYPL [JLC 84-260]*

Sosoo, Leonard. L'enseignement en Côte d'Ivoire / par Leonard Sosoo. [Abidjan? : s.n., 1980-1987] 2 v. : ill. ; 24 cm. Bibliography: v. 1, p. 82; v. 2, p. 304. CONTENTS.-- [t. 1.] Depuis les origines jusqu'en 1954.--t. 2. De 1954 à 1984.
1. Education - Ivory Coast - History. I. Title.
                          NYPL [Sc E 88-128]

Sotheby, Madeline. The Bob Marley story / Madeline Sotheby. London : Hutchinson Education, 1985. 64 p. ; 19 cm. (Ace)   ISBN 0-09-160031-6 (pbk) :   DDC 428.6/2 19
1. Marley, Bob - Juvenile literature. 2. Reggae musicians - Jamaica - Biography - Juvenile literature. I. Title. II. Series.
PE1121   *NYPL [Sc C 88-141]*

Sotheby's. African heritage . Cape Town , 1987. 24 p. :   *NYPL [Sc F 89-117]*

SOTHO LANGUAGE - DICTIONARIES - ENGLISH.
Mabille, A. (Adolphe), 1836-1894. Southern Sotho-English dictionary /. Morija, Lesotho , 1950 (1974 printing) xvi, 445 p. ;
PL8689.4 .M33 1974   *NYPL [Sc D 89-289]*

SOTHO LANGUAGE - TEXTS.
Chaphole, Sol. Dihaeya /. [Cape Town] , c1986. xiii, 68 p. ;   ISBN 0-7992-1048-X
                          NYPL [Sc D 88-1123]

SOTHO LITERATURE - HISTORY AND CRITICISM.
Chaphole, Sol. Dihaeya /. [Cape Town] , c1986. xiii, 68 p. ;   ISBN 0-7992-1048-X
                          NYPL [Sc D 88-1123]

Soto, Sara. Magia e historia en los "Cuentos negros," "Por qué" y "Ayapá" de Lydia Cabrera / Sara Soto. Miami, Fla., U.S.A. : Ediciones

Universal, 1988. 162 p. ; 21 cm. (Colección Ébano y canela) Bibliography: p. 155-162.   ISBN 0-89729-444-0   DDC 863 20
1. Cabrera, Lydia - Criticism and interpretation. 2. Magic in literature. I. Title.
PQ7389.C22 Z87 1988   *NYPL [Sc D 89-601]*

Soudan . Messaoud, Jir, 1938- Paris , c1987. 160 p., [12] p. of plates :   ISBN 2-7087-0491-5
                          NYPL [Sc D 88-1008]

Soudan. see Sudan.

Soukar, Michel.
L'île de braise et de pluie : théâtre / Michel Soukar. [Port-au-Prince?] : M. Soukar, 1984. 30 leaves ; 25 cm. Cover title.
I. Title.   *NYPL [Sc E 88-161]*

Seize ans de lutte pour un pays normal / Michel Soukar. 1ère éd. Port-au-Prince, Haïti : Impressions Magiques,c1987. v, 60 p. ; 21 cm.
1. Haiti - Politics and government - 1971-. I. Title.
                          NYPL [Sc D 88-511]

Soul clap hands and sing /. Marshall, Paule, 1929- Washington, D.C. , 1988, 1961. xlviii, 105 p. ;   ISBN 0-88258-155-4
                          NYPL [Sc D 88-1451]

SOUL MUSIC - HISTORY AND CRITICISM.
George, Nelson. Where did our love go? . New York , c1985. xviii, 250 p., [32] p. of plates : ISBN 0-312-86698-4 :   DDC 784.5/5/00973 19
ML3537 .G46 1985   *NYPL [*LE 86-1451]*

The sound of pestles and other stories /. Yeboah-Afari, Ajoa. Accra , 1986. 72 p. ;   ISBN 996-470-046-6   *NYPL [Sc C 88-352]*

Sounds & echoes /. Bakari, Ishaq Imruh. London , 1980. 45 p. ;   ISBN 0-907015-01-8
                          NYPL [Sc D 88-492]

Sounds and echoes. Bakari, Ishaq Imruh. Sounds & echoes /. London , 1980. 45 p. ; ISBN 0-907015-01-8   *NYPL [Sc D 88-492]*

La source interdite /. Ugochukwu, Françoise, 1949- Abidjan , Paris , c1984. 63 p. :
                          NYPL [Sc B 88-33]

La source [microform] : conte de Noel /. Colimon, Marie-Thérèse. [Port-au-Prince? , 1973?] (Port-au-Prine : Atelier Fardin) 17 p. :
                          NYPL [Sc Micro F-10983]

The source of African philosophy . Sumner, Claude. Stuttgart , 1986. 153 p. :   ISBN 3-515-04438-8   DDC 199/.63 19
B5409.M27 S86 1986   *NYPL [Sc E 89-260]*

Sous le masque de l'animal : essais sur le sacrifice en Afrique noire / textes réunis par Michel Carty. Paris : Presses Universitaires de France, c1987. 380 p. : ill., maps ; 24 cm. (Bibliothèque de l'Ecole des hautes études. Section des sciences religieuses . v. 88) Includes indexes. "Guide de recherche bibliographique". p. [319]-374.   ISBN 2-13-039831-6
1. Sacrifice - Africa, Sub-Saharan. I. Carty, Michel. II. Series.   *NYPL [Sc E 88-314]*

South Africa : no turning back / edited by Shaun Johnson ; foreword by Lord Bullock. Basingstoke, Hampshire : Macmillan ; in association with the David Davies Memorial Institute of International Studies, 1988. xxiii, 390 p. : maps ; 24 cm. Includes bibliographical references and index.   ISBN 0-333-47095-8 (hardcover)
1. Apartheid - South Africa. 2. South Africa - Politics and government - 1978-. I. Johnson, Shaun.
                          NYPL [Sc D 89-257]

South Africa : human rights and the rule of law / International Commission of Jurists ; edited by Geoffrey Bindman. London ; New York : Pinter, 1988. 159 p. : 2 forms ; 24 cm. Includes bibliographical references and index.   ISBN 0-86187-979-1 :   DDC 323.4/0968 19
1. Civil rights - South Africa. 2. Blacks - Legal status, laws, etc. - South Africa. I. Bindman, Geoffrey. II. International Commission of Jurists (1952-). III. Title.
                          NYPL [JLE 88-4543]

South Africa . Brickley, Carol. London , 1985. 50 p. :   ISBN 0-905400-06-2 :
                          NYPL [Sc D 89-361]

South Africa . Buthelezi, Gatsha. Lagos, Nigeria , c1986. xxxvii, 143 p. :   ISBN 978-242-308-4
                          NYPL [Sc C 88-269]

South Africa . Harsch, Ernest. New York , 1980.

352 p., [8] leaves of plates : ISBN 0-913460-78-8
DT763 .H29

South Africa . Louw, Leon. Bisho, Ciskei , 1986.
xvi, 238 p. : ISBN 0-620-09371-4 (pbk.) DDC
306/.0968 19
HN801.A8 L68 1986 *NYPL [Sc D 88-197]*

South Africa.
[Census of population (1936)]
Report on the sixth census of South Africa,
5th May, 1936, v. 7 : Occupations and
industries [microform] Pretoria : office of
Census and Statistics, 1941. lx, 119 p.
Afrikaans and English. With: Annual report/Chamber
of Mines of Rhodesia. Bulawaya, 1941--Annual
report/Dept. of Agriculture. Basutoland, 1941.
Microfilm. Washington: Library of Congress, [195-?].
1 reel; 35 mm.
*1. South Africa - Census, 6th, 1936. 2. South Africa -
Population. I. South Africa. Office of Census and
Statistics. II. Title.*
NYPL [Sc Micro R-4651 no.1]

[Laws, etc]
Native Land Act, 1913. Amendment Bill,
1927 [microform]. Representation of Natives
in Parliament Bill. Union Native Council Bill.
Coloured Persons Rights Bill, 1927. [S.l. :
Lovedale Institution Press, [1927?] 47 p. ; 18
cm. Cover title. Microfiche. New York: New York
Public Library, 198 . 1 microfiche: negative; 11 x 15
cm. (FSN Sc 019,069)
*1. Blacks - Legal status, laws, etc. - South Africa. I.
Title. II. Title: Representation of Natives in Parliament
Bill. III. Title: Union Native Council Bill. IV. Title:
Coloured Persons Rights Bill, 1927.*
NYPL [Sc Micro F-10937]

**South Africa and international relations between
the two World Wars .** Pienaar, Sara.
Johannesburg, 1987. 207 p. ; ISBN
0-85494-936-4 *NYPL [Sc D 88-1026]*

South Africa and nuclear proliferation . Moore, J.
D. L. (John Davey Lewis) New York , 1987.
xvii, 227 p. : ISBN 0-312-74698-9 : DDC
355.8/25119/0968 19
U264 .M66 1987 *NYPL [Sc D 88-765]*

South Africa and the Commonwealth [microform]
/. Nyerere, Julius Kambarage, Pres. Tanzania,
1922- [S.l. , 1971] 14 p. ;
NYPL [Sc Micro F-10922]

South Africa belongs to us . Meli, Francis, 1942-
Harare , 1988. xx, 258, [8] p. of plates :
NYPL [Sc D 89-308]

South Africa between reform and revolution /.
Callinicos, Alex. London , Chicago , 1988. 231
p. : ISBN 0-906224-46-2 *NYPL [JLD 89-489]*

SOUTH AFRICA - BIOGRAPHY.
Gastrow, Shelagh. Who's who in South African
politics /. Johannesburg , 1985. xiv, 347 p. :
ISBN 0-86975-280-4 (pbk.) DDC 968.06/092/2
B 19
DT779.954 .G37 1985
NYPL [Sc D 87-1109]

**South Africa. Bureau of Census and Statistics.
see South Africa. Office of Census and
Statistics.**

**South Africa. Census and Statistics, Office of. see
South Africa. Office of Census and Statistics.**

SOUTH AFRICA - CENSUS, 6TH, 1936.
South Africa. [Census of population (1936)]
Report on the sixth census of South Africa, 5th
May, 1936, v. 7 : Occupations and industries
[microform] Pretoria , 1941. lx, 119 p.
NYPL [Sc Micro R-4651 no.1]

SOUTH AFRICA - CHURCH HISTORY.
Oosthuizen, G. C. (Gerhardus Cornelis) The
birth of Christian Zionism in South Africa /.
KwaDlangezwa, South Africa , 1987. ii, 56 p. ;
ISBN 0-09-079580-2 DDC 289.9 19
BR1450 .O55 1987 *NYPL [Sc D 88-693]*

**SOUTH AFRICA - CHURCH HISTORY -
20TH CENTURY.**
Religion, intergroup relations, and social change
in South Africa /. New York , 1988. xii, 237
p. : ISBN 0-313-26360-4 (lib. bdg. : alk. paper)
DDC 306/.6/0968 19
DT763 .R393 1988 *NYPL [Sc D 89-305]*

**SOUTH AFRICA - CHURCH HISTORY -
SOURCES.**
Records from Natal, Lesotho, the Orange Free
State, and Mozambique concerning the history
of the Catholic Church in southern Africa /.

Roma, Lesotho [1974] 2 v. : DDC 282/.68 19
BV3625S67 R43 1974 *NYPL [Sc E 89-47]*

SOUTH AFRICA - CONSTITUTIONAL LAW.
El Mahmud-Okereke, N. O. E. (Noel Olufemi
Enuma), 1948- Beyond the Botha/Buthelezi
political debate . London , c1987. v, 177 p. :
ISBN 978-242-309-2 (pbk) : DDC 346.802/3 19
NYPL [Sc C 88-180]

South Africa. Consulate (New York) Prospects
and progress in South Afirca. New York :
Director of Information, South African
Consulate General, [1973?] 153 p. : ill. ; 20 cm.
Cover title. Bibliography: p. 151-153.
*1. South Africa - Economic conditions - 1966-. 2. South
Africa - Economic policy. I. Title.*
NYPL [JLD 79-3283]

**SOUTH AFRICA - DESCRIPTION AND
TRAVEL.**
Juta, Jan. Look out for the ostriches! New
York, 1949. xii, 177 p.
DT757 .J8 *NYPL [Sc D 89-90]*

**SOUTH AFRICA - DESCRIPTION AND
TRAVEL - TO 1800.**
Paterson, William, 1755-1810. Paterson's Cape
travels, 1777 to 1779 /. Johannesburg, [South
Africa] , c1980. 202 p. : ISBN 0-909079-12-9
(standard edition) *NYPL [Sc F 85-110]*

**SOUTH AFRICA - DESCRIPTION AND
TRAVEL - 1801-1900.**
Livingstone, David, 1813-1873. [Missionary
travels and researches in South Africa. Danish.]
Livingstones Reise : Syd-Afrika /.
Kjøbenhavn , 1858-1859. 2 v. :
NYPL [Sc E 88-47]

**SOUTH AFRICA - DESCRIPTION AND
TRAVEL - 1966-- GUIDE-BOOKS.**
Fries, Marianne. Südafrika, SWA/Namibia .
Frankfurt [am Main] , 1987. 550 p. : ISBN
3-87936-153-3 *NYPL [Sc B 88-18]*

**SOUTH AFRICA - ECONOMIC
CONDITIONS.**
Louw, Leon. South Africa . Bisho, Ciskei ,
1986. xvi, 238 p. : ISBN 0-620-09371-4 (pbk.)
DDC 306/.0968 19
HN801.A8 L68 1986 *NYPL [Sc D 88-197]*

**SOUTH AFRICA - ECONOMIC
CONDITIONS - TO 1918.**
Keegan, Timothy J. Rural transformations in
industrializing South Africa . Basingstoke ;
London , 1987. xviii, 302 p. : ISBN
0-333-41746-1 *NYPL [Sc D 88-1228]*

**SOUTH AFRICA - ECONOMIC
CONDITIONS - 1961-**
Davies, Robert H. The struggle for South
Africa . London , Atlantic Highlands, N.J. ,
1988. 2 v. : ISBN 0-86232-760-1 (v. 1) DDC
322/.0968 19
JQ1931 .D38 1988 *NYPL [Sc D 88-1369]*

Lemon, Anthony. Apartheid in transition /.
Aldershot, Hants , Brookfield, Vt. , c1987. xi,
414 p. : ISBN 0-566-00635-9
NYPL [Sc D 88-644]

McCartan, P. J. (Patrick John) The demand for
skilled labour in the Border, Ciskei, southern
Transkei regional economy /. Grahamstown
[1983] 50, xxii p. : ISBN 0-86810-058-7 (pbk.) :
DDC 331.12/3/0968792 19
HD5842.A6 M33 1983 *NYPL [Sc F 88-356]*

South Africa in southern Africa . Pretoria ,
1988. viii, 266 p. : ISBN 0-7983-0102-3
NYPL [Sc F 89-50]

Turner, Richard, 1941- The eye of the needle .
Maryknoll, N.Y. , 1978, c1972. xxiv, 173 p. ;
ISBN 0-88344-121-7. DDC 309.1/68/06
DT763 .T85 1978 *NYPL [JLD 84-744]*

**SOUTH AFRICA - ECONOMIC
CONDITIONS - 1966-**
South Africa. Consulate (New York) Prospects
and progress in South Afirca. New York
[1973?] 153 p. : *NYPL [JLD 79-3283]*

SOUTH AFRICA - ECONOMIC POLICY.
Regional restructuring under apartheid .
Johannesburg , 1987. xxii, 317 p. ; ISBN
0-86975-327-4 *NYPL [Sc D 89-16]*

South Africa. Consulate (New York) Prospects
and progress in South Afirca. New York
[1973?] 153 p. : *NYPL [JLD 79-3283]*

SOUTH AFRICA - ETHNIC RELATIONS.
The South African society . New York , c1987.

xv, 217 p. : ISBN 0-313-25724-8 (lib. bdg. : alk.
paper) DDC 306/.0968 19
HN801.A8 S68 1987 *NYPL [JLD 87-2390]*

SOUTH AFRICA - FICTION.
De Vries, Abraham H. Bliksoldate bloei nie /.
Kaapstad , 1975. 80 p. ; ISBN 0-7981-0640-9
PT6592.14.E9 B56 *NYPL [Sc D 88-673]*

Galgut, Damon, 1963- Small circle of beings /.
London , 1988. 221 p. ;
NYPL [Sc D 88-1342]

Havemann, Ernst. Bloodsong and other stories
of South Africa /. Boston , 1987. 134 p. ;
ISBN 0-395-43296-0 : DDC 813/.54 19
PR9199.3.H3642 B56 1987
NYPL [Sc D 88-209]

Karodia, Farida. Coming home and other
stories /. London , 1988. v, 185 p. ; ISBN
0-435-90738-7 (pbk)
PR9369.3.K3 *NYPL [Sc C 89-88]*

Langa, Mandla, 1950- Tenderness of blood /.
Harare , 1987. 427 p. ; ISBN 0-949225-30-4
NYPL [Sc C 89-102]

Somehow tenderness survives . New York ,
c1988. 147 p. ; ISBN 0-06-025022-4 : DDC [Fic]
19
PZ5 .S695 1988 *NYPL [Sc D 88-1461]*

Stone, David. Too deep then /. London , 1987.
vi, 114 p. ; ISBN 0-7453-0136-3 (cased) : DDC
823 19
PR9369.3.S *NYPL [Sc D 88-961]*

**SOUTH AFRICA - FOREIGN ECONOMIC
RELATIONS - UNITED STATES.**
United States. Congress. House. Committee on
International Relations. Subcommittee on
Africa. United States private investment in
South Africa . Washington , 1978. iv, 641 p. ;
DDC 332.6/7373/068
KF27 .I54914 1978d *NYPL [Sc E 88-92]*

**SOUTH AFRICA - FOREIGN OPINION,
AMERICAN.**
Parker, Aida. Secret U. S. war against South
Africa /. Johannesburg , c1977. 79 p. ;
NYPL [Sc D 88-277]

SOUTH AFRICA - FOREIGN RELATIONS.
Mahmud-Okereke, N. Enuma, 1948-
OAU--time to admit South Africa /. Lagos,
Nigeria , 1986. xxvi, 57, 190 p. : ISBN
978-242-302-5 *NYPL [Sc C 88-204]*

Pienaar, Sara. South Africa and international
relations between the two World Wars .
Johannesburg , 1987. 207 p. ; ISBN
0-85494-936-4 *NYPL [Sc D 88-1026]*

**SOUTH AFRICA - FOREIGN RELATIONS -
AFRICA, SOUTHERN.**
Poverty, policy, and food security in southern
Africa /. Boulder , 1988. xii, 291 p. : ISBN
1-555-87092-9 (lib. bdg.) : DDC 363.8/56/0968
19
HD9017.A26 P68 1988 *NYPL [Sc E 88-355]*

**SOUTH AFRICA - FOREIGN RELATIONS -
MOZAMBIQUE.**
Davies, Robert. South African strategy towards
Mozambique in the post-Nkomati period .
Uppsala , 1985. 71 p. ; ISBN 91-7106-238-6
(pbk.) DDC 327.68067/9 19
DT771.M85 D38 1985 *NYPL [Sc E 88-121]*

Magaia, Lina. [Dumba nengue. English.] Dumba
nengue, run for your life . Trenton, N.J. , 1988.
113 p. : ISBN 0-86543-073-X
NYPL [Sc D 88-1509]

**SOUTH AFRICA - FOREIGN RELATIONS -
UNITED STATES.**
Pomeroy, William J., 1916- Apartheid,
imperialism, and African freedom /. New
York , 1986. ix, 259 p. : ISBN 0-7178-0640-5 :
DDC 305.8/00968 19
E183.8.S6 P65 1986 *NYPL [Sc D 88-1147]*

Schümer, Martin. Die amerikanische Politik
gegenüber dem südlichen Afrika /. Bonn
[1986]. v, 183 p. ; ISBN 3-7713-0275-7
NYPL [Sc D 88-983]

United States. Congress. House. Committee on
Foreign Affairs. Subcommittee on International
Economic Policy and Trade. Controls on
exports to South Africa . Washington , 1983. iv,
321 p. ; DDC 382/.64/0973 19
KF27 .F6465 1982e *NYPL [Sc E 88-113]*

United States. Dept. of State. Advisory

Committee on South Africa. A U. S. policy toward South Africa . [Washington, D.C.] [1987] vi, 49 p. :
                    NYPL [Sc F 88-300]

SOUTH AFRICA - FOREIGN RELATIONS - UNITED STATES - CONGRESSES.
South Africa--the vital link /. Washington , c1976. 120 p. ;
                    NYPL [Sc F 89-129]

SOUTH AFRICA - FOREIGN RELATIONS - ZIMBABWE.
Ushewokunze, H. S. M. (Herbert Sylvester Masiyiwa), 1938- An agenda for Zimbabwe /. [Harare, Zimbabwe] c1984. vi, 198 p. ; ISBN 0-906041-67-8 DDC 361.6/1/096891 19
HX451.A6 U84 1984   *NYPL [Sc D 88-942]*

South Africa - Government. see South Africa - Politics and government.

SOUTH AFRICA - HISTORY.
Cukierman, Maurice. Afrique du Sud . Paris , c1987. 279 p. : ISBN 2-209-05983-6
                    NYPL [Sc D 88-756]

González, Carmen, 1940- Sobre los hombros ajenos /. La Habana , 1985. 119 p. ; DDC 968 19
DT766 .G66 1985   *NYPL [Sc D 88-416]*

Neffe, Dieter. Kämpfe im Süden Afrikas . Berlin , 1987. 64 p. : ISBN 3-327-00283-5
                    NYPL [Sc D 88-680]

A People's history of South Africa. Johannesburg , c1980- v. : ISBN 0-86975-119-0 (pbk. v. 1) DDC 968 19
DT766 .P43   *NYPL [JLM 85-439]*

Tsotsi, W. M. From chattel to wage slavery . Maseru , 1981. 136 p., [2] folded leaves of plates : DDC 306/.0968 19
DT763.6 .T76 1981   *NYPL [Sc D 89-22]*

SOUTH AFRICA - HISTORY - TO 1836 - FICTION.
Brink, André Philippus, 1935- An instant in the wind /. New York, N.Y., U. S. A. , 1985, c1976. 250 p. : ISBN 0-14-008014-7 (pbk.) : DDC 823 19
PR9369.3.B7 I5 1985   *NYPL [Sc C 88-281]*

SOUTH AFRICA - HISTORY - 1961-
Bernstein, Keith. Frontline Southern Africa /. London , c1988. x, 117 p. : ISBN 0-7470-3012-X (pbk) : DDC 968.06/3 19
HN800.A8   *NYPL [Sc E 89-122]*

Murray, Martin J. South Africa, time of agony, time of destiny . London , 1987. xii, 496 p.: ISBN 0-86091-146-2 *NYPL [JFD 87-8776]*

SOUTH AFRICA - HISTORY - DICTIONARIES.
Saunders, Christopher C. Historical dictionary of South Africa /. Metuchen, N.J. , 1983. xxviii, 241 p. : ISBN 0-8108-1629-6 DDC 968/.003/21 19
DT766 .S23 1983   *NYPL [*R-BN 89-3347]*

SOUTH AFRICA - HISTORY, MILITARY.
Neffe, Dieter. Kämpfe im Süden Afrikas . Berlin , 1987. 64 p. : ISBN 3-327-00283-5
                    NYPL [Sc D 88-680]

SOUTH AFRICA - HISTORY - SOURCES - BIBLIOGRAPHY - CATALOGS.
University of the Witwatersrand. Library. Guide to the archives and papers . Johannesburg , 1979. v, 100 p. : ISBN 0-85494-593-8
                    NYPL [Sc F 89-32]

SOUTH AFRICA - HISTORY - STUDY AND TEACHING.
Dean, Elizabeth. [History in black and white. Spanish.] Historia en blanco y negro . Barcelona , Paris , 1984. 196 p. ; ISBN 92-3-302092-4 (Unesco)
                    NYPL [Sc D 88-594]

SOUTH AFRICA - IMPRINTS.
Peters, Marguerite Andree. Bibliography of the Tswana language . Pretoria , 1982. 1 [i.e. L], 175 p., [3] leaves of plates : ISBN 0-7989-0116-0 DDC 015.68 19
Z3601 .P47 1982   *NYPL [Sc E 87-667]*

South Africa in black and white /. Kuus, Juhan. London , c1987. [190] p. : ISBN 0-245-54543-3 (pbk.)   *NYPL [MFX (Kuus) 89-1313]*

South Africa in question / edited by John Lonsdale. Cambridge, Cambridgeshire : African Studies Centre, University of Cambridge, in association with J. Currey ; Portsmouth, NH : Heinemann, c1988. x, 244 p. : maps ; 24 cm.

Includes bibliographies and index. ISBN 0-85255-325-0 DDC 305.8/00968 19
1. Apartheid - South Africa. 2. South Africa - Politics and government - 1978-. I. Lonsdale, John.
DT763 .S6428 1988   *NYPL [Sc D 88-841]*

South Africa in southern Africa : economic interaction / editors, Erich Leistner and Pieter Esterhuysen. Pretoria : Africa Institute of South Africa, 1988. viii, 266 p. : maps (some col.) ; 30 cm. (Research communications series . no. 51) Bibliography: p. 266. ISBN 0-7983-0102-3
1. South Africa - Economic conditions - 1961-. 2. Africa, Southern - Economic conditions - 1975-.
                    NYPL [Sc F 89-50]

South Africa, in transition to what? / Helen Kitchen, editor. New York : Praeger ; Washington, D.C. : Published with the Center for Strategic and International Studies, 1988. xii, 201 p. ; 24 cm. (The Washington papers, 0278-937X . 132) Includes index. ISBN 0-275-92975-2 (alk. paper) DDC 968.06/3 19
1. South Africa - Politics and government - 1978-. I. Kitchen, Helen A. II. Series.
DT779.952 .S654 1988   NYPL [Sc E 88-510]

SOUTH AFRICA - INDUSTRIES - LOCATION.
Regional restructuring under apartheid . Johannesburg , 1987. xxii, 317 p. ; ISBN 0-86975-327-4   *NYPL [Sc D 89-16]*

SOUTH AFRICA - MILITARY POLICY.
Brittain, Victoria. Hidden lives, hidden deaths . London , Boston , 1988. xvii, 189 p. : ISBN 0-571-13907-8 : DDC 355/.0335/68 19
UA856   *NYPL [JLD 88-4608]*

Moore, J. D. L. (John Davey Lewis) South Africa and nuclear proliferation . New York , 1987. xvii, 227 p. : ISBN 0-312-74698-9 : DDC 355.8/25119//0968 19
U264 .M66 1987   *NYPL [Sc D 88-765]*

SOUTH AFRICA - MILITARY RELATIONS - AFRICA, SOUTHERN.
Frontline Southern Africa . New York , 1988. xxxv, 530 p., [16] p. of leaves : ISBN 0-941423-08-5 : DDC 322.5/0968 19
DT747.S6 F76 1988   *NYPL [JLE 89-595]*

SOUTH AFRICA - OCCUPATIONS.
Hindson, D. Pass controls and the urban African proletariat in South Africa /. Johannesburg, South Africa , 1987. xii, 121 p. ; ISBN 0-86975-311-8   *NYPL [Sc D 88-956]*

South Africa. Office of Census and Statistics.
South Africa. [Census of population (1936)] Report on the sixth census of South Africa, 5th May, 1936, v. 7 : Occupations and industries [microform] Pretoria , 1941. lx, 119 p.
                    NYPL [Sc Micro R-4651 no.1]

SOUTH AFRICA - POETRY.
Serote, Mongane, 1944- A tough tale /. London , 1987. 48 p. : ISBN 0-904759-80-6 (pbk) : DDC 821 19
                    NYPL [Sc D 88-513]

SOUTH AFRICA - POLITICS AND GOVERNMENT - 20TH CENTURY.
Benson, Mary. A far cry /. London,England , 1989. 254 p., [4] leaves of plates : ISBN 0-670-82138-1   *NYPL [Sc E 89-228]*

Davies, Robert H. The struggle for South Africa . London , Atlantic Highlands, N.J. , 1988. 2 v. : ISBN 0-86232-760-1 (v. 1) DDC 322/.0968 19
JQ1931 .D38 1988   *NYPL [Sc D 88-1369]*

Meli, Francis, 1942- South Africa belongs to us . Harare , 1988. xx, 258, [8] p. of plates :
                    NYPL [Sc D 89-308]

Resistance and ideology in settler societies /. Johannesburg, Athens, Ohio , 1986. viii, 222 p. ; ISBN 0-86975-304-5
                    NYPL [Sc D 88-1093]

SOUTH AFRICA - POLITICS AND GOVERNMENT - 1961-
Boon, Rudolf. Over vijf jaar in Johannesburg-- . Amsterdam , 's-Gravenhage [Netherlands] , 1986. 223 p. ; ISBN 90-70509-53-9
                    NYPL [Sc D 89-167]

SOUTH AFRICA - POLITICS AND GOVERNMENT - 1961- - CONGRESSES.
South Africa--the vital link /. Washington , c1976. 120 p. ;
                    NYPL [Sc F 89-129]

SOUTH AFRICA - POLITICS AND GOVERNMENT - 1961-1978.
Parker, Aida. Secret U. S. war against South Africa /. Johannesburg , c1977. 79 p. ;
                    NYPL [Sc D 88-277]

Time for Azania [microform] [Toronto] , 1976. 89 p. : 17 cm.
DT770 .T55   NYPL [Sc Micro R-4849 no.1]

Turner, Richard, 1941- The eye of the needle . Maryknoll, N.Y. , 1978, c1972. xxiv, 173 p. ; ISBN 0-88344-121-7. DDC 309.1/68/06
DT763 .T85 1978   *NYPL [JLD 84-744]*

SOUTH AFRICA - POLITICS AND GOVERNMENT - 1978-
Buthelezi, Gatsha. South Africa . Lagos, Nigeria , c1986. xxxvii, 143 p. : ISBN 978-242-308-4   *NYPL [Sc C 88-269]*

Callinicos, Alex. South Africa between reform and revolution /. London , Chicago , 1988. 231 p. : ISBN 0-906224-46-2 *NYPL [JLD 89-489]*

Commonwealth Group of Eminent Persons. Mission to South Africa . Harmondsworth, Middlesex, Eng. , New York , 1986. 176 p. : ISBN 0-14-052384-7 : *NYPL [Sc C 88-116]*

El Mahmud-Okereke, N. O. E. (Noel Olufemi Enuma), 1948- Beyond the Botha/Buthelezi political debate . London , c1987. v, 177 p. : ISBN 978-242-309-2 (pbk) DDC 346.802/3 19
                    NYPL [Sc C 88-180]

Gastrow, Shelagh. Who's who in South African politics /. Johannesburg , 1985. xiv, 347 p. : ISBN 0-86975-280-4 (pbk.) DDC 968.06/092/2 B 19
DT779.954 .G37 1985
                    NYPL [Sc D 87-1109]

Mahmud-Okereke, N. Enuma, 1948- OAU--time to admit South Africa /. Lagos, Nigeria , 1986. xxvi, 57, 190 p. : ISBN 978-242-302-5   *NYPL [Sc C 88-204]*

Murray, Martin J. South Africa, time of agony, time of destiny . London , 1987. xii, 496 p.: ISBN 0-86091-146-2 *NYPL [JFD 87-8776]*

Phelan, John M. Apartheid media . Westport, Conn. , c1987. xi, 220 p. ; ISBN 0-88208-244-2 : DDC 323.44/5 19
PN4748.S58 P4 1987   *NYPL [JLD 87-4698]*

South Africa . Basingstoke, Hampshire , 1988. xxiii, 390 p. : ISBN 0-333-47095-8 (hardcover)
                    NYPL [Sc D 89-257]

South Africa in question /. Cambridge, Cambridgeshire , Portsmouth, NH , c1988. x, 244 p. : ISBN 0-85255-325-0 DDC 305.8/00968 19
DT763 .S6428 1988   *NYPL [Sc D 88-841]*

South Africa, in transition to what? /. New York , Washington, D.C. , 1988. xii, 201 p. ; ISBN 0-275-92975-2 (alk. paper) DDC 968.06/3 19
DT779.952 .S654 1988 NYPL [Sc E 88-510]

SOUTH AFRICA - POPULATION.
South Africa. [Census of population (1936)] Report on the sixth census of South Africa, 5th May, 1936, v. 7 : Occupations and industries [microform] Pretoria , 1941. lx, 119 p.
                    NYPL [Sc Micro R-4651 no.1]

SOUTH AFRICA - RACE RELATIONS - DRAMA.
Richard Attenborough's cry freedom . New York , 1987. [128] p. : ISBN 0-394-75838-2 DDC 791.43/72 19
PN1997.C885 A88 1987 NYPL [Sc G 89-17]

SOUTH AFRICA. - RACE RELATIONS - PICTORIAL WORKS.
Kuus, Juhan. South Africa in black and white /. London , c1987. [190] p. : ISBN 0-245-54543-3 (pbk.)   *NYPL [MFX (Kuus) 89-1313]*

SOUTH AFRICA - RACE RELATIONS - RELIGIOUS ASPECTS - CHRISTIANITY.
Religion, intergroup relations, and social change in South Africa /. New York , 1988. xii, 237 p. : ISBN 0-313-26360-4 (lib. bdg. : alk. paper) DDC 306/.6/0968 19
DT763 .R393 1988   *NYPL [Sc D 89-305]*

SOUTH AFRICA - RACE RELATIONS - STUDY AND TEACHING.
Dean, Elizabeth. [History in black and white. Spanish.] Historia en blanco y negro . Barcelona , Paris , 1984. 196 p. ; ISBN

92-3-302092-4 (Unesco)
NYPL [Sc D 88-594]

SOUTH AFRICA - RELATIONS - FOREIGN COUNTRIES.
Special report of the Director-General on the application of the declaration concerning the policy of apartheid in South Africa. Geneva , 1986. 186 p. : ISBN 92-2-105167-6 (pbk.) :
NYPL [Sc E 88-179]

SOUTH AFRICA - RELATIONS (GENERAL) WITH GREAT BRITAIN.
Nyerere, Julius Kambarage, Pres. Tanzania, 1922- South Africa and the Commonwealth [microform] /. [S.l. , 1971] 14 p. ;
NYPL [Sc Micro F-10922]

SOUTH AFRICA - RELATIONS - SWAZILAND.
Crush, Jonathan Scott, 1953- The struggle for Swazi labour, 1890-1920 /. Kingston, Ont. , 1987. xviii, 292 p., [9] p. of plates : ISBN 0-7735-0569-5   *NYPL [Sc E 89-150]*

South Africa (Republic) see South Africa.

SOUTH AFRICA - RURAL CONDITIONS.
Bundy, Colin. The rise and fall of the South African peasantry /. Cape Town , 1988. [21], 276 p. ; ISBN 0-520-03754-5
NYPL [Sc D 89-533]

SOUTH AFRICA - RURAL CONDITIONS - CASE STUDIES.
Keegan, Timothy J. Facing the storm . London , Athens , 1988. vi, 169 p. : ISBN 0-8214-0924-7 DDC 305.8/96068 19
HN801.A8 K44 1989   *NYPL [Sc D 89-233]*

SOUTH AFRICA - SOCIAL CONDITIONS.
Louw, Leon. South Africa . Bisho, Ciskei , 1986. xvi, 238 p. : ISBN 0-620-09371-4 (pbk.) DDC 306/.0968 19
HN801.A8 L68 1986   *NYPL [Sc D 88-197]*

SOUTH AFRICA - SOCIAL CONDITIONS - 1961-
Boon, Rudolf. Over vijf jaar in Johannesburg-- . Amsterdam , 's-Gravenhage [Netherlands] , 1986. 223 p. ; ISBN 90-70509-53-9
NYPL [Sc D 89-167]

Dreyer, Lynette, 1949- The modern African elite of South Africa /. Houndmills, Basingstoke, Hampshire , 1989. xii, 186 p. ; ISBN 0-333-46410-9   *NYPL [Sc D 89-306]*

Lemon, Anthony. Apartheid in transition /. Aldershot, Hants , Brookfield, Vt. , c1987. xi, 414 p. : ISBN 0-566-00635-9
NYPL [Sc D 88-644]

The South African society . New York , c1987. xv, 217 p. : ISBN 0-313-25724-8 (lib. bdg. : alk. paper) DDC 306/.0968 19
HN801.A8 S68 1987   *NYPL [JLD 87-2390]*

SOUTH AFRICA - SOCIAL CONDITIONS - PICTORIAL WORKS.
Kuus, Juhan. South Africa in black and white /. London , c1987. [190] p. : ISBN 0-245-54543-3 (pbk.)   *NYPL [MFX (Kuus) 89-1313]*

SOUTH AFRICA - SOCIAL POLICY.
Regional restructuring under apartheid . Johannesburg , 1987. xxii, 317 p. ; ISBN 0-86975-327-4   *NYPL [Sc D 89-16]*

South Africa. State Library. Peters, Marguerite Andree. Bibliography of the Tswana language . Pretoria , 1982. 1 [i.e. L], 175 p., [3] leaves of plates : ISBN 0-7989-0116-0 DDC 015.68 19
Z3601 .P47 1982   *NYPL [Sc E 87-667]*

South Africa. Statistics and Census, Office of. see South Africa. Office of Census and Statistics.

South Africa--the vital link / edited by Robert L. Schuettinger. Washington : Council on American Affairs, c1976. 120 p. ; 26 cm. Papers presented at a seminar on United States - South African relations in Washington, D.C. on July 20, 1976. Includes bibliographical references.
1. South Africa - Politics and government - 1961- - Congresses. 2. South Africa - Foreign relations - United States - Congresses. 3. United States - Foreign relations - South Africa - Congresses. I. Schuettinger, Robert Lindsay, 1936-. II. Council on American Affairs.
NYPL [Sc F 89-129]

South Africa, time of agony, time of destiny . Murray, Martin J. London , 1987. xii, 496 p.: ISBN 0-86091-146-2 *NYPL [JFD 87-8776]*

South Africa. University.
Documenta.
(19) Kotzé, D. A. Bibliography of official publications of the Black South African homelands /. Pretoria , 1979. xix, 80 p. : ISBN 0-86981-137-1 DDC 015.68
Z3607.H65 K67 J705.T3;
NYPL [Sc D 88-1197]

South African Homelands, South Africa. see Homelands, South Africa.

South African Institute of Race Relations.
Gaydon, Vanessa. Race against the ratios . Johannesburg, South Africa , 1987. 70 p. ; ISBN 0-86982-321-3   *NYPL [Sc F 88-322]*

South African labour bulletin.
The Independent trade unions, 1974-1984 . Johannesburg , 1987. xvi, 355 p. ; ISBN 0-86975-307-X   *NYPL [Sc D 88-1329]*

SOUTH AFRICAN LABOUR BULLETIN - INDEXES.
The Independent trade unions, 1974-1984 . Johannesburg , 1987. xvi, 355 p. ; ISBN 0-86975-307-X   *NYPL [Sc D 88-1329]*

SOUTH AFRICAN PROGRESSIVE REFORM PARTY.
Eglin, Colin. Die beginsels en belied van die Suid-Afrikaanse Progressiewe Reformisteparty [microform] /. [Cape Town , 1975] 12, 12 p. ;
NYPL [Sc Micro R-4094 no. 4]

SOUTH AFRICAN SHORT STORIES (ENGLISH) see **SHORT STORIES, SOUTH AFRICAN (ENGLISH)**

The South African society : realities and future prospects / Human Sciences Research Council. New York : Greenwood Press, c1987. xv, 217 p. : ill. ; 22 cm. (Contributions in ethnic studies, 0196-7088 . no. 21) "Final report of the Main Committee of the HSRC Investigation into Intergroup Relations"--Pref. Includes index. Bibliography: p. 179-186. ISBN 0-313-25724-8 (lib. bdg. : alk. paper) DDC 306/.0968 19
1. South Africa - Social conditions - 1961-. 2. South Africa - Ethnic relations. I. HSRC Investigation into Intergroup Relations. Main Committee. II. Series.
HN801.A8 S68 1987   *NYPL [JLD 87-2390]*

South African strategy towards Mozambique in the post-Nkomati period . Davies, Robert. Uppsala , 1985. 71 p. ; ISBN 91-7106-238-6 (pbk.) : DDC 327.68067/9 19
DT771.M85 D38 1985   *NYPL [Sc E 88-121]*

SOUTH AMERICAN INDIANS. see **INDIANS OF SOUTH AMERICA.**

SOUTH ASIANS - GREAT BRITAIN - SOCIAL CONDITIONS.
Britain's Black population . Aldershot, Hants, England , Brookfield, Vt., USA , c1988. xv, 298 p. ; ISBN 0-566-05179-6 : DDC 305.8/96/041 19
DA125.N4 B75 1988   *NYPL [Sc E 89-100]*

SOUTH ASIANS - HEALTH AND HYGIENE - ENGLAND - LONDON.
Donovan, Jenny, 1960- We don't buy sickness, it just comes . Aldershot, Hants, England , Brookfield, Vt., USA , c1986. xv, 294 p. ; ISBN 0-566-05201-6 : DDC 362.1/08996/0421 19
RA488.L8 D65 1986   *NYPL [Sc D 86-844]*

SOUTH ASIANS - MEDICAL CARE - ENGLAND - LONDON.
Donovan, Jenny, 1960- We don't buy sickness, it just comes . Aldershot, Hants, England , Brookfield, Vt., USA , c1986. xv, 294 p. ; ISBN 0-566-05201-6 : DDC 362.1/08996/0421 19
RA488.L8 D65 1986   *NYPL [Sc D 86-844]*

SOUTH CAROLINA - BIOGRAPHY.
Taylor, Susie King, b. 1848. [Reminiscences of my life in camp.] A Black woman's Civil War memoirs . New York , 1988. 154 p. : ISBN 0-910129-85-1 (pbk.) : DDC 973.7/415 B 19
E492.94 33rd .T3 1988
NYPL [Sc D 88-1473]

SOUTH CAROLINA - HISTORY - REVOLUTION, 1775-1783 - JUVENILE FICTION.
Allen, Merritt Parmelee. Battle lanterns /. New York , 1949. 278 p. ; *NYPL [Sc D 88-1106]*

SOUTH CAROLINA - RACE RELATIONS.
Hammond, James Henry, 1807-1864. Secret and sacred . New York , 1988. xxix, 342 p., [2] leaves of plates : ISBN 0-19-505308-7 DDC

975.7/03/0924 B 19
F273 .H24 1988   *NYPL [Sc E 88-513]*

Koger, Larry, 1958- Black slaveowners . Jefferson, N.C. , 1985. xiii, 286 p. ; ISBN 0-89950-160-5 : DDC 975.7/00496073 19
E445.S7 K64 1985   *NYPL [Sc E 88-473]*

SOUTH PHILADELPHIA (PHILADELPHIA, PA.) - SOCIAL CONDITIONS.
Rose, Dan. Black American street life . Philadelphia, Pa. , c1987. x, 278 p. : ISBN 0-8122-8071-7 DDC 974.8/1100496073 19
F158.9.N4 R67 1987   *NYPL [Sc E 88-76]*

SOUTH PHILADELPHIA (PHILADELPHIA, PA.) - SOCIAL LIFE AND CUSTOMS.
Rose, Dan. Black American street life . Philadelphia, Pa. , c1987. x, 278 p. : ISBN 0-8122-8071-7 DDC 974.8/1100496073 19
F158.9.N4 R67 1987   *NYPL [Sc E 88-76]*

SOUTH WEST AFRICA COMPANY - HISTORY.
Voeltz, Richard Andrew. German colonialism and the South West Africa Company, 1884-1914 /. Athens, Ohio , 1988. x, 133 p. : ISBN 0-89680-146-2 (pbk.) : DDC 325/.343/09688 19
JV2029.A5 S689 1988   *NYPL [JLD 88-3416]*

Southall, Geneva H. Blind Tom : the post-Civil War enslavement of a Black musical genius / by Geneva H. Southall. Minneapolis : Challenge Productions, 1979- v. : ill. ; 24 cm. Vol. 2 has title: The continuing enslavement of Blind Tom, the Black pianist-composer (1865-1887) Includes bibliographical references. DDC 786.1/092/4 B
1. Blind Tom, 1849-1908. 2. Pianists - United States - Biography. 3. Composers - United States - Biography. 4. Afro-American musicians - Biography. I. Title. II. Title: Continuing enslavement of Blind Tom, the Black pianist-composer (1865-1887).
ML417.B78 S7 1979
NYPL [Sc Ser.-L .S674]

Southall, Roger. Labour and unions in Asia and Africa . New York , 1988. x, 258 p. ; ISBN 0-312-01362-0 : DDC 331.88/095 19
HD6796 .L3 1988   *NYPL [Sc D 88-1393]*

SOUTHAMPTON INSURRECTION, 1831 - JUVENILE LITERATURE.
Bisson, Terry. Nat Turner /. New York , c1988. 111 p. : ISBN 1-555-46613-3 DDC 975.1/5503/0924 B 92 19
F232.S7 T873 1988   *NYPL [Sc E 88-454]*

Southern Africa. Brown, Alex. Ottawa [1973] 43 p.
DT746 .B76   *NYPL [JLD 75-1128]*

Southern Africa and Western security /. Hanks, Robert, 1923- Cambridge, Mass. , c1983. vii, 74 p. : ISBN 0-89549-055-2 : DDC 355/.033268 19
UA855.6 .H36 1983   *NYPL [Sc D 85-489]*

Southern Africa film guide [microform] New York : Africa Fund, [1982] 12 p. ; 28 cm. Cover title. Microfiche. New York: New York Public Library, 198 . 1 microfiche: negative; 11 x 15 cm. (FSN Sc 019,122)
1. Moving-pictures - Africa, Southern - Bibliography. 2. Africa in moving-pictures - Bibliography. I. AFRICA Fund.   *NYPL [Sc Micro F-11052]*

Southern African Development Coordination Conference. Southern African Development Coordination Conference. SADCC . Gaborone, Botswana , c1984. 24 p. : DDC 338.968 19
HC900 .S66 1984   *NYPL [Sc F 88-394]*

Southern African Development Coordination Conference. SADCC : Southern African Development Coordination Conference : a handbook. Gaborone, Botswana : SADCC Secretariat, c1984. 24 p. : ill. ; 21 x 30 cm. Cover title. DDC 338.968 19
1. Southern African Development Coordination Conference. I. Title. II. Title: Southern African Development Coordination Conference.
HC900 .S66 1984   *NYPL [Sc F 88-394]*

SOUTHERN AFRICAN DEVELOPMENT COORDINATION CONFERENCE.
SADCC . Tokyo, Japan : London ; xi, 256 p. ; ISBN 0-86232-748-2 : DDC 337.1/68 19
HC900 .S23 1987   *NYPL [Sc D 89-50]*

Southern African Development Coordination Conference. SADCC . Gaborone, Botswana , c1984. 24 p. : DDC 338.968 19
HC900 .S66 1984   *NYPL [Sc F 88-394]*

Southern African Society for Legislative Drafting. Aspects of legislative drafting /. KwaDlangezwa, South Africa , 1987. ix, 204 p. ; ISBN 0-907995-73-X *NYPL [Sc C 88-66]*

Southern African stories. The Penguin book of Southern African stories /. Harmondsworth, Middlesex, England , New York, N.Y., U. S.A. , 1985. 328 p. ; ISBN 0-14-007239-X (pbk.) : DDC 808.83/1 19
PL8014.S62 P46 1985 *NYPL [Sc C 88-270]*

Southern African Universities Social Science Conference.
Class formation and class struggle . [Roma? Lesotho] [1982] 211 p. ;
NYPL [Sc D 89-25]

Southern African Universities Social Science Conference. Conference (4th : 1981 : National University of Lesotho) Class formation and class struggle . [Roma? Lesotho] [1982] 211 p. ;
NYPL [Sc D 89-25]

Southern Black creative writers, 1829-1953 . Foster, Mamie Marie Booth. New York , 1988. xvii, 113 p. ; ISBN 0-313-26207-1 (lib. bdg. : alk. paper) DDC 016.81/09/896073 19
Z1229.N39 F67 1988 PS153.N5
NYPL [Sc E 88-495]

SOUTHERN CHRISTIAN LEADERSHIP CONFERENCE - HISTORY.
Peake, Thomas R., 1939- Keeping the dream alive . New York , 1987. xiv, 492 p. : ISBN 0-8204-0397-0 : DDC 323.42/3/06073 19
E185.61 .P4 1987 *NYPL [Sc D 88-444]*

Southern, Eileen. Readings in Black American music /. New York, c1983. xii, 338 p. : ISBN 0-393-95280-0 (pbk.) DDC 781.7/296073 19
ML3556 .R34 1983 *NYPL [Sc D 85-30]*

Southern food . Egerton, John. New York , c1987. v, 408 p. : ISBN 0-394-54494-3 DDC 641.5975 19
TX715 .E28 1987 *NYPL [JSE 87-1598]*

The Southern review and modern literature, 1935-1985 / edited by Lewis P. Simpson, James Olney, and Jo Gulledge. Baton Rouge : Louisiana State University Press, c1988. xvi, 238 p.: ill. ; 24 cm. (Southern literary studies) Contains most of the papers presented at the Conference on Southern Letters and Modern Literature, held at Louisiana State University in 1985, along with a few pieces from the Southern review. Bibliography: p. [237]-238. ISBN 0-8071-1424-3 : DDC 810/.9/975 19
1. Southern review (Baton Rouge, La.) - Congresses. 2. American literature - Louisiana - Baton Rouge - History and criticism - Congresses. 3. American literature - 20th century - History and criticism - Congresses. 4. American literature - Southern states - History and criticism - Congresses. 5. Literature publishing - Southern States - History - 20th century - Congresses. 6. Southern States - Intellectual life - 20th century - Congresses. I. Simpson, Lewis P. II. Olney, James. III. Gulledge, Jo. IV. Conference on Southern Letters and Modern Literature (1985 : Louisiana State University, Baton Rouge). V. Southern review (Baton Rouge, La.).
PS267.B3 S68 1987 *NYPL [Sc E 88-280]*

Southern review (Baton Rouge, La.)
The Southern review and modern literature, 1935-1985 /. Baton Rouge , c1988. xvi, 238 p.: ISBN 0-8071-1424-3 : DDC 810/.9/975 19
PS267.B3 S68 1987 *NYPL [Sc E 88-280]*

SOUTHERN REVIEW (BATON ROUGE, LA.) - CONGRESSES.
The Southern review and modern literature, 1935-1985 /. Baton Rouge , c1988. xvi, 238 p.: ISBN 0-8071-1424-3 : DDC 810/.9/975 19
PS267.B3 S68 1987 *NYPL [Sc E 88-280]*

Southern Sotho-English dictionary /. Mabille, A. (Adolphe), 1836-1894. Morija, Lesotho , 1950 (1974 printing) xvi, 445 p. ;
PL8689.4 .M33 1974 *NYPL [Sc D 89-289]*

SOUTHERN STATES - ECONOMIC CONDITIONS.
Beardsley, Edward H. A history of neglect . Knoxville , c1987. xvi, 383 p. : ISBN 0-87049-523-2 (alk. paper) : DDC 362.1/0425 19
RA448.5.N4 B33 1987 *NYPL [Sc E 87-625]*

Davis, Allison, 1902- Deep South. Los Angeles, CA , 1988. xxiii, 567 p. : ISBN 0-934934-26-6
NYPL [Sc E 89-45]

SOUTHERN STATES - FICTION.
Youngblood, Shay. The big mama stories /. Ithaca, N.Y. , c1989. 106 p. ; ISBN 0-932379-58-3 (alk. paper) : DDC 813/.54 19
PS3575.O8535 B5 1989
NYPL [Sc D 89-530]

SOUTHERN STATES - GENEALOGY.
Tregillis, Helen Cox. River roads to freedom . Bowie, Md. , 1988. 122 p. : ISBN 1-556-13120-8 DDC 929/.3/089960773 19
F540 .T7 1988 *NYPL [Sc D 88-1442]*

SOUTHERN STATES - HISTORY - 1775-1865.
Fredrickson, George M., 1934- The arrogance of race . Middletown, Conn. , c1988. viii, 310 p. ; ISBN 0-8195-5177-5 DDC 973/.0496 19
E441 .F77 1988 *NYPL [Sc E 88-487]*

Mathew, William M. Edmund Ruffin and the crisis of slavery in the Old South . Athens , c1988. xiv, 286 p. : ISBN 0-8203-1011-5 (alk. paper) DDC 306/.362/0924 19
F230.R932 M38 1988 *NYPL [JFE 88-3149]*

Southern States - History - Civil War, 1861-1865. see United States - History - Civil War, 1861-1865.

SOUTHERN STATES - HISTORY - 1865-1951.
Rouse, Jacqueline Anne. Lugenia Burns Hope, Black southern reformer /. Athens , c1989. xi, 182 p., [8] p. of plates : ISBN 0-8203-1082-4 (alk. paper) DDC 973/.0496073024 B 19
E185.97.H717 R68 1989
NYPL [Sc D 89-469]

SOUTHERN STATES - INTELLECTUAL LIFE - 20TH CENTURY - CONGRESSES.
The Southern review and modern literature, 1935-1985 /. Baton Rouge , c1988. xvi, 238 p.: ISBN 0-8071-1424-3 : DDC 810/.9/975 19
PS267.B3 S68 1987 *NYPL [Sc E 88-280]*

SOUTHERN STATES - JUVENILE FICTION.
Edwards, Pat, 1922- Little John and Plutie /. Boston , 1988. 172 p. ; ISBN 0-395-48223-2 DDC [Fic] 19
PZ7.E2637 Li 1988 *NYPL [Sc D 89-126]*

SOUTHERN STATES - POLITICS AND GOVERNMENT - 1951-
Contemporary southern politics /. Baton Rouge , c1988. 309 p. ; ISBN 0-8071-1386-7 (alk. paper) DDC 320.975 19
F216.2 .C59 1988 *NYPL [Sc E 88-522]*

SOUTHERN STATES - POLITICS AND GOVERNMENT - 1951- - CONGRESSES.
Blacks in southern politics /. New York , 1987. vii, 305 p. : ISBN 0-275-92655-9 (alk. paper) : DDC 323.1/196073/075 19
E185.92 .B58 1987 *NYPL [Sc E 88-196]*

SOUTHERN STATES - RACE RELATIONS.
Cooper, Anna J. (Anna Julia), 1858-1964. A voice from the South /. New York , 1988. liv, 304 p. ; ISBN 0-19-505246-3 (alk. paper) DDC 975/.00496073 19
E185.86 .C587 1988 *NYPL [IEC 88-1201]*

Neverdon-Morton, Cynthia, 1944- Afro-American women of the South and the advancement of the race, 1895-1925 /. Knoxville , c1989. 272 p. : ISBN 0-87049-583-6 (alk. paper) : DDC 305.4/8896073/075 19
E185.86 .N48 1989 *NYPL [Sc E 89-218]*

Peake, Thomas R., 1939- Keeping the dream alive . New York , 1987. xiv, 492 p. : ISBN 0-8204-0397-0 : DDC 323.42/3/06073 19
E185.61 .P4 1987 *NYPL [Sc D 88-444]*

Whitfield, Stephen J., 1942- A death in the Delta . New York , London , c1988. xiv, 193 p., [8] p. of plates : ISBN 0-02-935121-9 : DDC 345.73/02523 347.3052523 19
E185.61 .W63 1989 *NYPL [Sc E 89-140]*

SOUTHERN STATES - RACE RELATIONS - JUVENILE FICTION.
Edwards, Pat, 1922- Little John and Plutie /. Boston , 1988. 172 p. ; ISBN 0-395-48223-2 DDC [Fic] 19
PZ7.E2637 Li 1988 *NYPL [Sc D 89-126]*

Taylor, Mildred D. The friendship /. New York , 1987. 53 p. ; ISBN 0-8037-0418-6 (lib. bdg.) : DDC [Fic] 19
PZ7.T21723 Fr 1987 *NYPL [Sc D 88-126]*

SOUTHERN STATES - SOCIAL CONDITIONS.
Beardsley, Edward H. A history of neglect . Knoxville , c1987. xvi, 383 p. : ISBN

0-87049-523-2 (alk. paper) : DDC 362.1/0425 19
RA448.5.N4 B33 1987 *NYPL [Sc E 87-625]*

Davis, Allison, 1902- Deep South. Los Angeles, CA , 1988. xxiii, 567 p. : ISBN 0-934934-26-6
NYPL [Sc E 89-45]

SOUTHERN TENANT FARMERS' UNION - HISTORY.
Mitchell, H. L. (Harry Leland), 1906- Roll the union on . Chicago , 1987. 96 p. :
NYPL [Sc F 88-187]

Southwest Africa. see Namibia.

SOUTHWEST CONFERENCE (U. S.)
Pennington, Richard, 1952- Breaking the ice . Jefferson, N.C. , c1987. ix, 182 p. : ISBN 0-89950-295-4 : DDC 796.332/72/0973 19
GV939.A1 P46 1987 *NYPL [Sc E 88-35]*

SOUTHWESTERN STATES - RACE RELATIONS.
Pennington, Richard, 1952- Breaking the ice . Jefferson, N.C. , c1987. ix, 182 p. : ISBN 0-89950-295-4 : DDC 796.332/72/0973 19
GV939.A1 P46 1987 *NYPL [Sc E 88-35]*

Soviet-Egyptian relations, 1945-85 /. El Hussini, Mohrez Mahmoud, 1942- New York , 1987. xix, 276 p. : ISBN 0-312-74781-0 : DDC 327.47062 19
DK69.4.E3 E4 1987 *NYPL [Sc D 88-1031]*

Soviet foreign policy in Southern Africa . Vanneman, Peter. Pretoria, Republic of South Africa , 1982. 57 p. ; ISBN 0-7983-0078-7 (pbk.) DDC 327.68047 19
DT747.S65 V36 1982 NYPL [Sc D 88-1155]

SOVIET UNION - DESCRIPTION AND TRAVEL - 1970.
Odear, Godwin N. (Goodwin Nwafor), 1958- 336 hours in the hero cities of Russians . [Nigeria? , 1984?] 145, [17] p. of plates :
NYPL [Sc D 88-790]

SOVIET UNION - FOREIGN RELATIONS - 1945-
El Hussini, Mohrez Mahmoud, 1942- Soviet-Egyptian relations, 1945-85 /. New York , 1987. xix, 276 p. : ISBN 0-312-74781-0 : DDC 327.47062 19
DK69.4.E3 E4 1987 *NYPL [Sc D 88-1031]*

SOVIET UNION - FOREIGN RELATIONS - 1975-
Vanneman, Peter. Soviet foreign policy in Southern Africa . Pretoria, Republic of South Africa , 1982. 57 p. ; ISBN 0-7983-0078-7 (pbk.) DDC 327.68047 19
DT747.S65 V36 1982 NYPL [Sc D 88-1155]

SOVIET UNION - FOREIGN RELATIONS - AFRICA, NORTHEAST.
Sauldie, Madan M. Super powers in the Horn of Africa /. New York , c1987. ix, 252 p. ; ISBN 0-86590-092-2 DDC 320.960 19
DT367.8 .S28 1987 *NYPL [Sc D 89-488]*

SOVIET UNION - FOREIGN RELATIONS - AFRICA, SOUTHERN.
Vanneman, Peter. Soviet foreign policy in Southern Africa . Pretoria, Republic of South Africa , 1982. 57 p. ; ISBN 0-7983-0078-7 (pbk.) DDC 327.68047 19
DT747.S65 V36 1982 NYPL [Sc D 88-1155]

SOVIET UNION - FOREIGN RELATIONS - CARIBBEAN AREA.
Ashby, Timothy. The bear in the back yard . Lexington, Mass. , c1987. xii, 240 p. : ISBN 0-669-14768-0 (alk. paper) DDC 327.470729 19
F2178.S65 A84 1987 *NYPL [HNB 87-1399]*

SOVIET UNION - FOREIGN RELATIONS - EGYPT.
El Hussini, Mohrez Mahmoud, 1942- Soviet-Egyptian relations, 1945-85 /. New York , 1987. xix, 276 p. : ISBN 0-312-74781-0 : DDC 327.47062 19
DK69.4.E3 E4 1987 *NYPL [Sc D 88-1031]*

SOVIET UNION - RELATIONS - AFRICA - ADDRESSES, ESSAYS, LECTURES.
The USSR and Africa. Moscow , 1983. 205 p. ; DDC 303.4/8247/06 19
DT38.9.S65 U86 1983 *NYPL [Sc D 88-980]*

Sow, Alfâ Ibrâhîm. Introduction à la culture africaine. Spanish. Introducción a la cultura africana . Barcelona , Paris , 1982. 176 p. ; ISBN 92-3-301478-9 (Unesco)
NYPL [Sc D 88-600]

Sow, Ibrahima. see Sow, Alfâ Ibrâhîm.

Sow the wind . Alexander, Neville.
Johannesburg , c1985 (1987 printing) xi, 180
p. ; ISBN 0-947009-07-8 *NYPL [Sc D 88-196]*

Sowande, Bode. Flamingo and other plays / Bode
Şowande. Harlow, Essex : Longman, 1986. 183
p. ; 20 cm. (Longman African writers)
CONTENTS. - Flamingo--Afamako - the
workhorse--The masters and the frauds--Circus of
Freedom Square. ISBN 0-582-78630-4
I. Title.   *NYPL [Sc C 88-89]*

Sowell, Floyd. (illus) Gray, Genevieve. A kite for
Bennie. New York, 1972. [40] p. ISBN
0-07-024197-X DDC [Fic]
PZ7.G7774 Ki   *NYPL [Sc E 88-422]*

Sowell, Thomas, 1930- Patterns of black
excellence / Thomas Sowell. Washington :
Ethics and Public Policy Center, Georgetown
University, 1977. [26]-58 p. ; 23 cm. (Ethics and
public policy reprint . 5) Cover title. Reprinted from
the Public interest, no. 43, spring, 1976. Includes
bibliographical references.
*1. Intelligence levels - Afro-Americans. I. Georgetown
University, Washington, D. C. Ethics and Public Policy
Center. II. Title. III. Series.*
       NYPL [Sc D 89-588]

**SOWETO (AFRICA) - SOCIAL
CONDITIONS.**
Finnegan, William. Dateline Soweto . New
York , c1988. x. 244 p. : ISBN 0-06-015932-4 :
DDC 070/.92/4 B 19
PN4874.F45 A3 1989   *NYPL [JFE 88-2005]*

Soweto, my love /. Ramusi, Molapatene Collins.
New York , c1988. viii, 262 p. ; ISBN
0-8050-0263-4 DDC 968.06/092/4 B 19
DT779.955.R36 A3 1988
       NYPL [Sc E 89-95]

SOWETO (SOUTH AFRICA) - FICTION.
Tlali, Miriam. Soweto stories / . London , 1989.
xx, 162 p. ;   *NYPL [Sc C 89-140]*

**SOWETO (SOUTH AFRICA) - HISTORY -
PICTORIAL WORKS.**
Magubane, Peter. June 16 . Johannesburg ,
c1986. [85] p. : ISBN 0-947009-13-2 (pbk.) DDC
968.2/21 19
DT944.J66 S674 1986   *NYPL [Sc G 88-12]*

Soweto stories /. Tlali, Miriam. London , 1989.
xx, 162 p. ;   *NYPL [Sc C 89-140]*

Soyinka, Wole.
Avery-Coger, Greta Margaret Kay McCormick.
Index of subjects, proverbs, and themes in the
writings of Wole Soyinka /. New York , c1988.
xxii, 311 p. ; ISBN 0-313-25712-4 (lib. bdg. : alk.
paper) DDC 822 19
PR9387.9.S6 Z54 1988   *NYPL [Sc E 88-496]*

The lion and the jewel / Wole Soyinka. Harare,
Zimbabwe : ZPH Pub. House, 1986. 64
p. ; 19 cm. (ZPH writers series. 32) ISBN
0-949225-41-X :
1. Yorubas - Drama. I. Title. II. Series.
       NYPL [Sc C 89-107]

Mandela's earth and other poems / by Wole
Soyinka. 1st ed. New York, N.Y. : Random
House, 1988. 70 p. ; 22 cm. ISBN
0-394-57021-9 : DDC 821 19
I. Title.
PR9387.9.S6 M36 1988
       NYPL [Sc D 88-1480]

Requiem for a futurologist / Wole Soyinka.
London : Collings, 1985. [6], 56 p. ; 22 cm.
ISBN 0-86036-207-8
I. Title.   *NYPL [Sc D 89-355]*

[Season of anomy. French]
Une Saison d'anomie / Wole Soyinka ;
traduit de l'anglais par Etienne Galle. Paris :
P. Belfond, c1987. 326 p. ; 23 cm. Translation
of: Season of anomy. ISBN 2-7144-1999-2
*1. Nigeria - Fiction. 2. Nigeria - History - Civil War,
1967-1970 - Fiction. I. Title.*
       NYPL [Sc D 88-1000]

Three short plays. Dunton, C. P. Wole
Soyinka, three short plays : The swamp
dwellers, The strong breed, The trials of
Brother Jero ; notes / by C.P. Dunton.
Harlow, Essex, Beirut , 1982. 71 p. ; ISBN
0-582-78260-0 *NYPL [Sc D 88-159]*

**SOYINKA, WOLE - CRITICISM AND
INTERPRETATION.**
Galle, Etienne. L'homme vivant de Wole

Soyinka /. Paris , c1987. 270 p. ; ISBN
2-903871-88-4   *NYPL [Sc D 88-1128]*

Jones, Eldred D. The writing of Wole Soyinka
/. London , Portsmouth, N.H. , 1988. xiv, 242
p. ; ISBN 0-435-08021-0 (pbk. : U. S.) DDC 822
19
PR9387.9.S6 Z7 1988   *NYPL [Sc D 88-1134]*

Maduakor, Obi. Wole Soyinka . New York ,
c1987, 1986. xv, 339 p. : ISBN 0-8240-9141-8
(alk. paper) DDC 822 19
PR9387.9.S6 Z77 1987   *NYPL [Sc D 88-643]*

**SOYINKA, WOLE - DICTIONARIES,
INDEXES, ETC.**
Avery-Coger, Greta Margaret Kay McCormick.
Index of subjects, proverbs, and themes in the
writings of Wole Soyinka /. New York , c1988.
xxii, 311 p. ; ISBN 0-313-25712-4 (lib. bdg. : alk.
paper) DDC 822 19
PR9387.9.S6 Z54 1988   *NYPL [Sc E 88-496]*

SPACE AND TIME - JUVENILE FICTION.
Boston, L. M. (Lucy Maria), 1892- Treasure of
Green Knowe. New York [1958] 185 p. DDC
[Fic]
PZ7.B6497 Tr   *NYPL [Sc D 88-1497]*

SPACE FLIGHT - JUVENILE FICTION.
Wassermann, Selma. Moonbeam and Dan Starr.
Westchester, Ill., c1966. 64 p.
       NYPL [Sc D 89-398]

**SPACE FLIGHT TO THE MOON -
JUVENILE FICTION.**
Wassermann, Selma. Moonbeam finds a moon
stone. Chicago [1967] 96 p. DDC [Fic]
PE1119 .W3636   *NYPL [Sc D 88-1423]*

SPACE-TIMES. see SPACE AND TIME.

SPACE TRAVEL. see SPACE FLIGHT.

SPAIN - COLONIES - AFRICA.
Bonelli Rubio, Juan María. El problema de la
colonización [microform] . Madrid , 1945. 15
p. ;   *NYPL [Sc Micro F-11057]*

SPAIN - COLONIES - SOUTH AMERICA.
Pons, François Raymond Joseph de, 1751-1812.
Voyage à la partie orientale de la Terre-Ferme,
dans l'Amérique Méridionale, fait pendant les
années 1801, 1802, 1803 et 1804: contenant la
description de la capitainerie générale de
Carácas, composée des provinces de Vénézuéla,
Maracaïbo, Varinas, la Guiane Espagnole,
Cumana, et de l'île de la Marguerite ... Paris,
1806. 3 v.
F2311 .P79   *NYPL [Sc Rare F 88-77]*

SPAIN - COMMERCIAL POLICY.
Pons, François Raymond Joseph de, 1751-1812.
Voyage à la partie orientale de la Terre-Ferme,
dans l'Amérique Méridionale, fait pendant les
années 1801, 1802, 1803 et 1804: contenant la
description de la capitainerie générale de
Carácas, composée des provinces de Vénézuéla,
Maracaïbo, Varinas, la Guiane Espagnole,
Cumana, et de l'île de la Marguerite ... Paris,
1806. 3 v.
F2311 .P79   *NYPL [Sc Rare F 88-77]*

**SPAIN - DESCRIPTION AND TRAVEL -
1951-**
Wright, Richard, 1908-1960. Pagan Spain /.
London , 1960, c1957. 191 p. ;
       NYPL [Sc Rare F 88-65]

Spanel, Donald, 1952- Through ancient eyes :
Egyptian portraiture : an exhibition organized
for the Birmingham Museum of Art,
Birmingham, Alabama, April 21-July 31, 1988 /
by Donald Spanel. Birmingham, AL : The
Museum, 1988. xiii, 159 p. : ill. (some col.) ; 28
cm. Bibliography: p. 153-156. DDC 732/.8 19
*1. Portrait sculpture, Egyptian - Exhibitions. 2. Portrait
sculpture, Ancient - Egypt - Exhibitions. I. Birmingham
Museum of Art. II. Title.*
NB1296.2 .S63 1988
       NYPL [3-MAE 88-3366]

Spanish America. see Latin America.

**SPANISH AMERICAN FICTION - 19TH
CENTURY - HISTORY AND CRITICISM.**
Bueno, Salvador. El negro en la novela
hispanoamericana /. La Habana, Cuba , 1986.
294 p. ; DDC 863/.009/3520396 19
PQ7082.N7 B84 1986   *NYPL [Sc C 89-124]*

**SPANISH AMERICAN FICTION - 20TH
CENTURY - HISTORY AND CRITICISM.**
Bueno, Salvador. El negro en la novela
hispanoamericana /. La Habana, Cuba , 1986.

294 p. ; DDC 863/.009/3520396 19
PQ7082.N7 B84 1986   *NYPL [Sc C 89-124]*

**SPANISH AMERICAN POETRY - 20TH
CENTURY.**
The image of Black women in twentieth-century
South American poetry . Washington, D.C. ,
c1987. 250 p. ; ISBN 0-89410-275-3
       NYPL [Sc E 88-321]

**SPANISH AMERICAN POETRY - 20TH
CENTURY - TRANSLATIONS INTO
ENGLISH.**
The image of Black women in twentieth-century
South American poetry . Washington, D.C. ,
c1987. 250 p. ; ISBN 0-89410-275-3
       NYPL [Sc E 88-321]

SPANISH EXPLORERS. see EXPLORERS -
SPAIN.

**SPANISH LANGUAGE - DICTIONARIES -
TZOTZIL.**
Laughlin, Robert M. The great Tzotzil
dictionary of Santo Domingo Zinacantán .
Washington, D.C. , 1988. 3 v. (xiii, 1119 p.) :
DDC 497/.4 301 s 19
GN1 .S54 no. 31a PM4466.Z5
       NYPL [HBR 89-17311]

**SPANISH LANGUAGE - VENEZUELA -
FOREIGN WORDS AND PHRASES -
AFRICAN.**
Alvarez, Alexandra, 1946- Malabí
Maticulambí . Montevideo, Uruguay? , c1987.
191 p. ;   *NYPL [Sc D 88-1012]*

SPARRING. see BOXING.

Spearhead (Eldoret, Kenya) .
(no. 77) An African Chris[t]mas? /. Eldoret,
Kenya , 1983. 53 p. ; DDC 263/.91/096 19
BS2575.2 .A37 1983   *NYPL [Sc D 88-195]*

(no. 92) Amecea Liturgical Colloquium (1985 :
Catholic Higher Institute of Eastern Africa)
Liturgy . Eldoret, Kenya , 1986. viii, 78 p. :
       NYPL [Sc D 88-901]

(no. 94) Donders, Joseph G. War and rumours
of war . Eldoret, Kenya , 1986. 51 p. :
       NYPL [Sc D 88-1467]

SPEC. see Association of Research Libraries.
Systems and Procedures Exchange Center.

SPECIAL EDUCATION - NIGERIA.
Development of special education in Nigeria /.
Ibadan , 1988. ix, 132 p. ; ISBN 978-267-703-5
       NYPL [Sc E 89-70]

**SPECIAL EDUCATION - NIGERIA -
ADMINISTRATION.**
Ihenacho, Izuka John. Administrators of special
education . [Nigeria] , c1986. 208 p. ; ISBN
978-239-609-5 (pbk.) DDC 371.9/09669 19
LC3988.N6 144 1986   *NYPL [Sc C 89-145]*

SPECIAL EDUCATION - TANZANIA.
The development of special education in
Tanzania /. Dar es Salaam, Tanzania , c1984.
81 p. : ISBN 997-661-002-5
       NYPL [Sc C 89-127]

SPECIAL LIBRARIES. see LIBRARIES,
SPECIAL.

**Special report (Human Awareness Programme
(South Africa))** .
(no. 3) Human Awareness Programme (South
Africa) Black urban public road transport .
Grant Park [South Africa] [1982] 64 p. :
ISBN 0-620-05750-5 (pbk.) : DDC
388.4/1322/089968 19
HE5704.4.A6 H86 1982
       NYPL [Sc F 88-150]

**Special report of the Director-General on the
application of the declaration concerning the
policy of apartheid in South Africa.** Geneva :
International Labour Office, 1986. 186 p. : ill. ;
24 cm. At head of title: International Labour
Conference, 72nd session, 1986. ISBN 92-2-105167-6
(pbk.)
*1. South Africa - Relations - Foreign countries. I.
International Labour Office. II. International Labour
Conference (72nd : 1986 : Geneva, Switzerland). III.
Title: Apartheid in South Africa.*
       NYPL [Sc E 88-179]

**Special report of the directors of the African
Institution, made at the annual general
meeting, on the 12th of April, 1815** . African
Institution, London. London , 1815 (London :
Printed by Ellerton and Henderson) 157 p. ;
       NYPL [Sc Rare G 86-5]

Special reports (Institute for International Economics (U. S.)) .
(5) African debt and financing /. Washington, D.C. , 1986. 223 p. : ISBN 0-88132-044-7 : DDC 336.3/435/096 19
HJ8826 .A36 1986   **NYPL** *[JLE 87-3261]*

SPECIALIZED AGENCIES OF THE UNITED NATIONS. see INTERNATIONAL AGENCIES.

SPECIE. see GOLD.

Speech anthology, 1986-1987 / Jamaica Cultural Development Commission. [Kingston] : The Commission, [1986] 183 p. ; 28 cm. Cover title. DDC 820/.8 19
I. Jamaica Cultural Development Commission.
PN4228.J25 S6 1986   **NYPL** *[Sc F 88-303]*

Speech of Horace Mann, of Massachusetts, in the House of Representatives, Feb. 23, 1849; on slavery in the United States, and the slave trade in the District of Columbia. Mann, Horace, 1796-1859. Boston [1849]. [15] p. ;
E416 .M28   **NYPL** *[Sc Rare C 89-3]*

Speech of John C. Rutherfoord, of Goochland, in the House of Delegates of Virginia, on the removal from the Commonwealth of the free colored population . Rutherfoord, John Coles 1825-1866. Richmond , 1853. 20 p. ;
   NYPL *[Sc Rare C 89-10]*

Speech of Mr. Horace Mann, of Massachusetts, in the House of Representatives of the United States, June 30, 1848 . Mann, Horace, 1796-1859. [Boston] , 1848. 31 p. ;
   NYPL *[Sc Rare C 89-30]*

Speech of the Rev. Wm. H. Brisbane . Brisbane, William Henry, ca. 1803-1878. Hartford , 1840. 12 p. ;
   NYPL *[Sc Rare C 89-26]*

Speeches of Hayne and Webster in the United States Senate, on the resolution of Mr. Foot, January, 1830 . Hayne, Robert Young, 1791-1839. Boston , 1853. 115 p. ;
E381 .H424 1853   **NYPL** *[Sc Rare C 89-20]*

Spegg, Hans Ludwig. Volkstümliche Künste . Reinbek , c1986/87. 135 p. ;
   NYPL *[Sc D 89-238]*

SPELLS. see MAGIC; INCANTATIONS.

Spencer, F. Louise. A comprehensive approach to study and test taking / F. Louise Spencer. New York, N.Y. : Spencer-Strachan Publications, c1986. xii ; 22 cm. "Recommended for student and graduate nurses sitting for classroom and State Board examination." Bibliography: p. [59]
1. Nursing - Examinations. 2. Nursing - Study and teaching. I. Title.   **NYPL** *[Sc D 88-1168]*

Spencer, Ian R. G. The economic development of Kenya, 1895-1929 [microform] : a reconsideration / by Ian R. G. Spencer. [Nairobi] : University of Nairobi, Dept. of History, [1978] 14 p. ; 33 cm. (Staff seminar paper / University of Nairobi, Department of History. no. 6, 1978/79) Cover title. Includes bibliographical references. Microfilm. New York: New York Public Library, 1982. 1 microfilm reel; 35 mm. (MN *ZZ-23051)
1. Kenya - Economic conditions. I. Series: Nairobi. University. Dept. of History. Staff seminar paper, no. 6. II. Title.   **NYPL** *[Sc Micro R-4108 no.33]*

Spencer, Paul, 1932- The Maasai of Matapato : a study of rituals of rebellion / Paul Spencer. Bloomington : Indiana University Press in association with the International African Institute, London, c1988. xii, 296 p. : ill. ; 25 cm. (International African library) Includes bibliographical references and indexes. ISBN 0-253-33625-2 DDC 306/.08996 19
1. Masai (African people) - Social life and customs. 2. Masai (African people) - Rites and ceremonies. 3. Age groups - Kenya. 4. Matapatu (Kenya) - Social life and customs. I. Title. II. Series.
DT433.545.M33 S64 1988
   NYPL *[JFE 88-7115]*

Spider webs /. Millar, Margaret. New York , c1986. 323 p. ; ISBN 0-930330-76-5
   NYPL *[Sc C 88-350]*

The spider's web /. Koroma, Salia. Freetown , 1986. 134 p. :   **NYPL** *[Sc D 89-403]*

SPIES - FICTION. see SPY STORIES.

Spirit heads . Glantz, Stephan Hamilton. New York , 1987. 133 p. :   **NYPL** *[Sc F 88-103]*

SPIRIT POSSESSION.
Agosto de Muñoz, Nélida. El fenómeno de la posesión en la religión Vudú . Río Piedras, P.R. , 1975, c1974. 119 p. ; DDC 299/.64 19
BL2490 .A33 1975   **NYPL** *[TB (Caribbean monograph series no. 14)]*

Spiritual empowerment in Afro-American literature . Evans, James H., 1950- Lewiston, NY , 1987. 174 p. ; ISBN 0-88946-560-6 DDC 810/.9/896073 19
PS153.N5 E92 1987   **NYPL** *[Sc E 88-265]*

Spiritual narratives / with an introduction by Sue E. Houchins. New York : Oxford University Press, 1988. 489 p. in various pagings : port., music ; 17 cm. (The Schomburg library of nineteenth-century Black women writers) Includes bibliographical references. Reprint. Originally published: Boston : Friends of Freedom and Virtue, c1835. CONTENTS. - Productions of Mrs. Maria W. Stewart / presented to the First African Baptist Church & Society -- Religious experience and journal of Mrs. Jarena Lee -- A brand plucked from the fire / by Mrs. Julia A.J. Foote -- Twenty-year's experience of a missionary / by Virginia W. Broughton. ISBN 0-19-505266-8 (alk. paper) DDC 209/.22 B 19
1. Afro-American women - Biography. 2. Afro-American women - Religion. I. Houchins, Susan. II. Series.
BR1713 .S65 1988   **NYPL** *[JFC 88-2189]*

Spiritualité et libération en Afrique / sous la direction de Engelbert Mveng. Paris : L'Harmattan, c1987. 123 p. ; 22 cm. (Médiations religieuses) Includes bibliographical references.
1. Africa - Religion. 2. Christianity - Africa. I. Mveng, Engelbert. II. Series.   **NYPL** *[Sc D 88-1416]*

SPIRITUALS (SONGS) - HISTORY AND CRITICISM.
Finn, Julio. The bluesman . London , New York , 1986. 256 p., [8] p. of plates : ISBN 0-7043-2523-3   **NYPL** *[Sc E 88-181]*

Lovell, John, 1907- Black song . New York , 1986, c1972. xviii, 686 p. : ISBN 0-913729-53-1 (pbk.) DDC 783.6/7/09 19
ML3556 .L69 1986   **NYPL** *[Sc D 88-421]*

Oliver, Paul. The New Grove gospel, blues and jazz . New York , 1986. 395 p. [16] p. of plates : ISBN 0-393-01696-X
   NYPL *[JND 88-16]*

Spofford, Tim. Lynch Street : the May 1970 slayings at Jackson State College / Tim Spofford. Kent, Ohio : Kent State University Press, c1988. 219 p., [1] leaf of plates : ill. ; 24 cm. Includes index. Bibliography: p. 196-210. ISBN 0-87338-355-9 (alk. paper) DDC 976.2/51 19
1. Jackson State College. 2. Afro-Americans - Civil rights - Mississippi - Jackson. 3. Riots - Mississippi - Jackson. 4. Murder - Mississippi - Jackson. 5. Jackson, Miss. - Race relations. I. Title.
F349.J13 S66 1988   **NYPL** *[Sc E 89-27]*

SPOILS SYSTEMS. see CORRUPTION (IN POLITICS)

Spojené staty americké. see **United States.**

SPORT FISHING. see FISHING.

Sport im Kolonialismus, Kolonialismus im Sport . Rummelt, Peter. Köln , 1986. 341 p. : ISBN 3-7609-5213-5 DDC 796/.096 19
GV665 .R85 1986   **NYPL** *[Sc D 88-973]*

Sport science studies .
(1) Cheska, Alyce Taylor. Traditional games and dances in West African nations /. Schorndorf , 1987. 136 p. : ISBN 3-7780-6411-8 (pbk.) DDC 793.3/1966 19
GV1713.A358 C48 1987
   NYPL *[JFE 87-5517]*

SPORTS - AFRICA - HISTORY - 19TH CENTURY.
Rummelt, Peter. Sport im Kolonialismus, Kolonialismus im Sport . Köln , 1986. 341 p. : ISBN 3-7609-5213-5 DDC 796/.096 19
GV665 .R85 1986   **NYPL** *[Sc D 88-973]*

SPORTS - AFRICA - HISTORY - 20TH CENTURY.
Rummelt, Peter. Sport im Kolonialismus, Kolonialismus im Sport . Köln , 1986. 341 p. : ISBN 3-7609-5213-5 DDC 796/.096 19
GV665 .R85 1986   **NYPL** *[Sc D 88-973]*

SPORTS - EUROPE - HISTORY - 19TH CENTURY.
Rummelt, Peter. Sport im Kolonialismus, Kolonialismus im Sport . Köln , 1986. 341 p. :
ISBN 3-7609-5213-5 DDC 796/.096 19
GV665 .R85 1986   **NYPL** *[Sc D 88-973]*

SPORTS - SOCIAL ASPECTS - GREAT BRITAIN - COLONIES - HISTORY.
Pleasure, profit, proselytism . London, England , Totowa, NJ , 1988. 284 p. [8] p. ofplates : ISBN 0-7146-3289-9 : DDC 796/.0941 19
GV605 .P58 1988   **NYPL** *[JLE 88-1312]*

SPORTS - SOCIAL ASPECTS - GREAT BRITAIN - HISTORY.
Pleasure, profit, proselytism . London, England , Totowa, NJ , 1988. 284 p. [8] p. ofplates : ISBN 0-7146-3289-9 : DDC 796/.0941 19
GV605 .P58 1988   **NYPL** *[JLE 88-1312]*

SPORTS - SOCIAL ASPECTS - GREAT BRITAIN - HISTORY - 19TH CENTURY.
Pleasure, profit, proselytism . London, England , Totowa, NJ , 1988. 284 p. [8] p. ofplates : ISBN 0-7146-3289-9 : DDC 796/.0941 19
GV605 .P58 1988   **NYPL** *[JLE 88-1312]*

Die Sprache der Aithiopen im Lande Kusch /. Böhm, Gerhard. Wien , 1988. 206 p. : ISBN 3-85043-047-2   **NYPL** *[Sc D 88-1339]*

Die Sprache der Mauka . Ebermann, Erwin. Wien , 1986. 207 p. ; ISBN 3-85369-656-2
PL8491.95.I9 E24 1986
   NYPL *[Sc D 88-687]*

The spread of Islam in Uganda /. Kasozi, A. B. K. (Abdu Basajabaka Kawalya), 1942- Nairobi, Kenya , 1986. vi, 136 p., [4] p. of plates : ISBN 0-19-572596-4   **NYPL** *[Sc E 89-109]*

Springer, Nancy. They're all named Wildfire / by Nancy Springer. 1st ed. New York : Atheneum, 1989. 103 p. ; 22 cm. Jenny loses most of her friends and suffers the verbal abuse of classmates when she befriends a black girl who has moved with her family into Jenny's duplex and shares her interest in horses. ISBN 0-689-31450-7 DDC [Fic] 19
1. Horses - Juvenile fiction. 2. Afro-American children - Juvenile fiction. I. Title. II. Title: They are all named Wildfire.
PZ7.S76846 Th 1989   **NYPL** *[Sc D 89-498]*

Springer, Steve. Ostler, Scott. Winnin' times . New York , c1988. 304 p. ; ISBN 0-02-029591-X (pbk.) DDC 796.32/364/0979494 19
GV885.52.L67 O87 1986
   NYPL *[Sc D 89-106]*

Springtime bears /. Warren, Cathy. New York , c1986. [32] p. : ISBN 0-688-05905-8 DDC [E] 19
PZ7.W2514 Sp 1986   **NYPL** *[Sc D 87-622]*

Die Sprokiesboom en ander verhale uit Midde-Afrika. De Villiers, Helene. (comp) Kaapstad, 1970. 84 p.;
P214 .D43   **NYPL** *[Sc D 89-373]*

Spurlock, Jeanne. Black families in crisis . New York , c1988. xiv, 305 p. ; ISBN 0-87630-524-9 DDC 305.8/96073 19
E185.86 .B5254 1988   **NYPL** *[Sc E 89-155]*

SPY STORIES.
Teague, Bob. Agent K-13. Garden City, N.Y., c1974. 47 p. ; ISBN 0-385-08704-7 DDC [E]
PZ7.T21937 Ag   **NYPL** *[Sc E 88-587]*

Squandering Eden . Rosenblum, Mort. San Diego , c1987. x, 326 p., [32] p. of plates : ISBN 0-15-184860-2 : DDC 960/.3 19
GF701 .R67 1987   **NYPL** *[Sc E 88-24]*

Squatters and the roots of Mau Mau, 1905-63 /. Kanogo, Tabitha M. Athens , London , 1987. xviii, 206 p. : ISBN 0-8214-0873-9 DDC 307.3/36 19
HD1538.K4 K36 1987   **NYPL** *[Sc D 88-207]*

SQUATTERS - KENYA - HISTORY - 20TH CENTURY.
Kanogo, Tabitha M. Squatters and the roots of Mau Mau, 1905-63 /. Athens , London , 1987. xviii, 206 p. : ISBN 0-8214-0873-9 DDC 307.3/36 19
HD1538.K4 K36 1987   **NYPL** *[Sc D 88-207]*

SQUATTERS - SOUTH AFRICA - CAPE TOWN.
Cole, Josette. Crossroads . Johannesburg, South Africa , 1987. xii, 175 p., [25] p. of plates : ISBN 0-86975-318-5   **NYPL** *[Sc D 88-957]*

SROLOU, GABRIEL.
La Chanson populaire en Côte-d'Ivoire . Paris ,

c1986. 342 p., [12] p. of plates : ISBN
2-7087-0470-2 *NYPL [Sc D 88-1099]*

Staatliches Museum für Völkerkunde München.
Ndiaye, Iba, 1928- Iba N'Diaye, Gemälde,
Lavierungen, Zeichnungen =. München ,
c1987. 71 p. : ISBN 3-7774-4650-5
NYPL [Sc C 88-297]

Staber, Margrit. Jazz in Willisau . Luzern ,
c1978. 206 p. : ISBN 3-7239-0051-8 DDC
785.42/09494/5 19
ML3509.S9 J4 1978 *NYPL [Sc F 89-24]*

Stability and change in Africa [microform] d.
Nyerere, Julius Kambarage, Pres. Tanzania,
1922- Dar es Salaam , 1969. 15 p. :
NYPL [Sc Micro F-10986]

Stadt im Norden /. Graham, Lorenz B. [North
Town. German.] Stuttgart , 1973, c1965. 157
p. ; ISBN 3-8002-5087-X
NYPL [Sc D 88-1171]

Stafford, Joseph. The Black gourmet : favorite
Afro-American and Creole recipes from coast
to coast / by Joseph Stafford.1988 ed.,
completely rev. and expanded. Detroit : Harlo,
1988. 256 p., [6] leaves of plates : ill. (some
col.) ; 23 cm. Includes index. ISBN 0-9617123-0-9 :
I. Title. *NYPL [Sc D 88-1199]*

STAGE. see DRAMA; THEATER.

STAGE COSTUME. see COSTUME.

A stage for victory . Foster, William A. A.
Kingston, Jamaica, W.I. , 1985. 36 p. [32] p. of
plates : ISBN 976-8032-00-6
NYPL [Sc D 88-182]

Stainback, Berry. Robinson, Frank, 1935- Extra
innings /. New York , c1988. x, 270, [8] p. of
plates : ISBN 0-07-053183-8 DDC
796.357/08996073 19
GV863.A1 R582 1988 *NYPL [Sc E 88-382]*

Stam, Robert, 1941- Brazilian cinema /. Austin ,
1988. 373 p. : ISBN 0-292-70767-3
NYPL [Sc E 89-59]

Standley, Fred L. Critical essays on James
Baldwin /. Boston, Mass. , 1988. ix, 312 p. ;
ISBN 0-8161-8879-3 DDC PS3552.5409 19
PS3552.A45 Z88 1988 *NYPL [JFE 88-2203]*

Stanley, Diane. Shaka, king of the Zulus / Diane
Stanley and Peter Vennema ; illustrated by
Diane Stanley. New York : Morrow Junior
Books, c1988. [40] p. : col. ill. ; 29 cm. A
biography of the nineteenth-century military genius and
Zulu chief. Bibliography: p. [40] SCHOMBURG
CHILDREN'S COLLECTION. ISBN 0-688-07342-5
DDC 968.04/092/4 B 92 19
1. Chaka, Zulu chief, 1787?-1828 - Juvenile literature.
2. Zulus - Kings and rulers - Biography - Juvenile
literature. 3. Zulus - History. I. Vennema, Peter. II.
Schomburg Children's Collection. III. Title.
DT878.Z9 C565 1988 *NYPL [Sc F 88-358]*

Stanley Foundation.
Occasional paper.
([no.]14) Epstein, William, 1912- A
nuclear-weapon-free zone in Africa? /.
Muscatine, Iowa , 1977. 52 p. :
JX1974.7 .E553 *NYPL [JLK 75-198 [no.]14]*

Staples, Robert. The urban plantation : racism &
colonialism in the post civil rights era / Robert
Staples. Oakland, CA : Black Scholar Press,
c1987. 248 p. ; 22 cm. Includes bibliographical
references. ISBN 0-933296-13-4 (pbk.)
1. Racism - United States. 2. Afro-Americans -
Economic conditions. 3. Afro-Americans - Social
conditions. 4. United States - Race relations. I. Title.
NYPL [Sc D 88-1021]

Stapleton, Cris. African all-stars : the pop music
of a continent / Chris Stapleton and Chris
May ; Ill. by Andy Isham ; Photos. by Jak
Kilby. London : Quartet Books, 1987. 373 p.,
[16] p. of plates : ill., ports. ; 25 cm. Includes
index. Discography: p. 325-333. ISBN 0-7043-2504-7
1. Music - Africa - History and criticism. I. May, Cris.
II. Title. *NYPL [Sc E 88-137]*

Stappers, Leo. Substitutiv und Possessiv im Bantu
/ Leo Stappers ; überarbeitet, herausgegeben
und mit neuem Kartenmaterial versehen von
Hans-Ingolf Weier. Berlin : D. Reimer, [1986]
xix, 223 p. : maps ; 24 cm. (Mainzer
Afrika-Studien. Bd. 8) "Bantuklassifikation nach Guthrie
(1967-71)" (plastic sheet) laid in. Bibliography: p.
222-223. ISBN 3-496-00877-6 DDC 496/.3 19
1. Bantu languages - Pronoun. 2. Bantu languages -

Possessives. I. Weier, Hans-Ingolf. II. Title.
PL8025.1 .S73 1986 *NYPL [Sc E 88-360]*

Stares, Rodney. Ethnic minorities : their
involvement in MSC Special Programmes / by
Rodney Stares, David Imberg and John
McRobie. [London] : Special Programmes,
Manpower Services Commission, 1982. 62 p. ;
30 cm. (Research and development series . no. 6)
Cover title. ISBN 0-905932-32-3
1. Blacks - Employment - England. 2. Minorities -
Employment - England. I. Imberg, David. II. McRobie,
John. III. Great Britain. Manpower Services
Commission. IV. Title. *NYPL [Sc F 88-96]*

Starling, Marion Wilson, 1907. The slave
narrative : its place in American history /
Marion Wilson Starling.2nd ed. Washington,
D.C. : Howard University Press, 1988. xxx, 375
p. ; 24 cm. Originally presented as the author's thesis
(Ph.D.--New York University, 1946) Includes index.
Bibliography: p. [357]-363. ISBN 0-88258-165-1 :
DDC 973/.0496073 19
1. Slaves - United States - Biography - History and
criticism. 2. Slaves' writings, American - History and
criticism. 3. Afro-Americans - Biography - History and
criticism. 4. Biography (as a literary form). I. Title.
E444 .S8 1988 *NYPL [Sc E 89-185]*

Stars of the new curfew /. Okri, Ben. London ,
1988. 194 p. ; ISBN 0-436-33944-7 :
NYPL [Sc D 89-454]

Start your own school! / Institute for
Independent Education. Washington, D.C. :
Institute for Independent Education, 1988. vi,
68 p. : ill. ; 22 cm. "Ten school founders and
administrators tell how"- Cover. ISBN 0-941001-08-3
1. Private schools - United States. I. Institute for
Independent Education. *NYPL [Sc D 89-406]*

**STATE AND AGRICULTURE. see
AGRICULTURE AND STATE.**

**STATE AND CHURCH. see CHURCH AND
STATE.**

**STATE AND EDUCATION. see EDUCATION
AND STATE.**

**STATE AND ENVIRONMENT. see
ENVIRONMENTAL POLICY.**

STATE AND FAMILY. see FAMILY POLICY.

**STATE AND HIGHER EDUCATION. see
HIGHER EDUCATION AND STATE.**

State and industrial relations in Nigeria /.
Otobo, Dafe. Lagos , 1988. 192 p. ISBN
978-260-104-7 *NYPL [Sc D 89-523]*

STATE AND LABOR. see LABOR POLICY.

**STATE AND MASS MEDIA. see MASS
MEDIA POLICY.**

**STATE AND MEDICINE. see MEDICAL
POLICY.**

**STATE AND SCIENCE. see SCIENCE AND
STATE.**

**STATE AND TECHNOLOGY. see
TECHNOLOGY AND STATE.**

**State Convention of Colored Men (1856 :
Columbus, Ohio)** Proceedings of the State
Convention of Colored Men, held in the city of
Columbus, Ohio, Jan. 16th, 17th & 18th, 1856.
[Columbus? : s.n., 1856?] 8 p. ; 23 cm. Caption
title.
1. Afro-Americans - Ohio - Congresses. 2.
Afro-Americans - Legal status, laws, etc. - Ohio.
E185.93.O2 S84 1856
NYPL [Sc Rare F 89-23]

The state of Black Britain /. Haynes, Aaron,
1927- London , 1983. 160 p. ; ISBN
0-946455-01-5 *NYPL [Sc D 88-348]*

**State of Georgia v. Vincent Derek Mallory
M.D. .** Haith, Dorothy May. Washington ,
1988. 12 leaves ; *NYPL [Sc F 88-131]*

**The State of medicinal plants research in
Nigeria :** (proceedings of a workshop, Ife, 1986)
/ edited by Abayomi Sofowora. [Ibadan?] :
Ibandan University Press, c1986. vi, 404 p. :
ill. ; 24 cm. Proceedings of a workshop organized by
the African Biosciences Network, the Federal Ministry
of Science and Technology, Lagos, the Nigerian Society
of Pharmacognosy and the Drug Research and
Production Unit of the University of Ife. Includes
index. Includes bibliographical references. ISBN
978-302-850-2

1. Botany, Medical - Nigeria - Congresses. I. Sofowora,
Abayomi. II. African Biosciences Network.
NYPL [Sc E 88-305]

**STATE PLANNING. see REGIONAL
PLANNING.**

STATE RIGHTS.
Bestor, Arthur. State sovereignty and slavery .
Springfield, IL , 1961. 64 p. ;
NYPL [Sc E 87-669]

**STATE RIGHTS, NULLIFICATION AND
SECESSION. see NULLIFICATION.**

State sovereignty and slavery . Bestor, Arthur.
Springfield, IL , 1961. 64 p. ;
NYPL [Sc E 87-669]

**STATE, THE - MORAL AND ETHICAL
ASPECTS.**
Naranjit, Darryl. The righteous state /.
[Chaguanas? Trinidad] , c1987. ii, 225 p. ;
DDC 172 19
JA79 .N34 1987 *NYPL [Sc D 89-518]*

STATE, WELFARE. see WELFARE STATE.

STATES' RIGHTS. see STATE RIGHTS.

**STATES, SMALL - ECONOMIC
CONDITIONS - CASE STUDIES.**
Thomas, Clive Yolande. The poor and the
powerless . New York , 1988. xv, 396 p. :
ISBN 0-85345-743-3 : DDC 338.9/009729 19
HC151 .T56 1988 *NYPL [Sc D 88-763]*

STATESMEN - BRAZIL - BIOGRAPHY.
Nabuco, Joaquim, 1849-1910. Minha formação
/. Rio de Janeiro , 1957. 258 p. :
F2536 .N1425 1957 *NYPL [Sc D 87-1353]*

STATESMEN - GUINEA - BIOGRAPHY.
Kaké, Ibrahima Baba. Sékou Touré, le héros et
le tyran /. Paris , 1987. 254 p. :
NYPL [Sc D 88-468]

STATESMEN - KENYA - BIOGRAPHY.
Ng'weno, Hilary. The day Kenyatta died /.
Nairobi , 1978. 68 p., [1] leaf of plates ; ISBN
0-582-64283-3 DDC 967.6/204/0924 B 19
DT433.576.K46 N45 *NYPL [Sc F 89-28]*

STATESMEN - NIGERIA - BIOGRAPHY.
Adebo, Simeon O., 1913- Our international
years /. Ibadan , 1988. xi, 281 p., [10] p. of
plates : ISBN 987-246-025-7
NYPL [Sc D 89-75]

Babatope, Ebenezer. Awo & Nigeria . Ikeja
[Nigeria] , 1984. 97 p. : ISBN 3-7830-0100-0
NYPL [Sc D 88-1397]

Udo-Inyang, D. S. (Denis S.) The man--Sir
Justice Udo Udoma /. Calabar [Nigeria] [1985]
72 p. : ISBN 978-228-168-9 (pbk.) DDC
347.669/03534 B 346.69073534 B 19
LAW *NYPL [Sc D 88-776]*

**STATESMEN - SOUTH AFRICA -
BIOGRAPHY.**
Gastrow, Shelagh. Who's who in South African
politics /. Johannesburg , 1985. xiv, 347 p. :
ISBN 0-86975-280-4 (pbk.) DDC 968.06/092/2
B 19
DT779.954 .G37 1985
NYPL [Sc D 87-1109]

Plomer, William, 1903-1973. Cecil Rhodes /.
Cape Town , 1984. xvii, 179 p. ; ISBN
0-86486-018-8 *NYPL [Sc C 88-64]*

**STATESMEN - SOUTH AFRICA -
KWAZULU - BIOGRAPHY.**
Mzala. Gatsha Buthelezi . London , Atlantic
Highlands, N.J. , 1988. ix, 240 p. ; ISBN
0-86232-792-X DDC 968.4/9106/0924 B 19
DT878.Z9 B856 1988 *NYPL [Sc D 88-1324]*

STATESMEN - UGANDA - BIOGRAPHY.
Udo-Inyang, D. S. (Denis S.) The man--Sir
Justice Udo Udoma /. Calabar [Nigeria] [1985]
72 p. : ISBN 978-228-168-9 (pbk.) DDC
347.669/03534 B 346.69073534 B 19
LAW *NYPL [Sc D 88-776]*

The Status of Blacks in higher education / Ada
M. Elam, editor. Lanham, MD : University
Press of America ; [Washington, D.C.] :
NAFEO Research Institute, c1989. ix, 110 p. ;
23 cm. ISBN 0-8191-7286-3 (alk. paper) DDC
378/.008996073 19
1. Afro-Americans - Education (Higher). I. Elam, Ada
M. II. NAFEO Research Institute (U. S.).
LC2781 .S72 1988 *NYPL [Sc D 89-589]*

Statuts et programme d'action /. Front populaire (Burkina Faso) Ouagadougou [1988]. 47 p. ;
NYPL [Sc D 88-1452]

Staudt, Kathleen A. Women and the state in Africa /. Boulder, Colo. , c1989. ix, 229 p. ; ISBN 1-555-87082-1 (alk. paper) : DDC 305.4/2/096 19
HQ1236.5.A357 W65 1988
NYPL [Sc E 89-159]

Stealing the fire . Porter, Horace A., 1950- Middletown, Conn. , Scranton, Pa. , c1989. xviii, 220 p. ; ISBN 0-8195-5197-X : DDC 818/.5409 19
PS3552.A45 Z85 1989   NYPL [Sc D 89-468]

Steed, Robert P. Blacks in southern politics /. New York , 1987. vii, 305 p. : ISBN 0-275-92655-9 (alk. paper) : DDC 323.1/196073/075 19
E185.92 .B58 1987   NYPL [Sc E 88-196]

De steeg . Jongh, Edward Arthur de. [S.l.] , 1976. 148 p. ;
PT5881.2.O58 S7   NYPL [Sc D 88-1033]

Steele, B. Great Britain. Overseas Development Administration. Review of UK manpower and training aid to Nigeria /. [London? , 1984 or 1985] v, 72 p. :   *NYPL [Sc F 88-185]*

STEEPLECHASING - JUVENILE FICTION.
Willis, Priscilla D. The race between the flags /. New York , 1955. 177 p. :
NYPL [Sc D 88-1508]

Steinman, Beatrice. This railroad disappears. with pictures by Douglas Gorsline. New York, F. Watts [1958] 181 p. illus. 21 cm. SCHOMBURG CHILDREN'S COLLECTION.
1. Underground Railroad - Juvenile fiction. I. Gorsline, Douglas W., 1913-. II. Schomburg Children's Collection. III. Title.
PZ7.S8266 Th   NYPL [Sc D 89-391]

Stella, the princess /. Thompson, Roydon, 1911- Kingston, Jamaica, West Indies (9 Roselle Ave., Kingston 6) , 1984. 255 p. :   ISBN 976-8024-00-3 (pbk.)   DDC [Fic] 19
PZ7.T37199 St 1984   NYPL [Sc D 88-317]

STENCIL WORK.
Menten, Theodore. Ancient Egyptian cut and use stencils /. New York , 1978. [32] leaves : ISBN 0-486-23626-9 :   *NYPL [Sc F 88-366]*

Stephen, James, 1758-1832.
African Institution, London. Reasons for establishing a registry of slaves in the British colonies . London , 1815 (London : Printed by Ellerton and Henderson) 118 p. :
NYPL [Sc Rare G 86-4]

THE SLAVERY OF THE BRITISH WEST INDIA COLONIES DELINEATED.
West India slavery . Aberdeen , 1825. 24 p. ;
NYPL [Sc Rare G 86-34]

Stephenson, Anne N. Informal history of the Black people I have known in Halifax / by Anne N. Stephenson. [Halifax : A.N Stephenson], c1978. 99 p. : facsims. ; 23 cm.
Cover title: A history of the Black people I have known in Halifax.
1. Afro-Americans - North Carolina - Halifax - Genealogy. 2. Halifax (North Carolina) - Genealogy. I. Title. II. Title: History of the Black people I have known in Halifax.
NYPL [Sc D 88-1209]

Stephenson, Elie, 1944- Comme des gouttes de sang : poèmes / Elie Stephenson. Paris : Présence africaine, c1988. 95 p. ; 19 cm (Poésie) ISBN 2-7087-0509-1
I. Title.
PQ3959.2.S78 C65x 1988
NYPL [Sc C 89-156]

Steps for socio-political and religious change .
Eze, Sylvester Omumeka. [Nsukka?] 1987 (Nsukka : Chinedu Printers) 52 p. ;
NYPL [Sc C 89-53]

Stepto, Robert B. Wright, Jay. Selected poems of Jay Wright /. Princeton, N.J. , c1987. xv, 197 p. ; ISBN 0-691-06687-6 (alk. paper) : DDC 811/.54 19
PS3573.R5364 A6 1987
NYPL [JFD 87-6880]

Steptoe, John, 1950- Baby says / John Steptoe. New York : Lothrop, Lee & Shepard Books, 1988. [24] p. : col. ill. ; 22 cm. A little boy figures out how to get along with his baby brother.
SCHOMBURG CHILDREN'S COLLECTION. ISBN

0-688-07423-5   DDC [E] 19
1. Afro-American children - Juvenile fiction. I. Schomburg Children's Collection. II. Title.
PZ7.S8367 Bab 1988   NYPL [Sc D 88-1257]

Sterkenburg, J.J. Hinderink, J. (Jan) Agricultural commercialization and government policy in Africa /. London , New York , 1987. xii, 328 p. :   ISBN 0-7103-0205-3   *NYPL [Sc D 88-580]*

Stetter, Ernst. Senegal . Hamburg , 1983. xxxix, 392 p. :   ISBN 3-922887-28-7 (pbk.)   DDC 324.266/3 19
JQ3396.A91 S38 1983   NYPL [JLF 85-1341]

Stevens, Frank S. Black Australia / Frank Stevens. Sydney : Alternative Pub. Co-Operative, 1981. xviii, 248 p. : ill. ; 22 cm.
"Publications of Frank Stevens on aboriginal affairs": p. 237-242. Includes bibliographical references and index. ISBN 0-909188-43-2
1. Australian aborigines - Social conditions. 2. Australian aborigines - Economic conditions. I. Title.
NYPL [Sc D 88-1165]

Stevens, Jon Ellis. (illus) Gross, Mary Anne. (comp) Ah, man, you found me again. Boston [1972] x, 84 p. ;   ISBN 0-8070-1532-6   DDC 810/.8/09282
HQ792.U53 N53 1972   NYPL [Sc F 88-336]

Stevenson, Brenda. Forten, Charlotte L. [Journals.] The journals of Charlotte Forten Grimké /. New York , 1988. xlix, 609 p. ; ISBN 0-19-505238-2 (alk. paper)   DDC 371.1/0092/4 B 19
LA2317.F67 A3 1988   NYPL [JFC 88-2152]

Stevenson, Janet. Marian Anderson / by Janet Stevenson. Chicago : Encyclopaedia Britannica Press [1963] 189 p. : ports. ; 22 cm. (Britannica bookshelf: Great lives for young Americans) With author's autograph.
1. Anderson, Marian, 1902- Juvenile literature. 2. Singers - United States - Biography - Juvenile literature. 3. Afro-American singers - Biography - Juvenile literature. I. Title.
NYPL [Sc D 88-377]

Stevenson, Rosemary M. Index to Afro-American reference resources / compiled by Rosemary M. Stevenson. New York : Greenwood Press, 1988. xxvi, 315 p. ; 24 cm. (Bibliographies and indexes in Afro-American and African studies, 0742-6925 . no. 20) Includes indexes. Bibliography: p. [xv]-xxvi.   ISBN 0-313-24580-0 (lib. bdg. : alk. paper)   DDC 973/.0496073 19
1. Afro-Americans - Indexes. 2. Reference books - Afro-Americans - Indexes. 3. Blacks - Indexes. 4. Reference books - Blacks - Indexes. I. Title. II. Series.
Z1361.N39 S77 1988 E185
NYPL [Sc E 88-220]

Stevie Wonder /. Swenson, John. London , c1986. 160 p. :   ISBN 0-85965-076-6 (pbk.) : DDC 784.5/4/00924 B 19
ML410.W836 S9 1986b
NYPL [Sc F 88-363]

Stewart, John O. Drinkers, drummers, and decent folk : ethographic narratives of village Trinidad / John O. Stewart. Albany : State University of New York Press, c1989. xviii, 230 p. ; 23 cm. Bibliography: p. 227-230   ISBN 0-88706-829-4   DDC 306/.097298/3 19
1. Ethnology - Trinidad. 2. Trinidad - Social life and customs. I. Title.
GN564.T7 S74 1988   NYPL [Sc E 89-220]

Stewart, Rowena. A heritage discovered : Blacks in Rhode Island / by Rowena Stewart ; illustration and design by Lawrence Sykes. Providence, R.I. : Rhode Island Black Heritage Society, [1975] 39 p. : ill. ; 26 cm. Bibliography: p. 37.
1. Afro-Americans - Rhode Island - History. 2. Afro-Americans - Biography. 3. Rhode Island - History. I. Title. II. Title: Blacks in Rhode Island.
NYPL [Sc E 89-110]

Stick-in-the-mud . Ketchum, Jean, 1926- New York [c1953] unpaged :
NYPL [Sc C 88-375]

Stielow, Frederick J., 1946- Activism in American librarianship, 1962-1973 /. New York , 1987. x, 207 p. :   ISBN 0-313-24602-5 (lib. bdg. : alk. paper)   DDC 021 19
Z716.4 .A27 1987   NYPL [JFE 87-6266]

Stiles, Daniel. Ethnoarchaeology, a case-study with the Boni of Kenya [microform] / by Daniel Stiles. [Nairobi] : University of Nairobi, Dept. of History, [1979] 20 p. ; 33 cm. (Staff

seminar paper / University of Nairobi, Department of History. no. 16, 1978/79) Cover title. Bibliography: p. 16-20. Microfilm. New York: New York Public Library, 1982. 1 microfilm reel; 35 mm. (MN *ZZ-23051)
1. Ethnoarchaeology. 2. Bonis (African people). I. Series: Nairobi. University. Dept. of History. Staff seminar paper, no. 16. II. Title.
NYPL [Sc Micro R-4108 no. 36]

The still cry . Mahabir, Noor Kumar. Tacarigua, Trinidad , Ithaca, N.Y. , c1985. 191 p. :
NYPL [Sc D 88-401]

STILL, WILLIAM, 1821-1902.
Khan, Lurey. One day, Levin ... he be free. New York [1972] 231 p.   ISBN 0-525-36415-3 DDC 973.7/115 B 92
E450.S852 K45 1972   NYPL [Sc D 88-1116]

STILL, WILLIAM GRANT, 1895-
Arvey, Verna, 1910- William Grant Still. New York, 1939. 48 p.
ML410.S855 A8   NYPL [Sc D 89-3]

Stimmen der Weltkirche .
(Nr. 21) Die Bischofskonferenzen Angolas und Südafrikas zu Frieden und Gerechtigkeit in ihren Länder. Bonn , 1986. 54 p. :
NYPL [Sc D 88-929]

Stimson, James A. Carmines, Edward G. Issue evolution . Princeton, N.J. , c1989. xvii, 217 p. :   ISBN 0-691-07802-5 :   DDC 323.1/196073 19
E185.615 .C35 1989   NYPL [Sc E 89-214]

Stinetorf, Louise A. Elephant outlaw / by Louise A. Stinetorf ; pictures by Harper Johnson. Philadelphia : Lippincott, c1956. 173 p. : ill. ; 21 cm. SCHOMBURG CHILDREN'S COLLECTION.
1. Elephant hunting - Kenya - Juvenile fiction. 2. Kenya - Juvenile fiction. I. Schomburg Children's Collection. II. Title.   NYPL [Sc D 88-1167]

The sting of a queen bee /. Umegakwe, Onyedika Veronica. Onitsha , 1988. 121 p. :
NYPL [Sc C 89-11]

Stockwell, A. J. Porter, A. N. (Andrew N.) British imperial policy and decolonization, 1938-64 /. New York , 1987- v. :   ISBN 0-312-00554-7 (v. 1) :   DDC 325/.31/41 19
JV1018 .P66 1987   NYPL [Sc D 88-219]

Stolen moments /. Akeh, Afam. Lagos, Nigeria , 1988. 66 p. ;   ISBN 978-302-097-8
NYPL [Sc C 89-133]

Stolen moments /. Preston, John. Boston , 1985. 125 p. ;   ISBN 0-932870-71-6
NYPL [Sc D 88-3]

The stolen ruler. Johnson, Eric W. Philadelphia [1970] 64 p.   DDC [Fic]
PZ7.J631765 St   NYPL [Sc D 88-1114]

Stolz, Mary, 1920- Storm in the night / by Mary Stolz ; illustrated by Pat Cummings. 1st ed. New York : Harper & Row, c1988. [32] p. : col. ill. ; 23 x 29 cm. While sitting through a fearsome thunderstorm that has put the lights out, Thomas hears a story from Grandfather's boyhood, when Grandfather was afraid of thunderstorms. SCHOMBURG CHILDREN'S COLLECTION.   ISBN 0-06-025912-4 :   DDC [E] 19
1. Thunderstorms - Juvenile fiction. 2. Afro-American children - Juvenile fiction. I. Cummings, Pat. II. Schomburg Children's Collection. III. Title.
PZ7.S875854 St 1988   NYPL [Sc F 88-181]

STONE CARVING - ZIMBABWE.
Arnold, Marion I. Zimbabwean stone sculpture /. Bulawayo , 1986. xxvi, 234 p. :   ISBN 0-7974-0747-2   DDC 730/.96891 19
NB1209.Z55 A76 1986
NYPL [Sc D 89-326]

Stone, David. Too deep / David Stone. London : Pluto, 1987. vi, 114 p. ; 21 cm. (Pluto crime)   ISBN 0-7453-0136-3 (cased) :   DDC 823 19
1. South Africa - Fiction. I. Title.
PR9369.3.S   NYPL [Sc D 88-961]

Stone, Ruth M. Dried millet breaking : time, words, and song in the Woi epic of the Kpelle / Ruth M. Stone. Bloomington : Indiana University Press, c1988. xvi, 150 p., [5] p. of plates : ill. ; 25 cm. Includes index. Bibliography: p. [139]-145. ISBN 0-253-31818-1   DDC 896/.34 19
1. Epic poetry, Kpelle - History and criticism. I. Title.
PL8411.5 .S76 1988   NYPL [Sc E 88-519]

Stoneman, Colin. Zimbabwe : politics, economics, and society / Colin Stoneman and Lionel Cliffe. London ; New York : Pinter Publishers, 1989.

xxi, 210 p. : ill., maps ; 23 cm. (Marxist regimes series) Includes index. Bibliography: p. [196]-201.
ISBN 0-86187-454-4 : DDC 968.91 19
1. Zimbabwe - Politics and government. 2. Zimbabwe - Social conditions. 3. Zimbabwe - Economic conditions. I. Cliffe, Lionel. II. Title. III. Series.
JQ2929.A15 S76 1989 NYPL [Sc D 89-307]

STONEWORK, DECORATIVE. see SCULPTURE.

STORES, COOPERATIVE. see COOPERATIVE SOCIETIES.

STORIES. see LEGENDS; TALES.

Stories and songs from Sierra Leone .
(14) Koroma, Salia. The spider's web /. Freetown , 1986. 134 p. :
NYPL [Sc D 89-403]

(15) James, Frederick Bobor. The weaver birds /. Freetown [Sierra Leone] , 1986. 79 p. ;
DDC 822 19
PR9393.9.J36 W4 1986
NYPL [Sc D 89-517]

(19) Temne names and proverbs /. Freetown , 1986. 137 p. ; *NYPL [Sc D 89-489]*

(20) Rogers, Braima. Love without questions /. Freetown , 1986. 86 p. ;
NYPL [Sc D 89-415]

(21) Temne stories and songs /. Freetown, Sierra Leone , 1986. 96 p. :
NYPL [Sc D 89-427]

(23) Gbomba, Lele. The bossy wife /. Freetown , 1987. 91 p. :
NYPL [Sc D 89-429]

(26) Smith, Arthur E. E. Folktales from Freetown /. Freetown , 1987. 69 p. ;
NYPL [Sc D 89-413]

(28) Hinzen, Heribert. Koranko riddles, songs and stories /. Freetown , 1987. 69 p. :
NYPL [Sc D 89-416]

(31) Kissi stories and songs /. Freetown , 1987. 95 p. : *NYPL [Sc D 89-459]*

(32) Nyankume, Manty. The hunter /. Freetown , 1987. 68 p. :
NYPL [Sc D 89-414]

(6) Tucker, Musu Margaret. Harvest time stories /. Freetown , 1985. 55 p. :
NYPL [Sc D 89-9]

Stories from Central America.
Rohmer, Harriet. The invisible hunters . San Francisco, c1987. 32 p. : ISBN 0-89239-031-X :
DDC 398.2/08998 19
F1529.M9 R64 1987 NYPL [Sc E 88-241]

The stories Julian tells /. Cameron, Ann, 1943- New York : c1987, c1981. 71 p. : ISBN 0-394-82892-5 *NYPL [Sc C 89-93]*

Storm in the night /. Stolz, Mary, 1920- New York , c1988. [32] p. : ISBN 0-06-025912-4 :
DDC [E] 19
PZ7.S875854 St 1988 NYPL [Sc F 88-181]

Storms of the heart : an anthology of black arts & culture / edited by Kwesi Owusu. London : Camden, 1988. 308 p. : ill. ; 23 cm. Includes bibliographical references. ISBN 0-948491-30-2 (pbk) : DDC 700/.8996 19
1. Arts, Black - Great Britain. I. Owusu, Kwesi.
NYPL [Sc D 88-1364]

The story of Albert Schweitzer /. Daniel, Anita. New York , 1957. 179 p. :
NYPL [Sc D 88-379]

The story of the Ibibio Union . Udoma, Egbert Udo, Sir, 1917- Ibadan, Nigeria , 1987. xv, 590 p., [12] leaves of plates : ISBN 978-246-128-8
NYPL [Sc D 89-4]

The story of the old Calabar : a guide to the National Museum at the old Residency Calabar. [Lagos?] : National Commission for Museums and Monuments, c1986. 228 p. : ill., maps, ports. ; 22 cm.
1. Old Residency Museum (Calabar, Nigeria). 2. Calabar, Nigeria - History. I. Nigeria. National Commission for Museums and Monuments.
NYPL [Sc D 89-253]

Story telling. Baker, Augusta. Storytelling . New York , 1987. xvii, 182 p. : ISBN 0-8352-2336-1
DDC 808.06/8543 19
LB1042 .B34 1987 NYPL [Sc E 89-46]

Storytelling . Baker, Augusta. New York , 1987.

xvii, 182 p. : ISBN 0-8352-2336-1 DDC 808.06/8543 19
LB1042 .B34 1987 NYPL [Sc E 89-46]

STORYTELLING - UNITED STATES.
Baker, Augusta. Storytelling . New York , 1987. xvii, 182 p. : ISBN 0-8352-2336-1 DDC 808.06/8543 19
LB1042 .B34 1987 NYPL [Sc E 89-46]

Storyville to Harlem . Longstreet, Stephen, 1907- New Brunswick, N.J. , c1986. 211 p. : ISBN 0-8135-1174-7 : DDC 785.42/09 19
ML87 .L66 1986 NYPL [Sc G 87-4]

Stoute, Edward. Glimpses of old Barbados / by Edward A. Stoute. [Barbados] : Barbados National Trust, 1986. 156 p. ; 23 cm.
1. Barbados - History. 2. Barbados - Biography. 3. Barbados - Description and travel. I. Title.
NYPL [Sc D 88-394]

Stowe, Harriet Beecher, 1811-1896.
Dred : a tale of the great Dismal Swamp / by Harriet Beecher Stowe. Boston : Phillips, Sampson, 1856. 2 v. ; 20 cm.
1. Slavery - United States - Fiction. I. Title.
PZ3.S89 D NYPL [Sc Rare C 89-31]

Uncle Tom's cabin. Pictures and stories from Uncle Tom's cabin. Boston [c1853] [5],6-32p.
NYPL [Sc Rare C 89-1]

STOWE, HARRIET BEECHER, 1811-1896 - BIOGRAPHY - JUVENILE LITERATURE.
Jakoubek, Robert E. Harriet Beecher Stowe /. New York , c1989. 111 p. : ISBN 1-555-46680-X DDC 813/.3 B 92 19
PS2956 .J35 1989 NYPL [Sc E 89-144]

Strader, Jacob. Birney, James Gillespie, 1792-1857. Examination of the decision of the Supreme Court of the United States, in the case of Strader, Gorman and Armstrong vs. Christopher Graham . Cincinnati , 1852. iv, [1], 6-46, [1] p. ;
E450 .B57 NYPL [Sc Rare F 88-37]

Stranger in the storm. May, Charles Paul. London, New York [1972] 92 p. ISBN 0-200-71821-5 DDC [Fic]
PZ7.M4505 St NYPL [Sc D 88-1430]

Stranger to himself. Hansen, Joseph, 1923- Pretty boy dead . San Francisco , 1984. 203 p. ; ISBN 0-917342-48-8 : DDC 813/.54 19
PS3558.A513 P7 1984 NYPL [JFD 87-9537]

Strangers in Africa. Davis, Russell G. New York [1963] 149 p.
PZ7.D2993 St NYPL [Sc D 88-505]

Strasburg, Toni. Bernstein, Keith. Frontline Southern Africa /. London , c1988. x, 117 p. : ISBN 0-7470-3012-X (pbk) : DDC 968.06/3 19
HN800.A8 NYPL [Sc E 89-122]

Strategies for Nigerian development. Achebe, Chinua. The university and the leadership factor in Nigerian politics /. Enugu, Nigeria , c1988. 22 p. ; ISBN 978-226-907-7
NYPL [Sc D 89-28]

Strategy for political stability /. Nwankwo, Uchenna. Lagos , 1988. ix, 310 p. ;
NYPL [Sc D 89-539]

Strawberry dress escape /. Dragonwagon, Crescent. New York [1975] [32] p. : ISBN 0-684-13912-X : *NYPL [Sc F 88-126]*

Strawberry roan /. Lang, Don. New York , 1946. 218 p. : *NYPL [Sc D 88-646]*

Street life /. Macgoye, Marjorie Oludhe. Nairobi , 1987. 102 p. ; ISBN 996-646-362-3
NYPL [Sc C 89-4]

STREET NAMES - MICHIGAN - DETROIT.
Detroit public sites named for Blacks /. [[Detroit, Mich.] , c1987. xii, 62 p. ;
NYPL [Sc D 88-1183]

Stremplat, Axel V., 1941- Der l"andliche Arbeitskalender in der Regionalplanung Burundis / Axel V. Stremplat. Giessen : Zentrum für regionale Entwicklungsforschung der Justus-Liebig-Universität Giessen, 1984. 130 p. : ill., maps ; 21 cm. (Materialien des Zentrums für regionale Entwicklungsforschung der Justus-Liebig-Universität Giessen . Bd. 8) "Dezember 1984." Bibliography: p. [95]-100. ISBN 3-924840-08-3
1. Regional planning - Burundi - Musso-Buyogoma Region. 2. Seasonal labor - Burundi - Musso-Buyogoma Region. 3. Seasonal variations (Economics) - Burundi -

Musso-Buyogoma. I. Title. II. Series.
NYPL [Sc D 88-556]

STRESS IN CHILDREN.
Hendricks, Leo E. The effect of family size, child spacing and family density on stress in low income Black mothers and their preadolescent children [microform] /. 1977. 156 leaves. *NYPL [Sc Micro R-4684]*

Stressed out . Carn, John, 1947- Indianapolis, Ind. , c1988. vii, 148 p. ; ISBN 0-916967-03-4 :
NYPL [Sc D 89-423]

Stricklin, Joyce Occomy. Bonner, Marita, 1899-1971. Frye Street & environs . Boston , c1987. xxix, 286 p. ; ISBN 0-8070-6300-2 DDC 810/.8/0896073 19
PS3503 .O439 1987 NYPL [Sc D 88-683]

STRIKES AND LOCKOUTS - CONNECTICUT.
On strike for respect . Chicago , 1988. 94 p. ;
NYPL [Sc C 89-101]

STRIKES AND LOCKOUTS - SOUTH AFRICA.
Haarløv, Jens. Labour regulation and black workers' struggles in South Africa /. Uppsala , 1983. 80 p. ; ISBN 91-7106-213-0 (pbk). DDC 960 s 331.6/9/968 19
DT1 .N64 no. 68 HD6870.5
NYPL [JLD 87-1037]

STRIKES AND LOCKOUTS - TRINIDAD.
Craig, Susan. Smiles and blood . London , 1988. vii, 70 p., [4] p. of plates : ISBN 0-901241-81-4 (hard back)
NYPL [Sc D 89-418]

Strip-weaving traditions. Gilfoy, Peggy Stoltz. Patterns of life . Washington, D.C. , c1987. 95 p. : ISBN 0-87474-475-X (alk. paper) : DDC 746.1/4/088042 19
NK8989 .G55 1987 NYPL [Sc F 88-166]

Strong, Arline. (illus) Howell, Ruth Rea. A crack in the pavement. New York, 1970. [48] p.
DDC 500.9
PZ10.H7958 Cr NYPL [Sc E 88-154]

Strong, Kathy, 1950-
Bed and breakfast in the Caribbean / by Kathy Strong. 2nd ed. Chester, Conn. : Globe Pequot Press, c1987. ix, 278 p. : ill. ; 22 cm. Rev. ed. of: The Caribbean bed & breakfast book. c1985. "A Voyager book." Includes indexes. ISBN 0-87106-764-1 (pbk.) DDC 647/.94729 19
1. Bed and breakfast accommodations - Caribbean Area - Guide-books. I. Strong, Kathy, 1950- Caribbean bed & breakfast book. II. Title.
TX910.C25 S77 1987 NYPL [Sc D 88-1148]

Caribbean bed & breakfast book. Strong, Kathy, 1950- Bed and breakfast in the Caribbean / by Kathy Strong. 2nd ed. Chester, Conn. , c1987. ix, 278 p. : ISBN 0-87106-764-1 (pbk). DDC 647/.94729 19
TX910.C25 S77 1987 NYPL [Sc D 88-1148]

La structure bipartite de Jn 6, 26-71 . Kuzenzama, K. P. M. Kinshasa , 1987. 124 p. ;
NYPL [Sc E 88-374]

La structure foncière de la Martinique [microform] /. Desruisseaux, Jacques. [Montréal] [1975] 49 p. :
*HD459.Z8 M372 NYPL [*XME-7721]*

The struggle for black empowerment in New York City . Green, Charles (Charles St. Clair) New York , 1989. xvi, 183 p. : ISBN 0-275-92614-1 (alk. paper) : DDC 974.7/100496073 19
F128.9.N3 G74 1989 NYPL [Sc E 89-203]

The struggle for British interests in Barotseland, 1871-88 /. Sampson, Richard, 1922- [Man with a toothbrush in his hat.] Lusaka [198-?] v, 158 p. : DDC 968.94/01 19
DT963.72.W47 S25 1980z
NYPL [Sc D 88-381]

Struggle for development . Abucar, Mohamed. [S.l.] 1988 (Halifax, Nova Scotia: McCurdy Print. & Typesetting) xiv, 103 p. : ISBN 0-921201-04-4 *NYPL [Sc D 89-138]*

The struggle for South Africa . Davies, Robert H. London , Atlantic Highlands, N.J. , 1988. 2 v. : ISBN 0-86232-760-1 (v. 1) DDC 322/.0968 19
JQ1931 .D38 1988 NYPL [Sc D 88-1369]

The struggle for Swazi labor, 1890-1920. Crush, Jonathan Scott, 1953- The struggle for Swazi labour, 1890-1920 /. Kingston, Ont. , 1987.

xviii, 292 p., [9] p. of plates : ISBN
0-7735-0569-5 *NYPL [Sc E 89-150]*

The struggle for Swazi labour, 1890-1920 /.
Crush, Jonathan Scott, 1953- Kingston, Ont. ,
1987. xviii, 292 p., [9] p. of plates : ISBN
0-7735-0569-5 *NYPL [Sc E 89-150]*

Struggle in Babylon . Leech, Kenneth, 1939-
London , 1988. 253 p. ; ISBN 0-85969-577-8
(pbk) DDC 261.8/348/0941 19
NYPL [Sc D 89-176]

Strugnell, Ann.
Cameron, Ann, 1943- The stories Julian tells /.
New York : c1987, c1981. 71 p. : ISBN
0-394-82892-5 *NYPL [Sc C 89-93]*

Jensen, Virginia Allen. Sara and the door /.
Reading, Mass. , c1977. [32] p. : ISBN
0-201-03446-8 DDC [E]
PZ8.3.J425 Sar *NYPL [Sc B 89-17]*

Stubbs, Jean. Cuba : the test of time / by Jean
Stubbs. London : Latin America Bureau, 1989.
142 p. : ill., maps ; 21 cm. Bibliography: p. 142.
ISBN 0-906156-43-2 (cased) : DDC 972.91/064
19
1. Cuba - History - 1959-. I. Title.
F1788 *NYPL [Sc D 89-502]*

Stubbs, Joanna. (illus) Kaye, Geraldine, 1925-
Koto and the lagoon. New York [1969, c1967]
128 p. DDC [Fic]
PZ7.K212 Ko3 *NYPL [Sc D 89-159]*

Stuckey, Elma, 1907-
[Poems]
The collected poems of Elma Stuckey /
introduction by E.D. Hirsch, Jr. Chicago :
Precedent Pub., 1987. iv, 187 p. ; 24 cm.
ISBN 0-913750-49-2 DDC 811/.54 19
I. Hirsch, E. D. (Eric Donald), 1928-. II. Title.
PS3569.T83 A17 1987 *NYPL [Sc E 89-104]*

STUDENT AID - UNITED STATES.
Recruitment and retention of Black students in
higher education /. Lanham, MD , c1989. viii,
135 p. : ISBN 0-8191-7292-8 (alk. paper) DDC
378/.1982 19
LC2781 .R43 1989 *NYPL [Sc D 89-590]*

**STUDENT COUNSELORS - UNITED
STATES.**
Gary, Lawrence E. The delivery of mental
health services to Black children . Washington,
D.C. , 1982. vi, 111, 19 p. ;
NYPL [Sc F 88-66]

**STUDENT GUIDANCE. see PERSONNEL
SERVICE IN EDUCATION.**

**STUDENT MOVEMENTS - ETHIOPIA -
HISTORY.**
Balsvik, Randi Rønning. Haile Sellassie's
students . East Lansing, Mich. , c1985. xix, 363
p. : ill., maps ; DDC 378/.198/0963 19
LA1518.7 .B35 1985 *NYPL [Sc D 88-1403]*

**STUDENT PROTEST. see STUDENT
MOVEMENTS.**

**STUDENT UNREST. see STUDENT
MOVEMENTS.**

STUDENTS, INTERCHANCE OF.
Kullas, Ulrike. Lernen von der Dritten Welt? .
Saarbrücken , Fort Lauderdale , 1982. 174 p. :
ISBN 3-88156-233-8 *NYPL [Sc D 89-339]*

STUDENTS - NIGERIA - FICTION.
Agburum, Ezenwa. Broken graduate /. Orlu,
Imo State, Nigeria , 1986. 96 p. ;
NYPL [Sc C 88-193]

STUDENTS - PASTORAL COUNSELING OF.
Kiriswa, Benjamin. Christian counselling for
students /. Eldoret, Kenya , 1988. vi, 81 p. ;
NYPL [Sc D 89-350]

**STUDENTS - PERSONNEL WORK. see
PERSONNEL SERVICE IN EDUCATION.**

**STUDENTS, TRANSFER OF - UNITED
STATES.**
Richardson, Richard C. Fostering minority
access and achievement in higher education .
San Francisco, Calif. , c1987. xviii, 244 p. ;
ISBN 1-555-42053-2 (alk. paper) DDC 378/.052
19
LC3727 .R53 1987 *NYPL [Sc E 88-472]*

Studer, Elena F. S. de. La trata de negros en el
Río de la Plata durante el siglo XVIII / Elena
F.S. de Studer. Bs. As. [i.e. Buenos Aires] :
Libros de Hispanoamérica, [1984] 378 p., [27]
leaves of plates (some folded) : facsims., maps ;

23 cm. Facsims., maps, and tables inserted. Includes
index. Bibliography: p. 355-360. ISBN 950-9138-08-8
*1. Slavery - Rio de la Plata Region (Argentina and
Uruguay) - History - 18th century. 2. Slave-trade - Rio
de la Plata Region (Argentina and Uruguay) - History -
18th century. 3. Rio de la Plata Region (Argentina and
Uruguay) - History. I. Title.*
HT1123.R5 S78 1984 *NYPL [Sc E 87-419]*

**Studia Instituti Missiologici Societatis Verbi
Divini, 0562-2816 .**
(Nr. 38) Beken, Alain van der, 1935-
L'Evangile en Afrique, vécu et commenté par
des Bayaka /. Nettetal [Germany] , 1986. 328
p. ; ISBN 3-87787-204-2 :
BV3630.B69 B45 1986 *NYPL [Sc E 88-339]*

Studia linguarum Africae orientalis .
(Bd. 2) Haberland, Eike. Ibaddo ka-Ba'iso .
Heidelberg , 1988. 184 p. ; ISBN 3-533-04014-3
NYPL [Sc D 89-552]

(Bd. 3) Lamberti, Marcello. Kuliak and
Cushitic . Heidelberg , 1988. 157 p. :
NYPL [Sc D 89-330]

Studien über Asien, Afrika und Lateinamerika.
(Bd. 15) African studies. Berlin, 1973. xi, 400
p. *NYPL [JLK 73-249 Bd. 15]*

**Studien zur integrierten ländlichen Entwicklung,
0177-2503 .**
(6) Johnny, Michael. Informal credit for
integrated rural development in Sierra Leone /.
Hamburg , 1985. xviii, 212 p. : ISBN
3-87895-274-X (pbk.)
HG2146.5.S5 J63x 1985
NYPL [Sc D 88-766]

Studien zur Kulturkunde.
(Bd. 61) Lange, Werner J., 1946- History of the
Southern Gonga (Southwestern Ethiopia) /.
Wiesbaden , 1982. xvi, 348 p., [12] p. of
plates : ISBN 3-515-03399-8 (pbk.) : DDC
306/.08996 19
DT380.4.G66 L36 1982
NYPL [Sc E 88-379]

(Bd. 77) Jones, Adam. Brandenburg sources for
West African history, 1680-1700 /. Stuttgart ,
1985. xiv, 348 p., [14] p. of plates : ISBN
3-515-04315-2 *NYPL [Sc E 88-84]*

Studies in African political economy.
SADCC . Tokyo, Japan : London ; xi, 256 p. ;
ISBN 0-86232-748-2 : DDC 337.1/68 19
HC900 .S23 1987 *NYPL [Sc D 89-50]*

Studies in Black American literature .
(v. 3) Black feminist criticism and critical
theory /. Greenwood, Fla. , c1988. iii, 202 p. ;
ISBN 0-913283-25-8
NYPL [Sc D 88-1394]

Studies in Caribbean literature.
Ormerod, Beverley, 1937- An introduction to
the French Caribbean novel /. London ,
Portsmouth, N.H., USA , 1985. 152 p. ; ISBN
0-435-91839-7 (pbk.) DDC 843 19
PQ3944 .O76 1985 *NYPL [Sc D 88-1267]*

Studies in environment and history.
Harms, Robert. Games against nature .
Cambridge [Cambridgeshire] , New York ,
1987. xi, 276 p. : ISBN 0-521-34373-9 DDC
967/.24 19
DT546.245.N86 H37 1987
NYPL [Sc E 88-192]

Studies in jazz .
(no. 4) Brown, Scott E., 1960- James P.
Johnson . Metuchen, N.J. , 1986. viii, 500 p.,
[12] p. of plates : ISBN 0-8108-1887-6 DDC
786.1/092/4 B 19
ML417.J62 B76 1986 *NYPL [Sc D 88-1435]*

Studies in research.
Black youth futures . Leicester , 1987. ii, 113
p. : ISBN 0-86155-106-0 (pbk) : DDC
331.3/46/0941 19
HD8398 *NYPL [Sc D 89-175]*

Studies in Saramaccan language structure /
Mervyn C. Alleyne, editor. [Amsterdam] :
ATW, Universiteit van Amsterdam, 1987. viii,
112 p. ; 21 cm. (Caribbean culture studies . 2)
Includes bibliographies. ISBN 976-410-004-X
*1. Saramaccan laguages - Syntax. 2. Saramaccan
languages - Morphophonemics. I. Alleyne, Mervyn C.
II. Title.*
NYPL [Sc D 88-554]

Studies in the African novel / edited by Samuel
Omo Asein and Albert Olu Ashaolu. [Ibadan] :
Ibadan University Press, [1985?] viii, 258 p. ;
22 cm. (Modern essays on African literature . v. 1)

Ibadan literature series ; 4 Includes bibliographical
references and index.
*1. African fiction (English) - History and criticism. I.
Asein, S. O. II. Ashaolu, Albert Olu. III. Series.*
NYPL [Sc D 88-1316]

Studies of fishing on Lake Kariba /. Bouedillon,
M. F. C. [Harare] , 1985. 185 p. :
NYPL [Sc D 88-875]

Studio Museum in Harlem. Pindell, Howardena,
1943- Howardena Pindell . New York, NY
(144 W. 125th St., New York 10027) , c1986.
24 p. : DDC 709/.2/4 19
N6537.P49 A4 1986 *NYPL [Sc F 88-270]*

**A study of Negro periodicals in the United
States /.** Knox, Ellis Oneal. 1928. 77 leaves ;
NYPL [Sc F 88-264]

**A study of the inclusion of Black administrators
in American medical schools, 1968-78, and
their perception of their roles [microform] /.**
Logan, Harold G. 1982. v, 90 leaves ;
NYPL [Sc Micro R-4793]

**A study of the portrayal of Black Americans in
the dramatic literature of the United States
[microform] /.** Brenowitz, Ruth. 1969. 92
leaves. *NYPL [Sc Micro R-4691]*

**A study of the transition from white to Black
presidents at three selected schools founded by
the American Missionary Association
[microform] /.** Lundy, Harold Wayne. 1978.
676 leaves. *NYPL [Sc Micro R-4216]*

Stundenblätter Hansberry " A raisin in the sun"
/. Felber, Monika. Stuttgard , 1986. 85 p. :
ISBN 3-12-925163-4 *NYPL [Sc D 88-631]*

Stuttgarter geographische Studien, 0343-7906 .
(Bd. 95 95) Desertification in extremely arid
environments /. [Stuttgart] , 1980. 203 p., [1]
folded leaf of plates : ISBN 3-88028-095-9 (pbk.)
DDC 551.4 19
GB611 .D44 *NYPL [JFL 74-410 Bd. 95]*

Style, Colin. Mambo book of Zimbabwean Verse
in English /. Gweru, Zimbabwe , c986. xxix,
417 p. ; ISBN 0-86922-367-4 (pbk.)
NYPL [JFD 88-10986]

STYLE IN DRESS. see COSTUME.

Style, O-lan. Mambo book of Zimbabwean Verse
in English /. Gweru, Zimbabwe , c986. xxix,
417 p. ; ISBN 0-86922-367-4 (pbk.)
NYPL [JFD 88-10986]

**Stylistic boundaries among mobile
hunter-foragers /.** Sampson, C. Garth (Clavil
Garth)- 1941- Washington , c1988. 186 p. :
ISBN 0-87474-838-0 DDC 968/.004961 19
DT764.B8 S24 1988 *NYPL [Sc F 89-97]*

**Subject guide to research papers held by the
University of Zambia Library, Special
Collections Division (Lusaka Campus) /.**
University of Zambia. Library. Special
Collections Division. Lusaka, Zambia , 1986. v,
423 p. ; DDC 016.96894 19
Z5055.Z334 U558 1986 AS623.L84
NYPL [Sc F 88-353]

Sub-Saharan Africa . Gannon, Edmund J.
Washington , c1978. 185 p. :
NYPL [JFD 84-783]

Sub-Saharan African films and filmmakers .
Schmidt, Nancy J. London , 1988. 401 p. ;
ISBN 0-905450-32-9 : DDC 016.79143/096 19
NYPL [Sc D 89-196]

Subsistence and change . Massey, Garth.
Boulder , 1987. xvii, 238 p. : ISBN
0-8133-7294-1 (alk. paper) : DDC
338.1/0967/73 19
DT402.4.R35 M37 1987
NYPL [Sc D 88-298]

SUBSISTENCE ECONOMY - SOMALIA.
Massey, Garth. Subsistence and change .
Boulder , 1987. xvii, 238 p. : ISBN
0-8133-7294-1 (alk. paper) : DDC
338.1/0967/73 19
DT402.4.R35 M37 1987
NYPL [Sc D 88-298]

Substitutiv und Possessiv im Bantu /. Stappers,
Leo. Berlin [1986] xix, 223 p. : ISBN
3-496-00877-6 DDC 496/.3 19
PL8025.1 .S73 1986 *NYPL [Sc E 88-360]*

**Succession conflict within the Church of the
Nazarites, iBandla zamaNazaretha /.**
Oosthuizen, G. C. (Gerhardus Cornelis) Durban

[South Africa] [1981] 71 p. ; ISBN
0-949947-43-1 (pbk.) DDC 289.9 19
BX7068.7.Z5 O56 1981
NYPL [Sc F 87-351]

Such, David Glen. Music, metaphor and values
among avant-garde jazz musicians living in New
York City / by David Glen Such. 1985. ix, 307
leaves. : music ; 28 cm. Thesis(Ph. D.)--University
of California, Los Angeles, 1985. Typescript.
Bibliography: leaves. 287-307.
*1. Jazz musicians - New York (N.Y.). 2. Jazz music -
New York (N.Y.). I. Title.* *NYPL [Sc F 88-284]*

Such was the season . Major, Clarence. San
Francisco , c1987. 213 p. ; ISBN 0-916515-20-6 :
DDC 813/.54 19
PS3563.A39 S8 1987 *NYPL [Sc D 88-744]*

Suckale-Redlefsen, Gude. Mauritius, der heilige
Mohr / Gude Suckale-Redlefsen, unter
Mitarbeit von Robert Suckale ; Vorwort von
Ladislas Bugner ; [englische Übersetzung von
Vorwort und Einleitung von Genoveva Nitz] =
The Black Saint Maurice / Gude
Suckale-Redlefsen ; foreword by Ladislas Bugner ;
[English translation of the foreword and
introduction by Genoveva Nitz]. Houston :
Menil Foundation ; München : Schnell &
Steiner, c1987. 295 p. : ill. (some col.) ; 23 cm.
German and English. Includes index. Bibliography: p.
286-287. ISBN 0-939594-03-X DDC
704.9/4863/094 19
*1. Maurice, Saint, d. ca. 287 - Art. 2. Maurice, Saint, d.
ca. 287 - Cult - Europe. 3. Maurice, Saint, d. ca. 287 -
Art - Catalogs. 4. Blacks in art. 5. Art, European -
Catalogs. I. Suckale, Robert. II. Title. III. Title: Black
Saint Maurice.*
N8080.M38 S9 1987 *NYPL [Sc D 88-1357]*

Suckale, Robert. Suckale-Redlefsen, Gude.
Mauritius, der heilige Mohr /. Houston ,
München , c1987. 295 p. : ISBN 0-939594-03-X
DDC 704.9/4863/094 19
N8080.M38 S9 1987 *NYPL [Sc D 88-1357]*

Der Sudan : zwischen Schwarz-Afrika und der
arabischen Welt : Tagung, 22-24. Juni 1984,
Schlösschen Schönburg, Hofgeismar.
Hofgeismar : Evangelische Akademie von
Kurhessen-Waldeck, [1985?] 112 p. ; 21 cm.
*1. Sudan - Social conditions - Congresses. 2. Sudan -
Politics and government - Congresses. 3. Sudan -
Economic conditions - Congresses. I. Evangelische
Akademie Hofgeismar.* *NYPL [Sc D 88-737]*

SUDAN - ARMED FORCES - HISTORY.
Muhammad, Ahmad al-'Awad. Sudan Defence
Force . [Khartoum? , 198-?]. ([Khartoum?] :
Military Printing Press) 118 p. :
NYPL [Sc E 88-261]

Sudan Defence Force . Muhammad, Ahmad
al-'Awad. [Khartoum? , 198-?]. ([Khartoum?] :
Military Printing Press) 118 p. :
NYPL [Sc E 88-261]

SUDAN. DEFENCE FORCE - HISTORY.
Muhammad, Ahmad al-'Awad. Sudan Defence
Force . [Khartoum? , 198-?]. ([Khartoum?] :
Military Printing Press) 118 p. :
NYPL [Sc E 88-261]

SUDAN - ECONOMIC CONDITIONS.
Messaoud, Jir, 1938- Soudan . Paris , c1987.
160 p., [12] p. of plates : ISBN 2-7087-0491-5
NYPL [Sc D 88-1008]

**SUDAN - ECONOMIC CONDITIONS -
CONGRESSES.**
Der Sudan . Hofgeismar [1985?] 112 p. ;
NYPL [Sc D 88-737]

Sudan, Egyptian. see Sudan.

**SUDAN - EMIGRATION AND
IMMIGRATION.**
Bulcha, Mekuria. Flight and integration .
Uppsala, Sweden , c1988. 256 p. : ISBN
91-7106-279-3 *NYPL [Sc E 88-581]*

**Sudan - Government. see Sudan - Politics and
government.**

SUDAN - HISTORY.
Messaoud, Jir, 1938- Soudan . Paris , c1987.
160 p., [12] p. of plates : ISBN 2-7087-0491-5
NYPL [Sc D 88-1008]

SUDAN - HISTORY - 1899-1956.
Abdin, Hasan. Early Sudanese nationalism,
1919-1925 /. [Khartoum?] [1985?] iv, 167 p. :
DDC 962.4/03 19
DT156.7 .A23 1985 *NYPL [Sc E 88-335]*

Sudan Majlis al-Sha'b. al-Numayrī, Ja'far
Muḥammad. Text of address delivered by His
Excellency President Gaafar Mohamed
Nimeiry, at the opening sitting of the first
session of the second People's Assembly,
Khartoum, 24th May, 1974 [microform]
[Khartoum] [1974] 24 p., [1] p. of plates :
NYPL [Sc Micro F-11007]

Sudan. Maktab al-Isti'lamat al-Markazi. Basic
facts about the southern provinces of The
Sudan. Khartoum : Central Office of
Information, 1964. 114 p., [1] folded leaf :
map ; 21 cm. Includes bibliographical footnotes.
I. Title. *NYPL [Sc D 88-449]*

**SUDAN PEOPLE'S LIBERATION
MOVEMENT.**
Garang, John, 1945- John Garang speaks /.
London , New York , 1987. xii, 147 p. ; ISBN
0-7103-0268-1 *NYPL [Sc D 88-418]*

**SUDAN - POLITICS AND GOVERNMENT -
ADDRESSES, ESSAYS, LECTURES.**
al-Numayrī, Ja'far Muḥammad. Text of address
delivered by His Excellency President Gaafar
Mohamed Nimeiry, at the opening sitting of the
first session of the second People's Assembly,
Khartoum, 24th May, 1974 [microform]
[Khartoum] [1974] 24 p., [1] p. of plates :
NYPL [Sc Micro F-11007]

**SUDAN - POLITICS AND GOVERNMENT -
CONGRESSES.**
Der Sudan . Hofgeismar [1985?] 112 p. ;
NYPL [Sc D 88-737]

SUDAN (REGION) - CONGRESSES.
International Conference on the Central Bilad
al-Sudan Tradition and Adaptation (3rd : 1977 :
Khartum, Sudan) Third International
Conference on the Central Bilad al-Sudan
Tradition and Adaptation [microform]
[Khartum] [1977] 25, 13 p. ;
NYPL [Sc Micro F-10980]

SUDAN - SOCIAL CONDITIONS.
Folklore and National Development Symposium
(1981 : Khartoum, Sudan) Folklore and
development in the Sudan . Khartoum , 1985.
272 p. :
GR355.8 .F65 1981 *NYPL [Sc E 88-333]*

**SUDAN - SOCIAL CONDITIONS -
CONGRESSES.**
Der Sudan . Hofgeismar [1985?] 112 p. ;
NYPL [Sc D 88-737]

SUDAN - SOCIAL LIFE AND CUSTOMS.
Folklore and National Development Symposium
(1981 : Khartoum, Sudan) Folklore and
development in the Sudan . Khartoum , 1985.
272 p. :
GR355.8 .F65 1981 *NYPL [Sc E 88-333]*

Sudawa, Adamu Sandalo. Zuma (ga zaki, ga
harbi) / Adamu Sandalo Sudawa. Kano :
Triumph Pub. Co., 1987. 56 p. : ill. ; 23 cm.
ISBN 978-18-8000-7
1. Hausa language - Texts. I. Title.
NYPL [Sc D 88-1292]

Südafrika, SWA/Namibia . Fries, Marianne.
Frankfurt [am Main] , 1987. 550 p. : ISBN
3-87936-153-3 *NYPL [Sc B 88-18]*

Südafrika - Widerstand und Befreiungskampf :
Darstellung und Dokumente : mit einem
Anhang zur Rolle der Bundesrepublik /
[herausgegeben von] Rainer Falk.2.
durchgesehene und verb. Aufl. Köln :
Pahl-Rugenstein, 1987, c1986. 286 p. : map ;
19 cm. (Serie, Dritte Welt) Kleine Bibliothek
Bibliography: p. 285-286. ISBN 3-7609-1023-8
*1. National liberation movements - South Africa. 2.
Anti-apartheid movement - South Africa. I. Falk,
Rainer. II. Title. III. Series.* *NYPL [Sc C 88-190]*

Südafrikas schwieriger Weg : Erfahrungen einer
Studienreise / Herausgeber, Michael Brüne ...
[et al.]. Krefeld : SINUS, c1988. 167 p., [8] p.
of plates : ill. ; 21 cm. Bibliography: p. 163-165.
ISBN 3-88289-803-8
1. Apartheid - South Africa. I. Brüne, Michael.
NYPL [Sc D 89-548]

Sugar and modern slavery . Plant, Roger.
London , Atlantic Highlands, N.J. , c1987. xiv,
177 p. : ISBN 0-86232-572-2 : DDC
331.7/6361/097293 19
HD8039.S852 D657 1987
NYPL [Sc D 87-1240]

SUGAR BOUNTIES. see SUGAR TRADE.

SUGAR TRADE - HAITI - HISTORY.
Cauna, Jacques, 1948- Au temps des isles à
sucre . Paris , c1987. 285 p., [16] p. of plates :
ISBN 2-86537-186-5 *NYPL [Sc E 88-492]*

SUGAR TRADE - SURINAM - HISTORY.
Lamur, H. E. The production of sugar and the
reproduction of slaves at Vossenburg
(Suriname), 1705-1863 /. Amsterdam, The
Netherlands . 164 p. : ISBN *NYPL [Sc D 88-555]*

SUGAR TRADE - WEST INDIES, BRITISH.
An Address to Her Royal Highness the
Dutchess of York, against the use of sugar.
[London?] 1792. 20 p. ;
NYPL [Sc Rare G 86-31]

**SUGAR WORKERS - DOMINICAN
REPUBLIC.**
Plant, Roger. Sugar and modern slavery .
London , Atlantic Highlands, N.J. , c1987. xiv,
177 p. : ISBN 0-86232-572-2 : DDC
331.7/6361/097293 19
HD8039.S852 D657 1987
NYPL [Sc D 87-1240]

**SUGARCANE INDUSTRY - DOMINICAN
REPUBLIC.**
Plant, Roger. Sugar and modern slavery .
London , Atlantic Highlands, N.J. , c1987. xiv,
177 p. : ISBN 0-86232-572-2 : DDC
331.7/6361/097293 19
HD8039.S852 D657 1987
NYPL [Sc D 87-1240]

Suggs, Henry Lewis. P.B. Young, newspaperman :
race, politics, and journalism in the New South,
1910-1962 / Henry Lewis Suggs.
Charlottesville : University Press of Virginia,
1988. xxii, 254 p. : ill. ; 24 cm. Includes index.
Bibliography: p. 231-233. ISBN 0-8139-1178-8 DDC
070.4/1/0924 B 19
*1. Young, P. B. (Plummer Bernard), d. 1962. 2. Journal
and guide - History. 3. Afro-American journalists -
United States - Biography. 4. Afro-Americans -
Virginia - Norfolk - Social conditions. 5. Civil rights
movements - Virginia - Norfolk. 6. Norfolk (Virginia) -
Biography. 7. Norfolk (Virginia) - Race relations. I.
Title.*
PN4874.Y59 S84 1988 *NYPL [JFE 89-97]*

Sula /. Morrison, Toni. New York [1987],
c1973. 174 p. ; ISBN 0-452-26010-8 DDC
813/.54 19
PS3563.O8749 S8 1987
NYPL [Sc D 88-633]

Suliman, Hassan Sayed. The nationalist
movements in the Maghrib : a comparative
approach / Hassan Sayed Suliman. Uppsala :
Scandinavian Institute of African Studies, 1987.
87 p. ; 25 cm. (Scandinavian Institute of African
Studies. Research report. no. 78) Includes
bibliographical references. ISBN 91-7106-266-1
*1. National liberation movements - Tunisia. 2. National
liberation movements - Algeria. 3. National liberation
movements - Morocco. I. Series: Research report
(Nordiska Afrikainstitutet) , no. 78. II. Title.*
NYPL [Sc E 88-202]

Sullivan, Gerard. From school--to work : report
on the School Leaver Tracer Project / Gerard
Sullivan. Oxford : Cotswold Press, c1981. xvi,
190 p. : ill. ; 27 cm. At head of title: Swaziland
Government, Ministry of Education, Mbabane, March
1981. Includes bibliographical references. DDC
373.12/913/096813 19
*1. Dropouts - Swaziland. 2. Education - Economic
aspects - Swaziland. 3. Industry and education -
Swaziland. I. Swaziland. Ministry of Education. II.
Title.*
LC145.S78 S94 1981 *NYPL [Sc F 87-331]*

Sullivan, Sarah A. The animals talk to Gussie /
story by Sarah A. Sullivan, and Zoa C.
Sullivan ; illustrated by Emma Lossen. [S.l. :
s.n., c1951 (wilmington, N.C. : Garey-Mintz
Print.) 28 p. : col. ill. ; 28 cm. SCHOMBURG
CHILDREN'S COLLECTION.
*1. Children and animals - Juvenile poetry. I. Sullivan,
Zoa C. II. Schomburg Children's Collection. III. Title.*
NYPL [Sc F 89-2]

Sullivan, Zoa C. Sullivan, Sarah A. The animals
talk to Gussie /. [S.l. , c1951 (wilmington,
N.C. : Garey-Mintz Print.) 28 p. :
NYPL [Sc F 89-2]

SULTANS - CHAD - BIOGRAPHY.
Berre, Henri, 1911-1984. Sultans dadjo du Sila,
Tchad /. Paris , 1985. xiv, 119 p. : ISBN

2-222-03641-0 :   DDC 967/.4302/0922 B 19
DT546.472 .B47 1985   NYPL [Sc D 87-1421]

Sultans dadjo du Sila, Tchad /. Berre, Henri,
1911-1984. Paris , 1985. xiv, 119 p. :   ISBN
2-222-03641-0 :   DDC 967/.4302/0922 B 19
DT546.472 .B47 1985   NYPL [Sc D 87-1421]

The sultan's fool and other North African tales /.
Gilstrap, Robert. New York , c1958. 95 p. :
ISBN 931-40-0118-0   *NYPL [Sc E 88-548]*

Summary of old Arabics manuscripts. Résumés de
vieux manuscrits arabes. Zanzibar [Tanzania] ,
1981. x, 50 leaves ;   *NYPL [Sc B 88-10]*

A summer adventure /. Lewis, Richard W. New
York , c1962. 105 p. :   *NYPL [Sc D 89-405]*

Summer growing time. Kelley, Sally. New York
[1971] 125 p.   ISBN 0-670-68172-5   DDC [Fic]
PZ7.K2818 Su   NYPL [Sc D 89-88]

Summer Institute of Linguistics.
Publications in linguistics.
(publication no. 82) Malou, Job. Dinka vowel
system /. Dallas, TX , Arlington , 1988. x,
89 p. :   ISBN 0-88312-008-9
NYPL [Sc D 88-1445]

Sumner, Charles, 1811-1874. "He, being dead, yet
speaketh" : Charles Sumner's explanation in
reply to an assault : a speech prepared for the
United States Senate, March, 1871. Boston :
Lee and Shepard ; New York : C.T.
Dillingham, 1878. 29, 16 p. ; 19 cm. With: The
complete works of Charles Sumner, publisher's
advertisement. Running title: Personal relations with the
President and Secretary of State.
*1. Sumner, Charles, 1811-1874. 2. Grant, Ulysses S.
(Ulysses Simpson), 1822-1885. 3. Fish, Hamilton,
1808-1893. 4. Dominican Republic - Annexation to the
United States. I. Title. II. Title: Personal relations with
the President and Secretary of State. III. Title:
Explanation in reply to an assault.*
NYPL [Sc Rare C 89-4]

SUMNER, CHARLES, 1811-1874.
Sumner, Charles, 1811-1874. "He, being dead,
yet speaketh" . Boston , New York , 1878. 29,
16 p. ;   *NYPL [Sc Rare C 89-4]*

Sumner, Claude. The source of African
philosophy : the Ethiopian philosophy of man /
Claude Sumner. Stuttgart : F. Steiner Verlag
Wiesbaden, 1986. 153 p. : ill. ; 25 cm.
(Äthiopistische Forschungen. Bd. 20) Includes index.
Bibliography: p. [147]-148. ISBN 3-515-04438-8
DDC 199/.63 19
1. Philosophy, Ethiopian. I. Title. II. Series.
B5409.M27 S86 1986   NYPL [Sc E 89-260]

Sun records . Escott, Colin. Vollersode, W.
Germany , c1987. 240 p. :   ISBN 3-924787-09-3
(pbk.)   *NYPL [Sc D 89-243]*

SUN RECORDS.
Escott, Colin. Sun records . Vollersode, W.
Germany , c1987. 240 p. :   ISBN 3-924787-09-3
(pbk.)   *NYPL [Sc D 89-243]*

SUNDAR SINGH, 1889-1929.
Wawili, Rafiki. Sadhu Sundar Singh . London ,
1949. 48 p. ;   *NYPL [Sc C 89-111]*

SUNY series in Afro-American studies.
Walter, John C. (John Christopher), 1933- The
Harlem Fox . Albany, N.Y. , c1989. xv, 287
p. :   ISBN 0-88706-756-5   DDC 974.7/1043/0924 B
19
F128.5.J72 W35 1988   NYPL [Sc E 89-107]

Walters, Ronald W. Black presidential politics
in America . Albany , c1988. xvi, 255 p.   ISBN
0-88706-546-5   DDC 324.6/2/08996073 19
JK1924 .W34 1987   NYPL [Sc E 88-283]

Walton, Hanes, 1941- When the marching
stopped . Albany , c1988. xxiv, 263 p. :   ISBN
0-88706-687-9   DDC 353.0081/1 19
E185.615 .W325 1988   NYPL [Sc E 89-10]

Super powers in the Horn of Africa /. Sauldie,
Madan M. New York , c1987. ix, 252 p. ;
ISBN 0-86590-092-2   DDC 320.960 19
DT367.8 .S28 1987   NYPL [Sc D 89-488]

Supersticiones y buenos consejos /. Cabrera,
Lydia. Miami, Fla. , 1987. 62 p. :   ISBN
0-89729-433-5   *NYPL [Sc D 89-522]*

Supplement à la grammaire lomongo /. Hulstaert,
G. Mbandaka, Zaire , 1988. 127 p. ;
NYPL [Sc D 89-39]

Suppressing the Ku Klux Klan . Swinney,
Everette, 1923- New York , 1987. ix, 360 p. ;

ISBN 0-8240-8297-4 (alk. paper) :   DDC
342.73/0873 347.302873 19
KF4757 .S93 1987   NYPL [Sc D 88-653]

SUPREMACY OF LAW. see RULE OF LAW.

Sur terre et sur l'eau . Le Roy, Alexandre, abp.,
1854-1938. Tours , 1894. 350 p. :
NYPL [Sc F 88-13]

Surafrica. Madrid : IEPALA : Fundamentos,
1986. 160 p. : maps ; 21 cm. (Africa
internacional . 2) Bibliography: p. 156-160.
CONTENTS. -- Suráfrica, del siglo XVI as apartheid /
Ferrán Iniesta.--Historia del A.N.C. / Antonio
Santamaría.--Economía y apartheid / Rafael
Dobado.--El desarollo surafricano / Antonio
Santamaría.--El apartheid como factor desestabilizador
en Africa austral / Antoni Castel.-- / Juan
Bosch.--Documentos.   ISBN 84-245-0469-0;
84-85436-39-3
1. Apartheid - South Africa. I. Series.
NYPL [Sc D 88-296]

Suret-Canale, Jean.
[Essais d'histoire africaine. English]
Essays on African history : from the slave
trade to neocolonialism / Jean Suret-Canale ;
with a preface by Basil Davidson ; translated
from the French by Christopher Hurst.
London : Hurst, 1988. 242 p. : map ; 23 cm.
Includes index. Translation of: Essais d'histoire
africaine. Bibliography: p. 233-238.   ISBN
0-905838-43-2 :   DDC 960/.3 19
1. Africa, Sub-Saharan - History. I. Title.
DT29   NYPL [Sc D 88-1314]

**SURINAAMS NATIONAAL
BEVRIJDINGSLEGER.**
Helman, Albert. Blijf even staan! .
[Netherlands?] c1987. 41 p. :
NYPL [Sc D 88-1039]

SURINAM - FICTION.
Loy, Harry Jong, 1901-1984. Fosten tori /.
[Paramaribo] , c1987. v. :   ISBN 999-14-1010-4
NYPL [Sc D 88-921]

SURINAM - HISTORY - 1950-
Ooft, Benny Ch. Suriname, 10 jaar republiek /.
Nieuwegein , Paramaribo , 1985. 145 p. :   ISBN
90-71138-05-4   *NYPL [Sc E 88-361]*

Surinam. Nationale Voorlichtings Dienst.
Caribbean Desk. Suriname, een hoeksteen .
Paramaribo, Suriname [1985] iv [i.e. vi], iv [i.e.
vi], 108 p. :   *NYPL [Sc D 88-1124]*

**SURINAM - POLITICS AND
GOVERNMENT - 1950-**
Helman, Albert. Blijf even staan! .
[Netherlands?] c1987. 41 p. :
NYPL [Sc D 88-1039]

Suriname. see Suriname.

Suriname, a corner stone. Suriname, een
hoeksteen . Paramaribo, Suriname [1985] iv
[i.e. vi], iv [i.e. vi], 108 p. :
NYPL [Sc D 88-1124]

Suriname, een hoeksteen : een keiharde spier op
een schouder van ons Amerika. Paramaribo,
Suriname : Nationale Voorlichtings Dienst,
Caribbean Desk, [1985] iv [i.e. vi], iv [i.e. vi],
108 p. : ill., map ; 21 cm. Cover title: Suriname, a
corner stone. Dutch and English. Bibliography: p.
106-108.
*I. Surinam. Nationale Voorlichtings Dienst. Caribbean
Desk. II. Title: Suriname, a corner stone.*
NYPL [Sc D 88-1124]

Suriname, tien jaar republiek. Ooft, Benny Ch.
Suriname, 10 jaar republiek /. Nieuwegein ,
Paramaribo , 1985. 145 p. :   ISBN 90-71138-05-4
NYPL [Sc E 88-361]

Suriname, 10 jaar republiek /. Ooft, Benny Ch.
Nieuwegein , Paramaribo , 1985. 145 p. :   ISBN
90-71138-05-4   *NYPL [Sc E 88-361]*

**SURINAMESE - NETHERLANDS - SOCIAL
CONDITIONS.**
Lost illusions . London , 1988. x, 316 p. :
ISBN 0-415-00628-7
NYPL [Sc D 88-1300]

SURNAMES. see NAMES, PERSONAL.

**A survey of handicrafts in North East District,
1980** . Mackenzie, Bob. Gaborone , 1980. 61
p. :   *NYPL [Sc F 88-2]*

**A survey of preservation of library collections in
Kenya** /. Khayundi, Festus E. [Nairobi?] 1988.
iii, 36 leaves ;   *NYPL [Sc F 89-142]*

**SURVEYS, ECONOMIC. see ECONOMIC
SURVEYS.**

**SURVIVAL (HUMAN ECOLOGY) see
HUMAN ECOLOGY.**

Survival of the Black family . Jewell, K. Sue.
New York , 1988. x, 197 p. :   ISBN
0-275-92985-X (alk. paper)   DDC
306.8/5/08996073 19
HQ536 .J48 1988   NYPL [Sc E 89-153]

'Sus', a report on the Vagrancy Act 1824 /.
Demuth, Clare. London , 1978. 62 p. :
NYPL [Sc D 88-1174]

"Susanna," "Jeanie," and "The old folks at home" .
Austin, William W. Urbana [Ill.] , 1987. xxiv,
422 p. ;   ISBN 0-252-01476-6   DDC 784.5/0092/4
19
ML410.F78 A9 1987   NYPL [Sc E 88-465]

Sutton, Felix. Big game hunter : Carl Akeley / by
Felix Sutton. New York : Julian Messner, 1960.
192 p. ; 22 cm. Bibliography: p. 187-188.
*1. Akeley, Carl Ethan, 1864-1926 - Juvenile literature.
2. Naturalists - Africa - Biography - Juvenile literature.
3. Naturalists - United States - Biography - Juvenile
literature. I. Title.   NYPL [Sc D 88-659]*

Svoboda, Terese. Cleaned the crocodile's teeth .
Greenfield Center, N.Y. , c1985. ix, 104 p. :
ISBN 0-912678-63-1 (pbk.) :   DDC 784.4/9669
19
PL8576.N47 C54 1985   NYPL [Sc D 88-743]

SWA Namibia today / [text (Afrikaans), Rianne
Selle (editor), Marlien de Beer ; translation,
Amy Schoeman]. English [ed.] Windhoek :
Dept. of Governmental Affairs, Section Liaison
Services, 1988. 128 p. : col. ill. ; 21 cm. Cover
title. "March 1988."
*I. Selle, Rianne. II. De Beer, Marlien. III. Title:
Namibia today.   NYPL [Sc D 88-1359]*

**SWAHILI LANGUAGE - CONVERSATION
AND PHRASE BOOKS - ENGLISH.**
Leonard, Robert. Swahili phrasebook /. Yarra
Vic, Australia , Berkeley, CA , 1988, c1987.
101 p. :   ISBN 0-86442-025-0
NYPL [Sc B 88-62]

SWAHILI LANGUAGE - DICTIONARIES.
Zani, Zachariah M. Maneno yanayotatiza /.
Nairobi , c1983. xi, 112 ;
NYPL [Sc C 89-57]

**SWAHILI LANGUAGE - DICTIONARIES -
ENGLISH.**
Msamiati wa maneno ya kitheologia. Dodoma
[Tanzania] , c1979. iv, 47 p. ;
BR95 .M72 1979   NYPL [Sc C 88-149]

**SWAHILI LANGUAGE - GLOSSARIES,
VOCABULARIES, ETC.**
Attas, Ali. Kamusi ya kwanza . Nairobi , 1986.
169 p. :   ISBN 0-333-42702-5
NYPL [Sc E 89-125]

**SWAHILI LANGUAGE - SELF-
INSTRUCTION.**
Adam, Hassan. Kiswahili . Hamburg , 1987.
208 p. :   ISBN 3-87118-843-3
NYPL [Sc E 88-433]

**SWAHILI LANGUAGE - TEXT-BOOKS FOR
FOREIGN SPEAKERS - ENGLISH.**
Adam, Hassan. Kiswahili . Hamburg , 1987.
208 p. :   ISBN 3-87118-843-3
NYPL [Sc E 88-433]

SWAHILI LANGUAGE - TEXTS.
Burhani, Z. Mwisho wa kosa /. Nairobi , c1987.
269 p. ;   ISBN 996-649-731-5
NYPL [Sc C 89-3]

Cory, Hans. Sheria na kawaida za
Wanyamwezi. /. [S.l. , 195-?] ix, 91 p. ;
NYPL [Sc E 89-1]

Ganzel, Edi, 1946- Kitanzi /. Dar es Salaam
[1984] 80 p. ;
PL8704.G35 K57 1984   NYPL [Sc C 88-120]

Halimoja, Yusuf J. Bunge la jamhuri ya
muungano /. Dar es Salaam , 1981. 64 p. :
NYPL [Sc C 89-61]

Halimoja, Yusuf J. Nchi yetu Tanzania /. Dar
es Salaam , 1981. 70 p. :
NYPL [Sc C 89-55]

Halimoja, Yusuf J. Uhusiano wa nchi za nje /.
Dar es Salaam , 1981. 60 p. :
NYPL [Sc C 89-60]

Kasalama, Mark M. Kila mtu na wake /.

Peramiho, Tanzania , 1983. 55 p. : ISBN
997-663-006-9 *NYPL [Sc D 89-1]*

Kassam, Kassim Mussa. Shuga dedi /. Dar es
Salaam, Tanzania , c1984. 60 p. ; ISBN
997-692-101-2 *NYPL [Sc C 88-69]*

Kezilahabi, Euphrase. Gamba la nyoka /.
Arusha [Tanzania] , 1979, 1981 printing. 151
p. ; *NYPL [Sc C 88-167]*

Maganga, Dotto B. Bye Bye Umaskini ... /. Dar
es Salaam , 1986. 90 p. ;
NYPL [Sc C 88-232]

Mazrui, Alamin. Chembe cha moyo /. Nairobi ,
1988. xiv, 73 p. ; ISBN 996-646-366-6
NYPL [Sc C 89-75]

Mbogo, Emmanuel. Giza limeingia /. Dar es
Salaam , 1980. 98 p. ; ISBN 997-610-022-1
NYPL [Sc C 89-23]

Mbotela, James. Uhuru wa watumwa /.
Nairobi , 1956. viii, 102 p. ;
NYPL [Sc C 89-35]

Mkangi, Katama G. C. Mafuta /. Nairobi ,
1984. 92 p. ; *NYPL [Sc C 88-198]*

Mwakasungula, N. E. R. Sheria ya kashfa /.
Tabora, Tanzania , c1985. x, 77 p. ;
NYPL [Sc C 88-191]

Rajab, Hammie. Roho mkononi /. Dar es
Salaam , c1984. 113 p. ; ISBN 997-693-102-6
NYPL [Sc C 88-94]

Rajab, Hammie. Somo kaniponza /. Dar es
Salaam , c1984. 69 p. ; ISBN 997-693-103-4;
997-693-103-04
PL8704.R28 S66 1984 *NYPL [Sc C 88-57]*

Saffari, A. J. Harusi /. Dar es Salaam , c1984.
100 p. ; ISBN 997-693-203-0
NYPL [Sc C 89-89]

Somba, John Ndeti, 1930- Wananchi mashujaa
wa imani, Kangundo, Machakos /. Kijabe,
Kenya , 1985. 68 p. : *NYPL [Sc D 89-345]*

SWAHILI PHILOLOGY.

Mbaabu, Ireri. New horizons in Kiswahili .
Nairobi , 1985. 229 p. ; DDC 496/.392 19
PL8701 .M374 1985 *NYPL [Sc C 85-128]*

Swahili phrasebook /. Leonard, Robert. Yarra
Vic, Australia , Berkeley, CA , 1988, c1987.
101 p. : ISBN 0-86442-025-0
NYPL [Sc B 88-62]

SWAHILI - VOCABULARIES. see SWAHILI LANGUAGE - GLOSSARIES, VOCABULARIES, ETC.

Swann and the global dimension : education for
world citizenship / edited by Teame Mebrahtu
with Roger White and David Brockington.
Clifton, Bristol : Youth Education Service,
c1987. 104 p. ; 30 cm. "Some of the papers
presented at a conference organised by the Centre for
Overseas Studies of the School of Education, University
of Bristol ... during 6-8 January 1986." Includes
bibliographies.
*1. Great Britain. Committee of Inquiry into the
Education of Children from Ethnic Minority Groups.
Report. 2. Children of minorities - Education - Great
Britain. I. Teame Mebrahtu.*
NYPL [Sc F 88-257]

SWAPO.

Menschenrechte im Konflikt um
Südwestafrika/Namibia . Frankfurt a.M. , 1985.
56 p. : *NYPL [Sc F 88-162]*

Swatuk, Larry A. (Larry Anthony), 1957- Black,
David R. (David Ross), 1960- Foreign policy in
small states . Halifax, N.S. , 1988. viii, 83 p. :
ISBN 0-7703-0736-1 ; DDC 327.681068 19
NYPL [Sc D 89-564]

SWAZILAND - ECONOMIC CONDITIONS.

Crush, Jonathan Scott, 1953- The struggle for
Swazi labour, 1890-1920 /. Kingston, Ont. ,
1987. xviii, 292 p., [9] p. of plates : ISBN
0-7735-0569-5 *NYPL [Sc E 89-150]*

**Swaziland. Education, Ministry of. see Swaziland.
Ministry of Education.**

SWAZILAND - FOREIGN RELATIONS - AFRICA, SOUTHERN.

Black, David R. (David Ross), 1960- Foreign
policy in small states . Halifax, N.S. , 1988. viii,
83 p. : ISBN 0-7703-0736-1 ; DDC 327.681068 19
NYPL [Sc D 89-564]

Swaziland. Ministry of Education. Sullivan,
Gerard. From school--to work . Oxford , c1981.

xvi, 190 p. : DDC 373.12/913/096813 19
LC145.S78 S94 1981 *NYPL [Sc F 87-331]*

SWAZILAND - RELATIONS - SOUTH AFRICA.

Crush, Jonathan Scott, 1953- The struggle for
Swazi labour, 1890-1920 /. Kingston, Ont. ,
1987. xviii, 292 p., [9] p. of plates : ISBN
0-7735-0569-5 *NYPL [Sc E 89-150]*

SWAZILAND - SOCIAL CONDITIONS.

Crush, Jonathan Scott, 1953- The struggle for
Swazi labour, 1890-1920 /. Kingston, Ont. ,
1987. xviii, 292 p., [9] p. of plates : ISBN
0-7735-0569-5 *NYPL [Sc E 89-150]*

SWEDEN - RELATIONS - AFRICA.

Jinadu, Adele. Idealism and pragmatism as
aspects of Sweden's development policy in
Africa /. Lagos [1982?]. 107 p. ; ISBN
978-227-698-7 *NYPL [Sc D 88-355]*

Sweeney, James Johnson. Museum of Modern
Art (New York, N.Y.) African Negro art . New
York [c1935] 58 p. : *NYPL [Sc F 88-125]*

Sweet, Dovie Davis. Red light, green light : the
life of Garrett Morgan and his invention of the
stoplight / Dovie Davis Sweet ; illustrations by
Larry Sherman, adapted from sketches by
Charlotte Durante. Smithtown, N.Y. :
Exposition Press, 1978 (1980 printing) 39 p. :
ill. ; 21 cm. A brief biography of the black inventor.
SCHOMBURG CHILDREN'S COLLECTION. With
autograph of author. ISBN 0-682-49088-1
*1. Morgan, Garrett A., 1877-1963 - Juvenile literature.
2. Traffic signs and signals - Juvenile literature. 3.
Inventors - United States - Biography - Juvenile
literature. 4. Afro-American inventors - Biography -
Juvenile literature. I. Schomburg Children's Collection.
II. Title.* *NYPL [Sc D 89-70]*

Sweeting, Earl. African history : an illustrated
handbook / Earl Sweeting and Lez
Edmund.2nd ed. London : London Strategic
Policy Unit, 1988. 31 p. : col. ill. ; 23 cm.
Bibliography: p. 31.
1. Africa - History. I. Edmond, Lez. II. Title.
NYPL [Sc D 89-505]

Swenson, John. Stevie Wonder / John Swenson.
London : Plexus, c1986. 160 p. : ill. ; 28 cm.
Discography: p. 146-159. ISBN 0-85965-076-6 (pbk.) :
DDC 784.5/4/00924 B 19
*1. Wonder, Stevie. 2. Rock musicians - United States -
Biography. 3. Afro-American musicians - Biography. I.
Title.*
ML410.W836 S9 1986b
NYPL [Sc F 88-363]

SWINE (IN RELIGION, FOLK-LORE, ETC.)

'Isá 'Abd Allāh Muḥammad al-Mahdī, 1945-
?Vino el puerco para la humanidad?
[microform] . [Brooklyn , 197-?] 40 p. :
NYPL [Sc Micro R-4114 no. 12]

SWING MUSIC. see JAZZ MUSIC.

Swinney, Everette, 1923- Suppressing the Ku
Klux Klan : the enforcement of the
Reconstruction amendments, 1870-1877 /
Everette Swinney. New York : Garland, 1987.
ix, 360 p. ; 21 cm. (American legal and
constitutional history) Thesis (Ph. D.)--University of
Texas, 1966. Bibliography: p. 341-360. ISBN
0-8240-8297-4 (alk. paper) : DDC 342.73/0873
347.302873 19
*1. Ku-Klux Klan - History. 2. Afro-Americans - Civil
rights - History. 3. Civil rights - United States -
History. I. Title. II. Series.*
KF4757 .S93 1987 *NYPL [Sc D 88-653]*

Sylla, Yèro, 1942- Récit initiatique peul du
Maciña : étude ethno-linguistique / par Yero
Sylla. [Dakar] : Centre linguistique appliquée de
Dakar, 1975. vi, 113 p. ; 27 cm. (Les Langues
nationales au Sénégal) "No 62." Errata slip inserted.
Bibliography: p. 111-113.
*1. Fulah language - Texts. I. Centre de linguistique
appliquée de Dakar. II. Title. III. Series.*
NYPL [Sc F 87-257]

**Sylvain, Suzanne Comhaire- see Comhaire-
Sylvain, Suzanne.**

Sylvie-Line. Ti Dolfine et le filibo vert /
Sylvie-Line. Paris : Editions caribéennes, c1985.
123 p. : ill. ; 24 cm. (Jeunesse, lire) SCHOMBURG
CHILDREN'S COLLECTION. ISBN 2-903033-72-2
*1. Children - West Indies. I. Schomburg Children's
Collection. II. Title.* *NYPL [Sc E 88-358]*

SYMBOLISM.

Myer, Isaac, 1836-1902. Scarabs [microform].

New York, Leipzig, 1894. xxvii, 177 p.
DT62.S3 M8 *NYPL [Sc Micro R-3541]*

SYMBOLISM, CHRISTIAN. see CHRISTIAN ART AND SYMBOLISM.

SYMBOLS. see SIGNS AND SYMBOLS.

Symbols of ancestral groves. Onobrakpeya, Bruce.
Bruce Onobrakpeya--Symbols of ancestral
groves . [Mushin [Nigeria] , 1985. 252 p. :
ISBN 978-250-900-0 *NYPL [Sc F 88-169]*

Symbols of death . Aschwanden, Herbert, 1933-
Gweru, Zimbabwe , 1987. 389 p. ; ISBN
0-86922-390-9 *NYPL [Sc D 88-979]*

**Symposium Amilcar Cabral (1983 : Praia, Cape
Verde)** Pour Cabral : sympósium international
Amilcar Cabral, Praia, Cap-Vert, 17-20 janvier
1983. Paris : Présence africaine, 1987. 486 p. ;
23 cm. Proceedings of a conference organized by the
African Party for the Independence of Cape
Verde(PAICV) Includes bibliographical references.
ISBN 2-7087-0482-6
*1. Cabral, Amilcar - Congresses. 2. Guinea-Bissau -
History - Revolution, 1963-1974 - Congresses. I. Parti
africain de k'indépendance du Cap-Vert. II. Title.*
NYPL [Sc D 87-1429]

Symposium on race and class. Philadelphia : For
Black Scholars Publications, 1984. 62 p. ; 22
cm. Title from cover. Includes bibliographies.
CONTENTS. - The illusion of a Black middle class : a
socio-philosophical analysis / Thomas Gayle
Snowden.--The African-American and the quest for the
golden mean : (a psycho-historical analysis) / Edward
Sims.--Race or class ?: a new chapter in an old story /
Van S. Bird.
*1. Afro-Americans - Social conditions. 2.
Afro-Americans - Economic conditions. 3. Social
classes - United States. 4. United States - Race
relations. I. Snowden, Thomas Gayle. II. Sims, Edward.
III. Bird, Van S.* *NYPL [Sc D 88-2]*

**Symposium on the Peopling of Ancient Egypt
and the deciphering of Meroitic Script
(1974 : Cairo, Egypt)**
[Peuplement de l'Egipte ancienne et la
déchiffrement de l'écriture méroïtique.
Spanish]
Poblamiento del antiguo Egipto y
desciframiento de la escritura meroítica / J.
Vercoutter ... [et al.] Barcelona : Serbal ;
Paris : Unesco, 1983. 155 p. : map ; 21 cm.
(Colección de temas africanos . 16) Conference
organized by Unesco. Translation of: Le Peuplement
de l'Egipte ancienne et le déchiffrement de l'écriture
meroïtique. 1978. Includes bibliographies. ISBN
0-923301-60-5 (Unesco)
*1. Egyptians - Origin - Congresses. 2. Man,
Prehistoric - Egypt - Congresses. 3. Inscriptions,
Meroitic - Congresses. I. Vercoutter, Jean, 1911-. II.
Unesco. III. Title. IV. Series.*
NYPL [Sc D 88-603]

SYNCRETISM (CHRISTIANITY) see CHRISTIANITY AND OTHER RELIGIONS.

SYNDICALISM - SENEGAL.

Lo, Magatte, 1925- Syndicalisme et
participation responsable /. Paris [1987] 151
p. : ISBN 2-85802-885-0 *NYPL [Sc D 88-915]*

Syndicalisme et participation responsable /. Lo,
Magatte, 1925- Paris [1987] 151 p. : ISBN
2-85802-885-0 *NYPL [Sc D 88-915]*

**A system approach to the implications of
national school-leaver problems in Dahomey,
Ivory Coast, Niger, Togo and Upper Volta** .
African-American Institute. Washington , 1970.
1 v. (various pagings), [7] folded leaves :
NYPL [Sc F 88-84]

SYSTEMATIC THEOLOGY. see THEOLOGY, DOCTRINAL.

Systèmes fonciers à la ville et au village :
Afrique noire francophone / textes réunis et
présentés par R. Verdier et A. Rochegude ;
[auteurs], M. Bachelet ... [et al.]. Paris :
L'Harmattan, c1986. 296 p. ; 22 cm. (Collection
Alternatives paysannes) Includes bibliographical
references. CONTENTS. - Civilisations paysannes et
traditions juridiques / par Raymond Verdier -- De la
prééminence de l'usage du sol à l'émergence d'une
question foncière / par Jean-Pierre Raison -- De la
nécessité d'un droit des terres / par A. Rochegude --
La loi coloniale / par Bernard Moleur -- Etat et
domanialité / par A. Ley -- Réformes agro-foncières et
développement / par Michel Bachelet -- Les systèmes

d'exploitation du sol en Afrique sub-saharienne / par Robert Badouin -- Techniques de crédit, garanties foncières et développement / par Gérard Pince -- Dynamique des structures de la production et modernité / par A. Mignot -- Les Arabes et la terre au sud du lac Tchad / par Jean-Pierre Magnant -- Le problème foncier en milieu péri-urbain / par Michel Prouzet et Pierre-Claver Kobo. ISBN 2-85802-719-6 DDC 346.6704/32 346.706432 19
1. Land tenure - Law and legislation - Africa, Sub-Saharan. I. Verdier, Raymond. II. Rochegude, Anne. III. Bachelet, Michel. IV. Series.
LAW   **NYPL [Sc D 89-367]**

Systems and Procedures Exchange Center. see Association of Research Libraries. Systems and Procedures Exchange Center.

Taariikhdii daraawiishta iyo Sayid Maxamed Cabdulle Xasan, 1895-1921 /. Jaamac Cumar Ciise. Muqdisho , 1976. vii, 320 p., [2] leaves of plates :
DT404.3.M38 C55   **NYPL [Sc E 87-435]**

Taaw. Sembene, Ousmane, 1923- Niiwam, suivi de Taaw . Paris , c1987. 189 p. ; ISBN 2-7087-0486-9   **NYPL [Sc C 88-320]**

Tabane, Matthew Mathêthê. Peters, Marguerite Andree. Bibliography of the Tswana language . Pretoria , 1982. l [i.e. L], 175 p., [3] leaves of plates : ISBN 0-7989-0116-0 DDC 015.68 19
Z3601 .P47 1982   **NYPL [Sc E 87-667]**

Tabler, Edward C. Baines, Thomas, 1820-1875. Baines on the Zambezi 1858 to 1859 /. Johannesburg , c1982. 251 p. : ISBN 0-909079-17-X (Standard ed.)
NYPL [Sc F 83-34]

Tadi Liben. Planning and conducting training in communication / Tadi Liben and Abebe Brehanu. Nairobi, Kenya : Communications for Basic Services Regional Training Project, UNICEF Eastern and Southern Africa Regional Office, 1986. viii, 55 p. : ill. ; 30 cm.
(Community development workers' training series . 7) Bibliography: p. 55. DDC 307.1/4/0706 19
1. Communication in community development - Study and teaching - Africa. I. Abebe Brehanu. II. Communications for Basic Services Regional Training Project. III. Title. IV. Series.
HN780.Z9 C679 1986   **NYPL [Sc F 89-171]**

Tai Solarin's adventure . Omole, Wale, 1960- Ibadan , 1985. x, 90 p. : DDC 822 19
PR9387.9.O396 T3 1985
NYPL [Sc C 88-309]

Taiwo and her twin /. Schatz, Letta. New York , c1964- 128 p. :   **NYPL [Sc E 88-430]**

Takaya, B. J. The Kaduna mafia / B.J. Takaya and S.G. Tyoden. [Jos, Nigeria] : Jos University Press, c1987. viii, 146 p. ; 23 cm. Includes bibliographical references. ISBN 978-16-6045-7
1. Elite (Social sciences) - Nigeria. 2. Religion and politics - Nigeria. 3. Nigeria - Politics and government - 1960- I. Tyoden, S. G. II. Title.
NYPL [Sc D 88-736]

Take five . McClane, Kenneth A., 1951- New York , c1988. xviii, 278 p. ; ISBN 0-313-25761-2 (lib. bdg. : alk. paper) DDC 811/.54 19
PS3563.A26119 T35 1987
NYPL [Sc D 88-723]

The Takula tree. Fleming, Elizabeth P. Philadelphia, 1964. 175 p.
PZ7.F5995 Tak   **NYPL [Sc D 88-508]**

TAL, UMAR, 1794?-1864.
Robinson, David, 1938- [Holy war of Umar Tal. French.] La guerre sainte d'al-Hajj Umar . Paris , c1988. 413 p. : ISBN 2-86537-211-1
NYPL [Sc E 89-258]

Talbot, Toby. I am Maria. Illustrated by Eleanor Mill. [1st ed.] New York, Cowles Book Co. [1969] 28 p. col. illus. 24 cm. It takes a special incident to bring nine-year-old Maria out of her shell after her initial exposure to New York City.
SCHOMBURG CHILDREN'S COLLECTION ISBN 0-402-14031-1 DDC [Fic]
1. Hispanic American children - Juvenile fiction. I. Mill, Eleanor, illus. II. Schomburg Children's Collection. III. Title.
PZ7.T148 I   **NYPL [Sc E 88-531]**

TALES - AFRICA.
Contes et histoires d'Afrique. Dakar , c1977- v. : ISBN 2-7236-0159-5 (v. 1) DDC 741.5/967 19
PZ24.1 .C6328 1977   **NYPL [Sc F 87-184]**

TALES - AFRICA, CENTRAL.
Bernard, Alain. Contes et légendes de l'Afrique des grands lacs /. Arudy, France [1984] 79 p. : ISBN 2-86819-011-1   **NYPL [Sc D 88-309]**

TALES - AFRICA, EAST.
Elliot, Geraldine. Where the leopard passes . New York, 1987. x, 125 p. :
NYPL [Sc D 88-840]

Sharma, Veena. Folk tales of East Africa /. New Delhi , c1987. vii, 113 p. : ISBN 81-207-0228-X   **NYPL [Sc D 88-781]**

TALES - AFRICA, NORTH.
Gilstrap, Robert. The sultan's fool and other North African tales /. New York , c1958. 95 p. : ISBN 931-40-0118-0   **NYPL [Sc E 88-548]**

TALES - AFRICA - STRUCTURAL ANALYSIS.
Calame-Griaule, Geneviève. Des cauris au marché . [Paris] , c1987. 293 p., [12] p. of plates :   **NYPL [Sc E 88-327]**

TALES - AFRICA, WEST.
Afrikanische Fabeln und Mythen /. Frankfurt am Main , New York , c1987. vi, 233 p. ; ISBN 3-8204-8641-0 DDC 398.2/0966 19
GR350.3 .A35 1987   **NYPL [JFD 88-8333]**

Arkhurst, Joyce Cooper. More adventures of Spider . New York , c1972. 48 p. :
NYPL [Sc D 88-1449]

Contes du pays malinké . Paris , c1987. 238 p. : ISBN 2-86537-188-3   **NYPL [Sc C 88-151]**

TALES - AFRICA, WEST - STRUCTURAL ANALYSIS.
Calame-Griaule, Geneviève. Des cauris au marché . [Paris] , c1987. 293 p., [12] p. of plates :   **NYPL [Sc E 88-327]**

TALES - AFRICAN, SOUTHERN.
The Penguin book of Southern African stories /. Harmondsworth, Middlesex, England , New York, N.Y., U. S.A., 1985. 328 p. ; ISBN 0-14-007239-X (pbk.) : DDC 808.83/1 19
PL8014.S62 P46 1985   **NYPL [Sc C 88-270]**

TALES - ANTILLES, LESSER.
Ti-Chika-- et d'autres contes antillais /. Paris , c1985. 186 p. : ISBN 2-903033-62-5
NYPL [Sc E 88-123]

TALES - BENIN.
Bene gulmanceba =. Cotonou, R.P. du Bénin , 1983. 101 p., [1] leaf of plates : DDC 305.8/963 19
DT541.45.G87 B46 1983
NYPL [Sc D 88-202]

TALES, BURUNDI.
Bernard, Alain. Contes et légendes de l'Afrique des grands lacs /. Arudy, France [1984] 79 p. : ISBN 2-86819-011-1   **NYPL [Sc D 88-309]**

Légendes historiques du Burundi . Paris , Bujumbura , c1987. 286 p. : ISBN 2-86507-178-6
NYPL [Sc E 88-324]

TALES - CARIBBEAN AREA.
Parmasad, Kenneth Vidia. Indian folk tales of the Caribbean . Charlieville, Chaguanas, Trinidad and Tobago, West Indies , c1984. xxii, 131 p., [2] p. of plates : ISBN 976-8016-01-9 (pbk.) DDC 398.2/09729 19
GR120 .P37 1984   **NYPL [Sc D 88-400]**

TALES, FRENCH - BIBLIOGRAPHY.
Jardel, Jean Pierre. Le conte créole [microform] /. [Montréal] [1977] 37 p. ;
GR120 .J37   **NYPL [*XM-12281]**

TALES - GABON.
Epopée Mulombi /. [Libreville , 1986?] 138 p. ;
NYPL [Sc D 88-561]

TALES - GHANA.
Aardema, Verna. The sky-god stories /. New York , c1960. [50] p. :   **NYPL [Sc D 89-83]**

Appiah, Peggy. Tales of an Ashanti father /. Boston , 1989, c1967. 156 p. : ISBN 0-8070-8312-7 DDC 398.2/1/09667 19
PZ8.1.A647 Tal 1989   **NYPL [Sc E 89-87]**

Appiah, Peggy. Why there are so many roads /. Lagos , 1972. 62 p. :   **NYPL [Sc C 88-12]**

TALES - GUADELOUPE.
Gaspard, Albert. Les belles paroles d'Albert Gaspard /. Paris , c1987. 128 p. : ISBN 2-903033-91-9 :
MLCM 87/1949 (P)   **NYPL [JFE 88-5765]**

TALES - GUINEA-BISSAU.
Lubu ku lebri ku mortu . Bissau , 1988. 49 p. :
NYPL [Sc F 88-351]

TALES - GUYANA.
Bland, Joy. Teddy the toucan . Bridgetown, Barbados , 1987 ; (Barbados : Caribbean Graphic Production) 20 p. :
NYPL [Sc E 88-478]

TALES - JAPAN.
Bryan, Ashley. Sh-ko and his eight wicked brothers /. New York , 1988. [22] p. : ISBN 0-689-31446-9 DDC 398.2/1/0952 E 19
PZ8.B842 Sh 1988   **NYPL [Sc E 88-569]**

TALES, KENYA.
Njau, Rebeka. Kenya women heroes and their mystical power /. Nairobi , 1984- v. ; DDC 398/.09676/2 19
GR356.4 .N43 1984   **NYPL [Sc D 88-1052]**

TALES - LIBERIA.
Dee, Ruby. Two ways to count to ten . New York , c1988. [32] p. : ISBN 0-8050-0407-6 : DDC 398.2/096 E 19
PZ8.1.D378 Tw 1988   **NYPL [Sc F 88-311]**

TALES - MALI.
Kounta, Albakaye. Contes de Tombouctou et du Macina /. Paris , c1987- v. ; ISBN 2-85802-853-2 (v. 1) DDC 843 19
PQ3989.2.K577 C6 1987
NYPL [Sc D 88-1027]

TALES - NIGERIA.
Folk-tales from Igboland /. Ibadan, Nigeria , 1986. 90 p. ; ISBN 978-16-7467-9
NYPL [Sc D 88-758]

Great tales of the Yorubas /. Ibadan, Oyo State, Nigeria , 1987. 92 p. :
NYPL [Sc D 88-712]

Slater, Sandra. The dog, the bone, and the wind . Ibadan, Nigeria , c1986. 30 p. : ISBN 0-19-575567-7
MLCS 88/07439 (P)   **NYPL [Sc D 89-116]**

Tales of an Ashanti father /. Appiah, Peggy. Boston , 1989, c1967. 156 p. : ISBN 0-8070-8312-7 DDC 398.2/1/09667 19
PZ8.1.A647 Tal 1989   **NYPL [Sc E 89-87]**

TALES - RWANDA.
Contes du Rwanda . Paris , 1983. 174 p. : ISBN 2-85319-119-2   **NYPL [Sc C 88-83]**

Imigani "tima-ngiro" y'u Rwanda =. Butare , 1987. 267, [1] p. ;   **NYPL [Sc D 88-865]**

TALES - SAINT LUCIA.
Lee, Jacintha A. (Jacintha Anius) Give me some more sense /. Basingstoke , 1983. 40 p. : ISBN 0-333-46121-5 (pbk) : DDC 813 19
PZ8.1   **NYPL [Sc D 89-284]**

TALES - SIERRA LEONE.
Kissi stories and songs /. Freetown , 1987. 95 p. :   **NYPL [Sc D 89-459]**

Nyankume, Manty. The hunter /. Freetown , 1987. 68 p. :   **NYPL [Sc D 89-414]**

Smith, Arthur E. E. Folktales from Freetown /. Freetown, 1987. 69 p. ;
NYPL [Sc D 89-413]

Temne stories and songs /. Freetown, Sierra Leone , 1986. 96 p. :   **NYPL [Sc D 89-427]**

Tucker, Musu Margaret. Harvest time stories /. Freetown , 1985. 55 p. :   **NYPL [Sc D 89-9]**

TALES - SOUTH AFRICA.
De Villiers, Helene. (comp) Die Sprokiesboom en ander verhale uit Midde-Afrika. Kaapstad, 1970. 84 p.;
P214 .D43   **NYPL [Sc D 89-373]**

TALES - UGANDA.
Kalibala, E. Balintuma. Wakaima and the clay man . New York , 1946. 145 p. :
NYPL [Sc D 89-486]

TALES - UNITED STATES.
Lester, Julius. More tales of Uncle Remus . New York , c1988. xvi, 143 p. : ISBN 0-8037-0419-4 DDC 398.2/08996073 19
PZ8.1.L434 Mo 1988   **NYPL [Sc E 88-458]**

TALES, WEST INDIAN.
Iremonger, Lucille. West Indian folk-tales. London [1956] 64 p.
GR120 .I7   **NYPL [Sc C 89-157]**

Jardel, Jean Pierre. Le conte créole [microform] /. [Montréal] [1977] 37 p. ;
GR120 .J37   **NYPL [*XM-12281]**

TALES, WEST INDIAN - BIBLIOGRAPHY.
Jardel, Jean Pierre. Le conte créole [microform]
/. [Montréal] [1977] 37 p. ;
GR120 .J37   *NYPL [*XM-12281]*

TALES - WEST INDIES.
Sherlock, Philip Manderson, Sir. Ears and tails
and common sense: more stories from the
Caribbean. London , 1982. xvii, 121 p.
       NYPL [Sc D 88-1220]

Sherlock, Philip Manderson, Sir. The iguana's
tail. New York [1969] 97 p.   DDC 823 398.2
PZ8.1.S54 Ig   *NYPL [Sc D 89-59]*

TALES, YORUBA.
Benedict, Niyi. The tortoise & the dog . Ilupeju,
Lagos , 1988. 21 p. :   *NYPL [Sc E 88-599]*

TALES - ZAIRE.
Djungu-Simba Kamatenda, 1953- Autour du
feu . Kinshasa , 1984. 70 p. :   DDC
398.2/09675/1 19
GR357.82.W35 D48 1984
       NYPL [Sc C 88-272]

Les Maitresses du feu et de la cuisine .
Bandundu, République du Zaïre , 1983. 164 p. :
       NYPL [Sc F 88-308]

TALES - ZIMBABWE.
Chisiya, 1960- Afrikan lullaby . London , 1986.
60 p. :   ISBN 0-946918-45-7 (pbk) :   DDC
398.2/1/096891 19
PZ8.1   *NYPL [Sc D 88-436]*

**TALES - ZIMBABWE - COLLECTED
     WORKS.**
Ngano /. Harare, Zimbabwe , 1980- v. ;   ISBN
0-7974-0478-3 (pbk.) :
GR358.62.M3 N47 1980
       NYPL [Sc F 87-416]

Talis, Sara Joan. Oral histories of three
secondary school students in Tanzania /.
Lewiston/Queenston , 1987. 248 p. ;   ISBN
0-88946-179-1 (alk. paper) :   DDC 306/.0967/8
19
LA1842 .O73 1987   *NYPL [Sc E 88-267]*

Talk about a family /. Greenfield, Eloise. New
York , c1978. 60 p. :   ISBN 0-590-42247-2
       NYPL [Sc C 89-79]

The tall one . Olson, Gene. New York , 1957,
c1956. 211 p. ;   *NYPL [Sc D 89-428]*

Tambo, Oliver, 1919- Oliver Tambo and the
struggle against apartheid /. New Delhi ,
c1987. xii, 172 p., [1] leaf of plates :   ISBN
81-207-0779-6 :   DDC 323.1/196/068 19
DT763 .O57 1987   *NYPL [Sc D 88-1443]*

TAMBO, OLIVER, 1919-
Oliver Tambo and the struggle against apartheid
/. New Delhi , c1987. xii, 172 p., [1] leaf of
plates :   ISBN 81-207-0779-6 :   DDC
323.1/196/068 19
DT763 .O57 1987   *NYPL [Sc D 88-1443]*

TAMBOUCTOU (MALI) - HISTORY.
A History of the migration and the settlement
of the Baayo family from Timbuktu to Bijini in
Guine Bissau /. [Banjul? , 1987.] 71 p. :
       NYPL [Sc F 89-146]

TAMPA (FLA.) - RACE RELATIONS.
Ingalls, Robert P., 1941- Urban vigilantes in the
New South . Knoxville , c1988. xx, 286 p. :
  ISBN 0-87049-571-2 (alk. paper)   DDC
305.8/009759/65 19
F319.T2 I64 1988   *NYPL [Sc E 88-518]*

TAMPA, FLA. - SOCIAL CONDITIONS.
Ingalls, Robert P., 1941- Urban vigilantes in the
New South . Knoxville , c1988. xx, 286 p. :
  ISBN 0-87049-571-2 (alk. paper)   DDC
305.8/009759/65 19
F319.T2 I64 1988   *NYPL [Sc E 88-518]*

Le tana de Soumangourou /. Cissé,
Ahmed-Tidjani. Paris , 1988. 77 p. ;   ISBN
2-85586-036-9   *NYPL [Sc C 89-73]*

**Tananarive, Malagasy Republic. Université de
     Madagascar. Musée d'art et d'archéologie.
     Travaux et documents.**
(19) Rasamuel, David. Traditions orales et
archéologie de la basse Sahatorendrika .
[Antananarivo] , 1979. 287 p., [33] leaves of
plates :
DT469.M37 S247 1979   *NYPL [Sc F 88-79]*

Tanenhaus, Sam. Louis Armstrong / Sam
Tanenhaus. New York : Chelsea House
Publishers, c1989. 127 p. : ill., ports. ; 25 cm.

(Black Americans of achievement) Includes index. A
biography of the famous trumpeter who was one of the
first great improvisers in jazz history. Discography: p.
124. Bibliography: p. 125.   ISBN 1-555-46571-4
  DDC 785.42/092/4 B 92 19
*1. Armstrong, Louis, 1900-1971 - Juvenile literature. 2.
Jazz musicians - United States - Biography - Juvenile
literature. 3. Afro-American musicians - Biography -
Juvenile literature. I. Title. II. Series.*
ML3930.A75 T3 1989   *NYPL [Sc E 89-170]*

Taney, Roger Brooke, 1777-1864. Birney, James
Gillespie, 1792-1857. Examination of the
decision of the Supreme Court of the United
States, in the case of Strader, Gorman and
Armstrong vs. Christopher Graham .
Cincinnati , 1852. iv, [1], 6-46, [1] p. ;
E450 .B57   *NYPL [Sc Rare F 88-37]*

TANGANYIKA - DESCRIPTION & TRAVEL.
Perkins, Carol Morse. The shattered skull .
New York, 1965. 59 p.,
DT440 .P4   *NYPL [Sc E 88-145]*

**Tanganyika - Government. see Tanganyika -
Politics and government.**

**TANGANYIKA - POLITICS AND
     GOVERNMENT.**
Charsley, Simon R. The princes of Nyakyusa.
[Nairobi, 1969] xii, 125 p.   DDC 301.29/678
DT443 .C5   *NYPL [Sc D 88-975]*

Tangled up in blue /. Duplechan, Larry. New
York , 1989. 264 p. ;   ISBN 0-312-02650-1 :
  DDC 813/.54 19
PS3554.U55 T36 1989   *NYPL [Sc D 89-250]*

Tantara notsongaina /. Raharolahy, Elie.
[Antananarivo?] [1976] v. ;
       NYPL [Sc C 88-238]

Tanzania : crisis and struggle for survival / edited
by Jannik Boesen ... [et al.]. Uppsala :
Scandinavian Institute of African Studies ;
[Stockholm, Sweden : Distributed by
Almqvist & Wiksell International], 1986. 325
p. : ill. ; 24 cm. Includes bibliographies.   ISBN
91-7106-257-2 (pbk.)   DDC 330.9678/04 19
*1. Agriculture - Economic aspects - Tanzania. 2.
Tanzania - Economic conditions - 1964-. 3. Tanzania -
Social conditions - 1964-. I. Boesen, Jannik.*
HD2128.5 .T36 1986   *NYPL [Sc E 88-450]*

Tanzania.
[Katiba (1977)]
Katiba ya Jamhuri ya Muungano wa
Tanzania, ya mwaka 1977. Dar es Salaam,
Tanzania : Mpiga Chapa wa Serikali, 1985.
100 p. ; 24 cm. Cover title. Swahili and English.
"Toleo hili la Katiba ... limezingatia na kuweka
pamoja mabadiliko yote yaliyofanywa katika Katiba
ya Muungano tangu ilipotungwa mwaka 1977 hadi
tarehe 1 Machi 1985. Zile sheria tatu zilizotungwa
kwa ... kurahisisha marejeo." "1 Julai, 1985."
1. Tanzania - Constitutional law. I. Title.
       NYPL [Sc E 89-156]

Tanzania after Nyerere / edited by Michael
Hodd. London ; New York : Pinter Publishers,
c1988. ix, 197 p. ; 23 cm. Includes bibliographies
and index.   ISBN 0-86187-916-3 :   DDC 967.8/04 19
*1. Tanzania - Politics and government - 1964-. 2.
Tanzania - Economic conditions - 1964-. I. Hodd,
Michael.*
DT448.2 .T29 1988   *NYPL [Sc D 88-838]*

TANZANIA - ANTIQUITIES.
Potts, Richard, 1953- Early hominid activities
at Olduvai /. New York , c1988. xi, 396 p. :
  ISBN 0-202-01176-3 (lib. bdg.)   DDC 967.8 19
GN772.42.T34 P67 1988
       NYPL [Sc E 89-92]

**Tanzania - Archaeology. see Tanzania -
Antiquities.**

TANZANIA - BIOGRAPHY.
Hoyle, B. S. Gillman of Tanganyika,
1882-1946 . Aldershot, Hants. , Brookfield, Vt ,
1987. xvii, 448 p.   ISBN 0-566-05028-5
       NYPL [Sc D 89-86]

Tanzania. Capital Development Authority. 10
years of CDA. Dodoma [Tanzania] [1983] [2],
29 p. :   DDC 307.1/4/0967826 19
HT169.T332 D6213 1983
       NYPL [Sc F 89-61]

**TANZANIA. CAPITAL DEVELOPMENT
     AUTHORITY.**
10 years of CDA. Dodoma [Tanzania] [1983]

[2], 29 p. :   DDC 307.1/4/0967826 19
HT169.T332 D6213 1983
       NYPL [Sc F 89-61]

TANZANIA - CONSTITUTIONAL LAW.
Tanzania. [Katiba (1977)] Katiba ya Jamhuri ya
Muungano wa Tanzania, ya mwaka 1977. Dar
es Salaam, Tanzania , 1985. 100 p. ;
       NYPL [Sc E 89-156]

TANZANIA - DESCRIPTION AND TRAVEL.
Barns, Thomas Alexander, 1880- Across the
great craterland to the Congo . London , 1923.
271, [1] p., [64] leaves of plates, 2 folded
leaves :   *NYPL [Sc E 88-252]*

**TANZANIA - ECONOMIC CONDITIONS -
     1964-**
Tanzania . Uppsala [Stockholm, Sweden]
1986. 325 p. :   ISBN 91-7106-257-2 (pbk.)   DDC
330.9678/04 19
HD2128.5 .T36 1986   *NYPL [Sc E 88-450]*

Tanzania after Nyerere /. London , New York ,
c1988. ix, 197 p. ;   ISBN 0-86187-916-3 :   DDC
967.8/04 19
DT448.2 .T29 1988   *NYPL [Sc D 88-838]*

TANZANIA - ECONOMIC POLICY.
Okoko, Kimse A. B. Socialism and self-reliance
in Tanzania /. London , New York , 1987. xiii,
272 p. :   ISBN 0-7103-0269-X
       NYPL [Sc D 88-902]

TANZANIA - FICTION.
Kagwema, Prince, 1931- Society in the dock .
Dar es Salaam , c1984. viii, 147 p. :
997-691-803-8   *NYPL [Sc D 88-1515]*

Kezilahabi, Euphrase. Gamba la nyoka /.
Arusha [Tanzania] , 1979, 1981 printing. 151
p. ;   *NYPL [Sc C 88-167]*

TANZANIA - FOREIGN RELATIONS.
Halimoja, Yusuf J. Uhusiano na nchi za nje /.
Dar es Salaam , 1981. 60 p. :
       NYPL [Sc C 89-60]

**TANZANIA - FOREIGN RELATIONS -
     UNITED STATES.**
Wilson, Amrit, 1941- US foreign policy and
revolution . London , distributed in the USA by
Unwin Hyman, 1989. ix, 179 p. ;   ISBN
1-85305-051-2   *NYPL [Sc D 89-426]*

**Tanzania - Government. see Tanzania - Politics
and government.**

TANZANIA - HISTORY.
Martin, Denis-Constant. Tanzanie . Paris ,
c1988. 318 p. :   ISBN 2-7246-0550-0 (Presses de la
fondation nationale des sciences politiques)
       NYPL [Sc D 89-603]

Tanzania inavyojitawala .
(1) Halimoja, Yusuf J. Nchi yetu Tanzania /.
Dar es Salaam , 1981. 70 p. :
       NYPL [Sc C 89-55]

(16) Halimoja, Yusuf J. Uhusiano na nchi za
nje /. Dar es Salaam , 1981. 60 p. :
       NYPL [Sc C 89-60]

(18) Halimoja, Yusuf J. Bunge la jamhuri ya
muungano /. Dar es Salaam , 1981. 64 p. :
       NYPL [Sc C 89-61]

TANZANIA - JUVENILE LITERATURE.
Kaula, Edna Mason. The land and people of
Tanzania. Philadelphia [1972] 139 p.   ISBN
0-397-31270-9   DDC 916.78
DT438 .K33   *NYPL [Sc D 88-1112]*

**Tanzania Library Service.
Occasional paper.**
(no. 27) Kaungamno, Ezekiel E. The East
Africa library movement and its problems
[microform] /. Dar es Salaam [197-?] 6
leaves ;   *NYPL [Sc Micro R4094 no. 30]*

Tanzania Library Services Board. International
standard book numbering in Tanzania . Dar es
Salaam , 1982. 17 leaves ;   ISBN 997-665-006-X
(pbk.)   DDC 025.4/2 19
Z467.T36 I57 1982   *NYPL [Sc F 88-76]*

**TANZANIA - POLITICS AND
     GOVERNMENT - 1964-**
Kagwema, Prince, 1931- Quo vadis Tanzania .
Dar-es-Salaam , c1985. vii, 119 p. ;   ISBN
997-691-804-6   *NYPL [Sc D 89-11]*

Martin, Denis-Constant. Tanzanie . Paris ,
c1988. 318 p. :   ISBN 2-7246-0550-0 (Presses de la
fondation nationale des sciences politiques)
       NYPL [Sc D 89-603]

Okoko, Kimse A. B. Socialism and self-reliance in Tanzania /. London , New York , 1987. xiii, 272 p. : ISBN 0-7103-0269-X
NYPL [Sc D 88-902]

One party democracy. [Nairobi, 1967] 470 p. DDC 324/.678
JQ3519.A55 O5   NYPL [Sc D 88-976]

Selections from One party democracy. [Nairobi, 1967] 143 p. DDC 324/.678
JQ3519.A55 O53   NYPL [Sc D 87-1320]

Tanzania after Nyerere /. London , New York , c1988. ix, 197 p. ; ISBN 0-86187-916-3 : DDC 967.8/04 19
DT448.2 .T29 1988   NYPL [Sc D 88-838]

Wilson, Amrit, 1941- US foreign policy and revolution . London , distributed in the USA by Unwin Hyman, 1989. ix, 179 p. ; ISBN 1-85305-051-2   NYPL [Sc D 89-426]

TANZANIA - RACE RELATIONS.
Deux études sur les relations entre groupes ethniques. Spanish. Dos estudios sobre las relaciones entre grupos étnicos en África . Barcelona [Paris] , 1982. 174 p. ; ISBN 84-85000-41-9
DT549.42 .D4818 1982
NYPL [Sc D 88-651]

TANZANIA - SOCIAL CONDITIONS - 1964-
Martin, Denis-Constant. Tanzanie . Paris , c1988. 318 p. : ISBN 2-7246-0550-0 (Presses de la fondation nationale des sciences politiques)
NYPL [Sc D 89-603]

Tanzania . Uppsala [Stockholm, Sweden] 1986. 325 p. : ISBN 91-7106-257-2 (pbk.) DDC 330.9678/04 19
HD2128.5 .T36 1986   NYPL [Sc E 88-450]

TANZANIA - SOCIAL CONDITIONS - CASE STUDIES.
Oral histories of three secondary school students in Tanzania /. Lewiston/Queenston , 1987. 248 p. ; ISBN 0-88946-179-1 (alk. paper) : DDC 306/.0967/8 19
LA1842 .O73 1987   NYPL [Sc E 88-267]

TANZANIA - SOCIAL LIFE AND CUSTOMS - CASE STUDIES.
Oral histories of three secondary school students in Tanzania /. Lewiston/Queenston , 1987. 248 p. ; ISBN 0-88946-179-1 (alk. paper) : DDC 306/.0967/8 19
LA1842 .O73 1987   NYPL [Sc E 88-267]

Tanzanie . Martin, Denis-Constant. Paris , c1988. 318 p. : ISBN 2-7246-0550-0 (Presses de la fondation nationale des sciences politiques)
NYPL [Sc D 89-603]

TAP DANCING.
Haskins, James, 1941- Mr. Bojangles . New York , 1988. 336 p. : ISBN 0-688-07203-8 : DDC 793.3/2/0924 B 19
GV1785.R54 H37 1988
NYPL [Sc D 88-851]

TAPESTRY - HISTORY.
Thomas, Michel. [Histoire d'un art. English.] Textile art /. Geneva, Switzerland , New York , NY , 1985. 279 p. : ISBN 0-8478-0640-5 (Rizzoli) : DDC 746 19
NK8806 .T4813 1985
NYPL [3-MON+ 86-527]

Tappan, Lewis, 1788-1873. Letters respecting a book "dropped from the catalogue" of the American Sunday School Union in compliance with the dictation of the slave power. New York : American and Foreign Anti-Slavery Society. Wm. Harned, publishing agent, 1848. 36 p. ; 19 cm.
1. American Sunday-School Union. 2. Jacob and his sons, or The second part of a conversation between Mary and her mother. 3. Slavery - United States - Controversial literature - 1848. I. Title.
NYPL [Sc Rare C 89-11]

Tapping Nigeria's limitless cultural treasures / [edited by Frank Aig-Imoukhuede. Ikeja : Published for the National Festival Committee by the National Council for Arts & Culture, [1987?] 119 p., [2] leaves of plates : ill. (some col.) ; 32 cm. Cover title. On cover: NCAC festival souvenir. Includes bibliographical references.
1. Arts - Nigeria. 2. Nigeria - Civilization.
NYPL [Sc F 89-1]

Tar baby /. Morrison, Toni. New York , 1981. 305 p. ; ISBN 0-452-26012-4
NYPL [Sc D 88-1105]

Tarbé, Charles. Rapport sur les troubles de Saint-Domingue, fait à l'Assemblée nationale, par Charles Tarbé, député de la Seine inférieure, Au nom du Comité colonial ... imprimé par ordre l'Assemblée nationale. Paris, Impr. nationale, 1791-[1792] 4 v. 20 cm. CONTENTS. - [1. ptie.] Rapport ... le 10 déc. 1791.--2. ptie. Rapport ... le 10 jan. 1792.--3. ptie. Rapport ... le 29 fév. 1792.--Réplique à J. P. Brissot ... par Charles Tarbé ... sur les troubles de Saint-Domingue; prononcée à l'Assemblée nationale, le 22 nov. [i.e. mars] 1792.--Pièces justificatives du Rapport procés-verbaux, arrêtés, proclamations, &c. de l'Assemblée coloniale de la partie françoise de Saint-Domingue.--[1]-3. Suite des pièces justificatives relatives aux troubles de Saint-Domingue.
1. Haiti - History - Revolution, 1791-1804 - Sources. I. France. Assemblée nationale legislative, 1791-1792. II. Saint-Domingue. Assembl ee g en erale. III. Title.
F1921 .T17   NYPL [Sc Rare F 88-17]

Tardanico, Richard. Crises in the Caribbean basin . Beverly Hills [Calif.] , c1987. 263 p. ; ISBN 0-8039-2808-4 DDC 330.9729 19
HC151 .C75 1986   NYPL [JLD 87-3555]

Tardits, Claude. Princes & serviteurs du royaume . Paris , 1987. 225 p. : ISBN 2-901161-29-4   NYPL [Sc E 88-409]

Tarr, S. Byron, 1943- Dunn, D. Elwood. Liberia . Metuchen, N.J. , c1988. xii, 259 p. : ISBN 0-8108-2088-9 DDC 966.6/203 19
DT631 .D953 1988   NYPL [JFD 88-8633]

Taschenbuch für Südwestafrika, 1909 / unter Mitwirkung von Bartoschat ... [et al.] ; hrsg. von Philalethes Kuhn, Kurd Schwabe, Georg Fock. Berlin : Weicher, 1909. xviii, 490, 60 p., [4] fold. leaves of plates : ill. ; 17 cm. Includes bibliographical references and index.
1. Namibia - Description and travel - Addresses, essays, lectures. I. Kuhn, Philalethes, 1870-. II. Schwabe,Kurd, 1866-. III. Fock, Georg, 1867-.
NYPL [Sc B 89-24]

Tati-Loutard, J. B. Le récit de la mort / J.B. Tati Loutard. Paris : Présence africaine, c1987. 166 p. ; 20 cm. (Collection Ecrits) ISBN 2-7087-0492-3
1. Zaire - Fiction. I. Title.   NYPL [Sc D 88-923]

TAVERNS. see HOTELS, TAVERNS, ETC.

Taylor, Charles A. (Charles Andrew), 1950- Guide to multicultural resources / compiled and edited by Charles A. Taylor. 1987 ed. Madison, WI : Praxis Publications, c1987. ix, 512 p. : ill. ; 23 cm. Includes index. ISBN 0-935483-07-1 (pbk.)
1. Minorities - United States - Bibliography. 2. Minorities - United States - Societies, etc. - Directories. 3. United States - Ethnic relations - Bibliography. 4. United States - Ethnic relations - Societies, etc. - Directories. 5. United States - Race relations - Bibliography. 6. United States - Race relations - Societies, etc. - Directories. I. Title.
NYPL [Sc D 88-530]

Taylor, Douglas. Aspects of Dominican history /. Dominica, W.I. , 1972. 172 p. ;
NYPL [HRG 83-1714]

Taylor, James Lumpkin, 1892- A Portuguese-English dictionary [by] James L. Taylor. Rev., with corrections and additions by the author and Priscilla Clark Martin. Stanford, Calif. , Stanford University Press, 1970 [c1958] xx, 655 p. 26 cm. Bibliography: p. xvii-xviii. ISBN 0-8047-0480-5 DDC 469/.3/21
1. Portuguese language - Dictionaries - English. I. Martin, Priscilla Clark. II. Title.
PC5333 .T3 1970   NYPL [Sc E 81-99]

Taylor, Jane. Fielding's literary Africa / by Jane and Leah Taylor. 1st ed. New York, N.Y. : Fielding Travel Books, 1988. xv, 506 p. : ill., maps ; 21 cm. Includes index. ISBN 0-688-05071-9 DDC 960 19
1. Literary landmarks - Africa. 2. Africa - Description and travel - 1977-. I. Taylor, Leah. II. Title. III. Title: Literary Africa.
DT12.25 .T39 1988   NYPL [Sc D 88-1361]

Taylor, Jeremy, 1943- Masquerade : the visitor's introduction to Trinidad and Tobago / Jeremy Taylor ; with photographs by Mark Lyndersay. London : Macmillan, 1986. v, 135 p. : col. ill., maps. (Caribbean guides) ISBN 0-333-41985-5 (pbk) DDC 917.298/3044 19
1. Trinidad and Tobago - Description and travel - Guide-books. I. Title. II. Series.
F2122   NYPL [Sc D 88-837]

Taylor, Leah. Taylor, Jane. Fielding's literary Africa /. New York, N.Y. , 1988. xv, 506 p. : ISBN 0-688-05071-9 DDC 960 19
DT12.25 .T39 1988   NYPL [Sc D 88-1361]

Taylor, Liba. (ill) Griffin, Michael. A family in Kenya /. Minneapolis , 1988, c1987. 31 p. : ISBN 0-8225-1680-2 (lib. bdg.) : DDC 306.8/5/096762 19
HQ692.5 .G75 1988   NYPL [Sc C 89-6]

TAYLOR, MARSHALL W. (MARSHALL WILLIAM), B. 1878.
Ritchie, Andrew. Major Taylor . San Francisco , New York , 1988. 304 p., [32] p. of plates : ISBN 0-933201-14-1 (hardcover)
NYPL [Sc E 88-570]

Taylor, Mildred D. The friendship / Mildred D. Taylor ; pictures by Max Ginsburg. New York : Dial Books for Young Readers, 1987. 53 p. : ill. ; 23 cm. Four children witness a confrontation between an elderly man and a white storekeeper in rural Mississippi in the 1930s. SCHOMBURG CHILDREN'S COLLECTION. ISBN 0-8037-0418-6 (lib. bdg.) : DDC [Fic] 19
1. Afro-American children - Juvenile fiction. 2. Southern States - Race relations - Juvenile fiction. I. Ginsburg, Max, ill. II. Schomburg Children's Collection. III. Title.
PZ7.T21723 Fr 1987   NYPL [Sc D 88-126]

Taylor, Susie King, b. 1848.
TAYLOR, SUSIE KING, B. 1848.
Taylor, Susie King, b. 1848. [Reminiscences of my life in camp.] A Black woman's Civil War memoirs . New York , 1988. 154 p. : ISBN 0-910129-85-1 (pbk.) : DDC 973.7/415 B 19
E492.94 33rd .T3 1988
NYPL [Sc D 88-1473]

[Reminiscences of my life in camp]
A Black woman's Civil War memoirs : reminiscences of my life in camp with the 33rd U. S. Colored Troops, late 1st South Carolina Volunteers / Susie King Taylor ; edited by Patricia W. Romero ; with a new introduction by Willie Lee Rose.1st M. Wiener Pub. ed. New York : M. Wiener Pub., 1988. 154 p. : ill. ; 21 cm. Bibliography: p. 153-154. Reprint. Originally published: Reminiscences of my life in camp with the 33d United States Colored Troops, late 1st S.C. Volunteers. Boston : S.K. Taylor, 1902. With new introd. ISBN 0-910129-85-1 (pbk.) : DDC 973.7/415 B 19
1. Taylor, Susie King, b. 1848. 2. United States. Army. South Carolina Volunteers, First - Biography. 3. Afro-Americans - South Carolina - Biography. 4. United States - History - Civil War, 1861-1865 - Personal narratives. 5. United States - History - Civil War, 1861-1865 - Afro-Americans. 6. United States - History - Civil War, 1861-1865 - Participation, Afro-American. 7. South Carolina - Biography. I. Romero, Patricia W. II. Title. III. Title: Reminiscences of my life in camp with the 33rd U. S. Colored Troops, late 1st South Carolina Volunteers.
E492.94 33rd .T3 1988
NYPL [Sc D 88-1473]

Tchakoute, Paul, 1945- Samba : tragédie coloniale en 5 actes / Paul Tchakoute ; préface de Robert Cornevin. Bafoussam, Cameroun : Éditions de la Librairie populaire, 1980. 95 p. ; 18 cm. Errata slip inserted. Includes bibliographical references. DDC 842 19
I. Title.
PQ3989.2.T33 S2   NYPL [Sc C 89-164]

Tchicaya U Tam'si, 1931- Ces fruits si doux de l'arbre à pain : roman / Tchicaya U Tam'si. Paris : Seghers, c1987. 327 p. ; 21 cm. (Chemins d'identité) 2-221-05172-6 :
1. Congo (Brazzaville) - Fiction. I. Title. II. Series.
MLCS 87/5379 (P)   NYPL [Sc D 88-581]

Tchichellé Tchivéla, 1940- L'exil, ou, La tombe : nouvelles / Tchichellé Tchivéla. Paris : Pr'esence africaine, c1986. 239 p. ; 20 cm. (Collection Ecrits) ISBN 2-7087-0473-7
1. Africa - Fiction. I. Title. NYPL [Sc C 88-289]

Té-a sé kód lonbret nou. Prémie pati : Konnin tè ou /. Jean-Baptiste, Chavannes. [Port-au-Prince, Haiti?] [1978?] 63 p. :
NYPL [Sc D 87-1404]

TEA PLANTATION WORKERS - SOUTH AFRICA.
Whisson, Michael G., 1937- Cherchez la

femme. Grahamstown [South Africa] , 1985. 90 p. [3] leaves of plates : ISBN 0-86810-125-7 *NYPL [Sc F 87-433]*

TEA ROOMS. see RESTAURANTS, LUNCH ROOMS, ETC.

TEACHERS - BRAZIL - BIOGRAPHY.
Barbosa, Rogério Andrade. La-le-li-lo-luta . Rio de Janeiro , 1984. 124 p. ; DDC 371.1/0092/4 B 19
LA2365.B72 B37 1984 NYPL [Sc D 88-284]

TEACHERS - SUPPLY AND DEMAND - MALAWI.
Hanson, John Wagner. Secondary level teachers: supply and demand in Malawi. [East Lansing, 1969] xi, 73, [2] p.
LB2833.4.M3 H3 NYPL [JFM 72-62 no. 3]

TEACHERS - TRAINING OF.
Okafor, Festus C. Nigeria teacher education . Enugu, Nigeria , 1988. 173 p. : ISBN 978-15-6298-6 *NYPL [Sc D 89-180]*

TEACHERS, TRAINING OF - NIGERIA.
Issues in teacher education and science curriculum in Nigeria /. [Nigeria , 1986?] vi, 331 p. : DDC 370/.7/309669 19
LB1727.N5 I88 1986 NYPL [Sc D 88-125]
Okafor, Festus C. Nigeria teacher education . Enugu, Nigeria , 1988. 173 p. : ISBN 978-15-6298-6 *NYPL [Sc D 89-180]*

TEACHERS - TRAINING OF - SOUTH AFRICA.
Gaydon, Vanessa. Race against the ratios . Johannesburg, South Africa , 1987. 70 p. ;
ISBN 0-86982-321-3 *NYPL [Sc F 88-322]*

TEACHERS - UNITED STATES - BIOGRAPHY - JUVENILE LITERATURE.
Halasa, Malu. Mary McLeod Bethune /. New York , c1989. 111 p. : ISBN 1-555-46574-9 DDC 370/.92/4 B 92 19
E185.97.B34 H35 1989 NYPL [Sc E 88-616]

Teaching and research in philosophy in Africa.
Spanish. Enseñanza de la filosofía e investigación filosófica en Africa / E.P. Elungu ... [et. al.] 1a ed. Barcelona : Serbal ; París : Unesco, 1984. 339 p. ; 20 cm. (Colección de temas africanos . 20) "Este libro es fiel reflejo de las actas de la reunión de once expertos, convocada por la Unesco y que tuvo lugar en Nairobi, Kenia, del 24 al 27 de junio de 1980." -- Preface. Translation of: Teaching and research in philosophy in Africa. Includes bibliographical footnotes. ISBN 92-3-302126-6 (Unesco)
1. Philosophy - Study and teaching - Africa - Congresses. 2. Philosophy - Africa - Congresses. I. Elungu, P. E. A. II. Unesco. III. Title. IV. Series.
NYPL [Sc D 88-616]

Teaching literature in Africa . Ngara, Emmanuel. Harare, Zimbabwe , 1984. 76 p. ; ISBN 0-908300-09-3 : *NYPL [Sc D 89-383]*

Teague, Bob.
Agent K-13, the super-spy. Illustrated by Geoffrey Moss.1st ed. Garden City, N.Y., Doubleday c1974. 47 p., illus., 20 x 24 cm. K-13, the best spy in the secret service, must retrieve the deadly Crumble-Bomb from the world's greediest man who is holding it for ransom. SCHOMBURG CHILDREN'S COLLECTION. ISBN 0-385-08704-7 DDC [E]
1. Spy stories. I. Moss, Geoffrey, illus. II. Schomburg Children's Collection. III. Title.
PZ7.T21937 Ag NYPL [Sc E 88-587]

The flip side of soul : letters to my son / Bob Teague.1st ed. New York : Morrow, c1989. 201 p. ; 22 cm. ISBN 0-688-08260-2 DDC 305.8/96073 19
1. Teague, Bob - Correspondence. 2. Authors, American - 20th century - Correspondence. 3. Journalists - United States - Correspondence. 4. Fathers and sons - United States. 5. United States - Race relations. I. Title.
PS3570.E2 Z495 1989 NYPL [Sc D 89-303]

TEAGUE, BOB - CORRESPONDENCE.
Teague, Bob. The flip side of soul . New York , c1989. 201 p. ; ISBN 0-688-08260-2 DDC 305.8/96073 19
PS3570.E2 Z495 1989 NYPL [Sc D 89-303]

Teame Mebrahtu. Swann and the global dimension . Clifton, Bristol , c1987. 104 p. ;
NYPL [Sc F 88-257]

TEAROOMS. see RESTAURANTS, LUNCH ROOMS, ETC.

Teatero, William, 1953- John Anderson : fugitive slave / by William Teatero. [Kingston, Ont.] : Treasure Island Books, c1986. 183 p. : ill., ports. ; 24 cm. Includes bibliographical references. ISBN 0-9692685-0-5 : DDC 345.71/056/0924 19
1. Anderson, John, b. 1831? - Trials, litigation, etc. 2. Habeas corpus - Canada. 3. Extradition - Canada. 4. Fugitive slaves - Canada. I. Title.
NYPL [Sc E 89-113]

Technical and vocational training in Kenya and the harambee institutes of technology [microform] /. Godfrey, E. M. [Nairobi] , 1973. 58 p. ;
NYPL [Sc Micro R-4108 no. 24]

TECHNICAL ASSISTANCE - AFRICA, SOUTHERN - EVALUATION.
Aid & development in southern Africa . Trenton, N.J. [1988] xi, 148 p. : ISBN 0-86543-047-0 (pbk.) : DDC 338.968 19
HC900 .A53 1988 NYPL [Sc D 88-1455]

TECHNICAL ASSISTANCE, BRITISH - NIGERIA.
Great Britain. Overseas Development Administration. Review of UK manpower and training aid to Nigeria /. [London? , 1984 or 1985] v, 72 p. ; *NYPL [Sc F 88-185]*

TECHNICAL ASSISTANCE, FRENCH - AFRICA.
Freud, Claude. Quelle coopération? . Paris , c1988. 270 p. : ISBN 2-86537-203-0
HC800 .F74 1988 NYPL [Sc D 89-602]

TECHNICAL ASSISTANCE IN UNDERDEVELOPED AREAS. see TECHNICAL ASSISTANCE.

TECHNICAL EDUCATION - KENYA.
Godfrey, E. M. Technical and vocational training in Kenya and the harambee institutes of technology [microform] /. [Nairobi] , 1973. 58 p. ; *NYPL [Sc Micro R-4108 no. 24]*

TECHNICAL EDUCATION - SOUTH AFRICA.
Bot, Monica. Training on separate tracks . Braamfontein, Johannesburg , 1988. iv, 71 p. ; ISBN 0-86982-346-9 *NYPL [Sc D 89-81]*

TECHNICAL SCHOOLS. see TECHNICAL EDUCATION.

Technische Universität Berlin. Seminar für Landwirtschaftliche Entwicklung. Promoting smallholder cropping systems in Sierra Leone . Berlin , 1985. xiv, 227 p. :
NYPL [Sc D 88-817]

TECHNOLOGICAL INNOVATIONS - AFRICA, WEST.
Improved village technology for women's activities . Geneva , 1984. vi, 292 p. : ISBN 92-2-103818-1 *NYPL [JLF 85-625]*

TECHNOLOGY AND STATE - CARIBBEAN AREA.
Girvan, Norman, 1941- Technology policies for small developing economies . Mona, Jamaica , c1983. 224 p. : DDC 338.9729 19
T24.A1 G57 1983 NYPL [Sc E 88-260]

TECHNOLOGY AND STATE - DEVELOPING COUNTRIES.
Girvan, Norman, 1941- Technology policies for small developing economies . Mona, Jamaica , c1983. 224 p. : DDC 338.9729 19
T24.A1 G57 1983 NYPL [Sc E 88-260]

Technology policies for small developing economies . Girvan, Norman, 1941- Mona, Jamaica , c1983. 224 p. : DDC 338.9729 19
T24.A1 G57 1983 NYPL [Sc E 88-260]

Ted and Bobby look for something special.
Quigg, Jane. New York [1969] 42, [3] p. DDC [Fic]
PZ7.Q333 Te3 NYPL [Sc E 88-543]

Teddy the toucan . Bland, Joy. Bridgetown, Barbados , 1987 ; (Barbados : Caribbean Graphic Production) 20 p. :
NYPL [Sc E 88-478]

TEEN-AGERS. see YOUTH.

TEENAGE PREGNANCY - WASHINGTON (D. C.) - CASE STUDIES.
Dash, Leon. When children want children . New York , c1989. 270 p. : ISBN 0-688-06957-6 DDC 306.7/088055 19
HQ759.4 .D37 1989 NYPL [Sc E 89-151]

TEENAGERS - CORRESPONDENCE.
Warner, Malcolm-Jamal. Theo and me . New York , c1988. xiv, [16] p. of plates, 208 p. : ISBN 0-525-24694-0 DDC 791.45/028/0924 19
PN2287.W43 A3 1988 NYPL [Sc D 89-258]

Telchid, Sylviane. Ti-Chika-- et d'autres contes antillais /. Paris , c1985. 186 p. : ISBN 2-903033-62-5 *NYPL [Sc E 88-123]*

TELEVISION ACTORS AND ACTRESSES - UNITED STATES - BIOGRAPHY.
Warner, Malcolm-Jamal. Theo and me . New York , c1988. xiv, [16] p. of plates, 208 p. : ISBN 0-525-24694-0 DDC 791.45/028/0924 19
PN2287.W43 A3 1988 NYPL [Sc D 89-258]

Tell it as it is / [compiled] by G.O. Nzeribe and Ugochukwu Atuchi. Enugu [Nigeria] : Lenjon Printers, [1985?]- v. ; 19 cm. A collection of articles inspired largely by the Public Officers Protection Decree of 1984 (Decree No. 4). ISBN 978-247-202-6
1. Freedom of the press - Nigeria. 2. Censorship - Nigeria. 3. Nigeria - Politics and government - 1979-. I. Nzeribe, G. O. II. Atuchi, Ugochukwu.
NYPL [Sc C 88-183]

Tell me a story, Mama /. Johnson, Angela. New York , c1989. [32] p. : ISBN 0-531-05794-1 : DDC [E] 19
PZ7.J629 Te 1988 NYPL [Sc F 89-109]

Tell Pharaoh /. Mitchell, Loften. N.Y., N.Y. , c1986. viii, 60 p. : ISBN 0-88145-048-0
NYPL [Sc D 88-1187]

TELLI, DIALLO, 1925-1977.
Diallo, Amadou. La mort de Diallo Telli . Paris , 1983. 154 p., [8] p. of plates : ISBN 2-86537-072-0 *NYPL [Sc D 88-316]*

Telling memories among southern women : domestic workers and their employers in the segregated South / [edited by] Susan Tucker. Baton Rouge : Louisiana State University Press, c1988. xi, 279 p. : ill., ports. ; 24 cm. Photographic essay: p. [263]-279. Includes bibliographical references. ISBN 0-8071-1440-5 (alk. paper) : DDC 305.4/3 19
1. Women domestics - Southern States - Interviews. 2. Afro-American women - Southern States - Interviews. 3. Women domestics - Southern States - History - Sources. 4. Housewives - Southern States - Interviews. I. Tucker, Susan, 1950-. II. Title: Domestic workers and their employers in the segregated South.
HD6072.2.U52 A137 1988 NYPL [Sc E 89-124]

Temas acerca de la esclavitud : colectivo de autores / [Julio Le Riverend ... [et al.]. La Habana, Cuba : Editorial de Ciencias Sociales, 1988. 288 p. ; 18 cm. Includes bibliographical references. "Manuscritos existentes en la Biblioteca Nacional 'Jose Marti' acerca de la esclavitud" --p. 205-288.
1. Slavery - Cuba. I. Le Riverend, Julio.
NYPL [Sc C 89-118]

TEMNE (AFRICAN PEOPLE)
Temne stories and songs /. Freetown, Sierra Leone , 1986. 96 p. : *NYPL [Sc D 89-427]*

Temne names and proverbs / collected by Abou Bai-Sharka. Freetown : People's Educational Association of Sierra Leone, 1986. 137 p. ; 21 cm. (Stories and songs from Sierra Leone . 19)
1. Proverbs, Timne. 2. Timne language - Etymology. I. Bai-Sharka, Abon. II. Series.
NYPL [Sc D 89-489]

Temne stories and songs / collected by Ibrahim Bangura, Heribert Hinzen, Lansana Kamara. Freetown, Sierra Leone : People's Educational Association of Sierra Leone, 1986. 96 p. : ill. ; 21 cm. (Stories and songs from Sierra Leone . 21)
1. Temne (African people). 2. Tales - Sierra Leone. I. Bangura, Ibrahim. II. Hinzen, Heribert. III. Kamara, Lansana. IV. Series. *NYPL [Sc D 89-427]*

Tempels Placide, 1906- Ecrits polémiques et politiques [microform] / Placide Tempels ;reproduction anastatique par A.J. Smet. Kinshasa-Limete : Département de philosophie et religions africaines, Faculté de théologie catholique, 1979. 24 p. ; 21 cm. (Cours et documents. 3) Cover title. "Nouveau tisage." Microfiche. New York: New York Public Library, 198 . 1 microfiche: negative; 11 x 15 cm. (FSN Sc 019, 140)
1. Zaire. I. Smet, A.J. II. Title. III. Series.
NYPL [Sc Micro F-11131]

Ten little nigger boys /. St. Lo, Montague.

[London] , New York , 1904. [20] leaves, [20] leaves of plates : *NYPL [Sc Rare C 86-1]*

TEN LOST TRIBES OF ISRAEL. see LOST TRIBES OF ISRAEL.

Ten secret ingredients for inner strength. Amos, Wally. The power in you . New York , c1988. xiii, 217 p. ; ISBN 1-556-11093-6 :
NYPL [Sc D 89-266]

Ten super Sunday schools in the Black community. Smith, Sid. 10 super Sunday schools in the Black community /. Nashville, Tenn. , c1986. 178 p. : ISBN 0-8054-6252-X : DDC 268/.861/08996073 19
BV1523.A37 S65 1986 NYPL [Sc C 88-229]

Ten, ten the Bible ten . McCartney, Timothy O. Nassau, Bahamas , c1976. 192 p. :
NYPL [Sc E 88-425]

Ten years of CDA. 10 years of CDA. Dodoma [Tanzania] [1983] [2], 29 p. : DDC 307.1/4/0967826 19
HT169.T332 D6213 1983
NYPL [Sc F 89-61]

TENANT FARMING. see FARM TENANCY.

Tenderness of blood /. Langa, Mandla, 1950- Harare , 1987. 427 p. ; ISBN 0-949225-30-4
NYPL [Sc C 89-102]

Tentacles of the gods /. Fakunle, Victor. Oshogbo , 1984. 111 p. ;
NYPL [Sc C 88-280]

Tenth anniversary calendar /. University of Maiduguri. [Maiduguri, Nigeria?] , c1986. [xi], 480 p. : ISBN 978-232-315-2
NYPL [Sc E 88-298]

TENURE OF LAND. see LAND TENURE.

TENURE OF OFFICE. see CIVIL SERVICE.

Teodoro, Lourdes, 1946- Água-marinha : ou, Tempo sem palavra / Lourdes Teodoro ; capa e ilustração, Mihail Iwanow. Brasília : Teodoro : [distribuição, Livraria Galilei], 1978. 63 p. ; 22 cm.
I. Title.
PQ9698.3.E6985 A79 NYPL [Sc D 88-889]

Tercinet, Alain, 1935- West Coast jazz / Alain Tercinet. Marseille : Parenthèses, 1986. 358 p. : ill. ; 24 cm. (Epistrophy) Filmography: p. 303-304. Discography: p. 311-340. Includes indexes. Bibliography: p. 305-309. ISBN 2-86364-031-3
1. Jazz music - Pacific States. 2. Jazz musicians - Pacific States. I. Title. II. Series.
NYPL [Sc E 88-307]

Terminus floride . Fanks, Russell, 1940- Paris , 1987. 346 p. ; ISBN 2-7357-0059-3
NYPL [Sc E 88-126]

La terre et le pouvoir chez les Guin du sud-est du Togo /. Mignot, Alain. Paris , 1985. 288 p. : ISBN 2-85944-087-9 *NYPL [Sc E 88-383]*

La terre sara, terre tchadienne /. Magnant, Jean-Pierre, 1946- Paris , c1986. 380 p. : ISBN 2-85802-691-2
DT546.445.S27 M34 1986
NYPL [Sc D 89-101]

Terrell, Richard. West African interlude : a retrieval of personal experience / Richard Terrell. Salisbury, Wiltshire : M. Russell, 1988. 175 p. : map ; 23 cm. Includes bibliographical references and index.
1. Nigeria - Politics and government - To 1960. 2. Great Britain - Colonies - Africa. I. Title.
NYPL [Sc D 88-1371]

The terrible twos /. Reed, Ishmael, 1938- New York , 1988, c1982. 178 p. ; ISBN 0-689-70727-4 (pbk.) : DDC 813/.54 19
PS3568.E365 T4 1988 NYPL [Sc D 89-362]

Tervuren, Belgium. Musée royal de l'Afrique centrale.
Annals. Serie in -8 . Sciences humaines .
(no. 117) Reyntjens, Filip. Pouvoir et droit au Rwanda . Tervuren, Belgique , 1985. 584 p. ;
NYPL [Sc E 87-668]

Terzian, James P. The Jimmy Brown story / by James P. Terzian and Jim Benagh. New York : J. Messner, c1964. 190 p. : ill., ports. ; 22 cm. Includes index.
1. Brown, Jim, 1936-. 2. Afro-American football players - Juvenile biography. 3. Football players - Juvenile biography. I. Benagh, Jim, 1937-. II. Title.
NYPL [Sc D 89-432]

TEST MATCHES (CRICKET)
Lawrence, Bridgette. 100 great Westindian test cricketers . London , 1988. 231 p. : ISBN 1-87051-865-9 : DDC 796.35/865 19
GV928.W4 NYPL [Sc F 88-380]

Testes, études et documents .
(nos 4-5) Parépou, Alfred. Atipa . Paris , 1987. viii, 231 p. : ISBN 2-85802-965-2
NYPL [Sc E 88-18]

The testimony of Steve Biko /. Biko, Steve, 1946-1977. London , 1987, c1978. xxxv, 298 p. ;
NYPL [Sc C 89-126]

TESTS AND MEASUREMENTS IN EDUCATION. see EDUCATIONAL TESTS AND MEASUREMENTS.

TESTS, EDUCATIONAL. see EDUCATIONAL TESTS AND MEASUREMENTS.

Tetley, Brian. Amin, Mohamed, 1943- Kenya . London , 1988. 191 p. : ISBN 0-370-31225-2 : DDC 967.6/204/0222 19
DT433.52 NYPL [Sc G 88-33]

TETRODOTOXIN - PHYSIOLOGICAL EFFECT.
Davis, Wade. Passage of darkness . Chapel Hill , c1988. xx, 344 p. : ISBN 0-8078-1776-7 (alk. paper) DDC 299/.65 19
BL2530.H3 D37 1988 NYPL [Sc E 88-429]

Teubert-Seiwert, Bärbel, 1951- Parteipolitik in Kenya 1960-1969 / Bärbel Teubert-Seiwert. Frankfurt am Main ; New York : P. Lang, c1987. 428 p. ; 21 cm. (Berliner Studien zur Politik in Afrika, 0930-7303 . Bd. 7) Originally presented as the author's thesis (doctoral--Freie Universität Berlin, 1986). Bibliography: p. 394-427. ISBN 3-8204-0151-2 DDC 324.2676/2 19
1. Political parties - Kenya. 2. Kenya - Politics and government - To 1963. 3. Kenya - Politics and government - 1963-1978. I. Title. II. Series.
JQ2947.A979 .T48 1987
NYPL [Sc D 88-1141]

TEUSO LANGUAGES.
Lamberti, Marcello. Kuliak and Cushitic . Heidelberg , 1988. 157 p. :
NYPL [Sc D 89-330]

Texan. The Yankee slave-dealer, or, An abolitionist down South : a tale for the times : by a Texan. Nashville, Tenn. : The author, 1860. 368 p. ; 19 cm.
1. Slavery - United States - Fiction. I. Title. II. Title: Abolitionist down South.
NYPL [Sc Rare C 88-21]

Texas women . Winegarten, Ruthe. Austin, Tex. [1986] ix, 187 p. : ISBN 0-89015-532-1 : DDC 305.4/09764 19
HQ1438.T4 W56 1986 NYPL [Sc F 87-41]

TEXT-BOOK BIAS - UNITED STATES.
Thinking and rethinking U. S. history /. New York, N.Y. , c1988. 389 p. ;
NYPL [Sc F 89-130]

TEXT-BOOKS - SOUTH AFRICA - EVALUATION.
Dean, Elizabeth. [History in black and white. Spanish.] Historia en blanco y negro . Barcelona , Paris , 1984. 196 p. ; ISBN 92-3-302092-4 (Unesco)
NYPL [Sc D 88-594]

Text of address delivered by His Excellency President Gaafar Mohamed Nimeiry, at the opening sitting of the first session of the second People's Assembly, Khartoum, 24th May, 1974 [microform] al-Numayrī, Ja'far Muḥammad. [Khartoum] [1974] 24 p., [1] p. of plates : *NYPL [Sc Micro F-11007]*

Textes et documents sur l'histoire des populations du nord Togo / choisis par N.L. Gayibor. Lomé : Institut pédagogique national, [1978] iii, 70 p. : ill., maps ; 30 cm. "Février 1978." At head of title: Ministère de l'éducation nationale et de la recherche scientifique. Directions des enseignements des 2e et 3e degrés. Association des professeurs d'histoire & de géographie du Togo. Includes bibliographical references.
1. Ethnology - Togo. I. Gayibor, N. L. (Nicoué Lodjou). II. Association des professeurs d'histoire & de géographie du Togo. NYPL [Sc F 88-332]

Textile art /. Thomas, Michel. [Histoire d'un art. English.] Geneva, Switzerland , New York, NY , 1985. 279 p. : ISBN 0-8478-0640-5

(Rizzoli) : DDC 746 19
NK8806 .T4813 1985
NYPL [3-MON+ 86-527]

TEXTILE FABRICS - AFRICA, WEST - EXHIBITIONS.
Gilfoy, Peggy Stoltz. Patterns of life . Washington, D.C. , c1987. 95 p. : ISBN 0-87474-475-X (alk. paper) : DDC 746.1/4/088042 19
NK8989 .G55 1987 NYPL [Sc F 88-166]

TEXTILE FABRICS - HISTORY.
Thomas, Michel. [Histoire d'un art. English.] Textile art /. Geneva, Switzerland , New York, NY , 1985. 279 p. : ISBN 0-8478-0640-5 (Rizzoli) : DDC 746 19
NK8806 .T4813 1985
NYPL [3-MON+ 86-527]

TEXTILE FABRICS - TOGO - LOMÉ - MARKETING.
Cordonnier, Rita. Femmes africaines et commerce . Paris , 1987. 190 p. : ISBN 2-85802-901-6 *NYPL [Sc E 88-368]*

TEXTILE INDUSTRY - ZAMBIA.
Errington, Leah. Natural dyes of Zambia /. [Zambia? , between 1986 and 1988] (Ndola, Zambia : Mission Press) 35 p. :
NYPL [Sc B 89-23]

TEXTILE TRADE AND STATISTICS. see TEXTILE INDUSTRY; TEXTILE FABRICS.

TEXTILE WORKERS - DISEASES AND HYGIENE - SOUTHERN STATES - HISTORY - 20TH CENTURY.
Beardsley, Edward H. A history of neglect . Knoxville , c1987. xvi, 383 p. : ISBN 0-87049-523-2 (alk. paper) : DDC 362.1/0425 19
RA448.5.N4 B33 1987 NYPL [Sc E 87-625]

TEXTILE WORKERS - MEDICAL CARE - SOUTHERN STATES - HISTORY - 20TH CENTURY.
Beardsley, Edward H. A history of neglect . Knoxville , c1987. xvi, 383 p. : ISBN 0-87049-523-2 (alk. paper) : DDC 362.1/0425 19
RA448.5.N4 B33 1987 NYPL [Sc E 87-625]

Textos del Tercer Mundo.
Romero, Vicente, 1947- Guinea-Bissau y Cabo Verde . Madrid , 1981. 109 p. ; ISBN 84-85761-09-X DDC 966/.5702 19
DT613.78 .R66 1981 NYPL [Sc C 89-1]

Texts on Zulu religion : traditional Zulu ideas about God / [edited by] Irving Hexam. Lewiston, NY ; Queenston, Ont. : E. Mellon Press, 1987. 488 p. ; 24 cm. (African studies . v. 6) Includes index. ISBN 0-88946-181-3 : DDC 299/.683 19
1. Zulus - Religion. I. Hexham, Irving. II. Series: African studies (Lewiston, N.Y.) , v. 6.
BL2480.Z8 T48 1987 NYPL [Sc E 88-463]

Teytaud, Anton C. Sarah & Addie : 15 short West Indian plays / by Anton C. Teytaud ; illustrations by Anton Teytaud and Roy Brodhurst. [S.l. : s.n.], c1976 (Christiansted, St. Croix, V.I. : Crown Printing Co.) 68 p. : ill. ; 21 cm.
1. St. Croix, Virgin Islands - Drama. I. Title. II. Title: Sarah and Addie. NYPL [Sc D 87-340]

That new river train. Hawkinson, Lucy (Ozone) 1924- Chicago [c1970] [32] p. ISBN 0-8075-7823-1 DDC 781/.96
PZ8.3.H315 Th NYPL [Sc C 89-59]

That's jazz, der Sound des 20. Jahrhunderts : eine Ausstellung der Stadt Darmstadt / veranstaltet vom Institut Mathildenhöhe Darmstadt in Zusammenarbeit mit dem Internationalen Musikinstitut ... 29. Mai bis 28. August 1988 ; [Katalog, inhaltliche Disposition, Annette Hauber, Ekkehard Jost, Klaus Wolbert]. [Darmstadt : Die Stadt, 1988] xv, 723 p. : numerous ill. (some col.), music ; 30 cm. Includes bibliographical references. German and English. DDC 781/.57/0740341 19
1. Jazz music - Exhibitions. I. Hauber, Annette. II. Jost, Ekkehard. III. Wolbert, Klaus, 1940-. IV. Darmstadt (Germany). V. Institut Mathildenhöhe (Stadtmuseum Darmstadt). VI. Internationales Musikinstitut Darmstadt.
ML141.D3 I6 1988 NYPL [JMF 89-297]

The reception of negritude writers in the Federal Republic of Germany . Séphocle, Marie-Line. Ann Arbor, Mich. , c1987. vi, 121 p. ;
NYPL [Sc D 89-293]

THEATER - AFRICA, SUB-SAHARAN.
Ricard, Alain. L'invention du théâtre . Lausanne , c1986. 134 p. :
NYPL [Sc D 88-707]

THEATER - COSTUME. see COSTUME.

THEATER - CUBA - HISTORY.
Ortiz Fernández, Fernando, 1881-1969. Los bailes y el teatro de los negros en el folklore de Cuba /. Habana, Cuba , 1981. 602 p. :
NYPL [JME 82-163]

THEATER - HAITI.
Fouchard, Jean. Artistes et répertoire des scènes de Saint-Domingue /. Port-au-Prince, Haiti , 1988. 195 p. ; *NYPL [Sc D 89-410]*

Fouchard, Jean, 1912- Le théâtre à Saint-Domingue /. Port-au-Prince, Haiti , 1988. 294 p. : *NYPL [Sc D 89-419]*

THEATER - HAITI - TABLES.
Fouchard, Jean. Artistes et répertoire des scènes de Saint-Domingue /. Port-au-Prince, Haiti , 1988. 195 p. ; *NYPL [Sc D 89-410]*

THEATER MANAGEMENT - UNITED STATES.
Marshall, Alex C. (Alexander Charles) Representative directors, Black theatre productions, and practices at historically Black colleges and universities, 1968-1978 [microform] /. 1980. ix, 141 leaves.
NYPL [Sc Micro R-4807]

Le théâtre à Saint-Domingue /. Fouchard, Jean, 1912- Port-au-Prince, Haiti , 1988. 294 p. :
NYPL [Sc D 89-419]

Théâtre [microform]. Leconte, Vergniaud. [n. p., 1919] xi, 291 p. *NYPL [Sc Micro R-3541]*

THEATRE - NIGERIA.
Enekwe, Onuora Ossie. Igbo masks . Lagos , c1987. 164 p. : ISBN 978-17-3040-4
NYPL [Sc D 88-1238]

THEATRICAL COSTUME. see COSTUME.

THEATRICAL MUSIC. see MUSICAL REVUE, COMEDY, ETC.

Thee, Hannah /. De Angeli, Marguerite, 1899- New York , 1940. [88] p. :
NYPL [Sc D 88-635]

Their contribution ignored. London : NCRCB, c1988. 16 p. : ill., ports. ; 30 cm. Originally published as a series of articles, entitled 'The Black contribution ignored,' advanced in Dragons teeth issues 13-18." Bibliography: p. [17]
1. Blacks - Biography - Juvenile literature. I. National Committee on Racism in Children's Books (Great Britain). *NYPL [Sc F 89-165]*

Them next door [microform] . Wallace, G. L. New York , 1974. 36 p. :
NYPL [Sc Micro F-11011]

Themba and the crocodile /. Molony, Rowland. Harare , 1984. 74 p. : ISBN 0-582-58741-7
NYPL [Sc D 88-347]

Thememschwerpunkte im Werk Ayi Kwei Armahs /. Ogidan, Anna. Wien , 1988. ii, 202 p. : ISBN 3-85043-046-4
NYPL [Sc D 88-1035]

Theo and me . Warner, Malcolm-Jamal. New York , c1988. xiv, [16] p. of plates, 208 p. : ISBN 0-525-24694-0 DDC 791.45/028/0924 19
PN2287.W43 A3 1988 NYPL [Sc D 89-258]

Theodore II, Negus of Ethiopia, d. 1868. Correspondence. English & Arabic. Selections. 1979. Letters from Ethiopian rulers (early and mid-nineteenth century) : preserved in the British Library, the Public Record Office, Lambeth Palace, the National Army Museum, India Office Library and Records / translated by David L. Appleyard from Gi'iz and Amharic and by A.K. Irvine from Arabic ; and annoted by Richard K.P. Pankhurst ; with an appendix by Bairu Tafla. Oxford , New York , c1985. xvii, 197 p. : ISBN 0-19-726046-2 *NYPL [Sc E 88-262]*

Théodore, Oriol, 1942- L'idéologie blanche et l'aliénation des noirs / Oriol Théodore. Montréal : Kauss, [1983] 54 p. : ill. ; 20 cm. (Collection Diasporama. Essai) Bibliography: p. 53-54.

ISBN 2-89270-001-9
1. Black race. I. Title. II. Series.
NYPL [Sc C 89-103]

Theology and ministry in context and crisis . De Gruchy, John W. London , 1987, c1986. 183 p. ; ISBN 0-00-599969-3 *NYPL [Sc C 88-73]*

Theology and the Black experience : the Lutheran heritage interpreted by African and African-American theologians / edited by Albert Pero and Ambrose Moyo. Minneapolis : Augsburg Pub. House, c1988. 272 p. ; 22 cm. Papers presented at the Conference of International Black Lutherans held at the University of Zimbabwe in Sept. 1986. Bibliography: p. 249-263. ISBN 0-8066-2353-5 DDC 284.1/08996 19
1. Lutheran Church - Doctrines - Congresses. 2. Afro-American Lutherans - Congresses. I. Pero, Albert, 1935-. II. Moyo, Ambrose, 1943-. III. Conference of International Black Lutherans (1986 : University of Zimbabwe).
BX8065.2 .T48 1988 NYPL [Sc D 89-353]

THEOLOGY, CHRISTIAN. see THEOLOGY.

THEOLOGY - DICTIONARIES.
Msamiati wa maneno ya kitheologia. Dodoma [Tanzania] , c1979. iv, 47 p. ;
BR95 .M72 1979 NYPL [Sc C 88-149]

THEOLOGY - DICTIONARIES - SWAHILI.
Msamiati wa maneno ya kitheologia. Dodoma [Tanzania] , c1979. iv, 47 p. ;
BR95 .M72 1979 NYPL [Sc C 88-149]

THEOLOGY, DOCTRINAL - AFRICA.
Mbiti, John S. Bible and theology in African Christianity /. Nairobi , 1986. xiv, 248 p., [16] p. of plates : ISBN 0-19-572593-X
NYPL [Sc D 89-296]

Salvoldi, Valentino. [Africa, il vangelo ci appartiene. English.] Africa, the gospel belongs to us . Ndola [Zambia] , 1986. 187 p ;
NYPL [Sc D 89-568]

THEOLOGY, DOCTRINAL - AFRICA, SUB-SAHARAN.
Agossou, Jacob-Mèdéwalé Jacob. Christianisme africain . Paris , 1987. 217 p. ; ISBN 2-86537-184-0 *NYPL [Sc D 88-552]*

Rücker, Heribert. "Afrikanische Theologie" . Innsbruck , 1985. 271 p. ; ISBN 3-7022-1548-4
BT30.A438 R83 1985 NYPL [Sc D 88-868]

THEOLOGY, DOGMATIC. see THEOLOGY, DOCTRINAL.

THEOLOGY, PRACTICAL.
De Gruchy, John W. Theology and ministry in context and crisis . London , 1987, c1986. 183 p. ; ISBN 0-00-599969-3 *NYPL [Sc C 88-73]*

THEOLOGY, SYSTEMATIC. see THEOLOGY, DOCTRINAL.

Theory and practice of educational administration in Nigeria /. Udoh, Sunday. Jos, Nigeria , 1987. x, 347 p. : *NYPL [Sc E 88-295]*

There is confusion . Fauset, Jessie Redmon. London , 1924. 297 p.
PZ3 .F276.Th NYPL [Sc Rare C 88-20]

There's some of me in each day of life /. Mullins, Richard T. [S.l.] c1980. vi, 56 p. :
NYPL [Sc D 88-535]

A thesaurus of African languages . Mann, Michael. New York , 1987. 325 p. ; ISBN 0-905450-24-8 *NYPL [Sc F 88-142]*

These hi-fi priests . Onyeocha, Anthony Ekendu. Owerri [Nigeria] , 1985. 208 p. :
NYPL [Sc D 88-926]

Thésée, Françoise. Les Ibos de l'Amélie : destinée d'une cargaison de traite clandestine à la Martinique, 1822-1838 / Françoise Thésée. Paris : Éditions Caribéennes, c1986. 134 p., [8] p. of plates : ill. (some col.), maps (1 col.) ; 24 cm. (Kód yanm) Includes bibliographical references. ISBN 2-903033-86-2
1. Slave-trade - Martinique - History. 2. Igbo (African people). I. Title. II. Series. NYPL [Sc E 88-560]

THESES. see DISSERTATIONS, ACADEMIC.

Theses accepted by the Atlanta University Graduate School of Library Service, 1950-1975 /. Haith, Dorothy May. Huntsville, Al , 1977. v, 45 p. ;
Z666 .H25 NYPL [Sc D 88-69]

Theses on Caribbean topics, 1778-1968. Baa,

Enid M. San Juan, 1970. v, 146 p.
Z1501 .C33 no. 1 NYPL [JFL 74-576 no. 1]

Thesiger, Wilfred, 1910- The life of my choice / Wilfred Thesiger. London : Collins, 1987. 459 p., [32] p. of plates : ill., maps ; 24 cm. Includes index. ISBN 0-00-216194-X .
1. Thesiger, Wilfred, 1910-. 2. Adventure and adventurers - Great Britain - Biography. 3. Ethiopia - Description and travel. I. Title.
G525 .T415x 1987 NYPL [Sc E 88-222]

THESIGER, WILFRED, 1910-
Thesiger, Wilfred, 1910- The life of my choice /. London , 1987. 459 p., [32] p. of plates : ISBN 0-00-216194-X .
G525 .T415x 1987 NYPL [Sc E 88-222]

THESIS WRITING. see DISSERTATIONS, ACADEMIC.

They are all named Wildfire. Springer, Nancy. They're all named Wildfire /. New York , 1989. 103 p. ; ISBN 0-689-31450-7 DDC [Fic] 19
PZ7.S76846 Th 1989 NYPL [Sc D 89-498]

They looked for a city . Fluker, Walter E., 1951- Lanham, MD , c1989. xiv, 281 p. ; ISBN 0-8191-7262-6 (alk. paper) DDC 307/.092/2 19
BX6447 .F57 1988 NYPL [Sc D 89-492]

They stole it, but you must return it /. Williams, Richard, Ed. D. Rochester, New York , c1986. vii, 130 p. ; ISBN 0-938805-00-2 (pbk.) DDC 306.8/5/08996073 19
E185.86 .W49 1986 NYPL [Sc D 88-1308]

They're all named Wildfire /. Springer, Nancy. New York , 1989. 103 p. ; ISBN 0-689-31450-7 DDC [Fic] 19
PZ7.S76846 Th 1989 NYPL [Sc D 89-498]

A thief in the village /. Berry, James. New York , 1988, c1987. 148 p. ; ISBN 0-531-05745-3 DDC [Fic] 19
PZ7.B46173 Th 1988 NYPL [Sc D 88-1252]

Things ain't what they used to be . Young, Al, 1939- Berkeley , 1987. xvii, 233 p. : ISBN 0-88739-024-2 *NYPL [Sc D 88-704]*

Thinking and rethinking U. S. history / edited by Gerald Horne ; researched and compiled by Madelon Bedell and Howard Dodson ; developed by the Council on Interracial Books for Children. New York, N.Y. : Council on Interracial Books for Children, c1988. 389 p. ; 28 cm. Includes bibliographical references.
1. Afro-Americans - History - Study and teaching. 2. Text-book bias - United States. 3. United States - History - Textbooks. I. Horne, Gerald. II. Bedell, Madelon. III. Dodson, Howard. IV. Council on Interracial Books for Children. V. Title.
NYPL [Sc F 89-130]

Thiong'o, Ngugi Wa. see Ngugi Wa Thiong'o, 1938-

Third International Conference on the Central Bilad al-Sudan Tradition and Adaptation [microform] International Conference on the Central Bilad al-Sudan Tradition and Adaptation (3rd : 1977 : Khartum, Sudan) [Khartum] [1977] 25, 13 p. ;
NYPL [Sc Micro F-10980]

Third World books.
Rigby, Peter. Persistent pastoralists . London , Totowa, N.J. , 1985. x, 198 p. : ISBN 0-86232-226-X : DDC 305.8/9676 19
DT443.3.M37 R54 1985 NYPL [JLD 86-2309]

Third world impact / edited by arif Ali. 7th ed. London : Hansib, 1986. 272 p. : ill., facsims., ports. ; 30 cm. Includes index. ISBN 0-9506664-8-3
1. Minorities - Great Britain. 2. Minorities - Developing countries. 3. Great Britain - Race relations. I. Ali, Arif.
NYPL [Sc F 88-19]

The Third World in transition . Hesselberg, J. (Jan) Uppsala , Stockholm, Sweden , 1985. 256 p. : ISBN 91-7106-243-2 (pbk.) DDC 305.5/63 19
HD1538.B55 H47 1985
NYPL [Sc E 88-290]

Third World radical regimes . Lake, Anthony. New York , 1985. 54 p. : ISBN 0-87124-099-8
NYPL [ILH 86-805]

Third World, second sex, vol. 2 / compiled by Miranda Davies. London, UK : Atlantic Highlands, N.J., USA : Zed Books, 1987. viii, 284 p. : ill. ; 23 cm. (Women in the Third World) Bibliography: p. 283-284. ISBN 0-86232-752-0 (v. 2) : DDC 305.4/2/091724 19

1. Women - Developing countries - Social conditions. 2. Feminism - Developing countries. I. Davies, Miranda. II. Series.
HQ1870.9 .T48 1987   *NYPL [Sc D 88-931]*

Thirties, donnybrook decade in St. Louis public school power plants. Young, F. Weldon (Frank Weldon), 1902- The 30's, donnybrook decade in St. Louis public school power plants . St. Louis, Mo. , c1984. 96 p. : ISBN 0-87527-331-9 (pbk.)   DDC 621.31/2132/0924 B 19
TA140.Y68 A33 1984   *NYPL [Sc D 89-256]*

Thirty years a slave and four years in the White House. Keckley, Elizabeth, 1824-1907. Behind the scenes, or, Thirty years a slave, and four years in the White House /. New York , 1988. xxxvi, xvi, 371 p. : ISBN 0-19-505259-5   DDC 973.7/092/2 19
E457.15 .K26 1988   *NYPL [JFC 88-2194]*

This is Ile-Ife /. Eluyemi, Omotoso. [Ile-Ife] 1986 (Ile-Ife : Adesanmi Printing Works) 62 p. :   *NYPL [Sc D 89-27]*

This is Kano State. Kano State . [Kano] [1987]. 192 p. :   *NYPL [Sc F 89-37]*

This is Obukpa . Ugwu, D. C. Enugu, Nigeria, 1987. xii, 76 p. ; ISBN 978-15-6288-9
NYPL [Sc D 88-801]

This railroad disappears. Steinman, Beatrice. New York [1958] 181 p.
PZ7.S8266 Th   *NYPL [Sc D 89-391]*

This street's for me! Hopkins, Lee Bennett. New York [1970] [38] p.
PZ8.3.H776 Th   *NYPL [JFE 72-966]*

Thoby-Marcelin, Philippe, 1904-1975.
[Bête du Musseau. English]
The beast of the Haitian hills / Philippe Thoby-Marcelin and Pierre Marcelin ; translated by Peter C. Rhodes. San Francisco : City Lights Books, 1986. 179 p. ; 21 cm. Translation of: La bête du Musseau. ISBN 0-87286-189-9 (pbk.)   DDC 843 19
1. Haiti - Fiction. I. Marcelin, Pierre, 1908-. II. Title.
PQ3949.T45 B413 1986
NYPL [Sc D 88-199]

Thoeny, A. Robert. Toward Black undergraduate student equality in American higher education /. New York , 1988. xvii, 217 p. : ISBN 0-313-25616-0 (lib. bdg. : alk. paper)   DDC 378/.1982 19
LC2781 .T69 1988   *NYPL [Sc E 88-507]*

Thomas, Clive Yolande. The poor and the powerless : economic policy and change in the Caribbean / Clive Y. Thomas. New York : Monthly Review Press, 1988. xv, 396 p. : ill., map ; 22 cm. Includes index. Bibliography: p. 379-388. ISBN 0-85345-743-3 :   DDC 338.9/009729 19
1. Economic development - Case studies. 2. States, Small - Economic conditions - Case studies. 3. Caribbean Area - Economic policy - Case studies. I. Title.
HC151 .T56 1988   *NYPL [Sc D 88-763]*

Thomas, Howell. Practical exercises in Nigerian history / by H. Thomas. Ibadan : Oxford University Press, 1966. 104 p. : ill. ; 25 cm. Errata slip inserted.
1. Nigeria - History - Problems, exercises, etc. I. Title.
NYPL [Sc E 88-598]

Thomas, Ianthe, 1951- Willie blows a mean horn / by Ianthe Thomas ; pictures by Ann Toulmin-Rothe. 1st ed. New York : Harper & Row, c1981. 22 p. : col. ill. ; 24 cm. SCHOMBURG CHILDREN'S COLLECTION. ISBN 0-06-026106-4 :   DDC [E]
1. Afro-American musicians - Juvenile fiction. 2. Jazz musicians - Juvenile fiction. I. Toulmin-Rothe, Ann. II. Schomburg Children's Collection. III. Title.
PZ7.T36693 Wi   *NYPL [Sc E 89-22]*

Thomas, Joyce Carol. Journey / Joyce Carol Thomas. New York : Scholastic Inc., c1988. 153 p. ; 22 cm. ISBN 0-590-40627-2 :   DDC [Fic] 19
1. Afro-Americans - Fiction. 2. Horror stories, American. I. Title.
PZ7.T36696 Jo 1988   *NYPL [Sc D 89-235]*

Water girl / Joyce Carol Thomas. New York, N.Y. : Avon Books, c1986. 119 p. ; 18 cm. (An Avon/Flare book) Sequel to Marked by fire. ISBN 0-380-89532-3 :
1. Afro-American youth - California. I. Title.
NYPL [Sc C 88-115]

Thomas, Marie.
Hansel and Gretel (in the 1980's). 1984.
Grant, Micki. Croesus and the witch / adapted from a century-old Black fable by Vinnette Carroll ; music and lyrics by Micki Grant. Hansel and Gretel (in the 1980s) / by Marie Thomas ; music and lyrics by Micki Grant. New York, N.Y. , 1984. 67, [119] p. : ISBN 0-88145-024-3   *NYPL [Sc F 88-205]*

Thomas, Michel.
[Histoire d'un art. English]
Textile art / by Michel Thomas, Christine Mainguy, Sophie Pommier. Geneva, Switzerland : Skira ; New York, NY : Rizzoli, 1985. 279 p. : ill. (some col.) ; 34 cm. Translation of: Histoire d'un art. Includes index. Bibliography: p. 259-263. ISBN 0-8478-0640-5 (Rizzoli) :   DDC 746 19
1. Textile fabrics - History. 2. Tapestry - History. 3. Wall hangings - History. 4. Soft sculpture - History. I. Pommier, Sophie. II. Mainguy, Christine. III. Title.
NK8806 .T4813 1985
NYPL [3-MON+ 86-527]

Thomas, Veona. Never too late to love / by Veona Thomas. Saddle Brook, N. J. : Rejoti, 1987. 69 p. : ill. ; 22 cm. Cover title.
1. Afro-Americans - Fiction. I. Title.
NYPL [Sc D 87-1427]

Thompson, Alvin O. Emancipation I . Barbados , c1986. vii, 108 p., [1] leaf of plates : DDC 306/.362/0972981 19
HT1119.B35 E46 1986   *NYPL [Sc D 88-248]*

Thompson, Carol, 1954- Bassani, Ezio. Africa and the Renaissance . New York City , c1988. 255 p. : ISBN 0-945802-00-5 :   DDC 736/.62/096607401471 19
NK5989 .B37 1988   *NYPL [Sc F 89-30]*

Thompson, Julius Eric. The Black press in Mississippi, 1865-1985 : a directory / by Julius E. Thompson. West Cornwall, CT : Locust Hill Press, 1988. xxiv, 144 p. : ill. ; 23 cm. Includes indexes. ISBN 0-933951-16-7 (alk. paper) :   DDC 015.762035 19
1. Afro-American newspapers - Mississippi - Bibliography - Union lists. 2. Afro-American periodicals - Mississippi - Bibliography - Union lists. 3. Catalogs, Union - Mississippi. 4. Afro-American newspapers - Mississippi - Directories. I. Title.
Z1361.N39 T52 1988 PN4882.5
NYPL [Sc D 89-34]

Thompson, Kenneth, 1937- Illegitimacy in Kentucky / prepared by Kenneth H. Thompson, Jr. Frankfort, Ky. : Legislative Research Commission, 1961. 52 p. : ill. ; 28 cm. (Research report / Legislative Research Commission . no. 4) Includes bibliographical references.
1. Illegitimacy - Kentucky. I. Series: Research report (Kentucky. General Assembly. Legislative Research com mission) , no. 4. II. Title.
NYPL [Sc F 88-36]

Thompson, L. A. Rome and race : the University Lectures, 1981, University of Ibadan / by L.A. Thompson. [Ibadan : L.A. Thompson], 1987. iii, 114 p. ; 26 cm. (Floridula. 1) One of "a limited number of copies ... made available to readers in mimeographed form, with the permission of the University, pending the still expected publication by the University Press." - p. iii. Bibliography: p. [99]-114.
1. Body, Human - Social aspects - Rome. 2. Blacks - Rome. 3. Rome - Ethnic relations. 4. Rome - Race relations. I. Title.
NYPL [Sc F 88-173]

Thompson, Robert Farris.
Black gods and kings : Yoruba art at UCLA / by Robert Farris Thompson. Bloomington : Indiana University Press, 1976, c1971. 94 p. in various pagings : ill. (some col.) ; 29 cm. Includes bibliography. ISBN 0-253-31204-3 :   DDC 732/.2.
I. Title.
N7399.N52 Y66 1976   *NYPL [Sc F 77-167]*

Chefs-d'oeuvre inédits de l'Afrique noire /. Paris , 1987. 320 p. : ISBN 2-04-012941-3
NYPL [Sc G 88-10]

Thompson, Roydon, 1911- Stella, the princess / Roydon Thompson. Kingston, Jamaica, West Indies (9 Roselle Ave., Kingston 6) : R. Thompson, 1984. 255 p. : ill. ; 22 cm. Follows the adventures of a freed slave living in Jamaica with her son during the construction of the Kingston railway and Morant Bay Rebellion of the mid 1800's. ISBN 976-8024-00-5 (pbk.)   DDC [Fic] 19
1. Jamaica - History - To 1962 - Juvenile fiction. I.

Title.
PZ7.T37199 St 1984   *NYPL [Sc D 88-317]*

Thompson, Virginia McLean, 1903-
Historical dictionary of the People's Republic of the Congo / by Virginia Thompson and Richard Adloff. 2nd ed. Metuchen, N.J. : Scarecrow Press, 1984. xxi, 239 p. : ill. ; 23 cm. (African historical dictionaries. no. 2 2) Rev. ed. of: Historical dictionary of the People's Republic of the Congo (Congo-Brazzaville). 1974. Bibliography: p. 229-239. ISBN 0-8108-1716-0   DDC 967/.24 19
1. Congo (Brazzaville) - Dictionaries and encyclopedias. I. Adloff, Richard. II. Thompson, Virginia McLean, 1903- Historical dictionary of the People's Republic of the Congo (Congo-Brazzaville). III. Title. IV. Series.
DT546.215 .T47 1984   *NYPL [Sc D 85-104]*

Historical dictionary of the People's Republic of the Congo (Congo-Brazzaville)
Thompson, Virginia McLean, 1903- Historical dictionary of the People's Republic of the Congo / by Virginia Thompson and Richard Adloff. 2nd ed. Metuchen, N.J. , 1984. xxi, 239 p. : ISBN 0-8108-1716-0   DDC 967/.24 19
DT546.215 .T47 1984   *NYPL [Sc D 85-104]*

Thomson, Colin A., 1938- Born with a call : a biography of Dr. William Pearly Oliver, C.M. / by Colin A. Thompson. Dartmouth, Nova Scotia : Black Cultural Centre for Nova Scotia, 1986. 157 p., [8] p. of plates : ill., facsims., ports. ; 28 cm. Includes bibliographical footnotes and index.
1. Oliver, William Pearly. 2. Civil rights movements - Canada. 3. Blacks - Nova Scotia. 4. Clergy - Canada - Biography. I. Title.   *NYPL [Sc F 88-63]*

Thomson, Robert. Green gold : bananas and dependency in the Eastern Caribbean. London : Latin America Bureau, 1987. vii, 93 p. : ill. ; 21 cm. "Written by Robert Thomson with additional material by George Brizan ... [et al.]" -- Verso] of t.p. Bibliography: p. 91-93. ISBN 0-906156-26-2
1. Banana trade - Windward Islands. I. Brizan, George I. II. Title.   *NYPL [Sc D 88-66]*

Thorbecke, Erik, 1929- Greer, Joel William, 1948- Food poverty and consumption patterns in Kenya /. Geneva , 1986. xii, 170 p. : ISBN 92-2-105374-1 (pbk.) :   DDC 338.1/9/6762 19
HD9017.K42 G74 1986
NYPL [JLE 87-3435]

Thorns /. Philip, Marlene. Toronto, Ontario, Canada , 1980. 56 p. ; ISBN 0-88795-008-6
NYPL [Sc D 87-1425]

Thorpe, Robert.
A LETTER TO WILLIAM WILBERFORCE ... CONTAINING REMARKS ON THE REPORTS OF THE SIERRA LEONE COMPANY AND AFRICAN INSTITUTION.
African Institution, London. Special report of the directors of the African Institution, made at the annual general meeting, on the 12th of April, 1815 . London , 1815 (London : Printed by Ellerton and Henderson) 157 p. ;
NYPL [Sc Rare G 86-5]

Those other people /. Childress, Alice. New York , c1988. 186 p. : ISBN 0-399-21510-7 DDC [Fic] 19
PZ7.C4412 Th 1988   *NYPL [Sc D 89-327]*

Those years of drought and hunger . Zimunya, Musaemura. Gweru, Zimbabwe , 1982. 129 p. ; ISBN 0-86922-183-3 (pbk.) :   DDC 823 19
PR9390.8 .Z55 1982   *NYPL [Sc C 88-237]*

Thoughts on Nigeria /. Nwankwo, Arthur A. Enugu, Nigeria , 1986. xxii, 198 p. ; ISBN 987-15-6264-1   *NYPL [Sc E 88-448]*

Thoughts on the duty of the Episcopal Church, in relation to slavery . Jay, John, 1817-1894. New York , 1839. 11 p. ;
NYPL [Sc Rare F 88-25]

Three days in Nigeria /. Ogunmuyiwa, Adetokunbo. [Lagos? , 1988] (Lagos : Remckoye Press) 80 p. ;
NYPL [Sc D 89-535]

Three decades of medical research at the College of Medicine, Ibadan, Nigeria, 1948-1980 . De Cola, Freya D. Ibadan, Nigeria , 1984. xv, 208 p. ; ISBN 978-12-1157-1 (pbk.)   DDC 016.61 19
Z6661.N6 D4 1984 R824.181
NYPL [Sc E 89-160]

Three-fingered Jack. Earle, William. Obi, or, The history of Three-fingered Jack . London , 1800.

vi, [2], 232 p., [1] leaf of plates :
NYPL [Sc Rare C 88-3]

Three hundred thirty-six hours in the hero cities of Russians. Odear, Godwin N. (Goodwin Nwafor), 1958- 336 hours in the hero cities of Russians . [Nigeria? , 1984?] 145, [17] p. of plates :
NYPL [Sc D 88-790]

Three plays of our time. Baku, Shango. 3 plays of our time /. Belmont, Trinidad , 1984. 116 p. ;
NYPL [Sc D 88-971]

Three thousand three hundred thirty-three proverbs in Haitian Creole. Fayó, Néstor A. 3333 proverbs in Haitian Creole . Port-au-Prince, Haiti [1980?] 428 p. :
NYPL [Sc D 86-839]

Three Yoruba artists . Beier, Ulli. Bayreuth, W. Germany, c19. 93 p. ;
NYPL [Sc D 88-1325]

Through ancient eyes . Spanel, Donald, 1952- Birmingham, AL , 1988. xiii, 159 p. : DDC 732/.8 19
NB1296.2 .S63 1988
NYPL [3-MAE 88-3366]

Thunder /. Cooper, Page. Cleveland , 1954. 218 p.
NYPL [Sc D 88-661]

THUNDERSTORMS - JUVENILE FICTION.
Stolz, Mary, 1920- Storm in the night /. New York , c1988. [32] p. : ISBN 0-06-025912-4 : DDC [E] 19
PZ7.S875854 St 1988   *NYPL [Sc F 88-181]*

THURMAN, HOWARD, 1900-1981 - VIEWS ON COMMUNITY.
Fluker, Walter E., 1951- They looked for a city . Lanham, MD , c1989. xiv, 281 p. ; ISBN 0-8191-7262-6 (alk. paper) DDC 307/.092/2 19
BX6447 .F57 1988   *NYPL [Sc D 89-492]*

Ti-Chika-- et d'autres contes antillais / Sylviane Telchid. Paris : Editions caribéennes, c1985. 186 p. : ill. ; 24 cm. French Creole and French. ISBN 2-903033-62-5
1. Tales - Antilles, Lesser. I. Telchid, Sylviane.
NYPL [Sc E 88-123]

Ti Dolfine et le filibo vert /. Sylvie-Line. Paris , c1985. 123 p. : ISBN 2-903033-72-2
NYPL [Sc E 88-358]

Tickner, Vincent. The food problem / Vincent Tickner. London : Catholic Institute for International Relations, 1979. 78 p. ; 21 cm. (From Rhodesia to Zimbabwe. 8) Includes bibliographical references.
1. Food supply - Zimbabwe. I. Title. II. Series.
NYPL [Sc D 88-188]

TIE-DYEING - NIGERIA - EXHIBITIONS.
Okuboyejo, Betti. Adire, a living craft /. [Nigeria] , c1987. 55 p. :
NYPL [Sc C 89-16]

The ties that bind . Magubane, Bernard. Trenton, N.J. [1987] xi, [251] p. ; ISBN 0-86543-037-3 (pbk.) DDC 305.8/96073 19
E185.625 .M83 1987   *NYPL [Sc D 88-1348]*

Tight Spaces /. Scott, Kesho. San Francisco , 1987. 182 p. ; ISBN 0-933216-27-0
NYPL [Sc D 88-12]

TILL, EMMETT, 1941-1955.
Whitfield, Stephen J., 1942- A death in the Delta . New York , London , c1988. xiv, 193 p., [8] p. of plates : ISBN 0-02-935121-9 : DDC 345.73/02523 347.3052523 19
E185.61 .W63 1989   *NYPL [Sc E 89-140]*

TIMANI (AFRICAN PEOPLE) see TEMNE (AFRICAN PEOPLE)

Time for Azania [microform] [Toronto] : Norman Bethune Institute : distributed by National Publications Centre, 1976. 89 p. : ill. ; 21 cm. "From the PAC in Perspective series." Includes bibliographical references. Microfilm. New York : New York Public Library, 198 . 1 microfilm reel ; 35 mm. (MN *ZZ-29210) DDC 320.5/4/0968
1. Pan-Africanist Congress. 2. Nationalism - South Africa. 3. South Africa - Politics and government - 1961-1978. I. Norman Bethune Institute. II. Pan-Africanist Congress.
DT770 .T55   NYPL [Sc Micro R-4849 no.1]

Time of fearful night. Wellman, Alice. New York [1970] 158 p. DDC [Fic]
PZ7.W4578 Ti   *NYPL [Sc D 88-1431]*

Timeless search /. Eze, Okpu. [Lagos] [1985?] 51 p. :
NYPL [Sc C 88-170]

Timeless Tai /. Solarin, Tai. Lagos, Nigeria , 1985. x, 232 p. ;   *NYPL [Sc D 89-371]*

Timité, Bassori, 1933- Les eaux claires de ma source /Timité bassori ; et six autres nouvelles. Paris : Hatier, 1986. 127 p. ; 18 cm. (Collection Monde noir poche) A collection of prize-winning stories from the Concours radiophonique de la Meilleure Nouvelle de Langue Française.
CONTENTS. - Les eaux cloeres de ma source / Timité Bassori--Le maquisard / Flavier Bihina Bandolo.--La fille des eaux / Sada Weindé Ndiaye.--Le fils du propriétaire / Patrice Ndedi Penda.--L'aînée de la famille / Abdoua Kanta.--La papaye / Séverin Cécile Michel Abega. ISBN 2-218-07813-9
1. Short stories, African (French). I. Concours radiophonique de la meilleure nouvelle de langue française. II. Title. III. Series.
NYPL [Sc C 88-11]

TIMNE (AFRICAN PEOPLE) see TEMNE (AFRICAN PEOPLE)

TIMNE LANGUAGE - ETYMOLOGY.
Temne names and proverbs /. Freetown , 1986. 137 p. ;   *NYPL [Sc D 89-489]*

Tin Pan Alley . Jasen, David A. New York , c1988. xxiv, 312 p., [32] p. of plates : ISBN 1-556-11099-5 : DDC 784.5/00973 19
ML3477 .J34 1988   *NYPL [Sc E 88-562]*

Tinker, Edward Larocque, 1881- Gombo comes to Philadelphia / Edward Larocque Tinker. Worcester, Mass. : American Antiquarian Society. 1957. [10], 22 p. : ill. ; 25 cm. Includes facsim of.: Idylles et chansons, ou, Essais de poësie créole / par un habitant d'Hayti. Philadelphie : J. Edwards, 1811. 22 p. ; 25 cm. "Reprinted from the Proceedings of the American Antiquarian Society for April 1957"--T.p. verso.
1. Habitant d'Hayti. Idylles et chansons, ou, Essais de poësie créole. 2. Creole dialects, French - Haiti. 3. Haitian poetry (French Creole). I. Habitant d'Hayti. Idylles et chansons, ou, Essais de poësie créole. 1957. II. Title. III. Title: Idylles et chansons, ou, Essais de poësie créole. IV. Title: Idylles et chansons.
NYPL [Sc E 89-9]

TINUBU, EFUNROYE 1805-1887.
Yemitan, Oladipo. Madame Tinubu . Ibadan , 1987. x, 85 p. ; ISBN 978-15-4985-9
NYPL [Sc D 88-1382]

Tip off. Lunemann, Evelyn. Westchester, Ill. [1969] 70 p. DDC [Fic]
PZ7.L979115 Ti   *NYPL [Sc E 88-533]*

Tipsy /. Persaud, Pat. Kingston, Jamaica , c1986. [28] p. :
MLCS 87/7926 (P)   *NYPL [Sc F 88-255]*

'Tis so . Short, Sam B. Baton Rouge, La. , c1972. 114 p. :   *NYPL [Sc D 89-63]*

Titcomb, Caldwell. Varieties of black experience at Harvard . Cambridge [Mass.] , 1986. v, 180 p. ;
LD2160 .V37x 1986   *NYPL [Sc D 88-672]*

Titon, Jeff. Worlds of music . New York , c1984. xviii, 325 p. : ISBN 0-02-872600-6 DDC 781.7 19
ML3798 .W67 1984   *NYPL [Sc E 85-247]*

TITUBA - FICTION.
Condé, Maryse. Moi, Tituba, sorcière-- . Paris , c1986. 276 p. ; ISBN 2-7152-1440-5
NYPL [Sc E 88-97]

Titus, Hénec. Poèmes du maquis / Hénec Titus. [Port-au-Prince : Imp. des Antilles, 1986?] 60 p. : ill. ; 21 cm. On cover: Pour la Société haïtienne de pédiatric.
I. Title.
NYPL [Sc D 88-499]

Tiv bibliography /. Gundu, Gabriel A. Makurdi, Nigeria , 1985. xxvii, 72 p. :
NYPL [Sc E 88-537]

TIVI (AFRICAN PEOPLE) - BIBLIOGRAPHY.
Gundu, Gabriel A. Tiv bibliography /. Makurdi, Nigeria , 1985. xxvii, 72 p. :
NYPL [Sc E 88-537]

TIVI LANGUAGE - BIBLIOGRAPHY.
Gundu, Gabriel A. Tiv bibliography /. Makurdi, Nigeria , 1985. xxvii, 72 p. :
NYPL [Sc E 88-537]

Tlaleho ea maikutlo le likhothaletso tsa sechaba ka bokamoso ba thuto Lesotho. Lesotho. Ministry of Education. Report on the views and recommendations of the Basotho Nation regarding the future of education in Lesotho =.

Maseru, Lesotho , 1978. 167 p. :
NYPL [Sc F 88-354]

Tlali, Miriam. Soweto stories / Miriam Tlali ; with an introduction by Lauretta Ngcobo. London : Pandora Press, 1989. xx, 162 p. ; 20 cm.
1. Blacks - South Africa - Fiction. 2. Soweto (South Africa) - Fiction. I. Title.   *NYPL [Sc C 89-140]*

TLOKWA (AFRICAN PEOPLE) - BIOGRAPHY.
Ramusi, Molapatene Collins. Soweto, my love /. New York , c1988. viii, 262 p. ; ISBN 0-8050-0263-4 DDC 968.06/092/4 B 19
DT779.955.R36 A3 1988
NYPL [Sc E 89-95]

To Benji, with love /. Wilson, Mary, 1938- Chicago , c1987. p. cm. ISBN 0-910671-07-9 : DDC 977.3/11043/0924 B 19
F548.9.N4 W559 1987
NYPL [Sc D 88-1219]

To breathe and wait /. Partridge, Nancy. Gweru [Zimbabwe] , 1986. 242 p. ; ISBN 0-86922-379-8
NYPL [Sc C 88-130]

To build a new world [microform]. Burnham, Forbes, 1923- [Georgetown, Guyana] , 1980. 20 p. :   *NYPL [Sc Micro F-11021]*

"To Fulfill These Rights", White House Conference. see White House Conference "To Fulfill These Rights", Washington, D. C., 1966.

To hell with dying /. Walker, Alice, 1944- San Diego , 1987. [32] p. ; ISBN 0-15-289075-0 DDC [Fic] 19
PZ7.W15213 To 1987   *NYPL [Sc F 88-182]*

To make a poet Black /. Redding, J. Saunders (Jay Saunders), 1906- Ithaca , 1988. xxxii, 142 p. ; ISBN 0-8014-1982-4 (alk. paper) DDC 811/.009/896073 19
PS153.N5 R4 1988   *NYPL [Sc D 89-388]*

To mother with love /. Solarin, Tai. Ibadan , c1987. 302 p. : ISBN 978-19-1050-X
NYPL [Sc D 88-732]

To plan is to choose /. Whiteley, Wilfred Howell. Bloomington , 1973. vii, 50 p. ;
NYPL [Sc D 88-213]

To the inhabitants of Oneida County.
Colonization Society of the County of Oneida. [Utica, N.Y. , 1838?] 8 p. ;
NYPL [Sc Rare G 86-40]

Tobago . Archibald, Douglas, 1919- Port-of-Spain , 1987- v. : ISBN 976-8059-00-1
NYPL [Sc D 88-106]

TOBAGO - HISTORY.
Archibald, Douglas, 1919- Tobago . Port-of-Spain , 1987- v. : ISBN 976-8059-00-1
NYPL [Sc D 88-106]

Today's English . Le Boulch, Pierre. [Dakar] , 1968- v. ;   *NYPL [Sc F 87-274]*

Todd, William Mills, 1944- Pushkin and his friends . Cambridge , 1987. xii, 95 p. :
NYPL [Sc F 88-236]

Todi ya dinose /. Matsepe, O. K. Pretoria , 1968, 1982 printing. 50 p. ; ISBN 0-627-00818-6
PL8690.9.M36 T6   *NYPL [Sc D 89-607]*

Todo se derrumba /. Achebe, Chinua. [Things fall apart. Spanish.] Madrid , 1986. 198 p. ; ISBN 84-204-2323-8   *NYPL [Sc D 88-1415]*

TOGO - COMMERCE - GERMANY - HISTORY.
Ahadji, A. Relations commerciales entre l'Allemagne et le Togo, 1680-1914 /. Lomé [1984] 71 leaves ;
HF3568.T64 A42 1984   NYPL [Sc F 88-164]

TOGO - DESCRIPTION AND TRAVEL.
Packer, George. The village of waiting /. New York , 1988. 316 p. : ISBN 0-394-75754-8 : DDC 966/.81 19
DT582.27 .P33 1988   *NYPL [Sc D 88-1318]*

TOGO - FICTION.
Ami, Gad, 1958- Etrange héritage . Lomé , 1986, c1985. 155 p. ; ISBN 2-7236-0931-6
NYPL [Sc E 88-427]

Gomez, Koffi, 1941- Opération Marigot . Lomé , 1982. 146 p. ; ISBN 2-7236-0849-2
NYPL [Sc D 88-1306]

Medetognon-Benissan, Tétévi. Tourbillons /.

Lomé , 1984, c1985. 116 p. ;
NYPL [Sc D 89-210]

**TOGO - POLITICS AND GOVERNMENT -
1960-**
Agbodjan, Combévi. Institutions politiques et
organisation administrative du Togo /. [S.l. ,
between 1981 and 1984] 134 leaves, [1] folded
leaf of plates :   DDC 320.966/81 19
JQ3532 .A37 1981   NYPL [Sc D 88-224]

Toulabor, Comi M. Le Togo sous Éyadéma /.
Paris , c1986. 332 p. ;   ISBN 2-86537-150-6
NYPL [Sc D 88-261]

Le Togo sous Éyadéma /. Toulabor, Comi M.
Paris , c1986. 332 p. ;   ISBN 2-86537-150-6
NYPL [Sc D 88-261]

TOGOLESE POETRY (FRENCH)
Semences nouvelles . Lomé, Togo , 1986. 96
p. ;   *NYPL [Sc C 88-123]*

Togolezskaya Respublika. see Togo.

Tolbert-Rouchaleau, Jane. James Weldon Johnson
/ Jane Tolbert-Rouchaleau. New York : Chelsea
House, c1988. 110 p. : ill. : 24 cm. (Black
Americans of achievement) Includes index. A biography
of the author, civil rights leader, and co-founder of the
NAACP who blazed a trail for racial equality and
human rights through his songs, poems, speeches, and
other writings. Bibliography: p. 108.   ISBN
1-555-46596-X   DDC 818/.5209 B 92 19
*1. Johnson, James Weldon, 1871-1938 - Biography -
Juvenile literature. 2. Authors, American - 20th
century - Biography - Juvenile literature. 3. Civil rights
workers - United States - Biography - Juvenile
literature. 4. Afro-American authors - Biography -
Juvenile literature. I. Title. II. Series.*
PS3519.O2625 Z894 1988
NYPL [Sc E 88-164]

Tollett, Kenneth S. The right to education :
Reaganism, Reagonomics, or human capital?
Washington, D.C. : Institute for the Study of
Educational Policy, Howard University, 1983.
xiii, 77 p. ; 23 cm. (Occasional paper of the Institute
for the Study of Educational Policy . 1983, no.5)
Bibliography: p. 73-77.
*1. Right to education. 2. Educational equalization -
United States. 3. Education - United States - Aims and
objectives. I. Howard University. Institute for the study
of Educational Policy. II. Title. III. Series.*
NYPL [Sc D 87-1294]

Tom Adams . Hoyos, F. A. Basingstoke , 1988. x,
198 p., [32] p. of plates :   ISBN 0-333-46332-3
(pbk) :   DDC 972.98/1/00994 19
NYPL [Sc D 88-1275]

Tomaselli, Keyan G., 1948- The cinema of
apartheid : race and class in South African
films / Keyan Tomaselli. New York :
Smyrna/Lakeview Press, c1988. 300 p. ; 22 cm.
Includes index. Filmography: p. 261-278. Bibliography:
p. 243-259.   ISBN 0-918266-19-X (pbk.) :   DDC
384/.8/0968 19
*1. Motion pictures - South Africa - History. 2.
Apartheid - South Africa. I. Title.*
PN1993.5.S6 T58 1988
NYPL [Sc D 88-1242]

TOMBS - EGYPT.
Watson, Philip J. Egyptian pyramids and
mastaba tombs of the Old and Middle
Kingdoms /. Aylesbury, Bucks , 1987. 64 p. :
ISBN 0-85263-853-1
NYPL [Sc D 88-1259]

Tomlinson, Richard. Regional restructuring under
apartheid. Johannesburg , 1987. xxii, 317 p. ;
ISBN 0-86975-327-4   *NYPL [Sc D 89-16]*

Ton beau capitaine . Schwarz-Bart, Simone.
Paris , c1987. 57 p. ;   ISBN 2-02-009832-6
NYPL [Sc C 88-112]

**TONGA (ZAMBIAN PEOPLE) - ALCOHOL
USE.**
Colson, Elizabeth, 1917- For prayer and profit .
Stanford, Calif. , 1988. vi, 147 p. :   ISBN
0-8047-1444-4 (alk. paper) :   DDC 968.94 19
DT963.42 .C65 1988   NYPL [Sc D 88-1254]

Tongues untied : poems / by Dirg
Aaab-Richards ... [et al.] London : GMP ;
Boston, MA, USA : Distributed in North
America by Alyson Publications. 1987. 95 p. ;
20 cm. (Gay verse) Includes index.   ISBN
0-85449-053-1 (pbk)   DDC
821/.914/080920664 19
1. English poetry - 20th century. 2. Homosexuals'

writings. I. Aaab-Richards, Dirg. II. Series.
PR1178.H6   NYPL [JFD 88-7561]

Too deep then /. Stone, David. London , 1987.
vi, 114 p. ;   ISBN 0-7453-0136-3 (cased) :   DDC
823 19
PR9369.3.S   NYPL [Sc D 88-961]

Too young to be old . Hill, Pauline Anderson
Simmons. Seattle, Washington , c1981. xiv, 58
p. :   ISBN 0-89716-098-3
NYPL [Sc D 88-1214]

Toomer, Jean, 1894-1967.
TOOMER, JEAN, 1894-1967.
Shaw, Brenda Joyce. Jean Toomer's life search
for identity as realized in Cane [microform] /.
1975. 169 leaves.   *NYPL [Sc Micro R-4219]*

**TOOMER, JEAN, 1894-1967 - CRITICISM
AND INTERPRETATION.**
Jean Toomer . Washington, D.C. , c1988. xxi,
557 p. :   ISBN 0-88258-111-2 :   DDC 813/.52 19
PS3539.O478 Z68 1988
NYPL [Sc E 89-231]

CARE.
Shaw, Brenda Joyce. Jean Toomer's life
search for identity as realized in Cane
[microform] /. 1975. 169 leaves.
NYPL [Sc Micro R-4219]

[Poems. 1988]
The collected poems of Jean Toomer / edited
by Robert B. Jones and Margery Toomer
Latimer ; with an introduction and textual
notes by Robert B. Jones. Chapel Hill :
University of North Carolina Press, c1988.
xxxv, 111 p. ; 24 cm. "A publication history of
the poetry of Jean Toomer": p. 105-111.   ISBN
0-8078-1773-2 (hard) :   DDC 811/.52 19
*I. Jones, Robert B. II. Latimer, Margery Toomer. III.
Title.*
PS3539.O478 A17 1988
NYPL [Sc E 88-282]

Topics in African literature /. John, Elerius Edet.
Lagos , 1986. 3 v. ;   ISBN 978-244-610-6 (v. 1)
NYPL [Sc D 89-370]

Toppin, Edgar Allan, 1928- (joint author) Drisko,
Carol F. The unfinished march. Garden City,
N.Y. , 1967. 118 p. :   DDC 973.8 (j)
E185.6 .D7   NYPL [Sc D 88-1429]

Torkington, Percy Anthony Thomas, 1931- Love
with no regrets : from the Catholic priesthood
to an African marriage / by Tony Torkington.
Liverpool : Spennithorne, 1988. 232 p. ; 21 cm.
*1. Catholic Church - South Africa. 2. Apartheid - South
Africa. I. Title.   NYPL [Sc D 89-368]*

**Toronto, Ont. Norman Bethune Institute. see
Norman Bethune Institute.**

**TORONTO, ONT. - POLITICS AND
GOVERNMENT.**
Hubbard, Stephen, 1961- Against all odds .
Toronto , 1987. 140 p. :   ISBN 1-550-02013-7
(bound)   *NYPL [Sc D 88-985]*

Torrents, Nissa. José Martí, revolutionary
democrat /. London , 1986. xviii, 238 p. ;
ISBN 0-485-15018-2   *NYPL [JFD 86-9243]*

The tortoise & the dog . Benedict, Niyi. Ilupeju,
Lagos , 1988. 21 p. :   *NYPL [Sc E 88-599]*

La tortue qui chante . Zinsou, Sénouvo Agbota,
1946- Paris , 1987. 127 p. ;   ISBN 2-218-07842-3
NYPL [Sc C 88-8]

Torture /. Davis, Levaster. New York , c1987.
167 p. ;   ISBN 0-533-07293-X
NYPL [Sc D 88-517]

Totem voices : plays from the Black world
repertory / edited with an introduction by Paul
Carter Harrison.1st ed. New York : Grove
Press, 1989. lxiii, 523 p. ; 22 cm. CONTENTS. -
Mother/word / Paul Carter Harrison -- The stong breed
/ Wole Soyinka -- Shango de Ima / Pepe Carril --
Ti-Jean and his brothers / Derek Walcott -- A new
song / Zakes Mofokeng -- For colored girls who have
considered suicide when the rainbow is enuf / Ntozake
Shange -- Zooman and the sign / Charles Fuller -- Ma
Rainey's Black bottom / August Wilson -- Ameri/Cain
Gothic / Paul Carter Harrison.   ISBN 0-8021-1053-3 :
DDC 812/.54/080896 19
*1. English drama - Black authors. 2. Afro-Americans -
Drama. 3. Blacks - Drama. I. Harrison, Paul Carter,
1931-.*
PS628.N4 T68 1988   NYPL [Sc D 89-381]

Totime Mikeni. La démocratie nouvelle, ou,
projet pour le Zaïre / Totime Mikeni. Paris :

[Totime Mikeni, 1984?]. iii, 104 p. ; 21 cm.
Bibliography: p. 102-104.
*1. Zaire - Politics and government - 1960-. 2. Zaire -
Economic conditions. 3. Zaire - Culture. I. Title.*
NYPL [Sc D 88-720]

Toto and the aardvark. Linde, Freda. Garden
City, N.Y. [1969] 59 p.
PZ7.L6574 To   NYPL [JFE 72-633]

Touche pas à mon pote /. Désir, Harlem, 1959-
Paris [c1985] 148 p. ;   ISBN 2-246-36421-3 :
DDC 323.42/3/06044 19
DC34 .D47 1985   NYPL [Sc C 88-305]

A tough tale /. Serote, Mongane, 1944- London ,
1987. 48 p. ;   ISBN 0-904759-80-6 (pbk)   DDC
821 19   *NYPL [Sc D 88-513]*

Tougher than leather . Adler, B. New York ,
c1987. viii, 191 p., [14] p. of plates :   ISBN
0-451-15121-6 (pbk.) :   *NYPL [Sc C 88-271]*

Toulabor, Comi M. Le Togo sous Éyadéma /
Comi M. Toulabor. Paris : Éditions Karthala,
c1986. 332 p. ; 21 cm. (Collection Les Afriques)
Bibliography: p. [315]-325.   ISBN 2-86537-150-6
*1. Eyadéma, Gnassingbé. 2. Togo - Politics and
government - 1960-. I. Title. II. Series.*
NYPL [Sc D 88-261]

Toulmin-Rothe, Ann. Thomas, Ianthe, 1951-
Willie blows a mean horn /. New York , c1981.
22 p. :   ISBN 0-06-026106-4 :   DDC [E]
PZ7.T36693 Wi   NYPL [Sc E 89-22]

Tour Jamaica /. Morris, Margaret. Kingston,
Jamaica , 1985. 125 p. :   ISBN 976-612-001-3
NYPL [Sc F 88-283]

Tourbillons /. Medetognon-Benissan, Tétévi.
Lomé , 1984, c1985. 116 p. ;
NYPL [Sc D 89-210]

Touré, Ahmed Sékou, 1922- [Conférences,
discours, et rapports] Conakry, Impr. du
Gouvernement, [1958?]- v. illus., ports. 25 cm.
Black author. At head of title, v. 3-6, 8: République de
Guinée. Travail, justice, solidarité; v. 9: Parti
démocratique de Guinée. "Au nom de la Révolution."
Conférences hebdomadaires. On cover, v. 2: Territoire
de la Guinée. Author's name appears on t. p., v. 6, 10,
and 13, as Ahmed Sékou Touré; v. 15-, as A. S. Touré.
Vols. 3-5 published by Impr. nationale; v. 6, 17- , Impr.
nationale "Patrice Lumumba"; v. 8, 9, 15-16, Impr.
Patrice-Lumumba; v. 10, publisher not named.
CONTENTS. - t. 2. L'action politique du Parti
démocratique de Guinée pour l'émancipation
africaine.--t. 3. L'action politique du Parti démocratique
de Guinée pour l'émancipation africaine, anée 1959.--t.
4. La lutte du Parti démocratique de Guinée pour
l'émancipation africaine, du Ve congrès du P. D. G. au
discours devant les membres de l'O. N. U.--t. 5. La
planification économique.--t. 8. L'action politique du Parti
démocratique de Guinée en faveur de l'émancipation de
la jeunesse guinéenne.--t. 9. L'action politique du P. D.
G.; conférences des mois de janvier et février 1962.--t.
10. L'Afrique en marche. 4. éd.--t. 13. L'Afrique et la
révolution.--t.14. Plan septennal 1964-1971.--t. 15.
Défendre la révolution. 2. éd. 1969.--t. 16. Le pouvoir
populaire.--t. 17. La révolution culturelle.--t. 18.
Technique de la r'evolution.--t. 19. Promotion
N'krumah.-- t. 20. Towards a revolutionary economy for
the people. 3rd ed.-- t. 21. Promotion Mao
Tsé-Toung.--t. 22. Qualifier le pouvoire populaire.--t. 23.
Informer et former pour transformer.-- t. 24. Colloque
id'eologique international de Conakry.-- t. 25, pt. 1. The
United States of Africa.--t. 26. R'evolution et
religion.-- t. 27. Le plan quinquennal, 1981-1985.-- t. 28.
Exigences du d'eveloppement.--29. Le combat syndical.
*1. Parti démocratique de Guinée. 2. Africa - Politics
and government - 1960-. 3. Guinea - Politics and
government - 1958-1984.   NYPL [Sc F966.52-T]*

TOURÉ, AHMED SÉKOU, 1922-
Kaké, Ibrahima Baba. Sékou Touré, le héros et
le tyran /. Paris , 1987. 254 p. :
NYPL [Sc D 88-468]

Touré, Sékou, Pres. Guinea, 1922- Journée
nationale du premier novembre 1961
[microform] Conakry [1961?] 38 p. ;
NYPL [Sc Micro F-11002]

TOURISM. see TOURIST TRADE.

**Tourismus und selbstbestimmte Entwicklung-ein
Widerspruch** . Scherrer, Christian. Berlin ,
c1988. 270 p. :   ISBN 3-496-00955-1
NYPL [Sc D 88-1334]

TOURIST INDUSTRY. see TOURIST TRADE.

TOURIST TRADE - SENEGAL - CASAMANCE.
Scibilia, Muriel. La Casamance ouvre ses cases . Paris , c1986. 171, [1] p., [8] p. of plates :
ISBN 2-85802-676-9   *NYPL [Sc D 89-170]*

TOURIST TRADE - TANZANIA.
Scherrer, Christian. Tourismus und selbstbestimmte Entwicklung-ein Widerspruch . Berlin , c1988. 270 p. :   ISBN 3-496-00955-1
    NYPL [Sc D 88-1334]

TOURIST TRAFFIC. see TOURIST TRADE.

TOURISTS. see TOURIST TRADE.

Tourne la peau, elle sera noire . Berthold Saieh, Laïla. Port-au-Prince, Haiti , 1986. 67 p. :
    NYPL [Sc D 88-183]

Tourneux, Henry. Les Mbara et leur langue (Tchad) / Henry Tourneux, Christian Seignobos, et Francine Lafarge. Paris : SELAF (Société d'etudes linguistiques et anthropologiques de France), 1986. 319 p. : ill. (maps) ; 24 cm. (Langues et cultures Africaines, 0755-9305 . 6) Includes lexicons of Mbara-French and French-Mbara-English. Contains bibliographical notes and bibliography : p. 307-311.   ISBN 2-85297-188-7
1. Mbara (African people) - Language. 2. Chadic languages. 3. Chad - History. I. Seignobos, Christian. II. Lafarge, Francine. III. Series: Langues et cultures Africaines , 6. IV. Title.   *NYPL [Sc E 88-162]*

TOUSSAINT LOUVERTURE, 1743?-1803.
Fouchard, Jean, 1912- Regards sur l'histoire /. Port-au-Prince, Haiti , 1988. 222 p. :
    NYPL [Sc D 89-409]

TOUSSAINT, PIERRE, 1766-1853?
Lee, Hannah Farnham Sawyer, 1780-1865. Memoir of Pierre Toussaint. Boston, 1854. 124 p.
E189.97 T732   *NYPL [Sc Rare C 88-23]*

Toward Black undergraduate student equality in American higher education / edited by Michael T. Nettles, with the assistance of A. Robert Thoeny. New York : Greenwood Press, 1988. xvii, 217 p. : ill. ; 25 cm. (Contributions to the study of education, 0196-707X . no. 25) Includes bibliographies and index.   ISBN 0-313-25616-0 (lib. bdg. : alk. paper)   DDC 378/.1982 19
1. Afro-American college students - History. 2. Educational equalization - United States - History. I. Nettles, Michael T., 1955-. II. Thoeny, A. Robert. III. Series.
LC2781 .T69 1988   *NYPL [Sc E 88-507]*

Toward job adjustment . Granger, Lester Blackwell, 1896- [New York] [1941] 78 p. :
    NYPL [Sc D 88-178]

Toward reflective analysis of Black families : final report : Office of Child Development, grant #OHD-W=252 (75) / Jualynne Dodson, project director. [Atlanta] : Atlanta University School of Social Work, 1976. ii, 74 l. : ill., map ; 29 cm. "November, 1976."
1. Afro-Americans - Families. I. Dodson, Jualynne E. II. Atlanta University. School of Social Work. III. United States. Office of Child Development.
    NYPL [Sc F 88-224]

Towards a new people's order. San Fernando, Trinidad : Vanguard Pub. Co., c1988. 87 p. ; 21 cm. Cover title.
1. Trade-unions - Trinidad and Tobago. I. Oilfields Workers' Trade Union.   *NYPL [Sc D 88-1516]*

Towards a political economy of Nigeria . Ihonvbere, Julius Omozuanvbo. Aldershot, [England] ; Brookfield, [Vt.], USA : xi, 213 p. :
ISBN 0-566-05422-1 :   DDC 338.9669 19
HC1055 .I38 1988   *NYPL [Sc D 89-47]*

Towards the decolonization of the British educational system / Amon Saba Saakana, Adetokunbo Pearse, editors. London, England : Frontline Journal/Karnak House, 1986 128 p. : ill. ; 21 cm. Includes bibliographies.   ISBN 0-907015-32-8
1. Blacks - Great Britain - Education. 2. Discrimination in education - Great Britain. 3. Literature - Black authors - Study and teaching. I. Saakana, Amon Saba, 1948-. II. Pearse, Adetokunbo. III. Frontline Journal.
    NYPL [Sc D 88-1346]

Towarzystwo jezusowe. see Jesuits.

TOWN AND GOWN. see COMMUNITY AND COLLEGE.

TOWN CHURCHES. see CITY CHURCHES.

TOWN LIFE. see CITY AND TOWN LIFE.

TOWN MEETING. see LOCAL GOVERNMENT.

TOWN MUSICIANS. see MUSICIANS.

TOWN PLANNING. see CITY PLANNING.

TOWNS. see CITIES AND TOWNS.

Towns and villages of Trinidad and Tobago /. Anthony, Michael. St. James, Port of Spain , 1988. v., 342 p. :   *NYPL [Sc D 89-404]*

Townsend, Willa A. Gospel pearls . Nashville, Tenn. , c1921. [152] p. :
    NYPL [Sc C 86-222]

TOWNSHIP GOVERNMENT. see LOCAL GOVERNMENT.

Townships of the PWV /. Mashabela, Harry. Braamfontein, Johannesburg , 1988. 184 p. :
ISBN 0-86982-343-4   *NYPL [Sc D 89-155]*

Toxic wastes and race in the United States : a national report on the racial and socio-economic characteristics of communities with hazardous waste sites / Commission for Racial Justice, United Church of Christ. New York, N.Y. : Public Data Access : Inquiries to the Commission, 1987. xvi, 69 p. : maps ; 28 cm. Bibliography: p. 28-30.   DDC 363.7/28 19
1. Hazardous wastes - Environmental aspects - United States. 2. Hazardous waste sites - Environmental aspects - United States. 3. Minorities - Health and hygiene - United States. 4. Hazardous wastes - United States - Moral and ethical aspects. I. United Church of Christ. Commission for Racial Justice.
TD811.5 .T695 1987   *NYPL [JLF 88-1607]*

TOYS - JUVENILE FICTION.
Upton, Bertha, 1849-1912. Golliwogg in the African jungle . London , New York , 1909. 62, [2] p. :   *NYPL [Sc Rare F 89-16]*

Upton, Florence Kate, 1873-1922. The Golliwogg's bicycle club. London, 1967. [1] 62 p.
PZ8.3.U74 Go2   *NYPL [Sc D 88-252]*

Trabalho e vadiagem . Kowarick, Lúcio. São Paulo , 1987. 133 p. ;   *NYPL [Sc D 88-784]*

Os trabalhos e os dias /. Lopes da Silva, Baltasar, 1907- Praia, Cabo Verde , 1987. 83 p. :
    NYPL [Sc D 88-1500]

Tractatus de instauranda ethiopum salute.
Sandoval, Alonso dc, 1576-1652. Naturaleza, policia sagrada i profana, costumbres i ritos, disciplina i catechismo evangelico de todos etiopes /. En Sevilla , 1627. [23], 334 p., 81 leaves ;   *NYPL [Sc Rare F 82-70]*

Tracy, Steven C. (Steven Carl), 1954- Langston Hughes & the blues / Steven C. Tracy. Urbana : University of Illinois Press, c1988. xiii, 305 p. ; 24 cm. Includes index. Bibliography: p. [266]-278. Discography: p. [279]-291.   ISBN 0-252-01457-X (alk. paper)   DDC 818/.5209 19
1. Hughes, Langston, 1902-1967 - Knowledge - Folklore, mythology. 2. Blues (Songs, etc.) - United States - History and criticism. 3. Folk poetry, American - Afro-American authors - History and criticism. 4. Literature and folklore - United States - History - 20th century. 5. Folklore in literature. 6. Afro-Americans in literature. 7. Afro-Americans - Folklore. I. Title. II. Title: Langston Hughes and the blues.
PS3515.U274 Z8 1988   *NYPL [Sc E 88-506]*

TRADE. see BUSINESS; COMMERCE.

TRADE BARRIERS. see COMMERCIAL POLICY.

Trade unionism and colonial authority [microform] . Amolo, Milcah. [Nairobi] [1978] 16 p. ;   *NYPL [Sc Micro R-4108 no. 37]*

TRADE-UNIONS - AFRICA.
Labour and unions in Asia and Africa . New York , 1988. x, 258 p. ;   ISBN 0-312-01362-0 :   DDC 331.88/095 19
HD6796 .L3 1988   *NYPL [Sc D 88-1393]*

TRADE-UNIONS AND FOREIGN POLICY - NIGERIA - HISTORY.
Otobo, Dafe. Foreign interests and Nigerian trade unions /. Ibadan [Nigeria] , 1986. xxviii, 190 p. :   ISBN 978-12-9532-5 (pbk.)   DDC 331.88/09669 19
HD6885.5 .O87 1986   *NYPL [Sc E 88-557]*

TRADE-UNIONS - ASIA.
Labour and unions in Asia and Africa . New York , 1988. x, 258 p. ;   ISBN 0-312-01362-0 :

DDC 331.88/095 19
HD6796 .L3 1988   *NYPL [Sc D 88-1393]*

TRADE-UNIONS - BARBADOS - DIRECTORIES.
Blondel, Eaulin. Credit unions, co-operatives, trade unions, and friendly societies in Barbados . St. Augustine, Trinidad, Trinidad and Tobago [1986] v, 102 p. ;   DDC 334/.025/72981 19
HD3464.9.A6 B353 1986
    NYPL [Sc F 88-361]

TRADE-UNIONS - NAMIBIA.
Working under South African occupation . London , 1987. 56 p. ;   ISBN 0-904759-73-3 (pbk.) :   DDC 968 s 331.6/9/9688 19
DT746 .F3 no. 14 HD8808
    NYPL [Sc D 89-525]

TRADE-UNIONS - NIGERIA - HISTORY.
Otobo, Dafe. Foreign interests and Nigerian trade unions /. Ibadan [Nigeria] , 1986. xxviii, 190 p. :   ISBN 978-12-9532-5 (pbk.)   DDC 331.88/09669 19
HD6885.5 .O87 1986   *NYPL [Sc E 88-557]*

TRADE-UNIONS - PETROLEUM WORKERS - TRINIDAD AND TOBAGO.
Oilfields Workers' Trade Union. Our fight for people's ownership and control of the oil industry . [San Fernando] , 1982. 80 p. :
    NYPL [Sc D 88-1253]

TRADE-UNIONS - SIERRA LEONE - HISTORY.
Amolo, Milcah. Trade unionism and colonial authority [microform] . [Nairobi] [1978] 16 p. ;
    NYPL [Sc Micro R-4108 no. 37]

TRADE-UNIONS - SOUTH AFRICA.
Haarløv, Jens. Labour regulation and black workers' struggles in South Africa /. Uppsala , 1983. 80 p. ;   ISBN 91-7106-213-0 (pbk:)   DDC 960 s 331.6/9/968 19
DT1 .N64 no. 68 HD6870.5
    NYPL [JLD 87-1037]

The Independent trade unions, 1974-1984 . Johannesburg , 1987. xvi, 355 p. ;   ISBN 0-86975-307-X   *NYPL [Sc D 88-1329]*

TRADE-UNIONS - TRINIDAD AND TOBAGO.
Kambon, Khafra. For bread justice and freedom . London , 1988. xi, 353 p., [16] p. of plates :   *NYPL [Sc D 89-294]*

Towards a new people's order. San Fernando, Trinidad , c1988. 87 p. ;
    NYPL [Sc D 88-1516]

TRADE-UNIONS - UNITED STATES - FICTION.
Himes, Chester B., 1909- Lonely crusade . New York , c1986. x, 398 p. ;   ISBN 0-938410-37-7 (pbk.) :   DDC 813/.54 19
PS3515.I713 L6 1986   *NYPL [Sc D 88-1362]*

TRADE-UNIONS - UNITED STATES - AFRO-AMERICAN MEMBERSHIP - HISTORY.
Black workers . Philadelphia , 1989. xv, 733 p. ;   ISBN 0-87722-592-3   *NYPL [Sc E 89-206]*

Tradition africaine et rationalité moderne /. Elungu, P. E. A. Paris , c1987. 187 p. ;
    NYPL [Sc D 88-1101]

Tradition and transformation in Eastern Nigeria . Ekechi, Felix K., 1934- Kent, Ohio , c1989. xi, 256 p. ;   ISBN 0-87338-368-0 (alk. paper)   DDC 966.9/4 19
DT515.9.O87 E39 1989
    NYPL [Sc E 89-186]

TRADITION (LITERATURE) see INFLUENCE (LITERARY, ARTISTIC, ETC.)

TRADITION, ORAL. see ORAL TRADITION.

La Tradition orale, source de la littérature contemporaine en Afrique : colloque international / organisé par l'ICA et le PEN international avec le concours du PNUD et de l'UNESCO, à Dakar (Sénégal) du 24 au 29 janvier 1983. Dakar : Les Nouvelles éditions africaines, c1984. 201 p. : ill. ; 25 cm. At head of title: Institut culturel africain. French or English. Includes bibliographical references.   ISBN 2-7236-0899-9
1. African literature - Congresses. 2. Folk literature, African - Congresses. I. Institut culturel africain. II. PEN.   *NYPL [Sc E 89-55]*

Traditional arts of Africa.
McNaughton, Patrick R. The Mande
blacksmiths . Bloomington , c1988. xxiv, 241 p.,
[4] p. of plates : ISBN 0-253-33683-X DDC
306/.089963 19
DT551.45.M36 M38 1988
NYPL [Sc E 88-393]

**Traditional games and dances in West African
nations /.** Cheska, Alyce Taylor. Schorndorf ,
1987. 136 p. ; ISBN 3-7780-6411-8 (pbk.) DDC
793.3/1966 19
GV1713.A358 C48 1987
NYPL [JFE 87-5517]

**Traditional leadership as service among the Igbo
of Nigeria .** Dine, George Uchechukwu. Rome ,
1983. xvi, 316 p. ; DDC 299/.6 19
BL2480.I2 D56 1983   **NYPL [Sc E 88-329]**

Traditional Zambian pottery /. Lorenz, Bente.
London , 1989. 47 p. : ISBN 0-905788-75-3
NYPL [Sc C 89-141]

TRADITIONS. see LEGENDS.

**Traditions orales et archéologie de la basse
Sahatorendrika .** Rasamuel, David.
[Antananarivo] , 1979. 287 p., [33] leaves of
plates :
DT469.M37 S247 1979   **NYPL [Sc F 88-79]**

**TRAFFIC SIGNS AND SIGNALS -
    JUVENILE LITERATURE.**
Sweet, Dovie Davis. Red light, green light .
Smithtown, N.Y. , 1978 (1980 printing) 39 p. :
ISBN 0-682-49088-1   **NYPL [Sc D 89-70]**

El tráfico de esclavos con América . Vega Franco,
Marisa. Sevilla , 1984. x, 220 p. : ISBN
84-00-05675-2 DDC 382/.44/09729 19
HT985 .V44 1984   **NYPL [Sc C 89-132]**

The trail-driving rooster /. Gipson, Fred. New
York : Harper & Row, c1955. 79 p. :
NYPL [Sc D 88-427]

The train to Lulu's /. Howard, Elizabeth
Fitzgerald. New York , c1988. [32] p. : ISBN
0-02-744620-4 : DDC [E] 19
PZ7.H8327 Tr 1988   **NYPL [Sc F 88-219]**

Training in Health and Race (Project) Pearson,
Maggie. Racial equality and good practice
maternity care . London , 1985. 37 p. : ISBN
0-86082-610-4 (pbk) : DDC 362.1/982 19
RG964.G7   **NYPL [Sc F 88-393]**

**TRAINING, OCCUPATIONAL. see
    OCCUPATIONAL TRAINING.**

**Training of personnel for services to Black
families .** Dodson, Jualynne E. [Atlanta]
[1976] 1 v. (various foliations) ;
NYPL [Sc F 88-130]

Training on separate tracks . Bot, Monica.
Braamfontein, Johannesburg , 1988. iv, 71 p. ;
ISBN 0-86982-346-9   **NYPL [Sc D 89-81]**

**TRAINING, PHYSICAL. see PHYSICAL
    EDUCATION AND TRAINING.**

**TRAINING, VOCATIONAL. see
    OCCUPATIONAL TRAINING.**

Traite négrière du XVe au XIXe siècle. Spanish.
La trata negrera del siglo XV al XIX :
documentos de trabajo e informe de la reunión
de expertos organizada por la Unesco en Puerto
Principe, Haiti, del 31 de enero al 4 de febrero
de 1978. Barcelona : Serbal ; UNESCO, 1981.
379 p. : ill. ; 20 cm. (Colección de temas africanos)
Translation of: La traite négrière du XVe au XIXe
siècle. ISBN 92-3-301672-2
1. Slave trade - History - Congresses. I. Title. II. Series.
NYPL [Sc D 88-650]

Transafrica Forum (Organization) A
retrospective : Blacks in U. S. foreign policy.
[Washington, D.C.] : Transafrica Forum, c1987.
32 p. : chiefly ill., ports. ; 24 cm. Cover title.
Errata slip inserted.
*1. Afro-Americans - Political activity. 2. United States -
Foreign relations. 3. United States - Foreign relations -
Africa. 4. Africa - Foreign relations - United States. I.
Title. II. Title: Blacks in U. S. foreign policy.*
NYPL [Sc E 88-163]

**Transformation and continuity in revolutionary
Ethiopia /.** Clapham, Christopher S. Cambridge
[Cambridgeshire] , New York , 1988. xviii, 284
p. : ISBN 0-521-33441-1 DDC 963.07 19
JQ3752 .C55 1988   **NYPL [Sc E 88-446]**

TRANSITION (KAMPALA, UGANDA)
Benson, Peter. Black Orpheus, Transition, and

modern cultural awakening in Africa /.
Berkeley , c1986. xiii, 320 p. : ISBN
0-520-05418-0 DDC 820/.8 19
PL8000.B63 B4 1986   **NYPL [Sc E 88-354]**

**TRANSVAAL (SOUTH AFRICA) - HISTORY -
    SOURCES - BIBLIOGRAPHY -
    CATALOGS.**
University of the Witwatersrand. Library. Guide
to the archives and papers . Johannesburg ,
1979. v, 100 p. ; ISBN 0-85494-593-8
NYPL [Sc F 89-32]

Traore, Fathié. Mémoires d'autres temps / Traore
Fathié. Ouagadougou, Burkina Faso? : s.n.,
1984- (Ouagadougou : Presses africaines) v. ; 22
cm. CONTENTS. - t. 1. Les enfants du hasard. DDC
966/.25 19
*1. Traore, Fathié. 2. Intellectuals - Burkina Faso -
Biography. 3. Burkina Faso - Biography. 4. Burkina
Faso - Colonization. 5. Burkina Faso - Social life and
customs - 20th century. I. Title.*
CT2478.T73 A3 1984   **NYPL [Sc D 88-386]**

TRAORE, FATHIÉ.
Traore, Fathié. Mémoires d'autres temps /.
Ouagadougou, Burkina Faso? , 1984-
(Ouagadougou : Presses africaines) v. ; DDC
966/.25 19
CT2478.T73 A3 1984   **NYPL [Sc D 88-386]**

**La trata de negros en el Río de la Plata durante
el siglo XVIII /.** Studer, Elena F. S. de. Bs.
As. [i.e. Buenos Aires] [1984] 378 p., [27]
leaves of plates (some folded) : ISBN
950-9138-08-8
HT1123.R5 S78 1984   **NYPL [Sc E 87-419]**

La trata negrera del siglo XV al XIX . Traite
négrière du XVe au XIXe siècle. Spanish.
Barcelona , 1981. 379 p. : ISBN 92-3-301672-2
NYPL [Sc D 88-650]

**Travail et main-d'oeuvre au Cameroun sous
régime français, 1916-1952 /.** Kaptue, Léon.
Paris [c1986] 282 p. : ISBN 2-85802-655-6
NYPL [Sc D 88-1237]

**Travaux et documents (Université de Madagascar.
Musée d'art et d'archéologie) .**
(22) Raherisoanjato, Daniel. Origines et
évolution du Royaume de l'Arindrano jusqu'au
XIXe siècle . Antananarivo , 1984. 334 leaves :
DDC 969/.1 19
DT469.M37 A747 1984
NYPL [Sc F 88-390]

TRAVEL - BIBLIOGRAPHY.
Simony, Maggy, 1920- Traveler's reading
guides . Bayport, N.Y. , c1981-c1984. 3 v. ;
ISBN 0-9602050-1-2 (v. 1) : DDC 016.9104 19
Z6016.T7 S54 G151   **NYPL [Sc D 89-343]**

**TRAVEL IN LITERATURE -
    BIBLIOGRAPHY.**
Simony, Maggy, 1920- Traveler's reading
guides . Bayport, N.Y. , c1981-c1984. 3 v. ;
ISBN 0-9602050-1-2 (v. 1) : DDC 016.9104 19
Z6016.T7 S54 G151   **NYPL [Sc D 89-343]**

TRAVELERS - BIOGRAPHY.
St. John, James Augustus, 1801-1875. The lives
of celebrated travellers [microform]. New York,
1859-68. 3 v.   **NYPL [Sc Micro R-3541]**

Traveler's reading guides . Simony, Maggy, 1920-
Bayport, N.Y. , c1981-c1984. 3 v. ; ISBN
0-9602050-1-2 (v. 1) : DDC 016.9104 19
Z6016.T7 S54 G151   **NYPL [Sc D 89-343]**

**Travels in Egypt and Nubia, Syria and Asia
Minor .** Irby, Charles Leonard, 1789-1845.
London , 1985. xxxiii, 560 p., [6] leaves of
plates (3 folded) : ISBN 1-85077-082-4 : DDC
915.6/041 916.2/043 19
DS48 DT53   **NYPL [JFD 88-9340]**

Travels with Pegasus . Dodwell, Christina, 1951-
London , 1989. 208 p., [16] p. of plates : ISBN
0-340-42502-4 : DDC 916.6/04 19
NYPL [JFE 89-902]

Treacherous journey . Avraham, Shmuel, 1945-
New York, NY , 1986. xii, 178 p. : ISBN
0-933503-46-6 (jacket); 0-933503-46-5 : DDC
963/.004924 19
DS135.E75 A93 1986   **NYPL [Sc E 87-275]**

Treading the ebony path . Lewis, Marvin A.
Columbia , 1987. 142 p. ; ISBN 0-8262-0638-7
(alk. paper) DDC 863 19
PQ8172 .L49 1987   **NYPL [Sc D 88-443]**

Treasure of Green Knowe. Boston, L. M. (Lucy
Maria), 1892- New York [1958] 185 p. DDC

[Fic]
PZ7.B6497 Tr   **NYPL [Sc D 88-1497]**

**A treasury of African art from the Harrison
Eiteljorg Collection /.** Celenko, Theodore.
Bloomington , c1983. 239 p. : ISBN
0-253-11057-2 DDC 730/.0967/074013 19
NB1091.65 .C46 1983
NYPL [3-MADF+ 88-2098]

Trecento anni di jazz . De Stefano, Gildo.
Milano , 1986. 262 p., [16] leaves of plates :
NYPL [Sc D 88-1226]

Tregillis, Helen Cox. River roads to freedom :
fugitive slave notices and sheriff notices found
in Illinois sources / compiled by Helen Cox
Tregillis. Bowie, Md. : Heritage Bks., 1988. 122
p. : ill. ; 21 cm. Spine title: Fugitive slave notices,
Illinois. Includes index. Bibliography: p. 108-110.
ISBN 1-556-13120-8 DDC 929/.3/089960773 19
*1. Fugitive slaves - Illinois - Registers. 2.
Afro-Americans - Illinois - Genealogy. 3. Illinois -
Genealogy. 4. Southern States - Genealogy. I. Title. II.
Title: Fugitive slave notices, Illinois.*
F540 .T7 1988   **NYPL [Sc D 88-1442]**

Les tresseurs de corde . Pliya, Jean, 1931- Paris ,
1987. 239 p. ; ISBN 2-218-07841-X
NYPL [Sc C 88-9]

The trial of Mallam Ilya and other plays /.
Abdallah, Mohammed Ben. Accra , 1987. 165
p. ; ISBN 996-497-076-5
NYPL [Sc D 88-1491]

Trial of Pedro de Zulueta, Jun. . Zulueta, Pedro
de, Jr. London , 1844. lxxiv, 410 p. ;
NYPL [Sc Rare F 88-1]

TRIAL PRACTICE - UNITED STATES.
Chesler, Mark A. Social science in court .
Madison, Wis. , 1988. xiv, 286 p. ; ISBN
0-299-11620-4 : DDC 344.73/0798 347.304798
19
KF8925.D5 C48 1988   **NYPL [Sc E 89-187]**

**TRIALS (ASSAULT AND BATTERY) - NEW
    YORK (N.Y.)**
Fletcher, George P. A crime of self-defense .
New York , London , c1988. xi, 253 p. ; ISBN
0-02-910311-8 DDC 345.73/04 347.3054 19
KF224.G63 F54 1988   **NYPL [JLE 88-4737]**

**TRIALS (MURDER) - MISSISSIPPI -
    SUMNER.**
Whitfield, Stephen J., 1942- A death in the
Delta . New York , London , c1988. xiv, 193
p., [8] p. of plates : ISBN 0-02-935121-9 : DDC
345.73/02523 347.3052523 19
E185.61 .W63 1989   **NYPL [Sc E 89-140]**

**TRIALS (TERRORISM) - SOUTH AFRICA -
    PRETORIA.**
Biko, Steve, 1946-1977. The testimony of Steve
Biko /. London , 1987, c1978. xxxv, 298 p. ;
NYPL [Sc C 89-126]

Triaud, Jean Louis. Ḥājj 'Umar ibn Sa'īd al-Fūti,
1794?-1864. [Bayān mā waqa'a. French &
Arabic.] Voilà ce qui est arrivé . Paris , 1983.
261 p., [57] leaves of plates : ISBN 2-222-03216-4
NYPL [Sc F 88-211]

**Tribal structure of the Ngok Dinka of southern
Kordofan Province [microform] /.** Abu Sabah,
Mohammed Azim. Khartoum , 1978. 20
leaves ;   **NYPL [Sc Micro F-11037]**

Tribaliks . Lopes, Henri, 1937- London , 1987.
86 p. ; ISBN 0-435-90762-X
NYPL [Sc C 88-20]

The tribe Israel is no more [microform] /. 'Isá
'Abd Allāh Muḥammad al-Mahdī, 1945-
Brooklyn [197-?] 62 p. ;
NYPL [Sc Micro R-4114 no. 13]

TRIBES AND TRIBAL SYSTEM.
Bernardi, Bernardo. The social structure of the
kraal among the Zezuru in Musami (Southern
Rhodesia) [Cape Town] 1950. [2], 60, [1] .
DDC 572.9689
GN490 .B4   **NYPL [Sc F 88-349]**

**TRIBES AND TRIBAL SYSTEMS - SUDAN -
    KORDOFAN.**
Abu Sabah, Mohammed Azim. Tribal structure
of the Ngok Dinka of southern Kordofan
Province [microform] /. Khartoum , 1978. 20
leaves ;   **NYPL [Sc Micro F-11037]**

Tribute. Broodhagen, Karl R. The National
Cultural Foundation presents Tribute, an
exhibition of the sculpture of Karl Broodhagen .

[Barbados] [1985?] 16 p. :
MLCM 87/08440 (N)   *NYPL [Sc D 88-570]*

A Tribute to president Daniel T. Arap Moi.
Nairobi : Mecka Publicity for and on behalf of
Mombasa KANU Branch, 1988. 52 p. : ill.
(some col.), ports. ; 30 cm. Cover title.
*1. Moi, Daniel Arap, 1924-. 2. Kenya - Politics and
government - 1978-. 3. Kenya - Economic conditions -
1963-. I. Kenya African National Union.*
       NYPL [Sc F 89-113]

Tricky Tortoise /. Mwenye Hadithi. Boston ,
c1988. [32] p. : ISBN 0-316-33724-2 : DDC [E]
19
PZ7.M975 Tr 1988   *NYPL [Sc F 88-389]*

Trill, Carol. Dispossessed daughter of Africa / by
Carol Trill. London : Karia Press, 1988. 190
p. : port. ; 20 cm. ISBN 0-946918-42-2 (pbk.)
*1. Women, Black - Great Britain - Biograpy. 2. Blacks -
Great Britain - Biography. 3. Nigerians - Great Britain -
Biography. 4. Clergymen's wives - Great Britain -
Biography. I. Title.*   *NYPL [sc C 88-228]*

Trillo, Richard. The rough guide to Kenya /
written and researched by Richard Trillo ; with
additional research by Jackie Switzer, Rosemary
Mercer, and Marc Dubin ; maps by Teresa
Driver. London ; New York : Routledge &
Kegan Paul, 1987. 374 p. : maps ; 20 cm. (The
Rough guides) Includes index. Bibliography: p. 344-347.
ISBN 0-7102-0616-X (pbk.) DDC 916.76/2044
19
*1. Kenya - Description and travel - 1981- -
Guide-books. I. Title. II. Series.*
DT433.52 .T75 1986   *NYPL [Sc C 88-145]*

Trindade, Diamantino Fernandes. Linares,
Ronaldo Antonio. Xangô e inhaçã /. [São
Paulo] , c1987. 85 p. : *NYPL [Sc D 88-553]*

Trinidad : the land of the humming bird. Port of
Spain, Trinidad : [s.n., 193-?] [28] p. : chiefly
ill. ; 17 x 24 cm. "Specially printed in Great Britain
for the publishers, Port of Spain, Trinidad."
1. Trinidad. I. Title: Land of the hummingbird.
       NYPL [Sc B 88-2]

TRINIDAD.
Trinidad . Port of Spain, Trinidad [193-?] [28]
p. :   *NYPL [Sc B 88-2]*

Trinidad and Tobago /. Chambers, Frances.
Oxford, England , Santa Barbara, Calif. , c1986.
xv, 213 p. : ISBN 1-8150-9020-7
       NYPL [Sc D 89-33]

**TRINIDAD AND TOBAGO -
BIBLIOGRAPHY.**
Chambers, Frances. Trinidad and Tobago /.
Oxford, England , Santa Barbara, Calif. , c1986.
xv, 213 p. : ISBN 1-8150-9020-7
       NYPL [Sc D 89-33]

TRINIDAD AND TOBAGO. CONSTITUTION.
Trinidad and Tobago. Constitution Commission.
Thinking things over /. Trinidad , 1988. v, 94
p. ;   *NYPL [Sc D 89-8]*

Trinidad and Tobago. Constitution Commission.
Thinking things over / by the Constitution
Commission (1987) of the Republic of Trinidad
and Tobago. Trinidad : Govt. Printery, 1988. v,
94 p. ; 21 cm.
1. Trinidad and Tobago. Constitution.
       NYPL [Sc D 89-8]

**TRINIDAD AND TOBAGO - DESCRIPTION
AND TRAVEL - GUIDE-BOOKS.**
Taylor, Jeremy, 1943- Masquerade . London ,
1986. v, 135 p. : ISBN 0-333-41985-5 (pbk) :
DDC 917.298/3044 19
F2122   *NYPL [Sc D 88-837]*

Trinidad and Tobago dialect (plus) /. Haynes,
Martin De Coursey, 1939. San Fernando,
Trinidad , 1987. 215 p. ;
       NYPL [Sc D 88-860]

**TRINIDAD AND TOBAGO - ECONOMIC
CONDITIONS.**
Committee for Labour Solidarity. CLS speaks .
[Trinidad and Tobago] [1987] iii, 80 p. :
       NYPL [Sc D 88-969]

**TRINIDAD AND TOBAGO - EMIGRATION
AND IMMIGRATION.**
Ho, Christine G. T. The Caribbean connection .
c1985. xvi, 290 leaves : *NYPL [Sc F 88-234]*

TRINIDAD AND TOBAGO - FICTION.
Sharlowe. Requiem for a village ; Apartheid
love /. Trinidad , 1982. 78, 70 p. ;
       NYPL [Sc C 88-63]

TRINIDAD AND TOBAGO - HISTORY.
De Verteuil, Anthony. A history of Diego
Martin 1784-1884 /. Port of Spain, Trinidad ,
c1987. viii, 174 p., [96] p. of plates : ISBN
976-8054-10-7   *NYPL [Sc F 88-192]*

TRINIDAD AND TOBAGO - INDUSTRIES.
Trinidad & Tobago investment opportunities in
industry. Port-of-Spain, Trinidad , 1985. 40 p. ;
       NYPL [Sc F 88-94]

**Trinidad & Tobago investment opportunities in
industry.** Port-of-Spain, Trinidad : Trinidad &
Tobago Industrial Development Corporation,
1985. 40 p. ; 28 cm.
*1. Investments - Trinidad and Tobago. 2. Trinidad and
Tobago - Industries. I. Industrial Development
Corporation (Trinidad and Tobago). II. Title.*
       NYPL [Sc F 88-94]

**TRINIDAD AND TOBAGO LITERATURE
(ENGLISH)**
Mahabir, Noor Kumar. The still cry .
Tacarigua, Trinidad , Ithaca, N.Y. , c1985. 191
p. ;   *NYPL [Sc D 88-401]*

**TRINIDAD AND TOBAGO LITERATURE
(ENGLISH) - 20TH CENTURY -
HISTORY AND CRITICISM.**
Sander, Reinhard. The Trinidad awakening .
New York , 1988. xii, 168 p. ; ISBN
0-313-24562-2 (lib. bdg. : alk. paper) DDC
810/.9 19
PR9272 .S24 1988   *NYPL [Sc E 89-111]*

**TRINIDAD AND TOBAGO LITERATURE
(ENGLISH) - BIBLIOGRAPHY.**
Wharton-Lake, Beverly D. Creative literature of
Trinidad and Tobago . Washington, D.C. ,
1988. xi, 102 p. ; ISBN 0-8270-2709-5
       NYPL [Sc D 88-710]

**Trinidad and Tobago. Working Group on Special
Libraries/Information Network.** Directory of
special libraries/information units in Trinidad
and Tobago /. Port of Spain, Trinidad &
Tobago [1986] iv, 59 p. ; DDC
026/.00025/72983 19
Z753.T7 D57 1986   *NYPL [Sc D 88-1019]*

The Trinidad awakening . Sander, Reinhard. New
York , 1988. xii, 168 p. ; ISBN 0-313-24562-2
(lib. bdg. : alk. paper) DDC 810/.9 19
PR9272 .S24 1988   *NYPL [Sc E 89-111]*

TRINIDAD - ETHNIC RELATIONS.
Magid, Alvin, 1937- Urban nationalism .
Gainesville , 1988. x, 294 p. : ISBN
0-8130-0853-0 DDC 972.98/3 19
F2119 .M34 1988   *NYPL [HRG 88-1040]*

TRINIDAD - FICTION.
Lovelace, Earl. A brief conversion and other
stories / . Oxford [Eng.] , 1988. 141 p. ; ISBN
0-435-98882-4   *NYPL [Sc C 89-43]*

TRINIDAD - MISCELLANEA.
Jackman, Randolph, 1932- From slavery to
jouvert, 1975 /. [Port of Spain?] [1975] 68 p. ;
DDC 972.98/3 19
F2119 .J32   *NYPL [Sc C 89-5]*

**TRINIDAD - POPULATION - HISTORY -
18TH CENTURY.**
John, A. Meredith. The plantation slaves of
Trinidad ,1783-1816 . Cambridge [Eng.] , New
York , 1988. xvi, 259 p. : ISBN 0-521-36166-4
DDC 306/.362/0972983 19
HT1105.T6 J65 1988   *NYPL [Sc E 89-235]*

TRINIDAD - SOCIAL CONDITIONS.
Craig, Susan. Smiles and blood . London ,
1988. vii, 70 p., [4] p. of plates : ISBN
0-901241-81-4 (hard back)
       NYPL [Sc D 89-418]

TRINIDAD - SOCIAL LIFE AND CUSTOMS.
Stewart, John O. Drinkers, drummers, and
decent folk . Albany , c1989. xviii, 230 p. ;
ISBN 0-88706-829-4 DDC 306/.097298/3 19
GN564.T7 S74 1988   *NYPL [Sc E 89-220]*

**TRINIDAD - STATISTICS, VITAL -
HISTORY - 18TH CENTURY.**
John, A. Meredith. The plantation slaves of
Trinidad, 1783-1816 . Cambridge [Eng.] , New
York , 1988. xvi, 259 p. : ISBN 0-521-36166-4
DDC 306/.362/0972983 19
HT1105.T6 J65 1988   *NYPL [Sc E 89-235]*

TRINIDADIANS - VENEZUELA.
Díaz Sánchez, Ramón. [Mene. English.] Mene
/. Trinidad [193-?] (Trinidad : Multimedia
Production Center, Faculty of Education,
U.W.I.) 141 p. :   *NYPL [Sc D 89-544]*

**Trinta anos do Instituto Joaquim Nabuco de
Pesquisas Sociais.** 30 anos do Instituto Joaquim
Nabuco de Pesquisas Sociais /. Recife , 1981.
343 p. : ISBN 85-7019-008-5 DDC 300.72081 19
H67.R44 A13 1981   *NYPL [Sc D 88-871]*

Trono de vidro . Olinto, Antônio. Rio de Janeiro ,
1987. 382 p. ; ISBN 85-7007-110-8
       NYPL [Sc D 88-76]

**TROOPS, MERCENARY. see MERCENARY
TROOPS.**

Tropical Africa Advisory Group. Tropical Africa
Advisory Group trade mission to the Republic
of Ghana, 16-22 March 1985. [London] ([1
Victoria Street, SW1H OET]) [1985] iii, 64 p. :
DDC 330.9667/05 19
HC1060   *NYPL [Sc F 88-88]*

**Tropical Africa Advisory Group trade mission to
the Republic of Ghana, 16-22 March 1985.**
[London] ([1 Victoria Street, SW1H OET]) :
British Overseas Trade Board, [1985] iii, 64 p. :
2 maps ; 30 cm. Cover title. DDC 330.9667/05 19
*1. Investments, British - Ghana. 2. Ghana - Economic
conditions - 1979-. 3. Ghana - Commerce. I. Tropical
Africa Advisory Group.*
HC1060   *NYPL [Sc F 88-88]*

TROPICAL MEDICINE - AFRICA.
Monekosso, G L. Introductíon aux problèmes
de santé des peuples d'Afrique tropicale .
Yaoundé , 1978. 241 p. :
       NYPL [Sc E 86-437]

**TROPICAL MEDICINE - NIGERIA -
BIBLIOGRAPHY.**
De Cola, Freya D. Three decades of medical
research at the College of Medicine, Ibadan,
Nigeria, 1948-1980 . Ibadan, Nigeria , 1984. xv,
208 p. ; ISBN 978-12-1157-1 (pbk.) DDC 016.61
19
Z6661.N6 D4 1984 R824.N6
       NYPL [Sc E 89-160]

**TROPICS - DESCRIPTION AND TRAVEL -
VIEWS.**
Webb, Alex. Hot light/half-made worlds . New
York, N.Y. , 1986. 91 p. : ISBN 0-500-54116-7 :
DDC 779/.99090913 19
TR820.5 .W43 1986   *NYPL [Sc G 87-23]*

Trotman, Donald A. B. Report on human rights
in Grenada : a survey of political and civil
rights in Grenada during the period of
1970-1983 / by Donald Trotman and Keith
Friday. [Bustamante?] : Bustamante Institute of
Public and International Affairs, [198-] viii, 54
p. : ill. ; 22 cm. "Sponsored by the Bustamante
Institute of Public and International Affairs." DDC
323.4/9/09729845 19
*1. Civil rights - Grenada. I. Friday, Keith (Keith
Hudson Wellington), 1954-. II. Bustamante Institute of
Public and International Affairs. III. Title.*
JC599.G76 T76 1980z   *NYPL [Sc D 88-816]*

Trouillot, Hénock. Les limites du créole dans
notre enseignement / Henock Trouillot.
Port-au-Prince : [H.Trouillot] ; Imprimerie des
Antilles, 1980. 85 p. ; 21 cm. Bibliography: p. 85.
*1. French language - Haiti. 2. Creole dialects, French -
Haiti. I. Title.*   *NYPL [Sc D 88-1400]*

Troupin, Dominique. Contes du Rwanda . Paris ,
1983. 174 p. : ISBN 2-85319-119-2
       NYPL [Sc C 88-83]

Troxler, Niklaus. Jazz in Willisau . Luzern ,
c1978. 206 p. : ISBN 3-7239-0051-8 DDC
785.42/09494/5 19
ML3509.S9 J4 1978   *NYPL [Sc F 89-24]*

The true ballad of glorious Harriet Tubman /.
Cleghorn, Sarah Norcliffe, 1876-1959.
[Manchester, Vt. , c1933] 12 p. ;
       NYPL [Sc Rare C 89-6]

The true story of Noah (Pbuh) [microform] /.
'Isá 'Abd Allāh Muḥammad al-Mahdī, 1945-
Brooklyn, N.Y. [1978] 62 p. :
       NYPL [Sc Micro R-4114 no. 9]

**The true story of the Prophet Abraham (Pbuh)
[microform] /.** 'Isá 'Abd Allāh Muḥammad
al-Mahdī, 1945- Brooklyn, N.Y. [1980?] 96 p. :
       NYPL [Sc Micro R-4114 no. 7]

Truly Elizabeth /. Weiss, Edna S. Boston , 1957.
178 p.   *NYPL [Sc D 88-663]*

The trumpet parable . Nwankwo, Chimalum.
Enugu, Nigeria , 1987. 126 p. : ISBN
978-226-931-X   *NYPL [Sc B 89-16]*

Trumpeters.
Anigbedu, Laide. Hero's welcome /.
Yaba-Lagos, Nigeria , 1986. 141 p. ; ISBN
978-256-400-1 *NYPL [Sc C 88-283]*

TRUTH, SOJOURNER, D. 1883 - JUVENILE LITERATURE.
Ferris, Jeri. Walking the road to freedom .
Minneapolis , 1987. 64 p. : ISBN 0-87614-318-4
(lib. bdg.) : DDC 305.5/67/0924 B 92 19
E185.97.T8 F47 1987 *NYPL [Sc D 88-1046]*

Krass, Peter. Sojourner Truth /. New York ,
c1988. 110 p. : ISBN 1-555-46611-7 DDC
305.5/67/0924 B 92 19
E185.97.T8 K73 1988 *NYPL [Sc E 88-470]*

Tsado, Jacob. Nwosu, I. E. A guide to Christian
writing in Africa /. Enugu, Nigeria , 1987. 116
p. ; ISBN 978-262-606-6 *NYPL [Sc C 88-156]*

Tsaro-Wiwa, Ken. Basi and company : a modern
African folktale / Ken Saro-Wiwa. Port
Harcourt, Nigeria ; Epsom,Surrey : Saros
International, 1987. 216 p. ; 20 cm. ISBN
1-87071-600-0 (pbk) : DDC 823 19
1. Nigeria - Fiction. I. Title.
PR9387.9.S3 *NYPL [Sc C 88-224]*

Tschad--Land ohne Hoffnung? . Baar, Marius.
Bad Liebenzell , c1985. 190 p., [6] p. of plates :
ISBN 3-88002-270-4 *NYPL [Sc D 88-892]*

Tshiyembe Mwayila. Francophonie & géopolitique
africaine . Paris , c1987. 156 p. ; ISBN
2-906861-01-4 *NYPL [Sc D 88-1448]*

TSIMIHETY (MADAGASCAN PEOPLE)
Patrice, Tongasolo. Fomban-drazana Tsimihety
/. Fianarantsoa [Madagascar] , 1985. 383 p., [8]
p. of plates : *NYPL [Sc C 88-292]*

Tsonga-English dictionary /. Cuenod, R.
Braamfontein , 1967. 286 p. ;
NYPL [Sc D 88-89]

TSONGA LANGUAGE - DICTIONARIES - ENGLISH.
Cuenod, R. Tsonga-English dictionary /.
Braamfontein , 1967. 286 p. ;
NYPL [Sc D 88-89]

TSONGA LANGUAGE - TEXTS.
Schnorr von Carolsfeld, Julius, 1794-1872.
[Bibel in Bildern. Selections.] Bibele hi
swifaniso . Kensington, Tvl. , 1970. 64 p. :
NYPL [Sc E 89-180]

Tsotsi, W. M. From chattel to wage slavery : a
new approach to South African history / by
W.M. Tsotsi.1st ed. Maseru : Lesotho Print.
and Pub. Co., 1981. 136 p., [2] folded leaves of
plates : maps ; 21 cm. Includes bibliographical
references and index. DDC 306/.0968 19
1. Blacks - South Africa - History. 2. Blacks - South
Africa - Economic conditions. 3. Blacks - South
Africa - Social conditions. 4. South Africa - History. I.
Title.
DT763.6 .T76 1981 *NYPL [Sc D 89-22]*

TSWANA (AFRICAN PEOPLE) - RELIGION.
Dierks, Friedrich. Evangelium im afrikanischen
Kontext . Gütersloh , c1986. 206 p. : ISBN
3-579-00239-2 DDC 266/.0089963 19
BL2480.T76 D54 1986 *NYPL [Sc D 88-879]*

TSWANA IMPRINTS.
Peters, Marguerite Andree. Bibliography of the
Tswana language . Pretoria , 1982. 1 [i.e. L],
175 p., [3] leaves of plates : ISBN 0-7989-0116-0
DDC 015.68 19
Z3601 .P47 1982 *NYPL [Sc E 87-667]*

TSWANA LANGUAGE - BIBLIOGRAPHY.
Peters, Marguerite Andree. Bibliography of the
Tswana language . Pretoria , 1982. 1 [i.e. L],
175 p., [3] leaves of plates : ISBN 0-7989-0116-0
DDC 015.68 19
Z3601 .P47 1982 *NYPL [Sc E 87-667]*

Tu as rendez-vous avec le Diable /. Mességué,
Maurice. Paris , c1987. 219 p. ; ISBN
2-87679-008-4 *NYPL [Sc E 88-540]*

Tu aurais pu lui dire je t'aime /. Mucci, Floren's.
Port-au-Prince, Haiti [between 1985 and 1988]
85 p. ; *NYPL [Sc C 88-233]*

TUAREGS - PICTORIAL WORKS.
Durou, Jean Marc. Sahara . Marseille, France ,
1986. 155 p. : ISBN 2-902634-30-7
NYPL [Sc G 88-1]

Tubiana, Marie José. Des troupeaux et des
femmes : mariage et transferts de biens chez les
Beri (Zaghawa et Bideyat) du Tchad et du

Soudan / Marie-José Tubiana. Paris : Éditions
L'Harmattan, 1985. 390 p., [16] p. of plates :
ill. ; 24 cm. (Bibliothèque Peiresc . 4) "Ouvrage
publié avec le concours du Centre national de la
recherche scientifique". Includes indexes. Bibliography:
p. 361-369. ISBN 2-85802-554-9
1. Zaghawa - Rites and ceremonies. 2. Marriage - Chad.
I. Title. II. Series. *NYPL [Sc E 88-217]*

TUBMAN, HARRIET, 1815?-1913 - JUVENILE LITERATURE.
Ferris, Jeri. Go free or die . Minneapolis ,
1987. 63 p. : ISBN 0-87614-317-6 (lib. bdg.) :
DDC 305.5/67/0924 B 92 19
E444.T82 F47 1987 *NYPL [Sc D 88-620]*

TUBMAN, HARRIET, 1820?-1913 - POETRY.
Cleghorn, Sarah Norcliffe, 1876-1959. The true
ballad of glorious Harriet Tubman /.
[Manchester, Vt. , c1933] 12 p. ;
NYPL [Sc Rare C 89-6]

Tucker, Charlotte Maria, 1821-1893. Abbeokoeta;
or, De dageraad tusschen de keerkringen: eene
schets van het ontstaan en den vooruitgang der
zending in Yorriba. Uit het Engelsch naar den
vijfden druk vertaald, en tot op den jongsten
tijd bijgewerkt door T. M. Looman.
Amsterdam, H. Höveker, 1860. viii, 330 p.
plates (part col.) fold. maps. 19cm.
1. Abeokuta (Nigeria) - Description. 2. Missions to
Yorubas. I. Looman, Theodorus Matthijs, 1816-1900. II.
Title. *NYPL [Sc Rare C 88-25]*

TUCKER, LORENZO.
Grupenhoff, Richard, 1941- The black
Valentino . Metuchen, N.J. , 1988. xi, 188 p. :
ISBN 0-8108-2078-1 DDC 790.2/092/4 B 19
PN2287.T78 G78 1988
NYPL [Sc D 88-1029]

Tucker, Musu Margaret. Harvest time stories /
collected by Musu Margaret Tucker. Freetown :
People's Educational Association of Sierra
Leone, 1985. 55 p. : ill. ; 21 cm. (Stories and
songs from Sierra Leone. 6)
1. Tales - Sierra Leone. I. Title. II. Series.
NYPL [Sc D 89-9]

Tucker, Susan, 1950- Telling memories among
southern women . Baton Rouge , c1988. xi, 279
p. : ISBN 0-8071-1440-5 (alk. paper) : DDC
305.4/3 19
HD6072.2.U52 A137 1988
NYPL [Sc E 89-124]

**Tuislande, South Africa. see Homelands, South
Africa.**

Turian Cardozo, Jacqueline. On ne guérit pas de
son enfance / Jacqueline Turian Cardozo.
Port-au-Prince : Deschamps, 1987. 220 p., [1]
folded leaf plates : ports. ; 21 cm.
1. Turian Cardozo, Jacqueline. 2. Women - Haiti -
Biography. I. Title. *NYPL [Sc D 88-293]*

TURIAN CARDOZO, JACQUELINE.
Turian Cardozo, Jacqueline. On ne guérit pas
de son enfance /. Port-au-Prince , 1987. 220 p.,
[1] folded leaf plates : *NYPL [Sc D 88-293]*

Turirimbane . Rugamba, Sipiriyani. Butare,
Rwanda , 1987. 289 p. ;
NYPL [Sc D 88-1514]

TURKANA LANGUAGE - DICTIONARY - ENGLISH.
Barrett, Anthony. English-Turkana dictionary /.
Nairobi , 1988. xxx, 225 p. ; ISBN
0-333-44577-5 *NYPL [Sc D 89-437]*

Turkie, Alan. Know what I mean? : young men
from Lewisham discuss their lives and
experiences / edited by Alan Turkie. Leicester :
National Youth Bureau, 1982. 82 p. : ill. ; 22
cm. ISBN 0-86155-062-5 :
1. Minority youth - England - London. 2. Youth -
England - London. 3. Lewisham (London, England). I.
Title. *NYPL [Sc D 89-464]*

Turn the next corner. Alcock, Gudrun. New
York [1969] 160 p. DDC [Fic]
PZ7.A332 Tu *NYPL [Sc D 88-1471]*

Turner, Charles F., 1918- AIDS . Washington,
DC , 1989. xiii, 589 p. : ISBN 0-309-03976-2;
0-309-03976-2 (pbk). *NYPL [Sc D 89-342]*

Turner, Darwin T., 1931. Marshall, Paule, 1929-
Soul clap hands and sing /. Washington, D.C. ,
1988, 1961. xlviii, 105 p. ; ISBN 0-88258-155-4
NYPL [Sc D 88-1451]

Turner, Joyce Moore, 1920- Moore, Richard B.
(Richard Benjamin) Richard B. Moore,

Caribbean militant in Harlem . Bloomington ,
London , 1988. ix, 324 p. : ISBN 0-253-31299-0
DDC 970.004/96 19
F2183 .M66 1988 *NYPL [Sc E 89-148]*

TURNER, NAT, 1800?-1831 - JUVENILE LITERATURE.
Bisson, Terry. Nat Turner /. New York ,
c1988. 111 p. : ISBN 1-555-46613-3 DDC
975.5/5503/0924 B 92 19
F232.S7 T873 1988 *NYPL [Sc E 88-454]*

Turner, Richard, 1941- The eye of the needle :
toward participatory democracy in South Africa
/ Richard Turner ; pref. by Merrill Proudfoot
and Ronald Christenson.U. S. ed. Maryknoll,
N.Y. : Orbis Books, 1978, c1972. xxiv, 173 p. ;
21 cm. ISBN 0-88344-121-7. DDC 309.1/68/06
1. Church and race relations - South Africa. 2. South
Africa - Economic conditions - 1961-. 3. South Africa -
Politics and government - 1961-1978. I. Title.
DT763 .T85 1978 *NYPL [JLD 84-744]*

Turner, Ruth S. Ramusi, Molapatene Collins.
Soweto, my love /. New York , c1988. viii, 262
p. ; ISBN 0-8050-0263-4 DDC 968.06/092/4 B 19
DT779.955.R36 A3 1988
NYPL [Sc E 89-95]

TURNER, THOMAS WYATT.
Nickels, Marilyn Wenzke. Black Catholic
protest and the Federated Colored Catholics,
1917-1933 . New York , 1988. ix, 325 p. ;
ISBN 0-8240-4098-8 (alk. paper) : DDC
282/.73/08996073 19
BX1407.N4 N5 1988 *NYPL [Sc E 89-85]*

Turner, W. Burghardt, 1915- Moore, Richard B.
(Richard Benjamin) Richard B. Moore,
Caribbean militant in Harlem . Bloomington ,
London , 1988. ix, 324 p. : ISBN 0-253-31299-0
DDC 970.004/96 19
F2183 .M66 1988 *NYPL [Sc E 89-148]*

TURTLES - AFRICA - JUVENILE FICTION.
Mwenye Hadithi. Tricky Tortoise /. Boston ,
c1988. [32] p. : ISBN 0-316-33724-2 : DDC [E]
19
PZ7.M975 Tr 1988 *NYPL [Sc F 88-389]*

The Tuskegee airmen . Francis, Charles E.
Boston, MA , c1988. 300, [33] p. : ISBN
0-8283-1386-5 : DDC 940.54/4973 19
D790 .F637 1988 *NYPL [Sc E 89-164]*

Tutu . Du Boulay, Shirley. London , 1988. 286 p.,
[8] p. of plates : ISBN 0-340-41614-9 : DDC
283/.68/0924 19
BX5700.6.Z8T87 *NYPL [*R-ZPZ 88-3127]*

Tutu, Desmond.
Crying in the wilderness : the struggle for
justice in South Africa / Desmond Tutu ;
introduced and edited by John Webster ;
foreword by Trevor Huddleston.Rev. and
updated. London : Mowbray, 1986. xix, 124 p.,
[8] p. of plates : ill., 1 map, ports. ; 18 cm.
(Mowbrays popular Christian paperbacks) Bibliography:
p. 124. ISBN 0-264-67119-8 (pbk) : DDC 261.7 19
1. Apartheid - South Africa. I. Webster, John. II. Title.
DT737 *NYPL [Sc C 89-10]*

The words of Desmond Tutu / selected by
Naomi Tutu. 1st ed. New York : Newmarket
Press, c1989. 109 p. : ill. ; 21 cm. Bibliography: p.
105-107. ISBN 1-557-04038-9 (dust jacket) : DDC
283/.68 19
1. Tutu, Desmond - Quotations. I. Tutu, Naomi. II.
Title.
BX5700.6.Z8 T875 1989
NYPL [Sc D 89-495]

TUTU, DESMOND.
Du Boulay, Shirley. Tutu . London , 1988. 286
p., [8] p. of plates : ISBN 0-340-41614-9 : DDC
283/.68/0924 19
BX5700.6.Z8T87 *NYPL [*R-ZPZ 88-3127]*

TUTU, DESMOND - QUOTATIONS.
Tutu, Desmond. The words of Desmond Tutu
/. New York , c1989. 109 p. : ISBN
1-557-04038-9 (dust jacket) : DDC 283/.68 19
BX5700.6.Z8 T875 1989
NYPL [Sc D 89-495]

Tutu, Naomi. Tutu, Desmond. The words of
Desmond Tutu /. New York , c1989. 109 p. :
ISBN 1-557-04038-9 (dust jacket) : DDC
283/.68 19
BX5700.6.Z8 T875 1989
NYPL [Sc D 89-495]

Twaddle, Michael. Uganda now . Athens ,
London , 1988. 376 p. : ISBN 0-85255-315-3

(cased) :   DDC 967.6/104 19
HN800.U35   *NYPL [Sc D 88-1436]*

Tweed Gallery (New York (N.Y))
Black visions '87 . New York , 1987. 32 p. :
NYPL [Sc F 88-258]

Black visions '88 . New York [1988] 44 p. :
NYPL [Sc D 88-1200]

The twelve-day revolution /. Boro, Isaac. Benin
City, Nigeria , 1982. 158 p., [8] p. of plates :
ISBN 978-234-040-5   *NYPL [Sc C 88-109]*

Twelve million black voices. 12 million Black
voices /. New York , 1988, c1941. xx, 152 p. :
ISBN 0-938410-48-2 :   DDC 973/.0496073 19
E185.86 .A13 1988   *NYPL [Sc F 88-315]*

Twelve years a slave . Northup, Solomon, b.
1808. New York , 1857. 336 p. :
NYPL [Sc Rare C 89-34]

TWENTIETH CENTURY - FORECASTS.
Reclaiming the future . Oxford , Riverton,
N.J. , c1986. xvi, 197 p. :   ISBN 1-85148-010-2
(pbk.) :   DDC 303.4/96 19
DT4 .R43 1986   *NYPL [Sc D 88-584]*

Twenty-dollar horse /. Raferty, Gerald. Eau
Claire, Wisconsin , 1967, c1955. 192 p. :
NYPL [Sc D 88-664]

TWENTY-FIRST CENTURY - FORECASTS.
Reclaiming the future . Oxford , Riverton,
N.J. , c1986. xvi, 197 p. :   ISBN 1-85148-010-2
(pbk.) :   DDC 303.4/96 19
DT4 .R43 1986   *NYPL [Sc D 88-584]*

**Twenty five years of merchant banking in
Nigeria** /. Adewunmi, Wole. Akoka , 1985. xvi,
136 p. ;   ISBN 978-226-475-X :   DDC
332.66/09669 19
HG1971.N6 A34 1985
NYPL [Sc D 88-1020]

Twenty-five years of partnership. Uku, Patience
Essie Urutajirinere Blankson. 25 years of
partnership /. [Benin City, Nigeria , 1981?] 114
p. :   *NYPL [Sc D 88-380]*

Twenty-two reviews /. Heinecke, P. Kaduna,
[Nigeria] [1986?] 69 p. ;
NYPL [Sc E 88-284]

Twenty year's [!] experience of a missionary
[microform]. [Broughton, Virginia W] Chicago,
1907. 140 p.   *NYPL [Sc Micro R-1445]*

Twice condemned . Schwarz, Philip J., 1940-
Baton Rouge , c1988. xiv, 353 p. :   ISBN
0-8071-1401-4 (alk. paper)   DDC 346.75501/3
347.550613 19
KFV2801.6.S55 S39 1988
NYPL [Sc E 89-112]

TWINS.
Brüggemann, Anne. Amagdala und Akawuruk .
Hohenschäftlarn bei München , 1986. 264 p. :
ISBN 3-87673-106-2   *NYPL [Sc D 88-652]*

TWINS SEVEN-SEVEN.
Beier, Ulli. Three Yoruba artists . Bayreuth, W.
Germany , c19. 93 p. ;
NYPL [Sc D 88-1325]

Two and me makes three. Greene, Roberta. New
York [1970] [36] p.
PZ7.G843 Tw   *NYPL [Sc F 88-375]*

Two dogs and freedom : children of the townships
speak out. Johannesburg : Ravan Press/The
Open School, 1986. 55 p. : ill. ; 21 cm. A
collection of essays in which black South African school
children discuss the political strife in their country and
its effect on their daily lives.   ISBN 0-86975-301-0
(pbk.)
*1. Blacks - South Africa - Social conditions. 2.
Children - South Africa. 3. Children's writings, South
African (English). I. Open School (Johannesburg, South
Africa).*   *NYPL [Sc D 88-151]*

Two dogs and freedom : Black children of South
Africa speak out / from the Open School.1st
American ed. New York : Rosset & Co. ;
Distributed by H. Holt and Co., 1987. 55 p. :
ill. ; 23 cm. A collection of essays in which black
South African school children discuss the political strife
in their country and its effect on their daily lives.
ISBN 0-8050-0637-0 (pbk.) :   DDC
323.1/196/068 19
*1. Blacks - South Africa - Social conditions. 2.
Children - South Africa. 3. Children's writings, South
African (English). I. Open School (Johannesburg, South
Africa). II. Title: 2 dogs and freedom.*
DT763.6 .T96 1987   *NYPL [Sc D 88-422]*

Two thousand years of African Christianity /.
Hickey, Raymond. Ibadan, Nigeria , 1987. viii,
54 p. :   *NYPL [Sc C 88-207]*

Two ways to count to ten . Dee, Ruby. New
York , c1988. [32] p. :   ISBN 0-8050-0407-6 :
DDC 398.2/096 E 19
PZ8.1.D378 Tw 1988   *NYPL [Sc F 88-311]*

Two women on the Hudson River /. Cartey,
Tom. New York City , c1986. 414 p. ;
NYPL [Sc D 88-754]

Twum-Akwaboah, Edward. From pidginization to
creolization of Africanisms in Black American
English / Edward Twum-Akwaboah. [Los
Angeles : University of California, Los Angeles,
1973] 46 leaves ; 28 cm. "Fall, 1973"--Pref.
Bibliography: leaves 44-46.
*1. Black English. 2. English language - United States -
Foreign elements - African. 3. Afro-Americans -
Language. I. Title.*   *NYPL [Sc F 88-210]*

Tyoden, S. G. Takaya, B. J. The Kaduna mafia /.
[Jos, Nigeria] , c1987. viii, 146 p. ;   ISBN
978-16-6045-7   *NYPL [Sc D 88-736]*

Tyson, Jennifer. Claudia Jones, 1915-1964 : a
woman of our times / [researched and compiled
by Jennifer Tyson]. London : Camden Black
Sisters Publications, c1988. 16 p. : ill., ports. ;
21 x 30 cm. Bibliography: p. 16.
*1. Jones Claudia, 1915-1964. 2. Afro-American
women - Biography. 3. Women, Black - Biography. I.
Title.*   *NYPL [Sc D 89-553]*

**TZOTZIL LANGUAGE - DICTIONARIES -
ENGLISH.**
Laughlin, Robert M. The great Tzotzil
dictionary of Santo Domingo Zinacantán .
Washington, D.C. , 1988. 3 v. (xiii, 1119 p.) :
DDC 497/.4 301 s 19
GN1 .S54 no. 31a PM4466.Z5
NYPL [HBR 89-17311]

U. N. For corporate body represented by these
initials see: **United Nations.**

U. N. I. A. see **Universal Negro Improvement
Association.**

U. N. O. For corporate body represented by these
initials see: **United Nations.**

U. P. C. see **Union des populations du Cameroun.**

U. S. foreign policy and revolution. Wilson,
Amrit, 1941- US foreign policy and revolution .
London , distributed in the USA by Unwin
Hyman, 1989. ix, 179 p. :   ISBN 1-85305-051-2
NYPL [Sc D 89-426]

A U. S. policy toward South Africa . United
States. Dept. of State. Advisory Committee on
South Africa. [Washington, D.C.] [1987] vi, 49
p. :   *NYPL [Sc F 88-300]*

U. S.S.R. and Africa. The USSR and Africa.
Moscow , 1983. 205 p. ;   DDC 303.4/8247/06 19
DT38.9.S65 U86 1983   *NYPL [Sc D 88-980]*

U zibe mutu /. Mukuni, R. M., 1929- [Lusaka] ,
c1976. 54 p. :
PL8460.9.M77 U2 1976   *NYPL [Sc C 89-37]*

Udeaja, Philip. The way we are / by Philip
Udeaja. [Enugu, Anambra State, Nigeria] :
Udeaja, [1987?]. vii, 61 p. ; 18 cm.
1. Nigeria - Civilization. I. Title.
NYPL [Sc C 89-36]

Udo-Inyang, D. S. (Denis S.) The man--Sir
Justice Udo Udoma / by D.S. Udo-Inyang.
Calabar [Nigeria] : Wusen Press, [1985] 72 p. :
ill. ; 21 cm. Bibliography: p. 72.   ISBN
978-228-168-9 (pbk.)   DDC 347.669/03534 B
346.69073534 B 19
*1. Udoma, Egbert Udo, 1917-. 2. Judges - Nigeria -
Biography. 3. Judges - Uganda - Biography. 4.
Statesmen - Nigeria - Biography. 5. Statesmen -
Uganda - Biography. I. Title.*
LAW   *NYPL [Sc D 88-776]*

Udoakah, Nkereuwem. Government and the
media in Nigeria / Nkereuwem Udoakah.
Calabar, Nigeria : Centaur Publishers, c1988. x,
88 p. ; 18 cm. Bibliography: p. 83-86.   ISBN
978-231-603-2
*1. Mass media policy - Nigeria. 2. Freedom of speech -
Nigeria. I. Title.*   *NYPL [Sc C 89-51]*

Udoh, Sunday. Theory and practice of educational
administration in Nigeria / By S.U. Udoh and
G.O. Akpa. Rev. ed. Jos, Nigeria : Faculty of
Education, University of Jos, 1987. x, 347 p. :
ill. ; 24 cm. Bibliography: p. 337-347.

*1. School management and organization - Nigeria -
Textbooks. I. Akpa, G. O. II. Title.*
NYPL [Sc E 88-295]

Udoma, Egbert Udo, Sir, 1917- The story of the
Ibibio Union : its background, emergence, aims,
objectives and achievements : founded, 1927 :
amalgamated with the Ibibio Mainland
Association, 1928 : proscribed, 1966 : a
successful experiment at re-integration of a
people / by the Hon. Sir Udo Udoma. Ibadan,
Nigeria : Spectrum Books, 1987. xv, 590 p.,
[12] leaves of plates : ill., ports. ; 23 cm.
Includes index.   ISBN 978-246-128-8
*1. Ibibio Union. 2. Ibibio State Union. 3. Ibibios -
History. I. Title.*   *NYPL [Sc D 89-4]*

UDOMA, EGBERT UDO, 1917-
Udo-Inyang, D. S. (Denis S.) The man--Sir
Justice Udo Udoma /. Calabar [Nigeria] [1985]
72 p. :   ISBN 978-228-168-9 (pbk.)   DDC
347.669/03534 B 346.69073534 B 19
LAW   *NYPL [Sc D 88-776]*

Uduehi, Godfrey O. Public lands acquisition and
compensation practice in Nigeria / Godfrey O.
Uduehi. Ogba, Ikeja : John West Publications,
1987. xviii, 162 p. : ill. ; 22 cm. Includes
bibliographical references and index.   ISBN
978-16-3064-7
1. Land use - Nigeria. 2. Nigeria - Public lands. I. Title.
NYPL [Sc D 89-480]

Uganda.
[Constitution (1986)]
The Constitution of the Republic of Uganda.
Rev. ed. Kampala : Law Development
Centre, 1986. 121 p. ; 32 cm.
1. Uganda. Constitution. I. Title.
NYPL [Sc G 89-9]

UGANDA - TANZANIA WAR, 1978-1979.
Kiwanuka, M. S. M. Semakula. Amin and the
tragedy of Uganda /. München , 1979. ix, 201
p. :   *DT433.283 .K58*   *NYPL [L-10 9005 nr. 104]*

**UGANDA - ARMED FORCES - POLITICAL
ACTIVITY.**
Omara-Otunnu, Amii, 1952- Politics and the
military in Uganda, 1890-1985 /. Basingstoke,
Hampshire , 1987. xx, 218 p. :   ISBN
0-333-41980-4   *NYPL [JFD 87-8644]*

UGANDA. CONSTITUTION.
Uganda. [Constitution (1986)] The Constitution
of the Republic of Uganda. Kampala , 1986.
121 p. ;   *NYPL [Sc G 89-9]*

Uganda - Government. see **Uganda - Politics and
government.**

UGANDA - HISTORY.
Kasozi, A. B. K. (Abdu Basajabaka Kawalya),
1942- The spread of Islam in Uganda /.
Nairobi, Kenya , 1986. vi, 136 p., [4] p. of
plates :   ISBN 0-19-572596-4
NYPL [Sc E 89-109]

UGANDA - HISTORY - 1971-1979.
Kiwanuka, M. S. M. Semakula. Amin and the
tragedy of Uganda /. München , 1979. ix, 201
p. :   ISBN 3-8039-0177-4
DT433.283 .K58   *NYPL [L-10 9005 nr. 104]*

UGANDA - HISTORY - 1979-
Kiwanuka, M. S. M. Semakula. Amin and the
tragedy of Uganda /. München , 1979. ix, 201
p. :   ISBN 3-8039-0177-4
DT433.283 .K58   *NYPL [L-10 9005 nr. 104]*

Uganda now : between decay development /
edited by Holger Bernt Hansen & Michael
Twaddle. Athens : Ohio University Press ;
London : Currey, 1988. 376 p. : ill., maps ; 22
cm. Bibliography: p. 359-366.   ISBN 0-85255-315-3
(cased) :   DDC 967.6/104 19
*1. Uganda - Social conditions. I. Hansen, Holger Bernt.
II. Twaddle, Michael.*
HN800.U35   *NYPL [Sc D 88-1436]*

**UGANDA - POLITICS AND GOVERNMENT -
CONGRESSES.**
International Seminar on Internal Conflict
(1987 : Makerere, Uganda) Seminar papers on
internal conflicts in Uganda /. [Makerere,
Uganda , 1987]. 1 v. ;   *NYPL [Sc F 89-86]*

Uganda saints : the story of Uganda martyrs.
[Kampala? : s. n., 1969?] 39 p. : ill., map ; 26
cm. Cover title.
1. Christian saints - Uganda. 2. Martyrs - Uganda.
NYPL [Sc F 87-314]

UGANDA - SOCIAL CONDITIONS.
Uganda now . Athens , London , 1988. 376 p. :
ISBN 0-85255-315-3 (cased) : DDC 967.6/104
19
HN800.U35 **NYPL [Sc D 88-1436]**

Ugochukwu, Françoise, 1949- La source interdite
/ Françoise Ugochukwu. Abidjan : Les
Nouvelles Editions africaines ; Paris : EDICEF,
c1984. 63 p. : ill. ; 17 cm. SCHOMBURG
CHILDREN'S COLLECTION.
*1. Nigeria - Juvenile fiction. I. Schomburg Children's
Collection. II. Title.* **NYPL [Sc B 88-33]**

Ugwoke, Oliva Obinna. Onye ije awele / nke
Oliva Obinna Ugwoke. [Ihiala, Nigeria : Deo
Gratias Press, 198-?] iv, 77 p. ; 21 cm.
1. Igbo language - Texts. I. Title.
NYPL [Sc D 88-1040]

Ugwu, D. C. This is Obukpa : a history of typical
ancient Igbo state / D.C. Ugwu. Enugu,
Nigeria: Fourth Dimension Pub. Co., 1987. xii,
76 p. ; 21 cm. ISBN 978-15-6288-9
*1. Igbo (African people) - Social life and customs. 2.
Obukpa (Nigeria) - Social life and customs. I. Title.*
NYPL [Sc D 88-801]

Ugwuegbu, Denis C. E. Social research and
information gathering /. Lagos [1987?] v. 72
p. : **NYPL [Sc E 88-301]**

Uhuru wa watumwa /. Mbotela, James. Nairobi ,
1956. viii, 102 p. : **NYPL [Sc C 89-35]**

Uhusiano na nchi za nje /. Halimoja, Yusuf J.
Dar es Salaam , 1981. 60 p. :
NYPL [Sc C 89-60]

Ukaegbu, Chikwendu Christian, 1945- Nigeria in
search of a future /. Nsukka , 1986. vii, 155
p. ; ISBN 978-229-900-6 **NYPL [Sc D 88-884]**

Ukeje, B. Onyerisara. School and society in
Nigeria / by B.O. Ukeje. Enugu, Nigeria :
Fourth Dimensions Publishers, 1986. 129 p. ;
21 cm. Includes bibliographies. ISBN 978-15-6245-5
*1. Education - Nigeria. 2. Nigeria - Social conditions -
1960-. I. Title.* **NYPL [Sc D 88-1243]**

Ukoli, F. M. A. What science? . Ibadan , 1985.
xvii, 321 p. : ISBN 978-12-9118-4 (pbk.) DDC
507/.11669 19
Q183.4.N5 W48 1985 **NYPL [Sc E 88-402]**

Ukpabi, Sam C. The origins of the Nigerian
army : a history of the West African Frontier
Force, 1897-1914 / by Sam C. Ukpabi. Zaria,
Nigeria : Gaskiya Corp., 1987. 194 p. : fold.
map ; 23 cm. Bibliography: p. 169-194. ISBN
978-19-4128-6
*1. Great Britain. Army. West African Frontier Force. 2.
Africa, West - History, Military. I. Title.*
NYPL [Sc D 88-1489]

Ukpong, Ignatius I. The contributions of
expatriate and indigenous manpower to the
manufacturing industry in Nigeria : a
comparative evaluation / Ignatius I. Ukpong
and Emmanuel C. Anusionwu.[1st ed.]
[Calabar, Cross River State, Nigeria] : Scholars
Press, [c1986] ix, 61 p. ; 20 cm. Spine title:
Expatriate and indigenous manpower. Bibliography: p.
59-61. ISBN 978-227-526-3 DDC 331.12/57/09669
19
*1. Manpower policy - Nigeria. 2. Alien labor - Nigeria.
3. Nigeria - Manufactures. I. Anusionwu, Emmanuel
Chukwuma, 1946-. II. Title. III. Title: Expatriate and
indigenous manpower.*
HD5848.A6 U37 1986 **NYPL [Sc C 89-128]**

Uku, Patience Essie Urutajirinere Blankson. 25
years of partnership / by Patience Essie
Urutajirinere Blankson Uku. [Benin City,
Nigeria : P.E.B. Uku, 1981?] 114 p. : ill. ; 21
cm.
*1. Uku, Patience Essie Urutajirinere Blankson. 2.
Marriage - Nigeria. I. Title. II. Title: Twenty-five years
of partnership.* **NYPL [Sc D 88-380]**

**UKU, PATIENCE ESSIE URUTAJIRINERE
BLANKSON.**
Uku, Patience Essie Urutajirinere Blankson. 25
years of partnership /. [Benin City, Nigeria ,
1981?] 114 p. : **NYPL [Sc D 88-380]**

ULDEME (AFRICAN PEOPLE)
Colombel, Véronique de. Les Ouldémés du
Nord-Cameroun . Paris , 1987. [13]-74 p., [61]
p. of plates : ISBN 2-85297-199-2
NYPL [Sc E 89-244]

ULDEME (AFRICAN PEOPLE) - MUSIC.
Colombel, Véronique de. Les Ouldémés du
Nord-Cameroun . Paris , 1987. [13]-74 p., [61]

---

p. of plates : ISBN 2-85297-199-2
NYPL [Sc E 89-244]

ULDEME LANGUAGE.
Colombel, Véronique de. Les Ouldémés du
Nord-Cameroun . Paris , 1987. [13]-74 p., [61]
p. of plates : ISBN 2-85297-199-2
NYPL [Sc E 89-244]

ULDEME LANGUAGE - PHONOLOGY.
Colombel, Véronique de. Phonologie
quantitative et synthématique . Paris , 1986.
375 p., [31] p. of plates : ISBN 2-85297-192-5 :
DDC 493/.7 19
PL8753.5 .C65 1986 **NYPL [Sc E 89-72]**

The ultimate end of Pan-Africanism /. Oshisanya,
Samuel Adekoya. [Lagos], Nigeria , 1983] 105
p. : **NYPL [Sc E 86-472]**

ULTRALIGHT AIRCRAFT.
Dodwell, Christina, 1951- Travels with
Pegasus . London , 1989. 208 p., [16] p. of
plates : ISBN 0-340-42502-4 : DDC 916.6/04 19
NYPL [JFE 89-902]

Umeasiegbu, Rems Nna, 1943- Ask the
humorist . Enugu , 1986. 104 p. : ISBN
978-225-808-3 **NYPL [Sc C 88-240]**

Umegakwe, Onyedika Veronica. The sting of a
queen bee / Onyedika Veronica Umegakwe.
Onitsha : Etukokwu Press, 1988. 121 p. : ill. ;
19 cm.
I. Title. **NYPL [Sc C 89-11]**

Umeh, John Anenchukwu. The University of
Nigeria, 1960-1985 . Nsukka, Nigeria , 1986.
xviii, 657 p. : ISBN 978-229-913-8
NYPL [Sc F 88-198]

Umeh, Rich Enujioke. Why the cock became a
sacrificial animal / Rich Enujioke Umeh.
Enugu, Nigeria : Cecta, 1985. 38 p. : ill. ; 18 x
22 cm. SCHOMBURG CHILDREN'S
COLLECTION. ISBN 978-239-648-6
*1. Animals - Juvenile fiction. 2. Nigeria - Juvenile
fiction. I. Schomburg Children's Collection. II. Title.*
NYPL [Sc C 89-18]

Umezinwa, Willy A. From African symbols to
physics : the meaning of the snake symbol in
African novels and the implications for modern
physics / Willy A. Umezinwa and Alexander
O.E. Animalu. [Nigeria : s.n.], c1988. 71 p. :
ill. ; 24 cm.
*1. Signs and symbols - Africa. 2. Serpents in literature.
I. Animalu, Alexander O. E., 1938-. II. Title.*
NYPL [Sc E 89-36]

Umobuarie, D. O. Adventures of a bank inspector
/ by D.O. Umobuarie. Nigeria : King David
Writers T., 1988. 168 p. ; 21 cm. Errata slip
inserted. ISBN 978-300-323-2
*1. Banks and banking - Nigeria - Fiction. 2. Nigeria -
Fiction. I. Title.* **NYPL [Sc C 88-339]**

UMOJA. Moi's reign of terror . London , 1989.
88 p. : ISBN 1-87188-601-5
NYPL [Sc D 89-524]

Umukoro, G. Dean. The devil is white / by G.
Dean Umukoro. Kaduna, Nigeria : ROSAMAC,
1985. 161 p. ; 18 cm. Poems.
I. Title. **NYPL [Sc C 88-177]**

Unborn child /. Ikonné, Chidi, 1940- Owerri, Imo
State, 1987. v. 137 p. ; ISBN 978-267-124-X
NYPL [Sc C 88-359]

The uncertain sound. Gilbert, Herman Cromwell.
Chicago [1969] 349 p. DDC 813/.5/4
PZ4.G4647 Un PS3557.I342
NYPL [Sc D 88-1117]

Uncle Tom's picture book. Pictures and stories
from Uncle Tom's cabin. Boston [c1853]
[5],6-32p. **NYPL [Sc Rare C 89-1]**

Under the flambo . Worrell, Vernon, 1952-
Bridgetown, Barbados , 1986. ix, 84 p. : DDC
811 19
PR9230.9.W67 U5 1986
NYPL [Sc D 88-945]

**UNDERDEVELOPED AREAS -
CONGRESSES.**
Bishop, Maurice. Address of the Conference on
Development Problems of Small Island States,
July 13, 1981 /. [St. George's, Grenada , 1981]
9 p. ; **NYPL [Sc Micro R-4108 no.26]**

Bishop, Maurice. Imperialism is the real
problem [microform] . [st. George's], Grenada ,
1981. 13 leaves ;
NYPL [Sc Micro R-4108 no.27]

**UNDERDEVELOPED AREAS - ECONOMIC
ASSISTANCE. see ECONOMIC
ASSISTANCE.**

**UNDERDEVELOPED AREAS - RURAL
DEVELOPMENT. see RURAL
DEVELOPMENT.**

**UNDERDEVELOPED AREAS - TECHNICAL
ASSISTANCE. see TECHNICAL
ASSISTANCE.**

**UNDERGROUND, ANTI-COMMUNISM. see
ANTI-COMMUNIST MOVEMENTS.**

Underground escape /. Nevin, Evelyn C.
Philadelphia , c1926. 191 p. :
NYPL [Sc D 88-1506]

UNDERGROUND RAILROAD.
Bramble, Linda. Black fugitive slaves in early
Canada /. St. Catharines, Ont. , c1988. 93 p. :
ISBN 0-920277-16-0 DDC 973.7/115 19
NYPL [Sc E 89-121]

Khan, Lurey. One day, Levin ... he be free.
New York [1972] 231 p. ISBN 0-525-36415-3
DDC 973.7/115 B 92
E450.S852 K45 1972 **NYPL [Sc D 88-1116]**

UNDERGROUND RAILROAD - FICTION.
Haley, Alex. A different kind of Christmas /.
New York , 1988. 101 p. ; ISBN 0-385-26043-1 :
DDC 813/.54 19
PS3558.A3575 D54 1988
NYPL [Sc C 89-38]

Howard, Elizabeth. North winds blow free.
New York , 1949. 192 p. :
NYPL [Sc D 88-1498]

**UNDERGROUND RAILROAD - JUVENILE
FICTION.**
Bacmeister, Rhoda Warner, 1893- Voices in the
night /. Indianapolis , 1965. 117 p. :
NYPL [Sc D 88-382]

Clark, Margaret Goff. Freedom crossing. New
York [1969] 128 p. DDC [Fic]
PZ7.C5487 Fr **NYPL [Sc D 88-1121]**

Nevin, Evelyn C. Underground escape /.
Philadelphia , c1926. 191 p. :
NYPL [Sc D 88-1506]

Steinman, Beatrice. This railroad disappears.
New York [1958] 181 p.
PZ7.S8266 Th **NYPL [Sc D 89-391]**

Winter, Jeanette. Follow the drinking gourd /.
New York , c1988. [48] p. : ISBN
0-394-89694-7 : DDC [E] 19
PZ7.W7547 Fo 1988 **NYPL [Sc F 89-59]**

**UNDERGROUND RAILROAD - JUVENILE
LITERATURE.**
Ferris, Jeri. Go free or die . Minneapolis ,
1987. 63 p. : ISBN 0-87614-317-6 (lib. bdg.) :
DDC 305.5/67/0924 B 92 19
E444.T82 F47 1987 **NYPL [Sc D 88-620]**

**UNDERGROUND RAILROAD - NEW YORK
(STATE)**
Phelan, Helene C. And why not every man? .
Interlaken, New York , 1987. 247 p. : ISBN
0-9605836-4-5 **NYPL [Sc D 87-1420]**

Understanding African traditional religion /.
Adasu, Moses Orshio. Sherborne, Dorset,
England , 1985- v. ; ISBN 0-902129-68-6
NYPL [Sc D 88-856]

Understanding and preventing AIDS . Jennings,
Chris, 1954- Cambridge, MA (P.O. Box 2060,
Cambridge 02238-2060) , c1988. 230 p. : ISBN
0-936571-01-2 **NYPL [Sc F 88-239]**

Understanding crime . Chuck, Delroy H.
Bridgetown, Barbados [c1986] xi, 171 p. ;
ISBN 976-8043-00-8 (pbk.) DDC 364 19
HV6025 .C48 1986 **NYPL [Sc D 89-195]**

Understanding sanctions /. Hoile, David.
London , 1988. 80 p. : ISBN 1-87111-700-3
(pbk.) : DDC 337.68 19
HF1613.4 .H654 1988 **NYPL [Sc D 89-317]**

Understanding the Black family . Nobles, Wade
W. Oakland, California , 1984. 137 p. ; ISBN
0-939205-00-9 **NYPL [Sc D 88-697]**

Understanding the sixties [microform] . Harris,
Norman, 1951- 1980. 202 leaves.
NYPL [Sc Micro R-4680]

Underwood, David C. West African oil, will it
matter? / by David C. Underwood ; foreword
by Helen Kitchen. Washington, D.C. : Center
for Strategic and International Studies,

Georgetown University, c1983. vi, 57 p. : map ; 22 cm. (Significant issues series, 0736-7163 . v. 5, no. 6) Includes bibliographical references.   ISBN 0-89206-046-8 (pbk.)   DDC 333.8/232/0966 19
1. Petroleum industry and trade - Africa, West. I. Georgetown University. Center for Strategic and International Studies. II. Title. III. Series.
HD9577.A3582 U52 1983
NYPL [Sc D 88-888]

Underwood, Thomas A. Varieties of black experience at Harvard . Cambridge [Mass.] , 1986. v, 180 p. ;
LD2160 .V37x 1986   **NYPL [Sc D 88-672]**

Undugu Society of Kenya. Dallpe, Fabio. "You are a thief" . Nairobi, Kenya , 1987. 151 p. :
NYPL [Sc E 88-538]

UNEMPLOYED - NIGERIA - WESTERN STATE - STATISTICS.
Western State, Nigeria. Ministry of Economic Planning and Social Development. Statistics Division. Report of a sample survey of unemployment among school leavers [microform /. Ibadan [1966]- v. ;
NYPL [Sc Micro F-10938]

Unesco.
Affirmation de l'identité culturelle et la formation de la conscience nationale dans l'Afrique contemporaine. Spanish. La Afrimación de la identidad cultural y la formación de la coniencia nacional en el África contemporánea /. Barcelona , Paris , 1983. 220 p. ;   ISBN 84-85800-57-5   **NYPL [Sc D 88-597]**

Décolonisation de l'Afrique. Spanish. La Descolonización de Africa : Africa austral y el Cuerno de Africa . Barcelona , Paris , 1983. 197 p. ;   ISBN 92-3-301834-2 (Unesco)
NYPL [Sc D 88-590]

Deux études sur les relations entre groupes ethniques. Spanish. Dos estudios sobre las relaciones entre grupos étnicos en África . Barcelona [Paris] , 1982. 174 p. ;   ISBN 84-85000-41-9
DT549.42 .D4818 1982
NYPL [Sc D 88-651]

Fighting apartheid . London , 1988. 76 p. :   ISBN 0-904759-84-9 (pbk) :   DDC 323.1/68 19
DT763   **NYPL [Sc D 88-1092]**

Historiographie de l'Afrique australe. Spanish. La historiografía del Africa austral . Barcelona , Paris , 1983. 128 p. ;   ISBN 92-3-301775-3 (Unesco)   **NYPL [Sc D 88-598]**

Introduction à la culture africaine. Spanish. Introducción a la cultura africana . Barcelona , Paris , 1982. 176 p. ;   ISBN 92-3-301478-9 (Unesco)   **NYPL [Sc D 88-600]**

Jeunesse, tradition et développement en Afrique. Spanish. Juventud, tradición y desarrollo en Africa . Barcelona , Paris , 1982. 148 p. ;   ISBN 84-85800-29-X
NYPL [Sc D 88-592]

Pierson-Mathy, Paulette. [Naissance de l'Etat par la guerre de libération nationale. Spanish.] El nacimiento del estado por la guerra de liberación nacional . Barcelona : [Paris] : 1983. 178 p. ;   ISBN 92-3-301794-X (Unesco)
NYPL [Sc D 88-602]

Relations historiques à travers l'océan Indien. Spanish. Relaciones históricas a través del océano Índico . Barcelona , Paris , 1983. 224 p. ;   ISBN 84-85800-51-6   **NYPL [Sc D 88-593]**

Ross, D. H. Educating handicapped young people in eastern and southern Africa in 1981-83 /. Paris , 1988. 152 p. :   ISBN 92-3-102560-0   **NYPL [Sc E 88-534]**

Socio-political aspects of the palaver in some African countries. Spanish. Aspectos sociopolíticos del parlamento tradicional en algunos países africanos /. Barcelona , Paris , 1979. 95 p. ;   ISBN 84-85800-24-9
NYPL [Sc D 88-599]

Symposium on the Peopling of Ancient Egypt and the deciphering of Meroitic Script (1974 : Cairo, Egypt) [Peuplement de l'Egipte ancianne et la déchiffrement de l'écriture méroïtique. Spanish.] Poblamiento del antiguo Egipto y desciframiento de la escritura meroítica /. Barcelona , Paris , 1983. 155 p. :   ISBN 0-923301-60-5 (Unesco)
NYPL [Sc D 88-603]

Teaching and research in philosophy in Africa. Spanish. Enseñanza de la filosofía e investigación filosófica en África /. Barcelona , París , 1984. 339 p. ;   ISBN 92-3-302126-6 (Unesco)   **NYPL [Sc D 88-616]**

Unesco. International Scientific Committee for the Drafting of a General History of Africa. Africa from the seventh to the eleventh century /. London : Berkeley : xxv, 869 p. :   ISBN 0-435-94809-1   **NYPL [Sc E 88-384]**

the unexamined life . Gyekye, Kwame. Accra , 1988. 36 p. ;   ISBN 996-430-147-2
NYPL [Sc D 89-521]

The unfinished march. Drisko, Carol F. Garden City, N.Y. , 1967. 118 p. :   DDC 973.8 (j)
E185.6 .D7   **NYPL [Sc D 88-1429]**

UNIÃO NACIONAL PARA A INDEPENDÊNCIA TOTAL DE ANGOLA.
Savimbi, Jonas Malheiro. Por um futuro melhor /. Lisboa , 1986. 192 p. :   DDC 967/.304 19
DT611.8 .S28 1986   **NYPL [Sc D 88-771]**

UNICEF. Children, youth, women and development plans in West and Central Africa . Abidjan [1972?] 152 p. ;
NYPL [Sc E 88-105]

UNION CATALOGS. see CATALOGS, UNION.

UNION CHURCH (MONTRÉAL, QUÉBEC) - HISTORY.
Bertley, Leo W. Montreal's oldest black congregation . Pierrefonds, Quebec , c1976. 30 p. :
BX9882.8.M668 B47 1976
NYPL [Sc F 89-49]

Union des écrivains zaïrois. Cris intérieurs . Kinshasa/Gombe, Zaïre , 1986. 62 p. ;
MLCS 86/6102 (P)   **NYPL [Sc C 88-124]**

UNION DES POPULATIONS DU CAMEROUN.
Kengne Pokam, E (Emmanuel), 1941- Les Églises chrétiennes face à la montée du nationalisme camerounais /. Paris [1987] 202 p. ;   ISBN 2-85802-823-0   **NYPL [Sc D 88-437]**

Union géographique internationale. see International Geographical Union.

Union internationale des associations patronales catholiques. see International Christian Union of Business Executives.

Union Native Council Bill. South Africa. [Laws, etc.] Native Land Act, 1913. Amendment Bill, 1927 [microform]. Representation of Natives in Parliament Bill. Union Native Council Bill. Coloured Persons Rights Bill, 1927. [S.I. [1927?] 47 p. ;   **NYPL [Sc Micro F-10937]**

Union of South Africa. see South Africa.

UNIONS, TRADE. see TRADE-UNIONS.

Unité et lutte /. Cabral, Amílcar, 1921-1973. Paris , 1980. 329 p. ;   ISBN 2-7071-1171-6
NYPL [Sc C 88-125]

United Arab Republic (al-Iqlim al Misri) see Egypt.

United Arab Republic (Egyptian region) see Egypt.

United Arab Republic (Southern region) see Egypt.

United Church of Christ. Commission for Racial Justice. Toxic wastes and race in the United States . New York, N.Y. , 1987. xvi, 69 p. :   DDC 363.7/28 19
TD811.5 .T695 1987   **NYPL [JLF 88-1607]**

United Nations. Apartheid, Centre against. see United Nations. Centre against Apartheid.

United Nations. Centre against Apartheid. Apartheid, South Africa and international law . New York, NY , 1985. iv, 136 p. ;
NYPL [Sc F 88-289]

United Nations Centre for Human Settlements. The Role of women in the execution of low-income housing projects . Nairobi, Kenya , 1986. 64 p. :   ISBN 92-1-131005-9
NYPL [Sc F 88-225]

United Nations Council on Namibia. Namibia . Lusaka , 1987. 408 p. :   ISBN 998-211-001-2
NYPL [Sc E 89-132]

United Nations. Dept. of Political and Security Council Affairs. Centre against Apartheid. see United Nations. Centre against

Apartheid.

United Nations Fund for Population Activities. Oppong, Christine. Seven roles of women . Geneva , 1987. xi, 127 p. :
NYPL [Sc E 89-143]

UNITED NATIONS. GENERAL ASSEMBLY (13TH SPECIAL SESSION : 1986) - PUBLC OPINION.
Die UNO-Sondersitzung über Afrika 1986 in der afrikanischen Presse /. Hamburg , 1986. ii, 104 p. :   ISBN 3-923519-66-4
NYPL [Sc F 88-229]

United Nations. International Labor Office. see International Labor Office.

United Nations. International Labor Organization. see International Labor Organization.

UNITED NATIONS - NAMIBIA.
Namibia . Lusaka , 1987. 408 p. :   ISBN 998-211-001-2   **NYPL [Sc E 89-132]**

United Nations Organization. see United Nations.

United Nations - Specialized agencies. see International agencies.

United Nations. Sub-commission on Prevention of Discrimination and Protection of Minorities. Khalifa, Ahmad M. Adverse consequences for the enjoyment of human rights of political, military, economic, and other forms of assistance given to the racist and colonialist régime of South Africa /. New York , 1985. ii, 164, [30] p. ;   ISBN 92-1-154046-1 (pbk).   DDC 332.6/73/0968 19
HG5851.A3 K45 1985   **NYPL [Sc F 88-273]**

United Nations World Security Organization. see United Nations.

United Republic of Tanganyika and Zanzibar. see Tanzania.

United States.
ACT IN ADDITION TO THE ACTS PROHIBITING THE SLAVE TRADE.
United States. President (1817-1825 : Monroe) Message from the President of the United States, stating the interpretation which has been given to the act entitled An Act in Addition to the Acts Prohibiting the Slave Trade. Washington , 1819. 4 p. ;
NYPL [Sc Rare F 89-25]

Constitution of the U. S. see United States. Constitution.

UNITED STATES - 1815-1861.
Werner, John M., 1941- Reaping the bloody harvest . New York , 1986. 333 p. ;   ISBN 0-8240-8301-6 (alk. paper) :   DDC 973.5/6 19
E185 .W44 1986   **NYPL [Sc E 88-242]**

UNITED STATES. AIR FORCE - BIOGRAPHY.
McGovern, James R. Black Eagle, General Daniel "Chappie" James, Jr. /. University, AL , c1985. 204 p. :   ISBN 0-8173-0179-8   DDC 355/.0092/4 B 19
UG626.2.J36 M34 1985
NYPL [JFD 85-7082]

United States. Air Forces, Army. see United States. Army Air Forces.

United States. Air Service. see United States. Army Air Forces.

UNITED STATES - ARMED FORCES - AFRO-AMERICANS.
McGuire, Phillip, 1944- He, too, spoke for democracy . New York , c1988. xvii, 154 p. ;   ISBN 0-313-26115-6 (lib. bdg. : alk. paper)   DDC 355/.008996073 B 19
KF373.H38 M35 1988   **NYPL [Sc E 88-347]**

UNITED STATES. ARMY - AFRO-AMERICAN TROOPS.
Fletcher, Marvin. America's first Black general . Lawrence, Kan. , c1989. xix, 226 p. :   ISBN 0-7006-0381-6 (alk. paper) :   DDC 355/.008996073 B 19
U53.D38 F57 1989   **NYPL [Sc D 89-276]**

Smith, Graham. When Jim Crow met John Bull . London , c1987. 265 p. :   ISBN 1-85043-039-X   **NYPL [Sc D 88-55]**

UNITED STATES. ARMY - AFRO-AMERICAN TROOPS - HISTORY - 19TH CENTURY.

Cornish, Dudley Taylor. The sable arm .
Lawrence, Kan. , c1987. xviii, 342 p. ; ISBN
0-7006-0328-X (pbk.)   DDC 973.7/415 19
E540.N3 C77 1987   *NYPL [Sc D 88-850]*

**UNITED STATES. ARMY AIR FORCES -
BIOGRAPHY.**
Johnson, Hayden C. The Fighting 99th Air
Squadron, 1941-45 /. New York , c1987. 49
p. : ISBN 0-533-06879-7 : DDC 940.54/4973 19
D790 .J57 1987   *NYPL [Sc D 88-1192]*

**UNITED STATES. ARMY AIR FORCES.
FIGHTER SQUADRON, 99TH -
HISTORY.**
Johnson, Hayden C. The Fighting 99th Air
Squadron, 1941-45 /. New York , c1987. 49
p. : ISBN 0-533-06879-7 : DDC 940.54/4973 19
D790 .J57 1987   *NYPL [Sc D 88-1192]*

UNITED STATES. ARMY - BIOGRAPHY.
Fletcher, Marvin. America's first Black general .
Lawrence, Kan. , c1989. xix, 226 p. : ISBN
0-7006-0381-6 (alk. paper) :   DDC
355/.008996073 B 19
U53.D38 F57 1989   *NYPL [Sc D 89-276]*

**UNITED STATES. ARMY - HISTORY - CIVIL
WAR, 1861-1865.**
Burton, William L., 1928- Melting pot soldiers .
Ames, Iowa , 1988. x, 282 p. ; ISBN
0-8138-1115-5 DDC 973.7/4 19
E540.F6 B87 1988   *NYPL [IKC 88-730]*

**UNITED STATES. ARMY - MINORITIES -
HISTORY - 19TH CENTURY.**
Burton, William L., 1928- Melting pot soldiers .
Ames, Iowa , 1988. x, 282 p. ; ISBN
0-8138-1115-5 DDC 973.7/4 19
·*E540.F6 B87 1988*   *NYPL [IKC 88-730]*

**UNITED STATES. ARMY. SOUTH
CAROLINA VOLUNTEERS, FIRST -
BIOGRAPHY.**
Taylor, Susie King, b. 1848. [Reminiscences of
my life in camp.] A Black woman's Civil War
memoirs . New York , 1988. 154 p. : ISBN
0-910129-85-1 (pbk.) : DDC 973.7/415 B 19
E492.94 33rd .T3 1988
NYPL [Sc D 88-1473]

**United States. Bureau of International
Commerce.** A market for U. S. products in
the Ivory Coast / U. S. Dept. of Commerce,
Bureau of Tnternational Commerce.
Washington, D.C. : U. S. Govt. Print. Office,
[1966] viii, 87 p. : ill., maps ; 26 cm. "A U. S.
Dept. of Commerce publication. "A supplement to
International Commerce."
*1. United States - Commerce - Ivory Coast. 2. Ivory
Coast - Commerce - United States. 3. Ivory Coast -
Economic conditions. I. Title.*
NYPL [Sc F 89-79]

**United States. Bureau of Refugees, Freedmen
and Abandoned Lands.**
Records of the Assistant Commissioner for the
District of Columbia, Bureau of Refugees,
Freedmen, and Abandoned Lands, 1865-1869
[microform] 1865-1869. 42 bound v., 18 ft. of
unbound doc. Guide in the first reel. Microfilm.
Washington: National Archives and Records Service,
1978. 21 reels; 35 mm. (National Archives microfilm
publications, M1055)
*1. Reconstruction - District of Columbia - Sources. I.
Title.*   *NYPL [Sc Micro R-4644]*

Records of the Assistant Commissioner for the
State of Arkansas, Bureau of Refugees,
Freedmen, and Abandoned Lands, 1865-1869
[microform] 1865-1869. 24 v. Finding aid in the
first reel. Microfilm. Washington: National Archives
and Records Service, 1974. 52 reels; 35 mm. (National
Archives microfilm publications, M979)
*1. Freedmen in Arkansas - Sources. 2. Reconstruction -
Arkansas - Sources. I. Title.*
NYPL [Sc Micro R-4642]

Records of the Assistant Commissioner for the
state of North Carolina, Bureau of Refugees,
Freedmen, and Abandoned Lands, 1865-1870
[microform] 1865-1870. 20 ft. (32 v.) Finding aid
in the first reel. Microfilm. Washington: National
Archives and Records Service, 1972. 38 reels; 35 mm.
(National Archives microfilm publications, M843)
*1. Freedmen in North Carolina - Sources. 2. Refugees,
Southern - North Carolina - Sources. 3.
Reconstruction - North Carolina - Sources. I. Title.*
NYPL [Sc Micro R-4646]

Records of the Assistant Commissioner for the
State of Virginia, Bureau of Refugees,

Freedmen, and Abandoned Lands, 1865-1869
[microform] 1865-1869. 40 bound v., 51 ft. of
unbound doc. Guide in the first reel. Microfilm.
Washington: National Archives and Records Service,
1977. 67 reels; 35 mm. (National Archives microfilm
publications, M1048)
*1. Freedmen in Virginia - Sources. 2. Reconstruction -
Virginia - Sources. I. Title.*
NYPL [Sc Micro R-4648]

Records of the Superintendent of Education for
the District of Columbia, Bureau of Refugees,
Freedmen, and Abandoned Lands, 1865-1872
[microform] 1865-1872. 11 bound v., 15 ft. of
unbound doc. Guide in the first reel. Microfilm.
Washington: National Archives and Records Service,
1977. 24 reels; 35 mm. (National Archives microfilm
publications, M1056)
*1. Freedmen in District of Columbia - Sources. 2.
Reconstruction - District of Columbia - Sources. 3.
Afro-Americans - Education - District of Columbia -
History - Sources. I. Title.*
NYPL [Sc Micro R-4645]

Records of the Superintendent of Education for
the State of Arkansas, Bureau of Refugees,
Freedmen, and Abandoned Lands, 1865-1871
[microform] 1865-1871. 10 v. Finding aid in the
first reel. Microfilm. Washington: National Archives
and Records Service, 1974. 5 reels; 35 mm. (National
Archives microfilm publications, M980)
*1. Freedmen in Arkansas - Sources. 2. Reconstruction -
Arkansas - Sources. 3. Afro-Americans - Education -
Arkansas - History - Sources. I. Title.*
NYPL [Sc Micro R-4643]

Records of the Superintendent of Education for
the State of North Carolina, Bureau of
Refugees, Freedmen, and Abandoned Lands,
1865-1870 [microform] 1865-1870. 7 ft. (24 v.)
Finding aid in the first reel. Microfilm. Washington:
National Archives and Records Service, 1971, 16 reels;
35 mm. (National Archives microfilm publications,
M844)
*1. Freedmen in North Carolina - Sources. 2.
Reconstruction - North Carolina - Sources. 3.
Afro-Americans - Education - North Carolina -
History - Sources. I. Title.*
NYPL [Sc Micro R-4647]

**United States. Bureau of Refugees, Freedmen
and Abandoned Lands. Education Division.**
Records of the Education Division of the
Bureau of Refugees, Freedmen, and Abandoned
Lands, 1865-1871 [microform] 1865-1871. 23 v.
Finding aid in the first reel. Microfilm. Washington:
National Archives and Records Service, 1969. 35 reels;
35 mm. (National Archives microfilm publications,
M803)
*1. Freedmen in the Southern States - Sources. 2.
Afro-Americans - Education - Southern States -
History - Sources. 3. Reconstruction - Southern States -
Sources. I. Title.*   *NYPL [Sc Micro R-4641]*

**UNITED STATES. BUREAU OF REFUGEES,
FREEDMEN AND ABANDONED LANDS,
MEDICAL DEPARTMENT.**
Hasson, Gail Snowden. The medical activities
of the Freedmen's Bureau in Reconstruction
Alabama, 1865-1868 [microform] /. 1982. 252
leaves.   *NYPL [Sc Micro R-4681]*

**United States Catholic Conference. Dept. of
Education.** Faith and culture . Washington,
D.C. , c1987. 111 p. : ISBN 1-555-86994-7 (pbk.)
DDC 268/.82 19
BX1968 .F24 1987   *NYPL [Sc D 88-1059]*

**United States Catholic Conference. Education,
Dept. of.** see United States Catholic
Conference. Dept. of Education.

UNITED STATES - CENSUS, 10TH, 1880.
Nitchman, Paul E. Blacks in Ohio, 1880 in the
counties of ... /. [Decorah? Iowa] , c1985- v. ;
DDC 929/.3/089960730771 19
E185.93.O2 N57 1985
NYPL [APR (Ohio) 86-2025]

**United States. Children's Bureau.
Publication no. 451.**
Herzog, Elizabeth. About the poor .
[Washington] , 1967 [i.e. 1968] 85 p. DDC
362.5//0973
HC110.P6 H47   *NYPL [Sc E 88-67]*

United States. Civil Rights, Office for. see
United States. Dept. of Health, Education,
and Welfare. Office for Civil Rights.

**UNITED STATES - COMMERCE - IVORY
COAST.**

United States. Bureau of International
Commerce. A market for U. S. products in the
Ivory Coast /. Washington, D.C. [1966] viii,
87 p. :   *NYPL [Sc F 89-79]*

United States - Commerce - Statistics. see
United States - Commerce.

United States. Commissioner of Education. see
United States. Office of Education.

United States. Congress.
United States. President (1817-1825 : Monroe)
Message from the President of the United
States, stating the interpretation which has been
given to the act entitled An Act in Addition to
the Acts Prohibiting the Slave Trade.
Washington , 1819. 4 p. ;
NYPL [Sc Rare F 89-25]

**UNITED STATES. CONGRESS. HOUSE -
BIOGRAPHY - JUVENILE LITERATURE.**
Jakoubek, Robert E. Adam Clayton Powell, Jr.
/. New York , c1988. xiv, 252 p. : ISBN
1-555-46606-0 DDC 973/.0496073024 B 92 19
E748.P86 J35 1988   *NYPL [Sc E 88-372]*

**United States. Congress. House. Committee on
Foreign Affairs. Subcommittee on
International Economic Policy and Trade.**
Controls on exports to South Africa : hearings
before the Subcommittees on International
Economic Policy and Trade and on Africa of
the Committee on Foreign Affairs, House of
Representatives, Ninety-seventh Congress,
second session, February 9 and December 2,
1982. Washington : U. S. G.P.O., 1983. iv, 321
p. ; 24 cm. Item 1017-A, 1017-B (microfiche)
Includes bibliographical references. DDC
382/.64/0973 19
*1. Export controls - United States. 2. United States -
Foreign relations - South Africa. 3. South Africa -
Foreign relations - United States. I. Title.*
KF27 .F6465 1982e   *NYPL [Sc E 88-113]*

**United States. Congress. House. Committee on
International Relations. Subcommittee on
Africa.** United States private investment in
South Africa : hearings before the
Subcommittees on Africa and on International
Economic Policy and Trade of the Committee
on International Relations, House of
Representatives, Ninety-fifth Congress, second
session. Washington : U. S. Govt. Print. Off.,
1978. iv, 641 p. ; 24 cm. Hearings held June
27-Sept. 7, 1978. DDC 332.6/7373/068
*1. Investments, American - South Africa. 2. United
States - Foreign economic relations - South Africa. 3.
South Africa - Foreign economic relations - United
States. I. United States. Congress. House. Committee on
International Relations. Subcommittee on International
Economic Policy and Trade. II. Title.*
KF27 .I54914 1978d   *NYPL [Sc E 88-92]*

**United States. Congress. House. Committee on
International Relations. Subcommittee on
International Economic Policy and Trade.**
United States. Congress. House. Committee on
International Relations. Subcommittee on
Africa. United States private investment in
South Africa . Washington , 1978. iv, 641 p. ;
DDC 332.6/7373/068
KF27 .I54914 1978d   *NYPL [Sc E 88-92]*

**UNITED STATES. CONGRESS. HOUSE -
CONTESTED ELECTIONS.**
Ball, Thomas E. Julian Bond vs John Lewis .
Atlanta, Ga. , 1988. ix, 144 p. : ISBN
0-9621362-0-4   *NYPL [Sc E 88-582]*

**United States. Congress. House. Mission to
Southern Africa.** see United States. Congress.
House. Special Study Mission to Southern
Africa.

**United States. Congress. House of
Representatives.** see United States. Congress.
House.

**United States. Congress. House. Southern Africa,
Special Study Mission to.** see United States.
Congress. House. Special Study Mission to
Southern Africa.

**United States. Congress. House. Special Study
Mission to Southern Africa.** Diggs, Charles
C. Report of Special Study Mission to Southern
Africa, August 10-30, 1969/. Washington ,
1969. vi, 179 p. : DDC 301.29'68'073
DT733.D5   *NYPL [Sc E 89-39]*

**United States. Congress. House. Subcommittee
on Africa.** see United States. Congress.

House. Committee on International Relations. Subcommittee on Africa.

United States. Congress. House. Subcommittee on International Economic Policy. see United States. Congress. House. Committee on International Relations. Subcommittee on International Economic Policy and Trade.

United States. Congress. Library. see United States. Library of Congress.

UNITED STATES - CONSTITUTION - AMENDMENTS - 13TH.
Bross, William, 1813-1890. Illinois and the thirteenth amendment to the constitution of the United States. Chicago, 1884. 8 p.
NYPL [Sc Rare F 88-43]

UNITED STATES - CONSTITUTIONAL HISTORY.
Bestor, Arthur. State sovereignty and slavery . Springfield, IL , 1961. 64 p. ;
NYPL [Sc E 87-669]

Constitutional roots, rights, and responsibilities . New York , 1987. 152 p. ;
NYPL [Sc F 88-299]

UNITED STATES - CONSTITUTIONAL LAW.
A Less than perfect union . New York , 1988. vii, 424 p. ; ISBN 0-85345-738-7 : DDC 342.73/029 347.30229 19
KF4550.A2 L47 1987   *NYPL [Sc D 88-724]*

UNITED STATES - CONSTITUTIONAL LAW - CASES.
Joseph, Joel D. Black Mondays . Bethesda, MD , c1987. 286 p. : ISBN 0-915765-44-6 : DDC 347.73/26 347.30735 19
KF4549 .J67 1987   *NYPL [Sc D 88-963]*

United States. Dept. of Commerce. Bureau of International Commerce. see United States. Bureau of International Commerce.

United States. Dept. of Health and Human Services. Task Force on Black and Minority Health. Report of the Secretary's Task Force on Black & Minority Health. Washington, D.C. : U. S. Dept. of Health and Human Services, 1985-1986. 8 v. in 9 : ill. ; 28 cm. Vol. 1: August 1985. Vols. 3-8: January 1986. Includes bibliographies. CONTENTS. - v. 1. Executive summary -- v. 2. Crosscutting issues in minority health -- 3. Cancer -- v. 4. Cardiovascular and cerebrovascular disease (2 v.) -- v. 5. Homicide, suicide, and unintentional injuries -- v. 6. Infant mortality and low birthweight -- v. 7. Chemical dependency and diabetes -- v. 8. Hispanic health issues, Inventory of DHHS programs, Survey of non-federal community. DDC 362.1/08996073 19
1. Afro-Americans - Health and hygiene - United States. 2. Minorities - Health and hygiene - United States. 3. Afro-Americans - Health and hygiene - United States - Statistics. 4. Minorities - Health and hygiene - United States - Statistics. 5. Mortality - United States - Statistics. 6. United States - Statistics, Medical. I. Title.
RA448.5.N4 U55 1985 NYPL [JLM 86-589]

UNITED STATES. DEPT. OF HEALTH, EDUCATION, AND WELFARE. OFFICE FOR CIVIL RIGHTS.
Rebell, Michael A. Equality and education . Princeton, N.J. , c1985. x, 340 p. ; ISBN 0-691-07692-8 : DDC 344.747/0798 347.4704798 19
KFX2065 .R43 1985   *NYPL [JLD 85-3778]*

United States. Dept. of Health, Education, and Welfare. Office of Child Development. see United States. Office of Child Development.

United States. Dept. of Health Education, and Welfare. Office of Education. see United States. Office of Education.

United States. Dept. of State. Advisory Committee on South Africa. A U. S. policy toward South Africa : the report of the Secretary of State's Advisory Committee on South Africa. [Washington, D.C.] : U. S. Dept. of State, [1987] vi, 49 p. : ill., maps ; 28 cm. (Department of State publication. 9537 (Apr. 1987))
1. Apartheid - South Africa. 2. United States - Foreign relations - South Africa. 3. South Africa - Foreign relations - United States. I. Title. II. Title: United States policy toward South Africa. III. Series: Department of State publication, 9537. *NYPL [Sc F 88-300]*

United States. Dept. of the Interior. Office of Education. see United States. Office of Education.

UNITED STATES - ECONOMIC CONDITIONS - 1981-
Black economic progress . Washington, D.C. , Lanham, Md. , 1988. xi, 52 p. : ISBN 0-941410-69-2 (alk. paper) DDC 330.973/008996073 19
E185.8 .B496 1988   *NYPL [Sc E 89-154]*

UNITED STATES - ECONOMIC CONDITIONS - PHILOSOPHY.
Ideology and American experience . Washington, DC , c1986. vi, 264 p. ; ISBN 0-88702-015-1 : DDC 320.5/0973 19
E169.12 .I34 1986   *NYPL [Sc E 89-74]*

UNITED STATES - ECONOMIC POLICY - 1981-
The Politics of Latin American liberation theology . Washington, D.C. , c1988. xxi, 360 p. ; ISBN 0-88702-039-9 : DDC 261.7/09181/2 19
BT83.57 .P643 1988   *NYPL [Sc E 89-75]*

United States. Education Bureau. see United States. Office of Education.

United States. Education, Office of. see United States. Office of Education.

United States - Elections. see Elections - United States.

UNITED STATES - EMIGRATION AND IMMIGRATION - FICTION.
Fanks, Russell, 1940- Terminus floride . Paris , 1987. 346 p. ; ISBN 2-7357-0059-3
NYPL [Sc E 88-126]

UNITED STATES - EMIGRATION AND IMMIGRATION - GOVERNMENT POLICY.
The Caribbean exodus /. New York , 1987. vii, 293 p. ; ISBN 0-275-92182-4 (alk. paper) : DDC 325.729 19
JV7321 .C37 1986   *NYPL [JLE 87-1789]*

The Mariel injustice . Coral Gables, Fl. , c1987. 204 p. :
NYPL [Sc F 89-64]

UNITED STATES - ETHNIC RELATIONS.
Race and politics /. New York , 1985. 174 p. ; ISBN 0-8242-0700-9 (pbk.) : DDC 305.8/00973 19
E184.A1 R25 1985   *NYPL [8-SAD (Reference shelf. v.56, no.6)]*

UNITED STATES - ETHNIC RELATIONS - BIBLIOGRAPHY.
Taylor, Charles A. (Charles Andrew), 1950- Guide to multicultural resources /. Madison, WI , c1987. ix, 512 p. : ISBN 0-935483-07-1 (pbk.)   *NYPL [Sc D 88-530]*

UNITED STATES - ETHNIC RELATIONS - CONGRESSES.
National Conference on African American/Jewish American Relations (1983 : Savannah State College) Blacks and Jews . [Savannah, Ga.] [1983] iii, 58 p. ;
NYPL [Sc D 88-335]

UNITED STATES - ETHNIC RELATIONS - SOCIETIES, ETC. - DIRECTORIES.
Taylor, Charles A. (Charles Andrew), 1950- Guide to multicultural resources /. Madison, WI , c1987. ix, 512 p. : ISBN 0-935483-07-1 (pbk.)   *NYPL [Sc D 88-530]*

United States. Federal Security Agency. Office of Education. see United States. Office of Education.

United States. Foreign Affairs, Committee on (House) see United States. Congress. House. Committee on Foreign Affairs.

UNITED STATES - FOREIGN ECONOMIC RELATIONS - SOUTH AFRICA.
United States. Congress. House. Committee on International Relations. Subcommittee on Africa. United States private investment in South Africa . Washington , 1978. iv, 641 p. ; DDC 332.6/7373/068
KF27 .I54914 1978d   *NYPL [Sc E 88-92]*

UNITED STATES - FOREIGN RELATIONS.
Transafrica Forum (Organization) A retrospective . [Washington, D.C.] , c1987. 32 p. :   *NYPL [Sc E 88-163]*

UNITED STATES - FOREIGN RELATIONS - 1977-
Lake, Anthony. Third World radical regimes . New York , 1985. 54 p. : ISBN 0-87124-099-8
NYPL [ILH 86-805]

UNITED STATES - FOREIGN RELATIONS - 1981-
Schümer, Martin. Die amerikanische Politik gegenüber dem südlichen Afrika /. Bonn [1986]. v, 183 p. ; ISBN 3-7713-0275-7
NYPL [Sc D 88-983]

UNITED STATES - FOREIGN RELATIONS - AFRICA.
Transafrica Forum (Organization) A retrospective . [Washington, D.C.] , c1987. 32 p. :   *NYPL [Sc E 88-163]*

UNITED STATES - FOREIGN RELATIONS - AFRICA - ADDRESSES, ESSAYS, LECTURES.
African crisis areas and U. S. foreign policy /. Berkeley , c1985. xiv, 374 p. : ISBN 0-520-05548-9 (alk. paper) DDC 327.7306 19
DT38.7 .A39 1986   *NYPL [JLE 85-4182]*

UNITED STATES - FOREIGN RELATIONS - AFRICA, NORTHEAST.
Sauldie, Madan M. Super powers in the Horn of Africa /. New York , c1987. ix, 252 p. ; ISBN 0-86590-092-2 DDC 320.960 19
DT367.8 .S28 1987   *NYPL [Sc D 89-488]*

UNITED STATES - FOREIGN RELATIONS - AFRICA, SOUTHERN.
Schümer, Martin. Die amerikanische Politik gegenüber dem südlichen Afrika /. Bonn [1986]. v, 183 p. ; ISBN 3-7713-0275-7
NYPL [Sc D 88-983]

UNITED STATES - FOREIGN RELATIONS - DEVELOPING COUNTRIES.
Lake, Anthony. Third World radical regimes . New York , 1985. 54 p. : ISBN 0-87124-099-8
NYPL [ILH 86-805]

UNITED STATES - FOREIGN RELATIONS - HAITI.
Gousse, Edgard Js. Th. Non à une intervention américaine en Haïti /. Montréal , 1988. 74 p. ;
NYPL [Sc D 88-861]

UNITED STATES - FOREIGN RELATIONS - LATIN AMERICA.
The Politics of Latin American liberation theology . Washington, D.C. , c1988. xxi, 360 p. ; ISBN 0-88702-039-9 : DDC 261.7/09181/2 19
BT83.57 .P643 1988   *NYPL [Sc E 89-75]*

UNITED STATES - FOREIGN RELATIONS - NAMIBIA.
Pomeroy, William J., 1916- Apartheid, imperialism, and African freedom /. New York , 1986. ix, 259 p. : ISBN 0-7178-0640-5 : DDC 305.8/00968 19
E183.8.S6 P65 1986   *NYPL [Sc D 88-1147]*

UNITED STATES - FOREIGN RELATIONS - PHILOSOPHY.
Ideology and American experience . Washington, DC , c1986. vi, 264 p. ; ISBN 0-88702-015-1 : DDC 320.5/0973 19
E169.12 .I34 1986   *NYPL [Sc E 89-74]*

UNITED STATES - FOREIGN RELATIONS - SOUTH AFRICA.
Pomeroy, William J., 1916- Apartheid, imperialism, and African freedom /. New York , 1986. ix, 259 p. : ISBN 0-7178-0640-5 : DDC 305.8/00968 19
E183.8.S6 P65 1986   *NYPL [Sc D 88-1147]*

Schümer, Martin. Die amerikanische Politik gegenüber dem südlichen Afrika /. Bonn [1986]. v, 183 p. ; ISBN 3-7713-0275-7
NYPL [Sc D 88-983]

United States. Congress. House. Committee on Foreign Affairs. Subcommittee on International Economic Policy and Trade. Controls on exports to South Africa . Washington , 1983. iv, 321 p. ; DDC 382/.64/0973 19
KF27 .F6465 1982e   *NYPL [Sc E 88-113]*

United States. Dept. of State. Advisory Committee on South Africa. A U. S. policy toward South Africa . [Washington, D.C.] [1987] vi, 49 p. :   *NYPL [Sc F 88-300]*

UNITED STATES - FOREIGN RELATIONS - SOUTH AFRICA - CONGRESSES.
South Africa--the vital link . Washington , c1976. 120 p. ;   *NYPL [Sc F 89-129]*

UNITED STATES - FOREIGN RELATIONS - TANZANIA.
Wilson, Amrit, 1941- US foreign policy and revolution . London , distributed in the USA by Unwin Hyman, 1989. ix, 179 p. ; ISBN 1-85305-051-2   *NYPL [Sc D 89-426]*

United States. Freedmen's Bureau. see United States. Bureau of Refugees, Freedmen and Abandoned Lands.

United States - Government. see United States - Politics and government.

United States. Health and Human Services, Dept. of. see United States. Dept. of Health and Human Services.

UNITED STATES - HISTORY - REVOLUTION, 1775-1783.
Jamaica. Assembly. To the King's most Excellent Majesty in Council, the humble petition and memorial of the Assembly of Jamaica . Philadelphia: , 1775. 8 p. ;
NYPL [Sc Rare F 88-14]

UNITED STATES - HISTORY - CIVIL WAR, 1861-1865 - AFRO-AMERICANS.
Taylor, Susie King, b. 1848. [Reminiscences of my life in camp.] A Black woman's Civil War memoirs . New York , 1988. 154 p. : ISBN 0-910129-85-1 (pbk.) : DDC 973.7/415 B 19
E492.94 33rd .T3 1988
NYPL [Sc D 88-1473]

UNITED STATES - HISTORY - CIVIL WAR, 1861-1865 - HOSPITALS, CHARITIES, ETC.
Committee of Merchants for the Relief of Colored People, Suffering from the Late Riots in the City of New York. Report of the Committee of Merchants for the Relief of Colored People, Suffering from the Late Riots in the City of New York. New York , 1863. 48 p. ;
NYPL [Sc Rare F 89-2]

UNITED STATES - HISTORY - CIVIL WAR, 1861-1865 - PARTICIPATION, AFRO-AMERICAN.
Cornish, Dudley Taylor. The sable arm . Lawrence, Kan. , c1987. xviii, 342 p. ; ISBN 0-7006-0328-X (pbk.) DDC 973.7/415 19
E540.N3 C77 1987   *NYPL [Sc D 88-850]*

Smith, Marion Whitney. Beacon Hill's Colonel Robert Gould Shaw /. New York , 1986. 512 p. : ISBN 0-8062-2732-X
NYPL [Sc D 88-414]

Taylor, Susie King, b. 1848. [Reminiscences of my life in camp.] A Black woman's Civil War memoirs . New York , 1988. 154 p. : ISBN 0-910129-85-1 (pbk.) : DDC 973.7/415 B 19
E492.94 33rd .T3 1988
NYPL [Sc D 88-1473]

UNITED STATES - HISTORY - CIVIL WAR, 1861-1865 - PARTICIPATION, IMMIGRANT.
Burton, William L., 1928- Melting pot soldiers . Ames, Iowa , 1988. x, 282 p. ; ISBN 0-8138-1115-5 DDC 973.7/4 19
E540.F6 B87 1988   *NYPL [IKC 88-730]*

UNITED STATES - HISTORY - CIVIL WAR, 1861-1865 - PERSONAL NARRATIVES.
Taylor, Susie King, b. 1848. [Reminiscences of my life in camp.] A Black woman's Civil War memoirs . New York , 1988. 154 p. : ISBN 0-910129-85-1 (pbk.) : DDC 973.7/415 B 19
E492.94 33rd .T3 1988
NYPL [Sc D 88-1473]

UNITED STATES - HISTORY - CIVIL WAR, 1861-1865 - PUBLIC OPINION.
Jimerson, Randall C. The private Civil War . Baton Rouge, LA , 1988. xiv, 270 p., [8] p. of plates : ISBN 0-8071-1454-5 (alk. paper) : DDC 973.7 19
E468.9 .J55 1988   *NYPL [IKI 89-2276]*

UNITED STATES - HISTORY - CIVIL WAR, 1861-1865 - SERMONS.
Boardman, Henry Augustus, 1808-1880. What Christianity demands of us at the present crisis . Philadelphia , 1860. 28 p. ;
NYPL [Sc Rare F 88-52]

UNITED STATES - HISTORY - CIVIL WAR, 1861-1865 - SOCIAL ASPECTS.
Jimerson, Randall C. The private Civil War . Baton Rouge, LA , 1988. xiv, 270 p., [8] p. of plates : ISBN 0-8071-1454-5 (alk. paper) : DDC 973.7 19
E468.9 .J55 1988   *NYPL [IKI 89-2276]*

UNITED STATES - HISTORY - 1953-1961.
Branch, Taylor. Parting the waters . New York , c1988- v. : ISBN 0-671-46097-8 (v. 1) DDC 973/.0496073 19
E185.61 .B7914 1988   *NYPL [IEC 88-122]*

UNITED STATES - HISTORY - 1961-1969.
Hayden, Tom. Reunion . New York , c1988. xix, 539 p., [16] p. of plates ; ISBN 0-394-56533-9 : DDC 328.794/092/4 B 19
F866.4.H39 A3 1988   *NYPL [JFE 88-6231]*

UNITED STATES - HISTORY - BIBLIOGRAPHY.
Prucha, Francis Paul. Handbook for research in American history . Lincoln , c19. xiii, 289 p. ; ISBN 0-8032-3682-4 (alk. paper) DDC 016.973 19
Z1236 .P78 1987 E178   NYPL [Sc D 88-545]

United States - History, Economic. see United States - Economic conditions.

United States - History, Political. see United States - Politics and government.

UNITED STATES - HISTORY - TEXT-BOOKS - BIBLIOGRAPHY.
Sloan, Irving J. The Negro in modern American history textbooks . Chicago, Ill. , 1966. 47 p. ;
NYPL [Sc D 89-262]

UNITED STATES - HISTORY - TEXTBOOKS.
Thinking and rethinking U. S. history /. New York, N.Y. , c1988. 389 p. ;
NYPL [Sc F 89-130]

United States. House of Representatives. see United States. Congress. House.

United States - Immigration. see United States - Emigration and immigration.

UNITED STATES IN LITERATURE.
Dash, J. Michael. Haiti and the United States . Basingstoke, Hampshire , 1988. xv, 152 p. ; ISBN 0-333-45491-X
NYPL [Sc D 88-1358]

UNITED STATES - INTELLECTUAL LIFE - 1865-1918.
Meier, August, 1923- Negro thought in America, 1880-1915 . Ann Arbor , 1988, c1963. xii, 336 p. ; ISBN 0-472-64230-8 DDC 973/.0496073 19
E185.6 .M5 1988   *NYPL [Sc D 89-509]*

UNITED STATES - INTELLECTUAL LIFE - 20TH CENTURY.
Childs, John Brown. Leadership, conflict, and cooperation in Afro-American social thought /. Philadelphia , 1989. xii, 172 p. ; ISBN 0-87722-581-8 (alk. paper) : DDC 303.3/4/08996073 19
E185.6 .C534 1989   *NYPL [Sc D 89-497]*

United States. International Commerce, Bureau of. see United States. Bureau of International Commerce.

United States. Kerner Commission. The Kerner report : the 1968 report of the National Advisory Commission on Civil Disorders, with a preface by Fred R. Harris and a new introduction by Tom Wicker. New York, N.Y. : Pantheon books, 1988. xxvi, 513 p. ; 21 cm. Includes bibliographical references and index. ISBN 0-679-72078-2
1. Riots - United States. 2. United States - Race relations. I. Harris, Fred R. II. Wicker, Tom. III. Title. IV. Title: Report of the National Advisory Commission on Civil Disorders. V. Title: National Advisory Commission on Civil Disorders.
NYPL [Sc D 89-604]

UNITED STATES. KERNER COMMISSION.
Quiet riots . New York , 1988. xiii, 223 p. : ISBN 0-394-57473-7 : DDC 305.5/69/0973 19
HV4045 .Q54 1988   *NYPL [JLD 89-239]*

United States. Library of Congress. African Section. Witherell, Julian W. French-speaking central Africa. Washington, 1973. xiv, 314 p. ISBN 0-8444-0033-5
Z3692 .W5   *NYPL [JLF 74-197]*

United States. Library of Congress. General Reference and Bibliography Division. African Section. see United States. Library of Congress. African Section.

United States of Colombia. see Colombia.

United States. Office for Civil Rights. see United States. Dept. of Health, Education, and Welfare. Office for Civil Rights.

United States. Office of Child Development. Dodson, Jualynne E. Black stylization and implications for child welfare. Atlanta, Georgia , 1975. 1 v. (various pagings) ;
NYPL [Sc F 88-223]

Toward reflective analysis of Black families . [Atlanta] , 1976. ii, 74 l. ;
NYPL [Sc F 88-224]

United States. Office of Child Development. Children's Bureau. see United States. Children's Bureau.

United States. Office of Education. Bulletin, 1959.
(no. 20) Dale, George Allan, 1900- Education in the Republic of Haiti. [Washington] [1959] x, 180 p.,   *NYPL [Sc E 88-60]*

United States. Office of Minority Health. The Black American elderly . New York , c1988. xvi, 383 p. ; ISBN 0-8261-5810-2 DDC 362.1/9897/00973 19
RA448.5.N4 B56 1988   NYPL [JLE 88-5391]

United States. Office of the Under Secretary of Defense for Policy. Henze, Paul B., 1924- Rebels and separatists in Ethiopia . Santa Monica, CA , 1985. xv, 98 p. ; ISBN 0-8330-0696-7 DDC 963/.07 19
DT387.95 .H46 1986   NYPL [JFE 86-5101]

United States policy toward South Africa. United States. Dept. of State. Advisory Committee on South Africa. A U. S. policy toward South Africa . [Washington, D.C.] [1987] vi, 49 p. :
NYPL [Sc F 88-300]

UNITED STATES - POLITICS AND GOVERNMENT - 1783-1865.
Blanchard, Joshua Pollard, 1782-1868. Principles of the Revolution. Boston, 1855. 24 p.
JK216 .B63   *NYPL [Sc Rare F 88-40]*

UNITED STATES - POLITICS AND GOVERNMENT - 1829-1837.
Hayne, Robert Young, 1791-1839. Speeches of Hayne and Webster in the United States Senate, on the resolution of Mr. Foot, January, 1830 . Boston , 1853. 115 p. ;
E381 .H424 1853   NYPL [Sc Rare C 89-20]

UNITED STATES - POLITICS AND GOVERNMENT - 1857-1861.
Boardman, Henry Augustus, 1808-1880. What Christianity demands of us at the present crisis . Philadelphia , 1860. 28 p. ;
NYPL [Sc Rare F 88-52]

UNITED STATES - POLITICS AND GOVERNMENT - 1865-1877.
Benedict, Michael Les. The fruits of victory . Lanham, MD , c1986. xiii, 159 p. ; ISBN 0-8191-5557-8 (pbk. : alk. paper) : DDC 973.8 19
E668 .B462 1986   *NYPL [IKR 87-1888]*

Foner, Eric. Reconstruction, America's unfinished revolution, 1863-1877 /. New York , c1988. xxvii, 690 p., [8] p. of plates : ISBN 0-06-015851-4 : DDC 973.8 19
E668 .F66 1988   *NYPL [*R-IKR 88-5216]*

UNITED STATES - POLITICS AND GOVERNMENT - 1865-1877 - SOURCES.
Benedict, Michael Les. The fruits of victory . Lanham, MD , c1986. xiii, 159 p. ; ISBN 0-8191-5557-8 (pbk. : alk. paper) : DDC 973.8 19
E668 .B462 1986   *NYPL [IKR 87-1888]*

UNITED STATES - POLITICS AND GOVERNMENT - 20TH CENTURY - SOURCES - BIBLIOGRAPHY.
University of Iowa. Libraries. The right wing collection of the University of Iowa Libraries, 1918-1977 . Glen Rock, N.J. , 1978. v, 175 p. ; ISBN 0-667-00520-X DDC 016.3205/0973 19
Z7163 .U585 1978 JA1 NYPL [Sc F 86-176]

UNITED STATES - POLITICS AND GOVERNMENT - 1945-
Carmines, Edward G. Issue evolution . Princeton, N.J. , c1989. xvii, 217 p. : ISBN 0-691-07802-5 : DDC 323.1/196073 19
E185.615 .C35 1989   *NYPL [Sc E 89-214]*

Haines, Herbert H. Black radicals and the civil rights mainstream, 1954-1970 /. Knoxville , c19. xii, 231 p. ; ISBN 0-87049-563-1 (alk. paper) : DDC 305.8/96073 19
E185.615 .H25 1988   *NYPL [Sc E 88-511]*

UNITED STATES - POLITICS AND GOVERNMENT - 1969-1974.
Chisolm, Shirley, 1924- The good fight /. New York , c1973. 206 p. ;   *NYPL [Sc C 88-43]*

UNITED STATES - POLITICS AND GOVERNMENT - 1981-

Cavanagh, Thomas E. The impact of the Black electorate [microform] /. Washington, D.C. (1301 Pennsylvania Ave., N.W., Suite 400, Washington 20004) , 1984. v, 28 p. ; DDC 324.973/008996073 19

E185.615 .C364 1984   NYPL   [*Z-4913 no.8]

Smith, J. Owens. Blacks and American government . Dubuque, Iowa , c1987. xii, 148 p. : ISBN 0-8403-4407-4 (pbk.) DDC 323.1/196073 19

E185.615 .S576 1987   NYPL   [Sc E 89-193]

UNITED STATES - POLITICS AND GOVERNMENT - PHILOSOPHY.

Ideology and American experience . Washington, DC , c1986. vi, 264 p. ; ISBN 0-88702-015-1 : DDC 320.5/0973 19

E169.12 .I34 1986   NYPL   [Sc E 89-74]

UNITED STATES - POPULAR CULTURE - HISTORY - 20TH CENTURY.

Ogren, Kathy J. The jazz revolution . New York , 1989. vii, 221 p., [8] p. of plates : ISBN 0-19-505153-X (alk. paper) DDC 781/.57/0973 19

ML3508 .O37 1987   NYPL   [Sc D 89-451]

United States. President (1817-1825 : Monroe)
Message from the President of the United States, stating the interpretation which has been given to the act entitled An Act in Addition to the Acts Prohibiting the Slave Trade. Washington : Printed by Gales & Seaton, 1819. 4 p. ; 23 cm. At head of title: 11. "December 20, 1819. Read, and referred to the committee on so much of the message of the President ... as relates to the unlawful introduction of slaves into the United States." Addressed to the Senate and House and dated Washington, December 17th, 1819.
1. United States. Act in Addition to the Acts Prohibiting the Slave Trade. 2. Slave-trade - United States. I. Monroe, James, 1758-1831. II. United States. Congress. III. Title.   **NYPL   [Sc Rare F 89-25]**

United States. President, 1841-1845 (Tyler)
Colored mariners in ports of South Carolina. Message from the President of the United States transmitting the information required by a resolution of the House of Representatives of 2d February ultimo, in relation to an act of the Legislature of the State of South Carolina. directing the imprisonment of colored persons arriving from abroad in the ports of that State, &c. March 2, 1842. [Washington, D. C.: s. n.], 1842 18 p.; 25 cm. Caption title. At head of title: 27th Congress, 2d Session. Doc. No. 119, House of Representatives.
1. Afro-American merchant seamen - Legal status, laws, etc. - South Carolina. 2. Merchant seamen - Legal status,laws, etc. - South Carolina. I. Title.
NYPL   [Sc Rare F 88-23]

United States - Presidents. see Presidents - United States.

United States private investment in South Africa . United States. Congress. House. Committee on International Relations. Subcommittee on Africa. Washington , 1978. iv, 641 p. ; DDC 332.6/7373/068

KF27 .I54914 1978d   NYPL   [Sc E 88-92]

United States. Public Health Service. Dept. of Health and Human Services. see United States. Dept. of Health and Human Services.

UNITED STATES - RACE RELATIONAS.

Law, John, 1900- Black creatures of destiny /. [New York? , 198-?] 80 p. :
NYPL   [Sc D 89-208]

UNITED STATES - RACE RELATIONS.

Ashmore, Harry S. Hearts and minds . Cabin John, Md. , c1988. xviii, 513 p. ; ISBN 0-932020-58-5 (pbk. : alk. paper) DDC 305.8/96073 19

E185.61 .A83 1988   NYPL   [Sc D 89-382]

Bernheim, Nicole. Voyage en Amérique noire /. Paris , c1986. 254 p. ; ISBN 2-234-01886-2 : DDC 305.8/96073/073 19

E185.86 .B47 1986   NYPL   [Sc E 88-607]

Black workers . Philadelphia , 1989. xv, 733 p. ; ISBN 0-87722-592-3   *NYPL   [Sc E 89-206]*

Blauner, Bob. Black lives, white lives . Berkeley , c1989. xii, 347 p. ; ISBN 0-520-06261-2 (alk. paper) DDC 305.8/00973 19

E185.615 .B556 1989   NYPL   [Sc E 89-219]

Booker T. Washington and the "Atlanta compromise" /. Sharpsburg, Md. , c1987. 13 p. :
NYPL   [Sc F 88-386]

Boston, Thomas D. Race, class, and conservatism /. Boston , 1988. xix, 172 p. : ISBN 0-04-330368-4 (alk. paper) DDC 305.5/0973 19

HN90.S6 B67 1988   NYPL   [Sc D 89-107]

Bowen, David Warren, 1944- Andrew Johnson and the Negro /. Knoxville , c1989. xvi, 206 p. ; ISBN 0-87049-584-4 (alk. paper) DDC 973/.0496073 19

E667 .B65 1989   NYPL   [Sc D 89-508]

Cheek, William F., 1933- John Mercer Langston and the fight for Black freedom, 1829-65 /. Urbana , c1989. 478 p. ; ISBN 0-252-01550-9 (alk. paper) DDC 973/.0496073/0924 B 19

E185.97.L27 C48 1989   NYPL   [Sc E 89-255]

The Civil rights movement in America . Jackson , c1986. xii, 188 p. ; ISBN 0-87805-297-6 (alk. paper) DDC 323.1/196073 19

E185.615 .C585 1986   NYPL   [IEC 87-273]

Colaiaco, James A., 1945- Martin Luther King, Jr. . New York , 1988. x, 238 p. ; ISBN 0-312-02365-0 : DDC 323.4/092/4 B 19

E185.97.K5 C65 1988   NYPL   [Sc D 89-231]

Davis, Angela Yvonne, 1944- Women, culture, & politics /. New York, NY , 1989. xv, 238 p. ; ISBN 0-394-76976-8 : DDC 305.4/8896073 19

E185.86 .D382 1989   NYPL   [Sc D 89-275]

Denby, Charles. Indignant heart . Detroit , 1989, c1978. xvi, 303 p. : ISBN 0-8143-2219-0 (alk. paper) DDC 331.6/396073 B 19

HD8039.A82 U633 1989
NYPL   [Sc D 89-563]

Drimmer, Melvin. Issues in Black history . Dubuque, Iowa , c1987. xviii, 308 p. ; ISBN 0-8403-4174-1 (pbk.) DDC 973/.0496073 19

E185 .D715 1987   NYPL   [Sc E 88-107]

Fredrickson, George M., 1934- The arrogance of race . Middletown, Conn. , c1988. viii, 310 p. ; ISBN 0-8195-5177-5 DDC 973/.0496 19

E441 .F77 1988   NYPL   [Sc E 88-487]

Gross, Samuel R. Death & discrimination . Boston , c1989. xvi, 268 p. ; ISBN 1-555-53040-0 (alk. paper) : DDC 364.6/6/0973 19

HV8699.U5 G76 1989   NYPL   [Sc D 89-493]

Haines, Herbert H. Black radicals and the civil rights mainstream, 1954-1970 /. Knoxville , c19. xii, 231 p. : ISBN 0-87049-563-1 (alk. paper) : DDC 305.8/96073 19

E185.615 .H25 1988   NYPL   [Sc E 88-511]

Harap, Louis. Dramatic encounters . New York , c1987. xiv, 177 p. ; ISBN 0-313-25388-9 (lib. bdg. : alk. paper) DDC 810/.9/35203924 19

PS173.J4 H294 1987   NYPL   [*PZB 87-5243]

Harris, Abram Lincoln, 1899-1963. Race, radicalism, and reform . New Brunswick, U. S.A. , c1989. viii, 521 p. ; ISBN 0-88738-210-X DDC 305.8/96073 19

E185.8 .H27 1989   NYPL   [Sc E 89-166]

Horne, Gerald. Communist front? . Rutherford [N.J.] , London , c1988. 454 p. ; ISBN 0-8386-3285-8 (alk. paper) DDC 323.1/196073/073 19

E185.61 .H8 1988   NYPL   [Sc E 88-147]

Johnson, Edward Augustus, 1860-1944. Light ahead for the Negro . New York , 1904. vi, 132 p. ;
NYPL   [Sc Rare C 88-6]

Kaufman, Jonathan. Broken alliance . New York , c1988. 311 p. ; ISBN 0-684-18699-3 : DDC 305.8/00973 19

E185.615 .K33 1988   NYPL   [*PXY 88-4777]

La Farge, John, 1880-1963. Interracial justice . New York , 1937. xii, 226 p. ; DDC 325.260973

E185.61 .L25   NYPL   [Sc C 88-146]

Landry, Bart. The new Black middle class /. Berkeley , 1987. xi, 250 p. ; ISBN 0-520-05942-5 (alk. paper) DDC 305.8/96073 19

E185.86 .L35 1987   NYPL   [Sc D 87-1006]

Pomerance, Alan. Repeal of the blues /. Secaucus, N.J. , c1988. x, 264 p., [16] p. of plates : ISBN 0-8065-1105-2 : DDC

792/.08996073 19

PN1590.B53 P6 1988   NYPL   [Sc E 89-90]

Quarles, Benjamin. Black mosaic . Amherst, Mass. , 1988. 213 p. ; ISBN 0-87023-604-0 (alk. paper) DDC 973/.0496073 19

E185 .Q19 1988   NYPL   [Sc E 88-330]

Quiet riots . New York , 1988. xiii, 223 p. : ISBN 0-394-57473-7 : DDC 305.5/69/0973 19

HV4045 .Q54 1988   NYPL   [JLD 89-239]

Race and politics /. New York , 1985. 174 p. ; ISBN 0-8242-0700-9 (pbk.) : DDC 305.8/00973 19

E184.A1 R25 1985   NYPL   [8-SAD (Reference shelf. v.56, no.6)]

Shakur, Assata. Assata, an autobiography /. Westport, CT , 1987. xiv, 274 p. ; ISBN 0-88208-221-3 : DDC 973/.0496073024 19

E185.97.S53 A3 1987   NYPL   [Sc E 88-21]

Smith, William Gardner, 1926-1974. [Return to Black America. Frech.] L'Amérique noire. [Tournai, 1972] 149 p.   *NYPL   [IEC 79-113]*

Staples, Robert. The urban plantation . Oakland, CA , c1987. 248 p. ; ISBN 0-933296-13-4 (pbk.)
NYPL   [Sc D 88-1021]

Symposium on race and class. Philadelphia , 1984. 62 p. ;   *NYPL   [Sc D 88-2]*

Teague, Bob. The flip side of soul . New York , c1989. 201 p. ; ISBN 0-688-08260-2 DDC 305.8/96073 19

PS3570.E2 Z495 1989   NYPL   [Sc D 89-303]

United States. Kerner Commission. The Kerner report . New York, N.Y. , 1988. xxvi, 513 p. ; ISBN 0-679-72078-2   *NYPL   [Sc D 89-604]*

Werner, John M., 1941- Reaping the bloody harvest . New York , 1986. 333 p. ; ISBN 0-8240-8301-6 (alk. paper) : DDC 973.5/6 19

E185 .W44 1986   NYPL   [Sc E 88-242]

Which path to freedom? . Pomona, Calif. , c1986. iv, 60 p. ; DDC 973.7/114 19

E449 .W565 1986   NYPL   [Sc D 88-1154]

UNITED STATES - RACE RELATIONS - BIBLIOGRAPHY.

Taylor, Charles A. (Charles Andrew), 1950- Guide to multicultural resources /. Madison, WI , c1987. ix, 512 p. : ISBN 0-935483-07-1 (pbk.)   *NYPL   [Sc D 88-530]*

UNITED STATES - RACE RELATIONS - HISTORY.

Denby, Charles. Indignant heart . Boston , c1978. 295 p. : ISBN 0-89608-092-7 DDC 331.6/3/960730774340924 B 19

HD8039.A82 U633 1978
NYPL   [Sc D 88-853]

UNITED STATES - RACE RELATIONS - JUVENILE FICTION.

Chenfeld, Mimi Brodsky. The house at 12 Rose Street. London, New York, 1966. 157 p. DDC [Fic]

PZ7.C4183 Ho   NYPL   [Sc D 88-509]

Garden, Nancy. What happened in Marston. New York [1971] 190 p. DDC [Fic]

PZ7.G165 Wh   NYPL   [Sc D 89-98]

UNITED STATES - RACE RELATIONS - POLITICAL ASPECTS.

Carmines, Edward G. Issue evolution . Princeton, N.J. , c1989. xvii, 217 p. : ISBN 0-691-07802-5 : DDC 323.1/196073 19

E185.615 .C35 1989   NYPL   [Sc E 89-214]

UNITED STATES - RACE RELATIONS - SOCIETIES, ETC. - DIRECTORIES.

Taylor, Charles A. (Charles Andrew), 1950- Guide to multicultural resources /. Madison, WI , c1987. ix, 512 p. : ISBN 0-935483-07-1 (pbk.)   *NYPL   [Sc D 88-530]*

United States. Refugees, Freedmen and Abandoned Lands, Bureau of. see United States. Bureau of Refugees, Freedmen and Abandoned Lands.

UNITED STATES - RELATIONS - AFRICA.

Africa in the 1990s and beyond . Algonac, Mich. , 1988. 309 p. ; ISBN 0-917256-44-1 (pbk.) : DDC 303.4/8273/06 19

DT38 .A44 1988   NYPL   [Sc E 89-98]

Watson, Denton L. Reclaiming a heritage . New York, N.Y. , c1977. 63 p. ;
NYPL   [Sc F 89-78]

BLACK STUDIES: 1989

365   *University of Bradford. International Centre for Intercultural*

UNITED STATES - RELATIONS - AFRICA, SOUTHERN.
Diggs, Charles C. Report of Special Study Mission to Southern Africa, August 10-30, 1969/. Washington , 1969. vi, 179 p. : DDC 301.29'68'073
DT733.D5   *NYPL [Sc E 89-39]*

UNITED STATES - RELATIONS (GENERAL) WITH AFRICA - HISTORY.
Roark, J. L. American expansionism vs. European colonialism [microform] . [Nairobi] , 1976. 16 leaves ;
NYPL [Sc Micro R-4108 no. 34]

UNITED STATES - RELATIONS - HAITI.
Dash, J. Michael. Haiti and the United States . Basingstoke, Hampshire , 1988. xv, 152 p. ; ISBN 0-333-45491-X
NYPL [Sc D 88-1358]

UNITED STATES - RELATIONS - LIBERIA.
Johnson, Charles Spurgeon, 1893-1956. Bitter Canaan . New Brunswick, N.J. , c1987. lxxiii, 256 p. ; ISBN 0-88738-053-0 : DDC 966.6/2 19
DT631 .J59 1987   *NYPL [Sc E 88-351]*

UNITED STATES - RELATIONS - SOUTH AFRICA.
Parker, Aida. Secret U. S. war against South Africa /. Johannesburg , c1977. 79 p. ;
NYPL [Sc D 88-277]

UNITED STATES - RELIGION - 1960-
West, Cornel. Prophetic fragments /. Grand Rapids, Mich. , Trenton, N.J. , c1988. xi, 294 p. ; ISBN 0-8028-0308-3 : DDC 291/.0973 19
BL2525 .W42 1988   *NYPL [Sc E 88-401]*

United States. Social and Rehabilitation Service. Children's Bureau. see United States. Children's Bureau.

UNITED STATES - SOCIAL CONDITIONS - 1960-
Dilemmas of the new Black middle class /. [Pa.?] c1980. v, 100 p. ;
E185.86 .D54x 1980   *NYPL [Sc D 89-24]*

UNITED STATES - SOCIAL CONDITIONS - 1960-1980.
Hayden, Tom. Reunion . New York , c1988. xix, 539 p., [16] p. of plates ; ISBN 0-394-56533-9 : DDC 328.794/092/4 B 19
F866.4.H39 A3 1988   *NYPL [JFE 88-6231]*

UNITED STATES - SOCIAL CONDITIONS - 1980-
Black families in crisis . New York , c1988. xiv, 305 p. ; ISBN 0-87630-524-9 DDC 305.8/96073 19
E185.86 .B5254 1988   *NYPL [Sc E 89-155]*

United States. Social Security Administration. Children's Bureau. see United States. Children's Bureau.

United States. State Dept. see United States. Dept. of State.

UNITED STATES - STATISTICS, MEDICAL.
United States. Dept. of Health and Human Services. Task Force on Black and Minority Health. Report of the Secretary's Task Force on Black & Minority Health. Washington, D.C. , 1985-1986. 8 v. in 9 : DDC 362.1/08996073 19
RA448.5.N4 U55 1985   *NYPL [JLM 86-589]*

United States. War Dept. Army Air Forces. see United States. Army Air Forces.

United States. Welfare Administration. Children's Bureau. see United States. Children's Bureau.

UNITY PARTY OF NIGERIA.
Babatope, Ebenezer. Awo & Nigeria . Ikeja [Nigeria] , 1984. 97 p. ; ISBN 3-7830-0100-0
NYPL [Sc D 88-1397]

UNITY PARTY OF NIGERIA - ACCOUNTING.
Labode, Sakirudeen Tunji. Party power . Abeokuta, Nigeria , 1988. 244 p. ; ISBN 978-18-3008-5
NYPL [Sc C 88-376]

UNIVERSAL NEGRO IMPROVEMENT ASSOCIATION - HISTORY.
Barron, Charles. Look for me in the whirlwind . [Brooklyn, NY] , c1987. v, 60 p. : DDC 305.8/96073 19
E185.97.G3 B37 1987
NYPL [Sc D 88-1501]
Lewis, Rupert. Marcus Gavey, anti-colonial champion /. Trenton, New Jersey , 1988. 301

p. : ISBN 0-86543-061-6 (hard)
NYPL [Sc D 88-516]

UNIVERSAL NEGRO IMPROVEMENT ASSOCIATION - JUVENILE LITERATURE.
Lawler, Mary. Marcus Garvey /. New York , c1988. 110 p. : ISBN 1-555-46587-0 DDC 305.8/96073/024 B 92 19
E185.97.G3 L39 1988   *NYPL [Sc E 88-156]*

Universidad y planificación. see Santo Domingo. Universidad Autónoma. Publicaciones.

Universidade Eduardo Mondlane. Departamento de Arqueologia e Antropologia. Seminario Interdisciplinar de Antropologia (1st : 1982 : Maputo, Mozambique) Primeiro seminário interdisciplinar de antropologia /. Maputo , 1987. 153 p. ;   *NYPL [Sc F 88-172]*

Universität Kiel. Institut für Weltwirtschaft. Bibliothek.
Verzeichnis, Afrika bezogener Zeitschriften in Auswahl / Bibliothek des Instituts für Weltwirtschaft, Zentralbibliothek der Wirtschaftswissenschaften in der Bundesrepublik Deutschland. 4., erw. Aufl. Kiel : Die Bibliothek, 1984. 161 p., [117] columns ; 30 cm. "Stand 1. September 1984."
1. Universität Kiel. Institut für Weltwirtschaft. Bibliothek - Catalogs. 2. Africa - Periodicals - Bibliography - Catalogs. I. Title.
Z3503 .U54 1984 DT1   NYPL [Sc F 88-213]

UNIVERSITÄT KIEL. INSTITUT FÜR WELTWIRTSCHAFT. BIBLIOTHEK - CATALOGS.
Universität Kiel. Institut für Weltwirtschaft. Bibliothek. Verzeichnis, Afrika bezogener Zeitschriften in Auswahl /. Kiel , 1984. 161 p., [117] columns ;
Z3503 .U54 1984 DT1   NYPL [Sc F 88-213]

Université de Ouagadougou. Institut supérieur des langues, des lettres et des arts. Kam, Sié Alain. Cours de littérature orale . [Ouagadougou] [1988?] 1 v. (various pagings) :
NYPL [Sc F 89-118]

Université de Paris I: Panthéon-Sorbonne. Centre de recherches africaines. Histoire rurale. Bujumbura , Paris , 1984. v., 236 p. :
NYPL [Sc F 88-217]

Université de Paris X: Nanterre. Centre de recherches Caraïbes-Amériques. Lara, Oruno D. Le commandant Mortenol . Epinay, France , c1985. 275 p. : ISBN 2-905787-00-7
NYPL [Sc D 88-1085]

Université du Burundi. Faculté des lettres et sciences humaines. Histoire rurale. Bujumbura , Paris , 1984. v., 236 p. :
NYPL [Sc F 88-217]

UNIVERSITIES AND COLLEGES - AFRICA - DIRECTORIES.
African universities . Lagos, Nigeria , 1968. iii, 80 p. ;   *NYPL [Sc F 88-81]*

UNIVERSITIES AND COLLEGES - AFRICA, EASTERN.
Eastern and Southern African Universities Research Programme. University capacity in eastern & southern African countries /. London , Portsmouth, N.H. , c1987. xix, 259 p. : ISBN 0-85255-107-X : DDC 378.67 19
LA1503   *NYPL [Sc D 89-314]*

UNIVERSITIES AND COLLEGES - AFRICA, SOUTHERN.
Eastern and Southern African Universities Research Programme. University capacity in eastern & southern African countries /. London , Portsmouth, N.H. , c1987. xix, 259 p. : ISBN 0-85255-107-X : DDC 378.67 19
LA1503   *NYPL [Sc D 89-314]*

UNIVERSITIES AND COLLEGES - AFRICA, WEST - ADMINISTRATION.
Lévy, Denis. Problems of co-operation between the English- and French-speaking universities of West Africa [microform] . Freetown [Sierra Leone] [1961] 7 p. ;
NYPL [Sc Micro R-4094 no. 23]

UNIVERSITIES AND COLLEGES, AFRO-AMERICAN. see AFRO-AMERICAN UNIVERSITIES AND COLLEGES.

UNIVERSITIES AND COLLEGES - NIGERIA.
The University of Nigeria, 1960-1985 . Nsukka,

Nigeria , 1986. xviii, 657 p. : ISBN 978-229-913-8   *NYPL [Sc F 88-198]*
What science? . Ibadan , 1985. xvii, 321 p. : ISBN 978-12-9118-4 (pbk.) DDC 507/.11669 19
Q183.4.N5 W48 1985   NYPL [Sc E 88-402]

UNIVERSITIES AND COLLEGES - NIGERIA - ADMINISTRATION.
Aderounmu, Olusola. Managing the Nigerian education enterprise /. Ikeja, Lagos, Nigeria , 1986. 230 p. :   *NYPL [Sc F 88-171]*

UNIVERSITIES AND COLLEGES - NIGERIA - DRAMA.
Onwueme, Tess Akaeke. Mirror for campus /. Owerri , 1987. iii leaves, 76 p. ;
NYPL [Sc C 88-159]

UNIVERSITIES AND COLLEGES - UNITED STATES.
The Black/white colleges . Washington, D.C. , 1981. v, 46 p. :   *NYPL [Sc F 89-48]*

UNIVERSITIES AND COLLEGES - UNITED STATES - DIRECTORIES.
Minority student enrollments in higher education. Garrett Park, Md [1987] [73] p. ; ISBN 0-912048-49-2   *NYPL [Sc F 88-39]*

UNIVERSITY AND COMMUNITY. see COMMUNITY AND COLLEGE.

The University and the Great Hall complex [microform] . Kimble, David. [Zomba, Malawi , 1982] 17 p., [2] leaves of plates :
NYPL [Sc Micro F-11020]

The university and the leadership factor in Nigerian politics /. Achebe, Chinua. Enugu, Nigeria , c1988. 22 p. ; ISBN 978-226-907-7
NYPL [Sc D 89-28]

The University and the nation [microform] d. Kimble, David. [Zomba, Malawi , 1978] 16 p. ;
NYPL [Sc Micro F-11018]

University capacity in eastern & southern African countries /. Eastern and Southern African Universities Research Programme. London , Portsmouth, N.H. , c1987. xix, 259 p. : ISBN 0-85255-107-X : DDC 378.67 19
LA1503   *NYPL [Sc D 89-314]*

University capacity in eastern and southern African countries. Eastern and Southern African Universities Research Programme. University capacity in eastern & southern African countries /. London , Portsmouth, N.H. , c1987. xix, 259 p. : ISBN 0-85255-107-X : DDC 378.67 19
LA1503   *NYPL [Sc D 89-314]*

University College of Botswana. Institute of Adult Education. Mackenzie, Bob. A survey of handicrafts in North East District, 1980 . Gaborone , 1980. 61 p. :   *NYPL [Sc F 88-2]*

The University community in Malawi [microform] . Kimble, David. [Zomba, Malawi , between 1980 and 1983] 19 p. ;
NYPL [Sc Micro F-11019]

UNIVERSITY COOPERATION - AFRICA, WEST.
Lévy, Denis. Problems of co-operation between the English- and French-speaking universities of West Africa [microform] . Freetown [Sierra Leone] [1961] 7 p. ;
NYPL [Sc Micro R-4094 no. 23]

UNIVERSITY EXTENSION - UGANDA.
Kakooza, Teresa. The problems of the university's role in adult education in Uganda /. [Kampala?] , 1987. 20 p. ;
NYPL [Sc F 89-92]

University of Benin. Center for Social, Cultural, and Environmental Research. The Urban poor in Nigeria /. Ibadan, Nigeria , 1987. xvi, 413 p. : ISBN 978-16-7489-4
NYPL [Sc D 88-779]

UNIVERSITY OF BIRMINGHAM. LIBRARY - CATALOGS.
Church Missionary Society. Africa (Group 3) Committee. Catalogue of the papers of the missions of the Africa (Group 3) Committee /. London , 1981. 8 v. : DDC 266/.3 19
CD1069.L715 C47 1981   NYPL [Sc F 88-78]

University of Bradford. International Centre for Intercultural Studies. Educational attainments . London , New York , 1988. vii, 180 p. : ISBN 1-85000-308-4 : DDC

370.19/34/0941 19
LC3736.G6 E336 1988 **NYPL** *[Sc E 89-52]*

**UNIVERSITY OF CALIFORNIA, BERKELEY -
TRIALS, LITIGATION, ETC.**
Schwartz, Bernard, 1923- Behind Bakke . New
York , c1988. x, 266 p. ; ISBN 0-8147-7878-X :
DDC 347.73/0798 347.304798 19
KF228.B34 S39 1988 **NYPL** *[JLE 88-4158]*

**University of California, Los Angeles. African
Studies Center.** Women as food producers in
developing countries /. Los Angeles, CA ,
c1985. ix, 118 p. : ISBN 0-918456-56-8 : DDC
331.4/83/091724 19
HD6073.A292 D4485 1985
NYPL *[JLE 88-2659]*

**University of California, Los Angeles. Center for
Afro-American Studies.** Race, class, and
power in Brazil . Los Angeles , c1985. xi, 160
p. : ISBN 0-934934-22-3 : DDC 305.8/96/081 19
F2659.N4 R24 1985 **NYPL** *[JLE 88-2671]*

**University of California, Los Angeles. Museum of
Cultural History.** Crowley, Daniel J., 1921-
African myth and black reality in Bahian
Carnaval /. [Los Angeles, Calif.] [1984] 47 p. :
NYPL *[Sc F 86-281]*

**University of California publications. Near
Eastern studies** .
(v. 7, 9, 11) Leslau, Wolf. Ethiopians speak.
Berkeley, 1965- v.
PJ8998.5 .L4 **NYPL** *[Sc F 89-19]*

(v.7, etc) Leslau, Wolf. Ethiopians speak.
Berkeley, 1965- v.
PJ8998.5 .L4 **NYPL** *[Sc F 89-19]*

University of Cambridge. African Studies Centre.
Brown, Winifred. Marriage, divorce and
inheritance . Cambridge , 1988. xii,91 p. ;
ISBN 0-902993-23-2 (pbk) : DDC
346.76/106134/0880655 19
NYPL *[Sc D 88-1350]*

Fox, Christine. Asante brass casting .
Cambridge , 1988. xii, 112 p. : ISBN
0-902993-24-0 (pbk) : DDC 739.2/27667 19
NYPL *[Sc D 88-1434]*

**University of Cape Town. School of African Life
and Language.
Publications.**
Bleek, Dorothea Frances, d. 1948.
Comparative vocabularies of Bushman
languages /. Cambridge [Eng.] , 1929. 94 p.,
1 leaf of plates : DDC 496.232
PL8101 .B6 **NYPL** *[Sc E 88-89]*

University of Cross River State. Cultural
development and nation building . Ibadan ,
1986. xiv, 157 p. : ISBN 978-246-048-6 (pbk).
DDC 338.4/77/0096694 19
NX750.N6 C85 1986 **NYPL** *[Sc D 88-812]*

**University of Edinburgh. Centre of African
Studies.** African medicine in the modern
world . Edinburgh [1987] 222 p. : DDC
615.8/82/096 19
GR350 **NYPL** *[Sc D 87-1283]*

**University of Florida monographs. Social
sciences** .
(no. 72) Dirks, Robert, 1942- The Black
Saturnalia . Gainesville , c1987. xvii, 228 p., [7]
p. of plates : ISBN 0-8130-0843-3 (pbk. : alk.
paper) : DDC 394.2/68282/09729 19
GT4987.23 .D57 1987
NYPL *[L-10 5328 no.72]*

University of Ghana population studies.
(no. 4) West African Seminar on Population
Studies, University of Ghana, 1972.
Interdisciplinary approaches to population
studies . Legon , 1975. ix, 333 p. :
HB21 .W38 1972 **NYPL** *[JLD 78-861]*

(no. 9) Olusanya, P. Olufemi. Nursemaids and
the pill . Legon , 1981. xiii, 157 p. :
NYPL *[Sc E 89-249]*

University of Ibadan. College of Medicine.
De Cola, Freya D. Three decades of medical
research at the College of Medicine, Ibadan,
Nigeria, 1948-1980 . Ibadan, Nigeria , 1984. xv,
208 p. ; ISBN 978-12-1157-1 (pbk.) DDC 016.61
19
Z6661.N6 D4 1984 R824.N6
NYPL *[Sc E 89-160]*

**UNIVERSITY OF IBADAN. COLLEGE OF
MEDICINE - BIBLIOGRAPHY.**
De Cola, Freya D. Three decades of medical

research at the College of Medicine, Ibadan,
Nigeria, 1948-1980 . Ibadan, Nigeria , 1984. xv,
208 p. ; ISBN 978-12-1157-1 (pbk.) DDC 016.61
19
Z6661.N6 D4 1984 R824.N6
NYPL *[Sc E 89-160]*

UNIVERSITY OF IBADAN - HISTORY.
University of Ibadan 1948-88 . Ibadan,
Nigeria , 1988. iv, 46 p. : ISBN 978-16-7861-5
NYPL *[Sc E 89-246]*

University of Ibadan 1948-88 : fortieth
anniversary brochure. Ibadan, Nigeria : Evans
Brothers (Nigeria Publishers), 1988. iv, 46 p. :
ill., ports. ; 25 cm. "Thanks ... to Professor
Okpewho and all those who have helped." - Foreword.
ISBN 978-16-7861-5
1. University of Ibadan - History. I. Okpewho, Isidore.
NYPL *[Sc E 89-246]*

**University of Ife. Dept. of Demography and
Social Statistics.** Seminar on Internal
Migration in Nigeria (1975 : University of Ife)
Internal migration in Nigeria . [Ife] , 1976. iii,
300 p. : **NYPL** *[Sc E 88-489]*

**UNIVERSITY OF IFE - DISSERTATIONS -
ABSTRACTS.**
Hezekiah Oluwasanmi Library. Abstracts of
theses accepted by University of Ife, 1985 /.
Ile-Ife , 1986. ii, ii, 95 p. ;
NYPL *[Sc D 89-580]*

**University of Illinois at Urbana-Champaign.
African Studies Program.**
Curriculum-related handouts for teachers :
(complete set) : Fall 1981 / University of
Illinois at Urbana-Champaign. Urbana, Illinois :
the University, [1981] ca. 500 p. ; 28 cm.
Collection of materials produced between 1975 and
1981. Cover title. On cover: African studies. Includes
bibliographies.
1. Africa - Civilization - Study and teaching. I. Title. II.
Title: African studies. **NYPL** *[Sc F 88-215]*

University of Illinois Film Center. Film and
video resources about Africa available from the
University of Illinois Film Center /.
Champaign, Ill. [c1985] 34 p. : DDC 016.96 19
Z3501 .U64 1985 DT3 **NYPL** *[Sc F 88-335]*

University of Illinois Film Center.
Film and video resources about Africa available
from the University of Illinois Film Center / in
cooperation with the African Studies Program
at the University of Illinois at
Urbana-Champaign. Champaign, Ill. : The
Center, [c1985] 34 p. : ill., map, port. ; 28 cm.
(African outreach series . no. 5) Includes indexes.
Bibliography: p. 5. DDC 016.96 19
1. University of Illinois Film Center - Catalogs. 2.
Africa - Film catalogs. 3. Africa - Video tape catalogs.
I. University of Illinois at Urbana-Champaign. African
Studies Program. II. Title. III. Series.
Z3501 .U64 1985 DT3 **NYPL** *[Sc F 88-335]*

**UNIVERSITY OF ILLINOIS FILM CENTER -
CATALOGS.**
University of Illinois Film Center. Film and
video resources about Africa available from the
University of Illinois Film Center /.
Champaign, Ill. [c1985] 34 p. : DDC 016.96 19
Z3501 .U64 1985 DT3 **NYPL** *[Sc F 88-335]*

University of Iowa. Libraries.
The right wing collection of the University of
Iowa Libraries, 1918-1977 : a guide to the
microfilm collection. Glen Rock, N.J. :
Microfilming Corp. of America, 1978. v, 175
p. ; 29 cm. Includes indexes. ISBN 0-667-00520-X
DDC 016.3205/0973
1. University of Iowa. Libraries - Catalogs. 2.
Conservatism - United States - History - Sources -
Bibliography. 3. United States - Politics and
government - 20th century - Sources - Bibliography. I.
Title.
Z7163 .U585 1978 JA1 **NYPL** *[Sc F 86-176]*

**UNIVERSITY OF IOWA. LIBRARIES -
CATALOGS.**
University of Iowa. Libraries. The right wing
collection of the University of Iowa Libraries,
1918-1977 . Glen Rock, N.J. , 1978. v, 175 p. ;
ISBN 0-667-00520-X DDC 016.3205/0973
Z7163 .U585 1978 JA1 **NYPL** *[Sc F 86-176]*

UNIVERSITY OF KANSAS - BASKETBALL.
Woodling, Chuck. Against all odds . Lawrence,
KS , c1988. 138 p., [16] p. of plates : ISBN
0-7006-0387-5 (pbk.) : DDC

796.32/363/0978165 19
GV885.43.U52 W66 1988
NYPL *[JFF 89-236]*

University of Lagos. Conference Centre.
Producer/User Seminar on Household Statistics
and Indicators for Women in Development held
at the Conference Centre, University of Lagos,
August 11th-13th, 1986 /. [Lagos , 1986?] 2
v. ; 25 cm. **NYPL** *[Sc E 89-158]*

UNIVERSITY OF LAGOS - HISTORY.
A History of the University of Lagos,
1962-1987 /. Lagos, Nigeria , 1987. xiii, 600
p. : **NYPL** *[Sc F 89-82]*

University of Lagos series in education / edited
by E.O. Fagbamiye. Ikeja, Lagos : Nelson
Publishers, 1987- v. : ill. ; 22 cm. "Fagbamiye, E.
O. -editor-in-chief." Includes bibliographies.
CONTENTS. - V. 1. Introduction to education -- v. 2.
the art and science of education.
1. Education - Nigeria. 2. Education - Study and
teaching. I. Fagbamiye, E. O.
NYPL *[Sc D 89-149]*

**University of London. Development Planning
Unit.** The Role of women in the execution of
low-income housing projects . Nairobi, Kenya ,
1986. 64 p. : ISBN 92-1-131005-9
NYPL *[Sc E 88-225]*

University of Maiduguri.
Tenth anniversary calendar / University of
Maiduguri. [Maiduguri, Nigeria?] : University of
Maiduguri, c1986. [xi], 480 p. : ill., map,
ports. ; 25 cm. Cover title: Tenth anniversary
Commemorative calendar, 1975-1985. Includes index.
ISBN 978-232-315-2
1. University of Maiduguri - Anniversaries, etc. I.
University of Maiduguri. Tenth anniversary calendar,
1975-1985. II. Title. **NYPL** *[Sc E 88-298]*

Tenth anniversary calendar, 1975-1985.
University of Maiduguri. Tenth anniversary
calendar / University of Maiduguri.
[Maiduguri, Nigeria?] , c1986. [xi], 480 p. :
ISBN 978-232-315-2 **NYPL** *[Sc E 88-298]*

**UNIVERSITY OF MAIDUGURI -
ANNIVERSARIES, ETC.**
University of Maiduguri. Tenth anniversary
calendar /. [Maiduguri, Nigeria?] , c1986. [xi],
480 p. : ISBN 978-232-315-2
NYPL *[Sc E 88-298]*

**University of Manchester. Centre for Educational
Guidance and Special Needs.** Educational
attainments . London , New York , 1988. vii,
180 p. : ISBN 1-85000-308-4 : DDC
370.19/34/0941 19
LC3736.G6 E336 1988 **NYPL** *[Sc E 89-52]*

**University of Nairobi. Dept. of Land
Development.** Yahya, Saad, 1939-
English-Swahili glossary of technical terms for
valuers and land economists /. [Nairobi]
[1979] [8] leaves ; DDC 333/.003/21 19
HD107.7 .Y34 1979 **NYPL** *[Sc F 88-77]*

**University of Nairobi. Institute of African
Studies.** Socio-cultural profiles, Baringo
District . [Nairobi?] , 1986. xviii, 268 p. : DDC
967.6/27 19
DT434.B36 S63 1986 **NYPL** *[Sc F 88-230]*

UNIVERSITY OF NIGERIA, NSUKKA.
The University of Nigeria, 1960-1985 . Nsukka,
Nigeria , 1986. xviii, 657 p. : ISBN
978-229-913-8 **NYPL** *[Sc F 88-198]*

**University of Nigeria, Nsukka. Centre for Rural
Development and cooperatives.** Fifty years of
Nigerian cooperative movement /. Nsukka
[Nigeria] , 1986. iii, 64 p. :
NYPL *[Sc D 88-859]*

**UNIVERSITY OF NIGERIA, NSUKKA.
DIVISION OF EXTRA-MURAL
STUDIES.**
Odokara, E. O. Outreach . Nsukka [between
1976 and 1981] 67 p. : **NYPL** *[Sc E 88-275]*

**University of Nigeria, Nsukka. Faculty of the
Social Sciences.** Austerity and the Nigerian
society /. Nsukka , 1987. vi, 240 p. : ISBN
978-264-356-4 **NYPL** *[Sc D 89-205]*

The University of Nigeria, 1960-1985 : an
experiment in higher education / edited by
Emmanuel Obiechina, Chukwuemeka Ike, John
Anenechukwu Umeh. Nsukka, Nigeria :
University of Nigeria Press, 1986. xviii, 657 p. :
ill. ; 28 cm. Includes bibliographical references and
index. ISBN 978-229-913-8

1. University of Nigeria, Nsukka. 2. Universities and colleges - Nigeria. I. Obiechina, Emmanuel N., 1933-. II. Ike, Vincent Chukwuemeka, 1931-. III. Umeh, John Anenchukwu. **NYPL [Sc F 88-198]**

University of Oxford. Inter-faculty Committee on African Studies. The Ecology of survival . London, England ; Boulder, Colo. , 1988. xii, 339 p. : ISBN 0-8133-0727-9 (Westview) DDC 304.2/096 19
GF720 .E26 1988 **NYPL [Sc D 89-280]**

University of Pennsylvania. Afro-American Studies Program. Dilemmas of the new Black middle class /. [Pa.?] c1980. v, 100 p. ;
E185.86 .D54x 1980 **NYPL [Sc D 89-24]**

University of South Africa. Institute of Foreign and Comparative Law. Aspects of legislative drafting /. KwaDlangezwa, South Africa , 1987. ix, 204 p. ; ISBN 0-907995-73-X
NYPL [Sc C 88-66]

University of Southwestern Louisiana. University Art Museum. Baking in the sun . Lafayette , c1987. 146 p. : ISBN 0-295-96606-8
NYPL [Sc F 88-197]

University of the West Indies (Cave Hill, Barbados). History Dept. Emancipation I . Barbados , c1986. vii, 108 p., [1] leaf of plates : DDC 306/.362/0972981 19
HT1119.B35 E46 1986 **NYPL [Sc D 88-248]**

**University of the West Indies, Cave Hill, Barbados. Institute of Social and Economic Research.
Occasional papers.**
(no. 19) Emmanuel, Patrick. Political change and public opinion in Grenada 1979-1984 /. Cave Hill, Barbados , c1986. xii, 173 p. :
NYPL [JLM 79-1223 no.19]

University of the West Indies (Cave Hill, Barbados). nInstitute of Social and Economic Research. Duncan, Neville C. Women and politics in Barbados, 1948-1981 /. Cave Hill, Barbados , c1983. x, 68 p. ;
NYPL [Sc E 84-107]

University of the West Indies (Cave Hill, Barbados). Women and Development Unit. Research and Documentation Centre.
Inniss, Diana. A selected bibliography of materials and resources on women in the Caribbean available at WAND's Research and Documentation Centre /. Pinelands, St. Michael [Barbados] [1987] 119 p. ;
NYPL [Sc F 88-218]

UNIVERSITY OF THE WEST INDIES (CAVE HILL, BARBADOS). WOMEN AND DEVELOPMENT UNIT. RESEARCH AND DOCUMENTATION CENTRE - CATALOGS.
Inniss, Diana. A selected bibliography of materials and resources on women in the Caribbean available at WAND's Research and Documentation Centre /. Pinelands, St. Michael [Barbados] [1987] 119 p. ;
NYPL [Sc F 88-218]

University of the West Indies (Mona, Jamaica) Medical Library. Sickle cell disease [microform] : a selected bibliography from the literature available at the Medical Library, U.W.I. [Mona, Jamaica] : The Library, 1978. 24 leaves ; 22 cm. (UWI medical bibliography. no. 3) Cover title. Microfiche. New York: New York Public Library, 198 . 1 microfiche: negative; 11 x 15 cm. (FSN Sc 019,033)
1. Sickle cell anemia - Bibliography. I. Title.
NYPL [Sc Micro F-10935]

UNIVERSITY OF THE WEST INDIES (ST. AUGUSTINE, TRINIDAD AND TOBAGO) - HISTORY.
Rétout, Marie Thérèse. A light rising from the west /. Trinidad , 1985. xiii, 268 p. : DDC 378.7298/3 19
LE15.S7 R48 1985 **NYPL [Sc C 88-67]**

University of the Witwatersrand. African Studies Institute. Resistance and ideology in settler societies /. Johannesburg, Athens, Ohio , 1986. viii, 222 p. ; ISBN 0-86975-304-5
NYPL [Sc D 88-1093]

University of the Witwatersrand. Library. Guide to the archives and papers : cumulative supplement, 1975-1979, to the third revised edition, 1975 / compiled by Anna M. Cunningham. Johannesburg : Library, University

of the Witwatersrand, 1979. v, 100 p. ; 30 cm. Includes index. ISBN 0-85494-593-8
1. Manuscripts - South Africa - Transvaal - Catalogs. 2. Transvaal (South Africa) - History - Sources - Bibliography - Catalogs. 3. South Africa - History - Sources - Bibliography - Catalogs. I. Cunningham, Anna M. II. Title. **NYPL [Sc F 89-32]**

University of Virginia. Constitutional roots, rights, and responsibilities . New York , 1987. 152 p. ;
NYPL [Sc F 88-299]

University of Warwick. Centre for Caribbean Studies. India in the Caribbean /. London , 1987. 326 p. : ISBN 1-87051-805-5 (cased) : DDC 909/.09182/1081 19
NYPL [Sc D 88-997]

UNIVERSITY OF ZAMBIA - BIBLIOGRAPHY - CATALOGS.
University of Zambia. Library. Special Collections Division. Subject guide to research papers held by the University of Zambia Library, Special Collections Division (Lusaka Campus) /. Lusaka, Zambia , 1986. v, 423 p. ; DDC 016.96894 19
Z5055.Z334 U558 1986 AS623.L84
NYPL [Sc F 88-353]

Zambian papers. see Zambian papers.

**University of Zambia. Institute of Human Relations.
Occasional paper.**
(82/1 82/1) Inaugural addresses [microform] /. [Lusaka] , 1982. [39] p. ;
NYPL [Sc Micro R-4132 no. 23]

UNIVERSITY OF ZAMBIA. INSTITUTE OF HUMAN RELATIONS.
Inaugural addresses [microform] /. [Lusaka] , 1982. [39] p. ;
NYPL [Sc Micro R-4132 no. 23]

University of Zambia. Library. Special Collections Division.
Subject guide to research papers held by the University of Zambia Library, Special Collections Division (Lusaka Campus) / compiled by Augustine W.C. Msika ; with the assistance of Webster Katete and Clare Nkwanga. Lusaka, Zambia : University of Zambia Library, 1986. v, 423 p. ; 29 cm. (Occasional publications / University of Zambia Library . no. 3 (1986)) Includes index. DDC 016.96894 19
1. University of Zambia - Bibliography - Catalogs. 2. University of Zambia. Library. Special Collections Division - Catalogs. 3. Zambia - Bibliography - Catalogs. 4. Zambia - Imprints - Catalogs. I. Msika, Augustine W. C. II. Series: Occasional publications / University of Zambia Library , no. 3. III. Title.
Z5055.Z334 U558 1986 AS623.L84
NYPL [Sc F 88-353]

UNIVERSITY OF ZAMBIA. LIBRARY. SPECIAL COLLECTIONS DIVISION - CATALOGS.
University of Zambia. Library. Special Collections Division. Subject guide to research papers held by the University of Zambia Library, Special Collections Division (Lusaka Campus) /. Lusaka, Zambia , 1986. v, 423 p. ; DDC 016.96894 19
Z5055.Z334 U558 1986 AS623.L84
NYPL [Sc F 88-353]

UNIVERSITY PRESSES - AFRICA, WEST - ADDRESSES, ESSAYS, LECTURES.
Harris, John, librarian. Rapport sur la coopération inter-universitaire dans le domaine de l'impression et l'édition [microform] /. 1961. 12 p. ; **NYPL [Sc Micro R-4137 no. 44]**

UNMARRIED FATHERS - UNITED STATES.
Hendricks, Leo E. A comparative analysis of three select populations of Black unmarried adolescent fathers /. Washington, D.C. , 1982. ix, 129 p. :
NYPL [Sc F 88-222]

Die UNO-Sondersitzung über Afrika 1986 in der afrikanischen Presse / Klaus Hemstedt (Bearb.). Hamburg : Institut für Afrika-Kunde, 1986. ii, 104 p. : all facsims. ; 30 cm. (Aktueller Informationsdienst Afrika. Beiheft . 9) ISBN 3-923519-66-4
1. United Nations. General Assembly (13th Special Session : 1986) - Publc opinion. 2. Africa - Foreign opinion. 3. Africa - Economic conditions - 1960-. I. Hemstedt, Klaus. II. Series. **NYPL [Sc F 88-229]**

Unoh, Solomon O. Cultural development and nation building . Ibadan , 1986. xiv, 157 p. :

ISBN 978-246-048-6 (pbk.) DDC 338.4/77/0096694 19
NX750.N6 C85 1986 **NYPL [Sc D 88-812]**

Until the morning after . Awoonor, Kofi, 1935- Greenfield Center, NY , 1987. 216 p. ; ISBN 0-912678-69-0 **NYPL [Sc D 88-103]**

Up from polygamy /. Ilouno, Chukwuemeka. [Nigeria] c1985 (Enugu, Nigeria : Bema Press) 68 p. ; **NYPL [Sc C 88-294]**

Uplift . Washington Consulting Group. Salt Lake City , c1974. xviii, 465 p. ; ISBN 0-913420-38-7
HV547 .W38 1974 **NYPL [JLE 75-1370]**

Uppsala. Universitet. Nordiska Afrikainstitutet. see Nordiska Afrikainstitutet.

Uppsala. Universitet. Scandinavian Institute of African Studies. see Nordiska Afrikainstitutet.

Upscaling downtown . Williams, Brett. Ithaca [N.Y.] , 1988. xi, 157 p. : ISBN 0-8014-2106-3 (alk. paper) DDC 307.3/42/09753 19
HT177.W3 W55 1988 **NYPL [Sc E 88-387]**

Upton, Bertha, 1849-1912.
Golliwogg in the African jungle / pictures by Florence K. Upton ; verses by Bertha Upton. London ; New York : Longmans, Green, 1909. 62, [2] p. : col. ill. ; 22 x 28 cm. SCHOMBURG CHILDREN'S COLLECTION.
1. Toys - Juvenile fiction. I. Upton, Florence Kate, 1873-1922. II. Schomburg Children's Collection. III. Title. **NYPL [Sc Rare F 89-16]**

Upton, Florence Kate, 1873-1922. The Golliwogg's bicycle club. London, 1967. [1] 62 p.
PZ8.3.U74 Go2 **NYPL [Sc D 88-252]**

Upton, Florence Kate, 1873-1922.
The Golliwogg's bicycle club; pictures by Florence K. Upton, words by Bertha Upton. London, Longmans, 1967. [1] 62 p. col. illus. 13 1/2 x 20 1/2 cm. Reduced facsimile of 1st ed., originally published 1896. SCHOMBURG CHILDREN'S COLLECTION.
1. Toys - Juvenile fiction. I. Upton, Bertha, 1849-1912. II. Schomburg Children's Collection. III. Title.
PZ8.3.U74 Go2 **NYPL [Sc D 88-252]**

Upton, Bertha, 1849-1912. Golliwogg in the African jungle /. London , New York , 1909. 62, [2] p. : **NYPL [Sc Rare F 89-16]**

Uptown down home cookbook. Hovis, Gene. [Uptown down home cookbook.] Gene Hovis's uptown down home cookbook /. Boston , c1987. xii, 235 p. ; ISBN 0-316-37443-1 : DDC 641.5 19
TX715 .H8385 1987 **NYPL [Sc E 88-476]**

URANIUM INDUSTRY - GREAT BRITAIN.
Campaign Against the Namibian Uranium Contracts (Group) Namibia -- a contract to kill . London , 1986. 80 p. : ISBN 0-947905-02-2
NYPL [Sc D 88-795]

URANIUM INDUSTRY - NAMIBIA.
Campaign Against the Namibian Uranium Contracts (Group) Namibia -- a contract to kill . London , 1986. 80 p. : ISBN 0-947905-02-2
NYPL [Sc D 88-795]

URBAN CHURCHES. see CITY CHURCHES.

URBAN COUNCILS ASSOCIATION OF SOUTH AFRICA.
Atkinson, Doreen. The search for power and legitimacy in Black urban areas . Grahamstown [South Africa] [1984] 38, xix, v, [1] p. ; ISBN 0-86810-114-1 (pbk.) DDC 320.8/0968 19
JS7533.A8 A85 1984 **NYPL [Sc F 88-355]**

URBAN DESIGN. see CITY PLANNING.

URBAN DEVELOPMENT. see CITY PLANNING.

URBAN HOUSING. see HOUSING.

Urban, Joan, 1950- Richard Wright / Joan Urban. New York, N.Y. : Chelsea House Publishers, [1989] 111 p. : ill., ports. ; 25 cm. (Black Americans of achievement) Traces the life and achievements of the Black American novelist. Bibliography: p. 108. ISBN 1-555-46618-4 DDC 813/.52 19
1. Wright, Richard, 1908-1960 - Biography - Juvenile literature. 2. Authors, American - 20th century - Biography - Juvenile literature. 3. Afro-Americans - Intellectual life - Juvenile literature. 4.

Afro-Americans - Biography. I. Title. II. Series.
PS3545.R815 Z85 1989
NYPL [Sc E 89-196]

URBAN LIFE. see CITY AND TOWN LIFE.

Urban nationalism . Magid, Alvin, 1937-
Gainesville , 1988. x, 294 p. : ISBN
0-8130-0853-0 DDC 972.98/3 19
F2119 .M34 1988 *NYPL [HRG 88-1040]*

URBAN PLANNING. see CITY PLANNING.

The urban plantation . Staples, Robert. Oakland,
CA , c1987. 248 p. ; ISBN 0-933296-13-4 (pbk.)
NYPL [Sc D 88-1021]

URBAN POLICY - UNITED STATES.
Nelson, Kathryn P. Gentrification and
distressed cities . Madison, Wis. , 1988. xiii,
187 p. : ISBN 0-299-11160-1 : DDC 307.2 19
HT175 .N398 1987 *NYPL [JLE 88-3486]*

URBAN POOR - BRAZIL - HISTORY.
Hahner, June Edith, 1940- Poverty and
politics . Albuquerque , 1986. xvi, 415 p. :
ISBN 0-8263-0878-3 : DDC 305.5/69/0981 19
HC190.P6 H34 1986 *NYPL [JLE 86-4407]*

The Urban poor in Nigeria / edited by P. Kofo
Makinwa and A.O. Ozo ; with a foreword by
Adamu Baikie. Ibadan, Nigeria : Evans Brothers
(Nigeria Publishers), 1987. xvi, 413 p. : ill.,
maps ; 22 cm. A selection of papers presented at the
National Conference on the Urban Poor, organized by
the Centre for Social, Cultural and Environmental
Research (CenSCER) of the University of Benin, and
held 17-19 April 1984. Includes bibliographical
references. ISBN 978-16-7489-4
*1. Urban poor - Nigeria. I. Makinwa, P. Kofo. II. Ozo,
A. O. III. Baikie, Adamu. IV. University of Benin.
Center for Social, Cultural, and Environmental
Research. V. National Conference of the Urban Poor
(1984 : University of Benin).*
NYPL [Sc D 88-779]

URBAN POOR - NIGERIA.
The Urban poor in Nigeria /. Ibadan, Nigeria ,
1987. xvi, 413 p. : ISBN 978-16-7489-4
NYPL [Sc D 88-779]

URBAN POOR - UNITED STATES.
Quiet riots . New York , 1988. xiii, 223 p. :
ISBN 0-394-57473-7 : DDC 305.5/69/0973 19
HV4045 .Q54 1988 *NYPL [JLD 89-239]*

URBAN PROBLEMS. see URBAN POLICY.

**URBAN REDEVELOPMENT. see URBAN
RENEWAL.**

**URBAN RENEWAL - MICHIGAN -
DETROIT.**
Detroit, race and uneven development /.
Philadelphia , 1987. xii, 317 p. : ISBN
0-87722-485-4 (alk. paper) DDC
305.8/009774/34 19
HC108.D6 D47 1987 *NYPL [Sc E 88-205]*

URBAN RENEWAL - UNITED STATES.
Nelson, Kathryn P. Gentrification and
distressed cities . Madison, Wis. , 1988. xiii,
187 p. : ISBN 0-299-11160-1 : DDC 307.2 19
HT175 .N398 1987 *NYPL [JLE 88-3486]*

URBAN RENEWAL - WASHINGTON, D.C.
Williams, Brett. Upscaling downtown . Ithaca
[N.Y.] , 1988. xi, 157 p. : ISBN 0-8014-2106-3
(alk. paper) DDC 307.3/42/09753 19
HT177.W3 W55 1988 *NYPL [Sc E 88-387]*

Urban vigilantes in the New South . Ingalls,
Robert P., 1941- Knoxville , c1988. xx, 286 p. :
ISBN 0-87049-571-2 (alk. paper) DDC
305.8/009759/65 19
F319.T2 I64 1988 *NYPL [Sc E 88-518]*

URBANISM. see CITIES AND TOWNS.

URBANIZATION - BRAZIL - HISTORY.
Hahner, June Edith, 1940- Poverty and
politics . Albuquerque , 1986. xvi, 415 p. :
ISBN 0-8263-0878-3 : DDC 305.5/69/0981 19
HC190.P6 H34 1986 *NYPL [JLE 86-4407]*

**URBANIZATION - ETHIOPIA -
BAGEMDER - CASE STUDIES.**
Baker, Jonathan. The rural-urban dichotomy in
the developing world . Oslo . 372 p. : ISBN
82-00-07412-9
HC845.Z7 B343 1986 *NYPL [JFD 87-3176]*

**URBANIZATION - RELIGIOUS ASPECTS.
see CITY CHURCHES.**

URBANIZATION - SOUTH AFRICA.
Regional restructuring under apartheid .

Johannesburg , 1987. xxii, 317 p. ; ISBN
0-86975-327-4 *NYPL [Sc D 89-16]*

The Urhobo, the Isoko and the Itsekiri /.
Erivwo, Samuel U. Ibadan , 1979. vii, 144 p. :
NYPL [Sc D 88-769]

Urundi. see Burundi.

US foreign policy and revolution . Wilson, Amrit,
1941- London , distributed in the USA by
Unwin Hyman, 1989. ix, 179 p. ; ISBN
1-85305-051-2 *NYPL [Sc D 89-426]*

USE OF LAND. see LAND USE.

**Ushewokunze, H. S. M. (Herbert Sylvester
Masiyiwa), 1938-** An agenda for Zimbabwe /
by H.S.M. Ushewokunze. [Harare, Zimbabwe :
s.n.], c1984. vi, 198 p. ; 23 cm. ISBN
0-906041-67-8 DDC 361.6/1/096891 19
*1. Socialism - Zimbabwe. 2. Medical policy - Zimbabwe.
3. Zimbabwe - Politics and government - 1980-. 4.
Zimbabwe - Foreign relations - South Africa. 5. South
Africa - Foreign relations - Zimbabwe. I. Title.*
HX451.A6 U84 1984 *NYPL [Sc D 88-942]*

**Ushirika wa Vyuo vya Theologia vya Afrika ya
Mashariki. Kamati ya Vitabu vya Theologia
vya Kiswahili.** Msamiati wa maneno ya
kitheologia. Dodoma [Tanzania] , c1979. iv, 47
p. ;
BR95 .M72 1979 *NYPL [Sc C 88-149]*

Usman, Yusufu Bala, 1945- The manipulation of
religion in Nigeria, 1977-1987 / by Yusufu Bala
Usman. Kaduna, Nigeria : Vanguard, 1987. 153
p. ; 18 cm. ISBN 978-255-708-0
*1. Religion and politics - Nigeria. 2. Nigeria - Religion.
3. Nigeria - Politics and government - 1960-. I. Title.*
NYPL [Sc C 88-220]

**Usos e costumes do Rio de Janeiro nas figurinhas
de Guillobel** =. Guillobel, Joaquim Cândido,
1787-1859. [Curitiba?] [1978] [19] p., [25]
leaves of plates : DDC 981/.5
F2646.2 .G84 1978 *NYPL [Sc F 88-188]*

The USSR and Africa. Moscow : "Social Sciences
Today" Editorial Board, USSR Academy of
Sciences, 1983. 205 p. ; 22 cm. (African studies
by Soviet scholars . no. 3) Bibliography: p. 191-[201]
CONTENTS. - The October Revolution and the
destiny of Africa / An. Gromyko -- Problems of Africa
in the 1980s / E. Tarabrin -- The Soviet Union and the
liberated countries / L. Yablochkov -- Relations with
countries of socialist orientation in tropical Africa / N.
Gavrilov -- The USSR and strengthening of unity of
African peoples / N. Vysotskaya -- Assistance in
eliminating inter-African conflicts / M. Rait --
Soviet-African trade relations / G. Rubinstein --
Economic, scientific, and technical cooperation / Yu.
Ilyin -- Cooperation in the survey and development of
mineral resources / V. Lopatov -- The Soviet economy
and the developing countries (critique of bourgeois
concepts) / P. Sedov -- Traditions of Soviet-African
cooperation / G. Nersesov. DDC 303.4/8247/06 19
*1. Africa - Relations - Soviet Union - Addresses, essays,
lectures. 2. Soviet Union - Relations - Africa -
Addresses, essays, lectures. 3. Africa - Politics and
government - 1960- - Addresses, essays, lectures. 4.
Africa - Economic conditions - 1960- - Addresses,
essays, lectures. I. Izdatel'stvo nauka. Redaktsiiā
"Obshchestvennye nauki i souvremennost'.". II. Title: U.
S.S.R. and Africa. III. Series.*
DT38.9.S65 U86 1983 *NYPL [Sc D 88-980]*

**USUFRUCTUARY LEASES. see FARM
TENANCY.**

Utah Museum of Fine Arts. Museum voor
Volkenkunde (Rotterdam, Netherlands)
Expressions of belief . New York , 1988. 248
p. : ISBN 0-8478-0959-5 : DDC 730 19
N5310.75.H68 M876 1988
NYPL [Sc G 88-37]

UTILIZATION OF LAND. see LAND USE.

V.Y. Mudimbe . Mouralis, Bernard. Paris , c1988.
143 p., [2] leaves of plates : ISBN 2-7087-0506-7
NYPL [Sc D 89-251]

Vacation time . Giovanni, Nikki. New York ,
1980. 59 p. : ISBN 0-688-03657-0 DDC 811/.54
PS3557.I55 V3 *NYPL [Sc D 89-69]*

Vacher, Peter, 1937- Darensbourg, Joe,
1906-1985. [Telling it like it is.] Jazz odyssey .
Baton Rouge , 1988, c1987. vi, 231 p., [32] p.
of plates : ISBN 0-8071-1442-1 : DDC
788/.S65/0924 B 19
ML419.D35 A3 1988 *NYPL [Sc E 89-28]*

VAGRANCY - GREAT BRITAIN.
Demuth, Clare. 'Sus', a report on the Vagrancy
Act 1824 /. London , 1978. 62 p. :
NYPL [Sc D 88-1174]

VAI (AFRICAN PEOPLE)
Akpan, Monday B. African resistance in
Liberia . Bremen , 1988. 68 p. : ISBN
3-926771-01-1 *NYPL [Sc D 89-347]*

Valdés-Cruz, Rosa. Lo ancestral africano en la
narrativa de Lydia Cabrera / Rosa Valdés-Cruz.
1. ed. Barcelona : Vosgos, 1974. 113 p. ; 21 cm.
Bibliography: p. 108-113. ISBN 84-346-0082-X :
*1. Cabrera, Lydia. 2. Blacks - Cuba - Folklore. 3.
Folklore - Cuba. I. Title.*
PQ7389.C22 Z94 *NYPL [Sc D 89-36]*

Valdés-Cruz, Rosa E. see Valdés-Cruz, Rosa.

Valdés, Rosa E. see Valdés-Cruz, Rosa.

Valdman, Albert. Les Langues de l'Afrique
subsaharienne / . Paris , 1981. 2 v : ISBN
2-222-01720-3 : *NYPL [JFN 81-11 v.1]*

**Valente, Ana Lúcia E. F. (Ana Lúcia Eduardo
Farah)** Ser negro no Brasil hoje / Ana Lúcia
E.F. Valente. 1a ed. São Paulo, SP, Brasil :
Editora Moderna, 1987. 64 p. : ill. ; 21 cm.
(Projeto Passo à frente. Coleção Polêmica . 11)
"Sugestões de leitura": p. 64. DDC 305.8/96/081 19
*1. Blacks - Brazil - Social conditions. 2. Brazil - Race
relations. I. Title. II. Series.*
F2659.N4 V35 1987 *NYPL [HFB 88-2561]*

Valentin, Christophe. Sierra Leone / Christophe
et Emmanuel Valentin ; [texte, Franc Nichele ;
traduction, Mostyn Mowbray]. Paris, France :
Richer, c1985. 128 p. : chiefly ill. (some col.),
maps ; 31 cm. English and French. ISBN
2-901151-16-7 DDC 966/.404/0222 19
*1. Sierra Leone - Description and travel - 1981- -
Views. I. Valentin, Emmanuel. II. Nichele, Franc. III.
Title.*
DT516.19 .V35 1985 *NYPL [Sc G 89-10]*

Valentin, Emmanuel. Valentin, Christophe. Sierra
Leone /. Paris, France , c1985. 128 p. : ISBN
2-901151-16-7 DDC 966/.404/0222 19
DT516.19 .V35 1985 *NYPL [Sc G 89-10]*

The valentine box /. Lovelace, Maud Hart, 1892-
New York , 1966. [48] p. :
PZ7.L9561 Val *NYPL [Sc D 89-115]*

Valentine Museum. McGraw, Marie Tyler. In
bondage and freedom . Richmond, VA.
[Chapel Hill, N.C.] , 1988. 71 p. :
NYPL [Sc F 89-107]

VALENTINES - JUVENILE FICTION.
Lexau, Joan M. Don't be my valentine /. New
York, N.Y. , c1985. 64 p. : ISBN
0-06-023872-0 : DDC [E] 19
PZ7.L5895 Dp 1985 *NYPL [Sc D 89-58]*

Valle, Manuel del. Law and bilingual education :
a manual for the community / Manuel del
Valle, Rubén Franco, Camille Rodríguez. New
York : National Puerto Rican Task Force on
Educational Policy, 1978. i, 206 p. ; 28 cm.
Cover title. Written by members of the National Puerto
Rican Task Force on Educational Policy "in order to
help community workers become more familiar with ...
the litigation process." Includes bibliographical
references.
*1. Educational law and legislation - United States. 2.
Education, Bilingual - United States. 3. Puerto Ricans -
United States - Education. I. Franco, Rubén, joint
author. II. Rodríguez, Camille, joint author. III.
National Puerto Rican Task Force on Educational
Policy. IV. Title.* *NYPL [Sc F 88-357]*

La valse des chandelles /. Germeil, Castel.
[Haiti? , 198-?] 52 p. ; *NYPL [Sc C 88-295]*

Valsecchi, Silvestro. Africa che cambia : problemi
e prospettive dello sviluppo africano / [di]
Silvestro Valsecchi. Bologna : EMI, 1979. 204
p. ; 21 cm. DDC 337.6 19
*1. Africa - Economic conditions - 1960-. 2. Africa -
Foreign relations - 1960-. 3. Africa - Foreign economic
relations. I. Title.*
HC800 .V34 1979 *NYPL [Sc D 87-1375]*

Valtis, Laureine. Barbarie-l'espoir / Laureine
Valtis. Paris : Silex, c1986. 135 p. ; 22 cm.
Poems. ISBN 2-903871-76-0
I. Title.
MLCS 87/1686 (P) *NYPL [Sc D 88-232]*

**VALUATION OF LAND. see REAL
PROPERTY - VALUATION.**

Van de Geer, Roeland. Government and development in rural Lesotho / Roeland Van de Geer, Malcolm Wallis. Roma, Lesotho : National University of Lesotho, 1982, 1984 printing. 159 p. ; 23 cm. "Public Administration Research and Curriculum Development Project." Includes bibliographical references and index.
1. Local government - Lesotho. 2. Rural development - Lesotho. I. Wallis, Malcolm. II. Title.
E443 .V36 1988   NYPL [Sc D 89-52]

Van Deburg, William L. The slave drivers : black agricultural labor supervisors in the antebellum South / William L. Van Deburg. New York : Oxford University Press, 1988. xvii, 202 p. : ill. ; 21 cm. Reprint. Originally published: Westport, Conn. : Greenwood Press, 1979. (Contributions in Afro American and African studies ; no. 43) Includes index. Bibliography: p. [173]-194.   ISBN 0-19-505698-1 DDC 305.5/67/0975 19
1. Slave labor - Southern States. 2. Elite (Social sciences) - Southern States - History - 19th century. 3. Agricultural laborers - Southern States - History - 19th century. 4. Slavery - Southern States - Condition of slaves. 5. Plantation life - Southern States - History - 19th century. I. Title.
E443 .V36 1988   NYPL [Sc D 89-424]

Van den Bergh, N. J. C. Aspects of legislative drafting /. KwaDlangezwa, South Africa , 1987. ix, 204 p. ;   ISBN 0-907995-73-X
NYPL [Sc C 88-66]

Van der Post, Laurens. The lost world of the Kalahari : with The great and the little memory / a new epilogue / by Laurens Van der Post ; photographs by David Coulson with captions by the author. London : Chatto & Windus, 1988. 261 p. : col. ill. ; 30 cm.
1. San (African people). 2. Kalahari Desert. I. Coulson, David. II. Title.
NYPL [Sc F 88-381]

Van-Dúnem, Domingos. Dibundu / Domingos Van-Dúnem. Lisbon : Vega, [1988?] 84 p. ; 20 cm. (Colecção Outras obras)
1. Angola - Fiction. I. Title.
NYPL [Sc C 89-134]

Van-Dúnem, Domingos, 1925- Kuluka / Domingos Van-Dunem. Lisboa : Vega, [1988?] 87 p. ; 20 cm. (Colecção Outras obras)
1. Angola - Fiction. I. Title.
NYPL [Sc C 89-129]

Van Evrie, John H., 1814-1896. Negroes and negro "slavery"; the first, an inferior race--the latter, its normal condition. By J. H. Van Evrie. New York, Van Evrie, Horton & co., 1861. xvi, 339 p. incl. front. 20 cm. Introductory chapter published 1853 and 1854; rewritten for the present edition.
1. Slavery - United States - Controversial literature - 1853. 2. Slavery - Justification. I. Title.
E449 .V253   NYPL [Sc Rare C 88-22]

Van Sertima, Ivan. Black women in antiquity /. New Brunswick, [N.J.] , London , 1988. 192 p. :   ISBN 0-87855-982-5 *NYPL [Sc D 89-351]*

Van Stockum, Hilda, 1908- Mogo's flute / Hilda van Stockum ; drawings by Robin Jacques. New York : Viking Press, 1966. 88 p. : ill. ; 24 cm. SCHOMBURG CHILDREN'S COLLECTION.
1. Children - Kenya - Juvenile fiction. I. Jacques, Robin. II. Schomburg Children's Collection. III. Title.
PZ7.V36 Mo   NYPL [Sc E 88-176]

Vanneman, Peter. Soviet foreign policy in Southern Africa : problems and prospects / Peter Vanneman, W. Martin James III.1st ed. Pretoria, Republic of South Africa : Africa Institute of South Africa, 1982. 57 p. ; 27 cm. Includes bibliographical references.   ISBN 0-7983-0078-7 (pbk).   DDC 327.68047 19
1. Africa, Southern - Foreign relations - Soviet Union. 2. Soviet Union - Foreign relations - Africa, Southern. 3. Africa, Southern - Foreign relations - 1975-. 4. Soviet Union - Foreign relations - 1975-. 5. Africa, Southern - Strategic aspects. I. James, W. Martin. II. Title.
DT747.S65 V36 1982 NYPL [Sc D 88-1155]

Vansina, Jan. La légende du passé : traditions orales du Burundi / par Jan Vansina. Tervuren, Belgique : Musée royal de l'Afrique Centrale, 1972. ix, 257 p. : maps ; 27 cm. (Archief voor anthropologie ; nr. 16) Imprint in French and Flemish. Bibliography: p. 253-257.
1. Legends - Burundi. 2. Folklore - Burundi. I. Title. II. Series.
NYPL [Sc F 88-193]

Vanwell history project series.
Bramble, Linda. Black fugitive slaves in early

Canada /. St. Catharines, Ont. , c1988. 93 p. :   ISBN 0-920277-16-0   DDC 973.7/115 19
NYPL [Sc E 89-121]

VAQUEROS. see COWBOYS.

Variations plastiques. Fry, Jacqueline, 1923- Visual variations . Kingston, Canada , c1987. vii, 63 p. :   PS730/.0966/074011372 19
NB1098 .F79 1987   NYPL [Sc F 88-189]

VARIATIONS, SEASONAL. see SEASONAL VARIATIONS (ECONOMICS)

Varieties of black experience at Harvard : an anthology / edited by Werner Sollors, Thomas A. Underwood, and Caldwell Titcomb. Cambridge [Mass.] : Harvard University, Dept. of Afro-American Studies, 1986. v, 180 p. ; 24 cm. Includes index. Bibliography: p. [161]-173.
1. Harvard University - Students. 2. Harvard University - History. 3. Afro-Americans - Education (Higher) - Massachusetts - Cambridge. 4. Afro-American college students - Massachusetts - Cambridge. I. Sollors, Werner. II. Underwood, Thomas A. III. Titcomb, Caldwell.
LD2160 .V37x 1986   NYPL [Sc D 88-672]

Varieties of English around the world, 0172-7362. General series .
(v. 8) Focus on the Caribbean /. Amsterdam , Philadelphia , 1986. ix, 209 p. :   ISBN 90-272-4866-4 (pbk. : alk. paper) :   DDC 427/.9729 19
PM7874.C27 F6 1986   NYPL [JFD 87-3902]

VASCULAR PLANTS. see BOTANY.

Vassa, Gustavus. see Equiano, Olaudah, b. 1745.

Vast, Jean. Guide touristique de Saint-Louis du Senegal /. [Saint-Louis, Senegal , 197-?] 53 p. :
NYPL [Sc D 89-420]

Vaudou, sorciers, empoisonneurs . Pluchon, Pierre. Paris , c1987. 320 p. ;   ISBN 2-86537-185-9   *NYPL [Sc D 88-912]*

Vaughan-Richards, Alan. (joint author) Akinsemoyin, Kunle. Building Lagos /. Jersey, 1977, c1906. 76 p.:
NYPL [3-MQWW 79-2215]

VAULTS (SEPULCHRAL) see TOMBS.

Vega Franco, Marisa. El tráfico de esclavos con América : asientos de Grillo y Lomelín, 1663-1674 / Marisa Vega Franco ; prólogo de Enriqueta Vila Vilar.1a ed. Sevilla : Escuela de Estudios Hispano-Americanos de Sevilla, 1984. x, 220 p. : ill. ; 20 cm. (Publicaciones de la Escuela de Estudios Hispano-americanos de Sevilla. 297 (no. general)) Bibliography: p. [219]-220.   ISBN 84-00-05675-2   DDC 382/.44/09729 19
1. Grillo, Domingo, fl. 1663-1674. 2. Lomelín, Ambrosio, fl. 1663-1674. 3. Slave trade - History - 17th century. 4. Slave trade - Europe - History - 17th century. 5. Slave trade - Caribbean Area - History - 17th century. 6. Slave trade - Africa - History - 17th century. I. Title.
HT985 .V44 1984   NYPL [Sc C 89-132]

VEGETABLE KINGDOM. see BOTANY.

Veiga, Manuel. Oju d'agu / Manuel Veiga. Praia : Instituto Caboverdiano do Livro, c1987. 229 p. ; 21 cm.
1. Creole dialects, Portuguese - Cape Verde - Texts. 2. Cape Verde - Fiction. I. Title.
NYPL [Sc D 88-1413]

Les Veillées de chase d'Henri Guizard /. Goulphin, Fred. [Paris] , 1987. 235 p. ;   ISBN 2-08-065054-8   *NYPL [Sc D 88-28]*

Velde, Daniel Van de. Antilles Caraïbes /. Paris , c1982. 157 p. :   ISBN 2-7191-0177-0
NYPL [Sc F 88-347]

VENDA LANGUAGE - TEXTS.
Makuya, T. N. Dzimbava. Pretoria, 1972. 62 p.   ISBN 0-627-00110-6   *NYPL [JFD 76-2629]*

Vendler, Helen Hennessy. Voices & visions . New York , c1987. xxx, 528 p. :   ISBN 0-394-53520-0   *NYPL [JFE 87-5435]*

VENEZUELA.
Pons, François Raymond Joseph de, 1751-1812. Voyage à la partie orientale de la Terre-Ferme, dans l'Amérique Méridionale, fait pendant les années 1801, 1802, 1803 et 1804: contenant la description de la capitainerie générale de Carácas, composée des provinces de Vénézuéla, Maracaïbo, Varinas, la Guiane Espagnole, Cumana, et de l'île de la Marguerite ... Paris,

1806. 3 v.
F2311 .P79   NYPL [Sc Rare F 88-77]

VENEZUELAN FICTION - 20TH CENTURY - HISTORY AND CRITICISM.
Alvarez, Alexandra, 1946- Malabí Maticulambí . Montevideo, Uruguay? , c1987. 191 p. ;   *NYPL [Sc D 88-1012]*

Vengroenweghe, Daniel. Bobongo : la grande fête des Ekonda (Zaire) / par Daniel Vangroenweghe. Berlin : D. Reimer, c1988. xv, 332 p. : maps ; 24 cm. (Mainzer Afrika-Studien. Bd. 9) Bibliography: p. 317-323.   ISBN 3-496-00963-2
1. Ekonda (Bantu people). 2. Ekonda (Bantu people) - Funeral customs and rites. 3. Festivals - Zaire. 4. Ethnology - Zaire. I. Title.   NYPL [Sc E 88-343]

Vennema, Peter. Stanley, Diane. Shaka, king of the Zulus /. New York , c1988. [40] p. :   ISBN 0-688-07342-5   DDC 968.04/092/4 B 92 19
DT878.Z9 C565 1988   NYPL [Sc F 88-358]

Le vent des mornes . Villeronce, Guy. [Fort-de-France?] [1986] 80 p. :
MLCS 86/6603 (P)   NYPL [Sc D 89-557]

Vera, Maité, 1930-
[Memorias de un proyecto. Portuguese]
Memórias de um projecto / Maité Vera ; [tradução, Willy Waddington e João da Fonseca Amaral] Maputo : Instituto Nacional do Livro e do Disco, c[1980] 86 p. ; 21 cm. (Colecção Teatro. 2) "Rémio de teatro da União de Escritores e Artistas de Cuba, 1975."
I. Title.   NYPL [Sc D 88-628]

Vercoutter, Jean, 1911- Symposium on the Peopling of Ancient Egypt and the deciphering of Meroitic Script (1974 : Cairo, Egypt) [Peuplement de l'Egipte ancianne et la déchiffrement de l'écriture méroïtique. Spanish.] Poblamiento del antiguo Egipto y desciframiento de la escritura meroítica /. Barcelona , Paris , 1983. 155 p. :   ISBN 0-923301-60-5 (Unesco)
NYPL [Sc D 88-603]

Verdier, Raymond. Systèmes fonciers à la ville et au village . Paris , c1986. 296 p. ;   ISBN 2-85802-719-6   DDC 346.6704/32 346.706432 19
LAW   NYPL [Sc D 89-367]

Verenigde Staten. see United States.

Verger, Pierre. Cunha, Marianno Carneiro da, 1926-1980. Da senzala ao sobrado . São Paulo , SP , c1985. 185 p. :   ISBN 85-21-30173-1 :
NA1599.N5 C86 1985   NYPL [Sc E 88-565]

Verma, Gajendra K.
Educational attainments . London , New York , 1988. vii, 180 p. :   ISBN 1-85000-308-4 :   DDC 370.19/34/0941 19
LC3736.G6 E336 1988   NYPL [Sc E 89-52]

Race, training, and employment / Gajendra K. Verma and D.S. Darby. London ; New York : Falmer Press, 1987. vi, 134 p. : ill. ; 24 cm. Includes index. Bibliography: p. 131-132.   ISBN 1-85000-243-6 :   DDC 331.3/46/0941 19
1. Occupational training - Great Britain. 2. Youth - Employment - Great Britain. 3. Minorities - Employment - Great Britain. I. Darby, D. S. II. Title.
HD5715.5.G7 V47 1987
*NYPL [*QT 88-3245]*

VERNACULAR ARCHITECTURE - BURUNDI.
Acquier, Jean-Louis, 1946- Le Burundi /. Marseille, France , c1986. 129 p. :   ISBN 2-86364-030-5 :   DDC 728/.67/0967572 19
GT377.B94 A27 1986   NYPL [Sc E 88-568]

VERNACULAR ARCHITECTURE - LIBERIA - EXHIBITIONS.
Belcher, Max. A land and life remembered . Athens , Brockton, Mass. , c1988. [xii], 176 p. :   ISBN 0-8203-1085-9 (alk. paper)   DDC 720/.9666/2074014482 19
NA1599.L4 B4 1988   NYPL [Sc F 89-90]

Veröffentlichungen der Institute für Afrikanistik und Ägyptologie der Universität Wien .
(Nr. 36) Böhm, Gerhard. Khoe-kowap . Wien , 1985. 406 p. ;   ISBN 3-85043-036-7
PL8541 .B6 1985   NYPL [Sc D 89-365]

(Nr. 46) Ogidan, Anna. Thememschwerpunkte im Werk Ayi Kwei Armahs /. Wien , 1988. ii, 202 p. :   ISBN 3-85043-046-4
NYPL [Sc D 88-1035]

Verrier, Anthony. The road to Zimbabwe, 1890-1980 / Anthony Verrier. London : J.

Cape, 1986. xiv, 364 p., [8] p. of plates : ill.,
map ; 23 cm. Map on lining papers. Includes index.
Bibliography: p. 327-348. ISBN 0-224-02161-3
*1. Zimbabwe - History - 1890-1965. 2. Zimbabwe -
History - 1965-1980. I. Title.*
NYPL [Sc D 88-313]

Verschuur, Christine. Mozambique, dix ans de
solitude-- / By Christine Verschuur...[et al.]
Paris : L'Harmattan, c1986. 182 p. : map ; 22
cm. Includes bibliographical references. ISBN
2-85802-700-5
*1. Mozambique - Economic conditions. 2.
Mozambique - Social conditions - 1975-. I. Title.*
NYPL [Sc D 89-285]

Verses for emancipation . Clarke, A. M. [Port of
Spain , 1986] 41 p. ; DDC 811 19
PR9272.9.C53 V4 1986
NYPL [Sc D 88-981]

Versluis, Arthur, 1959- The Egyptian mysteries /
Arthur Versluis. London ; New York : Arkana,
1988. vi, 169 p. ; 20 cm. Includes index.
Bibliography: p. 165-166. ISBN 1-85063-087-9 (pbk.)
DDC 133 19
*1. Occultism. 2. Mysteries, Religious - Miscellanea. 3.
Egypt - Religion - Miscellanea. I. Title.*
BF1999 .V43 1988 *NYPL [Sc C 88-195]*

Verteuil, Anthony de. see De Verteuil, Anthony.

**Verzeichnis, Afrika bezogener Zeitschriften in
Auswahl /.** Universität Kiel. Institut für
Weltwirtschaft. Bibliothek. Kiel , 1984. 161 p.,
[117] columns ;
Z3503 .U54 1984 DT1 *NYPL [Sc F 88-213]*

Verzeichnis der Zeitschriftenbestände . Institut
für Afrika-Kunde (Hamburg, Germany).
Bibliothek. Hamburg , 1986. 100 p. ;
NYPL [Sc F 88-209]

VEST, ABRAHAM, B.1813.
Fitts, Hervey. Abraham Vest, or, The cast-off
restored. Boston, 1847. 142 p.
T275.V55 F5 1847 *NYPL [Sc Rare C 88-12]*

VICTIMOLOGY. see VICTIMS OF CRIMES.

**VICTIMS OF CRIMES - GEORGIA -
ATLANTA - CASE STUDIES.**
Dettlinger, Chet. The list /. Atlanta , c1983.
516 p., [4] p. of plates : ISBN 0-942894-04-9 :
DDC 364.1/523/09758231 19
HV6534.A7 D47 1983 *NYPL [Sc E 86-40]*

Victor, Gary, 1958- Albert Buron, ou, Profil d'une
"élite" / Gary Victor. [Port-au-Prince :
L'Imprimeur II, 1988] 230 p. ; 22 cm.
*1. Intellectuals - Haiti - Anecdotes, facetiae, satire, etc.
2. Elite (Social sciences) - Haiti - Anecdotes, facetiae,
satire, etc. 3. Haiti - Officials and employees -
Anecdotes, facetiae, satire, etc. I. Title.*
NYPL [Sc D 88-1005]

A vida brasileira no final do século XIX .
Renault, Delso. Rio de Janeiro ; Brasília : xi,
315 p. ; ISBN 85-03-00181-0
NYPL [HFB 87-2508]

A vida fora das fábricas . Decca, Maria
Auxiliadora Guzzo. Rio de Janeiro, RJ , 1987.
135 p. ; DDC 305.5/62/098161 19
HD8290.S32 D4 1987
NYPL [Sc D 88-1367]

Vidas novas /. Vieira, José Luandino, 1935-
[Porto?] [1975]. 109 p. :
NYPL [Sc E 89-14]

Vidauro, Morris. Rohmer, Harriet. The invisible
hunters . San Francisco , c1987. 32 p. : ISBN
0-89239-031-X : DDC 398.2/08998 19
F1529.M9 R64 1987 *NYPL [Sc E 88-241]*

**Vidrovitch, Catherine Coquery- see Coquery-
Vidrovitch, Catherine.**

Vie du sultan Mohamed Bakhit, 1856-1916 .
Bret, René-Joseph, d. 1940. Paris , 1987. [xvi],
258 p. ; ISBN 2-222-03901-0
NYPL [Sc D 89-364]

La vie politique sénégalaise (1789 - 1940) /.
Zuccarelli, François. Paris , c1987. 157 p. ;
ISBN 2-903182-23-X *NYPL [Sc E 88-342]*

La Vie quotidienne dans un district, 1913-1935 :
cahier journal du district d'Arivonimamo /
présentation de Dahy Rainibe. Antananarivo :
Université de Madagascar, 1984. 53 p., [6]
leaves of plates : ill. ; 27 cm. (Etudes et
documents / Université de Madagascar, Etablissement
d'enseignement supérieur des lettres . no 1) Cover title.
DDC 969/.1 19

*1. Arivonimamo (Madagascar : District) - History -
Sources. I. Rainibe, Dahy. II. Series: Etudes et
documents / Université de Madagascar, Etablissement
d'enseignement supérieur des lettres , no 1.*
DT469.M37 A758 1984
NYPL [Sc F 88-241]

La vie scélérate . Condé, Maryse. Paris , c1987.
333 p. ; *NYPL [Sc D 88-1102]*

Vieira, José Luandino, 1935- Vidas novas /
Luandino Vieira ; desenhos de José Rodrigues.
[Porto?] : Afrontamento, [1975]. 109 p. : ill. ;
23 cm. (Ficção Angola) Short stories.
1. Angola - Fiction. I. Title. *NYPL [Sc E 89-14]*

**VIETNAM CONFLICT, 1961-1975. see
VIETNAMESE CONFLICT, 1961-1975.**

**VIETNAM WAR, 1961-1975. see
VIETNAMESE CONFLICT, 1961-1975.**

**VIETNAMESE CONFLICT, 1961-1975 -
FICTION.**
Flowers, A. R. De mojo blues . New York ,
1986, c1985. 216 p. ; ISBN 0-525-24376-3 :
DDC 813/.54 19
PS3556.L598 D4 1986 *NYPL [JFD 86-3984]*

Wise, Leonard. Doc's legacy /. New York ,
c1986. 410 p. ; ISBN 0-931933-16-1
NYPL [JFE 86-5265]

**VIETNAMESE CONFLICT, 1961-1975 -
JUVENILE FICTION.**
Myers, Walter Dean, 1937- Fallen angels /.
New York , c1988. 309 p. : ISBN
0-590-40942-5 : DDC [Fic] 19
PZ7.M992 Fal 1988 *NYPL [Sc D 88-1136]*

**VIETNAMESE CONFLICT, 1961-1975 -
LITERATURE AND THE WAR.**
Harris, Norman, 1951- Connecting times .
Jackson , c1988. 197 p. ; ISBN 0-87805-335-2
(alk. paper) DDC 813/.54/093520396073 19
PS153.N5 H27 1988 *NYPL [Sc E 88-288]*

**VIETNAMESE WAR, 1961-1975. see
VIETNAMESE CONFLICT, 1961-1975.**

The view from within . Keepnews, Orrin. New
York , 1988. x, 238 p. ; ISBN 0-19-505284-6
DDC 785.42 19
ML3507 .K43 1988 *NYPL [Sc D 88-1453]*

**VIGILANTES - FLORIDA - TAMPA -
HISTORY.**
Ingalls, Robert P., 1941- Urban vigilantes in the
New South . Knoxville , c1988. xx, 286 p. :
ISBN 0-87049-571-2 (alk. paper) DDC
305.8/009759/65 19
F319.T2 I64 1988 *NYPL [Sc E 88-518]*

The village . Watson, Wilbur H. Atlanta, Ga. ,
c1989. xxii, 204 p. : ISBN 0-9621460-0-5 DDC
977.1/3200496073 20
F499.C69 N38 1989 *NYPL [Sc D 89-609]*

Village in Nigeria /. Barker, Carol. London , c19.
25 p. : ISBN 0-7136-2391-8 : DDC 966.9/05 19
DT515.8 .B29 1984 *NYPL [Sc D 88-605]*

The village of waiting /. Packer, George. New
York , 1988. 316 p. ; ISBN 0-394-75754-8 :
DDC 966/.81 19
DT582.27 .P33 1988 *NYPL [Sc D 88-1318]*

VILLAGES - CARIBBEAN AREA.
Rural development in the Caribbean /.
London , 1985. xxi, 246 p. ; ISBN 0-312-69599-3
NYPL [Sc D 88-1309]

**VILLAGES - SOUTH AFRICA -
HOMELANDS - CASE STUDIES.**
De Wet, C. J. Rural communities in transition .
Grahamstown [1983] iii, 113 p., [6] leaves of
plates : ISBN 0-86810-101-X (pbk.) DDC
307.7/2/0968 19
HD2130.5.Z9 H653 1983
NYPL [Sc F 88-328]

VILLAGES - SUDAN - ABYEI.
Salih, Mohamed Abdel Rahim M. Abeyi,
administration and public services [microform]
/. Khartoum , 1978. 27 leaves ;
NYPL [Sc Micro F-11039]

VILLAGES - TRINIDAD AND TOBAGO.
Anthony, Michael. Towns and villages of
Trinidad and Tobago /. St. James, Port of
Spain , 1988. v., 342 p. :
NYPL [Sc D 89-404]

VILLAS. see ARCHITECTURE, DOMESTIC.

Villeronce, Guy. Le vent des mornes : poèmes /
Guy Villeronce. [Fort-de-France?] : Impr.

Désormeaux, [1986] 80 p. : ill. ; 21 cm.
I. Title.
MLCS 86/6603 (P) *NYPL [Sc D 89-557]*

Vincent, Alan W. The bangy book : New Yorker
street boys : fotografien / Vincent Alan W.
Berlin : Vis-à-vis, 1988. [80] p. : ill. ; 28 cm. In
German, English, French and Italian. ISBN
3-924040-62-1
*1. Puerto Rican men - New York (N.Y.) - Photographs.
2. Afro-American men - New York (N.Y.) -
Photographs. I. Title.* *NYPL [Sc F 89-115]*

Vincent, Occélus. Brouillerie : comédie en un acte
[microform] / par Occélus Vincent.
Port-au-Prince : Editions Panorama, [1964] 54
p. ; 21 cm. Microfilm. New York : New York Public
library, 198 , 1 microfilm reel ; 35 mm. (MN
*ZZ-28635)
1. Haiti - Drama. I. Title.
NYPL [Sc Micro R-4840 no.6]

Vincileoni, Nicole. Comprendre l'oeuvre de
Bernard B. Dadié / Nicole Vincileoni. Issy les
Moulineaux : Classiques africains, c1986. 319
p.,[12] p. of plates : ill., ports., facsims. ; 21 cm.
(Classiques africains. no 860) Comprendre Bibliography:
p. 311-316. ISBN 2-85049-368-6
*1. Dadié, Bernard Binlin, 1916- - Criticism and
interpretation. I. Title. II. Series.*
NYPL [Sc D 88-721]

Vingt questions sur l'Afrique : des socialistes
répondent : document, Intervention de Lionel
Jospin (Dakar, 15 octobre 1987) / sous la
direction de Louis Le Pensec. Paris :
L'Harmattan, 1988. 238 p. ; 22 cm. ISBN
2-7384-0048-5
*1. Africa - Politics and government - 1960-. 2. Africa -
Economic conditions - 1960-. 3. Africa - Relations -
France. 4. France - Relations - Africa. I. Le Pensec,
Louis. II. Jospin, Lionel.* *NYPL [Sc D 88-1390]*

?Vino el puerco para la humanidad?
[microform] . 'Isá 'Abd Alláh Muhammad
al-Mahdi, 1945- [Brooklyn , 197-?] 40 p. :
NYPL [Sc Micro R-4114 no. 12]

Vinogradov, V. S. (Viktor Sergeevich) Muzyka
narodov Azii i Afriki /. Moskva , 1969- v. :
ML3740 .M9 *NYPL [Sc D 89-470]*

**VIOLENCE - FLORIDA - TAMPA -
HISTORY.**
Ingalls, Robert P., 1941- Urban vigilantes in the
New South . Knoxville , c1988. xx, 286 p. :
ISBN 0-87049-571-2 (alk. paper) DDC
305.8/009759/65 19
F319.T2 I64 1988 *NYPL [Sc E 88-518]*

VIOLENCE IN LITERATURE.
Lewis, Marvin A. Treading the ebony path .
Columbia , 1987. 142 p. ; ISBN 0-8262-0638-7
(alk. paper) DDC 863 19
PQ8172 .L49 1987 *NYPL [Sc D 88-443]*

VIOLENCE - JAMAICA.
The Jamaica Council for Human Rights speaks
[microform] [Kingston, Jamaica , 1981] 45 p. ;
NYPL [Sc Micro R-4132 no. 22]

Virago modern classics (London, England) .
(241) West, Dorothy, 1909- The living is easy
/. London , 1987, c1982. 362 p. ; ISBN
0-86068-753-8 *NYPL [Sc C 88-165]*

**Virgin Islands, British. see British Virgin
Islands.**

**Virgin Islands (British W. I.) see British Virgin
Islands.**

**Virgin Islands of Great Britain. see British
Virgin Islands.**

**VIRGIN ISLANDS OF THE UNITED
STATES - CHURCH HISTORY.**
Oldendorp, C. G. A. (Christian Georg
Andreas), 1721-1787. [Geschichte der Mission
der Evangelischen Brüder auf den caraibischen
Inseln S. Thomas, S. Croix und S. Jan.] C.G.A.
Oldendorps Geschichte der Mission der
Evangelischen Brüder auf den caraibischen
Inseln S. Thomas, S. Croix und S. Jan /.
Barby , 1777. 2 v. in 1 (1068 p.) : DDC
266/.46729722 19
BV2848.V5 O42 1777
NYPL [Sc Rare C 89-33]

**VIRGIN ISLANDS OF THE UNITED
STATES - HISTORY, JUVENILE.**
Moolenaar, Ruth. Facts or fantasy about Virgin
Islands history [microform] /. [Charlotte
Amalie] , 1978. 22, [1] p. ;
NYPL [Sc Micro F-10966]

Virginia Museum of Fine Arts. Wood, Peter H.,
1943- Winslow Homer's images of Blacks .
Austin , c1988. 144 p. :   ISBN 0-292-79047-3
(University of Texas Press)   DDC 759.13 19
ND237.H7 A4 1988a   *NYPL [Sc F 89-133]*

Visible now : Blacks in private schools / edited
by Diana T. Slaughter and Deborah J.
Johnson ; foreword by James P. Comer. New
York : Greenwood Press, 1988. xvi, 344 p. ; 25
cm. (Contributions in Afro-American and African
studies, 0069-9624 . no. 116) Includes index.
Bibliography: p. [321]-324.   ISBN 0-313-25926-7 (lib.
bdg. : alk. paper)   DDC 371/.02/0973 19
*1. Afro-American children - Education. 2. Private
schools - United States. I. Slaughter, Diana T. II.
Johnson, Deborah J. (Deborah Jean), 1958-. III. Series.*
LC2761 .V57 1988   *NYPL [Sc E 98-257]*

Visram, M. G. On a plantation in Kenya / M.G.
Visram. Mombasa, Kenya : M.G. Visram, 1987
(reprinted 1988) 164 p., [4] p. of plates :
ports. ; 18 cm.   ISBN 996-698-411-9
1. Plantation life - Kenya - Yoi. I. Title.
NYPL [Sc C 89-92]

Visser, Johanna, 1898- A list of books, articles
and government publications on the economy of
Nigeria, 1963 and 1964. Ibadan, Nigerian
Institute of Social and Economic Research,
1965. x, 81 p. 26 cm.
*1. Nigeria - Economic conditions - Bibliography. I.
Nigerian Institute of Social and Economic Research. II.
Title.*   *NYPL [Sc F 78-58]*

Vissions Foundation. (Washington, D.C.)
American visions Afro-American art, 1986 /.
Washington, D.C. , 1987. 57 p. :
NYPL [Sc F 87-438]

**Visual arts collections relating to Caribbean
cultures.** New York : Visual Arts Research and
Resource Center Relating to the Caribbean,
[198-?] 16 p. : ill. ; 22 cm.
*1. Art, Caribbean - Museums - Directories. I. Visual
Arts Research and Resource Center Relating to the
Caribbean.*   *NYPL [Sc D 88-1177]*

**Visual Arts Research and Resource Center
Relating to the Caribbean.** Visual arts
collections relating to Caribbean cultures. New
York [198-?] 16 p. :   *NYPL [Sc D 88-1177]*

Visual variations . Fry, Jacqueline, 1923-
Kingston, Canada , c1987. vii, 63 p. :   DDC
730/.0966/074011372 19
NB1098 .F79 1987   *NYPL [Sc F 88-189]*

Vitalité de la petite pêche tropicale . Bonnardel,
Régine. Paris , 1985. 104 p. :   ISBN
2-222-03678-X   *NYPL [Sc F 88-329]*

VOCALISTS. see SINGERS.

VOCATIONAL EDUCATION - KENYA.
Godfrey, E. M. Technical and vocational
training in Kenya and the harambee institutes
of technology [microform] /. [Nairobi] , 1973.
58 p. ;   *NYPL [Sc Micro R-4108 no. 24]*

VOCATIONAL EDUCATION - NIGERIA.
Makinde, Olu. Profile of career education /.
Ibadan, Oyo State, Nigeria , 1987. xv, 308 p. ;
ISBN 978-254-605-4   *NYPL [Sc D 89-177]*

Osuala, Esogwa C. A handbook of
vocational-technical education for Nigeria /.
Oruowulu-Obosi, Anambra State, Nigeria ,
1987. x, 173 p. ;   ISBN 0-9782341-9-1
NYPL [Sc D 88-729]

**VOCATIONAL GUIDANCE FOR GIRLS. see
VOCATIONAL GUIDANCE FOR
WOMEN.**

**VOCATIONAL GUIDANCE FOR
MINORITIES - CALIFORNIA.**
Gray, Mattie Evans. Images . Sacramento,
Calif. , c1988. 185 p. :   ISBN 0-8011-0782-2
NYPL [Sc F 89-134]

**VOCATIONAL GUIDANCE FOR WOMEN -
CALIFORNIA.**
Gray, Mattie Evans. Images . Sacramento,
Calif. , c1988. 185 p. :   ISBN 0-8011-0782-2
NYPL [Sc F 89-134]

**VOCATIONAL GUIDANCE - JUVENILE
LITERATURE.**
Haskins, James, 1941- Jobs in business and
office. New York [1974] 96 p. :   ISBN
0-688-75011-7   DDC 651/.023
HF5381.2 .H38   *NYPL [Sc E 89-16]*

**VOCATIONAL OPPORTUNITIES. see
VOCATIONAL GUIDANCE.**

Voeltz, Richard Andrew. German colonialism and
the South West Africa Company, 1884-1914 /
by Richard A. Voeltz. Athens, Ohio : Ohio
University, Center for International Studies,
1988. x, 133 p. : map ; 22 cm. (Monographs in
international studies. African series . no. 50)
Bibliography: p. 123-133.   ISBN 0-89680-146-2 (pbk.) :
DDC 325/.343/09688 19
*1. South West Africa Company - History. 2.
Corporations, British - Namibia - History. 3. Namibia -
History - 1884-1915. 4. Germany - Colonies - Africa -
History. I. Title. II. Series.*
JV2029.A5 S689 1988   *NYPL [JLD 88-3416]*

Vogel, Susan. The Art of collecting African art /.
New York , c1988. 64 p. :   DDC
730/.0967/07401471 19
N7391.65 .A78 1988   *NYPL [Sc G 88-36]*

Vogel, Susan Mullin. Bassani, Ezio. Africa and
the Renaissance . New York City , c1988. 255
p. :   ISBN 0-945802-00-5 :   DDC
736/.62/096607401471 19
NK5989 .B37 1988   *NYPL [Sc F 89-30]*

A voice from the South /. Cooper, Anna J. (Anna
Julia), 1858-1964. New York , 1988. liv, 304
p. ;   ISBN 0-19-505246-3 (alk. paper)   DDC
975/.00496073 19
E185.86 .C587 1988   *NYPL [IEC 88-1201]*

Voices & visions : the poet in America / edited
by Helen Vendler.1st ed. New York : Random
House, c1987. xxx, 528 p. : ill., ports. ; 25 cm.
Published in conjunction with a Public Broadcasting
System television series: Voices and visions. Includes
index. Bibliography: p. 507-511.   ISBN 0-394-53520-0
*1. American poetry - History and criticism. I. Vendler,
Helen Hennessy. II. Voices and visions (Television
program). III. Title: Voices and visions.*
NYPL [JFE 87-5435]

Voices and visions. Voices & visions . New York ,
c1987. xxx, 528 p. :   ISBN 0-394-53520-0
NYPL [JFE 87-5435]

Voices and visions (Television program) Voices &
visions . New York , c1987. xxx, 528 p. :
ISBN 0-394-53520-0   *NYPL [JFE 87-5435]*

Voices from Rini . Roux, Andre, 1954-
Grahamstown, South Africa , 1986. 107 p. ;
ISBN 0-86810-131-1   *NYPL [Sc F 88-216]*

**Voices from twentieth-century Africa : griots and
towncriers** / selected with an introduction by
Chinweizu. London : Boston : Faber, 1988. xl,
424 p. ; 24 cm. Includes indexes.   ISBN
0-571-14929-4 (cased) :   DDC 808.8/9896 19
*1. African literature - Translations into English. 2.
English literature - Translations from African literature.
I. Chinweizu.*   *NYPL [Sc D 89-174]*

Voices in exile : Jamaican texts of the 18th and
19th centuries / edited by Jean D'Costa and
Barbara Lalla. Tuscaloosa : University of
Alabama Press, c1989. xiv, 157 p. : ill. ; 24 cm.
Bibliography: p. 152-157.   ISBN 0-8173-0382-0   DDC
427/.97292 19
*1. Creole dialects, English - Jamaica - Texts. I. Lalla,
Barbara, 1949-.*
PM7874.J3 V65 1989   *NYPL [Sc E 89-207]*

Voices in the night /. Bacmeister, Rhoda Warner,
1893- Indianapolis , 1965. 117 p. :
NYPL [Sc D 88-382]

Voices of négritude . Finn, Julio. London ,
NewYork , 1988. 246 p. ;
NYPL [Sc E 88-494]

Voices of resistance.
Attaway, William. Blood on the forge /. New
York , c1987. 315 p. ;   ISBN 0-85345-722-0
(pbk.) :   DDC 813/.52 19
PS3501.T59 B55 1987
NYPL [Sc D 88-1438]

Les voies de la souveraineté . Bangou, Henri.
Paris , c1988. 144 p. ;   ISBN 2-87679-021-1
NYPL [Sc D 88-1001]

**Les voies du lyrisme dans les "Poèmes" de
Léopold Sédar Senghor (Chants d'ombre,
Hosties noires, Ethiopiques, Nocturnes).**
Jouanny, Robert A. Paris , 1986. 161 p. ;   ISBN
2-85203-026-8   *NYPL [Sc D 88-1026]*

Voilà ce qui est arrivé . Hājj 'Umar ibn Sa'īd
al-Fūtī, 1794?-1864. [Bayān mā waqa'a.
French & Arabic.] Paris , 1983. 261 p., [57] p.
of plates :   ISBN 2-222-03216-4
NYPL [Sc F 88-211]

Voix nouvelles en psychanalyse.
André, Jacques. L'inceste focal dans la famille
noire antillaise . Paris : Presses universitaires de
France, 1987. 396 p. ;   ISBN 2-13-040101-5
NYPL [Sc D 88-129]

**Volkstümliche Künste : Kunst, Kunsthandwerk,
Folklore aus Europa, Amerika, Afrika, Asien,
Ozeanien : Sammlung Rolf Italiaander** /
[Redaktion: Hans L. Spegg ... et al.] Reinbek :
Stiftung Rolf Italiaander/Hans Spegg, Museum
Rade am Schloss Reinbek, c1986/87. 135 p. :
ill. (some col.) ; 21 cm.
*1. Italiaander, Rolf, 1913- - Art collections - Catalogs.
2. Museum Rade am Schloss Reinbek - Catalogs. 3.
Folk art - Catalogs. 4. Art - Germany (West) -
Reinbek - Catalogs. 5. Art, African - Exhibitions -
Catalogs. I. Spegg, Hans Ludwig. II. Museum Rade am
Schloss Reinbek.*   *NYPL [Sc D 89-238]*

Voll, Klaus. Senegal . Hamburg , 1983. xxxix, 392
p. :   ISBN 3-922887-28-7 (pbk.)   DDC 324.266/3 19
JQ3396.A91 S38 1983   *NYPL [JLF 85-1341]*

Vollaard, Piet. Groenendijk, Paul. Adolf Loos .
Rotterdam , 1985. 39 p., [6] leaves of plates :
ISBN 90-6450-027-4   DDC 728.3/72/0228 19
NA1011.5.L6 G76 1985   *NYPL [Sc F 89-67]*

Voltaire, Frantz. Pouvoir noir en Haiti . Québec ,
1988. 393 p., 7 p. of plates :   ISBN
2-920862-11-1   *NYPL [Sc D 89-482]*

**VOLUNTARY ASSOCIATIONS. see
ASSOCIATIONS, INSTITUTIONS, ETC.**

**VOLUNTARY INSTITUTIONS. see
ASSOCIATIONS, INSTITUTIONS, ETC.**

VOLUNTEERS - SOMALIA.
Baez, Joan, 1913- One bowl of porridge . Santa
Barbara, Calif. , 1986, c1985. 94 p. :   ISBN
0-936784-12-1 (pbk.) :   DDC 363.8/83/096773
19
HV696.F6 B34 1986   *NYPL [Sc D 89-333]*

Vonck, Pol. An African Chris[t]mas? /. Eldoret,
Kenya , 1983. 53 p. ;   DDC 263/.91/096 19
BS2575.2 .A37 1983   *NYPL [Sc D 88-195]*

VOODOISM - HAITI.
Pluchon, Pierre. Vaudou, sorciers,
empoisonneurs . Paris , c1987. 320 p. ;   ISBN
2-86537-185-9   *NYPL [Sc D 88-912]*

VOODOOISM.
Agosto de Muñoz, Nélida. El fenómeno de la
posesión en la religión Vudú . Río Piedras,
P.R. , 1975, c1974. 119 p. ;   DDC 299/.64 19
BL2490 .A33 1975   *NYPL [TB (Caribbean
monograph series no. 14)]*

Hurbon, Laënnec. Dieu dans le vaudou haïtien
/. Port-au-Prince, Haïti , 1987. 268 p. ;   DDC
299/.67 19
BL2490 .H87 1987   *NYPL [Sc D 89-366]*

**VOODOOISM - HAITI - JACMEL -
FICTION.**
Dépestre, René. Hadriana dans tous mes rêves .
[Paris] , c1988. 195 p. ;   ISBN 2-07-071255-9
NYPL [Sc D 88-1004]

VOODOOISM - HAITI - MUSIC.
Dauphin, Claude, 1949- Musique du vaudou .
Sherbrooke, Québec, Canada [1986] 182 p. :
ISBN 2-89040-366-1 (pbk.)   DDC 783/.02/9967
19
ML3565 .D34 1986   *NYPL [Sc D 87-315]*

**VOODOOISM - HAITI - MUSIC - HISTORY
AND CRITICISM.**
Dauphin, Claude, 1949- Musique du vaudou .
Sherbrooke, Québec, Canada [1986] 182 p. :
ISBN 2-89040-366-1 (pbk.)   DDC 783/.02/9967
19
ML3565 .D34 1986   *NYPL [Sc D 87-315]*

**VOODOOISM IN ART - HAITI -
EXHIBITIONS.**
Haïti . Paris , 1988. 276 p. :
NYPL [Sc E 89-227]

**VOTING - UNITED STATES - HISTORY -
20TH CENTURY.**
Carmines, Edward G. Issue evolution .
Princeton, N.J. , c1989. xvii, 217 p. :   ISBN
0-691-07802-5 :   DDC 323.1/196073 19
E185.615 .C35 1989   *NYPL [Sc E 89-214]*

The vow /. Ogunyemi, Wale, 1939- London ,
1985. vi, 47 p. ;   ISBN 0-333-35819-8
NYPL [Sc D 88-1210]

Voyage à la partie orientale de la Terre-Ferme, dans l'Amérique Méridionale, fait pendant les années 1801, 1802, 1803 et 1804: contenant la description de la capitainerie générale de Carácas, composée des provinces de Vénézuéla, Maracaïbo, Varinas, la Guiane Espagnole, Cumana, et de l'île de la Marguerite ... Pons, François Raymond Joseph de, 1751-1812. Paris, 1806. 3 v.
F2311 .P79   *NYPL [Sc Rare F 88-77]*

Voyage en Amérique noire /. Bernheim, Nicole. Paris , c1986. 254 p. ; ISBN 2-234-01886-2 : DDC 305.8/96073/073 19
E185.86 .B47 1986   *NYPL [Sc E 88-607]*

A voyage to Saint Domingo, in the years 1788, 1789, and 1790. Wimpffen, François Alexandre Stanislaus, baron de. London, 1817 [i. e. 1797] 371 p.   *NYPL [Sc 917.294-W]*

VOYAGERS. see EXPLORERS.

VOYAGES AND TRAVEL IN LITERATURE. see TRAVEL IN LITERATURE.

Voyance . Métellus, Jean, 1937- Paris , c1985. 124 p. ; ISBN 2-218-07137-1
    NYPL [Sc C 88-100]

WAEMBU (BANTU PEOPLE) see EMBU (BANTU PEOPLE)

Wagner, Geoffrey. Red calypso : the Grenadian revolution and its aftermath / Geoffrey Wagner. Washington, D.C. : Regnery Gateway, c1988. 264 p. ; 21 cm. Includes bibliographical references. ISBN 0-89526-773-X
1. Grenada - Politics and government - 1974-. I. Title.
    NYPL [Sc D 89-301]

Wahlman, Maude Southwell. Baking in the sun . Lafayette , c1987. 146 p. : ISBN 0-295-96606-8
    NYPL [Sc F 88-197]

The WAI as an ideology of moral rectitude /. Ali, Sidi H. [Nigeria] 1985 (Lagos : Academy Press) 88 p. :   *NYPL [Sc D 88-869]*

Wailing the dead to sleep /. Roy, Lucinda. London , c1988. 75 p. ; ISBN 0-904521-43-3 (pbk)   *NYPL [Sc D 88-1294]*

Wait and see /. Bradman, Tony. New York, NY , 1988. [28] p. ; ISBN 0-19-520644-4 DDC [E] 19
PZ7.B7275 Wai 1988   *NYPL [Sc D 89-255]*

Wakaima and the clay man . Kalibala, E. Balintuma. New York , 1946. 145 p. :
    NYPL [Sc D 89-486]

WAKARANGA (AFRICAN PEOPLE) see KARANGA (AFRICAN PEOPLE)

Wakokin Hausa / [Na'ibi Sulaimanu ... et al.]. An sake bugawa (Rev. ed.) [Zaria : Gaskiya Corp.?], 1963. 32 p. ; 22 cm.
1. Hausa poetry. I. Wali, Na'ibi Sulaimanu.
    NYPL [Sc D 89-473]

Walcott, Derek. Midsummer / Derek Walcott. London ; Boston : Faber and Faber, 1984. 79 p. ; 20 cm. Poems. Includes index. ISBN 0-571-13180-8 (pbk.) : DDC 811 19
I. Title.
PR9272.9.W3 M5 1984b
    NYPL [Sc C 88-306]

Wali, Na'ibi Sulaimanu. Wakokin Hausa /. [[Zaria] 1963. 32 p. ;   *NYPL [Sc D 89-473]*

Waliggo, John Mary, 1942- A history of African priests : Katigondo Major Seminary 1911-1986 / John Mary Waliggo. Masaka, Uganda : Katigondo National Major Seminary, 1988. xi, 236 p., [16] p. of plates : ill., ports. ; 22 cm. Bibliography: p. 191-198.
1. Katigondo National Major Seminary - History. 2. Catholic Church - Clergy - Training of - Africa. I. Title.
    NYPL [Sc D 89-15]

A walk through the neighborhood. Ft. Lauderdale, Fla. : The Community Press, c1985. 88 p. : ill. ; 22 cm. "Written by new readers who are currently learning to read and write." -- p. 87.
1. Afro-Americans - Florida - Fort Lauderdale.
    NYPL [Sc D 88-1414]

Walker, Alice, 1944-
The color purple : a novel / by Alice Walker.1st ed. New York : Harcourt Brace Jovanovich, c1982. 245 p. ; 22 cm. ISBN 0-15-119153-0 : DDC 813/.54 19
1. Afro-Americans - Fiction. 2. Afro-American Women - Fiction. I. Title.
PS3573.A425 C6 1982
    NYPL [Sc Rare F 88-3]

The color purple / Alice Walker. London : Women's Press, 1983 (1986 [printing]) 245 p. : 1 port. ; 20 cm. Originally published: New York : Harcourt Brace, 1982. ISBN 0-7043-3905-6 (pbk) : DDC 813/.54 19
1. Afro-Americans - Fiction. 2. Afro-American Women - Fiction. I. Title.   *NYPL [Sc C 88-143]*

Living by the word : selected writings, 1973-1987 / by Alice Walker.1st ed. San Diego : Harcourt Brace Jovanovich, c1988. xxi, 196 p. ; 22 cm. ISBN 0-15-152900-0 : DDC 813/.54 19
I. Title.
PS3573.A425 A6 1988
    NYPL [Sc D 88-1014]

To hell with dying / by Alice Walker ; illustrated by Catherine Deeter. San Diego : Harcourt Brace Jovanovich, 1987. [32] p. : col. ill. ; 26 cm. The author relates how old Mr. Sweet, though often on the verge of dying, could always be revived by the loving attention that she and her brother gave him. SCHOMBURG CHILDREN'S COLLECTION. ISBN 0-15-289075-0 DDC [Fic] 19
1. Afro-Americans - Juvenile fiction. I. Deeter, Catherine, ill. II. Schomburg Children's Collection. III. Title.
PZ7.W15213 To 1987   *NYPL [Sc F 88-182]*

You can't keep a good woman down : stories / by Alice Walker. New York : Harcourt Brace Jovanovich, c1982, c1981. 167 p. ; 21 cm. (A Harvest/HBJ book) ISBN 0-15-699778-9
1. Afro-American Women - Fiction. I. Title.
    NYPL [Sc D 87-684]

Walker, Alice, 1844-
[Color purple. Portuguese]
A Cor púrpura / Alice Walker ; tradução de Paula Reis. Lisboa : Teorema, 1986. 244 p. ; 21 cm. Translation of: The color purple.
1. Afro-Americans - Fictions. 2. Afro-American Women - Fiction. I. Title.   *NYPL [Sc D 88-388]*

Walker, Dale.
Fool's paradise / Dale Walker. 1st ed. New York : Vintage Books, 1988. 242 p. ; 21 cm. (Vintage departures) ISBN 0-394-75818-8 (pbk.) : DDC 915.3/80453 19
1. Walker, Dale - Journeys - Saudi Arabia. 2. Saudi Arabia - Description and travel. I. Title.
DS208 .W35 1988   *NYPL [Sc D 88-1463]*

WALKER, DALE - JOURNEYS - SAUDI ARABIA.
Walker, Dale. Fool's paradise /. New York , 1988. 242 p. ; ISBN 0-394-75818-8 (pbk.) : DDC 915.3/80453 19
DS208 .W35 1988   *NYPL [Sc D 88-1463]*

Walker, David, 1785-1830. David Walker's appeal, in four articles, together with a preamble, to the coloured citizens of the world, but in particular, and very expressly, to those of the United States of America. Edited and with an introd. by Charles M. Wiltse. New York, Hill and Wang [1965] xii, 78 p. 21 cm. (American century series, AC73) Bibliographical footnotes. DDC 326.973
1. Slavery - United States - Controversial literature - 1830. I. Wiltse, Charles Maurice, 1907- ed. II. Title.
E446 .W178   *NYPL [Sc D 89-456]*

Walker, David A. C. Paterson of Cyrene : a biography / by David A.C. Walker. Gweru, Zimbabwe : Mambo Press, 1985. xi, 85 p. : ill. (some col.) ; 20 x 23 cm. Bibliography: p. 85. ISBN 0-86922-340-2 DDC 283/.3 B 19
1. Paterson, Edward George, 1895-1974. 2. Paterson, Edward George, 1895-1974 - Contributions in sculpture. 3. Church of the Province of Central Africa - Clergy - Biography. 4. Anglican Communion - Zimbabwe - Clergy - Biography. I. Title.
BX5700.4.Z8 P378 1985
    NYPL [Sc D 88-229]

Walker, Margaret, 1915- Richard Wright, daemonic genius : a portrait of the man, a critical look at his work / Margaret Walker. New York : Warner Books, c1988. xix, 428 p., [8] leaves of plates : ill. ; 24 cm. "An Amistad book." Includes bibliographic essay and index. ISBN 0-446-71001-6 DDC 813/.52 B 19
1. Wright, Richard, 1908-1960. 2. Novelists, American - 20th century - Biography. 3. Afro-American novelists - Biography.
PS3545.R815 Z892 1988
    NYPL [Sc E 88-604]

Walker, Paul Robert. Pride of Puerto Rico : the life of Roberto Clemente / by Paul Robert Walker.1st ed. San Diego : Harcourt Brace Jovanovich, c1988. 135 p. ; 24 cm. "Gulliver books." A biography of the baseball superstar from Puerto Rico who, before his untimely death in a 1972 airplane crash, was noted for his achievements on and off the baseball field. Bibliography: p. 134-135. ISBN 0-15-200562-5 DDC 796.357/092/4 B 92 19
1. Clemente, Roberto, 1934-1972 - Juvenile literature. 2. Pittsburgh Pirates (Baseball team) - Juvenile literature. 3. Baseball players - Puerto Rico - Biography - Juvenile literature. I. Title.
GV865.C45 W35 1988   *NYPL [Sc E 88-452]*

Walker's American history series for young people.
Hansen, Joyce. Out from this place /. New York , 1988. vi, 135 p. ; ISBN 0-8027-6816-4 DDC [Fic] 19
PZ7.H19825 Ou 1988   *NYPL [Sc D 88-1321]*

Walking a tight rope . Jose, Babatunde. Ibadan , 1987. xiii, 421 p. : ISBN 978-15-4911-4 (limp)
    NYPL [Sc E 88-296]

WALKING CATFISH - JUVENILE LITERATURE.
Ricciuti, Edward R. Donald and the fish that walked /. New York [1974] 62 p. : ISBN 0-06-024997-8 DDC 597/.52
QL638.C6 R52 1974   *NYPL [Sc D 88-447]*

Walking the road to freedom . Ferris, Jeri. Minneapolis , 1987. 64 p. : ISBN 0-87614-318-4 (lib. bdg.) : DDC 305.5/67/0924 B 92 19
E185.97.T8 F47 1987   *NYPL [Sc D 88-1046]*

WALL HANGINGS - HISTORY.
Thomas, Michel. [Histoire d'un art. English.] Textile art /. Geneva, Switzerland , New York, NY , 1985. 279 p. : ISBN 0-8478-0640-5 (Rizzoli) : DDC 746 19
NK8806 .T4813 1985
    NYPL [3-MON+ 86-527]

Wall, L. Lewis, 1950- Hausa medicine : illness and well-being in a West African culture / L. Lewis Wall. Durham, N.C. : Duke University Press, 1988. xxvii, 369 p. : ill. ; 24 cm. Includes index. Bibliography: p. [337]-356. ISBN 0-8223-0777-4 DDC 306 19
1. Hausa (African people) - Medicine. 2. Hausa (African people) - Social life and customs. I. Title.
DT515.45.H38 W35 1988
    NYPL [Sc E 88-363]

Wallace, G. L. Them next door [microform] : a play in one act / by G.L. Wallace. New York : S. French, 1974. 36 p. : ill. ; 19 cm. Microfiche. New York: New York Public Library, 198 . 1 microfiche: negative; 11 x 15 cm. (FSN Sc 019,077)
1. Afro-Americans - Drama. I. Title.
    NYPL [Sc Micro F-11011]

Wallace, George B., poet. The best of George B. Wallace : poet of the people : a collection of tropical, sacred ... compassion / introduction by Adrian Foreman. [Kingston, Jamaica : s.n.], 1982. 152 p. : ill. ports., music ; 22 cm. Pagination includes advertising matter.
I. Title.
MLCS 84/1847 (P)   *NYPL [JFD 85-8238]*

Wallace, John A. Getting to know Egypt, U.A.R. / by John A. Wallace ; illustrated by Haris Petie. New York : Coward McCann, c1961. 64 p. : ill. ; 23 cm. Examines the land, history, people, culture, and economic progress of one of the world's oldest countries. SCHOMBURG CHILDREN'S COLLECTION.
1. Egypt - Description and travel - Juvenile literature. I. Petie, Haris, illus. II. Schomburg Children's Collection. III. Title.   *NYPL [Sc D 88-569]*

Wallerstein, Immanuel Maurice, 1930- Africa and the modern world / Immanuel Wallerstein. Trenton, N.J. : Africa World Press, c1986. 209 p. ; 22 cm. Includes bibliographies. ISBN 0-86543-024-1 (pbk.) : DDC 337.6 19
1. Africa - Foreign economic relations. 2. Africa - Foreign relations. I. Title.
HF1611 .W35 1986   *NYPL [Sc D 89-378]*

Wallis, Malcolm. Van de Geer, Roeland. Government and development in rural Lesotho /. Roma, Lesotho , 1982, 1984 printing. 159 p. ;   *NYPL [Sc D 89-52]*

Walsh, William, 1916- Commonwealth literature. London, New York, Oxford University Press, 1973. vi, 150 p. 21 cm. Bibliography: [139]-142.
1. English literature - Commonwealth of Nations authors - History and criticism. I. Title.
    NYPL [*R-NCB 74-5085]

Walter, John C. (John Christopher), 1933- The Harlem Fox : J. Raymond Jones and Tammany, 1920-1970 / John C. Walter. Albany, N.Y. : State University of New York Press, c1989. xv, 287 p. : port. ; 23 cm. (SUNY series in Afro-American studies) Includes index. Bibliography: p. 263-267. ISBN 0-88706-756-5 DDC 974.7/1043/0924 B 19
1. Jones, J. Raymond (John Raymond), 1899-. 2. Politicians - New York (N.Y.) - Biography. 3. West Indian Americans - New York (N.Y.) - Biography. 4. Afro-Americans - New York (N.Y) - Biography. 5. Afro-Americans - New York (N.Y.) - Politics and government. 6. New York (N.Y.) - Politics and government - 1898-1951. 7. New York (N.Y.) - Politics and government - 1951-. I. Title. II. Series.
F128.5.J72 W35 1988 **NYPL** *[Sc E 89-107]*

Walter, Mildred Pitts. Lillie of Watts takes a giant step. Illustrated by Bonnie Helene Johnson. [1st ed.] Garden City, N.Y., Doubleday [1971] 187 p. illus. 22 cm. Lillie's first year at Pelham Junior High in Watts is exciting but she faces a difficult decision when the African Culture Club tries to get Malcolm X's birthday declared a holiday. SCHOMBURG CHILDREN'S COLLECTION. DDC [Fic]
1. Afro-Americans - Social conditions - Juvenile fiction. I. Johnson, Bonnie Helene, illus. II. Schomburg Children's Collection. III. Title.
PZ7.W17125 Lk **NYPL** *[Sc D 88-1119]*

Mariah loves rock / Mildred Pitts Walter. New York : Bradbury Press, c1988. 117 p. : ill. ; 20 cm. As fifth grade comes to an end, Mariah, who idolizes a famous rock star, experiences many misgivings, as does every member of her family, about the arrival of a half sister who is coming to live with them. SCHOMBURG CHILDREN'S COLLECTION. ISBN 0-02-792511-0 DDC [Fic] 19
1. Afro-American children - Juvenile fiction. I. Schomburg Children's Collection. II. Title.
PZ7.W17125 Mar 1988 **NYPL** *[Sc C 89-29]*

Walters, Melora. Jackson, Angela, 1951- The man with the white liver . New York City , 1987. [12] p. : ISBN 0-936556-16-1 DDC 811/.54 19
PS3560.A179 M3 1987 **NYPL** *[Sc F 89-14]*

Walters, Ronald W. Black presidential politics in America : a strategic approach / Ronald W. Walters. Albany : State University of New York Press, c1988. xvii, 255 p. ill. ; 24 cm. (SUNY series in Afro-American studies) Includes index. Bibliography: p. [243]-245. ISBN 0-88706-546-5 DDC 324.6/2/08996073 19
1. Afro-Americans - Suffrage - History. 2. Presidents - United States - Election - History. I. Title. II. Series.
JK1924 .W34 1987 **NYPL** *[Sc E 88-283]*

Walton, Hanes, 1941- When the marching stopped : the politics of civil rights regulatory agencies / Hanes Walton, Jr. Albany : State University of New York Press, c1988. xxiv, 263 p. : ill. ; 24 cm. (SUNY series in Afro-American studies) Includes index. Bibliography: p. 239-252. ISBN 0-88706-687-9 DDC 353.0081/1 19
1. Afro-Americans - Civil rights. 2. Civil rights - United States. 3. Administrative agencies - United States. I. Title. II. Series.
E185.615 .W325 1988 **NYPL** *[Sc E 89-10]*

Walton, William, 1784-1857. Silva, José Bonifácio de Andrada e, 1763-1838. Memoir addressed to the general, constituent and legislative Assembly of the empire of Brazil, on slavery! London , 1826 London : Printed by A. Redford and W. Robins) 60 p. ;
NYPL *[Sc Rare G 86-14]*

Wamala, Elizabeth. Makerere University. Library. Annotated list of theses submitted to Makerere University and held by Makerere University Library [microform] /. [Kampala?] , 1981. 89 leaves ; **NYPL** *[Sc Micro R-4840 no.13]*

Wananchi mashujaa wa imani, Kangundo, Machakos /. Somba, John Ndeti, 1930- Kijabe, Kenya , 1985. 68 p. : **NYPL** *[Sc D 89-345]*

Wanjala, Chris. Socio-cultural profiles, Baringo District . [Nairobi?] , 1986. xviii, 268 p. : DDC 967.6/27 19
DT434.B36 S63 1986 **NYPL** *[Sc F 88-230]*

Wanjui, J. B. From where I sit : views of an African executive / J.B. Wanjui. Nairobi, Kenya : East African Publishing House, 1986. xi, 88 p. ; 19 cm.

1. Kenya - Economic conditions - 1963-. 2. Africa, Sub-Saharan - Economic conditions - 1960-. I. Title.
NYPL *[Sc C 88-90]*

Wanono, Nadine. Ciné-rituel de femmes dogon / Nadine Wanono ; préface de Jean Rouch ; postface de Germaine Diéterlen. Paris : Editions du Centre national de la recherche scientifique, 1987. 138 p. : ill., map ; 24 cm. Bibliography: p. 129-131. ISBN 2-222-03961-4 (pbk)
1. Moving-pictures in ethnology. 2. Women, Dogon (African people) - Social life and customs. 3. Dogons (African people) - Social life and customs. I. Title.
NYPL *[Sc E 88-177]*

War Against Indiscipline as an ideology of moral rectitude. Ali, Sidi H. The WAI as an ideology of moral rectitude /. [Nigeria] 1985 (Lagos : Academy Press) 88 p. :
NYPL *[Sc D 88-869]*

WAR AND EMERGENCY POWERS - UNITED STATES.
Whiting, William, 1813-1873. The war powers of the President, and the legislative powers of Congress in relation to rebellion, treason and slavery /. Boston , 1863. vi, 143 p. :
NYPL *[Sc Rare C 89-17]*

WAR AND PEACE. see PEACE.

War and rumours of war . Donders, Joseph G. Eldoret, Kenya , 1986. 51 p. :
NYPL *[Sc D 88-1467]*

The war and slavery; and their relations to each other . Barrows, William, 1815-1891. Boston , 1863. 18 p. ; **NYPL** *[Sc Rare F 88-51]*

WAR - ECONOMIC ASPECTS - AFRICA, SUB-SAHARAN.
Disarmament and development . Lagos, Nigeria , 1986. ix, 117 p., 1 folded leaf : ISBN 978-13-2828-2 **NYPL** *[Sc D 88-783]*

WAR OF SECESSION (UNITED STATES) see UNITED STATES - HISTORY - CIVIL WAR, 1861-1865.

WAR POWERS. see WAR AND EMERGENCY POWERS.

The war powers of the President, and the legislative powers of Congress in relation to rebellion, treason and slavery /. Whiting, William, 1813-1873. Boston , 1863. vi, 143 p. ;
NYPL *[Sc Rare C 89-17]*

WAR - RELIGIOUS ASPECTS - CHRISTIANITY.
Donders, Joseph G. War and rumours of war . Eldoret, Kenya , 1986. 51 p. :
NYPL *[Sc D 88-1467]*

Ward, J. R. British West Indian slavery, 1750-1834 : the process of amelioration / J.R. Ward. Oxford [Oxfordshire] : Clarendon Press ; New York : Oxford University Press, c1988. x, 320 p. : ill. ; 24 cm. Includes index. Bibliography: p. [289]-309.
ISBN 0-19-820144-3 (Oxford University Press) : DDC 306/.362/09729 19
1. Slavery - West Indies, British - Condition of slaves - History. 2. Plantation life - West Indies, British - History. I. Title.
HT1092 .W37 1988 **NYPL** *[Sc D 88-1355]*

Poverty and progress in the Caribbean, 1800-1960 / prepared for the Economic History Society by J.R. Ward. Houndmills, Basingstoke, Hampshire : Macmillan, 1985. 82 p. : ill. ; 22 cm. (Studies in economic and social history) Includes index. Bibliography: p. 70-78. ISBN 0-333-37212-3 (pbk.) DDC 330.9729 19
1. Poor - Caribbean Area - History. 2. Caribbean Area - Economic conditions. I. Economic History Society. II. Title.
HC151 .W37 1985 **NYPL** *[JLD 86-2144]*

Ward, S. D. (supposed author) Remarks upon the controversy between the Commonwealth of Massachusetts and the State of South Carolina. Boston, 1845. 21 p.
F273 .R38 **NYPL** *[Sc Rare C 89-9]*

WAREGAS - FOLKLORE.
Djungu-Simba Kamatenda, 1953- Autour du feu . Kinshasa , 1984. 70 p. : DDC 398.2/09675/1 19
GR357.82.W35 D48 1984
NYPL *[Sc C 88-272]*

Warner-Lewis, Maureen. Garvey--Africa, Europe, the Americas /. Kingston, Jamaica , 1986. xi,

208 p., [4] p. of plates :
NYPL *[Sc D 88-1131]*

Warner, Malcolm-Jamal. Theo and me : growing up okay / Malcolm-Jamal Warner with Daniel Paisner.1st ed. New York : Dutton, c1988. xiv, [16] p. of plates, 208 p. : ports. ; 22 cm. The popular teenage television actor uses excerpts from his fan mail as a jumping-off point to discuss troublesome aspects of adolescence, including family life, dating, and drugs, with examples drawn from his own experiences on and off the set of "The Cosby Show." ISBN 0-525-24694-0 DDC 791.45/028/0924 19
1. Warner, Malcolm-Jamal. 2. Cosby show (Television program). 3. Teenagers - Correspondence. 4. Television actors and actresses - United States - Biography. I. Paisner, Daniel. II. Title.
PN2287.W43 A3 1988 **NYPL** *[Sc D 89-258]*

WARNER, MALCOLM-JAMAL.
Warner, Malcolm-Jamal. Theo and me . New York , c1988. xiv, [16] p. of plates, 208 p. : ISBN 0-525-24694-0 DDC 791.45/028/0924 19
PN2287.W43 A3 1988 **NYPL** *[Sc D 89-258]*

Warner, Peter, 1939- (illus) Westwood, Gwen. Narni of the desert. [Chicago, c1967] 93 p. DDC [Fic]
PZ7.W5275 Nar **NYPL** *[Sc D 88-1424]*

Warren, Cathy. Springtime bears / Cathy Warren ; illustrated by Pat Cummings. 1st ed. New York : Lothrop, Lee & Shepard Books, c1986. [32] p. : col. ill. ; 21 cm. After Mama Bear has played with her three babies all winter, her gruffness about spring cleaning makes them wonder if she still loves them. ISBN 0-688-05905-8 DDC [E] 19
1. Bears - Juvenile fiction. I. Cummings, Pat, ill. II. Title.
PZ7.W2514 Sp 1986 **NYPL** *[Sc D 87-622]*

Warren, Dennis M. Yoruba medicines / collected by D.M. Warren ; translated and revised by Anthony D. Buckley and J. Akintunde Ayandokun. Legon : Institute of African Studies, University of Ghana, 1971 [i.e. 1973] iii, 93, xii, p. ; 33 cm. "June 1973"--P. 1 of cover. DDC 615.8/99 19
1. Yorubas - Medicine. 2. Folk medicine - Nigeria - Formulae, receipts, prescriptions. I. Title.
DT515.45.Y67 W37 1973
NYPL *[Sc G 88-34]*

Warren, Ruth. The Nile; the story of pharaohs, farmers, and explorers. Illustrated by Victor Lazzaro. New York, McGraw-Hill [1968] 127 p. illus., map, ports. 24 cm. Describes the journey of the major tributaries of the Nile from Lake Victoria to the Mediterranean; examines the civilizations which have peopled her valley since the early Egyptian kingdoms; explains nineteenth-century exploration of the Nile, her monuments and her path into "darkest Africa"; and defines man's efforts to control the river today. Bibliography: p. 121-122. SCHOMBURG CHILDREN'S COLLECTION. DDC 916.2
1. Nile River Valley - Juvenile literature. I. Lazzaro, Victor, illus. II. Schomburg Children's Collection. III. Title.
DT115 .W33 **NYPL** *[Sc E 89-21]*

WARRI (NIGERIA) - HISTORY.
Ayomike, J. O. S. A history of Warri /. Benin City , 1988. xiii, 198 p. :
NYPL *[Sc D 88-1370]*

WARS. see WAR.

Was Christ really crucified? [microform] /. 'Isá 'Abd Allāh Muhammad al-Mahdi, 1945- Brooklyn, N.Y. [1980] 72 p. :
NYPL *[Sc Micro R-4114 no. 6]*

Washington, Booker T. 1856-1915.
Booker T. Washington and the "Atlanta compromise" /. Sharpsburg, Md. , c1987. 13 p. : **NYPL** *[Sc F 88-386]*

Booker T. Washington gives facts and condemns lynching in a statement telegraphed to the New York world. Baltimore : [s.n.], 1908. [3] p. ; 15 cm.
1. Lynching - United States. I. Title.
NYPL *[Sc Rare C 89-25]*

The Booker T. Washington papers. Louis R. Harlan, editor. Urbana, University of Illinois Press [1972- v. illus. 25 cm. Black author. Includes bibliographies. CONTENTS. - v. 1. The autobiographical writings. - v. 2. 1860-89. - v. 3. 1889-95. - v. 4. 1895-98. - v. 5. 1899-1900. - v. 6. 1901-2. - v. 7. 1903-4. - v. 9. 1906-8. v. 10. 1909-11. - v. 11. 1911-12. - v. 12. 1912-14. - v. 13. 1914-15. - v.

14. Cumulative index.
1. Afro-Americans - History - Sources. 2.
Afro-Americans - Correspondence. 3. Social reformers -
United States - Correspondence. I. Harlan, Louis R., ed.
II. Title. **NYPL [Sc B-Washington, B.]**

A new Negro for a new century; an accurate
and up-to-date record of the upward struggles
of the Negro race. The Spanish-American War,
causes of it; vivid descriptions of fierce battles;
superb heroism and daring deeds of the Negro
soldier ... Education, industrial schools, colleges,
universities and their relationship to the race
problem, by Booker T. Washington.
Reconstruction and industrial advancement, by
N. B. Wood. The colored woman and her part
in race regeneration ... by Fannie Barrier
Williams. Miami, Fla., Mnemosyne Pub. Inc.,
1969. 428 p. ports. 23 cm. Reprint of the 1900 ed.
DDC 301.45/22
1. Afro-Americans - History - Addresses, essays,
lectures. I. Wood, Norman Barton, 1857- joint author.
II. Williams, Fannie Barrier, joint author. III. Title.
E185 .W315 1969b **NYPL [Sc D 89-43]**

WASHINGTON, BOOKER T. 1856-1915.
Booker T. Washington and the "Atlanta
compromise" /. Sharpsburg, Md. , c1987. 13
p. : **NYPL [Sc F 88-386]**

Harlan, Louis R. Booker T. Washington . New
York , 1983. xiv, 548 p. : ISBN 0-19-503202-0 :
DDC 378/.111 B 19
E185.97.W4 H373 1983
NYPL [Sc E 83-233]

Harlan, Louis R. Booker T. Washington in
perspective . Jackson , c1988. xii, 210 p., [8] p.
of plates : ISBN 0-87805-374-3 (alk. paper) DDC
378/.111 B 19
E185.97.W4 H36 1988 **NYPL [Sc E 89-217]**

WASHINGTON, BOOKER T., 1856-1915 -
INFLUENCE.
Meier, August, 1923- Negro thought in
America, 1880-1915 . Ann Arbor , 1988,
c1963. xii, 336 p. : ISBN 0-472-64230-8 DDC
973/.0496073 19
E185.6 .M5 1988 **NYPL [Sc D 89-509]**

Washington Consulting Group. Uplift : what
people themselves can do / prepared by the
Washington Consulting Group, inc. Salt Lake
City : Olympus Pub. Co., c1974. xviii, 465 p. :
ill. ; 23 cm. At head of title: The United States
Jaycees Foundation. ISBN 0-913420-38-7
1. Self-help groups - United States - Case studies. I.
Title.
HV547 .W38 1974 **NYPL [JLE 75-1370]**

Washington, D. C. American Council on
Education. see **American Council on**
Education.

Washington, D. C. American University. see
American University, Washington, D. C.

Washington, D. C. Biblioteca Conmemorativa de
Colón. see **Columbus Memorial Library.**

Washington, D. C. Columbus Memorial Library.
see **Columbus Memorial Library.**

WASHINGTON, D. C. - GENEALOGY.
Sluby, Paul E. Holmead's Cemetery (Western
Burial Ground), Washington, D.C. /.
Washington, D.C. , 1985. iv, 68 leaves : DDC
929.5/09753 19
F193 .S582 1985 **NYPL [Sc D 88-109]**

Sluby, Paul E. Selected small cemeteries of
Washington, DC /. [Washington] , c1987. 84
p. : **NYPL [Sc D 88-780]**

Washington, D. C. Smithsonian Institution. see
Smithsonian Institution.

WASHINGTON (D.C.) - BUILDINGS,
STRUCTURES, ETC.
Seale, William. The president's house .
Washington, D.C. , 1986. 2 v. (xx, 1224 p. [80]
p. of plates : ISBN 0-912308-28-1 (set) DDC 975
19
F204.W5 S43 1986 **NYPL [Sc E 89-183]**

WASHINGTON, HAROLD, 1922-1987.
Roberts, Naurice. Harold Washington .
Chicago , 1988. 30 p. : ISBN 0-516-03657-2
DDC 977.3/1100496073024 B 92 19
F548.52.W36 R63 1988
NYPL [Sc E 88-501]

WASHINGTON, HAROLD, 1922-
Kleppner, Paul. Chicago divided . DeKalb, Ill. ,
c1985. xviii, 313 p. : ISBN 0-87580-106-4 :

DDC 324.9773/11043 19
F548.52.W36 K54 1984
NYPL [JFE 85-2533]

WASHINGTON, HAROLD, 1922-1987 -
JUVENILE LITERATURE.
Roberts, Naurice. Harold Washington .
Chicago , 1988. 30 p. : ISBN 0-516-03657-2
DDC 977.3/1100496073024 B 92 19
F548.52.W36 R63 1988
NYPL [Sc E 88-501]

WASHINGTON HIGHLANDS
(WASHINGTON, D.C.)
Dash, Leon. When children want children .
New York , c1989. 270 p. : ISBN 0-688-06957-6
DDC 306.7/088055 19
HQ759.4 .D37 1989 **NYPL [Sc E 89-151]**

Washington, Joseph R. Dilemmas of the new
Black middle class /. [Pa.?] c1980. v, 100 p. ;
E185.86 .D54x 1980 **NYPL [Sc D 89-24]**

The Washington papers, 0278-937X .
(132) South Africa, in transition to what? /.
New York , Washington, D.C. , 1988. xii, 201
p. ; ISBN 0-275-92975-2 (alk. paper) DDC
968.06/3 19
DT779.952 .S654 1988 **NYPL [Sc E 88-510]**

Washington Project for the Arts. Morrison,
Keith. Art in Washington and its
Afro-American presence 1940-1970 /.
Washington, D.C. , 1985. 109 p. :
NYPL [Sc F 88-34]

Washington, Valora. Black children and American
institutions : an ecological review and resource
guide / Valora Washington, Velma La Point.
New York : Garland, 1988. xv, 432 p. ; 23 cm.
(Garland reference library of social science. vol. 382.
vol. 16) Includes indexes. Bibliography: p. [205]-398.
ISBN 0-8240-8517-5 : DDC 305.2/3/08996073
19
1. Afro-American children - Bibliography. I. La Point,
Velma. II. Series: Garland reference library of social
science, v. 382. III. Title.
Z1361.N39 W34 1988 E185.86
NYPL [Sc D 89-385]

Wassermann, Jack.
Wassermann, Selma. Moonbeam and Dan Starr.
Westchester, Ill., c1966. 64 p.
NYPL [Sc D 89-398]

(joint author) Wassermann, Selma. Moonbeam
and the rocket ride. Chicago [c1965] 64 p.
PE1119 .W363 **NYPL [Sc D 89-92]**

(joint author) Wassermann, Selma. Moonbeam
finds a moon stone. Chicago [1967] 96 p. DDC
[Fic]
PE1119 .W3636 **NYPL [Sc D 88-1423]**

Wassermann, Selma.
Moonbeam and Dan Starr [by] Selma and Jack
Wassermann. Illus. [by] George Rohrer.
Westchester, Ill., Benefic Press c1966. 64 p. col.
illus. 23 cm. (The moonbeam books) Moonbeam, a
chimpanzee, climbs aboard a rocket and takes a trip on
a space ship. SCHOMBURG CHILDREN'S
COLLECTION.
1. Chimpanzees - Juvenile fiction. 2. Space flight -
Juvenile fiction. 3. Readers - 1950-. 1. Wassermann,
Jack. II. Rohrer, George. III. Schomburg Children's
Collection. IV. Title. **NYPL [Sc D 89-398]**

Moonbeam and the rocket ride [by] Selma and
Jack Wassermann. Illus. [by] George Rohrer.
Chicago, Benefic Press [c1965] 64 p. col. illus.
23 cm. (The moonbeam books) SCHOMBURG
CHILDREN'S COLLECTION.
1. Readers - 1950-. 2. Chimpanzees - Juvenile fiction. I.
Wassermann, Jack, joint author. II. Rohrer, George,
illus. III. Schomburg Children's Collection. IV. Title.
PE1119 .W363 **NYPL [Sc D 89-92]**

Moonbeam finds a moon stone [by] Selma and
Jack Wassermann. Illus. [by] George Rohrer.
Chicago, Benefic Press [1967] 96 p. col. illus.
23 cm. (The moonbeam books) An energetic little
chimp participates in the first space journey to the
moon. SCHOMBURG CHILDREN'S COLLECTION.
DDC [Fic]
1. Readers - 1950-. 2. Chimpanzees - Juvenile fiction. 3.
Space flight to the moon - Juvenile fiction. I.
Wassermann, Jack, joint author. II. Schomburg
Children's Collection. III. Title.
PE1119 .W3636 **NYPL [Sc D 88-1423]**

Wästberg, Per.
[Afrika, ett uppdrag. English]
Assignments in Africa : reflections,

descriptions, guesses / Per Wästberg ;
translated by Joan Tate. London : Olive
Press, 1986. viii, 231 p. ; 23 cm. Translation of:
Afrika, ett uppdrag. ISBN 0-946889-11-2 (pbk.)
1. Africa - Description and travel - 1951-. I. Title.
NYPL [JFD 87-7408]

WASTES, HAZARDOUS. see **HAZARDOUS**
WASTES.

The watchman /. Callender, Timothy. [St.
Michael, Barbados? , 1978?] [28] p. :
NYPL [Sc F 89-52]

Water girl /. Thomas, Joyce Carol. New York,
N.Y. , c1986. 119 p. : ISBN 0-380-89532-3 :
NYPL [Sc C 88-115]

Water song /. Weaver, Michael S, 1951-
Lexington, Kentucky , 1985. 73 p. : ISBN
0-912759-05-4 **NYPL [Sc D 88-175]**

WATER SPIRITS - MALI.
Gibbal, Jean Marie. Les Génies du fleuve /.
Paris , c1988. 257 p. : ISBN 2-85616-467-6
NYPL [Sc D 88-1287]

WATER-SUPPLY, RURAL - CAMEROON.
Müller, Hans-Peter. Die
Helvetas-Wasserversorgungen in Kamerun .
[Zürich , 1978] 94, 45 leaves ;
NYPL [Sc F 88-122]

Waterbury, John. The Political economy of risk
and choice in Senegal /. London, England ,
Totowa, N.J. , 1987. xv, 363 p. : ISBN
0-7146-3297-X : DDC 338.966/3 19
HC1045 .P65 1987 **NYPL [Sc E 87-360]**

Waterfield, Hermione. Miniature African
sculptures from the Herman collection /.
London , 1985. 64 p. : ISBN 0-7287-0454-4
NYPL [Sc D 89-41]

Waters, Enoch P., 1909- American diary : a
personal history of the Black press / by Enoch
P. Waters.1st ed. Chicago : Path Press :
Distributed by Chicago Review Press, c1987.
xxiii, 520 p. ; 24 cm. Includes index. ISBN
0-910671-01-X : DDC 070.4/1/0924 B 19
1. Waters, Enoch P., 1909-. 2. Journalists - United
States - Biography. 3. Afro-American journalists -
Biography. 4. Afro-American newspapers - History. I.
Title.
PN4874.W293 A33 1987
NYPL [Sc E 88-270]

WATERS, ENOCH P., 1909-
Waters, Enoch P., 1909- American diary .
Chicago , c1987. xxiii, 520 p. ; ISBN
0-910671-01-X : DDC 070.4/1/0924 B 19
PN4874.W293 A33 1987
NYPL [Sc E 88-270]

Waters, Grahame H. C. (Grahame Hugh
Clement), 1923- Geography of Kenya and
the East African region / Grahame Waters and
John Odero. London : Macmillan, 1986. 252
p. : ill., maps ; 25 cm. Includes index. ISBN
0-333-41564-7 (pbk) DDC 916.76 19
1. Africa, East - Description and travel - 1951-. I.
Odero, John. II. Title.
DT427 **NYPL [Sc E 88-370]**

Watkins, Frances Ellen. see **Harper, Frances**
Ellen Watkins, 1825-1911.

Watson, Denton L. Reclaiming a heritage : a
historical profile of the NAACP and Africa /
this document was prepared by Denton L.
Watson of the Public Relations Dept., NAACP.
New York, N.Y. : National Association for the
Advancement of Colored People, c1977. 63 p. :
ill. ; 28 cm. "March 1977."
1. National Association for the Advancement of
Colored People - History. 2. United States - Relations -
Africa. 3. Africa - Relations - United States. I. Title.
NYPL [Sc F 89-78]

Watson, Jane (Werner) 1915- The Niger: Africa's
river of mystery. Maps by Henri Fluchere.
Champaign, Ill., Garrard Pub. Co. [1971] 96 p.
illus., maps, ports. 24 cm. (Rivers of the world) A
profile of the Niger, Africa's 2600-mile river that flows
north for over half its course. Includes index.
SCHOMBURG CHILDREN'S COLLECTION ISBN
0-8116-6374-4 DDC 916.6/2
1. Niger River - Juvenile literature. I. Fluchere, Henri
André, 1914- illus. II. Schomburg Children's Collection.
III. Title.
DT360 .W38 **NYPL [Sc E 88-415]**

Watson, Norbert. The metaphor lays barren / by
Norbert Watson. [Toronto?] : N. Watson,

c1986. 86 p. ; 22 cm. Poems.
I. Title.   *NYPL [Sc D 88-493]*

Watson, Philip J.
Costume of ancient Egypt / Philip J. Watson ; drawings by Jack Cassin-Scott. New York : Chelsea House, 1987. 64 p., [8] p. of plates : ill. (some col.) ; 25 cm. "Costume of the ancient world"--CIP, t.p. verso. Includes index. Outlines the geography and history of Ancient Egypt and describes, in text and illustrations, the materials and methods used to make clothing and the typical styles of the era. Bibliography: p. 63. ISBN 1-555-46771-7 : DDC 391/.00932 19
1. Costume - Egypt - History. 2. Costume - History - To 500. I. Cassin-Scott, Jack. II. Title.
GT533 .W38 1987   *NYPL [Sc F 88-228]*

Egyptian pyramids and mastaba tombs of the Old and Middle Kingdoms / Philip J. Watson. Aylesbury, Bucks : Shire Publications, 1987. 64 p. : ill. ; 21 cm. (Shire Egyptology . 6) Includes index. Bibliography: p. 61. ISBN 0-85263-853-1
1. Tombs - Egypt. 2. Pyramids - Egypt. I. Title. II. Series.   *NYPL [Sc D 88-1259]*

WATSON, SAMUEL, FUGITIVE SLAVE.
The Address and reply on the presentation of a testimonial to S.P. Chase by the colored people of Cincinnati. Cincinnati , 1845. 35 p. ;
    NYPL [Sc Rare G 86-15]

Watson, Susan. Blacks in Detroit . Detroit , 1980. 111 p. :   *NYPL [Sc G 88-15]*

Watson, Wilbur H. The village : an oral historical and ethnographic study of a black community / by Wilbur H. Watson. Atlanta, Ga. : Village Vanguard, c1989. xxii, 204 p. : ill. ; 22 cm. Includes index. Bibliography: p. [189]-199. ISBN 0-9621460-0-5 DDC 977.1/3200496073 20
1. Afro-Americans - Ohio - Cleveland Region - Social life and customs. 2. Oral history. 3. Cleveland Region (Ohio) - Social life and customs. I. Title.
F499.C69 N38 1989   *NYPL [Sc D 89-609]*

Waweru, Mwaura. The siege / Mwaura Waweru. Nairobi : Kenya Literature Bureau, 1985. 273 p. ; 19 cm.
1. Africa - Fiction. I. Title.   *NYPL [Sc C 88-287]*

Wawili, Rafiki. Sadhu Sundar Singh : mwaminifu mkuu / Kimetungwa na Rafiki Wawili. London : Longmans, Green, 1949. 48 p. ; 19 cm. "The compilers thank Messrs. Hoddar & Stroughton, publishers of the Memoir of the Sadhu by C. F. Andrews, for permission to make this Swahili abridgement of this book"- T.p. verso.
1. Sundar Singh, 1889-1929. 2. Mystics - India - Biography. I. Andrews, Charles Freer, 1871-1940. Sadhu Sundar Singh. II. Title.
    NYPL [Sc C 89-111]

Way of death . Miller, Joseph Calder. Madison, Wis. , c1988. xxx, 770 p. : ISBN 0-299-11560-7 : DDC 382/.44/09469 19
HT1221 .M55 1988   *NYPL [Sc E 89-105]*

The way we are /. Udeaja, Philip. [Enugu, Anambra State, Nigeria] [1987?]. vii, 61 p. ;
    NYPL [Sc C 89-36]

Wayne State University. Archives of Labor and Urban Affairs. Guide to the Raya Dunayevskaya collection . Detroit, Mich. [1986?] 84 p. ;   *NYPL [Sc F 88-196]*

We build together. Rollins, Charlemae Hill. [Champaign, Ill. , 1967] xxviii, 71 p. ; DDC 016.818
Z1361.N39 R77 1967   *NYPL [Sc D 89-387]*

We don't buy sickness, it just comes . Donovan, Jenny, 1960- Aldershot, Hants, England , Brookfield, Vt., USA , c1986. xv, 294 p. ; ISBN 0-566-05201-6 : DDC 362.1/08996/0421 19
RA488.L8 D65 1986   *NYPL [Sc D 86-844]*

We killed Mangy-Dog. Honwana, Luís Bernardo, 1942- [Nós matámos o Cão-Tinhoso. English.] Harare, Zimbabwe , 1987. 117 p. ; ISBN 0-9792256-2-2 :   *NYPL [Sc C 89-106]*

The weary blues. Hughes, Langston, 1902-1967. New York, 1935, c1926. 109 p.
    NYPL [Sc Rare C 88-18]

The weaver birds /. James, Frederick Bobor. Freetown [Sierra Leone] , 1986. 79 p. ; DDC 822 19
PR9393.9.J36 W4 1986
    NYPL [Sc D 89-517]

Weaver, Michael S, 1951- Water song / Michael S. Weaver. Lexington, Kentucky : University of Kentucky, 1985. 73 p. : port. ; 22 cm. (Callaloo poetry series . v.5) Poems. With autograph of author. ISBN 0-912759-05-4
I. Title. II. Series.   *NYPL [Sc D 88-175]*

WEAVING, HAND. see HAND WEAVING.

Webb, Alex. Hot light / half-made worlds : photographs from the tropics / Alex Webb. New York, N.Y. : Thames and Hudson, 1986. 91 p. : col. ill. ; 28 x 32 cm. ISBN 0-500-54116-7 : DDC 779/.99090913 19
1. Photography, Documentary - Tropics. 2. Tropics - Description and travel - Views. I. Title.
TR820.5 .W43 1986   *NYPL [Sc G 87-23]*

Webb, Spud. Flying high / Spud Webb with Reid Slaughter. 1st ed. New York : Harper & Row, c1988. xv, 208 p., [16] p. of plates : ports. ; 22 cm. ISBN 0-06-015820-4 : DDC 796.32/3/0924 B 19
1. Webb, Spud. 2. Basketball players - United States - Biography. 3. Afro-American basketball players - Biography. I. Slaughter, Reid. II. Title.
GV884.W35 A3 1988   *NYPL [Sc D 89-375]*

WEBB, SPUD.
Webb, Spud. Flying high /. New York , c1988. xv, 208 p., [16] p. of plates : ISBN 0-06-015820-4 : DDC 796.32/3/0924 B 19
GV884.W35 A3 1988   *NYPL [Sc D 89-375]*

Webster, Daniel, 1782-1852. Hayne, Robert Young, 1791-1839. Speeches of Hayne and Webster in the United States Senate, on the resolution of Mr. Foot, January, 1830 . Boston , 1853. 115 p. ;
E381 .H424 1853   *NYPL [Sc Rare C 89-20]*

Webster, Derek. Wilber, Bob, 1928- Music was not enough /. New York , 1988. 216 p. [8] p. of plates : ISBN 0-19-520629-0
    NYPL [Sc E 89-6]

Webster, John. Tutu, Desmond. Crying in the wilderness . London , 1986. xix, 124 p., [8] p. of plates : ISBN 0-264-67119-8 (pbk) : DDC 261.7 19
DT737   *NYPL [Sc C 89-10]*

WEEKES, GEORGE.
Kambon, Khafra. For bread justice and freedom . London , 1988. xi, 353 p., [16] p. of plates :   *NYPL [Sc D 89-294]*

Weier, Hans-Ingolf. Stappers, Leo. Substitutiv und Possessiv im Bantu /. Berlin [1986] xix, 223 p. ; ISBN 3-496-00877-6 DDC 496/.3 19
PL8025.1 .S73 1986   *NYPL [Sc E 88-360]*

WEIGHT CONTROL OF OBESITY. see REDUCING.

Weil, Lisl. The funny old bag. New York , Parents' Magazine Press [1974] [40] p. col. illus. 24 cm. Big Howie gets his comcuppance at the same time the children finally find out what old Mr. Gugelhupf carries in his old black bag. SCHOMBURG CHILDREN'S COLLECTION. ISBN 0-8193-0717-3 DDC [E]
1. City and town life - Juvenile fiction. I. Schomburg Children's Collection. II. Title.
PZ7.W433 Fu   *NYPL [Sc E 88-529]*

Weingrod, Alex. Ethiopian Jews and Israel /. New Brunswick, NJ, U. S.A. , c1987. 159 p. : ISBN 0-88738-133-2 DDC 305.8/924/05694 19
DS113.8.F34 E84 1987   *NYPL [Sc E 88-73]*

Weinrich, A. K. H., 1933- [Women and racial discrimination in Rhodesia. Spanish]
La situación de la mujer en Zimbabue antes de la independencia / A.K.H. Weinrich. 1a ed. Barcelona : Serbal ; Paris : Unesco, 1984. 198 p. ; 21 cm. (Colección de temas africanos . 17) Translation of: La situation de la femme au Zimbabwe avant l'indépendence. 1981. Originally published in English as: Women and racial discrimination in Rhodesia. 1979. Bibliography: p. [195]-198. ISBN 92-3-301621-8 (Unesco)
1. Women - Zimbabwe. 2. Ethnology - Zimbabwe. I. Title. II. Series.   *NYPL [Sc D 88-615]*

Weir, LaVada. Howdy! Illustrated by William Hoey. Austin, Tex., Steck-Vaughn Co. [1972] 32 p. illus. 22 x 25 cm. Feeling lonely Luke puts on his cowboy hat and greets everyone he meets in the street. SCHOMBURG CHILDREN'S COLLECTION. ISBN 0-8114-7735-5 DDC [E]
1. Afro-American children - Juvenile fiction. I. Hoey, William, 1930- illus. II. Schomburg Children's

Collection. III. Title.
PZ7.W4415 Ho   *NYPL [Sc E 88-613]*

Weiss, Andrea. Before Stonewall : the making of a gay and lesbian community / by Andrea Weiss & Greta Schiller. Tallahassee, FL : Naiad Press, 1988. 86 p. : ill. ; 22 cm. "An illustrated historical guide to the Emmy Award-winning film." Bibliography: p. 80-81. ISBN 0-941483-20-7 : DDC 306.7/66/0973 19
1. Gay liberation movement - United States - History - 20th century. 2. Gays - United States - History - 20th century. I. Schiller, Greta. II. Title.
HQ76.8.U5 W43 1988   *NYPL [Sc D 88-1125]*

Weiss, Edna S. Truly Elizabeth / Edna S. Weiss ; illustrated by Beth Krush. Boston : Houghton Mifflin, 1957. 178 p. ill. ; 22 cm. Summary: A white Vermont girl begins life in New York City; among her new friends is a young Black boy. SCHOMBURG CHILDREN'S COLLECTION.
1. Afro-American children - New York (N.Y.) - Juvenile fiction. I. Krush, Beth. II. Schomburg Children's Collection. III. Title.
    NYPL [Sc D 88-663]

Weiss, Marianne. Senegal . Hamburg , 1983. xxxix, 392 p. : ISBN 3-922887-28-7 (pbk.) DDC 324.266/3 19
JQ3396.A91 S38 1983   *NYPL [JLF 85-1341]*

Weixlmann, Joseph. Black feminist criticism and critical theory /. Greenwood, Fla. , c1988. iii, 202 p. ; ISBN 0-913283-25-8
    NYPL [Sc D 88-1394]

Welfare Council of New York City. Section on Employment and Vocational Guidance.
Granger, Lester Blackwell, 1896- Toward job adjustment . [New York] [1941] 78 p. :
    NYPL [Sc D 88-178]

WELFARE RECIPIENTS - HOUSING - NEW YORK (N.Y.) - CASE STUDIES - JUVENILE LITERATURE.
Kaufman, Curt. Hotel boy /. New York , c1987. 40 p. : ISBN 0-689-31287-3 : DDC 307.3/36 19
HV4046.N6 K38 1987   *NYPL [Sc F 88-362]*

WELFARE STATE - CROSS-CULTURAL STUDIES.
Ethnic associations and the welfare state . New York , 1988. x, 299 p. : ISBN 0-231-05690-7 DDC 362.8 19
HV4005 .E86 1988   *NYPL [JLE 88-3846]*

The well-wishers /. Eager, Edward. New York , c1960. 191 p. :   *NYPL [Sc D 88-429]*

Wellman, Alice. Time of fearful night. New York, Putnam [1970] 158 p. 21 cm. An American youth and the son of an African chieftain draw courage from each other in facing the problems posed by their respective societies. DDC [Fic]
1. Angola - Juvenile fiction. I. Title.
PZ7.W4578 Ti   *NYPL [Sc D 88-1431]*

Wells, Jovita. A School for freedom . [Knoxville] , 1986. xiii, 60 p. :
    NYPL [Sc D 88-417]

WELLS, WILLIE, 1905-
Riley, James A. Dandy, Day and the Devil /. Cocoa, FL , 1987. xiii, 153 p. : ISBN 0-9614023-2-6   *NYPL [Sc D 88-104]*

Welmers, William Everett, 1916-
(joint author) Gay, John. Mathematics and logic in the Kpelle language. Ibadan, 1971. 152, 184 p.
PL8411.1 .G35   *NYPL [JFF 74-877]*

First course in Kpelle. Gay, John. Mathematics and logic in the Kpelle language, by John Gay and William Welmers; and, A first course in Kpelle, by William Welmers. Ibadan, 1971. 152, 184 p.
PL8411.1 .G35   *NYPL [JFF 74-877]*

Weltbund der Christlichen Vereine Junger Männer. see World Alliance of YMCAs.

Weltkirchenrat. see World Council of Churches.

Welz, Stephan. African heritage . Cape Town , 1987. 24 p. :   *NYPL [Sc F 89-117]*

Wendo Nguma. Dictionnaire français-yansi / Wendo Nguma. Bandundu, République du Zaïre : Ceeba, 1986. 274 p. ; 28 cm. (Publications / Ceeba . série III, vol. 14)
1. French language - Dictionaries - Yanzi. I. Series: Publications / Ceeba , série III, vol. 14. II. Title.
    NYPL [Sc F 88-318]

Wenzel, Jürgen. Im Land der dreizehn Monate : Bilder aus Athiopien / Jürgen Wenzel. [Rudolstadt] : Greifenverlag zu Rudolstadt, 1985. 200 p. : ill. (some col.) ; 24 cm.
I. Title. *NYPL [Sc E 88-286]*

A WEP study.
African and Asian Inter-regional Workshop on Strategies for Improving the Employment Conditions of Rural Women (1984 : Arusha, Tanzania) Resources, power and women . Geneva , 1985. ix, 82 p. ; ISBN 92-2-105009-2 (pbk.) : DDC 331.4/83/095 19
HD6207 .A78 1984 NYPL [JLF 87-1038]

Improved village technology for women's activities . Geneva , 1984. vi, 292 p. : ISBN 92-2-103818-1 *NYPL [JLF 85-625]*

Loutfi, Martha Fetherolf. Rural women . Geneva , c1980 (1985 printing) v, 81 p., [4] p. of plates : ISBN 92-2-102389-3 (pbk.).
NYPL [Sc E 89-67]

Rural small-scale industries and employment in Africa and Asia . Geneva , 1984. x, 159 p. ; ISBN 92-2-103513-1 (pbk.) : DDC 338.6/42/095 19
HD2346.A55 R87 1984
NYPL [JLE 84-3222]

Were, Wasambo. Drama festival plays /. London , Baltimore, Md. , 1986. iv, 92 p. ; ISBN 0-7131-8446-9 *NYPL [Sc D 88-638]*

Werner, Jane. see Watson, Jane (Werner) 1915-

Werner, John M., 1941- Reaping the bloody harvest : race riots in the United States during the age of Jackson, 1824-1849 / John M. Werner. New York : Garland, 1986. 333 p. ; 25 cm. (American legal and constitutional history) Rev. ed. of the author's thesis (Ph. D.) Bibliography: p. 309-333. ISBN 0-8240-8301-6 (alk. paper) : DDC 973.5/6 19
1. Afro-Americans - History - To 1863. 2. Riots - United States - History - 19th century. 3. Racism - United States - History - 19th century. 4. United States - Race relations. 5. United States - 1815-1861. I. Title. II. Series.
E185 .W44 1986 NYPL [Sc E 88-242]

Wes Montgomery /. Ingram, Adrian. Gateshead, Tyne and Wear, England , 1985. 127 p. : ISBN 0-9506224-9-4 *NYPL [Sc F 88-61]*

Wesley, Charles H. (Charles Harris), 1891- The history of the National Association of Colored Women's Clubs : a legacy of service / by Charles Harris Wesley.1st ed. Washington, D.C. (5808 16th St., N.W., Washington) : The Association, 1984. viii, 562 p. : ill., ports. ; 23 cm. Includes index. Bibliography: p. 535-537. DDC 369/.1 19
1. National Association of Colored Women's Clubs (U. S.) - History. I. Title.
E185.86.N36 W47 1984
NYPL [Sc D 88-725]

Wesley, Charles H., 1891- The history of Alpha Phi Alpha : a development in college life / Charles H. Wesley.[14th printing] Chicago : The Foundation Publishers, 1981, c1929. xiv, 567 p. : ill., ports., map, music ; 23 cm. Includes index.
1. Alpha Phi Alpha. 2. Afro-American college students. I. Title. II. Title: Development in college life.
NYPL [Sc D 89-135]

West Africa. see Africa, West - Bibliography.

West African interlude . Terrell, Richard. Salisbury, Wiltshire , 1988. 175 p. :
NYPL [Sc D 88-1371]

WEST AFRICAN LITERATURE (ENGLISH) - HISTORY AND CRITICISM.
Achebe, Chinua. Hopes and impediments . London , 1988. x, 130 p. ; ISBN 0-435-91000-0 (cased) : DDC 823/.914/09 19
PR881 NYPL [Sc D 88-1265]

West African oil, will it matter? /. Underwood, David C. Washington, D.C. , c1983. vi, 57 p. : ISBN 0-89206-046-8 (pbk.) DDC 333.8/232/0966 19
HD9577.A3582 U52 1983
NYPL [Sc D 88-888]

West African poetry . Fraser, Robert, 1947- Cambridge [Cambridgeshire] , New York , 1986. vii, 351 p. ; ISBN 0-521-30993-X DDC 809.1/00966 19
PL8014.W37 F73 1986
NYPL [JFE 86-4349]

WEST AFRICAN POETRY - HISTORY AND CRITICISM.
Fraser, Robert, 1947- West African poetry . Cambridge [Cambridgeshire] , New York , 1986. vii, 351 p. ; ISBN 0-521-30993-X DDC 809.1/00966 19
PL8014.W37 F73 1986
NYPL [JFE 86-4349]

West African Seminar on Population Studies, University of Ghana, 1972. Interdisciplinary approaches to population studies : proceedings of the West African Seminar on Population Studies, University of Ghana, Legon, 30 November-4 December 1972 / Abraham S. David, Ebenezer Laing, & Nelson O. Addo, editors. Legon : Population Dynamics Programme, University of Ghana, 1975. ix, 333 p. : ill. ; 23 cm. (University of Ghana population studies. no. 4) Includes bibliographies.
1. Population - Congresses. 2. Population research - Africa, West - Congresses. 3. Africa, West - Population - Congresses. 4. Ghana - Population - Congresses. I. David, A. S. II. Laing, E., 1931-. III. Addo, N. O. IV. Ghana. University, Legon. Population Dynamics Programme. V. Title. VI. Series.
HB21 .W38 1972 NYPL [JLD 78-861]

West African traditional religion /. Quarcoopome, T. N. O. Ibadan , 1987. viii, 200 p. ; ISBN 978-14-8223-8 *NYPL [Sc D 88-819]*

West Coast jazz /. Tercinet, Alain, 1935- Marseille , 1986. 358 p. : ISBN 2-86364-031-3
NYPL [Sc E 88-307]

West, Cornel. Prophetic fragments / Cornel West. Grand Rapids, Mich. : Eerdmans ; Trenton, N.J. : Africa World Press, c1988. xi, 294 p. ; 24 cm. Includes bibliographical references. ISBN 0-8028-0308-3 : DDC 291/.0973 19
1. Afro-Americans - Religion. 2. United States - Religion - 1960-. I. Title.
BL2525 .W42 1988 NYPL [Sc E 88-401]

West, Dorothy, 1909- The living is easy / Dorothy West ; with an afterword by Adelaide M. Cromwell. London : Virago, 1987, c1982. 362 p. ; 20 cm. (Virago modern classics . 241) ISBN 0-86068-753-8
1. Afro-Americans - Massachusetts - Boston - Fiction. 2. Afro-American Women - Fiction. 3. Boston - Fiction. I. Series: Virago modern classics (London, England) , 241. II. Title. *NYPL [Sc C 88-165]*

West India slavery : a review of The slavery of the British West India colonies delineated, as it exists both in law and practice, and compared with the slavery of other countries, ancient and modern. By James Stephen, Esq. Vol. 1 being a delineation of the state in point of law. Aberdeen : Printed by D. Chalmers for the Aberdeen Anti-Slavery Society, 1825. 24 p. ; 18 cm. Reprinted from the Edinburgh review, no. 82
1. Stephen, James, 1758-1832. The slavery of the British West India colonies delineated. 2. Slavery - West Indies, British. I. Title: Anti-Slavery Society.
NYPL [Sc Rare G 86-34]

The West Indian /. Cranmore, Frederick, 1948- Brooklyn , c1978. 122 p., [1] leaf of plates : DDC 813/.5/4
PZ4.C8893 We PR9320.9.C7
NYPL [Sc D 88-37]

WEST INDIAN AMERICANS IN LITERATURE.
Rahming, Melvin B., 1943- The evolution of the West Indian's image in the Afro-American novel /. Millwood, N.Y. , c1986. xix, 160 p. ; ISBN 0-8046-9339-0 DDC 813/.009/35203969729 19
PS153.N5 R3 1985 NYPL [JFD 86-6569]

WEST INDIAN AMERICANS - NEW YORK (N.Y.) - BIOGRAPHY.
Walter, John C. (John Christopher), 1933- The Harlem Fox . Albany, N.Y. , c1989. xv, 287 p. : ISBN 0-88706-756-5 DDC 974.7/1043/0924 B 19
F128.5.J72 W35 1988 NYPL [Sc E 89-107]

WEST INDIAN FICTION (FRENCH) - HISTORY AND CRITICISM.
Ormerod, Beverley, 1937- An introduction to the French Caribbean novel /. London , Portsmouth, N.H., USA , 1985. 152 p. ; ISBN 0-435-91839-7 (pbk.) DDC 843 19
PQ3944 .O76 1985 NYPL [Sc D 88-1267]

West Indian folk-tales. Iremonger, Lucille.

London [1956] 64 p.
GR120 .I7 NYPL [Sc C 89-157]

WEST INDIAN LITERATURE - BLACK AUTHORS - HISTORY AND CRITICISM.
Bernd, Zilá, 1944- Introdução à literatura negra /. Sao Paulo , 1988. 101 p. ;
NYPL [Sc D 89-188]

WEST INDIAN LITERATURE (ENGLISH) - 20TH CENTURY - HISTORY AND CRITICISM.
Sander, Reinhard. The Trinidad awakening . New York , 1988. xii, 168 p. ; ISBN 0-313-24562-2 (lib. bdg. : alk. paper) DDC 810/.9 19
PR9272 .S24 1988 NYPL [Sc E 89-111]

WEST INDIAN LITERATURE (ENGLISH) - BIBLIOGRAPHY.
Merriman, Stella E. Commonwealth Caribbean writers. Georgetown, Guyana, 1970. iv, 98 p.
NYPL [JFF 72-67]

WEST INDIAN LITERATURE (ENGLISH) - HISTORY AND CRITICISM.
Dabydeen, David. A reader's guide to West Indian and black British literature /. London , 1988. 182 p. ; ISBN 1-87051-835-7 (pbk) : DDC 810.9/9729 19
PR9210 NYPL [Sc C 88-363]

WEST INDIAN LITERATURE (FRENCH) - HISTORY AND CRITICISM.
Réception critique de la littérature africaine et antillaise d'expression française. Paris , 1979. 272 p. ; *NYPL [Sc E 87-557]*

WEST INDIAN POETRY (ENGLISH)
Mahabir, Noor Kumar. The still cry . Tacarigua, Trinidad , Ithaca, N.Y. , c1985. 191 p. ; *NYPL [Sc D 88-401]*

WEST-INDIAN SKETCHES, DRAWN FROM AUTHENTIC SOURCES.
Antidote to West-Indian sketches, drawn from authentic sources. London , 1816-1817. 7 nos. ;
NYPL [Sc Rare G 86-16]

WEST INDIAN TALES. see TALES, WEST INDIAN.

West Indians and their language /. Roberts, Peter A. Cambridge [Cambridgeshire] , New York , 1988. vii, 215 p. : ISBN 0-521-35136-7 DDC 427/.9729 19
P381.W47 R63 1988 NYPL [Sc E 88-331]

WEST INDIANS - CANADA - FICTION.
Philip, Marlene Nourbese. Harriet's daughter /. Toronto, Ontario , 1988. 150 p. ;
NYPL [Sc C 89-109]

A Shapely fire . Oakville, Ont. , c1987. 175 p. : ISBN 0-88962-345-7 *NYPL [Sc B 88-263]*

WEST INDIANS - ENGLAND - DRAMA.
Moffatt, Nigel D. Mamma Decemba /. London , 1987. 34 p. ; ISBN 0-571-14775-5 :
NYPL [Sc C 87-465]

WEST INDIANS - GREAT BRITAIN.
Forty winters on . [London] [1988?] 47 p. :
NYPL [Sc D 88-1202]

Pilkington, Edward. Beyond the mother country . London , 1988. 182 p. ; ISBN 1-85043-113-2 DDC 305.8/96/041 19
NYPL [Sc D 89-122]

Saunders, Dave. The West Indians in Britain /. London , 1984. 72 p. : ISBN 0-7134-4427-4
DA125.W4 S28x 1984 NYPL [Sc F 88-68]

WEST INDIANS - GREAT BRITAIN - BIOGRAPHY.
From where I stand /. London , 1987. 94 p. : ISBN 0-9956664-9-1 *NYPL [Sc C 88-30]*

WEST INDIANS - GREAT BRITAIN - SOCIAL CONDITIONS.
Britain's Black population . Aldershot, Hants, England , Brookfield, Vt., USA , c1988. xv, 298 p. ; ISBN 0-566-05179-6 : DDC 305.8/96/041 19
DA125.N4 B75 1988 NYPL [Sc E 89-100]

Dennis, Ferdinand, 1956- Behind the frontlines . London , 1988. xv, 216 p. ; ISBN 0-575-04098-X *NYPL [JLD 89-210]*

Lost illusions . London , 1988. x, 316 p. : ISBN 0-415-00628-7
NYPL [Sc D 88-1300]

The West Indians in Britain /. Saunders, Dave. London , 1984. 72 p. : ISBN 0-7134-4427-4
DA125.W4 S28x 1984 NYPL [Sc F 88-68]

WEST INDIANS IN LITERATURE.
Rahming, Melvin B., 1943- The evolution of
the West Indian's image in the Afro-American
novel /. Millwood, N.Y. , c1986. xix, 160 p. ;
ISBN 0-8046-9339-0 DDC
813/.009/35203969729 19
PS153.N5 R3 1985 *NYPL [JFD 86-6569]*

**WEST INDIANS IN THE UNITED STATES -
RELATIONS WITH AFRO-AMERICANS.
see AFRO-AMERICANS - RELATIONS
WITH WEST INDIANS.**

**WEST INDIANS - NETHERLANDS - SOCIAL
CONDITIONS.**
Lost illusions . London , 1988. x, 316 p. :
ISBN 0-415-00628-7
NYPL [Sc D 88-1300]

**WEST INDIANS - ONTARIO - TORONTO -
FICTION.**
Clarke, Austin, 1934- Nine men who laughed /.
Markham, Ontario, Canada , 1986. 225 p. ;
ISBN 0-14-008560-2 *NYPL [JFD 87-7697]*

**WEST INDIANS - SOCIAL LIFE AND
CUSTOMS - EXHIBITIONS.**
Nunley, John W. (John Wallace), 1945-
Caribbean festival arts . [Saint Louis] , 1988.
218 p. ; ISBN 0-295-96702-1 : DDC
394.2/5/07409729 19
GT4823 .N85 1988 *NYPL [Sc F 89-89]*

**WEST INDIANS - UNITED STATES -
FICTION.**
Cranmore, Frederick, 1948- The West Indian /.
Brooklyn , c1978. 122 p., [1] leaf of plates :
DDC 813/.5/4
PZ4.C8893 We PR9320.9.C7
NYPL [Sc D 88-37]

The West Indies as they are, or, A real picture
of slavery . Bickell, Richard. London , 1825.
xvi, 256 p. ; *NYPL [Sc Rare F 88-57]*

**WEST INDIES, BRITISH - EMIGRATION
AND IMMIGRATION - HISTORY.**
Newton, Velma. The silver men . Mona,
Kingston, Jamaica , 1984. xx, 218 p., [4] p. of
plates : DDC 325/.2729/07287 19
JV7429 .N49 1984 *NYPL [Sc D 89-478]*

**WEST INDIES, BRITISH - SOCIAL LIFE
AND CUSTOMS.**
Dirks, Robert, 1942- The Black Saturnalia .
Gainesville , c1987. xvii, 228 p., [7] p. of
plates : ISBN 0-8130-0843-3 (pbk. : alk. paper) :
DDC 394.2/68282/09729 19
GT4987.23 .D57 1987
NYPL [L-10 5328 no.72]

**WEST INDIES - DESCRIPTION AND
TRAVEL.**
Antilles Caraïbes /. Paris , c1982. 157 p. :
ISBN 2-7191-0177-0 *NYPL [Sc F 88-347]*

Berney, Henri-Maurice. Les Antillles . Paris ,
1977, c1972. 128 p. : ISBN 3-405-11035-1
NYPL [Sc F 89-34]

**WEST INDIES - DESCRIPTION AND
TRAVEL - 1981- - GUIDE-BOOKS.**
Runge, Jonathan. Rum and reggae . New
York , c1988. ix, 227 p. : ISBN 0-312-01509-7
(pbk.) : DDC 917.29/0452 19
F1613 .R86 1988 *NYPL [Sc D 88-1217]*

**WEST INDIES - DESCRIPTION AND
TRAVEL - EARLY WORKS TO 1800.**
Un Flibustier français dans la mer des Antilles
en 1618-1620 /. Clamart [France] , c1987. 263
p. : ISBN 2-9502053-0-5 *NYPL [Sc E 88-247]*

**WEST INDIES - DISCOVERY AND
EXPLORATION.**
Colón, Fernando, 1488-1539. [Historie.
English.] Christophe Colomb raconté par son
fils /. Paris , 1986. xviii, 265 p., [8] p. of
plates : ISBN 2-262-00387-4
NYPL [Sc D 88-504]

Un Flibustier français dans la mer des Antilles
en 1618-1620 /. Clamart [France] , c1987. 263
p. : ISBN 2-9502053-0-5 *NYPL [Sc E 88-247]*

WEST INDIES - DRAMA.
Baku, Shango. 3 plays of our time /. Belmont,
Trinidad , 1984. 116 p. ;
NYPL [Sc D 88-971]

WEST INDIES - ECONOMIC CONDITIONS.
Greenwood, R. (Robert) Emancipation to
emigration /. London , New York , 1980 (1985
printing) viii, 152 p. : ISBN 0-333-28148-9 (pbk.)

DDC 972.9 19
F1621 .G74 1984 *NYPL [Sc E 88-526]*

WEST INDIES - FICTION.
Humfrey, Michael. No tears for Massa's day /.
London , 1987. 192 p. ; ISBN 0-7195-4442-4 :
DDC 813 19
PR9265.9.H8 *NYPL [Sc D 88-623]*

Seaforth, Sybil. Growing up with Miss Milly /.
Ithaca, N.Y. , 1988. 129 p. ; ISBN
0-911565-04-3 *NYPL [Sc D 89-439]*

**WEST INDIES, FRENCH - BIBLIOGRAPHY -
CATALOGS.**
Archives de la Martinique. Bibliographie
relative aux Antilles . Fort-de-France , 1978-
v. ; DDC 016.97298/2 19
Z1502.F5 A72 1978 F2151
NYPL [Sc F 88-286]

**WEST INDIES, FRENCH - DESCRIPTION
AND TRAVEL - GUIDE-BOOKS.**
Calderon, Agostina. Evasions Antilles /.
[Pointe-à-Pitre , Paris , 1987] 223 p. :
NYPL [Sc D 88-998]

WEST INDIES, FRENCH - FICTION.
Burnet, Mireille. La chienne du quimboiseur /.
Paris , c1986. 126 p. ; ISBN 2-903033-81-1
NYPL [Sc D 89-168]

WEST INDIES, FRENCH - HISTORY.
Histoire des communes . [S.l.] , c1986. 6 v. :
ISBN 2-88218-800-4 (set) DDC 972.97/6 19
F2151 .H575 1986 *NYPL [Sc F 88-98]*

**WEST INDIES, FRENCH - HISTORY,
LOCAL.**
Histoire des communes . [S.l.] , c1986. 6 v. :
ISBN 2-88218-800-4 (set) DDC 972.97/6 19
F2151 .H575 1986 *NYPL [Sc F 88-98]*

**WEST INDIES, FRENCH - SOCIAL LIFE
AND CUSTOMS.**
Rosemain, Jacqueline, 1930- La musique dans
la société antillaise . Paris , c1986. 183 p. :
ISBN 2-85802-685-8 (pbk.)
NYPL [Sc E 88-394]

WEST INDIES - HISTORY.
Greenwood, R. (Robert) Emancipation to
emigration /. London , New York , 1980 (1985
printing) viii, 152 p. : ISBN 0-333-28148-9 (pbk.)
DDC 972.9 19
F1621 .G74 1984 *NYPL [Sc E 88-526]*

WEST INDIES - JUVENILE FICTION.
Olsen, Aileen. Bernadine and the water bucket
/. London , New York , 1966. [41] p. ;
NYPL [Sc F 88-99]

WEST INDIES - JUVENILE LITERATURE.
James, Winston. The Caribbean /. London ,
1984. 46 p. : ISBN 0-356-07105-7 : DDC 972.9
19
F2175 *NYPL [Sc F 88-128]*

WEST INDIES - LANGUAGES.
Roberts, Peter A. West Indians and their
language /. Cambridge [Cambridgeshire] , New
York , 1988. vii, 215 p. : ISBN 0-521-35136-7
DDC 427/.9729 19
P381.W47 R63 1988 *NYPL [Sc E 88-331]*

WEST INDIES - PANAMA - HISTORY.
Newton, Velma. The silver men . Mona,
Kingston, Jamaica , 1984. xx, 218 p., [4] p. of
plates : DDC 325/.2729/07287 19
JV7429 .N49 1984 *NYPL [Sc D 89-478]*

WEST INDIES - SOCIAL CONDITIONS.
Antilles Caraïbes /. Paris , c1982. 157 p. :
ISBN 2-7191-0177-0 *NYPL [Sc F 88-347]*

**WEST INDIES - SOCIAL LIFE AND
CUSTOMS.**
Caldwell, John C. Let's visit the West Indies.
London, Eng. , c1983. 96 p. : ISBN
0-222-00920-9 *NYPL [Sc D 89-19]*

West, John Hamilton. Gary, Lawrence E. The
delivery of mental health services to Black
children . Washington, D.C. , 1982. vi, 111, 19
p. ; *NYPL [Sc F 88-66]*

WEST (U. S.) - BIOGRAPHY.
Katz, William Loren. The Black West . Seattle,
WA , c1987. xiii, 348 p. : ISBN 0-940880-17-2
DDC 978/.00496073 19
E185.925 .K37 1987 *NYPL [Sc E 89-86]*

WEST (U. S.) - FICTION.
Davis, Levaster. Torture /. New York , c1987.
167 p. ; ISBN 0-533-07293-X
NYPL [Sc D 88-517]

WEST (U. S.) - HISTORY.
Katz, William Loren. The Black West /. Seattle,
WA , c1987. xiii, 348 p. : ISBN 0-940880-17-2
DDC 978/.00496073 19
E185.925 .K37 1987 *NYPL [Sc E 89-86]*

West Virginia. State College, Institute.
The public looks at higher education
[microform] : proceedings of faculty meeting,
January 28, 1959. Institute, W. Va. : The
College, 1959. 15 p. (West Virginia State College
bulletin. series 46, no. 5) Microfiche. New York:
New York Public Library, 198. 1 microfiche: negative; 11 x
15 cm. (FSN Sc 019,143)
*1. Public relations - Universities and colleges - West
Virginia. I. Title.* *NYPL [Sc Micro F-11,161]*

**WEST VIRGINIA. STATE COLLEGE,
INSTITUTE - FACULTY.**
Jordan, Lawrence V. Publications of the faculty
and staff of West Virginia State College
[microform] /. Institute , 1960. 23 p. ;
NYPL [Sc Micro F-11,160]

WESTBEECH, GEORGE.
Sampson, Richard, 1922- [Man with a
toothbrush in his hat.] The struggle for British
interests in Barotseland, 1871-88 /. Lusaka
[198-?] v, 158 p. : DDC 968.94/01 19
DT963.72.W47 S25 1980z
NYPL [Sc D 88-381]

WESTBROOK, JOHN.
Pennington, Richard, 1952- Breaking the ice .
Jefferson, N.C. , c1987. ix, 182 p. : ISBN
0-89950-295-4 : DDC 796.332/72/0973 19
GV939.A1 P46 1987 *NYPL [Sc E 88-35]*

Westchester County Historical Society. Caro,
Edythe Quinn. "The Hills" in the
mid-nineteenth century . Valhalla, New York ,
c1988. iii, 184 p. : *NYPL [Sc F 89-71]*

**WESTERN AND COUNTRY MUSIC. see
COUNTRY MUSIC.**

WESTERN ART. see ART.

Western Europe's migrant workers /. Power,
Jonathan, 1941- London , 1984. 35 p. : ISBN
0-08-030831-7 *NYPL [Sc F 88-231]*

WESTERN SAHARA - HISTORY - 1884-1975.
Oliver, Paula, 1962- Sáhara . Mallorca , 1987.
287 p. : ISBN 84-86366-56-9 DDC 964/.805 19
DT346.S7 O43 1987 *NYPL [Sc D 89-319]*

WESTERN SAHARA - HISTORY - 1975-
Oliver, Paula, 1962- Sáhara . Mallorca , 1987.
287 p. : ISBN 84-86366-56-9 DDC 964/.805 19
DT346.S7 O43 1987 *NYPL [Sc D 89-319]*

**WESTERN SAHARA - SOCIAL LIFE AND
CUSTOMS.**
Perregaux, Christiane. L'école sahraouie . Paris ,
c1987. 158 p., [8] p. of plates : ISBN
2-85802-942-3 DDC 372.964/8 19
LA2034.W47 P47 1987
NYPL [Sc D 89-401]

**Western State, Nigeria. Ministry of Economic
Planning and Social Development. Statistics
Division.** Report of a sample survey of
unemployment among school leavers
[microform / Ministry of Economic Planning
and Social Development, Statistics Division,
Ibadan, Western State of Nigeria. Ibadan : The
Division, [1966]- v. ; 25 cm. Cover title.
Microfiche. New York: New York Public Library, 198.
1 microfiche: negative; 11 x 15 cm. (FSN Sc 019,091)
*1. High school graduates - Employment - Nigeria -
Western State. 2. Elementary school students'
socio-economic status - Nigeria - Western State. 3.
Unemployed - Nigeria - Western State - Statistics. I.
Title.* *NYPL [Sc Micro F-10938]*

Westwood, Gwen. Narni of the desert. Illustrated
by Peter Warner. [Chicago] Rand McNally
[c1967] 93 p. illus. 21 cm. A little boy of the Bush
tribe of southern Africa wants most of all to be a
hunter. He catches a land tortoise, only to have it
escape, but ultimately leads his tribe to a great catch
which will feed his hungry peoples. SCHOMBURG
CHILDREN'S COLLECTION. DDC [Fic]
*1. San (African people) - Juvenile fiction. I. Warner,
Peter, 1939- illus. II. Schomburg Children's Collection.
III. Title.*
PZ7.W5275 Nar *NYPL [Sc D 88-1424]*

Wet, C. de. Bekker, S. B. Socio-economic survey
of the Amatola Basin . Grahamstown [South
Africa] Institute of Social and Economic
Rrsearch, 1981. 58, xxxxiv p. : ISBN
0-86810-073-0 *NYPL [Sc F 87-430]*

Wharton-Lake, Beverly D. Creative literature of Trinidad and Tobago ; a bibliography compiled by Beverly D. Wharton-Lake ; foreword by Val T. McComie. Washington, D.C. : Columbus Memorial Library, Organization of American States, 1988. xi, 102 p. ; 23 cm. (Hipólito Unanue bibliographic series . 4) Includes index. ISBN 0-8270-2709-5
1. Trinidad and Tobago literature (English) - Bibliography. I. Columbus Memorial Library. II. Title. III. Series. ***NYPL [Sc D 88-710]***

What are you figuring now? / Ferris, Jeri. Minneapolis , c1988. 64 p. ; ISBN 0-87614-331-1 (lib. bdg.) : DDC 520.92/4 B 92 19
QB36.B22 F47 1988 ***NYPL [Sc D 89-120]***

What Christianity demands of us at the present crisis . Boardman, Henry Augustus, 1808-1880. Philadelphia , 1860. 28 p. ;
NYPL [Sc Rare F 88-52]

What happened in Marston. Garden, Nancy. New York [1971] 190 p. DDC [Fic]
PZ7.G165 Wh ***NYPL [Sc D 89-98]***

What is apartheid? Geneva, Switzerland : World Alliance of Young Men's Christian Associations, [1986]. 72 p. : ill. ;23 cm.
1. Apartheid - South Africa. I. World Alliance of YMCAs. ***NYPL [Sc D 88-326]***

What school for Africa in the year 2000? /. Panafrican Conference on Education (1984 : Yaoundé, Cameroon) Morges, Switzerland [1984?] 190 p. ***NYPL [Sc D 88-611]***

What science? : problems of teaching and research in science in Nigerian universities / edited by F.M.A. Ukoli. Ibadan : Heinemann Educational Books (Nigeria) : Ibadan University Press, 1985. xvii, 321 p. : ill. ; 25 cm. Includes bibliographies. ISBN 978-12-9118-4 (pbk.) DDC 507/.11669 19
1. Science - Study and teaching (Higher) - Nigeria. 2. Research - Nigeria - Methodology. 3. Universities and colleges - Nigeria. I. Ukoli, F. M. A.
Q183.4.N5 W48 1985 ***NYPL [Sc E 88-402]***

What science knows about AIDS. [New York : Scientific American, Inc.], 1988. 152 p. : ill. ; 28 cm. Title from cover. Scientific American, v. 259, no. 4, Oct. 1988. "A single topic issue."
1. AIDS (Disease). ***NYPL [Sc F 89-163]***

Wheatle, Hiliary-Ann. Museums of the Institute of Jamaica / by Hiliary-Ann Wheatle and Joanne Creary ; edited by Lois Gayle. 1st ed. Kingston : JAMAL Foundation, 1982. 16 p. : ill. (chiefly col.) ; 21 cm.
1. Institute of Jamaica - Museums. 2. Museums - Jamaica. I. Creary, Joanne. II. Gayle, Lois. III. Title.
NYPL [Sc D 88-1173]

Wheatley, Phillis, 1753-1784.
[Works. 1988]
The collected works of Phillis Wheatley / edited with an essay by John C. Shields. New York : Oxford University Press, 1988. xl, 339 p. : port. ; 17 cm. (The Schomburg library of nineteenth-century Black women writers) Reprint. Originally published: London : Bell, c1773. ISBN 0-19-505241-2 (alk. paper) DDC 811/.1 19
1. Wheatley, Phillis, 1753-1784 - Correspondence. 2. Poets, American - 18th century - Correspondence. I. Shields, John, 1944-. II. Title. III. Series.
PS866 .W5 1988 ***NYPL [JFC 88-2142]***

[Poems]
The poems of Phillis Wheatley / edited with an introduction by Julian D. Mason, Jr. Rev. and enl. ed. Chapel Hill : University of North Carolina Press, c1989. xvi, 235 p. ; 24 cm. Includes index. Bibliography: p. 217-221. ISBN 0-8078-1835-6 (alk. paper) DDC 811/.1 19
I. Mason, Julian D. (Julian Dewey), 1931-. II. Title.
PS866 .W5 1989 ***NYPL [Sc E 89-205]***

WHEATLEY, PHILLIS, 1753-1784 - BIOGRAPHY - JUVENILE LITERATURE.
Richmond, M. A. (Merle A.) Phillis Wheatley /. New York , 1988. 111 p : ISBN 1-555-46683-4 DDC 811/.1 B 92 19
PS866.W5 Z683 1987 ***NYPL [Sc E 88-173]***

WHEATLEY, PHILLIS, 1753-1784 - CORRESPONDENCE.
Wheatley, Phillis, 1753-1784. [Works. 1988.] The collected works of Phillis Wheatley /. New York , 1988. xl, 339 p. : ISBN 0-19-505241-2 (alk. paper) DDC 811/.1 19
PS866 .W5 1988 ***NYPL [JFC 88-2142]***

When a child is motherless /. Okogba, Andrew. Benin City, Nigeria , 1987. v, 326 p. 19 cm.
ISBN 978-234-045-6 ***NYPL [Sc C 88-206]***

When borders don't divide : labor migration and refugee movements in the Americas / edited by Patricia R. Pessar.1st ed. Staten Island, N.Y. : Center for Migration Studies of New York, c1988. viii, 220 p. : ill. ; 24 cm. Includes bibliographical references and index. ISBN 0-934733-26-0 : DDC 325.8 19
1. Alien labor - America. 2. Refugees - America. 3. America - Emigration and immigration. I. Pessar, Patricia R.
JV7398 .W47 1988 ***NYPL [Sc E 89-169]***

When children want children . Dash, Leon. New York , c1989. 270 p. : ISBN 0-688-06957-6 DDC 306.7/088055 19
HQ759.4 .D37 1989 ***NYPL [Sc E 89-151]***

When Jim Crow met John Bull . Smith, Graham. London , c1987. 265 p. ; ISBN 1-85043-039-X
NYPL [Sc D 88-55]

When the denizen weeps . Lauture, Denize. [Cactus legend. Selections.] Bronx, N.Y. , c1988. vi, 98 p. ; ***NYPL [Sc D 89-80]***

When the marching stopped . Walton, Hanes, 1941- Albany , c1988. xxiv, 263 p. : ISBN 0-88706-687-9 DDC 353.0081/1 19
E185.615 .W325 1988 ***NYPL [Sc E 89-10]***

Where are the love poems for dictators? /. Miller, E. Ethelbert. Washington, DC , c1986. 91 p. : ISBN 0-940880-16-4 (pbk.) : DDC 811/.54 19
PS3563.I3768 W45 1986
NYPL [Sc D 88-383]

Where art is joy . Rodman, Selden, 1909- New York , c1988. 236 p. : ISBN 0-938291-01-7 : DDC 759.97294 19
N6606.5.P74 R64 1988
NYPL [3-MAM+ 89-6425]

Where did our love go? . George, Nelson. New York , c1985. xviii, 250 p., [32] p. of plates : ISBN 0-312-86698-4 : DDC 784.5/5/00973 19
ML3537 .G46 1985 ***NYPL [*LE 86-1451]***

Where shall we live? Commission on Race and Housing. Berkeley , 1958. ix, 77 p.
HD7293 .C6427 ***NYPL [Sc E 88-397]***

Where the good luck was. Molarsky, Osmond. New York [1970] 63 p. ISBN 0-8098-1158-8 DDC [Fic]
PZ7.M7317 Wh ***NYPL [Sc E 88-552]***

Where the leopard passes . Elliot, Geraldine. New York, 1987. x, 125 p. :
NYPL [Sc D 88-840]

Which path to freedom? : the Black anti-slavery debate, 1815-1860 / senior editor, Ralph E. Shaffer ; assistant editors, Ann Chiu ... [et al.]. Pomona, Calif. : School of Arts, California State Polytechnic University, c1986. iv, 60 p. ; 22 cm. DDC 973.7/114 19
1. Slavery - United States - Anti-slavery movements. 2. Afro-Americans - History - To 1863. 3. Abolitionists - United States - History - 19th century. 4. United States - Race relations. I. Shaffer, Ralph E. II. Chiu, Ann. III. California State Polytechnic University, Pomona. School of Arts.
E449 .W565 1986 ***NYPL [Sc D 88-1154]***

Whispers of dawn /. Bhajan, Selwyn. [Barbados? , c1978] (Barbados : Caribbean Graphics) iv, 52 p. :
MLCS 85/658 (P) ***NYPL [Sc D 88-792]***

Whisson, Michael G., 1937- Cherchez la femme: a study of the organisation of labour and the lives of workers on a tea estate / M.G. Whisson & C.W. Manona. Grahamstown [South Africa] : Institute of Social and Economic Research, Rhodes University, 1985. 90 p. [3] leaves of plates : ill. ; 30 cm. (Development studies . Working Paper no. 21) "February 1985." ISBN 0-86810-125-7
1. Tea plantation workers - South Africa. I. Manona, C. W. II. Title. III. Series. ***NYPL [Sc F 87-433]***

Whistelo, Alexander. (defendant) The Commissioners of the Alms-house, vs. Alexander Whistelo, a black man : being a remarkable case of bastardy, tried and adjudged by the Mayor, Recorder, and several aldermen, of the city of New York, under the act passed 6th March, 1801, for the relief of cities and towns from the maintenance of bastard children. New York : Published by David

Longworth, at the Shakspeare-Gallery, 1808. 56 p. ; 22 cm. Shaw & Shoemaker, 14750.
1. Afro-Americans - New York (N.Y.). 2. Almshouses - New York (N.Y.). 3. Illegitimacy - New York (N.Y.). 4. Paternity - New York (N.Y.). I. New York (N.Y.). Almshouse. II. New York (N.Y.). Commissioners of the Alms-house. III. Title. ***NYPL [Sc Rare F 88-21]***

WHITE FATHERS - MISSIONS - RWANDA.
Rutayisire, Paul. La christianisation du Rwanda (1900-1945) . Fribourg, Suisse , 1987. 571 p. : ISBN 2-8271-0371-0 (pbk.)
NYPL [Sc D 88-1510]

WHITE FATHERS - RWANDA - BIOGRAPHY.
Rutayisire, Paul. La christianisation du Rwanda (1900-1945) . Fribourg, Suisse , 1987. 571 p. : ISBN 2-8271-0371-0 (pbk.)
NYPL [Sc D 88-1510]

White, Garth. The development of Jamaican popular music with special reference to the music of Bob Marley : a bibliography / compiled by Garth White. Kingston : African-Caribbean Institute of Jamaica, 1982. 49 p. ; 28 cm. Cover title. Errata slip inserted. Music Division copy lacks errata slip. DDC 016.78/042/097292 19
1. Marley, Bob - Bibliography. 2. Music, Popular (Songs, etc.) - Jamaica - Bibliography. 3. Reggae music - Bibliography. I. Title.
ML120.J35 5 1982 ***NYPL [Sc F 87-61]***

White House Conference "To Fulfill These Rights", Washington, D. C., 1966. Major addresses at the White House Conference to Fulfill These Rights, June 1-2, 1966. [Washington, U. S. Govt. Print. Off., 1966] 66 p. 24 cm. Cover title: Speeches. Includes addresses by A. Philip Randolph, Thurgood Marshall, and Roy Wilkins. DDC 323.4/09174/96
1. Afro-Americans - Congresses. 2. Afro-Americans - Civil rights - Addresses, essays, lectures. I. Randolph, A. Philip (Asa Philip), 1889-. II. Marshall, Thurgood, 1908-. III. Wilkins, Roy, 1901-.
E185.615 .W45 1966c ***NYPL [Sc E 88-386]***

WHITE HOUSE (WASHINGTON, D.C.)
Seale, William. The president's house . Washington, D.C. , 1986. 2 v. (xx, 1224 p. [80] p. of plates : ISBN 0-912308-28-1 (set) DDC 975 19
F204.W5 S43 1986 ***NYPL [Sc E 89-183]***

White, J. M. Great Britain. Overseas Development Administration. Review of UK manpower and training aid to Nigeria /. [London? , 1984 or 1985] v, 72 p. :
NYPL [Sc F 88-185]

White, John, 1939- Billie Holiday, her life & times / John White. Tunbridge Wells, Kent : Spellmount Ltd. ; New York : Universe Books, 1987. 144 p. : ill. ; 26 cm. (Jazz life & times) Includes index. Bibliography: p. 136-142. ISBN 0-87663-668-7 (USA) DDC 784.5/3/00924 B 19
1. Holiday, Billie, 1915-1959. 2. Singers - United States - Biography. I. Title. II. Title: Billie Holiday, her life and times. III. Series.
ML420.H58 W5 1987 ***NYPL [JNF 88-88]***

White, Michael. (ill) Garlake, Peter S. Life at Great Zimbabwe /. Gweru, Zimbabwe , 1983, c1982. [36] p. : ISBN 0-86922-180-9 (pbk.) DDC 968.91 19
DT962.9.G73 G374 1983
NYPL [Sc F 88-175]

A white romance /. Hamilton, Virginia. New York , 1987. 191 p. ; ISBN 0-399-21213-2 : DDC [Fic] 19
PZ7.H1828 Wh 1987 ***NYPL [Sc D 88-221]***

White talk, black talk . Hewitt, Roger. Cambridge [Cambridgeshire] , New York , 1986. x, 253 p. ; ISBN 0-521-26239-9 DDC 401/.9/094216 19
P40.45.G7 H48 1986 ***NYPL [JFE 87-279]***

White, Welsh S., 1940- The death penalty in the eighties : an examination of the modern system of capital punishment / Welsh S. White. Ann Arbor : University of Michigan Press, c1987. 198 p. ; 24 cm. Includes bibliographies and index. ISBN 0-472-10088-2 (alk. paper) : DDC 345.73/0773 347.305773 19
1. Capital punishment - United States. I. Title.
KF9227.C2 W44 1987 ***NYPL [Sc E 88-129]***

Whiteley, Wilfred Howell. To plan is to choose / Wilfred H. Whiteley. Bloomington : Indiana University, African Studies Program, 1973. vii,

50 p. ; 23 cm. (Hans Wolff Memorial lecture)
Bibliography: p. 35-39. "Bibliography of the works of
Wilfred Howell Whiteley": p. 43-50.
1. Africa, East - Languages. I. Title.
NYPL [Sc D 88-213]

WHITES - AFRICA - BIOGRAPHY.
Boyles, Denis. African lives . New York ,
c1988. xi, 225 p., [8] p. of plates : ISBN
1-555-84034-5   DDC 960/.04034 19
DT16.W45 B69 1988   NYPL [Sc E 88-503]

**WHITES - AFRICA - SOCIAL LIFE AND
CUSTOMS.**
Boyles, Denis. African lives . New York ,
c1988. xi, 225 p., [8] p. of plates : ISBN
1-555-84034-5   DDC 960/.04034 19
DT16.W45 B69 1988   NYPL [Sc E 88-503]

Whitfield, Stephen J., 1942- A death in the
Delta : the story of Emmett Till / Stephen J.
Whitfield. New York : Free Press ; London :
Collier Macmillan, c1988. xiv, 193 p., [8] p. of
plates : ill. ; 24 cm. Includes index. Bibliography: p.
175-187.   ISBN 0-02-935121-9 :   DDC 345.73/02523
347.3052523 19
1. Milam, J. W. - Trials, litigation, etc. 2. Till, Emmett,
1941-1955. 3. Racism - Southern States - History - 20th
century. 4. Trials (Murder) - Mississippi - Sumner. 5.
Afro-Americans - Mississippi. 6. Southern States - Race
relations. I. Title.
E185.61 .W63 1989   NYPL [Sc E 89-140]

Whiting, William, 1813-1873. The war powers of
the President, and the legislative powers of
Congress in relation to rebellion, treason and
slavery / by William Whiting. 6th ed. Boston :
Published for the Emancipation League [by] J.
L. Shorey, 1863. vi, 143 p. ; 22 cm.
1. War and emergency powers - United States. I. Title.
NYPL [Sc Rare C 89-17]

Whitmore, George, 1945- Someone was here :
profiles in the AIDS epidemic / George
Whitmore. New York, N.Y. : New American
Library, c1988. 211 p. ; 23 cm. "NAL books."
ISBN 0-453-00601-9 :   DDC
362.1/969792/00924 19
1. AIDS (Disease) - Case studies. 2. AIDS (Disease) -
Social aspects. 3. AIDS (Disease) - Psychological
aspects. 4. AIDS (Disease) - Patients - Family
relationships. I. Title.
RC607.A26 W495 1988
NYPL [JLD 88-4435]

Whitney Houston /. Greenberg, Keith Elliot.
Minneapolis , c1988. 32 p. ; ISBN 0-8225-1619-5
(lib. bdg.) :   DDC 784.5/0092/4 B 92 19
ML3930.H7 G7 1988   NYPL [Sc D 88-1459]

Whittemore, Robert C. (Robert Clifton), 1921-
Ideology and American experience .
Washington, DC , c1986. vi, 294 p. ;   ISBN
0-88702-015-1 :   DDC 320.5/0973 19
E169.12 .I34 1986   NYPL [Sc E 89-74]

Whittier, John Greenleaf, 1807-1892.
Justice and expediency; or, Slavery considered
with a view to its rightful and effectual remedy,
abolition. By John G. Whittier ... New-York,
1833. [49]-63 p. 22 cm. (Anti-slavery reporter. v.1,
no.4)
1. Slavery in the United States - Controversial
literature - 1833. I. Title. II. Series.
E449 .A624   NYPL [Sc Rare F 98-1]

Pictures and stories from Uncle Tom's cabin.
Boston [c1853] [5],6-32p.
NYPL [Sc Rare C 89-1]

WHITTLING. see WOOD-CARVING.

Who are Lagosians? [microform] /. Akinsemoyin,
Kunle. [Lagos] 23 p. ;
NYPL [Sc Micro F-11129]

Who is Johnny? /. Gedö, Leopold. [Janiból Jonny
lesz. English.] New York , 1939. 242 p. :
NYPL [Sc D 88-1512]

Who is who in South African politics. Gastrow,
Shelagh. Who's who in South African politics /.
Johannesburg , 1985. xiv, 347 p. : ISBN
0-86975-280-4 (pbk.)   DDC 968.06/092/2 B 19
DT779.954 .G37 1985
NYPL [Sc D 87-1109]

Who was Marcus Garvey? /. ʿĪsá ʿAbd Allāh
Muḥammad al-Mahdī, 1945- [Brooklyn, N.Y.]
c1988. 101 p. :   *NYPL [Sc D 89-139]*

Who was Noble Drew Ali? /. Īs a Ābd All ah
Muḥammad al-Hahd i, 1945- [Brooklyn, N.Y.]
1988, c1980. 122 p. :   *NYPL [Sc D 89-74]*

Who was Noble Drew Ali? [microform] /. ʿĪsá
ʿAbd Allāh Muḥammad al-Mahdī, 1945-
Brooklyn, N.Y. [1980] 56 p. :
NYPL [Sc Micro R-4114 no. 10]

**Who was the prophet Muhammad? [microform]
/.** ʿĪsá ʿAbd Allāh Muḥammad al-Mahdī, 1945-
Brooklyn, N.Y. [1980] 96 p. :
NYPL [Sc Micro R-4114 no. 11]

Who'd a thought it . Leon, Eli. San Francisco,
CA , c1987. 87 p. :   *NYPL [Sc F 88-235]*

Who's who in South African politics /. Gastrow,
Shelagh. Johannesburg , 1985. xiv, 347 p. :
ISBN 0-86975-280-4 (pbk.)   DDC 968.06/092/2
B 19
DT779.954 .G37 1985
NYPL [Sc D 87-1109]

Whose side are you on? /. Moore, Emily. New
York , 1988. 133 p. ;   ISBN 0-374-38409-6
NYPL [Sc D 88-1330]

Why army rule? Proceedings of the colloquium
on Why army rule?. [Lagos? , 1986 or 19. 338
p. ;   *NYPL [Sc G 88-23]*

Why race riots [microform]? Brown, Earl Louis,
1900- [New York] 1944. cover-title, 31, [1] p.
F574.D4 B58   NYPL [Sc Micro R-3541]

Why the cock became a sacrificial animal /.
Umeh, Rich Enujioke. Enugu, Nigeria , 1985.
38 p. :   ISBN 978-239-648-6
NYPL [Sc C 89-18]

Why the sun was late /. Elkin, Benjamin. New
York , 1966. [40] p. :
PZ7.#426 Wh   NYPL [Sc F 88-105]

Why there are so many roads /. Appiah, Peggy.
Lagos , 1972. 62 p. :   *NYPL [Sc C 88-12]*

Why you should never be a Christian /. Sanni,
Ishaq Kunle. Ibadan, Nigeria , 1987. ix, 125 p. :
NYPL [Sc C 88-157]

**WHYTE, IKOLI HARCOURT, 1905-1977 -
DRAMA.**
Rotimi, Ola. Hopes of the living dead . Ibadan ,
c1988. xii, 112 p. ;   ISBN 978-246-013-3
NYPL [Sc C 89-138]

Wicker, Tom. United States. Kerner Commission.
The Kerner report . New York, N.Y. , 1988.
xxvi, 513 p. ;   ISBN 0-679-72078-2
NYPL [Sc D 89-604]

Wicomb, Zoë. You can't get lost in Cape Town /
Zo e Wicomb. New York : Pantheon Books,
c1987. 185 p. ; 21 cm. (A Pantheon modern writers
original)   ISBN 0-394-56030-2 :   DDC 823 19
1. Colored people (South Africa) - Fiction. 2. Cape
Town (South Africa) - Fiction. I. Title. II. Series.
PR9369.3.W53 Y6 1987
NYPL [Sc D 88-341]

Wideman, John Edgar.
The lynchers / John Edgar Wideman. 1st Owl
book ed. New York : H. Holt, 1986. 264 p. ;
21 cm.   ISBN 0-8050-0118-2 (pbk.) :   DDC 813/.54
19
1. Afro-Americans - Fiction. I. Title.
PS3573.I26 L9 1986   NYPL [Sc D 88-306]

Reuben : a novel / John Edgar Wideman.1st
ed. New York : H. Holt, c1987. 215 p. ; 24 cm.
ISBN 0-8050-0375-4   DDC 813/.54 19
1. Afro-Americans - Fiction. I. Title.
PS3573.I26 R4 1987   NYPL [JFE 88-3493]

Widgery, David. Beating time / David Widgery ;
design, Ruth Gregory, Andy Dark. London :
Chatto & Windus, 1986. 126 p. : ill. ; 23 cm. "A
Tigerstripe book." Includes index.   ISBN
0-7011-2985-9
1. Anti Nazi League (Great Britain). 2. National Front
(Great Britain). 3. Racism - Great Britain. 4. Rock
music - Social aspects - Great Britain. 5. Great Britain -
Race relations. I. Title.   *NYPL [JMD 88-112]*

Widmer, Charlotte. Afrika für dich . St. Gallen
[1986]. [43] p. :   *NYPL [Sc D 88-675]*

Widmer, Mary Lou. Garvey, Joan B. Beautiful
crescent . New Orleans, LA , c1988. 249 p. :
ISBN 0-9612960-0-3   *NYPL [Sc E 89-189]*

Wie ein Aas für Hunde . Mwangi, Meja, 1948-
[Carcase for hounds. German.]
Bornheim-Merten , 1987. 173 p. ;   ISBN
3-88977-136-X   *NYPL [Sc C 88-148]*

Wilber, Bob, 1928- Music was not enough / by
Bob Wilber ; assisted by Derek Webster. New
York : Oxford University Press, 1988. 216 p.

[8] p. of plates : ill. ; 25 cm. Includes discography
and index.   ISBN 0-19-520629-0
1. Jazz musicians - United States - Biography. I.
Webster, Derek. II. Title.   *NYPL [Sc E 89-6]*

WILBERFORCE UNIVERSITY.
Joiner, William A., 1868- A half century of
freedom of the Negro in Ohio. Xenia, Ohio
[1915] 134 p.   *NYPL [Sc Rare F 89-7]*

Wilcox, Thomas J. Burrell, Evelyn Patterson. Of
flesh and the spirit /. Bryn Mawr,
Pennsylvania , 1986. 101 p. :   ISBN
0-8059-3039-6   *NYPL [Sc D 88-300]*

Wild animal hunter /. Hubbard, Wynant Davis.
New York [1958] 148 p. :
NYPL [Sc D 88-1130]

WILD PLANTS, EDIBLE - KENYA.
Becker, Barbara. Wildpflanzen in der Ernährung
der Bevölkerung afrikanischer Trockengebiete .
Göttingen , 1984. iv, 341 p. :
NYPL [Sc D 88-682]

WILD PLANTS, EDIBLE - SENEGAL.
Becker, Barbara. Wildpflanzen in der Ernährung
der Bevölkerung afrikanischer Trockengebiete .
Göttingen , 1984. iv, 341 p. :
NYPL [Sc D 88-682]

**Wildpflanzen in der Ernährung der Bevölkerung
afrikanischer Trockengebiete .** Becker, Barbara.
Göttingen , 1984. iv, 341 p. :
NYPL [Sc D 88-682]

Wilkins, Frances. Let's visit The Gambia /
Frances Wilkins. London : Burke, 1985. 94 p. :
ill. (some col.), col. map ; 21 cm. Includes index.
ISBN 0-222-01129-7
1. Gambia - Social life and customs. I. Title.
NYPL [Sc D 88-405]

Wilkins, Roger W., 1932- Quiet riots . New
York , 1988. xiii, 223 p. :   ISBN 0-394-57473-7 :
DDC 305.5/69/0973 19
HV4045 .Q54 1988   NYPL [JLD 89-239]

Wilkins, Roy, 1901- White House Conference "To
Fulfill These Rights", Washington, D. C., 1966.
Major addresses at the White House
Conference to Fulfill These Rights, June 1-2,
1966. [Washington, 1966] 66 p.   DDC
323.4/09174/96
E185.615 .W45 1966c   NYPL [Sc E 88-386]

Wilkinson, William H. H. Granger, Lester
Blackwell, 1896- Toward job adjustment . [New
York] [1941] 78 p. :   *NYPL [Sc D 88-178]*

Will, pseud. see Lipkind, William, 1904-

Willaby /. Isadora, Rachel. New York , c1977.
[32] p. :   ISBN 0-02-747746-0   DDC [E]
PZ7.I763 Wi   NYPL [Sc F 88-374]

Willetts, Duncan. Amin, Mohamed, 1943- The
last of the Maasai . London , 1987. 185 p. :
ISBN 0-370-31097-7   *NYPL [Sc G 88-21]*

Willetts, Duncan, 1945- Amin, Mohamed, 1943-
Kenya . London , 1988. 191 p. :   ISBN
0-370-31225-2 :   DDC 967.6/204/0222 19
DT433.52   NYPL [Sc G 88-33]

William, Andy and Ramón. Buckley, Peter. 1966.
70 p.   *NYPL [Sc E 89-41]*

The William Smeal collection [microform].
1833-1908. ca. 100 items. Microfilm made from
originals located in the Glasgow Public Library.
Minutes, reports, correspondence, notes, articles and
pamplets concerned with the Glasgow Emancipation
Society and the anti-slavery movement in Britain.
Microfilm of mss. London : World Microfilms
Publications, 198? ll reels ; 35 mm.
1. Glasgow Emancipation Society (Strathclyde). 2.
Slavery - Great Britain - Anti-slavery movements -
Sources.   *NYPL [Sc Micro R-4837]*

Williams, Alfred Brockenbrough, 1856-1930. The
Liberian exodus; an account of voyage of the
first emigrants in the Bark "Azor" and their
reception at Monrovia, with a description of
Liberia - its customs and civilization, romances
and prospects; a series of letters from A. B.
Williams. Charleston, S.C., News and Courier
Book Presses, 1878. 62 p. 23 cm.
1. Afro-Americans - Colonization - Liberia. 2. Liberia -
Description and travel. 3. Sierra Leone - Description
and travel. I. Title.
E448 .W53   NYPL [Sc Rare F 88-58]

Williams, Brett. Upscaling downtown : stalled
gentrification in Washington, D.C. / Brett
Williams. Ithaca [N.Y.] : Cornell University

Press, 1988. xi, 157 p. : ill. ; 24 cm.
(Anthropology of contemporary issues) Includes index.
Bibliography: p. 145-153. ISBN 0-8014-2106-3 (alk.
paper) DDC 307.3/42/09753 19
*1. Urban renewal - Washington, D.C. 2. Central
business districts - Washington D. C. 3. Community
organization - Washington (D.C.). I. Title. II. Series.*
HT177.W3 W55 1988   **NYPL [Sc E 88-387]**

Williams, Carole A. The Black/white colleges .
Washington, D.C. , 1981. v, 46 p. :
          NYPL [Sc F 89-48]

Williams, David, 1913- Malami, Shehu, Alhaji.
Nigerian memories /. London , Ibadan , 1985.
xii, [139] p., [12] p. of plates : ISBN
978-16-7526-8 (Nigeria)
          NYPL [Sc D 88-532]

Williams, Eric Eustace, 1911- Clarke, A. M.
Verses for emancipation . [Port of Spain , 1986]
41 p. ; DDC 811 19
PR9272.9.C53 V4 1986
          NYPL [Sc D 88-981]

WILLIAMS, ERIC EUSTACE, 1911-
Clarke, A. M. Verses for emancipation . [Port
of Spain , 1986] 41 p. ; DDC 811 19
PR9272.9.C53 V4 1986
          NYPL [Sc D 88-981]

Williams, Fannie Barrier. (joint author)
Washington, Booker T. 1856-1915. A new
Negro for a new century. Miami, Fla., 1969.
428 p. DDC 301.45/22
E185 .W315 1969b   **NYPL [Sc D 89-43]**

Williams-Garcia, Ria. Blue tights / Ria
Williams-Garcia. 1st ed. New York : Lodestar
Books, c1987. 138 p. ; 22 cm. Growing up in a
city neighborhood, fifteen-year-old Joyce, unsure of
herself and not quite comfortable with her maturing
body, tries to find a place to belong and a way to
express herself through dance. ISBN 0-525-67234-6
DDC [Fic] 19
*1. Afro-American youth - Juvenile fiction. 2. Dancing -
New York (N.Y.) - Juvenile fiction. 3. City and town
life - Fiction. I. Title.*
PZ7.W6713 Bl 1987   **NYPL [Sc D 88-939]**

Williams, George Awoonor. see Awoonor, Kofi,
  1935-

Williams, Gwyneth, 1953- The dictionary of
contemporary politics of southern Africa /
Gwyneth Williams, Brian Hackland. London ;
New York : Routledge, 1988. xi, 339 p. : map ;
23 cm. (Dictionaries of contemporary politics)
Bibliography: p. [337]-339. ISBN 0-415-00245-1
DDC 320.968/03 19
*1. Africa, Southern - Politics and government -
Dictionaries. I. Hackland, Brian, 1951-. II. Title.*
JQ2720.A127 W55 1988   **NYPL [Sc D 89-2]**

Williams, John Alden. (ed) Islam. New York, G.
Braziller, 1961. 256 p. 21 cm. (Great religions of
modern man) Includes bibliography and index. DDC
297.082
I. Title.
BP161.2 .W5   **NYPL [Sc D 88-1044]**

Williams, John Alfred, 1925- !Click song : a
novel / by John A. Williams. New York :
Thunder's Mouth Press : Distributed by Persea
Books Inc., c1987. 430 p. ; 22 cm. ISBN
0-938410-43-1 : DDC 813/.54 19
*1. Afro-Americans - New York (N.Y.) - Fiction. I.
Title.*
PS3573.I4495 C5 1987
          NYPL [Sc D 88-1344]

Williams, Lincoln Octavious. Partial surrender :
race and resistance in the youth service /
Lincoln Octavious Williams. London ; New
York : Falmer Press, 1988. viii, 194 p. ; 25 cm.
(Issues in education and training series ; 10) Originally
presented as the author's thesis (M.A.)--King's College,
University of London. Includes index. Bibliography: p.
177-183. ISBN 1-85000-289-4 DDC
361.7/97/009421 19
*1. Social work with youth - England - London. 2.
Youth, Black - England - London - Attitudes. 3. Great
Britain - Race relations. I. Title. II. Series.*
HV1441.G8 L78 1988   **NYPL [Sc E 89-73]**

Williams, Richard, Ed. D. They stole it, but you
must return it / Richard Williams. Rochester,
New York : HEMA Pub., c1986. vii, 130 p. ;
22 cm. Bibliography: p. 127-130. ISBN
0-938805-00-2 (pbk.) DDC 306.8/5/08996073
19
1. Afro-Americans - Health and hygiene. I. Title.
E185.86 .W49 1986   **NYPL [Sc D 88-1308]**

Williams, Sherley Anne, 1944-
Dessa Rose / Sherley Anne Williams. 1st ed.
New York : W. Morrow, c1986. 236 p. ; 22
cm. ISBN 0-688-05113-8 : DDC 813/.54 19
*1. Slavery - United States - Fiction. 2. Women slaves -
United States - Fiction. I. Title.*
PS3573.I45546 D47 1986
          NYPL [JFD 86-8841]

Give birth to brightness; a thematic study in
neo-Black literature. New York, Dial Press,
1972. 252 p. 21 cm. Bibliography: p. 244-252.
*1. American literature - Afro-American authors -
History and criticism. I. Title.*
PS153.N5 W54   **NYPL [JFD 72-6307]**

A Williamsburg household /. Anderson, Joan.
New York, c1988. [48] p. : ISBN
     0-89919-516-4 : DDC [Fic] 19
PZ7.A5367 Wi 1988   **NYPL [Sc F 88-242]**

**WILLIAMSBURG (VA.) - SOCIAL LIFE AND
CUSTOMS - JUVENILE FICTION.**
Anderson, Joan. A Williamsburg household /.
New York, c1988. [48] p. : ISBN
     0-89919-516-4 : DDC [Fic] 19
PZ7.A5367 Wi 1988   **NYPL [Sc F 88-242]**

Williamson, Doug. Rosenblum, Mort. Squandering
Eden . San Diego , c1987. x, 326 p., [32] p. of
plates : ISBN 0-15-184860-2 : DDC 960/.3 19
GF701 .R67 1987   **NYPL [Sc E 88-24]**

Williamson, John, 1937- African debt and
financing /. Washington, D.C. , 1986. 223 p. :
     ISBN 0-88132-044-7 : DDC 336.3/435/096 19
HJ8826 .A36 1986   **NYPL [JLE 87-3261]**

Willie blows a mean horn /. Thomas, Ianthe,
1951- New York , c1981. 22 p. : ISBN
     0-06-026106-4 : DDC [E]
PZ7.T36693 Wi   **NYPL [Sc E 89-22]**

Willis, David P. Currents of health policy . New
York , 1987. 2 v. :   **NYPL [Sc D 88-1205]**

Willis, Priscilla D. The race between the flags /
Priscilla D. Willis ; illustrated by Carl Kidwell.
New York : Longmans, Green, 1955. 177 p. :
ill. ; 21 cm.
*1. Steeplechasing - Juvenile fiction. 2. Afro-American
youth - Juvenile fiction. I. Title.*
          NYPL [Sc D 88-1508]

Willis, R. Ellen. Harrison, Alice W., 1929- The
conservation of archival and library materials .
Metuchen, N.J. , 1982. xi, 190 p. ; ISBN
     0-8108-1523-0 DDC 025.8/4 19
Z701 .H28   **NYPL [Cons. Div. 84-252]**

Willis-Thomas, Deborah, 1948- An illustrated
bio-bibliography of Black photographers,
1940-1988 / Deborah Willis-Thomas. New
York : Garland, 1989. xiv, 483 p. : ill. ; 29 cm.
(Garland reference library of the humanities. vol. 760)
Includes index. Bibliography: p. 475-478. ISBN
     0-8240-8389-X (alk. paper) DDC 770/.92/2 19
*1. Photography - Bio-bibliography. 2. Afro-American
photographers. I. Title.*
TR139 .W55 1988   **NYPL [Sc F 89-156]**

Willmore, Brigid. Social development and rural
fieldwork . Zimbabwe [1986]. 96 p. ;
          NYPL [Sc D 88-1153]

Wills, A. J. (Alfred John) An introduction to the
history of central Africa : Zambia, Malawi, and
Zimbabwe / A.J. Wills.4th ed. Oxford
[Oxfordshire] ; New York : Oxford University
Press, 1985. xiii, 556 p. : maps ; 22 cm. Includes
index. Bibliography: p. [521]-533. ISBN
     0-19-873075-6 : DDC 968.9 19
*1. Zambia - History. 2. Malawi - History. 3.
Zimbabwe - History. I. Title.*
DT963.5 .W54 1985   **NYPL [Sc D 88-656]**

Wilma Rudolph /. Biracree, Tom, 1947- New
York , 1988. 111 p. : ISBN 1-555-46675-3 DDC
     796.4/2/0924 B 92 19
GV697.R8 B57 1988   **NYPL [Sc E 88-172]**

Wilmer, Valerie. The face of Black music ;
photographs / by Valerie Wilmer ; introduction
by Archie Shepp. New York : Da Capo Press,
1976. [118] p. : ill. ; 28 cm. ISBN
     0-306-70756-X. DDC 780/.92/2 B
*1. Afro-American musicians - Portraits. 2. Jazz
musicians - Portraits. I. Title.*
ML87 .W655   **NYPL [Sc F 88-207]**

Wilson, Amrit, 1941- US foreign policy and
revolution : the creation of Tanzania / Amrit
Wilson ; introduction by A.M. Babu. London :
Pluto Press ; distributed in the USA by Unwin
Hyman, 1989. ix, 179 p. ; 23 cm. Includes index.

ISBN 1-85305-051-2
*1. Tanzania - Politics and government - 1964-. 2.
United States - Foreign relations - Tanzania. 3.
Tanzania - Foreign relations - United States. 4.
Zanzibar - Politics and government - To 1964. I. Title.
II. Title: U. S. foreign policy and revolution.*
          NYPL [Sc D 89-426]

Wilson, Basil, 1943- Green, Charles (Charles St.
Clair) The struggle for black empowerment in
New York City . New York , 1989. xvi, 183
p. : ISBN 0-275-92614-1 (alk. paper) : DDC
     974.7/100496073 19
F128.9.N3 G74 1989   **NYPL [Sc E 89-203]**

WILSON, BENJAMIN, 1967-1984.
Wilson, Mary, 1938- To Benji, with love /.
Chicago , c1987. p. cm. ISBN 0-910671-07-9 :
DDC 977.3/11043/0924 B 19
F548.9.N4 W559 1987
          NYPL [Sc D 88-1219]

Wilson, David, 1818-1887. Northup, Solomon, b.
1808. Twelve years a slave . New York , 1857.
336 p. :   **NYPL [Sc Rare C 89-34]**

Wilson, Eileen B. Psychology and society .
[Ife?] , 1986. 212 p. ;   **NYPL [Sc E 88-432]**

Wilson, Ernest J. Ray, Walter I. The pilgrimage
of 2 friends . Silver Spring, Md. , 1984. v, 80
p. ;   **NYPL [Sc F 87-440]**

Wilson, James L. (James Lynwood) Clementine
Hunter, American folk artist / James L. Wilson.
Gretna : Pelican Pub. Co., 1988. 160 p. : ill. ;
23 x 27 cm. Includes index. Bibliography: p. 155-158.
     ISBN 0-88289-658-X DDC 759.13 B 19
*1. Hunter, Clementine. 2. Afro-American painting -
Louisiana - Natchitoches. 3. Primitivism in art -
Louisiana - Natchitoches. 4. Painting, Modern - 20th
century - Louisiana - Natchitoches. I. Title.*
ND237.H915 A4 1988   **NYPL [Sc F 89-94]**

Wilson, Johnniece Marshall. Oh, brother /
Johnniece Marshall Wilson. New York :
Scholastic, c1988. 121 p. ; 22 cm. Alex's older
brother bullies him, taking his bicycle and his money,
until Alex discovers a way to stand up for himself.
     ISBN 0-590-41363-5 : DDC [Fic] 19
1. Afro-American youth - Juvenile fiction. I. Title.
PZ7.W696514 Oh 1988
          NYPL [Sc D 88-699]

Wilson, Joy Carter. Poems for Afrika's children /
by Joy Carter Wilson. South Framingham,
Mass. : J. C. Wilson, c1975. 30 p. : ill., port. ;
22 x 28 cm. SCHOMBURG CHILDREN'S
COLLECTION.
I. Schomburg Children's Collection. II. Title.
          NYPL [Sc D 89-183]

Wilson, M. L. (Matthew Lawrence), 1960-
Chester Himes / M.L. Wilson. New York :
Chelsea House, c1988. 111 p. : ill. ; 25 cm.
(Black Americans of achievement) Includes index.
Bibliography: p. 108. ISBN 1-555-46591-9 DDC
     813/.54 B 92 19
*1. Himes, Chester B., 1909- - Biography - Juvenile
literature. 2. Novelists, American - 20th century -
Biography - Juvenile literature. 3. Novelists, American -
20th century - Biography. 4. Afro-American novelists -
Biography - Juvenile literature. I. Title. II. Series.*
PS3515.I713 Z93 1988 **NYPL [Sc E 88-373]**

Wilson, Mary, 1938-
To Benji, with love / by Mary Wilson with Lee
Blackwell. Chicago : Path Press : Distributed by
Chicago Review Press, c1987. p. cm. ISBN
     0-910671-07-9 : DDC 977.3/11043/0924 B 19
*1. Wilson, Benjamin, 1967-1984. 2. Wilson, Mary,
1938- - Family. 3. Afro-Americans - Illinois - Chicago -
Biography. 4. Murder - Illinois - Chicago. 5. Chicago
(Ill.) - Biography. I. Blackwell, Lee. II. Title.*
F548.9.N4 W559 1987
          NYPL [Sc D 88-1219]

WILSON, MARY, 1938- - FAMILY.
Wilson, Mary, 1938- To Benji, with love /.
Chicago , c1987. p. cm. ISBN 0-910671-07-9 :
DDC 977.3/11043/0924 B 19
F548.9.N4 W559 1987
          NYPL [Sc D 88-1219]

Wilson-Tagoe, Nana. Dabydeen, David. A
reader's guide to West Indian and black British
literature /. London , 1988. 182 p. ; ISBN
     1-87051-835-7 (pbk) DDC 810.9/9729 19
PR9210   **NYPL [Sc C 89-363]**

Wiltse, Charles Maurice, 1907- (ed) Walker,
David, 1785-1830. David Walker's appeal, in
four articles, together with a preamble, to the

coloured citizens of the world, but in particular, and very expressly, to those of the United States of America. New York [1965] xii, 78 p.
DDC 326.973
E446 .W178   *NYPL [Sc D 89-456]*

Wimpfen, François Alexandre Stanislaus, baron de. see **Wimpffen, François Alexandre Stanislaus, baron de.**

Wimpffen, Alexandre Stanislaus, baron de. see **Wimpffen, François Alexandre Stanislaus, baron de.**

Wimpffen, François Alexandre Stanislaus, baron de. A voyage to Saint Domingo, in the years 1788, 1789, and 1790. Translated from the original manuscript, which has never been published, by J. Wright. London, Printed for T. Cadell, Jr., W. Davies, and J. Wright, 1817 [i. e. 1797] 371 p. 1 fold. map. 22 cm. The French original was published in Paris, 1797, under title: Voyage à Saint-Domingue, pendant les années 1788, 1789 et 1790. FISHER COLLECTION
1. Haiti - Description and travel. I. Wright, John, 1770?-1844, tr. II. Title.
NYPL [Sc 917.294-W]

Winch, Julie, 1953- Philadelphia's Black elite : activism, accommodation, and the struggle for autonomy, 1781-1848 / Julie Winch. Philadelphia : Temple University Press, 1988. x, 240 p. ; 24 cm. Includes index. Bibliography: p.215-230. ISBN 0-87722-515-X (alk. paper) : DDC 974.8/1100496073 19
1. Afro-Americans - Pennsylvania - Philadelphia - History. 2. Elite (Social sciences) - Pennsylvania - Philadelphia - History. 3. Philadelphia (Pa.) - History. I. Title.
F158.9.N4 W56 1988   *NYPL [Sc E 88-198]*

Windeatt, Mary Fabyan, 1910- Lad of Lima : the story of Blessed Martin de Porres / by Mary Fabyan Windeatt. New York : Sheed & Ward, 1942. 152 p. : ill. ; 17 cm. SCHOMBURG CHILDREN'S COLLECTION.
1. Martin de Porres, Saint, 1579-1639 - Juvenile literature. 2. Christian saints - Peru - Biography - Juvenile literature. I. Schomburg Children's Collection. II. Title.   *NYPL [Sc D 88-1170]*

Window series.
(1) Brown, Alex. Southern Africa. Ottawa [1973] 43 p.
DT746 .B76   *NYPL [JLD 75-1128]*

Winds against my people /. Fashagba, S. O. Ilorin [198-] 57 p. :   *NYPL [Sc C 88-353]*

Windward Islands letters patent and additional instructions [microform] St. Lucia. [Saint Lucia? , 1955?] [17] p. ;
NYPL [Sc Micro F-10,886]

WINDWARD ISLANDS - POLITICS AND GOVERNMENT.
St. Lucia. Windward Islands letters patent and additional instructions [microform] [Saint Lucia? , 1955?] [17] p. ;
NYPL [Sc Micro F-10,886]

Winegarten, Ruthe. Texas women : a pictorial history : from Indians to astronauts / Ruthe Winegarten.1st ed. Austin, Tex. : Eakin Press, [1986] ix, 187 p. : ill. ; 29 cm. Includes index. Bibliography: p. 173-176. ISBN 0-89015-532-1 : DDC 305.4/09764 19
1. Women - Texas - History. 2. Women - Employment - Texas - History. 3. Women in politics - Texas - History. I. Title.
HQ1438.T4 W56 1986   *NYPL [Sc F 87-41]*

Winfield . Winfield, Dave, 1951- New York , c1988. 314 p., [22] p. of plates : ISBN 0-393-02467-9 : DDC 796.357/092/4 B 19
GV865.W57 A3 1988
NYPL [JFD 88-11493]

Winfield, Dave, 1951- Winfield : a player's life / Dave Winfield with Tom Parker. New York : Norton, c1988. 314 p., [22] p. of plates : ill. ; 22 cm. ISBN 0-393-02467-9 : DDC 796.357/092/4 B 19
1. Winfield, Dave, 1951-. 2. New York Yankees (Baseball team). 3. Baseball players - United States - Biography. 4. Afro-American baseball players - Biography. I. Parker, Tom, 1943-. II. Title.
GV865.W57 A3 1988
NYPL [JFD 88-11493]

WINFIELD, DAVE, 1951-
Winfield, Dave, 1951- Winfield . New York , c1988. 314 p., [22] p. of plates : ISBN

0-393-02467-9 : DDC 796.357/092/4 B 19
GV865.W57 A3 1988
NYPL [JFD 88-11493]

Winnie Mandela . Haskins, James, 1941- New York , c1988. 179 p., [12] p. of plates : ISBN 0-399-21515-8 DDC 968.06/092/4 B 92 19
DT779.955.M36 H38 1988
NYPL [Sc D 88-1138]

Winnin' times . Ostler, Scott. New York , c1988. 304 p. ; ISBN 0-02-029591-X (pbk.) DDC 796.32/364/0979494 19
GV885.52.L67 O87 1986
NYPL [Sc D 89-106]

Winslow Homer's images of Blacks . Wood, Peter H., 1943- Austin , c1988. 144 p. : ISBN 0-292-79047-3 (University of Texas Press) DDC 759.13 19
ND237.H7 A4 1988a   *NYPL [Sc F 89-133]*

Winston, Henry. Africa's struggle for freedom, the USA and the USSR . New York , 1972. 96 p. : ISBN 0-87898-096-2   *NYPL [Sc C 88-139]*

Winter epigrams & Epigrams to Ernesto Cardinal in defense of Claudia /. Brand, Dionne, 1953- Toronto , 1983. 38 p. ; ISBN 0-88795-022-1 :
NYPL [Sc D 88-1207]

Winter, Jeanette. Follow the drinking gourd / story and pictures by Jeanette Winter. New York : Knopf, c1988. [48] p. : col. ill., music ; 27 cm. By following the directions in a song, "The Drinking Gourd," taught them by an old sailor named Peg Leg Joe, runaway slaves journey north along the Underground Railroad to freedom in Canada. ISBN 0-394-89694-7 : DDC [E] 19
1. Fugitive slaves - United States - Juvenile fiction. 2. Underground Railroad - Juvenile fiction. I. Title.
PZ7.W7547 Fo 1988   *NYPL [Sc F 89-59]*

Wintz, Cary D., 1943- Black culture and the Harlem Renaissance / Cary D. Wintz. Houston, Tex. : Rice University Press, 1988. 277 p. ; 24 cm. Includes bibliographic notes and index. ISBN 0-89263-267-4 : DDC 810/.9/896073 19
1. American literature - Afro-American authors - History and criticism. 2. American literature - New York (N.Y.) - History and criticism. 3. American literature - 20th century - History and criticism. 4. Harlem Renaissance. 5. Afro-Americans in literature. 6. Afro-Americans - Intellectual life. 7. Afro-American arts - New York (N.Y.). I. Title.
PS153.N5 W57 1988   *NYPL [Sc E 89-106]*

Wise, Leonard. Doc's legacy / by Leonard Wise. New York : Richardson & Steirman, c1986. 410 p. ; 24 cm. ISBN 0-931933-16-1
1. Vietnamese Conflict, 1961-1975 - Fiction. 2. Iowa - Fiction. I. Title.   *NYPL [JFE 86-5265]*

WIT AND HUMOR, AFRO-AMERICAN. see **AFRO-AMERICAN WIT AND HUMOR.**

WIT AND HUMOR, JEWISH. see **JEWISH WIT AND HUMOR.**

The wit and wisdom of Fat Albert. Cosby, William H. New York [1973] [64] p. ISBN 0-525-61004-9 DDC 818/.5/407
PZ8.7.C6 Wi   *NYPL [Sc C 89-26]*

WITCHCRAFT - MALI.
McNaughton, Patrick R. The Mande blacksmiths . Bloomington , c1988. xxiv, 241 p., [4] p. of plates : ISBN 0-253-33683-X DDC 306/.089963 19
DT551.45.M36 M38 1988
NYPL [Sc E 88-393]

WITCHCRAFT - MASSACHUSETTS - SALEM - FICTION.
Condé, Maryse. Moi, Tituba, sorcière-- . Paris , c1986. 276 p. ; ISBN 2-7152-1440-5
NYPL [Sc E 88-97]

WITCHCRAFT - WEST INDIES.
Ebroïn, Ary. Quimbois, magie noire et sorcellerie aux Antilles . Paris , c1977. 239 p., [4] leaves of plates : DDC 133.4/09729
BF1622.W47 E26   *NYPL [Sc D 89-270]*

Witherell, Julian W. French-speaking central Africa; a guide to official publications in American libraries / compiled by Julian W. Witherell, African Section. Washington, General Reference and Bibliography Division, Library of Congress; [for sale by the Supt. of Docs., U. S. Govt. Print. Off.] 1973. xiv, 314 p. 26 cm. ISBN 0-8444-0033-5
1. Catalogs, Union - United States. 2. Africa, French-speaking Equatorial - Government publications - Bibliography - Union lists. 3. Zaire - Government

publications - Bibliography - Union lists. 4. Burundi - Government publications - Bibliography - Union lists. 5. Rwanda - Government publications - Bibliography - Union lists. I. United States. Library of Congress. African Section. II. Title.
Z3692 .W5   *NYPL [JLF 74-197]*

Within the plantation household . Fox-Genovese, Elizabeth, 1941- Chapel Hill , c1988. xvii, 544 p. : ISBN 0-8078-1808-9 (alk. paper) DDC 305.4/0975 19
HQ1438.A13 F69 1988   *NYPL [JLE 89-21]*

WITNESSES, EXPERT. see **EVIDENCE, EXPERT.**

Witnesses to tears . Gimba, Abubakar. Enugu , 1986. 170 p. ; ISBN 978-233-521-5
NYPL [Sc C 88-208]

The wizard's pride and other poems /. Egblewogbe, E. Y., 1934- Tema, Ghana , 1986, c1974. xiii, 40 p. ; ISBN 996-410-128-7
NYPL [Sc C 88-351]

Wo die Sonne wohnt /. Babing, Alfred. Berlin , 1985. 368 p. :   *NYPL [Sc D 89-72]*

Wo Menschen lachen und sich frauen . Balling, Adalbert Ludwig. Freiburg im Breisgau , c1986. 126 p. ; ISBN 3-451-08297-7
NYPL [Sc C 89-125]

Wolbert, Klaus, 1940- That's jazz, der Sound des 20. Jahrhunderts . [Darmstadt , 1988] xv, 723 p. : ISBN 781/.57/0740341 19
ML141.D3 I6 1988   *NYPL [JMF 89-297]*

Wole Soyinka . Maduakor, Obi. New York , c1987, 1986. xv, 339 p. : ISBN 0-8240-9141-8 (alk. paper) DDC 822 19
PR9387.9.S6 Z77 1987   *NYPL [Sc D 88-643]*

Wole Soyinka, three short plays . Dunton, C. P. Harlow, Essex , Beirut , 1982. 71 p. ; ISBN 0-582-78260-0   *NYPL [Sc D 88-159]*

Wolfe, David. Adult education in Antigua and Barbuda : a directory of opportunities and resources / compiled and edited by David Wolfe.2nd ed. St. John's, Antigua : U.W.I., Dept. of Extra-Mural Studies (Antigua), 1985. 61 p. ; 25 cm. Includes index. DDC 379/.97297/4 19
1. Adult education - Antigua and Barbuda - Directories. I. Title.
L912.A63 W65 1983   *NYPL [Sc E 88-119]*

Wolfe, Tom. The bonfire of the vanities / [Tom Wolfe]. New York : Farrar, Straus, 1987. 659 p. ; 25 cm. ISBN 0-374-11534-6 : DDC 813/.54 19
1. Afro-Americans - New York (N.Y.) - Fiction. 2. New York (N.Y.) - Fiction. I. Title.
PS3573.O526 B6 1987   *NYPL [Sc E 88-389]*

Wolff, Lester L. Diggs, Charles C. Report of Special Study Mission to Southern Africa, August 10-30, 1969/. Washington , 1969. vi, 179 p. : DDC 301.29'68'073
DT733.D5   *NYPL [Sc E 89-39]*

Woll, Allen. Black musical theatre : from Coontown to Dreamgirls / Allen Woll. Baton Rouge : Louisiana State University Press, c1989. xiv, 301 p. : ill. ; 24 cm. Includes index. Bibliography: p. [279]-285. ISBN 0-8071-1469-3 DDC 782.81/08996073 19
1. Musical revue, comedy, etc. - United States. 2. Afro-Americans - Music - History and criticism. I. Title.
ML1711 .W64 1989   *NYPL [Sc E 89-198]*

Woll, Allen L. Ethnic and racial images in American film and television : historical essays and bibliography / Allen L. Woll, Randall M. Miller. New York : Garland, 1987. xv, 408 p. ; 23 cm. (Garland reference library of social science. vol. 308) Includes indexes. ISBN 0-8240-8733-X (alk. paper) DDC 016.79143/09/093520693 19
1. Minorities in motion pictures - United States - Bibliography. 2. Minorities in television - United States - Bibliography. 3. Minorities in motion pictures - United States. 4. Minorities in television - United States. I. Miller, Randall M. II. Title.
Z5784.M9 W65 1987 PN1995.9.M56
NYPL [MFL 87-3104]

WOLOF LANGUAGE - PHONOLOGY.
Dialo, Amadou. Une phonologie du wolof /. [Dakar] , 1981. 60 leaves ;
NYPL [Sc F 86-167]

WOLOF LANGUAGE - TEXTS.
Diop, Adja Khady, 1922- Le Sénégal d'hier et
ses traditions /. [S.l.] [198-?] 61, 18 p. :
NYPL [Sc D 88-933]

WOLOFS - FICTION.
Diallo, Nafissatou, 1941- Fary, princess of Tiali
/. Washington, D.C., c1987. xi, 106 p. : ISBN
0-89410-411-X   *NYPL [Sc D 88-1366]*

Wolpe, Harold. Race, class & the apartheid state
/ Harold Wolpe. London : Currey, 1988. viii,
118 p. ; 22 cm. (Apartheid & society) Bibliography:
p. 114-118. ISBN 0-85255-319-6 (pbk.) DDC
305.8/968 19
*1. Apartheid - Social aspects - South Africa. I. Title. II.
Title: Race, class and the apartheid state.*
DT763   *NYPL [JLD 88-3222]*

WOMAN. see WOMEN.

The woman co-operator & development . Meghji,
Zakia. Nairobi , 1985. iv, 127 p. ; DDC
334/.088042 19
HD3561.9.A4 M44 1985
                    NYPL [Sc C 88-92]

Woman co-operator and development. Meghji,
Zakia. The woman co-operator & development .
Nairobi , 1985. iv, 127 p. ; DDC 334/.088042 19
HD3561.9.A4 M44 1985
                    NYPL [Sc C 88-92]

Woman in ancient Africa /. Loth, Heinrich. [Frau
im Alten Afrika. English.] Westport, Conn. ,
c1987. 189 p. : ISBN 0-88208-218-3 DDC
305.4/096 19
HQ1137.A35 L6813 1987
                    NYPL [Sc F 88-132]

Woman of ancient Africa /. Loth, Heinrich. [Frau
im Alten Afrika. English.] Westport, Conn. ,
c1987. 189 p. : ISBN 0-88208-218-3 DDC
305.4/096 19
HQ1137.A35 L6813 1987
                    NYPL [Sc F 88-114]

Woman of my uncle /. Lu, Gorzef. Lusaka ,
1985. iv, 236 p. ;
MLCS 87/7908 (P)   *NYPL [Sc C 89-94]*

Woman of the aeroplanes. Laing, B. Kojo.
London , 1988. 196 p. ; ISBN 0-434-40218-4 :
DDC 823 19   *NYPL [Sc E 89-120]*

A WomanSleuth mystery.
Komo, Dolores. Clio Browne . Freedom, Calif. ,
c1988. 193 p. ; ISBN 0-89594-320-4 (pbk.) :
DDC 813/.54 19
PS3561.O4545 C55 1988
                    NYPL [Sc C 89-50]

The Womanspirit sourcebook : a catalog of books,
periodicals, music, calendars & tarot cards,
organizations, video & audio tapes, bookstores,
interviews, meditations, art / [edited] by Patrice
Wynne.1st ed. San Francisco : Harper & Row,
c1988. xxv, 277 p. : ill. ; 28 cm. Includes index.
   ISBN 0-06-250982-9 (pbk.) : DDC 291/.088042
19
*1. Women - Religious life. 2. Women - Religious life -
Bibliography - Catalogs. 3. Women - Religious life -
Audio-visual aids - Catalogs. I. Wynne, Patrice.*
BL458 .W575 1988 *NYPL [Sc F 88-294]*

WOMEN - AFRICA - BIBLIOGRAPHY.
Bullwinkle, Davis. African women, a general
bibliography, 1976-1985 /. New York , 1989.
xx, 334 p. ; ISBN 0-313-26607-7 (lib. bdg. : alk.
paper) DDC 016.3054/096 19
Z7964.A3 B84 1989 HQ1787
                    NYPL [Sc E 89-173]

WOMEN - AFRICA - CONGRESSES.
Regional Seminar for Africa (Mogadishu :
1975) On African women's equality, role in
national liberation, development and peace .
[Mogadishu] , 1975. 123 p. :
                    NYPL [Sc E 88-138]

WOMEN - AFRICA - HISTORY.
Loth, Heinrich. [Frau im Alten Afrika. English.]
Woman in ancient Africa /. Westport, Conn. ,
c1987. 189 p. : ISBN 0-88208-218-3 DDC
305.4/096 19
HQ1137.A35 L6813 1987
                    NYPL [Sc F 88-132]

Loth, Heinrich. [Frau im Alten Afrika. English.]
Woman of ancient Africa /. Westport, Conn. ,
c1987. 189 p. : ISBN 0-88208-218-3 DDC
305.4/096 19
HQ1137.A35 L6813 1987
                    NYPL [Sc F 88-114]

Pala, Achola O. [Femme africaine dans la
société précoloniale. Spanish.] La mujer africana
en la sociedad precolonial /. Barcelona
[Paris?] , 1982. 238 p. ; ISBN 84-85800-35-4
(Serbal)   *NYPL [Sc D 88-833]*

**WOMEN - AFRICA, SOUTHERN -
   HISTORY - SOURCES.**
Women in development . Gaborone , 1984. 49,
4 p. :   *NYPL [Sc F 88-116]*

WOMEN - AFRICA, SUB-SAHARAN.
Children, youth, women and development plans
in West and Central Africa . Abidjan [1972?]
152 p. ;   *NYPL [Sc E 88-105]*

**WOMEN - AFRICA, SUB-SAHARAN -
   BIOGRAPHY.**
Life histories of African women /. London ,
Atlantic Highlands, NJ , 1988. 200 p. : ISBN
0-948660-04-X DDC 305.4/0967 19
HQ1787.A3 L54 1988
                    NYPL [Sc D 88-1469]

**WOMEN - AFRICA, SUB-SAHARAN -
   HISTORY.**
L'Histoire des femmes en Afrique /. Paris ,
c1987. 164 p. : ISBN 2-7384-0172-4
                    NYPL [Sc E 89-226]

**WOMEN - AFRICA, SUB-SAHARAN -
   SOCIAL CONDITIONS - CASE
   STUDIES.**
Life histories of African women /. London ,
Atlantic Highlands, NJ , 1988. 200 p. : ISBN
0-948660-04-X DDC 305.4/0967 19
HQ1787.A3 L54 1988
                    NYPL [Sc D 88-1469]

**WOMEN - AFRICA, WEST - ECONOMIC
   CONDITIONS.**
Improved village technology for women's
activities . Geneva , 1984. vi, 292 p. : ISBN
92-2-103818-1   *NYPL [JLF 85-625]*

**WOMEN, AFRO-AMERICAN. see AFRO-
   AMERICAN WOMEN.**

**WOMEN AGRICULTURAL LABORERS -
   DEVELOPING COUNTRIES.**
Women as food producers in developing
countries /. Los Angeles, CA , c1985. ix, 118
p. : ISBN 0-918456-56-8 : DDC 331.4/83/091724
19
HD6073.A292 D4485 1985
                    NYPL [JLE 88-2659]

Women and AIDS /. Richardson, Diane. New
York , 1988. 183 p. ; ISBN 0-416-01741-X :
DDC 616.9/792 19
RC607.A26 R53 1988 *NYPL [Sc D 88-987]*

Women and development in Lesotho /. Gay,
Judith S. [Maseru, Lesotho] 1982. 84, xxii p. :
                    NYPL [Sc F 89-136]

Women and economic development : local,
regional and national planning strategies /
edited and with an introduction by Kate Young.
Oxford [England] ; New York : Berg ; ix, 231
p. ; 22 cm. (Berg/Unesco studies in development
theory and policy) "Part of this work was published as
Women's concerns and planning ..." Includes
bibliographies. ISBN 0-85496-091-0 : DDC 305.4/2
19
*1. Women in development - Case studies. 2. Economic
development projects - Planning - Case studies. 3.
Economic development - Social aspects - Case studies.
I. Young, Kate. II. Women's concerns and planning. III.
Series.*
HQ1240 .W665 1988   *NYPL [JLD 89-559]*

Women and law in southern Africa / edited by
Alice Armstrong ; assisted by Welshman
Ncube. Harare, Zimbabwe : Zimbabwe
Publishing House, 1987. xiv, 281 p. : 1 map ;
21 cm. Includes bibliographies. ISBN 0-949225-48-7
*1. Women - Legal status, laws, etc. - Africa, Southern.
I. Armstrong, Alice.*   *NYPL [Sc D 89-297]*

**WOMEN AND LITERATURE - UNITED
   STATES.**
Drake, William. The first wave . New York ,
London , c1987. xxi, 314 p., [8] p. of plates :
   ISBN 0-02-533490-5 : DDC 811/.52/099287 19
PS151 .D7 1987   *NYPL [JFD 87-7537]*

Hull, Gloria T. Color, sex, and poetry .
Bloomington , c1987. xi, 240 p. : ISBN
0-253-34974-5 DDC 811/.52/099287 19
PS153.N5 H84 1987   *NYPL [Sc E 88-72]*

**WOMEN AND LITERATURE - UNITED
   STATES - HISTORY - 20TH CENTURY.**
Angelou, Maya. Conversations with Maya

Angelou /. Jackson , c1989. xvi, 246 p. ; ISBN
0-87805-361-1 (alk. paper) DDC 818/.5409 19
PS3551.N464 Z4635 1989
                    NYPL [Sc E 89-225]

Awkward, Michael. Inspiriting influences . New
York , 1989. x, 178 p. ; ISBN 0-231-06806-9
   DDC 813/.5/099287 19
PS153.N5 A94 1989   *NYPL [Sc E 89-188]*

Women and politics in Barbados, 1948-1981 /.
Duncan, Neville C. Cave Hill, Barbados ,
c1983. x, 68 p. ;   *NYPL [Sc E 84-107]*

Women and population : reports of the Kenya
NGO sub-committee workshops. [Nairobi?] :
Kenya NGO Organzing [sic] Committee,
Forum '85 of the World Conference of the
U.N. Decade for Women, [1985] 73 p. ; 30 cm.
(Report / Kenya NGO Organising Committee . no. 15)
In English; p. 46-49 in Swahili. DDC 363.9/6/096762
19
*1. Birth control - Kenya - Congresses. 2. Kenya -
Population policy - Congresses. I. Kenya NGO
Organising Committee--Forum '85. II. Series: Report
(Kenya NGO Organising Committee--Forum '85) , no.
15.*
HQ766.5.K4 W65 1985 *NYPL [Sc F 88-191]*

**WOMEN AND SOCIALISM - AFRICA -
   CONGRESSES.**
Regional Seminar for Africa (Mogadishu :
1975) On African women's equality, role in
national liberation, development and peace .
[Mogadishu] , 1975. 123 p. :
                    NYPL [Sc E 88-138]

Women and the state in Africa / edited by Jane
L. Parpart & Kathleen A. Staudt. Boulder,
Colo. : L. Rienner Publishers, c1989. ix, 229
p. ; 24 cm. Includes index. Bibliography: p. 203-224.
   ISBN 1-555-87082-1 (alk. paper) : DDC
305.4/2/096 19
*1. Sex role - Africa, Sub-Saharan. I. Parpart, Jane L. II.
Staudt, Kathleen A.*
HQ1236.5.A357 W65 1988
                    NYPL [Sc E 89-159]

Women and work. Gill, Margaret. Women, work,
and development /. Cave Hill, Barbados , 1984.
xviii, 129 p. ;   *NYPL [Sc E 85-274]*

Women as food producers in developing countries
/ edited by Jamie Monson and Marion Kalb.
Los Angeles, CA : UCLA African Studies
Center, c1985. ix, 118 p. : ill. ; 24 cm. Papers
presented at a workshop conference, sponsored by
UCLA African Studies Center and OEF International.
Includes bibliographies. ISBN 0-918456-56-8 : DDC
331.4/83/091724 19
*1. Women agricultural laborers - Developing countries.
I. Monson, Jamie. II. Kalb, Marion. III. University of
California, Los Angeles. African Studies Center. IV.
OEF International.*
HD6073.A292 D4485 1985
                    NYPL [JLE 88-2659]

**WOMEN AS SINGERS. see WOMEN
   SINGERS.**

**WOMEN ATHLETES - HISTORY - 20TH
   CENTURY.**
Blue, Adrianne. Faster, higher, further .
London , 1988. ix, 182 p. : ISBN 0-86068-648-5
(pbk.)
GV721.5 .B58x 1988   *NYPL [Sc E 89-82]*

**WOMEN AUTHORS, BLACKS - GREAT
   BRITAIN.**
Let it be told . London , 1987. 145, [1] p. ;
   ISBN 0-7453-0254-8 *NYPL [Sc E 88-125]*

WOMEN, BLACK - AFRICA - HISTORY.
Black women in antiquity /. New Brunswick,
[N.J.] , London , 1988. 192 p. : ISBN
0-87855-982-5   *NYPL [Sc D 89-351]*

WOMEN, BLACK - BIOGRAPHY.
Tyson, Jennifer. Claudia Jones, 1915-1964 .
London , c1988. 16 p. :
                    NYPL [Sc D 89-553]

**WOMEN, BLACK - EDUCATION - SOUTH
   AFRICA.**
Moya, Lily Patience. Not either an
experimental doll . Bloomington , c1987. xv,
217 p., [18] p. of plates : ISBN 0-253-34843-9
   DDC 968.05/6 19
HQ1800 .M69 1988   *NYPL [Sc D 89-282]*

WOMEN, BLACK - EGYPT - HISTORY.
Black women in antiquity /. New Brunswick,
[N.J.] , London , 1988. 192 p. : ISBN
0-87855-982-5   *NYPL [Sc D 89-351]*

WOMEN, BLACK - ENGLAND.
Sojourn /. London , 1988. 215 p. ;   ISBN
0-413-16440-3 (pbk) :   DDC 823/.914/08 19
NYPL [Sc C 89-81]

WOMEN, BLACK - ETHIOPIA - HISTORY.
Black women in antiquity /. New Brunswick,
[N.J.] , London , 1988. 192 p. :   ISBN
0-87855-982-5   *NYPL [Sc D 89-351]*

**WOMEN, BLACK - GREAT BRITAIN -
BIOGRAPHY.**
Trill, Carol. Dispossessed daughter of Africa /.
London , 1988. 190 p. :   ISBN 0-946918-42-2
(pbk.)   *NYPL [sc C 88-228]*

**WOMEN, BLACK - GREAT BRITAIN -
HISTORY.**
Bryan, Beverley, 1949- The heart of the race .
London , 1985. vi, 250 p. ;   ISBN 0-86068-361-3
(pbk.) :   DDC 305.4/8896041 19
DA125.N4 B78 1985   NYPL [Sc C 88-178]

**WOMEN, BLACK - GREAT BRITAIN -
POETRY.**
Benji. Scribe sistren . London , 1987. 72 p. ;
ISBN 0-903738-72-4   *NYPL [Sc D 88-686]*

**WOMEN, BLACK - GREAT BRITAIN -
SOCIAL LIFE AND CUSTOMS.**
Bryan, Beverley, 1949- The heart of the race .
London , 1985. vi, 250 p. ;   ISBN 0-86068-361-3
(pbk.) :   DDC 305.4/8896041 19
DA125.N4 B78 1985   NYPL [Sc C 88-178]

**WOMEN, BLACK - SOUTH AFRICA -
SOCIAL CONDITIONS.**
Kuzwayo, Ellen. [Call me woman. French.]
Femme et noire en Afrique du Sud /. Paris ,
c1985. 296, [8] p. of plates :   ISBN 2-221-05157-2
NYPL [Sc E 88-315]

**WOMEN, BLACK - SOUTH AMERICA -
POETRY.**
The image of Black women in twentieth-century
South American poetry . Washington, D.C. ,
c1987. 250 p. ;   ISBN 0-89410-275-3
NYPL [Sc E 88-321]

**WOMEN, BLACK - TRINIDAD AND
TOBAGO - BIOGRAPHY.**
Reddock, Rhoda. Elma Francois . London ,
1988. vii, 60 p., [8] p. of plates :   ISBN
0-901241-80-6 (Pbk.)   *NYPL [Sc D 89-77]*

WOMEN - BRAZIL - SEXUAL BEHAVIOUR.
Quintas, Fátima. Sexo e marginalidade .
Petrópolis :Vozes, 1986. 191 p. ;
NYPL [Sc D 88-1477]

WOMEN - BRAZIL - SOCIAL CONDITIONS.
Horta, Elisabeth Vorcaro. A mulher na cultura
brasileira /. Belo Horizonte , 1975. 122 p. ;
HQ1542 .H66   NYPL [Sc D 86-811]

**WOMEN - BRAZIL - SOCIOLOGICAL
ASPECTS.**
Quintas, Fátima. Sexo e marginalidade .
Petrópolis :Vozes, 1986. 191 p. ;
NYPL [Sc D 88-1477]

**WOMEN - CARIBBEAN AREA - ECONOMIC
CONDITIONS.**
Gill, Margaret. Women, work, and development
/. Cave Hill, Barbados , 1984. xviii, 129 p. ;
NYPL [Sc E 85-274]

WOMEN - CLOTHING. see COSTUME.

WOMEN - COSTUME. see COSTUME.

Women, culture, & politics /. Davis, Angela
Yvonne, 1944- New York, NY , 1989. xv, 238
p. ;   ISBN 0-394-76976-8 :   DDC 305.4/8896073 19
E185.86 .D382 1989   NYPL [Sc D 89-275]

**WOMEN - DEVELOPING COUNTRIES -
ECONOMIC CONDITIONS.**
Women, state, and ideology. Basingstoke,
Hampshire , c1987. xii, 245 p. :   ISBN
0-333-41389-X   *NYPL [JLD 87-2346]*

**WOMEN - DEVELOPING COUNTRIES -
SOCIAL CONDITIONS.**
Fisher, Maxine P., 1948- Women in the Third
World /. New York , 1989. 176 p. :   ISBN
0-531-10666-7   DDC 305.4/09172/4 19
HQ1870.9 .F57 1989   NYPL [Sc E 89-223]

Third World, second sex, vol. 2 /. London,
UK , Atlantic Highlands, N.J., USA , 1987. viii,
284 p. :   ISBN 0-86232-752-0 (v. 2) :   DDC
305.4/2/091724 19
HQ1870.9 .T48 1987   NYPL [Sc D 88-931]

Women, state, and ideology. Basingstoke,

Hampshire , c1987. xii, 245 p. :   ISBN
0-333-41389-X   *NYPL [JLD 87-2346]*

**WOMEN - DEVELOPING COUNTRIES -
SOCIAL CONDITIONS - JUVENILE
LITERATURE.**
Fisher, Maxine P., 1948- Women in the Third
World /. New York , 1989. 176 p. :   ISBN
0-531-10666-7   DDC 305.4/09172/4 19
HQ1870.9 .F57 1989   NYPL [Sc E 89-223]

**WOMEN, DOGON (AFRICAN PEOPLE) -
SOCIAL LIFE AND CUSTOMS.**
Wanono, Nadine. Ciné-rituel de femmes dogon
/. Paris , 1987. 138 p. :   ISBN 2-222-03961-4
(pbk)   *NYPL [Sc E 88-177]*

WOMEN DOMESTICS - KENYA.
Ndegwa, Rosemary. Maids, blessing or blight?
/. Nairobi, Kenya , c1987. x, 141 p. ;
NYPL [Sc D 89-399]

WOMEN DOMESTICS - NIGERIA.
Olusanya, P. Olufemi. Nursemaids and the pill .
Legon , 1981. xiii, 157 p. ;
NYPL [Sc E 89-249]

**WOMEN DOMESTICS - SOUTHERN
STATES - HISTORY - SOURCES.**
Telling memories among southern women .
Baton Rouge , c1988. xi, 279 p. :   ISBN
0-8071-1440-5 (alk. paper) :   DDC 305.4/3 19
HD6072.2.U52 A137 1988
NYPL [Sc E 89-124]

**WOMEN DOMESTICS - SOUTHERN
STATES - INTERVIEWS.**
Telling memories among southern women .
Baton Rouge , c1988. xi, 279 p. :   ISBN
0-8071-1440-5 (alk. paper) :   DDC 305.4/3 19
HD6072.2.U52 A137 1988
NYPL [Sc E 89-124]

WOMEN - DRESS. see COSTUME.

WOMEN - EDUCATION - GHANA.
Oppong, Christine. Seven roles of women .
Geneva , 1987. xi, 127 p. :
NYPL [Sc E 89-143]

**WOMEN, EGBA (AFRICAN PEOPLE) -
BIOGRAPHY.**
Yemitan, Oladipo. Madame Tinubu . Ibadan ,
1987. x, 85 p. :   ISBN 978-15-4985-9
NYPL [Sc D 88-1382]

**WOMEN - EMPLOYMENT - AFRICA, WEST -
CASE STUDIES.**
Sex roles, population and development in West
Africa . London , Portsmouth, N.H. , 1987. xiii,
242 p. ;   ISBN 0-435-08022-9   DDC 304.6/0966 19
HB3665.5.A3 S49 1988
NYPL [Sc E 88-318]

WOMEN - EMPLOYMENT - BARBADOS.
Gill, Margaret. Women, work, and development
/. Cave Hill, Barbados , 1984. xviii, 129 p. ;
NYPL [Sc E 85-274]

WOMEN - EMPLOYMENT - BRAZIL.
Horta, Elisabeth Vorcaro. A mulher na cultura
brasileira /. Belo Horizonte , 1975. 122 p. ;
HQ1542 .H66   NYPL [Sc D 86-811]

**WOMEN - EMPLOYMENT - CARIBBEAN
AREA.**
Gill, Margaret. Women, work, and development
/. Cave Hill, Barbados , 1984. xviii, 129 p. ;
NYPL [Sc E 85-274]

WOMEN - EMPLOYMENT - GHANA.
Oppong, Christine. Seven roles of women .
Geneva , 1987. xi, 127 p. :
NYPL [Sc E 89-143]

WOMEN - EMPLOYMENT - NIGERIA.
Women in the modern sector labour force in
Nigeria /. Lagos , 1985. viii, 254 p. ;   ISBN
978-301-560-5   *NYPL [Sc D 89-538]*

**WOMEN - EMPLOYMENT - TEXAS -
HISTORY.**
Winegarten, Ruthe. Texas women . Austin, Tex.
[1986] ix, 187 p. :   ISBN 0-89015-532-1 :   DDC
305.4/09764 19
HQ1438.T4 W56 1986   NYPL [Sc F 87-41]

WOMEN - EMPLOYMENT - TOGO - LOMÉ.
Cordonnier, Rita. Femmes africaines et
commerce . Paris , 1987. 190 p. :   ISBN
2-85802-901-6   *NYPL [Sc E 88-368]*

**WOMEN - EMPLOYMENT - UNITED
STATES - CONGRESSES.**
Black working women . Berkeley, Calif.
[1981?] vii, 222 p. :   *NYPL [Sc F 89-33]*

**WOMEN EVANGELISTS - UNITED STATES -
BIOGRAPHY.**
Smith, Amanda, 1837-1915. An autobiography .
New York , 1988. xlii, 506 p. [23] p. of plates :
ISBN 0-19-505261-7 (alk. paper)   DDC
269/.2/0924 B 19
BV3785.S56 A3 1988   NYPL [JFC 88-2154]

WOMEN - FICTION.
Youngblood, Shay. The big mama stories /.
Ithaca, N.Y. , c1989. 106 p. ;   ISBN
0-932379-58-3 (alk. paper) :   DDC 813/.54 19
PS3575.O8535 B5 1989
NYPL [Sc D 89-530]

WOMEN - GHANA.
Rocksloh-Papendieck, Barbara. Frauenarbeit am
Strassenrand Kenkeyküchen in Ghana /.
Hamburg , 1988. iii, 193 p. :   ISBN
3-923519-75-3   *NYPL [Sc D 89-575]*

WOMEN - HAITI - BIOGRAPHY.
Turian Cardozo, Jacqueline. On ne guérit pas
de son enfance /. Port-au-Prince , 1987. 220 p.,
[1] folded leaf plates :   *NYPL [Sc D 88-293]*

WOMEN - HAITI - FICTION.
Cazanove, Michèle. Présumée Solitude, ou,
Histoire d'une paysanne haïtienne . Paris ,
c1988. 178 p. ;   ISBN 2-260-00546-2
NYPL [Sc D 88-1406]

WOMEN, HEBREW. see WOMEN, JEWISH.

**WOMEN IMMIGRANTS - QUÉBEC -
MONTRÉAL.**
Histoires d'immigrées . Montréal , 1987. 275
p. ;   ISBN 2-89052-170-2   *NYPL [Sc D 88-346]*

Women in African literature today : a review /
editor, Eldred Durosimi Jones ; associate editor,
Eustace Palmer ; editorial assistant, Marjorie
Jones. London : Currey ; Trenton, N.J. : Africa
World Press, 1987. vi, 162 p. ;   22 cm. Includes
bibliographical references and index.
ISBN
0-85255-500-8 (pbk) :   DDC 809/.89287 19
*1. African literature - Women authors - History and
criticism. I. Jones, Eldred D. II. Palmer, Eustace. III.
Jones, Marjorie.*
PL8010   NYPL [Sc D 88-984]

**WOMEN IN COMMUNITY
DEVELOPMENT - DEVELOPING
COUNTRIES.**
The Role of women in the execution of
low-income housing projects . Nairobi, Kenya ,
1986. 64 p. :   ISBN 92-1-131005-9
NYPL [Sc F 88-225]

**WOMEN IN COOPERATIVE SOCIETIES -
AFRICA, SOUTHERN.**
Meghji, Zakia. The woman co-operator &
development . Nairobi , 1985. iv, 127 p. ;
DDC 334/.088042 19
HD3561.9.A4 M44 1985
NYPL [Sc C 88-92]

Women in development : press cuttings, 11
January 1983 - 22 December 1983 / National
Institute of Development Research &
Documentation (NIR) ; [Stella Bakwena,
documentalist]. Gaborone : University of
Botswana, 1984. 49, 4 p. : all facsims. ;   30 cm.
Cover title. "May 1984."
*1. Women - Africa, Southern - History - Sources. 2.
Feminism - Africa, Southern - History - Sources. I.
Bakwena, Stella. II. National Institute of Development
Research & Documentation (Botswana).*
NYPL [Sc F 88-116]

Women in development : Cross river experience /
editors, S.O. Jaja, E.B.E. Ndem, Kate Okon.
Calabar : Association of Media Women, Cross
River State, 1988. 153 p. : ill., map, ports. ;   22
cm. Includes bibliographical references.
*1. Women - Nigeria. 2. Women - Nigeria - Cross River
State. I. Jaja, S. O. II. Ndem, E. B. E. III. Okon, Kate.*
NYPL [Sc D 89-79]

**WOMEN IN DEVELOPMENT - AFRICA,
SOUTHERN.**
Meghji, Zakia. The woman co-operator &
development . Nairobi , 1985. iv, 127 p. ;
DDC 334/.088042 19
HD3561.9.A4 M44 1985
NYPL [Sc C 88-92]

**WOMEN IN DEVELOPMENT - AFRICA,
WEST - CASE STUDIES.**
Sex roles, population and development in West
Africa . London , Portsmouth, N.H. , 1987. xiii,

242 p. ; ISBN 0-435-08022-9 DDC 304.6/0966 19
HB3665.5.A3 S49 1988
NYPL [Sc E 88-318]

WOMEN IN DEVELOPMENT - CARIBBEAN AREA - BIBLIOGRAPHY - CATALOGS.
Inniss, Diana. A selected bibliography of materials and resources on women in the Caribbean available at WAND's Research and Documentation Centre /. Pinelands, St. Michael [Barbados] [1987] 119 p. ;
NYPL [Sc F 88-218]

WOMEN IN DEVELOPMENT - CASE STUDIES.
Women and economic development . Oxford [England] ; New York : ix, 231 p. ; ISBN 0-85496-091-0 : DDC 305.4/2 19
HQ1240 .W665 1988 *NYPL [JLD 89-559]*

WOMEN IN DEVELOPMENT - NIGERIA.
Nigerian women and development /. Ibadan, Nigeria , 1988. xv, 495 p. ; ISBN 978-12-1219-5
NYPL [Sc D 89-576]

Producer/User Seminar on Household Statistics and Indicators for Women in Development held at the Conference Centre, University of Lagos, August 11th-13th, 1986 /. [Lagos, 1986?] 2 v. ; 25 cm. *NYPL [Sc E 89-158]*

WOMEN IN POLITICS - BARBADOS.
Duncan, Neville C. Women and politics in Barbados, 1948-1981 /. Cave Hill, Barbados , c1983. x, 68 p. ; *NYPL [Sc E 84-107]*

WOMEN IN POLITICS - TEXAS - HISTORY.
Winegarten, Ruthe. Texas women . Austin, Tex. [1986] ix, 187 p. ; ISBN 0-89015-532-1 : DDC 305.4/09764 19
HQ1438.T4 W56 1986 *NYPL [Sc F 87-41]*

WOMEN IN PUBLIC LIFE - BARBADOS.
Duncan, Neville C. Women and politics in Barbados, 1948-1981 /. Cave Hill, Barbados , c1983. x, 68 p. ; *NYPL [Sc E 84-107]*

WOMEN IN RURAL DEVELOPMENT. ·
Loutfi, Martha Fetherolf. Rural women . Geneva , c1980 (1985 printing) v, 81 p., [4] p. of plates : ISBN 92-2-102389-3 (pbk.)
NYPL [Sc E 89-67]

WOMEN IN RURAL DEVELOPMENT - AFRICA.
Droy, I. Femmes et projets de développement rural en Afrique Sub-Saharienne . 1985. 557 p. :
NYPL [Sc D 88-778]

WOMEN IN RURAL DEVELOPMENT - AFRICA - CONGRESSES.
African and Asian Inter-regional Workshop on Strategies for Improving the Employment Conditions of Rural Women (1984 : Arusha, Tanzania) Resources, power and women . Geneva , 1985. ix, 82 p. ; ISBN 92-2-105009-2 (pbk.) : DDC 331.4/83/095 19
HD6207 .A78 1984 *NYPL [JLF 87-1038]*

WOMEN IN RURAL DEVELOPMENT - AFRICA, WEST.
Improved village technology for women's activities . Geneva , 1984. vi, 292 p. : ISBN 92-2-103818-1 *NYPL [JLF 85-625]*

WOMEN IN RURAL DEVELOPMENT - ASIA - CONGRESSES.
African and Asian Inter-regional Workshop on Strategies for Improving the Employment Conditions of Rural Women (1984 : Arusha, Tanzania) Resources, power and women . Geneva , 1985. ix, 82 p. ; ISBN 92-2-105009-2 (pbk.) : DDC 331.4/83/095 19
HD6207 .A78 1984 *NYPL [JLF 87-1038]*

WOMEN IN RURAL DEVELOPMENT - KENYA.
Pala, Achola O. A preliminary survey of avenues for and constraints on women's involvement in the development process in Kenya [microform] /. [Nairobi? , 1975] 26 p. ;
NYPL [Sc Micro R-4108 no.14]

WOMEN IN RURAL DEVELOPMENT - LESOTHO.
Gay, Judith S. Women and development in Lesotho /. [Maseru, Lesotho] 1982. 84, xxii p. : *NYPL [Sc F 89-136]*

Women in the Caribbean project .
(v. 3) Duncan, Neville C. Women and politics in Barbados, 1948-1981 /. Cave Hill, Barbados , c1983. x, 68 p. ; *NYPL [Sc E 84-107]*

(v. 6) Gill, Margaret. Women, work, and

development /. Cave Hill, Barbados , 1984. xviii, 129 p. ; *NYPL [Sc E 85-274]*

WOMEN IN THE MASS MEDIA INDUSTRY - MEDIA - DIRECTORIES.
Directory of media women in Kenya /. [Nairobi] [1985] 48 p. : DDC 001.51/02552 19
P94.5.W652 K43 1985 *NYPL [Sc F 88-370]*

Women in the modern sector labour force in Nigeria / edited by Tayo Fashoyin, Felicia Durojaiye Oyekanmi, and Eleanor R. Fapohunda. Lagos : Dept. of Industrial Relations & Personnel Management, Faculty of Business Administration, University of Lagos, 1985. viii, 254 p. ; 23 cm. Includes bibliographies. ISBN 978-301-560-5
1. Women - Employment - Nigeria. I. Fashoyin, Tayo. II. Oyekammi,Felicia Durojaiye. III. Fapohunda, Eleanor R. *NYPL [Sc D 89-538]*

WOMEN IN THE PROFESSIONS - NIGERIA - BENDEL STATE - BIOGRAPHY.
Ibuje, Joan, 1941- Famous women /. [Benin City, Nigeria] [1982] 60 p. : DDC 305.4/09669/3 19
HQ1815.5.Z8 B465 1982
NYPL [Sc D 88-1144]

Women in the Third World /. Fisher, Maxine P., 1948- New York , 1989. 176 p. : ISBN 0-531-10666-7 DDC 305.4/09172/4 19
HQ1870.9 .F57 1989 *NYPL [Sc E 89-223]*

Women in the Third World.
Third World, second sex, vol. 2 /. London, UK , Atlantic Highlands, N.J., USA , 1987. viii, 284 p. ; ISBN 0-86232-752-0 (v. 2) : DDC 305.4/2/091724 19
HQ1870.9 .T48 1987 *NYPL [Sc D 88-931]*

WOMEN - INFORMATION SERVICES - NEW YORK (N.Y.) - DIRECTORIES.
Library and information sources on women . New York , c1988. ix, 254 p. ; ISBN 0-935312-88-9 (pbk.) : DDC 305.4/025/7471 19
HQ1181.U5 L52 1987
*NYPL [*R-Econ. 88-4682]*

WOMEN, ISLAMIC. see WOMEN, MUSLIM.

WOMEN - JAMAICA - BIOGRAPHY.
Yard, Lionel M. Biography of Amy Ashwood Garvey, 1897-1969 . [S.l.] [198-?] vii, 233 p. :
NYPL [Sc E 88-541]

WOMEN JAZZ MUSICIANS - UNITED STATES - EXHIBITIONS.
Black visions '88 . New York [1988] 44 p. :
NYPL [Sc D 88-1200]

WOMEN, JEWISH - UNITED STATES.
Eckardt, A. Roy (Arthur Roy), 1918- Black-woman-Jew . Bloomington , c1989. 229 p. ; ISBN 0-253-31221-3 DDC 305.4/8896073 19
E185.86 .E28 1989 *NYPL [Sc E 89-209]*

WOMEN - KENYA.
Pala, Achola O. A preliminary survey of avenues for and constraints on women's involvement in the development process in Kenya [microform] /. [Nairobi? , 1975] 26 p. ;
NYPL [Sc Micro R-4108 no.14]

WOMEN - KENYA - BIOGRAPHY.
Njau, Rebeka. Kenya women heroes and their mystical power /. Nairobi , 1984- v. ; DDC 398/.09676/2 19
GR356.4 .N43 1984 *NYPL [Sc D 88-1052]*

WOMEN - KENYA - FOLKLORE.
Njau, Rebeka. Kenya women heroes and their mystical power /. Nairobi , 1984- v. ; DDC 398/.09676/2 19
GR356.4 .N43 1984 *NYPL [Sc D 88-1052]*

WOMEN - KENYA - HISTORY.
Pala, Achola O. [Femme africaine dans la société précoloniale. Spanish.] La mujer africana en la sociedad precolonial /. Barcelona [Paris?] , 1982. 238 p. ; ISBN 84-85800-35-4 (Serbal) *NYPL [Sc D 88-833]*

WOMEN - KENYA - SOCIAL CONDITIONS.
Women of Kenya . Nairobi [1985] v, 51 p., [2] p. of plates : DDC 305.4/09676/2 19
HQ1796.5 .W66 1985 *NYPL [Sc D 88-1247]*

WOMEN - KENYA - STATISTICS.
Women of Kenya . Nairobi [1985] v, 51 p., [2] p. of plates : DDC 305.4/09676/2 19
HQ1796.5 .W66 1985 *NYPL [Sc D 88-1247]*

WOMEN - LEGAL STATUS, LAWS, ETC. - AFRICA, SOUTHERN.

Women and law in southern Africa /. Harare, Zimbabwe , 1987. xiv, 281 p. : ISBN 0-949225-48-7 *NYPL [Sc D 89-297]*

WOMEN - LEGAL STATUS, LAWS, ETC. - GHANA.
Law and the status of women in Ghana. Addis Ababa , 1984. iii, 75 p. ; DDC 342.669/0878 346.6902878 19
LAW *NYPL [Sc F 88-274]*

WOMEN - MALI - HISTORY.
Pala, Achola O. [Femme africaine dans la société précoloniale. Spanish.] La mujer africana en la sociedad precolonial /. Barcelona [Paris?] , 1982. 238 p. ; ISBN 84-85800-35-4 (Serbal) *NYPL [Sc D 88-833]*

WOMEN, MASAI.
Mitzlaff, Ulrike von. Maasai-Frauen . München , 1988. 181 p. : ISBN 3-923804-23-7
NYPL [Sc D 89-551]

WOMEN MERCHANTS - GHANA.
Rocksloh-Papendieck, Barbara. Frauenarbeit am Strassenrand Kenkeyküchen in Ghana /. Hamburg , 1988. iii, 193 p. : ISBN 3-923519-75-3 *NYPL [Sc D 89-575]*

WOMEN MISSIONARIES - BIOGRAPHY.
[Broughton, Virginia W] Twenty year's [!] experience of a missionary [microform]. Chicago, 1907. 140 p.
NYPL [Sc Micro R-1445]

WOMEN, MUSLIM - AFRICA, SUB-SAHARAN - SOCIAL CONDITIONS - CASE STUDIES.
Life histories of African women /. London , Atlantic Highlands, NJ , 1988. 200 p. : ISBN 0-948660-04-X DDC 305.4/0967 19
HQ1787.A3 L54 1988
NYPL [Sc D 88-1469]

WOMEN, NEGRO. see AFRO-AMERICAN WOMEN.

WOMEN - NIGERIA.
Akpan, Ekwere Otu. The women's war of 1929 . Calabar, Nigeria , 1988. vii, 68 p. :
NYPL [Sc E 89-20]

Nigerian women and development /. Ibadan, Nigeria , 1988. xv, 495 p. ; ISBN 978-12-1219-5
NYPL [Sc D 89-576]

Women in development . Calabar , 1988. 153 p. : *NYPL [Sc D 89-79]*

WOMEN - NIGERIA - BENDEL STATE - BIOGRAPHY.
Ibuje, Joan, 1941- Famous women /. [Benin City, Nigeria] [1982] 60 p. : DDC 305.4/09669/3 19
HQ1815.5.Z8 B465 1982
NYPL [Sc D 88-1144]

WOMEN - NIGERIA - BIOGRAPHY.
Yemitan, Oladipo. Madame Tinubu . Ibadan, 1987. x, 85 p. : ISBN 978-15-4985-9
NYPL [Sc D 88-1382]

WOMEN - NIGERIA - CROSS RIVER STATE.
Women in development . Calabar , 1988. 153 p. : *NYPL [Sc D 89-79]*

WOMEN - OCCUPATIONS. see WOMEN - EMPLOYMENT.

Women of color in the United States . Redfern, Bernice, 1947- New York , 1989. vii, 156 p. ; ISBN 0-8240-5849-6 (alk. paper) DDC 016.3054/8/0973 19
Z7964.U49 R4 1989 HQ1410
NYPL [Sc D 89-562]

Women of Kenya : review and evaluation of progress. Nairobi : Kenya Literature Bureau, [1985] v, 51 p., [2] p. of plates : maps ; 21 cm. "End of decade, Nairobi, July, 1985." DDC 305.4/09676/2 19
1. Women - Kenya - Social conditions. 2. Women - Kenya - Statistics.
HQ1796.5 .W66 1985 *NYPL [Sc D 88-1247]*

WOMEN - PSYCHOLOGY.
Competition, a feminist taboo? /. New York , 1987. xvi, 260 p. ; ISBN 0-935312-74-9 (pbk.) : DDC 305.4/2 19
HQ1206 .C69 1987 *NYPL [JFE 88-6669]*

WOMEN - RELIGIOUS LIFE.
The Womanspirit sourcebook . San Francisco , c1988. xxv, 277 p. : ISBN 0-06-250982-9 (pbk.) : DDC 291/.088042 19
BL458 .W575 1988 *NYPL [Sc F 88-294]*

WOMEN - RELIGIOUS LIFE - AUDIO-VISUAL AIDS - CATALOGS.
The Womanspirit sourcebook . San Francisco , c1988. xxv, 277 p. : ISBN 0-06-250982-9 (pbk.) : DDC 291/.088042 19
BL458 .W575 1988   *NYPL [Sc F 88-294]*

WOMEN - RELIGIOUS LIFE - BIBLIOGRAPHY - CATALOGS.
The Womanspirit sourcebook . San Francisco , c1988. xxv, 277 p. : ISBN 0-06-250982-9 (pbk.) : DDC 291/.088042 19
BL458 .W575 1988   *NYPL [Sc F 88-294]*

WOMEN - RESEARCH - NEW YORK (N.Y.) - INFORMATION SERVICES - DIRECTORIES.
Library and information sources on women . New York , c1988. ix, 254 p. ; ISBN 0-935312-88-9 (pbk.) : DDC 305.4/025/7471 19
HQ1181.U5 L52 1987
                        *NYPL [*R-Econ. 88-4682]*

WOMEN - SEXUAL BEHAVIOR - LITERARY COLLECTIONS.
Deep down . Boston , c1988. xii, 330 p. ; ISBN 0-571-12957-9 : DDC 810/.8/03538 19
PS509.E7 D44 1988   *NYPL [Sc D 88-1080]*

WOMEN SINGERS - UNITED STATES - BIOGRAPHY.
Buckley, Gail Lumet, 1937- The Hornes . New York , 1986. 262 p. : ISBN 0-394-51306-1 : DDC 974.7/2300496073/00922 B 19
F129.B7 B83 1986   *NYPL [Sc E 86-286]*

WOMEN SLAVES - BRAZIL - HISTORY.
Giacomini, Sonia Maria. Mulher e escrava . Petrópolis , 1988. 95 p., [7] p. of plates :
HT1126 .G49 1988   *NYPL [Sc D 88-1283]*

WOMEN SLAVES - UNITED STATES - BIOGRAPHY.
Jacobs, Harriet A. (Harriet Ann), 1813-1897. Incidents in the life of a slave girl /. New York , 1988. xl, 306 p. ; ISBN 0-19-505243-9 (alk. paper) DDC 973/.0496024 B 19
E444.J17 A3 1988   *NYPL [JFC 88-2193]*

WOMEN SLAVES - UNITED STATES - FICTION.
Williams, Sherley Anne, 1944- Dessa Rose /. New York , c1986. 236 p. ; ISBN 0-688-05113-8 : DDC 813/.54 19
PS3573.I45546 D47 1986
                        NYPL [JFD 86-8841]

WOMEN SOCIAL REFORMERS - NIGERIA - BENDEL STATE - BIOGRAPHY.
Ibuje, Joan, 1941- Famous women /. [Benin City, Nigeria] [1982] 60 p. : DDC 305.4/09669/3 19
HQ1815.5.Z8 B465 1982
                        NYPL [Sc D 88-1144]

WOMEN - SOUTH AFRICA - CORRESPONDENCE.
Moya, Lily Patience. Not either an experimental doll . Bloomington , c1987. xv, 217 p., [18] p. of plates : ISBN 0-253-34843-9 DDC 968.05/6 19
HQ1800 .M69 1988   *NYPL [Sc D 89-282]*

WOMEN - SOUTH AFRICA - POLITICAL ACTIVITY.
Makhoere, Caesarina Khana. No child's play . London , 1988. 121 p. ; ISBN 0-7043-4111-5 :
                        NYPL [Sc C 88-333]

WOMEN - SOUTH AFRICA - SOCIAL CONDITIONS.
Kuzwayo, Ellen. [Call me woman. French.] Femme et noire en Afrique du Sud /. Paris , c1985. 296, [8] p. of plates : ISBN 2-221-05157-2
                        NYPL [Sc E 88-315]

WOMEN - SOUTHERN STATES - HISTORY.
Fox-Genovese, Elizabeth, 1941- Within the plantation household . Chapel Hill , c1988. xvii, 544 p. : ISBN 0-8078-1808-9 (alk. paper) DDC 305.4/0975 19
HQ1438.A13 F69 1988   *NYPL [JLE 89-21]*

Women, state, and ideology : studies from Africa and Asia / edited by Haleh Afshar. Basingstoke, Hampshire : Macmillan, c1987. xii, 245 p. : ill. ; 23 cm. Includes bibliographies and index. CONTENTS - Women and the state in Nigeria / Carolyne Dennis -- Women in Zimbabwe / Susie Jacobs and Tracy Howard -- The state and the regulation of marriage / Penelope R. Roberts -- Women, marriage, and the state in Iran / Haleh Afshar -- Family and state in Malaysian

industrialisation / Maila Stivens -- Gender and population in the People's Republic of China / Delia Davin -- Some state responses to male and female need in British India / Jocelyn Kynch -- Contaminating states / Patricia Jeffrey, Roger Jeffrey, Andrew Lyon -- Women and handicraft production in North India / Ann Weston -- Front and rear: the sexual division of labour in the Israeli Army / Nira Yuval-Davis -- Controlling women's access to political power / Carol Wolkowitz -- State, culture, and gender / Christine Pelzer-White. ISBN 0-333-41389-X
1. Women - Developing countries - Social conditions. 2. Women - Developing countries - Economic conditions. 3. Developing countries - Social policy. I. Afshar, Haleh, 1944-.   *NYPL [JLD 87-2346]*

WOMEN - TEXAS - HISTORY.
Winegarten, Ruthe. Texas women . Austin, Tex. [1986] ix, 187 p. : ISBN 0-89015-532-1 : DDC 305.4/09764 19
HQ1438.T4 W56 1986   *NYPL [Sc F 87-41]*

Women, work and development, 0253-2042 . (13) Oppong, Christine. Seven roles of women . Geneva , 1987. xi, 127 p. :
                        NYPL [Sc E 89-143]

WOMEN WORKERS. see WOMEN - EMPLOYMENT.

WOMEN - ZIMBABWE.
Weinrich, A. K. H., 1933- [Women and racial discrimination in Rhodesia. Spanish.] La situación de la mujer en Zimbabue antes de la independencia /. Barcelona , Paris , 1984. 198 p. ; ISBN 92-3-301621-8 (Unesco)
                        NYPL [Sc D 88-615]

WOMEN - ZIMBABWE - BIOGRAPHY.
Bond-Stewart, Kathy. Independence is not only for one sex /. Harare, Zimbabwe , 1987. 128 p. : ISBN 0-949225-50-9 *NYPL [Sc E 89-146]*

Nzenza, Sekai. Zimbabwean woman . London , 1988. 160 p. ;   *NYPL [Sc C 88-291]*

WOMEN - ZIMBABWE - SOCIAL CONDITIONS.
Bond-Stewart, Kathy. Independence is not only for one sex /. Harare, Zimbabwe , 1987. 128 p. : ISBN 0-949225-50-9 *NYPL [Sc E 89-146]*

WOMEN'S CLOTHING. see COSTUME.

Women's concerns and planning. Women and economic development . Oxford [England] ; New York : ix, 231 p. ; ISBN 0-85496-091-0 : DDC 305.4/2 19
HQ1240 .W665 1988   *NYPL [JLD 89-559]*

Women's interest and involvement in income generating activities . Narayan-Parker, Deepa. Gaborone, Botswana [1983] vi, 143, 3 p. ; DDC 331.4/09676/2 19
HD6210.5 .N37 1983   *NYPL [Sc F 88-312]*

WOMEN'S LIB. see FEMINISM.

WOMEN'S LIBERATION MOVEMENT. see FEMINISM.

The women's movement in the Black Baptist church, 1880-1920 /. Brooks, Evelyn, 1945- [Rochester, N.Y.] c1984. xiii, 342 leaves ;
                        NYPL [Sc D 88-938]

The women's war of 1929 . Akpan, Ekwere Otu. Calabar, Nigeria , 1988. vii, 68 p. :
                        NYPL [Sc E 89-20]

WONDER, STEVIE.
Swenson, John. Stevie Wonder /. London , c1986. 160 p. : ISBN 0-85965-076-6 (pbk.) : DDC 784.5/4/00924 B 19
ML410.W836 S9 1986b
                        NYPL [Sc F 88-363]

Wonderful adventures of Mrs. Seacole in many lands /. Seacole, Mary, 1805-1881. New York , 1988. xxxiv, xii, 200 p., [2] p. of plates : ISBN 0-19-505249-8 (alk. paper) DDC 947/.073 19
DK215 .S43 1988   *NYPL [JFC 88-2150]*

The wonders of Hwange /. Rushworth, David. Gweru, Zimbabwe , 1986. 35 p. : ISBN 0-86922-389-5   *NYPL [Sc F 89-43]*

Wondji, Christophe. La Chanson populaire en Côte-d'Ivoire . Paris , c1986. 342 p., [12] p. of plates : ISBN 2-7087-0470-2
                        NYPL [Sc D 88-1099]

Wonyu, Eugène, 1933- Le chrétien, les dons et la mission dans l'église africaine indépendante : réflexions d'un laïc / Eugène Wonyu. Douala : [s.n.], 1979. 68 p. ; 21 cm. DDC 285 19

1. Presbyterian Church in Cameroon. I. Title.
BX9162.C35 W66   *NYPL [Sc D 88-1399]*

WOOD-CARVING - AFRICA, SUB-SAHARAN - EXHIBITIONS.
Mother and child in African Sculpture . New York , 1987. [16] p. :   *NYPL [Sc F 88-3]*

WOOD-CARVING - JAMAICA.
Crooks, Merrise. Rocky, the woodcarver . Brimingham, England , 1984[reprinted 1987] 24 p. :   *NYPL [Sc D 88-1076]*

WOOD-CARVINGS. see WOOD-CARVING.

Wood, M. S. (Mary S.), 1805-1894.
Narratives of colored Americans. New York , 1877. 276 p. ;   *NYPL [Sc Rare C 88-4]*

Narratives of colored Americans. New York , 1882. 276 p. ;   *NYPL [Sc Rare C 88-26]*

Wood, Muriel. (illus) Fisher, Aileen Lucia, 1906- Animal jackets. [Glendale, Calif., 1973] 43 p. ISBN 0-8372-0861-0 DDC [E]
PZ8.3.F634 Ap   *NYPL [Sc F 88-87]*

Wood, Norman Barton, 1857- (joint author) Washington, Booker T. 1856-1915. A new Negro for a new century. Miami, Fla., 1969. 428 p. DDC 301.45/22
E185 .W315 1969b   *NYPL [Sc D 89-43]*

Wood, Peter H., 1943- Winslow Homer's images of Blacks : the Civil War and Reconstruction years / Peter H. Wood, Karen C.C. Dalton ; introduction by Richard J. Powell. Austin : Menil Collection : University of Texas Press, c1988. 144 p. : ill. (some col.) ; 28 cm. "Exhibition schedule, the Menil Collection, Houston 21 October 1988-8 January 1989, Virginia Museum of Fine Arts, Richmond 14 February-2 April 1989, North Carolina Museum of Art, Raleigh 6 May-2 July 1989"--Verso t.p. Bibliography: p. 108-123. ISBN 0-292-79047-3 (University of Texas Press) DDC 759.13 19
1. Homer, Winslow, 1836-1910 - Exhibitions. 2. Afro-Americans in art - Exhibitions. 3. Afro-Americans - History - 1863-1877 - Pictorial works - Exhibitions. I. Homer, Winslow, 1836-1910. II. Dalton, Karen C. C., 1948-. III. Menil Collection (Houston, Tex.). IV. Virginia Museum of Fine Arts. V. Title.
ND237.H7 A4 1988a   *NYPL [Sc F 89-133]*

Wooden, Wayne S. Men behind bars : sexual exploitation in prison / Wayne S. Wooden and Jay Parker. New York : Plenum Press, c1982. x, 264 p. : ill. ; 22 cm. Includes bibliographical references and index. ISBN 0-306-41074-5
1. Prisoners - Sexual behavior. I. Parker, Jay, 1945-. II. Title.   *NYPL [Sc D 89-249]*

WOODFUEL CONSUMPTION - AFRICA.
Leach, Gerald. Beyond the woodfuel crisis . London , 1988. [x], 309 p. : ISBN 1-85383-031-3 (pbk) : DDC 333.75 19
                        NYPL [Sc D 89-397]

Woodling, Chuck. Against all odds : how Kansas won the 1988 NCAA championship / Chuck Woodling. Lawrence, KS : Lawrence Journal-World : Distributed by the University Press of Kansas, c1988. 138 p., [16] p. of plates : ill. (some col.) ; 28 cm. ISBN 0-7006-0387-5 (pbk.) : DDC 796.32/363/0978165 19
1. University of Kansas - Basketball. I. Title.
GV885.43.U52 W66 1988
                        NYPL [JFF 89-236]

WOODS, DONALD, 1933- - DRAMA.
Richard Attenborough's cry freedom . New York , 1987. [128] p. : ISBN 0-394-75838-2 DDC 791.43/72 19
PN1997.C885 A88 1987 *NYPL [Sc G 89-17]*

WOODSON FAMILY.
Woodson, Minnie Shumate. The Sable curtain /. Washington, D.C. , 1987, c1985. 380, 12 p. : ISBN 0-943153-00-X
                        NYPL [Sc D 88-68]

Woodson, Minnie Shumate. The Sable curtain / Minnie Shumate Wooksson. Washington, D.C. : Stafford Lowery Press, 1987, c1985. 380, 12 p. : ill., maps ; 23 cm. Appendix (p. 1-12) describes genealogical research on Woodson. Includes bibliographical references. ISBN 0-943153-00-X
1. Woodson, Thomas - Fiction. 2. Woodson family. 3. Hemings family. 4. Afro-Americans - Genealogy. I. Title.   *NYPL [Sc D 88-68]*

WOODSON, THOMAS - FICTION.
Woodson, Minnie Shumate. The Sable curtain /. Washington, D.C. , 1987, c1985. 380, 12 p. : ISBN 0-943153-00-X   *NYPL [Sc D 88-68]*

Woody, Regina Llewellyn (Jones) Almena's dogs / by Regina Woody ; illustrated by Elton C. Fax. New York : Ariel Books, c1954. 240 p. : ill. ; 22 cm. SCHOMBURG CHILDREN'S COLLECTION.
1. Dogs - Juvenile fiction. 2. Afro-American children - Juvenile fiction. I. Fax, Elton, illus. II. Schomburg Children's Collection. III. Title.
NYPL [Sc D 88-648]

Worcester County Colonization Society. Report made at an adjourned meeting of the friends of the American Colonization Society, in Worcester County, held in Worcester, Dec. 8, 1830 / by a committee appointed for that purpose ; with the proceedings of the meeting, &c. Worcester : Printed by S.H. Colton, 1831. 20 p. ; 23 cm.
1. Afro-Americans - Colonization - Liberia. I. Title.
NYPL [Sc Rare G 86-29]

The words of Desmond Tutu /. Tutu, Desmond. New York , c1989. 109 p. : ISBN 1-557-04038-9 (dust jacket) : DDC 283/.68 19
BX5700.6.Z8 T875 1989
NYPL [Sc D 89-495]

WORK CAMPS - TANZANIA.
Kullas, Ulrike. Lernen von der Dritten Welt? . Saarbrücken , Fort Lauderdale , 1982. 174 p. : ISBN 3-88156-233-8   *NYPL [Sc D 89-339]*

The work of the Afro-American woman /. Mossell, N. F., Mrs., 1855- New York , 1988. xlii, 178 p. : ISBN 0-19-505265-X (alk. paper) DDC 305.8/96073 19
E185.86 .M65 1988   *NYPL [JFC 88-2155]*

Workable strategies to end Africa's poverty . Katapu, Agbeko. Syracuse, N.Y. , c1986. xxiv, 288 p. ; ISBN 0-944338-00-3 DDC 338.96 19
HC800 .K37 1988   *NYPL [Sc D 89-610]*

WORKERS. see LABOR AND LABORING CLASSES.

WORKERS PARTY OF JAMAICA.
Munroe, Trevor. The working class party . [Jamaica?] , 1983. 72 p. ; DDC 324.27292/075 19
JL639.A8 W676 1983 *NYPL [Sc D 88-1271]*

Working bibliography .
(no. 9) Henderson, Francine I. A guide to periodical articles about Botswana, 1965-80 /. Gaborone, Botswana , 1982. v, 147, 6 p. ; DDC 016.96811 19
Z3559 .H46 1982 DT791
NYPL [Sc F 88-161]

The working class party . Munroe, Trevor. [Jamaica?] , 1983. 72 p. ; DDC 324.27292/075 19
JL639.A8 W676 1983 *NYPL [Sc D 88-1271]*

WORKING-CLASSES. see LABOR AND LABORING CLASSES.

WORKING-GIRLS. see CHILDREN - EMPLOYMENT.

WORKING-MEN'S ASSOCIATIONS. see TRADE-UNIONS.

WORKING-MEN'S LUNCH ROOMS. see RESTAURANTS, LUNCH ROOMS, ETC.

Working paper (CREDU (Organization)) .
(no. 2) Patel, H. H. No master, no mortgage, no sale . Nairobi, Kenya , 1987. 61 p. columns ;   *NYPL [Sc F 88-297]*

Working paper (National Institute of Development Research & Documentation (Botswana)) .
(no. 44) Narayan-Parker, Deepa. Women's interest and involvement in income generating activities . Gaborone, Botswana [1983] vi, 143, 3 p. ; DDC 331.4/09676/2 19
HD6210.5 .N37 1983   *NYPL [Sc F 88-312]*

Working under South African occupation : labour in Namibia. London : International Defence & Aid Fund, 1987. 56 p. ; 21 cm. (Fact paper on Southern Africa . no. 14) Includes index. Bibliography: p. 47-48. ISBN 0-904759-73-3 (pbk.). DDC 968 s 331.6/9/9688 19
1. Labor and laboring classes - Namibia. 2. Blacks - Employment - Namibia. 3. Trade-unions - Namibia. 4. Namibia - Economic conditions. I. International Defence and Aid Fund. II. Series.
DT746 .F3 no. 14 HD8808
NYPL [Sc D 89-525]

WORKINGMEN. see LABOR AND LABORING CLASSES.

The works of Alice Dunbar-Nelson /. Dunbar-Nelson, Alice Moore, 1875-1935. [Works. 1988.] New York , 1988. 3 v. : ISBN 0-19-505250-1 (v. 1 : alk. paper) DDC 818/.5209 19
PS3507 .U6228 1988   *NYPL [JFC 88-2143]*

Workshop on Social Development, Rural Poverty, and Fieldwork Intervention (1986 : Harare, Zimbabwe) Social development and rural fieldwork . Zimbabwe [1986]. 96 p. ;
NYPL [Sc D 88-1153]

World Alliance of YMCAs. What is apartheid? Geneva, Switzerland [1986]. 72 p. :
NYPL [Sc D 88-326]

The World Book atlas. World Book, Inc. Chicago , c1988. 1 atlas (432 p.) : ill. (some col.), col. maps ; 38 cm. ISBN 0-7166-3181-4 : DDC 912 19
G1021 .W6735 1986   *NYPL [Sc Ref 89-1]*

World Book, Inc. The World Book atlas. Revised 1988 ed. Chicago : World Book, c1988. 1 atlas (432 p.) : ill. (some col.), col. maps ; 38 cm. Maps copyright by Rand McNally and Company and Istituto geografico De Agostini. Includes index and glossary. Bibliography: p. 302-303. CONTENTS. - Looking at earth's features -- Looking at earth's people and their lands -- Looking at earth as a planet -- Thematic maps -- Understanding maps -- Maps of the world -- Maps of the United States and Canada -- Geographical information and maps of the world index.
ISBN 0-7166-3181-4 : DDC 912 19
I. Rand McNally and Company. II. Istituto geografico De Agostini. III. Title.
G1021 .W6735 1986   *NYPL [Sc Ref 89-1]*

World Confederation of Organizations of the Teaching Professions. Panafrican Conference on Education (1984 : Yaoundé, Cameroon) What school for Africa in the year 2000? /. Morges, Switzerland [1984?] 190 p. ;
NYPL [Sc D 88-611]

World Council of Churches. Division of Inter-church Aid, Refugee and World Service. All Africa Conference of Churches. Special Agency for EPEAA. Ecumenical Programme for Emergency Action in Africa . Nairobi , 1967. [193] p. ;   *NYPL [Sc F 88-74]*

World Council of Churches. Inter-church Aid, Refugee and World Service, Division of. see World Council of Churches. Division of Inter-church Aid, Refugee and World Service.

WORLD ECONOMICS. see COMMERCIAL POLICY.

World Future Studies Federation. Reclaiming the future . Oxford , Riverton, N.J. , c1986. xvi, 197 p. ; ISBN 1-85148-010-2 (pbk.) : DDC 303.4/96 19
DT4 .R43 1986   *NYPL [Sc D 88-584]*

World landmark books.
(W-33) Daniel, Anita. The story of Albert Schweitzer /. New York , 1957. 179 p. :
NYPL [Sc D 88-379]

WORLD LITERATURE. see LITERATURE.

The world of Patience Gromes . Davis, Scott C., 1948- [Lexington, Ky.] , 1988. 222 p. ; ISBN 0-8131-1644-9 DDC 975.5/45100496073 19
F234.R59 N43 1988   *NYPL [Sc D 88-1302]*

The world of the Ogbanje /. Achebe, Chinwe. Enugu, Nigeria , 1986. iv, 68 p. : ISBN 978-15-6239-0 DDC 616.89/1 19
RC455.4.E8 A34 1986
NYPL [Sc D 88-1246]

World Peace Foundation. Africa in the 1990s and beyond . Algonac, Mich. , 1988. 309 p. : ISBN 0-917256-44-1 (pbk.) : DDC 303.4/8273/06 19
DT38 .A44 1988   *NYPL [Sc E 89-98]*

A World Peace Foundation Study.
Africa in the 1990s and beyond . Algonac, Mich. , 1988. 309 p. : ISBN 0-917256-44-1 (pbk.) : DDC 303.4/8273/06 19
DT38 .A44 1988   *NYPL [Sc E 89-98]*

WORLD POLITICS - 1955-1965 - CONGRESSES.
Appeal for world peace [microform] . Accra [1961?] 19 p. :   *NYPL [Sc Micro F-10978]*

World Social Prospects Study Association. Reclaiming the future . Oxford , Riverton,

N.J. , c1986. xvi, 197 p. : ISBN 1-85148-010-2 (pbk.) : DDC 303.4/96 19
DT4 .R43 1986   *NYPL [Sc D 88-584]*

WORLD WAR, 1914-1918 - BLACKS - SOUTH AFRICA.
Grunlingh, A. M., 1948- Fighting their own war . Johannesburg , 1987. x, 200 p. ; ISBN 0-86975-321-5   *NYPL [Sc D 88-897]*

WORLD WAR, 1914-1918 - CAMPAIGNS - AFRICA.
Farwell, Byron. The Great War in Africa 1914-1918 /. Harmondsworth , 1987. 382 p. : ISBN 0-670-80244-1 : DDC 940.4/16 19
D575   *NYPL [Sc D 88-834]*

WORLD WAR, 1914-1918 - PARTICIPATION, BLACK.
Grunlingh, A. M., 1948- Fighting their own war . Johannesburg , 1987. x, 200 p. ; ISBN 0-86975-321-5   *NYPL [Sc D 88-897]*

WORLD WAR, 1914-1918 - SOUTH AFRICA.
Grunlingh, A. M., 1948- Fighting their own war . Johannesburg , 1987. x, 200 p. ; ISBN 0-86975-321-5   *NYPL [Sc D 88-897]*

WORLD WAR, 1939-1945 - AERIAL OPERATIONS, AMERICAN.
Francis, Charles E. The Tuskegee airmen . Boston, MA , c1988. 300, [33] p. : ISBN 0-8283-1386-5 : DDC 940.54/4973 19
D790 .F637 1988   *NYPL [Sc E 89-164]*

Johnson, Hayden C. The Fighting 99th Air Squadron, 1941-45 /. New York , c1987. 49 p. : ISBN 0-533-06879-7 : DDC 940.54/4973 19
D790 .J57 1987   *NYPL [Sc D 88-1192]*

WORLD WAR, 1939-1945 - BLACKS - FICTION.
Doumbi-Fakoly. Morts pour la France /. Paris , 1983. 150 p. ; ISBN 2-86537-074-7
NYPL [Sc C 88-346]

WORLD WAR, 1939-1945 - MARTINIQUE - FICTION.
Confiant, Raphaël. Le nègre et l'amiral . Paris , c1988. 334 p. ; ISBN 2-246-40991-8
NYPL [Sc D 89-340]

WORLD WAR, 1939-1945 - PARTICIPATION, AFRO-AMERICAN.
Francis, Charles E. The Tuskegee airmen . Boston, MA , c1988. 300, [33] p. : ISBN 0-8283-1386-5 : DDC 940.54/4973 19
D790 .F637 1988   *NYPL [Sc E 89-164]*

McGuire, Phillip, 1944- He, too, spoke for democracy . New York , c1988. xvii, 154 p. ; ISBN 0-313-26115-6 (lib. bdg. : alk. paper) DDC 355/.008996073 B 19
KF373.H38 M35 1988   *NYPL [Sc E 88-347]*

Smith, Graham. When Jim Crow met John Bull . London , c1987. 265 p. ; ISBN 1-85043-039-X   *NYPL [Sc D 88-55]*

WORLD WAR, 1939-1945 - PARTICIPATION, AFRO-AMERICAN - FICTION.
Covin, David, 1940- Brown sky . Chicago , c1987. 274 p. ; ISBN 0-910671-11-7 : DDC 813/.54 19
PS3553.O875 B7 1987   *NYPL [JFD 88-427]*

World's Alliance of Young Men's Christian Associations. see World Alliance of YMCAs.

Worlds apart : an anthology of lesbian and gay science fiction and fantasy / edited by Camilla Decarnin, Eric Garber, and Lyn Paleo.1st ed. Boston, Mass. : Alyson Publications, 1986. 293 p. ; 21 cm. ISBN 0-932870-87-2 (pbk.) : DDC 813/.0876/08353 19
1. Homosexuality - Fiction. 2. Science fiction, American. 3. Fantastic fiction, American. 4. American fiction - 20th century. I. Decarnin, Camilla. II. Garber, Eric. III. Paleo, Lyn.
PS648.H57 W67 1986   *NYPL [JFD 87-7753]*

Worlds of music : an introduction to the music of the world's peoples / Jeff Todd Titon, general editor. New York : Schirmer Books, c1984. xviii, 325 p. : ill., music ; 25 cm. Includes bibliographical references and index. CONTENTS. - The music-culture as a world of music / by Mark Slobin and Jeff Todd Titon -- North America/Native America / by David P. McAllester -- Africa/Ghana / by James T. Koetting -- North America/Black America / by Jeff Todd Titon -- Europe/Peasant music-cultures of eastern Europe / by Mark Slobin -- India/South India / by David B. Reck -- South India/Instrument building and performance / by David B. Reck -- Discovering and documenting a world of music / by

David B. Reck, Mark Slobin, and Jeff Todd Titon.
ISBN 0-02-872600-6 DDC 781.7 19
*1. Ethnomusicology. 2. Music - History and criticism. I.
Titon, Jeff.*
ML3798 .W67 1984   *NYPL [Sc E 85-247]*

Wormley, Stanton L. (Stanton Lawrence), 1909-
Sluby, Paul E. Holmead's Cemetery (Western
Burial Ground), Washington, D.C. /.
Washington, D.C. , 1985. iv, 68 leaves :   DDC
929.5/09753 19
F193 .S582 1985   *NYPL [Sc D 88-109]*

Sluby, Paul E. Selected small cemeteries of
Washington, DC /. [Washington] , c1987. 84
p. :   *NYPL [Sc D 88-780]*

Worrell, Vernon, 1952- Under the flambo : poems
for children / Vernon Worrell. Bridgetown,
Barbados : V. Worrell, 1986. ix, 84 p. : ill. ; 23
cm. Includes index. A Barbadian poet writes of work,
nature, fishing, food, and generally the familiar life of
children in Barbados. Includes a glossary and activities
for a classroom. SCHOMBURG CHILDREN'S
COLLECTION.   DDC 811 19
*1. Children's poetry, Barbadian. 2. Barbadian poetry. 3.
Barbados - Poetry. I. Schomburg Children's Collection.
II. Title.*
PR9230.9.W67 U5 1986
                                  NYPL [Sc D 88-945]

Worth noting . Berman, Sanford, 1933- Jefferson,
N.C. , c1988. viii, 175 p. ;   ISBN 0-89950-304-7
(lib. bdg.) :   DDC 081 19
Z674 .B44 1988   *NYPL [JFE 88-5518]*

Wosornu, Lade. The casebook of Dr. O.P. Asem
/ by Lade Wosornu. Accra : Sedco, 1985- v, ;
19 cm. Plays. CONTENTS. - v. 1.The unattached, the
hooked, and the married.   ISBN 996-472-044-0
1. Health education - Nigeria - Drama. I. Title.
                                  NYPL [Sc C 89-91]

The wrath of Koma /. Mumba, Maurice
Kambishera. Nairobi , 1987. 153 p. ;   ISBN
996-646-342-6   *NYPL [Sc C 89-45]*

Wren, Robert M. Chinua Achebe, Things fall
apart / Robert M. Wren. London : Longman,
1980. vi, 56 p. ; 20 cm. (Longman guides to
literature)   ISBN 0-582-60109-6
*I. Achebe, Chinua. Things fall apart. II. Title. III.
Series.*   *NYPL [Sc C 88-88]*

Wright, Bruce, 1918- Black robes, white justice /
by Bruce Wright. Secaucus, N.J. : L. Stuart,
c1987. 214 p. ; 24 cm.   ISBN 0-8184-0422-1 :
  DDC 345.73/05/08996073 347.305508996073 19
*1. Wright, Bruce, 1918-. 2. Afro-American judges -
New York (N.Y.) - Biography. 3. Criminal courts -
New York (N.Y.). 4. Criminal justice, Administration
of - New York (N.Y.). 5. Race discrimination - New
York (N.Y.). I. Title.*
KF373.W67 A33 1987   *NYPL [JLE 87-2842]*

WRIGHT, BRUCE, 1918-
Wright, Bruce, 1918- Black robes, white justice
/. Secaucus, N.J. , c1987. 214 p. ;   ISBN
0-8184-0422-1 :   DDC 345.73/05/08996073
347.305508996073 19
KF373.W67 A33 1987   *NYPL [JLE 87-2842]*

Wright, Giles R. Afro-Americans in New Jersey :
a short history / Giles R. Wright. Trenton :
New Jersey Historical Commission, Dept. of
State, c1988. 100 p. : ill. ; 23 cm. Bibliography: p.
99-100.   ISBN 0-89743-075-1   DDC 974.9/00496073
19
*1. Afro-Americans - New Jersey - History. 2. New
Jersey - Race relations. I. Title.*
E185.93.N54 W75 1988
                                  NYPL [Sc D 89-529]

Wright, Jay. Selected poems of Jay Wright /
edited with an introduction by Robert B.
Stepto ; afterword by Harold Bloom. Princeton,
N.J. : Princeton University Press, c1987. xv,
197 p. ; 23 cm. (Princeton series of contemporary
poets)   ISBN 0-691-06687-6 (alk. paper)   DDC
811/.54 19
I. Stepto, Robert B. II. Title.
PS3573.R5364 A6 1987
                                  NYPL [JFD 87-6880]

Wright, John, 1770?-1844. (tr) Wimpffen,
François Alexandre Stanislaus, baron de. A
voyage to Saint Domingo, in the years 1788,
1789, and 1790. London, 1817 [i. e. 1797] 371
p.   *NYPL [Sc 917.294-W]*

Wright, Richard, 1908-1960.
Eight men. [1st ed.] Cleveland, World Pub. Co.
[1961] 250 p. 21 cm. Short stories.

1. Afro-American men - Fiction. I. Title.
PZ3.W9352 Ei   *NYPL [Sc Rare F 88-59]*

Eight men : stories / by Richard Wright ;
foreword by David Bradley. New York :
Thunder's Mouth Press : Distributed by Persea
Books Inc., c1987. xxv, 250 p. ; 22 cm.   ISBN
0-938410-39-3 :   DDC 813/.52 19
1. Afro-American men - Fiction. I. Title.
PS3545.R815 E4 1987 *NYPL [Sc D 89-376]*

NATIVE SON.
Joyce, Joyce Ann, 1949- Richard Wright's art
of tragedy /. Iowa City , 1986. xvii, 129 p. ;
  ISBN 0-87745-148-6   DDC 813/.52 19
PS3545.R815 N34 1986
                                  NYPL [JFD 87-289]

Pagan Spain / Richard Wright. London :
Bodley Head, 1960, c1957. 191 p. ; 22 cm.
1. Spain - Description and travel - 1951-. I. Title.
                                  NYPL [Sc Rare F 88-65]

12 million Black voices /. New York , 1988,
c1941. xx, 152 p. :   ISBN 0-938410-48-2 :   DDC
973/.0496073 19
E185.86 .A13 1988   *NYPL [Sc F 88-315]*

WRIGHT, RICHARD, 1908-1960.
Walker, Margaret, 1915- Richard Wright,
daemonic genius . New York , c1988. xix, 428
p., [8] leaves of plates :   ISBN 0-446-71001-6
  DDC 813/.52 B 19
PS3545.R815 Z892 1988
                                  NYPL [Sc E 88-604]

**WRIGHT, RICHARD, 1908-1960 - CRITICISM
AND INTERPRETATION.**
Benson, Brian Joseph. The short fiction of
Richard Wright [microform] /. 1972. 266
leaves.   *NYPL [Sc Micro R-4217]*

Liston, Carolyn Olivia. Black positivism through
character growth and development in the short
stories of Richard Wright [microform] /. 1982.
xii, 207 p.   *NYPL [Sc Micro R-4819]*

**WRIGHT, RICHARD, 1908-1960 -
BIOGRAPHY - JUVENILE LITERATURE.**
Urban, Joan, 1950- Richard Wright /. New
York, N.Y. [1989] 111 p. :   ISBN 1-555-46618-4
  DDC 813/.52 19
PS3545.R815 Z85 1989
                                  NYPL [Sc E 89-196]

Wright, Stephen, 1954-
Africa in world politics . Houndmills,
Basingstoke, Hampshire , 1987. xvi, 214 p. ;
  ISBN 0-333-39630-8 *NYPL [Sc D 88-220]*

Nigeria, the dilemmas ahead : a political risk
analysis / by Stephen Wright. London :
Economist Publications Ltd., Economist
Intelligence Unit, c1986. 88 p. : map ; 30 cm.
(EIU political risk series) Special report / Economist
Intelligence Unit ; no. 1072 "November 1986."
*1. Nigeria - Politics and government - 1960-. 2.
Nigeria - Economic conditions - 1960-. I. Series. II.
Series: EIU special report, no. 1072. III. Title.*
                                  NYPL [Sc F 88-137]

WRITERS' MARKETS. see AUTHORSHIP.

**WRITING (AUTHORSHIP) see
AUTHORSHIP; CREATIVE WRITING.**

The writing of Wole Soyinka /. Jones, Eldred D.
London , Portsmouth, N.H. , 1988. xiv, 242 p. ;
  ISBN 0-435-08021-0 (pbk. : U. S.)   DDC 822 19
PR9387.9.S6 Z7 1988   *NYPL [Sc D 88-1134]*

Wucher King, Joan. Historical dictionary of
Egypt / by Joan Wucher King. Metuchen,
N.J. : Scarecrow Press, 1984. xiii, 719 p. :
maps ; 23 cm. (African historical dictionaries. no. 36
36) Bibliography: p. 651-719.   ISBN 0-8108-1670-9
  DDC 962/.003/21 19
1. Egypt - History - Dictionaries. I. Title. II. Series.
DT45 .W83 1984   *NYPL [Sc D 85-101]*

**WUNDERMAN, LESTER - ART
COLLECTIONS - EXHIBITIONS.**
Ezra, Kate. Art of the Dogon . New York ,
1988. 116 p. :   ISBN 0-87099-507-3 :   DDC
730/.089963 19
N7399.M3 E97 1988   *NYPL [Sc F 88-160]*

Wymeersch, Patrick. Les Bin Kanyok : culture et
traditions, Rép. du Zaïre / Patrick Wymeersch.
Bandundu, République du Zaïre : Ceeba, 1983.
ix, 368 p. : ill. ; 30 cm. (Publications (Ceeba). Série
II . v. 84) Bibliography: p. 357-368.
1. Bin Kanyok (African people). 2. Zaire - Social life

and customs. 3. Zaire - Civilization. I. Series. II. Series:
Publications (Ceeba). Série II , v. 84. III. Title.
                                  NYPL [Sc F 89-41]

Wynes, Charles E. Charles Richard Drew : the
man and the myth / Charles E. Wynes.
Urbana : University of Illinois Press, c1988. xvi,
132 p., [14] p. of plates : ill. ; 24 cm. (Blacks in
the new world) Includes index. Bibliography: p.
121-123.   ISBN 0-252-01551-7   DDC 610/.92/4 B 19
*1. Drew, Charles Richard, 1904-1950. 2. Physicians -
United States - Biography. 3. Afro-American
physicians - Biography. I. Title. II. Series.*
R154.D75 W96 1988   *NYPL [Sc E 89-65]*

Wynne, Patrice. The Womanspirit sourcebook .
San Francisco , c1988. xxv, 277 p. :   ISBN
0-06-250982-9 (pbk.) :   DDC 291/.088042 19
BL458 .W575 1988   *NYPL [Sc F 88-294]*

Wyse, Akintola. The Krio of Sierra Leone : an
interpretive history / Akintola Wyse. London :
Hurst, 1989. xiii, 156 p. : ill. ; 23 cm.
(International library of Sierra Leone studies . 2)
Includes bibliography and index.   ISBN 1-85322-006-X
  DDC 966.4/04969729 19
1. Creoks (Sierra Leone) - History. I. Title.
                                  NYPL [Sc D 89-566]

X/self /. Brathwaite, Edward. Oxford
[Oxfordshire] , New York , 1987. vi, 131 p. ;
  ISBN 0-19-281987-9 (pbk.) :   DDC 811 19
PR9230.9.B68 X7 1987
                                  NYPL [JFD 87-5776]

Xango /. Fichte, Hubert. Frankfurt am Main ,
1981. 353 p. ;   ISBN 3-10-020701-7
                                  NYPL [Sc D 88-1481]

Xangô e inhaçã /. Linares, Ronaldo Antonio. [São
Paulo] , c1987. 85 p. ;   *NYPL [Sc D 88-553]*

Xitala Mati /. Muianga, Aldino, 1950- [Maputo?]
[1987?] 87 p. ;   *NYPL [Sc D 88-531]*

Yachir, F. Enjeux miniers en Afrique / Fayçal
Yachir ; préface de Samir Amin. Paris :
Karthala, c1987. 180 p. ; 22 cm. (Les Afriques)
  ISBN 2-86537-170-0
*1. Mineral industries - Africa. 2. Mines and mineral
resources - Africa. I. Series: Collection Les Afriques. II.
Title.*
HD9506.A382 Y34 1987
                                  NYPL [Sc D 89-194]

Yahya, Saad, 1939- English-Swahili glossary of
technical terms for valuers and land economists
/ Saad S. Yahya. [Nairobi] : Dept. of Land
Development, University of Nairobi, [1979] [8]
leaves ; 30 cm. "January 1979."   DDC 333/.003/21
19
*1. Land use - Dictionaries. 2. Real property -
Valuation - Dictionaries. 3. English language -
Dictionaries - Swahili. I. University of Nairobi. Dept. of
Land Development. II. Title.*
HD107.7 .Y34 1979   *NYPL [Sc F 88-77]*

**Ya'Ityoḟy a 'ortodoks taw aḥedo béta kerestiy
an.** The Church of Ethiopia, a panorama of
history and spiritual life. Addis Ababa,
Ethiopian Orthodox Church, 1970. iv, 97 p.
illus., map, ports. 22 cm. Cover title. Chairman of
Publication Committee: Sergew Hable Selassie. A
publication of the Ethiopian Orthodox Church.
*1. Ya'Ityoḟy a 'ortodoks taw aḥedo béta kerestiy an. I.
Sergew Hable Selassie, 1929-. II. Title.*
                                  NYPL [Sc D 89-386]

**YA'ITYOḞY A 'ORTODOKS TAW AḤEDO
BÉTA KERESTIY AN.**
Ya'Ityoḟy a 'ortodoks taw aḥedo béta kerestiy
an. The Church of Ethiopia. Addis Ababa,
1970. iv, 97 p.   *NYPL [Sc D 89-386]*

Yajima, Isao, 1945- Mode drawing / instructed
by Isao Yajima. Tokyo, Japan : Toshiro Kuze ;
Graphic-sha Pub. Co., 1986. 105 p. : chiefly
ill. ; 27 cm. Title on cover: Mode drawing, nude
[male]. Text in English and Japanese.   ISBN
4-7661-0394-7
*1. Figure drawing - Study and teaching. I. Title. II.
Title: Mode drawing, nude.*   *NYPL [Sc F 88-238]*

Yakubu, Balaraba Ramat. Budurwar zuciya /
Balaraba Ramat Yakubu. Zaria : Gaskiya Corp.,
1987. 87 p. ; 18 cm.
1. Hausa language - Texts. I. Title.
                                  NYPL [Sc C 88-301]

Yale strike of 1984-85. On strike for respect .
Chicago , 1988. 94 p. ;   *NYPL [Sc C 89-101]*

**The Yankee slave-dealer, or, An abolitionist down
South .** Texan. Nashville, Tenn. , 1860. 368 p. ;
                                  NYPL [Sc Rare C 88-21]

Yarbrough, Camille. The shimmershine queens / Camille Yarbrough. New York : G.P. Putnam's, c1988. 142 p. ; 22 cm. Two fifth graders try to uplift themselves and their classmates out of a less than beautiful urban present by encouraging dreams and the desire to achieve them. SCHOMBURG CHILDREN'S COLLECTION. ISBN 0-399-21465-8 DDC [Fic] 19
1. Afro-American children - Juvenile fiction. 2. Schools - Juvenile fiction. I. Schomburg Children's Collection. II. Title.
PZ7.Y1955 Sh 1988 **NYPL [Sc D 89-283]**

Yard, Lionel M. Biography of Amy Ashwood Garvey, 1897-1969 : co-founder of the Universal Negro Improvement Association / by Lionel M. Yard. [S.l.] : Associated Publishers, [198-?] vii, 233 p. : ill., ports. ; 24 cm. Includes index. Bibliography: p. v.
1. Garvey, Amy Ashwood, 1895-1969. 2. Women - Jamaica - Biography. 3. Back to Africa movement. I. Title. **NYPL [Sc E 88-541]**

Yardbird suite . Koch, Lawrence O. Bowling Green, Ohio , c1988. 336 p. : ISBN 0-87972-259-2 (clothbound)
NYPL [Sc E 89-48]

YATENGA (KINGDOM) - HISTORY.
Princes & serviteurs du royaume . Paris , 1987. 225 p. : ISBN 2-901161-29-4
NYPL [Sc E 88-409]

A year for my nation /. Awonge, Flora. Calabar , c1986. 99 p. :
MLCS 87/7812 (P) **NYPL [Sc C 88-155]**

Yeboah-Afari, Ajoa. The sound of pestles and other stories / Ajoa Yeboah-Afari. Accra : Afram Publications, 1986. 72 p. ; 18 cm. ISBN 996-470-046-6
1. Ghana - Fiction. I. Title. **NYPL [Sc C 88-352]**

Yemitan, Oladipo. Madame Tinubu : merchant and king-maker / Oladipo Yemitan. Ibadan : University Press, 1987. x, 85 p. : ill., map ; 21 cm. Bibliography: p. 80. ISBN 978-15-4985-9
1. Tinubu, Efunroye 1805-1887. 2. Politicians - Nigeria - Biography. 3. Women, Egba (African people) - Biography. 4. Women - Nigeria - Biography. I. Title. **NYPL [Sc D 88-1382]**

Yerrinton, James M. W. Anti-Slavery Meeting (1855 : Boston) The Boston mob of "gentlemen of property and standing." . Boston , 1855 (Boston : J.B. Yerrinton and Son, printers) 76 p. ;
E450.B74 **NYPL [Sc Rare F 88-44]**

Yesterday's people. Martin, Robert, 1929- Garden City, N.Y. [1970] 158 p. DDC 916.8/03
DT764.B8 M35 **NYPL [Sc F 88-248]**

Les yeux du volcan . Sony Lab'Ou Tansi. Paris , c1988. 191 p. ; ISBN 2-02-010082-7
NYPL [Sc D 89-237]

Yhdysvallat. see United States.

Ylla, 1910-1955. Animals in Africa / photographed by Ylla; text by L.S.B. Leakey. New York : Harper, 1953. 146 p. : ill. (some col.) ; 27 cm.
1. Zoology - Africa. 2. Animal behavior - Africa. I. Leakey, Louis Seymour Bazett, 1903-1972. II. Title.
NYPL [Sc F 88-127]

Yoka Lye Mudaba, 1947- Le fossoyeur / Yoka Lyé Mudaba ; et sept autres nouvelles. Paris : Hatier, 1986. 127 p. ; 18 cm. (Collection Monde noir poche) A collection of prize-winning stories from the Concours radiophonique de la meilleure nouvelle de langue française. CONTENTS. - Le fossoyeur / Yoka Lyé Mukaba.--Le rôle du tyan / Cheikh C. Sow.--Le corbillard / Kitia Touré.--La couture de Paris / Baba Moustapha.--Lese-majesté / Sony Lab'ou-Tansi.--L'ami-de-celui-qui-vient-apre's-le-directeur / Senouvo Asbota Zinsou.--Enterrement d'une jeunesse / Ibrahima Sall.--L'Île de Pharisie / Alexix Goma-Loufouma. ISBN 2-218-07830-9
1. Short stories, African (French). I. Concours radiophonique de la meilleure nouvelle de langue française. II. Title. III. Series.
NYPL [Sc C 88-10]

Yoruba . Bamgbose, Ayo. Lagos, Nigeria , 1986. xvii, 83 p. ; **NYPL [Sc D 88-1091]**

YORUBA (AFRICAN PEOPLE) - HISTORY - 19TH CENTURY.
Falola, Toyin. The military in nineteenth century Yoruba politics /. Ile-Ife [Nigeria] , c1984. 127 p. ; ISBN 978-13-6064-X (pbk.) DDC

966.9/004963 19
DT515.45.Y67 F35 1984
NYPL [Sc D 88-227]

YORUBA (AFRICAN PEOPLE) - POLITICS AND GOVERNMENT.
Falola, Toyin. The military in nineteenth century Yoruba politics /. Ile-Ife [Nigeria] , c1984. 127 p. ; ISBN 978-13-6064-X (pbk.) DDC 966.9/004963 19
DT515.45.Y67 F35 1984
NYPL [Sc D 88-227]

YORUBA (AFRICAN PEOPLE) - WARFARE.
Falola, Toyin. The military in nineteenth century Yoruba politics /. Ile-Ife [Nigeria] , c1984. 127 p. ; ISBN 978-13-6064-X (pbk.) DDC 966.9/004963 19
DT515.45.Y67 F35 1984
NYPL [Sc D 88-227]

Yoruba dun ka . Odedeyi, M. B. London , New York , 1965. 75 p. : **NYPL [Sc C 88-275]**

The Yoruba language . Adewole, Lawrence Olufemi. Hamburg , c1987. 182 p. ; ISBN 3-87118-842-5 **NYPL [Sc D 88-821]**

YORUBA LANGUAGE - BIBLIOGRAPHY.
Adewole, Lawrence Olufemi. The Yoruba language . Hamburg , c1987. 182 p. ; ISBN 3-87118-842-5 **NYPL [Sc D 88-821]**

YORUBA LANGUAGE - GRAMMAR.
Ìjìnlè èdè àti lítírés̩ Ibadan, Nigeria , 1986. vi, 109 p. : ISBN 978-16-7525-X
NYPL [Sc D 89-248]

YORUBA LANGUAGE - HISTORY.
Bamgbose, Ayo. Yoruba . Lagos, Nigeria , 1986. xvii, 83 p. ; **NYPL [Sc D 88-1091]**

YORUBA LANGUAGE - READERS.
Odedeyi, M. B. Yoruba dun ka . London , New York , 1965. 75 p. : **NYPL [Sc C 88-275]**

YORUBA LANGUAGE - TEXT-BOOKS.
Babalọlá, Adébóyè. Iwe ede yoruba . [Ikeja] [1968] 139 p. : **NYPL [Sc C 88-127]**

YORUBA LANGUAGE - TEXTS.
Ab Ibadan , 1986. vii. 108 p. : ISBN 978-245-824-4 **NYPL [Sc C 88-358]**
Adéwọlé, Lásún. Àláyé Akéwi /. Ìbàdàn , 1987. v. 90 p. ; ISBN 978-14-5062-2
NYPL [Sc C 88-217]
Akinlabí, Bánjọ. Nńkan Às̩írí /. Ibadan, Oyo State, Nigeria , 1985. 62 p. ; ISBN 978-14-1052-3 **NYPL [Sc D 88-1381]**
Akójọp Lagos , 1986. xi, 324 p., map, ports. ; ISBN 978-13-2563-1 **NYPL [Sc D 88-955]**
Àlàbá, 'Gbóyèga. Àkójọp Nigeria , 1985. 118 p. ; ISBN 978-227-101-2
NYPL [Sc D 88-1373]
Am Al Ibàdan, Nigeria , 1987, c1978. vi, 136 p. ; ISBN 978-16-7488-1 **NYPL [Sc D 88-952]**
Awóyele, Oyètúndé. Akéwì ló n'ìtàn . Ìbàdàn , 1987. iv, 97 p. ; ISBN 978-14-5044-4
NYPL [Sc C 88-216]
Babalọlá, Adébóyè. Àw on oríkì oríl`e /. Glasgow U.K. , 1967. 160 p. ;
NYPL [Sc C 89-112]
Babayemi, S. O. Content analysis of oríkì oríl [Ibadan , 198-?] xi, 352 p. ;
NYPL [Sc E 89-229]
Kenyo, Elisha Alademomi. Awon olori Yoruba ati isedale won /. Lagos, Nigeria , 1952. 96 p. :
NYPL [Sc D 88-818]
Ọpadọtun, 'Tunji. Aròf Ibàdàn , 1987. v, 82 p. ; ISBN 978-14-5069-X **NYPL [Sc C 88-218]**
Ọpadọtun, 'Tunji. Arokò . Ibadan , 1986. viii, 120 p. : ISBN 978-245-840-6
NYPL [Sc D 88-948]
Owolabi, Olu. Agbà tí ń y Ibàdàn, Nigeria , 1985. iii, 117 p. ; ISBN 978-16-7246-3
NYPL [Sc C 88-219]
Owolabi, Olu. Ija Ọr Ibadan, Nigeria , 1986, c1983. vi, 84 p. : ISBN 978-16-7245-5
NYPL [Sc D 88-954]
Ramos, Miguel. Ase omo osayin-- ewe aye /. [S.l.] , 1985, c1982. 113 p. ;
NYPL [Sc D 89-487]

YORUBA LANGUAGES - TEXTS.
Olabimtan, Afọlabi. B'ó ti gb` /. Ìbàdàn,

Nigeria , 1987, c1980. v. 83 p. ; ISBN 978-16-7487-3 **NYPL [Sc D 88-953]**

Yoruba medicines /. Warren, Dennis M. Legon , 1971 [i.e. 1973] iii, 93, xii, p. ; DDC 615.8/99 19
DT515.45.Y67 W37 1973
NYPL [Sc G 88-34]

Yoruba Muslim youth and Christian-sponsored education /. Noibi, D. O. S. Ijebu-Ode, Nigeria , 1987. 44 p. ; ISBN 978-253-020-4
NYPL [Sc D 89-537]

YORUBA PROVERBS. see PROVERBS, YORUBA.

YORUBA TALES. see TALES, YORUBA.

YORUBAS.
Akójọp Lagos , 1986. xi, 324 p., map, ports. ; ISBN 978-13-2563-1 **NYPL [Sc D 88-955]**

YORUBAS - CUBA.
Soledad, Rosalía de la. Ibo . Miami, Fla. , 1988. 278 p. ; ISBN 0-89729-468-8
NYPL [Sc D 89-436]

YORUBAS - DRAMA.
Soyinka, Wole. The lion and the jewel /. Harare, Zimbabwe , 1986. 64 p. ; ISBN 0-949225-41-X , **NYPL [Sc C 89-107]**

YORUBAS - FOLKLORE.
Great tales of the Yorubas /. Ibadan, Oyo State, Nigeria , 1987. 92 p. :
NYPL [Sc D 88-712]

YORUBAS - HISTORY.
Kenyo, Elisha Alademomi. Awon olori Yoruba ati isedale won /. Lagos, Nigeria , 1952. 96 p. :
NYPL [Sc D 88-818]
Smith, Robert, 1919- Kingdoms of the Yoruba /. London , 1988. xii, 174 p. : ISBN 0-85255-028-6 (cased) : DDC 966/.004963 19
DT513 **NYPL [Sc E 88-482]**

YORUBAS - JUVENILE FICTION.
Schatz, Letta. Taiwo and her twin /. New York , c1964- 128 p. : **NYPL [Sc E 88-430]**

YORUBAS - LEGENDS.
Morgan, Kemi. Legends from Yorubaland /. Ibadan, Nigeria , 1988. iii, 100 p. : ISBN 978-246-003-6 **NYPL [Sc C 88-344]**

YORUBAS - MEDICINE.
Warren, Dennis M. Yoruba medicines /. Legon , 1971 [i.e. 1973] iii, 93, xii, p. ; DDC 615.8/99 19
DT515.45.Y67 W37 1973
NYPL [Sc G 88-34]

YORUBAS - RELIGION.
Babayemi, S. O. Egúngún among the Ọyọ Yoruba /. Ibadan , c1980. ix, 123 p. :
BL2480.Y6 B33 1980 **NYPL [Sc D 88-1149]**
Dopamu, P. Adelumo. ÈS̩Ù . Nigeria , 1986. 99 p. ; ISBN 978-253-014-X
NYPL [Sc D 88-1375]
Gleason, Judith Illsley. Oya . Boston , 1987. viii, 304 p. : ISBN 0-87773-430-5 (pbk.) : DDC 299/.63 19
BL2480.Y6 G58 1987 **NYPL [Sc D 88-101]**
Ibie, Cromwell Osamaro. Ifism . Lagos, Nigeria , 1986. 251 p., [10] p. of plates :
NYPL [Sc E 89-19]
Noibi, D. O. S. Yoruba Muslim youth and Christian-sponsored education /. Ijebu-Ode, Nigeria , 1987. 44 p. ; ISBN 978-253-020-4
NYPL [Sc D 89-537]
Soledad, Rosalía de la. Ibo . Miami, Fla. , 1988. 278 p. ; ISBN 0-89729-468-8
NYPL [Sc D 89-436]

YORUBAS - SOCIAL LIFE AND CUSTOMS.
Kenyo, Elisha Alademomi. Awon olori Yoruba ati isedale won /. Lagos, Nigeria , 1952. 96 p. :
NYPL [Sc D 88-818]

Yoshimura, Fumio. (ill) Bryan, Ashley. Sh-ko and his eight wicked brothers /. New York , 1988. [22] p. : ISBN 0-689-31446-9 DDC 398.2/1/0952 E 19
PZ8.B842 Sh 1988 **NYPL [Sc E 88-569]**

"You are a thief". Dallape, Fabio. Nairobi, Kenya , 1987. 151 p. : **NYPL [Sc E 88-538]**

You CAN do something about AIDS / Sasha Alyson, editor. Boston : The Stop AIDS Project, 1988. 126 p. : ill. ; 18 cm. Bibliography: p. 116-120. ISBN 0-945972-00-8

1. AIDS (Disease). I. Alyson, Sasha.
NYPL [Sc C 88-290]

You can't get lost in Cape Town /. Wicomb, Zoë.
New York , c1987. 185 p. ; ISBN
0-394-56030-2 : DDC 823 19
PR9369.3.W53 Y6 1987
NYPL [Sc D 88-341]

You can't keep a good woman down . Walker,
Alice, 1944- New York , c1982, c1981. 167 p. ;
ISBN 0-15-699778-9   *NYPL [Sc D 87-684]*

You must remember this . Kisseloff, Jeff. San
Diego , c1989. xvii, 622 p., [16] p. of plates :
ISBN 0-15-187988-5 : DDC 974.7/1042 19
F128.5 .K55 1988
NYPL [Sc E 89-54]

You visit a dairy [and a] clothing factory /.
Meshover, Leonard. Chicago , c1965. 48 p. :
NYPL [Sc D 89-545]

Young, Al, 1939- Things ain't what they used to
be : musical memoirs / by Al Young. Berkeley :
Creaive Arts Book Co., 1987. xvii, 233 p. :
ports. ; 22 cm. "A Donald S. Ellis book". ISBN
0-88739-024-2
1. Jazz music - United States - History and criticism. 2.
Jazz musicians - United States. I. Title.
NYPL [Sc D 88-704]

Young, Ann Venture. The image of Black women
in twentieth-century South American poetry .
Washington, D.C. , c1987. 250 p. ; ISBN
0-89410-275-3   *NYPL [Sc E 88-321]*

Young, British, and Black . Fusco, Coco. Buffalo,
N.Y. , c1988. 65 p. : *NYPL [Sc D 88-1186]*

YOUNG, COLEMAN A.
Rich, Wilbur C. Coleman Young and Detroit
politics . Detroit, Mich. , 1989. 298 p. : ISBN
0-8143-2093-7 DDC 977.4/34043/0924 B 19
F474.D453 Y677 1989   *NYPL [Sc E 89-208]*

Young, F. Weldon (Frank Weldon), 1902- The
30's, donnybrook decade in St. Louis public
school power plants : a Geechee maverick's
quest in a Jim Crow city / F. Weldon Young.
St. Louis, Mo. : Nathan B. Young Historic
Memorial, c1984. 96 p. : ill. ; 23 cm. ISBN
0-87527-331-9 (pbk.) : DDC 621.31/2132/0924
B 19
1. Young, F. Weldon (Frank Weldon), 1902-. 2.
Afro-American engineers - Missouri - St. Louis -
Biography. I. Title. II. Title: Thirties, donnybrook
decade in St. Louis public school power plants.
TA140.Y68 A33 1984   NYPL [Sc D 89-256]

**YOUNG, F. WELDON (FRANK WELDON),
1902-**
Young, F. Weldon (Frank Weldon), 1902- The
30's, donnybrook decade in St. Louis public
school power plants . St. Louis, Mo. , c1984. 96
p. : ISBN 0-87527-331-9 (pbk.) : DDC
621.31/2132/0924 B 19
TA140.Y68 A33 1984   NYPL [Sc D 89-256]

Young, Kate. Women and economic
development . Oxford [England] ; New York :
ix, 231 p. ; ISBN 0-85496-091-0 ; DDC 305.4/2
19
HQ1240 .W665 1988   NYPL [JLD 89-559]

**Young Men's Christian Associations. Alianza
Mundial. see World Alliance of YMCAs.**

**Young Men's Christian Associations. Alliance
universelle. see World Alliance of YMCAs.**

**Young Men's Christian Associations. Weltbund.
see World Alliance of YMCAs.**

**Young Men's Christian Associations. World
Alliance. see World Alliance of YMCAs.**

**YOUNG, P. B. (PLUMMER BERNARD), D.
1962.**
Suggs, Henry Lewis. P.B. Young,
newspaperman . Charlottesville , 1988. xxii, 254
p. : ISBN 0-8139-1178-8 DDC 070.4/1/0924 B 19
PN4874.Y59 S84 1988   NYPL [JFE 89-97]

Young people of East and South Africa : their
stories in their own words / [compiled] by
Charles R. Joy.1st ed. New York : Duell, Sloan
and Pearce, c1962. vii, 211 p. ; 21 cm.
1. Youth - Africa, East - Biography - Juvenile literature.
2. Youth, Africa, Southern - Biography - Juvenile
literature. 3. Africa, East - Social life and customs -
Juvenile literature. 4. Africa, Southern - Social life and
customs - Juvenile literature. I. Joy, Charles Rhind,
1885-. II. Title.   *NYPL [Sc D 88-660]*

Youngblood, Shay. The big mama stories / by
Shay Youngblood. Ithaca, N.Y. : Firebrand

Books, c1989. 106 p. ; 22 cm. CONTENTS. -
Born with religion -- Snuff dippers -- An independent
woman -- Did my mama like to dance? -- Miss Rosa's
monkey -- Spit in the governor's tea -- The blues ain't
nothin but a good woman feelin bad -- Funny women --
Maggie Agatha Christmas St. Clair -- Uncle Buck loves
Jesus, sometime -- Watch the spirit move -- They tell
me, now I know. ISBN 0-932399-58-3 (alk. paper) :
DDC 813/.54 19
1. Afro-American women - Southern States - Fiction. 2.
Women - Fiction. 3. Southern States - Fiction. I. Title.
PS3575.O8535 B5 1989
NYPL [Sc D 89-530]

Younge, Gavin. Art of the South African
townships / Gavin Younge ; foreword by
Desmond M. Tutu. New York : Rizzoli, 1988.
96 p. : ill. (some col.) ; 27 cm. ISBN
0-8478-0973-0 (pbk.) : DDC 704/.03968 19
1. Art, Black - South Africa - Homelands. 2.
Eclecticism in art - South Africa - Homelands. I. Title.
N7394.H66 Y68 1988   NYPL [Sc F 88-364]

**YOUTH - AFRICA, EAST - BIOGRAPHY -
JUVENILE LITERATURE.**
Young people of East and South Africa . New
York , c1962. vii, 211 p. ;
NYPL [Sc D 88-660]

**YOUTH - AFRICA, SOUTHERN -
BIOGRAPHY - JUVENILE LITERATURE.**
Young people of East and South Africa . New
York , c1962. vii, 211 p. ;
NYPL [Sc D 88-660]

YOUTH - AFRICA, SUB-SAHARAN.
Children, youth, women and development plans
in West and Central Africa . Abidjan [1972?]
152 p. ;   *NYPL [Sc E 88-105]*

**YOUTH - AFRICA, SUB-SAHARAN -
CONGRESSES.**
Jeunesse, tradition et développement en
Afrique. Spanish. Juventud, tradición y
desarrollo en Africa . Barcelona , Paris , 1982.
148 p. ; ISBN 84-85800-29-X
NYPL [Sc D 88-592]

**YOUTH, BLACK - ENGLAND - LONDON -
ATTITUDES.**
Williams, Lincoln Octavious. Partial surrender .
London , New York , 1988. viii, 194 p. ; ISBN
1-85000-289-4 DDC 361.7/97/009421 19
HV1441.G8 L78 1988   NYPL [Sc E 89-73]

**YOUTH, BLACK - GREAT BRITAIN -
ECONOMIC CONDITIONS.**
Solomos, John. Black youth, racism and the
state . Cambridge [Cambridgeshire] , New
York , 1988. 284 p. ; ISBN 0-521-36019-6 DDC
305.8/96041 19
DA125.N4 S65 1988   NYPL [Sc E 88-606]

**YOUTH, BLACK - GREAT BRITAIN -
SOCIAL CONDITIONS.**
Solomos, John. Black youth, racism and the
state . Cambridge [Cambridgeshire] , New
York , 1988. 284 p. ; ISBN 0-521-36019-6 DDC
305.8/96041 19
DA125.N4 S65 1988   NYPL [Sc E 88-606]

YOUTH - EMPLOYMENT - AFRICA.
Livingstone, Ian. Youth employment & youth
employment programmes in Africa . Addis
Ababa , 1986. 9 v. : ISBN 92-2-105527-2 (pbk. :
v. 1) DDC 331.3/4/096 19
HD6276.A32 L58 1986 NYPL [Sc F 88-313]

**Youth employment & youth employment
programmes in Africa** . Livingstone, Ian. Addis
Ababa , 1986. 9 v. : ISBN 92-2-105527-2 (pbk. :
v. 1) DDC 331.3/4/096 19
HD6276.A32 L58 1986 NYPL [Sc F 88-313]

**Youth employment and youth employment
programmes in Africa.** Livingstone, Ian. Youth
employment & youth employment programmes
in Africa . Addis Ababa , 1986. 9 v. : ISBN
92-2-105527-2 (pbk. : v. 1) DDC 331.3/4/096
19
HD6276.A32 L58 1986 NYPL [Sc F 88-313]

YOUTH - EMPLOYMENT - BOTSWANA.
Langley, Ph. Managing the Botswana brigades .
Douala, U.R.C. [1983] 93 p. : DDC
658.3/12404/096811 19
HD5715.5.B55 L36 1983
NYPL [Sc E 88-483]

Martin, Anthony. Report on the brigades in
Botswana. [n.p., 1971?] 96 p.
HD6276.B6 M37   NYPL [JLF 74-1283]

**YOUTH - EMPLOYMENT - GREAT
BRITAIN.**
Verma, Gajendra K. Race, training, and
employment /. London , New York , 1987. vi,
134 p. ; ISBN 1-85000-243-6 : DDC
331.3/46/0941 19
HD5715.5.G7 V47 1987
*NYPL [*QT 88-3245]*

YOUTH - ENGLAND - LONDON.
Turkie, Alan. Know what I mean? . Leicester ,
1982. 82 p. : ISBN 0-86155-062-5 :
NYPL [Sc D 89-464]

**YOUTH - ENGLAND - LONDON -
LANGUAGE.**
Hewitt, Roger. White talk, black talk .
Cambridge [Cambridgeshire] , New York ,
1986. x, 253 p. ; ISBN 0-521-26239-9 DDC
401/.9/094216 19
P40.45.G7 H48 1986   NYPL [JFE 87-279]

YOUTH - GOVERNMENT POLICY - AFRICA.
Livingstone, Ian. Youth employment & youth
employment programmes in Africa . Addis
Ababa , 1986. 9 v. : ISBN 92-2-105527-2 (pbk. :
v. 1) DDC 331.3/4/096 19
HD6276.A32 L58 1986 NYPL [Sc F 88-313]

**YOUTH - LAW AND LEGISLATION. 009. see
CHILDREN - LEGAL STATUS, LAWS,
ETC.**

YOUTH - LITERARY COLLECTIONS.
Mississippi writers . Jackson , c1985- v. ; ISBN
0-87805-232-1 (pbk.) DDC 813/.008/09762 19
PS558.M7 M55 1985   NYPL [Sc E 88-316]

YOUTH MOVEMENT - NIGERIA.
Schärer, Therese, 1946- Das Nigerian Youth
Movement. Frankfurt am Main , New York ,
c1986. xiii, 376, A76 p., 3 leaves of plates :
ISBN 3-261-03567-6   *NYPL [Sc D 88-878]*

YOUTH - RELIGIOUS LIFE.
Jeunes intellectuels en recherche . Abidjan ,
c1982. 67 p. :   *NYPL [Sc D 88-925]*

**YOUTH - SAINT KITTS-NEVIS -
CONGRESSES.**
Saint Kitts-Nevis. National Youth Council. 1st
annual convention, September 1973 [microform]
/. St. Kitts [1973?] 26 p. ;
NYPL [Sc Micro F-10999]

**YOUTH TRAINING SCHEME (GREAT
BRITAIN)**
Black youth futures . Leicester , 1987. ii, 113
p. : ISBN 0-86155-106-0 (pbk) : DDC
331.3/46/0941 19
HD8398   *NYPL [Sc D 89-175]*

YOUTH - ZAIRE - KINSHASA.
Comhaire-Sylvain, Suzanne. Food and leisure
among the African youth of Leopoldville,
Belgian Congo. [Rondebosch] 1950. 124 p.
DDC 309.1675
HQ799.C6 C6   *NYPL [Sc G 89-2]*

Youths in revolt . Aderinlewo, 'Dele. Ibadan, Oyo
State, Nigeria , 1985. 63 p. : ISBN
978-18-0006-2   *NYPL [Sc C 88-293]*

YULU LANGUAGE.
Boyeldieu, Pascal. Les langues fer ("Kara") et
yulu du Nord centrafricain . Paris , 1987. 280
p. ; ISBN 2-7053-0342-1 *NYPL [Sc E 88-124]*

ZANU. see Zimbabwe African National Union.

ZAGHAWA - RITES AND CEREMONIES.
Tubiana, Marie José. Des troupeaux et des
femmes . Paris , 1985. 390 p., [16] p. of plates :
ISBN 2-85802-554-9 *NYPL [Sc E 88-217]*

ZAIRE.
Tempels Placide, 1906- Ecrits polémiques et
politiques [microform] /. Kinshasa-Limete ,
1979. 24 p. ;   *NYPL [Sc Micro F-11131]*

ZAIRE - BIOGRAPHY.
Mabi Mulumba. Cadres et dirigeants au Zaïre .
Kinshasa , 1986. 541 p. :
NYPL [Sc E 88-322]

ZAIRE - CIVILIZATION.
Wymeersch, Patrick. Les Bin Kanyok .
Bandundu, République du Zaïre , 1983. ix, 368
p. :   *NYPL [Sc F 89-41]*

ZAIRE - CULTURE.
Totime Mikeni. La démocratie nouvelle, ou,
projet pour le Zaïre /. Paris [1984?]. iii, 104
p. ;   *NYPL [Sc D 88-720]*

ZAIRE - DESCRIPTION AND TRAVEL.
Barns, Thomas Alexander, 1880- Across the

great craterland to the Congo . London , 1923.
271, [1] p., [64] leaves of plates, 2 folded
leaves :   *NYPL [Sc E 88-252]*

**ZAIRE - DESCRIPTION AND TRAVEL -
JUVENILE LITERATURE.**
Kittler, Glenn D. Let's travel in the Congo /.
Chicago , 1965, c1961. 85 p. :
                 NYPL [Sc F 89-7]

ZAIRE - ECONOMIC CONDITIONS.
Totime Mikeni. La démocratie nouvelle, ou,
projet pour le Zaïre /. Paris [1984?]. iii, 104
p. ;   *NYPL [Sc D 88-720]*

ZAIRE - FICTION.
Mudimbe, V. Y., 1941?- [Bel immonde.
English.] Before the birth of the moon /. New
York , c1989. 203 p. ; ISBN 0-671-66840-4 :
DDC 843 19
PQ3989.2.M77 B413 1989
                NYPL [Sc D 89-236]

Sony Lab'Ou Tansi. [Anté-peuple. English.] The
antipeople . London ; New York : 170 p. ;
ISBN 0-7145-2845-5 : DDC 843 19
PQ3989.2.S64 A813 1987
                NYPL [Sc D 88-835]

Tati-Loutard, J. B. Le récit de la mort /. Paris ,
c1987. 166 p. ; ISBN 2-7087-0492-3
                NYPL [Sc D 88-923]

**ZAIRE - GOVERNMENT PUBLICATIONS -
BIBLIOGRAPHY - UNION LISTS.**
Witherell, Julian W. French-speaking central
Africa. Washington, 1973. xiv, 314 p. ISBN
0-8444-0033-5
Z3692 .W5   *NYPL [JLF 74-197]*

ZAIRE - HISTORY - TO 1908.
Roark, J. L. American expansionism vs.
European colonialism [microform] . [Nairobi] ,
1976. 16 leaves :
                NYPL [Sc Micro R-4108 no. 34]

ZAIRE - JUVENILE FICTION.
Booth, Esma (Rideout) Kalena and Sana /.
New York , 1962. 152 p. :
                NYPL [Sc D 88-506]

Gatti, Attilio. Adventure in black and white /.
New York , 1943. 172 p. :
                NYPL [Sc D 88-1169]

Shacklett, Juanita Purvis. Boloji and Old Hippo
/. New York , c1959. 121 p. :
                NYPL [Sc D 88-1166]

**ZAIRE - POLITICS AND GOVERNMENT -
1960-**
Manya K'Omalowete a Djonga, 1950- Patrice
Lumumba, le Sankuru et l'Afrique . Lutry
[1985] 166 p. :   *NYPL [Sc D 88-1490]*

Totime Mikeni. La démocratie nouvelle, ou,
projet pour le Zaïre /. Paris [1984?]. iii, 104
p. ;   *NYPL [Sc D 88-720]*

**ZAIRE - POLITICS AND GOVERNMENT -
1960- - PICTORIAL WORKS.**
Mobutu, maréchal du Zaïre. Paris , c1985. 237
p. : ISBN 2-85258-389-5 DDC 967.5/103/0924 B
19
DT658.2.M62 M62 1985
                NYPL [Sc F 88-371]

**ZAIRE - PRESIDENTS - PICTORIAL
WORKS.**
Mobutu, maréchal du Zaïre. Paris , c1985. 237
p. : ISBN 2-85258-389-5 DDC 967.5/103/0924 B
19
DT658.2.M62 M62 1985
                NYPL [Sc F 88-371]

**ZAIRE - RELATIONS (GENERAL) WITH
THE UNITED STATES.**
Roark, J. L. American expansionism vs.
European colonialism [microform] . [Nairobi] ,
1976. 16 leaves :
                NYPL [Sc Micro R-4108 no. 34]

ZAIRE - SOCIAL LIFE AND CUSTOMS.
Wymeersch, Patrick. Les Bin Kanyok .
Bandundu, République du Zaïre , 1983. ix, 368
p. ;   *NYPL [Sc F 89-41]*

**ZAIRE - SOCIAL LIFE AND CUSTOMS -
JUVENILE LITERATURE.**
Elting, Mary, 1909- A Mongo homecoming.
New York [1969] 54 p. DDC 309.1/675
DT644 .E4   *NYPL [Sc E 88-578]*

ZAIRIAN LITERATURE (FRENCH)
Cris intérieurs . Kinshasa/Gombe, Zaïre , 1986.

62 p. ;
MLCS 86/6102 (P)   *NYPL [Sc C 88-124]*

Zakari, Maikorema. Contribution a l'histoire des
populations du sud-est nigérien : le cas du
Mangari, XVIe-XIXe s. / Maikorema Zakari.
Niamey : Institut de recherches en sciences
humaines, 1985. 246 p. : ill. ; 25 cm. (Études
nigériennes. no 53) Errata slip inserted. Bibliography: p.
221-242. ISBN 2-85921-053-9
1. Ethnology - Niger. 2. Niger - History. I. Title. II.
Series.   *NYPL [Sc E 88-328]*

Zamanin Nan Namu . Makarfi, M. Shu'aibu.
Zariya , 1959. 88 p. ;   *NYPL [Sc D 89-481]*

**ZAMBEZI RIVER - DESCRIPTION AND
TRAVEL.**
Baines, Thomas, 1820-1875. Baines on the
Zambezi 1858 to 1859 /. Johannesburg , c1982.
251 p. : ISBN 0-909079-17-X (Standard ed.)
                NYPL [Sc F 83-34]

Zambezia. Mutizwa-Mangiza, N. D. Community
development in pre-independence Zimbabwe .
Harare , c1985. iv, 79 p. : ISBN 0-86924-090-0
(pbk.) DDC 307.1/4/096891 19
HN802.Z9 C65 1985   *NYPL [JLD 88-3699]*

Zambezia. Supplement. Cottrell, C. B. Aspects of
the biogeography of southern African
butterflies . Salisbury [Zimbabwe] , c1978. viii,
100 p. ;
QL557.S65 C68 1978   *NYPL [Sc E 88-555]*

Zambeziana.
(v. 10 10) Kosmin, Barry Alexander. Majuta .
Gwelo, Zimbabwe , c1980. xii, 223 p., [32] p.
of plates :   *NYPL [Sc D 82-130]*

(v. 8) Dachs, Anthony J. The Catholic church
and Zimbabwe, 1879-1979 /. Gwelo , 1979. xiii,
260 p., [26] p. of plates : DDC 282/.6891 19
BX1682.Z55 D33 1979   *NYPL [Sc D 88-900]*

(vol. 8) Dachs, Anthony J. The Catholic church
and Zimbabwe, 1879-1979 /. Gwelo , 1979. xiii,
260 p., [26] p. of plates : DDC 282/.6891 19
BX1682.Z55 D33 1979   *NYPL [Sc D 88-900]*

(18) Cheater, Angela P. The politics of factory
organization . Gweru, Zimbabwe , c1986. xix,
156, [1] p. : ISBN 0-86922-374-7
                NYPL [Sc D 88-671]

Zambia . Burdette, Marcia M. (Marcia Muldrow)
Boulder, Colo. , 1988. xiv, 210 p. : ISBN
0-86531-617-1 (alk. paper) DDC 968.94/04 19
DT963 .B87 1988   *NYPL [Sc E 89-103]*

ZAMBIA.
Burdette, Marcia M. (Marcia Muldrow)
Zambia . Boulder, Colo. , 1988. xiv, 210 p. :
ISBN 0-86531-617-1 (alk. paper) DDC
968.94/04 19
DT963 .B87 1988   *NYPL [Sc E 89-103]*

Zambia Alliance of Women. Food for Africa .
[Lusaka?] [1985?] 68 p., [3] p. of plates :
TX360.A26 F67 1985   *NYPL [Sc F 89-40]*

ZAMBIA - ANTIQUITIES.
Phillipson, D. W. The prehistory of eastern
Zambia /. Nairobi , 1976. xi, 229 p., [21] leaves
of plates (5 fold.) : ISBN 0-500-97003-3 :
GN865.Z3 P48   *NYPL [JFF 79-1585]*

ZAMBIA - BIBLIOGRAPHY - CATALOGS.
University of Zambia. Library. Special
Collections Division. Subject guide to research
papers held by the University of Zambia
Library, Special Collections Division (Lusaka
Campus) /. Lusaka, Zambia , 1986. v, 423 p. ;
DDC 016.96894 19
Z5055.Z334 U558 1986 AS623.L84
                NYPL [Sc F 88-353]

ZAMBIA - COLONIAL INFLUENCE.
Hansen, Karen Tranberg. Distant companions .
Ithaca , 1989. xv, 321 p. : ISBN 0-8014-2217-5
(alk. paper) DDC 331.7/6164046/096894 19
HD6072.2.Z33 H36 1989
                NYPL [Sc E 89-215]

ZAMBIA - FICTION.
Lu, Georzef. Woman of my uncle /. Lusaka ,
1985. iv, 236 p. ;
MLCS 87/7908 (P)   *NYPL [Sc C 89-94]*

Moono, Muchimba Simuwana. The ring /.
Lusaka , 1985. 121 p. ;   *NYPL [Sc C 89-70]*

Zambia - Government. see Zambia - Politics and
government.

ZAMBIA - HISTORY.
Wills, A. J. (Alfred John) An introduction to

the history of central Africa . Oxford
[Oxfordshire] , New York , 1985. xiii, 556 p. :
ISBN 0-19-873075-6 : DDC 968.9 19
DT963.5 .W54 1985   *NYPL [Sc D 88-656]*

ZAMBIA - HISTORY - TO 1890.
Kayongo, Kabunda. Reciprocity and
interdependence . [Stockholm] , 1987. 189 p. :
ISBN 91-22-00891-8   *NYPL [Sc D 88-863]*

Sampson, Richard, 1922- [Man with a
toothbrush in his hat.] The struggle for British
interests in Barotseland, 1871-88 /. Lusaka
[198-?] v, 158 p. : DDC 968.94/01 19
DT963.72.W47 S25 1980z
                NYPL [Sc D 88-381]

ZAMBIA - IMPRINTS - CATALOGS.
University of Zambia. Library. Special
Collections Division. Subject guide to research
papers held by the University of Zambia
Library, Special Collections Division (Lusaka
Campus) /. Lusaka, Zambia , 1986. v, 423 p. ;
DDC 016.96894 19
Z5055.Z334 U558 1986 AS623.L84
                NYPL [Sc F 88-353]

**ZAMBIA - POLITICS AND GOVERNMENT -
1964-**
Lungu, Gatian F. Administrative
decentralisation in the Zambian bureaucracy .
Gweru, Zimbabwe , c1985. 85 p. :
                NYPL [Sc D 89-318]

ZAMBIA - RURAL CONDITIONS.
Hedlund, Hans G. B. Migration and change in
rural Zambia /. Uppsala , 1983. 107 p. : ISBN
91-7106-220-3 (pbk.) DDC 960 s 307/.2 19
DT1 .N64 no. 70 HB1955
                NYPL [JLD 85-587]

ZAMBIA - SOCIAL CONDITIONS.
Hansen, Karen Tranberg. Distant companions .
Ithaca , 1989. xv, 321 p. : ISBN 0-8014-2217-5
(alk. paper) DDC 331.7/6164046/096894 19
HD6072.2.Z33 H36 1989
                NYPL [Sc E 89-215]

Madu, Oliver V. Models of class domination in
plural societies of Central Africa /.
Washington , c1978. vi, 510 p. ;
                NYPL [Sc D 88-1067]

Zambia. University. see University of Zambia.

The Zambian Bill of Rights . Zimba, L. S.
(Lawrence S.) Nairobi, Kenya , 1984. x, 288
p. ; DDC 342.6894/085 346.8940285 19
LAW   *NYPL [Sc E 88-392]*

Zambian papers.
(no. 18) Lungu, Gatian F. Administrative
decentralisation in the Zambian bureaucracy .
Gweru, Zimbabwe , c1985. 85 p. :
                NYPL [Sc D 89-318]

Zander, Hans, 1937- Fisher, Aileen Lucia, 1906-
Seeds on the go /. [Los Angeles] , c1977. 43
p. : ISBN 0-8372-2400-4 DDC 582/.01/6
QK929 .F57   *NYPL [Sc F 88-344]*

Zandi and the wonderful pillow /. Chukwuka, J.
I. N. Lagos, Nigeria , 1977. 48 p. : ISBN
0-410-80099-6   *NYPL [Sc C 88-76]*

Zani, Zachariah M. Maneno yanayotatiza /
Zachariah M. Zani. Nairobi : Heinemann
Educational Books, c1983. xi, 112 ; 18 cm.
1. Swahili language - Dictionaries. I. Title.
                NYPL [Sc C 89-57]

**ZANZIBAR - POLITICS AND
GOVERNMENT - TO 1964.**
Wilson, Amrit, 1941- US foreign policy and
revolution . London , distributed in the USA by
Unwin Hyman, 1989. ix, 179 p. ; ISBN
1-85305-051-2   *NYPL [Sc D 89-426]*

ZEB secondary school Shona series.
Matindike, Gabriel A. Kuziva mbuya huudzwa
/. Harare, Zimbabwe , 1982- v. : ISBN
0-908300-01-8 (v. 1)
PL8681.2 .M37 1982   *NYPL [Sc D 88-385]*

Zehmer, Evangeline. Self portrait -- Bernard
Goss. [S.l. , 1967?] 28 p. :
                NYPL [Sc D 88-503]

Zeltner, J. C. Les pays du Tchad dans la
tourmente, 1880-1903 / Jean-Claude Zeltner.
Paris : L'Harmattan , c1988. 285 p. : geneal.
table, maps ; 22 cm. (Racines du présent) Includes
index. Bibliography: p. 273-277. ISBN 2-85802-914-8
1. Chad - History. I. Title.
                NYPL [Sc D 88-1408]

Zementskulpturen aus Nigeria : Sunday Jack Akpan, Aniedi Okon Akpan . Stuttgart : Institut für Auslandsbeziehungen, c1988. 70 p. : ill. (some col.) ; 29 cm. "Eine Ausstellung des Instituts für Auslandsbeziehungen und des IWALEWA-Hauses unter Mitwirkung des Goethe-Institutes Lagos." Bibliography: p. 23.
1. Akpan, A. O. (Aneidi Okon), ca. 1916- - Exhibitions. 2. Akpan, S. J. (Sunday Jack), ca. 1940- - Exhibitions. 3. Sculpture, Nigerian - Exhibitions. 4. Primitivism in art - Nigeria - Exhibitions. I. Akpan, A. O. (Aneidi Okon) ca. 1916-. II. Akpan, S. J. (Sunday Jack), ca. 1940-. III. Iwalewa-Haus Bayreuth. IV. Iwalewa-Haus Bayreuth.   *NYPL [Sc F 89-44]*

ZEZERU (AFRICAN PEOPLE)
Samkange, Stanlake John Thompson, 1922-Oral history . Harare, Zimbabwe , c1986. ii, 93 p. :   *NYPL [Sc D 89-586]*

ZEZERU LANGUAGE. see SHONA LANGUAGE.

Zhana. Sojourn /. London , 1988. 215 p. ; ISBN 0-413-16440-3 (pbk) :   DDC 823/.914/08 19   *NYPL [Sc C 89-81]*

Z'iednani Derzhavy Ameryky. see United States.

Ziégler, Jean. Morizot, Frédéric. Grenade, épices et poudre . Paris , c1988. 385 p., [8] leaves of plates :   ISBN 2-7384-0082-5   *NYPL [Sc E 89-49]*

Zimba, L. S. (Lawrence S.) The Zambian Bill of Rights : an historical and comparative study of human rights in Commonwealth Africa / L.S. Zimba. Nairobi, Kenya : East African Pub. House, 1984. x, 288 p. ; 24 cm. Originally presented as the author's thesis (Ph.D.--University of London, 1979) under title: The constitutional protection of fundamental rights and freedoms in Zambia. Bibliography: p. [235]-267.   DDC 342.6894/085 346.8940285 19
1. Civil rights - Zambia. 2. Civil rights - Africa. I. Title.
LAW   *NYPL [Sc E 88-392]*

Zimbabwe . Stoneman, Colin. London , New York , 1989. xxi, 210 p. :   ISBN 0-86187-454-4 : DDC 968.91 19
JQ2929.A15 S76 1989   *NYPL [Sc D 89-307]*

ZIMBABWE.
A Guide to Zimbabwe /. Gweru, [Zimbabwe] , 1986. 63 p. :   ISBN 91-7810-685-0   *NYPL [Sc C 88-371]*

Nelson, Harold D. Area handbook for Southern Rhodesia /. Washington , 1975. xiv, 394 p. *DT962 .N36*   *NYPL [JFE 75-2684]*

ZIMBABWE AFRICAN NATIONAL UNION.
Martin, David, 1936- The Chitepo assassination /. Harare, Zimbabwe , 1985. 134 p., [8] p. of plates :   ISBN 0-949225-04-5
   NYPL [Sc D 88-1244]

ZIMBABWE - ANTIQUITIES.
Garlake, Peter S. The painted caves . Harare, Zimbabwe , c1987. iv, 100 p., [8] p. of plates : ISBN 0-908309-00-7   *NYPL [Sc D 89-411]*

ZIMBABWE. ARMY - COMMANDO TROOPS - BIOGRAPHY.
Ollivier Patrick. Commandos de brousse /. Paris , 1985. 275 p., [8] p. of plates :   ISBN 2-246-35481-1   *NYPL [Sc E 87-222]*

ZIMBABWE - BIOGRAPHY.
Farquhar, June. Jairos Jiri . Gweru , 1987. 92 p. :   ISBN 0-86922-416-6   *NYPL [Sc D 89-38]*

ZIMBABWE - CHURCH HISTORY.
Dachs, Anthony J. The Catholic church and Zimbabwe, 1879-1979 /. Gwelo , 1979. xiii, 260 p., [26] p. of plates :   DDC 282/.6891 19
BX1682.Z55 D33 1979   *NYPL [Sc D 88-900]*

ZIMBABWE - COLONIAL INFLUENCE - ADDRESSES, ESSAYS, LECTURES.
Perspectives of independent development in Southern Africa . Berlin , 1980. xiv, 183 p. : DDC 338.9688 19
HC910 .P47   *NYPL [JLE 82-36]*

Zimbabwe Cooperative Craft Workshop. Garlake, Peter S. Life at Great Zimbabwe /. Gweru, Zimbabwe , 1983, c1982. [36] p. :   ISBN 0-86922-180-9 (pbk.)   DDC 968.91 19
DT962.9.G73 G374 1983
   NYPL [Sc F 88-175]

ZIMBABWE - DESCRIPTION AND TRAVEL - VIEWS.

Klöppel, Eberhard. In Simbabwe /. Leipzig , c1985. 160 p. :   ISBN 0-325-00113-0
   NYPL [Sc D 88-627]

ZIMBABWE - ECONOMIC CONDITIONS.
Stoneman, Colin. Zimbabwe . London , New York , 1989. xxi, 210 p. :   ISBN 0-86187-454-4 : DDC 968.91 19
JQ2929.A15 S76 1989   *NYPL [Sc D 89-307]*

ZIMBABWE - ECONOMIC CONDITIONS - TO 1965.
Phimister, I. R. (Ian R.) An economic and social history of Zimbabwe, 1890-1948 . London , New York , 1988. xii, 336 p. :   ISBN 0-582-64423-2   DDC 330.96891/02 19
HC910.Z9 S36 1987   *NYPL [Sc D 89-35]*

ZIMBABWE - ECONOMIC CONDITIONS - 1965-1980 - ADDRESSES, ESSAYS, LECTURES.
Perspectives of independent development in Southern Africa . Berlin , 1980. xiv, 183 p. : DDC 338.9688 19
HC910 .P47   *NYPL [JLE 82-36]*

ZIMBABWE - FICTION.
Dangarembga, Tsitsi. Nervous conditions /. London , 1988. 204 p. ;   ISBN 0-7043-4100-X (pbk) :   DDC 823 19
PR9390.9.D3   *NYPL [Sc C 88-278]*

Fairbairn, Bill, 1935- Run for freedom /. [Lusaka, Zambia] , 1984. 181 p. ;
   NYPL [Sc C 88-227]

Kawara, James. Sajeni Chimedza /. Gweru, [Zimbabwe] , 1984. 174 p. ;   ISBN 0-86922-327-5
   NYPL [Sc C 88-97]

Motsi, Daniel, 1964- The beast of fame /. Harare, Zimbabwe , 1987. 59 p. :   ISBN 0-949225-61-4 :   *NYPL [Sc C 89-100]*

Mutasa, Garikai. The contact /. Gweru, Zimbabwe , 1985. 125 p. ; ISBN 0-86922-355-0 (pbk.)
MLCS 86/13019 (P)   *NYPL [JFC 87-1040]*

Partridge, Nancy. To breathe and wait /. Gweru [Zimbabwe] , 1986. 242 p. ;   ISBN 0-86922-379-8   *NYPL [Sc C 88-130]*

Parwada, Batisai B., 1966- Shreds of darkness /. Gweru, Zimbabwe , 1987. 111 p. ;
   NYPL [Sc C 89-96]

ZIMBABWE - FOREIGN POLICY.
Patel, H. H. No master, no mortgage, no sale . Nairobi, Kenya , 1987. 61 p. columns ;
   NYPL [Sc F 88-297]

ZIMBABWE - FOREIGN RELATIONS - 1965-
Rhodesia alone /. Washington [1977?] 95 p. ; DDC 320.9/689/104
DT962.75 .R53   *NYPL [Sc E 88-95]*

ZIMBABWE - FOREIGN RELATIONS - SOUTH AFRICA.
Ushewokunze, H. S. M. (Herbert Sylvester Masiyiwa), 1938- An agenda for Zimbabwe /. [Harare, Zimbabwe] c1984. vi, 198 p. ;   ISBN 0-906041-67-8   DDC 361.6/1/096891 19
HX451.A6 U84 1984   *NYPL [Sc D 88-942]*

ZIMBABWE - HISTORY.
Babing, Alfred. Wo die Sonne wohnt /. Berlin , 1985. 368 p. :   *NYPL [Sc D 89-72]*

Samkange, Stanlake John Thompson, 1922-Oral history . Harare, Zimbabwe , c1986. ii, 93 p. :   *NYPL [Sc D 89-586]*

Wills, A. J. (Alfred John) An introduction to the history of central Africa . Oxford [Oxfordshire] , New York , 1985. xiii, 556 p. :   ISBN 0-19-873075-6 :   DDC 968.9 19
DT963.5 .W54 1985   *NYPL [Sc D 88-656]*

ZIMBABWE - HISTORY - 1890-1965.
Verrier, Anthony. The road to Zimbabwe, 1890-1980 /. London , 1986. xiv, 364 p., [8] p. of plates :   ISBN 0-224-02161-3
   NYPL [Sc D 88-313]

ZIMBABWE - HISTORY - 1965-1980.
Flower, Ken. Serving secretly . London , c1987. xxii, 330 p., [12] p. of plates :   ISBN 0-7195-4438-6   *NYPL [JFE 88-5776]*

Martin, David, 1936- The Chitepo assassination /. Harare, Zimbabwe , 1985. 134 p., [8] p. of plates :   ISBN 0-949225-04-5
   NYPL [Sc D 88-1244]

Verrier, Anthony. The road to Zimbabwe, 1890-1980 /. London , 1986. xiv, 364 p., [8] p.

of plates :   ISBN 0-224-02161-3
   NYPL [Sc D 88-313]

ZIMBABWE - HISTORY - 1965-1980 - FICTION.
McLoughlin, T. O. Karima /. Gweru, Zimbabwe , 1985. 211 p. ;   ISBN 0-86922-319-4 (pbk.)   DDC 823 19
PR9390.9.M35 K37 1985
   NYPL [JFC 86-1652]

ZIMBABWE - HISTORY - CHIMURENGA WAR, 1966-1980 - FICTION.
Hondo yeChimurenga . Gweru , 1984. 230 p. ; ISBN 0-86922-284-8   *NYPL [Sc C 89-110]*

ZIMBABWE - INDUSTRIES.
Cheater, Angela P. The politics of factory organization . Gweru, Zimbabwe , c1986. xix, 156, [1] p. :   ISBN 0-86922-374-7
   NYPL [Sc D 88-671]

ZIMBABWE - JUVENILE FICTION.
Molony, Rowland. Themba and the crocodile /. Harare , 1984. 74 p. :   ISBN 0-582-58741-7
   NYPL [Sc D 88-347]

ZIMBABWE - POETRY.
Chakarira chindunduma . Gweru, Zimbabwe , 1985. x, 78 p. ;   ISBN 0-86922-365-8
   NYPL [Sc D 88-439]

Nyamubaya, Freedom T. V. On the road again . Harare, Zimbabwe , 1986. 69 p. :   ISBN 0-949225-00-4   *NYPL [Sc C 88-136]*

ZIMBABWE - POLITICS AND GOVERNMENT.
Babing, Alfred. Wo die Sonne wohnt /. Berlin , 1985. 368 p. :   *NYPL [Sc D 89-72]*

Harris, Phil. [Reporting southern Africa. Spanish.] La información sobre Africa austral . Barcelona , Paris , 1984. 188 p. :   ISBN 92-3-301700-1 (Unesco)
   NYPL [Sc D 88-614]

Martin, David, 1936- The Chitepo assassination /. Harare, Zimbabwe , 1985. 134 p., [8] p. of plates :   ISBN 0-949225-04-5
   NYPL [Sc D 88-1244]

Stoneman, Colin. Zimbabwe . London , New York , 1989. xxi, 210 p. :   ISBN 0-86187-454-4 : DDC 968.91 19
JQ2929.A15 S76 1989   *NYPL [Sc D 89-307]*

ZIMBABWE - POLITICS AND GOVERNMENT - 1965-
Rhodesia alone /. Washington [1977?] 95 p. ; DDC 320.9/689/104
DT962.75 .R53   *NYPL [Sc E 88-95]*

ZIMBABWE - POLITICS AND GOVERNMENT - 1965-1979.
Flower, Ken. Serving secretly . London , c1987. xxii, 330 p., [12] p. of plates :   ISBN 0-7195-4438-6   *NYPL [JFE 88-5776]*

Front for the Liberation of Zimbabwe. Resolutions adopted by the inaugural congress of the Front for the Liberation of Zimbabwe, held from August 21 to September 5, 1972 [microform]. [S.1] [1972?] 3 leaves ;
   NYPL [Sc Micro R-4137 no.15]

ZIMBABWE - POLITICS AND GOVERNMENT - 1980-
Ushewokunze, H. S. M. (Herbert Sylvester Masiyiwa), 1938- An agenda for Zimbabwe /. [Harare, Zimbabwe] c1984. vi, 198 p. ;   ISBN 0-906041-67-8   DDC 361.6/1/096891 19
HX451.A6 U84 1984   *NYPL [Sc D 88-942]*

ZIMBABWE - SOCIAL CONDITIONS.
Stoneman, Colin. Zimbabwe . London , New York , 1989. xxi, 210 p. :   ISBN 0-86187-454-4 : DDC 968.91 19
JQ2929.A15 S76 1989   *NYPL [Sc D 89-307]*

ZIMBABWE - SOCIAL CONDITIONS - 1890-1965.
Phimister, I. R. (Ian R.) An economic and social history of Zimbabwe, 1890-1948 . London , New York , 1988. xii, 336 p. :   ISBN 0-582-64423-2   DDC 330.96891/02 19
HC910.Z9 S36 1987   *NYPL [Sc D 89-35]*

Zimbabwean drama . Zinyemba, Ranga M. Zimbabwe , 1986. 112 p. ;
   NYPL [JFC 87-1037]

ZIMBABWEAN DRAMA (ENGLISH) - HISTORY AND CRITICISM.
Zinyemba, Ranga M. Zimbabwean drama .

Zimbabwe , 1986. 112 p. ;
NYPL [JFC 87-1037]

**ZIMBABWEAN FICTION (ENGLISH) -
HISTORY AND CRITICISM.**
Zimunya, Musaemura. Those years of drought
and hunger . Gweru, Zimbabwe , 1982. 129 p. ;
ISBN 0-86922-183-3 (pbk.) :   DDC 823 19
PR9390.8 .Z55 1982   NYPL [Sc C 88-237]

ZIMBABWEAN POETRY (ENGLISH)
Mambo book of Zimbabwean Verse in English
/. Gweru, Zimbabwe , c986. xxix, 417 p. ;
ISBN 0-86922-367-4 (pbk.)
NYPL [JFD 88-10986]

**ZIMBABWEAN POETRY - TRANSLATION
INTO ENGLISH.**
Mambo book of Zimbabwean Verse in English
/. Gweru, Zimbabwe , c986. xxix, 417 p. ;
ISBN 0-86922-367-4 (pbk.)
NYPL [JFD 88-10986]

Zimbabwean stone sculpture /. Arnold, Marion I.
Bulawayo , 1986. xxvi, 234 p. :   ISBN
0-7974-0747-2   DDC 730/.96891 19
NB1209.Z55 A76 1986
NYPL [Sc D 89-326]

Zimbabwean woman . Nzenza, Sekai. London ,
1988. 160 p. ;   *NYPL [Sc C 88-291]*

Zimmerman, Diana.
Center for Migration Studies (U. S.) Refugees .
Staten Island, N.Y. , 1987. ix, 423 p. ;   ISBN
0-934733-34-1 (pbk.)   *NYPL [Sc F 89-60]*

A Directory of international migration study
centers, research programs, and library
resources /. Staten Island, N.Y. , 1987. ix, 299
p. ; ISBN 0-934733-18-X (pbk.) :   DDC 325/.07 19
JV6033 .C45 1987   NYPL [JLF 88-1452]

Zimunya, Musaemura.
Chakarira chindunduma . Gweru, Zimbabwe ,
1985. x, 78 p. ;   ISBN 0-86922-365-8
NYPL [Sc D 88-439]

Those years of drought and hunger : the birth
of African fiction in English in Zimbabwe /
Musaemura Bonas Zimunya. Gweru,
Zimbabwe : Mambo Press, 1982. 129 p. ; 18
cm. (Mambo writers series. English section. vol. 9)
Bibliography: p. 129.   ISBN 0-86922-183-3 (pbk.) :
DDC 823 19
*1. Zimbabwean fiction (English) - History and criticism.
I. Title.*
PR9390.8 .Z55 1982   NYPL [Sc C 88-237]

Zindi, Fred. Roots rocking in Zimbabwe / by
Fred Zindi. Gweru, Zimbabwe : Mambo Press,
1985. viii, 98 p., [32] p. of plates : ports. ; 21
cm.
*1. Popular music - Zimbabwe - History and criticism. I.
Title.*   *NYPL [Sc D 88-1323]*

Zinsou, Sénouvo Agbota, 1946- La tortue qui
chante : suivi de la femme du blanchisseur, et
Les aventures de Yévi au pays des monstres :
théâtre / Sénouvo Agbota Zinsou. Paris :
Hatier, 1987. 127 p. ; 18 cm. (Collection Monde
noir poche)   ISBN 2-218-07842-3
*I. Title. II. Title: Femme du blanchisseur. III. Title:
Aventures de Yévi au pays des monstres. IV. Series.*
NYPL [Sc C 88-8]

Zinyemba, Ranga M. Zimbabwean drama : a
study of Shona and English plays / by Ranga
M. Zinyemba. Zimbabwe : Mambo Press, 1986.
112 p. ; 18 cm. (Mambo writers series. English
section. vol. 25) Bibliography: p. 111-112.
*1. Zimbabwean drama (English) - History and criticism.
I. Title.*   *NYPL [JFC 87-1037]*

ZIONIST CHURCHES (AFRICA)
Daneel, M. L. (Marthinus L.) Quest for
belonging . Gweru, Zimbabwe , 1987. 310 p.,
[17] p. of plates :   ISBN 0-86922-426-3
NYPL [Sc D 88-1007]

Oosthuizen, G. C. (Gerhardus Cornelis) The
birth of Christian Zionism in South Africa /.
KwaDlangezwa, South Africa , 1987. ii, 56 p. ;
ISBN 0-09-079580-2   DDC 289.9 19
BR1450 .O55 1987   NYPL [Sc D 88-693]

Zistwar ek zedmo Sesel. Contes, devinettes et
jeux de mots des Seychelles =.
[Le-Mée-sur-Seine] [Paris] , c1983. 157 p. :
ISBN 2-86427-018-8   DDC 398.2/0969/6 19
GR360.S44 C66 1983   NYPL [Sc D 88-583]

ZOMBIISM - HAITI.
Davis, Wade. Passage of darkness . Chapel
Hill , c1988. xx, 344 p. :   ISBN 0-8078-1776-7

(alk. paper)   DDC 299/.65 19
BL2530.H3 D37 1988   NYPL [Sc E 88-429]

ZOMBIISM - HAITI - JACMEL - FICTION.
Dépestre, René. Hadriana dans tous mes rêves .
[Paris] , c1988. 195 p. ;   ISBN 2-07-071255-9
NYPL [Sc D 88-1004]

ZOOLOGY - AFRICA.
YllA, 1910-1955. Animals in Africa /. New
York , 1953. 146 p. :   *NYPL [Sc F 88-127]*

ZOOLOGY - BOTSWANA.
Owens, Mark. Cry of the Kalahari /. Boston,
Mass. , 1986, c1984. 535 p., [16] p. of plates :
ISBN 0-8161-3972-5 (lg. print) :   DDC
591.9681/1 19
QL337.K3 O95 1986   NYPL [Sc E 88-183]

ZOOLOGY - KALAHARI DESERT.
Owens, Mark. Cry of the Kalahari /. Boston,
Mass. , 1986, c1984. 535 p., [16] p. of plates :
ISBN 0-8161-3972-5 (lg. print) :   DDC
591.9681/1 19
QL337.K3 O95 1986   NYPL [Sc E 88-183]

Zora Neale Hurston / edited and with an
introduction by Harold Bloom. New York :
Chelsea House Publishers, 1986. viii, 192 p. ;
25 cm. (Modern critical views) Includes index.
Bibliography: p. 181-182.   ISBN 0-87754-627-4 (alk.
paper) :   DDC 813/.52 19
*1. Hurston, Zora Neale - Criticism and interpretation. I.
Bloom, Harold. II. Series.*
PS3515.U789 Z96 1986
NYPL [JFE 87-1592]

**Zora Neale Hurston's Their eyes were watching
God /** edited and with an introduction by
Harold Bloom. New York : Chelsea House
Publishers, 1987. vii, 130 p. ; 24 cm. (Modern
critical interpretations) Includes index. Bibliography: p.
121-123.   ISBN 1-555-46054-2 (alk. paper) :   DDC
813/.52 19
*1. Hurston, Zora Neale. Their eyes were watching God.
2. Afro-American women in literature. I. Bloom,
Harold. II. Series.*
PS3515.U789 T639 1987
NYPL [JFE 87-5315]

ZPH writers.
(29) Nyamubaya, Freedom T. V. On the road
again . Harare, Zimbabwe , 1986. 69 p. :   ISBN
0-949225-00-4   *NYPL [Sc C 88-136]*

ZPH writers series.
(31) Langa, Mandla, 1950- Tenderness of blood
/. Harare , 1987. 427 p. ;   ISBN 0-949225-30-4
NYPL [Sc D 89-102]

(32) Soyinka, Wole. The lion and the jewel /.
Harare, Zimbabwe , 1986. 64 p. ;   ISBN
0-949225-41-X :   *NYPL [Sc C 89-107]*

(35) Honwana, Luís Bernardo, 1942- [Nós
matámos o Cão-Tinhoso. English.] We killed
Mangy-Dog. Harare, Zimbabwe , 1987. 117 p. ;
ISBN 0-9792256-2-2 :   *NYPL [Sc C 89-106]*

Zuccarelli, François. La vie politique sénégalaise
(1789 - 1940) / François Zuccarelli. Paris :
CHEAM, c1987. 157 p. ; 24 cm. (Publications du
CHEAM, 0769-2161) Includes index. Bibliography: p.
153-[155]   ISBN 2-903182-23-X
*1. Senegal - Politics and government - To 1960. I. Title.
II. Series.*   *NYPL [Sc E 88-342]*

The Zulu blind boy's story. New York :
American Tract Society, [185-?] 16 p. ; 12 cm.
"No. 493."
1. Christian life. 2. Missions - South Africa.
NYPL [Sc Rare C 89-29]

ZULU WAR, 1879 - SOURCES.
Zululand at war, 1879 . Houghton, South
Africa , c1984. 299 p. :   ISBN 0-909079-23-4
NYPL [Sc F 85-153]

Zulueta, Pedro de, Jr. Trial of Pedro de Zulueta,
Jun. : on a charge of slave trading, under the 5
Geo. IV, Cap. 113, on Friday the 27th,
Saturday the 28th, and Monday the 30th of
October, 1843, at the Central Criminal Court,
Old Bailey, London ; a full report from the
short-hand notes of W. B. Gurney, Esq. ; with
an address to the merchants, manufacturers,
and traders of Great Britain / by Pedro de
Zulueta, Jun., ; and documents illustrative of
the case. London : C. Wood & Co., 1844. lxxiv,
410 p. ; 25 cm. Schomburg Center copy has clipping
of newspaper article affixed to fr ont flyleaf; the article
describes Cape Coast Castle (now Cape Coast, Ghana).
*1. Slave-trade - Africa. 2. Slave traders - Africa. I.
Gurney, William Brodie, 1777-1855. II. London.*

Central Criminal Court. III. Title.
NYPL [Sc Rare F 88-1]

Zululand at war, eighteen seventy-nine. Zululand
at war, 1879 . Houghton, South Africa , c1984.
299 p. :   ISBN 0-909079-23-4
NYPL [Sc F 85-153]

Zululand at war, 1879 : the conduct of the
Anglo-Zulu War / [edited by] Sonia Clarke.
Houghton, South Africa : Brenthurst Press,
c1984. 299 p. : ill. [some col.], maps, ports. ; 27
cm. (Brenthurst series. 10) "This printing is limited to
one thousand copies"--T.p. verso. Includes index.
Bibliography: p. 287-289.   ISBN 0-909079-23-4
*1. Zulu War, 1879 - Sources. I. Clarke, Sonia. II. Title:
Zululand at war, eighteen seventy-nine.*
NYPL [Sc F 85-153]

ZULUS - BIOGRAPHY.
Mzala. Gatsha Buthelezi . London , Atlantic
Highlands, N.J. , 1988. ix, 240 p. ;   ISBN
0-86232-792-X   DDC 968.4/9106/0924 B 19
DT878.Z9 B856 1988   NYPL [Sc D 88-1324]

ZULUS - HISTORY.
Stanley, Diane. Shaka, king of the Zulus /.
New York , c1988. [40] p. ;   ISBN 0-688-07342-5
DDC 968.04/092/4 B 92 19
DT878.Z9 C565 1988   NYPL [Sc F 88-358]

ZULUS - JUVENILE FICTION.
Mirsky, Reba Paeff. Nomusa and the new
magic. Chicago, 1962. 190 p.
PZ7.M675 No   NYPL [Sc E 89-175]

**ZULUS - KINGS AND RULERS -
BIOGRAPHY - JUVENILE LITERATURE.**
Stanley, Diane. Shaka, king of the Zulus /.
New York , c1988. [40] p. ;   ISBN 0-688-07342-5
DDC 968.04/092/4 B 92 19
DT878.Z9 C565 1988   NYPL [Sc F 88-358]

ZULUS - MEDICINE.
Schlosser, Katesa. Medizinen des Blitzzauberers
Laduma Madela . Kiel , 1984. 186 p., 64, [1] p.
of plates :   ISBN 3-88312-106-1   DDC
615.8/99/089963 19
DT878.Z9 S32 1984   NYPL [Sc E 87-271]

ZULUS - RELIGION.
Texts on Zulu religion . Lewiston, NY ,
Queenston, Ont. , 1987. 488 p. ;   ISBN
0-88946-181-3 :   DDC 299/.683 19
BL2480.Z8 T48 1987   NYPL [Sc E 88-463]

Zuma (ga zaki, ga harbi) /. Sudawa, Adamu
Sandalo. Kano , 1987. 56 p. :   ISBN
978-18-8000-7   *NYPL [Sc D 88-1292]*

Zvimba people of Zimbabwe. Samkange, Stanlake
John Thompson, 1922- Oral history . Harare,
Zimbabwe , c1986. ii, 93 p. :
NYPL [Sc D 89-586]

Zwi, Rose. Another year in Africa / Rose Zwi.
Johannesburg : Ravan Press, c1980. 172 p. ; 22
cm.   ISBN 0-86975-316-9
1. Jews - South Africa - Johannesburg - Fiction. I. Title.
NYPL [Sc D 88-1328]